The Bill James Handbook 2020

Baseball Info Solutions

www.baseballinfosolutions.com

Published by ACTA Sports

A Division of ACTA Publications

Cover Design by Tom A. Wright
Front Cover Photo by Benny Sieu, USA TODAY Sports
Back Cover Photo by Mitch Stringer, USA TODAY Sports

First Edition: November 2019

Published by:
ACTA Sports, a division of ACTA Publications
4848 North Clark Street
Chicago, IL 60640
(800) 397-2282
www.actasports.com www.actapublications.com

ISBN: 978-0-87946-678-7
ISSN: 1940-8668

Printed in the United States of America by McNaughton & Gunn

Dedication

This book is dedicated to the following people:

In memory of my mom: Thank you for giving me life, raising me in the church, and for teaching me to put others before myself. I miss you more each passing day and can't wait to see you again. Without you, I would not be where I am today.

To my dad and brothers: Thank you for continuing to give me the confidence to pursue my dreams. Your love and support have been greatly appreciated.

To my fiancé, Mariah: I thank God every day for allowing me to have met such an amazing woman. Thanks for putting up with my passion for sports.

And last, but certainly not least, to all my colleagues at Sports Info Solutions, both past and present: Thank you for all the great memories over these past five years. The countless hours of collecting and analyzing data drives the success of this company. I am excited to see what the future holds for all of you.

Play Like A Champion Today!

James Mehall

Table of Contents

Introduction.. 1
Who Would the Public Want To Go Into the Hall of Fame (by Bill James)........ 3
The Aesthetic Issues (by Bill James)... 23
Sneak Peek At *The Fielding Bible – Volume V*..................................... 49
Hall of Fame Monitor (by Bill James).. 59
Hall of Fame Value.. 65
Fathers and Sons... 75
Baseball Looks a Little Different in Japan.. 79
RBI Percentages (by Bill James).. 83
Starting Pitcher Rankings.. 91
Team Statistics.. 97
Team Efficiency Summary... 105
The Fielding Bible Awards (by Mark Simon).. 107
Defensive Runs Saved Leaders... 121
Strike Zone Runs Saved... 125
The Shift Update.. 127
Hits Lost and Gained to the Shift.. 131
Four-Outfielder Alignments... 135
Home Run Robberies.. 137
Career Register... 139
Fielding Statistics.. 387
Runs Saved Multi-Year Summary... 397
Injury Information.. 401
Baserunning... 405
Stolen Base Attempt Times.. 417
Pitchers' Repertoires.. 419
Relief Pitching... 435
Openers... 449
Pitchers Fielding & Holding Runners, and Hitters Pitching................... 451
Pitchers Hitting... 461
Lords of the Flies.. 465
Hard Hit Balls.. 469
Pinch Hitting.. 475
Manufactured Runs, Productive Outs, & Unproductive Outs................ 481
Managers Record... 485
Ballparks and Park Indices... 497
Lefty/Righty Statistics.. 513
Leaderboards.. 533
Win Shares.. 567
Instant Replay... 573
2020 Hitter Projections (by Bill James).. 575
2020 Pitcher Projections (by Bill James).. 589
Career Targets... 603
The 300-Win Candidates... 607
Baseball Glossary... 609
Minor League Abbreviation Key.. 623
Baseball Info Solutions... 627
Acknowledgments... 629

Introduction

Yet another amazing season of baseball will soon be behind us and written into the record books. A season that was celebrated as the 150th anniversary of Major League Baseball's first organization, the Cincinnati Red Stockings. For the first time in league history, four teams won at least 100 games—unfortunately for the Reds, they were not one of them (Houston Astros, Los Angeles Dodgers, Minnesota Twins and New York Yankees).

On September 11, Jonathan Villar of the Baltimore Orioles crushed a 443-foot home run that was the 6,106th league-wide home run, breaking the previous record set way back in 2017. By the end of the regular season, the final record-setting total was 6,776. Although quite productive, that's a lot of plate appearances without putting the ball in play.

Additionally, for the 12th straight year, the league set a new total season strikeout record with over 42,000. Now, that is a huge amount of plate appearances without getting the ball in play.

Attendance at the ballparks continued its decline, dropping another 1.7% from the 69.6 million in 2018 to 68.5 million this season. However, the league played its first-ever games in Europe at London Stadium between the Yankees and the Boston Red Sox, along with a game between the Kansas City Royals and the Detroit Tigers in Omaha, the first MLB game ever played in the state of Nebraska.

How much will a change of venue really impact a fairly steady decade-long decline? More importantly, what other alternative options may be available? Well, a little later in the *Handbook*, Bill James is prepared to share with you *50 ways to stop baseball from being swallowed up by home runs and strikeouts*.

Several readers of last year's *Handbook* had questions regarding the changes made to the register portion of the *Handbook*. Specifically, what are the new guidelines used for minor league (MiLB) stat-line inclusion?

First, all top-25 prospects have their MiLB stats, regardless of whether they played in MLB this past season. That means top prospects, such as Tampa Bay Rays shortstop Wander Franco and Los Angeles Angels outfielder Jo Adell, are in the *Handbook* register despite not playing in the majors.

Second, all other top-100 prospects will have their MiLB stats shown provided they played in the majors. If a player graduated from the top-100 list this year, they will have their minor league stats displayed. That means players such as New York Mets first baseman Pete Alonso and Los Angeles Dodgers shortstop Gavin Lux have their minor league history included. If someone graduated from the prospect lists last year or prior, they will not have their MiLB stats shown unless they played in the minors this year. This includes a player such as Atlanta Braves outfielder Ronald Acuna Jr.

Next, all MLB players will have their 2019 MiLB stats shown, provided they have batter stat lines from least 10 games or pitcher stat lines from at least five games. This prevents short stints in the minors (mostly rehab assignments) from being shown.

Fourth, a player will never have more than five years of MiLB stats shown in the register.

Finally, if a player plays at multiple levels below AA in the same year, then those stat lines are combined and shown as the level "Low."

Bill James and the rest of our advisory board all agreed that these guidelines ultimately improve the *Handbook*, allowing us to add new stats and analysis, along with more written research and opinion pieces by some of the industry's best minds.

As an additional resource to you, our valued reader, we have added a free-to-the-public stat area for billjamesonline.com providing over 50 different batting, pitching, team and league profiles. The annual league-level hitter and pitcher analysis that had previously been printed in the book is now available in the same public stat area, along with new individual player search capability.

We hope that you enjoy all that this year's *Handbook* has to offer.

Rob Dougherty
Coplay, PA
October 8, 2019

Who Would the Public Want
To Go Into the Hall of Fame

Bill James

This article is not about who deserves to go into the Hall of Fame; I have written about that dozens of times. This is not about who meets the standards of a Hall of Famer, nor is it about whether those standards should be higher or lower or Mr. In-Between. It is not about what the experts think, nor is it a poll of sportswriters. It is not about WHY the public likes one guy and doesn't like another guy, beyond generalizing about that to learn something from the study. It is simply about who the public would most like see go in.

Where do you go, to find the public? I went to Twitter. There are other publics. You can go to a public park and ask the people who are hanging out there who they think should be in the Hall of Fame. You can go to Buffalo Wild Wings. You can go to a public beach and cross-examine beautiful women in skimpy bikinis about who they want to get into the Hall of Fame, but I've found that you can frequently get arrested doing that; shoot, I'll probably get arrested just for making a joke about it. There's Publix Grocery Stores in Florida. Maybe they have them other places, too, I don't know; I just see them in Florida. I have found that if you ask people at Kauffman Stadium who should be in the Hall of Fame, they talk about Frank White and Dan the Man Quisenberry.

My point is that there are problems with any public you want to poll, including Twitter. Twitter gets you access to a lot of people, and Twitter has a really neat polling function, which is what I used, granting that Twitter is not an absolutely perfect source to poll the public, but it's what we've got.

I started by drawing up a list of everyone that I thought would have a reasonable Hall of Fame case, a reasonable dossier to present, Harold-Baines like, to the powers that be. I drew up a list of about 130 names, and then I went to my on-line readers (Bill James Online), and asked them to submit anyone else that they thought should be included. Eventually I got to 156 names. I tried to be all-inclusive, except that I didn't include anybody like Mike Trout or Ichiro or Pujols or Cabrera who is just TOO obvious; I didn't include them because if they were in a four-person poll, somebody in the poll would probably get 0%, and I had to mathematically analyze the results, and math hates zeroes. When you are studying ratios, extreme ratios are a pain in the slide rule.

I didn't intend to include anyone who didn't have a legitimate argument to be a Hall of Famer, and I didn't include anyone for whom I didn't think there was a legitimate argument that he WASN'T a Hall of Famer. In retrospect, I made some mistakes on both sides. I included some people who I wish that I had not included, because they have almost no public support as candidates, and I included a few people, like Adrian Beltre and Justin Verlander, who are just too obvious; the polling system would have worked better without them. But I didn't know, until I did the work, how one guy would poll as opposed to another.

I polled each candidate six times, each time comparing his Hall of Fame support to that of three other candidates. That makes 18 "position points" for each candidate. With 156 players being polled and four candidates in each poll, there were 39 polls in each round of voting. With six rounds of voting, that makes 234 polls.

Beginning on June 24, 2019 and ending September 25, I ran 234 Twitter polls, asking people which of these four men they thought was MOST deserving of being in the Hall of Fame. I found that it was virtually impossible to get many people to focus on THAT question rather than the other question that people more often debate, which is WHETHER a particular player is or is not worthy of the Hall of Fame. The usual Hall of Fame debate is framed "Is Fred Sluggerewski worthy of being in the Hall of Fame?" I was trying to get people NOT to ask that question and not to think about that question. I was trying to explain that "this is not about what the standard is or where the line should be or where you think anyone stands with regard to those standards. This is just about who is better qualified than who." Whether you are talking about Willie Mays, Honus Wagner, Hank Aaron and Walter Johnson or Mark Whiten, Mark Loretta, Mark DeRosa and Mark Hendrickson, one of the four must still be better qualified than the others. What I am trying to get you to tell me is, Which one?

I found that it was basically impossible to get people to address the question I was asking. If a poll had two or three strong candidates in there I would get about 1600 responses, generally, whereas if a poll did not have strong candidates I might struggle to get the 800 that I felt that I needed, because a lot of people wouldn't vote if they didn't feel that any of the four candidates was "qualified", and also, I'd get 20 responses to every poll telling me that none of these people was qualified and I should have a "None of the above option", which, you know. . . .I didn't suggest that any of the four WAS qualified, and I really don't have any interest in how many of you think none of the four was qualified; it doesn't have ANY relevance to what I was trying to study, which is who should be behind who else in line.

For the 234 polls I got a total of 289,416 votes, or 1,237 votes per poll. The average player in the average poll got 309 votes, and I was able to get the 800 votes that I felt were needed in all but 19 of the 234 polls, and was usually pretty close in the rest. I appreciate you all voting, if you did. Also, there were the fun people who would write back "Tony Oliva" when I was trying to poll four other outfielders. I asked people to cut that out, and, when they persisted, I started blocking anybody who did that, just because it was annoying, rude, and non-responsive.

Each poll was then analyzed by a set of 12 formulas, which had to be hand-entered, so that's a total of 2,808 formulas that had to be hand-entered. It was a long process and a lot of work, is my point, and I got pretty cranky in there because I don't usually work that hard. I think it was, by far, the largest and most extensive study ever of who the public WANTS to get into the Hall of Fame. That was my goal, anyway.

We'll use Jim Edmonds to illustrate the process. In the first round, which was organized by alphabetical order, Jim Edmonds was polled against Carlos Delgado, Negro League star pitcher John Donaldson, and 1947 National League MVP Bob Elliott. D's and E's. In the second poll Edmonds, born 6-27-1970, was polled against Sammy Sosa (born 11-12-1968), Gary Sheffield (11-18-1968), and Juan Gonzalez (10-20-1969). Players were polled in the second round in order of their birth, so that each man was polled against contemporary stars.

In the third round, Edmonds was polled against three other center fielders—Fred Lynn, Chet Lemon, and Bernie Williams. In the fourth, the goal was to poll candidates against other players from the same franchise, although this didn't quite work in Edmonds' case, because the number of players from a franchise doesn't always neatly divide by four, so you have to do the best you can. In the fourth round Edmonds was polled against Cardinal third baseman Ken

Boyer, but also 1920s St. Louis Browns' outfielder Ken Williams and San Francisco first baseman Will Clark. Clark was actually Edmonds' teammate at the end of Clark's career, although that wasn't why he was in the poll; that just worked out that way.

In the fifth round players were placed in polls based on their career WAR (Baseball Reference WAR); Edmonds, with 60.4 WAR, was polled against Bobby Abreu (60 WAR), Andy Pettitte (60.2 WAR), and Negro League Star John Beckwith, who has no WAR number, so we penciled him in at 60; he had to go somewhere. In the sixth and final poll, players were placed in groups based on their support in the previous five polls. Edmonds, with a previous Support Score of 124, was placed in a competition with Luis Tiant (121), Kenny Lofton (123), and Dave Parker (125). Also, there was a rule that no two players could be polled against one another more than once.

The idea was to measure the strength of Jim Edmonds' support—and every other player's support—by contrasting the support for each player with the support for 18 other players. Each of the 156 players was initially assigned a Support Score of 100, and then those 100 points were re-assigned, again and again and again, literally hundreds of times, until the data completely stopped moving, so that recalculating the results a thousand more times would not move anyone up or down by a point, nor by a hundredth of a point. For example, in the first poll, Jim Edmonds got 53% of the vote, whereas Carlos Delgado got 34%, John Donaldson 9%, and Bob Elliott got 4%.

At the start, Jim Edmonds would have 100 points, and Carlos Delgado would have 100 points. 200 points total. Edmonds beat Delgado, 53-34. If you split those 200 points in the ratio of 53 to 34, it works out to 122 points for Edmonds, 78 for Delgado, 122-78 being more or less the same ratio as 53-34.

Edmonds beat John Donaldson 53-9, so those 200 points are split 171-29, and Edmonds beat Elliott 53-4, so those 200 points are split 186-14. I am showing those numbers as integers, although of course I did not use integers in the calculations.

As Edmonds is later compared to 15 other players, however, so are Delgado, Donaldson and Elliott. It turns out that Donaldson and Elliott don't have very much support when they are compared to anybody. Bob Elliott—who was a really fine player in the 1930s and 1940s—got 4% of the vote in the first round, 4% in the second round, 9% in the third round, 4% in the fourth round, 2% in the fifth round, and only 18% in the sixth and final round, when he was being polled against three other players who had performed as badly in previous votes as he had. Elliott had almost no support in the voting, with a final Support Score of 8, with the average being 100.

By the end of the process, Edmonds' first-round results are evaluated in this way:

	Poll Result	Pct Result	Support Score	Total	Edmonds' Share
Jim Edmonds	53	.609	119	179	109
Carlos Delgado	34	.391	60	179	

	Poll Result	Pct Result	Support Score	Total	Edmonds' Share
Jim Edmonds	53	.855	119	137	117
John Donaldson	9	.145	18	137	

	Poll Result	Pct Result	Support Score	Total	Edmonds' Share
Jim Edmonds	53	.930	119	127	118
Bob Elliott	4	.070	8	127	

In other words, Edmonds is stronger than Delgado by a ratio of 53-34, stronger than Donaldson by a ratio of 53-9, and stronger than Elliott by a ratio of 53-4. As a result of that, Edmonds has three "position points" resulting from that poll, which are 109, 117 and 118. A position point is something that tells us where the player stands in relation to other players.

In the second round of the voting, Edmonds was matched against much stronger competition—Sammy Sosa, Gary Sheffield and Juan Gonzalez. He finished second in that group, getting 28% to Sheffield's 39%, with Sosa getting 27% and Juan Gone only 6%. That poll is evaluated in the following way:

	Poll Result	Pct Result	Support Score	Total	Edmonds' Share
Jim Edmonds	28	.418	119	256	107
Gary Sheffield	39	.582	137	256	

	Poll Result	Pct Result	Support Score	Total	Edmonds' Share
Jim Edmonds	28	.509	119	222	113
Sammy Sosa	27	.491	103	222	

	Poll Result	Pct Result	Support Score	Total	Edmonds' Share
Jim Edmonds	28	.824	119	155	128
Juan Gonzalez	6	.176	36	155	

Edmonds is weaker than Sheffield by a ratio of 39-28, but stronger than Sosa by a ratio of 28-27, and stronger than Gonzalez by a ratio of 28-6. His three position points from the second poll are 107, 113, and 128.

By the end of the process, Edmonds has 18 position points, which are:

From Poll 1, relative to Carlos Delgado:109
From Poll 1, relative to John Donaldson:117
From Poll 1, relative to Bob Elliott:118

From Poll 2, relative to Gary Sheffield:107
From Poll 2, relative to Sammy Sosa:113
From Poll 2, relative to Juan Gonzalez:128

From Poll 3, relative to Chet Lemon:120
From Poll 3, relative to Fred Lynn:118
From Poll 3, relative to Bernie Williams:125

From Poll 4, relative to Ken Boyer:127
From Poll 4, relative to Will Clark:126
From Poll 4, relative to Ken Williams:123

From Poll 5, relative to Bobby Abreu:125
From Poll 5, relative to John Beckwith:106
From Poll 5, relative to Andy Pettitte:126

From Poll 6, relative to Luis Tiant:118
From Poll 6, relative to Kenny Lofton:110
From Poll 6, relative to Dave Parker:104

The average of these 18 positioning points appears to be 118, but if you save all of the decimals and make a little adjustment at the end of each round of calculations so that the average of all 156 players remains at 100.000, then it works out to 119. Edmonds' Support Score is 119. I identified these here as polls 1, 2, 3, 4, 5 and 6, which is not the numbers of the polls but the numbers of the voting rounds; these were actually polls 10, 69, 101, 152, 184 and 226.

Let me try again to explain this. People kept telling me that I needed to include a "None of the above" option. But that option would address the issue of WHETHER the respondent thought that one of these players should be in the Hall of Fame. I'm not studying whether people think that one of these players or any of these players or all of these players should be in the Hall of Fame. That's the way that most people frame a similar question most of the time, but I was studying a different question. Understanding that, it is no more logical to include a "none of the above" option than it would be to include an "all of the above" option, or a "two of the above" option, or a "three of the above" option. Each one of THOSE inputs is exactly as relevant as the others—but the structure of a Twitter poll does not allow you to present ALL of those options, so it would be entirely improper for me to include any of them—quite apart from the fact that that's not what I am studying. If I had asked that question, I would have been (a) confusing the issue as to what it was that I was studying, and (b) simultaneously introducing a bias into the data—a bias toward artificially low estimates, since the respondent would have had the opportunity to say that NONE of these players should be in the Hall of Fame, but no opportunity to say that two of them or three of them or all four of them should be in.

The other theme of the study was that after every poll in which somebody's favorite player from the 1960s or the 1970s didn't do well, I would be hit with a barrage of complaints about "recency bias." Of course there IS some recency bias in a Twitter poll, but (a) many of the respondents grossly exaggerated how large that bias was, and (b) my point here is that I was studying WHO the public most wanted to see go into the Hall of Fame—not WHY they wanted them to go in.

Every form of information may be represented as a bias. If Cardinal fans vote for Jim Edmonds and Yankee fans vote for Bernie Williams, that may be represented as a competition of biases in favor of the Cardinals or the Yankees. When I poll a center fielder against a second baseman, you may have a bias for fielding or a bias for hitting or a bias for baserunning. If you rely on WAR numbers to decide who you would support, that may be a bias toward WAR. We are not testing pure knowledge; we are testing biases.

The theory of the study was to change the alignments repeatedly, pitting players against random players (alphabetically), against their contemporaries, against players from the same team, against players who played the same position, etc., so that the biases are rotated and the support for each player is tested in competition with multiple biases. I'll return to this subject in a moment.

I compare the process of measuring the "Support" for each player to estimating the number of gallons of water in a lake. You can't measure the size of a lake simply by measuring how wide it is and how long it is and how deep it is. If a lake is 20 miles wide at the widest spot, it could have an average width of 18 miles, or an average width of 3 miles. If a lake is 100 feet deep at the deepest spot, it could have an average depth of 95 feet, or of 10 feet. In order to estimate the size of the lake, you have to take many, many different measurements, measuring from one shore to the other at many different points.

This problem is like that. A player may have very wide support, but very shallow support—meaning that a lot of people like this guy, but that his support disappears when he is compared to other strong candidates—or he could have narrow but deep support, meaning that only a small number of people will vote for him but they will vote for him no matter who else is in the group. To really see how much support the player has, you have to measure it again and again, comparing one player to as many other players as you realistically can.

It doesn't exactly matter whether a player "wins" the poll or not. You can win a poll but get a number that hurts your overall score, if you don't meet your expectations for the poll, or you can finish last in a poll against strong competition but still get position points from that poll that help you overall. But there were 234 polls, of which:

54 were won by the player who was listed first on the "ballot",

53 were won by the player who was listed second,

60 were won by the player who was listed third, and

67 were won by the player who was listed fourth.

213 were won by the player who had the highest overall Support Score at the end of the process,

126 were won by the player who had the highest WAR, and

110 were won by the most recent player of the four.

The "213" figure is misleading, because the outcome of the poll is an input into the Support Score. There were a substantial number of cases—I believe about 25—in which the player who won the poll also had the highest Support Score, but only because he won that poll; if we ignored the results of that poll, he would not have had the highest Support Score. So the number there, 213, should be more like 185 or 190. To figure out exactly how many times that happened would be a huge project.

A little over half of the polls were won by the player who had the highest WAR, both because many people rely on WAR to decide who they like best, and because WAR correlates with other forms of evaluation. Even if no one had access to the WAR calculations except the man who does them, WAR would still tend to indicate who would win the poll.

I identified the "most recent player" as "the player who has played in the majors in the most recent season" or, if two players retired in the same season, as the player who was born most recently. 110 of the 234 polls were won by the most recent player, whereas, at random, this number would be 58 or 59.

Some of that discrepancy is explained by a recency bias on the part of the voters—but by no means all of it. The Most Recent Players won many of the polls because, in a disproportionate number of the polls, the most recent player actually was the best candidate in the group.

There are two reasons for that. The larger reason is that, in looking for candidates from the 1930s, the 1950s, the 1960s or 1970s, what I had to choose from was the ones who have been left out—the Babe Hermans and Bucky Walterses and Bob Johnsons, from the 1930s, and the Ken Boyers and Rusty Staubs and Jim Kaats from the 1960s. Those guys were tremendous players, but they're not the top players from their generation; they're not the Bob Gibsons and Sandy Koufaxes and Joe DiMaggios and Jimmie Foxxes and Roberto Clementes. Those guys have already been taken off the table.

The most recent generations of players are much less thoroughly picked over by repeated elections—thus, they tend to be stronger candidates. If Todd Helton wins a poll over Gil Hodges, old-timers will scream about recency bias— but Todd Helton, by any reasonable standard, was a greater player than Gil Hodges. If Scott Rolen wins a poll over Bill Madlock, someone will yell about recency bias—but Scott Rolen was twice the player that Bill Madlock was, honestly.

The second reason that this happened was that, in the second round of voting, when players were paired with other players based on when they were born, the BEST player would almost always outlast the others who were born at the same time by at least a year or two—thus, the best player would also be the most recent player.

The most recent player won the poll 110 times—but the most recent player also had the highest WAR of any of the four players 84 times. Again, at random, that would only have been 58, 59 times. There were a remarkable number of times in the voting when the most recent player was also the player in the group with the highest WAR, and yet that player did not win the poll. In Poll #16, Todd Helton was both the most recent player in the group and the player with the highest WAR, but he did not win the poll. In Poll #50, Vada Pinson was both the most recent player in the group and the player with the highest WAR, but he finished a distant third in the voting, getting only 16% of the vote. In Poll #83, Keith Hernandez was both the most recent player and the player with the most WAR, but he finished third in the poll.

In both polls 88 and 89, the four candidates finished in exactly reverse order of the recency bias, with the most recent player drawing the least support, and the least recent player drawing the most support. In Polls #119 and #187, Andruw Jones was both the most recent player and the player with the most WAR, but did not win the poll either time. In Polls #138 and #171, Torii Hunter both times was both the player with the most WAR and the most recent player, but did not win the poll either time. In Poll #140, a poll of Yankee players, Ron Guidry was both the most recent player and the player with the highest WAR, but did not win the poll. In Poll #146, Scott Rolen was both the most recent player and the player with the highest WAR, and also was the player with the highest Support Score overall, but somehow did not win that poll, losing to Mark McGwire. In Poll #148, Chase Utley was both the most recent player and the player with the highest WAR, but did not win the poll. In Poll #168, Omar Vizquel was both the most recent player and the player with the most WAR, but did not win the poll. In Poll #173, Jason Giambi was both the most recent player and the player with the highest WAR, but he finished third in the poll. In Poll #177 Jose Cruz was both the most recent player and the player with the most WAR; in Poll #179, Robin Ventura was. Neither one of them won. In Poll #210, Dustin Pedroia was both the player with the highest WAR and the most recent player, but finished tied for last in the voting. In Poll #223 (Andy Pettitte, Sammy Sosa, Vida Blue and Jeff Kent), Andy Pettitte was both the most recent player and the player with the highest WAR, but he finished last in the poll. In Poll #224, Will Clark was both the most player and the player with the highest WAR, but he finished dead last in the poll, with only 16%.

I am using WAR here only to say "It is reasonable to think." If a player has the highest WAR in a group of four players, it is reasonable to think that he may deserve to win the group. About half the time he does; about half the time he doesn't; it's reasonable either way—but my point is that there were actually a lot of polls that the most recent player might reasonably have won, but did not.

There WAS some recency bias in the voting; there is no doubt about that. There were some cases where we had players of comparable merit, one from the 1960s and one from the 21st century, and the 21st player would win by a huge margin. There were some poll results that you could not explain without reference to recency bias, but I just wanted to say that many people who participated in the exercise greatly exaggerated the effect.

Poll #95 was interesting, because in that poll, one player had the highest WAR, a second player had the highest Support Score, a third player was the most recent player—and the winner of the poll was the one guy who wasn't any of those things. The same thing happened in Poll #100, but #95 caught my eye because two of the players involved were contemporary shortstops, Dave Concepcion and Bert Campaneris.

By objective standards, Dave Concepcion does not seem to have been a better player than Bert Campaneris. Concepcion had 40.1 career WAR; Campaneris had 53.1. The two players were more or less contemporary; they were the opposing shortstops in the 1972 World Series. Concepcion was the shortstop on one of the great teams of that era, the Big Red Machine, who won two World Championships—but Campaneris was the shortstop on the Oakland A's team that won three consecutive World Championships just before the Reds won two.

I have pointed out in the past that Concepcion's career is somewhat parallel to that of Pee Wee Reese, the Hall of Fame shortstop from the Boys of Summer, and that Concepcion's role on the Big Red Machine is somewhat parallel to Reese's role on the Dodger teams—but Campaneris is also closely parallel to a Hall of Fame shortstop, Luis Aparicio; in fact, Luis Aparicio and Bert Campaneris are the only two significant players in baseball history whose skill sets are literally identical. I can show you their stats for most of the seasons of each player, and you absolutely cannot tell which one is which; they are exactly the same in every area in most seasons. Aparicio hit .262 in his career, .311 on base percentage, .343 slugging, .653 OPS, 82 OPS+, 55.8 WAR; Campaneris hit .259, same on base percentage (.311), same OPS (.653), higher OPS+ (89), 53.1 WAR. Aparicio had a .972 fielding percentage at shortstop; Campaneris, .964. Campaneris stole 140 more bases than Aparicio and played for three World Championship teams, while Aparicio played for one—yet Aparicio entered the Hall of Fame ballot at 28% and was elected in his sixth year on the ballot, while Campaneris got 3% of the vote and dropped off the ballot after one year.

In this voting, Dave Concepcion drew much more support than Campaneris, Concepcion finishing with a Support Score of 50, Campaneris with a Support Score of 25. When the two of them were polled against one another, Poll #95, Campaneris, who had the highest WAR of any of the four players (Concepcion, Campaneris, Rollins and Garciaparra), finished last in the voting, with just 12% of the vote. You can't really explain it; it's just something that happened.

Well, it is time to get into a systematic report on the results of the study. My goal was to do the first-ever serious, large-scale inventory of who the public would like to see step into Cooperstown, and you can think what you want to about it, but I believe that I accomplished that goal. Who does the public believe is most deserving of Hall of Fame recognition?

We could say that there are six levels of Hall of Fame support here:

a) Those who are overwhelmingly supported as Hall of Fame candidates (14 players),

b) Those who enjoyed strong support in the voting (30 players), and who would probably be above the Hall of Fame line in the opinions of the majority of voters, understanding that that was not the question addressed by the poll, and that different voters use widely different standards for how many players should be selected,

c) Those who are seen by the voters as being credible but marginal candidates, depending on where you draw the line (about 15 players),

d) Those who have significant support but probably not enough for us to put forward their names (about 22 players),

e) Those who have some support, but clearly not enough to make them viable candidates unless the electors look at them much different than the public does (about 33 players), and

f) Those who have really no significant Hall of Fame support with these voters, although they were very fine players (about 42 players).

Starting at the bottom, the 42 players who had basically no support, and their Support Scores in the voting, were the following:

First	Last	Support Score
Mark	Teixeira	24
Buddy	Bell	23
Babe	Herman	23
Jose	Cruz	22
Wes	Ferrell	21
Jack	Clark	21
Frank	Tanana	20
Vern	Stephens	19

First	Last	Support Score
Billy	Pierce	16
Jack	Glasscock	16
Sherry	Magee	15
Ken	Williams	15
Bucky	Walters	15
Bob	Johnson	14
Bob	Caruthers	14
Jim	McCormick	13

First	Last	Support Score
Sal	Bando	19
Stan	Hack	19
John	Donaldson	18
John	Beckwith	18
Bill	White	18
Luis	Gonzalez	17
Pete	Browning	17
Willie	Davis	17
Mickey	Vernon	17
Jason	Giambi	17
Dick	Groat	17
Jim	Fregosi	16
Rick	Reuschel	16

First	Last	Support Score
Camilo	Pascual	12
Chet	Lemon	12
Hank	Sauer	10
Al	Dark	10
Roy	White	10
Bob	Allison	8
Tony	Mullane	8
Dolph	Camilli	8
Bob	Elliott	8
Jackie	Jensen	8
Harry	Stovey	7
Buddy	Myer	6
Jimmy	Ryan	5

I feel, in a sense, that I owe these 42 men an apology. If I were starting the polls over, I would not include them in the list of players being polled. There are men in there that I would see as being worthy of Hall of Fame support. I did not know, until I did the polls, that they would have as little support as they did. I wouldn't want to embarrass anyone by drawing attention to his lack of Hall of Fame Support.

An average Support Score for a player is 100 points. A player with a Support Score of 5, then, would typically get 1% or 2% support in a poll of four players. Three players at 100 each, add 5, that's 305; 5 divided by 305 is 1 to 2%. And, in fact, that's about what Ryan and Myer usually got.

Mark Teixeira had a Support Score of 24, which translates to about 7 to 8% support in a typical poll. Mark Teixeira was a tremendous player. He hit .301 with 43 homers, 144 RBI in 2005, led the American League in Home Runs and RBI in 2009 (39 and 122) and in Runs Scored in 2010 (113). He was, other than Keith Hernandez, the best defensive first baseman that I ever saw. He was like a good third baseman playing first. He was incredibly quick, and he could dive for a line drive and somehow make it stick in his glove. I don't know how many doubles he took away from the Red Sox on balls ripped right down the first base line, but it had to be 20 or more. I really don't know why more people would not support his candidacy—and I could say the same about many of these players.

One thing we can learn from this list of players is that the public—the Twitter public—has no interest at all in seeing more 19th century players inducted into the Hall of Fame. Jim McCormick had 76.2 WAR, the 7th highest total of any of the 156 players listed in the polls. Tony Mullane had 66.5, Jack Glasscock had 61.6. Modern players with less than that are routinely selected. I know for a fact that a strong presentation on behalf of Harry Stovey was made to the Veteran's Committee or whatever they call it now just a couple of years ago, because a friend of mine who was on the panel asked me later whether he should have voted for that guy.

But I'm not here to say that the public is wrong. 19th century baseball does not meet any reasonable test of "major league" status. These players are long gone; everybody who saw them play died a long time ago. It is not apparent to me that anything would be accomplished by honoring their good numbers.

The next group of 33 players is those about whom we could say that they have SOME minority support for the Hall of Fame, but that, in general, the public does not support their election. Those 33 players, and the Support Scores calculated based on the voting, would be the following:

First	Last	Support Score
Ken	Boyer	47
Nomar	Garciaparra	47
John	Olerud	46
Kirk	Gibson	45
Willie	Randolph	45
Vada	Pinson	45
Jimmy	Rollins	44
Elston	Howard	44
Rusty	Staub	43
Maury	Wills	43
Bill	Freehan	43
Al	Oliver	43
Bill	Madlock	42
Mickey	Lolich	42
Reggie	Smith	39
Bartolo	Colon	38

First	Last	Support Score
Dustin	Pedroia	37
Torii	Hunter	37
Juan	Gonzalez	36
Norm	Cash	35
Julio	Franco	35
Jimmy	Wynn	35
David	Wright	33
Bill	Dahlen	31
Boog	Powell	29
Robin	Ventura	28
Eddie	Cicotte	27
Andrew	McCutchen	27
Ted	Kluszewski	27
Ron	Cey	26
Cesar	Cedeno	26
Johnny	Damon	25
Bert	Campaneris	25

As I said, Bert Campaneris—the lowest-ranking of those players—is, in my view, a deserving Hall of Fame candidate—but this article is not about what I think; it is about who the public would like to get into the Hall of Fame. You could make several pretty good teams out of that bunch of guys. A Support Score of 25 translates to about 8% of the vote in a four-man group of average strength; a Support Score of 47 would be 15-16% support in a typical poll.

The third group of 22 players would be those who have a significant level of Hall of Fame Support, but almost certainly not enough to get them elected if my Twitter followers were perfectly aligned with the Hall of Fame voters. These are those 22 players:

First	Last	Support Score
Dwight	Gooden	79
Billy	Wagner	79
Albert	Belle	78
Lance	Berkman	78
Ron	Guidry	77
Joe	Carter	73
Fred	Lynn	69
Dan	Quisenberry	68
Fernando	Valenzuela	67
Bernie	Williams	66
Carlos	Delgado	60

First	Last	Support Score
Graig	Nettles	58
Darrell	Evans	57
Kevin	Brown	57
Robinson	Cano	56
Jorge	Posada	56
Bobby	Bonds	55
Dave	Stieb	54
Bobby	Abreu	54
Steve	Garvey	54
Rafael	Palmeiro	53
Dave	Concepcion	50

A Support Score of 50 would translate to about 14% support in a poll group of average strength, while a Support Score of 79 would indicate about 21% support in a typical poll. But it all depends on who you are being polled against. Billy Wagner got 59% in Poll #158, when he was polled against Ted Kluszewski (Support Score: 27), Bob Allison (8), and Dick Groat (17), and he (Wagner) got 54% in Poll #134 (Willie Davis, Ron Cey and Jimmy Wynn.)

At the end of the polling, a participant wrote to me to say that Kenny Lofton had been "criminally underrated." Well, maybe—but if you trust WAR, maybe not. Lofton had 68.3 WAR, which puts him in the center of six players: Robinson Cano (69.6 WAR), Rick Reuschel (69.5), Tony Mullane (66.5), Lofton (68.3), Graig Nettles (68) and Kevin Brown (67.8). In our voting, Lofton had a Support Score of 124—compared to Cano (56), Reuschel (16), Mullane (8), Nettles (58) and Brown (57). He may have been underrated by other people at other times—but not in this poll.

Most of these 22 men are players who very reasonably could be elected to the Hall of Fame—but wouldn't be, if my Twitter followers were in charge of the deal.

There were 156 players in the polls, and so far we have accounted for 97 of them. That's leaves 59 players who perhaps could be considered to be valid Hall of Fame contenders. Let's think about the numbers a little bit. How many of these 59 players remaining are going to get into the Hall of Fame some time in the next 15 years?

Most of them. Two-thirds of them, probably. Think about it. The Hall of Fame selects about four players per year—4 in 2015, 2 in 2016, 3 in 2017, 6 in 2018, 6 in 2019, not counting managers and executives. 21 in five years.

Over the next 15 years, it is likely that the Hall of Fame will elect about 60 players. Almost all of those will be players who were on this list of 156 candidates. There will be a few players selected who are not listed here—have to leave room for Suzuki and Trout and Pujols and Cabrera—but, unless I have miscalculated somewhere, not very many. The top 59 players on this list. . . most of them are going to go in.

Most of the Top 59, but not necessarily most of the next group; most of the top two groups, but not necessarily this one. This is the group of 15 players that I listed earlier as "credible but marginal" candidates. Those 15 players, and their Support Scores in this voting, are as follows:

First	Last	Support Score
Keith	Hernandez	108
Will	Clark	106
Sammy	Sosa	103
Tommy	John	101
Chase	Utley	97
Andy	Pettitte	96
Vida	Blue	96
David	Cone	95

First	Last	Support Score
Tony	Oliva	94
Johan	Santana	92
Omar	Vizquel	90
Thurman	Munson	89
Curt	Flood	89
Bobby	Grich	83
Don	Newcombe	82

I suppose I should say: I'm not paying any attention to who is "eligible" to be elected. That's not what I'm doing. I am asking who the public would LIKE to see elected. Some guys aren't eligible now; they'll be eligible later. If they want to elect you, they can make you eligible. They've got committees for that.

Some of you will remember that in my previous Hall of Fame systems, which dealt with who SHOULD be selected, I designed the systems so that below 100 means you are not a Hall of Famer, above 100 means that you are, although 70-130 is usually a gray area.

I didn't do that here, but it sort of worked out the same way. An "average" score for a candidate is 100, but, because the Top Candidates have Support Scores of 500 and up, 108 of the 156 candidates have below-average scores. That means that only 48 of the 156 candidates have Support Scores over 100.

And how many of these men will be elected to the Hall of Fame, in the next 15 years? About the same number—about 48. If we assume that four men per year will be selected for the next fifteen years and that 80% of those are people who are on this list somewhere, that would mean that 48 of these guys are going to get elected. So we'll see how that works out.

These players—the Gray Area—have Support Scores ranging from 82 to 108. That represents about 21% to 27% support, in an average poll.

Now we move on to the 30 players that we can generally say that our Twitter voters, not universally of course, would like to see elected. That list is as follows:

First	Last	Support Score
Fred	McGriff	192
Joey	Votto	180
Curt	Schilling	178
Dale	Murphy	178
Orel	Hershiser	167
Yadier	Molina	165
Joe	Mauer	162
Buck	O'Neil	160
Zack	Greinke	160
Dick	Allen	143
Scott	Rolen	138
Andruw	Jones	137
Gary	Sheffield	137
Todd	Helton	136
Dwight	Evans	134

First	Last	Support Score
Buster	Posey	134
Dave	Parker	133
CC	Sabathia	132
Don	Mattingly	131
Gil	Hodges	128
Kenny	Lofton	124
Jim	Edmonds	119
Roger	Maris	119
Ted	Simmons	117
Bret	Saberhagen	115
Minnie	Minoso	114
Jeff	Kent	114
Luis	Tiant	113
Jim	Kaat	112
Mark	McGwire	111

I try only to advocate for one or two Hall of Fame candidates at a time. At the moment, the men at the top of my list are Minnie Minoso and Dwight Evans, and of course Buck O'Neil. Many of these players are candidates who, when they are elected, I will be glad to see them go in—Greinke and Mauer and Schilling and Posey and some others. Some of these are players whose election I definitely do NOT support, but again, this is not about who I think should be selected. This is about what the public thinks, as best I have been able to determine that.

Also, returning to the issue of recency bias, you can see, once we have compiled the results, that the list is not dominated by recent players. There are a lot of guys on there from the 50s, the 60s and 70s. (Did CC Sabathia come up in the 1950s, does anybody know? Seems like he has been around a long time.)

Anyway, that brings us to the top of the mountain: the 14 men whose selection is overwhelmingly favored by the Twitter respondents:

First	Last	Support Score
Barry	Bonds	1445
Justin	Verlander	772
Adrian	Beltre	742
Clayton	Kershaw	558
Roger	Clemens	473
Max	Scherzer	439
Pete	Rose	414

First	Last	Support Score
David	Ortiz	343
Joe	Jackson	335
Larry	Walker	292
Alex	Rodriguez	258
Lou	Whitaker	247
Manny	Ramirez	223
Carlos	Beltran	220

I'm not here to talk about PEDs or other scandals; I'm not here to debate the rightness or wrongness of steroid users or other scoundrels being admitted into the Hallowed Halls of Harry Hooper. However, the most striking thing about the list of players most-favored for Cooperstown selection is the concentration on the list of those who have been kicked out of baseball in gambling scandals (two) or kept out of the Hall of Fame in righteous indignation about PEDs, or suspended for some period of time for failing a PED test.

It would not be accurate to conclude, based on this voting, that the public does not care about PED use, or that it does not care about involvement in gambling scandals. That is not actually what the study shows. A more careful look at the data shows clearly that a substantial portion of the public DOES care about steroid use. Rafael Palmeiro had 3,000 hits and 569 home runs, and he has a Support Score of 53. Jason Giambi has a Support Score of 17. Carlos Delgado, who had monster years in the Steroid Era, has a Support Score of only 60, and Juan Gonzalez, 36. Obviously these players would have much higher Support Scores were there no steroid question marks attached to them, so obviously "the voters"—the public—does care about this issue.

But at the same time, only a fairly small percentage of the public wants to deny Hall of Fame status to Barry Bonds, Roger Clemens, Pete Rose, Joe Jackson, or other players of similar stature. Barry Bonds had poll results, in his six polls, of 80%, 72%, 77%, 73%, 59% and 54%, with the 59 and 54% figures being when he was matched against "clean" superstars like Adrian Beltre, Justin Verlander and Clayton Kershaw. In general, the Twitter public does feel that Bonds, Clemens, Rose, Shoeless Joe, A-Rod and Manny do belong in the Hall of Fame.

In closing, I wanted to post this list of how many polls were won by who. Two players, Barry Bonds and Pete Rose, won all six polls in which they were included. Rose never butted heads with Bonds because, while Rose won all of his polls, he didn't win by large enough margins against good enough competition to be in the top group of candidates with Bonds, Kershaw, Verlander, A-Rod, and Clemens.

Five players won five of their six polls—Adrian Beltre, Kershaw, Verlander, Larry Walker and Buck O'Neil. Most of those players won all of their polls except when they were matched against Barry Bonds.

Sixteen players won four of their polls—David Ortiz, Joe Jackson, Lou Whitaker, Max Scherzer, Roger Clemens, Alex Rodriguez, Dick Allen, Manny Ramirez, Dale Murphy, Fred McGriff, Roger Maris, Zack Greinke, Jim Edmonds, Mark McGwire, Orel Hershiser and Dwight Evans.

Fourteen players won three of their six polls—Curt Schilling, Gil Hodges, Kenny Lofton, Yadier Molina, Bobby Grich, Gary Sheffield, Minnie Minoso, Thurman Munson, Andy Pettitte, Bernie Williams, CC Sabathia, Jeff Kent, Joey Votto and Maury Wills.

Twenty-five players won two polls, forty-one players won one poll, and fifty-three players did not win a poll.

Thank you all for reading, and thank you for participating in the polls.

The Aesthetic Issues

Or

50 Ways to Stop Baseball from Being Swallowed up by Home Runs and Strikeouts

Bill James

Baseball absolutely cannot address its pace-of-play issues without doing three things:

(1) Stop batters from stepping out of the box between pitches,

(2) Limit mid-inning pitching changes, and

(3) Limit throws to first base.

Baseball in recent years has taken numerous actions that are sincerely intended to make the game move along more like a dance than like a funeral dirge. They've put a clock on this, put a clock on that, limited how many times a game you can do a few things. The games are longer and slower than they have ever been. It's like trying to put out a forest fire with cans of soda pop. "I've got 200 trees on fire in Sector 17, Captain. I need 24 cases of Dr. Pepper, immediately!" Unless you do the three things listed above, you are not addressing the problem; you are merely pretending that you are addressing the problem.

It is my experience that whenever you try to talk about whatever problems modern baseball has or might possibly have, people will begin lobbing issues at you from every conceivable direction like a vaudeville audience lobbing spoiled fruit at a tone-deaf comedian. Ticket prices, the cost of going to games, minor league salaries, games ending near or past midnight, too many commercials, too many strikeouts, empty seats, teams that aren't really trying to compete, games played in cold weather, shifting, too many pitching changes, kids playing video games rather than sports, too many wild cards, pitchers not being trained to go nine innings, the high cost of concessions and parking, World Series games being played in November, declining attendance, declining TV ratings. . .you name it; somebody sees it as a terrible problem.

On a sports talk show, this is great because it creates a long line of callers with an inexhaustible list of grievances. In a serious discussion, this is destructive. Understanding requires focus.

Baseball has essentially two sets of problems: there are the economic problems, and there are the aesthetic problems. The economic problems are far, far more serious than the aesthetic issues. The economic problems include the high cost of going to games, the salaries of minor league players, the fact that teams in smaller cities simply cannot afford to field competitive teams on a consistent basis, the unsold seats resulting from that. . . .it's a mess. Baseball economics are a train wreck, frankly; they're a train wreck running into a dumpster fire just outside of Chernobyl.

This article is not about the economic issues, serious as those are; this article is about the smaller and more solvable issues of the aesthetics of the game, which means putting on a show that people like to watch. I'm not suggesting that these issues are unconnected; they are quite certainly connected. It's like a man goes to the doctor; he's got bladder cancer, but also he has high blood pressure and emphysema. These problems are quite certainly connected, because you can't treat the cancer until you get the other issues under control. They're connected, but they are also distinct problems. Same thing; we have to get the patient healthy enough that we can deal with the really serious economic issues.

I am not saying that baseball is currently selling an ugly game or an aesthetically un-pleasing game. I will leave that up to you. You can like the modern game; you can hate it. It's your call. The essence of the aesthetic problem is this: that as baseball players have gotten to be bigger, stronger and better trained, two very narrow athletic skills have threatened to crowd out of the game a wider range of athletic attributes.

Perhaps the most amazing athletic feat that I have ever seen in baseball passed by so quickly that, as far as I know, it didn't even make ESPN's nightly roundup. It was Doug Glanville, playing center field for the Philadelphia Phillies about 2001. A deep drive was hit to the right field wall, Glanville racing toward right as the right fielder raced toward center. When Glanville and the right fielder were perhaps six feet apart, racing toward one another and avoiding collision, the ball came off of a post between the two of them, a little above their heads, and bounced toward center. Glanville had what seemed like a billionth of a second to react—and yet he did. He was racing toward the ball when the ball, probably moving more than 90 MPH, suddenly and unpredictably bounced right above his shoulder from a distance of perhaps three to five feet. It seemed completely impossible for him to react that quickly to the baseball, but he threw up his left hand, in that tiny fraction of a second, and caught the ball bouncing off the wall. It made no impact on the public; it attracted no attention—and yet when you watched the play in slow motion, it seemed to be beyond belief that he could do that.

That is athleticism. Athleticism is not simply the strength and the skill to hit a baseball a great distance, nor the strength, energy and co-ordination to throw a baseball 100 MPH and on target, not that those are not impressive athletic accomplishments. Athleticism also involves quickness, speed, grace, agility, reaction time, balance, and things which have no names like the ability to cope quickly with things that could not have been anticipated and the determination, the will, to overcome obstacles and overcome opponents when things seem to be going against you.

In baseball, it is most often in fielding that these wider-range athletic qualities come into the game; fielding, and sometimes baserunning. A ball in play creates a contest between a fielder and a baserunner, and in that contest players dive for baseballs, have to throw off-balance, have to make split-second decisions, have to recover to unexpected bounces and other unexpected events. They are required to display a wide array of athletic skills.

Historically, the essence of baseball has been in this contest between fielder and baserunner. A strikeout, historically, was the relatively rare event in which a batter failed so completely that he was unable even to create the contest between fielder and baserunner. The home run was the relatively rare event in which a batter succeeded so completely that he denied the fielder any chance to make the play. Over time, however, both strikeouts and home runs have been increasing in frequency. For a hundred years, the marginal events have been becoming more common, and the "central" events have been getting less common and less important.

In recent years these hundred-year trends have not only continued, but accelerated sharply. Home runs are no longer the exceptional offense; they are now the ordinary offense. Strikeouts are no longer the exceptional defense; they are now the ordinary defense, "defense" in the broader definition of "anything that prevents offense." Many people perceive this as a problem. The fact that older people perceive this as a problem is not in itself noteworthy; for more than a hundred years, many older fans have perceived EVERY change in the game as a problem. They're not all problems. But while many people perceive this as a problem, baseball attendance is also dropping at a steady pace. THAT is a problem. You can't get away from that one by saying "Oh, I like it this way."

Attendance is dropping because of aesthetic and economic problems, but also, there is a third aesthetic issue that is a part of the equation. The third issue is the pace of play and/or the length of the games. Athletic contests normally showcase action. People running around, jumping, throwing, spinning, falling. . .that kind of thing. Baseball games increasingly involve waiting around for things to happen. In my youth games were commonly played in two hours-and the old-timers were complaining about that being too long. In 2019 the average is 3 hours and 5 minutes, increasing by about one minute per year. More and more games now last four hours. It's an issue—the more so because there is less "action" than ever, action as it is traditionally thought of. People running around and jumping and diving and racing one another to see whether the ball or the batter gets to the base first.

Given this set of problems, people suggest crude and radical solutions to the problems. People suggest cutting games to seven innings. That's a nice idea—and, as the players and managers devise even more ways to waste the public's time, we can cut them to five innings, to three innings. Eventually we can play one-inning games with ten-minute commercial breaks between every pitch. Other people have suggested cutting the count to 3 balls for a walk and 2 for a strikeout, which, in fairness, is not AS bad an idea as the seven-inning game.

Crude and radical solutions to the problem are a very bad idea. The general purpose of this article is to argue ***against*** crude and radical solutions to the problems. The designated hitter rule was a crude and radical solution to what was then a problem. To return to the medical analogy, crude solutions are like doing eye surgery with a knife, which was common only a generation ago, or doing surgery with a bone saw, which. . . .let's move on. The point is that we do not need raw and heavy-handed solutions to these problems, whether or not you consider them to be problems. There are things you can do to solve these problems which would be, from the standpoint of the fan in the stands or watching on TV, virtually invisible. It may be that people adopt horrible, heavy-handed solutions because they fail to see that softer and lighter solutions are available to them.

Whether I actually have 50 proposed ways to solve these problems or not I am not sure; we'll find out as the article evolves. (Spoiler alert: he doesn't get there. Runs out of gas at 30.) There's a bunch of things I want to talk about, so let's get to them.

First of all, let's deal with the length of game/pace of play issues; the acronym there would be LOGPOPI, which you have to admit is a fun word. My first point: you absolutely cannot deal with this general issue unless you deal with (1) the number of pitching changes, and (2) players stepping out of the box between every pitch. Baseball in recent years has implemented a number of rules/restrictions designed to improve the pace of play, and they haven't done any good whatsoever; the average length of a game just goes up and up.

I shouldn't say it hasn't done any good at all; the limitation on visits to the mound is a good rule and it has helped to slow down the rate at which the problem has gotten worse. The problem is still getting worse. It puzzles me to no end that anyone would not understand why this is happening, or why anyone would imagine that things like between-inning pitch clocks and limitations on visits to the mound are actually going to solve the problem (if it is a problem; I guess that is up to you).

Look, the problem with pace of play/length of games is (1) batters stepping out of the box to re-focus between every pitch, and (2) constant and frankly unnecessary pitching changes. ***Unless you deal with those two issues, you are***

not, in fact, dealing with the problem. You are <u>*pretending*</u> that you are dealing with the problem. All that baseball has done so far is pretend that it is dealing with the problem.

It is contrary to the very nature of team sports to allow either the pitcher or the hitter to "get ready" for a pitch. Does a basketball team give the other team an opportunity to get set for a fast break? Should they? Does a soccer team allow the goalie a moment to get his mind and his equipment in just the right place before the other team attempts to score? Should they do that? Does a football game allow the defense to break out of a set position an instant before the snap, because they're not feeling comfortable? Should they do that?

Somehow we have lost track of the fact that the MOST basic nature of sports is forcing the other team to react when they are NOT prepared to react, when they have NOT cinched up their batting gloves nice and tight and got into just the right position in the batter's box and cleared their mind and thought through what the pitcher is likely to throw.

My first suggestions, then, are (1) prohibit players from stepping out of the batter's box after the at bat has begun, or (2) limit the number of times that a batter can step out of the batter's box after stepping in to the batter's box to, let's say, one per team per inning.

Actually, no rule change is necessary here; all that is really necessary is an umpiring policy change. When the batter steps out of the batter's box, he has to ask for time. If the umpire doesn't grant the time out, then the pitch is legal. You don't actually have to change the rules; all you actually have to do is stop calling timeout, unless there is an actual reason to call timeout. If you cut the number of unnecessary timeouts in a game down from 300 or whatever it is now to something less than 20, you'll have the pace of play problem halfway solved.

The pitching-change part of this problem is trickier, not because it is hard to solve but because there are so many good options as to how to solve it that it is hard to choose exactly the right one. Some people have suggested that we require the pitcher to complete his warmup throws in the bullpen, eliminate his eight throws to warm up once he gets to the mound. That is another of those pathetic suggestions that people make when they don't really want to solve the problem; they just like to pretend that they're working on it. Eliminating the pitcher's warm-up throws from the mound, frankly, isn't going to do a damned thing about the pace of the game; it will just squeeze a few seconds out in one space, and they'll go back on in another space. What you will ultimately have to do, if you don't want the average game to stretch out to four hours, is make a rule that limits mid-inning pitching changes.

Actually, there is such a rule likely coming already for 2020, Rule 5.10 (g); a pitcher has to face three batters or finish the inning. That's great, and it will help; let's see how much. There are many other options, but this is the one that I propose, #3 on my list. A team may make as many pitching changes as they want in a game, between innings. Also, any pitcher may be taken out of the game at any time after he has been charged with a run allowed in this inning.

Beyond those two situations, a team may remove a pitcher from the game in mid-inning without penalty once a game—and only once. You've got one free shot a game to remove a pitcher who has not given up a run in this inning from the mound in the middle of the inning—one.

After you have used your free shot, if you take out a pitcher who has not allowed a run to score in the inning, there's a penalty. What the penalty would be probably doesn't matter very much. The strategic advantage of constantly changing pitchers is so small that any on-field penalty that you impose to offset it would probably be enough to stop it from happening. If you just made a rule that a "ball" is added to next hitter, that might be enough. You make a second mid-inning pitching change, the next hitter starts with a 1-0 count. That might be enough, because many of the pitching changes are made to get a platoon advantage on the hitter, and the disadvantage of having a 1-0 count on the hitter is probably as large as the platoon advantage, I would guess.

Still, I would favor a stronger penalty. The penalty that I would suggest is, for second delay-of-game pitching change, the next hitter automatically takes first base—and all runners who are on base automatically move up one base, whether they are "forced" or not. That would clearly put a stop to it.

I think that is the BEST rule for the problem because it is non-invasive. In practice, nobody would take out a pitcher to invoke the penalty, so the fan would never know it was there. If you went to games, if you watched every game on TV, and if that rule was adopted but no one told you about it, you would never know that there was a new rule; you would just notice that there were a lot fewer delays for pitching changes this year, but you wouldn't be able to figure out why. That's why I like the rule.

There have been other ways proposed to limit the number of pitching changes. We could (#4) limit a team to using three pitchers in the first nine innings of a game, or (#5) limit a team to 11 pitchers on a roster, or (#6) limit the number of pitchers who can be used in a series—a maximum of seven pitchers in a three-game series, or ten pitchers in a four-game series, with an increase of one for each four extra innings if there are extra innings in the game. Those are OK ideas; I think they're a little bit crude, a little bit heavy-handed. We could (#7) make a rule prohibiting any pitcher from pitching in consecutive games. If that was the only rule on the table, I'd vote for it.

Another rule that has been proposed to control delay-of-game pitching changes (#8) is that if a pinch hitter is announced and the other team brings in a different pitcher, that the team at bat may withdraw the pinch hitter and may use him later in the game. In other words, being ANNOUNCED as the pinch hitter does not mean that he is "in the game", does not mean that the other player has been replaced. It merely signals an intention to put the other player in the game. He's not actually in the game until you throw him a pitch.

That's not a bad rule, I don't think, but it's not adequate to the abuse that it intends to curtail. It would eliminate 3% of the problem, 5% maybe. I would be in favor of the rule, but it leaves the problem 95% or 97% unsolved.

One thing that very obviously needs to be done, also doesn't require a rules change, is to (#9) start enforcing the rule that the pitcher is supposed to have his foot on the rubber when he delivers the pitch. We used to talk about pitchers throwing a 59-foot fastball, which was considered cheating. Nobody throws a 59-foot fastball anymore; the norm now is 57. The escalation in strikeouts has been caused to a significant extent by ignoring the rule (Rule 5.07).

One can see how this rule came to be ignored. If a pitcher pulls his foot off the rubber a fraction of a second early, the umpire really can't see that reliably. If umpires tried to call that—which they never do—they would get it wrong some-times, which would be embarrassing, and also it would mess with the normal sequence of play—sort of like the balk rule, only worse. Because the umpire actually can't see a 20th of a second early step-off, they never called it, so the time gap between leaving the rubber and the ball leaving the pitcher's hand has gotten wider and wider, now wide enough that you actually CAN see it, many times.

We need some sort of protocol for enforcing the rule in the least intrusive way that we can. One way to do that would be to have special umpires, retired umpires perhaps, study the video of the games after the fact, and mark those pitches which, in slow motion, can be seen to be illegal, and track the data, and publish the data. Some pitchers now are pulling the foot off early on 95% of their pitches, at least. You identify the worst offenders, give them a warning to stop it, and if they continue to do it, then you suspend them from pitching briefly. If they continue to abuse their leeway after being reinstated, then you suspend them for a little bit longer.

Another way to enforce it. . .I don't like this one as much, but it could be done and it would work. . .would be to allow the manager, once a game <u>and only after a strikeout,</u> to protest that the pitch was illegal. If you review the tape and find that the pitch was in fact illegal, that the pitcher was in fact not in contact with the pitching rubber when he released the pitch, then the strikeout is wiped out, the count reverts to 0-0, and the batter stands in again. That would work to an extent because, of course, the manager would save his challenge for the biggest moment of the game. Your cleanup hitter is up with a runner on second; he strikes out on an illegal pitch, you give him a do-over. It would be a pretty effective deterrent against the 57-foot fastball.

There has been some talk about moving the mound back by two feet or something, which. . . .whoever suggested that has probably never played baseball. Pitchers spend 15 years learning to make a slider break at just the right moment so that it breaks across the plate; if you move them back two feet, every breaking pitch is horribly off target, and you can't just fix that in spring training.

We DO need to move the pitcher's mound back (#10), but more like three inches. It wouldn't make a LOT of difference, but it would make a difference. It's invisible to the fan, basically, but it would give the batter about .002 more seconds to read the pitch. And if three inches doesn't do anything, then you can do another three inches in a couple of years. Moving the pitcher's mound back even a couple of inches would reduce strikeouts, because it would give the batter a tiny bit more time to react.

The thing is that skill levels evolve over time. Pitchers throw harder than they used to, and batters react more quickly and swing harder—but the evolution of pitchers toward harder throwing and the evolution of hitters toward quicker reactions are not perfectly aligned. They're not happening on precisely the same schedule. There is no reason in nature that they should be perfectly aligned, but the fact that they are not is driving strikeouts upward. Moving the pitcher's mound back a few inches just helps to re-align the reaction time with the evolution of skills.

Another rule that many of us would favor (#11) would be that if a starting pitcher is removed from the game before pitching five innings and before allowing four runs to score, that pitcher is ineligible to pitch again for eight days. In other words, you can't use an opener. The starting pitcher that you announce; he's your guy for five innings, unless he just doesn't have it today.

I would favor that rule, and here is why. First, I am generally against any rule that attempts to change baseball—but I am often in favor of rules that PRE-VENT changes to the game. I like baseball. I'm not opposed to changes across the board; some changes are good, and some are not good.

It is my belief *that baseball should be played in the way that the fans most like to see it played*. The use of "openers" seems to me to be, from the standpoint of the fan, an undesirable change. Going to the game to see Gaylord Perry start against Vida Blue, going to see Tom Seaver against Steve Carlton, going to see Dave Stewart beat Roger Clemens again, going to see Greg Maddux against Randy Johnson, going to see Pedro Martinez against Tim Hudson. . .that's baseball as we learned to love it—but so is seeing Pedro Martinez against some humpty named John Snyder. Pedro Martinez in 1999 went 23-4, and you know who beat him? All four losses were to opposing starting pitchers—John Snyder, Mike Thurman, Dave Eiland and Tim Hudson. Snyder finished the season 9-12 with a 6.68 ERA, but he beat Pedro Martinez when Pedro was having one of the greatest seasons of all time. Mike Thurman finished the season 7-11 with a 4.05 ERA, but he beat Pedro Martinez. Dave Eiland finished the season 4-8 with a 5.60 ERA, but he beat Pedro Martinez. That's baseball, to me.

Baseball has always followed the rule. . . .well, the lack of a rule. We have always followed the policy that if managers figure out a more effective way to do something and it changes the game, we allow that change to take place—and changes have in fact happened for 150 years.

That's fine, except when it isn't. This is a case when it isn't. You know why it isn't?

Because it forces the organization to sell anonymity. It's a new $100-million movie starring: Eight people that you've never heard of before, and will never hear from again. Some 22-year-old who throws 100 MPH goes out and pitches the first two innings; he's anonymous.

Identity is crucial to marketing baseball—just as it is to marketing movies, or television shows, or any other form of entertainment. Baseball cards, you remember? They create *identity* for the players. Fantasy baseball, you remember? It's based on having players that you can identify.

We haven't lost identity for the players, but we are, in fact, losing it. We're trying to sell the public a game of anonymous, limited talents. We are losing identity primarily in two ways: one, through running pitchers in and out of the game so that, as a fan, you don't know who in the hell that guy is on the mound, and second, by shuttling players back and forth between majors and minors.

That's another rules change that DEFINITELY needs to be made; #12. Teams now send players back and forth to the minor leagues quite literally on a daily basis, making the 25-man roster, in effect, a 32-man roster. You bring a pitcher up, work him for a couple of weeks, then you send him back out and let him rest up, regain maximum arm strength so that his 94-MPH fastball becomes a 97-MPH fastball for a week or so. One thing that definitely needs to be done: cut that out. *Baseball does not benefit from anonymous players. It benefits from identifiable players*. Do you sincerely question that principle?

My suggestion—still on #12—would be to limit each team to one roster move a week, except that perhaps three times during the year a team can use a "free roster move". If you get two players actually hurt in the same game, you can use your free move to deal with that. Otherwise, you've got one move a week, and let's say that you can save your move for one week (only), so that if a team does not make any roster move in one week they can make two the next.

Again, that's an invisible change, to the fan. If that rule was adopted and nobody told you it had been adopted, you would never know, because you don't see anything different. I should stress that I am not advocating that baseball make ALL of these changes. Baseball is, in fact, losing popularity; you can put your head in the sand and say it ain't so if you want to, I guess. What I am trying to get you to see is that, if baseball actually chooses to address the things that are causing soccer to become popular, there are many, many, many ways to do it. We don't have to make crude, heavy-handed changes to the game. We can make the game move along a lot faster, make it more fun to watch, by doing things that are basically invisible to the fan—and there are many, many different options in how to do that. That's what I am trying to say.

I mentioned at the top of the article that we needed to limit throws to first base by pitchers (#13). My preference in that area is so far out of the mainstream of ideas that I won't advocate for it here; I'd like to eliminate the balk rule and replace it with some better-thought-through idea of how the pitcher can defend against a base stealer. Setting that aside, what one could do (#13) is limit a pitcher to two throws to first base, per batter; if he makes a third unsuccessful throw to first base, the baserunner automatically advances.

The failure to have such a rule is simply an oversight. If you think about it, a pitcher has a limited number of ineffective throws that he can make to home plate. The limit is three. You make four ineffective throws to home plate, and the batter wins; the batter takes his base.

What sort of sense does it make to say that the pitcher has a limited number of wasted throws that he can make to try to get the batter out—which is the central focus of the game—but that if he wants to stand on the mound and make 15 ineffective throws to first base, that's fine. It *isn't* fine. It's disrespectful of the fans; it is disrespectful of the game.

Up until about 1915, baseball regularly adjusted its rules to fix problems like this, but it never addressed the waste-of-time-throws-to-first problem because there was no such problem at the time. If it had ever occurred to the people who ran baseball before the commissioner system came along that some jackass was going to stand on the mound and throw to first 15 times, it is absolutely clear that they would have prohibited it. They never prohibited it because it never happened.

After the commissioner system came along there were very few stolen base attempts in baseball for fifty years, basically, so waste-of-time throws to first didn't become a real problem until the late 1970s. By the time the problem arose the idiotic, self-destructive idea had taken hold that baseball was a perfect game in which the rules never needed to be adjusted for new realities. This paralyzed the game for 40 years, which frankly pitched baseball into a death spiral; we've just begun to escape that paralysis, and try to fight to save the game.

Another alternative there is (#14) to prohibit the pitcher from throwing to first base unless the runner off of first actually has at least a six-foot lead. You see it all the time; the pitcher just isn't quite ready to pitch, so he throws to first even though the runner has no lead and is no threat to steal. It's annoying. Another thing you could do would be to draw a little line six feet off of first base. As long as the baserunner keeps one foot on the first base side of that line, he's absolutely safe, because the pitcher *can't* throw to first if he doesn't cross that line. Again, it's an almost invisible rule to the fans, apart from the little hash mark, because the pitcher would almost never throw to first when he was not allowed to, and you never give a thought to what *doesn't* happen.

So far I have suggested 14 possible rules fixes or policy fixes, of which 12 could be considered to be pro-offense, pro-hitter, so let's balance the scales. The 15th rule change that seems to me to be worthy of consideration would be to move the batter's boxes one inch further away from home plate. There is now a six-inch separation between the plate and the batter's box; we could make it seven.

Batters now stand much, much closer to the plate than they did 40 years ago. The change can be traced back to batting helmets. Batting helmets became theoretically mandatory in the 1950s, but the rule was not strictly enforced until the 1970s; there were still batters hitting without batting helmets occasionally into the mid-1970s.

Historically, it was widely accepted for pitchers to intimidate hitters by throwing pitches up and in, forcing the hitter to stay away from the plate out of the fear of being hit. This was still somewhat accepted, still slightly accepted, when I started working for the Red Sox in 2002. I can remember even then hearing discussions about whether it was "time" to knock so-and-so off the plate; I can remember those discussions in 2003 to 2005. By 2009—ten years ago—it had become clearly, absolutely, and universally forbidden to talk about using intimidation to keep hitters off the plate.

If you work back in time, you can see that it was more and more acceptable, in the past, for the pitcher to try to intimidate the batter against standing too close to the plate. In 2003-2005, it was acceptable to do that if the hitter was "diving in" to the pitch. At that time you didn't have general, every-day, every-game intimidation of the hitters like you did in the days of Bob Gibson, Don Drysdale and Early Wynn. But hitters sometimes would look for an outside pitch and dive toward the outside pitch. The unwritten rule at that time was that when a hitter started diving into the pitch, you were allowed to remind him not to do that.

Bret Saberhagen (1984-2001) had quite exceptional control. Saberhagen would knock down one hitter every game, usually the first time through the order, occasionally in the second. Although he never talked about it, that I know of, he never forgot to do it; you could take it to the bank. One hitter in the early innings of every game was going to wind up on his butt. But that was mild compared to the pitchers of the previous generation, who would throw several deliberate brushback pitches every game.

The batter is now protected not only by batting helmets—and larger and better batting helmets than players had 20 years ago—but also by a variety of other pieces of protective equipment—shin guards and elbow guards and wraps and sleeves and batting gloves, and also by an ethic of the game which prohibits the use of intimidation by the pitcher. The batter now is very thoroughly protected, which is why Hit By Pitch totals have gone up; the hitter has less to be afraid of in being hit by a pitch.

If a hitter can stand right on top of the plate, that provides three advantages for him: (1) it makes it easier for him to get to an outside pitch, (2) it makes it easier for him to pull a pitch in the middle of the plate, and (3) it prevents the pitcher from working inside, since any inside pitch has a high probability of hitting the batter and putting him on base.

It's a critical part of the problem, or the Syndrome, or whatever you want to call it, the syndrome of almost every hitter standing right on top of the plate and trying to crush any pitch on the inside half of the plate. There are four things that you can do about it; three of these I am actually advocating. The fourth is just a suggestion. The three that I advocate (15-16-17 on our list) are:

15) Move the batter's box one inch away from the plate,

16) Actually enforce the rule requiring the batter to stay in the batter's box. Batters like to wipe out the lines that form the batter's box. Stop them from doing that. Use technology to enforce the rule if you have to. With modern sensing equipment, it can't be that hard to tell if a batter's feet are where they are supposed to be when the pitch is thrown.

I believe that the rule says that if a batter is out of the batter's box when he hits the ball, he's out. You couldn't actually enforce that rule; the league batting average would drop to .150 if you did. Batters have a foot or both feet out of the box when they hit the ball all the time. You can't rigorously enforce that rule because it's not a well-thought out rule, but you can call out hitters who (a) plant their feet outside the box, or (b) step WAY out of the box to hit the ball. It would make a huge difference if you just enforced the rule, because you would be allowing the pitchers to work inside.

17) Get rid of some of the "protective" gear. Of course, nobody wants to see batters get hurt, but batters played baseball for 100 years without shin guards and elbow guards and whatever you call those things they wear on their wrists; for that matter, they played for 100 years without batting helmets. If you cut down on the protective gear, you (a) will NOT increase injuries, and (b) will force the hitters to get off the plate.

I do favor the rules changes above; I believe that all three of those rules are necessary and appropriate to cut down on the home runs and on the strikeouts. #18 is just a suggestion, just an idea; let's see what you think. #18: Change the rule from "the batter takes first if he is hit with a pitch" to "the batter takes first if the pitcher throws a pitch that breaks the front plane of the batter's box," meaning of course the box in which the hitter is standing, not the one across the plate. Make the front line of the batter's box a little bit wider, a little bit brighter; let's say you put a yellow stripe next to the white stripe, so that it's more visible whether the ball has crossed that line, and also let's say that you bury a sensor in the ground beneath that that turns on a signal light somewhere if the ball is thrown over that line.

Not exactly advocating this rules change, but. . . .doesn't that rule actually make more sense? Why is it OK to throw at the hitter, if he is able to get out of the way? On the other side or the issue, why does the batter get first base if he leans over the plate and the ball hits his shoulder? Shouldn't the issue be where the pitcher throws the ball, rather than whether the batter is able to get out of the way?

I don't think that this rules change would either increase or decrease significantly the number of batters awarded first base; I think it would be about the same. It just would work against guys like Brandon Guyer who hang out over the plate in an effort to make the ball hit their shoulder. I think that's a positive.

Possible Rules Change #19 is an extension of #17, above: Whatever equipment the batter wears into the batter's box, he wears until he gets back to the dugout. You want to wear a shin guard, OK—but if you wear it into the batter's box, you wear it running the bases. If you wear a six-pound elbow guard to hit, OK, but you carry it around the bases.

I strongly favor this rule, because changing equipment is another of the things which is slowing down the game. Batters take 30-45 seconds, after they reach base, to unsnap all their gear, hand it to the first base coach, and put on their sliding gloves. They hit a double, they have to run half-way back to first base to trade equipment with the first base coach. I don't see the entertainment value of this. There is no entertainment value in this; it just slows down the game. I say:

put the fan's interest first. I'd go beyond that: ultimately, in order to survive, baseball is going to HAVE to put the fan's interest first. Ultimately, there will be no choice but to do that.

Baseball is being pulled in the direction that it is by more and more hitters making more and more efforts to hit home runs. Anything that you do that causes that not to work will cause that strategy to be gradually abandoned, and will bring back the other concept of offense: get on base, run the bases, advance the runners.

That concept underlies my suggested rules changes #20, #21 and #22. #20: Deaden the baseball a little bit. Raise the stitches; reduce the resiliency of the ball, something. Something that helps the pitchers. This is going to be done this winter, the winter of 2019-2020, so I don't know that we need to spend a full paragraph on the issue.

#21 has a similar purpose: put in place an agreement among the teams that every fence that creates a home run must be either 340 feet from home plate, or 20 feet high, one or the other. It's not really a very radical rule; it merely says that if you have a short home run distance, you have to put up a home run screen until the fence angles away from home plate a little bit.

#22 is similar but more radical. In one sense, it's a tiny, tiny little change; it merely requires that you change one digit in the rule book. Baseball rule 5.05 (b) (5) says that when "a fair ball passes over a fence or into the stands at a distance from home base of 250 feet or more. Such hit entitles the batter to a home run when he shall have touched all bases legally. A fair fly ball that passes out of the playing field at a point less than 250 feet from home base shall entitle the batter to advance to second base only."

Well, suppose that you changed the "2" there to a "3"; 250 feet becomes 350 feet. That's actually a rather profound change in the rule. The change would not require that teams re-configure their parks. What it would mean is that the foul pole and the home run pole are not necessarily the same thing. You have a foul pole, which determines whether the ball is fair or foul, but also, you have a "home run pole" which determines whether the ball is a home run or a double. A ball hit into the seats, but hit less than 350 feet, is not a home run; it's a double.

A lot of fans are going to hate that idea, because we've been raised all of our lives to think that a ball hit out of play has to be a home run. But it doesn't HAVE to be a home run; it could very well be just a double. I personally would like the rule, because it would get rid of a lot of cheap home runs, and if you get rid of cheap home runs then it becomes a less profitable gamble to try to hit home runs, which means that the smart play becomes to put the ball in play. I would like the rule, but I do understand that it is a radical and visible change to the game, and the promise of this article was not to do that, so. . .

Getting back to rules changes that would be essentially invisible to the fan, rule 3.02 (a), "The bat shall be a smooth, round stick not more than 2.61 inches in diameter at the thickest part and not more than 42 inches in length." The rule book states a maximum thickness of the bat, but no minimum thickness. Suppose that (#23) we changed the rule to read "The bat shall be a smooth, round stick not more than 2.61 inches in diameter at the thickest part, *not less than 1.50 inches in diameter at the thinnest part*, and not more than *41* inches in length."

You couldn't actually do that right away; you'd have to start at a minimum thickness of 1.00 inches and gradually walk it up to 1.50 inches (1.00 inches the first year, 1.05 inches the second year, 1.10 the third year, etc.) Bats when I can first remember, 1950s bats, were more than 1.50 inches at the thinnest part, but then they kept making them thinner and thinner. That's one reason they break as often as they do—not the only reason, but one of the reasons. The handles are a lot thinner.

The thin-handled bats are a part of the syndrome of everybody trying to hit home runs, and hitting home runs and striking out. The reasons that modern hitters like the thin-handled bat are (1) it puts more wood in the sweet spot, and (2) there is something that happens with the momentum of the swing. If you put more weight out at the end of the bat head and less weight near the hands, then you can generate more bat speed with the same amount of energy.

But the fact that hitters LIKE those bats doesn't mean that it is good for the game, from the standpoint of the fans. A thicker-handled bat is more of a put-the-ball-in-play bat, rather than a hit-the-ball-400-feet bat. If you gradually change the bats back to the older style of bats, in stages so small that they are invisible from the seats, then you are legislating against home runs and strikeouts, and in favor of putting the ball in play—but without doing anything that the fan can see. Again, I think the failure of the rules to address this issue is essentially an oversight. I think if the people who created the modern rules, 1870 to 1920. . .I believe that if they had ever foreseen that the whip-handled bats were coming, they would have put a minimum thickness of the bat into the rules a hundred years ago.

My suggested rules change #24 would be to create an economic incentive for teams to play at a better pace. The way it would work is something like this. You can create a simple formula that predicts or correlates with the time of a game; maybe you can't, but I sure as hell could. The base formula would be something like 2.5 times the number of half-innings in the game, plus 1 minute for each hitter who comes to the plate in the game. An average game might be 18 half-innings; that's 45 minutes, plus 80 batters, that's 125 minutes; the "schedule time" is 125 minutes, or 2:05.

Then you create a rewards system for the team, based on the distribution of TV money, or maybe based on allowable money to be spent in the free agent draft, or based on modifications of the payroll tax levels. . . whatever. If the game is actually played in 2:05, then that's ten points into the system for each team. If the game takes twice that long—4 hours and 10 minutes—then that's zero points into the system for each team. Between 2:05 and 4:10, each team gets some number of "pace of play credit points" between zero and ten. That part of the system would be easy to figure out.

Some of you who are not really paying attention will start to object that this would penalize teams for getting runners on base or for extra inning games, but that's not true at all. If you have extra baserunners that means necessarily and inevitably that you have extra hitters, and the base line is extended every time somebody gets on base. If you play a 12-inning game in which 110 batters go to the plate—such things do happen—then the base line would be not 2:05, but 2:50. There's a real problem with the proposal, but that's not it.

It creates an economic incentive for the team NOT to waste time. If, by playing at a crisp pace, the team is allowed to spend more money in the free agent draft, the front office will tell the manager "Hey, we're in 27th place in the pace of play points. We're going to be a big disadvantage after the draft if we don't move that along. You've got to get these guys to stop wasting time." A pitcher who works slowly on the mound is trying to sign a free agent contract; somebody tells him "You cost your team $1.6 million last year by pitching so slowly. We just can't afford that."

That's not actually how salary negotiations go; that's a naïve person's idea of how negotiations go. The way that negotiations REALLY go is, if you want the guy, you pay what the market says he costs. But anyway, the message WILL get through to the players that you're reducing your own market value if you waste time, because time is money.

Here's the real problem with the idea. In order to make it have very much impact, the amount of money involved would have to be enormous. Getting back to the pitcher who cost his team $1.6 million by dilly-dallying around on the mound. . .in order for that to be real, you'd have to have a $10 million delta per team; you'd have to have some teams getting $20 million MORE than other teams either out of the TV money or in allowable bonuses or whatever. And in order to have a $10 million standard deviation on the team level, you'd have to have a genuinely enormous pool of money—even for baseball, where enormous pools of money are the norm rather than the exception.

It might work, though; sometimes very small incentive pools can be surprisingly effective at changing behavior, particularly if the rewards for the behavior you are trying to get rid of are themselves not very significant.

That idea would encourage *teams* not to waste time, and would rely on the teams to pass the message on to the players. But one way to directly encourage *players* not to waste time would be to restore (and strengthen) the start-of-inning curfews. Many cities used to have curfews saying (by law) that a baseball team could not start an inning at 1:00 in the morning, and the leagues used to have curfews as well.

Suppose that you had a rule saying that no inning of a nine-inning game may start more than three and a half hours after the start of the game. In other words, if the game starts at 7:30, you can't start an inning after eleven o'clock, unless you are in extra innings by then, in which case you can continue to play.

I suggested three and a half hours, because I want the rule to be more-or-less invisible, but I absolutely believe that if you made the same rule but said two and half hours, 90% of games would be completed without any problem. Why? *Because baseball players do not want to have suspended games hanging over their heads*. Nobody wants to get to the park two hours early so that we can finish last night's game before we play today's game. If it's the last game of the series, that's WAY worse; if it is the last game of the series, then having a suspended game may mean the loss of an off day, or it may mean unnecessary travel AND the loss of an off day. A player who wastes time and causes the game to run past the curfew is going to be *really* unpopular with his teammates.

Of course, there are two problems with this proposed rule. One is that you probably couldn't put it in place without the acquiescence of the player's union, and the players wouldn't like it. The even worse problem is that it might occasionally cause a situation in which the fans who pay to see a game do not get to see the end of the game because it hits curfew. Three and a half hours, you're NEVER going to hit the curfew, so that's not really an issue; all it would mean is that there are no nine-inning games lasting four hours. That rule puts the burden of playing at a decent pace directly on the players—and I have no doubt that they would respond to the change, and, after a year or so, would be very glad that they had made the change. The players would enjoy having the games get over with an hour earlier, once they got used to the idea.

My proposed rules change #26 is almost off the topic, not quite: an umpire's decision on a stolen base attempt is not an appealable play. He's called safe, he's safe; he's called out, he's out.

You probably all know why that might be better. Replays on that particular play tend to expose little tiny things that the naked eye could never see. The runner's foot comes off the bag for a twentieth of a second; you can see it on replay, so they call him out. It seems silly to me; it seems silly to a lot of people. Changing that rule would save a little time, because (a) you wouldn't have appeal plays on those, and (b) you wouldn't have people holding up the game while they decide whether to appeal.

Now, #27. I have to say up front that I honestly and sincerely do favor this rules change, although I acknowledge that it violates the premise of this article, which is that we're talking about rules adjustments which are essentially invisible to the fans. This one isn't; it's a significant rules change.

The rule for the last 120 years or so has been, as all of you know, that a foul ball is a strike, unless it would be the third strike, in which case the foul ball is a non-event, unless it was bunt try, in which case it is a third strike after all.

That rule was fine 50 years ago. It was OK 20 years ago. It doesn't work anymore. It needs to be fixed.

The reason that the rule needs to be fixed is that the hitters have gotten too good for that rule to work the way it used to work. The pitchers today are dramatically better than the pitchers of 50 years ago at hitting the corners with the pitch. Because they are so much better at hitting the corners of the zone, there are many fewer pitches than there used to be in the heart of the zone.

Pitches in the heart of the zone tend to be put in play. Pitches on the edges of the zone tend to be fouled off. At the same time, the hitters have gotten to be dramatically better than they were 50 years ago at spoiling those on-the-black pitches. Comparing baseball now to baseball even 20 years ago, there are many, many more foul balls on two-strike pitches. It slows down the game.

This is what the rule needs to be, given the talents of modern players. When a batter has two strikes and fouls off a pitch, that's a non-event—once. But if he gets to two strikes and then fouls off <u>two</u> pitches, that's a strikeout.

The reason that the rule needs to be changed is that hitters today are simply too damned good at fouling off borderline pitches that they can't hit hard. They're not really trying to put them into play; they're trying to spoil them, foul them off and wait for the pitcher to make a mistake—or, alternatively, they guess wrong, spoil the pitch, and wait to see if they can guess right on the next pitch.

The game needs to tell them to cut it out, and put the ball in play. We need a moment of truth for the hitter, and that moment of truth needs to arrive quicker. Unfortunately, the short-term consequence of this rule—if it were to be adopted, which obviously it is not going to be anytime soon—but the short-term effect would be that strikeout totals would explode, and batting averages would drop. That's not what we want, to drive strikeouts up. We want to drive strikeouts down, and batting averages up.

But what I believe would happen is that strikeouts in the short term would go up so much that hitters would realize that they simply HAD to adjust. Hitters use a "safety swing" to protect themselves once it is too late to take a full cut at the ball—but the one-foul-allowed rule would limit the hitter's ability to do that, thus force him to rely on his regular swing. Once hitters realized that they HAD to adjust, they would cut down their swings, and learn to put the ball in play earlier in the sequence, rather than waiting until moment of truth arrives. The longer-term result would be fewer strikeouts, fewer home runs—and many fewer at bats taking eight or ten or twelve pitches.

Back to mainstream suggestions, #28: back off calling strikes on so many checked swings.

The way that checked swings were called changed very suddenly after video replay became available. Before 1980 cameras with instant replay were much more expensive relative to the overall production, so games were broadcast with two or three cameras, and there was no technology to quickly and routinely look at replays. Once video replay became common, umpires could see that batters often went further than they thought they had—further than the umpires thought they had—before their swings were checked. The percentage of checked swings which were called strikes shot up.

This has contributed a little bit more to the forest fire of strikeouts that we have seen—but why? What I think should be the rule is that if a batter is attempting to slow his bat down before the ball crosses the plate, it's a checked swing. I think too many checked swings are called strikes—and I know that broadcasters almost universally disagree with that, but they disagree with that because they almost universally accept that the line between checked swing and swing has been drawn in the correct place. What I am saying is that it HASN'T been drawn in the correct place, for the best interests of the game, which has too many strikeouts. I'd like to see it re-drawn—and anyway, like it or not, that is one thing that could be done to reduce the avalanche of strikeouts. Or forest fire; whatever.

Well, I am running out of ideas here, and well short of 50; I have one more which is pretty obvious. Suggestion #29: cut the pitcher's mound down by a couple of inches. A high mound feeds strikeouts, obviously. If you have more strikeouts than you want, you have a higher mound than you need.

My 30th and final suggestion is a suggestion not for the teams or for the players, but for the leagues, or for MLB. Set targets. Set goals—publicly identified, publicly acknowledged goals. My suggestion would be that MLB should adopt the following resolution:

> It is the goal of Major League baseball (1) that nine-inning baseball games should be played in an average of two hours, thirty minutes or less, (2) that there should be no more than .75 home runs per team per game, and (3) that there should be no more than 6.5 strikeouts per nine innings. If these goals are not met in any season, aggressive actions will be taken to return the game to its historically normal form.

You can think what you want to think about it, but this is what I believe. Everything that we love about baseball is in its history. It does not actually matter to any of us, in a practical sense, whether our beloved (Red Sox, Royals, Dodgers, Gators, Red-Baiters, Smog-Haters, Third-Raters). . .it does not actually matter to any of us, in a practical sense, whether they win or lose, whether they have a good year or whether they do not. We care about them because we care about them; that's all. There was something that happened in the past that created a thread, and we hang on to that thread until we die. If you invented a new game tomorrow that was better than baseball or basketball or football by every objective measure, you couldn't get 100 people a game to show up and watch, because it would have no history, and because it would have no history it would have no fans.

Whenever you separate baseball from its past, you are at risk of cutting that thread. In my youth, baseball teams hopped from city to city like toads in wet grass, jumping from Philadelphia to Kansas City to Oakland and Boston to Milwaukee to Atlanta. Some of it was necessary and appropriate; the teams had to go where the people had moved to—but it was problematic, at the same time, because it was leaving history behind. For a period of more than 20 years, baseball attendance per game actually declined. Teams were leaving behind fans, to try to convince people who were not fans that they should become fans. It takes a long time. It takes 40, 50 years to build a fan base.

When the strikes happened (1972, 1981, 1994-1995), that cut a lot of people loose from the thread. When the steroid era happened and players started hitting 65, 70 homers a year, that cut a lot of people loose from the thread.

A certain amount of change is necessary; it is fresh water flowing into the lake, and without that change, without that fresh water, the lake would turn stale. But at the same time, everything we love about the game is in its past. If it changes too quickly, too fast, it loses its past, and it will lose its fans.

People adopt radical and harmful "solutions" to problems—stuff like cutting the games to seven innings, or going to three balls for a walk and two for a strikeout, or banning defensive shifts—because they don't see that there are transparent, non-invasive ways to address the same issues. Let's try a scalpel before we bring out the bone saw.

When you say "No no no; baseball can never change, everything has to stay the same," what you are really doing is ignoring the changes that ARE happening. If you can't tweak the rules, if you don't tweak the rules, you're just rolling over and allowing the game to go weird on you. Baseball has very real problems, but the aesthetic problems can be solved at this point with aspirins and band aids and exercise programs and better nutrition. Let's look over the options, try to see the whole field of options, and fix what needs to be fixed.

Sneak Peek at *The Fielding Bible – Volume V*

John Dewan, Mark Simon and Brian Reiff

Coming in the spring of 2020: *The Fielding Bible – Volume V.* This is a continuation of the series that began in 2006. The most important part of this new volume is a major update to the Defensive Runs Saved (DRS) system.

In the Fielding Bible series Baseball Info Solutions' mission has been to continuously improve upon our understanding of defensive metrics. This new update of the DRS system will feature two major things:

1) Evaluating defensive performance for individual fielders on shift plays
2) Breaking the DRS system into PARTs

The current DRS system evaluates shift plays purely as team defense and attributes runs saved or lost to the team overall. With this update the new system will now also evaluate how individual players perform defensively on shifts. For example, when the shortstop is positioned to the right of second base, how does his range compare to other shortstops? Heretofore in the current system, a given shortstop's superlative range on shift plays was counted in Team DRS. In the new system, we will measure each shortstop separately and attribute positive and negative values based on his range and throwing on shift plays directly to the player.

PART stands for **P**ositioning, **A**ir Balls, **R**ange, and **T**hrowing. It allows us to break the Defensive Runs Saved system into parts. With the new system we can now isolate each of these elements to evaluate these individual skills for each fielder. One of the key aspects of this is isolating how well a player is positioned, which is largely controlled by his team, from the other components that go into making plays, which are under a player's control.

In 2013, Baseball Info Solutions began tracking pre-pitch infielder positioning from video, the first comprehensive effort of its kind. Building off that data, it was possible to construct this new system to evaluate infield defense.

An infielder's Defensive Runs Saved total is now the sum of

His **Air Ball** Runs Saved
His **Range** Runs Saved
His **Throwing** Runs Saved.

Positioning, which was combined with Range in the previous version of Defensive Runs Saved, is now its own component. In the new system Positioning is added to a team's Runs Saved total but is no longer part of a player's total.

However, we do note that individual players can have great instincts and can play a role in their own positioning, so we have elected to calculate and share individual Positioning numbers as well, even though they are no longer included in player totals in the new DRS system. While seasons before 2013 will consist of all four elements of PART, contemporary seasons include just the Air balls, Range, and Throwing (ART).

Results

Parse through the sneak peek leaderboards on the next few pages and you can see the impact the changes had on player's numbers. In some cases, the changes were small. In others, they were larger.

Let's look at one that was in-between. Cardinals second baseman Kolten Wong led his position with 14 Runs Saved under the current system. He remains on top of the leaderboard with 19 Runs Saved in the PART system.

Wong's team positioning numbers indicate the Cardinals did a good job knowing how to put him in the best position to make plays. But that is now factored out of his individual total. With positioning out of the mix, Wong received

Non-Shift Plays
7 Runs Saved for Range
-1 Runs Saved for Throwing

Shift Plays
10 Runs Saved for Range
3 Runs Saved for Throwing

Adding those four together gives Wong 19 Runs Saved. Wong loses a run for his defense against balls hit in the air but gets that run back from his work on Double Plays and our Good Fielding Play/Defensive Misplay & Errors system. Wong comes out of this with 19 Defensive Runs Saved.

For those wondering, Wong's excellent numbers in defensive shifts makes sense given that the Cardinals doubled their shift usage from last season and increased how often they got outs when ground balls and bunts were hit to the right of second base by left-handed batters against their shifts (from 77%, which ranked last in the majors in 2018 to 81%, which ranked 19th).

Let's look at one of the leaders with the most intrigue, Athletics third baseman Matt Chapman. Chapman goes from 18 Runs Saved in the current version to 34 in the new system using PART. In this case, PART strips out the penalty Chapman was getting for being positioned where he was.

The Athletics position their third baseman differently than other teams, playing him closer to the third base line. Chapman was able to make many highly-challenging plays along the line that others can't make because they don't have Chapman's arm. And he can recover enough to make plays going to his left as well. But he is now no longer penalized for balls hit that were impossible to reach because of where he was playing, that would have been more likely reachable from a typical third baseman position.

Chapman receives

Non-Shift Plays
11 Runs Saved for range*
10 Runs Saved for throwing*

Shift Plays
8 Runs Saved for range
1 Run Saved for throwing

Chapman receives a combined 21 Runs Saved here, up from 14 in the current version of Runs Saved.

Those take Chapman to 30 Runs Saved. He adds four more combining Good Fielding Plays & Misplays, Bunts, and Double Play Runs Saved. That gets him to 34 Runs Saved.

At shortstop, Javier Baez and Paul DeJong make big jumps, vaulting ahead of Nick Ahmed into the top two spots on the Runs Saved leaderboard. In both cases, this is a product of their work in shifts. Baez gets a 10-run boost and finished with 26 Runs Saved. DeJong jumps by 11 runs to 24. There's value to be found in playing your shortstop up the middle, to the right of second base, or in short right field (which the Cubs did with Baez) if that player can effectively make plays (which both do).

The order of the top five teams in Defensive Runs Saved changes only slightly, with the Astros moving up one spot to third place and the Cardinals dropping one to fourth. The Indians and Yankees received the biggest run boost, each increasing by 14 runs (the Yankees rank 20th in Runs Saved). The White Sox suffered the biggest negative run impact, dropping 14 runs (they rank 26th in Runs Saved).

Most Defensive Runs Saved – PART System

1. Dodgers   135
2. Diamondbacks   118
3. Astros   96
4. Cardinals   94
5. Indians   84

Fewest Defensive Runs Saved – PART System

30. Orioles   -97
29. Tigers   -90
T-27. Mets   -87
T-27 Mariners   -87
26. White Sox   -63

In Greater Detail

The crux of the PART system involves the estimation of three distinct out probabilities based on different sets of information combined with the binary outcome of the play (out, or not out). Those four points are defined as:

A – The chance that the play will be made given only information about the batted ball (trajectory, location, and velocity) and the batter (speed)

B – The chance that the play will be made given information about the batted ball (trajectory, location, and velocity), the batter (speed), and the initial positioning of the fielders relative to the ball in play

C – The chance that the play will be made at the point that the fielder obtains the ball given the distance he has to throw and how long he has to complete the play before the batter/runner reaches safely

D – Whether the play was made (1) or was not made (0)

The differences between these out probabilities represent the portion of a play attributable to positioning, range, and throwing, respectively.

Positioning = B - A
Range = C - B
Throwing = D - C

There were several other factors we chose to consider and handle differently in the new PART system.

One immediate benefit of the PART system is that we can now evaluate **infielders' performances on shift plays** rather than disregarding them entirely in Defensive Runs Saved, as the current system does.

Given the dramatic increases in shift usage in recent seasons, thousands of plays each year had been previously excluded from individual player ratings due to the current system's inability to separate the player and team positioning efforts from his range and throwing contributions on the play. Since the new system accomplishes just that, we can evaluate these plays without the results becoming unreasonable.

Also, the current system handles short liners similarly to how it handles pop-ups, even though they are very different kinds of plays. However, the new system now treats short liners very similarly to ground balls (specifically, hard ground balls) and separates the positioning, range, and throwing components identically on these plays. Pop ups are still treated separately and are not split into positioning, range, and throwing components but are included in Defensive Runs Saved totals.

One thing we often get asked about is fielder overlap (for example, is one player "stealing" plays from another?). Even if two fielders are in position to make the play, knowing their position, specifically their relative depth, can help us out. We can assume that shallower-positioned fielders have a chance to act on the play before deeper-positioned fielders.

This assumption allows us to make a statement about one fielder even though another fielder might have made the play. For example, a third baseman can get penalized for not making a play that goes by him, regardless of whether his shortstop teammate made the play and bailed him out or not. Achieving this additional independence is a big step for our accuracy in evaluating fielders in a neutral context, without the benefit/penalty of having a good or bad fielder next to them.

When we developed Defensive Runs Saved in early 2009 (in The Fielding Bible – Volume II) and evaluated the run impact of plays back to 2003, we found that each ground ball play saved an average of .75 runs for the team. However, we have updated the PART system to use a dynamic plays-to-runs multiplier rather than a static one. The new multiplier not only depends on the league's run environment but also on the type of batted ball being considered.

For instance, a hard grounder down the first base line can turn into a costly double or triple if not nabbed by the first baseman, while a grounder in the first base/second base hole is far more likely to trickle to the right fielder for a routine single. The PART system distinguishes between these plays and applies an appropriate multiplier for each.

Lastly, we should point out that every number is centered (the sums for every player at a position add to zero), because we're comparing each player to league-average performance. The exception is team positioning on shifts. That number represents how well teams were positioned on shifts as compared to a basis of all plays rather than just shifts (and therefore it shouldn't be centered).

Most Important Takeaways

> • Positioning is no longer factored into a player's
>   Defensive Runs Saved total
> • This system allows for the evaluation of all infield plays,
>   not just ones involving an unshifted defense
> • We have transitioned from evaluating "How often did a
>   player make that play?" to "How often did a player
>   make that play *given where he was positioned*?" with
>   the PART system
> • The result is a more accurate overall depiction of
>   defensive *performance*

Summary

When it comes to evaluating defense, we're not yet quite all of the way there, but we're getting closer. Each volume of The Fielding Bible is another step. The introduction of the PART system provides a more accurate reflection of defensive performance.

Take a look at the sneak-peek data on the accompanying pages and think about it from the perspective of having watched that team or player. Hopefully, you'll come away better informed about how well or poorly that player played in the field in 2019.

You're grounded

The Cardinals defense had the highest out rate on ground balls and bunts, converting 78% of them into outs in 2019. They were two percentage points ahead of the next-closest teams, the Dodgers and Astros.

Gio Gonzalez and Justin Verlander were the starting pitchers who benefited most. Their infields converted 82% of ground balls and bunts into outs."

New DRS System Sneak Peek

First Basemen - Regulars

| Player Info | | Team Positioning Runs Saved | | New Defensive Runs Saved | | | | | | | | | | | | Current DRS |
Player	Tm	No Shift	Shift	No Shift Rng	Thr	R/T	Shift Rng	Thr	R/T	ART Air	Rng	Thr	Totals ART	Other	Total	Total
Olson, Matt	Oak	-3	-1	13	1	14	3	-1	2	0	16	0	17	1	18	13
Walker, Christian	Ari	3	1	7	-2	5	8	-2	6	1	15	-4	11	0	11	9
Votto, Joey	Cin	-1	-1	3	4	7	2	1	3	0	5	5	10	0	10	7
Belt, Brandon	SF	5	2	-1	1	0	3	1	4	0	2	2	4	2	6	4
Gurriel, Yuli	Hou	0	1	1	0	2	4	0	5	-1	6	1	6	0	6	0
Cron, C.J.	Min	0	0	0	2	2	2	1	3	0	2	2	4	0	4	3
Murphy, Daniel	Col	1	-1	-2	2	0	3	0	2	0	1	2	2	1	3	2
Rizzo, Anthony	ChC	-2	-1	-1	0	-1	-2	-2	-3	1	-2	-1	-2	4	2	3
Thames, Eric	Mil	0	2	1	1	2	-1	0	0	0	0	1	2	0	2	2
Goldschmidt, Paul	StL	4	-1	-4	2	-1	-1	2	0	1	-5	4	0	1	1	4
Santana, Carlos	Cle	-1	1	3	-1	2	2	-1	1	0	5	-2	3	-2	1	-1
Freeman, Freddie	Atl	4	2	-2	1	-1	0	1	1	0	-2	2	0	1	1	5
Choi, Ji-Man	TB	-2	-1	0	-1	-1	0	-1	-1	0	0	-2	-2	2	0	-1
Hoskins, Rhys	Phi	-1	1	-2	0	-2	2	0	2	0	0	0	0	0	0	-2
Pujols, Albert	LAA	-1	-1	-3	0	-3	1	0	1	-1	-2	0	-3	2	-1	-1
Davis, Chris	Bal	-1	4	1	0	1	-2	-1	-2	0	-1	0	-1	0	-1	0
Hosmer, Eric	SD	-2	-2	2	-2	1	-1	0	0	0	2	-1	0	-3	-3	-4
O'Hearn, Ryan	KC	-1	0	-3	1	-2	0	0	0	0	-3	1	-2	-1	-3	-4
Alonso, Pete	NYM	-1	1	-3	2	-1	1	0	2	0	-2	3	1	-4	-3	-6
Smoak, Justin	Tor	-1	1	-3	1	-2	-6	1	-5	0	-9	2	-7	0	-7	-3
Abreu, Jose	CWS	1	2	-3	-1	-4	-5	1	-3	0	-8	1	-8	0	-8	-4
Bell, Josh	Pit	0	0	-1	-1	-2	-5	0	-5	0	-6	-1	-8	-1	-9	-5

Second Basemen - Regulars

| Player Info | | Team Positioning Runs Saved | | New Defensive Runs Saved | | | | | | | | | | | | Current DRS |
Player	Tm	No Shift	Shift	No Shift Rng	Thr	R/T	Shift Rng	Thr	R/T	ART Air	Rng	Thr	Totals ART	Other	Total	Total
Wong, Kolten	StL	8	5	7	-1	6	10	3	13	-1	17	2	18	1	19	14
Albies, Ozzie	Atl	-4	5	11	0	11	-2	-2	-4	2	9	-3	9	1	10	8
Sanchez, Yolmer	CWS	5	12	-6	7	0	-2	1	0	-1	-8	8	-1	6	5	11
Castro, Starlin	Mia	-2	6	3	1	5	2	-2	-1	-1	5	-1	3	0	3	-2
Schoop, Jonathan	Min	-1	8	1	0	2	-5	6	1	-2	-3	6	1	-1	0	0
Altuve, Jose	Hou	0	7	-2	1	-1	4	-2	3	-1	2	0	1	-2	-1	-2
Rengifo, Luis	LAA	1	6	1	1	2	-3	1	-2	1	-2	2	1	-2	-1	3
Frazier, Adam	Pit	5	5	-3	3	0	-3	0	-3	0	-6	4	-3	2	-1	6
McMahon, Ryan	Col	1	1	1	-1	1	-3	-2	-5	0	-2	-3	-4	1	-3	3
Hernandez, Cesar	Phi	4	0	1	0	1	-2	-3	-5	5	-1	-3	1	-4	-3	6
Cano, Robinson	NYM	0	2	-7	0	-6	1	0	1	-2	-6	0	-7	2	-5	-6
Gordon, Dee	Sea	-3	6	-2	1	-1	2	-1	1	-1	0	0	-2	-3	-5	-8
Kipnis, Jason	Cle	-1	5	-3	-1	-4	3	-2	0	-2	0	-4	-5	0	-5	-7
Dozier, Brian	Was	-1	2	0	-3	-3	-5	3	-2	-2	-5	0	-7	2	-5	-5
Panik, Joe	TOT	2	3	-4	2	-2	0	-1	-1	-1	-3	1	-3	-3	-6	-3
Odor, Rougned	Tex	-5	3	1	-4	-3	-1	-3	-4	0	0	-7	-7	0	-7	-8
Profar, Jurickson	Oak	-7	4	3	-5	-2	-10	-1	-12	5	-8	-6	-9	-5	-14	-10

New DRS System Sneak Peek

Third Basemen - Regulars

Player Info		Team Positioning Runs Saved		New Defensive Runs Saved												Current DRS Total
		No Shift	Shift	No Shift			Shift			ART			Totals			
Player	Tm	No Shift	Shift	Rng	Thr	R/T	Rng	Thr	R/T	Air	Rng	Thr	ART	Other	Total	Total
Chapman, Matt	Oak	-10	-3	11	10	21	8	1	9	0	19	11	30	4	34	18
Arenado, Nolan	Col	2	-3	6	0	7	8	3	12	0	14	4	18	0	18	8
Donaldson, Josh	Atl	-2	0	11	2	14	-3	1	-1	1	9	4	13	2	15	15
Bregman, Alex	Hou	0	-2	6	0	6	3	-1	1	0	9	-1	8	0	8	7
Longoria, Evan	SF	2	1	6	0	6	2	-1	0	1	7	-1	7	0	7	7
Carpenter, Matt	StL	-2	-2	1	2	3	5	-1	4	0	6	1	7	-1	6	0
Ramirez, Jose	Cle	1	-1	0	3	3	2	0	1	0	2	2	4	0	4	3
Seager, Kyle	Sea	-6	-2	-3	3	0	-5	3	-2	0	-7	6	-1	4	3	-1
Machado, Manny	SD	-2	0	4	0	5	-2	-1	-3	0	2	0	2	0	2	5
Escobar, Eduardo	Ari	4	2	-1	2	1	-3	1	-2	0	-4	3	-1	3	2	8
Rendon, Anthony	Was	2	0	-4	3	-1	0	0	0	0	-3	3	0	2	2	2
Urshela, Giovanny	NYY	-3	-5	2	-1	2	0	1	1	-1	3	0	2	-1	1	-4
Moustakas, Mike	Mil	-3	0	5	-3	2	-4	-1	-5	0	1	-4	-3	2	-1	0
Franco, Maikel	Phi	0	0	-2	-2	-4	3	-2	1	-1	1	-4	-4	2	-2	-3
Turner, Justin	LAD	0	1	0	-7	-7	2	2	4	0	1	-4	-3	0	-3	-7
Frazier, Todd	NYM	2	0	-6	2	-4	-3	0	-3	0	-9	2	-7	4	-3	1
Suarez, Eugenio	Cin	4	2	3	-3	0	-4	0	-4	0	0	-3	-3	-1	-4	2
Moncada, Yoan	CWS	-3	1	-5	3	-3	-4	3	-1	0	-9	6	-3	-1	-4	-7
Ruiz, Rio	Bal	0	0	1	0	1	-6	-2	-8	0	-5	-2	-7	2	-5	2
Dozier, Hunter	KC	-4	-1	-5	-1	-5	7	-2	5	0	2	-3	-1	-4	-5	-14
Cabrera, Asdrubal	TOT	0	0	-2	-3	-4	-1	1	0	0	-3	-2	-5	-1	-6	-4
Bryant, Kris	ChC	-1	-2	-5	1	-4	1	-2	-1	0	-4	-1	-5	-2	-7	-7
Sano, Miguel	Min	-2	-1	1	-3	-2	-6	0	-5	0	-4	-3	-7	0	-7	-5
Guerrero Jr., Vlad	Tor	6	1	-4	-2	-6	2	-3	-1	0	-1	-5	-7	-2	-9	-3
Devers, Rafael	Bos	4	1	-11	6	-5	1	-3	-2	0	-11	3	-8	-3	-11	-6
Moran, Colin	Pit	0	0	-10	-2	-12	-7	-2	-8	-1	-16	-4	-21	0	-21	-13

Shortstops - Regulars

Player Info		Team Positioning Runs Saved		New Defensive Runs Saved												Current DRS Total
		No Shift	Shift	No Shift			Shift			ART			Totals			
Player	Tm	No Shift	Shift	Rng	Thr	R/T	Rng	Thr	R/T	Air	Rng	Thr	ART	Other	Total	Total
Baez, Javier	ChC	-1	0	0	10	10	9	1	10	-1	9	12	19	7	26	15
DeJong, Paul	StL	0	-3	11	3	14	12	-1	11	-1	23	2	24	0	24	14
Ahmed, Nick	Ari	5	13	9	0	9	-1	7	6	2	8	7	17	0	17	18
Story, Trevor	Col	3	4	5	4	10	3	0	4	-1	9	5	12	4	16	17
Semien, Marcus	Oak	0	2	11	-7	4	9	2	11	5	21	-6	20	-6	14	5
Simmons, Andrelton	LAA	2	8	9	4	12	-3	3	0	0	6	7	13	-1	12	14
Lindor, Francisco	Cle	4	3	-3	4	1	5	0	5	1	2	3	7	4	11	9
Adames, Willy	TB	3	19	5	-1	4	2	1	3	1	7	0	8	3	11	13
Mondesi, Adalberto	KC	1	-2	6	0	6	-2	-1	-3	2	4	-1	5	2	7	10
Iglesias, Jose	Cin	1	3	4	1	5	-3	1	-2	1	1	2	4	2	6	8
Galvis, Freddy	TOT	-3	5	-1	-1	-2	0	2	3	1	-1	2	2	2	4	-2
Rojas, Miguel	Mia	3	5	3	4	7	-4	-1	-5	1	0	3	3	0	3	12
Swanson, Dansby	Atl	-5	0	-3	3	0	1	0	1	2	-2	3	3	0	3	-3
Seager, Corey	LAD	2	13	3	1	4	-6	3	-3	0	-3	4	0	3	3	9
Arcia, Orlando	Mil	-3	-1	7	-2	5	0	-4	-5	-1	7	-7	0	2	2	3
Turner, Trea	Was	-3	-1	-7	1	-5	5	1	7	-2	-2	3	-1	0	-1	-10
Andrus, Elvis	Tex	-2	5	0	1	0	-4	3	-1	0	-5	4	-1	-3	-4	-6
Segura, Jean	Phi	0	3	-1	-3	-4	1	0	2	-1	0	-2	-3	-1	-4	-5
Crawford, Brandon	SF	0	8	-1	4	2	1	-5	-4	-1	0	-2	-3	-2	-5	0
Crawford, J.P.	Sea	1	-2	-7	2	-5	-1	2	0	0	-8	3	-4	-1	-5	-5
Newman, Kevin	Pit	-3	3	-5	0	-5	0	-3	-3	1	-5	-3	-8	1	-7	-6
Polanco, Jorge	Min	1	7	3	-4	0	-3	-5	-8	0	0	-9	-8	1	-7	1
Rosario, Amed	NYM	-7	1	-9	6	-3	-4	2	-2	-3	-13	8	-9	-2	-11	-16
Anderson, Tim	CWS	2	3	-18	5	-13	-1	2	1	-2	-19	7	-15	3	-12	-9
Martin Jr., Richie	Bal	0	4	-4	-2	-6	-3	-3	-6	0	-7	-5	-12	-1	-13	-8
Bogaerts, Xander	Bos	-7	1	-9	-2	-11	-1	-1	-2	0	-10	-3	-14	-1	-15	-21

Hall of Fame Monitor

Bill James

The Hall of Fame Monitor is a method which traces its origins back to the 1970s, was remodeled in the 1980s and remodeled again a few years ago. The method is losing relevance over time, but we continue to follow it because it still represents to a certain extent the way that many people think.

What a younger person could not completely process is that, until the mid-1970s, the way that baseball statistics were translated into value was through statistical standards—absolutely, totally, completely, 100%, not 99%. There were no generally accepted or widely published evaluative methods. Of course players were evaluated in part by observation or "fan-scouting", but I am talking about the evaluation of a player's record. If a player met statistical standards or was close to meeting them—standards like a .300 batting average, 100 RBI, 200 hits, 20 wins for a pitcher—then he was regarded a good player. If he met many of those standards and met them on a regular basis, he was regarded as a star.

In modern baseball this becomes less true every year. In modern baseball fans pay less attention to those standards, and evaluate players based on WAR, OPS, OPS+, WHIP, Fielding Runs, Win Shares, Win Probability Added, and a wide variety of other measures. The older method survives, however, because (1) not every fan is a younger fan, and (2) not everybody believes in things like WAR, OPS, OPS+ and all the others.

The Hall of Fame Monitor evaluates in an organized fashion the things that USED to make a player a star—hitting 40 homers, winning a Gold Glove, playing in a World Series, making the All-Star game, hitting .300, getting 3,000 hits, hitting 500 homers, etc. The assumption of the method is that (a) each of those accomplishments makes a contribution toward putting a player in the Hall of Fame, and (b) by studying who is in the Hall and who isn't, we assign weight to each accomplishment—3 points for 100 RBI, 5 points for 200 hits, 2.5 points for hitting .300, etc. As the player goes through his career, we keep track of his total.

This method gives credit for some things, like playing for a World Championship team, winning a Gold Glove, and winning a Cy Young Award, which will be known to you by November 30th of this year, but which are unknown to us when the book went to press. Thus, the totals for certain players will have moved up a little bit since these numbers were figured.

The way the system works is, a player with less than 70 points is not (in general) a serious Hall of Fame candidate, if he retired today. A player with 70 to 99 points is a possible but unlikely Hall of Famer. A player with 100 to 130 points is a likely but not certain Hall of Famer, and a player with 130 or more points is a certain Hall of Famer unless he is touched by a scandal of some sort.

By this method, five active players may be considered to be near-certain Hall of Famers as of now—**Clayton Kershaw, Miguel Cabrera, Justin Verlander, Albert Pujols and Robinson Cano**. Because of Cano's PED suspension, we might pull him off the list and substitute the name of **Mike Trout**, who is at only 115 points that we know of, but (a) moving forward at a good rate, and (b) possibly even higher, if he wins the 2019 American League MVP Award.

As **CC Sabathia** took his last turn around the league in 2019, many commentators assigned him a Hall of Fame plaque. Our method does not show him to be a certain Hall of Famer. It shows him, at 97 points, to be a player who might go in or might not.   The nine most serious Hall of Fame candidates, other than the seven mentioned above, would be:

Bryce Harper and **Mookie Betts**, both 26 years old in mid-summer 2019, and with current totals of 60 and 56, moving upward rapidly.

Nolan Arenado, 28 years old and with 81 points, moving strongly upward every year.

Jose Altuve, 29 years old and with 96 points, in excellent shape to have a complete Hall of Fame resume by his early thirties.

Buster Posey, 32 years old and with 76 points, although not moving rapidly in recent years, and still needing to do some work.

Corey Kluber, David Price and Felix Hernandez, all of them 33 years old and all of them with 77 to 82 points, but all of them needing a comeback.

Max Scherzer, 34 years old, is a nearly certain Hall of Famer, with 125 points.

In addition to those nine we should mention four others. The recently retired **Ichiro Suzuki** appears to be a lock, with 158 points. **Ryan Braun** has 100 points, making him a borderline Hall of Famer; however, because of his PED suspension several years ago, his position may not be as strong as this number suggests. **Craig Kimbrel** is at 93 points; however, I would agree that his actual position is probably not as solid as the Hall of Fame monitor thinks that it is. **Zack Greinke**, 35 years old, shows here with 90 points; however, intuitively, it would seem to me that his position might be stronger than that. The method is a tool to make a comparison; it's not always right.

The chart below gives the Hall of Fame Monitor points for every active player who has 10 or more, arranged by age, and starting with the leaders in each age group.

Hall of Fame Monitor

Player	Age	2019	Career
Cody Bellinger	23	13	21
Roberto Osuna	24	9	24
Carlos Correa	24	0	11
Francisco Lindor	25	8	39
Alex Bregman	25	11	24
Edwin Diaz	25	3	24
Corey Seager	25	6	22
Rougned Odor	25	3	12
Ketel Marte	25	8	11
Joey Gallo	25	0	11
Addison Russell	25	0	10
Bryce Harper	26	8	60
Mookie Betts	26	10	56
Xander Bogaerts	26	14	42
Manny Machado	26	2	40
Jose Ramirez	26	2	27
Javier Baez	26	6	24
Trevor Story	26	9	22
Blake Snell	26	0	18
Aaron Nola	26	6	17
Matt Chapman	26	6	12
Trea Turner	26	4	12
Noah Syndergaard	26	2	12
Josh Bell	26	8	11
Tim Anderson	26	8	10
Gary Sanchez	26	3	10
Mike Trout	27	11	115
Kris Bryant	27	7	42
Christian Yelich	27	13	39
Eugenio Suarez	27	10	20
Nicholas Castellanos	27	7	20
Carlos Martinez	27	1	17
Felipe Vazquez	27	3	16
Aaron Judge	27	0	16
Jorge Soler	27	12	14
Eddie Rosario	27	7	14
Jonathan Schoop	27	0	14
Trey Mancini	27	7	10
Michael Wacha	27	0	10
Nolan Arenado	28	13	81
Gerrit Cole	28	21	44
Trevor Bauer	28	6	20
Marcell Ozuna	28	2	20
Ken Giles	28	2	15
Julio Teheran	28	1	15
Marcus Semien	28	10	14
J.T. Realmuto	28	5	14
Jonathan Villar	28	5	13
Ender Inciarte	28	0	13
Yasiel Puig	28	1	12
Max Muncy	28	8	10
Hansel Robles	28	5	10
Mike Clevinger	28	1	10
Jake Lamb	28	0	10
Joe Panik	28	0	10
Wil Myers	28	0	10
Jose Altuve	29	6	96
Madison Bumgarner	29	5	67
Giancarlo Stanton	29	0	56
Freddie Freeman	29	9	55
Anthony Rizzo	29	5	55
Anthony Rendon	29	14	40
Jeurys Familia	29	1	36
Eric Hosmer	29	1	35
Jean Segura	29	1	28
Kelvin Herrera	29	1	27

Player	Age	2019	Career
Starlin Castro	29	2	24
Trevor Rosenthal	29	0	24
George Springer	29	6	19
Jason Heyward	29	1	18
Brad Hand	29	4	17
Patrick Corbin	29	5	16
Kyle Hendricks	29	1	16
Andrelton Simmons	29	0	15
Raisel Iglesias	29	4	13
Sonny Gray	29	3	13
Will Smith	29	5	11
Scooter Gennett	29	0	11
Travis Shaw	29	0	11
Jackie Bradley Jr.	29	1	10
Mike Montgomery	29	0	10
Chris Sale	30	2	50
DJ LeMahieu	30	12	43
Rick Porcello	30	2	41
Stephen Strasburg	30	14	35
Cody Allen	30	0	33
Elvis Andrus	30	2	29
Whit Merrifield	30	13	28
Alex Colome	30	5	21
Mike Moustakas	30	5	20
Starling Marte	30	4	19
Jose Quintana	30	2	19
Chris Archer	30	0	18
Miles Mikolas	30	1	13
Eduardo Escobar	30	9	12
Shane Greene	30	4	12
Liam Hendriks	30	8	11
Hector Neris	30	4	11
Yasmani Grandal	30	4	11
Corey Dickerson	30	0	10
Clayton Kershaw	31	3	137
Craig Kimbrel	31	0	93
Paul Goldschmidt	31	4	69
Kenley Jansen	31	4	60
J.D. Martinez	31	10	51
Aroldis Chapman	31	5	51
Justin Upton	31	0	38
Dee Gordon	31	0	36
Jacob deGrom	31	10	35
Zack Britton	31	3	35
Khris Davis	31	1	33
Dallas Keuchel	31	0	33
Blake Treinen	31	1	20
Hector Rondon	31	1	18
Bryan Shaw	31	1	17
Mike Minor	31	5	16
Dellin Betances	31	0	16
Trevor Cahill	31	0	16
Mike Leake	31	2	15
Brandon Belt	31	1	15
Brad Boxberger	31	0	15
Wilson Ramos	31	2	13
Kyle Seager	31	0	13
Sam Dyson	31	1	12
David Peralta	31	0	12
Tommy Pham	31	2	11
Jeremy Jeffress	31	0	11
Buster Posey	32	1	76
Andrew McCutchen	32	0	52
Charlie Blackmon	32	10	51
Jose Abreu	32	10	47
Lance Lynn	32	6	33
Jay Bruce	32	0	33
Michael Brantley	32	7	32
Brian Dozier	32	0	32

Player	Age	2019	Career
Brandon Crawford	32	1	27
Pablo Sandoval	32	0	26
Jason Kipnis	32	1	24
Carlos Carrasco	32	0	20
Kirby Yates	32	15	19
Yu Darvish	32	2	19
Derek Holland	32	1	19
Wade Miley	32	2	14
Tanner Roark	32	1	13
Daniel Hudson	32	3	12
Jake McGee	32	0	12
Jeremy Hellickson	32	0	12
Hyun-Jin Ryu	32	7	11
Sean Doolittle	32	3	11
Ivan Nova	32	2	11
Josh Reddick	32	1	11
Alex Avila	32	0	11
Tommy Hunter	32	0	11
Justin Smoak	32	1	10
Felix Hernandez	**33**	**0**	**82**
David Price	33	0	80
Corey Kluber	33	0	77
Carlos Gonzalez	33	0	59
Josh Donaldson	33	6	53
Evan Longoria	33	1	49
Johnny Cueto	33	0	47
Greg Holland	33	0	45
Chris Davis	33	0	44
Adam Jones	33	1	43
Jake Arrieta	33	0	40
Wade Davis	33	1	37
Matt Carpenter	33	0	34
Gio Gonzalez	33	0	32
Carlos Santana	33	7	30
Lorenzo Cain	33	1	27
Asdrubal Cabrera	33	1	24
Jordan Zimmermann	33	0	24
Mark Trumbo	33	0	23
Steve Cishek	33	3	22
Dexter Fowler	33	1	22
Jonathan Lucroy	33	0	21
Todd Frazier	33	0	17
Ian Desmond	33	0	15
Matt Wieters	33	0	15
Jared Hughes	33	1	14
Homer Bailey	33	2	12
Carlos Gomez	33	0	12
Adam Ottavino	33	3	10
Brad Brach	33	1	10
Max Scherzer	**34**	**3**	**125**
Troy Tulowitzki	34	0	60
Mark Melancon	34	2	46
Matt Kemp	34	0	46
Melky Cabrera	34	0	40
Daniel Murphy	34	0	34
Ryan Zimmerman	34	0	34
Ian Kennedy	34	4	33
David Robertson	34	0	29
Jeff Samardzija	34	1	25
Tyler Clippard	34	1	25
Andrew Miller	34	2	24
Tony Watson	34	1	19
Pedro Strop	34	1	17
Justin Turner	34	3	14
Fernando Salas	34	0	14
Jon Jay	34	0	13
Will Harris	34	3	12
Yusmeiro Petit	34	3	11
Brandon Kintzler	34	2	11
Clay Buchholz	34	0	10
Dan Otero	34	0	10
Jonny Venters	34	0	10

Player	Age	2019	Career
Ryan Braun	**35**	**3**	**100**
Zack Greinke	35	8	90
Joey Votto	35	1	87
Dustin Pedroia	35	0	85
Jon Lester	35	2	81
Hanley Ramirez	35	0	76
Cole Hamels	35	1	56
Joakim Soria	35	1	34
Nick Markakis	35	0	34
Alex Gordon	35	1	32
Brian McCann	35	0	32
Martin Prado	35	0	28
Brett Gardner	35	3	21
Anibal Sanchez	35	1	19
Edwin Jackson	35	0	19
Joe Smith	35	0	19
Francisco Liriano	35	1	18
Luke Gregerson	35	0	17
Edinson Volquez	35	0	16
Mark Reynolds	35	0	16
Yuli Gurriel	35	9	13
Jed Lowrie	35	0	13
Clayton Richard	35	0	12
Howie Kendrick	35	0	12
Charlie Morton	35	4	11
Kurt Suzuki	35	0	11
Jerry Blevins	35	0	10
Tony Sipp	35	0	10
Miguel Cabrera	**36**	**1**	**190**
Justin Verlander	36	20	159
Robinson Cano	36	0	132
Yadier Molina	36	1	79
Edwin Encarnacion	36	1	65
Sergio Romo	36	3	39
Ervin Santana	36	0	35
Hunter Pence	36	0	34
Shin-Soo Choo	36	3	29
Russell Martin	36	0	24
Kendrys Morales	36	0	22
J.A. Happ	36	2	21
Darren O'Day	36	0	21
Jason Vargas	36	1	18
Zach Duke	36	0	14
Matt Albers	36	1	11
David Freese	36	0	10
Seunghwan Oh	36	0	10
Adam Wainwright	**37**	**2**	**75**
Ian Kinsler	37	0	49
Oliver Perez	37	1	16
CC Sabathia	**38**	**0**	**97**
Nelson Cruz	38	12	81
Curtis Granderson	38	0	63
Ben Zobrist	38	0	38
Rajai Davis	38	0	13
Pat Neshek	38	0	11
Albert Pujols	**39**	**1**	**243**
Fernando Rodney	**42**	**1**	**58**
Ichiro Suzuki	**45**	**0**	**158**

The Hall of Fame Value Standard

Mark Simon

Last year, Bill James introduced a stat known as Hall of Fame Value that combines Win Shares and Baseball-Reference's Wins Above Replacement to assess whether a player belongs in the Hall of Fame. A career value of about 500 generally indicates Hall of Fame worthiness for position players. Knowing that, we can look at some active position players to ascertain where they stand.

Active position players who have cleared the 500 threshold are Albert Pujols, Miguel Cabrera, Robinson Cano, Joey Votto, Yadier Molina, and Mike Trout. As for pitchers, Justin Verlander (520.8) and Zack Greinke (511.0) each crossed 500 points in 2019.

Yes, Trout is already Hall-of-Fame caliber even though he's not yet Hall of Fame-eligible. But good news, he will be once he steps on the field for the first time in 2020, his 10th MLB season. His combination of power (285 home runs), speed (200 stolen bases) and overall offensive ability (1.000 OPS) are at a legendary level. Though it may be a surprise that he's reached the number already, he's shown himself to be more than worthy.

You may also be surprised to see that Clayton Kershaw (473.2) and Max Scherzer (426.4) aren't quite there yet, though in Kershaw's case one more season like 2019 will push him over the line.

Transitioning to this year's ballot, Derek Jeter (702.6) may join teammate Mariano Rivera as a unanimous selection. There are two other newcomers whose numbers indicate Hall of Fame worthiness, despite public perception not necessarily matching up—Bobby Abreu (596.1) and Jason Giambi (527.1).

Abreu was a better player than you probably think he was. He hit .291/.395/.475 with 2,470 hits, 288 home runs and 400 stolen bases in an 18-

year career. He also ranks in the top-20 all-time in walks. The numbers indicate he's worth a closer look, and not immediate dismissal, by voters.

Giambi will be another candidate whose connections to PEDs likely cost him votes. He hit .277/.399/.516 with 440 home runs in 20 seasons.

In all, 14 players on this year's ballot cleared the 500-point mark, headed by Barry Bonds and Roger Clemens (for whom, like Giambi, other factors impact their candidacy). If you read Bill James' article on who the public would want to go in the Hall of Fame you'll see that the public really wants to see Barry Bonds and Roger Clemens in the Hall, despite PEDs. And they want Pete Rose and Shoeless Joe Jackson there as well. Another candidate on the ballot who was on Bill's last list of having overwhelming public support is Larry Walker.

Walker's 598.8 Hall of Fame Value is the second-highest among current candidates with no PED connection (Derek Jeter is first). Like one of his former teammates, Todd Helton, Walker is likely hurt by voter perception of the impact that playing at Coors Field had on his numbers. Nonetheless, his statistics are impressive, a .313/.400/.565 slash line, with 383 home runs and 230 stolen bases. He also won seven Gold Gloves. Walker has one last chance on the ballot, but his vote percentage needs to jump by more than 20 percentage points for him to get elected.

The Hall of Fame gives us plenty to talk about and plenty to analyze every year. Perhaps new voting analysis will make Walker or one of these other players the next Bert Blyleven or Edgar Martinez, for whom public and statistical support changed enough minds to lead to induction.

Hall of Fame Values by Age Group

Player	Age	2019 Season			Career		
		Win Shares	WAR	HoF Value	Win Shares	WAR	HoF Value
Soto, Juan	20	24	4.7	42.6	39	7.6	69.4
Acuna Jr., Ronald	21	28	5.5	50.0	47	9.6	85.4
Albies, Ozzie	22	29	4.8	48.1	55	9.9	94.4
Torres, Gleyber	22	28	3.9	43.7	47	6.8	74.4
Devers, Rafael	22	24	5.3	45.2	40	6.6	66.4
Bellinger, Cody	23	31	9.0	67.1	73	17.4	142.7
Flaherty, Jack	23	17	6.0	40.9	26	8.2	58.9
Correa, Carlos	24	13	2.9	24.6	95	21.0	178.9
Benintendi, Andrew	24	15	1.7	21.9	62	8.7	97.0
Osuna, Roberto	24	14	2.0	22.0	61	8.7	95.7
Marquez, German	24	13	3.8	28.2	41	12.6	91.3
Moncada, Yoan	24	23	4.6	41.4	42	8.1	74.5
Mazara, Nomar	24	10	0.7	12.7	52	1.8	59.2
Margot, Manuel	24	9	1.8	16.3	33	6.4	58.4
Ohtani, Shohei	24	12	2.5	21.8	32	5.2	52.8
Lindor, Francisco	25	19	4.7	38.0	111	28.6	225.3
Bregman, Alex	25	31	8.4	64.4	100	20.8	183.3
Seager, Corey	25	20	4.0	36.0	90	17.8	161.0
Marte, Ketel	25	29	6.9	56.8	67	13.9	122.8
Odor, Rougned	25	13	-0.3	11.9	79	6.4	104.4
Polanco, Jorge	25	26	5.7	48.8	61	10.2	101.8
Russell, Addison	25	5	0.1	5.5	53	12.1	101.4
Olson, Matt	25	21	5.1	41.3	49	12.0	97.1
DeJong, Paul	25	20	4.1	36.4	49	10.6	91.5
Severino, Luis	25	1	0.6	3.4	39	12.3	88.1
Gallo, Joey	25	11	3.0	22.9	42	8.1	74.6
Buxton, Byron	25	11	3.1	23.5	33	9.9	72.7
Berrios, Jose	25	13	3.3	26.2	35	7.5	65.2
Hader, Josh	25	16	2.6	26.4	36	6.6	62.2
Swanson, Dansby	25	15	0.9	18.6	44	3.7	58.8
Diaz, Edwin	25	3	-0.6	0.8	39	4.8	58.2
Betts, Mookie	26	25	6.8	52.3	147	42.0	314.9
Machado, Manny	26	18	3.1	30.3	159	36.9	306.7
Harper, Bryce	26	27	4.2	43.6	179	31.5	305.1
Ramirez, Jose	26	17	3.3	30.3	108	25.3	209.3
Bogaerts, Xander	26	25	5.2	45.8	117	19.9	196.8
Story, Trevor	26	22	6.4	47.8	74	17.8	145.0
Baez, Javier	26	19	4.8	38.2	75	16.6	141.6
Chapman, Matt	26	25	6.7	51.8	61	18.5	134.8
Nola, Aaron	26	14	3.9	29.7	55	19.6	133.5
Turner, Trea	26	19	2.4	28.5	78	12.8	129.0
Conforto, Michael	26	20	3.5	34.0	75	12.8	126.2
Sanchez, Gary	26	15	3.1	27.4	50	11.3	114.0
Syndergaard, Noah	26	9	2.2	17.8	49	15.4	110.4
Rodriguez, Eduardo	26	15	5.9	38.8	45	13.5	99.2
Kepler, Max	26	19	4.0	34.8	52	10.8	95.2
Sano, Miguel	26	17	3.1	29.3	62	8.0	93.9
Anderson, Tim	26	19	4.0	34.9	49	10.2	89.9
Snell, Blake	26	6	1.4	11.6	39	10.8	82.4
Bell, Josh	26	24	2.9	35.8	58	5.1	78.5
Freeland, Kyle	26	0	-0.8	-3.0	32	10.8	75.3
Schwarber, Kyle	26	18	2.3	27.0	53	4.9	73.5
Anderson, Brian	26	13	3.8	28.2	42	7.6	72.5
Sanchez, Aaron	26	2	-0.3	1.0	36	8.8	71.4
Davies, Zach	26	11	2.5	21.0	35	8.0	67.0
Santana, Domingo	26	11	0.4	12.8	49	4.2	65.8
Hoskins, Rhys	26	18	1.5	23.8	50	3.9	65.7
DeShields, Delino	26	10	1.3	15.3	44	5.4	65.6
Nimmo, Brandon	26	8	0.9	11.7	38	6.3	63.4
Franco, Maikel	26	7	-0.8	3.8	57	1.6	63.3
Smith, Mallex	26	8	-0.1	7.7	38	6.0	62.1
Castillo, Luis	26	16	4.4	33.5	28	8.5	62.1
Bradley, Archie	26	9	1.0	13.0	34	5.1	54.5
Bundy, Dylan	26	6	2.3	15.2	27	6.8	54.2
Rodon, Carlos	26	1	0.1	1.3	27	6.6	53.5
Walker, Taijuan	26	0	0.1	0.2	27	5.8	50.2

Hall of Fame Values by Age Group

Player	Age	2019 Season			Career		
		Win Shares	WAR	HoF Value	Win Shares	WAR	HoF Value
Trout, Mike	**27**	**33**	**8.3**	**66.1**	**299**	**72.5**	**589.0**
Yelich, Christian	27	33	7.1	61.3	156	33.6	290.2
Bryant, Kris	27	23	3.6	37.4	126	25.1	226.3
Suarez, Eugenio	27	21	4.5	38.8	93	15.3	154.0
Judge, Aaron	27	16	5.4	37.5	64	18.6	138.2
Castellanos, Nicholas	27	16	2.7	27.0	101	7.1	129.4
Schoop, Jonathan	27	9	1.6	15.5	76	13.2	128.9
Martinez, Carlos	27	9	0.8	12.4	66	15.2	126.8
Contreras, Willson	27	13	3.1	25.6	53	11.5	116.6
Pederson, Joc	27	17	3.3	30.1	69	10.8	112.4
Herrera, Odubel	27	2	-0.5	0.1	67	10.1	107.4
Rosario, Eddie	27	17	1.6	23.6	64	10.3	105.3
Grichuk, Randal	27	8	0.3	9.2	54	9.7	92.6
Sanchez, Yolmer	27	15	2.1	23.4	55	8.6	89.6
Polanco, Gregory	27	2	-0.6	-0.4	65	5.8	88.2
Hernandez, Kike	27	12	1.5	17.8	50	8.9	85.8
Vazquez, Felipe	27	13	2.8	24.3	51	8.2	83.9
Gray, Jon	27	12	4.0	28.0	39	10.6	81.4
Ray, Robbie	27	8	1.0	11.9	45	9.0	81.2
Frazier, Adam	27	15	2.7	25.9	45	7.8	76.0
Wacha, Michael	27	4	0.2	4.9	45	7.4	74.5
Flores, Wilmer	27	8	0.8	11.3	61	1.9	68.5
Narvaez, Omar	27	14	2.1	22.3	34	5.5	66.9
Mancini, Trey	27	17	3.3	30.4	43	5.9	66.5
McNeil, Jeff	27	24	5.0	43.9	35	7.4	64.6
Manaea, Sean	27	4	1.4	9.6	28	8.6	62.4
Soler, Jorge	27	18	3.7	32.6	45	4.3	62.1
Renfroe, Hunter	27	11	2.6	21.4	34	6.2	58.9
Taillon, Jameson	27	1	0.3	2.0	27	7.9	58.8
Lorenzen, Michael	27	12	2.4	21.6	31	6.0	55.0
Claudio, Alex	27	4	0.6	6.2	28	5.9	51.5
Arenado, Nolan	**28**	**24**	**5.7**	**46.9**	**151**	**38.7**	**305.8**
Realmuto, J.T.	28	22	4.4	39.5	96	17.6	198.4
Ozuna, Marcell	28	14	2.1	22.4	114	19.4	191.6
Semien, Marcus	28	36	8.1	68.5	108	20.6	190.2
Puig, Yasiel	28	16	1.3	21.3	107	20.0	187.0
Cole, Gerrit	28	22	6.8	49.2	87	24.0	183.0
Inciarte, Ender	28	7	0.6	9.2	85	19.2	161.7
Teheran, Julio	28	11	2.4	20.5	75	20.2	155.8
Wong, Kolten	28	24	4.7	42.7	88	15.6	150.4
Bauer, Trevor	28	11	1.5	17.0	65	15.6	127.6
Villar, Jonathan	28	19	4.0	34.9	78	12.1	126.3
Myers, Wil	28	10	-0.3	8.6	87	9.7	125.6
Stroman, Marcus	28	14	4.1	30.5	54	14.6	112.4
Taylor, Chris	28	13	2.4	22.5	60	11.9	107.7
Piscotty, Stephen	28	7	0.7	9.9	68	8.1	100.2
Garcia, Avisail	28	13	2.0	21.2	72	7.0	100.0
Panik, Joe	28	11	-0.2	10.1	72	6.7	98.7
Zunino, Mike	28	5	-0.1	4.7	52	7.0	95.9
Clevinger, Mike	28	14	4.2	30.8	44	12.6	94.4
Wood, Alex	28	0	-0.2	-1.0	48	11.4	93.5
Haniger, Mitch	28	7	1.4	12.7	50	10.7	92.9
Duffy, Matt	28	4	0.1	4.5	51	8.9	86.4
Barnhart, Tucker	28	9	0.6	11.4	49	5.7	85.9
Hamilton, Billy	28	3	0.3	4.2	52	8.4	85.5
Muncy, Max	28	22	5.7	44.9	46	9.7	84.9
Gausman, Kevin	28	1	-1.0	-3.2	43	10.3	84.0
Giles, Ken	28	11	2.4	20.8	52	7.9	83.6
Marisnick, Jake	28	7	1.2	12.0	37	10.5	78.8
Lamb, Jake	28	4	-0.3	2.9	51	6.3	76.0
Miller, Shelby	28	0	-0.9	-3.7	35	7.4	64.7
Diaz, Aledmys	28	7	1.4	12.4	41	5.5	63.2
Perez, Martin	28	6	0.2	6.9	39	5.5	61.0
Vazquez, Christian	28	15	2.2	24.0	37	3.2	59.2
Garver, Mitch	28	18	4.0	33.9	30	4.9	59.0
Rogers, Taylor	28	13	2.5	23.0	32	6.5	58.0
Matz, Steven	28	8	2.2	17.0	25	7.6	55.5
Boyd, Matthew	28	10	3.5	24.1	27	6.7	53.9
Spangenberg, Cory	28	2	0.3	3.0	37	3.5	51.0
Santana, Danny	28	15	2.3	24.4	40	2.5	50.2
Freeman, Freddie	**29**	**28**	**4.4**	**45.7**	**226**	**37.4**	**375.6**
Altuve, Jose	29	17	3.7	31.8	198	38.5	351.9
Stanton, Giancarlo	29	3	0.4	4.5	173	39.9	332.5

Hall of Fame Values by Age Group

| Player | Age | 2019 Season | | | Career | | |
		Win Shares	WAR	HoF Value	Win Shares	WAR	HoF Value
Rizzo, Anthony	29	25	3.9	40.6	187	32.7	317.6
Heyward, Jason	29	13	2.0	20.9	169	36.9	316.4
Bumgarner, Madison	29	11	2.8	22.4	124	37.1	272.4
Simmons, Andrelton	29	6	2.1	14.5	120	36.9	267.5
Rendon, Anthony	29	31	6.3	56.3	151	27.3	260.3
Castro, Starlin	29	11	0.8	14.0	157	18.1	229.5
Hosmer, Eric	29	17	-0.3	15.7	157	15.3	218.4
Springer, George	29	25	6.2	49.7	114	24.6	212.6
Segura, Jean	29	15	1.3	20.4	128	19.6	206.4
Kiermaier, Kevin	29	11	2.3	20.4	72	26.2	177.0
Gregorius, Didi	29	11	0.6	13.6	102	16.6	168.6
Hendricks, Kyle	29	12	3.9	27.6	68	19.6	146.2
Gray, Sonny	29	17	5.6	39.3	67	18.4	140.4
Corbin, Patrick	29	16	5.4	37.6	69	17.5	139.1
Hernandez, Cesar	29	16	2.5	25.9	96	10.1	136.5
Bradley Jr., Jackie	29	10	2.0	17.8	75	15.0	135.2
Gennett, Scooter	29	2	-0.7	-0.9	80	10.8	123.2
Iglesias, Jose	29	12	1.5	17.9	77	10.5	119.1
Galvis, Freddy	29	12	1.6	18.5	84	6.8	111.2
Hicks, Aaron	29	7	1.3	12.0	63	11.8	110.4
Odorizzi, Jake	29	12	3.6	26.4	56	13.3	109.0
Shaw, Travis	29	3	-0.9	-0.4	65	10.6	107.4
Herrera, Kelvin	29	1	-0.4	-0.6	61	9.7	100.0
Miller, Brad	29	6	1.4	11.8	68	7.6	98.3
McCann, James	29	16	3.8	31.0	51	6.6	92.7
Dietrich, Derek	29	9	0.9	12.7	69	5.7	91.8
Chatwood, Tyler	29	6	1.5	11.9	45	11.2	89.7
Cron, C.J.	29	12	1.4	17.6	65	6.1	89.3
Ahmed, Nick	29	17	4.5	35.1	48	10.3	89.2
Grossman, Robbie	29	11	1.0	15.1	61	5.1	81.3
Iglesias, Raisel	29	9	0.7	12.0	45	8.6	79.2
Familia, Jeurys	29	1	-0.4	-0.8	52	6.7	78.8
Wheeler, Zack	29	12	4.1	28.3	37	10.2	77.9
Hand, Brad	29	11	1.2	15.8	51	6.3	76.1
Salazar, Danny	29	0	0.1	0.3	37	9.6	75.5
Tejada, Ruben	29	0	-0.3	-1.2	59	3.6	73.2
Eovaldi, Nathan	29	1	0.1	1.4	35	9.1	71.4
Beckham, Tim	29	9	0.4	10.6	45	5.5	67.2
Smith, Will	29	14	2.2	22.7	43	4.4	60.8
Rosenthal, Trevor	29	0	-1.2	-4.8	42	4.6	60.4
Lugo, Seth	29	12	2.2	20.8	29	6.9	56.7
Givens, Mychal	29	5	0.6	7.4	31	6.3	56.4
DeSclafani, Anthony	29	10	2.6	20.4	27	6.8	54.4
Montgomery, Mike	29	3	0.2	3.8	28	6.4	53.6
Andrus, Elvis	**30**	**17**	**1.9**	**24.4**	**202**	**31.6**	**328.6**
Sale, Chris	30	7	2.3	16.3	144	45.3	325.2
Marte, Starling	30	21	2.9	32.6	131	29.1	247.6
Strasburg, Stephen	30	19	6.5	45.0	107	33.9	242.7
LeMahieu, DJ	30	33	6.0	57.1	131	23.5	225.0
Grandal, Yasmani	30	24	2.5	33.9	114	16.1	211.0
Quintana, Jose	30	6	0.7	9.0	89	24.6	187.4
Porcello, Rick	30	6	1.1	10.5	105	19.9	184.6
Eaton, Adam	30	16	1.6	22.2	108	18.9	183.8
Moustakas, Mike	30	19	3.2	31.8	107	17.1	175.5
Escobar, Eduardo	30	22	4.2	38.6	94	11.8	141.3
Tanaka, Masahiro	30	7	1.7	13.8	66	17.2	134.8
Dickerson, Corey	30	10	0.7	12.9	80	13.1	132.6
Merrifield, Whit	30	21	4.0	37.2	72	15.1	132.6
Pillar, Kevin	30	16	1.0	20.1	68	15.6	130.5
Gonzalez, Marwin	30	12	1.6	18.4	76	13.3	129.4
Duffy, Danny	30	7	1.8	14.1	63	16.0	127.0
Archer, Chris	30	3	0.8	6.3	62	13.6	116.5
Gyorko, Jedd	30	1	-0.5	-1.0	75	10.4	116.4
Allen, Cody	30	0	-0.2	-0.6	67	8.7	101.9
Paxton, James	30	9	2.1	17.6	47	12.8	98.2
Lagares, Juan	30	2	-0.7	-0.6	44	12.3	93.1
Pineda, Michael	30	9	2.4	18.8	45	11.0	89.2
Pomeranz, Drew	30	4	0.3	5.1	46	10.8	89.0
Adams, Matt	30	6	0.0	6.0	65	5.6	87.4
Hechavarria, Adeiny	30	8	0.9	11.6	65	5.5	86.8
Perez, Roberto	30	18	3.9	33.6	42	6.9	83.7
Harvey, Matt	30	0	-0.7	-2.7	40	10.3	81.2
Colome, Alex	30	12	1.0	15.9	54	6.6	80.6
Rojas, Miguel	30	12	2.4	21.5	41	9.0	77.0

Hall of Fame Values by Age Group

Player	Age	2019 Season			Career		
		Win Shares	WAR	HoF Value	Win Shares	WAR	HoF Value
Smyly, Drew	30	3	-0.4	1.4	38	9.2	74.8
d'Arnaud, Travis	30	15	1.0	19.1	49	3.3	73.9
Canha, Mark	30	19	4.5	36.9	44	6.2	68.7
Neris, Hector	30	13	1.7	20.0	40	6.4	65.7
Duvall, Adam	30	4	0.6	6.4	39	6.5	64.9
Pressly, Ryan	30	9	1.8	16.2	35	6.7	61.8
Moore, Matt	30	1	0.7	3.9	36	5.4	57.4
Leon, Sandy	30	3	-0.5	1.0	34	2.4	52.3
Martinez, Jose	30	8	-0.3	7.0	39	2.8	50.2
Kershaw, Clayton	**31**	**15**	**3.6**	**29.3**	**201**	**68.0**	**473.2**
Goldschmidt, Paul	31	21	2.8	32.3	214	43.1	386.3
Upton, Justin	31	4	-0.9	0.5	204	34.2	340.8
Seager, Kyle	31	11	2.4	20.5	170	30.4	291.7
Martinez, J.D.	31	22	3.3	35.4	152	23.9	247.4
Belt, Brandon	31	15	0.6	17.3	136	23.2	228.8
deGrom, Jacob	31	21	7.9	52.5	89	34.9	228.5
Ramos, Wilson	31	15	2.0	22.8	112	15.2	207.5
Kimbrel, Craig	31	0	-0.5	-2.1	125	19.6	203.5
Jansen, Kenley	31	10	0.2	10.6	122	16.0	186.0
Chapman, Aroldis	31	10	1.5	16.1	111	17.5	181.0
Pollock, A.J.	31	10	0.2	10.8	92	20.3	173.1
Calhoun, Kole	31	14	2.3	23.3	107	15.9	170.4
Keuchel, Dallas	31	7	2.0	14.9	78	20.3	159.2
Gordon, Dee	31	10	0.4	11.7	105	12.1	153.5
Leake, Mike	31	8	1.3	13.2	85	16.7	151.7
Chacin, Jhoulys	31	0	-0.8	-3.0	72	19.9	151.6
Gomes, Yan	31	8	1.3	13.0	72	12.9	147.2
Davis, Khris	31	8	-0.3	6.8	95	11.9	142.6
Harrison, Josh	31	1	-0.9	-2.8	89	13.1	141.3
Peralta, David	31	13	1.9	20.5	81	14.2	137.8
Britton, Zack	31	9	2.4	18.5	81	14.1	137.4
Minor, Mike	31	18	7.6	48.5	66	17.8	137.3
Pham, Tommy	31	17	3.7	31.7	66	14.6	124.4
Cahill, Trevor	31	2	-0.3	0.7	66	11.1	110.4
Martin, Leonys	31	3	-0.3	1.7	60	11.9	107.5
Betances, Dellin	31	0	0.0	0.2	58	11.6	104.6
Solarte, Yangervis	31	1	-0.2	0.2	73	6.2	97.8
Morrison, Logan	31	0	-0.2	-0.9	79	4.4	96.8
Cobb, Alex	31	0	-0.4	-1.6	50	11.6	96.4
Gibson, Kyle	31	7	0.4	8.5	51	9.9	90.5
Anderson, Brett	31	11	2.7	21.8	50	10.1	90.4
Holt, Brock	31	8	1.0	11.8	57	7.5	87.0
Anderson, Chase	31	7	1.7	14.0	46	8.5	79.9
Santiago, Hector	31	0	-0.3	-1.4	46	8.2	78.7
Treinen, Blake	31	4	-0.3	2.6	45	8.2	77.9
Bour, Justin	31	1	-0.5	-1.2	58	4.4	75.5
Rondon, Hector	31	5	0.8	8.3	52	5.8	75.2
Jeffress, Jeremy	31	2	-0.4	0.3	45	7.5	74.8
Shaw, Bryan	31	5	0.6	7.3	48	5.8	71.2
Richards, Garrett	31	0	-0.3	-1.1	42	7.0	70.2
Wilson, Justin	31	6	1.3	11.0	42	7.1	70.2
Dyson, Sam	31	7	0.9	10.6	47	5.4	68.8
Warren, Adam	31	1	-0.2	0.0	39	6.7	66.0
Kelly, Joe	31	3	-0.6	0.7	42	5.6	64.6
Maeda, Kenta	31	10	1.8	17.4	33	5.4	54.8
Peacock, Brad	31	6	1.3	11.3	30	5.7	52.8
Posey, Buster	**32**	**12**	**0.9**	**15.8**	**223**	**42.1**	**454.4**
McCutchen, Andrew	32	8	1.4	13.7	277	43.6	451.3
Brantley, Michael	32	21	4.6	39.2	158	27.2	266.9
Bruce, Jay	32	5	0.6	7.4	167	19.7	245.8
Dozier, Brian	32	11	0.7	13.7	142	24.5	239.9
Kipnis, Jason	32	13	0.5	14.8	147	22.2	235.9
Crawford, Brandon	32	13	0.6	15.3	136	23.6	230.4
Sandoval, Pablo	32	8	1.5	13.9	148	19.8	227.9
Abreu, Jose	32	20	2.4	29.6	137	21.2	221.8
Reddick, Josh	32	12	1.2	16.6	122	24.9	221.7
Blackmon, Charlie	32	21	2.3	30.0	146	18.2	218.8
Avila, Alex	32	6	1.4	11.4	102	15.9	197.1
Lynn, Lance	32	18	7.6	48.3	83	22.2	171.8
Carrasco, Carlos	32	3	0.3	4.2	82	20.7	165.0
Maybin, Cameron	32	8	1.5	13.8	105	14.8	164.4
Darvish, Yu	32	9	3.0	21.2	72	21.8	159.2
Parra, Gerardo	32	7	0.5	9.2	108	11.3	153.2

Hall of Fame Values by Age Group

Player	Age	2019 Season			Career		
		Win Shares	WAR	HoF Value	Win Shares	WAR	HoF Value
Castro, Jason	32	7	0.7	9.7	76	12.0	148.8
Castillo, Welington	32	5	-0.2	4.0	72	12.2	144.9
Roark, Tanner	32	9	2.0	17.2	67	19.5	144.8
Smoak, Justin	32	10	0.6	12.4	110	7.7	140.7
Forsythe, Logan	32	7	-0.2	6.2	76	12.5	126.1
Alonso, Yonder	32	1	-0.8	-2.0	89	8.4	122.8
Nova, Ivan	32	9	2.1	17.2	64	12.5	114.1
Ryu, Hyun-Jin	32	18	5.3	39.4	54	14.8	113.2
Miley, Wade	32	11	2.0	18.9	67	11.2	111.8
Hellickson, Jeremy	32	0	-0.3	-1.3	61	12.0	109.0
Hunter, Tommy	32	1	0.3	2.0	65	10.3	106.2
Mercer, Jordy	32	5	0.3	6.2	72	8.0	104.0
Doolittle, Sean	32	9	0.9	12.7	62	9.3	99.1
Cashner, Andrew	32	7	2.5	16.9	51	11.5	97.2
Holland, Derek	32	0	-1.2	-4.6	60	9.0	96.0
Maldonado, Martin	32	6	1.3	11.4	54	6.4	95.0
Beckham, Gordon	32	2	-0.6	-0.5	71	5.5	92.9
McHugh, Collin	32	4	0.4	5.6	51	9.4	88.4
Bourjos, Peter	32	0	-0.4	-1.6	45	9.1	81.4
McGee, Jake	32	2	0.4	3.6	50	7.1	78.2
Nunez, Eduardo	32	1	-1.5	-5.0	70	1.5	76.0
Hudson, Daniel	32	11	2.0	18.9	50	6.0	74.1
Ross, Tyson	32	0	-0.1	-0.2	41	7.3	70.1
Descalso, Daniel	32	2	-1.4	-3.7	62	0.5	64.0
Shoemaker, Matt	32	3	1.2	7.8	34	7.1	62.4
Thames, Eric	32	13	1.6	19.3	47	3.4	60.4
Phelps, David	32	3	0.7	5.6	36	5.4	57.7
Milone, Tommy	32	4	1.3	9.2	36	4.7	54.7
Pina, Manny	32	5	0.7	7.7	27	4.4	53.6
Kang, Jung Ho	32	1	-0.7	-1.8	29	5.8	52.1
Yates, Kirby	32	14	2.8	25.2	33	4.7	51.6
Vincent, Nick	32	2	0.2	3.0	31	5.0	51.1
Longoria, Evan	**33**	**14**	**2.4**	**23.7**	**232**	**54.2**	**448.9**
Hernandez, Felix	33	0	-0.7	-2.7	188	50.1	388.4
Donaldson, Josh	33	25	6.1	49.3	184	44.8	363.7
Santana, Carlos	33	24	4.5	42.0	190	30.5	328.9
Jones, Adam	33	9	-0.4	7.6	199	32.1	327.4
Cabrera, Asdrubal	33	16	1.7	22.7	202	28.1	314.6
Price, David	33	6	1.9	13.5	144	39.7	302.8
Cain, Lorenzo	33	11	2.8	22.3	144	36.9	291.5
Carpenter, Matt	33	11	0.8	14.3	181	26.7	287.8
Walker, Neil	33	7	0.6	9.6	171	21.2	255.9
Cueto, Johnny	33	0	0.0	0.0	126	32.3	255.4
Gonzalez, Carlos	33	1	-0.5	-1.1	154	24.1	250.2
Lucroy, Jonathan	33	5	-1.0	1.0	137	18.0	248.7
Wieters, Matt	33	5	0.5	6.8	133	18.4	247.9
Fowler, Dexter	33	17	1.7	23.6	168	19.6	246.2
Kluber, Corey	33	1	-0.4	-0.5	109	33.2	241.6
Gomez, Carlos	33	2	-0.4	0.4	136	24.9	235.6
Gonzalez, Gio	33	6	1.6	12.6	114	29.2	231.0
Frazier, Todd	33	18	2.2	26.8	122	26.0	225.9
Desmond, Ian	33	8	-1.6	1.5	152	14.8	211.0
Davis, Chris	33	2	-1.0	-1.9	140	14.5	198.0
Arrieta, Jake	33	6	0.9	9.8	93	25.5	195.0
Zimmermann, Jordan	33	0	-0.4	-1.5	84	21.3	169.2
Cervelli, Francisco	33	3	0.2	4.0	78	12.4	152.5
Davis, Wade	33	0	-1.3	-5.4	94	11.6	140.6
Trumbo, Mark	33	0	-0.3	-1.1	98	9.2	135.0
Cozart, Zack	33	1	-0.8	-2.2	70	15.8	133.2
Moreland, Mitch	33	8	1.3	13.0	94	8.9	129.4
Cishek, Steve	33	8	1.7	15.0	79	12.4	128.8
Holland, Greg	33	4	0.1	4.3	81	11.5	127.1
Duda, Lucas	33	0	-0.8	-3.2	95	7.3	124.0
Flowers, Tyler	33	6	-0.1	5.7	61	7.7	110.0
Ottavino, Adam	33	8	2.2	16.7	52	10.8	95.0
Chen, Wei-Yin	33	0	-1.1	-4.2	52	7.7	83.0
Bailey, Homer	33	10	1.9	17.5	59	5.9	82.7
Hughes, Jared	33	5	0.3	6.3	47	8.5	81.2
Sogard, Eric	33	15	2.6	25.3	51	7.4	80.7
Brach, Brad	33	2	-0.1	1.6	47	6.4	72.7
Joseph, Caleb	33	1	0.0	1.1	34	4.6	62.3
Jones, Nate	33	1	0.2	1.8	30	6.4	55.4
Swarzak, Anthony	33	3	0.0	3.2	32	4.8	51.4

Hall of Fame Values by Age Group

Player	Age	2019 Season			Career		
		Win Shares	WAR	HoF Value	Win Shares	WAR	HoF Value
Scherzer, Max	**34**	**16**	**5.8**	**39.1**	**185**	**60.3**	**426.4**
Tulowitzki, Troy	34	0	0.0	-0.2	186	44.1	362.6
Zimmerman, Ryan	34	3	-0.2	2.3	208	37.8	359.2
Kemp, Matt	34	0	-0.9	-3.6	214	21.1	298.6
Cabrera, Melky	34	6	-1.2	1.1	186	20.4	267.7
Murphy, Daniel	34	9	0.2	9.7	189	18.9	264.7
Turner, Justin	34	20	3.7	34.7	146	27.9	257.5
Joyce, Matt	34	8	0.9	11.5	107	14.9	166.7
Jay, Jon	34	4	-0.8	0.8	111	13.1	163.5
Robertson, David	34	0	0.0	-0.1	96	16.0	159.9
Kennedy, Ian	34	10	1.4	15.6	90	16.7	157.0
Clippard, Tyler	34	6	1.4	11.4	92	15.0	152.2
Buchholz, Clay	34	0	-0.3	-1.3	79	17.7	149.9
Dyson, Jarrod	34	10	1.3	15.2	68	16.5	134.0
Melancon, Mark	34	8	0.9	11.7	90	11.0	133.9
Samardzija, Jeff	34	11	2.9	22.5	72	15.0	132.0
Watson, Tony	34	3	0.2	3.9	67	11.9	114.5
Miller, Andrew	34	4	-0.4	2.2	71	8.0	103.1
Vogt, Stephen	34	11	1.2	15.8	56	8.1	102.5
Fiers, Mike	34	12	2.9	23.5	58	11.0	101.9
Rodriguez, Sean	34	3	0.4	4.5	62	8.8	97.2
Strop, Pedro	34	4	0.0	4.0	60	9.2	96.9
Harris, Will	34	10	2.1	18.3	46	7.8	77.1
Petit, Yusmeiro	34	10	2.2	18.8	46	6.6	72.6
Hernandez, David	34	0	-1.9	-7.4	51	4.6	69.5
Kintzler, Brandon	34	7	1.7	13.8	44	6.2	68.6
Tomlin, Josh	34	6	1.0	9.9	43	6.0	66.9
LeBlanc, Wade	34	3	0.3	4.4	37	5.5	59.0
Otero, Dan	34	1	0.0	1.1	32	5.1	52.4
Votto, Joey	**35**	**11**	**1.5**	**17.2**	**309**	**60.2**	**549.9**
Greinke, Zack	35	21	6.4	46.6	224	71.7	511.0
Braun, Ryan	35	15	1.8	22.2	276	48.2	468.8
Hamels, Cole	35	9	3.0	20.8	189	59.6	427.4
Pedroia, Dustin	35	0	-0.5	-1.9	216	51.7	422.6
McCann, Brian	35	7	0.3	8.2	222	31.8	417.9
Ramirez, Hanley	35	0	-0.2	-0.8	242	37.9	393.4
Markakis, Nick	35	11	0.8	14.1	243	33.0	374.9
Lester, Jon	35	8	1.7	14.8	175	45.5	357.1
Gardner, Brett	35	17	4.0	33.1	173	41.6	339.2
Gordon, Alex	35	13	1.2	17.8	178	36.4	323.8
Kendrick, Howie	35	12	2.6	22.6	191	32.9	322.4
Prado, Martin	35	1	-1.3	-4.0	155	28.1	267.5
Suzuki, Kurt	35	11	0.4	12.7	137	20.3	261.7
Sanchez, Anibal	35	11	3.3	24.1	100	26.8	207.2
Lowrie, Jed	35	0	-0.2	-0.6	131	17.5	200.9
Reynolds, Mark	35	1	-1.0	-3.2	149	7.4	178.4
Soria, Joakim	35	5	0.4	6.5	106	17.8	177.2
Liriano, Francisco	35	6	1.1	10.4	93	18.1	165.4
Smith, Joe	35	3	0.7	5.8	76	13.4	129.6
Chirinos, Robinson	35	11	3.8	26.2	56	12.9	129.1
Hundley, Nick	35	1	-0.4	-0.4	78	6.8	126.2
Jackson, Edwin	35	0	-2.4	-9.6	76	8.8	111.3
Estrada, Marco	35	0	-0.4	-1.6	58	12.4	107.6
Morton, Charlie	35	18	5.0	38.2	66	8.0	98.0
Gregerson, Luke	35	0	-0.1	-0.4	66	6.5	92.1
Gurriel, Yuli	35	20	3.2	32.8	59	8.0	91.2
Stammen, Craig	35	9	0.8	12.3	55	8.4	88.7
Volquez, Edinson	35	0	0.1	0.2	61	5.4	82.7
Blevins, Jerry	35	3	0.3	4.3	41	6.3	66.0
Rivera, Rene	35	1	-0.1	0.7	44	2.0	62.2
Chavez, Jesse	35	5	0.8	8.0	43	3.8	58.1
Sipp, Tony	35	1	0.1	1.2	35	5.1	55.4
Kelley, Shawn	35	5	0.8	8.3	37	4.3	54.2
Cabrera, Miguel	**36**	**9**	**0.0**	**9.0**	**402**	**69.6**	**680.2**
Cano, Robinson	36	7	0.3	8.0	344	69.6	622.3
Molina, Yadier	36	16	1.3	21.2	277	40.2	523.2
Verlander, Justin	36	23	7.8	54.1	237	71.0	520.8
Martin, Russell	36	7	0.8	10.1	199	38.0	418.3
Encarnacion, Edwin	36	18	2.7	29.0	238	34.9	377.8
Choo, Shin-Soo	36	18	1.6	24.3	224	34.7	362.8
Pence, Hunter	36	12	1.7	18.8	218	31.3	343.0
Santana, Ervin	36	0	-0.4	-1.6	134	25.9	237.7
Iannetta, Chris	36	2	-0.4	0.2	117	15.5	214.2

Hall of Fame Values by Age Group

Player	Age	2019 Season			Career		
		Win Shares	WAR	HoF Value	Win Shares	WAR	HoF Value
Freese, David	36	7	1.4	12.6	123	17.2	192.0
Happ, J.A.	36	6	1.2	10.7	97	21.7	183.9
Morales, Kendrys	36	1	-0.8	-2.3	124	13.0	175.8
Vargas, Jason	36	6	0.9	9.8	76	17.0	143.9
O'Day, Darren	36	1	0.2	1.7	71	16.5	137.0
Romo, Sergio	36	11	0.6	13.4	84	10.7	126.9
Duke, Zach	36	1	0.0	1.2	72	12.3	121.1
Pearce, Steve	36	0	-0.6	-2.4	69	9.7	108.0
Albers, Matt	36	4	-0.2	3.2	46	2.5	56.0
Mathis, Jeff	36	3	-1.6	-3.3	44	-0.6	50.1
Kinsler, Ian	37	4	-0.3	3.0	250	57.2	478.9
Wainwright, Adam	37	9	2.1	17.5	151	40.2	311.8
Perez, Oliver	37	4	0.4	5.7	69	10.7	111.7
Sabathia, CC	38	3	0.3	4.3	242	63.1	494.3
Granderson, Curtis	38	3	-0.6	0.8	244	47.3	433.1
Zobrist, Ben	38	3	-0.1	2.6	225	45.2	405.7
Cruz, Nelson	38	22	4.3	39.3	235	37.9	386.6
Davis, Rajai	38	1	-0.1	0.7	99	11.2	144.0
Neshek, Pat	38	1	-0.1	0.5	59	10.8	102.2
Pujols, Albert	39	10	0.4	11.7	487	100.3	888.1
Hill, Rich	39	5	1.4	10.4	64	13.6	118.3
Rodney, Fernando	42	3	-0.2	2.1	110	7.5	140.0
Suzuki, Ichiro	45	0	0.0	0.0	324	59.4	561.6

Potential Players on 2020 Hall of Fame Ballot

Player	Win Shares	WAR	HoF Value	HoF Monitor
Bonds, Barry	704	162.8	1355.2	267
Clemens, Roger	437	139.6	995.3	283
Jeter, Derek	413	72.4	702.6	197
Ramirez, Manny	408	69.3	685.4	169
Sheffield, Gary	430	60.5	672.1	103
Walker, Larry	308	72.7	598.8	118
Abreu, Bobby	356	60.0	596.1	76
Rolen, Scott	304	70.2	584.7	82
Schilling, Curt	252	79.6	570.4	122
Helton, Todd	318	61.2	562.8	128
Kent, Jeff	339	55.4	560.6	94
Sosa, Sammy	321	58.6	555.3	134
Jones, Andruw	276	62.8	527.2	57
Giambi, Jason	325	50.5	527.1	90
Pettitte, Andy	224	60.3	465.0	104
Vizquel, Omar	282	45.6	464.3	72
Furcal, Rafael	224	39.4	381.7	40
Konerko, Paul	254	27.7	364.9	57
Soriano, Alfonso	241	28.2	354.0	87
Chavez, Eric	188	37.5	338.0	27
Lee, Cliff	149	43.5	323.0	74
Dunn, Adam	235	17.4	304.6	47
Ibanez, Raul	213	20.4	294.7	30
Wagner, Billy	182	27.7	292.8	81
Roberts, Brian	165	30.4	286.5	37
Beckett, Josh	128	35.6	270.6	42
Pena, Carlos	155	25.1	255.6	21
Figgins, Chone	142	22.2	230.6	21
Scutaro, Marco	142	22.1	230.3	14
Overbay, Lyle	126	16.8	193.2	13
Bartlett, Jason	100	18.3	173.2	8
Penny, Brad	95	19.1	171.3	29
Ludwick, Ryan	114	11.2	158.8	12
Gonzalez, Alex	113	11.2	157.8	7
Valverde, Jose	107	11.5	152.8	50
Putz, J.J.	87	13.1	139.3	33
Wright, Jamey	87	9.1	123.4	14
McLouth, Nate	90	6.4	115.8	7
Saunders, Joe	69	8.6	103.3	15
Bell, Heath	69	7.1	97.4	34
Farnsworth, Kyle	72	6.2	96.6	17

Fathers and Sons

Mark Simon

A Guerrero excelled at the Home Run Derby.

A Biggio reached double figures in home runs and stolen bases.

A Yastrzemski stood in front of the Green Monster at Fenway Park.

No, this was not the 1970s, 1980s or 1990s. It was the 2019 season, in which a new generation of young stars lived up to their family legacies. This was a great year for sons and even a grandson of former major leaguers to make their mark in the major leagues for the first time.

Vladimir Guerrero Jr. (son of Vladimir)
The Blue Jays had three prominent sons of former major leaguers begin their big league careers.

The game was a challenge early on for one of the team's and game's top prospects, but in the shadow of the 2019 All-Star Game, Guerrero Jr. thrived.

At the Home Run Derby in Cleveland, he hit 91 home runs before falling to Pete Alonso in the finals. His father, Vladimir Guerrero, won the 2007 Home Run Derby.

Guerrero's season took a more positive turn after the Derby, as he fared better against the offspeed pitches that were a bugaboo in the early part of his season. He hit .293/.349/.452 in his last 62 games, besting his OPS in his first 61 games by 60 points. He'll try to carry that momentum into the Blue Jays' 2020 season.

Vladimir Guerrero Jr. – Season Highlights
- Finished 2nd at HR Derby (Hit 91 HR)
- Hit .293/.349/.452 after All-Star Break

Vladimir Guerrero – Career Highlights
- 2018 Baseball Hall of Fame inductee
- 449 HR (tied for 40th all-time)

Cavan Biggio (son of Craig)
Don't look at batting average when it comes to judging Biggio's first season. Though Biggio hit .234, he showed a great eye, modest power, and good baserunning instincts.

Biggio's 16% chase rate was the second-lowest in the majors among players with at least 250 plate appearances. His .364 on-base percentage bested the career mark of his father, Hall of Famer Craig Biggio, by one point.

Cavan scratched the surface of the 26-homer power he showed in Double-A in 2018 by hitting 16 home runs with the Blue Jays. He was perfect on the basepaths, with 14 steals in 14 attempts. Biggio also fared well in taking extra bases on hits and wild pitches, enough to finish tied for eighth in our Net Baserunning Gain stat (+ 33 bases).

Cavan Biggio – Season Highlights
- .364 OBP, 16% chase rate (2nd-lowest)
- 14-for-14 in SB attempts (T-8th in Net Baserunning Gain)

Craig Biggio – Career Highlights
- 2015 Baseball Hall of Fame inductee
- 3,060 hits, 668 doubles (5th all-time), 414 stolen bases

Bo Bichette (son of Dante)
Bichette was an instant star for the Blue Jays, as he set major league records by hitting a double in nine straight games and recording 15 extra-

base hits within the first 15 games of his career. He posted a .311/.358/.571 slashline in a season shortened to 46 games by a concussion.

Bichette showed he could catch up to major league fastballs, hitting .376 against them. That's league-leader caliber if maintained for a full season. He also played a respectable shortstop, saving three runs with his defense.

Bichette's presence made his team better. Toronto was 22-24 when he started, 45-71 when he didn't.

Bo Bichette – Season Highlights
- .311/.358/.571
- First player to double in nine straight games

Dante Bichette – Career Highlights
- .299 BA, 274 HR in 14 MLB seasons
- Runner-up for 1995 NL MVP (led NL with 40 HR, 128 RBI)

Fernando Tatis Jr. (son of Fernando)
When he was on the field, Tatis Jr. was one of the best players in baseball. Tatis hit .317/.379/.590 with 22 home runs and 16 stolen bases in 84 games but missed two long stretches due to injuries.

How impressive was Tatis? The last two players to match or better all three of his slashline stats in their debut season were Ted Williams (1939) and Albert Pujols (2001) (minimum 300 at-bats). Tatis' .969 OPS was 12 points better than his father's best season. Fernando Sr. had a .957 OPS in 1999, the year he hit two grand slams in the same inning.

Tatis Jr. didn't do that, but he did do just about everything else. Though he finished two runs below average in Defensive Runs Saved, he had his share of highlight-reel plays.

Fernando Tatis Jr. – Season Highlights
- .317/.379/.590
- 22 HR and 16 SB in 84 games

Fernando Tatis Sr. – Career Highlights
- .265 BA, 113 HR in 11 MLB seasons
- 34 HR in 1999 (including 2 grand slams in one inning)

Mike Yastrzemski (grandson of Carl)
One of the coolest moments of 2019 came when the Giants visited the Red Sox in September and Mike Yastrzemski got to walk around the Fenway Park outfield with his grandfather, who spent much of his Hall of Fame career in left field there.

For the younger Yastrzemski, homering that night capped an improbable rookie season. It was a long path to the majors but he found a home in the Giants outfield. He tied for the team lead in home runs with 21 and ranked second on the Giants in Defensive Runs Saved with eight.

Mike Yastrzemski established himself as one of the top hitters in the game against low pitches. He slugged .582 on pitches in the bottom-third of the strike zone or below. Only Mike Trout slugged better against those pitches (.623).

Mike Yastrzemski – Season Highlights
- 21 HR tied for team lead
- Homered in first game at Fenway Park

Carl Yastrzemski - Career Highlights
- Hall of Fame inductee, 1989
- 3,419 hits, 452 HR, all with Red Sox

These five join a long line of second and third-generation players thriving in the major leagues. At the top of that list is Cody Bellinger (son of Clay), who had himself an MVP-caliber year for the Dodgers this season. The level that Bellinger reached is one to which these young standouts can aspire.

Baseball Looks a Little Different in Japan

Joe Rosales

Earlier in this book, Bill wrote about the aesthetics of the game, how they're changing, and how we might be able to move things back toward a more fun and engaging version of how the game is played. Obviously, Bill was focused on baseball as it is currently being played at the professional level in the U.S. But, of course, baseball is a global game, and it can look very different in some of the other places where it's played.

The most prominent professional league outside of MLB is Nippon Professional Baseball, NPB, the highest level of baseball played in Japan. Some outstanding players have come over from Japan to play in the U.S. over the years—former MVPs like Ichiro Suzuki, pitchers that have thrown multiple no-hitters like Hideo Nomo, and young phenoms like Shohei Ohtani—all of whom began their careers playing in NPB.

Part of what we enjoy so much about Japanese imports to MLB is the visual flair that they often bring to the game relative to what we're used to. Ichiro seemed like he was already running to first base when swinging at the ball, and somehow he still managed to drive it just about wherever he wanted. Nomo had that distinct, exaggerated, drawn out, stretch-coil-pause-unleash delivery. Baseball offers a little more room for aesthetically varied techniques than other sports do, and it's great.

Given how meaningful Japanese baseball is to baseball globally and to MLB specifically, Baseball Info Solutions began collecting data on NPB at the start of the 2018 season. We use the same comprehensive methods to collect all the same detailed data and produce all the same advanced analytics, with the one exception being anything related to pitch charting. This allows for more extensive evaluation of players that might one day make the transition from NPB to MLB.

For example, BIS calculates Defensive Runs Saved numbers for NPB players. Prior to now, evaluation of a Japanese player's defensive abilities would have had to rely almost entirely on traditional scouting methods.

However, by collecting hit locations, trajectories, and timer data for NPB games, we can determine how difficult it actually is to make a given play and therefore how good a defender is at turning balls in play into outs.

And we don't just evaluate NPB players against themselves. Because DRS is a metric that is stated as a value relative to league average, if we choose MLB's league average as our basis of comparison, then we can measure NPB players on the same scale as MLB players. One example of this is Sosuke Genda, shortstop for the Seibu Lions. In 2018 he had 35 Runs Saved using an MLB basis. That put him on par with the performances of elite players like Nick Ahmed and Andrelton Simmons. While he followed that up with only 10 Runs Saved in 2019, that was still the best performance among shortstops in NPB.

Another example is Yoshitomo Tsutsugo, a 27-year-old outfielder on the Yokohama DeNA Baystars. He has announced that he will be posting this offseason to make the transition over to MLB. In 2018, Tsutsugoh hit 38 home runs for the Baystars, tying him for fifth-most in NPB along with former Seattle Mariner and Cincinnati Red Wladimir Balentien. That was accompanied by a .295 AVG/.393 OBP/.596 SLG batting line. In 2019, those numbers slipped a bit to .272/.388/.511 and 29 home runs (tied for 15th). Regardless, he's obviously one of the better hitters in NPB.

However, for any MLB team that might be considering bringing Tsutsugo on, it might also be useful to know that he recorded minus-9 and minus-6 DRS at his primary position of left field in 2018 and 2019, respectively. Plus, he played an additional 230 innings at third base in 2019, and recorded minus-7 DRS there. Again, those numbers are relative to MLB average at those positions, so they're already translated. There's a good chance that he could struggle defensively in MLB.

In addition to looking at specific players, BIS's NPB data allows for a more complete look at how differently the game is played between the two countries. The table at the end of this section highlights some of the more prominent differences between MLB and NPB.

Something that commonly gets associated with Japanese baseball is samurai culture and a sense of honor that players feel compelled to live up to through direct action. I have no idea how prevalent these ideas actually are, but it certainly is the case that NPB hitters seem more intent on putting the ball in play than their MLB counterparts.

In 2019, 35.1% of MLB plate appearances ended with a strikeout, a walk, or a homerun, whereas only 31.2% of plate appearance in NPB did so. That doesn't mean that NPB hitters were necessarily more aggressive, though. They actually had a slightly higher walk rate than MLB hitters—8.8% for NPB versus 8.5% for MLB—and they had a lower swing rate than MLB hitters—46.0% for NPB versus 47.1% for MLB.

However, NPB hitters were less likely to let the plate appearance end without putting the bat on the ball. They had a lower strikeout rate than MLB hitters—19.9% for NPB versus 23.0% for MLB—as well as a higher contact rate when they did swing—78.3% for NPB versus 75.5% for MLB.

In preparation for this new NPB data collection operation, John Dewan, his wife Sue Dewan, and I travelled to Japan to experience the atmosphere for ourselves. Anecdotally, I can tell you that Japanese hitters certainly take a different approach to a plate appearance than many of the foreign-born players playing in NPB, most of whom played professionally in the U.S. at either the Major League or Minor League level. Japanese hitters tend to have flatter swing paths and tend to make more of an effort to guide the bat toward contact. The foreign players tend to keep their weight back longer and tend to have longer swings, something that can lead to hitting for more power but also to more swings and misses.

In terms of analytics, NPB teams are starting to incorporate them into their strategy and player evaluation more than in the past, but they still don't do so at nearly the same levels as MLB teams. Take defensive shifts. In 2019, MLB teams employed 28,194 Full Ted Williams Shifts (three infielders on one side of second base) on balls that were put into play. NPB teams used just 85. If we include Partial Shifts as well—two or more fielders significantly out of position—MLB teams used 46,758 shifts on balls in play, whereas NPB teams employed only 496.

NPB still has a long way to go in order to fully embrace analytics, but teams there are beginning to allocate more of their budget toward new data sources, technologies, and analysts. Additionally, there are companies like Delta Inc, good friends of BIS, who are doing all they can to promote the use of baseball analytics. Delta is owned and run by Yusuke Okada, sometimes referred to as the Bill James of Japan. Delta has developed a very similar operation to what we do here at BIS with the goal of advancing the use of data and analytics in Japan.

Beyond NPB, there are many other prominent professional baseball leagues in the world that are producing outstanding baseball talent. BIS's next expansion is going to be into collecting data on the KBO—the Korean Baseball Organization—beginning in 2020 and backfilling to include at least 2019. Given the success of our NPB operation, our hope is to bring the same level of analytical insight and expertise to an even larger percentage of the baseball playing world.

NPB vs. MLB Comparison, 2019

Metric	League	Value
Strikeout Rate	NPB	19.9%
	MLB	23.0%
Walk Rate	NPB	8.8%
	MLB	8.5%
Home Run Rate	NPB	2.6%
	MLB	3.6%
Three True Outcome Rate	NPB	31.2%
	MLB	35.1%
Swing Rate	NPB	46.0%
	MLB	47.0%
Contact Rate	NPB	78.3%
	MLB	75.5%
Groundball Rate	NPB	47.9%
	MLB	43.4%
Line Drive Rate	NPB	19.0%
	MLB	21.1%
Flyball Rate	NPB	33.2%
	MLB	35.5%
Shifts on BIP	NPB	496
	MLB	46,758
GFP/DME	NPB	0.68
	MLB	0.72

RBI Percentages

Bill James

Everybody complains about the weather, but nobody ever does anything about it. It's an old saying, halfway a joke because, you know, what can you do about the weather? The parallel in baseball is that everybody complains about RBI, but nobody ever does anything to address the obvious problem, the obvious problem being that different players have different opportunities to drive in runs.

Eleven years ago I proposed a solution to this problem, which was to measure the RBI opportunities for each player. The simplest thing to do would be just to count each player's at bats with runners on base as chances to drive in runs. That doesn't work, because (a) you CAN drive in a run when there is no one on base, and (b) there's a big difference between a runner on third base with no one out and a runner on first base with two out. You can't count all of those things the same.

The next thing you can do is to look separately at plate appearances with runners on base and with runners in scoring position. That represents a higher level of granularity in the data, but it's not quite what we need. RBI Opportunities are the sum of actual RBI and missed RBI opportunities. We know what RBI are; it is not within our job description to re-define RBI. What we need is a workable definition of missed RBI opportunities.

Players are charged with missed RBI opportunities whenever they make an out without driving in a run. This charge can be any of four things: 1.00, .70, .40 or .10. Players are charged with

1.00 missed RBI opportunities for a runner left on third with less than two out,

.70 for a runner left on third base with two out,

.70 for a runner left on second base,

.40 for a runner left on first base, and

.10 for an out made with no one on base.

If a batter doesn't make an out but doesn't drive in a run, he is not charged with a missed opportunity. Let us suppose that a runner is on first base and the batter hits a double, but the runner from first does not score. Should that batter be charged with missing the opportunity to drive in a run?

Well, no, of course not, because that opportunity is still there. It hasn't been lost at all. The runner who was on first base is now on third, and now there is another runner on second. The situation isn't <u>worse</u>; it's better. It would not be right to charge a player with a missed opportunity when the opportunity has not been missed in any sense.

If you leave two runners on base without driving them in, they both count; in other words, if you leave runners on second and third with less than two out, that's a charge of 1.70 missed RBI opportunities.

This effort is, in a sense, parallel to what my friend John Dewan did with Blown Saves. "Saves" were invented in my lifetime; yeah, I know, I'm really old. But for twenty years after Saves were invented, it was very common for announcers to cast shade on them based on the fact that there were no "negative saves", no "failures" to balance the saves. It was a one-sided stat.

So John Dewan invented "Blown Saves", and we started counting them. It took a little while; for four or five years nobody paid much attention. Then Blown Saves gradually caught on, you started seeing Blown Save counts pretty much every time you saw Saves. Nobody complains about it being a one-sided Stat anymore, because it isn't.

In developing RBI Opportunities, I was trying to do sort of the same thing, and sort of the opposite. When I was young, RBI men had a similar mythology about them. Sometimes hitters who weren't all that Joe Carter whippy were mythologized by the media as superstars because they drove in runs. By 2008, however, the worm had turned. Young baseball fans didn't believe in RBI anymore, because they understood that all stats are only meaningful with context.

What I was really trying to do, in developing RBI Opportunities, was not to expose the stat, but to save it, to pass it on to younger baseball fans with a shield against the charge that RBI were merely a creation of opportunities.

Well, I have failed; I have failed so far, anyway. My own fault. My philosophy has always been that my ideas are orphans after I publish them. Sometimes they catch on; sometimes they don't. It's not up to me to decide which ones catch on and which ones drift away; it's up to the public.

That idea works sometimes, and sometimes it doesn't. With RBI Opportunities, what we really did was to calculate them and put them on my website, Bill James Online, where nobody ever saw them, because Bill James Online does not have very many subscribers to begin with, and those we have very rarely even take a look at the huge warehouse of oddball statistics that hide somewhere behind a button at the top of the screen.

A year ago, 2018, two of the very best RBI men in the major leagues were Mookie Betts, who drove in only 80 runs but had an RBI percentage of .455, and Mike Trout, who drove in only 79 runs but had an RBI percentage of .463. Mookie was used all year as a leadoff hitter, while Trout had mostly hit second, limiting the RBI chances for both men.

That was actually a remarkable thing, instructive about modern baseball—that two of the very best RBI men in baseball were not used to drive in runs. Hard to imagine that happening 20 years ago. And you know what? Nobody knew. By 2018, the public had so thoroughly lost interest in RBI that it didn't really matter.

I should have done more to promote the stat. I should have written about it in this book, I should have written about it on the website; I should have made reference to it on television when I happened to be on TV or in interviews with reporters when I talked to reporters. I didn't. We're publishing them here in an effort to give them a little bit of exposure.

A few notes about the stats on the following pages:

1) The standards for the stat are about the same as the standards for on base percentage. The major league on base percentage in 2019 was .323; the average RBI percentage in the chart below is .326, and the average would drop a couple of points if we included players with less than 150 at bats. The standard deviation of RBI percentage is higher than the standard deviation for on base percentage, so that RBI percentages of .400 or better are more common than on base percentages of .400.

2) The best RBI man in the majors in 2019, as you can see below, was Nelson Cruz of the Minnesota Twins.

3) Among the 22 men who drove in 100 runs in 2019, all were legitimately good RBI producers, all with RBI percentages of .393 or higher. Juan Soto was the only one who was under .400. No one, in 2019, drove in 100 runs because he just had a lot of chances to drive in runs.

4) Among players with 300 or more at bats, Billy Hamilton was by far the worst RBI producer in the major leagues, with an RBI percentage of .159. Martin Maldonado, Hamilton's teammate for most of the season, was second-worst, at .220. The poorest RBI producer with 400 or more at bats was Mallex Smith of Seattle, who drove in only 37 runs with 162.7 opportunities, or .227—oddly enough, the same as his batting average. Smith had significantly more chances to drive in runs than did Mitch Garver of Minnesota (144.4)—but Garver drove in 30 more runs.

5) The major league player who had the most opportunities to drive in runs in 2019 was Jose Abreu of the White Sox, with 302.3. Abreu had a very good .407 RBI Percentage, giving him 123 RBI. Generally speaking, the best RBI men almost always get the most chances to drive in runs. The cases like Mookie Betts and Mike Trout in 2018 are very much the exception, rather than the rule.

6) The major league leader in runs NOT driven in was Randal Grichuk of Toronto, who drove in 80 runs but had an RBI percentage of just .308. He missed 179.5 opportunities to drive in runs—the highest total in the major leagues.

7) Among major league players with 90 to 99 RBI, the best actual RBI producer was Christian Yelich (.463) and the worst was Albert Pujols (.371). Among those with 80 to 89 RBI, the best RBI producer was Edwin Encarnacion (.457), and the worst was Grichuk (.308). Among those with 70 to 79 RBI, the best RBI producer was Yordan Alvarez (.444) and the worst was Cesar Hernandez (.315). Among those with 60 to 69 RBI, the best RBI producer was Mitch Garver (.464) and the worst was Tommy Pham (.303).

8) There were 257 major league players in 2019 with 300 or more at bats. Among those 257 men, 50 had RBI percentages of .400 or better, 159 had RBI percentages in the .300s, and 48 had RBI percentages under .300.

RBI Percentages by Batter

Player	AB	RBI	RBI Opps	Pct
Cruz, Nelson	454	108	222.0	.486
Trout, Mike	470	104	220.3	.472
Smith, Will	170	42	89.9	.467
Garver, Mitch	311	67	144.4	.464
Yelich, Christian	489	97	209.3	.463
Rendon, Anthony	545	126	272.5	.462
Freeman, Freddie	597	121	264.4	.458
Encarnacion, Edwin	418	86	188.1	.457
Pence, Hunter	286	59	129.1	.457
LeMahieu, DJ	602	102	226.6	.450
Alvarez, Yordan	313	78	175.7	.444
Bell, Josh	527	116	261.5	.444
Bregman, Alex	554	112	252.4	.444
Dickerson, Corey	260	59	133.1	.443
Arenado, Nolan	588	118	268.0	.440
Harper, Bryce	573	114	259.4	.439
Springer, George	479	96	218.9	.439
Aquino, Aristides	205	47	107.5	.437
Bellinger, Cody	559	115	263.4	.437
Alonso, Pete	597	120	275.2	.436
Beaty, Matt	249	46	105.8	.435
Suzuki, Kurt	280	63	145.1	.434
Tatis Jr., Fernando	334	53	122.1	.434
Kepler, Max	524	90	208.4	.432
Acuna Jr., Ronald	626	101	234.8	.430
Meadows, Austin	530	89	207.1	.430
Blackmon, Charlie	580	86	200.8	.428
Semien, Marcus	657	92	216.1	.426
Soler, Jorge	589	117	275.6	.425
Marte, Ketel	569	92	217.8	.422
Rosario, Eddie	562	109	259.2	.421
Bogaerts, Xander	614	117	278.7	.420
Freese, David	162	29	69.1	.420
Devers, Rafael	647	115	275.1	.418
Muncy, Max	487	98	234.6	.418
McCutchen, Andrew	219	29	69.6	.417
Rizzo, Anthony	512	94	226.3	.415
Phegley, Josh	314	62	149.7	.414
Dietrich, Derek	251	43	104.3	.412
d'Arnaud, Travis	351	69	167.8	.411
Baez, Javier	531	85	207.1	.410
Escobar, Eduardo	636	118	287.7	.410
Martinez, J.D.	575	105	256.4	.410
McNeil, Jeff	510	75	182.8	.410
Olson, Matt	483	91	222.0	.410
Sano, Miguel	380	79	192.7	.410
Dahl, David	374	61	149.0	.409
Hosmer, Eric	619	99	242.2	.409
Abreu, Jose	634	123	302.3	.407
Gregorius, Didi	324	61	149.9	.407
Santana, Danny	474	81	199.5	.406
Pederson, Joc	450	74	182.5	.405
Contreras, Willson	360	64	158.5	.404
Suarez, Eugenio	575	103	255.2	.404
Urshela, Giovanny	442	74	183.9	.402
Chapman, Matt	583	91	227.4	.400
Frazier, Clint	225	38	95.1	.400
Gurriel, Yuli	564	104	260.3	.400
Murphy, Daniel	438	78	194.8	.400
Schwarber, Kyle	529	92	230.0	.400
Cabrera, Asdrubal	447	91	229.1	.397
Correa, Carlos	280	59	148.6	.397
Story, Trevor	588	85	214.2	.397
Nimmo, Brandon	199	29	73.3	.396
Luplow, Jordan	225	38	96.2	.395
Sanchez, Gary	396	77	195.1	.395
Donaldson, Josh	549	94	238.4	.394
Goldschmidt, Paul	597	97	246.8	.393
Soto, Juan	542	110	279.6	.393
Hechavarria, Adeiny	203	33	84.2	.392
Parra, Gerardo	274	48	122.4	.392
Torres, Gleyber	546	90	229.8	.392
Altuve, Jose	500	74	189.1	.391
Romine, Austin	228	35	89.5	.391
Odor, Rougned	522	93	238.4	.390
Riley, Austin	274	49	126.0	.389
Castillo, Welington	230	41	105.6	.388
Albies, Ozzie	640	86	222.2	.387
Betts, Mookie	597	80	206.9	.387
Diaz, Aledmys	210	40	103.4	.387
Kendrick, Howie	334	62	160.7	.386
Lowe, Brandon	296	51	132.2	.386
Beckham, Tim	304	47	122.1	.385
Cron, C.J.	458	78	202.7	.385
Seager, Corey	489	87	226.1	.385
Conforto, Michael	549	92	239.3	.384
Marte, Starling	539	82	213.4	.384
Miller, Brad	154	25	65.3	.383
Santana, Carlos	573	93	244.2	.381
Buxton, Byron	271	46	120.9	.380
Gardner, Brett	491	74	194.6	.380
Grisham, Trent	156	24	63.1	.380
Hernandez, Teoscar	417	65	171.0	.380
Gurriel Jr., Lourdes	314	50	131.8	.379
Moncada, Yoan	511	79	208.2	.379
Brantley, Michael	575	90	238.9	.377
Fowler, Dexter	487	67	178.2	.376
Braun, Ryan	459	75	199.8	.375
Gallo, Joey	241	49	130.8	.375
Nunez, Renato	541	90	240.2	.375
Bruce, Jay	310	59	157.7	.374
Healy, Ryon	169	26	69.6	.374
Mancini, Trey	602	97	259.5	.374
Seager, Kyle	393	63	168.6	.374
Laureano, Ramon	434	67	179.6	.373
Reyes, Franmil	494	81	217.3	.373
Calhoun, Willie	309	48	128.9	.372
Ramirez, Jose	482	83	223.3	.372
Tauchman, Mike	260	47	126.3	.372
Pujols, Albert	491	93	250.5	.371
Reynolds, Bryan	491	68	183.4	.371
Bryant, Kris	543	77	208.1	.370
Newman, Kevin	493	64	173.2	.370
Peralta, David	382	57	154.1	.370
Hicks, Aaron	221	36	98.1	.367
Judge, Aaron	378	55	150.0	.367
Santander, Anthony	380	59	160.6	.367
Austin, Tyler	154	24	65.7	.365
Moreland, Mitch	298	58	159.0	.365
Anderson, Brian	459	66	181.5	.364
Ozuna, Marcell	485	89	244.5	.364
Turner, Justin	479	67	184.0	.364
Camargo, Johan	232	32	88.1	.363
Biggio, Cavan	354	48	132.8	.361
Lamb, Jake	187	30	83.0	.361
Lindor, Francisco	598	74	205.1	.361
McMahon, Ryan	480	83	229.8	.361
Ramos, Wilson	473	73	202.2	.361
Mazara, Nomar	429	66	183.5	.360
Mondesi, Adalberto	415	62	172.4	.360
Guzman, Ronald	256	36	100.6	.358
Puig, Yasiel	555	84	234.7	.358
Jimenez, Eloy	468	79	221.5	.357
Jones, Adam	485	67	187.6	.357
Machado, Manny	587	85	238.3	.357
Franco, Maikel	389	56	157.5	.356

Player	AB	RBI	RBI Opps	Pct
Moustakas, Mike	523	87	244.4	.356
Ohtani, Shohei	384	62	174.2	.356
Taylor, Chris	366	52	146.2	.356
Murphy, Tom	260	40	112.7	.355
Pillar, Kevin	611	88	248.2	.355
Slater, Austin	168	21	59.2	.355
Yastrzemski, Mike	371	55	155.0	.355
Adams, Matt	310	56	158.4	.354
Aguilar, Jesus	314	50	141.4	.354
Casali, Curt	207	32	90.3	.354
Upton, Justin	219	40	113.0	.354
Dickerson, Alex	174	28	79.3	.353
Dozier, Hunter	523	84	238.0	.353
La Stella, Tommy	292	44	124.8	.353
Santana, Domingo	451	69	195.7	.353
Turner, Trea	521	57	161.7	.353
Naylor, Josh	253	32	91.0	.352
Perez, Roberto	389	63	179.0	.352
Canha, Mark	410	58	165.2	.351
Castellanos, Nicholas	615	73	207.8	.351
Polanco, Jorge	631	79	225.0	.351
Pollock, A.J.	308	47	134.0	.351
Voit, Luke	429	62	176.4	.351
Smoak, Justin	414	61	174.4	.350
Grandal, Yasmani	513	77	220.5	.349
Moran, Colin	466	80	229.4	.349
Bote, David	303	41	117.7	.348
France, Ty	184	24	69.0	.348
Desmond, Ian	443	65	187.4	.347
Freeman, Mike	177	24	69.2	.347
Smith Jr., Dwight	357	53	152.6	.347
Vogt, Stephen	255	40	115.2	.347
Frazier, Todd	447	67	193.9	.346
Ramirez, Harold	421	50	144.4	.346
Longoria, Evan	453	69	199.8	.345
Vogelbach, Daniel	462	76	220.2	.345
Bour, Justin	151	26	75.5	.344
Choi, Ji-Man	410	63	183.6	.343
Hernandez, Kike	414	64	186.4	.343
Hiura, Keston	314	49	143.0	.343
Mercado, Oscar	438	54	157.3	.343
Sandoval, Pablo	272	41	119.7	.343
Sogard, Eric	396	40	116.7	.343
Cooper, Garrett	381	50	146.2	.342
Gordon, Alex	556	76	222.4	.342
Rodriguez, Ronny	276	43	125.7	.342
Dean, Austin	178	21	61.6	.341
Duggar, Steven	261	28	82.0	.341
McKinney, Billy	251	28	82.2	.341
Renfroe, Hunter	440	64	187.7	.341
Chavis, Michael	347	58	170.5	.340
Gonzalez, Marwin	425	55	161.7	.340
Kipnis, Jason	458	65	191.4	.340
McCann, Brian	277	45	132.4	.340
Thames, Eric	396	61	179.3	.340
Crawford, J.P.	345	46	135.6	.339
Guerrero Jr., Vladimir	464	69	203.3	.339
McCann, James	439	60	176.9	.339
Ahmed, Nick	556	82	242.8	.338
Markakis, Nick	414	62	183.7	.338
Senzel, Nick	375	42	124.4	.338
Vazquez, Christian	482	72	213.1	.338
Farmer, Kyle	183	27	80.1	.337
Nola, Austin	238	31	92.1	.337
Castro, Starlin	636	86	256.2	.336
Haniger, Mitch	246	32	95.2	.336
Kelly, Carson	314	47	139.9	.336
Maybin, Cameron	239	32	95.8	.334
Severino, Pedro	305	44	131.8	.334

Player	AB	RBI	RBI Opps	Pct
DeJong, Paul	583	78	234.3	.333
Garcia, Avisail	489	72	216.3	.333
Wong, Kolten	478	59	177.2	.333
Flores, Wilmer	265	37	111.4	.332
Merrifield, Whit	681	74	223.0	.332
Solano, Donovan	215	23	69.3	.332
Chirinos, Robinson	366	58	175.4	.331
Diaz, Isan	179	23	69.5	.331
Gomes, Yan	314	43	129.8	.331
Vargas, Ildemaro	201	24	72.4	.331
Davis, Khris	481	73	221.2	.330
Galvis, Freddy	557	70	211.9	.330
Benintendi, Andrew	541	68	206.7	.329
Hoskins, Rhys	570	85	258.0	.329
Barnhart, Tucker	316	40	121.8	.328
Bichette, Bo	196	21	64.1	.328
Choo, Shin-Soo	563	61	186.2	.328
Ruiz, Rio	370	46	140.4	.328
Smith, Dominic	177	25	76.3	.328
Wieters, Matt	168	27	82.2	.328
Osuna, Jose	261	36	110.1	.327
Realmuto, J.T.	538	83	253.7	.327
Dixon, Brandon	391	52	159.5	.326
Kiermaier, Kevin	447	55	168.7	.326
Cabrera, Miguel	493	59	181.5	.325
Heyward, Jason	513	62	190.8	.325
Iglesias, Jose	504	59	181.3	.325
Molina, Yadier	419	57	175.3	.325
Zimmerman, Ryan	171	27	83.1	.325
Avila, Alex	164	24	74.4	.323
Joyce, Matt	200	23	71.3	.323
Villar, Jonathan	642	73	226.7	.322
Castro, Harold	354	38	118.4	.321
Rosario, Amed	616	72	224.6	.321
Verdugo, Alex	343	44	136.9	.321
Anderson, Tim	498	56	174.8	.320
Kemp, Tony	245	29	90.6	.320
Tellez, Rowdy	370	54	168.9	.320
Caratini, Victor	244	34	106.6	.319
Jansen, Danny	347	43	134.7	.319
Profar, Jurickson	459	67	210.2	.319
Robles, Victor	546	65	204.4	.318
Walker, Christian	529	73	229.3	.318
Calhoun, Kole	552	74	233.6	.317
Martinez, Jose	334	42	132.3	.317
Andrus, Elvis	600	72	227.8	.316
Arraez, Luis	326	28	88.7	.316
Kingery, Scott	458	55	173.9	.316
Swanson, Dansby	483	65	205.6	.316
Hernandez, Cesar	612	71	225.4	.315
Myers, Wil	435	53	168.3	.315
Gamel, Ben	311	33	105.2	.314
Segura, Jean	576	60	191.2	.314
Edman, Tommy	326	36	115.2	.313
Pinder, Chad	341	47	150.1	.313
Schoop, Jonathan	433	59	188.2	.313
Davis, J.D.	410	57	183.5	.311
Pina, Manny	158	25	80.7	.310
Alberto, Hanser	524	51	165.1	.309
Grichuk, Randal	586	80	259.5	.308
Naquin, Tyler	274	34	110.9	.307
Bradley Jr., Jackie	494	62	202.4	.306
Castro, Jason	237	30	98.2	.305
Crawford, Brandon	500	59	193.4	.305
Narvaez, Omar	428	55	180.2	.305
Alfaro, Jorge	431	57	187.5	.304
Pham, Tommy	567	68	224.6	.303
Cave, Jake	198	25	82.7	.302
Kang, Jung Ho	172	24	79.6	.302

Player	AB	RBI	RBI Opps	Pct
Goodwin, Brian	413	47	156.2	.301
Granderson, Curtis	317	34	112.9	.301
Piscotty, Stephen	357	44	146.1	.301
Dozier, Brian	416	50	166.7	.300
Garcia, Greg	311	31	103.3	.300
Urias, Luis	215	24	80.0	.300
Winker, Jesse	338	38	126.6	.300
Hedges, Austin	312	36	120.3	.299
Polanco, Gregory	153	17	57.0	.298
Reddick, Josh	501	56	187.8	.298
Bader, Harrison	347	39	131.5	.297
Adrianza, Ehire	202	22	74.6	.295
Diaz, Yandy	307	38	129.0	.295
Zobrist, Ben	150	17	57.7	.295
Cabrera, Melky	378	47	160.1	.294
Cuthbert, Cheslor	309	40	135.9	.294
Forsythe, Logan	317	39	132.7	.294
Inciarte, Ender	199	24	81.5	.294
Sisco, Chance	167	20	68.1	.294
Tapia, Raimel	426	44	149.8	.294
Davis, Chris	307	36	122.8	.293
Fletcher, David	596	49	167.4	.293
Alonso, Yonder	292	37	126.9	.292
Carpenter, Matt	416	46	157.6	.292
Smith, Kevan	191	20	68.5	.292
Allen, Greg	231	27	92.7	.291
Lowe, Nate	152	19	65.2	.291
Walker, Neil	337	38	130.7	.291
Berti, Jon	256	24	82.9	.290
Haseley, Adam	222	26	89.7	.290
Arcia, Orlando	494	59	204.2	.289
Belt, Brandon	526	57	197.8	.288
Holt, Brock	259	31	107.5	.288
Reyes, Victor	276	25	86.9	.288
Engel, Adam	227	26	90.5	.287
Frazier, Adam	554	50	174.4	.287
Margot, Manuel	398	37	128.7	.287
Wolters, Tony	359	42	146.6	.286
Astudillo, Willians	190	21	73.8	.285
Rojas, Miguel	483	46	161.2	.285
Russell, Addison	215	23	80.8	.285
Stewart, Christin	369	40	140.3	.285
Bauers, Jake	372	43	152.7	.282
Ervin, Phillip	236	23	81.6	.282
Moore, Dylan	247	28	99.9	.280
Cordell, Ryan	217	24	86.1	.279
Grossman, Robbie	420	38	136.2	.279
Wilkerson, Stevie	329	35	126.4	.277
Marisnick, Jake	292	34	123.3	.276
Lagares, Juan	258	27	98.2	.275
Lugo, Dawel	273	26	94.5	.275
Lucroy, Jonathan	293	36	131.4	.274
Adames, Willy	531	52	191.5	.272
Flowers, Tyler	271	34	125.1	.272
Barnes, Austin	212	25	92.3	.271
Votto, Joey	525	47	173.7	.271
Eaton, Adam	566	49	181.2	.270
Goodrum, Niko	423	45	166.6	.270
Drury, Brandon	418	41	153.2	.268
Peraza, Jose	376	33	123.7	.267
DeShields, Delino	357	32	120.2	.266
Hampson, Garrett	299	27	102.0	.265
Martin, Leonys	236	19	72.0	.264
Martin, Russell	209	20	75.9	.264
O'Hearn, Ryan	328	38	144.2	.264
Gordon, Dee	393	34	129.3	.263
Jones, JaCoby	298	26	98.7	.263
Leon, Sandy	172	19	72.2	.263
Plawecki, Kevin	158	17	64.6	.263

Player	AB	RBI	RBI Opps	Pct
Simmons, Andrelton	398	40	152.8	.262
Cano, Robinson	390	39	149.3	.261
Kinsler, Ian	258	22	84.5	.260
Candelario, Jeimer	335	32	123.6	.259
Mercer, Jordy	256	22	85.1	.259
Rengifo, Luis	357	33	127.4	.259
VanMeter, Josh	228	23	88.8	.259
Nunez, Eduardo	167	20	78.2	.256
Hicks, John	319	35	137.2	.255
Diaz, Elias	303	28	110.1	.254
Heredia, Guillermo	204	20	78.6	.254
Dyson, Jarrod	400	27	107.3	.252
Posey, Buster	405	38	152.3	.250
Locastro, Tim	212	17	68.4	.249
Zunino, Mike	266	32	128.7	.249
Cain, Lorenzo	562	46	193.2	.248
Long, Shed	152	15	60.6	.248
Panik, Joe	438	39	157.6	.247
Lopez, Nicky	379	30	122.9	.244
Mejia, Francisco	226	22	90.9	.242
Sanchez, Yolmer	496	43	178.0	.242
Almora Jr., Albert	339	32	133.7	.239
Greiner, Grayson	208	19	80.0	.238
Descalso, Daniel	168	15	63.5	.236
Robertson, Daniel	207	19	81.0	.235
Garcia, Leury	577	40	174.1	.230
White, Tyler	240	23	100.6	.229
Kiner-Falefa, Isiah	202	21	92.1	.228
Smith, Mallex	510	37	162.7	.227
Jay, Jon	165	9	40.4	.223
Martin Jr., Richie	283	23	103.0	.223
Munoz, Yairo	172	13	58.6	.222
Maldonado, Martin	333	27	122.9	.220
Owings, Chris	180	14	64.6	.217
Wendle, Joey	238	19	87.5	.217
Stallings, Jacob	191	13	60.5	.215
Morales, Kendrys	170	12	58.4	.205
Brinson, Lewis	226	15	75.0	.200
Perez, Hernan	232	18	91.6	.197
Rickard, Joey	168	10	50.7	.197
Prado, Martin	245	15	77.5	.194
Broxton, Keon	204	16	86.2	.186
Demeritte, Travis	169	10	53.8	.186
Beckham, Gordon	223	15	85.2	.176
Mathis, Jeff	228	12	68.7	.175
Starling, Bubba	186	12	68.4	.175
Shaw, Travis	230	16	93.4	.171
Hamilton, Billy	316	15	94.1	.159

Starting Pitcher Rankings

Andrew Kyne

How good was the starting rotation of the 107-win Houston Astros? By the Bill James *World's No. 1 Starting Pitcher Rankings*, Justin Verlander finished the season as the best starter in Major League Baseball, and teammate Gerrit Cole was right behind him.

Cole led the American League with a 2.50 ERA, with the veteran Verlander second at 2.58. They were the only pitchers to reach 300 strikeouts in 2019, well ahead of the rest of the field.

And to supplement that one-two punch, the Astros acquired Zack Greinke at the trade deadline, who finished at No. 8 in the rankings.

But, impressively, Houston isn't the only club with three pitchers in the top ten. The Nationals can also make that claim with Max Scherzer (No. 4), Stephen Strasburg (No. 5), and Patrick Corbin (No. 10).

Scherzer started the season at the very top of the list, and though he pitched extremely well, injuries forced him to his lowest innings total in a decade. Corbin continued his success from 2018, recording a 3.25 ERA over 33 starts in his first season as a National.

The biggest riser into the top ten was Jack Flaherty of the Cardinals, climbing from No. 72 to No. 6. It was a late push for Flaherty, who had an incredible run after the All-Star break. He led MLB with a 0.91 ERA and struck out 124 batters in 99 innings. The Cardinals won 10 of his final 14 starts en route to the National League Central title.

Sonny Gray made a significant jump from No. 75 to No. 14, cutting his ERA by more than two runs with the Reds. His rotation-mate Luis Castillo also made a big leap from No. 48 to No. 18. Trevor Bauer, who started the season at No. 6 in the rankings, joined the Cincinnati rotation at the trade deadline. Although Bauer fell to No. 19 by season's end, the Reds look to have a formidable staff heading into 2020.

The two biggest falls out of the top ten belonged to Cleveland's Corey Kluber and Carlos Carrasco. Kluber dropped from No. 5 to No. 38 in the rankings; Carrasco from No. 10 to No. 40. Between Bauer, Kluber, and Carrasco, the Indians' pitching did not go to plan in 2019. Yet the team still had two bright spots: Mike Clevinger posted a 2.71 ERA and finished No. 11, and Shane Bieber posted a 3.28 ERA and finished No. 22.

The following pages provide the rankings for baseball's top starting pitchers by month in 2019. For more details on the system, check out Bill's articles on the *World's No. 1 Starting Pitcher* on BillJamesOnline.com.

Record setting

Reds pitcher Luis Castillo induced misses on 34% of the swings against him. That is the highest rate for any pitcher who qualified for the ERA title in the 18 seasons in which that stat has been tracked by BIS.

Lower the qualifier to 100 innings and Blake Snell of the Rays set the high mark with a miss rate of 36% in 2019.

Starting Pitcher Rankings

Player	April 1 Score	Rank	May 1 Score	Rank	June 1 Score	Rank	July 1 Score	Rank	Aug 1 Score	Rank	Sept 1 Score	Rank	Sept 29 Score	Rank
Verlander, Justin	520.7	3	527.2	1	544.1	1	536.9	2	544.1	2	561.4	1	559.1	1
Cole, Gerrit	474.1	7	482.0	6	483.3	7	496.1	5	516.8	4	523.8	4	553.2	2
deGrom, Jacob	524.7	2	510.1	3	503.0	4	506.0	4	519.2	3	525.5	3	541.2	3
Scherzer, Max	541.9	1	525.4	2	525.7	2	553.8	1	552.7	1	541.1	2	531.8	4
Strasburg, Stephen	462.9	11	473.3	9	487.6	5	475.4	9	496.4	6	499.0	6	507.6	5
Flaherty, Jack	376.2	72	393.4	58	413.8	45	404.3	59	432.4	40	458.5	18	498.1	6
Sale, Chris	510.1	4	499.2	4	513.6	3	521.9	3	507.9	5	501.8	5	494.8	7
Greinke, Zack	458.2	12	478.3	7	484.3	6	489.3	6	494.3	7	483.5	10	493.1	8
Kershaw, Clayton	471.3	9	478.1	8	473.7	10	475.4	8	488.2	8	494.8	7	489.7	9
Corbin, Patrick	446.9	16	458.0	13	462.8	13	463.2	13	481.3	9	492.3	8	487.7	10
Clevinger, Mike	451.8	14	453.9	16	446.1	21	429.8	36	450.2	24	469.8	11	482.4	11
Nola, Aaron	472.3	8	454.8	15	461.1	16	465.3	11	476.8	11	491.6	9	477.5	12
Morton, Charlie	422.9	34	436.0	26	451.5	18	464.8	12	468.4	13	466.9	13	475.4	13
Gray, Sonny	374.1	75	396.9	53	407.0	55	412.5	49	438.0	35	465.8	14	474.4	14
Lynn, Lance	379.9	66	389.4	62	412.2	47	438.3	29	452.0	21	459.3	17	474.3	15
Buehler, Walker	396.3	51	404.5	50	418.8	41	445.7	25	447.6	25	467.4	12	464.8	16
Rodriguez, Eduardo	390.3	55	394.3	56	406.1	57	424.6	42	442.8	29	446.1	29	464.4	17
Castillo, Luis	405.9	48	435.2	29	440.1	24	451.2	19	460.6	15	457.2	19	461.0	18
Bauer, Trevor	482.4	6	491.7	5	477.0	8	485.6	7	480.2	10	452.8	21	460.9	19
Paxton, James	431.7	28	442.9	21	443.3	23	426.4	40	419.0	48	435.5	39	457.7	20
Hendricks, Kyle	446.6	17	438.0	24	466.1	11	459.1	15	468.8	12	460.3	15	457.4	21
Bieber, Shane	325.0	165	351.2	115	381.4	75	411.4	51	434.2	37	452.1	22	453.6	22
Ryu, Hyun-Jin	376.2	71	396.7	54	433.0	32	439.1	28	457.7	16	439.8	34	451.4	23
Giolito, Lucas	343.4	108	345.2	132	393.9	64	419.8	45	421.7	46	448.6	26	450.9	24
Berrios, Jose	430.9	29	440.6	23	439.7	26	455.7	17	463.5	14	443.5	31	450.4	25
Tanaka, Masahiro	450.7	15	447.0	19	458.8	17	466.8	10	442.0	31	451.8	24	449.2	26
Odorizzi, Jake	415.6	39	419.7	35	444.1	22	446.3	23	429.0	43	438.7	36	448.8	27
Teheran, Julio	436.2	23	434.4	30	448.6	20	435.1	31	452.3	20	459.5	16	448.7	28
Bumgarner, Madison	416.7	38	418.7	37	422.0	38	427.8	38	438.7	33	454.3	20	446.2	29
Ray, Robbie	430.1	30	435.9	28	437.0	29	440.4	27	452.6	19	451.9	23	445.4	30
Darvish, Yu	326.8	160	344.8	134	360.7	111	378.4	89	401.5	65	421.6	49	442.6	31
Minor, Mike	349.9	96	391.6	60	411.4	49	441.7	26	434.5	36	445.4	30	442.4	32
Snell, Blake	458.1	13	461.1	12	475.7	9	447.7	22	455.1	18	447.4	28	442.4	33
Marquez, German	443.9	18	456.9	14	461.9	14	449.7	21	450.7	22	448.5	27	441.5	34
Fiers, Mike	417.3	37	404.9	48	424.1	36	435.9	30	446.1	27	450.8	25	439.6	35
Wheeler, Zack	393.5	53	399.8	51	413.3	46	418.4	47	422.4	45	419.1	52	439.2	36
Syndergaard, Noah	413.8	41	404.9	49	416.8	42	420.0	44	433.6	38	435.1	40	435.9	37
Kluber, Corey	500.6	5	472.0	10	465.8	12	458.3	16	450.5	23	442.8	32	435.8	38
Happ, J.A.	434.5	26	436.7	25	437.5	28	426.0	41	421.4	47	422.2	47	434.1	39
Carrasco, Carlos	464.6	10	464.1	11	461.5	15	455.0	18	447.2	26	439.5	35	432.5	40
Hamels, Cole	437.0	22	450.7	18	438.8	27	463.1	14	456.1	17	437.9	38	431.8	41
Gray, Jon	403.8	50	413.6	46	423.5	37	431.7	34	439.2	32	438.5	37	431.5	42
Soroka, Mike	325.0	165	346.2	128	386.5	69	397.1	67	407.3	59	424.1	45	431.3	43
Hill, Rich	437.3	21	432.1	31	440.0	25	445.9	24	438.2	34	430.4	43	431.1	44
Sanchez, Anibal	375.0	73	375.2	75	389.8	68	408.7	52	415.4	51	422.1	48	430.5	45
Foltynewicz, Mike	430.0	31	416.2	42	409.3	51	403.1	61	395.3	74	401.4	70	429.7	46
Boyd, Matthew	392.0	54	416.7	41	435.5	31	434.3	32	442.2	30	434.6	41	428.2	47
Stroman, Marcus	369.1	81	389.2	63	396.5	62	406.2	55	417.9	49	415.7	57	426.6	48
Price, David	434.7	25	445.4	20	450.5	19	450.1	20	444.2	28	429.9	44	424.4	49
Mikolas, Miles	383.1	64	391.1	61	405.5	59	405.3	57	414.5	52	415.8	56	423.4	50
Porcello, Rick	412.6	45	414.7	43	421.0	39	429.9	35	412.6	54	422.8	46	423.0	51
Gonzales, Marco	361.3	89	380.0	68	379.6	78	381.2	83	397.6	71	401.9	69	421.1	52
Maeda, Kenta	362.4	88	368.6	79	395.1	63	406.7	54	411.9	55	420.7	51	420.7	53
DeSclafani, Anthony	325.0	165	352.7	109	352.0	130	370.1	108	387.7	90	400.7	71	419.5	54
Bundy, Dylan	371.4	76	373.5	77	397.2	61	397.6	66	394.0	80	407.9	61	417.2	55
Samardzija, Jeff	330.3	146	354.0	104	354.4	122	366.7	119	395.1	75	408.3	60	416.9	56
Anderson, Chase	405.8	49	394.0	57	393.4	66	395.5	69	416.7	50	403.7	67	415.1	57
Hudson, Dakota	325.1	162	327.8	180	352.2	127	367.3	115	370.0	108	413.2	58	413.2	58
Paddack, Chris	332.7	139	367.4	81	381.5	74	384.4	80	403.1	61	394.4	81	412.7	59
Roark, Tanner	393.6	52	394.6	55	414.0	44	423.8	43	410.0	56	420.8	50	412.5	60
Means, John			338.4	157	366.0	104	386.6	77	388.3	88	396.6	77	411.6	61
Lester, Jon	441.6	20	451.8	17	431.6	33	434.2	33	432.7	39	417.5	55	410.7	62
Alcantara, Sandy	336.8	120	334.0	165	354.3	123	365.5	120	360.9	124	387.2	94	410.7	63
Archer, Chris	421.6	35	419.2	36	406.0	58	408.6	53	409.7	58	417.6	54	410.6	64
Quintana, Jose	434.9	24	440.7	22	435.8	30	426.5	39	422.9	44	441.1	33	409.5	65
Pineda, Michael	333.1	135	332.9	167	355.3	120	372.9	102	392.6	82	405.6	64	408.2	66
Lucchesi, Joey	347.3	100	351.4	113	380.2	77	392.3	74	394.4	79	406.0	63	408.2	67
Gibson, Kyle	414.8	40	417.4	40	428.9	34	428.1	37	431.2	42	418.7	53	407.2	68
Matz, Steven	363.8	87	378.2	69	381.2	76	372.8	103	385.9	91	404.4	66	406.2	69
Davies, Zach	361.2	90	380.1	67	393.6	65	385.7	79	390.5	83	388.5	92	406.1	70
Gonzalez, Gio	406.4	47	397.3	52	407.8	54	400.6	63	400.5	67	398.9	75	405.2	71

Starting Pitcher Rankings

Player	April 1 Score	Rank	May 1 Score	Rank	June 1 Score	Rank	July 1 Score	Rank	Aug 1 Score	Rank	Sept 1 Score	Rank	Sept 29 Score	Rank
Bailey, Homer	325.0	165	344.5	135	348.7	136	373.7	97	372.5	107	387.3	93	404.6	72
Leake, Mike	384.4	63	380.8	66	391.4	67	397.7	65	409.8	57	396.1	79	404.4	73
Miley, Wade	367.3	83	381.5	65	400.7	60	411.4	50	431.6	41	430.8	42	404.2	74
Lopez, Reynaldo	377.0	69	384.0	64	378.5	79	383.5	81	400.8	66	399.2	73	404.2	75
Keuchel, Dallas	418.6	36	405.8	47	374.8	83	355.3	130	380.7	95	397.8	76	403.6	76
Keller, Brad	354.6	92	366.3	83	368.9	95	380.3	84	402.9	62	409.0	59	402.0	77
Nova, Ivan	385.2	61	364.6	89	371.5	90	377.9	91	394.9	77	409.6	58	400.8	78
Duffy, Danny	371.3	77	348.3	123	367.8	99	379.7	86	389.7	85	377.8	106	400.7	79
Kelly, Merrill	328.6	155	348.3	124	348.8	135	379.3	88	376.7	100	372.4	113	400.7	80
Sabathia, CC	408.2	46	414.6	44	415.4	43	416.5	48	406.7	60	403.3	68	400.6	81
Fried, Max	325.0	165	363.1	91	370.0	93	373.0	101	380.1	96	392.6	85	400.2	82
Woodruff, Brandon	328.7	152	341.0	147	377.0	81	399.1	64	401.9	63	394.1	83	398.2	83
Arrieta, Jake	424.9	33	428.5	32	426.7	35	419.0	46	414.1	53	404.9	65	397.9	84
Musgrove, Joe	325.0	165	358.2	95	349.3	133	367.1	117	383.3	93	386.7	95	397.6	85
Lyles, Jordan	325.0	165	350.2	118	371.0	91	369.4	111	356.1	134	381.1	100	397.4	86
German, Domingo	333.5	133	355.0	102	369.9	94	367.5	114	381.1	94	396.2	78	397.2	87
Junis, Jakob	370.1	78	376.3	72	382.7	72	386.9	76	401.7	64	406.3	62	396.8	88
Bassitt, Chris	325.0	165	344.0	139	361.3	109	373.6	99	388.4	87	399.0	74	394.6	89
Thornton, Trent	334.9	125	343.8	140	365.5	105	372.2	104	368.1	111	370.4	117	394.1	90
Gallen, Zac							334.0	182	361.9	123	379.8	104	393.4	91
Williams, Trevor	413.1	44	418.4	38	419.0	40	403.1	60	400.1	68	393.5	84	392.6	92
Chacin, Jhoulys	426.1	32	422.5	33	410.2	50	405.9	56	379.0	70	391.3	87	392.0	93
Anderson, Brett	333.8	130	339.7	152	357.4	116	370.2	107	379.8	97	384.7	97	391.7	94
Wainwright, Adam	324.1	464	346.0	131	352.1	128	367.9	113	375.7	101	378.7	105	391.2	95
Norris, Daniel	325.0	165	337.9	159	348.3	137	360.0	123	369.3	109	377.4	107	391.0	96
Chirinos, Yonny	335.5	124	357.3	97	373.1	88	393.3	73	395.1	76	394.1	82	390.7	97
Yarbrough, Ryan	329.9	149	325.0	190	332.8	172	346.2	150	366.9	114	399.2	72	390.6	98
Vargas, Jason	343.9	106	352.3	110	360.6	112	382.5	82	388.7	86	389.3	90	389.2	99
Freeland, Kyle	442.8	19	436.0	27	409.2	52	402.7	62	390.4	84	391.2	88	387.9	100
Plesac, Zach					331.1	178	359.9	124	373.5	105	380.7	101	387.4	101
Smith, Caleb	330.3	147	368.4	80	382.2	73	375.9	93	397.6	72	389.4	89	385.9	102
Lauer, Eric	333.0	136	344.1	138	358.2	115	368.2	112	364.1	117	374.6	111	385.4	103
Stanek, Ryne	345.5	103	365.4	86	385.1	70	395.0	70	399.9	69	392.1	86	385.1	104
Eflin, Zach	330.8	145	354.2	103	376.6	82	385.8	78	363.8	119	370.3	118	383.9	105
Taillon, Jameson	413.7	42	418.3	39	412.0	48	404.5	58	396.8	73	389.0	91	382.0	106
Montas, Frankie	333.8	131	347.2	125	373.5	86	395.7	68	387.9	89	380.2	103	381.0	107
Milone, Tommy	325.0	165	325.0	190	339.2	153	367.1	116	362.1	122	366.7	121	379.3	108
Heaney, Andrew	366.7	84	339.0	154	338.5	155	348.9	144	348.9	146	380.5	102	379.1	109
Lamet, Dinelson	325.0	165	325.0	190	325.0	210	325.0	219	337.8	171	362.9	126	378.2	110
Gausman, Kevin	413.2	43	420.6	34	408.7	53	393.5	72	394.8	78	384.8	96	378.0	111
Houser, Adrian			325.0	190	325.4	207	327.1	213	332.2	190	359.0	137	377.9	112
Cashner, Andrew	348.2	99	366.0	84	373.4	87	394.9	71	394.0	81	384.1	98	377.1	113
Turnbull, Spencer	328.6	154	356.4	99	374.1	85	379.6	87	373.6	104	368.3	119	376.9	114
Canning, Griffin			328.1	179	358.7	114	375.6	94	379.7	98	382.8	99	375.8	115
Wojciechowski, Asher	325.0	165	325.0	190	325.0	210	325.0	219	356.4	132	362.8	127	374.3	116
Young, Alex							331.1	196	350.5	141	359.9	134	373.9	117
Velasquez, Vince	342.1	109	359.1	94	351.0	131	353.1	137	365.9	116	370.6	116	373.3	118
Beede, Tyler	325.0	165	325.0	190	330.3	182	338.2	166	356.9	131	353.2	147	371.7	119
Font, Wilmer	325.0	165	325.0	190	325.0	210	325.0	219	325.0	231	365.2	125	371.5	120
Perez, Martin	325.0	165	351.8	112	366.3	103	373.7	98	374.9	103	371.6	115	371.5	121
Glasnow, Tyler	330.2	148	365.6	85	374.5	84	367.0	118	359.2	127	351.5	153	371.1	122
Richards, Trevor	340.3	114	351.3	114	368.6	98	376.4	92	368.8	110	373.2	112	370.5	123
Urena, Jose	389.3	57	393.0	59	407.0	56	391.5	75	383.7	92	376.0	109	369.0	124
Civale, Aaron							334.2	180	326.4	223	356.4	142	368.7	125
Plutko, Adam	325.0	165	325.0	190	328.0	192	343.9	154	349.3	143	366.1	123	368.7	126
Pena, Felix	325.1	163	347.0	126	367.0	102	369.7	109	378.2	99	375.5	110	368.5	127
Yamamoto, Jordan							352.4	139	359.6	126	362.3	128	368.0	128
Wacha, Michael	332.3	141	340.0	150	336.5	162	348.4	145	345.2	154	364.8	140	367.8	129
Mahle, Tyler	325.0	165	339.7	153	363.2	107	378.2	90	367.3	113	367.4	120	367.1	130
Manaea, Sean	376.3	70	346.3	127	325.0	210	325.0	219	325.0	231	334.1	194	366.7	131
Hernandez, Elieser	325.0	165	325.0	190	325.0	210	344.5	152	345.5	153	362.0	130	365.5	132
Smyly, Drew	15.5	473	325.0	190	333.7	170	325.0	219	343.6	155	345.1	162	364.9	133
LeBlanc, Wade	350.0	95	352.1	111	343.2	144	369.5	110	374.9	102	371.6	114	364.6	134
Waguespack, Jacob					328.7	186	325.0	219	337.0	173	356.7	141	364.3	135
Green, Chad	325.0	165	325.0	190	333.5	171	353.4	134	351.0	140	355.3	145	363.9	136
Stripling, Ross	343.5	107	364.6	88	356.9	117	353.2	136	364.0	118	361.4	131	363.0	137
Gonzalez, Chi Chi							25.4	504	332.2	191	324.8	504	362.4	138
Brault, Steven	325.0	165	325.0	190	337.5	158	354.1	133	352.7	136	376.4	108	362.3	139
Kikuchi, Yusei	334.8	126	343.2	142	355.0	121	349.0	143	356.2	133	362.2	129	360.9	140
Barria, Jaime	349.3	98	345.0	133	337.3	160	338.6	163	351.2	139	358.9	138	359.4	141
VerHagen, Drew	325.0	165	325.0	190	325.0	210	325.0	219	319.7	501	346.7	160	358.9	142
Skaggs, Tyler	342.1	110	353.5	106	367.1	101	380.1	85	373.3	106	365.6	124	358.6	143
Sandoval, Patrick											343.0	168	357.9	144
Quantrill, Cal			329.1	175	333.9	168	336.0	171	357.9	129	366.6	122	356.0	145

Starting Pitcher Rankings

Player	April 1 Score	Rank	May 1 Score	Rank	June 1 Score	Rank	July 1 Score	Rank	Aug 1 Score	Rank	Sept 1 Score	Rank	Sept 29 Score	Rank
Lopez, Pablo	328.7	151	346.0	129	355.4	119	370.6	106	362.9	121	352.5	150	355.8	146
Montgomery, Mike	325.0	165	325.0	190	325.0	210	325.0	219	325.6	227	352.9	148	354.9	147
Voth, Austin	325.0	165	325.0	190	325.0	210	333.3	184	338.7	168	331.0	205	354.6	148
Weaver, Luke	323.3	467	348.9	121	378.4	80	370.9	105	363.1	120	355.4	144	354.6	149
Ross, Joe	325.0	165	325.0	190	325.0	210	325.0	219	324.3	498	351.7	152	354.2	150
Dobnak, Randy													353.1	151
Peacock, Brad	336.4	121	341.1	146	371.6	89	375.0	95	367.7	112	360.0	133	353.0	152
Wisler, Matt	325.0	165	325.0	190	325.0	210	325.0	219	335.7	176	359.7	135	352.7	153
Sanchez, Aaron	332.8	137	354.0	105	361.2	110	334.8	176	348.9	145	359.1	136	352.1	154
Urquidy, Jose									338.6	169	332.1	201	351.8	155
Newcomb, Sean	380.2	65	376.6	71	368.8	97	374.2	96	366.4	115	358.7	139	351.7	156
Cease, Dylan									333.4	185	328.4	216	350.0	157
Allard, Kolby	325.0	165	325.0	190	325.0	210	325.0	219	325.0	231	346.1	161	349.0	158
Brooks, Aaron	21.6	472	326.3	187	325.0	210	325.0	219	330.7	196	341.2	171	348.9	159
Pomeranz, Drew	352.5	94	365.0	87	342.6	146	356.9	128	357.3	130	355.5	143	348.5	160
Melville, Tim	325.0	165	325.0	190	325.0	210	325.0	219	325.0	231	339.1	180	348.2	161
Hoffman, Jeff	325.0	165	327.5	182	328.4	189	336.1	170	333.3	186	328.4	217	348.1	162
Gonsolin, Tony							323.5	500	325.0	231	347.9	157	347.6	163
Hernandez, Felix	364.3	86	374.9	76	358.8	113	351.3	140	343.6	156	347.0	159	347.3	164
Eovaldi, Nathan	346.7	101	353.5	107	345.7	140	338.2	165	330.5	198	333.2	197	346.4	165
Agrazal, Dario							331.0	197	346.5	152	342.2	169	345.9	166
Severino, Luis	432.7	27	413.9	45	382.9	71	352.9	138	325.0	231	325.0	236	345.9	167
Pivetta, Nick	353.3	93	344.3	137	341.9	148	359.2	126	360.6	125	352.8	149	345.8	168
Zimmermann, Jordan	369.9	79	364.2	90	356.4	118	357.5	127	339.1	165	360.7	132	345.5	169
Sampson, Adrian	333.4	134	338.7	155	343.7	141	373.1	100	359.0	128	351.8	151	344.8	170
Peters, Dillon	325.0	165	325.0	190	325.0	210	325.0	219	331.3	194	348.7	154	343.7	171
Lopez, Jorge	326.7	161	342.6	144	338.7	154	332.0	191	325.0	231	333.3	196	343.4	172
Rodriguez, Dereck	346.0	102	355.7	101	352.8	126	346.5	148	342.6	158	343.1	167	343.1	173
Sparkman, Glenn	325.0	165	336.8	162	329.5	183	336.8	169	341.9	160	340.2	173	343.0	174
Webb, Logan											334.5	191	342.8	175
Jurado, Ariel	325.0	165	325.0	190	339.6	152	351.2	141	352.8	135	354.3	146	342.8	176
Dunn, Justin											341.8	177		
Strahm, Matt	319.6	471	350.2	117	370.1	92	362.9	121	350.4	142	348.6	155	341.6	178
Sheffield, Justus											324.6	505	341.6	179
Keller, Mitch						322.7	487	325.0	219	325.0	231	328.0	218	341.5	180
Detwiler, Ross	325.0	165	325.0	190	325.0	210	328.9	204	325.0	231	343.2	165	341.4	181
Fedde, Erick	325.0	165	332.0	169	340.4	151	343.5	155	341.3	162	347.9	156	340.9	182
Clarke, Taylor					328.6	188	332.3	189	341.6	161	338.1	181	340.8	183
Lakins, Travis													340.7	184
Zeuch, T.J.													340.2	185
Suarez, Jose							332.2	190	342.2	159	336.7	185	339.4	186
Mills, Alec	325.0	165	325.0	190	325.0	210	325.0	219	330.2	200	329.3	211	338.7	187
Smeltzer, Devin					335.6	164	331.5	195	329.9	203	332.2	200	338.2	188
Pruitt, Austin	325.0	165	325.0	190	325.0	210	325.0	219	325.0	231	337.2	182	338.0	189
Dugger, Robert											335.2	189	337.9	190
Ynoa, Gabriel	325.0	165	325.0	190	328.3	190	332.7	188	329.5	204	325.7	232	337.8	191
Anderson, Tyler	389.8	56	376.7	70	367.2	100	359.7	125	351.9	137	344.2	163	337.2	192
McKay, Brendan							334.8	177	332.4	189	329.2	212	337.0	193
Mengden, Daniel	344.0	105	325.0	190	340.9	149	344.1	153	351.4	138	343.7	164	336.7	194
Senzatela, Antonio	327.9	157	337.5	160	336.9	161	353.3	135	334.6	179	320.8	509	335.9	195
Buchholz, Clay	335.9	124	334.3	163	325.0	210	325.0	219	325.0	231	337.0	183	335.9	196
Cueto, Johnny	340.4	113	325.0	190	325.0	210	325.0	219	325.0	231	325.0	236	335.7	197
Lambert, Peter							334.0	181	346.5	151	343.1	166	335.3	198
Chavez, Jesse	325.0	165	325.0	190	338.3	156	361.4	122	349.1	144	341.4	170	334.4	199
Castillo, Diego	325.0	165	325.0	190	325.0	210	325.0	219	330.1	201	339.8	176	334.0	200
Wood, Alex	387.3	59	357.3	98	326.3	204	325.0	219	327.4	218	339.9	175	333.7	201
Estrada, Marco	385.2	62	371.0	78	363.2	106	355.7	129	348.0	147	340.2	172	333.2	202
Burke, Brock											347.8	158	333.1	203
Kittredge, Andrew	325.0	165	325.0	190	325.0	210	328.5	205	333.8	183	333.8	195	333.0	204
Anderson, Shaun					335.5	165	349.0	142	347.0	150	340.0	174	333.0	205
May, Dustin											339.6	177	332.6	206
Godley, Zack	378.4	68	376.1	73	368.9	96	354.8	132	347.0	149	339.3	179	332.3	207
Ramirez, Noe	325.0	165	325.0	190	325.0	210	335.8	174	334.6	178	331.8	202	331.8	208
Parker, Blake													331.7	209
Baez, Michel													331.5	210
Kay, Anthony													331.4	211
Ponce de Leon, Daniel	325.0	165	331.9	171	325.0	210	340.8	158	343.1	157	335.5	188	330.0	212
Farrell, Luke	325.0	165	325.0	190	325.0	210	325.0	219	325.0	231	325.0	236	330.0	213
Urias, Julio	333.5	132	342.8	143	335.0	166	335.9	173	330.4	199	325.0	236	329.9	214
Reid-Foley, Sean	323.5	466	325.0	190	325.0	210	329.4	203	331.8	193	336.7	184	329.7	215
Hernandez, Jonathan													329.5	216
Richards, Garrett	325.0	165	325.0	190	325.0	210	325.0	219	325.0	231	325.0	236	329.4	217
Valdez, Framber	325.0	165	325.0	190	325.0	210	338.5	164	327.8	216	331.2	203	329.4	218
Walker, Taijuan	325.0	165	325.0	190	325.0	210	325.0	219	325.0	231	325.0	236	329.4	219

Starting Pitcher Rankings

Player	April 1 Score	Rank	May 1 Score	Rank	June 1 Score	Rank	July 1 Score	Rank	Aug 1 Score	Rank	Sept 1 Score	Rank	Sept 29 Score	Rank
Montgomery, Jordan	325.0	165	325.0	190	325.0	210	325.0	219	325.0	231	325.0	236	329.3	220
Stashak, Cody													329.2	221
Tomlin, Josh	325.0	165	325.0	190	325.0	210	332.8	187	325.0	230	325.0	236	329.2	221
Shepherd, Chandler													329.2	223
Ruiz, Jose													328.9	224
Johnson, Brian	325.0	165	325.0	190	325.0	210	334.3	179	326.5	222	334.5	192	328.7	225
Beeks, Jalen	325.0	165	343.7	141	343.6	142	348.4	146	338.8	166	335.6	187	328.6	226
Poyner, Bobby													328.3	227
Palumbo, Joseph								325.0	219	325.0	231	325.0	236	328.0	228
Alexander, Tyler									335.9	175	336.0	186	327.9	229
Bolanos, Ronald													327.8	230
Stewart, Brock	325.0	165	325.0	190	325.0	210	325.0	219	325.0	231	334.8	190	327.8	231
Pannone, Thomas	332.8	138	327.4	183	325.0	210	325.0	219	331.2	195	334.4	193	327.7	232
Chen, Wei-Yin	337.4	116	325.0	190	325.0	210	325.0	219	325.0	231	333.0	198	327.3	233
Sims, Lucas	325.0	165	325.0	190	331.4	175	325.0	219	325.7	226	325.0	236	327.2	234
Ferguson, Caleb	325.0	165	325.0	190	325.0	210	325.0	219	325.0	231	325.0	236	326.7	235
Eickhoff, Jerad	325.0	165	340.2	149	353.4	125	348.0	147	340.3	163	332.5	199	325.5	236
McRae, Alex								325.0	219	318.7	503	325.0	236	325.4	237
Holland, Derek	365.5	85	375.8	74	362.5	108	355.0	131	347.3	148	339.5	178	325.1	238
Loaisiga, Jonathan	325.0	165	328.8	176	325.0	210	325.0	219	325.0	231	325.0	236	325.1	239
All Others													325.0	240

Team Statistics

Alex Vigderman

Welcome. You've reached (for my money) the best section in the *Bill James Handbook*, one with an unbeatable combination of breadth and depth.

You'll see stats from every team in every facet of the game. There are lots of stats you won't easily find in other places. And it starts with the most familiar and friendly face, the division standings. It feels like coming home.

Right when you open the door, you see that only two teams held control of first place in the AL West (the Astros and Mariners), and one of those teams ended up in last place in the division.

Then you walk past the foyer and into the living room, where you find that three teams in the American League went at least 17-2 against a division rival (Yankees vs. Orioles, Indians vs. Tigers, and Astros vs. Mariners).

There's a rattle in the kitchen, and it turns out that it was just another passed ball for the Braves, who led the league with 24.

You start to climb the stairs, but stop short, as you see that shortstops had the highest batting average of any position in 2019 (.269).

Kick your shoes off and stay a while. We've got everything you need right here.

2019 American League Standings

Overall

EAST Team	W-L	Pct	GB	D1	LD1	LLd	CENTRAL Team	W-L	Pct	GB	D1	LD1	LLd	WEST Team	W-L	Pct	GB	D1	LD1	LLd
New York Yankees	103-59	.636	0.0	135	9/29	11.5	Minnesota Twins	101-61	.623	0.0	174	9/29	11.5	Houston Astros	107-55	.660	0.0	161	9/29	10.5
Tampa Bay Rays	96-66	.593	7.0	54	6/14	5.5	Cleveland Indians	93-69	.574	8.0	10	8/12	1.0	Oakland Athletics	97-65	.599	10.0	0	-	0.0
Boston Red Sox	84-78	.519	19.0	0	-	0.0	Chicago White Sox	72-89	.447	28.5	0	-	0.0	Texas Rangers	78-84	.481	29.0	0	-	0.0
Toronto Blue Jays	67-95	.414	36.0	1	3/30	0.0	Kansas City Royals	59-103	.364	42.0	5	4/1	1.0	Los Angeles Angels	72-90	.444	35.0	0	-	0.0
Baltimore Orioles	54-108	.333	49.0	0	-	0.0	Detroit Tigers	47-114	.292	53.5	5	4/12	0.5	Seattle Mariners	68-94	.420	39.0	33	4/27	4.0

Wild Card Clinch Dates: Oakland 9/27, Tampa Bay 9/27. Division Clinch Dates: New York 9/17, Houston 9/20, Minnesota 9/25.
D1 = Number of days a team had at least a share of first place of their division; LD1 = Last date the team had at least a share of first place; LLd = The largest number of games that a team led their division by.

East Division

Tm	Home	Road	East	Cent	West	NL	LHS	RHS	Day	Night	Grass	Turf	1-Rn	5+Rn	Xinn	April	May	June	July	Aug	Sept	Pre	Post
NYY	57-24	46-35	54-22	18-15	19-14	12-8	33-18	70-41	42-21	61-38	93-46	10-13	18-19	32-16	7-4	17-12	20-7	17-9	14-11	21-9	14-11	57-31	46-28
TB	48-33	48-33	44-32	20-13	18-15	14-6	32-25	64-41	36-28	60-38	43-29	53-37	23-16	26-16	11-8	19-9	16-11	13-16	14-12	17-10	17-8	52-39	44-27
Bos	38-43	46-35	35-41	21-11	18-16	10-10	24-30	60-48	27-26	57-52	71-66	13-12	23-22	27-23	9-8	13-17	16-11	15-12	15-10	14-13	11-15	49-41	35-37
Tor	35-46	32-49	33-43	17-18	14-17	3-17	24-30	43-65	26-38	41-57	30-41	37-54	18-23	19-30	7-8	14-15	7-21	10-17	12-14	12-15	12-13	34-57	33-38
Bal	25-56	29-52	24-52	12-20	11-23	7-13	21-41	33-67	21-36	33-72	45-96	9-12	11-22	18-41	2-8	10-20	8-19	6-20	12-12	9-19	9-18	27-62	27-46

Central Division

Tm	Home	Road	East	Cent	West	NL	LHS	RHS	Day	Night	Grass	Turf	1-Rn	5+Rn	Xinn	April	May	June	July	Aug	Sept	Pre	Post
Min	46-35	55-26	20-12	50-26	23-11	8-12	22-17	79-44	34-24	67-37	95-60	6-1	23-12	35-13	5-7	17-10	21-8	15-12	13-11	17-11	18-9	56-33	45-28
Cle	49-32	44-37	18-16	48-28	19-13	8-12	33-22	60-47	34-26	59-43	91-65	2-4	15-16	29-24	6-7	16-12	12-17	17-9	18-6	16-13	14-12	50-38	43-31
CWS	39-41	33-48	15-18	38-37	13-20	6-14	28-27	44-62	26-39	46-50	67-84	4-2	14-18	20-30	4-4	12-16	14-15	11-13	7-17	14-16	13-14	42-44	30-45
KC	31-50	28-53	10-23	31-45	9-24	9-11	16-27	43-76	21-40	38-63	57-98	2-5	15-25	16-27	4-9	9-20	10-18	10-17	11-15	8-19	11-14	30-61	29-42
Det	22-59	25-55	14-19	22-53	6-27	5-15	13-24	34-90	22-47	25-67	44-110	3-4	14-22	6-40	6-10	13-14	9-19	5-20	5-20	8-21	7-20	28-58	19-56

West Division

Tm	Home	Road	East	Cent	West	NL	LHS	RHS	Day	Night	Grass	Turf	1-Rn	5+Rn	Xinn	April	May	June	July	Aug	Sept	Pre	Post
Hou	60-21	47-34	19-13	21-13	56-20	11-9	38-11	69-44	30-14	77-41	104-51	3-4	24-19	36-12	10-4	18-12	20-8	15-12	16-8	19-9	19-6	57-33	50-22
Oak	52-29	45-36	17-16	25-8	44-32	11-9	35-14	62-51	35-26	62-39	95-59	2-6	27-22	30-17	6-9	14-18	16-10	17-11	15-9	17-9	18-8	51-41	46-24
Tex	45-36	33-48	18-14	18-16	33-43	9-11	26-32	52-52	25-25	53-59	75-79	3-5	25-21	25-32	7-6	14-14	14-13	18-11	8-16	13-16	11-14	48-42	30-42
LAA	38-43	34-47	17-18	13-18	30-46	12-8	23-30	49-60	20-24	52-66	67-87	5-3	18-22	21-30	3-7	13-17	14-13	15-13	14-11	9-18	7-18	45-46	27-44
Sea	35-46	33-48	14-19	18-15	27-49	9-11	16-36	52-58	25-33	43-61	62-92	6-2	23-26	22-31	9-4	18-14	7-21	12-16	10-13	10-16	11-14	39-55	29-39

Team vs. Team Breakdown

	EAST NYY	TB	Bos	Tor	Bal	CENTRAL Min	Cle	CWS	KC	Det	WEST Hou	Oak	Tex	LAA	Sea
New York Yankees	-	12	14	11	17	4	3	3	5	3	3	2	3	5	6
Tampa Bay Rays	7	-	12	13	12	2	6	4	4	4	4	3	3	4	4
Boston Red Sox	5	7	-	11	12	3	3	5	5	5	2	4	4	4	4
Toronto Blue Jays	8	6	8	-	11	3	1	3	6	4	2	6	3	1	2
Baltimore Orioles	2	7	7	8	-	0	3	3	3	3	2	1	1	4	3
Minnesota Twins	2	5	3	4	6	-	9	13	14	14	4	3	6	5	5
Cleveland Indians	4	1	3	6	4	10	-	8	12	18	3	1	4	6	5
Chicago White Sox	4	2	2	4	3	6	11	-	9	12	4	1	4	2	2
Kansas City Royals	2	3	1	1	3	5	7	10	-	9	1	2	2	2	2
Detroit Tigers	3	2	2	3	3	5	1	6	10	-	1	1	0	3	1
Houston Astros	4	3	4	4	4	3	4	3	5	6	-	13	13	14	18
Oakland Athletics	4	4	3	0	6	4	5	5	5	6	8	-	13	13	10
Texas Rangers	3	3	3	3	6	1	3	3	5	6	6	6	-	10	11
Los Angeles Angels	2	3	3	6	3	1	0	5	4	3	5	6	9	-	10
Seattle Mariners	1	2	3	4	4	2	1	4	5	6	1	9	8	9	-

2019 National League Standings

Overall

EAST							CENTRAL							WEST						
Team	W-L	Pct	GB	D1	LD1	LLd	Team	W-L	Pct	GB	D1	LD1	LLd	Team	W-L	Pct	GB	D1	LD1	LLd
Atlanta Braves	97-65	.599	0.0	113	9/29	10.5	St Louis Cardinals	91-71	.562	0.0	68	9/29	4.5	Los Angeles Dodgers	106-56	.654	0.0	180	9/29	21.0
Washington Nationals	93-69	.574	4.0	0	-	0.0	Milwaukee Brewers	89-73	.549	2.0	37	7/5	3.0	Arizona Diamondbacks	85-77	.525	21.0	0	-	0.0
New York Mets	86-76	.531	11.0	15	4/25	1.0	Chicago Cubs	84-78	.519	7.0	84	8/22	3.5	San Francisco Giants	77-85	.475	29.0	0	-	0.0
Philadelphia Phillies	81-81	.500	16.0	68	6/11	4.0	Cincinnati Reds	75-87	.463	16.0	3	3/30	0.0	Colorado Rockies	71-91	.438	35.0	3	3/30	0.0
Miami Marlins	57-105	.352	40.0	0	-	0.0	Pittsburgh Pirates	69-93	.426	22.0	5	4/22	1.0	San Diego Padres	70-92	.432	36.0	12	4/16	3.0

Wild Card Clinch Dates: Washington 9/24, Milwaukee 9/25. Division Clinch Dates: Los Angeles 9/9, Atlanta 9/19, St Louis 9/28.
D1 = Number of days a team had at least a share of first place of their division; LD1 = Last date the team had at least a share of first place; LLd = The largest number of games that a team led their division

East Division

Tm	AT		VERSUS						CONDITIONS				GAME			MONTHLY						ALL-STAR	
	Home	Road	East	Cent	West	AL	LHS	RHS	Day	Night	Grass	Turf	1-Rn	5+Rn	XInn	April	May	June	July	Aug	Sept	Pre	Post
Atl	50-31	47-34	46-30	20-13	18-15	13-7	23-14	74-51	23-16	74-49	93-63	4-2	28-16	31-17	11-6	14-15	16-12	20-8	14-10	19-9	14-11	54-37	43-28
Was	50-31	43-38	44-32	17-15	18-16	14-6	24-17	69-52	38-24	54-49	92-67	1-2	17-21	29-19	4-6	12-16	12-17	18-8	15-10	19-7	17-11	47-42	46-27
NYM	48-33	38-43	40-36	14-19	17-16	15-5	18-23	68-53	28-23	58-53	85-74	1-2	24-23	21-17	7-9	15-14	13-15	10-18	14-8	17-11	17-10	40-50	46-26
Phi	45-36	36-45	36-40	20-13	14-19	11-9	18-25	63-56	26-25	55-56	80-79	1-2	20-20	27-25	7-6	16-13	17-11	11-16	12-11	13-14	12-16	47-43	34-38
Mia	30-51	27-54	24-52	10-24	14-18	9-11	18-24	39-81	18-29	39-76	56-101	1-4	16-28	16-36	7-9	8-21	11-15	13-14	9-15	7-22	9-18	33-55	24-50

Central Division

Tm	AT		VERSUS						CONDITIONS				GAME			MONTHLY						ALL-STAR	
	Home	Road	East	Cent	West	AL	LHS	RHS	Day	Night	Grass	Turf	1-Rn	5+Rn	XInn	April	May	June	July	Aug	Sept	Pre	Post
StL	50-31	41-40	18-15	46-30	18-15	9-11	18-16	73-55	36-21	55-50	90-69	1-2	25-22	26-17	8-4	19-10	9-18	13-13	16-9	18-9	16-12	44-44	47-27
Mil	49-32	40-41	21-11	45-31	15-19	8-12	25-24	64-49	34-25	55-48	86-72	3-1	27-18	18-22	7-8	17-14	15-12	13-13	12-13	12-14	20-7	47-44	42-29
ChC	50-31	33-48	17-17	37-39	18-14	12-8	14-18	70-60	40-28	44-50	82-77	2-1	19-27	32-18	4-9	15-12	16-12	14-15	12-11	16-12	11-16	47-43	37-35
Cin	41-40	34-47	17-17	33-43	16-16	9-11	17-23	58-64	23-40	52-47	73-86	2-1	24-33	20-19	7-8	12-17	15-13	11-13	13-13	13-16	12-15	41-46	34-41
Pit	35-46	34-47	11-21	29-47	17-17	12-8	16-27	53-66	23-35	46-58	68-91	1-2	19-25	18-39	7-11	13-14	15-14	11-15	8-18	12-16	10-16	44-45	25-48

West Division

Tm	AT		VERSUS						CONDITIONS				GAME			MONTHLY						ALL-STAR	
	Home	Road	East	Cent	West	AL	LHS	RHS	Day	Night	Grass	Turf	1-Rn	5+Rn	XInn	April	May	June	July	Aug	Sept	Pre	Post
LAD	59-22	47-34	23-10	22-11	51-25	10-10	30-22	76-34	31-11	75-45	101-49	5-7	27-22	41-12	6-4	20-12	19-7	18-10	14-10	17-11	18-6	60-32	46-24
Ari	44-37	41-40	17-17	16-16	38-38	14-6	25-19	60-58	27-28	58-49	37-38	48-39	24-26	32-20	9-9	17-13	11-17	15-13	11-12	16-11	15-11	46-45	39-32
SF	35-46	42-39	14-19	14-19	38-38	11-9	20-29	57-56	25-37	52-48	68-82	9-3	38-16	18-24	13-3	12-18	10-16	14-13	19-6	11-16	11-16	41-48	36-37
Col	43-38	28-53	16-17	15-18	32-44	8-12	25-36	46-55	27-28	44-63	66-84	5-7	26-26	18-32	10-6	13-17	16-10	15-13	6-19	9-19	12-13	44-45	27-46
SD	36-45	34-47	14-18	14-20	31-45	11-9	14-22	56-70	25-31	45-61	65-84	5-8	26-24	13-23	5-7	17-13	13-14	12-14	8-16	13-15	7-20	45-45	25-47

Team vs. Team Breakdown

	EAST					CENTRAL					WEST				
	Atl	Was	NYM	Phi	Mia	StL	Mil	ChC	Cin	Pit	LAD	Ari	SF	Col	SD
Atlanta Braves	-	11	11	9	15	4	4	5	3	5	2	3	5	3	5
Washington Nationals	8	-	7	14	15	2	2	4	5	4	3	3	5	4	3
New York Mets	8	12	-	7	13	2	1	2	4	5	2	5	3	4	3
Philadelphia Phillies	10	5	12	-	9	4	3	5	4	4	2	2	3	4	3
Miami Marlins	4	4	6	10	-	3	2	1	1	3	1	4	3	2	4
St Louis Cardinals	2	5	5	2	4	-	10	10	12	14	4	3	4	5	2
Milwaukee Brewers	3	4	5	4	5	9	-	10	11	15	3	5	2	2	3
Chicago Cubs	2	2	5	2	6	9	9	-	8	11	3	4	4	3	4
Cincinnati Reds	4	1	3	3	6	7	8	11	-	7	1	3	4	3	5
Pittsburgh Pirates	2	3	1	2	3	5	4	8	12	-	0	1	5	5	6
Los Angeles Dodgers	4	4	5	5	5	3	4	4	5	6	-	11	12	15	15
Arizona Diamondbacks	4	4	2	4	3	3	2	2	3	6	8	-	10	9	11
San Francisco Giants	2	1	4	4	3	3	4	2	3	2	7	9	-	12	10
Colorado Rockies	3	3	2	3	5	2	5	3	3	2	4	10	7	-	11
San Diego Padres	2	4	3	3	2	4	4	3	2	1	6	8	9	8	-

American League Batting

Tm	G	AB	H	2B	3B	HR	(Hm	Rd)	TB	R	RBI	TBB	IBB	SO	HBP	SH	SF	ShO	SB	CS	SB%	GDP	LOB	Avg	OBP	Slg
NYY	162	5583	1493	290	17	306	(143	163)	2735	943	904	569	18	1437	49	10	33	2	55	22	.71	113	1512	.267	.339	.490
Min	162	5732	1547	318	23	307	(137	170)	2832	939	906	525	21	1334	81	10	41	3	28	21	.57	101	1647	.270	.338	.494
Hou	162	5613	1538	323	28	288	(150	138)	2781	920	891	645	17	1166	66	10	57	6	67	27	.71	146	1727	.274	.352	.495
Bos	162	5770	1554	345	27	245	(118	127)	2688	901	857	590	36	1382	49	20	44	6	68	30	.69	127	1751	.269	.340	.466
Oak	162	5561	1384	292	23	257	(122	135)	2493	845	800	578	17	1338	87	7	36	3	49	21	.70	140	1630	.249	.327	.448
Tex	162	5540	1374	296	24	223	(114	109)	2387	810	765	534	18	1578	67	17	44	6	131	38	.78	98	1558	.248	.319	.431
TB	162	5628	1427	291	29	217	(99	118)	2427	769	730	542	20	1493	73	8	34	6	94	37	.72	114	1679	.254	.325	.431
LAA	162	5542	1368	268	21	220	(116	104)	2338	769	734	586	29	1276	67	4	42	11	65	20	.76	143	1696	.247	.324	.422
Cle	162	5425	1354	286	18	223	(107	116)	2345	769	731	563	30	1332	50	40	46	14	103	35	.75	110	1605	.250	.323	.432
Sea	162	5500	1305	254	28	239	(107	132)	2332	758	730	588	7	1581	58	14	37	11	115	47	.71	83	1585	.237	.316	.424
Bal	162	5596	1379	252	25	213	(114	99)	2320	729	698	462	8	1435	71	22	37	8	84	30	.74	111	1595	.246	.310	.415
Tor	162	5493	1299	270	21	247	(136	111)	2352	726	697	509	10	1514	45	14	28	12	51	20	.72	107	1494	.236	.305	.428
CWS	161	5529	1443	260	20	182	(90	92)	2289	708	676	378	13	1549	66	36	32	12	63	28	.69	114	1565	.261	.314	.414
KC	162	5496	1356	281	40	162	(62	100)	2203	691	655	456	17	1405	59	24	42	12	117	39	.75	113	1609	.247	.309	.401
Det	161	5549	1333	292	41	149	(64	85)	2154	582	556	391	14	1595	48	9	42	14	57	20	.74	108	1565	.240	.294	.388
AL	1214	83557	21154	4318	385	3478	(1679	1799)	36676	11859	11330	7916	275	21415	936	245	595	126	1147	435	.73	1728	24218	.253	.323	.439

American League Pitching

	HOW MUCH THEY PITCHED					WHAT THEY GAVE UP												THE RESULTS									
Tm	G	CG	Rel	IP	BFP	H	R	ER	HR	SH	SF	HB	TBB	IBB	SO	WP	Bk	W	L	Pct.	ShO	Sv-Op	Hld	OAvg	OOBP	OSlg	ERA
Hou	162	2	492	1462.1	5995	1205	640	595	230	11	30	41	448	0	1671	41	8	107	55	.660	14	47-67	97	.221	.283	.397	3.66
TB	162	0	603	1474.1	6086	1274	656	598	181	11	28	60	453	27	1621	59	7	96	66	.593	12	46-70	116	.230	.294	.386	3.65
Cle	162	6	522	1437.2	6008	1308	657	601	207	17	30	62	450	19	1508	42	2	93	69	.574	16	42-58	77	.240	.304	.419	3.76
Oak	162	1	547	1465.0	6153	1342	680	646	201	25	42	66	477	19	1299	74	4	97	65	.599	12	45-75	109	.242	.308	.404	3.97
NYY	162	1	545	1443.0	6133	1374	739	691	248	7	36	44	507	12	1534	55	5	103	59	.636	9	50-75	101	.248	.314	.439	4.31
Min	162	1	524	1463.1	6246	1456	754	680	198	20	40	61	452	10	1463	71	5	101	61	.623	10	50-72	102	.257	.316	.419	4.18
Bos	162	1	632	1471.0	6400	1423	828	768	215	18	38	76	605	22	1633	81	6	84	78	.519	8	33-61	82	.251	.330	.431	4.70
Tor	162	1	591	1440.1	6313	1450	828	767	228	11	36	69	604	25	1332	70	6	72	89	.447	7	33-43	72	.259	.337	.451	4.79
CWS	161	6	536	1412.2	6159	1438	832	769	238	20	38	51	582	30	1312	71	5	72	89	.447	7	33-49	73	.263	.337	.452	4.90
LAA	162	0	589	1442.2	6289	1417	868	820	267	12	43	82	576	11	1404	98	9	72	90	.444	2	32-46	72	.254	.331	.459	5.12
KC	162	1	520	1465.2	6307	1525	869	824	221	18	49	81	582	25	1230	59	5	59	103	.364	7	37-60	61	.273	.348	.456	5.20
Tex	162	4	499	1438.0	6354	1515	878	808	241	19	50	70	583	11	1379	68	3	78	84	.481	5	33-47	58	.269	.342	.464	5.06
Sea	162	3	538	1439.1	6268	1484	893	798	260	12	46	51	505	25	1239	75	4	68	94	.420	4	34-63	66	.263	.326	.469	4.99
Det	161	0	577	1433.0	6341	1555	915	835	250	25	46	69	536	24	1368	66	7	47	114	.292	3	31-56	65	.275	.342	.478	5.24
Bal	162	0	533	1443.0	6396	1544	981	897	305	10	46	80	561	11	1248	75	6	54	108	.333	5	27-54	57	.271	.342	.497	5.59
AL	1214	27	8248	21690.2	93448	21310	12018	11097	3490	236	598	963	7921	271	21241	1005	82	1198	1230	.493	125	573-896	1208	.255	.324	.442	4.60

American League Fielding

Team	G	Inn	PO	Ast	OFAst	E	(Throw	Field)	TC	DP	GDP	SB	CS	SB%	CPkof	PPkof	PB	UER	UERA	FPct
Houston	162	1462.1	4387	1353	15	71	41	30	5811	97	83	75	17	.82	0	4	7	45	0.28	.988
Kansas City	162	1425.0	4275	1505	27	73	34	39	5853	152	133	57	27	.68	1	4	10	45	0.28	.988
Oakland	162	1465.0	4395	1464	21	80	37	43	5939	123	114	83	41	.67	0	3	19	34	0.21	.987
Cleveland	162	1437.2	4313	1322	38	83	47	36	5718	111	89	53	28	.65	0	10	2	56	0.35	.985
Tampa Bay	162	1474.1	4423	1414	23	87	41	46	5924	129	107	75	35	.68	2	1	16	58	0.35	.985
Boston	162	1471.0	4413	1436	37	88	33	55	5937	115	97	70	31	.69	5	2	15	60	0.37	.985
Los Angeles	162	1442.2	4328	1469	19	92	37	55	5889	118	106	99	35	.74	1	8	11	48	0.30	.984
Toronto	162	1440.1	4321	1503	27	96	39	57	5920	141	111	74	36	.67	2	6	9	61	0.38	.984
New York	162	1443.0	4329	1347	22	102	49	53	5778	135	119	71	24	.75	4	1	13	48	0.30	.982
Texas	162	1438.0	4314	1364	18	105	47	58	5783	143	131	81	26	.76	2	5	11	70	0.44	.982
Baltimore	162	1443.0	4329	1442	20	108	59	49	5879	156	134	82	25	.77	2	2	16	84	0.52	.982
Detroit	161	1433.0	4299	1451	19	110	49	61	5860	127	107	97	37	.72	1	1	16	80	0.50	.981
Minnesota	162	1463.1	4390	1405	35	111	50	61	5906	129	107	71	16	.82	0	7	15	74	0.46	.981
Chicago	161	1412.2	4238	1525	35	117	50	67	5880	170	149	76	26	.75	2	2	13	40	0.40	.980
Seattle	162	1439.1	4318	1490	19	132	54	78	5940	146	132	83	26	.76	0	1	7	95	0.59	.978
American League	1214	21690.2	65072	21490	375	1455	667	788	88017	1992	1719	1147	430	.73	23	57	180	921	0.38	.983

National League Batting

Tm	G	AB	H	2B	3B	HR	(Hm	Rd)	TB	R	RBI	TBB	IBB	SO	HBP	SH	SF	ShO	SB	CS	SB%	GDP	LOB	Avg	OBP	Slg
LAD	162	5493	1414	302	20	279	(143	136)	2593	886	861	607	47	1356	81	55	45	6	57	10	.85	100	1684	.257	.338	.472
Was	162	5512	1460	298	27	231	(130	101)	2505	873	824	584	33	1308	81	48	42	8	116	29	.80	117	1659	.265	.342	.454
Atl	162	5560	1432	277	29	249	(131	118)	2514	855	824	619	39	1467	60	25	35	5	89	28	.76	104	1684	.258	.336	.452
Col	162	5660	1502	323	41	224	(132	92)	2579	835	803	489	25	1503	43	51	43	7	71	31	.70	111	1618	.265	.326	.456
ChC	162	5461	1378	270	26	256	(123	133)	2468	814	783	581	33	1460	83	30	39	8	45	24	.65	127	1591	.252	.331	.452
Ari	162	5633	1419	288	40	220	(97	123)	2447	813	778	540	36	1360	70	31	40	7	88	14	.86	120	1668	.252	.323	.434
NYM	162	5624	1445	280	17	242	(126	116)	2485	791	767	516	34	1384	95	28	27	9	56	27	.67	129	1714	.257	.328	.442
Phi	162	5571	1369	311	26	215	(123	92)	2377	774	742	562	47	1453	57	34	34	7	78	18	.81	97	1663	.246	.319	.427
Mil	162	5542	1366	279	17	250	(126	124)	2429	769	744	629	42	1563	72	20	38	8	101	25	.80	120	1705	.246	.329	.438
StL	162	5449	1337	246	24	210	(89	121)	2261	764	714	561	15	1420	76	40	39	9	116	29	.80	110	1660	.245	.322	.415
Pit	162	5657	1497	315	38	163	(70	93)	2377	758	722	425	41	1213	63	47	34	10	64	29	.69	119	1684	.265	.321	.420
Cin	162	5450	1328	235	27	227	(118	109)	2298	701	679	492	25	1436	89	30	33	11	80	38	.68	111	1595	.244	.315	.422
SD	162	5391	1281	224	24	219	(101	118)	2210	682	652	504	19	1581	55	37	31	8	70	37	.65	120	1509	.238	.308	.410
SF	162	5579	1332	300	26	167	(63	104)	2185	678	655	475	26	1435	50	24	42	17	47	28	.63	111	1632	.239	.302	.392
Mia	162	5512	1326	265	18	146	(68	78)	2065	615	593	395	16	1469	73	31	33	22	55	30	.65	139	1573	.241	.298	.375
NL	1215	83094	20886	4213	400	3298	(1640	1658)	35793	11608	11141	7979	478	21408	1048	531	555	142	1133	397	.74	1735	24639	.251	.323	.431

National League Pitching

Tm	G	CG	Rel	IP	BFP	H	R	ER	HR	SH	SF	HB	TBB	IBB	SO	WP	Bk	W	L	Pct.	ShO	Sv-Op	Hld	OAvg	OOBP	OSlg	ERA
LAD	162	3	545	1445.2	5913	1201	613	541	185	30	36	66	392	24	1519	40	7	106	56	.654	18	44-72	74	.223	.282	.379	3.37
StL	162	1	542	1444.0	6068	1284	662	609	191	27	38	69	545	41	1399	46	4	91	71	.562	14	52-73	97	.238	.314	.397	3.80
Cin	162	0	535	1438.0	6057	1270	711	668	214	36	31	58	536	31	1552	35	8	75	87	.463	10	46-69	85	.251	.323	.410	4.18
ChC	162	1	576	1442.0	6190	1377	717	657	195	29	49	80	534	16	1444	60	1	84	78	.519	10	38-66	71	.251	.323	.415	4.10
Was	162	1	530	1439.1	6134	1340	724	683	202	27	37	61	517	41	1511	53	5	93	69	.574	13	40-69	94	.244	.314	.412	4.27
NYM	162	3	502	1461.0	6232	1405	737	688	204	35	35	60	500	40	1520	47	2	86	76	.531	12	38-65	59	.251	.317	.418	4.24
Ari	162	0	557	1465.0	6230	1400	743	691	220	39	39	62	516	38	1427	49	4	85	77	.525	11	45-69	90	.251	.320	.432	4.25
Atl	162	1	575	1450.2	6243	1421	743	675	203	39	27	69	548	33	1393	70	3	97	65	.599	8	44-66	106	.256	.329	.419	4.19
Mil	162	0	588	1459.1	6251	1364	766	713	225	43	34	60	570	28	1497	41	3	89	73	.549	7	50-77	104	.246	.321	.425	4.40
SF	162	1	587	1469.0	6256	1395	773	715	227	41	33	65	519	26	1368	53	4	77	85	.475	8	41-63	86	.249	.318	.428	4.38
SD	162	0	543	1432.0	6160	1394	789	732	215	43	35	68	463	19	1475	60	6	70	92	.432	6	47-72	96	.251	.315	.430	4.60
Phi	162	3	564	1453.2	6274	1452	794	731	258	46	40	71	546	38	1392	45	7	81	81	.500	7	36-55	94	.261	.332	.453	4.53
Mia	162	2	539	1444.1	6247	1340	808	760	236	29	39	90	615	52	1378	71	6	57	105	.352	8	27-49	55	.245	.329	.435	4.74
Pit	162	1	550	1440.0	6391	1511	911	829	241	34	36	85	584	22	1443	50	4	69	93	.426	6	31-55	57	.268	.343	.470	5.18
Col	162	1	590	1448.2	6423	1576	958	895	270	42	43	57	589	33	1264	63	7	71	91	.438	5	28-51	62	.277	.348	.492	5.56
NL	1215	18	8323	21732.2	93069	20730	11449	10587	3286	540	552	1021	7974	482	21582	783	71	1231	1199	.507	143	607-971	1230	.250	.321	.428	4.38

National League Fielding

Team	G	Inn	PO	Ast	OFAst	E	(Throw	Field)	TC	DP	GDP	SB	CS	SB%	CPkof	PPkof	PB	UER	UERA	FPct
St Louis	162	1444.0	4332	1578	26	66	20	46	5976	170	139	34	19	.64	0	3	6	53	0.33	.989
Atlanta	162	1450.2	4352	1522	26	78	30	48	5952	156	134	76	20	.79	1	6	24	68	0.42	.987
Arizona	162	1465.0	4395	1560	25	86	40	46	6041	138	113	47	31	.60	2	3	6	52	0.32	.986
San Francisco	162	1469.0	4407	1536	28	90	35	55	6033	143	124	88	33	.73	2	0	7	58	0.36	.985
Washington	162	1439.1	4318	1374	20	87	32	55	5779	112	98	86	24	.78	3	5	16	41	0.26	.985
Cincinnati	162	1438.0	4314	1460	22	91	51	40	5865	125	105	88	26	.77	1	1	10	43	0.27	.984
Colorado	162	1448.2	4346	1758	22	97	45	52	6201	167	139	75	30	.71	1	3	8	63	0.39	.984
Philadelphia	162	1453.2	4361	1552	33	97	48	49	6010	139	116	66	50	.57	3	5	11	63	0.39	.984
Miami	162	1444.1	4333	1364	36	94	48	46	5791	135	113	57	24	.70	0	2	13	48	0.30	.984
Milwaukee	162	1459.1	4378	1395	23	97	49	48	5870	136	108	94	34	.73	1	1	10	53	0.33	.983
New York	162	1461.0	4383	1434	21	99	44	55	5916	129	116	139	22	.86	4	2	14	49	0.30	.983
Los Angeles	162	1445.2	4337	1428	27	106	50	56	5871	118	106	63	17	.79	2	2	11	72	0.45	.982
Chicago	162	1442.0	4326	1619	24	117	57	60	6062	133	133	91	25	.78	3	9	10	60	0.37	.981
San Diego	162	1432.0	4296	1386	28	116	61	55	5798	101	86	58	18	.76	0	4	6	57	0.36	.980
Pittsburgh	162	1440.0	4320	1493	20	121	58	63	5934	132	114	71	29	.71	7	4	17	82	0.51	.980
National League	1215	21732.2	65198	22459	381	1442	668	774	89099	2043	1744	1133	402	.74	30	50	169	862	0.36	.984

Team Pitching Staff Summary

Team	Starters				Bullpen					
	IP	ERA	ERA Rank	W-L	IP	ERA	ERA Rank	W-L	Sv-Opp	Sv Pct
Arizona Diamondbacks	867.1	4.23	13	56-51	597.2	4.26	12	29-26	45-69	65%
Atlanta Braves	873.0	4.20	12	60-46	577.2	4.21	11	37-19	44-66	67%
Baltimore Orioles	789.0	5.57	28	36-76	654.0	5.79	30	18-32	27-54	50%
Boston Red Sox	806.0	4.95	20	50-50	665.0	4.40	17	34-28	33-61	54%
Chicago Cubs	888.0	4.18	10	51-47	554.0	3.98	8	33-31	38-66	58%
Chicago White Sox	838.2	5.30	23	48-68	574.0	4.33	14	24-21	33-49	67%
Cincinnati Reds	883.1	4.12	9	48-54	554.2	4.28	13	27-33	46-69	67%
Cleveland Indians	930.1	3.81	6	62-51	507.1	3.76	3	31-18	42-58	72%
Colorado Rockies	842.1	5.87	30	45-62	606.1	5.18	28	26-29	28-51	55%
Detroit Tigers	792.0	5.51	27	23-81	641.0	4.94	24	24-33	31-56	55%
Houston Astros	907.1	3.61	3	79-37	555.0	3.75	2	28-18	47-67	70%
Kansas City Royals	860.0	5.30	23	39-70	565.0	5.07	27	20-33	37-60	62%
Los Angeles Angels	681.0	5.64	29	28-60	761.2	4.64	20	44-30	32-46	70%
Los Angeles Dodgers	893.2	3.11	1	62-32	552.0	3.85	4	44-24	44-72	61%
Miami Marlins	888.0	4.59	16	36-71	556.1	4.97	25	21-34	27-49	55%
Milwaukee Brewers	788.2	4.40	14	44-40	670.2	4.40	17	45-33	50-77	65%
Minnesota Twins	889.2	4.19	11	67-39	573.2	4.17	10	34-22	50-72	69%
New York Mets	941.1	3.84	7	54-44	519.2	4.99	26	32-32	38-65	58%
New York Yankees	778.1	4.51	15	60-38	664.2	4.08	9	43-21	50-75	67%
Oakland Athletics	886.0	4.02	8	68-37	579.0	3.89	7	29-28	45-75	60%
Philadelphia Phillies	869.2	4.64	17	49-52	584.0	4.38	16	32-29	36-55	65%
Pittsburgh Pirates	813.2	5.40	26	36-63	626.1	4.91	23	33-30	31-55	56%
San Diego Padres	813.0	4.66	18	41-59	619.0	4.59	19	29-33	47-72	65%
San Francisco Giants	849.0	4.77	19	39-66	620.0	3.85	4	38-19	41-63	65%
Seattle Mariners	745.0	5.21	21	36-56	694.1	4.77	22	32-38	34-63	54%
St Louis Cardinals	883.0	3.78	5	55-50	561.0	3.88	6	36-21	52-73	71%
Tampa Bay Rays	702.1	3.64	4	40-35	772.0	3.71	1	56-31	46-70	66%
Texas Rangers	808.0	5.37	25	45-60	630.0	4.73	21	33-24	33-47	70%
Toronto Blue Jays	711.1	5.25	22	26-68	729.0	4.35	15	41-27	33-43	77%
Washington Nationals	938.2	3.53	2	66-36	500.2	5.68	29	27-33	40-69	58%

Team Defense
Defensive Runs Saved by Position and Team

Team	P	C	1B	2B	3B	SS	LF	CF	RF	Shifts	Total
Los Angeles Dodgers	12	11	0	9	-1	9	17	2	29	48	136
Arizona Diamondbacks	6	13	8	-4	1	19	11	9	10	44	117
St Louis Cardinals	17	-2	6	16	7	16	0	16	-11	30	95
Houston Astros	-2	3	0	-1	8	1	17	11	17	35	89
Cleveland Indians	0	30	-2	1	3	8	6	7	1	16	70
Cincinnati Reds	9	11	6	1	3	12	-3	-1	7	13	58
Tampa Bay Rays	-6	7	-1	8	0	12	1	8	0	25	54
Philadelphia Phillies	6	10	-3	6	1	-2	16	1	11	7	53
San Francisco Giants	-4	8	6	2	5	-1	4	0	14	12	46
Oakland Athletics	0	-21	11	-10	21	4	20	-11	14	14	42
Atlanta Braves	4	5	5	8	13	-4	9	-2	-1	0	37
Milwaukee Brewers	-11	6	2	2	5	3	5	22	0	2	36
San Diego Padres	-7	22	-4	7	6	-2	5	-1	0	-7	19
Miami Marlins	5	-12	3	-1	7	11	-7	0	-7	12	11
Los Angeles Angels	-7	-13	2	-2	5	17	-18	7	1	19	11
Colorado Rockies	6	1	8	1	8	15	-10	-26	-11	16	8
Kansas City Royals	0	6	-6	11	-17	9	2	14	-11	-1	7
Washington Nationals	3	-10	1	-2	-1	-23	2	23	0	5	-2
Minnesota Twins	-1	-9	-3	-6	-1	-5	2	8	2	6	-7
Toronto Blue Jays	5	18	-6	-9	-2	1	-5	-8	-15	12	-9
Chicago Cubs	-6	-4	2	-2	-4	15	-2	-8	1	-5	-13
New York Yankees	-10	1	-9	-2	-4	-6	7	0	19	-14	-18
Boston Red Sox	2	3	0	-11	-12	-20	-6	-1	8	-3	-40
Chicago White Sox	-2	-9	-6	8	-6	-6	-16	0	-23	11	-49
Texas Rangers	-8	-9	-1	-5	-4	-8	-16	4	-12	10	-49
Pittsburgh Pirates	15	-8	-3	9	-16	-6	-5	-12	-23	-4	-53
Detroit Tigers	-11	-3	-1	-6	-5	-17	-12	-17	-12	1	-83
Seattle Mariners	-3	-14	-7	-13	-8	-20	0	-10	-12	1	-86
New York Mets	-22	-14	-5	-7	-5	-18	-11	-13	3	-1	-93
Baltimore Orioles	-21	-22	-1	-9	-1	-8	-12	-8	-10	-13	-105

Batting By Position

Pos	AB	H	2B	3B	HR	(Hm	Rd)	TB	R	RBI	TBB	IBB	SO	HBP	SH	SF	SB	CS	SB%	GDP	LOB	Avg	OBP	Slg
						BATTING											**BASERUNNING**					**PERCENTAGES**		
P	4490	574	74	4	25	(12	13)	731	227	234	156	0	2218	12	431	8	4	4	.50	55	1759	.128	.159	.163
C	17334	4123	795	32	694	(356	338)	7064	2130	2293	1614	94	4611	230	60	125	69	29	.70	436	5497	.238	.309	.408
1B	18462	4723	970	54	909	(475	434)	8528	2645	2872	2119	115	4779	230	2	138	89	41	.68	440	5584	.256	.338	.462
2B	18555	4759	917	109	617	(317	300)	7745	2494	2300	1580	59	4093	213	58	127	295	118	.71	332	5522	.256	.320	.417
3B	18658	4903	1005	83	855	(440	415)	8639	2729	2742	1865	94	4349	227	16	147	166	61	.73	434	5409	.263	.335	.463
SS	19004	5108	1084	121	676	(354	322)	8462	2761	2410	1533	70	4172	158	52	132	421	158	.73	393	5066	.269	.326	.445
LF	18731	4907	1039	119	796	(404	392)	8572	2762	2650	1806	63	4712	216	33	119	263	108	.71	371	5372	.262	.332	.458
CF	18390	4598	962	122	687	(352	335)	7865	2691	2229	1644	61	4921	281	79	114	528	152	.78	305	5020	.250	.319	.428
RF	18845	4960	995	90	858	(425	433)	8709	2888	2588	1945	110	4726	234	27	128	288	93	.76	377	5135	.263	.338	.462
DH	9237	2285	458	28	469	(236	233)	4206	1318	1397	1024	51	2608	114	1	71	69	27	.72	207	2666	.247	.328	.455
PH	4926	1099	232	23	190	(86	104)	1947	620	755	608	36	1618	69	17	41	31	22	.58	113	1819	.223	.315	.395
PR	3	1	0	0	0	(0	0)	1	202	1	1	0	0	0	0	0	57	19	.75	0	7	.333	.500	.333

Fielding By Position

Pos	Inn	PO	Ast	E	(Throw	Field)	TC	DP	GDP	FPct
P	43423.1	2535	4240	373	289	83	7148	324	264	.948
C	43423.1	43145	2238	300	196	92	45683	255	15	.993
1B	43423.1	37740	3031	301	79	201	41072	3674	231	.993
2B	43423.1	8026	11867	366	135	225	20259	2967	1045	.982
3B	43423.1	3392	9149	525	239	281	13066	962	709	.960
SS	43423.1	6008	12668	553	274	278	19229	2625	1348	.971
LF	43423.1	8530	256	158	39	116	8944	41	1	.982
CF	43423.1	11391	219	152	40	112	11762	51		.987
RF	43423.1	9503	281	169	44	121	9953	54		.983

Team Efficiency Summary

Brian Reiff

You won't find many leaderboards from the 2019 season that show the Houston Astros and Detroit Tigers next to each other. However, that's exactly what you'll see if you turn this page—the Astros and Tigers together as the two least efficient teams in the AL in 2019, at least in terms of converting their offensive and defensive production into wins.

The Tigers scored an MLB-low 582 runs, but based on their components of offensive production—e.g. singles, doubles, triples and home runs—they were expected to score 611 runs. Defensively, they allowed about as many runs as would have been expected. Based on their combined expected runs scored and runs allowed, the Tigers would have been expected to win 50 games, three more than the 47 they did win.

In contrast, the Astros scored the third-most runs in baseball. They, too, were expected to score more. Factoring in their defensive inefficiency as well gets them to 115 expected wins, eight more than they actually had.

Generally, when a team wins 100+ games, one would expect that they had to be efficient in getting there. After all, it's difficult enough to get to 100 wins, and even more so when your record is hampered by unlucky sequencing, poor baserunning, shoddy defense or any other of myriad reasons why a team might have been inefficient in winning games.

And yet, despite scoring fewer runs than expected and allowing more runs than expected, the Astros still finished with over 100 wins. The Los Angeles Dodgers, too, finished with over 100 wins despite being one of the most inefficient teams in their league. The only other 100-win teams this year, the New York Yankees and Minnesota Twins, did overperform by this metric, having played more like 95- and 98-win teams, respectively.

The tables in this section contain four different efficiency numbers for each team:

1. Offensive efficiency (Hit Eff): Comparison of the expected number of runs scored using components of production to the actual number of runs scored.

2. Defensive efficiency (Pit Eff): Comparison of the expected number of runs allowed using components of production to the actual number of runs allowed.

3. Runs efficiency (Runs Eff): Comparison of the expected number of wins based on actual runs scored and runs allowed to the actual number of wins.

4. Overall efficiency (Overall Eff): Comparison of the expected number of wins based on expected runs scored and allowed to the actual number of wins.

2019 American League Team Efficiency Summary

	RC	Runs	Hit Eff	Exp RA	RA	Pit Eff	Exp Wins	Wins	Runs Eff	Eff Wins	Wins	Overall Eff
Texas Rangers	753	810	108	882	878	100	74	78	105	68	78	114
New York Yankees	898	943	105	758	739	103	100	103	103	95	103	109
Chicago White Sox	696	708	102	831	832	100	68	72	106	66	72	108
Oakland Athletics	787	845	107	684	680	101	98	97	99	92	97	105
Cleveland Indians	746	769	103	665	657	101	94	93	99	90	93	103
Los Angeles Angels	741	769	104	854	868	98	71	72	101	70	72	103
Minnesota Twins	928	939	101	751	754	100	98	101	103	98	101	103
Toronto Blue Jays	692	726	105	830	828	100	70	67	95	66	67	101
Seattle Mariners	732	758	104	851	893	95	68	68	100	69	68	99
Tampa Bay Rays	773	769	99	613	656	94	94	96	102	99	96	97
Kansas City Royals	668	691	103	854	869	98	63	59	94	61	59	96
Baltimore Orioles	704	729	103	952	981	97	58	54	94	57	54	94
Boston Red Sox	886	901	102	800	828	97	88	84	96	89	84	94
Detroit Tigers	611	582	95	907	915	99	46	47	101	50	47	94
Houston Astros	954	920	96	607	640	95	109	107	98	115	107	93

2019 National League Team Efficiency Summary

	RC	Runs	Hit Eff	Exp RA	RA	Pit Eff	Exp Wins	Wins	Runs Eff	Eff Wins	Wins	Overall Eff
San Francisco Giants	639	678	106	743	773	96	70	77	109	69	77	112
Philadelphia Phillies	750	774	103	831	794	105	79	81	103	73	81	111
Atlanta Braves	839	855	102	752	743	101	92	97	105	90	97	108
Milwaukee Brewers	788	769	98	746	766	97	81	89	109	85	89	104
Pittsburgh Pirates	741	758	102	892	911	98	66	69	104	66	69	104
Colorado Rockies	813	835	103	925	958	97	70	71	102	71	71	101
St Louis Cardinals	731	764	105	643	662	97	93	91	98	91	91	100
San Diego Padres	656	682	104	750	789	95	69	70	101	70	70	100
Arizona Diamondbacks	780	813	104	738	743	99	88	85	96	85	85	99
New York Mets	789	791	100	729	737	99	87	86	99	87	86	98
Washington Nationals	851	873	103	703	724	97	96	93	97	96	93	97
Miami Marlins	588	615	105	780	808	97	59	57	96	59	57	97
Chicago Cubs	794	814	103	741	717	103	91	84	92	87	84	97
Los Angeles Dodgers	867	886	102	571	613	93	110	106	97	113	106	94
Cincinnati Reds	706	701	99	677	711	95	80	75	94	84	75	89

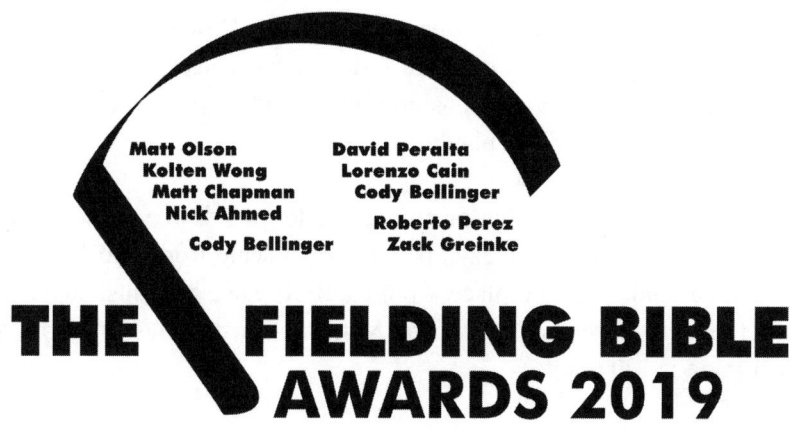

Matt Olson
Kolten Wong
Matt Chapman
Nick Ahmed
Cody Bellinger

David Peralta
Lorenzo Cain
Cody Bellinger

Roberto Perez
Zack Greinke

THE FIELDING BIBLE
AWARDS 2019

The Fielding Bible Awards 2019

Mark Simon

Both watching and playing great defense never gets old.

Some of the top defensive players in the game have aged a bit, but that didn't stop them from having outstanding seasons in 2019. This year's Fielding Bible Awards include four recipients who were 30 or older—Indians catcher Roberto Perez, Brewers center fielder Lorenzo Cain, Diamondbacks left fielder David Peralta, and Astros pitcher Zack Greinke.

The 33-year-old Cain and the 35-year-old Greinke (he'll be 36 by the time you read this) each won for the second straight season. They were joined as repeat winners by first baseman Matt Olson, second baseman Kolten Wong, and third baseman Matt Chapman.

Newly honored winners joining Peralta and Perez are shortstop Nick Ahmed and right fielder Cody Bellinger. Bellinger also won the Multi-Position award. He's the first player to win two Fielding Bible Awards in the same season.

Congratulations to all the winners!

Two new panelists, baseball journalists Joe Sheehan and Christina Kahrl, are now part of our 12-person expert voting panel. Meg Rowley, managing editor of Fangraphs.com, has been added as a tiebreaker voter. The panel awards 10 winners each year, one at each position plus an additional award that goes to the best defensive multi-position player.

Here's a refresher on how the awards are determined. We asked a panel of 12 experts to rank 10 players at each position on a scale from 1 to 10. A first-place vote gets 10 points, second place 9 points, third place 8 points, etc. Total up the points for each player and the player with the most points wins the award. A perfect score is 120 points.

Here are the Fielding Bible Awards for the 2019 season.

First Base – Matt Olson, Oakland Athletics

Olson won his second in a row, this time by unanimous selection. He is a difference-maker at first base for the Athletics, helping make their infield one of the best in baseball. Twelve of his 13 Defensive Runs Saved come from Range & Positioning. Only two other first basemen even reached five Range & Positioning Runs Saved. Olson is very surehanded, rating above average on balls hit down the line and in the hole. He does great work handling throws from shortstop Marcus Semien and third baseman Matt Chapman. Over the last two seasons, Olson has 67 Good Fielding Plays for throw handling. No other first baseman has more than 60.

Previous Winners:

2018	Matt Olson	2011	Albert Pujols
2017	Paul Goldschmidt	2010	Daric Barton
2016	Anthony Rizzo	2009	Albert Pujols
2015	Paul Goldschmidt	2008	Albert Pujols
2014	Adrian Gonzalez	2007	Albert Pujols
2013	Paul Goldschmidt	2006	Albert Pujols
2012	Mark Teixeira		

Second Base – Kolten Wong, St. Louis Cardinals

Kolten Wong has earned the title of best defensive second baseman the last two seasons, becoming an efficient machine when it comes to turning ground balls into outs. Last year he edged out DJ LeMahieu by five points. This time he was a unanimous selection. Wong stands out for getting outs on balls in the '34' hole that other second basemen don't reach. He also brings an aggressiveness to the position. Wong made 38 plays in which he sprinted to either reach a pop up or go after a ground ball, five more than any oher second baseman.

Previous Winners:

2018	Kolten Wong	2011	Dustin Pedroia
2017	DJ LeMahieu	2010	Chase Utley
2016	Dustin Pedroia	2009	Aaron Hill
2015	Ian Kinsler	2008	Brandon Phillips
2014	Dustin Pedroia	2007	Aaron Hill
2013	Dustin Pedroia	2006	Orlando Hudson
2012	Darwin Barney		

Third Base – Matt Chapman, Oakland Athletics

Chapman hasn't been around for that long, but his defensive work already merits mention with all-time greats. Chapman specializes in doubles denial. The Athletics allowed 97 ground balls hit within 10 feet of the third base line. Their third basemen (almost always Chapman) turned 76% of them into outs, a rate 20 percentage points above the MLB average. What's so impressive is that Chapman does this sort of thing while playing a mistake-free third base. He had the fewest Misplays & Errors on a per-inning basis of any third baseman. In the last three seasons Chapman has 66 Defensive Runs Saved. Nolan Arenado ranks second among third basemen with 33, half as many!

Previous Winners:

2018	Matt Chapman	2011	Adrian Beltre
2017	Nolan Arenado	2010	Evan Longoria
2016	Nolan Arenado	2009	Ryan Zimmerman
2015	Nolan Arenado	2008	Adrian Beltre
2014	Josh Donaldson	2007	Pedro Feliz
2013	Manny Machado	2006	Adrian Beltre
2012	Adrian Beltre		

Shortstop – Nick Ahmed, Arizona Diamondbacks

Ahmed ended Andrelton Simmons' six-year reign as a Fielding Bible Award winner. He edged Javier Baez by two points in an extremely tight vote. Ahmed's success doesn't come from making flashy plays like his positional counterparts. It comes on the strength of his throwing arm (he pitched in college) which allows him to make plays in the hole that other shortstops can't make. On the Sports Info Solutions Baseball Podcast, Ahmed expressed concern that good defenders outside major markets might get overlooked. He's not getting overlooked by our panel.

Previous Winners:

2018	Andrelton Simmons	2011	Troy Tulowitzki
2017	Andrelton Simmons	2010	Troy Tulowitzki
2016	Andrelton Simmons	2009	Jack Wilson
2015	Andrelton Simmons	2008	Jimmy Rollins
2014	Andrelton Simmons	2007	Troy Tulowitzki
2013	Andrelton Simmons	2006	Adam Everett
2012	Brendan Ryan		

Left Field – David Peralta, Arizona Diamondbacks

Speaking of close votes, left field went to our tiebreaker, which gave the award to Peralta over Michael Brantley of the Astros. Peralta tied Brantley and Mike Tauchman for the lead in Defensive Runs Saved among left fielders with 10. Those came largely from his being able to catch up to fly balls hit to the deepest part of the ballpark. He also had a positive value in Outfield Arm Runs Saved in left field for the first time in his career. Left field might not be the most glamorous position in the major leagues these days, but Peralta does what needs to be done to excel there.

Previous Winners:

2018	Alex Gordon	2011	Brett Gardner
2017	Brett Gardner	2010	Brett Gardner
2016	Starling Marte	2009	Carl Crawford
2015	Starling Marte	2008	Carl Crawford
2014	Alex Gordon	2007	Eric Byrnes
2013	Alex Gordon	2006	Carl Crawford
2012	Alex Gordon		

Center Field – Lorenzo Cain, Milwaukee Brewers

Center field is a physically challenging position. And it's one in which great players abound. That makes it highly impressive that Cain is the first center fielder to win a Fielding Bible Award in consecutive years since BIS introduced the award in 2006. Cain is all about chasing down well-hit fly balls. His five home run robberies matched the most in a season since we began tracking them in 2004 (Carlos Gomez had five in 2013, Josh Reddick matched Cain this season). Cain now has three Fielding Bible Awards. He took our first Multi-Positional honor in 2014.

Previous Winners:

2018	Lorenzo Cain	2011	Austin Jackson
2017	Byron Buxton	2010	Michael Bourn
2016	Kevin Pillar	2009	Franklin Gutierrez
2015	Kevin Kiermaier	2008	Carlos Beltran
2014	Juan Lagares	2007	Andruw Jones
2013	Carlos Gomez	2006	Carlos Beltran
2012	Mike Trout		

Right Field – Cody Bellinger, Los Angeles Dodgers

Bellinger racked up Defensive Runs Saved early in the season, setting a pace that was tough to match. His 19 Runs Saved matched Aaron Judge for the most at the position. Bellinger's winning ended a three-year award-winning run by Mookie Betts. Like Betts, Bellinger has great range and a terrific throwing arm. Bellinger, Betts and Brian Anderson of the Marlins tied for the lead among right fielders with five Outfield Arm Runs Saved. He's the first Dodgers outfielder to win a Fielding Bible Award.

Previous Winners:

2018	Mookie Betts	2011	Justin Upton
2017	Mookie Betts	2010	Ichiro Suzuki
2016	Mookie Betts	2009	Ichiro Suzuki
2015	Jason Heyward	2008	Franklin Gutierrez
2014	Jason Heyward	2007	Alex Rios
2013	Gerardo Parra	2006	Ichiro Suzuki
2012	Jason Heyward		

Catcher – Roberto Perez, Cleveland Indians

After trading Yan Gomes in the offseason, the Indians committed to Perez as their primary catcher. He ranked fourth in the majors in innings caught and every one was caught at a high level. Perez does everything you would want a catcher to do. He ranked second at the position in our pitch-framing metric (Strike Zone Runs Saved) and second in Catcher Block Rate and was above-average in basestealing deterrence. That led to him saving 29 runs, one shy of the most in a season for a catcher. Four different catchers have won a Fielding Bible Award the last four years, but Perez may have some staying power.

Previous Winners:

2018	Jeff Mathis	2011	Matt Wieters
2017	Martin Maldonado	2010	Yadier Molina
2016	Buster Posey	2009	Yadier Molina
2015	Buster Posey	2008	Yadier Molina
2014	Jonathan Lucroy	2007	Yadier Molina
2013	Yadier Molina	2006	Ivan Rodriguz
2012	Yadier Molina		

Pitcher – Zack Greinke, Houston Astros

Greinke won his second straight Fielding Bible Award because he kept busy. His 68 chances were a career-high and the most in the majors. He led the majors in putouts by a pitcher and tied for the lead in assists with Braves starter Max Fried. He ran away with the lead in double plays, being a part of 12. No other pitcher had more than five. Greinke is still spry, even after 16 years in the major leagues. He covers ground well off the mound. His defense is important to his overall success as a pitcher.

Previous Winners:

2018	Zack Greinke	2011	Mark Buehrle
2017	Dallas Keuchel	2010	Mark Buehrle
2016	Dallas Keuchel	2009	Mark Buehrle
2015	Dallas Keuchel	2008	Kenny Rogers
2014	Dallas Keuchel	2007	Johan Santana
2013	R.A. Dickey	2006	Greg Maddux
2012	Mark Buehrle		

Multi-Position – Cody Bellinger, Los Angeles Dodgers

In talking to Dodgers coach George Lombard earlier this season, he felt that Bellinger was capable of being the game's best defender in right field, center field, and first base. Bellinger might prove him correct someday. For now, he's good enough at all three to earn this award for multi-positional excellence. Bellinger had 19 Runs Saved in right field, four at first base, and three in center field. His 26 in total were good for second in the majors to Roberto Perez's 29. Bellinger has the range, the reflexes and the arm to handle whatever comes his way. He showed that and then some in 2019.

Previous Winners

2018	Javier Baez	2015	Ender Inciarte
2017	Javier Baez	2014	Lorenzo Cain
2016	Javier Baez		

Background of the Fielding Bible Awards

While the four volumes of *The Fielding Bible* put a lot of emphasis on the numbers, especially Defensive Runs Saved and the Plus-Minus system, we feel that visual observation and subjective judgment are still very important parts of determining the best defensive players. Also, we believe people have a right to know who is voting and all the players they are voting for. Therefore, in setting up the Fielding Bible Awards, we took the following steps:

1. *We appointed a panel of experts to vote*. We have a panel of twelve experts plus three "tie-breaker" ballots. (See below.)

2. *We rate everybody in one group.* The Gold Glove vote is divided into National League and American League. We make ours different by putting everybody together. Besides, is playing shortstop in the American League one thing and playing shortstop in the National League a different thing, or are they really very much the same thing? A few years back we had a great example of this decision. Without the Fielding Bible Award, Jack Wilson wins *nada*, because he switched leagues in mid-year. According to our panelists (and unlike the Gold Glove voters), Jack was the best fielding shortstop in baseball in 2009. Period. He deserved to be recognized for that.

3. *We use a ten-man ballot and a ten-point scale*. We use a ten-man ballot. We give ten points for first place, nine points for second place, etc, down to one point for tenth place. We feel strongly that a ten-man ballot with weighted positions leads to more accurate outcomes.

4. *We defined the list of candidates*. Only players who actually were regulars at the position are candidates. This eliminates the possibility of a vote going to somebody who wasn't really playing the position.

5. *We are publishing the balloting*. We summarize the voting at each position, clearly identifying whom everybody voted for. Publishing the actual vote totals encourages the voters to take their votes more seriously. Also, we feel the public will have more respect for the voting if they have more insight into the process.

A perfect score is 120 points. If all 12 voters place one player first on their ballot, he scores 120. Two players had perfect scores of 120 this year: Matt Olson and Kolten Wong.

Here are the tie-breaker rules, which came into play in our very first year (2006), in 2010, in 2016, and again this year. They are applied one at a time until we have a winner:

1. Most first-place votes wins.
2. Count the tie-breaker ballots, highest point tally wins.
3. Award goes to player with the higher defensive runs saved.

Ballots were due three days after the end of the regular season. Here is this year's panel:

Ben Lindbergh is a staff writer for *The Ringer*. He also hosts the *Effectively Wild* podcast for *FanGraphs*. He is a former staff writer for *FiveThirtyEight* and *Grantland*, a former editor-in-chief of *Baseball Prospectus*, and the *New York Times* bestselling co-author of *The MVP Machine: How Baseball's New Nonconformists Are Using Data to Build Better Players* and *The Only Rule Is It Has to Work: Our Wild Experiment Building a New Kind of Baseball Team*. He lives in New York City.

Since you have this book, you probably know **Bill James**, a baseball writer and analyst published for more than thirty years. Bill is the Senior Baseball Operations Advisor for the Boston Red Sox and the author of *The Man from the Train: The Solving of a Century-Old Serial Killer Mystery* (published in September 2017), which he co-wrote with his daughter, Rachel.

The **BIS Video Scouts** at Baseball Info Solutions (BIS) study every game of the season, multiple times, charting a huge list of valuable game details.

Chris Singleton played six seasons in the major leagues primarily as a center fielder. As a rookie, he led American League center fielders in Total Zone Fielding Runs Above Average. Chris has been a Major League broadcaster for the past 13 seasons and has been a color commentator/analyst on over 1,000 live games for the Chicago White Sox, ESPN Radio, and ESPN *Baseball Tonight*.

Christina Kahrl is a senior editor for MLB coverage at ESPN.com, a member of the Baseball Writers Association of America, and a voter for the Hall of Fame in Cooperstown. Before joining ESPN, she was a co-founder of the sabermetric think-tank *Baseball Prospectus*, where she was the Executive Editor of the website as well as managing editor of the group's bestselling annual. Long based out of Chicago, she now works from ESPN's main campus in Connecticut.

The man who created Strat-O-Matic Baseball, **Hal Richman**, continues to lead his company's annual in-depth analysis of each player's season. Hal cautions SOM players that his voting on this ballot may or may not reflect the eventual fielding ratings for players in his game. Ballots were due prior to the completion of his annual research effort to evaluate player defense.

Joe Sheehan writes for *Sports Illustrated*, *Baseball America*, and has published the Joe Sheehan Baseball Newsletter for a decade. He was one of the founding members of Baseball Prospectus. He has contributed to ESPN, *The Wall Street Journal*, *The Washington Post*, *Rotowire*, and many other publications in his 25-year career. His career DRS in Inwood Little League is confidential.

For over twenty-five years, BIS CEO and owner **John Dewan** has collected, analyzed, and published in-depth baseball statistics and analysis. He has focused his analytics work in baseball on defense and has authored or co-authored four volumes of *The Fielding Bible*.

Mark Simon is a senior research analyst at Baseball Info Solutions. Prior to that, he worked as a researcher for ESPN Stats & Information from 2002 to January 2018, including eight years on *Baseball Tonight*. He regularly wrote about baseball for ESPN.com and now contributes to *The Athletic*, as well as the Sports Info Solutions Blog (SportsInfoSolutionsBlog.com). He also hosts the Sports Info Solutions Baseball Podcast. His book, *Numbers Don't Lie: The Biggest Numbers in Yankees History* was published by Triumph Books in 2016.

Peter Gammons serves as an on-air and online analyst for MLB Network, MLB.com and NESN (New England Sports Network). He is the 56th recipient of the J. G. Taylor Spink Award for outstanding baseball writing given by the BBWAA (Baseball Writers Association of America).

Rob Neyer has been a working writer for more than 25 years, and most recently has contributed to *The New York Times*, Vice Sports, and Complex. When he's not writing, he's thinking about not writing. Rob will live in Portland, Oregon for as long as they let him.

Travis Sawchik is a sportswriter for *FiveThirtyEight*. He is the author of the *New York Times* best-selling book *Big Data Baseball: Math, Miracles, and the End of a 20-Year Losing Streak* and co-author of *The MVP Machine: How Baseball's New Nonconformists Are Using Data to Build Better Players*. He previously covered the Pittsburgh Pirates for the *Pittsburgh Tribune-Review*.

Our three tie-breakers are **Dan Casey**, veteran Video Scout and Senior Operations Analyst and MLB Coordinator at BIS, **Chris Dial**, who developed Runs Effectively Defended (RED), a component of the SABR Defensive Index, in 1997, and **Meg Rowley**, managing editor at *FanGraphs*.

Ichiro

Ichiro Suzuki closed his career by recording one Defensive Run Saved in right field in the two games the Mariners played in Japan. Ichiro ranks tied for second in Runs Saved in right field since the stat was first tracked in 2003. His 102 are tied with Mookie Betts, 39 behind Jason Heyward.

Fielding Bible Awards Voting

Below we show the final point tally for The Fielding Bible Awards in the 2019 season. We asked a panel of experts to complete a 10-man ballot ranking players from 1 to 10 based on their defensive abilities. We show the ranks in the tables below. We then awarded points in the same way as Major League Baseball's MVP voting: 10 points for a first place vote, 9 for second, etc., down to 1 point for 10th place. We cover all nine positions, looking at only their fielding work for the 2019 season. Position players are eligible if they played at least 600 innings while catchers require a minimum of 500 innings. Either can qualify with 10 Runs Saved, as well. Pitchers require a minimum of 120 innings pitched or 5 Runs Saved.

In 2014, we introduced a Multi-Position Award for fielders who are excellent defensive players but do not call any one position their home. For a player to qualify for the Multi-Position Award, he must have played at least 600 innings (or saved at least 10 runs) across all positions and played no more than 70 percent of those innings at any one position.

First Basemen

First Basemen	Ben	Bill	BIS Video Scouts	Chris	Christina	Hal	Joe	John	Mark	Peter	Rob	Travis	Total Points
Matt Olson	1	1	1	1	1	1	1	1	1	1	1	1	120
Joey Votto	2	8	2	3	5	6	7	2	2	4	3	3	85
Christian Walker	4	9	3	9	2	7	5	4	3	2	2	2	80
Paul Goldschmidt	9	2	5	4	4	2	3	5	8	3	6	5	76
Brandon Belt	3	5	7	2	6	5	6	3	4	8	4	4	73
Freddie Freeman	8	4	4	5	3	3	2	7	6	5	9	4	72
Anthony Rizzo		3	6	6	10	4	4	6		7	7	7	50
C.J. Cron	5	7	10					8	5	9	5		28
Ronald Guzman	7		9	10		8	8	9	7	6		8	27
Yuli Gurriel	6		8			10					8		12

Others receiving points: Mitch Moreland 7, Garrett Cooper 6, Matt Adams 5, Carlos Santana 5, Chris Davis 4, Michael Chavis 3, Eric Thames 2, Ji-Man Choi 2, Eric Hosmer 2, Peter Alonso 1

Second Basemen

Second Basemen	Ben	Bill	BIS Video Scouts	Chris	Christina	Hal	Joe	John	Mark	Peter	Rob	Travis	Total Points
Kolten Wong	1	1	1	1	1	1	1	1	1	1	1	1	120
Yolmer Sanchez	4	2	3	2	3	2	2	4	4	3	3	2	98
Ozzie Albies	2	4	2	3	2	4	5	2	5	2	2	4	95
DJ LeMahieu	5	8	4	8	6	3	3	3	3		9	9	60
Whit Merrifield		3	5	9	5	5	4	6	7		5	3	58
Adam Frazier	9	7	6	4		6	6	9	6	5	7	5	51
Cesar Hernandez		5	9	5	4	7	9			4		6	39
Kike Hernandez	3		7				8	5	2				30
Brandon Lowe	6	10	10			8	10	7	8			7	22
Ryan McMahon				7						6	6		14
Others receiving points: Hanser Alberto 14, Luis Rengifo 12, Jonathan Schoop 11, Jose Peraza 9, Max Muncy 8, Nicky Lopez 5, Cavan Biggio 5, Jose Altuve 5, Starlin Castro 3, Joe Panik 1													

Third Basemen

Third Basemen	Ben	Bill	BIS Video Scouts	Chris	Christina	Hal	Joe	John	Mark	Peter	Rob	Travis	Total Points
Matt Chapman	1	3	1	1	1	1	1	1	1	1	1	1	118
Nolan Arenado	2	1	2	3	2	2	2	2	2	2	2	2	108
Josh Donaldson	4		3	2	3	4	3	4	3	3	4	5	83
Alex Bregman	5	2	4	7	5	3	5	5	4	5	5	4	78
Evan Longoria	3	8	5	9	6	10	4	3	5	7	3	10	59
Manny Machado	10		8	4	4	5	8	8	7	6	8	9	44
Brian Anderson	8	4	7	5	7	7	7		6		9		39
David Fletcher	7	6	9	10				6		9	10	3	28
Jose Ramirez	9	10				8		7		10	6	7	20
Anthony Rendon		7	10		8	6	9	10	9				18
Others receiving points: Eduardo Escobar 17, Jeimer Candelario 16, Kyle Seager 14, Matt Carpenter 5, Asdrubal Cabrera 5, Yoan Moncada 3, Eugenio Suarez 2, Giovanny Urshela 2, Rafael Devers 1														

Shortstops

Shortstops	Ben	Bill	BIS Video Scouts	Chris	Christina	Hal	Joe	John	Mark	Peter	Rob	Travis	Total Points
Nick Ahmed	3	2	4	2	2	3	2	3	2	1	4	1	103
Javier Baez	1	6	1	3	1	5	6	1	1	3	1	2	101
Andrelton Simmons	5	1	2	4	3	1	1	4	4	4	5	4	94
Trevor Story	4	4	3	1	5	4	5	6	3	2	2	3	90
Paul DeJong	2	10	5	6	4	9	4	2	5	5	3	5	72
Francisco Lindor	7	3	6	5	9	2		7	6		7	6	52
Marcus Semien	6		7			10	3	5	7	9	6		35
Willy Adames	9	7	8	7	7		7	9	8		10	9	29
Miguel Rojas		8	9		6	8	9	10		6	8	10	25
Adalberto Mondesi		5	10	9	8	7				8	9	7	25
Others receiving points: Corey Seager 11, Jose Iglesias 11, Carlos Correa 6, Richie Martin Jr. 3, Gleyber Torres 2, Freddy Galvis 1														

Left Fielders

Left Fielders	Ben	Bill	BIS Video Scouts	Chris	Christina	Hal	Joe	John	Mark	Peter	Rob	Travis	Total Points
David Peralta	4	1	1	2	2	1	3	6	1	1	4	2	104
Michael Brantley	3	2	2	3	1	8	1	2	2	2	1	1	104
Mike Tauchman	1	5	3	1	3	4	2	1	3		7	3	88
Alex Gordon		8	6	5	9	2		3	5	3	2	6	61
Joc Pederson	5	3	5		4	7	5	8	7		6	5	55
Robbie Grossman	7	6	7	4	7				4	4		7	42
Chad Pinder	2		4			6	10	4			9	4	38
Marcell Ozuna			9		8	5	4	7	8	10	5	9	34
Tommy Pham				6	10		6	5	9	5	3		33
Juan Soto		7	10	7	5	10	9			9	10		21

Others receiving points: Bryan Reynolds 21, Mike Yastrzemski 20, Andrew Benintendi 17, Chris Taylor 5, Eddie Rosario 5, Ben Gamel 4, Jay Bruce 3, Jeff McNeil 3, Wil Myers 1, Curtis Granderson 1

Center Fielders

Center Fielders	Ben	Bill	BIS Video Scouts	Chris	Christina	Hal	Joe	John	Mark	Peter	Rob	Travis	Total Points
Lorenzo Cain	2	1	1	1	1	1	7	1	1	2	1	1	112
Victor Robles	1	7	2	2	3	4	1	3	2	3	2	4	98
Kevin Kiermaier	3	5	3	3	5	3	3	2	3	4	3	2	93
Byron Buxton	6	3	5	4	4	6	2	5	4	5	5	5	78
Harrison Bader	4		4	5	2	2	4	4	5	7	4	3	77
Jackie Bradley Jr.	7	4	8	9		7	8	7		1		9	39
Billy Hamilton	9	9	7	7	6	5	10	6			6	7	38
Oscar Mercado	5		6	6	8		6	10	6		8	6	38
Manuel Margot	10	2			9		5			10			19
Jake Marisnick		10		8	7	8			8	8			17

Others receiving points: Jarrod Dyson 16, Ketel Marte 8, George Springer 8, Kevin Pillar 8, Delino DeShields 5, Adam Engel 3, Mike Trout 2, Ramon Laureano 1

Right Fielders

Right Fielders	Ben	Bill	BIS Video Scouts	Chris	Christina	Hal	Joe	John	Mark	Peter	Rob	Travis	Total Points
Cody Bellinger	1	2	1	1	2	3	1	3	1	3	1	1	112
Mookie Betts	2	1	2	2	3	1	2	1	3	1	4	2	108
Aaron Judge	3	5	3	4	1	2	3	2	2	2	2	3	100
Jason Heyward	5	3	7	3	6	4	6	4	5	5	5	7	72
Hunter Renfroe	4		4	5	4	9	4	6	4		3	5	62
Josh Reddick	9	6	6	6	8	6	9	5	10	6	6	6	49
Max Kepler	7	4	9	10	7	7	5	8	7	9	10	4	45
Bryce Harper		7	5		5	8	8		6	4	7	8	41
Yasiel Puig			8	9			7	7	9	8			18
Tyler Naquin	8	8	10	7	10			10				9	15

Others receiving points: Avisail Garcia 14, Michael Conforto 10, Christian Yelich 7, Kole Calhoun 3, Stephen Piscotty 2, Anthony Santander 1, Adam Eaton 1

Catchers

Catchers	Ben	Bill	BIS Video Scouts	Chris	Christina	Hal	Joe	John	Mark	Peter	Rob	Travis	Total Points
Roberto Perez	1	2	2	1	3	1	1	1	1	1	1	1	116
Austin Hedges	2	4	1	2	1	2	2	2	2	2	2	2	108
Buster Posey	4	7	4	4	2	5	5	3	4	5	4	5	80
J.T. Realmuto	5	1	3	3	5	6	4		3	3	3		74
Danny Jansen	7	5	5	5	8	8	9	10	5	7	5	4	54
Yasmani Grandal	3		6		7		3			6	6	3	43
Mike Zunino	10	3		6	9	4		4	10	10	7		36
Christian Vazquez		6	8	8	6		7			4	9		29
Martin Maldonado		8	9	7		3		5	9			8	28
Tony Wolters		10	10	10		9		6	6	9	8		20

Others receiving points: Tyler Flowers 19, Jacob Stallings 19, Yan Gomes 8, Tucker Barnhart 7, Yadier Molina 6, Austin Barnes 5, Austin Romine 5, Josh Phegley 3

Pitchers

Pitchers	Ben	Bill	BIS Video Scouts	Chris	Christina	Hal	Joe	John	Mark	Peter	Rob	Travis	Total Points
Zack Greinke	1	1	2	4	4	1	1	1	1	1	1	3	111
Aaron Nola	6	3	3	2	3		4		7	3	2	1	76
Max Fried	5		1	3	9	10	10	4	3	5	3	2	66
Dallas Keuchel	10	10	7	1	1	2	2	6	2			7	62
Joe Musgrove		5	8	5	2	9			5	2	8	6	49
Marcus Stroman	2		5	9			3	2	4	10	4		49
Mike Soroka	4		4	10			9	5		6	6	4	40
Jack Flaherty	3		9				6	9	6		5		28
Hyun-Jin Ryu	9	6	6		7	8				9		5	27
Clayton Kershaw				6	6	7			9	4			23

Others receiving points: Julio Teheran 18, German Marquez 13, Mike Leake 12, Patrick Corbin 12, Clayton Richard 11, Adam Wainwright 9, Luis Castillo 8, Chris Stratton 8, Masahiro Tanaka 8, Miles Mikolas 7, Wade Miley 7, Jose Berrios 6, Lucas Giolito 4, Trevor Richards 3, Sonny Gray 3

Multi-Position

Multi-Position	Ben	Bill	BIS Video Scouts	Chris	Christina	Hal	Joe	John	Mark	Peter	Rob	Travis	Total Points
Cody Bellinger	1		1	1	1	1	5	1	1	1		1	96
Max Muncy	7	4	9	4					5	3	6	2	48
DJ LeMahieu	9		4			3	2	3	8	3		9	47
Hunter Renfroe	3		3	2			9	8	2				39
Mike Tauchman	4		5	3				9	4			3	38
Brian Anderson	8	3	6	6	8	9			6	5		10	38
Kike Hernandez	6	8	8				4	6		9	1		35
Whit Merrifield		5			2	4	3			6			35
David Fletcher	2		2			8		2		8			33
Marwin Gonzalez	5	6	7					4	9		4		31

Others receiving points: Ketel Marte 30, Alex Bregman 27, Jeff McNeil 24, Chris Taylor 18, Ronald Acuna Jr. 14, Scott Kingery 13, Jason Heyward 13, Adam Haseley 12, Alex Verdugo 12, George Springer 10, Danny Santana 9, Gleyber Torres 6, Chad Pinder 5, Dexter Fowler 5, Michael Chavis 4, Niko Goodrum 4, Bryan Reynolds 4, Tommy Edman 3, Mike Moustakas 3, Garrett Cooper 2, Brandon Drury 2

Defensive Runs Saved Leaders

Mark Simon

Of the 12 teams to record at least 25 Defensive Runs Saved this season, seven made the postseason and two others contended for a playoff spot into September. There is still a place for great defensive teams and players.

The Dodgers were the best with the gloves in 2019, recording 136 Runs Saved. Cody Bellinger led the way with 26, but the Dodgers don't have a lot of players dominating the leaderboards found on the accompanying pages. Their success comes from the multi-positional efforts of players like Max Muncy (13 Runs Saved) and Kiké Hernández (8 Runs Saved).

The Dodgers threatened the record for most Runs Saved in a season, set by the Diamondbacks when they had 157 in 2018. Arizona was good again in 2019, finishing second to the Dodgers with 117. Nick Ahmed topped shortstops for 2019, though he still ranks second to Andrelton Simmons on the three-year leaderboard.

One leaderboard worth checking out is the 2019 catchers list. Roberto Perez and Austin Hedges became the second pair of catchers to record 20 Runs Saved in a season in the last five years, joining Hedges and Martin Maldonado (2017).

All four infield positions had the same DRS leader in 2019 as they did in 2018 (save for Andrelton Simmons, who tied Nick Ahmed at shortstop last year). Despite missing the start of the season due to injury, Matt Olson led first basemen with 13 Runs Saved, four better than anyone else. That was the second-biggest gap between first and second place at a position.

All three outfield spots were led by different players in 2019 than those that led last season. One notable newcomer was rookie Nationals center fielder Victor Robles. To beat out the likes of Lorenzo Cain and Kevin Kiermaier, you have to earn it. Robles did so with 22 Runs Saved, including an MLB-leading nine from the deterrent value of his throwing arm. Robles can stand tall as one of the top defensive players to watch in years ahead.

Infield Runs Saved Leaders

First Basemen 3-Year Leaders		Second Basemen 3-Year Leaders		Third Basemen 3-Year Leaders		Shortstops 3-Year Leaders	
Olson, Matt	31	Wong, Kolten	32	Chapman, Matt	66	Simmons, Andrelton	67
Belt, Brandon	28	LeMahieu, DJ	31	Arenado, Nolan	33	Ahmed, Nick	42
Votto, Joey	27	Merrifield, Whit	20	Longoria, Evan	25	Russell, Addison	30
Goldschmidt, Paul	20	Sanchez, Yolmer	19	Gyorko, Jedd	23	Story, Trevor	29
Rizzo, Anthony	16	Kinsler, Ian	17	Donaldson, Josh	19	Lindor, Francisco	28
Freeman, Freddie	15	Albies, Ozzie	17	Shaw, Travis	15	DeJong, Paul	28
Aguilar, Jesus	12	Frazier, Adam	10	Machado, Manny	14	Rojas, Miguel	25
Moreland, Mitch	10	Forsythe, Logan	8	Frazier, Todd	13	Baez, Javier	19
Santana, Carlos	9	Wendle, Joey	8	Freese, David	10	Seager, Corey	17
Bellinger, Cody	8	Zobrist, Ben	6	Kiner-Falefa, Isiah	10	Crawford, Brandon	15

First Basemen 3-Year Trailers		Second Basemen 3-Year Trailers		Third Basemen 3-Year Trailers		Shortstops 3-Year Trailers	
Voit, Luke	-11	Murphy, Daniel	-33	Andujar, Miguel	-27	Bogaerts, Xander	-51
Cabrera, Miguel	-10	Nunez, Eduardo	-21	Moran, Colin	-22	Rosario, Amed	-31
Davis, Chris	-9	Cabrera, Asdrubal	-21	Dozier, Hunter	-20	Diaz, Aledmys	-19
Healy, Ryon	-8	Dozier, Brian	-17	Devers, Rafael	-20	Mercer, Jordy	-19
Gurriel, Yuli	-8	Panik, Joe	-15	Franco, Maikel	-19	Anderson, Tim	-17
Bell, Josh	-8	Kipnis, Jason	-14	Sano, Miguel	-16	Machado, Manny	-15

First Basemen 2019 Leaders		Second Basemen 2019 Leaders		Third Basemen 2019 Leaders		Shortstops 2019 Leaders	
Olson, Matt	13	Wong, Kolten	14	Chapman, Matt	18	Ahmed, Nick	18
Walker, Christian	9	Sanchez, Yolmer	11	Donaldson, Josh	15	Story, Trevor	17
Votto, Joey	7	Albies, Ozzie	8	Arenado, Nolan	8	Baez, Javier	15
Freeman, Freddie	5	Merrifield, Whit	7	Escobar, Eduardo	8	DeJong, Paul	14
Goldschmidt, Paul	4	Hernandez, Cesar	6	Anderson, Brian	8	Simmons, Andrelton	14
Belt, Brandon	4	Frazier, Adam	6	Longoria, Evan	7	Adames, Willy	13
Aguilar, Jesus	4	LeMahieu, DJ	5	Candelario, Jeimer	7	Rojas, Miguel	12
Rizzo, Anthony	3	Lowe, Brandon	5	Bregman, Alex	7	Mondesi, Adalberto	10
Cron, C.J.	3	Alberto, Hanser	5	Machado, Manny	5	Lindor, Francisco	9
Adams, Matt	3	Muncy, Max	5	Fletcher, David	5	Seager, Corey	9

First Basemen 2019 Trailers		Second Basemen 2019 Trailers		Third Basemen 2019 Trailers		Shortstops 2019 Trailers	
Voit, Luke	-6	Villar, Jonathan	-11	Dozier, Hunter	-14	Bogaerts, Xander	-21
Alonso, Pete	-6	Profar, Jurickson	-10	Moran, Colin	-13	Rosario, Amed	-16
Bell, Josh	-5	Gordon, Dee	-8	Turner, Justin	-7	Turner, Trea	-10
Vogelbach, Daniel	-4	Odor, Rougned	-8	Bryant, Kris	-7	Mercer, Jordy	-9
O'Hearn, Ryan	-4	Torres, Gleyber	-7	Moncada, Yoan	-7	Anderson, Tim	-9
Abreu, Jose	-4	Kipnis, Jason	-7	Lugo, Dawel	-6	Beckham, Tim	-8

Outfield Runs Saved Leaders

Left Fielders 3-Year Leaders		Center Fielders 3-Year Leaders		Right Fielders 3-Year Leaders	
Gardner, Brett	32	Kiermaier, Kevin	49	Betts, Mookie	66
Gordon, Alex	28	Cain, Lorenzo	45	Judge, Aaron	42
Duvall, Adam	26	Buxton, Byron	36	Heyward, Jason	28
Ozuna, Marcell	21	Bader, Harrison	26	Puig, Yasiel	24
Peralta, David	18	Margot, Manuel	23	Haniger, Mitch	21
Pinder, Chad	16	Dyson, Jarrod	22	Bellinger, Cody	21
Pham, Tommy	14	Robles, Victor	22	Reddick, Josh	20
Taylor, Chris	13	Inciarte, Ender	21	Renfroe, Hunter	17
Brantley, Michael	11	Hamilton, Billy	20	Kepler, Max	14
Parra, Gerardo	11	Taylor, Michael A.	18	Stanton, Giancarlo	11

Left Fielders 3-Year Trailers		Center Fielders 3-Year Trailers		Right Fielders 3-Year Trailers	
Kemp, Matt	-26	Jones, Adam	-30	Castellanos, Nicholas	-35
Dietrich, Derek	-18	Desmond, Ian	-17	Cabrera, Melky	-28
Choo, Shin-Soo	-17	McCutchen, Andrew	-17	Williams, Nick	-24
Smith Jr., Dwight	-17	Conforto, Michael	-16	Martinez, Jose	-17
Davis, Khris	-16	Pederson, Joc	-15	Soler, Jorge	-17
Cabrera, Melky	-14	Fowler, Dexter	-14	Palka, Daniel	-14

Left Fielders 2019 Leaders		Center Fielders 2019 Leaders		Right Fielders 2019 Leaders	
Peralta, David	10	Robles, Victor	22	Bellinger, Cody	19
Brantley, Michael	10	Cain, Lorenzo	20	Judge, Aaron	19
Tauchman, Mike	10	Kiermaier, Kevin	13	Betts, Mookie	15
Renfroe, Hunter	7	Bader, Harrison	13	Renfroe, Hunter	13
Pederson, Joc	6	Buxton, Byron	10	Harper, Bryce	9
Grossman, Robbie	4	Mercado, Oscar	9	Reddick, Josh	9
Riley, Austin	4	Hamilton, Billy	7	Heyward, Jason	7
Gamel, Ben	4	DeShields, Delino	6	Yastrzemski, Mike	7
McCutchen, Andrew	3	Margot, Manuel	6	Naquin, Tyler	6
Ozuna, Marcell	2	Marte, Ketel	6	Anderson, Brian	5

Left Fielders 2019 Trailers		Center Fielders 2019 Trailers		Right Fielders 2019 Trailers	
Upton, Justin	-13	Desmond, Ian	-19	Cabrera, Melky	-11
Smith Jr., Dwight	-12	Jones, JaCoby	-13	Reyes, Franmil	-11
Davis, J.D.	-11	Pollock, A.J.	-9	Grichuk, Randal	-10
Jimenez, Eloy	-11	Smith, Mallex	-9	Martinez, Jose	-9
Santana, Domingo	-10	Marte, Starling	-9	Castellanos, Nicholas	-9
Calhoun, Willie	-7	Hernandez, Teoscar	-7	Meadows, Austin	-8

Pitcher/Catcher Runs Saved Leaders

Pitchers 3-Year Leaders		Catchers 3-Year Leaders	
Keuchel, Dallas	17	Hedges, Austin	54
Greinke, Zack	15	Perez, Roberto	47
Teheran, Julio	15	Maldonado, Martin	33
Corbin, Patrick	13	Leon, Sandy	27
Leake, Mike	13	Grandal, Yasmani	27
Stroman, Marcus	12	Posey, Buster	26
Richard, Clayton	12	Pina, Manny	26
Musgrove, Joe	12	Zunino, Mike	25
Chatwood, Tyler	11	Mathis, Jeff	22
Tanaka, Masahiro	11	Flowers, Tyler	22

Pitchers 3-Year Trailers		Catchers 3-Year Trailers	
Syndergaard, Noah	-12	Lucroy, Jonathan	-40
Grace, Matt	-10	Narvaez, Omar	-39
Ottavino, Adam	-10	Diaz, Elias	-28
Gausman, Kevin	-10	Castillo, Welington	-25
Garcia, Luis	-9	Hundley, Nick	-25
Gaviglio, Sam	-9	Ramos, Wilson	-23

Pitchers 2019 Leaders		Catchers 2019 Leaders	
Fried, Max	6	Perez, Roberto	29
Nola, Aaron	5	Hedges, Austin	22
Soroka, Mike	5	Posey, Buster	14
Ryu, Hyun-Jin	5	Jansen, Danny	12
Musgrove, Joe	5	Realmuto, J.T.	11
Keuchel, Dallas	5	Zunino, Mike	9
Castillo, Luis	4	Wolters, Tony	8
Greinke, Zack	4	Maldonado, Martin	8
Kershaw, Clayton	4	Murphy, Tom	6
Marquez, German	4	Barnes, Austin	6

Pitchers 2019 Trailers		Catchers 2019 Trailers	
Syndergaard, Noah	-7	Diaz, Elias	-23
Darvish, Yu	-5	Narvaez, Omar	-20
Sabathia, CC	-4	Phegley, Josh	-14
Lester, Jon	-4	Suzuki, Kurt	-14
Gausman, Kevin	-4	Lucroy, Jonathan	-14
		Ramos, Wilson	-13

Strike Zone Runs Saved

Joe Rosales

During the 2019 season, an average of about 303 pitches were thrown in each game. That's about 150 pitches per team, 80 of which were generally not swung at. That's 80 chances for the catcher to influence the outcome of the game via his pitch framing skills. Compare that to the infrequency of things like stolen base attempts, blocking pitches in the dirt, or fielding bunts, and it's clear that pitch framing offers catchers the most opportunities to impact a game defensively.

With almost all MLB teams emphasizing good pitch framing these days, it is more difficult than ever for catchers to stand out from each other. In 2018, three catchers tied for the most Strike Zone Runs Saved with 10 each. However, in 2019, Austin Hedges of the Padres finished the season well clear of the field with 18 Runs Saved. The next best was Roberto Perez of the Indians, who had 11.

Hedges received 7,125 called pitches this past season. Based on factors such as the location of the pitch, the handedness of the batter, and how close the pitch came to hitting the catcher's target, Hedges would have been expected to get 2,243 of those pitches called strikes. In actuality, he got 2,393 strike calls. That's 150 Extra Strikes, a fantastic feat.

This past September, BIS had the opportunity to interview Hedges on its podcast (the Sports Info Solutions Baseball Podcast). In that interview, he shed some light on his dedication to the craft of pitch framing in discussing the drills that he has done since high school, the techniques he uses to receive pitches (keeping his thumb under the ball and catching the ball on the way up), and the relationships he has with his pitchers and the umpires. The most intriguing topic discussed in the interview is robot umpires, which MLB began testing in the Atlantic League this season. While the system still leaves the final ball/strike call up to the human umpire, it would be a potentially momentous change to the game. Analytics helped illuminate how effective pitch framing can be, an artful skill that may eventually find its impact reduced if robot umpires find traction at the MLB level.

2019 Catcher Strike Zone Runs Saved Leaders

Catcher	Called Pitches	Called Strikes			Runs Saved	
		Actual	Expected	Extra	Per 1,000 Called Pitches	Total
Hedges, Austin	7125	2393	2243	150	2.5	18
Perez, Roberto	8542	2783	2692	91	1.3	11
Flowers, Tyler	6226	1982	1899	83	1.6	10
Grandal, Yasmani	9840	2994	2920	74	0.9	9
Posey, Buster	7286	2334	2262	72	1.2	9
Vazquez, Christian	8861	2734	2678	56	0.8	7
Stassi, Max	3278	1066	1018	48	1.7	6
Jansen, Danny	7981	2425	2381	44	0.7	5
Barnes, Austin	4052	1394	1356	38	1.1	5
Zunino, Mike	5599	1841	1804	37	0.8	4
Plawecki, Kevin	3490	1165	1128	37	1.3	4
Smith, Will	3356	1085	1056	29	1.0	3
Pina, Manny	3255	977	948	29	1.0	3
Stallings, Jacob	3962	1258	1230	28	0.8	3
Leon, Sandy	4284	1411	1388	23	0.6	3
Maile, Luke	3200	949	929	20	0.7	2
Barnhart, Tucker	6905	2080	2061	19	0.3	2
Murphy, Tom	4980	1634	1616	18	0.4	2
Mejia, Francisco	3956	1259	1241	18	0.5	2
Caratini, Victor	3587	1181	1165	16	0.5	2
Gallagher, Cam	2909	941	925	16	0.7	2
Alfaro, Jorge	8647	2574	2558	16	0.2	2
Martin, Russell	3971	1291	1275	16	0.5	2
Casali, Curt	4479	1415	1400	15	0.4	2
McCann, Brian	5785	1708	1694	14	0.3	2
Kelly, Carson	6918	2164	2153	11	0.2	1
Greiner, Grayson	4519	1402	1392	10	0.3	1
Realmuto, J.T.	10131	3207	3197	10	0.1	1
Castro, Jason	5487	1770	1760	10	0.2	1
Romine, Austin	4925	1529	1524	5	0.1	1
d'Arnaud, Travis	5505	1800	1795	5	0.1	1
Garver, Mitch	5591	1784	1779	5	0.1	1
Nido, Tomas	2773	883	878	5	0.2	1
Molina, Yadier	8336	2669	2665	4	0.1	0
Avila, Alex	3714	1160	1156	4	0.1	0
Cervelli, Francisco	2668	865	862	3	0.2	0
Maldonado, Martin	7768	2413	2419	-6	-0.1	-1
Vogt, Stephen	3996	1167	1177	-10	-0.3	-1
McCann, James	7924	2375	2395	-20	-0.3	-2
Viloria, Meibrys	3170	948	970	-22	-0.8	-3
Sanchez, Gary	6697	2062	2084	-22	-0.4	-3
Mathis, Jeff	5879	1861	1891	-30	-0.6	-4
Contreras, Willson	7571	2394	2425	-31	-0.5	-4
Gomes, Yan	6875	2079	2112	-33	-0.6	-4
Smith, Kevan	4027	1219	1252	-33	-1.0	-4
Lucroy, Jonathan	6424	1946	1979	-33	-0.6	-4
Holaday, Bryan	2671	780	816	-36	-1.6	-4
Sisco, Chance	3459	1046	1083	-37	-1.3	-4
Iannetta, Chris	3203	939	977	-38	-1.4	-4
Hicks, John	4533	1419	1458	-39	-1.0	-5
Phegley, Josh	6996	2211	2253	-42	-0.7	-5
Wieters, Matt	3200	933	976	-43	-1.6	-5
Suzuki, Kurt	5413	1687	1731	-44	-1.0	-5
Wolters, Tony	7858	2375	2427	-52	-0.8	-6
Chirinos, Robinson	8259	2630	2683	-53	-0.8	-6
Castillo, Welington	3724	1081	1142	-61	-1.9	-7
Severino, Pedro	6935	1985	2052	-67	-1.2	-8
Narvaez, Omar	7440	2378	2448	-70	-1.1	-8
Ramos, Wilson	8963	2829	2903	-74	-1.0	-9
Diaz, Elias	6572	1978	2054	-76	-1.4	-9

Shift Update

Mark Simon

How does your brain react when you're watching a game and you see a ground ball hit up the middle, or halfway between first base and second base?

For many generations of baseball fans, the instantaneous reaction was one of "base hit." But for current baseball watchers, you can't presume anything anymore.

Defensive shifts increased by 35% from 2018, 49% among National League teams. There were more than 46,000 balls put in play against a defensive shift this season. That's nearly 20 times the number that there were at the start of the decade. Four teams doubled their shift total from last season to this season, including the overall leader in shift usage, the Orioles.

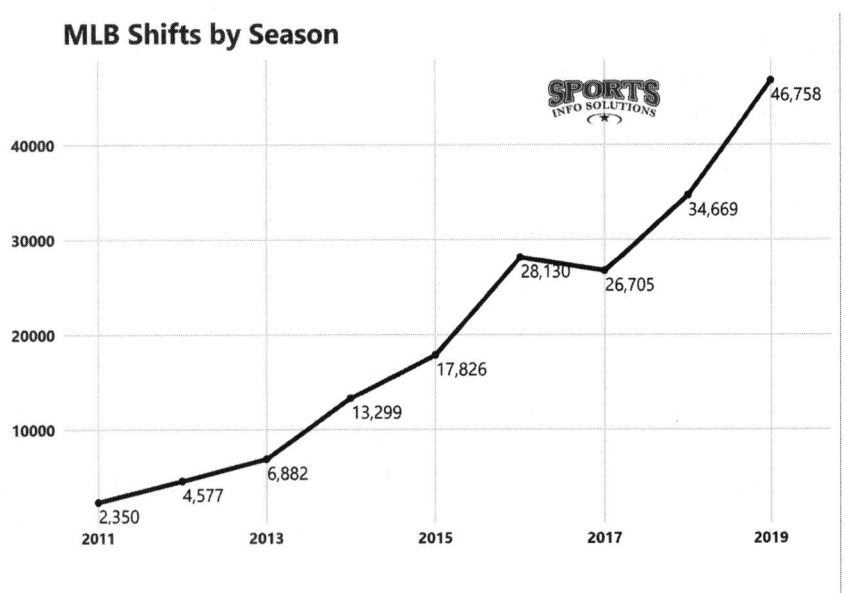

Do shifts work? This chart indicates that in aggregate, they do what they're meant to do.

MLB Runs Saved per 100 Shifts

Season	Shifts	Shift Runs Saved	Runs/100
2010	2,463	25	1.02
2011	2,350	28	1.19
2012	4,577	62	1.35
2013	6,882	117	1.70
2014	13,299	144	1.08
2015	17,826	238	1.34
2016	28,130	378	1.34
2017	26,705	346	1.30
2018	34,669	592	1.71
2019	46,758	622	1.33

The Diamondbacks and Astros seem to think so. They led their respective leagues in Shift Runs Saved. Justin Verlander probably thinks so. The Astros got an out on 72 of the 85 ground balls or bunts against Verlander when a shift was on. The 85% ground ball and bunt out rate for the Astros with Verlander on the mound was the highest for any team with any pitcher.

Two of the teams that got the greatest value out of shifting were the Diamondbacks and Cardinals. The Diamondbacks ranked second in the majors with 44 Shift Runs Saved. The Cardinals ranked fourth with 30. They ranked ninth and 18th in shift usage respectively. Both of these teams had very strong defensive infields regardless of whether they were shifting.

The Indians are another good example. They got outs on 73% of ground balls and bunts when playing a "normal" defense and an MLB-best 78% of ground balls and bunts when using a defensive shift.

The White Sox are a good example of how shift usage can help a below-average defensive infield. Their infielders combined to cost the team 10 runs defensively when playing straight-up but saved 11 runs when using defensive shifts.

In terms of improvement, the Phillies boosted their performance in defensive shifts considerably from 2018. They saved 7 runs with shifts in 2019 after shifts cost them 10 runs last season.

There is still room for teams to make better shifting decisions. Baseball Info Solutions' BIS-D software provides a recommendation for every player in MLB as to whether that player is a shift candidate or not. There were just north of 12,000 balls put in play by shift candidates against unshifted defenses (down from last year, when there were over 17,000). There were also more than 23,000 balls in play by non-shift candidates who were shifted, up from just over 15,500 last season.

Weighted* Batting Average on Groundballs and Short Line Drives, 2018–19

BIS-D Recommendation	No Shift	Shift	Difference
Shift Candidate	.268	.236	Helps by 32 points
Non-Shift Candidate	.270	.282	Hurts by 12 points

*The averages are weighted such that players with extreme shift tendencies (high or low) are not over-represented, thus separating the effect of the shift from batter quality.

The payoff is still there for teams that play the percentages and put fielders in the best place to field ground balls for each hitter. That often means using a shift.

In all, 25 of the 30 MLB teams increased their shift usage, same as 2018. The trendline continues to be pointing upwards in that regard. Get used to a different way of watching the game.

In the player stats table on the following page, GSL stands for Grounders and Short Liners, i.e. the plays that the shift is designed to defend.

Shifts Employed
American League

Team	2018	2019	Change
Baltimore Orioles	1206	2513	1307
Minnesota Twins	1722	2302	580
Tampa Bay Rays	1861	1962	101
Houston Astros	1714	1887	173
Toronto Blue Jays	1094	1735	641
New York Yankees	1449	1702	253
Detroit Tigers	1174	1507	333
Chicago White Sox	1855	1500	-355
Seattle Mariners	1337	1459	122
Texas Rangers	653	1426	773
Kansas City Royals	1382	1290	-92
Cleveland Indians	981	1195	214
Boston Red Sox	1020	1163	143
Los Angeles Angels	648	1007	359
Oakland Athletics	883	804	-79
Total	**18979**	**23452**	**4473**
Average	**1265**	**1563**	**298**

Shifts Employed
National League

Team	2018	2019	Change
Los Angeles Dodgers	1182	2329	1147
Miami Marlins	1189	2085	896
Pittsburgh Pirates	1395	2077	682
Colorado Rockies	1049	1891	842
Arizona Diamondbacks	1391	1873	482
Milwaukee Brewers	1462	1776	314
Cincinnati Reds	1075	1716	641
San Francisco Giants	933	1517	584
St Louis Cardinals	701	1453	752
Philadelphia Phillies	1321	1240	-81
San Diego Padres	506	1220	714
Atlanta Braves	997	1217	220
Washington Nationals	928	1051	123
New York Mets	1097	1027	-70
Chicago Cubs	464	834	370
Total	**15690**	**23306**	**7616**
Average	**1046**	**1554**	**508**

Top 30 Shifted Batters

Batter	Shifted PA	Shift Percent	Shift GSL BA	No Shift GSL BA
Freeman, Freddie	459	87.9	.227	.667
Rizzo, Anthony	449	93.0	.219	.333
Bellinger, Cody	448	91.1	.279	.600
Schwarber, Kyle	416	90.6	.215	.333
Belt, Brandon	415	88.5	.176	.364
Calhoun, Kole	401	88.9	.188	.200
Blackmon, Charlie	400	78.4	.300	.128
Rosario, Eddie	390	78.9	.255	.182
Santana, Carlos	384	76.8	.258	.268
Harper, Bryce	380	88.8	.252	.167
Kepler, Max	379	80.3	.205	.243
Moustakas, Mike	368	84.2	.226	.281
Olson, Matt	364	88.3	.161	.563
Vogelbach, Daniel	363	89.4	.164	.100
Hoskins, Rhys	361	80.4	.229	.429
Muncy, Max	359	88.2	.152	.476
Escobar, Eduardo	355	66.0	.216	.281
Gordon, Alex	353	73.1	.263	.263
Brantley, Michael	347	65.7	.268	.302
Choo, Shin-Soo	344	76.8	.274	.286
Albies, Ozzie	342	67.1	.268	.380
Odor, Rougned	341	82.4	.194	.280
Grichuk, Randal	337	70.6	.233	.263
Meadows, Austin	337	79.3	.317	.250
Conforto, Michael	334	75.7	.310	.095
Pederson, Joc	332	90.0	.257	.286
Devers, Rafael	328	62.0	.264	.309
Bradley Jr., Jackie	324	80.0	.197	.359
Heyward, Jason	321	75.2	.229	.302
Carpenter, Matt	317	83.6	.216	.500

Hits Lost and Gained to the Shift

Andrew Kyne

Despite suffering a hand injury early in the season, Matt Olson had another strong campaign for the 97-win Oakland A's. In addition to 13 Defensive Runs Saved at first base, Olson hit .267 with 36 home runs. However, that batting average could have been much higher—if not for infield shifts.

By Baseball Info Solutions' methodology, Olson lost approximately 27 hits to the shift in 2019. We calculate this by estimating how likely a play would have been made without a shift, based on batted ball type, velocity, and location, and comparing to the actual results with a shift.

While Olson also gained 11 hits thanks to shifts, his net difference of 16 hits was the most extreme loss in baseball this year. Another 16 hits for Olson would have raised his batting average from .267 to .300.

Such is life in Major League Baseball for pull-happy sluggers like Olson. Others who lost significantly more hits to the shift than they gained include Daniel Vogelbach, Freddie Freeman, Jay Bruce, Brandon Belt, and Bryce Harper.

Defensively, the Arizona Diamondbacks were the best team at deploying infield shifts in 2019. Opponents had a net loss of 75 hits when hitting into an Arizona shift. Other highly analytical teams like the Los Angeles Dodgers, Houston Astros, and Tampa Bay Rays also ranked in the top five.

Interestingly, opponents had a net gain of six hits when hitting into a shift against the New York Yankees. Every other defense at least broke even with shifting, and more than half of the teams saved at least 20 hits.

The following pages detail this information. In addition to hits lost and gained to the shift for batters, this year's book also includes data for pitchers and teams. Only players who had more than five net hits gained or lost to the shift are listed.

Hits Lost and Gained to the Shift for Batters

Player	2019 Season				Career Since 2010			
	Shifts	Lost	Gained	Net	Shifts	Lost	Gained	Net
Olson, Matt	272	27	11	16	702	64	39	25
Vogelbach, Daniel	246	24	9	15	309	30	14	16
Freeman, Freddie	373	35	21	14	1743	148	108	40
Bruce, Jay	189	18	4	14	1761	149	87	62
Belt, Brandon	332	22	9	13	1402	96	60	36
Harper, Bryce	300	30	17	13	1096	104	69	35
Calhoun, Kole	308	27	15	12	1351	138	81	57
Brantley, Michael	305	29	17	12	655	60	48	12
McCann, Brian	192	22	11	11	1897	165	93	72
Santana, Carlos	308	30	19	11	1817	162	100	62
Ramirez, Jose	242	20	9	11	568	43	26	17
Bell, Josh	230	26	15	11	552	57	40	17
Muncy, Max	254	24	14	10	479	44	22	22
Betts, Mookie	261	21	11	10	446	37	27	10
Profar, Jurickson	187	20	10	10	374	38	26	12
Odor, Rougned	245	22	12	10	1102	99	60	39
Rizzo, Anthony	354	32	22	10	2132	184	109	75
Seager, Kyle	246	18	8	10	1846	147	95	52
Ruiz, Rio	197	18	8	10	222	21	9	12
Tellez, Rowdy	192	19	9	10	229	21	12	9
Schwarber, Kyle	296	30	20	10	811	85	58	27
Stewart, Christin	190	16	7	9	212	17	8	9
Granderson, Curtis	198	19	10	9	1522	134	71	63
Smoak, Justin	222	20	11	9	1282	123	63	60
Frazier, Todd	228	20	11	9	662	50	31	19
Grichuk, Randal	265	25	16	9	538	41	37	4
Dietrich, Derek	117	11	3	8	460	37	24	13
Seager, Corey	224	20	12	8	574	46	36	10
Bradley Jr., Jackie	248	26	18	8	940	91	73	18
Morales, Kendrys	121	14	6	8	1466	155	90	65
Alvarez, Yordan	137	15	7	8	137	15	7	8
Benintendi, Andrew	231	20	13	7	680	51	44	7
Hoskins, Rhys	290	24	17	7	520	40	27	13
Ford, Mike	84	12	5	7	84	12	5	7
Camargo, Johan	80	10	3	7	168	18	9	9
Kipnis, Jason	215	17	10	7	610	49	34	15
Barnhart, Tucker	133	12	5	7	402	33	23	10
Carpenter, Matt	230	21	14	7	1114	89	47	42
Pujols, Albert	244	28	21	7	1613	184	104	80
Peralta, David	131	16	9	7	572	59	53	6
Moreland, Mitch	188	19	12	7	1513	141	89	52
Moustakas, Mike	315	25	18	7	1647	131	94	37
Cabrera, Asdrubal	204	16	9	7	836	65	44	21
Crawford, Brandon	185	17	10	7	547	47	39	8
Candelario, Jeimer	132	10	3	7	298	23	15	8
Guzman, Ronald	104	11	4	7	275	24	16	8
Severino, Pedro	75	9	2	7	82	9	3	6
Kepler, Max	291	21	14	7	778	57	44	13
Machado, Manny	114	15	9	6	374	41	27	14
Kiermaier, Kevin	173	16	10	6	473	42	37	5
Rendon, Anthony	118	9	3	6	213	17	9	8
Cano, Robinson	193	15	9	6	988	89	78	11
Avila, Alex	74	10	4	6	618	74	35	39
Walker, Neil	177	17	11	6	700	63	44	19
Trout, Mike	156	15	9	6	468	32	37	-5
McKinney, Billy	119	12	6	6	170	14	8	6
O'Hearn, Ryan	159	17	11	6	219	23	14	9
Kingery, Scott	101	9	3	6	140	11	5	6
Moran, Colin	234	19	13	6	444	37	27	10
Dixon, Brandon	80	2	8	-6	92	4	8	-4
Story, Trevor	186	11	17	-6	375	27	31	-4
Braun, Ryan	48	2	8	-6	132	11	15	-4
Holt, Brock	88	6	12	-6	241	20	27	-7
Blackmon, Charlie	334	23	29	-6	763	56	57	-1
Villar, Jonathan	90	5	11	-6	157	11	22	-11
Arenado, Nolan	167	10	16	-6	482	34	42	-8
Castellanos, Nicholas	200	14	21	-7	523	37	45	-8

Outs Gained and Lost to the Shift for Pitchers

Player	2019 Season				Career Since 2010			
	Shifts	Gained	Lost	Net	Shifts	Gained	Lost	Net
Kelly, Merrill	249	26	12	14	249	26	12	14
Leake, Mike	261	30	16	14	945	105	67	38
Castillo, Luis	228	30	17	13	392	45	26	19
Kershaw, Clayton	328	37	25	12	572	56	45	11
Hudson, Dakota	205	21	9	12	222	23	11	12
Mikolas, Miles	221	22	11	11	352	32	18	14
Lopez, Yoan	68	13	2	11	76	14	2	12
Jurado, Ariel	172	20	10	10	225	24	13	11
Marquez, German	247	24	14	10	515	43	38	5
Bieber, Shane	165	20	10	10	253	27	13	14
Anderson, Chase	199	19	10	9	810	67	42	25
Young, Alex	118	14	5	9	118	14	5	9
Chirinos, Yonny	290	27	18	9	473	42	31	11
Davies, Zach	281	25	16	9	829	76	64	12
Strasburg, Stephen	135	17	8	9	411	37	26	11
Ryu, Hyun-Jin	323	31	22	9	514	50	37	13
Musgrove, Joe	278	25	16	9	625	54	42	12
McHugh, Collin	110	13	4	9	919	81	52	29
Gray, Jon	173	19	10	9	579	50	35	15
Anderson, Shaun	118	15	7	8	118	15	7	8
Flaherty, Jack	191	17	9	8	266	21	11	10
Berrios, Jose	334	29	21	8	640	54	40	14
Barria, Jaime	117	13	5	8	184	16	7	9
Baez, Pedro	126	11	3	8	227	19	7	12
Means, John	226	15	7	8	227	15	8	7
Peacock, Brad	138	14	6	8	606	51	32	19
Wittgren, Nick	48	9	1	8	126	14	9	5
Foltynewicz, Mike	125	12	4	8	379	34	18	16
Zimmermann, Jordan	165	18	11	7	526	52	34	18
Yarbrough, Ryan	181	18	11	7	352	31	18	13
Stripling, Ross	152	16	9	7	377	41	29	12
Archer, Chris	168	15	8	7	953	83	64	19
Morton, Charlie	223	23	16	7	866	81	63	18
Pressly, Ryan	53	8	1	7	192	22	14	8
Thornton, Trent	224	16	9	7	224	16	9	7
Clarke, Taylor	131	14	7	7	131	14	7	7
Verlander, Justin	199	16	9	7	701	50	34	16
Miley, Wade	268	27	20	7	697	74	50	24
Guerra, Junior	98	10	4	6	477	43	29	14
Tanaka, Masahiro	349	33	27	6	1210	115	86	29
Urias, Julio	108	13	7	6	145	19	8	11
Pagan, Emilio	106	10	4	6	176	16	7	9
Maeda, Kenta	278	21	15	6	609	49	30	19
Gaviglio, Sam	167	19	13	6	375	39	24	15
Parker, Blake	79	8	2	6	174	17	8	9
Webb, Logan	50	7	1	6	50	7	1	6
Bettis, Chad	102	13	7	6	561	65	38	27
Odorizzi, Jake	218	19	13	6	1138	88	59	29
McFarland, T.J.	77	12	6	6	293	38	23	15
Greinke, Zack	306	29	23	6	931	85	59	26
Rodriguez, Richard	101	6	12	-6	144	8	15	-7
Jeffress, Jeremy	66	5	11	-6	235	27	27	0
Rogers, Taylor	94	7	13	-6	216	17	21	-4
Keller, Mitch	72	2	9	-7	72	2	9	-7
Armstrong, Shawn	94	3	10	-7	122	6	11	-5

Hits Lost and Gained to the Shift by Batting Team

Team	2019 Season				Totals Since 2010			
	Shifts	Lost	Gained	Net	Shifts	Lost	Gained	Net
Los Angeles Angels	1796	172	115	57	7145	699	453	246
Philadelphia Phillies	1596	152	101	51	6054	569	362	207
Atlanta Braves	1878	165	121	44	5910	505	387	118
Houston Astros	1628	149	107	42	5941	495	380	115
Oakland Athletics	1776	155	114	41	7617	618	500	118
Toronto Blue Jays	1869	150	110	40	7669	682	443	239
Cleveland Indians	1733	144	106	38	6971	594	431	163
Cincinnati Reds	1574	134	99	35	5920	510	391	119
Los Angeles Dodgers	1915	173	141	32	6717	594	439	155
Texas Rangers	1570	149	117	32	7529	708	541	167
Pittsburgh Pirates	1297	122	91	31	5014	456	365	91
Miami Marlins	865	84	54	30	3410	318	244	74
San Francisco Giants	1645	126	99	27	4490	349	273	76
Seattle Mariners	1477	113	86	27	7336	641	473	168
New York Yankees	1444	128	102	26	8155	733	497	236
Arizona Diamondbacks	1542	128	102	26	4339	400	313	87
Boston Red Sox	1778	150	126	24	8798	767	579	188
Detroit Tigers	1218	95	73	22	5184	453	361	92
Chicago Cubs	1879	165	143	22	7618	654	512	142
New York Mets	1507	127	106	21	6940	599	394	205
San Diego Padres	1337	112	97	15	4313	388	313	75
Washington Nationals	1330	97	82	15	5108	414	334	80
Tampa Bay Rays	1717	140	125	15	6737	582	459	123
Baltimore Orioles	1453	113	100	13	6772	581	473	108
Kansas City Royals	1337	107	95	12	6230	547	412	135
Minnesota Twins	1931	141	135	6	7133	583	498	85
Milwaukee Brewers	1503	114	108	6	4570	384	310	74
St Louis Cardinals	1363	100	97	3	4849	389	315	74
Chicago White Sox	1071	85	96	-11	4200	364	299	65
Colorado Rockies	1729	119	144	-25	4990	402	425	-23

Outs Gained and Lost to the Shift by Defensive Team

Team	2019 Season				Totals Since 2010			
	Shifts	Gained	Lost	Net	Shifts	Gained	Lost	Net
Arizona Diamondbacks	1873	192	117	75	5944	580	369	211
Los Angeles Dodgers	2329	217	149	68	5770	527	375	152
Houston Astros	1887	177	120	57	10426	908	681	227
St Louis Cardinals	1453	128	80	48	4235	377	281	96
Tampa Bay Rays	1962	181	137	44	10666	965	717	248
Toronto Blue Jays	1735	148	108	40	7027	597	436	161
Colorado Rockies	1891	166	128	38	6340	571	443	128
Los Angeles Angels	1007	94	61	33	5449	464	348	116
Cleveland Indians	1195	99	68	31	5783	508	318	190
Cincinnati Reds	1716	149	118	31	5771	498	356	142
Miami Marlins	2085	165	134	31	5535	433	365	68
San Francisco Giants	1517	128	101	27	5184	441	324	117
Oakland Athletics	804	68	45	23	5038	454	310	144
Minnesota Twins	2302	185	162	23	7152	597	467	130
Seattle Mariners	1459	120	100	20	7039	600	489	111
Texas Rangers	1426	117	97	20	5350	475	340	135
Chicago White Sox	1500	121	102	19	6718	581	457	124
Philadelphia Phillies	1240	101	85	16	4479	379	323	56
Atlanta Braves	1217	107	93	14	4717	436	343	93
Milwaukee Brewers	1776	156	143	13	8236	750	579	171
Washington Nationals	1051	79	66	13	4094	337	285	52
Detroit Tigers	1507	128	116	12	4763	429	308	121
Kansas City Royals	1290	108	100	8	5592	481	413	68
Boston Red Sox	1163	82	74	8	5398	445	318	127
Pittsburgh Pirates	2077	157	151	6	8680	733	632	101
New York Mets	1027	74	71	3	4257	348	274	74
Baltimore Orioles	2513	183	180	3	8190	683	526	157
Chicago Cubs	834	66	64	2	3359	286	208	78
San Diego Padres	1220	93	93	0	4296	392	296	96
New York Yankees	1702	122	128	-6	8171	703	594	109

Four-Outfielder Alignments

Andrew Kyne

Major League teams are constantly looking for a competitive edge. Fielder positioning has been a point of emphasis over the past decade, and Baseball Info Solutions has spent lots of time tracking and analyzing defensive shifts. While most of that research has been on the topic of infield shifts, teams are starting to do interesting things in the outfield as well.

An extreme way that teams have begun aligning themselves is with a fourth fielder in the outfield. BIS started tracking four-outfielder alignments in 2018, observing 37 on balls in play. In 2019, that number climbed to 101.

The majority of the 2019 alignments were played by the Tampa Bay Rays and Cincinnati Reds. The Minnesota Twins used the most alignments in 2018 but cut back on their usage this season.

The hitters who have had the most four-outfielder alignments played against them over the past two seasons include Justin Smoak, Joey Gallo, Brandon Belt, Lucas Duda, and Matt Olson.

These are all left-handed sluggers who hit a high proportion of their batted balls to the outfield. When they do hit one in the infield, it's very likely to be pulled. Thus, these types of hitters may tempt some defenses to take an infielder and put him in the outfield.

The following data tables show four-outfielder alignments by defensive team and batter for the last two seasons. This will be a trend to monitor in 2020 and beyond.

Four-Outfielder Alignments Employed
On Balls In Play

Team	2018	2019	Total
Tampa Bay Rays	2	48	50
Cincinnati Reds	0	35	35
Minnesota Twins	26	3	29
Arizona Diamondbacks	0	5	5
San Francisco Giants	0	5	5
Houston Astros	5	0	5
Toronto Blue Jays	0	3	3
Chicago Cubs	2	0	2
Los Angeles Dodgers	0	1	1
Seattle Mariners	0	1	1
Colorado Rockies	1	0	1
Oakland Athletics	1	0	1
MLB	37	101	138

Four-Outfielder Alignments By Batter
On Balls In Play (Minimum 2 BIP)

Batter	AB	H	2B	3B	BABIP	SlgBIP
Smoak, Justin	18	5	1	0	.278	.333
Gallo, Joey	14	6	1	0	.429	.500
Belt, Brandon	12	2	1	0	.167	.250
Duda, Lucas	11	3	0	0	.273	.273
Olson, Matt	11	4	1	0	.364	.455
Carpenter, Matt	9	5	0	1	.556	.778
Bellinger, Cody	5	3	2	0	.600	1.000
Moreland, Mitch	5	0	0	0	.000	.000
Seager, Corey	5	5	1	0	1.000	1.200
Biggio, Cavan	4	2	1	0	.500	.750
Freeman, Freddie	4	3	0	0	.750	.750
Grandal, Yasmani	4	2	0	0	.500	.500
Muncy, Max	4	1	0	0	.250	.250
Granderson, Curtis	3	0	0	0	.000	.000
Davis, Chris	2	0	0	0	.000	.000
Davis, Khris	2	1	0	0	.500	.500
Encarnacion, Edwin	2	1	0	0	.500	.500
Seager, Kyle	2	0	0	0	.000	.000
Thaiss, Matt	2	0	0	0	.000	.000

Home Run Robberies

Brian Reiff

One of my favorite sports-related comics comes from the site xkcd.com. It depicts two sports broadcasters sitting at a desk. One says, "A weighted random number generator just produced a new batch of numbers." The other replies, "Let's use them to build narratives!"

It's funnier if you see it.

In 2019, MLB set a record—at least since Baseball Info Solutions started tracking such things in 2004—with 69 home run robberies. That's an average of one per every 35 games, or a little bit over two per park per season. When dealing with any event that occurs so infrequently, it's difficult to argue that any narratives that arise from studying that data are anything but random. But let's take a look anyway.

Two players—Josh Reddick and Lorenzo Cain—each robbed five home runs this season, three more than any other player. In doing so, they tied the record for home run robberies in a season, set by Carlos Gomez back in 2013.

Thanks to Reddick's total, the Astros led all teams in home run robberies with seven. Cain's Brewers had six total robberies, as did the Yankees, who were led by Aaron Judge with two.

While Cain was busy robbing home runs, his teammate and fellow outfielder Christian Yelich found himself at the top of the other, less desirable leaderboard—hitters who were robbed the most. Two of Yelich's would-be home runs were pulled back in 2019, tied with five others—Jose Martinez, Eduardo Escobar, Lewis Brinson, Pete Alonso and Nick Senzel—for the most in MLB.

Home Run Robberies

Date	Matchup	Fielder	Pos	Pitcher	Batter	Inn.	Outs	Men On	Score
07/14/2019	Braves@Padres	Ronald Acuna Jr.	8	Mike Soroka	Manny Machado	5	2	1__	0-0
08/15/2019	Mets@Braves	Ronald Acuna Jr.	7	Josh Tomlin	J.D. Davis	6	0	___	9-2
09/27/2019	Cubs@Cardinals	Albert Almora Jr.	8	Alec Mills	Yadier Molina	4	0	___	0-0
04/21/2019	Dodgers@Brewers	Cody Bellinger	9	Pedro Baez	Christian Yelich	8	0	___	5-2
05/08/2019	Red Sox@Orioles	Jackie Bradley Jr.	8	Ryan Brasier	Trey Mancini	11	1	___	1-1
06/17/2019	Brewers@Padres	Ryan Braun	7	Freddy Peralta	Austin Hedges	6	0	___	0-2
06/28/2019	Phillies@Marlins	Jay Bruce	7	Edgar Garcia	Neil Walker	6	0	___	2-4
03/28/2019	Cardinals@Brewers	Lorenzo Cain	8	Josh Hader	Jose Martinez	9	2	___	4-5
04/15/2019	Cardinals@Brewers	Lorenzo Cain	8	Freddy Peralta	Matt Carpenter	2	2	_2_	2-0
04/26/2019	Brewers@Mets	Lorenzo Cain	8	Chase Anderson	Todd Frazier	2	2	___	0-0
07/18/2019	Brewers@Diamondbacks	Lorenzo Cain	8	Zach Davies	Eduardo Escobar	1	2	___	0-0
09/28/2019	Brewers@Rockies	Lorenzo Cain	8	Junior Guerra	Garrett Hampson	7	1	1__	2-0
07/26/2019	Rangers@Athletics	Delino DeShields	8	Lance Lynn	Chris Herrmann	2	0	1__	0-1
08/28/2019	Rangers@Angels	Delino DeShields	8	Ariel Jurado	Brian Goodwin	3	1	___	0-0
03/29/2019	Rockies@Marlins	Ian Desmond	8	D.J. Johnson	Lewis Brinson	8	0	___	2-1
08/03/2019	Giants@Rockies	Steven Duggar	8	Madison Bumgarner	Ian Desmond	5	1	_2_	4-5
06/26/2019	Dodgers@Diamondbacks	Jarrod Dyson	8	Stefan Crichton	Joc Pederson	7	2	___	2-8
09/18/2019	Blue Jays@Orioles	Derek Fisher	7	Clay Buchholz	Jonathan Villar	1	0	___	0-0
09/18/2019	Nationals@Cardinals	Dexter Fowler	9	Andrew Miller	Asdrubal Cabrera	8	1	12_	1-5
05/29/2019	Royals@White Sox	Leury Garcia	8	Reynaldo Lopez	Jorge Soler	4	1	___	1-7
08/28/2019	Twins@White Sox	Leury Garcia	8	Ross Detwiler	C.J. Cron	2	1	1__	0-1
07/16/2019	Rays@Yankees	Brett Gardner	7	CC Sabathia	Avisail Garcia	4	2	___	2-1
04/10/2019	Brewers@Angels	Brian Goodwin	8	Felix Pena	Yasmani Grandal	2	2	___	0-0
09/16/2019	Royals@Athletics	Alex Gordon	7	Glenn Sparkman	Jurickson Profar	2	0	___	1-2
07/14/2019	Mets@Marlins	Curtis Granderson	7	Sandy Alcantara	Pete Alonso	1	1	___	1-0
09/04/2019	Phillies@Reds	Adam Haseley	8	Blake Parker	Freddy Galvis	8	0	___	5-6
09/26/2019	Phillies@Nationals	Adam Haseley	8	Jason Vargas	Yan Gomes	1	2	1_3	0-1
09/19/2019	Blue Jays@Orioles	Austin Hays	8	Gabriel Ynoa	Vladimir Guerrero Jr.	4	1	___	2-1
06/30/2019	Cubs@Reds	Jason Heyward	9	Rowan Wick	Nick Senzel	7	0	1__	3-4
07/03/2019	Yankees@Mets	Aaron Hicks	8	Domingo German	Robinson Cano	6	1	___	4-1
07/04/2019	Tigers@White Sox	Eloy Jimenez	7	Reynaldo Lopez	Nicholas Castellanos	5	2	1__	3-2
05/09/2019	Braves@Diamondbacks	Adam Jones	9	Luke Weaver	Ronald Acuna Jr.	6	2	1__	1-1
06/29/2019	Nationals@Tigers	JaCoby Jones	8	Gregory Soto	Victor Robles	3	0	___	0-0
04/14/2019	White Sox@Yankees	Aaron Judge	9	Luis Cessa	Jose Abreu	5	0	123	4-2
08/31/2019	Athletics@Yankees	Aaron Judge	9	Cory Gearrin	Matt Chapman	10	2	___	3-3
08/12/2019	Rays@Padres	Kevin Kiermaier	8	Oliver Drake	Francisco Mejia	8	2	___	10-2
04/21/2019	Blue Jays@Athletics	Ramon Laureano	8	Brett Anderson	Teoscar Hernandez	2	0	1__	0-0
05/07/2019	Reds@Athletics	Ramon Laureano	8	Mike Fiers	Joey Votto	6	2	___	0-1
05/08/2019	Mets@Padres	Manuel Margot	8	Matt Strahm	Pete Alonso	6	2	___	2-2
08/27/2019	Dodgers@Padres	Manuel Margot	8	Robbie Erlin	Cody Bellinger	6	1	1__	8-0
08/29/2019	Pirates@Rockies	Starling Marte	8	Trevor Williams	Nolan Arenado	5	2	___	11-3
05/04/2019	Twins@Yankees	Cameron Maybin	9	J.A. Happ	Jonathan Schoop	4	2	12_	2-0
06/28/2019	Indians@Orioles	Oscar Mercado	8	Adam Plutko	Chance Sisco	4	2	___	0-8
09/02/2019	Rockies@Dodgers	Joc Pederson	9	Walker Buehler	Charlie Blackmon	5	0	1_3	4-10
05/04/2019	Giants@Reds	Kevin Pillar	8	Dereck Rodriguez	Nick Senzel	3	2	___	1-5
06/05/2019	Marlins@Brewers	Harold Ramirez	9	Sandy Alcantara	Lorenzo Cain	1	2	___	1-0
05/09/2019	Rangers@Astros	Josh Reddick	9	Roberto Osuna	Hunter Pence	9	1	1_3	2-4
06/04/2019	Astros@Mariners	Josh Reddick	9	Chris Devenski	Kyle Seager	8	1	1__	11-5
06/25/2019	Pirates@Astros	Josh Reddick	9	Gerrit Cole	Starling Marte	4	0	___	0-0
07/21/2019	Rangers@Astros	Josh Reddick	9	Rogelio Armenteros	Rougned Odor	2	1	1__	0-2
09/10/2019	Athletics@Astros	Josh Reddick	9	Chris Devenski	Khris Davis	4	2	___	17-2
05/12/2019	Pirates@Cardinals	Bryan Reynolds	7	Francisco Liriano	Jose Martinez	9	1	___	10-6
08/05/2019	Brewers@Pirates	Bryan Reynolds	7	Dario Agrazal	Mike Moustakas	2	0	___	1-0
04/20/2019	Twins@Orioles	Eddie Rosario	7	Jose Berrios	Chris Davis	6	0	___	6-3
06/08/2019	Orioles@Astros	Anthony Santander	9	Andrew Cashner	Yuli Gurriel	6	1	1_3	1-0
06/23/2019	Orioles@Mariners	Anthony Santander	9	Gabriel Ynoa	Domingo Santana	1	1	___	1-1
04/25/2019	Diamondbacks@Pirates	JB Shuck	7	Francisco Liriano	Eduardo Escobar	7	2	1__	5-0
04/23/2019	White Sox@Orioles	Dwight Smith Jr.	7	Andrew Cashner	Adam Engel	2	2	_2_	0-0
07/21/2019	Royals@Indians	Jorge Soler	9	Glenn Sparkman	Jason Kipnis	4	0	___	2-2
07/29/2019	Braves@Nationals	Juan Soto	7	Patrick Corbin	Adam Duvall	6	1	1_3	1-2
08/21/2019	Nationals@Pirates	Juan Soto	7	Patrick Corbin	Jose Osuna	4	2	___	6-0
05/13/2019	Astros@Tigers	George Springer	9	Brad Peacock	Niko Goodrum	1	0	___	0-0
05/15/2019	Astros@Tigers	Christin Stewart	7	Nick Ramirez	George Springer	4	2	_2_	3-1
08/17/2019	Marlins@Rockies	Raimel Tapia	8	German Marquez	Lewis Brinson	4	2	___	2-4
08/06/2019	Yankees@Orioles	Mike Tauchman	7	Stephen Tarpley	Pedro Severino	4	0	___	5-2
04/08/2019	Brewers@Angels	Mike Trout	8	Trevor Cahill	Christian Yelich	3	0	___	1-2
09/18/2019	Rangers@Astros	Kyle Tucker	9	Gerrit Cole	Scott Heineman	3	0	___	0-0
09/29/2019	Orioles@Red Sox	Stevie Wilkerson	9	Mychal Givens	Jackie Bradley Jr.	8	2	1__	4-4
07/28/2019	Giants@Padres	Mike Yastrzemski	9	Madison Bumgarner	Franmil Reyes	6	1	___	5-4

2019 Career Register

John Shirley

In the Career Register you will find the career statistics of every player who played in the majors this past season. Included here are all the traditional stats such as hits, home runs, strikeouts, etc. that provide the baseline for how players have performed over their careers. This year we removed Complete Games and Shutouts from pitching statistics due to the fact that starters are no longer expected to go nine innings. In place of these two statistics we now provide each pitcher's OPS allowed. (Complete Games and Shutouts can be found in the Leader Boards section of this book.)

Along with every player's Major League statistics, we also provide minor league statistics for some players. We also include five seasons of MiLB data for the top 25 prospects in baseball, even if they have yet to play in the majors, along with the top 100 prospects who played in MLB this year.

For minor league data below Double-A, if a player played at only one level in a given season, you will see that level explicitly specified. If a player played at multiple levels in a given season, his statistics will be grouped into a single row labeled Low.

For all levels, in instances where a player either pitched in fewer than five games or hit in fewer than 10 games at a given level, we do not include those lines in this book.

If a player led the AL or NL in a category, that number will appear in **boldface**.

Age is seasonal as of June 30, 2019.

For pitchers, BFP is Batters Facing Pitcher; TBB is Total Bases on Balls (or Total Walks, intentional and unintentional); Op is Save Opportunities; Hld is Holds.

For the various levels of Class-A ball, we have used "A+" to indicate High-A and "A-" to indicate Low-A. To help readers decode our minor league abbreviations, there is a legend in the back of the book.

A pronunciation guide is provided underneath the name of selected players.

In addition to a variety of traditional statistics, the Register also shows Runs Created (RC) for hitters and Component ERA (ERC) for pitchers. Runs Created is a comprehensive measurement of a player's offensive production distilled into a single number. It was originally developed by Bill James. Component ERA estimates what a pitcher's ERA should have been based on his raw pitching statistics and acts as a good indicator of whether a pitcher deserved the ERA he ended the season with. The details of the current formulas for both RC and ERC are in the Baseball Glossary at the back of the Handbook.

A player's total career numbers in the postseason appear on one line above his total regular season career numbers. Since we work hard to bring you this publication by November 1, postseason data from 2019 is not included. In addition, the Japanese baseball season extends a bit beyond our deadline, so the Japanese statistics for posted players will not include a complete record of their most recent games. Those numbers will be updated in the following year's handbook.

Looking For More?

If you like our work, there are other outlets at which you can find more of it.

The Sports Info Solutions Baseball Podcast features interviews with players (Nick Ahmed, Austin Hedges, Kevin Pillar) and notable people who work with analytics (David Cone, baseball writers Joe Sheehan and Tyler Kepner) and provides insight into different projects our R&D team is working on. It can be found wherever you subscribe to podcasts.

The Sports Info Solutions Blog (SportsInfoSolutionsBlog.com) features articles and research written by our R&D team and our Baseball Operations department. Topics include examinations of player and team performance, as well as statistical updates and leaderboards.

You can also follow us on Twitter at @sportsinfo_SIS and on Instagram at @sportsinfosolutions.

Fernando Abad

Pitches: L Bats: L Pos: RP-21   ah-BAHD   Ht: 6'1" Wt: 220 Born: 12/17/1985 Age: 34

Year	Team	Lg	G	GS	GF	IP	BFP	H	R	ER	HR	SH	SF	HB	TBB	IBB	SO	WP	W	L	Pct	Sv-Op Hld	Vel	OPS	ERC	ERA
2019 Scrmto	AAA		38	0	28	44.0	185	49	17	15	3	1	3	0	4	0	49	5	2	3	.400	13--	-	.684	3.21	3.07
2010 Hou	NL		22	0	6	19.0	76	14	6	6	3	0	1	0	5	0	12	0	0	1	.000	0-0	6	90	.636	2.49	2.84
2011 Hou	NL		29	0	1	19.2	99	28	18	16	5	1	2	1	9	0	15	0	1	4	.200	0-2	7	90	.946	8.06	7.32
2012 Hou	NL		37	6	8	46.0	208	57	27	26	6	2	1	3	19	1	38	4	0	6	.000	0-0	3	90	.892	6.13	5.09
2013 Was	NL		39	0	17	37.2	166	42	14	14	3	0	0	1	10	0	32	0	0	3	.000	0-1	2	93	.687	4.05	3.35
2014 Oak	AL		69	0	17	57.1	216	34	11	10	4	1	2	4	15	3	51	0	2	4	.333	0-2	9	92	.499	1.64	1.57
2015 Oak	AL		62	0	17	47.2	205	45	23	22	11	3	3	1	19	3	45	4	2	2	.500	0-3	1	91	.813	4.63	4.15
2016 2 Tms	AL		57	0	15	46.2	198	40	20	19	4	0	1	1	22	2	41	1	1	6	.143	1-5	8	91	.657	3.50	3.66
2017 Bos	AL		48	0	15	43.2	182	40	18	16	4	0	2	1	14	1	37	0	2	1	.667	1-2	2	92	.672	3.32	3.30
2019 SF	NL		21	0	1	13.0	49	9	6	6	2	0	0	0	3	0	9	1	0	2	.000	0-0	8	93	.571	2.26	4.15
16 Min	AL		39	0	8	34.0	138	27	11	10	2	0	1	0	14	2	29	0	1	4	.200	1-2	6	91	.614	2.72	2.65
16 Bos	AL		18	0	7	12.2	60	13	9	9	2	0	0	1	8	0	12	1	0	2	.000	0-3	2	92	.759	5.81	6.39
Postseason			1	0	0	0.1	1	0	0	0	0	0	0	0	0	0	0	0	0	0		0-0	0	95	.000	0.00	0.00
9 ML YEARS			384	6	97	330.2	1399	309	143	135	42	7	12	12	116	10	280	10	8	29	.216	2-15	46	91	.711	3.81	3.67

Bryan Abreu

Pitches: R Bats: R Pos: RP-7   Ht: 6'1" Wt: 204 Born: 4/22/1997 Age: 23

Year	Team	Lg	G	GS	GF	IP	BFP	H	R	ER	HR	SH	SF	HB	TBB	IBB	SO	WP	W	L	Pct	Sv-Op Hld	Vel	OPS	ERC	ERA
2019 CpChr	AA		20	13	3	76.2	337	60	45	43	6	1	4	7	48	0	101	16	6	2	.750	2--	-	.674	3.95	5.05
2019 Hou	AL		7	0	2	8.2	32	4	1	1	0	0	0	0	3	0	13	0	0	0	-	0-0	0	95	.391	1.05	1.04

Jose Abreu

Bats: R Throws: R Pos: 1B-125;DH-34   Ht: 6'3" Wt: 255 Born: 1/29/1987 Age: 33

Year	Team	Lg	G	AB	H	2B	3B	HR	(Hm	Rd)	TB	R	RBI	RC	TBB	IBB	SO	HBP	SH	SF	SB	CS	GDP	Avg	OBP	Slg	OPS
2014 CWS	AL		145	556	176	35	2	36	(15	21)	323	80	107	113	51	15	131	11	0	4	3	1	14	.317	.383	.581	.964
2015 CWS	AL		154	613	178	34	3	30	(16	14)	308	88	101	105	39	11	140	15	0	1	0	0	16	.290	.347	.502	.850
2016 CWS	AL		159	624	183	32	1	25	(15	10)	292	67	100	92	47	7	125	15	0	9	0	2	21	.293	.353	.468	.820
2017 CWS	AL		156	621	189	43	6	33	(16	17)	343	95	102	116	35	6	119	15	0	4	3	0	21	.304	.354	.552	.906
2018 CWS	AL		128	499	132	36	1	22	(11	11)	236	68	78	78	37	7	109	11	0	6	2	0	14	.265	.325	.473	.798
2019 CWS	AL		159	634	180	38	1	33	(15	18)	319	85	123	103	36	4	152	13	0	10	2	2	24	.284	.330	.503	.834
6 ML YEARS			901	3547	1038	218	14	179	(88	91)	1821	483	611	607	245	50	776	80	0	34	10	5	110	.293	.349	.513	.862

Ronald Acuna Jr.

Bats: R Throws: R Pos: CF-100;LF-46;RF-35;PH-2   Ht: 6'0" Wt: 180 Born: 12/18/1997 Age: 22

Year	Team	Lg	G	AB	H	2B	3B	HR	(Hm	Rd)	TB	R	RBI	RC	TBB	IBB	SO	HBP	SH	SF	SB	CS	GDP	Avg	OBP	Slg	OPS
2018 Atl	NL		111	433	127	26	4	26	(14	12)	239	78	64	83	45	2	123	6	0	3	16	5	4	.293	.366	.552	.917
2019 Atl	NL		156	626	175	22	2	41	(18	23)	324	127	101	122	76	4	188	9	0	1	37	9	8	.280	.365	.518	.883
Postseason			4	16	3	1	0	1	(1	0)	7	1	4	3	1	0	5	0	0	0	1	0	0	.188	.235	.438	.673
2 ML YEARS			267	1059	302	48	6	67	(32	35)	563	205	165	205	121	6	311	15	0	4	53	14	12	.285	.365	.532	.897

Jason Adam

Pitches: R Bats: R Pos: RP-23   Ht: 6'4" Wt: 225 Born: 8/4/1991 Age: 28

Year	Team	Lg	G	GS	GF	IP	BFP	H	R	ER	HR	SH	SF	HB	TBB	IBB	SO	WP	W	L	Pct	Sv-Op Hld	Vel	OPS	ERC	ERA
2019 Buffalo	AAA		11	0	8	14.0	56	10	7	4	2	0	1	0	5	1	20	0	1	3	.250	1--	-	.728	2.59	2.57
2018 KC	AL		31	0	14	32.1	142	30	22	22	9	0	2	3	15	1	37	4	0	3	.000	0-2	2	94	.871	5.56	6.12
2019 Tor	AL		23	0	2	21.2	91	15	8	7	1	0	3	3	10	1	18	1	3	0	1.000	0-1	4	94	.601	2.75	2.91
2 ML YEARS			54	0	16	54.0	233	45	30	29	10	0	5	6	25	2	55	5	3	3	.500	0-3	6	94	.768	4.38	4.83

Cristhian Adames

Bats: B Throws: R Pos: 2B-4;PH-4;3B-3;PR-1   Ht: 6'0" Wt: 185 Born: 7/26/1991 Age: 28

Year	Team	Lg	G	AB	H	2B	3B	HR	(Hm	Rd)	TB	R	RBI	RC	TBB	IBB	SO	HBP	SH	SF	SB	CS	GDP	Avg	OBP	Slg	OPS
2019 Iowa	AAA		12	39	10	2	0	2	(-	-)	18	9	6	7	8	0	7	0	0	1	1	0	1	.256	.375	.462	.837
2019 Scrmto	AAA		43	145	41	12	2	6	(-	-)	75	23	25	27	19	0	32	0	0	1	1	1	7	.283	.364	.517	.881
2014 Col	NL		7	15	1	0	0	0	(0	0)	1	1	0	0	0	0	5	0	0	0	0	0	1	.067	.067	.067	.133
2015 Col	NL		26	53	13	1	1	0	(0	0)	16	4	3	4	3	1	11	1	1	0	0	1	0	.245	.298	.302	.600
2016 Col	NL		121	225	49	7	3	2	(0	2)	68	25	17	17	24	0	47	4	3	0	2	3	5	.218	.304	.302	.607
2017 Col	NL		12	13	0	0	0	0	(0	0)	0	1	0	1	1	0	6	0	0	0	0	0	0	.000	.071	.000	.071
2019 SF	NL		10	22	7	1	0	0	(0	0)	8	1	2	4	2	0	8	0	0	0	0	0	0	.318	.375	.364	.739
5 ML YEARS			176	328	70	9	4	2	(0	2)	93	32	22	25	30	1	77	5	4	0	2	4	6	.213	.289	.284	.573

Willy Adames

Bats: R **Throws:** R **Pos:** SS-152;PH-2   **Ht:** 6'0" **Wt:** 205 **Born:** 9/2/1995 **Age:** 24

Year	Team	Lg	G	AB	H	2B	3B	HR	(Hm	Rd)	TB	R	RBI	RC	TBB	IBB	SO	HBP	SH	SF	SB	CS	GDP	Avg	OBP	Slg	OPS
2018	TB	AL	85	288	80	7	0	10	(7	3)	117	43	34	34	31	3	95	1	1	2	6	5	6	.278	.348	.406	.754
2019	TB	AL	152	531	135	25	1	20	(5	15)	222	69	52	60	46	1	153	3	3	1	4	2	9	.254	.317	.418	.735
	2 ML YEARS		237	819	215	32	1	30	(12	18)	339	112	86	94	77	4	248	4	4	3	10	7	15	.263	.328	.414	.742

Austin D Adams

Pitches: R **Bats:** R **Pos:** RP-15   **Ht:** 5'11" **Wt:** 205 **Born:** 8/19/1986 **Age:** 33

Year	Team	Lg	G	GS	GF	IP	BFP	H	R	ER	HR	SH	SF	HB	TBB	IBB	SO	WP	W	L	Pct	Sv-Op	Hld	Vel	OPS	ERC	ERA
2019	Roch	AAA	11	1	7	18.0	77	16	9	9	3	0	0	1	6	0	28	2	1	1	.500	1- -	-	-	.699	3.79	4.50
2019	Toledo	AAA	18	1	4	25.2	114	26	20	19	6	0	1	2	10	0	20	3	0	2	.000	1- -	-	-	.848	5.33	6.66
2014	Cle	AL	6	0	1	7.0	30	9	7	7	1	0	0	0	1	0	4	0	0	0	-	0-0	0	97	.851	5.04	9.00
2015	Cle	AL	28	0	9	33.1	149	37	15	14	2	2	0	0	13	0	23	1	2	0	1.000	1-1	0	97	.766	4.29	3.78
2016	Cle	AL	19	0	11	18.1	88	27	22	20	5	0	0	0	7	1	17	0	0	0	-	0-0	0	96	1.065	8.11	9.82
2019	2 Tms	AL	15	0	9	16.2	80	18	13	13	4	0	1	0	13	1	14	0	0	0	-	0-0	0	96	.918	7.10	7.02
19	Min	AL	2	0	1	2.2	15	4	5	5	2	0	0	0	3	0	5	0	0	0	-	0-0	0	95	1.300	16.82	16.88
19	Det	AL	13	0	8	14.0	65	14	8	8	2	0	1	0	10	1	9	0	0	0	-	0-0	0	97	.832	5.51	5.14
	4 ML YEARS		68	0	30	75.1	347	91	57	54	12	2	1	0	34	2	58	1	2	0	1.000	1-1	0	97	.885	5.85	6.45

Austin L Adams

Pitches: R **Bats:** R **Pos:** RP-28; SP-2   **Ht:** 6'3" **Wt:** 225 **Born:** 5/5/1991 **Age:** 29

Year	Team	Lg	G	GS	GF	IP	BFP	H	R	ER	HR	SH	SF	HB	TBB	IBB	SO	WP	W	L	Pct	Sv-Op	Hld	Vel	OPS	ERC	ERA
2019	Fresno	AAA	8	0	3	10.0	40	7	4	3	0	0	0	0	3	0	20	4	0	1	.000	1- -	-	-	.520	1.60	2.70
2017	Was	NL	6	0	3	5.0	29	4	4	2	0	0	1	1	8	0	10	1	0	0	-	0-0	0	95	.711	7.11	3.60
2018	Was	NL	2	0	0	1.0	7	1	0	0	0	0	0	0	3	0	0	0	0	0	-	0-0	0	95	.821	13.82	0.00
2019	2 Tms		30	2	3	32.0	130	20	14	14	4	0	1	1	16	0	53	4	2	2	.500	0-2	10	95	.615	2.77	3.94
19	Was	NL	1	0	0	1.0	6	0	1	1	0	0	0	1	2	0	2	2	0	0	-	0-0	0	94	.500	7.00	9.00
19	Sea	AL	29	2	3	31.0	124	20	13	13	4	0	1	0	14	0	51	2	2	2	.500	0-2	10	95	.614	2.62	3.77
	3 ML YEARS		38	2	6	38.0	166	25	18	16	4	0	2	2	27	0	63	5	2	2	.500	0-2	10	95	.644	3.60	3.79

Chance Adams

Pitches: R **Bats:** R **Pos:** RP-13   **Ht:** 6'1" **Wt:** 225 **Born:** 8/10/1994 **Age:** 25

Year	Team	Lg	G	GS	GF	IP	BFP	H	R	ER	HR	SH	SF	HB	TBB	IBB	SO	WP	W	L	Pct	Sv-Op	Hld	Vel	OPS	ERC	ERA
2019	S-WB	AAA	18	15	3	81.2	363	77	44	42	11	0	0	7	38	0	80	2	4	4	.500	1- -	-	-	.748	4.55	4.63
2018	NYY	AL	3	1	1	7.2	34	8	7	6	3	0	0	0	4	0	4	0	0	1	.000	0-0	0	93	.953	7.11	7.04
2019	NYY	AL	13	0	5	25.1	124	39	25	24	7	0	0	2	11	0	23	1	1	1	.500	1-1	0	92	1.068	9.56	8.53
	2 ML YEARS		16	1	6	33.0	158	47	32	30	10	0	0	2	15	0	27	1	1	2	.333	1-1	0	92	1.043	8.99	8.18

Matt Adams

Bats: L **Throws:** R **Pos:** 1B-79;PH-33;PR-1   **Ht:** 6'3" **Wt:** 245 **Born:** 8/31/1988 **Age:** 31

Year	Team	Lg	G	AB	H	2B	3B	HR	(Hm	Rd)	TB	R	RBI	RC	TBB	IBB	SO	HBP	SH	SF	SB	CS	GDP	Avg	OBP	Slg	OPS
2012	StL	NL	27	86	21	6	0	2	(1	1)	33	8	13	9	5	0	24	0	0	0	0	0	3	.244	.286	.384	.669
2013	StL	NL	108	296	84	14	0	17	(10	7)	149	46	51	49	23	0	80	0	0	0	0	1	9	.284	.335	.503	.839
2014	StL	NL	142	527	152	34	5	15	(8	7)	241	55	68	65	26	5	114	3	0	7	3	2	9	.288	.321	.457	.779
2015	StL	NL	60	175	42	9	0	5	(1	4)	66	14	24	16	10	1	41	0	0	1	1	0	1	.240	.280	.377	.657
2016	StL	NL	118	297	74	18	0	16	(11	5)	140	37	54	46	25	1	81	2	0	3	0	1	5	.249	.309	.471	.780
2017	2 Tms	NL	131	339	93	22	1	20	(12	8)	177	46	65	55	23	5	88	1	0	4	0	0	5	.274	.319	.522	.841
2018	2 Tms	NL	121	306	73	10	0	21	(12	9)	146	42	57	47	27	3	73	4	0	0	0	0	6	.239	.309	.477	.786
2019	Was	NL	111	310	70	14	0	20	(13	7)	144	42	56	42	20	1	115	2	0	1	0	0	7	.226	.276	.465	.741
17	StL	NL	31	48	14	2	0	1	(0	1)	19	4	7	6	4	0	17	0	0	1	0	0	0	.292	.340	.396	.735
17	Atl	NL	100	291	79	20	1	19	(12	7)	158	42	58	49	19	5	71	1	0	3	0	0	5	.271	.315	.543	.858
18	Was	NL	94	249	64	9	0	18	(11	7)	127	37	48	42	24	2	55	4	0	0	0	0	6	.257	.332	.510	.842
18	StL	NL	27	57	9	1	0	3	(1	2)	19	5	9	5	3	1	18	0	0	0	0	0	0	.158	.200	.333	.533
	Postseason		26	93	21	3	0	4	(3	1)	36	10	11	12	8	2	24	1	0	0	0	0	2	.226	.294	.387	.681
	8 ML YEARS		818	2336	609	127	6	116	(68	48)	1096	290	388	329	159	16	616	12	0	16	4	4	45	.261	.309	.469	.778

Jim Adduci

Bats: L **Throws:** L **Pos:** RF-1;PH-1   ah-DOO-see   **Ht:** 6'2" **Wt:** 210 **Born:** 5/15/1985 **Age:** 35

Year	Team	Lg	G	AB	H	2B	3B	HR	(Hm	Rd)	TB	R	RBI	RC	TBB	IBB	SO	HBP	SH	SF	SB	CS	GDP	Avg	OBP	Slg	OPS
2019	Iowa	AAA	105	359	108	23	0	12	(-	-)	167	59	58	57	21	1	89	1	1	4	10	4	7	.301	.338	.465	.803
2013	Tex	AL	17	31	8	1	0	0	(0	0)	9	2	0	3	3	0	9	0	0	0	2	0	0	.258	.324	.290	.614
2014	Tex	AL	44	101	17	3	0	1	(0	1)	23	13	8	6	10	0	27	0	1	2	3	1	2	.168	.239	.228	.467
2017	Det	AL	29	83	20	6	2	1	(0	1)	33	14	10	11	10	0	27	0	0	0	1	1	1	.241	.323	.398	.720
2018	Det	AL	59	176	47	8	2	3	(1	2)	68	19	21	20	6	0	45	0	2	1	1	0	2	.267	.290	.386	.676
2019	ChC	NL	2	5	0	0	0	0	(0	0)	0	0	0	0	0	0	3	0	0	0	0	0	0	.000	.000	.000	.000
	5 ML YEARS		151	396	92	18	4	5	(1	4)	133	48	39	40	29	0	111	0	3	3	7	2	5	.232	.283	.336	.619

Jo Adell

Bats: R Throws: R Pos: OF

Ht: 6'3" Wt: 215 Born: 4/8/1999 Age: 21

Year	Team	Lg	G	AB	H	2B	3B	HR	(Hm	Rd)	TB	R	RBI	RC	TBB	IBB	SO	HBP	SH	SF	SB	CS	GDP	Avg	OBP	Slg	OPS
2017	2 Tms	Low	49	203	66	11	8	5	(-	-)	108	43	30	37	14	1	49	3	1	1	8	2	3	.325	.376	.532	.908
2018	2 Tms	Low	82	333	100	26	4	18	(-	-)	188	69	71	52	26	0	89	7	0	3	13	3	7	.300	.360	.565	.925
2018	Mobile	AA	17	63	15	6	0	2	(-	-)	27	14	6	9	6	0	22	2	0	0	2	0	0	.238	.324	.429	.753
2019	Mobile	AA	43	159	49	15	0	8	(-	-)	88	28	23	35	19	0	41	3	0	1	6	0	7	.308	.390	.553	.944
2019	Salt Lk	AAA	27	121	32	11	0	0	(-	-)	43	22	8	14	10	0	43	0	0	0	1	0	0	.264	.321	.355	.676

Ehire Adrianza

eh-EE-ray ah-dree-AHN-zah

Bats: B Throws: R Pos: 3B-24;SS-24;1B-20;PH-11;PR-8;2B-7;RF-6;LF-1

Ht: 6'1" Wt: 195 Born: 8/21/1989 Age: 30

Year	Team	Lg	G	AB	H	2B	3B	HR	(Hm	Rd)	TB	R	RBI	RC	TBB	IBB	SO	HBP	SH	SF	SB	CS	GDP	Avg	OBP	Slg	OPS
2013	SF	NL	9	18	4	1	0	1	(0	1)	8	3	3	1	1	0	5	0	1	0	0	0	1	.222	.263	.444	.708
2014	SF	NL	53	97	23	6	0	0	(0	0)	29	10	5	6	5	1	22	1	2	1	1	1	2	.237	.279	.299	.578
2015	SF	NL	52	113	21	7	1	0	(0	0)	30	11	11	12	15	0	20	4	2	0	3	2	2	.186	.303	.265	.569
2016	SF	NL	40	63	16	2	0	2	(1	1)	24	3	7	6	2	0	13	2	4	0	0	1	0	.254	.299	.381	.679
2017	Min	AL	70	162	43	9	2	2	(0	2)	62	30	24	24	16	1	25	1	1	6	8	1	0	.265	.324	.383	.707
2018	Min	AL	114	335	84	23	1	6	(2	4)	127	42	39	38	24	2	82	1	4	2	5	1	4	.251	.301	.379	.680
2019	Min	AL	84	202	55	8	3	5	(3	2)	84	34	22	31	20	1	40	6	2	4	0	2	2	.272	.349	.416	.765
	Postseason		1	1	0	0	0	0	(0	0)	0	0	0	0	0	0	1	0	0	0	0	0	0	.000	.000	.000	.000
	7 ML YEARS		422	990	246	56	7	16	(6	10)	364	133	111	118	83	5	207	15	16	13	17	8	11	.248	.312	.368	.680

Dario Agrazal

Pitches: R Bats: R Pos: SP-14; RP-1

Ht: 6'2" Wt: 240 Born: 12/28/1994 Age: 25

Year	Team	Lg	G	GS	GF	IP	BFP	H	R	ER	HR	SH	SF	HB	TBB	IBB	SO	WP	W	L	Pct	Sv-Op Hld	Vel	OPS	ERC	ERA
2019	Indy	AAA	12	12	0	64.0	259	62	36	34	8	2	2	3	12	0	55	2	4	4	.500	0- -	-	.716	3.50	4.78
2019	Pit	NL	15	14	0	73.1	321	82	43	40	15	2	1	10	18	0	41	0	4	5	.444	0-0	0	91	.841	5.49	4.91

Jesus Aguilar

AGG-you-lahr

Bats: R Throws: R Pos: 1B-75;PH-44;DH-13;3B-2

Ht: 6'3" Wt: 250 Born: 6/30/1990 Age: 30

Year	Team	Lg	G	AB	H	2B	3B	HR	(Hm	Rd)	TB	R	RBI	RC	TBB	IBB	SO	HBP	SH	SF	SB	CS	GDP	Avg	OBP	Slg	OPS
2014	Cle	AL	19	33	4	0	0	0	(0	0)	4	2	3	0	4	0	13	0	0	1	0	0	1	.121	.211	.121	.332
2015	Cle	AL	7	19	6	1	0	0	(0	0)	7	0	2	4	0	0	7	1	0	0	0	0	0	.316	.350	.368	.718
2016	Cle	AL	9	6	0	0	0	0	(0	0)	0	0	0	0	0	0	1	0	0	0	0	0	0	.000	.000	.000	.000
2017	Mil	NL	133	279	74	15	2	16	(4	12)	141	40	52	47	25	1	94	4	0	3	0	0	8	.265	.331	.505	.837
2018	Mil	NL	149	492	135	25	0	35	(18	17)	265	80	108	82	58	3	143	6	0	10	0	0	19	.274	.352	.539	.890
2019	2 Tms		131	314	74	12	0	12	(5	7)	122	39	50	43	43	0	81	2	0	7	0	0	12	.236	.325	.389	.714
19	Mil	NL	94	222	50	9	0	8	(3	5)	83	26	34	28	31	0	59	2	0	4	0	0	11	.225	.320	.374	.694
19	TB	AL	37	92	24	3	0	4	(2	2)	39	13	16	15	12	0	22	0	0	3	0	0	1	.261	.336	.424	.760
	Postseason		10	37	8	3	0	2	(1	1)	17	5	5	3	3	1	15	0	0	0	0	0	0	.216	.275	.459	.734
	6 ML YEARS		448	1143	293	53	2	63	(27	36)	539	161	215	176	130	4	339	13	0	21	0	0	40	.256	.334	.472	.805

Nick Ahmed

Bats: R Throws: R Pos: SS-158;PH-2

Ht: 6'2" Wt: 195 Born: 3/15/1990 Age: 30

Year	Team	Lg	G	AB	H	2B	3B	HR	(Hm	Rd)	TB	R	RBI	RC	TBB	IBB	SO	HBP	SH	SF	SB	CS	GDP	Avg	OBP	Slg	OPS
2014	Ari	NL	25	70	14	2	0	1	(1	0)	19	9	4	3	3	0	10	0	2	0	0	1	2	.200	.233	.271	.504
2015	Ari	NL	134	421	95	17	6	9	(4	5)	151	49	34	38	29	1	81	1	5	3	4	5	4	.226	.275	.359	.634
2016	Ari	NL	90	284	62	9	1	4	(1	3)	85	26	20	18	15	3	58	4	2	3	5	2	9	.218	.265	.299	.564
2017	Ari	NL	53	167	42	8	1	6	(3	3)	70	24	21	18	10	3	39	1	0	0	3	4	3	.251	.298	.419	.717
2018	Ari	NL	153	516	121	33	5	16	(7	9)	212	61	70	62	40	2	109	2	1	5	5	4	15	.234	.290	.411	.700
2019	Ari	NL	158	556	141	33	6	19	(8	11)	243	79	82	73	52	1	113	4	1	12	8	2	15	.254	.316	.437	.753
	6 ML YEARS		613	2014	475	102	19	55	(24	31)	780	248	231	212	149	11	410	12	11	23	25	18	51	.236	.289	.387	.677

R.J. Alaniz

Pitches: R Bats: R Pos: RP-12

Ht: 6'4" Wt: 219 Born: 6/14/1991 Age: 29

Year	Team	Lg	G	GS	GF	IP	BFP	H	R	ER	HR	SH	SF	HB	TBB	IBB	SO	WP	W	L	Pct	Sv-Op Hld	Vel	OPS	ERC	ERA
2019	Tacom	AAA	10	0	6	12.2	63	18	10	9	3	0	1	0	7	1	23	2	2	1	.667	2- -	-	.997	8.12	6.39
2019	Lsvlle	AAA	25	0	16	27.2	122	25	11	9	1	1	1	4	11	1	31	1	1	2	.333	4- -	-	.626	3.51	2.93
2019	2 Tms		12	0	4	15.2	71	19	17	16	3	0	1	0	7	0	13	0	1	0	1.000	0-0	0	94	.890	6.27	9.19
19	Sea	AL	4	0	1	4.0	25	11	10	9	3	0	0	0	3	0	6	0	0	0	-	0-0	0	94	1.605	26.27	20.25
19	Cin	NL	8	0	3	11.2	46	8	7	7	0	0	1	0	4	0	7	0	1	0	1.000	0-0	0	93	.505	1.69	5.40

Matt Albers

Pitches: R **Bats:** L **Pos:** RP-67 **Ht:** 6'1" **Wt:** 225 **Born:** 1/20/1983 **Age:** 37

Year	Team	Lg	G	GS	GF	IP	BFP	H	R	ER	HR	SH	SF	HB	TBB	IBB	SO	WP	W	L	Pct	Sv-Op	Hld	Vel	OPS	ERC	ERA
2006	Hou	NL	4	2	0	15.0	66	17	10	10	1	2	0	0	7	0	11	0	0	2	.000	0-0	0	92	.796	4.97	6.00
2007	Hou	NL	31	18	2	110.2	508	127	77	72	18	6	8	7	50	6	71	7	4	11	.267	0-0	0	93	.859	5.76	5.86
2008	Bal	AL	28	3	5	49.0	208	43	21	19	4	1	3	2	22	1	26	1	3	3	.500	0-2	6	91	.655	3.62	3.49
2009	Bal	AL	56	0	13	67.0	309	80	43	41	3	5	2	2	36	3	49	3	3	6	.333	0-4	10	93	.797	5.41	5.51
2010	Bal	AL	62	0	19	75.2	329	78	41	38	6	3	0	2	34	5	49	2	5	3	.625	0-2	7	93	.726	4.35	4.52
2011	Bal	AL	56	0	10	64.2	289	62	35	34	7	4	2	5	31	1	68	2	4	4	.500	0-3	10	94	.733	4.44	4.73
2012	2 Tms		63	0	12	60.1	241	46	21	16	9	1	2	2	22	3	44	1	3	1	.750	0-6	9	94	.642	3.13	2.39
2013	Cle	AL	56	0	21	63.0	262	57	25	22	2	2	0	1	23	3	35	6	3	1	.750	0-0	1	93	.621	2.99	3.14
2014	Hou	AL	8	0	1	10.0	42	10	1	1	0	0	0	1	3	0	8	0	0	0	-	0-1	3	93	.675	3.46	0.90
2015	CWS	AL	30	0	5	37.1	149	31	6	5	3	0	3	1	9	2	28	0	2	0	1.000	0-0	6	90	.599	2.52	1.21
2016	CWS	AL	58	1	11	51.1	237	67	44	36	10	3	2	3	19	1	30	4	2	6	.250	0-4	13	92	.942	6.75	6.31
2017	Was	NL	63	0	23	61.0	233	35	12	11	6	0	1	4	17	0	63	0	7	2	.778	2-5	14	93	.520	1.76	1.62
2018	Mil	NL	34	0	10	34.1	157	45	29	28	10	0	3	2	12	2	32	1	3	3	.500	1-2	7	92	.962	7.46	7.34
2019	Mil	NL	67	0	13	59.2	258	53	34	34	8	2	2	3	29	3	57	2	8	6	.571	4-6	10	93	.728	4.16	5.13
12	Bos	AL	40	0	8	39.1	157	30	14	10	6	0	2	1	15	3	25	0	2	0	1.000	0-4	7	94	.653	3.16	2.29
12	Ari	NL	23	0	4	21.0	84	16	7	6	3	1	0	1	7	0	19	1	1	1	.500	0-2	2	93	.622	3.07	2.57
	Postseason		2	0	0	2.1	9	1	0	0	0	0	0	0	1	0	0	0	0	0	-	0-0	0	94	.347	1.08	0.00
	14 ML YEARS		616	24	145	759.0	3288	751	399	367	87	29	28	35	314	30	571	29	47	48	.495	7-35	96	93	.741	4.32	4.35

Hanser Alberto

HAHN-zer al-BAIR-tow

Bats: R **Throws:** R **Pos:** 2B-90;3B-66;PH-7;LF-3;PR-2;RF-1;DH-1 **Ht:** 5'11" **Wt:** 215 **Born:** 10/17/1992 **Age:** 27

Year	Team	Lg	G	AB	H	2B	3B	HR	(Hm	Rd)	TB	R	RBI	RC	TBB	IBB	SO	HBP	SH	SF	SB	CS	GDP	Avg	OBP	Slg	OPS
2015	Tex	AL	41	99	22	2	1	0	(0	0)	26	12	4	3	2	0	17	0	3	0	1	0	2	.222	.238	.263	.500
2016	Tex	AL	35	56	8	1	0	0	(0	0)	9	2	5	1	0	0	17	0	2	0	1	0	1	.143	.143	.161	.304
2018	Tex	AL	13	27	5	2	0	0	(0	0)	7	0	0	0	2	0	4	0	1	0	1	1	0	.185	.241	.259	.501
2019	Bal	AL	139	524	160	21	2	12	(9	3)	221	62	51	64	16	1	50	4	3	3	4	4	9	.305	.329	.422	.751
	Postseason		3	10	2	1	0	0	(0	0)	3	0	2	1	0	0	2	0	0	1	0	0	0	.200	.182	.300	.482
	4 ML YEARS		228	706	195	26	3	12	(9	3)	263	76	60	68	20	1	88	4	9	3	6	5	12	.276	.299	.373	.671

Ozzie Albies

Bats: B **Throws:** R **Pos:** 2B-158;PH-2 **Ht:** 5'8" **Wt:** 165 **Born:** 1/7/1997 **Age:** 23

Year	Team	Lg	G	AB	H	2B	3B	HR	(Hm	Rd)	TB	R	RBI	RC	TBB	IBB	SO	HBP	SH	SF	SB	CS	GDP	Avg	OBP	Slg	OPS
2017	Atl	NL	57	217	62	9	5	6	(1	5)	99	34	28	36	21	0	36	3	1	2	8	1	3	.286	.354	.456	.810
2018	Atl	NL	158	639	167	40	5	24	(9	15)	289	105	72	82	36	0	116	5	1	3	14	3	9	.261	.305	.452	.757
2019	Atl	NL	160	640	189	43	8	24	(12	12)	320	102	86	113	54	6	112	4	0	4	15	4	2	.295	.352	.500	.852
	Postseason		4	15	3	0	0	0	(0	0)	3	1	0	1	0	0	1	0	0	0	0	0	0	.200	.200	.200	.400
	3 ML YEARS		375	1496	418	92	18	54	(22	32)	708	241	186	231	111	6	264	12	2	9	37	8	14	.279	.332	.473	.806

Jorge Alcala

Pitches: R **Bats:** R **Pos:** RP-2 **Ht:** 6'3" **Wt:** 205 **Born:** 7/28/1995 **Age:** 24

Year	Team	Lg	G	GS	GF	IP	BFP	H	R	ER	HR	SH	SF	HB	TBB	IBB	SO	WP	W	L	Pct	Sv-Op	Hld	Vel	OPS	ERC	ERA
2019	Pnscla	AA	26	16	1	102.2	450	114	68	67	12	4	2	5	37	2	105	6	5	7	.417	0--	-	-	.810	4.88	5.87
2019	Roch	AAA	5	0	1	7.2	26	4	0	0	0	0	0	0	2	0	11	0	1	0	1.000	0--	-	-	.445	1.05	0.00
2019	Min	AL	2	0	2	1.2	7	1	0	0	0	0	0	0	1	0	1	0	0	0	-	0-0	0	94	.452	2.03	0.00

Sandy Alcantara

Pitches: R **Bats:** R **Pos:** SP-32 **Ht:** 6'4" **Wt:** 170 **Born:** 9/7/1995 **Age:** 24

Year	Team	Lg	G	GS	GF	IP	BFP	H	R	ER	HR	SH	SF	HB	TBB	IBB	SO	WP	W	L	Pct	Sv-Op	Hld	Vel	OPS	ERC	ERA
2017	StL	NL	8	0	3	8.1	39	9	6	4	2	0	0	0	6	0	10	0	0	0	-	0-0	0	98	.869	7.04	4.32
2018	Mia	NL	6	6	0	34.0	146	25	13	13	3	2	2	2	23	0	30	0	2	3	.400	0-0	0	95	.706	3.90	3.44
2019	Mia	NL	32	32	0	197.1	838	179	94	85	23	5	1	8	81	5	151	4	6	14	.300	0-0	0	96	.719	3.86	3.88
	3 ML YEARS		46	38	3	239.2	1023	213	113	102	28	7	3	10	110	5	191	4	8	17	.320	0-0	0	96	.723	3.97	3.83

Victor Alcantara

Pitches: R **Bats:** R **Pos:** RP-46 **Ht:** 6'2" **Wt:** 190 **Born:** 4/3/1993 **Age:** 27

Year	Team	Lg	G	GS	GF	IP	BFP	H	R	ER	HR	SH	SF	HB	TBB	IBB	SO	WP	W	L	Pct	Sv-Op	Hld	Vel	OPS	ERC	ERA
2019	Toledo	AAA	13	2	1	18.1	75	17	12	12	3	0	2	0	6	0	16	0	0	0	-	0--	-	-	.740	3.91	5.89
2017	Det	AL	6	0	2	7.1	39	12	7	7	1	0	1	2	4	0	5	1	0	0	-	0-0	0	92	.962	10.32	8.59
2018	Det	AL	27	0	8	30.0	119	25	8	8	6	0	3	0	6	0	21	2	1	1	.500	0-0	3	93	.680	2.84	2.40
2019	Det	AL	46	0	9	42.2	182	45	25	23	8	1	1	2	15	0	24	3	3	2	.600	0-3	10	93	.827	5.14	4.85
	3 ML YEARS		79	0	19	80.0	340	82	40	38	14	1	3	4	25	0	50	6	4	3	.571	0-3	13	93	.790	4.66	4.28

Scott Alexander

Pitches: L Bats: L Pos: RP-28
Ht: 6'2" Wt: 195 Born: 7/10/1989 Age: 30

		HOW MUCH PITCHED					WHAT HE GAVE UP											THE RESULTS								
Year Team	Lg	G	GS	GF	IP	BFP	H	R	ER	HR	SH	SF	HB	TBB	IBB	SO	WP	W	L	Pct	Sv-Op	Hld	Vel	OPS	ERC	ERA
2015 KC	AL	4	0	3	6.0	25	5	3	3	0	0	0	1	3	0	3	1	0	0	-	0-0	0	93	.598	3.67	4.50
2016 KC	AL	17	0	4	19.0	84	24	7	7	1	0	1	0	7	0	16	0	0	0	-	0-1	0	91	.790	5.24	3.32
2017 KC	AL	58	0	9	69.0	283	62	23	19	3	1	2	0	28	0	59	3	5	4	.556	4-6	9	93	.645	3.27	2.48
2018 LAD	NL	73	1	8	66.0	268	57	28	27	4	1	0	2	27	2	56	2	2	1	.667	3-6	21	93	.667	3.32	3.68
2019 LAD	NL	28	0	4	17.1	76	17	7	7	2	0	0	1	7	2	9	0	3	2	.600	0-0	6	93	.741	4.09	3.63
Postseason		4	0	1	2.1	10	1	2	2	0	0	0	0	2	0	2	1	0	0	-	0-0	0	92	.425	2.03	7.71
5 ML YEARS		180	1	28	177.1	736	165	68	63	10	2	3	4	72	4	143	6	10	7	.588	7-13	36	93	.678	3.58	3.20

Tyler Alexander

Pitches: L Bats: R Pos: SP-8; RP-5
Ht: 6'2" Wt: 200 Born: 7/14/1994 Age: 25

		HOW MUCH PITCHED					WHAT HE GAVE UP											THE RESULTS								
Year Team	Lg	G	GS	GF	IP	BFP	H	R	ER	HR	SH	SF	HB	TBB	IBB	SO	WP	W	L	Pct	Sv-Op	Hld	Vel	OPS	ERC	ERA
2019 Toledo	AAA	20	16	1	98.1	433	112	57	56	18	1	4	11	23	0	108	2	5	10	.333	0--	-	-	.853	5.25	5.13
2019 Det	AL	13	8	1	53.2	235	68	30	29	9	0	1	2	7	0	47	1	1	4	.200	0-0	0	91	.834	5.10	4.86

Jorge Alfaro

Bats: R Throws: R Pos: C-118;PH-14;1B-1;DH-1
Ht: 6'2" Wt: 225 Born: 6/11/1993 Age: 27

		BATTING																	RUNNING			AVERAGES			
Year Team	Lg	G	AB	H	2B	3B	HR	(Hm	Rd)	TB	R	RBI	RC	TBB	IBB	SO	HBP	SH	SF	SB	CS	GDP	Avg	OBP	Slg	OPS
2016 Phi	NL	6	16	2	0	0	0	(0	0)	2	0	0	0	1	1	8	0	0	0	0	0	0	.125	.176	.125	.301
2017 Phi	NL	29	107	34	6	0	5	(3	2)	55	12	14	20	3	1	33	4	0	0	0	0	2	.318	.360	.514	.874
2018 Phi	NL	108	344	90	16	2	10	(8	2)	140	35	37	44	18	6	138	14	0	1	3	0	2	.262	.324	.407	.731
2019 Mia	NL	130	431	113	14	1	18	(7	11)	183	44	57	53	22	1	154	10	0	2	4	4	12	.262	.312	.425	.736
4 ML YEARS		273	898	239	36	3	33	(18	15)	380	91	108	117	44	9	333	28	0	3	7	4	16	.266	.320	.423	.743

Anthony Alford

Bats: R Throws: R Pos: LF-6;RF-5;PH-5;PR-3;CF-2;DH-2
Ht: 6'1" Wt: 215 Born: 7/20/1994 Age: 25

		BATTING																	RUNNING			AVERAGES			
Year Team	Lg	G	AB	H	2B	3B	HR	(Hm	Rd)	TB	R	RBI	RC	TBB	IBB	SO	HBP	SH	SF	SB	CS	GDP	Avg	OBP	Slg	OPS
2019 Buffalo	AAA	76	282	73	16	3	7	(-	-)	116	46	37	42	31	0	94	5	1	0	22	8	4	.259	.343	.411	.754
2017 Tor	AL	4	8	1	1	0	0	(0	0)	2	0	0	0	0	0	3	0	0	0	0	0	0	.125	.125	.250	.375
2018 Tor	AL	13	19	2	0	0	0	(0	0)	2	3	1	1	2	0	9	0	0	0	1	0	0	.105	.190	.105	.296
2019 Tor	AL	16	28	5	0	0	1	(1	0)	8	3	1	2	1	0	11	1	0	0	2	0	0	.179	.233	.286	.519
3 ML YEARS		33	55	8	1	0	1	(1	0)	12	6	2	3	3	0	23	1	0	0	3	0	0	.145	.203	.218	.422

Kolby Allard

Pitches: L Bats: L Pos: SP-9
Ht: 6'1" Wt: 190 Born: 8/13/1997 Age: 22

		HOW MUCH PITCHED					WHAT HE GAVE UP											THE RESULTS								
Year Team	Lg	G	GS	GF	IP	BFP	H	R	ER	HR	SH	SF	HB	TBB	IBB	SO	WP	W	L	Pct	Sv-Op	Hld	Vel	OPS	ERC	ERA
2019 Gwnntt	AAA	20	20	0	110.0	465	119	60	51	15	3	5	2	36	0	98	2	7	5	.583	0--	-	-	.789	4.71	4.17
2018 Atl	NL	3	1	0	8.0	47	19	12	11	3	1	0	1	4	0	3	0	1	1	.500	0-0	0	89	1.253	17.45	12.38
2019 Tex	AL	9	9	0	45.1	208	52	26	25	3	0	1	2	19	0	33	1	4	2	.667	0-0	0	92	.742	4.82	4.96
2 ML YEARS		12	10	0	53.1	255	71	38	36	6	1	1	3	23	0	36	1	5	3	.625	0-0	0	92	.835	6.41	6.08

Austin Allen

Bats: L Throws: R Pos: C-19;PH-17;1B-2
Ht: 6'2" Wt: 220 Born: 1/16/1994 Age: 26

		BATTING																	RUNNING			AVERAGES			
Year Team	Lg	G	AB	H	2B	3B	HR	(Hm	Rd)	TB	R	RBI	RC	TBB	IBB	SO	HBP	SH	SF	SB	CS	GDP	Avg	OBP	Slg	OPS
2019 ElPaso	AAA	67	270	89	27	0	21	(-	-)	179	52	67	65	22	0	56	2	0	4	0	0	7	.330	.379	.663	1.042
2019 SD	NL	34	65	14	4	0	0	(0	0)	18	4	3	4	6	3	21	0	0	0	0	0	2	.215	.282	.277	.559

Cody Allen

Pitches: R Bats: R Pos: RP-25
Ht: 6'1" Wt: 210 Born: 11/20/1988 Age: 31

		HOW MUCH PITCHED					WHAT HE GAVE UP											THE RESULTS								
Year Team	Lg	G	GS	GF	IP	BFP	H	R	ER	HR	SH	SF	HB	TBB	IBB	SO	WP	W	L	Pct	Sv-Op	Hld	Vel	OPS	ERC	ERA
2019 Roch	AAA	7	1	1	8.0	34	7	5	3	1	1	0	0	5	0	7	0	0	2	.000	0--	-	-	.828	4.63	3.38
2012 Cle	AL	27	0	9	29.0	126	29	12	12	2	1	1	0	15	0	27	0	1	0	1.000	0-1	1	95	.710	4.39	3.72
2013 Cle	AL	77	0	12	70.1	301	62	22	19	7	4	4	1	26	2	88	9	6	1	.857	2-4	11	95	.679	3.24	2.43
2014 Cle	AL	76	0	44	69.2	279	48	21	16	7	2	2	1	26	5	91	4	6	4	.600	24-28	9	95	.601	2.32	2.07
2015 Cle	AL	70	0	58	69.1	286	56	26	23	2	1	2	2	25	2	99	9	2	5	.286	34-38	0	95	.596	2.51	2.99
2016 Cle	AL	67	0	55	68.0	264	41	23	19	8	3	2	0	27	2	87	3	3	5	.375	32-35	0	94	.584	2.14	2.51
2017 Cle	AL	69	0	55	67.1	282	57	24	22	9	1	0	2	21	0	92	9	3	7	.300	30-34	4	94	.619	3.18	2.94
2018 Cle	AL	70	0	45	67.0	289	58	35	35	11	1	0	4	33	2	80	3	4	6	.400	27-32	7	94	.740	4.35	4.70
2019 LAA	AL	25	0	13	23.0	116	24	16	16	9	0	1	0	20	0	29	3	0	2	.000	4-4	0	92	1.010	8.34	6.26
Postseason		17	0	9	20.1	91	18	9	7	2	0	0	1	10	3	35	1	0	0	-	7-7	1	94	.669	3.60	3.10
8 ML YEARS		481	0	291	463.2	1943	375	179	162	55	13	12	10	193	13	593	40	24	31	.436	153-176	32	95	.668	3.25	3.14

Greg Allen

Bats: B **Throws:** R **Pos:** LF-60;CF-18;PH-17;RF-13;PR-5   **Ht:** 6'0" **Wt:** 185 **Born:** 3/15/1993 **Age:** 27

Year Team	Lg	G	AB	H	2B	3B	HR	(Hm	Rd)	TB	R	RBI	RC	TBB	IBB	SO	HBP	SH	SF	SB	CS	GDP	Avg	OBP	Slg	OPS
2019 Clmbs	AAA	48	198	53	9	3	5	(-	-)	83	37	17	31	20	1	44	8	0	0	10	5	0	.268	.358	.419	.778
2017 Cle	AL	25	35	8	1	0	1	(0	1)	12	7	6	4	2	0	8	1	0	1	1	0	0	.229	.282	.343	.625
2018 Cle	AL	91	265	68	11	3	2	(1	1)	91	36	20	26	14	1	58	7	4	1	21	4	5	.257	.310	.343	.654
2019 Cle	AL	89	231	53	9	3	4	(0	4)	80	30	27	24	11	1	53	9	4	1	8	2	3	.229	.290	.346	.636
Postseason		3	1	0	0	0	0	(0	0)	0	0	0	0	0	0	0	0	0	0	0	0	1	.000	.000	.000	.000
3 ML YEARS		205	531	129	21	6	7	(1	6)	183	73	53	54	27	2	119	17	8	3	30	6	8	.243	.299	.345	.644

Logan Allen

Pitches: L **Bats:** R **Pos:** RP-5;SP-4   **Ht:** 6'3" **Wt:** 200 **Born:** 5/23/1997 **Age:** 23

Year Team	Lg	G	GS	GF	IP	BFP	H	R	ER	HR	SH	SF	HB	TBB	IBB	SO	WP	W	L	Pct	Sv-Op	Hld	Vel	OPS	ERC	ERA
2019 ElPaso	AAA	13	13	0	57.2	257	61	39	33	8	1	0	6	22	1	63	4	4	3	.571	0--	-	-	.776	5.00	5.15
2019 Clmbs	AAA	5	5	0	22.1	107	31	20	19	6	1	1	2	12	0	18	0	1	1	.500	0--	-	-	1.051	9.12	7.66
2019 2 Tms		9	4	3	27.2	127	36	20	19	4	2	1	2	13	0	17	0	2	3	.400	0-0	0	93	.958	7.07	6.18
19 SD	NL	8	4	2	25.1	118	33	20	19	4	2	1	2	13	0	14	0	2	3	.400	0-0	0	93	.974	7.39	6.75
19 Cle	AL	1	0	1	2.1	9	3	0	0	0	0	0	0	0	0	3	0	0	0	-	0-0	0	94	.778	3.75	0.00

Abraham Almonte

Bats: B **Throws:** R **Pos:** RF-9;PH-6;CF-3;PR-1   **Ht:** 5'9" **Wt:** 210 **Born:** 6/27/1989 **Age:** 31

Year Team	Lg	G	AB	H	2B	3B	HR	(Hm	Rd)	TB	R	RBI	RC	TBB	IBB	SO	HBP	SH	SF	SB	CS	GDP	Avg	OBP	Slg	OPS
2019 Reno	AAA	91	319	86	33	4	17	(-	-)	178	78	59	70	60	1	70	0	0	3	12	3	4	.270	.382	.558	.940
2013 Sea	AL	25	72	19	4	0	2	(1	1)	29	10	9	9	6	0	21	0	2	1	1	0	2	.264	.313	.403	.715
2014 2 Tms		59	204	47	10	1	3	(2	1)	68	19	15	18	12	0	60	1	2	1	4	3	5	.230	.275	.333	.609
2015 2 Tms		82	232	58	12	5	5	(4	1)	95	36	24	28	21	0	52	0	3	2	7	1	5	.250	.310	.409	.719
2016 Cle	AL	67	182	48	20	1	1	(1	0)	73	24	22	20	8	1	42	1	0	3	8	0	5	.264	.294	.401	.695
2017 Cle	AL	69	172	40	8	3	3	(2	1)	63	26	14	19	20	0	46	1	1	1	2	1	2	.233	.314	.366	.681
2018 KC	AL	50	134	24	1	2	3	(1	2)	38	15	9	5	15	0	36	0	1	1	2	2	6	.179	.260	.284	.544
2019 Ari	NL	17	31	9	3	1	1	(1	0)	17	11	4	6	7	0	8	0	0	0	0	0	1	.290	.421	.548	.969
14 Sea	AL	27	106	21	5	1	1	(0	1)	31	10	8	10	6	0	40	1	0	0	3	1	1	.198	.248	.292	.540
14 SD	NL	32	98	26	5	0	2	(2	0)	37	9	7	8	6	0	20	0	2	1	1	2	4	.265	.305	.378	.682
15 SD	NL	31	54	11	3	0	0	(0	0)	14	6	4	3	5	0	19	0	3	0	1	1	1	.204	.271	.259	.530
15 Cle	AL	51	178	47	9	5	5	(4	1)	81	30	20	25	16	0	33	0	0	2	6	0	4	.264	.321	.455	.776
7 ML YEARS		369	1027	245	58	13	18	(12	6)	383	141	97	105	89	1	265	3	9	10	24	7	26	.239	.298	.373	.671

Yency Almonte

Pitches: R **Bats:** B **Pos:** RP-28   **Ht:** 6'5" **Wt:** 217 **Born:** 6/4/1994 **Age:** 26

Year Team	Lg	G	GS	GF	IP	BFP	H	R	ER	HR	SH	SF	HB	TBB	IBB	SO	WP	W	L	Pct	Sv-Op	Hld	Vel	OPS	ERC	ERA
2019 Albq	AAA	30	0	23	30.0	147	29	21	14	2	0	1	1	26	2	32	3	2	3	.400	5--	-	-	.723	5.30	4.20
2018 Col	NL	14	0	3	14.2	60	15	5	3	1	0	1	0	4	0	14	1	0	0	-	0-0	3	95	.735	3.61	1.84
2019 Col	NL	28	0	6	34.0	157	39	22	21	7	1	0	2	14	0	29	1	0	1	.000	0-1	1	96	.860	5.73	5.56
2 ML YEARS		42	0	9	48.2	217	54	27	24	8	1	2	1	18	0	43	2	0	1	.000	0-1	4	96	.825	5.07	4.44

Albert Almora Jr.

Bats: R **Throws:** R **Pos:** CF-125;PH-21;PR-1   **Ht:** 6'2" **Wt:** 190 **Born:** 4/16/1994 **Age:** 26

Year Team	Lg	G	AB	H	2B	3B	HR	(Hm	Rd)	TB	R	RBI	RC	TBB	IBB	SO	HBP	SH	SF	SB	CS	GDP	Avg	OBP	Slg	OPS
2019 Iowa	AAA	13	49	11	3	1	0	(-	-)	16	6	2	4	4	0	7	0	1	0	2	1	2	.224	.283	.327	.610
2016 ChC	NL	47	112	31	9	1	3	(1	2)	51	14	14	16	5	0	20	0	0	0	0	0	5	.277	.308	.455	.763
2017 ChC	NL	132	299	89	18	1	8	(4	4)	133	39	46	44	19	1	53	0	3	2	1	0	8	.298	.338	.445	.782
2018 ChC	NL	152	444	127	24	1	5	(3	2)	168	62	41	51	24	1	83	3	2	6	1	3	12	.286	.323	.378	.701
2019 ChC	NL	130	339	80	11	1	12	(6	6)	129	41	32	25	16	4	62	1	5	2	2	1	8	.236	.271	.381	.651
Postseason		19	37	7	1	0	1	(0	1)	11	2	3	3	1	0	7	0	2	0	0	0	1	.189	.211	.297	.508
4 ML YEARS		461	1194	327	62	4	28	(14	14)	481	156	133	136	64	6	218	4	10	10	4	4	33	.274	.311	.403	.713

Pete Alonso

Bats: R **Throws:** R **Pos:** 1B-156;PH-7;DH-1   **Ht:** 6'3" **Wt:** 245 **Born:** 12/7/1994 **Age:** 25

Year Team	Lg	G	AB	H	2B	3B	HR	(Hm	Rd)	TB	R	RBI	RC	TBB	IBB	SO	HBP	SH	SF	SB	CS	GDP	Avg	OBP	Slg	OPS
2016 Bklyn	A-	30	109	35	12	1	5	(-	-)	64	20	21	23	11	0	22	1	0	2	0	1	2	.321	.382	.587	.969
2017 Stluci	A+	82	308	88	23	0	16	(-	-)	159	45	58	57	25	1	64	12	0	1	3	4	11	.286	.308	.455	.878
2017 Bnghtn	AA	11	45	14	4	1	2	(-	-)	26	7	5	8	2	0	7	0	0	0	0	0	0	.311	.340	.578	.918
2018 Bnghtn	AA	65	220	69	12	0	15	(-	-)	126	42	52	55	43	3	50	8	0	2	0	2	7	.314	.440	.573	1.012
2018 LsVgs	AAA	67	258	67	19	1	21	(-	-)	151	50	67	54	33	0	78	7	0	3	0	1	2	.260	.355	.585	.941
2019 NYM	NL	161	597	155	30	2	53	(27	26)	348	103	120	112	72	6	183	21	0	3	1	0	13	.260	.358	.583	.941

Yonder Alonso

Bats: L Throws: R Pos: PH-49;DH-41;1B-32   YONN-dur ah-LONN-zo   Ht: 6'1" Wt: 230 Born: 4/8/1987 Age: 33

Year	Team	Lg	G	AB	H	2B	3B	HR	(Hm	Rd)	TB	R	RBI	RC	TBB	IBB	SO	HBP	SH	SF	SB	CS	GDP	Avg	OBP	Slg	OPS
2010	Cin	NL	22	29	6	2	0	0	(0	0)	8	2	3	0	0	0	10	0	0	0	0	0	1	.207	.207	.276	.483
2011	Cin	NL	47	88	29	4	0	5	(2	3)	48	9	15	16	10	0	21	0	0	0	0	0	2	.330	.398	.545	.943
2012	SD	NL	155	549	150	39	0	9	(3	6)	216	47	62	71	62	9	101	3	1	4	3	0	14	.273	.348	.393	.741
2013	SD	NL	97	334	94	11	0	6	(4	2)	123	34	45	46	32	5	47	2	0	7	6	0	9	.281	.341	.368	.710
2014	SD	NL	84	267	64	19	1	7	(3	4)	106	27	27	26	17	1	36	1	0	3	6	1	8	.240	.285	.397	.682
2015	SD	NL	103	354	100	18	1	5	(3	2)	135	50	31	40	42	3	48	3	0	3	2	5	13	.282	.361	.381	.742
2016	Oak	AL	156	482	122	34	0	7	(3	4)	177	52	56	58	45	1	74	1	0	4	3	1	15	.253	.316	.367	.683
2017	2 Tms	AL	142	451	120	22	0	28	(17	11)	226	72	67	79	68	6	118	2	0	0	2	0	9	.266	.365	.501	.866
2018	Cle	AL	145	516	129	19	0	23	(12	11)	217	64	83	75	51	1	123	2	0	5	0	0	10	.250	.317	.421	.738
2019	2 Tms	AL	121	292	58	13	0	10	(4	6)	101	34	37	27	39	3	70	2	0	2	0	1	13	.199	.296	.346	.641
17	Oak	AL	100	319	85	17	0	22	(15	7)	168	52	49	59	50	6	88	2	0	0	1	0	6	.266	.369	.527	.896
17	Sea	AL	42	132	35	5	0	6	(2	4)	58	20	18	20	18	0	30	0	0	0	1	0	3	.265	.353	.439	.793
19	CWS	AL	67	219	39	6	0	7	(4	3)	66	23	27	17	29	2	53	1	0	2	0	1	8	.178	.275	.301	.576
19	Col	NL	54	73	19	7	0	3	(0	3)	35	11	10	10	10	1	17	1	0	0	0	0	5	.260	.357	.479	.837
	Postseason		2	6	0	0	0	0	(0	0)	0	0	0	0	0	0	4	0	0	0	0	0	0	.000	.000	.000	.000
	10 ML YEARS		1072	3362	872	181	2	100	(51	49)	1357	391	426	438	366	29	648	16	1	28	22	8	94	.259	.332	.404	.736

Dan Altavilla

Pitches: R Bats: R Pos: RP-17   all-ta-VILL-ah   Ht: 5'11" Wt: 200 Born: 9/8/1992 Age: 27

Year	Team	Lg	G	GS	GF	IP	BFP	H	R	ER	HR	SH	SF	HB	TBB	IBB	SO	WP	W	L	Pct	Sv-Op	Hld	Vel	OPS	ERC	ERA
2019	Tacom	AAA	14	0	1	14.0	67	11	13	13	0	0	0	4	11	0	25	1	2	1	.667	0--	-	-	.696	4.60	8.36
2019	Ark	AA	14	0	9	16.1	59	7	3	2	1	0	0	0	3	0	25	0	3	0	1.000	4--	-	-	.348	0.84	1.10
2016	Sea	AL	15	0	7	12.1	48	11	1	1	0	0	1	1	1	0	10	1	0	0	-	0-1	1	96	.560	2.09	0.73
2017	Sea	AL	41	0	13	46.2	203	43	27	22	9	0	4	1	20	1	52	9	1	1	.500	0-4	2	97	.765	4.38	4.24
2018	Sea	AL	22	0	3	20.2	85	11	7	6	2	0	0	2	15	0	23	4	3	2	.600	0-1	5	96	.609	3.27	2.61
2019	Sea	AL	17	0	3	14.2	64	9	9	9	1	1	1	0	12	1	18	2	2	1	.667	0-2	1	97	.613	3.20	5.52
	4 ML YEARS		95	0	26	94.1	400	74	44	38	12	1	6	4	48	2	103	16	6	4	.600	0-8	9	97	.685	3.65	3.63

Aaron Altherr

Bats: R Throws: R Pos: PH-21;CF-16;LF-14;PR-7;RF-6   ALL-tair   Ht: 6'5" Wt: 215 Born: 1/14/1991 Age: 29

Year	Team	Lg	G	AB	H	2B	3B	HR	(Hm	Rd)	TB	R	RBI	RC	TBB	IBB	SO	HBP	SH	SF	SB	CS	GDP	Avg	OBP	Slg	OPS
2019	Syrcse	AAA	28	74	20	5	1	4	(-	-)	39	9	13	14	10	0	16	3	0	1	3	2	4	.270	.375	.527	.902
2014	Phi	NL	2	5	0	0	0	0	(0	0)	0	0	0	0	0	0	2	0	0	0	0	0	0	.000	.000	.000	.000
2015	Phi	NL	39	137	33	11	4	5	(2	3)	67	25	22	23	16	0	41	5	1	2	6	2	3	.241	.338	.489	.827
2016	Phi	NL	57	198	39	6	0	4	(2	2)	57	23	22	20	23	2	69	6	0	0	7	2	4	.197	.300	.288	.587
2017	Phi	NL	107	372	101	24	5	19	(14	5)	192	58	65	55	32	2	104	7	0	1	5	4	12	.272	.340	.516	.856
2018	Phi	NL	105	243	44	11	1	8	(6	2)	81	28	38	30	36	0	91	4	0	2	3	2	13	.181	.295	.333	.628
2019	3 Tms	NL	49	61	5	2	0	1	(1	0)	10	8	3	1	3	0	25	1	0	1	0	0	1	.082	.154	.164	.300
19	Phi	NL	22	29	1	1	0	0	(0	0)	2	2	1	0	1	0	9	0	0	0	0	0	1	.034	.067	.069	.136
19	SF	NL	1	1	0	0	0	0	(0	0)	0	0	0	0	0	0	1	0	0	0	0	0	0	.000	.000	.000	.000
19	NYM	NL	26	31	4	1	0	1	(1	0)	8	6	2	1	2	0	15	1	0	1	0	0	0	.129	.200	.258	.458
	6 ML YEARS		359	1016	222	54	10	37	(25	12)	407	142	150	129	110	4	332	23	1	6	21	10	33	.219	.307	.401	.708

Jose Altuve

Bats: R Throws: R Pos: 2B-121;DH-2;PH-2;SS-1   al-TOO-vay   Ht: 5'6" Wt: 165 Born: 5/6/1990 Age: 30

Year	Team	Lg	G	AB	H	2B	3B	HR	(Hm	Rd)	TB	R	RBI	RC	TBB	IBB	SO	HBP	SH	SF	SB	CS	GDP	Avg	OBP	Slg	OPS
2011	Hou	NL	57	221	61	10	1	2	(2	0)	79	26	12	18	5	0	29	2	5	1	7	3	5	.276	.297	.357	.654
2012	Hou	NL	147	576	167	34	4	7	(4	3)	230	80	37	76	40	0	74	6	4	4	33	11	8	.290	.340	.399	.740
2013	Hou	AL	152	626	177	31	2	5	(4	1)	227	64	52	67	32	5	85	2	4	8	35	13	24	.283	.316	.363	.678
2014	Hou	AL	158	660	225	47	3	7	(4	3)	299	85	59	106	36	7	53	5	1	5	56	9	20	.341	.377	.453	.830
2015	Hou	AL	154	638	200	40	4	15	(9	6)	293	86	66	98	33	8	67	9	3	6	38	13	17	.313	.353	.459	.812
2016	Hou	AL	161	640	216	42	5	24	(15	9)	340	108	96	132	60	11	70	7	3	7	30	10	15	.338	.396	.531	.928
2017	Hou	AL	153	590	204	39	4	24	(9	15)	323	112	81	118	58	3	84	9	1	4	32	6	19	.346	.410	.547	.957
2018	Hou	AL	137	534	169	29	2	13	(7	6)	241	84	61	91	55	4	79	6	3	1	17	4	17	.316	.386	.451	.837
2019	Hou	AL	124	500	149	27	3	31	(15	16)	275	89	74	81	41	0	82	3	1	3	6	5	19	.298	.353	.550	.903
	Postseason		32	131	35	4	0	8	(7	1)	63	24	20	15	13	2	23	0	0	0	3	1	5	.267	.333	.481	.814
	9 ML YEARS		1243	4985	1568	299	28	128	(72	56)	2307	734	538	787	360	38	623	49	25	39	254	74	144	.315	.364	.463	.827

Jose Alvarado

Pitches: L Bats: L Pos: RP-34; SP-1   Ht: 6'2" Wt: 245 Born: 5/21/1995 Age: 25

Year	Team	Lg	G	GS	GF	IP	BFP	H	R	ER	HR	SH	SF	HB	TBB	IBB	SO	WP	W	L	Pct	Sv-Op	Hld	Vel	OPS	ERC	ERA
2017	TB	AL	35	0	6	29.2	123	24	12	12	1	2	1	0	9	1	29	2	0	3	.000	0-0	7	98	.570	2.19	3.64
2018	TB	AL	70	0	17	64.0	263	42	21	17	1	2	2	1	29	4	80	2	1	6	.143	8-12	32	97	.525	1.90	2.39
2019	TB	AL	35	1	16	30.0	146	29	18	16	2	3	2	0	27	3	39	8	1	6	.143	7-9	8	98	.751	5.28	4.80
	3 ML YEARS		140	1	39	123.2	532	95	51	45	4	7	5	1	65	8	148	12	2	15	.118	15-21	47	98	.595	2.71	3.27

Jose Alvarez

Pitches: L **Bats:** L **Pos:** RP-66; SP-1   **Ht:** 5'11" **Wt:** 180 **Born:** 5/6/1989 **Age:** 31

		HOW MUCH PITCHED					WHAT HE GAVE UP										THE RESULTS						
Year Team	Lg	G	GS	GF	IP	BFP	H	R	ER	HR	SH	SF	HB	TBB	IBB	SO	WP	W	L	Pct	Sv-Op Hld	Vel	OPS	ERC	ERA
2013 Det	AL	14	6	0	38.2	172	42	26	25	7	2	2	2	16	1	31	0	1	5	.167	0-0 2	89	.866	5.41	5.82
2014 LAA	AL	2	0	1	0.2	3	1	0	0	0	0	0	0	0	0	1	0	0	0	-	0-0 0	89	.667	4.47	0.00
2015 LAA	AL	64	0	18	67.0	283	58	29	26	5	0	1	5	23	4	59	1	4	3	.571	0-1 7	91	.642	3.13	3.49
2016 LAA	AL	64	0	12	57.1	256	71	29	22	4	1	1	1	15	4	51	2	1	3	.250	0-1 11	91	.745	4.55	3.45
2017 LAA	AL	64	0	12	48.2	203	50	23	21	7	1	0	0	12	5	45	1	0	3	.000	1-3 13	91	.733	3.78	3.88
2018 LAA	AL	76	0	5	63.0	261	51	20	19	3	2	0	2	22	2	59	1	6	4	.600	1-4 14	92	.613	2.59	2.71
2019 Phi	NL	67	1	11	59.0	255	66	25	22	8	1	3	1	18	4	51	3	3	4	.429	1-3 16	91	.766	4.61	3.36
Postseason		1	0	0	3.0	10	0	0	0	0	0	0	0	1	0	3	0	0	0	-	0-0 0	91	.100	0.13	0.00
7 ML YEARS		351	7	59	334.1	1433	339	152	135	34	7	7	11	106	20	297	8	15	22	.405	3-12 63	91	.717	3.86	3.63

Yordan Alvarez

Bats: L **Throws:** R **Pos:** DH-74;LF-10;PH-4   **Ht:** 6'5" **Wt:** 225 **Born:** 6/27/1997 **Age:** 23

		BATTING																	RUNNING			AVERAGES			
Year Team	Lg	G	AB	H	2B	3B	HR	(Hm | Rd)	TB	R	RBI	RC	TBB	IBB	SO	HBP	SH	SF	SB	CS	GDP	Avg	OBP	Slg	OPS
2017 2 Tms	Low	90	335	102	17	3	12	(- | -)	161	45	69	66	42	4	77	4	0	10	8	1	9	.304	.379	.481	.859
2018 CpChr	AA	43	169	55	13	0	12	(- | -)	104	39	46	39	19	2	45	0	0	2	5	2	1	.325	.389	.615	1.005
2018 Fresno	AAA	45	166	43	8	0	8	(- | -)	75	24	28	27	23	0	47	0	0	0	1	0	3	.259	.349	.452	.801
2019 RdRck	AAA	56	213	73	16	0	23	(- | -)	158	50	71	64	38	11	50	1	0	1	2	1	5	.343	.443	.742	1.184
2019 Hou	AL	87	313	98	26	0	27	(14 | 13)	205	58	78	72	52	4	94	2	0	2	0	0	9	.313	.412	.655	1.067

Adbert Alzolay

Pitches: R **Bats:** R **Pos:** SP-2; RP-2   **Ht:** 6'0" **Wt:** 179 **Born:** 3/1/1995 **Age:** 25

		HOW MUCH PITCHED					WHAT HE GAVE UP											THE RESULTS						
Year Team	Lg	G	GS	GF	IP	BFP	H	R	ER	HR	SH	SF	HB	TBB	IBB	SO	WP	W	L	Pct	Sv-Op Hld	Vel	OPS	ERC	ERA
2019 Iowa	AAA	15	15	0	65.1	282	53	34	32	10	0	1	4	31	2	91	3	2	4	.333	0- -	-	.686	3.83	4.41
2019 ChC	NL	4	2	1	12.1	60	13	10	10	4	0	0	1	9	0	13	0	1	1	.500	0-0 0	94	.923	7.80	7.30

Brett Anderson

Pitches: L **Bats:** L **Pos:** SP-31   **Ht:** 6'4" **Wt:** 230 **Born:** 2/1/1988 **Age:** 32

		HOW MUCH PITCHED					WHAT HE GAVE UP											THE RESULTS						
Year Team	Lg	G	GS	GF	IP	BFP	H	R	ER	HR	SH	SF	HB	TBB	IBB	SO	WP	W	L	Pct	Sv-Op Hld	Vel	OPS	ERC	ERA
2009 Oak	AL	30	30	0	175.1	735	180	94	79	20	4	4	3	45	1	150	0	11	11	.500	0-0 0	93	.711	3.84	4.06
2010 Oak	AL	19	19	0	112.1	470	112	41	35	6	3	2	7	22	2	75	4	7	6	.538	0-0 0	92	.655	3.16	2.80
2011 Oak	AL	13	13	0	83.1	356	86	40	37	8	4	1	7	25	1	61	0	3	6	.333	0-0 0	91	.721	4.20	4.00
2012 Oak	AL	6	6	0	35.0	137	29	11	10	1	0	0	1	7	1	25	1	4	2	.667	0-0 0	92	.565	2.13	2.57
2013 Oak	AL	16	5	4	44.2	200	51	32	30	5	1	0	0	21	1	46	0	1	4	.200	3-3 1	92	.794	5.27	6.04
2014 Col	NL	8	8	0	43.1	180	44	18	14	1	1	1	0	13	3	29	0	1	3	.250	0-0 0	90	.688	3.20	2.91
2015 LAD	NL	31	31	0	180.1	750	194	82	74	18	3	2	2	46	2	116	4	10	9	.526	0-0 0	91	.726	4.05	3.69
2016 LAD	NL	4	3	0	11.1	62	25	15	15	4	1	1	0	4	0	5	2	1	2	.333	0-0 0	91	1.208	14.27	11.91
2017 2 Tms		13	13	0	55.1	251	73	41	39	5	0	3	0	21	0	38	2	4	4	.500	0-0 0	91	.872	5.87	6.34
2018 Oak	AL	17	17	0	80.1	333	90	42	40	10	2	0	2	13	0	47	3	4	5	.444	0-0 0	90	.770	4.15	4.48
2019 Oak	AL	31	31	0	176.0	743	181	80	76	20	4	4	4	49	2	90	4	13	9	.591	0-0 0	91	.724	3.94	3.89
17 ChC	NL	6	6	0	22.0	111	34	22	20	2	0	1	0	12	0	16	1	2	2	.500	0-0 0	90	.986	7.85	8.18
17 Tor	AL	7	7	0	33.1	140	39	19	19	3	0	2	0	9	0	22	1	2	2	.500	0-0 0	91	.785	4.62	5.13
Postseason		3	2	1	9.1	40	10	7	7	1	0	0	0	3	0	10	1	1	1	.500	0-0 0	92	.730	4.23	6.75
11 ML YEARS		188	176	4	997.1	4217	1065	496	449	98	23	18	26	266	13	682	20	59	61	.492	3-3 1	91	.730	4.04	4.05

Brian Anderson

Bats: R **Throws:** R **Pos:** 3B-67;RF-55;PH-6;DH-1   **Ht:** 6'3" **Wt:** 185 **Born:** 5/19/1993 **Age:** 27

		BATTING																	RUNNING			AVERAGES			
Year Team	Lg	G	AB	H	2B	3B	HR	(Hm | Rd)	TB	R	RBI	RC	TBB	IBB	SO	HBP	SH	SF	SB	CS	GDP	Avg	OBP	Slg	OPS
2017 Mia	NL	25	84	22	7	1	0	(0 | 0)	31	11	8	11	10	0	28	0	0	1	0	0	1	.262	.337	.369	.706
2018 Mia	NL	156	590	161	34	4	11	(7 | 4)	236	87	65	94	62	2	129	16	0	2	2	4	18	.273	.357	.400	.757
2019 Mia	NL	126	459	120	33	1	20	(10 | 10)	215	57	66	72	44	1	114	14	0	3	5	1	15	.261	.342	.468	.811
3 ML YEARS		307	1133	303	74	6	31	(17 | 14)	482	155	139	177	116	3	271	30	0	6	7	5	34	.267	.349	.425	.775

Chase Anderson

Pitches: R **Bats:** R **Pos:** SP-27; RP-5   **Ht:** 6'1" **Wt:** 200 **Born:** 11/30/1987 **Age:** 32

		HOW MUCH PITCHED					WHAT HE GAVE UP											THE RESULTS						
Year Team	Lg	G	GS	GF	IP	BFP	H	R	ER	HR	SH	SF	HB	TBB	IBB	SO	WP	W	L	Pct	Sv-Op Hld	Vel	OPS	ERC	ERA
2014 Ari	NL	21	21	0	114.1	486	117	56	51	16	4	4	2	40	2	105	4	9	7	.563	0-0 0	91	.779	4.39	4.01
2015 Ari	NL	27	27	0	152.2	640	158	75	73	18	9	7		40	2	111	3	6	6	.500	0-0 0	92	.754	4.08	4.30
2016 Mil	NL	31	30	1	151.2	647	155	83	74	28	4	3	4	53	0	120	4	9	11	.450	0-0 0	91	.819	4.76	4.39
2017 Mil	NL	25	25	0	141.1	569	113	47	43	14	5	2	7	41	1	133	0	12	4	.750	0-0 0	93	.647	2.80	2.74
2018 Mil	NL	30	30	0	158.0	644	131	71	69	30	4	1	8	57	0	128	1	9	8	.529	0-0 0	92	.731	3.85	3.93
2019 Mil	NL	32	27	1	139.0	592	126	67	65	23	6	2	8	50	2	124	1	8	4	.667	0-0 0	93	.763	4.03	4.21
6 ML YEARS		166	160	2	857.0	3578	800	399	375	129	26	21	35	281	7	721	13	53	40	.570	0-0 0	92	.749	3.97	3.94

Cody Anderson

Pitches: R Bats: R Pos: RP-3; SP-2   **Ht:** 6'4" **Wt:** 240 **Born:** 9/14/1990 **Age:** 29

Year Team	Lg	G	GS	GF	IP	BFP	H	R	ER	HR	SH	SF	HB	TBB	IBB	SO	WP	W	L	Pct	Sv-Op	Hld	Vel	OPS	ERC	ERA
2019 Clmbs	AAA	6	6	0	23.2	98	25	12	12	3	0	0	3	7	0	21	2	0	2	.000	0--	-	-	.812	4.99	4.56
2015 Cle	AL	15	15	0	91.1	365	77	32	31	9	3	3	1	24	1	44	0	7	3	.700	0-0	0	92	.647	2.78	3.05
2016 Cle	AL	19	9	2	60.2	270	85	45	45	13	0	1	1	13	3	54	5	2	5	.286	0-0	0	94	.935	6.67	6.68
2019 Cle	AL	5	2	2	8.2	46	12	9	9	1	1	0	1	8	0	9	3	0	1	.000	0-1	0	94	.994	9.34	9.35
3 ML YEARS		39	26	4	160.2	681	174	86	85	23	4	4	3	45	4	107	8	9	9	.500	0-1	0	93	.786	4.47	4.76

Drew Anderson

Pitches: R Bats: R Pos: RP-2   **Ht:** 6'3" **Wt:** 185 **Born:** 3/22/1994 **Age:** 26

Year Team	Lg	G	GS	GF	IP	BFP	H	R	ER	HR	SH	SF	HB	TBB	IBB	SO	WP	W	L	Pct	Sv-Op	Hld	Vel	OPS	ERC	ERA
2019 LV	AAA	11	11	0	48.1	223	48	35	31	9	2	3	4	27	1	40	7	0	6	.000	0--	-	-	.791	5.54	5.77
2017 Phi	NL	2	0	1	2.1	14	6	7	6	0	0	1	0	1	0	2	0	0	0	-	0-0	0	94	1.167	13.44	23.14
2018 Phi	NL	5	1	1	12.2	59	17	7	7	0	0	0	2	2	0	11	0	0	1	.000	0-0	0	93	.792	4.81	4.97
2019 Phi	NL	2	0	1	6.0	30	6	5	5	1	0	0	0	6	2	6	0	0	0	-	0-0	0	93	.775	6.27	7.50
3 ML YEARS		9	1	3	21.0	103	29	19	18	1	0	1	2	9	2	19	0	0	1	.000	0-0	0	93	.839	6.08	7.71

Justin Anderson

Pitches: R Bats: L Pos: RP-54   **Ht:** 6'3" **Wt:** 230 **Born:** 9/28/1992 **Age:** 27

Year Team	Lg	G	GS	GF	IP	BFP	H	R	ER	HR	SH	SF	HB	TBB	IBB	SO	WP	W	L	Pct	Sv-Op	Hld	Vel	OPS	ERC	ERA
2018 LAA	AL	57	0	10	55.1	241	42	25	25	3	0	0	4	40	3	67	9	3	3	.500	4-6	22	97	.634	3.92	4.07
2019 LAA	AL	54	0	7	47.0	217	42	32	29	6	1	2	1	32	0	60	4	3	0	1.000	1-2	11	95	.778	4.74	5.55
2 ML YEARS		111	0	17	102.1	458	84	57	54	9	1	2	5	72	3	127	13	6	3	.667	5-8	33	96	.703	4.30	4.75

Nick Anderson

Pitches: R Bats: R Pos: RP-68   **Ht:** 6'5" **Wt:** 195 **Born:** 7/5/1990 **Age:** 29

Year Team	Lg	G	GS	GF	IP	BFP	H	R	ER	HR	SH	SF	HB	TBB	IBB	SO	WP	W	L	Pct	Sv-Op	Hld	Vel	OPS	ERC	ERA
2019 2 Tms		68	0	3	65.0	264	52	24	24	8	0	1	2	18	4	110	4	5	4	.556	1-5	16	96	.647	2.71	3.32
19 Mia	NL	45	0	3	43.2	186	40	19	19	5	0	1	1	16	3	69	2	2	4	.333	1-2	7	96	.705	3.53	3.92
19 TB	AL	23	0	0	21.1	78	12	5	5	3	0	0	1	2	1	41	2	3	0	1.000	0-3	9	96	.512	1.33	2.11

Shaun Anderson

Pitches: R Bats: R Pos: SP-16; RP-12   **Ht:** 6'4" **Wt:** 225 **Born:** 10/29/1994 **Age:** 25

Year Team	Lg	G	GS	GF	IP	BFP	H	R	ER	HR	SH	SF	HB	TBB	IBB	SO	WP	W	L	Pct	Sv-Op	Hld	Vel	OPS	ERC	ERA
2019 Scrmto	AAA	8	8	0	38.1	161	36	18	16	3	1	0	0	13	0	41	3	2	1	.667	0--	-	-	.714	3.36	3.76
2019 SF	NL	28	16	4	96.0	427	111	61	58	13	4	1	2	38	3	70	6	3	5	.375	2-2	1	93	.818	5.29	5.44

Tanner Anderson

Pitches: R Bats: R Pos: SP-5   **Ht:** 6'2" **Wt:** 203 **Born:** 5/27/1993 **Age:** 27

Year Team	Lg	G	GS	GF	IP	BFP	H	R	ER	HR	SH	SF	HB	TBB	IBB	SO	WP	W	L	Pct	Sv-Op	Hld	Vel	OPS	ERC	ERA
2019 LsVgs	AAA	21	16	1	96.0	444	121	66	64	21	0	4	5	41	0	59	1	9	5	.643	0--	-	-	.924	6.92	6.00
2018 Pit	NL	6	0	1	11.1	56	15	10	8	1	2	0	1	8	2	6	2	1	0	1.000	0-0	0	93	.911	7.31	6.35
2019 Oak	AL	5	5	0	22.1	105	30	16	15	4	0	0	0	7	1	18	3	0	3	.000	0-0	0	93	.809	6.06	6.04
2 ML YEARS		11	5	1	33.2	161	45	26	23	5	2	0	1	15	3	24	5	1	3	.250	0-0	0	93	.844	6.51	6.15

Tim Anderson

Bats: R Throws: R Pos: SS-122;PR-1   **Ht:** 6'1" **Wt:** 185 **Born:** 6/23/1993 **Age:** 27

Year Team	Lg	G	AB	H	2B	3B	HR	(Hm	Rd)	TB	R	RBI	RC	TBB	IBB	SO	HBP	SH	SF	SB	CS	GDP	Avg	OBP	Slg	OPS
2016 CWS	AL	99	410	116	22	6	9	(5	4)	177	57	30	45	13	0	117	1	6	1	10	2	15	.283	.306	.432	.738
2017 CWS	AL	146	587	151	26	4	17	(7	10)	236	72	56	59	13	0	162	3	2	1	15	1	13	.257	.276	.402	.679
2018 CWS	AL	153	567	136	28	3	20	(10	10)	230	77	64	58	30	2	149	4	2	3	26	8	15	.240	.281	.406	.687
2019 CWS	AL	123	498	167	32	0	18	(9	9)	253	81	56	77	15	0	109	3	0	2	17	5	12	.335	.357	.508	.865
4 ML YEARS		521	2062	570	108	13	64	(31	33)	896	287	206	239	71	2	537	11	10	7	68	16	55	.276	.303	.435	.738

Tyler Anderson

Pitches: L Bats: L Pos: SP-5   **Ht:** 6'3" **Wt:** 215 **Born:** 12/30/1989 **Age:** 30

Year Team	Lg	G	GS	GF	IP	BFP	H	R	ER	HR	SH	SF	HB	TBB	IBB	SO	WP	W	L	Pct	Sv-Op	Hld	Vel	OPS	ERC	ERA
2016 Col	NL	19	19	0	114.1	478	119	50	45	12	6	3	3	28	2	99	4	5	6	.455	0-0	0	91	.742	3.85	3.54
2017 Col	NL	17	15	1	86.0	362	88	48	46	16	5	2	2	26	0	81	6	6	6	.500	0-0	0	92	.820	4.57	4.81
2018 Col	NL	32	32	0	176.0	737	165	94	89	30	3	7	3	59	1	164	9	7	9	.438	0-0	0	92	.757	4.04	4.55
2019 Col	NL	5	5	0	20.2	106	33	27	27	8	2	2	0	11	0	23	0	0	3	.000	0-0	0	91	1.159	10.75	11.76
Postseason		2	1	0	7.0	28	6	3	3	1	0	0	0	2	0	6	0	0	1	.000	0-0	0	92	.709	3.21	3.86
4 ML YEARS		73	71	1	397.0	1683	405	219	207	66	16	14	8	124	3	367	19	18	24	.429	0-0	0	92	.791	4.40	4.69

Matt Andriese

Pitches: R **Bats:** R **Pos:** RP-54 — ANN-dreese — **Ht:** 6'2" **Wt:** 225 **Born:** 8/28/1989 **Age:** 30

Year	Team	Lg	G	GS	GF	IP	BFP	H	R	ER	HR	SH	SF	HB	TBB	IBB	SO	WP	W	L	Pct	Sv-Op	Hld	Vel	OPS	ERC	ERA
2015	TB	AL	25	8	8	65.2	282	69	32	30	8	1	3	2	18	1	49	2	3	5	.375	2-2	0	91	.728	4.08	4.11
2016	TB	AL	29	19	3	127.2	527	131	64	62	17	0	6	1	25	1	109	3	8	8	.500	1-1	4	92	.720	3.68	4.37
2017	TB	AL	18	17	1	86.0	374	90	48	43	16	0	1	4	28	1	76	3	5	5	.500	1-1	0	92	.795	4.80	4.50
2018	2 Tms		41	5	13	78.2	340	84	51	46	15	1	1	2	25	5	78	3	3	7	.300	0-0	1	92	.819	4.77	5.26
2019	Ari	NL	54	0	13	70.2	310	72	37	37	8	1	3	3	27	4	79	9	5	5	.500	1-4	4	93	.757	4.24	4.71
18	TB	AL	27	4	6	59.2	251	55	32	27	7	1	1	2	18	3	59	3	3	4	.429	0-0	1	92	.702	3.41	4.07
18	Ari	NL	14	1	7	19.0	89	29	19	19	8	0	0	0	7	2	19	0	0	3	.000	0-0	0	92	1.148	9.93	9.00
5 ML YEARS			167	49	38	428.2	1833	446	232	218	64	3	14	12	123	12	391	20	24	30	.444	5-8	9	92	.761	4.25	4.58

Elvis Andrus

Bats: R **Throws:** R **Pos:** SS-146;DH-1 — AHN-droos — **Ht:** 6'0" **Wt:** 200 **Born:** 8/26/1988 **Age:** 31

Year	Team	Lg	G	AB	H	2B	3B	HR	(Hm	Rd)	TB	R	RBI	RC	TBB	IBB	SO	HBP	SH	SF	SB	CS	GDP	Avg	OBP	Slg	OPS
2009	Tex	AL	145	480	128	17	8	6	(3	3)	179	72	40	65	40	0	77	6	12	3	33	6	4	.267	.329	.373	.702
2010	Tex	AL	148	588	156	15	3	0	(0	0)	177	88	35	79	64	0	96	5	17	0	32	15	6	.265	.342	.301	.643
2011	Tex	AL	150	587	164	27	3	5	(2	3)	212	96	60	76	56	0	74	5	16	1	37	12	17	.279	.347	.361	.708
2012	Tex	AL	158	629	180	31	9	3	(1	2)	238	85	62	92	57	0	96	5	17	3	21	10	15	.286	.349	.378	.727
2013	Tex	AL	156	620	168	17	4	4	(0	4)	205	91	67	72	52	1	97	4	16	6	42	8	19	.271	.328	.331	.659
2014	Tex	AL	157	619	163	35	1	2	(1	1)	206	72	41	59	46	0	96	3	9	7	27	15	21	.263	.314	.333	.647
2015	Tex	AL	160	596	154	34	2	7	(4	3)	213	69	62	68	46	1	78	2	8	9	25	9	14	.258	.309	.357	.667
2016	Tex	AL	147	506	153	31	7	8	(3	5)	222	75	69	87	47	2	70	4	4	7	24	8	18	.302	.362	.439	.800
2017	Tex	AL	158	643	191	44	4	20	(7	13)	303	100	88	104	38	0	101	9	3	4	25	10	18	.297	.337	.471	.808
2018	Tex	AL	97	395	101	20	3	6	(6	0)	145	53	33	44	28	0	66	3	0	2	5	3	8	.256	.308	.367	.675
2019	Tex	AL	147	600	165	27	4	12	(4	8)	236	81	72	76	34	1	96	4	0	10	31	8	16	.275	.313	.393	.707
Postseason			42	173	46	4	1	1	(0	1)	55	21	7	15	12	0	24	1	4	1	9	5	6	.266	.316	.318	.633
11 ML YEARS			1623	6263	1723	298	48	73	(31	42)	2336	882	629	822	508	5	947	44	100	52	302	104	156	.275	.331	.373	.704

Miguel Andujar

Bats: R **Throws:** R **Pos:** DH-8;3B-4 — **Ht:** 6'0" **Wt:** 215 **Born:** 3/2/1995 **Age:** 25

Year	Team	Lg	G	AB	H	2B	3B	HR	(Hm	Rd)	TB	R	RBI	RC	TBB	IBB	SO	HBP	SH	SF	SB	CS	GDP	Avg	OBP	Slg	OPS
2017	NYY	AL	5	7	4	2	0	0	(0	0)	6	0	4	4	1	0	0	0	0	0	1	0	0	.571	.625	.857	1.482
2018	NYY	AL	149	573	170	47	2	27	(16	11)	302	83	92	99	25	2	97	4	0	4	2	1	9	.297	.328	.527	.855
2019	NYY	AL	12	47	6	0	0	0	(0	0)	6	1	1	0	1	0	11	0	0	1	0	0	4	.128	.143	.128	.271
Postseason			4	10	2	0	0	0	(0	0)	2	0	0	1	2	0	2	0	0	0	0	0	1	.200	.333	.200	.533
3 ML YEARS			166	627	180	49	2	27	(16	11)	314	84	97	103	27	2	108	4	0	5	3	1	13	.287	.318	.501	.819

Aristides Aquino

Bats: R **Throws:** R **Pos:** RF-54;PH-2;1B-1 — **Ht:** 6'4" **Wt:** 220 **Born:** 4/22/1994 **Age:** 26

Year	Team	Lg	G	AB	H	2B	3B	HR	(Hm	Rd)	TB	R	RBI	RC	TBB	IBB	SO	HBP	SH	SF	SB	CS	GDP	Avg	OBP	Slg	OPS
2019	Lsvlle	AAA	78	294	88	13	1	28	(-	-)	187	56	53	65	23	0	81	4	0	2	5	1	5	.299	.356	.636	.992
2018	Cin	NL	1	1	0	0	0	0	(0	0)	0	0	0	0	0	0	1	0	0	0	0	0	0	.000	.000	.000	.000
2019	Cin	NL	56	205	53	8	0	19	(11	8)	118	31	47	39	16	2	60	2	0	2	7	0	5	.259	.316	.576	.891
2 ML YEARS			57	206	53	8	0	19	(11	8)	118	31	47	39	16	2	61	2	0	2	7	0	5	.257	.314	.573	.887

Victor Arano

Pitches: R **Bats:** R **Pos:** RP-3 — **Ht:** 6'2" **Wt:** 200 **Born:** 2/7/1995 **Age:** 25

Year	Team	Lg	G	GS	GF	IP	BFP	H	R	ER	HR	SH	SF	HB	TBB	IBB	SO	WP	W	L	Pct	Sv-Op	Hld	Vel	OPS	ERC	ERA
2017	Phi	NL	10	0	2	10.2	42	6	2	2	0	0	0	0	4	0	13	0	1	0	1.000	0-0	2	93	.475	1.35	1.69
2018	Phi	NL	60	0	14	59.1	246	54	19	18	6	0	2	1	17	4	60	1	1	2	.333	3-5	10	94	.673	3.12	2.73
2019	Phi	NL	3	0	1	4.2	16	2	2	2	1	0	1	0	2	0	7	0	1	0	1.000	0-0	0	93	.635	2.23	3.86
3 ML YEARS			73	0	17	74.2	304	62	23	22	7	0	3	1	23	4	80	1	3	2	.600	3-5	12	94	.644	2.77	2.65

Pedro Araujo

Pitches: R **Bats:** R **Pos:** RP-1 — **Ht:** 6'3" **Wt:** 215 **Born:** 7/2/1993 **Age:** 26

Year	Team	Lg	G	GS	GF	IP	BFP	H	R	ER	HR	SH	SF	HB	TBB	IBB	SO	WP	W	L	Pct	Sv-Op	Hld	Vel	OPS	ERC	ERA
2019	Bowie	AA	24	0	12	39.2	165	26	20	16	7	1	2	1	19	2	40	5	1	3	.250	0- -	-	-	.668	3.00	3.63
2018	Bal	AL	20	0	8	28.0	130	29	24	24	9	0	0	2	18	0	29	1	1	3	.250	0-0	0	92	.959	7.39	7.71
2019	Bal	AL	1	0	0	0.2	4	2	2	2	1	0	0	0	1	0	0	0	0	0	-	0-0	0	91	2.417	52.46	27.00
2 ML YEARS			21	0	8	28.2	134	31	26	26	10	0	0	2	19	0	29	1	1	3	.250	0-0	0	92	.999	8.07	8.16

Chris Archer

Pitches: R Bats: R Pos: SP-23

Ht: 6'2" Wt: 195 Born: 9/26/1988 Age: 31

Year Team	Lg	G	GS	GF	IP	BFP	H	R	ER	HR	SH	SF	HB	TBB	IBB	SO	WP	W	L	Pct	Sv-Op	Hld	Vel	OPS	ERC	ERA
2012 TB	AL	6	4	1	29.1	122	23	17	15	3	1	0	1	13	0	36	2	1	3	.250	0-0	0	94	.624	3.24	4.60
2013 TB	AL	23	23	0	128.2	525	107	49	46	15	1	5	8	38	2	101	7	9	7	.563	0-0	0	95	.660	3.13	3.22
2014 TB	AL	32	32	0	194.2	822	177	85	72	12	4	9	8	72	1	173	8	10	9	.526	0-0	0	95	.650	3.36	3.33
2015 TB	AL	34	34	0	212.0	868	175	85	76	19	2	2	3	66	0	252	13	12	13	.480	0-0	0	95	.613	2.79	3.23
2016 TB	AL	33	33	0	201.1	850	183	100	90	30	6	4	3	67	0	233	11	9	19	.321	0-0	0	94	.703	3.66	4.02
2017 TB	AL	34	34	0	201.0	852	193	101	91	27	1	2	5	60	0	249	15	10	12	.455	0-0	0	95	.710	3.75	4.07
2018 2 Tms		27	27	0	148.1	638	155	77	71	19	1	3	6	49	3	162	6	6	8	.429	0-0	0	95	.767	4.41	4.31
2019 Pit	NL	23	23	0	119.2	526	114	73	69	25	6	3	4	55	2	143	6	3	9	.250	0-0	0	94	.793	4.89	5.19
18 TB	AL	17	17	0	96.0	413	102	50	46	11	0	1	4	31	0	102	3	3	5	.375	0-0	0	95	.751	4.43	4.31
18 Pit	NL	10	10	0	52.1	225	53	27	25	8	1	2	2	18	3	60	3	3	3	.500	0-0	0	95	.796	4.36	4.30
Postseason		2	0	0	1.2	6	1	0	0	0	0	1	0	0	0	2	0	0	0	-	0-0	0	96	.367	0.75	0.00
8 ML YEARS		212	210	1	1235.0	5203	1127	587	530	150	22	28	38	420	8	1349	68	60	80	.429	0-0	0	95	.691	3.61	3.86

Orlando Arcia

Bats: R Throws: R Pos: SS-150;PH-5;PR-1

ARR-see-ya

Ht: 6'0" Wt: 165 Born: 8/4/1994 Age: 25

Year Team	Lg	G	AB	H	2B	3B	HR	(Hm	Rd)	TB	R	RBI	RC	TBB	IBB	SO	HBP	SH	SF	SB	CS	GDP	Avg	OBP	Slg	OPS
2016 Mil	NL	55	201	44	10	3	4	(2	2)	72	21	17	20	15	0	47	0	0	0	8	0	6	.219	.273	.358	.631
2017 Mil	NL	153	506	140	17	2	15	(8	7)	206	56	53	63	36	9	100	1	2	3	14	7	10	.277	.324	.407	.731
2018 Mil	NL	119	348	82	16	0	3	(2	1)	107	32	30	26	15	0	87	1	1	1	7	4	9	.236	.268	.307	.576
2019 Mil	NL	152	494	110	16	1	15	(6	9)	173	51	59	48	43	5	109	1	2	6	8	5	15	.223	.283	.350	.633
Postseason		10	33	11	0	0	3	(1	2)	20	7	4	4	1	1	4	0	0	0	0	0	1	.333	.353	.606	.959
4 ML YEARS		479	1549	376	59	6	37	(18	19)	558	160	159	157	109	14	343	3	5	10	37	16	40	.243	.292	.360	.652

Nolan Arenado

Bats: R Throws: R Pos: 3B-154;PH-2

ahr-eh-NOD-oh

Ht: 6'2" Wt: 215 Born: 4/16/1991 Age: 29

Year Team	Lg	G	AB	H	2B	3B	HR	(Hm	Rd)	TB	R	RBI	RC	TBB	IBB	SO	HBP	SH	SF	SB	CS	GDP	Avg	OBP	Slg	OPS
2013 Col	NL	133	486	130	29	4	10	(5	5)	197	49	52	48	23	1	72	1	2	2	2	0	16	.267	.301	.405	.706
2014 Col	NL	111	432	124	34	2	18	(16	2)	216	58	61	60	25	1	58	4	1	5	2	1	13	.287	.328	.500	.828
2015 Col	NL	157	616	177	43	4	42	(20	22)	354	97	130	116	34	13	110	4	0	11	2	5	17	.287	.323	.575	.898
2016 Col	NL	160	618	182	35	6	41	(25	16)	352	116	133	128	68	10	103	2	0	8	2	3	17	.294	.362	.570	.932
2017 Col	NL	159	606	187	43	7	37	(19	18)	355	100	130	130	62	9	106	4	1	6	3	2	21	.309	.373	.586	.959
2018 Col	NL	156	590	175	38	2	38	(23	15)	331	104	110	117	73	10	122	3	1	6	2	2	16	.297	.374	.561	.935
2019 Col	NL	155	588	185	31	2	41	(21	20)	343	102	118	123	62	11	93	4	0	8	3	2	14	.315	.379	.583	.962
Postseason		5	21	4	0	0	1	(0	1)	7	2	3	0	0	0	7	0	0	2	0	0	0	.190	.174	.333	.507
7 ML YEARS		1031	3936	1160	253	27	227	(129	98)	2148	626	734	722	347	55	664	22	5	46	16	15	114	.295	.351	.546	.897

Rogelio Armenteros

Pitches: R Bats: R Pos: RP-3; SP-2

roh-HELL-ee-oh

Ht: 6'1" Wt: 215 Born: 6/30/1994 Age: 26

Year Team	Lg	G	GS	GF	IP	BFP	H	R	ER	HR	SH	SF	HB	TBB	IBB	SO	WP	W	L	Pct	Sv-Op	Hld	Vel	OPS	ERC	ERA
2019 RdRck	AAA	19	18	0	84.1	365	90	48	45	14	2	5	1	31	0	85	2	6	7	.462	0- -	-	-	.824	4.89	4.80
2019 Hou	AL	5	2	2	18.0	75	17	9	8	1	0	0	0	5	0	18	0	1	1	.500	1-1	0	91	.608	2.99	4.00

Shawn Armstrong

Pitches: R Bats: R Pos: RP-55

Ht: 6'2" Wt: 225 Born: 9/11/1990 Age: 29

Year Team	Lg	G	GS	GF	IP	BFP	H	R	ER	HR	SH	SF	HB	TBB	IBB	SO	WP	W	L	Pct	Sv-Op	Hld	Vel	OPS	ERC	ERA
2015 Cle	AL	8	0	5	8.0	30	5	2	2	1	0	0	0	2	0	11	0	0	0	-	0-0	0	94	.590	1.84	2.25
2016 Cle	AL	10	0	2	10.2	44	9	3	3	1	1	0	0	5	2	7	1	0	0	-	0-0	0	92	.668	3.25	2.53
2017 Cle	AL	21	0	14	24.2	108	23	12	12	5	0	0	1	10	0	20	1	1	0	1.000	0-0	0	93	.737	4.50	4.38
2018 Sea	AL	14	0	3	14.2	57	9	2	2	1	0	2	3	3	1	15	0	0	1	.000	1-1	2	94	.569	1.91	1.23
2019 2 Tms	AL	55	0	10	58.0	271	66	38	37	8	1	3	4	29	1	63	4	1	1	.500	4-9	9	93	.815	5.74	5.74
19 Sea	AL	4	0	1	3.2	23	8	6	6	1	0	1	0	3	1	3	0	0	1	.000	0-0	0	93	1.268	16.16	14.73
19 Bal	AL	51	0	9	54.1	248	58	32	31	7	0	3	4	26	0	60	4	1	0	1.000	4-9	9	93	.777	5.14	5.13
5 ML YEARS		108	0	34	116.0	510	112	57	56	16	2	5	8	49	4	116	6	2	2	.500	5-10	11	93	.745	4.42	4.34

Randy Arozarena

Bats: R Throws: R Pos: RF-6;PR-6;CF-5;PH-5;LF-1

Ht: 5'11" Wt: 170 Born: 2/28/1995 Age: 25

Year Team	Lg	G	AB	H	2B	3B	HR	(Hm	Rd)	TB	R	RBI	RC	TBB	IBB	SO	HBP	SH	SF	SB	CS	GDP	Avg	OBP	Slg	OPS
2019 Sprgfld	AA	28	97	30	7	2	3	(-	-)	50	14	15	21	13	2	23	6	0	0	8	5	4	.309	.422	.515	.938
2019 Memp	AAA	64	246	88	18	2	12	(-	-)	146	51	38	60	24	0	48	11	0	2	9	7	5	.358	.435	.593	1.028
2019 StL	NL	19	20	6	1	0	1	(0	1)	10	4	2	3	2	0	4	1	0	0	2	1	0	.300	.391	.500	.891

Luis Arraez

Bats: L **Throws:** R **Pos:** 2B-49;LF-21;3B-17;SS-8;DH-5;PH-5;PR-1 **Ht:** 5'10" **Wt:** 177 **Born:** 4/9/1997 **Age:** 23

							BATTING												RUNNING			AVERAGES			
Year Team	Lg	G	AB	H	2B	3B	HR	(Hm Rd)	TB	R	RBI	RC	TBB	IBB	SO	HBP	SH	SF	SB	CS	GDP	Avg	OBP	Slg	OPS
2019 Pnscla	AA	38	146	50	6	1	0	(- -)	58	18	14	25	18	0	13	0	0	0	3	3	3	.342	.415	.397	.812
2019 Roch	AAA	16	66	23	4	0	0	(- -)	27	8	8	11	6	0	2	0	0	1	1	0	2	.348	.397	.409	.806
2019 Min	AL	92	326	109	20	1	4	(1 3)	143	54	28	59	36	1	29	1	0	3	2	2	2	.334	.399	.439	.838

Jake Arrieta

Pitches: R **Bats:** R **Pos:** SP-24 air-ee-ETT-uh **Ht:** 6'4" **Wt:** 225 **Born:** 3/6/1986 **Age:** 34

			HOW MUCH PITCHED				WHAT HE GAVE UP										THE RESULTS							
Year Team	Lg	G	GS	GF	IP	BFP	H	R	ER	HR	SH	SF	HB	TBB	IBB	SO	WP	W	L	Pct	Sv-Op	Hld	Vel	OPS	ERC	ERA
2010 Bal	AL	18	18	0	100.1	449	106	57	52	7	9	4	2	48	3	52	5	6	6	.500	0-0	0	93	.767	4.74	4.66
2011 Bal	AL	22	22	0	119.1	523	115	70	67	21	3	2	4	59	2	93	0	10	8	.556	0-0	0	92	.791	4.93	5.05
2012 Bal	AL	24	18	1	114.2	496	122	82	79	16	3	4	5	35	3	109	4	3	9	.250	0-0	1	93	.763	4.47	6.20
2013 2 Tms		14	14	0	75.1	324	59	41	40	9	2	3	5	41	1	60	1	5	4	.556	0-0	0	94	.718	3.82	4.78
2014 ChC	NL	25	25	0	156.2	614	114	46	44	5	5	3	3	41	2	167	8	10	5	.667	0-0	0	94	.535	1.85	2.53
2015 ChC	NL	33	33	0	229.0	870	150	52	45	10	4	1	6	48	2	236	6	22	6	.786	0-0	0	95	.507	1.53	1.77
2016 ChC	NL	31	31	0	197.1	795	138	72	68	16	2	1	6	76	1	190	16	18	8	.692	0-0	0	94	.583	2.45	3.10
2017 ChC	NL	30	30	0	168.1	707	150	82	66	23	1	4	10	55	3	163	14	14	10	.583	0-0	0	92	.716	3.64	3.53
2018 Phi	NL	31	31	0	172.2	724	165	93	76	21	1	8	7	57	0	138	11	10	11	.476	0-0	0	93	.724	3.92	3.96
2019 Phi	NL	24	24	0	135.2	594	149	76	70	21	5	4	7	51	3	110	7	8	8	.500	0-0	0	93	.799	5.19	4.64
13 Bal	AL	5	5	0	23.2	115	25	19	19	2	0	3	2	17	1	23	1	1	2	.333	0-0	0	94	.857	5.91	7.23
13 ChC	NL	9	9	0	51.2	213	34	22	21	7	2	0	3	24	0	37	0	4	2	.667	0-0	0	94	.648	2.94	3.66
Postseason		9	9	0	52.2	218	36	19	18	6	1	1	5	21	1	66	3	5	3	.625	0-0	0	94	.623	2.79	3.08
10 ML YEARS		252	246	1	1469.1	6096	1268	671	607	151	30	32	57	511	20	1318	72	106	75	.586	0-0	1	93	.673	3.30	3.72

Christian Arroyo

Bats: R **Throws:** R **Pos:** 3B-13;PH-2;2B-1 **Ht:** 6'1" **Wt:** 220 **Born:** 5/30/1995 **Age:** 25

							BATTING												RUNNING			AVERAGES			
Year Team	Lg	G	AB	H	2B	3B	HR	(Hm Rd)	TB	R	RBI	RC	TBB	IBB	SO	HBP	SH	SF	SB	CS	GDP	Avg	OBP	Slg	OPS
2019 Drham	AAA	33	121	38	9	1	8	(- -)	73	21	29	27	12	0	26	1	0	0	1	0	5	.314	.381	.603	.984
2017 SF	NL	34	125	24	5	0	3	(2 1)	38	9	14	7	8	1	32	1	0	1	1	2	4	.192	.244	.304	.548
2018 TB	AL	20	53	14	2	1	1	(1 0)	21	5	6	9	6	0	16	0	0	0	0	0	0	.264	.339	.396	.735
2019 TB	AL	16	50	11	2	0	2	(2 0)	19	8	7	6	5	0	18	1	1	0	0	0	0	.220	.304	.380	.684
3 ML YEARS		70	228	49	9	1	6	(5 1)	78	22	27	22	19	1	66	2	1	1	1	2	4	.215	.280	.342	.622

Humberto Arteaga

Bats: R **Throws:** R **Pos:** SS-36;2B-2;PH-2;3B-1 um-BARE-toh ar-teh-AH-gah **Ht:** 6'1" **Wt:** 160 **Born:** 1/23/1994 **Age:** 26

							BATTING												RUNNING			AVERAGES			
Year Team	Lg	G	AB	H	2B	3B	HR	(Hm Rd)	TB	R	RBI	RC	TBB	IBB	SO	HBP	SH	SF	SB	CS	GDP	Avg	OBP	Slg	OPS
2019 Omha	AAA	66	284	85	10	1	5	(- -)	112	39	26	38	12	0	34	3	2	1	11	5	11	.299	.333	.394	.728
2019 KC	AL	41	122	24	4	0	0	(0 0)	28	11	4	8	8	0	28	2	3	0	1	1	2	.197	.258	.230	.487

Willians Astudillo

Bats: R **Throws:** R **Pos:** C-21;1B-15;3B-13;RF-6;PH-6;LF-3;2B-2;DH-2;PR-1 **Ht:** 5'9" **Wt:** 225 **Born:** 10/14/1991 **Age:** 28

							BATTING												RUNNING			AVERAGES			
Year Team	Lg	G	AB	H	2B	3B	HR	(Hm Rd)	TB	R	RBI	RC	TBB	IBB	SO	HBP	SH	SF	SB	CS	GDP	Avg	OBP	Slg	OPS
2019 Roch	AAA	18	78	33	1	0	5	(- -)	49	18	19	19	2	0	2	2	0	1	1	1	1	.423	.446	.628	1.074
2018 Min	AL	30	93	33	4	1	3	(1 2)	48	9	21	17	2	0	3	1	0	1	0	0	4	.355	.371	.516	.887
2019 Min	AL	58	190	51	9	0	4	(1 3)	72	28	21	19	5	0	8	5	0	4	0	0	6	.268	.299	.379	.678
2 ML YEARS		88	283	84	13	1	7	(2 5)	120	37	42	36	7	0	11	6	0	5	0	0	10	.297	.322	.424	.746

Tyler Austin

Bats: R **Throws:** R **Pos:** PH-55;1B-23;LF-22;RF-3;DH-1 **Ht:** 6'2" **Wt:** 220 **Born:** 9/6/1991 **Age:** 28

							BATTING												RUNNING			AVERAGES			
Year Team	Lg	G	AB	H	2B	3B	HR	(Hm Rd)	TB	R	RBI	RC	TBB	IBB	SO	HBP	SH	SF	SB	CS	GDP	Avg	OBP	Slg	OPS
2019 SnAnt	AAA	15	54	18	3	0	4	(- -)	33	15	10	13	8	0	17	0	0	1	3	1	3	.333	.413	.611	1.024
2016 NYY	AL	31	83	20	3	0	5	(5 0)	38	7	12	12	7	0	36	0	0	0	1	0	1	.241	.300	.458	.758
2017 NYY	AL	20	40	9	2	0	2	(0 2)	17	4	8	6	4	0	17	0	0	2	0	0	1	.225	.283	.425	.708
2018 2 Tms	AL	69	244	56	10	0	17	(9 8)	117	34	47	34	19	0	95	0	0	3	1	2	3	.230	.287	.480	.767
2019 3 Tms		89	154	29	5	1	9	(5 4)	63	30	24	21	24	1	67	0	0	1	2	0	2	.188	.296	.409	.705
18 NYY	AL	34	121	27	6	0	8	(3 5)	57	16	23	19	8	0	53	0	0	1	1	1	2	.223	.280	.471	.751
18 Min	AL	35	123	29	4	0	9	(6 3)	60	18	24	15	11	0	42	0	0	2	0	1	1	.236	.294	.488	.782
19 Min	AL	2	4	1	1	0	0	(0 0)	2	1	0	1	1	0	3	0	0	0	0	0	0	.250	.400	.500	.900
19 SF	NL	70	130	24	2	1	8	(4 4)	52	24	20	16	17	0	57	0	0	1	1	0	1	.185	.279	.400	.679
19 Mil	NL	17	20	4	2	0	1	(1 0)	9	5	4	4	6	1	7	0	0	0	1	0	1	.200	.370	.450	.820
4 ML YEARS		209	521	114	20	1	33	(19 14)	235	75	91	73	54	1	215	0	0	6	4	2	7	.219	.292	.451	.743

Abiatal Avelino

Bats: R Throws: R Pos: PH-2;SS-1;LF-1   Ht: 5'11" Wt: 195 **Born:** 2/14/1995 **Age:** 25

Year	Team	Lg	G	AB	H	2B	3B	HR	(Hm	Rd)	TB	R	RBI	RC	TBB	IBB	SO	HBP	SH	SF	SB	CS	GDP	Avg	OBP	Slg	OPS
2019	Scrmto	AAA	121	473	134	24	8	12	(-	-)	210	70	62	68	23	2	84	0	3	3	17	5	10	.283	.315	.444	.759
2018	SF	NL	6	11	3	0	0	0	(0	0)	3	1	0	0	0	0	3	0	0	0	0	0	0	.273	.273	.273	.545
2019	SF	NL	4	7	2	0	0	0	(0	0)	2	0	1	1	1	0	3	0	0	0	0	0	0	.286	.375	.286	.661
	2 ML YEARS		10	18	5	0	0	0	(0	0)	5	1	1	1	1	0	6	0	0	0	0	0	0	.278	.316	.278	.594

Alex Avila

Bats: L Throws: R Pos: C-54;PH-9   ah-VEE-lah   Ht: 5'11" Wt: 210 **Born:** 1/29/1987 **Age:** 33

Year	Team	Lg	G	AB	H	2B	3B	HR	(Hm	Rd)	TB	R	RBI	RC	TBB	IBB	SO	HBP	SH	SF	SB	CS	GDP	Avg	OBP	Slg	OPS
2009	Det	AL	29	61	17	4	0	5	(4	1)	36	9	14	12	10	0	18	0	0	1	0	0	0	.279	.375	.590	.965
2010	Det	AL	104	294	67	12	0	7	(4	3)	100	28	31	26	36	0	71	2	1	0	2	2	12	.228	.316	.340	.656
2011	Det	AL	141	464	137	33	4	19	(10	9)	235	63	82	86	73	9	131	3	3	8	3	1	8	.295	.389	.506	.895
2012	Det	AL	116	367	89	21	2	9	(7	2)	141	42	48	53	61	2	104	2	2	2	0	0	12	.243	.352	.384	.736
2013	Det	AL	102	330	75	14	1	11	(7	4)	124	39	47	37	44	0	112	1	1	3	0	0	10	.227	.317	.376	.693
2014	Det	AL	124	390	85	22	0	11	(3	8)	140	44	47	48	61	1	151	3	1	2	0	3	6	.218	.327	.359	.686
2015	Det	AL	67	178	34	5	0	4	(2	2)	51	21	13	20	40	0	66	0	1	0	0	1	4	.191	.339	.287	.626
2016	CWS	AL	57	169	36	6	0	7	(5	2)	63	19	11	17	38	0	78	1	0	1	0	0	3	.213	.359	.373	.732
2017	2 Tms		112	311	82	13	1	14	(8	6)	139	41	49	55	62	2	120	1	1	1	0	1	10	.264	.387	.447	.834
2018	Ari	NL	80	194	32	6	0	7	(1	6)	59	13	20	17	37	2	90	1	0	2	0	0	4	.165	.299	.304	.603
2019	Ari	NL	63	164	34	8	0	9	(5	4)	69	22	24	23	36	7	68	1	0	0	1	0	8	.207	.353	.421	.774
17	Det	AL	77	219	60	11	0	11	(6	5)	104	30	32	37	43	2	80	1	0	1	0	1	6	.274	.394	.475	.869
17	ChC	NL	35	92	22	2	1	3	(2	1)	35	11	17	18	19	0	40	0	1	0	0	0	4	.239	.369	.380	.750
	Postseason		35	111	17	2	0	3	(2	1)	28	6	7	5	11	0	43	1	1	0	0	0	1	.153	.236	.252	.488
	11 ML YEARS		995	2922	688	144	8	103	(56	47)	1157	341	386	394	498	23	1009	15	10	20	8	8	77	.235	.348	.396	.744

Pedro Avila

Pitches: R Bats: R Pos: SP-1   AH-vee-lah   Ht: 5'11" Wt: 190 **Born:** 1/14/1997 **Age:** 23

			HOW MUCH PITCHED				WHAT HE GAVE UP										THE RESULTS							
Year	Team	Lg	G	GS	GF	IP	BFP	H	R	ER	HR	SH	SF	HB	TBB	IBB	SO	WP	W	L	Pct	Sv-Op Hld	Vel	OPS	ERC	ERA
2019	SD	NL	1	1	0	5.1	23	4	1	1	0	0	0	1	2	0	5	0	0	0	-	0-0 0	94	.504	2.60	1.69

Luis Avilan

Pitches: L Bats: L Pos: RP-45   ah-VEE-lan   Ht: 6'2" Wt: 220 **Born:** 7/19/1989 **Age:** 30

			HOW MUCH PITCHED				WHAT HE GAVE UP										THE RESULTS							
Year	Team	Lg	G	GS	GF	IP	BFP	H	R	ER	HR	SH	SF	HB	TBB	IBB	SO	WP	W	L	Pct	Sv-Op Hld	Vel	OPS	ERC	ERA
2012	Atl	NL	31	0	2	36.0	142	27	9	8	1	3	0	1	10	1	33	3	1	0	1.000	0-0 5	92	.547	2.00	2.00
2013	Atl	NL	75	0	7	65.0	256	40	12	11	1	1	1	4	22	2	38	3	5	0	1.000	0-2 27	93	.478	1.62	1.52
2014	Atl	NL	62	0	14	43.1	193	47	22	22	2	3	2	3	21	7	25	5	4	1	.800	0-2 8	93	.764	4.55	4.57
2015	2 Tms	NL	73	0	9	53.1	220	48	24	24	6	1	2	1	15	2	49	2	2	5	.286	0-3 17	94	.665	3.18	4.05
2016	LAD	NL	27	0	3	19.2	82	12	8	7	0	2	0	2	10	4	28	1	3	0	1.000	0-1 3	92	.491	1.84	3.20
2017	LAD	NL	61	0	5	46.0	194	42	16	15	2	0	0	1	22	3	52	1	2	3	.400	0-2 13	93	.703	3.57	2.93
2018	2 Tms	NL	70	0	9	45.1	197	44	22	19	3	1	1	2	18	3	51	2	2	1	.667	2-5 9	91	.692	3.70	3.77
2019	NYM	NL	45	0	8	32.0	141	33	18	18	5	0	0	3	14	0	30	2	4	0	1.000	0-0 3	90	.782	5.28	5.06
15	Atl	NL	50	0	7	37.2	154	35	15	15	4	0	1	0	10	2	31	1	2	4	.333	0-3 11	94	.670	3.16	3.58
15	LAD	NL	23	0	2	15.2	66	13	9	9	2	1	1	1	5	0	18	1	0	1	.000	0-0 6	94	.654	3.21	5.17
18	CWS	AL	58	0	7	39.2	172	40	20	17	2	1	1	2	14	2	46	2	2	1	.667	2-4 9	91	.685	3.68	3.86
18	Phi	NL	12	0	1	5.2	25	4	2	2	1	0	0	0	4	1	5	0	0	0	-	0-1 0	91	.749	3.81	3.18
	Postseason		11	0	2	7.2	31	7	0	0	0	0	1	0	2	1	6	1	0	0	-	0-1 2	93	.576	2.30	0.00
	8 ML YEARS		444	0	56	340.2	1425	293	131	124	20	11	6	17	132	22	306	19	23	10	.697	2-15 85	93	.644	3.10	3.28

Harrison Bader

Bats: R Throws: R Pos: CF-122;PH-11;PR-4   Ht: 6'0" Wt: 195 **Born:** 6/3/1994 **Age:** 26

Year	Team	Lg	G	AB	H	2B	3B	HR	(Hm	Rd)	TB	R	RBI	RC	TBB	IBB	SO	HBP	SH	SF	SB	CS	GDP	Avg	OBP	Slg	OPS
2019	Memp	AAA	16	63	20	3	0	7	(-	-)	44	23	15	18	8	0	16	4	0	0	3	0	1	.317	.427	.698	1.125
2017	StL	NL	32	85	20	3	0	3	(0	3)	32	10	10	10	5	1	25	1	0	1	2	1	1	.235	.283	.376	.659
2018	StL	NL	138	379	100	20	2	12	(2	10)	160	61	37	54	31	3	125	11	2	4	15	3	1	.264	.334	.422	.756
2019	StL	NL	128	347	71	14	3	12	(5	7)	127	54	39	41	46	4	117	10	1	2	11	3	3	.205	.314	.366	.680
	3 ML YEARS		298	811	191	37	5	27	(7	20)	319	125	86	105	82	8	266	22	3	7	28	7	5	.236	.320	.393	.713

Javier Baez

Bats: R Throws: R Pos: SS-129;PR-4;PH-3;DH-2;3B-1   BYE-ezz   Ht: 6'0" Wt: 190 **Born:** 12/1/1992 **Age:** 27

Year	Team	Lg	G	AB	H	2B	3B	HR	(Hm	Rd)	TB	R	RBI	RC	TBB	IBB	SO	HBP	SH	SF	SB	CS	GDP	Avg	OBP	Slg	OPS
2014	ChC	NL	52	213	36	6	0	9	(3	6)	69	25	20	12	15	0	95	1	0	0	5	1	5	.169	.227	.324	.551
2015	ChC	NL	28	76	22	6	0	1	(1	0)	31	4	4	5	4	1	24	0	0	0	1	2	0	.289	.325	.408	.733
2016	ChC	NL	142	421	115	19	1	14	(8	6)	178	50	59	53	15	3	108	11	1	2	12	3	8	.273	.314	.423	.737
2017	ChC	NL	145	469	128	24	2	23	(13	10)	225	75	75	66	30	15	144	1	6	2	10	3	10	.273	.317	.480	.796
2018	ChC	NL	160	606	176	40	9	34	(13	21)	336	101	**111**	96	29	8	167	5	1	4	21	9	10	.290	.326	.554	.881
2019	ChC	NL	138	531	149	38	4	29	(15	14)	282	89	85	82	28	3	156	0	0	2	11	7	16	.281	.316	.531	.847
	Postseason		34	114	26	5	0	5	(4	1)	46	12	14	13	5	0	38	0	0	1	7	0	3	.228	.258	.404	.662
	6 ML YEARS		665	2316	626	133	16	110	(53	57)	1121	344	354	317	121	30	694	18	8	10	60	25	49	.270	.310	.484	.794

Michel Baez

Pitches: R **Bats:** R **Pos:** RP-23; SP-1   BYE-ezz   **Ht:** 6'8" **Wt:** 220 **Born:** 1/21/1996 **Age:** 24

Year Team	Lg	G	GS	GF	IP	BFP	H	R	ER	HR	SH	SF	HB	TBB	IBB	SO	WP	W	L	Pct	Sv-Op	Hld	Vel	OPS	ERC	ERA
2019 Amrillo	AA	15	0	5	27.0	115	22	9	6	1	0	0	2	11	1	38	1	3	2	.600	1--	-	-	.598	2.86	2.00
2019 SD	NL	24	1	8	29.2	131	25	10	10	3	1	1	3	14	2	28	1	1	1	.500	0-0	0	96	.689	3.69	3.03

Pedro Baez

Pitches: R **Bats:** R **Pos:** RP-71   BYE-ezz   **Ht:** 6'0" **Wt:** 232 **Born:** 3/11/1988 **Age:** 32

Year Team	Lg	G	GS	GF	IP	BFP	H	R	ER	HR	SH	SF	HB	TBB	IBB	SO	WP	W	L	Pct	Sv-Op	Hld	Vel	OPS	ERC	ERA
2014 LAD	NL	20	0	8	24.0	92	16	7	7	3	1	1	0	5	1	18	0	0	0	-	0-0	5	95	.537	1.79	2.63
2015 LAD	NL	52	0	8	51.0	208	47	22	19	4	3	3	1	11	1	60	1	4	2	.667	0-3	11	97	.693	2.87	3.35
2016 LAD	NL	73	0	10	74.0	295	52	27	25	11	1	2	2	22	0	83	3	3	2	.600	0-2	23	97	.615	2.52	3.04
2017 LAD	NL	66	0	6	64.0	280	56	24	21	9	0	0	2	29	2	64	1	3	6	.333	0-3	23	97	.728	3.84	2.95
2018 LAD	NL	55	0	8	56.1	237	46	19	18	4	2	2	1	23	2	62	0	4	3	.571	0-1	7	96	.652	2.91	2.88
2019 LAD	NL	71	0	9	69.2	276	43	30	24	6	2	0	4	23	1	69	0	7	2	.778	1-7	25	96	.543	1.97	3.10
Postseason		21	0	1	21.0	88	13	13	9	3	1	0	2	12	1	22	0	1	0	1.000	0-0	2	97	.653	3.27	3.86
6 ML YEARS		337	0	49	339.0	1388	260	129	114	37	9	8	10	113	7	356	5	21	15	.583	1-16	94	96	.636	2.71	3.03

Sandy Baez

Pitches: R **Bats:** R **Pos:** RP-1   BYE-ezz   **Ht:** 6'2" **Wt:** 245 **Born:** 11/25/1993 **Age:** 26

Year Team	Lg	G	GS	GF	IP	BFP	H	R	ER	HR	SH	SF	HB	TBB	IBB	SO	WP	W	L	Pct	Sv-Op	Hld	Vel	OPS	ERC	ERA
2019 Toledo	AAA	18	0	3	22.0	106	27	19	18	1	0	2	0	14	0	18	5	1	0	1.000	0--	-	-	.820	5.84	7.36
2018 Det	AL	9	0	0	14.1	66	12	12	8	2	0	1	2	9	1	10	1	0	0	-	0-0	1	95	.737	4.67	5.02
2019 Det	AL	1	0	0	1.0	5	2	1	1	0	0	0	0	0	0	0	0	0	0	-	0-0	0	92	1.000	7.48	9.00
2 ML YEARS		10	0	0	15.1	71	14	13	9	2	0	1	2	9	1	10	1	0	0	-	0-0	1	95	.759	4.84	5.28

Homer Bailey

Pitches: R **Bats:** R **Pos:** SP-31   **Ht:** 6'4" **Wt:** 223 **Born:** 5/3/1986 **Age:** 34

Year Team	Lg	G	GS	GF	IP	BFP	H	R	ER	HR	SH	SF	HB	TBB	IBB	SO	WP	W	L	Pct	Sv-Op	Hld	Vel	OPS	ERC	ERA
2007 Cin	NL	9	9	0	45.1	205	43	32	29	3	1	6	3	28	1	28	1	4	2	.667	0-0	0	92	.758	4.61	5.76
2008 Cin	NL	8	8	0	36.1	180	59	36	32	8	5	2	0	17	1	18	4	0	6	.000	0-0	0	91	1.024	9.31	7.93
2009 Cin	NL	20	20	0	113.1	496	115	61	57	12	4	4	3	52	1	86	6	8	5	.615	0-0	0	94	.740	4.56	4.53
2010 Cin	NL	19	19	0	109.0	465	109	55	54	11	2	1	3	40	6	100	3	4	3	.571	0-0	0	93	.744	4.01	4.46
2011 Cin	NL	22	22	0	132.0	561	136	68	65	18	4	4	5	33	2	106	4	9	7	.563	0-0	0	92	.728	4.01	4.43
2012 Cin	NL	33	33	0	208.0	874	206	97	85	26	5	5	8	52	3	168	3	13	10	.565	0-0	0	92	.718	3.73	3.68
2013 Cin	NL	32	32	0	209.0	849	181	85	81	20	8	4	10	54	2	199	5	11	12	.478	0-0	0	94	.660	2.99	3.49
2014 Cin	NL	23	23	0	145.2	604	134	60	60	16	5	4	7	45	1	124	5	9	5	.643	0-0	0	94	.703	3.57	3.71
2015 Cin	NL	2	2	0	11.1	51	16	7	7	3	0	0	0	4	2	3	0	1	1	.500	0-0	0	91	1.009	7.64	5.56
2016 Cin	NL	6	6	0	23.0	111	35	19	17	2	0	2	2	7	0	27	1	2	3	.400	0-0	0	93	.816	7.04	6.65
2017 Cin	NL	18	18	0	91.0	420	112	67	65	11	5	2	8	42	2	67	4	6	9	.400	0-0	0	93	.875	6.26	6.43
2018 Cin	NL	20	20	0	106.1	494	141	82	72	23	5	3	2	33	9	75	2	1	14	.067	0-0	0	93	.901	6.32	6.09
2019 2 Tms	AL	31	31	0	163.1	696	162	84	83	21	2	5	4	53	1	149	4	13	9	.591	0-0	0	93	.719	4.01	4.57
19 KC	AL	18	18	0	90.0	389	89	49	48	12	1	3	2	38	0	81	2	7	6	.538	0-0	0	93	.741	4.45	4.80
19 Oak	AL	13	13	0	73.1	307	73	35	35	9	1	2	2	15	1	68	2	6	3	.667	0-0	0	93	.691	3.49	4.30
Postseason		2	1	0	9.0	32	3	1	1	0	1	1	1	1	0	12	0	0	0	-	0-0	0	94	.268	0.52	1.00
13 ML YEARS		243	243	0	1393.2	6006	1449	753	707	174	46	42	55	460	31	1150	42	80	86	.482	0-0	0	93	.754	4.33	4.57

Anthony Banda

Pitches: L **Bats:** L **Pos:** RP-3   **Ht:** 6'2" **Wt:** 225 **Born:** 8/10/1993 **Age:** 26

Year Team	Lg	G	GS	GF	IP	BFP	H	R	ER	HR	SH	SF	HB	TBB	IBB	SO	WP	W	L	Pct	Sv-Op	Hld	Vel	OPS	ERC	ERA
2019 Drham	AAA	9	4	0	28.1	120	28	19	19	7	1	0	1	11	0	27	0	2	3	.400	0--	-	-	.831	5.27	6.04
2017 Ari	NL	8	4	1	25.2	115	26	17	17	1	0	0	3	10	1	25	2	2	3	.400	0-0	0	94	.771	3.98	5.96
2018 TB	AL	3	1	0	14.2	56	12	6	6	1	1	1	0	3	0	10	0	1	0	1.000	0-0	0	95	.665	2.32	3.68
2019 TB	AL	3	0	1	4.0	18	6	3	3	0	0	0	0	0	0	2	0	0	0	-	0-0	0	93	.889	4.47	6.75
3 ML YEARS		14	5	3	44.1	189	44	26	26	2	1	1	3	13	1	37	2	3	3	.500	0-0	0	94	.752	3.46	5.28

Manny Banuelos

Pitches: L **Bats:** R **Pos:** SP-8; RP-8   ban-yoo-WAY-lohss   **Ht:** 5'10" **Wt:** 215 **Born:** 3/13/1991 **Age:** 29

Year Team	Lg	G	GS	GF	IP	BFP	H	R	ER	HR	SH	SF	HB	TBB	IBB	SO	WP	W	L	Pct	Sv-Op	Hld	Vel	OPS	ERC	ERA
2015 Atl	NL	7	6	0	26.1	121	30	17	15	4	0	2	1	12	0	19	1	1	4	.200	0-0	0	89	.825	6.01	5.13
2019 CWS	AL	16	8	4	50.2	235	60	39	39	12	1	2	1	33	3	44	2	3	4	.429	0-0	0	92	.932	7.52	6.93
2 ML YEARS		23	14	4	77.0	356	90	56	54	16	1	2	4	45	3	63	3	4	8	.333	0-0	0	91	.895	6.99	6.31

Luke Bard

Pitches: R **Bats:** R **Pos:** RP-29; SP-3   **Ht:** 6'3" **Wt:** 200 **Born:** 11/13/1990 **Age:** 29

			HOW MUCH PITCHED					WHAT HE GAVE UP										THE RESULTS						
Year Team	Lg	G	GS	GF	IP	BFP	H	R	ER	HR	SH	SF	HB	TBB	IBB	SO	WP	W	L	Pct	Sv-Op	Hld	Vel	OPS	ERC	ERA
2019 Salt Lk	AAA	16	1	8	19.0	94	28	20	15	4	0	0	1	10	0	26	2	2	4	.333	1--	-	-	.933	8.72	7.11
2018 LAA	AL	8	0	3	11.2	53	10	7	7	4	0	0	3	5	1	13	1	0	0	-	0-0	0	92	.829	5.95	5.40
2019 LAA	AL	32	3	5	49.0	199	41	27	26	8	0	1	5	13	1	40	5	3	3	.500	0-1	1	94	.691	3.52	4.78
2 ML YEARS		40	3	8	60.2	252	51	34	33	12	0	1	8	18	2	53	6	3	3	.500	0-1	1	94	.719	3.96	4.90

Scott Barlow

Pitches: R **Bats:** R **Pos:** RP-61   **Ht:** 6'3" **Wt:** 215 **Born:** 12/18/1992 **Age:** 27

			HOW MUCH PITCHED					WHAT HE GAVE UP										THE RESULTS						
Year Team	Lg	G	GS	GF	IP	BFP	H	R	ER	HR	SH	SF	HB	TBB	IBB	SO	WP	W	L	Pct	Sv-Op	Hld	Vel	OPS	ERC	ERA
2018 KC	AL	6	0	3	15.0	65	16	7	6	2	0	0	0	3	0	15	1	1	1	.500	0-0	0	91	.679	3.73	3.60
2019 KC	AL	61	0	7	70.1	310	64	33	33	6	2	1	3	37	3	92	5	3	3	.500	1-3	14	94	.735	4.03	4.22
2 ML YEARS		67	0	10	85.1	375	80	40	39	8	2	1	3	40	3	107	5	4	4	.500	1-3	14	93	.725	3.98	4.11

Austin Barnes

Bats: R **Throws:** R **Pos:** C-64;PH-12;2B-1   **Ht:** 5'10" **Wt:** 187 **Born:** 12/28/1989 **Age:** 30

			BATTING																	RUNNING			AVERAGES			
Year Team	Lg	G	AB	H	2B	3B	HR	(Hm	Rd)	TB	R	RBI	RC	TBB	IBB	SO	HBP	SH	SF	SB	CS	GDP	Avg	OBP	Slg	OPS
2019 OkCity	AAA	23	87	23	6	0	6	(-	-)	47	19	17	18	14	0	20	2	0	1	1	1	2	.264	.375	.540	.915
2015 LAD	NL	20	29	6	2	0	0	(0	0)	8	4	1	3	6	0	6	1	1	0	1	0	2	.207	.361	.276	.637
2016 LAD	NL	21	32	5	1	0	0	(0	0)	6	3	2	3	5	0	9	0	0	0	0	0	0	.156	.270	.188	.458
2017 LAD	NL	102	218	63	15	2	8	(6	2)	106	35	38	46	39	1	43	5	0	0	4	1	6	.289	.408	.486	.895
2018 LAD	NL	100	200	41	5	0	4	(2	2)	58	32	14	15	31	4	67	6	1	0	4	3	7	.205	.329	.290	.619
2019 LAD	NL	75	212	43	12	1	5	(4	1)	72	28	25	18	23	3	56	5	0	2	3	0	8	.203	.293	.340	.633
Postseason		27	76	12	2	0	1	(0	1)	17	9	7	4	7	0	25	1	0	1	1	0	2	.158	.235	.224	.459
5 ML YEARS		318	691	158	35	3	17	(12	5)	250	102	80	85	104	8	181	17	2	2	12	4	23	.229	.343	.362	.705

Jacob Barnes

Pitches: R **Bats:** R **Pos:** RP-32; SP-1   **Ht:** 6'2" **Wt:** 220 **Born:** 4/14/1990 **Age:** 30

			HOW MUCH PITCHED					WHAT HE GAVE UP										THE RESULTS						
Year Team	Lg	G	GS	GF	IP	BFP	H	R	ER	HR	SH	SF	HB	TBB	IBB	SO	WP	W	L	Pct	Sv-Op	Hld	Vel	OPS	ERC	ERA
2019 SnAnt	AAA	14	0	4	14.0	59	14	7	7	3	0	0	0	2	0	15	1	2	0	1.000	1--	-	-	.692	3.64	4.50
2016 Mil	NL	27	0	7	26.2	106	24	9	8	1	1	1	0	6	1	26	2	0	1	.000	1-1	0	95	.612	2.50	2.70
2017 Mil	NL	73	0	8	72.0	304	57	35	32	8	0	3	3	33	4	80	6	3	4	.429	2-7	24	97	.664	3.31	4.00
2018 Mil	NL	49	0	19	48.2	217	51	24	18	4	1	1	0	23	2	47	4	0	1	.000	2-4	4	95	.723	4.39	3.33
2019 2 Tms		33	1	6	32.2	160	36	30	27	7	0	2	0	22	1	32	3	1	5	.167	0-0	1	94	.840	6.34	7.44
19 Mil	NL	18	1	3	19.2	95	22	17	15	3	0	1	0	11	1	22	1	1	1	.500	0-0	1	94	.769	5.40	6.86
19 KC	AL	15	0	3	13.0	65	14	13	12	4	0	1	0	11	0	10	2	0	4	.000	0-0	0	94	.951	7.85	8.31
4 ML YEARS		182	1	40	180.0	787	168	98	85	20	2	7	3	84	8	185	15	4	11	.267	5-12	29	95	.708	3.99	4.25

Matt Barnes

Pitches: R **Bats:** R **Pos:** RP-70   **Ht:** 6'4" **Wt:** 210 **Born:** 6/17/1990 **Age:** 30

			HOW MUCH PITCHED					WHAT HE GAVE UP										THE RESULTS						
Year Team	Lg	G	GS	GF	IP	BFP	H	R	ER	HR	SH	SF	HB	TBB	IBB	SO	WP	W	L	Pct	Sv-Op	Hld	Vel	OPS	ERC	ERA
2014 Bos	AL	5	0	3	9.0	39	11	4	4	1	0	1	0	2	0	8	0	0	0	-	0-0	0	94	.861	4.72	4.00
2015 Bos	AL	32	2	7	43.0	199	56	28	26	9	2	0	2	15	0	39	4	3	4	.429	0-0	3	95	.887	6.66	5.44
2016 Bos	AL	62	0	13	66.2	287	62	32	30	6	2	1	3	31	1	71	4	4	3	.571	1-2	16	97	.709	4.06	4.05
2017 Bos	AL	70	0	15	69.2	287	57	31	30	7	1	3	1	28	0	83	3	7	3	.700	1-3	21	95	.655	3.20	3.88
2018 Bos	AL	62	0	8	61.2	265	47	25	25	5	0	2	2	31	1	96	8	6	4	.600	0-3	25	97	.624	3.08	3.65
2019 Bos	AL	70	0	14	64.1	285	51	29	27	8	0	1	2	38	2	110	13	5	4	.556	4-12	26	97	.666	3.81	3.78
Postseason		11	0	10.1	42	6	2	1	1	0	0	0	6	0	10	2	2	0	1.000	0-0	3	96	.536	2.55	0.87		
6 ML YEARS		301	2	60	314.1	1362	284	149	142	36	5	8	10	145	4	407	32	25	18	.581	6-20	91	96	.703	3.96	4.07

Tony Barnette

Pitches: R **Bats:** R **Pos:** RP-2   **Ht:** 6'1" **Wt:** 190 **Born:** 11/9/1983 **Age:** 36

			HOW MUCH PITCHED					WHAT HE GAVE UP										THE RESULTS						
Year Team	Lg	G	GS	GF	IP	BFP	H	R	ER	HR	SH	SF	HB	TBB	IBB	SO	WP	W	L	Pct	Sv-Op	Hld	Vel	OPS	ERC	ERA
2019 Iowa	AAA	13	0	0	11.2	43	6	3	3	1	0	0	1	2	0	12	1	1	0	1.000	0--	-	-	.484	1.31	2.31
2016 Tex	AL	53	0	9	60.1	246	54	16	14	4	1	2	4	16	1	49	6	7	3	.700	0-1	15	92	.638	3.06	2.09
2017 Tex	AL	50	0	7	57.1	252	64	36	35	7	0	6	2	22	4	57	4	2	1	.667	2-6	4	93	.809	4.91	5.49
2018 Tex	AL	22	0	5	26.1	104	19	11	7	2	0	0	2	5	0	26	0	2	0	1.000	0-0	1	93	.590	2.01	2.39
2019 ChC	NL	2	0	0	1.1	5	2	1	1	0	0	0	0	0	0	0	0	0	0	-	0-0	0	91	1.400	12.07	6.75
Postseason		3	0	0	4.0	15	3	0	0	0	0	0	0	0	0	1	0	0	0	-	0-0	0	92	.400	1.13	0.00
4 ML YEARS		127	0	21	145.1	607	139	64	57	14	1	8	8	43	5	132	10	11	4	.733	2-7	20	93	.707	3.61	3.53

Tucker Barnhart

Bats: L **Throws:** R **Pos:** C-102;PH-24;1B-3   **Ht:** 5'11" **Wt:** 192 **Born:** 1/7/1991 **Age:** 29

							BATTING															RUNNING			AVERAGES			
Year	Team	Lg	G	AB	H	2B	3B	HR	(Hm	Rd)	TB	R	RBI	RC	TBB	IBB	SO	HBP	SH	SF	SB	CS	GDP	Avg	OBP	Slg	OPS
2014	Cin	NL	21	54	10	0	0	1	(1	0)	13	3	1	2	4	1	10	0	0	0	0	0	0	.185	.241	.241	.482
2015	Cin	NL	81	242	61	9	0	3	(2	1)	79	23	18	22	25	5	45	2	2	3	0	1	10	.252	.324	.326	.650
2016	Cin	NL	115	377	97	23	1	7	(6	1)	143	34	51	51	36	8	72	2	2	3	1	0	12	.257	.323	.379	.702
2017	Cin	NL	121	370	100	24	2	7	(2	5)	149	26	44	50	42	11	68	3	5	3	4	0	12	.270	.347	.403	.750
2018	Cin	NL	138	460	114	21	3	10	(7	3)	171	50	46	48	54	2	96	2	3	3	0	4	13	.248	.328	.372	.699
2019	Cin	NL	114	316	73	14	0	11	(5	6)	120	32	40	40	44	7	83	2	1	1	1	0	5	.231	.328	.380	.708
	6 ML YEARS		590	1819	455	91	6	39	(23	16)	675	168	200	213	205	34	374	11	15	13	6	5	52	.250	.328	.371	.699

Steven Baron

Bats: R **Throws:** R **Pos:** C-5;PH-2   **Ht:** 6'0" **Wt:** 205 **Born:** 12/7/1990 **Age:** 29

							BATTING															RUNNING			AVERAGES			
Year	Team	Lg	G	AB	H	2B	3B	HR	(Hm	Rd)	TB	R	RBI	RC	TBB	IBB	SO	HBP	SH	SF	SB	CS	GDP	Avg	OBP	Slg	OPS
2019	Indy	AAA	45	133	24	3	0	2	(-	-)	33	17	8	8	13	0	38	2	1	0	0	0	2	.180	.264	.248	.512
2015	Sea	AL	4	11	0	0	0	0	(0	0)	0	0	0	0	0	0	2	0	0	0	0	0	0	.000	.000	.000	.000
2018	StL	NL	2	5	1	0	0	0	(0	0)	1	0	0	0	0	0	2	0	0	0	0	0	0	.200	.200	.200	.400
2019	Pit	NL	7	10	2	1	0	0	(0	0)	3	0	1	1	0	0	6	0	0	0	0	0	0	.200	.200	.300	.500
	3 ML YEARS		13	26	3	1	0	0	(0	0)	4	0	1	1	0	0	10	0	0	0	0	0	2	.115	.115	.154	.269

Kyle Barraclough

Pitches: R **Bats:** R **Pos:** RP-43   BAIR-ah-claw   **Ht:** 6'3" **Wt:** 225 **Born:** 5/23/1990 **Age:** 30

			HOW MUCH PITCHED					WHAT HE GAVE UP										THE RESULTS							
Year	Team	Lg	G	GS	GF	IP	BFP	H	R	ER	HR	SH	SF	HB	TBB	IBB	SO	WP	W	L	Pct	Sv-Op	Hld	Vel	OPS	ERC	ERA
2019	Hrsbrg	AA	7	0	3	9.2	37	4	2	2	0	0	0	0	5	0	14	0	0	1	.000	0- -	-		.399	1.23	1.86
2019	Scrmto	AAA	7	0	0	5.2	28	6	9	7	0	0	0	0	6	0	9	1	0	1	.000	0- -	-		.747	6.29	11.12
2015	Mia	NL	25	0	5	24.1	98	12	8	7	1	0	2	0	18	2	30	1	2	1	.667	0-1	6	96	.563	2.25	2.59
2016	Mia	NL	75	0	6	72.2	306	45	24	23	1	2	2	2	44	1	113	8	6	3	.667	0-4	29	96	.538	2.31	2.85
2017	Mia	NL	66	0	12	66.0	286	53	25	22	5	3	4	2	38	3	76	6	6	2	.750	1-5	22	95	.638	3.53	3.00
2018	Mia	NL	61	0	25	55.2	245	40	27	26	8	2	1	5	34	3	60	4	1	6	.143	10-17	10	94	.675	3.84	4.20
2019	2 Tms	NL	43	0	9	33.2	164	38	24	21	9	1	1	2	21	2	40	3	1	2	.333	0-3	8	93	.892	7.02	5.61
19	Was	NL	33	0	6	25.2	124	33	21	19	8	0	1	2	12	2	30	2	1	2	.333	0-2	8	93	.948	7.83	6.66
19	SF	NL	10	0	3	8.0	40	5	3	2	1	1	0	0	9	0	10	1	0	0	-	0-1	0	94	.692	4.59	2.25
	5 ML YEARS		270	0	57	252.1	1099	188	108	99	24	8	10	11	155	11	319	22	16	14	.533	11-30	75	95	.650	3.52	3.53

Tres Barrera

Bats: R **Throws:** R **Pos:** C-1;PH-1   **Ht:** 6'0" **Wt:** 215 **Born:** 9/15/1994 **Age:** 25

							BATTING															RUNNING			AVERAGES			
Year	Team	Lg	G	AB	H	2B	3B	HR	(Hm	Rd)	TB	R	RBI	RC	TBB	IBB	SO	HBP	SH	SF	SB	CS	GDP	Avg	OBP	Slg	OPS
2019	Hrsbrg	AA	101	357	89	24	0	8	(-	-)	137	42	46	47	36	1	69	5	1	4	1	2	9	.249	.323	.384	.707
2019	Was	NL	2	2	0	0	0	0	(0	0)	0	0	0	0	0	0	0	0	0	0	0	0	0	.000	.000	.000	.000

Franklin Barreto

Bats: R **Throws:** R **Pos:** 2B-17;SS-5;PR-4   **Ht:** 5'10" **Wt:** 200 **Born:** 2/27/1996 **Age:** 24

							BATTING															RUNNING			AVERAGES			
Year	Team	Lg	G	AB	H	2B	3B	HR	(Hm	Rd)	TB	R	RBI	RC	TBB	IBB	SO	HBP	SH	SF	SB	CS	GDP	Avg	OBP	Slg	OPS
2019	LsVgs	AAA	98	373	110	29	5	19	(-	-)	206	88	65	79	42	0	113	6	1	2	15	1	11	.295	.374	.552	.926
2017	Oak	AL	25	71	14	1	2	2	(1	1)	25	10	6	5	5	0	33	0	0	0	2	0	1	.197	.250	.352	.602
2018	Oak	AL	32	73	17	4	0	5	(1	4)	36	10	16	11	1	0	29	1	0	0	0	0	3	.233	.253	.493	.746
2019	Oak	AL	23	57	7	2	0	2	(1	1)	15	6	5	1	1	0	23	0	0	0	1	0	0	.123	.138	.263	.401
	3 ML YEARS		80	201	38	7	2	9	(3	6)	76	26	27	17	7	0	85	1	0	0	3	0	4	.189	.220	.378	.598

Aaron Barrett

Pitches: R **Bats:** R **Pos:** RP-3   **Ht:** 6'3" **Wt:** 230 **Born:** 1/2/1988 **Age:** 32

			HOW MUCH PITCHED					WHAT HE GAVE UP										THE RESULTS							
Year	Team	Lg	G	GS	GF	IP	BFP	H	R	ER	HR	SH	SF	HB	TBB	IBB	SO	WP	W	L	Pct	Sv-Op	Hld	Vel	OPS	ERC	ERA
2019	Hrsbrg	AA	50	0	43	52.1	218	39	20	16	6	1	0	5	16	0	62	1	0	2	.000	31- -	-	-	.608	2.75	2.75
2014	Was	NL	50	0	12	40.2	174	33	17	12	1	1	2	1	20	2	49	6	3	0	1.000	0-0	8	94	.605	2.87	2.66
2015	Was	NL	40	0	8	29.1	123	28	15	15	1	0	0	3	7	0	35	1	3	3	.500	0-3	10	94	.636	3.17	4.60
2019	Was	NL	3	0	0	2.1	16	5	4	4	1	0	0	0	4	0	1	1	0	0	-	0-0	0	92	1.229	21.72	15.43
	Postseason		2	0	0	0.1	3	1	0	0	0	0	0	0	2	1	0	1	0	0	-	0-0	0	94	3.000	44.72	0.00
	3 ML YEARS		93	0	20	72.1	313	66	36	31	3	1	2	4	31	2	85	8	6	3	.667	0-3	18	94	.647	3.44	3.86

Jake Barrett

Pitches: R **Bats:** R **Pos:** RP-2   **Ht:** 6'2" **Wt:** 240 **Born:** 7/22/1991 **Age:** 28

			HOW MUCH PITCHED					WHAT HE GAVE UP										THE RESULTS							
Year	Team	Lg	G	GS	GF	IP	BFP	H	R	ER	HR	SH	SF	HB	TBB	IBB	SO	WP	W	L	Pct	Sv-Op	Hld	Vel	OPS	ERC	ERA
2019	S-WB	AAA	10	0	7	15.1	59	10	2	2	0	0	0	0	4	0	20	1	0	1	.000	1- -	-		.474	1.40	1.17
2016	Ari	NL	68	0	12	59.1	250	47	25	23	6	0	3	3	28	4	56	4	1	2	.333	4-9	8	95	.682	3.33	3.49
2017	Ari	NL	28	0	5	27.0	121	27	18	15	7	0	2	0	15	2	26	1	1	1	.500	0-1	2	96	.847	5.75	5.00
2018	Ari	NL	7	0	5	7.0	30	8	4	4	1	0	0	0	2	0	6	1	0	1	.000	0-0	0	94	.833	4.80	5.14
2019	NYY	AL	2	0	2	3.2	19	6	6	6	2	0	0	0	2	0	4	0	0	0	-	0-0	0	93	1.245	12.57	14.73
	4 ML YEARS		105	0	24	97.0	420	88	53	48	16	0	5	3	47	6	92	6	2	4	.333	4-10	10	95	.767	4.38	4.45

Jaime Barria

Pitches: R **Bats:** R **Pos:** SP-13; RP-6   HIGH-may   **Ht:** 6'1" **Wt:** 210 **Born:** 7/18/1996 **Age:** 23

Year	Team	Lg	G	GS	GF	IP	BFP	H	R	ER	HR	SH	SF	HB	TBB	IBB	SO	WP	W	L	Pct	Sv-Op	Hld	Vel	OPS	ERC	ERA
2019	Salt Lk	AAA	10	10	0	48.1	227	73	53	52	16	0	2	2	10	0	44	0	3	3	.500	0--	-	-	1.074	8.32	9.68
2018	LAA	AL	26	26	0	129.1	537	117	50	49	17	0	0	6	47	0	98	3	10	9	.526	0-0	0	91	.719	3.89	3.41
2019	LAA	AL	19	13	1	82.2	365	92	61	59	24	0	2	2	27	0	75	1	4	10	.286	0-0	0	92	.903	5.85	6.42
	2 ML YEARS		45	39	1	212.0	902	209	111	108	41	0	2	8	74	0	173	4	14	19	.424	0-0	0	91	.794	4.64	4.58

Joey Bart

Bats: R **Throws:** R **Pos:** C   **Ht:** 6'3" **Wt:** 235 **Born:** 12/15/1996 **Age:** 23

Year	Team	Lg	G	AB	H	2B	3B	HR	(Hm	Rd)	TB	R	RBI	RC	TBB	IBB	SO	HBP	SH	SF	SB	CS	GDP	Avg	OBP	Slg	OPS
2018	2 Tms	Low	51	204	60	15	3	13	(-	-)	120	38	40	42	13	2	47	10	0	1	2	1	9	.294	.364	.588	.952
2019	SnJos	A+	57	234	62	10	2	12	(-	-)	112	37	37	36	14	0	50	3	0	0	5	2	10	.265	.315	.479	.793
2019	Rchmd	AA	22	79	25	4	1	4	(-	-)	43	9	11	14	7	1	21	0	0	1	0	2	2	.316	.368	.544	.912

Tyler Bashlor

Pitches: R **Bats:** R **Pos:** RP-24   **Ht:** 6'0" **Wt:** 195 **Born:** 4/16/1993 **Age:** 27

Year	Team	Lg	G	GS	GF	IP	BFP	H	R	ER	HR	SH	SF	HB	TBB	IBB	SO	WP	W	L	Pct	Sv-Op	Hld	Vel	OPS	ERC	ERA
2019	Syrcse	AAA	33	0	19	37.0	151	29	14	14	3	0	1	2	15	1	37	2	3	2	.600	8--	-	-	.718	3.05	3.41
2018	NYM	NL	24	0	6	32.0	135	26	16	15	6	1	0	3	12	0	25	1	0	3	.000	0-0	0	96	.726	3.89	4.22
2019	NYM	NL	24	0	7	22.0	103	21	17	17	6	1	1	0	17	2	20	0	0	3	.000	0-3	1	96	.861	6.46	6.95
	2 ML YEARS		48	0	13	54.0	238	47	33	32	12	2	1	3	29	2	45	1	0	6	.000	0-3	1	96	.783	4.90	5.33

Anthony Bass

Pitches: R **Bats:** R **Pos:** RP-44   **Ht:** 6'2" **Wt:** 200 **Born:** 11/1/1987 **Age:** 32

Year	Team	Lg	G	GS	GF	IP	BFP	H	R	ER	HR	SH	SF	HB	TBB	IBB	SO	WP	W	L	Pct	Sv-Op	Hld	Vel	OPS	ERC	ERA
2019	Lsvlle	AAA	19	0	16	20.1	80	13	7	5	1	0	2	0	6	1	19	0	1	1	.500	9--	-	-	.557	1.56	2.21
2011	SD	NL	27	3	6	48.1	198	41	9	9	3	2	0	1	21	1	24	1	2	0	1.000	0-0	4	93	.655	3.28	1.68
2012	SD	NL	24	15	3	97.0	411	89	59	51	10	2	2	1	39	3	80	5	2	8	.200	1-1	0	92	.719	3.65	4.73
2013	SD	NL	24	0	9	42.0	193	51	26	25	4	1	0	0	20	4	31	5	0	0	-	0-0	0	92	.829	5.41	5.36
2014	Hou	AL	21	0	8	27.0	119	32	20	19	6	0	1	2	7	1	7	2	1	1	.500	2-4	4	94	.840	5.74	6.33
2015	Tex	AL	33	0	9	64.0	272	66	33	32	5	3	3	1	20	1	45	1	0	0	-	0-1	0	93	.756	3.81	4.50
2017	Tex	AL	2	0	1	5.2	31	14	9	9	1	0	1	0	0	0	1	1	0	0	-	0-0	0	92	1.152	12.41	14.29
2018	ChC	AL	16	0	3	15.1	62	18	6	5	1	0	0	0	3	0	14	2	0	0	-	0-0	3	94	.729	4.26	2.93
2019	Sea	AL	44	0	14	48.0	189	30	20	19	5	2	1	1	17	2	43	6	2	4	.333	5-10	6	95	.560	2.04	3.56
	8 ML YEARS		191	18	53	347.1	1475	341	182	169	35	10	8	6	127	12	245	23	7	13	.350	8-16	18	93	.731	3.89	4.38

Chris Bassitt

Pitches: R **Bats:** R **Pos:** SP-25; RP-3   **Ht:** 6'5" **Wt:** 220 **Born:** 2/22/1989 **Age:** 31

Year	Team	Lg	G	GS	GF	IP	BFP	H	R	ER	HR	SH	SF	HB	TBB	IBB	SO	WP	W	L	Pct	Sv-Op	Hld	Vel	OPS	ERC	ERA
2014	CWS	AL	6	5	1	29.2	137	34	13	13	0	1	1	3	13	1	21	0	1	1	.500	0-0	0	92	.721	4.57	3.94
2015	Oak	AL	18	13	3	86.0	361	78	36	34	5	1	1	9	30	0	64	5	1	8	.111	0-0	0	93	.684	3.55	3.56
2016	Oak	AL	5	5	0	28.0	133	35	20	19	5	0	0	0	14	0	23	2	0	2	.000	0-0	0	93	.856	6.44	6.11
2018	Oak	AL	11	7	0	47.2	204	40	21	16	4	0	0	4	19	0	41	2	2	3	.400	0-0	0	92	.624	3.37	3.02
2019	Oak	AL	28	25	2	144.0	612	125	66	61	21	2	5	13	47	0	141	3	10	5	.667	0-0	0	94	.698	3.68	3.81
	5 ML YEARS		68	55	6	335.1	1447	312	156	143	35	4	7	29	123	1	290	12	14	19	.424	0-0	0	93	.701	3.90	3.84

Trevor Bauer

Pitches: R **Bats:** R **Pos:** SP-34   **Ht:** 6'1" **Wt:** 205 **Born:** 1/17/1991 **Age:** 29

Year	Team	Lg	G	GS	GF	IP	BFP	H	R	ER	HR	SH	SF	HB	TBB	IBB	SO	WP	W	L	Pct	Sv-Op	Hld	Vel	OPS	ERC	ERA
2012	Ari	NL	4	4	0	16.1	77	14	13	11	2	1	1	1	13	0	17	2	1	2	.333	0-0	0	92	.795	5.12	6.06
2013	Cle	AL	4	4	0	17.0	81	15	11	10	3	0	1	1	16	0	11	1	1	2	.333	0-0	0	93	.840	6.47	5.29
2014	Cle	AL	26	26	0	153.0	663	151	76	71	16	1	8	11	60	4	143	6	5	8	.385	0-0	0	94	.737	4.27	4.18
2015	Cle	AL	31	30	1	176.0	744	152	90	89	23	4	1	5	79	1	170	7	11	12	.478	0-0	0	93	.713	3.86	4.55
2016	Cle	AL	35	28	3	190.0	811	179	96	90	20	4	7	9	70	1	168	3	12	8	.600	0-0	0	93	.712	3.85	4.26
2017	Cle	AL	32	31	1	176.1	749	181	84	82	25	1	3	5	60	0	196	3	17	9	.654	0-0	0	94	.774	4.46	4.19
2018	Cle	AL	28	27	0	175.1	717	134	51	43	9	3	3	9	57	2	221	12	12	6	.667	1-1	0	95	.582	2.41	2.21
2019	2 Tms		34	34	0	213.0	911	184	118	106	34	5	5	19	82	0	253	10	11	13	.458	0-0	0	95	.743	4.00	4.48
19	Cle	AL	24	24	0	156.2	664	127	76	66	22	2	3	14	63	0	185	8	9	8	.529	0-0	0	95	.707	3.55	3.79
19	Cin	NL	10	10	0	56.1	247	57	42	40	12	3	2	5	19	0	68	2	2	5	.286	0-0	0	94	.841	5.02	6.39
	Postseason		10	6	1	26.0	116	31	16	11	4	0	1	0	8	1	32	1	1	4	.200	0-1	0	94	.832	5.06	3.81
	8 ML YEARS		194	184	6	1117.0	4753	1010	539	502	132	19	29	60	437	8	1179	44	70	60	.538	1-1	0	94	.715	3.85	4.04

Jake Bauers

Bats: L **Throws:** L **Pos:** LF-53;DH-35;1B-31;PH-7;PR-1   **Ht:** 6'1" **Wt:** 195 **Born:** 10/6/1995 **Age:** 24

							BATTING													RUNNING			AVERAGES			
Year	Team	Lg	G	AB	H	2B	3B	HR	(Hm | Rd)	TB	R	RBI	RC	TBB	IBB	SO	HBP	SH	SF	SB	CS	GDP	Avg	OBP	Slg	OPS
2019	Clmbs	AAA	24	89	22	7	0	3	(- | -)	38	13	15	14	14	0	26	0	0	0	8	2	2	.247	.350	.427	.776
2018	TB	AL	96	323	65	22	2	11	(7 | 4)	124	48	48	45	54	0	104	3	2	6	6	6	3	.201	.316	.384	.700
2019	Cle	AL	117	372	84	16	1	12	(5 | 7)	138	46	43	44	45	0	115	3	0	3	3	3	3	.226	.312	.371	.683
	2 ML YEARS		213	695	149	38	3	23	(12 | 11)	262	94	91	89	99	0	219	6	2	9	9	9	6	.214	.314	.377	.691

Gerson Bautista

Pitches: R **Bats:** R **Pos:** RP-6; SP-2   **Ht:** 6'3" **Wt:** 195 **Born:** 5/31/1995 **Age:** 25

			HOW MUCH PITCHED					WHAT HE GAVE UP										THE RESULTS							
Year	Team	Lg	G	GS	GF	IP	BFP	H	R	ER	HR	SH	SF	HB	TBB	IBB	SO	WP	W	L	Pct	Sv-Op	Hld	Vel	OPS	ERC	ERA
2019	Tacom	AAA	21	0	4	23.2	118	29	23	23	7	0	1	0	18	0	31	4	0	0	-	1- -	-	-	.962	8.74	8.75
2019	Mdest	A+	5	0	0	5.0	20	1	2	2	0	1	0	0	4	0	9	2	0	0	-	0- -	-	-	.330	1.13	3.60
2018	NYM	NL	5	0	5	4.1	25	8	6	6	2	0	2	0	5	0	3	1	0	1	.000	0-0	0	97	1.520	17.39	12.46
2019	Sea	AL	8	2	3	9.0	49	13	11	11	2	0	1	0	9	0	7	2	0	1	.000	0-0	0	98	1.039	10.42	11.00
	2 ML YEARS		13	2	8	13.1	74	21	17	17	4	0	3	0	14	0	10	3	0	2	.000	0-0	0	97	1.192	12.55	11.48

Matt Beaty

Bats: L **Throws:** R **Pos:** 1B-35;LF-34;PH-32;3B-9;RF-2;DH-2;PR-1   **Ht:** 6'0" **Wt:** 215 **Born:** 4/28/1993 **Age:** 27

							BATTING													RUNNING			AVERAGES			
Year	Team	Lg	G	AB	H	2B	3B	HR	(Hm	Rd)	TB	R	RBI	RC	TBB	IBB	SO	HBP	SH	SF	SB	CS	GDP	Avg	OBP	Slg	OPS
2019	OkCity	AAA	32	121	37	7	1	3	(-	-)	55	17	18	21	10	0	12	4	0	0	0	1	3	.306	.378	.455	.832
2019	LAD	NL	99	249	66	19	1	9	(5	4)	114	36	46	42	17	2	33	2	0	0	5	0	6	.265	.317	.458	.775

Gordon Beckham

Bats: R **Throws:** R **Pos:** 2B-39;SS-18;PR-12;DH-9;PH-8;3B-5;1B-4   **Ht:** 6'0" **Wt:** 190 **Born:** 9/16/1986 **Age:** 33

							BATTING													RUNNING			AVERAGES			
Year	Team	Lg	G	AB	H	2B	3B	HR	(Hm	Rd)	TB	R	RBI	RC	TBB	IBB	SO	HBP	SH	SF	SB	CS	GDP	Avg	OBP	Slg	OPS
2009	CWS	AL	103	378	102	28	1	14	(4	10)	174	58	63	61	41	0	65	6	1	4	7	4	10	.270	.347	.460	.808
2010	CWS	AL	131	444	112	25	2	9	(7	2)	168	58	49	52	37	0	92	7	6	4	6	9	.252	.317	.378	.695
2011	CWS	AL	150	499	115	23	0	10	(7	3)	168	60	44	48	35	0	111	13	7	3	5	3	6	.230	.296	.337	.633
2012	CWS	AL	151	525	123	24	0	16	(12	4)	195	62	60	58	40	0	89	7	8	2	5	4	10	.234	.296	.371	.668
2013	CWS	AL	103	371	99	22	1	5	(3	2)	138	46	24	36	28	2	56	4	1	4	5	1	10	.267	.322	.372	.694
2014	2 Tms		127	446	101	27	0	9	(4	5)	155	53	44	32	22	2	81	7	3	5	3	0	17	.226	.271	.348	.618
2015	CWS	AL	100	211	44	8	0	6	(3	3)	70	24	20	17	19	1	43	2	1	4	0	1	6	.209	.275	.332	.607
2016	2 Tms	NL	88	245	52	16	1	5	(2	3)	85	25	31	22	26	1	52	4	0	4	1	0	12	.212	.294	.347	.641
2017	Sea	AL	11	17	3	0	0	0	(0	0)	3	2	0	0	1	0	2	0	0	0	1	0	2	.176	.222	.176	.399
2018	Sea	AL	22	44	8	1	0	0	(0	0)	9	3	1	1	4	0	11	0	2	0	1	0	1	.182	.250	.205	.455
2019	Det	AL	83	223	48	13	2	6	(2	4)	83	29	15	17	13	0	68	4	0	5	3	1	6	.215	.271	.372	.643
	14 CWS		101	390	86	24	0	7	(3	4)	131	43	36	28	19	1	70	5	3	5	3	0	12	.221	.263	.336	.598
	14 LAA		26	56	15	3	0	2	(1	1)	24	10	8	4	3	1	11	2	0	0	0	0	5	.268	.328	.429	.756
	16 Atl	NL	85	240	52	16	1	5	(2	3)	85	25	30	22	26	1	50	4	0	3	1	0	12	.217	.300	.354	.655
	16 SF	NL	3	5	0	0	0	0	(0	0)	0	0	1	0	0	0	2	0	0	1	0	0	0	.000	.000	.000	.000
	Postseason		2	1	0	0	0	0	(0	0)	0	0	0	0	0	0	1	1	0	0	0	0	0	.000	.500	.000	.500
	11 ML YEARS		1069	3403	807	187	7	80	(44	36)	1248	420	351	344	266	6	670	54	29	30	35	20	89	.237	.300	.367	.667

Tim Beckham

Bats: R **Throws:** R **Pos:** SS-41;LF-13;3B-10;DH-9;2B-8;1B-5;PH-3;PR-2   **Ht:** 6'1" **Wt:** 205 **Born:** 1/27/1990 **Age:** 30

							BATTING													RUNNING			AVERAGES			
Year	Team	Lg	G	AB	H	2B	3B	HR	(Hm	Rd)	TB	R	RBI	RC	TBB	IBB	SO	HBP	SH	SF	SB	CS	GDP	Avg	OBP	Slg	OPS
2013	TB	AL	5	7	3	0	0	0	(0	0)	3	1	1	1	0	0	0	0	0	1	0	0	0	.429	.375	.429	.804
2015	TB	AL	83	203	45	7	4	9	(3	6)	87	24	37	26	13	0	69	3	0	4	3	1	3	.222	.274	.429	.702
2016	TB	AL	64	198	49	12	5	5	(1	4)	86	25	16	23	14	0	67	1	2	0	2	1	3	.247	.300	.434	.735
2017	2 Tms	AL	137	533	148	18	5	22	(9	13)	242	67	62	81	36	0	167	4	1	1	6	5	10	.278	.328	.454	.782
2018	Bal	AL	96	369	85	17	0	12	(6	6)	138	45	35	39	27	0	100	3	1	2	1	2	10	.230	.287	.374	.661
2019	Sea	AL	88	304	72	21	1	15	(9	6)	140	39	47	44	21	0	102	3	0	1	1	3	7	.237	.293	.461	.753
	17 TB	AL	87	317	82	5	3	12	(5	7)	129	31	36	39	24	0	110	2	1	1	5	4	8	.259	.314	.407	.721
	17 Bal	AL	50	216	66	13	2	10	(4	6)	113	36	26	42	12	0	57	2	0	0	1	1	2	.306	.348	.523	.871
	6 ML YEARS		473	1614	402	75	15	63	(28	35)	696	201	198	214	111	0	505	14	4	8	13	12	33	.249	.302	.431	.733

David Bednar

Pitches: R **Bats:** L **Pos:** RP-13   **Ht:** 6'1" **Wt:** 220 **Born:** 10/10/1994 **Age:** 25

			HOW MUCH PITCHED					WHAT HE GAVE UP										THE RESULTS							
Year	Team	Lg	G	GS	GF	IP	BFP	H	R	ER	HR	SH	SF	HB	TBB	IBB	SO	WP	W	L	Pct	Sv-Op	Hld	Vel	OPS	ERC	ERA
2019	Amrillo	AA	44	0	33	58.0	240	49	24	19	4	2	0	3	18	2	86	5	2	5	.286	14- -	-	-	.612	2.84	2.95
2019	SD	NL	13	0	4	11.0	48	10	8	8	3	2	1	0	5	0	14	0	0	2	.000	0-0	2	95	.876	4.89	6.55

Cam Bedrosian

Pitches: R Bats: R Pos: RP-52; SP-7   beh-DROH-zhee-ann   Ht: 6'1" Wt: 225 Born: 10/2/1991 Age: 28

Year Team	Lg	G	GS	GF	IP	BFP	H	R	ER	HR	SH	SF	HB	TBB	IBB	SO	WP	W	L	Pct	Sv-Op	Hld	Vel	OPS	ERC	ERA
2014 LAA	AL	17	0	4	19.1	93	23	17	14	2	0	1	0	12	1	20	1	0	1	.000	0-1	1	94	.801	5.88	6.52
2015 LAA	AL	34	0	10	33.1	156	40	21	20	3	1	2	2	19	2	34	2	1	0	1.000	0-0	1	94	.833	6.05	5.40
2016 LAA	AL	45	0	9	40.1	162	30	7	5	1	0	2	1	14	1	51	3	2	0	1.000	1-2	7	95	.532	2.25	1.12
2017 LAA	AL	48	0	13	44.2	190	41	26	22	5	1	1	0	17	1	53	7	6	5	.545	6-11	10	94	.705	3.56	4.43
2018 LAA	AL	71	0	7	64.0	271	63	30	27	7	1	1	2	26	0	57	1	5	4	.556	1-8	10	93	.738	4.31	3.80
2019 LAA	AL	59	7	5	61.1	258	48	30	22	7	0	1	3	22	0	64	9	3	3	.500	1-3	15	93	.619	2.96	3.23
6 ML YEARS		274	7	48	263.0	1130	245	131	110	25	3	9	9	110	5	279	23	17	13	.567	9-25	44	94	.693	3.83	3.76

Tyler Beede

Pitches: R Bats: R Pos: SP-22; RP-2   Ht: 6'3" Wt: 211 Born: 5/23/1993 Age: 27

Year Team	Lg	G	GS	GF	IP	BFP	H	R	ER	HR	SH	SF	HB	TBB	IBB	SO	WP	W	L	Pct	Sv-Op	Hld	Vel	OPS	ERC	ERA
2019 Scrmto	AAA	7	7	0	34.2	141	24	10	9	3	1	0	4	14	0	49	4	2	2	.500	0- -	-	92	.620	2.86	2.34
2018 SF	NL	2	2	0	7.2	40	9	7	7	0	0	0	1	8	0	9	0	0	1	.000	0-0	0	92	.869	7.41	8.22
2019 SF	NL	24	22	0	117.0	523	127	70	66	22	1	3	5	46	1	113	9	5	10	.333	0-0	0	94	.803	5.29	5.08
2 ML YEARS		26	24	0	124.2	563	136	77	73	22	1	3	6	54	1	122	9	5	11	.313	0-0	0	94	.808	5.44	5.27

Jalen Beeks

Pitches: L Bats: L Pos: RP-30; SP-3   Ht: 5'11" Wt: 200 Born: 7/10/1993 Age: 26

Year Team	Lg	G	GS	GF	IP	BFP	H	R	ER	HR	SH	SF	HB	TBB	IBB	SO	WP	W	L	Pct	Sv-Op	Hld	Vel	OPS	ERC	ERA
2018 2 Tms	AL	14	1	0	50.2	223	52	31	31	6	1	1	3	24	0	42	0	5	1	.833	0-0	0	92	.794	4.97	5.51
2019 TB	AL	33	3	5	104.1	464	115	56	50	12	1	5	9	40	1	89	3	6	3	.667	1-1	2	92	.789	5.07	4.31
18 Bos	AL	2	1	0	6.1	34	11	9	9	1	0	0	1	4	0	5	0	0	1	.000	0-0	0	91	1.160	11.16	12.79
18 TB	AL	12	0	0	44.1	189	41	22	22	5	1	1	2	20	0	37	0	5	0	1.000	0-0	0	92	.729	4.20	4.47
2 ML YEARS		47	4	5	155.0	687	167	87	81	18	2	6	12	64	1	131	3	11	4	.733	1-1	2	92	.791	5.04	4.70

Josh Bell

Bats: B Throws: R Pos: 1B-134;DH-7;PH-3   Ht: 6'4" Wt: 240 Born: 8/14/1992 Age: 27

Year Team	Lg	G	AB	H	2B	3B	HR	(Hm	Rd)	TB	R	RBI	RC	TBB	IBB	SO	HBP	SH	SF	SB	CS	GDP	Avg	OBP	Slg	OPS
2016 Pit	NL	45	128	35	8	0	3	(2	1)	52	18	19	18	21	0	19	0	0	3	0	1	4	.273	.368	.406	.775
2017 Pit	NL	159	549	140	26	6	26	(11	15)	256	75	90	86	66	4	117	1	0	4	2	4	15	.255	.334	.466	.800
2018 Pit	NL	148	501	131	31	4	12	(5	7)	206	74	62	73	77	2	104	0	0	5	2	5	12	.261	.357	.411	.768
2019 Pit	NL	143	527	146	37	3	37	(17	20)	300	94	116	112	74	13	118	5	0	7	0	1	11	.277	.367	.569	.936
4 ML YEARS		495	1705	452	102	13	78	(35	43)	814	261	287	289	238	19	358	6	0	19	4	11	42	.265	.354	.477	.831

Cody Bellinger

Bats: L Throws: L Pos: RF-115;1B-36;CF-25;PH-3   Ht: 6'4" Wt: 203 Born: 7/13/1995 Age: 24

Year Team	Lg	G	AB	H	2B	3B	HR	(Hm	Rd)	TB	R	RBI	RC	TBB	IBB	SO	HBP	SH	SF	SB	CS	GDP	Avg	OBP	Slg	OPS
2017 LAD	NL	132	480	128	26	4	39	(19	20)	279	87	97	94	64	13	146	1	0	3	10	3	5	.267	.352	.581	.933
2018 LAD	NL	162	557	145	28	7	25	(11	14)	262	84	76	88	69	9	151	3	0	3	14	1	7	.260	.343	.470	.814
2019 LAD	NL	156	558	170	34	3	47	(27	20)	351	121	115	124	95	21	108	3	0	4	15	5	10	.305	.406	.629	1.035
Postseason		31	116	20	5	1	4	(0	4)	39	15	13	9	8	0	45	0	0	0	5	1	1	.172	.226	.336	.562
3 ML YEARS		450	1595	443	88	14	111	(57	54)	892	292	288	306	228	43	405	7	0	10	39	9	22	.278	.368	.559	.928

Brandon Belt

Bats: L Throws: L Pos: 1B-144;PH-19;LF-14;RF-1   Ht: 6'4" Wt: 235 Born: 4/20/1988 Age: 32

Year Team	Lg	G	AB	H	2B	3B	HR	(Hm	Rd)	TB	R	RBI	RC	TBB	IBB	SO	HBP	SH	SF	SB	CS	GDP	Avg	OBP	Slg	OPS
2011 SF	NL	63	187	42	6	1	9	(2	7)	77	21	18	20	20	1	57	2	0	0	3	2	3	.225	.306	.412	.718
2012 SF	NL	145	411	113	27	6	7	(5	2)	173	47	56	63	54	5	106	3	0	4	12	2	2	.275	.360	.421	.781
2013 SF	NL	150	509	147	39	4	17	(6	11)	245	76	67	82	52	4	125	6	1	3	5	2	4	.289	.360	.481	.841
2014 SF	NL	61	214	52	8	0	12	(2	10)	96	30	27	24	18	2	64	2	0	1	3	1	4	.243	.306	.449	.755
2015 SF	NL	137	492	138	33	5	18	(5	13)	235	73	68	78	56	2	147	4	0	3	9	3	3	.280	.356	.478	.834
2016 SF	NL	156	542	149	41	8	17	(6	11)	257	77	82	105	104	4	148	5	0	4	0	4	7	.275	.394	.474	.868
2017 SF	NL	104	382	92	27	3	18	(8	10)	179	63	51	60	66	2	104	2	0	1	3	2	5	.241	.355	.469	.823
2018 SF	NL	112	399	101	18	2	14	(8	6)	165	50	46	63	49	6	107	6	0	2	4	0	2	.253	.342	.414	.756
2019 SF	NL	156	526	123	32	3	17	(5	12)	212	76	57	72	83	3	127	3	0	4	4	3	6	.234	.339	.403	.742
Postseason		37	127	29	2	2	2	(1	1)	41	14	13	16	21	1	40	0	0	3	1	2	0	.228	.331	.323	.654
9 ML YEARS		1084	3662	957	231	32	129	(47	82)	1639	513	472	567	502	29	985	33	1	23	43	19	36	.261	.354	.448	.801

Anthony Bemboom

Bats: L Throws: R Pos: C-25   Ht: 6'2" Wt: 200 Born: 1/18/1990 Age: 30

Year Team	Lg	G	AB	H	2B	3B	HR	(Hm	Rd)	TB	R	RBI	RC	TBB	IBB	SO	HBP	SH	SF	SB	CS	GDP	Avg	OBP	Slg	OPS
2019 Drham	AAA	14	47	10	3	0	1	(-	-)	16	7	6	3	2	0	10	0	0	1	0	1	2	.213	.240	.340	.580

Year Team	Lg	G	AB	H	2B	3B	HR	(Hm	Rd)	TB	R	RBI	RC	TBB	IBB	SO	HBP	SH	SF	SB	CS	GDP	Avg	OBP	Slg	OPS
2019 Salt Lk	AAA	16	57	18	1	2	2	(-	-)	29	7	10	11	7	0	9	0	0	0	0	0	0	.316	.391	.509	.899
2019 2 Tms	AL	25	54	7	1	0	1	(1	0)	11	2	4	1	1	0	21	0	1	0	0	0	0	.130	.145	.204	.349
19 TB	AL	3	5	2	1	0	0	(0	0)	3	0	1	1	0	0	2	0	0	0	0	0	0	.400	.400	.600	1.000
19 LAA	AL	22	49	5	0	0	1	(1	0)	8	2	3	0	1	0	19	0	1	0	0	0	0	.102	.120	.163	.283

Andrew Benintendi

Bats: L Throws: L Pos: LF-131;CF-12;PH-2;PR-1　　　　　　　　**Ht: 5'10" Wt: 170 Born: 7/6/1994 Age: 25**

Year Team	Lg	G	AB	H	2B	3B	HR	(Hm	Rd)	TB	R	RBI	RC	TBB	IBB	SO	HBP	SH	SF	SB	CS	GDP	Avg	OBP	Slg	OPS
2016 Bos	AL	34	105	31	11	1	2	(0	2)	50	16	14	20	10	0	25	1	1	0	1	0	0	.295	.359	.476	.835
2017 Bos	AL	151	573	155	26	1	20	(7	13)	243	84	90	96	70	7	112	6	1	8	20	5	16	.271	.352	.424	.776
2018 Bos	AL	148	579	168	41	6	16	(7	9)	269	103	87	105	71	1	106	2	2	7	21	3	9	.290	.366	.465	.830
2019 Bos	AL	138	541	144	40	5	13	(8	5)	233	72	68	88	59	1	140	1	3	5	10	3	6	.266	.343	.431	.774
Postseason		21	81	22	5	0	2	(1	1)	33	18	9	13	5	0	17	1	0	0	2	0	2	.272	.322	.407	.729
4 ML YEARS		471	1798	498	118	13	51	(22	29)	795	275	259	309	210	9	383	16	7	21	52	11	31	.277	.354	.442	.796

Travis Bergen

Pitches: L Bats: L Pos: RP-21　　　　　　　　**Ht: 6'1" Wt: 205 Born: 10/8/1993 Age: 26**

Year Team	Lg	G	GS	GF	IP	BFP	H	R	ER	HR	SH	SF	HB	TBB	IBB	SO	WP	W	L	Pct	Sv-Op	Hld	Vel	OPS	ERC	ERA
2019 Scrmto	AAA	15	0	1	16.2	73	13	9	7	2	0	0	0	10	0	15	0	0	0	-	1--	-	-	.728	3.69	3.78
2019 SF	NL	21	0	8	19.2	85	18	12	12	4	0	0	1	9	2	18	1	2	0	1.000	0-0	0	91	.823	4.62	5.49

Jose Berrios

Pitches: R Bats: R Pos: SP-32　　　　　beh-REE-ohs　　　　　**Ht: 6'0" Wt: 205 Born: 5/27/1994 Age: 26**

Year Team	Lg	G	GS	GF	IP	BFP	H	R	ER	HR	SH	SF	HB	TBB	IBB	SO	WP	W	L	Pct	Sv-Op	Hld	Vel	OPS	ERC	ERA
2016 Min	AL	14	14	0	58.1	281	74	56	52	12	2	0	5	35	0	49	1	3	7	.300	0-0	0	93	.932	7.85	8.02
2017 Min	AL	26	25	0	145.2	616	131	71	63	15	3	4	13	48	0	139	7	14	8	.636	0-0	0	93	.693	3.62	3.89
2018 Min	AL	32	32	0	192.1	797	159	83	82	25	2	4	13	61	1	202	2	12	11	.522	0-0	0	93	.665	3.26	3.84
2019 Min	AL	32	32	0	200.1	842	194	94	82	26	2	6	9	51	0	195	8	14	8	.636	0-0	0	93	.707	3.69	3.68
Postseason		1	0	0	3.0	14	5	3	3	1	0	0	0	0	0	4	0	0	1	.000	0-0	0	95	1.000	8.04	9.00
4 ML YEARS		104	103	0	596.2	2536	558	304	279	78	9	14	40	195	1	585	18	43	34	.558	0-0	0	93	.715	3.90	4.21

Jon Berti

Bats: R Throws: R Pos: SS-32;CF-21;3B-20;LF-7;PH-6;PR-3;RF-1　　　　**Ht: 5'10" Wt: 195 Born: 1/22/1990 Age: 30**

Year Team	Lg	G	AB	H	2B	3B	HR	(Hm	Rd)	TB	R	RBI	RC	TBB	IBB	SO	HBP	SH	SF	SB	CS	GDP	Avg	OBP	Slg	OPS
2019 NewOr	AAA	22	62	18	1	0	4	(-	-)	31	14	8	15	15	0	11	1	0	1	5	0	2	.290	.430	.500	.930
2018 Tor	AL	4	15	4	1	1	0	(0	0)	7	2	2	2	0	0	4	0	0	0	1	0	0	.267	.267	.467	.733
2019 Mia	NL	73	256	70	14	1	6	(3	3)	104	52	24	37	24	0	73	6	0	1	17	3	2	.273	.348	.406	.755
2 ML YEARS		77	271	74	15	2	6	(3	3)	111	54	26	39	24	0	77	6	0	1	18	3	2	.273	.344	.410	.754

Dellin Betances

Pitches: R Bats: R Pos: RP-1　　　　　DELL-inn buh-TAN-siss　　　　　**Ht: 6'8" Wt: 265 Born: 3/23/1988 Age: 32**

Year Team	Lg	G	GS	GF	IP	BFP	H	R	ER	HR	SH	SF	HB	TBB	IBB	SO	WP	W	L	Pct	Sv-Op	Hld	Vel	OPS	ERC	ERA
2011 NYY	AL	2	1	0	2.2	16	1	2	2	0	0	1	1	6	0	2	0	0	0	-	0-0	0	93	.625	7.94	6.75
2013 NYY	AL	6	0	3	5.0	26	9	6	6	1	0	0	0	2	0	10	0	0	0	-	0-0	0	96	.965	9.81	10.80
2014 NYY	AL	70	0	6	90.0	341	46	15	14	4	2	3	4	24	1	135	2	5	0	1.000	1-5	22	97	.442	1.24	1.40
2015 NYY	AL	74	0	17	84.0	332	45	17	14	6	1	1	3	40	2	131	9	6	4	.600	9-13	28	97	.510	1.94	1.50
2016 NYY	AL	73	0	20	73.0	299	54	31	25	5	1	1	1	28	0	126	6	3	6	.333	12-17	**28**	98	.577	2.48	3.08
2017 NYY	AL	66	0	21	59.2	261	29	20	19	3	1	0	11	44	0	100	5	3	6	.333	10-13	19	99	.538	2.86	2.87
2018 NYY	AL	66	0	15	66.2	272	44	22	20	7	3	1	5	26	2	115	4	4	6	.400	4-7	20	98	.578	2.51	2.70
2019 NYY	AL	1	0	0	0.2	2	0	0	0	0	0	0	0	0	0	2	0	0	0	-	0-0	0	94	.000	0.00	0.00
Postseason		9	0	3	11.0	47	6	4	4	0	0	1	0	7	1	17	1	1	1	.500	0-0	1	98	.482	1.72	3.27
8 ML YEARS		358	1	84	381.2	1549	228	113	100	26	8	7	25	170	5	621	26	21	22	.488	36-55	117	97	.534	2.17	2.36

Chad Bettis

Pitches: R Bats: R Pos: RP-36; SP-3　　　　　　　　**Ht: 6'0" Wt: 201 Born: 4/26/1989 Age: 31**

Year Team	Lg	G	GS	GF	IP	BFP	H	R	ER	HR	SH	SF	HB	TBB	IBB	SO	WP	W	L	Pct	Sv-Op	Hld	Vel	OPS	ERC	ERA
2013 Col	NL	16	8	0	44.2	208	55	34	28	6	3	1	2	20	2	30	2	1	3	.250	0-1	0	93	.859	5.95	5.64
2014 Col	NL	21	0	9	24.2	127	42	26	25	4	5	0	1	10	2	13	5	0	2	.000	0-1	1	93	1.020	8.84	9.12
2015 Col	NL	20	20	0	115.0	502	120	56	54	11	7	2	3	42	2	98	6	8	6	.571	0-0	0	92	.771	4.20	4.23
2016 Col	NL	32	32	0	186.0	814	204	107	99	22	10	3	7	59	5	138	4	14	8	.636	0-0	0	92	.775	4.51	4.79
2017 Col	NL	9	9	0	46.1	200	52	27	26	8	5	1	1	11	0	30	3	2	4	.333	0-0	0	90	.828	4.68	5.05
2018 Col	NL	27	20	2	120.1	518	121	72	67	18	5	5	5	47	3	80	3	5	2	.714	0-0	1	91	.791	4.60	5.01
2019 Col	NL	39	3	9	63.2	287	78	47	43	10	2	0	5	21	3	42	2	1	6	.143	1-3	4	93	.863	5.81	6.08
7 ML YEARS		164	92	20	600.2	2656	672	369	342	79	37	12	24	210	17	431	25	31	31	.500	1-5	9	92	.809	4.88	5.12

Mookie Betts

Bats: R **Throws:** R **Pos:** RF-132;CF-17;DH-7;PR-1   **Ht:** 5'9" **Wt:** 180 **Born:** 10/7/1992 **Age:** 27

Year Team	Lg	G	AB	H	2B	3B	HR	(Hm	Rd)	TB	R	RBI	RC	TBB	IBB	SO	HBP	SH	SF	SB	CS	GDP	Avg	OBP	Slg	OPS
2014 Bos	AL	52	189	55	12	1	5	(1	4)	84	34	18	30	21	0	31	2	1	0	7	3	2	.291	.368	.444	.812
2015 Bos	AL	145	597	174	42	8	18	(9	9)	286	92	77	100	46	1	82	2	3	6	21	6	2	.291	.341	.479	.820
2016 Bos	AL	158	672	214	42	5	31	(17	14)	359	122	113	130	49	1	80	2	0	7	26	4	12	.318	.363	.534	.897
2017 Bos	AL	153	628	166	46	2	24	(8	16)	288	101	102	115	77	9	79	2	0	5	26	3	9	.264	.344	.459	.803
2018 Bos	AL	136	520	180	47	5	32	(13	19)	333	**129**	80	134	81	8	91	8	0	5	30	6	5	**.346**	**.438**	**.640**	1.078
2019 Bos	AL	150	597	176	40	5	29	(17	12)	313	**135**	80	118	97	6	101	3	0	9	16	3	11	.295	.391	.524	.915
Postseason		21	88	20	7	0	1	(0	1)	30	16	4	8	10	4	17	1	0	0	2	0	1	.227	.313	.341	.654
6 ML YEARS		794	3203	965	229	26	139	(65	74)	1663	613	470	627	371	25	464	19	4	32	126	25	41	.301	.374	.519	.893

Joe Biagini

Pitches: R **Bats:** R **Pos:** RP-63   bee-ah-gee-nee   **Ht:** 6'5" **Wt:** 235 **Born:** 5/29/1990 **Age:** 30

Year Team	Lg	G	GS	GF	IP	BFP	H	R	ER	HR	SH	SF	HB	TBB	IBB	SO	WP	W	L	Pct	Sv-Op	Hld	Vel	OPS	ERC	ERA
2016 Tor	AL	60	0	12	67.2	295	69	28	23	3	2	3	5	19	1	62	3	4	3	.571	1-3	8	94	.678	3.52	3.06
2017 Tor	AL	44	18	3	119.2	517	125	78	71	15	0	2	2	42	0	97	6	3	13	.188	1-3	9	94	.752	4.38	5.34
2018 Tor	AL	50	4	7	72.0	328	96	50	48	14	0	1	6	24	0	53	8	4	7	.364	0-0	5	94	.913	7.04	6.00
2019 2 Tms	AL	63	0	15	64.2	281	71	35	33	14	1	0	1	26	3	60	3	3	2	.600	1-3	10	94	.864	5.60	4.59
19 Tor	AL	50	0	11	50.0	212	50	22	21	8	1	0	1	17	3	50	2	3	1	.750	1-3	10	94	.783	4.28	3.78
19 Hou	AL	13	0	4	14.2	69	21	13	12	6	0	0	0	9	0	10	1	0	1	.000	0-0	0	94	1.118	10.95	7.36
Postseason		6	0	0	7.1	26	3	0	0	0	0	0	0	1	0	6	1	0	0	-	0-1	0	94	.354	0.55	0.00
4 ML YEARS		217	22	37	324.0	1421	361	191	175	46	3	6	14	111	4	272	20	14	25	.359	3-9	32	94	.796	4.98	4.86

Bo Bichette

Bats: R **Throws:** R **Pos:** SS-42;DH-4   **Ht:** 6'0" **Wt:** 185 **Born:** 3/5/1998 **Age:** 22

Year Team	Lg	G	AB	H	2B	3B	HR	(Hm	Rd)	TB	R	RBI	RC	TBB	IBB	SO	HBP	SH	SF	SB	CS	GDP	Avg	OBP	Slg	OPS
2016 B Jays	R	22	82	35	9	2	4	(-	-)	60	21	36	24	6	0	17	0	0	3	3	0	1	.427	.451	.732	1.182
2017 2 Tms	Low	110	448	162	41	4	14	(-	-)	253	78	71	103	42	2	81	7	0	2	22	7	5	.362	.423	.565	.988
2018 Nham	AA	131	539	154	43	7	11	(-	-)	244	95	74	88	48	1	101	2	1	5	32	11	13	.286	.343	.453	.796
2019 Buffalo	AAA	56	222	61	16	2	8	(-	-)	105	34	32	36	19	0	48	1	1	1	15	5	2	.275	.333	.473	.806
2019 Tor	AL	46	196	61	18	0	11	(3	8)	112	32	21	32	14	0	50	1	0	1	4	4	2	.311	.358	.571	.930

Jesse Biddle

Pitches: L **Bats:** L **Pos:** RP-30   **Ht:** 6'5" **Wt:** 220 **Born:** 10/22/1991 **Age:** 28

Year Team	Lg	G	GS	GF	IP	BFP	H	R	ER	HR	SH	SF	HB	TBB	IBB	SO	WP	W	L	Pct	Sv-Op	Hld	Vel	OPS	ERC	ERA
2018 Atl	NL	60	0	14	63.2	266	50	26	22	6	2	1	3	31	5	67	2	6	1	.857	1-4	12	94	.654	3.31	3.11
2019 3 Tms		30	0	3	28.0	152	42	33	26	5	0	2	4	22	1	26	7	0	1	.000	0-1	5	94	.972	9.96	8.36
19 Atl	NL	15	0	1	11.2	64	18	11	7	1	0	0	0	10	1	11	3	0	1	.000	0-0	0	94	.882	8.75	5.40
19 Sea	AL	11	0	1	11.0	60	20	14	12	2	0	2	1	7	0	8	4	0	0	-	0-1	1	94	1.067	11.55	9.82
19 Tex	AL	4	0	1	5.1	28	4	8	7	2	0	0	3	5	0	7	0	0	0	-	0-0	0	93	.979	9.44	11.81
2 ML YEARS		90	0	17	91.2	418	92	59	48	11	2	3	7	53	6	93	9	6	2	.750	1-5	13	94	.768	5.15	4.71

Shane Bieber

Pitches: R **Bats:** R **Pos:** SP-33; RP-1   **Ht:** 6'3" **Wt:** 200 **Born:** 5/31/1995 **Age:** 25

Year Team	Lg	G	GS	GF	IP	BFP	H	R	ER	HR	SH	SF	HB	TBB	IBB	SO	WP	W	L	Pct	Sv-Op	Hld	Vel	OPS	ERC	ERA
2018 Cle	AL	20	19	0	114.2	485	130	60	58	13	0	4	2	23	0	118	5	11	5	.688	0-0	0	93	.787	4.23	4.55
2019 Cle	AL	34	33	1	214.1	859	186	86	78	31	2	1	6	40	1	259	6	15	8	.652	0-0	0	93	.663	2.94	3.28
2 ML YEARS		54	52	1	329.0	1344	316	146	136	44	2	5	8	63	1	377	11	26	13	.667	0-0	0	93	.708	3.38	3.72

Cavan Biggio

Bats: L **Throws:** R **Pos:** 2B-85;1B-8;RF-8;DH-4;LF-1;PH-1;PR-1   **Ht:** 6'2" **Wt:** 200 **Born:** 4/11/1995 **Age:** 25

Year Team	Lg	G	AB	H	2B	3B	HR	(Hm	Rd)	TB	R	RBI	RC	TBB	IBB	SO	HBP	SH	SF	SB	CS	GDP	Avg	OBP	Slg	OPS
2019 Buffalo	AAA	43	138	43	8	1	6	(-	-)	71	23	27	34	34	0	28	1	0	1	5	1	1	.312	.448	.514	.963
2019 Tor	AL	100	354	83	17	2	16	(9	7)	152	66	48	65	71	0	123	2	0	2	14	0	0	.234	.364	.429	.793

Greg Bird

Bats: L **Throws:** R **Pos:** 1B-10   **Ht:** 6'4" **Wt:** 220 **Born:** 11/9/1992 **Age:** 27

Year Team	Lg	G	AB	H	2B	3B	HR	(Hm	Rd)	TB	R	RBI	RC	TBB	IBB	SO	HBP	SH	SF	SB	CS	GDP	Avg	OBP	Slg	OPS
2015 NYY	AL	46	157	41	9	0	11	(5	6)	83	26	31	30	19	0	53	1	0	1	0	0	1	.261	.343	.529	.871
2017 NYY	AL	48	147	28	7	0	9	(8	1)	62	20	28	26	19	1	42	2	0	2	0	0	2	.190	.288	.422	.710
2018 NYY	AL	82	272	54	16	1	11	(7	4)	105	23	38	28	30	1	78	5	0	4	0	0	4	.199	.286	.386	.672
2019 NYY	AL	10	35	6	0	1	1	(1	0)	9	6	1	2	6	0	16	0	0	1	0	0	1	.171	.293	.257	.550
Postseason		14	44	11	2	0	3	(1	2)	22	5	6	10	12	1	18	1	0	0	0	0	0	.250	.421	.500	.921
4 ML YEARS		186	611	129	32	1	32	(21	11)	259	75	98	86	74	1	189	8	0	7	0	0	8	.211	.301	.424	.725

Kyle Bird

Pitches: L Bats: L Pos: RP-12   Ht: 6'2" Wt: 175 Born: 4/12/1993 Age: 27

		HOW MUCH PITCHED						WHAT HE GAVE UP										THE RESULTS						
Year	Team	Lg	G	GS	GF	IP	BFP	H	R	ER	HR	SH	SF	HB	TBB	IBB	SO	WP	W	L	Pct	Sv-Op	Hld	Vel	OPS	ERC	ERA
2019	Nashv	AAA	29	0	7	34.2	150	35	11	11	4	0	0	2	15	0	39	3	5	1	.833	2--	-	-	.738	4.69	2.86
2019	Tex	AL	12	0	5	12.2	65	11	11	11	5	0	0	2	15	0	10	2	0	0	-	1-1	0	91	.972	9.85	7.82

Braden Bishop

Bats: R Throws: R Pos: CF-20;LF-4;PR-3;RF-1   Ht: 6'1" Wt: 190 Born: 8/22/1993 Age: 26

			BATTING																		RUNNING			AVERAGES			
Year	Team	Lg	G	AB	H	2B	3B	HR	(Hm	Rd)	TB	R	RBI	RC	TBB	IBB	SO	HBP	SH	SF	SB	CS	GDP	Avg	OBP	Slg	OPS
2019	Tacom	AAA	43	185	51	15	0	8	(-	-)	90	29	31	33	23	0	44	2	0	1	2	2	1	.276	.360	.486	.847
2019	Sea	AL	27	56	6	0	0	0	(0	0)	6	3	4	1	3	0	21	0	1	0	0	0	0	.107	.153	.107	.260

Ty Blach

Pitches: L Bats: R Pos: SP-5; RP-2   block   Ht: 6'1" Wt: 213 Born: 10/20/1990 Age: 29

			HOW MUCH PITCHED						WHAT HE GAVE UP										THE RESULTS						
Year	Team	Lg	G	GS	GF	IP	BFP	H	R	ER	HR	SH	SF	HB	TBB	IBB	SO	WP	W	L	Pct	Sv-Op	Hld	Vel	OPS	ERC	ERA
2019	Scrmto	AAA	17	15	0	91.0	415	121	65	60	14	1	2	2	25	0	65	4	3	4	.429	0--	-	-	.848	5.95	5.93
2016	SF	NL	4	2	2	17.0	62	8	2	2	1	4	0	0	5	0	10	0	1	0	1.000	0-0	0	91	.445	1.18	1.06
2017	SF	NL	34	24	3	163.2	692	179	91	87	17	10	5	1	43	2	73	3	8	12	.400	0-0	0	90	.766	4.14	4.78
2018	SF	NL	47	13	13	118.2	512	133	62	56	8	8	1	1	41	4	75	1	6	7	.462	0-0	3	90	.746	4.35	4.25
2019	2 Tms		7	5	1	27.0	139	46	37	36	8	0	0	0	17	0	20	2	1	3	.250	0-0	0	90	1.125	11.59	12.00
19	SF	NL	2	0	1	6.1	36	14	10	10	2	0	0	0	4	0	3	0	0	0	-	0-0	0	91	1.188	15.61	14.21
19	Bal	AL	5	5	0	20.2	103	32	27	26	6	0	0	0	13	0	17	2	1	3	.250	0-0	0	90	1.104	10.41	11.32
	Postseason		2	0	1	3.1	11	2	0	0	0	0	0	0	0	0	3	0	1	0	1.000	0-0	0	92	.364	0.82	0.00
	4 ML YEARS		92	44	19	326.1	1405	366	192	181	34	19	6	2	106	6	178	6	16	22	.421	0-0	3	90	.780	4.55	4.99

Ray Black

Pitches: R Bats: R Pos: RP-17   Ht: 6'5" Wt: 225 Born: 6/26/1990 Age: 30

			HOW MUCH PITCHED						WHAT HE GAVE UP										THE RESULTS						
Year	Team	Lg	G	GS	GF	IP	BFP	H	R	ER	HR	SH	SF	HB	TBB	IBB	SO	WP	W	L	Pct	Sv-Op	Hld	Vel	OPS	ERC	ERA
2019	Scrmto	AAA	23	1	3	22.2	96	19	13	13	4	0	0	0	13	0	36	1	1	0	1.000	1--	-	-	.743	4.51	5.16
2019	SnAnt	AAA	6	0	2	6.0	21	1	2	1	0	1	1	0	2	0	9	0	0	0	-	1--	-	-	.268	0.36	1.50
2018	SF	NL	26	0	4	23.1	95	17	16	16	4	2	0	1	10	0	33	1	2	2	.500	0-1	1	98	.728	3.41	6.17
2019	2 Tms	NL	17	0	3	16.0	70	14	9	9	5	0	0	1	9	0	18	0	0	1	.000	0-2	2	98	.860	5.89	5.06
19	SF	NL	2	0	1	2.0	11	4	1	1	1	0	0	0	1	0	5	0	0	0	-	0-0	0	99	1.155	14.72	4.50
19	Mil	NL	15	0	2	14.0	59	10	8	8	4	0	0	1	8	0	13	0	0	1	.000	0-2	2	98	.802	4.82	5.14
	2 ML YEARS		43	0	7	39.1	165	31	25	25	9	2	0	2	19	0	51	1	2	3	.400	0-3	3	98	.784	4.37	5.72

Paul Blackburn

Pitches: R Bats: R Pos: RP-3; SP-1   Ht: 6'1" Wt: 200 Born: 12/4/1993 Age: 26

			HOW MUCH PITCHED						WHAT HE GAVE UP										THE RESULTS						
Year	Team	Lg	G	GS	GF	IP	BFP	H	R	ER	HR	SH	SF	HB	TBB	IBB	SO	WP	W	L	Pct	Sv-Op	Hld	Vel	OPS	ERC	ERA
2019	LsVgs	AAA	24	22	0	132.2	539	133	70	64	18	0	1	3	34	0	92	4	11	3	.786	0--	-	-	.753	4.00	4.34
2017	Oak	AL	10	10	0	58.2	238	58	22	21	5	0	0	1	16	0	22	1	3	1	.750	0-0	0	90	.686	3.62	3.22
2018	Oak	AL	6	6	0	27.2	119	33	23	22	2	0	2	2	6	0	19	1	2	3	.400	0-0	0	90	.794	4.62	7.16
2019	Oak	AL	4	1	1	11.0	57	19	14	13	3	1	1	1	4	0	8	1	0	2	.000	0-0	0	91	1.089	10.24	10.64
	3 ML YEARS		20	17	1	97.1	414	110	59	56	10	1	3	4	26	0	49	3	5	6	.455	0-0	0	90	.771	4.57	5.18

Charlie Blackmon

Bats: L Throws: L Pos: RF-135;PH-4;DH-2   Ht: 6'3" Wt: 220 Born: 7/1/1986 Age: 33

			BATTING																		RUNNING			AVERAGES			
Year	Team	Lg	G	AB	H	2B	3B	HR	(Hm	Rd)	TB	R	RBI	RC	TBB	IBB	SO	HBP	SH	SF	SB	CS	GDP	Avg	OBP	Slg	OPS
2011	Col	NL	27	98	25	1	0	1	(1	0)	29	9	8	10	3	1	8	0	1	0	5	1	2	.255	.277	.296	.573
2012	Col	NL	42	113	32	8	0	2	(1	1)	46	15	9	11	4	0	17	3	1	0	1	2	4	.283	.325	.407	.732
2013	Col	NL	82	246	76	17	2	6	(3	3)	115	35	22	35	7	0	49	3	2	0	7	0	1	.309	.336	.467	.803
2014	Col	NL	154	593	171	27	3	19	(13	6)	261	82	72	87	31	5	96	13	6	5	28	10	3	.288	.335	.440	.775
2015	Col	NL	157	614	176	31	9	17	(7	10)	276	93	58	95	46	2	112	13	5	4	43	13	4	.287	.347	.450	.797
2016	Col	NL	143	578	187	35	5	29	(12	17)	319	111	82	110	43	4	102	13	3	4	17	9	2	.324	.381	.552	.933
2017	Col	NL	159	644	213	35	14	37	(24	13)	387	137	104	151	65	9	135	10	3	3	14	10	4	.331	.399	.601	1.000
2018	Col	NL	156	626	182	31	7	29	(14	15)	314	119	70	110	59	2	134	8	1	2	12	4	10	.291	.358	.502	.860
2019	Col	NL	140	580	182	42	7	32	(22	10)	334	112	86	115	40	1	104	9	0	5	2	5	11	.314	.364	.576	.940
	Postseason		5	19	2	0	0	0	(0	0)	2	1	2	0	1	0	2	0	1	0	0	0	0	.105	.150	.105	.255
	9 ML YEARS		1060	4092	1244	227	47	172	(97	75)	2081	713	511	724	298	24	757	72	22	23	129	54	41	.304	.360	.509	.868

Alex Blandino

Bats: R Throws: R Pos: PH-11;2B-10;3B-4;1B-3;DH-1;PR-1   Ht: 6'0" Wt: 190 Born: 11/6/1992 Age: 27

			BATTING																		RUNNING			AVERAGES			
Year	Team	Lg	G	AB	H	2B	3B	HR	(Hm	Rd)	TB	R	RBI	RC	TBB	IBB	SO	HBP	SH	SF	SB	CS	GDP	Avg	OBP	Slg	OPS
2019	Lsvlle	AAA	70	239	59	13	1	5	(-	-)	89	36	24	38	40	0	73	14	0	0	1	3	5	.247	.386	.372	.758
2018	Cin	NL	69	128	30	4	0	1	(1	0)	37	14	8	10	13	1	41	4	2	0	0	0	4	.234	.324	.289	.613
2019	Cin	NL	23	36	9	1	0	1	(0	1)	13	6	3	6	10	0	14	2	0	2	0	0	1	.250	.420	.361	.781
	2 ML YEARS		92	164	39	5	0	2	(1	1)	50	20	11	16	23	1	55	6	2	2	0	0	5	.238	.349	.305	.654

Michael Blazek

Pitches: R Bats: R Pos: RP-4   BLAY-zek   Ht: 6'0" Wt: 205 Born: 3/16/1989 Age: 31

Year Team	Lg	G	GS	GF	IP	BFP	H	R	ER	HR	SH	SF	HB	TBB	IBB	SO	WP	W	L	Pct	Sv-Op	Hld	Vel	OPS	ERC	ERA
2019 Fresno	AAA	34	1	13	38.2	178	44	31	26	9	0	4	1	16	0	42	5	2	2	.500	1--	-	-	.870	5.87	6.05
2013 2 Tms	NL	18	0	7	17.1	84	16	12	11	3	1	1	1	13	0	14	0	0	1	.000	0-0	0	95	.759	5.57	5.71
2015 Mil	NL	45	0	17	55.2	222	40	17	15	3	1	2	1	18	1	47	3	5	3	.625	0-0	4	93	.557	2.11	2.43
2016 Mil	NL	41	0	7	41.1	201	52	31	26	7	1	4	2	27	3	36	2	3	1	.750	0-1	9	93	.932	7.31	5.66
2017 Mil	NL	5	1	2	8.2	37	12	9	8	6	1	0	0	1	0	7	0	0	1	.000	0-0	0	93	1.247	9.88	8.31
2019 Was	NL	4	0	3	5.0	26	6	4	4	1	0	0	0	5	0	0	0	0	0	-	0-0	0	95	.899	8.54	7.20
13 StL	NL	11	0	3	10.1	52	10	8	8	2	0	0	1	10	0	10	0	0	0	-	0-0	0	95	.818	7.25	6.97
13 Mil	NL	7	0	4	7.0	32	6	4	3	1	1	1	0	3	0	4	0	0	1	.000	0-0	0	94	.661	3.35	3.86
5 ML YEARS		113	1	36	128.0	570	126	73	64	20	4	7	4	64	4	104	5	8	6	.571	0-1	13	93	.779	4.83	4.50

Richard Bleier

Pitches: L Bats: L Pos: RP-52; SP-1   BLY-er   Ht: 6'3" Wt: 215 Born: 4/16/1987 Age: 33

Year Team	Lg	G	GS	GF	IP	BFP	H	R	ER	HR	SH	SF	HB	TBB	IBB	SO	WP	W	L	Pct	Sv-Op	Hld	Vel	OPS	ERC	ERA
2016 NYY	AL	23	0	8	23.0	92	20	6	5	0	0	1	1	4	0	13	0	0	0	-	0-0	2	89	.586	2.11	1.96
2017 Bal	AL	57	0	14	63.1	265	62	23	14	6	3	4	4	13	3	26	5	2	1	.667	0-0	3	89	.671	3.33	1.99
2018 Bal	AL	31	0	4	32.2	133	36	7	7	0	0	2	1	4	1	15	1	3	0	1.000	0-1	9	88	.673	3.05	1.93
2019 Bal	AL	53	1	13	55.1	235	65	34	33	6	1	2	4	8	2	30	1	3	0	1.000	4-5	5	89	.802	4.39	5.37
4 ML YEARS		164	1	39	174.1	725	183	70	59	12	4	9	10	29	6	84	7	8	1	.889	4-6	19	89	.703	3.43	3.05

Jerry Blevins

Pitches: L Bats: L Pos: RP-45   Ht: 6'6" Wt: 190 Born: 9/6/1983 Age: 36

Year Team	Lg	G	GS	GF	IP	BFP	H	R	ER	HR	SH	SF	HB	TBB	IBB	SO	WP	W	L	Pct	Sv-Op	Hld	Vel	OPS	ERC	ERA
2019 LsVgs	AAA	7	0	1	10.2	44	9	2	2	2	0	0	0	4	0	16	0	0	0	-	0--	-	-	.720	3.72	1.69
2007 Oak	AL	6	0	1	4.2	25	8	6	5	1	0	0	0	2	0	3	0	0	1	.000	0-0	0	91	.965	9.08	9.64
2008 Oak	AL	36	0	8	37.2	156	32	14	13	2	0	1	3	13	2	35	0	1	3	.250	0-1	5	91	.639	3.00	3.11
2009 Oak	AL	20	0	5	22.1	90	19	12	12	2	0	1	0	6	1	23	0	0	0	-	0-0	0	91	.651	4.84	4.84
2010 Oak	AL	63	0	9	48.2	220	54	20	20	7	3	1	1	18	1	46	0	2	1	.667	1-2	11	91	.758	4.81	3.70
2011 Oak	AL	26	0	11	28.1	122	24	14	9	2	3	2	1	14	1	26	0	0	0	-	0-0	0	89	.688	3.45	2.86
2012 Oak	AL	63	0	17	65.1	261	45	20	18	7	5	2	5	25	5	54	2	5	1	.833	1-1	14	90	.637	2.66	2.48
2013 Oak	AL	67	0	14	60.0	245	47	23	21	7	3	5	4	17	2	52	2	5	0	1.000	0-4	4	90	.651	2.78	3.15
2014 Was	NL	64	0	25	57.1	240	48	31	31	3	3	3	1	23	6	66	2	2	3	.400	0-0	9	91	.623	2.78	4.87
2015 NYM	NL	7	0	1	5.0	15	0	0	0	0	0	0	0	0	0	4	0	1	0	1.000	0-1	5	90	.000	0.00	0.00
2016 NYM	NL	73	0	8	42.0	178	36	14	13	4	2	3	1	15	3	52	1	4	2	.667	2-3	16	89	.627	3.02	2.79
2017 NYM	NL	75	0	5	49.0	217	43	16	16	4	0	1	4	24	2	69	2	6	0	1.000	1-8	19	89	.652	3.79	2.94
2018 NYM	NL	64	1	7	42.2	188	36	24	23	6	0	1	5	22	1	41	1	3	2	.600	1-1	8	89	.729	4.35	4.85
2019 Atl	NL	45	0	12	32.1	141	25	15	14	5	0	2	2	16	2	37	2	1	0	1.000	1-1	10	89	.685	3.61	3.90
Postseason		6	0	1	7.0	22	1	0	0	0	0	0	0	0	0	2	0	0	0	-	0-0	0	90	.091	0.05	0.00
13 ML YEARS		609	1	123	495.1	2098	417	209	195	50	18	23	27	195	26	508	12	30	13	.698	7-22	101	90	.665	3.30	3.54

Xander Bogaerts

Bats: R Throws: R Pos: SS-153;DH-1;PH-1   ZAN-derr BO-garts   Ht: 6'1" Wt: 210 Born: 10/1/1992 Age: 27

Year Team	Lg	G	AB	H	2B	3B	HR	(Hm	Rd)	TB	R	RBI	RC	TBB	IBB	SO	HBP	SH	SF	SB	CS	GDP	Avg	OBP	Slg	OPS
2013 Bos	AL	18	44	11	2	0	1	(0	1)	16	7	5	4	5	0	13	0	0	1	1	0	1	.250	.320	.364	.684
2014 Bos	AL	144	538	129	28	1	12	(7	5)	195	60	46	43	39	1	138	8	2	7	2	3	11	.240	.297	.362	.660
2015 Bos	AL	156	613	196	35	3	7	(5	2)	258	84	81	88	32	1	101	3	3	3	10	2	16	.320	.355	.421	.776
2016 Bos	AL	157	652	192	34	1	21	(11	10)	291	115	89	98	58	0	123	6	0	3	13	4	14	.294	.356	.446	.802
2017 Bos	AL	148	571	156	32	6	10	(4	6)	230	94	62	81	56	6	116	6	0	2	15	1	17	.273	.343	.403	.746
2018 Bos	AL	136	513	148	45	3	23	(15	8)	268	72	103	100	55	4	102	6	0	6	8	2	14	.288	.360	.522	.883
2019 Bos	AL	155	614	190	52	0	33	(17	16)	341	110	117	124	76	2	122	2	0	6	4	2	11	.309	.384	.555	.939
Postseason		33	114	25	5	1	2	(2	0)	38	17	10	11	14	1	25	0	0	2	0	0	4	.219	.300	.333	.633
7 ML YEARS		914	3545	1022	228	14	107	(59	48)	1599	542	503	538	321	14	715	31	5	28	53	14	84	.288	.350	.451	.801

Ronald Bolanos

Pitches: R Bats: R Pos: SP-3; RP-2   boh-LAHN-yos   Ht: 6'3" Wt: 220 Born: 8/23/1996 Age: 23

Year Team	Lg	G	GS	GF	IP	BFP	H	R	ER	HR	SH	SF	HB	TBB	IBB	SO	WP	W	L	Pct	Sv-Op	Hld	Vel	OPS	ERC	ERA
2019 Lk Els	A+	10	10	0	53.2	219	37	24	17	4	1	0	3	23	0	54	9	5	2	.714	0--	-	-	.570	2.61	2.85
2019 Amrillo	AA	15	13	1	76.2	326	71	39	36	7	0	1	10	30	0	88	7	8	5	.615	0--	-	-	.723	4.19	4.23
2019 SD	NL	5	3	0	19.2	88	17	13	13	3	0	1	1	12	0	19	1	0	2	.000	0-0	0	94	.800	4.68	5.95

Skye Bolt

Bats: B Throws: R Pos: CF-3;PH-3;RF-1   Ht: 6'2" Wt: 187 Born: 1/15/1994 Age: 26

Year Team	Lg	G	AB	H	2B	3B	HR	(Hm	Rd)	TB	R	RBI	RC	TBB	IBB	SO	HBP	SH	SF	SB	CS	GDP	Avg	OBP	Slg	OPS
2019 LsVgs	AAA	89	305	82	19	3	11	(-	-)	140	57	61	50	37	0	94	2	1	2	7	5	5	.269	.350	.459	.809
2019 Oak	AL	5	10	1	1	0	0	(0	0)	2	1	0	0	1	0	3	0	0	0	0	0	0	.100	.182	.200	.382

Jorge Bonifacio

Bats: R **Throws:** R **Pos:** RF-4;LF-1

Ht: 6'1" **Wt:** 225 **Born:** 6/4/1993 **Age:** 27

Year Team	Lg	G	AB	H	2B	3B	HR	(Hm	Rd)	TB	R	RBI	RC	TBB	IBB	SO	HBP	SH	SF	SB	CS	GDP	Avg	OBP	Slg	OPS
2019 Omha	AAA	117	451	100	18	5	20	(-	-)	188	67	62	55	38	1	121	4	0	7	6	4	5	.222	.284	.417	.701
2017 KC	AL	113	384	98	15	1	17	(8	9)	166	55	40	51	35	0	118	2	0	1	1	1	8	.255	.320	.432	.752
2018 KC	AL	69	236	53	16	2	4	(1	3)	85	31	23	29	29	1	71	2	1	2	0	1	3	.225	.312	.360	.672
2019 KC	AL	5	20	7	3	0	0	(0	0)	10	3	3	5	1	0	7	0	0	0	0	0	0	.350	.381	.500	.881
3 ML YEARS		187	640	158	34	3	21	(9	12)	261	89	66	85	65	1	196	4	1	3	1	2	11	.247	.319	.408	.727

Ryan Borucki

Pitches: L **Bats:** L **Pos:** SP-2

Ht: 6'4" **Wt:** 215 **Born:** 3/31/1994 **Age:** 26

Year Team	Lg	G	GS	GF	IP	BFP	H	R	ER	HR	SH	SF	HB	TBB	IBB	SO	WP	W	L	Pct	Sv-Op	Hld	Vel	OPS	ERC	ERA
2018 Tor	AL	17	17	0	97.2	415	96	48	42	7	3	2	2	33	3	67	2	4	6	.400	0-0	0	92	.705	3.58	3.87
2019 Tor	AL	2	2	0	6.2	40	15	10	8	2	0	0	0	6	0	6	0	0	1	.000	0-0	0	92	1.319	17.16	10.80
2 ML YEARS		19	19	0	104.1	455	111	58	50	9	3	2	2	39	3	73	2	4	7	.364	0-0	0	92	.757	4.26	4.31

Buddy Boshers

Pitches: L **Bats:** L **Pos:** RP-27; SP-1

bo-SHEERS

Ht: 6'3" **Wt:** 222 **Born:** 5/9/1988 **Age:** 32

Year Team	Lg	G	GS	GF	IP	BFP	H	R	ER	HR	SH	SF	HB	TBB	IBB	SO	WP	W	L	Pct	Sv-Op	Hld	Vel	OPS	ERC	ERA
2019 Buffalo	AAA	25	0	11	32.1	137	27	13	10	3	1	4	2	14	0	35	2	0	2	.000	5--	-		.687	3.50	2.78
2013 LAA	AL	25	0	1	15.1	63	13	8	8	0	0	0	1	8	1	13	0	0	0	-	0-0	6	93	.646	3.33	4.70
2016 Min	AL	37	0	9	36.0	152	35	21	17	3	0	3	1	7	1	37	1	2	0	1.000	0-0	2	92	.659	3.00	4.25
2017 Min	AL	38	0	1	35.0	153	37	20	19	7	1	2	2	10	1	28	2	1	0	1.000	0-0	3	91	.801	4.76	4.89
2019 Tor	AL	28	1	6	20.0	91	20	10	9	3	1	0	1	10	0	26	2	0	3	.000	0-0	4	93	.775	4.93	4.05
4 ML YEARS		128	1	17	106.1	459	105	59	53	13	2	5	5	35	3	104	5	3	3	.500	0-0	15	92	.727	3.98	4.49

David Bote

Bats: R **Throws:** R **Pos:** 3B-67;2B-50;PH-27;SS-9;PR-3;RF-1 BOH-tee

Ht: 6'1" **Wt:** 210 **Born:** 4/7/1993 **Age:** 27

Year Team	Lg	G	AB	H	2B	3B	HR	(Hm	Rd)	TB	R	RBI	RC	TBB	IBB	SO	HBP	SH	SF	SB	CS	GDP	Avg	OBP	Slg	OPS
2018 ChC	NL	74	184	44	9	2	6	(5	1)	75	23	33	26	19	1	60	4	0	3	3	4	3	.239	.319	.408	.727
2019 ChC	NL	127	303	78	17	0	11	(3	8)	128	47	41	44	44	4	93	7	0	2	5	1	11	.257	.362	.422	.785
Postseason		1	2	0	0	0	0	(0	0)	0	0	0	0	0	0	2	0	0	0	0	0	0	.000	.000	.000	.000
2 ML YEARS		201	487	122	26	2	17	(8	9)	203	70	74	70	63	5	153	11	0	5	8	5	14	.251	.346	.417	.763

Justin Bour

Bats: L **Throws:** R **Pos:** 1B-37;PH-14;DH-2

BOOR

Ht: 6'4" **Wt:** 270 **Born:** 5/28/1988 **Age:** 32

Year Team	Lg	G	AB	H	2B	3B	HR	(Hm	Rd)	TB	R	RBI	RC	TBB	IBB	SO	HBP	SH	SF	SB	CS	GDP	Avg	OBP	Slg	OPS
2019 Salt Lk	AAA	49	187	59	12	1	17	(-	-)	124	44	43	52	41	1	46	1	0	0	2	1	5	.316	.441	.663	1.104
2014 Mia	NL	39	74	21	3	0	1	(1	0)	27	10	11	13	9	1	19	0	0	0	0	0	0	.284	.361	.365	.726
2015 Mia	NL	129	409	107	20	0	23	(10	13)	196	42	73	58	34	3	101	2	0	1	0	0	19	.262	.321	.479	.800
2016 Mia	NL	90	280	74	12	1	15	(9	6)	133	35	51	44	38	9	56	0	0	3	0	0	8	.264	.349	.475	.824
2017 Mia	NL	108	377	109	18	0	25	(14	11)	202	52	83	71	47	7	95	1	0	4	1	0	10	.289	.366	.536	.902
2018 2 Tms	NL	141	423	96	13	1	20	(11	9)	171	49	59	57	73	6	124	2	0	3	2	0	10	.227	.341	.404	.746
2019 LAA	AL	52	151	26	5	0	8	(5	3)	55	18	26	14	17	0	52	1	0	1	0	0	7	.172	.259	.364	.623
18 Mia	NL	112	374	85	10	1	19	(11	8)	154	43	54	53	69	6	111	1	0	3	1	0	8	.227	.347	.412	.759
18 Phi	NL	29	49	11	3	0	1	(0	1)	17	6	5	4	4	0	13	1	0	0	1	0	2	.224	.296	.347	.643
6 ML YEARS		559	1714	433	71	2	92	(50	42)	784	206	303	257	218	26	447	6	0	12	3	0	54	.253	.337	.457	.794

Peter Bourjos

Bats: R **Throws:** R **Pos:** LF-12;CF-11;PR-4;PH-2;2B-1;DH-1 BORE-juss

Ht: 6'1" **Wt:** 190 **Born:** 3/31/1987 **Age:** 33

Year Team	Lg	G	AB	H	2B	3B	HR	(Hm	Rd)	TB	R	RBI	RC	TBB	IBB	SO	HBP	SH	SF	SB	CS	GDP	Avg	OBP	Slg	OPS
2010 LAA	AL	51	181	37	6	4	6	(1	5)	69	19	15	13	6	0	40	2	3	1	10	3	2	.204	.237	.381	.618
2011 LAA	AL	147	502	136	26	11	12	(7	5)	220	72	43	66	32	0	124	10	7	1	22	9	7	.271	.327	.438	.765
2012 LAA	AL	101	168	37	7	0	3	(1	2)	53	27	19	18	15	0	44	3	6	3	3	1	2	.220	.291	.315	.606
2013 LAA	AL	55	175	48	3	3	3	(1	2)	66	26	12	19	10	0	43	6	4	1	6	0	8	.274	.333	.377	.710
2014 StL	NL	119	264	61	9	5	4	(2	2)	92	32	24	27	20	1	78	4	5	1	9	3	5	.231	.294	.348	.643
2015 StL	NL	117	195	39	8	3	4	(2	2)	65	32	13	14	19	4	59	6	4	1	5	8	2	.200	.290	.333	.623
2016 Phi	NL	123	355	89	20	7	5	(1	4)	138	40	23	33	17	2	91	4	6	1	6	4	6	.251	.292	.389	.681
2017 TB	NL	100	188	42	9	3	5	(2	3)	72	27	15	16	12	0	53	1	1	1	5	4	2	.223	.272	.383	.655
2018 Atl	NL	36	44	9	2	1	1	(0	1)	16	5	4	3	2	0	15	0	1	0	0	0	0	.205	.239	.364	.603
2019 LAA	AL	26	44	4	1	0	0	(0	0)	5	4	2	1	1	0	15	0	0	1	2	0	1	.091	.109	.114	.222
Postseason		5	2	0	0	0	0	(0	0)	0	0	0	0	0	0	1	0	0	0	0	0	0	.000	.000	.000	.000
10 ML YEARS		875	2116	502	91	37	43	(17	26)	796	284	170	209	134	7	562	36	37	11	68	32	35	.237	.293	.376	.669

James Bourque

Pitches: R Bats: R Pos: RP-1   **Ht: 6'4" Wt: 215 Born: 7/9/1993 Age: 26**

			HOW MUCH PITCHED					WHAT HE GAVE UP											THE RESULTS							
Year Team	Lg	G	GS	GF	IP	BFP	H	R	ER	HR	SH	SF	HB	TBB	IBB	SO	WP	W	L	Pct	Sv-Op	Hld	Vel	OPS	ERC	ERA
2019 Hrsbrg	AA	14	0	9	20.1	83	17	5	3	1	0	0	1	6	0	33	0	3	0	1.000	6--	-	-	.579	2.68	1.33
2019 Fresno	AAA	33	0	5	43.2	203	41	29	27	6	1	2	4	30	0	53	8	4	1	.800	3--	-	-	.781	5.49	5.56
2019 Was	NL	1	0	0	0.2	6	3	4	4	0	0	0	0	2	0	0	0	0	0	-	0-0	0	96	2.083	49.74	54.00

Matt Bowman

Pitches: R Bats: R Pos: RP-27   **Ht: 6'0" Wt: 185 Born: 5/31/1991 Age: 29**

			HOW MUCH PITCHED					WHAT HE GAVE UP											THE RESULTS							
Year Team	Lg	G	GS	GF	IP	BFP	H	R	ER	HR	SH	SF	HB	TBB	IBB	SO	WP	W	L	Pct	Sv-Op	Hld	Vel	OPS	ERC	ERA
2019 Lsvlle	AAA	29	0	12	39.0	156	28	11	9	1	0	0	0	18	2	35	1	1	1	.500	4--	-	92	.623	2.34	2.08
2016 StL	NL	59	0	12	67.2	281	59	31	26	4	1	1	1	20	2	52	0	2	5	.286	0-1	13	92	.659	2.71	3.46
2017 StL	NL	75	0	10	58.2	247	52	29	26	4	2	4	5	18	2	46	1	3	6	.333	2-5	23	91	.659	3.15	3.99
2018 StL	NL	22	0	5	23.0	109	29	16	16	4	2	1	1	11	3	26	1	0	2	.000	0-2	5	92	.894	6.39	6.26
2019 Cin	NL	27	0	10	32.0	137	27	15	13	2	0	2	0	13	3	25	0	2	0	1.000	0-0	0	93	.628	2.78	3.66
4 ML YEARS		183	0	37	181.1	774	167	91	81	14	5	8	7	62	10	149	2	7	13	.350	2-8	41	92	.672	3.28	4.02

Brad Boxberger

Pitches: R Bats: R Pos: RP-29   **Ht: 6'2" Wt: 205 Born: 5/27/1988 Age: 32**

			HOW MUCH PITCHED					WHAT HE GAVE UP											THE RESULTS							
Year Team	Lg	G	GS	GF	IP	BFP	H	R	ER	HR	SH	SF	HB	TBB	IBB	SO	WP	W	L	Pct	Sv-Op	Hld	Vel	OPS	ERC	ERA
2019 Hrsbrg	AA	8	0	3	8.2	35	6	2	1	0	0	1	0	3	0	11	1	1	1	.500	1--	-	-	.483	1.68	1.04
2019	AAA	5	0	2	5.1	31	5	7	7	2	0	0	0	5	1	8	0	0	0	-	0--	-	-	1.215	14.38	11.81
2012 SD	NL	24	0	4	27.2	120	22	12	8	3	0	1	2	18	1	33	0	0	0	-	0-0	1	92	.734	4.28	2.60
2013 SD	NL	18	0	6	22.0	94	19	9	7	3	3	2	0	13	0	24	0	0	1	.000	1-1	0	92	.760	4.43	2.86
2014 TB	AL	63	0	10	64.2	247	34	17	17	9	2	2	4	20	0	104	3	5	2	.714	2-5	18	93	.538	1.84	2.37
2015 TB	AL	69	0	53	63.0	271	54	29	26	9	2	1	2	32	5	74	5	4	10	.286	**41-47**	2	93	.703	4.01	3.71
2016 TB	AL	27	0	3	24.1	114	23	13	13	3	0	1	2	19	1	22	0	4	3	.571	0-3	7	92	.734	5.75	4.81
2017 TB	AL	30	0	10	29.1	121	23	11	11	4	1	1	1	11	3	40	1	4	4	.500	0-2	5	92	.665	3.03	3.38
2018 Ari	NL	60	0	45	53.1	235	44	30	26	9	2	1	0	32	4	71	3	3	7	.300	32-40	1	91	.732	4.27	4.39
2019 KC	AL	29	0	9	26.2	122	25	16	16	3	0	1	0	17	0	27	1	1	3	.250	1-4	0	90	.751	4.83	5.40
8 ML YEARS		320	0	140	311.0	1324	244	137	124	43	10	10	10	162	14	395	13	21	30	.412	77-102	34	92	.687	3.72	3.59

Matthew Boyd

Pitches: L Bats: L Pos: SP-32   **Ht: 6'3" Wt: 234 Born: 2/2/1991 Age: 29**

			HOW MUCH PITCHED					WHAT HE GAVE UP											THE RESULTS							
Year Team	Lg	G	GS	GF	IP	BFP	H	R	ER	HR	SH	SF	HB	TBB	IBB	SO	WP	W	L	Pct	Sv-Op	Hld	Vel	OPS	ERC	ERA
2015 2 Tms	AL	13	12	0	57.1	252	71	50	48	17	1	3	1	20	0	43	4	1	6	.143	0-0	0	91	.979	7.04	7.53
2016 Det	AL	20	18	1	97.1	412	97	51	49	17	0	3	4	29	0	82	1	6	5	.545	0-0	0	91	.765	4.35	4.53
2017 Det	AL	26	25	0	135.0	605	157	84	79	18	3	6	3	53	3	110	2	6	11	.353	0-0	0	92	.826	5.28	5.27
2018 Det	AL	31	31	0	170.1	709	146	87	83	27	2	6	11	51	0	159	6	9	13	.409	0-0	0	90	.704	3.53	4.39
2019 Det	AL	32	32	0	185.1	788	178	101	94	39	4	4	8	50	1	238	6	9	12	.429	0-0	0	92	.766	4.18	4.56
15 Tor	AL	2	2	0	6.2	36	15	11	11	5	0	1	0	1	0	7	2	0	2	.000	0-0	0	91	1.327	17.16	14.85
15 Det	AL	11	10	0	50.2	216	56	39	37	12	1	2	1	19	0	36	2	1	4	.200	0-0	0	91	.918	5.88	6.57
5 ML YEARS		122	118	1	645.1	2766	649	373	353	118	10	22	27	203	4	632	19	31	47	.397	0-0	0	91	.783	4.49	4.92

Brad Brach

Pitches: R Bats: R Pos: RP-58   BROCK   **Ht: 6'6" Wt: 215 Born: 4/12/1986 Age: 34**

			HOW MUCH PITCHED					WHAT HE GAVE UP											THE RESULTS							
Year Team	Lg	G	GS	GF	IP	BFP	H	R	ER	HR	SH	SF	HB	TBB	IBB	SO	WP	W	L	Pct	Sv-Op	Hld	Vel	OPS	ERC	ERA
2011 SD	NL	9	0	4	7.0	38	9	5	4	0	0	0	1	7	4	11	1	0	2	.000	0-0	0	93	.747	6.51	5.14
2012 SD	NL	67	0	13	66.2	280	50	28	28	11	1	3	2	33	7	75	4	2	4	.333	0-1	15	92	.674	3.47	3.78
2013 SD	NL	33	0	6	31.0	141	36	15	11	3	0	3	0	19	0	31	4	1	0	1.000	0-0	2	92	.819	6.03	3.19
2014 Bal	AL	46	0	8	62.1	254	48	24	22	6	2	4	1	25	1	54	2	7	1	.875	0-0	8	93	.640	2.90	3.18
2015 Bal	AL	62	0	12	79.1	324	57	25	24	7	3	2	0	38	3	89	1	5	3	.625	1-2	14	94	.627	2.78	2.72
2016 Bal	AL	71	0	16	79.0	311	57	23	18	7	0	3	0	25	1	92	4	10	4	.714	2-7	24	94	.578	2.27	2.05
2017 Bal	AL	67	0	36	68.0	275	51	27	24	7	1	3	0	26	1	70	4	4	5	.444	18-24	9	95	.620	2.70	3.18
2018 2 Tms		69	0	32	62.2	289	72	32	25	5	1	1	1	28	2	60	3	2	4	.333	12-16	11	94	.754	4.85	3.59
2019 2 Tms	NL	58	0	6	54.1	242	57	33	33	4	1	4	1	31	2	60	3	5	4	.556	0-3	6	94	.774	4.94	5.47
18 Bal	AL	42	0	24	39.0	185	50	24	21	4	0	1	0	19	1	38	1	1	2	.333	11-13	3	93	.830	5.96	4.85
18 Atl	NL	27	0	8	23.2	104	22	8	4	1	0	1	1	9	1	22	2	1	2	.333	1-3	8	95	.620	3.19	1.52
19 ChC	NL	42	0	6	39.2	181	42	27	27	3	0	4	1	28	1	45	3	4	3	.571	0-2	4	94	.811	5.66	6.13
19 NYM	NL	16	0	0	14.2	61	15	6	6	1	1	0	0	3	1	15	0	1	1	.500	0-1	2	94	.668	3.12	3.68
Postseason		5	0	0	5.0	24	5	1	1	1	0	0	0	5	1	5	0	1	0	1.000	0-1	0	94	.890	7.14	1.80
9 ML YEARS		482	0	133	510.1	2154	437	212	189	50	9	23	6	232	21	542	26	36	27	.571	33-53	89	94	.675	3.48	3.33

Chasen Bradford

Pitches: R Bats: R Pos: RP-12   **Ht: 6'1" Wt: 229 Born: 8/5/1989 Age: 30**

			HOW MUCH PITCHED					WHAT HE GAVE UP											THE RESULTS							
Year Team	Lg	G	GS	GF	IP	BFP	H	R	ER	HR	SH	SF	HB	TBB	IBB	SO	WP	W	L	Pct	Sv-Op	Hld	Vel	OPS	ERC	ERA
2019 Tacom	AAA	5	0	5	5.1	26	5	5	4	2	0	0	1	3	0	2	0	0	0	-	1--	-	-	.937	6.86	6.75

			HOW MUCH PITCHED					WHAT HE GAVE UP											THE RESULTS						
Year	Team	Lg	G	GS	GF	IP	BFP	H	R	ER	HR	SH	SF	HB	TBB	IBB	SO	WP	W	L	Pct	Sv-Op	Hld	Vel	OPS	ERC	ERA
2017	NYM	NL	28	0	7	33.2	143	30	17	14	3	0	1	0	13	1	27	1	2	0	1.000	0-0	2	91	.657	3.26	3.74
2018	Sea	AL	46	0	15	53.2	231	55	23	22	9	0	2	5	14	1	38	1	5	0	1.000	0-0	2	91	.758	4.46	3.69
2019	Sea	AL	12	0	6	16.2	69	17	9	9	6	0	1	0	4	0	11	1	0	0	-	1-1	1	91	.898	5.34	4.86
3 ML YEARS			86	0	28	104.0	443	102	49	45	18	0	4	5	31	2	76	3	7	0	1.000	1-1	6	91	.748	4.21	3.89

Archie Bradley

Pitches: R **Bats:** R **Pos:** RP-65; SP-1   **Ht:** 6'4" **Wt:** 225 **Born:** 8/10/1992 **Age:** 27

			HOW MUCH PITCHED					WHAT HE GAVE UP											THE RESULTS						
Year	Team	Lg	G	GS	GF	IP	BFP	H	R	ER	HR	SH	SF	HB	TBB	IBB	SO	WP	W	L	Pct	Sv-Op	Hld	Vel	OPS	ERC	ERA
2015	Ari	NL	8	8	0	35.2	161	36	23	23	3	1	1	2	22	1	23	0	2	3	.400	0-0	0	92	.768	5.12	5.80
2016	Ari	NL	26	26	0	141.2	638	154	84	79	16	2	7	4	67	8	143	7	8	9	.471	0-0	0	92	.802	4.96	5.02
2017	Ari	NL	63	0	13	73.0	290	55	14	14	4	1	1	1	21	2	79	0	3	3	.500	1-7	25	96	.567	2.14	1.73
2018	Ari	NL	76	0	8	71.2	296	62	30	29	9	1	0	4	20	1	75	2	4	5	.444	3-11	34	96	.672	3.24	3.64
2019	Ari	NL	66	1	32	71.2	317	67	30	28	5	2	2	5	36	2	87	0	4	5	.444	18-21	7	96	.714	4.10	3.52
Postseason			3	0	1	6.0	28	6	3	2	2	0	0	0	3	0	5	0	0	0	-	0-0	1	96	.841	5.84	3.00
5 ML YEARS			239	35	53	393.2	1702	374	181	173	37	7	11	16	166	14	407	9	21	25	.457	22-39	66	94	.719	3.94	3.96

Bobby Bradley

Bats: L **Throws:** R **Pos:** DH-8;1B-5;PH-2   **Ht:** 6'1" **Wt:** 225 **Born:** 5/29/1996 **Age:** 24

			BATTING																	RUNNING			AVERAGES			
Year	Team	Lg	G	AB	H	2B	3B	HR	(Hm	Rd)	TB	R	RBI	RC	TBB	IBB	SO	HBP	SH	SF	SB	CS	GDP	Avg	OBP	Slg	OPS
2019	Clmbs	AAA	107	402	106	23	0	33	(-	-)	228	65	74	78	46	2	153	4	0	1	0	0	8	.264	.344	.567	.912
2019	Cle	AL	15	45	8	5	0	1	(1	0)	16	4	4	1	4	0	20	0	0	0	0	0	2	.178	.245	.356	.600

Jackie Bradley Jr.

Bats: L **Throws:** R **Pos:** CF-144;PH-4;RF-3;PR-1   **Ht:** 5'10" **Wt:** 200 **Born:** 4/19/1990 **Age:** 30

			BATTING																	RUNNING			AVERAGES			
Year	Team	Lg	G	AB	H	2B	3B	HR	(Hm	Rd)	TB	R	RBI	RC	TBB	IBB	SO	HBP	SH	SF	SB	CS	GDP	Avg	OBP	Slg	OPS
2013	Bos	AL	37	95	18	5	0	3	(2	1)	32	18	10	8	10	0	31	2	0	0	2	0	1	.189	.280	.337	.617
2014	Bos	AL	127	384	76	19	2	1	(1	0)	102	45	30	27	31	1	121	5	1	2	8	0	10	.198	.265	.266	.531
2015	Bos	AL	74	221	55	17	4	10	(5	5)	110	43	43	41	27	0	69	3	1	3	3	0	5	.249	.335	.498	.832
2016	Bos	AL	156	558	149	30	7	26	(12	14)	271	94	87	86	63	5	143	10	0	5	9	2	10	.267	.349	.486	.835
2017	Bos	AL	133	482	118	19	3	17	(6	11)	194	58	63	70	48	4	124	9	0	2	8	3	8	.245	.323	.402	.726
2018	Bos	AL	144	474	111	33	4	13	(4	9)	191	76	59	67	46	3	137	11	0	4	17	1	6	.234	.314	.403	.717
2019	Bos	AL	147	494	111	28	3	21	(10	11)	208	69	62	61	56	3	155	12	3	2	8	6	6	.225	.317	.421	.738
Postseason			21	65	12	2	0	4	(1	3)	26	7	15	12	9	0	22	2	0	0	1	2	2	.185	.303	.400	.703
7 ML YEARS			818	2708	638	151	23	91	(40	51)	1108	403	354	360	281	16	780	52	5	18	55	12	46	.236	.317	.409	.727

Michael Brantley

Bats: L **Throws:** L **Pos:** LF-120;DH-25;RF-9;PH-5   **Ht:** 6'2" **Wt:** 200 **Born:** 5/15/1987 **Age:** 33

			BATTING																	RUNNING			AVERAGES			
Year	Team	Lg	G	AB	H	2B	3B	HR	(Hm	Rd)	TB	R	RBI	RC	TBB	IBB	SO	HBP	SH	SF	SB	CS	GDP	Avg	OBP	Slg	OPS
2009	Cle	AL	28	112	35	4	0	0	(0	0)	39	10	11	16	8	0	19	0	1	0	4	4	3	.313	.358	.348	.707
2010	Cle	AL	72	297	73	9	3	3	(2	1)	97	38	22	32	22	0	38	0	4	2	10	2	6	.246	.296	.327	.623
2011	Cle	AL	114	451	120	24	4	7	(4	3)	173	63	46	56	34	2	76	3	3	5	13	5	11	.266	.318	.384	.702
2012	Cle	AL	149	552	159	37	4	6	(3	3)	222	63	60	76	53	12	56	0	0	4	12	9	7	.288	.348	.402	.750
2013	Cle	AL	151	556	158	26	3	10	(9	1)	220	66	73	86	40	1	67	4	3	8	17	4	11	.284	.332	.396	.728
2014	Cle	AL	156	611	200	45	2	20	(11	9)	309	94	97	114	52	4	56	8	0	5	23	1	16	.327	.385	.506	.890
2015	Cle	AL	137	529	164	45	0	15	(9	6)	254	68	84	94	60	8	51	2	0	5	15	1	14	.310	.379	.480	.859
2016	Cle	AL	11	39	9	2	0	0	(0	0)	11	5	7	5	3	1	6	0	0	1	1	0	1	.231	.279	.282	.561
2017	Cle	AL	90	338	101	20	1	9	(6	3)	150	47	52	51	31	3	50	2	0	4	11	1	8	.299	.357	.444	.801
2018	Cle	AL	143	570	176	36	2	17	(9	8)	267	89	76	86	48	0	60	5	1	6	12	3	15	.309	.364	.468	.832
2019	Hou	AL	148	575	179	40	2	22	(12	10)	289	88	90	103	51	3	66	7	0	4	3	2	21	.311	.372	.503	.875
Postseason			7	25	4	0	0	0	(0	0)	4	0	1	1	2	0	5	0	0	1	0	0	1	.160	.214	.160	.374
11 ML YEARS			1199	4630	1374	288	21	109	(65	44)	2031	631	618	719	402	34	545	31	12	44	121	32	113	.297	.354	.439	.792

Rob Brantly

Bats: L **Throws:** R **Pos:** PH-1   **Ht:** 6'1" **Wt:** 195 **Born:** 7/14/1989 **Age:** 30

			BATTING																	RUNNING			AVERAGES			
Year	Team	Lg	G	AB	H	2B	3B	HR	(Hm	Rd)	TB	R	RBI	RC	TBB	IBB	SO	HBP	SH	SF	SB	CS	GDP	Avg	OBP	Slg	OPS
2019	LV	AAA	82	236	74	13	2	6	(-	-)	109	32	28	45	32	4	29	4	0	0	0	0	7	.314	.404	.462	.866
2012	Mia	NL	31	100	29	8	0	3	(1	2)	46	14	8	14	13	2	16	0	0	0	1	1	1	.290	.372	.460	.832
2013	Mia	NL	67	223	47	9	0	1	(1	0)	59	11	18	14	15	1	53	2	0	3	0	0	6	.211	.263	.265	.528
2015	CWS	AL	14	33	4	1	0	1	(1	0)	8	3	6	1	2	0	8	0	0	1	0	0	1	.121	.167	.242	.409
2017	CWS	AL	14	31	9	1	0	2	(1	1)	16	4	5	7	3	0	14	2	0	0	0	0	2	.290	.389	.516	.905
2019	Phi	NL	1	1	0	0	0	0	(0	0)	0	0	0	0	0	0	1	0	0	0	0	0	0	.000	.000	.000	.000
5 ML YEARS			127	388	89	19	0	7	(4	3)	129	32	37	36	33	3	92	4	0	4	1	1	10	.229	.294	.332	.626

Ryan Brasier

Pitches: R Bats: R Pos: RP-62   BRAY-zhur   Ht: 6'0" Wt: 225 Born: 8/26/1987 Age: 32

Year	Team	Lg	G	GS	GF	IP	BFP	H	R	ER	HR	SH	SF	HB	TBB	IBB	SO	WP	W	L	Pct	Sv-Op	Hld	Vel	OPS	ERC	ERA
2019	Pwtckt	AAA	10	0	2	9.1	36	6	1	1	1	0	0	2	1	0	13	0	2	0	1.000	0--	-	-	.523	2.05	0.96
2013	LAA	AL	7	0	7	9.0	35	7	2	2	1	0	1	0	4	0	7	0	0	0		0-0	0	94	.648	3.37	2.00
2018	Bos	AL	34	0	5	33.2	124	19	6	6	2	1	5	0	7	0	29	1	2	0	1.000	0-2	10	97	.482	1.26	1.60
2019	Bos	AL	62	0	15	55.2	241	51	33	30	9	0	3	3	21	1	61	3	2	4	.333	7-11	9	96	.722	4.06	4.85
	Postseason		9	0	0	8.2	39	7	1	1	0	0	1	1	5	0	7	1	0	0		0-0	5	96	.583	3.31	1.04
	3 ML YEARS		103	0	27	98.1	400	77	41	38	12	1	9	3	32	1	97	4	4	4	.500	7-13	19	96	.641	2.88	3.48

Steven Brault

Pitches: L Bats: L Pos: SP-19; RP-6   Ht: 6'0" Wt: 195 Born: 4/29/1992 Age: 28

Year	Team	Lg	G	GS	GF	IP	BFP	H	R	ER	HR	SH	SF	HB	TBB	IBB	SO	WP	W	L	Pct	Sv-Op	Hld	Vel	OPS	ERC	ERA
2016	Pit	NL	8	7	0	33.1	166	45	26	18	5	3	0	2	17	1	29	1	0	3	.000	0-0	0	91	.893	6.99	4.86
2017	Pit	NL	11	4	2	34.2	162	41	21	18	3	2	1	2	14	1	23	0	1	0	1.000	1-1	0	92	.790	5.06	4.67
2018	Pit	NL	45	5	6	91.2	413	84	51	47	10	3	1	8	57	4	82	9	6	3	.667	0-0	3	93	.747	4.84	4.61
2019	Pit	NL	25	19	1	113.1	505	117	69	65	15	3	0	7	53	2	100	7	4	6	.400	0-0	0	92	.791	5.00	5.16
	4 ML YEARS		89	35	9	273.0	1246	287	167	148	33	11	2	19	141	8	234	17	11	12	.478	1-1	3	92	.790	5.19	4.88

Ryan Braun

Bats: R Throws: R Pos: LF-110;PH-31;DH-3;RF-2   Ht: 6'2" Wt: 205 Born: 11/17/1983 Age: 36

Year	Team	Lg	G	AB	H	2B	3B	HR	(Hm	Rd)	TB	R	RBI	RC	TBB	IBB	SO	HBP	SH	SF	SB	CS	GDP	Avg	OBP	Slg	OPS
2007	Mil	NL	113	451	146	26	6	34	(17	17)	286	91	97	94	29	1	112	7	0	5	15	5	13	.324	.370	.634	1.004
2008	Mil	NL	151	611	174	39	7	37	(23	14)	338	92	106	100	42	4	129	6	0	4	14	4	13	.285	.335	.553	.888
2009	Mil	NL	158	635	203	39	6	32	(15	17)	350	113	114	133	57	1	121	13	0	3	20	6	6	.320	.386	.551	.937
2010	Mil	NL	157	619	188	45	6	25	(13	12)	310	101	103	104	56	1	105	6	0	3	14	3	17	.304	.365	.501	.866
2011	Mil	NL	150	563	187	38	6	33	(16	17)	336	109	111	124	58	2	93	5	0	3	33	6	9	.332	.397	.597	.994
2012	Mil	NL	154	598	191	36	3	41	(24	17)	356	108	112	125	63	15	128	11	0	5	30	7	12	.319	.391	.595	.987
2013	Mil	NL	61	225	67	14	2	9	(5	4)	112	30	38	39	27	7	56	0	0	1	4	5	8	.298	.372	.498	.869
2014	Mil	NL	135	530	141	30	6	19	(8	11)	240	68	81	74	41	3	113	6	0	3	11	5	17	.266	.324	.453	.777
2015	Mil	NL	140	506	144	27	3	25	(8	17)	252	87	84	91	54	4	115	4	0	3	24	4	20	.285	.356	.498	.854
2016	Mil	NL	135	511	156	23	3	30	(15	15)	275	80	91	93	46	10	98	4	0	3	16	5	20	.305	.365	.538	.903
2017	Mil	NL	104	380	102	28	2	17	(7	10)	185	58	52	53	38	2	76	3	0	4	12	4	15	.268	.336	.487	.823
2018	Mil	NL	125	405	103	25	1	20	(8	12)	190	59	64	65	34	5	85	2	0	3	11	5	8	.254	.313	.469	.782
2019	Mil	NL	144	459	131	31	2	22	(9	13)	232	70	75	75	34	1	105	8	0	3	11	1	15	.285	.343	.505	.849
	Postseason		25	100	34	11	0	2	(2	0)	51	9	16	18	6	0	26	1	0	1	3	0	0	.340	.380	.510	.890
	13 ML YEARS		1727	6493	1933	401	48	344	(168	176)	3462	1066	1128	1170	579	56	1336	75	0	43	215	60	173	.298	.360	.533	.893

John Brebbia

Pitches: R Bats: L Pos: RP-66   Ht: 6'1" Wt: 185 Born: 5/30/1990 Age: 30

Year	Team	Lg	G	GS	GF	IP	BFP	H	R	ER	HR	SH	SF	HB	TBB	IBB	SO	WP	W	L	Pct	Sv-Op	Hld	Vel	OPS	ERC	ERA
2017	StL	NL	50	0	13	51.2	209	37	15	14	8	1	0	5	11	3	51	2	0	0		0-1	5	94	.640	2.45	2.44
2018	StL	NL	45	0	17	50.2	209	43	18	18	5	1	2	0	16	2	60	1	3	3	.500	2-2	5	95	.647	2.85	3.20
2019	StL	NL	66	0	22	72.2	304	59	31	29	6	0	1	3	27	2	87	0	3	4	.429	0-1	12	93	.626	2.93	3.59
	3 ML YEARS		161	0	52	175.0	722	139	64	61	19	2	3	8	54	7	198	3	6	7	.462	2-4	22	94	.636	2.77	3.14

Alex Bregman

Bats: R Throws: R Pos: 3B-99;SS-65;DH-6   Ht: 6'0" Wt: 180 Born: 3/30/1994 Age: 26

Year	Team	Lg	G	AB	H	2B	3B	HR	(Hm	Rd)	TB	R	RBI	RC	TBB	IBB	SO	HBP	SH	SF	SB	CS	GDP	Avg	OBP	Slg	OPS
2016	Hou	AL	49	201	53	13	3	8	(3	5)	96	31	34	37	15	0	52	0	0	1	2	0	1	.264	.313	.478	.791
2017	Hou	AL	155	556	158	39	5	19	(9	10)	264	88	71	87	55	2	97	7	1	7	17	5	15	.284	.352	.475	.827
2018	Hou	AL	157	594	170	51	1	31	(16	15)	316	105	103	135	96	2	85	12	0	3	10	4	15	.286	.394	.532	.926
2019	Hou	AL	156	554	164	37	2	41	(16	25)	328	122	112	126	119	2	83	9	0	8	5	1	9	.296	.423	.592	1.015
	Postseason		26	96	22	5	0	6	(4	2)	45	19	15	12	16	1	14	3	0	1	1	1	2	.229	.353	.469	.822
	4 ML YEARS		517	1905	545	140	11	99	(44	55)	1004	346	320	385	285	6	317	28	1	19	34	10	40	.286	.384	.527	.911

Brandon Brennan

Pitches: R Bats: R Pos: RP-44   Ht: 6'4" Wt: 220 Born: 7/26/1991 Age: 28

Year	Team	Lg	G	GS	GF	IP	BFP	H	R	ER	HR	SH	SF	HB	TBB	IBB	SO	WP	W	L	Pct	Sv-Op	Hld	Vel	OPS	ERC	ERA
2019	Tacom	AAA	9	0	2	8.2	32	5	1	1	1	0	0	1	4	0	10	0	1	0	1.000	0--	-	-	.609	2.95	1.04
2019	Sea	AL	44	0	7	47.1	196	34	25	24	6	0	3	0	24	4	47	6	3	6	.333	0-2	8	95	.651	3.03	4.56

Colten Brewer

Pitches: R **Bats:** R **Pos:** RP-58　　　　　　**Ht:** 6'4" **Wt:** 230 **Born:** 10/29/1992 **Age:** 27

Year Team	Lg	G	GS	GF	IP	BFP	H	R	ER	HR	SH	SF	HB	TBB	IBB	SO	WP	W	L	Pct	Sv-Op	Hld	Vel	OPS	ERC	ERA
2019 Pwtckt	AAA	9	0	2	11.0	56	14	9	6	2	1	0	2	7	0	10	3	2	3	.400	0- -	-	-	.918	8.03	4.91
2018 SD	NL	11	0	5	9.2	49	15	10	6	0	0	0	0	7	0	10	1	1	0	1.000	0-0	0	93	.878	8.08	5.59
2019 Bos	AL	58	0	8	54.2	253	59	26	25	6	1	3	2	34	1	52	9	1	2	.333	0-1	6	93	.804	5.63	4.12
2 ML YEARS		69	0	13	64.1	302	74	36	31	6	1	3	2	41	1	62	10	2	2	.500	0-1	6	93	.816	5.99	4.34

Austin Brice

Pitches: R **Bats:** R **Pos:** RP-36　　　　　　**Ht:** 6'4" **Wt:** 235 **Born:** 6/19/1992 **Age:** 28

Year Team	Lg	G	GS	GF	IP	BFP	H	R	ER	HR	SH	SF	HB	TBB	IBB	SO	WP	W	L	Pct	Sv-Op	Hld	Vel	OPS	ERC	ERA
2016 Mia	NL	15	0	2	14.0	59	9	12	11	2	0	0	2	5	1	14	0	0	1	.000	0-0	1	94	.598	2.63	7.07
2017 Cin	NL	22	0	4	32.2	137	33	18	18	6	1	1	3	7	0	26	0	0	0	-	0-0	1	94	.756	4.38	4.96
2018 Cin	NL	33	0	8	37.1	162	39	26	24	9	1	1	3	13	6	32	1	2	3	.400	0-0	3	94	.876	5.26	5.79
2019 Mia	NL	36	0	10	44.2	199	37	21	17	7	0	1	7	18	2	46	2	1	0	1.000	0-1	6	93	.676	3.92	3.43
4 ML YEARS		106	0	24	128.2	557	118	77	70	24	2	3	15	43	9	118	3	3	4	.429	0-1	11	94	.746	4.26	4.90

Jeff Brigham

Pitches: R **Bats:** R **Pos:** RP-32　　　　　　**Ht:** 6'0" **Wt:** 200 **Born:** 2/16/1992 **Age:** 28

Year Team	Lg	G	GS	GF	IP	BFP	H	R	ER	HR	SH	SF	HB	TBB	IBB	SO	WP	W	L	Pct	Sv-Op	Hld	Vel	OPS	ERC	ERA
2019 NewOr	AAA	17	0	6	24.0	89	9	5	4	0	0	1	2	8	1	30	1	0	1	.000	2- -	-	-	.355	0.91	1.50
2018 Mia	NL	4	4	0	16.1	77	16	11	11	2	0	3	2	13	0	12	0	0	4	.000	0-0	0	93	.860	6.35	6.06
2019 Mia	NL	32	0	10	38.1	161	36	20	19	8	0	1	1	14	2	39	6	3	2	.600	1-2	4	97	.765	4.43	4.46
2 ML YEARS		36	4	10	54.2	238	52	31	30	10	0	4	3	27	2	51	6	3	6	.333	1-2	4	95	.796	5.01	4.94

Lewis Brinson

Bats: R **Throws:** R **Pos:** CF-60;RF-11;PH-7;PR-1　　　　**Ht:** 6'3" **Wt:** 195 **Born:** 5/8/1994 **Age:** 26

Year Team	Lg	G	AB	H	2B	3B	HR	(Hm Rd)	TB	R	RBI	RC	TBB	IBB	SO	HBP	SH	SF	SB	CS	GDP	Avg	OBP	Slg	OPS
2019 NewOr	AAA	81	296	80	15	4	16	(- -)	151	56	56	56	32	0	100	10	0	0	16	5	5	.270	.361	.510	.871
2017 Mil	NL	21	47	5	0	1	2	(0 2)	13	2	3	4	7	1	17	1	0	0	1	0	0	.106	.236	.277	.513
2018 Mil	NL	109	382	76	10	5	11	(2 9)	129	31	42	29	17	2	120	4	0	2	2	1	6	.199	.240	.338	.577
2019 Mia	NL	75	226	39	9	1	0	(0 0)	50	15	15	10	13	1	74	6	2	1	1	1	8	.173	.236	.221	.457
3 ML YEARS		205	655	120	19	7	13	(2 11)	192	48	60	43	37	4	211	11	2	3	4	2	14	.183	.238	.293	.531

Socrates Brito

Bats: L **Throws:** L **Pos:** RF-12;CF-4;LF-1;PH-1;PR-1　　BREE-tow　　**Ht:** 6'2" **Wt:** 205 **Born:** 9/6/1992 **Age:** 27

Year Team	Lg	G	AB	H	2B	3B	HR	(Hm Rd)	TB	R	RBI	RC	TBB	IBB	SO	HBP	SH	SF	SB	CS	GDP	Avg	OBP	Slg	OPS
2019 Buffalo	AAA	97	394	111	28	7	16	(- -)	201	66	67	66	29	1	97	0	1	4	11	7	4	.282	.328	.510	.838
2015 Ari	NL	18	33	10	3	1	0	(0 0)	15	5	1	5	1	0	7	0	0	0	1	0	0	.303	.324	.455	.778
2016 Ari	NL	40	95	17	3	1	4	(1 3)	34	10	12	6	2	0	23	0	0	0	2	0	3	.179	.196	.358	.554
2018 Ari	NL	24	40	7	0	0	1	(1 0)	10	3	3	1	3	0	9	0	0	1	0	1	0	.175	.227	.250	.477
2019 Tor	AL	17	39	3	0	1	0	(0 0)	5	5	2	1	4	0	17	0	0	0	0	0	2	.077	.163	.128	.291
4 ML YEARS		99	207	37	6	3	5	(2 3)	64	23	18	13	10	0	56	0	0	1	3	1	5	.179	.216	.309	.525

Zack Britton

Pitches: L **Bats:** L **Pos:** RP-66　　　　　　**Ht:** 6'3" **Wt:** 195 **Born:** 12/22/1987 **Age:** 32

Year Team	Lg	G	GS	GF	IP	BFP	H	R	ER	HR	SH	SF	HB	TBB	IBB	SO	WP	W	L	Pct	Sv-Op	Hld	Vel	OPS	ERC	ERA
2011 Bal	AL	28	28	0	154.1	666	162	93	79	12	8	7	1	62	3	97	7	11	11	.500	0-0	0	92	.735	4.24	4.61
2012 Bal	AL	12	11	0	60.1	270	61	37	34	6	0	1	2	32	3	53	4	5	3	.625	0-0	0	92	.756	4.70	5.07
2013 Bal	AL	8	7	0	40.0	182	52	23	22	4	1	1	1	17	1	18	1	2	3	.400	0-0	0	92	.837	6.14	4.95
2014 Bal	AL	71	0	49	76.1	285	46	17	14	4	3	0	1	23	0	62	0	3	2	.600	37-41	7	95	.500	1.62	1.65
2015 Bal	AL	64	0	58	65.2	253	51	16	14	3	0	0	1	14	1	79	5	4	1	.800	36-40	0	96	.547	2.02	1.92
2016 Bal	AL	69	0	63	67.0	254	38	7	4	1	1	0	0	18	3	74	10	2	1	.667	47-47	0	96	.430	1.08	0.54
2017 Bal	AL	38	0	30	37.1	161	39	12	12	1	1	1	0	18	1	29	4	2	1	.667	15-17	0	96	.690	4.18	2.89
2018 2 Tms	AL	41	0	21	40.2	169	29	16	14	3	0	1	3	21	0	34	7	2	0	1.000	7-10	9	95	.605	3.13	3.10
2019 NYY	AL	66	0	15	61.1	245	38	13	13	3	2	1	2	32	1	53	3	3	1	.750	3-7	29	95	.545	2.32	1.91
18 Bal	AL	16	0	11	15.2	63	11	6	6	1	0	0	1	10	0	13	2	1	0	1.000	4-5	1	94	.676	3.63	3.45
18 NYY	AL	25	0	10	25.0	106	18	10	8	2	0	1	2	11	0	21	5	1	0	1.000	3-5	8	95	.564	2.84	2.88
Postseason		10	0	4	9.2	46	10	5	5	2	1	0	0	7	2	9	0	0	0	-	2-2	1	95	.904	5.93	4.66
9 ML YEARS		397	46	236	603.0	2485	516	234	206	37	15	13	10	237	13	499	41	34	23	.596	145-162	45	94	.636	3.10	3.07

Aaron Brooks

Pitches: R **Bats:** R **Pos:** SP-18; RP-11　　　　　　**Ht:** 6'4" **Wt:** 230 **Born:** 4/27/1990 **Age:** 30

Year Team	Lg	G	GS	GF	IP	BFP	H	R	ER	HR	SH	SF	HB	TBB	IBB	SO	WP	W	L	Pct	Sv-Op	Hld	Vel	OPS	ERC	ERA
2014 KC	AL	2	1	0	2.2	24	12	13	13	1	0	1	2	3	0	2	0	0	1	.000	0-0	0	92	1.764	44.02	43.88
2015 2 Tms	AL	13	9	3	55.1	250	73	41	41	9	3	2	4	14	0	38	0	3	4	.429	0-0	0	92	.888	6.17	6.67
2018 Oak	AL	3	0	2	2.2	10	1	0	0	0	0	0	0	2	0	1	0	0	0	-	0-0	0	92	.425	1.70	0.00
2019 2 Tms	AL	29	18	8	110.0	482	118	72	69	21	1	1	10	34	0	82	4	6	8	.429	0-0	0	92	.830	5.15	5.65

Year Team	Lg	G	GS	GF	IP	BFP	H	R	ER	HR	SH	SF	HB	TBB	IBB	SO	WP	W	L	Pct	Sv-Op	Hld	Vel	OPS	ERC	ERA
15 KC	AL	2	0		4.1	18	6	3	3	0	0	0	0	3	0	3	0	0	0	-	0-0	0	91	1.000	4.08	6.23
15 Oak	AL	11	9	1	51.0	232	67	38	38	9	3	2	4	14	0	35	0	3	4	.429	0-0	0	92	.878	6.35	6.71
19 Oak	AL	15	6	7	50.1	215	49	29	28	12	0	0	4	14	0	43	1	2	3	.400	0-0	0	92	.799	4.68	5.01
19 Bal	AL	14	12	1	59.2	267	69	43	41	9	1	1	6	20	0	39	3	4	5	.444	0-0	0	92	.855	5.54	6.18
4 ML YEARS		47	28	14	170.2	766	204	126	123	31	4	4	16	53	0	123	4	9	13	.409	0-0	0	92	.871	5.87	6.49

Mike Brosseau

Bats: R **Throws:** R **Pos:** 2B-26;3B-18;RF-6;PH-6;LF-5;PR-4;1B-1;DH-1   **Ht:** 5'10" **Wt:** 215 **Born:** 3/15/1994 **Age:** 26

Year Team	Lg	G	AB	H	2B	3B	HR	(Hm	Rd)	TB	R	RBI	RC	TBB	IBB	SO	HBP	SH	SF	SB	CS	GDP	Avg	OBP	Slg	OPS
2019 Drham	AAA	73	270	82	21	1	16	(-	-)	153	53	60	59	34	0	58	8	0	3	2	3	10	.304	.394	.567	.960
2019 TB	AL	51	132	36	7	0	6	(2	4)	61	17	16	18	7	0	39	2	1	0	1	0	3	.273	.319	.462	.781

Seth Brown

Bats: L **Throws:** L **Pos:** LF-23;PH-6;1B-4   **Ht:** 6'3" **Wt:** 220 **Born:** 7/13/1992 **Age:** 27

Year Team	Lg	G	AB	H	2B	3B	HR	(Hm	Rd)	TB	R	RBI	RC	TBB	IBB	SO	HBP	SH	SF	SB	CS	GDP	Avg	OBP	Slg	OPS
2019 LsVgs	AAA	112	451	134	29	6	37	(-	-)	286	101	104	100	38	1	127	4	0	7	8	1	3	.297	.352	.634	.986
2019 Oak	AL	26	75	22	8	2	0	(0	0)	34	11	13	13	7	0	23	1	0	0	1	0	2	.293	.361	.453	.815

Keon Broxton

Bats: R **Throws:** R **Pos:** CF-65;LF-21;PR-11;RF-9;PH-7;DH-3   **Ht:** 6'3" **Wt:** 195 **Born:** 5/7/1990 **Age:** 30

Year Team	Lg	G	AB	H	2B	3B	HR	(Hm	Rd)	TB	R	RBI	RC	TBB	IBB	SO	HBP	SH	SF	SB	CS	GDP	Avg	OBP	Slg	OPS
2015 Pit	NL	7	2	0	0	0	0	(0	0)	0	3	0	0	0	0	1	0	0	0	1	1	0	.000	.000	.000	.000
2016 Mil	NL	75	207	50	10	1	9	(2	7)	89	28	19	32	36	0	88	0	1	2	23	4	2	.242	.354	.430	.784
2017 Mil	NL	143	414	91	15	4	20	(10	10)	174	66	49	46	40	1	175	7	1	1	21	7	3	.220	.299	.420	.719
2018 Mil	NL	51	78	14	2	2	4	(0	4)	32	15	11	9	11	0	28	0	0	0	5	1	0	.179	.281	.410	.691
2019 3 Tms		100	204	34	4	0	6	(2	4)	56	24	16	11	20	0	104	1	1	2	10	6	5	.167	.242	.275	.517
19 NYM	NL	34	49	7	1	0	0	(0	0)	8	5	2	1	4	0	22	0	0	0	4	1	1	.143	.208	.163	.371
19 Bal	AL	37	103	21	3	0	4	(2	2)	36	14	9	9	8	0	49	0	1	0	4	1	4	.204	.261	.350	.611
19 Sea	AL	29	52	6	0	0	2	(0	2)	12	5	5	1	8	0	33	1	0	2	2	4	0	.115	.238	.231	.469
Postseason		2	2	1	0	0	1	(0	1)	4	1	1	0	0	0	1	0	0	0	0	0	0	.500	.500	2.000	2.500
5 ML YEARS		376	905	189	31	7	39	(14	25)	351	136	95	98	107	1	396	8	3	3	60	19	10	.209	.297	.388	.685

Jay Bruce

Bats: L **Throws:** L **Pos:** LF-37;RF-24;PH-20;1B-16;DH-7   **Ht:** 6'3" **Wt:** 225 **Born:** 4/3/1987 **Age:** 33

Year Team	Lg	G	AB	H	2B	3B	HR	(Hm	Rd)	TB	R	RBI	RC	TBB	IBB	SO	HBP	SH	SF	SB	CS	GDP	Avg	OBP	Slg	OPS
2008 Cin	NL	108	413	105	17	1	21	(13	8)	187	63	52	49	33	1	110	4	0	2	4	6	8	.254	.314	.453	.767
2009 Cin	NL	101	345	77	15	2	22	(13	9)	162	47	58	47	38	2	75	2	1	1	3	3	5	.223	.303	.470	.773
2010 Cin	NL	148	509	143	23	5	25	(19	6)	251	80	70	71	58	5	136	1	0	5	5	4	12	.281	.353	.493	.846
2011 Cin	NL	157	585	150	27	2	32	(16	16)	277	84	97	96	71	14	158	5	1	2	8	7	8	.256	.341	.474	.814
2012 Cin	NL	155	560	141	35	5	34	(21	13)	288	89	99	85	62	11	155	4	0	7	9	3	5	.252	.327	.514	.841
2013 Cin	NL	160	626	164	43	1	30	(16	14)	299	89	109	88	63	13	185	2	0	5	7	3	9	.262	.329	.478	.807
2014 Cin	NL	137	493	107	21	1	18	(10	8)	184	71	66	54	44	5	149	2	1	5	12	3	8	.217	.281	.373	.654
2015 Cin	NL	157	580	131	35	4	26	(13	13)	252	72	87	61	58	8	145	2	0	9	9	5	10	.226	.294	.434	.729
2016 2 Tms	NL	147	539	135	27	6	33	(17	16)	273	74	99	87	44	7	126	3	0	3	4	2	14	.250	.309	.506	.815
2017 2 Tms	NL	146	555	141	29	2	36	(15	21)	282	82	101	94	57	0	139	2	0	3	1	1	11	.254	.324	.508	.832
2018 NYM	NL	94	319	71	18	1	9	(3	6)	118	31	37	44	41	4	75	0	0	1	2	3	3	.223	.310	.370	.680
2019 2 Tms		98	310	67	17	0	26	(8	18)	162	43	59	36	19	0	82	1	0	3	1	0	5	.216	.261	.523	.784
16 Cin	NL	97	370	98	22	6	25	(14	11)	207	60	80	67	27	3	83	2	0	3	4	2	11	.265	.316	.559	.875
16 NYM	NL	50	169	37	5	0	8	(3	5)	66	14	19	20	17	4	43	1	0	0	0	0	3	.219	.294	.391	.685
17 NYM	NL	103	406	104	20	0	29	(11	18)	211	61	75	68	39	0	102	1	0	2	0	1	9	.256	.321	.520	.841
17 Cle	AL	43	149	37	9	2	7	(4	3)	71	21	26	26	18	0	37	1	0	1	1	0	2	.248	.331	.477	.808
19 Sea	AL	47	165	35	11	0	14	(5	9)	88	27	28	19	16	0	53	1	0	2	1	0	1	.212	.283	.533	.816
19 Phi	NL	51	145	32	6	0	12	(3	9)	74	16	31	17	3	0	29	0	0	1	0	0	4	.221	.235	.510	.745
Postseason		15	52	13	3	0	4	(2	2)	28	8	10	7	6	0	13	1	0	1	0	1	0	.250	.333	.538	.872
12 ML YEARS		1608	5834	1432	307	30	312	(164	148)	2735	825	934	812	588	70	1535	28	3	46	65	40	98	.245	.315	.469	.784

Kris Bryant

Bats: R **Throws:** R **Pos:** 3B-115;RF-27;LF-23;1B-3;DH-3;PH-2   **Ht:** 6'5" **Wt:** 230 **Born:** 1/4/1992 **Age:** 28

Year Team	Lg	G	AB	H	2B	3B	HR	(Hm	Rd)	TB	R	RBI	RC	TBB	IBB	SO	HBP	SH	SF	SB	CS	GDP	Avg	OBP	Slg	OPS
2015 ChC	NL	151	559	154	31	5	26	(21	5)	303	87	99	104	77	0	**199**	9	0	5	13	4	7	.275	.369	.488	.858
2016 ChC	NL	155	603	176	35	3	39	(17	**22)**	334	**121**	102	120	75	5	154	18	0	3	8	5	3	.292	.385	.554	.939
2017 ChC	NL	151	549	162	38	4	29	(18	11)	295	111	73	113	95	5	128	15	0	6	7	5	8	.295	.409	.537	.946
2018 ChC	NL	102	389	106	28	3	13	(7	6)	179	59	52	65	48	6	107	17	0	3	2	4	5	.272	.374	.460	.834
2019 ChC	NL	147	543	153	35	1	31	(15	16)	283	108	77	107	74	1	145	15	0	2	4	0	10	.282	.382	.521	.903
Postseason		37	145	35	8	1	6	(4	2)	63	17	16	18	13	0	50	1	0	0	1	0	3	.241	.308	.434	.743
5 ML YEARS		706	2643	751	167	16	138	(78	60)	1364	486	403	509	369	17	733	74	0	19	34	18	33	.284	.385	.516	.901

Clay Buchholz

Pitches: R **Bats:** L **Pos:** SP-12 BUCK-holtz **Ht:** 6'3" **Wt:** 190 **Born:** 8/14/1984 **Age:** 35

Year Team	Lg	G	GS	GF	IP	BFP	H	R	ER	HR	SH	SF	HB	TBB	IBB	SO	WP	W	L	Pct	Sv-Op	Hld	Vel	OPS	ERC	ERA
2007 Bos	AL	4	3	0	22.2	88	14	6	4	0	0	1	1	10	0	22	0	3	1	.750	0-0	0	91	.508	1.90	1.59
2008 Bos	AL	16	15	0	76.0	357	93	63	57	11	0	3	2	41	1	72	2	2	9	.182	0-0	0	93	.844	6.40	6.75
2009 Bos	AL	16	16	0	92.0	399	91	44	43	13	2	3	2	36	1	68	1	7	4	.636	0-0	0	94	.729	4.31	4.21
2010 Bos	AL	28	28	0	173.2	711	142	55	45	9	5	5	5	67	1	120	7	17	7	.708	0-0	0	94	.615	2.88	2.33
2011 Bos	AL	14	14	0	82.2	353	76	34	32	10	1	4	2	31	1	60	3	6	3	.667	0-0	0	93	.706	3.72	3.48
2012 Bos	AL	29	29	0	189.1	802	187	104	96	25	5	9	12	64	2	129	2	11	8	.579	0-0	0	92	.757	4.29	4.56
2013 Bos	AL	16	16	0	108.1	416	75	23	21	4	1	2	1	36	0	96	1	12	1	.923	0-0	0	92	.546	2.00	1.74
2014 Bos	AL	28	28	0	170.1	737	182	108	101	17	3	4	10	54	2	132	8	8	11	.421	0-0	0	92	.751	4.37	5.34
2015 Bos	AL	18	18	0	113.1	469	114	48	41	6	1	2	5	23	0	107	3	7	7	.500	0-0	0	92	.664	3.23	3.26
2016 Bos	AL	37	21	7	139.1	588	130	80	74	21	2	6	5	55	1	93	1	8	10	.444	0-0	2	92	.742	4.23	4.78
2017 Phi	NL	2	2	0	7.1	40	16	10	10	1	0	2	0	3	0	5	0	1	0	1.000	0-0	0	91	1.161	12.26	12.27
2018 Ari	NL	16	16	0	98.1	393	80	25	22	9	0	4	3	22	1	81	1	7	2	.778	0-0	0	92	.620	2.49	2.01
2019 Tor	AL	12	12	0	59.0	254	72	44	43	13	0	1	1	16	1	39	1	2	5	.286	0-0	0	89	.918	5.91	6.56
Postseason		6	6	0	29.2	133	34	15	14	4	1	0	2	10	1	24	2	0	1	.000	0-0	0	92	.807	5.10	4.25
13 ML YEARS		236	218	7	1332.1	5607	1272	644	589	139	20	46	49	458	11	1024	30	90	69	.566	0-0	2	92	.710	3.81	3.98

Ryan Buchter

Pitches: L **Bats:** L **Pos:** RP-64 BOOK-ter **Ht:** 6'4" **Wt:** 232 **Born:** 2/13/1987 **Age:** 33

Year Team	Lg	G	GS	GF	IP	BFP	H	R	ER	HR	SH	SF	HB	TBB	IBB	SO	WP	W	L	Pct	Sv-Op	Hld	Vel	OPS	ERC	ERA
2014 Atl	NL	1	0	1	1.0	3	0	0	0	0	0	0	0	1	0	1	0	1	0	1.000	0-0	0	92	.333	1.26	0.00
2016 SD	NL	67	0	10	63.0	247	34	20	20	4	0	2	2	31	3	78	3	3	0	1.000	1-2	20	92	.559	1.94	2.86
2017 2 Tms	NL	71	0	12	65.1	268	44	25	21	10	0	3	4	26	1	65	0	4	3	.571	1-3	20	93	.642	2.86	2.89
2018 Oak	AL	54	0	4	39.1	163	32	17	12	4	1	1	0	15	1	41	1	6	0	1.000	0-0	16	92	.646	2.96	2.75
2019 Oak	AL	64	0	7	45.1	198	42	16	15	8	3	3	2	23	2	50	1	1	1	.500	0-4	12	93	.799	4.77	2.98
17 SD	NL	42	0	5	38.1	161	28	15	13	7	0	1	1	18	0	47	0	3	3	.500	1-3	15	93	.696	3.48	3.05
17 KC	AL	29	0	7	27.0	107	16	10	8	3	0	2	3	8	1	18	0	1	0	1.000	0-0	5	93	.561	2.03	2.67
5 ML YEARS		257	0	33	214.0	879	152	78	68	26	4	9	8	96	7	235	5	15	4	.789	2-9	68	93	.653	2.96	2.86

Walker Buehler

Pitches: R **Bats:** R **Pos:** SP-30 **Ht:** 6'2" **Wt:** 185 **Born:** 7/28/1994 **Age:** 25

Year Team	Lg	G	GS	GF	IP	BFP	H	R	ER	HR	SH	SF	HB	TBB	IBB	SO	WP	W	L	Pct	Sv-Op	Hld	Vel	OPS	ERC	ERA
2017 LAD	NL	8	0	2	9.1	44	11	8	8	2	0	0	0	8	1	12	1	1	0	1.000	0-0	0	98	.932	8.22	7.71
2018 LAD	NL	24	23	0	137.1	541	95	43	40	12	2	3	6	37	1	151	4	8	5	.615	0-1	0	96	.556	2.10	2.62
2019 LAD	NL	30	30	0	182.1	737	153	77	66	20	2	6	7	37	0	215	4	14	4	.778	0-0	0	97	.636	2.66	3.26
Postseason		4	4	0	23.2	89	16	10	10	3	1	0	0	4	1	29	1	0	1	.000	0-0	0	98	.596	1.74	3.80
3 ML YEARS		62	53	2	329.0	1322	259	128	114	34	4	9	13	82	2	378	9	23	9	.719	0-1	1	97	.613	2.55	3.12

Madison Bumgarner

Pitches: L **Bats:** R **Pos:** SP-34 **Ht:** 6'4" **Wt:** 242 **Born:** 8/1/1989 **Age:** 30

Year Team	Lg	G	GS	GF	IP	BFP	H	R	ER	HR	SH	SF	HB	TBB	IBB	SO	WP	W	L	Pct	Sv-Op	Hld	Vel	OPS	ERC	ERA
2009 SF	NL	4	1	1	10.0	40	8	2	2	2	1	1	0	3	1	10	0	0	0	-	0-0	0	89	.739	3.14	1.80
2010 SF	NL	18	18	0	111.0	472	119	40	37	11	0	4	5	26	2	86	1	7	6	.538	0-0	0	91	.732	3.98	3.00
2011 SF	NL	33	33	0	204.2	844	202	82	73	12	12	4	5	46	5	191	0	13	13	.500	0-0	0	91	.670	3.14	3.21
2012 SF	NL	32	32	0	208.1	849	183	87	78	23	7	4	7	49	6	191	3	16	11	.593	0-0	0	91	.670	2.95	3.37
2013 SF	NL	31	31	0	201.1	803	146	68	62	15	10	4	6	62	6	199	6	13	9	.591	0-0	0	91	.577	2.23	2.77
2014 SF	NL	33	33	0	217.1	873	194	81	72	21	9	5	6	43	3	219	4	18	10	.643	0-0	0	92	.653	2.83	2.98
2015 SF	NL	32	32	0	218.1	869	181	73	71	21	5	4	7	39	2	234	1	18	9	.667	0-0	0	92	.612	2.43	2.93
2016 SF	NL	34	34	0	226.2	912	179	79	69	26	3	6	8	54	0	251	4	15	9	.625	0-0	0	92	.619	2.57	2.74
2017 SF	NL	17	17	0	111.0	450	101	41	41	17	2	1	3	20	3	101	0	4	9	.308	0-0	0	91	.704	3.14	3.32
2018 SF	NL	21	21	0	129.2	551	118	51	47	14	5	3	5	43	3	109	3	6	7	.462	0-0	0	91	.694	3.44	3.26
2019 SF	NL	34	34	0	207.2	844	191	99	90	30	5	5	10	43	3	203	3	9	9	.500	0-0	0	91	.717	3.38	3.90
Postseason		16	14	1	102.1	398	74	25	24	8	6	1	5	18	2	87	0	8	3	.727	1-1	0	92	.544	1.88	2.11
11 ML YEARS		289	286	1	1846.0	7507	1622	703	642	192	59	41	62	428	34	1794	25	119	92	.564	0-0	0	91	.659	2.92	3.13

Aaron Bummer

Pitches: L **Bats:** L **Pos:** RP-58 **Ht:** 6'3" **Wt:** 200 **Born:** 9/21/1993 **Age:** 26

Year Team	Lg	G	GS	GF	IP	BFP	H	R	ER	HR	SH	SF	HB	TBB	IBB	SO	WP	W	L	Pct	Sv-Op	Hld	Vel	OPS	ERC	ERA
2019 Charltt	AAA	5	0	1	7.2	32	7	2	2	0	2	0	1	2	0	6	1	0	0	-	0- -	-	-	.667	2.92	2.35
2017 CWS	AL	30	0	3	22.0	91	13	11	11	4	1	1	1	15	1	17	1	1	3	.250	0-1	7	93	.692	3.70	4.50
2018 CWS	AL	37	0	9	31.2	144	40	19	15	1	0	0	1	10	0	35	7	0	1	1.000	0-1	2	93	.730	4.80	4.26
2019 CWS	AL	58	0	5	67.2	262	43	17	16	4	1	0	3	24	2	60	4	0	0	-	1-3	27	96	.520	1.99	2.13
3 ML YEARS		125	0	17	121.1	497	96	47	42	9	2	1	5	49	3	112	12	1	4	.200	1-5	36	95	.612	2.97	3.12

Dylan Bundy

Pitches: R **Bats:** B **Pos:** SP-30   **Ht:** 6'1" **Wt:** 200 **Born:** 11/15/1992 **Age:** 27

Year	Team	Lg	G	GS	GF	IP	BFP	H	R	ER	HR	SH	SF	HB	TBB	IBB	SO	WP	W	L	Pct	Sv-Op	Hld	Vel	OPS	ERC	ERA
2012	Bal	AL	2	0	2	1.2	6	1	0	0	0	0	0	0	1	0	0	0	0	0	-	0-0	0	94	.533	2.46	0.00
2016	Bal	AL	36	14	6	109.2	474	109	52	49	18	1	1	6	42	4	104	0	10	6	.625	0-0	3	94	.766	4.61	4.02
2017	Bal	AL	28	28	0	169.2	698	152	82	80	26	0	7	5	51	0	152	0	13	9	.591	0-0	0	92	.721	3.68	4.24
2018	Bal	AL	31	31	0	171.2	750	188	116	104	41	3	2	6	54	1	184	6	8	16	.333	0-0	0	92	.855	5.39	5.45
2019	Bal	AL	30	30	0	161.2	700	161	95	86	29	1	7	6	58	0	162	7	7	14	.333	0-0	0	91	.784	4.57	4.79
	5 ML YEARS		127	103	8	614.1	2628	611	345	319	114	5	17	25	206	5	602	13	38	45	.458	0-0	3	92	.784	4.54	4.67

Nick Burdi

Pitches: R **Bats:** R **Pos:** RP-11   **Ht:** 6'3" **Wt:** 225 **Born:** 1/19/1993 **Age:** 27

Year	Team	Lg	G	GS	GF	IP	BFP	H	R	ER	HR	SH	SF	HB	TBB	IBB	SO	WP	W	L	Pct	Sv-Op	Hld	Vel	OPS	ERC	ERA
2018	Pit	NL	2	0	1	1.1	10	3	4	3	1	0	0	0	2	0	2	0	0	0	-	0-0	0	96	1.250	22.77	20.25
2019	Pit	NL	11	0	3	8.2	40	11	9	9	1	0	0	0	3	0	17	1	2	1	.667	0-1	0	97	.836	5.40	9.35
	2 ML YEARS		13	0	4	10.0	50	14	13	12	2	0	0	0	5	0	19	1	2	1	.667	0-1	0	97	.913	7.42	10.80

Brock Burke

Pitches: L **Bats:** L **Pos:** SP-6   **Ht:** 6'4" **Wt:** 180 **Born:** 8/4/1996 **Age:** 23

Year	Team	Lg	G	GS	GF	IP	BFP	H	R	ER	HR	SH	SF	HB	TBB	IBB	SO	WP	W	L	Pct	Sv-Op	Hld	Vel	OPS	ERC	ERA
2019	Frisco	AA	9	9	0	45.1	182	34	19	16	2	0	3	2	11	0	49	2	3	5	.375	0--	-	-	.584	2.01	3.18
2019	Tex	AL	6	6	0	26.2	120	30	22	22	6	1	1	2	11	0	14	0	0	2	.000	0-0	0	92	.876	6.15	7.43

Corbin Burnes

Pitches: R **Bats:** R **Pos:** RP-28; SP-4   **Ht:** 6'3" **Wt:** 205 **Born:** 10/22/1994 **Age:** 25

Year	Team	Lg	G	GS	GF	IP	BFP	H	R	ER	HR	SH	SF	HB	TBB	IBB	SO	WP	W	L	Pct	Sv-Op	Hld	Vel	OPS	ERC	ERA
2019	SnAnt	AAA	8	7	0	22.1	104	29	21	21	2	0	0	2	9	0	25	0	0	1	.000	0--	-	-	.804	6.17	8.46
2018	Mil	NL	30	0	6	38.0	152	27	11	11	4	1	1	3	11	2	35	2	7	0	1.000	1-2	3	95	.595	2.42	2.61
2019	Mil	NL	32	4	8	49.0	235	70	52	48	17	3	0	0	20	0	70	2	1	5	.167	1-1	4	95	1.011	8.65	8.82
	Postseason		6	0	1	9.0	31	4	2	2	0	0	0	1	1	0	11	0	1	0	1.000	0-0	1	96	.400	0.81	2.00
	2 ML YEARS		62	4	14	87.0	387	97	63	59	21	4	1	3	31	2	105	4	8	5	.615	2-3	7	95	.848	5.66	6.10

Ryan Burr

Pitches: R **Bats:** R **Pos:** RP-15; SP-1   **Ht:** 6'4" **Wt:** 225 **Born:** 5/28/1994 **Age:** 26

Year	Team	Lg	G	GS	GF	IP	BFP	H	R	ER	HR	SH	SF	HB	TBB	IBB	SO	WP	W	L	Pct	Sv-Op	Hld	Vel	OPS	ERC	ERA
2018	CWS	AL	8	0	1	9.2	44	12	8	8	3	1	0	1	6	1	6	0	0	0	-	0-0	0	95	1.109	9.13	7.45
2019	CWS	AL	16	1	2	19.2	86	17	13	10	3	1	2	0	8	0	20	0	1	1	.500	0-0	0	95	.707	3.54	4.58
	2 ML YEARS		24	1	3	29.1	130	29	21	18	6	2	2	1	14	1	26	0	1	1	.500	0-0	0	95	.839	5.14	5.52

Drew Butera

Bats: R **Throws:** R **Pos:** C-14;1B-3;PH-1   bue-TARE-ah   **Ht:** 6'1" **Wt:** 205 **Born:** 8/9/1983 **Age:** 36

Year	Team	Lg	G	AB	H	2B	3B	HR	(Hm	Rd)	TB	R	RBI	RC	TBB	IBB	SO	HBP	SH	SF	SB	CS	GDP	Avg	OBP	Slg	OPS
2019	Albq	AAA	67	223	67	16	2	9	(-	-)	114	38	40	46	33	2	55	2	0	4	2	0	4	.300	.389	.511	.901
2010	Min	AL	49	142	28	6	1	2	(0	2)	42	12	13	7	4	0	25	4	3	0	0	0	5	.197	.237	.296	.533
2011	Min	AL	93	234	39	9	1	2	(1	1)	56	19	23	11	11	0	42	2	6	1	0	0	7	.167	.210	.239	.449
2012	Min	AL	42	111	22	6	0	1	(1	0)	31	7	5	6	9	0	26	2	0	0	0	0	3	.198	.270	.279	.550
2013	2 Tms		6	10	1	0	0	0	(0	0)	1	0	0	0	0	0	5	0	0	0	0	0	0	.100	.100	.100	.200
2014	LAD	NL	61	170	32	6	1	3	(0	3)	49	16	14	10	17	1	41	2	1	2	0	0	1	.188	.267	.288	.555
2015	2 Tms	AL	55	107	21	3	0	1	(0	1)	27	9	5	6	6	0	26	2	5	0	0	1	0	.196	.252	.252	.505
2016	KC	AL	56	123	35	10	1	4	(0	4)	59	18	16	15	8	0	36	0	2	0	0	0	2	.285	.328	.480	.808
2017	KC	AL	75	163	37	4	1	3	(1	2)	52	18	14	18	12	0	41	1	1	0	0	0	0	.227	.284	.319	.603
2018	2 Tms		62	163	31	9	0	3	(2	1)	49	13	21	13	15	0	39	2	0	2	0	0	4	.190	.264	.301	.564
2019	Col	NL	16	43	7	3	0	0	(0	0)	10	6	3	1	4	0	14	0	1	1	0	0	2	.163	.229	.233	.462
13	Min	AL	2	3	0	0	0	0	(0	0)	0	0	0	0	0	0	1	0	0	0	0	0	0	.000	.000	.000	.000
13	LAD	NL	4	7	1	0	0	0	(0	0)	1	0	0	0	0	0	4	0	0	0	0	0	0	.143	.143	.143	.286
15	LAA	AL	10	21	4	0	0	0	(0	0)	4	3	0	0	0	0	2	0	0	0	0	1	0	.190	.190	.190	.381
15	KC	AL	45	86	17	3	0	1	(0	1)	23	6	5	6	6	0	24	2	5	0	0	0	0	.198	.266	.267	.533
18	KC	AL	52	149	28	9	0	2	(1	1)	43	11	18	10	13	0	37	2	0	2	0	0	4	.188	.259	.289	.548
18	Col	AL	10	14	3	0	0	1	(1	0)	6	2	3	3	2	0	2	0	0	0	0	0	0	.214	.313	.429	.741
	Postseason		4	3	0	0	0	0	(0	0)	0	0	0	0	0	0	2	0	0	0	0	0	0	.000	.400	.000	.400
	10 ML YEARS		515	1266	253	56	5	19	(5	14)	376	118	114	87	86	1	295	15	19	8	0	1	24	.200	.257	.297	.554

Ty Buttrey

Pitches: R **Bats:** L **Pos:** RP-72   **Ht:** 6'6" **Wt:** 240 **Born:** 3/31/1993 **Age:** 27

Year	Team	Lg	G	GS	GF	IP	BFP	H	R	ER	HR	SH	SF	HB	TBB	IBB	SO	WP	W	L	Pct	Sv-Op	Hld	Vel	OPS	ERC	ERA
2018	LAA	AL	16	0	4	16.1	70	15	7	6	0	1	1	0	5	0	20	0	0	1	.000	4-6	6	96	.591	2.52	3.31
2019	LAA	AL	72	0	6	72.1	309	69	34	32	8	0	2	5	23	0	84	6	6	7	.462	2-6	26	97	.690	3.83	3.98
	2 ML YEARS		88	0	10	88.2	379	84	41	38	8	1	3	5	28	0	104	6	6	8	.429	6-12	32	97	.672	3.57	3.86

Byron Buxton

Bats: R **Throws:** R **Pos:** CF-86;PR-3;DH-1 **Ht:** 6'2" **Wt:** 190 **Born:** 12/18/1993 **Age:** 26

Year	Team	Lg	G	AB	H	2B	3B	HR	(Hm	Rd)	TB	R	RBI	RC	TBB	IBB	SO	HBP	SH	SF	SB	CS	GDP	Avg	OBP	Slg	OPS
2015	Min	AL	46	129	27	7	1	2	(0	2)	42	16	6	10	6	0	44	1	2	0	2	2	1	.209	.250	.326	.576
2016	Min	AL	92	298	67	19	6	10	(6	4)	128	44	38	33	23	0	118	3	4	3	10	2	2	.225	.284	.430	.714
2017	Min	AL	140	462	117	14	6	16	(8	8)	191	69	51	63	38	2	150	4	5	2	29	1	1	.253	.314	.413	.728
2018	Min	AL	28	90	14	4	0	0	(0	0)	18	8	4	4	3	0	28	0	1	0	5	0	1	.156	.183	.200	.383
2019	Min	AL	87	271	71	30	4	10	(4	6)	139	48	46	44	19	1	68	2	2	1	14	3	3	.262	.314	.513	.827
	Postseason		1	2	0	0	0	0	(0	0)	0	0	1	0	0	0	1	0	0	0	1	0	0	.000	.000	.000	.000
5 ML YEARS			393	1250	296	74	17	38	(18	20)	518	185	145	154	89	3	408	10	14	6	60	8	8	.237	.292	.414	.706

Asdrubal Cabrera

Bats: B **Throws:** R **Pos:** 3B-98;2B-31;PH-5;1B-3;PR-1   azz-DRUE-bull   **Ht:** 6'0" **Wt:** 205 **Born:** 11/13/1985 **Age:** 34

Year	Team	Lg	G	AB	H	2B	3B	HR	(Hm	Rd)	TB	R	RBI	RC	TBB	IBB	SO	HBP	SH	SF	SB	CS	GDP	Avg	OBP	Slg	OPS
2007	Cle	AL	45	159	45	9	2	3	(1	2)	67	30	22	27	17	0	29	2	5	3	0	0	7	.283	.354	.421	.775
2008	Cle	AL	114	352	91	20	0	6	(5	1)	129	48	47	48	46	2	77	4	11	5	4	4	8	.259	.346	.366	.713
2009	Cle	AL	131	523	161	42	4	6	(4	2)	229	81	68	81	44	1	89	1	10	3	17	4	13	.308	.361	.438	.799
2010	Cle	AL	97	381	105	16	1	3	(2	1)	132	39	29	46	25	0	60	5	11	3	6	4	10	.276	.326	.346	.673
2011	Cle	AL	151	604	165	32	3	25	(13	12)	278	87	92	100	44	5	119	11	4	4	17	5	10	.273	.332	.460	.792
2012	Cle	AL	143	555	150	35	1	16	(10	6)	235	70	68	74	52	3	99	6	1	2	9	4	18	.270	.338	.423	.762
2013	Cle	AL	136	508	123	35	2	14	(8	6)	204	66	64	51	35	1	114	8	6	5	9	3	10	.242	.299	.402	.700
2014	2 Tms		146	553	133	31	4	14	(6	8)	214	74	61	57	49	2	108	7	1	6	10	2	15	.241	.307	.387	.694
2015	TB	AL	143	505	134	28	5	15	(7	8)	217	66	58	53	36	4	107	3	1	6	6	3	14	.265	.315	.430	.744
2016	NYM	NL	141	521	146	30	1	23	(18	5)	247	65	62	76	38	3	103	7	0	2	5	1	14	.280	.336	.474	.810
2017	NYM	NL	135	479	134	32	0	14	(5	9)	208	66	59	70	50	1	83	5	1	5	3	2	19	.280	.351	.434	.785
2018	2 Tms	NL	147	546	143	36	1	23	(10	13)	250	68	75	77	41	1	119	3	0	2	0	0	16	.262	.316	.458	.774
2019	2 Tms		131	447	116	25	1	18	(13	5)	197	69	91	79	57	2	103	3	0	7	4	0	9	.260	.342	.441	.783
14	Cle	AL	97	378	93	22	2	9	(5	4)	146	54	40	36	27	1	79	7	0	4	7	2	11	.246	.305	.386	.692
14	Was	NL	49	175	40	9	2	5	(1	4)	68	20	21	21	22	1	29	0	1	2	3	0	4	.229	.312	.389	.700
18	NYM	NL	98	375	104	23	1	18	(7	11)	183	48	58	57	29	1	81	1	0	2	0	0	12	.277	.329	.488	.817
18	Phi	NL	49	171	39	13	0	5	(3	2)	67	20	17	20	12	0	38	2	0	0	0	0	4	.228	.286	.392	.678
19	Tex	AL	93	323	76	15	0	12	(11	1)	127	45	51	47	38	1	85	3	0	4	4	0	6	.235	.318	.393	.711
19	Was	NL	38	124	40	10	1	6	(2	4)	70	24	40	32	19	1	18	0	0	3	0	0	3	.323	.404	.565	.969
	Postseason		17	68	14	1	0	2	(2	0)	21	7	8	6	3	0	18	0	3	1	0	0	3	.206	.236	.309	.545
13 ML YEARS			1660	6133	1646	371	25	180	(102	78)	2607	829	796	839	534	25	1210	65	51	53	90	32	163	.268	.331	.425	.756

Genesis Cabrera

Pitches: L **Bats:** L **Pos:** RP-11; SP-2 **Ht:** 6'2" **Wt:** 190 **Born:** 10/10/1996 **Age:** 23

			HOW MUCH PITCHED						WHAT HE GAVE UP										THE RESULTS							
Year	Team	Lg	G	GS	GF	IP	BFP	H	R	ER	HR	SH	SF	HB	TBB	IBB	SO	WP	W	L	Pct	Sv-Op	Hld	Vel	OPS	ERC	ERA
2019	Memp	AAA	20	18	0	99.0	434	107	68	65	20	3	0	5	39	0	106	4	5	6	.455	0- -	-	-	.852	5.54	5.91
2019	StL	NL	13	2	5	20.1	99	23	16	11	2	1	1	2	11	0	19	1	0	2	.000	1-1	1	96	.760	5.53	4.87

Melky Cabrera

Bats: B **Throws:** L **Pos:** RF-74;PH-44;LF-24;DH-2 **Ht:** 5'10" **Wt:** 210 **Born:** 8/11/1984 **Age:** 35

Year	Team	Lg	G	AB	H	2B	3B	HR	(Hm	Rd)	TB	R	RBI	RC	TBB	IBB	SO	HBP	SH	SF	SB	CS	GDP	Avg	OBP	Slg	OPS
2005	NYY	AL	6	19	4	0	0	0	(0	0)	4	1	0	0	0	0	2	0	0	0	0	0	0	.211	.211	.211	.421
2006	NYY	AL	130	460	129	26	2	7	(3	4)	180	75	50	68	56	3	59	2	5	1	12	5	9	.280	.360	.391	.752
2007	NYY	AL	150	545	149	24	8	8	(4	4)	213	66	73	70	43	0	68	5	10	9	13	5	14	.273	.327	.391	.718
2008	NYY	AL	129	414	103	12	1	8	(4	4)	141	42	37	37	29	5	58	3	4	3	9	2	11	.249	.301	.341	.641
2009	NYY	AL	154	485	133	28	1	13	(9	4)	202	66	68	69	43	4	59	4	4	4	10	2	15	.274	.336	.416	.752
2010	Atl	NL	147	458	117	27	3	4	(1	3)	162	50	42	45	42	11	64	1	5	3	7	1	8	.255	.317	.354	.671
2011	KC	AL	155	658	201	44	5	18	(6	12)	309	102	87	92	35	3	94	1	7	5	20	10	12	.305	.339	.470	.809
2012	SF	NL	113	459	159	25	10	11	(2	9)	237	84	60	83	36	4	63	0	1	5	13	5	8	**.346**	.390	.516	.906
2013	Tor	AL	88	344	96	15	2	3	(3	0)	124	39	30	39	23	0	47	0	2	3	2	2	7	.279	.322	.360	.682
2014	Tor	AL	139	568	171	35	3	16	(6	10)	260	81	73	84	43	3	67	3	2	5	6	2	19	.301	.351	.458	.808
2015	CWS	AL	158	629	172	36	2	12	(6	6)	248	70	77	81	40	2	88	2	2	**10**	3	0	18	.273	.314	.394	.709
2016	CWS	AL	151	591	175	42	5	14	(6	8)	269	70	86	89	47	2	69	0	3	5	2	0	17	.296	.345	.455	.800
2017	2 Tms		156	620	177	30	2	17	(9	8)	262	78	85	83	36	1	74	2	2	6	1	2	15	.285	.324	.423	.746
2018	Cle	AL	78	250	70	17	0	6	(1	5)	105	28	39	34	20	0	38	3	0	5	1	1	10	.280	.335	.420	.755
2019	Pit	NL	133	378	106	22	1	7	(3	4)	151	43	47	43	17	3	41	1	1	0	2	0	14	.280	.313	.399	.713
17	CWS	AL	98	397	117	17	0	13	(8	5)	173	54	56	59	25	1	52	1	2	3	0	0	3	.295	.336	.436	.771
17	KC	AL	58	223	60	13	2	4	(1	3)	89	24	29	24	11	0	22	1	0	3	1	2	12	.269	.303	.399	.702
	Postseason		25	83	17	2	0	1	(0	1)	22	8	7	5	3	0	16	0	2	0	0	0	0	.205	.233	.265	.498
15 ML YEARS			1887	6878	1962	383	45	144	(64	80)	2867	895	854	917	510	41	891	27	48	64	101	37	181	.285	.334	.417	.751

Miguel Cabrera

Bats: R **Throws:** R **Pos:** DH-107;1B-26;PH-3 **Ht:** 6'4" **Wt:** 249 **Born:** 4/18/1983 **Age:** 37

Year	Team	Lg	G	AB	H	2B	3B	HR	(Hm	Rd)	TB	R	RBI	RC	TBB	IBB	SO	HBP	SH	SF	SB	CS	GDP	Avg	OBP	Slg	OPS
2003	Fla	NL	87	314	84	21	3	12	(7	5)	147	39	62	51	25	3	84	2	4	1	0	2	12	.268	.325	.468	.793
2004	Fla	NL	160	603	177	31	1	33	(14	19)	309	101	112	92	68	5	148	6	0	8	5	2	20	.294	.366	.512	.879
2005	Fla	NL	158	613	198	43	2	33	(11	22)	344	106	116	108	64	12	125	2	0	6	1	0	20	.323	.385	.561	.947
2006	Fla	NL	158	576	195	50	2	26	(15	11)	327	112	114	132	86	27	108	10	0	4	9	6	18	.339	.430	.568	.998
2007	Fla	NL	157	588	188	38	2	34	(19	15)	332	91	119	122	79	23	127	5	1	7	2	1	17	.320	.401	.565	.965

Year	Team	Lg	G	AB	H	2B	3B	HR	(Hm	Rd)	TB	R	RBI	RC	TBB	IBB	SO	HBP	SH	SF	SB	CS	GDP	Avg	OBP	Slg	OPS
																								BATTING	**RUNNING**	**AVERAGES**	
2008	Det	AL	160	616	180	36	2	37	(19	18)	331	85	127	109	56	6	126	3	0	9	1	0	16	.292	.349	.537	.887
2009	Det	AL	160	611	198	34	0	34	(19	15)	334	96	103	114	68	14	107	5	0	1	6	2	22	.324	.396	.547	.942
2010	Det	AL	150	548	180	45	1	38	(17	21)	341	111	126	122	89	32	95	3	0	8	3	3	17	.328	.420	.622	1.042
2011	Det	AL	161	572	197	48	0	30	(15	15)	335	111	105	141	108	22	89	3	0	5	2	1	24	.344	.448	.586	1.033
2012	Det	AL	161	622	205	40	0	44	(28	16)	377	109	139	123	66	17	98	3	0	6	4	1	28	.330	.393	.606	.999
2013	Det	AL	148	555	193	26	1	44	(17	27)	353	103	137	146	90	19	94	5	0	2	3	0	19	.348	.442	.636	1.078
2014	Det	AL	159	611	191	52	1	25	(13	12)	320	101	109	110	60	10	117	3	0	11	1	1	19	.313	.371	.524	.895
2015	Det	AL	119	429	145	28	1	18	(7	11)	229	64	76	93	77	15	82	3	0	2	1	1	19	.338	.440	.534	.974
2016	Det	AL	158	595	188	31	1	38	(20	18)	335	92	108	106	75	15	116	4	0	5	0	0	26	.316	.393	.563	.956
2017	Det	AL	130	469	117	22	0	16	(11	5)	187	50	60	55	54	6	110	3	0	3	0	1	15	.249	.329	.399	.728
2018	Det	AL	38	134	40	11	0	3	(2	1)	60	17	22	23	22	4	27	0	0	1	0	0	6	.299	.395	.448	.843
2019	Det	AL	136	493	139	21	0	12	(5	7)	196	41	59	72	48	4	108	3	0	5	0	0	18	.282	.346	.398	.744
	Postseason		55	205	57	10	0	13	(4	9)	106	29	38	34	27	7	48	2	1	0	3	0	7	.278	.368	.517	.885
	17 ML YEARS		2400	8949	2815	577	17	477	(239	238)	4857	1429	1694	1719	1135	234	1761	63	5	84	38	21	318	.315	.392	.543	.935

Trevor Cahill

Pitches: R **Bats:** R **Pos:** RP-26; SP-11   KAY-hill   **Ht:** 6'4" **Wt:** 230 **Born:** 3/1/1988 **Age:** 32

Year	Team	Lg	G	GS	GF	IP	BFP	H	R	ER	HR	SH	SF	HB	TBB	IBB	SO	WP	W	L	Pct	Sv-Op	Hld	Vel	OPS	ERC	ERA
			HOW MUCH PITCHED					**WHAT HE GAVE UP**											**THE RESULTS**								
2009	Oak	AL	32	32	0	178.2	773	185	99	92	27	4	7	4	72	1	90	5	10	13	.435	0-0	0	90	.810	4.79	4.63
2010	Oak	AL	30	30	0	196.2	783	155	73	65	19	3	6	6	63	1	118	2	18	8	.692	0-0	0	90	.619	2.81	2.97
2011	Oak	AL	34	34	0	207.2	901	214	102	96	19	8	6	8	82	1	147	15	12	14	.462	0-0	0	89	.738	4.34	4.16
2012	Ari	NL	32	32	0	200.0	839	184	93	84	16	12	6	11	74	0	156	10	13	12	.520	0-0	0	89	.706	3.66	3.78
2013	Ari	NL	26	25	1	146.2	636	143	70	65	13	9	9	6	65	2	102	17	8	10	.444	0-0	0	89	.745	4.19	3.99
2014	Ari	NL	32	17	8	110.2	499	123	76	69	9	6	3	4	55	2	105	5	3	12	.200	1-2	0	90	.791	5.11	5.61
2015	2 Tms		26	3	6	43.1	187	44	27	26	4	3	1	2	16	1	36	2	1	3	.250	0-0	2	92	.725	4.15	5.40
2016	ChC	NL	50	1	16	65.2	284	49	22	20	7	0	0	5	35	3	66	3	4	4	.500	0-1	4	92	.621	3.42	2.74
2017	2 Tms		21	14	1	84.0	381	91	50	46	16	2	0	3	45	1	87	16	4	3	.571	0-0	1	91	.850	5.97	4.93
2018	Oak	AL	21	20	0	110.0	450	90	52	46	8	3	3	5	41	0	100	8	7	4	.636	0-0	0	92	.653	3.05	3.76
2019	LAA	AL	37	11	12	102.1	455	111	71	68	25	0	4	6	39	0	81	14	4	9	.308	0-0	0	92	.880	5.78	5.98
15	Atl	NL	15	3	6	26.1	124	36	23	22	2	2	1	1	11	1	14	1	0	3	.000	0-0	0	91	.843	6.22	7.52
15	ChC	NL	11	0	0	17.0	63	8	4	4	2	1	0	1	5	0	22	1	1	0	1.000	0-0	2	93	.494	1.52	2.12
17	SD	NL	11	11	0	61.0	263	58	29	25	6	1	0	3	24	1	72	14	4	3	.571	0-0	0	91	.712	3.92	3.69
17	KC	AL	10	3	1	23.0	118	33	21	21	10	1	0	0	21	0	15	2	0	0	-	0-0	1	91	1.180	12.52	8.22
	Postseason		6	0	1	5.1	24	7	2	2	0	1	0	0	0	0	8	1	1	1	.500	0-1	2	94	.783	3.29	3.38
	11 ML YEARS		341	219	44	1445.2	6188	1389	735	677	163	50	45	60	587	12	1088	97	84	92	.477	1-3	7	90	.738	4.16	4.21

Lorenzo Cain

Bats: R **Throws:** R **Pos:** CF-143;PH-9   **Ht:** 6'2" **Wt:** 205 **Born:** 4/13/1986 **Age:** 34

Year	Team	Lg	G	AB	H	2B	3B	HR	(Hm	Rd)	TB	R	RBI	RC	TBB	IBB	SO	HBP	SH	SF	SB	CS	GDP	Avg	OBP	Slg	OPS
												BATTING									**RUNNING**			**AVERAGES**			
2010	Mil	NL	43	147	45	11	1	1	(1	0)	61	17	13	23	9	0	28	1	0	1	7	1	1	.306	.348	.415	.763
2011	KC	AL	6	22	6	1	0	0	(0	0)	7	4	1	2	1	0	4	0	0	0	0	0	0	.273	.304	.318	.623
2012	KC	AL	61	222	59	9	2	7	(3	4)	93	27	31	32	15	0	56	3	0	4	10	0	4	.266	.316	.419	.734
2013	KC	AL	115	399	100	21	3	4	(3	1)	139	54	46	46	33	2	90	4	1	3	14	6	10	.251	.310	.348	.658
2014	KC	AL	133	471	142	29	4	5	(3	2)	194	55	53	67	24	2	108	4	0	3	28	5	9	.301	.339	.412	.751
2015	KC	AL	140	551	169	34	6	16	(9	7)	263	101	72	90	37	4	98	12	0	4	28	6	16	.307	.361	.477	.838
2016	KC	AL	103	397	114	19	1	9	(3	6)	162	56	56	53	31	3	84	2	0	4	14	5	15	.287	.339	.408	.747
2017	KC	AL	155	584	175	27	5	15	(3	12)	257	86	49	90	54	1	100	5	0	2	26	2	20	.300	.363	.440	.803
2018	Mil	NL	141	539	166	25	2	10	(4	6)	225	90	38	94	71	1	94	6	0	4	30	7	10	.308	.395	.417	.813
2019	Mil	NL	148	562	146	30	0	11	(7	4)	209	75	48	61	50	0	106	6	0	4	18	8	14	.260	.325	.372	.697
	Postseason		41	167	47	11	0	1	(0	1)	61	28	20	29	19	3	35	1	1	2	8	2	1	.281	.354	.365	.720
	10 ML YEARS		1045	3894	1122	206	24	78	(36	42)	1610	565	407	558	325	13	768	45	0	30	175	40	99	.288	.347	.413	.761

Kole Calhoun

Bats: L **Throws:** L **Pos:** RF-150;PH-4;CF-2   **Ht:** 5'10" **Wt:** 215 **Born:** 10/14/1987 **Age:** 32

Year	Team	Lg	G	AB	H	2B	3B	HR	(Hm	Rd)	TB	R	RBI	RC	TBB	IBB	SO	HBP	SH	SF	SB	CS	GDP	Avg	OBP	Slg	OPS
												BATTING									**RUNNING**			**AVERAGES**			
2012	LAA	AL	21	23	4	1	0	0	(0	0)	5	2	1	0	2	1	6	0	0	0	1	0	0	.174	.240	.217	.457
2013	LAA	AL	58	195	55	7	2	8	(5	3)	90	29	32	33	21	0	41	1	0	5	2	2	6	.282	.347	.462	.808
2014	LAA	AL	127	493	134	31	3	17	(7	10)	222	90	58	75	38	0	104	2	2	2	5	3	5	.272	.325	.450	.776
2015	LAA	AL	159	630	161	23	2	26	(16	10)	266	78	83	85	45	1	164	5	2	4	4	1	6	.256	.308	.422	.731
2016	LAA	AL	157	594	161	35	5	18	(7	11)	260	91	75	93	67	0	118	6	0	5	2	3	10	.271	.348	.438	.786
2017	LAA	AL	155	569	139	23	2	19	(8	11)	223	77	71	85	71	4	134	8	0	6	5	1	10	.244	.333	.392	.725
2018	LAA	AL	137	491	102	18	2	19	(9	10)	181	71	57	53	53	2	133	1	0	6	6	2	9	.208	.283	.369	.652
2019	LAA	AL	152	552	128	29	1	33	(16	17)	258	92	74	77	70	1	162	7	0	2	4	1	14	.232	.325	.467	.792
	Postseason		3	15	5	0	0	0	(0	0)	5	1	0	1	0	0	1	0	0	0	0	0	0	.333	.333	.333	.667
	8 ML YEARS		966	3547	884	167	17	140	(68	72)	1505	530	451	501	367	15	862	30	4	30	29	13	60	.249	.322	.424	.747

Willie Calhoun

Bats: L **Throws:** R **Pos:** LF-71;DH-7;PH-5;PR-1   **Ht:** 5'8" **Wt:** 187 **Born:** 11/4/1994 **Age:** 25

Year	Team	Lg	G	AB	H	2B	3B	HR	(Hm	Rd)	TB	R	RBI	RC	TBB	IBB	SO	HBP	SH	SF	SB	CS	GDP	Avg	OBP	Slg	OPS
												BATTING									**RUNNING**			**AVERAGES**			
2019	Nashv	AAA	41	138	41	8	0	8	(-	-)	73	23	28	32	32	0	24	1	1	0	1	1	4	.297	.433	.529	.962

Year Team	Lg	G	AB	H	2B	3B	HR	(Hm	Rd)	TB	R	RBI	RC	TBB	IBB	SO	HBP	SH	SF	SB	CS	GDP	Avg	OBP	Slg	OPS
2017 Tex	AL	13	34	9	0	0	1	(1	0)	12	3	4	6	2	0	7	1	0	0	0	0	0	.265	.324	.353	.677
2018 Tex	AL	35	99	22	5	0	2	(1	1)	33	8	11	11	6	0	24	1	0	2	0	0	2	.222	.269	.333	.602
2019 Tex	AL	83	309	83	14	1	21	(8	13)	162	51	48	49	23	0	53	3	0	2	0	0	5	.269	.323	.524	.848
3 ML YEARS		131	442	114	19	1	24	(10	14)	207	62	63	66	31	0	84	5	0	4	0	0	7	.258	.311	.468	.780

Johan Camargo

Bats: B **Throws:** R **Pos:** PH-39;SS-25;3B-18;LF-11;RF-5;PR-5;2B-4;1B-1;DH-1   **Ht:** 6'0" **Wt:** 195 **Born:** 12/13/1993 **Age:** 26

Year Team	Lg	G	AB	H	2B	3B	HR	(Hm	Rd)	TB	R	RBI	RC	TBB	IBB	SO	HBP	SH	SF	SB	CS	GDP	Avg	OBP	Slg	OPS
2019 Gwnntt	AAA	14	58	28	6	0	2	(-	-)	40	10	15	18	5	0	12	1	0	0	0	0	0	.483	.531	.690	1.221
2017 Atl	NL	82	241	72	21	2	4	(2	2)	109	30	27	32	12	2	51	0	2	1	0	0	5	.299	.331	.452	.783
2018 Atl	NL	134	464	126	27	1	19	(7	12)	212	63	76	72	51	4	108	6	0	3	1	1	13	.272	.349	.457	.806
2019 Atl	NL	98	232	54	12	1	7	(2	5)	89	31	32	27	15	2	43	0	1	0	1	0	5	.233	.279	.384	.663
Postseason		4	15	0	0	0	0	(0	0)	0	1	0	0	1	0	5	0	0	0	0	0	1	.000	.063	.000	.063
3 ML YEARS		314	937	252	60	4	30	(11	19)	410	124	135	131	78	8	202	6	3	4	2	1	23	.269	.328	.438	.765

Jeimer Candelario

Bats: B **Throws:** R **Pos:** 3B-69;1B-20;DH-4;PH-4   **Ht:** 6'1" **Wt:** 221 **Born:** 11/24/1993 **Age:** 26

Year Team	Lg	G	AB	H	2B	3B	HR	(Hm	Rd)	TB	R	RBI	RC	TBB	IBB	SO	HBP	SH	SF	SB	CS	GDP	Avg	OBP	Slg	OPS
2019 Toledo	AAA	39	153	49	10	2	9	(-	-)	90	30	33	36	22	0	35	3	0	0	0	0	1	.320	.416	.588	1.004
2016 ChC	NL	5	11	1	0	0	0	(0	0)	1	0	0	0	2	1	5	1	0	0	0	0	0	.091	.286	.091	.377
2017 2 Tms		38	127	36	9	0	3	(2	1)	54	18	16	19	13	0	30	2	0	0	0	0	3	.283	.359	.425	.784
2018 Det	AL	144	539	121	28	3	19	(10	9)	212	78	54	64	66	1	160	9	0	5	3	2	4	.224	.317	.393	.710
2019 Det	AL	94	335	68	17	2	8	(4	4)	113	33	32	35	43	1	99	7	0	1	3	1	3	.203	.306	.337	.643
17 ChC	NL	11	33	5	2	0	1	(0	1)	10	2	3	1	1	0	12	2	0	0	0	0	1	.152	.222	.303	.525
17 Det	AL	27	94	31	7	0	2	(2	0)	44	16	13	18	12	0	18	0	0	0	0	0	2	.330	.406	.468	.874
4 ML YEARS		281	1012	226	54	5	30	(16	14)	380	129	102	118	124	3	294	19	0	6	6	3	10	.223	.318	.375	.693

Mark Canha

Bats: R **Throws:** R **Pos:** CF-56;RF-27;DH-16;1B-15;LF-10;PH-10;PR-1   CAN-uh   **Ht:** 6'2" **Wt:** 212 **Born:** 2/15/1989 **Age:** 31

Year Team	Lg	G	AB	H	2B	3B	HR	(Hm	Rd)	TB	R	RBI	RC	TBB	IBB	SO	HBP	SH	SF	SB	CS	GDP	Avg	OBP	Slg	OPS
2015 Oak	AL	124	441	112	22	3	16	(8	8)	188	61	70	62	33	0	96	8	0	3	7	2	9	.254	.315	.426	.742
2016 Oak	AL	16	41	5	0	0	3	(1	2)	14	4	6	0	0	0	20	1	1	1	0	1	1	.122	.140	.341	.481
2017 Oak	AL	57	173	36	13	1	5	(3	2)	66	16	14	13	7	0	56	6	0	1	2	0	5	.208	.262	.382	.644
2018 Oak	AL	122	365	91	22	0	17	(8	9)	164	60	52	52	34	3	88	10	0	2	1	2	11	.249	.328	.449	.778
2019 Oak	AL	126	410	112	16	3	26	(15	11)	212	80	58	80	67	1	107	18	0	2	3	2	10	.273	.396	.517	.913
Postseason		1	1	0	0	0	0	(0	0)	0	0	0	0	0	0	1	0	0	0	0	0	0	.000	.000	.000	.000
5 ML YEARS		445	1430	356	73	7	67	(35	32)	644	221	200	207	141	4	367	43	1	9	13	7	36	.249	.333	.450	.783

Griffin Canning

Pitches: R **Bats:** R **Pos:** SP-17; RP-1   **Ht:** 6'2" **Wt:** 180 **Born:** 5/11/1996 **Age:** 24

Year Team	Lg	G	GS	GF	IP	BFP	H	R	ER	HR	SH	SF	HB	TBB	IBB	SO	WP	W	L	Pct	Sv-Op	Hld	Vel	OPS	ERC	ERA
2018 Mobile	AA	10	10	0	45.2	180	27	11	10	2	0	1	1	19	0	49	4	1	0	1.000	0- -	-	-	.488	1.82	1.97
2018 Salt Lk	AAA	13	13	0	59.0	261	68	36	36	6	1	3	4	22	0	64	2	3	3	.500	0- -	-	-	.838	5.22	5.49
2019 LAA	AL	18	17	1	90.1	384	80	46	46	14	1	4	8	30	0	96	9	5	6	.455	0-0	0	94	.739	3.87	4.58

Robinson Cano

Bats: L **Throws:** R **Pos:** 2B-99;PH-7;DH-2   kuh-NOE   **Ht:** 6'0" **Wt:** 210 **Born:** 10/22/1982 **Age:** 37

Year Team	Lg	G	AB	H	2B	3B	HR	(Hm	Rd)	TB	R	RBI	RC	TBB	IBB	SO	HBP	SH	SF	SB	CS	GDP	Avg	OBP	Slg	OPS
2005 NYY	AL	132	522	155	34	4	14	(5	9)	239	78	62	59	16	1	68	3	7	3	1	3	16	.297	.320	.458	.778
2006 NYY	AL	122	482	165	41	1	15	(9	6)	253	62	78	74	18	3	54	2	1	5	5	2	19	.342	.365	.525	.890
2007 NYY	AL	160	617	189	41	7	19	(10	9)	301	93	97	94	39	5	85	8	1	4	4	5	19	.306	.353	.488	.841
2008 NYY	AL	159	597	162	35	3	14	(7	7)	245	70	72	64	26	3	65	5	1	5	2	4	18	.271	.305	.410	.715
2009 NYY	AL	161	637	204	48	2	25	(14	11)	331	103	85	79	30	2	63	3	0	4	5	7	22	.320	.352	.520	.871
2010 NYY	AL	160	626	200	41	3	29	(16	13)	334	103	109	118	57	14	77	8	0	5	3	2	19	.319	.381	.534	.914
2011 NYY	AL	159	623	188	46	7	28	(16	12)	332	104	118	111	38	11	96	12	0	8	8	2	18	.302	.349	.533	.882
2012 NYY	AL	161	627	196	48	1	33	(22	11)	345	105	94	110	61	10	96	7	0	2	3	2	22	.313	.379	.550	.929
2013 NYY	AL	160	605	190	41	0	27	(11	16)	312	81	107	120	65	16	85	6	0	5	7	1	18	.314	.383	.516	.899
2014 Sea	AL	157	595	187	37	2	14	(9	5)	270	77	82	106	61	20	68	6	0	3	10	3	19	.314	.382	.454	.836
2015 Sea	AL	156	624	179	34	1	21	(11	10)	278	82	79	84	43	5	107	3	0	4	2	6	26	.287	.334	.446	.779
2016 Sea	AL	161	655	195	33	2	39	(17	22)	349	107	103	100	47	8	100	8	0	5	0	1	18	.298	.350	.533	.882
2017 Sea	AL	150	592	166	33	0	23	(11	12)	268	79	97	96	49	8	85	4	0	3	1	0	18	.280	.338	.453	.791
2018 Sea	AL	80	310	94	22	0	10	(5	5)	146	44	50	55	32	2	47	4	0	2	0	0	9	.303	.374	.471	.845
2019 NYM	NL	107	390	100	28	0	13	(6	7)	167	46	39	40	25	3	69	5	0	3	0	0	16	.256	.307	.428	.736
Postseason		51	203	45	10	3	8	(5	3)	85	22	33	23	11	3	28	2	0	1	0	2	7	.222	.267	.419	.686
15 ML YEARS		2185	8502	2570	562	33	324	(169	155)	4170	1234	1272	1310	607	111	1165	84	10	61	51	38	277	.302	.352	.490	.843

Matt Carasiti

Pitches: R **Bats:** R **Pos:** RP-6; SP-5   **Ht:** 6'3" **Wt:** 210 **Born:** 7/23/1991 **Age:** 28

Year	Team	Lg	G	GS	GF	IP	BFP	H	R	ER	HR	SH	SF	HB	TBB	IBB	SO	WP	W	L	Pct	Sv-Op	Hld	Vel	OPS	ERC	ERA
2019	Iowa	AAA	16	0	5	27.0	114	20	11	8	1	0	2	3	11	0	23	5	1	1	.500	1--	-	-	.584	2.68	2.67
2019	Tacom	AAA	15	0	13	16.1	75	19	11	9	3	0	0	0	7	0	17	2	1	0	1.000	4--	-	-	.817	5.64	4.96
2016	Col	NL	19	0	7	15.2	83	25	17	16	1	0	2	3	11	0	17	2	1	0	1.000	0-0	2	94	1.052	9.75	9.19
2019	Sea	AL	11	5	2	9.2	43	11	6	5	2	0	1	0	5	0	10	4	0	1	.000	0-0	0	95	.886	6.36	4.66
	2 ML YEARS		30	5	9	25.1	126	36	23	21	3	0	3	3	16	0	27	6	1	1	.500	0-0	2	95	.994	8.46	7.46

Victor Caratini

Bats: B **Throws:** R **Pos:** C-59;1B-23;PH-23;3B-2   **Ht:** 6'1" **Wt:** 215 **Born:** 8/17/1993 **Age:** 26

								BATTING													RUNNING			AVERAGES			
Year	Team	Lg	G	AB	H	2B	3B	HR	(Hm	Rd)	TB	R	RBI	RC	TBB	IBB	SO	HBP	SH	SF	SB	CS	GDP	Avg	OBP	Slg	OPS
2017	ChC	NL	31	59	15	3	0	1	(0	1)	21	6	2	3	4	1	13	3	0	0	0	0	3	.254	.333	.356	.689
2018	ChC	NL	76	181	42	7	0	2	(1	1)	55	21	21	15	12	0	42	4	2	1	0	0	5	.232	.293	.304	.597
2019	ChC	NL	95	244	65	11	0	11	(4	7)	109	31	34	35	29	0	59	3	0	3	1	0	6	.266	.348	.447	.794
	Postseason		1	1	0	0	0	0	(0	0)	0	0	0	0	0	0	0	0	0	0	0	0	0	.000	.000	.000	.000
	3 ML YEARS		202	484	122	21	0	14	(5	9)	185	58	57	53	45	1	114	10	2	4	1	0	14	.252	.326	.382	.708

Shane Carle

Pitches: R **Bats:** R **Pos:** RP-6   carl   **Ht:** 6'4" **Wt:** 210 **Born:** 8/30/1991 **Age:** 28

Year	Team	Lg	G	GS	GF	IP	BFP	H	R	ER	HR	SH	SF	HB	TBB	IBB	SO	WP	W	L	Pct	Sv-Op	Hld	Vel	OPS	ERC	ERA
2019	Gwnntt	AAA	20	1	4	33.1	151	39	20	19	2	1	1	0	14	2	31	3	4	2	.667	0--	-	-	.805	4.67	5.13
2019	Nashv	AAA	7	0	1	6.2	36	13	7	6	0	0	0	0	3	0	4	1	1	0	1.000	0--	-	-	.899	9.16	8.10
2017	Col	NL	3	0	3	4.0	19	6	3	3	1	0	0	0	0	0	4	1	0	0	-	0-0	0	94	.842	5.94	6.75
2018	Atl	NL	53	0	8	63.0	259	50	22	20	2	1	4	1	27	7	43	2	4	1	.800	1-2	14	95	.616	2.56	2.86
2019	Atl	NL	6	0	0	9.1	49	11	10	10	3	0	0	3	9	2	6	0	0	0	-	0-0	0	95	1.145	10.85	9.64
	3 ML YEARS		62	0	11	76.1	327	67	35	33	6	1	4	4	36	9	53	3	4	1	.800	1-2	14	95	.704	3.56	3.89

David Carpenter

Pitches: R **Bats:** R **Pos:** RP-4   **Ht:** 6'3" **Wt:** 250 **Born:** 7/15/1985 **Age:** 34

Year	Team	Lg	G	GS	GF	IP	BFP	H	R	ER	HR	SH	SF	HB	TBB	IBB	SO	WP	W	L	Pct	Sv-Op	Hld	Vel	OPS	ERC	ERA
2019	Nashv	AAA	39	0	38	38.2	154	30	8	7	3	1	1	2	13	0	42	0	2	0	1.000	21--	-	-	.623	2.79	1.63
2011	Hou	NL	34	0	12	27.2	125	28	9	9	3	4	1	4	13	7	29	2	1	3	.250	1-2	3	94	.809	4.62	2.93
2012	2 Tms		33	0	9	32.1	163	51	31	29	5	2	0	2	16	4	31	2	0	2	.000	0-1	2	94	.953	8.52	8.07
2013	Atl	NL	56	0	14	65.2	256	45	13	13	5	2	4	3	20	3	74	4	4	1	.800	0-0	12	95	.558	2.12	1.78
2014	Atl	NL	65	0	14	61.0	259	61	27	24	5	1	1	3	16	0	67	1	6	4	.600	3-6	19	96	.663	3.59	3.54
2015	2 Tms		30	0	5	24.2	107	25	12	11	4	3	1	1	9	1	15	1	0	1	.000	0-2	6	95	.810	4.54	4.01
2019	Tex	AL	4	0	2	3.1	19	4	4	2	0	0	0	0	4	0	2	0	0	0	-	0-0	0	93	.821	7.07	5.40
12	Hou	NL	30	0	8	29.2	143	43	21	20	4	2	0	1	14	3	27	2	0	2	.000	0-1	2	94	.895	7.38	6.07
12	Tor	AL	3	0	1	2.2	20	8	10	9	1	0	0	1	2	1	4	0	0	0	-	0-0	0	94	1.374	22.64	30.38
15	NYY	AL	22	0	2	18.2	82	20	11	10	3	3	1	1	7	1	11	0	0	1	.000	0-2	5	95	.869	4.97	4.82
15	Was	NL	8	0	3	6.0	25	5	1	1	1	0	0	0	2	0	4	1	0	0	-	0-0	4	95	.628	3.28	1.50
	Postseason		3	0	1	2.2	12	3	4	4	2	0	0	0	1	0	3	0	0	1	.000	0-1	1	96	1.242	9.34	13.50
	6 ML YEARS		222	0	56	214.2	929	214	96	88	22	12	7	13	78	15	218	10	11	11	.500	4-11	42	95	.723	4.06	3.69

Matt Carpenter

Bats: L **Throws:** R **Pos:** 3B-107;PH-21;1B-4;DH-2   **Ht:** 6'3" **Wt:** 205 **Born:** 11/26/1985 **Age:** 34

								BATTING													RUNNING			AVERAGES			
Year	Team	Lg	G	AB	H	2B	3B	HR	(Hm	Rd)	TB	R	RBI	RC	TBB	IBB	SO	HBP	SH	SF	SB	CS	GDP	Avg	OBP	Slg	OPS
2011	StL	NL	7	15	1	1	0	0	(0	0)	2	0	0	0	4	0	4	0	0	0	0	0	0	.067	.263	.133	.396
2012	StL	NL	114	296	87	22	5	6	(3	3)	137	44	46	46	34	2	63	3	0	7	1	1	10	.294	.365	.463	.828
2013	StL	NL	157	626	199	55	7	11	(6	5)	301	126	78	119	72	1	98	9	3	7	3	3	4	.318	.392	.481	.873
2014	StL	NL	158	595	162	33	2	8	(4	4)	223	99	59	93	95	2	111	8	2	9	5	3	3	.272	.375	.375	.750
2015	StL	NL	154	574	156	44	3	28	(13	15)	290	101	84	108	81	5	151	6	0	4	4	3	5	.272	.365	.505	.871
2016	StL	NL	129	473	128	36	6	21	(9	12)	239	81	68	87	81	6	108	5	3	4	0	4	4	.271	.380	.505	.885
2017	StL	NL	145	497	120	31	2	23	(9	14)	224	91	69	94	109	4	125	9	2	5	2	1	5	.241	.384	.451	.835
2018	StL	NL	156	564	145	42	0	36	(13	23)	295	111	81	107	102	17	158	6	0	4	4	1	0	.257	.374	.523	.897
2019	StL	NL	129	416	94	20	2	15	(8	7)	163	59	46	61	63	0	129	7	1	5	6	1	3	.226	.334	.392	.726
	Postseason		39	136	33	8	1	6	(4	2)	61	20	16	19	11	0	39	1	0	2	1	0	1	.243	.300	.449	.749
	9 ML YEARS		1149	4056	1092	284	27	148	(65	83)	1874	712	531	715	641	37	947	53	11	45	25	17	34	.269	.372	.462	.835

Ryan Carpenter

Pitches: L **Bats:** L **Pos:** SP-9   **Ht:** 6'5" **Wt:** 230 **Born:** 8/22/1990 **Age:** 29

Year	Team	Lg	G	GS	GF	IP	BFP	H	R	ER	HR	SH	SF	HB	TBB	IBB	SO	WP	W	L	Pct	Sv-Op	Hld	Vel	OPS	ERC	ERA
2019	Toledo	AAA	14	14	0	77.0	334	77	45	45	11	0	4	8	26	0	76	1	5	7	.417	0--	-	-	.809	4.56	5.26
2018	Det	AL	6	5	0	22.1	107	34	19	18	8	0	2	3	4	0	15	0	1	2	.333	0-0	0	90	1.026	8.93	7.25
2019	Det	AL	9	9	0	40.2	197	61	46	42	12	0	2	2	13	0	25	0	1	6	.143	0-0	0	90	1.014	8.48	9.30
	2 ML YEARS		15	14	0	63.0	304	95	65	60	20	0	4	5	17	0	40	0	2	8	.200	0-0	0	90	1.018	8.64	8.57

Carlos Carrasco

Pitches: R Bats: R Pos: SP-12; RP-11   Ht: 6'4" Wt: 224 Born: 3/21/1987 Age: 33

			HOW MUCH PITCHED					WHAT HE GAVE UP											THE RESULTS								
Year Team	Lg	G	GS	GF	IP	BFP	H	R	ER	HR	SH	SF	HB	TBB	IBB	SO	WP	W	L	Pct	Sv-Op	Hld	Vel	OPS	ERC	ERA
2009 Cle	AL	5	5	0	22.1	112	40	23	22	6	0	1	0	11	1	11	0	0	4	.000	0-0	0	92	1.125	11.36	8.87
2010 Cle	AL	7	7	0	44.2	188	47	20	19	6	2	1	1	14	1	38	1	2	2	.500	0-0	0	93	.816	4.42	3.83
2011 Cle	AL	21	21	0	124.2	536	130	68	64	15	3	7	4	40	3	85	3	8	9	.471	0-0	0	92	.754	4.24	4.62
2013 Cle	AL	15	7	5	46.2	218	64	36	35	4	2	3	1	18	2	30	2	1	4	.200	0-0	0	95	.864	6.11	6.75
2014 Cle	AL	40	14	12	134.0	529	103	40	38	7	2	3	3	29	1	140	4	8	7	.533	1-1	0	95	.543	2.00	2.55
2015 Cle	AL	30	30	0	183.2	730	154	75	74	18	1	6	5	43	2	216	5	14	12	.538	0-0	0	95	.646	2.72	3.63
2016 Cle	AL	25	25	0	146.1	599	134	64	54	21	1	3	3	34	2	150	4	11	8	.579	0-0	0	94	.711	3.31	3.32
2017 Cle	AL	32	32	0	200.0	798	173	73	73	21	1	6	10	46	2	226	10	18	6	.750	0-0	0	94	.674	2.99	3.29
2018 Cle	AL	32	30	1	192.0	784	173	78	72	21	4	5	6	43	4	231	9	17	10	.630	0-0	0	93	.669	3.02	3.38
2019 Cle	AL	23	12	3	80.0	341	92	48	47	18	2	2	2	16	1	96	2	6	7	.462	1-2	0	93	.867	5.11	5.29
Postseason		2	2	0	11.0	44	9	2	2	0	1	0	1	4	0	10	0	0	1	.000	0-0	0	94	.562	2.79	1.64
10 ML YEARS		230	183	21	1174.1	4835	1110	525	498	137	18	37	35	294	19	1223	40	85	69	.552	2-3	0	94	.706	3.43	3.82

Curt Casali

Bats: R Throws: R Pos: C-67;PH-19;1B-4;DH-1;PR-1   cuh-SAL-ee   Ht: 6'3" Wt: 225 Born: 11/9/1988 Age: 31

			BATTING																RUNNING			AVERAGES			
Year Team	Lg	G	AB	H	2B	3B	HR	(Hm Rd)	TB	R	RBI	RC	TBB	IBB	SO	HBP	SH	SF	SB	CS	GDP	Avg	OBP	Slg	OPS
2014 TB	AL	30	72	12	3	0	0	(0 0)	15	10	3	3	8	0	23	2	2	0	0	0	2	.167	.268	.208	.477
2015 TB	AL	38	101	24	6	0	10	(7 3)	60	13	18	14	8	0	34	2	1	1	0	0	2	.238	.304	.594	.898
2016 TB	AL	84	226	42	10	0	8	(3 5)	76	23	25	18	25	1	82	2	3	0	0	0	2	.186	.273	.336	.609
2017 TB	AL	9	9	3	0	0	1	(1 0)	6	2	3	2	3	0	3	0	0	1	0	0	0	.333	.462	.667	1.128
2018 Cin	NL	52	140	41	10	0	4	(2 2)	63	15	16	17	12	1	32	2	1	1	0	2	5	.293	.355	.450	.805
2019 Cin	NL	84	207	52	9	0	8	(2 6)	85	24	32	24	25	1	59	1	0	3	0	0	1	.251	.331	.411	.741
6 ML YEARS		297	755	174	38	0	31	(15 16)	305	87	97	78	81	3	233	9	7	6	0	2	12	.230	.310	.404	.714

Andrew Cashner

Pitches: R Bats: R Pos: SP-23; RP-19   Ht: 6'6" Wt: 235 Born: 9/11/1986 Age: 33

			HOW MUCH PITCHED					WHAT HE GAVE UP											THE RESULTS								
Year Team	Lg	G	GS	GF	IP	BFP	H	R	ER	HR	SH	SF	HB	TBB	IBB	SO	WP	W	L	Pct	Sv-Op	Hld	Vel	OPS	ERC	ERA
2010 ChC	NL	53	0	9	54.1	248	55	31	29	8	6	2	4	30	5	50	4	2	6	.250	0-1	16	96	.795	5.22	4.80
2011 ChC	NL	7	1	0	10.2	39	3	2	2	1	0	0	0	4	0	8	0	0	0	-	0-0	1	95	.351	0.91	1.69
2012 SD	NL	33	5	5	46.1	196	42	23	22	5	3	1	1	19	1	52	2	3	4	.429	0-4	6	98	.688	3.73	4.27
2013 SD	NL	31	26	2	175.0	707	151	68	60	12	6	3	4	47	3	128	5	10	9	.526	0-0	1	95	.639	2.74	3.09
2014 SD	NL	19	19	0	123.1	506	110	42	35	7	3	4	1	29	3	93	2	5	7	.417	0-0	0	94	.623	2.57	2.55
2015 SD	NL	31	31	0	184.2	804	200	111	89	19	8	6	6	66	2	165	3	6	16	.273	0-0	0	95	.772	4.53	4.34
2016 2 Tms	NL	28	27	1	132.0	588	142	83	77	19	6	5	7	60	3	112	3	5	11	.313	0-0	0	94	.849	5.28	5.25
2017 Tex	AL	28	28	0	166.2	704	156	75	63	15	2	5	9	64	0	86	10	11	11	.500	0-0	0	93	.692	3.86	3.40
2018 Bal	AL	28	28	0	153.0	681	177	97	90	25	1	3	3	65	3	99	6	4	15	.211	0-0	0	92	.856	5.69	5.29
2019 2 Tms	AL	42	23	3	150.0	650	144	84	78	19	1	3	4	58	0	108	8	11	8	.579	1-1	4	94	.742	4.14	4.68
16 SD	NL	16	16	0	79.1	347	80	47	42	13	4	3	6	30	0	67	1	4	7	.364	0-0	0	94	.821	4.80	4.76
16 Mia	NL	12	11	1	52.2	241	62	36	35	6	2	2	1	30	3	45	2	1	4	.200	0-0	0	93	.889	6.01	5.98
19 Bal	AL	17	17	0	96.1	400	86	45	41	11	0	2	1	29	0	66	4	9	3	.750	0-0	0	94	.665	3.23	3.83
19 Bos	AL	25	6	3	53.2	236	58	39	37	8	1	1	3	29	0	42	4	2	5	.286	1-1	4	95	.878	5.98	6.20
10 ML YEARS		300	188	20	1196.0	5109	1180	616	545	130	36	32	39	442	20	901	43	57	87	.396	1-6	28	94	.738	4.07	4.10

Nicholas Castellanos

Bats: R Throws: R Pos: RF-137;LF-11;DH-11   cahs-teh-YAHN-ohs   Ht: 6'4" Wt: 203 Born: 3/4/1992 Age: 28

			BATTING																RUNNING			AVERAGES			
Year Team	Lg	G	AB	H	2B	3B	HR	(Hm Rd)	TB	R	RBI	RC	TBB	IBB	SO	HBP	SH	SF	SB	CS	GDP	Avg	OBP	Slg	OPS
2013 Det	AL	11	18	5	0	0	0	(0 0)	5	1	0	1	0	0	1	0	0	0	0	0	0	.278	.278	.278	.556
2014 Det	AL	148	533	138	31	4	11	(6 5)	210	50	66	63	36	3	140	3	0	7	2	2	7	.259	.306	.394	.700
2015 Det	AL	154	549	140	33	6	15	(6 9)	230	42	73	66	39	1	152	1	0	6	0	3	21	.255	.303	.419	.721
2016 Det	AL	110	411	117	25	4	18	(5 13)	204	54	58	67	28	1	111	3	0	5	1	1	4	.285	.331	.496	.827
2017 Det	AL	157	614	167	36	10	26	(14 12)	301	73	101	97	41	0	142	5	0	5	4	5	12	.272	.320	.490	.811
2018 Det	AL	157	620	185	46	5	23	(10 13)	310	88	89	110	49	5	151	6	0	3	2	1	8	.298	.354	.500	.854
2019 2 Tms		151	615	178	58	3	27	(11 16)	323	100	73	94	41	1	143	5	0	3	2	2	12	.289	.337	.525	.863
19 Det	AL	100	403	110	37	3	11	(3 8)	186	57	37	54	31	1	96	3	0	2	2	1	7	.273	.328	.462	.790
19 ChC	NL	51	212	68	21	0	16	(8 8)	137	43	36	40	10	0	47	2	0	1	0	1	5	.321	.356	.646	1.002
Postseason		3	10	1	0	0	1	(0 1)	4	1	1	0	2	1	1	0	0	0	0	0	0	.100	.250	.400	.650
7 ML YEARS		888	3360	930	229	32	120	(52 68)	1583	408	460	498	234	11	840	23	0	29	11	14	64	.277	.326	.471	.797

Diego Castillo

Pitches: R Bats: R Pos: RP-59; SP-6   Ht: 6'3" Wt: 250 Born: 1/18/1994 Age: 26

			HOW MUCH PITCHED					WHAT HE GAVE UP											THE RESULTS								
Year Team	Lg	G	GS	GF	IP	BFP	H	R	ER	HR	SH	SF	HB	TBB	IBB	SO	WP	W	L	Pct	Sv-Op	Hld	Vel	OPS	ERC	ERA
2018 TB	AL	43	11	5	56.2	222	36	21	20	6	0	0	2	18	0	65	5	4	2	.667	0-2	10	98	.554	2.09	3.18
2019 TB	AL	65	6	18	68.2	290	59	32	26	8	1	1	5	26	4	81	5	5	8	.385	8-10	17	98	.685	3.53	3.41
2 ML YEARS		108	17	23	125.1	512	95	53	46	14	1	1	7	44	4	146	10	9	10	.474	8-12	27	98	.628	2.85	3.30

Jose Castillo

Pitches: L Bats: L Pos: RP-1   Ht: 6'5" Wt: 246 Born: 1/10/1996 Age: 24

			HOW MUCH PITCHED					WHAT HE GAVE UP										THE RESULTS						
Year	Team	Lg	G	GS	GF	IP	BFP	H	R	ER	HR	SH	SF	HB	TBB	IBB	SO	WP	W	L	Pct	Sv-Op Hld	Vel	OPS	ERC	ERA
2019	2 Tms	Low	7	2	1	6.2	26	4	3	3	1	0	0	1	1	0	15	0	0	1	.000	0- - -	-	.606	1.94	4.05
2018	SD	NL	37	0	5	38.1	150	23	14	14	3	0	0	3	12	1	52	1	3	3	.500	0-1 12	95	.520	1.87	3.29
2019	SD	NL	1	0	0	0.2	4	0	0	0	0	0	0	1	1	0	2	1	0	0	-	0-0 0	95	.500	7.00	0.00
	2 ML YEARS		38	0	5	39.0	154	23	14	14	3	0	0	4	13	1	54	2	3	3	.500	0-1 12	95	.523	1.96	3.23

Luis Castillo

Pitches: R Bats: R Pos: SP-32   Ht: 6'2" Wt: 190 Born: 12/12/1992 Age: 27

			HOW MUCH PITCHED					WHAT HE GAVE UP										THE RESULTS						
Year	Team	Lg	G	GS	GF	IP	BFP	H	R	ER	HR	SH	SF	HB	TBB	IBB	SO	WP	W	L	Pct	Sv-Op Hld	Vel	OPS	ERC	ERA
2017	Cin	NL	15	15	0	89.1	359	64	32	31	11	4	3	3	32	1	98	2	3	7	.300	0-0 0	97	.638	2.70	3.12
2018	Cin	NL	31	31	0	169.2	708	158	89	81	28	3	6	5	49	1	165	4	10	12	.455	0-0 0	96	.732	3.80	4.30
2019	Cin	NL	32	32	0	190.2	781	139	76	72	22	6	1	7	79	0	226	5	15	8	.652	0-0 0	96	.633	2.94	3.40
	3 ML YEARS		78	78	0	449.2	1848	361	197	184	61	13	10	15	160	2	489	11	28	27	.509	0-0 0	96	.673	3.21	3.68

Welington Castillo

Bats: R Throws: R Pos: C-48;DH-20;PH-9   WELL-ing-tunn   Ht: 5'10" Wt: 220 Born: 4/24/1987 Age: 33

			BATTING																		RUNNING			AVERAGES			
Year	Team	Lg	G	AB	H	2B	3B	HR	(Hm	Rd)	TB	R	RBI	RC	TBB	IBB	SO	HBP	SH	SF	SB	CS	GDP	Avg	OBP	Slg	OPS
2010	ChC	NL	7	20	6	4	0	1	(0	1)	13	3	5	3	1	0	7	0	0	0	0	0	0	.300	.333	.650	.983
2011	ChC	NL	4	13	2	0	0	0	(0	0)	2	0	0	0	0	0	4	0	0	0	0	0	1	.154	.154	.154	.308
2012	ChC	NL	52	170	45	11	0	5	(4	1)	71	16	22	22	17	2	51	2	0	1	0	0	4	.265	.337	.418	.754
2013	ChC	NL	113	380	104	23	0	8	(1	7)	151	41	32	44	34	3	97	11	1	2	2	0	13	.274	.349	.397	.746
2014	ChC	NL	110	380	90	19	0	13	(7	6)	148	28	46	44	26	0	102	7	2	2	0	0	7	.237	.296	.389	.686
2015	3 Tms		110	342	81	15	1	19	(7	12)	155	42	57	41	25	1	92	6	0	5	0	0	12	.237	.296	.453	.750
2016	Ari	NL	113	416	110	24	0	14	(8	6)	176	41	68	58	33	3	121	4	0	4	2	0	5	.264	.322	.423	.745
2017	Bal	AL	96	341	96	11	0	20	(13	7)	167	44	53	52	22	0	97	0	0	2	0	0	10	.282	.323	.490	.813
2018	CWS	AL	49	170	44	7	0	6	(3	3)	69	17	15	16	9	0	46	2	0	0	1	0	7	.259	.304	.406	.710
2019	CWS	AL	72	230	48	12	0	12	(5	7)	96	19	41	30	16	0	74	3	0	2	0	0	8	.209	.267	.417	.684
15	ChC	NL	24	43	7	2	0	2	(1	1)	15	5	5	5	3	1	12	1	0	0	0	0	0	.163	.234	.349	.583
15	Sea		6	25	4	0	0	0	(0	0)	4	3	2	0	1	0	5	0	0	2	0	0	2	.160	.179	.160	.339
15	Ari	NL	80	274	70	13	1	17	(6	11)	136	34	50	39	21	0	75	5	0	3	0	0	10	.255	.317	.496	.813
	10 ML YEARS		726	2462	626	126	1	98	(48	50)	1048	251	339	310	183	9	691	35	3	18	5	0	67	.254	.313	.426	.738

Wilkin Castillo

Bats: B Throws: R Pos: C-2   Ht: 6'0" Wt: 215 Born: 6/1/1984 Age: 36

			BATTING																		RUNNING			AVERAGES			
Year	Team	Lg	G	AB	H	2B	3B	HR	(Hm	Rd)	TB	R	RBI	RC	TBB	IBB	SO	HBP	SH	SF	SB	CS	GDP	Avg	OBP	Slg	OPS
2019	NewOr	AAA	58	196	49	9	2	6	(-	-)	80	23	24	26	16	2	30	1	1	0	5	1	4	.250	.310	.408	.718
2008	Cin	NL	18	32	9	1	0	0	(0	0)	10	6	1	3	1	0	5	0	1	0	0	0	0	.281	.303	.313	.616
2009	Cin	NL	4	3	2	0	0	0	(0	0)	2	0	1	1	0	0	0	0	0	0	0	0	0	.667	.667	.667	1.333
2019	Mia	NL	2	7	1	1	0	0	(0	0)	2	0	2	1	0	0	3	0	0	0	0	0	0	.143	.143	.286	.429
	3 ML YEARS		24	42	12	2	0	0	(0	0)	14	6	4	5	1	0	8	0	1	0	0	0	0	.286	.302	.333	.636

Harold Castro

Bats: L Throws: R Pos: 2B-34;CF-30;3B-10;LF-8;RF-7;PH-6;DH-4;SS-2;PR-2;1B-1   Ht: 6'0" Wt: 180 Born: 11/30/1993 Age: 26

			BATTING																		RUNNING			AVERAGES			
Year	Team	Lg	G	AB	H	2B	3B	HR	(Hm	Rd)	TB	R	RBI	RC	TBB	IBB	SO	HBP	SH	SF	SB	CS	GDP	Avg	OBP	Slg	OPS
2019	Toledo	AAA	31	122	40	5	1	4	(-	-)	59	20	25	20	9	0	26	0	2	1	1	3	5	.328	.371	.484	.855
2018	Det	AL	6	10	3	0	0	0	(0	0)	3	2	0	1	0	0	2	0	0	0	0	0	0	.300	.300	.300	.600
2019	Det	AL	97	354	103	10	4	5	(2	3)	136	30	38	44	9	0	86	0	2	4	4	2	6	.291	.305	.384	.689
	2 ML YEARS		103	364	106	10	4	5	(2	3)	139	32	38	45	9	0	88	0	2	4	5	2	6	.291	.305	.382	.687

Jason Castro

Bats: L Throws: R Pos: C-78;PH-1   Ht: 6'3" Wt: 215 Born: 6/18/1987 Age: 33

			BATTING																		RUNNING			AVERAGES			
Year	Team	Lg	G	AB	H	2B	3B	HR	(Hm	Rd)	TB	R	RBI	RC	TBB	IBB	SO	HBP	SH	SF	SB	CS	GDP	Avg	OBP	Slg	OPS
2010	Hou	NL	67	195	40	8	1	2	(1	1)	56	26	8	12	22	2	41	0	0	0	0	0	4	.205	.286	.287	.573
2012	Hou	NL	87	257	66	15	2	6	(3	3)	103	29	29	33	31	2	61	1	2	4	0	0	8	.257	.334	.401	.735
2013	Hou	AL	120	435	120	35	1	18	(13	5)	211	63	56	76	50	3	130	2	0	4	2	1	4	.276	.350	.485	.835
2014	Hou	AL	126	465	103	21	2	14	(10	4)	170	43	56	45	34	1	151	9	1	3	1	0	11	.222	.286	.366	.651
2015	Hou	AL	104	337	71	19	0	11	(8	3)	123	38	31	29	33	1	115	2	0	3	0	0	5	.211	.283	.365	.648
2016	Hou	AL	113	329	69	16	3	11	(5	6)	124	41	32	34	45	0	123	1	1	0	2	1	9	.210	.307	.377	.684
2017	Min	AL	110	356	86	22	0	10	(6	4)	138	49	47	45	45	1	108	4	1	1	0	0	10	.242	.333	.388	.720
2018	Min	AL	19	63	9	3	0	1	(0	1)	15	4	3	1	9	0	26	1	0	1	0	0	2	.143	.257	.238	.495
2019	Min	AL	79	237	55	9	0	13	(7	6)	103	39	30	31	33	0	88	3	1	1	0	0	2	.232	.332	.435	.767
	Postseason		7	19	1	0	0	0	(0	0)	1	1	2	0	2	0	11	0	0	0	0	0	2	.053	.143	.053	.195
	9 ML YEARS		825	2674	619	148	9	86	(53	33)	1043	332	292	306	302	10	843	23	6	17	5	2	53	.231	.313	.390	.703

Miguel Castro

Pitches: R **Bats:** R **Pos:** RP-65   **Ht:** 6'7" **Wt:** 205 **Born:** 12/24/1994 **Age:** 25

			HOW MUCH PITCHED					WHAT HE GAVE UP										THE RESULTS						
Year	Team	Lg	G	GS	GF	IP	BFP	H	R	ER	HR	SH	SF	HB	TBB	IBB	SO	WP	W	L	Pct	Sv-Op	Hld	Vel	OPS	ERC	ERA
2015	2 Tms		18	0	12	17.2	83	21	13	12	4	0	2	0	10	2	18	2	0	3	.000	4-6	1	96	.937	6.61	6.11
2016	Col	NL	19	0	4	14.2	67	18	10	10	3	1	0	1	5	0	12	0	0	0	-	0-1	7	96	.880	6.21	6.14
2017	Bal	AL	39	1	8	66.1	274	53	29	26	8	3	4	2	28	4	38	2	3	3	.500	0-0	1	96	.682	3.27	3.53
2018	Bal	AL	63	1	16	86.1	376	75	41	38	9	0	3	5	50	7	57	9	2	7	.222	0-2	5	96	.714	4.22	3.96
2019	Bal	AL	65	0	28	73.1	319	63	42	38	10	0	6	0	41	3	71	11	1	3	.250	2-5	9	97	.712	4.08	4.66
15	Tor	AL	13	0	9	12.1	57	15	7	6	2	0	2	0	6	2	12	2	0	2	.000	4-6	1	96	.688	5.86	4.38
15	Col	NL	5	0	3	5.1	26	6	6	6	2	0	0	0	4	0	6	0	0	1	.000	0-0	0	96	1.112	8.41	10.13
	5 ML YEARS		204	2	68	258.1	1119	230	135	124	34	4	15	8	134	16	196	24	6	16	.273	6-14	23	96	.732	4.19	4.32

Starlin Castro

Bats: R **Throws:** R **Pos:** 2B-117;3B-45;SS-3;PH-2   STARR-linn   **Ht:** 6'2" **Wt:** 230 **Born:** 3/24/1990 **Age:** 30

						BATTING															RUNNING			AVERAGES			
Year	Team	Lg	G	AB	H	2B	3B	HR	(Hm	Rd)	TB	R	RBI	RC	TBB	IBB	SO	HBP	SH	SF	SB	CS	GDP	Avg	OBP	Slg	OPS
2010	ChC	NL	125	463	139	31	5	3	(1	2)	189	53	41	56	29	7	71	6	4	4	10	8	14	.300	.347	.408	.755
2011	ChC	NL	158	674	207	36	9	10	(4	6)	291	91	66	93	35	2	96	2	0	4	22	9	20	.307	.341	.432	.773
2012	ChC	NL	162	646	183	29	12	14	(7	7)	278	78	78	91	36	5	100	4	0	5	25	13	15	.283	.323	.430	.753
2013	ChC	NL	161	666	163	34	2	10	(9	1)	231	59	44	55	30	0	129	7	1	1	9	6	21	.245	.284	.347	.631
2014	ChC	NL	134	528	154	33	1	14	(3	11)	231	58	65	72	35	4	100	4	0	2	4	4	18	.292	.339	.438	.777
2015	ChC	NL	151	547	145	23	2	11	(3	8)	205	52	69	54	21	6	91	5	1	4	5	5	18	.265	.296	.375	.671
2016	NYY	AL	151	577	156	29	1	21	(15	6)	250	63	70	69	24	1	118	3	1	5	4	0	15	.270	.300	.433	.734
2017	NYY	AL	112	443	133	18	1	16	(10	6)	201	66	63	69	23	1	93	4	0	3	2	0	9	.300	.338	.454	.792
2018	Mia	NL	154	593	165	32	2	12	(7	5)	237	76	54	70	48	3	124	0	0	6	6	4	18	.278	.329	.400	.729
2019	Mia	NL	162	636	172	31	4	22	(11	11)	277	68	86	77	28	2	111	3	0	9	2	2	23	.270	.300	.436	.736
	Postseason		22	84	17	4	0	1	(1	0)	24	7	3	6	3	1	15	1	0	0	0	0	1	.202	.239	.286	.524
	10 ML YEARS		1470	5773	1617	296	39	133	(70	63)	2390	664	636	706	309	31	1033	38	7	43	89	51	171	.280	.319	.414	.733

Willi Castro

Bats: B **Throws:** R **Pos:** SS-29;PH-1;PR-1   **Ht:** 6'1" **Wt:** 205 **Born:** 4/24/1997 **Age:** 23

						BATTING															RUNNING			AVERAGES			
Year	Team	Lg	G	AB	H	2B	3B	HR	(Hm	Rd)	TB	R	RBI	RC	TBB	IBB	SO	HBP	SH	SF	SB	CS	GDP	Avg	OBP	Slg	OPS
2019	Toledo	AAA	119	465	140	28	8	11	(-	-)	217	75	62	83	37	0	110	14	3	6	17	4	4	.301	.366	.467	.833
2019	Det	AL	30	100	23	6	1	1	(1	0)	34	10	8	9	6	0	34	2	1	1	0	1	4	.230	.284	.340	.624

Jake Cave

Bats: L **Throws:** L **Pos:** RF-45;CF-23;LF-10;PR-5;PH-4;DH-1   **Ht:** 6'0" **Wt:** 200 **Born:** 12/4/1992 **Age:** 27

						BATTING															RUNNING			AVERAGES			
Year	Team	Lg	G	AB	H	2B	3B	HR	(Hm	Rd)	TB	R	RBI	RC	TBB	IBB	SO	HBP	SH	SF	SB	CS	GDP	Avg	OBP	Slg	OPS
2019	Roch	AAA	48	196	69	18	4	7	(-	-)	116	37	39	44	15	0	50	0	0	3	5	0	5	.352	.393	.592	.984
2018	Min	AL	91	283	75	16	2	13	(6	7)	134	54	45	46	18	2	102	3	2	3	2	1	2	.265	.313	.473	.786
2019	Min	AL	72	198	51	11	2	8	(3	5)	90	28	25	27	21	0	71	8	0	1	0	0	5	.258	.351	.455	.805
	2 ML YEARS		163	481	126	27	4	21	(9	12)	224	82	70	73	39	2	173	11	2	4	2	1	7	.262	.329	.466	.795

Dylan Cease

Pitches: R **Bats:** R **Pos:** SP-14   **Ht:** 6'2" **Wt:** 190 **Born:** 12/28/1995 **Age:** 24

			HOW MUCH PITCHED					WHAT HE GAVE UP										THE RESULTS						
Year	Team	Lg	G	GS	GF	IP	BFP	H	R	ER	HR	SH	SF	HB	TBB	IBB	SO	WP	W	L	Pct	Sv-Op	Hld	Vel	OPS	ERC	ERA
2015	Cubs	R	11	8	0	24.0	101	12	12	7	0	0	0	2	16	0	25	9	1	2	.333	0- -	-	-	.454	2.06	2.63
2016	Eugene	A-	12	12	0	44.2	182	27	14	11	1	0	1	2	25	0	66	4	2	0	1.000	0- -	-	-	.537	2.29	2.22
2017	2 Tms	Low	22	22	0	93.1	388	74	40	34	3	2	4	3	44	0	126	10	1	10	.091	0- -	-	-	.612	2.94	3.28
2018	WinSa	A+	13	13	0	71.2	290	52	31	23	5	3	1	3	28	0	82	5	9	2	.818	0- -	-	-	.583	2.59	2.89
2018	Brham	AA	10	10	0	52.1	202	30	11	10	3	0	1	0	22	0	78	3	3	0	1.000	0- -	-	-	.509	1.79	1.72
2019	Charllt	AAA	15	15	0	68.1	304	75	39	34	4	2	3	3	32	0	73	7	5	2	.714	0- -	-	-	.754	4.83	4.48
2019	CWS	AL	14	14	0	73.0	326	78	51	47	15	0	1	2	35	1	81	4	4	7	.364	0-0	0	97	.839	5.70	5.79

Brett Cecil

Pitches: L **Bats:** R **Pos:** P   SEE-sill   **Ht:** 6'3" **Wt:** 235 **Born:** 7/2/1986 **Age:** 33

			HOW MUCH PITCHED					WHAT HE GAVE UP										THE RESULTS						
Year	Team	Lg	G	GS	GF	IP	BFP	H	R	ER	HR	SH	SF	HB	TBB	IBB	SO	WP	W	L	Pct	Sv-Op	Hld	Vel	OPS	ERC	ERA
2009	Tor	AL	18	17	1	93.1	422	116	59	55	17	0	2	5	38	0	69	0	7	4	.636	0-0	0	91	.894	6.53	5.30
2010	Tor	AL	28	28	0	172.2	726	175	87	81	18	1	6	1	54	2	117	7	15	7	.682	0-0	0	90	.733	3.88	4.22
2011	Tor	AL	20	20	0	123.2	532	122	68	65	22	3	5	6	42	1	87	1	4	11	.267	0-0	0	88	.779	4.47	4.73
2012	Tor	AL	21	9	2	61.1	270	70	40	39	11	3	3	3	23	0	51	0	2	4	.333	0-0	1	89	.855	5.68	5.72
2013	Tor	AL	60	0	12	60.2	250	44	20	19	4	3	2	3	23	3	70	5	5	1	.833	1-3	11	92	.594	2.42	2.82
2014	Tor	AL	66	0	17	53.1	234	46	16	16	2	0	3	1	27	4	76	1	2	3	.400	5-7	24	93	.627	3.16	2.70
2015	Tor	AL	63	0	24	54.1	214	39	17	15	4	1	0	2	13	3	70	4	5	5	.500	5-8	9	92	.562	1.95	2.48
2016	Tor	AL	54	0	8	36.2	157	39	17	16	6	1	1	2	8	0	45	0	1	7	.125	0-4	9	92	.742	4.33	3.93
2017	StL	NL	73	0	12	67.1	277	67	31	29	7	0	5	0	16	3	66	3	2	4	.333	1-7	13	92	.714	3.41	3.88
2018	StL	NL	40	0	7	32.2	157	39	27	25	5	0	3	0	25	5	19	1	1	1	.500	0-0	0	90	.904	6.96	6.89
	Postseason		8	0	0	6.0	21	1	0	0	0	1	0	0	4	0	6	0	0	1	-	0-1	1	92	.313	0.90	0.00
	10 ML YEARS		443	74	83	756.0	3239	757	382	360	96	12	30	23	269	21	670	22	44	47	.484	12-29	67	90	.749	4.19	4.29

Xavier Cedeno

Pitches: L **Bats:** L **Pos:** RP-5   seh-DAYN-yo   **Ht:** 5'11" **Wt:** 210 **Born:** 8/26/1986 **Age:** 33

Year	Team	Lg	G	GS	GF	IP	BFP	H	R	ER	HR	SH	SF	HB	TBB	IBB	SO	WP	W	L	Pct	Sv-Op	Hld	Vel	OPS	ERC	ERA
2019	Tenn	AA	7	0	1	5.0	28	8	4	4	0	0	0	1	4	0	7	1	0	1	.000	0--	-	-	.856	9.25	7.20
2019	Iowa	AAA	9	0	1	7.0	34	8	3	3	0	0	0	1	7	0	3	2	1	0	1.000	0--	-	-	.849	6.73	3.86
2011	Hou	NL	3	0	0	1.2	11	7	5	5	2	0	0	0	0	0	0	0	0	0	-	0-0	0	88	1.818	43.10	27.00
2012	Hou	NL	44	0	12	31.0	138	30	15	13	3	2	3	1	14	1	36	3	0	1	.000	1-3	6	89	.704	4.05	3.77
2013	2 Tms		16	0	3	12.1	60	15	12	9	0	1	0	2	8	0	9	0	0	0	-	0-0	2	89	.811	6.24	6.57
2014	Was	NL	9	0	4	7.0	30	10	4	3	1	0	0	0	0	0	5	0	0	0	-	0-0	0	91	.833	5.27	3.86
2015	2 Tms		66	0	10	46.0	189	40	13	12	4	0	0	2	14	2	47	6	4	1	.800	1-3	19	90	.614	3.05	2.35
2016	TB	AL	54	0	7	41.1	174	36	17	17	2	1	2	0	13	1	43	3	3	4	.429	0-5	19	88	.597	2.62	3.70
2017	Hou	AL	9	0	0	3.0	21	7	5	4	3	1	0	0	4	1	0	0	1	1	.500	0-3	0	88	1.550	8.91	12.00
2018	2 Tms		48	0	4	33.1	140	26	10	9	1	0	0	0	16	1	34	4	2	0	1.000	1-2	11	86	.590	2.67	2.43
2019	ChC	NL	5	0	0	2.0	13	4	0	0	0	0	0	0	3	1	1	0	0	0	-	0-0	0	86	1.138	12.98	0.00
13	Hou	AL	5	0	0	6.1	37	10	11	8	0	1	0	2	7	0	3	0	0	0	-	0-0	0	88	1.046	11.27	11.37
13	Was	NL	11	0	3	6.0	23	5	1	1	0	0	0	0	1	0	6	0	0	0	-	0-0	2	91	.488	1.84	1.50
15	Was	NL	5	0	1	3.0	15	3	2	2	1	0	0	1	2	0	4	2	0	0	-	0-2	0	90	.900	8.41	6.00
15	TB	AL	61	0	9	43.0	174	37	11	10	3	0	0	1	12	2	43	4	4	1	.800	1-1	19	89	.592	2.74	2.09
18	CWS	AL	33	0	4	25.1	106	19	9	8	1	0	0	0	13	1	28	3	2	0	1.000	1-2	7	86	.614	2.70	2.84
18	Mil	NL	15	0	0	8.0	34	7	1	1	0	0	0	0	3	0	6	1	0	0	-	0-0	4	87	.520	2.58	1.13
	Postseason		4	0	0	1.0	7	3	2	2	0	0	0	0	1	1	1	0	0	0	-	0-0	0	88	1.071	16.67	18.00
9 ML YEARS			254	0	41	177.2	776	175	81	72	16	5	5	5	72	7	175	16	10	7	.588	3-16	57	89	.695	3.94	3.65

Juan Centeno

Bats: L **Throws:** R **Pos:** C-5;PH-3;DH-1   sen-TAIN-no   **Ht:** 5'9" **Wt:** 195 **Born:** 11/16/1989 **Age:** 30

Year	Team	Lg	G	AB	H	2B	3B	HR	(Hm	Rd)	TB	R	RBI	RC	TBB	IBB	SO	HBP	SH	SF	SB	CS	GDP	Avg	OBP	Slg	OPS
2019	Pwtckt	AAA	81	266	66	15	0	4	(-	-)	93	27	40	32	24	1	47	6	2	3	2	0	15	.248	.321	.350	.671
2013	NYM	NL	4	10	3	0	0	0	(0	0)	3	0	1	1	0	0	1	0	0	0	0	0	0	.300	.300	.300	.600
2014	NYM	NL	10	30	6	1	0	0	(0	0)	6	1	2	2	3	0	5	0	0	0	0	0	2	.200	.273	.200	.473
2015	Mil	NL	10	21	1	1	0	0	(0	0)	2	0	0	0	2	0	7	0	0	0	0	0	0	.048	.130	.095	.226
2016	Min	AL	55	176	46	12	1	3	(1	2)	69	16	25	20	12	0	38	1	3	0	0	0	8	.261	.312	.392	.704
2017	Hou	AL	22	52	12	0	0	2	(2	0)	18	5	4	4	4	1	12	1	1	0	0	0	2	.231	.286	.346	.632
2018	Tex	AL	10	37	6	1	0	1	(0	1)	10	3	3	3	1	0	7	0	0	0	0	0	2	.162	.184	.270	.454
2019	Bos	AL	7	15	2	0	0	0	(0	0)	2	0	2	1	2	0	2	1	0	0	1	0	0	.133	.278	.133	.411
	Postseason		1	0	0	0	0	0	(0	0)	0	0	0	0	0	0	0	0	0	0	0	0	0	-	-	-	-
7 ML YEARS			118	341	76	14	1	6	(3	3)	110	25	37	28	24	1	72	2	4	0	1	0	14	.223	.278	.323	.601

Francisco Cervelli

Bats: R **Throws:** R **Pos:** C-41;PH-4;1B-3;DH-1   sir-VEL-lee   **Ht:** 6'1" **Wt:** 210 **Born:** 3/6/1986 **Age:** 34

Year	Team	Lg	G	AB	H	2B	3B	HR	(Hm	Rd)	TB	R	RBI	RC	TBB	IBB	SO	HBP	SH	SF	SB	CS	GDP	Avg	OBP	Slg	OPS
2008	NYY	AL	3	5	0	0	0	0	(0	0)	0	0	0	0	0	0	3	0	0	0	0	0	1	.000	.000	.000	.000
2009	NYY	AL	42	94	28	4	0	1	(0	1)	35	13	11	11	2	0	11	0	4	1	0	3	1	.298	.309	.372	.682
2010	NYY	AL	93	266	72	11	3	0	(0	0)	89	27	38	40	33	1	42	6	8	4	1	1	7	.271	.359	.335	.694
2011	NYY	AL	43	124	33	4	0	4	(2	2)	49	17	22	17	9	0	29	2	1	1	4	1	4	.266	.324	.395	.719
2012	NYY	AL	3	1	0	0	0	0	(0	0)	0	1	0	0	1	0	1	0	0	0	0	0	0	.000	.500	.000	.500
2013	NYY	AL	17	52	14	3	0	3	(3	0)	26	12	8	9	8	0	9	1	0	0	0	0	1	.269	.377	.500	.877
2014	NYY	AL	49	146	44	11	1	2	(1	1)	63	18	13	19	11	0	41	5	0	0	0	0	5	.301	.370	.432	.802
2015	Pit	NL	130	451	133	17	5	7	(6	1)	181	56	43	62	46	1	94	8	4	1	1	1	12	.295	.370	.401	.771
2016	Pit	NL	101	326	86	14	1	1	(0	1)	105	42	33	40	56	1	72	6	0	5	6	2	14	.264	.377	.322	.699
2017	Pit	NL	81	265	66	13	2	5	(2	3)	98	31	31	30	32	0	65	6	0	1	2	0	7	.249	.342	.370	.712
2018	Pit	NL	104	332	86	15	3	12	(5	7)	143	39	57	60	51	1	84	15	2	4	2	3	7	.259	.378	.431	.809
2019	2 Tms	NL	48	141	30	8	1	3	(1	2)	49	15	12	11	13	0	41	5	1	0	1	0	7	.213	.302	.348	.649
19	Pit	NL	34	109	21	3	0	1	(0	1)	27	11	5	4	9	0	31	4	1	0	1	0	4	.193	.279	.248	.526
19	Atl	NL	14	32	9	5	1	2	(1	1)	22	4	7	7	4	0	10	1	0	0	0	0	3	.281	.378	.688	1.066
	Postseason		4	6	1	0	0	0	(0	0)	1	0	0	0	0	0	2	1	0	0	0	0	0	.167	.286	.167	.452
12 ML YEARS			714	2203	592	100	16	38	(20	18)	838	271	268	299	262	4	491	54	20	17	16	13	66	.269	.358	.380	.738

Yoenis Cespedes

Bats: R **Throws:** R **Pos:** OF   yo-EHN-ess SESS-peh-des   **Ht:** 5'10" **Wt:** 220 **Born:** 10/18/1985 **Age:** 34

Year	Team	Lg	G	AB	H	2B	3B	HR	(Hm	Rd)	TB	R	RBI	RC	TBB	IBB	SO	HBP	SH	SF	SB	CS	GDP	Avg	OBP	Slg	OPS
2012	Oak	AL	129	487	142	25	5	23	(11	12)	246	70	82	90	43	5	102	7	0	3	16	4	9	.292	.356	.505	.861
2013	Oak	AL	135	529	127	21	4	26	(14	12)	234	74	80	65	37	5	137	5	0	3	7	7	8	.240	.294	.442	.737
2014	2 Tms	AL	152	600	156	36	6	22	(13	9)	270	89	100	85	35	3	128	3	0	7	7	2	13	.260	.301	.450	.751
2015	2 Tms	AL	159	633	184	42	6	35	(10	25)	343	105	105	103	33	5	141	5	0	5	7	5	14	.291	.328	.542	.870
2016	NYM	NL	132	479	134	25	1	31	(14	17)	254	72	86	83	51	8	108	7	0	6	3	1	14	.280	.354	.530	.884
2017	NYM	NL	81	291	85	17	2	17	(5	12)	157	46	42	44	26	5	61	2	0	2	0	1	7	.292	.352	.540	.892
2018	NYM	NL	38	141	37	6	0	9	(4	5)	70	20	29	24	13	2	50	1	0	2	1	0	3	.262	.325	.496	.821
14	Oak	AL	101	399	102	26	3	17	(11	6)	185	62	67	55	28	3	80	1	0	4	3	2	8	.256	.303	.464	.767
14	Bos	AL	51	201	54	10	3	5	(2	3)	85	27	33	30	7	0	48	2	0	3	4	0	5	.269	.296	.423	.719
15	Det	AL	102	403	118	28	2	18	(5	13)	204	62	61	58	19	2	87	1	0	4	3	4	9	.293	.323	.506	.829
15	NYM	NL	57	230	66	14	4	17	(5	12)	139	39	44	45	14	3	54	4	0	1	4	1	5	.287	.337	.604	.942
	Postseason		25	98	26	3	1	3	(2	1)	40	11	14	14	3	0	25	1	0	1	3	0	1	.265	.291	.408	.699
7 ML YEARS			826	3160	865	172	24	163	(71	92)	1574	472	524	494	238	33	727	30	0	28	43	20	66	.274	.328	.498	.826

Luis Cessa

Pitches: R **Bats:** R **Pos:** RP-43 — SESS-uh — **Ht:** 6'0" **Wt:** 210 **Born:** 4/25/1992 **Age:** 28

Year Team	Lg	G	GS	GF	IP	BFP	H	R	ER	HR	SH	SF	HB	TBB	IBB	SO	WP	W	L	Pct	Sv-Op	Hld	Vel	OPS	ERC	ERA
2016 NYY	AL	17	9	5	70.1	285	64	36	34	16	1	1	3	14	0	46	2	4	4	.500	0-0	0	95	.744	3.81	4.35
2017 NYY	AL	10	5	2	36.0	160	36	21	19	7	0	0	3	17	0	30	2	0	3	.000	0-0	0	96	.829	5.43	4.75
2018 NYY	AL	16	5	6	44.2	195	51	27	26	5	1	0	0	13	0	39	7	1	4	.200	2-2	0	95	.761	4.50	5.24
2019 NYY	AL	43	0	14	81.0	343	75	42	37	14	0	4	3	31	1	75	1	2	1	.667	1-1	0	94	.751	4.26	4.11
4 ML YEARS		86	19	27	232.0	983	226	126	116	42	2	5	9	75	1	190	12	7	12	.368	3-3	4	95	.763	4.35	4.50

Jhoulys Chacin

Pitches: R **Bats:** R **Pos:** SP-24; RP-1 — yoo-LEES cha-SEEN — **Ht:** 6'3" **Wt:** 215 **Born:** 1/7/1988 **Age:** 32

Year Team	Lg	G	GS	GF	IP	BFP	H	R	ER	HR	SH	SF	HB	TBB	IBB	SO	WP	W	L	Pct	Sv-Op	Hld	Vel	OPS	ERC	ERA
2009 Col	NL	9	1	3	11.0	48	6	6	6	1	1	0	0	11	0	13	2	0	1	.000	0-0	0	91	.667	3.87	4.91
2010 Col	NL	28	21	2	137.1	583	114	64	50	10	6	5	9	61	5	138	4	9	11	.450	0-0	0	91	.650	3.33	3.28
2011 Col	NL	31	31	0	194.0	827	168	87	78	20	5	3	4	87	1	150	7	11	14	.440	0-0	0	91	.707	3.61	3.62
2012 Col	NL	14	14	0	69.0	314	80	35	34	10	1	1	2	32	0	45	3	3	5	.375	0-0	0	90	.821	5.73	4.43
2013 Col	NL	31	31	0	197.1	816	188	82	76	11	3	7	3	61	3	126	5	14	10	.583	0-0	0	90	.685	3.26	3.47
2014 Col	NL	11	11	0	63.1	272	63	38	38	8	2	3	1	28	1	42	4	1	7	.125	0-0	0	88	.790	4.52	5.40
2015 Ari	NL	5	4	0	26.2	111	24	11	10	4	1	0	0	10	0	21	0	2	1	.667	0-0	0	89	.729	3.80	3.38
2016 2 Tms		34	22	5	144.0	632	153	81	77	14	4	6	5	55	4	119	8	6	8	.429	0-0	0	91	.745	4.42	4.81
2017 SD	NL	32	32	0	180.1	765	157	87	78	19	6	6	14	72	5	153	7	13	10	.565	0-0	0	91	.693	3.67	3.89
2018 Mil	NL	35	35	0	192.2	796	153	83	75	18	8	9	11	71	3	156	5	15	8	.652	0-0	0	90	.655	3.01	3.50
2019 2 Tms		25	24	0	103.1	470	115	73	69	25	4	4	5	46	1	101	3	3	12	.200	0-0	0	90	.877	6.13	6.01
16 Atl	NL	5	5	0	26.2	117	29	17	16	4	2	1	0	8	0	27	0	1	2	.333	0-0	0	89	.756	4.42	5.40
16 LAA	AL	29	17	5	117.1	515	124	64	61	10	2	5	5	47	4	92	8	5	6	.455	0-0	0	91	.742	4.42	4.68
19 Mil	NL	19	19	0	88.2	403	99	61	57	19	4	4	5	39	1	80	3	3	10	.231	0-0	0	90	.857	5.96	5.79
19 Bos	AL	6	5	0	14.2	67	16	12	12	6	0	0	0	7	0	21	0	0	2	.000	0-0	0	90	.993	7.12	7.36
Postseason		3	3	0	12.1	51	9	2	2	1	0	0	0	6	1	9	0	2	1	.667	0-0	0	91	.627	2.72	1.46
11 ML YEARS		255	226	10	1319.0	5634	1221	642	591	140	41	44	54	534	23	1064	48	77	87	.470	0-0	0	90	.718	3.87	4.03

Andrew Chafin

Pitches: L **Bats:** R **Pos:** RP-77 — **Ht:** 6'2" **Wt:** 225 **Born:** 6/17/1990 **Age:** 30

Year Team	Lg	G	GS	GF	IP	BFP	H	R	ER	HR	SH	SF	HB	TBB	IBB	SO	WP	W	L	Pct	Sv-Op	Hld	Vel	OPS	ERC	ERA
2014 Ari	NL	3	3	0	14.0	60	13	6	6	0	2	0	1	8	1	10	2	0	1	.000	0-0	0	91	.685	3.92	3.86
2015 Ari	NL	66	0	6	75.0	306	56	23	23	3	3	2	1	30	6	58	2	5	1	.833	2-2	16	92	.587	2.30	2.76
2016 Ari	NL	32	0	1	22.2	98	22	18	17	1	1	0	1	11	1	28	2	0	1	.000	0-1	6	93	.703	4.01	6.75
2017 Ari	NL	71	0	12	51.1	221	48	21	20	5	2	1	2	21	3	61	1	1	0	1.000	0-0	17	94	.699	3.78	3.51
2018 Ari	NL	77	0	13	49.1	211	41	18	17	0	0	3	2	25	1	53	3	1	6	.143	0-0	17	94	.621	2.99	3.10
2019 Ari	NL	77	0	6	52.2	225	52	23	22	6	3	0	2	18	0	68	2	2	2	.500	0-4	23	94	.691	4.03	3.76
Postseason		3	0	1	0.2	3	2	1	1	0	0	0	0	0	0	0	0	1	0	1.000	0-0	0	94	1.333	19.55	13.50
6 ML YEARS		326	3	38	265.0	1121	232	109	105	15	11	6	9	113	12	278	12	9	11	.450	2-7	79	93	.652	3.27	3.57

Yu-Cheng Chang

Bats: R **Throws:** R **Pos:** 3B-25;SS-8;PH-3 — **Ht:** 6'1" **Wt:** 180 **Born:** 8/18/1995 **Age:** 24

Year Team	Lg	G	AB	H	2B	3B	HR	(Hm	Rd)	TB	R	RBI	RC	TBB	IBB	SO	HBP	SH	SF	SB	CS	GDP	Avg	OBP	Slg	OPS
2019 Clmbs	AAA	68	253	64	15	1	9	(-	-)	108	45	39	36	26	1	67	1	0	3	4	1	5	.253	.322	.427	.748
2019 Cle	AL	28	73	13	2	1	1	(0	1)	20	8	6	5	11	0	22	0	0	0	0	0	4	.178	.286	.274	.560

Aroldis Chapman

Pitches: L **Bats:** L **Pos:** RP-60 — ah-ROLL-diss — **Ht:** 6'4" **Wt:** 212 **Born:** 2/28/1988 **Age:** 32

Year Team	Lg	G	GS	GF	IP	BFP	H	R	ER	HR	SH	SF	HB	TBB	IBB	SO	WP	W	L	Pct	Sv-Op	Hld	Vel	OPS	ERC	ERA
2010 Cin	NL	15	0	3	13.1	51	9	4	3	0	0	0	0	5	0	19	2	2	2	.500	0-1	4	100	.492	1.82	2.03
2011 Cin	NL	54	0	13	50.0	207	24	21	20	2	1	0	2	41	0	71	4	4	1	.800	1-3	13	98	.534	2.69	3.60
2012 Cin	NL	68	0	52	71.2	276	35	13	12	4	0	1	4	23	0	122	6	5	5	.500	38-43	6	98	.450	1.35	1.51
2013 Cin	NL	68	0	55	63.2	258	37	18	18	7	1	0	3	29	0	112	6	4	5	.444	38-43	0	98	.544	2.33	2.54
2014 Cin	NL	54	0	44	54.0	202	21	12	12	1	1	1	2	24	0	106	4	0	3	.000	36-38	0	100	.406	1.18	2.00
2015 Cin	NL	65	0	54	66.1	278	43	13	12	3	0	2	5	33	1	116	7	4	4	.500	33-36	0	99	.527	2.45	1.63
2016 2 Tms		59	0	52	58.0	222	32	12	10	2	0	1	0	18	0	90	8	4	1	.800	36-39	0	100	.452	1.33	1.55
2017 NYY	AL	52	0	42	50.1	210	37	20	18	3	0	1	3	20	2	69	5	4	3	.571	22-26	1	100	.584	2.53	3.22
2018 NYY	AL	55	0	43	51.1	212	24	15	14	2	0	0	5	30	0	93	9	3	0	1.000	32-34	1	99	.493	1.94	2.45
2019 NYY	AL	60	0	53	57.0	235	38	18	14	9	0	3	1	25	0	85	6	3	2	.600	37-42	0	98	.537	2.21	2.21
16 NYY	AL	31	0	29	31.1	120	20	8	7	2	0	0	0	8	0	44	2	3	0	1.000	20-21	0	100	.519	1.59	2.01
16 ChC	NL	28	0	23	26.2	102	12	4	3	0	0	1	0	10	0	46	6	1	1	.500	16-18	0	101	.370	1.04	1.01
Postseason		27	0	20	31.1	129	24	11	8	1	1	1	2	11	1	45	2	2	2	.500	7-11	0	100	.579	2.40	2.30
10 ML YEARS		550	0	411	535.2	2151	300	146	133	27	3	9	25	248	3	883	55	33	26	.559	273-305	25	99	.504	1.91	2.23

Matt Chapman

Bats: R **Throws:** R **Pos:** 3B-156   **Ht:** 6'0" **Wt:** 220 **Born:** 4/28/1993 **Age:** 27

									BATTING													RUNNING			AVERAGES			
Year	Team	Lg	G	AB	H	2B	3B	HR	(Hm	Rd)	TB	R	RBI	RC	TBB	IBB	SO	HBP	SH	SF		SB	CS	GDP	Avg	OBP	Slg	OPS
2017	Oak	AL	84	290	68	23	2	14	(8	6)	137	39	40	42	32	0	92	2	0	2		0	3	2	.234	.313	.472	.785
2018	Oak	AL	145	547	152	42	6	24	(8	16)	278	100	68	94	58	0	146	9	0	2		1	2	18	.278	.356	.508	.864
2019	Oak	AL	156	583	145	36	3	36	(21	15)	295	102	91	109	73	0	147	11	0	3		1	1	12	.249	.342	.506	.848
	Postseason		1	5	1	0	0	0	(0	0)	1	0	0	0	0	0	0	0	0	0		0	0	0	.200	.200	.200	.400
	3 ML YEARS		385	1420	365	101	11	74	(37	37)	710	241	199	245	163	0	385	22	0	7		2	6	32	.257	.341	.500	.841

JT Chargois

Pitches: R **Bats:** B **Pos:** RP-21   SHAHG-wah   **Ht:** 6'3" **Wt:** 200 **Born:** 12/3/1990 **Age:** 29

			HOW MUCH PITCHED					WHAT HE GAVE UP											THE RESULTS							
Year	Team	Lg	G	GS	GF	IP	BFP	H	R	ER	HR	SH	SF	HB	TBB	IBB	SO	WP		W	L	Pct	Sv-Op Hld	Vel	OPS	ERC	ERA
2019	OkCity	AAA	27	0	18	32.2	135	27	12	10	3	1	0	1	16	0	37	2		1	2	.333	4- - -	-	.670	3.66	2.76
2016	Min	AL	25	0	10	23.0	100	25	12	12	0	0	1	1	12	0	17	3		1	1	.500	0-0 2	96	.752	4.67	4.70
2018	LAD	NL	39	0	4	32.1	135	26	13	12	4	1	0	2	15	3	40	0		3	4	.333	0-4 7	95	.697	3.58	3.34
2019	LAD	NL	21	0	9	21.1	88	21	16	15	4	0	4	2	5	2	28	0		1	0	1.000	0-0 0	96	.825	4.28	6.33
	3 ML YEARS		85	0	23	76.2	323	72	41	39	8	1	5	5	32	5	85	6		4	5	.444	0-4 9	96	.749	4.11	4.58

Tyler Chatwood

Pitches: R **Bats:** R **Pos:** RP-33; SP-5   **Ht:** 6'0" **Wt:** 185 **Born:** 12/16/1989 **Age:** 30

			HOW MUCH PITCHED					WHAT HE GAVE UP											THE RESULTS							
Year	Team	Lg	G	GS	GF	IP	BFP	H	R	ER	HR	SH	SF	HB	TBB	IBB	SO	WP		W	L	Pct	Sv-Op Hld	Vel	OPS	ERC	ERA
2011	LAA	AL	27	25	0	142.0	633	166	81	75	14	6	3	6	71	4	74	3		6	11	.353	0-0 0	93	.830	5.78	4.75
2012	Col	NL	19	12	3	64.2	294	74	43	39	9	4	2	0	33	2	41	4		5	6	.455	1-1 0	94	.836	5.62	5.43
2013	Col	NL	20	20	0	111.1	476	118	44	39	5	2	4	4	41	5	66	10		8	5	.615	0-0 0	93	.711	4.05	3.15
2014	Col	NL	4	4	0	24.0	101	21	13	12	4	0	2	2	8	0	20	2		1	0	1.000	0-0 0	95	.711	3.91	4.50
2016	Col	NL	27	27	0	158.0	669	147	75	68	15	2	3	5	70	2	117	7		12	9	.571	0-0 0	92	.723	4.01	3.87
2017	Col	NL	33	25	3	147.2	631	136	79	77	20	4	3	4	77	2	120	12		8	15	.348	1-1 0	95	.788	4.58	4.69
2018	ChC	NL	24	20	4	103.2	486	92	62	61	9	5	4	7	95	1	85	8		4	6	.400	0-0 0	93	.774	5.72	5.30
2019	ChC	NL	38	5	9	76.2	324	65	33	32	8	1	1	5	37	0	74	8		5	3	.625	2-4 3	96	.685	3.92	3.76
	8 ML YEARS		192	138	19	828.0	3614	819	430	403	84	24	22	33	432	16	597	54		49	55	.471	4-6 3	93	.764	4.74	4.38

Jesse Chavez

Pitches: R **Bats:** R **Pos:** RP-39; SP-9   CHAH-vezz   **Ht:** 6'2" **Wt:** 175 **Born:** 8/21/1983 **Age:** 36

			HOW MUCH PITCHED					WHAT HE GAVE UP											THE RESULTS							
Year	Team	Lg	G	GS	GF	IP	BFP	H	R	ER	HR	SH	SF	HB	TBB	IBB	SO	WP		W	L	Pct	Sv-Op Hld	Vel	OPS	ERC	ERA
2008	Pit	NL	15	0	6	15.0	74	20	11	11	2	3	1	0	9	2	16	2		0	1	.000	0-2 0	94	.900	6.76	6.60
2009	Pit	NL	73	0	24	67.1	286	69	33	30	11	1	1	1	22	3	47	5		1	4	.200	0-4 15	94	.783	4.39	4.01
2010	2 Tms		51	0	26	62.2	280	69	44	41	11	5	3	1	23	7	45	2		5	5	.500	0-1 6	95	.834	4.85	5.89
2011	KC	AL	4	0	3	7.2	39	12	9	9	3	0	0	0	5	0	8	0		0	0	-	0-0 0	93	1.112	11.48	10.57
2012	2 Tms	AL	13	2	3	24.2	123	34	29	27	7	0	1	3	11	1	30	1		1	1	.500	0-0 0	93	.983	8.32	9.85
2013	Oak	AL	35	0	16	57.1	248	50	27	25	3	6	2	3	20	4	55	5		2	4	.333	1-2 1	92	.620	2.85	3.92
2014	Oak	AL	32	21	5	146.0	621	142	64	56	17	1	4	5	49	3	136	7		8	8	.500	0-0 0	91	.692	3.89	3.45
2015	Oak	AL	30	26	3	157.0	672	164	78	73	18	4	6	2	48	2	136	3		7	15	.318	1-1 0	91	.730	4.08	4.18
2016	2 Tms		62	0	9	67.0	282	71	36	33	12	0	1	2	18	3	63	1		2	2	.500	0-3 10	93	.779	4.56	4.43
2017	LAA	AL	38	21	6	138.0	586	148	83	82	28	0	2	2	45	2	119	1		7	11	.389	0-1 1	92	.826	5.06	5.35
2018	2 Tms		62	0	26	95.1	377	84	28	27	13	0	2	0	17	1	92	1		5	2	.714	5-6 7	93	.645	2.84	2.55
2019	Tex		48	9	5	78.0	337	82	48	42	12	1	2	5	22	0	72	1		3	5	.375	1-2 8	91	.787	4.52	4.85
10	Atl	NL	28	0	16	36.2	162	40	24	24	6	3	2	1	12	3	29	0		3	2	.600	0-0 0	95	.812	4.65	5.89
10	KC	AL	23	0	10	26.0	118	29	20	17	5	2	1	0	11	4	16	2		2	3	.400	0-1 6	94	.864	5.13	5.88
12	Tor	AL	9	2	2	21.1	102	25	22	20	6	0	1	2	10	1	27	0		1	1	.500	0-0 0	93	.925	6.90	8.44
12	Oak	AL	4	0	1	3.1	21	9	7	7	1	0	0	1	1	0	3	1		0	0	-	0-0 0	93	1.261	18.70	18.90
16	Tor	AL	39	0	6	41.1	173	43	22	21	9	0	1	2	10	0	42	1		1	2	.333	0-2 7	93	.799	4.75	4.57
16	LAD	NL	23	0	3	25.2	109	28	14	12	3	0	0	0	8	3	21	0		1	0	1.000	0-0 0	93	.746	4.24	4.21
18	Tex	AL	30	0	15	56.1	234	58	23	22	10	0	1	0	12	1	50	1		1	1	.750	1-1 3	93	.747	4.00	3.51
18	ChC	NL	32	0	11	39.0	143	26	5	5	3	0	1	0	5	0	42	0		2	1	.667	4-5 4	93	.480	1.47	1.15
	Postseason		1	0	0	1.0	3	1	0	0	0	0	0	0	0	0	0	0		0	0	-	0-0 0	93	.667	2.79	0.00
	12 ML YEARS		463	79	132	916.0	3925	945	490	456	137	21	25	24	289	28	819	29		41	58	.414	8-22 48	93	.757	4.32	4.48

Michael Chavis

Bats: R **Throws:** R **Pos:** 1B-49;2B-45;3B-5;PH-4;DH-1;PR-1   **Ht:** 5'10" **Wt:** 216 **Born:** 8/11/1995 **Age:** 24

									BATTING													RUNNING			AVERAGES			
Year	Team	Lg	G	AB	H	2B	3B	HR	(Hm	Rd)	TB	R	RBI	RC	TBB	IBB	SO	HBP	SH	SF		SB	CS	GDP	Avg	OBP	Slg	OPS
2019	Pwtckt	AAA	21	70	18	4	0	7	(-	-)	43	11	11	14	8	0	21	0	0	1		0	0	1	.257	.329	.614	.943
2019	Bos	AL	95	347	88	10	1	18	(10	8)	154	46	58	47	31	2	127	4	0	0		2	1	11	.254	.322	.444	.766

Wei-Yin Chen

Pitches: L **Bats:** R **Pos:** RP-45   way-yin   **Ht:** 6'0" **Wt:** 200 **Born:** 7/21/1985 **Age:** 34

			HOW MUCH PITCHED					WHAT HE GAVE UP											THE RESULTS							
Year	Team	Lg	G	GS	GF	IP	BFP	H	R	ER	HR	SH	SF	HB	TBB	IBB	SO	WP		W	L	Pct	Sv-Op Hld	Vel	OPS	ERC	ERA
2012	Bal	AL	32	32	0	192.2	818	186	97	86	29	5	8	5	57	0	154	2		12	11	.522	0-0 0	91	.729	3.88	4.02
2013	Bal	AL	23	23	0	137.0	572	142	62	62	17	2	6	2	39	2	104	3		7	7	.500	0-0 0	91	.761	4.11	4.07
2014	Bal	AL	31	31	0	185.2	772	193	77	73	23	5	4	3	35	2	136	2		16	6	.727	0-0 0	92	.727	3.67	3.54
2015	Bal	AL	31	31	0	191.1	792	192	78	71	28	5	8	5	41	0	153	3		11	8	.579	0-0 0	91	.758	3.80	3.34

Year	Team	Lg	G	GS	GF	IP	BFP	H	R	ER	HR	SH	SF	HB	TBB	IBB	SO	WP	W	L	Pct	Sv-Op	Hld	Vel	OPS	ERC	ERA
			HOW MUCH PITCHED					WHAT HE GAVE UP											THE RESULTS								
2016	Mia	NL	22	22	0	123.1	520	134	69	68	22	3	4	3	24	0	100	1	5	5	.500	0-0	0	91	.789	4.38	4.96
2017	Mia	NL	9	5	1	33.0	132	25	14	14	3	0	1	1	9	0	25	1	2	1	.667	0-0	0	91	.612	2.39	3.82
2018	Mia	NL	26	26	0	133.1	572	131	75	71	19	5	7	1	47	6	111	4	6	12	.333	0-0	0	91	.749	4.01	4.79
2019	Mia	NL	45	0	14	68.1	307	87	54	50	15	2	2	5	18	2	63	2	0	1	.000	0-0	3	91	.918	6.31	6.59
Postseason			3	3	0	15.1	69	22	9	8	2	0	0	0	2	0	10	0	1	1	.500	0-0	0	91	.811	5.68	4.70
8 ML YEARS			219	170	15	1064.2	4485	1090	526	495	156	27	40	25	270	12	846	18	59	51	.536	0-0	3	91	.757	4.03	4.18

Robinson Chirinos

Bats: R **Throws:** R **Pos:** C-112;PH-2   chee-REE-nos   **Ht:** 6'1" **Wt:** 210 **Born:** 6/5/1984 **Age:** 36

Year	Team	Lg	G	AB	H	2B	3B	HR	(Hm	Rd)	TB	R	RBI	RC	TBB	IBB	SO	HBP	SH	SF	SB	CS	GDP	Avg	OBP	Slg	OPS
2011	TB	AL	20	55	12	2	0	1	(1	0)	17	4	7	5	5	0	13	0	0	0	0	0	0	.218	.283	.309	.592
2013	Tex	AL	13	28	5	3	0	0	(0	0)	8	3	0	0	2	0	6	0	0	0	0	0	1	.179	.233	.286	.519
2014	Tex	AL	93	306	73	15	0	13	(6	7)	127	36	40	38	17	1	71	7	4	4	0	1	4	.239	.290	.415	.705
2015	Tex	AL	78	233	54	16	1	10	(4	6)	102	33	34	28	28	0	62	5	5	2	0	0	4	.232	.325	.438	.762
2016	Tex	AL	57	147	33	11	0	9	(1	8)	71	21	20	21	15	0	44	5	1	2	0	1	4	.224	.314	.483	.797
2017	Tex	AL	88	263	67	13	1	17	(10	7)	133	46	38	44	34	0	79	10	1	1	1	0	5	.255	.360	.506	.866
2018	Tex	AL	113	360	80	15	1	18	(10	8)	151	48	65	66	45	0	140	19	0	2	2	0	7	.222	.338	.419	.757
2019	Hou	AL	114	366	87	22	1	17	(10	7)	162	57	58	55	51	1	125	13	2	5	1	2	11	.238	.347	.443	.790
Postseason			4	11	3	0	0	1	(0	1)	6	1	3	3	1	0	2	0	0	0	0	0	0	.273	.333	.545	.879
8 ML YEARS			576	1758	411	97	4	85	(42	43)	771	248	262	257	197	2	540	59	13	16	4	4	36	.234	.329	.439	.767

Yonny Chirinos

Pitches: R **Bats:** R **Pos:** SP-18; RP-8   chih-REE-nos   **Ht:** 6'2" **Wt:** 240 **Born:** 12/26/1993 **Age:** 26

Year	Team	Lg	G	GS	GF	IP	BFP	H	R	ER	HR	SH	SF	HB	TBB	IBB	SO	WP	W	L	Pct	Sv-Op	Hld	Vel	OPS	ERC	ERA
2018	TB	AL	18	7	2	89.2	370	84	40	35	7	2	7	5	25	2	75	5	5	5	.500	0-0	0	94	.687	3.36	3.51
2019	TB	AL	26	18	0	133.1	530	112	61	57	23	0	1	3	28	1	114	4	9	5	.643	0-0	0	94	.683	3.05	3.85
2 ML YEARS			44	25	2	223.0	900	196	101	92	30	2	8	8	53	3	189	9	14	10	.583	0-0	0	94	.685	3.18	3.71

Lonnie Chisenhall

Bats: L **Throws:** R **Pos:** OF   CHIZ-en-hall   **Ht:** 6'2" **Wt:** 190 **Born:** 10/4/1988 **Age:** 31

Year	Team	Lg	G	AB	H	2B	3B	HR	(Hm	Rd)	TB	R	RBI	RC	TBB	IBB	SO	HBP	SH	SF	SB	CS	GDP	Avg	OBP	Slg	OPS
2011	Cle	AL	66	212	54	13	0	7	(2	5)	88	27	22	24	8	1	49	1	1	1	1	0	3	.255	.284	.415	.699
2012	Cle	AL	43	142	38	6	1	5	(4	1)	61	16	16	18	8	0	27	1	0	0	2	1	2	.268	.311	.430	.741
2013	Cle	AL	94	289	65	17	0	11	(4	7)	115	30	36	31	16	0	56	2	1	0	1	0	8	.225	.270	.398	.668
2014	Cle	AL	142	478	134	29	1	13	(6	7)	204	62	59	69	39	3	99	8	4	3	3	1	8	.280	.343	.427	.770
2015	Cle	AL	106	333	82	19	1	7	(3	4)	124	38	44	39	23	3	69	1	2	3	4	1	0	.246	.294	.372	.667
2016	Cle	AL	126	385	110	25	5	8	(4	4)	169	43	57	61	23	2	70	3	3	4	6	0	4	.286	.328	.439	.767
2017	Cle	AL	82	236	68	17	1	12	(6	6)	123	34	53	46	25	2	55	3	3	3	2	2	2	.288	.360	.521	.881
2018	Cle	AL	29	84	27	6	1	1	(1	0)	38	11	9	13	8	1	12	2	1	0	1	0	2	.321	.394	.452	.846
Postseason			19	51	12	0	0	1	(1	0)	15	5	5	4	2	0	18	3	1	1	0	0	1	.235	.298	.294	.592
8 ML YEARS			688	2159	578	132	10	64	(29	35)	922	261	296	301	150	12	437	21	15	14	20	5	33	.268	.320	.427	.747

Ji-Man Choi

Bats: L **Throws:** R **Pos:** 1B-103;PH-20;DH-16;PR-1   gee-man choy   **Ht:** 6'1" **Wt:** 250 **Born:** 5/19/1991 **Age:** 29

Year	Team	Lg	G	AB	H	2B	3B	HR	(Hm	Rd)	TB	R	RBI	RC	TBB	IBB	SO	HBP	SH	SF	SB	CS	GDP	Avg	OBP	Slg	OPS
2016	LAA	AL	54	112	19	4	0	5	(3	2)	38	9	12	8	16	1	27	0	0	1	2	4	2	.170	.271	.339	.611
2017	NYY	AL	6	15	4	1	0	2	(2	0)	11	2	5	3	2	0	5	0	0	1	0	0	0	.267	.333	.733	1.067
2018	2 Tms		61	190	50	14	1	10	(5	5)	96	25	32	30	26	1	55	3	0	2	2	0	1	.263	.357	.505	.863
2019	TB	AL	127	410	107	20	2	19	(8	11)	188	54	63	68	64	2	108	6	0	7	2	3	7	.261	.363	.459	.822
18	Mil	NL	12	30	7	2	0	2	(2	0)	15	4	5	5	2	1	14	0	0	0	0	0	1	.233	.281	.500	.781
18	TB	AL	49	160	43	12	1	8	(5	3)	81	21	27	25	24	0	41	3	0	2	2	0	0	.269	.370	.506	.877
4 ML YEARS			248	727	180	39	3	36	(18	18)	333	90	112	109	108	4	195	9	0	11	6	7	11	.248	.347	.458	.805

Shin-Soo Choo

Bats: L **Throws:** L **Pos:** DH-61;RF-42;LF-40;PH-10   SHIN-sue CHEW   **Ht:** 5'11" **Wt:** 210 **Born:** 7/13/1982 **Age:** 37

Year	Team	Lg	G	AB	H	2B	3B	HR	(Hm	Rd)	TB	R	RBI	RC	TBB	IBB	SO	HBP	SH	SF	SB	CS	GDP	Avg	OBP	Slg	OPS
2005	Sea	AL	10	18	1	0	0	0	(0	0)	1	1	1	0	3	0	4	0	0	0	0	0	0	.056	.190	.056	.246
2006	2 Tms	AL	49	157	44	12	3	3	(2	1)	71	23	22	24	18	2	50	2	1	1	5	3	3	.280	.360	.452	.812
2007	Cle	AL	6	17	5	0	0	0	(0	0)	5	5	5	3	2	1	5	0	0	1	0	1	0	.294	.350	.294	.644
2008	Cle	AL	94	317	98	28	3	14	(10	4)	174	68	66	72	44	4	78	5	0	4	4	3	5	.309	.397	.549	.946
2009	Cle	AL	156	583	175	38	6	20	(11	9)	285	87	86	111	78	5	151	17	0	7	21	2	9	.300	.394	.489	.883
2010	Cle	AL	144	550	165	31	2	22	(8	14)	266	81	90	106	83	11	118	11	0	2	22	7	11	.300	.401	.484	.885
2011	Cle	AL	85	313	81	11	3	8	(7	1)	122	37	36	38	36	3	78	6	0	3	12	5	7	.259	.344	.390	.733
2012	Cle	AL	155	598	169	43	2	16	(8	8)	264	88	67	96	73	0	150	14	0	1	21	7	10	.283	.373	.441	.815
2013	Cin	NL	154	569	162	34	2	21	(10	11)	263	107	54	111	112	5	133	26	3	2	20	11	3	.285	.423	.462	.885
2014	Tex	AL	123	455	110	19	1	13	(5	8)	170	58	40	54	58	3	131	12	0	4	3	4	9	.242	.340	.374	.714
2015	Tex	AL	149	555	153	32	3	22	(12	10)	257	94	82	99	76	1	147	15	2	5	4	2	7	.276	.375	.463	.838
2016	Tex	AL	48	178	43	7	0	7	(2	5)	71	27	17	25	25	1	46	7	0	0	6	3	1	.242	.357	.399	.756
2017	Tex	AL	149	544	142	20	1	22	(9	13)	230	96	78	97	77	1	134	7	3	5	12	3	18	.261	.357	.423	.780
2018	Tex	AL	146	560	148	30	1	21	(7	14)	243	83	62	94	92	2	156	10	1	2	6	1	11	.264	.377	.434	.810

BATTING / RUNNING / AVERAGES (continued)

Year Team	Lg	G	AB	H	2B	3B	HR	(Hm Rd)	TB	R	RBI	RC	TBB	IBB	SO	HBP	SH	SF	SB	CS	GDP	Avg	OBP	Slg	OPS
2019 Tex	AL	151	563	149	31	2	24	(12 12)	256	93	61	103	78	3	165	18	0	1	15	1	6	.265	.371	.455	.826
06 Sea	AL	4	11	1	1	0	0	(0 0)	2	0	0	0	0	0	4	1	0	0	0	0	1	.091	.167	.182	.348
06 Cle	AL	45	146	43	11	3	3	(2 1)	69	23	22	24	18	2	46	1	1	1	5	3	2	.295	.373	.473	.846
Postseason		7	27	6	0	0	2	(0 2)	12	6	4	3	1	0	9	1	1	0	0	0	0	.222	.276	.444	.720
15 ML YEARS		1619	5977	1645	336	29	213	(103 110)	2678	948	767	1033	855	42	1546	150	10	38	151	53	100	.275	.377	.448	.826

Adam Cimber

Pitches: R Bats: R Pos: RP-68
Ht: 6'4" Wt: 195 Born: 8/15/1990 Age: 29

Year Team	Lg	G	GS	GF	IP	BFP	H	R	ER	HR	SH	SF	HB	TBB	IBB	SO	WP	W	L	Pct	Sv-Op	Hld	Vel	OPS	ERC	ERA
2018 2 Tms		70	0	16	68.1	284	68	28	26	5	2	2	6	17	9	58	1	3	8	.273	0-1	12	87	.743	3.49	3.42
2019 Cle	AL	68	0	12	56.2	244	56	29	28	6	1	2	4	19	2	41	0	6	3	.667	1-3	19	85	.720	4.01	4.45
18 SD	NL	42	0	10	48.1	192	42	19	17	2	1	2	2	10	3	51	0	3	5	.375	0-1	5	86	.644	2.42	3.17
18 Cle	AL	28	0	6	20.0	92	26	9	9	3	1	0	4	7	6	7	1	0	3	.000	0-0	7	87	.957	6.53	4.05
Postseason		2	0	1	2.0	8	2	1	1	0	0	0	0	1	0	0	0	0	0	-	0-0	0	87	.661	4.15	4.50
2 ML YEARS		138	0	28	125.0	528	124	57	54	11	3	4	10	36	11	99	1	9	11	.450	1-4	31	86	.732	3.73	3.89

Steve Cishek

Pitches: R Bats: R Pos: RP-70
SEE-sheck
Ht: 6'6" Wt: 215 Born: 6/18/1986 Age: 34

Year Team	Lg	G	GS	GF	IP	BFP	H	R	ER	HR	SH	SF	HB	TBB	IBB	SO	WP	W	L	Pct	Sv-Op	Hld	Vel	OPS	ERC	ERA
2010 Fla	NL	3	0	2	4.1	15	1	0	0	0	0	0	0	1	0	3	0	0	0	-	0-0	0	93	.276	0.35	0.00
2011 Fla	NL	45	0	21	54.2	229	45	18	16	1	3	0	3	19	7	55	5	2	1	.667	3-3	2	93	.591	2.38	2.63
2012 Mia	NL	68	0	36	63.2	275	54	26	19	3	3	2	6	29	6	68	1	5	2	.714	15-19	13	92	.663	3.28	2.69
2013 Mia	NL	69	0	62	69.2	281	53	19	18	3	3	3	2	22	6	74	1	4	6	.400	34-36	1	92	.568	2.15	2.33
2014 Mia	NL	67	0	55	65.1	275	58	26	23	3	5	3	1	21	2	84	1	4	5	.444	39-43	0	92	.643	2.78	3.17
2015 2 Tms	NL	59	0	23	55.1	243	55	26	22	4	1	2	1	27	3	48	1	2	6	.250	4-9	6	91	.720	4.17	3.58
2016 Sea	AL	62	0	40	64.0	258	44	21	20	8	1	0	4	21	2	76	4	4	6	.400	25-32	9	91	.600	2.51	2.81
2017 2 Tms	NL	49	0	11	44.2	174	26	10	10	3	0	1	3	14	1	41	3	3	2	.600	1-4	15	90	.491	1.70	2.01
2018 ChC	NL	80	0	10	70.1	288	45	19	17	5	2	1	9	28	4	78	2	4	3	.571	4-7	25	90	.593	2.39	2.18
2019 ChC	NL	70	0	23	64.0	267	48	22	21	7	0	2	7	29	1	57	4	4	6	.400	7-11	11	91	.642	3.44	2.95
15 Mia	NL	32	0	15	32.0	144	37	19	16	2	1	2	0	14	3	28	0	2	6	.250	3-7	3	91	.782	4.66	4.50
15 StL	NL	27	0	8	23.1	99	18	7	6	2	0	0	1	13	0	20	1	0	0	-	1-2	3	91	.629	3.53	2.31
17 Sea	AL	23	0	8	20.0	80	13	7	7	3	0	1	1	7	1	15	1	1	1	.500	1-4	6	90	.601	2.48	3.15
17 TB	AL	26	0	3	24.2	94	13	3	3	0	0	0	2	7	0	26	2	2	1	.667	0-0	9	91	.399	1.25	1.09
Postseason		1	0	0	0.2	1	0	0	0	0	0	0	0	0	0	0	0	0	0	-	0-0	0	92	.000	0.00	0.00
10 ML YEARS		572	0	283	556.0	2305	429	187	166	37	18	14	36	211	32	584	22	32	37	.464	132-164	82	91	.614	2.72	2.69

Jose Cisnero

Pitches: R Bats: R Pos: RP-35
siss-NEHR-oh
Ht: 6'3" Wt: 245 Born: 4/11/1989 Age: 31

Year Team	Lg	G	GS	GF	IP	BFP	H	R	ER	HR	SH	SF	HB	TBB	IBB	SO	WP	W	L	Pct	Sv-Op	Hld	Vel	OPS	ERC	ERA
2019 Toledo	AAA	32	2	23	40.0	177	36	14	12	3	1	0	2	21	0	49	1	1	2	.333	7--	-	-	.695	3.97	2.70
2013 Hou	AL	28	0	11	43.2	198	49	23	20	5	0	2	1	22	5	41	1	2	2	.500	0-2	5	93	.826	5.21	4.12
2014 Hou	AL	5	0	1	4.2	25	8	5	5	0	0	1	0	4	0	5	0	0	0	-	0-1	0	94	.930	9.79	9.64
2019 Det	AL	35	0	10	35.1	162	35	21	17	5	2	2	3	19	3	40	1	0	4	.000	0-2	4	96	.805	4.99	4.33
3 ML YEARS		68	0	22	83.2	385	92	49	42	10	2	5	4	45	8	86	2	2	6	.250	0-5	9	94	.824	5.36	4.52

Nick Ciuffo

Bats: L Throws: R Pos: C-3
Ht: 6'0" Wt: 200 Born: 3/7/1995 Age: 25

Year Team	Lg	G	AB	H	2B	3B	HR	(Hm Rd)	TB	R	RBI	RC	TBB	IBB	SO	HBP	SH	SF	SB	CS	GDP	Avg	OBP	Slg	OPS
2019 Drham	AAA	34	123	28	7	1	2	(- -)	43	14	16	12	9	0	37	0	0	2	1	1	2	.228	.276	.350	.626
2018 TB	AL	16	37	7	1	0	1	(1 0)	11	3	5	4	3	0	12	1	2	1	0	0	1	.189	.262	.297	.559
2019 TB	AL	3	6	1	0	0	0	(0 0)	1	0	0	0	0	0	3	0	0	0	0	0	0	.167	.167	.167	.333
2 ML YEARS		19	43	8	1	0	1	(1 0)	12	3	5	4	3	0	15	1	2	1	0	0	1	.186	.250	.279	.529

Aaron Civale

Pitches: R Bats: R Pos: SP-10
Ht: 6'2" Wt: 215 Born: 6/12/1995 Age: 25

Year Team	Lg	G	GS	GF	IP	BFP	H	R	ER	HR	SH	SF	HB	TBB	IBB	SO	WP	W	L	Pct	Sv-Op	Hld	Vel	OPS	ERC	ERA
2019 Akron	AA	5	5	0	30.1	121	26	9	9	3	0	2	1	6	0	24	1	4	0	1.000	0--	-	-	.666	2.70	2.67
2019 Clmbs	AAA	8	8	0	42.1	176	38	13	10	4	1	1	2	9	0	46	2	3	1	.750	0--	-	-	.636	2.90	2.13
2019 Cle	AL	10	10	0	57.2	227	44	18	15	4	1	5	1	16	0	46	2	3	4	.429	0-0	0	93	.638	2.31	2.34

Taylor Clarke

Pitches: R Bats: R Pos: SP-15; RP-8
Ht: 6'4" Wt: 200 Born: 5/13/1993 Age: 27

Year Team	Lg	G	GS	GF	IP	BFP	H	R	ER	HR	SH	SF	HB	TBB	IBB	SO	WP	W	L	Pct	Sv-Op	Hld	Vel	OPS	ERC	ERA
2019 Reno	AAA	8	8	0	36.2	164	41	27	27	6	2	2	1	17	0	28	4	3	1	.750	0--	-	-	.885	5.67	6.63
2019 Ari	NL	23	15	3	84.2	369	86	55	50	23	1	5	6	30	0	68	3	5	5	.500	1-1	0	94	.882	5.50	5.31

Emmanuel Clase

Pitches: R Bats: R Pos: RP-20; SP-1　　　　Ht: 6'2" Wt: 206 Born: 3/18/1998 Age: 22

Year Team	Lg	G	GS	GF	IP	BFP	H	R	ER	HR	SH	SF	HB	TBB	IBB	SO	WP	W	L	Pct	Sv-Op	Hld	Vel	OPS	ERC	ERA
2019 Frisco	AA	33	1	20	37.2	153	34	15	14	1	1	0	0	8	0	39	6	1	2	.333	11--	-	-	.554	2.38	3.35
2019 DwnEast	A+	6	0	5	7.0	25	4	0	0	0	0	0	0	1	0	11	0	2	0	1.000	1--	-	-	.367	0.97	0.00
2019 Tex	AL	21	1	7	23.1	94	20	8	6	2	0	0	1	6	0	21	1	2	3	.400	1-1	4	99	.678	2.89	2.31

Alex Claudio

Pitches: L Bats: L Pos: RP-83　　　　Ht: 6'3" Wt: 180 Born: 1/31/1992 Age: 28

Year Team	Lg	G	GS	GF	IP	BFP	H	R	ER	HR	SH	SF	HB	TBB	IBB	SO	WP	W	L	Pct	Sv-Op	Hld	Vel	OPS	ERC	ERA
2014 Tex	AL	15	0	5	12.1	54	14	4	4	0	0	0	0	4	0	14	0	0	0	-	0-0	0	84	.693	3.79	2.92
2015 Tex	AL	18	0	6	15.2	66	12	6	5	4	0	2	1	6	2	13	1	1	1	.500	0-1	3	84	.762	3.74	2.87
2016 Tex	AL	39	0	15	51.2	217	55	19	16	2	0	2	1	10	0	34	0	4	1	.800	0-0	2	85	.662	3.28	2.79
2017 Tex	AL	70	1	38	82.2	323	71	26	23	5	1	3	2	15	4	56	0	4	2	.667	11-15	7	87	.591	2.37	2.50
2018 Tex	AL	66	1	20	68.1	299	91	35	34	4	3	3	3	13	3	41	0	4	2	.667	1-3	14	86	.827	5.03	4.48
2019 Mil	NL	83	0	9	62.0	267	57	29	28	8	1	3	6	24	2	44	1	2	2	.500	0-3	22	86	.751	4.12	4.06
Postseason		2	0	0	5.0	18	3	0	0	0	0	0	0	3	0	0	0	0	0	-	0-0	0	86	.600	2.46	0.00
6 ML YEARS		291	2	93	292.2	1226	300	119	110	23	5	13	13	72	11	202	2	15	8	.652	12-22	48	86	.709	3.62	3.38

Mike Clevinger

Pitches: R Bats: R Pos: SP-21　　　　Ht: 6'4" Wt: 215 Born: 12/21/1990 Age: 29

Year Team	Lg	G	GS	GF	IP	BFP	H	R	ER	HR	SH	SF	HB	TBB	IBB	SO	WP	W	L	Pct	Sv-Op	Hld	Vel	OPS	ERC	ERA
2016 Cle	AL	17	10	3	53.0	233	50	31	31	8	0	1	0	29	0	50	2	3	3	.500	0-0	0	93	.768	4.72	5.26
2017 Cle	AL	27	21	1	121.2	502	92	46	42	13	1	0	3	60	2	137	3	12	6	.667	0-0	0	92	.667	3.29	3.11
2018 Cle	AL	32	32	0	200.0	810	164	71	67	21	0	1	4	67	0	207	4	13	8	.619	0-0	0	94	.655	3.02	3.02
2019 Cle	AL	21	21	0	126.0	499	96	38	38	10	0	1	2	37	0	169	0	13	4	.765	0-0	0	95	.602	2.41	2.71
Postseason		7	1	3	12.0	57	8	7	6	3	0	1	0	12	0	15	1	0	0	-	0-0	0	95	.857	5.95	4.50
4 ML YEARS		97	84	4	500.2	2044	402	186	178	52	1	3	9	193	2	563	9	41	21	.661	0-0	0	94	.658	3.09	3.20

Tyler Clippard

Pitches: R Bats: R Pos: RP-50; SP-3　　　　Ht: 6'3" Wt: 200 Born: 2/14/1985 Age: 35

Year Team	Lg	G	GS	GF	IP	BFP	H	R	ER	HR	SH	SF	HB	TBB	IBB	SO	WP	W	L	Pct	Sv-Op	Hld	Vel	OPS	ERC	ERA
2007 NYY	AL	6	6	0	27.0	124	29	19	19	6	0	0	0	17	1	18	2	3	1	.750	0-0	0	88	.876	6.37	6.33
2008 Was	NL	2	2	0	10.1	48	12	5	5	2	0	0	0	7	1	8	1	1	1	.500	0-0	0	89	.957	6.90	4.35
2009 Was	NL	41	0	8	60.1	246	36	20	18	9	3	1	1	32	1	67	1	4	2	.667	0-1	3	90	.633	2.79	2.69
2010 Was	NL	78	0	18	91.0	378	69	33	31	8	3	7	2	41	4	112	1	11	8	.579	1-11	23	92	.646	2.91	3.07
2011 Was	NL	72	0	8	88.1	329	48	18	18	11	4	3	0	26	2	104	1	3	0	1.000	0-7	38	93	.535	1.61	1.83
2012 Was	NL	74	0	42	72.2	307	55	32	30	7	3	4	2	29	2	84	5	2	6	.250	32-37	13	93	.621	2.73	3.72
2013 Was	NL	72	0	6	71.0	275	37	19	19	9	2	1	4	24	1	73	2	6	3	.667	0-3	33	92	.517	1.79	2.41
2014 Was	NL	75	0	6	70.1	278	47	22	17	5	2	2	1	23	1	82	0	7	4	.636	1-7	40	92	.541	1.98	2.18
2015 2 Tms		69	0	36	71.0	301	49	25	23	8	1	2	4	31	2	64	6	5	4	.556	19-25	8	92	.599	2.72	2.92
2016 2 Tms		69	0	17	63.0	262	54	27	25	10	1	0	1	26	2	72	5	4	6	.400	3-6	25	91	.716	3.80	3.57
2017 3 Tms	AL	67	0	23	60.1	264	47	33	32	10	3	3	2	31	1	72	11	2	8	.200	5-11	9	91	.711	3.73	4.77
2018 Tor	AL	73	1	22	68.2	285	57	29	28	13	2	2	2	23	0	85	7	4	3	.571	7-13	15	91	.719	3.57	3.67
2019 Cle	AL	53	3	7	62.0	241	38	20	20	8	2	1	7	15	0	64	3	1	0	1.000	0-0	8	90	.608	2.13	2.90
15 Oak	AL	37	0	30	38.2	167	25	12	12	3	0	1	2	21	1	38	1	1	3	.250	17-21	0	91	.567	2.62	2.79
15 NYM	NL	32	0	6	32.1	134	24	13	11	5	1	1	2	10	1	26	5	4	1	.800	2-4	8	92	.637	2.82	3.06
16 Ari	NL	40	0	10	37.2	155	34	18	18	7	1	0	0	15	0	46	1	2	3	.400	1-3	13	91	.764	4.23	4.30
16 NYY	AL	29	0	7	25.1	107	20	9	7	3	0	0	1	11	2	26	4	2	3	.400	2-3	12	92	.646	3.19	2.49
17 NYY	AL	40	0	7	36.1	158	28	21	20	7	3	1	1	19	1	42	5	1	5	.167	1-6	8	91	.735	3.88	4.95
17 CWS	AL	11	0	7	10.0	44	8	2	2	0	0	1	0	5	0	12	3	1	1	.500	2-2	0	91	.585	2.56	1.80
17 Hou	AL	16	0	9	14.0	62	11	10	10	3	0	1	1	7	0	18	3	0	2	.000	2-3	1	90	.740	4.19	6.43
Postseason		14	0	1	12.2	53	9	6	6	2	1	0	0	5	0	11	1	0	1	.000	0-0	8	92	.673	2.77	4.26
13 ML YEARS		751	12	193	816.0	3338	578	302	285	106	26	26	26	325	18	905	45	53	46	.535	68-121	215	91	.635	2.79	3.14

Alex Cobb

Pitches: R Bats: R Pos: SP-3　　　　Ht: 6'3" Wt: 205 Born: 10/7/1987 Age: 32

Year Team	Lg	G	GS	GF	IP	BFP	H	R	ER	HR	SH	SF	HB	TBB	IBB	SO	WP	W	L	Pct	Sv-Op	Hld	Vel	OPS	ERC	ERA
2011 TB	AL	9	9	0	52.2	224	49	21	20	3	0	1	1	21	1	37	2	3	2	.600	0-0	0	91	.655	3.44	3.42
2012 TB	AL	23	23	0	136.1	569	130	67	61	11	3	6	9	40	2	106	8	11	9	.550	0-0	0	90	.690	3.56	4.03
2013 TB	AL	22	22	0	143.1	578	120	46	44	13	1	2	2	45	4	134	5	11	3	.786	0-0	0	91	.644	2.92	2.76
2014 TB	AL	27	27	0	166.1	681	142	56	53	11	4	4	10	47	1	149	8	10	9	.526	0-0	0	92	.619	2.87	2.87
2016 TB	AL	5	5	0	22.0	104	32	22	21	5	1	1	0	7	0	16	0	1	2	.333	0-0	0	90	.968	7.40	8.59
2017 TB	AL	29	29	0	179.1	742	175	78	73	22	2	1	6	44	2	128	8	12	10	.545	0-0	0	92	.709	3.64	3.66
2018 Bal	AL	28	28	0	152.1	661	172	93	83	24	2	6	4	43	5	102	4	5	15	.250	0-0	0	92	.814	4.81	4.90
2019 Bal	AL	3	3	0	12.1	60	21	16	15	9	0	0	0	2	0	8	0	0	2	.000	0-0	0	92	1.297	12.47	10.95
Postseason		2	2	0	11.2	51	13	3	2	0	0	0	0	3	0	10	1	1	0	1.000	0-0	0	92	.695	3.75	1.54
8 ML YEARS		146	146	0	864.2	3619	841	399	370	98	13	21	33	249	15	680	35	53	52	.505	0-0	0	91	.713	3.73	3.85

A.J. Cole

Pitches: R **Bats:** R **Pos:** RP-25 **Ht:** 6'5" **Wt:** 238 **Born:** 1/5/1992 **Age:** 28

Year	Team	Lg	G	GS	GF	IP	BFP	H	R	ER	HR	SH	SF	HB	TBB	IBB	SO	WP	W	L	Pct	Sv-Op	Hld	Vel	OPS	ERC	ERA
2019	Clmbs	AAA	13	0	8	17.0	63	10	6	6	2	0	1	1	5	0	21	3	0	1	.000	2--	-		.593	2.05	3.18
2015	Was	NL	3	1	1	9.1	44	14	11	6	1	1	1	0	1	1	9	1	0	0	-	1-1	0	90	.812	5.38	5.79
2016	Was	NL	8	8	0	38.1	168	37	24	22	7	0	3	2	14	1	39	1	1	2	.333	0-0	0	91	.779	4.39	5.17
2017	Was	NL	11	8	0	52.0	229	51	23	22	8	3	1	3	27	0	44	2	3	5	.375	0-0	0	93	.799	5.15	3.81
2018	2 Tms		32	2	14	48.1	221	55	38	33	15	2	1	0	22	1	59	2	4	2	.667	0-1	0	93	.928	6.57	6.14
2019	Cle	AL	25	0	9	26.0	118	31	16	11	4	1	2	0	8	0	30	0	3	1	.750	1-1	0	94	.819	5.03	3.81
18	Was	NL	4	2	1	10.1	53	16	15	15	6	2	0	0	6	0	10	0	1	1	.500	0-0	0	92	1.298	12.42	13.06
18	NYY	AL	28	0	13	38.0	168	39	23	18	9	0	1	0	16	1	49	2	3	1	.750	0-1	0	94	.817	5.17	4.26
	5 ML YEARS		79	19	24	174.0	780	188	112	94	35	7	8	5	72	3	181	6	11	10	.524	2-3	0	93	.836	5.36	4.86

Gerrit Cole

Pitches: R **Bats:** R **Pos:** SP-33 **Ht:** 6'4" **Wt:** 225 **Born:** 9/8/1990 **Age:** 29

Year	Team	Lg	G	GS	GF	IP	BFP	H	R	ER	HR	SH	SF	HB	TBB	IBB	SO	WP	W	L	Pct	Sv-Op	Hld	Vel	OPS	ERC	ERA
2013	Pit	NL	19	19	0	117.1	469	109	43	42	7	5	2	3	28	0	100	4	10	7	.588	0-0	0	96	.638	3.02	3.22
2014	Pit	NL	22	22	0	138.0	571	127	58	56	11	10	0	9	40	1	138	9	11	5	.688	0-0	0	95	.693	3.37	3.65
2015	Pit	NL	32	32	0	208.0	832	183	71	60	11	7	6	10	44	1	202	7	19	8	.704	0-0	0	96	.623	2.66	2.60
2016	Pit	NL	21	21	0	116.0	506	131	57	50	7	4	6	6	36	3	98	5	7	10	.412	0-0	0	95	.754	4.35	3.88
2017	Pit	NL	33	33	0	203.0	849	199	98	96	31	5	1	4	55	1	196	7	12	12	.500	0-0	0	96	.739	3.89	4.26
2018	Hou	AL	32	32	0	200.1	799	143	68	64	19	2	3	7	64	0	276	6	15	5	.750	0-0	0	97	.600	2.40	2.88
2019	Hou	AL	33	33	0	212.1	817	142	66	59	29	1	3	3	48	3	326	4	20	5	.800	0-0	0	97	.579	2.02	2.50
	Postseason		5	5	0	29.0	112	20	13	12	5	0	0	0	5	0	31	0	2	3	.400	0-0	0	97	.588	2.03	3.72
	7 ML YEARS		192	192	0	1195.0	4843	1034	461	427	115	34	21	42	315	6	1336	45	94	52	.644	0-0	0	96	.656	2.97	3.22

Taylor Cole

Pitches: R **Bats:** R **Pos:** RP-32; SP-6 **Ht:** 6'1" **Wt:** 200 **Born:** 8/20/1989 **Age:** 30

Year	Team	Lg	G	GS	GF	IP	BFP	H	R	ER	HR	SH	SF	HB	TBB	IBB	SO	WP	W	L	Pct	Sv-Op	Hld	Vel	OPS	ERC	ERA
2019	Salt Lk	AAA	16	0	8	20.2	93	29	12	12	5	0	0	0	6	0	24	0	3	0	1.000	3--	-		.986	7.30	5.23
2017	Tor	AL	1	0	0	1.0	10	6	4	4	0	0	0	1	1	0	1	0	0	0	-	0-0	0	93	1.675	55.76	36.00
2018	LAA	AL	18	2	4	36.0	135	20	11	11	3	1	1	3	12	0	39	1	4	2	.667	0-0	0	93	.541	1.91	2.75
2019	LAA	AL	38	6	9	51.2	231	58	35	34	2	0	2	2	24	4	50	3	3	4	.429	0-0	4	93	.763	4.63	5.92
	3 ML YEARS		57	8	13	88.2	376	84	50	49	5	1	3	6	37	4	90	4	7	6	.538	0-0	4	93	.706	3.82	4.97

Tim Collins

Pitches: L **Bats:** L **Pos:** RP-9 **Ht:** 5'7" **Wt:** 170 **Born:** 8/21/1989 **Age:** 30

Year	Team	Lg	G	GS	GF	IP	BFP	H	R	ER	HR	SH	SF	HB	TBB	IBB	SO	WP	W	L	Pct	Sv-Op	Hld	Vel	OPS	ERC	ERA
2019	Iowa	AAA	28	0	6	27.0	117	20	16	14	7	1	1	0	16	3	37	0	1	3	.250	1--	-	-	.765	4.23	4.67
2019	Lsvlle	AAA	5	0	1	4.0	18	5	3	3	0	0	0	0	3	1	3	1	1	0	1.000	0--	-	-	.911	6.14	6.75
2011	KC	AL	68	0	18	67.0	295	52	28	27	5	3	1	2	48	2	60	3	4	4	.500	0-1	11	92	.681	3.95	3.63
2012	KC	AL	72	0	9	69.2	295	55	29	26	8	3	1	2	34	8	93	1	5	4	.556	0-4	11	93	.692	3.29	3.36
2013	KC	AL	66	0	8	53.1	233	49	26	21	3	2	2	0	28	1	52	0	3	6	.333	0-5	21	93	.677	3.74	3.54
2014	KC	AL	22	0	9	21.0	90	18	9	9	2	3	1	2	11	0	15	1	0	3	.000	0-1	1	92	.712	4.20	3.86
2018	Was	NL	38	0	5	22.2	99	23	11	11	5	0	0	0	12	0	21	1	0	0	-	0-0	4	92	.825	5.70	4.37
2019	ChC	NL	9	0	3	8.2	38	9	3	3	1	0	1	0	3	0	4	0	0	0	-	0-0	0	92	.757	4.09	3.12
	Postseason		4	0	2	5.2	26	6	2	2	0	1	0	1	2	0	7	1	0	0	-	0-0	0	92	.724	4.05	3.18
	6 ML YEARS		275	0	52	242.1	1050	206	106	97	24	14	6	6	136	11	245	8	12	17	.414	0-11	48	93	.703	3.90	3.60

Zack Collins

Bats: L **Throws:** R **Pos:** DH-14;C-10;PH-2;1B-1 **Ht:** 6'3" **Wt:** 220 **Born:** 2/6/1995 **Age:** 25

Year	Team	Lg	G	AB	H	2B	3B	HR	(Hm Rd)	TB	R	RBI	RC	TBB	IBB	SO	HBP	SH	SF	SB	CS	GDP	Avg	OBP	Slg	OPS
2019	Charltt	AAA	88	294	83	19	1	19	(- -)	161	56	74	67	62	1	98	3	0	8	0	0	2	.282	.403	.548	.951
2019	CWS	AL	27	86	16	3	1	3	(0 3)	30	10	12	11	14	1	39	1	0	0	0	0	1	.186	.307	.349	.656

Alex Colome

Pitches: R **Bats:** R **Pos:** RP-62
COHL-oh-may
Ht: 6'1" **Wt:** 220 **Born:** 12/31/1988 **Age:** 31

Year	Team	Lg	G	GS	GF	IP	BFP	H	R	ER	HR	SH	SF	HB	TBB	IBB	SO	WP	W	L	Pct	Sv-Op	Hld	Vel	OPS	ERC	ERA
2013	TB	AL	3	3	0	16.0	71	14	8	4	2	0	0	1	9	0	12	1	1	1	.500	0-0	0	95	.715	4.41	2.25
2014	TB	AL	5	3	1	23.2	97	19	7	7	1	0	2	0	10	0	13	3	2	0	1.000	0-0	0	94	.590	2.77	2.66
2015	TB	AL	43	13	6	109.2	457	112	50	48	9	2	7	4	31	4	88	8	8	5	.615	0-5	8	94	.698	3.78	3.94
2016	TB	AL	57	0	48	56.2	226	43	12	12	6	0	0	2	15	1	71	1	2	4	.333	37-40	1	95	.572	2.46	1.91
2017	TB	AL	65	0	53	66.2	281	57	27	24	4	3	6	3	23	7	58	4	2	3	.400	47-53	1	95	.636	2.79	3.24
2018	2 Tms		70	0	24	68.0	282	59	26	23	7	0	1	3	21	2	72	10	7	5	.583	12-17	30	95	.645	3.15	3.04
2019	CWS	AL	62	0	54	61.0	249	42	28	19	7	2	3	1	23	2	55	4	4	5	.444	30-33	0	94	.617	2.43	2.80
18	TB	AL	23	0	21	21.2	97	24	12	10	1	0	1	0	8	1	23	4	2	5	.286	11-13	0	95	.728	3.99	4.15
18	Sea	AL	47	0	3	46.1	185	35	14	13	6	0	0	3	13	1	49	6	5	0	1.000	1-4	30	95	.601	2.77	2.53
	7 ML YEARS		305	19	185	401.2	1663	346	158	137	36	7	18	14	132	16	369	31	26	23	.531	126-148	40	95	.644	3.07	3.07

Christian Colon

Bats: R **Throws:** R **Pos:** PH-8;2B-3 co-LONE **Ht:** 5'10" **Wt:** 195 **Born:** 5/14/1989 **Age:** 31

Year	Team	Lg	G	AB	H	2B	3B	HR	(Hm	Rd)	TB	R	RBI	RC	TBB	IBB	SO	HBP	SH	SF	SB	CS	GDP	Avg	OBP	Slg	OPS
2014	KC	AL	21	45	15	5	1	0	(0	0)	22	8	6	9	3	0	4	0	1	0	2	0	1	.333	.375	.489	.864
2015	KC	AL	43	107	31	5	0	0	(0	0)	36	8	6	12	11	0	17	0	1	0	3	2	2	.290	.356	.336	.692
2016	KC	AL	54	147	34	6	0	1	(1	0)	43	13	13	13	11	0	31	2	1	0	0	1	4	.231	.294	.293	.586
2017	2 Tms		24	50	8	1	0	0	(0	0)	9	4	0	0	5	1	10	0	2	0	0	0	4	.160	.236	.180	.416
2019	Cin	NL	8	6	3	0	0	0	(0	0)	3	1	1	2	0	0	0	2	0	0	0	0	0	.500	.625	.500	1.125
17	KC	AL	7	17	3	0	0	0	(0	0)	3	1	0	0	1	0	3	0	1	0	0	0	2	.176	.222	.176	.399
17	Mia		17	33	5	1	0	0	(0	0)	6	3	0	0	4	1	7	0	1	0	0	0	2	.152	.243	.182	.425
	Postseason		3	2	2	0	0	0	(0	0)	2	2	2	2	0	0	0	0	1	0	1	0	0	1.000	1.000	1.000	2.000
	5 ML YEARS		150	355	91	17	1	1	(1	0)	113	34	26	36	30	1	62	4	5	0	5	3	11	.256	.321	.318	.640

Michael Conforto

Bats: L **Throws:** R **Pos:** RF-132;CF-39;PH-5 **Ht:** 6'1" **Wt:** 215 **Born:** 3/1/1993 **Age:** 27

Year	Team	Lg	G	AB	H	2B	3B	HR	(Hm	Rd)	TB	R	RBI	RC	TBB	IBB	SO	HBP	SH	SF	SB	CS	GDP	Avg	OBP	Slg	OPS
2015	NYM	NL	56	174	47	14	0	9	(4	5)	88	30	26	29	17	0	39	1	0	2	0	1	4	.270	.335	.506	.841
2016	NYM	NL	109	304	67	21	1	12	(7	5)	126	38	42	35	36	2	89	5	0	3	2	1	6	.220	.310	.414	.725
2017	NYM	NL	109	373	104	20	1	27	(16	11)	207	72	68	77	57	5	113	8	0	2	2	0	3	.279	.384	.555	.939
2018	NYM	NL	153	543	132	25	1	28	(11	17)	243	78	82	87	84	8	159	7	0	4	3	4	10	.243	.350	.448	.797
2019	NYM	NL	151	549	141	29	1	33	(16	17)	271	90	92	97	84	5	149	10	0	5	7	2	11	.257	.363	.494	.856
	Postseason		12	30	6	0	0	3	(2	1)	15	3	6	5	1	0	8	1	0	0	0	0	0	.200	.235	.500	.735
	5 ML YEARS		578	1943	491	109	4	109	(56	53)	935	308	310	325	278	20	549	31	0	16	14	8	34	.253	.353	.481	.834

Adam Conley

Pitches: L **Bats:** L **Pos:** RP-60 **Ht:** 6'3" **Wt:** 200 **Born:** 5/24/1990 **Age:** 30

Year	Team	Lg	G	GS	GF	IP	BFP	H	R	ER	HR	SH	SF	HB	TBB	IBB	SO	WP	W	L	Pct	Sv-Op	Hld	Vel	OPS	ERC	ERA
2015	Mia	NL	15	11	1	67.0	281	65	28	28	7	1	4	3	21	1	59	0	4	1	.800	0-0	0	91	.723	3.80	3.76
2016	Mia	NL	25	25	0	133.1	584	125	59	57	13	7	3	11	62	7	124	9	8	6	.571	0-0	0	91	.738	4.21	3.85
2017	Mia	NL	22	20	1	102.2	463	114	74	70	19	8	2	8	42	4	72	5	8	8	.500	0-0	0	90	.852	5.63	6.14
2018	Mia	NL	52	0	5	50.2	202	37	25	23	5	1	3	1	18	1	50	3	3	4	.429	3-5	16	95	.642	2.57	4.09
2019	Mia	NL	60	0	18	60.2	283	76	45	44	10	2	1	3	29	6	53	2	2	11	.154	2-4	6	95	.908	6.45	6.53
	5 ML YEARS		174	56	25	414.1	1813	417	231	222	54	19	13	26	172	19	358	19	25	30	.455	5-9	22	92	.780	4.58	4.82

Willson Contreras

Bats: R **Throws:** R **Pos:** C-99;PH-3;1B-2;RF-2;LF-1;DH-1;PR-1 **Ht:** 6'1" **Wt:** 210 **Born:** 5/13/1992 **Age:** 28

Year	Team	Lg	G	AB	H	2B	3B	HR	(Hm	Rd)	TB	R	RBI	RC	TBB	IBB	SO	HBP	SH	SF	SB	CS	GDP	Avg	OBP	Slg	OPS
2016	ChC	NL	76	252	71	14	1	12	(8	4)	123	33	35	41	26	0	67	4	0	1	2	2	7	.282	.357	.488	.845
2017	ChC	NL	117	377	104	21	0	21	(10	11)	188	50	74	76	45	2	98	3	1	2	5	4	13	.276	.356	.499	.855
2018	ChC	NL	138	474	118	27	5	10	(6	4)	185	50	54	58	53	2	121	13	2	2	4	1	14	.249	.339	.390	.730
2019	ChC	NL	105	360	98	18	2	24	(15	9)	192	57	64	62	38	2	102	9	0	2	1	2	4	.272	.355	.533	.888
	Postseason		28	74	17	2	0	3	(2	1)	28	9	7	11	12	1	21	0	0	0	0	0	0	.230	.337	.378	.716
	4 ML YEARS		436	1463	391	80	8	67	(39	28)	688	190	227	237	162	6	388	29	3	7	12	9	38	.267	.350	.470	.821

Sam Coonrod

Pitches: R **Bats:** R **Pos:** RP-33 **Ht:** 6'2" **Wt:** 225 **Born:** 9/22/1992 **Age:** 27

Year	Team	Lg	G	GS	GF	IP	BFP	H	R	ER	HR	SH	SF	HB	TBB	IBB	SO	WP	W	L	Pct	Sv-Op	Hld	Vel	OPS	ERC	ERA
2019	Scrmto	AAA	33	1	13	32.1	154	41	27	25	4	1	0	0	18	0	43	3	2	4	.333	3--	-	-	.882	6.44	6.96
2019	SF	NL	33	0	9	27.2	114	19	11	11	3	1	0	4	15	1	20	2	5	1	.833	0-1	0	97	.655	3.63	3.58

Garrett Cooper

Bats: R **Throws:** R **Pos:** 1B-73;RF-31;PH-6;DH-2 **Ht:** 6'6" **Wt:** 230 **Born:** 12/25/1990 **Age:** 29

Year	Team	Lg	G	AB	H	2B	3B	HR	(Hm	Rd)	TB	R	RBI	RC	TBB	IBB	SO	HBP	SH	SF	SB	CS	GDP	Avg	OBP	Slg	OPS
2017	NYY	AL	13	43	14	5	1	0	(0	0)	21	3	6	6	1	0	12	0	0	1	0	0	0	.326	.333	.488	.822
2018	Mia	NL	14	33	7	1	0	0	(0	0)	8	2	2	3	4	0	12	1	0	0	0	0	1	.212	.316	.242	.558
2019	Mia	NL	107	381	107	16	1	15	(6	9)	170	52	50	57	33	0	110	5	0	2	0	0	10	.281	.344	.446	.791
	3 ML YEARS		134	457	128	22	2	15	(6	9)	199	57	58	66	38	0	134	6	0	3	0	0	11	.280	.341	.435	.777

Patrick Corbin

Pitches: L **Bats:** L **Pos:** SP-33 **Ht:** 6'3" **Wt:** 210 **Born:** 7/19/1989 **Age:** 30

Year	Team	Lg	G	GS	GF	IP	BFP	H	R	ER	HR	SH	SF	HB	TBB	IBB	SO	WP	W	L	Pct	Sv-Op	Hld	Vel	OPS	ERC	ERA
2012	Ari	NL	22	17	3	107.0	454	117	56	54	14	2	5	4	25	2	86	1	6	8	.429	1-1	0	91	.782	4.31	4.54
2013	Ari	NL	32	32	0	208.1	860	189	81	79	19	8	1	9	54	1	178	13	14	8	.636	0-0	0	92	.671	3.14	3.41
2015	Ari	NL	16	16	0	85.0	357	91	34	34	9	2	1	2	17	0	78	4	6	5	.545	0-0	0	92	.743	3.82	3.60
2016	Ari	NL	36	24	6	155.2	701	177	109	89	24	6	5	5	66	2	131	9	5	13	.278	1-1	2	92	.825	5.47	5.15

Year	Team	Lg	G	GS	GF	IP	BFP	H	R	ER	HR	SH	SF	HB	TBB	IBB	SO	WP	W	L	Pct	Sv-Op Hld	Vel	OPS	ERC	ERA
2017	Ari	NL	33	32	0	189.2	826	208	97	85	26	4	5	3	61	8	178	10	14	13	.519	0-0 0	92	.792	4.55	4.03
2018	Ari	NL	33	33	0	200.0	800	162	70	70	15	3	2	5	48	3	246	8	11	7	.611	0-0 0	91	.607	2.41	3.15
2019	Was	NL	33	33	0	202.0	835	169	81	73	24	8	8	3	70	2	238	4	14	7	.667	0-0 0	92	.668	3.15	3.25
7 ML YEARS			205	187	9	1147.2	4833	1113	528	484	131	33	27	31	341	18	1135	49	70	61	.534	2-2 2	92	.718	3.68	3.80

Ryan Cordell

Bats: R **Throws:** R **Pos:** RF-72;CF-19;PH-8;PR-6;LF-2 **Ht:** 6'4" **Wt:** 195 **Born:** 3/31/1992 **Age:** 28

Year	Team	Lg	G	AB	H	2B	3B	HR	(Hm	Rd)	TB	R	RBI	RC	TBB	IBB	SO	HBP	SH	SF	SB	CS	GDP	Avg	OBP	Slg	OPS
2019	Charltt		14	51	14	5	1	1	(-	-)	24	8	6	7	4	0	17	0	0	0	1	1	0	.275	.327	.471	.798
2018	CWS	AL	19	37	4	1	0	1	(0	1)	8	3	4	0	0	0	15	1	0	2	0	0	0	.108	.125	.216	.341
2019	CWS	AL	97	217	48	8	0	7	(3	4)	77	22	24	21	19	0	69	3	6	2	3	1	2	.221	.290	.355	.645
2 ML YEARS			116	254	52	9	0	8	(3	5)	85	25	28	21	19	0	84	4	6	4	3	1	2	.205	.267	.335	.602

Franchy Cordero

Bats: L **Throws:** R **Pos:** CF-5;RF-4;PH-2 **Ht:** 6'3" **Wt:** 175 **Born:** 9/2/1994 **Age:** 25

Year	Team	Lg	G	AB	H	2B	3B	HR	(Hm	Rd)	TB	R	RBI	RC	TBB	IBB	SO	HBP	SH	SF	SB	CS	GDP	Avg	OBP	Slg	OPS
2019	ElPaso	AAA	11	46	10	2	1	3	(-	-)	23	7	8	6	4	0	19	1	0	0	0	0	1	.217	.294	.500	.794
2017	SD	NL	30	92	21	3	3	3	(3	0)	39	15	9	9	6	0	44	0	1	0	1	1	0	.228	.276	.424	.699
2018	SD	NL	40	139	33	5	1	7	(3	4)	61	19	19	19	14	0	55	0	1	0	5	2	1	.237	.307	.439	.746
2019	SD	NL	9	15	5	1	0	0	(0	0)	6	2	1	3	4	0	7	0	0	1	1	0	0	.333	.450	.400	.850
3 ML YEARS			79	246	59	9	4	10	(6	4)	106	36	29	31	24	0	106	0	2	1	7	3	1	.240	.306	.431	.737

Jimmy Cordero

Pitches: R **Bats:** R **Pos:** RP-31 **Ht:** 6'4" **Wt:** 222 **Born:** 10/19/1991 **Age:** 28

Year	Team	Lg	G	GS	GF	IP	BFP	H	R	ER	HR	SH	SF	HB	TBB	IBB	SO	WP	W	L	Pct	Sv-Op Hld	Vel	OPS	ERC	ERA
2019	Fresno	AAA	12	0	3	15.0	71	17	12	10	3	0	0	0	9	0	17	4	0	1	.000	3- -	-	.882	6.33	6.00
2019	Charltt	AAA	13	0	12	17.2	68	14	1	1	0	0	0	1	2	0	14	2	3	1	.750	4- -	-	.481	1.65	0.51
2018	Was	NL	22	0	3	19.0	94	23	13	12	2	0	0	2	12	2	12	0	1	2	.333	0-1 0	98	.794	6.39	5.68
2019	2 Tms	AL	31	0	7	37.1	146	26	12	12	4	0	0	3	11	0	31	1	1	1	.500	0-0 4	97	.615	2.52	2.89
19	Tor	AL	1	0	1	1.1	5	2	1	1	1	0	0	0	0	0	0	0	0	1	.000	0-0 0	97	1.400	12.07	6.75
19	CWS	AL	30	0	6	36.0	141	24	11	11	3	0	0	3	11	0	31	1	1	0	1.000	0-0 4	97	.584	2.27	2.75
2 ML YEARS			53	0	10	56.1	240	49	25	24	6	0	0	5	23	2	43	1	2	3	.400	0-1 4	98	.684	3.74	3.83

Carlos Correa

Bats: R **Throws:** R **Pos:** SS-75 coh-RAY-uh **Ht:** 6'4" **Wt:** 215 **Born:** 9/22/1994 **Age:** 25

Year	Team	Lg	G	AB	H	2B	3B	HR	(Hm	Rd)	TB	R	RBI	RC	TBB	IBB	SO	HBP	SH	SF	SB	CS	GDP	Avg	OBP	Slg	OPS
2015	Hou	AL	99	387	108	22	1	22	(12	10)	198	52	68	68	40	2	78	1	0	4	14	4	10	.279	.345	.512	.857
2016	Hou	AL	153	577	158	36	3	20	(8	12)	260	76	96	93	75	5	139	5	0	3	13	3	12	.274	.361	.451	.811
2017	Hou	AL	109	422	133	25	1	24	(11	13)	232	82	84	86	53	5	92	2	0	4	2	1	12	.315	.391	.550	.941
2018	Hou	AL	110	402	96	20	1	15	(7	8)	163	60	65	49	53	3	111	2	0	11	3	0	17	.239	.323	.405	.728
2019	Hou	AL	75	280	78	16	1	21	(11	10)	159	42	59	52	35	0	75	2	0	4	1	0	8	.279	.358	.568	.926
Postseason			32	126	35	7	0	8	(5	3)	66	15	24	22	10	0	28	1	0	0	0	0	2	.278	.336	.524	.860
5 ML YEARS			546	2068	573	119	7	102	(49	53)	1012	312	372	348	256	15	495	12	0	26	33	8	59	.277	.356	.489	.845

Nestor Cortes

Pitches: L **Bats:** R **Pos:** RP-32; SP-1 **Ht:** 5'11" **Wt:** 210 **Born:** 12/10/1994 **Age:** 25

Year	Team	Lg	G	GS	GF	IP	BFP	H	R	ER	HR	SH	SF	HB	TBB	IBB	SO	WP	W	L	Pct	Sv-Op Hld	Vel	OPS	ERC	ERA
2019	S-WB	AAA	7	6	0	39.2	157	29	17	17	3	1	1	1	11	0	42	0	2	2	.500	0- -	-	.598	2.19	3.86
2018	Bal	AL	4	0	3	4.2	26	10	4	4	2	0	0	4	0	3	0	0	0	0	-	0-0 0	88	1.357	18.44	7.71
2019	NYY	AL	33	1	7	66.2	298	75	44	42	16	0	2	1	28	1	69	1	5	1	.833	0-1 1	90	.843	5.97	5.67
2 ML YEARS			37	1	10	71.1	324	85	48	46	18	0	2	1	32	1	72	1	5	1	.833	0-1 1	89	.883	6.65	5.80

Ryan Court

Bats: R **Throws:** R **Pos:** 1B-7;LF-3;RF-2;PH-2 **Ht:** 6'2" **Wt:** 210 **Born:** 5/28/1988 **Age:** 32

Year	Team	Lg	G	AB	H	2B	3B	HR	(Hm	Rd)	TB	R	RBI	RC	TBB	IBB	SO	HBP	SH	SF	SB	CS	GDP	Avg	OBP	Slg	OPS
2019	Tacom	AAA	54	190	49	10	2	11	(-	-)	96	40	48	37	32	0	63	2	0	4	2	0	2	.258	.364	.505	.869
2019	Sea	AL	12	24	5	1	0	1	(1	0)	9	1	5	3	1	0	11	0	0	0	0	0	0	.208	.240	.375	.615

Dylan Covey

Pitches: R **Bats:** R **Pos:** SP-12; RP-6 COE-vee **Ht:** 6'1" **Wt:** 220 **Born:** 8/14/1991 **Age:** 28

Year	Team	Lg	G	GS	GF	IP	BFP	H	R	ER	HR	SH	SF	HB	TBB	IBB	SO	WP	W	L	Pct	Sv-Op Hld	Vel	OPS	ERC	ERA
2019	Charltt	AAA	13	11	1	51.0	217	59	19	16	6	0	1	1	9	0	46	4	2	1	.667	0- -	-	.779	4.27	2.82

Year	Team	Lg	G	GS	GF	IP	BFP	H	R	ER	HR	SH	SF	HB	TBB	IBB	SO	WP	W	L	Pct	Sv-Op	Hld	Vel	OPS	ERC	ERA
2017	CWS	AL	18	12	4	70.0	309	83	60	60	20	1	1	1	34	1	41	6	0	7	.000	0-0	0	93	.979	7.33	7.71
2018	CWS	AL	27	21	2	121.2	542	129	81	70	13	**5**	3	2	52	4	91	5	5	14	.263	0-0	0	94	.735	4.53	5.18
2019	CWS	AL	18	12	2	58.2	280	75	54	52	12	3	1	3	28	2	41	3	1	8	.111	0-1	0	94	.889	6.95	7.98
	3 ML YEARS		63	45	8	250.1	1131	287	195	182	45	9	5	6	114	7	173	14	6	29	.171	0-1	0	94	.839	5.83	6.54

Kaleb Cowart

Bats: B **Throws:** R **Pos:** 3B-6;2B-3;PR-1 **Ht:** 6'3" **Wt:** 225 **Born:** 6/2/1992 **Age:** 28

						BATTING																RUNNING			AVERAGES			
Year	Team	Lg	G	AB	H	2B	3B	HR	(Hm	Rd)	TB	R	RBI	RC	TBB	IBB	SO	HBP	SH	SF	SB	CS	GDP	Avg	OBP	Slg	OPS
2019	Salt Lk	AAA	85	287	83	15	4	8	(-	-)	130	42	60	45	25	1	55	1	1	3	3	4	4	.289	.345	.453	.798
2019	Mobile	AA	15	39	7	1	0	1	(-	-)	11	4	2	2	2	0	11	0	0	0	0	0	2	.179	.214	.282	.496
2015	LAA	AL	34	46	8	2	0	1	(1	0)	13	8	4	3	5	0	19	0	1	0	1	1	1	.174	.255	.283	.538
2016	LAA	AL	31	85	15	4	0	1	(0	1)	22	8	8	3	0	0	23	1	0	1	0	0	1	.176	.184	.259	.443
2017	LAA	AL	50	102	23	5	1	3	(2	1)	39	18	11	11	10	1	28	3	2	0	4	2	4	.225	.313	.382	.695
2018	LAA	AL	47	112	15	7	1	1	(0	1)	27	7	10	7	10	0	44	1	0	1	1	0	2	.134	.210	.241	.451
2019	LAA	AL	9	25	4	3	0	0	(0	0)	7	1	1	0	1	0	7	0	0	0	1	0	2	.160	.192	.280	.472
	5 ML YEARS		171	370	65	21	2	6	(3	3)	108	42	34	24	26	1	121	5	3	2	7	3	10	.176	.238	.292	.530

Zack Cozart

Bats: R **Throws:** R **Pos:** 3B-31;SS-5;PH-3;PR-2;2B-1   COE-zart **Ht:** 6'0" **Wt:** 205 **Born:** 8/12/1985 **Age:** 34

						BATTING																RUNNING			AVERAGES			
Year	Team	Lg	G	AB	H	2B	3B	HR	(Hm	Rd)	TB	R	RBI	RC	TBB	IBB	SO	HBP	SH	SF	SB	CS	GDP	Avg	OBP	Slg	OPS
2011	Cin	NL	11	37	12	0	0	2	(0	2)	18	6	3	3	0	0	6	0	1	0	0	0	2	.324	.324	.486	.811
2012	Cin	NL	138	561	138	33	4	15	(6	9)	224	72	35	51	31	0	113	3	2	3	4	0	11	.246	.288	.399	.687
2013	Cin	NL	151	567	144	30	3	12	(7	5)	216	74	63	56	26	2	102	2	13	**10**	0	0	18	.254	.284	.381	.665
2014	Cin	NL	147	506	112	18	5	4	(1	3)	152	48	38	36	25	3	79	7	5	0	7	0	13	.221	.268	.300	.568
2015	Cin	NL	53	194	50	10	1	9	(4	5)	89	28	28	23	14	1	29	2	1	3	3	3	4	.258	.310	.459	.769
2016	Cin	NL	121	464	117	28	2	16	(7	9)	197	67	50	53	37	3	84	2	1	4	4	1	9	.252	.308	.425	.732
2017	Cin	NL	122	438	130	24	7	24	(12	12)	240	80	63	87	62	0	78	3	0	4	3	0	5	.297	.385	.548	.933
2018	LAA	AL	58	224	49	13	2	5	(2	3)	81	29	18	17	19	0	42	7	0	3	0	0	7	.219	.296	.362	.658
2019	LAA	AL	38	97	12	2	0	0	(0	0)	14	4	7	1	5	0	16	2	0	3	0	0	2	.124	.178	.144	.322
	Postseason		6	24	5	0	0	0	(0	0)	5	2	0	1	3	0	5	1	0	0	0	0	0	.208	.321	.208	.530
	9 ML YEARS		839	3088	764	158	24	87	(41	46)	1231	408	305	327	219	9	549	28	23	30	21	4	71	.247	.300	.399	.699

Dylan Cozens

Bats: L **Throws:** L **Pos:** PH-1 **Ht:** 6'6" **Wt:** 235 **Born:** 5/31/1994 **Age:** 26

						BATTING																RUNNING			AVERAGES			
Year	Team	Lg	G	AB	H	2B	3B	HR	(Hm	Rd)	TB	R	RBI	RC	TBB	IBB	SO	HBP	SH	SF	SB	CS	GDP	Avg	OBP	Slg	OPS
2019	LV	AAA	23	78	13	1	2	6	(-	-)	36	20	15	13	20	0	42	0	0	1	5	2	0	.167	.333	.462	.795
2018	Phi	NL	26	38	6	2	0	1	(0	1)	11	2	2	2	6	0	24	0	0	0	1	0	0	.158	.273	.289	.562
2019	Phi	NL	1	1	0	0	0	0	(0	0)	0	0	0	0	0	0	0	0	0	0	0	0	0	.000	.000	.000	.000
	2 ML YEARS		27	39	6	2	0	1	(0	1)	11	2	2	2	6	0	24	0	0	0	1	0	0	.154	.267	.282	.549

Brandon Crawford

Bats: L **Throws:** R **Pos:** SS-142;PH-8 **Ht:** 6'2" **Wt:** 227 **Born:** 1/21/1987 **Age:** 33

						BATTING																RUNNING			AVERAGES			
Year	Team	Lg	G	AB	H	2B	3B	HR	(Hm	Rd)	TB	R	RBI	RC	TBB	IBB	SO	HBP	SH	SF	SB	CS	GDP	Avg	OBP	Slg	OPS
2011	SF	NL	66	196	40	5	2	3	(0	3)	58	22	21	20	23	1	31	0	1	0	1	3	4	.204	.288	.296	.584
2012	SF	NL	143	435	108	26	3	4	(1	3)	152	44	45	40	33	6	95	3	2	3	1	4	4	.248	.304	.349	.653
2013	SF	NL	149	499	124	24	3	9	(2	7)	181	52	43	42	42	6	96	5	1	3	1	2	10	.248	.311	.363	.674
2014	SF	NL	153	491	121	20	10	10	(4	6)	191	54	69	72	59	10	129	2	2	10	5	3	4	.246	.324	.389	.713
2015	SF	NL	143	507	130	33	4	21	(8	13)	234	65	84	69	39	9	119	11	0	4	6	4	18	.256	.321	.462	.782
2016	SF	NL	155	553	152	28	11	12	(4	8)	238	67	84	82	57	10	115	4	0	9	7	0	13	.275	.342	.430	.772
2017	SF	NL	144	518	131	34	1	14	(6	8)	209	58	77	61	42	3	113	1	0	9	3	5	18	.253	.305	.403	.709
2018	SF	NL	151	531	135	28	2	14	(7	7)	209	63	54	60	50	13	122	8	0	5	4	5	12	.254	.325	.394	.719
2019	SF	NL	147	500	114	24	2	11	(2	9)	175	58	59	55	53	5	117	3	0	4	3	2	10	.228	.304	.350	.654
	Postseason		38	127	30	6	1	1	(0	1)	41	13	17	14	15	2	32	0	1	2	2	0	2	.236	.313	.323	.635
	9 ML YEARS		1251	4230	1055	222	38	98	(34	64)	1647	483	536	501	398	63	937	37	6	47	31	28	93	.249	.316	.389	.706

J.P. Crawford

Bats: L **Throws:** R **Pos:** SS-93 **Ht:** 6'2" **Wt:** 180 **Born:** 1/11/1995 **Age:** 25

						BATTING																RUNNING			AVERAGES			
Year	Team	Lg	G	AB	H	2B	3B	HR	(Hm	Rd)	TB	R	RBI	RC	TBB	IBB	SO	HBP	SH	SF	SB	CS	GDP	Avg	OBP	Slg	OPS
2019	Tacom	AAA	31	116	37	7	0	3	(-	-)	53	20	15	24	20	1	25	1	0	1	3	0	1	.319	.420	.457	.877
2017	Phi	NL	23	70	15	4	1	0	(0	0)	21	8	6	9	16	0	22	0	0	1	1	0	1	.214	.356	.300	.656
2018	Phi	NL	49	117	25	6	3	3	(2	1)	46	17	12	17	13	0	37	5	2	0	2	0	2	.214	.319	.393	.712
2019	Sea	AL	93	345	78	21	4	7	(4	3)	128	43	46	46	43	0	83	2	3	3	5	3	4	.226	.313	.371	.684
	3 ML YEARS		165	532	118	31	8	10	(6	4)	195	68	64	72	72	0	142	7	5	4	8	3	7	.222	.320	.367	.687

Stefan Crichton

Pitches: R Bats: R Pos: RP-28　　　　　　　CRY-ton　　　　　　　Ht: 6'3" Wt: 200 Born: 2/29/1992 Age: 28

			HOW MUCH PITCHED					WHAT HE GAVE UP										THE RESULTS							
Year	Team	Lg	G	GS	GF	IP	BFP	H	R	ER	HR	SH	SF	HB	TBB	IBB	SO	WP	W	L	Pct	Sv-Op	Hld	Vel	OPS	ERC	ERA
2019	Reno	AAA	36	0	9	57.1	235	52	24	23	4	0	2	4	15	0	52	5	4	3	.571	1- -	-	-	.643	3.16	3.61
2017	Bal	AL	8	0	1	12.1	62	26	11	11	2	0	1	0	4	0	8	2	0	0	-	0-0	1	94	1.151	12.21	8.03
2019	Ari	NL	28	0	9	30.1	123	23	12	12	3	0	0	2	8	1	33	1	1	0	1.000	0-0	3	93	.578	2.47	3.56
	2 ML YEARS		36	0	10	42.2	185	49	23	23	5	0	1	2	12	1	41	3	1	0	1.000	0-0	4	93	.770	4.77	4.85

Kyle Crick

Pitches: R Bats: L Pos: RP-52　　　　　　　　　　　　　　Ht: 6'4" Wt: 220 Born: 11/30/1992 Age: 27

			HOW MUCH PITCHED					WHAT HE GAVE UP										THE RESULTS							
Year	Team	Lg	G	GS	GF	IP	BFP	H	R	ER	HR	SH	SF	HB	TBB	IBB	SO	WP	W	L	Pct	Sv-Op	Hld	Vel	OPS	ERC	ERA
2017	SF	NL	30	0	14	32.1	134	22	13	11	2	1	0	1	17	1	28	6	0	0	-	0-0	1	96	.596	2.68	3.06
2018	Pit	NL	64	0	13	60.1	255	45	18	16	3	1	1	7	23	3	65	9	3	2	.600	2-3	16	96	.569	2.63	2.39
2019	Pit	NL	52	0	9	49.0	226	41	30	27	10	0	1	7	35	1	61	1	3	7	.300	0-6	13	95	.799	5.73	4.96
	3 ML YEARS		146	0	36	141.2	615	108	61	54	15	2	2	15	75	5	154	16	6	9	.400	2-9	30	96	.657	3.63	3.43

C.J. Cron

Bats: R Throws: R Pos: 1B-117;PH-6;DH-4　　　　　CROHN　　　　　Ht: 6'4" Wt: 235 Born: 1/5/1990 Age: 30

			BATTING																			RUNNING			AVERAGES			
Year	Team	Lg	G	AB	H	2B	3B	HR	(Hm	Rd)	TB	R	RBI	RC	TBB	IBB	SO	HBP	SH	SF	SB	CS	GDP	Avg	OBP	Slg	OPS
2014	LAA	AL	79	242	62	12	1	11	(5	6)	109	28	37	35	10	0	61	1	0	0	0	0	10	.256	.289	.450	.739
2015	LAA	AL	113	378	99	17	1	16	(11	5)	166	37	51	46	17	1	82	5	0	3	3	1	9	.262	.300	.439	.739
2016	LAA	AL	116	407	113	25	2	16	(7	9)	190	51	69	66	24	1	75	7	0	5	2	3	9	.278	.325	.467	.792
2017	LAA	AL	100	339	84	14	1	16	(8	8)	148	39	56	51	22	0	96	7	0	3	2	2	5	.248	.305	.437	.741
2018	TB	AL	140	501	127	28	1	30	(11	19)	247	68	74	65	37	2	145	17	0	5	1	2	11	.253	.323	.493	.816
2019	Min	AL	125	458	116	24	0	25	(10	15)	215	51	78	66	29	3	107	10	0	2	0	0	13	.253	.311	.469	.780
	Postseason		3	9	1	1	0	0	(0	0)	2	0	0	0	2	0	4	0	0	0	0	0	0	.111	.273	.222	.495
	6 ML YEARS		673	2325	601	120	6	114	(52	62)	1075	274	365	329	139	7	566	47	0	18	9	8	57	.258	.311	.462	.774

Kevin Cron

Bats: R Throws: R Pos: PH-24;1B-12;DH-4;3B-1　　　CROHN　　　　　Ht: 6'5" Wt: 250 Born: 2/17/1993 Age: 27

			BATTING																			RUNNING			AVERAGES			
Year	Team	Lg	G	AB	H	2B	3B	HR	(Hm	Rd)	TB	R	RBI	RC	TBB	IBB	SO	HBP	SH	SF	SB	CS	GDP	Avg	OBP	Slg	OPS
2019	Reno	AAA	82	305	101	20	1	38	(-	-)	237	81	105	97	61	5	77	6	0	2	1	2	7	.331	.449	.777	1.226
2019	Ari	NL	39	71	15	4	0	6	(2	4)	37	12	16	11	4	0	28	2	0	1	0	1	2	.211	.269	.521	.790

Nelson Cruz

Bats: R Throws: R Pos: DH-114;PH-6　　　　　　　　　　　Ht: 6'2" Wt: 230 Born: 7/1/1980 Age: 39

			BATTING																			RUNNING			AVERAGES			
Year	Team	Lg	G	AB	H	2B	3B	HR	(Hm	Rd)	TB	R	RBI	RC	TBB	IBB	SO	HBP	SH	SF	SB	CS	GDP	Avg	OBP	Slg	OPS
2005	Mil	NL	8	5	1	1	0	0	(0	0)	2	1	0	1	2	0	0	0	0	0	0	0	0	.200	.429	.400	.829
2006	Tex	AL	41	130	29	3	0	6	(3	3)	50	15	22	18	7	0	32	0	0	1	0	1	1	.223	.261	.385	.645
2007	Tex	AL	96	307	72	15	2	9	(4	5)	118	35	34	32	21	1	87	2	1	1	2	4	5	.235	.287	.384	.671
2008	Tex	AL	31	115	38	9	1	7	(4	3)	70	19	26	30	17	2	28	1	0	0	3	1	1	.330	.421	.609	1.030
2009	Tex	AL	128	462	120	21	1	33	(18	15)	242	75	76	72	49	6	118	2	0	2	20	4	9	.260	.332	.524	.856
2010	Tex	AL	108	399	127	31	3	22	(13	9)	230	60	78	77	38	5	81	1	1	6	17	4	12	.318	.374	.576	.950
2011	Tex	AL	124	475	125	28	1	29	(19	10)	242	64	87	79	33	1	116	2	0	3	9	5	8	.263	.312	.509	.821
2012	Tex	AL	159	585	152	45	0	24	(18	6)	269	86	90	80	48	2	140	5	0	4	8	4	7	.260	.319	.460	.779
2013	Tex	AL	109	413	110	18	0	27	(13	14)	209	49	76	69	35	2	109	4	0	4	5	1	14	.266	.327	.506	.833
2014	Bal	AL	159	613	166	32	2	**40**	(15	25)	322	87	108	93	55	8	140	5	0	5	4	5	17	.271	.333	.525	.859
2015	Sea	AL	152	590	178	22	1	44	(17	27)	334	90	93	108	59	9	164	5	0	1	3	2	6	.302	.369	.566	.936
2016	Sea	AL	155	589	169	27	1	43	(17	26)	327	96	105	101	62	5	159	9	0	7	2	0	15	.287	.360	.555	.915
2017	Sea	AL	155	556	160	28	0	39	(19	20)	305	91	**119**	112	70	7	140	12	0	7	1	1	15	.288	.375	.549	.924
2018	Sea	AL	144	519	133	18	1	37	(21	16)	264	70	97	90	55	5	122	14	0	3	1	0	15	.256	.342	.509	.850
2019	Min	AL	120	454	141	26	0	41	(21	20)	290	81	108	102	56	8	131	7	0	3	0	1	14	.311	.392	.639	1.031
	Postseason		41	154	45	10	0	16	(10	6)	103	31	34	35	12	2	36	1	0	0	1	1	4	.292	.347	.669	1.016
	15 ML YEARS		1689	6212	1721	324	13	401	(202	199)	3274	919	1119	1064	607	61	1567	69	2	47	76	32	139	.277	.346	.527	.873

Johnny Cueto

Pitches: R Bats: R Pos: SP-4　　　　　　　　KWAY-toe　　　　　　Ht: 5'11" Wt: 229 Born: 2/15/1986 Age: 34

			HOW MUCH PITCHED					WHAT HE GAVE UP										THE RESULTS							
Year	Team	Lg	G	GS	GF	IP	BFP	H	R	ER	HR	SH	SF	HB	TBB	IBB	SO	WP	W	L	Pct	Sv-Op	Hld	Vel	OPS	ERC	ERA
2008	Cin	NL	31	31	0	174.0	769	178	101	93	29	5	5	**14**	68	1	158	6	9	14	.391	0-0	0	93	.803	4.95	4.81
2009	Cin	NL	30	30	0	171.1	740	172	90	84	24	5	3	14	61	0	132	4	11	11	.500	0-0	0	93	.780	4.57	4.41
2010	Cin	NL	31	31	0	185.2	780	181	79	75	19	9	3	9	56	5	138	5	12	7	.632	0-0	0	93	.727	3.75	3.64
2011	Cin	NL	24	24	0	156.0	631	123	51	40	8	10	4	10	47	0	104	5	9	5	.643	0-0	0	93	.593	2.55	2.31
2012	Cin	NL	33	**33**	0	217.0	888	205	73	67	15	6	6	12	49	5	170	1	19	9	.679	0-0	0	93	.667	3.13	2.78
2013	Cin	NL	11	11	0	60.2	242	46	20	19	7	2	1	1	18	1	51	1	5	2	.714	0-0	0	92	.607	2.57	2.82
2014	Cin	NL	34	**34**	0	243.2	961	169	69	61	22	7	1	15	65	2	**242**	1	20	9	.690	0-0	0	93	.574	2.18	2.25
2015	2 Tms		32	32	0	212.0	866	194	87	81	21	5	4	8	46	1	176	0	11	13	.458	0-0	0	93	.675	3.06	3.44
2016	SF	NL	32	32	0	219.2	881	195	71	68	15	7	3	8	45	1	198	3	18	5	.783	0-0	0	91	.633	2.71	2.79
2017	SF	NL	25	25	0	147.1	648	160	77	74	22	7	3	8	53	2	136	4	8	8	.500	0-0	0	91	.814	4.97	4.52
2018	SF	NL	9	9	0	53.0	214	46	19	19	8	3	0	5	13	0	38	2	3	2	.600	0-0	0	89	.702	3.55	3.23
2019	SF	NL	4	4	0	16.0	67	11	9	9	3	2	0	0	9	0	13	1	1	2	.333	0-0	0	91	.754	3.58	5.06

Year Team	Lg	G	GS	GF	IP	BFP	H	R	ER	HR	SH	SF	HB	TBB	IBB	SO	WP	W	L	Pct	Sv-Op	Hld	Vel	OPS	ERC	ERA
15 Cin	NL	19	19	0	130.2	516	93	42	38	11	4	3	6	29	1	120	0	7	6	.538	0-0	0	93	.577	2.00	2.62
15 KC	AL	13	13	0	81.1	350	101	45	43	10	1	1	2	17	0	56	0	4	7	.364	0-0	0	92	.818	5.05	4.76
Postseason		8	8	0	41.2	170	33	22	21	7	1	1	1	12	0	32	0	2	4	.333	0-0	0	93	.646	3.02	4.54
12 ML YEARS		296	296	0	1856.1	7687	1680	746	690	193	72	33	104	530	18	1556	33	126	87	.592	0-0	0	93	.689	3.37	3.35

Noel Cuevas

Bats: R Throws: R Pos: LF-1   Ht: 6'2" Wt: 224 Born: 10/2/1991 Age: 28

Year Team	Lg	G	AB	H	2B	3B	HR	(Hm	Rd)	TB	R	RBI	RC	TBB	IBB	SO	HBP	SH	SF	SB	CS	GDP	Avg	OBP	Slg	OPS
2019 Albq	AAA	60	205	57	12	3	5	(-	-)	90	35	33	33	24	0	46	2	1	1	3	3	6	.278	.358	.439	.797
2018 Col	NL	75	146	34	4	1	2	(0	2)	46	16	10	12	6	1	24	1	0	0	1	0	1	.233	.268	.315	.583
2019 Col	NL	1	2	0	0	0	0	(0	0)	0	0	0	0	0	0	0	0	0	0	0	0	0	.000	.000	.000	.000
2 ML YEARS		76	148	34	4	1	2	(0	2)	46	16	10	12	6	1	24	1	0	0	1	0	1	.230	.265	.311	.575

Charlie Culberson

Bats: R Throws: R Pos: PH-59;LF-36;RF-11;1B-10;SS-7;PR-3;3B-1   Ht: 6'0" Wt: 200 Born: 4/10/1989 Age: 31

Year Team	Lg	G	AB	H	2B	3B	HR	(Hm	Rd)	TB	R	RBI	RC	TBB	IBB	SO	HBP	SH	SF	SB	CS	GDP	Avg	OBP	Slg	OPS
2012 SF	NL	6	22	3	0	0	0	(0	0)	3	0	1	0	0	1	7	0	1	0	0	0	0	.136	.136	.136	.273
2013 Col	NL	47	99	29	5	0	2	(0	2)	40	12	12	13	4	1	23	0	0	1	5	1	5	.293	.317	.404	.721
2014 Col	NL	95	210	41	7	2	3	(2	1)	61	17	24	14	12	2	62	5	4	2	2	2	6	.195	.253	.290	.544
2016 LAD	NL	34	67	20	3	0	1	(1	0)	26	6	7	9	1	0	13	0	0	0	1	0	2	.299	.309	.388	.697
2017 LAD	NL	15	13	2	1	0	0	(0	0)	3	0	1	0	2	0	4	0	0	0	0	0	2	.154	.267	.231	.497
2018 Atl	NL	113	296	80	18	2	12	(5	7)	138	47	45	50	21	5	85	4	0	1	4	2	5	.270	.326	.466	.792
2019 Atl	NL	108	135	35	5	2	5	(3	2)	59	14	20	11	6	0	44	1	1	1	0	1	5	.259	.294	.437	.731
Postseason		18	35	10	2	1	1	(1	0)	17	5	2	5	1	1	9	0	1	1	0	0	0	.286	.297	.486	.783
7 ML YEARS		418	842	210	39	6	23	(11	12)	330	96	110	97	46	8	238	10	6	5	12	6	25	.249	.295	.392	.686

John Curtiss

Pitches: R Bats: R Pos: RP-1   Ht: 6'5" Wt: 220 Born: 4/5/1993 Age: 27

Year Team	Lg	G	GS	GF	IP	BFP	H	R	ER	HR	SH	SF	HB	TBB	IBB	SO	WP	W	L	Pct	Sv-Op	Hld	Vel	OPS	ERC	ERA
2019 Salt Lk	AAA	13	0	2	21.1	96	20	14	14	4	0	1	1	13	0	29	4	2	0	1.000	1--	-	-	.811	5.41	5.91
2019 LV	AAA	9	1	1	12.1	66	20	15	15	5	0	0	0	9	2	15	0	0	1	.000	0--	-	-	1.159	11.78	10.95
2017 Min	AL	9	0	4	8.2	38	9	8	8	2	0	0	1	2	0	10	2	0	0	-	0-0	0	95	.802	4.89	8.31
2018 Min	AL	8	0	2	6.1	30	8	4	4	0	0	0	0	4	1	7	3	0	1	.000	0-0	0	94	.900	5.47	5.68
2019 LAA	AL	1	0	1	2.1	12	2	1	1	0	0	0	0	3	0	1	0	0	0	-	0-0	0	92	.750	5.73	3.86
3 ML YEARS		18	0	7	17.1	80	19	13	13	2	0	0	1	9	1	18	5	0	1	.000	0-0	0	94	.834	5.30	6.75

Cheslor Cuthbert

Bats: R Throws: R Pos: 1B-46;3B-40;PH-10;DH-1   CHESS-lohr   Ht: 6'1" Wt: 210 Born: 11/16/1992 Age: 27

Year Team	Lg	G	AB	H	2B	3B	HR	(Hm	Rd)	TB	R	RBI	RC	TBB	IBB	SO	HBP	SH	SF	SB	CS	GDP	Avg	OBP	Slg	OPS
2019 Omha	AAA	51	197	61	17	1	8	(-	-)	104	25	35	38	17	1	46	3	0	2	0	0	10	.310	.370	.528	.898
2015 KC	AL	19	46	10	2	1	1	(1	0)	17	6	8	6	4	0	9	0	0	0	0	0	0	.217	.280	.370	.650
2016 KC	AL	128	475	130	28	1	12	(4	8)	196	49	46	57	32	0	96	0	1	2	2	0	14	.274	.318	.413	.731
2017 KC	AL	58	143	33	7	0	2	(1	1)	46	10	18	11	9	0	39	0	0	1	0	0	2	.231	.275	.322	.596
2018 KC	AL	30	103	20	2	0	3	(2	1)	31	11	7	4	11	0	23	2	0	1	0	1	5	.194	.282	.301	.583
2019 KC	AL	87	309	76	14	0	9	(5	4)	117	24	40	35	19	1	67	2	0	0	1	0	14	.246	.294	.379	.673
5 ML YEARS		322	1076	269	53	2	27	(13	14)	407	100	119	113	75	1	234	4	1	4	3	1	35	.250	.300	.378	.679

David Dahl

Bats: L Throws: R Pos: CF-40;LF-39;RF-24;PH-8   Ht: 6'2" Wt: 200 Born: 4/1/1994 Age: 26

Year Team	Lg	G	AB	H	2B	3B	HR	(Hm	Rd)	TB	R	RBI	RC	TBB	IBB	SO	HBP	SH	SF	SB	CS	GDP	Avg	OBP	Slg	OPS
2016 Col	NL	63	222	70	12	4	7	(3	4)	111	42	24	35	15	0	59	0	0	0	5	0	3	.315	.359	.500	.859
2018 Col	NL	77	249	68	11	3	16	(13	3)	133	31	48	43	19	4	68	1	0	2	5	3	4	.273	.325	.534	.859
2019 Col	NL	100	374	113	28	5	15	(9	6)	196	67	61	70	28	0	110	4	2	5	4	4	3	.302	.353	.524	.877
Postseason		3	11	0	0	0	0	(0	0)	0	0	0	0	0	0	3	0	0	0	0	0	0	.000	.000	.000	.000
3 ML YEARS		240	845	251	51	12	38	(25	13)	440	140	133	148	62	4	237	5	2	7	14	7	10	.297	.346	.521	.867

Travis d'Arnaud

Bats: R Throws: R Pos: C-85;1B-21;PH-13;DH-4;PR-1   dar-NO   Ht: 6'2" Wt: 210 Born: 2/10/1989 Age: 31

Year Team	Lg	G	AB	H	2B	3B	HR	(Hm	Rd)	TB	R	RBI	RC	TBB	IBB	SO	HBP	SH	SF	SB	CS	GDP	Avg	OBP	Slg	OPS
2013 NYM	NL	31	99	20	3	0	1	(1	0)	26	4	5	6	12	0	21	0	0	1	0	0	3	.202	.286	.263	.548
2014 NYM	NL	108	385	93	22	3	13	(5	8)	160	48	41	39	32	5	64	2	1	1	1	0	15	.242	.302	.416	.718
2015 NYM	NL	67	239	64	14	1	12	(6	6)	116	31	41	36	23	0	49	4	0	2	0	0	7	.268	.340	.485	.825
2016 NYM	NL	75	251	62	7	0	4	(4	0)	81	27	15	17	19	1	50	3	2	1	0	0	7	.247	.307	.323	.629
2017 NYM	NL	112	348	85	19	1	16	(5	11)	154	39	57	41	23	3	59	2	0	3	0	0	12	.244	.293	.443	.735
2018 NYM	NL	4	15	3	0	0	1	(1	0)	6	1	3	2	1	0	5	0	0	0	0	0	4	.200	.250	.400	.650
2019 3 Tms		103	351	88	16	0	16	(6	10)	152	52	69	59	32	0	85	2	0	6	0	1	4	.251	.312	.433	.745
19 NYM	NL	10	23	2	0	0	0	(0	0)	2	2	2	0	2	0	5	0	0	0	0	0	1	.087	.160	.087	.247

Year	Team	Lg	G	AB	H	2B	3B	HR	(Hm	Rd)	TB	R	RBI	RC	TBB	IBB	SO	HBP	SH	SF	SB	CS	GDP	Avg	OBP	Slg	OPS
									BATTING												RUNNING			AVERAGES			
19	LAD	NL	1	1	0	0	0	0	(0	0)	0	0	0	0	0	0	0	0	0	0	0	0	0	.000	.000	.000	.000
19	TB	AL	92	327	86	16	0	16	(6	10)	150	50	67	59	30	0	80	2	0	6	0	1	3	.263	.323	.459	.782
	Postseason		14	55	10	1	0	3	(2	1)	20	5	7	3	0	0	17	1	0	1	0	0	2	.182	.193	.364	.557
	7 ML YEARS		500	1688	415	81	5	63	(28	35)	695	202	231	200	142	9	333	13	3	14	1	1	48	.246	.307	.412	.719

Yu Darvish

Pitches: R **Bats:** R **Pos:** SP-31   YOO DARR-vish   **Ht:** 6'5" **Wt:** 220 **Born:** 8/16/1986 **Age:** 33

Year	Team	Lg	G	GS	GF	IP	BFP	H	R	ER	HR	SH	SF	HB	TBB	IBB	SO	WP	W	L	Pct	Sv-Op	Hld	Vel	OPS	ERC	ERA
			HOW MUCH PITCHED					WHAT HE GAVE UP											THE RESULTS								
2012	Tex	AL	29	29	0	191.1	816	156	89	83	14	2	7	10	89	1	221	8	16	9	.640	0-0	0	93	.659	3.31	3.90
2013	Tex	AL	32	32	0	209.2	841	145	68	66	26	0	5	8	80	1	277	7	13	9	.591	0-0	0	93	.611	2.70	2.83
2014	Tex	AL	22	22	0	144.1	605	133	54	49	13	1	2	2	49	1	182	14	10	7	.588	0-0	0	92	.679	3.39	3.06
2016	Tex	AL	17	17	0	100.1	416	81	43	38	12	0	4	3	31	1	132	6	7	5	.583	0-0	0	93	.636	2.87	3.41
2017	2 Tms		31	31	0	186.2	766	159	83	80	27	2	3	6	58	1	209	12	10	12	.455	0-0	0	94	.689	3.35	3.86
2018	ChC	NL	8	8	0	40.0	180	36	24	22	7	1	1	4	21	0	49	2	1	3	.250	0-0	0	94	.766	4.88	4.95
2019	ChC	NL	31	31	0	178.2	731	140	82	79	33	4	3	11	56	1	229	11	6	8	.429	0-0	0	94	.695	3.35	3.98
17	Tex	AL	22	22	0	137.0	564	115	63	61	20	1	3	5	45	0	148	9	6	9	.400	0-0	0	94	.689	3.39	4.01
17	LAD	NL	9	9	0	49.2	202	44	20	19	7	1	0	1	13	1	61	3	4	3	.571	0-0	0	94	.690	3.27	3.44
	Postseason		6	6	0	26.1	114	27	19	17	8	1	2	3	4	0	25	0	2	4	.333	0-0	0	94	.839	4.91	5.81
	7 ML YEARS		170	170	0	1051.0	4355	850	443	417	132	9	26	44	384	6	1299	60	63	53	.543	0-0	0	93	.666	3.23	3.57

Zach Davies

Pitches: R **Bats:** R **Pos:** SP-31   **Ht:** 6'0" **Wt:** 155 **Born:** 2/7/1993 **Age:** 27

Year	Team	Lg	G	GS	GF	IP	BFP	H	R	ER	HR	SH	SF	HB	TBB	IBB	SO	WP	W	L	Pct	Sv-Op	Hld	Vel	OPS	ERC	ERA
			HOW MUCH PITCHED					WHAT HE GAVE UP											THE RESULTS								
2015	Mil	NL	6	6	0	34.0	139	26	14	14	2	1	0	0	15	0	24	0	3	2	.600	0-0	0	89	.614	2.74	3.71
2016	Mil	NL	28	28	0	163.1	682	166	79	72	20	3	4	6	38	0	135	3	11	7	.611	0-0	0	89	.728	3.83	3.97
2017	Mil	NL	33	33	0	191.1	817	204	90	83	20	7	5	9	55	3	124	2	17	9	.654	0-0	0	90	.755	4.24	3.90
2018	Mil	NL	13	13	0	66.0	280	67	36	35	8	0	5	4	21	3	49	1	2	7	.222	0-0	0	90	.768	4.22	4.77
2019	Mil	NL	31	31	0	159.2	672	155	73	63	20	7	5	2	51	0	102	4	10	7	.588	0-0	0	88	.729	3.83	3.55
	Postseason		1	0	1	1.0	4	1	0	0	0	0	0	0	0	0	1	0	0	0	-	0-0	0	91	.750	1.95	0.00
	5 ML YEARS		111	111	0	614.1	2590	618	292	267	70	18	19	21	180	6	434	10	43	32	.573	0-0	0	89	.735	3.94	3.91

Austin Davis

Pitches: L **Bats:** L **Pos:** RP-14   **Ht:** 6'4" **Wt:** 245 **Born:** 2/3/1993 **Age:** 27

Year	Team	Lg	G	GS	GF	IP	BFP	H	R	ER	HR	SH	SF	HB	TBB	IBB	SO	WP	W	L	Pct	Sv-Op	Hld	Vel	OPS	ERC	ERA
			HOW MUCH PITCHED					WHAT HE GAVE UP											THE RESULTS								
2019	LV	AAA	37	0	11	52.1	222	43	17	16	2	2	3	1	24	2	64	1	4	1	.800	3- -	2		.622	2.91	2.75
2018	Phi	NL	32	0	10	34.2	151	35	20	16	4	1	4	2	12	1	38	4	1	2	.333	0-0	2	93	.812	4.17	4.15
2019	Phi	NL	14	0	7	20.2	98	22	15	15	6	0	0	3	14	1	24	0	0	0	-	0-0	0	94	.929	7.79	6.53
	2 ML YEARS		46	0	17	55.1	249	57	35	31	10	1	4	5	26	2	62	4	1	2	.333	0-0	2	93	.857	5.44	5.04

Chris Davis

Bats: L **Throws:** R **Pos:** 1B-97;PH-11;RF-1;DH-1;PR-1   **Ht:** 6'3" **Wt:** 230 **Born:** 3/17/1986 **Age:** 34

Year	Team	Lg	G	AB	H	2B	3B	HR	(Hm	Rd)	TB	R	RBI	RC	TBB	IBB	SO	HBP	SH	SF	SB	CS	GDP	Avg	OBP	Slg	OPS
									BATTING												RUNNING			AVERAGES			
2008	Tex	AL	80	295	84	23	2	17	(8	9)	162	51	55	44	20	1	88	1	0	1	1	2	5	.285	.331	.549	.880
2009	Tex	AL	113	391	93	15	1	21	(11	10)	173	48	59	50	24	2	150	2	0	2	0	0	6	.238	.284	.442	.726
2010	Tex	AL	45	120	23	9	0	1	(0	1)	35	7	4	5	15	3	40	0	0	1	3	0	3	.192	.279	.292	.571
2011	2 Tms		59	199	53	12	0	5	(2	3)	80	25	19	23	11	1	63	0	0	0	1	0	4	.266	.305	.402	.707
2012	Bal	AL	139	515	139	20	0	33	(22	11)	258	75	85	85	37	6	169	7	0	3	2	3	8	.270	.326	.501	.827
2013	Bal	AL	160	584	167	42	1	53	(28	25)	370	103	138	134	72	12	199	10	0	7	4	1	4	.286	.370	.634	1.004
2014	Bal	AL	127	450	88	16	0	26	(13	13)	182	65	72	58	60	9	173	9	1	5	2	1	2	.196	.300	.404	.704
2015	Bal	AL	160	573	150	31	0	47	(29	18)	322	100	117	117	84	6	208	8	0	5	2	3	6	.262	.361	.562	.923
2016	Bal	AL	157	566	125	21	0	38	(17	21)	260	99	84	82	88	3	219	8	0	3	1	0	6	.221	.332	.459	.792
2017	Bal	AL	128	456	98	15	1	26	(15	11)	193	65	61	55	61	4	195	3	0	4	1	1	7	.215	.309	.423	.732
2018	Bal	AL	128	470	79	12	0	16	(10	6)	139	40	49	36	41	2	192	7	0	4	2	0	4	.168	.243	.296	.539
2019	Bal	AL	105	307	55	9	0	12	(5	7)	100	26	36	29	39	1	139	3	0	3	0	0	6	.179	.276	.326	.601
11	Tex	AL	28	76	19	3	0	3	(1	2)	31	9	6	7	5	0	24	0	0	0	0	0	2	.250	.296	.408	.704
11	Bal	AL	31	123	34	9	0	2	(1	1)	49	16	13	16	6	1	39	0	0	0	1	0	2	.276	.310	.398	.708
	Postseason		7	27	5	0	0	0	(0	0)	5	1	2	1	2	0	11	1	0	0	0	0	0	.185	.267	.185	.452
	12 ML YEARS		1401	4926	1154	225	5	295	(160	135)	2274	704	779	718	552	50	1835	58	1	38	19	11	62	.234	.316	.462	.778

J.D. Davis

Bats: R **Throws:** R **Pos:** LF-79;PH-35;3B-31;DH-1   **Ht:** 6'3" **Wt:** 225 **Born:** 4/27/1993 **Age:** 27

Year	Team	Lg	G	AB	H	2B	3B	HR	(Hm	Rd)	TB	R	RBI	RC	TBB	IBB	SO	HBP	SH	SF	SB	CS	GDP	Avg	OBP	Slg	OPS
									BATTING												RUNNING			AVERAGES			
2017	Hou	AL	25	62	14	4	0	4	(2	2)	30	8	7	4	4	0	20	1	0	1	1	1	3	.226	.279	.484	.763
2018	Hou	AL	42	103	18	2	0	1	(0	1)	23	9	5	3	10	0	29	0	0	0	0	0	3	.175	.248	.223	.471
2019	NYM	NL	140	410	126	22	1	22	(16	6)	216	65	57	66	38	2	97	3	0	2	3	0	14	.307	.369	.527	.895
	3 ML YEARS		207	575	158	28	1	27	(18	9)	269	82	69	73	52	2	146	4	0	3	4	1	20	.275	.338	.468	.805

Jaylin Davis

Bats: R Throws: R Pos: RF-15;DH-1;PH-1 Ht: 6'1" Wt: 190 Born: 7/1/1994 Age: 25

							BATTING													RUNNING			AVERAGES			
Year	Team	Lg	G	AB	H	2B	3B	HR	(Hm | Rd)	TB	R	RBI	RC	TBB	IBB	SO	HBP	SH	SF	SB	CS	GDP	Avg	OBP	Slg	OPS
2019	Pnscla	AA	58	212	58	9	0	10	(- | -)	97	34	25	39	36	0	64	2	0	1	7	3	5	.274	.382	.458	.840
2019	Roch	AAA	41	154	51	11	1	15	(- | -)	109	39	42	41	15	1	46	4	0	0	2	0	6	.331	.405	.708	1.112
2019	Scrmto	AAA	27	102	34	6	0	10	(- | -)	70	21	27	27	14	1	28	1	0	0	1	1	1	.333	.419	.686	1.105
2019	SF	NL	17	42	7	0	0	1	(1 | 0)	10	2	3	1	3	0	11	2	0	0	1	2	1	.167	.255	.238	.493

Johnny Davis

Bats: B Throws: R Pos: PR-6;CF-2;LF-1 Ht: 5'10" Wt: 180 Born: 4/26/1990 Age: 30

							BATTING													RUNNING			AVERAGES			
Year	Team	Lg	G	AB	H	2B	3B	HR	(Hm	Rd)	TB	R	RBI	RC	TBB	IBB	SO	HBP	SH	SF	SB	CS	GDP	Avg	OBP	Slg	OPS
2019	TB	AL	8	4	1	0	1	0	(0	0)	3	5	0	1	0	0	2	0	0	0	0	0	0	.250	.250	.750	1.000

Jonathan Davis

Bats: R Throws: R Pos: CF-33;RF-2;PH-2;PR-2;LF-1;DH-1 Ht: 5'8" Wt: 190 Born: 5/12/1992 Age: 28

							BATTING													RUNNING			AVERAGES			
Year	Team	Lg	G	AB	H	2B	3B	HR	(Hm	Rd)	TB	R	RBI	RC	TBB	IBB	SO	HBP	SH	SF	SB	CS	GDP	Avg	OBP	Slg	OPS
2019	Buffalo	AAA	82	294	77	19	3	10	(5	6)	132	64	36	54	40	1	83	17	1	0	13	4	4	.262	.382	.449	.831
2018	Tor	AL	20	25	5	1	0	0	(0	0)	6	3	0	0	1	0	6	1	0	0	3	0	2	.200	.259	.240	.499
2019	Tor	AL	37	83	15	1	0	2	(1	1)	22	8	6	5	5	0	24	5	1	1	3	1	1	.181	.266	.265	.531
	2 ML YEARS		57	108	20	2	0	2	(1	1)	28	11	6	5	6	0	30	6	1	1	6	1	3	.185	.264	.259	.524

Khris Davis

Bats: R Throws: R Pos: DH-123;PH-6;LF-4 Ht: 5'11" Wt: 203 Born: 12/21/1987 Age: 32

							BATTING													RUNNING			AVERAGES			
Year	Team	Lg	G	AB	H	2B	3B	HR	(Hm	Rd)	TB	R	RBI	RC	TBB	IBB	SO	HBP	SH	SF	SB	CS	GDP	Avg	OBP	Slg	OPS
2013	Mil	NL	56	136	38	10	0	11	(5	6)	81	27	27	25	11	0	34	5	0	1	3	0	4	.279	.353	.596	.949
2014	Mil	NL	144	501	122	37	2	22	(12	10)	229	70	69	58	32	0	122	10	0	6	4	1	13	.244	.299	.457	.756
2015	Mil	NL	121	392	97	16	2	27	(16	11)	198	54	66	57	44	1	122	1	0	3	6	2	9	.247	.323	.505	.828
2016	Oak	AL	150	555	137	24	2	42	(19	23)	291	85	102	77	42	0	166	8	0	5	1	2	19	.247	.307	.524	.831
2017	Oak	AL	153	566	140	28	1	43	(26	17)	299	91	110	98	73	1	195	6	0	7	4	0	20	.247	.336	.528	.864
2018	Oak	AL	151	576	142	28	1	**48**	(23	**25**)	316	98	123	104	59	5	175	12	0	7	0	0	16	.247	.326	.549	.874
2019	Oak	AL	133	481	106	11	0	23	(9	14)	186	61	73	60	47	3	146	3	0	2	0	0	11	.220	.293	.387	.679
	Postseason		1	4	1	0	0	1	(0	1)	4	1	2	1	0	0	2	0	0	0	0	0	0	.250	.250	1.000	1.250
	7 ML YEARS		908	3207	782	154	8	216	(110	106)	1600	486	570	479	308	10	960	45	0	31	18	5	92	.244	.316	.499	.815

Rajai Davis

RAH-jay

Bats: R Throws: R Pos: PH-17;LF-11;PR-5;RF-3 Ht: 5'10" Wt: 195 Born: 10/19/1980 Age: 39

							BATTING													RUNNING			AVERAGES			
Year	Team	Lg	G	AB	H	2B	3B	HR	(Hm	Rd)	TB	R	RBI	RC	TBB	IBB	SO	HBP	SH	SF	SB	CS	GDP	Avg	OBP	Slg	OPS
2019	Syrcse	AAA	84	310	89	8	3	8	(-	-)	127	47	28	45	17	0	72	6	2	2	20	6	2	.287	.334	.410	.744
2006	Pit	NL	20	14	2	1	0	0	(0	0)	3	1	0	0	2	0	3	0	1	0	1	3	0	.143	.250	.214	.464
2007	2 Tms	NL	75	190	53	11	2	1	(0	1)	71	32	9	26	21	1	28	4	3	1	22	6	1	.279	.361	.374	.735
2008	2 Tms		113	214	52	5	4	3	(0	3)	74	30	19	24	8	0	40	1	2	1	29	6	1	.243	.272	.346	.618
2009	Oak	AL	125	390	119	27	5	3	(1	2)	165	65	48	63	29	0	70	7	2	4	41	12	12	.305	.360	.423	.784
2010	Oak	AL	143	525	149	28	3	5	(5	0)	198	66	52	62	26	0	78	4	1	5	50	11	10	.284	.320	.377	.697
2011	Tor	AL	95	320	76	21	6	1	(1	0)	112	44	29	32	15	0	63	1	1	1	34	11	4	.238	.273	.350	.623
2012	Tor	AL	142	447	115	24	3	8	(5	3)	169	64	43	59	29	3	102	6	1	4	46	**13**	8	.257	.309	.378	.687
2013	Tor	AL	108	331	86	16	2	6	(3	3)	124	49	24	36	21	0	67	5	1	2	45	6	8	.260	.312	.375	.687
2014	Det	AL	134	461	130	27	2	8	(4	4)	185	64	51	62	22	0	75	5	3	3	36	11	7	.282	.320	.401	.721
2015	Det	AL	112	341	88	16	11	8	(6	2)	150	55	30	37	22	0	76	3	1	3	18	8	5	.258	.306	.440	.746
2016	Cle	AL	134	454	113	23	2	12	(3	9)	176	74	48	62	33	0	106	5	1	2	**43**	6	9	.249	.306	.388	.693
2017	2 Tms	AL	117	336	79	19	2	5	(3	2)	117	56	20	29	27	1	83	1	1	1	29	7	12	.235	.293	.348	.641
2018	Cle	AL	101	196	44	6	1	1	(0	1)	55	33	6	12	11	0	48	4	4	1	21	7	2	.224	.278	.281	.559
2019	NYM	NL	29	25	5	2	0	1	(1	0)	10	4	8	3	1	0	5	0	0	0	0	1	0	.200	.231	.400	.631
	07 Pit	NL	24	48	13	2	1	0	(0	0)	17	6	2	6	7	0	3	0	1	1	5	2	1	.271	.357	.354	.711
	07 SF	NL	51	142	40	9	1	1	(0	1)	54	26	7	20	14	1	25	4	2	0	17	4	0	.282	.363	.380	.743
	08 SF	NL	12	18	1	0	0	0	(0	0)	1	2	0	0	1	0	6	0	0	0	4	0	0	.056	.105	.056	.161
	08 Oak	AL	101	196	51	5	4	3	(0	3)	73	28	19	24	7	0	34	1	2	1	25	6	1	.260	.288	.372	.660
	17 Oak	AL	100	300	70	17	2	5	(3	2)	106	49	18	26	26	1	70	0	1	1	26	6	10	.233	.294	.353	.647
	17 Bos	AL	17	36	9	2	0	0	(0	0)	11	7	2	3	1	0	13	1	0	0	3	1	2	.250	.289	.306	.595
	Postseason		19	40	7	1	0	1	(1	0)	11	4	4	5	1	0	9	1	0	1	4	0	1	.175	.209	.275	.484
	14 ML YEARS		1448	4244	1111	226	43	62	(32	30)	1609	637	387	507	267	5	844	46	22	28	415	108	79	.262	.311	.379	.690

Rookie Davis

Pitches: R Bats: R Pos: RP-4; SP-1 Ht: 6'5" Wt: 255 Born: 4/29/1993 Age: 27

			HOW MUCH PITCHED					WHAT HE GAVE UP										THE RESULTS							
Year	Team	Lg	G	GS	GF	IP	BFP	H	R	ER	HR	SH	SF	HB	TBB	IBB	SO	WP	W	L	Pct	Sv-Op	Hld	Vel	OPS	ERC	ERA
2019	Indy	AAA	13	9	1	52.2	232	61	33	33	9	0	2	1	22	0	40	1	1	6	.143	0--	-		.860	5.81	5.64
2017	Cin	NL	7	6	0	24.0	123	38	25	23	7	2	1	1	14	0	20	3	1	3	.250	0-0	0	92	1.086	10.42	8.63
2019	Pit	NL	5	1	2	10.2	51	12	8	8	3	2	1	0	8	0	10	1	0	1	.000	0-0	0	91	1.033	7.78	6.75
	2 ML YEARS		12	7	2	34.2	174	50	33	31	10	4	2	1	22	0	30	4	1	4	.200	0-0	0	92	1.071	9.59	8.05

Taylor Davis

Bats: R **Throws:** R **Pos:** C-6;1B-1   **Ht:** 5'10" **Wt:** 200 **Born:** 11/28/1989 **Age:** 30

							BATTING													RUNNING			AVERAGES			
Year Team	Lg	G	AB	H	2B	3B	HR	(Hm	Rd)	TB	R	RBI	RC	TBB	IBB	SO	HBP	SH	SF	SB	CS	GDP	Avg	OBP	Slg	OPS
2019 Iowa	AAA	61	204	48	4	0	5	(-	-)	67	21	23	25	31	1	38	1	4	1	0	0	10	.235	.338	.328	.666
2017 ChC	NL	8	13	3	1	0	0	(0	0)	4	1	1	2	0	0	4	0	0	0	0	0	0	.231	.231	.308	.538
2018 ChC	NL	5	5	2	0	0	0	(0	0)	2	0	2	0	0	0	1	0	0	1	0	0	0	.400	.333	.400	.733
2019 ChC	NL	7	18	3	0	0	1	(1	0)	6	2	4	2	2	0	4	0	0	0	0	0	0	.167	.250	.333	.583
3 ML YEARS		20	36	8	1	0	1	(1	0)	12	3	7	4	2	0	9	0	0	1	0	0	0	.222	.256	.333	.590

Wade Davis

Pitches: R **Bats:** R **Pos:** RP-50   **Ht:** 6'5" **Wt:** 227 **Born:** 9/7/1985 **Age:** 34

		HOW MUCH PITCHED					WHAT HE GAVE UP											THE RESULTS							
Year Team	Lg	G	GS	GF	IP	BFP	H	R	ER	HR	SH	SF	HB	TBB	IBB	SO	WP	W	L	Pct	Sv-Op	Hld	Vel	OPS	ERC	ERA
2009 TB	AL	6	6	0	36.1	150	33	19	15	2	0	0	0	13	1	36	1	2	2	.500	0-0	0	92	.640	3.12	3.72
2010 TB	AL	29	29	0	168.0	722	165	77	76	24	8	0	5	62	2	113	4	12	10	.545	0-0	0	92	.756	4.25	4.07
2011 TB	AL	29	29	0	184.0	795	190	96	91	23	5	7	8	63	1	105	6	11	10	.524	0-0	0	91	.771	4.38	4.45
2012 TB	AL	54	0	15	70.1	284	48	20	19	5	0	1	0	29	2	87	2	3	0	1.000	0-1	6	94	.570	2.25	2.43
2013 KC	AL	31	24	2	135.1	618	169	89	80	15	1	5	4	58	2	114	7	8	11	.421	0-0	0	92	.822	5.88	5.32
2014 KC	AL	71	0	11	72.0	279	38	8	8	0	0	1	3	23	0	109	1	9	2	.818	3-6	33	96	.408	1.23	1.00
2015 KC	AL	69	0	24	67.1	251	33	8	7	3	0	2	0	20	1	78	1	8	1	.889	17-18	18	96	.451	1.16	0.94
2016 KC	AL	45	0	40	43.1	176	33	9	9	0	0	0	3	16	0	47	4	2	1	.667	27-30	0	95	.537	2.35	1.87
2017 ChC	NL	59	0	56	58.2	242	39	16	15	6	1	0	3	28	1	79	7	4	2	.667	32-33	0	94	.600	2.77	2.30
2018 Col	NL	69	0	63	65.1	261	43	31	30	8	0	0	2	26	0	78	6	3	6	.333	**43-49**	0	94	.615	2.56	4.13
2019 Col	NL	50	0	32	42.2	206	51	42	41	7	0	0	2	29	0	42	1	1	6	.143	15-18	0	93	.872	7.12	8.65
Postseason		30	1	14	40.0	160	29	9	8	5	0	0	0	18	0	57	2	4	0	1.000	8-8	3	95	.639	3.05	1.80
11 ML YEARS		512	88	243	943.1	3984	842	415	391	93	10	22	30	367	10	888	40	63	51	.553	137-155	57	93	.685	3.55	3.73

Grant Dayton

Pitches: L **Bats:** L **Pos:** RP-14   **Ht:** 6'2" **Wt:** 210 **Born:** 11/25/1987 **Age:** 32

		HOW MUCH PITCHED					WHAT HE GAVE UP											THE RESULTS							
Year Team	Lg	G	GS	GF	IP	BFP	H	R	ER	HR	SH	SF	HB	TBB	IBB	SO	WP	W	L	Pct	Sv-Op	Hld	Vel	OPS	ERC	ERA
2019 Gwnntt	AAA	22	0	9	26.2	103	20	9	9	6	1	1	1	4	0	41	0	0	1	.000	0--	-	-	.662	2.70	3.04
2016 LAD	NL	25	0	6	26.1	101	14	7	6	4	0	1	0	6	0	39	0	0	1	.000	0-2	6	92	.495	1.56	2.05
2017 LAD	NL	29	0	6	23.2	102	19	13	13	5	1	3	0	12	1	20	0	1	1	.500	0-1	4	91	.749	4.02	4.94
2019 Atl	NL	14	0	4	12.0	51	12	5	4	4	0	0	0	4	0	14	0	0	1	.000	0-1	1	91	.824	5.42	3.00
Postseason		7	0	1	3.1	18	6	3	3	1	0	0	0	2	0	6	0	0	0	-	0-0	1	93	1.132	11.76	8.10
3 ML YEARS		68	0	10	62.0	254	45	25	23	13	1	3	1	22	1	73	0	1	3	.250	0-4	11	92	.661	3.11	3.34

Yonathan Daza

Bats: R **Throws:** R **Pos:** CF-24;PH-16;LF-3;RF-3;PR-1   **Ht:** 6'2" **Wt:** 210 **Born:** 2/28/1994 **Age:** 26

							BATTING													RUNNING			AVERAGES			
Year Team	Lg	G	AB	H	2B	3B	HR	(Hm	Rd)	TB	R	RBI	RC	TBB	IBB	SO	HBP	SH	SF	SB	CS	GDP	Avg	OBP	Slg	OPS
2019 Albq	AAA	89	387	141	30	4	11	(-	-)	212	67	48	81	25	0	52	2	2	2	12	9	5	.364	.404	.548	.952
2019 Col	NL	44	97	20	1	1	0	(0	0)	23	7	3	5	7	0	21	0	0	1	1	0	2	.206	.257	.237	.494

Chase De Jong

Pitches: R **Bats:** L **Pos:** RP-1   **Ht:** 6'4" **Wt:** 205 **Born:** 12/29/1993 **Age:** 26

		HOW MUCH PITCHED					WHAT HE GAVE UP											THE RESULTS							
Year Team	Lg	G	GS	GF	IP	BFP	H	R	ER	HR	SH	SF	HB	TBB	IBB	SO	WP	W	L	Pct	Sv-Op	Hld	Vel	OPS	ERC	ERA
2019 Roch	AAA	13	10	0	45.1	233	72	53	49	16	1	1	4	26	0	30	3	0	5	.000	0--	-	-	1.117	11.29	9.73
2017 Sea	AL	7	4	2	28.1	125	31	20	20	5	1	1	0	13	0	13	0	0	3	.000	0-1	0	90	.837	5.49	6.35
2018 Min	AL	4	4	0	17.2	74	18	9	7	3	0	0	0	6	0	13	2	1	1	.500	0-0	0	89	.810	4.53	3.57
2019 Min	AL	1	0	1	1.0	9	3	4	4	1	0	0	0	3	0	0	0	0	0	-	0-0	0	91	1.667	44.28	36.00
3 ML YEARS		12	8	3	47.0	208	52	33	31	9	1	1	0	22	0	26	2	1	4	.200	0-1	0	90	.857	5.73	5.94

Jose De Leon

Pitches: R **Bats:** R **Pos:** RP-3   **Ht:** 6'1" **Wt:** 220 **Born:** 8/7/1992 **Age:** 27

		HOW MUCH PITCHED					WHAT HE GAVE UP											THE RESULTS							
Year Team	Lg	G	GS	GF	IP	BFP	H	R	ER	HR	SH	SF	HB	TBB	IBB	SO	WP	W	L	Pct	Sv-Op	Hld	Vel	OPS	ERC	ERA
2019 Drham	AAA	17	13	2	51.1	222	41	20	20	4	0	2	6	27	0	73	2	2	1	.667	1--	-	-	.686	3.77	3.51
2016 LAD	NL	4	4	0	17.0	80	19	17	12	5	3	1	3	7	1	15	0	2	0	1.000	0-0	0	92	.937	6.82	6.35
2017 TB	AL	1	0	0	2.2	15	4	3	3	1	0	0	0	3	0	2	2	1	0	1.000	0-0	0	92	1.133	12.97	10.13
2019 TB	AL	3	0	1	4.0	21	3	2	1	0	0	0	2	3	1	7	1	1	0	1.000	0-0	0	92	.568	4.23	2.25
3 ML YEARS		8	4	1	23.2	116	26	22	16	6	3	1	5	13	2	24	3	4	0	1.000	0-0	0	92	.900	7.04	6.08

Enyel De Los Santos

Pitches: R **Bats:** R **Pos:** RP-4; SP-1   **Ht:** 6'3" **Wt:** 170 **Born:** 12/25/1995 **Age:** 24

		HOW MUCH PITCHED					WHAT HE GAVE UP											THE RESULTS							
Year Team	Lg	G	GS	GF	IP	BFP	H	R	ER	HR	SH	SF	HB	TBB	IBB	SO	WP	W	L	Pct	Sv-Op	Hld	Vel	OPS	ERC	ERA
2019 LV	AAA	19	19	0	94.0	396	81	52	46	16	2	5	4	35	3	83	4	5	7	.417	0--	-	-	.738	3.78	4.40
2018 Phi	NL	7	2	2	19.0	81	19	10	10	2	1	1	0	8	0	15	1	1	0	1.000	0-0	0	95	.836	4.54	4.74
2019 Phi	NL	5	1	3	11.0	46	13	9	9	4	0	0	1	5	0	9	1	0	1	.000	0-0	0	93	1.001	8.11	7.36
2 ML YEARS		12	3	5	30.0	127	32	19	19	6	1	1	1	13	0	24	2	1	1	.500	0-0	0	94	.897	5.77	5.70

Austin Dean

Bats: R **Throws:** R **Pos:** LF-44;PH-15;1B-5;RF-5;PR-1 **Ht:** 6'1" **Wt:** 190 **Born:** 10/14/1993 **Age:** 26

Year	Team	Lg	G	AB	H	2B	3B	HR	(Hm	Rd)	TB	R	RBI	RC	TBB	IBB	SO	HBP	SH	SF	SB	CS	GDP	Avg	OBP	Slg	OPS
2019	NewOr	AAA	73	252	85	19	1	18	(-	-)	160	48	57	60	28	0	52	0	0	2	4	3	5	.337	.401	.635	1.036
2018	Mia	NL	34	113	25	4	0	4	(2	2)	41	16	14	12	7	0	22	2	0	0	1	0	1	.221	.279	.363	.642
2019	Mia	NL	64	178	40	14	0	6	(4	2)	72	17	21	16	9	1	47	0	1	1	0	2	5	.225	.261	.404	.665
	2 ML YEARS		98	291	65	18	0	10	(6	4)	113	33	35	28	16	1	69	2	1	1	1	2	6	.223	.268	.388	.656

Jacob deGrom

Pitches: R **Bats:** L **Pos:** SP-32 duh-GRAHM **Ht:** 6'4" **Wt:** 180 **Born:** 6/19/1988 **Age:** 32

Year	Team	Lg	G	GS	GF	IP	BFP	H	R	ER	HR	SH	SF	HB	TBB	IBB	SO	WP	W	L	Pct	Sv-Op	Hld	Vel	OPS	ERC	ERA
2014	NYM	NL	22	22	0	140.1	565	117	44	42	7	5	3	1	43	2	144	1	9	6	.600	0-0	0	93	.613	2.57	2.69
2015	NYM	NL	30	30	0	191.0	751	149	59	54	16	10	7	2	38	2	205	6	14	8	.636	0-0	0	95	.574	2.13	2.54
2016	NYM	NL	24	24	0	148.0	604	142	53	50	15	5	3	3	36	0	143	4	7	8	.467	0-0	0	93	.685	3.40	3.04
2017	NYM	NL	31	31	0	201.1	827	180	87	79	28	3	5	2	59	5	239	7	15	10	.600	0-0	0	95	.682	3.36	3.53
2018	NYM	NL	32	32	0	217.0	835	152	48	41	10	3	5	5	46	3	269	2	10	9	.526	0-0	0	96	.521	**1.67**	**1.70**
2019	NYM	NL	32	32	0	204.0	804	154	59	55	19	5	3	7	44	1	**255**	2	11	8	.579	0-0	0	97	.580	**2.21**	2.43
	Postseason		4	4	0	25.0	105	21	8	8	2	2	0	0	8	1	29	0	3	1	.750	0-0	0	96	.608	2.65	2.88
	6 ML YEARS		171	171	0	1101.2	4386	894	350	321	95	31	26	20	266	13	1255	22	66	49	.574	0-0	0	95	.605	2.48	2.62

Paul DeJong

Bats: R **Throws:** R **Pos:** SS-157;PH-3 **Ht:** 6'0" **Wt:** 200 **Born:** 8/2/1993 **Age:** 26

Year	Team	Lg	G	AB	H	2B	3B	HR	(Hm	Rd)	TB	R	RBI	RC	TBB	IBB	SO	HBP	SH	SF	SB	CS	GDP	Avg	OBP	Slg	OPS
2017	StL	NL	108	417	119	26	1	25	(11	14)	222	55	65	57	21	1	124	4	0	1	1	0	8	.285	.325	.532	.857
2018	StL	NL	115	436	105	25	1	19	(4	15)	189	68	68	67	36	2	123	12	0	5	1	1	6	.241	.313	.433	.746
2019	StL	NL	159	583	136	31	1	30	(10	20)	259	97	78	76	62	1	149	13	0	6	9	5	15	.233	.318	.444	.762
	3 ML YEARS		382	1436	360	82	3	74	(25	49)	670	220	211	200	119	4	396	29	0	12	11	6	29	.251	.318	.467	.785

Miguel Del Pozo

Pitches: L **Bats:** L **Pos:** RP-17 **Ht:** 6'1" **Wt:** 180 **Born:** 10/14/1992 **Age:** 27

Year	Team	Lg	G	GS	GF	IP	BFP	H	R	ER	HR	SH	SF	HB	TBB	IBB	SO	WP	W	L	Pct	Sv-Op	Hld	Vel	OPS	ERC	ERA
2019	Nashv	AAA	38	0	11	45.2	206	53	27	26	5	0	1	4	21	1	65	5	2	3	.400	1--	-	-	.834	5.77	5.12
2019	LAA	AL	17	0	1	9.1	45	10	11	11	3	1	1	0	8	0	11	0	1	1	.500	0-0	0	95	.981	8.30	10.61

Nicky Delmonico

Bats: L **Throws:** R **Pos:** LF-21;PH-4;1B-1 **Ht:** 6'3" **Wt:** 230 **Born:** 7/12/1992 **Age:** 27

Year	Team	Lg	G	AB	H	2B	3B	HR	(Hm	Rd)	TB	R	RBI	RC	TBB	IBB	SO	HBP	SH	SF	SB	CS	GDP	Avg	OBP	Slg	OPS
2019	Charllt	AAA	17	63	18	7	0	3	(-	-)	34	13	10	13	10	1	12	1	0	2	1	0	0	.286	.382	.540	.921
2017	CWS	AL	43	141	37	4	0	9	(3	6)	68	25	23	23	23	0	31	2	0	0	2	0	5	.262	.373	.482	.856
2018	CWS	AL	88	284	61	11	5	8	(7	1)	106	31	25	30	27	1	80	6	0	1	1	2	5	.215	.296	.373	.669
2019	CWS	AL	21	63	13	2	0	1	(1	0)	18	6	6	7	4	0	25	1	0	0	0	1	1	.206	.265	.286	.550
	3 ML YEARS		152	488	111	17	5	18	(11	7)	192	62	54	60	54	1	136	9	0	1	3	3	13	.227	.315	.393	.709

Travis Demeritte

Bats: R **Throws:** R **Pos:** RF-47;PH-1;PR-1 **Ht:** 6'0" **Wt:** 180 **Born:** 9/30/1994 **Age:** 25

Year	Team	Lg	G	AB	H	2B	3B	HR	(Hm	Rd)	TB	R	RBI	RC	TBB	IBB	SO	HBP	SH	SF	SB	CS	GDP	Avg	OBP	Slg	OPS
2019	Gwnntt	AAA	96	339	97	28	2	20	(-	-)	189	68	73	73	51	0	106	6	1	2	4	3	5	.286	.387	.558	.944
2019	Det	AL	48	169	38	7	2	3	(2	1)	58	24	10	13	14	0	63	1	1	1	3	0	3	.225	.286	.343	.630

Daniel Descalso

Bats: L **Throws:** R **Pos:** 2B-45;PH-38;3B-3;DH-2;PR-2;1B-1 dess-CAL-so **Ht:** 5'10" **Wt:** 190 **Born:** 10/19/1986 **Age:** 33

Year	Team	Lg	G	AB	H	2B	3B	HR	(Hm	Rd)	TB	R	RBI	RC	TBB	IBB	SO	HBP	SH	SF	SB	CS	GDP	Avg	OBP	Slg	OPS
2019	Iowa	AAA	10	27	4	0	0	2	(-	-)	10	5	4	3	5	0	8	1	0	0	0	0	2	.148	.303	.370	.673
2010	StL	NL	11	34	9	2	0	0	(0	0)	11	6	4	5	2	0	6	1	0	0	1	0	0	.265	.324	.324	.648
2011	StL	NL	148	326	86	20	3	1	(1	0)	115	35	28	40	33	9	65	3	10	3	2	2	3	.264	.334	.353	.687
2012	StL	NL	143	374	85	10	7	4	(0	4)	121	41	26	29	37	3	83	5	7	3	6	3	5	.227	.303	.324	.627
2013	StL	NL	123	328	78	25	1	5	(1	4)	120	43	43	40	22	5	56	3	3	2	6	3	7	.238	.290	.366	.656
2014	StL	NL	104	161	39	11	0	0	(0	0)	50	20	10	15	20	0	33	2	1	0	1	3	2	.242	.333	.311	.644
2015	Col	NL	101	185	38	3	2	5	(1	4)	60	22	22	14	20	6	45	0	4	0	1	2	3	.205	.283	.324	.607
2016	Col	NL	99	250	66	12	2	8	(3	5)	106	38	38	45	34	3	56	1	0	4	3	0	2	.264	.349	.424	.773
2017	Ari	NL	131	344	80	16	5	10	(7	3)	136	47	51	49	48	0	89	4	0	2	4	0	6	.233	.332	.395	.727
2018	Ari	NL	138	349	83	22	4	13	(5	8)	152	54	57	57	64	2	110	2	0	7	0	1	2	.238	.353	.436	.789
2019	ChC	NL	82	168	29	5	1	2	(0	2)	42	20	15	16	23	0	57	0	1	1	2	1	3	.173	.271	.250	.521
	Postseason		48	93	21	3	0	4	(3	1)	36	19	9	8	8	3	23	0	5	1	2	0	2	.226	.284	.387	.671
	10 ML YEARS		1080	2519	593	126	25	48	(18	30)	913	326	294	310	303	28	600	21	26	22	26	15	33	.235	.320	.362	.683

Anthony DeSclafani

Pitches: R Bats: R Pos: SP-31   DEE-skla-fa-nee   Ht: 6'1" Wt: 195 Born: 4/18/1990 Age: 30

		HOW MUCH PITCHED					WHAT HE GAVE UP											THE RESULTS						
Year Team	Lg	G	GS	GF	IP	BFP	H	R	ER	HR	SH	SF	HB	TBB	IBB	SO	WP	W	L	Pct	Sv-Op Hld	Vel	OPS	ERC	ERA
2014 Mia	NL	13	5	4	33.0	146	40	23	23	4	4	3	2	5	0	26	2	2	2	.500	0-0 0	93	.801	4.56	6.27
2015 Cin	NL	31	31	0	184.2	785	194	93	83	17	10	5	5	55	1	151	6	9	13	.409	0-0 0	93	.742	4.00	4.05
2016 Cin	NL	20	20	0	123.1	507	120	51	45	16	7	3	4	30	2	105	6	9	5	.643	0-0 0	93	.723	3.67	3.28
2018 Cin	NL	21	21	0	115.0	484	118	68	63	24	5	4	2	30	2	108	4	7	8	.467	0-0 0	94	.792	4.47	4.93
2019 Cin	NL	31	31	0	166.2	696	151	77	72	29	5	3	4	49	5	167	2	9	9	.500	0-0 0	95	.717	3.66	3.89
5 ML YEARS		116	108	4	622.2	2618	623	312	286	90	31	18	17	169	14	557	20	36	37	.493	0-0 0	93	.744	3.96	4.13

Delino DeShields

Bats: R Throws: R Pos: CF-112;PR-7;PH-5;DH-1   Ht: 5'9" Wt: 200 Born: 8/16/1992 Age: 27

		BATTING																	RUNNING			AVERAGES			
Year Team	Lg	G	AB	H	2B	3B	HR	(Hm Rd)	TB	R	RBI	RC	TBB	IBB	SO	HBP	SH	SF	SB	CS	GDP	Avg	OBP	Slg	OPS
2019 Nashv	AAA	15	66	17	3	0	3	(- -)	29	10	11	11	8	0	17	0	1	0	8	0	1	.258	.338	.439	.777
2015 Tex	AL	121	425	111	22	10	2	(2 0)	159	83	37	66	53	1	101	3	7	4	25	8	1	.261	.344	.374	.718
2016 Tex	AL	74	182	38	7	0	4	(0 4)	57	36	13	16	15	0	54	2	3	1	8	3	1	.209	.275	.313	.588
2017 Tex	AL	120	376	101	15	2	6	(5 1)	138	75	22	54	44	0	109	3	13	4	29	8	2	.269	.347	.367	.714
2018 Tex	AL	106	334	72	14	1	2	(1 1)	94	52	22	38	43	0	83	4	12	1	20	4	1	.216	.310	.281	.591
2019 Tex	AL	118	357	89	15	4	4	(3 1)	124	42	32	51	38	0	100	3	8	2	24	6	8	.249	.325	.347	.672
Postseason		5	24	7	3	0	0	(0 0)	10	4	2	4	0	0	2	0	0	0	1	0	0	.292	.292	.417	.708
5 ML YEARS		539	1674	411	73	17	18	(11 7)	572	288	126	225	193	1	447	14	43	12	106	29	13	.246	.326	.342	.668

Ian Desmond

Bats: R Throws: R Pos: CF-74;LF-44;PH-24;DH-2   Ht: 6'3" Wt: 220 Born: 9/20/1985 Age: 34

		BATTING																	RUNNING			AVERAGES			
Year Team	Lg	G	AB	H	2B	3B	HR	(Hm Rd)	TB	R	RBI	RC	TBB	IBB	SO	HBP	SH	SF	SB	CS	GDP	Avg	OBP	Slg	OPS
2009 Was	NL	21	82	23	7	2	4	(2 2)	46	9	12	10	5	0	14	0	1	1	1	0	2	.280	.318	.561	.879
2010 Was	NL	154	525	141	27	4	10	(8 2)	206	59	65	58	28	3	109	5	9	7	17	5	9	.269	.308	.392	.700
2011 Was	NL	154	584	148	27	5	8	(7 1)	209	65	49	65	35	2	139	4	11	5	25	10	9	.253	.298	.358	.656
2012 Was	NL	130	513	150	33	2	25	(16 9)	262	72	73	73	30	1	113	3	0	1	21	6	17	.292	.335	.511	.845
2013 Was	NL	158	600	168	38	3	20	(10 10)	272	77	80	81	43	3	145	5	2	5	21	6	16	.280	.331	.453	.784
2014 Was	NL	154	593	151	26	3	24	(12 12)	255	73	91	78	46	0	183	6	0	3	24	5	17	.255	.313	.430	.743
2015 Was	NL	156	583	136	27	2	19	(11 8)	224	69	62	59	45	0	187	3	6	4	13	5	9	.233	.290	.384	.674
2016 Tex	AL	156	625	178	29	3	22	(10 12)	279	107	86	92	44	2	160	6	0	3	21	6	11	.285	.335	.446	.782
2017 Col	NL	95	339	93	11	1	7	(2 5)	127	47	40	47	24	1	87	4	2	4	15	4	13	.274	.326	.375	.701
2018 Col	NL	160	555	131	21	8	22	(8 14)	234	82	88	75	53	0	146	6	1	4	20	6	17	.236	.307	.422	.729
2019 Col	NL	140	443	113	31	4	20	(11 9)	212	64	65	59	34	1	119	2	1	2	3	3	12	.255	.310	.479	.788
Postseason		17	70	16	2	0	0	(0 0)	18	5	2	3	1	0	18	0	0	0	2	0	0	.229	.239	.257	.497
11 ML YEARS		1478	5442	1432	277	37	181	(97 84)	2326	724	711	697	387	13	1402	43	33	39	181	56	132	.263	.315	.427	.742

Odrisamer Despaigne

Pitches: R Bats: R Pos: SP-3   oh-DREE-sa-mehr des-PAHN-yay   Ht: 6'0" Wt: 200 Born: 4/4/1987 Age: 33

		HOW MUCH PITCHED					WHAT HE GAVE UP											THE RESULTS						
Year Team	Lg	G	GS	GF	IP	BFP	H	R	ER	HR	SH	SF	HB	TBB	IBB	SO	WP	W	L	Pct	Sv-Op Hld	Vel	OPS	ERC	ERA
2019 Lsvlle	AAA	8	8	0	41.1	176	40	21	18	5	0	2		16	0	40	1	3	2	.600	0- - -	-	.728	4.25	3.92
2019 Charllt	AAA	16	14	1	83.0	355	83	31	30	6	1	5	6	28	0	84	6	5	4	.556	0- - -	-	.689	3.96	3.25
2014 SD	NL	16	16	0	96.1	404	85	44	36	6	8	1	5	32	0	65	0	4	7	.364	0-0 0	91	.638	3.12	3.36
2015 SD	NL	34	18	5	125.2	547	142	82	81	17	8	3	9	32	3	69	7	5	9	.357	0-0 0	91	.802	4.75	5.80
2016 2 Tms		19	0	8	30.1	135	36	21	20	3	0	2	1	16	1	17	0	0	2	.000	0-2 1	93	.884	6.02	5.93
2017 Mia	NL	18	8	5	58.1	254	57	31	26	3	2	2	3	24	1	31	1	2	3	.400	1-1 1	92	.688	3.81	4.01
2018 2 Tms		19	5	2	39.0	188	52	34	29	4	1	4	2	19	1	35	0	2	3	.400	0-1 0	93	.860	6.52	6.69
2019 CWS	AL	3	3	0	13.1	68	24	14	14	3	0	1	1	7	0	7	0	0	2	.000	0-0 0	93	1.149	11.71	9.45
16 Bal	AL	16	0	5	27.1	122	32	18	17	3	0	1	1	15	1	17	0	0	2	.000	0-2 1	93	.889	6.11	5.60
16 Mia	NL	3	0	3	3.0	13	4	3	3	0	0	1	0	1	0	0	0	0	0	-	0-0 0	92	.839	5.24	9.00
18 Mia	NL	11	1	2	20.1	91	22	16	12	1	1	2	1	8	0	18	0	2	0	1.000	0-1 0	92	.737	4.19	5.31
18 LAA	AL	8	4	0	18.2	97	30	18	17	3	0	2	1	11	0	17	0	0	3	.000	0-0 0	93	.975	9.37	8.20
6 ML YEARS		109	50	20	363.0	1596	396	226	206	36	19	13	21	130	6	224	8	13	26	.333	1-4 2	91	.771	4.64	5.11

Ross Detwiler

Pitches: L Bats: R Pos: SP-12; RP-6   DETT-why-lerr   Ht: 6'5" Wt: 210 Born: 3/6/1986 Age: 34

		HOW MUCH PITCHED					WHAT HE GAVE UP											THE RESULTS						
Year Team	Lg	G	GS	GF	IP	BFP	H	R	ER	HR	SH	SF	HB	TBB	IBB	SO	WP	W	L	Pct	Sv-Op Hld	Vel	OPS	ERC	ERA
2019 Charllt	AAA	8	8	0	43.0	174	44	19	19	11	0	0	2	11	0	35	1	1	2	.333	0- - -	-	.831	5.15	3.98
2007 Was	NL	1	0	1	1.0	4	0	0	0	0	0	0	0	0	0	1	0	0	0	-	0-0 0	93	.000	0.00	0.00
2009 Was	NL	15	14	0	75.2	341	87	43	42	3	4	1	2	33	3	43	4	1	6	.143	0-0 0	91	.767	4.65	5.00
2010 Was	NL	8	5	1	29.2	135	34	22	14	5	2	0	1	14	1	17	1	1	3	.250	0-0 0	90	.826	5.83	4.25
2011 Was	NL	15	10	0	66.0	277	63	26	22	7	7	3	3	20	2	41	2	4	5	.444	0-0 1	92	.704	3.64	3.00
2012 Was	NL	33	27	1	164.1	686	149	75	62	15	8	3	5	52	0	105	4	10	8	.556	0-0 1	93	.681	3.30	3.40
2013 Was	NL	13	13	0	71.1	316	92	37	32	5	4	1	5	14	2	39	0	2	7	.222	0-0 0	92	.811	4.96	4.04
2014 Was	NL	47	0	15	63.0	274	68	34	28	5	4	3	6	21	4	39	3	2	3	.400	1-2 3	93	.734	4.36	4.00
2015 2 Tms		41	7	7	58.1	288	82	51	47	10	1	4	6	36	1	41	3	1	5	.167	0-2 2	92	.984	6.11	7.25
2016 2 Tms		16	7	0	48.2	220	59	34	33	5	0	1	1	19	0	26	3	2	4	.333	0-1 0	92	.806	5.37	6.10
2018 Sea	AL	1	0	0	6.0	23	8	3	3	1	0	1	0	2	0	2	0	0	1	.000	0-0 0	90	.985	7.59	4.50
2019 CWS	AL	18	12	2	69.2	315	86	54	51	20	2	1	3	27	3	46	1	3	5	.375	0-0 0	91	.942	7.05	6.59
15 Tex	AL	17	7	4	43.0	208	62	37	34	9	1	3	3	20	0	28	3	0	5	.000	0-1 1	91	.991	8.35	7.12
15 Atl	NL	24	0	3	15.1	80	20	14	13	1	0	1	3	16	1	13	0	1	0	1.000	0-0 0	93	.954	9.42	7.63

Year Team	Lg	G	GS	GF	IP	BFP	H	R	ER	HR	SH	SF	HB	TBB	IBB	SO	WP	W	L	Pct	Sv-Op	Hld	Vel	OPS	ERC	ERA
16 Cle	AL	7	0	0	4.2	21	3	3	3	1	0	1	0	4	0	3	0	0	0	-	0-1	0	91	.833	4.60	5.79
16 Oak	AL	9	7	0	44.0	199	56	31	30	4	0	0	1	15	0	23	3	2	4	.333	0-0	0	92	.804	5.46	6.14
Postseason		1	1	0	6.0	25	3	1	0	0	1	1	0	3	1	2	0	0	0	-	0-0	0	92	.400	1.21	0.00
11 ML YEARS		208	95	27	653.2	2879	728	379	334	76	32	18	31	238	16	400	21	26	47	.356	1-5	7	92	.789	4.88	4.60

Chris Devenski

Pitches: R **Bats:** R **Pos:** RP-60; SP-1 **Ht:** 6'3" **Wt:** 210 **Born:** 11/13/1990 **Age:** 29

Year Team	Lg	G	GS	GF	IP	BFP	H	R	ER	HR	SH	SF	HB	TBB	IBB	SO	WP	W	L	Pct	Sv-Op	Hld	Vel	OPS	ERC	ERA
2016 Hou	AL	48	5	16	108.1	408	79	26	26	4	1	1	3	20	0	104	2	4	4	.500	1-1	5	92	.551	1.74	2.16
2017 Hou	AL	62	0	10	80.2	316	50	26	24	11	0	1	2	26	3	100	2	8	5	.615	4-10	24	94	.588	2.10	2.68
2018 Hou	AL	50	1	8	47.1	196	42	23	22	9	1	1	3	13	1	51	1	2	3	.400	2-5	18	94	.719	3.79	4.18
2019 Hou	AL	61	1	19	69.0	298	69	39	37	13	1	3	3	21	0	72	2	2	3	.400	0-1	7	95	.784	4.42	4.83
Postseason		10	0	2	8.0	36	9	8	8	2	0	1	0	3	0	8	0	1	0	1.000	0-1	3	95	.927	5.67	9.00
4 ML YEARS		221	7	53	305.1	1218	240	114	109	37	3	6	11	80	4	327	7	16	15	.516	7-17	54	94	.644	2.70	3.21

Rafael Devers

Bats: L **Throws:** R **Pos:** 3B-152;PH-4;SS-1;DH-1 **Ht:** 6'0" **Wt:** 237 **Born:** 10/24/1996 **Age:** 23

Year Team	Lg	G	AB	H	2B	3B	HR	(Hm	Rd)	TB	R	RBI	RC	TBB	IBB	SO	HBP	SH	SF	SB	CS	GDP	Avg	OBP	Slg	OPS
2017 Bos	AL	58	222	63	14	0	10	(6	4)	107	34	30	34	18	3	57	0	0	0	3	1	5	.284	.338	.482	.819
2018 Bos	AL	121	450	108	24	0	21	(9	12)	195	59	66	47	38	6	121	0	0	2	5	2	9	.240	.298	.433	.731
2019 Bos	AL	156	647	201	54	4	32	(13	19)	359	129	115	119	48	7	119	4	1	2	8	8	8	.311	.361	.555	.916
Postseason		15	45	14	0	0	3	(2	1)	23	10	14	10	5	0	17	0	0	1	1	0	1	.311	.373	.511	.884
3 ML YEARS		335	1319	372	92	4	63	(28	35)	661	222	211	200	104	16	297	4	1	4	16	11	22	.282	.335	.501	.837

Aledmys Diaz

Bats: R **Throws:** R **Pos:** 1B-26;2B-25;3B-19;PH-9;SS-5;LF-4;PR-3;DH-2   ah-LED-mees   **Ht:** 6'1" **Wt:** 195 **Born:** 8/1/1990 **Age:** 29

Year Team	Lg	G	AB	H	2B	3B	HR	(Hm	Rd)	TB	R	RBI	RC	TBB	IBB	SO	HBP	SH	SF	SB	CS	GDP	Avg	OBP	Slg	OPS
2016 StL	NL	111	404	121	28	3	17	(7	10)	206	71	65	75	41	6	60	7	2	6	4	4	10	.300	.369	.510	.879
2017 StL	NL	79	286	74	17	0	7	(5	2)	112	31	20	27	13	1	42	0	1	1	4	1	9	.259	.290	.392	.682
2018 Tor	AL	130	422	111	26	0	18	(7	11)	191	55	55	50	23	2	62	3	0	4	3	4	9	.263	.303	.453	.756
2019 Hou	AL	69	210	57	12	1	9	(5	4)	98	36	40	36	26	1	28	5	0	6	2	0	10	.271	.356	.467	.823
4 ML YEARS		389	1322	363	83	4	51	(24	27)	607	193	180	188	103	10	192	15	3	17	13	9	38	.275	.330	.459	.789

Edwin Diaz

Pitches: R **Bats:** R **Pos:** RP-66 **Ht:** 6'3" **Wt:** 165 **Born:** 3/22/1994 **Age:** 26

Year Team	Lg	G	GS	GF	IP	BFP	H	R	ER	HR	SH	SF	HB	TBB	IBB	SO	WP	W	L	Pct	Sv-Op	Hld	Vel	OPS	ERC	ERA
2016 Sea	AL	49	0	23	51.2	217	45	16	16	5	0	0	0	15	2	88	6	0	4	.000	18-21	13	97	.627	3.05	2.79
2017 Sea	AL	66	0	52	66.0	278	44	28	24	10	1	2	3	32	2	89	3	4	6	.400	34-39	2	97	.619	3.01	3.27
2018 Sea	AL	73	0	65	73.1	280	41	17	16	5	0	0	6	17	0	124	3	0	4	.000	57-61	0	97	.470	1.49	1.96
2019 NYM	NL	66	0	48	58.0	254	58	36	36	15	1	2	4	22	3	99	3	2	7	.222	26-33	1	97	.834	5.31	5.59
4 ML YEARS		254	0	188	249.0	1029	188	97	92	35	2	4	16	86	7	400	15	6	21	.222	135-154	16	97	.632	2.99	3.33

Elias Diaz

Bats: R **Throws:** R **Pos:** C-96;PH-10;PR-1   Eh-lee-ahs   **Ht:** 6'1" **Wt:** 220 **Born:** 11/17/1990 **Age:** 29

Year Team	Lg	G	AB	H	2B	3B	HR	(Hm	Rd)	TB	R	RBI	RC	TBB	IBB	SO	HBP	SH	SF	SB	CS	GDP	Avg	OBP	Slg	OPS
2015 Pit	NL	2	2	0	0	0	0	(0	0)	0	0	0	0	0	0	1	0	0	0	0	0	0	.000	.000	.000	.000
2016 Pit	NL	1	4	0	0	0	0	(0	0)	0	0	1	0	0	0	1	0	0	0	0	0	0	.000	.000	.000	.000
2017 Pit	NL	64	188	42	14	0	1	(0	1)	59	18	19	15	11	0	38	0	0	1	1	0	8	.223	.265	.314	.579
2018 Pit	NL	82	252	72	12	0	10	(3	7)	114	33	34	36	21	1	40	1	0	3	0	1	4	.286	.339	.452	.792
2019 Pit	NL	101	303	73	14	0	2	(2	0)	93	31	28	30	23	0	56	2	1	3	0	0	11	.241	.296	.307	.603
5 ML YEARS		250	749	187	40	0	13	(5	8)	266	82	82	81	55	1	136	3	1	7	1	1	23	.250	.301	.355	.656

Isan Diaz

Bats: L **Throws:** R **Pos:** 2B-48;PH-1 **Ht:** 5'10" **Wt:** 185 **Born:** 5/27/1996 **Age:** 24

Year Team	Lg	G	AB	H	2B	3B	HR	(Hm	Rd)	TB	R	RBI	RC	TBB	IBB	SO	HBP	SH	SF	SB	CS	GDP	Avg	OBP	Slg	OPS
2019 NewOr	AAA	102	377	115	21	2	26	(-	-)	218	89	70	84	49	3	96	7	2	0	5	4	4	.305	.395	.578	.973
2019 Mia	NL	49	179	31	5	2	5	(2	3)	55	17	23	19	19	0	59	2	0	1	0	3	2	.173	.259	.307	.566

Jairo Diaz

Pitches: R **Bats:** R **Pos:** RP-56   HIGH-row   **Ht:** 6'0" **Wt:** 200 **Born:** 5/27/1991 **Age:** 29

Year Team	Lg	G	GS	GF	IP	BFP	H	R	ER	HR	SH	SF	HB	TBB	IBB	SO	WP	W	L	Pct	Sv-Op	Hld	Vel	OPS	ERC	ERA
2019 Albq	AAA	16	0	10	20.0	77	12	1	1	0	0	0	1	6	0	22	1	1	0	1.000	6-	-	-	.447	1.44	0.45
2014 LAA	AL	5	0	2	5.2	24	4	2	2	0	1	0	0	3	0	8	0	0	0	-	0-0	0	97	.592	2.29	3.18

Year	Team	Lg	G	GS	GF	IP	BFP	H	R	ER	HR	SH	SF	HB	TBB	IBB	SO	WP	W	L	Pct	Sv-Op	Hld	Vel	OPS	ERC	ERA
2015	Col	NL	21	0	5	19.0	78	16	6	5	2	0	0	0	6	0	18	0	0	1	.000	0-1	7	97	.615	2.93	2.37
2017	Col	NL	4	0	3	5.0	30	12	6	5	0	0	0	1	5	0	2	0	0	0	-	0-0	0	97	1.267	17.54	9.00
2019	Col	NL	56	0	20	57.2	245	56	34	29	7	0	1	2	19	0	63	4	6	4	.600	5-8	7	97	.745	3.92	4.53
	4 ML YEARS		86	0	30	87.1	377	88	48	41	9	0	2	3	33	0	91	4	6	5	.545	5-9	14	97	.748	4.20	4.23

Miguel Diaz

Pitches: R **Bats:** R **Pos:** RP-5   **Ht:** 6'0" **Wt:** 214 **Born:** 11/28/1994 **Age:** 25

Year	Team	Lg	G	GS	GF	IP	BFP	H	R	ER	HR	SH	SF	HB	TBB	IBB	SO	WP	W	L	Pct	Sv-Op	Hld	Vel	OPS	ERC	ERA
2019	Amrillo	AA	6	4	0	22.2	97	21	11	11	9	0	0	0	8	0	33	1	2	1	.667	0--	-	-	.872	5.37	4.37
2017	SD	NL	31	3	8	41.2	192	44	35	34	11	2	2	3	25	0	33	5	1	1	.500	0-0	0	96	.929	6.87	7.34
2018	SD	NL	11	0	4	18.2	85	16	11	10	2	0	2	0	12	2	30	1	1	0	1.000	0-0	0	96	.738	3.94	4.82
2019	SD	NL	5	0	2	6.1	29	9	5	5	1	0	0	2	4	0	4	1	0	0	-	0-0	1	95	1.068	7.78	7.11
	3 ML YEARS		47	3	14	66.2	306	69	51	49	14	2	4	5	38	2	67	7	2	1	.667	0-0	1	96	.890	6.07	6.62

Yandy Diaz

Bats: R **Throws:** R **Pos:** 3B-50;1B-22;DH-16;PR-1   **Ht:** 6'2" **Wt:** 215 **Born:** 8/8/1991 **Age:** 28

Year	Team	Lg	G	AB	H	2B	3B	HR	(Hm	Rd)	TB	R	RBI	RC	TBB	IBB	SO	HBP	SH	SF	SB	CS	GDP	Avg	OBP	Slg	OPS
2017	Cle	AL	49	156	41	8	1	0	(0	0)	51	25	13	18	21	0	35	1	0	1	2	0	5	.263	.352	.327	.679
2018	Cle	AL	39	109	34	5	2	1	(1	0)	46	15	15	16	11	1	19	0	0	0	0	0	6	.312	.375	.422	.797
2019	TB	AL	79	307	82	20	1	14	(7	7)	146	53	38	38	35	1	61	1	0	4	2	2	9	.267	.340	.476	.816
	Postseason		1	3	1	1	0	0	(0	0)	2	0	0	1	0	0	1	0	0	0	0	0	0	.333	.333	.667	1.000
	3 ML YEARS		167	572	157	33	4	15	(8	7)	243	93	66	72	67	2	115	2	0	5	4	2	20	.274	.350	.425	.775

Yennsy Diaz

Pitches: R **Bats:** R **Pos:** RP-1   **Ht:** 6'1" **Wt:** 202 **Born:** 11/15/1996 **Age:** 23

Year	Team	Lg	G	GS	GF	IP	BFP	H	R	ER	HR	SH	SF	HB	TBB	IBB	SO	WP	W	L	Pct	Sv-Op	Hld	Vel	OPS	ERC	ERA
2019	Nham	AA	26	24	2	144.1	609	125	71	60	12	7	5	9	53	0	116	9	11	9	.550	0--	-	-	.664	3.34	3.74
2019	Tor	AL	1	0	0	0.2	7	1	2	2	0	0	0	0	4	0	0	0	0	0	-	0-0	0	96	1.048	31.81	27.00

Alex Dickerson

Bats: L **Throws:** L **Pos:** LF-50;PH-29;RF-1   **Ht:** 6'3" **Wt:** 235 **Born:** 5/26/1990 **Age:** 30

Year	Team	Lg	G	AB	H	2B	3B	HR	(Hm	Rd)	TB	R	RBI	RC	TBB	IBB	SO	HBP	SH	SF	SB	CS	GDP	Avg	OBP	Slg	OPS
2019	ElPaso	AAA	26	94	35	5	1	5	(-	-)	57	17	20	25	14	0	18	4	0	1	0	0	3	.372	.469	.606	1.075
2015	SD	NL	11	8	2	0	0	0	(0	0)	2	0	0	0	0	0	3	0	0	0	0	0	1	.250	.250	.250	.500
2016	SD	NL	84	253	65	16	2	10	(5	5)	115	39	37	40	26	2	44	4	0	2	5	1	5	.257	.333	.455	.788
2019	2 Tms	NL	68	174	48	13	3	6	(4	2)	85	29	28	27	13	1	42	2	0	1	1	1	5	.276	.332	.489	.820
19	SD	NL	12	19	3	0	0	0	(0	0)	3	1	2	2	0	0	7	0	0	0	0	0	0	.158	.158	.158	.316
19	SF	NL	56	155	45	13	3	6	(4	2)	82	28	26	25	13	1	35	2	0	1	1	1	5	.290	.351	.529	.880
	3 ML YEARS		163	435	115	29	5	16	(9	7)	202	68	65	67	39	3	89	6	0	3	6	2	11	.264	.331	.464	.796

Corey Dickerson

Bats: L **Throws:** R **Pos:** LF-65;PH-15   **Ht:** 6'1" **Wt:** 210 **Born:** 5/22/1989 **Age:** 31

Year	Team	Lg	G	AB	H	2B	3B	HR	(Hm	Rd)	TB	R	RBI	RC	TBB	IBB	SO	HBP	SH	SF	SB	CS	GDP	Avg	OBP	Slg	OPS
2013	Col	NL	69	194	51	13	5	5	(4	1)	89	32	17	23	16	0	41	0	1	2	2	2	1	.263	.316	.459	.775
2014	Col	NL	131	436	136	27	6	24	(15	9)	247	74	76	79	37	6	101	1	0	4	8	7	6	.312	.364	.567	.931
2015	Col	NL	65	224	68	18	2	10	(5	5)	120	30	31	39	10	0	56	0	1	3	0	1	3	.304	.333	.536	.869
2016	TB	AL	148	510	125	36	3	24	(7	17)	239	57	70	59	33	6	134	2	0	2	0	2	12	.245	.293	.469	.761
2017	TB	AL	150	588	166	33	4	27	(14	13)	288	84	62	87	35	6	152	3	0	2	4	3	11	.282	.325	.490	.815
2018	Pit	NL	135	504	151	35	7	13	(4	9)	239	65	55	69	21	4	80	4	0	4	8	3	14	.300	.330	.474	.804
2019	2 Tms	NL	78	260	79	28	2	12	(6	6)	147	33	59	50	16	4	56	0	0	3	1	0	4	.304	.341	.565	.906
19	Pit	NL	44	127	40	18	0	4	(0	4)	70	20	25	24	13	4	23	0	0	2	1	0	3	.315	.373	.551	.924
19	Phi	NL	34	133	39	10	2	8	(6	2)	77	13	34	26	3	0	33	0	0	1	0	0	1	.293	.307	.579	.886
	7 ML YEARS		776	2716	776	190	29	115	(55	60)	1369	375	370	406	168	26	620	10	1	17	23	18	51	.286	.328	.504	.832

Phillip Diehl

Pitches: L **Bats:** L **Pos:** RP-10   **Ht:** 6'2" **Wt:** 180 **Born:** 7/16/1994 **Age:** 25

Year	Team	Lg	G	GS	GF	IP	BFP	H	R	ER	HR	SH	SF	HB	TBB	IBB	SO	WP	W	L	Pct	Sv-Op	Hld	Vel	OPS	ERC	ERA
2019	Hrtfrd	AA	11	0	2	13.1	47	5	0	0	0	0	0	1	3	0	12	0	0	0	-	0--	-	-	.354	0.76	0.00
2019	Albq	AAA	39	0	10	45.1	197	54	35	34	16	0	1	0	15	0	52	1	2	1	.667	0--	-	-	.975	6.94	6.75
2019	Col	NL	10	0	2	7.1	35	10	6	6	1	0	0	1	2	0	8	1	0	0	-	0-0	0	91	.934	6.41	7.36

Jake Diekman

Pitches: L Bats: L Pos: RP-76   DEEK-man   Ht: 6'4" Wt: 200 Born: 1/21/1987 Age: 33

			HOW MUCH PITCHED				WHAT HE GAVE UP												THE RESULTS						
Year	Team	Lg	G	GS	GF	IP	BFP	H	R	ER	HR	SH	SF	HB	TBB	IBB	SO	WP	W	L	Pct	Sv-Op	Hld	Vel	OPS	ERC	ERA
2012	Phi	NL	32	0	7	27.1	131	25	17	12	1	1	0	3	20	3	35	1	1	1	.500	0-1	4	95	.696	4.45	3.95
2013	Phi	NL	45	0	11	38.1	164	34	15	11	1	2	1	0	16	2	41	2	1	4	.200	0-1	11	96	.598	2.89	2.58
2014	Phi	NL	73	0	19	71.0	313	66	36	30	4	2	7	3	35	5	100	7	5	5	.500	0-4	18	97	.692	3.73	3.80
2015	2 Tms		67	0	7	58.1	260	53	28	26	5	0	0	3	31	0	69	2	2	1	.667	0-3	16	96	.689	4.11	4.01
2016	Tex	AL	66	0	14	53.0	221	36	22	20	4	0	2	3	26	1	59	3	4	2	.667	4-5	26	95	.594	2.72	3.40
2017	Tex	AL	11	0	2	10.2	45	4	3	3	1	0	2	0	10	1	13	0	0	0	-	1-1	5	95	.523	2.58	2.53
2018	2 Tms		71	0	15	53.1	243	49	33	28	4	0	2	6	31	2	66	3	1	2	.333	2-3	17	95	.717	4.46	4.73
2019	2 Tms		76	0	5	62.0	282	49	34	32	3	1	3	11	39	1	84	6	1	7	.125	0-2	31	96	.668	4.00	4.65
15	Phi	NL	41	0	6	36.2	175	40	23	21	3	0	0	2	24	0	49	1	2	1	.667	0-2	6	96	.773	5.60	5.15
15	Tex	AL	26	0	1	21.2	85	13	5	5	2	0	0	1	7	0	20	1	0	0	-	0-1	10	97	.520	1.89	2.08
18	Tex	AL	47	0	10	39.0	172	31	18	16	2	0	2	3	23	1	48	0	1	1	.500	2-3	14	95	.651	3.53	3.69
18	Ari	NL	24	0	5	14.1	71	18	15	12	2	0	0	3	8	1	18	3	0	1	.000	0-0	3	96	.875	7.29	7.53
19	KC	AL	48	0	4	41.2	188	33	23	22	3	0	1	8	23	0	63	4	0	6	.000	0-2	18	96	.667	3.97	4.75
19	Oak	AL	28	0	1	20.1	94	16	11	10	0	1	2	3	16	1	21	2	1	1	.500	0-0	13	96	.668	4.05	4.43
	Postseason		6	0	2	7.0	29	7	4	4	1	0	0	0	2	1	6	0	0	0	-	0-0	1	97	.755	3.76	5.14
	8 ML YEARS		441	0	80	374.0	1659	316	188	162	23	6	17	29	208	15	467	24	15	22	.405	7-20	128	96	.665	3.72	3.90

Derek Dietrich

Bats: L Throws: R Pos: 2B-58;PH-38;1B-21;LF-16;DH-2;3B-1   DEE-trick   Ht: 6'0" Wt: 205 Born: 7/18/1989 Age: 30

							BATTING													RUNNING			AVERAGES			
Year	Team	Lg	G	AB	H	2B	3B	HR	(Hm	Rd)	TB	R	RBI	RC	TBB	IBB	SO	HBP	SH	SF	SB	CS	GDP	Avg	OBP	Slg	OPS
2013	Mia	NL	57	215	46	10	2	9	(3	6)	87	32	23	24	11	1	56	7	0	0	1	0	1	.214	.275	.405	.679
2014	Mia	NL	49	158	36	6	2	5	(1	4)	61	31	17	22	13	0	38	10	2	0	1	0	1	.228	.326	.386	.712
2015	Mia	NL	90	250	64	14	3	10	(3	7)	114	38	24	32	23	2	65	13	0	3	0	2	4	.256	.346	.456	.802
2016	Mia	NL	128	351	98	20	5	7	(3	4)	149	39	42	57	32	2	84	24	0	5	1	0	6	.279	.374	.425	.798
2017	Mia	NL	135	406	101	22	5	13	(7	6)	172	56	53	59	36	5	98	18	0	4	1	0	4	.249	.334	.424	.758
2018	Mia	NL	149	499	132	26	2	16	(4	12)	210	72	45	63	29	2	140	21	0	2	2	0	5	.265	.330	.421	.751
2019	Cin	NL	113	251	47	8	2	19	(12	7)	116	41	43	45	28	2	74	25	0	1	1	1	2	.187	.328	.462	.790
	7 ML YEARS		721	2130	524	106	21	79	(33	46)	909	309	247	302	172	14	555	118	2	15	6	4	23	.246	.334	.427	.761

Wilmer Difo

Bats: B Throws: R Pos: SS-33;3B-6;PH-5;2B-2   DEE-fo   Ht: 5'11" Wt: 200 Born: 4/2/1992 Age: 28

							BATTING													RUNNING			AVERAGES			
Year	Team	Lg	G	AB	H	2B	3B	HR	(Hm	Rd)	TB	R	RBI	RC	TBB	IBB	SO	HBP	SH	SF	SB	CS	GDP	Avg	OBP	Slg	OPS
2019	Fresno	AAA	61	233	70	14	3	4	(-	-)	102	48	30	39	25	0	51	1	1	1	13	5	4	.300	.369	.438	.807
2015	Was	NL	15	11	2	0	0	0	(0	0)	2	1	0	0	0	0	2	0	0	0	0	0	0	.182	.182	.182	.364
2016	Was	NL	31	58	16	3	0	1	(1	0)	22	14	7	9	8	1	12	0	0	0	3	0	0	.276	.364	.379	.743
2017	Was	NL	124	332	90	10	4	5	(3	2)	123	47	21	34	24	6	74	1	5	3	10	1	7	.271	.319	.370	.690
2018	Was	NL	148	408	94	14	7	7	(5	2)	143	55	42	38	39	5	82	2	3	4	10	3	8	.230	.298	.350	.649
2019	Was	NL	43	131	33	2	0	2	(1	1)	41	15	8	15	12	3	29	0	1	0	0	1	2	.252	.315	.313	.628
	Postseason		3	3	0	0	0	0	(0	0)	0	0	0	0	0	0	1	0	0	0	0	0	0	.000	.000	.000	.000
	5 ML YEARS		361	940	235	29	11	15	(10	5)	331	132	78	96	83	15	199	3	9	7	23	5	17	.250	.311	.352	.663

Nick Dini

Bats: R Throws: R Pos: C-20;PH-1   Ht: 5'8" Wt: 180 Born: 7/27/1993 Age: 26

							BATTING													RUNNING			AVERAGES			
Year	Team	Lg	G	AB	H	2B	3B	HR	(Hm	Rd)	TB	R	RBI	RC	TBB	IBB	SO	HBP	SH	SF	SB	CS	GDP	Avg	OBP	Slg	OPS
2019	Omha	AAA	58	186	55	11	0	13	(-	-)	105	34	36	39	21	1	29	2	2	2	7	2	4	.296	.370	.565	.934
2019	KC	AL	20	56	11	3	0	2	(0	2)	20	11	6	8	4	0	18	2	1	1	0	0	1	.196	.270	.357	.627

Brandon Dixon

Bats: R Throws: R Pos: 1B-61;LF-26;DH-15;PH-8;PR-8;RF-7;3B-4;2B-3;CF-1   Ht: 6'2" Wt: 215 Born: 1/29/1992 Age: 28

							BATTING													RUNNING			AVERAGES			
Year	Team	Lg	G	AB	H	2B	3B	HR	(Hm	Rd)	TB	R	RBI	RC	TBB	IBB	SO	HBP	SH	SF	SB	CS	GDP	Avg	OBP	Slg	OPS
2019	Toledo	AAA	11	46	8	0	0	1	(-	-)	11	6	3	1	0	0	16	0	0	0	0	0	0	.174	.174	.239	.413
2018	Cin	NL	74	118	21	6	0	5	(2	3)	42	14	10	2	6	0	43	0	0	0	0	0	2	.178	.218	.356	.574
2019	Det	AL	118	391	97	20	4	15	(5	10)	170	41	52	50	21	0	136	4	0	4	5	1	5	.248	.290	.435	.725
	2 ML YEARS		192	509	118	26	4	20	(7	13)	212	55	62	52	27	0	179	4	0	4	5	1	7	.232	.274	.417	.690

Randy Dobnak

Pitches: R Bats: R Pos: SP-5; RP-4   Ht: 6'1" Wt: 230 Born: 1/17/1995 Age: 25

			HOW MUCH PITCHED				WHAT HE GAVE UP												THE RESULTS						
Year	Team	Lg	G	GS	GF	IP	BFP	H	R	ER	HR	SH	SF	HB	TBB	IBB	SO	WP	W	L	Pct	Sv-Op	Hld	Vel	OPS	ERC	ERA
2019	Pnscla	AA	11	10	0	66.2	263	58	23	19	6	2	1	2	6	0	61	2	4	2	.667	0- -	-	-	.608	2.28	2.57
2019	Roch	AAA	9	7	0	46.0	182	28	12	11	0	1	1	2	18	0	34	3	5	2	.714	0- -	-	-	.484	1.64	2.15
2019	Min	AL	9	5	4	28.1	118	27	9	5	1	0	0	3	5	0	23	0	2	1	.667	1-1	0	93	.597	2.93	1.59

Seranthony Dominguez

Pitches: R Bats: R Pos: RP-27   Ht: 6'1" Wt: 185 Born: 11/25/1994 Age: 25

Year Team	Lg	G	GS	GF	IP	BFP	H	R	ER	HR	SH	SF	HB	TBB	IBB	SO	WP	W	L	Pct	Sv-Op	Hld	Vel	OPS	ERC	ERA
2018 Phi	NL	53	0	24	58.0	231	32	19	19	4	0	1	4	22	2	74	10	2	5	.286	16-20	14	98	.501	1.74	2.95
2019 Phi	NL	27	0	2	24.2	110	24	13	11	3	1	0	1	12	0	29	1	3	0	1.000	0-2	9	97	.725	4.52	4.01
2 ML YEARS		80	0	26	82.2	341	56	32	30	7	1	1	5	34	2	103	11	5	5	.500	16-22	23	98	.573	2.48	3.27

Josh Donaldson

Bats: R Throws: R Pos: 3B-148;PH-6;DH-1   Ht: 6'1" Wt: 210 Born: 12/8/1985 Age: 34

Year Team	Lg	G	AB	H	2B	3B	HR	(Hm	Rd)	TB	R	RBI	RC	TBB	IBB	SO	HBP	SH	SF	SB	CS	GDP	Avg	OBP	Slg	OPS
2010 Oak	AL	14	32	5	1	0	1	(0	1)	9	1	4	3	2	0	12	0	0	0	0	0	0	.156	.206	.281	.487
2012 Oak	AL	75	274	66	16	0	9	(3	6)	109	34	33	33	14	0	61	5	0	1	4	1	6	.241	.289	.398	.687
2013 Oak	AL	158	579	174	37	3	24	(13	11)	289	89	93	112	76	2	110	6	1	6	5	2	15	.301	.384	.499	.883
2014 Oak	AL	158	608	155	31	2	29	(11	18)	277	93	98	105	76	5	130	7	0	4	8	0	16	.255	.342	.456	.798
2015 Tor	AL	158	620	184	41	2	41	(24	17)	352	122	123	131	73	0	133	6	2	10	6	0	16	.297	.371	.568	.939
2016 Tor	AL	155	577	164	32	5	37	(21	16)	317	122	99	121	109	6	119	9	2	3	7	1	16	.284	.404	.549	.953
2017 Tor	AL	113	415	112	21	0	33	(14	19)	232	65	78	98	76	1	111	3	0	2	2	2	5	.270	.385	.559	.944
2018 2 Tms	AL	52	187	46	14	0	8	(4	4)	84	30	23	32	31	2	54	0	0	1	2	0	3	.246	.352	.449	.801
2019 Atl	NL	155	549	142	33	0	37	(22	15)	286	96	94	103	100	2	155	8	0	2	4	2	13	.259	.379	.521	.900
18 Tor	AL	36	137	32	11	0	5	(2	3)	58	22	16	24	21	2	44	0	0	1	2	0	1	.234	.333	.423	.757
18 Cle	AL	16	50	14	3	0	3	(2	1)	26	8	7	8	10	0	10	0	0	0	0	0	2	.280	.400	.520	.920
Postseason		34	131	36	10	0	4	(3	1)	58	17	13	21	13	1	35	1	0	0	1	0	2	.275	.345	.443	.788
9 ML YEARS		1038	3841	1048	226	12	219	(112	107)	1955	652	645	738	557	18	885	44	5	29	38	8	90	.273	.369	.509	.878

Sean Doolittle

Pitches: L Bats: L Pos: RP-63   Ht: 6'2" Wt: 204 Born: 9/26/1986 Age: 33

Year Team	Lg	G	GS	GF	IP	BFP	H	R	ER	HR	SH	SF	HB	TBB	IBB	SO	WP	W	L	Pct	Sv-Op	Hld	Vel	OPS	ERC	ERA
2012 Oak	AL	44	0	7	47.1	191	40	18	16	3	2	2	0	11	1	60	0	2	1	.667	1-2	18	94	.611	2.36	3.04
2013 Oak	AL	70	0	11	69.0	266	53	24	24	4	3	2	0	13	1	60	2	5	5	.500	2-7	26	94	.573	2.00	3.13
2014 Oak	AL	61	0	40	62.2	236	38	19	19	5	2	1	0	8	1	89	0	2	4	.333	22-26	5	94	.459	1.23	2.73
2015 Oak	AL	12	0	7	13.2	57	12	6	6	1	0	1	0	5	0	15	0	1	0	1.000	4-5	1	92	.651	3.10	3.95
2016 Oak	AL	44	0	13	39.0	155	33	14	14	6	4	0	0	8	2	45	1	2	3	.400	4-6	10	95	.705	2.79	3.23
2017 2 Tms		53	0	34	51.1	197	34	18	16	5	0	3	0	10	1	62	3	2	0	1.000	24-26	9	95	.517	1.62	2.81
2018 Was	NL	43	0	35	45.0	163	21	8	8	3	0	0	2	6	1	60	1	3	3	.500	25-26	1	94	.391	0.93	1.60
2019 Was	NL	63	0	55	60.0	260	63	27	27	11	1	0	2	15	2	66	0	6	5	.545	29-35	2	93	.772	4.32	4.05
17 Oak	AL	23	0	6	21.1	79	12	8	8	3	0	1	0	2	0	31	1	1	0	1.000	3-4	8	94	.467	1.23	3.38
17 Was	AL	30	0	28	30.0	118	22	10	8	2	0	2	0	8	1	31	2	1	0	1.000	21-22	1	95	.551	1.99	2.40
Postseason		11	0	4	12.0	50	11	6	4	1	3	1	0	2	0	15	0	0	1	.000	1-4	5	95	.618	2.53	3.00
8 ML YEARS		390	0	202	388.0	1525	294	134	130	38	12	7	6	76	9	457	7	23	21	.523	111-133	72	94	.583	2.08	3.02

Kyle Dowdy

Pitches: R Bats: R Pos: RP-12; SP-1   Ht: 6'1" Wt: 195 Born: 2/3/1993 Age: 27

Year Team	Lg	G	GS	GF	IP	BFP	H	R	ER	HR	SH	SF	HB	TBB	IBB	SO	WP	W	L	Pct	Sv-Op	Hld	Vel	OPS	ERC	ERA
2019 Nashv	AAA	8	1	0	12.1	60	13	12	9	0	0	0	3	10	0	11	5	1	1	.500	0- -	-	-	.816	6.33	6.57
2019 Akron	AA	7	3	0	29.0	120	25	10	8	2	0	1	1	11	0	27	4	1	1	.500	0- -	-	-	.663	3.22	2.48
2019 Tex	AL	13	1	2	22.1	110	26	20	18	4	1	2	1	18	1	17	3	2	1	.667	0-1	0	95	.890	7.50	7.25

Brian Dozier

Bats: R Throws: R Pos: 2B-123;PH-14   DOE-zhur   Ht: 5'11" Wt: 200 Born: 5/15/1987 Age: 33

Year Team	Lg	G	AB	H	2B	3B	HR	(Hm	Rd)	TB	R	RBI	RC	TBB	IBB	SO	HBP	SH	SF	SB	CS	GDP	Avg	OBP	Slg	OPS
2012 Min	AL	84	316	74	11	1	6	(4	2)	105	33	33	24	16	0	58	1	4	3	9	2	10	.234	.271	.332	.603
2013 Min	AL	147	558	136	33	4	18	(8	10)	231	72	66	74	51	0	120	6	3	4	14	7	14	.244	.312	.414	.726
2014 Min	AL	156	598	145	33	1	23	(11	12)	249	112	71	87	89	1	129	9	3	8	21	7	8	.242	.345	.416	.762
2015 Min	AL	157	628	148	39	4	28	(13	15)	279	101	77	87	61	2	148	7	0	8	12	4	10	.236	.307	.444	.751
2016 Min	AL	155	615	165	35	5	42	(21	21)	336	104	99	102	61	6	138	8	2	5	18	2	12	.268	.340	.546	.886
2017 Min	AL	152	617	167	30	4	34	(18	16)	307	106	93	106	78	6	141	8	0	2	16	7	11	.271	.359	.498	.856
2018 2 Tms		151	553	119	30	3	21	(14	7)	216	81	72	69	70	1	129	4	0	5	12	3	12	.215	.305	.391	.696
2019 Was	NL	135	416	99	20	0	20	(10	10)	179	54	50	58	61	2	105	4	0	1	3	4	11	.238	.340	.430	.771
18 Min	AL	104	410	93	21	2	16	(5	11)	166	65	52	47	46	1	96	3	0	3	8	3	7	.227	.307	.405	.712
18 LAD		47	143	26	9	0	5	(2	3)	50	16	20	22	24	0	33	1	0	2	4	0	5	.182	.300	.350	.650
Postseason		12	20	4	0	0	1	(0	1)	7	4	3	2	6	0	6	1	0	0	1	1	0	.200	.407	.350	.757
8 ML YEARS		1137	4301	1053	231	21	192	(92	100)	1902	663	561	607	487	18	968	47	12	36	105	36	88	.245	.326	.442	.768

Hunter Dozier

Bats: R Throws: R Pos: 3B-100;RF-20;DH-15;1B-7;PH-1   DOE-zhur   Ht: 6'4" Wt: 220 Born: 8/22/1991 Age: 28

Year Team	Lg	G	AB	H	2B	3B	HR	(Hm	Rd)	TB	R	RBI	RC	TBB	IBB	SO	HBP	SH	SF	SB	CS	GDP	Avg	OBP	Slg	OPS
2016 KC	AL	8	19	4	1	0	0	(0	0)	5	4	1	1	2	0	8	0	0	0	0	0	0	.211	.286	.263	.549
2018 KC	AL	102	362	83	19	4	11	(5	6)	143	36	34	26	24	0	109	1	0	1	2	3	12	.229	.278	.395	.673
2019 KC	AL	139	523	146	29	10	26	(8	18)	273	75	84	91	55	2	148	3	0	5	2	2	9	.279	.348	.522	.870
3 ML YEARS		249	904	233	49	14	37	(13	24)	421	115	119	118	81	2	265	4	0	6	4	5	21	.258	.320	.466	.785

Oliver Drake

Pitches: R **Bats:** R **Pos:** RP-50   Ht: 6'4" Wt: 215 Born: 1/13/1987 Age: 33

			HOW MUCH PITCHED					WHAT HE GAVE UP										THE RESULTS							
Year	Team	Lg	G	GS	GF	IP	BFP	H	R	ER	HR	SH	SF	HB	TBB	IBB	SO	WP	W	L	Pct	Sv-Op Hld	Vel	OPS	ERC	ERA
2019	Drhm	AAA	19	2	14	23.2	95	20	13	13	2	0	1	1	7	0	40	0	1	2	.333	6-- -	-	.644	2.99	4.94
2015	Bal	AL	13	0	5	15.2	72	16	7	5	1	0	2	0	9	0	17	3	0	0	-	0-0 2	91	.708	4.50	2.87
2016	Bal	AL	14	0	5	18.0	74	11	11	8	2	1	0	0	7	0	21	1	1	0	1.000	0-1 0	90	.595	2.01	4.00
2017	2 Tms		64	0	15	56.0	251	63	31	29	6	3	0	0	25	2	62	3	3	5	.375	1-4 5	92	.808	4.96	4.66
2018	5 Tms		44	0	19	47.2	209	52	29	28	4	1	0	1	17	1	51	5	1	1	.500	0-1 1	92	.758	4.33	5.29
2019	TB	AL	50	0	9	56.0	219	36	20	20	9	0	0	1	19	1	70	1	5	2	.714	2-3 10	94	.612	2.43	3.21
17	Bal	AL	3	0	1	3.1	18	6	3	3	0	0	0	0	3	0	3	1	0	0	-	0-0 0	92	1.033	10.76	8.10
17	Mil	NL	61	0	14	52.2	233	57	28	26	6	3	0	0	22	2	59	2	3	5	.375	1-4 5	92	.791	4.63	4.44
18	Mil	NL	11	0	3	12.2	58	14	9	9	0	1	0	0	8	1	15	2	1	0	1.000	0-1 0	92	.794	4.71	6.39
18	Cle	AL	4	0	0	4.1	22	7	6	6	0	0	0	1	1	0	4	0	0	0	-	0-0 0	93	.859	7.03	12.46
18	LAA	AL	8	0	6	8.2	40	15	5	5	2	0	0	0	1	0	8	0	0	1	.000	0-0 0	93	.990	8.66	5.19
18	Tor	AL	2	0	2	1.2	9	4	3	3	0	0	0	0	0	0	2	1	0	0	-	0-0 0	92	1.333	10.16	16.20
18	Min	AL	19	0	8	20.1	80	12	6	5	2	0	0	0	7	0	22	2	0	0	-	0-0 1	92	.511	1.77	2.21
5 ML YEARS			185	0	53	193.1	825	178	98	90	22	5	2	2	77	4	221	13	10	8	.556	3-9 18	92	.715	3.71	4.19

Brandon Drury

Bats: R **Throws:** R **Pos:** 3B-65;RF-18;2B-16;1B-12;LF-8;SS-5;PH-4;DH-2;PR-1 DROO-ree   Ht: 6'2" Wt: 215 Born: 8/21/1992 Age: 27

					BATTING															RUNNING			AVERAGES			
Year	Team	Lg	G	AB	H	2B	3B	HR	(Hm	Rd)	TB	R	RBI	RC	TBB	IBB	SO	HBP	SH	SF	SB	CS	GDP	Avg	OBP	Slg	OPS
2015	Ari	NL	20	56	12	3	0	2	(0	2)	21	3	8	4	2	0	8	1	0	0	0	0	5	.214	.254	.375	.629
2016	Ari	NL	134	461	130	31	1	16	(12	4)	211	59	53	59	31	2	100	3	0	4	1	1	14	.282	.329	.458	.786
2017	Ari	NL	135	445	119	37	2	13	(7	6)	199	41	63	62	28	1	103	5	0	2	1	1	9	.267	.317	.447	.764
2018	2 Tms	AL	26	77	13	4	0	1	(0	1)	20	5	10	7	7	0	20	2	0	0	0	0	5	.169	.256	.260	.516
2019	Tor	AL	120	418	91	21	1	15	(9	6)	159	43	41	37	25	0	113	1	0	3	0	1	6	.218	.262	.380	.642
18	NYY	AL	18	51	9	2	0	1	(0	1)	14	2	7	5	5	0	12	1	0	0	0	0	4	.176	.263	.275	.538
18	Tor	AL	8	26	4	2	0	0	(0	0)	6	3	3	2	2	0	8	1	0	0	0	0	1	.154	.241	.231	.472
Postseason			3	6	1	0	0	1	(0	1)	4	1	3	1	0	0	2	0	0	0	0	0	2	.167	.167	.667	.833
5 ML YEARS			435	1457	365	96	4	47	(28	19)	610	151	175	169	93	3	344	12	0	9	2	3	39	.251	.299	.419	.718

Mauricio Dubon

Bats: R **Throws:** R **Pos:** 2B-22;SS-10;PH-2   Ht: 6'0" Wt: 160 Born: 7/19/1994 Age: 25

					BATTING															RUNNING			AVERAGES			
Year	Team	Lg	G	AB	H	2B	3B	HR	(Hm	Rd)	TB	R	RBI	RC	TBB	IBB	SO	HBP	SH	SF	SB	CS	GDP	Avg	OBP	Slg	OPS
2019	SnAnt	AAA	98	404	120	22	1	16	(-	-)	192	59	47	63	18	2	59	4	1	0	9	6	6	.297	.333	.475	.809
2019	Scrmto	AAA	25	99	32	4	0	4	(-	-)	48	23	9	18	10	0	9	1	0	0	1	2	0	.323	.391	.485	.876
2019	2 Tms	NL	30	106	29	5	0	4	(2	2)	46	12	9	11	5	0	20	0	0	0	3	1	3	.274	.306	.434	.740
19	Mil	NL	2	2	0	0	0	0	(0	0)	0	0	0	0	0	0	1	0	0	0	0	0	0	.000	.000	.000	.000
19	SF	NL	28	104	29	5	0	4	(2	2)	46	12	9	11	5	0	19	0	0	0	3	1	3	.279	.312	.442	.754

Lucas Duda

Bats: L **Throws:** R **Pos:** 1B-19;DH-14;PH-7   DOO-duh   Ht: 6'4" Wt: 255 Born: 2/3/1986 Age: 34

					BATTING															RUNNING			AVERAGES			
Year	Team	Lg	G	AB	H	2B	3B	HR	(Hm	Rd)	TB	R	RBI	RC	TBB	IBB	SO	HBP	SH	SF	SB	CS	GDP	Avg	OBP	Slg	OPS
2019	Omha	AAA	12	42	12	3	0	1	(-	-)	18	6	4	6	4	1	13	0	0	0	0	0	2	.286	.348	.429	.776
2019	Gwnntt	AAA	16	57	8	1	0	1	(-	-)	12	3	5	2	6	0	21	2	0	3	0	0	1	.140	.235	.211	.446
2010	NYM	NL	29	84	17	6	0	4	(3	1)	35	11	13	5	6	0	22	1	0	1	0	0	2	.202	.261	.417	.678
2011	NYM	NL	100	301	88	21	3	10	(2	8)	145	38	50	44	33	3	57	7	1	5	1	0	5	.292	.370	.482	.852
2012	NYM	NL	121	401	96	15	0	15	(9	6)	156	43	57	58	51	0	120	4	0	3	1	0	5	.239	.329	.389	.718
2013	NYM	NL	100	318	71	16	0	15	(9	6)	132	42	33	38	55	4	102	9	0	2	0	3	1	.223	.352	.415	.767
2014	NYM	NL	153	514	130	27	0	30	(14	16)	247	74	92	91	69	8	135	9	0	4	3	2	9	.253	.349	.481	.830
2015	NYM	NL	135	471	115	33	0	27	(19	8)	229	67	73	69	66	7	138	14	0	3	0	2	12	.244	.352	.486	.838
2016	NYM	NL	47	153	35	7	0	7	(4	3)	63	20	23	18	15	2	36	2	0	0	0	0	1	.229	.302	.412	.714
2017	2 Tms		127	423	92	28	0	30	(15	15)	210	50	64	57	60	6	135	6	0	2	0	0	9	.217	.322	.496	.818
2018	2 Tms		107	328	79	14	1	14	(7	7)	137	35	50	44	28	2	102	8	0	3	1	0	5	.241	.313	.418	.731
2019	KC	AL	39	105	18	4	0	4	(1	3)	34	7	15	8	11	1	32	1	0	2	0	0	3	.171	.252	.324	.576
17	NYM	NL	75	252	62	21	0	17	(11	6)	134	30	37	37	37	4	73	2	0	0	0	0	6	.246	.347	.532	.879
17	TB	AL	52	171	30	7	0	13	(4	9)	76	20	27	20	23	2	62	4	0	2	0	0	3	.175	.285	.444	.729
18	KC	AL	87	310	75	12	1	13	(7	6)	128	34	48	42	24	2	95	8	0	3	1	0	4	.242	.310	.413	.723
18	Atl	NL	20	18	4	2	0	1	(0	1)	9	1	2	2	4	0	7	0	0	0	0	0	1	.222	.364	.500	.864
Postseason			17	50	11	2	0	1	(0	1)	16	3	8	7	5	0	21	0	1	1	0	0	0	.220	.286	.320	.606
10 ML YEARS			958	3098	741	171	4	156	(83	73)	1388	387	470	432	394	33	879	61	1	27	6	7	52	.239	.334	.448	.782

Tyler Duffey

Pitches: R **Bats:** R **Pos:** RP-58   Ht: 6'3" Wt: 220 Born: 12/27/1990 Age: 29

					HOW MUCH PITCHED					WHAT HE GAVE UP										THE RESULTS					
Year	Team	Lg	G	GS	GF	IP	BFP	H	R	ER	HR	SH	SF	HB	TBB	IBB	SO	WP	W	L	Pct	Sv-Op Hld	Vel	OPS	ERC	ERA
2019	Roch	AAA	7	0	2	13.2	53	8	2	2	0	1	0	1	5	0	22	1	0	0	-	1-- -	-	.487	1.60	1.32
2015	Min	AL	10	10	0	58.0	242	56	20	20	4	3	0	1	20	0	53	1	5	1	.833	0-0 0	90	.702	3.51	3.10
2016	Min	AL	26	26	0	133.0	596	167	103	95	25	2	2	6	32	3	114	9	9	12	.429	0-0 0	90	.876	5.66	6.43
2017	Min	AL	56	0	7	71.0	310	79	41	39	9	1	3	1	18	5	67	4	2	3	.400	1-3 12	92	.721	4.17	4.94
2018	Min	AL	19	1	4	25.0	107	26	22	20	6	0	2	1	4	0	19	2	2	2	.500	0-0 2	93	.830	4.29	7.20
2019	Min	AL	58	0	12	57.2	238	44	23	16	8	1	1	3	14	1	82	3	5	1	.833	0-2 15	94	.595	2.55	2.50
5 ML YEARS			169	37	23	344.2	1493	372	209	190	52	7	8	11	88	9	335	19	23	19	.548	1-5 29	92	.768	4.32	4.96

Danny Duffy

Pitches: L Bats: L Pos: SP-23   Ht: 6'3" Wt: 205 Born: 12/21/1988 Age: 31

Year	Team	Lg	G	GS	GF	IP	BFP	H	R	ER	HR	SH	SF	HB	TBB	IBB	SO	WP	W	L	Pct	Sv-Op	Hld	Vel	OPS	ERC	ERA
2011	KC	AL	20	20	0	105.1	474	119	66	66	15	2	2	5	51	1	87	4	4	8	.333	0-0	0	93	.864	5.76	5.64
2012	KC	AL	6	6	0	27.2	121	26	13	12	2	0	0	0	18	1	28	0	2	2	.500	0-0	0	95	.771	4.58	3.90
2013	KC	AL	5	5	0	24.1	104	19	5	5	0	0	0	1	14	0	22	2	2	0	1.000	0-0	0	94	.608	3.02	1.85
2014	KC	AL	31	25	1	149.1	606	113	52	42	12	3	4	5	53	2	113	5	9	12	.429	0-0	1	93	.605	2.62	2.53
2015	KC	AL	30	24	1	136.2	588	137	64	62	15	3	5	9	53	0	102	11	7	8	.467	1-1	2	94	.746	4.44	4.08
2016	KC	AL	42	26	5	179.2	731	163	71	70	27	4	2	7	42	0	188	0	12	3	.800	0-0	1	95	.710	3.44	3.51
2017	KC	AL	24	24	0	146.1	609	143	67	62	13	6	2	4	41	0	130	2	9	10	.474	0-0	0	93	.709	3.55	3.81
2018	KC	AL	28	28	0	155.0	692	161	86	84	23	2	6	4	70	1	141	14	8	12	.400	0-0	0	93	.767	4.90	4.88
2019	KC	AL	23	23	0	130.2	555	125	69	63	21	0	3	8	46	0	115	4	7	6	.538	0-0	0	92	.760	4.35	4.34
	Postseason		9	0	1	10.2	44	10	6	6	2	1	1	0	4	0	14	0	2	0	1.000	0-0	0	95	.878	4.35	5.06
	9 ML YEARS		209	181	7	1055.0	4480	1006	493	466	128	20	24	43	388	5	926	46	60	61	.496	1-1	4	93	.731	4.02	3.98

Matt Duffy

Bats: R Throws: R Pos: 3B-46;SS-1   Ht: 6'2" Wt: 190 Born: 1/15/1991 Age: 29

Year	Team	Lg	G	AB	H	2B	3B	HR	(Hm	Rd)	TB	R	RBI	RC	TBB	IBB	SO	HBP	SH	SF	SB	CS	GDP	Avg	OBP	Slg	OPS
2019	2 Tms	Low	10	24	6	1	1	1	(-	-)	12	5	2	4	5	0	2	2	0	0	0	0	1	.250	.419	.500	.919
2014	SF	NL	34	60	16	2	0	0	(0	0)	18	5	8	8	1	0	14	2	1	1	0	1	1	.267	.302	.300	.602
2015	SF	NL	149	573	169	28	6	12	(7	5)	245	77	77	84	30	0	96	5	2	2	12	0	22	.295	.334	.428	.762
2016	2 Tms		91	333	86	14	2	5	(1	4)	119	41	28	30	23	0	53	4	2	4	8	5	13	.258	.310	.357	.668
2018	TB	AL	132	503	148	22	1	4	(0	4)	184	59	44	72	47	1	93	7	1	2	12	6	12	.294	.361	.366	.727
2019	TB	AL	46	147	37	8	0	1	(0	1)	48	12	12	19	19	0	29	2	0	1	0	1	4	.252	.343	.327	.670
16	SF	NL	70	257	65	11	2	4	(1	3)	92	32	21	23	20	0	40	4	2	3	8	4	9	.253	.313	.358	.671
16	TB	AL	21	76	21	3	0	1	(0	1)	27	9	7	7	3	0	13	0	0	1	0	1	4	.276	.300	.355	.655
	Postseason		8	6	1	0	0	0	(0	0)	1	2	0	0	0	0	2	0	1	0	0	0	0	.167	.167	.167	.333
	5 ML YEARS		452	1616	456	74	9	22	(8	14)	614	194	169	213	120	1	285	20	6	9	32	13	52	.282	.338	.380	.718

Steven Duggar

Bats: L Throws: R Pos: CF-39;RF-34;PH-3   Ht: 6'2" Wt: 189 Born: 11/4/1993 Age: 26

Year	Team	Lg	G	AB	H	2B	3B	HR	(Hm	Rd)	TB	R	RBI	RC	TBB	IBB	SO	HBP	SH	SF	SB	CS	GDP	Avg	OBP	Slg	OPS
2019	Scrmto	AAA	23	83	28	6	1	3	(-	-)	45	24	13	20	18	0	21	1	0	0	2	3	1	.337	.461	.542	1.003
2018	SF	NL	41	141	36	11	1	2	(1	1)	55	20	17	19	10	1	44	0	0	1	5	1	0	.255	.303	.390	.693
2019	SF	NL	73	261	61	12	2	4	(1	3)	89	26	28	29	16	0	78	1	0	3	1	4	1	.234	.278	.341	.619
	2 ML YEARS		114	402	97	23	3	6	(2	4)	144	46	45	48	26	1	122	1	0	4	6	5	1	.241	.286	.358	.645

Robert Dugger

Pitches: R Bats: R Pos: SP-7   Ht: 6'2" Wt: 180 Born: 7/3/1995 Age: 24

Year	Team	Lg	G	GS	GF	IP	BFP	H	R	ER	HR	SH	SF	HB	TBB	IBB	SO	WP	W	L	Pct	Sv-Op	Hld	Vel	OPS	ERC	ERA
2019	Jaxnvl	AA	13	13	0	70.2	292	57	31	26	6	4	0	7	21	0	73	1	6	6	.500	0--	-	-	.634	2.93	3.31
2019	NewOr	AAA	10	10	0	53.1	246	74	49	45	12	0	3	3	17	0	49	2	2	4	.333	0--	-	-	.983	7.38	7.59
2019	Mia	NL	7	7	0	34.1	156	33	26	22	6	1	3	5	17	1	25	2	0	4	.000	0-0	0	90	.824	5.29	5.77

Zach Duke

Pitches: L Bats: L Pos: RP-30   Ht: 6'2" Wt: 210 Born: 4/19/1983 Age: 37

Year	Team	Lg	G	GS	GF	IP	BFP	H	R	ER	HR	SH	SF	HB	TBB	IBB	SO	WP	W	L	Pct	Sv-Op	Hld	Vel	OPS	ERC	ERA
2005	Pit	NL	14	14	0	84.2	341	79	20	17	3	2	3	1	23	2	58	1	8	2	.800	0-0	0	89	.651	2.96	1.81
2006	Pit	NL	34	34	0	215.1	935	255	116	107	17	13	4	7	68	6	117	8	10	15	.400	0-0	0	87	.799	4.82	4.47
2007	Pit	NL	20	19	0	107.1	482	161	74	66	14	2	4	3	25	2	41	0	3	8	.273	0-0	0	88	.941	6.96	5.53
2008	Pit	NL	31	31	0	185.0	829	230	111	99	19	14	4	7	47	1	87	2	5	14	.263	0-0	0	89	.812	4.99	4.82
2009	Pit	NL	32	32	0	213.0	891	231	101	96	23	18	10	3	49	0	106	2	11	16	.407	0-0	0	89	.764	4.05	4.06
2010	Pit	NL	29	29	0	159.0	730	231	115	101	25	9	6	4	51	2	96	4	8	15	.348	0-0	0	87	.881	6.22	5.72
2011	Ari	NL	21	9	5	76.2	338	101	42	42	6	3	3	1	19	0	32	1	3	4	.429	1-1	0	87	.820	5.27	4.93
2012	Was	NL	8	0	3	13.2	56	11	2	2	0	0	0	0	4	0	10	0	1	0	1.000	0-0	0	89	.556	2.00	1.32
2013	2 Tms	NL	26	1	3	31.1	142	39	23	21	3	2	2	1	10	3	18	2	1	2	.333	0-0	1	89	.806	5.04	6.03
2014	Mil	NL	74	0	13	58.2	238	49	19	16	3	0	4	0	17	1	74	3	5	1	.833	0-4	12	90	.578	2.46	2.45
2015	CWS	AL	71	0	14	60.2	255	47	26	23	9	2	1	3	32	4	66	0	3	6	.333	1-3	26	89	.724	3.82	3.41
2016	2 Tms		81	0	13	61.0	258	48	16	16	2	3	1	4	29	3	68	4	2	1	.667	2-5	26	90	.612	2.93	2.36
2017	StL	NL	27	0	1	18.1	74	13	8	8	3	0	0	2	6	2	12	2	1	1	.500	0-0	6	89	.647	2.95	3.93
2018	2 Tms	AL	72	0	11	52.0	240	57	28	24	1	2	1	6	21	4	51	3	5	5	.500	0-3	17	88	.701	4.22	4.15
2019	Cin	NL	30	0	4	23.1	106	21	13	13	4	1	1	2	18	1	18	0	3	1	.750	0-0	4	89	.843	5.98	5.01
13	Was	NL	12	1	1	20.2	101	31	22	20	2	2	1	1	8	3	11	1	1	1	.500	0-0	0	88	.915	6.83	8.71
13	Cin	NL	14	0	2	10.2	41	8	1	1	1	0	0	0	2	0	7	1	0	1	.000	0-0	1	90	.552	2.01	0.84
16	CWS	AL	53	0	9	37.2	159	31	11	11	2	2	1	2	16	3	42	2	0	1	1.000	1-4	20	90	.653	2.97	2.63
16	StL	NL	28	0	4	23.1	99	17	5	5	0	1	0	2	13	0	26	2	0	1	.000	1-1	6	90	.543	2.85	1.93
18	Min	AL	45	0	8	37.1	178	44	19	15	0	1	1	5	15	4	39	3	3	4	.429	0-3	12	88	.689	4.48	3.62
18	Sea	AL	27	0	3	14.2	62	13	9	9	1	1	0	1	6	0	12	0	2	1	.667	0-0	5	89	.735	3.57	5.52
	15 ML YEARS		570	169	67	1360.0	5915	1554	714	651	132	72	38	45	419	31	854	32	69	91	.431	4-16	92	88	.783	4.63	4.31

Ryan Dull

Pitches: R Bats: R Pos: RP-11 Ht: 5'9" Wt: 185 Born: 10/2/1989 Age: 30

Year	Team	Lg	G	GS	GF	IP	BFP	H	R	ER	HR	SH	SF	HB	TBB	IBB	SO	WP	W	L	Pct	Sv-Op	Hld	Vel	OPS	ERC	ERA
2019	LsVgs	AAA	30	0	13	39.2	174	43	28	24	6	0	2	1	13	1	50	1	1	4	.200	4- -	-	-	.815	4.64	5.45
2015	Oak	AL	13	0	3	17.0	66	12	8	8	4	0	1	0	6	1	16	0	1	2	.333	1-2	2	91	.713	3.19	4.24
2016	Oak	AL	70	0	9	74.1	290	50	23	20	10	0	5	1	15	4	73	6	5	5	.500	3-6	15	91	.577	1.84	2.42
2017	Oak	AL	49	0	4	42.0	177	37	30	24	7	0	1	3	16	1	45	6	2	2	.500	0-2	20	91	.724	4.08	5.14
2018	Oak	AL	28	0	3	25.1	100	22	12	12	3	1	1	0	7	0	21	3	0	0	-	0-0	4	91	.713	3.13	4.26
2019	3 Tms	AL	11	0	6	12.2	71	25	19	18	5	1	1	1	7	0	15	1	0	0	-	0-0	1	91	1.291	14.18	12.79
19	Oak	AL	7	0	4	9.0	51	19	13	12	4	1	1	1	4	0	8	1	0	0	-	0-0	1	91	1.321	15.34	12.00
19	NYY	AL	3	0	1	2.1	15	5	5	5	0	0	0	0	3	0	4	0	0	0	-	0-0	0	91	1.283	14.38	19.29
19	Tor	AL	1	0	1	1.1	5	1	1	1	1	0	0	0	0	0	3	0	0	0	-	0-0	0	91	1.000	4.25	6.75
5 ML YEARS			171	0	25	171.1	704	146	92	82	29	2	9	5	51	6	170	16	8	9	.471	4-10	42	91	.708	3.39	4.31

Justin Dunn

Pitches: R Bats: R Pos: SP-4 Ht: 6'2" Wt: 185 Born: 9/22/1995 Age: 24

Year	Team	Lg	G	GS	GF	IP	BFP	H	R	ER	HR	SH	SF	HB	TBB	IBB	SO	WP	W	L	Pct	Sv-Op	Hld	Vel	OPS	ERC	ERA
2016	Bklyn	A-	11	8	2	30.0	126	25	11	5	1	0	1	5	10	0	35	2	1	1	.500	0- -	-	-	.608	3.13	1.50
2017	Stluci	A+	20	16	2	95.1	433	101	66	53	5	3	5	7	48	2	75	13	5	6	.455	0- -	-	-	.752	4.70	5.00
2018	Stluci	A+	9	9	0	45.2	197	43	17	12	2	2	0	3	15	0	51	2	2	3	.400	0- -	-	-	.624	3.28	2.36
2018	Bnghtn	AA	15	15	0	89.2	379	85	49	42	7	5	4	4	37	1	105	6	6	5	.545	0- -	-	-	.696	3.93	4.22
2019	Ark	AA	25	25	0	131.2	553	118	62	52	13	0	4	9	39	0	158	9	9	5	.643	0- -	-	-	.663	3.35	3.55
2019	Sea	AL	4	4	0	6.2	30	2	2	2	0	0	2	0	9	0	5	0	0	0	-	0-0	0	92	.472	3.04	2.70

Mike Dunn

Pitches: L Bats: L Pos: RP-28 Ht: 6'0" Wt: 212 Born: 5/23/1985 Age: 35

Year	Team	Lg	G	GS	GF	IP	BFP	H	R	ER	HR	SH	SF	HB	TBB	IBB	SO	WP	W	L	Pct	Sv-Op	Hld	Vel	OPS	ERC	ERA
2009	NYY	AL	4	0	3	4.0	20	3	3	3	1	0	0	0	5	0	5	1	0	0	-	0-0	0	93	.800	7.17	6.75
2010	Atl	NL	25	0	5	19.0	88	15	4	4	1	0	0	0	17	2	27	2	2	0	1.000	0-0	1	95	.659	4.19	1.89
2011	Fla	NL	72	0	11	63.0	267	51	28	24	9	4	2	2	31	2	68	3	5	6	.455	0-4	15	94	.723	3.77	3.43
2012	Mia	NL	60	0	8	44.0	208	49	31	24	3	2	4	0	29	8	47	2	0	3	.000	1-6	18	94	.806	5.10	4.91
2013	Mia	NL	75	0	15	67.2	282	53	21	20	5	1	3	0	28	4	72	2	3	4	.429	2-5	18	94	.604	2.68	2.66
2014	Mia	NL	75	0	15	57.0	245	47	25	20	4	4	1	4	22	1	67	2	10	6	.625	1-4	22	95	.635	3.03	3.16
2015	Mia	NL	72	0	9	54.0	235	46	27	27	6	0	1	2	29	1	65	2	2	5	.286	0-3	23	95	.712	3.96	4.50
2016	Mia	NL	51	0	5	42.1	176	43	16	16	5	1	2	3	11	0	38	2	6	1	.857	0-4	8	94	.735	4.13	3.40
2017	Col	NL	68	0	10	50.1	220	43	25	25	8	0	3	0	28	0	57	4	5	1	.833	0-1	19	92	.730	4.24	4.47
2018	Col	NL	25	0	6	17.0	83	22	17	17	1	0	1	0	18	0	12	1	0	0	-	0-0	5	92	.966	8.90	9.00
2019	Col	NL	28	0	2	17.2	75	17	14	14	4	0	4	0	6	0	15	2	1	0	1.000	0-1	2	91	.830	4.46	7.13
Postseason			3	0	0	1.1	6	2	0	0	0	0	0	0	0	0	2	0	0	0	-	0-1	0	94	.667	4.47	0.00
11 ML YEARS			555	0	89	436.0	1899	389	211	194	47	12	21	11	224	18	473	23	34	26	.567	4-28	131	94	.716	3.99	4.00

Jon Duplantier

Pitches: R Bats: L Pos: RP-12; SP-3 Ht: 6'4" Wt: 225 Born: 7/11/1994 Age: 25

Year	Team	Lg	G	GS	GF	IP	BFP	H	R	ER	HR	SH	SF	HB	TBB	IBB	SO	WP	W	L	Pct	Sv-Op	Hld	Vel	OPS	ERC	ERA
2019	Reno	AAA	13	11	0	38.0	168	31	25	22	1	2	3	2	28	0	44	3	1	2	.333	0- -	-	-	.698	4.07	5.21
2019	Ari	NL	15	3	5	36.2	163	39	18	18	2	1	1	5	18	1	34	2	1	1	.500	1-1	0	92	.774	5.11	4.42

Montana DuRapau

Pitches: R Bats: R Pos: RP-12; SP-2 Ht: 5'11" Wt: 175 Born: 3/27/1992 Age: 28

Year	Team	Lg	G	GS	GF	IP	BFP	H	R	ER	HR	SH	SF	HB	TBB	IBB	SO	WP	W	L	Pct	Sv-Op	Hld	Vel	OPS	ERC	ERA
2019	Indy	AAA	37	0	20	46.1	175	21	13	11	3	1	2	2	14	1	57	1	2	1	.667	10- -	-	-	.463	1.21	2.14
2019	Pit	NL	14	2	6	17.1	90	27	24	18	4	0	0	2	9	0	22	0	0	1	.000	0-0	0	92	1.017	9.54	9.35

Adam Duvall

Bats: R Throws: R Pos: LF-31;PH-10;RF-2 Ht: 6'1" Wt: 215 Born: 9/4/1988 Age: 31

Year	Team	Lg	G	AB	H	2B	3B	HR	(Hm	Rd)	TB	R	RBI	RC	TBB	IBB	SO	HBP	SH	SF	SB	CS	GDP	Avg	OBP	Slg	OPS
2019	Gwnntt	AAA	101	369	98	20	4	32	(-	-)	222	74	93	81	48	4	86	10	0	2	1	0	9	.266	.364	.602	.965
2014	SF	NL	28	73	14	2	0	3	(2	1)	25	8	5	4	3	0	20	1	0	0	0	0	0	.192	.234	.342	.576
2015	Cin	NL	27	64	14	2	0	5	(3	2)	31	6	9	9	6	1	26	2	0	0	0	0	0	.219	.306	.484	.790
2016	Cin	NL	150	552	133	31	6	33	(16	17)	275	85	103	80	41	1	164	6	0	8	6	5	7	.241	.297	.498	.795
2017	Cin	NL	157	587	146	37	3	31	(12	19)	282	78	99	75	39	1	170	10	0	11	5	3	11	.249	.301	.480	.782
2018	2 Tms	NL	138	384	75	20	0	15	(8	7)	140	48	61	37	37	3	117	5	0	1	2	2	9	.195	.274	.365	.639
2019	Atl	NL	41	120	32	4	1	10	(4	6)	68	17	19	19	7	0	39	2	0	1	0	0	0	.267	.315	.567	.882
18	Cin	NL	105	331	68	19	0	15	(8	7)	132	40	61	37	34	3	100	4	0	1	2	2	8	.205	.286	.399	.685
18	Atl	NL	33	53	7	1	0	0	(0	0)	8	8	0	0	3	0	17	1	0	0	0	0	1	.132	.193	.151	.344
6 ML YEARS			541	1780	414	96	10	97	(45	52)	821	242	296	224	133	6	536	26	0	21	13	10	27	.233	.292	.461	.754

Jarrod Dyson

Bats: L **Throws:** R **Pos:** CF-103;RF-21;LF-16;PH-12;PR-7   juh-ROD   **Ht:** 5'10" **Wt:** 165 **Born:** 8/15/1984 **Age:** 35

Year Team	Lg	G	AB	H	2B	3B	HR	(Hm	Rd)	TB	R	RBI	RC	TBB	IBB	SO	HBP	SH	SF	SB	CS	GDP	Avg	OBP	Slg	OPS
2010 KC	AL	18	57	12	4	2	1	(1	0)	23	11	5	9	6	0	16	0	2	0	9	1	2	.211	.286	.404	.689
2011 KC	AL	26	44	9	1	0	0	(0	0)	10	8	3	7	7	0	14	0	1	1	11	1	0	.205	.308	.227	.535
2012 KC	AL	102	292	76	8	5	0	(0	0)	94	52	9	36	30	1	56	1	4	3	30	5	5	.260	.328	.322	.650
2013 KC	AL	87	213	55	9	4	2	(2	0)	78	30	17	28	21	1	45	1	3	1	34	6	4	.258	.326	.366	.692
2014 KC	AL	120	260	70	4	4	1	(1	0)	85	33	24	32	22	0	52	0	6	2	36	7	5	.269	.324	.327	.651
2015 KC	AL	90	200	50	8	6	2	(2	0)	76	31	18	25	14	0	37	4	6	1	26	3	3	.250	.311	.380	.691
2016 KC	AL	107	299	83	14	8	1	(1	0)	116	46	25	45	26	2	39	3	8	1	30	7	4	.278	.340	.388	.728
2017 Sea	AL	111	346	87	13	8	5	(2	3)	121	56	30	40	28	2	55	10	4	2	28	7	3	.251	.324	.350	.674
2018 Ari	NL	67	206	39	4	2	2	(0	2)	53	29	12	19	27	2	34	0	3	1	16	3	3	.189	.282	.257	.539
2019 Ari	NL	130	400	92	11	2	7	(1	6)	128	65	27	52	47	0	86	2	1	2	30	4	1	.230	.313	.320	.633
Postseason		19	20	2	0	0	0	(0	0)	2	3	0	0	2	0	6	0	1	0	4	2	1	.100	.182	.100	.282
10 ML YEARS		858	2317	573	76	36	21	(10	11)	784	361	170	293	228	8	434	21	38	14	250	44	30	.247	.319	.338	.657

Sam Dyson

Pitches: R **Bats:** R **Pos:** RP-61   **Ht:** 6'1" **Wt:** 212 **Born:** 5/7/1988 **Age:** 32

		HOW MUCH PITCHED						WHAT HE GAVE UP												THE RESULTS							
Year Team	Lg	G	GS	GF	IP	BFP	H	R	ER	HR	SH	SF	HB	TBB	IBB	SO	WP	W	L	Pct	Sv-Op	Hld	Vel	OPS	ERC	ERA
2012 Tor	AL	2	0	0	0.2	8	4	3	3	0	0	0	0	2	0	1	0	0	0		0-0	0	92	1.750	56.02	40.50
2013 Mia	NL	5	1	1	11.0	54	16	12	11	2	1	1	1	5	1	5	0	0	2	.000	0-0	1	92	.959	7.96	9.00
2014 Mia	NL	31	0	12	42.0	181	41	14	10	1	2	0	3	15	4	33	1	3	1	.750	0-1	0	96	.653	3.36	2.14
2015 2 Tms		75	0	16	75.1	309	65	26	22	4	4	1	4	21	1	71	8	5	4	.556	2-4	21	96	.603	2.77	2.63
2016 Tex	AL	73	0	53	70.1	285	63	19	19	5	1	0	3	23	0	55	3	3	2	.600	38-43	10	95	.658	3.32	2.43
2017 2 Tms		55	0	34	54.2	260	67	41	37	8	1	0	3	30	7	34	2	4	10	.286	14-21	4	95	.860	6.34	6.09
2018 SF	NL	74	0	16	70.1	273	56	23	21	5	1	3	3	20	1	56	2	4	3	.571	3-8	15	94	.652	2.66	2.69
2019 2 Tms		61	0	8	62.1	249	53	26	23	6	3	0	3	13	0	55	1	5	1	.833	2-4	23	94	.637	2.75	3.32
15 Mia	NL	44	0	10	44.0	190	41	21	18	3	3	1	3	17	1	41	6	3	3	.500	0-2	9	96	.658	3.63	3.68
15 Tex	AL	31	0	6	31.1	119	24	5	4	1	1	0	1	4	0	30	2	2	1	.667	2-2	12	96	.520	1.68	1.15
17 Tex	AL	17	0	8	16.2	91	31	23	20	6	0	0	0	12	3	7	1	1	6	.143	0-4	3	95	1.156	13.30	10.80
17 SF	NL	38	0	26	38.0	169	36	18	17	2	1	0	3	18	4	27	1	3	4	.429	14-17	1	95	.700	3.80	4.03
19 SF	NL	49	0	8	51.0	196	39	17	14	3	3	0	3	7	0	47	0	4	1	.800	2-3	17	94	.565	1.93	2.47
19 Min	AL	12	0	0	11.1	53	14	9	9	3	0	0	0	6	0	8	1	1	0	1.000	0-1	6	94	.909	7.33	7.15
Postseason		5	0	2	4.2	21	6	1	1	1	0	0	0	1	1	3	0	0	0	-	1-2	0	97	.783	5.32	1.93
8 ML YEARS		376	1	140	386.2	1619	365	164	146	31	13	5	20	129	14	310	17	24	23	.511	59-81	73	95	.689	3.57	3.40

Ryan Eades

Pitches: R **Bats:** R **Pos:** RP-8   **Ht:** 6'2" **Wt:** 210 **Born:** 12/15/1991 **Age:** 28

		HOW MUCH PITCHED						WHAT HE GAVE UP												THE RESULTS							
Year Team	Lg	G	GS	GF	IP	BFP	H	R	ER	HR	SH	SF	HB	TBB	IBB	SO	WP	W	L	Pct	Sv-Op	Hld	Vel	OPS	ERC	ERA
2019 Roch	AAA	29	2	8	50.2	221	59	32	31	7	0	1	0	16	0	63	3	4	3	.571	3--	-	-	.830	4.98	5.51
2019 2 Tms	AL	8	0	4	11.1	50	11	3	3	2	0	1	0	6	0	10	0	0	1	.000	0-1	1	92	.825	5.47	2.38
19 Min	AL	2	0	0	3.2	16	4	0	0	0	0	0	0	2	0	5	0	0	0	-	0-0	0	93	.732	4.58	0.00
19 Bal	AL	6	0	4	7.2	34	7	3	3	2	0	1	0	4	0	5	0	0	1	.000	0-1	1	91	.870	5.86	3.52

Adam Eaton

Bats: L **Throws:** L **Pos:** RF-139;LF-7;PH-7   **Ht:** 5'9" **Wt:** 176 **Born:** 12/6/1988 **Age:** 31

		BATTING																		RUNNING			AVERAGES			
Year Team	Lg	G	AB	H	2B	3B	HR	(Hm	Rd)	TB	R	RBI	RC	TBB	IBB	SO	HBP	SH	SF	SB	CS	GDP	Avg	OBP	Slg	OPS
2012 Ari	NL	22	85	22	3	2	2	(1	1)	35	19	5	13	14	0	15	3	1	0	2	3	0	.259	.382	.412	.794
2013 Ari	NL	66	250	63	10	4	3	(2	1)	90	40	22	27	17	0	44	6	3	1	5	2	4	.252	.314	.360	.674
2014 CWS	AL	123	486	146	26	10	1	(1	0)	195	76	35	77	43	0	83	5	2	2	15	9	4	.300	.362	.401	.763
2015 CWS	AL	153	610	175	28	9	14	(6	8)	263	98	56	96	58	2	131	14	5	2	18	8	5	.287	.361	.431	.792
2016 CWS	AL	157	619	176	29	9	14	(7	7)	265	91	59	92	63	2	115	14	7	3	14	5	6	.284	.362	.428	.790
2017 Was	NL	23	91	27	7	1	2	(1	1)	42	24	13	19	14	0	18	1	0	1	3	1	0	.297	.393	.462	.854
2018 Was	NL	95	319	96	18	1	5	(1	4)	131	55	33	58	38	0	64	11	2	0	9	1	2	.301	.394	.411	.805
2019 Was	NL	151	566	158	25	7	15	(8	7)	242	103	49	88	65	0	106	13	9	3	15	3	8	.279	.365	.428	.792
8 ML YEARS		790	3026	863	146	43	56	(27	29)	1263	506	272	470	312	4	576	67	29	12	81	32	29	.285	.363	.417	.781

Tommy Edman

Bats: B **Throws:** R **Pos:** 3B-55;2B-29;PH-15;RF-12;LF-1;CF-1   **Ht:** 5'10" **Wt:** 180 **Born:** 5/9/1995 **Age:** 25

		BATTING																		RUNNING			AVERAGES			
Year Team	Lg	G	AB	H	2B	3B	HR	(Hm	Rd)	TB	R	RBI	RC	TBB	IBB	SO	HBP	SH	SF	SB	CS	GDP	Avg	OBP	Slg	OPS
2019 Memp	AAA	49	197	60	12	4	7	(-	-)	101	39	29	38	15	0	33	2	2	2	9		2	.305	.356	.513	.869
2019 StL	NL	92	326	99	17	7	11	(4	7)	163	59	36	52	16	0	61	7	0	0	15	1	3	.304	.350	.500	.850

Jon Edwards

Pitches: R **Bats:** R **Pos:** RP-9   **Ht:** 6'5" **Wt:** 240 **Born:** 1/8/1988 **Age:** 32

		HOW MUCH PITCHED						WHAT HE GAVE UP												THE RESULTS							
Year Team	Lg	G	GS	GF	IP	BFP	H	R	ER	HR	SH	SF	HB	TBB	IBB	SO	WP	W	L	Pct	Sv-Op	Hld	Vel	OPS	ERC	ERA
2019 Clmbs	AAA	41	0	12	49.0	217	43	25	23	7	2	0	0	26	2	62	5	6	1	.857	3--	-	-	.712	4.03	4.22
2014 Tex	AL	9	0	3	8.1	43	13	5	4	0	0	0	1	5	0	9	2	0	0	-	0-0	1	95	.820	7.97	4.32
2015 2 Tms		22	0	7	16.2	75	12	8	8	4	0	2	0	16	0	22	2	0	0	-	0-0	2	94	.829	5.92	4.32
2018 Cle	AL	9	0	0	8.2	37	6	4	3	2	0	0	0	4	0	10	0	0	0	-	0-0	0	95	.695	3.32	3.12

		HOW MUCH PITCHED					WHAT HE GAVE UP											THE RESULTS						
Year Team	Lg	G	GS	GF	IP	BFP	H	R	ER	HR	SH	SF	HB	TBB	IBB	SO	WP	W	L	Pct	Sv-Op	Hld	Vel	OPS	ERC	ERA
2019 Cle	AL	9	0	3	8.0	36	5	2	2	2	0	0	2	6	0	5	0	2	0	1.000	0-0	0	93	.825	5.51	2.25
15 Tex	AL	11	0	2	6.0	31	6	4	4	1	0	1	0	8	0	6	1	0	0	-	0-0	2	94	.906	8.67	6.00
15 SD	NL	11	0	5	10.2	44	6	4	4	3	0	1	0	8	0	16	1	0	0	-	0-0	0	94	.775	4.41	3.38
4 ML YEARS		49	0	13	41.2	191	36	19	17	8	0	2	3	31	0	46	4	2	0	1.000	0-0	3	94	.799	5.68	3.67

Carl Edwards Jr.

Pitches: R Bats: R Pos: RP-22   Ht: 6'3" Wt: 170 Born: 9/3/1991 Age: 28

		HOW MUCH PITCHED					WHAT HE GAVE UP											THE RESULTS						
Year Team	Lg	G	GS	GF	IP	BFP	H	R	ER	HR	SH	SF	HB	TBB	IBB	SO	WP	W	L	Pct	Sv-Op	Hld	Vel	OPS	ERC	ERA
2019 Iowa	AAA	14	0	0	14.2	62	12	6	5	2	0	0	0	6	0	14	0	2	0	1.000	0- -	-		.665	3.30	3.07
2015 ChC	NL	5	0	3	4.2	19	3	3	2	0	0	0	0	3	0	4	0	0	0		0-0	0	93	.566	2.50	3.86
2016 ChC	NL	36	0	10	36.0	138	15	15	15	4	0	2	0	14	1	52	5	0	1	.000	2-3	6	95	.456	1.33	3.75
2017 ChC	NL	73	0	8	66.1	262	29	22	22	6	1	1	4	38	2	94	4	5	4	.556	0-4	25	95	.503	1.99	2.98
2018 ChC	NL	58	0	4	52.0	222	36	17	15	2	1	0	0	32	1	67	4	3	2	.600	0-2	23	95	.583	2.75	2.60
2019 2 Tms	NL	22	0	4	17.0	78	12	17	16	3	0	1	1	13	0	19	4	1	1	.500	0-2	4	94	.683	4.48	8.47
19 ChC	NL	20	0	3	15.1	64	8	11	10	3	0	1	1	9	0	17	2	1	1	.500	0-2	4	94	.621	3.05	5.87
19 SD	NL	2	0	1	1.2	14	4	6	6	0	0	0	0	4	0	2	2	0	0		0-0	0	94	.971	20.14	32.40
Postseason		15	0	0	11.0	48	7	8	8	1	1	0	0	10	0	12	2	1	2	.333	0-1	5	95	.632	4.04	6.55
5 ML YEARS		194	0	27	176.0	719	95	74	70	15	2	4	5	100	4	236	17	9	8	.529	2-11	58	95	.540	2.28	3.58

Zach Eflin

Pitches: R Bats: R Pos: SP-28; RP-4   Ht: 6'6" Wt: 215 Born: 4/8/1994 Age: 26

		HOW MUCH PITCHED					WHAT HE GAVE UP											THE RESULTS						
Year Team	Lg	G	GS	GF	IP	BFP	H	R	ER	HR	SH	SF	HB	TBB	IBB	SO	WP	W	L	Pct	Sv-Op	Hld	Vel	OPS	ERC	ERA
2016 Phi	NL	11	11	0	63.1	272	67	42	39	12	4	1	4	17	1	31	1	3	5	.375	0-0	0	92	.828	4.49	5.54
2017 Phi	NL	11	11	0	64.1	280	79	45	44	16	2	5	5	12	0	35	2	1	5	.167	0-0	0	93	.896	6.00	6.16
2018 Phi	NL	24	24	0	128.0	548	130	69	62	16	5	4	3	37	4	123	4	11	8	.579	0-0	0	94	.746	3.90	4.36
2019 Phi	NL	32	28	3	163.1	705	172	88	75	28	6	3	6	48	5	129	1	10	13	.435	0-0	0	94	.775	4.53	4.13
4 ML YEARS		78	74	3	419.0	1805	448	244	220	72	14	16	15	114	10	318	8	25	31	.446	0-0	0	93	.793	4.54	4.73

Jerad Eickhoff

Pitches: R Bats: R Pos: SP-10; RP-2   EYE-koff   Ht: 6'4" Wt: 245 Born: 7/2/1990 Age: 29

		HOW MUCH PITCHED					WHAT HE GAVE UP											THE RESULTS						
Year Team	Lg	G	GS	GF	IP	BFP	H	R	ER	HR	SH	SF	HB	TBB	IBB	SO	WP	W	L	Pct	Sv-Op	Hld	Vel	OPS	ERC	ERA
2015 Phi	NL	8	8	0	51.0	203	40	16	15	5	0	1	4	13	0	49	1	3	3	.500	0-0	0	91	.621	2.40	2.65
2016 Phi	NL	33	33	0	197.1	811	187	88	80	30	6	10	8	42	2	167	6	11	14	.440	0-0	0	91	.740	3.56	3.65
2017 Phi	NL	24	24	0	128.0	576	142	74	67	16	3	9	5	53	4	118	6	4	8	.333	0-0	0	90	.794	5.00	4.71
2018 Phi	NL	3	1	1	5.1	26	10	4	4	1	0	0	0	0	0	11	0	0	1	.000	0-0	0	91	1.038	8.28	6.75
2019 Phi	NL	12	10	1	58.1	245	58	37	37	18	3	0	2	18	0	51	0	3	4	.429	1-1	0	89	.885	5.33	5.71
5 ML YEARS		80	76	2	440.0	1861	437	219	203	70	12	20	15	126	6	396	13	21	30	.412	1-1	0	91	.767	4.11	4.15

Roenis Elias

Pitches: L Bats: L Pos: RP-48   roh-EN-ees ehl-LEE-us   Ht: 6'1" Wt: 205 Born: 8/1/1988 Age: 31

		HOW MUCH PITCHED					WHAT HE GAVE UP											THE RESULTS						
Year Team	Lg	G	GS	GF	IP	BFP	H	R	ER	HR	SH	SF	HB	TBB	IBB	SO	WP	W	L	Pct	Sv-Op	Hld	Vel	OPS	ERC	ERA
2014 Sea	AL	29	29	0	163.2	693	151	77	70	16	4	4	11	64	3	143	6	10	12	.455	0-0	0	92	.713	3.89	3.85
2015 Sea	AL	22	20	0	115.1	490	106	57	53	15	1	4	9	44	1	97	1	5	8	.385	0-0	1	92	.730	4.10	4.14
2016 Bos	AL	3	1	2	7.2	41	15	11	11	2	0	0	0	5	1	3	0	0	1	.000	0-0	0	93	1.210	13.11	12.91
2017 Bos	AL	1	0	1	0.1	2	0	0	0	0	0	0	0	1	0	1	0	0	0		0-0	0	92	.500	7.00	0.00
2018 Sea	AL	23	4	13	51.0	210	46	17	15	1	0	3	1	16	1	34	3	3	1	.750	0-0	0	94	.642	2.76	2.65
2019 2 Tms	NL	48	0	28	50.0	216	46	32	22	10	1	1	1	18	1	47	1	4	2	.667	14-17	2	94	.728	4.09	3.96
19 Sea	AL	44	0	28	47.0	203	41	28	19	8	1	1	1	17	1	45	1	4	2	.667	14-16	1	94	.686	3.61	3.64
19 Was	NL	4	0	0	3.0	13	5	4	3	2	0	0	0	1	0	2	0	0	0		0-1	1	94	1.378	14.71	9.00
6 ML YEARS		126	54	44	388.0	1652	364	194	171	44	6	12	22	148	7	325	11	22	24	.478	14-17	3	92	.723	3.98	3.97

Chris Ellis

Pitches: R Bats: L Pos: RP-1   Ht: 6'5" Wt: 205 Born: 9/22/1992 Age: 27

		HOW MUCH PITCHED					WHAT HE GAVE UP											THE RESULTS						
Year Team	Lg	G	GS	GF	IP	BFP	H	R	ER	HR	SH	SF	HB	TBB	IBB	SO	WP	W	L	Pct	Sv-Op	Hld	Vel	OPS	ERC	ERA
2019 Memp	AAA	40	7	5	79.0	385	98	65	63	13	1	1	8	47	1	82	11	5	5	.500	1- -	-	-	.898	7.20	7.18
2019 KC	AL	1	0	1	1.0	5	1	0	0	0	0	0	0	1	0	0	0	0	0		0-0	0	93	.650	5.48	0.00

Jake Elmore

Bats: R Throws: R Pos: PH-9; LF-5; 3B-4; RF-3; 2B-1   Ht: 5'10" Wt: 180 Born: 6/15/1987 Age: 33

		BATTING																		RUNNING			AVERAGES			
Year Team	Lg	G	AB	H	2B	3B	HR	(Hm	Rd)	TB	R	RBI	RC	TBB	IBB	SO	HBP	SH	SF	SB	CS	GDP	Avg	OBP	Slg	OPS
2019 Indy	AAA	109	367	118	31	0	6	(-	-)	167	56	35	64	37	5	55	5	1	4	3	8	11	.322	.387	.455	.842
2012 Ari	NL	30	68	13	4	0	0	(0	0)	17	1	7	3	5	0	6	0	0	0	0	0	1	.191	.247	.250	.497
2013 Hou	AL	52	120	29	4	0	2	(1	1)	39	16	6	13	13	0	20	0	2	1	1	6	1	.242	.313	.325	.638
2014 Cin	NL	5	11	2	0	0	0	(0	0)	2	0	0	0	1	0	4	0	0	0	0	0	0	.182	.250	.182	.432

Year Team	Lg	G	AB	H	2B	3B	HR	(Hm	Rd)	TB	R	RBI	RC	TBB	IBB	SO	HBP	SH	SF	SB	CS	GDP	Avg	OBP	Slg	OPS
2015 TB	AL	51	141	29	5	0	2	(2	0)	40	10	16	10	12	1	25	0	2	3	1	1	6	.206	.263	.284	.547
2016 Mil	NL	59	78	17	2	0	0	(0	0)	19	7	4	7	17	1	17	2	2	2	2	3	1	.218	.371	.244	.615
2019 Pit	NL	20	47	10	1	0	0	(0	0)	11	3	4	3	2	0	8	0	0	0	0	1	0	.213	.245	.234	.479
6 ML YEARS		217	465	100	16	0	4	(3	1)	128	37	37	36	50	2	80	2	6	4	4	11	9	.215	.292	.275	.567

Edwin Encarnacion

Bats: R **Throws:** R **Pos:** 1B-57;DH-51;2B-1;PH-1   **Ht:** 6'1" **Wt:** 230 **Born:** 1/7/1983 **Age:** 37

Year Team	Lg	G	AB	H	2B	3B	HR	(Hm	Rd)	TB	R	RBI	RC	TBB	IBB	SO	HBP	SH	SF	SB	CS	GDP	Avg	OBP	Slg	OPS
2005 Cin	NL	69	211	49	16	0	9	(3	6)	92	25	31	24	20	2	60	3	0	0	3	0	8	.232	.308	.436	.744
2006 Cin	NL	117	406	112	33	1	15	(7	8)	192	60	72	66	41	3	78	13	0	3	6	3	9	.276	.359	.473	.831
2007 Cin	NL	139	502	145	25	1	16	(10	6)	220	66	76	86	39	4	86	14	0	1	8	1	5	.289	.356	.438	.794
2008 Cin	NL	146	506	127	29	1	26	(15	11)	236	75	68	72	61	1	102	10	0	5	1	0	13	.251	.340	.466	.807
2009 2 Tms		85	293	66	11	2	13	(5	8)	120	35	39	37	37	0	67	5	0	3	2	1	5	.225	.320	.410	.729
2010 Tor	AL	96	332	81	16	0	21	(7	14)	160	47	51	41	29	1	60	2	0	4	1	0	9	.244	.305	.482	.787
2011 Tor	AL	134	481	131	36	0	17	(14	3)	218	70	55	67	43	2	77	3	0	3	8	2	17	.272	.334	.453	.787
2012 Tor	AL	151	542	152	24	0	42	(23	19)	302	93	110	124	84	12	94	11	0	7	13	3	6	.280	.384	.557	.941
2013 Tor	AL	142	530	144	29	1	36	(12	24)	283	90	104	102	82	7	62	4	0	5	7	1	20	.272	.370	.534	.904
2014 Tor	AL	128	477	128	27	2	34	(19	15)	261	75	98	86	62	6	82	2	0	1	2	0	5	.268	.354	.547	.901
2015 Tor	AL	146	528	146	31	0	39	(18	21)	294	94	111	110	77	5	98	9	0	10	3	2	14	.277	.372	.557	.929
2016 Tor	AL	160	601	158	34	0	42	(20	22)	318	99	127	104	87	3	138	5	0	8	2	0	22	.263	.357	.529	.886
2017 Cle	AL	157	554	143	20	1	38	(15	23)	279	96	107	102	104	5	133	5	0	5	2	0	18	.258	.377	.504	.881
2018 Cle	AL	137	500	123	16	1	32	(16	16)	237	74	107	85	63	2	132	8	0	7	3	0	14	.246	.336	.474	.810
2019 2 Tms	AL	109	418	102	18	0	34	(17	17)	222	81	86	84	58	1	103	7	0	3	0	1	4	.244	.344	.531	.875
09 Cin	NL	43	139	29	6	1	5	(3	2)	52	10	16	19	24	0	38	2	0	1	1	1	3	.209	.333	.374	.707
09 Tor	NL	42	154	37	5	1	8	(2	6)	68	25	23	18	13	0	29	3	0	1	1	0	2	.240	.306	.442	.748
19 Sea	AL	65	241	58	7	0	21	(9	12)	128	48	49	52	41	0	55	4	0	3	0	1	3	.241	.356	.531	.888
19 NYY	AL	44	177	44	11	0	13	(8	5)	94	33	37	32	17	1	48	3	0	0	0	0	1	.249	.325	.531	.856
Postseason		26	92	22	3	0	4	(3	1)	37	12	14	14	14	5	20	1	0	0	0	0	2	.239	.346	.402	.748
15 ML YEARS		1916	6881	1807	365	10	414	(201	213)	3434	1080	1242	1190	887	54	1372	101	0	65	61	14	182	.263	.352	.499	.851

Adam Engel

Bats: R **Throws:** R **Pos:** CF-86;PR-5;PH-3   **Ht:** 6'2" **Wt:** 210 **Born:** 12/9/1991 **Age:** 28

Year Team	Lg	G	AB	H	2B	3B	HR	(Hm	Rd)	TB	R	RBI	RC	TBB	IBB	SO	HBP	SH	SF	SB	CS	GDP	Avg	OBP	Slg	OPS
2019 Charllt	AAA	64	248	67	13	4	9	(-	-)	115	43	29	42	22	0	62	7	0	0	13	3	4	.270	.347	.464	.810
2017 CWS	AL	97	301	50	11	3	6	(4	2)	85	34	21	16	19	0	117	8	8	0	8	1	1	.166	.235	.282	.517
2018 CWS	AL	143	429	101	17	4	6	(4	2)	144	49	29	31	18	0	129	8	7	1	16	8	1	.235	.279	.336	.614
2019 CWS	AL	89	227	55	10	2	6	(3	3)	87	26	26	26	14	0	78	6	1	0	3	3	5	.242	.304	.383	.687
3 ML YEARS		329	957	206	38	9	18	(11	7)	316	109	76	73	51	0	324	22	16	1	27	12	7	.215	.271	.330	.601

Nathan Eovaldi

Pitches: R **Bats:** R **Pos:** SP-12; RP-11   eh-VOLL-dee   **Ht:** 6'2" **Wt:** 225 **Born:** 2/13/1990 **Age:** 30

Year Team	Lg	G	GS	GF	IP	BFP	H	R	ER	HR	SH	SF	HB	TBB	IBB	SO	WP	W	L	Pct	Sv-Op	Hld	Vel	OPS	ERC	ERA
2011 LAD	NL	10	6	1	34.2	146	28	14	14	2	2	0	2	20	0	23	0	1	2	.333	0-0	1	94	.667	3.75	3.63
2012 2 Tms	NL	22	22	0	119.1	526	133	59	57	10	1	6	3	47	3	78	1	4	13	.235	0-0	0	94	.771	4.67	4.30
2013 Mia	NL	18	18	0	106.1	451	100	44	40	7	6	1	1	40	3	78	3	4	6	.400	0-0	0	96	.681	3.41	3.39
2014 Mia	NL	33	33	0	199.2	854	223	107	97	14	9	5	7	43	5	142	6	6	14	.300	0-0	0	96	.732	3.89	4.37
2015 NYY	AL	27	27	0	154.1	673	175	72	72	10	3	3	3	49	0	121	8	14	3	.824	0-0	0	97	.716	4.34	4.20
2016 NYY	AL	24	21	2	124.2	525	123	66	66	23	1	1	1	40	2	97	5	9	8	.529	0-0	0	97	.778	4.30	4.76
2018 2 Tms	AL	22	21	0	111.0	455	105	55	47	14	1	4	3	20	1	101	4	6	7	.462	0-0	0	97	.685	3.18	3.81
2019 Bos	AL	23	12	2	67.2	302	72	46	45	16	1	2	3	35	0	70	6	2	1	.667	0-1	4	98	.875	6.26	5.99
12 LAD	NL	10	10	0	56.1	241	63	27	26	5	0	3	0	20	2	34	1	1	6	.143	0-0	0	94	.771	4.54	4.15
12 Mia	NL	12	12	0	63.0	285	70	32	31	5	1	3	3	27	1	44	0	3	7	.300	0-0	0	94	.770	4.79	4.43
18 TB	AL	10	10	0	57.0	224	48	27	27	11	0	2	1	8	1	53	1	3	4	.429	0-0	0	97	.682	2.85	4.26
18 Bos	AL	12	11	0	54.0	231	57	28	20	3	1	2	2	12	0	48	3	3	3	.500	0-0	0	97	.687	3.48	3.33
Postseason		6	2	1	22.1	85	15	5	4	1	1	0	0	3	0	16	0	2	1	.667	0-0	2	99	.449	1.34	1.61
8 ML YEARS		179	160	5	917.2	3932	959	463	438	96	24	22	23	294	14	710	33	46	54	.460	0-1	5	96	.738	4.14	4.30

Robbie Erlin

Pitches: L **Bats:** R **Pos:** RP-36; SP-1   **Ht:** 6'0" **Wt:** 190 **Born:** 10/8/1990 **Age:** 29

Year Team	Lg	G	GS	GF	IP	BFP	H	R	ER	HR	SH	SF	HB	TBB	IBB	SO	WP	W	L	Pct	Sv-Op	Hld	Vel	OPS	ERC	ERA
2019 ElPaso	AAA	10	0	3	15.1	73	26	15	15	2	1	1	2	2	0	14	3	0	1	.000	1--	-		.984	8.16	8.80
2013 SD	NL	11	9	2	54.2	227	53	26	25	6	3	1	0	15	0	40	3	3	3	.500	0-0	0	90	.698	3.50	4.12
2014 SD	NL	13	11	1	61.1	264	71	34	34	6	2	4	1	15	1	46	4	4	5	.444	0-0	0	90	.787	4.39	4.99
2015 SD	NL	3	3	0	17.0	65	16	9	9	1	0	0	1	2	0	10	1	1	2	.333	0-0	0	90	.663	2.84	4.76
2016 SD	NL	3	2	0	15.2	58	12	7	7	3	0	0	0	3	0	13	2	1	2	.333	0-0	0	88	.750	2.77	4.02
2018 SD	NL	39	12	8	109.0	439	112	57	51	12	3	5	0	12	0	88	2	4	7	.364	0-0	1	90	.695	3.20	4.21
2019 SD	NL	37	1	10	55.1	251	72	36	33	6	1	3	1	15	0	52	3	0	1	.000	0-1	5	91	.789	5.37	5.37
6 ML YEARS		106	38	21	313.0	1304	336	169	159	34	9	13	3	62	1	249	15	13	20	.394	0-1	6	90	.733	3.81	4.57

Phillip Ervin

Bats: R **Throws:** R **Pos:** LF-61;PH-29;CF-25;RF-17;PR-2   **Ht:** 5'10" **Wt:** 207 **Born:** 7/15/1992 **Age:** 27

					BATTING														RUNNING			AVERAGES			
Year Team	Lg	G	AB	H	2B	3B	HR	(Hm	Rd)	TB	R	RBI	RC	TBB	IBB	SO	HBP	SH	SF	SB	CS	GDP	Avg	OBP	Slg	OPS
2019 Lsvlle	AAA	40	145	42	8	1	6	(-	-)	70	27	26	27	19	0	34	5	0	3	6	6	2	.290	.384	.483	.866
2017 Cin	NL	28	58	15	2	0	3	(1	2)	26	8	10	10	4	0	15	1	1	0	4	1	1	.259	.317	.448	.766
2018 Cin	NL	78	218	55	10	1	7	(3	4)	88	27	31	27	20	1	60	5	0	4	6	1	5	.252	.324	.404	.728
2019 Cin	NL	94	236	64	11	7	7	(3	4)	110	30	23	32	18	0	63	4	0	2	4	3	4	.271	.331	.466	.797
3 ML YEARS		200	512	134	23	8	17	(7	10)	224	65	64	69	42	1	138	10	1	6	14	5	10	.262	.326	.438	.764

Eduardo Escobar

Bats: B **Throws:** R **Pos:** 3B-144;2B-33;PH-3;DH-1   **Ht:** 5'10" **Wt:** 185 **Born:** 1/5/1989 **Age:** 31

					BATTING														RUNNING			AVERAGES			
Year Team	Lg	G	AB	H	2B	3B	HR	(Hm	Rd)	TB	R	RBI	RC	TBB	IBB	SO	HBP	SH	SF	SB	CS	GDP	Avg	OBP	Slg	OPS
2011 CWS	AL	9	7	2	0	0	0	(0	0)	2	0	0	1	0	0	1	0	0	0	0	0	0	.286	.286	.286	.571
2012 2 Tms	AL	50	131	28	4	1	0	(0	0)	34	18	9	12	11	0	31	1	2	1	3	0	0	.214	.278	.260	.537
2013 Min	AL	66	165	39	5	2	3	(2	1)	57	23	10	14	11	0	34	0	2	1	0	2	0	.236	.282	.345	.628
2014 Min	AL	133	433	119	35	2	6	(2	4)	176	52	37	53	24	1	93	2	4	2	1	1	6	.275	.315	.406	.721
2015 Min	AL	127	409	107	31	4	12	(2	10)	182	48	58	55	28	1	86	2	2	5	2	3	7	.262	.309	.445	.754
2016 Min	AL	105	352	83	14	2	6	(3	3)	119	32	37	38	21	1	72	1	2	1	1	3	7	.236	.280	.338	.618
2017 Min	AL	129	457	116	16	5	21	(12	9)	205	62	73	72	33	3	98	5	1	3	5	1	5	.254	.309	.449	.758
2018 2 Tms	AL	151	566	154	48	3	23	(9	14)	277	75	84	93	52	8	126	5	0	8	2	4	12	.272	.334	.489	.824
2019 Ari	NL	158	636	171	29	10	35	(18	17)	325	94	118	108	50	3	130	3	0	10	5	1	8	.269	.320	.511	.831
12 CWS	AL	36	87	18	4	1	0	(0	0)	24	14	3	7	9	0	23	0	1	0	2	0	0	.207	.281	.276	.557
12 Min	AL	14	44	10	0	0	0	(0	0)	10	4	6	5	2	0	8	1	1	1	1	0	0	.227	.271	.227	.498
18 Min	AL	97	368	101	37	3	15	(7	8)	189	45	63	70	34	6	91	3	0	3	1	3	7	.274	.338	.514	.852
18 Ari	NL	54	198	53	11	0	8	(2	6)	88	30	21	23	18	2	35	2	0	5	1	1	5	.268	.327	.444	.772
Postseason		1	4	2	0	0	0	(0	0)	2	0	0	0	0	0	0	0	0	0	0	0	0	.500	.500	.500	1.000
9 ML YEARS		928	3156	819	182	29	106	(48	58)	1377	404	426	446	230	17	671	19	13	31	19	15	45	.260	.311	.436	.747

Luis Escobar

Pitches: R **Bats:** R **Pos:** RP-4   **Ht:** 6'1" **Wt:** 205 **Born:** 5/30/1996 **Age:** 24

		HOW MUCH PITCHED					WHAT HE GAVE UP										THE RESULTS							
Year Team	Lg	G	GS	GF	IP	BFP	H	R	ER	HR	SH	SF	HB	TBB	IBB	SO	WP	W	L	Pct	Sv-Op Hld	Vel	OPS	ERC	ERA
2019 Bradtn	A+	10	0	5	13.1	54	6	0	0	0	0	0	2	6	0	15	4	0	0	-	3-- -	-	.397	1.47	0.00
2019 Indy	AAA	24	5	5	55.0	241	54	27	25	7	1	1	2	32	0	57	3	2	1	.667	1-- -	-	.806	5.20	4.09
2019 Pit	NL	4	0	2	5.2	29	10	5	5	1	1	1	1	4	0	2	1	0	0	-	0-0 0	95	1.218	12.92	7.94

Tom Eshelman

Pitches: R **Bats:** R **Pos:** RP-6; SP-4   **Ht:** 6'3" **Wt:** 210 **Born:** 6/20/1994 **Age:** 26

		HOW MUCH PITCHED					WHAT HE GAVE UP										THE RESULTS							
Year Team	Lg	G	GS	GF	IP	BFP	H	R	ER	HR	SH	SF	HB	TBB	IBB	SO	WP	W	L	Pct	Sv-Op Hld	Vel	OPS	ERC	ERA
2019 Rdng	AA	6	6	0	28.2	133	43	22	20	4	1	0	0	6	0	26	2	0	3	.000	0-- -	-	.855	6.51	6.28
2019 Norfolk	AAA	7	6	1	38.1	167	43	21	20	6	1	1	2	7	0	28	0	2	1	.667	0-- -	-	.756	4.39	4.70
2019 Bal	AL	10	4	2	36.0	164	47	31	26	12	0	2	1	11	1	22	0	1	2	.333	0-0 0	86	.953	7.35	6.50

Carlos Estevez

Pitches: R **Bats:** R **Pos:** RP-71   **Ht:** 6'6" **Wt:** 275 **Born:** 12/28/1992 **Age:** 27

		HOW MUCH PITCHED					WHAT HE GAVE UP										THE RESULTS							
Year Team	Lg	G	GS	GF	IP	BFP	H	R	ER	HR	SH	SF	HB	TBB	IBB	SO	WP	W	L	Pct	Sv-Op Hld	Vel	OPS	ERC	ERA
2016 Col	NL	63	0	26	55.0	246	50	32	32	6	1	4	5	28	4	59	3	3	7	.300	11-18 11	97	.728	4.23	5.24
2017 Col	NL	35	0	9	32.1	149	39	21	20	3	1	0	1	14	2	31	1	5	0	1.000	0-0 6	97	.778	5.31	5.57
2019 Col	NL	71	0	13	72.0	308	70	34	30	12	1	3	1	23	1	81	1	2	2	.500	0-2 11	98	.756	4.03	3.75
Postseason		1	0	0	0.1	2	1	1	1	0	0	0	0	0	0	1	0	0	0	-	0-0 0	99	1.000	14.52	27.00
3 ML YEARS		169	0	48	159.1	703	159	87	82	21	3	7	7	65	7	171	5	10	9	.526	11-20 28	97	.752	4.36	4.63

Marco Estrada

Pitches: R **Bats:** R **Pos:** SP-5   **Ht:** 6'0" **Wt:** 180 **Born:** 7/5/1983 **Age:** 36

		HOW MUCH PITCHED					WHAT HE GAVE UP										THE RESULTS							
Year Team	Lg	G	GS	GF	IP	BFP	H	R	ER	HR	SH	SF	HB	TBB	IBB	SO	WP	W	L	Pct	Sv-Op Hld	Vel	OPS	ERC	ERA
2008 Was	NL	11	0	3	12.2	63	17	13	11	4	0	0	2	5	1	10	0	0	0	-	0-1 3	90	.952	8.13	7.82
2009 Was	NL	4	1	1	7.1	33	6	6	5	1	1	0	0	4	0	9	1	0	1	.000	0-0 0	90	.741	3.67	6.14
2010 Mil	NL	7	1	0	11.1	58	14	13	12	3	1	0	1	6	0	13	2	0	0	-	0-0 0	91	.908	7.17	9.53
2011 Mil	NL	43	7	12	92.2	381	83	45	42	11	7	1	2	29	2	88	4	4	8	.333	0-3 4	91	.700	3.39	4.08
2012 Mil	NL	29	23	0	138.1	562	129	62	56	18	7	3	0	29	0	143	4	5	7	.417	0-0 1	90	.703	3.18	3.64
2013 Mil	NL	21	21	0	128.0	512	109	56	55	19	3	2	2	29	0	118	3	7	4	.636	0-0 0	89	.670	3.01	3.87
2014 Mil	NL	39	18	3	150.2	624	137	77	73	29	4	4	3	44	0	127	2	7	6	.538	0-0 0	89	.752	3.85	4.36
2015 Tor	AL	34	28	3	181.0	725	134	67	63	24	2	3	5	55	2	131	2	13	8	.619	0-0 0	89	.633	2.64	3.13
2016 Tor	AL	29	29	0	176.0	723	132	73	68	23	0	3	4	65	1	165	5	9	9	.500	0-0 0	88	.639	2.88	3.48
2017 Tor	AL	33	33	0	186.0	806	186	104	103	31	0	6	2	71	0	176	1	10	9	.526	0-0 0	90	.785	4.48	4.98
2018 Tor	AL	28	28	0	143.2	627	155	91	90	29	1	7	2	50	0	103	3	7	14	.333	0-0 0	89	.852	5.09	5.64
2019 Oak	AL	5	5	0	23.2	106	23	19	18	7	0	0	3	8	0	11	2	0	2	.000	0-0 0	87	.858	5.41	6.85
Postseason		10	6	2	47.2	180	36	15	14	5	2	0	0	4	0	43	1	3	3	.500	0-0 0	89	.581	1.73	2.64
12 ML YEARS		283	194	22	1251.1	5220	1125	626	596	199	26	29	26	395	6	1094	29	62	68	.477	0-4 8	89	.726	3.65	4.29

Thairo Estrada

Bats: R **Throws:** R **Pos:** 2B-17;SS-9;PR-7;PH-3;LF-2;RF-2;DH-1   **Ht:** 5'10" **Wt:** 190 **Born:** 2/22/1996 **Age:** 24

Year Team	Lg	G	AB	H	2B	3B	HR	(Hm	Rd)	TB	R	RBI	RC	TBB	IBB	SO	HBP	SH	SF	SB	CS	GDP	Avg	OBP	Slg	OPS
2019 S-WB	AAA	60	241	64	17	2	8	(-	-)	109	39	32	35	14	0	50	3	0	1	3	1	3	.266	.313	.452	.765
2019 NYY	AL	35	64	16	3	0	3	(1	2)	28	12	12	12	3	0	15	1	1	0	4	0	1	.250	.294	.438	.732

Peter Fairbanks

Pitches: R **Bats:** R **Pos:** RP-21   **Ht:** 6'6" **Wt:** 219 **Born:** 12/16/1993 **Age:** 26

		HOW MUCH PITCHED					WHAT HE GAVE UP										THE RESULTS							
Year Team	Lg	G	GS	GF	IP	BFP	H	R	ER	HR	SH	SF	HB	TBB	IBB	SO	WP	W	L	Pct	Sv-Op	Hld	Vel	OPS	ERC	ERA
2019 DwnEast	A+	11	0	5	12.1	51	10	4	4	0	0	0	0	4	0	15	0	1	0	1.000	2- -	-		.551	2.13	2.92
2019 Frisco	AA	6	0	3	7.1	24	2	0	0	0	0	0	0	0	0	14	0	1	0	1.000	0- -	-		.167	0.17	0.00
2019 Nashv	AAA	7	0	0	6.1	31	10	8	8	1	1	1	0	2	0	11	1	0	0	-	0- -	-		.919	7.54	11.37
2019 Drham	AAA	16	1	7	17.2	75	15	11	10	3	0	1	0	6	0	30	2	1	2	.333	0- -	-		.677	3.35	5.09
2019 2 Tms	AL	21	0	3	21.0	99	25	20	16	5	0	0	0	10	0	28	2	2	3	.400	2-2	3	97	.882	6.37	6.86
19 Tex	AL	8	0	0	8.2	41	8	10	9	4	0	0	0	7	0	15	1	0	2	.000	0-0	0	97	.954	8.04	9.35
19 TB	AL	13	0	3	12.1	58	17	10	7	1	0	0	0	3	0	13	1	2	1	.667	2-2	3	98	.836	5.26	5.11

Jeurys Familia

Pitches: R **Bats:** R **Pos:** RP-66   jer-ISS fa-MEAL-ya   **Ht:** 6'3" **Wt:** 240 **Born:** 10/10/1989 **Age:** 30

		HOW MUCH PITCHED					WHAT HE GAVE UP										THE RESULTS							
Year Team	Lg	G	GS	GF	IP	BFP	H	R	ER	HR	SH	SF	HB	TBB	IBB	SO	WP	W	L	Pct	Sv-Op	Hld	Vel	OPS	ERC	ERA
2012 NYM	NL	8	1	4	12.1	52	10	8	8	0	0	0	0	9	0	10	0	0	0	-	0-0	0	96	.644	3.76	5.84
2013 NYM	NL	9	0	3	10.2	52	12	5	5	2	2	0	0	9	1	8	3	0	0	-	1-1	0	95	.908	7.20	4.22
2014 NYM	NL	76	0	16	77.1	322	59	26	19	3	4	2	2	32	5	73	9	2	5	.286	5-10	23	96	.587	2.45	2.21
2015 NYM	NL	76	0	65	78.0	308	59	16	16	6	1	1	2	19	1	86	4	2	2	.500	43-48	1	97	.569	2.19	1.85
2016 NYM	NL	78	0	67	77.2	321	63	25	22	1	2	1	1	31	6	84	3	3	4	.429	51-56	0	96	.574	2.44	2.55
2017 NYM	NL	26	0	15	24.2	111	21	14	12	1	2	2	1	15	3	25	1	2	2	.500	6-7	2	96	.636	3.48	4.38
2018 2 Tms		70	0	36	72.0	302	60	26	25	3	0	1	2	28	1	83	2	8	6	.571	18-24	7	96	.601	2.81	3.13
2019 NYM	NL	66	0	14	60.0	274	62	39	38	7	2	1	3	42	4	63	3	4	2	.667	0- -	14	96	.831	5.84	5.70
18 NYM	NL	40	0	29	40.2	171	36	13	13	1	0	1	2	14	1	43	1	4	4	.500	17-21	1	96	.616	2.88	2.88
18 Oak	AL	30	0	7	31.1	131	24	13	12	2	0	0	0	14	0	40	1	4	2	.667	1-3	6	97	.581	2.73	3.45
Postseason		14	0	11	16.2	60	7	5	4	2	0	0	0	3	0	11	0	0	1	.000	5-8	0	96	.412	0.97	2.16
8 ML YEARS		409	1	220	412.2	1742	346	159	145	23	13	8	11	185	21	432	25	21	21	.500	124-150	47	96	.635	3.11	3.16

Jake Faria

Pitches: R **Bats:** R **Pos:** RP-16   **Ht:** 6'4" **Wt:** 225 **Born:** 7/30/1993 **Age:** 26

		HOW MUCH PITCHED					WHAT HE GAVE UP										THE RESULTS							
Year Team	Lg	G	GS	GF	IP	BFP	H	R	ER	HR	SH	SF	HB	TBB	IBB	SO	WP	W	L	Pct	Sv-Op	Hld	Vel	OPS	ERC	ERA
2019 Drham	AAA	23	7	3	59.2	250	55	29	27	8	0	0	0	26	0	74	2	6	2	.750	1- -	-		.753	4.11	4.07
2019 SnAnt	AAA	6	0	2	7.2	34	8	2	2	1	0	0	0	5	0	8	0	1	1	.500	0- -	-		.831	5.80	2.35
2017 TB	AL	16	14	1	86.2	357	71	35	33	11	1	4	5	31	0	84	6	5	4	.556	0-0	0	92	.677	3.37	3.43
2018 TB	AL	17	12	1	65.0	281	60	39	39	4	0	3	3	33	1	50	2	4	4	.500	0-0	0	92	.776	4.58	5.40
2019 2 Tms		16	0	4	18.2	95	28	15	14	5	0	1	1	12	0	19	3	0	1	.000	0-0	2	94	1.049	10.00	6.75
19 TB	AL	7	0	1	10.0	47	10	3	3	2	0	0	0	7	0	11	0	0	0	-	0-0	0	94	.837	5.94	2.70
19 Mil	NL	9	0	3	8.2	48	18	12	11	3	0	1	1	5	0	8	3	0	1	.000	0-0	2	93	1.256	15.43	11.42
3 ML YEARS		49	26	6	170.1	733	159	89	86	25	1	8	9	76	1	153	11	9	9	.500	0-0	2	92	.762	4.47	4.54

Buck Farmer

Pitches: R **Bats:** L **Pos:** RP-72; SP-1   **Ht:** 6'4" **Wt:** 232 **Born:** 2/20/1991 **Age:** 29

		HOW MUCH PITCHED					WHAT HE GAVE UP										THE RESULTS							
Year Team	Lg	G	GS	GF	IP	BFP	H	R	ER	HR	SH	SF	HB	TBB	IBB	SO	WP	W	L	Pct	Sv-Op	Hld	Vel	OPS	ERC	ERA
2014 Det	AL	4	2	1	9.1	46	12	12	12	2	0	0	2	5	0	11	0	0	1	.000	0-0	0	93	1.054	8.29	11.57
2015 Det	AL	14	5	0	40.1	186	53	35	33	10	1	1	3	17	2	24	1	0	4	.000	0-0	0	93	.986	7.65	7.36
2016 Det	AL	14	1	7	29.1	131	25	15	15	4	1	1	1	20	1	27	2	0	1	.000	0-0	0	93	.771	4.71	4.60
2017 Det	AL	11	11	0	48.0	219	55	38	36	9	0	2	4	20	0	49	1	5	5	.500	0-0	0	92	.843	5.99	6.75
2018 Det	AL	66	1	12	69.1	308	67	34	32	6	1	2	1	41	1	57	2	3	4	.429	0-0	7	94	.754	4.61	4.15
2019 Det	AL	73	1	8	67.2	288	62	32	28	8	4	4	5	24	2	73	4	6	6	.500	0-3	15	95	.743	3.81	3.72
6 ML YEARS		182	21	28	264.0	1178	274	166	156	39	7	10	16	127	6	241	10	14	21	.400	0-3	22	93	.819	5.21	5.32

Kyle Farmer

Bats: R **Throws:** R **Pos:** 2B-41;PH-39;1B-18;C-15;3B-12;SS-1;DH-1;PR-1   **Ht:** 6'0" **Wt:** 214 **Born:** 8/17/1990 **Age:** 29

Year Team	Lg	G	AB	H	2B	3B	HR	(Hm	Rd)	TB	R	RBI	RC	TBB	IBB	SO	HBP	SH	SF	SB	CS	GDP	Avg	OBP	Slg	OPS
2017 LAD	NL	20	20	6	1	0	0	(0	0)	7	1	2	1	0	0	3	0	0	0	0	0	2	.300	.300	.350	.650
2018 LAD	NL	39	68	16	4	1	0	(0	0)	22	1	9	7	5	1	15	3	0	1	0	0	1	.235	.312	.324	.635
2019 Cin	NL	97	183	42	6	0	9	(6	3)	75	22	27	22	10	1	59	3	0	1	4	1	1	.230	.279	.410	.689
Postseason		5	4	0	0	0	0	(0	0)	0	0	1	0	0	0	2	0	0	1	0	0	0	.000	.000	.000	.000
3 ML YEARS		156	271	64	11	1	9	(6	3)	104	24	38	30	15	2	77	6	0	2	4	1	4	.236	.289	.384	.673

Luke Farrell

Pitches: R Bats: L Pos: RP-8; SP-1   Ht: 6'6" Wt: 210 Born: 6/7/1991 Age: 29

			HOW MUCH PITCHED					WHAT HE GAVE UP											THE RESULTS						
Year Team	Lg	G	GS	GF	IP	BFP	H	R	ER	HR	SH	SF	HB	TBB	IBB	SO	WP	W	L	Pct	Sv-Op Hld	Vel	OPS	ERC	ERA
2019 Frisco	AA	5	0	1	8.2	31	2	2	1	0	0	0	1	4	0	12	1	0	0	-	0- - -	-	.380	0.89	1.04
2017 2 Tms		10	1	3	13.0	61	12	8	8	2	0	0	0	10	0	9	0	0	0	-	0-0 1	91	.753	5.40	5.54
2018 ChC	NL	20	2	8	31.1	141	30	22	18	7	0	1	1	16	2	39	1	3	4	.429	0-1 1	92	.797	5.09	5.17
2019 Tex	AL	9	1	3	13.1	48	6	4	4	3	0	1	0	3	0	12	0	1	0	1.000	0-0 0	92	.574	1.49	2.70
17 KC	AL	1	1	0	2.2	18	7	5	5	1	0	0	0	3	0	2	0	0	0	-	0-0 0	90	1.289	21.83	16.88
17 Cin	NL	9	0	3	10.1	43	5	3	3	1	0	0	0	7	0	7	0	0	0	-	0-0 1	91	.529	2.34	2.61
3 ML YEARS		39	4	14	57.2	250	48	34	30	12	0	2	1	29	2	60	1	4	4	.500	0-1 2	92	.743	4.24	4.68

Erick Fedde

Pitches: R Bats: R Pos: SP-12; RP-9   Ht: 6'4" Wt: 195 Born: 2/25/1993 Age: 27

			HOW MUCH PITCHED					WHAT HE GAVE UP											THE RESULTS						
Year Team	Lg	G	GS	GF	IP	BFP	H	R	ER	HR	SH	SF	HB	TBB	IBB	SO	WP	W	L	Pct	Sv-Op Hld	Vel	OPS	ERC	ERA
2019 Hrsbrg	AA	5	4	0	24.2	99	18	9	7	2	2	0	1	5	0	27	1	2	0	1.000	0- - -	-	.517	1.95	2.55
2017 Was	NL	3	3	0	15.1	76	25	16	16	5	2	0	1	8	2	15	0	0	1	.000	0-0 0	93	1.106	11.01	9.39
2018 Was	NL	11	11	0	50.1	217	55	31	31	8	1	2	0	22	1	46	0	2	4	.333	0-0 0	94	.846	5.32	5.54
2019 Was	NL	21	12	3	78.0	334	81	39	39	11	4	2	2	33	2	41	1	4	2	.667	0-0 0	92	.802	4.88	4.50
3 ML YEARS		35	26	3	143.2	627	161	86	86	24	7	4	3	63	5	102	1	6	7	.462	0-0 0	93	.853	5.62	5.39

Tim Federowicz

Bats: R Throws: R Pos: C-29   fed-er-oh-vich   Ht: 5'10" Wt: 215 Born: 8/5/1987 Age: 32

							BATTING													RUNNING			AVERAGES			
Year Team	Lg	G	AB	H	2B	3B	HR	(Hm Rd)	TB	R	RBI	RC	TBB	IBB	SO	HBP	SH	SF		SB	CS	GDP	Avg	OBP	Slg	OPS
2019 Clmbs	AAA	26	90	25	6	0	2	(- -)	37	7	13	13	11	0	23	0	1	1		0	0	3	.278	.353	.411	.764
2019 Nashv	AAA	16	57	8	0	0	1	(- -)	11	5	8	1	4	0	16	0	0	2		0	0	4	.140	.190	.193	.383
2011 LAD	NL	7	13	2	0	0	0	(0 0)	2	0	1	1	2	0	4	1	0	0		0	0	0	.154	.313	.154	.466
2012 LAD	NL	3	3	1	0	0	0	(0 0)	1	0	0	1	1	0	2	0	0	0		0	0	0	.333	.500	.333	.833
2013 LAD	NL	56	160	37	8	0	4	(1 3)	57	12	16	9	10	5	56	0	2	1		0	0	5	.231	.275	.356	.631
2014 LAD	NL	23	71	8	3	0	1	(0 1)	14	2	5	0	3	0	18	1	2	1		0	0	3	.113	.158	.197	.355
2016 ChC	NL	17	31	6	2	0	0	(0 0)	8	3	3	2	1	0	12	0	0	1		0	0	0	.194	.212	.258	.470
2017 SF	NL	13	13	3	0	0	2	(1 1)	9	3	3	3	1	0	4	0	0	0		0	0	1	.231	.286	.692	.978
2018 2 Tms		15	40	9	4	0	1	(1 0)	16	5	4	5	2	0	16	0	0	0		0	0	0	.225	.262	.400	.662
2019 Tex	AL	29	75	12	2	0	4	(4 0)	26	6	7	4	5	0	31	0	0	0		1	0	0	.160	.213	.347	.559
18 Hou	AL	10	34	7	3	0	0	(0 0)	10	4	2	2	1	0	13	0	0	0		0	0	0	.206	.229	.294	.523
18 Cin	NL	5	6	2	1	0	1	(1 0)	6	1	2	3	1	0	3	0	0	0		0	0	0	.333	.429	1.000	1.429
8 ML YEARS		163	406	78	19	0	12	(7 5)	133	31	39	25	25	5	143	2	7	3		1	0	12	.192	.241	.328	.568

Ryan Feierabend

Pitches: L Bats: L Pos: SP-1; RP-1   FEAR-ahh-bend   Ht: 6'3" Wt: 225 Born: 8/22/1985 Age: 34

			HOW MUCH PITCHED					WHAT HE GAVE UP											THE RESULTS						
Year Team	Lg	G	GS	GF	IP	BFP	H	R	ER	HR	SH	SF	HB	TBB	IBB	SO	WP	W	L	Pct	Sv-Op Hld	Vel	OPS	ERC	ERA
2019 Buffalo	AAA	14	12	0	68.1	297	77	47	42	19	1	2	1	21	0	53	1	6	5	.545	0- - -	-	.890	5.79	5.53
2006 Sea	AL	4	2	2	17.0	73	15	7	7	3	1	0	0	7	0	11	1	0	1	.000	0-0 0	90	.721	3.91	3.71
2007 Sea	AL	13	9	0	49.1	236	73	44	44	10	0	2	4	23	2	27	3	1	6	.143	0-0 0	88	1.018	8.71	8.03
2008 Sea	AL	8	8	0	39.2	183	59	34	34	7	1	1	1	14	0	26	1	1	4	.200	0-0 0	88	.997	7.83	7.71
2014 Tex	AL	6	0	0	7.1	36	12	5	5	0	1	1	0	2	1	4	1	0	0	-	0-0 1	89	.900	6.10	6.14
2019 Tor	AL	2	1	1	5.2	29	11	7	7	2	0	0	0	1	0	4	1	0	1	.000	0-0 0	86	1.092	11.09	11.12
5 ML YEARS		33	20	3	119.0	557	170	97	97	22	3	4	5	47	3	72	7	2	12	.143	0-0 1	88	.969	7.61	7.34

Michael Feliz

Pitches: R Bats: R Pos: RP-57; SP-1   Ht: 6'4" Wt: 240 Born: 6/28/1993 Age: 27

			HOW MUCH PITCHED					WHAT HE GAVE UP											THE RESULTS						
Year Team	Lg	G	GS	GF	IP	BFP	H	R	ER	HR	SH	SF	HB	TBB	IBB	SO	WP	W	L	Pct	Sv-Op Hld	Vel	OPS	ERC	ERA
2019 Indy	AAA	10	0	6	15.0	65	13	2	2	1	1	1	1	7	1	22	0	0	0	-	2- - -	-	.655	3.49	1.20
2015 Hou	AL	5	0	5	8.0	38	9	7	7	2	0	0	1	4	0	7	0	0	0	-	0-0 0	94	.884	6.79	7.88
2016 Hou	AL	47	0	17	65.0	270	55	33	32	10	0	2	0	22	0	95	0	8	1	.889	0-3 5	95	.659	3.32	4.43
2017 Hou	AL	46	0	13	48.0	218	53	31	30	8	0	4	0	22	1	70	7	4	2	.667	0-2 5	96	.854	5.28	5.63
2018 Pit	NL	47	0	7	47.2	217	49	33	30	6	0	3	3	23	0	55	3	1	2	.333	0-2 12	95	.776	4.92	5.66
2019 Pit	NL	58	1	5	56.1	239	44	27	25	11	1	1	2	27	1	73	0	4	4	.500	0-1 3	95	.720	3.91	3.99
5 ML YEARS		203	1	47	225.0	982	210	131	124	37	1	10	6	98	2	300	16	17	9	.654	0-8 22	95	.751	4.33	4.96

Caleb Ferguson

Pitches: L Bats: R Pos: RP-44; SP-2   Ht: 6'3" Wt: 226 Born: 7/2/1996 Age: 23

			HOW MUCH PITCHED					WHAT HE GAVE UP											THE RESULTS						
Year Team	Lg	G	GS	GF	IP	BFP	H	R	ER	HR	SH	SF	HB	TBB	IBB	SO	WP	W	L	Pct	Sv-Op Hld	Vel	OPS	ERC	ERA
2019 OkCity	AAA	13	1	2	15.1	58	9	3	3	1	0	0	0	5	0	27	1	0	0	-	1- - -	-	.543	1.63	1.76
2018 LAD	NL	29	3	7	49.0	202	43	21	19	8	0	0	3	12	1	59	1	7	2	.778	2-3 5	94	.688	3.42	3.49
2019 LAD	NL	46	2	5	44.2	204	39	26	24	7	1	3	6	27	2	54	1	1	2	.333	0-0 4	94	.774	4.99	4.84
Postseason		6	0	0	3.0	10	0	0	0	0	0	0	0	1	0	3	0	0	0	-	0-0 1	95	.100	0.13	0.00
2 ML YEARS		75	5	12	93.2	406	82	47	43	15	1	3	9	39	3	113	2	8	4	.667	2-3 9	94	.731	4.16	4.13

Jose Fernandez

Pitches: L **Bats:** L **Pos:** RP-4 **Ht:** 6'3" **Wt:** 215 **Born:** 2/13/1993 **Age:** 27

Year Team	Lg	G	GS	GF	IP	BFP	H	R	ER	HR	SH	SF	HB	TBB	IBB	SO	WP	W	L	Pct	Sv-Op	Hld	Vel	OPS	ERC	ERA
2019 Toledo	AAA	27	1	6	34.2	155	40	24	23	5	0	0	0	16	0	24	1	1	1	.500	0--	-	-	.865	5.62	5.97
2019 Erie	AA	11	3	4	26.0	114	30	16	12	4	2	1	0	7	1	19	1	1	3	.250	1--	-	-	.830	4.68	4.15
2018 Tor	AL	13	0	1	10.1	45	10	7	7	2	0	0	0	4	0	6	0	0	0	-	0-0	2	94	.750	4.40	6.10
2019 Det	AL	4	0	0	3.2	23	6	8	7	1	0	1	1	5	1	2	0	0	0	-	0-0	0	93	1.209	14.74	17.18
2 ML YEARS		17	0	1	14.0	68	16	15	14	3	0	1	1	9	1	8	0	0	0	-	0-0	2	94	.891	6.87	9.00

Junior Fernandez

Pitches: R **Bats:** R **Pos:** RP-13 **Ht:** 6'1" **Wt:** 180 **Born:** 3/2/1997 **Age:** 23

Year Team	Lg	G	GS	GF	IP	BFP	H	R	ER	HR	SH	SF	HB	TBB	IBB	SO	WP	W	L	Pct	Sv-Op	Hld	Vel	OPS	ERC	ERA
2019 PlmBh	A+	9	0	8	11.2	51	8	2	2	0	0	0	1	8	0	11	1	0	0	-	4--	-	-	.548	3.03	1.54
2019 Sprgfld	AA	18	0	11	29.0	115	18	6	5	0	0	1	1	11	1	42	5	1	1	.500	5--	-	-	.457	1.59	1.55
2019 Memp	AAA	18	0	5	24.1	102	17	6	4	0	0	0	2	11	0	27	1	2	1	.667	2--	-	-	.541	2.30	1.48
2019 StL	NL	13	0	5	11.2	54	9	7	7	2	0	0	4	6	0	16	2	0	1	.000	0-3	0	97	.693	5.01	5.40

Matt Festa

Pitches: R **Bats:** R **Pos:** RP-20 **Ht:** 6'2" **Wt:** 195 **Born:** 3/11/1993 **Age:** 27

Year Team	Lg	G	GS	GF	IP	BFP	H	R	ER	HR	SH	SF	HB	TBB	IBB	SO	WP	W	L	Pct	Sv-Op	Hld	Vel	OPS	ERC	ERA
2019 Tacom	AAA	23	0	14	30.2	128	23	11	9	3	0	0	1	14	0	33	1	1	1	.500	5--	-	-	.660	3.05	2.64
2018 Sea	AL	8	1	0	8.1	40	13	2	2	0	0	1	2	2	0	4	2	0	0	-	0-0	1	93	.859	6.44	2.16
2019 Sea	AL	20	0	10	22.1	101	20	15	14	5	1	2	2	12	1	21	1	0	2	.000	0-2	3	93	.874	5.12	5.64
2 ML YEARS		28	1	10	30.2	141	33	17	16	5	1	2	3	14	1	25	3	0	2	.000	0-2	4	93	.868	5.48	4.70

Mike Fiers

FIRES

Pitches: R **Bats:** R **Pos:** SP-33 **Ht:** 6'2" **Wt:** 202 **Born:** 6/15/1985 **Age:** 35

Year Team	Lg	G	GS	GF	IP	BFP	H	R	ER	HR	SH	SF	HB	TBB	IBB	SO	WP	W	L	Pct	Sv-Op	Hld	Vel	OPS	ERC	ERA
2011 Mil	NL	2	0	2	2.0	10	2	0	0	0	0	0	0	3	0	2	0	0	0	-	0-0	0	88	.786	8.25	0.00
2012 Mil	NL	23	22	1	127.2	539	125	56	53	12	4	4	2	36	0	135	4	9	10	.474	0-0	0	88	.694	3.50	3.74
2013 Mil	NL	11	3	4	22.1	103	28	20	18	8	1	2	0	6	0	15	1	1	4	.200	0-0	0	88	.972	6.65	7.25
2014 Mil	NL	14	10	1	71.2	274	46	19	17	7	2	1	0	17	1	76	1	6	5	.545	0-0	0	90	.531	1.68	2.13
2015 2 Tms		31	30	0	180.1	761	162	83	74	24	3	8	6	64	5	180	8	7	10	.412	0-0	0	89	.713	3.64	3.69
2016 Hou	AL	31	30	0	168.2	724	187	89	84	26	3	5	7	42	0	134	17	11	8	.579	0-0	0	90	.801	4.66	4.48
2017 Hou	AL	29	28	0	153.1	671	157	95	89	32	3	1	13	62	0	146	11	8	10	.444	0-0	0	90	.827	5.44	5.22
2018 2 Tms		31	30	0	172.0	714	166	71	68	32	1	2	8	37	1	139	4	12	8	.600	0-0	0	89	.746	3.90	3.56
2019 Oak	AL	33	33	0	184.2	754	166	82	80	30	4	5	9	53	0	126	13	15	4	.789	0-0	0	90	.712	3.76	3.90
15 Mil	NL	21	21	0	118.0	509	117	57	51	14	3	6	5	43	5	121	6	5	9	.357	0-0	0	89	.749	4.11	3.89
15 Hou	AL	10	9	0	62.1	252	45	26	23	10	0	2	1	21	0	59	2	2	1	.667	0-0	0	90	.643	2.78	3.32
18 Det	AL	21	21	0	119.0	502	121	49	46	20	1	1	5	26	1	87	2	7	6	.538	0-0	0	89	.749	4.04	3.48
18 Oak	AL	10	9	0	53.0	212	45	22	22	12	0	1	3	11	0	52	2	5	2	.714	0-0	0	90	.740	3.57	3.74
Postseason		1	0	0	1.0	4	1	1	1	0	1	1	0	0	0	0	0	0	0	-	0-0	0	90	1.333	1.95	9.00
9 ML YEARS		205	186	8	1082.2	4550	1039	515	483	171	21	28	45	320	7	953	59	69	59	.539	0-0	0	89	.742	4.00	4.02

Heath Fillmyer

Pitches: R **Bats:** R **Pos:** RP-9; SP-3 **Ht:** 6'1" **Wt:** 195 **Born:** 5/16/1994 **Age:** 26

Year Team	Lg	G	GS	GF	IP	BFP	H	R	ER	HR	SH	SF	HB	TBB	IBB	SO	WP	W	L	Pct	Sv-Op	Hld	Vel	OPS	ERC	ERA
2019 Omha	AAA	19	10	2	49.1	219	48	28	28	8	0	1	5	26	0	51	2	2	3	.400	0--	-	-	.799	5.40	5.11
2018 KC	AL	17	13	2	82.1	344	78	41	39	11	0	4	2	32	0	57	3	4	2	.667	0-0	0	93	.721	4.17	4.26
2019 KC	AL	12	3	2	22.1	109	28	20	20	6	0	3	3	12	0	15	1	0	2	.000	0-0	1	92	.955	8.08	8.06
2 ML YEARS		29	16	4	104.2	453	106	61	59	17	0	7	5	44	0	72	4	4	4	.500	0-0	1	92	.775	4.95	5.07

Derek Fisher

Bats: L **Throws:** R **Pos:** LF-38;RF-9;PR-6;DH-5;PH-4;CF-3 **Ht:** 6'3" **Wt:** 205 **Born:** 8/21/1993 **Age:** 26

Year Team	Lg	G	AB	H	2B	3B	HR	(Hm	Rd)	TB	R	RBI	RC	TBB	IBB	SO	HBP	SH	SF	SB	CS	GDP	Avg	OBP	Slg	OPS
2019 RdRck	AAA	60	224	64	9	1	14	(-	-)	117	44	36	48	40	1	67	4	1	3	8	3	3	.286	.401	.522	.924
2017 Hou	AL	53	146	31	4	1	5	(3	2)	52	21	17	18	17	1	54	3	0	3	3	3	1	.212	.307	.356	.663
2018 Hou	AL	42	79	13	2	2	4	(2	2)	31	13	11	4	5	0	42	0	0	2	2	0	0	.165	.209	.392	.602
2019 2 Tms		57	146	27	4	1	7	(4	3)	54	23	17	13	21	0	57	0	0	0	5	1	3	.185	.287	.370	.657
19 Hou	AL	17	53	12	2	1	1	(0	1)	19	9	5	7	7	0	14	0	0	0	4	1	0	.226	.317	.358	.675
19 Tor	AL	40	93	15	2	0	6	(4	2)	35	14	12	6	14	0	43	0	0	0	1	0	3	.161	.271	.376	.647
Postseason		5	0	0	0	0	0	(0	0)	0	1	0	0	1	0	0	0	0	1	0	0	0	-	1.000	-	-
3 ML YEARS		152	371	71	10	4	16	(9	7)	137	57	45	35	43	1	153	3	0	2	10	4	4	.191	.279	.369	.649

Jack Flaherty

Pitches: R **Bats:** R **Pos:** SP-33   **Ht:** 6'4" **Wt:** 205 **Born:** 10/15/1995 **Age:** 24

		HOW MUCH PITCHED					WHAT HE GAVE UP											THE RESULTS							
Year	Team	Lg	G	GS	GF	IP	BFP	H	R	ER	HR	SH	SF	HB	TBB	IBB	SO	WP	W	L	Pct	Sv-Op	Hld	Vel	OPS	ERC	ERA
2017	StL	NL	6	5	0	21.1	94	23	15	15	4	0	2	1	10	1	20	0	0	2	.000	0-0	0	93	.843	5.71	6.33
2018	StL	NL	28	28	0	151.0	615	108	59	56	20	2	1	11	59	3	182	6	8	9	.471	0-0	0	93	.635	3.01	3.34
2019	StL	NL	33	33	0	196.1	772	135	62	60	25	3	3	7	55	2	231	6	11	8	.579	0-0	0	94	.591	2.31	2.75
	3 ML YEARS		67	66	0	368.2	1481	266	136	131	49	5	6	19	124	6	433	12	19	19	.500	0-0	0	93	.625	2.77	3.20

Ryan Flaherty

Bats: L **Throws:** R **Pos:** 3B-11;2B-2;PH-1;PR-1   **Ht:** 6'3" **Wt:** 205 **Born:** 7/27/1986 **Age:** 33

							BATTING															RUNNING			AVERAGES			
Year	Team	Lg	G	AB	H	2B	3B	HR	(Hm	Rd)	TB	R	RBI	RC	TBB	IBB	SO	HBP	SH	SF	SB	CS	GDP	Avg	OBP	Slg	OPS
2019	Clmbs	AAA	113	414	109	23	2	19	(-	-)	193	66	73	73	65	7	121	3	1	3	2	2	8	.263	.365	.466	.831
2012	Bal	AL	77	153	33	2	1	6	(3	3)	55	15	19	15	6	0	43	3	3	1	1	0	3	.216	.258	.359	.617
2013	Bal	AL	85	246	55	11	0	10	(6	4)	96	28	27	27	19	3	62	5	1	0	2	0	2	.224	.293	.390	.683
2014	Bal	AL	102	281	62	15	1	7	(7	0)	100	33	32	34	22	2	68	5	3	1	1	0	3	.221	.288	.356	.644
2015	Bal	AL	91	267	54	8	3	9	(2	7)	95	34	31	24	26	2	81	4	2	2	0	0	8	.202	.281	.356	.637
2016	Bal	AL	74	157	34	7	0	3	(3	0)	50	16	15	18	17	1	48	0	1	1	2	0	1	.217	.291	.318	.610
2017	Bal	AL	23	38	8	1	0	0	(0	0)	9	5	4	5	4	0	10	1	0	0	0	0	0	.211	.302	.237	.539
2018	Atl	NL	81	161	35	6	0	2	(1	1)	47	17	13	14	18	4	41	1	1	1	4	2	5	.217	.298	.292	.590
2019	Cle	AL	14	21	3	2	0	0	(0	0)	5	4	1	0	0	0	7	0	1	0	0	0	1	.143	.143	.238	.381
	Postseason		13	34	9	0	0	2	(0	2)	15	5	5	4	4	0	9	0	0	0	0	0	0	.265	.342	.441	.783
	8 ML YEARS		547	1324	284	52	5	37	(22	15)	457	152	142	137	112	12	360	19	12	6	10	2	23	.215	.284	.345	.629

David Fletcher

Bats: R **Throws:** R **Pos:** 3B-90;2B-42;SS-39;LF-21;RF-2;PR-1   **Ht:** 5'9" **Wt:** 185 **Born:** 5/31/1994 **Age:** 26

							BATTING															RUNNING			AVERAGES			
Year	Team	Lg	G	AB	H	2B	3B	HR	(Hm	Rd)	TB	R	RBI	RC	TBB	IBB	SO	HBP	SH	SF	SB	CS	GDP	Avg	OBP	Slg	OPS
2018	LAA	AL	80	284	78	18	2	1	(1	0)	103	35	25	35	15	0	34	3	3	2	3	0	7	.275	.316	.363	.678
2019	LAA	AL	154	596	173	30	4	6	(3	3)	229	83	49	89	55	2	64	0	1	1	8	3	8	.290	.350	.384	.734
	2 ML YEARS		234	880	251	48	6	7	(4	3)	332	118	74	124	70	2	98	3	4	3	11	3	15	.285	.339	.377	.716

Chris Flexen

Pitches: R **Bats:** R **Pos:** RP-8; SP-1   **Ht:** 6'3" **Wt:** 250 **Born:** 7/1/1994 **Age:** 25

				HOW MUCH PITCHED					WHAT HE GAVE UP											THE RESULTS						
Year	Team	Lg	G	GS	GF	IP	BFP	H	R	ER	HR	SH	SF	HB	TBB	IBB	SO	WP	W	L	Pct	Sv-Op	Hld	Vel	OPS	ERC	ERA
2019	Syrcse	AAA	26	14	4	78.2	345	94	41	39	11	2	3	2	21	0	92	2	5	3	.625	0--	-		.821	5.06	4.46
2017	NYM	NL	14	9	1	48.0	233	62	44	42	11	1	2	2	35	0	36	1	3	6	.333	0-0	0	92	.981	8.75	7.88
2018	NYM	NL	4	1	2	6.1	40	14	13	9	2	0	0	1	6	1	3	0	0	2	.000	0-0	0	93	1.283	17.26	12.79
2019	NYM	NL	9	1	4	13.2	70	15	12	10	1	0	1	0	13	2	10	1	0	3	.000	0-0	0	94	.829	6.12	6.59
	3 ML YEARS		27	11	7	68.0	343	91	69	61	14	1	3	3	54	3	49	2	3	11	.214	0-0	0	93	.986	8.92	8.07

Wilmer Flores

Bats: R **Throws:** R **Pos:** 2B-64;PH-23;1B-16   **Ht:** 6'3" **Wt:** 205 **Born:** 8/6/1991 **Age:** 28

							BATTING															RUNNING			AVERAGES			
Year	Team	Lg	G	AB	H	2B	3B	HR	(Hm	Rd)	TB	R	RBI	RC	TBB	IBB	SO	HBP	SH	SF	SB	CS	GDP	Avg	OBP	Slg	OPS
2013	NYM	NL	27	95	20	5	0	1	(0	1)	28	8	13	7	5	0	23	0	0	1	0	0	1	.211	.248	.295	.542
2014	NYM	NL	78	259	65	13	1	6	(4	2)	98	28	29	25	12	2	31	1	1	1	1	0	6	.251	.286	.378	.664
2015	NYM	NL	137	483	127	22	0	16	(8	8)	197	55	59	58	19	2	63	4	2	2	0	1	12	.263	.295	.408	.703
2016	NYM	NL	103	307	82	14	0	16	(12	4)	144	38	49	39	23	0	48	2	0	3	1	1	9	.267	.319	.469	.788
2017	NYM	NL	110	336	91	17	1	18	(9	9)	164	42	52	39	17	1	54	3	0	6	1	1	14	.271	.307	.488	.795
2018	NYM	NL	126	386	103	25	0	11	(4	7)	161	43	51	51	29	1	42	5	0	9	0	0	8	.267	.319	.417	.736
2019	Ari	NL	89	265	84	18	0	9	(6	3)	129	31	37	38	15	0	31	4	0	1	0	0	9	.317	.361	.487	.848
	Postseason		13	41	8	2	1	0	(0	0)	12	4	0	5	5	2	9	1	1	0	1	0	1	.195	.298	.293	.591
	7 ML YEARS		670	2131	572	114	2	77	(43	34)	921	245	290	257	120	6	292	19	3	23	3	3	59	.268	.310	.432	.742

Dylan Floro

Pitches: R **Bats:** L **Pos:** RP-50   **Ht:** 6'2" **Wt:** 203 **Born:** 12/27/1990 **Age:** 29

				HOW MUCH PITCHED					WHAT HE GAVE UP											THE RESULTS						
Year	Team	Lg	G	GS	GF	IP	BFP	H	R	ER	HR	SH	SF	HB	TBB	IBB	SO	WP	W	L	Pct	Sv-Op	Hld	Vel	OPS	ERC	ERA
2019	OkCity	AAA	6	0	0	4.1	20	3	3	1	0	0	0	0	4	0	5	0	0	0	-	0--	-		.600	3.50	2.08
2016	TB	AL	12	0	4	15.0	72	23	8	7	0	0	1	0	5	1	14	2	0	1	.000	0-0	0	93	.813	5.96	4.20
2017	ChC	NL	3	0	2	9.2	45	15	7	7	2	0	0	1	2	0	6	0	0	0	-	0-0	0	91	.971	8.12	6.52
2018	2 Tms	NL	54	0	20	64.0	271	57	17	16	3	3	3	1	23	6	58	1	6	3	.667	0-0	7	93	.634	2.85	2.25
2019	LAD	NL	50	0	4	46.2	201	46	25	22	4	2	1	2	14	5	42	1	5	3	.625	0-3	6	94	.685	3.44	4.24
18	Cin	NL	25	0	13	36.1	159	39	12	11	2	2	3	0	12	3	27	0	3	2	.600	0-0	1	93	.726	3.69	2.72
18	LAD	NL	29	0	7	27.2	112	18	5	5	1	1	0	1	11	3	31	1	3	1	.750	0-0	6	94	.503	1.84	1.63
	Postseason		8	0	2	7.0	29	6	3	3	0	0	0	0	4	2	8	0	0	1	.000	0-0	0	93	.665	2.91	3.86
	4 ML YEARS		119	0	30	135.1	589	141	57	52	9	5	5	4	44	12	120	4	11	7	.611	0-3	13	93	.700	3.70	3.46

Tyler Flowers

Bats: R **Throws:** R **Pos:** C-83;PH-4;PR-1   **Ht:** 6'4" **Wt:** 260 **Born:** 1/24/1986 **Age:** 34

									BATTING													RUNNING			AVERAGES			
Year	Team	Lg	G	AB	H	2B	3B	HR	(Hm	Rd)	TB	R	RBI	RC	TBB	IBB	SO	HBP	SH	SF	SB	CS	GDP	Avg	OBP	Slg	OPS
2009	CWS	AL	10	16	3	1	0	0	(0	0)	4	3	0	2	3	0	8	1	0	0	0	0	1	.188	.350	.250	.600
2010	CWS	AL	8	11	1	0	0	0	(0	0)	1	2	0	1	4	0	5	0	0	0	0	0	0	.091	.333	.091	.424
2011	CWS	AL	38	110	23	5	1	5	(3	2)	45	13	16	13	14	0	38	3	0	2	0	1	2	.209	.310	.409	.719
2012	CWS	AL	52	136	29	6	0	7	(5	2)	56	19	13	13	12	0	56	4	1	0	2	1	2	.213	.296	.412	.708
2013	CWS	AL	84	256	50	11	0	10	(7	3)	91	24	24	14	14	1	94	4	0	1	0	1	9	.195	.247	.355	.603
2014	CWS	AL	127	407	98	16	1	15	(7	8)	161	42	50	43	25	0	159	8	1	1	0	1	10	.241	.297	.396	.693
2015	CWS	AL	112	331	79	12	0	9	(3	6)	118	21	39	36	21	0	104	6	2	1	0	1	8	.239	.295	.356	.652
2016	Atl	NL	83	281	76	18	0	8	(5	3)	118	27	41	46	29	1	91	11	0	4	0	0	3	.270	.357	.420	.777
2017	Atl	NL	99	317	89	16	0	12	(6	6)	141	41	49	50	31	1	82	20	0	2	0	1	6	.281	.378	.445	.823
2018	Atl	NL	82	251	57	9	0	8	(5	3)	90	34	30	33	35	0	76	9	0	1	0	0	6	.227	.341	.359	.700
2019	Atl	NL	85	271	62	11	3	11	(7	4)	112	36	34	31	31	3	105	6	0	2	0	0	8	.229	.319	.413	.733
	Postseason		3	7	1	0	0	0	(0	0)	1	1	0	0	1	0	3	0	0	0	0	0	0	.143	.250	.143	.393
	11 ML YEARS		780	2387	567	105	5	85	(48	37)	937	262	296	282	219	6	818	72	4	14	2	6	55	.238	.319	.393	.711

Brian Flynn

Pitches: L **Bats:** L **Pos:** RP-10; SP-1   **Ht:** 6'7" **Wt:** 255 **Born:** 4/19/1990 **Age:** 30

			HOW MUCH PITCHED					WHAT HE GAVE UP										THE RESULTS							
Year	Team	Lg	G	GS	GF	IP	BFP	H	R	ER	HR	SH	SF	HB	TBB	IBB	SO	WP	W	L	Pct	Sv-Op	Hld	Vel	OPS	ERC	ERA
2019	Omha	AAA	11	5	0	43.1	195	47	25	23	7	2	0	2	18	0	42	3	4	4	.500	0--	-	-	.750	4.96	4.78
2013	Mia	NL	4	4	0	18.0	88	27	17	17	4	2	0	0	13	0	15	3	0	2	.000	0-0	0	91	1.068	10.17	8.50
2014	Mia	NL	2	1	0	7.0	35	12	7	7	0	0	0	0	3	0	6	1	0	1	.000	0-0	0	90	.929	7.75	9.00
2016	KC	AL	36	1	11	55.1	221	38	19	16	5	4	1	1	23	0	44	8	1	2	.333	0-0	2	93	.598	2.55	2.60
2017	KC	AL	1	0	0	2.1	8	3	1	1	0	0	0	0	0	0	0	0	0	0	-	0-0	0	93	1.250	4.29	3.86
2018	KC	AL	48	0	10	75.2	336	87	37	34	5	1	2	3	35	3	47	5	3	5	.375	1-2	4	92	.790	5.15	4.04
2019	KC	AL	11	1	3	29.1	139	38	18	17	2	3	2	3	17	2	22	2	2	2	.500	0-0	0	91	.891	6.79	5.22
	6 ML YEARS		102	7	24	187.2	827	205	99	92	16	10	5	7	91	5	134	19	6	12	.333	1-2	6	92	.795	5.07	4.41

Mike Foltynewicz

fohl-tuh-neh-vich   **Ht:** 6'4" **Wt:** 200 **Born:** 10/7/1991 **Age:** 28

Pitches: R **Bats:** R **Pos:** SP-21

			HOW MUCH PITCHED					WHAT HE GAVE UP										THE RESULTS							
Year	Team	Lg	G	GS	GF	IP	BFP	H	R	ER	HR	SH	SF	HB	TBB	IBB	SO	WP	W	L	Pct	Sv-Op	Hld	Vel	OPS	ERC	ERA
2019	Gwnntt	AAA	10	10	0	51.1	217	49	24	22	1	1	3	2	17	0	45	2	5	1	.833	0--	-	-	.670	3.17	3.86
2014	Hou	AL	16	0	9	18.2	84	23	11	11	3	0	0	0	7	0	14	3	0	1	.000	0-0	0	97	.864	5.80	5.30
2015	Atl	NL	18	15	1	86.2	399	112	63	55	17	2	6	4	29	0	77	3	4	6	.400	0-0	1	95	.896	6.43	5.71
2016	Atl	NL	22	22	0	123.1	525	125	61	59	18	5	4	6	35	2	111	13	9	5	.643	0-0	0	95	.761	4.18	4.31
2017	Atl	NL	29	28	0	154.0	692	169	86	82	20	11	2	10	59	2	143	4	10	13	.435	0-0	0	95	.795	4.97	4.79
2018	Atl	NL	31	31	0	183.0	744	130	65	58	17	2	1	6	68	3	202	7	13	10	.565	0-0	0	96	.600	2.49	2.85
2019	Atl	NL	21	21	0	117.0	491	109	65	59	23	5	1	2	37	2	105	5	8	6	.571	0-0	0	95	.764	4.05	4.54
	Postseason		2	2	0	6.0	31	5	5	5	2	1	0	1	7	1	10	0	0	1	.000	0-0	0	96	1.024	8.49	7.50
	6 ML YEARS		137	117	10	682.2	2935	668	351	324	98	25	14	28	235	9	652	35	44	41	.518	0-0	2	96	.750	4.16	4.27

Wilmer Font

FAHNT   **Ht:** 6'4" **Wt:** 250 **Born:** 5/24/1990 **Age:** 30

Pitches: R **Bats:** R **Pos:** RP-31; SP-17

			HOW MUCH PITCHED					WHAT HE GAVE UP										THE RESULTS							
Year	Team	Lg	G	GS	GF	IP	BFP	H	R	ER	HR	SH	SF	HB	TBB	IBB	SO	WP	W	L	Pct	Sv-Op	Hld	Vel	OPS	ERC	ERA
2012	Tex	AL	3	0	1	2.0	10	0	2	2	0	0	0	0	4	0	1	1	0	0	-	0-0	0	95	.400	3.47	9.00
2013	Tex	AL	2	0	2	1.1	7	1	0	0	0	0	0	0	2	0	0	0	0	0	-	0-0	0	95	.629	5.91	0.00
2017	LAD	NL	3	0	2	3.2	22	7	7	7	2	0	0	0	4	0	3	0	0	0	-	0-0	0	94	1.389	17.78	17.18
2018	3 Tms		19	5	8	44.0	192	46	29	29	12	0	0	1	16	1	36	1	2	3	.400	0-1	0	94	.842	5.46	5.93
2019	3 Tms		48	17	6	84.1	356	78	42	42	17	0	2	3	29	2	95	2	4	5	.444	0-1	2	94	.797	4.24	4.48
18	LAD	NL	6	0	6	10.1	48	18	13	13	5	0	0	0	1	1	7	0	0	2	.000	0-1	0	93	1.119	10.58	11.32
18	Oak	AL	4	0	2	6.2	37	13	11	11	5	0	0	0	4	0	9	1	0	0	-	0-0	0	94	1.369	17.41	14.85
18	TB	AL	9	5	0	27.0	107	15	5	5	2	0	0	1	11	0	20	0	2	1	.667	0-0	0	95	.526	1.83	1.67
19	TB	AL	10	0	3	14.0	60	15	9	9	2	0	0	0	5	0	18	1	1	0	1.000	0-0	1	94	.806	4.68	5.79
19	NYM	NL	15	3	1	31.0	134	29	17	17	8	0	0	2	13	1	24	1	1	2	.333	0-1	0	94	.858	5.14	4.94
19	Tor	AL	23	14	2	39.1	162	34	16	16	7	0	2	1	11	1	53	0	2	3	.400	0-0	1	95	.743	3.42	3.66
	5 ML YEARS		75	22	18	135.1	587	132	80	80	31	0	2	4	55	3	135	4	6	8	.429	0-2	2	94	.827	4.95	5.32

Mike Ford

Bats: L **Throws:** R **Pos:** 1B-29;DH-13;PH-12   **Ht:** 6'0" **Wt:** 225 **Born:** 7/4/1992 **Age:** 27

									BATTING													RUNNING			AVERAGES			
Year	Team	Lg	G	AB	H	2B	3B	HR	(Hm	Rd)	TB	R	RBI	RC	TBB	IBB	SO	HBP	SH	SF	SB	CS	GDP	Avg	OBP	Slg	OPS
2019	S-WB	AAA	79	294	89	20	0	23	(-	-)	178	59	60	70	46	2	55	5	0	4	0	1	8	.303	.401	.605	1.007
2019	NYY	AL	50	143	37	7	0	12	(2	10)	80	30	25	27	17	2	28	3	0	0	0	0	0	.259	.350	.559	.909

Logan Forsythe

Bats: R Throws: R Pos: 1B-46;3B-33;SS-15;PH-9;2B-8;PR-2   Ht: 6'1" Wt: 205 Born: 1/14/1987 Age: 33

Year Team	Lg	G	AB	H	2B	3B	HR	(Hm Rd)	TB	R	RBI	RC	TBB	IBB	SO	HBP	SH	SF	SB	CS	GDP	Avg	OBP	Slg	OPS
2011 SD	NL	62	150	32	9	1	0	(0 0)	43	12	12	15	12	3	33	3	2	2	3	1	3	.213	.281	.287	.568
2012 SD	NL	91	315	86	13	3	6	(5 1)	123	45	26	37	28	0	57	6	0	1	8	2	6	.273	.343	.390	.733
2013 SD	NL	75	220	47	6	1	6	(2 4)	73	22	19	16	19	2	54	2	1	1	6	1	5	.214	.281	.332	.613
2014 TB	AL	110	301	67	12	1	6	(2 4)	99	32	26	26	25	0	71	4	2	4	2	0	9	.223	.287	.329	.616
2015 TB	AL	153	540	152	33	2	17	(8 9)	240	69	68	73	55	2	111	14	0	6	9	4	12	.281	.359	.444	.804
2016 TB	AL	127	511	135	24	4	20	(12 8)	227	76	52	74	46	0	127	8	0	2	6	8	6	.264	.333	.444	.778
2017 LAD	NL	119	361	81	19	0	6	(4 2)	118	56	36	45	69	1	109	4	0	5	3	2	12	.224	.351	.327	.678
2018 2 Tms		120	371	86	16	0	2	(1 1)	108	37	27	40	41	1	83	3	0	1	3	0	10	.232	.313	.291	.604
2019 Tex	AL	101	317	72	17	1	7	(2 5)	112	38	39	41	44	0	100	3	0	2	2	0	8	.227	.325	.353	.678
18 LAD	NL	70	193	40	10	0	2	(1 1)	56	18	13	15	17	1	43	0	0	1	2	0	5	.207	.270	.290	.560
18 Min	AL	50	178	46	6	0	0	(0 0)	52	19	14	25	24	0	40	3	0	0	1	0	9	.258	.356	.292	.648
Postseason		14	37	11	2	0	0	(0 0)	13	9	6	8	9	3	7	0	0	0	2	1	1	.297	.435	.351	.786
9 ML YEARS		958	3086	758	149	13	70	(36 34)	1143	387	305	367	339	9	745	47	5	24	42	16	73	.246	.327	.370	.698

Dexter Fowler

Bats: B Throws: R Pos: RF-118;CF-58;PH-11;PR-1   Ht: 6'5" Wt: 195 Born: 3/22/1986 Age: 34

Year Team	Lg	G	AB	H	2B	3B	HR	(Hm Rd)	TB	R	RBI	RC	TBB	IBB	SO	HBP	SH	SF	SB	CS	GDP	Avg	OBP	Slg	OPS
2008 Col	NL	13	26	4	0	0	0	(0 0)	4	3	0	0	0	0	5	1	0	0	1	0	0	.154	.185	.154	.339
2009 Col	NL	135	433	115	29	10	4	(2 2)	176	73	34	68	67	1	116	1	14	3	27	10	4	.266	.363	.406	.770
2010 Col	NL	132	439	114	20	14	6	(5 1)	180	73	36	68	57	0	104	2	7	0	13	8	5	.260	.347	.410	.757
2011 Col	NL	125	481	128	35	15	5	(3 2)	208	84	45	79	68	3	130	6	7	1	12	9	6	.266	.363	.432	.796
2012 Col	NL	143	454	136	18	11	13	(10 3)	215	72	53	81	68	1	128	0	6	2	12	5	5	.300	.389	.474	.863
2013 Col	NL	119	415	109	18	3	12	(7 5)	169	71	42	62	65	1	105	6	4	2	19	9	5	.263	.369	.407	.776
2014 Hou	AL	116	434	120	21	4	8	(5 3)	173	61	35	65	66	2	108	3	1	1	11	4	6	.276	.375	.399	.774
2015 ChC	NL	156	596	149	29	8	17	(11 6)	245	102	46	77	84	1	154	5	2	3	20	7	4	.250	.346	.411	.757
2016 ChC	NL	125	456	126	25	7	13	(6 7)	204	84	48	83	79	0	124	11	1	4	13	4	3	.276	.393	.447	.840
2017 StL	NL	118	420	111	22	9	18	(11 7)	205	68	64	74	63	6	101	4	0	4	7	3	10	.264	.363	.488	.851
2018 StL	NL	90	289	52	10	0	8	(4 4)	86	40	31	27	38	0	75	3	0	4	5	2	2	.180	.278	.298	.576
2019 StL	NL	150	487	116	24	1	19	(9 10)	199	69	67	81	74	1	142	8	1	4	5	5	6	.238	.346	.409	.754
Postseason		30	122	31	7	0	5	(3 2)	53	18	11	14	5	0	26	1	2	2	2	1	1	.254	.285	.434	.719
12 ML YEARS		1422	4930	1280	251	82	123	(71 52)	2064	800	501	765	729	16	1292	50	43	28	147	67	56	.260	.359	.419	.778

Jake Fraley

Bats: L Throws: L Pos: CF-11;PH-2;RF-1   Ht: 6'0" Wt: 195 Born: 5/25/1995 Age: 25

Year Team	Lg	G	AB	H	2B	3B	HR	(Hm Rd)	TB	R	RBI	RC	TBB	IBB	SO	HBP	SH	SF	SB	CS	GDP	Avg	OBP	Slg	OPS
2019 Ark	AA	61	230	72	15	2	11	(- -)	124	40	47	48	23	2	55	5	0	1	16	5	3	.313	.386	.539	.925
2019 Tacom	AAA	38	152	42	12	3	8	(- -)	84	28	33	28	11	1	34	3	0	2	6	2	1	.276	.333	.553	.886
2019 Sea	AL	12	40	6	2	0	0	(0 0)	8	3	1	2	0	0	14	1	0	0	0	0	0	.150	.171	.200	.371

Ty France

Bats: R Throws: R Pos: 3B-36;2B-21;PH-21;1B-1   Ht: 6'0" Wt: 205 Born: 7/13/1994 Age: 25

Year Team	Lg	G	AB	H	2B	3B	HR	(Hm Rd)	TB	R	RBI	RC	TBB	IBB	SO	HBP	SH	SF	SB	CS	GDP	Avg	OBP	Slg	OPS
2019 ElPaso	AAA	76	296	118	27	1	27	(- -)	228	83	89	97	30	1	51	18	0	4	1	0	4	.399	.477	.770	1.247
2019 SD	NL	69	184	43	8	1	7	(4 3)	74	20	24	25	9	0	49	7	0	1	0	2	8	.234	.294	.402	.696

Enderson Franco

Pitches: R Bats: R Pos: RP-5   Ht: 6'2" Wt: 180 Born: 12/29/1992 Age: 27

Year Team	Lg	G	GS	GF	IP	BFP	H	R	ER	HR	SH	SF	HB	TBB	IBB	SO	WP	W	L	Pct	Sv-Op Hld	Vel	OPS	ERC	ERA
2019 Scrmto	AAA	26	22	0	113.0	505	139	80	75	24	2	1	5	36	1	98	6	6	5	.545	0- --		.894	6.15	5.97
2019 SF	NL	5	0	2	5.1	20	4	2	2	1	0	0	0	1	0	4	0	0	0	-	0-0 1	96	.671	2.59	3.38

Maikel Franco

Bats: R Throws: R Pos: 3B-110;PH-14;1B-2;PR-1   MY-kell   Ht: 6'1" Wt: 215 Born: 8/26/1992 Age: 27

Year Team	Lg	G	AB	H	2B	3B	HR	(Hm Rd)	TB	R	RBI	RC	TBB	IBB	SO	HBP	SH	SF	SB	CS	GDP	Avg	OBP	Slg	OPS
2019 LV	AAA	12	40	7	2	1	2	(- -)	17	5	6	5	5	0	7	1	0	0	0	0	1	.175	.283	.425	.708
2014 Phi	NL	16	56	10	2	0	0	(0 0)	12	5	5	1	1	0	13	1	0	0	0	0	1	.179	.190	.214	.404
2015 Phi	NL	80	304	85	22	1	14	(7 7)	151	45	50	48	26	2	52	4	0	1	1	0	8	.280	.343	.497	.840
2016 Phi	NL	152	581	148	23	1	25	(10 15)	248	67	88	74	40	7	106	5	0	4	1	1	13	.255	.306	.427	.733
2017 Phi	NL	154	575	132	29	1	24	(14 10)	235	66	76	53	41	3	95	2	0	5	0	0	21	.230	.281	.409	.690
2018 Phi	NL	131	433	117	17	1	22	(10 12)	202	48	68	55	29	7	62	0	0	3	1	0	15	.270	.314	.467	.780
2019 Phi	NL	123	389	91	17	0	17	(13 4)	159	48	56	44	36	19	61	0	0	3	0	0	14	.234	.297	.409	.705
6 ML YEARS		656	2338	583	110	4	102	(54 48)	1007	279	343	275	173	38	389	11	0	17	3	1	72	.249	.302	.431	.733

Wander Franco

Bats: B Throws: R Pos: SS   Ht: 5'10" Wt: 189 Born: 3/1/2001 Age: 19

							BATTING												RUNNING			AVERAGES			
Year	Team	Lg	G	AB	H	2B	3B	HR	(Hm | Rd)	TB	R	RBI	RC	TBB	IBB	SO	HBP	SH	SF	SB	CS	GDP	Avg	OBP	Slg	OPS
2018	Prnctn	R+	61	242	85	10	7	11	(- | -)	142	46	57	57	27	1	19	2	0	2	4	3	5	.351	.418	.587	1.004
2019	2 Tms	Low	114	425	139	27	7	9	(- | -)	207	82	53	89	56	3	35	2	0	12	18	14	6	.327	.398	.487	.885

Caleb Frare

Pitches: L Bats: L Pos: RP-5   Ht: 6'1" Wt: 210 Born: 7/8/1993 Age: 26

			HOW MUCH PITCHED					WHAT HE GAVE UP										THE RESULTS							
Year	Team	Lg	G	GS	GF	IP	BFP	H	R	ER	HR	SH	SF	HB	TBB	IBB	SO	WP	W	L	Pct	Sv-Op	Hld	Vel	OPS	ERC	ERA
2019	Charllt	AAA	21	0	7	22.1	109	22	20	19	5	0	0	3	19	0	34	3	2	1	.667	1--	-	-	.909	7.43	7.66
2019	2 Tms	Low	6	0	0	6.0	25	3	2	1	0	0	0	0	4	0	8	0	0	0		0--	-	-	.470	1.79	1.50
2018	CWS	AL	11	0	1	7.0	31	6	4	4	0	0	0	1	4	0	9	1	0	1	.000	0-0	2	94	.586	3.77	5.14
2019	CWS	AL	5	0	1	2.2	14	2	3	3	1	0	0	0	4	0	3	2	0	0		0-0	0	92	.929	9.44	10.13
2 ML YEARS			16	0	2	9.2	45	8	7	7	1	0	0	1	8	0	12	3	0	1	.000	0-0	2	93	.683	5.21	6.52

Adam Frazier

Bats: L Throws: R Pos: 2B-142;PH-13   Ht: 5'10" Wt: 180 Born: 12/14/1991 Age: 28

									BATTING											RUNNING			AVERAGES			
Year	Team	Lg	G	AB	H	2B	3B	HR	(Hm	Rd)	TB	R	RBI	RC	TBB	IBB	SO	HBP	SH	SF	SB	CS	GDP	Avg	OBP	Slg	OPS
2016	Pit	NL	66	146	44	8	1	2	(2	0)	60	21	11	23	12	0	26	1	0	1	4	1	0	.301	.356	.411	.767
2017	Pit	NL	121	406	112	20	6	6	(2	4)	162	55	53	61	36	2	57	8	1	3	9	5	9	.276	.344	.399	.743
2018	Pit	NL	113	318	88	23	2	10	(6	4)	145	52	35	49	29	2	53	3	1	1	1	3	3	.277	.342	.456	.798
2019	Pit	NL	152	554	154	33	7	10	(5	5)	231	80	50	72	40	4	75	9	4	1	5	5	6	.278	.336	.417	.753
4 ML YEARS			452	1424	398	84	16	28	(15	13)	598	208	149	205	117	8	211	21	6	6	19	14	18	.279	.342	.420	.762

Clint Frazier

Bats: R Throws: R Pos: RF-36;LF-17;DH-15;PH-4;PR-1   Ht: 6'1" Wt: 190 Born: 9/6/1994 Age: 25

									BATTING											RUNNING			AVERAGES			
Year	Team	Lg	G	AB	H	2B	3B	HR	(Hm	Rd)	TB	R	RBI	RC	TBB	IBB	SO	HBP	SH	SF	SB	CS	GDP	Avg	OBP	Slg	OPS
2019	S-WB	AAA	61	247	61	20	1	8	(-	-)	107	35	26	33	17	0	56	4	0	1	1	2	5	.247	.305	.433	.738
2017	NYY	AL	39	134	31	9	4	4	(3	1)	60	16	17	17	7	0	43	0	0	1	1	0	2	.231	.268	.448	.715
2018	NYY	AL	15	34	9	3	0	0	(0	0)	12	9	1	3	5	0	13	2	0	0	0	0	3	.265	.390	.353	.743
2019	NYY	AL	69	225	60	14	0	12	(5	7)	110	31	38	40	16	1	70	2	0	3	1	2	2	.267	.317	.489	.806
3 ML YEARS			123	393	100	26	4	16	(8	8)	182	56	56	60	28	1	126	4	0	4	2	2	7	.254	.308	.463	.771

Todd Frazier

Bats: R Throws: R Pos: 3B-120;PH-12;1B-3;DH-3   Ht: 6'3" Wt: 220 Born: 2/12/1986 Age: 34

									BATTING											RUNNING			AVERAGES			
Year	Team	Lg	G	AB	H	2B	3B	HR	(Hm	Rd)	TB	R	RBI	RC	TBB	IBB	SO	HBP	SH	SF	SB	CS	GDP	Avg	OBP	Slg	OPS
2019	Stluci	A+	11	37	8	0	0	1	(-	-)	11	3	8	4	6	1	8	0	0	0	1	0	2	.216	.326	.297	.623
2011	Cin	NL	41	112	26	5	0	6	(2	4)	49	17	15	13	7	0	27	2	0	0	1	0	2	.232	.289	.438	.727
2012	Cin	NL	128	422	115	26	6	19	(10	9)	210	55	67	59	36	1	103	3	0	4	3	2	9	.273	.331	.498	.829
2013	Cin	NL	150	531	124	29	3	19	(12	7)	216	63	73	67	50	1	125	14	2	3	6	5	14	.234	.314	.407	.721
2014	Cin	NL	157	597	163	22	1	29	(20	9)	274	88	80	84	52	2	139	7	0	4	20	8	9	.273	.336	.459	.795
2015	Cin	NL	157	619	158	43	1	35	(19	16)	308	82	89	73	44	3	137	7	1	7	13	8	19	.255	.309	.498	.806
2016	CWS	AL	158	590	133	21	0	40	(16	24)	274	89	98	71	64	1	163	4	1	7	15	5	11	.225	.302	.464	.767
2017	2 Tms	AL	147	474	101	19	1	27	(9	18)	203	74	76	69	83	2	125	14	0	5	4	3	10	.213	.344	.428	.772
2018	NYM	NL	115	408	87	18	0	18	(10	8)	159	54	59	48	48	1	112	8	0	8	9	4	10	.213	.303	.390	.693
2019	NYM	NL	133	447	112	19	2	21	(10	11)	198	63	67	70	40	1	106	12	0	0	1	2	9	.251	.329	.443	.772
17	CWS	AL	81	280	58	15	0	16	(5	11)	121	41	44	39	48	1	71	4	0	3	4	3	4	.207	.328	.432	.761
17	NYY	AL	66	194	43	4	1	11	(4	7)	82	33	32	30	35	1	54	10	0	2	0	0	6	.222	.365	.423	.788
Postseason			18	53	10	3	0	1	(1	0)	16	6	6	5	5	0	13	0	0	0	0	1	0	.189	.259	.302	.561
9 ML YEARS			1186	4200	1019	202	14	214	(108	106)	1891	585	624	554	424	12	1037	71	4	38	72	37	93	.243	.320	.450	.770

Kyle Freeland

Pitches: L Bats: L Pos: SP-22   Ht: 6'4" Wt: 201 Born: 5/14/1993 Age: 27

			HOW MUCH PITCHED					WHAT HE GAVE UP										THE RESULTS							
Year	Team	Lg	G	GS	GF	IP	BFP	H	R	ER	HR	SH	SF	HB	TBB	IBB	SO	WP	W	L	Pct	Sv-Op	Hld	Vel	OPS	ERC	ERA
2019	Albq	AAA	6	6	0	29.2	143	40	31	29	4	4	1	0	16	0	28	1	0	4	.000	0-	-	-	.960	6.97	8.80
2017	Col	NL	33	28	0	156.0	688	169	78	71	17	14	7	8	63	4	107	1	11	11	.500	0-0	0	92	.792	4.83	4.10
2018	Col	NL	33	33	0	202.1	844	182	64	64	17	5	6	6	70	2	173	2	17	7	.708	0-0	0	92	.666	3.33	2.85
2019	Col	NL	22	22	0	104.1	473	126	85	78	25	2	4	2	39	3	79	4	3	11	.214	0-0	0	92	.909	6.23	6.73
Postseason			1	1	0	6.2	24	4	0	0	0	0	0	1	0	6	0	0	0			0-0	0	93	.382	1.06	0.00
3 ML YEARS			88	83	0	462.2	2005	477	227	213	59	21	17	16	172	9	359	7	31	29	.517	0-0	0	92	.766	4.45	4.14

Freddie Freeman

Bats: L Throws: R Pos: 1B-158;PH-1   Ht: 6'5" Wt: 220 Born: 9/12/1989 Age: 30

									BATTING											RUNNING			AVERAGES			
Year	Team	Lg	G	AB	H	2B	3B	HR	(Hm	Rd)	TB	R	RBI	RC	TBB	IBB	SO	HBP	SH	SF	SB	CS	GDP	Avg	OBP	Slg	OPS
2010	Atl	NL	20	24	4	1	0	1	(0	1)	8	3	1	0	0	0	8	0	0	0	0	0	1	.167	.167	.333	.500
2011	Atl	NL	157	571	161	32	0	21	(9	12)	256	67	76	79	53	3	142	6	0	5	4	4	15	.282	.346	.448	.795
2012	Atl	NL	147	540	140	33	2	23	(12	11)	246	91	94	82	64	4	129	7	0	9	2	0	10	.259	.340	.456	.796
2013	Atl	NL	147	551	176	27	2	23	(16	7)	276	89	109	124	66	10	121	7	0	5	1	0	10	.319	.396	.501	.897

Year	Team	Lg	G	AB	H	2B	3B	HR	(Hm	Rd)	TB	R	RBI	RC	TBB	IBB	SO	HBP	SH	SF	SB	CS	GDP	Avg	OBP	Slg	OPS
2014	Atl	NL	162	607	175	43	4	18	(7	11)	280	93	78	101	90	4	145	8	0	3	3	4	18	.288	.386	.461	.847
2015	Atl	NL	118	416	115	27	0	18	(5	13)	196	62	66	77	56	4	98	7	0	2	1	1	6	.276	.370	.471	.841
2016	Atl	NL	158	589	178	43	6	34	(15	19)	335	102	91	119	89	18	171	10	0	5	6	1	12	.302	.400	.569	.968
2017	Atl	NL	117	440	135	35	2	28	(11	17)	258	84	71	93	65	14	95	7	0	2	8	5	9	.307	.403	.586	.989
2018	Atl	NL	162	618	191	44	4	23	(13	10)	312	94	98	115	76	12	132	7	0	6	10	3	11	.309	.388	.505	.892
2019	Atl	NL	158	597	176	34	2	38	(22	16)	328	113	121	126	87	11	127	6	0	2	6	3	17	.295	.389	.549	.938
Postseason			9	36	12	2	0	1	(1	0)	17	5	1	4	3	0	8	0	0	0	0	0	0	.333	.385	.472	.857
10 ML YEARS			1346	4953	1451	319	22	227	(110	117)	2495	798	805	916	646	80	1168	65	0	39	43	21	109	.293	.379	.504	.883

Mike Freeman

Bats: L **Throws:** R **Pos:** 2B-33;3B-18;PH-13;SS-9;LF-6;PR-6;DH-2 **Ht:** 6'0" **Wt:** 195 **Born:** 8/4/1987 **Age:** 32

Year	Team	Lg	G	AB	H	2B	3B	HR	(Hm	Rd)	TB	R	RBI	RC	TBB	IBB	SO	HBP	SH	SF	SB	CS	GDP	Avg	OBP	Slg	OPS
2016	2 Tms		21	22	5	1	0	0	(0	0)	6	1	1	1	2	0	7	0	0	0	0	0	2	.227	.292	.273	.564
2017	3 Tms		35	60	6	2	0	1	(1	0)	11	6	1	2	6	1	19	0	0	0	0	0	1	.100	.182	.183	.365
2018	ChC	NL	1	0	0	0	0	0	(0	0)	0	0	0	0	0	0	0	0	1	0	0	0	0				
2019	Cle	AL	75	177	49	8	0	4	(3	1)	69	27	24	28	22	0	61	4	6	4	1	2	2	.277	.362	.390	.752
16	Ari	NL	8	9	0	0	0	0	(0	0)	0	0	0	0	2	0	5	0	0	0	0	0	1	.000	.182	.000	.182
16	Sea	AL	13	13	5	1	0	0	(0	0)	6	1	1	1	0	0	2	0	0	0	0	0	1	.385	.385	.462	.846
17	Sea	AL	16	30	2	0	0	1	(1	0)	5	3	1	0	4	1	9	0	0	0	0	0	0	.067	.176	.167	.343
17	LAD	NL	4	5	0	0	0	0	(0	0)	0	0	0	0	0	0	2	0	0	0	0	0	0	.000	.000	.000	.000
17	ChC	NL	15	25	4	2	0	0	(0	0)	6	3	0	2	2	0	8	0	0	0	0	0	1	.160	.222	.240	.462
4 ML YEARS			132	259	60	11	0	5	(4	1)	86	34	26	31	30	1	87	4	7	4	1	2	5	.232	.316	.332	.649

Sam Freeman

Pitches: L **Bats:** R **Pos:** RP-1 **Ht:** 5'11" **Wt:** 180 **Born:** 6/24/1987 **Age:** 33

Year	Team	Lg	G	GS	GF	IP	BFP	H	R	ER	HR	SH	SF	HB	TBB	IBB	SO	WP	W	L	Pct	Sv-Op	Hld	Vel	OPS	ERC	ERA
2019	Salt Lk	AAA	35	0	8	52.2	255	77	48	41	11	2	4	0	29	0	42	5	1	1	.500	2--	-	-	.996	8.61	7.01
2019	Fresno	AAA	5	0	1	6.0	23	4	0	0	0	0	0	1	1	0	11	0	0	0	-	1--	-	-	.451	1.64	0.00
2012	StL	NL	24	0	7	20.0	86	17	13	12	2	1	0	1	10	0	18	0	0	2	.000	0-0	2	93	.654	3.84	5.40
2013	StL	NL	13	0	2	12.1	50	8	3	3	0	1	0	0	5	0	8	2	1	0	1.000	0-0	1	95	.515	1.67	2.19
2014	StL	NL	44	0	9	38.0	169	34	13	11	2	1	1	4	19	0	35	3	2	0	1.000	0-0	11	94	.638	3.89	2.61
2015	Tex	AL	54	0	10	38.1	171	31	13	13	4	0	1	3	25	0	40	0	0	0	-	0-0	12	94	.683	4.31	3.05
2016	Mil	NL	7	0	4	7.2	44	13	11	11	2	0	2	0	9	0	8	1	0	0	-	0-0	0	94	1.136	13.79	12.91
2017	Atl	NL	58	0	5	60.0	254	48	19	17	3	1	1	3	27	2	59	2	2	0	1.000	0-3	12	95	.592	2.97	2.55
2018	Atl	NL	63	0	4	50.1	216	41	26	24	3	1	2	2	32	2	58	4	3	5	.375	0-3	9	95	.667	3.85	4.29
2019	LAA	AL	1	0	0	2.0	11	3	1	1	1	0	0	0	2	0	0	0	0	0	-	0-0	0	93	1.121	13.58	4.50
Postseason			1	0	0	0.0	2	0	0	0	0	0	0	0	2	0	0	0	0	0	-	0-0	0	94	-	-	-
8 ML YEARS			264	0	41	228.2	1001	195	99	92	17	5	7	13	129	4	226	12	8	7	.533	0-6	47	94	.661	3.90	3.62

David Freese

Bats: R **Throws:** R **Pos:** 1B-50;PH-36;DH-3;3B-2 FREEZE **Ht:** 6'2" **Wt:** 213 **Born:** 4/28/1983 **Age:** 37

Year	Team	Lg	G	AB	H	2B	3B	HR	(Hm	Rd)	TB	R	RBI	RC	TBB	IBB	SO	HBP	SH	SF	SB	CS	GDP	Avg	OBP	Slg	OPS
2009	StL	NL	17	31	10	2	0	1	(0	1)	15	3	7	4	2	0	7	0	0	1	0	0	1	.323	.353	.484	.837
2010	StL	NL	70	240	71	12	1	4	(3	1)	97	28	36	36	21	0	59	4	4	1	1	1	7	.296	.361	.404	.765
2011	StL	NL	97	333	99	16	1	10	(6	4)	147	41	55	50	24	0	75	4	0	2	1	0	18	.297	.350	.441	.791
2012	StL	NL	144	501	147	25	1	20	(8	12)	234	70	79	79	57	2	122	7	0	2	3	3	19	.293	.372	.467	.839
2013	StL	NL	138	462	121	26	1	9	(4	5)	176	53	60	48	47	1	106	9	0	3	1	2	25	.262	.340	.381	.721
2014	LAA	AL	134	462	120	25	1	10	(6	4)	177	53	55	55	38	0	124	6	0	5	1	3	10	.260	.321	.383	.704
2015	LAA	AL	121	424	109	27	0	14	(9	5)	178	53	56	60	31	0	107	12	0	3	1	1	12	.257	.323	.420	.743
2016	Pit	NL	141	437	118	23	0	13	(5	8)	180	63	55	65	45	2	142	10	0	0	0	0	15	.270	.352	.412	.764
2017	Pit	NL	130	426	112	16	0	10	(7	3)	158	44	52	63	58	5	116	15	0	4	0	1	10	.263	.368	.371	.739
2018	2 Tms	NL	113	280	83	12	2	11	(4	7)	132	38	51	44	24	1	72	5	0	3	0	0	10	.296	.359	.471	.830
2019	LAD	NL	79	162	51	13	0	11	(5	6)	97	35	29	33	23	0	44	1	0	0	0	0	7	.315	.403	.599	1.002
18	Pit	NL	94	241	68	10	1	9	(3	6)	107	29	42	32	18	1	56	3	0	3	0	0	10	.282	.336	.444	.780
18	LAD	NL	19	39	15	2	1	2	(1	1)	25	9	9	12	6	0	16	2	0	0	0	0	0	.385	.489	.641	1.130
Postseason			65	196	57	16	2	10	(5	5)	107	24	36	36	20	2	52	4	0	2	0	1	9	.291	.365	.546	.911
11 ML YEARS			1184	3758	1041	197	7	113	(57	56)	1591	481	535	533	370	11	974	73	4	24	8	11	134	.277	.351	.423	.775

David Freitas

Bats: R **Throws:** R **Pos:** PH-16;C-1 **Ht:** 6'3" **Wt:** 225 **Born:** 3/18/1989 **Age:** 31

Year	Team	Lg	G	AB	H	2B	3B	HR	(Hm	Rd)	TB	R	RBI	RC	TBB	IBB	SO	HBP	SH	SF	SB	CS	GDP	Avg	OBP	Slg	OPS
2019	SnAnt	AAA	85	310	120	21	0	12	(-	-)	177	51	76	78	42	2	49	2	0	3	0	1	18	.387	.459	.571	1.030
2017	Atl	NL	6	17	4	2	0	0	(0	0)	6	2	2	1	0	0	4	0	0	0	0	0	1	.235	.235	.353	.588
2018	Sea	AL	36	93	20	6	0	1	(0	1)	29	9	5	7	8	0	25	0	1	0	0	0	2	.215	.277	.312	.589
2019	2 Tms		17	15	1	0	0	0	(0	0)	1	2	1	0	4	0	5	0	0	1	0	0	1	.067	.250	.067	.317
19	Sea	AL	1	2	0	0	0	0	(0	0)	0	1	1	0	1	0	0	0	0	0	0	0	0	.000	.250	.000	.250
19	Mil	NL	16	13	1	0	0	0	(0	0)	1	1	0	0	3	0	5	0	0	1	0	0	1	.077	.250	.077	.327
3 ML YEARS			59	125	25	8	0	1	(0	1)	36	13	8	8	12	0	34	0	1	1	0	0	4	.200	.268	.288	.556

Max Fried

Pitches: L **Bats:** L **Pos:** SP-30; RP-3 **Ht:** 6'4" **Wt:** 190 **Born:** 1/18/1994 **Age:** 26

Year	Team	Lg	G	GS	GF	IP	BFP	H	R	ER	HR	SH	SF	HB	TBB	IBB	SO	WP	W	L	Pct	Sv-Op	Hld	Vel	OPS	ERC	ERA
2017	Atl	NL	9	4	4	26.0	121	30	15	11	3	0	0	4	12	1	22	0	1	1	.500	0-0	0	92	.818	5.92	3.81
2018	Atl	NL	14	5	5	33.2	142	26	12	11	3	2	2	2	20	0	44	2	1	4	.200	0-0	1	93	.688	3.84	2.94
2019	Atl	NL	33	30	1	165.2	702	174	80	74	21	3	2	5	47	3	173	11	17	6	.739	0-0	0	94	.743	4.22	4.02
	Postseason		4	0	0	2.1	8	1	1	1	1	0	0	0	1	0	1	0	0	0	-	0-0	0	96	.821	3.41	3.86
	3 ML YEARS		56	39	10	225.1	965	230	107	96	27	5	4	11	79	4	239	13	19	11	.633	0-0	1	94	.745	4.35	3.83

Jace Fry

Pitches: L **Bats:** L **Pos:** RP-68 **Ht:** 6'1" **Wt:** 190 **Born:** 7/9/1993 **Age:** 26

Year	Team	Lg	G	GS	GF	IP	BFP	H	R	ER	HR	SH	SF	HB	TBB	IBB	SO	WP	W	L	Pct	Sv-Op	Hld	Vel	OPS	ERC	ERA
2017	CWS	AL	11	0	3	6.2	36	12	8	8	1	0	0	0	5	1	3	3	0	0	-	0-0	0	94	1.085	10.97	10.80
2018	CWS	AL	59	1	12	51.1	214	37	28	25	4	2	0	1	20	0	70	5	2	3	.400	4-5	16	93	.567	2.43	4.38
2019	CWS	AL	68	0	6	55.0	251	44	33	29	7	2	1	3	43	3	68	4	3	4	.429	0-2	11	92	.733	4.74	4.75
	3 ML YEARS		138	1	21	113.0	501	93	69	62	12	4	1	4	68	4	141	12	5	7	.417	4-7	27	93	.686	3.93	4.94

Paul Fry

Pitches: L **Bats:** L **Pos:** RP-66 **Ht:** 6'0" **Wt:** 190 **Born:** 7/26/1992 **Age:** 27

Year	Team	Lg	G	GS	GF	IP	BFP	H	R	ER	HR	SH	SF	HB	TBB	IBB	SO	WP	W	L	Pct	Sv-Op	Hld	Vel	OPS	ERC	ERA
2018	Bal	AL	35	0	11	37.2	159	33	20	14	1	0	0	4	15	0	36	3	1	2	.333	2-4	9	91	.613	3.34	3.35
2019	Bal	AL	66	0	8	57.1	255	54	39	34	7	1	0	6	29	1	55	2	1	9	.100	3-8	11	91	.752	4.72	5.34
	2 ML YEARS		101	0	19	95.0	414	87	59	48	8	1	0	10	44	1	91	5	2	11	.154	5-12	20	91	.698	4.16	4.55

Josh Fuentes

Bats: R **Throws:** R **Pos:** PH-13;1B-11;3B-2 **Ht:** 6'2" **Wt:** 209 **Born:** 2/19/1993 **Age:** 27

Year	Team	Lg	G	AB	H	2B	3B	HR	(Hm	Rd)	TB	R	RBI	RC	TBB	IBB	SO	HBP	SH	SF	SB	CS	GDP	Avg	OBP	Slg	OPS
2019	Albq	AAA	101	402	102	23	2	17	(-	-)	180	66	64	55	25	1	118	2	4	4	1	1	8	.254	.298	.448	.746
2019	Col	NL	24	55	12	1	0	3	(2	1)	22	8	7	4	1	0	20	0	0	0	1	0	0	.218	.232	.400	.632

Carson Fulmer

Pitches: R **Bats:** R **Pos:** RP-18; SP-2 **Ht:** 6'0" **Wt:** 195 **Born:** 12/13/1993 **Age:** 26

Year	Team	Lg	G	GS	GF	IP	BFP	H	R	ER	HR	SH	SF	HB	TBB	IBB	SO	WP	W	L	Pct	Sv-Op	Hld	Vel	OPS	ERC	ERA
2019	Charllt	AAA	24	0	7	34.0	152	31	21	18	2	0	1	0	21	0	51	6	1	2	.333	1--	-	-	.704	4.08	4.76
2016	CWS	AL	8	0	4	11.2	53	12	11	11	2	0	0	2	7	0	10	2	0	2	.000	0-1	0	93	.873	6.57	8.49
2017	CWS	AL	7	5	0	23.1	101	16	10	10	4	1	0	2	13	0	19	0	3	1	.750	0-0	0	93	.639	3.71	3.86
2018	CWS	AL	9	8	1	32.1	164	37	32	29	8	1	2	5	24	0	29	2	2	4	.333	0-0	0	93	.935	8.08	8.07
2019	CWS	AL	20	2	3	27.1	133	26	22	19	5	0	3	3	20	0	25	1	1	2	.333	0-0	1	94	.780	6.01	6.26
	4 ML YEARS		44	15	8	94.2	451	91	75	69	19	2	5	12	64	0	83	5	6	9	.400	0-1	1	93	.815	6.15	6.56

Michael Fulmer

Pitches: R **Bats:** R **Pos:** P **Ht:** 6'3" **Wt:** 246 **Born:** 3/15/1993 **Age:** 27

Year	Team	Lg	G	GS	GF	IP	BFP	H	R	ER	HR	SH	SF	HB	TBB	IBB	SO	WP	W	L	Pct	Sv-Op	Hld	Vel	OPS	ERC	ERA
2016	Det	AL	26	26	0	159.0	647	136	57	54	16	4	2	9	42	1	132	1	11	7	.611	0-0	0	95	.652	3.02	3.06
2017	Det	AL	25	25	0	164.2	676	150	80	70	13	3	8	8	40	2	114	3	10	12	.455	0-0	0	96	.644	3.04	3.83
2018	Det	AL	24	24	0	132.1	558	128	75	69	19	1	2	5	46	1	110	1	3	12	.200	0-0	0	96	.758	4.18	4.69
	3 ML YEARS		75	75	0	456.0	1881	414	212	193	48	8	12	22	128	4	356	5	24	31	.436	0-0	0	95	.680	3.35	3.81

Drew Gagnon

Pitches: R **Bats:** R **Pos:** RP-18 GAHN-yo **Ht:** 6'4" **Wt:** 215 **Born:** 6/26/1990 **Age:** 30

Year	Team	Lg	G	GS	GF	IP	BFP	H	R	ER	HR	SH	SF	HB	TBB	IBB	SO	WP	W	L	Pct	Sv-Op	Hld	Vel	OPS	ERC	ERA
2019	Syrcse	AAA	15	15	0	88.2	362	78	29	23	12	1	0	5	17	1	72	6	6	5	.545	0--	-	-	.658	3.03	2.33
2018	NYM	NL	5	1	0	12.0	56	15	11	7	2	2	0	2	5	0	8	2	2	1	.667	0-0	0	92	.854	6.97	5.25
2019	NYM	NL	18	0	8	23.2	117	34	26	22	11	0	0	2	7	0	17	2	3	1	.750	0-1	0	92	1.043	9.21	8.37
	2 ML YEARS		23	1	8	35.2	173	49	37	29	13	2	0	4	12	0	25	4	5	2	.714	0-1	0	92	.987	8.49	7.32

Rocky Gale

Bats: R **Throws:** R **Pos:** C-4;PH-1 **Ht:** 6'1" **Wt:** 185 **Born:** 2/22/1988 **Age:** 32

Year	Team	Lg	G	AB	H	2B	3B	HR	(Hm	Rd)	TB	R	RBI	RC	TBB	IBB	SO	HBP	SH	SF	SB	CS	GDP	Avg	OBP	Slg	OPS
2019	OkCity	AAA	30	100	25	4	1	2	(-	-)	37	12	14	11	7	0	24	1	0	1	1	0	2	.250	.303	.370	.673
2019	Drham	AAA	17	62	20	2	0	0	(-	-)	22	6	6	7	2	0	9	0	0	0	0	0	2	.323	.344	.355	.699
2015	SD	NL	11	10	1	0	0	0	(0	0)	1	0	0	0	0	0	1	0	0	0	0	0	1	.100	.100	.100	.200

Year	Team	Lg	G	AB	H	2B	3B	HR	(Hm	Rd)	TB	R	RBI	RC	TBB	IBB	SO	HBP	SH	SF	SB	CS	GDP	Avg	OBP	Slg	OPS
											BATTING										RUNNING			AVERAGES			
2017	SD	NL	3	10	1	0	0	1	(1	0)	4	1	2	1	0	0	2	0	0	0	0	0	0	.100	.100	.400	.500
2018	LAD	NL	3	2	0	0	0	0	(0	0)	0	0	0	0	0	0	1	0	0	0	0	0	0	.000	.000	.000	.000
2019	LAD	NL	5	15	2	0	0	0	(0	0)	2	1	0	0	0	0	7	0	0	0	0	0	1	.133	.133	.133	.267
4 ML YEARS			22	37	4	0	0	1	(1	0)	7	2	2	1	0	0	11	0	0	0	0	0	2	.108	.108	.189	.297

Cam Gallagher

Bats: R Throws: R Pos: C-44;PH-2　　　　　　　　　　　　Ht: 6'3" Wt: 230 Born: 12/6/1992 Age: 27

Year	Team	Lg	G	AB	H	2B	3B	HR	(Hm	Rd)	TB	R	RBI	RC	TBB	IBB	SO	HBP	SH	SF	SB	CS	GDP	Avg	OBP	Slg	OPS
											BATTING										RUNNING			AVERAGES			
2017	KC	AL	13	24	6	1	0	1	(0	1)	10	2	5	4	3	0	4	0	0	0	0	0	1	.250	.333	.417	.750
2018	KC	AL	22	63	13	3	0	1	(1	0)	19	5	7	5	3	0	15	1	1	1	0	0	1	.206	.250	.302	.552
2019	KC	AL	45	126	30	7	0	3	(2	1)	46	14	12	14	11	0	28	3	1	1	0	1	3	.238	.312	.365	.677
3 ML YEARS			80	213	49	11	0	5	(3	2)	75	21	24	23	17	0	47	4	2	2	0	1	5	.230	.297	.352	.649

Giovanny Gallegos

Pitches: R Bats: R Pos: RP-66　　　　　　　gah-YAY-gohss　　　　　　Ht: 6'2" Wt: 210 Born: 8/14/1991 Age: 28

Year	Team	Lg	G	GS	GF	IP	BFP	H	R	ER	HR	SH	SF	HB	TBB	IBB	SO	WP	W	L	Pct	Sv-Op	Hld	Vel	OPS	ERC	ERA
				HOW MUCH PITCHED				WHAT HE GAVE UP											THE RESULTS							
2017	NYY	AL	16	0	7	20.1	88	21	12	11	3	1	1	0	5	1	22	1	0	1	.000	0-1	0	94	.740	3.76	4.87
2018	2 Tms		6	0	4	11.1	45	11	5	5	2	1	0	0	3	0	12	0	0	0	-	1-1	0	94	.782	4.10	3.97
2019	StL	NL	66	0	10	74.0	279	44	19	19	9	0	1	3	16	2	93	3	3	2	.600	1-4	19	94	.546	1.66	2.31
18	NYY	AL	4	0	2	10.0	40	10	5	5	2	1	0	0	3	0	10	0	0	0	-	1-1	0	94	.833	4.63	4.50
18	StL	NL	2	0	2	1.1	5	1	0	0	0	0	0	0	0	0	2	0	0	0	-	0-0	0	95	.400	1.13	0.00
3 ML YEARS			88	0	21	105.2	412	76	36	35	14	2	2	3	24	3	127	4	3	3	.500	2-6	19	94	.612	2.26	2.98

Zac Gallen

Pitches: R Bats: R Pos: SP-15　　　　　　　　　　　　Ht: 6'2" Wt: 191 Born: 8/3/1995 Age: 24

Year	Team	Lg	G	GS	GF	IP	BFP	H	R	ER	HR	SH	SF	HB	TBB	IBB	SO	WP	W	L	Pct	Sv-Op	Hld	Vel	OPS	ERC	ERA
				HOW MUCH PITCHED				WHAT HE GAVE UP											THE RESULTS							
2019	NewOr	AAA	14	14	0	91.1	333	48	21	18	10	1	0	1	17	0	112	0	9	1	.900	0- -			.492	1.29	1.77
2019	2 Tms	NL	15	15	0	80.0	334	62	26	25	8	0	1	4	36	1	96	3	3	6	.333	0-0	0	93	.660	3.24	2.81
19	Mia	NL	7	7	0	36.1	151	25	12	11	3	0	0	2	18	1	43	1	1	3	.250	0-0	0	92	.603	2.83	2.72
19	Ari	NL	8	8	0	43.2	183	37	14	14	5	0	1	2	18	0	53	2	2	3	.400	0-0	0	93	.707	3.60	2.89

Joey Gallo

Bats: L Throws: R Pos: CF-38;LF-34;DH-7　　　　　　　　　　　　Ht: 6'5" Wt: 235 Born: 11/19/1993 Age: 26

Year	Team	Lg	G	AB	H	2B	3B	HR	(Hm	Rd)	TB	R	RBI	RC	TBB	IBB	SO	HBP	SH	SF	SB	CS	GDP	Avg	OBP	Slg	OPS
											BATTING										RUNNING			AVERAGES			
2015	Tex	AL	36	108	22	3	1	6	(4	2)	45	16	14	13	15	3	57	0	0	0	3	0	0	.204	.301	.417	.717
2016	Tex	AL	17	25	1	0	0	1	(1	0)	4	2	1	0	5	0	19	0	0	0	1	0	0	.040	.200	.160	.360
2017	Tex	AL	145	449	94	18	3	41	(22	19)	241	85	80	84	75	1	196	8	0	0	7	2	3	.209	.333	.537	.869
2018	Tex	AL	148	500	103	24	1	40	(23	17)	249	82	92	80	74	4	207	3	0	0	3	4	3	.206	.312	.498	.810
2019	Tex	AL	70	241	61	15	1	22	(13	9)	144	54	49	50	52	4	114	2	1	1	4	2	0	.253	.389	.598	.986
5 ML YEARS			416	1323	281	60	6	110	(63	47)	683	239	236	227	221	12	593	13	1	1	18	8	6	.212	.331	.516	.847

Isaac Galloway

Bats: R Throws: R Pos: CF-13;LF-4;PH-4;RF-2;PR-1　　　　　　　　　　　Ht: 6'2" Wt: 205 Born: 10/10/1989 Age: 30

Year	Team	Lg	G	AB	H	2B	3B	HR	(Hm	Rd)	TB	R	RBI	RC	TBB	IBB	SO	HBP	SH	SF	SB	CS	GDP	Avg	OBP	Slg	OPS
											BATTING										RUNNING			AVERAGES			
2019	NewOr	AAA	32	103	23	5	0	7	(-	-)	49	19	16	12	2	0	41	2	1	0	3	1	1	.223	.252	.476	.728
2018	Mia	NL	43	64	13	3	0	3	(0	3)	25	7	7	7	9	0	21	0	1	0	1	1	0	.203	.301	.391	.692
2019	Mia	NL	19	54	9	1	0	0	(0	0)	10	6	1	2	0	0	17	0	0	0	2	0	0	.167	.167	.185	.352
2 ML YEARS			62	118	22	4	0	3	(0	3)	35	13	8	9	9	0	38	0	1	0	3	1	0	.186	.244	.297	.541

Freddy Galvis

Bats: B Throws: R Pos: SS-110;2B-32;PH-7;DH-5　　　　　　　GAL-viss　　　　　　Ht: 5'10" Wt: 185 Born: 11/14/1989 Age: 30

Year	Team	Lg	G	AB	H	2B	3B	HR	(Hm	Rd)	TB	R	RBI	RC	TBB	IBB	SO	HBP	SH	SF	SB	CS	GDP	Avg	OBP	Slg	OPS
											BATTING										RUNNING			AVERAGES			
2012	Phi	NL	58	190	43	15	1	3	(3	0)	69	14	24	14	7	0	29	0	3	0	0	0	6	.226	.254	.363	.617
2013	Phi	NL	70	205	48	5	4	6	(4	2)	79	13	19	20	13	2	45	1	3	0	1	0	5	.234	.283	.385	.668
2014	Phi	NL	43	119	21	3	1	4	(2	2)	38	14	12	9	8	0	30	0	0	1	1	0	0	.176	.227	.319	.546
2015	Phi	NL	151	559	147	14	5	7	(6	1)	192	63	50	64	30	1	103	3	7	4	10	1	11	.263	.302	.343	.645
2016	Phi	NL	158	584	141	26	3	20	(11	9)	233	61	67	59	25	6	136	3	8	4	17	6	16	.241	.274	.399	.673
2017	Phi	NL	162	608	155	29	6	12	(10	2)	232	71	61	77	45	2	111	4	2	4	14	5	12	.255	.309	.382	.690
2018	SD	NL	162	602	149	31	5	13	(5	8)	229	62	67	65	45	2	147	2	1	6	8	6	8	.248	.299	.380	.680
2019	2 Tms	NL	147	557	145	28	1	23	(9	14)	244	67	70	69	28	1	145	1	1	2	4	2	14	.260	.296	.438	.734
19	Tor	AL	115	450	120	24	1	18	(7	11)	200	55	54	56	21	1	112	0	1	1	4	1	11	.267	.299	.444	.743
19	Cin	NL	32	107	25	4	0	5	(2	3)	44	12	16	13	7	0	33	1	0	1	0	1	3	.234	.284	.411	.696
8 ML YEARS			951	3424	849	151	26	88	(50	38)	1316	365	370	377	201	14	746	14	25	21	55	20	72	.248	.291	.384	.675

Ben Gamel

Bats: L **Throws:** L **Pos:** LF-70;PH-40;RF-23;CF-22;PR-2   **Ht:** 5'11" **Wt:** 185 **Born:** 5/17/1992 **Age:** 28

							BATTING															RUNNING			AVERAGES			
Year	Team	Lg	G	AB	H	2B	3B	HR	(Hm	Rd)	TB	R	RBI	RC	TBB	IBB	SO	HBP	SH	SF	SB	CS	GDP	Avg	OBP	Slg	OPS
2016	2 Tms	AL	33	48	9	2	0	1	(0	1)	14	9	5	4	6	0	16	0	3	0	0	0	1	.188	.278	.292	.569
2017	Sea	AL	134	509	140	27	5	11	(5	6)	210	68	59	68	36	1	122	1	1	3	4	1	8	.275	.322	.413	.735
2018	Sea	AL	101	257	70	14	4	1	(1	0)	95	37	19	38	31	1	61	4	0	1	7	3	4	.272	.358	.370	.728
2019	Mil	NL	134	311	77	18	0	7	(4	3)	116	47	33	40	40	2	104	3	0	2	2	2	0	.248	.337	.373	.710
16	NYY	AL	6	8	1	0	0	0	(0	0)	1	1	0	0	1	0	1	0	1	0	0	0	1	.125	.222	.125	.347
16	Sea	AL	27	40	8	2	0	1	(0	1)	13	8	5	4	5	0	15	0	2	0	0	0	0	.200	.289	.325	.614
4 ML YEARS			402	1125	296	61	9	20	(10	10)	435	161	116	150	113	4	303	8	4	6	13	6	13	.263	.333	.387	.720

John Gant

Pitches: R **Bats:** R **Pos:** RP-64   **Ht:** 6'3" **Wt:** 200 **Born:** 8/6/1992 **Age:** 27

			HOW MUCH PITCHED					WHAT HE GAVE UP										THE RESULTS							
Year	Team	Lg	G	GS	GF	IP	BFP	H	R	ER	HR	SH	SF	HB	TBB	IBB	SO	WP	W	L	Pct	Sv-Op	Hld	Vel	OPS	ERC	ERA
2016	Atl	NL	20	7	6	50.0	227	54	32	27	7	3	2	2	21	3	49	4	1	4	.200	0-0	0	92	.831	4.97	4.86
2017	StL	NL	7	1	1	17.1	76	17	9	9	4	0	1	1	10	1	11	0	0	1	.000	0-0	0	93	.884	6.01	4.67
2018	StL	NL	26	19	1	114.0	487	91	54	44	9	2	4	2	57	3	95	5	7	6	.538	0-0	0	93	.646	3.21	3.47
2019	StL	NL	64	0	13	66.1	269	51	29	27	4	0	0	0	34	1	60	1	11	1	.917	3-6	18	96	.639	3.09	3.66
4 ML YEARS			117	28	21	247.2	1054	213	124	107	24	5	7	5	122	8	215	10	19	12	.613	3-6	18	94	.700	3.70	3.89

Aramis Garcia

Bats: R **Throws:** R **Pos:** C-11;1B-5;PH-3   **Ht:** 6'2" **Wt:** 220 **Born:** 1/12/1993 **Age:** 27

							BATTING															RUNNING			AVERAGES			
Year	Team	Lg	G	AB	H	2B	3B	HR	(Hm	Rd)	TB	R	RBI	RC	TBB	IBB	SO	HBP	SH	SF	SB	CS	GDP	Avg	OBP	Slg	OPS
2019	Scrmto	AAA	89	332	90	20	2	16	(-	-)	162	52	55	55	34	0	114	3	1	1	0	2	11	.271	.343	.488	.831
2018	SF	NL	19	63	18	1	0	4	(2	2)	31	8	9	8	2	0	31	0	0	0	0	0	1	.286	.308	.492	.800
2019	SF	NL	18	42	6	1	0	2	(2	0)	13	5	5	2	4	1	21	0	0	0	0	0	1	.143	.217	.310	.527
2 ML YEARS			37	105	24	2	0	6	(4	2)	44	13	14	10	6	1	52	0	0	0	0	0	2	.229	.270	.419	.689

Avisail Garcia

Bats: R **Throws:** R **Pos:** RF-92;DH-24;CF-12;PH-3   ah-vee-SAH-eel   **Ht:** 6'4" **Wt:** 250 **Born:** 6/12/1991 **Age:** 29

							BATTING															RUNNING			AVERAGES			
Year	Team	Lg	G	AB	H	2B	3B	HR	(Hm	Rd)	TB	R	RBI	RC	TBB	IBB	SO	HBP	SH	SF	SB	CS	GDP	Avg	OBP	Slg	OPS
2012	Det	AL	23	47	15	0	0	0	(0	0)	15	7	3	5	3	1	10	1	0	0	0	2	1	.319	.373	.319	.692
2013	2 Tms	AL	72	244	69	7	3	7	(3	4)	103	31	31	30	9	0	59	1	0	2	3	3	8	.283	.309	.422	.731
2014	CWS	AL	46	172	42	8	0	7	(2	5)	71	19	29	20	14	1	44	2	0	2	4	1	5	.244	.305	.413	.718
2015	CWS	AL	148	553	142	17	2	13	(8	5)	202	66	59	58	36	3	141	8	0	4	7	7	13	.257	.309	.365	.675
2016	CWS	AL	120	413	101	18	2	12	(5	7)	159	59	51	56	34	0	115	4	0	2	4	4	9	.245	.307	.385	.692
2017	CWS	AL	136	518	171	27	5	18	(9	9)	262	75	80	96	33	5	111	9	0	1	5	3	14	.330	.380	.506	.885
2018	CWS	AL	93	356	84	11	2	19	(6	13)	156	47	49	38	20	2	102	4	0	5	3	1	9	.236	.281	.438	.719
2019	TB	AL	125	489	138	25	2	20	(13	7)	227	61	72	70	31	2	125	7	0	3	10	4	15	.282	.332	.464	.796
13	Det	AL	30	83	20	3	1	2	(1	1)	31	12	10	7	4	0	21	0	0	1	0	1	3	.241	.273	.373	.646
13	CWS	AL	42	161	49	4	2	5	(2	3)	72	19	21	23	5	0	38	1	0	1	3	2	5	.304	.327	.447	.775
Postseason			12	23	6	1	0	0	(0	0)	7	0	4	4	2	0	5	0	0	0	1	0	0	.261	.320	.304	.624
8 ML YEARS			763	2792	762	113	16	96	(46	50)	1195	365	374	373	180	14	707	36	0	19	36	25	74	.273	.323	.428	.751

Bryan Garcia

Pitches: R **Bats:** R **Pos:** RP-7   **Ht:** 6'1" **Wt:** 203 **Born:** 4/19/1995 **Age:** 25

			HOW MUCH PITCHED					WHAT HE GAVE UP										THE RESULTS							
Year	Team	Lg	G	GS	GF	IP	BFP	H	R	ER	HR	SH	SF	HB	TBB	IBB	SO	WP	W	L	Pct	Sv-Op	Hld	Vel	OPS	ERC	ERA
2019	Toledo	AAA	31	0	3	33.1	138	26	12	11	4	0	0	0	14	0	33	0	3	0	1.000	0- -	-	-	.677	3.09	2.97
2019	Det	AL	7	0	1	6.2	33	9	9	9	1	0	0	0	5	1	7	1	0	0	-	0-1	1	94	.924	7.88	12.15

Edgar Garcia

Pitches: R **Bats:** R **Pos:** RP-37   **Ht:** 6'1" **Wt:** 180 **Born:** 10/4/1996 **Age:** 23

			HOW MUCH PITCHED					WHAT HE GAVE UP										THE RESULTS							
Year	Team	Lg	G	GS	GF	IP	BFP	H	R	ER	HR	SH	SF	HB	TBB	IBB	SO	WP	W	L	Pct	Sv-Op	Hld	Vel	OPS	ERC	ERA
2019	LV	AAA	25	0	15	29.0	108	15	8	8	4	0	1	0	8	2	38	0	2	1	.667	8- -	-	-	.505	1.57	2.48
2019	Phi	NL	37	0	9	39.0	172	38	25	25	11	1	2	0	26	2	45	4	2	0	1.000	0-0	2	94	.906	6.55	5.77

Greg Garcia

Bats: L **Throws:** R **Pos:** 2B-74;PH-46;3B-13;SS-9;1B-1;LF-1;DH-1   **Ht:** 6'0" **Wt:** 190 **Born:** 8/8/1989 **Age:** 30

							BATTING															RUNNING			AVERAGES			
Year	Team	Lg	G	AB	H	2B	3B	HR	(Hm	Rd)	TB	R	RBI	RC	TBB	IBB	SO	HBP	SH	SF	SB	CS	GDP	Avg	OBP	Slg	OPS
2014	StL	NL	14	14	2	1	0	0	(0	0)	3	2	1	1	1	0	6	3	0	0	0	0	0	.143	.333	.214	.548
2015	StL	NL	49	75	18	5	0	2	(1	1)	29	7	4	7	10	1	12	1	1	0	0	0	2	.240	.337	.387	.724
2016	StL	NL	99	214	59	11	0	3	(0	3)	79	33	17	31	38	4	50	4	0	1	1	1	3	.276	.393	.369	.762
2017	StL	NL	133	241	61	9	2	2	(1	1)	80	27	20	30	37	0	64	6	5	1	2	1	6	.253	.365	.332	.697
2018	StL	NL	114	181	40	6	0	3	(0	3)	55	15	15	18	20	1	37	4	1	2	3	1	2	.221	.309	.304	.613
2019	StL	NL	134	311	77	13	4	4	(0	4)	110	52	31	45	53	1	83	5	1	2	0	2	4	.248	.364	.354	.718
Postseason			3	3	0	0	0	0	(0	0)	0	0	0	0	0	0	1	0	0	0	0	0	0	.000	.000	.000	.000
6 ML YEARS			543	1036	257	45	6	14	(2	12)	356	136	88	132	159	7	252	23	8	6	6	5	18	.248	.359	.344	.702

Jarlin Garcia

Pitches: L Bats: L Pos: RP-53   HAR-lin   Ht: 6'3" Wt: 215 Born: 1/18/1993 Age: 27

Year	Team	Lg	G	GS	GF	IP	BFP	H	R	ER	HR	SH	SF	HB	TBB	IBB	SO	WP	W	L	Pct	Sv-Op	Hld	Vel	OPS	ERC	ERA
2019	NewOr	AAA	7	0	4	9.1	36	6	2	2	1	0	0	0	4	0	11	0	2	0	1.000	0- -	-		.622	2.49	1.93
2017	Mia	NL	68	0	14	53.1	225	47	29	28	6	2	2	4	17	0	42	5	1	2	.333	0-1	15	94	.695	3.46	4.73
2018	Mia	NL	29	7	3	66.0	278	59	37	36	16	1	2	0	28	3	40	0	3	3	.500	0-0	2	92	.792	4.52	4.91
2019	Mia	NL	53	0	11	50.2	206	40	17	17	4	1	2	2	16	2	39	4	4	2	.667	0-1	6	93	.602	2.61	3.02
	3 ML YEARS		150	7	28	170.0	709	146	83	81	26	4	6	6	61	5	121	9	8	7	.533	0-2	23	93	.706	3.60	4.29

Leury Garcia

lay-OOH-ree

Bats: B Throws: R Pos: CF-80;RF-45;LF-24;SS-19;2B-2;PH-2;PR-2;3B-1;DH-1   Ht: 5'8" Wt: 180 Born: 3/18/1991 Age: 29

Year	Team	Lg	G	AB	H	2B	3B	HR	(Hm	Rd)	TB	R	RBI	RC	TBB	IBB	SO	HBP	SH	SF	SB	CS	GDP	Avg	OBP	Slg	OPS
2013	2 Tms	AL	45	101	20	1	1	0	(0	0)	23	10	2	4	7	0	34	0	2	1	7	2	0	.198	.248	.228	.475
2014	CWS	AL	74	145	24	3	0	1	(0	1)	30	13	6	0	5	1	48	0	4	1	11	1	6	.166	.192	.207	.399
2015	CWS	AL	18	14	3	0	0	0	(0	0)	3	0	1	2	1	0	7	0	0	0	1	0	0	.214	.267	.214	.481
2016	CWS	AL	18	48	11	1	1	1	(1	0)	17	6	5	5	1	0	13	1	0	0	2	1	0	.229	.260	.354	.614
2017	CWS	AL	87	300	81	15	2	9	(5	4)	127	41	33	39	13	0	69	8	3	2	8	5	4	.270	.316	.423	.739
2018	CWS	AL	82	258	70	7	4	4	(2	2)	97	23	32	38	9	0	69	3	4	1	12	1	2	.271	.303	.376	.679
2019	CWS	AL	140	577	161	27	3	8	(6	2)	218	93	40	60	21	0	139	6	11	3	15	5	6	.279	.310	.378	.688
13	Tex	AL	25	52	10	0	1	0	(0	0)	12	8	1	2	3	0	16	0	2	0	1	0	0	.192	.236	.231	.467
13	CWS	AL	20	49	10	1	0	0	(0	0)	11	2	1	2	4	0	18	0	0	1	6	2	0	.204	.259	.224	.484
	7 ML YEARS		464	1443	370	54	11	23	(14	9)	515	186	119	148	57	1	379	18	24	8	56	15	18	.256	.292	.357	.649

Luis Garcia

Pitches: R Bats: R Pos: RP-62; SP-2   Ht: 6'2" Wt: 240 Born: 1/30/1987 Age: 33

Year	Team	Lg	G	GS	GF	IP	BFP	H	R	ER	HR	SH	SF	HB	TBB	IBB	SO	WP	W	L	Pct	Sv-Op	Hld	Vel	OPS	ERC	ERA
2013	Phi	NL	24	0	6	31.1	138	27	15	13	3	0	0	1	23	0	23	3	1	1	.500	0-0	1	94	.764	4.85	3.73
2014	Phi	NL	13	0	5	14.0	69	14	12	10	2	1	0	0	13	0	12	4	1	0	1.000	0-0	0	95	.815	6.43	6.43
2015	Phi	NL	72	0	14	66.2	304	72	28	26	4	3	2	0	37	8	63	6	4	6	.400	2-4	16	96	.748	4.59	3.51
2016	Phi	NL	17	0	7	15.1	76	21	11	11	2	0	1	1	8	1	14	2	1	1	.500	0-1	1	97	.895	7.04	6.46
2017	Phi	NL	66	0	16	71.1	295	61	22	21	3	1	2	0	26	5	60	9	2	5	.286	2-7	14	97	.593	2.69	2.65
2018	Phi	NL	59	0	7	46.0	204	49	31	31	4	0	1	4	18	1	51	7	3	1	.750	1-4	13	97	.773	4.63	6.07
2019	LAA	AL	64	2	18	62.0	278	61	35	30	13	1	2	5	33	1	57	7	2	1	.667	1-3	6	97	.800	5.68	4.35
	7 ML YEARS		315	2	73	306.2	1364	305	154	142	31	6	8	11	158	16	280	38	14	15	.483	6-19	51	96	.741	4.56	4.17

Rico Garcia

Pitches: R Bats: R Pos: SP-1; RP-1   Ht: 5'11" Wt: 190 Born: 1/10/1994 Age: 26

Year	Team	Lg	G	GS	GF	IP	BFP	H	R	ER	HR	SH	SF	HB	TBB	IBB	SO	WP	W	L	Pct	Sv-Op	Hld	Vel	OPS	ERC	ERA
2019	Hrtfrd	AA	13	13	0	68.0	258	41	16	14	4	0	4	2	23	0	87	3	8	2	.800	0- -	-	-	.540	1.80	1.85
2019	Albq	AAA	13	13	0	61.1	284	77	52	47	14	3	3	0	28	0	51	4	2	4	.333	0- -	-	-	.910	6.81	6.90
2019	Col	NL	2	1	1	6.0	30	9	7	7	3	0	0	0	5	0	2	0	0	1	.000	0-0	0	90	1.307	13.57	10.50

Robel Garcia

Bats: B Throws: R Pos: 2B-18;PH-10;LF-5;PR-2;RF-1;DH-1   Ht: 6'0" Wt: 168 Born: 3/28/1993 Age: 27

Year	Team	Lg	G	AB	H	2B	3B	HR	(Hm	Rd)	TB	R	RBI	RC	TBB	IBB	SO	HBP	SH	SF	SB	CS	GDP	Avg	OBP	Slg	OPS
2019	Tenn	AA	22	78	23	5	0	6	(-	-)	46	12	26	17	12	0	22	1	0	1	1	1	0	.295	.391	.590	.981
2019	Iowa	AAA	76	260	73	12	2	21	(-	-)	152	51	52	54	30	1	98	4	0	2	3	3	1	.281	.361	.585	.946
2019	ChC	NL	31	72	15	2	2	5	(1	4)	36	8	11	9	7	0	35	0	0	1	0	0	2	.208	.275	.500	.775

Yimi Garcia

Pitches: R Bats: R Pos: RP-64   YIM-ee   Ht: 6'0" Wt: 225 Born: 8/18/1990 Age: 29

Year	Team	Lg	G	GS	GF	IP	BFP	H	R	ER	HR	SH	SF	HB	TBB	IBB	SO	WP	W	L	Pct	Sv-Op	Hld	Vel	OPS	ERC	ERA
2014	LAD	NL	8	0	5	10.0	36	6	2	2	2	0	0	0	1	0	9	0	0	0		0-0	1	92	.537	1.59	1.80
2015	LAD	NL	59	1	15	56.2	225	44	23	21	8	0	2	2	10	1	68	1	3	5	.375	1-6	11	93	.595	2.40	3.34
2016	LAD	NL	9	0	1	8.1	35	9	3	3	0	2	2	1	1	0	4	0	0	0		0-2	1	93	.644	3.23	3.24
2018	LAD	NL	25	0	3	22.1	101	29	18	14	7	0	0	2	4	1	19	0	1	2	.333	0-1	2	94	.957	6.74	5.64
2019	LAD	NL	64	0	22	62.1	247	40	28	25	15	1	1	6	14	2	66	1	1	4	.200	0-3	4	94	.671	2.65	3.61
	Postseason		1	0	0	1.0	4	0	0	0	0	0	0	0	1	0	3	0	0	0		0-0	0	94	.250	0.95	0.00
	5 ML YEARS		165	1	46	159.2	644	128	74	65	32	3	5	11	30	4	166	2	5	11	.313	1-12	19	94	.680	3.02	3.66

Brett Gardner

Bats: L Throws: L Pos: CF-98;LF-45;PH-3;DH-1;PR-1   Ht: 5'11" Wt: 195 Born: 8/24/1983 Age: 36

Year	Team	Lg	G	AB	H	2B	3B	HR	(Hm	Rd)	TB	R	RBI	RC	TBB	IBB	SO	HBP	SH	SF	SB	CS	GDP	Avg	OBP	Slg	OPS
2008	NYY	AL	42	127	29	5	2	0	(0	0)	38	18	16	17	8	0	30	2	3	1	13	1	0	.228	.283	.299	.582
2009	NYY	AL	108	248	67	6	6	3	(1	2)	94	48	23	38	26	0	40	3	6	1	26	5	3	.270	.345	.379	.724
2010	NYY	AL	150	477	132	20	7	5	(5	0)	181	97	47	77	79	1	101	5	5	3	47	9	6	.277	.383	.379	.762
2011	NYY	AL	159	510	132	19	8	7	(4	3)	188	87	36	77	60	1	93	8	8	2	49	13	5	.259	.345	.369	.713

Year Team	Lg	G	AB	H	2B	3B	HR	(Hm	Rd)	TB	R	RBI	RC	TBB	IBB	SO	HBP	SH	SF	SB	CS	GDP	Avg	OBP	Slg	OPS
2012 NYY	AL	16	31	10	2	0	0	(0	0)	12	7	3	7	5	0	7	0	1	0	2	2	0	.323	.417	.387	.804
2013 NYY	AL	145	539	147	33	10	8	(6	2)	224	81	52	88	52	1	127	8	7	3	24	8	8	.273	.344	.416	.759
2014 NYY	AL	148	555	142	25	8	17	(8	9)	234	87	58	81	56	0	134	6	13	6	21	5	3	.256	.327	.422	.749
2015 NYY	AL	151	571	148	26	3	16	(12	4)	228	94	66	90	68	1	135	6	8	3	20	5	8	.259	.343	.399	.742
2016 NYY	AL	148	547	143	22	6	7	(5	2)	198	80	41	77	70	0	106	8	4	5	16	4	6	.261	.351	.362	.713
2017 NYY	AL	151	594	157	26	4	21	(11	10)	254	96	63	95	72	2	122	8	5	3	23	5	4	.264	.350	.428	.778
2018 NYY	AL	140	530	125	20	7	12	(5	7)	195	95	45	70	65	0	107	5	4	5	16	2	6	.236	.322	.368	.690
2019 NYY	AL	141	491	123	26	7	28	(12	16)	247	86	74	77	52	0	108	4	0	3	10	2	6	.251	.325	.503	.829
Postseason		52	129	26	3	0	1	(1	0)	32	16	12	9	10	0	33	1	3	3	6	3	2	.202	.259	.248	.507
12 ML YEARS		1499	5220	1355	230	68	124	(69	55)	2093	876	524	794	613	6	1110	63	64	35	267	61	55	.260	.342	.401	.743

Kyle Garlick

Bats: R Throws: R Pos: PH-18;LF-12;RF-5;PR-1 **Ht: 6'1" Wt: 210 Born: 1/26/1992 Age: 28**

Year Team	Lg	G	AB	H	2B	3B	HR	(Hm	Rd)	TB	R	RBI	RC	TBB	IBB	SO	HBP	SH	SF	SB	CS	GDP	Avg	OBP	Slg	OPS
2019 OkCity	AAA	81	271	85	25	2	23	(-	-)	183	54	59	66	25	1	85	6	0	2	2	1	11	.314	.382	.675	1.057
2019 LAD	NL	30	48	12	4	0	3	(2	1)	25	8	6	7	5	1	19	0	0	0	0	0	0	.250	.321	.521	.842

Dustin Garneau

Bats: R Throws: R Pos: C-34;PH-2;1B-1 GARR-noh **Ht: 6'2" Wt: 205 Born: 8/13/1987 Age: 32**

Year Team	Lg	G	AB	H	2B	3B	HR	(Hm	Rd)	TB	R	RBI	RC	TBB	IBB	SO	HBP	SH	SF	SB	CS	GDP	Avg	OBP	Slg	OPS
2019 Salt Lk	AAA	26	83	19	8	0	6	(-	-)	45	16	13	16	11	0	28	4	0	0	0	0	6	.229	.347	.542	.889
2015 Col	NL	22	70	11	3	0	2	(0	2)	20	6	8	5	6	2	14	0	0	0	0	0	2	.157	.224	.286	.509
2016 Col	NL	24	68	16	6	0	1	(0	1)	25	7	6	6	6	0	22	0	0	1	0	0	1	.235	.293	.368	.661
2017 2 Tms		41	112	21	8	0	2	(1	1)	35	10	9	6	12	0	36	1	1	0	0	0	3	.188	.272	.313	.585
2018 CWS	AL	1	2	1	0	0	0	(0	0)	1	0	1	1	1	0	0	0	0	0	0	0	0	.500	.667	.500	1.167
2019 2 Tms		35	86	21	5	0	3	(1	2)	35	14	14	15	10	0	22	4	0	0	0	0	1	.244	.350	.407	.757
17 Col	NL	22	68	14	7	0	1	(1	0)	24	5	6	4	4	0	24	1	1	0	0	0	1	.206	.260	.353	.613
17 Oak	AL	19	44	7	1	0	1	(0	1)	11	5	3	2	8	0	12	0	0	0	0	0	2	.159	.288	.250	.538
19 LAA	AL	28	69	16	3	0	2	(1	1)	25	11	7	9	8	0	18	4	0	0	0	0	1	.232	.346	.362	.708
19 Oak	AL	7	17	5	2	0	1	(0	1)	10	3	7	6	2	0	4	0	0	0	0	0	0	.294	.368	.588	.957
5 ML YEARS		123	338	70	22	0	8	(2	6)	116	37	38	33	35	2	94	5	1	1	0	0	7	.207	.290	.343	.633

Amir Garrett

Pitches: L Bats: R Pos: RP-69 **Ht: 6'5" Wt: 228 Born: 5/3/1992 Age: 28**

	HOW MUCH PITCHED					WHAT HE GAVE UP										THE RESULTS							
Year Team	Lg	G	GS	GF	IP	BFP	H	R	ER	HR	SH	SF	HB	TBB	IBB	SO	WP	W	L	Pct	Sv-Op	Hld	Vel	OPS	ERC	ERA
2017 Cin	NL	16	14	0	70.2	321	74	60	58	23	1	3	2	40	2	63	1	3	8	.273	0-0	1	92	.937	6.86	7.39
2018 Cin	NL	66	0	7	63.0	264	56	30	30	8	1	1	3	25	3	71	3	1	2	.333	0-2	21	95	.734	3.81	4.29
2019 Cin	NL	69	0	4	56.0	246	44	22	20	7	0	0	4	35	1	78	5	5	3	.625	0-3	22	95	.695	4.19	3.21
3 ML YEARS		151	14	11	189.2	831	174	112	108	38	2	4	9	100	6	212	9	9	13	.409	0-5	44	94	.801	5.01	5.12

Reed Garrett

Pitches: R Bats: R Pos: RP-13 **Ht: 6'2" Wt: 210 Born: 1/2/1993 Age: 27**

	HOW MUCH PITCHED					WHAT HE GAVE UP										THE RESULTS							
Year Team	Lg	G	GS	GF	IP	BFP	H	R	ER	HR	SH	SF	HB	TBB	IBB	SO	WP	W	L	Pct	Sv-Op	Hld	Vel	OPS	ERC	ERA
2019 Nashv	AAA	34	0	14	40.1	183	48	23	22	4	0	2	2	19	1	40	4	1	3	.250	2--	-	-	.796	5.72	4.91
2019 Det	AL	13	0	5	15.1	77	24	15	14	3	0	0	1	13	0	10	0	0	0	-	0-1	0	96	1.144	11.60	8.22

Ryan Garton

Pitches: R Bats: R Pos: RP-2 **Ht: 5'10" Wt: 190 Born: 12/5/1989 Age: 30**

	HOW MUCH PITCHED					WHAT HE GAVE UP										THE RESULTS							
Year Team	Lg	G	GS	GF	IP	BFP	H	R	ER	HR	SH	SF	HB	TBB	IBB	SO	WP	W	L	Pct	Sv-Op	Hld	Vel	OPS	ERC	ERA
2019 Tacom	AAA	39	1	4	65.1	277	57	33	29	9	0	2	0	30	0	77	3	4	2	.667	1--	-	-	.710	3.87	3.99
2016 TB	AL	37	0	14	39.1	171	44	20	19	5	1	0	0	11	2	33	2	1	2	.333	1-1	2	92	.732	4.33	4.35
2017 2 Tms	AL	20	0	6	22.0	90	18	12	12	4	1	1	0	6	0	16	2	0	1	.000	0-1	1	93	.684	3.07	4.91
2019 Sea	AL	2	0	0	3.0	14	4	4	4	2	0	0	0	1	0	1	0	0	0	-	0-0	0	92	1.203	10.06	12.00
17 TB	AL	7	0	3	10.1	48	13	10	10	3	1	0	0	5	0	9	2	0	1	.000	0-1	0	93	.978	7.49	8.71
17 Sea	AL	13	0	3	11.2	42	5	2	2	1	0	1	0	1	0	7	0	0	0	-	0-0	1	92	.368	0.71	1.54
3 ML YEARS		59	0	20	64.1	275	66	36	35	11	2	1	0	18	2	50	4	1	3	.250	1-2	3	92	.741	4.12	4.90

Mitch Garver

Bats: R Throws: R Pos: C-82;PH-14;DH-4;1B-1 **Ht: 6'1" Wt: 220 Born: 1/15/1991 Age: 29**

Year Team	Lg	G	AB	H	2B	3B	HR	(Hm	Rd)	TB	R	RBI	RC	TBB	IBB	SO	HBP	SH	SF	SB	CS	GDP	Avg	OBP	Slg	OPS
2017 Min	AL	23	46	9	1	3	0	(0	0)	16	5	3	5	6	0	15	0	0	0	0	0	1	.196	.288	.348	.636
2018 Min	AL	103	302	81	19	2	7	(4	3)	125	38	45	45	29	2	72	2	1	1	0	0	8	.268	.335	.414	.749
2019 Min	AL	93	311	85	16	1	31	(16	15)	196	70	67	71	41	0	87	5	0	2	0	0	5	.273	.365	.630	.995
3 ML YEARS		219	659	175	36	6	38	(20	18)	337	113	115	121	76	2	174	7	1	3	0	0	14	.266	.346	.511	.858

Kevin Gausman

Pitches: R **Bats:** L **Pos:** SP-17; RP-14   GAHZ-man   **Ht:** 6'3" **Wt:** 190 **Born:** 1/6/1991 **Age:** 29

			HOW MUCH PITCHED				WHAT HE GAVE UP										THE RESULTS						
Year	Team	Lg	G	GS	GF	IP	BFP	H	R	ER	HR	SH	SF	HB	TBB	IBB	SO	WP	W	L	Pct	Sv-Op	Hld	Vel	OPS	ERC	ERA
2013	Bal	AL	20	5	3	47.2	201	51	30	30	8	2	1	0	13	2	49	4	3	5	.375	0-2	2	96	.792	4.41	5.66
2014	Bal	AL	20	20	0	113.1	476	111	48	45	7	3	7	1	38	0	88	9	7	7	.500	0-0	0	95	.685	3.52	3.57
2015	Bal	AL	25	17	1	112.1	470	109	56	53	17	2	3	2	29	1	103	7	4	7	.364	0-0	1	95	.739	3.74	4.25
2016	Bal	AL	30	30	0	179.2	757	183	76	72	28	4	3	5	47	1	174	8	9	12	.429	0-0	0	95	.742	4.13	3.61
2017	Bal	AL	34	**34**	0	186.2	816	208	99	97	29	1	3	5	71	0	179	8	11	12	.478	0-0	0	95	.808	5.24	4.68
2018	2 Tms		31	31	0	183.2	776	189	85	80	26	0	4	7	50	1	148	6	10	11	.476	0-0	0	94	.753	4.19	3.92
2019	2 Tms	NL	31	17	6	102.1	451	113	71	65	15	7	6	5	32	3	114	2	3	9	.250	0-0	2	94	.792	4.76	5.72
18	Bal	AL	21	21	0	124.0	534	139	62	61	21	0	2	5	32	0	104	6	5	8	.385	0-0	0	94	.806	4.88	4.43
18	Atl	NL	10	10	0	59.2	242	50	23	19	5	0	2	2	18	1	44	0	5	3	.625	0-0	0	94	.635	2.87	2.87
19	Atl	NL	16	16	0	80.0	360	92	60	55	12	6	6	4	27	2	85	2	3	7	.300	0-0	0	94	.814	5.14	6.19
19	Cin	NL	15	1	6	22.1	91	21	11	10	3	1	0	1	5	1	29	0	0	2	.000	0-0	2	95	.705	3.46	4.03
	Postseason		4	0	1	10.0	37	6	3	3	1	0	1	0	4	0	11	0	0	0	-	0-0	0	97	.583	2.21	2.70
	7 ML YEARS		191	154	10	925.2	3947	964	465	442	130	19	27	25	280	8	855	44	47	63	.427	0-2	5	95	.759	4.32	4.30

Sam Gaviglio

Pitches: R **Bats:** R **Pos:** RP-52   **Ht:** 6'2" **Wt:** 205 **Born:** 5/22/1990 **Age:** 30

			HOW MUCH PITCHED				WHAT HE GAVE UP										THE RESULTS						
Year	Team	Lg	G	GS	GF	IP	BFP	H	R	ER	HR	SH	SF	HB	TBB	IBB	SO	WP	W	L	Pct	Sv-Op	Hld	Vel	OPS	ERC	ERA
2017	2 Tms	AL	16	13	1	74.1	313	76	41	36	16	1	2	3	26	1	49	1	4	5	.444	0-0	0	89	.849	5.11	4.36
2018	Tor	AL	26	24	1	123.2	548	140	77	73	21	4	4	3	38	1	105	6	3	10	.231	0-0	0	88	.804	5.01	5.31
2019	Tor	AL	52	0	9	95.2	392	85	51	49	18	1	3	4	22	0	88	0	4	2	.667	0-0	3	89	.718	3.53	4.61
17	Sea	AL	12	11	1	62.1	259	63	37	32	15	1	2	2	21	1	40	1	3	5	.375	0-0	0	89	.866	5.16	4.62
17	KC	AL	4	2	0	12.0	54	13	4	4	1	0	0	1	5	0	9	0	1	0	1.000	0-0	0	89	.769	4.80	3.00
	3 ML YEARS		94	37	11	293.2	1253	301	169	158	55	6	9	11	86	2	242	7	11	17	.393	0-0	3	88	.788	4.54	4.84

Cory Gearrin

Pitches: R **Bats:** R **Pos:** RP-64; SP-2   GARE-inn   **Ht:** 6'1" **Wt:** 205 **Born:** 4/14/1986 **Age:** 34

			HOW MUCH PITCHED				WHAT HE GAVE UP										THE RESULTS						
Year	Team	Lg	G	GS	GF	IP	BFP	H	R	ER	HR	SH	SF	HB	TBB	IBB	SO	WP	W	L	Pct	Sv-Op	Hld	Vel	OPS	ERC	ERA
2011	Atl	NL	18	0	4	18.1	85	17	16	16	0	0	1	2	12	4	25	1	1	1	.500	0-1	3	90	.722	3.84	7.85
2012	Atl	NL	22	0	7	20.0	80	17	4	4	1	0	0	2	5	0	20	2	0	1	.000	0-1	4	91	.642	2.86	1.80
2013	Atl	NL	37	0	12	31.0	133	30	13	13	2	1	0	4	16	2	23	3	2	1	.667	1-3	1	88	.754	4.73	3.77
2015	SF	NL	7	0	0	3.2	13	1	2	2	0	0	0	0	1	0	5	0	0	0	-	0-0	3	93	.237	0.47	4.91
2016	SF	NL	56	0	10	48.1	197	42	24	23	4	0	2	1	14	2	45	1	3	2	.600	3-7	15	92	.650	2.89	4.28
2017	SF	NL	68	0	21	68.0	285	50	16	15	4	1	2	7	35	4	64	3	4	3	.571	0-0	8	92	.645	3.15	1.99
2018	3 Tms		62	0	12	57.1	248	56	24	24	7	1	0	6	21	1	53	4	2	1	.667	1-3	9	92	.741	4.39	3.77
2019	2 Tms	AL	66	2	8	55.1	241	55	25	25	5	0	1	4	25	1	47	4	1	3	.250	0-0	13	91	.732	4.50	4.07
18	SF	NL	35	0	8	30.0	137	33	14	14	5	1	0	3	13	1	31	0	1	1	.500	1-3	2	92	.810	5.61	4.20
18	Tex	AL	21	0	3	21.1	82	13	6	6	2	0	0	2	6	0	20	1	1	0	1.000	0-0	7	92	.540	2.02	2.53
18	Oak	AL	6	0	1	6.0	29	10	4	4	0	0	0	1	2	0	2	3	0	0	-	0-0	0	92	.987	8.08	6.00
19	Sea	AL	48	2	3	41.1	180	38	18	18	3	0	1	4	21	1	39	4	0	2	.000	0-0	11	91	.701	4.26	3.92
19	NYY	AL	18	0	5	14.0	61	17	7	7	2	0	0	0	4	0	8	0	1	1	.500	0-0	2	91	.818	5.22	4.50
	8 ML YEARS		336	2	74	302.0	1282	268	124	122	23	3	6	26	129	14	282	18	13	12	.520	5-15	56	91	.693	3.71	3.64

Scooter Gennett

Bats: L **Throws:** R **Pos:** 2B-36;PH-7   jen-ETT   **Ht:** 5'10" **Wt:** 185 **Born:** 5/1/1990 **Age:** 30

			BATTING																		RUNNING			AVERAGES			
Year	Team	Lg	G	AB	H	2B	3B	HR	(Hm	Rd)	TB	R	RBI	RC	TBB	IBB	SO	HBP	SH	SF	SB	CS	GDP	Avg	OBP	Slg	OPS
2013	Mil	NL	69	213	69	11	2	6	(0	6)	102	29	21	35	10	0	42	1	5	1	2	1	0	.324	.356	.479	.834
2014	Mil	NL	137	440	127	31	3	9	(6	3)	191	55	54	59	22	5	67	0	8	4	6	3	11	.289	.320	.434	.754
2015	Mil	NL	114	375	99	18	4	6	(5	1)	143	42	29	36	12	5	68	4	0	0	1	3	11	.264	.294	.381	.675
2016	Mil	NL	136	498	131	30	1	14	(8	6)	205	58	56	61	38	1	114	2	1	2	8	1	11	.263	.317	.412	.728
2017	Cin	NL	141	461	136	22	3	27	(16	11)	245	80	97	81	30	1	114	4	0	2	3	2	15	.295	.342	.531	.874
2018	Cin	NL	154	584	181	30	3	23	(10	13)	286	86	92	89	42	3	125	4	3	5	4	2	14	.310	.357	.490	.847
2019	2 Tms	NL	42	133	30	7	0	2	(1	1)	43	15	11	9	2	0	41	2	0	2	0	0	1	.226	.245	.323	.568
19	Cin	NL	21	69	15	3	0	0	(0	0)	18	4	5	4	1	0	20	1	0	1	0	0	0	.217	.236	.261	.497
19	SF	NL	21	64	15	4	0	2	(1	1)	25	11	6	5	1	0	21	1	0	1	0	0	1	.234	.254	.391	.644
	7 ML YEARS		793	2704	773	149	16	87	(46	41)	1215	365	360	370	156	15	571	17	17	16	24	12	63	.286	.327	.449	.776

Mike Gerber

Bats: L **Throws:** R **Pos:** LF-5;RF-5;PH-4;PR-1   **Ht:** 6'0" **Wt:** 190 **Born:** 7/8/1992 **Age:** 27

			BATTING																		RUNNING			AVERAGES			
Year	Team	Lg	G	AB	H	2B	3B	HR	(Hm	Rd)	TB	R	RBI	RC	TBB	IBB	SO	HBP	SH	SF	SB	CS	GDP	Avg	OBP	Slg	OPS
2019	Scrmto	AAA	119	464	143	41	1	26	(-	-)	264	95	83	94	39	0	140	7	0	3	5	4	10	.308	.368	.569	.937
2018	Det	AL	18	42	4	1	0	0	(0	0)	5	2	2	0	4	0	21	0	0	1	0	0	1	.095	.170	.119	.289
2019	SF	NL	12	24	1	1	0	0	(0	0)	2	0	0	0	2	0	15	0	0	0	0	0	0	.042	.115	.083	.199
	2 ML YEARS		30	66	5	2	0	0	(0	0)	7	2	2	0	6	0	36	0	0	1	0	0	1	.076	.151	.106	.257

Domingo German

Pitches: R **Bats:** R **Pos:** SP-24; RP-3 — hair-MAHN — **Ht:** 6'2" **Wt:** 175 **Born:** 8/4/1992 **Age:** 27

Year Team	Lg	G	GS	GF	IP	BFP	H	R	ER	HR	SH	SF	HB	TBB	IBB	SO	WP	W	L	Pct	Sv-Op	Hld	Vel	OPS	ERC	ERA
2017 NYY	AL	7	0	5	14.1	62	11	6	5	1	1	1	0	9	0	18	3	0	1	.000	0-0	0	96	.661	3.44	3.14
2018 NYY	AL	21	14	2	85.2	375	81	55	53	15	0	2	5	33	0	102	7	2	6	.250	0-0	0	95	.774	4.39	5.57
2019 NYY	AL	27	24	0	143.0	594	125	69	64	30	1	1	5	39	0	153	5	18	4	**.818**	0-0	0	94	.727	3.69	4.03
3 ML YEARS		55	38	7	243.0	1031	217	130	122	46	2	4	10	81	0	273	15	20	11	.645	0-0	0	94	.740	3.93	4.52

Ian Gibaut

Pitches: R **Bats:** R **Pos:** RP-10 — jih-BOH — **Ht:** 6'3" **Wt:** 250 **Born:** 11/19/1993 **Age:** 26

Year Team	Lg	G	GS	GF	IP	BFP	H	R	ER	HR	SH	SF	HB	TBB	IBB	SO	WP	W	L	Pct	Sv-Op	Hld	Vel	OPS	ERC	ERA
2019 Drham	AAA	11	1	7	10.1	49	7	4	4	0	1	0	1	10	0	16	1	1	0	1.000	4--	-	-	.591	3.91	3.48
2019 Nashv	AAA	6	0	1	5.2	28	8	5	5	0	0	0	0	4	0	6	0	0	1	.000	0--	-	-	.762	7.05	7.94
2019 2 Tms	AL	10	0	1	14.1	64	12	9	9	1	0	2	1	10	1	16	1	1	1	.500	0-0	0	95	.732	4.28	5.65
19 TB	AL	1	0	1	2.0	9	1	2	2	0	0	1	0	2	0	2	0	0	0	-	0-0	0	95	.667	2.80	9.00
19 Tex	AL	9	0	0	12.1	55	11	7	7	1	0	1	1	8	1	14	1	1	1	.500	0-0	0	95	.741	4.54	5.11

Kyle Gibson

Pitches: R **Bats:** R **Pos:** SP-29; RP-5 — **Ht:** 6'6" **Wt:** 215 **Born:** 10/23/1987 **Age:** 32

Year Team	Lg	G	GS	GF	IP	BFP	H	R	ER	HR	SH	SF	HB	TBB	IBB	SO	WP	W	L	Pct	Sv-Op	Hld	Vel	OPS	ERC	ERA
2013 Min	AL	10	10	0	51.0	238	69	38	37	7	0	2	5	20	0	29	4	2	4	.333	0-0	0	92	.874	6.98	6.53
2014 Min	AL	31	31	0	179.1	757	178	91	89	12	4	3	2	57	0	107	11	13	12	.520	0-0	0	91	.679	3.54	4.47
2015 Min	AL	32	32	0	194.2	821	186	88	83	18	6	6	7	65	6	145	7	11	11	.500	0-0	0	92	.698	3.63	3.84
2016 Min	AL	25	25	0	147.1	653	175	89	83	20	3	4	4	55	3	104	9	6	11	.353	0-0	0	91	.820	5.47	5.07
2017 Min	AL	29	29	0	158.0	693	182	93	89	24	1	2	6	60	0	121	4	12	10	.545	0-0	0	92	.826	5.53	5.07
2018 Min	AL	32	32	0	196.2	826	177	88	79	23	3	2	4	79	2	179	8	10	13	.435	0-0	0	93	.701	3.75	3.62
2019 Min	AL	34	29	0	160.0	706	175	99	86	23	3	2	7	56	0	160	8	13	7	.650	0-1	2	93	.782	4.88	4.84
7 ML YEARS		193	188	0	1087.0	4694	1142	586	546	127	20	26	35	392	11	845	51	67	68	.496	0-1	2	92	.753	4.47	4.52

Ken Giles

Pitches: R **Bats:** R **Pos:** RP-53 — **Ht:** 6'3" **Wt:** 210 **Born:** 9/20/1990 **Age:** 29

Year Team	Lg	G	GS	GF	IP	BFP	H	R	ER	HR	SH	SF	HB	TBB	IBB	SO	WP	W	L	Pct	Sv-Op	Hld	Vel	OPS	ERC	ERA
2014 Phi	NL	44	0	11	45.2	166	25	7	6	1	2	1	0	11	1	64	1	3	1	.750	1-1	13	97	.450	1.15	1.18
2015 Phi	NL	69	0	28	70.0	298	59	23	14	2	1	2	1	25	2	87	1	6	3	.667	15-20	12	97	.569	2.53	1.80
2016 Hou	AL	69	0	24	65.2	286	60	32	30	8	2	1	2	25	1	102	14	2	5	.286	15-20	18	97	.709	3.66	4.11
2017 Hou	AL	63	0	55	62.2	247	44	16	16	4	1	2	1	21	0	83	3	1	3	.250	34-38	2	98	.566	2.17	2.30
2018 2 Tms	AL	55	0	42	50.1	212	54	28	26	6	1	0	1	7	0	53	2	0	3	.000	26-26	1	97	.722	3.59	4.65
2019 Tor	AL	53	0	44	53.0	208	36	11	11	5	0	0	1	17	1	83	2	2	3	.400	23-24	0	97	.574	2.10	1.87
18 Hou	AL	34	0	24	30.2	129	36	17	17	2	0	0	0	3	0	31	1	0	2	.000	12-12	1	97	.723	3.59	4.99
18 Tor	AL	21	0	18	19.2	83	18	11	9	4	1	0	1	4	0	22	1	0	1	.000	14-14	0	97	.722	3.58	4.12
Postseason		7	0	4	7.2	40	12	10	10	3	0	0	0	5	1	10	3	0	2	.000	2-3	0	98	1.111	10.90	11.74
6 ML YEARS		353	0	204	347.1	1417	278	117	103	26	7	6	5	106	5	472	23	14	18	.438	114-129	46	97	.607	2.52	2.67

Sean Gilmartin

Pitches: L **Bats:** L **Pos:** SP-1 — **Ht:** 6'2" **Wt:** 205 **Born:** 5/8/1990 **Age:** 30

Year Team	Lg	G	GS	GF	IP	BFP	H	R	ER	HR	SH	SF	HB	TBB	IBB	SO	WP	W	L	Pct	Sv-Op	Hld	Vel	OPS	ERC	ERA
2019 Norfolk	AAA	32	3	7	66.0	270	54	32	29	8	0	1	3	23	0	74	4	3	3	.500	0--	-	-	.687	3.25	3.95
2015 NYM	NL	50	1	13	57.1	235	50	17	17	2	2	1	2	18	5	54	1	3	2	.600	0-1	2	89	.626	2.67	2.67
2016 NYM	NL	14	1	3	17.2	79	21	14	14	4	1	0	1	7	1	11	0	0	1	.000	0-0	1	88	.872	6.99	7.13
2017 NYM	NL	2	0	1	3.1	19	8	5	5	2	1	1	0	1	0	4	1	0	0	-	0-0	0	90	1.375	17.83	13.50
2018 Bal	AL	12	0	2	27.0	113	23	9	9	4	0	0	2	11	0	15	0	1	1	.500	0-0	0	88	.729	3.98	3.00
2019 Bal	AL	2	1	0	2.1	16	7	5	5	2	0	0	0	2	0	1	0	0	1	.000	0-0	0	90	1.563	29.43	19.29
Postseason		1	0	1	0.2	2	0	0	0	0	0	0	0	0	0	0	0	0	0	-	0-0	0	89	.000	0.00	0.00
5 ML YEARS		79	3	19	107.2	462	109	50	50	14	4	2	5	39	6	85	2	4	5	.444	0-1	3	89	.754	4.35	4.18

Kevin Ginkel

Pitches: R **Bats:** L **Pos:** RP-25 — **Ht:** 6'4" **Wt:** 210 **Born:** 3/24/1994 **Age:** 26

Year Team	Lg	G	GS	GF	IP	BFP	H	R	ER	HR	SH	SF	HB	TBB	IBB	SO	WP	W	L	Pct	Sv-Op	Hld	Vel	OPS	ERC	ERA
2019 Jacksn	AA	14	0	12	16.2	65	9	6	4	2	2	0	1	5	0	26	2	1	2	.333	5--	-	-	.501	1.72	2.16
2019 Reno	AAA	15	0	12	16.2	67	10	3	3	2	0	0	0	8	0	36	2	1	0	1.000	6--	-	-	.608	2.42	1.62
2019 Ari	NL	25	0	4	24.1	96	15	7	4	2	0	0	0	9	0	28	2	3	0	1.000	2-2	8	94	.532	1.91	1.48

Lucas Giolito

Pitches: R Bats: R Pos: SP-29   jee-oh-LEE-toh   Ht: 6'6" Wt: 245 Born: 7/14/1994 Age: 25

Year	Team	Lg	G	GS	GF	IP	BFP	H	R	ER	HR	SH	SF	HB	TBB	IBB	SO	WP	W	L	Pct	Sv-Op	Hld	Vel	OPS	ERC	ERA
2016	Was	NL	6	4	1	21.1	101	26	18	16	7	0	1	4	12	0	11	1	0	1	.000	0-0	0	93	.988	8.14	6.75
2017	CWS	AL	7	7	0	45.1	179	31	14	12	8	1	0	3	12	0	34	2	3	3	.500	0-0	0	92	.645	2.63	2.38
2018	CWS	AL	32	32	0	173.1	775	166	123	118	27	1	5	15	90	2	125	13	10	13	.435	0-0	0	92	.794	5.05	6.13
2019	CWS	AL	29	29	0	176.2	705	131	69	67	24	1	3	4	57	1	228	6	14	9	.609	0-0	0	94	.646	2.75	3.41
	4 ML YEARS		74	72	1	416.2	1760	354	224	213	66	3	8	23	171	3	398	22	27	26	.509	0-0	0	93	.730	3.90	4.60

Mychal Givens

Pitches: R Bats: R Pos: RP-58   michael   Ht: 6'0" Wt: 210 Born: 5/13/1990 Age: 30

Year	Team	Lg	G	GS	GF	IP	BFP	H	R	ER	HR	SH	SF	HB	TBB	IBB	SO	WP	W	L	Pct	Sv-Op	Hld	Vel	OPS	ERC	ERA
2015	Bal	AL	22	0	5	30.0	117	20	7	6	1	1	1	1	6	0	38	0	2	0	1.000	0-0	4	94	.538	1.49	1.80
2016	Bal	AL	66	0	8	74.2	313	59	28	26	6	2	1	6	36	2	96	3	8	2	.800	0-1	13	94	.664	3.44	3.13
2017	Bal	AL	69	0	8	78.2	315	57	24	24	10	0	0	5	25	1	88	2	8	1	.889	0-5	21	96	.617	2.74	2.75
2018	Bal	AL	69	0	32	76.2	317	61	37	34	4	1	3	3	30	4	79	4	0	7	.000	9-13	15	95	.622	2.72	3.99
2019	Bal	AL	58	0	33	63.0	260	49	35	32	13	0	2	2	26	1	86	5	2	6	.250	11-19	7	95	.722	3.74	4.57
	Postseason		1	0	0	2.1	6	0	0	0	0	0	0	0	0	0	3	0	0	0	-	0-0	0	96	.000	0.00	0.00
	5 ML YEARS		284	0	86	323.0	1322	246	131	122	34	4	7	17	123	8	387	14	20	16	.556	20-38	60	95	.643	2.95	3.40

Tyler Glasnow

Pitches: R Bats: L Pos: SP-12   Ht: 6'8" Wt: 230 Born: 8/23/1993 Age: 26

Year	Team	Lg	G	GS	GF	IP	BFP	H	R	ER	HR	SH	SF	HB	TBB	IBB	SO	WP	W	L	Pct	Sv-Op	Hld	Vel	OPS	ERC	ERA
2016	Pit	NL	7	4	0	23.1	105	22	13	11	2	1	0	3	13	0	24	2	0	2	.000	0-0	0	94	.774	4.80	4.24
2017	Pit	NL	15	13	0	62.0	305	81	61	53	13	4	1	2	44	2	56	3	2	7	.222	0-0	1	95	.997	8.32	7.69
2018	2 Tms		45	11	9	111.2	468	89	55	53	15	0	1	4	53	3	136	12	2	7	.222	0-0	4	97	.688	3.62	4.27
2019	TB	AL	12	12	0	60.2	230	40	13	12	4	0	1	0	14	0	76	2	6	1	.857	0-0	0	97	.509	1.63	1.78
18	PIT	NL	34	0	9	56.0	243	47	28	27	5	0	0	1	34	2	72	7	1	2	.333	0-0	4	97	.698	3.95	4.34
18	TB	AL	11	11	0	55.2	225	42	27	26	10	0	1	3	19	1	64	5	1	5	.167	0-0	0	97	.676	3.26	4.20
	4 ML YEARS		79	40	9	257.2	1108	232	142	129	34	5	3	9	124	5	292	19	10	17	.370	0-0	5	96	.739	4.20	4.51

Zack Godley

Pitches: R Bats: R Pos: RP-24; SP-9   Ht: 6'3" Wt: 240 Born: 4/21/1990 Age: 30

Year	Team	Lg	G	GS	GF	IP	BFP	H	R	ER	HR	SH	SF	HB	TBB	IBB	SO	WP	W	L	Pct	Sv-Op	Hld	Vel	OPS	ERC	ERA
2015	Ari	NL	9	6	1	36.2	150	29	13	13	4	1	1	3	17	1	34	2	5	1	.833	0-0	0	91	.688	3.67	3.19
2016	Ari	NL	27	9	1	74.2	335	86	54	53	13	7	1	4	25	4	60	5	5	4	.556	0-1	0	91	.844	5.31	6.39
2017	Ari	NL	26	25	1	155.0	627	124	61	58	15	6	2	5	53	2	165	13	8	9	.471	0-0	0	92	.657	2.92	3.37
2018	Ari	NL	33	32	0	178.1	791	177	103	94	16	8	8	12	81	2	185	17	15	11	.577	0-0	0	90	.733	4.40	4.74
2019	2 Tms		33	9	10	92.0	407	96	62	61	14	3	2	5	42	2	70	3	4	5	.444	2-2	0	90	.824	5.17	5.97
19	Ari	NL	27	9	9	76.0	338	81	55	54	12	3	2	4	35	2	58	3	3	5	.375	2-2	0	90	.834	5.35	6.39
19	Tor	AL	6	0	1	16.0	69	15	7	7	2	0	0	1	7	0	12	0	1	0	1.000	0-0	0	90	.776	4.34	3.94
	Postseason		1	0	0	5.0	22	4	3	2	0	1	0	0	2	0	5	1	0	0	-	0-0	0	90	.496	2.18	3.60
	5 ML YEARS		128	81	13	536.2	2310	512	293	279	62	25	14	29	218	11	514	40	37	30	.552	2-3	0	91	.742	4.15	4.68

Ryan Goins

Bats: L Throws: R Pos: 3B-23;SS-14;PH-11;RF-7;1B-2;PR-2;LF-1;DH-1   GO-inns   Ht: 5'10" Wt: 180 Born: 2/13/1988 Age: 32

Year	Team	Lg	G	AB	H	2B	3B	HR	(Hm Rd)	TB	R	RBI	RC	TBB	IBB	SO	HBP	SH	SF	SB	CS	GDP	Avg	OBP	Slg	OPS
2019	Charllt	AAA	83	273	88	23	2	10	(- -)	145	47	48	58	39	0	77	1	1	2	3	3	3	.322	.406	.531	.937
2013	Tor	AL	34	119	30	5	0	2	(2 0)	41	11	8	11	2	0	28	0	0	0	0	1	1	.252	.264	.345	.609
2014	Tor	AL	67	181	34	6	3	1	(1 0)	49	14	15	7	5	0	42	0	6	1	0	1	4	.188	.209	.271	.479
2015	Tor	AL	128	376	94	16	4	5	(4 1)	133	52	45	48	39	0	83	1	7	5	2	1	12	.250	.318	.354	.672
2016	Tor	AL	77	183	34	9	2	3	(1 2)	56	13	12	9	9	0	48	1	3	0	1	1	6	.186	.228	.306	.534
2017	Tor	AL	143	418	99	21	1	9	(3 6)	149	37	62	53	31	0	96	1	0	5	3	2	14	.237	.286	.356	.643
2018	KC	AL	41	115	26	8	1	0	(0 0)	36	10	6	7	4	0	29	0	1	0	0	0	2	.226	.252	.313	.565
2019	CWS	AL	52	144	36	6	1	2	(1 1)	50	13	10	16	17	1	44	1	1	0	0	1	7	.250	.333	.347	.681
	Postseason		14	41	6	1	0	1	(1 0)	10	5	5	3	2	0	14	0	3	0	0	0	2	.146	.186	.244	.430
	7 ML YEARS		542	1536	353	71	12	22	(12 10)	514	150	158	151	107	1	370	3	23	11	6	6	46	.230	.279	.335	.614

Paul Goldschmidt

Bats: R Throws: R Pos: 1B-159;PH-3   Ht: 6'3" Wt: 225 Born: 9/10/1987 Age: 32

Year	Team	Lg	G	AB	H	2B	3B	HR	(Hm Rd)	TB	R	RBI	RC	TBB	IBB	SO	HBP	SH	SF	SB	CS	GDP	Avg	OBP	Slg	OPS
2011	Ari	NL	48	156	39	9	1	8	(2 6)	74	28	26	26	20	0	53	0	0	4	4	0	4	.250	.333	.474	.808
2012	Ari	NL	145	514	147	43	1	20	(10 10)	252	82	82	86	60	4	130	4	0	9	18	3	9	.286	.359	.490	.850
2013	Ari	NL	160	602	182	36	3	36	(17 19)	332	103	125	131	99	19	145	0	0	5	15	7	25	.302	.401	.551	.952
2014	Ari	NL	109	406	122	39	1	19	(10 9)	220	75	69	83	64	10	110	2	0	3	9	3	10	.300	.396	.542	.938
2015	Ari	NL	159	567	182	38	2	33	(13 20)	323	103	110	135	118	29	151	2	0	7	21	5	16	.321	.435	.570	1.005
2016	Ari	NL	158	579	172	33	3	24	(15 9)	283	106	95	113	110	15	150	7	0	8	32	5	14	.297	.411	.489	.899
2017	Ari	NL	155	558	166	34	3	36	(20 16)	314	117	120	131	94	15	147	8	0	4	18	5	14	.297	.404	.563	.966

Year Team	Lg	G	AB	H	2B	3B	HR	(Hm Rd)	TB	R	RBI	RC	TBB	IBB	SO	HBP	SH	SF	SB	CS	GDP	Avg	OBP	Slg	OPS
2018 Ari	NL	158	593	172	35	5	33	(12 21)	316	95	83	118	90	11	173	6	0	0	7	4	7	.290	.389	.533	.922
2019 StL	NL	161	597	155	25	1	34	(17 17)	284	97	97	103	78	2	166	2	0	3	3	1	11	.260	.346	.476	.821
Postseason		8	32	10	0	0	4	(2 2)	22	6	11	7	3	0	9	1	0	0	1	0	1	.313	.389	.688	1.076
9 ML YEARS		1253	4572	1337	292	20	243	(116 127)	2398	806	807	926	733	105	1225	34	0	40	127	33	110	.292	.391	.524	.916

Yan Gomes

Bats: R Throws: R Pos: C-93;PH-4;1B-1   YAHN GOHMS   Ht: 6'2" Wt: 215 Born: 7/19/1987 Age: 32

Year Team	Lg	G	AB	H	2B	3B	HR	(Hm Rd)	TB	R	RBI	RC	TBB	IBB	SO	HBP	SH	SF	SB	CS	GDP	Avg	OBP	Slg	OPS
2012 Tor	AL	43	98	20	4	0	4	(3 1)	36	9	13	11	6	0	32	3	1	3	0	0	3	.204	.264	.367	.631
2013 Cle	AL	88	293	86	18	2	11	(6 5)	141	45	38	42	18	0	67	7	0	4	2	0	12	.294	.345	.481	.826
2014 Cle	AL	135	485	135	25	3	21	(9 12)	229	61	74	65	24	3	120	3	0	6	0	0	13	.278	.313	.472	.785
2015 Cle	AL	95	363	84	22	0	12	(5 7)	142	38	45	25	13	1	104	7	0	6	0	0	11	.231	.267	.391	.659
2016 Cle	AL	74	251	42	11	1	9	(4 5)	82	22	34	18	9	0	69	2	0	2	0	0	7	.167	.201	.327	.527
2017 Cle	AL	105	341	79	15	0	14	(5 9)	136	43	56	41	31	0	99	8	1	2	0	0	9	.232	.309	.399	.708
2018 Cle	AL	112	403	107	26	0	16	(5 11)	181	52	48	47	21	2	119	8	0	3	0	0	4	.266	.313	.449	.762
2019 Was	NL	97	314	70	16	0	12	(8 4)	122	36	43	39	38	6	84	5	0	1	2	0	7	.223	.316	.389	.704
Postseason		11	22	6	2	0	0	(0 0)	8	3	1	3	3	1	8	0	0	0	0	0	1	.273	.360	.364	.724
8 ML YEARS		749	2548	623	137	6	99	(45 54)	1069	306	351	288	160	12	694	43	2	27	4	0	66	.245	.297	.420	.717

Carlos Gomez

Bats: R Throws: R Pos: CF-22;LF-13;RF-7;PH-5;PR-2   Ht: 6'3" Wt: 220 Born: 12/4/1985 Age: 34

Year Team	Lg	G	AB	H	2B	3B	HR	(Hm Rd)	TB	R	RBI	RC	TBB	IBB	SO	HBP	SH	SF	SB	CS	GDP	Avg	OBP	Slg	OPS
2019 Syrcse	AAA	35	126	34	9	1	6	(- -)	63	16	22	20	8	0	29	4	0	2	5	5	1	.270	.329	.500	.829
2007 NYM	NL	58	125	29	3	0	2	(1 1)	38	14	12	11	8	2	27	3	0	3	12	3	6	.232	.288	.304	.592
2008 Min	AL	153	577	149	24	7	7	(3 4)	208	79	59	66	25	0	142	7	3	2	33	11	7	.258	.296	.360	.657
2009 Min	AL	137	315	72	15	5	3	(1 2)	106	51	28	33	22	0	72	4	7	1	14	7	1	.229	.287	.337	.623
2010 Mil	NL	97	291	72	11	3	5	(3 2)	104	38	24	28	17	1	72	4	6	0	18	3	10	.247	.298	.357	.655
2011 Mil	NL	94	231	52	11	3	8	(4 4)	93	37	24	25	15	0	64	2	8	2	16	2	2	.225	.276	.403	.679
2012 Mil	NL	137	415	108	19	4	19	(11 8)	192	72	51	59	20	1	98	8	6	3	37	6	6	.260	.305	.463	.768
2013 Mil	NL	147	536	152	27	10	24	(15 9)	271	80	73	81	37	2	146	10	1	6	40	7	11	.284	.338	.506	.843
2014 Mil	NL	148	574	163	34	4	23	(13 10)	274	95	73	98	47	0	141	19	1	3	34	12	10	.284	.356	.477	.833
2015 2 Tms		115	435	111	29	1	12	(6 6)	178	61	56	63	31	1	101	7	3	1	17	9	5	.255	.314	.409	.724
2016 2 Tms	AL	118	411	95	22	1	13	(8 5)	158	45	53	54	34	2	136	5	3	0	18	5	11	.231	.298	.384	.682
2017 Tex	AL	105	368	94	23	1	17	(12 5)	170	51	51	55	31	0	127	19	3	5	13	5	3	.255	.340	.462	.802
2018 TB	AL	118	360	75	15	2	9	(5 4)	121	42	32	36	25	0	103	21	2	0	12	3	6	.208	.298	.336	.634
2019 NYM	NL	34	86	17	3	0	3	(2 1)	29	10	10	11	7	0	30	3	2	1	4	1	3	.198	.278	.337	.616
15 Mil	NL	74	286	75	20	1	8	(6 2)	121	42	43	45	23	0	70	5	0	0	7	6	4	.262	.328	.423	.751
15 Hou	NL	41	149	36	9	0	4	(0 4)	57	19	13	18	8	1	31	2	3	1	10	3	1	.242	.288	.383	.670
16 Hou	AL	85	295	62	16	1	5	(2 3)	95	27	29	29	21	2	100	4	3	0	13	2	11	.210	.272	.322	.594
16 Tex	AL	33	116	33	6	0	8	(6 2)	63	18	24	25	13	0	36	1	0	0	5	3	0	.284	.362	.543	.905
Postseason		18	46	11	0	0	3	(1 2)	20	7	6	6	2	0	13	2	2	0	3	1	0	.239	.300	.435	.735
13 ML YEARS		1461	4724	1189	236	41	145	(84 61)	1942	675	546	620	319	9	1259	112	45	27	268	74	75	.252	.313	.411	.724

Jeanmar Gomez

Pitches: R Bats: R Pos: RP-16   JENN-marr   Ht: 6'3" Wt: 215 Born: 2/10/1988 Age: 32

Year Team	Lg	G	GS	GF	IP	BFP	H	R	ER	HR	SH	SF	HB	TBB	IBB	SO	WP	W	L	Pct	Sv-Op	Hld	Vel	OPS	ERC	ERA
2010 Cle	AL	11	11	0	57.2	265	73	36	30	7	0	3	2	22	3	34	1	4	5	.444	0-0	0	91	.841	5.75	4.68
2011 Cle	AL	11	10	0	58.1	259	73	31	29	6	0	2	1	15	1	31	2	5	3	.625	0-0	0	90	.804	4.99	4.47
2012 Cle	AL	20	17	1	90.2	395	95	66	60	15	2	7	4	34	5	47	2	5	8	.385	0-0	0	90	.810	4.83	5.96
2013 Pit	NL	34	6	4	80.2	333	65	35	30	6	4	6	3	28	3	53	6	3	0	1.000	0-0	0	91	.617	2.75	3.35
2014 Pit	NL	44	0	20	62.0	270	70	24	22	6	3	2	2	23	7	38	2	2	2	.500	1-1	2	91	.810	4.70	3.19
2015 Phi	NL	65	0	21	74.2	319	82	28	25	4	1	4	2	17	4	50	3	2	3	.400	0-3	7	91	.697	3.63	3.01
2016 Phi	NL	70	0	59	68.2	297	78	38	37	6	0	3	2	22	2	47	3	3	5	.375	37-43	1	91	.762	4.58	4.85
2017 Phi	NL	18	0	12	22.1	100	31	19	18	7	2	0	2	7	2	21	1	3	2	.600	2-3	0	91	1.037	8.41	7.25
2018 CWS	AL	20	0	5	25.0	114	29	15	13	3	1	3	1	10	1	27	0	0	2	.000	0-1	6	92	.809	5.16	4.68
2019 Tex	AL	16	0	1	15.1	73	23	15	14	2	0	2	1	6	0	10	2	1	0	1.000	0-0	0	91	.973	7.76	8.22
Postseason		1	0	0	4.0	17	3	2	0	0	1	0	0	2	0	0	0	0	0	-	0-0	0	92	.598	2.40	0.00
10 ML YEARS		315	46	130	555.1	2425	619	307	278	62	13	32	20	184	28	358	22	28	30	.483	40-51	19	91	.780	4.62	4.51

Tony Gonsolin

Pitches: R Bats: R Pos: SP-6; RP-5   Ht: 6'3" Wt: 205 Born: 5/14/1994 Age: 26

Year Team	Lg	G	GS	GF	IP	BFP	H	R	ER	HR	SH	SF	HB	TBB	IBB	SO	WP	W	L	Pct	Sv-Op	Hld	Vel	OPS	ERC	ERA
2019 OkCity	AAA	13	13	0	41.1	191	41	25	20	4	0	2	3	21	0	50	3	2	4	.333	0- --	-	-	.734	4.55	4.35
2019 LAD	NL	11	6	1	40.0	163	26	15	13	4	0	1	1	15	0	37	2	4	2	.667	1-1	0	94	.580	2.21	2.93

Marco Gonzales

Pitches: L **Bats:** L **Pos:** SP-34   **Ht:** 6'1" **Wt:** 195 **Born:** 2/16/1992 **Age:** 28

Year	Team	Lg	G	GS	GF	IP	BFP	H	R	ER	HR	SH	SF	HB	TBB	IBB	SO	WP	W	L	Pct	Sv-Op	Hld	Vel	OPS	ERC	ERA
2014	StL	NL	10	5	0	34.2	156	32	16	16	4	0	1	1	21	1	31	0	4	2	.667	0-0	1	90	.737	4.59	4.15
2015	StL	NL	1	1	0	2.2	16	7	4	4	1	0	1	0	1	0	1	0	0	0	-	0-0	0	89	1.286	17.70	13.50
2017	2 Tms		11	8	1	40.0	185	59	27	27	8	0	1	1	11	0	32	2	1	1	.500	0-0	0	92	.924	7.40	6.08
2018	Sea	AL	29	29	0	166.2	686	172	76	74	17	1	4	6	32	0	145	2	13	9	.591	0-0	0	90	.720	3.65	4.00
2019	Sea	AL	34	**34**	0	203.0	866	210	106	90	23	1	**9**	6	56	1	147	2	16	13	.552	0-0	0	89	.736	3.96	3.99
17	StL	NL	1	1	0	3.1	16	6	5	5	3	0	0	0	0	0	2	0	0	0	-	0-0	0	91	1.500	13.65	13.50
17	Sea	AL	10	7	1	36.2	169	53	22	22	5	0	1	1	11	0	30	2	1	1	.500	0-0	0	92	.865	6.82	5.40
	Postseason		6	0	0	6.0	24	4	3	3	0	1	0	0	2	0	4	0	2	1	.667	0-1	0	91	.451	1.57	4.50
	5 ML YEARS		85	77	1	447.0	1909	480	229	211	53	2	16	14	121	2	356	6	34	25	.576	0-0	1	90	.754	4.24	4.25

Carlos Gonzalez

Bats: L **Throws:** L **Pos:** LF-20;RF-17;DH-9;PH-2   **Ht:** 6'1" **Wt:** 220 **Born:** 10/17/1985 **Age:** 34

Year	Team	Lg	G	AB	H	2B	3B	HR	(Hm	Rd)	TB	R	RBI	RC	TBB	IBB	SO	HBP	SH	SF	SB	CS	GDP	Avg	OBP	Slg	OPS
2008	Oak	AL	85	302	73	22	1	4	(3	1)	109	31	26	30	13	1	81	0	1	7	4	1	7	.242	.273	.361	.634
2009	Col	NL	89	278	79	14	7	13	(7	6)	146	53	29	42	28	3	70	3	5	3	16	4	3	.284	.353	.525	.878
2010	Col	NL	145	587	**197**	34	9	34	(26	8)	**351**	111	117	118	40	8	135	2	0	7	26	8	9	**.336**	.376	.598	.974
2011	Col	NL	127	481	142	27	3	26	(16	10)	253	92	92	95	48	8	105	7	0	6	20	5	11	.295	.363	.526	.889
2012	Col	NL	135	518	157	31	5	22	(13	9)	264	89	85	88	56	11	115	2	0	3	20	5	11	.303	.371	.510	.881
2013	Col	NL	110	391	118	23	6	26	(12	14)	231	72	70	69	41	2	118	1	0	3	21	3	7	.302	.367	.591	.958
2014	Col	NL	70	260	62	15	1	11	(5	6)	112	35	38	32	19	2	70	1	0	1	3	0	7	.238	.292	.431	.723
2015	Col	NL	153	554	150	25	2	40	(24	16)	299	87	97	94	46	6	133	1	1	6	2	0	11	.271	.325	.540	.864
2016	Col	NL	150	584	174	42	2	25	(18	7)	295	87	100	99	46	6	129	1	0	1	2	2	10	.298	.350	.505	.855
2017	Col	NL	136	470	123	34	0	14	(8	6)	199	72	57	58	56	3	119	2	0	6	3	0	9	.262	.339	.423	.762
2018	Col	NL	132	463	128	32	4	16	(10	6)	216	71	64	68	37	4	113	1	0	3	5	2	5	.276	.329	.467	.796
2019	2 Tms		45	145	29	3	0	3	(1	2)	41	21	10	8	18	1	52	1	0	2	0	3	3	.200	.289	.283	.572
19	Cle	AL	30	105	22	1	0	2	(0	2)	29	13	7	6	10	0	33	1	0	1	0	1	2	.210	.282	.276	.558
19	ChC	NL	15	40	7	2	0	1	(1	0)	12	8	3	2	8	1	19	0	0	1	0	2	1	.175	.306	.300	.606
	Postseason		9	34	14	2	1	1	(1	0)	21	5	2	6	4	0	7	0	0	0	2	1	0	.412	.474	.618	1.091
	12 ML YEARS		1377	5033	1432	302	40	234	(143	91)	2516	821	785	801	448	55	1240	22	7	41	122	33	93	.285	.343	.500	.843

Chi Chi Gonzalez

Pitches: R **Bats:** R **Pos:** SP-12; RP-2   **Ht:** 6'3" **Wt:** 215 **Born:** 1/15/1992 **Age:** 28

Year	Team	Lg	G	GS	GF	IP	BFP	H	R	ER	HR	SH	SF	HB	TBB	IBB	SO	WP	W	L	Pct	Sv-Op	Hld	Vel	OPS	ERC	ERA
2019	Albq	AAA	16	15	0	87.0	396	105	64	59	15	2	2	6	36	0	76	3	4	5	.444	0--	-	-	.862	6.25	6.10
2015	Tex	AL	14	10	1	67.0	280	49	33	29	6	1	2	3	32	1	30	2	4	6	.400	0-0	0	91	.632	3.00	3.90
2016	Tex	AL	3	3	0	10.1	62	21	13	10	1	0	1	0	9	0	7	0	0	2	.000	0-0	0	91	.984	12.48	8.71
2019	Col	NL	14	12	0	63.0	278	59	39	37	11	3	1	1	33	0	46	1	2	6	.250	0-0	0	92	.784	4.78	5.29
	Postseason		1	0	0	1.2	8	2	1	1	1	0	0	0	2	0	0	0	0	0	-	0-0	0	93	1.333	15.09	5.40
	3 ML YEARS		31	25	1	140.1	620	129	85	76	18	4	4	4	74	1	83	3	6	14	.300	0-0	0	92	.735	4.39	4.87

Erik Gonzalez

Bats: R **Throws:** R **Pos:** SS-26;3B-16;PH-5;LF-4;PR-4;CF-1   **Ht:** 6'3" **Wt:** 205 **Born:** 8/31/1991 **Age:** 28

Year	Team	Lg	G	AB	H	2B	3B	HR	(Hm	Rd)	TB	R	RBI	RC	TBB	IBB	SO	HBP	SH	SF	SB	CS	GDP	Avg	OBP	Slg	OPS
2019	Indy	AAA	20	78	15	3	1	1	(-	-)	23	6	10	4	3	0	29	0	0	0	1	1	1	.192	.222	.295	.517
2016	Cle	AL	21	16	5	0	0	0	(0	0)	5	2	0	1	1	0	8	0	0	0	0	1	0	.313	.353	.313	.665
2017	Cle	AL	60	110	28	6	0	4	(1	3)	46	18	11	9	3	0	37	0	1	1	1	2	1	.255	.272	.418	.690
2018	Cle	AL	81	136	36	10	1	1	(1	0)	51	17	16	14	5	0	34	2	0	0	3	0	0	.265	.301	.375	.676
2019	Pit	NL	53	142	36	4	1	1	(1	0)	45	15	6	7	9	3	37	1	3	1	4	1	5	.254	.301	.317	.618
	Postseason		2	2	0	0	0	0	(0	0)	0	0	0	0	0	0	0	0	0	0	0	0	0	.000	.000	.000	.000
	4 ML YEARS		215	404	105	20	2	6	(2	4)	147	52	33	31	18	3	116	3	4	2	8	4	6	.260	.295	.364	.659

Gio Gonzalez

Pitches: L **Bats:** R **Pos:** SP-17; RP-2   JEE-oh   **Ht:** 6'0" **Wt:** 205 **Born:** 9/19/1985 **Age:** 34

Year	Team	Lg	G	GS	GF	IP	BFP	H	R	ER	HR	SH	SF	HB	TBB	IBB	SO	WP	W	L	Pct	Sv-Op	Hld	Vel	OPS	ERC	ERA
2008	Oak	AL	10	7	3	34.0	163	32	34	29	9	2	1	3	25	1	34	1	1	4	.200	0-0	0	90	.911	6.54	7.68
2009	Oak	AL	20	17	0	98.2	455	113	68	63	14	2	3	1	56	2	109	2	6	7	.462	0-0	0	92	.846	5.96	5.75
2010	Oak	AL	33	33	0	200.2	851	171	75	72	15	5	2	4	92	1	171	4	15	9	.625	0-0	0	92	.644	3.39	3.23
2011	Oak	AL	32	32	0	202.0	864	175	81	70	17	3	2	8	**91**	1	197	6	16	12	.571	0-0	0	92	.654	3.56	3.12
2012	Was	NL	32	32	0	199.1	822	149	69	64	9	9	7	5	76	3	207	10	**21**	8	.724	0-0	0	93	.582	2.37	2.89
2013	Was	NL	32	32	0	195.2	819	169	79	73	17	7	1	2	76	1	192	4	11	8	.579	0-0	0	93	.668	3.23	3.36
2014	Was	NL	27	27	0	158.2	653	134	66	63	10	7	4	3	56	0	162	2	10	10	.500	0-0	0	92	.647	2.91	3.57
2015	Was	NL	31	31	0	175.2	758	181	79	74	8	3	**9**	4	69	3	169	4	11	8	.579	0-0	0	92	.711	3.92	3.79
2016	Was	NL	32	32	0	177.1	765	179	98	90	19	8	5	9	59	2	171	7	11	11	.500	0-0	0	91	.730	4.08	4.57
2017	Was	NL	32	32	0	201.0	827	158	69	66	21	7	3	7	**79**	5	188	7	15	9	.625	0-0	0	90	.642	3.05	2.96
2018	2 Tms	NL	32	32	0	171.0	746	167	84	80	17	3	**9**	2	80	2	148	5	10	11	.476	0-0	0	90	.734	4.23	4.21
2019	Mil	NL	19	17	0	87.1	366	76	36	34	9	4	0	0	37	0	78	5	3	2	.600	0-0	0	89	.709	3.50	3.50
18	Was	NL	27	27	0	145.2	646	153	77	74	15	3	8	2	70	2	126	4	7	11	.389	0-0	0	90	.769	4.75	4.57
18	Mil	NL	5	5	0	25.1	100	14	7	6	2	0	1	0	10	0	22	1	3	0	1.000	0-0	0	92	.510	1.67	2.13
	Postseason		8	8	0	29.1	131	23	18	16	4	1	1	0	21	0	27	4	0	0	-	0-0	0	92	.739	4.48	4.91
	12 ML YEARS		332	324	3	1901.1	8089	1704	838	778	165	60	46	48	796	21	1826	57	130	99	.568	0-0	0	92	.683	3.57	3.68

Marwin Gonzalez

MARR-win

Bats: B **Throws:** R **Pos:** RF-44;3B-40;1B-21;LF-18;PH-4;DH-3;2B-2;SS-1   **Ht:** 6'1" **Wt:** 205 **Born:** 3/14/1989 **Age:** 31

							BATTING													RUNNING			AVERAGES			
Year	Team	Lg	G	AB	H	2B	3B	HR	(Hm | Rd)	TB	R	RBI	RC	TBB	IBB	SO	HBP	SH	SF	SB	CS	GDP	Avg	OBP	Slg	OPS
2012	Hou	NL	80	205	48	13	0	2	(1 | 1)	67	21	12	12	13	0	29	0	1	0	3	3	9	.234	.280	.327	.607
2013	Hou	AL	72	204	45	8	0	4	(2 | 2)	65	22	14	10	9	0	37	0	8	1	6	2	5	.221	.252	.319	.571
2014	Hou	AL	103	285	79	15	1	6	(3 | 3)	114	33	23	26	17	0	58	4	4	0	2	4	6	.277	.327	.400	.727
2015	Hou	AL	120	344	96	18	1	12	(6 | 6)	152	44	34	39	16	0	74	3	7	0	4	5	9	.279	.317	.442	.759
2016	Hou	AL	141	484	123	26	3	13	(8 | 5)	194	55	51	47	22	1	118	5	6	1	12	6	16	.254	.293	.401	.694
2017	Hou	AL	134	455	138	34	0	23	(15 | 8)	241	67	90	93	49	4	99	6	3	2	8	3	8	.303	.377	.530	.907
2018	Hou	AL	145	489	121	25	3	16	(5 | 11)	200	61	68	61	53	3	126	4	5	2	2	3	14	.247	.324	.409	.733
2019	Min	AL	114	425	112	19	0	15	(5 | 10)	176	52	55	58	31	2	98	6	0	1	0	1	7	.264	.322	.414	.736
	Postseason		30	97	22	6	0	3	(1 | 2)	37	10	13	8	7	2	26	4	0	0	0	2	1	.227	.306	.381	.687
	8 ML YEARS		909	2891	762	158	8	91	(50 | 41)	1209	355	347	346	210	10	639	27	34	7	38	26	74	.264	.319	.418	.737

Niko Goodrum

Bats: B **Throws:** R **Pos:** SS-38;2B-22;LF-20;1B-18;CF-8;RF-5;DH-4;PH-3;3B-1   **Ht:** 6'3" **Wt:** 218 **Born:** 2/28/1992 **Age:** 28

							BATTING													RUNNING			AVERAGES			
Year	Team	Lg	G	AB	H	2B	3B	HR	(Hm	Rd)	TB	R	RBI	RC	TBB	IBB	SO	HBP	SH	SF	SB	CS	GDP	Avg	OBP	Slg	OPS
2017	Min	AL	11	17	1	0	0	0	(0	0)	1	1	0	0	1	0	10	0	0	0	0	0	0	.059	.111	.059	.170
2018	Det	AL	131	444	109	29	3	16	(8	8)	192	55	53	63	42	1	132	4	0	2	12	4	9	.245	.315	.432	.747
2019	Det	AL	112	423	105	27	5	12	(4	8)	178	61	45	50	46	1	138	1	0	2	12	3	7	.248	.322	.421	.743
	3 ML YEARS		254	884	215	56	8	28	(12	16)	371	117	98	113	89	2	280	5	0	4	24	7	16	.243	.315	.420	.734

Brian Goodwin

Bats: L **Throws:** R **Pos:** LF-68;CF-39;PH-21;RF-17;PR-3;DH-2   **Ht:** 6'0" **Wt:** 200 **Born:** 11/2/1990 **Age:** 29

							BATTING													RUNNING			AVERAGES			
Year	Team	Lg	G	AB	H	2B	3B	HR	(Hm	Rd)	TB	R	RBI	RC	TBB	IBB	SO	HBP	SH	SF	SB	CS	GDP	Avg	OBP	Slg	OPS
2016	Was	NL	22	42	12	4	1	0	(0	0)	18	1	5	6	2	0	14	0	0	0	0	0	1	.286	.318	.429	.747
2017	Was	NL	74	251	63	21	1	13	(9	4)	125	41	30	31	23	2	69	1	0	3	6	0	3	.251	.313	.498	.811
2018	2 Tms		75	159	38	6	2	4	(2	4)	62	20	25	27	16	0	57	3	1	1	4	2	0	.239	.318	.390	.708
2019	LAA	AL	136	413	108	29	3	17	(10	7)	194	65	47	57	38	2	129	3	1	3	7	3	3	.262	.326	.470	.796
18	Was	NL	48	65	13	1	0	3	(1	2)	23	9	12	10	10	0	26	2	1	1	3	1	0	.200	.321	.354	.674
18	KC		27	94	25	5	0	3	(1	2)	39	11	13	17	6	0	31	1	0	0	1	1	0	.266	.317	.415	.732
	Postseason		1	0	0	0	0	0	(0	0)	0	0	0	0	0	0	0	0	0	0	0	0	0	-	-	-	-
	4 ML YEARS		307	865	221	60	5	36	(21	15)	399	127	107	121	79	4	269	7	2	7	17	5	7	.255	.320	.461	.782

Nick Goody

Pitches: R **Bats:** R **Pos:** RP-39   **Ht:** 5'11" **Wt:** 200 **Born:** 7/6/1991 **Age:** 28

			HOW MUCH PITCHED					WHAT HE GAVE UP											THE RESULTS						
Year	Team	Lg	G	GS	GF	IP	BFP	H	R	ER	HR	SH	SF	HB	TBB	IBB	SO	WP	W	L	Pct	Sv-Op	Hld	Vel	OPS	ERC	ERA
2019	Clmbs	AAA	21	0	6	24.1	115	28	23	21	8	1	1	2	13	1	34	3	0	1	.000	0- -	-	-	.979	7.55	7.77
2015	NYY	AL	7	0	5	5.2	26	6	3	3	0	0	0	1	3	0	3	0	0	0	-	0-0	0	91	.794	4.90	4.76
2016	NYY	AL	27	0	10	29.0	128	30	15	15	7	1	1	1	12	1	34	0	0	0	-	0-0	0	91	.878	5.42	4.66
2017	Cle	AL	56	0	14	54.2	221	39	20	17	7	1	0	3	20	2	72	4	1	2	.333	0-0	6	92	.632	2.78	2.80
2018	Cle	AL	12	0	1	11.2	58	15	9	9	4	0	0	1	5	1	12	1	0	2	.000	0-1	2	91	1.016	7.63	6.94
2019	Cle	AL	39	0	6	40.2	173	30	18	16	7	0	2	0	22	1	50	0	3	2	.600	0-0	10	93	.690	3.59	3.54
	5 ML YEARS		141	0	36	141.2	606	120	65	60	25	2	3	6	62	5	171	5	4	6	.400	0-1	18	92	.745	3.98	3.81

Alex Gordon

Bats: L **Throws:** R **Pos:** LF-146;DH-2;PH-2   **Ht:** 6'1" **Wt:** 225 **Born:** 2/10/1984 **Age:** 36

							BATTING													RUNNING			AVERAGES			
Year	Team	Lg	G	AB	H	2B	3B	HR	(Hm	Rd)	TB	R	RBI	RC	TBB	IBB	SO	HBP	SH	SF	SB	CS	GDP	Avg	OBP	Slg	OPS
2007	KC	AL	151	543	134	36	4	15	(8	7)	223	60	60	69	41	4	137	13	1	2	14	4	12	.247	.314	.411	.725
2008	KC	AL	134	493	128	35	1	16	(9	7)	213	72	59	71	66	5	120	6	1	5	9	2	8	.260	.351	.432	.783
2009	KC	AL	49	164	38	6	0	6	(2	4)	62	28	22	16	21	0	43	2	1	1	5	0	5	.232	.324	.378	.703
2010	KC	AL	74	242	52	10	0	8	(5	3)	86	34	20	23	34	1	62	2	2	1	1	5	9	.215	.315	.355	.671
2011	KC	AL	151	611	185	45	4	23	(12	11)	307	101	87	103	67	2	139	7	0	3	17	8	9	.303	.376	.502	.879
2012	KC	AL	161	642	189	51	5	14	(6	8)	292	93	72	94	73	3	140	3	0	3	10	5	14	.294	.368	.455	.822
2013	KC	AL	156	633	168	27	6	20	(10	10)	267	90	81	90	52	7	141	9	0	6	11	3	4	.265	.327	.422	.749
2014	KC	AL	156	563	150	34	1	19	(11	8)	243	87	74	95	65	5	126	11	0	4	12	3	11	.266	.351	.432	.783
2015	KC	AL	104	354	96	18	0	13	(4	9)	153	40	48	60	49	7	92	14	0	5	2	5	2	.271	.377	.432	.809
2016	KC	AL	128	445	98	16	2	17	(8	9)	169	62	40	48	52	3	148	8	0	1	8	1	9	.220	.312	.380	.692
2017	KC	AL	148	476	99	20	2	9	(6	3)	150	52	45	45	45	3	126	14	2	4	7	4	7	.208	.293	.315	.608
2018	KC	AL	141	506	124	24	0	13	(2	11)	187	56	54	66	50	4	124	10	0	2	12	2	7	.245	.324	.370	.694
2019	KC	AL	150	556	148	31	1	13	(5	8)	220	77	76	81	51	4	100	19	1	6	5	3	13	.266	.345	.396	.741
	Postseason		31	108	24	10	0	3	(1	2)	43	17	17	13	14	2	30	4	0	0	4	0	3	.222	.333	.398	.731
	13 ML YEARS		1703	6228	1609	353	26	186	(85	101)	2572	852	738	861	666	48	1498	118	8	43	113	45	110	.258	.339	.413	.752

Dee Gordon

Bats: L Throws: R Pos: 2B-111;PR-5;PH-4;SS-2;DH-1   Ht: 5'11" Wt: 170 Born: 4/22/1988 Age: 32

Year	Team	Lg	G	AB	H	2B	3B	HR	(Hm	Rd)	TB	R	RBI	RC	TBB	IBB	SO	HBP	SH	SF	SB	CS	GDP	Avg	OBP	Slg	OPS
2011	LAD	NL	56	224	68	9	2	0	(0	0)	81	34	11	25	7	0	27	0	2	0	24	7	1	.304	.325	.362	.686
2012	LAD	NL	87	303	69	9	2	1	(0	1)	85	38	17	22	20	0	62	3	2	2	32	10	5	.228	.280	.281	.561
2013	LAD	NL	38	94	22	1	1	1	(0	0)	28	9	6	9	10	2	21	1	1	0	10	2	0	.234	.314	.298	.612
2014	LAD	NL	148	609	176	24	12	2	(2	0)	230	92	34	76	31	0	107	4	3	3	64	19	3	.289	.326	.378	.704
2015	Mia	NL	145	615	205	24	8	4	(2	2)	257	88	46	94	25	2	91	2	6	5	58	20	6	.333	.359	.418	.776
2016	Mia	NL	79	325	87	7	6	1	(1	0)	109	47	14	33	18	1	55	0	1	1	30	7	4	.268	.305	.335	.641
2017	Mia	NL	158	653	201	20	9	2	(0	2)	245	114	33	81	25	0	93	10	2	4	60	16	7	.308	.341	.375	.716
2018	Sea	AL	141	556	149	17	8	4	(2	2)	194	62	36	50	9	0	80	9	9	5	30	12	10	.268	.288	.349	.637
2019	Sea	AL	117	393	108	12	6	3	(0	3)	141	36	34	51	18	1	61	1	3	6	22	5	8	.275	.304	.359	.663
	Postseason		6	17	3	0	0	0	(0	0)	3	0	2	0	2	0	6	0	0	0	1	1	1	.176	.263	.176	.440
	9 ML YEARS		969	3772	1085	123	54	18	(8	10)	1370	520	231	441	163	6	597	30	29	26	330	98	44	.288	.320	.363	.683

MacKenzie Gore

Pitches: L Bats: L Pos: P   Ht: 6'3" Wt: 195 Born: 2/24/1999 Age: 21

			HOW MUCH PITCHED				WHAT HE GAVE UP										THE RESULTS							
Year	Team	Lg	G	GS	GF	IP	BFP	H	R	ER	HR	SH	SF	HB	TBB	IBB	SO	WP	W	L	Pct	Sv-Op	Hld	Vel	OPS	ERC	ERA
2017	Padres	R	7	7	0	21.1	84	14	5	3	0	0	0	1	7	0	34	1	0	1	.000	0- -	-	-	.499	1.67	1.27
2018	FtWyn	A	16	16	0	60.2	261	61	35	30	5	0	2	5	18	0	74	9	2	5	.286	0- -	-	-	.698	3.89	4.45
2019	Lk Els	A+	15	15	0	79.1	288	36	9	9	4	1	3	2	20	0	110	4	7	1	.875	0- -	-	-	.420	1.07	1.02
2019	Amrillo	AA	5	5	0	21.2	90	20	10	10	3	0	1	1	8	0	25	2	2	1	.667	0- -	-	-	.735	4.09	4.15

Terrance Gore

Bats: R Throws: R Pos: PR-16;RF-10;LF-9;CF-4;DH-2;PH-2   Ht: 5'7" Wt: 165 Born: 6/8/1991 Age: 29

Year	Team	Lg	G	AB	H	2B	3B	HR	(Hm	Rd)	TB	R	RBI	RC	TBB	IBB	SO	HBP	SH	SF	SB	CS	GDP	Avg	OBP	Slg	OPS
2019	S-WB	AAA	21	55	9	3	1	0	(-	-)	14	8	1	6	12	0	17	1	1	0	3	0	0	.164	.324	.255	.578
2014	KC	AL	11	1	0	0	0	0	(0	0)	0	5	0	1	0	0	0	1	0	0	5	0	0	.000	.500	.000	.500
2015	KC	AL	9	3	0	0	0	0	(0	0)	0	1	0	0	0	0	1	1	0	0	3	0	0	.000	.250	.000	.250
2016	KC	AL	17	3	0	0	0	0	(0	0)	0	6	0	0	0	0	1	0	0	0	11	2	0	.000	.000	.000	.000
2017	KC	AL	12	4	0	0	0	0	(0	0)	0	2	0	0	1	0	2	0	0	0	2	2	0	.000	.200	.000	.200
2018	ChC	NL	14	5	1	0	0	0	(0	0)	1	5	0	1	0	0	1	0	0	0	6	0	0	.200	.200	.200	.400
2019	KC	AL	37	51	14	2	1	0	(0	0)	18	13	1	8	6	0	18	1	0	0	13	5	0	.275	.362	.353	.715
	Postseason		9	2	0	0	0	0	(0	0)	0	3	0	0	0	0	2	0	0	0	5	1	0	.000	.000	.000	.000
	6 ML YEARS		100	67	15	2	1	0	(0	0)	19	32	1	10	7	0	23	3	0	0	40	9	0	.224	.325	.284	.608

Phil Gosselin

Bats: R Throws: R Pos: PH-35;LF-6;SS-5;3B-1   GAHSS-eh-lin   Ht: 6'1" Wt: 200 Born: 10/3/1988 Age: 31

Year	Team	Lg	G	AB	H	2B	3B	HR	(Hm	Rd)	TB	R	RBI	RC	TBB	IBB	SO	HBP	SH	SF	SB	CS	GDP	Avg	OBP	Slg	OPS
2019	LV	AAA	78	296	93	20	5	8	(-	-)	147	54	47	61	46	0	61	3	2	6	3	2	2	.314	.405	.497	.901
2013	Atl	NL	4	6	2	0	0	0	(0	0)	2	2	0	1	1	1	2	0	0	0	0	0	0	.333	.429	.333	.762
2014	Atl	NL	46	128	34	4	0	1	(1	0)	41	17	3	10	5	0	27	2	1	0	2	2	1	.266	.304	.320	.624
2015	2 Tms		44	106	33	9	1	3	(2	1)	53	19	15	22	9	0	16	2	0	1	2	1	2	.311	.373	.500	.873
2016	Ari	NL	122	220	61	12	1	2	(1	1)	81	26	13	24	15	0	46	1	2	2	3	0	0	.277	.324	.368	.692
2017	2 Tms		40	48	7	2	0	0	(0	0)	9	3	2	0	2	0	12	0	0	1	0	1	1	.146	.180	.188	.368
2018	Cin	NL	20	24	3	0	0	1	(1	0)	6	5	2	2	4	1	8	0	0	0	0	0	1	.125	.250	.250	.500
2019	Phi	NL	44	65	17	3	0	0	(0	0)	20	5	7	8	3	0	16	0	0	0	0	0	1	.262	.294	.308	.602
15	Atl	NL	20	40	13	4	0	0	(0	0)	17	2	2	6	2	0	5	0	0	0	2	0	0	.325	.357	.425	.782
15	Ari	NL	24	66	20	5	1	3	(2	1)	36	17	13	16	7	0	11	2	0	1	0	1	2	.303	.382	.545	.927
17	Pit	NL	28	40	6	1	0	0	(0	0)	7	3	2	0	2	0	9	0	0	0	0	0	1	.150	.190	.175	.365
17	Tex	AL	12	8	1	1	0	0	(0	0)	2	0	0	0	0	0	3	0	0	0	0	0	0	.125	.125	.250	.375
	7 ML YEARS		320	597	157	30	2	7	(5	2)	212	77	42	67	39	2	127	5	3	3	7	4	6	.263	.312	.355	.667

Daniel Gossett

Pitches: R Bats: R Pos: P   Ht: 6'2" Wt: 185 Born: 11/13/1992 Age: 27

			HOW MUCH PITCHED				WHAT HE GAVE UP										THE RESULTS							
Year	Team	Lg	G	GS	GF	IP	BFP	H	R	ER	HR	SH	SF	HB	TBB	IBB	SO	WP	W	L	Pct	Sv-Op	Hld	Vel	OPS	ERC	ERA
2017	Oak	AL	18	18	0	91.1	414	116	67	62	21	2	2	0	31	0	72	10	4	11	.267	0-0	0	91	.906	6.38	6.11
2018	Oak	AL	5	5	0	24.1	102	25	14	14	5	0	0	1	8	0	12	1	0	3	.000	0-0	0	93	.828	5.01	5.18
	2 ML YEARS		23	23	0	115.2	516	141	81	76	26	2	2	1	39	0	84	11	4	14	.222	0-0	0	92	.890	6.08	5.91

Trevor Gott

Pitches: R Bats: R Pos: RP-50   Ht: 6'0" Wt: 185 Born: 8/26/1992 Age: 27

			HOW MUCH PITCHED				WHAT HE GAVE UP										THE RESULTS							
Year	Team	Lg	G	GS	GF	IP	BFP	H	R	ER	HR	SH	SF	HB	TBB	IBB	SO	WP	W	L	Pct	Sv-Op	Hld	Vel	OPS	ERC	ERA
2015	LAA	AL	48	0	7	47.2	202	43	18	16	2	2	3	3	16	3	27	1	4	2	.667	0-4	14	96	.625	3.03	3.02
2016	Was	NL	9	0	1	6.0	28	6	1	1	0	0	0	1	3	1	6	0	0	0	-	0-0	1	94	.690	3.93	1.50
2017	Was	NL	4	0	1	3.0	23	11	10	10	1	0	0	0	3	1	3	1	1	0	1.000	0-0	0	95	1.359	28.38	30.00
2018	Was	NL	20	0	5	19.0	84	19	13	12	4	0	2	2	10	1	15	2	0	2	.000	0-0	2	95	.869	5.94	5.68
2019	SF	NL	50	0	6	52.2	214	41	26	26	4	1	4	2	17	0	57	1	7	0	1.000	1-2	1	95	.597	2.61	4.44
	5 ML YEARS		131	0	20	128.1	551	120	68	65	11	3	9	8	49	6	108	5	12	4	.750	1-6	18	95	.684	3.71	4.56

Matt Grace

Pitches: L Bats: L Pos: RP-50; SP-1   Ht: 6'4" Wt: 215 Born: 12/14/1988 Age: 31

Year Team	Lg	G	GS	GF	IP	BFP	H	R	ER	HR	SH	SF	HB	TBB	IBB	SO	WP	W	L	Pct	Sv-Op	Hld	Vel	OPS	ERC	ERA
2015 Was	NL	26	0	5	17.0	84	26	11	8	0	0	2	1	8	2	14	1	2	1	.667	0-2	4	91	.855	6.71	4.24
2016 Was	NL	5	0	1	3.0	10	1	0	0	0	0	0	0	0	0	4	0	0	0	-	0-0	0	89	.200	0.25	0.00
2017 Was	NL	40	1	11	50.0	215	50	25	24	3	3	3	3	18	4	31	2	1	0	1.000	2-2	4	91	.702	3.76	4.32
2018 Was	NL	56	0	12	59.2	247	55	22	19	5	1	2	2	13	2	48	1	1	1	.500	0-0	8	91	.638	2.90	2.87
2019 Was	NL	51	1	12	46.2	206	61	34	33	11	1	2	2	10	0	35	1	1	2	.333	0-0	4	91	.916	6.39	6.36
5 ML YEARS		178	2	41	176.1	762	193	92	84	19	5	9	8	49	8	132	5	5	4	.556	2-4	20	91	.750	4.29	4.29

Yasmani Grandal

Bats: B Throws: R Pos: C-137;1B-20;PH-9;DH-1   yahz-MAH-nee gran-DAHL   Ht: 6'1" Wt: 235 Born: 11/8/1988 Age: 31

Year Team	Lg	G	AB	H	2B	3B	HR	(Hm	Rd)	TB	R	RBI	RC	TBB	IBB	SO	HBP	SH	SF	SB	CS	GDP	Avg	OBP	Slg	OPS
2012 SD	NL	60	192	57	7	1	8	(3	5)	90	28	36	37	31	1	39	1	0	2	0	0	8	.297	.394	.469	.863
2013 SD	NL	28	88	19	8	0	1	(1	0)	30	13	9	12	18	2	18	1	0	1	0	0	1	.216	.352	.341	.693
2014 LAD	NL	128	377	85	19	1	15	(7	8)	151	47	49	45	58	1	115	2	0	6	3	0	7	.225	.327	.401	.728
2015 LAD	NL	115	355	83	12	0	16	(8	8)	143	43	47	47	65	1	92	2	1	3	0	1	16	.234	.353	.403	.756
2016 LAD	NL	126	390	89	14	1	27	(20	7)	186	49	72	63	64	1	116	2	0	1	1	3	11	.228	.339	.477	.816
2017 LAD	NL	129	438	108	27	0	22	(13	9)	201	50	58	48	40	0	130	0	1	3	0	1	10	.247	.308	.459	.767
2018 LAD	NL	140	440	106	23	2	24	(11	13)	205	65	68	65	72	1	124	3	0	3	2	1	12	.241	.349	.466	.815
2019 Mil	NL	153	513	126	26	2	28	(13	15)	240	79	77	94	109	2	139	5	0	5	5	1	16	.246	.380	.468	.848
Postseason		32	75	8	1	0	2	(2	0)	15	3	6	3	16	0	35	0	1	0	0	0	2	.107	.264	.200	.464
8 ML YEARS		879	2793	673	136	7	141	(76	65)	1246	374	416	411	457	9	773	16	2	24	11	7	81	.241	.348	.446	.794

Curtis Granderson

Bats: L Throws: R Pos: LF-85;PH-59;RF-6;DH-1   Ht: 6'1" Wt: 200 Born: 3/16/1981 Age: 39

Year Team	Lg	G	AB	H	2B	3B	HR	(Hm	Rd)	TB	R	RBI	RC	TBB	IBB	SO	HBP	SH	SF	SB	CS	GDP	Avg	OBP	Slg	OPS
2004 Det	AL	9	25	6	1	1	0		9	2	0	2	3	0	8	0	0	0	0	0	1	.240	.321	.360	.681
2005 Det	AL	47	162	44	6	3	8	(5	3)	80	18	20	26	10	0	43	0	2	0	1	1	2	.272	.314	.494	.808
2006 Det	AL	159	596	155	31	9	19	(7	12)	261	90	68	89	66	4	174	7	6	8	8	5	4	.260	.335	.438	.773
2007 Det	AL	158	612	185	38	23	23	(10	13)	338	122	74	106	52	3	141	5	5	2	26	1	3	.302	.361	.552	.913
2008 Det	AL	141	553	155	26	13	22	(11	11)	273	112	66	100	71	1	111	3	1	1	12	4	7	.280	.365	.494	.858
2009 Det	AL	160	631	157	23	8	30	(10	20)	286	91	71	92	72	4	141	2	3	2	20	6	1	.249	.327	.453	.780
2010 NYY	AL	136	466	115	17	7	24	(14	10)	218	76	67	71	53	3	116	2	4	3	12	2	3	.247	.324	.468	.792
2011 NYY	AL	156	583	153	26	10	41	(21	20)	322	136	119	113	85	0	169	12	4	7	25	10	12	.262	.364	.552	.916
2012 NYY	AL	160	596	138	18	4	43	(26	17)	293	102	106	92	75	4	195	5	1	7	10	3	5	.232	.319	.492	.811
2013 NYY	AL	61	214	49	13	2	7	(2	5)	87	31	15	23	27	1	69	1	2	1	8	2	1	.229	.317	.407	.723
2014 NYM	NL	155	564	128	27	2	20	(7	13)	219	73	66	70	79	1	141	6	0	5	8	4	1	.227	.326	.388	.714
2015 NYM	NL	157	580	150	33	2	26	(12	14)	265	98	70	104	91	3	151	7	0	4	11	6	3	.259	.364	.457	.821
2016 NYM	NL	150	545	129	24	5	30	(13	17)	253	88	59	69	74	7	130	9	0	5	4	2	10	.237	.335	.464	.799
2017 2 Tms	NL	147	449	95	24	3	26	(7	19)	203	74	64	64	71	2	123	4	0	3	6	2	5	.212	.323	.452	.775
2018 2 Tms		123	343	83	22	2	13	(5	8)	148	60	38	51	54	1	106	4	1	1	2	1	2	.242	.351	.431	.782
2019 Mia	NL	138	317	58	17	1	12	(8	4)	113	44	34	32	41	1	98	3	0	2	0	3	3	.183	.281	.356	.637
17 NYM	NL	111	337	77	22	3	19	(6	13)	162	58	52	56	53	2	90	2	0	3	4	2	4	.228	.334	.481	.815
17 LAD	NL	36	112	18	2	0	7	(1	6)	41	16	12	8	18	0	33	2	0	0	2	0	1	.161	.288	.366	.654
18 Tor	AL	104	302	74	21	1	11	(4	7)	130	48	35	44	42	1	96	3	1	1	2	1	3	.245	.342	.430	.772
18 Mil	NL	19	41	9	1	1	2	(1	1)	18	12	3	7	12	0	10	1	0	0	0	0	0	.220	.407	.439	.846
Postseason		64	210	47	9	3	9	(6	3)	89	27	30	36	29	1	56	1	1	3	9	3	2	.224	.317	.424	.741
16 ML YEARS		2057	7236	1800	346	95	344	(158	186)	3368	1217	937	1104	924	31	1916	67	30	49	153	50	64	.249	.337	.465	.803

Brusdar Graterol

Pitches: R Bats: R Pos: RP-10   Ht: 6'1" Wt: 265 Born: 8/26/1998 Age: 21

Year Team	Lg	G	GS	GF	IP	BFP	H	R	ER	HR	SH	SF	HB	TBB	IBB	SO	WP	W	L	Pct	Sv-Op	Hld	Vel	OPS	ERC	ERA
2017 2 Tms	Low	10	7	0	40.0	157	26	12	12	2	0	0	3	13	0	45	3	4	1	.800	0--	-	-	.523	2.02	2.70
2018 2 Tms	Low	19	19	0	102.0	419	89	34	31	3	0	2	9	28	0	107	8	8	4	.667	0--	-	-	.606	2.82	2.74
2019 Pnscla	AA	12	9	1	52.2	205	32	10	10	2	1	1	3	21	0	50	2	6	0	1.000	1--	-	-	.537	1.96	1.71
2019 Min	AL	10	0	4	9.2	40	10	5	5	1	0	1	1	2	1	10	2	1	1	.500	0-0		99	.714	3.90	4.66

Juan Graterol

Bats: R Throws: R Pos: C-5;PH-1   Ht: 6'1" Wt: 205 Born: 2/14/1989 Age: 31

Year Team	Lg	G	AB	H	2B	3B	HR	(Hm	Rd)	TB	R	RBI	RC	TBB	IBB	SO	HBP	SH	SF	SB	CS	GDP	Avg	OBP	Slg	OPS
2019 Lsvlle	AAA	58	209	52	8	1	2	(-	-)	68	19	26	21	14	0	18	2	0	1	0	1	11	.249	.301	.325	.626
2016 LAA	AL	9	14	4	2	0	0	(0	0)	6	2	3	1	0	0	3	0	1	0	0	0	0	.286	.286	.429	.714
2017 LAA	AL	48	84	17	4	0	0	(0	0)	21	5	10	0	1	0	13	0	0	2	0	0	4	.202	.207	.250	.457
2018 2 Tms		4	8	2	0	0	0	(0	0)	2	2	0	1	1	0	0	0	0	0	0	0	0	.250	.333	.250	.583
2019 Cin	NL	6	18	4	0	0	0	(0	0)	4	1	1	1	0	0	4	0	0	0	0	0	0	.222	.222	.222	.444
18 LAA	AL	1	1	1	0	0	0	(0	0)	1	0	0	0	0	0	0	0	0	0	0	0	0	1.000	1.000	1.000	2.000
18 Min	AL	3	7	1	0	0	0	(0	0)	1	2	0	0	1	0	0	0	0	0	0	0	0	.143	.250	.143	.393
4 ML YEARS		67	124	27	6	0	0	(0	0)	33	10	14	3	2	0	20	0	1	2	0	0	4	.218	.227	.266	.493

227

Kendall Graveman

Pitches: R **Bats:** R **Pos:** P **Ht:** 6'2" **Wt:** 200 **Born:** 12/21/1990 **Age:** 29

Year Team	Lg	G	GS	GF	IP	BFP	H	R	ER	HR	SH	SF	HB	TBB	IBB	SO	WP	W	L	Pct	Sv-Op	Hld	Vel	OPS	ERC	ERA
2014 Tor	AL	5	0	1	4.2	18	4	2	2	0	0	0	0	0	0	4	1	0	0	-	0-0	0	93	.556	1.44	3.86
2015 Oak	AL	21	21	0	115.2	502	126	57	52	15	1	2	5	38	0	77	4	6	9	.400	0-0	0	91	.761	4.72	4.05
2016 Oak	AL	31	31	0	186.0	786	196	87	85	22	2	6	7	47	2	108	2	10	11	.476	0-0	0	93	.734	4.08	4.11
2017 Oak	AL	19	19	0	105.1	444	114	50	49	12	0	1	4	32	1	70	5	6	4	.600	0-0	0	93	.780	4.53	4.19
2018 Oak	AL	7	7	0	34.1	158	44	32	29	9	0	0	1	13	0	27	2	1	5	.167	0-0	0	94	.909	7.04	7.60
5 ML YEARS		83	78	1	446.0	1908	484	228	217	58	3	9	17	130	3	286	14	23	29	.442	0-0	0	93	.764	4.53	4.38

Jon Gray

Pitches: R **Bats:** R **Pos:** SP-25; RP-1 **Ht:** 6'4" **Wt:** 227 **Born:** 11/5/1991 **Age:** 28

Year Team	Lg	G	GS	GF	IP	BFP	H	R	ER	HR	SH	SF	HB	TBB	IBB	SO	WP	W	L	Pct	Sv-Op	Hld	Vel	OPS	ERC	ERA
2015 Col	NL	9	9	0	40.2	185	52	26	25	4	2	4	2	14	2	40	3	0	2	.000	0-0	0	94	.856	5.60	5.53
2016 Col	NL	29	29	0	168.0	712	153	92	86	18	5	5	12	59	2	185	1	10	10	.500	0-0	0	95	.703	3.71	4.61
2017 Col	NL	20	20	0	110.1	461	113	47	45	10	2	2	2	30	0	112	3	10	4	.714	0-0	0	96	.716	3.76	3.67
2018 Col	NL	31	31	0	172.1	743	180	102	98	27	4	3	6	52	1	183	6	12	9	.571	0-0	0	95	.773	4.44	5.12
2019 Col	NL	26	25	1	150.0	637	147	70	64	19	7	3	4	56	4	150	7	11	8	.579	0-0	0	96	.766	4.16	3.84
Postseason		1	1	0	1.1	11	7	4	4	1	0	0	0	0	0	2	0	0	1	.000	0-0	0	97	1.818	43.52	27.00
5 ML YEARS		115	114	1	641.1	2738	645	337	318	78	20	17	26	211	9	670	26	43	33	.566	0-0	0	95	.749	4.14	4.46

Sonny Gray

Pitches: R **Bats:** R **Pos:** SP-31 **Ht:** 5'10" **Wt:** 192 **Born:** 11/7/1989 **Age:** 30

Year Team	Lg	G	GS	GF	IP	BFP	H	R	ER	HR	SH	SF	HB	TBB	IBB	SO	WP	W	L	Pct	Sv-Op	Hld	Vel	OPS	ERC	ERA
2013 Oak	AL	12	10	0	64.0	261	51	22	19	4	0	3	0	20	0	67	2	5	3	.625	0-0	0	93	.570	2.42	2.67
2014 Oak	AL	33	33	0	219.0	899	187	84	75	15	8	5	7	74	2	183	15	14	10	.583	0-0	0	93	.627	2.99	3.08
2015 Oak	AL	31	31	0	208.0	831	166	71	63	17	1	4	2	59	0	169	13	14	7	.667	0-0	0	93	.590	2.53	2.73
2016 Oak	AL	22	22	0	117.0	517	133	80	74	18	0	7	2	42	0	94	15	5	11	.313	0-0	0	93	.818	5.16	5.69
2017 2 Tms	AL	27	27	0	162.1	678	139	79	64	19	1	2	3	57	1	153	11	10	12	.455	0-0	0	93	.668	3.26	3.55
2018 NYY	AL	30	23	2	130.1	582	138	73	71	14	1	5	8	57	0	123	9	11	9	.550	0-0	0	93	.768	4.85	4.90
2019 Cin	NL	31	31	0	175.1	708	122	59	56	17	6	5	7	68	1	205	7	11	8	.579	0-0	0	93	.605	2.57	2.87
17 Oak	AL	16	16	0	97.0	400	84	48	37	8	0	2	1	30	0	94	7	6	5	.545	0-0	0	93	.644	2.93	3.43
17 NYY	AL	11	11	0	65.1	278	55	31	27	11	1	0	2	27	1	59	4	4	7	.364	0-0	0	93	.702	3.77	3.72
Postseason		4	4	0	21.1	90	14	8	7	2	1	0	2	12	1	18	2	0	2	.000	0-0	0	93	.615	3.09	2.95
7 ML YEARS		186	177	2	1076.0	4476	936	468	422	104	17	31	29	377	4	994	72	70	60	.538	0-0	0	93	.660	3.26	3.53

Chad Green

Pitches: R **Bats:** L **Pos:** RP-39; SP-15 **Ht:** 6'3" **Wt:** 210 **Born:** 5/24/1991 **Age:** 29

Year Team	Lg	G	GS	GF	IP	BFP	H	R	ER	HR	SH	SF	HB	TBB	IBB	SO	WP	W	L	Pct	Sv-Op	Hld	Vel	OPS	ERC	ERA
2016 NYY	AL	12	8	4	45.2	198	49	26	24	12	1	1	1	15	0	52	1	2	4	.333	1-1	0	94	.852	5.46	4.73
2017 NYY	AL	40	1	4	69.0	253	34	14	14	4	2	1	2	17	0	103	3	5	0	1.000	0-1	9	96	.454	1.20	1.83
2018 NYY	AL	63	0	3	75.2	298	64	22	21	9	0	3	1	15	2	94	3	8	3	.727	0-4	12	96	.641	2.67	2.50
2019 NYY	AL	54	15	10	69.0	295	66	35	32	10	0	3	6	19	0	98	2	4	4	.500	2-2	4	96	.735	3.95	4.17
Postseason		7	0	1	12.1	54	10	6	5	1	1	1	1	6	1	11	0	1	0	1.000	0-0	0	96	.699	3.34	3.65
4 ML YEARS		169	24	21	259.1	1044	213	97	91	35	3	8	10	66	2	347	9	19	11	.633	3-8	25	96	.662	2.95	3.16

Zach Green

Bats: R **Throws:** R **Pos:** 3B-5;PH-3 **Ht:** 6'3" **Wt:** 210 **Born:** 3/7/1994 **Age:** 26

Year Team	Lg	G	AB	H	2B	3B	HR	(Hm	Rd)	TB	R	RBI	RC	TBB	IBB	SO	HBP	SH	SF	SB	CS	GDP	Avg	OBP	Slg	OPS
2019 Scrmto	AAA	72	252	71	18	1	25	(-	-)	166	43	64	62	39	1	99	3	0	3	1	0	5	.282	.380	.659	1.039
2019 SF	NL	8	14	2	1	0	0	(0	0)	3	1	1	1	2	0	6	0	0	0	0	0	2	.143	.250	.214	.464

Shane Greene

Pitches: R **Bats:** R **Pos:** RP-65 **Ht:** 6'4" **Wt:** 197 **Born:** 11/17/1988 **Age:** 31

Year Team	Lg	G	GS	GF	IP	BFP	H	R	ER	HR	SH	SF	HB	TBB	IBB	SO	WP	W	L	Pct	Sv-Op	Hld	Vel	OPS	ERC	ERA
2014 NYY	AL	15	14	0	78.2	345	81	38	33	8	0	1	6	29	0	81	1	5	4	.556	0-0	0	93	.715	4.43	3.78
2015 Det	AL	18	16	1	83.2	373	103	67	64	13	2	4	6	27	4	50	1	4	8	.333	0-0	0	92	.897	5.83	6.88
2016 Det	AL	50	3	4	60.1	256	58	39	39	3	2	2	4	22	1	59	0	5	4	.556	2-3	16	94	.680	3.65	5.82
2017 Det	AL	71	0	26	67.2	283	50	21	20	6	0	1	4	34	4	73	1	4	3	.571	9-13	14	95	.631	3.14	2.66
2018 Det	AL	66	0	58	63.1	279	68	39	36	12	0	3	3	19	1	65	3	4	6	.400	32-38	1	94	.787	4.80	5.12
2019 2 Tms		65	0	37	62.2	252	46	22	16	8	1	1	3	17	1	64	0	0	3	.000	23-28	10	93	.598	2.51	2.30
19 NYY	AL	38	0	32	38.0	151	21	11	5	7	1	0	1	12	1	43	0	0	2	.000	22-25	0	93	.504	1.70	1.18
19 Atl	NL	27	0	5	24.2	101	25	11	11	3	0	1	2	5	0	21	0	0	1	.000	1-3	10	92	.736	3.97	4.01
6 ML YEARS		285	33	126	416.1	1788	406	226	208	50	5	12	26	148	11	392	6	22	28	.440	66-82	40	93	.730	4.12	4.50

Luke Gregerson

Pitches: R **Bats:** L **Pos:** RP-6   **Ht:** 6'3" **Wt:** 205 **Born:** 5/14/1984 **Age:** 36

Year	Team	Lg		HOW MUCH PITCHED					WHAT HE GAVE UP											THE RESULTS					
			G	GS	GF	IP	BFP	H	R	ER	HR	SH	SF	HB	TBB	IBB	SO	WP	W	L	Pct	Sv-Op	Hld	Vel	OPS	ERC	ERA
2019	Sprgfld	AA	6	0	0	6.0	21	3	1	1	0	0	0	0	0	0	7	1	0	0	-	0- -			.333	0.54	1.50
2009	SD	NL	72	0	7	75.0	318	62	29	27	3	3	1	3	31	9	93	4	2	4	.333	1-7	27	91	.615	2.72	3.24
2010	SD	NL	80	0	9	78.1	297	47	30	28	8	1	1	1	18	2	89	0	4	7	.364	2-7	40	91	.524	1.56	3.22
2011	SD	NL	61	0	11	55.2	241	57	23	17	2	5	1	2	19	3	34	2	3	3	.500	0-4	16	90	.681	3.55	2.75
2012	SD	NL	77	0	15	71.2	294	57	19	19	7	5	0	3	21	3	72	3	2	0	1.000	9-13	24	89	.612	2.64	2.39
2013	SD	NL	73	0	17	66.1	268	49	24	20	3	4	1	4	18	2	64	1	6	8	.429	4-9	25	88	.572	2.07	2.71
2014	Oak	AL	72	0	17	72.1	284	58	20	17	6	3	1	1	15	3	59	6	5	5	.500	3-11	22	88	.604	2.25	2.12
2015	Hou	AL	64	0	53	61.0	239	48	24	21	5	2	0	2	10	2	59	1	7	3	.700	31-36	0	89	.573	2.09	3.10
2016	Hou	AL	59	0	25	57.2	230	38	23	21	5	0	2	2	18	2	67	6	4	3	.571	15-21	15	89	.589	1.99	3.28
2017	Hou	AL	65	0	17	61.0	263	62	31	31	13	1	1	0	20	4	70	5	2	3	.400	1-4	18	90	.790	4.50	4.57
2018	StL	NL	17	0	4	12.2	57	14	10	10	2	0	0	0	6	0	12	2	0	0	-	0-0	2	88	.841	5.39	7.11
2019	StL	NL	6	0	3	5.2	27	11	5	5	0	0	0	0	1	0	2	0	0	0	-	0-0	0	87	.944	8.51	7.94
	Postseason		10	0	5	8.1	36	5	1	1	1	0	0	1	5	0	13	2	0	0	-	3-3	1	90	.572	3.20	1.08
	11 ML YEARS		646	0	174	617.1	2518	503	238	216	54	24	8	18	177	30	621	30	35	36	.493	66-112	189	89	.625	2.62	3.15

Didi Gregorius

Bats: L **Throws:** R **Pos:** SS-80;DH-1;PR-1   dee-dee greh-GORE-ee-us   **Ht:** 6'3" **Wt:** 205 **Born:** 2/18/1990 **Age:** 30

Year	Team	Lg				BATTING																	RUNNING			AVERAGES		
			G	AB	H	2B	3B	HR	(Hm	Rd)	TB	R	RBI	RC	TBB	IBB	SO	HBP	SH	SF	SB	CS	GDP	Avg	OBP	Slg	OPS
2012	Cin	NL	8	20	6	0	0	0	(0	0)	6	1	2	2	0	0	5	0	1	0	0	0	0	.300	.300	.300	.600
2013	Ari	NL	103	357	90	16	3	7	(3	4)	133	47	28	42	37	5	65	6	2	1	0	2	4	.252	.332	.373	.704
2014	Ari	NL	80	270	61	9	5	6	(3	3)	98	35	27	37	22	3	52	3	2	3	3	0	1	.226	.290	.363	.653
2015	NYY	AL	155	525	139	24	2	9	(6	3)	194	57	56	64	33	0	85	11	3	6	5	3	4	.265	.318	.370	.688
2016	NYY	AL	153	562	155	32	2	20	(11	9)	251	68	70	71	19	2	82	6	5	5	7	1	9	.276	.304	.447	.751
2017	NYY	AL	136	534	153	27	0	25	(12	13)	255	73	87	84	25	1	70	3	0	7	3	1	7	.287	.318	.478	.796
2018	NYY	AL	134	504	135	23	5	27	(19	8)	249	89	86	79	48	3	69	7	1	9	10	6	8	.268	.335	.494	.829
2019	NYY	AL	82	324	77	14	2	16	(6	10)	143	47	61	45	17	1	53	1	0	2	2	1	5	.238	.276	.441	.718
	Postseason		19	68	17	2	1	3	(1	2)	30	7	10	10	7	3	16	0	1	1	0	0	0	.250	.316	.441	.757
	8 ML YEARS		851	3096	816	145	19	110	(60	50)	1329	417	417	424	201	15	481	37	14	32	30	14	38	.264	.313	.429	.742

Grayson Greiner

Bats: R **Throws:** R **Pos:** C-58   **Ht:** 6'6" **Wt:** 239 **Born:** 10/11/1992 **Age:** 27

Year	Team	Lg				BATTING																	RUNNING			AVERAGES		
			G	AB	H	2B	3B	HR	(Hm	Rd)	TB	R	RBI	RC	TBB	IBB	SO	HBP	SH	SF	SB	CS	GDP	Avg	OBP	Slg	OPS
2019	Toledo	AAA	13	48	12	1	0	2	(-	-)	19	8	4	6	4	0	16	1	0	0	0	0	2	.250	.321	.396	.717
2018	Det	AL	30	96	21	6	0	0	(0	0)	27	9	12	13	17	0	32	0	0	3	0	1	0	.219	.328	.281	.609
2019	Det	AL	58	208	42	5	1	5	(1	4)	64	18	19	15	13	0	70	1	1	1	0	0	5	.202	.251	.308	.559
	2 ML YEARS		88	304	63	11	1	5	(1	4)	91	27	31	28	30	0	102	1	1	4	0	1	5	.207	.277	.299	.577

Zack Greinke

Pitches: R **Bats:** R **Pos:** SP-33   GRAIN-key   **Ht:** 6'2" **Wt:** 200 **Born:** 10/21/1983 **Age:** 36

Year	Team	Lg		HOW MUCH PITCHED					WHAT HE GAVE UP											THE RESULTS					
			G	GS	GF	IP	BFP	H	R	ER	HR	SH	SF	HB	TBB	IBB	SO	WP	W	L	Pct	Sv-Op	Hld	Vel	OPS	ERC	ERA
2004	KC	AL	24	24	0	145.0	599	143	64	64	26	3	2	8	26	3	100	1	8	11	.421	0-0	0	89	.752	3.85	3.97
2005	KC	AL	33	33	0	183.0	829	233	125	118	23	4	4	13	53	0	114	4	5	17	.227	0-0	0	90	.846	5.71	5.80
2006	KC	AL	3	0	1	6.1	28	7	3	3	1	0	0	0	3	2	5	0	1	0	1.000	0-0	0	93	.757	4.93	4.26
2007	KC	AL	52	14	7	122.0	507	122	52	50	12	3	4	3	36	5	106	3	7	7	.500	1-1	12	94	.747	3.77	3.69
2008	KC	AL	32	32	0	202.1	851	202	87	78	21	2	4	4	56	1	183	8	13	10	.565	0-0	0	93	.715	3.68	3.47
2009	KC	AL	33	33	0	229.1	915	195	64	55	11	8	3	4	51	0	242	5	16	8	.667	0-0	0	94	.611	2.39	2.16
2010	KC	AL	33	33	0	220.0	919	219	114	102	18	6	7	7	55	1	181	4	10	14	.417	0-0	0	93	.696	3.48	4.17
2011	Mil	NL	28	28	0	171.2	715	161	82	73	19	6	1	4	45	0	201	10	16	6	.727	0-0	0	93	.708	3.35	3.83
2012	2 Tms		34	34	0	212.1	868	200	84	82	18	7	2	2	54	0	200	8	15	5	.750	0-0	0	92	.663	3.17	3.48
2013	LAD	NL	28	28	0	177.2	717	152	54	52	13	13	1	7	46	1	148	5	15	4	.789	0-0	0	92	.647	2.78	2.63
2014	LAD	NL	32	32	0	202.1	821	190	69	61	19	2	4	2	43	3	207	12	17	8	.680	0-0	0	92	.660	3.03	2.71
2015	LAD	NL	32	32	0	222.2	843	148	43	41	14	6	2	5	40	1	200	7	19	3	.864	0-0	0	92	.507	1.56	1.66
2016	Ari	NL	26	26	0	158.2	667	161	80	77	23	7	4	0	41	3	134	4	13	7	.650	0-0	0	91	.750	3.86	4.37
2017	Ari	NL	32	32	0	202.1	801	172	80	72	25	4	3	0	45	0	215	12	17	7	.708	0-0	0	91	.659	2.79	3.20
2018	Ari	NL	33	33	0	207.2	839	181	77	74	28	3	3	6	43	3	199	4	15	11	.577	0-0	0	90	.665	2.96	3.21
2019	2 Tms		33	33	0	208.2	810	175	73	68	21	5	4	4	30	2	187	2	18	5	.783	0-0	0	90	.623	2.39	2.93
12	Mil	NL	21	21	0	123.0	504	120	49	47	7	3	0	0	28	0	122	4	9	3	.750	0-0	0	92	.653	3.02	3.44
12	LAA	AL	13	13	0	89.1	364	80	35	35	11	4	2	2	26	0	78	4	6	2	.750	0-0	0	92	.679	3.38	3.53
19	Ari	NL	23	23	0	146.0	562	117	48	47	15	4	3	3	21	2	135	1	10	4	.714	0-0	0	90	.614	2.22	2.90
19	Hou	AL	10	10	0	62.2	248	58	25	21	6	1	1	1	9	0	52	1	8	1	.889	0-0	0	92	.644	2.79	3.02
	Postseason		11	11	0	67.0	274	60	33	30	9	2	4	2	15	0	59	1	3	4	.429	0-0	0	92	.685	3.16	4.03
	16 ML YEARS		488	447	8	2872.0	11729	2661	1151	1070	292	79	48	69	667	25	2622	86	205	123	.625	1-1	12	92	.679	3.15	3.35

Randal Grichuk

Bats: R **Throws:** R **Pos:** RF-92;CF-62;DH-10;PH-2;PR-1   GRICH-ick   **Ht:** 6'2" **Wt:** 213 **Born:** 8/13/1991 **Age:** 28

Year	Team	Lg				BATTING																	RUNNING			AVERAGES		
			G	AB	H	2B	3B	HR	(Hm	Rd)	TB	R	RBI	RC	TBB	IBB	SO	HBP	SH	SF	SB	CS	GDP	Avg	OBP	Slg	OPS
2014	StL	NL	47	110	27	6	1	3	(2	1)	44	11	8	7	5	0	31	0	1	0	0	2	4	.245	.278	.400	.678
2015	StL	NL	103	323	89	23	7	17	(10	7)	177	49	47	47	22	2	110	4	0	1	4	2	6	.276	.329	.548	.877
2016	StL	NL	132	446	107	29	3	24	(12	12)	214	66	68	62	28	0	141	3	0	1	5	4	9	.240	.289	.480	.769
2017	StL	NL	122	412	98	25	3	22	(13	9)	195	53	59	47	26	3	133	2	0	2	6	1	9	.238	.285	.473	.758

Year	Team	Lg	G	AB	H	2B	3B	HR	(Hm	Rd)	TB	R	RBI	RC	TBB	IBB	SO	HBP	SH	SF	SB	CS	GDP	Avg	OBP	Slg	OPS
2018	Tor	AL	124	424	104	32	1	25	(17	8)	213	60	61	61	27	0	122	8	0	3	3	2	5	.245	.301	.502	.803
2019	Tor	AL	151	586	136	29	5	31	(19	12)	268	75	80	68	35	0	163	5	0	2	2	1	20	.232	.280	.457	.738
Postseason			13	43	8	0	0	3	(1	2)	17	5	4	2	1	0	17	0	0	0	0	0	0	.186	.205	.395	.600
6 ML YEARS			679	2301	561	144	20	122	(73	49)	1111	314	323	292	143	5	700	22	1	9	20	12	53	.244	.293	.483	.776

Trent Grisham

Bats: L **Throws:** L **Pos:** CF-21;LF-17;RF-16;PH-13   **Ht:** 6'0" **Wt:** 205 **Born:** 11/1/1996 **Age:** 23

Year	Team	Lg	G	AB	H	2B	3B	HR	(Hm	Rd)	TB	R	RBI	RC	TBB	IBB	SO	HBP	SH	SF	SB	CS	GDP	Avg	OBP	Slg	OPS
2015	2 Tms	Low	55	207	64	7	6	2	(-	-)	89	39	21	42	39	2	44	3	2	1	25	8	5	.309	.424	.430	.854
2016	Wisc	A	59	221	51	15	2	2	(-	-)	76	27	24	26	37	0	68	2	2	0	5	10	3	.231	.346	.344	.690
2017	Carlina	A+	133	457	102	21	6	8	(-	-)	159	78	45	72	98	2	141	3	5	6	38	5	3	.223	.360	.348	.708
2018	Biloxi	AA	107	335	78	10	2	7	(-	-)	113	45	31	47	63	0	87	2	3	2	11	3	6	.233	.356	.337	.693
2019	Biloxi	AA	63	236	60	14	3	13	(-	-)	119	34	41	46	44	4	50	1	0	2	6	4	2	.254	.371	.504	.875
2019	SnAnt	AAA	34	134	51	8	3	13	(-	-)	104	37	30	44	23	1	22	0	1	0	6	1	2	.381	.471	.776	1.247
2019	Mil	NL	51	156	36	6	2	6	(3	3)	64	24	24	20	20	0	48	4	0	3	1	0	3	.231	.328	.410	.738

Robbie Grossman

Bats: B **Throws:** L **Pos:** LF-112;PH-26;RF-20;CF-1   **Ht:** 6'0" **Wt:** 215 **Born:** 9/16/1989 **Age:** 30

Year	Team	Lg	G	AB	H	2B	3B	HR	(Hm	Rd)	TB	R	RBI	RC	TBB	IBB	SO	HBP	SH	SF	SB	CS	GDP	Avg	OBP	Slg	OPS
2013	Hou	AL	63	257	69	14	0	4	(3	1)	95	29	21	37	23	0	70	2	6	7	6	7	2	.268	.332	.370	.702
2014	Hou	AL	103	360	84	14	2	6	(2	4)	120	42	37	48	55	1	105	2	3	2	9	3	7	.233	.337	.333	.670
2015	Hou	AL	24	49	7	2	0	1	(1	0)	12	7	5	4	5	0	17	0	0	0	0	0	0	.143	.222	.245	.467
2016	Min	AL	99	332	93	19	1	11	(8	3)	147	49	37	52	55	0	96	2	0	2	3	3	3	.280	.386	.443	.828
2017	Min	AL	119	382	94	22	1	9	(5	4)	145	62	45	58	67	0	79	3	2	2	3	1	6	.246	.361	.380	.741
2018	Min	AL	129	396	108	27	1	5	(2	3)	152	50	48	62	60	0	83	2	2	5	0	1	2	.273	.367	.384	.751
2019	Oak	AL	138	420	101	21	3	6	(2	4)	146	57	38	58	59	2	86	1	0	2	9	4	7	.240	.334	.348	.682
Postseason			1	4	0	0	0	0	(0	0)	0	0	0	0	0	0	3	0	0	0	0	0	0	.000	.000	.000	.000
7 ML YEARS			675	2196	556	119	8	42	(23	19)	817	296	231	319	324	3	536	12	12	12	29	19	27	.253	.351	.372	.723

Zac Grotz

Pitches: R **Bats:** R **Pos:** RP-14   **Ht:** 6'2" **Wt:** 195 **Born:** 2/17/1993 **Age:** 27

Year	Team	Lg	G	GS	GF	IP	BFP	H	R	ER	HR	SH	SF	HB	TBB	IBB	SO	WP	W	L	Pct	Sv-Op	Hld	Vel	OPS	ERC	ERA
2019	Ark	AA	26	6	8	57.1	225	47	18	16	4	1	1	3	11	1	69	5	4	4	.500	1--	-	-	.579	2.40	2.51
2019	Sea	AL	14	0	4	17.1	73	14	9	8	0	0	1	1	8	1	18	6	1	0	1.000	0-0	1	92	.585	2.73	4.15

Deivy Grullon

Bats: R **Throws:** R **Pos:** C-2;PH-2   **Ht:** 6'1" **Wt:** 180 **Born:** 2/17/1996 **Age:** 24

Year	Team	Lg	G	AB	H	2B	3B	HR	(Hm	Rd)	TB	R	RBI	RC	TBB	IBB	SO	HBP	SH	SF	SB	CS	GDP	Avg	OBP	Slg	OPS
2019	LV	AAA	108	407	115	24	0	21	(-	-)	202	55	77	73	45	0	133	2	0	3	1	0	5	.283	.354	.496	.851
2019	Phi	NL	4	9	1	1	0	0	(0	0)	2	0	1	0	0	0	2	0	0	0	0	0	1	.111	.111	.222	.333

Robert Gsellman

Pitches: R **Bats:** R **Pos:** RP-52   guh-ZELL-man   **Ht:** 6'4" **Wt:** 205 **Born:** 7/18/1993 **Age:** 26

Year	Team	Lg	G	GS	GF	IP	BFP	H	R	ER	HR	SH	SF	HB	TBB	IBB	SO	WP	W	L	Pct	Sv-Op	Hld	Vel	OPS	ERC	ERA
2016	NYM	NL	8	7	0	44.2	185	42	12	12	1	4	2	1	15	2	42	1	4	2	.667	0-0	0	94	.639	3.05	2.42
2017	NYM	NL	25	22	1	119.2	549	138	85	69	17	4	2	8	42	3	82	4	8	7	.533	0-1	1	93	.807	5.16	5.19
2018	NYM	NL	68	0	24	80.0	345	76	44	38	8	3	5	5	28	6	70	1	6	3	.667	13-19	15	94	.700	3.69	4.28
2019	NYM	NL	52	0	9	63.2	277	64	36	33	7	1	2	6	23	2	60	4	2	3	.400	1-5	7	95	.766	4.36	4.66
4 ML YEARS			153	29	34	308.0	1356	320	177	152	33	12	11	20	108	13	254	10	20	15	.571	14-25	23	94	.749	4.29	4.44

Reymin Guduan

Pitches: L **Bats:** L **Pos:** RP-7   **Ht:** 6'4" **Wt:** 205 **Born:** 3/16/1992 **Age:** 28

Year	Team	Lg	G	GS	GF	IP	BFP	H	R	ER	HR	SH	SF	HB	TBB	IBB	SO	WP	W	L	Pct	Sv-Op	Hld	Vel	OPS	ERC	ERA
2019	RdRck	AAA	23	0	13	27.1	131	29	14	8	1	0	4	1	18	0	32	5	3	1	.750	2--	-	-	.746	4.93	2.63
2017	Hou	AL	22	0	3	16.0	83	24	14	14	1	0	0	0	12	0	16	3	0	0	-	0-0	1	95	.899	8.22	7.88
2018	Hou	AL	3	0	2	3.1	11	1	1	1	0	0	0	0	0	0	4	0	0	0	-	0-0	0	95	.455	0.66	2.70
2019	Hou	AL	7	0	3	5.1	27	8	7	7	3	0	1	0	4	0	6	0	1	0	1.000	0-1	0	96	1.263	13.32	11.81
3 ML YEARS			32	0	8	24.2	121	33	22	22	5	0	1	0	16	0	26	3	1	0	1.000	0-1	1	95	.934	8.01	8.03

Deolis Guerra

Pitches: R **Bats:** R **Pos:** RP-1

day-OH-lis

Ht: 6'5" **Wt:** 245 **Born:** 4/17/1989 **Age:** 31

Year Team	Lg	G	GS	GF	IP	BFP	H	R	ER	HR	SH	SF	HB	TBB	IBB	SO	WP	W	L	Pct	Sv-Op	Hld	Vel	OPS	ERC	ERA
2019 SnAnt	AAA	45	1	10	66.2	256	43	19	14	5	1	0	2	16	1	88	3	4	0	1.000	0--	-	-	.530	1.68	1.89
2015 Pit	NL	10	0	4	16.2	74	26	12	12	5	0	0	1	3	0	17	2	2	0	1.000	0-0	0	91	1.077	8.96	6.48
2016 LAA	AL	44	0	11	53.1	220	52	23	19	6	1	1	2	7	0	36	2	3	0	1.000	0-4	5	90	.671	3.08	3.21
2017 LAA	AL	19	0	5	25.0	105	20	13	13	4	0	1	0	12	0	22	2	2	2	.500	0-1	0	92	.729	3.70	4.68
2019 Mil	NL	1	0	0	0.2	6	4	4	4	1	0	1	0	0	0	0	0	0	0	-	0-0	0	92	2.067	61.64	54.00
4 ML YEARS		74	0	20	95.2	405	102	52	48	16	1	3	3	22	0	75	6	7	2	.778	0-5	5	91	.780	4.37	4.52

Javier Guerra

Pitches: R **Bats:** L **Pos:** RP-8

Ht: 5'11" **Wt:** 155 **Born:** 9/25/1995 **Age:** 24

Year Team	Lg	G	GS	GF	IP	BFP	H	R	ER	HR	SH	SF	HB	TBB	IBB	SO	WP	W	L	Pct	Sv-Op	Hld	Vel	OPS	ERC	ERA
2019 Lk Els	A+	17	0	6	17.0	66	13	7	7	2	0	0	6	5	0	23	0	0	0	-	1--	-	-	.633	2.65	3.71
2019 SD	NL	8	0	1	8.2	36	7	5	5	3	0	1	0	3	0	6	0	0	0	-	0-0	0	98	.840	4.29	5.19

Javy Guerra

Pitches: R **Bats:** R **Pos:** RP-51

Ht: 6'1" **Wt:** 216 **Born:** 10/31/1985 **Age:** 34

Year Team	Lg	G	GS	GF	IP	BFP	H	R	ER	HR	SH	SF	HB	TBB	IBB	SO	WP	W	L	Pct	Sv-Op	Hld	Vel	OPS	ERC	ERA
2019 Buffalo	AAA	5	0	2	7.1	28	4	2	2	0	0	0	0	4	0	6	0	0	1	.000	1--	-	-	.577	1.79	2.45
2011 LAD	NL	47	0	38	46.2	195	37	12	12	2	3	1	3	18	1	38	2	2	2	.500	21-23	0	94	.608	2.73	2.31
2012 LAD	NL	45	0	17	45.0	196	44	13	13	1	4	2	1	23	5	37	1	2	3	.400	8-13	4	93	.685	3.76	2.60
2013 LAD	NL	9	0	5	10.2	55	15	9	8	1	0	1	1	6	0	12	0	0	0	-	0-0	0	93	.826	7.24	6.75
2014 CWS	AL	42	0	10	46.1	198	41	15	15	3	2	4	5	20	5	38	2	2	4	.333	1-6	7	94	.696	3.60	2.91
2015 CWS	AL	3	0	0	1.2	7	2	0	0	0	0	0	0	1	0	0	0	0	0	-	0-0	1	92	.762	5.91	0.00
2016 LAA	AL	7	0	1	6.1	30	5	4	4	1	0	0	1	7	1	4	1	0	0	-	0-0	0	92	.842	6.80	5.68
2017 Mia	NL	16	0	5	21.0	88	23	8	7	2	1	0	0	7	1	12	0	1	1	.500	0-1	0	92	.757	4.40	3.00
2018 Mia	NL	32	0	12	35.2	162	42	27	22	4	2	1	3	12	2	30	3	1	1	.500	1-1	5	93	.835	5.12	5.55
2019 2 Tms	NL	51	0	21	67.2	287	67	36	35	10	1	1	1	17	3	57	3	3	1	.750	2-2	5	93	.724	3.68	4.66
19 Tor	AL	11	0	6	14.0	59	12	6	6	1	1	0	1	5	1	15	0	0	0	-	1-1	1	93	.714	3.10	3.86
19 Was	NL	40	0	15	53.2	228	55	30	29	9	0	1	0	12	2	42	3	3	1	.750	1-1	4	93	.726	3.83	4.86
9 ML YEARS		252	0	109	281.0	1218	276	124	116	24	13	10	15	111	18	228	12	11	12	.478	33-46	18	93	.721	3.96	3.72

Junior Guerra

Pitches: R **Bats:** R **Pos:** RP-72

Ht: 6'0" **Wt:** 205 **Born:** 1/16/1985 **Age:** 35

Year Team	Lg	G	GS	GF	IP	BFP	H	R	ER	HR	SH	SF	HB	TBB	IBB	SO	WP	W	L	Pct	Sv-Op	Hld	Vel	OPS	ERC	ERA
2015 CWS	AL	3	0	3	4.0	18	7	3	3	1	0	0	0	1	1	3	1	0	0	-	0-0	0	94	1.033	9.70	6.75
2016 Mil	NL	20	20	0	121.2	492	94	40	38	10	3	2	3	43	2	100	7	9	3	.750	0-0	0	93	.633	2.68	2.81
2017 Mil	NL	21	14	2	70.1	314	61	44	40	18	1	1	4	43	0	67	5	1	4	.200	0-0	0	93	.817	5.53	5.12
2018 Mil	NL	31	26	1	141.0	611	143	74	64	19	5	4	4	55	0	136	11	6	9	.400	0-0	1	93	.767	4.49	4.09
2019 Mil	NL	72	0	11	83.2	344	58	35	33	11	3	2	4	36	2	77	5	9	5	.643	3-11	20	95	.639	2.90	3.55
Postseason		2	0	2	4.2	15	2	1	1	0	0	0	0	0	0	5	1	0	1	.000	0-0	0	94	.267	0.43	1.93
5 ML YEARS		147	60	17	420.2	1779	363	196	178	59	12	9	15	178	5	383	29	25	21	.543	3-11	21	93	.716	3.82	3.81

Tayron Guerrero

Pitches: R **Bats:** R **Pos:** RP-52

ty-ROHN

Ht: 6'8" **Wt:** 210 **Born:** 1/9/1991 **Age:** 29

Year Team	Lg	G	GS	GF	IP	BFP	H	R	ER	HR	SH	SF	HB	TBB	IBB	SO	WP	W	L	Pct	Sv-Op	Hld	Vel	OPS	ERC	ERA
2016 SD	NL	1	0	1	2.0	9	3	1	1	0	0	0	0	1	0	0	0	0	0	-	0-0	0	95	.944	7.26	4.50
2018 Mia	NL	60	0	11	58.0	268	64	40	35	8	0	1	3	30	1	68	8	1	3	.250	0-4	9	99	.797	5.56	5.43
2019 Mia	NL	52	0	10	46.0	216	42	34	32	7	0	3	6	36	0	43	9	1	2	.333	0-4	6	99	.804	6.10	6.26
3 ML YEARS		113	0	22	106.0	493	109	75	68	15	0	4	9	67	1	111	17	2	5	.286	0-8	15	99	.803	5.82	5.77

Vladimir Guerrero Jr.

Bats: R **Throws:** R **Pos:** 3B-96;DH-24;PH-5

Ht: 6'2" **Wt:** 250 **Born:** 3/16/1999 **Age:** 21

Year Team	Lg	G	AB	H	2B	3B	HR	(Hm	Rd)	TB	R	RBI	RC	TBB	IBB	SO	HBP	SH	SF	SB	CS	GDP	Avg	OBP	Slg	OPS
2016 Bluefld	R+	62	236	64	12	3	8	(-	-)	106	32	46	41	33	1	35	2	0	5	15	5	3	.271	.359	.449	.808
2017 2 Tms	Low	119	437	141	28	2	13	(-	-)	212	84	76	94	76	3	62	7	0	7	8	4	15	.323	.425	.485	.910
2018 Nham	AA	61	234	94	19	1	14	(-	-)	157	48	60	64	21	5	27	4	1	6	3	3	3	.402	.449	.671	1.120
2018 Buffalo	AAA	30	110	37	7	0	6	(-	-)	62	15	16	25	15	0	10	1	0	2	0	0	4	.336	.414	.564	.978
2019 Tor	AL	123	464	126	26	2	15	(5	10)	201	52	69	67	46	0	91	2	0	2	0	1	17	.272	.339	.433	.772

Taylor Guerrieri

Pitches: R **Bats:** R **Pos:** RP-20

Ht: 6'2" **Wt:** 210 **Born:** 12/1/1992 **Age:** 27

Year Team	Lg	G	GS	GF	IP	BFP	H	R	ER	HR	SH	SF	HB	TBB	IBB	SO	WP	W	L	Pct	Sv-Op	Hld	Vel	OPS	ERC	ERA
2019 Nashv	AAA	23	2	3	36.1	152	36	15	14	1	0	0	1	15	0	39	3	1	3	.250	0--	-	-	.666	3.81	3.47
2018 Tor	AL	9	0	5	9.2	44	9	5	5	1	0	0	3	4	0	8	2	0	0	-	0-0	0	92	.688	5.00	4.66
2019 Tex	AL	20	0	5	26.1	123	26	19	17	3	0	0	2	22	0	27	2	0	0	-	0-3	3	94	.861	6.36	5.81
2 ML YEARS		29	0	10	36.0	167	35	24	22	4	0	0	5	26	0	35	4	0	0	-	0-3	3	93	.814	5.98	5.50

Taylor Guilbeau

Pitches: L **Bats:** L **Pos:** RP-17   **Ht:** 6'4" **Wt:** 180 **Born:** 5/12/1993 **Age:** 27

			HOW MUCH PITCHED					WHAT HE GAVE UP										THE RESULTS							
Year	Team	Lg	G	GS	GF	IP	BFP	H	R	ER	HR	SH	SF	HB	TBB	IBB	SO	WP	W	L	Pct	Sv-Op	Hld	Vel	OPS	ERC	ERA
2019	Hrsbrg	AA	27	0	8	35.0	141	27	10	9	1	1	1	2	10	0	44	4	1	2	.333	0--	-	-	.562	2.24	2.31
2019	Fresno	AAA	7	0	3	8.2	39	10	5	5	0	0	0	1	5	0	6	0	2	0	1.000	0--	-	-	.804	5.63	5.19
2019	Tacom	AAA	5	0	1	5.0	19	3	1	1	0	0	0	0	2	0	5	2	0	0	-	0--	-	-	.616	1.59	1.80
2019	Sea	AL	17	0	1	12.1	51	10	6	5	2	0	0	1	3	1	7	0	0	0	-	0-2	3	94	.657	2.99	3.65

Luis Guillorme

Bats: L **Throws:** R **Pos:** PH-25;2B-8;SS-8;3B-5;PR-4;DH-1 ghee-YOR-may   **Ht:** 5'10" **Wt:** 195 **Born:** 9/27/1994 **Age:** 25

			BATTING															RUNNING			AVERAGES			
Year	Team	Lg	G	AB	H	2B	3B	HR	(Hm | Rd)	TB	R	RBI	RC	TBB	IBB	SO	HBP	SH	SF	SB	CS	GDP	Avg	OBP	Slg	OPS
2019	Syrcse	AAA	69	228	70	12	0	7	(- | -)	103	33	32	44	39	0	42	3	3	3	4	4	5	.307	.410	.452	.862
2018	NYM	NL	35	67	14	2	0	0	(0 | 0)	16	4	5	6	7	0	3	0	0	0	1	0	1	.209	.284	.239	.523
2019	NYM	NL	45	61	15	4	0	1	(1 | 0)	22	8	3	5	7	0	14	0	2	0	0	0	2	.246	.324	.361	.684
	2 ML YEARS		80	128	29	6	0	1	(1 | 0)	38	12	8	11	14	0	17	0	2	0	1	0	3	.227	.303	.297	.600

Yuli Gurriel

Bats: R **Throws:** R **Pos:** 1B-110;3B-42;2B-4;DH-1;PH-1 yoo-lee goo-REE-el   **Ht:** 6'0" **Wt:** 190 **Born:** 6/9/1984 **Age:** 36

			BATTING															RUNNING			AVERAGES			
Year	Team	Lg	G	AB	H	2B	3B	HR	(Hm | Rd)	TB	R	RBI	RC	TBB	IBB	SO	HBP	SH	SF	SB	CS	GDP	Avg	OBP	Slg	OPS
2016	Hou	AL	36	130	34	7	0	3	(1 | 2)	50	13	15	13	5	0	12	1	0	1	1	1	7	.262	.292	.385	.677
2017	Hou	AL	139	529	158	43	1	18	(8 | 10)	257	69	75	83	22	1	62	7	0	6	3	2	12	.299	.332	.486	.817
2018	Hou	AL	136	537	156	33	1	13	(10 | 3)	230	70	85	88	23	0	63	6	0	7	5	1	22	.291	.323	.428	.751
2019	Hou	AL	144	564	168	40	2	31	(19 | 12)	305	85	104	98	37	2	65	5	0	6	5	3	12	.298	.343	.541	.884
	Postseason		26	100	28	9	1	3	(2 | 1)	48	10	11	17	9	1	15	0	0	0	0	0	1	.280	.339	.480	.819
	4 ML YEARS		455	1760	516	123	4	65	(38 | 27)	842	237	279	282	87	3	202	19	0	20	14	7	53	.293	.330	.478	.808

Lourdes Gurriel Jr.

Bats: R **Throws:** R **Pos:** LF-63;2B-9;DH-9;1B-3;PH-3 goo-REE-el   **Ht:** 6'3" **Wt:** 215 **Born:** 10/10/1993 **Age:** 26

			BATTING															RUNNING			AVERAGES			
Year	Team	Lg	G	AB	H	2B	3B	HR	(Hm | Rd)	TB	R	RBI	RC	TBB	IBB	SO	HBP	SH	SF	SB	CS	GDP	Avg	OBP	Slg	OPS
2019	Buffalo	AAA	31	123	34	13	0	4	(- | -)	59	18	26	17	3	0	23	3	0	1	0	2	4	.276	.308	.480	.787
2018	Tor	AL	65	249	70	8	0	11	(6 | 5)	111	30	35	30	9	1	59	2	1	2	1	2	4	.281	.309	.446	.755
2019	Tor	AL	84	314	87	19	2	20	(10 | 10)	170	52	50	51	20	0	86	5	1	3	6	4	2	.277	.327	.541	.869
	2 ML YEARS		149	563	157	27	2	31	(16 | 15)	281	82	85	81	29	1	145	7	2	5	7	6	6	.279	.320	.499	.819

Jandel Gustave

Pitches: R **Bats:** R **Pos:** RP-23 hahn-DELL goo-STAH-vay   **Ht:** 6'2" **Wt:** 210 **Born:** 10/12/1992 **Age:** 27

			HOW MUCH PITCHED					WHAT HE GAVE UP										THE RESULTS							
Year	Team	Lg	G	GS	GF	IP	BFP	H	R	ER	HR	SH	SF	HB	TBB	IBB	SO	WP	W	L	Pct	Sv-Op	Hld	Vel	OPS	ERC	ERA
2019	Scrmto	AAA	29	1	19	26.1	118	28	19	18	5	0	1	1	12	0	25	1	2	2	.500	7--	-	-	.819	5.47	6.15
2016	Hou	AL	14	0	4	15.1	60	13	6	6	2	0	0	0	4	0	16	2	1	0	1.000	0-0	0	97	.676	3.04	3.52
2017	Hou	AL	6	0	2	5.0	25	5	4	3	0	0	0	0	7	0	2	0	0	0	-	0-0	0	96	.813	7.65	5.40
2019	SF	NL	23	0	4	24.1	99	18	11	8	1	1	3	0	9	0	14	0	0	0	-	1-2	4	96	.566	2.22	2.96
	3 ML YEARS		43	0	10	44.2	184	36	21	17	3	1	3	0	20	0	32	2	1	0	1.000	1-2	4	96	.637	3.04	3.43

Kelvin Gutierrez

Bats: R **Throws:** R **Pos:** 3B-18;DH-2   **Ht:** 6'3" **Wt:** 215 **Born:** 8/28/1994 **Age:** 25

			BATTING															RUNNING			AVERAGES			
Year	Team	Lg	G	AB	H	2B	3B	HR	(Hm | Rd)	TB	R	RBI	RC	TBB	IBB	SO	HBP	SH	SF	SB	CS	GDP	Avg	OBP	Slg	OPS
2019	Omha	AAA	75	286	82	9	2	9	(- | -)	122	41	43	49	35	0	71	3	0	3	12	1	8	.287	.367	.427	.794
2019	KC	AL	20	73	19	2	1	1	(1 | 0)	26	4	11	9	5	0	24	0	0	1	1	0	2	.260	.304	.356	.660

Ronald Guzman

Bats: L **Throws:** L **Pos:** 1B-81;PH-7;DH-1   **Ht:** 6'5" **Wt:** 225 **Born:** 10/20/1994 **Age:** 25

			BATTING															RUNNING			AVERAGES			
Year	Team	Lg	G	AB	H	2B	3B	HR	(Hm | Rd)	TB	R	RBI	RC	TBB	IBB	SO	HBP	SH	SF	SB	CS	GDP	Avg	OBP	Slg	OPS
2019	Nashv	AAA	30	117	36	8	0	5	(- | -)	59	22	16	23	17	1	31	1	0	0	0	0	2	.308	.400	.504	.904
2018	Tex	AL	123	387	91	18	2	16	(7 | 9)	161	46	58	55	33	2	121	7	0	1	1	0	8	.235	.306	.416	.722
2019	Tex	AL	87	256	56	20	0	10	(2 | 8)	106	34	36	36	32	1	87	3	0	4	1	2	7	.219	.308	.414	.723
	2 ML YEARS		210	643	147	38	2	26	(9 | 17)	267	80	94	91	65	3	208	10	0	5	2	2	15	.229	.307	.415	.722

Jedd Gyorko

Bats: R **Throws:** R **Pos:** PH-36;3B-21;1B-8;2B-3;DH-1;PR-1 JERK-oh   **Ht:** 5'10" **Wt:** 215 **Born:** 9/23/1988 **Age:** 31

			BATTING															RUNNING			AVERAGES			
Year	Team	Lg	G	AB	H	2B	3B	HR	(Hm | Rd)	TB	R	RBI	RC	TBB	IBB	SO	HBP	SH	SF	SB	CS	GDP	Avg	OBP	Slg	OPS
2013	SD	NL	125	486	121	26	0	23	(13 | 10)	216	62	63	48	33	1	123	4	0	2	1	1	14	.249	.301	.444	.745
2014	SD	NL	111	400	84	17	1	10	(7 | 3)	133	37	51	42	36	1	100	4	0	3	3	2	8	.210	.280	.333	.612
2015	SD	NL	128	421	104	15	0	16	(9 | 7)	167	34	57	46	27	1	107	5	0	5	0	1	13	.247	.297	.397	.694
2016	StL	NL	128	400	97	9	1	30	(12 | 18)	198	58	59	54	37	1	96	0	0	1	0	0	11	.243	.306	.495	.801
2017	StL	NL	125	426	116	21	2	20	(9 | 11)	201	52	67	65	47	1	105	1	0	7	6	2	12	.272	.341	.472	.813

Year Team	Lg	G	AB	H	2B	3B	HR	(Hm	Rd)	TB	R	RBI	RC	TBB	IBB	SO	HBP	SH	SF	SB	CS	GDP	Avg	OBP	Slg	OPS
2018 StL	NL	125	351	92	19	1	11	(6	5)	146	49	47	53	44	0	77	3	0	4	2	0	12	.262	.346	.416	.762
2019 2 Tms	NL	62	92	16	1	0	2	(1	1)	23	6	9	7	9	0	24	0	0	0	2	0	3	.174	.248	.250	.498
19 StL	NL	38	56	11	0	0	2	(1	1)	17	5	7	7	6	0	14	0	0	0	2	0	1	.196	.274	.304	.578
19 LAD	NL	24	36	5	1	0	0	(0	0)	6	1	2	0	3	0	10	0	0	0	0	0	2	.139	.205	.167	.372
7 ML YEARS		804	2576	630	108	5	112	(57	55)	1084	298	353	315	233	5	632	17	0	22	14	6	73	.245	.309	.421	.730

Eric Haase

Bats: R Throws: R Pos: C-8;PH-3;DH-2 **Ht:** 5'10" **Wt:** 210 **Born:** 12/18/1992 **Age:** 27

Year Team	Lg	G	AB	H	2B	3B	HR	(Hm	Rd)	TB	R	RBI	RC	TBB	IBB	SO	HBP	SH	SF	SB	CS	GDP	Avg	OBP	Slg	OPS
2019 Clmbs	AAA	102	350	79	12	3	28	(-	-)	181	67	60	59	42	0	142	5	1	3	1	1	3	.226	.315	.517	.832
2018 Cle	AL	9	16	2	0	0	0	(0	0)	2	0	1	1	0	0	6	1	0	0	0	0	1	.125	.176	.125	.301
2019 Cle	AL	10	16	1	0	0	1	(0	1)	4	1	3	1	1	0	8	0	0	0	0	0	0	.063	.118	.250	.368
2 ML YEARS		19	32	3	0	0	1	(0	1)	6	1	4	2	1	0	14	1	0	0	0	0	1	.094	.147	.188	.335

Josh Hader

Pitches: L Bats: L Pos: RP-61 **Ht:** 6'3" **Wt:** 185 **Born:** 4/7/1994 **Age:** 26

Year Team	Lg	G	GS	GF	IP	BFP	H	R	ER	HR	SH	SF	HB	TBB	IBB	SO	WP	W	L	Pct	Sv-Op	Hld	Vel	OPS	ERC	ERA
2017 Mil	NL	35	0	2	47.2	188	25	11	11	4	1	4	2	22	1	68	0	2	3	.400	0-1	12	94	.554	2.09	2.08
2018 Mil	NL	55	0	14	81.1	306	36	23	22	9	1	2	1	30	0	143	0	6	1	.857	12-17	21	95	.484	1.45	2.43
2019 Mil	NL	61	0	46	75.2	289	41	24	22	15	0	0	4	20	2	138	0	3	5	.375	37-44	6	96	.591	1.98	2.62
Postseason		7	0	1	10.0	35	5	0	0	0	1	0	0	0	0	16	0	0	0	-	0-0	2	96	.328	0.71	0.00
3 ML YEARS		151	0	62	204.2	783	102	58	55	28	2	3	9	72	3	349	0	11	9	.550	49-62	39	95	.541	1.76	2.42

Sam Haggerty

Bats: B Throws: R Pos: PR-8;PH-3;2B-1;RF-1 **Ht:** 5'11" **Wt:** 175 **Born:** 5/26/1994 **Age:** 26

Year Team	Lg	G	AB	H	2B	3B	HR	(Hm	Rd)	TB	R	RBI	RC	TBB	IBB	SO	HBP	SH	SF	SB	CS	GDP	Avg	OBP	Slg	OPS
2019 Bnghtn	AA	68	247	64	8	5	2	(-	-)	88	39	13	38	40	0	78	4	0	1	19	4	4	.259	.370	.356	.726
2019 Syrcse	AAA	12	42	13	4	1	1	(-	-)	22	9	9	9	4	1	10	1	2	0	4	0	0	.310	.383	.524	.907
2019 NYM	NL	11	4	0	0	0	0	(0	0)	0	2	0	0	0	0	3	0	0	0	0	0	0	.000	.000	.000	.000

Jesse Hahn

Pitches: R Bats: R Pos: RP-6 **Ht:** 6'4" **Wt:** 215 **Born:** 7/30/1989 **Age:** 30

Year Team	Lg	G	GS	GF	IP	BFP	H	R	ER	HR	SH	SF	HB	TBB	IBB	SO	WP	W	L	Pct	Sv-Op	Hld	Vel	OPS	ERC	ERA
2014 SD	NL	14	12	2	73.1	306	57	26	25	4	3	1	2	32	1	70	4	7	4	.636	0-0	0	91	.623	2.91	3.07
2015 Oak	AL	16	16	0	96.2	406	88	46	36	5	1	2	8	25	1	64	7	6	6	.500	0-0	0	92	.623	3.00	3.35
2016 Oak	AL	9	9	0	46.1	203	57	32	31	8	1	1	0	19	1	23	2	2	4	.333	0-0	0	94	.860	6.22	6.02
2017 Oak	AL	14	13	1	69.2	316	78	46	41	4	3	6	3	27	0	55	2	3	6	.333	0-0	0	94	.748	4.46	5.30
2019 KC	AL	6	0	2	4.2	27	7	7	7	1	0	0	0	6	1	7	0	0	1	.000	0-0	0	95	1.053	11.57	13.50
5 ML YEARS		59	50	5	290.2	1258	287	157	140	22	8	10	15	109	4	219	15	18	21	.462	0-0	0	93	.701	3.91	4.33

David Hale

Pitches: R Bats: R Pos: RP-20 **Ht:** 6'2" **Wt:** 210 **Born:** 9/27/1987 **Age:** 32

Year Team	Lg	G	GS	GF	IP	BFP	H	R	ER	HR	SH	SF	HB	TBB	IBB	SO	WP	W	L	Pct	Sv-Op	Hld	Vel	OPS	ERC	ERA
2019 S-WB	AAA	7	7	0	32.2	145	36	17	15	3	1	2	2	10	0	30	1	3	2	.600	0-	-	-	.764	4.39	4.13
2013 Atl	NL	2	2	0	11.0	46	11	1	1	0	0	0	0	1	0	14	0	1	0	1.000	0-0	0	91	.572	2.18	0.82
2014 Atl	NL	45	6	13	87.1	383	89	38	32	5	1	3	3	39	8	44	5	4	5	.444	0-0	4	91	.714	4.05	3.30
2015 Col	NL	17	12	0	78.1	346	95	56	53	14	3	2	2	20	2	61	11	5	5	.500	0-0	0	90	.861	5.33	6.09
2016 Col	NL	2	0	0	2.0	12	4	3	3	1	0	0	0	2	0	1	0	0	0	-	0-0	0	90	1.200	17.51	13.50
2018 2 Tms	AL	4	0	1	13.2	62	16	7	7	3	0	0	1	5	0	8	0	0	0	-	0-0	0	91	.891	6.11	4.61
2019 NYY	AL	20	0	10	37.2	157	39	13	13	2	0	1	1	7	1	23	2	3	0	1.000	2-2	0	93	.712	3.19	3.11
18 NYY	AL	3	0	1	10.2	46	12	3	3	2	0	0	1	1	0	6	0	0	0	-	0-0	0	91	.804	4.42	2.53
18 Min	AL	1	0	0	3.0	16	4	4	4	1	0	0	0	4	0	2	0	0	0	-	0-0	0	92	1.167	13.17	12.00
Postseason		1	0	1	0.1	1	0	0	0	0	0	0	0	0	0	0	0	0	0	-	0-0	0	92	.000	0.00	0.00
6 ML YEARS		90	20	24	230.0	1006	254	118	109	25	4	6	7	74	11	151	18	13	10	.565	2-2	4	91	.775	4.44	4.27

Matt Hall

Pitches: L Bats: L Pos: RP-16 **Ht:** 6'0" **Wt:** 200 **Born:** 7/23/1993 **Age:** 26

Year Team	Lg	G	GS	GF	IP	BFP	H	R	ER	HR	SH	SF	HB	TBB	IBB	SO	WP	W	L	Pct	Sv-Op	Hld	Vel	OPS	ERC	ERA
2019 Toledo	AAA	25	13	5	86.2	392	102	58	51	16	1	2	3	31	0	106	6	5	4	.556	0-	-	-	.852	5.64	5.30
2018 Det	AL	5	0	2	8.0	48	19	16	13	1	0	2	1	3	0	5	2	0	0	-	0-0	0	89	1.146	13.40	14.63
2019 Det	AL	16	0	7	23.1	113	28	20	20	4	0	0	1	15	1	27	1	0	1	.000	0-1	0	90	.853	6.87	7.71
2 ML YEARS		21	0	9	31.1	161	47	36	33	5	0	2	2	18	1	32	3	0	1	.000	0-1	0	90	.941	8.45	9.48

Cole Hamels

Pitches: L **Bats:** L **Pos:** SP-27   **Ht:** 6'4" **Wt:** 205 **Born:** 12/27/1983 **Age:** 36

Year	Team	Lg	G	GS	GF	IP	BFP	H	R	ER	HR	SH	SF	HB	TBB	IBB	SO	WP	W	L	Pct	Sv-Op	Hld	Vel	OPS	ERC	ERA
			HOW MUCH PITCHED					**WHAT HE GAVE UP**											**THE RESULTS**								
2006	Phi	NL	23	23	0	132.1	558	117	66	60	19	6	8	3	48	4	145	5	9	8	.529	0-0	0	91	.730	3.61	4.08
2007	Phi	NL	28	28	0	183.1	743	163	72	69	25	5	5	3	43	4	177	5	15	5	.750	0-0	0	90	.686	3.12	3.39
2008	Phi	NL	33	33	0	227.1	914	193	89	78	28	6	2	1	53	7	196	0	14	10	.583	0-0	0	90	.657	2.76	3.09
2009	Phi	NL	32	32	0	193.2	814	206	95	93	24	7	5	5	43	4	168	1	10	11	.476	0-0	0	90	.755	3.98	4.32
2010	Phi	NL	33	33	0	208.2	856	185	74	71	26	7	0	8	61	5	211	3	12	11	.522	0-0	0	92	.693	3.36	3.06
2011	Phi	NL	32	31	0	216.0	850	169	68	67	19	9	3	5	44	2	194	3	14	9	.609	0-0	0	92	.596	2.23	2.79
2012	Phi	NL	31	31	0	215.1	867	190	80	73	24	6	4	3	52	3	216	3	17	6	.739	0-0	0	91	.661	2.98	3.05
2013	Phi	NL	33	33	0	220.0	905	205	94	88	21	11	3	9	50	5	202	4	8	14	.364	0-0	0	92	.699	3.15	3.60
2014	Phi	NL	30	30	0	204.2	829	176	60	56	14	7	7	8	59	3	198	6	9	9	.500	0-0	0	92	.641	2.88	2.46
2015	2 Tms		32	32	0	212.1	880	190	88	86	22	6	2	10	62	3	215	9	13	8	.619	0-0	0	93	.669	3.28	3.65
2016	Tex	AL	32	32	0	200.2	848	185	83	74	24	1	2	8	77	1	200	4	15	5	.750	0-0	0	93	.699	3.90	3.32
2017	Tex	AL	24	24	0	148.0	614	125	74	69	18	0	2	11	53	1	105	6	11	6	.647	0-0	0	92	.693	3.54	4.20
2018	2 Tms		32	32	0	190.2	806	176	93	80	29	1	4	19	65	0	188	7	9	12	.429	0-0	0	92	.746	4.23	3.78
2019	ChC	NL	27	27	0	141.2	617	141	64	60	17	4	6	7	56	1	143	1	7	7	.500	0-0	0	91	.740	4.35	3.81
15	Phi	NL	20	20	0	128.2	537	113	53	52	12	5	1	6	39	3	137	7	6	7	.462	0-0	0	92	.645	3.13	3.64
15	Tex	AL	12	12	0	83.2	343	77	35	34	10	1	1	4	23	0	78	2	7	1	.875	0-0	0	93	.705	3.54	3.66
18	Tex	AL	20	20	0	114.1	502	115	70	60	23	0	3	12	42	0	114	6	5	9	.357	0-0	0	91	.811	5.13	4.72
18	ChC	NL	12	12	0	76.1	304	61	23	20	6	1	1	7	23	0	74	1	4	3	.571	0-0	0	93	.639	2.95	2.36
	Postseason		17	16	0	100.1	411	83	45	38	12	4	2	2	27	2	93	1	7	6	.538	0-0	0	92	.653	2.79	3.41
	14 ML YEARS		422	421	0	2694.2	11101	2421	1100	1024	310	76	53	100	766	43	2558	57	163	121	.574	0-0	0	92	.688	3.32	3.42

Billy Hamilton

Bats: B **Throws:** R **Pos:** CF-114;PH-8;PR-7;DH-1   **Ht:** 6'0" **Wt:** 160 **Born:** 9/9/1990 **Age:** 29

Year	Team	Lg	G	AB	H	2B	3B	HR	(Hm	Rd)	TB	R	RBI	RC	TBB	IBB	SO	HBP	SH	SF	SB	CS	GDP	Avg	OBP	Slg	OPS
						BATTING															**RUNNING**			**AVERAGES**			
2013	Cin	NL	13	19	7	2	0	0	(0	0)	9	9	1	5	2	0	4	0	1	0	13	1	0	.368	.429	.474	.902
2014	Cin	NL	152	563	141	25	8	6	(3	3)	200	72	48	64	34	0	117	1	9	4	56	23	1	.250	.292	.355	.648
2015	Cin	NL	114	412	93	8	3	4	(2	2)	119	56	28	32	28	0	75	1	9	4	57	8	5	.226	.274	.289	.563
2016	Cin	NL	119	411	107	19	3	3	(2	1)	141	69	17	46	36	0	93	1	11	1	58	8	5	.260	.321	.343	.664
2017	Cin	NL	139	582	144	17	11	4	(3	1)	195	85	38	62	44	0	133	0	5	2	59	13	5	.247	.299	.335	.634
2018	Cin	NL	153	504	119	16	9	4	(4	0)	165	74	29	51	46	0	132	1	1	4	34	10	5	.236	.299	.327	.626
2019	2 Tms		119	316	69	14	2	0	(0	0)	87	41	15	29	32	1	87	0	3	2	22	6	1	.218	.289	.275	.564
19	KC	AL	93	275	58	12	2	0	(0	0)	74	32	12	22	25	0	74	0	3	2	18	5	1	.211	.275	.269	.544
19	Atl	NL	26	41	11	2	0	0	(0	0)	13	9	3	7	7	1	13	0	0	0	4	1	0	.268	.375	.317	.692
	7 ML YEARS		809	2807	680	101	36	21	(14	7)	916	406	176	289	222	1	641	4	39	17	299	69	18	.242	.297	.326	.623

J. D. Hammer

Pitches: R **Bats:** R **Pos:** RP-20   **Ht:** 6'3" **Wt:** 215 **Born:** 7/12/1994 **Age:** 25

Year	Team	Lg	G	GS	GF	IP	BFP	H	R	ER	HR	SH	SF	HB	TBB	IBB	SO	WP	W	L	Pct	Sv-Op	Hld	Vel	OPS	ERC	ERA
			HOW MUCH PITCHED					**WHAT HE GAVE UP**											**THE RESULTS**								
2019	Rdng	AA	13	0	4	20.1	81	17	7	4	1	0	0	0	4	1	26	1	1	0	1.000	2--	-	-	.610	2.09	1.77
2019	LV	AAA	17	0	5	15.2	81	20	22	22	4	1	1	0	15	0	16	0	2	2	.500	0--	-	-	1.031	9.50	12.64
2019	Phi	NL	20	0	7	19.0	81	15	8	8	2	0	0	0	12	0	13	1	1	0	1.000	0-1	0	94	.710	3.92	3.79

Garrett Hampson

Bats: R **Throws:** R **Pos:** 2B-50;CF-31;PH-18;SS-15;LF-2;PR-1   **Ht:** 5'11" **Wt:** 188 **Born:** 10/10/1994 **Age:** 25

Year	Team	Lg	G	AB	H	2B	3B	HR	(Hm	Rd)	TB	R	RBI	RC	TBB	IBB	SO	HBP	SH	SF	SB	CS	GDP	Avg	OBP	Slg	OPS
						BATTING															**RUNNING**			**AVERAGES**			
2019	Albq	AAA	26	109	29	9	1	2	(-	-)	46	15	9	15	5	0	25	2	1	0	7	2	4	.266	.310	.422	.732
2018	Col	NL	24	40	11	3	1	0	(0	0)	16	3	4	9	7	0	12	1	0	0	2	0	0	.275	.396	.400	.796
2019	Col	NL	105	299	74	9	4	8	(1	7)	115	40	27	29	24	1	88	0	2	2	15	3	2	.247	.302	.385	.686
	Postseason		2	1	0	0	0	0	(0	0)	0	1	0	0	0	0	0	0	0	0	0	0	0	.000	.000	.000	.000
	2 ML YEARS		129	339	85	12	5	8	(1	7)	131	43	31	38	31	1	100	1	2	2	17	3	2	.251	.314	.386	.700

Brad Hand

Pitches: L **Bats:** L **Pos:** RP-60   **Ht:** 6'3" **Wt:** 220 **Born:** 3/20/1990 **Age:** 30

Year	Team	Lg	G	GS	GF	IP	BFP	H	R	ER	HR	SH	SF	HB	TBB	IBB	SO	WP	W	L	Pct	Sv-Op	Hld	Vel	OPS	ERC	ERA
			HOW MUCH PITCHED					**WHAT HE GAVE UP**											**THE RESULTS**								
2011	Fla	NL	12	12	0	60.0	263	53	32	28	10	4	3	1	35	1	38	0	1	8	.111	0-0	0	90	.789	4.68	4.20
2012	Mia	NL	1	1	0	3.2	23	6	7	7	1	0	0	0	6	1	3	0	0	1	.000	0-0	0	90	1.169	14.74	17.18
2013	Mia	NL	7	2	2	20.2	82	13	7	7	2	0	0	0	8	0	15	1	1	1	.500	0-0	0	93	.553	2.10	3.05
2014	Mia	NL	32	16	5	111.0	474	112	56	54	10	6	2	2	39	3	67	5	3	8	.273	1-1	0	92	.732	3.91	4.38
2015	Mia	NL	38	12	7	93.1	408	107	55	55	9	5	2	3	32	1	67	2	4	7	.364	0-0	2	92	.784	4.83	5.30
2016	SD	NL	82	0	16	89.1	364	63	32	29	8	2	1	7	36	4	111	7	4	4	.500	1-7	21	93	.589	2.44	2.92
2017	SD	NL	72	0	32	79.1	311	54	20	19	9	1	1	7	20	1	104	1	3	4	.429	21-26	16	94	.580	2.30	2.16
2018	2 Tms		69	0	42	72.0	301	52	28	22	8	2	0	9	28	2	106	2	2	5	.286	32-39	10	94	.656	3.03	2.75
2019	Cle	AL	60	0	54	57.1	242	53	21	21	6	1	0	4	18	5	84	0	6	4	.600	34-39	0	93	.695	3.50	3.30
18	SD	NL	41	0	31	44.1	186	33	21	15	5	1	0	7	15	1	65	1	2	4	.333	24-29	3	94	.672	3.09	3.05
18	Cle	AL	28	0	11	27.2	115	19	7	7	3	1	0	2	13	1	41	1	0	1	.000	8-10	7	93	.632	2.94	2.28
	Postseason		2	0	1	1.2	9	3	2	2	1	0	0	0	1	1	4	1	0	0	-	0-0	0	93	1.194	13.35	10.80
	9 ML YEARS		373	43	158	586.2	2468	513	258	242	63	21	10	27	222	18	595	21	24	42	.364	89-112	49	92	.691	3.50	3.71

Mitch Haniger

Bats: R Throws: R Pos: RF-43;CF-24;DH-1;PR-1   **Ht: 6'2" Wt: 215 Born: 12/23/1990 Age: 29**

Year Team	Lg	G	AB	H	2B	3B	HR	(Hm	Rd)	TB	R	RBI	RC	TBB	IBB	SO	HBP	SH	SF	SB	CS	GDP	Avg	OBP	Slg	OPS
2016 Ari	NL	34	109	25	2	1	5	(4	1)	44	9	17	16	12	2	27	1	0	1	0	0	3	.229	.309	.404	.713
2017 Sea	AL	96	369	104	25	2	16	(6	10)	181	58	47	55	31	0	93	9	1	0	5	4	9	.282	.352	.491	.843
2018 Sea	AL	157	596	170	38	4	26	(12	14)	294	90	93	102	70	4	148	10	0	7	8	2	8	.285	.366	.493	.859
2019 Sea	AL	63	246	54	13	1	15	(7	8)	114	46	32	35	30	1	81	5	0	2	4	0	3	.220	.314	.463	.778
4 ML YEARS		350	1320	353	78	8	62	(29	33)	633	203	189	208	143	7	349	25	1	10	17	6	23	.267	.348	.480	.827

Alen Hanson

Bats: B Throws: R Pos: 2B-8;RF-5;PH-3;PR-3;1B-2;DH-2;LF-1   **Ht: 6'0" Wt: 170 Born: 10/22/1992 Age: 27**

Year Team	Lg	G	AB	H	2B	3B	HR	(Hm	Rd)	TB	R	RBI	RC	TBB	IBB	SO	HBP	SH	SF	SB	CS	GDP	Avg	OBP	Slg	OPS
2019 Buffalo	AAA	48	166	31	3	1	3	(-	-)	45	19	18	10	9	0	39	1	3	1	7	2	4	.187	.232	.271	.503
2016 Pit	NL	27	31	7	1	0	0	(0	0)	8	5	1	1	2	1	5	0	0	0	2	1	0	.226	.273	.258	.531
2017 2 Tms		106	217	48	9	3	4	(3	1)	75	36	11	14	12	0	52	1	1	3	11	3	5	.221	.262	.346	.607
2018 SF	NL	110	294	74	17	5	8	(3	5)	125	36	39	38	9	0	71	1	3	3	7	3	4	.252	.274	.425	.699
2019 Tor	AL	18	43	7	0	0	0	(0	0)	7	5	4	3	3	1	17	1	0	1	1	0	0	.163	.229	.163	.392
17 Pit	NL	37	57	11	0	2	0	(0	0)	15	8	1	2	2	0	9	0	0	0	2	1	0	.193	.220	.263	.483
17 CWS	AL	69	160	37	9	1	4	(3	1)	60	28	10	12	10	0	43	1	1	3	9	2	5	.231	.276	.375	.651
4 ML YEARS		261	585	136	27	8	12	(6	6)	215	82	55	56	26	2	145	3	4	7	21	7	9	.232	.266	.368	.633

Ian Happ

Bats: B Throws: R Pos: PH-19;LF-15;2B-13;CF-13;3B-8;RF-8;1B-7   **Ht: 6'0" Wt: 205 Born: 8/12/1994 Age: 25**

Year Team	Lg	G	AB	H	2B	3B	HR	(Hm	Rd)	TB	R	RBI	RC	TBB	IBB	SO	HBP	SH	SF	SB	CS	GDP	Avg	OBP	Slg	OPS
2019 Iowa	AAA	99	359	87	18	1	16	(-	-)	155	66	53	61	65	0	113	4	0	1	9	2	0	.242	.364	.432	.795
2017 ChC	NL	115	364	92	17	3	24	(15	9)	187	62	68	57	39	5	129	4	2	4	8	4	12	.253	.328	.514	.842
2018 ChC	NL	142	387	90	19	2	15	(7	8)	158	56	44	56	70	9	167	3	0	2	8	4	6	.233	.353	.408	.761
2019 ChC	NL	58	140	37	7	1	11	(4	7)	79	25	30	30	15	0	39	0	0	1	2	0	1	.264	.333	.564	.898
Postseason		6	7	1	0	0	0	(0	0)	1	0	0	0	2	0	5	0	0	0	0	0	0	.143	.333	.143	.476
3 ML YEARS		315	891	219	43	6	50	(26	24)	424	143	142	143	124	14	335	7	2	7	18	8	19	.246	.340	.476	.816

J.A. Happ

Pitches: L Bats: L Pos: SP-30; RP-1   JAY   **Ht: 6'5" Wt: 205 Born: 10/19/1982 Age: 37**

Year Team	Lg	HOW MUCH PITCHED					WHAT HE GAVE UP												THE RESULTS							
		G	GS	GF	IP	BFP	H	R	ER	HR	SH	SF	HB	TBB	IBB	SO	WP	W	L	Pct	Sv-Op	Hld	Vel	OPS	ERC	ERA
2007 Phi	NL	1	1	0	4.0	21	7	5	5	3	0	0	2	0	5	0		0	1	.000	0-0	0	88	1.323	15.13	11.25
2008 Phi	NL	8	4	1	31.2	138	28	13	13	3	2	1	1	14	1	26	1	1	0	1.000	0-0	1	89	.658	3.55	3.69
2009 Phi	NL	35	23	4	166.0	685	149	55	54	20	7	6	5	56	2	119	2	12	4	.750	0-0	0	90	.710	3.57	2.93
2010 2 Tms	NL	16	16	0	87.1	374	73	37	33	8	5	4	1	47	1	70	4	6	4	.600	0-0	0	90	.688	3.69	3.40
2011 Hou	NL	28	28	0	156.1	698	157	103	93	21	12	8	2	83	5	134	3	6	15	.286	0-0	0	90	.806	4.86	5.35
2012 2 Tms	NL	28	24	3	144.2	627	147	79	77	19	9	4	2	56	1	144	7	10	11	.476	0-0	1	90	.787	4.37	4.79
2013 Tor	AL	18	18	0	92.2	415	91	53	47	10	1	3	2	45	0	77	5	5	7	.417	0-0	1	91	.734	4.36	4.56
2014 Tor	AL	30	26	2	158.0	673	160	79	74	22	1	5	2	51	0	133	1	11	11	.500	0-0	1	93	.770	4.17	4.22
2015 2 Tms	AL	32	31	0	172.0	717	173	71	69	16	2	0	2	45	4	151	6	11	8	.579	0-0	2	92	.698	3.56	3.61
2016 Tor	AL	32	32	0	195.0	796	168	72	69	22	2	2	6	60	0	163	3	20	4	.833	0-0	0	92	.665	3.22	3.18
2017 Tor	AL	25	25	0	145.1	626	145	64	57	18	1	4	0	46	1	142	4	10	11	.476	0-0	0	92	.700	3.81	3.53
2018 2 Tms	AL	31	31	0	177.2	733	150	81	72	27	2	2	9	51	0	193	4	17	6	.739	0-0	0	92	.677	3.32	3.65
2019 NYY	AL	31	30	0	161.1	678	160	88	88	34	0	2	5	49	1	140	3	12	8	.600	0-0	1	91	.785	4.57	4.91
10 Phi	NL	3	3	0	15.1	70	13	4	3	1	1	1	0	12	0	9	1	1	0	1.000	0-0	0	89	.702	4.40	1.76
10 Hou	NL	13	13	0	72.0	304	60	33	30	7	4	3	1	35	1	61	3	5	4	.556	0-0	0	90	.684	3.53	3.75
12 Hou	NL	18	18	0	104.1	457	112	58	56	17	7	2	1	39	0	98	5	7	9	.438	0-0	0	90	.818	4.86	4.83
12 Tor	AL	10	6	3	40.1	170	35	21	21	2	2	2	1	17	1	46	2	3	2	.600	0-0	1	91	.701	3.16	4.69
15 Sea	AL	21	20	0	108.2	468	121	58	56	13	1	0	2	32	3	82	4	4	6	.400	0-0	0	92	.764	4.49	4.64
15 Pit	NL	11	11	0	63.1	249	52	13	13	3	1	0	0	13	1	69	2	7	2	.778	0-0	0	92	.577	2.12	1.85
18 Tor	AL	20	20	0	114.0	475	99	61	53	17	1	1	4	35	0	130	1	10	6	.625	0-0	0	92	.677	3.43	4.18
18 NYY	AL	11	11	0	63.2	258	51	20	19	10	1	1	5	16	0	63	3	7	0	1.000	0-0	0	92	.676	3.11	2.69
Postseason		11	4	0	21.1	102	29	13	13	3	0	0	0	11	0	21	1	1	2	.333	0-0	1	91	.843	7.03	5.48
13 ML YEARS		315	289	10	1692.0	7181	1608	800	751	223	44	41	37	605	16	1497	43	121	90	.573	0-0	2	91	.729	3.93	3.99

Blaine Hardy

Pitches: L Bats: L Pos: RP-39   **Ht: 6'2" Wt: 218 Born: 3/14/1987 Age: 33**

Year Team	Lg	HOW MUCH PITCHED					WHAT HE GAVE UP												THE RESULTS							
		G	GS	GF	IP	BFP	H	R	ER	HR	SH	SF	HB	TBB	IBB	SO	WP	W	L	Pct	Sv-Op	Hld	Vel	OPS	ERC	ERA
2014 Det	AL	38	0	7	39.0	167	34	12	11	1	1	2	1	20	3	31	1	2	1	.667	0-1	4	89	.611	3.28	2.54
2015 Det	AL	70	0	11	61.1	265	61	23	21	3	3	4	1	22	2	55	5	5	3	.625	0-3	13	88	.704	3.38	3.08
2016 Det	AL	21	0	10	25.2	112	25	11	10	2	1	0	0	12	1	20	1	1	0	1.000	0-0	0	88	.707	3.95	3.51
2017 Det	AL	35	0	9	33.1	156	46	24	22	7	0	4	0	13	1	28	1	1	0	1.000	0-0	6	90	.925	7.12	5.94
2018 Det	AL	30	13	0	86.0	351	79	37	34	10	1	4	2	22	1	66	2	4	5	.444	1-1	2	88	.698	3.30	3.56
2019 Det	AL	39	0	3	44.1	182	38	24	22	10	1	4	0	13	0	29	3	1	1	.500	0-0	7	88	.751	3.66	4.47
6 ML YEARS		233	13	45	289.2	1233	283	131	120	32	7	18	4	102	8	229	13	14	10	.583	1-5	32	89	.726	3.84	3.73

Bryce Harper

Bats: L **Throws:** R **Pos:** RF-152;PH-3;DH-2 **Ht:** 6'3" **Wt:** 220 **Born:** 10/16/1992 **Age:** 27

								BATTING												RUNNING			AVERAGES			
Year	Team	Lg	G	AB	H	2B	3B	HR	(Hm | Rd)	TB	R	RBI	RC	TBB	IBB	SO	HBP	SH	SF	SB	CS	GDP	Avg	OBP	Slg	OPS
2012	Was	NL	139	533	144	26	9	22	(10 | 12)	254	98	59	82	56	0	120	2	3	3	18	6	8	.270	.340	.477	.817
2013	Was	NL	118	424	116	24	3	20	(13 | 7)	206	71	58	73	61	4	94	5	3	4	11	4	4	.274	.368	.486	.854
2014	Was	NL	100	352	96	10	2	13	(5 | 8)	149	41	32	43	38	4	104	1	3	1	2	2	6	.273	.344	.423	.768
2015	Was	NL	153	521	172	38	1	42	(23 | 19)	338	118	99	138	124	15	131	5	0	4	6	4	15	.330	.460	.649	1.109
2016	Was	NL	147	506	123	24	2	24	(12 | 12)	223	84	86	90	108	20	117	3	0	10	21	10	11	.243	.373	.441	.814
2017	Was	NL	111	420	134	27	1	29	(12 | 17)	250	95	87	93	68	11	99	1	0	3	4	2	5	.319	.413	.595	1.008
2018	Was	NL	159	550	137	34	0	34	(17 | 17)	273	103	100	111	130	16	169	6	0	9	13	3	7	.249	.393	.496	.889
2019	Phi	NL	157	573	149	36	1	35	(20 | 15)	292	98	114	125	99	11	178	6	0	4	15	3	10	.260	.372	.510	.882
	Postseason		19	76	16	4	1	5	(3 | 2)	37	12	10	12	11	1	23	1	0	1	4	0	0	.211	.315	.487	.801
	8 ML YEARS		1084	3879	1071	219	19	219	(112 | 107)	1985	708	635	755	684	81	1012	29	9	38	90	34	76	.276	.385	.512	.897

Ryne Harper

Pitches: R **Bats:** R **Pos:** RP-61 **Ht:** 6'3" **Wt:** 215 **Born:** 3/27/1989 **Age:** 31

			HOW MUCH PITCHED					WHAT HE GAVE UP										THE RESULTS						
Year	Team	Lg	G	GS	GF	IP	BFP	H	R	ER	HR	SH	SF	HB	TBB	IBB	SO	WP	W	L	Pct	Sv-Op	Hld	Vel	OPS	ERC	ERA
2019	Min	AL	61	0	7	54.1	225	54	25	23	7	0	3	1	10	0	50	5	4	2	.667	1-4	12	89	.709	3.44	3.81

Will Harris

Pitches: R **Bats:** R **Pos:** RP-68 **Ht:** 6'4" **Wt:** 240 **Born:** 8/28/1984 **Age:** 35

			HOW MUCH PITCHED					WHAT HE GAVE UP										THE RESULTS						
Year	Team	Lg	G	GS	GF	IP	BFP	H	R	ER	HR	SH	SF	HB	TBB	IBB	SO	WP	W	L	Pct	Sv-Op	Hld	Vel	OPS	ERC	ERA
2012	Col	NL	20	0	10	17.2	89	27	18	16	3	2	1	1	6	1	19	4	1	1	.500	0-0	3	91	.922	7.39	8.15
2013	Ari	NL	61	0	11	52.2	217	50	17	17	3	0	4	2	15	1	53	4	4	1	.800	0-1	4	92	.661	3.25	2.91
2014	Ari	NL	29	0	8	29.0	120	27	14	14	3	1	1	2	9	2	35	1	0	3	.000	0-1	3	92	.740	3.62	4.34
2015	Hou	AL	68	0	18	71.0	276	42	18	15	8	2	1	1	22	1	68	2	5	5	.500	2-6	13	92	.525	1.79	1.90
2016	Hou	AL	66	0	19	64.0	255	52	17	16	3	1	2	1	15	1	69	4	1	2	.333	12-15	28	92	.560	2.21	2.25
2017	Hou	AL	46	0	5	45.1	177	37	15	15	7	0	0	0	7	0	52	1	3	2	.600	2-4	20	92	.613	2.52	2.98
2018	Hou	AL	61	0	11	56.2	230	48	22	22	3	1	1	2	14	1	64	6	5	3	.625	0-3	16	92	.591	2.50	3.49
2019	Hou	AL	68	0	10	60.0	229	42	14	10	6	1	0	0	14	0	62	3	4	1	.800	4-5	26	88	.540	1.99	1.50
	Postseason		11	0	1	8.0	40	15	7	6	1	0	0	0	2	0	5	3	0	1	.000	0-1	4	92	1.004	9.15	6.75
	8 ML YEARS		419	0	92	396.1	1593	325	135	125	36	8	10	9	102	7	422	25	23	18	.561	20-35	113	92	.608	2.60	2.84

Josh Harrison

Bats: R **Throws:** R **Pos:** 2B-34;PR-2;DH-1 **Ht:** 5'8" **Wt:** 185 **Born:** 7/8/1987 **Age:** 32

								BATTING												RUNNING			AVERAGES			
Year	Team	Lg	G	AB	H	2B	3B	HR	(Hm	Rd)	TB	R	RBI	RC	TBB	IBB	SO	HBP	SH	SF	SB	CS	GDP	Avg	OBP	Slg	OPS
2011	Pit	NL	65	195	53	13	2	1	(1	0)	73	21	16	19	3	0	24	0	5	1	4	1	6	.272	.281	.374	.656
2012	Pit	NL	104	249	58	9	5	3	(1	2)	86	34	16	22	10	0	37	7	7	3	7	3	3	.233	.279	.345	.624
2013	Pit	NL	60	88	22	1	2	3	(1	2)	36	10	14	11	2	0	10	3	2	0	2	0	4	.250	.290	.409	.699
2014	Pit	NL	143	520	164	38	7	13	(4	9)	255	77	52	84	22	1	81	4	2	2	18	7	6	.315	.347	.490	.837
2015	Pit	NL	114	418	120	29	1	4	(2	2)	163	57	28	48	19	1	71	7	3	2	10	8	4	.287	.327	.390	.717
2016	Pit	NL	131	487	138	25	7	4	(2	2)	189	57	59	61	18	0	76	5	4	8	19	4	10	.283	.311	.388	.699
2017	Pit	NL	128	486	132	26	2	16	(9	7)	210	66	47	65	28	2	90	23	2	3	12	4	5	.272	.339	.432	.771
2018	Pit	NL	97	344	86	13	1	8	(3	5)	125	41	37	42	18	1	68	5	2	5	3	0	8	.250	.293	.363	.656
2019	Det	AL	36	137	24	7	1	1	(1	0)	36	10	8	3	6	0	27	2	0	2	4	2	0	.175	.218	.263	.480
	Postseason		4	7	2	0	0	0	(0	0)	2	1	0	0	0	0	2	1	0	0	0	1	0	.286	.375	.286	.661
	9 ML YEARS		878	2924	797	161	28	53	(24	29)	1173	373	277	355	126	5	484	56	27	26	79	29	46	.273	.313	.401	.714

Donnie Hart

Pitches: L **Bats:** L **Pos:** RP-5 **Ht:** 5'11" **Wt:** 180 **Born:** 9/6/1990 **Age:** 29

			HOW MUCH PITCHED					WHAT HE GAVE UP										THE RESULTS						
Year	Team	Lg	G	GS	GF	IP	BFP	H	R	ER	HR	SH	SF	HB	TBB	IBB	SO	WP	W	L	Pct	Sv-Op	Hld	Vel	OPS	ERC	ERA
2019	SnAnt	AAA	40	0	5	37.1	169	43	21	17	3	2	0	0	13	1	30	0	4	3	.571	3--	-	-	.731	4.40	4.10
2019	Syrcse	AAA	8	0	0	7.1	34	11	5	5	2	0	0	0	1	0	3	0	0	0	-	0--	-	-	.959	7.12	6.14
2016	Bal	AL	22	0	3	18.1	71	12	1	1	1	2	1	0	6	1	12	0	0	0	-	0-0	4	88	.519	1.76	0.49
2017	Bal	AL	51	0	12	43.2	190	48	19	18	5	0	1	4	13	0	29	1	2	0	1.000	0-2	5	88	.755	4.75	3.71
2018	Bal	AL	20	0	3	19.1	99	31	13	12	2	0	1	0	12	0	13	0	0	0	-	0-0	0	88	.923	8.79	5.59
2019	2 Tms	NL	5	0	2	7.2	29	4	0	0	0	0	0	0	4	1	3	0	0	0	-	0-0	0	87	.436	1.49	0.00
19	Mil	NL	4	0	2	6.2	26	4	0	0	0	0	0	0	4	1	3	0	0	0	-	0-0	0	87	.490	1.99	0.00
19	NYM	NL	1	0	0	1.0	3	0	0	0	0	0	0	0	0	0	0	0	0	0	-	0-0	0	87	.000	0.00	0.00
	Postseason		1	0	0	0.1	1	0	0	0	0	0	0	0	0	0	0	0	0	0	-	0-0	0	88	.000	0.00	0.00
	4 ML YEARS		98	0	20	89.0	389	95	33	31	8	2	3	4	35	2	57	1	2	0	1.000	0-2	10	88	.732	4.54	3.13

Geoff Hartlieb

Pitches: R **Bats:** R **Pos:** RP-29 **Ht:** 6'5" **Wt:** 235 **Born:** 12/9/1993 **Age:** 26

			HOW MUCH PITCHED					WHAT HE GAVE UP										THE RESULTS						
Year	Team	Lg	G	GS	GF	IP	BFP	H	R	ER	HR	SH	SF	HB	TBB	IBB	SO	WP	W	L	Pct	Sv-Op	Hld	Vel	OPS	ERC	ERA
2019	Indy	AAA	26	0	10	39.2	163	31	11	11	0	0	2	0	15	0	50	5	4	1	.800	3--	-	-	.584	2.19	2.50
2019	Pit	NL	29	0	10	35.0	171	52	35	35	8	1	4	0	18	0	38	5	0	1	.000	0-0	2	96	1.020	8.67	9.00

Hunter Harvey

Pitches: R **Bats:** R **Pos:** RP-7   **Ht:** 6'3" **Wt:** 175 **Born:** 12/9/1994 **Age:** 25

Year	Team	Lg	G	GS	GF	IP	BFP	H	R	ER	HR	SH	SF	HB	TBB	IBB	SO	WP	W	L	Pct	Sv-Op	Hld	Vel	OPS	ERC	ERA
2019	Bowie	AA	14	11	1	59.0	257	63	40	34	14	0	0	6	21	0	61	2	2	5	.286	1- -	-	-	.859	5.83	5.19
2019	Norfolk	AAA	12	0	0	16.2	70	13	8	8	2	1	0	1	5	0	22	0	1	1	.500	0- -	-	-	.656	2.78	4.32
2019	Bal	AL	7	0	1	6.1	26	3	1	1	1	0	0	0	4	0	11	0	1	0	1.000	0-1	1	98	.678	2.51	1.42

Joe Harvey

Pitches: R **Bats:** R **Pos:** RP-18   **Ht:** 6'2" **Wt:** 235 **Born:** 1/9/1992 **Age:** 28

Year	Team	Lg	G	GS	GF	IP	BFP	H	R	ER	HR	SH	SF	HB	TBB	IBB	SO	WP	W	L	Pct	Sv-Op	Hld	Vel	OPS	ERC	ERA
2019	S-WB	AAA	22	0	18	26.0	111	15	10	9	4	1	0	2	15	0	38	3	0	1	.000	9- -	-	-	.657	3.04	3.12
2019	Albq	AAA	9	0	3	8.2	43	12	10	10	5	0	2	0	5	0	10	1	0	1	.000	1- -	-	-	1.173	11.11	10.38
2019	2 Tms		18	0	7	18.0	84	18	11	10	3	0	1	2	13	0	17	0	1	0	1.000	0-0	0	95	.834	6.48	5.00
19	NYY	AL	9	0	4	10.0	48	11	6	5	1	0	1	1	7	0	11	0	1	0	1.000	0-0	0	95	.832	6.28	4.50
19	Col	NL	9	0	3	8.0	36	7	5	5	2	0	0	1	6	0	6	0	0	0	-	0-0	0	95	.837	6.71	5.63

Matt Harvey

Pitches: R **Bats:** R **Pos:** SP-12   **Ht:** 6'4" **Wt:** 220 **Born:** 3/27/1989 **Age:** 31

Year	Team	Lg	G	GS	GF	IP	BFP	H	R	ER	HR	SH	SF	HB	TBB	IBB	SO	WP	W	L	Pct	Sv-Op	Hld	Vel	OPS	ERC	ERA
2019	LsVgs	AAA	5	3	1	17.0	67	13	6	6	2	0	0	0	5	0	21	0	1	0	1.000	0- -	-	95	.640	2.60	3.18
2012	NYM	NL	10	10	0	59.1	245	42	19	18	5	3	3	3	26	0	70	3	3	5	.375	0-0	0	95	.631	2.75	2.73
2013	NYM	NL	26	26	0	178.1	690	135	46	45	7	5	4	4	31	1	191	2	9	5	.643	0-0	0	96	.530	1.76	2.27
2015	NYM	NL	29	29	0	189.1	755	156	62	57	18	7	2	5	37	2	188	4	13	8	.619	0-0	0	96	.609	2.44	2.71
2016	NYM	NL	17	17	0	92.2	402	111	55	50	8	5	4	1	25	1	76	4	4	10	.286	0-0	0	94	.797	4.65	4.86
2017	NYM	NL	19	18	0	92.2	431	110	70	69	21	3	2	6	47	3	67	6	5	7	.417	0-0	0	94	.890	6.87	6.70
2018	2 Tms		32	28	2	155.0	663	165	87	85	27	6	5	6	37	2	131	2	7	9	.438	0-0	0	94	.783	4.42	4.94
2019	LAA	AL	12	12	0	59.2	266	63	48	47	13	1	4	3	29	0	39	3	3	5	.375	0-0	0	93	.887	5.91	7.09
18	NYM	NL	8	4	2	27.0	123	33	21	21	6	2	2	1	9	0	20	1	0	2	.000	0-0	0	93	.906	6.10	7.00
18	Cin	NL	24	24	0	128.0	540	132	66	64	21	4	3	5	28	2	111	1	7	7	.500	0-0	0	94	.756	4.08	4.50
	Postseason		4	4	0	26.2	109	21	10	9	2	0	1	1	8	1	27	0	2	0	1.000	0-0	0	95	.578	2.49	3.04
	7 ML YEARS		145	140	2	827.0	3452	782	387	371	99	30	24	28	232	9	762	24	44	49	.473	0-0	0	95	.705	3.57	4.04

Adam Haseley

Bats: L **Throws:** L **Pos:** CF-40;LF-22;RF-10;PH-3;PR-1   **Ht:** 6'1" **Wt:** 195 **Born:** 4/12/1996 **Age:** 24

Year	Team	Lg	G	AB	H	2B	3B	HR	(Hm	Rd)	TB	R	RBI	RC	TBB	IBB	SO	HBP	SH	SF	SB	CS	GDP	Avg	OBP	Slg	OPS
2019	Rdng	AA	44	165	44	8	2	8	(-	-)	80	30	21	29	21	1	35	2	0	2	4	2	4	.267	.353	.485	.837
2019	LV	AAA	18	68	20	6	0	2	(-	-)	32	8	9	12	8	1	14	1	1	0	1	1	1	.294	.377	.471	.847
2019	Phi	NL	67	222	59	14	0	5	(3	2)	88	30	26	28	14	1	60	5	1	0	4	0	7	.266	.324	.396	.720

Ke'Bryan Hayes

Bats: R **Throws:** R **Pos:** 3B   **Ht:** 6'1" **Wt:** 210 **Born:** 1/28/1997 **Age:** 23

Year	Team	Lg	G	AB	H	2B	3B	HR	(Hm	Rd)	TB	R	RBI	RC	TBB	IBB	SO	HBP	SH	SF	SB	CS	GDP	Avg	OBP	Slg	OPS
2015	2 Tms	Low	56	185	57	5	1	0	(-	-)	64	32	20	31	28	1	31	6	4	4	8	2	2	.308	.408	.346	.754
2016	2 Tms	Low	67	252	67	13	1	6	(-	-)	100	27	37	32	17	1	52	6	3	4	6	5	5	.266	.323	.397	.719
2017	Bradtn	A+	108	421	117	16	7	2	(-	-)	153	66	43	60	41	0	76	4	12	4	27	5	12	.278	.345	.363	.708
2018	Altna	AA	117	437	128	31	7	7	(-	-)	194	64	47	77	57	0	84	4	4	6	12	5	10	.293	.375	.444	.819
2019	Indy	AAA	110	427	113	30	2	10	(-	-)	177	64	53	64	43	0	90	5	1	4	12	1	8	.265	.336	.415	.751

Austin Hays

Bats: R **Throws:** R **Pos:** CF-20;PH-4   **Ht:** 6'1" **Wt:** 195 **Born:** 7/5/1995 **Age:** 24

Year	Team	Lg	G	AB	H	2B	3B	HR	(Hm	Rd)	TB	R	RBI	RC	TBB	IBB	SO	HBP	SH	SF	SB	CS	GDP	Avg	OBP	Slg	OPS
2019	Bowie	AA	14	56	15	5	0	3	(-	-)	29	9	11	9	5	0	11	0	0	0	3	1	3	.268	.328	.518	.846
2019	Norfolk	AAA	59	240	61	16	1	10	(-	-)	109	43	27	33	11	0	61	6	0	0	6	4	5	.254	.304	.454	.758
2019	2 Tms	Low	14	55	11	2	0	4	(-	-)	25	8	10	6	2	0	11	2	0	1	1	0	1	.200	.250	.455	.705
2017	Bal	AL	20	60	13	3	0	1	(0	1)	19	4	8	5	2	0	16	0	0	1	0	0	2	.217	.238	.317	.555
2019	Bal	AL	21	68	21	6	0	4	(2	2)	39	12	13	16	7	0	13	0	0	0	2	0	0	.309	.373	.574	.947
	2 ML YEARS		41	128	34	9	0	5	(2	3)	58	16	21	21	9	0	29	0	0	1	2	0	2	.266	.312	.453	.765

Ryon Healy

Bats: R **Throws:** R **Pos:** 3B-44;1B-11   **Ht:** 6'5" **Wt:** 225 **Born:** 1/10/1992 **Age:** 28

Year	Team	Lg	G	AB	H	2B	3B	HR	(Hm	Rd)	TB	R	RBI	RC	TBB	IBB	SO	HBP	SH	SF	SB	CS	GDP	Avg	OBP	Slg	OPS
2016	Oak	AL	72	269	82	20	0	13	(8	5)	141	36	37	43	12	1	60	1	1	0	0	0	7	.305	.337	.524	.861
2017	Oak	AL	149	576	156	29	0	25	(14	11)	260	66	78	75	23	0	142	4	0	2	0	1	16	.271	.302	.451	.754
2018	Sea	AL	133	493	116	15	0	24	(15	9)	203	51	73	52	27	0	113	2	0	2	0	0	21	.235	.277	.412	.688
2019	Sea	AL	47	169	40	16	0	7	(2	5)	77	24	26	23	13	0	40	1	0	4	0	0	1	.237	.289	.456	.744
	4 ML YEARS		401	1507	394	80	0	69	(39	30)	681	177	214	193	75	1	355	8	1	8	0	1	45	.261	.298	.452	.750

Andrew Heaney

Pitches: L Bats: L Pos: SP-18
HEE-nee

Ht: 6'2" Wt: 200 Born: 6/5/1991 Age: 29

Year	Team	Lg	G	GS	GF	IP	BFP	H	R	ER	HR	SH	SF	HB	TBB	IBB	SO	WP	W	L	Pct	Sv-Op	Hld	Vel	OPS	ERC	ERA
2014	Mia	NL	7	5	2	29.1	126	32	19	19	6	2	0	3	7	0	20	2	0	3	.000	0-0	0	90	.847	5.17	5.83
2015	LAA	AL	18	18	0	105.2	438	99	41	41	9	1	3	6	28	1	78	4	6	4	.600	0-0	0	91	.679	3.35	3.49
2016	LAA	AL	1	1	0	6.0	25	7	4	4	2	0	0	0	0	0	7	0	0	1	.000	0-0	0	91	.840	4.78	6.00
2017	LAA	AL	5	5	0	21.2	101	27	17	17	12	2	0	0	9	0	27	2	1	2	.333	0-0	0	92	1.108	8.99	7.06
2018	LAA	AL	30	30	0	180.0	749	171	91	83	27	2	5	8	45	0	180	9	9	10	.474	0-0	0	92	.719	3.73	4.15
2019	LAA	AL	18	18	0	95.1	409	93	53	52	20	0	2	7	30	1	118	4	4	6	.400	0-0	0	93	.772	4.63	4.91
	6 ML YEARS		79	77	2	438.0	1848	429	225	216	76	7	10	24	119	2	430	21	20	26	.435	0-0	0	92	.753	4.17	4.44

Taylor Hearn

Pitches: L Bats: L Pos: SP-1

Ht: 6'5" Wt: 210 Born: 8/30/1994 Age: 25

Year	Team	Lg	G	GS	GF	IP	BFP	H	R	ER	HR	SH	SF	HB	TBB	IBB	SO	WP	W	L	Pct	Sv-Op	Hld	Vel	OPS	ERC	ERA
2019	Tex	AL	1	1	0	0.1	8	3	5	4	0	0	0	0	4	0	0	0	0	1	.000	0-0	0	92	1.875	131.5	108.0

Adeiny Hechavarria

a-DAY-nee hetch-a-VA-ree-a

Bats: R Throws: R Pos: 2B-29;SS-27;PH-21;3B-9;PR-3;DH-1

Ht: 6'0" Wt: 195 Born: 4/15/1989 Age: 31

									BATTING										RUNNING			AVERAGES			
Year	Team	Lg	G	AB	H	2B	3B	HR	(Hm | Rd)	TB	R	RBI	RC	TBB	IBB	SO	HBP	SH	SF	SB	CS	GDP	Avg	OBP	Slg	OPS
2019	Syrcse	AAA	25	92	32	9	0	0	(- | -)	41	15	17	16	6	1	14	1	0	3	2	1	1	.348	.382	.446	.828
2012	Tor	AL	41	126	32	8	0	2	(1 | 1)	46	10	15	15	4	0	32	1	5	1	0	0	2	.254	.280	.365	.645
2013	Mia	NL	148	543	123	14	8	3	(1 | 2)	162	30	42	37	30	1	96	0	4	1	11	10	19	.227	.267	.298	.565
2014	Mia	NL	146	536	148	20	10	1	(0 | 1)	191	53	34	49	26	5	86	1	4	6	7	5	21	.276	.308	.356	.664
2015	Mia	NL	130	470	132	17	6	5	(3 | 2)	176	54	48	49	23	4	78	2	0	4	7	2	18	.281	.315	.374	.689
2016	Mia	NL	155	508	120	17	6	3	(1 | 2)	158	52	38	40	33	7	73	1	2	3	1	0	10	.236	.283	.311	.594
2017	2 Tms		97	330	86	14	5	8	(4 | 4)	134	37	30	36	13	1	67	1	2	2	4	1	7	.261	.289	.406	.695
2018	3 Tms		94	296	73	11	0	6	(2 | 4)	102	34	31	24	16	2	58	0	2	7	2	0	7	.247	.279	.345	.624
2019	2 Tms	NL	84	203	49	12	1	9	(6 | 3)	90	34	33	29	14	0	48	3	0	1	3	1	3	.241	.299	.443	.742
17	Mia	NL	20	65	18	2	1	1	(0 | 1)	25	8	6	8	1	0	9	0	1	0	0	0	1	.277	.288	.385	.672
17	TB	AL	77	265	68	12	4	7	(4 | 3)	109	29	24	28	12	1	58	1	1	2	4	1	6	.257	.289	.411	.701
18	TB	AL	61	217	56	7	0	3	(2 | 1)	72	29	26	22	12	1	37	0	2	6	1	0	4	.258	.289	.332	.621
18	Pit	NL	15	43	10	4	0	1	(0 | 1)	17	2	3	0	3	1	11	0	0	1	0	0	3	.233	.277	.395	.672
18	NYY	AL	18	36	7	0	0	2	(0 | 2)	13	3	2	2	1	0	10	0	0	0	1	0	0	.194	.216	.361	.577
19	NYM	NL	60	142	29	7	0	5	(4 | 1)	51	20	18	13	8	0	33	1	0	0	3	1	2	.204	.252	.359	.611
19	Atl	NL	24	61	20	5	1	4	(2 | 2)	39	14	15	16	6	0	15	2	0	1	0	0	1	.328	.400	.639	1.039
	Postseason		4	3	0	0	0	0	(0 | 0)	0	0	0	0	1	0	0	0	0	0	0	0	0	.000	.250	.000	.250
	8 ML YEARS		895	3012	763	113	36	37	(18 | 19)	1059	304	271	279	159	20	538	9	19	25	35	19	87	.253	.290	.352	.642

Austin Hedges

Bats: R Throws: R Pos: C-95;PH-7;3B-2

Ht: 6'1" Wt: 206 Born: 8/18/1992 Age: 27

									BATTING										RUNNING			AVERAGES			
Year	Team	Lg	G	AB	H	2B	3B	HR	(Hm	Rd)	TB	R	RBI	RC	TBB	IBB	SO	HBP	SH	SF	SB	CS	GDP	Avg	OBP	Slg	OPS
2015	SD	NL	56	137	23	6	0	3	(2	1)	34	13	11	7	8	1	38	1	3	3	0	0	1	.168	.215	.248	.463
2016	SD	NL	8	24	3	1	0	0	(0	0)	4	2	1	0	0	0	7	1	0	1	0	1	0	.125	.154	.167	.321
2017	SD	NL	120	387	83	17	0	18	(9	9)	154	36	55	39	23	3	122	3	1	3	4	1	10	.214	.262	.398	.660
2018	SD	NL	91	303	70	14	2	14	(5	9)	130	29	37	28	21	3	90	1	0	1	3	0	9	.231	.282	.429	.711
2019	SD	NL	102	312	55	9	0	11	(3	8)	97	28	36	28	27	3	109	5	2	1	1	0	3	.176	.252	.311	.563
	5 ML YEARS		377	1163	234	43	2	46	(19	27)	419	108	140	102	79	10	366	11	6	9	8	2	23	.201	.257	.360	.617

Scott Heineman

Bats: R Throws: R Pos: CF-9;RF-8;LF-6;1B-4

Ht: 6'1" Wt: 215 Born: 12/4/1992 Age: 27

									BATTING										RUNNING			AVERAGES			
Year	Team	Lg	G	AB	H	2B	3B	HR	(Hm	Rd)	TB	R	RBI	RC	TBB	IBB	SO	HBP	SH	SF	SB	CS	GDP	Avg	OBP	Slg	OPS
2019	Nashv	AAA	42	159	54	6	2	8	(-	-)	88	34	25	35	17	0	45	4	0	2	4	3	6	.340	.412	.553	.966
2019	Tex	AL	25	75	16	6	0	2	(1	1)	28	8	7	7	9	0	20	1	0	0	1	2	3	.213	.306	.373	.679

Tyler Heineman

Bats: B Throws: R Pos: PH-3;C-2

Ht: 5'11" Wt: 205 Born: 6/19/1991 Age: 29

									BATTING										RUNNING			AVERAGES			
Year	Team	Lg	G	AB	H	2B	3B	HR	(Hm	Rd)	TB	R	RBI	RC	TBB	IBB	SO	HBP	SH	SF	SB	CS	GDP	Avg	OBP	Slg	OPS
2019	Reno	AAA	25	80	26	5	1	3	(-	-)	42	16	13	17	9	0	14	2	0	0	0	0	2	.325	.407	.525	.932
2019	NewOr	AAA	48	164	56	12	2	10	(-	-)	102	26	25	39	12	0	21	3	3	0	4	0	2	.341	.397	.622	1.019
2019	Mia	NL	5	11	3	1	0	1	(0	1)	7	1	2	3	0	0	4	0	1	0	0	0	0	.273	.273	.636	.909

Ben Heller

Pitches: R Bats: R Pos: RP-6
Ht: 6'3" Wt: 205 Born: 8/5/1991 Age: 28

Year Team	Lg	G	GS	GF	IP	BFP	H	R	ER	HR	SH	SF	HB	TBB	IBB	SO	WP	W	L	Pct	Sv-Op	Hld	Vel	OPS	ERC	ERA
2019 S-WB	AAA	9	4	1	11.0	39	5	1	1	0	0	0	1	3	0	13	1	0	0	-	1--	-	-	.374	1.11	0.82
2016 NYY	AL	10	0	4	7.0	40	11	5	5	3	0	0	2	4	1	6	0	1	0	1.000	0-1	1	96	1.101	11.69	6.43
2017 NYY	AL	9	0	4	11.0	43	5	1	1	0	1	0	0	6	0	9	1	1	0	1.000	0-0	0	95	.450	1.40	0.82
2019 NYY	AL	6	0	1	7.1	28	6	1	1	1	1	0	0	3	1	9	0	0	0	-	0-0	0	93	.750	3.49	1.23
3 ML YEARS		25	0	9	25.1	111	22	7	7	4	1	1	2	13	2	24	1	2	0	1.000	0-1	1	95	.762	4.37	2.49

Jeremy Hellickson

Pitches: R Bats: R Pos: SP-8; RP-1
Ht: 6'1" Wt: 190 Born: 4/8/1987 Age: 33

Year Team	Lg	G	GS	GF	IP	BFP	H	R	ER	HR	SH	SF	HB	TBB	IBB	SO	WP	W	L	Pct	Sv-Op	Hld	Vel	OPS	ERC	ERA
2019 Nats	R	5	4	0	16.2	70	11	4	4	1	1	1	5	2	0	22	0	1	1	.500	0--	-	-	.523	2.03	2.16
2010 TB	AL	10	4	0	36.1	149	32	14	14	5	0	1	2	8	2	33	2	4	0	1.000	0-1	0	91	.666	3.10	3.47
2011 TB	AL	29	29	0	189.0	774	146	64	62	21	1	2	4	72	8	117	8	13	10	.565	0-0	0	91	.660	2.89	2.95
2012 TB	AL	31	31	0	177.0	741	163	68	61	25	4	3	4	59	3	124	5	10	11	.476	0-0	0	91	.710	3.73	3.10
2013 TB	AL	32	31	1	174.0	737	185	103	100	24	2	5	4	50	0	135	7	12	10	.545	0-0	0	91	.775	4.40	5.17
2014 TB	AL	13	13	0	63.2	281	71	35	32	8	0	1	2	21	1	54	0	1	5	.167	0-0	0	90	.759	4.70	4.52
2015 Ari	NL	27	27	0	146.0	636	151	79	75	22	8	6	6	43	3	121	5	9	12	.429	0-0	0	90	.781	4.25	4.62
2016 Phi	NL	32	32	0	189.0	772	173	86	78	24	4	6	6	45	0	154	6	12	10	.545	0-0	0	90	.709	3.31	3.71
2017 2 Tms		30	30	0	164.0	695	160	105	99	35	5	7	8	47	2	96	4	8	11	.421	0-0	0	90	.808	4.43	5.43
2018 Was	NL	19	19	0	91.1	370	78	41	35	11	2	1	8	20	1	65	2	5	3	.625	0-0	0	90	.677	3.08	3.45
2019 Was	NL	9	8	1	39.0	183	47	31	27	9	1	1	1	20	1	30	1	2	3	.400	0-0	0	88	.899	6.79	6.23
17 Phi	NL	20	20	0	112.1	472	111	62	59	22	5	5	6	30	2	65	3	6	5	.545	0-0	0	90	.810	4.35	4.73
17 Bal	AL	10	10	0	51.2	223	49	43	40	13	0	2	2	17	0	31	1	2	6	.250	0-0	0	90	.805	4.60	6.97
Postseason		2	2	0	5.0	22	5	3	3	3	0	0	0	3	0	1	0	0	1	.000	0-0	0	91	1.100	8.99	5.40
10 ML YEARS		232	224	2	1269.1	5338	1206	626	583	184	27	33	45	385	21	929	48	76	75	.503	0-1	0	90	.738	3.84	4.13

Ryan Helsley

Pitches: R Bats: R Pos: RP-24
Ht: 6'1" Wt: 195 Born: 7/18/1994 Age: 25

Year Team	Lg	G	GS	GF	IP	BFP	H	R	ER	HR	SH	SF	HB	TBB	IBB	SO	WP	W	L	Pct	Sv-Op	Hld	Vel	OPS	ERC	ERA
2019 Memp	AAA	17	7	3	37.1	155	29	20	19	3	1	1	0	20	0	41	3	2	3	.400	1--	-	-	.657	3.32	4.58
2019 StL	NL	24	0	4	36.2	153	34	13	12	5	1	1	0	12	2	32	2	2	0	1.000	0-1	1	98	.734	3.56	2.95

Heath Hembree

Pitches: R Bats: R Pos: RP-45
HEHM-bree
Ht: 6'4" Wt: 210 Born: 1/13/1989 Age: 31

Year Team	Lg	G	GS	GF	IP	BFP	H	R	ER	HR	SH	SF	HB	TBB	IBB	SO	WP	W	L	Pct	Sv-Op	Hld	Vel	OPS	ERC	ERA
2013 SF	NL	9	0	2	7.2	29	4	0	0	0	0	0	0	2	0	12	0	0	0	-	0-0	0	92	.392	1.02	0.00
2014 Bos	AL	6	0	3	10.0	43	11	5	5	1	0	0	0	5	2	6	1	0	0	-	0-0	0	92	.846	4.94	4.50
2015 Bos	AL	22	0	9	25.1	106	25	10	10	5	0	0	0	9	2	46	1	2	0	1.000	0-1	1	94	.795	4.46	3.55
2016 Bos	AL	38	0	8	51.0	223	51	23	15	6	0	1	0	17	1	47	0	4	1	.800	0-2	5	94	.695	3.78	2.65
2017 Bos	AL	62	0	8	62.0	271	72	29	25	10	1	2	1	18	0	70	2	2	3	.400	0-3	14	95	.803	5.07	3.63
2018 Bos	AL	67	0	10	60.0	260	53	30	28	10	0	5	1	27	1	76	4	4	1	.800	0-3	20	95	.734	4.05	4.20
2019 Bos	AL	45	0	14	39.2	173	34	20	17	7	0	0	3	18	2	46	2	1	0	1.000	2-3	4	94	.772	4.18	3.86
Postseason		4	0	2	4.2	16	0	0	0	0	0	0	0	5	0	3	0	0	0	-	0-0	0	94	.313	1.27	0.00
7 ML YEARS		249	0	54	255.2	1105	250	117	100	39	1	8	5	96	8	272	10	13	5	.722	2-11	44	94	.750	4.21	3.52

Kyle Hendricks

Pitches: R Bats: R Pos: SP-30
Ht: 6'3" Wt: 190 Born: 12/7/1989 Age: 30

Year Team	Lg	G	GS	GF	IP	BFP	H	R	ER	HR	SH	SF	HB	TBB	IBB	SO	WP	W	L	Pct	Sv-Op	Hld	Vel	OPS	ERC	ERA
2014 ChC	NL	13	13	0	80.1	321	72	24	22	4	4	1	4	15	2	47	0	7	2	.778	0-0	0	88	.610	2.61	2.46
2015 ChC	NL	32	32	0	180.0	739	166	82	79	17	6	0	4	43	1	167	3	8	7	.533	0-0	0	88	.677	3.18	3.95
2016 ChC	NL	31	30	0	190.0	745	142	53	45	15	4	3	8	44	3	170	5	16	8	.667	0-0	0	88	.581	**2.19**	**2.13**
2017 ChC	NL	24	24	0	139.2	570	126	49	47	17	6	1	2	40	1	123	0	7	5	.583	0-0	0	86	.670	3.34	3.03
2018 ChC	NL	33	33	0	199.0	812	184	82	76	22	7	7	9	44	4	161	0	14	11	.560	0-0	0	87	.685	3.22	3.44
2019 ChC	NL	30	30	0	177.0	730	168	78	68	19	8	5	9	32	1	150	1	11	10	.524	0-0	0	87	.687	3.17	3.46
Postseason		11	10	0	51.1	214	48	19	17	9	2	1	2	13	1	48	0	2	3	.400	0-0	0	88	.724	3.75	2.98
6 ML YEARS		163	162	0	966.0	3917	858	368	337	94	35	17	40	218	12	818	9	63	43	.594	0-0	0	87	.656	2.96	3.14

Liam Hendriks

Pitches: R Bats: R Pos: RP-73; SP-2
Ht: 6'0" Wt: 225 Born: 2/10/1989 Age: 31

Year Team	Lg	G	GS	GF	IP	BFP	H	R	ER	HR	SH	SF	HB	TBB	IBB	SO	WP	W	L	Pct	Sv-Op	Hld	Vel	OPS	ERC	ERA
2011 Min	AL	4	4	0	23.1	100	29	16	16	3	0	0	0	6	0	16	1	0	2	.000	0-0	0	90	.866	5.26	6.17
2012 Min	AL	16	16	0	85.1	381	106	61	53	17	3	1	4	26	3	50	4	1	8	.111	0-0	0	90	.890	6.03	5.59
2013 Min	AL	10	8	1	47.1	224	67	39	36	10	0	2	3	14	1	34	1	1	3	.250	0-0	0	91	.907	7.16	6.85
2014 2 Tms	AL	9	6	0	32.2	143	38	21	19	3	0	2	3	7	0	23	1	1	2	.333	0-0	0	91	.786	4.56	5.23
2015 Tor	AL	58	0	14	64.2	261	59	23	21	3	0	2	2	11	1	71	4	5	0	1.000	0-2	5	95	.605	2.51	2.92
2016 Oak	AL	53	0	10	64.2	275	69	31	27	6	0	4	1	14	3	71	3	0	4	.000	0-1	10	94	.704	3.63	3.76
2017 Oak	AL	70	0	13	64.0	273	57	34	30	7	0	1	0	23	0	78	6	4	2	.667	1-4	16	95	.663	3.30	4.22
2018 Oak	AL	25	8	1	24.0	104	25	11	11	3	0	1	1	10	0	22	1	0	1	.000	0-0	0	94	.759	4.82	4.13

Year Team	Lg	G	GS	GF	IP	BFP	H	R	ER	HR	SH	SF	HB	TBB	IBB	SO	WP	W	L	Pct	Sv-Op	Hld	Vel	OPS	ERC	ERA
2019 Oak	AL	75	2	41	85.0	332	61	18	17	5	2	3	2	21	5	124	7	4	4	.500	25-32	8	96	.564	1.86	1.80
14 Tor	AL	3	3	0	13.1	57	12	9	9	3	0	0	2	4	0	8	0	1	0	1.000	0-0	0	91	.767	4.58	6.08
14 KC	AL	6	3	0	19.1	86	26	12	10	0	0	2	1	3	0	15	1	0	2	.000	0-0	1	92	.799	4.52	4.66
Postseason		4	1	1	6.0	23	6	5	5	1	0	1	0	1	0	3	0	0	1	.000	0-0	0	96	.781	3.87	7.50
9 ML YEARS		320	44	80	491.0	2093	511	254	230	57	5	17	16	132	13	489	28	16	26	.381	26-39	40	93	.735	3.97	4.22

Guillermo Heredia

Bats: R Throws: L Pos: CF-41;RF-28;LF-14;PH-9;PR-9;DH-1   ghee-YAIR-moh   Ht: 5'10" Wt: 195 Born: 1/31/1991 **Age: 29**

Year Team	Lg	G	AB	H	2B	3B	HR	(Hm	Rd)	TB	R	RBI	RC	TBB	IBB	SO	HBP	SH	SF	SB	CS	GDP	Avg	OBP	Slg	OPS
2016 Sea	AL	45	92	23	3	0	1	(1	0)	29	12	12	12	12	0	15	2	1	0	1	1	1	.250	.349	.315	.664
2017 Sea	AL	123	386	96	16	0	6	(4	2)	130	43	24	37	27	2	64	11	1	1	1	5	9	.249	.315	.337	.652
2018 Sea	AL	125	292	69	14	1	5	(1	4)	100	29	19	33	32	0	52	4	7	2	2	4	4	.236	.318	.342	.661
2019 TB	AL	89	204	46	13	0	5	(1	4)	74	31	20	20	18	0	60	6	2	1	2	2	4	.225	.306	.363	.668
4 ML YEARS		382	974	234	46	1	17	(7	10)	333	115	75	102	89	2	191	23	11	4	6	12	18	.240	.317	.342	.659

Jimmy Herget

Pitches: R Bats: R Pos: RP-5   Ht: 6'3" Wt: 170 Born: 9/9/1993 **Age: 26**

Year Team	Lg	G	GS	GF	IP	BFP	H	R	ER	HR	SH	SF	HB	TBB	IBB	SO	WP	W	L	Pct	Sv-Op	Hld	Vel	OPS	ERC	ERA
2019 Lsvlle	AAA	48	0	16	58.2	251	41	22	19	7	0	1	2	36	1	68	3	3	4	.429	2--	-	-	.650	3.48	2.91
2019 Cin	NL	5	0	4	6.1	26	8	3	3	2	0	0	0	3	0	0	0	0	0	-	0-0	0	93	1.119	8.76	4.26

Michael Hermosillo

Bats: R Throws: R Pos: LF-14;CF-5;RF-2;PR-1   air-moh-SEE-yo   Ht: 6'0" Wt: 205 Born: 1/17/1995 **Age: 25**

Year Team	Lg	G	AB	H	2B	3B	HR	(Hm	Rd)	TB	R	RBI	RC	TBB	IBB	SO	HBP	SH	SF	SB	CS	GDP	Avg	OBP	Slg	OPS
2019 Salt Lk	AAA	62	259	63	8	3	15	(-	-)	122	51	43	41	26	0	88	9	0	2	6	4	3	.243	.331	.471	.802
2018 LAA	AL	31	57	12	4	0	1	(1	0)	19	7	1	3	3	0	17	2	0	0	0	1	0	.211	.274	.333	.608
2019 LAA	AL	18	36	5	1	1	0	(0	0)	8	7	3	3	5	0	19	4	0	1	2	0	1	.139	.304	.222	.527
2 ML YEARS		49	93	17	5	1	1	(1	0)	27	14	4	6	8	0	36	6	0	1	2	1	1	.183	.287	.290	.577

Cesar Hernandez

Bats: B Throws: R Pos: 2B-157;PH-4   Ht: 5'10" Wt: 160 Born: 5/23/1990 **Age: 30**

Year Team	Lg	G	AB	H	2B	3B	HR	(Hm	Rd)	TB	R	RBI	RC	TBB	IBB	SO	HBP	SH	SF	SB	CS	GDP	Avg	OBP	Slg	OPS
2013 Phi	NL	34	121	35	5	0	0	(0	0)	40	17	10	13	9	0	26	1	0	0	0	3	2	.289	.344	.331	.674
2014 Phi	NL	66	114	27	2	0	1	(1	0)	32	13	4	7	9	1	33	0	1	1	1	1	1	.237	.290	.281	.571
2015 Phi	NL	127	405	110	20	4	1	(1	0)	141	57	35	52	40	1	86	2	4	1	19	5	6	.272	.339	.348	.687
2016 Phi	NL	155	547	161	14	11	6	(4	2)	215	67	39	82	66	4	116	2	5	2	17	13	6	.294	.371	.393	.764
2017 Phi	NL	128	511	150	26	6	9	(6	3)	215	85	34	80	61	1	104	4	0	1	15	5	8	.294	.373	.421	.793
2018 Phi	NL	161	605	153	15	3	15	(7	8)	219	91	60	85	95	4	155	4	1	3	19	6	12	.253	.356	.362	.718
2019 Phi	NL	161	612	171	31	3	14	(7	7)	250	77	71	82	45	4	100	6	0	4	9	2	9	.279	.333	.408	.741
7 ML YEARS		832	2915	807	113	27	46	(26	20)	1112	407	253	401	325	15	620	19	11	12	80	35	44	.277	.352	.381	.733

Darwinzon Hernandez

Pitches: L Bats: L Pos: RP-28; SP-1   Ht: 6'2" Wt: 245 Born: 12/17/1996 **Age: 23**

Year Team	Lg	G	GS	GF	IP	BFP	H	R	ER	HR	SH	SF	HB	TBB	IBB	SO	WP	W	L	Pct	Sv-Op	Hld	Vel	OPS	ERC	ERA
2019 Portlnd	AA	10	9	0	40.1	188	33	28	23	2	1	0	3	32	0	59	7	1	4	.200	0--	-	-	.719	4.39	5.13
2019 Pwtckt	AAA	7	3	0	17.0	77	10	9	9	2	0	0	4	16	0	20	1	1	2	.333	0--	-	-	.740	5.06	4.76
2019 Bos	AL	29	1	2	30.1	147	27	18	15	1	1	0	3	26	1	57	4	0	1	.000	0-0	2	96	.725	4.90	4.45

David Hernandez

Pitches: R Bats: R Pos: RP-47   Ht: 6'3" Wt: 245 Born: 5/13/1985 **Age: 35**

Year Team	Lg	G	GS	GF	IP	BFP	H	R	ER	HR	SH	SF	HB	TBB	IBB	SO	WP	W	L	Pct	Sv-Op	Hld	Vel	OPS	ERC	ERA
2019 S-WB	AAA	8	0	2	7.0	35	5	7	6	1	0	1	1	8	0	11	2	0	1	.000	0--	-	-	.760	6.16	7.71
2009 Bal	AL	20	19	0	101.1	462	118	62	61	27	2	3	1	46	0	68	3	4	10	.286	0-0	0	93	.912	6.55	5.42
2010 Bal	AL	41	8	16	79.1	348	72	40	38	9	1	3	4	42	4	72	9	8	8	.500	2-6	2	94	.733	4.28	4.31
2011 Ari	NL	74	0	28	69.1	291	49	27	26	4	3	2	2	30	1	77	7	5	3	.625	11-14	23	95	.561	2.40	3.38
2012 Ari	NL	72	0	21	68.1	278	48	21	19	4	0	1	3	22	1	98	4	2	3	.400	4-10	25	95	.544	2.10	2.50
2013 Ari	NL	62	0	12	62.1	263	50	33	31	10	2	0	4	24	4	66	6	5	6	.455	2-8	15	95	.702	3.45	4.48
2015 Ari	NL	40	0	7	33.2	144	33	18	16	6	1	0	3	11	0	33	1	1	5	.167	0-0	7	94	.778	4.62	4.28
2016 Phi	NL	70	0	16	72.2	322	77	31	31	11	1	1	2	32	5	80	6	3	4	.429	1-3	15	94	.785	4.95	3.84
2017 2 Tms		64	0	15	55.0	214	48	20	19	4	1	2	1	9	0	52	5	3	1	.750	2-4	18	94	.611	2.50	3.11
2018 Cin	NL	57	0	6	64.0	254	46	20	18	6	2	0	5	17	1	65	3	5	2	.714	0-6	15	93	.635	2.37	2.53
2019 Cin	NL	47	0	8	42.2	198	53	39	38	7	1	3	1	20	3	53	1	2	5	.286	2-5	12	94	.913	6.25	8.02
17 LAA	AL	38	0	10	36.1	140	29	10	9	0	1	0	1	8	0	37	3	1	0	1.000	1-2	8	94	.535	1.96	2.23
17 Ari	NL	26	0	5	18.2	74	19	10	10	4	0	2	0	1	0	15	2	2	1	.667	1-2	10	94	.749	3.55	4.82
Postseason		6	0	1	6.2	23	3	2	2	1	0	0	0	0	0	6	0	0	0	-	0-0	0	95	.478	0.77	2.70
10 ML YEARS		547	27	129	648.2	2774	594	311	297	88	14	15	26	253	19	664	45	38	47	.447	24-56	132	94	.725	3.91	4.12

Elieser Hernandez

Pitches: R Bats: R Pos: SP-15; RP-6   Ht: 6'0" Wt: 210 Born: 5/3/1995 Age: 25

			HOW MUCH PITCHED					WHAT HE GAVE UP									THE RESULTS						
Year	Team	Lg	G	GS	GF	IP	BFP	H	R	ER	HR	SH	SF	HB	TBB	IBB	SO	WP	W	L	Pct	Sv-Op Hld	Vel	OPS	ERC	ERA
2019 NewOr	AAA	9	9	0	48.0	201	35	8	6	0	0	0	7	14	0	69	1	3	1	.750	0- -	-	.534	2.10	1.13
2018 Mia	NL	32	6	6	65.2	284	68	38	38	11	3	2	2	27	3	45	1	2	7	.222	0-0	2	91	.809	4.94	5.21
2019 Mia	NL	21	15	1	82.1	353	76	49	46	20	3	1	9	26	1	85	2	3	5	.375	0-0	0	91	.820	4.69	5.03
2 ML YEARS		53	21	7	148.0	637	144	87	84	31	6	3	11	53	4	130	3	5	12	.294	0-0	2	91	.815	4.80	5.11

Felix Hernandez

Pitches: R Bats: R Pos: SP-15   Ht: 6'3" Wt: 225 Born: 4/8/1986 Age: 34

Year	Team	Lg	G	GS	GF	IP	BFP	H	R	ER	HR	SH	SF	HB	TBB	IBB	SO	WP	W	L	Pct	Sv-Op Hld	Vel	OPS	ERC	ERA
2005 Sea	AL	12	12	0	84.1	328	61	26	25	5	1	2	2	23	0	77	3	4	4	.500	0-0	0	96	.546	2.08	2.67
2006 Sea	AL	31	31	0	191.0	816	195	105	96	23	2	3	6	60	2	176	11	12	14	.462	0-0	0	95	.729	4.11	4.52
2007 Sea	AL	30	30	0	190.1	808	209	88	83	20	6	1	3	53	4	165	7	14	7	.667	0-0	0	96	.751	4.27	3.92
2008 Sea	AL	31	31	0	200.2	857	198	85	77	17	4	6	8	80	7	175	8	9	11	.450	0-0	0	95	.727	4.05	3.45
2009 Sea	AL	34	34	0	238.2	977	200	81	66	15	6	11	8	71	0	217	17	19	5	.792	0-0	0	94	.605	2.72	2.49
2010 Sea	AL	34	34	0	249.2	1001	194	80	63	17	6	3	8	70	1	232	14	13	12	.520	0-0	0	94	.585	2.39	2.27
2011 Sea	AL	33	33	0	233.2	964	218	99	90	19	3	7	7	67	0	222	12	14	14	.500	0-0	0	93	.660	3.31	3.47
2012 Sea	AL	33	33	0	232.0	939	209	84	79	14	2	2	12	56	0	223	13	13	9	.591	0-0	0	92	.629	2.94	3.06
2013 Sea	AL	31	31	0	204.1	823	185	74	69	15	4	6	3	46	1	216	13	12	10	.545	0-0	0	92	.644	2.82	3.04
2014 Sea	AL	34	34	0	236.0	912	170	68	56	16	4	5	5	46	1	248	16	15	6	.714	0-0	0	92	.546	1.81	2.14
2015 Sea	AL	31	31	0	201.2	826	180	80	79	23	4	4	9	58	0	191	10	18	9	.667	0-0	0	92	.682	3.37	3.53
2016 Sea	AL	25	25	0	153.1	655	138	76	65	19	3	0	10	65	0	122	6	11	8	.579	0-0	0	90	.718	4.07	3.82
2017 Sea	AL	16	16	0	86.2	368	86	46	42	17	1	1	6	26	0	78	8	6	5	.545	0-0	0	90	.791	4.62	4.36
2018 Sea	AL	29	28	0	155.2	685	159	107	96	27	3	4	12	59	0	125	11	8	14	.364	0-0	0	89	.798	4.94	5.55
2019 Sea	AL	15	15	0	71.2	325	85	58	51	17	1	1	6	25	0	57	5	1	8	.111	0-0	0	90	.909	6.34	6.40
15 ML YEARS		419	418	0	2729.2	11284	2487	1157	1037	264	50	56	105	805	16	2524	156	169	136	.554	0-0	0	93	.673	3.33	3.42

Gorkys Hernandez

Bats: R Throws: R Pos: RF-7;LF-6;PR-3;CF-2;PH-2;DH-1   GORE-keez   Ht: 6'1" Wt: 196 Born: 9/7/1987 Age: 32

			BATTING																	RUNNING			AVERAGES			
Year	Team	Lg	G	AB	H	2B	3B	HR	(Hm	Rd)	TB	R	RBI	RC	TBB	IBB	SO	HBP	SH	SF	SB	CS	GDP	Avg	OBP	Slg	OPS
2019 Pwtckt	AAA	123	430	94	15	3	16	(-	-)	163	75	53	58	62	0	146	4	2	6	20	6	8	.219	.319	.379	.698
2012 2 Tms	NL	70	156	30	2	3	3	(2	1)	47	18	13	15	13	0	42	3	1	0	7	2	2	.192	.267	.301	.569
2015 Pit	NL	8	5	0	0	0	0	(0	0)	0	0	0	0	0	0	0	0	0	0	1	0	0	.000	.000	.000	.000
2016 SF	NL	26	54	14	5	0	2	(1	1)	25	7	4	5	3	0	11	0	0	0	0	1	0	.259	.298	.463	.761
2017 SF	NL	128	310	79	20	1	0	(0	0)	101	40	22	31	31	3	73	3	2	2	12	4	6	.255	.327	.326	.652
2018 SF	NL	142	414	97	16	2	15	(7	8)	162	52	40	38	27	1	113	4	2	4	8	5	14	.234	.285	.391	.676
2019 Bos	AL	20	49	7	1	2	0	(0	0)	12	5	2	3	5	0	14	0	2	1	1	0	0	.143	.218	.245	.463
12 Pit	NL	25	24	2	0	0	0	(0	0)	2	2	2	0	1	0	5	1	0	0	2	0	1	.083	.154	.083	.237
12 Mia	NL	45	132	28	2	3	3	(2	1)	45	16	11	15	12	0	37	2	1	0	5	2	1	.212	.288	.341	.629
Postseason		3	6	1	0	0	0	(0	0)	1	0	0	0	0	0	2	0	0	0	0	1	0	.167	.167	.167	.333
6 ML YEARS		394	988	227	44	8	20	(10	10)	347	122	81	92	79	4	253	10	7	7	29	12	22	.230	.292	.351	.643

Jonathan Hernandez

Pitches: R Bats: R Pos: RP-7; SP-2   Ht: 6'2" Wt: 175 Born: 7/6/1996 Age: 23

			HOW MUCH PITCHED					WHAT HE GAVE UP									THE RESULTS						
Year	Team	Lg	G	GS	GF	IP	BFP	H	R	ER	HR	SH	SF	HB	TBB	IBB	SO	WP	W	L	Pct	Sv-Op Hld	Vel	OPS	ERC	ERA
2019 Frisco	AA	22	16	1	96.0	418	100	58	55	11	0	1	5	38	1	95	11	5	9	.357	0- -	-	.775	4.64	5.16
2019 Tex	AL	9	2	1	16.2	78	14	10	8	3	0	1	0	13	0	19	1	2	1	.667	0-0	1	97	.721	5.09	4.32

Kike Hernandez

kee-KAY

Bats: R Throws: R Pos: 2B-85;PH-22;CF-20;RF-17;SS-11;LF-10;1B-2;3B-1;PR-1   Ht: 5'11" Wt: 192 Born: 8/24/1991 Age: 28

			BATTING																	RUNNING			AVERAGES			
Year	Team	Lg	G	AB	H	2B	3B	HR	(Hm	Rd)	TB	R	RBI	RC	TBB	IBB	SO	HBP	SH	SF	SB	CS	GDP	Avg	OBP	Slg	OPS
2014 2 Tms		42	121	30	6	3	3	(1	2)	51	13	14	18	12	0	21	1	0	0	0	1	1	.248	.321	.421	.742
2015 LAD	NL	76	202	62	12	2	7	(2	5)	99	24	22	32	11	0	46	2	1	2	0	2	3	.307	.346	.490	.836
2016 LAD	NL	109	216	41	8	0	7	(5	2)	70	25	18	16	28	1	64	0	0	0	2	0	3	.190	.283	.324	.607
2017 LAD	NL	140	297	64	24	2	11	(7	4)	125	46	37	39	41	2	80	0	1	3	3	0	4	.215	.308	.421	.729
2018 LAD	NL	145	402	103	17	3	21	(14	7)	189	67	52	58	50	5	78	1	4	5	3	0	3	.256	.336	.470	.806
2019 LAD	NL	130	414	98	19	1	17	(8	9)	170	57	64	57	36	3	97	6	0	4	4	0	9	.237	.304	.411	.715
14 Hou	AL	24	81	23	4	2	1	(1	0)	34	10	8	14	8	0	11	0	0	0	0	1	0	.284	.348	.420	.768
14 Mia	NL	18	40	7	2	1	2	(0	2)	17	3	6	4	4	0	10	1	0	0	0	0	1	.175	.267	.425	.692
Postseason		38	87	17	1	0	5	(2	3)	33	12	11	10	15	2	24	1	0	0	3	2	2	.195	.320	.379	.700
6 ML YEARS		642	1652	398	86	11	66	(37	29)	704	232	207	220	178	11	386	10	6	14	12	2	23	.241	.316	.426	.742

Marco Hernandez

Bats: L Throws: R Pos: 2B-48;PH-19;PR-4;DH-3;SS-2   Ht: 6'0" Wt: 200 Born: 9/6/1992 Age: 27

							BATTING														RUNNING			AVERAGES			
Year	Team	Lg	G	AB	H	2B	3B	HR	(Hm	Rd)	TB	R	RBI	RC	TBB	IBB	SO	HBP	SH	SF	SB	CS	GDP	Avg	OBP	Slg	OPS
2019	Salem	A+	21	78	23	7	0	0	(-	-)	30	15	9	12	8	0	9	3	0	2	1	1	0	.295	.374	.385	.758
2019	Pwtckt	AAA	35	137	39	12	0	2	(-	-)	57	23	11	17	6	1	32	0	0	3	3	2	3	.285	.308	.416	.724
2016	Bos	AL	40	51	15	1	0	1	(0	1)	19	11	5	6	5	0	10	0	0	0	1	0	0	.294	.357	.373	.730
2017	Bos	AL	21	58	16	3	0	0	(0	0)	19	7	2	4	1	0	15	1	0	0	0	1	0	.276	.300	.328	.628
2019	Bos	AL	61	148	37	7	0	2	(0	2)	50	18	11	10	3	0	42	3	1	0	1	2	1	.250	.279	.338	.617
	Postseason		2	0	0	0	0	0	(0	0)	0	0	0	0	0	0	0	0	0	0	0	0	0	-	-	-	-
	3 ML YEARS		122	257	68	11	0	3	(0	3)	88	36	18	20	9	0	67	4	1	0	2	3	1	.265	.300	.342	.642

Teoscar Hernandez

Bats: R Throws: R Pos: CF-79;LF-46;PH-9;DH-2;PR-2   tay-OH-skar   Ht: 6'2" Wt: 205 Born: 10/15/1992 Age: 27

							BATTING														RUNNING			AVERAGES			
Year	Team	Lg	G	AB	H	2B	3B	HR	(Hm	Rd)	TB	R	RBI	RC	TBB	IBB	SO	HBP	SH	SF	SB	CS	GDP	Avg	OBP	Slg	OPS
2019	Buffalo	AAA	19	75	19	0	1	5	(-	-)	36	11	11	12	6	1	21	1	0	1	3	0	1	.253	.313	.480	.793
2016	Hou	AL	41	100	23	7	0	4	(1	3)	42	15	11	11	11	1	28	0	0	1	0	2	5	.230	.304	.420	.724
2017	2 Tms		27	88	23	6	0	8	(5	3)	53	16	20	15	6	0	36	0	0	1	0	1	0	.261	.305	.602	.908
2018	Tor	AL	134	476	114	29	7	22	(9	13)	223	67	57	60	41	0	163	3	0	3	5	5	14	.239	.302	.468	.771
2019	Tor	AL	125	417	96	19	2	26	(15	11)	197	58	65	67	45	1	153	1	0	1	6	3	8	.230	.306	.472	.778
17	Hou	AL	1	0	0	0	0	0	(0	0)	0	0	0	0	0	0	0	0	0	0	0	0	0	-	-	-	-
17	Tor	AL	26	88	23	6	0	8	(5	3)	53	16	20	15	6	0	36	0	0	1	0	1	0	.261	.305	.602	.908
	4 ML YEARS		327	1081	256	61	9	60	(30	30)	515	156	153	153	103	2	380	4	0	6	11	11	27	.237	.304	.476	.780

Kelvin Herrera

Pitches: R Bats: R Pos: RP-57   Ht: 5'10" Wt: 200 Born: 12/31/1989 Age: 30

			HOW MUCH PITCHED					WHAT HE GAVE UP										THE RESULTS							
Year	Team	Lg	G	GS	GF	IP	BFP	H	R	ER	HR	SH	SF	HB	TBB	IBB	SO	WP	W	L	Pct	Sv-Op	Hld	Vel	OPS	ERC	ERA
2011	KC	AL	2	0	0	2.0	9	2	3	3	1	1	0	1	0	0	0	0	0	1	.000	0-0	1	96	1.232	7.30	13.50
2012	KC	AL	76	0	10	84.1	344	79	24	22	4	5	0	2	21	6	77	3	4	3	.571	3-4	19	99	.643	2.84	2.35
2013	KC	AL	59	0	16	58.1	245	48	27	25	9	0	3	2	21	2	74	5	5	7	.417	2-4	20	98	.701	3.35	3.86
2014	KC	AL	70	0	12	70.0	285	54	12	11	0	4	0	3	26	0	59	1	4	3	.571	0-1	20	98	.561	2.31	1.41
2015	KC	AL	72	0	8	69.2	286	52	23	21	5	1	5	2	26	1	64	4	4	3	.571	0-7	21	98	.578	2.53	2.71
2016	KC	AL	72	0	23	72.0	283	57	23	22	6	1	1	3	12	0	86	3	2	6	.250	12-15	26	97	.590	2.20	2.75
2017	KC	AL	64	0	48	59.1	259	60	33	28	9	1	2	1	20	2	56	2	3	3	.500	26-31	4	97	.786	4.17	4.25
2018	2 Tms		48	0	32	44.1	184	43	12	12	6	1	0	1	10	0	38	0	2	3	.400	17-19	2	97	.689	3.54	2.44
2019	CWS	AL	57	0	16	51.1	235	60	36	35	8	1	2	1	23	6	53	8	3	3	.500	1-3	6	96	.821	5.50	6.14
18	KC	AL	27	0	21	25.2	95	19	3	3	2	1	0	0	2	0	22	0	1	1	.500	14-16	0	96	.506	1.58	1.05
18	Was	NL	21	0	11	18.2	89	24	9	9	4	0	0	1	8	0	16	0	1	2	.333	3-3	2	97	.894	6.88	4.34
	Postseason		22	0		28.2	115	21	5	4	0	0	1	0	10	0	38	0	2	0	1.000	0-0	6	98	.491	1.90	1.26
	9 ML YEARS		520	0	165	511.1	2130	455	193	179	48	15	13	16	159	17	507	26	27	32	.458	61-84	119	98	.666	3.16	3.15

Odubel Herrera

Bats: L Throws: R Pos: CF-37;PH-5   oh-DOO-bull   Ht: 5'11" Wt: 205 Born: 12/29/1991 Age: 28

							BATTING														RUNNING			AVERAGES			
Year	Team	Lg	G	AB	H	2B	3B	HR	(Hm	Rd)	TB	R	RBI	RC	TBB	IBB	SO	HBP	SH	SF	SB	CS	GDP	Avg	OBP	Slg	OPS
2015	Phi	NL	147	495	147	30	3	8	(4	4)	207	64	41	66	28	0	129	8	5	1	16	8	6	.297	.344	.418	.762
2016	Phi	NL	159	583	167	21	6	15	(7	8)	245	87	49	93	63	7	134	6	2	2	25	7	6	.286	.361	.420	.781
2017	Phi	NL	138	526	148	42	3	14	(8	6)	238	67	56	63	31	4	126	4	0	2	8	5	13	.281	.325	.452	.778
2018	Phi	NL	148	550	140	19	3	22	(13	9)	231	64	71	71	38	3	122	7	1	1	5	2	11	.255	.310	.420	.730
2019	Phi	NL	39	126	28	10	1	1	(1	0)	43	12	16	13	11	0	33	1	0	1	2	2	0	.222	.288	.341	.629
	5 ML YEARS		631	2280	630	122	16	60	(33	27)	964	294	233	306	171	14	544	26	8	7	56	24	36	.276	.333	.423	.756

Rosell Herrera

Bats: B Throws: R Pos: PH-26;CF-25;RF-15;LF-13;PR-6;2B-1;3B-1;SS-1   Ht: 6'3" Wt: 195 Born: 10/16/1992 Age: 27

							BATTING														RUNNING			AVERAGES			
Year	Team	Lg	G	AB	H	2B	3B	HR	(Hm	Rd)	TB	R	RBI	RC	TBB	IBB	SO	HBP	SH	SF	SB	CS	GDP	Avg	OBP	Slg	OPS
2019	NewOr	AAA	48	165	51	11	1	5	(-	-)	79	21	24	29	14	0	32	1	0	0	2	1	1	.309	.367	.479	.845
2018	2 Tms		86	278	65	14	3	1	(0	1)	88	25	20	25	19	0	57	2	1	2	3	5	6	.234	.286	.317	.602
2019	Mia	NL	63	105	21	6	0	2	(1	1)	33	10	11	9	11	1	27	2	1	0	4	1	2	.200	.286	.314	.602
18	Cin	NL	11	13	2	0	0	0	(0	0)	2	0	0	0	0	0	5	0	0	0	0	1	0	.154	.154	.154	.308
18	KC	AL	75	265	63	14	3	1	(0	1)	86	25	20	25	19	0	52	2	1	2	3	4	6	.238	.292	.325	.616
	2 ML YEARS		149	383	86	20	3	3	(1	2)	121	35	31	34	30	1	84	4	2	2	7	6	8	.225	.286	.316	.602

Chris Herrmann

Bats: L Throws: R Pos: C-25;PH-5;LF-3   HERR-men   Ht: 6'0" Wt: 200 Born: 11/24/1987 Age: 32

							BATTING														RUNNING			AVERAGES			
Year	Team	Lg	G	AB	H	2B	3B	HR	(Hm	Rd)	TB	R	RBI	RC	TBB	IBB	SO	HBP	SH	SF	SB	CS	GDP	Avg	OBP	Slg	OPS
2019	LsVgs	AAA	13	51	17	3	1	4	(-	-)	34	14	13	12	6	0	18	0	0	1	0	0	0	.333	.397	.667	1.063
2012	Min	AL	7	18	1	0	0	0	(0	0)	1	0	1	0	1	0	5	0	0	0	0	0	0	.056	.105	.056	.161
2013	Min	AL	57	157	32	7	0	4	(1	3)	51	16	18	15	18	0	49	0	3	0	0	1	3	.204	.286	.325	.611
2014	Min	AL	33	75	16	3	0	0	(0	0)	19	8	4	5	4	0	17	0	0	0	1	0	2	.213	.253	.253	.506
2015	Min	AL	45	103	15	5	1	2	(2	0)	28	13	10	8	7	0	37	2	1	0	0	0	1	.146	.214	.272	.486
2016	Ari	NL	56	148	42	5	4	6	(3	3)	73	21	28	31	16	1	44	0	1	1	4	0	2	.284	.352	.493	.845

Year	Team	Lg	G	AB	H	2B	3B	HR	(Hm	Rd)	TB	R	RBI	RC	TBB	IBB	SO	HBP	SH	SF	SB	CS	GDP	Avg	OBP	Slg	OPS
2017	Ari	NL	106	226	41	7	0	10	(7	3)	78	35	27	26	29	0	67	0	0	1	5	0	1	.181	.273	.345	.619
2018	Sea	AL	36	76	18	4	2	2	(2	0)	32	6	7	9	10	0	24	0	0	0	0	0	0	.237	.322	.421	.743
2019	Oak	AL	30	84	17	3	0	1	(1	0)	23	9	8	6	9	0	29	0	1	0	0	0	4	.202	.280	.274	.553
8 ML YEARS			370	887	182	34	7	25	(16	9)	305	108	103	100	94	1	272	2	6	3	10	1	13	.205	.282	.344	.626

David Hess

Pitches: R Bats: R Pos: SP-14; RP-9   Ht: 6'2" Wt: 180 Born: 7/10/1993 Age: 26

Year	Team	Lg	G	GS	GF	IP	BFP	H	R	ER	HR	SH	SF	HB	TBB	IBB	SO	WP	W	L	Pct	Sv-Op	Hld	Vel	OPS	ERC	ERA
2019	Norfolk	AAA	13	4	1	41.1	175	41	21	21	7	1	0	0	12	1	47	1	3	2	.600	1- -	-	-	.768	3.99	4.57
2018	Bal	AL	21	19	1	103.1	454	106	64	56	22	1	4	8	37	2	74	3	3	10	.231	0-0	0	92	.821	5.12	4.88
2019	Bal	AL	23	14	5	80.0	365	94	73	63	28	3	3	2	30	0	68	1	1	10	.091	0-0	0	93	.957	6.87	7.09
2 ML YEARS			44	33	6	183.1	819	200	137	119	50	4	7	10	67	2	142	4	4	20	.167	0-0	0	92	.882	5.87	5.84

Jason Heyward

Bats: L Throws: L Pos: RF-105;CF-84;PH-7   Ht: 6'5" Wt: 240 Born: 8/9/1989 Age: 30

Year	Team	Lg	G	AB	H	2B	3B	HR	(Hm	Rd)	TB	R	RBI	RC	TBB	IBB	SO	HBP	SH	SF	SB	CS	GDP	Avg	OBP	Slg	OPS
2010	Atl	NL	142	520	144	29	5	18	(9	9)	237	83	72	96	91	2	128	10	0	2	11	6	13	.277	.393	.456	.849
2011	Atl	NL	128	396	90	18	2	14	(5	9)	154	50	42	49	51	4	93	4	0	3	9	2	7	.227	.319	.389	.708
2012	Atl	NL	158	587	158	30	6	27	(9	18)	281	93	82	87	58	1	152	2	0	5	21	8	4	.269	.335	.479	.814
2013	Atl	NL	104	382	97	22	1	14	(10	4)	163	67	38	55	48	1	73	8	1	0	2	4	7	.254	.349	.427	.776
2014	Atl	NL	149	573	155	26	3	11	(5	6)	220	74	58	84	67	3	98	6	0	3	20	4	2	.271	.351	.384	.735
2015	StL	NL	154	547	160	33	4	13	(5	8)	240	79	60	78	56	4	90	2	0	3	23	3	13	.293	.359	.439	.797
2016	ChC	NL	142	530	122	27	1	7	(3	4)	172	61	49	53	54	0	93	5	1	2	11	4	12	.230	.306	.325	.631
2017	ChC	NL	126	432	112	15	4	11	(4	7)	168	59	59	60	41	1	67	3	2	2	4	4	8	.259	.326	.389	.715
2018	ChC	NL	127	440	119	23	4	8	(5	3)	174	67	57	67	42	1	60	2	2	2	1	1	7	.270	.335	.395	.731
2019	ChC	NL	147	513	129	20	4	21	(8	13)	220	78	62	74	68	5	110	5	0	3	8	3	12	.251	.343	.429	.772
Postseason			38	121	18	3	1	2	(0	2)	29	8	7	5	7	2	35	2	0	0	4	0	2	.149	.208	.240	.447
10 ML YEARS			1377	4920	1286	243	34	144	(63	81)	2029	711	579	703	576	22	964	47	6	23	110	39	85	.261	.343	.412	.755

Aaron Hicks

Bats: B Throws: R Pos: CF-58;DH-1;PH-1   Ht: 6'1" Wt: 202 Born: 10/2/1989 Age: 30

Year	Team	Lg	G	AB	H	2B	3B	HR	(Hm	Rd)	TB	R	RBI	RC	TBB	IBB	SO	HBP	SH	SF	SB	CS	GDP	Avg	OBP	Slg	OPS
2013	Min	AL	81	281	54	11	3	8	(3	5)	95	37	27	25	24	0	84	2	4	2	9	3	0	.192	.259	.338	.597
2014	Min	AL	69	186	40	8	0	1	(0	1)	51	22	18	22	36	0	56	0	2	1	4	3	2	.215	.341	.274	.615
2015	Min	AL	97	352	90	18	3	11	(6	5)	140	48	33	45	34	2	56	2	0	2	13	3	6	.256	.323	.398	.721
2016	NYY	AL	123	327	71	13	6	8	(7	1)	110	32	31	28	30	1	68	0	1	3	3	4	7	.217	.281	.336	.617
2017	NYY	AL	88	301	80	18	6	15	(12	3)	143	54	52	52	51	0	67	3	1	5	10	5	8	.266	.372	.475	.847
2018	NYY	AL	137	480	119	18	3	27	(15	12)	224	90	79	94	90	1	111	3	2	6	11	2	1	.248	.366	.467	.833
2019	NYY	AL	59	221	52	10	0	12	(4	8)	98	41	36	34	31	0	72	0	0	1	1	2	2	.235	.325	.443	.769
Postseason			16	55	11	3	0	1	(0	1)	17	6	6	7	5	0	15	0	0	0	0	0	1	.200	.267	.309	.576
7 ML YEARS			654	2148	506	89	10	82	(47	35)	861	324	276	300	296	4	524	10	10	22	51	22	26	.236	.328	.401	.729

John Hicks

Bats: R Throws: R Pos: C-60;1B-29;PH-11;DH-2;PR-1   Ht: 6'2" Wt: 230 Born: 8/31/1989 Age: 30

Year	Team	Lg	G	AB	H	2B	3B	HR	(Hm	Rd)	TB	R	RBI	RC	TBB	IBB	SO	HBP	SH	SF	SB	CS	GDP	Avg	OBP	Slg	OPS
2015	Sea	AL	17	32	2	1	0	0	(0	0)	3	1	1	0	1	0	18	0	1	0	1	1	0	.063	.091	.094	.185
2016	Det	AL	1	2	1	0	0	0	(0	0)	2	1	0	0	0	0	0	0	0	0	0	0	0	.500	.500	1.000	1.500
2017	Det	AL	60	173	46	12	0	6	(3	3)	76	25	22	25	13	0	51	3	0	1	2	1	5	.266	.326	.439	.766
2018	Det	AL	81	288	75	12	1	9	(2	7)	116	35	32	35	22	0	84	0	1	9	1	1	9	.260	.312	.403	.715
2019	Det	AL	95	319	67	15	0	13	(6	7)	121	29	35	21	13	0	109	0	0	1	1	1	7	.210	.240	.379	.620
5 ML YEARS			254	814	191	41	1	28	(11	17)	318	91	90	81	49	0	262	3	2	3	4	4	21	.235	.280	.391	.670

Jordan Hicks

Pitches: R Bats: R Pos: RP-29   Ht: 6'2" Wt: 185 Born: 9/6/1996 Age: 23

Year	Team	Lg	G	GS	GF	IP	BFP	H	R	ER	HR	SH	SF	HB	TBB	IBB	SO	WP	W	L	Pct	Sv-Op	Hld	Vel	OPS	ERC	ERA
2018	StL	NL	73	0	20	77.2	339	59	33	31	2	0	2	8	45	2	70	9	3	4	.429	6-13	24	101	.587	3.24	3.59
2019	StL	NL	29	0	21	28.2	110	16	10	10	2	0	0	1	11	0	31	2	2	2	.500	14-15	3	101	.510	1.80	3.14
2 ML YEARS			102	0	41	106.1	449	75	43	41	4	0	2	9	56	2	101	11	5	6	.455	20-28	27	101	.568	2.84	3.47

Kyle Higashioka

Bats: R Throws: R Pos: C-18   Ht: 6'1" Wt: 205 Born: 4/20/1990 Age: 30

Year	Team	Lg	G	AB	H	2B	3B	HR	(Hm	Rd)	TB	R	RBI	RC	TBB	IBB	SO	HBP	SH	SF	SB	CS	GDP	Avg	OBP	Slg	OPS
2019	S-WB	AAA	70	241	67	13	0	20	(-	-)	140	42	56	48	24	1	53	3	0	2	0	0	7	.278	.348	.581	.929
2017	NYY	AL	9	18	0	0	0	0	(0	0)	0	2	0	0	2	0	6	0	0	0	0	0	0	.000	.100	.000	.100
2018	NYY	AL	29	72	12	2	0	3	(3	0)	23	6	6	2	6	0	16	1	0	0	0	0	2	.167	.241	.319	.560
2019	NYY	AL	18	56	12	5	0	3	(0	3)	26	8	11	7	0	0	26	0	0	1	0	0	1	.214	.211	.464	.675
3 ML YEARS			56	146	24	7	0	6	(3	3)	49	16	17	9	8	0	48	1	0	1	0	0	3	.164	.212	.336	.547

Trevor Hildenberger

Pitches: R **Bats:** R **Pos:** RP-22 **Ht:** 6'2" **Wt:** 211 **Born:** 12/15/1990 **Age:** 29

			HOW MUCH PITCHED					WHAT HE GAVE UP											THE RESULTS						
Year Team	Lg	G	GS	GF	IP	BFP	H	R	ER	HR	SH	SF	HB	TBB	IBB	SO	WP	W	L	Pct	Sv-Op	Hld	Vel	OPS	ERC	ERA
2019 Roch	AAA	14	0	7	19.0	79	19	11	10	2	1	0	1	4	0	15	1	1	0	1.000	2- -	-		.705	3.60	4.74
2017 Min	AL	37	0	8	42.0	170	38	15	15	4	1	1	4	6	2	44	1	3	3	.500	1-3	12	89	.664	2.87	3.21
2018 Min	AL	73	0	20	73.0	319	75	46	44	12	3	3	2	26	9	70	2	4	6	.400	7-11	17	90	.803	4.37	5.42
2019 Min	AL	22	0	5	16.1	88	30	19	19	2	0	2	3	7	0	15	1	2	2	.500	1-1	6	88	1.033	10.46	10.47
Postseason		1	0	0	1.1	7	1	1	1	0	0	0	0	2	1	0	0	0	0	-	0-0	0	91	.629	4.29	6.75
3 ML YEARS		132	0	33	131.1	577	143	80	78	18	4	6	9	39	11	129	4	9	11	.450	9-15	35	89	.796	4.53	5.35

Rich Hill

Pitches: L **Bats:** L **Pos:** SP-13 **Ht:** 6'5" **Wt:** 221 **Born:** 3/11/1980 **Age:** 40

			HOW MUCH PITCHED					WHAT HE GAVE UP											THE RESULTS						
Year Team	Lg	G	GS	GF	IP	BFP	H	R	ER	HR	SH	SF	HB	TBB	IBB	SO	WP	W	L	Pct	Sv-Op	Hld	Vel	OPS	ERC	ERA
2005 ChC	NL	10	4	1	23.2	115	25	24	24	3	1	0	1	17	1	21	0	0	2	.000	0-0	0	90	.794	5.81	9.13
2006 ChC	NL	17	16	1	99.1	417	83	51	46	15	8	3	2	39	1	90	3	6	7	.462	0-0	0	90	.725	3.59	4.17
2007 ChC	NL	32	32	0	195.0	812	170	89	85	27	9	4	12	63	3	183	1	11	8	.579	0-0	0	89	.699	3.56	3.92
2008 ChC	NL	5	5	0	19.2	89	13	9	9	2	0	2	1	18	0	15	1	1	0	1.000	0-0	0	88	.683	4.38	4.12
2009 Bal	AL	14	13	0	57.2	275	68	53	50	7	2	2	1	40	2	46	1	3	3	.500	0-0	0	88	.886	6.55	7.80
2010 Bos	AL	6	0	0	4.0	18	5	0	0	0	0	0	0	1	0	3	0	1	0	1.000	0-0	1	89	.627	4.05	0.00
2011 Bos	AL	9	0	3	8.0	30	3	0	0	0	0	0	1	3	0	12	1	0	0	-	0-0	3	91	.349	1.10	0.00
2012 Bos	AL	25	0	3	19.2	83	17	4	4	0	0	0	0	11	1	21	0	1	0	1.000	0-0	6	92	.685	3.24	1.83
2013 Cle	AL	63	0	38	38.2	182	38	30	27	3	1	2	2	29	6	51	6	1	2	.333	0-2	13	91	.719	5.07	6.28
2014 2 Tms	AL	16	0	2	5.1	29	7	2	2	0	0	0	1	6	1	9	1	0	0	-	0-0	1	90	.801	8.55	3.38
2015 Bos	AL	4	4	0	29.0	106	14	5	5	2	0	0	0	5	0	36	0	2	1	.667	0-0	0	90	.410	1.13	1.55
2016 2 Tms		20	20	0	110.1	439	77	29	26	4	1	2	8	33	0	129	0	12	5	.706	0-0	0	90	.530	2.04	2.12
2017 LAD	NL	25	25	0	135.2	552	99	51	50	18	4	2	9	49	1	166	2	12	8	.600	0-0	0	89	.639	2.96	3.32
2018 LAD	NL	25	24	0	132.2	547	108	57	54	20	4	1	8	41	3	150	2	11	5	.688	0-0	0	90	.689	3.24	3.66
2019 LAD	NL	13	13	0	58.2	242	48	20	16	10	4	1	4	18	2	72	0	4	1	.800	0-0	0	90	.689	3.40	2.45
14 LAA	AL	2	0	0	0.0	4	1	1	1	0	0	0	0	3	0	0	1	0	0	-	0-0	0	92	2.000	-	-
14 NYY	AL	14	0	2	5.1	25	6	1	1	0	0	0	1	3	1	9	0	0	0	-	0-0	1	90	.686	5.10	1.69
16 Oak	AL	14	14	0	76.0	311	55	22	19	2	0	1	8	28	0	90	0	9	3	.750	0-0	0	90	.559	2.44	2.25
16 LAD	NL	6	6	0	34.1	128	22	7	7	2	1	1	0	5	0	39	0	3	2	.600	0-0	0	90	.461	1.34	1.83
Postseason		12	11	1	50.1	221	39	17	17	5	3	0	4	28	3	63	1	1	2	.333	0-0	0	90	.638	3.58	3.04
15 ML YEARS		284	156	13	937.1	3936	775	424	398	112	34	19	52	373	21	1004	18	65	42	.607	0-2	24	90	.678	3.44	3.82

Tim Hill

Pitches: L **Bats:** R **Pos:** RP-46 **Ht:** 6'2" **Wt:** 200 **Born:** 2/10/1990 **Age:** 30

			HOW MUCH PITCHED					WHAT HE GAVE UP											THE RESULTS						
Year Team	Lg	G	GS	GF	IP	BFP	H	R	ER	HR	SH	SF	HB	TBB	IBB	SO	WP	W	L	Pct	Sv-Op	Hld	Vel	OPS	ERC	ERA
2019 Omha	AAA	27	0	14	29.2	119	26	7	7	2	0	0	2	6	0	30	0	1	1	.500	3- -	-		.634	2.77	2.12
2018 KC	AL	70	0	9	45.2	198	46	28	23	4	2	1	2	14	0	42	0	1	4	.200	2-4	13	91	.691	3.77	4.53
2019 KC	AL	46	0	4	39.2	161	31	17	16	4	1	0	4	13	2	39	0	2	0	1.000	1-2	9	90	.636	3.01	3.63
2 ML YEARS		116	0	13	85.1	359	77	45	39	8	3	1	6	27	2	81	0	3	4	.429	3-6	22	91	.666	3.41	4.11

Sam Hilliard

Bats: L **Throws:** L **Pos:** CF-17;RF-6;PH-6;LF-5 **Ht:** 6'5" **Wt:** 238 **Born:** 2/21/1994 **Age:** 26

							BATTING												RUNNING			AVERAGES			
Year Team	Lg	G	AB	H	2B	3B	HR	(Hm	Rd)	TB	R	RBI	RC	TBB	IBB	SO	HBP	SH	SF	SB	CS	GDP	Avg	OBP	Slg	OPS
2019 Albq	AAA	126	500	131	29	7	35	(-	-)	279	109	101	96	54	1	164	2	0	3	22	5	7	.262	.335	.558	.893
2019 Col	NL	27	77	21	4	2	7	(5	2)	50	13	13	17	9	0	23	1	0	0	2	0	1	.273	.356	.649	1.006

Yoshihisa Hirano

Pitches: R **Bats:** R **Pos:** RP-62 **Ht:** 6'1" **Wt:** 185 **Born:** 3/8/1984 **Age:** 36

			HOW MUCH PITCHED					WHAT HE GAVE UP											THE RESULTS						
Year Team	Lg	G	GS	GF	IP	BFP	H	R	ER	HR	SH	SF	HB	TBB	IBB	SO	WP	W	L	Pct	Sv-Op	Hld	Vel	OPS	ERC	ERA
2018 Ari	NL	75	0	10	66.1	262	49	22	18	6	1	1	2	23	4	59	6	4	3	.571	3-7	32	91	.615	2.55	2.44
2019 Ari	NL	62	0	11	53.0	233	51	31	28	7	1	2	3	22	2	61	2	5	5	.500	1-6	15	91	.723	4.26	4.75
2 ML YEARS		137	0	21	119.1	495	100	53	46	13	2	3	5	45	6	120	8	9	8	.529	4-13	47	91	.666	3.28	3.47

Keston Hiura

Bats: R **Throws:** R **Pos:** 2B-81;PH-3 **Ht:** 5'11" **Wt:** 190 **Born:** 8/2/1996 **Age:** 23

							BATTING												RUNNING			AVERAGES			
Year Team	Lg	G	AB	H	2B	3B	HR	(Hm	Rd)	TB	R	RBI	RC	TBB	IBB	SO	HBP	SH	SF	SB	CS	GDP	Avg	OBP	Slg	OPS
2017 2 Tms	Low	42	167	62	14	7	4	(-	-)	102	32	33	39	13	0	37	4	0	3	2	2	2	.371	.422	.611	1.033
2018 Carlina	A+	50	206	66	16	3	7	(-	-)	109	38	23	39	14	1	47	7	0	1	4	6	4	.320	.382	.529	.911
2018 Biloxi	AA	73	279	76	18	2	6	(-	-)	116	36	20	40	22	0	56	6	0	0	11	5	13	.272	.339	.416	.755
2019 SnAnt	AAA	57	213	70	16	1	19	(-	-)	145	44	46	56	23	2	64	6	0	1	7	2	3	.329	.407	.681	1.088
2019 Mil	NL	84	314	95	23	2	19	(10	9)	179	51	49	53	25	1	107	8	0	1	9	3	6	.303	.368	.570	.938

Nico Hoerner

Bats: R Throws: R Pos: SS-17;2B-1;CF-1;PH-1

Ht: 5'11" Wt: 200 Born: 5/13/1997 Age: 23

Year	Team	Lg	G	AB	H	2B	3B	HR	(Hm	Rd)	TB	R	RBI	RC	TBB	IBB	SO	HBP	SH	SF	SB	CS	GDP	Avg	OBP	Slg	OPS
2018	3 Tms	Low	14	49	16	2	2	2	(-	-)	28	10	6	12	9	0	4	2	0	0	6	1	2	.327	.450	.571	1.021
2019	Tenn	AA	70	268	76	16	3	3	(-	-)	107	37	22	38	21	0	31	4	0	1	8	4	5	.284	.344	.399	.743
2019	ChC	NL	20	78	22	1	1	3	(3	0)	34	13	17	14	3	1	11	0	0	1	0	0	3	.282	.305	.436	.741

Jeff Hoffman

Pitches: R Bats: R Pos: SP-15

Ht: 6'5" Wt: 227 Born: 1/8/1993 Age: 27

			HOW MUCH PITCHED					WHAT HE GAVE UP									THE RESULTS							
Year	Team	Lg	G	GS	GF	IP	BFP	H	R	ER	HR	SH	SF	HB	TBB	IBB	SO	WP	W	L	Pct	Sv-Op	Hld	Vel	OPS	ERC	ERA
2019	Albq	AAA	17	16	0	85.1	394	105	73	73	19	1	3	9	30	0	98	5	6	8	.429	0--	-	-	.893	6.59	7.70
2016	Col	NL	8	6	0	31.1	147	37	29	17	7	1	0	0	17	1	22	4	0	4	.000	0-0	0	94	.881	6.55	4.88
2017	Col	NL	23	16	3	99.1	440	106	66	65	15	3	5	4	40	1	82	2	6	5	.545	0-0	0	94	.833	4.97	5.89
2018	Col	NL	6	1	1	8.2	44	15	9	9	0	0	0	0	7	1	5	1	0	0	-	0-0	1	93	.986	9.88	9.35
2019	Col	NL	15	15	0	70.0	315	77	51	51	21	3	2	4	34	3	68	2	2	6	.250	0-0	0	94	.957	6.81	6.56
	4 ML YEARS		52	38	4	209.1	946	235	155	142	43	7	7	8	98	6	177	9	8	15	.348	0-0	1	94	.889	6.00	6.11

Bryan Holaday

Bats: R Throws: R Pos: C-38;PH-4

HAHL-ih-daye

Ht: 6'0" Wt: 214 Born: 11/19/1987 Age: 32

Year	Team	Lg	G	AB	H	2B	3B	HR	(Hm	Rd)	TB	R	RBI	RC	TBB	IBB	SO	HBP	SH	SF	SB	CS	GDP	Avg	OBP	Slg	OPS
2019	NewOr	AAA	35	93	23	7	0	2	(-	-)	36	8	12	16	17	2	12	5	1	2	1	1	5	.247	.385	.387	.772
2012	Det	AL	6	12	3	1	0	0	(0	0)	4	3	0	1	0	0	2	0	1	0	0	0	0	.250	.250	.333	.583
2013	Det	AL	16	27	8	1	0	1	(1	0)	12	8	2	3	2	0	3	1	3	0	0	0	0	.296	.367	.444	.811
2014	Det	AL	62	156	36	5	1	0	(0	0)	43	14	15	11	8	0	37	1	2	4	1	1	4	.231	.266	.276	.542
2015	Det	AL	24	64	18	5	0	2	(1	1)	29	3	13	9	1	0	13	0	0	0	0	0	0	.281	.292	.453	.745
2016	2 Tms	AL	44	117	27	7	1	2	(1	1)	42	17	14	14	7	0	28	2	1	2	0	1	1	.231	.281	.359	.640
2017	Det	AL	13	29	7	2	0	0	(0	0)	9	1	2	2	0	0	1	0	0	0	0	0	2	.241	.241	.310	.552
2018	Mia	NL	61	151	31	5	0	1	(0	1)	39	7	16	10	10	2	29	2	1	2	0	0	4	.205	.261	.258	.519
2019	Mia	NL	43	115	32	6	0	4	(0	4)	50	12	12	14	11	2	21	1	1	1	0	1	5	.278	.344	.435	.779
16	Tex	AL	30	84	20	6	1	2	(1	1)	34	14	13	12	5	0	16	2	1	2	0	1	0	.238	.290	.405	.695
16	Bos	AL	14	33	7	1	0	0	(0	0)	8	3	1	2	2	0	12	0	0	0	0	0	1	.212	.257	.242	.500
	Postseason		1	2	0	0	0	0	(0	0)	0	0	0	0	0	0	1	0	0	0	0	0	0	.000	.000	.000	.000
	8 ML YEARS		269	671	162	32	2	10	(3	7)	228	65	74	64	39	4	134	7	9	9	1	3	16	.241	.287	.340	.626

Jonathan Holder

Pitches: R Bats: R Pos: RP-33; SP-1

Ht: 6'2" Wt: 235 Born: 6/9/1993 Age: 27

			HOW MUCH PITCHED					WHAT HE GAVE UP									THE RESULTS							
Year	Team	Lg	G	GS	GF	IP	BFP	H	R	ER	HR	SH	SF	HB	TBB	IBB	SO	WP	W	L	Pct	Sv-Op	Hld	Vel	OPS	ERC	ERA
2019	S-WB	AAA	9	0	3	12.1	52	13	5	4	1	1	1	0	2	0	15	1	1	1	.500	2--	-	-	.648	3.25	2.92
2016	NYY	AL	8	0	1	8.1	36	8	5	5	1	0	1	0	4	0	5	0	0	0	-	0-0	0	93	.753	4.34	5.40
2017	NYY	AL	37	0	12	39.1	171	45	17	17	5	0	1	3	8	1	40	2	1	1	.500	0-2	3	93	.770	4.54	3.89
2018	NYY	AL	60	1	14	66.0	272	53	27	23	4	2	2	1	19	3	60	1	1	3	.250	0-0	7	93	.589	2.31	3.14
2019	NYY	AL	34	1	8	41.1	181	43	32	29	8	0	0	2	11	1	46	0	5	2	.714	0-2	4	92	.762	4.44	6.31
	Postseason		1	0	0	2.0	9	2	1	1	0	0	0	0	1	0	1	0	0	0	-	0-0	0	92	.708	3.63	4.50
	4 ML YEARS		139	2	35	155.0	660	149	81	74	18	3	6	6	42	5	151	3	7	6	.538	0-4	14	93	.693	3.50	4.30

Derek Holland

Pitches: L Bats: B Pos: RP-43; SP-8

Ht: 6'2" Wt: 213 Born: 10/9/1986 Age: 33

			HOW MUCH PITCHED					WHAT HE GAVE UP									THE RESULTS							
Year	Team	Lg	G	GS	GF	IP	BFP	H	R	ER	HR	SH	SF	HB	TBB	IBB	SO	WP	W	L	Pct	Sv-Op	Hld	Vel	OPS	ERC	ERA
2009	Tex	AL	33	21	0	138.1	611	160	98	94	26	2	3	4	47	0	107	3	8	13	.381	0-1	2	93	.856	5.52	6.12
2010	Tex	AL	14	10	2	57.1	253	55	30	26	6	0	2	4	24	0	54	0	3	4	.429	0-0	1	92	.727	4.17	4.08
2011	Tex	AL	32	32	0	198.0	843	201	97	87	22	1	3	6	67	1	162	2	16	5	.762	0-0	0	94	.724	4.15	3.95
2012	Tex	AL	29	27	0	175.1	730	162	100	91	32	5	4	3	52	0	145	1	12	7	.632	0-0	0	93	.745	3.86	4.67
2013	Tex	AL	33	33	0	213.0	894	210	90	81	20	8	9	3	64	0	189	9	10	9	.526	0-0	0	94	.711	3.64	3.42
2014	Tex	AL	6	5	0	37.0	145	34	8	6	0	2	1	0	5	1	25	1	2	0	1.000	0-0	0	92	.601	2.07	1.46
2015	Tex	AL	10	10	0	58.2	245	59	32	32	11	3	1	5	17	2	41	1	4	3	.571	0-0	0	93	.828	4.31	4.91
2016	Tex	AL	22	20	0	107.1	461	116	62	59	15	1	2	2	35	2	67	2	7	9	.438	0-0	0	92	.770	4.61	4.95
2017	CWS	AL	29	26	0	135.0	626	156	106	93	31	1	3	8	75	2	104	7	7	14	.333	0-0	0	91	.918	6.96	6.20
2018	SF	NL	36	30	1	171.1	727	154	74	68	19	9	7	4	67	6	169	2	7	9	.438	0-0	0	93	.718	3.58	3.57
2019	2 Tms	NL	51	8	19	84.1	376	82	61	57	20	7	2	4	45	2	82	1	2	5	.286	0-1	2	92	.852	5.64	6.08
19	SF	NL	31	7	10	68.2	308	68	49	45	17	6	2	4	35	2	71	0	2	4	.333	0-0	0	92	.860	5.73	5.90
19	ChC	NL	20	1	9	15.2	68	14	12	12	3	1	0	0	10	0	11	1	0	1	.000	0-1	2	94	.814	5.23	6.89
	Postseason		14	5	2	37.2	161	37	23	21	10	0	0	1	16	0	24	2	3	1	.750	0-0	2	94	.870	5.47	5.02
	11 ML YEARS		295	222	23	1375.2	5911	1389	758	694	202	39	37	43	498	16	1145	29	78	78	.500	0-2	5	93	.771	4.44	4.54

Greg Holland

Pitches: R **Bats:** R **Pos:** RP-40   **Ht:** 5'10" **Wt:** 205 **Born:** 11/20/1985 **Age:** 34

Year Team	Lg		HOW MUCH PITCHED					WHAT HE GAVE UP												THE RESULTS						
		G	GS	GF	IP	BFP	H	R	ER	HR	SH	SF	HB	TBB	IBB	SO	WP	W	L	Pct	Sv-Op	Hld	Vel	OPS	ERC	ERA
2019 Hrsbrg	AA	8	0	2	9.0	34	4	1	0	0	0	0	0	3	0	9	3	1	0	1.000	0--	-	-	.399	0.95	0.00
2010 KC	AL	15	0	10	18.2	87	23	15	14	3	1	0	0	8	0	23	2	0	1	.000	0-0	0	96	.835	5.88	6.75
2011 KC	AL	46	0	15	60.0	233	37	13	12	3	1	1	1	19	3	74	7	5	1	.833	4-6	18	95	.521	1.60	1.80
2012 KC	AL	67	0	36	67.0	289	58	22	22	2	4	3	0	34	7	91	3	7	4	.636	16-20	9	96	.653	3.07	2.96
2013 KC	AL	68	0	61	67.0	255	40	11	9	3	1	1	0	18	1	103	2	2	1	.667	47-50	1	96	.479	1.41	1.21
2014 KC	AL	65	0	60	62.1	240	37	13	10	3	1	1	0	20	0	90	9	1	3	.250	46-48	0	96	.472	1.54	1.44
2015 KC	AL	48	0	40	44.2	193	39	20	19	2	3	1	0	26	1	49	7	3	2	.600	32-37	0	94	.692	3.68	3.83
2017 Col	NL	61	0	58	57.1	235	40	24	23	7	0	1	1	26	1	70	7	3	6	.333	**41-45**	1	93	.623	2.86	3.61
2018 2 Tms	NL	56	0	13	46.1	212	43	30	24	2	1	0	1	32	2	47	0	2	2	.500	3-6	6	93	.697	4.33	4.66
2019 Ari	NL	40	0	27	35.2	152	25	18	18	5	0	2	0	24	2	41	6	1	2	.333	17-22	5	92	.687	3.71	4.54
18 StL	NL	32	0	7	25.0	132	34	28	22	1	1	0	0	22	2	22	0	0	2	.000	0-3	2	93	.859	7.32	7.92
18 Was	NL	24	0	6	21.1	80	9	2	2	1	0	0	1	10	0	25	0	2	0	1.000	3-3	4	93	.438	1.48	0.84
Postseason		12	0	11	11.2	49	7	3	3	0	0	0	0	6	2	15	1	0	0	-	7-7	0	95	.475	1.54	2.31
9 ML YEARS		466	0	320	459.0	1896	342	166	151	30	12	10	3	207	17	588	43	24	22	.522	206-234	35	95	.605	2.66	2.96

Clay Holmes

Pitches: R **Bats:** R **Pos:** RP-35   **Ht:** 6'5" **Wt:** 225 **Born:** 3/27/1993 **Age:** 27

Year Team	Lg		HOW MUCH PITCHED					WHAT HE GAVE UP												THE RESULTS						
		G	GS	GF	IP	BFP	H	R	ER	HR	SH	SF	HB	TBB	IBB	SO	WP	W	L	Pct	Sv-Op	Hld	Vel	OPS	ERC	ERA
2019 Indy	AAA	10	0	4	15.2	80	17	15	11	1	1	2	1	15	1	13	0	2	1	.667	1--	-	-	.811	6.51	6.32
2018 Pit	NL	11	4	4	26.1	117	30	21	20	2	0	1	2	23	1	21	4	1	3	.250	0-1	0	94	.824	6.99	6.84
2019 Pit	NL	35	0	10	50.0	240	45	36	31	5	0	0	9	36	1	56	4	1	2	.333	0-1	1	94	.743	5.32	5.58
2 ML YEARS		46	4	16	76.1	369	75	57	51	7	0	1	11	59	2	77	8	2	5	.286	0-2	1	94	.771	5.88	6.01

Brock Holt

Bats: L **Throws:** R **Pos:** 2B-60;PH-12;1B-11;SS-6;RF-6;3B-4;LF-4;DH-1;PR-1   **Ht:** 5'10" **Wt:** 180 **Born:** 6/11/1988 **Age:** 32

Year Team	Lg		BATTING																RUNNING			AVERAGES			
		G	AB	H	2B	3B	HR	(Hm | Rd)	TB	R	RBI	RC	TBB	IBB	SO	HBP	SH	SF	SB	CS	GDP	Avg	OBP	Slg	OPS
2012 Pit	NL	24	65	19	2	1	0	(0 | 0)	23	6	3	10	4	0	14	0	2	1	0	0	1	.292	.329	.354	.682
2013 Bos	AL	26	59	12	2	0	0	(0 | 0)	14	9	11	7	7	0	4	0	3	3	1	0	0	.203	.275	.237	.513
2014 Bos	AL	106	449	126	23	5	4	(1 | 3)	171	68	29	56	33	0	98	2	5	3	12	2	7	.281	.331	.381	.711
2015 Bos	AL	129	454	127	27	6	2	(1 | 1)	172	56	45	65	46	0	97	3	4	2	8	1	7	.280	.349	.379	.727
2016 Bos	AL	94	290	74	16	0	7	(4 | 3)	111	45	34	36	27	0	58	3	1	3	4	3	5	.255	.322	.383	.705
2017 Bos	AL	64	140	28	6	0	0	(0 | 0)	34	20	7	12	19	0	34	3	0	2	2	1	3	.200	.305	.243	.548
2018 Bos	AL	109	321	89	18	2	7	(3 | 4)	132	41	46	48	37	2	73	7	0	2	7	7	7	.277	.362	.411	.774
2019 Bos	AL	87	259	77	14	2	3	(1 | 2)	104	38	31	40	28	1	57	4	0	4	1	0	4	.297	.369	.402	.771
Postseason		12	37	11	3	1	2	(0 | 2)	22	8	7	7	4	0	6	1	0	1	1	0	1	.297	.381	.595	.976
8 ML YEARS		639	2037	552	108	16	23	(10 | 13)	761	283	206	274	201	3	435	22	15	20	35	14	34	.271	.340	.374	.714

Rhys Hoskins

Bats: R **Throws:** R **Pos:** 1B-158;DH-2   **Ht:** 6'4" **Wt:** 225 **Born:** 3/17/1993 **Age:** 27

Year Team	Lg		BATTING																RUNNING			AVERAGES			
		G	AB	H	2B	3B	HR	(Hm | Rd)	TB	R	RBI	RC	TBB	IBB	SO	HBP	SH	SF	SB	CS	GDP	Avg	OBP	Slg	OPS
2017 Phi	NL	50	170	44	7	0	18	(10 | 8)	105	37	48	45	37	1	46	3	0	2	2	0	2	.259	.396	.618	1.014
2018 Phi	NL	153	558	137	38	0	34	(20 | 14)	277	89	96	97	87	2	150	9	0	5	5	3	7	.246	.354	.496	.850
2019 Phi	NL	160	570	129	33	5	29	(16 | 13)	259	86	85	97	**116**	6	173	11	0	6	2	2	10	.226	.364	.454	.819
3 ML YEARS		363	1298	310	78	5	81	(46 | 35)	641	212	229	239	240	9	369	23	0	13	9	5	19	.239	.364	.494	.858

Eric Hosmer

Bats: L **Throws:** L **Pos:** 1B-157;PH-3;DH-1   HOZZ-mer   **Ht:** 6'4" **Wt:** 225 **Born:** 10/24/1989 **Age:** 30

Year Team	Lg		BATTING																RUNNING			AVERAGES			
		G	AB	H	2B	3B	HR	(Hm | Rd)	TB	R	RBI	RC	TBB	IBB	SO	HBP	SH	SF	SB	CS	GDP	Avg	OBP	Slg	OPS
2011 KC	AL	128	523	153	27	3	19	(3 | 16)	243	66	78	71	34	7	82	1	0	5	11	5	13	.293	.334	.465	.799
2012 KC	AL	152	535	124	22	2	14	(8 | 6)	192	65	60	61	56	4	95	2	0	5	16	1	10	.232	.304	.359	.663
2013 KC	AL	159	623	188	34	3	17	(10 | 7)	279	86	79	88	51	4	100	1	1	4	11	4	15	.302	.353	.448	.801
2014 KC	AL	131	503	136	35	1	9	(4 | 5)	200	54	58	62	35	4	93	3	0	6	4	2	12	.270	.318	.398	.716
2015 KC	AL	158	599	178	33	5	18	(10 | 8)	275	98	93	94	61	6	108	3	1	3	7	3	16	.297	.363	.459	.822
2016 KC	AL	158	605	161	24	1	25	(8 | 17)	262	80	104	87	57	5	132	1	0	4	5	3	18	.266	.328	.433	.761
2017 KC	AL	162	603	192	31	1	25	(16 | 9)	300	98	94	116	66	3	104	0	0	2	6	1	20	.318	.385	.498	.882
2018 SD	NL	157	613	155	31	2	18	(10 | 8)	244	72	69	77	62	10	142	1	0	1	7	4	18	.253	.322	.398	.720
2019 SD	NL	160	619	164	29	2	22	(11 | 11)	263	72	99	87	40	3	163	3	0	5	0	3	12	.265	.310	.425	.735
Postseason		31	123	34	5	1	3	(1 | 2)	50	18	29	21	12	2	33	0	0	3	1	1	1	.276	.333	.407	.740
9 ML YEARS		1365	5223	1451	266	20	167	(81 | 86)	2258	691	734	743	462	46	1019	15	2	35	67	26	134	.278	.336	.432	.768

Adrian Houser

Pitches: R **Bats:** R **Pos:** SP-18; RP-17   HOW-zer   **Ht:** 6'4" **Wt:** 235 **Born:** 2/2/1993 **Age:** 27

Year Team	Lg		HOW MUCH PITCHED					WHAT HE GAVE UP												THE RESULTS						
		G	GS	GF	IP	BFP	H	R	ER	HR	SH	SF	HB	TBB	IBB	SO	WP	W	L	Pct	Sv-Op	Hld	Vel	OPS	ERC	ERA
2015 Mil	NL	2	0	2	2.0	8	1	0	0	0	0	0	0	2	0	0	0	0	0	-	0-0	0	94	.542	3.21	0.00
2018 Mil	NL	7	0	5	13.2	59	13	5	5	0	0	0	1	7	0	8	1	0	0	-	0-0	0	94	.728	3.89	3.29
2019 Mil	NL	35	18	7	111.1	462	101	49	46	14	3	3	5	37	2	117	2	6	7	.462	0-0	1	94	.710	3.68	3.72
3 ML YEARS		44	18	14	127.0	529	115	54	51	14	3	3	6	46	2	125	3	6	7	.462	0-0	1	94	.710	3.71	3.61

Sam Howard

Pitches: L Bats: R Pos: RP-20 Ht: 6'3" Wt: 170 Born: 3/5/1993 Age: 27

Year Team	Lg	G	GS	GF	IP	BFP	H	R	ER	HR	SH	SF	HB	TBB	IBB	SO	WP	W	L	Pct	Sv-Op	Hld	Vel	OPS	ERC	ERA
2019 Albq	AAA	42	0	16	50.2	216	50	23	22	5	0	0	2	23	2	62	3	4	1	.800	1--	-	-	.735	4.43	3.91
2018 Col	NL	4	0	4	4.0	20	5	1	1	0	0	1	0	3	0	1	0	0	0	-	0-0	0	92	.888	7.36	2.25
2019 Col	NL	20	0	3	19.0	91	21	16	14	5	2	0	3	10	0	23	2	2	0	1.000	0-0	0	93	.895	7.04	6.63
2 ML YEARS		24	0	7	23.0	111	26	17	15	5	2	0	4	13	0	24	2	2	0	1.000	0-0	0	92	.894	7.14	5.87

James Hoyt

Pitches: R Bats: R Pos: RP-8 Ht: 6'6" Wt: 230 Born: 9/30/1986 Age: 33

Year Team	Lg	G	GS	GF	IP	BFP	H	R	ER	HR	SH	SF	HB	TBB	IBB	SO	WP	W	L	Pct	Sv-Op	Hld	Vel	OPS	ERC	ERA
2019 Clmbs	AAA	40	2	22	42.0	190	46	17	16	3	0	1	4	20	2	48	8	2	0	1.000	4--	-	-	.768	5.05	3.43
2016 Hou	AL	22	0	7	22.0	91	16	12	11	5	1	1	1	9	1	28	3	1	1	.500	0-1	1	93	.707	3.55	4.50
2017 Hou	AL	43	0	7	49.1	211	51	24	24	7	0	0	2	14	0	66	4	1	0	1.000	0-0	7	93	.748	4.25	4.38
2018 Hou	AL	1	0	0	0.1	3	1	0	0	0	0	0	0	1	0	0	0	0	0	-	0-0	0	93	1.167	29.63	0.00
2019 Cle	AL	8	0	2	8.1	32	6	2	2	2	0	0	0	2	0	10	0	0	0	-	0-0	1	94	.717	2.87	2.16
4 ML YEARS		74	0	16	80.0	337	74	38	37	14	1	1	3	26	1	104	7	2	1	.667	0-1	9	93	.738	4.00	4.16

Wei-Chieh Huang

way-chay hwong

Pitches: R Bats: R Pos: RP-4 Ht: 6'1" Wt: 170 Born: 9/26/1993 Age: 26

Year Team	Lg	G	GS	GF	IP	BFP	H	R	ER	HR	SH	SF	HB	TBB	IBB	SO	WP	W	L	Pct	Sv-Op	Hld	Vel	OPS	ERC	ERA
2019 Frisco	AA	6	1	2	9.2	37	7	2	2	2	0	0	0	2	0	14	1	1	0	1.000	0--	-	-	.615	2.57	1.86
2019 Nashv	AAA	18	3	1	31.0	140	24	23	21	5	0	0	3	25	0	42	4	1	2	.333	0--	-	-	.764	5.34	6.10
2019 Tex	AL	4	0	1	5.2	32	8	5	2	0	0	0	1	5	0	2	3	0	0	-	0-0	0	93	.899	7.98	3.18

Dakota Hudson

Pitches: R Bats: R Pos: SP-32; RP-1 Ht: 6'5" Wt: 215 Born: 9/15/1994 Age: 25

Year Team	Lg	G	GS	GF	IP	BFP	H	R	ER	HR	SH	SF	HB	TBB	IBB	SO	WP	W	L	Pct	Sv-Op	Hld	Vel	OPS	ERC	ERA
2018 StL	NL	26	0	2	27.1	118	19	9	8	0	0	2	1	18	0	19	2	4	1	.800	0-0	11	96	.559	2.82	2.63
2019 StL	NL	33	32	1	174.2	757	160	80	65	22	3	7	9	86	8	136	5	16	7	.696	1-1	0	94	.742	4.32	3.35
2 ML YEARS		59	32	3	202.0	875	179	89	73	22	3	9	10	104	8	155	7	20	8	.714	1-1	11	94	.718	4.11	3.25

Daniel Hudson

Pitches: R Bats: R Pos: RP-68; SP-1 Ht: 6'3" Wt: 225 Born: 3/9/1987 Age: 33

Year Team	Lg	G	GS	GF	IP	BFP	H	R	ER	HR	SH	SF	HB	TBB	IBB	SO	WP	W	L	Pct	Sv-Op	Hld	Vel	OPS	ERC	ERA
2009 CWS	AL	6	2	1	18.2	82	16	9	7	3	0	1	1	9	0	14	1	1	1	.500	0-0	0	93	.711	4.15	3.38
2010 2 Tms		14	14	0	95.1	372	68	26	26	8	2	2	4	27	1	84	5	8	2	.800	0-0	0	93	.579	2.26	2.45
2011 Ari	NL	33	33	0	222.0	921	217	98	86	17	6	6	8	50	1	169	4	16	12	.571	0-0	0	93	.694	3.26	3.49
2012 Ari	NL	9	9	0	45.1	202	62	37	37	9	2	1	0	12	0	37	2	3	2	.600	0-0	0	93	.910	6.56	7.35
2014 Ari	NL	3	0	0	2.2	13	4	4	4	0	0	0	0	0	0	2	0	0	1	.000	0-0	0	95	.769	4.08	13.50
2015 Ari	NL	64	1	13	67.2	290	64	34	29	7	1	3	0	25	2	71	5	4	3	.571	4-6	20	96	.691	3.58	3.86
2016 Ari	NL	70	0	17	60.1	268	65	40	35	6	0	0	4	22	3	58	5	3	2	.600	5-7	17	96	.753	4.51	5.22
2017 Pit	NL	71	0	18	61.2	271	57	34	30	7	1	2	5	33	1	66	4	2	7	.222	0-2	21	96	.761	4.63	4.38
2018 LAD	NL	40	1	11	46.0	197	38	25	21	6	0	0	4	18	1	44	3	3	2	.600	0-1	3	95	.653	3.54	4.11
2019 2 Tms		69	1	25	73.0	304	56	25	20	8	1	5	4	27	2	71	2	9	3	.750	8-12	11	96	.650	2.91	2.47
10 CWS	AL	3	3	0	15.2	71	17	11	11	1	1	1	0	11	0	14	2	1	1	.500	0-0	0	93	.797	5.69	6.32
10 Ari	NL	11	11	0	79.2	301	51	15	15	7	1	1	4	16	1	70	3	7	1	.875	0-0	0	92	.531	1.70	1.69
19 Tor	AL	45	1	11	48.0	207	38	18	16	5	1	3	3	23	0	48	1	6	3	.667	2-4	8	96	.678	3.45	3.00
19 Was	NL	24	0	14	25.0	97	18	7	4	3	0	2	1	4	2	23	1	3	0	1.000	6-8	3	96	.593	1.93	1.44
Postseason		1	1	0	5.1	24	9	5	5	1	0	0	0	0	0	6	0	1	0	.000	0-0	0	95	1.042	7.35	8.44
10 ML YEARS		379	61	85	692.2	2920	647	332	295	71	13	20	30	223	11	616	31	49	35	.583	17-28	72	94	.699	3.57	3.83

Joe Hudson

Bats: R Throws: R Pos: PH-1 Ht: 6'0" Wt: 210 Born: 5/21/1991 Age: 29

Year Team	Lg	G	AB	H	2B	3B	HR	(Hm	Rd)	TB	R	RBI	RC	TBB	IBB	SO	HBP	SH	SF	SB	CS	GDP	Avg	OBP	Slg	OPS
2019 Memp	AAA	60	197	44	5	1	10	(-	-)	81	24	30	25	20	0	69	1	0	4	0	0	10	.223	.293	.411	.704
2018 LAA	AL	8	12	2	1	0	0	(0	0)	3	0	1	0	0	0	0	0	0	0	0	0	0	.167	.167	.250	.417
2019 StL	NL	1	1	0	0	0	0	(0	0)	0	0	0	0	0	0	1	0	0	0	0	0	0	.000	.000	.000	.000
2 ML YEARS		9	13	2	1	0	0	(0	0)	3	0	1	0	0	0	1	0	0	0	0	0	0	.154	.154	.231	.385

Jared Hughes

Pitches: R Bats: R Pos: RP-72 Ht: 6'7" Wt: 240 Born: 7/4/1985 Age: 34

Year Team	Lg	G	GS	GF	IP	BFP	H	R	ER	HR	SH	SF	HB	TBB	IBB	SO	WP	W	L	Pct	Sv-Op	Hld	Vel	OPS	ERC	ERA
2011 Pit	NL	12	0	1	11.0	46	9	5	5	1	1	0	0	4	0	10	0	0	1	.000	0-0	2	93	.630	2.85	4.09
2012 Pit	NL	66	0	20	75.2	316	65	30	24	7	1	0	5	22	4	50	5	2	2	.500	2-4	11	92	.677	2.99	2.85
2013 Pit	NL	29	0	8	32.0	148	37	17	17	2	2	1	2	16	1	23	2	2	3	.400	0-0	3	92	.786	5.27	4.78
2014 Pit	NL	63	0	16	64.1	256	51	21	14	4	6	2	6	19	5	36	2	7	5	.583	0-2	13	92	.609	2.68	1.96
2015 Pit	NL	76	0	11	67.0	284	70	21	17	6	4	7	6	19	2	36	3	3	1	.750	0-3	21	93	.720	3.93	2.28

			HOW MUCH PITCHED					WHAT HE GAVE UP												THE RESULTS						
Year	Team	Lg	G	GS	GF	IP	BFP	H	R	ER	HR	SH	SF	HB	TBB	IBB	SO	WP	W	L	Pct	Sv-Op	Hld	Vel	OPS	ERC	ERA
2016	Pit	NL	67	0	18	59.1	257	62	24	20	6	4	2	5	22	3	34	5	1	1	.500	1-3	4	93	.794	4.55	3.03
2017	Mil	NL	67	0	15	59.2	244	49	21	20	4	2	0	6	24	5	48	6	5	3	.625	1-4	12	93	.723	3.27	3.02
2018	Cin	NL	72	0	23	78.2	298	57	17	17	4	1	3	2	23	2	59	5	4	3	.571	7-11	15	92	.566	2.16	1.94
2019	2 Tms	NL	72	0	13	71.1	289	57	37	32	13	4	1	2	27	1	54	1	5	5	.500	1-4	7	91	.725	3.61	4.04
19	Cin	NL	47	0	12	48.1	199	41	27	22	6	3	1	2	19	0	34	0	3	4	.429	1-3	3	91	.707	3.63	4.10
19	Phi	NL	25	0	1	23.0	90	16	10	10	7	1	0	0	8	1	20	1	2	1	.667	0-1	4	92	.763	3.50	3.91
Postseason			1	0	0	1.0	7	3	2	2	0	0	0	0	1	0	1	0	0	0	-	0-0	0	93	1.071	19.55	18.00
9 ML YEARS			524	0	125	519.0	2138	457	193	166	44	27	13	35	176	23	350	29	29	24	.547	12-31	88	92	.691	3.36	2.88

Danny Hultzen

Pitches: L **Bats:** L **Pos:** RP-6   **Ht:** 6'3" **Wt:** 210 **Born:** 11/28/1989 **Age:** 30

			HOW MUCH PITCHED					WHAT HE GAVE UP												THE RESULTS						
Year	Team	Lg	G	GS	GF	IP	BFP	H	R	ER	HR	SH	SF	HB	TBB	IBB	SO	WP	W	L	Pct	Sv-Op	Hld	Vel	OPS	ERC	ERA
2019	Iowa	AAA	14	0	5	14.1	59	4	2	2	0	0	1	3	9	0	23	1	0	1	.000	3- -	-	-	.380	1.43	1.26
2019	ChC	NL	6	0	0	3.1	18	4	0	0	0	0	0	1	2	0	5	0	0	0	-	0-0	0	93	.656	5.90	0.00

Nick Hundley

Bats: R **Throws:** R **Pos:** C-30;PH-1   **Ht:** 6'0" **Wt:** 203 **Born:** 9/8/1983 **Age:** 36

			BATTING																		RUNNING			AVERAGES			
Year	Team	Lg	G	AB	H	2B	3B	HR	(Hm	Rd)	TB	R	RBI	RC	TBB	IBB	SO	HBP	SH	SF	SB	CS	GDP	Avg	OBP	Slg	OPS
2019	LV	AAA	12	32	4	1	0	1	(-	-)	8	2	3	0	2	0	17	0	0	2	0	0	1	.125	.167	.250	.417
2008	SD	NL	60	198	47	7	1	5	(4	1)	71	21	24	17	11	0	52	2	0	5	0	0	1	.237	.278	.359	.636
2009	SD	NL	78	256	61	15	2	8	(4	4)	104	23	30	33	28	1	76	1	1	3	5	1	2	.238	.313	.406	.719
2010	SD	NL	85	273	68	18	2	8	(7	1)	114	33	43	37	25	0	66	1	2	6	0	5	8	.249	.308	.418	.726
2011	SD	NL	82	281	81	16	5	9	(6	3)	134	34	29	40	22	3	74	4	0	1	1	1	5	.288	.347	.477	.824
2012	SD	NL	58	204	32	7	1	3	(1	2)	50	14	22	6	15	2	56	2	1	3	0	3	4	.157	.219	.245	.464
2013	SD	NL	114	373	87	19	0	13	(6	7)	145	35	44	36	26	5	98	5	1	3	1	0	7	.233	.290	.389	.679
2014	2 Tms		83	218	53	7	0	6	(4	2)	78	18	22	21	10	0	63	0	2	3	1	0	3	.243	.273	.358	.631
2015	Col	NL	103	366	110	21	5	10	(7	3)	171	45	43	44	21	0	76	1	0	1	5	6	8	.301	.339	.467	.807
2016	Col	NL	83	289	75	20	1	10	(4	6)	127	30	48	41	25	3	65	1	1	1	0	0	12	.260	.320	.439	.759
2017	SF	NL	101	287	70	23	0	9	(4	5)	120	27	35	25	12	2	81	0	2	2	0	0	6	.244	.272	.418	.691
2018	SF	NL	96	282	68	13	2	10	(6	4)	115	34	31	31	22	2	85	1	0	0	2	1	8	.241	.298	.408	.706
2019	Oak	AL	31	70	14	3	1	2	(0	2)	25	5	5	1	2	0	18	1	0	1	0	0	7	.200	.233	.357	.590
14	SD	NL	33	59	16	3	0	1	(1	0)	22	1	3	5	0	0	13	0	0	0	0	0	1	.271	.271	.373	.644
14	Bal	AL	50	159	37	4	0	5	(3	2)	56	17	19	16	10	0	50	0	2	3	1	0	2	.233	.273	.352	.625
Postseason			5	15	1	0	0	0	(0	0)	1	0	1	0	0	0	5	0	0	0	0	0	0	.067	.067	.067	.133
12 ML YEARS			974	3097	766	169	20	93	(53	40)	1254	319	376	332	219	18	810	19	10	28	15	18	69	.247	.299	.405	.703

Tommy Hunter

Pitches: R **Bats:** R **Pos:** RP-5   **Ht:** 6'3" **Wt:** 250 **Born:** 7/3/1986 **Age:** 33

			HOW MUCH PITCHED					WHAT HE GAVE UP												THE RESULTS						
Year	Team	Lg	G	GS	GF	IP	BFP	H	R	ER	HR	SH	SF	HB	TBB	IBB	SO	WP	W	L	Pct	Sv-Op	Hld	Vel	OPS	ERC	ERA
2008	Tex	AL	3	3	0	11.0	63	23	20	20	4	0	4	0	3	0	9	0	0	2	.000	0-0	0	91	1.144	12.66	16.36
2009	Tex	AL	19	19	0	112.0	475	113	55	51	13	2	1	2	33	2	64	6	9	6	.600	0-0	0	89	.736	3.86	4.10
2010	Tex	AL	23	22	0	128.0	536	126	55	53	21	3	2	3	33	0	68	1	13	4	.765	0-0	0	90	.740	3.95	3.73
2011	2 Tms	AL	20	11	2	84.2	367	100	50	44	12	2	2	4	15	1	45	0	4	4	.500	0-1	1	92	.782	4.65	4.68
2012	Bal	AL	33	20	5	133.2	573	161	85	81	32	3	6	4	27	2	77	0	7	8	.467	0-1	0	92	.864	5.63	5.45
2013	Bal	AL	68	0	20	86.1	336	71	28	27	11	1	0	2	14	1	68	0	6	5	.545	4-6	21	96	.617	2.53	2.81
2014	Bal	AL	60	0	24	60.2	241	55	22	20	4	1	2	1	12	3	45	2	3	2	.600	11-17	12	96	.643	2.65	2.97
2015	2 Tms	AL	58	0	17	60.1	249	61	29	28	7	1	3	1	14	2	47	2	4	2	.667	1-2	7	96	.711	3.65	4.18
2016	2 Tms	AL	33	0	8	34.0	139	35	13	12	1	1	0	2	8	1	23	0	2	2	.500	0-1	1	94	.678	3.43	3.18
2017	TB	AL	61	0	11	58.2	228	43	18	17	6	0	0	1	14	0	64	2	3	5	.375	1-1	25	96	.588	2.21	2.61
2018	Phi	NL	65	0	10	64.0	270	65	28	27	6	1	1	3	15	1	51	1	5	4	.556	4-6	25	96	.745	3.62	3.80
2019	Phi	NL	5	0	1	5.1	18	2	0	0	0	0	0	0	0	0	5	0	0	0	-	0-0	1	94	.222	0.31	0.00
11	Tex	AL	8	0	2	15.1	62	12	6	5	1	1	1	0	5	0	10	0	1	1	.500	0-1	1	93	.570	2.44	2.93
11	Bal	AL	12	11	0	69.1	305	88	44	39	11	1	1	4	10	1	35	0	3	3	.500	0-0	1	92	.823	5.19	5.06
15	Bal	AL	39	0	12	44.2	180	41	19	18	3	1	3	1	11	2	32	2	2	2	.500	0-1	6	96	.650	2.92	3.63
15	ChC	NL	19	0	5	15.2	69	20	10	10	4	0	0	0	3	0	15	0	2	0	1.000	1-1	1	97	.864	5.91	5.74
16	Cle	AL	21	0	5	21.2	90	21	10	9	1	1	0	2	5	1	17	0	2	2	.500	0-1	1	94	.668	3.22	3.74
16	Bal	AL	12	0	3	12.1	49	14	3	3	0	0	0	0	3	0	6	0	0	0	-	0-0	1	95	.695	3.82	2.19
Postseason			7	3	2	14.1	65	19	8	7	2	0	2	1	2	0	15	0	0	2	.000	0-0	0	92	.888	5.35	4.40
12 ML YEARS			448	75	98	838.2	3495	855	403	380	117	15	17	24	188	13	566	14	56	44	.560	21-35	93	93	.736	3.87	4.08

Chris Iannetta

Bats: R **Throws:** R **Pos:** C-45;PH-10;DH-1   eye-ah-NETT-ah   **Ht:** 6'0" **Wt:** 230 **Born:** 4/8/1983 **Age:** 37

			BATTING																		RUNNING			AVERAGES			
Year	Team	Lg	G	AB	H	2B	3B	HR	(Hm	Rd)	TB	R	RBI	RC	TBB	IBB	SO	HBP	SH	SF	SB	CS	GDP	Avg	OBP	Slg	OPS
2006	Col	NL	21	77	20	4	0	2	(0	2)	30	12	10	9	13	2	17	1	1	1	0	1	1	.260	.370	.390	.759
2007	Col	NL	67	197	43	8	3	4	(1	3)	69	22	27	27	29	3	58	5	1	2	0	0	3	.218	.330	.350	.681
2008	Col	NL	104	333	88	22	2	18	(11	7)	168	50	65	65	56	0	92	14	2	2	0	0	6	.264	.390	.505	.895
2009	Col	NL	93	289	66	15	2	16	(8	8)	133	41	52	47	43	3	75	11	1	6	0	0	4	.228	.344	.460	.804
2010	Col	NL	61	188	37	6	1	9	(7	2)	72	20	27	21	30	2	48	4	0	1	1	0	4	.197	.318	.383	.701
2011	Col	NL	112	345	82	17	1	14	(10	4)	143	51	55	62	70	5	89	5	2	4	6	3	10	.238	.370	.414	.785
2012	LAA	AL	79	221	53	6	1	9	(3	6)	88	27	26	26	29	0	60	2	0	1	1	3	4	.240	.332	.398	.730
2013	LAA	AL	115	325	73	15	0	11	(1	10)	121	40	39	44	68	2	100	2	0	3	0	1	8	.225	.358	.372	.731
2014	LAA	AL	108	306	77	22	0	7	(6	1)	120	41	43	56	54	3	91	8	0	5	3	0	3	.252	.373	.392	.765
2015	LAA	AL	92	272	51	10	0	10	(3	7)	91	28	34	27	41	1	83	1	0	3	0	1	11	.188	.293	.335	.628

Year	Team	Lg	G	AB	H	2B	3B	HR	(Hm	Rd)	TB	R	RBI	RC	TBB	IBB	SO	HBP	SH	SF	SB	CS	GDP	Avg	OBP	Slg	OPS
2016	Sea	AL	94	295	62	14	0	7	(5	2)	97	23	24	27	38	0	83	2	1	2	0	0	4	.210	.303	.329	.631
2017	Ari	NL	89	272	69	19	0	17	(7	10)	139	38	43	46	37	0	87	6	0	1	0	0	3	.254	.354	.511	.865
2018	Col	NL	110	299	67	13	1	11	(7	4)	115	36	36	35	50	5	87	7	1	3	0	0	13	.224	.345	.385	.730
2019	Col	NL	52	144	32	10	0	6	(4	2)	60	20	21	16	18	3	54	1	0	1	0	0	9	.222	.311	.417	.728
Postseason			9	24	1	0	0	1	(1	0)	4	1	1	0	1	0	8	0	0	0	0	0	0	.042	.080	.167	.247
14 ML YEARS			1197	3563	820	181	11	141	(73	68)	1446	449	502	509	576	29	1024	69	9	36	11	10	83	.230	.345	.406	.751

Jose Iglesias

Bats: R **Throws:** R **Pos:** SS-144;PH-6   ee-GLAY-see-us   **Ht:** 5'11" **Wt:** 194 **Born:** 1/5/1990 **Age:** 30

Year	Team	Lg	G	AB	H	2B	3B	HR	(Hm	Rd)	TB	R	RBI	RC	TBB	IBB	SO	HBP	SH	SF	SB	CS	GDP	Avg	OBP	Slg	OPS
2011	Bos	AL	10	6	2	0	0	0	(0	0)	2	3	0	0	0	0	2	0	0	0	0	0	0	.333	.333	.333	.667
2012	Bos	AL	25	68	8	2	0	1	(0	1)	13	5	2	0	4	0	16	3	2	0	1	0	2	.118	.200	.191	.391
2013	2 Tms		109	350	106	16	2	3	(1	2)	135	39	29	45	15	0	60	11	4	2	5	2	7	.303	.349	.386	.735
2015	Det	AL	120	416	125	17	3	2	(1	2)	154	44	23	47	25	2	44	6	4	3	11	8	10	.300	.347	.370	.717
2016	Det	AL	137	467	119	26	0	4	(1	3)	157	57	32	47	28	1	50	8	7	3	7	4	12	.255	.306	.336	.643
2017	Det	AL	130	463	118	33	1	6	(4	2)	171	56	54	54	21	0	65	1	3	1	7	4	6	.255	.288	.369	.657
2018	Det	AL	125	432	116	31	3	5	(3	2)	168	43	48	60	19	0	47	8	3	2	15	6	11	.269	.310	.389	.699
2019	Cin	NL	146	504	145	21	3	11	(9	2)	205	62	59	61	20	3	70	3	1	2	6	6	17	.288	.318	.407	.724
13	Bos	AL	63	215	71	10	2	1	(0	1)	88	27	19	34	11	0	30	6	0	2	3	1	4	.330	.376	.409	.785
13	Det	AL	46	135	35	6	0	2	(1	1)	47	12	10	11	4	0	30	5	4	0	2	1	3	.259	.306	.348	.654
Postseason			11	26	6	0	0	0	(0	0)	6	2	1	0	1	0	5	1	3	0	0	1	1	.231	.286	.231	.516
8 ML YEARS			802	2706	739	146	12	32	(19	13)	1005	309	247	314	132	6	354	40	24	13	52	30	65	.273	.315	.371	.687

Raisel Iglesias

Pitches: R **Bats:** R **Pos:** RP-68   rye-SELL   **Ht:** 6'2" **Wt:** 188 **Born:** 1/4/1990 **Age:** 30

Year	Team	Lg	G	GS	GF	IP	BFP	H	R	ER	HR	SH	SF	HB	TBB	IBB	SO	WP	W	L	Pct	Sv-Op	Hld	Vel	OPS	ERC	ERA
2015	Cin	NL	18	16	1	95.1	395	81	45	44	11	4	0	7	28	0	104	2	3	7	.300	0-0	0	92	.682	3.24	4.15
2016	Cin	NL	37	5	15	78.1	325	63	22	22	7	1	2	5	26	1	83	3	3	2	.600	6-8	7	93	.623	2.90	2.53
2017	Cin	NL	63	0	57	76.0	306	57	22	21	5	1	1	1	27	1	92	1	3	3	.500	28-30	0	96	.576	2.43	2.49
2018	Cin	NL	66	0	57	72.0	291	52	22	19	12	1	2	2	25	2	80	2	2	5	.286	30-34	0	95	.644	2.88	2.38
2019	Cin	NL	68	0	55	67.0	279	61	31	31	12	1	1	2	21	4	89	3	3	12	.200	34-40	3	95	.743	3.81	4.16
5 ML YEARS			252	21	185	388.2	1596	314	142	137	47	8	6	17	127	8	448	11	14	29	.326	98-112	10	94	.654	3.04	3.17

Ender Inciarte

Bats: L **Throws:** L **Pos:** CF-63;PH-3;PR-1   END-er in-see-ARR-tay   **Ht:** 5'11" **Wt:** 190 **Born:** 10/29/1990 **Age:** 29

Year	Team	Lg	G	AB	H	2B	3B	HR	(Hm	Rd)	TB	R	RBI	RC	TBB	IBB	SO	HBP	SH	SF	SB	CS	GDP	Avg	OBP	Slg	OPS
2014	Ari	NL	118	418	116	18	2	4	(1	3)	150	54	27	49	25	0	53	0	4	0	19	3	3	.278	.318	.359	.677
2015	Ari	NL	132	524	159	27	5	6	(1	5)	214	73	45	69	26	0	58	4	2	5	21	10	8	.303	.338	.408	.747
2016	Atl	NL	131	522	152	24	7	3	(1	2)	199	85	29	58	45	5	68	4	5	2	16	7	8	.291	.351	.381	.732
2017	Atl	NL	158	662	201	27	5	11	(6	5)	271	93	57	95	49	3	94	0	3	4	22	9	8	.304	.350	.409	.759
2018	Atl	NL	156	597	158	27	6	10	(3	7)	227	83	61	70	49	1	86	6	4	4	28	14	6	.265	.325	.380	.705
2019	Atl	NL	65	199	49	11	2	5	(2	3)	79	30	24	32	26	2	41	4	0	1	7	1	1	.246	.343	.397	.740
Postseason			4	13	3	0	0	0	(0	0)	3	0	0	0	1	0	4	0	1	0	0	0	0	.231	.231	.231	.462
6 ML YEARS			760	2922	835	134	27	39	(14	25)	1140	418	243	373	220	11	400	18	18	16	113	44	34	.286	.338	.390	.728

Cole Irvin

Pitches: L **Bats:** L **Pos:** RP-13;SP-3   **Ht:** 6'4" **Wt:** 180 **Born:** 1/31/1994 **Age:** 26

Year	Team	Lg	G	GS	GF	IP	BFP	H	R	ER	HR	SH	SF	HB	TBB	IBB	SO	WP	W	L	Pct	Sv-Op	Hld	Vel	OPS	ERC	ERA
2019	LV	AAA	17	16	0	93.2	401	113	46	41	13	2	3	2	14	1	65	2	6	1	.857	0--	-	-	.776	4.58	3.94
2019	Phi	NL	16	3	1	41.2	181	45	28	27	7	1	2	3	13	1	31	1	2	1	.667	1-1	0	90	.796	4.96	5.83

Alex Jackson

Bats: R **Throws:** R **Pos:** C-4   **Ht:** 6'2" **Wt:** 215 **Born:** 12/25/1995 **Age:** 24

Year	Team	Lg	G	AB	H	2B	3B	HR	(Hm	Rd)	TB	R	RBI	RC	TBB	IBB	SO	HBP	SH	SF	SB	CS	GDP	Avg	OBP	Slg	OPS
2019	Gwnntt	AAA	85	306	70	9	0	28	(-	-)	163	52	65	52	20	0	118	18	0	1	1	0	6	.229	.313	.533	.846
2019	Atl	NL	4	13	0	0	0	0	(0	0)	0	0	0	0	1	1	5	1	0	0	0	0	1	.000	.133	.000	.133

Drew Jackson

Bats: R **Throws:** R **Pos:** CF-2;PH-2;LF-1   **Ht:** 6'2" **Wt:** 200 **Born:** 7/28/1993 **Age:** 26

Year	Team	Lg	G	AB	H	2B	3B	HR	(Hm	Rd)	TB	R	RBI	RC	TBB	IBB	SO	HBP	SH	SF	SB	CS	GDP	Avg	OBP	Slg	OPS
2019	OkCity	AAA	85	273	57	10	1	6	(-	-)	87	40	28	27	31	1	92	5	1	1	9	5	6	.209	.300	.319	.619
2019	Bal	AL	3	3	0	0	0	0	(0	0)	0	0	0	0	1	0	1	0	0	0	0	0	0	.000	.250	.000	.250

Edwin Jackson

Pitches: R Bats: R Pos: SP-13; RP-5 Ht: 6'2" Wt: 215 Born: 9/9/1983 Age: 36

Year	Team	Lg	G	GS	GF	IP	BFP	H	R	ER	HR	SH	SF	HB	TBB	IBB	SO	WP	W	L	Pct	Sv-Op	Hld	Vel	OPS	ERC	ERA
2003	LAD	NL	4	3	0	22.0	91	17	6	6	2	1	1	1	11	1	19	3	2	1	.667	0-0	0	94	.673	3.36	2.45
2004	LAD	NL	8	5	1	24.2	113	31	20	20	7	1	0	0	11	1	16	0	2	1	.667	0-0	0	93	.949	7.21	7.30
2005	LAD	NL	7	6	0	28.2	134	31	22	20	2	0	2	1	17	0	13	2	2	2	.500	0-0	0	92	.769	5.13	6.28
2006	TB	AL	23	1	7	36.1	174	42	27	22	2	2	2	1	25	0	27	3	0	0	-	0-0	0	95	.826	5.86	5.45
2007	TB	AL	32	31	0	161.0	755	195	116	103	19	5	6	4	88	3	128	7	5	15	.250	0-0	0	94	.837	6.11	5.76
2008	TB	AL	32	31	0	183.1	792	199	91	90	23	3	3	2	77	1	108	7	14	11	.560	0-1	0	94	.796	4.99	4.42
2009	Det	AL	33	33	0	214.0	890	200	93	86	27	4	2	5	70	3	161	6	13	9	.591	0-0	0	95	.726	3.72	3.62
2010	2 Tms		32	32	0	209.1	902	214	111	104	21	6	4	6	78	4	181	20	10	12	.455	0-0	0	94	.735	4.20	4.47
2011	2 Tms		32	31	1	199.2	861	225	92	84	16	15	6	2	62	4	148	9	12	9	.571	0-0	0	94	.768	4.34	3.79
2012	Was	NL	31	31	0	189.2	790	173	90	85	23	9	8	2	58	5	168	3	10	11	.476	0-0	0	93	.719	3.36	4.03
2013	ChC	NL	31	31	0	175.1	777	197	110	97	16	8	3	5	59	7	135	14	8	18	.308	0-0	0	93	.775	4.46	4.98
2014	ChC	NL	28	27	0	140.2	633	168	105	99	18	6	4	3	63	3	123	9	6	15	.286	0-0	0	93	.869	5.75	6.33
2015	2 Tms	NL	47	0	18	55.2	228	44	25	19	4	1	3	1	21	1	40	5	4	3	.571	1-2	5	94	.622	2.75	3.07
2016	2 Tms	NL	21	13	3	84.0	373	92	56	55	14	2	4	1	41	3	61	6	5	7	.417	0-0	0	92	.857	5.55	5.89
2017	2 Tms		16	13	0	76.0	339	86	53	44	20	4	3	0	29	2	60	3	5	6	.455	0-0	0	93	.891	5.87	5.21
2018	Oak	AL	17	17	0	92.0	381	75	37	34	12	2	1	2	37	1	68	5	6	3	.667	0-0	0	93	.687	3.37	3.33
2019	2 Tms	AL	18	13	0	67.2	336	105	81	72	23	0	2	3	32	0	52	6	3	10	.231	0-0	0	93	1.102	10.14	9.58
10	Ari	NL	21	21	0	134.1	587	141	80	77	13	6	2	5	60	2	104	13	6	10	.375	0-0	0	94	.775	4.72	5.16
10	CWS	AL	11	11	0	75.0	315	73	31	27	8	0	2	1	18	2	77	7	4	2	.667	0-0	0	95	.663	3.32	3.24
11	CWS	AL	19	19	0	121.2	522	134	55	53	8	6	4	0	39	2	97	7	7	7	.500	0-0	0	95	.735	4.10	3.92
11	StL	NL	13	12	1	78.0	339	91	37	31	8	9	2	2	23	2	51	2	5	2	.714	0-0	0	94	.820	4.73	3.58
15	ChC	NL	23	0	11	31.0	134	30	14	11	0	1	2	1	12	1	23	3	2	1	.667	0-1	0	94	.637	3.19	3.19
15	Atl	NL	24	0	7	24.2	94	14	11	8	4	0	1	0	9	0	17	2	2	2	.500	1-1	5	94	.602	2.16	2.92
16	Mia	NL	8	0	3	10.2	47	13	7	7	2	0	0	0	6	1	7	1	0	1	.000	0-0	0	93	.916	7.01	5.91
16	SD	NL	13	13	0	73.1	326	79	49	48	12	2	4	1	35	2	54	5	5	6	.455	0-0	0	92	.848	5.35	5.89
17	Bal	AL	3	0	0	5.0	29	11	7	4	2	1	0	0	4	0	2	0	0	0	-	0-0	0	92	1.411	17.51	7.20
17	Was	NL	13	13	0	71.0	310	75	46	40	18	3	3	0	25	2	58	3	5	6	.455	0-0	0	94	.845	5.19	5.07
19	Tor	AL	8	5	0	28.1	144	49	41	35	12	0	0	2	13	0	19	3	1	5	.167	0-0	0	93	1.235	12.49	11.12
19	Det	AL	10	8	0	39.1	192	56	40	37	11	0	2	1	19	0	33	3	2	5	.286	0-0	0	93	1.002	8.55	8.47
	Postseason		9	5	2	28.0	124	30	17	17	6	2	0	0	15	1	23	0	1	2	.333	0-0	1	95	.920	5.97	5.46
17 ML YEARS			412	318	30	1960.0	8569	2094	1135	1040	249	69	54	39	779	39	1508	108	107	133	.446	1-3	5	94	.789	4.72	4.78

Jay Jackson

Pitches: R Bats: R Pos: RP-28 Ht: 6'1" Wt: 195 Born: 10/27/1987 Age: 32

Year	Team	Lg	G	GS	GF	IP	BFP	H	R	ER	HR	SH	SF	HB	TBB	IBB	SO	WP	W	L	Pct	Sv-Op	Hld	Vel	OPS	ERC	ERA
2019	SnAnt	AAA	34	0	26	40.2	160	28	10	6	1	4	0	1	10	1	54	2	5	2	.714	8--	-	-	.484	1.59	1.33
2015	SD	NL	6	0	4	4.1	20	7	3	3	0	0	0	0	1	0	4	0	0	0	-	0-0	0	95	.874	6.40	6.23
2019	Mil	NL	28	0	9	30.1	132	22	15	15	6	1	2	2	18	1	47	0	1	0	1.000	0-0	2	94	.724	4.15	4.45
2 ML YEARS			34	0	10	34.2	152	29	18	18	6	1	2	2	19	1	51	0	1	0	1.000	0-0	2	94	.745	4.41	4.67

Luke Jackson

Pitches: R Bats: R Pos: RP-70 Ht: 6'2" Wt: 210 Born: 8/24/1991 Age: 28

Year	Team	Lg	G	GS	GF	IP	BFP	H	R	ER	HR	SH	SF	HB	TBB	IBB	SO	WP	W	L	Pct	Sv-Op	Hld	Vel	OPS	ERC	ERA
2015	Tex	AL	7	0	4	6.1	27	5	3	3	1	0	0	0	2	0	6	1	0	0	-	0-0	0	96	.619	2.81	4.26
2016	Tex	AL	8	0	2	11.2	62	22	14	14	4	0	1	0	8	0	3	0	0	0	-	0-0	0	94	1.201	13.93	10.80
2017	Atl	NL	43	0	17	50.2	224	55	26	26	4	1	2	4	19	4	33	4	2	0	1.000	0-0	1	95	.759	4.50	4.62
2018	Atl	NL	35	0	11	40.2	184	41	22	20	3	1	2	2	21	3	46	6	1	2	.333	1-2	3	94	.742	4.39	4.43
2019	Atl	NL	70	0	35	72.2	315	76	34	31	10	1	0	2	26	4	106	3	9	2	.818	18-25	9	96	.733	4.46	3.84
5 ML YEARS			163	0	69	182.0	812	199	99	94	22	3	5	8	76	11	194	14	12	4	.750	19-27	13	95	.773	4.90	4.65

Josh James

Pitches: R Bats: R Pos: RP-48; SP-1 Ht: 6'3" Wt: 206 Born: 3/8/1993 Age: 27

Year	Team	Lg	G	GS	GF	IP	BFP	H	R	ER	HR	SH	SF	HB	TBB	IBB	SO	WP	W	L	Pct	Sv-Op	Hld	Vel	OPS	ERC	ERA
2018	Hou	AL	6	3	0	23.0	91	15	6	6	3	0	0	2	7	0	29	0	2	0	1.000	0-0	2	97	.605	2.45	2.35
2019	Hou	AL	49	1	18	61.1	266	46	34	32	10	0	0	4	35	0	100	6	5	1	.833	1-3	6	97	.694	4.02	4.70
	Postseason		2	0	0	4.2	21	6	4	4	1	0	0	2	0	0	7	0	1	0	1.000	0-0	0	99	.960	6.98	7.71
2 ML YEARS			55	4	18	84.1	357	61	40	38	13	0	0	6	42	0	129	6	7	1	.875	1-3	8	97	.671	3.57	4.06

Travis Jankowski

Bats: L Throws: R Pos: PH-13; PR-6; CF-5; RF-5; LF-2 Ht: 6'2" Wt: 185 Born: 6/15/1991 Age: 29

Year	Team	Lg	G	AB	H	2B	3B	HR	(Hm	Rd)	TB	R	RBI	RC	TBB	IBB	SO	HBP	SH	SF	SB	CS	GDP	Avg	OBP	Slg	OPS
2019	ElPaso	AAA	39	160	50	7	0	0	(-	-)	57	27	12	25	21	0	32	1	0	1	7	2	7	.313	.393	.356	.750
2015	SD	NL	34	90	19	2	2	0	(0	2)	31	9	12	10	4	0	24	0	2	0	2	1	1	.211	.245	.344	.589
2016	SD	NL	131	335	82	13	2	2	(1	1)	105	53	12	34	42	0	100	2	3	0	30	12	5	.245	.332	.313	.646
2017	SD	NL	27	75	14	2	0	0	(0	0)	16	10	1	5	9	0	28	1	2	0	4	0	2	.187	.282	.213	.496
2018	SD	NL	117	347	90	12	3	4	(3	1)	120	45	17	42	37	0	73	1	2	0	24	7	7	.259	.332	.346	.678
2019	SD	NL	25	22	4	0	0	0	(0	0)	4	4	0	0	2	0	4	0	0	0	2	2	0	.182	.250	.182	.432
5 ML YEARS			334	869	209	29	7	8	(4	4)	276	121	42	91	94	0	229	4	9	0	62	22	15	.241	.317	.318	.635

Danny Jansen

Bats: R Throws: R Pos: C-103;DH-4;PH-3   Ht: 6'2" Wt: 230 Born: 4/15/1995 Age: 25

Year	Team	Lg	G	AB	H	2B	3B	HR	(Hm	Rd)	TB	R	RBI	RC	TBB	IBB	SO	HBP	SH	SF	SB	CS	GDP	Avg	OBP	Slg	OPS
2015 2 Tms		Low	53	181	38	9	0	5	(-	-)	62	23	30	19	21	0	27	3	0	2	2	0	2	.210	.300	.343	.642
2016 2 Tms		Low	57	197	43	7	0	1	(-	-)	53	18	25	19	23	0	42	6	0	2	7	1	3	.218	.316	.269	.585
2017 Dnedin		A+	31	122	45	6	0	5	(-	-)	66	19	18	27	8	0	14	4	1	1	0	0	3	.369	.422	.541	.963
2017 Nham		AA	52	179	52	15	1	2	(-	-)	75	23	20	31	22	2	19	5	1	3	1	0	5	.291	.378	.419	.797
2017 Buffalo		AAA	21	67	22	4	1	3	(-	-)	37	8	10	15	11	1	7	0	0	0	0	0	0	.328	.423	.552	.975
2018 Buffalo		AAA	88	298	82	21	1	12	(-	-)	141	45	58	59	44	1	49	14	1	3	5	0	7	.275	.390	.473	.863
2018 Tor		AL	31	81	20	6	0	3	(1	2)	35	12	8	14	9	0	17	4	0	1	0	0	1	.247	.347	.432	.779
2019 Tor		AL	107	347	72	12	1	13	(8	5)	125	41	43	40	31	1	79	4	1	1	0	1	8	.207	.279	.360	.640
2 ML YEARS			138	428	92	18	1	16	(9	7)	160	53	51	54	40	1	96	8	1	2	0	1	9	.215	.293	.374	.667

Kenley Jansen

Pitches: R Bats: B Pos: RP-62   KEN-lee JANN-sen   Ht: 6'5" Wt: 265 Born: 9/30/1987 Age: 32

| | | | HOW MUCH PITCHED | | | | | WHAT HE GAVE UP | | | | | | | | | | THE RESULTS | | | | | | | |
Year	Team	Lg	G	GS	GF	IP	BFP	H	R	ER	HR	SH	SF	HB	TBB	IBB	SO	WP	W	L	Pct	Sv-Op	Hld	Vel	OPS	ERC	ERA
2010 LAD		NL	25	0	8	27.0	109	12	2	2	1	0	1	0	15	1	41	1	1	0	1.000	4-4	4	94	.422	1.40	0.67
2011 LAD		NL	51	0	13	53.2	218	30	17	17	3	0	1	2	26	0	96	0	2	1	.667	5-6	9	93	.494	1.96	2.85
2012 LAD		NL	65	0	40	65.0	252	33	18	17	6	0	1	3	22	1	99	3	5	3	.625	25-32	8	92	.504	1.55	2.35
2013 LAD		NL	75	0	45	76.2	292	48	16	16	6	0	0	3	18	1	111	2	4	3	.571	28-32	16	92	.509	1.65	1.88
2014 LAD		NL	68	0	57	65.1	268	55	20	20	5	1	2	0	19	2	101	2	2	3	.400	44-49	0	94	.610	2.60	2.76
2015 LAD		NL	54	0	50	52.1	200	33	14	14	6	0	2	2	8	0	80	0	2	1	.667	36-38	1	93	.513	1.58	2.41
2016 LAD		NL	71	0	63	68.2	251	35	14	14	4	3	1	2	11	2	104	1	3	2	.600	47-53	0	94	.446	1.03	1.83
2017 LAD		NL	65	0	57	68.1	258	44	11	10	5	0	0	2	7	0	109	2	5	0	1.000	**41**-42	1	93	.476	1.35	1.32
2018 LAD		NL	69	0	59	71.2	289	54	28	24	13	0	1	2	17	1	82	0	1	5	.167	38-42	0	92	.635	2.68	3.01
2019 LAD		NL	62	0	51	63.0	263	51	28	26	9	0	3	4	16	0	80	2	5	3	.625	33-41	0	92	.653	2.92	3.71
Postseason			39	0	31	47.2	184	24	12	11	5	0	0	3	15	2	68	0	1	1	.500	16-19	1	94	.499	1.55	2.08
10 ML YEARS			605	0	443	611.2	2400	395	168	160	57	5	11	21	159	8	903	13	30	21	.588	301-339	39	93	.537	1.83	2.35

Jon Jay

Bats: L Throws: L Pos: RF-33;LF-13;DH-2;PH-2   Ht: 5'11" Wt: 195 Born: 3/15/1985 Age: 35

Year	Team	Lg	G	AB	H	2B	3B	HR	(Hm	Rd)	TB	R	RBI	RC	TBB	IBB	SO	HBP	SH	SF	SB	CS	GDP	Avg	OBP	Slg	OPS
2019 Charllt		AAA	13	53	19	2	0	0	(-	-)	21	8	6	8	2	0	10	0	0	0	1	0	2	.358	.382	.396	.778
2010 StL		NL	105	287	86	19	2	4	(2	2)	121	47	27	40	24	0	50	3	8	1	2	4	5	.300	.359	.422	.780
2011 StL		NL	159	455	135	24	2	10	(5	5)	193	56	37	56	28	1	81	7	9	4	6	7	11	.297	.344	.424	.768
2012 StL		NL	117	443	135	22	4	4	(3	1)	177	70	40	65	34	3	71	15	5	1	19	7	9	.305	.373	.400	.773
2013 StL		NL	157	443	135	21	2	7	(2	5)	203	75	67	74	52	7	103	14	9	5	10	5	13	.276	.351	.370	.721
2014 StL		NL	140	413	125	16	3	3	(0	3)	156	52	46	57	28	3	78	**20**	3	4	6	3	17	.303	.372	.378	.750
2015 StL		NL	79	210	44	5	1	1	(0	1)	54	25	10	11	19	5	36	11	3	2	0	2	7	.210	.306	.257	.563
2016 SD		NL	90	347	101	26	1	2	(1	1)	135	49	26	55	19	0	78	6	1	0	2	0	5	.291	.339	.389	.728
2017 ChC		NL	141	379	112	18	3	2	(1	1)	142	65	34	58	37	3	80	12	3	2	6	2	11	.296	.374	.375	.749
2018 2 Tms			143	527	141	19	7	3	(2	1)	183	74	40	64	33	0	95	18	5	3	4	3	11	.268	.330	.347	.678
2019 CWS		AL	47	165	44	8	0	0	(0	0)	52	12	9	23	8	0	30	3	5	1	0	0	1	.267	.311	.315	.626
18 KC		AL	59	238	73	9	2	1	(1	0)	89	28	18	31	19	0	39	3	4	2	3	2	4	.307	.363	.374	.737
18 Ari		NL	84	289	68	10	5	2	(1	1)	94	46	22	33	14	0	56	15	1	1	1	1	7	.235	.304	.325	.629
Postseason			67	213	48	6	1	0	(0	0)	56	26	16	23	19	1	36	8	6	2	5	2	5	.225	.310	.263	.573
10 ML YEARS			1178	3774	1074	184	25	36	(16	20)	1416	525	336	503	282	22	702	109	55	23	55	33	90	.285	.350	.375	.725

Jeremy Jeffress

Pitches: R Bats: R Pos: RP-48   JEFF-ress   Ht: 6'0" Wt: 205 Born: 9/21/1987 Age: 32

| | | | HOW MUCH PITCHED | | | | | WHAT HE GAVE UP | | | | | | | | | | THE RESULTS | | | | | | | |
Year	Team	Lg	G	GS	GF	IP	BFP	H	R	ER	HR	SH	SF	HB	TBB	IBB	SO	WP	W	L	Pct	Sv-Op	Hld	Vel	OPS	ERC	ERA
2010 Mil		NL	10	0	5	10.0	42	8	4	3	0	0	0	0	6	1	8	1	1	0	1.000	0-0	0	95	.676	2.96	2.70
2011 KC		AL	14	0	6	15.1	67	12	8	8	1	2	0	0	11	0	13	1	1	1	.500	1-2	0	97	.706	3.87	4.70
2012 KC		AL	13	0	6	13.1	73	19	14	10	0	0	0	0	13	0	13	1	0	0		0-0	0	95	.838	7.87	6.75
2013 Tor		AL	10	0	3	10.1	43	8	1	1	1	0	0	0	5	0	12	0	1	0	1.000	0-0	0	97	.592	3.17	0.87
2014 2 Tms			32	0	12	32.0	135	35	10	10	1	3	1	2	10	2	29	1	1	1	.500	0-1	6	96	.709	4.06	2.81
2015 Mil		NL	72	0	8	68.0	285	64	22	20	5	3	0	3	22	5	67	4	5	0	1.000	0-5	23	95	.666	3.36	2.65
2016 2 Tms			59	0	41	58.0	241	55	17	15	2	2	1	4	18	3	42	3	3	2	.600	27-28	6	95	.656	3.26	2.33
2017 2 Tms			61	1	12	65.1	295	73	35	34	10	1	1	2	34	4	51	6	5	2	.714	0-1	8	94	.830	5.75	4.68
2018 Mil		NL	73	0	24	76.2	299	49	12	11	5	1	1	1	27	4	89	4	8	1	.889	15-20	18	95	.530	1.87	1.29
2019 Mil		NL	48	0	12	52.0	225	54	32	29	5	2	0	5	17	0	46	1	3	4	.429	1-4	12	94	.734	4.40	5.02
14 Tor		AL	3	0	3	3.1	21	8	4	4	0	0	1	2	3	0	4	0	0	0		0-0	0	96	1.219	19.06	10.80
14 Mil		NL	29	0	9	28.2	114	27	6	6	1	3	0	0	7	2	25	1	1	1	.500	0-1	6	97	.624	2.75	1.88
16 Mil		NL	47	0	40	44.2	190	45	13	11	2	2	1	4	11	3	35	0	2	2	.500	27-28	0	96	.662	3.38	2.22
16 Tex		AL	12	0	1	13.1	51	10	4	4	0	0	0	0	7	0	7	3	1	0	1.000	0-0	6	94	.629	2.84	2.70
17 Tex		AL	39	0	10	40.2	183	49	25	24	8	0	1	2	19	2	29	3	1	2	.333	0-0	4	94	.898	6.63	5.31
17 Mil		NL	22	1	2	24.2	112	24	10	10	2	1	0	0	15	2	22	3	4	0	1.000	0-1	4	95	.716	4.39	3.65
Postseason			9	0	2	9.0	48	17	7	6	2	0	1	0	5	0	12	0	0	1	.000	1-3	2	95	1.054	11.67	6.00
10 ML YEARS			392	1	129	401.0	1705	377	155	141	30	14	5	17	163	19	370	22	28	11	.718	44-61	73	95	.688	3.73	3.16

Dan Jennings

Pitches: L Bats: L Pos: RP-8

Ht: 6'3" Wt: 215 Born: 4/17/1987 Age: 33

		HOW MUCH PITCHED					WHAT HE GAVE UP											THE RESULTS						
Year	Team	Lg	G	GS	GF	IP	BFP	H	R	ER	HR	SH	SF	HB	TBB	IBB	SO	WP	W	L	Pct	Sv-Op Hld	Vel	OPS	ERC	ERA
2012	Mia	NL	22	0	4	19.0	86	18	5	4	2	0	0	2	11	1	8	0	1	0	1.000	0-0	2	90	.771	4.85	1.89
2013	Mia	NL	47	0	6	40.2	171	39	17	17	1	0	2	0	16	2	38	3	2	4	.333	0-2	1	92	.714	3.27	3.76
2014	Mia	NL	47	0	12	40.1	182	45	11	6	3	2	3	0	17	1	38	2	0	2	.000	0-2	3	93	.738	4.50	1.34
2015	CWS	AL	53	0	17	56.1	244	55	28	25	3	4	1	0	24	6	46	4	2	3	.400	0-0	4	92	.664	3.52	3.99
2016	CWS	AL	64	0	15	60.2	259	57	18	14	1	2	6	3	28	0	46	4	4	3	.571	1-3	10	91	.679	3.65	2.08
2017	2 Tms	AL	77	0	12	62.2	267	53	27	24	8	0	1	1	31	7	51	3	3	1	.750	0-2	14	92	.667	3.68	3.45
2018	Mil	NL	72	1	11	64.1	271	66	27	23	6	4	3	1	23	1	45	2	4	5	.444	1-3	11	91	.758	4.14	3.22
2019	Was	NL	8	0	0	4.2	32	8	8	7	1	0	0	1	7	2	9	1	1	2	.333	0-2	0	91	.958	13.65	13.50
17	CWS	AL	48	0	8	44.1	185	35	20	17	6	0	1	1	19	4	38	0	3	1	.750	0-1	7	92	.642	3.22	3.45
17	TB	AL	29	0	4	18.1	82	18	7	7	2	0	0	0	12	3	13	3	0	0	-	0-1	7	92	.723	4.83	3.44
8 ML YEARS			390	1	77	348.2	1512	341	141	120	25	12	16	8	157	20	281	19	17	20	.459	2-14	45	92	.711	3.96	3.10

Williams Jerez

Pitches: L Bats: L Pos: RP-12

heh-REHZ

Ht: 6'4" Wt: 205 Born: 5/16/1992 Age: 28

		HOW MUCH PITCHED					WHAT HE GAVE UP											THE RESULTS						
Year	Team	Lg	G	GS	GF	IP	BFP	H	R	ER	HR	SH	SF	HB	TBB	IBB	SO	WP	W	L	Pct	Sv-Op Hld	Vel	OPS	ERC	ERA
2019	Scrmto	AAA	47	0	12	56.0	235	46	33	24	6	1	1	3	16	0	61	6	4	4	.500	2- -	-	-	.656	2.85	3.86
2018	LAA	AL	17	0	1	15.0	71	17	14	10	3	0	0	0	8	0	15	2	0	0	-	0-1	3	95	.812	5.95	6.00
2019	2 Tms	AL	12	0	4	10.1	48	12	5	5	2	0	0	0	9	0	9	2	1	0	1.000	0-0	1	94	1.002	8.33	4.35
19	SF	NL	6	0	3	6.2	29	7	2	2	1	0	0	0	6	0	4	2	1	0	1.000	0-0	1	94	.970	7.68	2.70
19	Pit	NL	6	0	1	3.2	19	5	3	3	1	0	0	0	3	0	5	0	0	0	-	0-0	0	94	1.046	9.47	7.36
2 ML YEARS			29	0	5	25.1	119	29	19	15	5	0	0	0	17	0	24	4	1	0	1.000	0-1	4	95	.887	6.87	5.33

Jake Jewell

Pitches: R Bats: R Pos: RP-18

Ht: 6'3" Wt: 200 Born: 5/16/1993 Age: 27

		HOW MUCH PITCHED					WHAT HE GAVE UP											THE RESULTS						
Year	Team	Lg	G	GS	GF	IP	BFP	H	R	ER	HR	SH	SF	HB	TBB	IBB	SO	WP	W	L	Pct	Sv-Op Hld	Vel	OPS	ERC	ERA
2019	Salt Lk	AAA	34	0	19	37.2	169	42	25	22	3	1	0	3	17	0	41	4	4	4	.500	8- -	-	-	.781	5.18	5.26
2018	LAA	AL	3	0	1	2.0	11	2	2	2	0	0	0	2	1	0	1	1	0	1	.000	0-0	0	96	.830	7.45	9.00
2019	LAA	AL	18	0	7	26.1	114	28	20	20	8	0	1	3	8	0	23	0	0	0	-	0-0	1	94	.901	6.10	6.84
2 ML YEARS			21	0	8	28.1	125	30	22	22	8	0	1	5	9	0	24	1	0	1	.000	0-0	1	95	.897	6.25	6.99

Eduardo Jimenez

Pitches: R Bats: R Pos: RP-8

Ht: 6'2" Wt: 225 Born: 4/4/1995 Age: 25

		HOW MUCH PITCHED					WHAT HE GAVE UP											THE RESULTS						
Year	Team	Lg	G	GS	GF	IP	BFP	H	R	ER	HR	SH	SF	HB	TBB	IBB	SO	WP	W	L	Pct	Sv-Op Hld	Vel	OPS	ERC	ERA
2019	Toledo	AAA	41	0	14	54.2	223	39	23	18	5	0	1	7	18	0	51	3	4	3	.571	2- -	-	-	.637	2.74	2.96
2019	Det	AL	8	0	2	10.2	49	12	7	7	1	0	0	0	5	0	8	1	0	0	-	0-0	0	93	.779	4.90	5.91

Eloy Jimenez

Bats: R Throws: R Pos: LF-114;DH-8

Ht: 6'4" Wt: 205 Born: 11/27/1996 Age: 23

							BATTING															RUNNING			AVERAGES			
Year	Team	Lg	G	AB	H	2B	3B	HR	(Hm	Rd)	TB	R	RBI	RC	TBB	IBB	SO	HBP	SH	SF	SB	CS	GDP	Avg	OBP	Slg	OPS
2015	Eugene	A-	57	232	66	10	0	7	(-	-)	97	36	33	32	15	0	43	1	0	2	3	2	0	.284	.328	.418	.746
2016	Sbend	A	112	432	142	40	3	14	(-	-)	230	65	81	80	25	3	94	4	0	3	8	3	7	.329	.369	.532	.901
2017	Brham	AA	18	68	24	5	0	3	(-	-)	38	11	7	14	5	1	16	0	0	0	1	1	1	.353	.397	.559	.956
2017	2 Tms	Low	71	265	80	17	3	16	(-	-)	151	43	58	54	30	5	56	1	0	0	2	2	10	.302	.375	.570	.945
2018	Brham	AA	53	205	65	15	2	10	(-	-)	114	36	42	41	18	0	39	1	0	4	0	0	6	.317	.368	.556	.925
2018	Charllt	AAA	55	211	75	13	1	12	(-	-)	126	28	33	47	14	2	30	2	0	1	0	1	8	.355	.399	.597	.996
2019	CWS	AL	122	468	125	18	2	31	(12	19)	240	69	79	68	30	0	134	4	0	2	0	0	11	.267	.315	.513	.828

Joe Jimenez

Pitches: R Bats: R Pos: RP-66

Ht: 6'3" Wt: 272 Born: 1/17/1995 Age: 25

		HOW MUCH PITCHED					WHAT HE GAVE UP											THE RESULTS						
Year	Team	Lg	G	GS	GF	IP	BFP	H	R	ER	HR	SH	SF	HB	TBB	IBB	SO	WP	W	L	Pct	Sv-Op Hld	Vel	OPS	ERC	ERA
2017	Det	AL	24	0	12	19.0	99	31	28	26	4	0	1	2	9	0	17	0	0	2	.000	0-1	0	95	.999	9.60	12.32
2018	Det	AL	68	0	17	62.2	267	53	34	30	5	0	2	3	22	3	78	3	5	4	.556	3-7	23	96	.645	2.95	4.31
2019	Det	AL	66	0	29	59.2	257	56	33	29	13	0	0	4	23	1	82	1	4	7	.364	9-14	15	95	.797	4.74	4.37
3 ML YEARS			158	0	52	141.1	623	140	95	85	22	0	3	9	54	4	177	4	9	13	.409	12-22	38	95	.763	4.49	5.41

Connor Joe

Bats: R Throws: R Pos: LF-5;PH-3

Ht: 6'0" Wt: 205 Born: 8/16/1992 Age: 27

							BATTING															RUNNING			AVERAGES			
Year	Team	Lg	G	AB	H	2B	3B	HR	(Hm	Rd)	TB	R	RBI	RC	TBB	IBB	SO	HBP	SH	SF	SB	CS	GDP	Avg	OBP	Slg	OPS
2019	OkCity	AAA	105	360	108	26	1	15	(-	-)	181	82	68	81	72	0	81	10	0	4	1	2	10	.300	.426	.503	.929
2019	SF	NL	8	15	1	0	0	0	(0	0)	1	1	0	0	1	0	5	0	0	0	0	0	1	.067	.125	.067	.192

Brian Johnson

Pitches: L Bats: L Pos: RP-14; SP-7   Ht: 6'4" Wt: 235 Born: 12/7/1990 Age: 29

			HOW MUCH PITCHED					WHAT HE GAVE UP										THE RESULTS							
Year	Team	Lg	G	GS	GF	IP	BFP	H	R	ER	HR	SH	SF	HB	TBB	IBB	SO	WP	W	L	Pct	Sv-Op	Hld	Vel	OPS	ERC	ERA
2019	Pwtckt	AAA	6	3	0	14.2	61	13	6	6	1	0	0	1	8	0	19	1	1	0	1.000	0--	-	-	.707	4.31	3.68
2015	Bos	AL	1	1	0	4.1	19	3	4	4	0	0	1	0	4	0	3	0	0	1	.000	0-0	0	88	.583	3.72	8.31
2017	Bos	AL	5	5	0	27.0	121	32	13	13	5	0	0	0	8	1	21	0	2	0	1.000	0-0	0	87	.817	5.16	4.33
2018	Bos	AL	38	13	10	99.1	434	104	49	46	16	0	0	1	38	0	87	1	4	5	.444	0-1	1	89	.773	4.73	4.17
2019	Bos	AL	21	7	3	40.1	193	53	29	27	6	2	0	0	23	3	31	5	1	3	.250	0-0	0	89	.934	6.91	6.02
	4 ML YEARS		65	26	13	171.0	767	192	95	90	27	2	1	1	73	4	142	6	7	9	.438	0-1	1	88	.816	5.27	4.74

DJ Johnson

Pitches: R Bats: L Pos: RP-28   Ht: 6'4" Wt: 230 Born: 8/30/1989 Age: 30

			HOW MUCH PITCHED					WHAT HE GAVE UP										THE RESULTS							
Year	Team	Lg	G	GS	GF	IP	BFP	H	R	ER	HR	SH	SF	HB	TBB	IBB	SO	WP	W	L	Pct	Sv-Op	Hld	Vel	OPS	ERC	ERA
2019	Albq	AAA	40	0	16	48.0	218	62	31	30	8	2	1	1	16	2	67	3	4	1	.800	3--	-	-	.851	6.04	5.63
2018	Col	NL	7	0	3	6.1	27	6	3	3	0	0	0	0	2	0	9	0	1	0	1.000	0-0	0	94	.536	2.73	4.26
2019	Col	NL	28	0	7	25.0	116	23	14	14	1	0	1	3	19	2	24	4	0	2	.000	0-0	4	93	.743	4.93	5.04
	Postseason		1	0	0	0.2	3	1	0	0	0	0	0	0	0	0	2	0	0	0	-	0-0	0	95	.667	4.47	0.00
	2 ML YEARS		35	0	10	31.1	143	29	17	17	1	0	1	3	21	2	33	4	1	2	.333	0-0	4	94	.701	4.46	4.88

Adam Jones

Bats: R Throws: R Pos: RF-130;PH-14;CF-1   Ht: 6'2" Wt: 215 Born: 8/1/1985 Age: 34

			BATTING																			RUNNING			AVERAGES			
Year	Team	Lg	G	AB	H	2B	3B	HR	(Hm	Rd)	TB	R	RBI	RC	TBB	IBB	SO	HBP	SH	SF	SB	CS	GDP	Avg	OBP	Slg	OPS
2006	Sea	AL	32	74	16	4	0	1	(0	1)	23	6	8	4	2	0	22	0	0	0	3	1	3	.216	.237	.311	.548
2007	Sea	AL	41	65	16	2	1	2	(1	1)	26	16	4	5	4	0	21	1	1	0	2	1	0	.246	.300	.400	.700
2008	Bal	AL	132	477	129	21	7	9	(4	5)	191	61	57	56	23	0	108	7	2	5	10	3	12	.270	.311	.400	.711
2009	Bal	AL	119	473	131	22	3	19	(11	8)	216	83	70	71	36	3	93	7	0	3	10	4	13	.277	.335	.457	.792
2010	Bal	AL	149	581	165	25	5	19	(9	10)	257	76	69	72	23	1	119	13	2	2	7	7	17	.284	.325	.442	.767
2011	Bal	AL	151	567	159	26	2	25	(19	6)	264	68	83	77	29	2	113	9	1	12	12	4	16	.280	.319	.466	.785
2012	Bal	AL	162	648	186	39	3	32	(15	17)	327	103	82	101	34	0	126	13	0	2	16	7	15	.287	.334	.505	.839
2013	Bal	AL	160	653	186	35	4	33	(17	16)	322	100	108	101	25	4	136	8	0	3	14	3	15	.285	.318	.493	.811
2014	Bal	AL	159	644	181	30	2	29	(14	15)	302	88	96	92	19	1	133	12	0	7	7	1	11	.281	.311	.469	.780
2015	Bal	AL	137	546	147	25	3	27	(10	17)	259	74	82	73	24	3	102	8	0	3	3	1	21	.269	.308	.474	.782
2016	Bal	AL	152	619	164	19	0	29	(14	15)	270	86	83	82	39	2	115	5	1	8	2	0	13	.265	.310	.436	.746
2017	Bal	AL	147	597	170	28	1	26	(17	9)	278	82	73	89	27	1	113	7	1	3	2	1	18	.285	.322	.466	.787
2018	Bal	AL	145	580	163	35	0	15	(6	9)	243	54	63	70	24	1	93	5	0	4	7	1	21	.281	.313	.419	.732
2019	Ari	NL	137	485	126	25	1	16	(6	10)	201	66	67	60	31	2	101	8	0	3	2	1	15	.260	.313	.414	.728
	Postseason		14	58	9	0	0	1	(1	0)	12	7	4	3	3	0	16	1	0	1	1	0	1	.155	.206	.207	.413
	14 ML YEARS		1823	7009	1939	336	29	282	(153	129)	3179	963	945	953	340	20	1395	103	8	55	97	35	190	.277	.317	.454	.771

JaCoby Jones

Bats: R Throws: R Pos: CF-85;PH-2;PR-1   Ht: 6'2" Wt: 201 Born: 5/10/1992 Age: 28

			BATTING																			RUNNING			AVERAGES			
Year	Team	Lg	G	AB	H	2B	3B	HR	(Hm	Rd)	TB	R	RBI	RC	TBB	IBB	SO	HBP	SH	SF	SB	CS	GDP	Avg	OBP	Slg	OPS
2016	Det	AL	13	28	6	3	0	0	(0	0)	9	3	2	2	0	0	12	0	0	0	0	0	1	.214	.214	.321	.536
2017	Det	AL	56	141	24	3	1	3	(2	1)	38	14	13	7	9	0	65	4	0	0	6	2	5	.170	.240	.270	.510
2018	Det	AL	129	429	89	22	6	11	(8	3)	156	54	34	36	24	0	142	11	1	2	13	5	9	.207	.266	.364	.630
2019	Det	AL	88	298	70	19	3	11	(7	4)	128	39	26	35	27	2	94	6	1	1	7	2	6	.235	.310	.430	.740
	4 ML YEARS		286	896	189	47	10	25	(17	8)	331	110	75	80	60	2	313	21	2	3	26	9	21	.211	.276	.369	.645

Nate Jones

Pitches: R Bats: R Pos: RP-13   Ht: 6'5" Wt: 220 Born: 1/28/1986 Age: 34

			HOW MUCH PITCHED					WHAT HE GAVE UP										THE RESULTS							
Year	Team	Lg	G	GS	GF	IP	BFP	H	R	ER	HR	SH	SF	HB	TBB	IBB	SO	WP	W	L	Pct	Sv-Op	Hld	Vel	OPS	ERC	ERA
2012	CWS	AL	65	0	11	71.2	301	67	19	19	4	2	4	1	32	3	65	5	8	0	1.000	0-3	7	98	.686	3.67	2.39
2013	CWS	AL	70	0	17	78.0	315	69	40	36	5	3	6	1	26	1	89	8	4	5	.444	0-4	16	98	.659	3.09	4.15
2014	CWS	AL	2	0	0	0.0	5	2	4	4	0	0	0	0	3	0	0	0	0	0	-	0-1	0	96	2.500	-	-
2015	CWS	AL	19	0	3	19.0	72	12	7	7	5	2	0	0	6	0	27	0	2	2	.500	0-1	6	98	.665	2.87	3.32
2016	CWS	AL	71	0	11	70.2	274	48	20	18	7	2	2	3	15	3	80	7	5	3	.625	3-12	28	97	.552	1.87	2.29
2017	CWS	AL	11	0	1	11.2	49	9	3	3	1	1	0	1	6	1	15	1	1	0	1.000	0-0	4	97	.675	3.43	2.31
2018	CWS	AL	33	0	15	30.0	137	28	14	10	4	1	1	3	15	0	32	2	2	2	.500	5-8	6	97	.723	4.59	3.00
2019	CWS	AL	13	0	5	10.1	47	10	4	4	2	0	0	1	7	1	10	2	0	1	.000	1-1	2	95	.793	6.10	3.48
	8 ML YEARS		284	0	63	291.1	1200	245	111	101	28	11	13	10	110	9	318	25	22	13	.629	9-30	69	97	.661	3.24	3.12

Caleb Joseph

Bats: R Throws: R Pos: C-16;PH-3   Ht: 6'3" Wt: 180 Born: 6/18/1986 Age: 34

			BATTING																			RUNNING			AVERAGES			
Year	Team	Lg	G	AB	H	2B	3B	HR	(Hm	Rd)	TB	R	RBI	RC	TBB	IBB	SO	HBP	SH	SF	SB	CS	GDP	Avg	OBP	Slg	OPS
2019	Reno	AAA	48	162	43	12	1	7	(-	-)	78	29	26	26	13	0	44	2	0	2	0	0	3	.265	.324	.481	.806
2014	Bal	AL	82	246	51	9	0	9	(4	5)	87	22	28	22	17	0	69	3	6	3	0	1	6	.207	.264	.354	.618
2015	Bal	AL	100	320	75	16	1	11	(5	6)	126	38	49	44	27	2	72	3	1	0	0	0	6	.234	.299	.394	.693
2016	Bal	AL	49	132	23	3	0	0	(0	0)	26	7	0	0	7	0	28	0	2	0	0	0	6	.174	.216	.197	.413
2017	Bal	AL	89	254	65	14	1	8	(3	5)	105	31	28	28	10	0	72	1	1	0	0	0	7	.256	.287	.413	.700

Year Team	Lg	G	AB	H	2B	3B	HR	(Hm	Rd)	TB	R	RBI	RC	TBB	IBB	SO	HBP	SH	SF	SB	CS	GDP	Avg	OBP	Slg	OPS
2018 Bal	AL	82	265	58	14	2	3	(1	2)	85	28	17	19	10	0	68	3	1	1	2	1	3	.219	.254	.321	.575
2019 Ari	NL	20	38	8	2	0	0	(0	0)	10	5	3	3	1	0	10	1	1	0	1	0	0	.211	.250	.263	.513
Postseason		3	9	2	0	0	0	(0	0)	2	0	1	1	0	0	4	0	0	1	0	0	0	.222	.200	.222	.422
6 ML YEARS		422	1255	280	58	4	31	(13	18)	439	131	125	116	72	2	319	11	14	5	2	2	29	.223	.270	.350	.620

Corban Joseph

Bats: L **Throws:** R **Pos:** 2B-13;PH-11;3B-3;RF-1;DH-1   **Ht:** 6'0" **Wt:** 185 **Born:** 10/28/1988 **Age:** 31

Year Team	Lg	G	AB	H	2B	3B	HR	(Hm	Rd)	TB	R	RBI	RC	TBB	IBB	SO	HBP	SH	SF	SB	CS	GDP	Avg	OBP	Slg	OPS
2019 LsVgs	AAA	97	383	142	35	4	13	(-	-)	224	63	73	90	33	1	46	4	0	5	0	0	7	.371	.421	.585	1.006
2013 NYY	AL	2	6	1	1	0	0	(0	0)	2	1	0	1	1	0	1	0	0	0	0	0	0	.167	.286	.333	.619
2018 Bal	AL	14	18	4	1	0	0	(0	0)	5	1	3	1	1	0	5	0	0	0	0	0	0	.222	.263	.278	.541
2019 3 Tms		28	64	10	3	0	1	(1	0)	16	5	7	1	3	0	12	0	0	1	0	0	2	.156	.191	.250	.441
19 Oak	AL	11	37	7	2	0	1	(1	0)	12	4	5	1	2	0	5	0	0	1	0	0	1	.189	.225	.324	.549
19 SF	NL	8	16	1	0	0	0	(0	0)	1	0	2	0	1	0	6	0	0	0	0	0	0	.063	.118	.063	.180
19 Pit	NL	9	11	2	1	0	0	(0	0)	3	1	0	0	0	0	1	0	0	0	0	0	1	.182	.182	.273	.455
3 ML YEARS		44	88	15	5	0	1	(1	0)	23	7	10	3	5	0	18	0	0	1	0	0	2	.170	.213	.261	.474

Matt Joyce

Bats: L **Throws:** R **Pos:** PH-87;RF-33;DH-6;LF-4   **Ht:** 6'2" **Wt:** 200 **Born:** 8/3/1984 **Age:** 35

Year Team	Lg	G	AB	H	2B	3B	HR	(Hm	Rd)	TB	R	RBI	RC	TBB	IBB	SO	HBP	SH	SF	SB	CS	GDP	Avg	OBP	Slg	OPS
2008 Det	AL	92	242	61	16	3	12	(6	6)	119	40	33	36	31	0	65	2	0	2	0	2	3	.252	.339	.492	.831
2009 TB	AL	11	32	6	1	0	3	(2	1)	16	3	7	5	3	0	7	1	0	1	1	0	0	.188	.270	.500	.770
2010 TB	AL	77	216	52	15	3	10	(4	6)	103	30	40	41	40	2	55	2	0	3	2	2	2	.241	.360	.477	.837
2011 TB	AL	141	462	128	32	2	19	(11	8)	221	69	75	77	49	9	106	4	0	7	13	1	7	.277	.347	.478	.825
2012 TB	AL	124	399	96	18	3	17	(4	13)	171	55	59	59	55	4	102	6	1	1	4	3	10	.241	.341	.429	.769
2013 TB	AL	140	413	97	22	0	18	(8	10)	173	61	47	51	59	0	87	2	0	7	7	3	8	.235	.328	.419	.747
2014 TB	AL	140	418	106	23	2	9	(2	7)	160	51	52	52	62	4	111	4	0	9	2	5	11	.254	.349	.383	.732
2015 LAA	AL	93	247	43	12	1	5	(4	1)	72	17	21	15	30	1	67	4	1	2	0	3	5	.174	.272	.291	.564
2016 Pit	NL	140	231	56	10	1	13	(10	3)	107	45	42	47	59	4	67	3	0	1	1	1	9	.242	.403	.463	.866
2017 Oak	AL	141	469	114	33	0	25	(11	14)	222	78	68	70	66	0	113	2	0	7	4	1	10	.243	.335	.473	.808
2018 Oak	AL	83	207	43	9	0	7	(2	5)	73	34	15	20	35	2	53	1	1	2	0	2	3	.208	.322	.353	.675
2019 Atl	NL	129	200	59	10	0	7	(4	3)	90	32	23	39	38	0	45	0	0	0	3	5	5	.295	.408	.450	.858
Postseason		12	32	5	1	0	1	(0	1)	9	1	4	3	1	0	13	0	0	0	1	0	0	.156	.182	.281	.463
12 ML YEARS		1311	3536	861	201	15	145	(68	77)	1527	515	482	512	527	26	878	31	3	41	34	23	71	.243	.343	.432	.775

Aaron Judge

Bats: R **Throws:** R **Pos:** RF-92;DH-10;PH-2   **Ht:** 6'7" **Wt:** 282 **Born:** 4/26/1992 **Age:** 28

Year Team	Lg	G	AB	H	2B	3B	HR	(Hm	Rd)	TB	R	RBI	RC	TBB	IBB	SO	HBP	SH	SF	SB	CS	GDP	Avg	OBP	Slg	OPS
2016 NYY	AL	27	84	15	2	0	4	(3	1)	29	10	10	6	9	0	42	1	0	1	0	1	2	.179	.263	.345	.608
2017 NYY	AL	155	542	154	24	3	**52**	(33	19)	340	**128**	114	**131**	**127**	11	**208**	5	0	4	9	4	15	.284	.422	.627	1.049
2018 NYY	AL	112	413	115	22	0	27	(18	9)	218	77	67	82	76	3	152	4	0	5	6	3	10	.278	.392	.528	.919
2019 NYY	AL	102	378	103	18	1	27	(11	16)	204	75	55	70	64	4	141	3	0	1	3	2	11	.272	.381	.540	.921
Postseason		18	67	17	4	0	7	(4	3)	42	15	15	15	12	0	30	0	0	0	0	1	1	.254	.367	.627	.994
4 ML YEARS		396	1417	387	66	4	110	(65	45)	791	290	246	289	276	18	543	13	0	11	18	10	38	.273	.394	.558	.952

Jakob Junis

Pitches: R **Bats:** R **Pos:** SP-31   **Ht:** 6'2" **Wt:** 225 **Born:** 9/16/1992 **Age:** 27

		HOW MUCH PITCHED					WHAT HE GAVE UP										THE RESULTS							
Year Team	Lg	G	GS	GF	IP	BFP	H	R	ER	HR	SH	SF	HB	TBB	IBB	SO	WP	W	L	Pct	Sv-Op	Hld	Vel	OPS	ERC	ERA
2017 KC	AL	20	16	1	98.1	422	101	52	47	15	3	3	9	25	1	80	3	9	3	.750	0-0	0	91	.762	4.36	4.30
2018 KC	AL	30	30	0	177.0	758	182	94	86	32	4	8	15	43	1	164	9	9	12	.429	0-0	0	91	.773	4.49	4.37
2019 KC	AL	31	31	0	175.1	771	192	108	102	31	0	5	11	58	1	164	4	9	14	.391	0-0	0	92	.807	5.14	5.24
3 ML YEARS		81	77	1	450.2	1951	475	254	235	78	7	16	35	126	3	408	16	27	29	.482	0-0	0	91	.784	4.71	4.69

Ariel Jurado

Pitches: R **Bats:** R **Pos:** SP-18; RP-14   hoo-RAH-doh   **Ht:** 6'1" **Wt:** 180 **Born:** 1/30/1996 **Age:** 24

		HOW MUCH PITCHED					WHAT HE GAVE UP										THE RESULTS							
Year Team	Lg	G	GS	GF	IP	BFP	H	R	ER	HR	SH	SF	HB	TBB	IBB	SO	WP	W	L	Pct	Sv-Op	Hld	Vel	OPS	ERC	ERA
2018 Tex	AL	12	8	0	54.2	241	66	36	36	7	1	0	0	18	1	22	0	5	5	.500	0-0	0	92	.809	5.29	5.93
2019 Tex	AL	32	18	3	122.1	541	148	94	79	21	5	9	4	36	1	81	3	7	11	.389	0-0	1	92	.876	5.54	5.81
2 ML YEARS		44	26	3	177.0	782	214	130	115	28	6	9	4	54	2	103	3	12	16	.429	0-0	1	92	.855	5.43	5.85

Tommy Kahnle

Pitches: R **Bats:** R **Pos:** RP-72   KAIN-lee   **Ht:** 6'1" **Wt:** 235 **Born:** 8/7/1989 **Age:** 30

		HOW MUCH PITCHED					WHAT HE GAVE UP										THE RESULTS							
Year Team	Lg	G	GS	GF	IP	BFP	H	R	ER	HR	SH	SF	HB	TBB	IBB	SO	WP	W	L	Pct	Sv-Op	Hld	Vel	OPS	ERC	ERA
2014 Col	NL	54	0	7	68.2	285	51	39	32	7	2	3	1	31	2	63	7	2	1	.667	0-2	8	95	.628	2.91	4.19
2015 Col	NL	36	0	8	33.1	155	31	22	18	3	1	2	0	28	1	39	3	0	1	.000	2-3	10	96	.778	5.31	4.86
2016 CWS	AL	29	0	12	27.1	119	21	8	8	2	0	0	0	20	3	25	3	0	1	.000	1-2	4	97	.678	3.74	2.63
2017 2 Tms	AL	69	0	17	62.2	256	53	20	18	4	1	4	2	17	1	96	5	2	4	.333	0-6	15	98	.606	2.63	2.59

254

			HOW MUCH PITCHED					WHAT HE GAVE UP											THE RESULTS					
Year Team	Lg	G	GS	GF	IP	BFP	H	R	ER	HR	SH	SF	HB	TBB	IBB	SO	WP	W	L	Pct	Sv-Op Hld	Vel	OPS	ERC	ERA
2018 NYY	AL	24	0	7	23.1	107	23	22	17	3	0	2	0	15	0	30	2	2	0	1.000	1-2 2	95	.811	5.11	6.56
2019 NYY	AL	72	0	5	61.1	248	45	27	25	9	0	1	2	20	0	88	8	3	2	.600	0-5 27	96	.635	2.79	3.67
17 CWS	AL	37	0	10	36.0	141	28	12	10	3	1	2	0	7	1	60	2	1	3	.250	0-4 7	98	.571	2.04	2.50
17 NYY	AL	32	0	7	26.2	115	25	8	8	1	0	2	2	10	0	36	3	1	1	.500	0-2 8	98	.648	3.47	2.70
Postseason		7	0	3	11.1	39	6	3	3	1	0	0	0	2	0	10	0	0	0	-	1-1 1	98	.502	1.25	2.38
6 ML YEARS		284	0	56	276.2	1170	224	138	118	28	4	12	5	131	7	341	28	9	9	.500	4-20 66	96	.665	3.35	3.84

Jung Ho Kang

Bats: R **Throws:** R **Pos:** 3B-44;PH-16;SS-15   GAHNG   **Ht:** 6'0" **Wt:** 210 **Born:** 4/5/1987 **Age:** 33

								BATTING												RUNNING			AVERAGES			
Year Team	Lg	G	AB	H	2B	3B	HR	(Hm	Rd)	TB	R	RBI	RC	TBB	IBB	SO	HBP	SH	SF	SB	CS	GDP	Avg	OBP	Slg	OPS
2015 Pit	NL	126	421	121	24	2	15	(5	10)	194	60	58	60	28	0	99	17	0	1	5	4	10	.287	.355	.461	.816
2016 Pit	NL	103	318	81	19	0	21	(10	11)	163	45	62	47	36	1	79	14	0	2	3	1	11	.255	.354	.513	.867
2018 Pit	NL	3	6	2	0	0	0	(0	0)	2	0	0	1	0	0	1	0	0	0	0	0	0	.333	.333	.333	.667
2019 Pit	NL	65	172	29	7	1	10	(6	4)	68	15	24	13	11	0	60	1	0	1	0	0	4	.169	.222	.395	.617
4 ML YEARS		297	917	233	50	3	46	(21	25)	427	120	144	121	75	1	239	32	0	4	8	5	25	.254	.331	.466	.796

James Karinchak

Pitches: R **Bats:** R **Pos:** RP-5   **Ht:** 6'3" **Wt:** 230 **Born:** 9/22/1995 **Age:** 24

			HOW MUCH PITCHED					WHAT HE GAVE UP											THE RESULTS					
Year Team	Lg	G	GS	GF	IP	BFP	H	R	ER	HR	SH	SF	HB	TBB	IBB	SO	WP	W	L	Pct	Sv-Op Hld	Vel	OPS	ERC	ERA
2019 Akron	AA	10	0	8	10.0	36	2	0	0	0	0	0	0	2	0	24	3	0	0	-	6- - -	-	.175	0.25	0.00
2019 Clmbs	AAA	17	0	3	17.1	78	14	10	9	2	0	0	0	13	0	42	2	1	1	.500	2- - -	-	.654	4.44	4.67
2019 Cle	AL	5	0	4	5.1	22	3	1	1	0	0	1	0	1	0	8	2	0	0	-	0-0 0	97	.382	0.90	1.69

Nate Karns

Pitches: R **Bats:** R **Pos:** SP-2; RP-2   **Ht:** 6'3" **Wt:** 225 **Born:** 11/25/1987 **Age:** 32

			HOW MUCH PITCHED					WHAT HE GAVE UP											THE RESULTS					
Year Team	Lg	G	GS	GF	IP	BFP	H	R	ER	HR	SH	SF	HB	TBB	IBB	SO	WP	W	L	Pct	Sv-Op Hld	Vel	OPS	ERC	ERA
2019 2 Tms	Low	6	6	0	7.0	31	4	4	4	0	0	1	0	6	0	4	2	0	0	-	0- - -	-	.573	2.69	5.14
2013 Was	NL	3	3	0	12.0	61	17	11	10	5	1	0	1	6	0	11	0	0	1	.000	0-0 0	93	1.060	9.80	7.50
2014 TB	AL	2	2	0	12.0	49	7	6	6	3	0	0	2	4	0	13	0	1	1	.500	0-0 0	93	.661	3.12	4.50
2015 TB	AL	27	26	0	147.0	621	132	62	60	19	3	4	5	56	1	145	15	7	5	.583	0-0 0	92	.699	3.77	3.67
2016 Sea	AL	22	15	2	94.1	417	95	55	54	11	0	2	3	45	1	101	5	6	2	.750	1-1 0	93	.760	4.65	5.15
2017 KC	AL	9	8	0	45.1	188	41	21	21	9	0	0	2	13	1	51	2	2	2	.500	0-0 0	93	.743	3.91	4.17
2019 Bal	AL	4	2	1	5.1	25	7	1	0	0	0	0	1	3	0	5	1	0	1	.000	0-0 0	91	.821	6.91	0.00
6 ML YEARS		67	56	3	316.0	1361	299	156	151	47	4	6	14	127	3	326	23	16	12	.571	1-1 0	92	.741	4.28	4.30

Anthony Kay

Pitches: L **Bats:** L **Pos:** SP-2; RP-1   **Ht:** 6'0" **Wt:** 218 **Born:** 3/21/1995 **Age:** 25

			HOW MUCH PITCHED					WHAT HE GAVE UP											THE RESULTS					
Year Team	Lg	G	GS	GF	IP	BFP	H	R	ER	HR	SH	SF	HB	TBB	IBB	SO	WP	W	L	Pct	Sv-Op Hld	Vel	OPS	ERC	ERA
2019 Bnghtn	AA	12	12	0	66.1	262	38	18	11	2	2	1	5	23	0	70	1	7	3	.700	0- - -	-	.472	1.62	1.49
2019 Syrcse	AAA	7	7	0	31.1	140	40	23	23	7	3	0	3	11	1	26	0	1	3	.250	0- - -	-	.980	7.09	6.61
2019 Buffalo	AAA	7	7	0	36.0	159	33	21	10	3	0	0	2	22	0	39	1	2	2	.500	0- - -	-	.744	4.60	2.50
2019 Tor	AL	3	2	0	14.0	63	15	9	9	0	0	0	1	5	0	13	1	1	0	1.000	0-0 0	93	.649	3.75	5.79

Keone Kela

Pitches: R **Bats:** R **Pos:** RP-32   KEY-oh-nee KELL-uh   **Ht:** 6'1" **Wt:** 210 **Born:** 4/16/1993 **Age:** 27

			HOW MUCH PITCHED					WHAT HE GAVE UP											THE RESULTS					
Year Team	Lg	G	GS	GF	IP	BFP	H	R	ER	HR	SH	SF	HB	TBB	IBB	SO	WP	W	L	Pct	Sv-Op Hld	Vel	OPS	ERC	ERA
2015 Tex	AL	68	0	11	60.1	243	52	18	16	4	1	0	0	18	0	68	6	7	5	.583	1-4 22	96	.615	2.79	2.39
2016 Tex	AL	35	0	2	34.0	150	30	23	23	6	2	1	3	17	0	45	2	5	1	.833	0-1 15	96	.779	4.68	6.09
2017 Tex	AL	39	0	13	38.2	151	18	12	12	4	0	0	1	17	1	51	1	4	1	.800	2-3 11	96	.479	1.64	2.79
2018 2 Tms		54	0	36	52.0	212	38	19	19	5	1	1	0	19	2	66	6	3	4	.429	24-26 4	97	.605	2.43	3.29
2019 Pit	NL	32	0	8	29.2	119	19	7	7	3	0	0	0	11	0	33	1	2	0	1.000	1-5 6	96	.606	2.23	2.12
18 Tex	AL	38	0	31	36.2	152	28	14	14	3	1	1	0	14	1	44	4	3	3	.500	24-25 0	97	.602	2.55	3.44
18 Pit	NL	16	0	5	15.1	60	10	5	5	2	0	0	0	5	1	22	2	0	1	.000	0-1 4	97	.614	2.12	2.93
Postseason		4	0	1	4.2	16	1	1	1	1	0	0	0	2	0	3	0	1	0	1.000	0-1 1	97	.473	1.27	1.93
5 ML YEARS		228	0	70	214.2	875	157	79	77	22	4	2	5	82	3	263	16	21	11	.656	28-39 58	96	.615	2.67	3.23

Jarred Kelenic

Bats: L **Throws:** L **Pos:** CF   **Ht:** 6'0" **Wt:** 196 **Born:** 7/16/1999 **Age:** 20

								BATTING												RUNNING			AVERAGES			
Year Team	Lg	G	AB	H	2B	3B	HR	(Hm	Rd)	TB	R	RBI	RC	TBB	IBB	SO	HBP	SH	SF	SB	CS	GDP	Avg	OBP	Slg	OPS
2018 2 Tms	Low	56	220	63	10	6	6	(-	-)	103	42	42	40	26	0	50	4	0	1	15	1	1	.286	.371	.468	.839
2019 2 Tms	Low	96	360	108	27	4	17	(-	-)	194	69	51	75	42	0	94	3	0	3	17	7	4	.300	.375	.539	.914
2019 Ark	AA	21	83	21	4	1	6	(-	-)	45	11	17	15	8	0	17	0	0	1	3	0	2	.253	.315	.542	.857

Brad Keller

Pitches: R Bats: R Pos: SP-28   Ht: 6'5" Wt: 230 Born: 7/27/1995 Age: 24

Year	Team	Lg	G	GS	GF	IP	BFP	H	R	ER	HR	SH	SF	HB	TBB	IBB	SO	WP	W	L	Pct	Sv-Op	Hld	Vel	OPS	ERC	ERA
2018	KC	AL	41	20	2	140.1	583	133	50	48	7	0	3	2	50	1	96	8	9	6	.600	0-2	5	94	.653	3.39	3.08
2019	KC	AL	28	28	0	165.1	709	154	80	77	15	1	5	9	70	2	122	9	7	14	.333	0-0	0	93	.711	3.94	4.19
	2 ML YEARS		69	48	2	305.2	1292	287	130	125	22	1	8	11	120	3	218	17	16	20	.444	0-2	5	94	.684	3.69	3.68

Kyle Keller

Pitches: R Bats: R Pos: RP-10   Ht: 6'4" Wt: 200 Born: 4/28/1993 Age: 27

Year	Team	Lg	G	GS	GF	IP	BFP	H	R	ER	HR	SH	SF	HB	TBB	IBB	SO	WP	W	L	Pct	Sv-Op	Hld	Vel	OPS	ERC	ERA
2019	NewOr	AAA	37	0	17	54.0	224	44	31	27	8	1	0	0	21	1	73	2	2	3	.400	10-	-	-	.692	3.30	4.50
2019	Mia	NL	10	0	4	10.2	46	5	4	4	3	0	0	2	8	0	11	0	0	0	-	0-0	0	95	.715	4.53	3.38

Mitch Keller

Pitches: R Bats: R Pos: SP-11   Ht: 6'2" Wt: 210 Born: 4/4/1996 Age: 24

Year	Team	Lg	G	GS	GF	IP	BFP	H	R	ER	HR	SH	SF	HB	TBB	IBB	SO	WP	W	L	Pct	Sv-Op	Hld	Vel	OPS	ERC	ERA
2015	Brstol	R+	6	6	0	19.2	101	25	18	12	1	1	0	3	16	0	25	2	0	3	.000	0-	-	-	.835	7.62	5.49
2016	2 Tms	Low	24	24	0	130.1	511	101	36	34	4	3	2	11	19	0	138	10	9	5	.643	0-	-	-	.562	1.91	2.35
2017	2 Tms	Low	17	17	0	81.1	322	59	29	27	5	2	2	8	21	0	71	7	6	3	.667	0-	-	-	.552	2.29	2.99
2017	Altna	AA	6	6	0	34.2	142	25	14	12	2	1	1	2	11	0	45	0	2	2	.500	0-	-	-	.569	2.23	3.12
2018	Altna	AA	14	14	0	86.0	342	64	29	26	7	1	1	0	32	0	76	6	9	2	.818	0-	-	-	.632	2.57	2.72
2018	Indy	AAA	10	10	0	52.1	236	59	34	28	3	1	1	1	22	0	57	1	3	2	.600	0-	-	-	.771	4.59	4.82
2019	Indy	AAA	19	19	0	103.2	436	94	44	41	9	5	2	7	35	0	123	5	7	5	.583	0-	-	-	.695	3.52	3.56
2019	Pit	NL	11	11	0	48.0	227	72	41	38	6	1	2	1	16	0	65	2	1	5	.167	0-0	0	95	.940	7.13	7.13

Shawn Kelley

Pitches: R Bats: R Pos: RP-50   Ht: 6'2" Wt: 237 Born: 4/26/1984 Age: 36

Year	Team	Lg	G	GS	GF	IP	BFP	H	R	ER	HR	SH	SF	HB	TBB	IBB	SO	WP	W	L	Pct	Sv-Op	Hld	Vel	OPS	ERC	ERA
2009	Sea	AL	41	0	12	46.0	191	45	23	23	9	2	2	3	9	1	41	2	5	4	.556	0-4	9	93	.742	4.02	4.50
2010	Sea	AL	22	0	7	25.0	112	26	11	11	5	0	0	1	12	2	26	0	3	1	.750	0-0	3	93	.841	5.38	3.96
2011	Sea	AL	10	0	2	12.2	47	7	0	0	0	0	0	0	3	1	10	0	0	0	.417	0-0	1	91	1.01	0.00	
2012	Sea	AL	47	0	10	44.1	190	43	20	16	5	4	3	0	15	6	45	2	2	4	.333	0-2	6	92	.717	3.49	3.25
2013	NYY	AL	57	0	13	53.1	227	47	28	26	8	0	2	0	23	2	71	8	4	2	.667	0-1	11	92	.729	3.80	4.39
2014	NYY	AL	59	0	15	51.2	220	45	26	26	5	3	1	1	20	4	67	3	3	6	.333	4-7	12	92	.663	3.20	4.53
2015	SD	NL	53	0	14	51.1	205	41	18	14	4	0	4	0	15	4	63	0	2	2	.500	0-0	7	92	.596	2.40	2.45
2016	Was	NL	67	0	26	58.0	224	41	19	17	9	0	2	0	11	2	80	2	3	2	.600	7-9	13	92	.635	2.06	2.64
2017	Was	NL	33	0	18	26.0	121	29	21	21	12	0	0	1	11	1	25	2	3	2	.600	4-6	2	92	.963	7.40	7.27
2018	2 Tms		54	0	15	49.0	190	33	16	16	7	0	2	1	11	3	50	2	2	0	1.000	0-2	4	91	.618	2.01	2.94
2019	Tex	AL	50	0	23	47.1	205	55	27	26	12	2	1	2	11	2	43	2	5	2	.714	11-15	6	92	.885	5.55	4.94
18	Was	NL	35	0	12	32.1	128	26	12	12	7	0	1	1	5	1	32	0	1	0	1.000	0-1	1	91	.729	2.85	3.34
18	Oak	AL	19	0	3	16.2	62	7	4	4	0	0	1	0	6	2	18	2	1	0	1.000	0-1	3	91	.373	0.85	2.16
	Postseason		3	0	0	2.2	10	2	0	0	0	0	0	0	0	0	3	0	0	0	-	0-0	1	93	.600	1.13	0.00
	11 ML YEARS		493	0	155	464.2	1932	412	209	196	76	11	17	9	141	28	521	23	32	25	.561	26-46	74	92	.715	3.46	3.80

Trevor Kelley

Pitches: R Bats: R Pos: RP-10   Ht: 6'2" Wt: 210 Born: 10/20/1993 Age: 26

Year	Team	Lg	G	GS	GF	IP	BFP	H	R	ER	HR	SH	SF	HB	TBB	IBB	SO	WP	W	L	Pct	Sv-Op	Hld	Vel	OPS	ERC	ERA
2019	Pwtckt	AAA	52	0	31	65.1	268	51	18	13	8	2	3	6	21	3	63	4	5	5	.500	12-	-	-	.649	3.05	1.79
2019	Bos	AL	10	0	3	8.1	40	9	8	8	2	0	4	0	5	0	6	2	0	3	.000	0-0	0	89	.963	6.15	8.64

Carson Kelly

Bats: R Throws: R Pos: C-101;PH-15;3B-1   Ht: 6'2" Wt: 220 Born: 7/14/1994 Age: 25

Year	Team	Lg	G	AB	H	2B	3B	HR	(Hm	Rd)	TB	R	RBI	RC	TBB	IBB	SO	HBP	SH	SF	SB	CS	GDP	Avg	OBP	Slg	OPS
2016	StL	NL	10	13	2	1	0	0	(0	0)	3	1	1	0	0	0	2	1	0	0	0	0	0	.154	.214	.231	.445
2017	StL	NL	34	69	12	3	0	0	(0	0)	15	5	6	4	5	0	11	1	0	0	0	0	3	.174	.240	.217	.457
2018	StL	NL	19	35	4	0	0	0	(0	0)	4	1	3	1	3	0	7	1	3	0	0	0	0	.114	.205	.114	.319
2019	Ari	NL	111	314	77	19	0	18	(4	14)	150	46	47	46	48	10	79	2	0	1	0	0	11	.245	.348	.478	.826
	4 ML YEARS		174	431	95	23	0	18	(4	14)	172	53	57	51	56	10	99	5	3	1	0	0	14	.220	.316	.399	.716

Joe Kelly

Pitches: R Bats: R Pos: RP-55   Ht: 6'1" Wt: 174 Born: 6/9/1988 Age: 32

Year	Team	Lg	G	GS	GF	IP	BFP	H	R	ER	HR	SH	SF	HB	TBB	IBB	SO	WP	W	L	Pct	Sv-Op	Hld	Vel	OPS	ERC	ERA
2012	StL	NL	24	16	4	107.0	457	112	50	42	10	4	1	3	36	2	75	4	5	7	.417	0-0	0	94	.740	4.17	3.53
2013	StL	NL	37	15	8	124.0	532	124	42	37	10	2	2	5	44	4	79	3	10	5	.667	0-1	2	95	.694	3.88	2.69
2014	2 Tms		17	17	0	96.1	415	88	48	45	8	2	4	7	42	0	66	3	6	4	.600	0-0	0	95	.693	3.92	4.20
2015	Bos	AL	25	25	0	134.1	587	145	76	72	15	0	5	6	49	0	110	9	10	6	.625	0-0	0	95	.769	4.68	4.82
2016	Bos	AL	20	6	6	40.0	188	44	23	23	5	0	4	2	24	0	48	0	4	0	1.000	0-1	2	96	.828	5.80	5.18
2017	Bos	AL	54	0	14	58.0	238	42	19	18	3	0	2	1	27	1	52	4	4	1	.800	0-4	13	99	.573	2.61	2.79

Year	Team	Lg	G	GS	GF	IP	BFP	H	R	ER	HR	SH	SF	HB	TBB	IBB	SO	WP	W	L	Pct	Sv-Op	Hld	Vel	OPS	ERC	ERA
2018	Bos	AL	73	0	9	65.2	285	57	34	32	4	0	4	5	32	0	68	4	4	2	.667	2-7	21	98	.662	3.70	4.39
2019	LAD	NL	55	0	13	51.1	226	49	31	26	6	0	0	3	22	2	62	10	5	4	.556	1-6	8	98	.711	4.16	4.56
14	StL	NL	7	7	0	35.0	156	41	19	17	3	1	1	3	10	0	25	3	2	2	.500	0-0		95	.774	4.82	4.37
14	Bos	AL	10	10	0	61.1	259	47	29	28	5	1	3	4	32	0	41	0	4	2	.667	0-0		95	.641	3.43	4.11
	Postseason		25	4	1	47.0	193	38	15	13	2	1	0	2	13	1	41	4	3	2	.600	0-0	2	97	.553	2.34	2.49
	8 ML YEARS		305	79	54	676.2	2928	661	323	295	61	8	22	32	276	9	560	37	48	29	.623	3-19	46	96	.713	4.08	3.92

Merrill Kelly

Pitches: R Bats: R Pos: SP-32　　　　　　　　　　　　Ht: 6'2" Wt: 190 Born: 10/14/1988 Age: 31

				HOW MUCH PITCHED				WHAT HE GAVE UP											THE RESULTS							
Year	Team	Lg	G	GS	GF	IP	BFP	H	R	ER	HR	SH	SF	HB	TBB	IBB	SO	WP	W	L	Pct	Sv-Op	Hld	Vel	OPS	ERC	ERA
2019	Ari	NL	32	32	0	183.1	777	184	95	90	29	2	5	2	57	4	158	4	13	14	.481	0-0	0	92	.761	4.16	4.42

Matt Kemp

Bats: R Throws: R Pos: LF-17;PH-4　　　　　　　　　　　Ht: 6'4" Wt: 225 Born: 9/23/1984 Age: 35

									BATTING											RUNNING			AVERAGES			
Year	Team	Lg	G	AB	H	2B	3B	HR	(Hm	Rd)	TB	R	RBI	RC	TBB	IBB	SO	HBP	SH	SF	SB	CS	GDP	Avg	OBP	Slg	OPS
2006	LAD	NL	52	154	39	7	1	7	(4	3)	69	30	23	20	9	1	53	0	0	3	6	0	1	.253	.289	.448	.737
2007	LAD	NL	98	292	100	12	5	10	(9	1)	152	47	42	49	16	0	66	1	0	3	10	5	6	.342	.373	.521	.894
2008	LAD	NL	155	606	176	38	5	18	(14	4)	278	93	76	86	46	6	153	1	1	3	35	11	11	.290	.340	.459	.799
2009	LAD	NL	159	606	180	25	7	26	(13	13)	297	97	101	100	52	6	139	3	0	6	34	8	14	.297	.352	.490	.842
2010	LAD	NL	162	602	150	25	6	28	(15	13)	271	82	89	74	53	4	170	4	0	9	19	15	14	.249	.310	.450	.760
2011	LAD	NL	161	602	195	33	4	39	(19	20)	353	115	126	126	74	24	159	6	0	7	40	11	16	.324	.399	.586	.986
2012	LAD	NL	106	403	122	22	2	23	(13	10)	217	74	69	75	40	8	103	3	0	3	9	4	10	.303	.367	.538	.906
2013	LAD	NL	73	263	71	15	0	6	(0	6)	104	35	33	27	22	3	76	2	0	3	9	0	11	.270	.328	.395	.723
2014	LAD	NL	150	541	156	38	3	25	(17	8)	274	77	89	79	52	3	145	0	0	6	8	5	21	.287	.346	.506	.852
2015	SD	NL	154	596	158	31	3	23	(13	10)	264	80	100	81	39	0	147	5	0	8	12	2	17	.265	.312	.443	.755
2016	2 Tms	NL	156	623	167	39	0	35	(14	21)	311	89	108	85	36	6	156	1	0	12	1	0	17	.268	.304	.499	.803
2017	Atl	NL	115	438	121	23	1	19	(7	12)	203	47	64	46	27	5	99	0	0	1	0	2	25	.276	.318	.463	.781
2018	LAD	NL	146	462	134	25	0	21	(11	10)	222	62	85	80	36	2	115	1	0	7	0	0	14	.290	.338	.481	.818
2019	Cin	NL	20	60	12	2	0	1	(1	0)	17	4	5	3	1	0	19	0	0	1	0	0	2	.200	.210	.283	.493
16	SD	NL	100	409	107	24	0	23	(8	15)	200	54	69	58	16	3	100	0	0	6	0	0	8	.262	.285	.489	.774
16	Atl	NL	56	214	60	15	0	12	(6	6)	111	35	39	27	20	3	56	1	0	6	1	0	9	.280	.336	.519	.855
	Postseason		33	102	24	4	0	4	(2	2)	40	7	10	3	6	1	34	0	0	1	0	2	4	.235	.275	.392	.667
	14 ML YEARS		1707	6248	1780	335	37	281	(150	131)	3032	932	1010	934	503	68	1600	26	1	72	183	63	179	.285	.337	.485	.822

Tony Kemp

Bats: L Throws: R Pos: 2B-43;PH-38;LF-20;CF-12;DH-6;RF-3;PR-2　　　　Ht: 5'6" Wt: 165 Born: 10/31/1991 Age: 28

									BATTING											RUNNING			AVERAGES			
Year	Team	Lg	G	AB	H	2B	3B	HR	(Hm	Rd)	TB	R	RBI	RC	TBB	IBB	SO	HBP	SH	SF	SB	CS	GDP	Avg	OBP	Slg	OPS
2016	Hou	AL	59	120	26	4	3	1	(1	0)	39	15	7	11	14	0	27	0	1	1	2	1	5	.217	.296	.325	.621
2017	Hou	AL	17	37	8	1	0	0	(0	0)	9	6	4	4	1	0	5	1	0	0	1	0	0	.216	.256	.243	.500
2018	Hou	AL	97	255	67	15	0	6	(1	5)	100	37	30	41	32	1	44	3	3	1	9	3	7	.263	.351	.392	.743
2019	2 Tms	NL	110	245	52	9	4	8	(7	1)	93	31	29	28	23	1	47	6	1	4	4	4	4	.212	.291	.380	.671
19	Hou	AL	66	163	37	6	2	7	(6	1)	68	23	17	18	16	1	29	4	1	2	4	3	2	.227	.308	.417	.725
19	ChC	NL	44	82	15	3	2	1	(1	0)	25	8	12	10	7	0	18	2	0	2	0	1	2	.183	.258	.305	.563
	Postseason		6	14	4	1	0	1	(1	0)	8	3	1	3	5	0	3	0	0	0	0	0	0	.286	.474	.571	1.045
	4 ML YEARS		283	657	153	29	7	15	(9	6)	241	89	70	84	70	2	123	10	5	6	16	8	16	.233	.314	.367	.680

Howie Kendrick

Bats: R Throws: R Pos: 1B-48;PH-41;2B-23;3B-15;DH-7　　　　　　Ht: 5'11" Wt: 220 Born: 7/12/1983 Age: 36

									BATTING											RUNNING			AVERAGES			
Year	Team	Lg	G	AB	H	2B	3B	HR	(Hm	Rd)	TB	R	RBI	RC	TBB	IBB	SO	HBP	SH	SF	SB	CS	GDP	Avg	OBP	Slg	OPS
2006	LAA	AL	72	267	76	21	1	4	(2	2)	111	25	30	32	9	2	44	4	0	3	6	0	5	.285	.314	.416	.730
2007	LAA	AL	88	338	109	24	2	5	(3	2)	152	55	39	41	9	2	61	4	1	1	5	4	15	.322	.347	.450	.796
2008	LAA	AL	92	340	104	26	2	3	(1	2)	143	43	37	50	12	3	58	4	1	4	11	4	8	.306	.333	.421	.754
2009	LAA	AL	105	374	109	21	3	10	(5	5)	166	61	61	58	20	1	71	4	2	0	11	4	8	.291	.334	.444	.778
2010	LAA	AL	158	616	172	41	4	10	(4	6)	251	67	75	81	28	2	94	5	4	5	14	4	16	.279	.313	.407	.721
2011	LAA	AL	140	537	130	30	6	18	(5	13)	249	86	63	69	33	3	119	10	3	0	14	6	18	.285	.338	.464	.802
2012	LAA	AL	147	550	158	32	3	8	(4	4)	220	57	67	65	29	1	115	4	6	5	14	6	26	.287	.325	.400	.725
2013	LAA	AL	122	478	142	21	4	13	(9	4)	210	55	54	57	23	5	89	6	3	3	6	3	16	.297	.335	.439	.775
2014	LAA	AL	157	617	181	33	5	7	(0	7)	245	85	75	94	48	8	110	4	3	2	14	5	15	.293	.347	.397	.744
2015	LAD	NL	117	464	137	22	2	9	(6	3)	190	64	54	62	27	1	82	2	1	1	6	2	17	.295	.336	.409	.746
2016	LAD	NL	146	487	124	26	2	8	(3	5)	178	65	40	55	50	2	96	3	0	3	10	2	20	.255	.326	.366	.691
2017	2 Tms	NL	91	305	96	16	3	9	(4	5)	145	40	41	47	22	0	68	5	0	2	12	5	8	.315	.368	.475	.844
2018	Was	NL	40	152	46	14	0	4	(3	1)	72	17	12	15	5	1	29	2	0	1	1	1	6	.303	.331	.474	.805
2019	Was	NL	121	334	115	23	1	17	(10	7)	191	61	62	58	27	1	49	4	0	5	2	1	11	.344	.395	.572	.966
17	Phi	NL	39	141	48	8	1	2	(0	2)	64	16	16	23	11	0	30	3	0	1	8	3	4	.340	.397	.454	.851
17	Was	NL	52	164	48	8	2	7	(4	3)	81	24	25	24	11	0	38	2	0	1	4	2	4	.293	.343	.494	.837
	Postseason		33	105	22	4	1	2	(1	1)	34	11	6	6	3	1	23	0	2	1	4	0	3	.210	.229	.324	.553
	14 ML YEARS		1596	5859	1722	350	38	125	(59	66)	2523	781	710	784	342	32	1085	61	24	35	126	47	189	.294	.337	.431	.768

Ian Kennedy

Pitches: R Bats: R Pos: RP-63 **Ht: 6'0" Wt: 205 Born: 12/19/1984 Age: 35**

Year	Team	Lg	G	GS	GF	IP	BFP	H	R	ER	HR	SH	SF	HB	TBB	IBB	SO	WP	W	L	Pct	Sv-Op	Hld	Vel	OPS	ERC	ERA
2007	NYY	AL	3	3	0	19.0	77	13	6	4	1	0	0	0	9	0	15	0	1	0	1.000	0-0	0	89	.565	2.42	1.89
2008	NYY	AL	10	9	1	39.2	194	50	37	36	5	1	4	1	26	0	27	3	0	4	.000	0-0	0	89	.917	6.93	8.17
2009	NYY	AL	1	0	0	1.0	6	0	0	0	0	0	0	0	2	0	1	0	0	0	.500	0-0	1	92	.500	7.00	0.00
2010	Ari	NL	32	32	0	194.0	810	163	87	82	26	11	5	10	70	2	168	16	9	10	.474	0-0	0	89	.696	3.47	3.80
2011	Ari	NL	33	33	0	222.0	900	186	73	71	19	9	9	9	55	0	198	11	21	4	.840	0-0	0	90	.641	2.71	2.88
2012	Ari	NL	33	33	0	208.1	899	216	101	93	28	13	5	14	55	4	187	5	15	12	.556	0-0	0	90	.775	4.18	4.02
2013	2 Tms	NL	31	31	0	181.1	794	180	108	99	27	8	5	12	73	1	163	10	7	10	.412	0-0	0	90	.781	4.64	4.91
2014	SD	NL	33	33	0	201.0	846	189	85	81	16	9	8	4	70	4	207	11	13	13	.500	0-0	0	92	.698	3.47	3.63
2015	SD	NL	30	30	0	168.1	713	166	95	80	31	8	2	7	52	4	174	5	9	15	.375	0-0	0	91	.816	4.37	4.44
2016	KC	AL	33	33	0	195.2	818	173	81	80	33	1	5	13	66	1	184	4	11	11	.500	0-0	0	92	.722	3.94	3.68
2017	KC	AL	30	30	0	154.0	655	143	99	92	34	1	6	5	61	2	131	4	5	13	.278	0-0	0	92	.804	4.64	5.38
2018	KC	AL	22	22	0	119.2	518	125	66	62	20	4	2	1	40	2	105	4	3	9	.250	0-0	0	92	.779	4.51	4.66
2019	KC	AL	63	0	51	63.1	266	64	24	24	6	3	0	1	17	1	73	3	3	2	.600	30-34	1	94	.675	3.63	3.41
13	Ari	NL	21	21	0	124.0	549	128	79	72	18	8	5	10	48	1	108	9	3	8	.273	0-0	0	90	.798	4.82	5.23
13	SD	NL	10	10	0	57.1	245	52	29	27	9	0	2	2	25	0	55	1	4	2	.667	0-0	0	90	.744	4.26	4.24
	Postseason		2	2	0	12.2	57	13	6	6	1	0	2	3	3	0	8	1	0	1	.000	0-0	0	92	.782	4.25	4.26
13 ML YEARS			354	289	52	1767.1	7496	1668	862	804	246	68	51	78	596	21	1633	76	97	103	.485	30-34	2	91	.741	3.94	4.09

Max Kepler

Bats: L Throws: L Pos: RF-84;CF-60;PH-4;DH-2;PR-1 **Ht: 6'4" Wt: 220 Born: 2/10/1993 Age: 27**

Year	Team	Lg	G	AB	H	2B	3B	HR	(Hm	Rd)	TB	R	RBI	RC	TBB	IBB	SO	HBP	SH	SF	SB	CS	GDP	Avg	OBP	Slg	OPS
2015	Min	AL	3	7	1	0	0	0	(0	0)	1	0	0	0	0	0	3	0	0	0	0	0	0	.143	.143	.143	.286
2016	Min	AL	113	396	93	20	2	17	(8	9)	168	52	63	52	42	3	93	3	1	5	6	2	2	.235	.309	.424	.734
2017	Min	AL	147	511	124	32	2	19	(9	10)	217	67	69	68	47	2	114	6	1	3	6	1	5	.243	.312	.425	.737
2018	Min	AL	156	532	119	30	4	20	(12	8)	217	80	58	65	71	2	96	5	0	3	4	5	8	.224	.319	.408	.727
2019	Min	AL	134	524	132	32	0	36	(17	19)	272	98	90	90	60	0	99	8	0	4	1	5	5	.252	.336	.519	.855
	Postseason		1	3	1	1	0	0	(-	-)	2	0	0	1	1	0	0	0	0	0	0	0	0	.333	.500	.667	1.167
5 ML YEARS			553	1970	469	114	8	92	(46	46)	875	297	280	275	220	7	405	22	2	15	17	13	20	.238	.319	.444	.763

Clayton Kershaw

Pitches: L Bats: L Pos: SP-28; RP-1 **Ht: 6'4" Wt: 226 Born: 3/19/1988 Age: 32**

Year	Team	Lg	G	GS	GF	IP	BFP	H	R	ER	HR	SH	SF	HB	TBB	IBB	SO	WP	W	L	Pct	Sv-Op	Hld	Vel	OPS	ERC	ERA
2008	LAD	NL	22	21	0	107.2	470	109	51	51	11	3	3	1	52	3	100	7	5	5	.500	0-0	1	94	.756	4.53	4.26
2009	LAD	NL	31	30	1	171.0	701	119	55	53	7	11	2	1	91	4	185	11	8	8	.500	0-0	0	94	.588	2.60	2.79
2010	LAD	NL	32	32	0	204.1	848	160	73	66	13	8	4	7	81	9	212	5	13	10	.565	0-0	0	93	.615	2.72	2.91
2011	LAD	NL	33	33	0	233.1	912	174	66	59	15	11	2	3	54	4	248	5	21	5	.808	0-0	0	93	.554	2.00	2.28
2012	LAD	NL	33	33	0	227.2	901	170	70	64	16	18	4	5	63	5	229	6	14	9	.609	0-0	0	93	.593	2.20	2.53
2013	LAD	NL	33	33	0	236.0	908	164	55	48	11	8	3	3	52	2	232	12	16	9	.640	0-0	0	93	.521	1.65	1.83
2014	LAD	NL	27	27	0	198.1	749	139	42	39	9	6	1	2	31	0	239	7	21	3	.875	0-0	0	93	.521	1.53	1.77
2015	LAD	NL	33	33	0	232.2	890	163	62	55	15	4	0	5	42	1	301	9	16	7	.696	0-0	0	93	.521	1.67	2.13
2016	LAD	NL	21	21	0	149.0	544	97	31	28	8	4	1	2	11	1	172	5	12	4	.750	0-0	0	93	.472	1.23	1.69
2017	LAD	NL	27	27	0	175.0	679	136	49	45	23	4	3	0	30	0	202	4	18	4	.818	0-0	0	93	.604	2.27	2.31
2018	LAD	NL	26	26	0	161.1	650	139	55	49	17	3	2	2	29	0	155	10	9	5	.643	0-0	0	91	.630	2.56	2.73
2019	LAD	NL	29	28	0	178.1	706	145	63	60	28	6	1	2	41	0	189	7	16	5	.762	0-0	0	90	.664	2.86	3.03
	Postseason		30	24	2	152.0	615	122	78	73	22	5	5	2	44	5	165	10	9	10	.474	1-1	1	93	.647	2.88	4.32
12 ML YEARS			347	344	1	2274.2	8958	1715	672	617	173	86	26	33	577	27	2464	88	169	74	.695	0-0	1	93	.580	2.18	2.44

Dallas Keuchel

Pitches: L Bats: L Pos: SP-19 KY-kull **Ht: 6'3" Wt: 205 Born: 1/1/1988 Age: 32**

Year	Team	Lg	G	GS	GF	IP	BFP	H	R	ER	HR	SH	SF	HB	TBB	IBB	SO	WP	W	L	Pct	Sv-Op	Hld	Vel	OPS	ERC	ERA
2012	Hou	NL	16	16	0	85.1	377	93	56	50	14	9	3	1	39	1	38	2	3	8	.273	0-0	0	88	.823	5.39	5.27
2013	Hou	AL	31	22	2	153.2	682	184	96	88	20	2	3	5	52	3	123	7	6	10	.375	0-0	2	89	.812	5.33	5.15
2014	Hou	AL	29	29	0	200.0	808	187	71	64	11	4	5	7	48	2	146	7	12	9	.571	0-0	0	90	.655	3.02	2.93
2015	Hou	AL	33	33	0	232.0	911	185	68	64	17	1	3	2	51	0	216	9	20	8	.714	0-0	0	90	.575	2.26	2.48
2016	Hou	AL	26	26	0	168.0	701	168	88	85	20	2	1	2	48	1	144	9	9	12	.429	0-0	0	89	.736	3.84	4.55
2017	Hou	AL	23	23	0	145.2	584	116	50	47	15	1	0	2	47	0	125	1	14	5	.737	0-0	0	89	.619	2.82	2.90
2018	Hou	AL	34	34	0	204.2	874	211	92	85	18	3	9	2	58	0	153	9	12	11	.522	0-0	0	89	.704	3.71	3.74
2019	Atl	NL	19	19	0	112.2	487	115	50	47	16	5	0	9	39	1	91	6	8	8	.500	0-0	0	88	.764	4.62	3.75
	Postseason		10	9	1	51.2	212	43	20	19	5	3	1	0	16	2	48	1	4	2	.667	0-0	0	90	.636	2.74	3.31
8 ML YEARS			211	202	2	1302.0	5424	1259	571	531	131	27	24	30	382	8	1036	50	84	71	.542	0-0	2	89	.697	3.60	3.67

Carter Kieboom

Bats: R Throws: R Pos: SS-10;PH-1 **Ht: 6'2" Wt: 190 Born: 9/3/1997 Age: 22**

Year	Team	Lg	G	AB	H	2B	3B	HR	(Hm	Rd)	TB	R	RBI	RC	TBB	IBB	SO	HBP	SH	SF	SB	CS	GDP	Avg	OBP	Slg	OPS
2016	Nats	R	36	135	33	8	4	4	(-	-)	61	22	25	20	12	0	43	5	0	3	1	2	4	.244	.323	.452	.774
2017	3 Tms	Low	61	219	65	16	0	9	(-	-)	108	41	35	43	32	3	42	4	0	0	3	2	5	.297	.396	.493	.889
2018	Ptomc	A+	61	245	73	15	0	11	(-	-)	121	48	46	49	36	0	50	1	0	3	6	1	5	.298	.386	.494	.880
2018	Hrsbrg	AA	62	248	66	16	1	5	(-	-)	99	36	23	34	22	0	59	2	0	1	3	1	5	.266	.330	.399	.729
2019	Fresno	AAA	109	412	125	24	3	16	(-	-)	203	79	79	87	68	1	100	9	0	5	5	2	11	.303	.409	.493	.902
2019	Was	NL	11	39	5	0	0	2	(2	0)	11	4	2	0	4	1	16	0	0	0	0	0	0	.128	.209	.282	.491

Kevin Kiermaier

Bats: L Throws: R Pos: CF-125;PH-8;PR-1   KEER-my-urr   Ht: 6'1" Wt: 210 Born: 4/22/1990 Age: 30

Year	Team	Lg	G	AB	H	2B	3B	HR	(Hm	Rd)	TB	R	RBI	RC	TBB	IBB	SO	HBP	SH	SF	SB	CS	GDP	Avg	OBP	Slg	OPS
2013	TB	AL	1	0	0	0	0	0	(0	0)	0	0	0	0	0	0	0	0	0	0	0	0	0	-	-	-	-
2014	TB	AL	108	331	87	16	8	10	(4	6)	149	35	35	37	23	2	71	3	5	2	5	4	3	.263	.315	.450	.765
2015	TB	AL	151	505	133	25	12	10	(5	5)	212	62	40	66	24	0	95	2	2	2	18	5	7	.263	.298	.420	.718
2016	TB	AL	105	366	90	20	2	12	(5	7)	150	55	37	54	40	1	74	7	0	1	21	3	5	.246	.331	.410	.741
2017	TB	AL	98	380	105	15	3	15	(8	7)	171	56	39	53	31	2	99	5	4	1	16	7	3	.276	.338	.450	.788
2018	TB	AL	88	332	72	12	9	7	(4	3)	123	44	29	30	25	2	91	6	2	2	10	5	4	.217	.282	.370	.653
2019	TB	AL	129	447	102	20	7	14	(7	7)	178	60	55	56	26	2	104	5	1	1	19	5	8	.228	.278	.398	.676
Postseason			1	0	0	0	0	0	(0	0)	0	0	0	0	0	0	0	0	0	0	0	0	0	-	-	-	-
7 ML YEARS			680	2361	589	108	41	68	(33	35)	983	312	235	296	169	9	534	28	14	9	89	29	30	.249	.306	.416	.723

Yusei Kikuchi

Pitches: L Bats: L Pos: SP-32   Ht: 6'0" Wt: 194 Born: 6/17/1991 Age: 29

Year	Team	Lg	G	GS	GF	IP	BFP	H	R	ER	HR	SH	SF	HB	TBB	IBB	SO	WP	W	L	Pct	Sv-Op	Hld	Vel	OPS	ERC	ERA
2019	Sea	AL	32	32	0	161.2	721	195	109	98	36	0	5	6	50	0	116	5	6	11	.353	0-0	0	92	.888	5.97	5.46

Craig Kimbrel

Pitches: R Bats: R Pos: RP-23   KIM-brull   Ht: 6'0" Wt: 210 Born: 5/28/1988 Age: 32

Year	Team	Lg	G	GS	GF	IP	BFP	H	R	ER	HR	SH	SF	HB	TBB	IBB	SO	WP	W	L	Pct	Sv-Op	Hld	Vel	OPS	ERC	ERA
2010	Atl	NL	21	0	7	20.2	88	9	2	1	0	0	0	0	16	1	40	4	4	0	1.000	1-1	2	95	.437	1.72	0.44
2011	Atl	NL	79	0	64	77.0	306	48	19	18	3	1	2	1	32	1	127	4	4	3	.571	46-54	0	96	.499	1.88	2.10
2012	Atl	NL	63	0	56	62.2	231	27	7	7	3	0	0	2	14	0	116	5	3	1	.750	42-45	0	97	.358	0.93	1.01
2013	Atl	NL	68	0	60	67.0	258	39	10	9	4	0	0	3	20	2	98	3	4	3	.571	50-54	0	97	.487	1.58	1.21
2014	Atl	NL	63	0	54	61.2	244	30	13	11	2	3	0	2	26	0	95	6	0	3	.000	47-51	0	97	.430	1.41	1.61
2015	SD	NL	61	0	53	59.1	239	40	19	17	6	0	0	1	22	1	87	4	4	2	.667	39-43	0	97	.569	2.31	2.58
2016	Bos	AL	57	0	47	53.0	220	28	22	20	4	1	1	4	30	0	83	6	2	6	.250	31-33	1	97	.539	2.32	3.40
2017	Bos	AL	67	0	51	69.0	254	33	11	11	6	1	0	4	14	0	126	5	5	0	1.000	35-39	0	98	.444	1.21	1.43
2018	Bos	AL	63	0	57	62.1	247	31	19	19	7	1	0	2	31	0	96	7	5	1	.833	42-47	0	97	.565	2.07	2.74
2019	ChC	NL	23	0	17	20.2	96	21	15	15	9	0	1	2	12	0	30	0	0	4	.000	13-16	0	96	1.019	7.90	6.53
Postseason			19	0	15	20.2	87	14	10	9	2	0	1	3	12	0	25	2	0	1	.000	7-7	1	98	.671	3.64	3.92
10 ML YEARS			565	0	466	553.1	2183	306	137	128	44	7	4	21	217	5	898	44	31	23	.574	346-383	4	97	.507	1.79	2.08

Isiah Kiner-Falefa

Bats: R Throws: R Pos: C-38;3B-25;DH-1;PH-1;PR-1   Ht: 5'10" Wt: 176 Born: 3/23/1995 Age: 25

Year	Team	Lg	G	AB	H	2B	3B	HR	(Hm	Rd)	TB	R	RBI	RC	TBB	IBB	SO	HBP	SH	SF	SB	CS	GDP	Avg	OBP	Slg	OPS
2019	Frisco	AA	17	60	17	4	0	2	(-	-)	27	7	11	11	8	0	9	2	0	1	1	0	1	.283	.380	.450	.830
2018	Tex	AL	111	356	93	18	2	4	(0	4)	127	43	34	34	28	1	62	6	5	1	7	5	14	.261	.325	.357	.682
2019	Tex	AL	65	202	48	12	1	1	(0	1)	65	23	21	18	14	0	49	4	1	1	3	0	9	.238	.299	.322	.620
2 ML YEARS			176	558	141	30	3	5	(0	5)	192	66	55	52	42	1	111	10	6	2	10	5	23	.253	.315	.344	.659

Michael King

Pitches: R Bats: R Pos: RP-1   Ht: 6'3" Wt: 210 Born: 5/25/1995 Age: 25

Year	Team	Lg	G	GS	GF	IP	BFP	H	R	ER	HR	SH	SF	HB	TBB	IBB	SO	WP	W	L	Pct	Sv-Op	Hld	Vel	OPS	ERC	ERA
2019	NYY	AL	1	0	0	2.0	9	2	1	0	0	0	0	0	0	0	1	0	0	0	-	0-0	0	92	.444	1.68	0.00

Scott Kingery

Bats: R Throws: R Pos: CF-65;3B-41;SS-18;2B-10;LF-10;PH-8;RF-1   Ht: 5'10" Wt: 180 Born: 4/29/1994 Age: 26

Year	Team	Lg	G	AB	H	2B	3B	HR	(Hm	Rd)	TB	R	RBI	RC	TBB	IBB	SO	HBP	SH	SF	SB	CS	GDP	Avg	OBP	Slg	OPS
2018	Phi	NL	147	452	102	23	2	8	(6	2)	153	55	35	39	24	1	126	3	0	5	10	3	2	.226	.267	.338	.605
2019	Phi	NL	126	458	118	34	4	19	(10	9)	217	64	55	63	34	1	147	5	1	2	15	4	3	.258	.315	.474	.788
2 ML YEARS			273	910	220	57	6	27	(16	11)	370	119	90	102	58	2	273	8	1	7	25	7	5	.242	.291	.407	.698

Nick Kingham

Pitches: R Bats: R Pos: RP-21; SP-4   Ht: 6'5" Wt: 235 Born: 11/8/1991 Age: 28

Year	Team	Lg	G	GS	GF	IP	BFP	H	R	ER	HR	SH	SF	HB	TBB	IBB	SO	WP	W	L	Pct	Sv-Op	Hld	Vel	OPS	ERC	ERA
2018	Pit	NL	18	15	1	76.0	342	79	50	44	18	4	2	5	26	3	69	3	5	7	.417	0-0	0	92	.837	5.07	5.21
2019	2 Tms		25	4	5	55.2	259	78	45	45	11	5	0	0	25	1	46	3	4	2	.667	1-1	0	92	1.004	7.63	7.28
19	Pit	NL	14	4	3	34.2	170	54	38	38	7	5	0	0	17	0	32	1	1	1	.500	1-1	0	91	1.079	8.47	9.87
19	Tor	AL	11	0	2	21.0	89	24	7	7	4	0	0	0	8	1	14	2	3	1	.750	0-0	0	92	.866	5.68	3.00
2 ML YEARS			43	19	6	131.2	601	157	95	89	29	9	2	5	51	4	115	6	9	9	.500	1-1	0	92	.908	6.11	6.08

Tyler Kinley

Pitches: R Bats: R Pos: RP-52   Ht: 6'4" Wt: 205 Born: 1/31/1991 Age: 29

Year	Team	Lg	G	GS	GF	IP	BFP	H	R	ER	HR	SH	SF	HB	TBB	IBB	SO	WP	W	L	Pct	Sv-Op	Hld	Vel	OPS	ERC	ERA
			HOW MUCH PITCHED					**WHAT HE GAVE UP**											**THE RESULTS**								
2019	NewOr	AAA	14	0	5	15.2	57	4	3	3	1	0	1	0	7	0	19	0	0	1	.000	2--	-	-	.356	0.90	1.72
2018	2 Tms		13	0	4	11.0	57	15	15	15	2	0	0	1	8	2	13	3	0	0	-	0-0	0	97	.942	8.25	12.27
2019	Mia	NL	52	0	13	49.1	221	43	20	20	5	1	2	1	36	2	46	3	3	1	.750	1-3	1	95	.723	4.71	3.65
18	Min	AL	4	0	3	3.1	23	9	9	9	2	0	0	0	4	0	4	2	0	0	-	0-0	0	96	1.407	25.66	24.30
18	Min	NL	9	0	1	7.2	34	6	6	6	0	0	0	1	4	2	9	1	0	0	-	0-0	0	97	.634	2.62	7.04
2 ML YEARS			65	0	17	60.1	278	58	35	35	7	1	2	2	44	4	59	6	3	1	.750	1-3	1	95	.768	5.32	5.22

Ian Kinsler

Bats: R Throws: R Pos: 2B-72;PH-19;PR-1   Ht: 6'0" Wt: 200 Born: 6/22/1982 Age: 38

Year	Team	Lg	G	AB	H	2B	3B	HR	(Hm	Rd)	TB	R	RBI	RC	TBB	IBB	SO	HBP	SH	SF	SB	CS	GDP	Avg	OBP	Slg	OPS
			BATTING																		**RUNNING**			**AVERAGES**			
2006	Tex	AL	120	423	121	27	1	14	(10	4)	192	65	55	65	40	1	64	3	1	7	11	4	12	.286	.347	.454	.801
2007	Tex	AL	130	483	127	22	2	20	(12	8)	213	96	61	79	62	2	83	9	8	4	23	2	14	.263	.355	.441	.796
2008	Tex	AL	121	518	165	41	4	18	(4	14)	268	102	71	106	45	1	67	6	7	7	26	2	12	.319	.375	.517	.892
2009	Tex	AL	144	566	143	32	4	31	(20	11)	276	101	86	99	59	0	77	6	3	6	31	5	9	.253	.327	.488	.814
2010	Tex	AL	103	391	112	20	1	9	(4	5)	161	73	45	59	56	2	57	7	2	4	15	5	11	.286	.382	.412	.794
2011	Tex	AL	155	620	158	34	4	32	(16	16)	296	121	77	100	89	2	71	8	4	2	30	4	17	.255	.355	.477	.832
2012	Tex	AL	157	655	168	42	5	19	(14	5)	277	105	72	83	60	0	90	10	1	5	21	9	14	.256	.326	.423	.749
2013	Tex	AL	136	545	151	31	2	13	(5	8)	225	85	72	84	51	0	59	8	3	7	15	11	5	.277	.344	.413	.757
2014	Det	AL	161	**684**	188	40	4	17	(9	8)	287	100	92	89	29	1	79	5	3	5	15	4	20	.275	.307	.420	.727
2015	Det	AL	154	624	185	35	7	11	(6	5)	267	94	73	81	43	0	80	3	0	5	10	6	13	.296	.342	.428	.770
2016	Det	AL	153	618	178	29	4	28	(13	15)	299	117	83	105	45	0	115	13	0	3	14	6	5	.288	.348	.484	.831
2017	Det	AL	139	551	130	25	3	22	(12	10)	227	90	52	68	55	2	86	7	0	0	14	5	9	.236	.313	.412	.725
2018	2 Tms		128	487	117	26	0	14	(7	7)	185	66	48	57	40	0	64	4	0	3	16	7	15	.240	.301	.380	.681
2019	SD	NL	87	258	56	12	0	9	(6	3)	95	28	22	23	19	0	54	3	0	1	2	4	5	.217	.278	.368	.646
18	LAA	AL	91	355	85	20	0	13	(7	6)	144	49	32	42	30	0	40	4	0	2	9	4	10	.239	.304	.406	.710
18	Bos	AL	37	132	32	6	0	1	(0	1)	41	17	16	15	10	0	24	0	0	1	7	3	5	.242	.294	.311	.604
Postseason			48	168	46	10	1	4	(1	3)	70	22	23	27	25	1	33	1	1	1	7	5	4	.274	.369	.417	.786
14 ML YEARS			1888	7423	1999	416	41	257	(138	119)	3268	1243	909	1098	693	11	1046	92	32	59	243	74	161	.269	.337	.440	.777

Brandon Kintzler

Pitches: R Bats: R Pos: RP-62   Ht: 6'0" Wt: 194 Born: 8/1/1984 Age: 35

Year	Team	Lg	G	GS	GF	IP	BFP	H	R	ER	HR	SH	SF	HB	TBB	IBB	SO	WP	W	L	Pct	Sv-Op	Hld	Vel	OPS	ERC	ERA
			HOW MUCH PITCHED					**WHAT HE GAVE UP**											**THE RESULTS**								
2010	Mil	NL	7	0	2	7.1	33	10	6	6	2	1	0	0	4	1	9	1	0	1	.000	0-0	0	93	1.045	8.67	7.36
2011	Mil	NL	9	0	3	14.2	61	14	9	6	3	0	2	0	3	0	15	0	1	1	.500	0-0	0	93	.725	3.65	3.68
2012	Mil	NL	14	0	1	16.2	72	18	7	7	1	0	0	0	7	1	14	1	3	0	1.000	0-0	2	93	.732	4.30	3.78
2013	Mil	NL	71	0	11	77.0	305	66	26	23	2	4	2	1	16	2	58	1	3	3	.500	0-4	26	92	.567	2.21	2.69
2014	Mil	NL	64	0	13	58.1	239	62	22	21	8	4	1	0	16	3	31	1	3	3	.500	0-3	8	92	.781	4.28	3.24
2015	Mil	NL	7	0	4	7.0	36	12	6	5	1	0	0	0	5	0	7	1	0	1	.000	0-0	0	91	1.021	10.76	6.43
2016	Min	AL	54	0	36	54.1	224	59	22	19	5	0	0	2	8	1	35	0	0	2	.000	17-20	1	93	.705	3.68	3.15
2017	2 Tms		72	0	45	71.2	288	66	25	24	5	1	2	3	16	2	39	1	4	3	.571	29-35	10	93	.638	2.99	3.03
2018	2 Tms	NL	70	0	15	60.2	263	67	31	31	5	1	2	4	22	5	43	1	3	3	.500	2-5	19	93	.787	4.62	4.60
2019	ChC	NL	62	0	10	57.0	227	45	18	17	5	0	1	4	13	3	48	0	3	3	.500	1-3	17	93	.632	2.47	2.68
17	Min	AL	45	0	41	45.1	182	41	15	14	3	0	2	2	11	1	27	1	2	2	.500	28-32	0	93	.626	2.97	2.78
17	Was	NL	27	0	4	26.0	106	25	10	10	2	1	0	1	5	1	12	0	2	1	.667	1-3	10	93	.659	3.04	3.46
18	Was	NL	45	0	8	42.2	175	40	17	17	2	1	0	3	13	3	31	1	1	2	.333	2-5	15	92	.689	3.28	3.59
18	ChC	NL	25	0	7	18.0	88	27	14	14	3	0	2	1	9	2	12	0	2	1	.667	0-0	4	93	.986	8.26	7.00
Postseason			3	0	1	3.1	12	1	2	2	0	1	0	1	2	0	2	0	0	1	.000	0-0	0	93	.614	1.96	5.40
10 ML YEARS			430	0	140	424.1	1748	419	172	159	37	11	10	14	110	18	299	7	20	20	.500	49-70	83	93	.697	3.51	3.37

Jason Kipnis

KIP-niss

Bats: L Throws: R Pos: 2B-117;DH-4   Ht: 5'11" Wt: 200 Born: 4/3/1987 Age: 33

Year	Team	Lg	G	AB	H	2B	3B	HR	(Hm	Rd)	TB	R	RBI	RC	TBB	IBB	SO	HBP	SH	SF	SB	CS	GDP	Avg	OBP	Slg	OPS
			BATTING																		**RUNNING**			**AVERAGES**			
2011	Cle	AL	36	136	37	9	1	7	(3	4)	69	24	19	22	11	0	34	2	0	1	5	0	0	.272	.333	.507	.841
2012	Cle	AL	152	591	152	22	4	14	(5	9)	224	86	76	88	67	2	109	5	3	6	31	7	12	.257	.335	.379	.714
2013	Cle	AL	149	564	160	36	4	17	(7	10)	255	86	84	99	76	3	143	3	5	10	30	7	10	.284	.366	.452	.818
2014	Cle	AL	129	500	120	25	1	6	(3	3)	165	61	41	44	50	2	100	2	1	2	22	3	15	.240	.310	.330	.640
2015	Cle	AL	141	565	171	43	7	9	(6	3)	255	86	52	92	57	6	107	9	4	6	12	8	5	.303	.372	.451	.823
2016	Cle	AL	156	610	168	41	4	23	(13	10)	286	91	82	90	60	0	146	6	5	7	15	3	21	.275	.343	.469	.811
2017	Cle	AL	90	336	78	25	0	12	(5	7)	139	43	35	42	28	0	71	2	2	5	6	2	0	.232	.291	.414	.705
2018	Cle	AL	147	530	122	28	1	18	(13	5)	206	65	75	80	60	1	112	7	1	3	7	1	5	.230	.315	.389	.704
2019	Cle	AL	121	458	112	23	1	17	(6	11)	188	52	65	63	40	2	88	2	5	6	7	2	7	.245	.304	.410	.715
Postseason			24	96	19	3	1	4	(2	2)	36	9	9	9	2	0	30	1	0	0	0	0	1	.198	.222	.375	.597
9 ML YEARS			1121	4290	1120	252	23	123	(61	62)	1787	594	529	620	449	16	910	38	26	46	135	33	75	.261	.333	.417	.750

Andrew Kittredge

Pitches: R Bats: R Pos: RP-30; SP-7   Ht: 6'1" Wt: 235 Born: 3/17/1990 Age: 30

Year Team	Lg	G	GS	GF	IP	BFP	H	R	ER	HR	SH	SF	HB	TBB	IBB	SO	WP	W	L	Pct	Sv-Op	Hld	Vel	OPS	ERC	ERA
		HOW MUCH PITCHED					**WHAT HE GAVE UP**											**THE RESULTS**								
2019 Drham	AAA	27	1	19	37.1	142	24	9	8	3	1	1	2	6	1	55	1	2	1	.667	6- -	-		.500	1.55	1.93
2017 TB	AL	15	0	2	15.1	66	13	4	3	2	1	0	0	6	1	14	1	0	1	.000	0-0	1	94	.665	3.19	1.76
2018 TB	AL	33	3	4	38.1	181	54	34	33	7	1	2	1	17	5	30	1	3	2	.600	0-0	0	93	.956	7.35	7.75
2019 TB	AL	37	7	10	49.2	210	51	25	23	7	0	2	2	12	0	58	2	1	0	1.000	0-0	2	95	.717	4.03	4.17
3 ML YEARS		85	10	16	103.1	457	118	63	59	16	2	4	3	35	6	102	4	4	3	.571	0-0	3	94	.803	5.05	5.14

Branden Kline

Pitches: R Bats: R Pos: RP-34   Ht: 6'3" Wt: 210 Born: 9/29/1991 Age: 28

Year Team	Lg	G	GS	GF	IP	BFP	H	R	ER	HR	SH	SF	HB	TBB	IBB	SO	WP	W	L	Pct	Sv-Op	Hld	Vel	OPS	ERC	ERA
		HOW MUCH PITCHED					**WHAT HE GAVE UP**											**THE RESULTS**								
2019 Norfolk	AAA	18	0	7	21.0	101	27	17	16	4	0	0	0	13	0	27	3	1	1	.500	2- -	-		.907	7.45	6.86
2019 Bal	AL	34	0	8	41.0	183	44	28	27	9	1	1	1	19	0	34	3	1	4	.200	0-1	5	96	.860	5.76	5.93

Corey Kluber

Pos: SP-7   CLUE-burr   Ht: 6'4" Wt: 215 Born: 4/10/1986 Age: 34
Pitches: R Bats: R

Year Team	Lg	G	GS	GF	IP	BFP	H	R	ER	HR	SH	SF	HB	TBB	IBB	SO	WP	W	L	Pct	Sv-Op	Hld	Vel	OPS	ERC	ERA
		HOW MUCH PITCHED					**WHAT HE GAVE UP**											**THE RESULTS**								
2011 Cle	AL	3	0	2	4.1	25	6	4	4	0	0	0	2	3	0	5	1	0	0	-	0-0	0	92	.740	8.12	8.31
2012 Cle	AL	12	12	0	63.0	281	76	44	36	9	1	0	4	18	0	54	2	2	5	.286	0-0	0	93	.834	5.38	5.14
2013 Cle	AL	26	24	1	147.1	608	153	67	63	15	4	2	5	33	0	136	1	11	5	.688	0-0	0	93	.729	3.83	3.85
2014 Cle	AL	34	**34**	0	235.2	951	207	72	64	14	5	2	6	51	3	269	3	**18**	9	.667	0-0	0	93	.624	2.57	2.44
2015 Cle	AL	32	32	0	222.0	886	189	92	86	22	7	4	11	45	3	245	6	9	**16**	.360	0-0	0	93	.650	2.74	3.49
2016 Cle	AL	32	32	0	215.0	860	170	82	75	22	6	2	7	57	1	227	5	18	9	.667	0-0	0	92	.631	2.62	3.14
2017 Cle	AL	29	29	0	203.2	777	141	56	51	21	3	1	5	36	2	265	4	**18**	4	.818	0-0	0	93	.556	**1.83**	**2.25**
2018 Cle	AL	33	33	0	**215.0**	842	179	75	69	25	2	2	3	34	0	222	2	20	7	.741	0-0	0	92	.624	2.47	2.89
2019 Cle	AL	7	7	0	35.2	168	44	26	23	4	1	1	3	15	0	38	1	2	3	.400	0-0	0	92	.824	5.87	5.80
Postseason		9	9	0	45.1	194	44	20	20	10	0	1	5	13	0	47	0	4	3	.571	0-0	0	92	.787	4.75	3.97
9 ML YEARS		208	203	3	1341.2	5398	1165	518	471	132	29	14	46	292	9	1461	25	98	58	.628	0-0	0	93	.649	2.82	3.16

Andrew Knapp

Bats: B Throws: R Pos: C-43;PH-34;1B-1   Ht: 6'1" Wt: 195 Born: 11/9/1991 Age: 28

Year Team	Lg	G	AB	H	2B	3B	HR	(Hm	Rd)	TB	R	RBI	RC	TBB	IBB	SO	HBP	SH	SF	SB	CS	GDP	Avg	OBP	Slg	OPS
		BATTING																		**RUNNING**			**AVERAGES**			
2017 Phi	NL	56	171	44	8	1	3	(2	1)	63	26	13	20	31	4	56	0	0	2	1	0	5	.257	.368	.368	.736
2018 Phi	NL	84	187	37	6	2	4	(1	3)	59	19	15	15	24	1	75	2	1	1	1	0	2	.198	.294	.316	.610
2019 Phi	NL	74	136	29	9	0	2	(0	2)	44	12	8	11	18	2	51	3	3	0	0	0	2	.213	.318	.324	.642
3 ML YEARS		214	494	110	23	3	9	(3	6)	166	57	36	46	73	7	182	5	4	3	2	0	9	.223	.327	.336	.663

Corey Knebel

Pitches: R Bats: R Pos: P   kuh-NAY-bull   Ht: 6'4" Wt: 220 Born: 11/26/1991 Age: 28

Year Team	Lg	G	GS	GF	IP	BFP	H	R	ER	HR	SH	SF	HB	TBB	IBB	SO	WP	W	L	Pct	Sv-Op	Hld	Vel	OPS	ERC	ERA
		HOW MUCH PITCHED					**WHAT HE GAVE UP**											**THE RESULTS**								
2014 Det	AL	8	0	4	8.2	39	11	7	6	0	0	0	0	3	0	11	1	0	0	-	0-0	0	94	.776	4.65	6.23
2015 Mil	NL	48	0	15	50.1	209	44	18	18	8	0	0	2	17	1	58	1	0	0	-	0-1	3	95	.744	3.69	3.22
2016 Mil	NL	35	0	7	32.2	145	32	20	17	3	0	1	1	16	3	38	1	1	4	.200	2-4	13	95	.708	4.18	4.68
2017 Mil	NL	76	0	48	76.0	309	48	15	15	6	0	0	2	40	5	126	2	1	4	.200	39-45	11	97	.568	2.51	1.78
2018 Mil	NL	57	0	29	55.1	223	38	23	22	7	0	1	4	22	0	88	0	4	3	.571	16-19	6	97	.659	2.90	3.58
Postseason		9	0	1	10.0	33	2	1	1	0	0	0	1	3	0	14	0	1	0	1.000	1-1	3	97	.320	0.55	0.90
5 ML YEARS		224	0	103	223.0	925	173	83	78	24	0	2	9	98	9	321	5	6	11	.353	57-69	33	96	.662	3.19	3.15

Andrew Knizner

Bats: R Throws: R Pos: C-16;PH-2;PR-2;1B-1   KIZZ-ner   Ht: 6'1" Wt: 200 Born: 2/3/1995 Age: 25

Year Team	Lg	G	AB	H	2B	3B	HR	(Hm	Rd)	TB	R	RBI	RC	TBB	IBB	SO	HBP	SH	SF	SB	CS	GDP	Avg	OBP	Slg	OPS
		BATTING																		**RUNNING**			**AVERAGES**			
2019 Memp	AAA	66	246	68	10	0	12	(-	-)	114	41	34	42	24	1	37	8	0	2	2	0	6	.276	.357	.463	.821
2019 StL	NL	18	53	12	2	0	2	(1	1)	20	7	7	7	4	0	14	1	0	0	2	0	3	.226	.293	.377	.670

Matt Koch

Pitches: R Bats: L Pos: RP-9   cook   Ht: 6'3" Wt: 215 Born: 11/2/1990 Age: 29

Year Team	Lg	G	GS	GF	IP	BFP	H	R	ER	HR	SH	SF	HB	TBB	IBB	SO	WP	W	L	Pct	Sv-Op	Hld	Vel	OPS	ERC	ERA
		HOW MUCH PITCHED					**WHAT HE GAVE UP**											**THE RESULTS**								
2019 Reno	AAA	21	17	1	100.0	464	135	86	82	21	3	3	2	30	0	81	4	5	10	.333	0- -	-		.940	6.57	7.38
2016 Ari	NL	7	2	4	18.0	69	9	4	4	1	1	0	2	4	0	10	0	1	1	.500	1-1	0	92	.463	1.29	2.00
2017 Ari	NL	1	0	0	0.0	3	2	3	3	0	0	0	0	1	0	0	0	0	0	-	0-0	0	92	2.500		
2018 Ari	NL	19	14	4	86.2	360	88	43	40	19	2	1	6	22	1	50	3	5	5	.500	0-0	0	91	.816	4.79	4.15
2019 Ari	NL	9	0	5	20.2	96	29	21	21	8	0	0	5	4	0	9	1	0	0	-	0-0	0	92	1.097	9.26	9.15
4 ML YEARS		36	16	13	125.1	528	128	71	68	28	3	1	13	31	1	69	4	6	6	.500	1-1	0	92	.830	4.95	4.88

Adam Kolarek

Pitches: L Bats: L Pos: RP-80   **Ht: 6'3" Wt: 215 Born: 1/14/1989 Age: 31**

Year Team	Lg	G	GS	GF	IP	BFP	H	R	ER	HR	SH	SF	HB	TBB	IBB	SO	WP	W	L	Pct	Sv-Op	Hld	Vel	OPS	ERC	ERA
2017 TB	AL	12	0	5	8.1	40	9	6	6	2	1	0	4	4	2	4	1	1	0	1.000	0-0	2	88	.984	7.84	6.48
2018 TB	AL	31	0	5	34.1	141	38	15	15	0	0	1	1	5	1	19	0	1	0	1.000	2-4	10	90	.685	3.14	3.93
2019 2 Tms		80	0	18	55.0	229	48	22	20	7	0	0	3	16	4	45	1	6	3	.667	1-1	17	89	.669	3.23	3.27
19 TB	AL	54	0	15	43.1	184	39	19	19	6	0	0	3	14	4	36	1	4	3	.571	1-1	14	89	.700	3.58	3.95
19 LAD	NL	26	0	3	11.2	45	9	3	1	1	0	0	0	2	0	9	0	2	0	1.000	0-0	3	89	.547	2.01	0.77
3 ML YEARS		123	0	28	97.2	410	95	43	41	9	1	1	8	25	7	68	2	8	3	.727	3-5	29	89	.702	3.54	3.78

Michael Kopech

Pitches: R Bats: R Pos: P   **Ht: 6'3" Wt: 205 Born: 4/30/1996 Age: 24**

Year Team	Lg	G	GS	GF	IP	BFP	H	R	ER	HR	SH	SF	HB	TBB	IBB	SO	WP	W	L	Pct	Sv-Op	Hld	Vel	OPS	ERC	ERA
2015 Grnvlle	A	16	15	0	65.0	270	53	25	19	2	1	2	8	27	0	70	2	4	5	.444	0- -	-		.646	3.22	2.63
2016 2 Tms	Low	12	12	0	56.1	225	29	15	13	1	0	1	5	33	0	86	11	4	1	.800	0- -	-		.497	2.11	2.08
2017 Brham	AA	22	22	0	119.1	488	77	45	38	6	0	3	6	60	0	155	8	8	7	.533	0- -	-		.570	2.48	2.87
2018 Charltt	AAA	24	24	0	126.1	543	101	58	52	9	3	6	13	60	0	170	12	7	7	.500	0- -	-		.658	3.45	3.70

Kevin Kramer

Bats: L Throws: R Pos: PH-8;LF-7;RF-7;2B-3   **Ht: 6'0" Wt: 200 Born: 10/3/1993 Age: 26**

Year Team	Lg	G	AB	H	2B	3B	HR	(Hm	Rd)	TB	R	RBI	RC	TBB	IBB	SO	HBP	SH	SF	SB	CS	GDP	Avg	OBP	Slg	OPS
2019 Indy	AAA	113	393	102	30	1	10	(-	-)	164	49	54	57	43	0	116	5	0	7	4	5	7	.260	.335	.417	.752
2018 Pit	NL	21	37	5	0	0	0	(0	0)	5	5	4	1	2	0	20	0	0	1	0	0	0	.135	.175	.135	.310
2019 Pit	NL	22	42	7	1	0	0	(0	0)	8	5	5	3	6	0	17	0	0	2	0	1	0	.167	.260	.190	.450
2 ML YEARS		43	79	12	1	0	0	(0	0)	13	10	9	4	8	0	37	0	0	3	0	1	0	.152	.222	.165	.387

Erik Kratz

Bats: R Throws: R Pos: C-17;PH-4   **Ht: 6'4" Wt: 250 Born: 6/15/1980 Age: 40**

Year Team	Lg	G	AB	H	2B	3B	HR	(Hm	Rd)	TB	R	RBI	RC	TBB	IBB	SO	HBP	SH	SF	SB	CS	GDP	Avg	OBP	Slg	OPS
2019 S-WB	AAA	46	154	46	10	0	7	(-	-)	77	27	31	29	17	0	21	3	0	2	1	0	8	.299	.375	.500	.875
2010 Pit	NL	9	34	4	0	0	0	(0	0)	4	2	1	0	2	0	9	0	0	0	0	0	0	.118	.167	.118	.284
2011 Phi	NL	2	6	2	1	0	0	(0	0)	3	0	0	1	0	0	1	0	0	0	0	0	0	.333	.333	.500	.833
2012 Phi	NL	50	141	35	9	0	9	(6	3)	71	14	26	20	11	2	34	2	0	3	0	0	2	.248	.306	.504	.809
2013 Phi	NL	68	197	42	7	0	9	(5	4)	76	21	26	15	18	4	45	1	0	2	0	0	11	.213	.280	.386	.666
2014 2 Tms	AL	47	110	24	4	0	5	(1	4)	43	12	13	7	4	1	22	0	0	1	0	0	4	.218	.243	.391	.634
2015 2 Tms		16	26	5	2	0	0	(0	0)	7	3	3	1	1	0	5	0	0	1	0	0	0	.192	.214	.269	.484
2016 2 Tms		33	85	8	2	0	1	(1	0)	13	3	4	0	1	0	32	0	1	0	0	0	3	.094	.105	.153	.258
2017 NYY	AL	4	2	2	1	0	0	(0	0)	3	0	2	2	0	0	0	0	0	0	0	0	0	1.000	1.000	1.500	2.500
2018 Mil	NL	67	203	48	6	0	6	(2	4)	72	18	23	16	6	0	40	7	1	2	1	0	8	.236	.280	.355	.634
2019 2 Tms		21	49	5	2	0	1	(1	0)	10	1	3	2	2	0	14	2	0	0	0	0	0	.102	.170	.204	.374
14 Tor	AL	34	81	16	3	0	3	(1	2)	28	8	10	5	3	0	12	0	0	0	0	0	3	.198	.226	.346	.572
14 KC	AL	13	29	8	1	0	2	(0	2)	15	4	3	2	1	1	10	0	0	1	0	0	1	.276	.290	.517	.808
15 KC	AL	4	4	0	0	0	0	(0	0)	0	0	0	1	0	0	2	0	0	1	0	0	0	.000	.000	.000	.000
15 Phi	NL	12	22	5	2	0	0	(0	0)	7	3	2	1	1	0	3	0	0	0	0	0	0	.227	.261	.318	.579
16 Hou	AL	15	29	2	1	0	0	(0	0)	3	0	0	0	1	0	14	0	0	0	0	0	1	.069	.100	.103	.203
16 Pit	NL	18	56	6	1	0	1	(1	0)	10	3	4	0	0	0	18	0	1	0	0	0	2	.107	.107	.179	.286
19 SF	NL	15	32	4	2	0	1	(1	0)	9	1	3	2	2	0	6	2	0	0	0	0	0	.125	.222	.281	.503
19 TB	AL	6	17	1	0	0	0	(0	0)	1	0	0	0	0	0	8	0	0	0	0	0	0	.059	.059	.059	.118
Postseason		9	24	7	2	0	0	(0	0)	9	2	3	2	1	0	6	1	0	0	0	0	1	.292	.346	.375	.721
10 ML YEARS		317	853	175	34	0	31	(16	15)	302	74	101	64	45	7	202	12	2	9	1	0	28	.205	.252	.354	.606

Chad Kuhl

Pitches: R Bats: R Pos: P   cool   **Ht: 6'3" Wt: 216 Born: 9/10/1992 Age: 27**

Year Team	Lg	G	GS	GF	IP	BFP	H	R	ER	HR	SH	SF	HB	TBB	IBB	SO	WP	W	L	Pct	Sv-Op	Hld	Vel	OPS	ERC	ERA
2016 Pit	NL	14	14	0	70.2	301	73	34	33	7	2	2	4	20	0	53	2	5	4	.556	0-0	0	93	.757	4.04	4.20
2017 Pit	NL	31	31	0	157.1	680	159	81	76	17	6	4	6	72	7	142	8	8	11	.421	0-0	0	96	.793	4.60	4.35
2018 Pit	NL	16	16	0	85.0	373	89	47	43	14	6	6	4	33	1	81	7	5	5	.500	0-0	0	95	.806	4.94	4.55
3 ML YEARS		61	61	0	313.0	1354	321	162	152	38	14	12	14	125	8	276	17	18	20	.474	0-0	0	95	.788	4.57	4.37

Joel Kuhnel

Pitches: R Bats: R Pos: RP-11   **Ht: 6'5" Wt: 260 Born: 2/19/1995 Age: 25**

Year Team	Lg	G	GS	GF	IP	BFP	H	R	ER	HR	SH	SF	HB	TBB	IBB	SO	WP	W	L	Pct	Sv-Op	Hld	Vel	OPS	ERC	ERA
2019 Chatt	AA	25	0	17	35.2	142	26	10	9	5	0	5	0	8	3	30	2	3	2	.600	10- -	-		.581	2.10	2.27
2019 Lsvlle	AAA	16	0	11	18.0	73	13	5	4	1	0	0	0	8	0	20	1	2	1	.667	4- -	-		.580	2.52	2.00
2019 Cin	NL	11	0	2	9.2	42	8	5	5	1	0	0	0	5	0	9	0	1	0	1.000	0-0	1	96	.634	3.53	4.66

Tommy La Stella

Bats: L **Throws:** R **Pos:** 2B-46;3B-30;PH-4;1B-3;DH-3;PR-1   **Ht:** 5'11" **Wt:** 180 **Born:** 1/31/1989 **Age:** 31

Year	Team	Lg	G	AB	H	2B	3B	HR	(Hm	Rd)	TB	R	RBI	RC	TBB	IBB	SO	HBP	SH	SF	SB	CS	GDP	Avg	OBP	Slg	OPS
2014	Atl	NL	93	319	80	16	1	1	(1	0)	101	22	31	36	36	2	40	1	3	1	2	1	8	.251	.328	.317	.644
2015	ChC	NL	33	67	18	6	0	1	(1	0)	27	4	11	10	5	0	7	1	0	1	2	0	1	.269	.324	.403	.727
2016	ChC	NL	74	148	40	12	1	2	(1	1)	60	17	11	20	18	1	27	2	0	0	0	1	2	.270	.357	.405	.763
2017	ChC	NL	73	125	36	8	0	5	(0	5)	59	18	22	24	20	1	18	2	0	2	0	0	3	.288	.389	.472	.861
2018	ChC	NL	123	169	45	8	0	1	(0	1)	56	23	19	17	17	1	27	2	0	0	0	1	5	.266	.340	.331	.672
2019	LAA	AL	80	292	86	8	0	16	(11	5)	142	49	44	43	20	0	28	3	0	0	0	0	8	.295	.346	.486	.832
	Postseason		12	13	0	0	0	0	(0	0)	0	0	0	0	1	0	4	0	0	0	0	0	0	.000	.071	.000	.071
	6 ML YEARS		476	1120	305	58	2	26	(14	12)	445	133	138	150	116	5	147	11	3	4	4	3	27	.272	.345	.397	.743

Juan Lagares

Bats: R **Throws:** R **Pos:** CF-125;PH-14;PR-9   luh-GAR-ess   **Ht:** 6'1" **Wt:** 215 **Born:** 3/17/1989 **Age:** 31

Year	Team	Lg	G	AB	H	2B	3B	HR	(Hm	Rd)	TB	R	RBI	RC	TBB	IBB	SO	HBP	SH	SF	SB	CS	GDP	Avg	OBP	Slg	OPS
2013	NYM	NL	121	392	95	21	5	4	(1	3)	138	35	34	36	20	4	96	2	5	2	6	3	6	.242	.281	.352	.633
2014	NYM	NL	116	416	117	24	3	4	(2	2)	159	46	47	53	20	1	87	7	3	6	13	4	6	.281	.321	.382	.703
2015	NYM	NL	143	441	114	16	5	6	(2	4)	158	47	41	51	16	2	87	4	1	3	7	3	6	.259	.289	.358	.647
2016	NYM	NL	79	142	34	7	2	3	(2	1)	54	15	9	12	11	1	27	2	4	1	4	2	4	.239	.301	.380	.682
2017	NYM	NL	94	252	63	16	2	3	(1	2)	92	37	15	20	14	0	56	3	2	1	7	3	6	.250	.296	.365	.661
2018	NYM	NL	30	59	20	1	1	0	(0	0)	23	9	6	10	3	1	9	1	0	1	3	1	2	.339	.375	.390	.765
2019	NYM	NL	133	258	55	12	1	5	(2	3)	84	38	27	23	22	4	75	2	2	1	4	1	8	.213	.279	.326	.605
	Postseason		13	23	8	2	0	0	(0	0)	10	7	0	3	1	0	3	0	1	0	2	0	0	.348	.375	.435	.810
	7 ML YEARS		716	1960	498	97	19	25	(10	15)	708	227	179	205	106	13	437	21	17	15	44	17	38	.254	.297	.361	.659

Brady Lail

Pitches: R **Bats:** R **Pos:** RP-1   **Ht:** 6'2" **Wt:** 205 **Born:** 8/9/1993 **Age:** 26

	HOW MUCH PITCHED						WHAT HE GAVE UP										THE RESULTS							
Year	Team	Lg	G	GS	GF	IP	BFP	H	R	ER	HR	SH	SF	HB	TBB	IBB	SO	WP	W	L	Pct	Sv-Op Hld	Vel	OPS	ERC	ERA
2019	S-WB	AAA	11	0	6	15.2	71	19	14	13	3	0	1	3	3	0	17	0	1	1	.500	0-- -	-	.883	5.89	7.47
2019	Trntn	AA	14	1	6	31.0	121	18	6	6	1	1	0	0	12	0	47	1	3	1	.750	1-- -	-	.491	1.58	1.74
2019	NYY	AL	1	0	0	2.2	10	2	3	3	1	0	0	0	1	0	2	0	0	0	-	0-0 0	92	.856	4.74	10.13

Travis Lakins

Pitches: R **Bats:** R **Pos:** RP-13; SP-3   **Ht:** 6'1" **Wt:** 180 **Born:** 6/29/1994 **Age:** 26

	HOW MUCH PITCHED						WHAT HE GAVE UP										THE RESULTS							
Year	Team	Lg	G	GS	GF	IP	BFP	H	R	ER	HR	SH	SF	HB	TBB	IBB	SO	WP	W	L	Pct	Sv-Op Hld	Vel	OPS	ERC	ERA
2019	Pwtckt	AAA	40	1	16	45.0	201	46	25	23	4	2	0	2	23	1	42	5	3	4	.429	6-- -	-	.753	4.71	4.60
2019	Bos	AL	16	3	4	23.1	102	23	11	10	1	0	2	1	10	1	18	1	0	1	.000	0-0 1	94	.738	3.78	3.86

Ryan LaMarre

Bats: R **Throws:** L **Pos:** CF-12;RF-2;PH-2;DH-1   la-MARR   **Ht:** 6'1" **Wt:** 210 **Born:** 11/21/1988 **Age:** 31

Year	Team	Lg	G	AB	H	2B	3B	HR	(Hm	Rd)	TB	R	RBI	RC	TBB	IBB	SO	HBP	SH	SF	SB	CS	GDP	Avg	OBP	Slg	OPS
2019	Gwnntt	AAA	112	405	126	24	8	9	(-	-)	193	55	53	74	38	0	118	9	0	3	19	9	7	.311	.380	.477	.857
2015	Cin	NL	21	25	2	0	0	0	(0	0)	2	2	0	0	0	0	9	0	1	0	0	0	1	.080	.080	.080	.160
2016	Bos	AL	6	5	0	0	0	0	(0	0)	0	1	0	0	1	0	2	0	0	0	0	0	1	.000	.167	.000	.167
2017	Oak	AL	3	7	0	0	0	0	(0	0)	0	0	0	0	1	0	3	0	0	0	0	0	0	.000	.125	.000	.125
2018	2 Tms	AL	76	165	46	11	0	2	(0	2)	63	15	18	19	10	0	53	2	0	3	2	2	3	.279	.322	.382	.704
2019	Min	AL	14	23	5	0	0	2	(1	1)	11	3	3	3	3	0	5	0	0	0	1	1	0	.217	.308	.478	.786
18	Min	AL	43	99	26	5	0	0	(0	0)	31	7	8	11	8	0	33	1	0	1	1	1	3	.263	.321	.313	.634
18	CWS	AL	33	66	20	6	0	2	(0	2)	32	8	10	8	2	0	20	1	0	2	1	1	0	.303	.324	.485	.809
	5 ML YEARS		120	225	53	11	0	4	(1	3)	76	21	21	22	15	0	72	2	1	3	3	3	5	.236	.286	.338	.623

Jake Lamb

Bats: L **Throws:** R **Pos:** 3B-36;1B-24;PH-24;DH-1   **Ht:** 6'3" **Wt:** 215 **Born:** 10/9/1990 **Age:** 29

Year	Team	Lg	G	AB	H	2B	3B	HR	(Hm	Rd)	TB	R	RBI	RC	TBB	IBB	SO	HBP	SH	SF	SB	CS	GDP	Avg	OBP	Slg	OPS
2019	Reno	AAA	12	39	7	2	0	1	(-	-)	12	5	7	4	7	0	12	0	0	0	0	0	0	.179	.304	.308	.612
2014	Ari	NL	37	126	29	4	1	4	(2	2)	47	15	11	7	6	0	37	0	1	0	1	1	4	.230	.263	.373	.636
2015	Ari	NL	107	350	92	15	5	6	(1	5)	135	38	34	39	36	3	97	1	0	3	3	2	5	.263	.331	.386	.716
2016	Ari	NL	151	523	130	31	9	29	(19	10)	266	81	91	84	64	5	154	3	0	4	6	1	13	.249	.332	.509	.840
2017	Ari	NL	149	536	133	30	4	30	(16	14)	261	89	105	90	87	13	152	7	0	5	6	4	15	.248	.357	.487	.844
2018	Ari	NL	56	207	46	8	0	6	(3	3)	72	34	31	26	26	0	65	1	0	4	1	2	4	.222	.307	.348	.655
2019	Ari	NL	78	187	36	8	2	6	(3	3)	66	26	30	27	32	1	55	5	0	2	1	0	4	.193	.323	.353	.676
	Postseason		4	13	6	0	0	0	(0	0)	6	4	0	1	0	0	2	0	0	0	0	0	0	.462	.462	.462	.923
	6 ML YEARS		578	1929	466	96	21	81	(44	37)	847	283	302	273	251	22	560	17	0	19	18	10	45	.242	.331	.439	.770

Peter Lambert

Pitches: R Bats: R Pos: SP-19 Ht: 6'2" Wt: 185 Born: 4/18/1997 Age: 23

Year Team	Lg	G	GS	GF	IP	BFP	H	R	ER	HR	SH	SF	HB	TBB	IBB	SO	WP	W	L	Pct	Sv-Op	Hld	Vel	OPS	ERC	ERA
2019 Albq	AAA	11	11	0	60.1	257	63	34	34	10	0	2	0	16	0	51	3	2	2	.500	0- -	-	-	.751	4.20	5.07
2019 Col	NL	19	19	0	89.1	420	119	74	72	18	4	3	6	36	3	57	5	3	7	.300	0-0	0	93	.958	7.11	7.25

Dinelson Lamet

Pitches: R Bats: R Pos: SP-14 Ht: 6'4" Wt: 187 Born: 7/18/1992 Age: 27

Year Team	Lg	G	GS	GF	IP	BFP	H	R	ER	HR	SH	SF	HB	TBB	IBB	SO	WP	W	L	Pct	Sv-Op	Hld	Vel	OPS	ERC	ERA
2017 SD	NL	21	21	0	114.1	485	88	63	58	18	1	5	6	54	2	139	9	7	8	.467	0-0	0	95	.707	3.64	4.57
2019 SD	NL	14	14	0	73.0	313	62	38	33	12	2	2	5	30	0	105	6	3	5	.375	0-0	0	96	.721	3.95	4.07
2 ML YEARS		35	35	0	187.1	798	150	101	91	30	3	7	11	84	2	244	15	10	13	.435	0-0	0	95	.712	3.76	4.37

Eric Lauer

Pitches: L Bats: R Pos: SP-29; RP-1 Ht: 6'3" Wt: 205 Born: 6/3/1995 Age: 25

Year Team	Lg	G	GS	GF	IP	BFP	H	R	ER	HR	SH	SF	HB	TBB	IBB	SO	WP	W	L	Pct	Sv-Op	Hld	Vel	OPS	ERC	ERA
2018 SD	NL	23	23	0	112.0	504	127	61	54	15	4	2	6	46	2	100	2	6	7	.462	0-0	0	91	.800	5.33	4.34
2019 SD	NL	30	29	0	149.2	651	158	82	74	20	3	3	5	51	4	138	4	8	10	.444	0-0	0	92	.760	4.47	4.45
2 ML YEARS		53	52	0	261.2	1155	285	143	128	35	7	5	11	97	6	238	6	14	17	.452	0-0	0	92	.777	4.83	4.40

Ramon Laureano

Bats: R Throws: R Pos: CF-110; RF-13; PH-3 Ht: 5'11" Wt: 200 Born: 7/15/1994 Age: 25

Year Team	Lg	G	AB	H	2B	3B	HR	(Hm	Rd)	TB	R	RBI	RC	TBB	IBB	SO	HBP	SH	SF	SB	CS	GDP	Avg	OBP	Slg	OPS
2018 Oak	AL	48	156	45	12	1	5	(4	1)	74	27	19	29	16	0	50	2	0	2	7	1	0	.288	.358	.474	.832
2019 Oak	AL	123	434	125	29	0	24	(13	11)	226	79	67	69	27	0	123	11	1	8	13	2	7	.288	.340	.521	.860
Postseason		1	3	0	0	0	0	(0	0)	0	0	0	0	1	0	2	0	0	0	0	0	0	.000	.250	.000	.250
2 ML YEARS		171	590	170	41	1	29	(17	12)	300	106	86	98	43	0	173	13	1	10	20	3	7	.288	.345	.508	.853

Ryan Lavarnway

luh-VARN-way

Bats: R Throws: R Pos: C-5 Ht: 6'4" Wt: 240 Born: 8/7/1987 Age: 32

Year Team	Lg	G	AB	H	2B	3B	HR	(Hm	Rd)	TB	R	RBI	RC	TBB	IBB	SO	HBP	SH	SF	SB	CS	GDP	Avg	OBP	Slg	OPS
2019 S-WB	AAA	35	108	23	2	0	3	(-	-)	34	13	19	13	17	0	26	3	0	1	0	0	3	.213	.333	.315	.648
2019 Lsvlle	AAA	13	40	9	2	0	3	(-	-)	20	6	7	6	6	0	9	0	0	1	0	0	4	.225	.319	.500	.819
2011 Bos	AL	17	39	9	2	0	2	(0	2)	17	5	8	4	4	0	10	0	0	0	0	0	1	.231	.302	.436	.738
2012 Bos	AL	46	153	24	8	0	2	(0	2)	38	11	12	4	11	0	41	0	0	2	0	0	4	.157	.211	.248	.459
2013 Bos	AL	25	77	23	7	0	1	(1	0)	33	8	14	11	2	0	17	2	0	1	0	0	3	.299	.329	.429	.758
2014 Bos	AL	9	10	0	0	0	0	(0	0)	0	0	0	0	0	0	3	0	0	1	0	0	1	.000	.000	.000	.000
2015 2 Tms		37	94	18	6	0	2	(0	2)	30	6	6	4	12	1	28	0	0	0	0	0	5	.191	.283	.319	.602
2017 Oak	AL	6	11	3	1	0	0	(0	0)	4	0	2	2	1	0	3	1	0	0	0	0	0	.273	.385	.364	.748
2018 Pit	NL	6	6	4	1	0	0	(0	0)	5	1	1	2	0	0	1	0	0	0	0	0	0	.667	.667	.833	1.500
2019 Cin	NL	5	18	5	2	0	2	(2	0)	13	4	7	5	1	0	5	0	0	0	0	0	0	.278	.316	.722	1.038
15 Bal	AL	10	28	3	1	0	0	(0	0)	4	1	0	0	4	0	7	0	0	0	0	0	4	.107	.219	.143	.362
15 Atl	NL	27	66	15	5	0	2	(0	2)	26	5	6	4	8	1	21	0	0	0	0	0	1	.227	.311	.394	.705
8 ML YEARS		151	408	86	27	0	9	(3	6)	140	35	50	32	31	1	108	3	0	3	0	0	15	.211	.270	.343	.613

Derek Law

Pitches: R Bats: R Pos: RP-54; SP-4 Ht: 6'3" Wt: 215 Born: 9/14/1990 Age: 29

Year Team	Lg	G	GS	GF	IP	BFP	H	R	ER	HR	SH	SF	HB	TBB	IBB	SO	WP	W	L	Pct	Sv-Op	Hld	Vel	OPS	ERC	ERA
2019 Buffalo	AAA	8	0	5	10.2	42	7	3	2	1	0	0	0	3	0	17	1	2	1	.667	2- -	-	-	.495	1.84	1.69
2016 SF	NL	61	0	12	55.0	214	44	13	13	5	0	0	0	9	0	50	1	4	2	.667	1-2	14	93	.570	1.93	2.13
2017 SF	NL	41	0	12	37.1	168	45	21	21	5	2	2	2	14	2	35	5	4	1	.800	4-6	5	94	.840	5.60	5.06
2018 SF	NL	7	0	4	13.1	66	16	13	11	2	0	1	1	8	0	12	1	1	0	1.000	0-0	0	94	.861	6.55	7.43
2019 Tor	AL	58	4	18	68.0	285	61	36	33	8	2	2	3	40	3	67	7	1	2	.333	5-6	8	94	.804	5.40	4.90
Postseason		3	0	0	2.1	11	1	1	1	0	0	0	0	1	0	3	0	0	0	-	0-0	0	94	.282	0.88	3.86
4 ML YEARS		167	4	46	166.1	733	166	83	78	18	4	5	6	71	5	164	14	10	5	.667	10-14	27	94	.746	4.28	4.22

Mike Leake

LEEK

Pitches: R Bats: R Pos: SP-32 Ht: 5'10" Wt: 170 Born: 11/12/1987 Age: 32

Year Team	Lg	G	GS	GF	IP	BFP	H	R	ER	HR	SH	SF	HB	TBB	IBB	SO	WP	W	L	Pct	Sv-Op	Hld	Vel	OPS	ERC	ERA
2010 Cin	NL	24	22	0	138.1	604	158	77	65	19	7	3	3	49	2	91	2	8	4	.667	0-0	0	89	.804	5.12	4.23
2011 Cin	NL	29	26	2	167.2	693	159	74	72	23	3	6	8	38	3	118	2	12	9	.571	0-0	0	89	.714	3.53	3.86
2012 Cin	NL	30	30	0	179.0	757	201	97	91	26	6	7	3	41	3	116	3	8	9	.471	0-0	0	90	.805	4.60	4.58
2013 Cin	NL	31	31	0	192.1	801	193	78	72	21	8	5	6	48	4	122	2	14	7	.667	0-0	0	90	.719	3.69	3.37
2014 Cin	NL	33	33	0	214.1	902	217	93	88	23	7	7	13	50	3	164	4	11	13	.458	0-0	0	91	.730	3.77	3.70
2015 2 Tms	NL	30	30	0	192.0	778	174	80	79	22	6	3	3	49	5	119	6	11	10	.524	0-0	0	91	.686	3.18	3.70
2016 StL	NL	30	30	0	176.2	757	203	101	92	20	5	10	7	30	1	125	7	9	12	.429	0-0	0	91	.756	4.22	4.69
2017 2 Tms	NL	31	31	0	186.0	782	201	93	81	20	6	6	9	37	3	130	3	10	13	.435	0-0	0	90	.742	3.99	3.92
2018 Sea	AL	31	31	0	185.2	784	207	98	90	23	4	3	6	34	3	119	2	10	10	.500	0-0	0	89	.762	4.15	4.36

Year Team	Lg	HOW MUCH PITCHED					WHAT HE GAVE UP												THE RESULTS								
		G	GS	GF	IP	BFP	H	R	ER	HR	SH	SF	HB	TBB	IBB	SO	WP	W	L	Pct	Sv-Op	Hld	Vel	OPS	ERC	ERA
2019 2 Tms		32	32	0	197.0	835	227	114	94	41	2	3	10	27	2	127	2	12	11	.522	0-0	0	88	.823	4.83	4.29
15 Cin	NL	21	21	0	136.2	556	123	55	54	14	6	2	2	34	4	90	3	9	5	.643	0-0	0	91	.666	3.01	3.56
15 SF	NL	9	9	0	55.1	222	51	25	25	8	0	1	1	15	1	29	3	2	5	.286	0-0	0	91	.736	3.61	4.07
17 StL		26	26	0	154.0	654	169	83	72	19	6	6	7	35	3	103	2	7	12	.368	0-0	0	90	.761	4.29	4.21
17 Sea	AL	5	5	0	32.0	128	32	10	9	1	0	0	2	2	0	27	1	3	1	.750	0-0	0	90	.652	2.64	2.53
19 Sea	AL	22	22	0	137.0	576	153	78	65	26	1	1	4	19	1	100	2	9	8	.529	0-0	0	88	.796	4.39	4.27
19 Ari	NL	10	10	0	60.0	259	74	36	29	15	1	2	6	8	1	27	0	3	3	.500	0-0	0	89	.882	5.89	4.35
Postseason		1	1	0	4.1	20	6	5	5	2	1	0	0	2	0	1	0	0	1	.000	0-0	0	90	1.303	10.00	10.38
10 ML YEARS		301	296	2	1829.0	7693	1940	905	824	238	51	53	68	403	29	1231	33	105	98	.517	0-0	0	90	.754	4.06	4.05

Wade LeBlanc

Pitches: L Bats: L Pos: RP-18; SP-8 | lah-BLAHNK | Ht: 6'3" Wt: 205 Born: 8/7/1984 Age: 35

Year Team	Lg	HOW MUCH PITCHED					WHAT HE GAVE UP												THE RESULTS								
		G	GS	GF	IP	BFP	H	R	ER	HR	SH	SF	HB	TBB	IBB	SO	WP	W	L	Pct	Sv-Op	Hld	Vel	OPS	ERC	ERA
2008 SD	NL	5	4	0	21.1	104	29	19	19	7	1	0	0	15	2	14	0	1	3	.250	0-0	0	86	1.086	9.57	8.02
2009 SD	NL	9	9	0	46.1	194	35	19	19	6	3	1	4	19	1	30	0	3	1	.750	0-0	0	85	.669	3.28	3.69
2010 SD	NL	26	25	0	146.0	625	157	69	69	24	7	2	2	51	5	110	2	8	12	.400	0-0	0	87	.818	4.84	4.25
2011 SD	NL	14	14	0	79.2	339	84	42	41	7	3	3	1	28	1	51	1	5	6	.455	0-0	0	87	.757	4.21	4.63
2012 Mia	NL	25	9	1	68.2	284	71	30	28	7	5	1	1	19	1	43	1	2	5	.286	0-0	1	87	.729	3.94	3.67
2013 2 Tms		17	7	1	55.0	259	72	40	33	7	2	1	3	20	3	33	0	1	5	.167	0-0	0	86	.855	5.97	5.40
2014 2 Tms	AL	11	3	3	29.2	121	27	13	13	2	0	2	2	7	2	21	1	1	1	.500	0-0	0	88	.625	2.96	3.94
2016 2 Tms		19	8	7	62.0	252	59	30	26	14	0	2	0	11	0	51	0	4	0	1.000	2-2	1	87	.776	3.72	3.77
2017 Pit	NL	50	0	18	68.0	283	64	35	34	10	1	1	1	17	1	54	2	5	2	.714	1-3	4	87	.717	3.48	4.50
2018 Sea	AL	32	27	5	162.0	662	151	74	67	24	1	4	3	40	1	130	1	9	5	.643	0-0	0	87	.712	3.52	3.72
2019 Sea	AL	26	8	4	121.1	532	145	80	77	28	1	1	1	31	1	92	0	6	7	.462	0-0	0	86	.867	5.55	5.71
13 Mia	NL	13	7	0	48.2	222	63	30	28	6	2	1	2	15	2	31	0	1	5	.167	0-0	0	86	.834	5.67	5.18
13 Hou	AL	4	0	1	6.1	37	9	10	5	1	0	0	1	5	1	2	0	0	0	-	0-0	0	87	.986	8.25	7.11
14 LAA	AL	10	3	2	28.2	114	25	11	11	2	0	1	1	6	1	21	1	1	1	.500	0-0	0	88	.601	2.63	3.45
14 NYY	AL	1	0	1	1.0	7	2	2	2	0	0	1	1	1	1	0	0	0	0	-	0-0	0	89	1.071	13.81	18.00
16 Sea	AL	11	8	3	50.0	208	52	27	25	14	0	0	0	9	0	41	0	3	0	1.000	1-1	0	87	.841	4.58	4.50
16 Pit	NL	8	0	4	12.0	44	7	3	1	0	0	2	0	2	0	10	0	1	0	1.000	1-1	1	87	.455	1.03	0.75
11 ML YEARS		234	114	39	860.0	3655	894	451	426	136	24	18	18	258	18	629	8	45	47	.489	3-5	6	86	.779	4.38	4.46

Jose Leclerc

Pitches: R Bats: R Pos: RP-67; SP-3 | leh-KLURK | Ht: 6'0" Wt: 190 Born: 12/19/1993 Age: 26

Year Team	Lg	HOW MUCH PITCHED					WHAT HE GAVE UP												THE RESULTS								
		G	GS	GF	IP	BFP	H	R	ER	HR	SH	SF	HB	TBB	IBB	SO	WP	W	L	Pct	Sv-Op	Hld	Vel	OPS	ERC	ERA
2016 Tex	AL	12	0	5	15.0	66	11	4	3	0	0	1	0	13	2	15	1	0	0	-	0-0	0	94	.710	3.46	1.80
2017 Tex	AL	47	0	15	45.2	200	23	21	20	4	0	0	3	40	1	60	5	2	3	.400	2-3	10	96	.585	3.28	3.94
2018 Tex	AL	59	0	21	57.2	223	24	16	10	4	1	0	3	25	1	85	2	2	3	.400	12-16	15	95	.431	1.21	1.56
2019 Tex	AL	70	3	40	68.2	299	52	34	33	7	3	2	6	39	1	100	7	2	4	.333	14-18	7	97	.701	3.68	4.33
4 ML YEARS		188	3	81	187.0	788	110	75	66	12	7	3	12	117	5	260	15	6	10	.375	28-37	32	96	.596	2.68	3.18

DJ LeMahieu

Bats: R Throws: R Pos: 2B-75;3B-52;1B-40;DH-1;PH-1;PR-1 | la-MAY-hugh | Ht: 6'4" Wt: 215 Born: 7/13/1988 Age: 31

Year Team	Lg	BATTING																		RUNNING			AVERAGES			
		G	AB	H	2B	3B	HR	Hm	Rd	TB	R	RBI	RC	TBB	IBB	SO	HBP	SH	SF	SB	CS	GDP	Avg	OBP	Slg	OPS
2011 ChC	NL	37	60	15	2	0	0	(0	0)	17	3	4	3	1	0	12	0	1	0	0	0	2	.250	.262	.283	.546
2012 Col	NL	81	229	68	12	4	2	(1	1)	94	26	22	28	13	4	42	0	3	2	1	2	8	.297	.332	.410	.742
2013 Col	NL	109	404	113	21	3	2	(1	1)	146	39	28	42	19	2	67	1	7	3	18	7	13	.280	.311	.361	.673
2014 Col	NL	149	494	132	15	5	5	(2	3)	172	59	42	47	33	7	97	2	7	2	10	10	13	.267	.315	.348	.663
2015 Col	NL	150	564	170	21	5	6	(3	3)	219	85	61	75	50	4	107	1	3	2	23	3	20	.301	.358	.388	.746
2016 Col	NL	146	552	192	32	8	11	(7	4)	273	104	66	104	66	2	80	3	8	6	11	7	19	.348	.416	.495	.911
2017 Col	NL	155	609	189	28	4	8	(3	5)	249	95	64	87	59	1	90	6	3	5	6	5	24	.310	.374	.409	.783
2018 Col	NL	128	533	147	32	2	15	(4	11)	228	90	62	72	37	0	82	2	2	7	6	5	14	.276	.321	.428	.749
2019 NYY	AL	145	602	197	33	2	26	(19	7)	312	109	102	122	46	0	90	2	1	4	5	2	14	.327	.375	.518	.893
Postseason		5	20	3	2	0	0	(0	0)	5	0	0	1	3	0	5	0	0	1	0	0	1	.150	.261	.250	.511
9 ML YEARS		1100	4047	1223	196	33	75	(40	35)	1710	610	451	580	324	20	667	17	35	31	80	41	127	.302	.354	.423	.776

Sandy Leon

Bats: B Throws: R Pos: C-65;1B-1;PH-1 | lay-OHN | Ht: 5'10" Wt: 225 Born: 3/13/1989 Age: 31

Year Team	Lg	BATTING																		RUNNING			AVERAGES			
		G	AB	H	2B	3B	HR	Hm	Rd	TB	R	RBI	RC	TBB	IBB	SO	HBP	SH	SF	SB	CS	GDP	Avg	OBP	Slg	OPS
2012 Was	NL	12	30	8	2	0	0	(0	0)	10	2	2	2	4	0	11	2	0	0	0	0	1	.267	.389	.333	.722
2013 Was	NL	2	1	0	0	0	0	(0	0)	0	0	0	0	0	0	0	0	0	0	0	0	0	.000	.000	.000	.000
2014 Was	NL	20	64	10	1	0	1	(0	1)	14	7	3	2	6	0	20	0	0	1	0	0	1	.156	.229	.219	.447
2015 Bos	AL	41	114	21	2	0	0	(0	0)	23	8	3	1	7	1	28	1	6	0	0	1	4	.184	.238	.202	.439
2016 Bos	AL	78	252	78	17	2	7	(3	4)	120	36	35	44	23	1	67	2	4	2	0	0	4	.310	.369	.476	.845
2017 Bos	AL	85	271	61	14	0	7	(3	4)	96	32	39	32	25	1	74	1	1	3	0	0	5	.225	.290	.354	.644
2018 Bos	AL	89	265	47	12	0	5	(2	3)	74	30	22	17	15	0	75	4	3	1	1	0	6	.177	.232	.279	.511
2019 Bos	AL	65	172	33	3	0	5	(2	3)	51	14	19	15	13	0	47	1	4	1	0	0	0	.192	.251	.297	.548
Postseason		15	31	8	1	0	1	(0	1)	12	2	3	4	2	0	11	0	1	0	0	0	1	.258	.303	.387	.690
8 ML YEARS		392	1169	258	51	2	25	(11	14)	388	129	123	113	93	3	322	11	18	7	1	1	21	.221	.283	.332	.615

Dominic Leone

Pitches: R **Bats:** R **Pos:** RP-40

LEE-own

Ht: 5'11" **Wt:** 210 **Born:** 10/26/1991 **Age:** 28

		HOW MUCH PITCHED					WHAT HE GAVE UP											THE RESULTS						
Year Team	Lg	G	GS	GF	IP	BFP	H	R	ER	HR	SH	SF	HB	TBB	IBB	SO	WP	W	L	Pct	Sv-Op	Hld	Vel	OPS	ERC	ERA
2019 Memp	AAA	23	0	5	31.2	130	20	10	10	3	0	0	2	14	0	42	4	1	0	1.000	0--	-	-	.610	2.48	2.84
2014 Sea	AL	57	0	3	66.1	272	52	18	16	4	1	3	3	25	3	70	4	8	2	.800	0-2	7	95	.624	2.71	2.17
2015 2 Tms		13	0	6	15.0	74	19	15	14	2	0	1	1	9	2	9	2	0	5	.000	0-1	1	93	.884	6.63	8.40
2016 Ari	NL	25	0	8	27.0	131	45	21	19	7	0	3	1	12	1	23	4	0	1	.000	0-1	0	93	1.095	10.37	6.33
2017 Tor	AL	65	0	6	70.1	279	51	22	20	6	0	3	0	23	3	81	8	3	0	1.000	1-5	11	94	.625	2.25	2.56
2018 StL	NL	29	0	8	24.0	106	27	12	12	3	1	3	0	8	3	26	0	1	2	.333	0-2	5	94	.727	4.43	4.50
2019 StL	NL	40	0	11	40.2	180	39	28	25	9	1	1	0	22	2	46	1	1	0	1.000	1-2	0	94	.822	5.20	5.53
15 Sea	AL	10	0	5	11.1	54	11	9	8	1	0	0	0	9	2	7	2	0	4	.000	0-0	1	93	.770	4.93	6.35
15 Ari	NL	3	0	1	3.2	20	8	6	6	1	0	1	1	0	0	2	0	0	1	.000	0-1	0	93	1.172	12.63	14.73
6 ML YEARS		229	0	42	243.1	1042	233	116	106	31	3	14	5	99	14	255	19	13	10	.565	2-13	24	94	.746	4.06	3.92

Jon Lester

Pitches: L **Bats:** L **Pos:** SP-31

Ht: 6'4" **Wt:** 240 **Born:** 1/7/1984 **Age:** 36

		HOW MUCH PITCHED					WHAT HE GAVE UP											THE RESULTS						
Year Team	Lg	G	GS	GF	IP	BFP	H	R	ER	HR	SH	SF	HB	TBB	IBB	SO	WP	W	L	Pct	Sv-Op	Hld	Vel	OPS	ERC	ERA
2006 Bos	AL	15	15	0	81.1	367	91	43	43	7	2	8	5	43	1	60	5	7	2	.778	0-0	0	90	.814	5.52	4.76
2007 Bos	AL	12	11	0	63.0	275	61	33	32	10	1	5	1	31	0	50	1	4	0	1.000	0-0	0	90	.753	4.78	4.57
2008 Bos	AL	33	33	0	210.1	874	202	78	75	14	6	3	10	66	1	152	3	16	6	.727	0-0	0	92	.688	3.55	3.21
2009 Bos	AL	32	32	0	203.1	843	186	80	77	20	2	6	3	64	1	225	6	15	8	.652	0-0	0	94	.667	3.35	3.41
2010 Bos	AL	32	32	0	208.0	861	167	81	75	14	4	6	10	83	0	225	6	19	9	.679	0-0	0	93	.628	3.00	3.25
2011 Bos	AL	31	31	0	191.2	799	166	77	74	20	2	2	11	75	0	182	4	15	9	.625	0-0	0	93	.690	3.62	3.47
2012 Bos	AL	33	33	0	205.1	876	216	117	110	25	5	7	4	68	2	166	6	9	14	.391	0-0	0	93	.773	4.36	4.82
2013 Bos	AL	33	33	0	213.1	903	209	94	89	19	1	1	7	67	0	177	5	15	8	.652	0-0	0	93	.703	3.69	3.75
2014 2 Tms	AL	32	32	0	219.2	885	194	76	60	16	6	5	5	48	0	220	3	16	11	.593	0-0	0	92	.635	2.70	2.46
2015 ChC	NL	32	32	0	205.0	828	183	83	76	16	5	4	7	47	0	207	4	11	12	.478	0-0	0	92	.661	2.88	3.34
2016 ChC	NL	32	32	0	202.2	796	154	57	55	21	4	4	6	52	0	197	4	19	5	.792	0-0	0	92	.602	2.47	2.44
2017 ChC	NL	32	32	0	180.2	763	179	101	87	26	4	4	4	60	3	180	3	13	8	.619	0-0	0	91	.750	4.16	4.33
2018 ChC	NL	32	32	0	181.2	761	174	75	67	24	7	3	6	64	1	149	4	18	6	.750	0-0	0	91	.733	4.07	3.32
2019 ChC	NL	31	31	0	171.2	764	205	101	85	26	5	4	5	52	0	165	3	13	10	.565	0-0	0	90	.815	5.27	4.46
14 Bos	AL	21	21	0	143.0	580	128	52	40	9	5	2	4	32	0	149	2	10	7	.588	0-0	0	92	.637	2.73	2.52
14 Oak	AL	11	11	0	76.2	305	66	24	20	7	1	3	1	16	0	71	1	6	4	.600	0-0	0	91	.632	2.65	2.35
Postseason		26	22	2	154.0	610	117	46	43	15	6	2	3	40	0	133	4	9	7	.563	0-0	0	93	.594	2.37	2.51
14 ML YEARS		412	411	0	2537.2	10595	2387	1096	1005	258	54	62	84	820	8	2355	61	190	108	.638	0-0	0	92	.700	3.62	3.56

Kyle Lewis

Bats: R **Throws:** R **Pos:** RF-17;CF-2;PH-1

Ht: 6'4" **Wt:** 210 **Born:** 7/13/1995 **Age:** 24

		BATTING																			RUNNING			AVERAGES			
Year Team	Lg	G	AB	H	2B	3B	HR	(Hm	Rd)	TB	R	RBI	RC	TBB	IBB	SO	HBP	SH	SF	SB	CS	GDP	Avg	OBP	Slg	OPS
2019 Ark	AA	122	457	120	25	2	11	(-	-)	182	61	62	65	56	1	152	1	0	3	3	2	5	.263	.342	.398	.741
2019 Sea	AL	18	71	19	5	0	6	(4	2)	42	10	13	13	3	0	29	0	0	1	0	0	0	.268	.293	.592	.885

Royce Lewis

Bats: R **Throws:** R **Pos:** SS

Ht: 6'2" **Wt:** 200 **Born:** 6/5/1999 **Age:** 21

		BATTING																			RUNNING			AVERAGES			
Year Team	Lg	G	AB	H	2B	3B	HR	(Hm	Rd)	TB	R	RBI	RC	TBB	IBB	SO	HBP	SH	SF	SB	CS	GDP	Avg	OBP	Slg	OPS
2017 2 Tms	Low	54	204	57	8	3	4	(-	-)	83	54	27	38	25	0	33	9	0	1	18	3	3	.279	.381	.407	.788
2018 2 Tms	Low	121	483	141	29	3	14	(-	-)	218	83	74	65	43	1	84	4	1	4	28	8	8	.292	.352	.451	.803
2019 FtMyrs	A+	94	383	91	17	3	10	(-	-)	144	55	35	46	27	1	90	3	0	5	16	8	5	.238	.289	.376	.665
2019 Pnscla	AA	33	134	31	9	1	2	(-	-)	48	18	14	15	11	0	33	1	0	2	6	2	0	.231	.291	.358	.649

Domingo Leyba

Bats: B **Throws:** R **Pos:** PH-15;2B-8;SS-2;3B-1

Ht: 5'11" **Wt:** 160 **Born:** 9/11/1995 **Age:** 24

		BATTING																			RUNNING			AVERAGES			
Year Team	Lg	G	AB	H	2B	3B	HR	(Hm	Rd)	TB	R	RBI	RC	TBB	IBB	SO	HBP	SH	SF	SB	CS	GDP	Avg	OBP	Slg	OPS
2019 Reno	AAA	112	457	137	36	3	19	(-	-)	236	85	77	82	32	1	78	6	0	3	0	2	8	.300	.351	.516	.868
2019 Ari	NL	21	25	7	2	1	0	(0	0)	11	6	5	5	4	0	9	0	0	1	0	0	0	.280	.367	.440	.807

Tzu-Wei Lin

Bats: L **Throws:** R **Pos:** 2B-8;SS-2;CF-1;PH-1;PR-1

zoo-way

Ht: 5'9" **Wt:** 155 **Born:** 2/15/1994 **Age:** 26

		BATTING																			RUNNING			AVERAGES			
Year Team	Lg	G	AB	H	2B	3B	HR	(Hm	Rd)	TB	R	RBI	RC	TBB	IBB	SO	HBP	SH	SF	SB	CS	GDP	Avg	OBP	Slg	OPS
2019 Pwtckt	AAA	59	224	55	11	1	4	(-	-)	80	30	22	26	21	0	58	0	3	2	6	2	7	.246	.308	.357	.665
2017 Bos	AL	25	56	15	0	2	0	(0	0)	19	7	2	7	9	0	17	0	1	0	1	1	0	.268	.369	.339	.709
2018 Bos	AL	37	65	16	6	1	1	(0	1)	27	15	6	8	8	0	17	0	0	0	0	1	0	.246	.329	.415	.744
2019 Bos	AL	13	20	4	2	0	0	(0	0)	6	3	1	2	2	0	6	0	0	0	1	1	0	.200	.273	.300	.573
3 ML YEARS		75	141	35	8	3	1	(0	1)	52	25	9	17	19	0	40	0	1	0	2	3	0	.248	.338	.369	.706

Francisco Lindor

Bats: B Throws: R Pos: SS-137;DH-5;PH-1 lin-DOHR **Ht: 5'11" Wt: 190 Born: 11/14/1993 Age: 26**

Year Team	Lg	G	AB	H	2B	3B	HR	(Hm	Rd)	TB	R	RBI	RC	TBB	IBB	SO	HBP	SH	SF	SB	CS	GDP	Avg	OBP	Slg	OPS
2015 Cle	AL	99	390	122	22	4	12	(8	4)	188	50	51	64	27	0	69	1	13	7	12	2	12	.313	.353	.482	.835
2016 Cle	AL	158	604	182	30	3	15	(6	9)	263	99	78	87	57	3	88	5	5	15	19	5	18	.301	.358	.435	.794
2017 Cle	AL	159	651	178	44	4	33	(16	17)	329	99	89	107	60	6	93	4	5	3	15	3	11	.273	.337	.505	.842
2018 Cle	AL	158	661	183	42	2	38	(20	18)	343	129	92	117	70	7	107	8	3	3	25	10	5	.277	.352	.519	.871
2019 Cle	AL	143	598	170	40	2	32	(14	18)	310	101	74	89	46	9	98	3	1	6	22	5	13	.284	.335	.518	.854
Postseason		23	87	24	3	0	5	(4	1)	42	10	12	14	8	2	24	0	1	0	1	3	2	.276	.337	.483	.820
5 ML YEARS		717	2904	835	178	15	130	(64	66)	1433	478	384	464	260	25	455	21	25	34	93	25	59	.288	.347	.493	.840

Francisco Liriano

Pitches: L Bats: L Pos: RP-69 **Ht: 6'3" Wt: 218 Born: 10/26/1983 Age: 36**

Year Team	Lg	G	GS	GF	IP	BFP	H	R	ER	HR	SH	SF	HB	TBB	IBB	SO	WP	W	L	Pct	Sv-Op	Hld	Vel	OPS	ERC	ERA
2005 Min	AL	6	4	2	23.2	93	19	15	15	4	0	0	0	7	0	33	0	1	2	.333	0-0		95	.687	3.15	5.70
2006 Min	AL	28	16	2	121.0	473	89	31	29	9	4	2	1	32	0	144	9	12	3	.800	1-1		95	.567	2.12	2.16
2008 Min	AL	14	14	0	76.0	329	74	40	33	7	2	3	1	32	1	67	3	6	4	.600	0-0	0	91	.719	3.97	3.91
2009 Min	AL	29	24	2	136.2	609	147	93	88	21	5	6	6	65	0	122	5	5	13	.278	0-0	0	92	.830	5.46	5.80
2010 Min	AL	31	31	0	191.2	806	184	77	77	9	6	2	10	58	0	201	10	14	10	.583	0-0	0	94	.670	3.34	3.62
2011 Min	AL	26	24	0	134.1	591	125	81	76	14	0	6	7	75	1	112	9	9	10	.474	0-0	0	92	.726	4.58	5.09
2012 2 Tms		34	28	2	156.2	693	143	97	93	19	4	8	7	85	5	167	11	6	12	.333	0-0	1	93	.741	4.47	5.34
2013 Pit	NL	26	26	0	161.0	666	134	54	54	9	3	1	0	63	0	163	7	16	8	.667	0-0	0	93	.611	2.86	3.02
2014 Pit	NL	29	29	0	162.1	691	130	68	61	13	6	5	4	81	3	175	12	7	10	.412	0-0	0	93	.645	3.28	3.38
2015 Pit	NL	31	31	0	186.2	773	155	75	70	15	2	1	5	70	1	205	10	12	7	.632	0-0	0	93	.631	3.04	3.38
2016 2 Tms		31	29	0	163.0	731	157	98	85	26	7	6	9	85	1	168	9	8	13	.381	0-0	0	93	.773	4.96	4.69
2017 2 Tms	AL	38	18	3	97.0	439	105	66	61	11	2	3	4	53	2	85	5	6	7	.462	0-0	6	93	.824	5.43	5.66
2018 Det	AL	27	26	0	133.2	586	127	84	68	19	0	5	5	73	0	110	9	5	12	.294	0-0	0	92	.771	4.90	4.58
2019 Pit	NL	69	0	8	70.0	301	60	32	27	8	2	2	3	35	1	63	1	5	3	.625	0-4	12	93	.710	3.93	3.47
12 Min	AL	22	17	2	100.0	440	89	63	59	12	2	7	4	55	4	109	6	3	10	.231	0-0	1	93	.730	4.27	5.31
12 CWS		12	11	0	56.2	253	54	34	34	7	2	1	3	32	1	58	5	3	2	.600	0-0	0	93	.759	4.83	5.40
16 Pit	NL	21	21	0	113.2	523	115	76	69	19	7	5	7	69	1	116	8	6	11	.353	0-0	0	92	.814	5.71	5.46
16 Tor	AL	10	8	0	49.1	208	42	22	16	7	0	1	2	16	0	52	1	2	2	.500	0-0	0	93	.675	3.34	2.92
17 Tor	AL	18	18	0	82.2	375	91	57	54	11	2	3	2	43	1	74	4	6	5	.545	0-0	0	93	.832	5.49	5.88
17 Hou	AL	20	0	3	14.1	64	14	9	7	0	0	0	2	10	1	11	1	0	2	.000	0-0	6	94	.772	5.00	4.40
Postseason		11	3	3	25.0	103	18	12	11	2	0	0	2	9	0	21	3	2	1	.667	0-0	0	94	.619	2.60	3.96
14 ML YEARS		419	300	19	1813.2	7781	1649	911	837	184	43	50	62	816	15	1815	100	112	114	.496	1-5	20	93	.705	3.91	4.15

Zack Littell

Pitches: R Bats: R Pos: RP-29 lah-TELL **Ht: 6'4" Wt: 220 Born: 10/5/1995 Age: 24**

Year Team	Lg	G	GS	GF	IP	BFP	H	R	ER	HR	SH	SF	HB	TBB	IBB	SO	WP	W	L	Pct	Sv-Op	Hld	Vel	OPS	ERC	ERA
2019 Roch	AAA	20	7	4	63.0	265	55	29	26	11	0	2	4	25	0	68	4	3	3	.500	1--	-	-	.728	4.01	3.71
2018 Min	AL	8	2	1	20.1	101	25	17	14	3	1	1	4	11	0	14	0	0	2	.000	0-0	0	92	.924	7.09	6.20
2019 Min	AL	29	0	7	37.0	146	34	12	11	4	1	0	0	9	1	32	0	6	0	1.000	0-1	1	94	.708	3.18	2.68
2 ML YEARS		37	2	8	57.1	247	59	29	25	7	2	1	4	20	1	46	0	6	2	.750	0-1	1	93	.793	4.50	3.92

Ben Lively

Pitches: R Bats: R Pos: RP-1 **Ht: 6'4" Wt: 190 Born: 3/5/1992 Age: 28**

Year Team	Lg	G	GS	GF	IP	BFP	H	R	ER	HR	SH	SF	HB	TBB	IBB	SO	WP	W	L	Pct	Sv-Op	Hld	Vel	OPS	ERC	ERA
2019 Omha	AAA	17	3	6	42.0	185	41	20	19	7	0	0	3	19	1	41	0	4	1	.800	3--	-	-	.752	4.89	4.07
2019 Reno	AAA	7	7	0	30.1	136	36	17	17	7	0	1	0	11	0	35	1	2	1	.667	0--	-	-	.854	5.95	5.04
2017 Phi	NL	15	15	0	88.2	372	90	45	42	13	2	3	8	24	1	52	1	4	7	.364	0-0	0	91	.813	4.42	4.26
2018 2 Tms		10	5	1	30.1	145	41	19	19	4	0	1	3	15	1	27	0	0	3	.000	0-0	0	91	.899	7.30	5.64
2019 KC	AL	1	0	1	1.0	6	3	3	3	1	0	0	0	0	0	1	0	0	0	-	0-0	0	92	1.500	25.51	27.00
18 Phi	NL	5	5	0	23.2	115	34	18	18	4	0	1	3	10	1	22	0	0	2	.000	0-0	0	91	.953	7.91	6.85
18 KC	AL	5	0	1	6.2	30	7	1	1	0	0	0	0	5	0	5	0	0	1	.000	0-0	0	93	.680	5.17	1.35
3 ML YEARS		26	20	2	120.0	523	134	67	64	18	2	4	11	39	2	80	1	4	10	.286	0-0	0	91	.846	5.26	4.80

Jonathan Loaisiga

Pitches: R Bats: R Pos: RP-11; SP-4 **Ht: 5'11" Wt: 165 Born: 11/2/1994 Age: 25**

Year Team	Lg	G	GS	GF	IP	BFP	H	R	ER	HR	SH	SF	HB	TBB	IBB	SO	WP	W	L	Pct	Sv-Op	Hld	Vel	OPS	ERC	ERA
2019 S-WB	AAA	5	4	0	15.2	68	14	11	11	3	0	1	1	5	0	19	2	0	2	.000	0--	-	-	.770	3.89	6.32
2018 NYY	AL	9	4	2	24.2	108	26	17	14	3	0	0	0	12	0	33	0	2	0	1.000	0-0	0	96	.789	4.97	5.11
2019 NYY	AL	15	4	3	31.2	139	31	16	16	6	0	4	1	16	0	37	1	2	2	.500	0-1	0	97	.820	5.21	4.55
2 ML YEARS		24	8	5	56.1	247	57	33	30	9	0	4	1	28	0	70	1	4	2	.667	0-1	0	97	.806	5.11	4.79

Tim Locastro

Bats: R **Throws:** R **Pos:** LF-34;RF-25;CF-20;PH-19;PR-8   **Ht:** 6'1" **Wt:** 200 **Born:** 7/14/1992 **Age:** 27

								BATTING													RUNNING			AVERAGES			
Year Team	Lg	G	AB	H	2B	3B	HR	(Hm	Rd)	TB	R	RBI	RC	TBB	IBB	SO	HBP	SH	SF	SB	CS	GDP	Avg	OBP	Slg	OPS
2019 Reno	AAA	31	123	37	11	2	8	(-	-)	76	35	21	30	10	0	24	9	1	0	9	1	0	.301	.394	.618	1.012
2017 LAD	NL	3	1	0	0	0	0	(0	0)	0	0	0	0	0	0	0	0	0	0	1	0	0	.000	.000	.000	.000
2018 LAD	NL	18	11	2	1	0	0	(0	0)	3	6	0	2	2	0	5	1	0	0	4	0	0	.182	.357	.273	.630
2019 Ari	AL	91	212	53	12	2	1	(0	1)	72	38	17	35	14	0	44	22	1	1	17	0	1	.250	.357	.340	.697
3 ML YEARS		112	224	55	13	2	1			75	44	17	37	16	0	49	23	1	1	22	0	1	.246	.356	.335	.691

Walker Lockett

Pitches: R **Bats:** R **Pos:** RP-5; SP-4   **Ht:** 6'5" **Wt:** 225 **Born:** 5/3/1994 **Age:** 26

			HOW MUCH PITCHED					WHAT HE GAVE UP										THE RESULTS							
Year Team	Lg	G	GS	GF	IP	BFP	H	R	ER	HR	SH	SF	HB	TBB	IBB	SO	WP	W	L	Pct	Sv-Op	Hld	Vel	OPS	ERC	ERA
2019 Syrcse	AAA	11	10	0	59.0	261	75	29	24	5	0	2	2	11	1	39	2	3	3	.500	0--	-	-	.788	4.72	3.66
2018 SD	NL	4	3	1	15.0	76	22	16	16	4	0	0	0	10	1	12	0	0	3	.000	0-0	0	93	1.042	9.39	9.60
2019 NYM	NL	9	4	1	22.2	103	33	21	21	6	1	0	1	6	0	16	1	1	1	.500	0-0	0	93	1.003	7.99	8.34
2 ML YEARS		13	7	2	37.2	179	55	37	37	10	1	0	1	16	1	28	1	1	4	.200	0-0	0	93	1.019	8.55	8.84

Shed Long

Bats: L **Throws:** R **Pos:** 2B-24;LF-16;PH-2;3B-1;DH-1;PR-1   **Ht:** 5'8" **Wt:** 184 **Born:** 8/22/1995 **Age:** 24

								BATTING													RUNNING			AVERAGES			
Year Team	Lg	G	AB	H	2B	3B	HR	(Hm	Rd)	TB	R	RBI	RC	TBB	IBB	SO	HBP	SH	SF	SB	CS	GDP	Avg	OBP	Slg	OPS
2019 Tacom	AAA	56	226	62	7	4	9	(-	-)	104	38	36	34	20	0	65	1	2	1	1	3	3	.274	.335	.460	.795
2019 Sea	AL	42	152	40	12	1	5	(1	4)	69	21	15	19	16	0	40	0	0	0	3	3	1	.263	.333	.454	.787

Evan Longoria

Bats: R **Throws:** R **Pos:** 3B-119;PH-12   **Ht:** 6'1" **Wt:** 215 **Born:** 10/7/1985 **Age:** 34

								BATTING													RUNNING			AVERAGES			
Year Team	Lg	G	AB	H	2B	3B	HR	(Hm	Rd)	TB	R	RBI	RC	TBB	IBB	SO	HBP	SH	SF	SB	CS	GDP	Avg	OBP	Slg	OPS
2008 TB	AL	122	448	122	31	2	27	(18	9)	238	67	85	72	46	4	122	6	0	8	7	0	8	.272	.343	.531	.874
2009 TB	AL	157	584	164	44	0	33	(16	17)	307	100	113	102	72	11	140	8	0	7	9	0	27	.281	.364	.526	.889
2010 TB	AL	151	574	169	46	5	22	(10	12)	291	96	104	99	72	12	124	5	0	10	15	5	15	.294	.372	.507	.879
2011 TB	AL	133	483	118	26	1	31	(14	17)	239	78	99	91	80	6	93	6	0	5	3	2	11	.244	.355	.495	.850
2012 TB	AL	74	273	79	14	0	17	(8	9)	144	39	55	55	33	6	61	3	0	3	2	3	14	.289	.369	.527	.896
2013 TB	AL	160	614	165	39	3	32	(15	17)	306	91	88	90	70	10	162	3	0	6	1	0	16	.269	.343	.498	.842
2014 TB	AL	162	624	158	26	1	22	(12	10)	252	83	91	83	57	11	133	9	1	9	5	0	15	.253	.320	.404	.724
2015 TB	AL	160	604	163	35	1	21	(10	11)	263	74	73	77	51	8	132	6	0	9	3	1	11	.270	.328	.435	.764
2016 TB	AL	160	633	173	41	4	36	(17	19)	330	81	98	95	42	6	144	3	0	7	0	3	13	.273	.318	.521	.840
2017 TB	AL	156	613	160	36	2	20	(10	10)	260	71	86	81	46	3	109	6	0	12	6	1	18	.261	.313	.424	.737
2018 SF	NL	125	480	117	25	4	16	(4	12)	198	51	54	46	22	3	101	5	0	5	3	1	14	.244	.281	.413	.694
2019 SF	NL	129	453	115	19	2	20	(6	14)	198	59	69	63	43	1	112	7	0	5	3	1	14	.254	.325	.437	.762
Postseason		30	115	22	5	0	9	(4	5)	54	16	21	13	11	0	38	0	0	0	1	0	4	.191	.262	.470	.731
12 ML YEARS		1689	6383	1703	382	25	297	(140	157)	3026	890	1015	954	634	81	1433	67	1	86	57	17	173	.267	.335	.474	.809

Tim Lopes

Bats: R **Throws:** R **Pos:** LF-33;PH-7;2B-3;RF-3;DH-3;PR-1   **Ht:** 5'11" **Wt:** 180 **Born:** 6/24/1994 **Age:** 26

								BATTING													RUNNING			AVERAGES			
Year Team	Lg	G	AB	H	2B	3B	HR	(Hm	Rd)	TB	R	RBI	RC	TBB	IBB	SO	HBP	SH	SF	SB	CS	GDP	Avg	OBP	Slg	OPS
2019 Tacom	AAA	95	374	113	31	2	10	(-	-)	178	59	60	68	36	0	72	3	0	7	26	9	7	.302	.362	.476	.838
2019 Sea	AL	41	111	30	7	0	1	(1	0)	40	11	12	16	15	0	29	1	0	1	6	3	1	.270	.359	.360	.720

Jorge Lopez

Pitches: R **Bats:** R **Pos:** RP-21; SP-18   **Ht:** 6'3" **Wt:** 195 **Born:** 2/10/1993 **Age:** 27

			HOW MUCH PITCHED					WHAT HE GAVE UP										THE RESULTS							
Year Team	Lg	G	GS	GF	IP	BFP	H	R	ER	HR	SH	SF	HB	TBB	IBB	SO	WP	W	L	Pct	Sv-Op	Hld	Vel	OPS	ERC	ERA
2015 Mil	NL	2	2	0	10.0	46	14	6	6	0	0	0	1	5	0	10	1	1	1	.500	0-0	0	94	.687	6.87	5.40
2017 Mil	NL	1	0	1	2.0	10	4	1	1	0	0	0	0	1	0	0	0	0	0	-	0-0	0	95	1.056	10.75	4.50
2018 2 Tms		17	7	8	53.2	234	57	30	30	6	0	2	1	22	1	38	3	2	5	.286	0-0	0	94	.763	4.64	5.03
2019 KC	AL	39	18	8	123.2	548	140	94	87	27	0	7	10	42	0	109	6	4	9	.308	1-2	0	94	.864	5.85	6.33
18 Mil	NL	10	0	8	19.2	85	16	6	6	1	0	1	0	13	1	15	1	0	1	.000	0-0	0	94	.665	3.66	2.75
18 KC	AL	7	7	0	34.0	149	41	24	24	5	0	1	1	9	0	23	2	2	4	.333	0-0	0	93	.813	5.20	6.35
4 ML YEARS		59	27	17	189.1	838	215	131	124	33	0	9	12	70	1	157	10	7	15	.318	1-2	0	94	.838	5.61	5.89

Nicky Lopez

Bats: L **Throws:** R **Pos:** 2B-76;SS-33;DH-1;PH-1;PR-1   **Ht:** 5'11" **Wt:** 175 **Born:** 3/13/1995 **Age:** 25

								BATTING													RUNNING			AVERAGES			
Year Team	Lg	G	AB	H	2B	3B	HR	(Hm	Rd)	TB	R	RBI	RC	TBB	IBB	SO	HBP	SH	SF	SB	CS	GDP	Avg	OBP	Slg	OPS
2019 Omha	AAA	31	116	41	6	1	3	(-	-)	58	27	13	27	20	0	5	2	0	0	9	3	2	.353	.457	.500	.957
2019 KC	AL	103	379	91	22	2	2	(1	1)	123	44	30	38	18	0	51	1	4	0	1	1	5	.240	.276	.325	.601

Pablo Lopez

Pitches: R Bats: L Pos: SP-21 Ht: 6'3" Wt: 200 Born: 3/7/1996 Age: 24

Year	Team	Lg	G	GS	GF	IP	BFP	H	R	ER	HR	SH	SF	HB	TBB	IBB	SO	WP	W	L	Pct	Sv-Op	Hld	Vel	OPS	ERC	ERA
2018	Mia	NL	10	10	0	58.2	247	56	28	27	8	1	2	4	18	5	46	2	2	4	.333	0-0	0	92	.745	3.88	4.14
2019	Mia	NL	21	21	0	111.1	469	111	64	63	15	4	2	11	27	3	95	6	5	8	.385	0-0	0	94	.756	4.07	5.09
	2 ML YEARS		31	31	0	170.0	716	167	92	90	23	5	4	15	45	8	141	8	7	12	.368	0-0	0	93	.752	4.00	4.76

Reynaldo Lopez

Pitches: R Bats: R Pos: SP-33 ray-NAHL-doh Ht: 6'1" Wt: 200 Born: 1/4/1994 Age: 26

Year	Team	Lg	G	GS	GF	IP	BFP	H	R	ER	HR	SH	SF	HB	TBB	IBB	SO	WP	W	L	Pct	Sv-Op	Hld	Vel	OPS	ERC	ERA
2016	Was	NL	11	6	1	44.0	201	47	27	24	4	3	2	0	22	2	42	5	5	3	.625	0-0	1	96	.772	4.60	4.91
2017	CWS	AL	8	8	0	47.2	207	49	29	25	7	0	2	1	14	0	30	3	3	3	.500	0-0	0	94	.741	4.12	4.72
2018	CWS	AL	32	32	0	188.2	799	165	88	82	25	0	9	10	75	1	151	7	7	10	.412	0-0	0	95	.713	3.80	3.91
2019	CWS	AL	33	33	0	184.0	809	203	119	110	35	2	5	8	65	0	169	5	10	15	.400	0-0	0	95	.833	5.33	5.38
	Postseason		1	0	0	2.0	9	2	1	1	0	0	0	0	1	0	3	0				0-0	0	96	.708	3.63	4.50
	4 ML YEARS		84	79	1	464.1	2016	464	263	241	71	5	18	19	176	3	392	20	25	31	.446	0-0	1	95	.770	4.50	4.67

Yoan Lopez

Pitches: R Bats: R Pos: RP-70 Ht: 6'3" Wt: 185 Born: 1/2/1993 Age: 27

Year	Team	Lg	G	GS	GF	IP	BFP	H	R	ER	HR	SH	SF	HB	TBB	IBB	SO	WP	W	L	Pct	Sv-Op	Hld	Vel	OPS	ERC	ERA
2018	Ari	NL	10	0	5	9.0	35	7	3	3	2	1	0	0	1	0	11	0	0	0	-	0-0	1	97	.720	2.47	3.00
2019	Ari	NL	70	0	13	60.2	246	52	27	23	11	1	4	0	17	2	42	1	2	7	.222	1-4	21	96	.728	3.32	3.41
	2 ML YEARS		80	0	18	69.2	281	59	30	26	13	2	4	0	18	2	53	1	2	7	.222	1-4	22	96	.727	3.21	3.36

Michael Lorenzen

Pitches: R Bats: R Pos: RP-73 Ht: 6'3" Wt: 217 Born: 1/4/1992 Age: 28

Year	Team	Lg	G	GS	GF	IP	BFP	H	R	ER	HR	SH	SF	HB	TBB	IBB	SO	WP	W	L	Pct	Sv-Op	Hld	Vel	OPS	ERC	ERA
2015	Cin	NL	27	21	1	113.1	515	131	70	68	18	2	1	6	57	6	83	4	4	9	.308	0-0	1	94	.882	6.09	5.40
2016	Cin	NL	35	0	4	50.0	202	41	16	16	5	0	6	6	13	0	48	2	2	1	.667	0-2	10	96	.630	3.11	2.88
2017	Cin	NL	70	0	14	83.0	361	78	43	41	9	2	1	4	34	5	80	12	8	4	.667	2-7	18	96	.695	3.89	4.45
2018	Cin	NL	45	3	10	81.0	344	78	32	28	6	2	3	3	34	2	54	2	4	2	.667	1-2	8	95	.707	3.95	3.11
2019	Cin	NL	73	0	16	83.1	343	68	29	27	9	4	2	2	28	1	85	2	1	4	.200	7-11	21	97	.644	2.96	2.92
	5 ML YEARS		250	24	45	410.2	1765	396	190	180	47	10	7	21	166	14	350	22	19	20	.487	10-22	58	95	.734	4.17	3.94

Aaron Loup

Pitches: L Bats: L Pos: RP-4 LOOP Ht: 5'11" Wt: 210 Born: 12/19/1987 Age: 32

Year	Team	Lg	G	GS	GF	IP	BFP	H	R	ER	HR	SH	SF	HB	TBB	IBB	SO	WP	W	L	Pct	Sv-Op	Hld	Vel	OPS	ERC	ERA
2012	Tor	AL	33	0	3	30.2	117	26	10	9	0	2	1	0	2	0	21	1	0	2	.000	0-1	6	92	.547	1.59	2.64
2013	Tor	AL	64	0	12	69.1	282	66	23	19	5	2	4	7	13	4	53	2	4	6	.400	2-3	8	92	.670	3.20	2.47
2014	Tor	AL	71	0	15	68.2	283	50	25	24	4	3	3	6	30	5	56	5	4	4	.500	4-8	13	92	.647	2.75	3.15
2015	Tor	AL	60	0	6	42.1	186	47	24	21	6	4	3	6	7	0	46	0	2	5	.286	0-4	9	93	.776	4.54	4.46
2016	Tor	AL	21	0	2	14.1	62	15	8	8	2	0	3	3	4	0	15	3	0	0	-	0-1	1	91	.855	5.13	5.02
2017	Tor	AL	70	0	8	57.2	265	59	27	24	4	5	0	6	29	5	64	3	2	3	.400	0-0	6	92	.722	4.56	3.75
2018	2 Tms		59	0	8	39.2	183	48	23	20	4	0	3	4	14	0	44	0	0	0	-	0-0	11	92	.805	5.45	4.54
2019	SD	NL	4	0	1	3.1	14	2	0	0	0	0	1	1	1	0	5	0	0	0	-	0-0	1	92	.558	2.03	0.00
18	Tor	AL	50	0	7	35.2	166	44	21	18	4	0	3	3	13	0	42	0	0	0	-	0-0	9	92	.824	5.63	4.54
18	Phi	NL	9	0	1	4.0	17	4	2	2	0	0	0	1	1	0	2	0	0	0	-	0-0	2	91	.620	3.88	4.50
	Postseason		4	0	0	2.0	7	1	1	1	0	0	0	0	2	0	1	0	0	0	-	0-0	0	91	.629	3.75	4.50
	8 ML YEARS		382	0	55	326.0	1392	313	140	125	25	14	15	33	100	14	304	14	12	20	.375	6-17	55	92	.704	3.66	3.45

Richard Lovelady

Pitches: L Bats: L Pos: RP-25 Ht: 6'0" Wt: 175 Born: 7/7/1995 Age: 24

Year	Team	Lg	G	GS	GF	IP	BFP	H	R	ER	HR	SH	SF	HB	TBB	IBB	SO	WP	W	L	Pct	Sv-Op	Hld	Vel	OPS	ERC	ERA
2019	Omha	AAA	24	0	13	26.1	112	26	11	9	1	3	2	2	7	2	29	0	1	2	.333	4--	-	-	.648	3.22	3.08
2019	KC	AL	25	0	5	20.0	96	30	17	17	2	1	1	1	8	2	17	1	0	3	.000	0-1	2	94	.952	7.18	7.65

Brandon Lowe

Bats: L Throws: R Pos: 2B-69;PH-9;1B-5;RF-5;DH-3;LF-2 LAOW Ht: 5'10" Wt: 185 Born: 7/6/1994 Age: 25

Year	Team	Lg	G	AB	H	2B	3B	HR	(Hm	Rd)	TB	R	RBI	RC	TBB	IBB	SO	HBP	SH	SF	SB	CS	GDP	Avg	OBP	Slg	OPS
2016	BG	A	107	379	94	15	3	5	(-	-)	130	67	42	51	60	1	77	5	3	6	6	3	6	.248	.357	.343	.700
2017	Charltt	A+	90	315	98	34	3	9	(-	-)	165	62	46	67	47	2	65	3	0	2	6	3	2	.311	.403	.524	.927
2017	Mont	AA	24	95	24	5	1	2	(-	-)	37	8	12	10	2	0	26	1	1	2	1	1	0	.253	.290	.389	.659
2018	Mont	AA	54	199	58	17	1	8	(-	-)	101	37	41	42	35	1	55	3	0	3	8	2	3	.291	.400	.508	.908
2018	Drham	AAA	46	181	55	14	0	14	(-	-)	111	36	35	40	22	0	47	1	0	1	0	1	1	.304	.380	.613	.994
2018	TB	AL	43	129	30	6	2	6	(2	4)	58	16	25	21	16	0	38	2	0	1	2	1	3	.233	.324	.450	.774
2019	TB	AL	82	296	80	17	2	17	(8	9)	152	42	51	50	25	0	113	5	0	1	5	0	1	.270	.336	.514	.850
	2 ML YEARS		125	425	110	23	4	23	(10	13)	210	58	76	71	41	0	151	7	0	2	7	1	4	.259	.333	.494	.827

Nate Lowe

Bats: L **Throws:** R **Pos:** 1B-21;DH-17;PH-12;3B-4   **Ht:** 6'4" **Wt:** 245 **Born:** 7/7/1995 **Age:** 24

Year	Team	Lg	G	AB	H	2B	3B	HR	(Hm	Rd)	TB	R	RBI	RC	TBB	IBB	SO	HBP	SH	SF	SB	CS	GDP	Avg	OBP	Slg	OPS
2019	Drham	AAA	93	329	95	24	0	16	(-	-)	167	63	63	74	72	1	82	4	0	1	1	0	11	.289	.421	.508	.929
2019	TB	AL	50	152	40	8	0	7	(4	3)	69	24	19	19	13	0	50	2	0	2	0	0	4	.263	.325	.454	.779

Jed Lowrie

Bats: B **Throws:** R **Pos:** PH-9   LAU-ree   **Ht:** 6'0" **Wt:** 180 **Born:** 4/17/1984 **Age:** 36

Year	Team	Lg	G	AB	H	2B	3B	HR	(Hm	Rd)	TB	R	RBI	RC	TBB	IBB	SO	HBP	SH	SF	SB	CS	GDP	Avg	OBP	Slg	OPS
2019	Syrcse	AAA	12	44	11	1	0	2	(-	-)	18	7	3	5	4	0	12	0	0	0	0	0	0	.250	.313	.409	.722
2008	Bos	AL	81	260	67	25	3	2	(0	2)	104	34	46	35	35	0	68	1	2	8	1	0	8	.258	.339	.400	.739
2009	Bos	AL	32	68	10	2	0	2	(1	1)	18	5	11	5	6	0	20	0	0	2	0	0	0	.147	.211	.265	.475
2010	Bos	AL	55	171	49	14	0	9	(3	6)	90	31	24	32	25	0	25	1	0	0	1	1	2	.287	.381	.526	.907
2011	Bos	AL	88	309	78	14	4	6	(3	3)	118	40	36	33	23	2	60	2	1	6	1	1	6	.252	.303	.382	.685
2012	Hou	NL	97	340	83	18	0	16	(9	7)	149	43	42	45	43	0	65	2	0	2	2	0	3	.244	.331	.438	.769
2013	Oak	AL	154	603	175	45	2	15	(7	8)	269	80	75	88	50	3	91	2	3	4	1	0	17	.290	.344	.446	.791
2014	Oak	AL	136	502	125	29	3	6	(4	2)	178	59	50	52	51	5	79	5	2	6	0	0	14	.249	.321	.355	.676
2015	Hou	AL	69	230	51	14	0	9	(5	4)	92	35	30	29	28	5	43	3	0	2	1	0	3	.222	.312	.400	.712
2016	Oak	AL	87	338	89	12	1	2	(1	1)	109	30	27	36	26	0	65	1	0	4	0	0	10	.263	.314	.322	.637
2017	Oak	AL	153	567	157	49	3	14	(8	6)	254	86	69	94	73	2	100	2	0	3	0	1	10	.277	.360	.448	.808
2018	Oak	AL	157	596	159	37	1	23	(4	19)	267	78	99	106	78	1	128	3	0	3	0	0	8	.267	.353	.448	.801
2019	NYM	NL	9	7	0	0	0	0	(0	0)	0	0	0	0	1	0	4	0	0	0	0	0	0	.000	.125	.000	.125
	Postseason		23	64	9	2	0	1	(0	1)	14	7	5	4	7	0	17	1	1	1	0	0	1	.141	.233	.219	.452
	12 ML YEARS		1118	3991	1043	259	17	104	(45	59)	1648	521	509	555	439	18	748	22	8	40	7	3	81	.261	.335	.413	.748

Josh Lucas

Pitches: R **Bats:** R **Pos:** RP-9   **Ht:** 6'6" **Wt:** 185 **Born:** 11/5/1990 **Age:** 29

			HOW MUCH PITCHED					WHAT HE GAVE UP									THE RESULTS							
Year	Team	Lg	G	GS	GF	IP	BFP	H	R	ER	HR	SH	SF	HB	TBB	IBB	SO	WP	W	L	Pct	Sv-Op	Hld	Vel	OPS	ERC	ERA
2019	Norfolk	AAA	20	2	12	23.2	111	29	19	18	4	0	1	2	12	0	19	0	0	2	.000	2- --	-	-	.898	6.81	6.85
2017	StL	NL	5	0	2	7.1	32	7	3	3	2	0	0	1	4	0	7	1	0	0	-	0-0	0	93	.931	6.58	3.68
2018	Oak	AL	8	1	4	14.1	66	16	11	10	1	0	0	1	9	0	14	0	0	0	-	0-0	0	91	.823	5.85	6.28
2019	Bal	AL	9	0	4	15.2	69	14	12	10	2	0	3	0	7	0	16	0	0	0	-	1-1	0	90	.677	3.71	5.74
	3 ML YEARS		22	1	10	37.1	167	37	26	23	5	0	3	2	20	0	37	1	0	0	-	1-1	0	91	.783	5.05	5.54

Joey Lucchesi

Pitches: L **Bats:** L **Pos:** SP-30   loo-KAY-zee   **Ht:** 6'5" **Wt:** 204 **Born:** 6/6/1993 **Age:** 27

			HOW MUCH PITCHED					WHAT HE GAVE UP									THE RESULTS							
Year	Team	Lg	G	GS	GF	IP	BFP	H	R	ER	HR	SH	SF	HB	TBB	IBB	SO	WP	W	L	Pct	Sv-Op	Hld	Vel	OPS	ERC	ERA
2018	SD	NL	26	26	0	130.0	548	125	63	59	23	3	4	4	43	2	145	4	8	9	.471	0-0	0	90	.766	4.24	4.08
2019	SD	NL	30	30	0	163.2	686	144	78	76	23	5	4	2	56	0	158	8	10	10	.500	0-0	0	90	.702	3.48	4.18
	2 ML YEARS		56	56	0	293.2	1234	269	141	135	46	8	8	6	99	2	303	12	18	19	.486	0-0	0	90	.731	3.81	4.14

Elvis Luciano

Pitches: R **Bats:** R **Pos:** RP-25   **Ht:** 6'3" **Wt:** 200 **Born:** 2/15/2000 **Age:** 20

			HOW MUCH PITCHED					WHAT HE GAVE UP									THE RESULTS							
Year	Team	Lg	G	GS	GF	IP	BFP	H	R	ER	HR	SH	SF	HB	TBB	IBB	SO	WP	W	L	Pct	Sv-Op	Hld	Vel	OPS	ERC	ERA
2019	Tor	AL	25	0	9	33.2	159	36	20	20	4	0	1	3	24	1	27	4	1	0	1.000	0-0	0	94	.847	6.28	5.35

Jonathan Lucroy

Bats: R **Throws:** R **Pos:** C-87;1B-9;PH-8;DH-3   LOO-croy   **Ht:** 6'0" **Wt:** 200 **Born:** 6/13/1986 **Age:** 34

Year	Team	Lg	G	AB	H	2B	3B	HR	(Hm	Rd)	TB	R	RBI	RC	TBB	IBB	SO	HBP	SH	SF	SB	CS	GDP	Avg	OBP	Slg	OPS
2010	Mil	NL	75	277	70	9	0	4	(4	0)	91	24	26	23	18	1	44	1	0	1	4	2	9	.253	.300	.329	.628
2011	Mil	NL	136	430	114	16	1	12	(8	4)	168	45	59	50	29	0	99	2	4	3	2	1	7	.265	.313	.391	.703
2012	Mil	NL	96	316	101	17	4	12	(7	5)	162	46	58	61	22	1	44	4	1	3	4	1	12	.320	.368	.513	.881
2013	Mil	NL	147	521	146	26	6	18	(9	9)	237	59	82	78	46	2	69	5	0	8	9	1	16	.280	.340	.455	.795
2014	Mil	NL	153	585	176	53	2	13	(6	7)	272	73	69	90	66	3	71	2	0	2	4	4	13	.301	.373	.465	.837
2015	Mil	NL	103	371	98	20	3	7	(3	4)	145	51	43	46	36	0	64	1	1	6	1	0	18	.264	.326	.391	.717
2016	2 Tms		142	490	143	24	3	24	(15	9)	245	67	81	74	47	5	100	3	0	4	5	0	16	.292	.355	.500	.855
2017	2 Tms		123	423	112	21	3	6	(2	4)	157	45	40	53	46	6	51	8	0	4	1	0	16	.265	.345	.371	.716
2018	Oak	AL	126	415	100	21	1	4	(1	3)	135	41	51	44	29	1	65	3	1	6	0	0	12	.241	.291	.325	.617
2019	2 Tms		101	293	68	10	1	8	(6	2)	104	30	36	32	27	1	51	5	0	3	0	0	17	.232	.305	.355	.660
	16 Mil	NL	95	338	101	17	3	13	(9	4)	163	48	50	46	33	3	70	1	0	4	5	0	12	.299	.359	.482	.841
	16 Tex	AL	47	152	42	7	0	11	(6	5)	82	19	31	28	14	2	30	2	0	0	0	0	4	.276	.345	.539	.885
	17 Tex	AL	77	281	68	15	0	4	(0	4)	95	27	27	28	19	0	32	4	0	2	1	0	10	.242	.297	.338	.635
	17 Col	NL	46	142	44	6	3	2	(2	0)	62	18	13	25	27	6	19	4	0	2	0	0	6	.310	.429	.437	.865
	19 LAA	AL	74	240	58	8	1	7	(5	2)	89	28	30	28	21	0	39	4	0	3	0	0	15	.242	.310	.371	.681
	19 ChC	NL	27	53	10	2	0	1	(1	0)	15	2	6	4	6	1	12	1	0	0	0	0	2	.189	.283	.283	.566
	Postseason		15	51	12	3	0	1	(1	0)	18	6	6	5	1	0	12	0	0	0	0	0	0	.235	.250	.353	.603
	10 ML YEARS		1202	4121	1128	216	24	108	(61	47)	1716	481	545	551	366	20	658	34	7	40	30	9	136	.274	.335	.416	.751

Dawel Lugo

Bats: R Throws: R Pos: 3B-73;PR-4;DH-2;PH-1   Ht: 6'0" Wt: 220 Born: 12/31/1994 Age: 25

| | | | | | BATTING | | | | | | | | | | | | | | | | RUNNING | | | AVERAGES | | | |
Year Team	Lg	G	AB	H	2B	3B	HR	(Hm	Rd)	TB	R	RBI	RC	TBB	IBB	SO	HBP	SH	SF	SB	CS	GDP	Avg	OBP	Slg	OPS
2019 Toledo	AAA	68	282	94	21	4	5	(-	-)	138	46	41	50	15	2	52	3	0	3	6	3	8	.333	.370	.489	.859
2018 Det	AL	27	94	20	4	1	1	(0	1)	29	10	8	10	7	0	20	0	0	0	0	0	2	.213	.267	.309	.576
2019 Det	AL	77	273	67	11	4	6	(3	3)	104	28	26	22	8	1	59	3	0	4	0	0	8	.245	.271	.381	.652
2 ML YEARS		104	367	87	15	5	7	(3	4)	133	38	34	32	15	1	79	3	0	4	0	0	10	.237	.270	.362	.632

Seth Lugo

Pitches: R Bats: R Pos: RP-61   Ht: 6'4" Wt: 225 Born: 11/17/1989 Age: 30

| | | HOW MUCH PITCHED | | | | WHAT HE GAVE UP | | | | | | | | | | THE RESULTS | | | | | | | |
Year Team	Lg	G	GS	GF	IP	BFP	H	R	ER	HR	SH	SF	HB	TBB	IBB	SO	WP	W	L	Pct	Sv-Op Hld	Vel	OPS	ERC	ERA
2016 NYM	NL	17	8	2	64.0	260	49	19	19	7	8	4	4	21	3	45	1	5	2	.714	0-0 0	92	.666	2.81	2.67
2017 NYM	NL	19	18	1	101.1	436	114	57	53	13	2	5	2	25	1	85	2	7	5	.583	0-0 0	91	.770	4.43	4.71
2018 NYM	NL	54	5	13	101.1	410	81	36	30	9	1	5	2	28	4	103	2	3	4	.429	3-4 11	94	.595	2.49	2.66
2019 NYM	NL	61	0	14	80.0	314	56	28	24	8	1	1	5	16	4	104	2	7	4	.636	6-11 21	94	.562	1.97	2.70
4 ML YEARS		151	31	30	346.2	1420	300	140	126	37	12	15	13	90	12	337	7	22	15	.595	9-15 32	93	.654	2.95	3.27

Jordan Luplow

Bats: R Throws: R Pos: RF-42;LF-34;PH-22;CF-4;DH-3   Ht: 6'1" Wt: 195 Born: 9/26/1993 Age: 26

| | | | | | BATTING | | | | | | | | | | | | | | | | RUNNING | | | AVERAGES | | | |
Year Team	Lg	G	AB	H	2B	3B	HR	(Hm	Rd)	TB	R	RBI	RC	TBB	IBB	SO	HBP	SH	SF	SB	CS	GDP	Avg	OBP	Slg	OPS
2019 Clmbs	AAA	13	45	14	3	0	2	(-	-)	23	12	7	11	10	0	14	2	0	0	2	1	4	.311	.456	.511	.967
2017 Pit	NL	27	78	16	3	1	3	(3	0)	30	6	11	8	6	0	22	2	0	1	0	1	4	.205	.276	.385	.660
2018 Pit	NL	37	92	17	1	3	3	(3	0)	33	16	7	4	10	0	18	1	0	0	2	2	7	.185	.272	.359	.631
2019 Cle	AL	85	225	62	15	1	15	(8	7)	124	42	38	42	33	0	61	2	0	1	3	2	7	.276	.372	.551	.923
3 ML YEARS		149	395	95	19	5	21	(14	7)	187	64	56	54	49	0	101	5	0	2	5	5	18	.241	.330	.473	.804

Gavin Lux

Bats: L Throws: R Pos: 2B-22;PH-4   Ht: 6'2" Wt: 190 Born: 11/23/1997 Age: 22

| | | | | | BATTING | | | | | | | | | | | | | | | | RUNNING | | | AVERAGES | | | |
Year Team	Lg	G	AB	H	2B	3B	HR	(Hm	Rd)	TB	R	RBI	RC	TBB	IBB	SO	HBP	SH	SF	SB	CS	GDP	Avg	OBP	Slg	OPS
2016 2 Tms	Low	56	223	66	13	5	0	(-	-)	89	41	21	37	28	0	51	1	0	1	2	0	4	.296	.375	.399	.775
2017 Gt Lks	A	111	434	106	14	8	7	(-	-)	157	68	39	57	56	0	88	3	3	5	27	10	6	.244	.331	.362	.693
2018 Rcuca	A+	88	358	116	23	7	11	(-	-)	186	64	48	79	43	0	68	1	0	2	11	7	3	.324	.396	.520	.916
2018 Tulsa	AA	28	105	34	4	1	4	(-	-)	52	21	9	21	14	2	20	1	0	0	2	2	2	.324	.408	.495	.904
2019 Tulsa	AA	64	259	81	7	4	13	(-	-)	135	45	37	51	28	1	60	0	0	0	7	3	1	.313	.375	.521	.896
2019 OkCity	AAA	49	199	78	18	4	13	(-	-)	143	54	39	61	33	0	42	0	0	0	3	2	2	.392	.478	.719	1.197
2019 LAD	NL	23	75	18	4	1	2	(0	2)	30	12	9	10	7	0	24	0	0	0	2	0	0	.240	.305	.400	.705

Jesus Luzardo

Pitches: L Bats: L Pos: RP-6   Ht: 6'0" Wt: 209 Born: 9/30/1997 Age: 22

| | | HOW MUCH PITCHED | | | | WHAT HE GAVE UP | | | | | | | | | | THE RESULTS | | | | | | | |
Year Team	Lg	G	GS	GF	IP	BFP	H	R	ER	HR	SH	SF	HB	TBB	IBB	SO	WP	W	L	Pct	Sv-Op Hld	Vel	OPS	ERC	ERA
2017 3 Tms	Low	12	11	0	43.1	171	35	9	8	2	1	0	3	5	0	48	3	2	1	.667	0- - -	-	.549	1.97	1.66
2018 Mdlnd	AA	16	16	0	78.2	310	58	22	20	5	2	3	2	18	0	86	2	7	3	.700	0- - -	-	.579	2.03	2.29
2019 LsVgs	AAA	7	7	0	31.0	131	29	12	11	3	1	1	0	8	0	34	3	1	1	.500	0- - -	-	.673	3.06	3.19
2019 Oak	AL	6	0	2	12.0	46	5	2	2	1	0	0	1	3	0	16	2	0	0	-	2-2 2	96	.434	1.13	1.50

Jordan Lyles

Pitches: R Bats: R Pos: SP-28   Ht: 6'5" Wt: 230 Born: 10/19/1990 Age: 29

| | | HOW MUCH PITCHED | | | | WHAT HE GAVE UP | | | | | | | | | | THE RESULTS | | | | | | | |
Year Team	Lg	G	GS	GF	IP	BFP	H	R	ER	HR	SH	SF	HB	TBB	IBB	SO	WP	W	L	Pct	Sv-Op Hld	Vel	OPS	ERC	ERA
2011 Hou	NL	20	15	2	94.0	415	107	61	56	14	7	1	5	26	1	67	0	2	8	.200	0-0 0	90	.817	4.87	5.36
2012 Hou	NL	25	25	0	141.1	628	159	97	80	20	6	4	5	42	4	99	2	5	12	.294	0-0 0	92	.772	4.67	5.09
2013 Hou	AL	27	25	1	141.2	642	165	98	88	17	0	3	11	49	1	93	5	7	9	.438	1-1 0	92	.801	5.20	5.59
2014 Col	NL	22	22	0	126.2	546	127	64	61	12	4	3	8	46	1	90	6	7	4	.636	0-0 0	91	.750	4.17	4.33
2015 Col	NL	10	10	0	49.0	212	54	32	28	2	3	1	3	19	1	30	2	2	5	.286	0-0 0	92	.751	4.51	5.14
2016 Col	NL	40	5	7	58.2	273	69	46	38	4	1	2	4	28	2	32	5	4	5	.444	1-4 3	93	.790	5.32	5.83
2017 2 Tms	NL	38	5	12	69.2	324	96	61	60	16	2	1	4	22	1	55	4	1	5	.167	0-0 2	94	.948	7.24	7.75
2018 2 Tms	NL	35	8	10	87.2	371	83	42	40	12	3	4	3	28	3	84	5	3	4	.429	0-0 2	94	.718	3.78	4.11
2019 2 Tms	NL	28	28	0	141.0	599	131	72	65	25	2	3	1	55	2	146	4	12	8	.600	0-0 0	93	.767	4.18	4.15
17 Col	NL	33	0	12	46.2	211	61	37	36	11	1	1	4	12	1	33	2	0	2	.000	0-0 2	94	.921	6.72	6.94
17 SD	NL	5	5	0	23.0	113	35	24	24	5	1	0	0	10	0	22	2	1	3	.250	0-0 0	93	1.000	8.31	9.39
18 SD	NL	24	8	5	71.1	300	71	35	34	12	3	3	1	19	0	62	4	2	4	.333	0-0 2	93	.741	4.03	4.29
18 Mil	NL	11	0	5	16.1	71	12	7	6	0	0	1	2	9	3	22	1	1	0	1.000	0-0 0	94	.612	2.63	3.31
19 Pit	NL	17	17	0	82.1	361	88	53	49	16	1	1	1	33	1	90	4	5	7	.417	0-0 0	93	.853	5.20	5.36
19 Mil	NL	11	11	0	58.2	238	43	19	16	9	1	2	0	22	1	56	0	7	1	.875	0-0 0	93	.636	2.87	2.45
9 ML YEARS		245	143	32	909.2	4010	991	573	516	122	28	22	44	315	16	696	33	43	60	.417	2-5 8	92	.787	4.76	5.11

Lance Lynn

Pitches: R Bats: B Pos: SP-33 Ht: 6'5" Wt: 280 Born: 5/12/1987 Age: 33

			HOW MUCH PITCHED					WHAT HE GAVE UP										THE RESULTS							
Year	Team	Lg	G	GS	GF	IP	BFP	H	R	ER	HR	SH	SF	HB	TBB	IBB	SO	WP	W	L	Pct	Sv-Op	Hld	Vel	OPS	ERC	ERA
2011	StL	NL	18	2	2	34.2	136	25	12	12	3	1	0	1	11	1	40	1	1	1	.500	1-2	3	93	.591	2.37	3.12
2012	StL	NL	35	29	2	176.0	744	168	76	74	16	4	3	10	64	3	180	3	18	7	.720	0-0	1	93	.728	3.87	3.78
2013	StL	NL	33	33	0	201.2	856	189	92	89	14	11	8	11	76	0	198	6	15	10	.600	0-0	0	92	.701	3.67	3.97
2014	StL	NL	33	33	0	203.2	866	185	72	62	13	6	4	7	72	1	181	7	15	10	.600	0-0	0	92	.662	3.24	2.74
2015	StL	NL	31	31	0	175.1	751	172	66	59	13	9	2	5	68	5	167	2	12	11	.522	0-0	0	92	.708	3.83	3.03
2017	StL	NL	33	33	0	186.1	776	151	80	71	27	9	3	10	78	5	153	2	11	8	.579	0-0	0	92	.707	3.62	3.43
2018	2 Tms	AL	31	29	0	156.2	700	163	87	83	14	0	2	6	76	3	161	5	10	10	.500	0-0	0	93	.744	4.68	4.77
2019	Tex	AL	33	33	0	208.1	875	195	89	85	21	1	6	8	59	0	246	18	16	11	.593	0-0	0	94	.689	3.41	3.67
18	Min	AL	20	20	0	102.1	469	105	61	58	12	0	2	6	62	3	100	3	7	8	.467	0-0	0	93	.780	5.38	5.10
18	NYY	AL	11	9	0	54.1	231	58	26	25	2	0	0	0	14	0	61	2	3	2	.600	0-0	0	93	.676	3.44	4.14
	Postseason		26	7	3	54.1	244	59	33	29	6	2	3	1	28	5	52	0	5	4	.556	0-0	3	94	.792	5.06	4.80
	8 ML YEARS		247	223	4	1342.2	5704	1248	574	535	121	41	28	58	504	18	1326	44	98	68	.590	1-2	4	93	.701	3.68	3.59

Tyler Lyons

Pitches: L Bats: L Pos: RP-14 Ht: 6'4" Wt: 210 Born: 2/21/1988 Age: 32

			HOW MUCH PITCHED					WHAT HE GAVE UP										THE RESULTS							
Year	Team	Lg	G	GS	GF	IP	BFP	H	R	ER	HR	SH	SF	HB	TBB	IBB	SO	WP	W	L	Pct	Sv-Op	Hld	Vel	OPS	ERC	ERA
2019	Indy	AAA	35	0	12	45.2	181	34	20	17	4	1	1	1	16	0	55	4	4	3	.571	3- -	-	-	.629	2.62	3.35
2013	StL	NL	12	8	1	53.0	223	49	29	28	5	1	0	3	16	0	43	0	2	4	.333	0-0	0	90	.725	3.46	4.75
2014	StL	NL	11	4	1	36.2	155	33	23	18	4	1	2	1	11	2	36	0	0	4	.000	0-0	0	90	.677	3.29	4.42
2015	StL	NL	17	8	1	60.0	255	59	29	25	12	3	2	1	15	0	60	4	3	1	.750	0-0	0	90	.751	4.04	3.75
2016	StL	NL	30	0	10	48.0	187	35	18	18	9	1	1	0	14	0	46	2	2	0	1.000	0-0	4	91	.667	2.83	3.38
2017	StL	NL	50	0	12	54.0	220	39	17	17	3	1	3	7	20	2	68	1	4	1	.800	3-4	15	90	.608	2.68	2.83
2018	StL	NL	27	0	2	16.2	83	24	16	16	3	1	2	2	8	2	19	2	1	0	1.000	0-2	9	89	.986	7.98	8.64
2019	2 Tms		14	0	7	12.2	54	13	9	9	4	0	0	1	5	2	17	0	1	2	.333	0-0	1	90	.956	6.07	6.39
19	Pit	NL	3	0	2	4.0	20	6	5	5	1	0	0	0	3	1	5	0	1	1	.500	0-0	1	90	1.156	9.83	11.25
19	NYY	AL	11	0	5	8.2	34	7	4	4	3	0	0	1	2	1	12	0	0	1	.000	0-0	0	90	.843	4.41	4.15
	7 ML YEARS		161	20	34	281.0	1177	252	141	131	40	8	9	16	89	8	289	9	13	12	.520	3-6	29	90	.722	3.65	4.20

Manny Machado

Bats: R Throws: R Pos: 3B-119;SS-37;PH-2 muh-CHAH-doe Ht: 6'3" Wt: 215 Born: 7/6/1992 Age: 27

						BATTING														RUNNING			AVERAGES			
Year	Team	Lg	G	AB	H	2B	3B	HR	(Hm	Rd)	TB	R	RBI	RC	TBB	IBB	SO	HBP	SH	SF	SB	CS	GDP	Avg	OBP	Slg	OPS
2012	Bal	AL	51	191	50	8	3	7	(7	0)	85	24	26	29	9	0	38	0	1	0	2	0	6	.262	.294	.445	.739
2013	Bal	AL	156	667	189	51	3	14	(5	9)	288	88	71	87	29	0	113	2	9	3	6	7	15	.283	.314	.432	.746
2014	Bal	AL	82	327	91	14	0	12	(9	3)	141	38	32	44	20	2	68	3	2	2	2	0	13	.278	.324	.431	.755
2015	Bal	AL	162	633	181	30	1	35	(21	14)	318	102	86	107	70	2	111	4	2	4	20	8	17	.286	.359	.502	.861
2016	Bal	AL	157	640	188	40	1	37	(18	19)	341	105	96	103	48	9	120	3	0	5	0	3	14	.294	.343	.533	.876
2017	Bal	AL	156	630	163	33	1	33	(22	11)	297	81	95	94	50	3	115	1	0	9	9	4	17	.259	.310	.471	.782
2018	2 Tms		162	632	188	35	3	37	(24	13)	340	84	107	115	70	18	104	2	0	5	14	2	26	.297	.367	.538	.905
2019	SD	NL	156	587	150	21	2	32	(15	17)	271	81	85	86	65	3	128	6	0	3	5	3	24	.256	.334	.462	.796
18	Bal	AL	96	365	115	21	1	24	(17	7)	210	48	65	74	45	12	51	0	0	3	8	1	14	.315	.387	.575	.963
18	LAD		66	267	73	14	2	13	(7	6)	130	36	42	41	25	6	53	2	0	2	6	1	12	.273	.338	.487	.825
	Postseason		23	89	19	3	0	4	(1	3)	34	11	14	8	6	2	24	1	2	1	1	0	5	.213	.268	.382	.650
	8 ML YEARS		1082	4307	1200	232	14	207	(121	86)	2081	603	598	665	361	37	797	21	14	32	58	27	132	.279	.335	.483	.818

Kenta Maeda

Pitches: R Bats: R Pos: SP-26; RP-11 mah-AY-duh Ht: 6'1" Wt: 184 Born: 4/11/1988 Age: 32

			HOW MUCH PITCHED					WHAT HE GAVE UP										THE RESULTS							
Year	Team	Lg	G	GS	GF	IP	BFP	H	R	ER	HR	SH	SF	HB	TBB	IBB	SO	WP	W	L	Pct	Sv-Op	Hld	Vel	OPS	ERC	ERA
2016	LAD	NL	32	32	0	175.2	716	150	72	68	20	0	3	8	50	6	179	6	16	11	.593	0-0	0	90	.649	3.09	3.48
2017	LAD	NL	29	25	1	134.1	557	121	68	63	22	6	4	5	34	1	140	4	13	6	.684	1-1	0	92	.714	3.48	4.22
2018	LAD	NL	39	20	4	125.1	532	115	58	53	13	2	3	5	43	4	153	2	8	10	.444	2-2	5	92	.706	3.51	3.81
2019	LAD	NL	37	26	3	153.2	624	114	70	69	22	2	3	4	51	1	169	3	10	8	.556	3-3	4	92	.642	2.79	4.04
	Postseason		20	3	2	28.0	124	26	12	12	2	0	0	2	12	2	32	2	2	1	.667	0-0	3	93	.713	3.65	3.86
	4 ML YEARS		137	103	8	589.0	2429	500	268	253	77	10	13	22	178	12	641	15	47	35	.573	6-6	9	91	.675	3.19	3.87

Matt Magill

Pitches: R Bats: R Pos: RP-50 Ht: 6'3" Wt: 210 Born: 11/10/1989 Age: 30

			HOW MUCH PITCHED					WHAT HE GAVE UP										THE RESULTS							
Year	Team	Lg	G	GS	GF	IP	BFP	H	R	ER	HR	SH	SF	HB	TBB	IBB	SO	WP	W	L	Pct	Sv-Op	Hld	Vel	OPS	ERC	ERA
2019	Roch	AAA	5	1	2	5.1	20	2	1	1	0	0	0	0	1	0	8	0	1	0	1.000	1- -	-	-	.308	0.53	1.69
2013	LAD	NL	6	6	0	27.2	137	27	25	20	6	1	2	1	28	1	26	1	0	2	.000	0-0	0	91	.869	7.48	6.51
2016	Cin	NL	5	0	2	4.1	20	5	3	3	1	1	0	0	5	0	1	0	0	0	-	0-0	0	93	1.098	10.68	6.23
2018	Min	AL	40	0	9	56.2	249	58	24	24	11	1	3	3	23	0	56	0	3	3	.500	0-1	6	95	.809	5.13	3.81
2019	2 Tms	AL	50	0	20	50.2	229	51	31	23	7	2	2	2	20	3	64	5	5	2	.714	5-7	1	95	.760	4.24	4.09
19	Min	AL	28	0	8	28.1	133	30	21	14	4	1	1	2	15	1	36	2	2	0	1.000	0-0	0	95	.830	5.30	4.45
19	Sea	AL	22	0	12	22.1	96	21	10	9	3	1	1	0	5	2	28	3	3	2	.600	5-7	1	95	.667	2.98	3.63
	4 ML YEARS		101	6	31	139.1	635	141	83	70	25	5	6	6	76	4	147	6	8	7	.533	5-8	7	94	.813	5.39	4.52

Tyler Mahle

Pitches: R Bats: R Pos: SP-25   Ht: 6'3" Wt: 210 Born: 9/29/1994 Age: 25

			HOW MUCH PITCHED					WHAT HE GAVE UP										THE RESULTS						
Year	Team	Lg	G	GS	GF	IP	BFP	H	R	ER	HR	SH	SF	HB	TBB	IBB	SO	WP	W	L	Pct	Sv-Op	Hld	Vel	OPS	ERC	ERA
2017	Cin	NL	4	4	0	20.0	92	19	6	6	0	2	0	4	11	1	14	1	1	2	.333	0-0	0	93	.684	4.27	2.70
2018	Cin	NL	23	23	0	112.0	507	125	68	62	22	5	3	3	53	7	110	1	7	9	.438	0-0	0	92	.848	5.77	4.98
2019	Cin	NL	25	25	0	129.2	556	136	82	74	25	2	2	6	34	0	129	2	3	12	.200	0-0	0	93	.775	4.61	5.14
3 ML YEARS			52	52	0	261.2	1155	280	156	142	47	9	5	13	98	8	253	4	11	23	.324	0-0	0	93	.800	5.09	4.88

Mikie Mahtook

Bats: R Throws: R Pos: CF-7;PR-2;LF-1;DH-1   MIKE-ee MAH-took   Ht: 6'1" Wt: 216 Born: 11/30/1989 Age: 30

							BATTING												RUNNING			AVERAGES			
Year	Team	Lg	G	AB	H	2B	3B	HR	(Hm | Rd)	TB	R	RBI	RC	TBB	IBB	SO	HBP	SH	SF	SB	CS	GDP	Avg	OBP	Slg	OPS
2019	Toledo	AAA	98	354	92	17	1	21	(- | -)	174	64	56	64	51	1	106	5	1	4	14	7	6	.260	.357	.492	.849
2015	TB	AL	41	105	31	5	1	9	(3 | 6)	65	22	19	22	6	0	31	3	1	0	4	3	0	.295	.351	.619	.970
2016	TB	AL	65	185	36	9	0	3	(1 | 2)	54	16	11	5	7	0	68	2	1	1	0	1	2	.195	.231	.292	.523
2017	Det	AL	109	348	96	15	6	12	(6 | 6)	159	50	38	48	23	0	79	6	0	2	6	0	4	.276	.330	.457	.787
2018	Det	AL	67	223	45	4	2	9	(3 | 6)	80	24	29	24	21	1	66	3	0	3	4	1	3	.202	.276	.359	.635
2019	Det	AL	9	23	0	0	0	0	(0 | 0)	0	0	0	0	2	0	11	0	0	0	0	0	0	.000	.080	.000	.080
5 ML YEARS			291	884	208	33	9	33	(13 | 20)	358	112	97	99	59	1	255	14	2	6	14	5	9	.235	.292	.405	.697

Luke Maile

Bats: R Throws: R Pos: C-44   MAY-lee   Ht: 6'3" Wt: 225 Born: 2/6/1991 Age: 29

							BATTING												RUNNING			AVERAGES			
Year	Team	Lg	G	AB	H	2B	3B	HR	(Hm | Rd)	TB	R	RBI	RC	TBB	IBB	SO	HBP	SH	SF	SB	CS	GDP	Avg	OBP	Slg	OPS
2015	TB	AL	15	35	6	3	0	0	(0 | 0)	9	2	2	0	0	0	8	0	0	0	0	0	3	.171	.171	.257	.429
2016	TB	AL	42	119	27	7	0	3	(2 | 1)	43	10	15	11	4	1	36	0	3	0	0	0	0	.227	.252	.361	.613
2017	Tor	AL	46	130	19	5	0	2	(1 | 1)	30	10	7	2	3	0	35	2	0	1	1	0	2	.146	.176	.231	.407
2018	Tor	AL	68	202	50	13	1	3	(2 | 1)	74	22	27	28	25	0	67	2	0	2	2	0	4	.248	.333	.366	.700
2019	Tor	AL	45	119	18	2	1	2	(2 | 0)	28	9	9	4	8	0	33	0	2	0	1	0	1	.151	.205	.235	.440
5 ML YEARS			216	605	120	30	2	10	(7 | 3)	184	53	60	45	40	1	179	4	5	3	4	0	12	.198	.252	.304	.556

Martin Maldonado

Bats: R Throws: R Pos: C-103;PH-2;1B-1   mar-TEEN   Ht: 6'0" Wt: 230 Born: 8/16/1986 Age: 33

							BATTING												RUNNING			AVERAGES			
Year	Team	Lg	G	AB	H	2B	3B	HR	(Hm | Rd)	TB	R	RBI	RC	TBB	IBB	SO	HBP	SH	SF	SB	CS	GDP	Avg	OBP	Slg	OPS
2011	Mil	NL	3	1	0	0	0	0	(0 | 0)	0	0	0	0	0	0	1	0	0	0	0	0	0	.000	.000	.000	.000
2012	Mil	NL	78	233	62	9	0	8	(6 | 2)	95	22	30	28	17	0	56	2	4	0	1	1	5	.266	.321	.408	.729
2013	Mil	NL	67	183	31	7	1	4	(1 | 3)	52	13	22	14	13	1	53	3	3	0	0	0	7	.169	.236	.284	.520
2014	Mil	NL	52	111	26	5	0	4	(2 | 2)	43	14	16	14	11	1	32	3	1	0	0	0	4	.234	.320	.387	.707
2015	Mil	NL	79	229	48	7	0	4	(4 | 0)	67	19	22	20	23	3	65	1	1	2	0	1	6	.210	.282	.293	.575
2016	Mil	NL	76	208	42	7	0	8	(6 | 2)	73	21	21	23	35	9	56	6	3	1	1	0	6	.202	.332	.351	.683
2017	LAA	AL	138	429	95	19	1	14	(5 | 9)	158	43	38	37	15	1	119	18	8	1	0	2	12	.221	.276	.368	.645
2018 2 Tms		AL	119	373	84	18	1	9	(2 | 7)	131	39	44	38	16	0	98	11	2	2	0	1	8	.225	.276	.351	.627
2019 3 Tms		AL	105	333	71	19	0	12	(8 | 4)	126	46	27	29	32	1	86	6	2	1	0	0	11	.213	.293	.378	.671
18 LAA		AL	78	265	59	14	0	5	(2 | 3)	88	24	32	30	13	0	73	10	1	1	0	1	3	.223	.284	.332	.616
18 Hou		AL	41	108	25	4	1	4	(0 | 4)	43	15	12	8	3	0	25	1	1	1	0	0	5	.231	.257	.398	.655
19 KC		AL	74	238	54	15	0	6	(2 | 4)	87	26	17	21	17	0	55	5	2	1	0	0	9	.227	.291	.366	.657
19 ChC		NL	4	11	0	0	0	0	(0 | 0)	0	0	0	0	2	1	5	0	0	0	0	0	0	.000	.154	.000	.154
19 Hou		AL	27	84	17	4	0	6	(6 | 0)	39	20	10	8	13	0	26	1	0	0	0	0	2	.202	.316	.464	.781
Postseason			7	19	2	1	0	1	(1 | 0)	6	3	1	0	0	0	7	1	1	0	0	0	2	.105	.150	.316	.466
9 ML YEARS			717	2100	459	91	3	63	(34 | 29)	745	217	220	203	162	16	566	50	24	7	2	5	54	.219	.289	.355	.644

Sean Manaea

Pitches: L Bats: R Pos: SP-5   muh-NIE-uh   Ht: 6'5" Wt: 245 Born: 2/1/1992 Age: 28

			HOW MUCH PITCHED					WHAT HE GAVE UP										THE RESULTS						
Year	Team	Lg	G	GS	GF	IP	BFP	H	R	ER	HR	SH	SF	HB	TBB	IBB	SO	WP	W	L	Pct	Sv-Op	Hld	Vel	OPS	ERC	ERA
2019	LsVgs	AAA	5	5	0	28.0	105	16	11	10	5	0	0	1	6	0	43	1	3	1	.750	0- -	-	-	.582	1.83	3.21
2016	Oak	AL	25	24	0	144.2	594	135	65	62	20	4	4	4	37	1	124	3	7	9	.438	0-0	0	92	.713	3.53	3.86
2017	Oak	AL	29	29	0	158.2	692	167	88	77	18	2	10	5	55	1	140	8	12	10	.545	0-0	0	92	.763	4.51	4.37
2018	Oak	AL	27	27	0	160.2	654	141	67	64	21	4	2	8	32	1	108	9	12	9	.571	0-0	0	90	.663	3.02	3.59
2019	Oak	AL	5	5	0	29.2	109	16	4	4	3	0	0	2	7	0	30	1	4	0	1.000	0-0	0	90	.509	1.58	1.21
4 ML YEARS			86	85	0	493.2	2049	459	224	207	62	9	8	24	131	3	402	21	35	28	.556	0-0	0	91	.703	3.53	3.77

Trey Mancini

Bats: R Throws: R Pos: RF-87;1B-56;DH-17;LF-6;PH-1   Ht: 6'4" Wt: 215 Born: 3/18/1992 Age: 28

							BATTING												RUNNING			AVERAGES			
Year	Team	Lg	G	AB	H	2B	3B	HR	(Hm | Rd)	TB	R	RBI	RC	TBB	IBB	SO	HBP	SH	SF	SB	CS	GDP	Avg	OBP	Slg	OPS
2016	Bal	AL	5	14	5	1	0	3	(3 | 0)	15	3	5	5	0	0	4	0	0	0	0	0	0	.357	.400	1.071	1.471
2017	Bal	AL	147	543	159	26	4	24	(11 | 13)	265	65	78	90	33	1	139	6	0	4	1	0	12	.293	.338	.488	.826
2018	Bal	AL	156	582	141	23	3	24	(13 | 11)	242	69	58	55	44	1	153	5	0	5	0	1	17	.242	.299	.416	.715
2019	Bal	AL	154	602	175	38	2	35	(18 | 17)	322	106	97	101	63	3	143	9	0	5	1	0	22	.291	.364	.535	.899
4 ML YEARS			462	1741	480	88	9	86	(45 | 41)	844	243	238	251	140	5	439	21	0	14	2	1	51	.276	.335	.485	.819

Joe Mantiply

Pitches: L **Bats:** R **Pos:** RP-1   **Ht:** 6'4" **Wt:** 215 **Born:** 3/1/1991 **Age:** 29

		HOW MUCH PITCHED						WHAT HE GAVE UP										THE RESULTS							
Year Team	Lg	G	GS	GF	IP	BFP	H	R	ER	HR	SH	SF	HB	TBB	IBB	SO	WP	W	L	Pct	Sv-Op	Hld	Vel	OPS	ERC	ERA
2019 Lsvlle	AAA	18	0	3	29.0	115	26	12	12	2	0	2	2	3	0	26	1	0	0	-	1--	-	-	.658	2.51	3.72
2019 S-WB	AAA	6	0	0	9.1	40	11	6	5	3	0	0	1	1	0	7	0	0	0	-	0--	-	-	.813	5.28	4.82
2016 Det	AL	5	0	3	2.2	16	7	5	5	1	1	0	0	2	1	2	0	0	0	-	0-0	0	88	1.446	19.98	16.88
2019 NYY	AL	1	0	0	3.0	14	3	3	3	1	0	0	0	2	0	2	0	1	0	1.000	0-0	0	89	1.024	6.85	9.00
2 ML YEARS		6	0	3	5.2	30	10	8	8	2	1	0	0	4	1	4	0	1	0	1.000	0-0	0	88	1.243	12.59	12.71

Dillon Maples

Pitches: R **Bats:** R **Pos:** RP-14   **Ht:** 6'2" **Wt:** 230 **Born:** 5/9/1992 **Age:** 28

		HOW MUCH PITCHED						WHAT HE GAVE UP										THE RESULTS							
Year Team	Lg	G	GS	GF	IP	BFP	H	R	ER	HR	SH	SF	HB	TBB	IBB	SO	WP	W	L	Pct	Sv-Op	Hld	Vel	OPS	ERC	ERA
2019 Iowa	AAA	38	0	14	43.0	188	21	19	18	1	0	1	6	36	0	79	5	4	4	.500	7--	-	-	.542	2.91	3.77
2017 ChC	NL	6	0	1	5.1	27	6	6	6	0	0	0	0	6	0	11	1	0	0	-	0-0	0	97	.825	6.99	10.13
2018 ChC	NL	9	0	1	5.1	29	7	7	7	2	0	0	2	5	0	9	2	1	0	1.000	0-0	0	97	1.210	12.98	11.81
2019 ChC	NL	14	0	3	11.2	54	6	7	7	2	0	0	4	10	0	18	0	1	0	1.000	0-0	0	97	.670	4.99	5.40
3 ML YEARS		29	0	5	22.1	110	19	20	20	4	0	0	6	21	0	38	3	2	0	1.000	0-0	0	97	.852	7.21	8.06

Nick Margevicius

Pitches: L **Bats:** L **Pos:** SP-12; RP-5   mahr-GAH-vih-chus   **Ht:** 6'5" **Wt:** 220 **Born:** 6/18/1996 **Age:** 24

		HOW MUCH PITCHED						WHAT HE GAVE UP										THE RESULTS							
Year Team	Lg	G	GS	GF	IP	BFP	H	R	ER	HR	SH	SF	HB	TBB	IBB	SO	WP	W	L	Pct	Sv-Op	Hld	Vel	OPS	ERC	ERA
2019 Amrillo	AA	12	12	0	69.0	287	75	35	33	14	0	1	1	13	0	53	4	4	4	.500	0--	-	-	.810	4.53	4.30
2019 SD	NL	17	12	1	57.0	263	73	46	43	12	3	0	3	19	1	42	1	2	6	.250	0-0	0	88	.912	6.43	6.79

Manuel Margot

Bats: R **Throws:** R **Pos:** CF-135; PH-22; PR-4   mar-GOH   **Ht:** 5'11" **Wt:** 180 **Born:** 9/28/1994 **Age:** 25

				BATTING																	RUNNING			AVERAGES			
Year Team	Lg	G	AB	H	2B	3B	HR	(Hm	Rd)	TB	R	RBI	RC	TBB	IBB	SO	HBP	SH	SF	SB	CS	GDP	Avg	OBP	Slg	OPS
2016 SD	NL	10	37	9	4	1	0	(0	0)	15	4	3	5	0	0	7	0	0	0	2	0	0	.243	.243	.405	.649
2017 SD	NL	126	487	128	18	7	13	(7	6)	199	53	39	55	35	0	106	2	1	4	17	7	6	.263	.313	.409	.721
2018 SD	NL	141	477	117	26	8	8	(5	3)	183	50	51	56	32	4	88	2	1	7	11	10	9	.245	.292	.384	.675
2019 SD	NL	151	398	93	19	3	12	(3	9)	154	59	37	47	38	1	88	2	3	0	20	4	6	.234	.304	.387	.691
4 ML YEARS		428	1399	347	67	19	33	(15	18)	551	166	130	163	105	5	289	6	5	11	50	21	21	.248	.301	.394	.695

Jake Marisnick

Bats: R **Throws:** R **Pos:** CF-109; PR-10; PH-7; DH-6   mah-RIZ-nick   **Ht:** 6'4" **Wt:** 220 **Born:** 3/30/1991 **Age:** 29

				BATTING																	RUNNING			AVERAGES			
Year Team	Lg	G	AB	H	2B	3B	HR	(Hm	Rd)	TB	R	RBI	RC	TBB	IBB	SO	HBP	SH	SF	SB	CS	GDP	Avg	OBP	Slg	OPS
2013 Mia	NL	40	109	20	2	1	1	(1	0)	27	6	5	7	6	0	27	1	1	1	3	1	1	.183	.231	.248	.478
2014 2 Tms		65	221	55	8	0	3	(3	0)	72	21	19	19	8	3	67	3	2	3	11	3	2	.249	.281	.326	.607
2015 Hou	AL	133	339	80	15	4	9	(4	5)	130	46	36	40	18	0	105	5	6	4	24	9	2	.236	.281	.383	.665
2016 Hou	AL	118	287	60	18	1	5	(1	4)	95	40	21	23	16	0	83	3	4	1	10	5	4	.209	.257	.331	.588
2017 Hou	AL	106	230	56	10	0	16	(10	6)	114	50	35	31	20	1	90	6	2	1	9	4	5	.243	.319	.496	.815
2018 Hou	AL	103	213	45	8	1	10	(2	8)	85	34	28	24	15	1	84	4	1	1	6	2	6	.211	.275	.399	.674
2019 Hou	AL	120	292	68	16	3	10	(5	5)	120	46	34	31	17	0	95	6	3	0	10	3	6	.233	.289	.411	.700
14 Mia	NL	14	48	8	0	0	0	(0	0)	8	3	0	1	3	1	19	0	0	0	5	0	0	.167	.216	.167	.382
14 Hou	AL	51	173	47	8	0	3	(3	0)	64	18	19	18	5	2	48	3	2	3	6	3	2	.272	.299	.370	.669
Postseason		9	10	3	1	0	0	(0	0)	4	1	0	2	0	0	3	0	0	0	1	0	0	.300	.300	.400	.700
7 ML YEARS		685	1691	384	77	10	54	(26	28)	643	243	178	175	100	5	551	28	19	11	73	27	26	.227	.280	.380	.660

Nick Markakis

Bats: L **Throws:** L **Pos:** RF-103; LF-9; PH-6; DH-1   mar-KAY-kiss   **Ht:** 6'1" **Wt:** 210 **Born:** 11/17/1983 **Age:** 36

				BATTING																	RUNNING			AVERAGES			
Year Team	Lg	G	AB	H	2B	3B	HR	(Hm	Rd)	TB	R	RBI	RC	TBB	IBB	SO	HBP	SH	SF	SB	CS	GDP	Avg	OBP	Slg	OPS
2006 Bal	AL	147	491	143	25	2	16	(9	7)	220	72	62	67	43	3	72	3	3	2	2	0	15	.291	.351	.448	.799
2007 Bal	AL	161	637	191	43	3	23	(15	8)	309	97	112	103	61	5	112	5	1	6	18	6	22	.300	.362	.485	.848
2008 Bal	AL	157	595	182	48	1	20	(11	9)	292	106	87	113	99	7	113	2	0	1	10	7	10	.306	.406	.491	.897
2009 Bal	AL	161	642	188	45	2	18	(8	10)	291	94	101	97	56	0	98	3	0	10	6	2	12	.293	.347	.453	.801
2010 Bal	AL	160	629	187	45	3	12	(8	4)	274	79	60	99	73	9	93	2	0	5	7	2	18	.297	.370	.436	.805
2011 Bal	AL	160	641	182	31	1	15	(8	7)	260	72	73	90	62	6	75	7	0	6	12	3	16	.284	.351	.406	.756
2012 Bal	AL	104	420	125	28	3	13	(9	4)	198	59	54	69	42	3	51	4	0	5	1	1	11	.298	.363	.471	.834
2013 Bal	AL	160	634	172	24	0	10	(6	4)	226	89	59	66	55	3	76	3	0	8	1	2	17	.271	.329	.356	.685
2014 Bal	AL	155	642	177	27	1	14	(8	6)	248	81	50	82	62	4	84	4	0	2	4	2	10	.276	.342	.386	.729
2015 Atl	NL	156	612	181	38	1	3	(1	2)	230	73	53	81	70	11	83	3	0	1	2	1	17	.296	.370	.376	.746
2016 Atl	NL	158	599	161	38	0	13	(7	6)	238	67	89	82	71	9	101	5	0	9	0	2	16	.269	.346	.397	.744
2017 Atl	NL	160	593	163	39	1	8	(4	4)	228	76	76	77	68	8	110	6	0	3	0	2	16	.275	.354	.384	.738
2018 Atl	NL	162	623	185	43	2	14	(4	10)	274	78	93	96	72	10	80	1	0	9	1	1	20	.297	.366	.440	.806
2019 Atl	NL	116	414	118	25	2	9	(4	5)	174	61	62	60	47	1	59	2	0	6	2	0	11	.285	.356	.420	.776
Postseason		11	43	9	1	0	1	(1	0)	13	5	3	4	4	0	5	0	0	0	1	0	0	.209	.277	.302	.579
14 ML YEARS		2117	8172	2355	499	22	188	(103	85)	3462	1104	1031	1182	881	79	1207	50	4	73	66	31	209	.288	.358	.424	.782

Parker Markel

Pitches: R Bats: R Pos: RP-20   Ht: 6'5" Wt: 240 Born: 9/15/1990 Age: 29

		HOW MUCH PITCHED					WHAT HE GAVE UP										THE RESULTS							
Year	Team	Lg	G	GS	GF	IP	BFP	H	R	ER	HR	SH	SF	HB	TBB	IBB	SO	WP	W	L	Pct	Sv-Op	Hld	Vel	OPS	ERC	ERA
2019	Ark	AA	5	0	3	7.2	27	2	0	0	0	0	0	0	2	0	18	0	2	0	1.000	1--	-	-	.228	0.44	0.00
2019	Tacom	AAA	22	0	19	27.2	119	13	9	8	3	1	1	2	21	0	44	11	2	0	1.000	8--	-	-	.550	2.86	2.60
2019	2 Tms		20	0	8	22.0	110	26	21	19	6	0	0	3	17	1	24	2	0	1	.000	0-0	0	96	.985	8.74	7.77
19	Sea	AL	5	0	0	4.2	28	10	9	8	3	0	0	1	4	0	3	1	0	0	-	0-0	0	96	1.449	21.44	15.43
19	Pit	NL	15	0	8	17.1	82	16	12	11	3	0	0	2	13	1	21	1	0	1	.000	0-0	0	96	.826	5.93	5.71

German Marquez

Pitches: R Bats: R Pos: SP-28   hair-MAHN   Ht: 6'1" Wt: 225 Born: 2/22/1995 Age: 25

		HOW MUCH PITCHED					WHAT HE GAVE UP										THE RESULTS							
Year	Team	Lg	G	GS	GF	IP	BFP	H	R	ER	HR	SH	SF	HB	TBB	IBB	SO	WP	W	L	Pct	Sv-Op	Hld	Vel	OPS	ERC	ERA
2016	Col	NL	6	3	0	20.2	98	28	12	12	2	2	1	3	6	0	15	0	1	1	.500	0-0	0	93	.932	6.21	5.23
2017	Col	NL	29	29	0	162.0	701	174	82	79	25	5	4	8	49	3	147	6	11	7	.611	0-0	0	95	.806	4.67	4.39
2018	Col	NL	33	33	0	196.0	817	179	90	82	24	2	6	8	57	5	230	8	14	11	.560	0-0	0	95	.698	3.45	3.77
2019	Col	NL	28	28	0	174.0	721	174	96	92	29	6	4	5	35	0	175	14	12	5	.706	0-0	0	95	.740	3.86	4.76
	Postseason		1	1	0	5.0	22	7	2	2	1	0	0	0	1	0	5	0	0	1	.000	0-0	0	96	.840	6.52	3.60
	4 ML YEARS		96	93	0	552.2	2337	555	280	265	80	15	15	24	147	8	567	28	38	24	.613	0-0	0	95	.753	4.03	4.32

Deven Marrero

Bats: R Throws: R Pos: PH-3;SS-2;3B-1;PR-1   Ht: 6'0" Wt: 190 Born: 8/25/1990 Age: 29

			BATTING																	RUNNING			AVERAGES			
Year	Team	Lg	G	AB	H	2B	3B	HR	(Hm	Rd)	TB	R	RBI	RC	TBB	IBB	SO	HBP	SH	SF	SB	CS	GDP	Avg	OBP	Slg	OPS
2019	NewOr	AAA	112	383	94	16	2	15	(-	-)	159	55	42	55	43	1	100	1	3	1	10	1	12	.245	.322	.415	.738
2015	Bos	AL	25	53	12	0	0	1	(0	1)	15	8	3	4	3	0	19	0	0	0	2	1	0	.226	.268	.283	.551
2016	Bos	AL	13	12	1	0	0	0	(0	0)	1	0	0	0	2	0	5	0	0	0	0	0	0	.083	.214	.083	.298
2017	Bos	AL	71	171	36	9	0	4	(1	3)	57	32	27	18	12	0	61	0	3	2	5	0	8	.211	.259	.333	.593
2018	Ari	NL	49	78	13	1	1	0	(0	0)	16	11	7	4	6	0	23	0	0	1	3	0	5	.167	.224	.205	.429
2019	Mia	NL	5	5	0	0	0	0	(0	0)	0	0	0	0	0	0	3	0	0	0	0	0	0	.000	.000	.000	.000
	Postseason		1	2	0	0	0	0	(0	0)	0	0	0	0	0	0	2	0	0	0	0	0	0	.000	.000	.000	.000
	5 ML YEARS		163	319	62	10	1	5	(1	4)	89	51	37	26	23	0	111	0	3	3	10	1	13	.194	.246	.279	.525

Evan Marshall

Pitches: R Bats: R Pos: RP-55   Ht: 6'2" Wt: 225 Born: 4/18/1990 Age: 30

		HOW MUCH PITCHED					WHAT HE GAVE UP										THE RESULTS							
Year	Team	Lg	G	GS	GF	IP	BFP	H	R	ER	HR	SH	SF	HB	TBB	IBB	SO	WP	W	L	Pct	Sv-Op	Hld	Vel	OPS	ERC	ERA
2019	Charllt	AAA	9	0	4	10.0	37	8	0	0	0	1	0	0	1	0	13	1	3	0	1.000	2--	-	-	.479	1.56	0.00
2014	Ari	NL	57	0	11	49.1	210	50	17	15	3	2	1	2	17	3	54	3	4	4	.500	0-1	19	94	.709	3.76	2.74
2015	Ari	NL	13	0	4	13.1	61	20	9	9	3	0	0	0	5	1	7	1	0	2	.000	0-2	2	94	.999	8.27	6.08
2016	Ari	NL	15	0	8	15.1	79	28	18	15	2	0	0	1	8	2	9	1	0	1	.000	0-0	1	93	1.083	10.46	8.80
2017	Sea	AL	6	0	2	7.2	38	12	8	8	1	0	0	0	5	1	4	0	0	0	-	0-0	0	94	.993	8.94	9.39
2018	Cle	AL	10	0	1	7.0	37	12	6	6	0	0	0	1	4	0	9	1	0	0	-	0-1	3	93	.866	9.01	7.71
2019	CWS	AL	55	0	2	50.2	209	42	16	14	5	0	1	0	24	2	41	1	4	2	.667	0-4	19	94	.669	3.45	2.49
	6 ML YEARS		156	0	28	143.1	634	164	74	67	14	2	2	4	63	9	124	7	8	9	.471	0-8	44	94	.797	5.16	4.21

Ketel Marte

Bats: B Throws: R Pos: CF-96;2B-83;SS-11;PH-3   kuh-TELL marr-TAY   Ht: 6'1" Wt: 165 Born: 10/12/1993 Age: 26

			BATTING																	RUNNING			AVERAGES			
Year	Team	Lg	G	AB	H	2B	3B	HR	(Hm	Rd)	TB	R	RBI	RC	TBB	IBB	SO	HBP	SH	SF	SB	CS	GDP	Avg	OBP	Slg	OPS
2015	Sea	AL	57	219	62	14	3	2	(1	1)	88	25	17	33	24	0	43	0	2	2	8	4	1	.283	.351	.402	.753
2016	Sea	AL	119	437	113	21	2	1	(1	0)	141	55	33	41	18	0	84	2	3	6	11	5	10	.259	.287	.323	.610
2017	Ari	NL	73	223	58	11	2	5	(1	4)	88	30	18	27	29	3	37	1	0	2	3	1	3	.260	.345	.395	.740
2018	Ari	NL	153	520	135	26	12	14	(8	6)	227	68	59	67	54	3	79	3	1	2	6	1	12	.260	.332	.437	.768
2019	Ari	NL	144	569	187	36	9	32	(13	19)	337	97	92	121	53	2	86	4	0	2	10	2	7	.329	.389	.592	.981
	Postseason		4	17	7	0	2	1	(0	1)	14	4	2	4	0	0	5	0	0	0	0	0	0	.412	.412	.824	1.235
	5 ML YEARS		546	1968	555	108	28	54	(24	30)	881	275	219	289	178	8	329	10	6	14	38	13	33	.282	.342	.448	.790

Starling Marte

Bats: R Throws: R Pos: CF-130;PR-2;PH-1   marr-TAY   Ht: 6'1" Wt: 190 Born: 10/9/1988 Age: 31

			BATTING																	RUNNING			AVERAGES			
Year	Team	Lg	G	AB	H	2B	3B	HR	(Hm	Rd)	TB	R	RBI	RC	TBB	IBB	SO	HBP	SH	SF	SB	CS	GDP	Avg	OBP	Slg	OPS
2012	Pit	NL	47	167	43	3	6	5	(3	2)	73	18	17	21	8	0	50	3	2	2	12	5	5	.257	.300	.437	.737
2013	Pit	NL	135	510	143	26	10	12	(5	7)	225	83	35	74	25	2	138	24	6	1	41	15	6	.280	.343	.441	.784
2014	Pit	NL	135	495	144	29	6	13	(5	8)	224	73	56	70	33	0	131	17	0	0	30	11	5	.291	.356	.453	.808
2015	Pit	NL	153	579	166	30	2	19	(10	9)	257	84	81	81	27	3	123	19	3	5	30	10	14	.287	.337	.444	.780
2016	Pit	NL	129	489	152	34	5	9	(2	7)	223	71	46	77	23	5	104	16	1	0	47	12	8	.311	.362	.456	.818
2017	Pit	NL	77	309	85	7	2	7	(5	2)	117	48	31	46	20	0	63	8	0	2	21	4	5	.275	.333	.379	.712
2018	Pit	NL	145	559	155	32	5	20	(8	12)	257	81	72	83	35	2	109	8	1	3	33	14	11	.277	.327	.460	.787
2019	Pit	NL	132	539	159	31	6	23	(9	14)	271	97	82	95	25	1	94	16	2	4	25	6	15	.295	.342	.503	.845
	Postseason		8	32	4	1	0	1	(0	1)	8	2	1	1	1	0	7	1	0	0	1	0	2	.125	.176	.250	.426
	8 ML YEARS		953	3647	1047	192	42	108	(47	61)	1647	555	420	547	196	13	812	111	15	17	239	77	69	.287	.341	.452	.793

Brett Martin

Pitches: L **Bats:** L **Pos:** RP-49; SP-2   **Ht:** 6'4" **Wt:** 190 **Born:** 4/28/1995 **Age:** 25

			HOW MUCH PITCHED					WHAT HE GAVE UP												THE RESULTS						
Year	Team	Lg	G	GS	GF	IP	BFP	H	R	ER	HR	SH	SF	HB	TBB	IBB	SO	WP	W	L	Pct	Sv-Op	Hld	Vel	OPS	ERC	ERA
2019	Nashv	AAA	10	0	2	12.2	51	10	1	1	0	0	0	0	4	0	19	0	0	0	-	1--	-	-	.551	2.06	0.71
2019	Tex	AL	51	2	7	62.1	280	72	38	33	7	0	3	2	18	2	62	3	2	3	.400	0-1	4	94	.745	4.54	4.76

Chris Martin

Pitches: R **Bats:** R **Pos:** RP-58   **Ht:** 6'8" **Wt:** 215 **Born:** 6/2/1986 **Age:** 34

			HOW MUCH PITCHED					WHAT HE GAVE UP												THE RESULTS						
Year	Team	Lg	G	GS	GF	IP	BFP	H	R	ER	HR	SH	SF	HB	TBB	IBB	SO	WP	W	L	Pct	Sv-Op	Hld	Vel	OPS	ERC	ERA
2014	Col	NL	16	0	1	15.2	69	22	12	12	2	0	0	0	4	0	14	1	0	0	-	0-0	3	94	.915	6.30	6.89
2015	NYY	AL	24	0	8	20.2	99	28	13	13	2	0	0	1	6	1	18	3	0	2	.000	1-1	5	94	.777	5.52	5.66
2018	Tex	AL	46	0	8	41.2	177	46	21	21	5	0	1	3	5	2	37	4	1	5	.167	0-3	14	95	.722	3.85	4.54
2019	2 Tms		58	0	20	55.2	216	52	23	21	9	0	2	0	5	0	65	0	1	3	.250	4-6	18	96	.675	2.98	3.40
19	Tex	AL	38	0	15	38.0	147	35	13	13	8	0	1	0	4	0	43	0	0	2	.000	4-5	12	96	.716	3.27	3.08
19	Atl	NL	20	0	5	17.2	69	17	10	8	1	0	1	0	1	0	22	0	1	1	.500	0-1	6	95	.589	2.36	4.08
4 ML YEARS			144	0	37	133.2	561	148	69	67	18	0	3	4	20	3	134	8	2	10	.167	5-10	40	95	.737	4.00	4.51

Corbin Martin

Pitches: R **Bats:** R **Pos:** SP-5   **Ht:** 6'2" **Wt:** 200 **Born:** 12/28/1995 **Age:** 24

			HOW MUCH PITCHED					WHAT HE GAVE UP												THE RESULTS						
Year	Team	Lg	G	GS	GF	IP	BFP	H	R	ER	HR	SH	SF	HB	TBB	IBB	SO	WP	W	L	Pct	Sv-Op	Hld	Vel	OPS	ERC	ERA
2019	RdRck	AAA	9	8	0	37.1	158	33	13	13	2	2	0	2	18	0	45	1	2	1	.667	0--	-	-	.715	3.72	3.13
2019	Hou	AL	5	5	0	19.1	92	23	14	12	8	0	0	0	12	0	19	1	1	1	.500	0-0	0	95	1.030	8.64	5.59

Jason Martin

Bats: L **Throws:** R **Pos:** LF-12;PH-4;PR-4;CF-3   **Ht:** 5'9" **Wt:** 185 **Born:** 9/5/1995 **Age:** 24

			BATTING																		RUNNING			AVERAGES			
Year	Team	Lg	G	AB	H	2B	3B	HR	(Hm	Rd)	TB	R	RBI	RC	TBB	IBB	SO	HBP	SH	SF	SB	CS	GDP	Avg	OBP	Slg	OPS
2019	Indy	AAA	101	370	96	25	5	8	(-	-)	155	47	50	49	29	1	79	1	2	4	9	6	3	.259	.312	.419	.731
2019	Pit	NL	20	36	9	2	0	0	(0	0)	11	5	2	5	4	0	10	0	0	0	2	0	0	.250	.325	.306	.631

Leonys Martin

Bats: L **Throws:** R **Pos:** CF-65   lay-OH-nees mar-TEEN   **Ht:** 6'2" **Wt:** 200 **Born:** 3/6/1988 **Age:** 32

			BATTING																		RUNNING			AVERAGES			
Year	Team	Lg	G	AB	H	2B	3B	HR	(Hm	Rd)	TB	R	RBI	RC	TBB	IBB	SO	HBP	SH	SF	SB	CS	GDP	Avg	OBP	Slg	OPS
2011	Tex	AL	8	8	3	1	0	0	(0	0)	4	2	0	1	0	0	1	0	0	0	0	0	0	.375	.375	.500	.875
2012	Tex	AL	24	46	8	5	2	0	(0	0)	17	6	6	4	4	0	12	0	1	0	3	0	2	.174	.235	.370	.605
2013	Tex	AL	147	457	119	21	6	8	(3	5)	176	66	49	58	28	0	104	8	12	3	36	9	6	.260	.313	.385	.698
2014	Tex	AL	155	533	146	13	7	7	(4	3)	194	68	40	64	39	3	114	2	7	2	31	12	4	.274	.325	.364	.689
2015	Tex	AL	95	288	63	12	0	5	(1	4)	90	26	25	22	16	1	69	2	3	1	14	5	5	.219	.264	.313	.576
2016	Sea	AL	143	518	128	17	3	15	(7	8)	196	72	47	64	44	0	149	3	4	7	24	6	10	.247	.306	.378	.684
2017	2 Tms		49	128	22	3	1	3	(2	1)	36	14	9	7	8	1	33	2	0	0	7	4	2	.172	.232	.281	.513
2018	2 Tms	AL	84	318	81	15	3	11	(6	5)	135	48	33	39	30	1	77	3	0	2	7	4	2	.255	.323	.425	.747
2019	Cle	AL	65	236	47	7	0	9	(1	8)	81	32	19	21	21	0	78	4	3	0	4	5	1	.199	.276	.343	.619
17	Sea	AL	34	115	20	2	1	3	(2	1)	33	12	8	5	5	1	29	2	0	0	6	4	2	.174	.221	.287	.508
17	ChC	NL	15	13	2	1	0	0	(0	0)	3	2	1	2	3	0	4	0	0	0	1	0	0	.154	.313	.231	.543
18	Det	AL	78	303	76	15	3	9	(4	5)	124	45	29	37	29	1	75	3	0	1	7	3	1	.251	.321	.409	.731
18	Cle	AL	6	15	5	0	0	2	(2	0)	11	3	4	2	1	0	2	0	0	1	0	1	1	.333	.353	.733	1.086
Postseason			5	3	0	0	0	0	(0	0)	0	1	0	0	0	0	1	0	0	0	0	0	0	.000	.000	.000	.000
9 ML YEARS			770	2532	617	94	22	58	(24	34)	929	334	228	280	190	6	637	24	30	16	126	45	32	.244	.301	.367	.668

Russell Martin

Bats: R **Throws:** R **Pos:** C-60;PH-20;3B-7   **Ht:** 5'10" **Wt:** 215 **Born:** 2/15/1983 **Age:** 37

			BATTING																		RUNNING			AVERAGES			
Year	Team	Lg	G	AB	H	2B	3B	HR	(Hm	Rd)	TB	R	RBI	RC	TBB	IBB	SO	HBP	SH	SF	SB	CS	GDP	Avg	OBP	Slg	OPS
2006	LAD	NL	121	415	117	26	4	10	(8	2)	181	65	65	58	45	8	57	4	1	3	10	5	17	.282	.355	.436	.792
2007	LAD	NL	151	540	158	32	3	19	(8	11)	253	87	87	84	67	1	89	7	0	6	21	9	16	.293	.374	.469	.843
2008	LAD	NL	155	553	155	25	0	13	(6	7)	219	87	69	89	90	8	83	5	0	2	18	6	16	.280	.385	.396	.781
2009	LAD	NL	143	505	126	19	0	7	(4	3)	166	63	53	62	69	9	80	11	2	1	11	6	18	.250	.352	.329	.680
2010	LAD	NL	97	331	82	13	0	5	(2	3)	110	45	26	40	48	7	61	4	1	3	6	2	7	.248	.347	.332	.679
2011	NYY	AL	125	417	99	17	0	18	(8	10)	170	57	65	56	50	1	81	5	1	3	8	2	19	.237	.324	.408	.732
2012	NYY	AL	133	422	89	18	0	21	(13	8)	170	50	53	50	53	0	95	8	2	0	6	1	13	.211	.311	.403	.713
2013	Pit	NL	127	438	99	21	0	15	(6	9)	165	51	55	47	58	2	108	8	1	1	9	5	13	.226	.327	.377	.703
2014	Pit	NL	111	379	110	20	0	11	(8	3)	163	45	67	66	59	5	78	15	2	5	4	4	16	.290	.402	.430	.832
2015	Tor	AL	129	441	106	23	2	23	(13	10)	202	76	77	66	53	1	106	8	0	5	4	5	22	.240	.329	.458	.787
2016	Tor	AL	137	455	105	16	0	20	(8	12)	181	62	74	69	64	1	148	10	1	5	2	1	12	.231	.335	.398	.733
2017	Tor	AL	91	307	68	12	0	13	(8	5)	119	49	35	35	50	0	83	7	1	0	1	2	13	.221	.343	.388	.731
2018	Tor	AL	90	289	56	8	0	10	(4	6)	94	37	25	35	56	0	82	7	0	0	0	3	7	.194	.338	.325	.663
2019	LAD	NL	83	209	46	5	0	6	(2	4)	69	29	20	28	30	3	60	8	0	2	1	0	1	.220	.337	.330	.667
Postseason			57	195	36	8	0	5	(3	2)	59	22	18	15	24	0	52	9	0	2	1	0	5	.185	.300	.303	.603
14 ML YEARS			1693	5701	1416	255	9	191	(92	99)	2262	803	771	785	792	46	1211	107	12	36	101	51	190	.248	.349	.397	.746

Richie Martin Jr.

Bats: R Throws: R Pos: SS-117;PR-6;PH-2;DH-1   Ht: 5'11" Wt: 190 Born: 12/22/1994 Age: 25

						BATTING													RUNNING			AVERAGES			
Year	Team	Lg	G	AB	H	2B	3B	HR	(Hm | Rd)	TB	R	RBI	RC	TBB	IBB	SO	HBP	SH	SF	SB	CS	GDP	Avg	OBP	Slg	OPS
2019	Bal	AL	120	283	59	8	3	6	(3 | 3)	91	29	23	17	14	0	83	6	5	1	10	1	6	.208	.260	.322	.581

Carlos Martinez

Pitches: R Bats: R Pos: RP-48   Ht: 6'0" Wt: 190 Born: 9/21/1991 Age: 28

			HOW MUCH PITCHED					WHAT HE GAVE UP										THE RESULTS							
Year	Team	Lg	G	GS	GF	IP	BFP	H	R	ER	HR	SH	SF	HB	TBB	IBB	SO	WP	W	L	Pct	Sv-Op Hld	Vel	OPS	ERC	ERA
2013	StL	NL	21	1	5	28.1	124	31	16	16	1	1	1	3	9	1	24	0	2	1	.667	1-1	3	97	.704	4.20	5.08
2014	StL	NL	57	7	13	89.1	386	90	41	40	4	7	1	4	36	8	84	8	2	4	.333	1-6	17	97	.713	3.79	4.03
2015	StL	NL	31	29	1	179.2	755	168	65	60	13	9	4	8	63	5	184	8	14	7	.667	0-0	1	95	.687	3.51	3.01
2016	StL	NL	31	31	0	195.1	809	169	68	66	15	2	2	11	70	1	174	8	16	9	.640	0-0	0	96	.643	3.29	3.04
2017	StL	NL	32	32	0	205.0	858	179	93	83	27	4	2	8	71	3	217	9	12	11	.522	0-0	0	96	.694	3.51	3.64
2018	StL	NL	33	18	9	118.2	521	100	48	41	5	7	4	11	60	4	117	5	8	6	.571	5-5	3	94	.647	3.46	3.11
2019	StL	NL	48	0	38	48.1	200	39	18	17	2	1	1	3	18	1	53	2	4	2	.667	24-27	3	96	.590	2.77	3.17
	Postseason		16	0	1	16.2	65	10	6	6	0	1	1	1	7	1	13	1	0	1	.000	0-0	5	97	.518	1.70	3.24
	7 ML YEARS		253	118	66	864.2	3653	776	349	323	67	31	15	48	327	23	853	40	58	40	.592	31-39	27	95	.671	3.47	3.36

J.D. Martinez

Bats: R Throws: R Pos: DH-107;RF-24;LF-15;PH-2   Ht: 6'3" Wt: 220 Born: 8/21/1987 Age: 32

						BATTING													RUNNING			AVERAGES			
Year	Team	Lg	G	AB	H	2B	3B	HR	(Hm	Rd)	TB	R	RBI	RC	TBB	IBB	SO	HBP	SH	SF	SB	CS	GDP	Avg	OBP	Slg	OPS
2011	Hou	NL	53	208	57	13	0	6	(3	3)	88	29	35	30	13	1	48	2	0	3	0	1	4	.274	.319	.423	.742
2012	Hou	NL	113	395	95	14	3	11	(5	6)	148	34	55	45	40	0	96	1	0	2	0	2	18	.241	.311	.375	.685
2013	Hou	AL	86	296	74	17	0	7	(4	3)	112	24	36	29	10	0	82	0	0	3	2	0	8	.250	.272	.378	.650
2014	Det	AL	123	441	139	30	3	23	(13	10)	244	57	76	75	30	5	126	3	0	6	6	3	8	.315	.358	.553	.912
2015	Det	AL	158	596	168	33	2	38	(20	18)	319	93	102	100	53	7	178	5	0	3	3	2	11	.282	.344	.535	.879
2016	Det	AL	120	460	141	35	2	22	(13	9)	246	69	68	77	49	2	128	3	0	5	1	2	13	.307	.373	.535	.908
2017	2 Tms		119	432	131	26	3	45	(27	18)	298	85	104	92	53	8	128	0	0	4	4	0	23	.303	.376	.690	1.066
2018	Bos	AL	150	569	188	37	2	43	(26	17)	358	111	130	138	69	11	146	4	0	7	6	1	19	.330	.402	.629	1.031
2019	Bos	AL	146	575	175	33	2	36	(18	18)	320	98	105	117	72	9	138	4	0	5	2	0	19	.304	.383	.557	.939
17	Det	AL	57	200	61	13	2	16	(11	5)	126	38	39	39	29	5	54	0	0	3	2	0	10	.305	.388	.630	1.018
17	Ari	AL	62	232	70	13	1	29	(16	13)	172	47	65	53	24	3	74	0	0	1	2	0	13	.302	.366	.741	1.107
	Postseason		21	77	22	3	0	6	(1	5)	43	10	20	18	11	3	21	0	0	2	0	1	1	.286	.367	.558	.925
	9 ML YEARS		1068	3972	1168	238	17	231	(129	102)	2133	600	711	703	389	43	1070	22	0	38	24	11	123	.294	.357	.537	.894

Jose Martinez

Bats: R Throws: R Pos: RF-75;PH-42;DH-8;LF-7   Ht: 6'6" Wt: 215 Born: 7/25/1988 Age: 31

						BATTING													RUNNING			AVERAGES			
Year	Team	Lg	G	AB	H	2B	3B	HR	(Hm	Rd)	TB	R	RBI	RC	TBB	IBB	SO	HBP	SH	SF	SB	CS	GDP	Avg	OBP	Slg	OPS
2016	StL	NL	12	16	7	1	0	0	(0	0)	8	4	1	4	2	0	1	0	0	0	0	0	0	.438	.500	.500	1.000
2017	StL	NL	106	272	84	13	1	14	(8	6)	141	47	46	47	32	2	60	0	1	2	4	0	9	.309	.379	.518	.897
2018	StL	NL	152	534	163	30	4	17	(9	8)	244	64	83	89	49	0	104	2	2	3	0	3	15	.305	.364	.457	.821
2019	StL	NL	128	334	90	13	2	10	(3	7)	137	45	42	46	35	0	82	2	0	2	3	0	14	.269	.340	.410	.751
	4 ML YEARS		398	1156	344	57	3	41	(20	21)	530	160	172	186	118	2	247	4	3	7	7	3	38	.298	.363	.458	.821

Nick Martini

Bats: L Throws: L Pos: LF-26;PH-7;DH-1   Ht: 5'11" Wt: 205 Born: 6/27/1990 Age: 30

						BATTING													RUNNING			AVERAGES			
Year	Team	Lg	G	AB	H	2B	3B	HR	(Hm	Rd)	TB	R	RBI	RC	TBB	IBB	SO	HBP	SH	SF	SB	CS	GDP	Avg	OBP	Slg	OPS
2019	LsVgs	AAA	70	274	90	18	0	8	(-	-)	132	57	42	59	49	1	51	3	0	3	0	0	8	.328	.432	.482	.913
2018	Oak	AL	55	152	45	9	3	1	(1	0)	63	26	19	30	21	1	36	5	0	1	0	0	0	.296	.397	.414	.811
2019	2 Tms		32	93	21	4	1	1	(0	1)	30	8	7	14	14	0	26	1	0	1	0	0	0	.226	.330	.323	.653
19	Oak	AL	6	11	1	0	0	1	(0	1)	4	1	2	2	2	0	5	0	0	0	0	0	0	.091	.231	.364	.594
19	SD	NL	26	82	20	4	1	0	(0	0)	26	7	5	12	12	0	21	1	0	1	0	0	0	.244	.344	.317	.661
	Postseason		1	4	1	0	0	0	(0	0)	1	0	0	0	0	0	2	0	0	0	0	0	0	.250	.250	.250	.500
	2 ML YEARS		87	245	66	13	4	2	(1	1)	93	34	26	44	35	1	62	6	0	2	0	0	0	.269	.372	.380	.751

James Marvel

Pitches: R Bats: R Pos: SP-4   Ht: 6'4" Wt: 205 Born: 9/17/1993 Age: 26

			HOW MUCH PITCHED					WHAT HE GAVE UP										THE RESULTS							
Year	Team	Lg	G	GS	GF	IP	BFP	H	R	ER	HR	SH	SF	HB	TBB	IBB	SO	WP	W	L	Pct	Sv-Op Hld	Vel	OPS	ERC	ERA
2019	Altna	AA	17	17	0	101.2	412	85	36	35	6	2	4	10	24	2	83	2	9	5	.643	0--	-	-	.634	2.70	3.10
2019	Indy	AAA	11	11	0	60.2	245	46	19	18	4	4	1	3	22	1	53	5	7	0	1.000	0--	-	-	.634	2.65	2.67
2019	Pit	NL	4	4	0	17.1	84	25	16	16	4	2	0	2	6	0	9	0	0	3	.000	0-0	0	91	1.024	8.04	8.31

Jeff Mathis

Bats: R **Throws:** R **Pos:** C-86   **Ht:** 6'0" **Wt:** 205 **Born:** 3/31/1983 **Age:** 37

Year	Team	Lg	G	AB	H	2B	3B	HR	(Hm	Rd)	TB	R	RBI	RC	TBB	IBB	SO	HBP	SH	SF	SB	CS	GDP	Avg	OBP	Slg	OPS
2005	LAA	AL	5	3	1	0	0	0	(0	0)	1	1	0	0	0	0	1	0	0	0	0	0	0	.333	.333	.333	.667
2006	LAA	AL	23	55	8	2	0	2	(1	1)	16	9	6	4	7	1	14	0	0	1	0	0	0	.145	.238	.291	.529
2007	LAA	AL	59	171	36	12	0	4	(3	1)	60	24	23	13	15	0	49	2	3	4	0	1	3	.211	.276	.351	.627
2008	LAA	AL	94	283	55	8	0	9	(4	5)	90	35	42	33	30	4	90	3	8	4	2	2	1	.194	.275	.318	.593
2009	LAA	AL	84	237	50	8	0	5	(3	2)	73	26	28	24	22	0	73	4	8	1	2	3	2	.211	.288	.308	.596
2010	LAA	AL	68	205	40	6	1	3	(2	1)	57	19	18	10	6	0	59	1	3	3	3	0	3	.195	.219	.278	.497
2011	LAA	AL	93	247	43	12	0	3	(1	2)	64	18	22	12	15	2	75	2	14	3	1	2	3	.174	.225	.259	.484
2012	Tor	AL	71	211	46	13	0	8	(5	3)	83	25	27	18	9	0	68	0	6	1	1	0	2	.218	.249	.393	.642
2013	Mia	NL	73	232	42	7	1	5	(3	2)	66	14	29	15	21	4	76	1	1	0	0	0	5	.181	.251	.284	.535
2014	Mia	NL	64	175	35	7	0	2	(1	1)	48	12	12	11	15	2	64	0	5	0	0	0	2	.200	.263	.274	.537
2015	Mia	NL	32	93	15	4	1	2	(1	1)	27	9	12	3	7	1	24	0	0	3	0	0	2	.161	.214	.290	.504
2016	Mia	NL	41	126	30	4	1	2	(0	2)	42	12	15	10	4	0	36	1	1	0	0	0	1	.238	.267	.333	.601
2017	Ari	NL	60	186	40	10	2	2	(2	0)	60	13	11	14	14	1	61	2	1	0	1	0	6	.215	.277	.323	.600
2018	Ari	NL	69	195	39	9	1	1	(1	0)	53	15	20	15	20	1	66	0	1	2	0	0	7	.200	.272	.272	.544
2019	Tex	NL	88	228	36	9	0	2	(1	1)	51	17	12	9	15	1	87	0	0	1	1	0	2	.158	.209	.224	.433
	Postseason		13	29	11	5	0	1	(0	1)	19	3	4	5	1	0	8	0	1	0	0	0	0	.379	.400	.655	1.055
	15 ML YEARS		924	2647	516	111	7	50	(28	22)	791	249	277	191	200	17	843	16	51	24	11	8	39	.195	.254	.299	.552

Phil Maton

Pitches: R **Bats:** R **Pos:** RP-30   **Ht:** 6'3" **Wt:** 220 **Born:** 3/25/1993 **Age:** 27

Year	Team	Lg	G	GS	GF	IP	BFP	H	R	ER	HR	SH	SF	HB	TBB	IBB	SO	WP	W	L	Pct	Sv-Op	Hld	Vel	OPS	ERC	ERA
2019	ElPaso	AAA	13	0	5	18.2	78	17	6	6	2	1	1	2	6	1	30	0	2	1	.667	2- -	-		.707	3.74	2.89
2019	Clmbs	AAA	9	0	3	10.2	39	5	3	3	1	0	0	0	4	0	17	0	0	1	.000	3- -	-		.459	1.50	2.53
2017	SD	NL	46	0	12	43.0	180	41	23	20	10	0	0	1	14	0	46	0	3	2	.600	1-1	8	93	.778	4.56	4.19
2018	SD	NL	45	0	12	47.1	214	50	25	23	3	2	1	2	23	1	55	4	0	2	.000	0-1	3	91	.757	4.55	4.37
2019	2 Tms		30	0	13	36.2	163	38	27	25	7	2	0	2	12	0	33	3	0	0	-	0-0	2	91	.806	4.72	6.14
19	SD	NL	21	0	5	24.1	115	34	22	21	6	2	0	1	6	0	20	1	0	0	-	0-0	2	91	.948	6.90	7.77
19	Cle	AL	9	0	8	12.1	48	4	5	4	1	0	0	1	6	0	13	2	0	0	-	0-0	0	90	.449	1.36	2.92
	3 ML YEARS		121	0	37	127.0	557	129	75	68	20	4	1	5	49	1	134	7	3	4	.429	1-2	13	92	.779	4.62	4.82

Steven Matz

Pitches: L **Bats:** R **Pos:** SP-30; RP-2   **Ht:** 6'2" **Wt:** 200 **Born:** 5/29/1991 **Age:** 29

Year	Team	Lg	G	GS	GF	IP	BFP	H	R	ER	HR	SH	SF	HB	TBB	IBB	SO	WP	W	L	Pct	Sv-Op	Hld	Vel	OPS	ERC	ERA
2015	NYM	NL	6	6	0	35.2	149	34	9	9	4	1	1	1	10	0	34	0	4	0	1.000	0-0	0	94	.650	3.55	2.27
2016	NYM	NL	22	22	0	132.1	547	129	53	50	14	8	1	5	31	2	129	3	9	8	.529	0-0	0	94	.689	3.49	3.40
2017	NYM	NL	13	13	0	66.2	298	83	46	45	12	3	1	3	19	2	48	1	2	7	.222	0-0	0	93	.860	5.78	6.08
2018	NYM	NL	30	30	0	154.0	654	134	77	68	25	6	2	10	58	2	152	0	5	11	.313	0-0	0	93	.730	3.91	3.97
2019	NYM	NL	32	30	0	160.1	691	163	83	75	27	5	1	7	52	7	153	3	11	10	.524	0-0	1	93	.777	4.44	4.21
	Postseason		3	3	0	14.2	64	17	6	6	0	0	0	0	4	1	13	0	0	1	.000	0-0	0	94	.678	3.60	3.68
	5 ML YEARS		103	101	0	549.0	2339	543	268	247	82	23	6	26	170	13	516	7	31	36	.463	0-0	1	93	.746	4.15	4.05

Dustin May

Pitches: R **Bats:** R **Pos:** RP-10; SP-4   **Ht:** 6'6" **Wt:** 180 **Born:** 9/6/1997 **Age:** 22

Year	Team	Lg	G	GS	GF	IP	BFP	H	R	ER	HR	SH	SF	HB	TBB	IBB	SO	WP	W	L	Pct	Sv-Op	Hld	Vel	OPS	ERC	ERA
2016	Ddgrs	R	10	6	1	30.1	135	37	16	13	0	0	1	3	4	0	34	3	0	1	.000	1- -	-	-	.696	3.82	3.86
2017	2 Tms	Low	25	24	0	134.0	566	127	63	54	8	3	2	9	27	0	128	10	9	6	.600	0- -	-	-	.638	2.95	3.63
2018	Rcuca	A+	17	17	0	98.1	407	91	42	36	9	2	2	8	17	0	94	6	7	3	.700	0- -	-	-	.641	3.03	3.29
2018	Tulsa	AA	6	6	0	34.1	145	27	14	14	0	0	0	4	12	0	28	4	2	2	.500	0- -	-	-	.560	2.48	3.67
2019	Tulsa	AA	15	15	0	79.1	333	71	41	33	5	3	3	7	20	0	86	8	3	5	.375	0- -	-	-	.627	3.00	3.74
2019	OkCity	AAA	5	5	0	27.1	114	21	8	7	0	1	0	5	9	0	24	1	3	0	1.000	0- -	-	-	.562	2.60	2.30
2019	LAD	NL	14	4	0	34.2	141	33	17	14	2	0	0	4	5	0	32	0	2	3	.400	0-1	4	96	.639	3.06	3.63

Trevor May

Pitches: R **Bats:** R **Pos:** RP-65   **Ht:** 6'5" **Wt:** 240 **Born:** 9/23/1989 **Age:** 30

Year	Team	Lg	G	GS	GF	IP	BFP	H	R	ER	HR	SH	SF	HB	TBB	IBB	SO	WP	W	L	Pct	Sv-Op	Hld	Vel	OPS	ERC	ERA
2014	Min	AL	10	9	0	45.2	213	59	41	40	7	0	1	2	22	1	44	3	3	6	.333	0-0	0	92	.900	6.80	7.88
2015	Min	AL	48	16	9	114.2	492	127	53	51	11	3	4	4	26	2	110	4	8	9	.471	0-2	7	93	.752	4.06	4.00
2016	Min	AL	44	0	10	42.2	187	39	26	25	7	0	0	2	17	1	60	10	2	2	.500	0-2	6	94	.757	4.07	5.27
2018	Min	AL	24	1	6	25.1	103	21	9	9	4	2	0	1	5	0	36	1	4	1	.800	3-3	5	94	.646	2.85	3.20
2019	Min	AL	65	0	13	64.1	266	43	24	21	8	0	3	3	26	1	79	3	5	3	.625	2-4	17	96	.587	2.59	2.94
	5 ML YEARS		191	26	38	292.2	1261	289	153	146	37	5	8	12	96	5	329	21	22	21	.512	5-11	35	94	.735	4.00	4.49

Cameron Maybin

Bats: R Throws: R Pos: LF-46;RF-36;PH-4;CF-3;PR-3;DH-2   Ht: 6'3" Wt: 215 Born: 4/4/1987 Age: 33

Year Team	Lg	G	AB	H	2B	3B	HR	(Hm	Rd)	TB	R	RBI	RC	TBB	IBB	SO	HBP	SH	SF	SB	CS	GDP	Avg	OBP	Slg	OPS
2019 Clmbs	AAA	14	51	11	3	0	0	(-	-)	14	4	5	6	13	0	20	2	0	1	1	2	1	.216	.388	.275	.663
2007 Det	AL	24	49	7	3	0	1	(0	1)	13	8	2	2	3	0	21	1	0	0	5	0	1	.143	.208	.265	.473
2008 Fla	NL	8	32	16	2	0	0	(0	0)	18	9	2	8	3	0	8	0	1	0	4	0	0	.500	.543	.563	1.105
2009 Fla	NL	54	176	44	12	2	4	(1	3)	72	30	13	15	17	1	51	1	4	1	1	3	2	.250	.318	.409	.727
2010 Fla	NL	82	291	68	7	3	8	(5	3)	105	46	28	37	24	1	92	5	1	1	9	2	4	.234	.302	.361	.663
2011 SD	NL	137	516	136	24	8	9	(2	7)	203	82	40	69	44	2	125	2	4	2	40	8	6	.264	.323	.393	.716
2012 SD	NL	147	507	123	20	5	8	(3	5)	177	67	45	52	44	1	110	4	3	3	26	7	12	.243	.306	.349	.656
2013 SD	NL	14	51	8	1	0	1	(0	1)	12	7	5	0	4	1	9	1	1	0	4	1	3	.157	.232	.235	.467
2014 SD	NL	95	251	59	13	4	1	(0	1)	83	24	15	22	19	2	56	1	0	1	4	3	8	.235	.290	.331	.621
2015 Atl	NL	141	505	135	18	2	10	(5	5)	187	65	59	64	45	1	102	1	1	3	23	6	16	.267	.327	.370	.697
2016 Det	AL	94	349	110	14	5	4	(3	1)	146	65	43	60	36	0	69	3	2	1	15	6	8	.315	.383	.418	.801
2017 2 Tms	AL	114	395	90	20	2	10	(3	4)	144	63	35	51	51	1	94	2	1	1	33	8	12	.228	.318	.365	.683
2018 2 Tms	NL	129	342	85	14	2	4	(2	2)	115	32	28	38	38	1	75	2	0	2	10	5	7	.249	.326	.336	.662
2019 NYY	AL	82	239	68	17	0	11	(5	6)	118	48	32	36	30	0	72	0	0	0	9	6	5	.285	.364	.494	.858
17 LAA	AL	93	336	79	19	1	6	(2	4)	118	57	22	42	48	1	78	2	0	1	29	5	11	.235	.333	.351	.685
17 Hou	AL	21	59	11	1	1	4	(1	3)	26	6	13	9	3	0	16	0	1	0	4	3	1	.186	.226	.441	.666
18 Mia	NL	99	251	63	12	1	3	(2	1)	86	20	20	29	32	1	55	2	0	2	8	5	3	.251	.338	.343	.681
18 Sea	AL	30	91	22	2	1	1	(0	1)	29	12	8	9	6	0	20	0	0	0	2	0	4	.242	.289	.319	.607
Postseason		6	7	2	0	0	0	(0	0)	2	2	0	2	1	0	1	0	0	0	1	0	0	.286	.375	.286	.661
13 ML YEARS		1121	3703	949	165	33	71	(29	42)	1393	546	347	454	358	11	884	23	18	15	183	55	83	.256	.324	.376	.701

Mike Mayers

Pitches: R Bats: R Pos: RP-16   MY-erz   Ht: 6'3" Wt: 200 Born: 12/6/1991 Age: 28

Year Team	Lg	G	GS	GF	IP	BFP	H	R	ER	HR	SH	SF	HB	TBB	IBB	SO	WP	W	L	Pct	Sv-Op	Hld	Vel	OPS	ERC	ERA
2019 Memp	AAA	20	1	10	20.0	86	21	10	7	4	0	0	0	7	0	24	1	0	1	.000	6--	-	-	.832	4.88	3.15
2016 StL	NL	4	1	0	5.1	35	16	16	16	3	0	1	1	3	0	2	0	1	1	.500	0-0	0	93	1.438	25.90	27.00
2017 StL	NL	3	0	1	4.2	25	8	8	6	2	0	2	0	4	1	3	0	0	0	-	0-0	0	94	1.427	13.79	11.57
2018 StL	NL	50	0	15	51.2	226	59	28	27	7	3	3	1	15	1	49	4	2	1	.667	1-1	6	96	.822	4.72	4.70
2019 StL	NL	16	0	4	19.0	88	21	14	14	3	0	0	1	11	2	16	1	0	1	.000	0-0	1	95	.888	5.90	6.63
4 ML YEARS		73	1	20	80.2	374	104	66	63	15	3	6	3	33	4	70	5	3	3	.500	1-1	7	95	.931	6.57	7.03

Jack Mayfield

Bats: R Throws: R Pos: SS-21;2B-5;PH-2;PR-2;3B-1   Ht: 5'11" Wt: 190 Born: 9/30/1990 Age: 29

Year Team	Lg	G	AB	H	2B	3B	HR	(Hm	Rd)	TB	R	RBI	RC	TBB	IBB	SO	HBP	SH	SF	SB	CS	GDP	Avg	OBP	Slg	OPS
2019 RdRck	AAA	100	380	109	26	1	26	(-	-)	215	78	79	77	37	0	78	5	0	9	7	1	11	.287	.350	.566	.916
2019 Hou	AL	26	64	10	5	0	2	(0	2)	21	8	5	3	1	0	16	0	0	0	0	0	0	.156	.169	.328	.497

Tim Mayza

Pitches: L Bats: L Pos: RP-68   Ht: 6'3" Wt: 220 Born: 1/15/1992 Age: 28

Year Team	Lg	G	GS	GF	IP	BFP	H	R	ER	HR	SH	SF	HB	TBB	IBB	SO	WP	W	L	Pct	Sv-Op	Hld	Vel	OPS	ERC	ERA
2017 Tor	AL	19	0	7	17.0	79	24	15	13	3	0	0	0	4	0	27	0	1	0	1.000	0-0	2	94	.874	6.27	6.88
2018 Tor	AL	37	0	9	35.2	151	33	13	13	3	0	0	2	14	4	40	2	2	0	1.000	0-0	1	94	.695	3.61	3.28
2019 Tor	AL	68	0	5	51.1	227	45	29	28	8	1	2	1	27	2	55	4	1	3	.250	0-1	18	94	.741	4.20	4.91
3 ML YEARS		124	0	21	104.0	457	102	57	54	14	1	2	3	45	6	122	6	4	3	.571	0-1	21	94	.750	4.32	4.67

Nomar Mazara

Bats: L Throws: L Pos: RF-101;DH-8;PH-8   Ht: 6'4" Wt: 215 Born: 4/26/1995 Age: 25

Year Team	Lg	G	AB	H	2B	3B	HR	(Hm	Rd)	TB	R	RBI	RC	TBB	IBB	SO	HBP	SH	SF	SB	CS	GDP	Avg	OBP	Slg	OPS
2016 Tex	AL	145	516	137	13	3	20	(7	13)	216	59	64	67	39	1	112	6	0	7	0	2	12	.266	.320	.419	.739
2017 Tex	AL	148	554	140	30	2	20	(11	9)	234	64	101	87	55	6	127	4	0	3	2	2	12	.253	.323	.422	.745
2018 Tex	AL	128	489	126	25	1	20	(15	5)	213	61	77	67	40	2	116	4	0	3	1	0	13	.258	.317	.436	.753
2019 Tex	AL	116	429	115	27	1	19	(8	11)	201	69	66	60	28	2	108	6	0	6	4	1	5	.268	.318	.469	.786
Postseason		2	6	1	0	0	0	(0	0)	1	1	0	0	0	0	3	0	0	0	0	0	0	.167	.167	.167	.333
4 ML YEARS		537	1988	518	95	7	79	(41	38)	864	253	308	281	162	11	463	20	0	19	7	5	42	.261	.320	.435	.754

Chris Mazza

Pitches: R Bats: R Pos: RP-9   Ht: 6'4" Wt: 180 Born: 10/17/1989 Age: 30

Year Team	Lg	G	GS	GF	IP	BFP	H	R	ER	HR	SH	SF	HB	TBB	IBB	SO	WP	W	L	Pct	Sv-Op	Hld	Vel	OPS	ERC	ERA
2019 Syrcse	AAA	14	13	0	76.0	301	65	33	31	6	3	1	3	18	0	62	3	3	3	.500	0--	-	-	.655	2.79	3.67
2019 NYM	NL	9	0	6	16.1	74	21	10	10	0	0	1	4	5	0	11	0	1	1	.500	0-0	0	92	.905	5.81	5.51

Ryan McBroom

Bats: R **Throws:** L **Pos:** RF-12;1B-6;PH-4;LF-3   **Ht:** 6'3" **Wt:** 235 **Born:** 4/9/1992 **Age:** 28

								BATTING											RUNNING			AVERAGES			
Year Team	Lg	G	AB	H	2B	3B	HR	(Hm | Rd)	TB	R	RBI	RC	TBB	IBB	SO	HBP	SH	SF	SB	CS	GDP	Avg	OBP	Slg	OPS
2019 S-WB	AAA	117	413	130	29	0	26	(- | -)	237	87	66	94	58	3	100	6	0	5	2	2	9	.315	.402	.574	.976
2019 KC	AL	23	75	22	5	0	0	(0 | 0)	27	8	6	7	7	0	25	1	0	0	0	0	3	.293	.361	.360	.721

Brian McCann

Bats: L **Throws:** R **Pos:** C-83;PH-4   **Ht:** 6'3" **Wt:** 225 **Born:** 2/20/1984 **Age:** 36

								BATTING											RUNNING			AVERAGES			
Year Team	Lg	G	AB	H	2B	3B	HR	(Hm | Rd)	TB	R	RBI	RC	TBB	IBB	SO	HBP	SH	SF	SB	CS	GDP	Avg	OBP	Slg	OPS
2005 Atl	NL	59	180	50	7	0	5	(2 | 3)	72	20	23	25	18	5	26	1	4	1	1	1	5	.278	.345	.400	.745
2006 Atl	NL	130	442	147	34	0	24	(10 | 14)	253	61	93	94	41	8	54	3	0	6	2	0	12	.333	.388	.572	.961
2007 Atl	NL	139	504	136	38	0	18	(6 | 12)	228	51	92	68	35	7	74	5	2	6	0	1	19	.270	.320	.452	.772
2008 Atl	NL	145	509	153	42	1	23	(10 | 13)	266	68	87	84	57	4	64	4	0	3	5	0	17	.301	.373	.523	.896
2009 Atl	NL	138	488	137	35	1	21	(12 | 9)	237	63	94	83	49	3	83	5	3	6	4	1	17	.281	.349	.486	.834
2010 Atl	NL	143	479	129	25	0	21	(13 | 8)	217	63	77	76	74	10	98	9	0	4	5	2	12	.269	.375	.453	.828
2011 Atl	NL	128	466	126	19	0	24	(15 | 9)	217	51	71	76	57	14	89	2	0	2	3	2	10	.270	.351	.466	.817
2012 Atl	NL	121	439	101	14	0	20	(11 | 9)	175	44	67	45	44	7	76	1	0	3	3	0	15	.230	.300	.399	.698
2013 Atl	NL	102	356	91	13	0	20	(12 | 8)	164	43	57	51	39	3	66	5	0	2	0	1	9	.256	.336	.461	.796
2014 NYY	AL	140	495	115	15	1	23	(19 | 4)	201	57	75	58	32	1	77	7	0	4	0	0	16	.232	.286	.406	.692
2015 NYY	AL	135	465	108	15	1	26	(16 | 10)	203	68	94	77	52	3	97	11	0	7	0	0	7	.232	.320	.437	.756
2016 NYY	AL	130	429	104	13	0	20	(11 | 9)	177	56	58	51	54	2	99	7	0	2	1	0	15	.242	.335	.413	.748
2017 Hou	AL	97	349	84	12	1	18	(7 | 11)	152	47	62	46	38	3	58	7	0	5	1	0	9	.241	.323	.436	.759
2018 Hou	AL	63	189	40	3	0	7	(3 | 4)	64	22	23	19	19	0	40	6	0	2	0	1	7	.212	.301	.339	.640
2019 Atl	NL	85	277	69	9	0	12	(7 | 5)	114	28	45	36	31	1	53	2	0	6	0	0	10	.249	.323	.412	.734
Postseason		34	112	19	3	0	4	(3 | 1)	34	7	16	11	9	0	36	4	0	1	0	0	2	.170	.254	.304	.558
15 ML YEARS		1755	6067	1590	294	5	282	(154 | 128)	2740	742	1018	889	640	71	1054	75	9	59	25	9	180	.262	.337	.452	.789

James McCann

Bats: R **Throws:** R **Pos:** C-106;DH-13;PH-2   **Ht:** 6'3" **Wt:** 225 **Born:** 6/13/1990 **Age:** 30

								BATTING											RUNNING			AVERAGES			
Year Team	Lg	G	AB	H	2B	3B	HR	(Hm | Rd)	TB	R	RBI	RC	TBB	IBB	SO	HBP	SH	SF	SB	CS	GDP	Avg	OBP	Slg	OPS
2014 Det	AL	9	12	3	1	0	0	(0 | 0)	4	2	0	1	0	0	2	0	0	0	1	0	0	.250	.250	.333	.583
2015 Det	AL	114	401	106	18	5	7	(5 | 2)	155	32	41	34	16	0	90	3	4	1	0	1	17	.264	.297	.387	.683
2016 Det	AL	105	344	76	9	1	12	(7 | 5)	123	31	48	30	23	0	109	2	1	3	0	1	12	.221	.272	.358	.629
2017 Det	AL	106	352	89	14	2	13	(8 | 5)	146	39	49	46	26	0	89	9	1	3	1	0	8	.253	.318	.415	.733
2018 Det	AL	118	427	94	16	0	8	(5 | 3)	134	31	39	31	26	0	116	2	0	2	0	3	9	.220	.267	.314	.581
2019 CWS	AL	118	439	120	26	1	18	(8 | 10)	202	62	60	67	30	1	137	6	1	0	4	1	10	.273	.328	.460	.789
6 ML YEARS		570	1975	488	84	9	58	(33 | 25)	764	197	237	209	121	1	543	22	7	9	6	6	56	.247	.297	.387	.683

Kevin McCarthy

Pitches: R **Bats:** R **Pos:** RP-56   **Ht:** 6'3" **Wt:** 215 **Born:** 2/22/1992 **Age:** 28

		HOW MUCH PITCHED					WHAT HE GAVE UP										THE RESULTS							
Year Team	Lg	G	GS	GF	IP	BFP	H	R	ER	HR	SH	SF	HB	TBB	IBB	SO	WP	W	L	Pct	Sv-Op	Hld	Vel	OPS	ERC	ERA
2019 Omha	AAA	13	0	9	16.2	70	19	7	7	0	1	0	0	5		15	0	0	0	-	3--		-	.770	3.89	3.78
2016 KC	AL	10	0	1	8.1	41	11	8	6	1	1	0	0	5		7	0	1	0	1.000	0-1	0	94	.857	6.83	6.48
2017 KC	AL	33	0	14	45.0	196	50	23	16	4	1	1	0	13	0	27	1	1	0	1.000	0-0	1	93	.704	4.13	3.20
2018 KC	AL	65	0	10	72.0	293	70	28	26	7	0	1	2	20	2	46	2	5	4	.556	0-4	15	92	.703	3.62	3.25
2019 KC	AL	56	0	14	60.1	268	68	31	30	4	2	4	2	21	6	38	2	4	2	.667	1-5	6	91	.756	4.26	4.48
4 ML YEARS		164	0	39	185.2	798	199	90	78	16	4	6	4	59	8	118	5	11	6	.647	1-10	22	92	.729	4.09	3.78

Reggie McClain

Pitches: R **Bats:** R **Pos:** RP-12; SP-2   **Ht:** 6'2" **Wt:** 180 **Born:** 11/16/1992 **Age:** 27

		HOW MUCH PITCHED					WHAT HE GAVE UP										THE RESULTS							
Year Team	Lg	G	GS	GF	IP	BFP	H	R	ER	HR	SH	SF	HB	TBB	IBB	SO	WP	W	L	Pct	Sv-Op	Hld	Vel	OPS	ERC	ERA
2019 Mdest	A+	6	0	1	16.0	58	9	1	1	1	0	0	0	0	0	18	4	0	0	-	0--	-	-	.397	0.82	0.56
2019 Tacom	AAA	17	1	8	41.0	165	29	20	15	3	0	2	2	18	0	34	3	3	4	.429	2--	-	-	.598	2.76	3.29
2019 Ark	AA	6	2	1	15.2	57	6	2	2	0	1	1	2	4	0	20	2	0	0	-	0--	-	-	.378	0.91	1.15
2019 Sea	AL	14	2	6	21.0	95	22	14	14	2	0	0	0	13	0	11	1	1	1	.500	0-1	0	94	.795	5.24	6.00

Lance McCullers Jr.

Pitches: R **Bats:** L **Pos:** P   **Ht:** 6'1" **Wt:** 205 **Born:** 10/2/1993 **Age:** 26

		HOW MUCH PITCHED					WHAT HE GAVE UP										THE RESULTS							
Year Team	Lg	G	GS	GF	IP	BFP	H	R	ER	HR	SH	SF	HB	TBB	IBB	SO	WP	W	L	Pct	Sv-Op	Hld	Vel	OPS	ERC	ERA
2015 Hou	AL	22	22	0	125.2	520	106	49	45	10	0	3	5	43	2	129	8	6	7	.462	0-0	0	94	.659	3.02	3.22
2016 Hou	AL	14	14	0	81.0	352	80	29	29	5	0	0	0	45	1	106	9	6	5	.545	0-0	0	94	.736	4.42	3.22
2017 Hou	AL	22	22	0	118.2	512	114	61	56	8	2	2	11	40	1	132	8	7	4	.636	0-0	0	94	.696	3.71	4.25
2018 Hou	AL	25	22	0	128.1	527	100	60	55	12	1	4	7	50	0	142	14	10	6	.625	0-0	1	94	.653	3.05	3.86
Postseason		11	4	1	32.0	127	19	10	9	2	0	0	6	13	0	30	2	1	0	1.000	1-1	1	94	.558	2.53	2.53
4 ML YEARS		83	80	0	453.2	1911	400	199	185	35	3	9	23	178	4	509	39	29	22	.569	0-0	1	94	.681	3.45	3.67

Andrew McCutchen

Bats: R **Throws:** R **Pos:** LF-52;CF-15;DH-1   **Ht:** 5'11" **Wt:** 195 **Born:** 10/10/1986 **Age:** 33

								BATTING												RUNNING			AVERAGES			
Year	Team	Lg	G	AB	H	2B	3B	HR	(Hm | Rd)	TB	R	RBI	RC	TBB	IBB	SO	HBP	SH	SF	SB	CS	GDP	Avg	OBP	Slg	OPS
2009	Pit	NL	108	433	124	26	9	12	(8 | 4)	204	74	54	78	54	2	83	2	0	4	22	5	3	.286	.365	.471	.836
2010	Pit	NL	154	570	163	35	5	16	(8 | 8)	256	94	56	86	70	1	89	5	1	7	33	10	6	.286	.365	.449	.814
2011	Pit	NL	158	572	148	34	5	23	(10 | 13)	261	87	89	102	89	3	126	9	2	6	23	10	7	.259	.364	.456	.820
2012	Pit	NL	157	593	**194**	29	6	31	(15 | 16)	328	107	96	125	70	13	132	5	0	5	20	12	9	.327	.400	.553	.953
2013	Pit	NL	157	583	185	38	5	21	(9 | 12)	296	97	84	105	78	12	101	9	0	4	27	10	13	.317	.404	.508	.911
2014	Pit	NL	146	548	172	38	6	25	(10 | 15)	297	89	83	**109**	84	8	115	10	0	6	18	3	9	.314	**.410**	.542	**.952**
2015	Pit	NL	157	566	165	36	3	23	(13 | 10)	276	91	96	120	98	12	133	12	0	9	11	5	9	.292	.401	.488	.889
2016	Pit	NL	153	598	153	26	3	24	(10 | 14)	257	81	79	83	69	7	143	5	0	3	6	7	15	.256	.336	.430	.766
2017	Pit	NL	156	570	159	30	2	28	(9 | 19)	277	94	88	98	73	5	116	4	0	3	11	5	10	.279	.363	.486	.849
2018	2 Tms		155	569	145	30	3	20	(7 | 13)	241	83	65	88	95	1	145	11	0	7	14	9	12	.255	.368	.424	.792
2019	Phi	NL	59	219	56	12	1	10	(5 | 5)	100	45	29	41	43	0	55	0	0	0	2	1	1	.256	.378	.457	.834
18	SF	NL	130	482	123	28	2	15	(5 | 10)	200	65	55	70	73	1	123	7	0	6	13	6	11	.255	.357	.415	.772
18	NYY	AL	25	87	22	2	1	5	(2 | 3)	41	18	10	18	22	0	22	4	0	1	1	3	1	.253	.421	.471	.892
	Postseason		13	46	11	1	0	0	(0 | 0)	12	5	1	3	7	1	7	0	0	0	0	0	1	.239	.340	.261	.600
11 ML YEARS			1560	5821	1664	334	48	233	(104 | 129)	2793	942	819	1035	823	64	1238	72	3	54	187	77	94	.286	.378	.480	.858

T.J. McFarland

Pitches: L **Bats:** L **Pos:** RP-51   **Ht:** 6'3" **Wt:** 220 **Born:** 6/8/1989 **Age:** 31

			HOW MUCH PITCHED					WHAT HE GAVE UP											THE RESULTS						
Year	Team	Lg	G	GS	GF	IP	BFP	H	R	ER	HR	SH	SF	HB	TBB	IBB	SO	WP	W	L	Pct	Sv-Op	Hld	Vel	OPS	ERC	ERA
2013	Bal	AL	38	1	8	74.2	331	83	37	35	7	2	1	0	28	5	58	2	4	1	.800	0-0	0	88	.737	4.40	4.22
2014	Bal	AL	37	1	14	58.2	255	70	22	18	2	5	0	4	13	2	34	0	4	2	.667	0-0	5	91	.739	4.23	2.76
2015	Bal	AL	30	0	7	40.1	188	52	26	22	4	0	0	0	18	5	26	3	2	2	.500	0-0	3	92	.814	5.68	4.91
2016	Bal	AL	16	0	2	24.2	112	33	19	19	3	0	3	2	10	2	7	1	2	2	.500	0-3	0	92	.928	6.74	6.93
2017	Ari	NL	43	1	22	54.0	241	65	42	32	4	2	3	2	17	6	29	2	4	5	.444	0-0	2	92	.757	4.65	5.33
2018	Ari	NL	47	0	21	72.0	292	64	18	16	4	1	1	0	22	3	42	0	2	2	.500	1-1	9	91	.631	2.82	2.00
2019	Ari	NL	51	0	13	56.0	250	71	35	30	6	2	2	1	20	5	35	1	0	0	-	0-0	9	89	.842	5.53	4.82
7 ML YEARS			262	3	87	380.1	1669	438	199	172	30	12	10	9	128	28	231	11	18	14	.563	1-4	20	90	.758	4.52	4.07

Jake McGee

Pitches: L **Bats:** L **Pos:** RP-45   **Ht:** 6'4" **Wt:** 237 **Born:** 8/6/1986 **Age:** 33

			HOW MUCH PITCHED					WHAT HE GAVE UP											THE RESULTS						
Year	Team	Lg	G	GS	GF	IP	BFP	H	R	ER	HR	SH	SF	HB	TBB	IBB	SO	WP	W	L	Pct	Sv-Op	Hld	Vel	OPS	ERC	ERA
2010	TB	AL	8	0	3	5.0	20	2	1	1	0	0	0	0	3	0	6	0	0	0	-	0-0	0	94	.426	1.32	1.80
2011	TB	AL	37	0	9	28.0	124	30	14	14	5	1	0	0	12	1	27	0	5	2	.714	0-0	4	95	.801	5.09	4.50
2012	TB	AL	69	0	13	55.1	212	33	13	12	3	0	2	1	11	4	73	3	5	2	.714	0-2	19	96	.452	1.26	1.95
2013	TB	AL	71	0	6	62.2	260	52	28	28	8	1	3	1	22	5	75	4	5	3	.625	1-5	27	96	.659	3.07	4.02
2014	TB	AL	73	0	31	71.1	274	48	15	15	2	1	1	2	16	1	90	1	5	2	.714	19-23	14	96	.486	1.55	1.89
2015	TB	AL	39	0	6	37.1	147	27	11	10	3	0	1	1	8	1	48	1	1	2	.333	6-10	19	95	.544	1.92	2.41
2016	Col	NL	57	0	25	45.2	205	56	25	24	9	0	0	3	16	1	38	4	2	3	.400	15-19	4	93	.887	6.26	4.73
2017	Col	NL	62	0	13	57.1	229	47	23	23	4	1	1	1	16	0	58	5	0	2	.000	3-6	20	95	.624	2.59	3.61
2018	Col	NL	61	0	9	51.1	227	59	39	37	10	2	0	2	16	1	47	5	2	4	.333	1-3	14	94	.883	5.38	6.49
2019	Col	NL	45	0	10	41.1	180	47	25	20	11	0	3	3	11	1	35	0	0	2	.000	0-2	4	94	.903	5.83	4.35
	Postseason		6	0	1	3.2	18	3	2	2	0	1	0	1	3	1	3	0	0	1	.000	0-0	2	96	.643	4.24	4.91
10 ML YEARS			522	0	125	455.1	1878	401	194	184	55	6	11	14	131	15	497	23	25	22	.532	45-70	125	95	.678	3.20	3.64

Kyle McGowin

Pitches: R **Bats:** R **Pos:** RP-6; SP-1   **Ht:** 6'3" **Wt:** 195 **Born:** 11/27/1991 **Age:** 28

			HOW MUCH PITCHED					WHAT HE GAVE UP											THE RESULTS						
Year	Team	Lg	G	GS	GF	IP	BFP	H	R	ER	HR	SH	SF	HB	TBB	IBB	SO	WP	W	L	Pct	Sv-Op	Hld	Vel	OPS	ERC	ERA
2019	Fresno	AAA	11	11	0	60.2	256	59	28	26	8	1	0	4	17	1	68	0	7	2	.778	0--	-	-	.758	3.92	3.86
2019	Hrsbrg	AA	6	6	0	32.1	124	22	10	9	2	0	1	1	9	0	36	2	1	1	.500	0--	-	-	.532	1.96	2.51
2018	Was	NL	5	1	2	7.2	34	6	5	5	2	0	1	0	5	0	8	2	0	0	-	0-0	0	91	.824	4.90	5.87
2019	Was	NL	7	1	4	16.0	76	22	19	18	7	1	1	1	4	0	18	4	0	0	-	1-1	0	91	1.012	8.33	10.13
2 ML YEARS			12	2	6	23.2	110	28	24	23	9	1	2	1	9	0	26	6	0	0	-	1-1	0	91	.957	7.17	8.75

Reese McGuire

Bats: L **Throws:** R **Pos:** C-30;PH-2   **Ht:** 6'0" **Wt:** 215 **Born:** 3/2/1995 **Age:** 25

									BATTING											RUNNING			AVERAGES			
Year	Team	Lg	G	AB	H	2B	3B	HR	(Hm	Rd)	TB	R	RBI	RC	TBB	IBB	SO	HBP	SH	SF	SB	CS	GDP	Avg	OBP	Slg	OPS
2019	Buffalo	AAA	72	243	60	12	1	5	(-	-)	89	30	29	31	25	2	44	2	2	5	4	0	5	.247	.316	.366	.683
2018	Tor	AL	14	31	9	3	0	2	(1	1)	18	5	4	5	2	0	9	0	0	0	1	0	0	.290	.333	.581	.914
2019	Tor	AL	30	97	29	7	0	5	(4	1)	51	14	11	14	7	0	18	0	0	0	0	0	1	.299	.346	.526	.872
2 ML YEARS			44	128	38	10	0	7	(5	2)	69	19	15	19	9	0	27	0	0	0	1	0	1	.297	.343	.539	.882

Collin McHugh

Pitches: R **Bats:** R **Pos:** RP-27; SP-8   mick-HYOO   **Ht:** 6'2" **Wt:** 190 **Born:** 6/19/1987 **Age:** 33

Year	Team	Lg	G	GS	GF	IP	BFP	H	R	ER	HR	SH	SF	HB	TBB	IBB	SO	WP	W	L	Pct	Sv-Op	Hld	Vel	OPS	ERC	ERA
2012	NYM	NL	8	4	1	21.1	99	27	21	18	5	2	1	2	8	2	17	0	0	4	.000	0-0	0	90	1.044	6.83	7.59
2013	2 Tms	NL	7	5	2	26.0	125	45	29	29	6	2	2	0	5	0	11	0	0	4	.000	0-0	0	90	1.053	8.82	10.04
2014	Hou	AL	25	25	0	154.2	619	117	53	47	11	8	4	6	41	1	157	6	11	9	.550	0-0	0	92	.588	2.34	2.73
2015	Hou	AL	32	32	0	203.2	859	207	89	88	19	5	4	9	53	2	171	5	19	7	.731	0-0	0	90	.705	3.75	3.89
2016	Hou	AL	33	33	0	184.2	796	206	92	89	25	1	5	5	54	1	177	9	13	10	.565	0-0	0	90	.790	4.69	4.34
2017	Hou	AL	12	12	0	63.1	271	62	27	25	7	0	0	5	20	0	62	4	5	2	.714	0-0	0	90	.747	4.02	3.55
2018	Hou	AL	58	0	18	72.1	283	45	18	16	6	1	1	5	21	0	94	0	6	2	.750	0-1	12	92	.542	1.92	1.99
2019	Hou	AL	35	8	8	74.2	317	62	41	39	12	0	3	3	30	0	82	0	4	5	.444	0-0	4	91	.733	3.67	4.70
13	NYM	NL	3	1	2	7.0	34	12	8	8	2	0	1	0	3	0	3	0	0	1	.000	0-0	0	91	1.141	10.77	10.29
13	Col	NL	4	4	0	19.0	91	33	21	21	4	2	1	0	2	0	8	0	0	3	.000	0-0	0	90	1.021	8.14	9.95
	Postseason		8	2	3	20.0	77	11	8	8	3	0	0	2	6	0	14	0	2	1	.667	0-0	0	91	.551	2.12	3.60
	8 ML YEARS		210	119	29	800.2	3369	771	370	351	93	17	20	35	232	6	771	24	58	43	.574	0-1	16	91	.718	3.72	3.95

Brendan McKay

Pitches: L **Bats:** L **Pos:** SP-11; RP-2   **Ht:** 6'2" **Wt:** 212 **Born:** 12/18/1995 **Age:** 24

Year	Team	Lg	G	GS	GF	IP	BFP	H	R	ER	HR	SH	SF	HB	TBB	IBB	SO	WP	W	L	Pct	Sv-Op	Hld	Vel	OPS	ERC	ERA
2017	HudVal	A-	6	6	0	20.0	73	10	4	4	3	1	0	0	5	0	21	1	1	0	1.000	0- -	-	-	.507	1.48	1.80
2018	3 Tms	Low	19	17	0	78.1	299	55	22	21	3	2	1	1	14	0	103	0	5	2	.714	0- -	-	-	.511	1.56	2.41
2019	Mont	AA	8	7	0	41.2	156	25	6	6	2	0	1	1	9	0	62	3	3	0	1.000	0- -	-	-	.466	1.40	1.30
2019	Drham	AAA	7	6	0	32.0	122	17	4	3	1	1	1	2	9	0	40	0	3	0	1.000	0- -	-	-	.452	1.34	0.84
2019	TB	AL	13	11	0	49.0	216	53	32	28	8	1	1	0	16	0	56	0	2	4	.333	0-0	0	94	.796	4.59	5.14

David McKay

Pitches: R **Bats:** R **Pos:** RP-25   **Ht:** 6'3" **Wt:** 205 **Born:** 3/31/1995 **Age:** 25

Year	Team	Lg	G	GS	GF	IP	BFP	H	R	ER	HR	SH	SF	HB	TBB	IBB	SO	WP	W	L	Pct	Sv-Op	Hld	Vel	OPS	ERC	ERA
2019	Tacom	AAA	30	0	11	43.2	201	31	26	25	4	2	2	10	31	2	71	4	3	1	.750	1- -	-	-	.676	4.33	5.15
2019	2 Tms	AL	25	0	11	26.1	115	20	17	16	3	0	0	1	17	1	34	2	0	0	-	0-1	1	94	.681	3.87	5.47
19	Det	AL	18	0	6	19.1	81	15	12	12	2	0	0	1	9	1	29	2	0	0	-	0-1	1	94	.647	3.27	5.59
19	Sea	AL	7	0	5	7.0	34	5	5	4	1	0	0	0	8	0	5	0	0	0	-	0-0	0	93	.767	5.59	5.14

Billy McKinney

Bats: L **Throws:** L **Pos:** RF-43;LF-29;PH-12;1B-9;DH-3;PR-3   **Ht:** 6'1" **Wt:** 205 **Born:** 8/23/1994 **Age:** 25

Year	Team	Lg	G	AB	H	2B	3B	HR	(Hm	Rd)	TB	R	RBI	RC	TBB	IBB	SO	HBP	SH	SF	SB	CS	GDP	Avg	OBP	Slg	OPS
2019	Buffalo	AAA	36	129	35	8	4	4	(-	-)	63	17	20	25	22	1	25	2	0	1	1	1	1	.271	.383	.488	.871
2018	2 Tms	AL	38	119	30	7	0	6	(5	1)	55	14	13	14	11	0	33	1	0	1	1	0	0	.252	.318	.462	.780
2019	Tor	AL	84	251	54	14	1	12	(7	5)	106	37	28	35	19	0	73	2	2	2	0	2	0	.215	.274	.422	.696
18	NYY	AL	2	4	1	0	0	0	(0	0)	1	0	0	0	0	0	1	0	0	0	0	0	0	.250	.250	.250	.500
18	Tor	AL	36	115	29	7	0	6	(5	1)	54	14	13	14	11	0	32	1	0	1	1	0	0	.252	.320	.470	.790
	2 ML YEARS		122	370	84	21	1	18	(12	6)	161	51	41	49	30	0	106	3	2	3	1	2	0	.227	.288	.435	.723

Ryan McMahon

Bats: L **Throws:** R **Pos:** 2B-113;3B-22;1B-19;PH-14   **Ht:** 6'2" **Wt:** 208 **Born:** 12/14/1994 **Age:** 25

Year	Team	Lg	G	AB	H	2B	3B	HR	(Hm	Rd)	TB	R	RBI	RC	TBB	IBB	SO	HBP	SH	SF	SB	CS	GDP	Avg	OBP	Slg	OPS
2017	Col	NL	17	19	3	1	0	0	(0	0)	4	2	1	1	5	0	5	0	0	0	0	0	1	.158	.333	.211	.544
2018	Col	NL	91	181	42	9	1	5	(4	1)	68	17	19	23	18	2	64	2	0	1	1	0	0	.232	.307	.376	.683
2019	Col	NL	141	480	120	22	1	24	(18	6)	216	70	83	69	56	1	160	1	1	1	5	1	14	.250	.329	.450	.779
	Postseason		4	3	0	0	0	0	(0	0)	0	0	0	0	1	0	1	0	0	0	0	1	0	.000	.250	.000	.250
	3 ML YEARS		249	680	165	32	2	29	(22	7)	288	89	103	93	79	3	229	3	1	2	6	1	15	.243	.323	.424	.747

Jeff McNeil

Bats: L **Throws:** R **Pos:** LF-71;RF-42;2B-37;3B-31;PH-7   **Ht:** 6'1" **Wt:** 195 **Born:** 4/8/1992 **Age:** 28

Year	Team	Lg	G	AB	H	2B	3B	HR	(Hm	Rd)	TB	R	RBI	RC	TBB	IBB	SO	HBP	SH	SF	SB	CS	GDP	Avg	OBP	Slg	OPS
2018	NYM	NL	63	225	74	11	6	3	(1	2)	106	35	19	39	14	1	24	5	4	0	7	1	2	.329	.381	.471	.852
2019	NYM	NL	133	510	162	38	1	23	(9	14)	271	83	75	103	35	2	75	21	0	1	5	6	5	.318	.384	.531	.916
	2 ML YEARS		196	735	236	49	7	26	(10	16)	377	118	94	142	49	3	99	26	4	1	12	7	7	.321	.383	.513	.896

Alex McRae

Pitches: R **Bats:** R **Pos:** RP-9; SP-2   **Ht:** 6'2" **Wt:** 220 **Born:** 4/6/1993 **Age:** 27

Year	Team	Lg	G	GS	GF	IP	BFP	H	R	ER	HR	SH	SF	HB	TBB	IBB	SO	WP	W	L	Pct	Sv-Op	Hld	Vel	OPS	ERC	ERA
2019	Indy	AAA	22	22	0	114.1	502	128	70	66	20	3	3	5	43	0	101	5	7	8	.467	0- -	-	-	.844	5.48	5.20
2018	Pit	NL	2	0	0	6.1	32	8	4	4	0	0	0	1	5	0	5	2	0	1	.000	0-0	0	92	.899	7.08	5.68
2019	Pit	NL	11	2	3	26.2	132	36	30	26	9	0	0	3	16	1	19	2	0	4	.000	0-0	0	93	1.027	9.60	8.78
	2 ML YEARS		13	2	3	33.0	164	44	34	30	9	0	0	4	21	1	24	4	0	5	.000	0-0	0	93	1.003	9.14	8.18

Austin Meadows

Bats: L Throws: L Pos: RF-57;DH-44;LF-34;PH-8;CF-3   Ht: 6'3" Wt: 220 Born: 5/3/1995 Age: 25

								BATTING										RUNNING			AVERAGES			
Year Team	Lg	G	AB	H	2B	3B	HR	(Hm | Rd)	TB	R	RBI	RC	TBB	IBB	SO	HBP	SH	SF	SB	CS	GDP	Avg	OBP	Slg	OPS
2018 2 Tms		59	178	51	9	2	6	(3 | 3)	82	19	17	23	10	2	40	1	0	2	5	1	1	.287	.325	.461	.785
2019 TB	AL	138	530	154	29	7	33	(13 | 20)	296	83	89	103	54	6	131	7	0	0	12	5	3	.291	.364	.558	.922
18 Pit	NL	49	154	45	8	2	5	(2 | 3)	72	16	13	20	8	2	35	1	0	2	4	1	1	.292	.327	.468	.795
18 TB	AL	10	24	6	1	0	1	(1 | 0)	10	3	4	3	2	0	5	0	0	0	1	0	0	.250	.308	.417	.724
2 ML YEARS		197	708	205	38	9	39	(16 | 23)	378	102	106	126	64	8	171	8	0	2	17	6	4	.290	.354	.534	.888

John Means

Pitches: L Bats: L Pos: SP-27; RP-4   Ht: 6'3" Wt: 230 Born: 4/24/1993 Age: 27

		HOW MUCH PITCHED					WHAT HE GAVE UP										THE RESULTS							
Year Team	Lg	G	GS	GF	IP	BFP	H	R	ER	HR	SH	SF	HB	TBB	IBB	SO	WP	W	L	Pct	Sv-Op	Hld	Vel	OPS	ERC	ERA
2018 Bal	AL	1	0	0	3.1	16	6	5	5	1	0	0	0	0	0	4	0	0	0	-	0-0	0	90	1.125	8.70	13.50
2019 Bal	AL	31	27	1	155.0	637	138	68	62	23	0	3	5	38	0	121	5	12	11	.522	0-0	0	92	.702	3.31	3.60
2 ML YEARS		32	27	1	158.1	653	144	73	67	24	0	3	5	38	0	125	5	12	11	.522	0-0	0	92	.713	3.40	3.81

Adalberto Mejia

Pitches: L Bats: R Pos: RP-35   ah-dahl-BAIR-toe meh-HEE-yah   Ht: 6'3" Wt: 195 Born: 6/20/1993 Age: 27

		HOW MUCH PITCHED					WHAT HE GAVE UP										THE RESULTS							
Year Team	Lg	G	GS	GF	IP	BFP	H	R	ER	HR	SH	SF	HB	TBB	IBB	SO	WP	W	L	Pct	Sv-Op	Hld	Vel	OPS	ERC	ERA
2016 Min	AL	1	0	0	2.1	13	5	2	2	0	0	1	0	1	0	0	0	0	0	-	0-0	0	90	1.098	10.38	7.71
2017 Min	AL	21	21	0	98.0	443	110	52	49	13	0	3	5	44	4	85	2	4	7	.364	0-0	0	92	.822	5.37	4.50
2018 Min	AL	5	4	1	22.1	92	17	5	5	1	1	1	2	9	0	13	2	2	0	1.000	0-0	0	92	.561	2.82	2.01
2019 3 Tms		35	0	4	31.1	145	33	25	23	4	0	1	0	21	0	30	3	0	2	.000	0-1	4	93	.925	5.69	6.61
19 Min	AL	13	0	2	15.1	71	16	16	15	1	0	0	0	12	0	15	1	0	2	.000	0-1	2	93	.894	6.83	8.80
19 LAA	AL	20	0	2	13.0	57	9	6	5	1	0	0	0	8	0	13	0	0	0	-	0-0	2	92	.625	2.95	3.46
19 StL	NL	2	0	0	3.0	17	8	3	3	0	0	0	0	1	0	2	2	0	0	-	0-0	0	92	1.154	14.52	9.00
4 ML YEARS		62	25	5	154.0	693	165	84	79	18	1	6	7	75	4	128	7	6	9	.400	0-1	4	93	.792	5.10	4.62

Erick Mejia

Bats: B Throws: R Pos: CF-7;PH-2;2B-1;SS-1;PR-1   Ht: 5'11" Wt: 155 Born: 11/9/1994 Age: 25

								BATTING										RUNNING			AVERAGES			
Year Team	Lg	G	AB	H	2B	3B	HR	(Hm	Rd)	TB	R	RBI	RC	TBB	IBB	SO	HBP	SH	SF	SB	CS	GDP	Avg	OBP	Slg	OPS
2019 Omha	AAA	128	495	134	22	6	7	(-	-)	189	83	63	69	50	0	103	3	5	3	19	6	4	.271	.339	.382	.721
2019 KC	AL	9	22	5	1	0	0	(0	0)	6	3	4	3	4	0	7	0	0	1	0	0	1	.227	.333	.273	.606

Francisco Mejia

Bats: B Throws: R Pos: C-60;PH-19;LF-4;DH-2   Ht: 5'10" Wt: 180 Born: 10/27/1995 Age: 24

								BATTING										RUNNING			AVERAGES			
Year Team	Lg	G	AB	H	2B	3B	HR	(Hm	Rd)	TB	R	RBI	RC	TBB	IBB	SO	HBP	SH	SF	SB	CS	GDP	Avg	OBP	Slg	OPS
2019 ElPaso	AAA	18	63	23	8	2	4	(-	-)	47	14	12	18	5	0	10	2	0	3	0	0	3	.365	.411	.746	1.157
2017 Cle	AL	11	13	2	0	0	0	(0	0)	2	1	1	0	1	1	3	0	0	0	0	0	0	.154	.214	.154	.368
2018 2 Tms		21	56	10	2	0	3	(1	2)	21	6	8	5	5	0	19	1	0	0	0	0	0	.179	.258	.375	.633
2019 SD	NL	79	226	60	11	2	8	(3	5)	99	27	22	27	13	1	56	4	0	1	1	1	6	.265	.316	.438	.754
18 Cle	AL	1	2	0	0	0	0	(0	0)	0	0	0	0	2	0	0	0	0	0	0	0	0	.000	.500	.000	.500
18 SD	NL	20	54	10	2	0	3	(1	2)	21	6	8	5	3	0	19	1	0	0	0	0	0	.185	.241	.389	.630
3 ML YEARS		111	295	72	13	2	11	(4	7)	122	34	31	32	19	2	78	5	0	1	1	1	8	.244	.300	.414	.714

Seth Mejias-Brean

Bats: R Throws: R Pos: PH-7;1B-5;SS-3;3B-2   Ht: 6'2" Wt: 216 Born: 4/5/1991 Age: 29

								BATTING										RUNNING			AVERAGES			
Year Team	Lg	G	AB	H	2B	3B	HR	(Hm	Rd)	TB	R	RBI	RC	TBB	IBB	SO	HBP	SH	SF	SB	CS	GDP	Avg	OBP	Slg	OPS
2019 ElPaso	AAA	117	411	130	18	3	11	(-	-)	187	69	66	70	33	1	79	3	0	1	4	2	8	.316	.371	.455	.826
2019 SD	NL	14	30	7	2	0	2	(1	1)	15	3	5	5	3	0	9	0	0	0	0	0	1	.233	.303	.500	.803

Mark Melancon

Pitches: R Bats: R Pos: RP-66   muh-LANN-sun   Ht: 6'2" Wt: 215 Born: 3/28/1985 Age: 35

		HOW MUCH PITCHED					WHAT HE GAVE UP										THE RESULTS							
Year Team	Lg	G	GS	GF	IP	BFP	H	R	ER	HR	SH	SF	HB	TBB	IBB	SO	WP	W	L	Pct	Sv-Op	Hld	Vel	OPS	ERC	ERA
2009 NYY	AL	13	0	4	16.1	74	13	8	7	0	0	0	4	10	0	10	3	0	1	.000	0-1	0	93	.665	3.94	3.86
2010 2 Tms		22	0	4	21.1	90	19	13	10	2	0	1	1	8	0	22	2	2	0	1.000	0-1	8	93	.674	3.53	4.22
2011 Hou	NL	71	0	47	74.1	309	65	28	23	5	2	0	2	26	6	66	1	8	4	.667	20-25	3	93	.631	2.98	2.78
2012 Bos	AL	41	0	17	45.0	194	45	31	31	8	1	2	3	12	1	41	2	0	2	.000	1-2	3	93	.754	4.24	6.20
2013 Pit	NL	72	0	24	71.0	279	60	15	11	1	0	1	1	8	0	70	6	3	2	.600	16-21	26	93	.511	1.78	1.39
2014 Pit	NL	72	0	48	71.0	277	51	15	15	2	1	1	3	11	1	71	3	3	5	.375	33-37	14	93	.473	1.54	1.90
2015 Pit	NL	78	0	63	76.2	293	57	22	19	4	1	1	2	14	2	62	3	3	2	.600	51-53	1	92	.541	1.82	2.23
2016 2 Tms		75	0	67	71.1	270	52	16	13	3	0	2	1	12	0	65	4	2	2	.500	47-51	0	92	.511	1.66	1.64
2017 SF	NL	32	0	18	30.0	130	37	16	15	3	0	0	1	6	0	29	2	1	2	.333	11-16	5	92	.794	4.78	4.50
2018 SF	NL	41	0	8	39.0	174	48	18	14	2	0	0	1	8	2	31	4	1	4	.200	3-7	8	92	.771	4.94	4.23
2019 2 Tms		66	0	34	67.1	284	71	28	27	4	0	1	2	18	2	68	4	5	2	.714	12-12	5	92	.678	3.69	3.61
10 NYY	AL	2	0	2	4.0	19	7	5	4	1	0	1	0	0	0	3	0	0	0	-	0-0	0	93	.980	7.95	9.00
10 Hou	NL	20	0	2	17.1	71	12	8	6	1	0	0	1	8	0	19	2	2	0	1.000	0-1	8	93	.586	2.65	3.12
16 Pit	NL	45	0	39	41.2	163	31	10	7	2	0	2	1	9	0	38	1	1	1	.500	30-33	0	92	.516	1.89	1.51

Year Team	Lg	G	GS	GF	IP	BFP	H	R	ER	HR	SH	SF	HB	TBB	IBB	SO	WP	W	L	Pct	Sv-Op	Hld	Vel	OPS	ERC	ERA
16 Was	NL	30	0	28	29.2	107	21	6	6	1	0	0	0	3	0	27	3	1	1	.500	17-18	0	92	.503	1.41	1.82
19 SF	NL	43	0	16	46.1	195	49	19	18	3	0	1	2	16	2	44	3	4	2	.667	1-1	5	92	.724	4.18	3.50
19 Atl	NL	23	0	18	21.0	89	22	9	9	1	0	0	0	2	0	24	1	1	0	1.000	11-11	0	93	.580	2.69	3.86
Postseason		10	0	7	10.0	40	9	4	4	2	0	0	0	3	2	8	0	1	0	1.000	1-2	0	93	.705	3.62	3.60
11 ML YEARS		583	0	334	583.1	2374	518	210	185	34	5	9	21	139	14	535	34	28	26	.519	194-226	72	93	.611	2.72	2.85

Keury Mella

Pitches: R **Bats:** R **Pos:** RP-2   **Ht:** 6'2" **Wt:** 200 **Born:** 8/2/1993 **Age:** 26

Year Team	Lg	G	GS	GF	IP	BFP	H	R	ER	HR	SH	SF	HB	TBB	IBB	SO	WP	W	L	Pct	Sv-Op	Hld	Vel	OPS	ERC	ERA
2019 Lsvlle	AAA	27	27	0	142.2	640	160	93	80	22	1	3	11	56	0	102	4	8	14	.364	0--	-	-	.832	5.48	5.05
2017 Cin	NL	2	0	1	4.0	19	5	3	3	1	0	0	0	2	1	1	0	0	0	-	0-0	0	96	.957	6.56	6.75
2018 Cin	NL	4	0	1	9.1	48	13	9	9	4	2	0	1	8	0	8	1	0	0	-	0-0	0	94	1.262	12.40	8.68
2019 Cin	NL	2	0	1	3.2	18	5	3	3	0	0	0	0	2	1	4	0	0	0	-	0-0	0	95	.826	5.31	7.36
3 ML YEARS		8	0	3	17.0	85	23	15	15	5	2	0	1	12	2	13	1	0	0	-	0-0	0	95	1.091	9.32	7.94

Tim Melville

Pitches: R **Bats:** R **Pos:** SP-7   **Ht:** 6'4" **Wt:** 225 **Born:** 10/9/1989 **Age:** 30

Year Team	Lg	G	GS	GF	IP	BFP	H	R	ER	HR	SH	SF	HB	TBB	IBB	SO	WP	W	L	Pct	Sv-Op	Hld	Vel	OPS	ERC	ERA
2019 Albq	AAA	18	17	0	96.1	444	113	64	58	24	2	2	8	40	2	94	5	10	5	.667	0--	-	-	.892	6.57	5.42
2016 Cin	NL	3	2	0	9.0	54	16	12	11	5	2	0	1	9	0	8	1	0	1	.000	0-0	0	91	1.310	16.62	11.00
2017 2 Tms		3	1	1	5.2	30	7	8	7	1	0	0	1	6	0	7	0	0	1	.000	0-0	0	94	.988	9.95	11.12
2019 Col	NL	7	7	0	33.1	143	34	18	18	9	2	2	1	14	0	24	1	2	3	.400	0-0	0	89	.880	5.76	4.86
17 Min	AL	1	1	0	3.1	18	4	5	5	1	0	0	1	3	0	4	0	0	1	.000	0-0	0	94	1.016	10.42	13.50
17 SD	NL	2	0	1	2.1	12	3	3	2	0	0	0	0	3	0	3	0	0	0		0-0	0	94	.944	9.14	7.71
3 ML YEARS		13	10	1	48.0	227	57	38	36	15	4	2	3	29	0	39	2	2	5	.286	0-0	0	91	.992	8.13	6.75

Yohander Mendez

Pitches: L **Bats:** L **Pos:** RP-3   yo-HAHN-dair   **Ht:** 6'5" **Wt:** 200 **Born:** 1/17/1995 **Age:** 25

Year Team	Lg	G	GS	GF	IP	BFP	H	R	ER	HR	SH	SF	HB	TBB	IBB	SO	WP	W	L	Pct	Sv-Op	Hld	Vel	OPS	ERC	ERA
2019 Nashv	AAA	5	0	0	7.1	29	3	4	4	1	1	0	2	2	0	15	0	0	1	.000	0--	-	-	.542	1.82	4.91
2016 Tex	AL	2	0	0	3.0	17	5	6	6	0	0	0	0	2	0	0	0	0	0	-	0-0	0	91	.878	7.72	18.00
2017 Tex	AL	7	0	0	12.1	52	13	9	7	3	0	0	1	3	0	7	0	0	1	.000	0-0	1	93	.869	5.19	5.11
2018 Tex	AL	8	5	1	27.2	121	28	18	17	4	0	0	1	15	0	18	0	2	2	.500	0-0	0	92	.789	5.16	5.53
2019 Tex	AL	3	0	0	4.2	21	4	3	3	2	0	0	0	5	0	8	0	1	0	1.000	0-0	0	94	1.054	9.49	5.79
4 ML YEARS		20	5	1	47.2	211	50	36	33	9	0	0	1	25	0	33	0	3	3	.500	0-0	1	92	.841	5.72	6.23

Danny Mendick

Bats: R **Throws:** R **Pos:** SS-5;DH-4;2B-3;3B-3;PH-3;PR-3   **Ht:** 5'10" **Wt:** 189 **Born:** 9/28/1993 **Age:** 26

Year Team	Lg	G	AB	H	2B	3B	HR	(Hm	Rd)	TB	R	RBI	RC	TBB	IBB	SO	HBP	SH	SF	SB	CS	GDP	Avg	OBP	Slg	OPS
2019 Charltt	AAA	133	477	133	26	1	17	(-	-)	212	75	64	83	66	0	96	5	3	7	19	8	20	.279	.368	.444	.812
2019 CWS	AL	16	39	12	0	0	2	(2	0)	18	6	4	6	1	0	11	0	0	0	0	0	1	.308	.325	.462	.787

Conner Menez

Pitches: L **Bats:** L **Pos:** RP-5; SP-3   **Ht:** 6'3" **Wt:** 205 **Born:** 5/29/1995 **Age:** 25

Year Team	Lg	G	GS	GF	IP	BFP	H	R	ER	HR	SH	SF	HB	TBB	IBB	SO	WP	W	L	Pct	Sv-Op	Hld	Vel	OPS	ERC	ERA
2019 Rchmd	AA	11	11	0	59.2	234	37	22	18	5	0	3	4	20	0	70	3	3	3	.500	0--	-	-	.570	2.07	2.72
2019 Scrmto	AAA	12	11	0	61.1	270	60	33	33	12	2	1	3	30	1	84	2	3	1	.750	0--	-	-	.830	5.21	4.84
2019 SF	NL	8	3	2	17.0	73	13	10	10	4	1	1	0	12	0	22	2	0	1	.000	0-0	0	91	.805	5.06	5.29

Daniel Mengden

Pitches: R **Bats:** R **Pos:** SP-9; RP-4   MENG-den   **Ht:** 6'1" **Wt:** 225 **Born:** 2/19/1993 **Age:** 27

Year Team	Lg	G	GS	GF	IP	BFP	H	R	ER	HR	SH	SF	HB	TBB	IBB	SO	WP	W	L	Pct	Sv-Op	Hld	Vel	OPS	ERC	ERA
2019 LsVgs	AAA	13	10	1	64.0	270	56	37	30	8	0	2	2	20	2	61	3	4	3	.571	0--	-	-	.691	3.23	4.22
2016 Oak	AL	14	14	0	72.0	332	83	54	52	9	2	1	4	33	0	71	5	2	9	.182	0-0	0	92	.819	5.56	6.50
2017 Oak	AL	7	7	0	43.0	169	36	16	15	6	1	2	0	9	0	29	2	3	2	.600	0-0	0	92	.650	2.78	3.14
2018 Oak	AL	22	17	0	115.2	476	103	58	52	18	4	2	3	26	0	72	6	7	6	.538	0-0	0	92	.699	3.22	4.05
2019 Oak	AL	13	9	2	59.2	260	59	32	32	7	0	1	0	27	0	42	1	5	2	.714	1-1	0	91	.753	4.34	4.83
4 ML YEARS		56	47	2	290.1	1237	281	160	151	40	7	6	7	95	0	214	14	17	19	.472	1-1	0	92	.736	3.94	4.68

Oscar Mercado

Bats: R **Throws:** R **Pos:** CF-82;LF-24;RF-9;PH-5;PR-4;DH-1   **Ht:** 6'2" **Wt:** 197 **Born:** 12/16/1994 **Age:** 25

Year Team	Lg	G	AB	H	2B	3B	HR	(Hm	Rd)	TB	R	RBI	RC	TBB	IBB	SO	HBP	SH	SF	SB	CS	GDP	Avg	OBP	Slg	OPS
2019 Clmbs	AAA	30	119	35	10	1	4	(-	-)	59	24	15	25	16	0	32	4	1	0	14	3	1	.294	.396	.496	.891
2019 Cle	AL	115	438	118	25	3	15	(11	4)	194	70	54	69	28	0	84	5	7	4	15	4	9	.269	.318	.443	.761

Jordy Mercer

Bats: R Throws: R Pos: SS-59;2B-8;1B-5;3B-1;DH-1;PH-1   Ht: 6'3" Wt: 210 Born: 8/27/1986 Age: 33

							BATTING														RUNNING			AVERAGES			
Year	Team	Lg	G	AB	H	2B	3B	HR	(Hm	Rd)	TB	R	RBI	RC	TBB	IBB	SO	HBP	SH	SF	SB	CS	GDP	Avg	OBP	Slg	OPS
2019	Toledo	AAA	12	43	10	3	0	0	(-	0)	13	11	4	5	5	0	6	2	0	0	0	0	1	.233	.340	.302	.642
2012	Pit	NL	42	62	13	5	1	1	(1	0)	23	7	5	6	4	0	14	1	0	1	0	1	0	.210	.265	.371	.636
2013	Pit	NL	103	333	95	22	2	8	(1	7)	145	33	27	46	22	6	62	4	5	1	3	2	7	.285	.336	.435	.772
2014	Pit	NL	149	506	129	27	2	12	(3	9)	196	56	55	45	35	12	89	4	5	5	4	1	14	.255	.305	.387	.693
2015	Pit	NL	116	394	96	21	0	3	(0	3)	126	34	34	34	27	7	73	2	4	3	3	2	7	.244	.293	.320	.613
2016	Pit	NL	149	519	133	22	3	11	(4	7)	194	66	59	58	51	8	83	5	7	2	1	1	11	.256	.328	.374	.701
2017	Pit	NL	145	502	128	24	5	14	(9	5)	204	52	58	60	51	13	88	3	0	2	0	4	16	.255	.326	.406	.733
2018	Pit	NL	117	394	99	29	2	6	(1	5)	150	43	39	41	32	9	87	6	1	3	2	0	12	.251	.315	.381	.696
2019	Det	AL	74	256	69	16	0	9	(4	5)	112	24	22	28	13	1	57	2	0	0	0	0	4	.270	.310	.438	.747
	Postseason		7	14	2	0	0	0	(0	0)	2	0	0	0	1	1	5	0	0	0	0	0	0	.143	.200	.143	.343
	8 ML YEARS		895	2966	762	166	15	64	(19	45)	1150	315	299	318	235	56	553	27	22	17	13	11	71	.257	.316	.388	.703

Whit Merrifield

Bats: R Throws: R Pos: 2B-82;RF-61;CF-17;DH-8;1B-5;LF-4   Ht: 6'0" Wt: 195 Born: 1/24/1989 Age: 31

							BATTING														RUNNING			AVERAGES			
Year	Team	Lg	G	AB	H	2B	3B	HR	(Hm	Rd)	TB	R	RBI	RC	TBB	IBB	SO	HBP	SH	SF	SB	CS	GDP	Avg	OBP	Slg	OPS
2016	KC	AL	81	311	88	22	3	2	(2	0)	122	44	29	38	19	1	72	0	1	1	8	3	1	.283	.323	.392	.716
2017	KC	AL	145	587	169	32	6	19	(13	6)	270	80	78	88	29	0	88	6	1	7	34	8	13	.288	.324	.460	.784
2018	KC	AL	158	632	192	43	3	12	(5	7)	277	88	60	103	61	2	114	6	2	6	45	10	12	.304	.367	.438	.806
2019	KC	AL	162	681	206	41	10	16	(4	12)	315	105	74	114	45	5	126	5	0	4	20	10	8	.302	.348	.463	.811
	4 ML YEARS		546	2211	655	138	22	49	(24	25)	984	317	241	343	154	8	400	17	4	18	107	31	34	.296	.344	.445	.789

Keynan Middleton

Pitches: R Bats: R Pos: RP-11   Ht: 6'3" Wt: 215 Born: 9/12/1993 Age: 26

			HOW MUCH PITCHED					WHAT HE GAVE UP									THE RESULTS						
Year	Team	Lg	G	GS	GF	IP	BFP	H	R	ER	HR	SH	SF	HB	TBB	IBB	SO	WP	W	L	Pct	Sv-Op	Hld	Vel	OPS	ERC	ERA
2019 2 Tms	Low	5	3	0	4.2	20	2	0	0	0	0	0	0	3	0	11	0	0	0		0--	-	-	.426	1.42	0.00
2019 Salt Lk	AAA	5	0	0	4.1	19	2	1	1	0	0	0	0	3	0	5	0	0	0		0--	-	-	.451	1.60	2.08
2017	LAA	AL	64	0	17	58.1	246	60	25	25	11	0	2	0	18	2	63	2	6	1	.857	3-5	10	97	.791	4.47	3.86
2018	LAA	AL	16	0	9	17.2	71	14	4	4	1	0	1	1	9	1	16	1	0	0		6-7	2	96	.688	3.42	2.04
2019	LAA	AL	11	0	0	7.2	33	4	1	1	0	0	0	0	7	0	6	1	0	0		0-0	0	94	.564	2.72	1.17
	3 ML YEARS		91	0	26	83.2	350	78	30	30	12	0	3	1	34	3	85	4	6	1	.857	9-12	12	96	.752	4.11	3.23

Miles Mikolas

Pitches: R Bats: R Pos: SP-32   MIKE-uh-liss   Ht: 6'5" Wt: 220 Born: 8/23/1988 Age: 31

			HOW MUCH PITCHED					WHAT HE GAVE UP									THE RESULTS						
Year	Team	Lg	G	GS	GF	IP	BFP	H	R	ER	HR	SH	SF	HB	TBB	IBB	SO	WP	W	L	Pct	Sv-Op	Hld	Vel	OPS	ERC	ERA
2012	SD	NL	25	0	9	32.1	144	32	15	13	4	2	0	2	15	0	23	2	2	1	.667	0-1	1	93	.761	4.65	3.62
2013	SD	NL	2	0	1	1.2	7	0	0	0	0	0	0	1	1	0	1	0	0	0		0-0	0	94	.286	1.30	0.00
2014	Tex	AL	10	10	0	57.1	255	64	43	41	8	1	2	4	18	2	38	0	2	5	.286	0-0	0	93	.769	4.85	6.44
2018	StL	NL	32	32	0	200.2	808	186	70	63	16	8	4	7	29	4	146	2	18	4	.818	0-0	0	94	.628	2.70	2.83
2019	StL	NL	32	32	0	184.0	764	193	90	85	27	3	7	12	32	1	144	5	9	14	.391	0-0	0	94	.761	4.08	4.16
	5 ML YEARS		101	74	10	476.0	1978	475	218	202	55	14	13	26	95	7	352	9	31	24	.564	0-1	1	94	.706	3.59	3.82

Wade Miley

Pitches: L Bats: L Pos: SP-33   MY-lee   Ht: 6'0" Wt: 220 Born: 11/13/1986 Age: 33

			HOW MUCH PITCHED					WHAT HE GAVE UP									THE RESULTS						
Year	Team	Lg	G	GS	GF	IP	BFP	H	R	ER	HR	SH	SF	HB	TBB	IBB	SO	WP	W	L	Pct	Sv-Op	Hld	Vel	OPS	ERC	ERA
2011	Ari	NL	8	7	0	40.0	180	48	20	20	6	3	1	0	18	0	25	1	4	2	.667	0-0	0	90	.873	5.90	4.50
2012	Ari	NL	32	29	0	194.2	807	193	79	72	14	8	3	2	37	0	144	6	16	11	.593	0-0	0	91	.685	3.05	3.33
2013	Ari	NL	33	33	0	202.2	847	201	88	80	21	6	2	4	66	4	147	13	10	10	.500	0-0	0	91	.727	3.88	3.55
2014	Ari	NL	33	33	0	201.1	866	207	103	97	23	8	9	4	75	3	183	9	8	12	.400	0-0	0	91	.746	4.31	4.34
2015	Bos	AL	32	32	0	193.2	831	201	98	96	17	3	2	4	64	0	147	10	11	11	.500	0-0	0	91	.740	4.01	4.46
2016 2 Tms	AL	30	30	0	166.0	711	187	100	99	25	2	5	6	49	1	137	6	9	13	.409	0-0	0	90	.808	4.98	5.37
2017	Bal	AL	32	32	0	157.1	728	179	104	98	25	1	6	4	93	1	142	1	8	15	.348	0-0	0	91	.841	6.27	5.61
2018	Mil	NL	16	16	0	80.2	338	71	28	23	3	5	1	5	27	1	50	1	5	2	.714	0-0	0	91	.636	2.98	2.57
2019	Hou	AL	33	33	0	167.1	720	164	83	74	23	2	5	5	61	0	140	4	14	6	.700	0-0	0	90	.726	4.19	3.98
16	Sea	AL	19	19	0	112.0	469	117	62	62	18	2	3	3	34	1	82	5	7	8	.467	0-0	0	90	.786	4.58	4.98
16	Bal	AL	11	11	0	54.0	242	70	38	37	7	0	2	3	15	0	55	3	2	5	.286	0-0	0	90	.850	5.83	6.17
	Postseason		4	4	0	14.2	58	10	2	2	1	0	0	0	4	0	9	0	0	0		0-0	0	91	.519	1.79	1.23
	9 ML YEARS		249	245	0	1403.2	6028	1451	703	659	157	38	34	34	490	10	1115	53	85	82	.509	0-0	0	91	.748	4.26	4.23

Andrew Miller

Pitches: L Bats: L Pos: RP-73   Ht: 6'7" Wt: 205 Born: 5/21/1985 Age: 35

			HOW MUCH PITCHED					WHAT HE GAVE UP									THE RESULTS						
Year	Team	Lg	G	GS	GF	IP	BFP	H	R	ER	HR	SH	SF	HB	TBB	IBB	SO	WP	W	L	Pct	Sv-Op	Hld	Vel	OPS	ERC	ERA
2006	Det	AL	8	0	3	10.1	51	8	9	7	0	0	0	2	10	0	6	1	0	1	.000	0-0	1	94	.700	4.79	6.10
2007	Det	AL	13	13	0	64.0	309	73	43	40	8	3	1	7	39	0	56	4	5	5	.500	0-0	0	92	.821	6.31	5.63
2008	Fla	NL	29	20	1	107.1	492	120	78	70	7	10	7	4	56	4	89	6	6	10	.375	0-0	2	91	.798	5.04	5.87
2009	Fla	NL	20	14	1	80.0	366	85	52	43	7	6	4	2	43	1	59	10	3	5	.375	0-0	1	91	.792	4.90	4.84
2010	Fla	NL	9	7	1	32.2	171	51	34	31	6	5	2	1	26	2	28	5	1	5	.167	0-0	0	91	1.054	10.20	8.54
2011	Bos	AL	17	12	2	65.0	310	77	43	40	8	6	5	3	41	0	50	2	6	3	.667	0-0	0	93	.857	6.48	5.54

Year	Team	Lg	G	GS	GF	IP	BFP	H	R	ER	HR	SH	SF	HB	TBB	IBB	SO	WP	W	L	Pct	Sv-Op	Hld	Vel	OPS	ERC	ERA
2012	Bos	AL	53	0	4	40.1	169	28	15	15	3	0	3	2	20	1	51	1	3	2	.600	0-0	13	95	.588	2.76	3.35
2013	Bos	AL	37	0	11	30.2	135	25	12	9	3	1	0	2	17	0	48	2	1	2	.333	0-1	6	95	.624	3.83	2.64
2014	2 Tms	AL	73	0	15	62.1	242	33	16	14	3	2	2	5	17	2	103	3	5	5	.500	1-2	22	94	.456	1.36	2.02
2015	NYY	AL	60	0	53	61.2	246	33	16	14	5	1	2	5	20	1	100	2	3	2	.600	36-38	0	94	.475	1.61	2.04
2016	2 Tms	AL	70	0	23	74.1	275	42	13	12	8	1	1	2	9	0	123	1	10	1	.909	12-14	25	95	.487	1.27	1.45
2017	Cle	AL	57	0	6	62.2	244	31	11	10	3	2	1	5	21	0	95	1	4	3	.571	2-4	27	94	.440	1.42	1.44
2018	Cle	AL	37	0	5	34.0	133	31	16	16	3	0	0	5	16	1	45	1	2	4	.333	2-5	10	93	.729	4.19	4.24
2019	StL	NL	73	0	11	54.2	236	45	32	27	11	0	1	8	27	1	70	4	5	6	.455	6-11	28	92	.739	4.81	4.45
14	Bos	AL	50	0	12	42.1	170	25	13	11	2	2	2	4	13	2	69	2	3	5	.375	0-0	13	94	.492	1.62	2.34
14	Bal	AL	23	0	3	20.0	72	8	3	3	1	0	0	1	4	0	34	1	2	0	1.000	1-2	9	94	.375	0.86	1.35
16	NYY	AL	44	0	16	45.1	172	28	8	7	5	1	1	2	7	0	77	0	6	1	.857	9-11	16	95	.521	1.55	1.39
16	Cle	AL	26	0	7	29.0	103	14	5	5	3	0	0	0	2	0	46	1	4	0	1.000	3-3	9	95	.433	0.87	1.55
Postseason			22	0	2	33.0	126	18	4	4	3	1	1	1	11	1	48	1	2	1	.667	1-2	7	95	.508	1.64	1.09
14 ML YEARS			556	66	136	780.0	3400	682	390	348	75	37	29	53	362	13	923	41	54	54	.500	59-75	135	93	.690	3.80	4.02

Brad Miller

Bats: L **Throws:** R **Pos:** PH-36;3B-19;LF-16;2B-13;SS-1;RF-1;PR-1　　**Ht:** 6'2" **Wt:** 215 **Born:** 10/18/1989 **Age:** 30

Year	Team	Lg	G	AB	H	2B	3B	HR	(Hm	Rd)	TB	R	RBI	RC	TBB	IBB	SO	HBP	SH	SF	SB	CS	GDP	Avg	OBP	Slg	OPS
2019	S-WB	AAA	41	136	40	9	1	10	(-	-)	81	31	29	31	24	1	40	1	0	2	1	3	2	.294	.399	.596	.994
2013	Sea	AL	76	306	81	11	6	8	(3	5)	128	41	36	41	24	0	52	1	2	2	5	3	2	.265	.318	.418	.737
2014	Sea	AL	123	367	81	15	4	10	(4	6)	134	47	36	41	34	2	95	2	3	3	4	2	2	.221	.288	.365	.653
2015	Sea	AL	144	438	113	22	4	11	(6	5)	176	44	46	58	47	0	101	2	4	6	13	4	7	.258	.329	.402	.730
2016	TB	AL	152	548	133	29	6	30	(22	8)	264	73	81	74	47	0	149	3	0	3	6	4	5	.243	.304	.482	.786
2017	TB	AL	110	338	68	13	3	9	(6	3)	114	43	40	37	63	4	110	2	0	4	5	3	5	.201	.327	.337	.664
2018	2 Tms		75	230	57	13	2	7	(6	2)	95	21	29	27	22	1	82	0	0	2	0	0	4	.248	.311	.413	.724
2019	2 Tms		79	154	40	6	1	13	(6	7)	87	26	25	26	15	0	45	1	0	2	2	0	2	.260	.329	.565	.894
18	TB	AL	48	156	40	10	1	5	(3	2)	67	16	21	18	16	0	51	0	0	2	0	0	2	.256	.322	.429	.751
18	Mil	NL	27	74	17	3	1	2	(2	0)	28	5	8	9	6	1	31	0	0	0	0	0	2	.230	.288	.378	.666
19	Cle	AL	13	36	9	3	0	1	(0	1)	15	4	4	7	4	0	10	0	0	0	1	0	0	.250	.325	.417	.742
19	Phi	NL	66	118	31	3	1	12	(6	6)	72	22	21	19	11	0	35	1	0	0	1	0	2	.263	.331	.610	.941
7 ML YEARS			759	2381	573	109	26	88	(52	36)	998	295	293	304	252	7	634	11	9	20	35	16	27	.241	.314	.419	.733

Ian Miller

Bats: L **Throws:** R **Pos:** CF-8;LF-2;RF-2;PR-1　　**Ht:** 6'0" **Wt:** 175 **Born:** 2/21/1992 **Age:** 28

Year	Team	Lg	G	AB	H	2B	3B	HR	(Hm	Rd)	TB	R	RBI	RC	TBB	IBB	SO	HBP	SH	SF	SB	CS	GDP	Avg	OBP	Slg	OPS
2019	Tacom	AAA	106	390	106	27	5	11	(-	-)	175	64	54	68	45	1	81	6	0	4	29	5	6	.269	.351	.449	.799
2019	Roch	AAA	15	60	14	3	1	0	(-	-)	19	8	4	7	6	0	8	2	0	1	6	2	1	.233	.319	.317	.636
2019	Min	AL	12	17	3	1	0	0	(0	0)	4	2	1	1	0	0	3	0	0	0	0	0	0	.176	.176	.235	.412

Justin Miller

Pitches: R **Bats:** R **Pos:** RP-17　　**Ht:** 6'3" **Wt:** 215 **Born:** 6/13/1987 **Age:** 33

Year	Team	Lg	G	GS	GF	IP	BFP	H	R	ER	HR	SH	SF	HB	TBB	IBB	SO	WP	W	L	Pct	Sv-Op	Hld	Vel	OPS	ERC	ERA
2019	Hrsbrg	AA	6	0	0	5.2	21	3	3	2	1	0	0	0	0	0	6	0	0	1	.000	0- -	-	-	.550	0.99	3.18
2019	Fresno	AAA	9	0	2	12.2	50	9	4	4	3	0	0	0	3	0	16	0	0	0		0- -	-	-	.751	2.69	2.84
2014	Det	AL	8	0	4	12.1	53	14	9	7	2	1	2	0	2	0	5	0	1	0	1.000	0-0	0	92	.829	4.21	5.11
2015	Col	NL	34	0	9	33.1	129	21	15	15	2	0	0	0	11	0	38	2	3	3	.500	1-2	7	94	.553	1.75	4.05
2016	Col	NL	40	0	13	42.2	194	50	27	27	6	0	3	2	20	0	45	3	1	1	.500	0-0	1	93	.885	5.92	5.70
2018	Was	NL	51	0	10	52.1	215	42	22	21	10	1	2	2	17	1	60	1	7	1	.875	2-3	11	94	.705	3.41	3.61
2019	Was	NL	17	0	5	15.2	65	16	8	7	5	1	0	2	4	0	11	0	1	0	1.000	0-1	4	92	.878	5.94	4.02
5 ML YEARS			150	0	41	156.1	656	143	81	77	25	3	7	6	54	1	159	6	13	5	.722	3-6	23	93	.754	3.96	4.43

Shelby Miller

Pitches: R **Bats:** R **Pos:** RP-11; SP-8　　**Ht:** 6'3" **Wt:** 225 **Born:** 10/10/1990 **Age:** 29

Year	Team	Lg	G	GS	GF	IP	BFP	H	R	ER	HR	SH	SF	HB	TBB	IBB	SO	WP	W	L	Pct	Sv-Op	Hld	Vel	OPS	ERC	ERA
2019	SnAnt	AAA	5	5	0	20.2	92	17	13	11	1	0	1	1	16	0	20	1	1	2	.333	0- -	-	-	.707	4.42	4.79
2012	StL	NL	6	1	1	13.2	54	9	2	2	0	0	0	1	4	0	16	0	1	0	1.000	0-0	1	93	.463	1.65	1.32
2013	StL	NL	31	31	0	173.1	722	152	65	59	20	7	3	5	57	0	169	2	15	9	.625	0-0	0	94	.670	3.34	3.06
2014	StL	NL	32	31	0	183.0	764	160	78	76	22	7	4	2	73	4	127	4	10	9	.526	0-0	0	93	.698	3.56	3.74
2015	Atl	NL	33	33	0	205.1	860	183	82	69	13	8	4	6	73	8	171	5	6	17	.261	0-0	0	94	.663	3.12	3.02
2016	Ari	NL	20	20	0	101.0	460	127	72	69	14	3	3	2	42	3	70	3	3	12	.200	0-0	0	93	.867	6.03	6.15
2017	Ari	NL	4	4	0	22.0	99	20	10	10	1	0	0	0	12	1	20	1	2	2	.500	0-0	0	95	.668	3.53	4.09
2018	Ari	NL	5	4	0	16.0	79	24	21	19	5	0	1	0	8	0	19	1	0	4	.000	0-0	1	94	1.048	9.35	10.69
2019	Tex	AL	19	8	4	44.0	220	58	46	42	8	0	4	3	29	1	30	1	1	3	.250	0-1	1	94	.908	7.95	8.59
Postseason			5	2	0	13.2	61	16	8	8	1	1	1	1	6	0	12	0	0	0		0-0	0	94	.768	5.46	5.27
8 ML YEARS			150	132	5	758.1	3258	733	376	346	83	25	19	19	298	17	622	17	38	56	.404	0-1	3	94	.724	3.99	4.11

Alec Mills

Pitches: R Bats: R Pos: RP-5; SP-4   Ht: 6'4" Wt: 190 Born: 11/30/1991 Age: 28

Year Team	Lg	G	GS	GF	IP	BFP	H	R	ER	HR	SH	SF	HB	TBB	IBB	SO	WP	W	L	Pct	Sv-Op	Hld	Vel	OPS	ERC	ERA
2019 Iowa	AAA	19	18	0	104.0	447	116	62	59	17	4	3	2	30	1	96	2	6	4	.600	0--	-	-	.795	4.84	5.11
2016 KC	AL	3	0	2	3.1	19	3	5	5	0	0	0	1	5	0	4	0	0	0	-	0-0	0	92	.858	8.02	13.50
2018 ChC	NL	7	2	1	18.0	71	11	8	8	1	0	0	0	7	0	23	1	0	1	.000	0-0	0	91	.550	1.80	4.00
2019 ChC	NL	9	4	3	36.0	152	31	11	11	5	0	0	7	11	0	42	0	1	0	1.000	1-1	0	90	.718	4.03	2.75
3 ML YEARS		19	6	6	57.1	242	45	24	24	6	0	0	8	23	0	69	1	1	1	.500	1-1	0	90	.679	3.50	3.77

Hoby Milner

Pitches: L Bats: L Pos: RP-4   Ht: 6'3" Wt: 175 Born: 1/13/1991 Age: 29

Year Team	Lg	G	GS	GF	IP	BFP	H	R	ER	HR	SH	SF	HB	TBB	IBB	SO	WP	W	L	Pct	Sv-Op	Hld	Vel	OPS	ERC	ERA
2019 Drham	AAA	50	0	28	61.2	243	47	25	21	7	1	2	2	13	3	89	2	3	3	.500	12--	-	-	.572	2.28	3.06
2017 Phi	NL	37	0	5	31.1	139	30	7	7	2	2	1	4	16	3	22	0	0	0	-	0-1	7	89	.736	4.39	2.01
2018 2 Tms		14	0	3	7.1	38	9	8	6	3	0	0	1	5	1	8	0	0	0	-	0-0	1	89	.988	9.22	7.36
2019 TB	AL	4	0	1	3.2	17	4	3	3	0	0	0	1	1	0	3	0	0	0	-	0-0	1	88	.820	4.28	7.36
18 Phi	NL	10	0	2	4.2	25	6	4	4	1	0	0	1	3	1	4	0	0	0	-	0-0	0	89	.829	7.79	7.71
18 TB	AL	4	0	1	2.2	13	3	4	2	2	0	0	0	2	0	4	0	0	0	-	0-0	1	89	1.294	11.59	6.75
3 ML YEARS		55	0	9	42.1	194	43	18	16	5	2	1	6	22	4	33	0	0	0	-	0-1	9	89	.793	5.17	3.40

Tommy Milone

mah-LONE

Pitches: L Bats: L Pos: RP-17; SP-6   Ht: 6'0" Wt: 215 Born: 2/16/1987 Age: 33

Year Team	Lg	G	GS	GF	IP	BFP	H	R	ER	HR	SH	SF	HB	TBB	IBB	SO	WP	W	L	Pct	Sv-Op	Hld	Vel	OPS	ERC	ERA
2019 Tacom	AAA	9	8	0	49.1	211	49	26	21	7	0	1	2	12	0	43	0	4	2	.667	0--	-	-	.722	3.78	3.83
2011 Was	NL	5	5	0	26.0	110	28	11	11	2	3	2	2	4	2	15	0	1	1	.500	0-0	0	88	.742	3.55	3.81
2012 Oak	AL	31	31	0	190.0	791	207	90	79	24	3	3	4	36	2	137	2	13	10	.565	0-0	0	88	.738	4.04	3.74
2013 Oak	AL	28	26	0	156.1	667	160	83	72	25	0	6	2	39	2	126	1	12	9	.571	0-0	0	87	.738	3.98	4.14
2014 2 Tms	AL	22	21	1	118.0	519	128	63	55	16	1	2	5	37	2	75	0	6	4	.600	0-0	0	87	.763	4.55	4.19
2015 Min	AL	24	23	1	128.2	543	128	64	56	17	6	7	1	36	1	91	3	9	5	.643	1-1	0	88	.731	3.79	3.92
2016 Min	AL	19	12	3	69.1	311	84	53	44	15	4	3	1	22	3	49	3	3	5	.375	0-0	1	88	.857	5.77	5.71
2017 2 Tms	NL	17	8	2	48.1	221	65	43	41	15	2	0	0	14	3	38	0	1	3	.250	1-1	0	88	.970	7.12	7.63
2018 Was	NL	5	4	1	26.1	118	37	17	17	7	2	2	1	1	0	23	0	1	1	.500	0-0	0	87	.917	6.17	5.81
2019 Sea	AL	23	6	0	111.2	453	102	61	59	24	0	5	2	23	2	94	1	4	10	.286	0-0	0	87	.765	3.63	4.76
14 Oak	AL	16	16	0	96.1	405	91	42	38	12	1	2	4	26	2	61	0	6	3	.667	0-0	0	87	.705	3.53	3.55
14 Min	AL	6	5	1	21.2	114	37	21	17	4	0	0	1	11	0	14	0	0	1	.000	0-0	0	87	.969	9.76	7.06
17 Mil	NL	6	3	1	21.0	93	29	15	15	6	0	0	0	2	0	16	0	1	0	1.000	1-1	0	88	.905	6.32	6.43
17 NYM	NL	11	5	1	27.1	128	36	28	26	9	2	0	0	12	3	22	0	0	3	.000	0-0	0	88	1.021	7.74	8.56
Postseason		1	1	0	6.0	25	5	1	1	0	0	0	1	1	0	6	1	0	0	-	0-0	0	88	.584	2.26	1.50
9 ML YEARS		174	136	8	874.2	3733	939	485	434	145	21	30	18	212	17	648	10	50	47	.515	2-2	1	87	.773	4.35	4.47

Juan Minaya

Pitches: R Bats: R Pos: RP-22   Ht: 6'4" Wt: 210 Born: 9/18/1990 Age: 29

Year Team	Lg	G	GS	GF	IP	BFP	H	R	ER	HR	SH	SF	HB	TBB	IBB	SO	WP	W	L	Pct	Sv-Op	Hld	Vel	OPS	ERC	ERA
2019 Charlt	AAA	24	0	18	34.0	149	32	18	14	4	3	0	3	15	1	41	9	4	3	.571	6--	-	-	.741	4.33	3.71
2016 CWS	AL	11	0	3	10.1	47	10	6	5	0	0	0	2	5	0	6	0	1	0	1.000	0-0	0	94	.712	4.19	4.35
2017 CWS	AL	40	0	20	43.2	184	38	22	22	7	0	1	4	20	0	51	2	3	2	.600	9-10	2	94	.765	4.51	4.53
2018 CWS	AL	52	0	9	46.2	209	39	19	17	3	0	0	3	29	3	58	9	2	2	.500	1-4	8	95	.673	3.84	3.28
2019 CWS	AL	22	0	8	27.2	126	31	13	12	4	0	0	2	12	0	27	3	0	0	-	0-0	0	93	.857	5.51	3.90
4 ML YEARS		125	0	40	128.1	566	118	60	56	14	0	1	11	66	3	142	14	6	4	.600	10-14	10	94	.748	4.45	3.93

Mike Minor

Pitches: L Bats: R Pos: SP-32   Ht: 6'4" Wt: 210 Born: 12/26/1987 Age: 32

Year Team	Lg	G	GS	GF	IP	BFP	H	R	ER	HR	SH	SF	HB	TBB	IBB	SO	WP	W	L	Pct	Sv-Op	Hld	Vel	OPS	ERC	ERA
2010 Atl	NL	9	8	1	40.2	185	53	28	27	6	1	3	1	11	0	43	0	3	2	.600	0-0	0	91	.880	5.71	5.98
2011 Atl	NL	15	15	0	82.2	361	93	39	38	7	3	1	1	30	5	77	2	5	3	.625	0-0	0	91	.785	4.51	4.14
2012 Atl	NL	30	30	0	179.1	728	151	88	82	26	8	8	5	56	7	145	3	11	10	.524	0-0	0	90	.702	3.28	4.12
2013 Atl	NL	32	32	0	204.2	820	177	79	73	22	5	6	1	46	2	181	5	13	9	.591	0-0	0	90	.657	2.76	3.21
2014 Atl	NL	25	25	0	145.1	637	165	77	77	21	6	2	6	44	2	120	5	6	12	.333	0-0	0	90	.798	4.93	4.77
2017 KC	AL	65	0	13	77.2	307	57	23	22	5	3	1	1	22	3	88	5	6	6	.500	6-9	17	94	.585	2.07	2.55
2018 Tex	AL	28	28	0	157.0	640	138	76	73	25	1	6	8	38	1	132	3	12	8	.600	0-0	0	93	.733	3.40	4.18
2019 Tex	AL	32	32	0	208.1	863	190	86	83	30	3	6	7	68	1	200	2	14	10	.583	0-0	0	93	.704	3.78	3.59
Postseason		1	1	0	6.1	26	8	1	1	0	1	0	0	1	0	5	0	1	0	1.000	0-0	0	92	.777	4.11	1.42
8 ML YEARS		236	170	14	1095.2	4541	1024	496	475	142	30	33	30	315	21	986	25	70	60	.538	6-9	17	91	.718	3.58	3.90

A.J. Minter

Pitches: L Bats: L Pos: RP-36 Ht: 6'0" Wt: 215 Born: 9/2/1993 Age: 26

Year	Team	Lg	G	GS	GF	IP	BFP	H	R	ER	HR	SH	SF	HB	TBB	IBB	SO	WP	W	L	Pct	Sv-Op	Hld	Vel	OPS	ERC	ERA
2019	Gwnntt	AAA	20	0	13	22.2	94	24	11	9	4	0	0	0	3	0	30	1	2	2	.500	5--	-	-	.716	3.80	3.57
2017	Atl	NL	16	0	3	15.0	60	13	5	5	1	0	0	0	2	0	26	0	0	1	.000	0-0	5	96	.595	2.15	3.00
2018	Atl	NL	65	0	31	61.1	260	57	23	22	3	1	1	2	22	1	69	5	4	3	.571	15-17	12	97	.642	3.27	3.23
2019	Atl	NL	36	0	12	29.1	147	36	23	23	3	1	1	1	23	5	35	5	3	4	.429	5-7	5	96	.857	6.73	7.06
	Postseason		2	0	1	2.0	8	1	0	0	0	0	0	0	1	0	3	1	0	0	-	0-0	1	97	.393	1.41	0.00
	3 ML YEARS		117	0	46	105.2	467	106	51	50	7	2	2	3	47	6	130	10	7	8	.467	20-24	22	96	.701	4.00	4.26

Casey Mize

Pitches: R Bats: R Pos: P Ht: 6'3" Wt: 220 Born: 5/1/1997 Age: 23

Year	Team	Lg	G	GS	GF	IP	BFP	H	R	ER	HR	SH	SF	HB	TBB	IBB	SO	WP	W	L	Pct	Sv-Op	Hld	Vel	OPS	ERC	ERA
2018	2 Tms	Low	5	5	0	13.2	55	13	6	6	2	0	0	2	3	0	14	0	0	1	.000	0--	-	-	.747	4.23	3.95
2019	Lkland	A+	6	6	0	30.2	107	11	3	3	0	1	0	1	5	0	30	0	2	0	1.000	0--	-	-	.300	0.55	0.88
2019	Erie	AA	15	15	0	78.2	323	69	30	28	5	1	3	6	18	0	76	0	6	3	.667	0--	-	-	.635	2.82	3.20

Yadier Molina

Bats: R Throws: R Pos: C-111;1B-4;PH-3;3B-1 YAH-dee-air Ht: 5'11" Wt: 205 Born: 7/13/1982 Age: 37

Year	Team	Lg	G	AB	H	2B	3B	HR	(Hm	Rd)	TB	R	RBI	RC	TBB	IBB	SO	HBP	SH	SF	SB	CS	GDP	Avg	OBP	Slg	OPS
2004	StL	NL	51	135	36	6	0	2	(1	1)	48	12	15	15	13	3	20	0	2	1	0	1	4	.267	.329	.356	.684
2005	StL	NL	114	385	97	15	1	8	(6	2)	138	36	49	46	23	3	30	2	8	3	2	3	10	.252	.295	.358	.654
2006	StL	NL	129	417	90	26	0	6	(2	4)	134	29	49	35	26	2	41	8	8	2	1	2	15	.216	.274	.321	.595
2007	StL	NL	111	353	97	15	0	6	(4	2)	130	30	40	38	34	5	43	3	2	4	1	1	18	.275	.340	.368	.708
2008	StL	NL	124	444	135	18	0	7	(2	5)	174	37	56	57	32	4	29	1	3	5	0	2	21	.304	.349	.392	.740
2009	StL	NL	140	481	141	23	1	6	(5	1)	184	45	54	64	50	2	39	6	6	1	9	3	27	.293	.366	.383	.749
2010	StL	NL	136	465	122	19	0	6	(1	5)	159	34	62	55	42	6	51	7	2	5	8	4	19	.262	.329	.342	.671
2011	StL	NL	139	475	145	32	1	14	(5	9)	221	55	65	64	33	4	44	1	5	4	4	5	21	.305	.349	.465	.814
2012	StL	NL	138	505	159	28	0	22	(9	13)	253	65	76	91	45	4	55	5	3	5	12	3	10	.315	.373	.501	.874
2013	StL	NL	136	505	161	44	0	12	(5	7)	241	68	80	84	30	4	55	3	0	3	3	2	14	.319	.359	.477	.836
2014	StL	NL	110	404	114	21	0	7	(3	4)	156	40	38	47	28	4	55	6	1	6	1	1	14	.282	.333	.386	.719
2015	StL	NL	136	488	132	23	2	4	(3	1)	171	34	61	48	32	3	59	0	1	9	3	1	16	.270	.310	.350	.660
2016	StL	NL	147	534	164	38	1	8	(4	4)	228	56	58	74	39	1	63	6	0	2	3	2	22	.307	.360	.427	.787
2017	StL	NL	136	501	137	27	1	18	(7	11)	220	60	82	67	28	4	74	4	1	9	9	4	14	.273	.312	.439	.751
2018	StL	NL	123	459	120	20	0	20	(3	17)	200	55	74	65	29	0	66	9	0	6	4	3	15	.261	.314	.436	.750
2019	StL	NL	113	419	113	24	0	10	(4	6)	167	45	57	56	23	0	58	5	0	5	6	0	14	.270	.312	.399	.711
	Postseason		89	315	90	17	0	3	(2	1)	116	25	31	32	25	5	38	1	1	1	1	1	11	.286	.339	.368	.707
	16 ML YEARS		1983	6970	1963	379	7	156	(64	92)	2824	701	916	906	507	49	782	66	42	70	66	37	254	.282	.333	.405	.738

Yoan Moncada

Bats: B Throws: R Pos: 3B-129;DH-1;PH-1 yo-AHN Ht: 6'2" Wt: 205 Born: 5/27/1995 Age: 25

Year	Team	Lg	G	AB	H	2B	3B	HR	(Hm	Rd)	TB	R	RBI	RC	TBB	IBB	SO	HBP	SH	SF	SB	CS	GDP	Avg	OBP	Slg	OPS
2016	Bos	AL	8	19	4	1	0	0	(0	0)	5	3	1	1	0	0	12	0	0	0	0	0	0	.211	.250	.263	.513
2017	CWS	AL	54	199	46	8	2	8	(4	4)	82	31	22	27	29	0	74	3	0	0	3	2	0	.231	.338	.412	.750
2018	CWS	AL	149	578	136	32	6	17	(10	7)	231	73	61	73	67	1	217	1	2	2	12	6	4	.235	.315	.400	.714
2019	CWS	AL	132	511	161	34	5	25	(16	9)	280	83	79	90	40	2	154	4	1	3	10	3	1	.315	.367	.548	.915
	4 ML YEARS		343	1307	347	75	13	50	(30	20)	598	190	163	194	137	3	457	8	3	5	25	11	5	.265	.338	.458	.795

Adalberto Mondesi

Bats: B Throws: R Pos: SS-100;DH-2;PH-1 Ht: 6'1" Wt: 190 Born: 7/27/1995 Age: 24

Year	Team	Lg	G	AB	H	2B	3B	HR	(Hm	Rd)	TB	R	RBI	RC	TBB	IBB	SO	HBP	SH	SF	SB	CS	GDP	Avg	OBP	Slg	OPS
2016	KC	AL	47	135	25	1	3	2	(0	2)	38	16	13	9	6	0	48	2	6	0	9	1	1	.185	.231	.281	.512
2017	KC	AL	25	53	9	1	0	1	(1	0)	13	4	3	0	3	0	22	0	4	0	5	2	2	.170	.214	.245	.460
2018	KC	AL	75	275	76	13	3	14	(7	7)	137	47	37	39	11	0	77	1	3	7	32	7	2	.276	.306	.498	.804
2019	KC	AL	102	415	109	20	10	9	(4	5)	176	58	62	60	19	0	132	0	3	6	43	7	6	.263	.291	.424	.715
	Postseason		1	1	0	0	0	0	(0	0)	0	0	0	0	0	0	1	0	0	0	0	0	0	.000	.000	.000	.000
	4 ML YEARS		249	878	219	35	16	26	(12	14)	364	125	115	108	39	0	279	3	16	7	89	17	11	.249	.282	.415	.696

Frankie Montas

Pitches: R Bats: R Pos: SP-16 MOHN-tahs Ht: 6'2" Wt: 245 Born: 3/21/1993 Age: 27

Year	Team	Lg	G	GS	GF	IP	BFP	H	R	ER	HR	SH	SF	HB	TBB	IBB	SO	WP	W	L	Pct	Sv-Op	Hld	Vel	OPS	ERC	ERA
2015	CWS	AL	7	2	2	15.0	66	14	8	8	1	0	0	0	9	1	20	0	0	2	.000	0-0	0	97	.699	4.16	4.80
2017	Oak	AL	23	0	5	32.0	152	39	25	25	10	0	0	3	20	0	36	1	1	1	.500	0-0	1	98	.974	8.72	7.03
2018	Oak	AL	13	11	1	65.0	283	74	34	28	5	2	3	2	21	0	43	5	5	4	.556	0-0	0	96	.796	4.55	3.88
2019	Oak	AL	16	16	0	96.0	394	84	35	28	8	0	2	4	23	1	103	5	9	2	.818	0-0	0	97	.646	2.82	2.63
	4 ML YEARS		59	29	8	208.0	895	211	102	89	24	2	5	9	73	2	202	11	15	9	.625	0-0	1	97	.751	4.24	3.85

Rafael Montero

Pitches: R **Bats:** R **Pos:** RP-22 **Ht:** 6'0" **Wt:** 185 **Born:** 10/17/1990 **Age:** 29

			HOW MUCH PITCHED				WHAT HE GAVE UP										THE RESULTS						
Year	Team	Lg	G	GS	GF	IP	BFP	H	R	ER	HR	SH	SF	HB	TBB	IBB	SO	WP	W	L	Pct	Sv-Op	Hld	Vel	OPS	ERC	ERA
2019	Rngrs	R	5	3	1	7.0	23	2	0	0	0	0	0	0	0	0	12	0	0	0	-	0--	-	-	.217	0.19	0.00
2019	Frisco	AA	5	2	0	9.0	45	15	7	7	0	0	1	1	2	1	15	0	0	0	-	0--	-	-	.888	6.59	7.00
2014	NYM	NL	10	8	1	44.1	194	44	21	20	8	0	0	0	23	0	42	0	1	3	.250	0-0	0	92	.825	5.16	4.06
2015	NYM	NL	5	1	1	10.0	46	9	6	5	0	1	0	0	5	3	13	0	0	1	.000	0-0	1	92	.661	2.50	4.50
2016	NYM	NL	9	3	1	19.0	93	23	17	17	4	0	0	0	16	1	20	2	0	1	.000	0-0	0	93	.965	8.15	8.05
2017	NYM	NL	34	18	4	119.0	550	141	75	73	12	9	8	5	67	5	114	6	5	11	.313	0-0	0	94	.832	5.63	5.52
2019	Tex	AL	22	0	6	29.0	113	23	8	8	5	0	0	2	5	0	34	0	2	0	1.000	0-1	7	96	.671	2.89	2.48
	5 ML YEARS		80	30	13	221.1	996	240	127	123	29	10	8	7	116	9	223	8	8	16	.333	0-1	8	93	.816	5.41	5.00

Jordan Montgomery

Pitches: L **Bats:** L **Pos:** SP-1; RP-1 **Ht:** 6'6" **Wt:** 225 **Born:** 12/27/1992 **Age:** 27

			HOW MUCH PITCHED				WHAT HE GAVE UP										THE RESULTS						
Year	Team	Lg	G	GS	GF	IP	BFP	H	R	ER	HR	SH	SF	HB	TBB	IBB	SO	WP	W	L	Pct	Sv-Op	Hld	Vel	OPS	ERC	ERA
2017	NYY	AL	29	29	0	155.1	649	140	72	67	21	2	3	1	51	0	144	7	9	7	.563	0-0	0	92	.684	3.50	3.88
2018	NYY	AL	6	6	0	27.1	116	25	11	11	3	0	0	0	12	0	23	0	2	0	1.000	0-0	0	90	.675	3.85	3.62
2019	NYY	AL	2	1	0	4.0	19	7	3	3	1	0	0	0	0	0	5	0	0	0	-	0-0	0	92	1.053	7.95	6.75
	3 ML YEARS		37	36	0	186.2	784	172	86	81	25	2	3	1	63	0	172	7	11	7	.611	0-0	0	92	.692	3.63	3.91

Mike Montgomery

Pitches: L **Bats:** L **Pos:** RP-20; SP-13 **Ht:** 6'5" **Wt:** 215 **Born:** 7/1/1989 **Age:** 30

			HOW MUCH PITCHED				WHAT HE GAVE UP										THE RESULTS						
Year	Team	Lg	G	GS	GF	IP	BFP	H	R	ER	HR	SH	SF	HB	TBB	IBB	SO	WP	W	L	Pct	Sv-Op	Hld	Vel	OPS	ERC	ERA
2015	Sea	AL	16	16	0	90.0	395	92	49	46	11	0	0	4	37	1	64	10	4	6	.400	0-0	0	91	.754	4.56	4.60
2016	2 Tms		49	7	18	100.0	414	79	33	28	8	3	2	10	38	2	92	10	4	5	.444	0-0	5	94	.652	3.13	2.52
2017	ChC	NL	44	14	11	130.2	540	103	52	49	10	5	2	8	55	4	100	7	7	8	.467	3-3	1	92	.632	3.09	3.38
2018	ChC	NL	38	19	6	124.0	534	131	58	55	10	3	4	7	39	4	86	4	5	6	.455	0-0	0	92	.724	4.11	3.99
2019	2 Tms		33	13	6	91.0	402	113	55	50	18	3	1	4	34	1	69	3	3	9	.250	0-1	3	92	.914	6.53	4.95
16	Sea	AL	32	2	13	61.2	250	49	18	16	3	2	1	6	18	2	54	5	3	4	.429	0-0	3	94	.617	2.61	2.34
16	ChC	NL	17	5	5	38.1	164	30	15	12	5	1	1	4	20	0	38	5	1	1	.500	0-0	2	93	.708	4.01	2.82
19	ChC	NL	20	0	6	27.0	123	35	18	17	6	1	1	0	13	1	18	0	1	2	.333	0-1	3	93	1.004	7.31	5.67
19	KC	AL	13	13	0	64.0	279	78	37	33	12	2	0	4	21	0	51	3	2	7	.222	0-0	0	92	.876	6.21	4.64
	Postseason		16	0	5	18.2	95	28	14	13	3	1	2	0	11	1	15	3	1	1	.500	1-1	2	93	.970	8.19	6.27
	5 ML YEARS		180	69	41	535.2	2285	518	247	228	57	14	9	33	203	12	411	34	23	34	.404	3-4	9	92	.729	4.12	3.83

Andrew Moore

Pitches: R **Bats:** R **Pos:** SP-1 **Ht:** 6'0" **Wt:** 195 **Born:** 6/2/1994 **Age:** 26

			HOW MUCH PITCHED				WHAT HE GAVE UP										THE RESULTS						
Year	Team	Lg	G	GS	GF	IP	BFP	H	R	ER	HR	SH	SF	HB	TBB	IBB	SO	WP	W	L	Pct	Sv-Op	Hld	Vel	OPS	ERC	ERA
2019	Drham	AAA	5	4	0	17.1	91	29	26	25	9	0	0	2	10	0	10	0	0	2	.000	0--	-	-	1.248	13.73	12.98
2019	Ark	AA	5	5	0	28.0	108	24	12	12	1	0	1	0	4	0	29	0	2	1	.667	0--	-	-	.599	2.06	3.86
2019	Tacom	AAA	13	8	1	54.0	252	71	52	48	14	1	2	2	17	0	36	1	0	5	.000	0--	-	-	.950	6.83	8.00
2017	Sea	AL	11	9	1	59.0	243	60	36	35	14	0	4	1	8	0	31	0	1	5	.167	0-1	0	91	.784	4.04	5.34
2019	Sea	AL	1	1	0	4.2	20	6	4	4	2	0	0	0	1	0	2	0	0	0	-	0-0	0	91	1.087	7.64	7.71
	2 ML YEARS		12	10	1	63.2	263	66	40	39	16	0	4	1	9	0	33	0	1	5	.167	0-1	0	91	.807	4.28	5.51

Dylan Moore

Bats: R **Throws:** R **Pos:** SS-31;LF-31;2B-18;3B-14;PR-13;RF-11;1B-5;CF-4;PH-4;DH-3 **Ht:** 6'0" **Wt:** 200 **Born:** 8/2/1992 **Age:** 27

			BATTING																RUNNING			AVERAGES		
Year	Team	Lg	G	AB	H	2B	3B	HR	(Hm | Rd)	TB	R	RBI	RC	TBB	IBB	SO	HBP	SH	SF	SB	CS	GDP	Avg	OBP	Slg	OPS
2019	Sea	AL	113	247	51	14	2	9	(6 | 3)	96	31	28	29	25	0	93	9	1	0	11	9	6	.206	.302	.389	.691

Matt Moore

Pitches: L **Bats:** L **Pos:** SP-2 **Ht:** 6'3" **Wt:** 210 **Born:** 6/18/1989 **Age:** 31

			HOW MUCH PITCHED				WHAT HE GAVE UP										THE RESULTS						
Year	Team	Lg	G	GS	GF	IP	BFP	H	R	ER	HR	SH	SF	HB	TBB	IBB	SO	WP	W	L	Pct	Sv-Op	Hld	Vel	OPS	ERC	ERA
2011	TB	AL	3	1	0	9.1	40	9	3	3	1	0	0	0	3	0	15	2	1	0	1.000	0-0	1	96	.651	3.54	2.89
2012	TB	AL	31	31	0	177.1	759	158	85	75	18	3	4	7	81	5	175	8	11	11	.500	0-0	0	94	.706	3.83	3.81
2013	TB	AL	27	27	0	150.1	642	119	58	55	14	5	6	4	76	1	143	17	17	4	.810	0-0	0	92	.655	3.36	3.29
2014	TB	AL	2	2	0	10.0	44	10	3	3	1	0	0	0	5	0	6	0	0	2	.000	0-0	0	92	.777	4.48	2.70
2015	TB	AL	12	12	0	63.0	278	74	40	38	9	0	3	4	23	1	46	6	3	4	.429	0-0	0	92	.839	5.63	5.43
2016	2 Tms		33	33	0	198.1	838	184	93	90	25	4	4	6	72	1	178	6	13	12	.520	0-0	0	93	.694	3.83	4.08
2017	SF	NL	32	31	1	174.1	790	200	116	107	27	4	4	8	67	3	148	10	6	15	.286	0-0	0	92	.835	5.35	5.52
2018	Tex	AL	39	12	10	102.0	471	128	82	77	19	1	4	5	41	1	86	6	3	8	.273	0-1	2	92	.911	6.43	6.79
2019	Det	AL	2	2	0	10.0	33	3	0	0	0	0	0	0	1	0	9	0	0	0	-	0-0	0	93	.215	0.32	0.00
16	TB	AL	21	21	0	130.0	549	125	62	59	20	3	2	5	40	0	109	3	7	7	.500	0-0	0	93	.716	4.02	4.08
16	SF	NL	12	12	0	68.1	289	59	31	31	5	1	2	1	32	1	69	3	6	5	.545	0-0	0	93	.651	3.47	4.08
	Postseason		5	3	0	24.1	97	14	11	9	2	0	1	2	8	1	25	2	1	1	.500	0-0	0	93	.550	1.78	3.33
	9 ML YEARS		181	151	11	894.2	3895	885	480	448	114	19	25	33	369	12	806	55	54	56	.491	0-1	3	93	.752	4.38	4.51

289

Kendrys Morales

Bats: B **Throws:** R **Pos:** 1B-33;DH-16;PH-7   KEN-dreez   **Ht:** 6'1" **Wt:** 242 **Born:** 6/20/1983 **Age:** 37

Year	Team	Lg	G	AB	H	2B	3B	HR	(Hm	Rd)	TB	R	RBI	RC	TBB	IBB	SO	HBP	SH	SF	SB	CS	GDP	Avg	OBP	Slg	OPS
2006	LAA	AL	57	197	46	10	1	5	(1	4)	73	21	22	19	17	1	28	0	0	1	1	1	11	.234	.293	.371	.664
2007	LAA	AL	43	119	35	10	0	4	(2	2)	57	12	15	15	6	2	21	1	0	0	0	1	5	.294	.333	.479	.812
2008	LAA	AL	27	61	13	2	0	3	(0	3)	24	7	8	3	4	0	7	1	0	0	0	1	3	.213	.273	.393	.666
2009	LAA	AL	152	566	173	43	2	34	(21	13)	322	86	108	105	46	10	117	2	0	8	3	7	15	.306	.355	.569	.924
2010	LAA	AL	51	193	56	5	0	11	(7	4)	94	29	39	34	12	3	31	5	0	1	0	1	5	.290	.346	.487	.833
2012	LAA	AL	134	484	132	26	1	22	(10	12)	226	61	73	68	31	1	116	4	0	3	0	1	11	.273	.320	.467	.787
2013	Sea	AL	156	602	167	34	0	23	(12	11)	270	64	80	85	49	6	114	5	0	1	0	0	21	.277	.336	.449	.785
2014	2 Tms	AL	98	367	80	20	0	8	(4	4)	124	28	42	29	27	3	68	3	0	4	0	0	12	.218	.274	.338	.612
2015	KC	AL	158	569	165	41	2	22	(10	12)	276	81	106	98	58	4	103	8	0	4	0	0	24	.290	.362	.485	.847
2016	KC	AL	154	558	147	24	0	30	(12	18)	261	65	93	86	48	2	120	7	0	5	0	0	20	.263	.327	.468	.795
2017	Tor	AL	150	557	139	25	0	28	(13	15)	248	67	85	71	43	2	132	5	0	3	0	0	22	.250	.308	.445	.753
2018	Tor	AL	130	413	103	15	0	21	(12	9)	181	47	57	54	50	5	95	3	0	5	2	3	15	.249	.331	.438	.769
2019	2 Tms	AL	53	170	33	2	1	2	(1	1)	43	16	12	14	26	0	26	4	0	1	0	0	6	.194	.313	.253	.566
14	Min	AL	39	154	36	11	0	1	(0	1)	50	12	18	11	6	1	27	0	0	2	0	0	4	.234	.259	.325	.584
14	Sea	AL	59	213	44	9	0	7	(4	3)	74	16	24	18	21	2	41	3	0	2	0	0	8	.207	.285	.347	.632
19	Oak	AL	34	108	22	1	1	1	(0	1)	28	9	7	10	14	0	20	3	0	1	0	0	3	.204	.310	.259	.569
19	NYY	AL	19	62	11	1	0	1	(1	0)	15	7	5	4	12	0	6	1	0	0	0	0	3	.177	.320	.242	.562
	Postseason		32	98	22	1	0	6	(4	2)	41	8	17	12	6	0	20	1	0	2	0	0	1	.224	.271	.418	.689
13 ML YEARS			1363	4856	1289	257	7	213	(105	108)	2199	584	740	681	417	39	978	48	0	36	6	15	170	.265	.327	.453	.780

Brian Moran

Pitches: L **Bats:** L **Pos:** RP-10   **Ht:** 6'4" **Wt:** 230 **Born:** 9/30/1988 **Age:** 31

Year	Team	Lg	G	GS	GF	IP	BFP	H	R	ER	HR	SH	SF	HB	TBB	IBB	SO	WP	W	L	Pct	Sv-Op	Hld	Vel	OPS	ERC	ERA
2019	NewOr	AAA	43	1	11	60.0	252	45	25	21	6	2	0	7	26	2	77	4	2	3	.400	0- -	-	-	.653	3.26	3.15
2019	Mia	NL	10	0	0	6.1	29	6	3	3	1	1	0	2	2	1	10	0	1	0	1.000	0-1	2	84	.857	4.74	4.26

Colin Moran

Bats: L **Throws:** R **Pos:** 3B-121;PH-23;2B-11;1B-8;LF-2   **Ht:** 6'4" **Wt:** 205 **Born:** 10/1/1992 **Age:** 27

Year	Team	Lg	G	AB	H	2B	3B	HR	(Hm	Rd)	TB	R	RBI	RC	TBB	IBB	SO	HBP	SH	SF	SB	CS	GDP	Avg	OBP	Slg	OPS
2016	Hou	AL	9	23	3	1	0	0	(0	0)	4	1	2	0	1	0	8	1	0	0	0	0	4	.130	.200	.174	.374
2017	Hou	AL	7	11	4	0	1	0	(0	1)	9	3	3	4	1	0	1	0	0	0	0	0	0	.364	.417	.818	1.235
2018	Pit	NL	144	415	115	19	1	11	(5	6)	169	49	58	55	39	4	82	4	0	7	0	2	6	.277	.340	.407	.747
2019	Pit	NL	149	466	129	30	1	13	(6	7)	200	46	80	69	30	4	117	3	0	4	0	1	13	.277	.322	.429	.751
4 ML YEARS			309	915	251	50	3	25	(11	14)	382	99	143	128	71	8	208	8	0	11	0	3	23	.274	.328	.417	.746

Adrian Morejon

Pitches: L **Bats:** L **Pos:** RP-3; SP-2   moh-ray-HOHN   **Ht:** 6'0" **Wt:** 175 **Born:** 2/27/1999 **Age:** 21

Year	Team	Lg	G	GS	GF	IP	BFP	H	R	ER	HR	SH	SF	HB	TBB	IBB	SO	WP	W	L	Pct	Sv-Op	Hld	Vel	OPS	ERC	ERA
2019	Amrillo	AA	16	16	0	36.0	154	29	20	17	3	0	1	3	15	0	44	2	0	4	.000	0- -	-	-	.676	3.24	4.25
2019	SD	NL	5	2	1	8.0	42	15	9	9	1	0	0	0	3	0	9	0	0	0	-	0-0	0	96	1.044	9.51	10.13

Mitch Moreland

Bats: L **Throws:** L **Pos:** 1B-85;PH-14;DH-4   **Ht:** 6'2" **Wt:** 230 **Born:** 9/6/1985 **Age:** 34

Year	Team	Lg	G	AB	H	2B	3B	HR	(Hm	Rd)	TB	R	RBI	RC	TBB	IBB	SO	HBP	SH	SF	SB	CS	GDP	Avg	OBP	Slg	OPS
2010	Tex	AL	47	145	37	4	0	9	(3	6)	68	20	25	27	25	5	36	1	0	2	3	1	3	.255	.364	.469	.833
2011	Tex	AL	134	464	120	22	1	16	(7	9)	192	60	51	56	39	6	92	4	2	3	2	2	9	.259	.320	.414	.733
2012	Tex	AL	114	327	90	18	0	15	(10	5)	153	41	50	46	23	5	71	1	2	4	1	1	8	.275	.321	.468	.789
2013	Tex	AL	147	462	107	24	1	23	(10	13)	202	60	60	55	45	1	117	3	0	8	0	0	11	.232	.299	.437	.736
2014	Tex	AL	52	167	41	9	1	2	(1	1)	58	18	23	20	12	0	43	1	2	2	0	0	7	.246	.297	.347	.644
2015	Tex	AL	132	471	131	27	0	23	(9	14)	227	51	85	74	32	2	112	7	0	5	1	0	9	.278	.330	.482	.812
2016	Tex	AL	147	460	107	21	0	22	(13	9)	194	49	60	56	35	5	118	8	0	0	1	0	8	.233	.298	.422	.720
2017	Bos	AL	149	508	125	34	0	22	(10	12)	225	73	79	69	57	6	120	6	0	5	0	1	14	.246	.326	.443	.769
2018	Bos	AL	124	404	99	23	4	15	(6	9)	175	57	68	60	50	2	102	0	0	5	2	0	12	.245	.325	.433	.758
2019	Bos	AL	91	298	75	17	1	19	(8	11)	151	48	58	44	34	0	74	1	0	2	1	0	12	.252	.328	.507	.835
	Postseason		48	127	31	9	0	4	(3	1)	52	15	18	20	12	1	30	2	1	0	0	0	3	.244	.319	.409	.729
10 ML YEARS			1137	3706	932	199	8	166	(77	89)	1645	477	559	512	352	32	885	32	6	36	11	5	93	.251	.319	.444	.763

Adam Morgan

Pitches: L **Bats:** L **Pos:** RP-40   **Ht:** 6'1" **Wt:** 200 **Born:** 2/27/1990 **Age:** 30

Year	Team	Lg	G	GS	GF	IP	BFP	H	R	ER	HR	SH	SF	HB	TBB	IBB	SO	WP	W	L	Pct	Sv-Op	Hld	Vel	OPS	ERC	ERA
2015	Phi	NL	15	15	0	84.1	352	88	45	42	14	1	3	4	17	0	49	2	5	7	.417	0-0	0	89	.775	4.21	4.48
2016	Phi	NL	23	21	1	113.1	507	141	81	76	23	3	4	4	29	3	95	2	2	11	.154	0-0	0	91	.880	5.72	6.04
2017	Phi	NL	37	0	6	54.2	229	51	25	25	10	0	0	0	18	2	63	1	3	3	.500	0-1	6	94	.737	3.92	4.12
2018	Phi	NL	67	0	9	49.1	214	49	25	21	5	0	2	0	22	3	50	3	0	2	.000	1-4	14	94	.698	4.14	3.83
2019	Phi	NL	40	0	0	29.2	120	20	14	13	4	0	0	3	10	1	29	0	3	3	.500	0-2	19	93	.621	2.68	3.94
5 ML YEARS			182	36	16	331.1	1422	349	190	177	56	4	9	11	96	9	286	8	13	26	.333	1-7	39	91	.783	4.51	4.81

Mike Morin

MORE-in

Pitches: R **Bats:** R **Pos:** RP-52   **Ht:** 6'4" **Wt:** 220 **Born:** 5/3/1991 **Age:** 29

Year	Team	Lg	G	GS	GF	IP	BFP	H	R	ER	HR	SH	SF	HB	TBB	IBB	SO	WP	W	L	Pct	Sv-Op	Hld	Vel	OPS	ERC	ERA
2019	Roch	AAA	8	1	5	12.0	50	11	4	3	1	0	0	0	3	0	12	0	0	1	.000	1--	-	-	.599	2.89	2.25
2014	LAA	AL	60	0	10	59.0	246	51	22	19	3	2	4	3	19	6	54	3	4	4	.500	0-2	9	92	.629	2.76	2.90
2015	LAA	AL	47	0	10	35.1	151	36	28	25	3	2	2	2	9	2	41	0	4	2	.667	1-1	5	92	.720	3.61	6.37
2016	LAA	AL	60	0	8	55.2	227	52	31	27	6	2	1	1	15	1	49	1	2	2	.500	0-1	12	91	.677	3.37	4.37
2017	2 Tms	AL	16	0	8	20.0	93	29	16	16	3	1	2	1	5	1	16	0	0	0	-	0-0	0	91	.916	6.64	7.20
2018	Sea	AL	3	0	1	4.0	18	6	3	3	1	0	1	0	1	1	6	0	0	0	-	0-1	0	91	1.014	5.30	6.75
2019	2 Tms	AL	52	0	13	50.2	210	46	29	26	6	2	1	4	10	0	26	2	1	3	.250	1-2	8	91	.672	3.19	4.62
17	LAA	AL	10	0	3	14.1	65	21	11	11	3	1	1	1	2	1	10	0	0	0	-	0-0	0	91	.958	6.84	6.91
17	KC	AL	6	0	5	5.2	28	8	5	5	0	0	1	0	3	0	6	0	0	0	-	0-0	0	90	.810	6.06	7.94
19	Min	AL	23	0	10	22.2	92	20	11	8	3	0	0	2	2	0	11	0	0	0	-	1-1	1	91	.647	2.75	3.18
19	Phi	AL	29	0	3	28.0	118	26	18	18	3	2	1	2	8	0	15	2	1	3	.250	0-1	7	91	.691	3.56	5.79
	Postseason		1	0	0	1.0	6	3	2	2	1	0	1	0	0	0	1	1	0	0	-	0-0	0	93	1.700	25.51	18.00
	6 ML YEARS		238	0	50	224.2	945	220	129	116	21	9	11	11	59	11	192	6	11	11	.500	2-7	34	91	.700	3.50	4.65

Max Moroff

Bats: B **Throws:** R **Pos:** 2B-10;SS-10;PH-3;PR-3;3B-2   **Ht:** 5'10" **Wt:** 190 **Born:** 5/13/1993 **Age:** 27

Year	Team	Lg	G	AB	H	2B	3B	HR	(Hm	Rd)	TB	R	RBI	RC	TBB	IBB	SO	HBP	SH	SF	SB	CS	GDP	Avg	OBP	Slg	OPS
2019	Clmbs	AAA	34	108	23	4	0	4	(-	-)	39	20	8	16	26	0	34	2	0	0	1	2	5	.213	.375	.361	.736
2016	Pit	NL	2	2	0	0	0	0	(0	0)	0	0	0	0	0	0	2	0	0	0	0	0	0	.000	.000	.000	.000
2017	Pit	NL	56	120	24	4	1	3	(3	0)	39	19	21	15	16	0	43	2	1	1	0	1	0	.200	.302	.325	.627
2018	Pit	NL	26	59	11	1	0	3	(2	1)	21	7	9	7	7	1	24	1	0	0	0	0	0	.186	.284	.356	.640
2019	Cle	AL	20	32	4	1	0	1	(1	0)	8	3	4	1	2	0	16	0	1	0	1	0	0	.125	.176	.250	.426
	4 ML YEARS		104	213	39	6	1	7	(6	1)	68	29	34	23	25	1	85	3	2	1	1	1	0	.183	.277	.319	.596

Reyes Moronta

Pitches: R **Bats:** R **Pos:** RP-56   **Ht:** 5'11" **Wt:** 241 **Born:** 1/6/1993 **Age:** 27

Year	Team	Lg	G	GS	GF	IP	BFP	H	R	ER	HR	SH	SF	HB	TBB	IBB	SO	WP	W	L	Pct	Sv-Op	Hld	Vel	OPS	ERC	ERA
2017	SF	NL	7	0	1	6.2	29	6	2	2	1	0	0	0	5	1	11	0	0	0	-	0-1	0	96	.656	3.74	2.70
2018	SF	NL	69	0	9	65.0	262	34	20	18	4	1	3	0	37	4	79	5	5	2	.714	1-6	12	97	.507	1.93	2.49
2019	SF	NL	56	0	5	56.2	246	41	19	18	4	1	1	3	33	1	70	3	3	7	.300	0-5	15	97	.612	3.18	2.86
	3 ML YEARS		132	0	15	128.1	537	81	41	38	9	2	4	3	73	6	160	8	8	9	.471	1-12	27	97	.564	2.55	2.66

Logan Morrison

Bats: L **Throws:** L **Pos:** PH-25;1B-3;DH-1   **Ht:** 6'3" **Wt:** 245 **Born:** 8/25/1987 **Age:** 32

Year	Team	Lg	G	AB	H	2B	3B	HR	(Hm	Rd)	TB	R	RBI	RC	TBB	IBB	SO	HBP	SH	SF	SB	CS	GDP	Avg	OBP	Slg	OPS
2019	S-WB	AAA	43	152	44	11	0	15	(-	-)	100	29	37	32	8	0	26	4	0	0	1	1	5	.289	.341	.658	.999
2019	LV	AAA	18	59	21	5	0	3	(-	-)	35	7	12	14	7	0	12	2	0	1	0	0	1	.356	.435	.593	1.028
2010	Fla	NL	62	244	69	20	7	2	(1	1)	109	43	18	41	41	0	51	2	0	0	0	1	4	.283	.390	.447	.837
2011	Fla	NL	123	462	114	25	4	23	(12	11)	216	54	72	55	54	3	99	5	0	4	2	1	9	.247	.330	.468	.797
2012	Mia	NL	93	296	68	15	1	11	(4	7)	118	30	36	27	31	2	58	4	0	3	1	0	9	.230	.308	.399	.707
2013	Mia	NL	85	293	71	13	4	6	(1	5)	110	32	36	37	38	5	56	2	0	0	0	0	10	.242	.333	.375	.709
2014	Sea	AL	99	336	88	20	0	11	(7	4)	141	41	38	46	24	1	59	3	0	2	5	2	9	.262	.315	.420	.735
2015	Sea	AL	146	457	103	15	3	17	(7	10)	175	47	54	53	47	5	81	4	1	2	8	4	7	.225	.302	.383	.685
2016	TB	AL	107	353	84	18	1	14	(6	8)	146	45	43	50	37	1	89	6	0	2	4	2	4	.238	.319	.414	.733
2017	TB	AL	149	512	126	22	1	38	(11	27)	264	75	85	77	81	8	149	5	0	3	2	0	12	.246	.353	.516	.868
2018	Min	AL	95	318	59	13	0	15	(9	6)	117	41	39	31	34	0	80	6	0	1	1	0	3	.186	.276	.368	.644
2019	Phi	NL	29	35	7	1	0	2	(1	1)	14	5	3	4	3	0	10	0	0	0	0	0	1	.200	.263	.400	.663
	10 ML YEARS		988	3306	789	162	21	139	(59	80)	1410	413	424	421	390	25	732	37	1	17	23	10	68	.239	.324	.426	.751

Brandon Morrow

Pitches: R **Bats:** R **Pos:** P   **Ht:** 6'3" **Wt:** 205 **Born:** 7/26/1984 **Age:** 35

Year	Team	Lg	G	GS	GF	IP	BFP	H	R	ER	HR	SH	SF	HB	TBB	IBB	SO	WP	W	L	Pct	Sv-Op	Hld	Vel	OPS	ERC	ERA
2007	Sea	AL	60	0	18	63.1	289	56	29	29	3	4	4	1	50	5	66	4	3	4	.429	0-2	18	95	.723	4.47	4.12
2008	Sea	AL	45	5	24	64.2	265	40	26	24	10	1	0	0	34	1	75	5	3	4	.429	10-12	3	95	.611	2.84	3.34
2009	Sea	AL	26	10	9	69.2	313	66	38	34	10	1	2	0	44	1	63	3	2	4	.333	6-8	1	95	.755	4.99	4.39
2010	Tor	AL	26	26	0	146.1	629	136	76	73	17	2	4	6	66	0	178	8	10	7	.588	0-0	0	93	.725	3.99	4.49
2011	Tor	AL	30	30	0	179.1	777	162	103	94	21	4	9	12	69	1	203	12	11	11	.500	0-0	0	94	.705	3.79	4.72
2012	Tor	AL	21	21	0	124.2	504	98	45	41	12	1	3	2	41	0	108	3	10	7	.588	0-0	0	93	.635	2.73	2.96
2013	Tor	AL	10	10	0	54.1	242	63	39	34	12	0	3	1	18	1	42	1	2	3	.400	0-0	0	94	.880	5.63	5.63
2014	Tor	AL	13	6	2	33.1	148	37	21	21	2	1	0	0	18	0	30	1	1	3	.250	0-0	1	94	.832	5.09	5.67
2015	SD	NL	5	5	0	33.0	126	29	10	10	3	1	1	0	7	0	23	0	2	0	1.000	0-0	0	93	.681	2.84	2.73
2016	SD	NL	18	0	2	16.0	68	19	4	3	2	2	1	0	3	1	8	0	1	0	1.000	0-1	2	94	.769	4.40	1.69
2017	LAD	NL	45	0	10	43.2	170	31	10	10	0	0	0	1	9	1	50	2	6	0	1.000	2-3	10	98	.454	1.48	2.06
2018	ChC	NL	35	0	30	30.2	122	24	5	5	2	0	0	1	9	0	31	1	0	0	-	22-24	0	98	.555	2.49	1.47
	Postseason		14	0	0	13.2	53	11	6	6	3	0	0	0	2	0	12	1	0	0	-	0-1	5	98	.696	2.79	3.95
	12 ML YEARS		334	113	95	859.0	3653	761	406	378	88	17	27	27	368	11	877	40	51	43	.543	40-50	35	94	.698	3.68	3.96

Charlie Morton

Pitches: R Bats: R Pos: SP-33   Ht: 6'5" Wt: 215 Born: 11/12/1983 Age: 36

			HOW MUCH PITCHED					WHAT HE GAVE UP												THE RESULTS							
Year	Team	Lg	G	GS	GF	IP	BFP	H	R	ER	HR	SH	SF	HB	TBB	IBB	SO	WP	W	L	Pct	Sv-Op	Hld	Vel	OPS	ERC	ERA
2008	Atl	NL	16	15	0	74.2	345	80	56	51	9	5	4	2	41	2	48	2	4	8	.333	0-0	0	91	.816	5.21	6.15
2009	Pit	NL	18	18	0	97.0	416	102	49	49	7	1	5	4	40	0	62	4	5	9	.357	0-0	0	91	.761	4.56	4.55
2010	Pit	NL	17	17	0	79.2	382	112	79	67	15	6	6	7	26	3	59	5	2	12	.143	0-0	0	93	.908	7.10	7.57
2011	Pit	NL	29	29	0	171.2	769	186	82	73	6	12	6	13	77	5	110	9	10	10	.500	0-0	0	91	.737	4.52	3.83
2012	Pit	NL	9	9	0	50.1	223	62	30	26	5	9	2	2	11	1	25	4	2	6	.250	0-0	0	90	.812	4.74	4.65
2013	Pit	NL	20	20	0	116.0	493	113	51	42	6	6	2	16	36	1	85	5	7	4	.636	0-0	0	93	.683	3.84	3.26
2014	Pit	NL	26	26	0	157.1	666	143	76	65	9	7	5	19	57	2	126	8	6	12	.333	0-0	0	91	.682	3.64	3.72
2015	Pit	NL	23	23	0	129.0	563	137	77	69	13	4	0	12	41	6	96	2	9	9	.500	0-0	0	92	.769	4.41	4.81
2016	Phi	NL	4	4	0	17.1	71	15	8	8	1	1	0	0	8	0	19	1	1	1	.500	0-0	0	94	.651	3.42	4.15
2017	Hou	AL	25	25	0	146.2	617	125	65	59	14	2	2	13	50	1	163	4	14	7	.667	0-0	0	95	.692	3.34	3.62
2018	Hou	AL	30	30	0	167.0	695	130	63	58	18	1	4	16	64	0	201	4	15	3	.833	0-0	0	96	.659	3.25	3.13
2019	TB	AL	33	33	0	194.2	790	154	71	66	15	1	3	12	57	0	240	5	16	6	.727	0-0	0	94	.623	2.67	3.05
	Postseason		7	6	1	31.1	131	26	16	16	3	1	0	3	12	0	31	3	2	2	.500	0-0	0	95	.672	3.46	4.60
	12 ML YEARS		250	249	0	1401.1	6030	1359	707	633	118	51	35	117	508	21	1234	53	91	87	.511	0-0	0	93	.720	3.97	4.07

Mike Moustakas

Bats: L Throws: R Pos: 3B-105;2B-47;PH-6;DH-1   moo-STOCK-us   Ht: 6'0" Wt: 225 Born: 9/11/1988 Age: 31

						BATTING														RUNNING			AVERAGES			
Year	Team	Lg	G	AB	H	2B	3B	HR	(Hm	Rd)	TB	R	RBI	RC	TBB	IBB	SO	HBP	SH	SF	SB	CS	GDP	Avg	OBP	Slg	OPS
2011	KC	AL	89	338	89	18	1	5	(3	2)	124	26	30	31	22	0	51	1	2	2	2	0	5	.263	.309	.367	.675
2012	KC	AL	149	563	136	34	1	20	(10	10)	232	69	73	64	39	4	124	7	0	5	5	2	4	.242	.296	.412	.708
2013	KC	AL	136	472	110	26	0	12	(5	7)	172	42	42	35	32	1	83	5	1	4	2	4	13	.233	.287	.364	.651
2014	KC	AL	140	457	97	21	1	15	(5	10)	165	45	54	44	35	1	74	3	1	4	1	0	12	.212	.271	.361	.632
2015	KC	AL	147	549	156	34	1	22	(9	13)	258	73	82	85	43	1	76	13	4	5	1	2	14	.284	.348	.470	.817
2016	KC	AL	27	104	25	6	0	7	(4	3)	52	12	13	10	9	0	13	0	0	0	0	1	5	.240	.301	.500	.801
2017	KC	AL	148	555	151	24	0	38	(14	24)	289	75	85	77	34	7	94	3	0	6	0	0	18	.272	.314	.521	.835
2018	2 Tms		152	573	144	33	1	28	(14	14)	263	66	95	89	49	5	103	7	0	6	4	1	13	.251	.315	.459	.774
2019	Mil	NL	143	523	133	30	1	35	(14	21)	270	80	87	82	53	5	98	6	0	2	3	0	12	.254	.329	.516	.845
	18 KC	AL	98	378	94	21	1	20	(9	11)	177	46	62	54	30	3	63	5	0	4	3	0	10	.249	.309	.468	.778
	18 Mil	NL	54	195	50	12	0	8	(5	3)	86	20	33	35	19	2	40	2	0	2	1	1	3	.256	.326	.441	.767
	Postseason		41	157	34	5	0	6	(3	3)	57	17	18	15	9	3	30	1	1	1	0	0	2	.217	.262	.363	.625
	9 ML YEARS		1131	4134	1041	226	6	182	(78	104)	1825	488	561	517	316	24	716	45	8	34	18	10	96	.252	.310	.441	.751

Cedric Mullins II

Bats: B Throws: L Pos: CF-22;PH-2   Ht: 5'8" Wt: 175 Born: 10/1/1994 Age: 25

						BATTING														RUNNING			AVERAGES			
Year	Team	Lg	G	AB	H	2B	3B	HR	(Hm	Rd)	TB	R	RBI	RC	TBB	IBB	SO	HBP	SH	SF	SB	CS	GDP	Avg	OBP	Slg	OPS
2019	Norfolk	AAA	66	268	55	8	2	5	(-	-)	82	40	24	24	25	0	51	1	6	4	13	4	4	.205	.272	.306	.578
2019	Bowie	AA	51	199	54	11	0	5	(-	-)	80	35	18	32	22	1	31	1	0	4	20	3	4	.271	.341	.402	.743
2018	Bal	AL	45	170	40	9	0	4	(1	3)	61	23	11	17	17	0	37	2	2	0	2	3	1	.235	.312	.359	.671
2019	Bal	AL	22	64	6	0	2	0	(0	0)	10	7	4	1	4	0	14	3	2	1	1	0	2	.094	.181	.156	.337
	2 ML YEARS		67	234	46	9	2	4	(1	3)	71	30	15	18	21	0	51	5	4	1	3	3	3	.197	.276	.303	.579

Max Muncy

Bats: L Throws: R Pos: 2B-70;1B-65;3B-35;PH-9   Ht: 6'0" Wt: 218 Born: 8/25/1990 Age: 29

						BATTING														RUNNING			AVERAGES			
Year	Team	Lg	G	AB	H	2B	3B	HR	(Hm	Rd)	TB	R	RBI	RC	TBB	IBB	SO	HBP	SH	SF	SB	CS	GDP	Avg	OBP	Slg	OPS
2015	Oak	AL	45	102	21	8	1	3	(1	2)	40	14	9	9	9	0	31	0	0	1	0	0	0	.206	.268	.392	.660
2016	Oak	AL	51	113	21	2	0	2	(1	1)	29	13	8	10	20	1	24	0	0	0	0	0	2	.186	.308	.257	.565
2018	LAD	NL	137	395	104	17	2	35	(20	15)	230	75	79	87	79	6	131	5	0	2	3	0	4	.263	.391	.582	.973
2019	LAD	NL	141	487	122	22	1	35	(13	22)	251	101	98	93	90	1	149	8	0	4	4	1	5	.251	.374	.515	.889
	Postseason		16	50	10	1	0	3	(2	1)	20	10	6	9	12	0	23	0	0	0	1	0	0	.200	.355	.400	.755
	4 ML YEARS		374	1097	268	49	4	75	(35	40)	550	203	194	199	198	8	335	13	0	7	7	1	11	.244	.364	.501	.866

Andres Munoz

Pitches: R Bats: R Pos: RP-22   Ht: 6'2" Wt: 165 Born: 1/16/1999 Age: 21

			HOW MUCH PITCHED					WHAT HE GAVE UP												THE RESULTS							
Year	Team	Lg	G	GS	GF	IP	BFP	H	R	ER	HR	SH	SF	HB	TBB	IBB	SO	WP	W	L	Pct	Sv-Op	Hld	Vel	OPS	ERC	ERA
2019	Amrillo	AA	16	0	7	16.2	75	9	10	4	1	1	1	3	11	0	34	3	0	2	.000	4- -	-	-	.616	2.81	2.16
2019	ElPaso	AAA	19	0	6	19.0	80	16	8	8	3	1	0	4	7	0	24	3	3	2	.600	2- -	-	-	.798	4.45	3.79
2019	SD	NL	22	0	3	23.0	97	16	10	10	2	1	0	0	11	0	30	1	1	1	.500	1-2	8	100	.611	2.59	3.91

Yairo Munoz

JYE-roh MOON-yohs

Bats: R Throws: R Pos: PH-37;3B-21;SS-17;RF-12;LF-11;CF-7;2B-4;PR-3   Ht: 6'1" Wt: 201 Born: 1/23/1995 Age: 25

						BATTING														RUNNING			AVERAGES			
Year	Team	Lg	G	AB	H	2B	3B	HR	(Hm	Rd)	TB	R	RBI	RC	TBB	IBB	SO	HBP	SH	SF	SB	CS	GDP	Avg	OBP	Slg	OPS
2018	StL	NL	108	293	81	16	0	8	(1	7)	121	39	42	46	30	7	71	4	0	2	5	6	3	.276	.350	.413	.763
2019	StL	NL	88	172	46	7	1	2	(0	2)	61	20	13	19	7	0	37	1	0	1	8	3	5	.267	.298	.355	.653
	2 ML YEARS		196	465	127	23	1	10	(1	9)	182	59	55	65	37	7	108	5	0	3	13	9	8	.273	.331	.391	.723

Daniel Murphy

Bats: L **Throws:** R **Pos:** 1B-110;PH-26;DH-4;2B-3   **Ht:** 6'1" **Wt:** 221 **Born:** 4/1/1985 **Age:** 35

Year	Team	Lg	G	AB	H	2B	3B	HR	(Hm	Rd)	TB	R	RBI	RC	TBB	IBB	SO	HBP	SH	SF	SB	CS	GDP	Avg	OBP	Slg	OPS
2008	NYM	NL	49	131	41	9	3	2	(1	1)	62	24	17	26	18	1	28	1	0	1	0	2	4	.313	.397	.473	.871
2009	NYM	NL	155	508	135	38	4	12	(7	5)	217	60	63	60	38	4	69	0	4	6	4	2	13	.266	.313	.427	.741
2011	NYM	NL	109	391	125	28	2	6	(2	4)	175	49	49	57	24	2	42	3	3	2	5	5	14	.320	.362	.448	.809
2012	NYM	NL	156	571	166	40	3	6	(1	5)	230	62	65	78	36	5	82	1	0	4	10	2	12	.291	.332	.403	.735
2013	NYM	NL	161	658	188	38	4	13	(6	7)	273	92	78	86	32	2	95	2	0	5	23	3	13	.286	.319	.415	.733
2014	NYM	NL	143	596	172	37	2	9	(4	5)	240	79	57	78	39	3	86	2	0	5	13	5	15	.289	.332	.403	.734
2015	NYM	NL	130	499	140	38	2	14	(7	7)	224	56	73	71	31	10	38	2	0	6	2	2	15	.281	.322	.449	.770
2016	Was	NL	142	531	184	**47**	5	25	(10	15)	316	88	104	115	35	10	57	8	0	8	5	3	4	**.347**	**.390**	**.595**	**.985**
2017	Was	NL	144	534	172	**43**	3	23	(6	17)	290	94	93	103	52	14	77	4	0	3	2	0	16	.322	.384	.543	.928
2018	2 Tms	NL	91	328	98	15	0	12	(5	7)	149	40	42	49	20	2	40	0	0	3	3	0	5	.299	.336	.454	.790
2019	Col	NL	132	438	122	35	1	13	(3	10)	198	56	78	64	32	1	74	2	0	4	1	1	10	.279	.328	.452	.780
18	Was	NL	56	190	57	9	0	6	(3	3)	84	17	29	27	13	2	17	0	0	2	1	0	4	.300	.341	.442	.784
18	ChC	NL	35	138	41	6	0	6	(2	4)	65	23	13	22	7	0	23	0	0	1	2	0	1	.297	.329	.471	.800
	Postseason		25	97	30	3	0	8	(4	4)	57	21	19	22	15	4	21	0	0	1	3	2	1	.309	.398	.588	.986
	11 ML YEARS		1412	5185	1543	368	29	135	(52	83)	2374	700	719	787	357	54	688	25	7	47	68	25	121	.298	.343	.458	.801

John Ryan Murphy

Bats: R **Throws:** R **Pos:** C-19;PH-6   **Ht:** 5'11" **Wt:** 205 **Born:** 5/13/1991 **Age:** 29

Year	Team	Lg	G	AB	H	2B	3B	HR	(Hm	Rd)	TB	R	RBI	RC	TBB	IBB	SO	HBP	SH	SF	SB	CS	GDP	Avg	OBP	Slg	OPS
2019	Reno	AAA	36	124	31	7	0	9	(-	-)	65	26	26	20	12	1	34	0	0	0	0	0	1	.250	.316	.524	.840
2019	Gwnntt	AAA	14	47	8	0	0	1	(-	-)	11	5	3	1	2	0	13	1	0	0	0	0	2	.170	.220	.234	.454
2013	NYY	AL	16	26	4	1	0	0	(0	0)	5	3	1	0	1	0	9	0	0	0	0	0	0	.154	.185	.192	.377
2014	NYY	AL	32	81	23	4	0	1	(1	0)	30	7	9	10	4	0	22	0	0	0	0	0	0	.284	.318	.370	.688
2015	NYY	AL	67	155	43	9	1	3	(1	2)	63	21	14	17	12	0	43	1	1	3	0	0	4	.277	.327	.406	.734
2016	Min	AL	26	82	12	3	0	1	(1	0)	18	4	3	0	5	0	19	0	2	1	0	0	3	.146	.193	.220	.413
2017	Ari	NL	5	7	1	1	0	0	(0	0)	2	0	1	0	0	0	1	0	0	0	0	0	1	.143	.143	.286	.429
2018	Ari	NL	87	208	42	9	0	9	(4	5)	78	19	24	17	11	1	71	1	2	1	0	0	1	.202	.244	.375	.619
2019	2 Tms	NL	26	63	11	3	0	4	(1	3)	26	9	7	5	6	0	28	0	1	0	0	0	0	.175	.246	.413	.659
19	Ari	NL	25	62	11	3	0	4	(1	3)	26	9	7	5	6	0	28	0	1	0	0	0	0	.177	.250	.419	.669
19	Atl	NL	1	1	0	0	0	0	(0	0)	0	0	0	0	0	0	0	0	0	0	0	0	0	.000	.000	.000	.000
	7 ML YEARS		259	622	136	30	1	18	(8	10)	222	63	59	49	39	1	193	2	6	5	0	0	9	.219	.265	.357	.622

Sean Murphy

Bats: R **Throws:** R **Pos:** C-18;PH-3;DH-2   **Ht:** 6'3" **Wt:** 232 **Born:** 10/10/1994 **Age:** 25

Year	Team	Lg	G	AB	H	2B	3B	HR	(Hm	Rd)	TB	R	RBI	RC	TBB	IBB	SO	HBP	SH	SF	SB	CS	GDP	Avg	OBP	Slg	OPS
2016	2 Tms	Low	23	79	18	1	0	2	(-	-)	25	11	7	8	9	0	12	0	0	0	1	0	6	.228	.307	.316	.623
2017	Stcktn	A+	45	165	49	11	0	9	(-	-)	87	22	26	29	11	0	33	1	0	1	0	0	9	.297	.343	.527	.870
2017	Mdlnd	AA	53	191	40	7	0	4	(-	-)	59	25	22	18	21	0	34	1	2	2	0	0	9	.209	.288	.309	.597
2018	Mdlnd	AA	68	257	74	26	2	8	(-	-)	128	51	43	47	23	2	47	6	1	2	3	0	9	.288	.358	.498	.856
2019	LsVgs	AAA	31	120	37	6	1	10	(-	-)	75	25	30	28	15	0	31	2	0	3	0	1	2	.308	.386	.625	1.011
2019	2 Tms	Low	10	30	7	2	0	1	(-	-)	12	9	1	4	7	1	5	0	0	0	0	0	3	.233	.378	.400	.778
2019	Oak	AL	20	53	13	5	0	4	(1	3)	30	14	8	7	6	0	16	1	0	0	0	0	3	.245	.333	.566	.899

Tom Murphy

Bats: R **Throws:** R **Pos:** C-67;DH-5;PH-3;LF-1   **Ht:** 6'1" **Wt:** 218 **Born:** 4/3/1991 **Age:** 29

Year	Team	Lg	G	AB	H	2B	3B	HR	(Hm	Rd)	TB	R	RBI	RC	TBB	IBB	SO	HBP	SH	SF	SB	CS	GDP	Avg	OBP	Slg	OPS
2015	Col	NL	11	35	9	1	0	3	(3	0)	19	5	9	9	4	1	10	0	0	0	0	0	0	.257	.333	.543	.876
2016	Col	NL	21	44	12	2	0	5	(5	0)	29	8	13	10	4	0	19	1	0	0	1	0	2	.273	.347	.659	1.006
2017	Col	NL	12	24	1	1	0	0	(0	0)	2	1	1	0	2	1	9	0	0	0	0	0	0	.042	.115	.083	.199
2018	Col	NL	37	93	21	7	1	2	(1	1)	36	5	11	8	3	1	44	0	0	0	0	1	2	.226	.250	.387	.637
2019	Sea	AL	76	260	71	12	1	18	(6	12)	139	32	40	43	19	0	87	1	0	1	2	0	0	.273	.324	.535	.858
	5 ML YEARS		157	456	114	23	2	28	(15	13)	225	51	74	70	32	3	169	2	0	1	3	1	4	.250	.301	.493	.795

Harrison Musgrave

Pitches: L **Bats:** L **Pos:** RP-10   **Ht:** 6'1" **Wt:** 206 **Born:** 3/3/1992 **Age:** 28

			HOW MUCH PITCHED					WHAT HE GAVE UP										THE RESULTS							
Year	Team	Lg	G	GS	GF	IP	BFP	H	R	ER	HR	SH	SF	HB	TBB	IBB	SO	WP	W	L	Pct	Sv-Op Hld	Vel	OPS	ERC	ERA
2019	Albq	AAA	21	1	5	24.0	131	51	29	27	5	0	1	0	12	1	23	1	0	2	.000	0- - -	-	1.184	13.03	10.13
2018	Col	NL	35	0	8	44.2	185	36	23	23	7	0	1	1	22	2	32	2	2	3	.400	0-0 5	91	.791	3.88	4.63
2019	Col	NL	10	0	4	10.0	47	9	4	4	0	0	1	0	7	1	12	1	0	0	-	0-0 0	91	.648	3.55	3.60
	Postseason		2	0	0	0.2	6	1	1	1	0	0	0	0	3	1	2	0	0	0	-	0-0 0	92	1.000	19.57	13.50
	2 ML YEARS		45	0	12	54.2	232	45	27	27	7	0	2	1	29	3	44	3	2	3	.400	0-0 5	91	.763	3.83	4.45

Joe Musgrove

Pitches: R **Bats:** R **Pos:** SP-31; RP-1   **Ht:** 6'5" **Wt:** 230 **Born:** 12/4/1992 **Age:** 27

		HOW MUCH PITCHED					WHAT HE GAVE UP											THE RESULTS								
Year Team	Lg	G	GS	GF	IP	BFP	H	R	ER	HR	SH	SF	HB	TBB	IBB	SO	WP	W	L	Pct	Sv-Op	Hld	Vel	OPS	ERC	ERA
2016 Hou	AL	11	10	1	62.0	256	59	28	28	9	0	1	3	16	0	55	0	4	4	.500	0-0	0	92	.758	3.80	4.06
2017 Hou	AL	38	15	5	109.1	462	117	59	58	18	5	2	4	28	1	98	4	7	8	.467	2-4	5	93	.798	4.54	4.77
2018 Pit	NL	19	19	0	115.1	486	113	56	52	12	3	5	8	23	3	100	5	6	9	.400	0-0	0	93	.687	3.40	4.06
2019 Pit	NL	32	31	0	170.1	718	168	98	84	21	1	6	9	39	1	157	2	11	12	.478	0-0	1	92	.738	3.66	4.44
Postseason		7	0	3	6.2	27	6	6	6	3	0	1	0	1	1	3	0	1	0	1.000	0-0	1	95	.859	4.35	8.10
4 ML YEARS		100	75	6	457.0	1922	457	241	222	60	9	14	24	106	5	410	11	28	33	.459	2-4	6	93	.742	3.81	4.37

Wil Myers

Bats: R **Throws:** R **Pos:** LF-98;CF-66;PH-25;1B-7;RF-5;3B-2;PR-2   **Ht:** 6'3" **Wt:** 205 **Born:** 12/10/1990 **Age:** 29

							BATTING													RUNNING			AVERAGES			
Year Team	Lg	G	AB	H	2B	3B	HR	(Hm	Rd)	TB	R	RBI	RC	TBB	IBB	SO	HBP	SH	SF	SB	CS	GDP	Avg	OBP	Slg	OPS
2013 TB	AL	88	335	98	23	0	13	(5	8)	160	50	53	52	33	6	91	1	0	4	5	2	10	.293	.354	.478	.831
2014 TB	AL	87	325	72	14	0	6	(2	4)	104	37	35	32	34	3	90	0	0	2	6	1	10	.222	.294	.320	.614
2015 SD	NL	60	225	57	13	1	8	(3	5)	96	40	29	35	27	0	55	1	0	0	5	2	2	.253	.336	.427	.763
2016 SD	NL	157	599	155	29	4	28	(18	10)	276	99	94	97	68	1	160	4	0	5	28	6	12	.259	.336	.461	.797
2017 SD	NL	155	567	138	29	3	30	(8	22)	263	80	74	80	70	3	180	5	0	7	20	6	15	.243	.328	.464	.792
2018 SD	NL	83	312	79	25	1	11	(6	5)	139	39	39	45	30	1	94	0	0	1	13	1	10	.253	.318	.446	.763
2019 SD	NL	155	435	104	22	1	18	(9	9)	182	58	53	54	51	0	168	2	1	1	16	7	12	.239	.321	.418	.739
Postseason		5	20	2	0	0	0	(0	0)	2	0	0	0	1	0	7	0	0	0	0	0	0	.100	.143	.100	.243
7 ML YEARS		785	2798	703	155	10	114	(51	63)	1220	403	377	395	313	14	838	13	1	20	93	25	71	.251	.327	.436	.763

Tyler Naquin

Bats: L **Throws:** R **Pos:** RF-68;LF-15;PH-9;DH-3;PR-2   NAY-kwin   **Ht:** 6'2" **Wt:** 195 **Born:** 4/24/1991 **Age:** 29

							BATTING													RUNNING			AVERAGES			
Year Team	Lg	G	AB	H	2B	3B	HR	(Hm	Rd)	TB	R	RBI	RC	TBB	IBB	SO	HBP	SH	SF	SB	CS	GDP	Avg	OBP	Slg	OPS
2016 Cle	AL	116	321	95	18	5	14	(9	5)	165	52	43	53	36	4	112	4	2	2	6	3	4	.296	.372	.514	.886
2017 Cle	AL	19	37	8	2	0	0	(0	0)	10	4	1	2	2	0	9	0	0	1	0	1	1	.216	.250	.270	.520
2018 Cle	AL	61	174	46	7	0	3	(0	3)	62	22	23	21	6	1	42	2	0	1	1	1	1	.264	.295	.356	.651
2019 Cle	AL	89	274	79	19	0	10	(6	4)	128	34	34	36	14	2	66	2	2	2	4	2	8	.288	.325	.467	.792
Postseason		11	23	4	2	0	0	(0	0)	6	0	2	1	1	1	14	0	1	0	0	0	0	.174	.208	.261	.469
4 ML YEARS		285	806	228	46	5	27	(15	12)	365	112	101	112	58	7	229	8	4	6	11	7	14	.283	.335	.453	.788

Omar Narvaez

Bats: L **Throws:** R **Pos:** C-98;PH-21;DH-19;2B-1   nar-VAH-es   **Ht:** 5'11" **Wt:** 220 **Born:** 2/10/1992 **Age:** 28

							BATTING													RUNNING			AVERAGES			
Year Team	Lg	G	AB	H	2B	3B	HR	(Hm	Rd)	TB	R	RBI	RC	TBB	IBB	SO	HBP	SH	SF	SB	CS	GDP	Avg	OBP	Slg	OPS
2016 CWS	AL	34	101	27	4	0	1	(1	0)	34	13	10	15	14	1	14	0	0	0	0	0	0	.267	.350	.337	.687
2017 CWS	AL	90	253	70	10	0	2	(2	0)	86	23	14	33	38	1	45	1	3	0	0	0	8	.277	.373	.340	.713
2018 CWS	AL	97	280	77	14	1	9	(4	5)	120	30	30	43	38	1	65	2	2	0	0	2	5	.275	.366	.429	.794
2019 Sea	AL	132	428	119	12	0	22	(13	9)	197	63	55	66	47	1	92	4	0	3	0	0	5	.278	.353	.460	.813
4 ML YEARS		353	1062	293	40	1	34	(20	14)	437	129	109	157	137	4	216	7	5	5	0	2	18	.276	.361	.411	.772

Josh Naylor

Bats: L **Throws:** L **Pos:** LF-33;RF-31;PH-30;DH-4   **Ht:** 5'11" **Wt:** 250 **Born:** 6/22/1997 **Age:** 23

							BATTING													RUNNING			AVERAGES			
Year Team	Lg	G	AB	H	2B	3B	HR	(Hm	Rd)	TB	R	RBI	RC	TBB	IBB	SO	HBP	SH	SF	SB	CS	GDP	Avg	OBP	Slg	OPS
2019 ElPaso	AAA	54	223	70	20	1	10	(-	-)	122	51	42	47	28	1	30	0	0	1	1	0	6	.314	.389	.547	.936
2019 SD	NL	94	253	63	15	0	8	(4	4)	102	29	32	36	25	1	64	0	0	1	1	1	4	.249	.315	.403	.719

Kristopher Negron

neh-GRONE

Bats: R **Throws:** R **Pos:** RF-12;CF-8;PH-8;LF-6;PR-6;3B-4;SS-4;2B-3   **Ht:** 6'0" **Wt:** 190 **Born:** 2/1/1986 **Age:** 34

							BATTING													RUNNING			AVERAGES			
Year Team	Lg	G	AB	H	2B	3B	HR	(Hm	Rd)	TB	R	RBI	RC	TBB	IBB	SO	HBP	SH	SF	SB	CS	GDP	Avg	OBP	Slg	OPS
2019 Tacom	AAA	82	306	95	15	4	12	(-	-)	154	62	61	63	41	0	91	5	0	4	11	3	6	.310	.396	.503	.899
2012 Cin	NL	4	4	1	0	0	0	(0	0)	1	2	0	1	1	0	2	0	0	0	0	0	0	.250	.400	.250	.650
2014 Cin	NL	49	144	39	10	1	6	(3	3)	69	19	17	23	12	0	40	1	1	0	5	0	2	.271	.331	.479	.810
2015 Cin	NL	43	93	13	2	0	0	(0	0)	15	5	2	2	9	0	23	3	2	0	2	0	2	.140	.238	.161	.399
2017 Ari	NL	14	25	4	1	0	0	(0	0)	5	3	1	1	4	0	7	1	1	0	0	0	1	.160	.300	.200	.500
2018 2 Tms		20	32	7	0	0	1	(0	1)	10	6	4	3	1	0	9	0	0	0	2	0	1	.219	.242	.313	.555
2019 2 Tms		40	77	19	1	0	2	(0	2)	26	12	8	8	5	1	26	0	0	0	1	1	1	.247	.293	.338	.630
18 Ari	NL	2	3	1	0	0	0	(0	0)	1	0	1	1	0	0	0	0	0	0	0	0	0	.333	.333	.333	.667
18 Sea	AL	18	29	6	0	0	1	(0	1)	9	6	3	2	1	0	9	0	0	0	2	0	1	.207	.233	.310	.544
19 Sea	AL	10	23	5	0	0	0	(0	0)	5	3	1	1	2	0	9	0	0	0	0	0	0	.217	.280	.217	.497
19 LAD	NL	30	54	14	1	0	2	(0	2)	21	9	7	7	3	1	17	0	0	0	1	1	1	.259	.298	.389	.687
6 ML YEARS		170	375	83	14	1	9	(3	6)	126	47	32	38	32	1	107	5	4	0	10	1	7	.221	.291	.336	.627

Jimmy Nelson

Pitches: R **Bats:** R **Pos:** RP-7; SP-3   **Ht:** 6'6" **Wt:** 250 **Born:** 6/5/1989 **Age:** 31

Year	Team	Lg	G	GS	GF	IP	BFP	H	R	ER	HR	SH	SF	HB	TBB	IBB	SO	WP	W	L	Pct	Sv-Op	Hld	Vel	OPS	ERC	ERA
2019	SnAnt	AAA	16	4	1	40.1	178	33	24	21	4	0	0	3	24	0	57	8	3	2	.600	0--	-	-	.681	4.08	4.69
2013	Mil	NL	4	1	0	10.0	37	2	1	1	0	0	1	0	5	0	8	1	0	0	-	0-0	0	94	.286	0.64	0.90
2014	Mil	NL	14	12	1	69.1	311	82	42	38	6	1	2	8	19	0	57	4	2	9	.182	0-0	0	94	.793	4.96	4.93
2015	Mil	NL	30	30	0	177.1	752	163	89	81	18	4	7	13	65	4	148	11	11	13	.458	0-0	0	93	.704	3.79	4.11
2016	Mil	NL	32	32	0	179.1	807	186	108	92	25	7	4	17	86	2	140	8	8	16	.333	0-0	0	93	.791	5.29	4.62
2017	Mil	NL	29	29	0	175.1	728	171	75	68	16	4	2	9	48	1	199	6	12	6	.667	0-0	0	94	.689	3.64	3.49
2019	Mil	NL	10	3	2	22.0	105	25	18	17	4	0	0	2	17	1	26	1	0	2	.000	0-0	0	93	.966	7.63	6.95
	6 ML YEARS		119	107	3	633.1	2740	629	333	297	69	16	16	49	240	8	578	31	33	46	.418	0-0	0	93	.740	4.34	4.22

Hector Neris

Pitches: R **Bats:** R **Pos:** RP-68   NAIR-ess   **Ht:** 6'2" **Wt:** 215 **Born:** 6/14/1989 **Age:** 31

Year	Team	Lg	G	GS	GF	IP	BFP	H	R	ER	HR	SH	SF	HB	TBB	IBB	SO	WP	W	L	Pct	Sv-Op	Hld	Vel	OPS	ERC	ERA
2014	Phi	NL	1	0	1	1.0	3	0	0	0	0	0	0	0	0	0	1	0	1	0	1.000	0-0	0	93	.000	0.00	0.00
2015	Phi	NL	32	0	8	40.1	170	38	19	17	8	1	0	4	10	0	41	3	2	2	.500	0-0	2	93	.772	4.21	3.79
2016	Phi	NL	79	0	13	80.1	328	59	26	23	9	1	2	3	30	3	102	4	4	4	.500	2-6	28	94	.620	2.73	2.58
2017	Phi	NL	74	0	56	74.2	320	68	26	25	9	1	2	6	26	3	86	2	4	5	.444	26-29	4	95	.689	3.74	3.01
2018	Phi	NL	53	0	28	47.2	203	46	27	27	11	2	0	1	16	1	76	5	1	3	.250	11-14	4	95	.803	4.55	5.10
2019	Phi	NL	68	0	49	67.2	275	45	24	22	10	1	2	6	24	1	89	2	3	6	.333	28-34	2	95	.613	2.74	2.93
	6 ML YEARS		307	0	155	311.2	1299	256	122	114	47	6	6	20	106	8	395	16	15	20	.429	67-83	40	94	.683	3.40	3.29

Pat Neshek

Pitches: R **Bats:** B **Pos:** RP-20   NEE-sheck   **Ht:** 6'3" **Wt:** 220 **Born:** 9/4/1980 **Age:** 39

Year	Team	Lg	G	GS	GF	IP	BFP	H	R	ER	HR	SH	SF	HB	TBB	IBB	SO	WP	W	L	Pct	Sv-Op	Hld	Vel	OPS	ERC	ERA
2006	Min	AL	32	0	3	37.0	138	23	9	9	6	0	1	0	6	0	53	0	4	2	.667	0-2	10	91	.531	1.58	2.19
2007	Min	AL	74	0	20	70.1	278	44	25	23	7	4	5	2	27	5	74	2	7	2	.778	0-3	15	90	.591	2.12	2.94
2008	Min	AL	15	0	3	13.1	56	12	7	7	2	1	0	1	4	1	15	0	0	1	.000	0-2	6	89	.751	3.29	4.73
2010	Min	AL	11	0	3	9.0	43	7	5	5	1	0	0	1	8	0	9	0	0	1	.000	0-1	1	86	.696	5.13	5.00
2011	SD	NL	25	0	13	24.2	112	19	12	11	4	1	0	1	22	1	20	1	1	1	.500	0-0	6	86	.742	5.37	4.01
2012	Oak	AL	24	0	5	19.2	77	10	3	3	3	0	2	1	6	1	16	1	2	1	.667	0-2	4	89	.530	1.66	1.37
2013	Oak	AL	45	0	17	40.1	177	40	17	15	6	0	3	0	15	2	29	1	2	1	.667	0-0	1	89	.738	4.06	3.35
2014	StL	NL	71	0	17	67.1	255	44	14	14	4	2	2	2	9	2	68	1	7	2	.778	6-10	25	90	.480	1.38	1.87
2015	Hou	AL	66	0	8	54.2	223	49	25	22	8	4	1	2	12	1	51	1	3	6	.333	1-4	28	90	.709	3.23	3.62
2016	Hou	AL	60	0	9	47.0	185	33	17	16	6	3	1	0	11	7	43	1	2	2	.500	0-0	18	89	.606	1.89	3.06
2017	2 Tms		71	0	7	62.1	235	48	13	11	3	1	2	0	6	0	69	0	5	3	.625	1-5	23	90	.536	1.60	1.59
2018	Phi	NL	30	0	8	24.1	101	23	9	7	2	1	1	0	5	1	15	1	3	2	.600	5-6	8	89	.663	2.80	2.59
2019	Phi	NL	20	0	6	18.0	79	23	11	10	5	0	1	0	9	0	20	0	0	1	.000	3-3	6	88	.856	5.61	5.00
17	Phi	NL	43	0	5	40.1	148	28	5	5	2	1	1	0	5	0	45	0	3	2	.600	1-3	10	90	.501	1.45	1.12
17	Col	NL	28	0	2	22.0	87	20	8	6	1	0	1	0	1	0	24	0	2	1	.667	0-2	13	90	.594	1.94	2.45
	Postseason		14	0	4	11.2	45	8	5	5	2	0	0	0	1	0	12	0	0	2	.000	0-1	3	91	.564	1.66	3.86
	13 ML YEARS		544	0	119	488.0	1959	375	167	153	57	17	20	9	133	21	471	9	36	25	.590	16-38	143	90	.621	2.49	2.82

Sheldon Neuse

Bats: R **Throws:** R **Pos:** 2B-20;3B-5;DH-1   **Ht:** 6'0" **Wt:** 218 **Born:** 12/10/1994 **Age:** 25

Year	Team	Lg	G	AB	H	2B	3B	HR	(Hm	Rd)	TB	R	RBI	RC	TBB	IBB	SO	HBP	SH	SF	SB	CS	GDP	Avg	OBP	Slg	OPS
2019	LsVgs	AAA	126	498	158	32	2	27	(-	-)	275	99	102	104	56	1	132	4	0	2	3	3	9	.317	.389	.552	.941
2019	Oak	AL	25	56	14	3	0	0	(0	0)	17	3	7	5	4	0	19	0	0	1	0	0	2	.250	.295	.304	.599

Dovydas Neverauskas

Pitches: R **Bats:** R **Pos:** RP-10   **Ht:** 6'3" **Wt:** 225 **Born:** 1/14/1993 **Age:** 27

Year	Team	Lg	G	GS	GF	IP	BFP	H	R	ER	HR	SH	SF	HB	TBB	IBB	SO	WP	W	L	Pct	Sv-Op	Hld	Vel	OPS	ERC	ERA
2019	Indy	AAA	36	0	20	52.0	225	51	30	29	8	1	2	1	22	2	73	2	3	4	.429	9--	-	-	.763	4.46	5.02
2017	Pit	NL	24	0	11	25.1	105	24	11	11	4	1	0	1	8	0	17	2	1	1	.500	0-1	2	97	.749	4.09	3.91
2018	Pit	NL	25	0	8	27.0	119	30	25	24	9	0	1	1	10	0	27	2	0	0	-	0-1	2	97	.943	6.52	8.00
2019	Pit	NL	10	0	3	9.1	53	15	11	11	2	0	1	2	7	1	10	1	0	0	-	0-0	1	96	1.081	10.85	10.61
	3 ML YEARS		59	0	22	61.2	277	69	47	46	15	1	2	4	25	1	54	5	1	1	.500	0-2	5	97	.894	6.12	6.71

Jake Newberry

Pitches: R **Bats:** R **Pos:** RP-27   **Ht:** 6'2" **Wt:** 195 **Born:** 11/20/1994 **Age:** 25

Year	Team	Lg	G	GS	GF	IP	BFP	H	R	ER	HR	SH	SF	HB	TBB	IBB	SO	WP	W	L	Pct	Sv-Op	Hld	Vel	OPS	ERC	ERA
2019	Omha	AAA	22	0	9	28.0	125	29	13	12	3	2	2	0	14	1	30	3	2	2	.500	0--	-	-	.770	4.64	3.86
2018	KC	AL	14	0	3	13.1	60	13	8	7	3	0	0	0	9	0	11	1	2	0	1.000	0-0	1	94	.857	6.10	4.73
2019	KC	AL	27	0	6	31.0	137	29	13	13	7	0	3	1	16	2	29	0	1	0	1.000	0-1	4	94	.849	5.08	3.77
	2 ML YEARS		41	0	9	44.1	197	42	21	20	10	0	3	1	25	2	40	1	3	0	1.000	0-1	5	94	.851	5.38	4.06

Sean Newcomb

Pitches: L Bats: L Pos: RP-51; SP-4   Ht: 6'5" Wt: 255 Born: 6/12/1993 Age: 27

				HOW MUCH PITCHED					WHAT HE GAVE UP											THE RESULTS						
Year	Team	Lg	G	GS	GF	IP	BFP	H	R	ER	HR	SH	SF	HB	TBB	IBB	SO	WP	W	L	Pct	Sv-Op	Hld	Vel	OPS	ERC	ERA
2017 Atl		NL	19	19	0	100.0	456	100	51	48	10	5	3	6	57	6	108	3	4	9	.308	0-0	0	94	.780	4.85	4.32
2018 Atl		NL	31	30	0	164.0	696	137	74	71	18	4	3	1	81	1	160	4	12	9	.571	0-0	0	93	.679	3.62	3.90
2019 Atl		NL	55	4	4	68.1	293	61	28	24	8	0	2	3	29	1	65	4	6	3	.667	1-3	16	94	.692	3.83	3.16
Postseason			2	1	0	4.2	17	2	2	1	0	1	0	0	3	0	2	0	0	0	-	0-0	0	96	.466	1.67	1.93
3 ML YEARS			105	53	4	332.1	1445	298	153	143	36	9	8	10	167	8	333	11	22	21	.512	1-3	16	94	.713	4.03	3.87

Kevin Newman

Bats: R Throws: R Pos: SS-104;2B-23;PH-7;3B-6;PR-4;LF-2   Ht: 6'0" Wt: 195 Born: 8/4/1993 Age: 26

								BATTING														RUNNING			AVERAGES			
Year	Team	Lg	G	AB	H	2B	3B	HR	(Hm	Rd)	TB	R	RBI	RC	TBB	IBB	SO	HBP	SH	SF	SB	CS	GDP	Avg	OBP	Slg	OPS
2018 Pit		NL	31	91	19	2	0	0	(0	0)	21	7	6	5	4	1	23	1	0	1	0	1	2	.209	.247	.231	.478
2019 Pit		NL	130	493	152	20	6	12	(3	9)	220	61	64	73	28	2	62	7	2	1	16	8	5	.308	.353	.446	.800
2 ML YEARS			161	584	171	22	6	12	(3	9)	241	68	70	78	32	3	85	8	2	2	16	9	7	.293	.337	.413	.750

Juan Nicasio

Pitches: R Bats: R Pos: RP-47   nih-KAH-see-oh   Ht: 6'4" Wt: 252 Born: 8/31/1986 Age: 33

				HOW MUCH PITCHED					WHAT HE GAVE UP											THE RESULTS						
Year	Team	Lg	G	GS	GF	IP	BFP	H	R	ER	HR	SH	SF	HB	TBB	IBB	SO	WP	W	L	Pct	Sv-Op	Hld	Vel	OPS	ERC	ERA
2011 Col		NL	13	13	0	71.2	299	73	35	33	8	1	0	1	18	3	58	1	4	4	.500	0-0	0	94	.735	3.69	4.14
2012 Col		NL	11	11	0	58.0	257	72	37	34	7	3	1	1	22	1	54	4	2	3	.400	0-0	0	93	.861	5.74	5.28
2013 Col		NL	31	31	0	157.2	703	168	97	90	17	6	1	5	64	7	119	6	9	9	.500	0-0	0	92	.785	4.52	5.14
2014 Col		NL	33	14	7	93.2	409	107	59	56	19	5	2	1	31	1	63	3	6	6	.500	0-0	1	93	.860	5.43	5.38
2015 LAD		NL	53	1	12	58.1	260	59	25	25	1	3	0	1	32	6	65	2	1	3	.250	1-3	14	95	.742	4.00	3.86
2016 Pit		NL	52	12	9	118.0	513	117	64	59	15	5	7	7	45	3	138	3	10	7	.588	0-2	6	94	.774	4.33	4.50
2017 3 Tms		NL	76	0	15	72.1	291	58	22	21	5	1	0	2	20	2	72	1	5	5	.500	6-10	21	95	.610	2.46	2.61
2018 Sea		AL	46	0	6	42.0	183	53	30	28	6	0	4	2	5	0	53	0	1	6	.143	1-7	19	94	.828	4.90	6.00
2019 Phi		NL	47	0	10	47.1	217	57	27	25	4	1	2	2	21	5	45	0	2	3	.400	1-2	10	94	.810	5.29	4.75
17 Pit		NL	65	0	8	60.0	243	49	20	19	4	1	0	2	18	2	60	1	2	5	.286	2-6	21	95	.617	2.62	2.85
17 Phi		NL	2	0	0	1.1	4	0	0	0	0	0	0	0	0	0	1	0	1	0	1.000	0-0	0	96	.000	0.00	0.00
17 StL		NL	9	0	7	11.0	44	9	2	2	1	0	0	0	2	0	11	0	2	0	1.000	4-4	0	95	.631	2.23	1.64
9 ML YEARS			362	82	59	719.0	3132	764	396	371	82	25	17	22	258	28	667	20	40	46	.465	9-24	71	93	.779	4.43	4.64

Tomas Nido

Bats: R Throws: R Pos: C-48;PH-4   Ht: 6'0" Wt: 210 Born: 4/12/1994 Age: 26

								BATTING														RUNNING			AVERAGES			
Year	Team	Lg	G	AB	H	2B	3B	HR	(Hm	Rd)	TB	R	RBI	RC	TBB	IBB	SO	HBP	SH	SF	SB	CS	GDP	Avg	OBP	Slg	OPS
2019 Syrcse		AAA	12	38	11	1	0	0	(-	-)	12	3	4	3	1	0	13	0	0	1	0	0	1	.289	.300	.316	.616
2017 NYM		NL	5	10	3	1	0	0	(0	0)	4	0	3	2	0	0	2	0	0	0	0	0	0	.300	.300	.400	.700
2018 NYM		NL	34	84	14	3	0	1	(1	0)	20	10	9	2	4	0	27	0	0	2	0	0	4	.167	.200	.238	.438
2019 NYM		NL	50	136	26	5	0	4	(2	2)	43	9	14	5	7	2	37	0	1	0	0	0	4	.191	.231	.316	.547
3 ML YEARS			89	230	43	9	0	5	(3	2)	67	19	26	9	11	2	66	0	1	2	0	0	8	.187	.222	.291	.514

Brandon Nimmo

Bats: L Throws: R Pos: CF-43;LF-38;PH-8;RF-6   NIH-moe   Ht: 6'3" Wt: 207 Born: 3/27/1993 Age: 27

								BATTING														RUNNING			AVERAGES			
Year	Team	Lg	G	AB	H	2B	3B	HR	(Hm	Rd)	TB	R	RBI	RC	TBB	IBB	SO	HBP	SH	SF	SB	CS	GDP	Avg	OBP	Slg	OPS
2019 Syrcse		AAA	10	35	7	2	0	1	(-	-)	12	10	6	5	8	0	8	1	0	0	3	0	0	.200	.364	.343	.706
2016 NYM		NL	32	73	20	1	0	1	(1	0)	24	12	6	9	6	0	20	1	0	0	0	0	0	.274	.338	.329	.666
2017 NYM		NL	69	177	46	11	1	5	(3	2)	74	26	21	26	33	1	60	2	1	2	2	0	3	.260	.379	.418	.797
2018 NYM		NL	140	433	114	28	8	17	(8	9)	209	77	47	84	80	2	140	22	0	0	9	6	8	.263	.404	.483	.886
2019 NYM		NL	69	199	44	11	1	8	(2	6)	81	34	29	38	46	2	71	5	1	3	3	0	1	.221	.375	.407	.783
4 ML YEARS			310	882	224	51	10	31	(14	17)	388	149	103	157	165	5	291	30	2	5	14	6	12	.254	.387	.440	.827

Hector Noesi

Pitches: R Bats: R Pos: RP-8; SP-4   noh-EH-see   Ht: 6'3" Wt: 205 Born: 1/26/1987 Age: 33

				HOW MUCH PITCHED					WHAT HE GAVE UP											THE RESULTS						
Year	Team	Lg	G	GS	GF	IP	BFP	H	R	ER	HR	SH	SF	HB	TBB	IBB	SO	WP	W	L	Pct	Sv-Op	Hld	Vel	OPS	ERC	ERA
2019 NewOr		AAA	21	21	0	125.0	509	112	54	53	27	6	3	5	30	0	133	0	11	4	.733	0- -	-	-	.751	3.82	3.82
2011 NYY		AL	30	2	14	56.1	247	63	29	28	6	1	2	2	22	4	45	4	2	2	.500	0-0	0	93	.785	4.85	4.47
2012 Sea		AL	22	18	4	106.2	453	107	71	69	21	3	7	2	39	1	68	1	2	12	.143	0-0	0	93	.826	4.77	5.82
2013 Sea		AL	12	1	4	27.1	134	42	21	20	3	1	1	1	12	4	21	2	0	1	.000	0-0	0	94	.935	7.45	6.59
2014 3 Tms		AL	33	27	3	172.1	733	180	98	91	28	4	7	2	56	1	123	9	8	12	.400	0-0	0	93	.774	4.55	4.75
2015 CWS		AL	10	5	4	32.2	154	41	26	25	7	0	0	1	17	1	22	3	0	4	.000	0-0	0	93	.920	7.08	6.89
2019 Mia		NL	12	4	3	27.2	124	30	26	26	7	1	1	1	14	0	24	2	0	3	.000	0-0	0	93	.955	6.41	8.46
14 Sea		AL	2	0	2	1.0	6	2	3	3	1	0	1	0	0	0	2	1	0	1	.000	0-0	0	94	1.733	13.47	27.00
14 Tex		AL	3	0	1	5.1	28	11	7	7	0	0	0	0	2	0	4	0	0	0	-	0-0	0	93	1.195	9.94	11.81
14 CWS		AL	28	27	0	166.0	699	167	88	81	27	4	6	2	54	1	117	8	8	11	.421	0-0	0	93	.749	4.34	4.39
6 ML YEARS			119	57	32	423.0	1845	463	271	259	72	10	18	9	160	11	303	21	12	34	.261	0-0	4	93	.824	5.14	5.51

Stephen Nogosek

Pitches: R **Bats:** R **Pos:** RP-7   **Ht:** 6'2" **Wt:** 205 **Born:** 1/11/1995 **Age:** 25

Year	Team	Lg	G	GS	GF	IP	BFP	H	R	ER	HR	SH	SF	HB	TBB	IBB	SO	WP	W	L	Pct	Sv-Op	Hld	Vel	OPS	ERC	ERA
2019	Bnghtn	AA	11	0	6	19.0	78	13	4	2	0	0	2	0	12	0	20	0	0	0	-	1- -	-		.555	2.66	0.95
2019	Syrcse	AAA	24	0	8	31.1	117	12	5	4	1	0	0	2	13	0	30	2	3	0	1.000	2- -	-		.388	1.21	1.15
2019	NYM	NL	7	0	6	6.2	34	12	8	8	2	0	1	0	2	0	6	0	0	1	.000	0-0	0	95	1.057	10.23	10.80

Aaron Nola

Pitches: R **Bats:** R **Pos:** SP-34   **Ht:** 6'2" **Wt:** 195 **Born:** 6/4/1993 **Age:** 27

Year	Team	Lg	G	GS	GF	IP	BFP	H	R	ER	HR	SH	SF	HB	TBB	IBB	SO	WP	W	L	Pct	Sv-Op	Hld	Vel	OPS	ERC	ERA
2015	Phi	NL	13	13	0	77.2	318	74	31	31	11	1	1	2	19	1	68	0	6	2	.750	0-0	0	91	.703	3.62	3.59
2016	Phi	NL	20	20	0	111.0	483	116	68	59	10	5	4	6	29	3	121	0	6	9	.400	0-0	0	90	.712	3.80	4.78
2017	Phi	NL	27	27	0	168.0	693	154	67	66	18	2	0	2	49	2	184	1	12	11	.522	0-0	0	92	.679	3.30	3.54
2018	Phi	NL	33	33	0	212.1	831	149	57	56	17	6	4	7	58	3	224	4	17	6	.739	0-0	0	92	.570	2.09	2.37
2019	Phi	NL	34	**34**	0	202.1	**852**	176	91	87	27	4	2	11	80	3	229	3	12	7	.632	0-0	0	93	.708	3.79	3.87
	5 ML YEARS		127	127	0	771.1	3177	669	314	299	83	18	11	28	235	12	826	10	53	35	.602	0-0	0	92	.666	3.17	3.49

Austin Nola

Bats: R **Throws:** R **Pos:** 1B-59;2B-15;C-7;3B-4;PH-3;LF-1;RF-1   **Ht:** 6'0" **Wt:** 195 **Born:** 12/28/1989 **Age:** 30

Year	Team	Lg	G	AB	H	2B	3B	HR	(Hm	Rd)	TB	R	RBI	RC	TBB	IBB	SO	HBP	SH	SF	SB	CS	GDP	Avg	OBP	Slg	OPS
2019	Tacom	AAA	55	196	64	15	1	7	(-	-)	102	36	37	43	29	0	40	2	0	2	4	1	7	.327	.415	.520	.935
2019	Sea	AL	79	238	64	12	1	10	(1	9)	108	37	31	34	23	1	63	4	1	1	1	0	8	.269	.342	.454	.796

Jake Noll

Bats: R **Throws:** R **Pos:** PH-5;1B-2;3B-1   **Ht:** 6'2" **Wt:** 195 **Born:** 3/8/1994 **Age:** 26

Year	Team	Lg	G	AB	H	2B	3B	HR	(Hm	Rd)	TB	R	RBI	RC	TBB	IBB	SO	HBP	SH	SF	SB	CS	GDP	Avg	OBP	Slg	OPS
2019	Fresno	AAA	118	456	130	24	0	11	(-	-)	187	69	54	63	26	0	89	4	0	3	5	2	12	.285	.327	.410	.737
2019	Was	NL	8	12	2	1	0	0	(0	0)	3	1	2	1	1	0	4	0	0	0	0	0	0	.167	.231	.250	.481

Daniel Norris

Pitches: L **Bats:** L **Pos:** SP-29; RP-3   **Ht:** 6'2" **Wt:** 185 **Born:** 4/25/1993 **Age:** 27

Year	Team	Lg	G	GS	GF	IP	BFP	H	R	ER	HR	SH	SF	HB	TBB	IBB	SO	WP	W	L	Pct	Sv-Op	Hld	Vel	OPS	ERC	ERA
2014	Tor	AL	5	1	2	6.2	30	5	4	4	1	0	1	0	5	0	4	0	0	0	-	0-0	1	91	.667	4.31	5.40
2015	2 Tms	AL	13	13	0	60.0	251	53	31	25	9	1	4	2	19	0	45	3	3	2	.600	0-0	0	92	.732	3.55	3.75
2016	Det	AL	14	13	1	69.1	302	75	30	26	10	0	3	0	22	0	71	1	4	2	.667	0-0	0	93	.762	4.46	3.38
2017	Det	AL	22	18	1	101.2	460	120	64	60	12	2	3	3	44	3	86	1	5	8	.385	0-0	0	93	.840	5.48	5.31
2018	Det	AL	11	8	0	44.1	200	46	28	28	8	1	2	2	19	0	51	2	0	5	.000	0-0	0	90	.791	5.06	5.68
2019	Det	AL	32	29	0	144.1	610	154	75	72	25	**5**	3	4	38	0	125	5	3	13	.188	0-0	0	91	.797	4.58	4.49
	15	Tor	AL	5	5	0	23.1	103	23	11	10	3	1	2	2	12	0	18	2	1	1	.500	0-0	0	91	.816	5.10	3.86
	15	Det	AL	8	8	0	36.2	148	30	20	15	6	0	2	0	7	0	27	1	2	1	.667	0-0	0	92	.674	2.64	3.68
	6 ML YEARS		97	82	4	426.1	1853	453	232	215	65	9	16	11	147	3	382	12	15	30	.333	0-0	1	92	.790	4.67	4.54

James Norwood

Pitches: R **Bats:** R **Pos:** RP-9   **Ht:** 6'2" **Wt:** 215 **Born:** 12/24/1993 **Age:** 26

Year	Team	Lg	G	GS	GF	IP	BFP	H	R	ER	HR	SH	SF	HB	TBB	IBB	SO	WP	W	L	Pct	Sv-Op	Hld	Vel	OPS	ERC	ERA
2019	Iowa	AAA	45	0	28	57.2	240	40	31	27	9	0	2	2	31	2	81	11	3	2	.600	6- -	-		.690	3.43	4.21
2018	ChC	NL	11	0	5	11.0	54	14	7	5	0	0	2	0	5	0	10	1	0	1	.000	0-0	2	98	.714	4.59	4.09
2019	ChC	NL	9	0	3	9.1	44	9	4	3	1	0	0	0	8	0	11	1	0	1	.000	0-0	0	96	.803	5.76	2.89
	2 ML YEARS		20	0	8	20.1	98	23	11	8	1	0	2	0	13	0	21	2	0	2	.000	0-0	2	97	.753	5.20	3.54

Jacob Nottingham

Bats: R **Throws:** R **Pos:** C-6;PH-4;1B-1   **Ht:** 6'2" **Wt:** 230 **Born:** 4/3/1995 **Age:** 25

Year	Team	Lg	G	AB	H	2B	3B	HR	(Hm	Rd)	TB	R	RBI	RC	TBB	IBB	SO	HBP	SH	SF	SB	CS	GDP	Avg	OBP	Slg	OPS
2019	SnAnt	AAA	83	290	67	21	0	5	(-	-)	103	40	40	36	28	1	95	9	0	5	7	1	8	.231	.313	.355	.668
2018	Mil	NL	9	20	4	1	0	0	(0	0)	5	2	0	1	4	0	8	0	0	0	0	0	0	.200	.333	.250	.583
2019	Mil	NL	9	6	2	0	0	1	(0	1)	5	1	4	3	0	0	2	1	0	0	0	0	0	.333	.429	.833	1.262
	2 ML YEARS		18	26	6	1	0	1	(0	1)	10	3	4	4	4	0	10	1	0	0	0	0	0	.231	.355	.385	.739

Ivan Nova

Pitches: R **Bats:** R **Pos:** SP-34   ee-VAHN   **Ht:** 6'5" **Wt:** 250 **Born:** 1/12/1987 **Age:** 33

Year	Team	Lg	G	GS	GF	IP	BFP	H	R	ER	HR	SH	SF	HB	TBB	IBB	SO	WP	W	L	Pct	Sv-Op	Hld	Vel	OPS	ERC	ERA
2010	NYY	AL	10	7	3	42.0	185	44	22	21	4	1	1	1	17	2	26	2	1	2	.333	0-1	0	93	.729	4.31	4.50
2011	NYY	AL	28	27	1	165.1	704	163	74	68	13	2	6	6	57	3	98	11	16	4	.800	0-0	0	93	.706	3.76	3.70
2012	NYY	AL	28	28	0	170.1	748	194	100	95	28	3	6	10	56	3	153	6	12	8	.600	0-0	0	93	.860	5.32	5.02
2013	NYY	AL	23	20	2	139.1	586	135	49	48	14	9	3	14	44	3	116	3	9	6	.600	0-0	0	93	.678	3.77	3.10

Year	Team	Lg	G	GS	GF	IP	BFP	H	R	ER	HR	SH	SF	HB	TBB	IBB	SO	WP	W	L	Pct	Sv-Op	Hld	Vel	OPS	ERC	ERA
2014	NYY	AL	4	4	0	20.2	96	32	19	19	6	0	2	2	6	0	12	1	2	2	.500	0-0	0	92	1.033	9.40	8.27
2015	NYY	AL	17	17	0	94.0	413	99	54	53	13	3	2	7	33	0	63	5	6	11	.353	0-0	0	93	.793	4.75	5.07
2016	2 Tms		32	26	3	162.0	684	175	81	75	23	5	4	9	28	1	127	10	12	8	.600	1-1	0	93	.778	4.12	4.17
2017	Pit	NL	31	31	0	187.0	785	203	96	86	29	7	3	7	36	2	131	8	11	14	.440	0-0	0	93	.781	4.27	4.14
2018	Pit	NL	29	29	0	161.0	683	171	82	75	26	4	2	4	35	4	114	9	9	9	.500	0-0	0	93	.769	4.15	4.19
2019	CWS	AL	34	34	0	187.0	806	225	107	98	30	2	4	9	47	1	114	7	11	12	.478	0-0	0	92	.833	5.40	4.72
16	NYY	AL	21	15	3	97.1	421	107	54	53	19	1	2	6	25	1	75	7	7	6	.538	1-1	0	92	.827	4.98	4.90
16	Pit	NL	11	11	0	64.2	263	68	27	22	4	4	4	3	3	0	52	3	5	2	.714	0-0	0	93	.699	2.93	3.06
Postseason			2	1	0	8.1	34	7	4	4	2	0	0	0	4	0	8	0	1	1	.500	0-0	0	92	.790	4.66	4.32
10 ML YEARS			236	223	9	1328.2	5690	1441	684	638	181	29	35	69	359	19	954	62	89	76	.539	1-2	0	93	.781	4.51	4.32

Dom Nunez

Bats: L **Throws:** R **Pos:** C-14;PH-2   **Ht:** 6'0" **Wt:** 175 **Born:** 1/17/1995 **Age:** 25

Year	Team	Lg	G	AB	H	2B	3B	HR	(Hm	Rd)	TB	R	RBI	RC	TBB	IBB	SO	HBP	SH	SF	SB	CS	GDP	Avg	OBP	Slg	OPS
2019	Albq	AAA	61	213	52	14	1	17	(-	-)	119	43	42	45	35	1	69	6	0	3	2	0	1	.244	.362	.559	.921
2019	Col	NL	16	39	7	3	0	2	(2	0)	16	4	4	2	3	0	17	0	0	1	0	0	0	.179	.233	.410	.643

Eduardo Nunez

Bats: R **Throws:** R **Pos:** 2B-31;PH-13;DH-12;3B-8;SS-6;PR-5   **Ht:** 6'0" **Wt:** 195 **Born:** 6/15/1987 **Age:** 33

Year	Team	Lg	G	AB	H	2B	3B	HR	(Hm	Rd)	TB	R	RBI	RC	TBB	IBB	SO	HBP	SH	SF	SB	CS	GDP	Avg	OBP	Slg	OPS
2010	NYY	AL	30	50	14	1	0	1	(0	1)	18	12	7	8	3	0	2	0	0	0	5	0	4	.280	.321	.360	.681
2011	NYY	AL	112	309	82	18	2	5	(2	3)	119	38	30	42	22	2	37	0	6	1	22	6	6	.265	.313	.385	.698
2012	NYY	AL	38	89	26	4	1	1	(1	0)	35	14	11	15	6	0	12	1	0	4	11	2	1	.292	.330	.393	.723
2013	NYY	AL	90	304	79	17	4	3	(2	1)	113	38	28	31	20	1	51	3	4	5	10	3	3	.260	.307	.372	.679
2014	Min	AL	72	204	51	7	4	4	(4	0)	78	26	24	21	5	0	31	1	3	0	9	3	7	.250	.271	.382	.654
2015	Min	AL	72	188	53	14	1	4	(3	1)	81	23	20	25	12	0	29	1	2	1	8	4	1	.282	.327	.431	.758
2016	2 Tms		141	553	159	24	4	16	(8	8)	239	73	67	74	29	3	88	5	2	6	40	10	8	.288	.325	.432	.758
2017	2 Tms		114	467	146	33	0	12	(5	7)	215	60	58	76	18	0	54	3	1	2	24	7	11	.313	.341	.460	.801
2018	Bos	AL	127	480	127	23	3	10	(6	4)	186	56	44	47	16	0	69	2	1	3	7	2	17	.265	.289	.388	.677
2019	Bos	AL	60	167	38	7	0	2	(2	0)	51	13	20	13	4	0	27	0	1	2	5	1	6	.228	.243	.305	.548
16	Min	AL	91	371	110	15	1	12	(6	6)	163	49	47	54	15	0	58	3	2	5	27	6	6	.296	.325	.439	.764
16	SF	NL	50	182	49	9	3	4	(2	2)	76	24	20	20	14	3	30	2	0	1	13	4	2	.269	.327	.418	.744
17	SF	NL	76	302	93	21	0	4	(1	3)	126	37	31	45	12	0	29	1	1	2	18	5	8	.308	.334	.417	.752
17	Bos	AL	38	165	53	12	0	8	(4	4)	89	23	27	31	6	0	25	2	0	0	6	2	3	.321	.353	.539	.892
Postseason			18	41	9	2	1	2	(1	1)	19	5	5	5	2	0	5	0	0	0	2	0	0	.220	.256	.463	.719
10 ML YEARS			856	2811	775	148	19	58	(31	27)	1135	353	309	352	135	6	400	16	20	24	141	38	64	.276	.310	.404	.714

Renato Nunez

Bats: R **Throws:** R **Pos:** DH-109;1B-24;PH-13;3B-9;LF-1   **Ht:** 6'1" **Wt:** 220 **Born:** 4/4/1994 **Age:** 26

Year	Team	Lg	G	AB	H	2B	3B	HR	(Hm	Rd)	TB	R	RBI	RC	TBB	IBB	SO	HBP	SH	SF	SB	CS	GDP	Avg	OBP	Slg	OPS
2016	Oak	AL	9	15	2	0	0	0	(0	0)	2	0	1	0	0	0	3	0	0	0	0	0	0	.133	.133	.133	.267
2017	Oak	AL	8	15	3	0	0	1	(0	1)	6	1	3	3	1	0	8	0	0	0	0	0	0	.200	.250	.400	.650
2018	2 Tms		73	236	61	14	0	8	(0	8)	99	28	22	26	19	0	62	4	0	2	0	0	4	.258	.322	.419	.741
2019	Bal	AL	151	541	132	24	0	31	(16	15)	249	72	90	81	44	1	143	10	0	4	1	1	9	.244	.311	.460	.771
18	Tex	AL	13	36	6	1	0	1	(0	1)	10	2	2	1	3	0	12	1	0	1	0	0	0	.167	.244	.278	.522
18	Bal	AL	60	200	55	13	0	7	(0	7)	89	26	20	25	16	0	50	3	0	1	0	0	4	.275	.336	.445	.781
4 ML YEARS			241	807	198	38	0	40	(16	24)	356	101	116	110	64	1	216	14	0	6	1	1	13	.245	.310	.441	.751

Scott Oberg

Pitches: R **Bats:** R **Pos:** RP-49   **Ht:** 6'2" **Wt:** 203 **Born:** 3/13/1990 **Age:** 30

Year	Team	Lg	G	GS	GF	IP	BFP	H	R	ER	HR	SH	SF	HB	TBB	IBB	SO	WP	W	L	Pct	Sv-Op	Hld	Vel	OPS	ERC	ERA
2015	Col	NL	64	0	11	58.1	259	58	35	33	10	3	1	6	31	2	44	6	3	4	.429	1-3	15	95	.839	5.60	5.09
2016	Col	NL	24	0	9	26.0	113	26	15	15	3	0	1	6	11	2	20	3	1	1	.500	1-2	5	95	.713	4.33	5.19
2017	Col	NL	66	0	12	58.1	265	70	35	32	4	1	2	2	24	2	55	3	0	1	.000	0-1	14	96	.800	5.11	4.94
2018	Col	NL	56	0	7	58.2	228	45	17	16	4	0	2	3	12	0	57	3	8	1	.889	0-4	14	95	.571	2.20	2.45
2019	Col	NL	49	0	18	56.0	223	39	18	14	5	0	1	0	23	2	58	3	6	1	.857	5-8	8	94	.569	2.46	2.25
Postseason			5	0	1	4.1	17	4	2	2	0	0	0	0	0	0	12	1	1	0	1.000	0-0	0	97	.588	1.64	4.15
5 ML YEARS			259	0	57	257.1	1088	238	120	110	26	4	6	12	101	8	234	18	18	8	.692	7-18	52	95	.703	3.82	3.85

Peter O'Brien

Bats: R **Throws:** R **Pos:** RF-10;LF-4;1B-1;PH-1   **Ht:** 6'4" **Wt:** 235 **Born:** 7/15/1990 **Age:** 29

Year	Team	Lg	G	AB	H	2B	3B	HR	(Hm	Rd)	TB	R	RBI	RC	TBB	IBB	SO	HBP	SH	SF	SB	CS	GDP	Avg	OBP	Slg	OPS
2019	NewOr	AAA	75	255	56	8	0	17	(-	-)	115	41	45	37	36	2	107	0	0	0	0	1	2	.220	.316	.451	.767
2015	Ari	NL	8	10	4	1	0	1	(1	0)	8	1	3	3	2	0	5	0	0	0	0	0	0	.400	.500	.800	1.300
2016	Ari	NL	28	64	9	1	0	5	(2	3)	25	6	9	3	3	2	27	0	0	0	0	0	2	.141	.179	.391	.570
2018	Mia	NL	22	66	18	5	0	4	(1	3)	35	8	10	10	7	0	22	0	0	1	0	0	2	.273	.338	.530	.868
2019	Mia	NL	14	42	7	1	0	1	(0	1)	11	2	4	2	4	0	19	1	0	0	1	0	2	.167	.255	.262	.517
4 ML YEARS			72	182	38	8	0	11	(4	7)	79	17	26	18	16	2	73	1	0	1	1	0	6	.209	.275	.434	.709

Darren O'Day

Pitches: R **Bats:** R **Pos:** RP-8   **Ht:** 6'4" **Wt:** 220 **Born:** 10/22/1982 **Age:** 37

			HOW MUCH PITCHED					WHAT HE GAVE UP										THE RESULTS							
Year	Team	Lg	G	GS	GF	IP	BFP	H	R	ER	HR	SH	SF	HB	TBB	IBB	SO	WP	W	L	Pct	Sv-Op Hld	Vel	OPS	ERC	ERA
2008	LAA	AL	30	0	17	43.1	194	49	24	22	2	2	1	4	14	6	29	1	0	1	.000	0-0 1	87	.719	4.20	4.57
2009	2 Tms		68	0	15	58.2	233	41	14	12	3	1	3	5	18	1	56	1	2	1	.667	2-2 20	85	.543	2.20	1.84
2010	Tex	AL	72	0	14	62.0	240	43	15	14	5	1	3	5	12	5	45	0	6	2	.750	0-2 22	86	.548	1.93	2.03
2011	Tex	AL	16	0	7	16.2	74	17	10	10	7	1	1	2	5	0	18	0	0	1	.000	0-0 3	84	.929	6.45	5.40
2012	Bal	AL	69	0	10	67.0	263	49	17	17	6	3	1	3	14	2	69	0	7	1	.875	0-2 15	85	.613	2.06	2.28
2013	Bal	AL	68	0	18	62.0	247	47	16	15	7	1	1	5	15	1	59	1	5	3	.625	2-6 20	86	.617	2.60	2.18
2014	Bal	AL	68	0	18	68.2	271	42	14	13	6	1	2	8	19	4	73	0	5	2	.714	4-8 25	87	.550	1.92	1.70
2015	Bal	AL	68	0	19	65.1	257	47	13	11	5	0	1	5	14	1	82	0	6	2	.750	6-11 18	87	.540	2.09	1.52
2016	Bal	AL	34	0	16	31.0	131	25	13	13	6	0	0	1	13	2	38	0	3	1	.750	3-5 10	86	.717	3.70	3.77
2017	Bal	AL	64	0	16	60.1	240	41	24	23	8	0	1	3	24	2	76	0	2	3	.400	2-4 17	88	.609	2.79	3.43
2018	Bal	AL	20	0	10	20.0	83	18	9	8	3	0	0	3	4	1	27	0	0	2	.000	2-4 4	87	.722	3.61	3.60
2019	Atl	NL	8	0	0	5.1	21	3	1	1	0	0	0	1	1	0	6	0	0	0	-	0-0 0	87	.554	1.35	1.69
09	NYM	NL	4	0	1	3.0	17	5	2	0	0	0	1	1	1	0	2	0	0	0	-	0-0 0	84	.769	7.72	0.00
09	Tex	NL	64	0	14	55.2	216	36	12	12	3	1	2	4	17	1	54	1	2	1	.667	2-2 20	85	.526	1.95	1.94
	Postseason		21	0	1	16.0	61	11	8	8	4	1	0	1	3	0	16	0	0	3	.000	0-0 5	86	.661	2.80	4.50
	12 ML YEARS		585	0	150	560.1	2254	422	170	159	58	10	14	45	153	22	578	3	36	19	.655	21-44 155	86	.612	2.58	2.55

Rougned Odor

Bats: L **Throws:** R **Pos:** 2B-137;PH-7;DH-3   ROOG-ned oh-DORE   **Ht:** 5'11" **Wt:** 195 **Born:** 2/3/1994 **Age:** 26

			BATTING																		RUNNING			AVERAGES			
Year	Team	Lg	G	AB	H	2B	3B	HR	(Hm	Rd)	TB	R	RBI	RC	TBB	IBB	SO	HBP	SH	SF	SB	CS	GDP	Avg	OBP	Slg	OPS
2014	Tex	AL	114	386	100	14	7	9	(4	5)	155	39	48	46	17	1	71	5	6	3	4	7	7	.259	.297	.402	.698
2015	Tex	AL	120	426	111	21	9	16	(7	9)	198	54	61	62	23	2	79	14	2	5	6	7	3	.261	.316	.465	.781
2016	Tex	AL	150	605	164	33	4	33	(17	16)	304	89	88	77	19	0	135	4	0	4	14	7	6	.271	.296	.502	.798
2017	Tex	AL	162	607	124	21	3	30	(18	12)	241	79	75	61	32	5	162	8	0	4	15	6	13	.204	.252	.397	.649
2018	Tex	AL	129	474	120	23	2	18	(10	8)	201	76	63	67	43	2	127	11	2	5	12	12	5	.253	.326	.424	.751
2019	Tex	AL	145	522	107	30	1	30	(15	15)	229	77	93	77	52	2	178	5	1	1	11	9	4	.205	.283	.439	.721
	Postseason		8	28	7	1	0	2	(0	2)	14	9	4	5	3	0	5	2	0	0	0	0	0	.250	.364	.500	.864
	6 ML YEARS		820	3020	726	142	26	136	(71	65)	1328	414	428	390	186	12	752	47	11	22	62	48	38	.240	.293	.440	.733

Jake Odorizzi

Pitches: R **Bats:** R **Pos:** SP-30   oh-duh-RIZZ-ee   **Ht:** 6'2" **Wt:** 190 **Born:** 3/27/1990 **Age:** 30

			HOW MUCH PITCHED					WHAT HE GAVE UP											THE RESULTS							
Year	Team	Lg	G	GS	GF	IP	BFP	H	R	ER	HR	SH	SF	HB	TBB	IBB	SO	WP	W	L	Pct	Sv-Op Hld	Vel	OPS	ERC	ERA
2012	KC	AL	2	2	0	7.1	34	8	4	4	1	0	0	0	4	0	4	0	0	1	.000	0-0 0	90	.820	5.34	4.91
2013	TB	AL	7	4	2	29.2	122	28	13	13	3	0	1	2	8	0	22	1	0	1	.000	1-1 0	91	.744	3.62	3.94
2014	TB	AL	31	31	0	168.0	719	156	79	77	20	3	8	5	59	0	174	3	11	13	.458	0-0 0	90	.692	3.68	4.13
2015	TB	AL	28	28	0	169.1	700	149	65	63	18	4	3	3	46	0	150	5	9	9	.500	0-0 0	91	.680	3.02	3.35
2016	TB	AL	33	33	0	187.2	773	170	80	77	29	3	6	4	54	3	166	3	10	6	.625	0-0 0	92	.715	3.56	3.69
2017	TB	AL	28	28	0	143.1	604	117	80	66	30	2	7	2	61	1	127	1	10	8	.556	0-0 0	92	.736	3.91	4.14
2018	Min	AL	32	32	0	164.1	711	151	89	82	20	4	4	8	70	3	162	1	7	10	.412	0-0 0	91	.743	4.02	4.49
2019	Min	AL	30	30	0	159.0	658	139	65	62	16	4	4	4	53	0	178	4	15	7	.682	0-0 0	93	.671	3.25	3.51
	8 ML YEARS		191	188	2	1028.2	4321	918	475	444	137	20	33	28	355	7	983	18	62	55	.530	1-1 0	91	.708	3.58	3.88

Brian O'Grady

Bats: L **Throws:** R **Pos:** PH-12;CF-11;LF-6;1B-2;DH-1   **Ht:** 6'2" **Wt:** 215 **Born:** 5/17/1992 **Age:** 28

			BATTING																		RUNNING			AVERAGES			
Year	Team	Lg	G	AB	H	2B	3B	HR	(Hm	Rd)	TB	R	RBI	RC	TBB	IBB	SO	HBP	SH	SF	SB	CS	GDP	Avg	OBP	Slg	OPS
2019	Lsvlle	AAA	112	429	120	30	1	28	(-	-)	236	71	77	87	51	2	136	4	0	4	20	4	1	.280	.359	.550	.909
2019	Cin	NL	28	42	8	2	1	2	(0	2)	18	4	3	4	4	0	17	2	0	0	0	0	0	.190	.292	.429	.720

Seunghwan Oh

Pitches: R **Bats:** R **Pos:** RP-21   sing-whan   **Ht:** 5'10" **Wt:** 205 **Born:** 7/15/1982 **Age:** 37

			HOW MUCH PITCHED					WHAT HE GAVE UP											THE RESULTS							
Year	Team	Lg	G	GS	GF	IP	BFP	H	R	ER	HR	SH	SF	HB	TBB	IBB	SO	WP	W	L	Pct	Sv-Op Hld	Vel	OPS	ERC	ERA
2016	StL	NL	76	0	35	79.2	313	55	20	17	5	2	1	2	18	3	103	3	6	3	.667	19-23 14	93	.510	1.69	1.92
2017	StL	NL	62	0	38	59.1	264	68	31	27	10	3	4	3	15	9	54	1	1	6	.143	20-24 7	93	.794	4.65	4.10
2018	2 Tms		73	0	10	68.1	274	52	21	20	8	0	4	4	17	1	79	3	6	3	.667	3-9 21	92	.620	2.56	2.63
2019	Col	NL	21	0	5	18.1	88	29	19	19	6	0	0	0	6	0	16	2	3	1	.750	0-1 5	91	.983	9.28	9.33
18	Tor	AL	48	0	7	47.0	189	37	14	14	5	0	3	3	10	1	55	1	4	3	.571	2-5 13	92	.617	2.49	2.68
18	Col	AL	25	0	3	21.1	85	15	7	6	3	0	1	1	7	0	24	2	2	0	1.000	1-4 8	92	.626	2.70	2.53
	Postseason		3	0	0	3.0	15	3	2	2	1	0	0	0	4	2	2	0	0	0	-	0-0 0	91	.900	5.70	6.00
	4 ML YEARS		232	0	88	225.2	939	204	91	83	29	5	9	9	56	13	252	9	16	13	.552	42-57 45	92	.666	3.19	3.31

Ryan O'Hearn

Bats: L **Throws:** L **Pos:** 1B-94;PH-12;LF-2;DH-2   **Ht:** 6'3" **Wt:** 200 **Born:** 7/26/1993 **Age:** 26

			BATTING																		RUNNING			AVERAGES			
Year	Team	Lg	G	AB	H	2B	3B	HR	(Hm	Rd)	TB	R	RBI	RC	TBB	IBB	SO	HBP	SH	SF	SB	CS	GDP	Avg	OBP	Slg	OPS
2019	Omha	AAA	35	129	38	10	1	9	(-	-)	77	20	28	29	17	1	31	2	0	1	0	0	2	.295	.383	.597	.979
2018	KC	AL	44	149	39	10	2	12	(5	7)	89	23	30	33	20	0	45	1	0	0	0	0	0	.262	.353	.597	.950
2019	KC	AL	105	328	64	13	1	14	(6	8)	121	32	38	25	39	1	99	1	0	2	0	1	7	.195	.281	.369	.650
	2 ML YEARS		149	477	103	23	3	26	(11	15)	210	55	68	58	59	1	144	2	0	2	0	1	7	.216	.304	.440	.744

Shohei Ohtani

Bats: L **Throws:** R **Pos:** DH-92;PH-15   **Ht:** 6'4" **Wt:** 210 **Born:** 7/5/1994 **Age:** 25

Year	Team	Lg	G	AB	H	2B	3B	HR	(Hm	Rd)	TB	R	RBI	RC	TBB	IBB	SO	HBP	SH	SF	SB	CS	GDP	Avg	OBP	Slg	OPS
2018	LAA	AL	114	326	93	21	2	22	(15	7)	184	59	61	70	37	2	102	2	0	1	10	4	2	.285	.361	.564	.925
2019	LAA	AL	106	384	110	20	5	18	(11	7)	194	51	62	68	33	1	110	2	0	4	12	3	6	.286	.343	.505	.848
	2 ML YEARS		220	710	203	41	7	40	(26	14)	378	110	123	138	70	3	212	4	0	5	22	7	8	.286	.351	.532	.883

Shohei Ohtani

Pitches: R **Bats:** L **Pos:** P   **Ht:** 6'4" **Wt:** 210 **Born:** 7/5/1994 **Age:** 25

Year	Team	Lg	G	GS	GF	IP	BFP	H	R	ER	HR	SH	SF	HB	TBB	IBB	SO	WP	W	L	Pct	Sv-Op	Hld	Vel	OPS	ERC	ERA
2018	LAA	AL	10	10	0	51.2	211	38	19	19	6	0	1	1	22	0	63	5	4	2	.667	0-0	0	97	.621	2.96	3.31

Matt Olson

Bats: L **Throws:** R **Pos:** 1B-127   **Ht:** 6'5" **Wt:** 230 **Born:** 3/29/1994 **Age:** 26

Year	Team	Lg	G	AB	H	2B	3B	HR	(Hm	Rd)	TB	R	RBI	RC	TBB	IBB	SO	HBP	SH	SF	SB	CS	GDP	Avg	OBP	Slg	OPS
2016	Oak	AL	11	21	2	1	0	0	(0	0)	3	3	0	1	7	0	4	0	0	0	0	0	1	.095	.321	.143	.464
2017	Oak	AL	59	189	49	2	0	24	(12	12)	123	33	45	40	22	1	60	5	0	0	0	0	6	.259	.352	.651	1.003
2018	Oak	AL	162	580	143	33	0	29	(14	15)	263	85	84	86	70	3	163	8	0	2	2	1	13	.247	.335	.453	.788
2019	Oak	AL	127	483	129	26	0	36	(13	23)	263	73	91	92	51	7	138	12	0	1	0	0	11	.267	.351	.545	.896
	Postseason		1	2	0	0	0	0	(0	0)	0	0	0	0	2	0	0	0	0	0	0	0	0	.000	.500	.000	.500
	4 ML YEARS		359	1273	323	62	0	89	(39	50)	652	194	220	219	150	11	365	25	0	3	2	1	31	.254	.343	.512	.855

Tyler Olson

Pitches: L **Bats:** R **Pos:** RP-39   **Ht:** 6'3" **Wt:** 205 **Born:** 10/2/1989 **Age:** 30

Year	Team	Lg	G	GS	GF	IP	BFP	H	R	ER	HR	SH	SF	HB	TBB	IBB	SO	WP	W	L	Pct	Sv-Op	Hld	Vel	OPS	ERC	ERA
2015	Sea	AL	11	0	4	13.1	65	18	8	8	2	2	0	1	10	7	8	0	1	1	.500	0-0	1	89	1.056	7.64	5.40
2016	NYY	AL	1	0	1	2.2	13	3	2	2	0	0	1	0	2	0	0	0	0	0	-	0-0	0	88	.885	5.24	6.75
2017	Cle	AL	30	0	4	20.0	77	13	0	0	1	0	1	1	6	0	18	0	1	0	1.000	1-1	8	89	.481	1.62	0.00
2018	Cle	AL	43	0	5	27.1	118	26	16	15	4	0	0	1	12	2	40	1	2	1	.667	0-0	5	89	.756	4.15	4.94
2019	Cle	AL	39	0	8	30.2	140	34	15	15	3	0	1	2	16	2	28	2	1	1	.500	0-1	1	87	.809	5.36	4.40
	Postseason		3	0	0	2.0	7	1	0	0	0	0	1	0	0	0	2	0	0	0	-	0-0	0	90	.476	0.54	0.00
	5 ML YEARS		124	0	22	94.0	413	94	41	40	9	3	2	4	46	11	94	3	5	3	.625	1-2	15	88	.770	4.41	3.83

Tyler O'Neill

Bats: R **Throws:** R **Pos:** LF-33;PH-17;RF-8;CF-3;PR-3   **Ht:** 5'11" **Wt:** 210 **Born:** 6/22/1995 **Age:** 25

Year	Team	Lg	G	AB	H	2B	3B	HR	(Hm	Rd)	TB	R	RBI	RC	TBB	IBB	SO	HBP	SH	SF	SB	CS	GDP	Avg	OBP	Slg	OPS
2019	Memp	AAA	41	151	40	5	0	11	(-	-)	78	26	26	26	14	0	51	0	0	1	3	0	3	.265	.325	.517	.842
2018	StL	NL	61	130	33	5	0	9	(6	3)	65	29	23	24	7	0	57	3	0	2	2	0	0	.254	.303	.500	.803
2019	StL	NL	60	141	37	6	0	5	(4	1)	58	18	16	19	10	0	53	0	0	0	1	0	3	.262	.311	.411	.723
	2 ML YEARS		121	271	70	11	0	14	(10	4)	123	47	39	43	17	0	110	3	0	2	3	0	3	.258	.307	.454	.761

Ryan O'Rourke

Pitches: L **Bats:** R **Pos:** RP-2   **Ht:** 6'3" **Wt:** 230 **Born:** 4/30/1988 **Age:** 32

Year	Team	Lg	G	GS	GF	IP	BFP	H	R	ER	HR	SH	SF	HB	TBB	IBB	SO	WP	W	L	Pct	Sv-Op	Hld	Vel	OPS	ERC	ERA
2019	Syrcse	AAA	36	2	13	44.0	188	39	21	16	4	0	0	1	23	2	47	4	2	3	.400	2--	-	-	.695	3.94	3.27
2019	Roch	AAA	7	0	3	12.0	55	7	6	6	0	0	0	1	12	0	14	3	2	1	.667	0--	-	-	.554	3.56	4.50
2015	Min	AL	28	0	7	22.0	97	16	15	15	3	1	1	0	15	2	24	2	0	0	-	0-0	0	91	.660	3.69	6.14
2016	Min	AL	26	0	6	25.0	101	18	13	11	3	2	1	1	10	0	24	2	0	1	.000	0-0	0	90	.615	2.91	3.96
2019	NYM	NL	2	0	0	1.1	6	0	0	0	0	0	0	0	3	0	1	0	0	0	-	0-0	0	92	.500	5.11	0.00
	3 ML YEARS		56	0	13	48.1	204	34	28	26	6	3	2	1	28	2	49	4	0	1	.000	0-0	0	90	.637	3.34	4.84

Rafael Ortega

Bats: L **Throws:** R **Pos:** LF-20;PH-10;RF-6;CF-3   **Ht:** 5'11" **Wt:** 160 **Born:** 5/15/1991 **Age:** 29

Year	Team	Lg	G	AB	H	2B	3B	HR	(Hm	Rd)	TB	R	RBI	RC	TBB	IBB	SO	HBP	SH	SF	SB	CS	GDP	Avg	OBP	Slg	OPS
2019	Gwnntt	AAA	111	431	123	34	3	21	(-	-)	226	83	58	85	59	1	95	2	0	1	14	7	1	.285	.373	.524	.898
2012	Col	NL	2	4	2	0	0	0	(0	0)	2	0	0	2	1	0	2	1	0	0	1	0	0	.500	.667	.500	1.167
2016	LAA	AL	66	185	43	8	0	1	(0	1)	54	24	16	19	13	0	23	0	3	0	8	3	5	.232	.283	.292	.575
2018	Mia	NL	41	133	31	3	1	0	(0	0)	36	10	7	10	10	0	23	0	0	0	5	2	5	.233	.287	.271	.557
2019	Atl	NL	34	88	18	3	0	2	(1	1)	27	7	10	8	8	0	22	0	0	0	3	0	2	.205	.271	.307	.578
	4 ML YEARS		143	410	94	14	1	3	(1	2)	119	41	33	39	32	0	70	1	3	0	17	5	12	.229	.287	.290	.577

Luis Ortiz

Pitches: R Bats: R Pos: SP-1   Ht: 6'3" Wt: 230 Born: 9/22/1995 Age: 24

			HOW MUCH PITCHED					WHAT HE GAVE UP											THE RESULTS						
Year Team	Lg	G	GS	GF	IP	BFP	H	R	ER	HR	SH	SF	HB	TBB	IBB	SO	WP	W	L	Pct	Sv-Op	Hld	Vel	OPS	ERC	ERA
2019 Norfolk	AAA	14	14	0	66.1	306	77	56	47	15	3	4	2	31	1	47	2	3	7	.300	0--	-	-	.878	6.30	6.38
2018 Bal	AL	2	1	0	2.1	18	7	6	4	0	0	1	0	3	0	0	1	0	1	.000	0-0	0	92	1.341	19.79	15.43
2019 Bal	AL	1	1	0	3.1	18	4	4	4	2	0	0	0	5	0	3	0	0	1	.000	0-0	0	94	1.346	15.85	10.80
2 ML YEARS		3	2	0	5.2	36	11	10	8	2	0	1	0	8	0	3	1	0	2	.000	0-0	0	93	1.343	17.59	12.71

Josh Osich

Pitches: L Bats: L Pos: RP-57   OH-sitch   Ht: 6'3" Wt: 232 Born: 9/3/1988 Age: 31

			HOW MUCH PITCHED					WHAT HE GAVE UP											THE RESULTS						
Year Team	Lg	G	GS	GF	IP	BFP	H	R	ER	HR	SH	SF	HB	TBB	IBB	SO	WP	W	L	Pct	Sv-Op	Hld	Vel	OPS	ERC	ERA
2015 SF	NL	35	0	6	28.2	120	24	12	7	4	1	1	0	8	0	27	2	2	0	1.000	0-2	11	96	.633	2.88	2.20
2016 SF	NL	59	0	9	36.1	160	31	20	19	7	1	0	3	19	1	25	2	1	3	.250	0-3	18	95	.769	4.65	4.71
2017 SF	NL	54	0	12	43.1	201	48	32	30	7	1	0	1	27	1	43	5	3	2	.600	0-1	6	95	.839	6.18	6.23
2018 SF	NL	12	0	6	12.0	61	20	11	11	2	0	0	2	7	0	10	3	0	0		0-1	2	95	1.052	10.94	8.25
2019 CWS	AL	57	0	14	67.2	272	62	38	35	15	0	1	0	15	1	61	3	4	0	1.000	0-1	2	94	.752	3.72	4.66
5 ML YEARS		217	0	43	188.0	814	185	113	102	35	3	2	6	76	3	166	15	10	5	.667	0-8	39	95	.781	4.72	4.88

Jose Osuna

Bats: R Throws: R Pos: 1B-31;PH-30;RF-23;3B-19;LF-2   Ht: 6'2" Wt: 240 Born: 12/12/1992 Age: 27

							BATTING													RUNNING			AVERAGES			
Year Team	Lg	G	AB	H	2B	3B	HR	(Hm Rd)	TB	R	RBI	RC	TBB	IBB	SO	HBP	SH	SF	SB	CS	GDP	Avg	OBP	Slg	OPS
2019 Indy	AAA	19	71	19	7	1	2	(- -)	34	13	13	13	9	0	22	2	0	1	2	0	4	.268	.361	.479	.840
2017 Pit	NL	104	215	50	13	4	7	(3 4)	92	31	30	19	9	0	40	2	0	1	0	0	10	.233	.269	.428	.697
2018 Pit	NL	51	106	24	9	4	3	(2 1)	42	14	11	8	3	0	22	1	0	1	0	0	2	.226	.252	.396	.648
2019 Pit	NL	95	261	69	20	0	10	(4 6)	119	41	36	33	18	0	48	1	0	4	0	0	6	.264	.310	.456	.766
3 ML YEARS		250	582	143	42	4	20	(9 11)	253	86	77	60	30	0	110	4	0	6	0	0	18	.246	.285	.435	.719

Roberto Osuna

Pitches: R Bats: R Pos: RP-66   Ht: 6'2" Wt: 215 Born: 2/7/1995 Age: 25

			HOW MUCH PITCHED					WHAT HE GAVE UP											THE RESULTS						
Year Team	Lg	G	GS	GF	IP	BFP	H	R	ER	HR	SH	SF	HB	TBB	IBB	SO	WP	W	L	Pct	Sv-Op	Hld	Vel	OPS	ERC	ERA
2015 Tor	AL	68	0	39	69.2	271	48	21	20	7	1	2	1	16	2	75	5	1	6	.143	20-23	7	96	.591	1.89	2.58
2016 Tor	AL	72	0	61	74.0	288	55	23	22	9	1	3	3	14	4	82	4	4	3	.571	36-42	0	96	.603	2.20	2.68
2017 Tor	AL	66	0	58	64.0	249	46	26	24	3	1	2	3	9	0	83	4	3	4	.429	39-49	0	95	.507	1.61	3.38
2018 2 Tms	AL	38	0	31	38.0	150	33	10	10	1	0	1	4	4	0	32	3	2	2	.500	21-22	2	95	.578	2.27	2.37
2019 Hou	AL	66	0	56	65.0	253	45	20	19	8	1	1	2	12	0	73	1	4	3	.571	**38-44**	0	97	.555	1.95	2.63
18 Tor	AL	15	0	13	15.1	63	16	5	5	0	0	0	2	1	0	13	1	0	0		9-10	0	95	.618	2.90	2.93
18 Hou	AL	23	0	18	22.2	87	17	5	5	1	0	1	2	3	0	19	2	2	2	.500	12-12	2	95	.549	1.87	1.99
Postseason		18	0	15	23.1	85	12	7	7	2	0	0	2	2	0	21	1	1	1	.500	3-3	0	96	.460	1.12	2.70
5 ML YEARS		310	0	245	310.2	1211	227	100	95	28	4	9	13	55	6	345	17	14	18	.438	154-180	9	96	.567	1.96	2.75

Corey Oswalt

Pitches: R Bats: R Pos: RP-2   Ht: 6'5" Wt: 250 Born: 9/3/1993 Age: 26

			HOW MUCH PITCHED					WHAT HE GAVE UP											THE RESULTS						
Year Team	Lg	G	GS	GF	IP	BFP	H	R	ER	HR	SH	SF	HB	TBB	IBB	SO	WP	W	L	Pct	Sv-Op	Hld	Vel	OPS	ERC	ERA
2019 Syrcse	AAA	16	16	0	86.2	352	84	35	28	9	1	0	2	15	0	79	1	10	4	.714	0--	-	-	.668	3.17	2.91
2018 NYM	NL	17	12	2	64.2	282	69	43	42	14	1	0	4	20	1	45	4	3	3	.500	0-0	1	90	.806	5.14	5.85
2019 NYM	NL	2	0	0	6.2	34	9	9	9	1	0	0	0	6	1	5	0	0	1	.000	0-0	0	92	1.013	8.55	12.15
2 ML YEARS		19	12	2	71.1	316	78	52	51	15	1	0	4	26	2	50	4	3	4	.429	0-0	1	91	.827	5.45	6.43

Dan Otero

Pitches: R Bats: R Pos: RP-25   oh-TEHR-oh   Ht: 6'3" Wt: 205 Born: 2/19/1985 Age: 35

			HOW MUCH PITCHED					WHAT HE GAVE UP											THE RESULTS						
Year Team	Lg	G	GS	GF	IP	BFP	H	R	ER	HR	SH	SF	HB	TBB	IBB	SO	WP	W	L	Pct	Sv-Op	Hld	Vel	OPS	ERC	ERA
2019 Clmbs	AAA	11	0	2	12.1	43	5	1	1	1	0	0	0	1	0	8	0	0	0	-	0--	-	-	.354	0.66	0.73
2012 SF	NL	12	0	4	12.1	57	19	11	8	0	0	0	2	2	1	8	1	0	0		0-0	0	90	.894	6.18	5.84
2013 Oak	AL	33	0	8	39.0	159	42	7	6	0	1	0	0	6	1	27	0	2	0	1.000	0-1	8	90	.613	2.90	1.38
2014 Oak	AL	72	0	14	86.2	349	80	24	22	4	4	3	2	15	7	45	1	8	2	.800	1-4	12	90	.609	2.46	2.28
2015 Oak	AL	41	0	6	46.2	204	64	35	35	7	1	3	2	6	2	28	1	4	2	.333	0-1	2	90	.886	5.70	6.75
2016 Cle	AL	62	0	20	70.2	269	54	14	12	2	3	0	0	10	1	57	2	5	1	.833	1-2	3	90	.526	1.60	1.53
2017 Cle	AL	52	0	14	60.0	242	63	23	19	6	1	1	0	9	4	38	0	3	0	1.000	0-0	1	90	.693	3.36	2.85
2018 Cle	AL	61	0	19	58.2	247	69	36	34	12	0	0	3	8	2	43	0	2	1	.667	1-3	1	90	.826	4.66	5.22
2019 Cle	AL	25	0	4	29.2	131	42	17	16	6	0	0	1	3	0	16	1	0	0		0-0	1	89	.879	6.24	4.85
Postseason		12	0	2	14.2	57	15	5	5	2	1	0	0	1	0	5	0	0	1	.000	0-0	1	91	.722	3.26	3.07
8 ML YEARS		358	0	89	403.2	1658	433	167	152	37	10	7	10	56	19	262	6	22	8	.733	3-11	28	90	.706	3.47	3.39

Adam Ottavino

Pitches: R **Bats:** B **Pos:** RP-73   ott-tah-VEE-no   **Ht:** 6'5" **Wt:** 220 **Born:** 11/22/1985 **Age:** 34

			HOW MUCH PITCHED				WHAT HE GAVE UP										THE RESULTS							
Year	Team	Lg	G	GS	GF	IP	BFP	H	R	ER	HR	SH	SF	HB	TBB	IBB	SO	WP	W	L	Pct	Sv-Op	Hld	Vel	OPS	ERC	ERA
2010	StL	NL	5	3	0	22.1	110	37	21	21	5	1	0	0	9	1	12	1	0	2	.000	0-0	0	93	1.072	9.22	8.46
2012	Col	NL	53	0	6	79.0	339	76	42	40	9	3	1	1	34	7	81	8	5	1	.833	0-2	6	94	.717	4.01	4.56
2013	Col	NL	51	0	5	78.1	335	73	27	23	5	6	4	2	31	5	78	9	1	3	.250	0-0	8	91	.672	3.42	2.64
2014	Col	NL	75	0	16	65.0	272	67	26	26	6	2	3	4	16	1	70	4	1	4	.200	1-6	21	94	.735	3.87	3.60
2015	Col	NL	10	0	5	10.1	35	3	0	0	0	0	0	1	2	0	13	0	1	0	1.000	3-3	3	96	.265	0.56	0.00
2016	Col	NL	34	0	19	27.0	107	18	9	8	3	0	0	2	7	0	35	4	1	3	.250	7-12	4	94	.528	2.17	2.67
2017	Col	NL	63	0	11	53.1	243	48	30	30	8	0	3	4	39	2	63	8	2	3	.400	0-2	21	94	.786	5.51	5.06
2018	Col	NL	75	0	16	77.2	309	41	25	21	5	1	5	6	36	5	112	7	6	4	.600	6-11	34	94	.509	1.89	2.43
2019	NYY	AL	73	0	7	66.1	283	47	17	14	5	0	3	2	40	3	88	3	6	5	.545	2-9	28	94	.624	3.13	1.90
	Postseason		3	0	1	3.2	18	3	2	2	0	0	0	0	3	1	3	2	0	1	.000	0-1	0	95	.639	3.10	4.91
	9 ML YEARS		439	3	85	479.1	2033	410	197	183	46	13	19	22	214	24	552	44	23	25	.479	19-45	125	94	.678	3.55	3.44

Chris Owings

Bats: R **Throws:** R **Pos:** 2B-25;3B-13;SS-10;PR-9;CF-7;RF-6;PH-6;LF-2   **Ht:** 5'10" **Wt:** 185 **Born:** 8/12/1991 **Age:** 28

						BATTING																RUNNING			AVERAGES			
Year	Team	Lg	G	AB	H	2B	3B	HR	(Hm	Rd)	TB	R	RBI	RC	TBB	IBB	SO	HBP	SH	SF	SB	CS	GDP	Avg	OBP	Slg	OPS
2019	Pwtckt	AAA	44	163	53	11	0	11	(-	-)	97	26	34	35	15	0	50	2	1	2	6	4	0	.325	.385	.595	.980
2013	Ari	NL	20	55	16	5	0	0	(0	0)	21	5	5	7	6	1	10	0	0	0	2	0	0	.291	.361	.382	.742
2014	Ari	NL	91	310	81	15	6	6	(1	5)	126	34	26	38	16	0	67	2	2	2	8	1	4	.261	.300	.406	.706
2015	Ari	NL	147	515	117	27	5	4	(3	1)	166	59	43	41	26	3	144	1	7	3	16	4	9	.227	.264	.322	.587
2016	Ari	NL	119	437	121	24	11	5	(5	0)	182	52	49	60	20	4	87	5	2	2	21	2	8	.277	.315	.416	.731
2017	Ari	NL	97	362	97	25	1	12	(8	4)	160	41	51	48	17	0	87	1	2	4	12	2	3	.268	.299	.442	.741
2018	Ari	NL	106	281	58	15	0	4	(3	1)	85	34	22	25	24	4	75	2	0	2	11	4	4	.206	.272	.302	.574
2019	2 Tms		67	180	25	6	1	3	(0	3)	42	13	14	7	14	0	78	2	0	0	5	2	2	.139	.209	.233	.443
19	KC	AL	41	135	18	4	1	2	(0	2)	30	9	9	4	8	0	55	2	0	0	4	1	1	.133	.193	.222	.415
19	Bos	AL	26	45	7	2	0	1	(0	1)	12	4	5	3	6	0	23	0	0	0	1	1	1	.156	.255	.267	.522
	7 ML YEARS		647	2140	515	117	24	34	(20	14)	782	238	210	226	123	12	548	13	13	13	75	15	30	.241	.284	.365	.650

Marcell Ozuna

Bats: R **Throws:** R **Pos:** LF-129;PH-1   oh-ZUNE-uh   **Ht:** 6'1" **Wt:** 225 **Born:** 11/12/1990 **Age:** 29

						BATTING																RUNNING			AVERAGES			
Year	Team	Lg	G	AB	H	2B	3B	HR	(Hm	Rd)	TB	R	RBI	RC	TBB	IBB	SO	HBP	SH	SF	SB	CS	GDP	Avg	OBP	Slg	OPS
2013	Mia	NL	70	275	73	17	4	3	(0	3)	107	31	32	35	13	0	57	2	1	0	5	1	6	.265	.303	.389	.693
2014	Mia	NL	153	565	152	26	5	23	(12	11)	257	72	85	74	41	1	164	1	0	5	3	1	12	.269	.317	.455	.772
2015	Mia	NL	123	459	119	27	0	10	(2	8)	176	47	44	48	30	1	110	3	0	2	2	3	10	.259	.308	.383	.691
2016	Mia	NL	148	557	148	23	6	23	(17	6)	252	75	76	69	43	2	115	4	0	4	0	3	11	.266	.321	.452	.773
2017	Mia	NL	159	613	191	30	2	37	(22	15)	336	93	124	117	64	4	144	0	0	2	1	3	18	.312	.376	.548	.924
2018	StL	NL	148	582	163	16	2	23	(13	10)	252	69	88	86	38	2	110	3	0	4	3	0	10	.280	.325	.433	.758
2019	StL	NL	130	485	117	23	1	29	(13	16)	229	80	89	73	62	2	114	1	0	1	12	2	21	.241	.328	.472	.800
	7 ML YEARS		931	3536	963	162	20	148	(74	74)	1609	467	538	502	291	12	814	14	1	18	26	13	88	.272	.329	.455	.784

Cristian Pache

Bats: R **Throws:** R **Pos:** CF   PAH-chay   **Ht:** 6'2" **Wt:** 185 **Born:** 11/19/1998 **Age:** 21

						BATTING																RUNNING			AVERAGES			
Year	Team	Lg	G	AB	H	2B	3B	HR	(Hm	Rd)	TB	R	RBI	RC	TBB	IBB	SO	HBP	SH	SF	SB	CS	GDP	Avg	OBP	Slg	OPS
2016	2 Tms	Low	57	220	68	4	7	0	(-	-)	86	28	21	30	13	0	24	1	1	1	11	5	5	.309	.349	.391	.740
2017	Rome	A	119	469	132	13	8	0	(-	-)	161	60	42	57	39	1	104	0	4	2	32	14	6	.281	.335	.343	.679
2018	Florida	A+	93	369	105	20	5	8	(-	-)	159	46	40	49	15	2	69	0	0	2	7	6	5	.285	.311	.431	.742
2018	Missi	AA	29	104	27	3	1	1	(-	-)	35	10	7	9	5	0	28	0	0	0	2	1	1	.260	.294	.337	.630
2019	Missi	AA	104	392	109	28	8	11	(-	-)	186	50	53	61	34	1	104	4	1	2	8	11	7	.278	.340	.474	.815
2019	Gwnntt	AAA	26	95	26	8	1	1	(-	-)	39	13	8	13	9	0	18	1	0	0	0	0	3	.274	.337	.411	.747

Chris Paddack

Pitches: R **Bats:** R **Pos:** SP-26   **Ht:** 6'4" **Wt:** 195 **Born:** 1/8/1996 **Age:** 24

			HOW MUCH PITCHED				WHAT HE GAVE UP											THE RESULTS								
Year	Team	Lg	G	GS	GF	IP	BFP	H	R	ER	HR	SH	SF	HB	TBB	IBB	SO	WP	W	L	Pct	Sv-Op	Hld	Vel	OPS	ERC	ERA
2015	Mrlns	R	11	7	0	45.1	180	37	14	11	1	2	1	1	7	0	39	3	4	3	.571	0--	-	-	.525	1.83	2.18
2016	2 Tms	Low	9	9	0	42.1	153	20	4	4	2	1	0	3	5	0	71	0	2	0	1.000	0--	-	-	.393	0.93	0.85
2018	Lk Els	A+	10	10	0	52.1	203	43	13	13	3	1	0	4	4	0	83	0	4	1	.800	0--	-	-	.575	2.03	2.24
2018	SnAnt	AA	7	7	0	37.2	137	23	8	8	1	0	0	2	4	1	37	2	3	2	.600	0--	-	-	.490	1.17	1.91
2019	SD	NL	26	26	0	140.2	568	107	58	52	23	4	3	6	31	1	153	1	9	7	.563	0-0	0	94	.635	2.62	3.33

Emilio Pagan

Pitches: R **Bats:** L **Pos:** RP-66   **Ht:** 6'3" **Wt:** 205 **Born:** 5/7/1991 **Age:** 29

			HOW MUCH PITCHED				WHAT HE GAVE UP											THE RESULTS								
Year	Team	Lg	G	GS	GF	IP	BFP	H	R	ER	HR	SH	SF	HB	TBB	IBB	SO	WP	W	L	Pct	Sv-Op	Hld	Vel	OPS	ERC	ERA
2017	Sea	AL	34	0	9	50.1	196	39	20	18	7	1	2	1	8	0	56	1	2	3	.400	0-1	8	94	.610	2.32	3.22
2018	Oak	AL	55	0	17	62.0	262	55	30	30	13	0	1	3	19	1	63	5	3	1	.750	0-0	6	94	.767	3.92	4.35
2019	TB	AL	66	0	29	70.0	267	45	19	18	12	0	1	1	13	1	96	3	4	2	.667	20-28	7	96	.590	1.91	2.31
	3 ML YEARS		155	0	55	182.1	725	139	69	66	32	1	4	5	40	2	215	7	9	6	.600	20-29	21	94	.659	2.67	3.26

Daniel Palka

Bats: L **Throws:** L **Pos:** RF-23;PH-7;DH-3;1B-1;PR-1   **Ht:** 6'2" **Wt:** 220 **Born:** 10/28/1991 **Age:** 28

Year Team	Lg	G	AB	H	2B	3B	HR	(Hm	Rd)	TB	R	RBI	RC	TBB	IBB	SO	HBP	SH	SF	SB	CS	GDP	Avg	OBP	Slg	OPS
2019 Charllt	AAA	106	395	104	23	0	27	(-	-)	208	83	72	80	72	4	109	0	0	4	2	0	8	.263	.374	.527	.900
2018 CWS	AL	124	417	100	15	3	27	(11	16)	202	56	67	54	30	3	153	2	0	0	2	1	7	.240	.294	.484	.778
2019 CWS	AL	30	84	9	0	0	2	(2	0)	15	4	4	0	8	0	35	1	0	0	0	1	3	.107	.194	.179	.372
2 ML YEARS		154	501	109	15	3	29	(13	16)	217	60	71	54	38	3	188	3	0	0	2	2	10	.218	.277	.433	.710

Joseph Palumbo

Pitches: L **Bats:** L **Pos:** SP-4; RP-3   **Ht:** 6'1" **Wt:** 168 **Born:** 10/26/1994 **Age:** 25

Year Team	Lg	G	GS	GF	IP	BFP	H	R	ER	HR	SH	SF	HB	TBB	IBB	SO	WP	W	L	Pct	Sv-Op Hld	Vel	OPS	ERC	ERA
2019 Frisco	AA	11	10	0	53.2	224	43	21	19	5	1	1	2	25	0	69	0	0	0	-	0-- -	-	.704	3.39	3.19
2019 Nashv	AAA	6	6	0	27.0	102	13	9	8	4	0	0	1	10	0	39	1	3	0	1.000	0-- -	-	.554	1.83	2.67
2019 Tex	AL	7	4	0	16.2	81	21	17	17	7	1	0	2	8	0	21	0	0	3	.000	0-0 0	94	1.073	8.98	9.18

Joe Panik

Bats: L **Throws:** R **Pos:** 2B-118;PH-28   PAN-ick   **Ht:** 6'1" **Wt:** 200 **Born:** 10/30/1990 **Age:** 29

Year Team	Lg	G	AB	H	2B	3B	HR	(Hm	Rd)	TB	R	RBI	RC	TBB	IBB	SO	HBP	SH	SF	SB	CS	GDP	Avg	OBP	Slg	OPS
2014 SF	NL	73	269	82	10	2	1	(0	1)	99	31	18	33	16	0	33	0	1	1	0	0	4	.305	.343	.368	.711
2015 SF	NL	100	382	119	27	2	8	(4	4)	174	59	37	60	38	0	42	5	3	2	3	2	7	.312	.378	.455	.833
2016 SF	NL	127	464	111	21	7	10	(3	7)	176	67	62	56	50	5	47	4	3	5	5	0	14	.239	.315	.379	.695
2017 SF	NL	138	511	147	28	5	10	(0	10)	215	60	53	73	46	4	54	5	3	8	4	1	10	.288	.347	.421	.768
2018 SF	NL	102	358	91	14	1	4	(1	3)	119	38	24	31	26	3	30	3	1	4	2	2	10	.254	.307	.332	.639
2019 2 Tms	NL	142	438	107	21	2	5	(1	4)	147	50	39	51	43	2	47	4	2	4	4	2	6	.244	.315	.336	.651
19 SF	NL	103	344	81	17	1	3	(0	3)	109	33	27	37	36	2	38	3	1	4	4	2	5	.235	.310	.317	.627
19 NYM	NL	39	94	26	4	1	2	(1	1)	38	17	12	14	7	0	9	1	1	0	0	0	1	.277	.333	.404	.738
Postseason		21	86	23	4	2	1	(1	0)	34	10	10	11	7	0	10	0	1	1	0	0	1	.267	.319	.395	.714
6 ML YEARS		682	2422	657	121	19	38	(9	29)	930	305	233	304	219	14	253	21	13	26	20	7	51	.271	.334	.384	.718

Thomas Pannone

Pitches: L **Bats:** L **Pos:** RP-30; SP-7   **Ht:** 6'0" **Wt:** 200 **Born:** 4/28/1994 **Age:** 26

Year Team	Lg	G	GS	GF	IP	BFP	H	R	ER	HR	SH	SF	HB	TBB	IBB	SO	WP	W	L	Pct	Sv-Op Hld	Vel	OPS	ERC	ERA
2019 Buffalo	AAA	8	6	0	33.2	142	25	12	12	4	0	2	2	15	0	41	0	3	1	.750	0-- -	-	.653	3.17	3.21
2018 Tor	AL	12	6	2	43.0	181	37	20	20	7	1	3	2	15	0	29	0	4	1	.800	0-0 0	88	.719	3.68	4.19
2019 Tor	AL	37	7	8	73.0	325	73	51	50	13	0	2	6	31	1	69	6	3	6	.333	0-0 1	90	.793	5.01	6.16
2 ML YEARS		49	13	10	116.0	506	110	71	70	20	1	5	8	46	1	98	6	7	7	.500	0-0 1	89	.766	4.50	5.43

Blake Parker

Pitches: R **Bats:** R **Pos:** RP-58; SP-2   **Ht:** 6'3" **Wt:** 225 **Born:** 6/19/1985 **Age:** 35

Year Team	Lg	G	GS	GF	IP	BFP	H	R	ER	HR	SH	SF	HB	TBB	IBB	SO	WP	W	L	Pct	Sv-Op Hld	Vel	OPS	ERC	ERA
2012 ChC	NL	7	0	0	6.0	32	10	7	4	3	0	0	0	5	1	6	0	0	0	-	0-0 0	92	1.172	14.02	6.00
2013 ChC	NL	49	0	18	46.1	195	39	17	14	4	0	1	2	15	1	55	2	1	2	.333	1-1 7	92	.626	2.91	2.72
2014 ChC	NL	18	0	10	21.0	91	24	13	12	3	0	1	0	4	0	24	1	1	1	.500	0-0 1	91	.784	4.24	5.14
2016 2 Tms	AL	17	0	5	17.1	79	17	9	9	1	0	0	2	9	1	15	0	1	0	1.000	1-1 0	92	.707	4.41	4.67
2017 LAA	AL	71	0	17	67.1	254	40	20	19	7	1	4	1	16	0	86	4	3	3	.500	8-11 15	94	.527	1.60	2.54
2018 LAA	AL	67	0	41	66.1	276	63	24	24	12	0	1	3	19	1	70	8	2	1	.667	14-17 6	92	.751	4.10	3.26
2019 2 Tms		60	2	21	61.1	255	53	32	31	13	2	2	3	22	0	65	4	3	3	.500	10-11 13	91	.746	4.15	4.55
16 Sea	AL	1	0	0	1.0	5	1	0	0	0	0	0	0	1	0	0	0	0	0	-	0-0 0	93	.650	5.48	0.00
16 NYY	AL	16	0	5	16.1	74	16	9	9	1	0	0	2	8	1	15	0	1	0	1.000	1-1 0	92	.711	4.35	4.96
19 Min	AL	37	0	19	36.1	157	34	18	17	7	0	1	2	16	0	34	4	1	2	.333	10-11 9	92	.773	4.79	4.21
19 Phi	NL	23	2	2	25.0	98	19	14	14	6	2	1	1	6	0	31	0	2	1	.667	0-0 4	91	.703	3.24	5.04
7 ML YEARS		289	2	112	285.2	1182	246	122	113	43	3	9	11	90	4	321	19	11	10	.524	34-41 42	92	.692	3.46	3.56

Jarrett Parker

Bats: L **Throws:** L **Pos:** LF-5   **Ht:** 6'4" **Wt:** 225 **Born:** 1/1/1989 **Age:** 31

Year Team	Lg	G	AB	H	2B	3B	HR	(Hm	Rd)	TB	R	RBI	RC	TBB	IBB	SO	HBP	SH	SF	SB	CS	GDP	Avg	OBP	Slg	OPS
2019 Salt Lk	AAA	96	346	92	19	1	24	(-	-)	185	71	76	75	72	4	125	3	0	3	2	1	8	.266	.394	.535	.929
2015 SF	NL	21	49	17	2	0	6	(1	5)	37	11	14	12	5	0	21	0	0	0	1	1	1	.347	.407	.755	1.163
2016 SF	NL	63	127	30	3	1	5	(3	2)	50	22	14	17	19	1	44	5	0	0	1	3	3	.236	.358	.394	.751
2017 SF	NL	51	166	41	12	2	4	(2	2)	69	14	23	22	10	2	54	1	0	2	2	1	2	.247	.294	.416	.709
2019 LAA	AL	5	12	0	0	0	0	(0	0)	0	1	0	0	3	0	8	0	0	0	0	0	0	.000	.200	.000	.200
4 ML YEARS		140	354	88	17	3	15	(6	9)	156	48	51	51	37	3	127	6	0	0	3	3	6	.249	.330	.441	.771

Gerardo Parra

heh-RAHR-doh PAR-uh

Bats: L **Throws:** L **Pos:** PH-52;RF-34;LF-24;1B-14;CF-12;2B-1;3B-1;PR-1 **Ht:** 5'11" **Wt:** 210 **Born:** 5/6/1987 **Age:** 33

Year	Team	Lg	G	AB	H	2B	3B	HR	(Hm	Rd)	TB	R	RBI	RC	TBB	IBB	SO	HBP	SH	SF	SB	CS	GDP	Avg	OBP	Slg	OPS
2009	Ari	NL	120	455	132	21	8	5	(4	1)	184	59	60	58	25	1	89	1	4	6	5	7	18	.290	.324	.404	.729
2010	Ari	NL	133	364	95	19	6	3	(1	2)	135	31	30	38	23	10	76	2	3	1	1	0	8	.261	.308	.371	.679
2011	Ari	NL	141	445	130	20	8	8	(3	5)	190	55	46	71	43	16	82	3	0	2	15	1	8	.292	.357	.427	.784
2012	Ari	NL	133	385	105	21	2	7	(5	2)	151	58	36	50	33	4	77	4	6	2	15	9	4	.273	.335	.392	.727
2013	Ari	NL	156	601	161	43	4	10	(6	4)	242	79	48	69	48	3	100	3	7	4	10	10	12	.268	.323	.403	.726
2014	2 Tms		150	529	138	22	4	9	(3	6)	195	64	40	46	32	5	100	5	6	2	9	7	10	.261	.308	.369	.677
2015	2 Tms		155	547	159	36	5	14	(8	6)	247	83	51	71	28	3	92	5	4	5	14	4	8	.291	.328	.452	.780
2016	Col	NL	102	368	93	27	3	7	(5	2)	147	45	39	29	9	1	73	1	1	2	6	4	16	.253	.271	.399	.671
2017	Col	NL	115	392	121	24	1	10	(6	4)	177	56	71	56	20	0	67	4	0	9	2	5	13	.309	.341	.452	.793
2018	Col	NL	142	401	114	17	0	6	(3	3)	149	52	53	57	32	3	75	5	2	3	11	4	6	.284	.342	.372	.714
2019	2 Tms		119	274	64	14	1	9	(4	5)	107	38	48	38	19	3	59	5	1	2	8	3	7	.234	.293	.391	.684
14	Ari	NL	104	406	105	18	3	6	(2	4)	147	51	30	37	24	3	72	4	4	2	5	5	6	.259	.305	.362	.667
14	Mil	NL	46	123	33	4	1	3	(1	2)	48	13	10	9	8	2	28	1	2	0	4	2	4	.268	.318	.390	.708
15	Mil	NL	100	323	106	24	5	9	(4	5)	167	53	31	47	20	2	57	3	1	4	9	3	7	.328	.369	.517	.886
15	Bal	NL	55	224	53	12	0	5	(4	1)	80	30	20	24	8	1	35	2	3	1	5	1	1	.237	.268	.357	.625
19	SF	NL	30	86	17	3	0	1	(0	1)	23	8	6	7	8	2	18	2	0	1	2	1	0	.198	.278	.267	.546
19	Was	NL	89	188	47	11	1	8	(4	4)	84	30	42	31	11	1	41	3	1	1	6	2	7	.250	.300	.447	.747
	Postseason		9	30	7	1	0	0	(0	0)	8	3	1	2	2	0	8	0	0	0	0	0	0	.233	.281	.267	.548
11 ML YEARS			1466	4761	1312	264	42	88	(48	40)	1924	620	522	583	312	49	890	38	34	38	96	54	110	.276	.323	.404	.727

Wes Parsons

Pitches: R **Bats:** R **Pos:** RP-32 **Ht:** 6'5" **Wt:** 204 **Born:** 9/6/1992 **Age:** 27

Year	Team	Lg	G	GS	GF	IP	BFP	H	R	ER	HR	SH	SF	HB	TBB	IBB	SO	WP	W	L	Pct	Sv-Op	Hld	Vel	OPS	ERC	ERA
2019	Gwnntt	AAA	27	0	12	56.2	240	58	24	18	1	2	2	4	21	0	54	3	2	3	.400	4--	-	-	.698	3.90	2.86
2018	Atl	NL	1	0	0	5.0	23	6	4	4	1	0	1	0	3	1	3	0	0	1	.000	0-0	0	91	.918	6.67	7.20
2019	2 Tms		32	0	5	34.2	157	32	24	21	6	2	3	2	29	2	26	2	1	2	.333	0-0	2	93	.861	6.38	5.45
19	Atl	NL	17	0	3	15.1	64	11	7	6	2	0	2	1	13	0	12	0	1	2	.333	0-0	1	93	.745	5.17	3.52
19	Col	NL	15	0	2	19.1	93	21	17	15	4	2	1	1	16	2	14	2	0	0	-	0-0	1	94	.938	7.36	6.98
2 ML YEARS			33	0	5	39.2	180	38	28	25	7	2	4	2	32	3	29	2	1	3	.250	0-0	2	93	.869	6.42	5.67

James Paxton

Pitches: L **Bats:** L **Pos:** SP-29 **Ht:** 6'4" **Wt:** 235 **Born:** 11/6/1988 **Age:** 31

Year	Team	Lg	G	GS	GF	IP	BFP	H	R	ER	HR	SH	SF	HB	TBB	IBB	SO	WP	W	L	Pct	Sv-Op	Hld	Vel	OPS	ERC	ERA
2013	Sea	AL	4	4	0	24.0	94	15	5	4	2	0	0	0	7	2	21	0	3	0	1.000	0-0	0	95	.533	1.61	1.50
2014	Sea	AL	13	13	0	74.0	303	60	29	25	3	3	1	1	29	2	59	7	6	4	.600	0-0	0	95	.612	2.69	3.04
2015	Sea	AL	13	13	0	67.0	297	67	34	29	8	0	3	0	29	1	56	5	3	4	.429	0-0	0	94	.704	4.22	3.90
2016	Sea	AL	20	20	0	121.0	511	134	62	51	9	0	6	1	24	3	117	5	6	7	.462	0-0	0	97	.717	3.70	3.79
2017	Sea	AL	24	24	0	136.0	552	113	47	45	9	1	5	3	37	1	156	15	12	5	.706	0-0	0	95	.602	2.56	2.98
2018	Sea	AL	28	28	0	160.1	645	134	67	67	23	2	2	1	42	0	208	8	11	6	.647	0-0	0	95	.662	2.98	3.76
2019	NYY	AL	29	29	0	150.2	633	138	71	64	23	2	4	2	55	0	186	7	15	6	.714	0-0	0	95	.732	3.90	3.82
7 ML YEARS			131	131	0	733.0	3035	661	315	285	77	8	21	8	223	9	803	47	56	32	.636	0-0	0	95	.670	3.23	3.50

Joel Payamps

Pitches: R **Bats:** R **Pos:** RP-2 **Ht:** 6'2" **Wt:** 200 **Born:** 4/7/1994 **Age:** 26

Year	Team	Lg	G	GS	GF	IP	BFP	H	R	ER	HR	SH	SF	HB	TBB	IBB	SO	WP	W	L	Pct	Sv-Op	Hld	Vel	OPS	ERC	ERA
2019	Reno	AAA	8	8	0	38.0	167	41	22	21	6	2	1	1	16	0	30	2	2	2	.500	0--	-	-	.828	5.20	4.97
2019	Jacksn	AA	7	7	0	40.2	160	40	17	13	2	0	1	0	2	0	39	2	3	4	.429	0--	-	-	.606	2.38	2.88
2019	Ari	NL	2	0	1	4.0	17	4	2	2	0	1	0	0	3	0	3	0	0	0	-	0-0	0	93	.745	5.14	4.50

Pedro Payano

Pitches: R **Bats:** R **Pos:** SP-4; RP-2 **Ht:** 6'2" **Wt:** 170 **Born:** 9/27/1994 **Age:** 25

Year	Team	Lg	G	GS	GF	IP	BFP	H	R	ER	HR	SH	SF	HB	TBB	IBB	SO	WP	W	L	Pct	Sv-Op	Hld	Vel	OPS	ERC	ERA
2019	Frisco	AA	8	8	0	42.2	173	30	21	21	3	0	1	3	18	0	49	6	3	1	.750	0--	-	-	.619	2.71	4.43
2019	Nashv	AAA	11	10	0	41.1	198	42	33	25	8	1	1	6	28	0	44	3	2	3	.400	0--	-	-	.886	6.59	5.44
2019	Tex	AL	6	4	0	22.0	103	26	17	14	3	1	0	1	15	0	17	1	1	2	.333	0-0	0	94	.900	7.00	5.73

James Pazos

pah-ZOHSS

Pitches: L **Bats:** R **Pos:** RP-12 **Ht:** 6'2" **Wt:** 235 **Born:** 5/5/1991 **Age:** 29

Year	Team	Lg	G	GS	GF	IP	BFP	H	R	ER	HR	SH	SF	HB	TBB	IBB	SO	WP	W	L	Pct	Sv-Op	Hld	Vel	OPS	ERC	ERA
2019	LV	AAA	7	0	3	7.1	38	8	6	5	0	0	0	1	7	2	4	1	0	1	.000	2--	-	-	.754	5.79	6.14
2019	Albq	AAA	39	0	11	44.0	219	69	45	43	8	1	2	2	23	2	42	2	1	3	.250	1--	-	-	.997	9.05	8.80
2015	NYY	AL	11	0	1	5.0	21	3	0	0	0	1	0	0	3	0	3	1	0	0	-	0-0	0	94	.476	2.03	0.00
2016	NYY	AL	7	0	1	3.1	17	7	5	5	2	0	0	0	1	0	3	0	1	0	1.000	0-0	0	95	1.408	16.29	13.50

Year	Team	Lg	G	GS	GF	IP	BFP	H	R	ER	HR	SH	SF	HB	TBB	IBB	SO	WP	W	L	Pct	Sv-Op	Hld	Vel	OPS	ERC	ERA
2017	Sea	AL	59	0	7	53.2	240	51	30	23	7	1	4	5	24	0	65	4	4	5	.444	0-3	10	96	.723	4.49	3.86
2018	Sea	AL	60	0	4	50.0	211	47	19	16	4	0	2	5	15	1	45	2	4	1	.800	0-2	19	94	.683	3.61	2.88
2019	Col	NL	12	0	0	10.1	39	7	2	2	1	0	0	0	4	1	10	0	0	0	-	0-0	3	94	.596	2.37	1.74
5 ML YEARS			149	0	13	122.1	528	115	56	46	14	2	6	10	47	2	126	7	9	6	.600	0-5	32	95	.711	4.08	3.38

Brad Peacock

Pitches: R **Bats:** R **Pos:** SP-15; RP-8   **Ht:** 6'1" **Wt:** 210 **Born:** 2/2/1988 **Age:** 32

Year	Team	Lg	G	GS	GF	IP	BFP	H	R	ER	HR	SH	SF	HB	TBB	IBB	SO	WP	W	L	Pct	Sv-Op	Hld	Vel	OPS	ERC	ERA
2019	RdRck	AAA	5	1	0	3.2	24	6	9	9	1	0	0	0	7	0	4	0	0	0	-	0- -	-		1.248	16.81	22.09
2011	Was	NL	3	2	0	12.0	48	7	1	1	0	0	0	0	6	0	4	1	2	0	1.000	0-1	-	93	.437	1.71	0.75
2013	Hou	AL	18	14	1	83.1	365	78	51	48	15	1	1	3	37	0	77	4	5	6	.455	0-0	2	93	.779	4.54	5.18
2014	Hou	AL	28	24	3	131.2	589	136	80	69	20	0	6	4	70	4	119	6	4	9	.308	0-0	1	92	.801	5.29	4.72
2015	Hou	AL	1	1	0	5.0	22	5	3	3	0	0	1	1	2	0	3	0	0	1	.000	0-0	0	90	.808	4.20	5.40
2016	Hou	AL	10	5	3	31.2	127	21	15	13	6	0	0	0	14	0	28	2	0	1	.000	0-0	0	92	.700	3.04	3.69
2017	Hou	AL	34	21	7	132.0	546	100	46	44	10	1	0	3	57	0	161	6	13	2	**.867**	0-0	0	92	.615	2.83	3.00
2018	Hou	AL	61	1	20	65.0	272	56	26	25	11	0	1	3	20	0	96	5	3	5	.375	3-6	10	93	.722	3.55	3.46
2019	Hou	AL	23	15	1	91.2	383	78	43	42	15	0	3	5	31	0	96	1	7	6	.538	0-0	0	92	.725	3.65	4.12
Postseason			7	1	1	12.1	55	13	7	7	2	0	0	1	4	0	16	1	0	0	-	1-1	1	93	.827	4.74	5.11
8 ML YEARS			178	83	35	552.1	2352	481	265	245	77	2	12	19	237	4	584	25	34	30	.531	3-7	13	92	.720	3.86	3.99

Steve Pearce

Bats: R **Throws:** R **Pos:** 1B-19;DH-5;LF-4;PH-4   **Ht:** 5'11" **Wt:** 200 **Born:** 4/13/1983 **Age:** 37

Year	Team	Lg	G	AB	H	2B	3B	HR	(Hm	Rd)	TB	R	RBI	RC	TBB	IBB	SO	HBP	SH	SF	SB	CS	GDP	Avg	OBP	Slg	OPS
2007	Pit	NL	23	68	20	5	1	0	(0	0)	27	13	6	9	5	0	12	0	0	0	2	1	2	.294	.342	.397	.740
2008	Pit	NL	37	109	27	7	0	4	(0	4)	46	6	15	13	5	0	22	3	0	2	2	0	1	.248	.294	.422	.716
2009	Pit	NL	60	165	34	13	1	4	(3	1)	61	19	16	17	21	0	43	0	0	2	1	0	2	.206	.296	.370	.665
2010	Pit	NL	15	29	8	2	1	0	(0	0)	12	4	5	5	7	0	6	0	0	2	0	0	0	.276	.395	.414	.809
2011	Pit	NL	50	94	19	2	0	1	(1	0)	24	8	10	5	7	1	21	1	1	2	0	0	6	.202	.260	.255	.515
2012	3 Tms		61	159	38	8	1	4	(2	2)	60	16	26	24	20	1	41	3	2	4	1	2	4	.239	.328	.377	.705
2013	Bal	AL	44	119	31	7	0	4	(3	1)	50	14	13	20	15	2	25	4	0	1	0	0	3	.261	.362	.420	.782
2014	Bal	AL	102	338	99	26	0	21	(12	9)	188	51	49	66	40	1	76	4	0	1	5	0	4	.293	.373	.556	.930
2015	Bal	AL	92	294	64	13	1	15	(7	8)	124	42	40	33	23	1	69	7	0	1	1	1	11	.218	.289	.422	.711
2016	2 Tms	AL	85	264	76	13	1	13	(6	7)	130	35	35	43	34	2	54	3	0	1	0	3	5	.288	.374	.492	.867
2017	Tor	AL	92	313	79	17	1	13	(6	7)	137	38	37	39	27	1	68	5	0	3	0	0	11	.252	.319	.438	.757
2018	2 Tms	AL	76	215	61	14	1	11	(6	5)	110	35	42	49	29	0	41	5	0	2	0	0	2	.284	.378	.512	.890
2019	Bos	AL	29	89	16	4	0	1	(0	1)	23	9	9	3	7	0	31	1	0	0	0	0	5	.180	.245	.258	.503
12	Bal	AL	28	71	18	4	0	3	(2	1)	31	8	14	12	8	0	17	0	2	2	0	1	1	.254	.321	.437	.758
12	Hou	AL	21	63	16	4	1	0	(0	0)	22	2	8	9	7	1	16	3	0	2	1	1	3	.254	.347	.349	.696
12	NYY	AL	12	25	4	0	0	1	(0	1)	7	6	4	3	5	0	8	0	0	0	0	0	0	.160	.300	.280	.580
16	TB	AL	60	204	63	11	1	10	(4	6)	106	26	29	37	26	2	40	1	0	1	0	3	4	.309	.388	.520	.908
16	Bal	AL	25	60	13	2	0	3	(2	1)	24	9	6	6	8	0	14	2	0	0	0	0	1	.217	.329	.400	.729
18	Tor	AL	26	79	23	6	0	4	(0	4)	41	16	16	19	7	0	14	0	0	0	0	0	0	.291	.349	.519	.868
18	Bos	AL	50	136	38	8	1	7	(6	1)	69	19	26	30	22	0	27	5	0	2	0	0	1	.279	.394	.507	.901
Postseason			20	65	15	3	0	4	(0	4)	30	16	12	12	11	0	11	1	0	0	0	0	0	.231	.351	.462	.812
13 ML YEARS			766	2256	572	131	8	91	(46	45)	992	290	303	326	240	8	509	36	3	19	13	7	53	.254	.332	.440	.772

Nate Pearson

Pitches: R **Bats:** R **Pos:** P   **Ht:** 6'6" **Wt:** 245 **Born:** 8/20/1996 **Age:** 23

Year	Team	Lg	G	GS	GF	IP	BFP	H	R	ER	HR	SH	SF	HB	TBB	IBB	SO	WP	W	L	Pct	Sv-Op	Hld	Vel	OPS	ERC	ERA
2017	2 Tms	Low	8	8	0	20.0	71	7	2	2	0	0	0	0	5	0	26	2	0	0	-	0- -	-	-	.305	0.61	0.90
2019	Dnedin	A+	6	6	0	21.0	75	10	2	2	2	0	0	0	3	0	35	0	3	0	1.000	0- -	-	-	.409	0.99	0.86
2019	Nham	AA	16	16	0	62.2	244	41	18	18	4	0	0	2	21	0	69	6	1	4	.200	0- -	-	-	.538	2.02	2.59

Joc Pederson

Bats: L **Throws:** L **Pos:** LF-84;RF-39;PH-32;1B-20;CF-2;DH-2;PR-1   JOCK   **Ht:** 6'1" **Wt:** 220 **Born:** 4/21/1992 **Age:** 28

Year	Team	Lg	G	AB	H	2B	3B	HR	(Hm	Rd)	TB	R	RBI	RC	TBB	IBB	SO	HBP	SH	SF	SB	CS	GDP	Avg	OBP	Slg	OPS
2014	LAD	NL	18	28	4	0	0	0	(0	0)	4	1	0	1	9	0	11	0	1	0	0	0	1	.143	.351	.143	.494
2015	LAD	NL	151	480	101	19	1	26	(13	13)	200	67	54	62	92	6	170	9	2	5	4	7	5	.210	.346	.417	.763
2016	LAD	NL	137	406	100	26	0	25	(13	12)	201	64	68	71	63	4	130	4	1	2	6	2	5	.246	.352	.495	.847
2017	LAD	NL	102	273	58	20	0	11	(8	3)	111	44	35	35	39	1	68	10	0	1	4	3	7	.212	.331	.407	.738
2018	LAD	NL	148	395	98	27	3	25	(13	12)	206	65	56	55	40	3	85	4	1	3	1	5	6	.248	.321	.522	.843
2019	LAD	NL	149	450	112	16	3	36	(24	12)	242	83	74	82	50	2	111	12	0	2	1	1	4	.249	.339	.538	.876
Postseason			43	102	24	6	0	6	(4	2)	48	18	11	14	10	2	38	3	1	0	2	0	1	.235	.322	.471	.792
6 ML YEARS			705	2032	473	108	7	123	(71	52)	964	324	287	306	293	16	575	39	5	10	16	18	28	.233	.339	.474	.813

Dustin Pedroia

Bats: R **Throws:** R **Pos:** 2B-4;DH-2   peh-DROY-uh   **Ht:** 5'9" **Wt:** 175 **Born:** 8/17/1983 **Age:** 36

Year	Team	Lg	G	AB	H	2B	3B	HR	(Hm	Rd)	TB	R	RBI	RC	TBB	IBB	SO	HBP	SH	SF	SB	CS	GDP	Avg	OBP	Slg	OPS
2006	Bos	AL	31	89	17	4	0	2	(1	1)	27	5	7	3	7	0	7	1	1	0	0	1	1	.191	.258	.303	.561
2007	Bos	AL	139	520	165	39	1	8	(5	3)	230	86	50	79	47	1	42	7	5	2	7	1	8	.317	.380	.442	.823
2008	Bos	AL	157	653	213	54	2	17	(7	10)	322	118	83	107	50	1	52	7	7	9	20	1	17	.326	.376	.493	.869
2009	Bos	AL	154	626	185	48	1	15	(10	5)	280	115	72	104	74	3	45	5	3	6	20	8	19	.296	.371	.447	.819
2010	Bos	AL	75	302	87	24	1	12	(4	8)	149	53	41	52	37	1	38	4	2	6	9	1	7	.288	.367	.493	.860
2011	Bos	AL	159	635	195	37	3	21	(13	8)	301	102	91	114	86	6	85	1	2	7	26	8	12	.307	.387	.474	.861
2012	Bos	AL	141	563	163	39	3	15	(9	6)	253	81	65	84	48	3	60	5	1	6	20	6	9	.290	.347	.449	.797
2013	Bos	AL	160	641	193	42	2	9	(7	2)	266	91	84	99	73	4	75	3	0	7	17	5	24	.301	.372	.415	.787
2014	Bos	AL	135	551	153	33	0	7	(2	5)	207	72	53	65	51	1	75	1	0	6	6	6	13	.278	.337	.376	.712
2015	Bos	AL	93	381	111	19	1	12	(7	5)	168	46	42	55	38	1	51	2	1	3	2	2	6	.291	.356	.441	.797
2016	Bos	AL	154	633	201	36	1	15	(7	8)	284	105	74	100	61	0	73	0	1	3	7	4	20	.318	.376	.449	.825
2017	Bos	AL	105	406	119	19	0	7	(4	3)	159	46	62	65	49	4	48	2	2	4	4	3	11	.293	.369	.392	.760
2018	Bos	AL	3	11	1	0	0	0	(0	0)	1	1	0	0	2	0	1	0	0	0	0	0	0	.091	.231	.091	.322
2019	Bos	AL	6	20	2	0	0	0	(0	0)	2	1	1	0	1	0	2	0	0	0	0	0	0	.100	.143	.100	.243
	Postseason		51	206	48	14	0	5	(2	3)	77	32	25	23	23	0	32	2	1	2	3	1	4	.233	.313	.374	.687
	14 ML YEARS		1512	6031	1805	394	15	140	(73	67)	2649	922	725	927	624	25	654	38	25	59	138	46	154	.299	.365	.439	.805

Felix Pena

Pitches: R **Bats:** R **Pos:** RP-15; SP-7   **Ht:** 6'2" **Wt:** 220 **Born:** 2/25/1990 **Age:** 30

			HOW MUCH PITCHED					WHAT HE GAVE UP										THE RESULTS							
Year	Team	Lg	G	GS	GF	IP	BFP	H	R	ER	HR	SH	SF	HB	TBB	IBB	SO	WP	W	L	Pct	Sv-Op	Hld	Vel	OPS	ERC	ERA
2016	ChC	NL	11	0	2	9.0	35	5	4	4	1	0	0	0	3	1	13	1	0	0	-	1-1	2	93	.479	1.57	4.00
2017	ChC	NL	25	0	15	34.1	155	35	21	20	8	0	0	2	18	1	37	3	1	0	1.000	0-0	1	94	.866	5.88	5.24
2018	LAA	AL	19	17	1	92.2	389	87	45	43	12	1	4	4	28	0	85	7	3	5	.375	0-0	0	92	.699	3.73	4.18
2019	LAA	AL	22	7	1	96.1	407	80	56	49	16	0	1	6	34	0	101	8	8	3	.727	0-0	1	92	.696	3.60	4.58
	4 ML YEARS		77	24	19	232.1	986	207	126	116	37	1	5	12	83	2	236	19	12	8	.600	1-1	4	92	.716	3.87	4.49

Hunter Pence

Bats: R **Throws:** R **Pos:** DH-46;LF-16;PH-14;RF-8   **Ht:** 6'4" **Wt:** 230 **Born:** 4/13/1983 **Age:** 37

Year	Team	Lg	G	AB	H	2B	3B	HR	(Hm	Rd)	TB	R	RBI	RC	TBB	IBB	SO	HBP	SH	SF	SB	CS	GDP	Avg	OBP	Slg	OPS
2007	Hou	NL	108	456	147	30	9	17	(7	10)	246	57	69	77	26	0	95	1	0	1	11	5	10	.322	.360	.539	.899
2008	Hou	NL	157	595	160	34	4	25	(14	11)	277	78	83	82	40	2	124	4	0	3	11	10	14	.269	.318	.466	.783
2009	Hou	NL	159	585	165	26	5	25	(14	11)	276	76	72	80	58	1	109	1	0	3	14	11	25	.282	.346	.472	.818
2010	Hou	NL	156	614	173	29	3	25	(14	11)	283	93	91	89	41	2	105	0	0	3	18	9	11	.282	.325	.461	.786
2011	2 Tms	NL	154	606	190	38	5	22	(5	17)	304	84	97	102	56	3	124	1	0	5	8	2	15	.314	.370	.502	.871
2012	2 Tms	NL	160	617	156	26	4	24	(9	15)	262	87	104	81	56	2	145	7	1	7	5	2	14	.253	.319	.425	.743
2013	SF	NL	162	629	178	35	5	27	(10	17)	304	91	99	91	52	3	115	3	0	3	22	3	17	.283	.339	.483	.822
2014	SF	NL	162	650	180	29	10	20	(5	15)	289	106	74	96	52	3	130	3	0	3	13	6	13	.277	.332	.445	.777
2015	SF	NL	52	207	57	13	1	9	(3	6)	99	30	40	28	16	0	48	0	0	0	4	1	8	.275	.327	.478	.806
2016	SF	NL	106	395	114	23	1	13	(6	7)	178	58	57	65	43	1	95	1	0	3	1	1	10	.289	.357	.451	.808
2017	SF	NL	134	493	128	13	5	13	(4	9)	190	55	67	68	40	1	102	2	0	4	2	3	8	.260	.315	.385	.701
2018	SF	NL	97	235	53	11	1	4	(2	2)	78	19	24	20	11	1	59	0	0	2	5	1	1	.226	.258	.332	.590
2019	Tex	AL	83	286	85	17	1	18	(7	11)	158	53	59	61	26	0	69	2	0	2	6	1	2	.297	.358	.552	.910
11	Hou	NL	100	399	123	26	4	11	(4	7)	188	49	62	63	30	1	86	1	0	2	7	1	7	.308	.356	.471	.828
11	Phi	NL	54	207	67	12	1	11	(1	10)	116	35	35	39	26	2	38	0	0	3	1	1	8	.324	.394	.560	.954
12	Phi	NL	101	398	108	15	2	17	(7	10)	178	59	59	50	37	1	85	3	0	2	4	2	13	.271	.336	.447	.784
12	SF	NL	59	219	48	11	2	7	(2	5)	84	28	45	31	19	1	60	4	1	5	1	0	1	.219	.287	.384	.671
	Postseason		43	169	43	8	0	2	(0	2)	57	23	16	14	12	1	33	0	0	1	4	3	3	.254	.302	.337	.639
	13 ML YEARS		1690	6368	1786	324	54	242	(100	142)	2944	887	936	940	517	19	1320	25	1	39	120	55	148	.280	.335	.462	.797

David Peralta

Bats: L **Throws:** L **Pos:** LF-93;PH-6;DH-1   **Ht:** 6'1" **Wt:** 210 **Born:** 8/14/1987 **Age:** 32

Year	Team	Lg	G	AB	H	2B	3B	HR	(Hm	Rd)	TB	R	RBI	RC	TBB	IBB	SO	HBP	SH	SF	SB	CS	GDP	Avg	OBP	Slg	OPS
2014	Ari	NL	88	329	94	12	9	8	(5	3)	148	40	36	38	16	0	60	1	1	1	6	3	9	.286	.320	.450	.770
2015	Ari	NL	149	462	144	26	10	17	(8	9)	241	61	78	83	44	2	107	4	0	7	9	4	7	.312	.371	.522	.893
2016	Ari	NL	48	171	43	9	5	4	(3	1)	74	23	15	15	8	1	42	3	0	1	2	0	3	.251	.295	.433	.728
2017	Ari	NL	140	525	154	31	3	14	(8	6)	233	82	57	77	43	1	94	6	0	3	8	4	7	.293	.352	.444	.796
2018	Ari	NL	146	560	164	25	5	30	(16	14)	289	75	87	104	48	4	124	4	0	2	4	0	14	.293	.352	.516	.868
2019	Ari	NL	99	382	105	29	3	12	(6	6)	176	48	57	62	35	3	87	5	0	1	0	0	9	.275	.343	.461	.804
	Postseason		4	18	4	0	0	0	(0	0)	4	2	0	1	1	0	1	0	0	0	0	0	1	.222	.263	.222	.485
	6 ML YEARS		670	2429	704	132	35	85	(46	39)	1161	329	330	379	194	11	514	23	1	15	29	11	49	.290	.346	.478	.824

Freddy Peralta

Pitches: R **Bats:** R **Pos:** RP-31; SP-8   **Ht:** 5'11" **Wt:** 175 **Born:** 6/4/1996 **Age:** 24

			HOW MUCH PITCHED					WHAT HE GAVE UP										THE RESULTS							
Year	Team	Lg	G	GS	GF	IP	BFP	H	R	ER	HR	SH	SF	HB	TBB	IBB	SO	WP	W	L	Pct	Sv-Op	Hld	Vel	OPS	ERC	ERA
2018	Mil	NL	16	14	1	78.1	321	49	37	37	8	1	1	4	40	1	96	3	6	4	.600	0-0	0	91	.622	2.71	4.25
2019	Mil	NL	39	8	3	85.0	382	87	58	50	15	3	1	2	37	1	115	3	7	3	.700	1-2	5	94	.790	4.86	5.29
	Postseason		1	0	0	3.0	12	0	0	0	0	0	0	0	3	0	6	0	0	0	-	0-0	0	92	.250	0.95	0.00
	2 ML YEARS		55	22	4	163.1	703	136	95	87	23	4	2	6	77	2	211	6	13	7	.650	1-2	5	92	.714	3.79	4.79

Wandy Peralta

Pitches: L Bats: L Pos: RP-47 Ht: 6'0" Wt: 220 Born: 7/27/1991 Age: 28

Year	Team	Lg	G	GS	GF	IP	BFP	H	R	ER	HR	SH	SF	HB	TBB	IBB	SO	WP	W	L	Pct	Sv-Op	Hld	Vel	OPS	ERC	ERA
2019	Lsvlle	AAA	12	0	0	11.0	44	11	4	4	0	0	0	1	1	0	7	0	0	0	-	0- -	-		.653	2.68	3.27
2016	Cin	NL	10	0	3	7.1	39	11	7	7	1	0	0	1	7	0	5	0	0	0	-	0-0	2	95	1.036	10.93	8.59
2017	Cin	NL	69	0	10	64.2	263	53	28	27	8	2	3	1	24	1	57	4	3	4	.429	0-2	16	96	.681	3.24	3.76
2018	Cin	NL	59	0	6	45.1	227	58	32	27	2	1	1	2	31	2	31	0	2	2	.500	0-0	7	96	.783	6.37	5.36
2019	2 Tms	NL	47	0	11	39.2	172	40	25	25	11	0	3	2	16	3	32	0	1	1	.500	0-1	3	95	.860	5.56	5.67
19	Cin	NL	39	0	11	34.0	151	36	23	23	10	0	3	2	15	3	27	0	1	1	.500	0-1	2	95	.893	6.17	6.09
19	SF	NL	8	0	0	5.2	21	4	2	2	1	0	0	0	1	0	5	0	0	0	-	0-0	1	95	.638	2.27	3.18
4 ML YEARS			185	0	30	157.0	701	162	92	86	22	3	7	6	78	6	125	4	6	7	.462	0-3	28	96	.777	5.04	4.93

Wily Peralta

Pitches: R Bats: R Pos: RP-42 Ht: 6'1" Wt: 255 Born: 5/8/1989 Age: 31

Year	Team	Lg	G	GS	GF	IP	BFP	H	R	ER	HR	SH	SF	HB	TBB	IBB	SO	WP	W	L	Pct	Sv-Op	Hld	Vel	OPS	ERC	ERA
2012	Mil	NL	6	5	1	29.0	113	24	8	8	0	3	0	0	11	0	23	1	2	1	.667	0-0	0	96	.601	2.61	2.48
2013	Mil	NL	32	32	0	183.1	802	187	107	89	19	11	3	7	73	3	129	12	11	15	.423	0-0	0	95	.722	4.32	4.37
2014	Mil	NL	32	32	0	198.2	838	198	88	78	23	9	3	7	61	0	154	7	17	11	.607	0-0	0	96	.714	3.98	3.53
2015	Mil	NL	20	20	0	108.2	478	130	60	57	14	4	3	4	37	2	60	5	5	10	.333	0-0	0	94	.844	5.40	4.72
2016	Mil	NL	23	23	0	127.2	554	152	73	69	19	6	4	3	43	1	93	0	7	11	.389	0-0	0	95	.855	5.52	4.86
2017	Mil	NL	19	8	4	57.1	269	73	51	50	10	1	3	1	32	2	52	5	5	4	.556	0-0	0	96	.947	7.07	7.85
2018	KC	AL	37	0	30	34.1	149	28	14	14	4	1	2	1	23	1	35	4	1	0	1.000	14-14	1	96	.737	4.37	3.67
2019	KC	AL	42	0	23	40.1	176	45	28	26	7	1	2	2	19	1	24	0	2	4	.333	2-5	5	94	.864	6.01	5.80
8 ML YEARS			211	120	58	779.1	3379	837	429	391	96	36	20	25	299	10	570	34	50	56	.472	16-19	6	95	.781	4.78	4.52

Jose Peraza

per-AH-zuh

Bats: R Throws: R Pos: 2B-78;SS-39;LF-33;PH-28;3B-5;CF-5;PR-2 Ht: 6'0" Wt: 196 Born: 4/30/1994 Age: 26

Year	Team	Lg	G	AB	H	2B	3B	HR	(Hm	Rd)	TB	R	RBI	RC	TBB	IBB	SO	HBP	SH	SF	SB	CS	GDP	Avg	OBP	Slg	OPS
2015	LAD	NL	7	22	4	1	1	0	(0	0)	7	3	1	2	2	1	2	0	1	0	3	0	0	.182	.250	.318	.568
2016	Cin	NL	72	241	78	8	2	3	(1	2)	99	25	25	32	7	0	33	5	0	3	21	10	3	.324	.352	.411	.762
2017	Cin	NL	143	487	126	9	4	5	(3	2)	158	50	37	43	20	1	70	7	3	1	23	8	7	.259	.297	.324	.622
2018	Cin	NL	157	632	182	31	4	14	(7	7)	263	85	58	79	29	4	75	9	8	5	23	6	12	.288	.326	.416	.742
2019	Cin	NL	141	376	90	18	2	6	(4	2)	130	37	33	34	17	0	58	8	0	2	7	6	9	.239	.285	.346	.631
5 ML YEARS			520	1758	480	67	13	28	(15	13)	657	200	154	190	75	6	238	29	12	11	77	30	31	.273	.312	.374	.686

Luis Perdomo

Pitches: R Bats: R Pos: RP-46; SP-1 Ht: 6'2" Wt: 185 Born: 5/9/1993 Age: 27

Year	Team	Lg	G	GS	GF	IP	BFP	H	R	ER	HR	SH	SF	HB	TBB	IBB	SO	WP	W	L	Pct	Sv-Op	Hld	Vel	OPS	ERC	ERA
2019	ElPaso	AAA	11	0	4	15.0	69	21	6	3	1	1	1	4	0	17	0	2	1	.667	1--	-	-	.931	7.03	3.60
2016	SD	NL	35	20	8	146.2	662	187	99	93	23	0	4	7	46	7	105	10	9	10	.474	0-0	0	94	.847	5.91	5.71
2017	SD	NL	29	29	0	163.2	716	182	97	85	17	3	2	8	65	3	118	11	8	11	.421	0-0	0	94	.784	5.00	4.67
2018	SD	NL	12	10	2	44.2	217	62	37	35	4	1	2	3	22	2	39	4	1	6	.143	0-0	0	93	.895	6.86	7.05
2019	SD	NL	47	1	13	72.0	296	69	34	32	6	2	0	2	18	1	55	3	2	4	.333	0-1	7	94	.675	3.29	4.00
4 ML YEARS			123	60	23	427.0	1891	500	267	245	50	6	8	20	151	13	317	28	20	31	.392	0-1	7	94	.801	5.19	5.16

Cionel Perez

see-oh-NEHL

Pitches: L Bats: L Pos: RP-5 Ht: 5'11" Wt: 170 Born: 4/21/1996 Age: 24

Year	Team	Lg	G	GS	GF	IP	BFP	H	R	ER	HR	SH	SF	HB	TBB	IBB	SO	WP	W	L	Pct	Sv-Op	Hld	Vel	OPS	ERC	ERA
2019	RdRck	AAA	13	10	1	47.0	213	53	30	28	6	1	1	3	24	0	43	1	2	1	.667	0--	-	-	.818	5.84	5.36
2018	Hou	AL	8	0	3	11.1	45	6	5	5	3	0	0	0	7	0	12	0	0	0	-	0-0	0	95	.684	3.56	3.97
2019	Hou	AL	5	0	3	9.0	40	11	10	10	3	0	0	0	2	0	7	0	1	1	.500	0-0	0	95	.904	6.18	10.00
2 ML YEARS			13	0	6	20.1	85	17	15	15	6	0	0	0	9	0	19	0	1	1	.500	0-0	0	95	.793	4.68	6.64

Hernan Perez

air-NAHN

Bats: R Throws: R Pos: 2B-45;SS-21;PH-19;3B-14;RF-7;1B-5;LF-3;PR-2 Ht: 6'1" Wt: 215 Born: 3/26/1991 Age: 29

Year	Team	Lg	G	AB	H	2B	3B	HR	(Hm	Rd)	TB	R	RBI	RC	TBB	IBB	SO	HBP	SH	SF	SB	CS	GDP	Avg	OBP	Slg	OPS
2019	SnAnt	AAA	27	107	31	10	0	5	(-	-)	56	18	19	22	14	0	23	0	0	0	6	0	4	.290	.372	.523	.895
2012	Det	AL	2	2	1	0	0	0	(0	0)	1	1	0	0	0	0	0	0	0	0	0	0	0	.500	.500	.500	1.000
2013	Det	AL	34	66	13	0	1	0	(0	0)	15	13	5	4	2	0	15	0	2	1	1	0	2	.197	.217	.227	.445
2014	Det	AL	8	5	1	0	0	0	(0	0)	1	1	0	0	0	0	1	0	0	0	0	0	0	.200	.333	.200	.533
2015	2 Tms		112	263	64	15	2	1	(0	1)	86	14	21	23	5	1	59	0	3	1	5	1	6	.243	.257	.327	.584
2016	Mil	NL	123	404	110	18	3	13	(7	6)	173	50	56	56	18	0	94	1	3	4	34	7	8	.272	.302	.428	.730
2017	Mil	NL	136	432	112	19	3	14	(7	7)	179	47	51	49	20	1	79	0	2	4	13	4	8	.259	.289	.414	.704
2018	Mil	NL	132	316	80	11	2	9	(5	4)	122	36	29	33	17	1	71	0	0	1	11	3	6	.253	.290	.386	.676
2019	Mil	NL	91	232	53	11	0	8	(3	5)	88	29	18	22	11	0	66	0	2	1	5	1	9	.228	.262	.379	.642

								BATTING														RUNNING			AVERAGES			
Year	Team	Lg	G	AB	H	2B	3B	HR	(Hm	Rd)	TB	R	RBI	RC	TBB	IBB	SO	HBP	SH	SF	SB	CS	GDP	Avg	OBP	Slg	OPS
15	Det	AL	22	33	2	0	0	0	(0	0)	2	1	0	0	1	0	11	0	0	0	1	0	2	.061	.088	.061	.149
15	Mil	NL	90	230	62	15	2	1	(0	1)	84	13	21	23	4	1	48	0	3	1	4	1	4	.270	.281	.365	.646
	Postseason		13	16	3	2	0	0	(0	0)	5	1	2	1	1	0	3	0	0	1	2	2	1	.188	.222	.313	.535
	8 ML YEARS		638	1720	434	74	11	45	(22	23)	665	191	180	177	74	3	385	1	12	12	69	16	37	.252	.282	.387	.668

Martin Perez

Pitches: L **Bats:** L **Pos:** SP-29; RP-3   mar-TEEN   **Ht:** 6'0" **Wt:** 200 **Born:** 4/4/1991 **Age:** 29

			HOW MUCH PITCHED					WHAT HE GAVE UP										THE RESULTS							
Year	Team	Lg	G	GS	GF	IP	BFP	H	R	ER	HR	SH	SF	HB	TBB	IBB	SO	WP	W	L	Pct	Sv-Op	Hld	Vel	OPS	ERC	ERA
2012	Tex	AL	12	6	2	38.0	177	47	26	23	3	1	1	2	15	1	25	5	1	4	.200	0-0	0	92	.819	5.33	5.45
2013	Tex	AL	20	20	0	124.1	529	129	55	50	15	2	3	3	37	0	84	9	10	6	.625	0-0	0	93	.728	4.14	3.62
2014	Tex	AL	8	8	0	51.1	207	50	25	25	3	1	0	1	19	1	35	1	4	3	.571	0-0	0	90	.743	3.82	4.38
2015	Tex	AL	14	14	0	78.2	339	88	45	39	3	0	3	2	24	1	48	1	3	6	.333	0-0	0	92	.729	4.04	4.46
2016	Tex	AL	33	33	0	198.2	855	205	110	97	18	9	8	4	76	0	103	3	10	11	.476	0-0	0	93	.741	4.24	4.39
2017	Tex	AL	32	32	0	185.0	811	221	108	99	23	4	3	6	63	3	115	4	13	12	.520	0-0	0	93	.812	5.35	4.82
2018	Tex	AL	22	15	3	85.1	397	116	68	59	16	1	5	2	36	1	52	3	2	7	.222	0-1	2	93	.916	7.19	6.22
2019	Min	AL	32	29	0	165.1	737	184	104	94	23	3	5	3	67	1	135	3	10	7	.588	0-0	0	92	.785	5.07	5.12
	Postseason		1	1	0	5.0	21	6	4	4	0	1	0	0	3	1	2	0	0	1	.000	0-0	0	92	.921	5.47	7.20
	8 ML YEARS		173	157	5	926.2	4052	1040	541	486	104	21	28	23	337	8	597	29	53	56	.486	0-1	2	93	.781	4.85	4.72

Michael Perez

Bats: L **Throws:** R **Pos:** C-20;1B-2;PH-2   **Ht:** 5'10" **Wt:** 195 **Born:** 8/7/1992 **Age:** 27

								BATTING														RUNNING			AVERAGES			
Year	Team	Lg	G	AB	H	2B	3B	HR	(Hm	Rd)	TB	R	RBI	RC	TBB	IBB	SO	HBP	SH	SF	SB	CS	GDP	Avg	OBP	Slg	OPS
2019	Drham	AAA	54	184	45	7	0	13	(-	-)	91	23	42	31	28	0	51	0	0	4	0	2	4	.245	.338	.495	.833
2018	TB	AL	24	74	21	5	0	1	(0	1)	29	9	11	9	3	0	19	0	1	2	0	0	0	.284	.304	.392	.696
2019	TB	AL	22	46	10	5	0	0	(0	0)	15	6	2	6	8	0	19	1	0	0	0	0	0	.217	.345	.326	.672
	2 ML YEARS		46	120	31	10	0	1	(0	1)	44	15	13	15	11	0	38	1	1	2	0	0	0	.258	.321	.367	.688

Oliver Perez

Pitches: L **Bats:** L **Pos:** RP-67   **Ht:** 6'3" **Wt:** 225 **Born:** 8/15/1981 **Age:** 38

			HOW MUCH PITCHED					WHAT HE GAVE UP										THE RESULTS							
Year	Team	Lg	G	GS	GF	IP	BFP	H	R	ER	HR	SH	SF	HB	TBB	IBB	SO	WP	W	L	Pct	Sv-Op	Hld	Vel	OPS	ERC	ERA
2002	SD	NL	16	15	0	90.0	387	71	37	35	13	6	3	5	48	1	94	3	4	5	.444	0-0	0	91	.702	3.93	3.50
2003	2 Tms	NL	24	24	0	126.2	579	129	80	77	22	5	2	4	77	3	141	7	4	10	.286	0-0	0	93	.830	5.66	5.47
2004	Pit	NL	30	30	0	196.0	805	145	71	65	22	9	5	9	81	2	239	2	12	10	.545	0-0	0	93	.655	2.99	2.98
2005	Pit	NL	20	20	0	103.0	471	102	68	67	23	5	4	6	70	1	97	3	7	5	.583	0-0	0	91	.874	6.44	5.85
2006	2 Tms	NL	22	22	0	112.2	529	129	90	82	20	5	10	6	68	0	102	5	3	13	.188	0-0	0	90	.865	6.62	6.55
2007	NYM	NL	29	29	0	177.0	765	153	90	70	22	4	9	7	79	1	174	6	15	10	.600	0-0	0	91	.696	3.76	3.56
2008	NYM	NL	34	34	0	194.0	847	167	100	91	24	9	7	11	105	4	180	9	10	7	.588	0-0	0	91	.725	4.21	4.22
2009	NYM	NL	14	14	0	66.0	324	69	51	50	12	5	4	4	58	2	62	2	3	4	.429	0-0	0	90	.897	7.16	6.82
2010	NYM	NL	17	7	4	46.1	234	54	37	35	9	1	3	4	42	3	37	4	0	5	.000	0-0	0	88	.935	8.27	6.80
2012	Sea	AL	33	0	6	29.2	123	27	7	7	1	1	1	0	10	2	24	2	1	3	.250	0-2	5	94	.628	2.82	2.12
2013	Sea	AL	61	0	22	53.0	229	50	23	22	6	1	0	1	26	3	74	1	3	3	.500	2-3	8	92	.731	4.23	3.74
2014	Ari	NL	68	0	11	58.2	256	50	25	19	5	4	0	7	24	2	76	3	3	4	.429	0-1	15	91	.679	3.53	2.91
2015	2 Tms	AL	70	0	15	41.0	183	39	24	19	4	1	0	4	15	2	51	3	2	4	.333	0-3	10	92	.681	3.81	4.17
2016	Was	NL	64	0	7	40.0	182	38	22	22	4	1	1	7	20	3	46	5	2	3	.400	0-1	15	92	.751	4.72	4.95
2017	Was	NL	50	0	8	33.0	143	32	17	17	4	0	1	4	12	2	39	1	0	0		1-1	12	93	.772	4.32	4.64
2018	Cle	AL	51	0	1	32.1	120	17	6	5	1	0	1	2	7	3	43	1	1	1	.500	0-0	15	92	.417	1.12	1.39
2019	Cle	AL	67	0	4	40.2	173	38	20	18	5	0	1	3	12	2	48	1	2	4	.333	1-5	22	92	.733	3.64	3.98
03	SD	NL	19	19	0	103.2	473	103	65	62	20	4	2	3	65	2	117	6	4	7	.364	0-0	0	92	.836	5.74	5.38
03	Pit	NL	5	5	0	23.0	106	26	15	15	2	1	0	1	12	1	24	1	0	3	.000	0-0	0	93	.806	5.29	5.87
06	Pit	NL	15	15	0	76.0	364	88	64	56	13	5	8	3	51	0	61	4	2	10	.167	0-0	0	90	.877	6.85	6.63
06	NYM	NL	7	7	0	36.2	165	41	26	26	7	0	2	3	17	0	41	1	1	3	.250	0-0	0	91	.838	6.16	6.38
15	Ari	NL	48	0	11	29.0	128	25	12	10	2	1	0	4	11	1	37	2	2	1	.667	0-3	7	92	.627	3.38	3.10
15	Hou	AL	22	0	4	12.0	55	14	12	9	2	0	0	0	4	1	14	1	0	3	.000	0-0	3	92	.798	4.89	6.75
	Postseason		10	2	1	16.1	69	17	7	7	3	3	0	2	5	1	10	0	2	0	1.000	0-0	3	93	.855	5.13	3.86
	17 ML YEARS		670	195	78	1440.0	6350	1310	768	701	197	56	50	84	754	36	1527	58	72	91	.442	4-16	102	91	.750	4.50	4.38

Roberto Perez

Bats: R **Throws:** R **Pos:** C-118;DH-1   **Ht:** 5'11" **Wt:** 220 **Born:** 12/23/1988 **Age:** 31

								BATTING														RUNNING			AVERAGES			
Year	Team	Lg	G	AB	H	2B	3B	HR	(Hm	Rd)	TB	R	RBI	RC	TBB	IBB	SO	HBP	SH	SF	SB	CS	GDP	Avg	OBP	Slg	OPS
2014	Cle	AL	29	85	23	5	0	1	(1	0)	31	10	4	8	5	0	26	0	5	0	0	0	2	.271	.311	.365	.676
2015	Cle	AL	70	184	42	9	1	7	(4	3)	74	30	21	24	33	1	64	2	5	2	0	0	9	.228	.348	.402	.751
2016	Cle	AL	61	153	28	6	1	3	(1	2)	45	14	17	17	23	0	44	0	5	3	0	0	4	.183	.285	.294	.579
2017	Cle	AL	73	217	45	12	0	8	(6	2)	81	22	38	26	26	0	71	0	4	1	0	1	4	.207	.291	.373	.664
2018	Cle	AL	62	179	30	9	1	2	(1	1)	47	16	19	12	21	0	70	1	7	2	1	0	6	.168	.256	.263	.519
2019	Cle	AL	119	389	93	19	1	24	(12	12)	176	46	63	56	45	1	127	4	7	4	0	0	12	.239	.321	.452	.774
	Postseason		19	53	11	1	0	4	(3	1)	24	6	9	7	9	0	18	0	2	0	0	0	0	.208	.323	.453	.775
	6 ML YEARS		414	1207	261	50	4	45	(25	20)	454	138	162	143	153	2	402	7	33	12	1	1	37	.216	.305	.376	.681

Salvador Perez

Bats: R Throws: R Pos: C   Ht: 6'4" Wt: 240 Born: 5/10/1990 Age: 30

Year Team	Lg	G	AB	H	2B	3B	HR	(Hm	Rd)	TB	R	RBI	RC	TBB	IBB	SO	HBP	SH	SF	SB	CS	GDP	Avg	OBP	Slg	OPS
2011 KC	AL	39	148	49	8	2	3	(1	2)	70	20	21	26	7	0	20	1	0	2	0	0	5	.331	.361	.473	.834
2012 KC	AL	76	289	87	16	0	11	(3	8)	136	38	39	36	12	3	27	1	0	3	0	0	14	.301	.328	.471	.798
2013 KC	AL	138	496	145	25	3	13	(6	7)	215	48	79	77	21	2	63	4	0	5	0	0	13	.292	.323	.433	.757
2014 KC	AL	150	578	150	28	2	17	(8	9)	233	57	70	55	22	2	85	3	0	3	1	0	22	.260	.289	.403	.692
2015 KC	AL	142	531	138	25	0	21	(9	12)	226	52	70	60	13	4	82	4	0	5	1	0	23	.260	.280	.426	.706
2016 KC	AL	139	514	127	28	2	22	(11	11)	225	57	64	61	22	3	119	8	0	2	0	0	12	.247	.288	.438	.725
2017 KC	AL	129	471	126	24	1	27	(6	21)	233	57	80	65	17	3	95	5	0	5	1	0	23	.268	.297	.495	.792
2018 KC	AL	129	510	120	23	0	27	(11	16)	224	52	80	58	17	0	108	12	0	5	1	1	19	.235	.274	.439	.713
Postseason		31	116	27	4	0	5	(3	2)	46	14	14	10	5	0	19	3	0	0	0	0	3	.233	.282	.397	.679
8 ML YEARS		942	3537	942	177	10	141	(55	86)	1562	381	503	438	131	17	599	38	0	30	4	1	131	.266	.297	.442	.739

Dillon Peters

Pitches: L Bats: L Pos: SP-12; RP-5   Ht: 5'11" Wt: 190 Born: 8/31/1992 Age: 27

Year Team	Lg	G	GS	GF	IP	BFP	H	R	ER	HR	SH	SF	HB	TBB	IBB	SO	WP	W	L	Pct	Sv-Op	Hld	Vel	OPS	ERC	ERA
2019 Salt Lk	AAA	13	11	1	57.0	256	74	44	41	11	0	4	1	17	0	55	3	4	1	.800	0- -	-	91	.915	6.23	6.47
2017 Mia	NL	6	6	0	31.1	139	32	18	18	3	0	0	2	19	1	27	3	1	2	.333	0-0	0	91	.771	5.38	5.17
2018 Mia	NL	7	5	2	27.2	129	34	22	22	4	1	1	1	15	0	17	3	2	2	.500	0-0	0	91	.868	6.59	7.16
2019 LAA	AL	17	12	1	72.0	327	85	50	43	18	1	2	5	26	1	55	1	4	4	.500	0-0	0	91	.926	6.34	5.38
3 ML YEARS		30	23	3	131.0	595	151	90	83	25	2	3	8	60	2	99	7	7	8	.467	0-0	0	91	.879	6.18	5.70

Dustin Peterson

Bats: R Throws: R Pos: LF-9;PR-3;CF-2;RF-2;1B-1;DH-1;PH-1   Ht: 6'2" Wt: 210 Born: 9/10/1994 Age: 25

Year Team	Lg	G	AB	H	2B	3B	HR	(Hm	Rd)	TB	R	RBI	RC	TBB	IBB	SO	HBP	SH	SF	SB	CS	GDP	Avg	OBP	Slg	OPS
2019 Toledo	AAA	79	301	86	13	0	11	(-	-)	132	31	49	42	14	0	78	1	0	3	1	1	11	.286	.317	.439	.755
2018 Atl	NL	2	2	0	0	0	0	(0	0)	0	0	0	0	0	0	1	0	0	0	0	0	0	.000	.000	.000	.000
2019 Det	AL	17	44	10	4	0	0	(0	0)	14	3	6	3	2	0	14	1	0	0	1	0	1	.227	.277	.318	.595
2 ML YEARS		19	46	10	4	0	0	(0	0)	14	3	6	3	2	0	15	1	0	0	1	0	1	.217	.265	.304	.570

Jace Peterson

Bats: L Throws: R Pos: LF-18;3B-9;2B-5;PH-5;RF-1   JAYCE   Ht: 6'0" Wt: 215 Born: 5/9/1990 Age: 30

Year Team	Lg	G	AB	H	2B	3B	HR	(Hm	Rd)	TB	R	RBI	RC	TBB	IBB	SO	HBP	SH	SF	SB	CS	GDP	Avg	OBP	Slg	OPS
2019 Norfolk	AAA	90	326	102	25	5	10	(-	-)	167	58	46	69	46	0	56	2	0	3	13	6	6	.313	.398	.512	.910
2014 SD	NL	27	53	6	0	0	0	(0	0)	6	3	0	0	2	1	18	1	2	0	2	0	1	.113	.161	.113	.274
2015 Atl	NL	152	528	126	23	5	6	(1	5)	177	55	52	56	56	4	120	3	7	3	12	10	5	.239	.314	.335	.649
2016 Atl	NL	115	350	89	16	1	7	(3	4)	128	45	29	42	52	2	69	1	2	5	5	5	9	.254	.350	.366	.715
2017 Atl	NL	89	186	40	9	2	2	(2	0)	59	15	17	20	27	3	48	1	1	0	3	0	4	.215	.318	.317	.635
2018 2 Tms	AL	96	210	42	13	2	3	(2	1)	68	21	28	26	31	0	58	3	1	1	13	3	8	.200	.310	.324	.634
2019 Bal	AL	29	100	22	3	1	2	(2	0)	33	14	11	13	6	0	24	1	0	1	4	1	1	.220	.269	.330	.599
18 NYY	AL	3	10	3	0	0	0	(0	0)	3	0	0	1	1	0	3	0	0	0	0	1	0	.300	.364	.300	.664
18 Bal	AL	93	200	39	13	2	3	(2	1)	65	21	28	25	30	0	55	3	1	1	13	2	8	.195	.308	.325	.633
6 ML YEARS		508	1427	325	64	11	20	(10	10)	471	153	137	157	174	10	337	10	13	8	39	19	28	.228	.314	.330	.644

Tim Peterson

Pitches: R Bats: R Pos: RP-6   Ht: 6'1" Wt: 215 Born: 2/22/1991 Age: 29

Year Team	Lg	G	GS	GF	IP	BFP	H	R	ER	HR	SH	SF	HB	TBB	IBB	SO	WP	W	L	Pct	Sv-Op	Hld	Vel	OPS	ERC	ERA
2019 Syrcse	AAA	41	0	28	55.0	216	42	19	18	7	0	1	4	13	1	54	2	2	6	.250	9- -	-	90	.645	2.46	2.95
2018 NYM	NL	22	0	9	27.2	118	29	19	19	8	1	0	1	5	2	25	0	2	2	.500	0-0	3	90	.795	4.67	6.18
2019 NYM	NL	6	0	2	7.1	35	7	4	4	1	0	0	1	7	1	3	3	0	0	-	0-0	0	90	.836	6.90	4.91
2 ML YEARS		28	0	11	35.0	153	36	23	23	9	1	0	2	12	3	28	3	2	2	.500	0-0	3	90	.807	5.18	5.91

Yusmeiro Petit

Pitches: R Bats: R Pos: RP-80   yooz-MAIR-oh peh-TEET   Ht: 6'1" Wt: 255 Born: 11/22/1984 Age: 35

Year Team	Lg	G	GS	GF	IP	BFP	H	R	ER	HR	SH	SF	HB	TBB	IBB	SO	WP	W	L	Pct	Sv-Op	Hld	Vel	OPS	ERC	ERA
2006 Fla	NL	15	1	5	26.1	129	46	28	28	7	1	0	0	7	1	20	0	1	1	.500	0-0	0	89	1.125	10.07	9.57
2007 Ari	NL	14	10	2	57.0	243	58	30	29	12	1	1	0	18	1	40	0	3	4	.429	0-0	0	87	.830	4.56	4.58
2008 Ari	NL	19	8	6	56.1	229	45	29	27	12	4	2	1	14	2	42	3	3	5	.375	0-0	0	87	.704	3.08	4.31
2009 Ari	NL	23	17	2	89.2	407	102	62	58	19	3	0	0	34	1	74	3	3	10	.231	0-0	0	87	.837	5.44	5.82
2012 SF	NL	1	1	0	4.2	22	7	2	2	0	1	0	0	4	0	1	1	0	0	-	0-0	0	88	.936	9.14	3.86
2013 SF	NL	8	7	0	48.0	196	46	19	19	4	2	0	0	11	1	47	0	4	1	.800	0-0	0	88	.660	3.08	3.56
2014 SF	NL	39	12	14	117.0	461	97	51	48	12	0	3	1	22	5	133	0	5	5	.500	0-0	0	89	.635	2.40	3.69
2015 SF	NL	42	1	15	76.0	316	75	32	31	11	1	6	1	15	2	59	3	1	1	.500	1-1	0	88	.743	3.48	3.67
2016 Was	NL	36	1	16	62.0	265	67	33	31	12	3	1	0	15	3	49	3	3	5	.375	1-2	1	89	.793	4.42	4.50
2017 LAA	AL	60	1	10	91.1	354	69	32	28	9	1	1	1	18	4	101	0	5	2	.714	4-5	14	90	.571	2.07	2.76
2018 Oak	AL	74	0	12	93.0	368	76	32	31	13	1	5	0	18	4	76	1	7	3	.700	0-2	16	89	.649	2.52	3.00
2019 Oak	AL	80	0	6	83.0	308	57	25	25	11	1	3	0	10	0	71	2	5	3	.625	0-1	29	89	.579	1.71	2.71
Postseason		4	0	0	12.2	47	7	2	2	0	0	0	0	4	1	13	1	3	0	1.000	0-0	0	88	.467	1.18	1.42
12 ML YEARS		411	59	88	804.1	3298	745	375	357	122	19	23	4	188	24	713	16	40	40	.500	6-11	60	88	.713	3.33	3.99

Jake Petricka

Pitches: R **Bats:** R **Pos:** RP-6 puh-TRICH-kuh **Ht:** 6'5" **Wt:** 220 **Born:** 6/5/1988 **Age:** 32

Year	Team	Lg	G	GS	GF	IP	BFP	H	R	ER	HR	SH	SF	HB	TBB	IBB	SO	WP	W	L	Pct	Sv-Op	Hld	Vel	OPS	ERC	ERA
2019	SnAnt	AAA	16	0	7	19.0	72	14	5	4	0	0	0	0	4	1	22	1	1	1	.500	3- -	-	-	.529	1.54	1.89
2019	Nashv	AAA	24	0	11	26.2	120	29	16	15	3	0	1	1	11	0	29	3	1	1	.500	4- -	-	-	.781	4.80	5.06
2013	CWS	AL	16	0	3	19.1	85	20	7	7	0	1	1	1	10	1	10	4	1	1	.500	0-1	0	93	.688	4.18	3.26
2014	CWS	AL	67	0	33	73.0	307	67	24	24	3	3	4	2	33	4	55	2	1	6	.143	14-18	10	94	.671	3.52	2.96
2015	CWS	AL	62	0	18	52.0	220	56	21	21	2	3	1	1	18	4	33	2	4	3	.571	2-3	12	94	.716	3.91	3.63
2016	CWS	AL	9	0	1	8.0	39	8	5	4	1	1	0	0	8	0	7	3	0	0	-	0-0	1	94	.854	6.76	4.50
2017	CWS	AL	27	0	7	25.2	122	39	21	20	6	0	1	1	6	0	26	3	1	1	.500	0-1	3	94	.947	7.66	7.01
2018	Tor	AL	41	0	5	45.2	208	59	28	23	6	1	0	5	16	0	41	5	3	1	.750	0-0	1	95	.897	6.44	4.53
2019	Mil	NL	6	0	6	8.0	36	6	3	3	0	0	1	0	6	1	3	1	0	0	-	0-0	0	93	.644	3.00	3.38
	7 ML YEARS		228	0	73	231.2	1017	255	109	102	18	9	8	10	97	10	175	20	10	12	.455	16-23	27	94	.770	4.74	3.96

Tommy Pham

Bats: R **Throws:** R **Pos:** LF-123;DH-21;PH-1 FAM **Ht:** 6'1" **Wt:** 215 **Born:** 3/8/1988 **Age:** 32

Year	Team	Lg	G	AB	H	2B	3B	HR	(Hm	Rd)	TB	R	RBI	RC	TBB	IBB	SO	HBP	SH	SF	SB	CS	GDP	Avg	OBP	Slg	OPS
2014	StL	NL	6	2	0	0	0	0	(0	0)	0	0	0	0	0	0	2	0	0	0	0	0	0	.000	.000	.000	.000
2015	StL	NL	52	153	41	7	5	5	(1	4)	73	28	18	26	19	1	41	0	0	1	2	0	1	.268	.347	.477	.824
2016	StL	NL	78	159	36	7	0	9	(3	6)	70	26	17	21	20	1	71	3	1	0	2	2	3	.226	.324	.440	.764
2017	StL	NL	128	444	136	22	2	23	(6	17)	231	95	73	93	71	0	117	10	2	3	25	7	18	.306	.411	.520	.931
2018	2 Tms		137	494	136	18	6	21	(9	12)	229	102	63	76	67	2	140	6	0	3	15	7	18	.275	.367	.464	.830
2019	TB		145	567	155	33	2	21	(11	10)	255	77	68	86	81	4	123	5	0	1	25	4	22	.273	.369	.450	.818
18	StL	NL	98	351	87	11	0	14	(8	8)	140	67	41	45	42	1	97	2	0	1	10	6	12	.248	.331	.399	.730
18	TB	AL	39	143	49	7	6	7	(3	4)	89	35	22	31	25	1	43	4	0	2	5	1	6	.343	.448	.622	1.071
	Postseason		3	5	1	0	0	1	(1	0)	4	1	2	0	0	0	2	0	0	0	0	0	0	.200	.200	.800	1.000
	6 ML YEARS		546	1819	504	87	15	79	(30	49)	858	328	239	302	258	8	494	24	3	8	69	20	62	.277	.373	.472	.844

Josh Phegley

Bats: R **Throws:** R **Pos:** C-106;PH-8;PR-1 FEG-lee **Ht:** 5'10" **Wt:** 225 **Born:** 2/12/1988 **Age:** 32

Year	Team	Lg	G	AB	H	2B	3B	HR	(Hm	Rd)	TB	R	RBI	RC	TBB	IBB	SO	HBP	SH	SF	SB	CS	GDP	Avg	OBP	Slg	OPS
2013	CWS	AL	65	204	42	7	0	4	(2	2)	61	14	22	12	5	0	41	0	2	2	2	0	6	.206	.223	.299	.522
2014	CWS	AL	11	37	8	2	0	3	(3	0)	19	4	7	2	0	0	9	0	0	1	0	0	0	.216	.211	.514	.724
2015	Oak	AL	73	225	56	16	1	9	(6	3)	101	27	34	32	14	0	51	3	0	1	0	0	5	.249	.300	.449	.749
2016	Oak	AL	26	78	20	6	0	1	(1	0)	29	11	10	8	5	0	13	2	0	1	0	0	4	.256	.314	.372	.686
2017	Oak	AL	57	149	30	11	0	3	(0	3)	50	14	10	11	9	0	26	2	0	1	0	1	4	.201	.255	.336	.590
2018	Oak	AL	39	93	19	7	0	2	(1	1)	32	13	15	8	6	0	27	1	0	2	0	0	3	.204	.255	.344	.599
2019	Oak	AL	106	314	75	18	0	12	(4	8)	129	44	62	40	15	0	63	6	2	5	0	1	11	.239	.282	.411	.693
	7 ML YEARS		377	1100	250	67	1	34	(17	17)	421	127	160	113	54	0	232	14	4	13	2	2	33	.227	.269	.383	.652

David Phelps

Pitches: R **Bats:** R **Pos:** RP-40; SP-1 **Ht:** 6'3" **Wt:** 200 **Born:** 10/9/1986 **Age:** 33

Year	Team	Lg	G	GS	GF	IP	BFP	H	R	ER	HR	SH	SF	HB	TBB	IBB	SO	WP	W	L	Pct	Sv-Op	Hld	Vel	OPS	ERC	ERA
2012	NYY	AL	33	11	5	99.2	414	81	38	37	14	4	3	6	38	2	96	2	4	4	.500	0-0	2	91	.682	3.48	3.34
2013	NYY	AL	22	12	3	86.2	376	88	50	48	8	1	2	5	35	1	79	2	6	5	.545	0-1	1	90	.749	4.38	4.98
2014	NYY	AL	32	17	5	113.0	497	115	62	55	13	4	7	6	47	2	92	2	5	5	.500	1-1	5	90	.753	4.52	4.38
2015	Mia	NL	23	19	1	112.0	482	119	59	56	11	2	5	4	33	0	77	2	4	8	.333	0-0	0	90	.729	4.13	4.50
2016	Mia	NL	64	5	6	86.2	352	61	23	22	6	1	2	2	38	6	114	0	7	6	.538	4-10	25	94	.582	2.47	2.28
2017	2 Tms		54	0	5	55.2	238	51	23	21	5	2	2	1	26	3	62	0	4	5	.444	0-8	21	94	.693	3.82	3.40
2019	2 Tms		41	1	4	34.1	147	31	14	13	5	0	1	1	17	1	36	3	2	1	.667	1-5	5	93	.755	4.36	3.41
17	Mia	NL	44	0	4	47.0	197	42	20	18	5	2	1	0	21	3	51	0	2	4	.333	0-6	18	94	.699	3.68	3.45
17	Sea	AL	10	0	1	8.2	41	9	3	3	0	0	1	1	5	0	11	0	2	1	.667	0-2	3	94	.660	4.54	3.12
19	Tor	AL	17	1	1	17.1	71	14	7	7	3	0	0	1	7	1	18	1	0	0	-	0-2	4	92	.754	3.77	3.63
19	ChC	NL	24	0	3	17.0	76	17	7	6	2	0	1	0	10	0	18	2	2	1	.667	1-3	1	93	.755	4.98	3.18
	Postseason		3	0	1	3.1	19	7	4	3	0	0	0	0	1	0	2	0	0	2	.000	0-0	0	90	1.032	8.97	8.10
	7 ML YEARS		269	65	29	588.0	2506	546	269	252	62	14	18	26	233	15	556	11	32	34	.485	6-25	59	91	.707	3.86	3.86

Brett Phillips

Bats: L **Throws:** R **Pos:** CF-23;PR-4;LF-3;RF-3;PH-2 **Ht:** 6'0" **Wt:** 185 **Born:** 5/30/1994 **Age:** 26

Year	Team	Lg	G	AB	H	2B	3B	HR	(Hm	Rd)	TB	R	RBI	RC	TBB	IBB	SO	HBP	SH	SF	SB	CS	GDP	Avg	OBP	Slg	OPS
2019	Omha	AAA	105	333	80	8	13	18	(-	-)	168	75	54	71	72	2	118	3	4	2	22	1	4	.240	.378	.505	.883
2017	Mil	NL	37	87	24	3	0	4	(2	2)	39	9	12	14	9	2	34	1	1	0	5	0	0	.276	.351	.448	.799
2018	2 Tms		51	134	25	4	3	2	(1	1)	41	15	11	10	11	0	61	1	0	1	1	1	2	.187	.262	.306	.558
2019	KC	AL	30	65	9	2	0	2	(1	1)	17	7	6	2	10	0	23	0	2	2	3	0	1	.138	.247	.262	.508
18	Mil	NL	15	22	4	0	1	0	(0	0)	6	2	4	2	2	0	11	0	0	0	0	0	1	.182	.250	.273	.523
18	KC	AL	36	112	21	4	2	2	(1	1)	35	13	7	8	9	0	50	1	0	1	1	1	1	.188	.252	.313	.565
	3 ML YEARS		118	286	58	9	3	8	(4	4)	97	31	29	26	30	2	118	2	3	3	9	1	4	.203	.280	.339	.620

Evan Phillips

Pitches: R Bats: R Pos: RP-25 Ht: 6'2" Wt: 215 Born: 9/11/1994 Age: 25

Year	Team	Lg	G	GS	GF	IP	BFP	H	R	ER	HR	SH	SF	HB	TBB	IBB	SO	WP	W	L	Pct	Sv-Op	Hld	Vel	OPS	ERC	ERA
2019	Norfolk	AAA	27	0	11	39.2	171	35	18	17	2	0	1	3	17	0	44	5	1	2	.333	1- -	-	-	.655	3.47	3.86
2018	2 Tms		9	1	4	11.2	59	13	19	17	5	0	0	1	10	0	8	1	0	1	.000	0-0	0	94	1.073	9.76	13.11
2019	Bal	AL	25	0	2	28.0	140	32	20	20	2	1	2	5	20	0	40	2	0	1	.000	0-0	3	94	.821	6.59	6.43
18	Atl	NL	4	0	4	6.1	29	6	6	6	3	0	0	0	4	0	3	0	0	0		0-0	0	94	.985	7.41	8.53
18	Bal	AL	5	1	0	5.1	30	7	13	11	2	0	0	1	6	0	5	1	0	1	.000	0-0	0	94	1.162	12.53	18.56
	2 ML YEARS		34	1	6	39.2	199	45	39	37	7	1	2	6	30	0	48	3	0	2	.000	0-0	3	94	.897	7.52	8.39

Kevin Pillar

Bats: R Throws: R Pos: CF-133;RF-27;PH-4;PR-2   pih-LAHR   Ht: 6'0" Wt: 210 Born: 1/4/1989 Age: 31

							BATTING															RUNNING			AVERAGES			
Year	Team	Lg	G	AB	H	2B	3B	HR	(Hm	Rd)	TB	R	RBI	RC	TBB	IBB	SO	HBP	SH	SF	SB	CS	GDP	Avg	OBP	Slg	OPS
2013	Tor	AL	36	102	21	4	0	3	(1	2)	34	11	13	9	4	0	29	2	2	0	0	1	0	.206	.250	.333	.583
2014	Tor	AL	53	116	31	9	0	2	(2	0)	46	19	7	8	4	0	28	1	0	1	1	2	3	.267	.295	.397	.692
2015	Tor	AL	159	586	163	31	2	12	(6	6)	234	76	56	73	28	1	85	5	4	5	25	4	9	.278	.314	.399	.713
2016	Tor	AL	146	548	146	35	2	7	(3	4)	206	59	53	66	24	0	90	6	3	3	14	6	12	.266	.303	.376	.679
2017	Tor	AL	154	587	150	37	1	16	(6	10)	237	72	42	58	33	0	95	6	3	3	15	6	13	.256	.300	.404	.704
2018	Tor	AL	142	512	129	40	2	15	(11	4)	218	65	59	59	18	0	98	6	0	6	14	3	8	.252	.282	.426	.708
2019	2 Tms		161	611	158	37	3	21	(11	10)	264	83	88	76	18	4	89	9	0	7	14	5	15	.259	.287	.432	.719
19	Tor	AL	5	16	1	0	0	0	(0	0)	1	1	1	0	0	0	3	0	0	1	0	0	0	.063	.059	.063	.121
19	SF	NL	156	595	157	37	3	21	(11	10)	263	82	87	76	18	4	86	9	0	6	14	5	15	.264	.293	.442	.735
	Postseason		20	74	15	6	0	2	(0	2)	27	7	8	8	5	1	14	0	0	1	3	1	1	.203	.250	.365	.615
	7 ML YEARS		851	3062	798	193	10	76	(40	36)	1239	385	318	349	129	5	514	35	12	25	83	27	60	.261	.296	.405	.701

Manny Pina

Bats: R Throws: R Pos: C-53;PH-24;3B-1   PEEN-yah   Ht: 6'0" Wt: 215 Born: 6/5/1987 Age: 33

							BATTING															RUNNING			AVERAGES			
Year	Team	Lg	G	AB	H	2B	3B	HR	(Hm	Rd)	TB	R	RBI	RC	TBB	IBB	SO	HBP	SH	SF	SB	CS	GDP	Avg	OBP	Slg	OPS
2011	KC	AL	4	14	3	2	0	0	(0	0)	5	2	0	1	1	0	2	0	0	0	0	0	1	.214	.267	.357	.624
2012	KC	AL	1	2	0	0	0	0	(0	0)	0	0	0	0	0	0	0	0	0	0	0	0	0	.000	.000	.000	.000
2016	Mil	NL	33	71	18	4	0	2	(1	1)	28	4	12	8	10	0	15	0	0	0	0	1	2	.254	.346	.394	.740
2017	Mil	NL	107	330	92	21	0	9	(6	3)	140	45	43	46	20	0	79	5	1	3	2	0	8	.279	.327	.424	.751
2018	Mil	NL	98	306	77	13	2	9	(6	3)	121	39	28	27	21	3	62	5	1	4	2	0	13	.252	.307	.395	.702
2019	Mil	NL	76	158	36	8	0	7	(5	2)	65	10	25	20	16	1	50	4	0	1	0	0	1	.228	.313	.411	.724
	Postseason		5	7	3	1	0	0	(0	0)	4	1	0	3	5	0	1	0	0	0	0	0	0	.429	.667	.571	1.238
	6 ML YEARS		319	881	226	48	2	27	(18	9)	359	100	108	102	68	4	208	14	2	8	4	1	25	.257	.317	.407	.725

Chad Pinder

Bats: R Throws: R Pos: LF-46;RF-34;PH-26;2B-21;3B-17;CF-5;SS-3;1B-2;DH-2;PR-2   Ht: 6'2" Wt: 207 Born: 3/29/1992 Age: 28

							BATTING															RUNNING			AVERAGES			
Year	Team	Lg	G	AB	H	2B	3B	HR	(Hm	Rd)	TB	R	RBI	RC	TBB	IBB	SO	HBP	SH	SF	SB	CS	GDP	Avg	OBP	Slg	OPS
2016	Oak	AL	22	51	12	4	0	1	(0	1)	19	4	4	5	3	0	14	0	0	1	0	0	1	.235	.273	.373	.645
2017	Oak	AL	87	282	67	15	1	15	(10	5)	129	36	42	37	18	0	92	5	0	3	2	1	7	.238	.292	.457	.750
2018	Oak	AL	110	298	77	12	1	13	(6	7)	130	43	27	35	27	1	88	6	2	0	0	2	4	.258	.332	.436	.769
2019	Oak	AL	124	341	82	21	0	13	(6	7)	142	45	47	43	20	0	88	5	1	3	0	1	11	.240	.290	.416	.706
	4 ML YEARS		343	972	238	52	2	42	(22	20)	420	128	120	120	68	1	282	16	3	7	2	4	23	.245	.303	.432	.735

Michael Pineda

Pitches: R Bats: R Pos: SP-26   pah-NAY-dah   Ht: 6'7" Wt: 280 Born: 1/18/1989 Age: 31

Year	Team	Lg	G	GS	GF	IP	BFP	H	R	ER	HR	SH	SF	HB	TBB	IBB	SO	WP	W	L	Pct	Sv-Op	Hld	Vel	OPS	ERC	ERA
2011	Sea	AL	28	28	0	171.0	696	133	76	71	18	4	3	5	55	1	173	9	9	10	.474	0-0	0	95	.621	2.73	3.74
2014	NYY	AL	13	13	0	76.1	290	56	18	16	5	2	1	0	7	0	59	3	5	5	.500	0-0	0	92	.526	1.51	1.89
2015	NYY	AL	27	27	0	160.2	668	176	83	78	21	4	6	3	21	0	156	4	12	10	.545	0-0	0	93	.752	3.82	4.37
2016	NYY	AL	32	32	0	175.2	756	184	98	94	27	0	3	6	53	1	207	7	6	12	.333	0-0	0	94	.784	4.45	4.82
2017	NYY	AL	17	17	0	96.1	410	103	55	47	20	0	4	2	21	0	92	5	8	4	.667	0-0	0	94	.769	4.52	4.39
2019	Min	AL	26	26	0	146.0	600	141	68	65	23	2	7	5	28	1	140	8	11	5	.688	0-0	0	93	.721	3.58	4.01
	6 ML YEARS		143	143	0	826.0	3420	793	398	371	114	12	24	21	185	3	827	36	51	46	.526	0-0	0	94	.710	3.51	4.04

Ricardo Pinto

Pitches: R Bats: R Pos: RP-2   Ht: 6'0" Wt: 195 Born: 1/20/1994 Age: 26

Year	Team	Lg	G	GS	GF	IP	BFP	H	R	ER	HR	SH	SF	HB	TBB	IBB	SO	WP	W	L	Pct	Sv-Op	Hld	Vel	OPS	ERC	ERA
2019	Drham	AAA	24	4	2	104.2	447	96	49	48	18	2	4	9	46	1	96	12	10	5	.667	0- -	-		.775	4.71	4.13
2017	Phi	NL	25	0	6	29.2	147	39	28	26	7	3	2	1	17	1	25	1	1	2	.333	0-2	2	95	.951	7.70	7.89
2019	TB	AL	2	0	1	2.1	13	4	4	4	1	0	0	0	2	0	0	0	0	0	-	0-0	0	95	1.189	13.74	15.43
	2 ML YEARS		27	0	7	32.0	160	43	32	30	8	3	2	1	19	1	25	1	1	2	.333	0-2	2	95	.971	8.10	8.44

Jose Pirela

Bats: R Throws: R Pos: PH-9;LF-4;RF-3   Ht: 6'0" Wt: 220 Born: 11/21/1989 Age: 30

Year	Team	Lg	G	AB	H	2B	3B	HR	(Hm	Rd)	TB	R	RBI	RC	TBB	IBB	SO	HBP	SH	SF	SB	CS	GDP	Avg	OBP	Slg	OPS
2019	ElPaso	AAA	55	221	78	13	2	18	(-	-)	149	50	59	55	17	2	51	1	0	2	0	1	2	.353	.401	.674	1.075
2019	LV	AAA	33	121	34	9	0	4	(-	-)	55	19	14	18	8	2	25	1	0	0	2	0	0	.281	.331	.455	.785
2014	NYY	AL	7	24	8	1	2	0	(0	0)	13	6	3	4	1	0	4	0	0	0	0	0	1	.333	.360	.542	.902
2015	NYY	AL	37	74	17	3	0	1	(1	0)	23	7	5	3	2	0	16	1	0	1	1	0	4	.230	.247	.311	.558
2016	SD	NL	15	39	6	2	0	0	(0	0)	8	2	0	0	1	0	9	0	1	0	0	1	0	.154	.175	.205	.380
2017	SD	NL	83	312	90	25	4	10	(5	5)	153	43	40	50	27	0	71	2	1	2	4	3	8	.288	.347	.490	.837
2018	SD	NL	146	438	109	23	2	5	(1	4)	151	54	34	47	30	1	89	3	0	2	6	3	10	.249	.305	.345	.645
2019	2 Tms		14	22	4	1	0	1	(0	1)	8	1	2	4	2	0	7	0	0	0	0	0	0	.182	.250	.364	.614
19	SD	NL	2	5	0	0	0	0	(0	0)	0	0	0	0	0	0	3	0	0	0	0	0	1	.000	.000	.000	.000
19	Phi	NL	12	17	4	1	0	1	(0	1)	8	1	2	4	2	0	4	0	0	0	0	0	0	.235	.316	.471	.786
	6 ML YEARS		302	909	234	55	8	17	(7	10)	356	113	82	108	63	1	196	5	3	5	11	7	24	.257	.308	.392	.699

Stephen Piscotty

Bats: R Throws: R Pos: RF-90;DH-2;PH-1   Ht: 6'4" Wt: 205 Born: 1/14/1991 Age: 29

Year	Team	Lg	G	AB	H	2B	3B	HR	(Hm	Rd)	TB	R	RBI	RC	TBB	IBB	SO	HBP	SH	SF	SB	CS	GDP	Avg	OBP	Slg	OPS
2015	StL	NL	63	233	71	15	4	7	(4	3)	115	29	39	41	20	2	56	1	0	2	2	1	7	.305	.359	.494	.853
2016	StL	NL	153	582	159	35	3	22	(13	9)	266	86	85	97	51	0	133	12	1	2	7	5	14	.273	.343	.457	.800
2017	StL	NL	107	341	80	16	1	9	(1	8)	125	40	39	43	52	2	87	5	0	3	3	6	11	.235	.342	.367	.708
2018	Oak	AL	151	546	146	41	0	27	(10	17)	268	78	88	87	42	0	114	12	0	5	2	0	21	.267	.331	.491	.821
2019	Oak	AL	93	357	89	17	1	13	(8	5)	147	46	44	42	29	0	84	3	1	3	2	0	13	.249	.309	.412	.720
	Postseason		5	19	6	1	0	3	(1	2)	16	5	6	8	3	0	10	0	0	0	0	0	0	.316	.409	.842	1.251
	5 ML YEARS		567	2059	545	124	9	78	(36	42)	921	279	295	310	194	4	474	33	2	15	16	12	66	.265	.336	.447	.783

Nick Pivetta

Pitches: R Bats: R Pos: RP-17; SP-13   Ht: 6'5" Wt: 220 Born: 2/14/1993 Age: 27

Year	Team	Lg	G	GS	GF	IP	BFP	H	R	ER	HR	SH	SF	HB	TBB	IBB	SO	WP	W	L	Pct	Sv-Op	Hld	Vel	OPS	ERC	ERA
2019	LV	AAA	9	6	0	41.0	166	23	14	14	2	1	2	1	22	0	58	3	5	1	.833	0--	-		.515	2.08	3.07
2017	Phi	NL	26	26	0	133.0	584	144	91	89	25	4	7	4	57	0	140	11	8	10	.444	0-0	0	94	.846	5.52	6.02
2018	Phi	NL	33	32	1	164.0	694	163	91	87	24	8	5	5	51	0	188	8	7	14	.333	0-0	0	95	.743	4.15	4.77
2019	Phi	NL	30	13	8	93.2	421	103	64	56	20	4	4	4	39	2	89	4	4	6	.400	1-1	1	95	.866	5.67	5.38
	3 ML YEARS		89	71	9	390.2	1699	410	246	232	69	16	16	13	147	2	417	23	19	30	.388	1-1	1	95	.808	4.97	5.34

Kevin Plawecki

Bats: R Throws: R Pos: C-57;PH-4;1B-1;DH-1;PR-1   plah-WEH-kee   Ht: 6'2" Wt: 220 Born: 2/26/1991 Age: 29

Year	Team	Lg	G	AB	H	2B	3B	HR	(Hm	Rd)	TB	R	RBI	RC	TBB	IBB	SO	HBP	SH	SF	SB	CS	GDP	Avg	OBP	Slg	OPS
2015	NYM	NL	73	233	51	9	0	3	(1	2)	69	18	21	22	17	4	60	4	1	3	0	0	4	.219	.280	.296	.576
2016	NYM	NL	48	132	26	6	0	1	(0	1)	35	6	11	11	17	2	33	2	0	0	0	0	1	.197	.298	.265	.563
2017	NYM	NL	37	100	26	5	0	3	(3	0)	40	11	13	15	14	2	17	3	0	1	1	0	2	.260	.364	.400	.764
2018	NYM	NL	79	238	50	13	2	7	(5	2)	88	33	30	25	28	2	65	9	1	1	0	1	12	.210	.315	.370	.685
2019	Cle	AL	60	158	35	10	0	3	(3	0)	54	13	17	14	12	0	31	3	0	1	0	1	4	.222	.287	.342	.629
	5 ML YEARS		297	861	188	43	2	17	(12	5)	286	81	92	87	88	10	206	21	2	6	1	2	23	.218	.304	.332	.636

Zach Plesac

Pitches: R Bats: R Pos: SP-21   Ht: 6'3" Wt: 220 Born: 1/21/1995 Age: 25

Year	Team	Lg	G	GS	GF	IP	BFP	H	R	ER	HR	SH	SF	HB	TBB	IBB	SO	WP	W	L	Pct	Sv-Op	Hld	Vel	OPS	ERC	ERA
2019	Akron	AA	6	6	0	37.1	137	23	4	4	0	0	0	0	6	0	34	0	1	1	.500	0--	-	-	.433	1.11	0.96
2019	Cle	AL	21	21	0	115.2	475	102	52	49	19	2	0	3	40	0	88	1	8	6	.571	0-0	0	94	.744	3.82	3.81

Adam Plutko

Pitches: R Bats: R Pos: SP-20; RP-1   Ht: 6'3" Wt: 215 Born: 10/3/1991 Age: 28

Year	Team	Lg	G	GS	GF	IP	BFP	H	R	ER	HR	SH	SF	HB	TBB	IBB	SO	WP	W	L	Pct	Sv-Op	Hld	Vel	OPS	ERC	ERA
2016	Cle	AL	2	0	1	3.2	18	5	3	3	1	0	0	0	2	0	3	1	0	0	-	0-0	0	91	.951	8.17	7.36
2018	Cle	AL	17	12	4	76.2	326	78	45	45	21	1	2	1	23	1	60	3	4	5	.444	1-1	0	91	.869	5.00	5.28
2019	Cle	AL	21	20	0	109.1	462	115	61	59	22	0	2	4	26	2	78	0	7	5	.583	0-0	0	91	.802	4.55	4.86
	3 ML YEARS		40	32	5	189.2	806	198	109	107	44	1	4	5	51	3	141	4	11	10	.524	1-1	0	91	.832	4.80	5.08

Colin Poche

Pitches: L Bats: L Pos: RP-51   Ht: 6'3" Wt: 235 Born: 1/17/1994 Age: 26

Year	Team	Lg	G	GS	GF	IP	BFP	H	R	ER	HR	SH	SF	HB	TBB	IBB	SO	WP	W	L	Pct	Sv-Op	Hld	Vel	OPS	ERC	ERA
2019	Drham	AAA	20	2	1	27.1	122	32	20	19	4	0	1	0	9	0	48	1	2	2	.500	0--	-	-	.747	5.03	6.26
2019	TB	AL	51	0	8	51.2	207	33	27	27	9	1	0	5	19	1	72	2	5	5	.500	2-6	16	93	.650	2.88	4.70

Gregory Polanco

Bats: L Throws: L Pos: RF-36;PH-6;DH-1   puh-LAHN-ko   Ht: 6'5" Wt: 235 Born: 9/14/1991 Age: 28

Year	Team	Lg	G	AB	H	2B	3B	HR	(Hm	Rd)	TB	R	RBI	RC	TBB	IBB	SO	HBP	SH	SF	SB	CS	GDP	Avg	OBP	Slg	OPS
2019	Indy	AAA	13	45	12	4	0	1	(-	-)	19	5	11	8	9	0	16	0	0	0	2	0	0	.267	.389	.422	.811
2014	Pit	NL	89	277	65	9	0	7	(5	2)	95	50	33	32	30	1	59	0	2	2	14	5	1	.235	.307	.343	.650
2015	Pit	NL	153	593	152	35	6	9	(6	3)	226	83	52	73	55	6	121	1	1	2	27	10	5	.256	.320	.381	.701
2016	Pit	NL	144	527	136	34	4	22	(9	13)	244	79	86	73	53	6	119	0	1	6	17	6	13	.258	.323	.463	.786
2017	Pit	NL	108	379	95	20	0	11	(7	4)	148	39	35	39	27	4	60	3	0	1	8	1	5	.251	.305	.391	.695
2018	Pit	NL	130	461	117	32	6	23	(12	11)	230	75	81	76	61	5	117	3	0	7	12	2	11	.254	.340	.499	.839
2019	Pit	NL	42	153	37	8	1	6	(3	3)	65	23	17	17	12	1	49	1	0	0	3	1	4	.242	.301	.425	.726
	Postseason		1	4	0	0	0	0	(0	0)	0	0	0	0	0	0	2	0	0	0	0	0	0	.000	.000	.000	.000
	6 ML YEARS		666	2390	602	138	17	78	(42	36)	1008	349	304	310	238	23	525	8	4	18	81	25	39	.252	.320	.422	.741

Jorge Polanco

Bats: B Throws: R Pos: SS-142;DH-11;PH-3   puh-LAHN-ko   Ht: 5'11" Wt: 200 Born: 7/5/1993 Age: 26

Year	Team	Lg	G	AB	H	2B	3B	HR	(Hm	Rd)	TB	R	RBI	RC	TBB	IBB	SO	HBP	SH	SF	SB	CS	GDP	Avg	OBP	Slg	OPS
2014	Min	AL	5	6	2	1	1	0	(0	0)	5	2	3	4	2	0	2	0	0	0	0	0	0	.333	.500	.833	1.333
2015	Min	AL	4	10	3	0	0	0	(0	0)	3	1	1	3	2	0	1	0	0	0	1	0	0	.300	.417	.300	.717
2016	Min	AL	69	245	69	15	4	4	(1	3)	104	24	27	36	17	0	46	3	2	3	4	3	3	.282	.332	.424	.757
2017	Min	AL	133	488	125	30	3	13	(4	9)	200	60	74	68	41	1	78	2	7	6	13	5	7	.256	.313	.410	.723
2018	Min	AL	77	302	87	18	3	6	(1	5)	129	38	42	50	25	0	62	2	3	1	7	7	5	.288	.345	.427	.773
2019	Min	AL	153	631	186	40	7	22	(9	13)	306	107	79	112	60	2	116	4	2	7	4	3	11	.295	.356	.485	.841
	Postseason		1	4	1	0	0	0	(0	0)	1	2	0	0	1	0	2	0	0	0	0	0	0	.250	.400	.250	.650
	6 ML YEARS		441	1682	472	104	18	45	(15	30)	747	232	226	273	147	3	305	11	14	17	29	18	26	.281	.339	.444	.783

A.J. Pollock

Bats: R Throws: R Pos: CF-62;LF-18;PH-8;DH-1   Ht: 6'1" Wt: 212 Born: 12/5/1987 Age: 32

Year	Team	Lg	G	AB	H	2B	3B	HR	(Hm	Rd)	TB	R	RBI	RC	TBB	IBB	SO	HBP	SH	SF	SB	CS	GDP	Avg	OBP	Slg	OPS
2012	Ari	NL	31	81	20	4	1	2	(2	0)	32	8	8	9	9	1	11	0	1	2	1	2	2	.247	.315	.395	.710
2013	Ari	NL	137	443	119	28	5	8	(3	5)	181	64	38	58	33	1	82	2	3	1	12	3	5	.269	.322	.409	.730
2014	Ari	NL	75	265	80	19	6	7	(7	0)	132	41	24	43	19	0	46	2	1	0	14	3	4	.302	.353	.498	.851
2015	Ari	NL	157	609	192	39	6	20	(9	11)	303	111	76	106	53	0	89	2	0	9	39	7	19	.315	.367	.498	.865
2016	Ari	NL	12	41	10	0	0	2	(2	0)	16	9	4	5	4	0	8	0	0	0	4	0	1	.244	.326	.390	.716
2017	Ari	NL	112	425	113	33	6	14	(9	5)	200	73	49	66	35	1	71	6	0	0	20	6	8	.266	.330	.471	.801
2018	Ari	NL	113	413	106	21	5	21	(11	10)	200	61	65	57	31	2	100	8	1	7	13	2	6	.257	.316	.484	.800
2019	LAD	NL	86	308	82	15	1	15	(9	6)	144	49	47	50	23	1	74	7	0	4	5	1	7	.266	.327	.468	.795
	Postseason		4	14	3	1	1	1	(0	1)	9	3	3	3	2	0	4	0	0	0	0	0	0	.214	.313	.643	.955
	8 ML YEARS		723	2585	722	159	30	89	(50	39)	1208	416	311	394	208	6	481	27	6	23	108	24	52	.279	.337	.467	.804

Drew Pomeranz

Pitches: L Bats: R Pos: RP-28; SP-18   POMM-er-anze   Ht: 6'6" Wt: 240 Born: 11/22/1988 Age: 31

Year	Team	Lg	G	GS	GF	IP	BFP	H	R	ER	HR	SH	SF	HB	TBB	IBB	SO	WP	W	L	Pct	Sv-Op	Hld	Vel	OPS	ERC	ERA
2011	Col	NL	4	4	0	18.1	77	19	11	11	0	1	0	1	5	0	13	1	2	1	.667	0-0	0	90	.700	3.36	5.40
2012	Col	NL	22	22	0	96.2	434	97	57	53	14	8	4	4	46	2	83	8	2	9	.182	0-0	0	91	.775	4.78	4.93
2013	Col	NL	8	4	0	21.2	105	25	15	15	4	1	1	4	19	1	19	0	0	4	.000	0-0	0	91	.951	8.04	6.23
2014	Oak	AL	20	10	4	69.0	278	51	22	18	7	1	0	1	26	0	64	0	5	4	.556	0-0	0	91	.586	2.70	2.35
2015	Oak	AL	53	9	9	86.0	357	71	44	35	8	4	5	3	31	1	82	2	5	6	.455	3-6	12	91	.651	3.05	3.66
2016	2 Tms		31	30	1	170.2	703	137	65	63	22	3	3	1	65	3	186	10	11	12	.478	0-0	0	90	.658	3.13	3.32
2017	Bos	AL	32	32	0	173.2	740	166	69	64	19	2	6	4	69	0	174	6	17	6	.739	0-0	0	91	.712	4.00	3.32
2018	Bos	AL	26	11	5	74.0	344	87	53	50	12	0	3	4	44	1	64	4	2	6	.250	0-0	1	89	.894	6.73	6.08
2019	2 Tms	NL	46	18	4	104.0	455	105	58	56	21	2	2	4	44	0	137	1	2	10	.167	2-2	12	93	.804	5.13	4.85
16	SD	NL	17	17	0	102.0	411	67	30	28	8	2	3	1	41	2	115	7	8	7	.533	0-0	0	90	.555	2.17	2.47
16	Bos	AL	14	13	1	68.2	292	70	35	35	14	1	0	0	24	1	71	3	3	5	.375	0-0	0	91	.799	4.73	4.59
19	SF	NL	21	17	0	77.2	355	89	51	49	17	2	1	4	36	0	92	1	2	9	.182	0-0	0	92	.872	6.32	5.68
19	Mil	NL	25	1	4	26.1	100	16	7	7	4	0	1	0	8	0	45	0	0	1	.000	2-2	12	94	.570	2.07	2.39
	Postseason		3	1	0	5.2	29	9	6	6	3	1	0	0	3	1	8	0	1	0	1.000	0-0	0	93	1.229	11.60	9.53
	9 ML YEARS		242	140	23	814.0	3493	758	394	365	107	22	24	23	349	8	824	32	46	58	.442	5-8	25	91	.728	4.13	4.04

Daniel Ponce de Leon

Pitches: R Bats: R Pos: SP-8; RP-5   Ht: 6'3" Wt: 200 Born: 1/16/1992 Age: 28

Year	Team	Lg	G	GS	GF	IP	BFP	H	R	ER	HR	SH	SF	HB	TBB	IBB	SO	WP	W	L	Pct	Sv-Op	Hld	Vel	OPS	ERC	ERA
2019	Memp	AAA	16	16	0	84.1	358	62	30	27	7	1	2	6	43	1	86	6	8	4	.667	0- -	-	-	.625	3.19	2.88
2018	StL	NL	11	4	2	33.0	132	24	10	10	2	0	1	1	13	0	31	0	0	2	.000	1-1	0	93	.596	2.54	2.73
2019	StL	NL	13	8	1	48.2	203	36	21	20	6	0	1	2	26	3	52	2	1	2	.333	0-0	0	93	.666	3.46	3.70
	2 ML YEARS		24	12	3	81.2	335	60	31	30	8	0	2	3	39	3	83	2	1	4	.200	1-1	0	93	.638	3.08	3.31

313

Sean Poppen

Pitches: R **Bats:** R **Pos:** RP-4   **Ht:** 6'3" **Wt:** 205 **Born:** 3/15/1994 **Age:** 26

Year	Team	Lg	G	GS	GF	IP	BFP	H	R	ER	HR	SH	SF	HB	TBB	IBB	SO	WP	W	L	Pct	Sv-Op	Hld	Vel	OPS	ERC	ERA
2019	Roch	AAA	12	9	0	61.0	266	53	29	26	4	0	1	6	27	0	68	4	5	1	.833	0- -	-		.675	3.61	3.84
2019	Pnscla	AA	8	7	0	28.2	131	30	16	14	0	0	1	4	17	0	39	1	2	3	.400	0- -	-		.720	4.97	4.40
2019	Min	AL	4	0	3	8.1	36	10	7	7	1	0	0	0	5	0	9	0	0	0	-	0-0	0	95	.997	6.83	7.56

Rick Porcello

Pitches: R **Bats:** R **Pos:** SP-32   pore-SELL-oh   **Ht:** 6'5" **Wt:** 205 **Born:** 12/27/1988 **Age:** 31

Year	Team	Lg	G	GS	GF	IP	BFP	H	R	ER	HR	SH	SF	HB	TBB	IBB	SO	WP	W	L	Pct	Sv-Op	Hld	Vel	OPS	ERC	ERA
2009	Det	AL	31	31	0	170.2	720	176	81	75	23	4	2	3	52	0	89	6	14	9	.609	0-0	0	91	.738	4.24	3.96
2010	Det	AL	27	27	0	162.2	700	188	96	89	18	1	2	7	38	2	84	11	10	12	.455	0-0	0	91	.752	4.56	4.92
2011	Det	AL	31	31	0	182.0	784	210	103	96	18	5	5	8	46	1	104	12	14	9	.609	0-0	0	90	.774	4.57	4.75
2012	Det	AL	31	31	0	176.1	783	226	101	90	16	2	3	6	44	3	107	6	10	12	.455	0-0	0	92	.808	5.16	4.59
2013	Det	AL	32	29	1	177.0	736	185	87	85	18	4	3	3	42	4	142	6	13	8	.619	0-0	0	91	.709	3.79	4.32
2014	Det	AL	32	31	1	204.2	840	211	89	78	18	3	4	4	41	4	129	0	15	13	.536	0-0	0	90	.712	3.50	3.43
2015	Bos	AL	28	28	0	172.0	737	196	103	94	25	2	5	10	38	0	149	12	9	15	.375	0-0	0	91	.787	4.76	4.92
2016	Bos	AL	33	33	0	223.0	890	193	85	78	23	2	3	13	32	0	189	3	22	4	.846	0-0	0	90	.635	2.64	3.15
2017	Bos	AL	33	33	0	203.1	885	236	125	105	38	1	6	6	48	1	181	5	11	17	.393	0-0	0	91	.826	5.04	4.65
2018	Bos	AL	33	33	0	191.1	808	177	97	91	27	3	6	16	48	0	190	3	17	7	.708	0-0	0	90	.698	3.64	4.28
2019	Bos	AL	32	32	0	174.1	768	198	114	107	31	3	1	6	45	2	143	5	14	12	.538	0-0	0	90	.809	4.87	5.52
	Postseason		16	7	5	40.0	174	44	23	21	6	0	2	5	7	2	34	2	1	3	.250	0-0	2	92	.803	4.47	4.73
	11 ML YEARS		343	339	2	2037.1	8651	2196	1081	988	255	30	40	82	474	17	1507	69	149	118	.558	0-0	0	91	.749	4.19	4.36

Buster Posey

Bats: R **Throws:** R **Pos:** C-101;PH-11;1B-4;DH-2   **Ht:** 6'1" **Wt:** 210 **Born:** 3/27/1987 **Age:** 33

Year	Team	Lg	G	AB	H	2B	3B	HR	(Hm	Rd)	TB	R	RBI	RC	TBB	IBB	SO	HBP	SH	SF	SB	CS	GDP	Avg	OBP	Slg	OPS
2009	SF	NL	7	17	2	0	0	0	(0	0)	2	1	0	0	0	0	4	0	0	0	0	0	0	.118	.118	.118	.235
2010	SF	NL	108	406	124	23	2	18	(6	12)	205	58	67	70	30	5	55	4	0	3	0	2	12	.305	.357	.505	.862
2011	SF	NL	45	162	46	5	0	4	(1	3)	63	17	21	26	18	3	30	4	0	1	3	0	4	.284	.368	.389	.756
2012	SF	NL	148	530	178	39	1	24	(7	17)	291	78	103	111	69	7	96	2	0	9	1	1	19	.336	.408	.549	.957
2013	SF	NL	148	520	153	34	1	15	(8	7)	234	61	72	77	60	8	70	8	0	7	2	1	15	.294	.371	.450	.821
2014	SF	NL	147	547	170	28	2	22	(11	11)	268	72	89	94	47	5	69	3	0	8	0	1	16	.311	.364	.490	.854
2015	SF	NL	150	557	177	28	0	19	(6	13)	262	74	95	96	56	10	52	3	0	7	2	0	17	.318	.379	.470	.849
2016	SF	NL	146	539	155	33	2	14	(7	7)	234	82	80	82	64	7	68	3	0	8	6	1	18	.288	.362	.434	.796
2017	SF	NL	140	494	158	34	0	12	(3	9)	228	62	67	84	61	13	66	8	0	5	6	1	17	.320	.400	.462	.861
2018	SF	NL	105	398	113	22	1	5	(4	1)	152	47	41	58	45	3	53	3	0	2	3	2	12	.284	.359	.382	.741
2019	SF	NL	114	405	104	24	0	7	(1	6)	149	43	38	49	34	1	71	4	1	1	0	0	18	.257	.320	.368	.688
	Postseason		53	206	51	4	0	4	(1	3)	67	17	23	21	23	5	41	1	0	2	1	1	4	.248	.323	.325	.649
	11 ML YEARS		1258	4575	1380	270	9	140	(54	86)	2088	595	673	747	484	62	634	42	1	51	23	9	148	.302	.370	.456	.826

Brooks Pounders

Pitches: R **Bats:** R **Pos:** RP-7   **Ht:** 6'5" **Wt:** 265 **Born:** 9/26/1990 **Age:** 29

Year	Team	Lg	G	GS	GF	IP	BFP	H	R	ER	HR	SH	SF	HB	TBB	IBB	SO	WP	W	L	Pct	Sv-Op	Hld	Vel	OPS	ERC	ERA
2019	Clmbs	AAA	24	0	6	35.0	133	19	9	9	4	0	1	3	11	1	46	1	2	1	.667	1- -	-		.536	1.88	2.31
2019	Syrcse	AAA	19	1	1	21.1	104	29	19	18	4	1	2	4	9	1	20	4	1	2	.333	0- -	-		.930	7.77	7.59
2016	KC	AL	13	0	6	12.2	58	19	13	13	6	0	1	0	3	0	13	0	2	1	.667	0-0	1	93	1.083	9.56	9.24
2017	LAA	AL	11	0	10	10.1	54	17	12	12	4	1	0	1	5	1	12	0	1	0	1.000	0-0	0	93	1.157	11.15	10.45
2018	Col	NL	14	0	11	15.1	72	25	13	13	3	0	0	2	2	0	17	1	0	1	.000	0-1	0	92	1.065	8.30	7.63
2019	NYM	NL	7	0	3	7.1	34	9	5	5	1	1	0	1	2	0	5	1	1	0	1.000	0-0	0	92	.864	5.58	6.14
	4 ML YEARS		45	0	30	45.2	218	70	43	43	14	2	1	4	12	1	47	2	4	2	.667	0-1	1	92	1.061	8.83	8.47

Bobby Poyner

Pitches: L **Bats:** L **Pos:** RP-12; SP-1   **Ht:** 6'0" **Wt:** 205 **Born:** 12/1/1992 **Age:** 27

Year	Team	Lg	G	GS	GF	IP	BFP	H	R	ER	HR	SH	SF	HB	TBB	IBB	SO	WP	W	L	Pct	Sv-Op	Hld	Vel	OPS	ERC	ERA
2019	Pwtckt	AAA	43	1	15	57.1	249	47	27	24	9	2	3	3	27	2	70	3	2	5	.286	6- -	-		.718	3.82	3.77
2018	Bos	AL	20	0	4	22	93	22	8	8	4	1	1	2	3	0	24	0	1	0	1.000	0-0	5	90	.770	3.79	3.22
2019	Bos	AL	13	1	2	11.2	49	10	9	9	2	0	0	1	5	0	11	0	0	1	.000	0-0	0	89	.792	4.33	6.94
	2 ML YEARS		33	1	6	34.0	142	32	17	17	6	1	1	3	8	0	35	0	1	1	.500	0-0	5	90	.778	3.97	4.50

Martin Prado

Bats: R **Throws:** R **Pos:** PH-49;1B-40;3B-22;DH-2   mar-TEEN PRAH-doe   **Ht:** 6'0" **Wt:** 215 **Born:** 10/27/1983 **Age:** 36

Year	Team	Lg	G	AB	H	2B	3B	HR	(Hm	Rd)	TB	R	RBI	RC	TBB	IBB	SO	HBP	SH	SF	SB	CS	GDP	Avg	OBP	Slg	OPS
2006	Atl	NL	24	42	11	1	1	1	(1	0)	17	3	9	9	5	0	7	0	2	0	0	0	2	.262	.340	.405	.745
2007	Atl	NL	28	59	17	3	0	0	(0	0)	20	5	2	6	3	0	6	0	0	0	0	0	0	.288	.323	.339	.662
2008	Atl	NL	78	228	73	18	4	2	(1	1)	105	36	33	39	21	0	29	1	2	2	3	1	3	.320	.377	.461	.838
2009	Atl	NL	128	450	138	38	0	11	(4	7)	209	64	49	57	36	1	59	2	11	4	1	3	17	.307	.358	.464	.822
2010	Atl	NL	140	599	184	40	3	15	(4	11)	275	100	66	86	40	2	86	3	3	6	5	3	13	.307	.350	.459	.809
2011	Atl	NL	129	551	143	26	2	13	(9	4)	212	66	57	57	34	1	52	1	1	7	4	8	16	.260	.302	.385	.687
2012	Atl	NL	156	617	186	42	6	10	(6	4)	270	81	70	96	58	2	69	2	4	9	17	4	19	.301	.359	.438	.796

			BATTING																	RUNNING			AVERAGES			
Year Team	Lg	G	AB	H	2B	3B	HR	(Hm Rd)	TB	R	RBI	RC	TBB	IBB	SO	HBP	SH	SF	SB	CS	GDP	Avg	OBP	Slg	OPS
2013 Ari	NL	155	609	172	36	2	14	(7 7)	254	79	82	72	47	2	53	2	0	6	3	5	29	.282	.333	.417	.750
2014 2 Tms		143	536	151	26	4	12	(7 5)	221	62	58	66	26	0	80	7	0	4	3	1	20	.282	.321	.412	.733
2015 Mia	NL	129	500	144	22	2	9	(5 4)	197	52	63	70	37	4	68	5	1	8	1	0	9	.288	.338	.394	.732
2016 Mia	NL	153	600	183	37	3	8	(6 2)	250	70	75	89	49	4	69	4	0	5	2	2	24	.305	.359	.417	.775
2017 Mia	NL	37	140	35	9	0	2	(0 2)	50	13	12	8	6	0	22	0	0	1	0	0	4	.250	.279	.357	.636
2018 Mia	NL	54	197	48	9	0	1	(0 1)	60	16	18	17	11	0	35	1	0	0	1	1	5	.244	.287	.305	.592
2019 Mia	NL	104	245	57	9	0	2	(0 2)	72	26	15	16	12	0	41	0	0	3	0	0	10	.233	.265	.294	.559
14 Ari	NL	106	403	109	17	4	5	(3 2)	149	44	42	43	23	0	57	6	0	4	2	1	17	.270	.317	.370	.686
14 NYY	AL	37	133	42	9	0	7	(4 3)	72	18	16	23	3	0	23	1	0	0	1	0	3	.316	.336	.541	.877
Postseason		1	5	1	0	0	0	(0 0)	1	0	0	0	0	0	1	0	0	0	0	0	0	.200	.200	.200	.400
14 ML YEARS		1458	5373	1542	316	27	100	(50 50)	2212	664	609	688	385	16	676	28	24	51	40	28	171	.287	.335	.412	.747

Ryan Pressly

Pitches: R Bats: R Pos: RP-55   Ht: 6'3" Wt: 210 Born: 12/15/1988 Age: 31

		HOW MUCH PITCHED					WHAT HE GAVE UP											THE RESULTS							
Year Team	Lg	G	GS	GF	IP	BFP	H	R	ER	HR	SH	SF	HB	TBB	IBB	SO	WP	W	L	Pct	Sv-Op	Hld	Vel	OPS	ERC	ERA
2013 Min	AL	49	0	18	76.2	315	71	37	33	5	2	3	0	27	1	49	7	3	3	.500	0-0	1	93	.677	3.31	3.87
2014 Min	AL	25	0	5	28.1	122	30	10	9	3	2	3	1	8	1	14	1	2	0	1.000	0-1	2	93	.779	3.98	2.86
2015 Min	AL	27	0	6	27.2	119	27	9	9	0	1	1	0	12	1	22	2	3	2	.600	0-0	4	94	.645	3.31	2.93
2016 Min	AL	72	0	10	75.1	328	79	34	31	8	4	2	2	23	2	67	7	6	7	.462	1-6	13	95	.725	4.01	3.70
2017 Min	AL	57	0	10	61.1	252	52	34	32	10	2	1	3	19	5	61	5	2	3	.400	0-1	6	96	.697	3.41	4.70
2018 2 Tms	AL	77	0	11	71.0	292	57	21	20	6	1	2	3	22	1	101	8	2	1	.667	2-8	21	96	.604	2.71	2.54
2019 Hou	AL	55	0	8	54.1	211	37	15	14	6	0	1	0	12	0	72	4	2	3	.400	3-8	31	96	.543	1.85	2.32
18 Min	AL	51	0	7	47.2	208	46	19	18	5	1	2	2	19	1	69	6	1	1	.500	0-4	8	96	.699	3.99	3.40
18 Hou	AL	26	0	4	23.1	84	11	2	2	1	0	0	1	3	0	32	2	1	0	1.000	2-4	13	96	.379	0.88	0.77
Postseason		5	0	0	5.0	20	1	1	1	0	0	0	0	3	0	7	1	0	0	-	0-0	3	96	.259	0.76	1.80
7 ML YEARS		362	0	68	394.2	1639	353	160	148	38	12	13	9	123	12	386	34	20	19	.513	6-24	78	95	.664	3.18	3.38

David Price

Pitches: L Bats: L Pos: SP-22   Ht: 6'5" Wt: 215 Born: 8/26/1985 Age: 34

		HOW MUCH PITCHED					WHAT HE GAVE UP											THE RESULTS							
Year Team	Lg	G	GS	GF	IP	BFP	H	R	ER	HR	SH	SF	HB	TBB	IBB	SO	WP	W	L	Pct	Sv-Op	Hld	Vel	OPS	ERC	ERA
2008 TB	AL	5	1	0	14.0	57	9	4	3	1	0	1	1	4	0	12	0	0	0	-	0-0	1	94	.501	1.86	1.93
2009 TB	AL	23	23	0	128.1	557	119	72	63	17	3	2	4	54	0	102	2	10	7	.588	0-0	0	93	.716	4.05	4.42
2010 TB	AL	32	31	0	208.2	861	170	71	63	15	4	3	5	79	1	188	5	19	6	.760	0-0	0	95	.637	2.91	2.72
2011 TB	AL	34	34	0	224.1	918	192	93	87	22	4	7	9	63	5	218	2	12	13	.480	0-0	0	95	.659	2.97	3.49
2012 TB	AL	31	31	0	211.0	836	173	63	60	16	2	3	5	59	2	205	8	20	5	.800	0-0	0	96	.602	2.67	2.56
2013 TB	AL	27	27	0	186.2	740	178	78	69	16	1	2	3	27	0	151	6	10	8	.556	0-0	0	94	.661	2.89	3.33
2014 2 Tms	AL	34	34	0	248.1	1009	230	100	90	25	4	3	5	38	1	271	2	15	12	.556	0-0	0	93	.647	2.79	3.26
2015 2 Tms	AL	32	32	0	220.1	888	190	70	60	17	4	8	3	47	2	225	4	18	5	.783	0-0	0	94	.621	2.54	2.45
2016 Bos	AL	35	35	0	230.0	951	227	106	102	30	8	7	7	50	1	228	4	17	9	.654	0-0	0	93	.721	3.43	3.99
2017 Bos	AL	16	11	1	74.2	317	65	30	28	8	0	2	4	24	0	76	2	6	3	.667	0-0	0	94	.652	3.25	3.38
2018 Bos	AL	30	30	0	176.0	722	151	75	70	21	1	4	10	50	0	177	1	16	7	.696	0-0	0	93	.691	3.38	3.58
2019 Bos	AL	22	22	0	107.1	458	109	57	51	15	0	1	3	32	0	128	3	7	5	.583	0-0	0	92	.755	4.13	4.28
14 TB	AL	23	23	0	170.2	689	156	68	59	20	3	3	5	23	1	189	2	11	8	.579	0-0	0	93	.647	2.79	3.11
14 Det	AL	11	11	0	77.2	320	74	32	31	5	1	0	0	15	0	82	0	4	4	.500	0-0	0	93	.647	2.77	3.59
15 Det	AL	21	21	0	146.0	592	133	50	41	13	4	5	3	29	2	138	3	9	4	.692	0-0	0	94	.654	2.83	2.53
15 Tor	AL	11	11	0	74.1	296	57	20	19	4	0	3	0	18	0	87	1	9	1	.900	0-0	0	95	.555	2.00	2.30
Postseason		23	14	5	99.1	414	91	53	51	16	0	2	3	28	1	91	1	5	9	.357	1-1	0	94	.707	3.65	4.62
12 ML YEARS		321	311	1	2029.2	8314	1813	819	746	207	31	43	59	527	12	1981	39	150	80	.652	0-0	2	94	.663	3.09	3.31

Jurickson Profar

JURR-ick-sun PRO-farr

Bats: B Throws: R Pos: 2B-124;DH-8;PH-8;LF-7;PR-3;1B-1   Ht: 6'0" Wt: 190 Born: 2/20/1993 Age: 27

							BATTING														RUNNING			AVERAGES			
Year Team	Lg	G	AB	H	2B	3B	HR	(Hm Rd)	TB	R	RBI	RC	TBB	IBB	SO	HBP	SH	SF	SB	CS	GDP	Avg	OBP	Slg	OPS
2012 Tex	AL	9	17	3	2	0	1	(0 1)	8	2	2	1	0	0	4	0	0	0	0	0	1	.176	.176	.471	.647
2013 Tex	AL	85	286	67	11	0	6	(3 3)	96	30	26	30	26	0	63	5	6	1	2	4	1	.234	.308	.336	.644
2016 Tex	AL	90	272	65	6	3	5	(4 1)	92	35	20	30	30	0	61	3	2	0	2	1	7	.239	.321	.338	.660
2017 Tex	AL	22	58	10	2	0	0	(0 0)	12	8	5	5	9	0	14	1	2	0	1	1	0	.172	.294	.207	.501
2018 Tex	AL	146	524	133	35	6	20	(11 9)	240	82	77	88	54	1	88	12	0	4	10	0	9	.254	.335	.458	.793
2019 Oak	AL	139	459	100	24	2	20	(11 9)	188	65	67	58	48	2	75	8	0	3	9	1	12	.218	.301	.410	.711
Postseason		1	1	1	0	0	0	(0 0)	1	0	0	0	0	0	0	0	0	0	0	0	0	1.000	1.000	1.000	2.000
6 ML YEARS		491	1616	378	80	11	52	(29 23)	636	222	197	212	167	3	305	29	10	8	24	7	30	.234	.315	.394	.709

Austin Pruitt

Pitches: R Bats: R Pos: RP-12; SP-2   Ht: 5'10" Wt: 185 Born: 8/31/1989 Age: 30

		HOW MUCH PITCHED					WHAT HE GAVE UP											THE RESULTS							
Year Team	Lg	G	GS	GF	IP	BFP	H	R	ER	HR	SH	SF	HB	TBB	IBB	SO	WP	W	L	Pct	Sv-Op	Hld	Vel	OPS	ERC	ERA
2019 Drham	AAA	18	6	1	48.1	216	61	31	29	9	0	3	1	12	0	51	1	3	3	.500	0- -	-	-	.848	5.65	5.40
2017 TB	AL	30	8	7	83.0	371	103	55	49	11	0	5		22	2	66	4	7	5	.583	1-2	1	92	.827	5.36	5.31
2018 TB	AL	23	0	11	69.2	291	72	40	36	7	1	4	1	16	0	42	1	2	3	.400	4-5	0	92	.712	3.67	4.65
2019 TB	AL	14	2	4	47.0	193	47	23	23	7	2	2	0	12	2	39	1	3	0	1.000	0-0	0	92	.761	3.84	4.40
3 ML YEARS		67	10	22	199.2	855	222	118	108	25	4	6	6	50	4	147	6	12	8	.600	5-7	1	92	.773	4.40	4.87

Cesar Puello

Bats: R **Throws:** R **Pos:** CF-20;LF-12;RF-10;PH-4;PR-1   PWAY-oh   **Ht:** 6'2" **Wt:** 220 **Born:** 4/1/1991 **Age:** 29

Year Team	Lg	G	AB	H	2B	3B	HR	(Hm Rd)	TB	R	RBI	RC	TBB	IBB	SO	HBP	SH	SF	SB	CS	GDP	Avg	OBP	Slg	OPS
2019 Salt Lk	AAA	43	135	40	7	0	7	(- -)	68	26	27	30	22	1	37	10	0	0	2	1	2	.296	.431	.504	.935
2017 2 Tms	AL	17	34	7	0	0	0	(0 0)	7	6	3	3	4	0	12	1	0	0	2	0	2	.206	.308	.206	.514
2019 2 Tms		44	125	31	5	0	4	(1 3)	48	14	18	19	10	1	38	11	1	0	0	0	2	.248	.356	.384	.740
17 LAA	AL	1	4	1	0	0	0	(0 0)	1	0	1	1	0	0	1	0	0	0	2	0	0	.250	.250	.250	.500
17 TB	AL	16	30	6	0	0	0	(0 0)	6	6	2	2	4	0	11	1	0	0	0	0	0	.200	.314	.200	.514
19 LAA	AL	12	41	16	3	0	3	(1 2)	28	6	12	15	3	0	8	6	0	0	0	0	1	.390	.500	.683	1.183
19 Mia	NL	32	84	15	2	0	1	(0 1)	20	8	6	4	7	1	30	5	1	0	0	0	1	.179	.281	.238	.519
2 ML YEARS		61	159	38	5	0	4	(1 3)	55	20	21	22	14	1	50	12	1	0	2	0	4	.239	.346	.346	.692

Yasiel Puig

Bats: R **Throws:** R **Pos:** RF-146;PH-4;DH-1   yah-SEE-el PWEEG   **Ht:** 6'2" **Wt:** 240 **Born:** 12/7/1990 **Age:** 29

Year Team	Lg	G	AB	H	2B	3B	HR	(Hm Rd)	TB	R	RBI	RC	TBB	IBB	SO	HBP	SH	SF	SB	CS	GDP	Avg	OBP	Slg	OPS
2013 LAD	NL	104	382	122	21	2	19	(9 10)	204	66	42	62	36	6	97	11	0	3	11	8	6	.319	.391	.534	.925
2014 LAD	NL	148	558	165	37	9	16	(8 8)	268	92	69	95	67	3	124	12	2	1	11	7	7	.296	.382	.480	.863
2015 LAD	NL	79	282	72	12	3	11	(6 5)	123	30	38	35	26	1	66	2	0	1	3	3	1	.255	.322	.436	.758
2016 LAD	NL	104	334	88	14	2	11	(6 5)	139	45	45	46	24	0	74	7	0	3	5	2	10	.263	.323	.416	.740
2017 LAD	NL	152	499	131	24	2	28	(14 14)	243	72	74	73	64	8	100	2	0	5	15	6	21	.263	.346	.487	.833
2018 LAD	NL	125	405	108	21	1	23	(6 17)	200	60	63	57	36	2	87	1	0	2	15	5	15	.267	.327	.494	.820
2019 2 Tms		149	555	148	30	2	24	(10 14)	254	76	84	86	44	1	133	8	0	4	19	7	13	.267	.327	.458	.785
19 Cin	NL	100	373	94	15	1	22	(10 12)	177	51	61	54	23	1	89	5	0	3	14	5	9	.252	.302	.475	.777
19 Cle		49	182	54	15	1	2	(0 2)	77	25	23	32	21	0	44	3	0	1	5	2	4	.297	.377	.423	.800
Postseason		58	182	51	6	3	5	(3 2)	78	23	23	23	17	3	46	3	0	0	2	4	7	.280	.351	.429	.780
7 ML YEARS		861	3015	834	159	21	132	(59 73)	1431	441	415	454	297	21	681	43	2	19	79	38	73	.277	.348	.475	.823

Albert Pujols

Bats: R **Throws:** R **Pos:** 1B-98;DH-29;PH-4;3B-1   POO-holes   **Ht:** 6'3" **Wt:** 235 **Born:** 1/16/1980 **Age:** 40

Year Team	Lg	G	AB	H	2B	3B	HR	(Hm Rd)	TB	R	RBI	RC	TBB	IBB	SO	HBP	SH	SF	SB	CS	GDP	Avg	OBP	Slg	OPS
2001 StL	NL	161	590	194	47	4	37	(18 19)	360	112	130	132	69	6	93	9	1	7	1	3	21	.329	.403	.610	1.013
2002 StL	NL	157	590	185	40	2	34	(14 20)	331	118	127	121	72	13	69	9	0	4	2	4	20	.314	.394	.561	.955
2003 StL	NL	157	591	212	51	1	43	(21 22)	394	137	124	160	79	12	65	10	0	5	5	1	13	.359	.439	.667	1.106
2004 StL	NL	154	592	196	51	2	46	(18 28)	389	133	123	143	84	12	52	7	0	9	5	5	21	.331	.415	.657	1.072
2005 StL	NL	161	591	195	38	2	41	(23 18)	360	129	117	139	97	27	65	9	0	3	16	2	19	.330	.430	.609	1.039
2006 StL	NL	143	535	177	33	1	49	(24 25)	359	119	137	146	92	28	50	4	0	3	7	2	20	.331	.431	.671	1.102
2007 StL	NL	158	565	185	38	1	32	(12 20)	321	99	103	118	99	22	58	7	0	8	2	6	27	.327	.429	.568	.997
2008 StL	NL	148	524	187	44	0	37	(19 18)	342	100	116	130	104	34	54	5	0	8	7	3	16	.357	.462	.653	1.114
2009 StL	NL	160	568	186	45	1	47	(22 25)	374	124	135	145	115	44	64	9	0	8	16	4	23	.327	.443	.658	1.101
2010 StL	NL	159	587	183	39	1	42	(17 25)	350	115	118	131	103	38	76	4	0	6	14	4	23	.312	.414	.596	1.011
2011 StL	NL	147	579	173	29	0	37	(16 21)	313	105	99	100	61	15	58	4	0	7	9	1	29	.299	.366	.541	.906
2012 LAA	AL	154	607	173	50	0	30	(14 16)	313	85	105	100	52	16	76	5	0	6	8	1	19	.285	.343	.516	.859
2013 LAA	AL	99	391	101	19	0	17	(8 9)	171	49	64	54	40	8	55	5	0	7	1	1	18	.258	.330	.437	.767
2014 LAA	AL	159	633	172	37	1	28	(13 15)	295	89	105	86	48	11	71	5	0	9	5	1	28	.272	.324	.466	.790
2015 LAA	AL	157	602	147	22	0	40	(20 20)	289	85	95	82	50	10	72	6	0	3	5	3	15	.244	.307	.480	.787
2016 LAA	AL	152	593	159	19	0	31	(18 13)	271	71	119	91	49	6	75	2	0	6	4	0	24	.268	.323	.457	.780
2017 LAA	AL	149	593	143	17	0	23	(13 10)	229	53	101	66	37	5	93	2	0	4	3	0	26	.241	.286	.386	.672
2018 LAA	AL	117	465	114	20	0	19	(10 9)	191	50	64	55	28	3	65	2	0	3	1	0	12	.245	.289	.411	.700
2019 LAA	AL	131	491	120	22	0	23	(9 14)	211	55	93	69	43	1	68	3	0	8	3	0	21	.244	.305	.430	.734
Postseason		77	279	90	18	1	19	(7 12)	167	55	54	68	49	20	40	5	0	1	1	2	6	.323	.431	.599	1.030
19 ML YEARS		2823	10687	3202	661	16	656	(309 347)	5863	1828	2075	2068	1322	311	1279	107	1	114	114	41	395	.300	.379	.549	.927

A.J. Puk

Pitches: L **Bats:** L **Pos:** RP-10   **Ht:** 6'7" **Wt:** 238 **Born:** 4/25/1995 **Age:** 25

Year Team	Lg	G	GS	GF	IP	BFP	H	R	ER	HR	SH	SF	HB	TBB	IBB	SO	WP	W	L	Pct	Sv-Op	Hld	Vel	OPS	ERC	ERA
2016 Vrmnt	A-	10	10	0	32.2	137	23	18	11	0	0	1	0	12	0	40	3	0	4	.000	0--	-	-	.489	1.72	3.03
2017 Stcktn	A+	14	11	1	61.0	254	44	28	25	1	0	2	4	23	0	98	2	4	5	.444	0--	-	-	.564	2.19	3.69
2017 Mdlnd	AA	13	13	0	64.0	279	64	34	31	2	0	1	3	25	0	86	7	2	5	.286	0--	-	-	.674	3.71	4.36
2019 Mdlnd	AA	6	1	0	8.1	35	9	4	4	2	0	0	0	3	0	13	3	0	0	-	0--	-	-	.843	5.59	4.32
2019 LsVgs	AAA	9	0	2	11.0	44	7	7	6	3	0	0	1	3	0	16	1	4	1	.800	0--	-	-	.675	3.00	4.91
2019 Oak	AL	10	0	0	11.1	47	10	4	4	1	0	0	0	5	0	13	2	2	0	1.000	0-1	2	97	.652	3.60	3.18

Cal Quantrill

Pitches: R **Bats:** L **Pos:** SP-18; RP-5   **Ht:** 6'3" **Wt:** 208 **Born:** 2/10/1995 **Age:** 25

Year Team	Lg	G	GS	GF	IP	BFP	H	R	ER	HR	SH	SF	HB	TBB	IBB	SO	WP	W	L	Pct	Sv-Op	Hld	Vel	OPS	ERC	ERA
2019 ElPaso	AAA	7	7	0	35.2	158	38	21	18	3	0	3	2	12	1	33	1	4	2	.667	0--	-	-	.755	4.18	4.54
2019 SD	NL	23	18	0	103.0	443	106	61	59	15	2	3	3	28	2	89	3	6	8	.429	0-0	1	94	.741	4.07	5.16

Jose Quijada

Pitches: L **Bats:** L **Pos:** RP-34   kee-HAH-dah   **Ht:** 5'11" **Wt:** 203 **Born:** 11/9/1995 **Age:** 24

			HOW MUCH PITCHED				WHAT HE GAVE UP										THE RESULTS						
Year	Team	Lg	G	GS	GF	IP	BFP	H	R	ER	HR	SH	SF	HB	TBB	IBB	SO	WP	W	L	Pct	Sv-Op	Hld	Vel	OPS	ERC	ERA
2019	NewOr	AAA	22	0	9	29.1	130	27	18	14	5	0	1	3	12	0	35	2	1	0	1.000	4- -	-	-	.744	4.47	4.30
2019	Mia	NL	34	0	9	29.2	144	27	20	19	10	1	0	4	26	3	44	2	2	3	.400	1-2	4	93	.974	7.81	5.76

Roman Quinn

Bats: B **Throws:** R **Pos:** CF-34;PH-11;PR-2   **Ht:** 5'10" **Wt:** 170 **Born:** 5/14/1993 **Age:** 27

					BATTING															RUNNING			AVERAGES			
Year	Team	Lg	G	AB	H	2B	3B	HR	(Hm	Rd)	TB	R	RBI	RC	TBB	IBB	SO	HBP	SH	SF	SB	CS	GDP	Avg	OBP	Slg	OPS
2016	Phi	NL	15	57	15	4	0	0	(0	0)	19	10	6	9	8	0	19	2	2	0	5	1	0	.263	.373	.333	.706
2018	Phi	NL	50	131	34	6	4	2	(1	1)	54	13	12	15	10	0	35	1	1	0	10	4	1	.260	.317	.412	.729
2019	Phi	NL	44	108	23	3	1	4	(3	1)	40	18	11	15	12	0	34	1	1	0	8	0	2	.213	.298	.370	.668
	3 ML YEARS		109	296	72	13	5	6	(4	2)	113	41	29	39	30	0	88	4	4	0	23	5	3	.243	.321	.382	.703

Jose Quintana

Pitches: L **Bats:** R **Pos:** SP-31; RP-1   KIN-tahn-ah   **Ht:** 6'1" **Wt:** 220 **Born:** 1/24/1989 **Age:** 31

			HOW MUCH PITCHED					WHAT HE GAVE UP											THE RESULTS							
Year	Team	Lg	G	GS	GF	IP	BFP	H	R	ER	HR	SH	SF	HB	TBB	IBB	SO	WP	W	L	Pct	Sv-Op	Hld	Vel	OPS	ERC	ERA
2012	CWS	AL	25	22	2	136.1	568	142	62	57	14	5	1	3	42	4	81	10	6	6	.500	0-0	0	90	.754	4.13	3.76
2013	CWS	AL	33	33	0	200.0	832	188	83	78	23	3	6	5	56	2	164	2	9	7	.563	0-0	0	91	.695	3.47	3.51
2014	CWS	AL	32	32	0	200.1	830	197	87	74	10	4	6	2	52	3	178	7	9	11	.450	0-0	0	92	.662	3.15	3.32
2015	CWS	AL	32	32	0	206.1	862	218	81	77	16	4	4	8	44	4	177	5	9	10	.474	0-0	0	92	.722	3.67	3.36
2016	CWS	AL	32	32	0	208.0	837	192	76	74	22	2	2	4	50	1	181	10	13	12	.520	0-0	0	92	.687	3.23	3.20
2017	2 Tms		32	32	0	188.2	790	170	92	87	23	1	3	10	61	4	207	8	11	11	.500	0-0	0	92	.701	3.57	4.15
2018	ChC	NL	32	32	0	174.1	739	162	81	78	25	8	2	3	68	3	158	3	13	11	.542	0-0	0	92	.737	4.00	4.03
2019	ChC	NL	32	31	0	171.0	745	191	100	89	20	5	**13**	2	46	0	152	11	13	9	.591	0-0	0	91	.763	4.32	4.68
17	CWS	AL	18	18	0	104.1	444	98	55	52	14	1	2	2	40	1	109	7	4	8	.333	0-0	0	92	.735	3.97	4.49
17	ChC	NL	14	14	0	84.1	346	72	37	35	9	0	1	8	21	3	98	1	7	3	.700	0-0	0	92	.659	3.08	3.74
	Postseason		4	3	0	13.1	57	11	9	8	1	0	2	0	5	0	12	0	0	1	.000	0-0	1	92	.621	2.76	5.40
	8 ML YEARS		250	246	2	1485.0	6203	1460	662	614	153	32	37	37	419	21	1298	56	83	77	.519	0-0	0	92	.713	3.65	3.72

Tanner Rainey

Pitches: R **Bats:** R **Pos:** RP-52   **Ht:** 6'2" **Wt:** 235 **Born:** 12/25/1992 **Age:** 27

			HOW MUCH PITCHED					WHAT HE GAVE UP											THE RESULTS							
Year	Team	Lg	G	GS	GF	IP	BFP	H	R	ER	HR	SH	SF	HB	TBB	IBB	SO	WP	W	L	Pct	Sv-Op	Hld	Vel	OPS	ERC	ERA
2019	Fresno	AAA	16	0	8	18.0	82	16	8	8	1	0	0	1	12	0	32	3	2	2	.500	2- -	-	-	.716	4.32	4.00
2018	Cin	NL	8	0	2	7.0	45	13	19	19	4	0	1	0	12	1	7	0	0	0	-	0-0	0	98	1.462	21.19	24.43
2019	Was	NL	52	0	7	48.1	214	32	22	21	6	2	0	4	38	2	74	7	2	3	.400	0-3	9	98	.696	4.13	3.91
	2 ML YEARS		60	0	9	55.1	259	45	41	40	10	2	1	4	50	3	81	7	2	3	.400	0-3	9	98	.821	5.86	6.51

Erasmo Ramirez

Pitches: R **Bats:** R **Pos:** RP-1   eh-RASS-moh   **Ht:** 5'10" **Wt:** 215 **Born:** 5/2/1990 **Age:** 30

			HOW MUCH PITCHED					WHAT HE GAVE UP											THE RESULTS							
Year	Team	Lg	G	GS	GF	IP	BFP	H	R	ER	HR	SH	SF	HB	TBB	IBB	SO	WP	W	L	Pct	Sv-Op	Hld	Vel	OPS	ERC	ERA
2019	Pwtckt	AAA	27	24	1	125.1	537	125	75	66	18	1	5	5	43	0	95	6	6	8	.429	0- -	-	-	.770	4.31	4.74
2012	Sea	AL	16	8	2	59.0	238	47	26	22	6	1	5	3	12	1	48	0	1	3	.250	0-0	0	93	.616	2.42	3.36
2013	Sea	AL	14	13	0	72.1	321	79	44	40	12	0	3	3	26	0	57	0	5	3	.625	0-0	0	92	.772	5.04	4.98
2014	Sea	AL	17	14	0	75.1	338	82	44	44	13	1	1	6	34	2	60	3	1	6	.143	0-0	0	91	.815	5.68	5.26
2015	TB	AL	34	27	5	163.1	666	145	73	68	16	1	9	9	40	0	126	3	11	6	.647	0-0	0	91	.655	3.11	3.75
2016	TB	AL	64	1	13	90.2	378	90	39	38	14	7	2	4	26	5	63	7	7	11	.389	2-6	15	91	.766	4.13	3.77
2017	2 Tms	AL	37	19	4	131.1	539	123	70	64	22	2	7	2	31	2	109	1	5	6	.455	1-2	6	90	.733	3.58	4.39
2018	Sea	AL	10	10	0	45.2	202	52	35	33	14	0	4	3	12	0	33	0	2	4	.333	0-0	0	90	.916	6.02	6.50
2019	Bos	AL	1	0	1	3.0	15	4	4	4	2	1	0	1	1	0	1	0	0	0	-	0-0	0	90	1.345	12.01	12.00
17	TB	AL	26	8	4	69.1	282	66	39	37	10	1	2	1	16	1	55	1	4	3	.571	1-2	6	92	.719	3.53	4.80
17	Sea	AL	11	11	0	62.0	257	57	31	27	12	1	5	1	15	1	54	0	1	3	.250	0-0	0	92	.749	3.62	3.92
	8 ML YEARS		193	92	25	640.2	2697	622	335	313	99	13	23	31	182	10	497	14	32	39	.451	3-8	21	91	.739	4.01	4.40

Hanley Ramirez

Bats: R **Throws:** R **Pos:** DH-15;PH-2   **Ht:** 6'2" **Wt:** 235 **Born:** 12/23/1983 **Age:** 36

					BATTING															RUNNING			AVERAGES			
Year	Team	Lg	G	AB	H	2B	3B	HR	(Hm	Rd)	TB	R	RBI	RC	TBB	IBB	SO	HBP	SH	SF	SB	CS	GDP	Avg	OBP	Slg	OPS
2005	Bos	AL	2	2	0	0	0	0			0	0	0	0	0	0	2	0	0	0	0	0	0	.000	.000	.000	.000
2006	Fla	NL	158	633	185	46	11	17	(9	8)	304	119	59	101	56	0	128	4	5	2	51	15	7	.292	.353	.480	.833
2007	Fla	NL	154	639	212	48	6	29	(15	14)	359	125	81	115	52	3	95	7	4	4	51	14	10	.332	.386	.562	.948
2008	Fla	NL	153	589	177	34	4	33	(17	16)	318	**125**	67	116	92	9	122	8	0	4	35	12	5	.301	.400	.540	.940
2009	Fla	NL	151	576	197	42	1	24	(17	7)	313	101	106	122	61	14	101	9	1	5	27	8	9	**.342**	.410	.543	.954
2010	Fla	NL	142	543	163	28	2	21	(15	6)	258	92	76	90	64	12	93	7	0	5	32	10	14	.300	.378	.475	.853
2011	Fla	NL	92	338	82	16	0	10	(5	5)	128	55	45	46	44	3	66	2	1	0	20	10	6	.243	.333	.379	.712
2012	2 Tms	NL	157	604	155	29	4	24	(11	13)	264	79	92	81	54	4	132	6	0	3	21	7	17	.257	.322	.437	.759
2013	LAD	NL	86	304	105	25	2	20	(8	12)	194	62	57	69	27	3	52	3	0	2	10	2	5	.345	.402	.638	1.040
2014	LAD	NL	128	449	127	35	0	13	(8	5)	201	64	71	69	56	2	84	6	0	1	14	5	10	.283	.369	.448	.817
2015	Bos	AL	105	401	100	12	1	19	(8	11)	171	59	53	47	21	2	71	4	0	4	6	3	11	.249	.291	.426	.717
2016	Bos	AL	147	549	157	28	1	30	(19	11)	277	81	111	94	60	5	120	7	0	4	9	5	17	.286	.361	.505	.866
2017	Bos	AL	133	496	120	24	0	23	(10	13)	213	58	62	55	51	8	116	4	0	3	1	3	15	.242	.320	.429	.750

Year Team	Lg	G	AB	H	2B	3B	HR	(Hm	Rd)	TB	R	RBI	RC	TBB	IBB	SO	HBP	SH	SF	SB	CS	GDP	Avg	OBP	Slg	OPS
2018 Bos	AL	44	177	45	7	0	6	(2	4)	70	25	29	26	14	0	35	2	0	2	4	1	9	.254	.313	.395	.708
2019 Cle	AL	16	49	9	1	0	2	(1	1)	16	4	8	4	8	0	17	0	0	0	0	0	0	.184	.298	.327	.625
12 Mia	NL	93	353	87	18	2	14	(7	7)	151	49	48	42	37	1	72	3	0	2	14	4	11	.246	.322	.428	.749
12 LAD	NL	64	251	68	11	2	10	(4	6)	113	30	44	39	17	3	60	3	0	1	7	3	6	.271	.324	.450	.774
Postseason		20	71	27	9	1	1	(0	1)	41	9	14	15	7	3	13	2	0	0	2	0	2	.380	.450	.577	1.027
15 ML YEARS		1668	6349	1834	375	32	271	(142	129)	3086	1049	917	1035	660	65	1234	71	11	36	281	93	137	.289	.360	.486	.847

Harold Ramirez

Bats: R Throws: R Pos: LF-61;RF-55;CF-27;PH-14   **Ht: 5'10" Wt: 220 Born: 9/6/1994 Age: 25**

Year Team	Lg	G	AB	H	2B	3B	HR	(Hm	Rd)	TB	R	RBI	RC	TBB	IBB	SO	HBP	SH	SF	SB	CS	GDP	Avg	OBP	Slg	OPS
2019 NewOr	AAA	31	110	39	12	1	4	(-	-)	65	19	14	24	6	0	19	4	0	0	1	1	2	.355	.408	.591	.999
2019 Mia	NL	119	421	116	20	3	11	(5	6)	175	54	50	52	18	1	91	5	0	1	2	1	8	.276	.312	.416	.728

JC Ramirez

Pitches: R Bats: R Pos: RP-5   **Ht: 6'5" Wt: 250 Born: 8/16/1988 Age: 31**

Year Team	Lg	G	GS	GF	IP	BFP	H	R	ER	HR	SH	SF	HB	TBB	IBB	SO	WP	W	L	Pct	Sv-Op	Hld	Vel	OPS	ERC	ERA
2019 Salt Lk	AAA	12	8	2	41.0	187	49	32	30	7	0	1	4	18	0	26	4	1	2	.333	0--	-	-	.898	6.45	6.59
2013 Phi	NL	18	0	2	24.0	116	30	22	20	6	1	4	0	15	1	16	0	0	1	.000	0-0	3	94	.975	7.59	7.50
2015 2 Tms		20	0	6	23.2	106	25	14	14	3	0	0	1	11	3	16	1	1	2	.333	0-3	5	95	.764	4.79	5.32
2016 2 Tms		70	0	16	78.2	335	77	41	38	12	2	7	4	22	2	59	7	3	4	.429	2-6	13	96	.713	3.97	4.35
2017 LAA	AL	27	24	1	147.1	620	149	72	68	21	3	4	6	49	1	105	5	11	10	.524	0-1	0	96	.761	4.42	4.15
2018 LAA	AL	2	2	0	6.2	33	7	8	7	3	0	0	1	7	0	4	0	0	2	.000	0-0	0	93	1.078	10.36	9.45
2019 LAA	AL	5	0	3	8.0	34	8	4	4	1	0	0	1	1	0	4	1	0	0	-	0-0	0	91	.825	3.58	4.50
15 Ari	NL	12	0	4	15.1	63	15	7	7	1	0	0	0	4	2	11	1	1	1	.500	0-2	2	95	.641	3.04	4.11
15 Sea	AL	8	0	2	8.1	43	10	7	7	2	0	0	1	7	1	5	0	0	1	.000	0-1	0	96	.961	8.47	7.56
16 Cin	NL	27	0	7	32.1	139	35	24	23	7	1	3	0	9	2	28	3	1	3	.250	1-4	1	96	.787	4.74	6.40
16 LAA	AL	43	0	9	46.1	196	42	17	15	5	1	4	4	13	0	31	4	2	1	.667	1-2	12	97	.659	3.45	2.91
6 ML YEARS		142	26	28	288.1	1244	296	161	151	46	6	15	12	105	7	204	14	15	19	.441	2-10	18	96	.777	4.67	4.71

Jose Ramirez

Bats: B Throws: R Pos: 3B-126;DH-3;PH-1   **Ht: 5'9" Wt: 190 Born: 9/17/1992 Age: 27**

Year Team	Lg	G	AB	H	2B	3B	HR	(Hm	Rd)	TB	R	RBI	RC	TBB	IBB	SO	HBP	SH	SF	SB	CS	GDP	Avg	OBP	Slg	OPS
2013 Cle	AL	15	12	4	0	1	0	(0	0)	6	5	0	2	2	0	2	0	0	0	1	0	0	.333	.429	.500	.929
2014 Cle	AL	68	237	62	10	2	2	(1	1)	82	27	17	25	13	0	35	1	**13**	2	10	1	3	.262	.300	.346	.646
2015 Cle	AL	97	315	69	14	3	6	(1	5)	107	50	27	28	32	0	39	1	5	2	10	4	5	.219	.291	.340	.631
2016 Cle	AL	152	565	176	46	3	11	(8	3)	261	84	76	101	44	1	62	4	1	4	22	7	10	.312	.363	.462	.825
2017 Cle	AL	152	585	186	**56**	6	29	(10	19)	341	107	83	113	52	5	69	3	0	5	17	5	13	.318	.374	.583	.957
2018 Cle	AL	157	578	156	38	4	39	(19	20)	319	110	105	130	106	15	80	8	0	6	34	6	2	.270	.387	.552	.939
2019 Cle	AL	129	482	123	33	3	23	(8	15)	231	68	83	80	52	3	74	2	0	6	24	4	8	.255	.327	.479	.806
Postseason		23	87	17	2	0	1	(0	1)	22	8	4	4	6	1	18	0	0	0	0	1	2	.195	.247	.253	.500
7 ML YEARS		770	2774	776	197	22	110	(47	63)	1347	451	391	479	301	24	361	19	19	25	117	28	41	.280	.351	.486	.837

Neil Ramirez

Pitches: R Bats: R Pos: RP-21; SP-1   **Ht: 6'4" Wt: 215 Born: 5/25/1989 Age: 31**

Year Team	Lg	G	GS	GF	IP	BFP	H	R	ER	HR	SH	SF	HB	TBB	IBB	SO	WP	W	L	Pct	Sv-Op	Hld	Vel	OPS	ERC	ERA
2019 Clmbs	AAA	25	0	4	29.1	130	28	17	16	7	0	1	3	11	0	45	1	2	1	.667	2--	-	-	.784	5.01	4.91
2014 ChC	NL	50	0	10	43.2	177	29	11	7	2	0	0	2	17	0	53	3	3	3	.500	3-5	16	94	.550	2.12	1.44
2015 ChC	NL	19	0	4	14.0	60	12	5	5	1	0	2	0	6	0	15	2	1	0	1.000	0-0	2	93	.685	3.14	3.21
2016 3 Tms		18	0	7	24.0	107	22	16	16	8	0	3	0	18	2	24	5	0	0	-	0-0	1	92	.967	6.88	6.00
2017 2 Tms	NL	29	0	9	31.1	153	35	30	25	6	0	3	1	21	0	44	3	0	1	.000	0-1	2	93	.826	6.51	7.18
2018 Cle	AL	47	0	9	41.2	180	36	21	21	9	1	0	3	18	1	51	0	0	3	.000	0-1	13	95	.774	4.46	4.54
2019 2 Tms	AL	22	1	3	25.0	112	26	16	15	7	0	2	0	15	0	24	1	0	1	.000	0-0	2	94	.924	6.63	5.40
16 ChC	NL	8	0	4	7.2	35	5	4	4	1	0	2	0	8	2	10	3	0	0	-	0-0	1	92	.771	4.41	4.70
16 Mil	NL	2	0	0	1.2	7	2	2	2	2	0	0	0	0	0	3	0	0	0	-	0-0	0	92	1.429	10.43	10.80
16 Min	AL	8	0	3	14.2	65	15	10	10	5	0	1	0	10	0	11	2	0	0	-	0-0	0	92	.996	7.60	6.14
17 SF	NL	9	0	2	10.1	53	15	15	10	2	0	1	1	4	0	18	2	0	0	-	0-0	1	93	.888	7.47	8.71
17 NYM	NL	20	0	7	21.0	100	20	15	15	4	0	2	0	17	0	26	1	0	1	.000	0-1	1	93	.790	6.04	6.43
19 Cle	AL	16	0	3	16.2	75	18	11	10	5	0	2	0	9	0	18	0	0	1	.000	0-0	2	95	.938	6.70	5.40
19 Tor	AL	6	1	0	8.1	37	8	5	5	2	0	0	0	6	0	6	1	0	0	-	0-0	0	94	.895	6.46	5.40
6 ML YEARS		185	1	42	179.2	789	160	99	89	33	1	10	6	95	3	211	14	4	8	.333	3-7	36	94	.771	4.65	4.46

Nick Ramirez

Pitches: L Bats: L Pos: RP-46   **Ht: 6'3" Wt: 240 Born: 8/1/1989 Age: 30**

Year Team	Lg	G	GS	GF	IP	BFP	H	R	ER	HR	SH	SF	HB	TBB	IBB	SO	WP	W	L	Pct	Sv-Op	Hld	Vel	OPS	ERC	ERA
2019 Det	AL	46	0	7	79.2	348	76	45	36	11	1	3	1	35	4	74	6	5	4	.556	0-1	1	90	.748	4.16	4.07

Noe Ramirez

Pitches: R Bats: R Pos: RP-44; SP-7   no-AY   Ht: 6'3" Wt: 205 Born: 12/22/1989 Age: 30

Year	Team	Lg	G	GS	GF	IP	BFP	H	R	ER	HR	SH	SF	HB	TBB	IBB	SO	WP	W	L	Pct	Sv-Op	Hld	Vel	OPS	ERC	ERA
2015	Bos	AL	17	0	3	13.0	61	13	12	6	3	0	0	2	7	0	13	1	0	1	.000	0-0	4	90	.803	6.15	4.15
2016	Bos	AL	14	0	7	13.0	61	16	9	9	4	0	2	2	8	1	15	0	0	0	-	0-0	0	90	1.059	9.08	6.23
2017	2 Tms	AL	12	0	1	13.0	49	6	5	4	2	0	0	0	5	0	14	0	0	0	-	0-0	0	90	.520	1.68	2.77
2018	LAA	AL	69	1	12	83.1	353	75	43	42	15	0	0	6	30	3	95	4	7	5	.583	1-4	5	90	.750	4.16	4.54
2019	LAA	AL	51	7	10	67.2	280	59	30	30	9	0	1	5	20	1	79	2	5	4	.556	0-0	3	89	.698	3.48	3.99
17	Bos	AL	2	0	1	4.2	18	3	2	2	2	0	0	0	1	0	4	0	0	0	-	0-0	0	89	.752	3.21	3.86
17	LAA	AL	10	0	0	8.1	31	3	3	2	0	0	0	0	4	0	10	0	0	0	-	0-0	0	90	.374	1.02	2.16
5 ML YEARS			163	8	33	190.0	804	169	99	91	33	0	3	15	70	5	216	7	12	10	.545	1-4	12	90	.743	4.14	4.31

Yefry Ramirez

Pitches: R Bats: R Pos: RP-12; SP-1   Jefry   Ht: 6'2" Wt: 215 Born: 11/28/1993 Age: 26

Year	Team	Lg	G	GS	GF	IP	BFP	H	R	ER	HR	SH	SF	HB	TBB	IBB	SO	WP	W	L	Pct	Sv-Op	Hld	Vel	OPS	ERC	ERA
2019	Indy	AAA	15	5	3	45.0	203	42	28	26	5	2	0	2	29	0	58	3	1	4	.200	0- -	-	-	.781	4.94	5.20
2018	Bal	AL	17	12	2	65.1	294	64	44	43	11	2	3	4	36	1	62	5	1	8	.111	0-0	0	93	.802	5.30	5.92
2019	2 Tms	AL	13	1	7	24.1	119	30	24	20	4	0	2	4	16	0	27	2	0	2	.000	0-0	0	93	.936	7.91	7.40
19	Bal	AL	4	1	2	10.1	49	11	9	8	2	0	2	2	9	0	11	1	0	2	.000	0-0	0	93	1.005	8.56	6.97
19	Pit	NL	9	0	5	14.0	70	19	15	12	2	0	0	2	7	0	16	1	0	0	-	0-0	0	93	.892	7.45	7.71
2 ML YEARS			30	13	9	89.2	413	94	68	63	15	2	5	8	52	1	89	7	1	10	.091	0-0	0	93	.840	5.98	6.32

Edubray Ramos

Pitches: R Bats: R Pos: RP-20   eh-DOO-bray   Ht: 6'0" Wt: 160 Born: 12/19/1992 Age: 27

Year	Team	Lg	G	GS	GF	IP	BFP	H	R	ER	HR	SH	SF	HB	TBB	IBB	SO	WP	W	L	Pct	Sv-Op	Hld	Vel	OPS	ERC	ERA
2019	LV	AAA	10	0	6	10.0	38	6	3	2	1	0	0	1	4	0	8	0	2	0	1.000	6- -	-	-	.593	2.55	1.80
2016	Phi	NL	42	0	6	40.0	160	36	18	17	5	1	0	0	11	1	40	1	1	3	.250	0-2	15	95	.687	3.28	3.83
2017	Phi	NL	59	0	18	57.2	256	57	29	27	4	2	1	0	28	3	75	5	2	7	.222	0-3	9	94	.699	3.97	4.21
2018	Phi	NL	52	0	10	42.2	174	34	14	11	4	1	1	1	15	2	42	4	3	1	.750	1-2	12	93	.603	2.81	2.32
2019	Phi	NL	20	0	6	15.0	69	19	10	9	5	0	0	1	7	1	11	3	1	0	1.000	0-2	2	92	1.014	8.21	5.40
4 ML YEARS			173	0	40	155.1	659	146	71	64	18	4	2	2	61	7	168	13	7	11	.389	1-9	38	94	.704	3.82	3.71

Wilson Ramos

Bats: R Throws: R Pos: C-124;PH-24;DH-2   Ht: 6'1" Wt: 245 Born: 8/10/1987 Age: 32

Year	Team	Lg	G	AB	H	2B	3B	HR	(Hm	Rd)	TB	R	RBI	RC	TBB	IBB	SO	HBP	SH	SF	SB	CS	GDP	Avg	OBP	Slg	OPS
2010	2 Tms		22	79	22	7	0	1	(1	0)	32	5	5	10	2	0	12	1	0	0	0	0	2	.278	.305	.405	.710
2011	Was	NL	113	389	104	22	1	15	(8	7)	173	48	52	43	38	8	76	2	4	2	0	2	19	.267	.334	.445	.779
2012	Was	NL	25	83	22	2	0	3	(1	2)	33	11	10	12	12	2	19	0	0	1	0	0	1	.265	.354	.398	.752
2013	Was	NL	78	287	78	9	0	16	(6	10)	135	29	59	40	15	1	42	0	0	1	0	1	12	.272	.307	.470	.777
2014	Was	NL	88	341	91	12	0	11	(3	8)	136	32	47	35	17	2	57	0	0	3	0	0	17	.267	.299	.399	.698
2015	Was	NL	128	475	109	16	0	15	(10	5)	170	41	68	39	21	2	101	0	0	8	0	0	16	.229	.258	.358	.616
2016	Was	NL	131	482	148	25	0	22	(12	10)	239	58	80	78	35	2	79	2	0	4	0	0	17	.307	.354	.496	.850
2017	TB	AL	64	208	54	6	0	11	(3	8)	93	19	35	27	10	2	36	0	0	3	0	0	11	.260	.290	.447	.737
2018	2 Tms		111	382	117	22	1	15	(6	9)	186	39	70	70	32	2	80	0	0	2	0	0	20	.306	.358	.487	.845
2019	NYM	NL	141	473	136	19	0	14	(8	6)	197	52	73	70	44	5	69	4	0	3	1	0	16	.288	.351	.416	.768
10	Min	AL	7	27	8	3	0	0	(0	0)	11	2	1	3	0	0	3	1	0	0	0	0	1	.296	.321	.407	.729
10	Was	NL	15	52	14	4	0	1	(1	0)	21	3	4	7	2	0	9	0	0	0	0	0	1	.269	.296	.404	.700
18	TB	AL	78	293	87	14	0	14	(6	8)	143	30	53	50	22	1	61	0	0	0	0	0	17	.297	.346	.488	.834
18	Phi	NL	33	89	30	8	1	1	(0	1)	43	9	17	20	10	1	19	0	0	2	0	0	3	.337	.396	.483	.879
	Postseason		4	17	2	0	0	0	(0	0)	2	1	0	1	1	0	6	0	1	0	0	0	1	.118	.167	.118	.284
10 ML YEARS			901	3199	881	140	2	123	(58	65)	1394	334	499	424	226	26	571	9	4	27	1	3	131	.275	.322	.436	.758

Matt Ramsey

Pitches: R Bats: R Pos: RP-1   Ht: 5'11" Wt: 210 Born: 9/24/1989 Age: 30

Year	Team	Lg	G	GS	GF	IP	BFP	H	R	ER	HR	SH	SF	HB	TBB	IBB	SO	WP	W	L	Pct	Sv-Op	Hld	Vel	OPS	ERC	ERA
2019	Salt Lk	AAA	12	0	8	13.2	67	16	12	8	0	0	1	1	8	0	15	2	0	3	.000	0- -	-	-	.706	5.07	5.27
2019	LAA	AL	1	0	1	1.0	3	0	0	0	0	0	0	0	0	0	1	0	0	0	-	0-0	0	92	.000	0.00	0.00

Rangel Ravelo

Bats: R Throws: R Pos: PH-22;1B-9   RAHN-hel   Ht: 6'1" Wt: 225 Born: 4/24/1992 Age: 28

Year	Team	Lg	G	AB	H	2B	3B	HR	(Hm	Rd)	TB	R	RBI	RC	TBB	IBB	SO	HBP	SH	SF	SB	CS	GDP	Avg	OBP	Slg	OPS
2019	Memp	AAA	95	334	100	20	1	12	(-	-)	158	50	56	62	37	1	61	9	0	1	0	1	9	.299	.383	.473	.856
2019	StL	NL	29	39	8	2	0	2	(1	1)	16	4	7	4	3	0	12	0	0	1	0	0	1	.205	.256	.410	.666

Robbie Ray

Pitches: L **Bats:** L **Pos:** SP-33   **Ht:** 6'2" **Wt:** 195 **Born:** 10/1/1991 **Age:** 28

Year	Team	Lg	G	GS	GF	IP	BFP	H	R	ER	HR	SH	SF	HB	TBB	IBB	SO	WP	W	L	Pct	Sv-Op	Hld	Vel	OPS	ERC	ERA
2014	Det	AL	9	6	1	28.2	136	43	26	26	5	1	1	0	11	0	19	2	1	4	.200	0-0	1	91	.993	7.72	8.16
2015	Ari	NL	23	23	0	127.2	545	121	56	50	9	7	6	8	49	3	119	2	5	12	.294	0-0	0	93	.731	3.75	3.52
2016	Ari	NL	32	32	0	174.1	776	185	105	95	24	3	2	6	71	4	218	8	8	15	.348	0-0	0	94	.770	4.78	4.90
2017	Ari	NL	28	28	0	162.0	665	116	57	52	23	4	3	5	71	3	218	8	15	5	.750	0-0	0	94	.646	3.08	2.89
2018	Ari	NL	24	24	0	123.2	526	97	55	54	19	1	1	5	70	3	165	1	6	2	.750	0-0	0	94	.706	4.08	3.93
2019	Ari	NL	33	33	0	174.1	747	150	91	84	30	11	4	5	84	5	235	7	12	8	.600	0-0	0	92	.766	4.19	4.34
	Postseason		2	1	0	6.2	30	6	5	5	0	0	0	1	4	0	9	4	0	1	.000	0-0	0	94	.647	4.14	6.75
	6 ML YEARS		149	146	1	790.2	3395	712	390	361	110	27	17	29	356	18	974	32	47	46	.505	0-0	1	94	.738	4.11	4.11

Raudy Read

Bats: R **Throws:** R **Pos:** C-4;PH-2   **Ht:** 6'0" **Wt:** 170 **Born:** 10/29/1993 **Age:** 26

Year	Team	Lg	G	AB	H	2B	3B	HR	(Hm	Rd)	TB	R	RBI	RC	TBB	IBB	SO	HBP	SH	SF	SB	CS	GDP	Avg	OBP	Slg	OPS
2019	Fresno	AAA	82	306	84	17	3	20	(-	-)	167	52	60	53	17	3	58	3	0	2	1	1	10	.275	.317	.546	.863
2017	Was	NL	8	11	3	0	0	0	(0	0)	3	1	0	1	0	0	3	0	0	0	0	0	0	.273	.273	.273	.545
2019	Was	NL	6	11	1	0	0	0	(0	0)	1	0	0	0	0	0	5	0	0	0	0	0	1	.091	.091	.091	.182
	2 ML YEARS		14	22	4	0	0	0	(0	0)	4	1	0	1	0	0	8	0	0	0	0	0	1	.182	.182	.182	.364

J.T. Realmuto

Bats: R **Throws:** R **Pos:** C-133;PH-12;1B-4;DH-1   ray-al-MOO-toh   **Ht:** 6'1" **Wt:** 210 **Born:** 3/18/1991 **Age:** 29

Year	Team	Lg	G	AB	H	2B	3B	HR	(Hm	Rd)	TB	R	RBI	RC	TBB	IBB	SO	HBP	SH	SF	SB	CS	GDP	Avg	OBP	Slg	OPS
2014	Mia	NL	11	29	7	1	1	0	(0	0)	10	4	9	4	1	0	8	0	0	0	0	0	2	.241	.267	.345	.611
2015	Mia	NL	126	441	114	21	7	10	(6	4)	179	49	47	44	19	2	70	2	1	4	8	4	11	.259	.290	.406	.696
2016	Mia	NL	137	509	154	31	0	11	(3	8)	218	60	48	63	28	1	100	5	0	3	12	4	12	.303	.343	.428	.771
2017	Mia	NL	141	532	148	31	5	17	(5	12)	240	68	65	74	36	4	106	8	0	3	8	2	13	.278	.332	.451	.783
2018	Mia	NL	125	477	132	30	3	21	(8	13)	231	74	74	74	38	0	104	10	0	4	3	2	9	.277	.340	.484	.825
2019	Phi	NL	145	538	148	36	3	25	(16	9)	265	92	83	78	41	2	123	5	0	8	9	1	12	.275	.328	.493	.820
	6 ML YEARS		685	2526	703	150	19	84	(38	46)	1143	347	326	337	163	9	511	30	1	22	40	13	59	.278	.327	.452	.779

Josh Reddick

Bats: L **Throws:** R **Pos:** RF-119;LF-29;CF-9;PH-9;1B-4;DH-4;PR-1   **Ht:** 6'2" **Wt:** 195 **Born:** 2/19/1987 **Age:** 33

Year	Team	Lg	G	AB	H	2B	3B	HR	(Hm	Rd)	TB	R	RBI	RC	TBB	IBB	SO	HBP	SH	SF	SB	CS	GDP	Avg	OBP	Slg	OPS
2009	Bos	AL	27	59	10	4	0	2	(0	2)	20	5	4	4	2	0	17	1	0	0	0	0	0	.169	.210	.339	.549
2010	Bos	AL	29	62	12	3	1	1	(1	0)	20	5	5	1	1	0	15	0	0	0	1	0	1	.194	.206	.323	.529
2011	Bos	AL	87	254	71	18	3	7	(2	5)	116	41	28	33	19	1	50	1	0	4	1	2	1	.280	.327	.457	.784
2012	Oak	AL	156	611	148	29	5	32	(18	14)	283	85	85	73	55	8	151	2	1	4	11	1	15	.242	.305	.463	.768
2013	Oak	AL	114	385	87	19	2	12	(2	10)	146	54	56	53	46	1	86	2	1	7	9	2	4	.226	.307	.379	.686
2014	Oak	AL	109	363	96	16	7	12	(5	7)	162	53	54	54	28	0	63	1	0	3	1	1	3	.264	.316	.446	.763
2015	Oak	AL	149	526	143	25	4	20	(7	13)	236	67	77	83	49	1	65	0	1	2	10	2	7	.272	.333	.449	.781
2016	2 Tms		115	398	112	17	1	10	(5	5)	161	53	37	54	39	5	56	0	0	1	8	3	6	.281	.345	.405	.749
2017	Hou	AL	134	477	150	34	4	13	(6	7)	231	77	82	88	43	1	72	0	1	12	7	3	9	.314	.363	.484	.847
2018	Hou	AL	134	433	105	13	2	17	(6	11)	173	63	47	50	49	3	77	0	1	2	7	2	9	.242	.318	.400	.718
2019	Hou	AL	141	501	138	19	3	14	(6	8)	205	57	56	65	36	1	66	0	1	9	5	2	9	.275	.319	.409	.728
16	Oak	AL	68	243	72	11	1	8	(3	5)	109	33	28	42	28	5	34	0	0	1	5	0	7	.296	.368	.449	.816
16	LAD	NL	47	155	40	6	0	2	(2	0)	52	20	9	12	11	0	22	0	0	0	3	3	1	.258	.307	.335	.643
	Postseason		47	155	34	3	0	3	(0	3)	46	16	10	12	13	2	35	0	0	6	3	0	6	.219	.280	.297	.577
	11 ML YEARS		1195	4069	1072	197	32	140	(58	82)	1753	560	531	558	367	21	718	7	6	44	60	18	66	.263	.322	.431	.753

A.J. Reed

Bats: L **Throws:** L **Pos:** DH-9;1B-4;PH-1   **Ht:** 6'4" **Wt:** 275 **Born:** 5/10/1993 **Age:** 27

Year	Team	Lg	G	AB	H	2B	3B	HR	(Hm	Rd)	TB	R	RBI	RC	TBB	IBB	SO	HBP	SH	SF	SB	CS	GDP	Avg	OBP	Slg	OPS
2019	RdRck	AAA	56	192	43	11	0	12	(-	-)	90	33	35	31	27	1	67	4	0	2	0	0	7	.224	.329	.469	.798
2019	Charllt	AAA	10	39	7	1	0	1	(-	-)	11	3	2	2	2	0	17	1	0	0	0	0	2	.179	.238	.282	.520
2016	Hou	AL	45	122	20	3	0	3	(2	1)	32	11	8	7	18	0	48	0	0	1	0	0	1	.164	.270	.262	.532
2017	Hou	AL	2	6	0	0	0	0	(0	0)	0	0	0	0	0	0	1	0	0	0	0	0	0	.000	.000	.000	.000
2018	Hou	AL	1	3	0	0	0	0	(0	0)	0	0	0	0	0	0	1	0	0	0	0	0	0	.000	.000	.000	.000
2019	CWS	AL	14	44	6	0	0	1	(0	1)	9	1	4	1	4	0	21	0	0	1	0	0	1	.136	.204	.205	.409
	4 ML YEARS		62	175	26	3	0	4	(2	2)	41	12	12	8	22	0	71	0	0	2	0	0	2	.149	.241	.234	.475

Cody Reed

Pitches: L **Bats:** L **Pos:** RP-3   **Ht:** 6'5" **Wt:** 230 **Born:** 4/15/1993 **Age:** 27

Year	Team	Lg	G	GS	GF	IP	BFP	H	R	ER	HR	SH	SF	HB	TBB	IBB	SO	WP	W	L	Pct	Sv-Op	Hld	Vel	OPS	ERC	ERA
2019	Lsvlle	AAA	18	0	7	20.2	80	13	6	6	1	0	0	1	8	0	25	1	1	2	.333	0--	-	-	.557	2.08	2.61
2016	Cin	NL	10	10	0	47.2	230	67	47	39	12	1	1	4	19	2	43	2	0	7	.000	0-0	0	93	.968	8.00	7.36
2017	Cin	NL	12	1	3	17.2	79	11	11	10	3	0	0	0	19	3	17	2	1	1	.500	1-1	0	94	.780	4.97	5.09
2018	Cin	NL	17	7	2	43.0	188	45	21	19	5	2	2	2	15	0	42	2	1	3	.250	0-0	0	92	.729	4.41	3.98
2019	Cin	NL	3	0	1	6.1	25	6	1	1	0	0	0	0	1	1	7	1	0	0		0-0	0	94	.530	2.11	1.42
	4 ML YEARS		42	18	6	114.2	522	129	80	69	20	3	3	6	54	6	109	7	2	11	.154	1-1	1	93	.833	5.78	5.42

Michael Reed

Bats: R Throws: R Pos: LF-2;RF-2   Ht: 6'0" Wt: 215 Born: 11/18/1992 Age: 27

							BATTING													RUNNING			AVERAGES			
Year	Team	Lg	G	AB	H	2B	3B	HR	(Hm | Rd)	TB	R	RBI	RC	TBB	IBB	SO	HBP	SH	SF	SB	CS	GDP	Avg	OBP	Slg	OPS
2019	Scrmto	AAA	15	53	12	4	0	1	(- | -)	19	8	9	6	7	0	21	0	0	0	2	0	2	.226	.317	.358	.675
2015	Mil	NL	7	6	2	1	0	0	(0 | 0)	3	2	0	1	0	0	3	0	0	0	0	0	0	.333	.333	.500	.833
2016	Mil	NL	8	22	4	0	0	0	(0 | 0)	4	3	0	1	2	0	7	0	0	0	1	0	1	.182	.250	.182	.432
2018	Atl	NL	7	7	2	0	0	0	(0 | 0)	2	1	0	0	0	0	3	0	0	0	0	0	0	.286	.286	.286	.571
2019	SF	NL	4	8	0	0	0	0	(0 | 0)	0	0	0	0	0	0	6	0	0	0	0	0	0	.000	.000	.000	.000
	4 ML YEARS		26	43	8	1	0	0	(0 | 0)	9	6	0	2	2	0	19	0	0	0	1	0	1	.186	.222	.209	.432

Sean Reid-Foley

Pitches: R Bats: R Pos: SP-6; RP-3   Ht: 6'3" Wt: 220 Born: 8/30/1995 Age: 24

			HOW MUCH PITCHED				WHAT HE GAVE UP										THE RESULTS							
Year	Team	Lg	G	GS	GF	IP	BFP	H	R	ER	HR	SH	SF	HB	TBB	IBB	SO	WP	W	L	Pct	Sv-Op	Hld	Vel	OPS	ERC	ERA
2019	Buffalo	AAA	20	19	0	89.0	414	78	71	64	13	1	3	9	65	0	105	6	3	5	.375	0- -	-	-	.782	5.39	6.47
2018	Tor	AL	7	7	0	33.1	150	31	23	19	6	0	1	1	21	0	42	3	2	4	.333	0-0	0	94	.794	5.32	5.13
2019	Tor	AL	9	6	0	31.2	150	33	20	15	5	0	1	2	21	0	28	3	2	4	.333	0-0	0	93	.818	6.01	4.26
	2 ML YEARS		16	13	0	65.0	300	64	43	34	11	0	2	3	42	0	70	6	4	8	.333	0-0	0	93	.806	5.66	4.71

Zac Reininger

Pitches: R Bats: B Pos: RP-24; SP-1   Ht: 6'3" Wt: 190 Born: 1/28/1993 Age: 27

			HOW MUCH PITCHED				WHAT HE GAVE UP										THE RESULTS							
Year	Team	Lg	G	GS	GF	IP	BFP	H	R	ER	HR	SH	SF	HB	TBB	IBB	SO	WP	W	L	Pct	Sv-Op	Hld	Vel	OPS	ERC	ERA
2019	Toledo	AAA	33	4	7	57.1	256	65	28	26	7	2	1	0	26	0	51	1	4	3	.571	0- -	-	-	.830	5.26	4.08
2017	Det	AL	10	0	3	9.2	47	16	8	8	3	0	1	0	3	0	5	2	0	0	-	0-0	0	95	.988	8.63	7.45
2018	Det	AL	18	0	6	21.1	100	28	18	18	5	0	1	0	9	2	18	2	1	0	1.000	0-0	0	94	.959	6.84	7.59
2019	Det	AL	25	1	7	28.0	140	44	28	27	11	0	2	0	16	1	17	1	0	3	.000	0-0	1	94	1.215	11.07	8.68
	3 ML YEARS		53	1	16	59.0	287	88	54	53	19	0	4	0	28	3	40	5	1	3	.250	0-0	1	94	1.087	9.07	8.08

Anthony Rendon

Bats: R Throws: R Pos: 3B-146;2B-1   ren-DOAN   Ht: 6'1" Wt: 200 Born: 6/6/1990 Age: 30

							BATTING													RUNNING			AVERAGES			
Year	Team	Lg	G	AB	H	2B	3B	HR	(Hm	Rd)	TB	R	RBI	RC	TBB	IBB	SO	HBP	SH	SF	SB	CS	GDP	Avg	OBP	Slg	OPS
2013	Was	NL	98	351	93	23	1	7	(3	4)	139	40	35	43	31	3	69	5	2	5	1	1	7	.265	.329	.396	.725
2014	Was	NL	153	613	176	39	6	21	(10	11)	290	111	83	97	58	2	104	5	2	5	17	3	11	.287	.351	.473	.824
2015	Was	NL	80	311	82	16	0	5	(3	2)	113	43	25	39	36	0	70	4	0	4	1	2	8	.264	.344	.363	.707
2016	Was	NL	156	567	153	38	2	20	(11	9)	255	91	85	95	65	2	117	7	0	8	12	6	5	.270	.348	.450	.797
2017	Was	NL	147	508	153	41	1	25	(14	11)	271	81	100	115	84	6	82	7	0	6	7	2	7	.301	.403	.533	.937
2018	Was	NL	136	529	163	**44**	2	24	(10	14)	283	88	92	99	55	5	82	5	0	8	2	1	5	.308	.374	.535	.909
2019	Was	NL	146	545	174	**44**	3	34	(20	14)	326	117	**126**	**130**	80	8	86	12	0	9	5	1	13	.319	.412	.598	1.010
	Postseason		14	56	13	1	0	2	(1	1)	20	5	6	7	7	1	9	0	0	0	1	0	0	.232	.317	.357	.675
	7 ML YEARS		916	3424	994	245	15	136	(71	65)	1677	571	546	618	409	26	610	45	4	45	45	16	56	.290	.369	.490	.859

Hunter Renfroe

Bats: R Throws: R Pos: RF-86;LF-67;PH-21;CF-4   Ht: 6'1" Wt: 220 Born: 1/28/1992 Age: 28

							BATTING													RUNNING			AVERAGES			
Year	Team	Lg	G	AB	H	2B	3B	HR	(Hm	Rd)	TB	R	RBI	RC	TBB	IBB	SO	HBP	SH	SF	SB	CS	GDP	Avg	OBP	Slg	OPS
2016	SD	NL	11	35	13	3	0	4	(4	0)	28	8	14	10	1	1	5	0	0	0	0	0	1	.371	.389	.800	1.189
2017	SD	NL	122	445	103	25	1	26	(14	12)	208	51	58	48	27	1	140	6	0	1	3	0	4	.231	.284	.467	.751
2018	SD	NL	117	403	100	23	1	26	(13	13)	203	53	68	58	30	2	109	3	0	5	2	1	9	.248	.302	.504	.805
2019	SD	NL	140	440	95	19	1	33	(14	19)	215	64	64	57	46	1	154	2	0	6	5	0	6	.216	.289	.489	.778
	4 ML YEARS		390	1323	311	70	3	89	(45	44)	654	176	204	173	104	5	408	11	0	12	10	1	20	.235	.294	.494	.788

Luis Rengifo

Bats: B Throws: R Pos: 2B-104;SS-12;PR-3;PH-1   ren-HEE-foh   Ht: 5'10" Wt: 195 Born: 2/26/1997 Age: 23

							BATTING													RUNNING			AVERAGES			
Year	Team	Lg	G	AB	H	2B	3B	HR	(Hm	Rd)	TB	R	RBI	RC	TBB	IBB	SO	HBP	SH	SF	SB	CS	GDP	Avg	OBP	Slg	OPS
2019	Salt Lk	AAA	27	110	30	4	1	5	(-	-)	51	16	14	17	11	0	24	0	0	1	3	3	2	.273	.336	.464	.800
2019	LAA	AL	108	357	85	18	3	7	(1	6)	130	44	33	45	40	0	93	5	1	3	2	5	6	.238	.321	.364	.685

Alex Reyes

Pitches: R Bats: R Pos: RP-4   Ht: 6'3" Wt: 175 Born: 8/29/1994 Age: 25

			HOW MUCH PITCHED				WHAT HE GAVE UP										THE RESULTS							
Year	Team	Lg	G	GS	GF	IP	BFP	H	R	ER	HR	SH	SF	HB	TBB	IBB	SO	WP	W	L	Pct	Sv-Op	Hld	Vel	OPS	ERC	ERA
2019	Memp	AAA	10	7	1	28.0	132	27	24	23	5	2	3	1	24	0	38	3	1	3	.250	0- -	-	-	.871	6.58	7.39
2016	StL	NL	12	5	3	46.0	189	33	8	8	1	0	0	1	23	1	52	3	4	1	.800	1-1	0	97	.578	2.43	1.57
2018	StL	NL	1	1	0	4.0	15	3	0	0	0	0	0	1	2	0	2	0	0	0	-	0-0	0	95	.650	3.97	0.00
2019	StL	NL	4	0	0	3.0	17	2	5	5	1	0	1	0	6	0	1	1	0	1	.000	0-0	2	97	.971	10.79	15.00
	3 ML YEARS		17	6	3	53.0	221	38	13	13	2	1	2	1	31	1	55	4	4	2	.667	1-1	3	96	.609	2.92	2.21

Franmil Reyes

Bats: R **Throws:** R **Pos:** RF-86;DH-47;PH-17   **Ht:** 6'5" **Wt:** 275 **Born:** 7/7/1995 **Age:** 24

Year Team	Lg	G	AB	H	2B	3B	HR	(Hm	Rd)	TB	R	RBI	RC	TBB	IBB	SO	HBP	SH	SF	SB	CS	GDP	Avg	OBP	Slg	OPS
2018 SD	NL	87	261	73	9	0	16	(8	8)	130	36	31	37	24	0	80	0	0	0	0	0	5	.280	.340	.498	.838
2019 2 Tms		150	494	123	19	0	37	(25	12)	253	69	81	71	47	1	156	0	0	7	0	0	15	.249	.310	.512	.822
19 SD	NL	99	321	82	9	0	27	(17	10)	172	43	46	41	29	1	93	0	0	4	0	0	12	.255	.314	.536	.849
19 Cle	AL	51	173	41	10	0	10	(8	2)	81	26	35	30	18	0	63	0	0	3	0	0	3	.237	.304	.468	.772
2 ML YEARS		237	755	196	28	0	53	(33	20)	383	105	112	108	71	1	236	0	0	7	0	0	20	.260	.321	.507	.828

Gerardo Reyes

Pitches: R **Bats:** R **Pos:** RP-27   **Ht:** 5'11" **Wt:** 160 **Born:** 5/13/1993 **Age:** 27

		HOW MUCH PITCHED					WHAT HE GAVE UP										THE RESULTS							
Year Team	Lg	G	GS	GF	IP	BFP	H	R	ER	HR	SH	SF	HB	TBB	IBB	SO	WP	W	L	Pct	Sv-Op	Hld	Vel	OPS	ERC	ERA
2019 ElPaso	AAA	34	0	16	45.1	191	39	22	18	8	0	1	2	20	0	61	1	4	2	.667	3--	-	-	.766	4.22	3.57
2019 SD	NL	27	0	9	26.0	117	24	22	22	3	1	2	3	11	1	38	3	4	0	1.000	0-1	1	97	.738	4.10	7.62

Pablo Reyes

Bats: R **Throws:** R **Pos:** PH-25;LF-19;RF-19;CF-11;2B-7;3B-2;SS-2;PR-1   **Ht:** 5'8" **Wt:** 175 **Born:** 9/5/1993 **Age:** 26

Year Team	Lg	G	AB	H	2B	3B	HR	(Hm	Rd)	TB	R	RBI	RC	TBB	IBB	SO	HBP	SH	SF	SB	CS	GDP	Avg	OBP	Slg	OPS
2019 Indy	AAA	51	175	50	15	0	10	(-	-)	95	22	30	32	13	0	37	2	1	0	5	3	2	.286	.342	.543	.885
2018 Pit	NL	18	58	17	2	0	3	(0	3)	28	9	7	7	5	0	11	0	0	0	0	1	2	.293	.349	.483	.832
2019 Pit	NL	71	143	29	7	2	2	(1	1)	46	18	19	16	13	0	36	1	0	0	1	1	0	.203	.274	.322	.596
2 ML YEARS		89	201	46	9	2	5	(1	4)	74	27	26	23	18	0	47	1	0	0	1	2	2	.229	.295	.368	.664

Victor Reyes

Bats: B **Throws:** R **Pos:** CF-37;LF-21;RF-9;PH-2;PR-1   **Ht:** 6'5" **Wt:** 215 **Born:** 10/5/1994 **Age:** 25

Year Team	Lg	G	AB	H	2B	3B	HR	(Hm	Rd)	TB	R	RBI	RC	TBB	IBB	SO	HBP	SH	SF	SB	CS	GDP	Avg	OBP	Slg	OPS
2019 Toledo	AAA	74	289	88	19	1	10	(-	-)	139	50	58	46	14	1	50	1	0	4	10	6	6	.304	.334	.481	.815
2018 Det	AL	100	212	47	5	3	1	(0	1)	61	35	12	12	5	0	46	0	1	1	9	1	4	.222	.239	.288	.526
2019 Det	AL	69	276	84	16	5	3	(2	1)	119	29	25	35	14	0	64	0	0	2	9	3	5	.304	.336	.431	.767
2 ML YEARS		169	488	131	21	8	4	(2	2)	180	64	37	47	19	0	110	0	1	3	18	4	9	.268	.294	.369	.663

Bryan Reynolds

Bats: B **Throws:** R **Pos:** LF-79;RF-31;CF-25;PH-8;PR-1   **Ht:** 6'3" **Wt:** 205 **Born:** 1/27/1995 **Age:** 25

Year Team	Lg	G	AB	H	2B	3B	HR	(Hm	Rd)	TB	R	RBI	RC	TBB	IBB	SO	HBP	SH	SF	SB	CS	GDP	Avg	OBP	Slg	OPS
2019 Indy	AAA	13	49	18	1	1	5	(-	-)	36	10	11	14	7	0	11	0	0	0	3	2	1	.367	.446	.735	1.181
2019 Pit	NL	134	491	154	37	4	16	(8	8)	247	83	68	89	46	0	121	6	0	3	3	2	9	.314	.377	.503	.880

Mark Reynolds

Bats: R **Throws:** R **Pos:** PH-46;1B-32;DH-1   **Ht:** 6'2" **Wt:** 220 **Born:** 8/3/1983 **Age:** 36

Year Team	Lg	G	AB	H	2B	3B	HR	(Hm	Rd)	TB	R	RBI	RC	TBB	IBB	SO	HBP	SH	SF	SB	CS	GDP	Avg	OBP	Slg	OPS
2007 Ari	NL	111	366	102	20	4	17	(7	10)	181	62	62	62	37	4	129	5	1	5	0	1	5	.279	.349	.495	.843
2008 Ari	NL	152	539	129	28	3	28	(13	15)	247	87	97	82	64	0	204	3	1	6	11	2	10	.239	.320	.458	.779
2009 Ari	NL	155	578	150	30	1	44	(19	25)	314	98	102	94	76	3	223	5	0	3	24	9	8	.260	.349	.543	.892
2010 Ari	NL	145	499	99	17	2	32	(21	11)	216	79	85	77	83	7	211	9	0	5	7	4	8	.198	.320	.433	.753
2011 Bal	AL	155	534	118	27	1	37	(17	20)	258	84	86	77	75	2	196	7	0	4	6	4	11	.221	.323	.483	.806
2012 Bal	AL	135	457	101	26	0	23	(11	12)	196	65	69	68	73	2	159	6	0	2	1	3	19	.221	.335	.429	.763
2013 2 Tms	AL	135	445	98	14	0	21	(9	12)	175	55	67	55	51	1	154	5	0	3	3	1	9	.220	.306	.393	.699
2014 Mil	NL	130	378	74	9	0	22	(9	13)	149	47	45	41	47	3	122	3	1	4	5	1	8	.196	.287	.394	.681
2015 StL	NL	140	382	88	21	2	13	(4	9)	152	35	48	38	44	2	121	4	0	2	2	3	10	.230	.315	.398	.713
2016 Col	NL	118	393	111	24	0	14	(8	6)	177	61	53	60	42	1	112	4	0	2	1	2	6	.282	.356	.450	.806
2017 Col	NL	148	520	139	22	1	30	(21	9)	253	82	97	88	69	0	175	1	0	3	2	1	12	.267	.352	.487	.839
2018 Was	NL	86	206	51	8	0	13	(7	6)	98	26	40	28	24	1	64	2	0	8	0	0	8	.248	.328	.476	.803
2019 Col	NL	78	135	23	7	0	4	(3	1)	42	13	20	16	22	0	57	2	0	3	2	0	3	.170	.290	.311	.601
13 Cle	AL	99	335	72	8	0	15	(8	7)	125	40	48	39	43	1	123	3	0	3	3	0	7	.215	.307	.373	.680
13 NYY	AL	36	110	26	6	0	6	(1	5)	50	15	19	16	8	0	31	2	0	0	0	1	2	.236	.300	.455	.755
Postseason		17	55	7	0	0	2	(1	1)	13	3	4	2	3	0	20	3	0	0	1	0	2	.127	.213	.236	.449
13 ML YEARS		1688	5432	1283	253	14	298	(149	149)	2458	794	871	786	707	26	1927	56	3	45	64	31	117	.236	.328	.453	.780

Jacob Rhame

Pitches: R **Bats:** R **Pos:** RP-5   RAME   **Ht:** 6'1" **Wt:** 215 **Born:** 3/16/1993 **Age:** 27

		HOW MUCH PITCHED					WHAT HE GAVE UP										THE RESULTS							
Year Team	Lg	G	GS	GF	IP	BFP	H	R	ER	HR	SH	SF	HB	TBB	IBB	SO	WP	W	L	Pct	Sv-Op	Hld	Vel	OPS	ERC	ERA
2019 Syrcse	AAA	20	0	10	19.2	83	19	13	12	4	0	2	0	6	1	25	1	3	2	.600	3--	-		.768	4.10	5.49
2017 NYM	NL	9	0	2	9.0	45	12	9	9	2	1	1	0	7	0	7	0	1	1	.500	0-0	0	95	1.071	8.82	9.00
2018 NYM	NL	30	0	15	32.1	140	38	21	21	8	2	0	1	8	2	28	0	1	2	.333	1-2	2	96	.899	5.60	5.85
2019 NYM	NL	5	0	3	6.1	30	3	4	3	1	1	0	0	9	0	5	0	0	1	.000	0-0	0	95	.814	5.60	4.26
3 ML YEARS		44	0	20	47.2	215	53	34	33	11	4	1	1	24	2	40	0	2	4	.333	1-2	2	96	.926	6.22	6.23

Clayton Richard

Pitches: L Bats: L Pos: SP-10   Ht: 6'5" Wt: 240 Born: 9/12/1983 Age: 36

		HOW MUCH PITCHED			WHAT HE GAVE UP									THE RESULTS						
Year Team	Lg	G GS GF	IP	BFP	H	R	ER	HR SH SF HB	TBB IBB	SO	WP	W	L	Pct	Sv-Op	Hld	Vel	OPS	ERC	ERA
2008 CWS	AL	13 8 3	47.2	215	61	37	32	5 0 1 0	13 2	29	1	2	5	.286	0-0	0	90	.802	5.06	6.04
2009 2 Tms		38 26 3	153.0	663	154	81	75	17 8 5 3	71 0	114	7	9	5	.643	0-0	0	92	.756	4.60	4.41
2010 SD	NL	33 33 0	201.2	861	206	89	84	16 6 2 4	78 6	153	4	14	9	.609	0-0	0	91	.718	4.09	3.75
2011 SD	NL	18 18 0	99.2	427	104	52	43	8 4 1 2	38 2	53	3	5	9	.357	0-0	0	90	.741	4.22	3.88
2012 SD	NL	33 33 0	218.2	910	228	110	97	31 3 6 6	42 4	107	4	14	14	.500	0-0	0	91	.739	3.87	3.99
2013 SD	NL	12 11 1	52.2	239	65	44	41	13 6 1 0	21 1	24	0	2	5	.286	0-0	0	90	.947	6.55	7.01
2015 ChC	NL	23 3 0	42.1	181	47	18	18	3 0 0 1	7 1	22	4	4	2	.667	0-0	2	91	.714	3.56	3.83
2016 2 Tms	NL	36 9 9	67.2	306	81	35	25	4 0 3 2	31 3	41	3	3	4	.429	1-1	1	91	.761	5.24	3.33
2017 SD	NL	32 32 0	197.1	858	240	114	105	24 6 5 8	59 6	151	7	8	15	.348	0-0	0	91	.842	5.33	4.79
2018 SD	NL	27 27 0	158.2	682	159	98	94	19 5 3 10	60 1	108	7	7	11	.389	0-0	0	90	.770	4.44	5.33
2019 Tor	AL	10 10 0	45.1	201	53	33	30	9 0 1 4	18 0	22	3	1	5	.167	0-0	0	90	.896	6.37	5.96
09 CWS	AL	26 14 3	89.0	387	94	50	46	10 3 4 3	37 0	66	5	4	3	.571	0-0	0	92	.770	4.76	4.65
09 SD	NL	12 12 0	64.0	276	60	31	29	7 5 1 0	34 0	48	2	5	2	.714	0-0	0	92	.737	4.38	4.08
16 ChC	NL	25 0 9	14.0	72	23	14	10	0 0 2 2	7 3	7	1	0	1	.000	1-1	1	92	.871	7.74	6.43
16 SD	NL	11 9 0	53.2	234	58	21	15	4 0 1 0	24 0	34	2	3	3	.500	0-0	0	90	.728	4.61	2.52
Postseason		8 0 0	11.0	42	8	1	1	0 0 0 0	4 0	9	0	0	0	-	0-0	2	92	.496	2.05	0.82
11 ML YEARS		275 210 16	1284.2	5543	1398	711	644	149 38 28 40	438 26	824	43	69	84	.451	1-1	3	91	.775	4.61	4.51

Garrett Richards

Pitches: R Bats: R Pos: SP-3   Ht: 6'3" Wt: 210 Born: 5/27/1988 Age: 32

		HOW MUCH PITCHED			WHAT HE GAVE UP									THE RESULTS						
Year Team	Lg	G GS GF	IP	BFP	H	R	ER	HR SH SF HB	TBB IBB	SO	WP	W	L	Pct	Sv-Op	Hld	Vel	OPS	ERC	ERA
2019 3 Tms	Low	5 5 0	9.1	51	12	12	11	1 0 0 1	11 0	13	2	0	1	.000	0- -	-	-	.906	9.68	10.61
2011 LAA	AL	7 3 2	14.0	62	16	11	9	4 0 0 0	7 0	9	2	0	2	.000	0-0	0	95	.989	6.97	5.79
2012 LAA	AL	30 9 4	71.0	318	77	46	37	7 2 4 3	34 1	47	2	4	3	.571	1-3	5	95	.793	5.04	4.69
2013 LAA	AL	47 17 6	145.0	620	151	73	67	12 9 3 1	44 4	101	11	7	8	.467	1-2	5	95	.699	3.78	4.16
2014 LAA	AL	26 26 0	168.2	678	124	51	49	5 0 3 7	51 1	164	22	13	4	.765	0-0	0	96	.529	2.06	2.61
2015 LAA	AL	32 32 0	207.1	865	181	94	84	20 6 10 5	76 2	176	17	15	12	.556	0-0	0	95	.664	3.32	3.65
2016 LAA	AL	6 6 0	34.2	148	31	16	9	2 2 0 1	15 1	34	3	1	3	.250	0-0	0	96	.683	3.39	2.34
2017 LAA	AL	6 6 0	27.2	108	18	8	7	1 1 0 0	7 0	27	2	0	2	.000	0-0	0	96	.494	1.49	2.28
2018 LAA	AL	16 16 0	76.1	324	64	43	31	11 1 0 1	34 0	87	15	5	4	.556	0-0	0	96	.688	3.69	3.66
2019 SD	NL	3 3 0	8.2	41	10	8	8	2 1 0 0	6 0	11	1	0	1	.000	0-0	0	95	1.076	7.31	8.31
9 ML YEARS		173 118 12	753.1	3164	672	350	301	64 22 20 18	274 9	656	75	45	39	.536	2-5	10	96	.663	3.32	3.60

Trevor Richards

Pitches: R Bats: R Pos: SP-23; RP-7   Ht: 6'2" Wt: 190 Born: 5/15/1993 Age: 27

		HOW MUCH PITCHED			WHAT HE GAVE UP									THE RESULTS						
Year Team	Lg	G GS GF	IP	BFP	H	R	ER	HR SH SF HB	TBB IBB	SO	WP	W	L	Pct	Sv-Op	Hld	Vel	OPS	ERC	ERA
2018 Mia	NL	25 25 0	126.1	547	121	65	62	15 5 4 5	54 5	130	8	4	9	.308	0-0	0	91	.754	4.18	4.42
2019 2 Tms	NL	30 23 1	135.1	580	127	63	61	19 5 4 5	56 6	127	4	6	12	.333	0-0	1	91	.749	4.16	4.06
19 Mia	NL	23 20 1	112.0	483	104	56	56	16 4 4 5	51 6	103	4	3	12	.200	0-0	1	91	.759	4.32	4.50
19 TB	AL	7 3 0	23.1	97	23	7	5	3 1 0 0	5 0	24	0	3	0	1.000	0-0	0	90	.698	3.43	1.93
2 ML YEARS		55 48 1	261.2	1127	248	128	123	34 10 8 10	110 11	257	12	10	21	.323	0-0	1	91	.751	4.17	4.23

Joey Rickard

Bats: R Throws: L Pos: LF-26;RF-25;CF-16;PH-11;PR-3;DH-1   Ht: 6'1" Wt: 185 Born: 5/21/1991 Age: 29

		BATTING																RUNNING			AVERAGES			
Year Team	Lg	G	AB	H	2B	3B	HR	(Hm Rd)	TB	R	RBI	RC	TBB IBB	SO	HBP SH SF	SB	CS	GDP	Avg	OBP	Slg	OPS
2019 Norfolk	AAA	18	64	13	5	0	4	(- -)	30	10	10	11	11 0	16	2 0 0	1	0	1	.203	.338	.469	.806
2019 Scrmto	AAA	46	172	64	15	2	6	(- -)	101	45	23	41	18 0	27	2 0 3	0	2	5	.372	.431	.587	1.018
2016 Bal	AL	85	257	69	13	0	5	(2 3)	97	32	19	32	18 0	54	2 3 2	4	1	3	.268	.319	.377	.696
2017 Bal	AL	111	261	63	15	0	4	(2 2)	90	29	19	20	9 0	63	4 2 1	8	1	6	.241	.276	.345	.621
2018 Bal	AL	79	213	52	10	1	8	(6 2)	88	27	23	22	15 0	55	2 0 0	4	2	3	.244	.300	.413	.713
2019 2 Tms		68	168	38	9	2	3	(2 1)	60	14	10	20	18 1	50	3 0 0	4	2	1	.226	.312	.357	.669
19 Bal	AL	42	118	24	7	2	2	(1 1)	41	10	6	15	14 1	33	3 0 0	3	2	0	.203	.304	.347	.651
19 SF	NL	26	50	14	2	0	1	(1 0)	19	4	4	5	4 0	17	0 0 0	1	0	1	.280	.333	.380	.713
4 ML YEARS		343	899	222	47	3	20	(13 7)	335	102	71	94	60 1	222	11 5 3	20	6	13	.247	.301	.373	.674

J.T. Riddle

Bats: L Throws: R Pos: CF-31;PH-13;SS-12;PR-2   Ht: 6'1" Wt: 180 Born: 10/12/1991 Age: 28

		BATTING																RUNNING			AVERAGES			
Year Team	Lg	G	AB	H	2B	3B	HR	(Hm Rd)	TB	R	RBI	RC	TBB IBB	SO	HBP SH SF	SB	CS	GDP	Avg	OBP	Slg	OPS
2019 NewOr	AAA	32	121	29	10	1	4	(- -)	53	22	19	15	6 1	20	1 1 2	3	0	3	.240	.277	.438	.715
2017 Mia	NL	70	228	57	13	1	3	(2 1)	81	20	31	24	12 2	50	0 2 5	0	0	6	.250	.282	.355	.637
2018 Mia	NL	102	308	71	10	4	9	(4 5)	116	28	36	31	20 1	67	0 3 1	0	3	4	.231	.277	.377	.653
2019 Mia	NL	51	132	25	6	0	6	(3 3)	49	15	12	7	5 1	42	2 0 0	0	0	3	.189	.230	.371	.601
3 ML YEARS		223	668	153	29	5	18	(9 9)	246	63	79	62	37 4	159	2 5 6	0	5	13	.229	.269	.368	.638

Austin Riley

Bats: R **Throws:** R **Pos:** LF-58;PH-10;1B-6;3B-5;RF-2;DH-1;PR-1   **Ht:** 6'3" **Wt:** 220 **Born:** 4/2/1997 **Age:** 23

Year Team	Lg	G	AB	H	2B	3B	HR	(Hm Rd)	TB	R	RBI	RC	TBB	IBB	SO	HBP	SH	SF	SB	CS	GDP	Avg	OBP	Slg	OPS
2015 2 Tms	Low	60	217	66	14	1	12	(- -)	118	36	40	45	26	1	65	6	0	3	2	2	5	.304	.389	.544	.933
2016 Rome	A	129	495	134	39	2	20	(- -)	237	68	80	80	39	0	147	3	0	6	3	3	11	.271	.324	.479	.803
2017 Florida	A+	81	306	77	10	1	12	(- -)	125	43	47	40	23	0	74	5	0	5	0	2	4	.252	.310	.408	.718
2017 Missi	AA	48	178	56	9	1	8	(- -)	91	28	27	36	20	0	50	3	0	2	2	0	3	.315	.389	.511	.900
2018 Missi	AA	27	99	33	10	3	6	(- -)	67	17	20	24	8	2	28	2	0	0	0	0	2	.333	.394	.677	1.071
2018 Gwnntt	AAA	75	291	82	17	0	12	(- -)	135	41	47	48	26	2	95	4	0	3	1	0	3	.282	.346	.464	.810
2019 Gwnntt	AAA	44	174	51	13	0	15	(- -)	109	39	41	38	20	0	39	0	0	0	0	0	6	.293	.366	.626	.992
2019 Atl	NL	80	274	62	11	1	18	(11 7)	129	41	49	38	16	3	108	5	0	2	0	2	4	.226	.279	.471	.750

Edwin Rios

Bats: L **Throws:** R **Pos:** PH-18;1B-12;3B-5;LF-1;DH-1   **Ht:** 6'3" **Wt:** 220 **Born:** 4/21/1994 **Age:** 26

Year Team	Lg	G	AB	H	2B	3B	HR	(Hm Rd)	TB	R	RBI	RC	TBB	IBB	SO	HBP	SH	SF	SB	CS	GDP	Avg	OBP	Slg	OPS
2019 OkCity	AAA	104	393	106	23	2	31	(- -)	226	72	91	77	37	0	153	8	0	6	2	2	3	.270	.340	.575	.915
2019 LAD	NL	28	47	13	2	1	4	(0 4)	29	10	8	10	9	0	21	0	0	0	0	0	1	.277	.393	.617	1.010

Yacksel Rios

Pitches: R **Bats:** R **Pos:** RP-14   **Ht:** 6'3" **Wt:** 185 **Born:** 6/27/1993 **Age:** 27

Year Team	Lg	G	GS	GF	IP	BFP	H	R	ER	HR	SH	SF	HB	TBB	IBB	SO	WP	W	L	Pct	Sv-Op	Hld	Vel	OPS	ERC	ERA
2019 LV	AAA	31	0	15	34.0	165	38	31	28	4	2	4	3	22	1	37	3	1	3	.250	7--	-	-	.827	6.08	7.41
2019 Indy	AAA	9	0	3	15.1	67	19	4	4	2	0	0	1	4	0	12	2	0	0	-	1--	-	-	.826	5.52	2.35
2017 Phi	NL	13	0	7	16.1	73	15	8	8	4	1	0	0	9	1	17	0	1	0	1.000	0-0	0	94	.825	5.06	4.41
2018 Phi	NL	36	0	10	36.0	165	43	28	27	6	0	1	2	15	2	36	2	3	2	.600	0-0	2	96	.853	5.90	6.75
2019 2 Tms	NL	14	0	5	13.0	65	16	13	10	4	1	2	3	8	0	12	1	1	0	1.000	0-0	1	96	1.049	9.16	6.92
19 Phi	NL	4	0	3	2.2	19	6	7	4	2	1	1	1	3	0	2	1	0	0	-	0-0	0	96	1.632	24.00	13.50
19 Pit	NL	10	0	2	10.1	46	10	6	6	2	0	1	2	5	0	10	0	1	0	1.000	0-0	1	96	.843	5.87	5.23
3 ML YEARS		63	0	22	65.1	303	74	49	45	14	2	3	5	32	3	65	3	5	2	.714	0-0	3	96	.886	6.30	6.20

Rene Rivera

Bats: R **Throws:** R **Pos:** C-8;PH-1   ruh-NAY   **Ht:** 5'10" **Wt:** 215 **Born:** 7/31/1983 **Age:** 36

Year Team	Lg	G	AB	H	2B	3B	HR	(Hm Rd)	TB	R	RBI	RC	TBB	IBB	SO	HBP	SH	SF	SB	CS	GDP	Avg	OBP	Slg	OPS
2019 Syrcse	AAA	98	355	90	13	0	25	(- -)	178	53	73	58	31	0	103	5	1	4	0	0	16	.254	.319	.501	.820
2004 Sea	AL	2	3	0	0	0	0	(0 0)	0	0	0	0	0	0	1	0	0	0	0	0	0	.000	.000	.000	.000
2005 Sea	AL	16	48	19	3	0	1	(0 1)	25	3	6	8	1	0	11	0	1	0	0	0	0	.396	.408	.521	.929
2006 Sea	AL	35	99	15	4	0	2	(1 1)	25	8	4	4	3	0	29	1	3	0	1	0	2	.152	.184	.253	.437
2011 Min	AL	45	104	15	3	0	1	(0 1)	21	9	5	3	8	0	32	1	0	1	0	0	2	.144	.211	.202	.412
2013 SD	NL	23	67	17	3	1	0	(0 0)	22	4	7	6	2	1	16	0	0	2	0	0	1	.254	.268	.328	.596
2014 SD	NL	103	294	74	18	1	11	(1 10)	127	27	44	41	27	3	76	3	3	2	0	0	6	.252	.319	.432	.751
2015 TB	AL	110	298	53	14	0	5	(4 1)	82	16	26	16	11	0	86	3	5	2	0	0	4	.178	.273	.275	.489
2016 NYM	NL	65	185	41	4	0	6	(4 2)	63	12	26	19	16	3	54	3	1	2	0	0	4	.222	.291	.341	.632
2017 2 Tms	NL	74	218	55	9	0	10	(5 5)	94	23	35	29	14	3	70	3	1	1	0	1	4	.252	.305	.431	.736
2018 2 Tms		33	86	20	4	0	4	(2 2)	36	8	11	8	4	0	35	1	0	0	0	0	3	.233	.275	.419	.693
2019 NYM	NL	9	17	4	0	0	1	(1 0)	7	2	3	4	3	0	4	0	0	0	0	0	3	.235	.350	.412	.762
17 NYM	NL	54	174	40	4	0	8	(3 5)	68	15	23	18	9	3	54	3	0	1	0	1	3	.230	.278	.391	.669
17 ChC	NL	20	44	15	5	0	2	(2 0)	26	8	12	11	5	0	16	0	1	0	0	0	1	.341	.408	.591	.999
18 LAA	AL	30	82	20	4	0	4	(2 2)	36	8	11	8	4	0	32	1	0	0	0	0	3	.244	.287	.439	.726
18 Atl	NL	3	4	0	0	0	0	(0 0)	0	0	0	0	0	0	3	0	0	0	0	0	0	.000	.000	.000	.000
Postseason		1	3	1	0	0	0	(0 0)	1	0	0	0	0	0	0	0	0	0	0	0	0	.333	.333	.333	.667
11 ML YEARS		515	1419	313	62	2	41	(18 23)	502	112	167	138	89	10	414	15	14	10	1	1	26	.221	.272	.354	.626

Yadiel Rivera

YA-dee-el

Bats: R **Throws:** R **Pos:** PH-12;3B-8;SS-8;1B-4;RF-3;PR-3;2B-2;CF-1   **Ht:** 6'3" **Wt:** 185 **Born:** 5/2/1992 **Age:** 28

Year Team	Lg	G	AB	H	2B	3B	HR	(Hm Rd)	TB	R	RBI	RC	TBB	IBB	SO	HBP	SH	SF	SB	CS	GDP	Avg	OBP	Slg	OPS
2019 NewOr	AAA	82	300	88	11	1	14	(- -)	143	38	46	44	6	0	81	2	2	2	15	6	10	.293	.310	.477	.786
2015 Mil	NL	7	14	1	0	0	0	(0 0)	1	0	0	0	0	0	4	0	1	0	0	0	0	.071	.071	.071	.143
2016 Mil	NL	35	66	14	4	0	0	(0 0)	18	12	3	3	2	0	20	0	3	0	1	0	4	.212	.235	.273	.508
2017 Mil	NL	1	2	0	0	0	0	(0 0)	0	0	0	0	0	0	1	0	0	0	0	0	0	.000	.000	.000	.000
2018 Mia	NL	111	139	24	3	0	1	(0 1)	30	13	9	7	19	3	51	0	0	2	2	1	3	.173	.269	.216	.485
2019 Mia	NL	34	60	11	2	0	0	(0 0)	13	8	3	5	6	0	20	0	0	0	2	0	1	.183	.258	.217	.474
5 ML YEARS		188	281	50	9	0	1	(0 1)	62	33	15	15	27	3	96	0	4	2	4	1	8	.178	.248	.221	.469

Anthony Rizzo

Bats: L Throws: L Pos: 1B-146;PH-2 **Ht: 6'3" Wt: 240 Born: 8/8/1989 Age: 30**

Year	Team	Lg	G	AB	H	2B	3B	HR	(Hm	Rd)	TB	R	RBI	RC	TBB	IBB	SO	HBP	SH	SF	SB	CS	GDP	Avg	OBP	Slg	OPS
2011	SD	NL	49	128	18	8	1	1	(1	0)	31	9	9	7	21	1	46	4	0	1	2	1	2	.141	.281	.242	.523
2012	ChC	NL	87	337	96	15	0	15	(7	8)	156	44	48	57	27	1	62	3	0	1	3	2	7	.285	.342	.463	.805
2013	ChC	NL	160	606	141	40	2	23	(13	10)	254	71	80	74	76	7	127	6	0	2	6	5	12	.233	.323	.419	.742
2014	ChC	NL	140	524	150	28	1	32	(14	18)	276	89	78	99	73	7	116	15	0	4	5	4	8	.286	.386	.527	.913
2015	ChC	NL	160	586	163	38	3	31	(11	20)	300	94	101	115	78	9	105	30	0	7	17	6	9	.278	.387	.512	.899
2016	ChC	NL	155	583	170	43	4	32	(12	20)	317	94	109	119	74	8	108	16	0	3	3	5	13	.292	.385	.544	.928
2017	ChC	NL	157	572	156	32	3	32	(15	17)	290	99	109	116	91	11	90	24	0	4	10	4	21	.273	.392	.507	.899
2018	ChC	NL	153	566	160	29	1	25	(13	12)	266	74	101	97	70	15	80	20	0	9	6	4	11	.283	.376	.470	.846
2019	ChC	NL	146	512	150	29	3	27	(13	14)	266	89	94	111	71	3	86	27	0	3	5	2	15	.293	.405	.520	.924
	Postseason		37	138	30	6	0	6	(3	3)	54	16	18	16	12	2	35	4	0	0	2	0	4	.217	.299	.391	.690
	9 ML YEARS		1207	4414	1204	262	18	218	(99	119)	2156	663	729	795	581	62	820	145	0	33	57	33	98	.273	.373	.488	.862

Tanner Roark

Pitches: R Bats: R Pos: SP-31 ROW-ark **Ht: 6'2" Wt: 240 Born: 10/5/1986 Age: 33**

Year	Team	Lg	G	GS	GF	IP	BFP	H	R	ER	HR	SH	SF	HB	TBB	IBB	SO	WP	W	L	Pct	Sv-Op	Hld	Vel	OPS	ERC	ERA
2013	Was	NL	14	5	1	53.2	204	38	11	9	1	3	2	0	11	0	40	0	7	1	.875	0-0	1	93	.473	1.54	1.51
2014	Was	NL	31	31	0	198.2	798	178	64	63	16	5	2	6	39	1	138	0	15	10	.600	0-0	0	91	.632	2.76	2.85
2015	Was	NL	40	12	8	111.0	467	119	55	54	17	4	4	5	26	3	70	0	4	7	.364	1-2	4	93	.784	4.39	4.38
2016	Was	NL	34	33	0	210.0	855	173	72	66	17	10	1	13	73	4	172	6	16	10	.615	0-0	1	92	.634	3.08	2.83
2017	Was	NL	32	30	0	181.1	776	178	105	94	23	3	2	6	64	5	166	3	13	11	.542	0-0	0	92	.729	4.06	4.67
2018	Was	NL	31	30	1	180.1	760	181	90	87	24	4	6	10	50	3	146	5	9	15	.375	0-0	0	91	.741	4.07	4.34
2019	2 Tms		31	31	0	165.1	722	180	84	80	28	0	2	13	51	1	158	0	10	10	.500	0-0	0	92	.806	5.05	4.35
19	Cin	NL	21	21	0	110.1	484	119	55	52	14	0	1	9	38	1	108	0	6	7	.462	0-0	0	92	.774	4.84	4.24
19	Oak	AL	10	10	0	55.0	238	61	29	28	14	0	1	4	13	0	50	3	4	3	.571	0-0	0	92	.868	5.44	4.58
	Postseason		3	1	1	7.0	35	10	3	3	2	0	0	1	3	1	4	0	0	1	.000	0-0	0	94	.916	8.56	3.86
	7 ML YEARS		213	172	10	1100.1	4582	1047	481	453	126	29	19	53	314	17	890	17	74	64	.536	1-2	6	92	.703	3.66	3.71

Luis Robert

Bats: R Throws: R Pos: CF **Ht: 6'3" Wt: 185 Born: 8/3/1997 Age: 22**

Year	Team	Lg	G	AB	H	2B	3B	HR	(Hm	Rd)	TB	R	RBI	RC	TBB	IBB	SO	HBP	SH	SF	SB	CS	GDP	Avg	OBP	Slg	OPS
2018	3 Tms	Low	50	186	50	11	3	0	(-	-)	67	31	17	18	12	0	52	7	1	2	15	4	1	.269	.333	.360	.694
2019	WinSa	A+	19	75	34	5	3	8	(-	-)	69	21	24	30	4	0	20	5	0	0	8	2	1	.453	.512	.920	1.432
2019	Brham	AA	56	226	71	16	3	8	(-	-)	117	43	29	43	13	0	54	4	1	0	21	5	3	.314	.362	.518	.880
2019	Charltt	AAA	47	202	60	10	5	16	(-	-)	128	44	39	43	11	0	55	5	0	5	7	3	6	.297	.341	.634	.974

Daniel Robertson

Bats: R Throws: R Pos: 3B-43;2B-26;SS-16;PH-5;PR-2 **Ht: 5'11" Wt: 200 Born: 3/22/1994 Age: 26**

Year	Team	Lg	G	AB	H	2B	3B	HR	(Hm	Rd)	TB	R	RBI	RC	TBB	IBB	SO	HBP	SH	SF	SB	CS	GDP	Avg	OBP	Slg	OPS
2019	Drham	AAA	28	104	27	1	0	2	(-	-)	34	11	9	14	16	0	25	3	0	0	1	0	6	.260	.374	.327	.701
2017	TB	AL	75	218	45	7	2	5	(4	1)	71	22	19	23	29	0	73	4	1	2	1	1	5	.206	.308	.326	.634
2018	TB	AL	88	282	74	16	0	9	(5	4)	117	46	34	40	43	0	77	13	0	2	2	2	7	.262	.382	.415	.797
2019	TB	AL	74	207	44	9	1	2	(0	2)	61	23	19	16	24	0	59	6	0	0	2	2	10	.213	.312	.295	.607
	3 ML YEARS		237	707	163	32	3	16	(9	7)	249	91	72	79	96	0	209	23	1	4	5	5	22	.231	.340	.352	.692

David Robertson

Pitches: R Bats: R Pos: RP-7 **Ht: 5'11" Wt: 195 Born: 4/9/1985 Age: 35**

Year	Team	Lg	G	GS	GF	IP	BFP	H	R	ER	HR	SH	SF	HB	TBB	IBB	SO	WP	W	L	Pct	Sv-Op	Hld	Vel	OPS	ERC	ERA
2008	NYY	AL	25	0	8	30.1	131	29	18	18	3	0	3	0	15	2	36	6	4	0	1.000	0-0	0	91	.690	4.12	5.34
2009	NYY	AL	45	0	20	43.2	191	36	19	16	4	0	0	1	23	1	63	6	2	1	.667	1-1	5	92	.685	3.51	3.30
2010	NYY	AL	64	0	10	61.1	273	59	26	26	5	5	3	3	33	6	71	7	4	5	.444	1-3	14	92	.721	4.29	3.82
2011	NYY	AL	70	0	8	66.2	272	40	9	8	1	1	0	1	35	6	100	6	4	0	1.000	1-4	34	93	.506	1.85	1.08
2012	NYY	AL	65	0	17	60.2	248	52	19	18	5	0	1	1	19	0	81	1	2	7	.222	2-5	30	92	.638	2.95	2.67
2013	NYY	AL	70	0	9	66.1	262	51	15	15	5	3	0	2	18	1	77	1	5	1	.833	3-5	33	92	.584	2.37	2.04
2014	NYY	AL	63	0	55	64.1	259	45	23	22	7	1	0	1	23	2	96	0	4	5	.444	39-44	0	92	.588	2.41	3.08
2015	CWS	AL	60	0	53	63.1	250	46	27	24	7	0	0	1	13	2	86	4	6	5	.545	34-41	0	92	.573	2.00	3.41
2016	CWS	AL	62	0	48	62.1	267	53	24	24	6	3	2	1	32	4	75	1	5	3	.625	37-44	0	92	.684	3.63	3.47
2017	2 Tms	AL	61	0	34	68.1	264	35	14	14	6	0	1	3	23	5	98	7	9	2	.818	14-16	8	92	.488	1.50	1.84
2018	NYY	AL	69	0	11	69.2	283	46	30	25	7	4	1	0	26	1	91	1	8	3	.727	5-9	21	92	.595	2.15	3.23
2019	Phi	NL	7	0	3	6.2	33	8	4	4	1	0	0	0	6	0	6	0	0	1	.000	0-0	2	92	.869	7.88	5.40
17	CWS	AL	31	0	28	33.1	132	21	10	10	4	0	0	2	11	3	47	3	4	2	.667	13-14	0	91	.577	2.14	2.70
17	NYY	AL	30	0	6	35.0	132	14	4	4	2	0	1	1	12	2	51	4	5	0	1.000	1-2	8	92	.399	1.05	1.03
	Postseason		30	0	9	33.2	136	26	13	13	4	1	0	1	10	3	40	2	5	0	1.000	0-1	3	92	.637	2.59	3.48
	12 ML YEARS		661	0	276	663.2	2733	500	228	214	57	17	11	14	266	30	880	40	53	33	.616	137-172	147	92	.611	2.68	2.90

Drew Robinson

Bats: L **Throws:** R **Pos:** PH-5;CF-1;RF-1 **Ht:** 6'1" **Wt:** 200 **Born:** 4/20/1992 **Age:** 28

Year	Team	Lg	G	AB	H	2B	3B	HR	(Hm	Rd)	TB	R	RBI	RC	TBB	IBB	SO	HBP	SH	SF	SB	CS	GDP	Avg	OBP	Slg	OPS
2019	Memp	AAA	55	189	50	7	2	6	(-	-)	79	28	28	34	36	3	71	3	3	3	10	3	2	.265	.385	.418	.803
2017	Tex	AL	48	107	24	5	0	6	(3	3)	47	11	13	12	14	0	42	0	0	0	0	2	2	.224	.314	.439	.753
2018	Tex	AL	47	109	20	3	0	3	(2	1)	32	20	9	12	16	0	57	0	0	0	2	1	0	.183	.288	.294	.582
2019	StL	NL	5	7	1	0	0	0	(0	0)	1	1	0	0	0	0	3	0	0	0	0	0	0	.143	.143	.143	.286
	3 ML YEARS		100	223	45	8	0	9	(5	4)	80	32	22	24	30	0	102	0	0	0	2	3	2	.202	.296	.359	.655

Hansel Robles

Pitches: R **Bats:** R **Pos:** RP-70; SP-1 **Ht:** 6'0" **Wt:** 220 **Born:** 8/13/1990 **Age:** 29

Year	Team	Lg	G	GS	GF	IP	BFP	H	R	ER	HR	SH	SF	HB	TBB	IBB	SO	WP	W	L	Pct	Sv-Op	Hld	Vel	OPS	ERC	ERA
2015	NYM	NL	57	0	7	54.0	217	37	27	22	8	1	1	2	18	1	61	2	4	3	.571	0-4	12	96	.659	2.57	3.67
2016	NYM	NL	68	0	15	77.2	331	69	32	30	7	1	5	1	36	4	85	3	6	4	.600	1-3	13	95	.703	3.62	3.48
2017	NYM	NL	46	0	9	56.2	247	47	31	31	10	3	2	5	29	2	60	2	7	5	.583	0-2	5	95	.750	4.38	4.92
2018	2 Tms		53	0	14	56.0	242	53	26	23	9	2	3	2	25	1	59	2	2	3	.400	2-3	8	96	.771	4.53	3.70
2019	LAA	AL	71	1	51	72.2	283	58	20	20	6	2	3	0	16	1	75	4	5	1	.833	23-27	2	97	.595	2.28	2.48
18	NYM	NL	16	0	3	19.2	88	21	11	11	7	1	1	1	10	1	23	1	2	2	.500	0-0	2	95	.981	7.12	5.03
18	LAA	AL	37	0	11	36.1	154	32	15	12	2	1	2	1	15	0	36	1	0	1	.000	2-3	6	97	.654	3.27	2.97
	Postseason		3	0	2	3.0	9	0	0	0	0	0	0	0	0	0	4	0	0	0	-	0-0	0	97	.000	0.00	0.00
	5 ML YEARS		295	1	96	317.0	1320	264	136	126	40	9	14	10	124	9	340	13	24	16	.600	26-39	40	96	.693	3.40	3.58

Victor Robles

Bats: R **Throws:** R **Pos:** CF-141;RF-15;PH-5 **Ht:** 6'0" **Wt:** 190 **Born:** 5/19/1997 **Age:** 23

Year	Team	Lg	G	AB	H	2B	3B	HR	(Hm	Rd)	TB	R	RBI	RC	TBB	IBB	SO	HBP	SH	SF	SB	CS	GDP	Avg	OBP	Slg	OPS
2017	Was	NL	13	24	6	1	2	0	(0	0)	11	2	4	3	0	0	6	2	1	0	0	1	2	.250	.308	.458	.766
2018	Was	NL	21	59	17	3	1	3	(2	1)	31	8	10	10	4	0	12	2	0	1	3	2	2	.288	.348	.525	.874
2019	Was	NL	155	546	139	33	3	17	(10	7)	229	86	65	79	35	3	140	25	6	5	28	9	6	.255	.326	.419	.745
	Postseason		2	1	0	0	0	0	(0	0)	0	1	0	0	0	0	1	0	0	0	0	0	0	.000	.000	.000	.000
	3 ML YEARS		189	629	162	37	6	20	(12	8)	271	96	79	92	39	3	158	29	7	6	31	12	10	.258	.327	.431	.758

Brady Rodgers

Pitches: R **Bats:** R **Pos:** RP-3 **Ht:** 6'2" **Wt:** 210 **Born:** 9/17/1990 **Age:** 29

Year	Team	Lg	G	GS	GF	IP	BFP	H	R	ER	HR	SH	SF	HB	TBB	IBB	SO	WP	W	L	Pct	Sv-Op	Hld	Vel	OPS	ERC	ERA
2019	RdRck	AAA	10	8	1	49.1	209	48	21	21	8	0	0	1	18	0	35	1	4	0	1.000	0- -		-	.757	4.34	3.83
2016	Hou	AL	5	1	2	8.1	48	15	14	14	0	0	1	1	7	0	3	0	0	1	.000	0-0	0	90	1.069	10.43	15.12
2019	Hou	AL	3	0	2	5.0	25	7	9	9	4	0	0	0	3	0	4	1	0	0	-	0-0	0	91	1.309	13.32	16.20
	2 ML YEARS		8	1	4	13.1	73	22	23	23	4	0	1	1	10	0	7	1	0	1	.000	0-0	0	90	1.157	11.80	15.53

Brendan Rodgers

Bats: R **Throws:** R **Pos:** 2B-16;SS-9;PH-3 **Ht:** 6'0" **Wt:** 180 **Born:** 8/9/1996 **Age:** 23

Year	Team	Lg	G	AB	H	2B	3B	HR	(Hm	Rd)	TB	R	RBI	RC	TBB	IBB	SO	HBP	SH	SF	SB	CS	GDP	Avg	OBP	Slg	OPS
2015	GdJunc	R+	37	143	39	8	2	3	(-	-)	60	22	20	20	15	0	37	0	0	1	4	3	1	.273	.340	.420	.759
2016	Ashvll	A	110	442	124	31	0	19	(-	-)	212	73	73	78	35	0	98	8	2	4	6	3	3	.281	.342	.480	.821
2017	Lancst	A+	51	222	86	21	3	12	(-	-)	149	44	47	55	6	0	35	4	0	4	2	1	3	.387	.407	.671	1.078
2017	Hrtfrd	AA	38	150	39	5	0	6	(-	-)	62	20	17	19	8	0	36	6	0	0	2	6	6	.260	.323	.413	.737
2018	Hrtfrd	AA	95	357	98	23	2	17	(-	-)	176	49	62	63	30	1	76	9	1	5	12	3	9	.275	.342	.493	.835
2018	Albq	AAA	19	69	16	4	0	0	(-	-)	20	5	5	5	1	0	16	2	0	0	0	0	3	.232	.264	.290	.554
2019	Albq	AAA	37	143	50	10	1	9	(-	-)	89	34	21	34	14	1	27	2	0	1	0	0	0	.350	.413	.622	1.035
2019	Col	NL	25	76	17	2	0	0	(0	0)	19	8	7	5	4	0	27	1	0	0	0	0	2	.224	.272	.250	.522

Fernando Rodney

Pitches: R **Bats:** R **Pos:** RP-55 **Ht:** 5'11" **Wt:** 240 **Born:** 3/18/1977 **Age:** 43

Year	Team	Lg	G	GS	GF	IP	BFP	H	R	ER	HR	SH	SF	HB	TBB	IBB	SO	WP	W	L	Pct	Sv-Op	Hld	Vel	OPS	ERC	ERA
2019	Fresno	AAA	9	0	7	8.0	43	8	5	4	1	0	1	1	9	1	11	3	0	2	.000	0- -		-	.794	7.17	4.50
2002	Det	AL	20	0	10	18.0	89	25	15	12	2	2	1	0	10	2	10	0	1	3	.250	0-4	0	95	.889	6.77	6.00
2003	Det	AL	27	0	11	29.2	143	35	20	20	2	3	3	1	17	1	33	0	1	3	.250	3-6	3	98	.774	5.46	6.07
2005	Det	AL	39	0	26	44.0	185	39	14	14	5	2	0	2	17	3	42	2	2	3	.400	9-15	3	93	.707	3.59	2.86
2006	Det	AL	63	0	30	71.2	304	51	36	28	6	2	0	8	34	4	65	3	7	4	.636	7-11	18	94	.608	3.01	3.52
2007	Det	AL	48	0	12	50.2	223	46	27	24	5	4	2	3	21	0	54	4	2	6	.250	1-3	12	93	.698	3.74	4.26
2008	Det	AL	38	0	25	40.1	188	34	22	22	3	1	2	3	30	5	49	3	0	6	.000	13-19	5	95	.733	4.29	4.91
2009	Det	AL	73	0	65	75.2	330	70	38	37	8	4	2	2	41	4	61	5	2	5	.286	37-38	0	96	.731	4.31	4.40
2010	LAA	AL	72	0	30	68.0	308	70	33	32	4	1	0	5	35	1	53	4	4	3	.571	14-21	21	96	.739	4.63	4.24
2011	LAA	AL	39	0	15	32.0	150	26	18	16	1	3	0	3	28	0	26	2	3	5	.375	3-7	10	96	.672	4.66	4.50
2012	TB	AL	76	0	65	74.2	282	43	9	5	2	4	2	3	15	1	76	4	2	2	.500	48-50	0	96	.417	1.22	0.60
2013	TB	AL	68	0	55	66.2	290	53	27	25	3	1	1	1	36	3	82	4	5	4	.556	37-45	0	96	.634	3.22	3.38
2014	Sea	AL	69	0	64	66.1	286	61	24	21	3	4	1	3	28	3	76	4	1	6	.143	48-51	0	95	.646	3.42	2.85
2015	2 Tms		68	0	32	62.2	277	59	36	33	9	1	1	8	29	3	58	6	7	5	.583	16-23	9	95	.776	4.76	4.74
2016	2 Tms	NL	67	0	41	65.1	283	54	27	25	5	3	1	5	37	3	74	5	2	4	.333	25-28	8	94	.668	3.85	3.44
2017	Ari	NL	61	0	53	55.1	231	40	29	26	3	2	1	2	26	3	65	7	5	4	.556	39-45	0	95	.582	2.60	4.23

Year	Team	Lg	HOW MUCH PITCHED					WHAT HE GAVE UP											THE RESULTS							
			G	GS	GF	IP	BFP	H	R	ER	HR	SH	SF	HB	TBB	IBB	SO	WP	W	L	Pct	Sv-Op	Hld	Vel	OPS	ERC	ERA
2018	2 Tms	AL	68	0	40	64.1	285	62	27	24	7	0	2	3	32	1	70	6	4	3	.571	25-32	7	94	.703	4.46	3.36
2019	2 Tms		55	0	16	47.2	210	49	31	30	5	0	0	0	28	1	49	6	0	5	.000	2-6	17	94	.762	5.12	5.66
15	Sea	AL	54	0	28	50.2	227	51	32	32	8	1	1	5	25	3	43	5	5	5	.500	16-22	7	95	.820	5.25	5.68
15	ChC	NL	14	0	4	12.0	50	8	4	1	1	0	0	3	4	0	15	1	2	0	1.000	0-1	2	94	.579	2.88	0.75
16	SD	NL	28	0	24	28.2	109	13	2	1	0	0	0	2	12	0	33	1	0	1	.000	17-17	0	94	.406	1.30	0.31
16	Mia	NL	39	0	17	36.2	174	41	25	24	5	3	1	3	25	3	41	4	2	3	.400	8-11	8	94	.840	6.45	5.89
18	Min		46	0	39	43.2	192	42	18	15	5	0	2	2	19	1	50	2	3	2	.600	25-31	0	94	.677	4.23	3.09
18	Oak	AL	22	0	1	20.2	93	20	9	9	2	0	0	1	13	0	20	4	1	1	.500	0-1	7	94	.758	5.02	3.92
19	Oak	AL	17	0	8	14.1	70	20	15	15	0	0	0	0	12	0	14	2	0	2	.000	0-1	0	93	.940	9.18	9.42
19	Was	AL	38	0	8	33.1	140	29	16	15	3	0	0	0	16	1	35	4	0	3	.000	2-5	17	94	.676	3.62	4.05
Postseason			14	0	3	12.2	60	12	11	9	1	3	0	1	10	1	18	2	1	0	1.000	0-2	3	95	.817	5.28	6.39
17 ML YEARS			951	0	590	933.0	4064	817	433	394	73	37	19	52	464	38	943	65	48	71	.403	327-404	113	95	.677	3.74	3.80

Carlos Rodon

roh-DON

Pitches: L Bats: L Pos: SP-7   Ht: 6'3" Wt: 235 Born: 12/10/1992 Age: 27

Year	Team	Lg	HOW MUCH PITCHED					WHAT HE GAVE UP											THE RESULTS							
			G	GS	GF	IP	BFP	H	R	ER	HR	SH	SF	HB	TBB	IBB	SO	WP	W	L	Pct	Sv-Op	Hld	Vel	OPS	ERC	ERA
2015	CWS	AL	26	23	1	139.1	607	130	63	58	11	6	5	8	71	0	139	7	9	6	.600	0-0	0	93	.725	4.25	3.75
2016	CWS	AL	28	28	0	165.0	715	176	82	74	23	4	6	6	54	3	168	11	9	10	.474	0-0	0	93	.763	4.57	4.04
2017	CWS	AL	12	12	0	69.1	297	64	35	32	12	1	2	3	31	0	76	4	2	5	.286	0-0	0	93	.770	4.57	4.15
2018	CWS	AL	20	20	0	120.2	511	97	61	56	15	0	2	12	55	1	90	4	6	8	.429	0-0	0	93	.698	3.80	4.18
2019	CWS	AL	7	7	0	34.2	158	33	22	20	4	0	2	1	17	0	46	5	3	2	.600	0-0	0	92	.714	4.19	5.19
5 ML YEARS			93	90	1	529.0	2288	500	263	240	65	11	17	30	228	4	519	31	29	31	.483	0-0	0	93	.736	4.28	4.08

Dereck Rodriguez

Pitches: R Bats: R Pos: SP-16; RP-12   Ht: 6'1" Wt: 215 Born: 6/5/1992 Age: 28

Year	Team	Lg	HOW MUCH PITCHED					WHAT HE GAVE UP											THE RESULTS							
			G	GS	GF	IP	BFP	H	R	ER	HR	SH	SF	HB	TBB	IBB	SO	WP	W	L	Pct	Sv-Op	Hld	Vel	OPS	ERC	ERA
2019	Scrmto	AAA	6	6	0	29.2	122	26	18	12	4	0	1	1	10	0	28	1	3	0	1.000	0- -	-		.712	3.58	3.64
2018	SF	NL	21	19	1	118.1	487	98	43	37	9	2	3	7	36	2	89	1	6	4	.600	0-0	0	91	.667	2.84	2.81
2019	SF	NL	28	16	4	99.0	439	108	74	62	21	3	0	2	36	0	71	1	6	11	.353	0-0	0	91	.827	5.28	5.64
2 ML YEARS			49	35	5	217.1	926	206	117	99	30	5	3	9	72	2	160	2	12	15	.444	0-0	0	91	.743	3.90	4.10

Eduardo Rodriguez

Pitches: L Bats: L Pos: SP-34   Ht: 6'2" Wt: 220 Born: 4/7/1993 Age: 27

Year	Team	Lg	HOW MUCH PITCHED					WHAT HE GAVE UP											THE RESULTS							
			G	GS	GF	IP	BFP	H	R	ER	HR	SH	SF	HB	TBB	IBB	SO	WP	W	L	Pct	Sv-Op	Hld	Vel	OPS	ERC	ERA
2015	Bos	AL	21	21	0	121.2	522	120	55	52	13	5	4	4	37	1	98	4	10	6	.625	0-0	0	94	.701	3.73	3.85
2016	Bos	AL	20	20	0	107.0	458	99	58	56	16	1	4	3	40	1	100	0	3	7	.300	0-0	0	93	.728	3.96	4.71
2017	Bos	AL	25	24	1	137.1	582	126	66	64	19	1	3	5	50	1	150	1	6	7	.462	0-0	0	93	.736	3.87	4.19
2018	Bos	AL	27	23	0	129.2	553	119	56	55	16	0	3	6	52	1	146	1	13	5	.722	0-0	0	93	.681	3.63	3.82
2019	Bos	AL	34	34	0	203.1	859	195	88	86	24	2	5	7	75	2	213	3	19	6	.760	0-0	0	93	.714	4.03	3.81
Postseason			8	1	2	10.0	44	7	9	9	2	0	0	2	5	1	11	0	0	0	-	0-0	1	94	.697	4.04	8.10
5 ML YEARS			127	122	1	699.0	2974	659	323	313	88	9	19	23	247	6	707	9	51	31	.622	0-0	0	93	.712	3.86	4.03

Jefry Rodriguez

Pitches: R Bats: R Pos: SP-8; RP-2   Ht: 6'6" Wt: 232 Born: 7/26/1993 Age: 26

Year	Team	Lg	HOW MUCH PITCHED					WHAT HE GAVE UP											THE RESULTS							
			G	GS	GF	IP	BFP	H	R	ER	HR	SH	SF	HB	TBB	IBB	SO	WP	W	L	Pct	Sv-Op	Hld	Vel	OPS	ERC	ERA
2019	Clmbs	AAA	5	3	0	21.2	88	16	10	10	1	0	0	0	11	0	16	2	1	0	1.000	0- -	-		.580	2.81	4.15
2018	Was	NL	14	8	1	52.0	233	43	35	33	8	3	1	3	37	5	39	2	3	3	.500	0-0	0	95	.784	4.81	5.71
2019	Cle	AL	10	8	1	46.2	203	48	26	24	5	1	3	0	21	1	33	4	1	5	.167	0-0	0	94	.769	4.49	4.63
2 ML YEARS			24	16	2	98.2	436	91	61	57	13	4	4	3	58	6	72	6	4	8	.333	0-0	0	94	.777	4.66	5.20

Jose Rodriguez

Pitches: R Bats: R Pos: RP-8; SP-1   Ht: 6'2" Wt: 175 Born: 8/29/1995 Age: 24

Year	Team	Lg	HOW MUCH PITCHED					WHAT HE GAVE UP											THE RESULTS							
			G	GS	GF	IP	BFP	H	R	ER	HR	SH	SF	HB	TBB	IBB	SO	WP	W	L	Pct	Sv-Op	Hld	Vel	OPS	ERC	ERA
2019	Mobile	AA	5	5	0	17.1	82	24	15	14	2	1	0	1	6	0	24	0	0	2	.000	0- -	-		.896	6.43	7.27
2019	Salt Lk	AAA	18	2	3	44.1	201	48	33	31	7	1	2	1	22	0	45	2	3	3	.500	2- -	-		.801	5.43	6.29
2019	LAA	AL	9	1	2	19.2	84	17	6	6	5	0	0	0	11	0	13	1	0	1	.000	0-0	0	93	.785	5.14	2.75

Richard Rodriguez

Pitches: R Bats: R Pos: RP-72   Ht: 6'4" Wt: 230 Born: 3/4/1990 Age: 30

Year	Team	Lg	HOW MUCH PITCHED					WHAT HE GAVE UP											THE RESULTS							
			G	GS	GF	IP	BFP	H	R	ER	HR	SH	SF	HB	TBB	IBB	SO	WP	W	L	Pct	Sv-Op	Hld	Vel	OPS	ERC	ERA
2017	Bal	AL	5	0	1	5.2	31	12	9	9	4	0	0	1	3	1	3	0	0	0	-	0-0	0	94	1.516	19.81	14.29
2018	Pit	NL	63	0	20	69.1	279	55	19	19	5	1	1	5	19	3	88	11	4	3	.571	0-0	15	93	.596	2.58	2.47
2019	Pit	NL	72	0	12	65.1	285	65	30	27	14	0	1	2	23	3	63	1	4	5	.444	1-5	16	93	.751	4.62	3.72
3 ML YEARS			140	0	33	140.1	595	132	58	55	23	1	2	8	45	7	154	12	8	8	.500	1-5	31	93	.717	4.01	3.53

Ronny Rodriguez

Bats: R **Throws:** R **Pos:** 2B-31;SS-20;1B-13;PH-12;DH-7;3B-6;PR-2;LF-1   **Ht:** 6'0" **Wt:** 200 **Born:** 4/17/1992 **Age:** 28

Year	Team	Lg	G	AB	H	2B	3B	HR	(Hm	Rd)	TB	R	RBI	RC	TBB	IBB	SO	HBP	SH	SF	SB	CS	GDP	Avg	OBP	Slg	OPS
2019	Toledo	AAA	44	172	55	9	2	11	(-	-)	101	33	31	34	6	0	41	1	0	2	5	0	3	.320	.343	.587	.930
2018	Det	AL	62	191	42	7	0	5	(3	2)	64	17	20	18	10	0	42	0	3	2	2	0	7	.220	.256	.335	.591
2019	Det	AL	84	276	61	12	3	14	(6	8)	121	29	43	26	13	0	82	0	0	5	3	1	5	.221	.252	.438	.690
	2 ML YEARS		146	467	103	19	3	19	(9	10)	185	46	63	44	23	0	124	0	3	7	5	1	12	.221	.254	.396	.650

Sean Rodriguez

Bats: R **Throws:** R **Pos:** PH-32;3B-24;SS-11;LF-8;RF-4;2B-3;CF-2;1B-1;DH-1;PR-1   **Ht:** 6'0" **Wt:** 200 **Born:** 4/26/1985 **Age:** 35

Year	Team	Lg	G	AB	H	2B	3B	HR	(Hm	Rd)	TB	R	RBI	RC	TBB	IBB	SO	HBP	SH	SF	SB	CS	GDP	Avg	OBP	Slg	OPS
2019	LV	AAA	12	45	12	2	1	4	(-	-)	28	7	12	9	3	0	19	1	0	0	0	0	0	.267	.327	.622	.949
2008	LAA	AL	59	167	34	8	1	3	(2	1)	53	18	10	12	14	0	55	3	2	1	3	1	3	.204	.276	.317	.593
2009	LAA	AL	12	25	5	0	0	2	(0	2)	11	4	4	2	3	0	7	0	0	1	0	0	2	.200	.276	.440	.716
2010	TB	AL	118	343	86	19	2	9	(5	4)	136	53	40	38	21	1	97	8	5	1	13	3	10	.251	.308	.397	.705
2011	TB	AL	131	373	83	20	3	8	(4	4)	133	45	36	41	38	2	87	4	4	5	11	7	8	.223	.323	.357	.679
2012	TB	AL	112	301	64	14	1	6	(3	3)	98	36	32	32	27	1	75	3	8	3	5	0	7	.213	.281	.326	.607
2013	TB	AL	96	195	48	10	1	5	(2	3)	75	21	23	21	17	0	59	5	3	2	1	3	3	.246	.320	.385	.704
2014	TB	AL	96	237	50	13	3	12	(7	5)	105	30	41	29	10	0	66	6	3	3	2	1	3	.211	.258	.443	.701
2015	Pit	NL	139	224	55	12	1	4	(2	2)	81	25	17	17	5	0	63	6	5	0	2	2	9	.246	.281	.362	.642
2016	Pit	NL	140	300	81	16	1	18	(7	11)	153	49	56	53	33	2	102	5	1	3	2	1	6	.270	.349	.510	.859
2017	2 Tms	NL	54	132	22	2	0	5	(2	3)	39	18	8	8	16	1	57	4	1	0	1	0	3	.167	.276	.295	.572
2018	Pit	NL	66	150	25	5	1	5	(1	4)	47	21	19	14	22	1	60	1	0	0	1	0	1	.167	.277	.313	.591
2019	Phi	NL	76	112	25	5	0	4	(3	1)	42	24	12	14	19	0	41	3	4	1	1	1	2	.223	.348	.375	.723
17	Atl	NL	15	37	6	1	0	2	(0	2)	13	6	3	4	8	1	19	1	1	0	1	0	1	.162	.326	.351	.677
17	Pit	NL	39	95	16	1	0	3	(2	1)	26	12	5	4	8	0	38	3	0	0	0	0	2	.168	.255	.274	.528
	Postseason		13	28	5	1	0	1	(0	1)	9	6	2	1	2	0	5	0	0	0	0	0	0	.179	.233	.321	.555
	12 ML YEARS		1099	2559	578	124	14	81	(39	42)	973	344	298	281	225	8	769	62	37	17	42	19	57	.226	.302	.380	.682

Chaz Roe

Pitches: R **Bats:** R **Pos:** RP-71   ROW   **Ht:** 6'5" **Wt:** 190 **Born:** 10/9/1986 **Age:** 33

			HOW MUCH PITCHED					WHAT HE GAVE UP											THE RESULTS							
Year	Team	Lg	G	GS	GF	IP	BFP	H	R	ER	HR	SH	SF	HB	TBB	IBB	SO	WP	W	L	Pct	Sv-Op	Hld	Vel	OPS	ERC	ERA
2013	Ari	NL	21	0	4	22.1	95	18	10	10	3	2	1	0	13	3	24	1	1	0	1.000	0-2	1	91	.726	3.78	4.03
2014	NYY	AL	3	0	2	2.0	13	3	3	2	0	0	1	0	3	0	4	1	0	0	-	0-0	0	91	1.239	9.89	9.00
2015	Bal	AL	36	0	6	41.1	177	44	19	19	4	1	1	1	17	2	38	0	4	2	.667	0-1	4	93	.798	4.62	4.14
2016	2 Tms		30	0	11	29.2	124	22	12	12	2	0	2	1	14	1	37	1	2	0	1.000	0-1	3	93	.672	2.82	3.64
2017	2 Tms		12	0	3	10.2	44	7	5	3	1	0	0	1	5	0	13	1	0	0	-	0-0	1	93	.585	2.84	2.53
2018	TB	AL	61	0	6	50.1	203	35	21	20	6	1	0	8	16	1	53	1	1	3	.250	1-2	31	92	.629	2.90	3.58
2019	TB	AL	71	0	11	51.0	229	49	27	23	3	0	1	1	31	2	65	3	1	3	.250	1-5	23	92	.704	4.36	4.06
16	Bal	AL	9	0	6	9.2	44	8	4	4	2	0	0	0	7	0	11	1	1	0	1.000	0-0	1	92	.800	5.07	3.72
16	Atl	NL	21	0	5	20.0	80	14	8	8	0	0	2	1	7	1	26	0	1	0	1.000	0-1	3	93	.604	1.86	3.60
17	Atl	NL	3	0	0	2.0	13	3	4	2	0	0	0	1	2	0	1	0	0	0	-	0-0	1	93	.762	9.89	9.00
17	TB	AL	9	0	3	8.2	31	4	1	1	1	0	0	0	3	0	12	1	0	0	-	0-0	1	93	.512	1.51	1.04
	7 ML YEARS		234	0	43	207.1	885	178	97	89	19	4	6	12	99	9	234	8	9	8	.529	2-11	63	92	.705	3.73	3.86

Jake Rogers

Bats: R **Throws:** R **Pos:** C-34;DH-1   **Ht:** 6'1" **Wt:** 205 **Born:** 4/18/1995 **Age:** 25

Year	Team	Lg	G	AB	H	2B	3B	HR	(Hm	Rd)	TB	R	RBI	RC	TBB	IBB	SO	HBP	SH	SF	SB	CS	GDP	Avg	OBP	Slg	OPS
2019	Erie	AA	28	86	26	3	1	5	(-	-)	46	17	21	21	19	0	26	3	0	4	0	0	1	.302	.429	.535	.963
2019	Toledo	AAA	48	166	37	10	1	9	(-	-)	76	29	31	25	18	0	53	6	1	0	0	0	2	.223	.321	.458	.779
2019	Det	AL	35	112	14	3	0	4	(3	1)	29	11	8	4	13	0	51	1	2	0	0	0	3	.125	.222	.259	.481

Josh Rogers

Pitches: L **Bats:** L **Pos:** RP-5   **Ht:** 6'3" **Wt:** 220 **Born:** 7/10/1994 **Age:** 25

			HOW MUCH PITCHED					WHAT HE GAVE UP											THE RESULTS							
Year	Team	Lg	G	GS	GF	IP	BFP	H	R	ER	HR	SH	SF	HB	TBB	IBB	SO	WP	W	L	Pct	Sv-Op	Hld	Vel	OPS	ERC	ERA
2019	Norfolk	AAA	11	11	0	55.0	254	86	53	52	18	0	1	2	10	0	33	1	2	6	.250	0--	-	-	1.075	8.71	8.51
2018	Bal	AL	3	3	0	11.2	56	17	11	11	2	0	1	0	5	0	6	0	1	2	.333	0-0	0	90	.953	7.52	8.49
2019	Bal	AL	5	0	1	14.1	69	18	14	14	7	0	0	4	6	0	5	0	0	1	.000	0-0	0	89	1.118	10.35	8.79
	2 ML YEARS		8	3	1	26.0	125	35	25	25	9	0	1	4	11	0	11	0	1	3	.250	0-0	0	89	1.042	9.06	8.65

Taylor Rogers

Pitches: L **Bats:** L **Pos:** RP-60   **Ht:** 6'3" **Wt:** 190 **Born:** 12/17/1990 **Age:** 29

			HOW MUCH PITCHED					WHAT HE GAVE UP											THE RESULTS							
Year	Team	Lg	G	GS	GF	IP	BFP	H	R	ER	HR	SH	SF	HB	TBB	IBB	SO	WP	W	L	Pct	Sv-Op	Hld	Vel	OPS	ERC	ERA
2016	Min	AL	57	0	8	61.1	264	63	29	27	7	0	1	5	16	3	64	1	3	1	.750	0-1	9	93	.719	3.99	3.96
2017	Min	AL	69	0	7	55.2	237	52	20	19	6	2	0	3	21	5	49	1	7	3	.700	0-4	30	93	.693	3.76	3.07
2018	Min	AL	72	0	18	68.1	260	49	20	20	3	1	3	2	16	3	75	0	1	2	.333	2-4	18	93	.553	1.83	2.63
2019	Min	AL	60	0	36	69.0	278	58	20	20	8	3	0	6	11	2	90	2	2	4	.333	30-36	10	95	.625	2.70	2.61
	Postseason		1	0	0	0.1	1	0	0	0	0	0	0	0	0	0	1	0	0	0	-	0-0	0	95	.000	0.00	0.00
	4 ML YEARS		258	0	57	254.1	1039	222	89	86	24	6	4	16	64	13	278	4	13	10	.565	32-44	67	93	.646	2.98	3.04

Tyler Rogers

Pitches: R Bats: R Pos: RP-17

Ht: 6'5" Wt: 187 Born: 12/17/1990 Age: 29

Year	Team	Lg	G	GS	GF	IP	BFP	H	R	ER	HR	SH	SF	HB	TBB	IBB	SO	WP	W	L	Pct	Sv-Op	Hld	Vel	OPS	ERC	ERA
2019	Scrmto	AAA	49	1	12	62.0	270	59	31	29	6	1	0	4	28	2	55	0	4	2	.667	5- -	-	-	.725	4.20	4.21
2019	SF	NL	17	0	4	17.2	70	12	3	2	0	1	0	1	3	0	16	1	2	0	1.000	0-2	5	82	.463	1.37	1.02

Josh Rojas

Bats: L Throws: R Pos: LF-33;RF-6;PH-3;2B-1

Ht: 6'1" Wt: 185 Born: 6/30/1994 Age: 26

Year	Team	Lg	G	AB	H	2B	3B	HR	(Hm	Rd)	TB	R	RBI	RC	TBB	IBB	SO	HBP	SH	SF	SB	CS	GDP	Avg	OBP	Slg	OPS
2019	CpChr	AA	44	171	55	13	2	8	(-	-)	96	29	30	38	22	1	28	2	0	0	13	6	3	.322	.405	.561	.967
2019	RdRck	AAA	53	210	65	16	3	12	(-	-)	123	49	39	50	30	0	36	3	0	1	19	4	5	.310	.402	.586	.987
2019	Ari	NL	41	138	30	7	0	2	(2	0)	43	17	16	15	18	0	41	1	0	0	4	2	3	.217	.312	.312	.624

Miguel Rojas

Bats: R Throws: R Pos: SS-125;1B-6;PH-4;2B-3

Ht: 5'11" Wt: 195 Born: 2/24/1989 Age: 31

Year	Team	Lg	G	AB	H	2B	3B	HR	(Hm	Rd)	TB	R	RBI	RC	TBB	IBB	SO	HBP	SH	SF	SB	CS	GDP	Avg	OBP	Slg	OPS
2014	LAD	NL	85	149	27	3	0	1	(0	1)	33	16	9	6	10	1	28	2	1	0	0	0	5	.181	.242	.221	.464
2015	Mia	NL	60	142	40	7	1	1	(1	0)	52	13	17	15	11	1	16	0	2	2	0	1	4	.282	.329	.366	.695
2016	Mia	NL	123	194	48	12	0	1	(0	1)	63	27	14	14	11	2	27	1	6	2	2	1	10	.247	.288	.325	.613
2017	Mia	NL	90	272	79	16	2	1	(1	0)	102	37	26	32	27	5	32	4	1	2	2	1	6	.290	.361	.375	.736
2018	Mia	NL	153	488	123	13	0	11	(4	7)	169	44	53	51	24	2	69	9	2	4	6	3	23	.252	.297	.346	.643
2019	Mia	NL	132	483	137	29	1	5	(3	2)	183	52	46	63	32	2	62	5	1	5	9	5	15	.284	.331	.379	.710
	Postseason		1	1	0	0	0	0	(0	0)	0	0	0	0	0	0	0	0	0	0	0	0	0	.000	.000	.000	.000
	6 ML YEARS		643	1728	454	80	4	20	(9	11)	602	189	165	181	115	13	234	21	13	15	19	11	63	.263	.314	.348	.662

Jordan Romano

Pitches: R Bats: R Pos: RP-17

Ht: 6'4" Wt: 200 Born: 4/21/1993 Age: 27

Year	Team	Lg	G	GS	GF	IP	BFP	H	R	ER	HR	SH	SF	HB	TBB	IBB	SO	WP	W	L	Pct	Sv-Op	Hld	Vel	OPS	ERC	ERA
2019	Buffalo	AAA	24	3	13	37.2	166	37	26	24	8	0	1	4	14	0	53	2	2	2	.500	5- -	-	-	.787	5.06	5.73
2019	Tor	AL	17	0	2	15.1	75	17	14	13	4	0	4	0	9	0	21	0	0	2	.000	0-0	5	95	.884	7.90	7.63

Sal Romano

Pitches: R Bats: L Pos: RP-12

Ht: 6'5" Wt: 255 Born: 10/12/1993 Age: 26

Year	Team	Lg	G	GS	GF	IP	BFP	H	R	ER	HR	SH	SF	HB	TBB	IBB	SO	WP	W	L	Pct	Sv-Op	Hld	Vel	OPS	ERC	ERA
2019	Lsvlle	AAA	43	5	10	69.1	300	72	38	33	6	0	3	3	26	2	76	8	4	8	.333	1- -	-	-	.751	4.26	4.28
2017	Cin	NL	16	16	0	87.0	384	91	49	43	9	6	6	4	37	2	73	5	5	8	.385	0-0	0	95	.799	4.61	4.45
2018	Cin	NL	39	25	1	145.2	644	155	92	86	23	3	4	4	53	6	105	7	8	11	.421	0-0	2	94	.784	4.69	5.31
2019	Cin	NL	12	0	4	16.1	77	22	14	14	4	0	1	1	8	1	16	1	1	0	1.000	2-2	1	96	1.029	8.05	7.71
	3 ML YEARS		67	41	5	249.0	1105	268	155	143	36	9	11	9	98	9	194	13	14	19	.424	2-2	3	95	.806	4.86	5.17

Fernando Romero

Pitches: R Bats: R Pos: RP-15

Ht: 6'0" Wt: 215 Born: 12/24/1994 Age: 25

Year	Team	Lg	G	GS	GF	IP	BFP	H	R	ER	HR	SH	SF	HB	TBB	IBB	SO	WP	W	L	Pct	Sv-Op	Hld	Vel	OPS	ERC	ERA
2019	Roch	AAA	35	1	11	57.2	254	53	36	28	7	1	1	7	29	1	63	12	2	4	.333	4- -	-	-	.731	4.68	4.37
2018	Min	AL	11	11	0	55.2	247	60	31	29	6	2	4	7	19	1	45	7	3	3	.500	0-0	0	95	.770	4.83	4.69
2019	Min	AL	15	0	7	14.0	72	19	12	11	2	0	0	1	11	1	18	5	0	1	.000	0-0	1	97	.914	8.37	7.07
	2 ML YEARS		26	11	7	69.2	319	79	43	40	8	2	4	8	30	2	63	12	3	4	.429	0-0	1	96	.802	5.50	5.17

Austin Romine

Bats: R Throws: R Pos: C-70;PH-2

ROW-mine

Ht: 6'1" Wt: 220 Born: 11/22/1988 Age: 31

Year	Team	Lg	G	AB	H	2B	3B	HR	(Hm	Rd)	TB	R	RBI	RC	TBB	IBB	SO	HBP	SH	SF	SB	CS	GDP	Avg	OBP	Slg	OPS
2011	NYY	AL	9	19	3	0	0	0	(0	0)	3	2	0	0	1	0	5	0	0	0	0	0	0	.158	.200	.158	.358
2013	NYY	AL	60	135	28	9	0	1	(0	1)	40	15	10	8	8	0	37	1	3	1	1	0	7	.207	.255	.296	.551
2014	NYY	AL	7	13	3	1	0	0	(0	0)	4	2	1	2	0	0	4	0	0	0	0	0	0	.231	.231	.308	.538
2015	NYY	AL	1	2	0	0	0	0	(0	0)	0	0	0	0	0	0	0	0	0	0	0	0	0	.000	.000	.000	.000
2016	NYY	AL	62	165	40	11	0	4	(1	3)	63	17	26	19	7	1	31	0	1	3	1	0	7	.242	.269	.382	.650
2017	NYY	AL	80	229	50	9	1	2	(2	0)	67	19	21	18	16	0	57	2	2	3	0	0	7	.218	.272	.293	.565
2018	NYY	AL	77	242	59	12	0	10	(3	7)	101	30	42	32	17	0	67	2	1	3	1	0	10	.244	.295	.417	.713
2019	NYY	AL	73	228	64	12	0	8	(2	6)	100	29	35	30	10	0	50	0	1	1	1	1	7	.281	.310	.439	.748
	Postseason		3	2	0	0	0	0	(0	0)	0	0	0	0	0	0	0	0	0	0	0	0	0	.000	.000	.000	.000
	8 ML YEARS		369	1033	247	54	1	25	(8	17)	378	114	135	109	59	1	251	5	8	11	4	1	38	.239	.281	.366	.647

Sergio Romo

Pitches: R **Bats:** R **Pos:** RP-65

Ht: 5'11" **Wt:** 185 **Born:** 3/4/1983 **Age:** 37

Year Team	Lg	G	GS	GF	IP	BFP	H	R	ER	HR	SH	SF	HB	TBB	IBB	SO	WP	W	L	Pct	Sv-Op	Hld	Vel	OPS	ERC	ERA
2008 SF	NL	29	0	8	34.0	130	16	13	8	3	2	1	3	8	1	33	0	3	1	.750	0-0	5	89	.470	1.27	2.12
2009 SF	NL	45	0	9	34.0	143	30	15	15	1	2	0	1	11	0	41	2	5	2	.714	2-2	10	90	.631	2.76	3.97
2010 SF	NL	68	0	13	62.0	247	46	16	15	6	2	2	4	14	2	70	0	5	3	.625	0-4	21	89	.599	2.26	2.18
2011 SF	NL	65	0	16	48.0	175	29	8	8	2	2	0	0	5	1	70	0	3	1	.750	1-2	23	89	.458	1.08	1.50
2012 SF	NL	69	0	27	55.1	215	37	11	11	5	2	0	3	10	1	63	2	4	2	.667	14-15	23	88	.525	1.72	1.79
2013 SF	NL	65	0	52	60.1	250	53	20	17	5	1	1	1	12	3	58	1	5	8	.385	38-43	0	88	.614	2.47	2.54
2014 SF	NL	64	0	35	58.0	230	43	24	24	9	2	0	4	12	2	59	2	6	4	.600	23-28	11	88	.622	2.54	3.72
2015 SF	NL	70	0	14	57.1	230	51	20	19	3	2	0	1	10	2	71	4	0	5	.000	2-4	34	87	.622	2.37	2.98
2016 SF	NL	40	0	13	30.2	117	26	9	9	5	0	0	0	7	1	33	1	1	0	1.000	4-4	14	86	.709	3.13	2.64
2017 2 Tms		55	0	12	55.2	224	42	23	22	9	0	1	1	19	2	59	2	3	1	.750	0-1	11	86	.661	2.97	3.56
2018 TB	AL	73	5	39	67.1	284	65	31	31	11	2	2	2	20	0	75	2	3	4	.429	25-33	9	86	.718	4.02	4.14
2019 2 Tms		65	0	33	60.1	249	50	27	23	7	0	4	2	17	3	60	3	2	1	.667	20-23	17	86	.649	2.83	3.43
17 LAD	NL	30	0	8	25.0	108	23	17	17	7	0	0	0	12	1	31	0	1	1	.500	0-0	7	87	.845	5.15	6.12
17 TB	AL	25	0	4	30.2	116	19	6	5	2	0	1	1	7	1	28	2	2	0	1.000	0-1	4	86	.494	1.54	1.47
19 Mia	NL	38	0	28	37.2	156	33	18	15	4	0	3	0	13	3	33	2	2	0	1.000	17-18	1	86	.673	3.12	3.58
19 Min	AL	27	0	5	22.2	93	17	9	8	3	0	1	2	4	0	27	1	0	1	.000	3-5	16	86	.608	2.35	3.18
Postseason		27	0	13	23.1	90	18	8	8	3	0	0	0	3	0	22	1	3	1	.750	4-7	4	88	.567	2.06	3.09
12 ML YEARS		708	5	271	623.0	2494	488	217	202	66	17	11	22	145	18	692	19	40	32	.556	129-159	178	88	.613	2.44	2.92

Hector Rondon

Pitches: R **Bats:** R **Pos:** RP-61; SP-1

rohn-DOHN

Ht: 6'3" **Wt:** 230 **Born:** 2/26/1988 **Age:** 32

Year Team	Lg	G	GS	GF	IP	BFP	H	R	ER	HR	SH	SF	HB	TBB	IBB	SO	WP	W	L	Pct	Sv-Op	Hld	Vel	OPS	ERC	ERA
2013 ChC	NL	45	0	14	54.2	242	52	29	29	6	4	3	3	25	5	44	4	2	1	.667	0-1	2	94	.737	4.10	4.77
2014 ChC	NL	64	0	44	63.1	255	52	21	17	2	1	0	1	15	0	63	0	4	4	.500	29-33	1	96	.526	2.10	2.42
2015 ChC	NL	72	0	47	70.0	281	55	19	13	4	3	1	3	15	2	69	5	6	4	.600	30-34	6	96	.568	2.12	1.67
2016 ChC	NL	54	0	35	51.0	200	42	20	20	8	1	2	2	8	0	58	3	2	3	.400	18-23	7	96	.641	2.75	3.53
2017 ChC	NL	61	0	14	57.1	237	50	30	27	10	1	0	1	20	0	69	3	4	1	.800	0-3	15	96	.724	3.77	4.24
2018 Hou	AL	63	0	26	59.0	250	58	22	21	4	0	0	0	20	2	67	1	2	5	.286	15-22	9	97	.695	3.47	3.20
2019 Hou	AL	62	1	5	60.2	257	56	25	25	10	1	1	4	20	0	48	0	3	2	.600	0-3	19	97	.754	4.08	3.71
Postseason		17	0	11	15.0	62	20	7	7	4	0	0	0	2	0	13	0	1	1	.500	2-2	1	97	.955	6.52	4.20
7 ML YEARS		421	1	185	416.0	1722	365	166	152	44	10	8	13	123	9	418	16	23	20	.535	92-119	56	96	.661	3.13	3.29

Jose Rondon

rohn-DOHN

Bats: R **Throws:** R **Pos:** 2B-19;SS-15;3B-13;PH-9;DH-6;PR-3;LF-2;1B-1

Ht: 6'1" **Wt:** 195 **Born:** 3/3/1994 **Age:** 26

Year Team	Lg	G	AB	H	2B	3B	HR	(Hm	Rd)	TB	R	RBI	RC	TBB	IBB	SO	HBP	SH	SF	SB	CS	GDP	Avg	OBP	Slg	OPS
2019 Norfolk	AAA	21	73	16	4	0	2	(-	-)	26	9	12	8	10	0	22	0	0	1	1	0	1	.219	.313	.356	.669
2016 SD	NL	8	25	3	0	0	0	(0	0)	3	1	1	1	1	0	4	0	0	0	0	0	1	.120	.154	.120	.274
2018 CWS	AL	42	100	23	6	0	6	(2	4)	47	15	14	11	7	0	30	0	0	0	2	1	3	.230	.280	.470	.750
2019 2 Tms	AL	56	143	28	3	0	3	(3	0)	40	10	9	7	11	0	38	2	1	0	0	0	4	.196	.263	.280	.543
19 CWS	AL	55	142	28	3	0	3	(3	0)	40	10	9	7	11	0	38	2	1	0	0	0	4	.197	.265	.282	.546
19 Bal	AL	1	1	0	0	0	0	(0	0)	0	0	0	0	0	0	0	0	0	0	0	0	0	.000	.000	.000	.000
3 ML YEARS		106	268	54	9	0	9	(5	4)	90	26	24	19	19	0	72	2	1	0	2	1	8	.201	.260	.336	.595

Adonis Rosa

Pitches: R **Bats:** R **Pos:** RP-1

Ht: 6'1" **Wt:** 170 **Born:** 11/17/1994 **Age:** 25

Year Team	Lg	G	GS	GF	IP	BFP	H	R	ER	HR	SH	SF	HB	TBB	IBB	SO	WP	W	L	Pct	Sv-Op	Hld	Vel	OPS	ERC	ERA
2019 S-WB	AAA	13	8	0	60.1	259	65	33	26	9	2	1	1	14	0	51	1	6	0	1.000	0- -	-	-	.776	4.19	3.88
2019 Trntn	AA	12	5	1	43.0	184	41	22	22	3	1	2	0	19	0	37	0	3	1	.750	0- -	-	-	.754	3.79	4.60
2019 NYY	AL	1	0	1	2.0	7	1	1	1	0	0	0	0	0	0	2	0	0	0	-	0-0	0	90	.714	1.73	4.50

Amed Rosario

Bats: R **Throws:** R **Pos:** SS-152;PH-4;LF-1;DH-1

Ht: 6'2" **Wt:** 189 **Born:** 11/20/1995 **Age:** 24

Year Team	Lg	G	AB	H	2B	3B	HR	(Hm	Rd)	TB	R	RBI	RC	TBB	IBB	SO	HBP	SH	SF	SB	CS	GDP	Avg	OBP	Slg	OPS
2017 NYM	NL	46	165	41	4	4	4	(1	3)	65	16	10	14	3	0	49	2	0	0	7	1	5	.248	.271	.394	.665
2018 NYM	NL	154	554	142	26	8	9	(4	5)	211	76	51	60	29	4	119	3	3	3	24	11	9	.256	.295	.381	.676
2019 NYM	NL	157	616	177	30	7	15	(8	7)	266	75	72	79	31	2	124	3	2	3	19	**10**	13	.287	.323	.432	.755
3 ML YEARS		357	1335	360	60	19	28	(13	15)	542	167	133	153	63	6	292	8	5	6	50	24	25	.270	.305	.406	.711

Eddie Rosario

Bats: L **Throws:** R **Pos:** LF-124;RF-11;CF-3;DH-3;PH-3

Ht: 6'1" **Wt:** 180 **Born:** 9/28/1991 **Age:** 28

Year Team	Lg	G	AB	H	2B	3B	HR	(Hm	Rd)	TB	R	RBI	RC	TBB	IBB	SO	HBP	SH	SF	SB	CS	GDP	Avg	OBP	Slg	OPS
2015 Min	AL	122	453	121	18	15	13	(10	3)	208	60	50	58	15	3	118	0	3	5	11	6	5	.267	.289	.459	.748
2016 Min	AL	92	335	90	17	2	10	(4	6)	141	52	32	35	12	2	91	2	2	3	5	2	4	.269	.295	.421	.716
2017 Min	AL	151	542	157	33	2	27	(20	7)	275	79	78	77	35	1	106	0	4	8	9	8	10	.290	.328	.507	.836

Year	Team	Lg	G	AB	H	2B	3B	HR	(Hm	Rd)	TB	R	RBI	RC	TBB	IBB	SO	HBP	SH	SF	SB	CS	GDP	Avg	OBP	Slg	OPS
2018	Min	AL	138	559	161	31	2	24	(15	9)	268	87	77	79	30	5	104	0	1	2	8	2	4	.288	.323	.479	.803
2019	Min	AL	137	562	155	28	1	32	(12	20)	281	91	109	88	22	2	86	0	0	6	3	1	10	.276	.300	.500	.800
	Postseason		1	3	1	0	0	1	(0	1)	4	1	2		1	0	1	0	0	0	0	0	0	.333	.500	1.333	1.833
	5 ML YEARS		640	2451	684	127	22	106	(61	45)	1173	369	346	337	114	13	505	2	10	22	36	19	33	.279	.309	.479	.788

Randy Rosario

Pitches: L Bats: L Pos: RP-19   **Ht: 6'1" Wt: 200 Born: 5/18/1994 Age: 26**

			HOW MUCH PITCHED					WHAT HE GAVE UP										THE RESULTS						
Year	Team	Lg	G	GS	GF	IP	BFP	H	R	ER	HR	SH	SF	HB	TBB	IBB	SO	WP	W	L	Pct	Sv-Op	Hld	Vel	OPS	ERC	ERA
2019	Iowa	AAA	31	0	15	37.2	177	46	20	13	5	0	0	1	14	0	31	5	1	2	.333	4--	-	-	.777	5.37	3.11
2017	Min	AL	2	0	1	2.1	15	7	8	8	1	0	0	1	0	0	2	0	0	0	-	0-0	0	94	1.390	21.70	30.86
2018	ChC	NL	44	0	8	46.2	200	47	22	19	5	0	0	0	22	2	30	1	4	0	1.000	1-2	8	93	.721	4.49	3.66
2019	2 Tms		19	0	4	14.1	63	15	9	7	2	0	0	0	5	0	13	3	2	0	1.000	0-1	0	94	.748	4.31	4.40
19	ChC	NL	13	0	2	10.2	49	12	8	7	2	0	0	0	5	0	10	2	1	0	1.000	0-1	0	94	.824	5.61	5.91
19	KC	AL	6	0	2	3.2	14	3	1	0	0	0	0	0	0	0	3	1	1	0	1.000	0-0	0	94	.500	1.32	0.00
	Postseason		1	0	0	0.1	2	0	0	0	0	0	0	0	1	0	0	0	0	0	-	0-0	0	94	.500	7.00	0.00
	3 ML YEARS		65	0	13	63.1	278	69	39	34	8	0	0	1	27	2	45	4	6	0	1.000	1-3	8	93	.765	4.95	4.83

Trevor Rosenthal

Pitches: R Bats: R Pos: RP-22   **Ht: 6'2" Wt: 230 Born: 5/29/1990 Age: 30**

			HOW MUCH PITCHED					WHAT HE GAVE UP										THE RESULTS						
Year	Team	Lg	G	GS	GF	IP	BFP	H	R	ER	HR	SH	SF	HB	TBB	IBB	SO	WP	W	L	Pct	Sv-Op	Hld	Vel	OPS	ERC	ERA
2019	Hrsbrg	AA	10	0	0	9.1	47	9	6	6	2	0	0	3	7	0	11	1	0	1	.000	0--	-		.891	7.45	5.79
2019	Toledo	AAA	6	0	0	5.1	31	8	6	6	0	0	0	0	6	0	9	1	0	0	-	0--	-		1.151	13.93	10.13
2012	StL	NL	19	0	7	22.2	89	14	7	7	2	1	0	1	7	0	25	1	0	2	.000	0-0	3	98	.513	1.89	2.78
2013	StL	NL	74	0	15	75.1	311	63	25	22	4	3	0	6	20	0	108	3	2	4	.333	3-8	29	97	.608	2.68	2.63
2014	StL	NL	72	0	59	70.1	308	57	25	25	2	2	4	4	42	5	87	1	2	6	.250	45-51	2	97	.641	3.36	3.20
2015	StL	NL	68	0	57	68.2	287	62	16	16	3	1	0	1	25	3	83	7	2	4	.333	48-51	0	98	.619	3.04	2.10
2016	StL	NL	45	0	27	40.1	197	48	22	20	3	1	0	3	29	0	56	0	2	4	.333	14-18	0	97	.792	6.49	4.46
2017	StL	NL	50	0	16	47.2	202	37	20	18	3	1	3	2	20	0	76	2	3	4	.429	11-13	12	98	.572	2.80	3.40
2019	2 Tms		22	0	8	15.1	85	11	24	23	0	1	1	4	26	0	17	9	0	1	.000	0-0	2	98	.715	7.67	13.50
19	Was	NL	12	0	5	6.1	43	8	16	16	0	0	1	3	15	0	5	5	0	1	.000	0-0	1	98	.938	15.78	22.74
19	Det	AL	10	0	3	9.0	42	3	8	7	0	1	0	1	11	0	12	4	0	0	-	0-0	1	98	.504	3.04	7.00
	Postseason		23	0	15	26.0	102	15	2	2	0	0	0	0	11	3	42	1	1	0	1.000	7-9	2	98	.475	1.41	0.69
	7 ML YEARS		350	0	189	340.1	1479	292	139	131	17	10	8	21	169	8	452	23	11	25	.306	121-141	48	97	.638	3.49	3.46

Joe Ross

Pitches: R Bats: R Pos: RP-18; SP-9   **Ht: 6'4" Wt: 220 Born: 5/21/1993 Age: 27**

			HOW MUCH PITCHED					WHAT HE GAVE UP										THE RESULTS						
Year	Team	Lg	G	GS	GF	IP	BFP	H	R	ER	HR	SH	SF	HB	TBB	IBB	SO	WP	W	L	Pct	Sv-Op	Hld	Vel	OPS	ERC	ERA
2019	Fresno	AAA	8	8	0	40.0	171	48	21	19	2	4	0	3	12	0	32	4	2	3	.400	0--	-	-	.792	4.59	4.28
2015	Was	NL	16	13	0	76.2	314	64	33	31	7	3	1	2	21	0	69	1	5	5	.500	0-0	0	93	.628	2.74	3.64
2016	Was	NL	19	19	0	105.0	447	108	43	40	9	7	3	6	29	3	93	2	7	5	.583	0-0	0	93	.713	3.84	3.43
2017	Was	NL	13	13	0	73.2	323	88	44	41	16	5	0	1	20	2	68	2	5	3	.625	0-0	0	91	.867	5.54	5.01
2018	Was	NL	3	3	0	16.0	68	17	10	9	3	0	0	2	4	0	7	0	0	2	.000	0-0	0	93	.870	5.09	5.06
2019	Was	NL	27	9	3	64.0	295	74	41	39	7	3	1	4	33	1	57	2	4	4	.500	0-2	2	94	.829	5.79	5.48
	Postseason		1	1	0	2.2	15	3	4	4	1	0	0	2	2	0	3	0	0	0	-	0-0	0	94	1.103	12.09	13.50
	5 ML YEARS		78	57	4	335.1	1447	351	171	160	42	18	5	15	107	6	294	7	21	19	.525	0-2	2	93	.760	4.35	4.29

Tyson Ross

Pitches: R Bats: R Pos: SP-7   **Ht: 6'6" Wt: 245 Born: 4/22/1987 Age: 33**

			HOW MUCH PITCHED					WHAT HE GAVE UP										THE RESULTS						
Year	Team	Lg	G	GS	GF	IP	BFP	H	R	ER	HR	SH	SF	HB	TBB	IBB	SO	WP	W	L	Pct	Sv-Op	Hld	Vel	OPS	ERC	ERA
2010	Oak	AL	26	2	9	39.1	169	39	24	24	4	1	4	0	20	0	32	5	1	4	.200	1-2	2	93	.754	4.60	5.49
2011	Oak	AL	9	6	1	36.0	145	33	12	11	1	1	0	0	13	1	24	2	3	3	.500	0-0	0	92	.617	3.09	2.75
2012	Oak	AL	18	13	3	73.1	342	96	56	53	7	3	3	5	37	3	46	2	2	11	.154	0-0	0	92	.870	6.68	6.50
2013	SD	NL	35	16	8	125.0	504	100	51	44	8	3	5	7	44	4	119	7	3	8	.273	0-0	0	94	.627	2.84	3.17
2014	SD	NL	31	31	0	195.2	811	165	75	61	13	10	4	9	72	2	195	12	13	14	.481	0-0	0	93	.634	3.07	2.81
2015	SD	NL	33	33	0	196.0	823	172	78	71	9	3	3	8	84	3	212	14	10	12	.455	0-0	0	93	.652	3.33	3.26
2016	SD	NL	1	1	0	5.1	27	9	8	7	0	0	0	0	5	1	5	1	0	1	.000	0-0	0	92	.986	8.24	11.81
2017	Tex	AL	12	10	0	49.0	238	53	46	42	7	0	1	6	37	0	36	4	3	3	.500	0-0	0	92	.856	6.88	7.71
2018	2 Tms		31	23	0	149.2	634	132	73	69	17	3	6	7	62	4	122	4	8	9	.471	0-0	0	91	.712	3.74	4.15
2019	Det	AL	7	7	0	35.1	162	41	28	24	7	0	1	1	18	0	25	1	1	5	.167	0-0	0	90	.863	6.38	6.11
18	SD	NL	22	22	0	123.1	530	112	64	61	16	1	4	7	52	3	107	4	6	9	.400	0-0	0	91	.729	4.04	4.45
18	StL	NL	9	1	0	26.1	104	20	9	8	1	2	2	0	10	1	15	0	2	0	1.000	0-0	0	92	.627	2.38	2.73
	10 ML YEARS		203	142	21	904.2	3855	840	451	406	73	24	27	45	388	17	816	52	44	70	.386	1-2	2	93	.700	3.87	4.04

Zac Rosscup

Pitches: L Bats: R Pos: RP-28   ROSS-cup   **Ht: 6'2" Wt: 220 Born: 6/9/1988 Age: 32**

			HOW MUCH PITCHED					WHAT HE GAVE UP										THE RESULTS						
Year	Team	Lg	G	GS	GF	IP	BFP	H	R	ER	HR	SH	SF	HB	TBB	IBB	SO	WP	W	L	Pct	Sv-Op	Hld	Vel	OPS	ERC	ERA
2019	OkCity	AAA	9	0	2	8.2	35	8	6	6	1	0	1	0	3	0	14	1	0	1	.000	1--	-		.798	3.70	6.23
2019	Memp	AAA	8	0	1	8.0	46	7	4	4	0	0	1	0	15	1	9	3	0	0	-	0--	-		.712	7.87	4.50
2013	ChC	NL	10	0	3	6.2	30	3	1	1	1	0	0	0	7	1	7	0	0	0	-	0-0	0	93	.638	3.56	1.35
2014	ChC	NL	18	0	5	13.1	66	14	14	14	0	0	0	0	12	1	21	0	1	0	1.000	0-0	1	92	.875	6.54	9.45

Year Team	Lg	G	GS	GF	IP	BFP	H	R	ER	HR	SH	SF	HB	TBB	IBB	SO	WP	W	L	Pct	Sv-Op	Hld	Vel	OPS	ERC	ERA
2015 ChC	NL	33	0	6	26.2	118	26	13	13	5	2	0	0	13	0	29	1	2	1	.667	0-2	6	93	.860	4.85	4.39
2017 2 Tms	NL	10	0	2	7.2	32	9	4	4	2	0	0	0	0	0	10	0	0	0	-	0-0	1	93	.806	4.37	4.70
2018 LAD	NL	17	0	5	11.1	47	9	6	6	3	0	0	0	4	0	20	0	0	1	.000	0-1	1	92	.718	3.75	4.76
2019 3 Tms		28	0	2	18.0	94	22	15	10	2	0	0	0	19	1	26	3	2	0	1.000	0-1	5	92	.863	8.06	5.00
17 ChC	NL	1	0	0	0.2	2	0	0	0	0	0	0	0	0	0	0	0	0	0	-	0-0	0	93	.000	0.00	0.00
17 Col	NL	9	0	2	7.0	30	9	4	4	2	0	0	0	0	0	10	0	0	0	-	0-0	1	93	.862	5.20	5.14
19 Sea	AL	19	0	1	14.0	69	13	8	5	1	0	0	0	14	1	20	2	2	0	1.000	0-1	5	92	.719	5.54	3.21
19 Tor	AL	2	0	0	1.0	8	3	4	3	0	0	0	0	2	0	2	0	0	0	-	0-0	0	93	1.292	24.59	27.00
19 LAD	NL	7	0	1	3.0	17	6	3	2	1	0	0	0	3	0	4	1	0	0	-	0-0	0	93	1.244	16.63	6.00
6 ML YEARS		116	0	23	83.2	387	83	53	48	15	2	0	0	55	3	113	4	5	2	.714	0-4	14	93	.827	5.52	5.16

Jose Ruiz

Pitches: R **Bats:** R **Pos:** RP-39; SP-1　　　　**Ht:** 6'1" **Wt:** 190 **Born:** 10/21/1994 **Age:** 25

Year Team	Lg	G	GS	GF	IP	BFP	H	R	ER	HR	SH	SF	HB	TBB	IBB	SO	WP	W	L	Pct	Sv-Op	Hld	Vel	OPS	ERC	ERA
2019 Charllt	AAA	11	0	8	14.1	58	9	2	2	0	0	0	1	7	0	15	1	0	0	-	7--	-	-	.533	2.11	1.26
2017 SD	NL	1	0	1	1.0	4	0	0	0	0	0	0	0	1	0	1	0	0	0	-	0-0	0	95	.250	0.95	0.00
2018 CWS	AL	6	0	2	4.1	21	5	2	2	1	0	0	0	3	0	6	2	0	0	-	0-0	0	96	.825	7.12	4.15
2019 CWS	AL	40	1	16	40.0	198	56	27	25	6	2	2	2	24	2	35	4	1	4	.200	0-1	1	96	.924	7.89	5.63
3 ML YEARS		47	1	19	45.1	223	61	29	27	7	2	2	2	28	2	42	6	1	4	.200	0-1	1	96	.903	7.62	5.36

Keibert Ruiz

Bats: B **Throws:** R **Pos:** C　　　　**Ht:** 6'0" **Wt:** 200 **Born:** 7/20/1998 **Age:** 21

Year Team	Lg	G	AB	H	2B	3B	HR	(Hm	Rd)	TB	R	RBI	RC	TBB	IBB	SO	HBP	SH	SF	SB	CS	GDP	Avg	OBP	Slg	OPS
2016 2 Tms	Low	56	222	83	22	3	2	(-	-)	117	33	48	47	15	0	27	3	0	5	0	0	5	.374	.412	.527	.939
2017 2 Tms	Low	101	376	119	22	3	8	(-	-)	170	58	51	70	25	2	53	4	1	5	0	0	12	.316	.361	.452	.813
2018 Tulsa	AA	101	377	100	14	0	12	(-	-)	150	44	47	51	26	1	33	9	0	3	0	1	14	.265	.325	.398	.723
2019 Tulsa	AA	76	276	70	9	0	4	(-	-)	91	33	25	33	28	2	21	4	0	2	0	0	10	.254	.329	.330	.659

Rio Ruiz

Bats: L **Throws:** R **Pos:** 3B-114;PH-24;1B-12;2B-1;DH-1;PR-1　　　　**Ht:** 6'1" **Wt:** 215 **Born:** 5/22/1994 **Age:** 26

Year Team	Lg	G	AB	H	2B	3B	HR	(Hm	Rd)	TB	R	RBI	RC	TBB	IBB	SO	HBP	SH	SF	SB	CS	GDP	Avg	OBP	Slg	OPS
2016 Atl	NL	5	7	2	0	1	0	(0	0)	4	1	2	2	0	0	2	0	0	0	1	0	0	.286	.286	.571	.857
2017 Atl	NL	53	150	29	5	0	4	(2	2)	46	22	19	15	19	1	41	1	0	3	1	0	4	.193	.283	.307	.590
2018 Atl	NL	14	12	1	0	0	0	(0	0)	1	1	0	0	2	0	5	1	0	0	0	0	0	.083	.267	.083	.350
2019 Bal	AL	127	370	86	13	2	12	(6	6)	139	35	46	50	40	0	88	0	1	2	0	1	12	.232	.306	.376	.682
4 ML YEARS		199	539	118	18	3	16	(8	8)	190	59	67	67	61	1	136	2	1	5	2	1	16	.219	.298	.353	.651

Nick Rumbelow

Pitches: R **Bats:** R **Pos:** RP-3　　　　**Ht:** 6'0" **Wt:** 190 **Born:** 9/6/1991 **Age:** 28

Year Team	Lg	G	GS	GF	IP	BFP	H	R	ER	HR	SH	SF	HB	TBB	IBB	SO	WP	W	L	Pct	Sv-Op	Hld	Vel	OPS	ERC	ERA
2019 Tacom	AAA	19	0	8	25.1	128	37	26	23	5	0	2	2	15	0	22	2	3	2	.600	0--	-	-	1.009	8.89	8.17
2019 Syrcse	AAA	5	0	0	6.1	31	11	3	3	1	0	0	0	2	0	6	0	0	0	-	0--	-	-	.937	8.89	4.26
2015 NYY	AL	17	0	6	15.2	68	16	8	7	2	0	0	0	5	1	15	2	1	1	.500	0-0	0	93	.722	3.87	4.02
2018 Sea	AL	13	0	6	17.2	77	19	12	12	6	0	1	1	6	1	16	2	0	0	-	0-0	1	93	.917	6.19	6.11
2019 Sea	AL	3	0	1	1.1	9	3	4	4	2	0	0	0	1	0	2	1	0	0	-	1-1	0	94	1.569	25.83	27.00
3 ML YEARS		33	0	13	34.2	154	38	24	23	10	0	1	1	12	2	33	5	1	1	.500	1-1	1	93	.867	5.72	5.97

Chris Rusin

Pitches: L **Bats:** L **Pos:** RP-2　　　RUSS-inn　　　**Ht:** 6'2" **Wt:** 198 **Born:** 10/22/1986 **Age:** 33

Year Team	Lg	G	GS	GF	IP	BFP	H	R	ER	HR	SH	SF	HB	TBB	IBB	SO	WP	W	L	Pct	Sv-Op	Hld	Vel	OPS	ERC	ERA
2019 Albq	AAA	22	10	2	65.2	299	83	48	36	7	2	4	3	21	2	42	5	3	4	.429	0--	-	-	.810	5.43	4.93
2012 ChC	NL	7	7	0	29.2	135	38	22	21	4	0	0	3	11	0	21	0	2	3	.400	0-0	0	88	.881	6.46	6.37
2013 ChC	NL	13	13	0	66.1	282	66	30	29	8	1	1	3	24	3	36	1	2	6	.250	0-0	0	88	.750	4.21	3.93
2014 ChC	NL	4	0	2	12.2	58	16	10	10	1	1	0	0	5	1	8	1	0	0	-	0-0	0	88	.830	5.24	7.11
2015 Col	NL	24	22	0	131.2	594	170	88	78	19	2	0	3	41	5	86	2	6	10	.375	0-0	0	90	.867	5.80	5.33
2016 Col	NL	29	7	1	84.1	350	82	36	35	5	7	0	3	23	2	69	4	3	5	.375	0-1	3	90	.706	3.30	3.74
2017 Col	NL	60	0	7	85.0	340	75	31	25	9	2	3	3	19	1	71	4	5	1	.833	2-3	12	91	.645	2.99	2.65
2018 Col	NL	49	0	11	54.2	241	56	42	37	7	1	3	2	26	1	47	4	2	3	.400	0-1	7	90	.785	4.88	6.09
2019 Col	NL	2	0	0	1.0	9	5	4	4	1	0	1	0	1	0	0	0	0	0	-	0-0	0	89	2.095	50.97	36.00
Postseason		5	0	2	6.1	26	4	0	0	0	0	0	0	4	1	5	0	0	0	-	0-0	0	90	.580	2.13	0.00
8 ML YEARS		188	49	21	465.1	2009	508	263	239	54	14	8	17	150	13	338	16	20	28	.417	2-5	22	90	.780	4.54	4.62

Addison Russell

Bats: R **Throws:** R **Pos:** 2B-63;SS-21;PH-8;PR-1 **Ht:** 6'0" **Wt:** 200 **Born:** 1/23/1994 **Age:** 26

								BATTING											RUNNING			AVERAGES			
Year Team	Lg	G	AB	H	2B	3B	HR	(Hm Rd)	TB	R	RBI	RC	TBB	IBB	SO	HBP	SH	SF	SB	CS	GDP	Avg	OBP	Slg	OPS
2019 Iowa	AAA	27	96	27	6	0	7	(- -)	54	25	26	21	14	0	25	5	0	4	1	2	3	.281	.387	.563	.949
2015 ChC	NL	142	475	115	29	1	13	(8 5)	185	60	54	53	42	2	149	3	1	2	4	3	8	.242	.307	.389	.696
2016 ChC	NL	151	525	125	25	3	21	(11 10)	219	67	95	73	55	6	135	12	0	6	5	1	11	.238	.321	.417	.738
2017 ChC	NL	110	352	84	21	3	12	(5 7)	147	52	43	40	29	5	91	4	0	0	2	1	5	.239	.304	.418	.722
2018 ChC	NL	130	420	105	21	1	5	(2 3)	143	52	38	46	40	2	99	2	1	2	4	0	7	.250	.317	.340	.657
2019 ChC	NL	82	215	51	4	1	9	(4 5)	84	25	23	23	20	2	58	3	1	2	2	0	7	.237	.308	.391	.699
Postseason		31	110	22	4	1	4	(0 4)	40	9	19	12	4	1	29	1	1	1	2	0	1	.200	.233	.364	.596
5 ML YEARS		615	1987	480	100	9	60	(30 30)	778	256	253	235	186	17	532	24	3	12	17	5	38	.242	.312	.392	.704

Adley Rutschman

Bats: B **Throws:** R **Pos:** C **Ht:** 6'2" **Wt:** 216 **Born:** 2/6/1998 **Age:** 22

								BATTING											RUNNING			AVERAGES			
Year Team	Lg	G	AB	H	2B	3B	HR	(Hm Rd)	TB	R	RBI	RC	TBB	IBB	SO	HBP	SH	SF	SB	CS	GDP	Avg	OBP	Slg	OPS
2019 3 Tms	Low	37	130	33	8	1	4	(- -)	55	19	26	20	20	1	27	1	0	3	1	0	2	.254	.351	.423	.774

Kyle Ryan

Pitches: L **Bats:** L **Pos:** RP-73 **Ht:** 6'5" **Wt:** 215 **Born:** 9/25/1991 **Age:** 28

		HOW MUCH PITCHED					WHAT HE GAVE UP										THE RESULTS							
Year Team	Lg	G	GS	GF	IP	BFP	H	R	ER	HR	SH	SF	HB	TBB	IBB	SO	WP	W	L	Pct	Sv-Op	Hld	Vel	OPS	ERC	ERA
2014 Det	AL	6	1	0	10.1	41	10	3	3	0	0	0	0	2	0	4	0	2	0	1.000	0-0	0	89	.626	2.57	2.61
2015 Det	AL	16	6	3	56.1	237	60	29	28	9	2	1	1	20	0	30	1	2	4	.333	0-0	0	88	.795	4.94	4.47
2016 Det	AL	56	0	14	55.2	226	48	21	19	2	2	1	3	15	5	35	1	4	2	.667	0-1	4	89	.636	2.55	3.07
2017 Det	AL	8	0	0	5.2	29	9	5	5	0	0	1	0	7	1	1	0	0	0	-	0-1	4	90	1.028	11.19	7.94
2019 ChC	NL	73	0	12	61.0	260	55	26	24	5	0	3	1	29	2	58	1	4	2	.667	0-2	14	90	.669	3.75	3.54
5 ML YEARS		159	7	30	189.0	793	182	84	79	16	4	6	5	73	8	128	3	12	8	.600	0-4	22	89	.708	3.84	3.76

Hyun-Jin Ryu

he-YUN-jin ree-YOO

Pitches: L **Bats:** R **Pos:** SP-29 **Ht:** 6'3" **Wt:** 255 **Born:** 3/25/1987 **Age:** 33

		HOW MUCH PITCHED					WHAT HE GAVE UP										THE RESULTS							
Year Team	Lg	G	GS	GF	IP	BFP	H	R	ER	HR	SH	SF	HB	TBB	IBB	SO	WP	W	L	Pct	Sv-Op	Hld	Vel	OPS	ERC	ERA
2013 LAD	NL	30	30	0	192.0	783	182	67	64	15	7	3	1	49	4	154	5	14	8	.636	0-0	0	90	.660	3.13	3.00
2014 LAD	NL	26	26	0	152.0	631	152	60	57	8	6	2	3	29	2	139	2	14	7	.667	0-0	0	91	.658	3.00	3.38
2016 LAD	NL	1	1	0	4.2	24	8	6	6	1	0	0	0	2	1	4	0	0	1	.000	0-0	0	90	1.144	9.03	11.57
2017 LAD	NL	25	24	1	126.2	541	128	58	53	22	4	1	4	45	3	116	4	5	9	.357	1-1	0	90	.792	4.61	3.77
2018 LAD	NL	15	15	0	82.1	324	68	23	18	9	1	0	1	15	1	89	0	7	3	.700	0-0	0	90	.622	2.45	1.97
2019 LAD	NL	29	29	0	182.2	723	160	53	47	17	8	2	4	24	2	163	0	14	5	.737	0-0	0	91	.622	2.45	**2.32**
Postseason		7	7	0	35.0	145	37	16	16	2	0	0	0	6	1	29	0	2	2	.500	0-0	0	92	.663	3.18	4.11
6 ML YEARS		126	125	1	740.1	3026	698	267	245	72	26	8	13	164	13	665	11	54	33	.621	1-1	0	90	.673	3.12	2.98

CC Sabathia

Pitches: L **Bats:** L **Pos:** SP-22; RP-1 **Ht:** 6'6" **Wt:** 300 **Born:** 7/21/1980 **Age:** 39

		HOW MUCH PITCHED					WHAT HE GAVE UP										THE RESULTS							
Year Team	Lg	G	GS	GF	IP	BFP	H	R	ER	HR	SH	SF	HB	TBB	IBB	SO	WP	W	L	Pct	Sv-Op	Hld	Vel	OPS	ERC	ERA
2001 Cle	AL	33	33	0	180.1	763	149	93	88	19	3	5	7	95	1	171	7	17	5	.773	0-0	0	-	.701	3.86	4.39
2002 Cle	AL	33	33	0	210.0	891	198	109	102	17	5	10	4	88	2	149	6	13	11	.542	0-0	0	92	.714	3.74	4.37
2003 Cle	AL	30	30	0	197.2	832	190	85	79	19	10	4	6	66	3	141	4	13	9	.591	0-0	0	94	.720	3.70	3.60
2004 Cle	AL	30	30	0	188.0	787	176	90	86	20	3	6	7	72	3	139	1	11	10	.524	0-0	0	94	.737	3.91	4.12
2005 Cle	AL	31	31	0	196.2	823	185	92	88	19	6	3	7	62	1	161	7	15	10	.600	0-0	0	94	.684	3.55	4.03
2006 Cle	AL	28	28	0	192.2	802	182	83	69	17	8	5	7	44	3	172	3	12	11	.522	0-0	0	94	.657	3.13	3.22
2007 Cle	AL	34	**34**	0	241.0	975	238	94	86	20	6	6	8	37	1	209	1	19	7	.731	0-0	0	93	.684	3.12	3.21
2008 2 Tms		35	35	0	253.0	1023	223	85	76	19	6	7	9	59	1	251	2	17	10	.630	0-0	0	94	.625	2.78	2.70
2009 NYY	AL	34	34	0	230.0	938	197	96	86	18	4	9	9	67	7	197	5	**19**	8	.704	0-0	0	94	.653	2.89	3.37
2010 NYY	AL	34	34	0	237.2	970	209	92	84	20	5	8	7	74	6	197	8	**21**	7	.750	0-0	0	93	.656	3.11	3.18
2011 NYY	AL	33	33	0	237.1	**985**	230	87	79	17	8	7	7	61	4	230	2	19	8	.704	0-0	0	94	.666	3.27	3.00
2012 NYY	AL	28	28	0	200.0	833	184	89	75	22	4	3	8	44	2	197	4	15	6	.714	0-0	0	92	.666	3.10	3.38
2013 NYY	AL	32	32	0	211.0	908	224	**122**	112	28	4	8	4	65	5	175	7	14	13	.519	0-0	0	91	.770	4.32	4.78
2014 NYY	AL	8	8	0	46.0	209	58	31	27	10	1	1	4	10	0	48	2	3	4	.429	0-0	0	90	.875	5.98	5.28
2015 NYY	AL	29	29	0	167.1	726	188	92	88	28	5	6	6	50	3	137	5	6	10	.375	0-0	0	90	.797	5.01	4.73
2016 NYY	AL	30	30	0	179.2	768	172	83	78	22	5	2	9	65	1	152	2	9	12	.429	0-0	0	90	.713	4.04	3.91
2017 NYY	AL	27	27	0	148.2	623	139	64	61	21	2	0	5	50	1	120	5	14	5	.737	0-0	0	91	.715	3.90	3.69
2018 NYY	AL	29	29	0	153.0	665	150	72	62	19	0	3	11	51	0	140	3	9	7	.563	0-0	0	90	.715	4.10	3.65
2019 NYY	AL	23	22	0	107.1	468	112	64	59	27	2	1	3	39	0	107	0	5	8	.385	0-0	0	89	.843	5.36	4.95
08 Cle	AL	18	18	0	122.1	507	117	54	52	13	3	3	3	34	1	123	1	6	8	.429	0-0	0	94	.698	3.52	3.83
08 Mil	NL	17	17	0	130.2	516	106	31	24	6	3	4	6	25	0	128	1	11	2	.846	0-0	0	94	.553	2.13	1.65
Postseason		24	23	0	129.1	581	137	67	62	15	6	1	7	63	9	121	5	10	7	.588	0-0	0	94	.807	4.99	4.31
19 ML YEARS		561	560	0	3577.1	14989	3404	1623	1485	382	94	93	123	1099	44	3093	74	251	161	.609	0-0	0	93	.702	3.63	3.74

Casey Sadler

Pitches: R **Bats:** R **Pos:** RP-32; SP-1 **Ht:** 6'3" **Wt:** 205 **Born:** 7/13/1990 **Age:** 29

| | | HOW MUCH PITCHED | | | | | WHAT HE GAVE UP | | | | | | | | | | | THE RESULTS | | | | | | | | |
Year Team	Lg	G	GS	GF	IP	BFP	H	R	ER	HR	SH	SF	HB	TBB	IBB	SO	WP	W	L	Pct	Sv-Op	Hld	Vel	OPS	ERC	ERA
2019 Drhm	AAA	11	3	2	32.2	136	30	13	10	5	0	0	2	5	0	44	2	1	1	.500	1--	-	-	.706	3.16	2.76
2014 Pit	NL	6	0	2	10.1	49	12	9	9	0	0	2	1	5	0	7	1	0	1	.000	0-0	0	92	.782	4.80	7.84
2015 Pit	NL	1	1	0	5.0	19	4	2	2	1	0	0	0	1	0	5	0	1	0	1.000	0-0	0	91	.763	2.98	3.60
2018 Pit	NL	2	0	1	4.1	25	9	7	4	0	0	0	0	3	0	3	1	0	0	-	0-0	0	92	1.116	11.14	8.31
2019 2 Tms		33	1	16	46.1	194	41	14	11	5	2	1	4	13	2	31	0	4	0	1.000	1-2	2	93	.664	3.30	2.14
19 TB	AL	9	0	8	19.1	79	16	5	4	2	0	0	1	5	0	11	0	0	0	-	0-0	0	93	.621	2.83	1.86
19 LAD	NL	24	1	8	27.0	115	25	9	7	3	2	1	3	8	2	20	0	4	0	1.000	1-2	2	94	.695	3.64	2.33
4 ML YEARS		42	2	19	66.0	287	66	32	26	6	2	3	5	22	2	46	2	5	1	.833	1-2	2	93	.730	3.96	3.55

Connor Sadzeck

Pitches: R **Bats:** R **Pos:** RP-20 **Ht:** 6'7" **Wt:** 240 **Born:** 10/1/1991 **Age:** 28

| | | HOW MUCH PITCHED | | | | | WHAT HE GAVE UP | | | | | | | | | | | THE RESULTS | | | | | | | | |
Year Team	Lg	G	GS	GF	IP	BFP	H	R	ER	HR	SH	SF	HB	TBB	IBB	SO	WP	W	L	Pct	Sv-Op	Hld	Vel	OPS	ERC	ERA
2018 Tex	AL	13	2	1	9.1	45	6	2	1	0	0	0	1	11	1	7	1	0	0	-	0-0	5	97	.612	4.40	0.96
2019 Sea	AL	20	0	10	23.2	107	18	10	7	3	0	0	2	15	1	27	4	0	1	.000	1-2	1	96	.672	3.97	2.66
2 ML YEARS		33	2	11	33.0	152	24	12	8	3	0	0	3	26	2	34	5	0	1	.000	1-2	6	96	.658	4.12	2.18

Tyler Saladino

Bats: R **Throws:** R **Pos:** SS-13;LF-7;3B-6;PH-6;2B-3 **Ht:** 6'0" **Wt:** 200 **Born:** 7/20/1989 **Age:** 30

| | | BATTING | | | | | | | | | | | | | | | | | RUNNING | | | AVERAGES | | | |
Year Team	Lg	G	AB	H	2B	3B	HR	(Hm Rd)	TB	R	RBI	RC	TBB	IBB	SO	HBP	SH	SF	SB	CS	GDP	Avg	OBP	Slg	OPS
2019 SnAnt	AAA	79	265	76	19	2	17	(- -)	150	51	64	59	41	0	67	2	0	2	8	1	10	.287	.384	.566	.950
2015 CWS	AL	68	236	53	6	4	4	(4 0)	79	33	20	19	12	0	51	2	3	1	8	2	9	.225	.267	.335	.602
2016 CWS	AL	93	298	84	14	0	8	(5 3)	122	33	38	38	13	0	62	3	2	3	11	5	11	.282	.315	.409	.725
2017 CWS	AL	79	253	45	9	2	0	(0 0)	58	23	10	13	23	0	67	3	2	0	5	4	5	.178	.254	.229	.484
2018 2 Tms		58	126	31	4	0	5	(2 3)	50	13	16	13	9	0	41	1	2	1	2	2	3	.246	.299	.397	.696
2019 Mil	NL	28	65	8	0	0	2	(1 1)	14	7	8	3	5	0	26	1	0	0	2	0	1	.123	.197	.215	.413
18 CWS	AL	6	8	2	1	0	0	(0 0)	3	2	0	0	0	0	3	0	1	0	0	0	0	.250	.250	.375	.625
18 Mil	NL	52	118	29	3	0	5	(2 3)	47	11	16	13	9	0	38	1	1	1	2	2	3	.246	.302	.398	.701
5 ML YEARS		326	978	221	33	6	19	(12 7)	323	109	92	86	62	0	247	10	9	5	28	13	29	.226	.278	.330	.608

Fernando Salas

Pitches: R **Bats:** R **Pos:** RP-3
SAH-lahss **Ht:** 6'2" **Wt:** 200 **Born:** 5/30/1985 **Age:** 35

| | | HOW MUCH PITCHED | | | | | WHAT HE GAVE UP | | | | | | | | | | | THE RESULTS | | | | | | | | |
Year Team	Lg	G	GS	GF	IP	BFP	H	R	ER	HR	SH	SF	HB	TBB	IBB	SO	WP	W	L	Pct	Sv-Op	Hld	Vel	OPS	ERC	ERA
2019 LV	AAA	18	0	2	23.1	95	24	12	11	3	0	1	0	7	0	21	1	1	1	.500	1--	-	-	.786	4.23	4.24
2010 StL	NL	27	0	11	30.2	133	28	13	12	4	1	1	0	15	2	29	2	0	0	-	0-1	1	91	.748	4.03	3.52
2011 StL	NL	68	0	46	75.0	295	50	20	19	7	3	0	2	21	3	75	2	5	6	.455	24-30	6	91	.566	1.94	2.28
2012 StL	NL	65	0	23	58.2	256	56	28	28	5	5	0	1	27	5	60	1	1	4	.200	0-3	7	92	.720	3.85	4.30
2013 StL	NL	27	0	14	28.0	118	27	15	14	3	1	4	1	6	1	22	2	0	3	.000	0-2	2	90	.715	3.22	4.50
2014 LAA	AL	57	0	11	58.2	239	50	22	22	5	4	1	1	14	4	61	1	5	0	1.000	0-1	8	91	.637	2.54	3.38
2015 LAA	AL	72	0	13	63.2	269	61	34	30	8	5	4	3	12	5	74	3	5	2	.714	0-2	17	91	.716	3.17	4.24
2016 2 Tms		75	0	24	73.2	293	63	32	32	12	0	2	0	19	1	64	1	3	7	.300	6-11	20	91	.699	3.19	3.91
2017 2 Tms		61	0	11	58.2	263	67	39	34	7	5	7	0	22	6	56	4	2	2	.500	0-1	12	91	.786	4.68	5.22
2018 Ari	NL	41	0	12	40.0	170	40	20	20	5	2	1	0	13	4	30	2	4	4	.500	0-0	3	90	.727	3.91	4.50
2019 Phi	NL	3	0	2	2.2	15	8	2	2	1	0	0	0	2	0	3	0	0	0	-	0-0	0	90	1.333	19.92	6.75
16 LAA	AL	58	0	22	56.1	231	52	28	28	9	0	2	0	19	1	45	0	3	6	.333	6-11	13	91	.750	3.87	4.47
16 NYM	NL	17	0	2	17.1	62	11	4	4	3	0	0	0	0	0	19	1	0	1	.000	0-0	7	91	.516	1.36	2.08
17 NYM	NL	48	0	7	45.0	214	60	35	30	7	4	3	0	20	6	47	4	1	2	.333	0-1	11	91	.862	6.32	6.00
17 LAA	AL	13	0	4	13.2	49	7	4	4	0	1	4	0	2	0	9	0	1	0	1.000	0-0	1	90	.449	0.81	2.63
Postseason		18	0	3	20.1	83	16	10	8	2	0	0	0	4	1	18	1	0	1	.000	0-0	4	91	.595	2.05	3.54
10 ML YEARS		496	0	167	489.2	2051	450	225	213	57	26	21	9	149	31	474	21	25	28	.472	30-51	76	91	.700	3.32	3.91

Danny Salazar

Pitches: R **Bats:** R **Pos:** SP-1
SAL-uh-zarr **Ht:** 6'0" **Wt:** 195 **Born:** 1/11/1990 **Age:** 30

| | | HOW MUCH PITCHED | | | | | WHAT HE GAVE UP | | | | | | | | | | | THE RESULTS | | | | | | | | |
Year Team	Lg	G	GS	GF	IP	BFP	H	R	ER	HR	SH	SF	HB	TBB	IBB	SO	WP	W	L	Pct	Sv-Op	Hld	Vel	OPS	ERC	ERA
2019 Akron	AA	5	4	0	8.1	40	8	5	5	1	0	0	1	6	0	7	2	0	1	.000	0--	-	-	.799	5.64	5.40
2013 Cle	AL	10	10	0	52.0	211	44	18	18	7	1	0	0	15	0	65	3	2	3	.400	0-0	0	96	.655	3.05	3.12
2014 Cle	AL	20	20	0	110.0	474	117	57	52	13	1	5	3	35	4	120	3	6	8	.429	0-0	0	95	.751	4.30	4.25
2015 Cle	AL	30	30	0	185.0	757	156	79	71	23	3	4	7	53	1	195	3	14	10	.583	0-0	0	95	.673	3.10	3.45
2016 Cle	AL	25	25	0	137.1	584	121	61	59	16	0	4	2	63	3	161	9	11	6	.647	0-0	0	95	.697	3.80	3.87
2017 Cle	AL	23	19	3	103.0	439	94	51	49	14	1	3	3	44	0	145	6	5	6	.455	0-0	0	95	.721	4.09	4.28
2019 Cle	AL	1	1	0	4.0	17	4	2	2	2	0	0	0	3	0	2	0	0	1	.000	0-0	0	86	1.197	9.66	4.50
Postseason		4	1	0	8.2	38	5	4	3	1	0	0	0	6	1	11	1	0	1	.000	0-0	0	96	.571	2.69	3.12
6 ML YEARS		109	105	3	591.1	2482	536	268	251	75	6	16	15	213	8	688	24	38	34	.528	0-0	0	95	.704	3.68	3.82

Chris Sale

Pitches: L **Bats:** L **Pos:** SP-25 — SAIL — **Ht:** 6'6" **Wt:** 180 **Born:** 3/30/1989 **Age:** 31

Year	Team	Lg	G	GS	GF	IP	BFP	H	R	ER	HR	SH	SF	HB	TBB	IBB	SO	WP	W	L	Pct	Sv-Op	Hld	Vel	OPS	ERC	ERA
2010	CWS	AL	21	0	8	23.1	92	15	5	5	2	1	0	0	10	0	32	1	2	1	.667	4-4	2	96	.546	2.30	1.93
2011	CWS	AL	58	0	17	71.0	288	52	22	22	6	3	0	2	27	3	79	2	2	2	.500	8-10	16	95	.612	2.55	2.79
2012	CWS	AL	30	29	0	192.0	772	167	66	65	19	1	3	6	51	5	192	6	17	8	.680	0-1	0	92	.660	3.00	3.05
2013	CWS	AL	30	30	0	214.1	866	184	81	73	23	2	4	14	46	2	226	8	11	14	.440	0-0	0	93	.636	2.92	3.07
2014	CWS	AL	26	26	0	174.0	685	129	48	42	13	2	3	11	39	2	208	3	12	4	.750	0-0	0	94	.567	2.18	2.17
2015	CWS	AL	31	31	0	208.2	854	185	88	79	23	2	3	13	42	0	274	7	13	11	.542	0-0	0	94	.649	3.00	3.41
2016	CWS	AL	32	32	0	226.2	907	190	88	84	27	5	3	17	45	2	233	2	17	10	.630	0-0	0	93	.651	2.88	3.34
2017	Bos	AL	32	32	0	214.1	851	165	73	69	24	2	4	8	43	0	308	3	17	8	.680	0-0	0	94	.603	2.33	2.90
2018	Bos	AL	27	27	0	158.0	617	102	39	37	11	0	4	14	34	0	237	4	12	4	.750	0-0	0	95	.532	1.76	2.11
2019	Bos	AL	25	25	0	147.1	612	123	80	72	24	2	4	13	37	0	218	2	6	11	.353	0-0	0	93	.695	3.31	4.40
	Postseason		7	4	1	25.0	107	24	16	16	5	0	0	1	9	0	36	0	1	2	.333	0-0	1	94	.751	4.54	5.76
10 ML YEARS			312	232	25	1629.2	6544	1312	590	548	172	20	28	98	374	14	2007	38	109	73	.599	12-15	18	94	.625	2.67	3.03

Jeff Samardzija

Pitches: R **Bats:** R **Pos:** SP-32 — suh-MAHR-jah — **Ht:** 6'5" **Wt:** 240 **Born:** 1/23/1985 **Age:** 35

Year	Team	Lg	G	GS	GF	IP	BFP	H	R	ER	HR	SH	SF	HB	TBB	IBB	SO	WP	W	L	Pct	Sv-Op	Hld	Vel	OPS	ERC	ERA
2008	ChC	NL	26	0	6	27.2	124	24	12	7	0	1	1	1	15	2	25	2	1	0	1.000	1-4	3	95	.599	3.08	2.28
2009	ChC	NL	20	2	7	34.2	161	46	29	29	7	4	1	1	15	1	21	2	1	3	.250	0-0	0	94	.981	7.13	7.53
2010	ChC	NL	7	3	0	19.1	100	21	22	18	4	0	0	2	20	1	9	1	2	2	.500	0-0	0	93	.930	8.45	8.38
2011	ChC	NL	75	0	18	88.0	380	64	35	29	5	3	2	5	50	3	87	8	8	4	.667	0-2	13	95	.613	3.05	2.97
2012	ChC	NL	28	28	0	174.2	723	157	79	74	20	5	4	4	56	2	180	10	9	13	.409	0-0	0	95	.698	3.41	3.81
2013	ChC	NL	33	33	0	213.2	914	210	109	103	25	4	2	8	78	3	214	11	8	13	.381	0-0	0	95	.736	4.11	4.34
2014	2 Tms		33	33	0	219.2	879	191	86	73	20	3	7	10	43	3	202	10	7	13	.350	0-0	0	94	.646	2.74	2.99
2015	CWS	AL	32	32	0	214.0	910	228	122	118	29	4	9	12	49	0	163	5	11	13	.458	0-0	0	94	.765	4.24	4.96
2016	SF	NL	32	32	0	203.1	829	190	88	86	24	6	4	1	54	4	167	2	12	11	.522	0-0	0	94	.710	3.36	3.81
2017	SF	NL	32	32	0	207.2	847	204	107	102	30	4	4	6	32	1	205	2	9	15	.375	0-0	0	94	.734	3.43	4.42
2018	SF	NL	10	10	0	44.2	207	47	32	31	6	1	4	2	26	1	30	2	1	5	.167	0-0	0	92	.789	5.45	6.25
2019	SF	NL	32	32	0	181.1	740	152	78	71	28	4	4	6	49	4	140	5	11	12	.478	0-0	0	92	.692	3.14	3.52
14	ChC	NL	17	17	0	108.0	449	99	44	34	7	3	4	6	31	3	103	6	2	7	.222	0-0	0	94	.672	3.14	2.83
14	Oak		16	16	0	111.2	430	92	42	39	13	0	3	4	12	0	99	4	5	6	.455	0-0	0	95	.619	2.34	3.14
	Postseason		2	1	0	3.0	17	8	5	5	0	0	0	1	0	1	0	0	0	1	.000	0-0	0	96	1.217	14.52	15.00
12 ML YEARS			360	237	31	1628.2	6814	1534	799	741	198	39	42	58	487	25	1443	60	80	104	.435	1-6	16	94	.717	3.64	4.09

Adrian Sampson

Pitches: R **Bats:** R **Pos:** RP-20; SP-15 — **Ht:** 6'2" **Wt:** 210 **Born:** 10/7/1991 **Age:** 28

Year	Team	Lg	G	GS	GF	IP	BFP	H	R	ER	HR	SH	SF	HB	TBB	IBB	SO	WP	W	L	Pct	Sv-Op	Hld	Vel	OPS	ERC	ERA
2016	Sea	AL	1	1	0	4.2	21	8	4	4	2	0	0	0	1	0	2	0	0	1	.000	0-0	0	91	1.129	11.33	7.71
2018	Tex	AL	5	4	0	23.0	96	24	13	11	6	0	1	2	4	0	15	2	0	3	.000	0-0	0	91	.829	4.92	4.30
2019	Tex	AL	35	15	4	125.1	563	156	86	82	29	0	2	9	36	1	101	4	6	8	.429	0-0	0	93	.925	6.36	5.89
3 ML YEARS			41	20	4	153.0	680	188	103	97	37	0	3	11	41	1	118	6	6	12	.333	0-0	0	92	.918	6.27	5.71

Aaron Sanchez

Pitches: R **Bats:** R **Pos:** SP-27 — **Ht:** 6'4" **Wt:** 210 **Born:** 7/1/1992 **Age:** 27

Year	Team	Lg	G	GS	GF	IP	BFP	H	R	ER	HR	SH	SF	HB	TBB	IBB	SO	WP	W	L	Pct	Sv-Op	Hld	Vel	OPS	ERC	ERA
2014	Tor	AL	24	0	6	33.0	121	14	5	4	1	2	0	1	9	0	27	1	2	2	.500	3-3	7	97	.367	0.96	1.09
2015	Tor	AL	41	11	4	92.1	380	74	35	33	9	2	1	3	44	2	61	8	7	6	.538	0-1	10	95	.666	3.47	3.22
2016	Tor	AL	30	30	0	192.0	790	161	69	64	15	1	2	5	63	0	161	5	15	2	.882	0-0	0	95	.625	2.90	3.00
2017	Tor	AL	8	8	0	36.0	167	42	24	17	6	0	1	0	20	0	24	1	1	3	.250	0-0	0	95	.836	6.36	4.25
2018	Tor	AL	20	20	0	105.0	474	106	62	57	11	0	4	7	58	2	86	4	4	6	.400	0-0	0	94	.768	5.02	4.89
2019	2 Tms	AL	27	27	0	131.1	605	145	92	86	20	0	4	11	68	2	115	7	5	14	.263	0-0	0	94	.828	5.88	5.89
19	Tor	AL	23	23	0	112.2	524	131	82	76	15	0	3	10	59	2	99	7	3	14	.176	0-0	0	94	.835	6.16	6.07
19	Hou	AL	4	4	0	18.2	81	14	10	10	5	0	1	1	9	0	16	0	2	0	1.000	0-0	0	92	.782	4.22	4.82
	Postseason		11	2	1	19.0	77	12	8	7	2	2	0	0	8	0	16	1	2	0	1.000	0-0	0	96	.565	2.24	3.32
6 ML YEARS			150	96	10	589.2	2537	542	287	261	62	5	11	28	262	6	474	26	34	33	.507	3-4	17	95	.707	4.02	3.98

Adrian Sanchez

Bats: R **Throws:** R **Pos:** PH-18;3B-6;2B-4;PR-3;SS-2;1B-1;LF-1 — **Ht:** 6'0" **Wt:** 216 **Born:** 8/16/1990 **Age:** 29

Year	Team	Lg	G	AB	H	2B	3B	HR	(Hm	Rd)	TB	R	RBI	RC	TBB	IBB	SO	HBP	SH	SF	SB	CS	GDP	Avg	OBP	Slg	OPS
2019	Hrsbrg	AA	69	256	81	19	1	6	(-	-)	120	43	36	45	19	2	39	3	0	4	11	5	8	.316	.365	.469	.834
2017	Was	NL	34	71	19	7	0	0	(0	0)	26	6	11	9	1	0	25	1	2	0	0	2	2	.268	.288	.366	.654
2018	Was	NL	28	58	16	2	1	0	(0	0)	20	8	3	5	1	0	8	0	0	0	0	0	0	.276	.288	.345	.633
2019	Was	NL	28	31	7	0	0	0	(0	0)	7	3	1	1	1	0	10	0	0	0	0	0	0	.226	.250	.226	.476
3 ML YEARS			90	160	42	9	1	0	(0	0)	53	17	15	15	3	0	43	1	2	0	0	2	2	.263	.280	.331	.612

Anibal Sanchez

Pitches: R Bats: R Pos: SP-30   ah-NEE-bahl   Ht: 6'0" Wt: 205 Born: 2/27/1984 Age: 36

						HOW MUCH PITCHED					WHAT HE GAVE UP											THE RESULTS							
Year	Team	Lg	G	GS	GF	IP	BFP	H	R	ER	HR	SH	SF	HB	TBB	IBB	SO	WP	W	L	Pct	Sv-Op	Hld	Vel	OPS	ERC	ERA
2006	Fla	NL	18	17	0	114.1	469	90	39	36	9	3	1	4	46	1	72	4	10	3	.769	0-0	0	91	.635	2.96	2.83
2007	Fla	NL	6	6	0	30.0	151	43	17	16	3	2	2	2	19	1	14	3	2	1	.667	0-0	0	90	.930	7.90	4.80
2008	Fla	NL	10	10	0	51.2	241	54	35	32	7	4	2	6	27	2	50	1	2	5	.286	0-0	0	90	.788	5.40	5.57
2009	Fla	NL	16	16	0	86.0	383	84	39	37	10	2	2	1	46	5	71	0	4	8	.333	0-0	0	91	.756	4.51	3.87
2010	Fla	NL	32	32	0	195.0	841	192	89	77	10	13	3	7	70	5	157	7	13	12	.520	0-0	0	91	.680	3.56	3.55
2011	Fla	NL	32	32	0	196.1	830	187	85	80	20	12	1	5	64	8	202	4	8	9	.471	0-0	0	92	.711	3.57	3.67
2012	2 Tms		31	31	0	195.2	820	200	95	84	20	5	7	5	48	3	167	7	9	13	.409	0-0	0	92	.716	3.70	3.86
2013	Det	AL	29	29	0	182.0	746	156	56	52	9	4	4	2	54	1	202	7	14	8	.636	0-0	0	93	.616	2.63	**2.57**
2014	Det	AL	22	21	0	126.0	514	108	55	48	4	3	4	3	30	1	102	5	8	5	.615	0-0	0	92	.599	2.35	3.43
2015	Det	AL	25	25	0	157.0	660	152	89	87	29	5	2	1	49	1	138	5	10	10	.500	0-0	0	92	.768	4.14	4.99
2016	Det	AL	35	26	3	153.1	668	171	108	100	30	4	6	5	53	1	135	7	7	13	.350	0-0	0	91	.828	5.40	5.87
2017	Det	AL	28	17	6	105.1	482	139	81	75	26	2	3	4	29	1	104	5	3	7	.300	0-0	0	91	.906	6.66	6.41
2018	Atl	NL	25	24	0	136.2	553	106	48	43	15	7	3	4	42	0	135	4	7	6	.538	0-0	0	91	.633	2.71	2.83
2019	Was	NL	30	30	0	166.0	712	153	77	71	22	1	2	4	58	10	134	1	11	8	.579	0-0	0	90	.709	3.59	3.85
12	Mia	NL	19	19	0	121.0	504	119	59	53	12	4	5	2	33	2	110	4	5	7	.417	0-0	0	91	.717	3.55	3.94
12	Det	AL	12	12	0	74.2	316	81	36	31	8	1	2	3	15	1	57	3	4	6	.400	0-0	0	93	.714	3.95	3.74
	Postseason		8	7	0	43.1	181	36	17	15	7	0	1	0	15	1	46	4	2	5	.286	0-0	1	92	.688	3.25	3.12
	14 ML YEARS		339	316	9	1895.1	8070	1835	913	838	214	67	42	53	635	40	1683	60	108	108	.500	0-0	0	91	.717	3.80	3.98

Gary Sanchez

Bats: R Throws: R Pos: C-90;DH-15;PH-5   Ht: 6'2" Wt: 230 Born: 12/2/1992 Age: 27

								BATTING													RUNNING			AVERAGES			
Year	Team	Lg	G	AB	H	2B	3B	HR	(Hm	Rd)	TB	R	RBI	RC	TBB	IBB	SO	HBP	SH	SF	SB	CS	GDP	Avg	OBP	Slg	OPS
2015	NYY	AL	2	2	0	0	0	0	(0	0)	0	0	0	0	0	0	1	0	0	0	0	0	0	.000	.000	.000	.000
2016	NYY	AL	53	201	60	12	0	20	(10	10)	132	34	42	40	24	2	57	2	0	2	1	0	5	.299	.376	.657	1.032
2017	NYY	AL	122	471	131	20	0	33	(15	18)	250	79	90	81	40	1	120	10	0	4	2	1	9	.278	.345	.531	.876
2018	NYY	AL	89	323	60	17	0	18	(8	10)	131	51	53	41	46	0	94	3	0	2	1	0	10	.186	.291	.406	.697
2019	NYY	AL	106	396	92	12	1	34	(19	15)	208	62	77	64	40	3	125	9	0	1	0	1	3	.232	.316	.525	.841
	Postseason		18	71	14	3	0	5	(2	3)	32	8	13	7	2	0	24	0	0	2	0	0	2	.197	.213	.451	.664
	5 ML YEARS		372	1393	343	61	1	105	(52	53)	721	226	262	226	150	6	397	24	0	9	4	2	27	.246	.328	.518	.846

Sixto Sanchez

Pitches: R Bats: R Pos: P   Ht: 6'0" Wt: 185 Born: 7/29/1998 Age: 21

						HOW MUCH PITCHED					WHAT HE GAVE UP											THE RESULTS							
Year	Team	Lg	G	GS	GF	IP	BFP	H	R	ER	HR	SH	SF	HB	TBB	IBB	SO	WP	W	L	Pct	Sv-Op	Hld	Vel	OPS	ERC	ERA
2016	Phillies	R	11	11	0	54.0	194	33	4	3	0	1	1	2	8	0	44	1	5	0	1.000	0- -	-	-	.377	1.18	0.50
2017	2 Tms	Low	18	18	0	95.0	375	73	35	32	2	2	3	4	18	0	84	5	5	7	.417	0- -	-	-	.519	1.81	3.03
2018	Clrwtr	A+	8	8	0	46.2	188	39	14	13	1	0	1	2	11	0	45	0	4	3	.571	0- -	-	-	.604	2.28	2.51
2019	Jaxnvl	AA	18	18	0	103.0	411	87	33	29	5	2	0	3	19	0	97	0	8	4	.667	0- -	-	-	.600	2.26	2.53

Yolmer Sanchez

Bats: B Throws: R Pos: 2B-149;PH-4;PR-2   Ht: 5'11" Wt: 185 Born: 6/29/1992 Age: 28

								BATTING													RUNNING			AVERAGES			
Year	Team	Lg	G	AB	H	2B	3B	HR	(Hm	Rd)	TB	R	RBI	RC	TBB	IBB	SO	HBP	SH	SF	SB	CS	GDP	Avg	OBP	Slg	OPS
2014	CWS	AL	28	100	25	5	0	0	(0	0)	30	6	5	5	3	0	25	0	0	1	1	1	1	.250	.269	.300	.569
2015	CWS	AL	120	389	87	23	1	5	(2	3)	127	40	31	30	19	0	81	5	6	1	2	2	9	.224	.268	.326	.595
2016	CWS	AL	53	154	32	9	1	4	(2	2)	55	15	21	14	5	0	42	1	2	1	0	1	1	.208	.236	.357	.593
2017	CWS	AL	141	484	129	19	8	12	(8	4)	200	63	59	68	35	2	111	4	7	4	8	9	10	.267	.319	.413	.732
2018	CWS	AL	155	600	145	34	10	8	(4	4)	223	62	55	72	49	0	138	8	2	3	14	6	9	.242	.306	.372	.678
2019	CWS	AL	149	496	125	20	4	2	(0	2)	159	59	43	55	44	1	117	5	7	3	5	4	7	.252	.318	.321	.638
	6 ML YEARS		646	2223	543	110	24	31	(16	15)	794	245	214	244	155	3	514	23	24	13	30	23	37	.244	.299	.357	.656

Pablo Sandoval

Bats: B Throws: R Pos: PH-50;3B-45;1B-23;DH-4   Ht: 5'11" Wt: 268 Born: 8/11/1986 Age: 33

								BATTING													RUNNING			AVERAGES			
Year	Team	Lg	G	AB	H	2B	3B	HR	(Hm	Rd)	TB	R	RBI	RC	TBB	IBB	SO	HBP	SH	SF	SB	CS	GDP	Avg	OBP	Slg	OPS
2008	SF	NL	41	145	50	10	1	3	(1	2)	71	24	24	24	4	1	14	1	0	4	0	0	4	.345	.357	.490	.847
2009	SF	NL	153	572	189	44	5	25	(13	12)	318	79	90	113	52	13	83	4	0	5	5	5	10	.330	.387	.556	.943
2010	SF	NL	152	563	151	34	3	13	(9	4)	230	61	63	55	47	12	81	1	0	5	3	2	26	.268	.323	.409	.732
2011	SF	NL	117	426	134	26	3	23	(7	16)	235	55	70	72	32	9	63	0	1	7	2	4	12	.315	.357	.552	.909
2012	SF	NL	108	396	112	25	2	12	(7	5)	177	59	63	60	38	4	59	1	0	7	1	1	13	.283	.342	.447	.789
2013	SF	NL	141	525	146	27	2	14	(6	8)	219	52	79	78	47	5	79	6	0	6	0	0	16	.278	.341	.417	.758
2014	SF	NL	157	588	164	26	3	16	(9	7)	244	68	73	78	39	6	85	4	0	7	0	0	16	.279	.324	.415	.739
2015	Bos	AL	126	470	115	25	1	10	(4	6)	172	43	47	46	25	1	73	7	1	2	0	0	14	.245	.292	.366	.658
2016	Bos	AL	3	6	0	0	0	0	(0	0)	0	0	0	0	1	0	4	0	0	0	0	0	0	.000	.143	.000	.143
2017	2 Tms		79	259	57	11	0	9	(4	5)	95	27	32	20	16	0	53	1	0	3	0	1	11	.220	.265	.367	.632
2018	SF	NL	92	230	57	10	1	9	(6	3)	96	22	40	31	19	2	52	2	0	1	0	0	9	.248	.310	.417	.727
2019	SF	NL	108	272	73	23	0	14	(6	8)	138	42	41	38	18	2	67	1	2	3	1	0	5	.268	.313	.507	.820
17	Bos	AL	32	99	21	2	0	4	(2	2)	35	10	12	9	8	0	24	0	0	1	0	1	4	.212	.269	.354	.622
17	SF	NL	47	160	36	9	0	5	(2	3)	60	17	20	11	8	0	29	1	0	2	0	0	7	.225	.263	.375	.638
	Postseason		39	154	53	13	0	6	(3	3)	84	21	20	27	10	3	22	2	0	1	0	0	7	.344	.389	.545	.935
	12 ML YEARS		1277	4452	1248	261	21	148	(72	76)	1995	532	622	615	338	55	713	28	4	50	12	13	144	.280	.332	.448	.780

Patrick Sandoval

Pitches: L Bats: L Pos: SP-9; RP-1   Ht: 6'3" Wt: 190 Born: 10/18/1996 Age: 23

Year	Team	Lg	G	GS	GF	IP	BFP	H	R	ER	HR	SH	SF	HB	TBB	IBB	SO	WP	W	L	Pct	Sv-Op	Hld	Vel	OPS	ERC	ERA
2019	Mobile	AA	5	4	1	20.0	83	14	10	8	1	0	0	0	7	0	32	7	0	3	.000	0- -	-	-	.536	1.94	3.60
2019	Salt Lk	AAA	15	15	0	60.1	302	84	62	43	7	1	1	2	35	0	66	4	4	4	.500	0- -	-	-	.908	7.31	6.41
2019	LAA	AL	10	9	0	39.1	169	35	22	22	6	2	1	1	19	0	42	4	0	4	.000	0-0	0	93	.754	4.28	5.03

Miguel Sano

Bats: R Throws: R Pos: 3B-91;1B-9;DH-6;PH-3   sah-NO   Ht: 6'4" Wt: 272 Born: 5/11/1993 Age: 27

Year	Team	Lg	G	AB	H	2B	3B	HR	(Hm	Rd)	TB	R	RBI	RC	TBB	IBB	SO	HBP	SH	SF	SB	CS	GDP	Avg	OBP	Slg	OPS
2015	Min	AL	80	279	75	17	1	18	(10	8)	148	46	52	62	53	1	119	1	0	2	1	1	4	.269	.385	.530	.916
2016	Min	AL	116	437	103	22	1	25	(11	14)	202	57	66	62	54	1	178	1	0	3	1	0	8	.236	.319	.462	.781
2017	Min	AL	114	424	112	15	2	28	(12	16)	215	75	77	71	54	5	173	4	0	1	0	0	12	.264	.352	.507	.859
2018	Min	AL	71	266	53	14	0	13	(7	6)	106	32	41	28	31	0	115	0	0	2	0	0	7	.199	.281	.398	.679
2019	Min	AL	105	380	94	19	2	34	(14	20)	219	76	79	74	55	0	159	3	0	1	0	1	5	.247	.346	.576	.923
	5 ML YEARS		486	1786	437	87	6	118	(54	64)	890	286	315	297	247	7	744	9	0	9	2	2	36	.245	.338	.498	.836

Carlos Santana

Bats: B Throws: R Pos: 1B-135;DH-23   Ht: 5'11" Wt: 210 Born: 4/8/1986 Age: 34

Year	Team	Lg	G	AB	H	2B	3B	HR	(Hm	Rd)	TB	R	RBI	RC	TBB	IBB	SO	HBP	SH	SF	SB	CS	GDP	Avg	OBP	Slg	OPS
2010	Cle	AL	46	150	39	13	0	6	(2	4)	70	23	22	25	37	2	29	1	0	4	3	0	3	.260	.401	.467	.868
2011	Cle	AL	155	552	132	35	2	27	(14	13)	252	84	79	81	97	7	133	2	0	7	5	3	15	.239	.351	.457	.808
2012	Cle	AL	143	507	128	27	2	18	(7	11)	213	72	76	77	91	4	101	3	0	8	3	5	21	.252	.365	.420	.785
2013	Cle	AL	154	541	145	39	1	20	(12	8)	246	75	74	93	93	6	110	4	0	4	3	1	7	.268	.377	.455	.832
2014	Cle	AL	152	541	125	25	0	27	(13	14)	231	68	85	88	113	5	124	3	0	3	5	2	13	.231	.365	.427	.792
2015	Cle	AL	154	550	127	29	2	19	(6	13)	217	72	85	80	108	8	122	3	0	5	11	3	20	.231	.357	.395	.752
2016	Cle	AL	158	582	151	31	3	34	(20	14)	290	89	87	104	99	0	99	2	0	5	5	2	18	.259	.366	.498	.865
2017	Cle	AL	154	571	148	37	3	23	(11	12)	260	90	79	89	88	6	94	6	0	2	5	1	11	.259	.363	.455	.818
2018	Phi	NL	161	560	128	28	2	24	(13	11)	232	82	86	87	110	6	93	1	0	8	2	1	12	.229	.352	.414	.766
2019	Cle	AL	158	573	161	30	1	34	(19	15)	295	110	93	114	108	12	108	3	0	2	4	0	13	.281	.397	.515	.911
	Postseason		21	75	16	2	0	4	(1	3)	30	8	8	10	11	0	16	1	0	0	0	0	0	.213	.322	.400	.722
	10 ML YEARS		1435	5127	1284	294	16	232	(117	115)	2306	765	766	838	944	56	1013	28	0	48	46	18	133	.250	.367	.450	.817

Danny Santana

Bats: B Throws: R Pos: 1B-44;CF-27;2B-17;LF-16;RF-15;PH-12;SS-9;3B-8;PR-2;DH-1   Ht: 5'11" Wt: 185 Born: 11/7/1990 Age: 29

Year	Team	Lg	G	AB	H	2B	3B	HR	(Hm	Rd)	TB	R	RBI	RC	TBB	IBB	SO	HBP	SH	SF	SB	CS	GDP	Avg	OBP	Slg	OPS
2014	Min	AL	101	405	129	27	7	7	(3	4)	191	70	40	72	19	0	98	3	2	1	20	4	3	.319	.353	.472	.824
2015	Min	AL	91	261	56	10	5	0	(0	0)	76	30	21	16	6	1	68	3	7	0	8	4	7	.215	.241	.291	.532
2016	Min	AL	75	233	56	10	2	2	(0	2)	76	29	14	18	12	0	55	1	1	1	12	9	1	.240	.279	.326	.606
2017	2 Tms		82	168	34	10	2	4	(3	1)	60	19	23	17	8	1	41	1	1	0	7	0	3	.202	.243	.357	.600
2018	Atl	NL	15	28	5	3	0	0	(0	0)	8	4	2	2	3	0	11	1	0	0	1	0	1	.179	.281	.286	.567
2019	Tex	AL	130	474	134	23	6	28	(19	9)	253	81	81	83	25	2	151	6	0	5	21	6	8	.283	.324	.534	.857
17	Min	AL	13	25	5	1	0	1	(1	0)	9	3	1	0	1	0	8	0	0	0	1	0	1	.200	.231	.360	.591
17	Atl	NL	69	143	29	9	2	3	(2	1)	51	16	22	17	7	1	33	1	1	0	6	0	2	.203	.245	.357	.602
	6 ML YEARS		494	1569	414	83	22	41	(25	16)	664	233	181	208	73	4	424	15	11	7	69	24	22	.264	.302	.423	.725

Dennis Santana

Pitches: R Bats: R Pos: RP-3   Ht: 6'2" Wt: 190 Born: 4/12/1996 Age: 24

Year	Team	Lg	G	GS	GF	IP	BFP	H	R	ER	HR	SH	SF	HB	TBB	IBB	SO	WP	W	L	Pct	Sv-Op	Hld	Vel	OPS	ERC	ERA
2019	OkCity	AAA	27	17	3	93.1	444	111	84	72	16	1	1	9	53	0	105	12	5	9	.357	0- -	-	-	.901	6.87	6.94
2018	LAD	NL	1	0	0	3.2	19	6	5	5	0	1	0	1	1	0	4	1	1	0	1.000	0-0	0	93	1.007	7.52	12.27
2019	LAD	NL	3	0	1	5.0	27	6	4	4	1	0	1	2	4	0	6	1	0	0	-	0-0	0	93	.994	9.44	7.20
	2 ML YEARS		4	0	1	8.2	46	12	9	9	1	1	1	3	5	0	10	2	1	0	1.000	0-0	0	93	1.000	8.62	9.35

Domingo Santana

Bats: R Throws: R Pos: LF-59;RF-42;DH-17;PH-6   Ht: 6'5" Wt: 220 Born: 8/5/1992 Age: 27

Year	Team	Lg	G	AB	H	2B	3B	HR	(Hm	Rd)	TB	R	RBI	RC	TBB	IBB	SO	HBP	SH	SF	SB	CS	GDP	Avg	OBP	Slg	OPS
2014	Hou	AL	6	17	0	0	0	0	(0	0)	0	1	0	0	1	0	14	0	0	0	0	0	0	.000	.056	.000	.056
2015	2 Tms		52	160	38	7	0	8	(3	5)	69	20	26	28	20	0	63	5	0	2	4	1	2	.238	.337	.431	.768
2016	Mil	NL	77	246	63	14	0	11	(3	8)	110	34	32	36	32	0	91	2	0	1	2	3	7	.256	.345	.447	.792
2017	Mil	NL	151	525	146	29	0	30	(19	11)	265	88	85	98	73	2	178	6	0	3	15	4	12	.278	.371	.505	.875
2018	Mil	NL	85	211	56	14	1	5	(4	1)	87	21	20	24	20	1	77	1	0	3	1	1	3	.265	.328	.412	.740
2019	Sea	AL	121	451	114	20	1	21	(9	12)	199	63	69	64	50	1	164	2	0	2	8	3	11	.253	.329	.441	.770
15	Hou	AL	14	39	10	2	0	2	(0	2)	18	6	8	8	2	0	17	1	0	0	2	1	1	.256	.310	.462	.771
15	Mil	NL	38	121	28	5	0	6	(3	3)	51	14	18	20	18	0	46	4	0	2	2	0	1	.231	.345	.421	.766
	Postseason		10	8	2	1	0	0	(0	0)	3	1	3	2	2	1	5	0	0	0	1	0	0	.250	.400	.375	.775
	6 ML YEARS		492	1610	417	84	2	75	(38	37)	730	227	232	250	196	4	587	16	0	11	30	12	35	.259	.343	.453	.797

Edgar Santana

Pitches: R Bats: R Pos: P   Ht: 6'2" Wt: 195 Born: 10/16/1991 Age: 28

Year Team	Lg	G	GS	GF	IP	BFP	H	R	ER	HR	SH	SF	HB	TBB	IBB	SO	WP	W	L	Pct	Sv-Op	Hld	Vel	OPS	ERC	ERA
2017 Pit	NL	19	0	2	18.0	81	16	8	7	2	1	0	1	12	1	20	0	0	0	-	0-0	2	95	.780	4.72	3.50
2018 Pit	NL	69	0	11	66.1	271	61	25	24	7	1	1	3	12	2	54	3	3	4	.429	0-7	20	95	.659	2.96	3.26
2 ML YEARS		88	0	13	84.1	352	77	33	31	9	2	1	4	24	3	74	3	3	4	.429	0-7	22	95	.686	3.32	3.31

Ervin Santana

Pitches: R Bats: R Pos: SP-3   Ht: 6'2" Wt: 175 Born: 12/12/1982 Age: 37

Year Team	Lg	G	GS	GF	IP	BFP	H	R	ER	HR	SH	SF	HB	TBB	IBB	SO	WP	W	L	Pct	Sv-Op	Hld	Vel	OPS	ERC	ERA
2019 Syrcse	AAA	15	15	0	82.0	369	97	51	49	11	2	1	4	32	2	54	10	4	4	.500	0--	-	-	.820	5.54	5.38
2005 LAA	AL	23	23	0	133.2	583	139	73	69	17	1	4	8	47	2	99	4	12	8	.600	0-0	0	93	.781	4.51	4.65
2006 LAA	AL	33	33	0	204.0	846	181	106	97	21	4	10	11	70	2	141	10	16	8	.667	0-0	0	93	.707	3.51	4.28
2007 LAA	AL	28	26	1	150.0	675	174	103	96	26	3	2	8	58	3	126	7	7	14	.333	0-0	0	92	.854	5.69	5.76
2008 LAA	AL	32	32	0	219.0	897	198	89	85	23	3	5	8	47	2	214	5	16	7	.696	0-0	0	92	.651	3.00	3.49
2009 LAA	AL	24	23	0	139.2	614	159	83	78	24	2	1	10	47	4	107	4	8	8	.500	0-0	1	92	.833	5.47	5.03
2010 LAA	AL	33	33	0	222.2	954	221	104	97	27	8	8	12	73	2	169	11	17	10	.630	0-0	0	92	.744	4.10	3.92
2011 LAA	AL	33	33	0	228.2	949	207	95	86	26	4	7	8	72	4	178	10	11	12	.478	0-0	0	93	.693	3.45	3.38
2012 LAA	AL	30	30	0	178.0	764	165	109	102	39	2	2	9	61	2	133	4	9	13	.409	0-0	0	92	.774	4.38	5.16
2013 KC	AL	32	32	0	211.0	859	190	85	76	26	2	3	6	51	3	161	6	9	10	.474	0-0	0	92	.668	3.19	3.24
2014 Atl	NL	31	31	0	196.0	817	193	90	86	16	12	12	4	63	4	179	9	14	10	.583	0-0	0	92	.724	3.68	3.95
2015 Min	AL	17	17	0	108.0	457	104	50	48	12	4	2	4	36	2	82	3	7	5	.583	0-0	0	92	.729	3.82	4.00
2016 Min	AL	30	30	0	181.1	748	168	78	68	19	1	5	4	53	2	149	11	7	11	.389	0-0	0	93	.682	3.39	3.38
2017 Min	AL	33	33	0	211.1	860	177	85	77	31	4	4	8	61	2	167	12	16	8	.667	0-0	0	93	.678	3.21	3.28
2018 Min	AL	5	5	0	24.2	114	31	22	22	9	0	3	2	9	0	16	0	0	1	.000	0-0	0	89	1.038	7.88	8.03
2019 CWS	AL	3	3	0	13.1	64	19	14	14	6	0	2	0	6	0	5	1	0	2	.000	0-0	0	90	1.212	9.79	9.45
Postseason		9	3	3	24.2	112	24	21	18	6	1	1	3	11	1	14	0	2	2	.500	0-0	0	94	.811	5.47	6.57
15 ML YEARS		387	384	1	2421.1	10205	2326	1186	1101	322	50	70	102	754	34	1926	97	149	127	.540	0-0	1	93	.732	3.90	4.09

Anthony Santander

Bats: B Throws: R Pos: RF-50;LF-40;CF-24;DH-3;PH-1   Ht: 6'2" Wt: 190 Born: 10/19/1994 Age: 25

Year Team	Lg	G	AB	H	2B	3B	HR	(Hm	Rd)	TB	R	RBI	RC	TBB	IBB	SO	HBP	SH	SF	SB	CS	GDP	Avg	OBP	Slg	OPS
2019 Norfolk	AAA	48	193	50	15	0	5	(-	-)	80	30	28	25	13	1	38	2	0	1	3	2	3	.259	.311	.415	.726
2017 Bal	AL	13	30	8	3	0	0	(0	0)	11	1	2	2	0	0	8	0	0	1	0	0	0	.267	.258	.367	.625
2018 Bal	AL	33	101	20	5	1	1	(0	1)	30	8	6	10	6	0	21	1	0	1	1	0	1	.198	.250	.297	.547
2019 Bal	AL	93	380	99	20	1	20	(10	10)	181	46	59	55	19	0	86	2	1	3	1	2	1	.261	.297	.476	.773
3 ML YEARS		139	511	127	28	2	21	(10	11)	222	55	67	67	25	0	115	3	1	4	2	2	2	.249	.285	.434	.720

Hector Santiago

Pitches: L Bats: R Pos: RP-17; SP-2   Ht: 6'0" Wt: 215 Born: 12/16/1987 Age: 32

Year Team	Lg	G	GS	GF	IP	BFP	H	R	ER	HR	SH	SF	HB	TBB	IBB	SO	WP	W	L	Pct	Sv-Op	Hld	Vel	OPS	ERC	ERA
2019 Syrcse	AAA	8	7	0	43.0	181	32	17	16	5	1	0	0	23	0	38	0	3	1	.750	0--	-	-	.637	3.31	3.35
2019 Charltt	AAA	7	7	0	37.0	159	45	25	24	9	0	2	3	9	0	33	1	1	4	.200	0--	-	-	.938	6.33	5.84
2011 CWS	AL	2	0	1	5.1	18	1	0	0	0	0	0	0	1	1	2	1	0	0	-	0-0	0	94	.170	0.16	0.00
2012 CWS	AL	42	4	19	70.1	306	54	26	26	10	2	1	7	40	1	79	5	4	1	.800	4-6	4	93	.680	4.11	3.33
2013 CWS	AL	34	23	4	149.0	656	137	69	59	17	3	3	15	72	2	137	2	4	9	.308	0-0	0	92	.739	4.43	3.56
2014 LAA	AL	30	24	2	127.1	544	120	63	53	15	1	3	3	53	3	108	5	6	9	.400	0-0	1	91	.698	4.02	3.75
2015 LAA	AL	33	32	0	180.2	776	156	80	72	29	4	4	10	71	5	162	1	9	9	.500	0-0	0	90	.723	3.82	3.59
2016 2 Tms	AL	33	33	0	182.0	785	169	100	95	33	5	6	5	79	0	144	3	13	10	.565	0-0	0	91	.774	4.48	4.70
2017 Min	AL	15	14	1	70.1	311	70	44	44	15	0	1	5	31	0	51	0	4	8	.333	0-0	0	91	.782	5.33	5.63
2018 CWS	AL	49	7	27	102.0	460	101	54	50	16	1	3	5	60	3	103	1	6	3	.667	2-2	0	91	.807	5.38	4.41
2019 2 Tms	AL	19	2	11	33.2	163	42	26	25	8	0	1	0	22	0	40	0	1	1	.500	0-0	0	92	.950	7.71	6.68
16 LAA	AL	22	22	0	120.2	515	104	61	57	20	3	4	4	57	0	107	2	10	4	.714	0-0	0	91	.736	4.20	4.25
16 Min	AL	11	11	0	61.1	270	65	39	38	13	2	2	1	22	0	37	1	3	6	.333	0-0	0	91	.843	5.05	5.58
19 NYM	NL	8	0	6	8.0	38	10	6	6	1	0	0	0	5	0	6	0	1	0	1.000	0-0	0	92	.940	6.73	6.75
19 CWS	AL	11	2	5	25.2	125	32	20	19	7	0	1	0	17	0	34	0	0	1	.000	0-0	0	92	.953	8.01	6.66
Postseason		1	0	0	1.1	7	1	2	2	1	0	0	0	2	0	1	0	0	0	-	0-0	0	91	1.229	12.98	13.50
9 ML YEARS		257	139	65	920.2	4019	850	462	424	143	16	22	50	429	15	826	18	47	50	.485	6-8	5	91	.750	4.48	4.14

Josh Sborz

Pitches: R Bats: R Pos: RP-7   Ht: 6'3" Wt: 215 Born: 12/17/1993 Age: 26

Year Team	Lg	G	GS	GF	IP	BFP	H	R	ER	HR	SH	SF	HB	TBB	IBB	SO	WP	W	L	Pct	Sv-Op	Hld	Vel	OPS	ERC	ERA
2019 OkCity	AAA	46	0	14	50.0	217	56	30	26	2	2	2	0	14	0	68	6	4	3	.571	3--	-	-	.736	3.81	4.68
2019 LAD	NL	7	0	6	9.0	40	10	8	8	2	0	1	0	4	0	7	0	0	1	.000	0-0	0	95	.921	5.84	8.00

Scott Schebler

Bats: L Throws: R Pos: CF-24;PH-5;LF-3;RF-1   SHEB-ler   Ht: 6'0" Wt: 228 Born: 10/6/1990 Age: 29

								BATTING													RUNNING			AVERAGES			
Year	Team	Lg	G	AB	H	2B	3B	HR	(Hm	Rd)	TB	R	RBI	RC	TBB	IBB	SO	HBP	SH	SF	SB	CS	GDP	Avg	OBP	Slg	OPS
2019	Lsvlle	AAA	53	194	42	6	0	5	(-	-)	63	18	17	17	12	1	51	4	0	2	0	1	2	.216	.274	.325	.598
2015	LAD	NL	19	36	9	0	0	3	(1	2)	18	6	4	4	3	1	13	1	0	0	2	1	0	.250	.325	.500	.825
2016	Cin	NL	82	257	68	12	2	9	(5	4)	111	36	40	36	19	2	59	6	0	0	2	4	5	.265	.330	.432	.762
2017	Cin	NL	141	473	110	25	2	30	(13	17)	229	63	67	58	39	5	125	14	0	5	5	3	7	.233	.307	.484	.791
2018	Cin	NL	107	380	97	19	0	17	(7	10)	167	55	49	47	39	1	99	9	0	2	4	2	5	.255	.337	.439	.777
2019	Cin	NL	30	81	10	2	0	2	(1	1)	18	11	7	3	14	0	27	0	0	0	0	1	3	.123	.253	.222	.475
	5 ML YEARS		379	1227	294	58	4	61	(27	34)	543	171	167	148	114	9	323	30	0	7	13	11	20	.240	.318	.443	.760

Max Scherzer

Pitches: R Bats: R Pos: SP-27   SHERR-zer   Ht: 6'3" Wt: 215 Born: 7/27/1984 Age: 35

			HOW MUCH PITCHED					WHAT HE GAVE UP											THE RESULTS							
Year	Team	Lg	G	GS	GF	IP	BFP	H	R	ER	HR	SH	SF	HB	TBB	IBB	SO	WP	W	L	Pct	Sv-Op	Hld	Vel	OPS	ERC	ERA
2008	Ari	NL	16	7	2	56.0	237	48	24	19	5	4	2	5	21	1	66	2	0	4	.000	0-0	0	94	.649	3.45	3.05
2009	Ari	NL	30	30	0	170.1	741	166	94	78	20	5	6	10	63	1	174	5	9	11	.450	0-0	0	94	.751	4.12	4.12
2010	Det	AL	31	31	0	195.2	800	174	84	76	20	5	5	7	70	1	184	8	12	11	.522	0-0	0	93	.700	3.56	3.50
2011	Det	AL	33	33	0	195.0	833	207	101	96	29	3	7	7	56	1	174	12	15	9	.625	0-0	0	93	.781	4.48	4.43
2012	Det	AL	32	32	0	187.2	787	179	82	78	23	5	1	5	60	2	231	2	16	7	.696	0-0	0	94	.721	3.77	3.74
2013	Det	AL	32	32	0	214.1	836	152	73	69	18	2	8	4	56	0	240	6	21	3	.875	0-0	0	93	.583	2.07	2.90
2014	Det	AL	33	33	0	220.1	904	196	80	77	18	4	8	6	63	1	252	10	18	5	.783	0-0	0	93	.663	3.04	3.15
2015	Was	NL	33	33	0	228.2	899	176	74	71	27	11	2	5	34	2	276	10	14	12	.538	0-0	0	94	.600	2.21	2.79
2016	Was	NL	34	34	0	228.1	902	165	77	75	31	7	3	6	56	2	284	2	20	7	.741	0-0	0	94	.619	2.35	2.96
2017	Was	NL	31	31	0	200.2	780	126	62	56	22	4	1	11	55	2	268	4	16	6	.727	0-0	0	94	.566	1.98	2.51
2018	Was	NL	33	33	0	220.2	866	150	66	62	23	4	2	12	51	4	300	4	18	7	.720	0-0	0	94	.580	2.02	2.53
2019	Was	NL	27	27	0	172.1	693	144	59	56	18	0	2	7	33	2	243	0	11	7	.611	0-0	0	95	.637	2.58	2.92
	Postseason		16	13	0	82.0	338	60	37	34	8	2	0	7	31	2	100	4	4	5	.444	0-0	1	94	.646	2.84	3.73
	12 ML YEARS		365	356	2	2290.0	9278	1883	876	813	254	54	47	85	618	19	2692	65	170	89	.656	0-0	0	94	.653	2.84	3.20

Brian Schlitter

Pitches: R Bats: R Pos: RP-6   Ht: 6'3" Wt: 238 Born: 12/21/1985 Age: 34

			HOW MUCH PITCHED					WHAT HE GAVE UP											THE RESULTS							
Year	Team	Lg	G	GS	GF	IP	BFP	H	R	ER	HR	SH	SF	HB	TBB	IBB	SO	WP	W	L	Pct	Sv-Op	Hld	Vel	OPS	ERC	ERA
2019	LsVgs	AAA	35	1	23	42.2	184	51	25	22	6	1	1	1	11	0	31	3	4	1	.800	11--	-		.785	5.10	4.64
2010	ChC	NL	7	0	3	8.0	48	18	11	11	2	0	0	1	5	1	7	0	0	1	.000	0-0	0	93	1.167	15.07	12.38
2014	ChC	NL	61	0	5	56.1	242	58	29	26	2	5	1	2	19	4	31	0	2	3	.400	0-4	12	93	.682	3.57	4.15
2015	ChC	NL	10	0	3	7.1	35	12	6	6	2	0	0	0	2	0	4	0	1	2	.333	0-2	0	95	1.006	8.97	7.36
2019	Oak	AL	6	0	3	9.2	41	12	4	4	0	0	0	0	4	0	6	1	0	0		0-0	0	93	.796	5.12	3.72
	4 ML YEARS		84	0	14	81.1	366	100	50	47	6	5	1	3	30	5	48	1	3	6	.333	0-6	12	93	.790	5.15	5.20

Jonathan Schoop

Bats: R Throws: R Pos: 2B-113;PH-6;DH-4;PR-2   SCOPE   Ht: 6'1" Wt: 225 Born: 10/16/1991 Age: 28

								BATTING													RUNNING			AVERAGES			
Year	Team	Lg	G	AB	H	2B	3B	HR	(Hm	Rd)	TB	R	RBI	RC	TBB	IBB	SO	HBP	SH	SF	SB	CS	GDP	Avg	OBP	Slg	OPS
2013	Bal	AL	5	14	4	0	0	1	(1	0)	7	5	1	1	1	0	2	0	0	0	0	0	2	.286	.333	.500	.833
2014	Bal	AL	137	455	95	18	0	16	(5	11)	161	48	45	32	13	0	122	8	5	0	2	0	12	.209	.244	.354	.598
2015	Bal	AL	86	305	85	17	0	15	(9	6)	147	34	39	40	9	0	79	4	1	2	2	0	9	.279	.306	.482	.788
2016	Bal	AL	162	615	164	38	1	25	(13	12)	279	82	82	72	21	0	137	8	0	3	1	2	16	.267	.298	.454	.752
2017	Bal	AL	160	622	182	35	0	32	(18	14)	313	92	105	100	35	0	142	11	0	7	1	0	20	.293	.338	.503	.841
2018	2 Tms		131	473	110	22	1	21	(12	9)	197	61	61	45	19	2	115	4	1	4	1	1	11	.233	.266	.416	.682
2019	Min	AL	121	433	111	23	1	23	(7	16)	205	61	59	52	20	1	116	10	0	1	1	1	13	.256	.304	.473	.777
18	Bal	AL	85	349	85	18	1	17	(9	8)	156	45	40	34	12	1	74	3	1	2	0	1	8	.244	.273	.447	.720
18	Mil	NL	46	124	25	4	0	4	(3	1)	41	16	21	11	7	1	41	1	0	2	1	0	3	.202	.246	.331	.577
	Postseason		12	33	4	1	0	0	(0	0)	5	3	2	2	3	0	8	0	0	0	2	0	1	.121	.194	.152	.346
	7 ML YEARS		802	2917	751	153	3	133	(65	68)	1309	383	392	342	118	3	713	45	7	17	8	4	83	.257	.295	.449	.744

John Schreiber

Pitches: R Bats: R Pos: RP-13   Ht: 6'3" Wt: 220 Born: 3/5/1994 Age: 26

			HOW MUCH PITCHED					WHAT HE GAVE UP											THE RESULTS							
Year	Team	Lg	G	GS	GF	IP	BFP	H	R	ER	HR	SH	SF	HB	TBB	IBB	SO	WP	W	L	Pct	Sv-Op	Hld	Vel	OPS	ERC	ERA
2019	Erie	AA	5	0	4	7.0	29	4	2	2	1	0	0	0	3	0	12	0	0	0		0--	-		.626	2.11	2.57
2019	Toledo	AAA	48	0	14	59.1	238	39	22	15	4	0	5	3	14	0	70	4	6	4	.600	4--	-		.561	2.12	2.28
2019	Det	AL	13	0	3	13.0	59	16	9	9	3	0	0	1	4	0	19	1	2	0	1.000	0-1	1	92	.837	6.34	6.23

Jaime Schultz

Pitches: R Bats: R Pos: RP-4   Ht: 5'10" Wt: 205 Born: 6/20/1991 Age: 29

			HOW MUCH PITCHED					WHAT HE GAVE UP											THE RESULTS							
Year	Team	Lg	G	GS	GF	IP	BFP	H	R	ER	HR	SH	SF	HB	TBB	IBB	SO	WP	W	L	Pct	Sv-Op	Hld	Vel	OPS	ERC	ERA
2019	OkCity	AAA	47	1	12	47.2	221	52	38	31	3	1	1	2	27	1	62	4	2	3	.400	4--	-		.763	5.05	5.85
2018	TB	AL	22	1	7	30.1	125	18	19	19	6	0	2	3	17	0	35	1	2	2	.500	0-0	2	95	.702	3.59	5.64
2019	LAD	NL	4	0	3	5.0	22	6	4	4	1	0	0	0	3	0	3	0	0	0		0-0	0	96	.988	7.41	7.20
	2 ML YEARS		26	1	10	35.1	147	24	23	23	7	0	2	3	20	0	38	1	2	2	.500	0-0	2	95	.746	4.06	5.86

Kyle Schwarber

Bats: L **Throws:** R **Pos:** LF-140;PH-14;DH-2;C-1   SHWAR-burr   **Ht:** 6'0" **Wt:** 235 **Born:** 3/5/1993 **Age:** 27

Year	Team	Lg	G	AB	H	2B	3B	HR	(Hm	Rd)	TB	R	RBI	RC	TBB	IBB	SO	HBP	SH	SF	SB	CS	GDP	Avg	OBP	Slg	OPS
2015	ChC	NL	69	232	57	6	1	16	(7	9)	113	52	43	39	36	1	77	4	0	1	3	3	4	.246	.355	.487	.842
2016	ChC	NL	2	4	0	0	0	0	(0	0)	0	0	0	0	1	0	2	0	0	0	0	0	0	.000	.200	.000	.200
2017	ChC	NL	129	422	89	16	1	30	(18	12)	197	67	59	55	59	1	150	5	0	0	1	1	6	.211	.315	.467	.782
2018	ChC	NL	137	428	102	14	3	26	(11	15)	200	64	61	65	78	20	140	1	1	2	4	3	6	.238	.356	.467	.823
2019	ChC	NL	155	529	132	29	3	38	(18	20)	281	82	92	92	70	5	156	5	0	6	2	3	6	.250	.339	.531	.871
	Postseason		22	62	19	1	0	6	(4	2)	38	10	11	12	10	0	18	0	0	0	1	0	1	.306	.403	.613	1.016
	5 ML YEARS		492	1615	380	65	8	110	(54	56)	791	265	255	251	244	27	525	15	1	9	10	10	22	.235	.339	.490	.829

Frank Schwindel

Bats: R **Throws:** R **Pos:** 1B-5;PH-2   **Ht:** 6'1" **Wt:** 215 **Born:** 6/29/1992 **Age:** 28

Year	Team	Lg	G	AB	H	2B	3B	HR	(Hm	Rd)	TB	R	RBI	RC	TBB	IBB	SO	HBP	SH	SF	SB	CS	GDP	Avg	OBP	Slg	OPS
2019	Omha	AAA	19	70	13	4	0	1	(-	-)	20	8	10	4	4	0	13	1	0	1	0	1	3	.186	.237	.286	.523
2019	Erie	AA	46	171	44	8	0	5	(-	-)	67	21	24	21	11	0	27	3	0	3	0	0	2	.257	.309	.392	.700
2019	Toledo	AAA	28	113	37	7	0	9	(-	-)	71	21	33	24	6	0	19	0	0	0	0	0	1	.327	.361	.628	.990
2019	KC	AL	6	15	1	0	0	0	(0	0)	1	0	0	0	0	0	2	0	0	0	0	0	0	.067	.067	.067	.133

Robby Scott

Pitches: L **Bats:** R **Pos:** RP-11   **Ht:** 6'3" **Wt:** 220 **Born:** 8/29/1989 **Age:** 30

Year	Team	Lg	G	GS	GF	IP	BFP	H	R	ER	HR	SH	SF	HB	TBB	IBB	SO	WP	W	L	Pct	Sv-Op	Hld	Vel	OPS	ERC	ERA
2019	Reno	AAA	41	0	8	48.0	225	42	40	37	10	1	3	4	35	1	61	2	3	0	1.000	1- -	-	-	.823	5.69	6.94
2016	Bos	AL	7	0	1	6.0	25	6	0	0	1	0	0	2	2	0	5	1	1	0	1.000	0-0	1	87	.606	3.19	0.00
2017	Bos	AL	57	0	12	35.2	141	22	16	15	7	0	2	3	13	1	31	3	2	1	.667	0-2	12	89	.660	2.85	3.79
2018	Bos	AL	9	0	4	6.2	40	10	6	6	2	0	0	5	5	2	8	0	0	1	.000	0-0	1	89	1.133	13.30	8.10
2019	Ari	NL	11	0	1	7.1	37	8	4	4	1	1	0	0	7	0	9	0	1	0	1.000	0-0	0	88	.899	7.05	4.91
	4 ML YEARS		84	0	18	55.2	243	46	26	25	10	2	2	8	27	3	53	4	4	2	.667	0-2	14	88	.763	4.49	4.04

Tanner Scott

Pitches: L **Bats:** R **Pos:** RP-28   **Ht:** 6'2" **Wt:** 220 **Born:** 7/22/1994 **Age:** 25

Year	Team	Lg	G	GS	GF	IP	BFP	H	R	ER	HR	SH	SF	HB	TBB	IBB	SO	WP	W	L	Pct	Sv-Op	Hld	Vel	OPS	ERC	ERA
2019	Norfolk	AAA	30	0	23	45.1	185	35	21	15	2	0	2	2	15	1	57	5	3	4	.429	7- -	-	-	.594	2.39	2.98
2017	Bal	AL	2	0	1	1.2	9	2	2	2	0	0	0	0	2	0	2	0	0	0	-	0-0	0	98	.873	7.49	10.80
2018	Bal	AL	53	0	8	53.1	240	55	33	32	6	1	1	1	28	1	76	7	3	3	.500	0-3	5	97	.777	4.86	5.40
2019	Bal	AL	28	0	5	26.1	122	28	17	14	4	0	0	2	19	2	37	2	1	1	.500	0-1	2	96	.847	6.54	4.78
	3 ML YEARS		83	0	14	81.1	371	85	52	48	10	1	1	3	49	3	115	9	4	4	.500	0-4	7	97	.802	5.44	5.31

Tayler Scott

Pitches: R **Bats:** R **Pos:** RP-11; SP-2   **Ht:** 6'3" **Wt:** 185 **Born:** 6/1/1992 **Age:** 28

Year	Team	Lg	G	GS	GF	IP	BFP	H	R	ER	HR	SH	SF	HB	TBB	IBB	SO	WP	W	L	Pct	Sv-Op	Hld	Vel	OPS	ERC	ERA
2019	Tacom	AAA	20	0	3	35.0	152	32	25	25	4	0	1	2	19	1	47	4	3	2	.600	1- -	-	-	.749	4.53	6.43
2019	Norfolk	AAA	13	0	8	16.0	61	11	1	1	0	0	1	0	3	0	21	3	0	0	-	6- -	-	-	.458	1.35	0.56
2019	2 Tms		13	2	6	16.1	93	31	28	26	6	0	0	4	11	0	14	2	0	0	-	0-0	0	95	1.174	15.16	14.33
19	Sea	AL	5	2	1	7.2	41	11	10	8	1	0	0	2	6	0	7	0	0	0	-	0-0	0	95	.948	9.89	9.39
19	Bal	AL	8	0	5	8.2	52	20	18	18	5	0	0	2	5	0	7	2	0	0	-	0-0	0	94	1.341	20.19	18.69

Corey Seager

Bats: L **Throws:** R **Pos:** SS-132;PH-7   SEE-gurr   **Ht:** 6'4" **Wt:** 215 **Born:** 4/27/1994 **Age:** 26

Year	Team	Lg	G	AB	H	2B	3B	HR	(Hm	Rd)	TB	R	RBI	RC	TBB	IBB	SO	HBP	SH	SF	SB	CS	GDP	Avg	OBP	Slg	OPS
2015	LAD	NL	27	98	33	8	1	4	(3	1)	55	17	17	19	14	1	19	1	0	0	2	0	2	.337	.425	.561	.986
2016	LAD	NL	157	627	193	40	5	26	(18	8)	321	105	72	110	54	5	133	4	0	2	3	3	12	.308	.365	.512	.877
2017	LAD	NL	145	539	159	33	0	22	(12	10)	258	85	77	104	67	5	131	4	0	3	4	2	14	.295	.375	.479	.854
2018	LAD	NL	26	101	27	5	1	2	(1	1)	40	13	13	17	11	1	17	2	0	1	0	0	2	.267	.348	.396	.744
2019	LAD	NL	134	489	133	44	1	19	(9	10)	236	82	87	81	44	3	98	4	0	4	1	0	8	.272	.335	.483	.817
	Postseason		26	98	21	3	1	3	(1	2)	35	12	10	8	10	0	33	1	0	1	1	0	1	.214	.291	.357	.648
	5 ML YEARS		489	1854	545	130	8	73	(43	30)	910	302	266	331	190	15	398	15	0	10	10	5	38	.294	.362	.491	.853

Kyle Seager

Bats: L **Throws:** R **Pos:** 3B-104;PH-2;DH-1   SEE-gurr   **Ht:** 6'0" **Wt:** 210 **Born:** 11/3/1987 **Age:** 32

Year	Team	Lg	G	AB	H	2B	3B	HR	(Hm	Rd)	TB	R	RBI	RC	TBB	IBB	SO	HBP	SH	SF	SB	CS	GDP	Avg	OBP	Slg	OPS
2011	Sea	AL	53	182	47	13	0	3	(0	3)	69	22	13	16	13	0	36	2	2	2	3	1	4	.258	.312	.379	.691
2012	Sea	AL	155	594	154	35	1	20	(5	15)	251	62	86	88	46	1	110	5	2	4	13	5	9	.259	.316	.423	.738
2013	Sea	AL	160	615	160	32	2	22	(8	14)	262	79	69	90	68	1	122	7	0	5	9	3	6	.260	.338	.426	.764
2014	Sea	AL	159	590	158	27	4	25	(16	9)	268	71	96	96	52	3	118	8	1	3	7	5	12	.268	.334	.454	.788
2015	Sea	AL	161	623	166	37	0	26	(7	19)	281	85	74	75	54	6	98	5	0	4	6	6	17	.266	.328	.451	.779
2016	Sea	AL	158	597	166	36	3	30	(11	19)	298	89	99	110	69	10	108	8	0	2	3	1	18	.278	.359	.499	.859

Year	Team	Lg	G	AB	H	2B	3B	HR	(Hm	Rd)	TB	R	RBI	RC	TBB	IBB	SO	HBP	SH	SF	SB	CS	GDP	Avg	OBP	Slg	OPS
2017	Sea	AL	154	578	144	33	1	27	(12	15)	260	72	88	84	58	6	110	8	0	6	2	1	6	.249	.323	.450	.773
2018	Sea	AL	155	583	129	36	1	22	(8	14)	233	62	78	59	38	3	138	1	0	4	2	2	10	.221	.273	.400	.673
2019	Sea	AL	106	393	94	19	1	23	(10	13)	184	55	63	57	44	0	86	4	0	2	2	2	12	.239	.321	.468	.789
9 ML YEARS			1261	4755	1218	268	13	198	(77	121)	2106	597	666	675	442	30	926	52	5	32	47	26	96	.256	.324	.443	.767

Jean Segura

Bats: R Throws: R Pos: SS-142;PH-3 GENE seg-ER-uh **Ht: 5'10" Wt: 205 Born: 3/17/1990 Age: 30**

Year	Team	Lg	G	AB	H	2B	3B	HR	(Hm	Rd)	TB	R	RBI	RC	TBB	IBB	SO	HBP	SH	SF	SB	CS	GDP	Avg	OBP	Slg	OPS
2012	2 Tms		45	151	39	4	3	0	(0	0)	49	19	14	16	13	3	23	0	1	1	7	1	1	.258	.315	.325	.640
2013	Mil	NL	146	588	173	20	10	12	(7	5)	249	74	49	72	25	1	84	6	2	2	44	13	17	.294	.329	.423	.752
2014	Mil	NL	146	513	126	14	6	5	(3	2)	167	61	31	45	28	5	70	4	10	2	20	9	13	.246	.289	.326	.614
2015	Mil	NL	142	560	144	16	5	6	(4	2)	188	57	50	57	13	2	93	6	3	2	25	6	14	.257	.281	.336	.616
2016	Ari	NL	153	637	203	41	7	20	(12	8)	318	102	64	107	39	1	101	12	4	2	33	10	6	.319	.368	.499	.867
2017	Sea	AL	125	524	157	30	2	11	(7	4)	224	80	45	71	34	3	83	6	0	1	22	8	14	.300	.349	.427	.776
2018	Sea	AL	144	586	178	29	3	10	(7	3)	243	91	63	77	32	2	69	4	4	6	20	11	17	.304	.341	.415	.755
2019	Phi	NL	144	576	161	37	4	12	(9	3)	242	79	60	79	30	1	73	8	1	3	10	2	11	.280	.323	.420	.743
12	LAA	AL	1	3	0	0	0	0	(0	0)	0	0	0	0	0	0	2	0	0	0	0	0	0	.000	.000	.000	.000
12	Mil	NL	44	148	39	4	3	0	(0	0)	49	19	14	16	13	3	21	0	1	1	7	1	1	.264	.321	.331	.652
8 ML YEARS			1045	4135	1181	191	40	76	(49	27)	1680	563	376	524	214	18	596	46	25	19	181	60	93	.286	.326	.406	.733

Sam Selman

Pitches: L Bats: R Pos: RP-10 **Ht: 6'3" Wt: 190 Born: 11/14/1990 Age: 29**

Year	Team	Lg	G	GS	GF	IP	BFP	H	R	ER	HR	SH	SF	HB	TBB	IBB	SO	WP	W	L	Pct	Sv-Op	Hld	Vel	OPS	ERC	ERA
2019	Scrmto	AAA	39	1	10	48.0	185	25	13	11	4	0	2	1	16	0	81	0	3	2	.600	0--	-	-	.480	1.51	2.06
2019	SF	NL	10	0	3	10.1	44	6	5	5	2	1	0	2	6	0	10	0	0	0	-	0-1	1	90	.697	3.89	4.35

Marcus Semien

Bats: R Throws: R Pos: SS-161 SIM-ee-inn **Ht: 6'0" Wt: 195 Born: 9/17/1990 Age: 29**

Year	Team	Lg	G	AB	H	2B	3B	HR	(Hm	Rd)	TB	R	RBI	RC	TBB	IBB	SO	HBP	SH	SF	SB	CS	GDP	Avg	OBP	Slg	OPS
2013	CWS	AL	21	69	18	4	0	2	(2	0)	28	7	7	7	1	0	22	0	0	1	2	2	1	.261	.268	.406	.673
2014	CWS	AL	64	231	54	10	2	6	(4	2)	86	30	28	31	21	0	70	1	2	0	3	0	6	.234	.300	.372	.673
2015	Oak	AL	155	556	143	23	7	15	(5	10)	225	65	45	57	42	1	132	1	1	1	11	5	16	.257	.310	.405	.715
2016	Oak	AL	159	568	135	27	2	27	(10	17)	247	72	75	77	51	1	139	0	1	1	10	2	12	.238	.300	.435	.735
2017	Oak	AL	85	342	85	19	1	10	(5	5)	136	53	40	48	38	0	85	2	1	3	12	1	3	.249	.325	.398	.722
2018	Oak	AL	159	632	161	35	2	15	(6	9)	245	89	70	85	61	1	131	1	2	7	14	6	12	.255	.318	.388	.706
2019	Oak	AL	162	657	187	43	7	33	(15	18)	343	123	92	136	87	2	102	2	0	1	10	8	11	.285	.369	.522	.892
Postseason			1	3	1	0	0	0	(0	0)	1	0	0	0	1	0	1	0	0	0	0	0	0	.333	.500	.333	.833
7 ML YEARS			805	3055	783	161	21	108	(47	61)	1310	439	357	441	301	5	681	7	7	14	62	24	61	.256	.323	.429	.752

Antonio Senzatela

Pitches: R Bats: R Pos: SP-25 **Ht: 6'1" Wt: 246 Born: 1/21/1995 Age: 25**

Year	Team	Lg	G	GS	GF	IP	BFP	H	R	ER	HR	SH	SF	HB	TBB	IBB	SO	WP	W	L	Pct	Sv-Op	Hld	Vel	OPS	ERC	ERA
2019	Albq	AAA	7	7	0	34.1	151	45	23	22	7	1	1	1	10	0	12	3	1	1	.500	0--	-	-	.910	6.59	5.77
2017	Col	NL	36	20	3	134.2	564	128	72	70	18	4	5	4	47	1	102	1	10	5	.667	0-0	1	94	.756	4.00	4.68
2018	Col	NL	23	13	2	90.1	390	94	45	44	10	1	3	3	30	1	69	1	6	6	.500	0-0	0	94	.763	4.22	4.38
2019	Col	NL	25	25	0	124.2	582	161	99	93	19	4	3	4	57	5	76	1	11	11	.500	0-0	0	94	.890	6.53	6.71
Postseason			1	1	0	5.0	19	3	2	2	1	0	0	0	2	0	1	2	0	0	-	0-0	0	94	.616	2.72	3.60
3 ML YEARS			84	58	5	349.2	1536	383	216	207	47	9	11	11	134	7	247	3	27	22	.551	0-0	1	94	.808	4.92	5.33

Nick Senzel

Bats: R Throws: R Pos: CF-96;PH-7;PR-3;2B-1 **Ht: 6'1" Wt: 205 Born: 6/29/1995 Age: 25**

Year	Team	Lg	G	AB	H	2B	3B	HR	(Hm	Rd)	TB	R	RBI	RC	TBB	IBB	SO	HBP	SH	SF	SB	CS	GDP	Avg	OBP	Slg	OPS
2016	2 Tms	Low	68	243	74	24	3	7	(-	-)	125	41	40	48	38	1	54	3	1	5	18	7	5	.305	.398	.514	.912
2017	Dytona	A+	62	246	75	26	2	4	(-	-)	117	41	31	44	23	2	54	3	0	0	9	2	0	.305	.371	.476	.847
2017	Pnscla	AA	57	209	71	14	1	10	(-	-)	117	40	34	46	26	0	43	0	0	0	5	4	3	.340	.413	.560	.973
2018	Lsvlle	AAA	44	171	53	12	2	6	(-	-)	87	23	25	34	19	1	39	1	0	2	8	2	2	.310	.378	.509	.887
2019	Cin	NL	104	375	96	20	4	12	(7	5)	160	55	42	49	30	0	101	3	0	1	14	5	6	.256	.315	.427	.742

Luis Severino

Pitches: R Bats: R Pos: SP-3 **Ht: 6'2" Wt: 215 Born: 2/20/1994 Age: 26**

Year	Team	Lg	G	GS	GF	IP	BFP	H	R	ER	HR	SH	SF	HB	TBB	IBB	SO	WP	W	L	Pct	Sv-Op	Hld	Vel	OPS	ERC	ERA
2015	NYY	AL	11	11	0	62.1	255	53	21	20	9	0	0	2	22	0	56	2	5	3	.625	0-0	0	95	.705	3.57	2.89
2016	NYY	AL	22	11	3	71.0	312	78	48	46	11	0	0	3	25	1	66	3	3	8	.273	0-0	1	96	.812	5.00	5.83
2017	NYY	AL	31	31	0	193.1	783	150	73	64	21	3	2	6	51	0	230	6	14	6	.700	0-0	0	98	.603	2.53	2.98

			HOW MUCH PITCHED						WHAT HE GAVE UP									THE RESULTS								
Year Team	Lg	G	GS	GF	IP	BFP	H	R	ER	HR	SH	SF	HB	TBB	IBB	SO	WP	W	L	Pct	Sv-Op	Hld	Vel	OPS	ERC	ERA
2018 NYY	AL	32	32	0	191.1	780	173	76	72	19	1	2	5	46	0	220	8	19	8	.704	0-0	0	98	.666	3.06	3.39
2019 NYY	AL	3	3	0	12.0	48	6	2	2	0	0	0	1	6	0	17	0	1	1	.500	0-0	0	96	.442	1.62	1.50
Postseason		6	6	0	23.0	105	22	16	16	5	1	0		14	0	21	0	1	2	.333	0-0	0	98	.776	5.43	6.26
5 ML YEARS		99	88	3	530.0	2178	460	220	204	60	4	4	17	150	1	589	19	42	26	.618	0-0	1	97	.664	3.12	3.46

Pedro Severino

Bats: R **Throws:** R **Pos:** C-89;PH-6;DH-3 **Ht:** 6'1" **Wt:** 219 **Born:** 7/20/1993 **Age:** 26

						BATTING															RUNNING			AVERAGES			
Year Team	Lg	G	AB	H	2B	3B	HR	(Hm	Rd)	TB	R	RBI	RC	TBB	IBB	SO	HBP	SH	SF	SB	CS	GDP	Avg	OBP	Slg	OPS
2015 Was	NL	2	4	1	1	0	0	(0	0)	2	1	0	0	0	0	1	0	0	0	0	0	0	.250	.250	.500	.750
2016 Was	NL	16	28	9	2	0	2	(1	1)	17	6	4	5	5	0	3	1	0	0	0	0	0	.321	.441	.607	1.048
2017 Was	NL	17	29	5	1	0	0	(0	0)	6	0	3	2	2	1	10	0	0	0	0	0	0	.172	.226	.207	.433
2018 Was	NL	70	190	32	9	0	2	(2	0)	47	14	15	12	18	4	47	4	0	1	1	0	3	.168	.254	.247	.501
2019 Bal	AL	96	305	76	13	0	13	(7	6)	128	37	44	39	29	0	73	4	1	2	3	1	5	.249	.321	.420	.740
Postseason		4	10	1	1	0	0	(0	0)	2	1	0	0	0	0	3	0	0	0	0	0	0	.100	.100	.200	.300
5 ML YEARS		201	556	123	26	0	17	(10	7)	200	58	66	58	54	5	134	9	1	3	4	1	8	.221	.299	.360	.659

Paul Sewald

Pitches: R **Bats:** R **Pos:** RP-17 **Ht:** 6'3" **Wt:** 207 **Born:** 5/26/1990 **Age:** 30

			HOW MUCH PITCHED				WHAT HE GAVE UP											THE RESULTS								
Year Team	Lg	G	GS	GF	IP	BFP	H	R	ER	HR	SH	SF	HB	TBB	IBB	SO	WP	W	L	Pct	Sv-Op	Hld	Vel	OPS	ERC	ERA
2019 Syrcse	AAA	41	0	10	51.0	217	56	23	19	6	0	1	4	15	1	52	3	3	3	.500	3--	-	-	.767	4.76	3.35
2017 NYM	NL	57	0	12	65.1	275	58	36	33	8	3	3	3	21	2	69	3	0	6	.000	0-3	13	91	.706	3.41	4.55
2018 NYM	NL	46	0	9	56.1	253	62	39	38	8	3	1	1	23	2	58	1	0	7	.000	2-4	2	90	.820	4.93	6.07
2019 NYM	NL	17	0	6	19.2	80	18	10	10	3	1	1	1	3	0	22	0	1	1	.500	1-1	0	91	.724	3.17	4.58
3 ML YEARS		120	0	27	141.1	608	138	85	81	19	6	7	5	47	4	149	4	1	14	.067	3-8	15	91	.756	3.97	5.16

Justin Shafer

Pitches: R **Bats:** R **Pos:** RP-34 **Ht:** 6'2" **Wt:** 195 **Born:** 9/18/1992 **Age:** 27

			HOW MUCH PITCHED				WHAT HE GAVE UP											THE RESULTS								
Year Team	Lg	G	GS	GF	IP	BFP	H	R	ER	HR	SH	SF	HB	TBB	IBB	SO	WP	W	L	Pct	Sv-Op	Hld	Vel	OPS	ERC	ERA
2019 Buffalo	AAA	24	0	17	30.2	129	29	14	12	3	0	2	1	8	0	35	3	0	2	.000	7--	-	-	93	.659	3.31	3.52
2018 Tor	AL	6	0	1	8.1	39	6	4	3	1	0	0	1	7	0	2	0	0	0	-	0-0	0	93	.714	4.72	3.24
2019 Tor	AL	34	0	11	39.2	182	41	19	17	6	1	0	1	25	4	39	1	2	1	.667	1-1	3	94	.854	5.52	3.86
2 ML YEARS		40	0	12	48.0	221	47	23	20	7	1	0	2	32	4	41	1	2	1	.667	1-1	3	94	.831	5.38	3.75

Bryan Shaw

Pitches: R **Bats:** B **Pos:** RP-70 **Ht:** 6'1" **Wt:** 232 **Born:** 11/8/1987 **Age:** 32

			HOW MUCH PITCHED				WHAT HE GAVE UP											THE RESULTS								
Year Team	Lg	G	GS	GF	IP	BFP	H	R	ER	HR	SH	SF	HB	TBB	IBB	SO	WP	W	L	Pct	Sv-Op	Hld	Vel	OPS	ERC	ERA
2011 Ari	NL	33	0	8	28.1	122	30	9	8	2	0	0	4	8	1	24	1	1	0	1.000	0-0	9	91	.699	4.31	2.54
2012 Ari	NL	64	0	19	59.1	252	60	29	23	4	4	2	2	24	3	41	4	1	6	.143	2-4	10	92	.747	4.08	3.49
2013 Cle	AL	70	0	11	75.0	316	60	31	27	4	4	2	4	28	2	73	5	7	3	.700	1-5	12	91	.586	2.71	3.24
2014 Cle	AL	80	0	16	76.1	313	61	26	22	6	5	2	2	22	4	64	4	5	5	.500	2-9	24	93	.602	2.45	2.59
2015 Cle	AL	74	0	19	64.0	265	59	24	21	8	1	0	1	19	1	54	3	3	3	.500	2-6	23	92	.693	3.47	2.95
2016 Cle	AL	75	0	9	66.2	275	56	26	24	8	2	1	1	28	3	69	2	2	5	.286	1-4	25	93	.686	3.47	3.24
2017 Cle	AL	79	0	16	76.2	312	71	36	30	5	1	1	0	22	3	73	3	4	6	.400	3-6	26	94	.653	3.01	3.52
2018 Col	NL	61	0	14	54.2	257	70	43	36	9	1	3	1	28	1	54	8	4	6	.400	0-5	13	93	.896	6.79	5.93
2019 Col	NL	70	0	18	72.0	311	69	44	43	12	1	1	5	29	1	58	1	3	2	.600	1-6	12	93	.798	4.61	5.38
Postseason		19	0	2	22.0	89	19	8	6	2	0	1	0	6	3	22	1	2	1	.667	0-0	5	95	.622	2.63	2.45
9 ML YEARS		606	0	130	573.0	2423	536	268	234	58	19	12	20	208	19	510	31	30	36	.455	12-45	154	93	.702	3.69	3.68

Chris Shaw

Bats: L **Throws:** R **Pos:** PH-14;1B-4;DH-1 **Ht:** 6'3" **Wt:** 226 **Born:** 10/20/1993 **Age:** 26

						BATTING															RUNNING			AVERAGES			
Year Team	Lg	G	AB	H	2B	3B	HR	(Hm	Rd)	TB	R	RBI	RC	TBB	IBB	SO	HBP	SH	SF	SB	CS	GDP	Avg	OBP	Slg	OPS
2019 Rchmd	AA	45	160	46	9	2	7	(-	-)	80	25	24	29	19	1	33	2	0	1	2	2	1	.288	.368	.500	.868
2019 Scrmto	AAA	75	282	84	18	1	21	(-	-)	167	52	70	58	20	1	78	6	0	2	0	0	4	.298	.355	.592	.947
2018 SF	NL	22	54	10	2	0	1	(0	1)	15	2	7	5	7	0	23	0	0	0	1	0	0	.185	.274	.278	.552
2019 SF	NL	16	18	1	0	0	0	(0	0)	1	0	0	0	2	0	8	0	0	0	0	0	0	.056	.150	.056	.206
2 ML YEARS		38	72	11	2	0	1	(0	1)	16	2	7	5	9	0	31	0	0	1	1	0	0	.153	.244	.222	.466

Travis Shaw

Bats: L **Throws:** R **Pos:** 3B-71;PH-18;1B-6;2B-2 **Ht:** 6'4" **Wt:** 230 **Born:** 4/16/1990 **Age:** 30

						BATTING															RUNNING			AVERAGES			
Year Team	Lg	G	AB	H	2B	3B	HR	(Hm	Rd)	TB	R	RBI	RC	TBB	IBB	SO	HBP	SH	SF	SB	CS	GDP	Avg	OBP	Slg	OPS
2019 SnAnt	AAA	42	133	38	4	0	12	(-	-)	78	27	33	35	36	0	37	2	0	3	3	1	0	.286	.437	.586	1.023
2015 Bos	AL	65	226	61	10	0	13	(8	5)	110	31	36	35	18	1	57	2	0	1	0	1	1	.270	.327	.487	.813
2016 Bos	AL	145	480	116	34	2	16	(7	9)	202	63	71	64	43	4	133	3	0	4	5	1	10	.242	.306	.421	.726
2017 Mil	NL	144	538	147	34	1	31	(13	18)	276	84	101	93	60	6	138	4	1	3	10	0	20	.273	.349	.513	.862

Year Team	Lg	G	AB	H	2B	3B	HR	(Hm	Rd)	TB	R	RBI	RC	TBB	IBB	SO	HBP	SH	SF	SB	CS	GDP	Avg	OBP	Slg	OPS
								BATTING												**RUNNING**			**AVERAGES**			
2018 Mil	NL	152	498	120	23	0	32	(16	16)	239	73	86	84	78	6	108	4	1	6	5	2	7	.241	.345	.480	.825
2019 Mil	NL	86	230	36	5	0	7	(3	4)	62	22	16	11	36	3	89	4	0	0	0	0	5	.157	.281	.270	.551
Postseason		11	32	9	2	1	1	(1	0)	16	2	2	3	4	1	10	0	0	0	1	0	0	.281	.361	.500	.861
5 ML YEARS		592	1972	480	106	3	99	(47	52)	889	273	310	287	235	20	525	17	2	15	20	4	43	.243	.327	.451	.778

Mike Shawaryn

Pitches: R Bats: R Pos: RP-14   Ht: 6'2" Wt: 200 Born: 9/17/1994 Age: 25

Year Team	Lg	G	GS	GF	IP	BFP	H	R	ER	HR	SH	SF	HB	TBB	IBB	SO	WP	W	L	Pct	Sv-Op	Hld	Vel	OPS	ERC	ERA
					HOW MUCH PITCHED				**WHAT HE GAVE UP**											**THE RESULTS**						
2019 Pwtckt	AAA	26	14	1	89.2	383	76	48	45	13	0	5	6	49	0	76	7	1	2	.333	0- -	-	-	.760	4.50	4.52
2019 Bos	AL	14	0	4	20.1	103	26	22	22	5	0	1	5	13	0	29	1	0	0	-	0-0	0	92	.987	9.15	9.74

Justus Sheffield

Pitches: L Bats: L Pos: SP-7; RP-1   Ht: 6'0" Wt: 200 Born: 5/13/1996 Age: 24

Year Team	Lg	G	GS	GF	IP	BFP	H	R	ER	HR	SH	SF	HB	TBB	IBB	SO	WP	W	L	Pct	Sv-Op	Hld	Vel	OPS	ERC	ERA
					HOW MUCH PITCHED				**WHAT HE GAVE UP**											**THE RESULTS**						
2019 Tacom	AAA	12	12	0	55.0	263	59	47	42	12	0	1	1	41	0	48	4	2	6	.250	0- -	-	-	.870	6.90	6.87
2019 Ark	AA	12	12	0	78.0	305	62	20	19	4	1	2	0	18	0	85	3	5	3	.625	0- -	-	-	.577	2.14	2.19
2018 NYY	AL	3	0	2	2.2	14	4	3	3	1	0	0	0	3	0	0	1	0	0	-	0-0	0	94	1.227	13.94	10.13
2019 Sea	AL	8	7	0	36.0	168	44	22	22	5	1	0	3	18	0	37	3	0	1	.000	0-0	0	93	.881	6.51	5.50
2 ML YEARS		11	7	2	38.2	182	48	25	25	6	1	0	3	21	0	37	4	0	1	.000	0-0	0	93	.906	6.96	5.82

Chandler Shepherd

Pitches: R Bats: R Pos: SP-3; RP-2   Ht: 6'3" Wt: 185 Born: 8/25/1992 Age: 27

Year Team	Lg	G	GS	GF	IP	BFP	H	R	ER	HR	SH	SF	HB	TBB	IBB	SO	WP	W	L	Pct	Sv-Op	Hld	Vel	OPS	ERC	ERA
					HOW MUCH PITCHED				**WHAT HE GAVE UP**											**THE RESULTS**						
2019 Pwtckt	AAA	8	7	0	29.2	163	53	43	33	11	0	5	16	0	30	1	0	5	.000	0- -	-	-	1.151	12.91	10.01	
2019 Norfolk	AAA	14	12	0	72.1	313	75	41	37	8	1	1	1	23	0	73	4	3	5	.375	0- -	-	-	.718	4.03	4.60
2019 Bal	AL	5	3	1	19.0	84	23	15	14	5	0	0	2	6	0	17	2	0	0	-	0-0	0	92	.935	6.85	6.63

Jimmie Sherfy

Pitches: R Bats: R Pos: RP-17   Ht: 6'0" Wt: 175 Born: 12/27/1991 Age: 28

Year Team	Lg	G	GS	GF	IP	BFP	H	R	ER	HR	SH	SF	HB	TBB	IBB	SO	WP	W	L	Pct	Sv-Op	Hld	Vel	OPS	ERC	ERA
					HOW MUCH PITCHED				**WHAT HE GAVE UP**											**THE RESULTS**						
2019 Reno	AAA	35	0	26	35.0	157	32	17	14	2	1	0	2	21	1	49	1	2	3	.400	12- -	-	-	.729	4.21	3.60
2017 Ari	NL	11	0	2	10.2	37	5	0	0	0	0	2	0	2	0	9	0	2	0	1.000	1-1	2	94	.418	0.80	0.00
2018 Ari	NL	15	0	4	16.1	69	8	3	3	1	0	2	2	10	1	17	0	0	0	-	0-0	1	93	.490	2.24	1.65
2019 Ari	NL	17	0	4	18.1	83	23	12	12	4	1	0	1	5	0	22	0	1	0	1.000	1-2	0	92	.867	6.10	5.89
Postseason		2	0	1	1.0	8	5	4	4	0	0	0	0	0	0	1	0	0	0	-	0-0	0	93	1.625	30.85	36.00
3 ML YEARS		43	0	9	45.1	189	36	15	15	5	1	2	3	17	1	48	0	3	0	1.000	2-3	3	93	.647	3.15	2.98

Matt Shoemaker

Pitches: R Bats: R Pos: SP-5   SHOO-may-kerr   Ht: 6'2" Wt: 225 Born: 9/27/1986 Age: 33

Year Team	Lg	G	GS	GF	IP	BFP	H	R	ER	HR	SH	SF	HB	TBB	IBB	SO	WP	W	L	Pct	Sv-Op	Hld	Vel	OPS	ERC	ERA
					HOW MUCH PITCHED				**WHAT HE GAVE UP**											**THE RESULTS**						
2013 LAA	AL	1	1	0	5.0	19	2	0	0	0	0	0	0	2	0	5	1	0	0	-	0-0	0	91	.328	0.95	0.00
2014 LAA	AL	27	20	5	136.0	543	122	49	46	14	3	5	4	24	0	124	5	16	4	.800	0-0	0	91	.658	2.84	3.04
2015 LAA	AL	25	24	1	135.1	569	135	70	67	24	4	4	4	35	2	116	3	7	10	.412	0-0	0	90	.758	4.12	4.46
2016 LAA	AL	27	27	0	160.0	668	166	71	69	18	2	5	7	30	1	143	2	9	13	.409	0-0	0	91	.723	3.71	3.88
2017 LAA	AL	14	14	0	77.2	326	73	41	39	15	1	1	4	28	0	69	2	6	3	.667	0-0	0	92	.788	4.52	4.52
2018 LAA	AL	7	7	0	31.0	130	29	17	17	3	0	0	1	10	0	33	3	2	2	.500	0-0	0	91	.694	3.54	4.94
2019 Tor	AL	5	5	0	28.2	108	16	7	5	3	0	0	1	9	0	24	1	3	0	1.000	0-0	0	91	.547	1.77	1.57
Postseason		1	1	0	6.0	23	5	1	1	0	1	0	0	0	0	6	0	0	0	-	0-0	0	91	.500	1.37	1.50
7 ML YEARS		106	98	6	573.2	2363	543	255	243	77	10	15	21	138	3	514	17	43	32	.573	0-0	0	91	.713	3.55	3.81

Chasen Shreve

Pitches: L Bats: L Pos: RP-3   CHAY-sen shreev   Ht: 6'4" Wt: 195 Born: 7/12/1990 Age: 29

Year Team	Lg	G	GS	GF	IP	BFP	H	R	ER	HR	SH	SF	HB	TBB	IBB	SO	WP	W	L	Pct	Sv-Op	Hld	Vel	OPS	ERC	ERA
					HOW MUCH PITCHED				**WHAT HE GAVE UP**											**THE RESULTS**						
2019 Memp	AAA	51	0	21	60.0	245	45	25	23	6	0	0	3	26	0	68	3	2	2	.500	3- -	-	-	.640	3.12	3.45
2014 Atl	NL	15	0	4	12.1	50	10	1	1	0	1	0	0	3	0	15	1	0	0	-	0-0	2	91	.526	1.88	0.73
2015 NYY	AL	59	0	13	58.1	251	49	21	20	10	2	0	1	33	2	64	4	6	2	.750	0-1	10	91	.738	4.39	3.09
2016 NYY	AL	37	0	11	33.0	142	29	19	19	8	1	0	3	13	0	33	0	2	1	.667	1-1	1	92	.823	4.70	5.18
2017 NYY	AL	44	0	15	45.1	198	35	20	19	8	0	2	0	25	3	58	4	4	1	.800	0-1	1	93	.712	3.71	3.77
2018 2 Tms		60	0	20	52.2	235	53	28	23	11	0	4	1	27	0	62	2	3	4	.429	1-1	6	92	.832	5.43	3.93
2019 StL	NL	3	0	1	2.0	10	2	2	2	0	0	0	1	1	0	2	0	1	0	1.000	0-0	1	91	.900	5.48	9.00
18 NYY	AL	40	0	17	38.0	170	39	23	18	8	0	2	1	18	0	46	2	2	2	.500	1-1	3	92	.831	5.40	4.26
18 StL	NL	20	0	3	14.2	65	14	5	5	3	0	2	0	9	0	16	0	1	2	.333	0-0	3	92	.835	5.52	3.07
6 ML YEARS		218	0	63	203.2	886	178	91	84	37	4	6	6	102	5	234	11	16	8	.667	2-4	21	92	.760	4.39	3.71

JB Shuck

Bats: L **Throws:** L **Pos:** RF-10;PH-9;LF-7;CF-3;PR-2;DH-1   **Ht:** 5'11" **Wt:** 195 **Born:** 6/18/1987 **Age:** 33

								BATTING												RUNNING			AVERAGES			
Year Team	Lg	G	AB	H	2B	3B	HR	(Hm	Rd)	TB	R	RBI	RC	TBB	IBB	SO	HBP	SH	SF	SB	CS	GDP	Avg	OBP	Slg	OPS
2019 Indy	AAA	61	142	38	12	2	3	(-	-)	63	17	14	22	16	0	17	0	0	0	3	1	2	.268	.342	.444	.785
2011 Hou	NL	37	81	22	2	1	0	(0	0)	26	9	3	9	11	1	7	0	0	0	2	0	3	.272	.359	.321	.680
2013 LAA	AL	129	437	128	20	3	2	(1	1)	160	60	39	54	27	0	54	1	6	7	8	4	10	.293	.331	.366	.697
2014 2 Tms	AL	38	110	16	1	0	2	(1	1)	23	12	9	3	3	1	12	0	1	0	2	0	1	.145	.168	.209	.377
2015 CWS	AL	79	143	38	8	2	0	(0	0)	50	15	15	20	16	0	16	1	3	2	7	5	2	.266	.340	.350	.689
2016 CWS	AL	81	224	46	5	2	4	(2	2)	67	27	14	12	12	0	21	1	3	1	3	3	5	.205	.248	.299	.547
2018 Mia	NL	70	130	25	3	1	0	(0	0)	30	10	4	3	10	1	22	1	1	0	2	2	1	.192	.255	.231	.486
2019 Pit	NL	27	47	10	0	1	0	(0	0)	12	4	2	5	8	0	10	1	1	0	1	1	0	.213	.339	.255	.595
14 LAA	AL	22	84	14	1	0	2	(1	1)	21	10	9	3	3	1	11	0	1	0	2	0	0	.167	.195	.250	.445
14 Cle	AL	16	26	2	0	0	0	(0	0)	2	2	0	0	0	0	1	0	0	0	0	0	1	.077	.077	.077	.154
7 ML YEARS		461	1172	285	39	10	8	(4	4)	368	137	86	106	87	3	142	5	15	10	25	15	22	.243	.296	.314	.610

Magneuris Sierra

Bats: L **Throws:** L **Pos:** CF-9;RF-5;PH-2;PR-2   **Ht:** 5'11" **Wt:** 160 **Born:** 4/7/1996 **Age:** 24

								BATTING												RUNNING			AVERAGES			
Year Team	Lg	G	AB	H	2B	3B	HR	(Hm	Rd)	TB	R	RBI	RC	TBB	IBB	SO	HBP	SH	SF	SB	CS	GDP	Avg	OBP	Slg	OPS
2019 Jaxnvl	AA	48	181	51	8	2	1	(-	-)	66	21	7	24	13	0	32	2	1	0	7	1	0	.282	.337	.365	.701
2019 NewOr	AAA	81	336	91	11	7	6	(-	-)	134	56	21	42	15	0	58	1	0	0	26	10	2	.271	.304	.399	.703
2017 StL	NL	22	60	19	0	0	0	(0	0)	19	10	5	10	4	0	14	0	0	0	2	2	0	.317	.359	.317	.676
2018 Mia	NL	54	147	28	3	0	0	(0	0)	31	10	7	6	6	1	39	0	3	0	3	2	0	.190	.222	.211	.433
2019 Mia	NL	15	40	14	1	1	0	(0	0)	17	5	1	5	2	0	7	0	0	0	3	3	0	.350	.381	.425	.806
3 ML YEARS		91	247	61	4	1	0	(0	0)	67	25	13	21	12	1	60	0	3	0	8	7	0	.247	.282	.271	.553

Andrelton Simmons

Bats: R **Throws:** R **Pos:** SS-102;DH-1;PR-1   ANN-drel-ton   **Ht:** 6'2" **Wt:** 195 **Born:** 9/4/1989 **Age:** 30

								BATTING												RUNNING			AVERAGES			
Year Team	Lg	G	AB	H	2B	3B	HR	(Hm	Rd)	TB	R	RBI	RC	TBB	IBB	SO	HBP	SH	SF	SB	CS	GDP	Avg	OBP	Slg	OPS
2012 Atl	NL	49	166	48	8	2	3	(3	0)	69	17	19	23	12	1	21	1	0	3	1	0	5	.289	.335	.416	.751
2013 Atl	NL	157	606	150	27	6	17	(5	12)	240	76	59	60	40	1	55	3	5	4	6	5	16	.248	.296	.396	.692
2014 Atl	NL	146	540	132	18	4	7	(3	4)	179	44	46	41	32	4	60	0	2	2	4	5	25	.244	.286	.331	.617
2015 Atl	NL	147	535	142	23	2	4	(2	2)	181	60	44	48	39	6	48	6	1	2	5	3	19	.265	.321	.338	.660
2016 LAA	AL	124	448	126	22	2	4	(4	0)	164	48	44	52	28	0	38	2	1	4	10	1	16	.281	.324	.366	.690
2017 LAA	AL	158	589	164	38	2	14	(10	4)	248	77	69	91	47	0	67	3	0	8	19	6	20	.278	.331	.421	.752
2018 LAA	AL	146	554	162	26	5	11	(1	10)	231	68	75	80	35	2	44	5	1	5	10	2	17	.292	.337	.417	.754
2019 LAA	AL	103	398	105	19	0	7	(5	2)	145	47	40	36	24	1	37	2	0	0	10	2	21	.264	.309	.364	.673
Postseason		5	16	4	1	0	0	(0	0)	5	0	2	1	2	0	3	0	1	0	0	0	1	.250	.333	.313	.646
8 ML YEARS		1030	3836	1029	181	23	67	(33	34)	1457	437	396	431	257	15	370	22	10	28	65	24	139	.268	.316	.380	.696

Lucas Sims

Pitches: R **Bats:** R **Pos:** RP-20; SP-4   **Ht:** 6'2" **Wt:** 225 **Born:** 5/10/1994 **Age:** 26

		HOW MUCH PITCHED					WHAT HE GAVE UP											THE RESULTS								
Year Team	Lg	G	GS	GF	IP	BFP	H	R	ER	HR	SH	SF	HB	TBB	IBB	SO	WP	W	L	Pct	Sv-Op	Hld	Vel	OPS	ERC	ERA
2019 Lsvlle	AAA	16	16	0	79.0	340	69	43	40	9	2	2	6	36	0	102	1	5	0	1.000	0--	-	-	.726	4.00	4.56
2017 Atl	NL	14	10	1	57.2	255	64	37	36	9	5	1	4	23	2	44	0	3	6	.333	0-0	1	92	.869	5.43	5.62
2018 2 Tms	NL	9	0	2	15.2	77	15	13	13	3	0	0	2	13	1	16	0	0	0	-	0-1	0	92	.825	6.59	7.47
2019 Cin	NL	24	4	2	43.0	177	31	22	22	8	1	1	2	19	0	57	1	2	1	.667	0-0	3	94	.711	3.49	4.60
18 Atl	NL	6	0	2	10.1	52	12	9	9	2	0	0	1	8	1	10	0	0	0	-	0-1	0	93	.869	7.45	7.84
18 Cin	NL	3	0	0	5.1	25	3	4	4	1	0	0	1	5	0	6	0	0	0	-	0-0	0	92	.728	5.00	6.75
3 ML YEARS		47	14	5	116.1	509	110	72	71	20	6	2	8	55	3	117	1	5	7	.417	0-1	4	93	.807	4.84	5.49

Tony Sipp

Pitches: L **Bats:** L **Pos:** RP-36   **Ht:** 6'0" **Wt:** 190 **Born:** 7/12/1983 **Age:** 36

		HOW MUCH PITCHED					WHAT HE GAVE UP											THE RESULTS								
Year Team	Lg	G	GS	GF	IP	BFP	H	R	ER	HR	SH	SF	HB	TBB	IBB	SO	WP	W	L	Pct	Sv-Op	Hld	Vel	OPS	ERC	ERA
2009 Cle	AL	46	0	8	40.0	168	27	16	13	5	3	1	0	25	2	48	3	2	0	1.000	0-0	9	92	.682	3.29	2.93
2010 Cle	AL	70	0	16	63.0	266	48	30	29	12	3	2	2	39	3	69	4	2	2	.500	1-3	15	92	.770	4.42	4.14
2011 Cle	AL	69	0	17	62.1	251	45	22	21	10	1	2	0	24	3	57	2	6	3	.667	0-1	24	91	.664	2.87	3.03
2012 Cle	AL	63	0	7	55.0	233	47	29	27	9	2	1	1	23	1	51	3	1	2	.333	1-2	12	91	.739	3.80	4.42
2013 Ari	NL	56	0	11	37.2	175	35	22	20	6	3	1	3	22	2	42	3	3	2	.600	0-2	3	90	.780	4.90	4.78
2014 Hou	AL	56	0	13	50.2	198	28	19	19	5	2	0	0	17	2	63	3	4	3	.571	4-6	11	92	.517	1.57	3.38
2015 Hou	AL	60	0	12	54.1	216	41	13	12	5	2	1	1	15	1	62	4	3	4	.429	0-3	13	91	.606	2.34	1.99
2016 Hou	AL	60	0	13	43.2	195	52	26	24	12	0	1	1	18	0	40	0	1	2	.333	1-2	12	91	.953	6.80	4.95
2017 Hou	AL	46	0	12	37.1	165	36	25	24	8	1	1	1	16	2	39	1	0	1	.000	0-0	4	91	.830	4.72	5.79
2018 Hou	AL	54	0	8	38.2	151	27	8	8	1	0	2	1	13	0	42	2	3	1	.750	0-0	10	92	.583	2.00	1.86
2019 Was	NL	36	0	7	21.0	92	19	12	11	1	0	3	1	9	0	18	1	1	2	.333	0-1	9	91	.644	3.39	4.71
Postseason		9	0	1	6.2	27	2	1	0	0	0	0	0	4	0	7	0	0	1	.000	0-1	3	91	.309	1.01	0.00
11 ML YEARS		616	0	124	503.2	2110	405	222	208	74	17	15	11	221	16	531	26	26	22	.542	7-20	122	91	.710	3.51	3.72

Chance Sisco

Bats: L Throws: R Pos: C-52;PH-5;DH-3;1B-1   Ht: 6'2" Wt: 195 Born: 2/24/1995 Age: 25

Year	Team	Lg	G	AB	H	2B	3B	HR	(Hm	Rd)	TB	R	RBI	RC	TBB	IBB	SO	HBP	SH	SF	SB	CS	GDP	Avg	OBP	Slg	OPS
2019	Norfolk	AAA	45	168	49	10	0	10	(-	-)	89	31	37	35	20	0	44	7	0	1	0	0	4	.292	.388	.530	.918
2017	Bal	AL	10	18	6	2	0	2	(1	1)	14	3	4	6	3	0	7	1	0	0	0	0	0	.333	.455	.778	1.232
2018	Bal	AL	63	160	29	8	0	2	(2	0)	43	13	16	13	13	0	66	11	0	0	1	0	2	.181	.288	.269	.557
2019	Bal	AL	59	167	35	7	0	8	(3	5)	66	29	20	21	22	0	61	9	0	0	0	1	5	.210	.333	.395	.729
	3 ML YEARS		132	345	70	17	0	12	(6	6)	123	45	40	40	38	0	134	21	0	0	1	1	7	.203	.319	.357	.676

Tyler Skaggs

Pitches: L Bats: L Pos: SP-15   Ht: 6'4" Wt: 225 Born: 7/13/1991 Age: 27

Year	Team	Lg	G	GS	GF	IP	BFP	H	R	ER	HR	SH	SF	HB	TBB	IBB	SO	WP	W	L	Pct	Sv-Op	Hld	Vel	OPS	ERC	ERA
2012	Ari	NL	6	6	0	29.1	133	30	20	19	6	1	0	2	13	0	21	1	1	3	.250	0-0	0	89	.785	5.31	5.83
2013	Ari	NL	7	7	0	38.2	170	38	23	22	7	0	2	2	15	2	36	2	2	3	.400	0-0	0	89	.780	4.56	5.12
2014	LAA	AL	18	18	0	113.0	464	107	59	54	9	2	5	4	30	1	86	7	5	5	.500	0-0	0	92	.674	3.31	4.30
2016	LAA	AL	10	10	0	49.2	219	51	23	23	5	0	3	2	23	0	50	0	3	4	.429	0-0	0	93	.750	4.67	4.17
2017	LAA	AL	16	16	0	85.0	365	90	46	43	13	0	2	6	28	0	76	5	2	6	.250	0-0	0	92	.790	4.88	4.55
2018	LAA	AL	24	24	0	125.1	533	127	60	56	14	0	4	5	40	0	129	2	8	10	.444	0-0	0	91	.736	4.10	4.02
2019	LAA	AL	15	15	0	79.2	335	73	41	38	9	1	2	2	28	0	78	2	7	7	.500	0-0	0	91	.689	3.62	4.29
	7 ML YEARS		96	96	0	520.2	2219	516	272	255	63	4	18	23	177	3	476	19	28	38	.424	0-0	0	91	.732	4.13	4.41

Eric Skoglund

Pitches: L Bats: L Pos: SP-4; RP-2   Ht: 6'7" Wt: 210 Born: 10/26/1992 Age: 27

Year	Team	Lg	G	GS	GF	IP	BFP	H	R	ER	HR	SH	SF	HB	TBB	IBB	SO	WP	W	L	Pct	Sv-Op	Hld	Vel	OPS	ERC	ERA
2019	Omha	AAA	11	11	0	63.0	278	79	45	43	12	1	2	5	17	0	43	3	2	4	.333	0--	-	-	.875	6.18	6.14
2017	KC	AL	7	5	1	18.0	93	30	20	19	2	0	1	0	12	0	14	0	1	2	.333	0-0	0	92	1.027	9.63	9.50
2018	KC	AL	14	13	0	70.0	293	66	41	40	12	0	0	6	19	0	49	3	1	6	.143	0-0	0	91	.781	4.11	5.14
2019	KC	AL	6	4	0	21.0	101	30	21	21	5	0	2	1	9	0	4	0	0	3	.000	0-0	0	90	1.014	8.15	9.00
	3 ML YEARS		27	22	1	109.0	487	126	82	80	19	0	3	7	40	0	67	3	2	11	.154	0-0	0	91	.875	5.70	6.61

Matt Skole

Bats: L Throws: R Pos: DH-11;1B-9;PH-7   Ht: 6'4" Wt: 220 Born: 7/30/1989 Age: 30

Year	Team	Lg	G	AB	H	2B	3B	HR	(Hm	Rd)	TB	R	RBI	RC	TBB	IBB	SO	HBP	SH	SF	SB	CS	GDP	Avg	OBP	Slg	OPS
2019	Charllt	AAA	92	314	78	15	0	21	(-	-)	156	65	56	64	70	4	99	2	0	5	0	0	6	.248	.384	.497	.880
2018	CWS	AL	4	11	3	0	0	1	(0	1)	6	2	1	2	2	0	3	0	0	0	0	0	0	.273	.385	.545	.930
2019	CWS	AL	27	72	15	2	0	0	(0	0)	17	7	6	4	7	0	31	0	0	1	0	0	0	.208	.275	.236	.511
	2 ML YEARS		31	83	18	2	0	1	(0	1)	23	9	7	6	9	0	34	0	0	1	0	0	0	.217	.290	.277	.567

Austin Slater

Bats: R Throws: R Pos: RF-46;PH-23;1B-8;LF-2;2B-1   Ht: 6'2" Wt: 197 Born: 12/13/1992 Age: 27

Year	Team	Lg	G	AB	H	2B	3B	HR	(Hm	Rd)	TB	R	RBI	RC	TBB	IBB	SO	HBP	SH	SF	SB	CS	GDP	Avg	OBP	Slg	OPS
2019	Scrmto	AAA	70	240	74	17	0	12	(-	-)	127	47	45	57	46	1	69	9	0	1	6	2	9	.308	.436	.529	.965
2017	SF	NL	34	117	33	3	1	3	(0	3)	47	15	16	17	8	0	29	2	0	0	0	0	3	.282	.339	.402	.740
2018	SF	NL	74	199	50	6	1	1	(0	1)	61	21	23	23	20	2	69	5	0	1	7	0	5	.251	.333	.307	.640
2019	SF	NL	68	168	40	9	3	5	(2	3)	70	20	21	28	22	1	59	2	0	0	1	0	1	.238	.333	.417	.750
	3 ML YEARS		176	484	123	18	5	9	(2	7)	178	56	60	68	50	3	157	9	0	1	8	0	9	.254	.335	.368	.702

Aaron Slegers

Pitches: R Bats: R Pos: RP-1   Ht: 6'10" Wt: 245 Born: 9/4/1992 Age: 27

Year	Team	Lg	G	GS	GF	IP	BFP	H	R	ER	HR	SH	SF	HB	TBB	IBB	SO	WP	W	L	Pct	Sv-Op	Hld	Vel	OPS	ERC	ERA
2019	Drham	AAA	26	15	4	112.1	488	130	72	63	22	1	3	7	28	1	80	4	6	7	.462	0--	-	-	.849	5.35	5.05
2017	Min	AL	4	3	0	15.1	63	12	12	11	3	0	0	0	6	0	9	0	0	1	.000	0-0	0	91	.689	3.48	6.46
2018	Min	AL	4	2	1	13.2	60	17	8	8	3	0	0	1	2	0	6	0	1	1	.500	0-0	0	90	.877	5.59	5.27
2019	TB	AL	1	0	1	3.0	12	3	1	1	1	0	0	1	0	0	0	0	0	0	-	1-1	0	90	.879	5.79	3.00
	3 ML YEARS		9	5	2	32.0	135	32	21	20	7	0	0	2	8	0	15	0	1	2	.333	1-1	0	90	.791	4.55	5.63

Devin Smeltzer

Pitches: L Bats: R Pos: SP-6; RP-5   Ht: 6'3" Wt: 195 Born: 9/7/1995 Age: 24

Year	Team	Lg	G	GS	GF	IP	BFP	H	R	ER	HR	SH	SF	HB	TBB	IBB	SO	WP	W	L	Pct	Sv-Op	Hld	Vel	OPS	ERC	ERA
2019	Pnscla	AA	5	5	0	30.0	108	19	3	2	0	0	0	1	3	0	33	0	3	1	.750	0--	-	-	.425	1.12	0.60
2019	Roch	AAA	15	14	0	74.1	306	68	32	30	14	2	0	3	19	0	71	4	1	4	.200	0--	-	-	.746	3.80	3.63
2019	Min	AL	11	6	2	49.0	202	50	23	21	8	0	0	1	12	0	38	1	2	2	.500	1-1	1	89	.777	4.18	3.86

Burch Smith

Pitches: R Bats: R Pos: RP-17 **Ht:** 6'4" **Wt:** 225 **Born:** 4/12/1990 **Age:** 30

			HOW MUCH PITCHED					WHAT HE GAVE UP											THE RESULTS						
Year	Team	Lg	G	GS	GF	IP	BFP	H	R	ER	HR	SH	SF	HB	TBB	IBB	SO	WP	W	L	Pct	Sv-Op	Hld	Vel	OPS	ERC	ERA
2019	SnAnt	AAA	15	15	0	77.1	314	49	22	20	6	0	0	6	37	0	85	2	6	3	.667	0- -	-		.592	2.63	2.33
2013	SD	NL	10	7	3	36.1	167	39	26	26	9	1	0	0	21	1	46	0	1	3	.250	0-0	0	92	.899	6.27	6.44
2018	KC	AL	38	6	16	78.0	358	90	60	60	15	2	4	4	40	2	77	0	1	6	.143	0-0	1	93	.873	6.38	6.92
2019	2 Tms	NL	17	0	6	21.1	106	26	14	13	3	1	0	1	14	2	20	1	0	1	.000	0-1	0	93	.857	6.56	5.48
19	Mil	NL	7	0	4	12.2	65	16	11	11	3	0	0	1	10	2	14	1	0	1	.000	0-0	0	93	.952	8.37	7.82
19	SF	NL	10	0	2	8.2	41	10	3	2	0	1	0	0	4	0	6	0	0	0	-	0-1	0	93	.711	4.19	2.08
	3 ML YEARS		65	13	25	135.2	631	155	100	99	27	4	4	5	75	5	143	1	2	10	.167	0-1	1	93	.878	6.38	6.57

Caleb Smith

Pitches: L Bats: R Pos: SP-28 **Ht:** 6'2" **Wt:** 205 **Born:** 7/28/1991 **Age:** 28

			HOW MUCH PITCHED					WHAT HE GAVE UP											THE RESULTS						
Year	Team	Lg	G	GS	GF	IP	BFP	H	R	ER	HR	SH	SF	HB	TBB	IBB	SO	WP	W	L	Pct	Sv-Op	Hld	Vel	OPS	ERC	ERA
2017	NYY	AL	9	2	6	18.2	86	21	16	16	4	0	1	0	10	1	18	1	0	1	.000	0-0	0	94	.854	6.09	7.71
2018	Mia	NL	16	16	0	77.1	326	63	36	36	10	2	2	3	33	2	88	0	5	6	.455	0-0	0	93	.694	3.46	4.19
2019	Mia	NL	28	28	0	153.1	646	128	82	77	33	2	5	6	60	2	168	6	10	11	.476	0-0	0	92	.755	4.01	4.52
	3 ML YEARS		53	46	6	249.1	1058	212	134	129	47	4	8	9	103	5	274	7	15	18	.455	0-0	0	92	.744	3.99	4.66

Dominic Smith

Bats: L Throws: L Pos: PH-39;1B-36;LF-32;RF-1 **Ht:** 6'0" **Wt:** 239 **Born:** 6/15/1995 **Age:** 25

			BATTING																				RUNNING			AVERAGES			
Year	Team	Lg	G	AB	H	2B	3B	HR	(Hm	Rd)	TB	R	RBI	RC	TBB	IBB	SO	HBP	SH	SF				SB	CS	GDP	Avg	OBP	Slg	OPS
2017	NYM	NL	49	167	33	6	0	9	(4	5)	66	17	26	19	14	0	49	1	0	1				0	0	5	.198	.262	.395	.658
2018	NYM	NL	56	143	32	11	1	5	(4	1)	60	14	11	9	4	0	47	2	0	0				0	0	2	.224	.255	.420	.675
2019	NYM	NL	89	177	50	10	0	11	(3	8)	93	35	25	26	19	0	44	1	0	0				1	2	5	.282	.355	.525	.881
	3 ML YEARS		194	487	115	27	1	25	(11	14)	219	66	62	54	37	0	140	4	0	1				1	2	12	.236	.295	.450	.745

Joe Smith

Pitches: R Bats: R Pos: RP-28 **Ht:** 6'2" **Wt:** 205 **Born:** 3/22/1984 **Age:** 36

			HOW MUCH PITCHED					WHAT HE GAVE UP											THE RESULTS						
Year	Team	Lg	G	GS	GF	IP	BFP	H	R	ER	HR	SH	SF	HB	TBB	IBB	SO	WP	W	L	Pct	Sv-Op	Hld	Vel	OPS	ERC	ERA
2007	NYM	NL	54	0	14	44.1	205	48	18	17	3	2	0	7	21	4	45	2	3	2	.600	0-0	10	86	.757	5.04	3.45
2008	NYM	NL	82	0	12	63.1	271	51	28	25	4	4	0	4	31	4	52	1	6	3	.667	0-3	18	89	.658	3.23	3.55
2009	Cle	AL	37	0	5	34.0	142	30	16	13	4	1	1	0	13	0	30	2	0	0	-	0-1	10	90	.707	3.49	3.44
2010	Cle	AL	53	0	7	40.0	170	30	18	17	4	1	0	1	24	2	32	0	2	2	.500	0-1	17	91	.659	3.53	3.83
2011	Cle	AL	71	0	13	67.0	267	52	16	15	1	2	2	2	21	1	45	2	3	3	.500	0-3	16	90	.541	2.19	2.01
2012	Cle	AL	72	0	12	67.0	278	53	27	22	4	1	1	2	25	4	53	1	7	4	.636	0-3	21	89	.594	2.60	2.96
2013	Cle	AL	70	0	20	63.0	259	54	17	16	5	3	0	3	23	2	54	3	6	2	.750	3-8	25	90	.643	3.23	2.29
2014	LAA	AL	76	0	26	74.2	285	45	16	15	4	3	0	6	15	3	68	4	7	2	.778	15-19	18	89	.491	1.47	1.81
2015	LAA	AL	70	0	13	65.1	271	64	26	26	4	2	1	2	19	4	57	1	5	5	.500	5-9	32	88	.684	3.36	3.58
2016	2 Tms		54	0	19	52.0	217	47	20	20	8	1	1	6	18	3	40	0	2	5	.286	6-9	7	88	.716	4.19	3.46
2017	2 Tms		59	0	3	54.0	214	46	20	20	4	1	1	1	10	1	71	0	3	0	1.000	1-2	21	89	.601	2.40	3.33
2018	Hou	AL	56	0	13	45.2	180	34	20	19	7	0	2	2	12	0	46	1	5	1	.833	0-2	11	88	.645	2.75	3.74
2019	Hou	AL	28	0	4	25.0	96	19	6	5	2	0	0	0	5	0	22	0	1	0	1.000	0-1	4	88	.569	2.04	1.80
16	2 Tms	AL	38	0	16	37.2	160	36	16	16	4	1	1	5	13	3	25	0	1	4	.200	6-9	6	88	.697	4.15	3.82
16	ChC	NL	16	0	3	14.1	57	11	4	4	4	0	0	1	5	0	15	0	1	1	.500	0-0	1	89	.769	4.20	2.51
17	Tor	AL	38	0	1	35.2	144	30	13	13	3	1	1	1	10	1	51	0	3	0	1.000	0-1	13	89	.623	2.78	3.28
17	Cle	AL	21	0	2	18.1	70	16	7	7	1	0	0	0	0	0	20	0	0	0	-	1-1	8	89	.557	1.72	3.44
	Postseason		8	0	3	5.1	20	2	1	1	1	0	0	0	1	1	6	0	0	1	.000	0-0	0	89	.413	0.89	1.69
	13 ML YEARS		782	0	161	695.1	2855	573	248	230	54	21	9	36	237	28	615	17	50	29	.633	30-61	210	89	.631	2.93	2.98

Josh A. Smith

Pitches: R Bats: R Pos: RP-16; SP-2 **Ht:** 6'2" **Wt:** 220 **Born:** 8/7/1987 **Age:** 32

			HOW MUCH PITCHED					WHAT HE GAVE UP											THE RESULTS						
Year	Team	Lg	G	GS	GF	IP	BFP	H	R	ER	HR	SH	SF	HB	TBB	IBB	SO	WP	W	L	Pct	Sv-Op	Hld	Vel	OPS	ERC	ERA
2019	Pwtckt	AAA	13	12	0	67.1	296	82	44	41	9	0	2	3	20	0	70	2	5	3	.625	0- -	-	-	.831	5.44	5.48
2015	Cin	NL	9	7	0	32.2	161	42	27	25	5	0	2	5	23	3	30	0	0	4	.000	0-0	0	90	.926	7.82	6.89
2016	Cin	NL	32	2	8	59.2	260	57	32	31	11	1	1	1	26	1	48	1	3	3	.500	0-0	1	91	.757	4.56	4.68
2017	Oak	AL	26	0	15	35.0	151	35	20	19	3	0	1	0	15	1	25	1	2	1	.667	0-0	1	91	.805	4.06	4.89
2019	Bos	AL	18	2	13	31.0	139	36	22	20	10	0	0	3	8	1	29	0	0	3	.000	1-2	0	91	.885	6.34	5.81
	4 ML YEARS		85	11	36	158.1	711	170	101	95	29	1	4	9	70	6	132	2	5	11	.313	1-2	2	91	.831	5.44	5.40

Josh D. Smith

Pitches: L Bats: L Pos: RP-14 **Ht:** 6'3" **Wt:** 200 **Born:** 10/11/1989 **Age:** 30

			HOW MUCH PITCHED					WHAT HE GAVE UP											THE RESULTS						
Year	Team	Lg	G	GS	GF	IP	BFP	H	R	ER	HR	SH	SF	HB	TBB	IBB	SO	WP	W	L	Pct	Sv-Op	Hld	Vel	OPS	ERC	ERA
2019	Clmbs	AAA	41	0	18	52.2	220	32	17	16	7	1	2	5	24	2	74	5	8	1	.889	6- -	-		.608	2.66	2.73
2019	2 Tms		14	0	6	12.2	64	11	9	9	0	0	1	3	11	2	14	0	0	0	-	0-0	0	91	.738	4.72	6.39
19	Cle	AL	8	0	3	8.1	43	8	5	5	0	0	0	2	8	1	12	0	0	0	-	0-0	0	91	.782	5.76	5.40
19	Mia	NL	6	0	3	4.1	21	3	4	4	0	0	1	1	3	1	2	0	0	0	-	0-0	0	90	.646	2.92	8.31

Kevan Smith

Bats: R Throws: R Pos: C-59;DH-6;PH-4;PR-2　　　　　　　　　Ht: 6'4" Wt: 240 Born: 6/28/1988 Age: 32

									BATTING												RUNNING			AVERAGES			
Year Team	Lg	G	AB	H	2B	3B	HR	(Hm	Rd)	TB	R	RBI	RC	TBB	IBB	SO	HBP	SH	SF	SB	CS	GDP	Avg	OBP	Slg	OPS
2016 CWS	AL	7	16	2	0	0	0	(0	0)	2	2	0	0	0	0	6	0	0	0	0	0	1	.125	.125	.125	.250
2017 CWS	AL	87	276	78	17	0	4	(4	0)	107	23	30	29	9	0	46	3	2	3	0	0	9	.283	.309	.388	.697
2018 CWS	AL	52	171	50	6	0	3	(1	2)	65	21	21	25	10	0	18	5	0	1	1	0	5	.292	.348	.380	.728
2019 LAA	AL	67	191	48	12	0	5	(1	4)	75	21	20	19	16	0	37	3	0	1	2	0	8	.251	.318	.393	.710
4 ML YEARS		213	654	178	35	0	12	(6	6)	249	67	71	73	35	0	107	11	2	5	3	0	23	.272	.318	.381	.698

Mallex Smith

Bats: L Throws: R Pos: CF-106;RF-28;LF-5;PH-2;DH-1;PR-1　　　　　　　Ht: 5'10" Wt: 180 Born: 5/6/1993 Age: 27

									BATTING												RUNNING			AVERAGES			
Year Team	Lg	G	AB	H	2B	3B	HR	(Hm	Rd)	TB	R	RBI	RC	TBB	IBB	SO	HBP	SH	SF	SB	CS	GDP	Avg	OBP	Slg	OPS
2019 Tacom	AAA	10	45	15	3	0	1	(-	-)	21	8	6	9	3	0	4	0	0	0	7	0	0	.333	.375	.467	.842
2016 Atl	NL	72	189	45	7	4	3	(0	3)	69	28	22	26	20	0	48	2	3	1	16	8	3	.238	.316	.365	.681
2017 TB	AL	81	256	69	8	4	2	(2	0)	91	33	12	30	23	0	62	0	2	1	16	5	2	.270	.329	.355	.684
2018 TB	AL	141	480	142	27	10	2	(1	1)	195	65	40	74	47	0	98	8	7	2	40	12	11	.296	.367	.406	.773
2019 Sea	AL	134	510	116	19	9	6	(4	2)	171	70	37	56	42	0	141	11	2	1	46	9	7	.227	.300	.335	.635
4 ML YEARS		428	1435	372	61	27	13	(7	6)	526	196	111	186	132	0	349	21	14	5	118	34	23	.259	.330	.367	.696

Will Smith

Pitches: L Bats: R Pos: RP-63　　　　　　　　　　　　　　　Ht: 6'5" Wt: 248 Born: 7/10/1989 Age: 30

			HOW MUCH PITCHED					WHAT HE GAVE UP										THE RESULTS						
Year Team	Lg	G	GS	GF	IP	BFP	H	R	ER	HR	SH	SF	HB	TBB	IBB	SO	WP	W	L	Pct	Sv-Op Hld	Vel	OPS	ERC	ERA
2012 KC	AL	16	16	0	89.2	396	111	54	53	12	2	5	1	33	1	59	4	6	9	.400	0-0 0	90	.853	5.75	5.32
2013 KC	AL	19	1	4	33.1	131	24	16	12	6	0	4	1	7	0	43	0	2	1	.667	0-3 6	91	.631	2.47	3.24
2014 Mil	NL	78	0	6	65.2	286	62	31	27	6	1	1	3	31	6	86	7	1	3	.250	1-6 30	93	.737	4.02	3.70
2015 Mil	NL	76	0	11	63.1	264	52	23	19	5	1	2	1	24	1	91	5	7	2	.778	0-4 20	93	.649	2.91	2.70
2016 2 Tms		53	0	4	40.1	167	31	19	15	3	1	1	1	18	1	48	3	2	4	.333	0-5 23	92	.637	2.92	3.35
2018 SF	NL	54	0	27	53.0	210	37	18	15	3	2	2	0	15	4	71	2	2	3	.400	14-18 6	93	.533	1.74	2.55
2019 SF	NL	63	0	52	65.1	257	46	20	20	10	0	1	0	21	2	96	3	6	0	1.000	34-38 0	93	.618	2.54	2.76
16 Mil	NL	27	0	3	22.0	92	18	13	9	3	1	1	1	9	1	22	3	1	3	.250	0-4 12	92	.708	3.48	3.68
16 SF	NL	26	0	1	18.1	75	13	6	6	0	0	0	0	9	0	26	0	1	1	.500	0-1 11	92	.551	2.26	2.95
Postseason		2	0	0	1.1	5	1	1	0	0	0	0	0	0	0	1	0	0	1	.000	0-1 0	93	.400	1.13	0.00
7 ML YEARS		359	17	104	410.2	1711	363	181	161	45	7	16	7	149	15	494	24	26	22	.542	49-74 85	92	.689	3.39	3.53

Will Smith

Bats: R Throws: R Pos: C-46;PH-7;DH-1　　　　　　　　　　Ht: 5'10" Wt: 195 Born: 3/28/1995 Age: 25

									BATTING												RUNNING			AVERAGES			
Year Team	Lg	G	AB	H	2B	3B	HR	(Hm	Rd)	TB	R	RBI	RC	TBB	IBB	SO	HBP	SH	SF	SB	CS	GDP	Avg	OBP	Slg	OPS
2019 OkCity	AAA	62	224	60	11	2	20	(-	-)	135	48	54	52	40	1	49	3	0	3	1	0	5	.268	.381	.603	.984
2019 LAD	NL	54	170	43	9	0	15	(7	8)	97	30	42	38	18	1	52	5	0	3	2	0	3	.253	.337	.571	.907

Dwight Smith Jr.

Bats: L Throws: R Pos: LF-86;PH-11;DH-7;PR-1　　　　　　　Ht: 6'0" Wt: 210 Born: 10/26/1992 Age: 27

									BATTING												RUNNING			AVERAGES			
Year Team	Lg	G	AB	H	2B	3B	HR	(Hm	Rd)	TB	R	RBI	RC	TBB	IBB	SO	HBP	SH	SF	SB	CS	GDP	Avg	OBP	Slg	OPS
2019 Norfolk	AAA	11	45	14	2	0	3	(-	-)	25	9	12	9	3	0	8	1	0	0	0	0	1	.311	.367	.556	.923
2017 Tor	AL	12	27	10	2	0	0	(0	0)	12	2	1	4	1	0	10	1	0	0	0	0	0	.370	.414	.444	.858
2018 Tor	AL	35	65	17	8	0	2	(1	1)	31	9	8	10	7	0	13	2	0	1	0	0	1	.262	.347	.477	.824
2019 Bal	AL	101	357	86	16	3	13	(7	6)	147	46	53	55	26	0	82	4	1	4	5	1	8	.241	.297	.412	.708
3 ML YEARS		148	449	113	26	3	15	(8	7)	190	57	62	69	34	0	105	7	1	5	6	1	9	.252	.311	.423	.734

Justin Smoak

Bats: B Throws: L Pos: 1B-89;DH-30;PH-3　　SMOKE　　　　Ht: 6'4" Wt: 220 Born: 12/5/1986 Age: 33

									BATTING												RUNNING			AVERAGES			
Year Team	Lg	G	AB	H	2B	3B	HR	(Hm	Rd)	TB	R	RBI	RC	TBB	IBB	SO	HBP	SH	SF	SB	CS	GDP	Avg	OBP	Slg	OPS
2010 2 Tms	AL	100	348	76	14	0	13	(4	9)	129	40	48	42	46	4	91	0	0	3	1	0	9	.218	.307	.371	.678
2011 Sea	AL	123	427	100	24	0	15	(10	5)	169	38	55	55	55	4	105	3	0	4	1	0	10	.234	.323	.396	.719
2012 Sea	AL	132	483	105	14	0	19	(4	15)	176	49	51	50	49	2	111	1	0	2	1	0	12	.217	.290	.364	.654
2013 Sea	AL	131	454	108	19	0	20	(9	11)	187	53	50	60	64	1	119	2	0	1	0	0	11	.238	.334	.412	.746
2014 Sea	AL	80	248	50	13	0	7	(4	3)	84	28	30	23	24	0	66	2	0	1	0	1	8	.202	.275	.339	.614
2015 Tor	AL	132	296	67	16	1	18	(8	10)	139	44	59	49	29	0	86	2	0	1	0	0	10	.226	.299	.470	.768
2016 Tor	AL	126	299	65	10	0	14	(10	4)	117	33	34	33	40	1	112	2	0	0	1	0	7	.217	.314	.391	.705
2017 Tor	AL	158	560	151	29	1	38	(19	19)	296	85	90	100	73	3	128	2	0	2	0	1	17	.270	.355	.529	.883
2018 Tor	AL	147	505	122	34	0	25	(11	14)	231	67	77	86	83	2	156	3	0	3	0	1	11	.242	.350	.457	.808
2019 Tor	AL	121	414	86	16	0	22	(13	9)	168	54	61	64	79	3	106	6	0	1	0	0	11	.208	.342	.406	.748
10 Tex	AL	70	235	49	10	0	8	(4	4)	83	29	34	30	38	4	57	0	0	2	1	0	6	.209	.316	.353	.670
10 Sea	AL	30	113	27	4	0	5	(0	5)	46	11	14	12	8	0	34	0	0	1	0	0	3	.239	.287	.407	.694
Postseason		11	10	0	0	0	0	(0	0)	0	0	0	0	0	0	5	0	0	0	0	0	0	.000	.000	.000	.000
10 ML YEARS		1250	4034	930	189	2	191	(92	99)	1696	491	555	562	542	20	1080	23	0	19	3	3	106	.231	.324	.420	.744

Drew Smyly

Pitches: L Bats: L Pos: SP-21; RP-4

SMY-lee

Ht: 6'3" Wt: 190 Born: 6/13/1989 Age: 31

Year	Team	Lg	HOW MUCH PITCHED					WHAT HE GAVE UP											THE RESULTS						
			G	GS	GF	IP	BFP	H	R	ER	HR	SH	SF	HB	TBB	IBB	SO	WP	W	L	Pct	Sv-Op	Hld	Vel	OPS	ERC	ERA
2012	Det	AL	23	18	0	99.1	416	93	49	44	12	2	3	2	33	1	94	3	4	3	.571	0-0	1	92	.732	3.68	3.99
2013	Det	AL	63	0	9	76.0	303	62	20	20	4	0	1	1	17	1	81	5	6	0	1.000	2-6	21	91	.601	2.21	2.37
2014	2 Tms	AL	28	25	0	153.0	618	136	57	55	18	1	3	1	42	2	133	8	9	10	.474	0-0	1	90	.688	3.17	3.24
2015	TB	AL	12	12	0	66.2	275	58	24	23	11	1	1	1	20	0	77	2	5	2	.714	0-0	0	90	.701	3.45	3.11
2016	TB	AL	30	30	0	175.1	738	174	103	95	32	5	11	2	49	2	167	10	7	12	.368	0-0	0	90	.763	4.13	4.88
2019	2 Tms	AL	25	21	1	114.0	514	126	83	79	32	2	2	2	55	0	120	7	4	7	.364	1-1	0	91	.916	6.49	6.24
14	Det	AL	21	18	0	105.1	445	111	48	46	14	0	3	1	31	1	89	4	6	9	.400	0-0	1	90	.770	4.26	3.93
14	TB	AL	7	7	0	47.2	173	25	9	9	4	1	0	0	11	1	44	4	3	1	.750	0-0	0	90	.476	1.28	1.70
19	Tex	AL	13	9	1	51.1	251	64	49	48	19	0	2	1	34	0	52	5	1	5	.167	1-1	0	91	1.021	8.95	8.42
19	Phi	NL	12	12	0	62.2	263	62	34	31	13	2	0	1	21	0	68	2	3	2	.600	0-0	0	92	.820	4.64	4.45
	Postseason		10	0	1	7.0	30	3	3	2	0	0	0	0	6	1	7	0	1	0	1.000	0-0	2	91	.467	1.81	2.57
6 ML YEARS			181	106	10	684.1	2864	649	336	316	109	11	21	9	216	6	672	35	35	34	.507	3-7	23	91	.745	3.91	4.16

Cy Sneed

Pitches: R Bats: R Pos: RP-8

Ht: 6'4" Wt: 215 Born: 10/1/1992 Age: 27

Year	Team	Lg	HOW MUCH PITCHED					WHAT HE GAVE UP											THE RESULTS						
			G	GS	GF	IP	BFP	H	R	ER	HR	SH	SF	HB	TBB	IBB	SO	WP	W	L	Pct	Sv-Op	Hld	Vel	OPS	ERC	ERA
2019	RdRck	AAA	19	9	6	81.2	333	71	40	38	13	4	4	3	24	0	71	2	7	6	.538	1- -	-	-	.717	3.53	4.19
2019	Hou	AL	8	0	4	21.1	93	26	13	13	5	1	0	0	5	0	23	0	0	1	.000	0-0	0	93	.866	5.64	5.48

Blake Snell

Pitches: L Bats: L Pos: SP-23

Ht: 6'4" Wt: 215 Born: 12/4/1992 Age: 27

Year	Team	Lg	HOW MUCH PITCHED					WHAT HE GAVE UP											THE RESULTS						
			G	GS	GF	IP	BFP	H	R	ER	HR	SH	SF	HB	TBB	IBB	SO	WP	W	L	Pct	Sv-Op	Hld	Vel	OPS	ERC	ERA
2016	TB	AL	19	19	0	89.0	401	93	44	35	5	2	2	0	51	0	98	6	6	8	.429	0-0	0	94	.728	4.69	3.54
2017	TB	AL	24	24	0	129.1	547	113	65	58	15	4	1	0	59	1	119	8	5	7	.417	0-0	0	94	.707	3.71	4.04
2018	TB	AL	31	31	0	180.2	700	112	41	38	16	2	3	1	64	2	221	13	21	5	.808	0-0	0	96	.554	1.95	1.89
2019	TB	AL	23	23	0	107.0	441	96	53	51	14	0	1	1	40	1	147	11	6	8	.429	0-0	0	96	.702	3.72	4.29
4 ML YEARS			97	97	0	506.0	2089	414	203	182	50	8	7	2	214	4	585	38	38	28	.576	0-0	0	95	.658	3.21	3.24

Chad Sobotka

Pitches: R Bats: R Pos: RP-32

Ht: 6'7" Wt: 225 Born: 7/10/1993 Age: 26

Year	Team	Lg	HOW MUCH PITCHED					WHAT HE GAVE UP											THE RESULTS						
			G	GS	GF	IP	BFP	H	R	ER	HR	SH	SF	HB	TBB	IBB	SO	WP	W	L	Pct	Sv-Op	Hld	Vel	OPS	ERC	ERA
2019	Gwnntt	AAA	17	0	5	20.2	90	23	11	11	3	0	0	2	4	0	32	1	2	1	.667	2- -	-	-	.715	4.54	4.79
2018	Atl	NL	14	0	5	14.1	58	5	3	3	2	1	0	0	9	2	21	3	1	0	1.000	0-0	1	97	.496	1.64	1.88
2019	Atl	NL	32	0	5	29.0	134	28	22	20	6	0	0	3	19	0	38	3	0	0	-	0-0	6	96	.820	6.19	6.21
	Postseason		3	0	1	2.1	13	2	4	3	1	0	1	0	4	0	0	0	0	0	-	0-0	1	97	1.087	11.75	11.57
2 ML YEARS			46	0	10	43.1	192	33	25	23	8	1	0	3	28	2	59	6	1	0	1.000	0-0	7	96	.723	4.47	4.78

Eric Sogard

Bats: L Throws: R Pos: 2B-74;DH-16;PH-13;3B-6;RF-6;SS-4;LF-1;PR-1

SO-guard

Ht: 5'10" Wt: 185 Born: 5/22/1986 Age: 34

Year	Team	Lg	BATTING																			RUNNING			AVERAGES			
			G	AB	H	2B	3B	HR	(Hm	Rd)	TB	R	RBI	RC	TBB	IBB	SO	HBP	SH	SF	SB	CS	GDP	Avg	OBP	Slg	OPS
2010	Oak	AL	4	7	3	0	0	0	(0	0)	3	0	0	1	2	0	1	0	0	0	0	1	0	.429	.556	.429	.984
2011	Oak	AL	27	70	14	3	0	2	(0	2)	23	7	4	3	6	0	13	0	0	0	0	2	0	.200	.243	.329	.572
2012	Oak	AL	37	102	17	3	1	2	(0	2)	28	8	7	7	5	0	17	0	1	0	2	0	1	.167	.206	.275	.480
2013	Oak	AL	130	368	98	24	3	2	(0	2)	134	45	35	43	27	2	51	1	5	4	10	5	4	.266	.322	.364	.686
2014	Oak	AL	117	291	65	10	0	1	(1	0)	78	38	22	27	31	0	37	1	4	2	11	4	6	.223	.298	.268	.567
2015	Oak	AL	120	372	92	12	3	1	(1	0)	113	40	37	36	23	1	50	2	3	1	6	1	9	.247	.294	.304	.598
2017	Mil	NL	94	249	68	15	1	3	(2	1)	94	37	18	37	45	2	37	4	1	0	3	3	7	.273	.393	.378	.770
2018	Mil	NL	55	97	13	3	0	0	(0	0)	16	7	2	2	12	1	23	2	1	0	3	0	3	.134	.241	.165	.406
2019	2 Tms	AL	110	396	115	23	2	13	(8	5)	181	59	40	67	38	2	63	2	3	3	8	0	4	.290	.353	.457	.810
19	Tor	AL	73	287	86	17	2	10	(6	4)	137	45	30	52	29	0	47	1	3	3	6	0	2	.300	.363	.477	.840
19	TB	AL	37	109	29	6	0	3	(2	1)	44	14	10	15	9	2	16	1	0	0	2	0	2	.266	.328	.404	.731
	Postseason		5	13	1	0	0	0	(0	0)	1	0	0	0	1	0	3	0	1	0	0	0	0	.077	.143	.077	.220
9 ML YEARS			694	1952	485	93	10	24	(12	12)	670	241	165	223	187	8	292	16	19	11	43	14	36	.248	.318	.343	.661

Nick Solak

Bats: R Throws: R Pos: DH-17;3B-11;2B-5;PH-1

Ht: 5'11" Wt: 190 Born: 1/11/1995 Age: 25

Year	Team	Lg	BATTING																			RUNNING			AVERAGES			
			G	AB	H	2B	3B	HR	(Hm	Rd)	TB	R	RBI	RC	TBB	IBB	SO	HBP	SH	SF	SB	CS	GDP	Avg	OBP	Slg	OPS
2019	Drham	AAA	85	301	80	13	1	17	(-	-)	146	56	47	53	39	0	80	4	0	4	3	2	8	.266	.353	.485	.838
2019	Nashv	AAA	30	118	41	6	0	10	(-	-)	77	23	27	28	6	0	25	2	1	1	2	0	0	.347	.386	.653	1.038
2019	Tex	AL	33	116	34	6	1	5	(3	2)	57	19	17	25	15	1	29	4	0	0	2	0	2	.293	.393	.491	.884

Donovan Solano

Bats: R **Throws:** R **Pos:** 2B-36;PH-33;SS-19;3B-2;DH-1   sol-ON-oh   **Ht:** 5'10" **Wt:** 205 **Born:** 12/17/1987 **Age:** 32

Year Team	Lg	G	AB	H	2B	3B	HR	(Hm Rd)	TB	R	RBI	RC	TBB	IBB	SO	HBP	SH	SF	SB	CS	GDP	Avg	OBP	Slg	OPS
2019 Scrmto	AAA	24	87	28	4	0	2	(- -)	38	12	16	15	9	0	11	1	0	0	0	0	2	.322	.392	.437	.829
2012 Mia	NL	93	285	84	11	3	2	(0 2)	107	29	28	35	21	1	58	2	3	5	7	0	5	.295	.342	.375	.717
2013 Mia	NL	102	361	90	13	1	3	(0 3)	114	33	34	38	23	3	57	7	2	2	3	1	11	.249	.305	.316	.621
2014 Mia	NL	111	310	78	11	1	3	(1 2)	100	26	28	35	19	0	61	3	7	1	1	2	5	.252	.300	.323	.623
2015 Mia	NL	55	90	17	3	1	0	(0 0)	22	6	7	3	1	0	18	2	1	0	0	0	4	.189	.215	.244	.459
2016 NYY	AL	9	22	5	2	0	1	(0 1)	10	5	2	3	1	0	3	0	0	0	0	0	0	.227	.261	.455	.715
2019 SF	NL	81	215	71	13	1	4	(0 4)	98	27	23	36	10	0	49	1	0	2	0	1	4	.330	.360	.456	.815
6 ML YEARS		451	1283	345	53	7	13	(1 12)	451	126	122	150	75	4	246	15	13	10	11	4	29	.269	.315	.352	.666

Yangervis Solarte

yahn-HAIR-vees so-LAHR-tay

Bats: B **Throws:** R **Pos:** 2B-10;LF-9;PH-9;SS-4;3B-2   **Ht:** 5'11" **Wt:** 205 **Born:** 7/3/1987 **Age:** 32

Year Team	Lg	G	AB	H	2B	3B	HR	(Hm Rd)	TB	R	RBI	RC	TBB	IBB	SO	HBP	SH	SF	SB	CS	GDP	Avg	OBP	Slg	OPS
2019 NewOr	AAA	15	51	16	2	1	1	(- -)	23	7	9	8	3	0	7	0	0	1	0	0	2	.314	.345	.451	.796
2014 2 Tms		131	469	122	19	1	10	(5 5)	173	56	48	59	53	1	58	4	3	6	0	1	13	.260	.336	.369	.705
2015 SD	NL	152	526	142	33	4	14	(5 9)	225	63	63	74	34	0	56	6	2	3	1	0	15	.270	.320	.428	.748
2016 SD	NL	109	405	116	26	1	15	(4 11)	189	55	71	68	30	1	63	5	0	3	1	1	7	.286	.341	.467	.808
2017 SD	NL	128	466	119	21	0	18	(8 10)	194	49	64	59	37	4	61	5	0	4	3	0	18	.255	.314	.416	.731
2018 Tor	AL	122	468	106	20	0	17	(12 5)	177	50	54	42	31	1	72	3	1	3	1	3	21	.226	.277	.378	.655
2019 SF	NL	28	73	15	5	0	1	(1 0)	23	9	7	5	4	1	16	0	1	0	0	0	4	.205	.247	.315	.562
14 NYY	AL	75	252	64	14	0	6	(3 3)	96	26	31	33	30	0	34	3	1	3	0	0	8	.254	.337	.381	.718
14 SD	NL	56	217	58	5	1	4	(2 2)	77	30	17	26	23	1	24	1	2	3	0	1	5	.267	.336	.355	.691
6 ML YEARS		670	2407	620	124	6	75	(35 40)	981	282	307	307	189	8	326	23	7	19	6	5	78	.258	.315	.408	.723

Jorge Soler

HOR-hay so-LAIR

Bats: R **Throws:** R **Pos:** DH-107;RF-56;PH-1   **Ht:** 6'4" **Wt:** 230 **Born:** 2/25/1992 **Age:** 28

Year Team	Lg	G	AB	H	2B	3B	HR	(Hm Rd)	TB	R	RBI	RC	TBB	IBB	SO	HBP	SH	SF	SB	CS	GDP	Avg	OBP	Slg	OPS
2014 ChC	NL	24	89	26	8	1	5	(1 4)	51	11	20	15	6	0	24	0	0	2	1	0	3	.292	.330	.573	.903
2015 ChC	NL	101	366	96	18	1	10	(7 3)	146	39	47	43	32	5	121	3	0	3	3	1	9	.262	.324	.399	.723
2016 ChC	NL	86	227	54	9	0	12	(6 6)	99	37	31	31	31	0	66	3	0	3	0	0	5	.238	.333	.436	.769
2017 KC	AL	35	97	14	5	0	2	(2 0)	25	7	6	5	12	1	36	1	0	0	0	0	5	.144	.245	.258	.503
2018 KC	AL	61	223	59	18	0	9	(4 5)	104	27	28	32	28	0	69	4	0	2	3	1	6	.265	.354	.466	.820
2019 KC	AL	162	589	156	33	1	48	(21 27)	335	95	117	109	73	3	178	10	0	4	3	1	16	.265	.354	.569	.922
Postseason		15	32	11	3	1	3	(2 1)	25	6	5	9	9	0	9	0	0	0	0	0	1	.344	.488	.781	1.269
6 ML YEARS		469	1591	405	91	3	86	(42 44)	760	216	249	235	182	9	494	21	0	14	10	3	44	.255	.336	.478	.814

Joakim Soria

Pitches: R **Bats:** R **Pos:** RP-70; SP-1   wah-KEEM SORE-ee-uh   **Ht:** 6'3" **Wt:** 200 **Born:** 5/18/1984 **Age:** 36

		HOW MUCH PITCHED					WHAT HE GAVE UP											THE RESULTS							
Year Team	Lg	G	GS	GF	IP	BFP	H	R	ER	HR	SH	SF	HB	TBB	IBB	SO	WP	W	L	Pct	Sv-Op	Hld	Vel	OPS	ERC	ERA
2007 KC	AL	62	0	38	69.0	270	46	20	19	3	1	3	1	19	3	75	2	2	3	.400	17-21	9	91	.510	1.63	2.48
2008 KC	AL	63	0	57	67.1	260	39	13	12	5	2	2	6	19	1	66	1	2	3	.400	42-45	0	91	.503	1.72	1.60
2009 KC	AL	47	0	41	53.0	222	44	14	13	5	1	2	2	16	1	69	3	3	2	.600	30-33	0	92	.614	2.80	2.21
2010 KC	AL	66	0	56	65.2	270	53	13	13	4	3	4	2	16	1	71	3	1	2	.333	43-46	0	92	.568	2.27	1.78
2011 KC	AL	60	0	47	60.1	256	60	29	27	7	3	2	2	17	0	60	1	5	5	.500	28-35	0	91	.709	3.80	4.03
2013 Tex	AL	26	0	9	23.2	101	18	10	10	2	1	0	1	14	2	28	2	1	0	1.000	0-0	6	91	.624	3.45	3.80
2014 2 Tms	AL	48	0	37	44.1	182	38	19	16	2	1	2	2	6	2	48	1	2	4	.333	18-20	1	90	.605	2.04	3.25
2015 2 Tms	AL	72	0	40	67.2	272	55	20	19	8	1	1	2	19	1	64	5	3	1	.750	24-30	11	92	.628	2.87	2.53
2016 KC	AL	70	0	18	66.2	293	70	31	30	10	4	2	2	27	0	68	2	5	8	.385	1-8	20	93	.800	4.86	4.05
2017 KC	AL	59	0	10	56.0	232	49	24	23	1	0	1	1	20	2	64	4	4	3	.571	1-8	20	93	.592	2.73	3.70
2018 2 Tms	AL	66	0	29	60.2	255	53	24	21	4	1	3	1	17	1	75	2	3	4	.429	16-21	13	92	.619	2.68	3.12
2019 Oak	AL	71	1	21	69.0	278	51	33	33	9	1	2	3	20	1	79	5	2	4	.333	1-6	21	93	.608	2.61	4.30
14 Tex	AL	35	0	32	33.1	133	25	12	10	0	1	1	1	4	1	42	0	1	3	.250	17-19	0	90	.521	1.38	2.70
14 Det	AL	13	0	5	11.0	49	13	7	6	2	0	1	1	2	1	6	1	1	1	.500	1-1	1	91	.838	4.92	4.91
15 Det	AL	43	0	35	41.0	165	32	13	13	8	1	0	2	11	1	36	0	3	1	.750	23-26	0	92	.665	3.15	2.85
15 Pit	NL	29	0	5	26.2	107	23	7	6	0	0	1	0	8	0	28	5	0	0	-	1-4	11	92	.571	2.39	2.03
18 CWS	AL	40	0	29	38.2	164	35	13	11	2	1	0	1	10	1	49	1	0	3	.000	16-19	2	92	.591	2.68	2.56
18 Mil	NL	26	0	0	22.0	91	18	11	10	2	0	0	0	6	0	26	1	3	1	.750	0-2	11	93	.668	2.69	4.09
Postseason		10	0	2	6.2	35	9	9	9	0	0	0	0	6	1	11	0	1	1	.500	0-1	1	93	.842	6.88	12.15
12 ML YEARS		710	1	403	703.1	2891	576	250	236	60	19	21	26	209	15	767	31	33	39	.458	221-273	101	92	.616	2.72	3.02

Mike Soroka

Pitches: R **Bats:** R **Pos:** SP-29   suh-ROH-kah   **Ht:** 6'5" **Wt:** 225 **Born:** 8/4/1997 **Age:** 22

		HOW MUCH PITCHED					WHAT HE GAVE UP											THE RESULTS							
Year Team	Lg	G	GS	GF	IP	BFP	H	R	ER	HR	SH	SF	HB	TBB	IBB	SO	WP	W	L	Pct	Sv-Op	Hld	Vel	OPS	ERC	ERA
2015 2 Tms	Low	10	9	0	34.0	143	33	14	12	0	0	0	4	5	0	37	1	0	2	.000	0- -	-	-	.585	2.70	3.18
2016 Rome	A	25	24	0	143.0	585	130	58	48	3	7	5	9	32	0	125	8	9	9	.500	0- -	-	-	.623	2.67	3.02
2017 Missi	AA	26	26	0	153.2	627	133	58	47	10	9	3	10	34	0	125	7	11	8	.579	0- -	-	-	.626	2.71	2.75
2018 Gwnntt	AAA	5	5	0	27.0	104	20	6	6	0	0	0		6	0	31	1	2	1	.667	0- -	-	-	.505	1.61	2.00
2018 Atl	NL	5	5	0	25.2	113	30	14	10	1	1	1	0	7	0	21	2	2	1	.667	0-0	0	93	.744	4.02	3.51
2019 Atl	NL	29	29	0	174.2	701	153	56	52	14	3	2	7	41	1	142	3	13	4	.765	0-0	0	92	.628	2.86	2.68
2 ML YEARS		34	34	0	200.1	814	183	70	62	15	4	3	7	48	1	163	5	15	5	.750	0-0	0	93	.644	3.00	2.79

Edmundo Sosa

Bats: R Throws: R Pos: PH-6;2B-4;PR-1   Ht: 5'11" Wt: 170 Born: 3/6/1996 Age: 24

Year	Team	Lg	G	AB	H	2B	3B	HR	(Hm	Rd)	TB	R	RBI	RC	TBB	IBB	SO	HBP	SH	SF	SB	CS	GDP	Avg	OBP	Slg	OPS
2019	Memp	AAA	118	453	132	18	5	17	(-	-)	211	70	62	71	17	0	96	16	4	6	2	3	9	.291	.335	.466	.801
2018	StL	NL	3	2	0	0	0	0	(0	0)	0	0	0	0	1	0	1	0	0	0	0	0	0	.000	.333	.000	.333
2019	StL	NL	8	8	2	0	0	0	(0	0)	2	2	0	1	1	0	2	1	0	0	1	0	0	.250	.400	.250	.650
	2 ML YEARS		11	10	2	0	0	0	(0	0)	2	3	0	1	2	0	3	1	0	0	1	0	0	.200	.385	.200	.585

Gregory Soto

Pitches: L Bats: L Pos: RP-26; SP-7   Ht: 6'1" Wt: 240 Born: 2/11/1995 Age: 25

Year	Team	Lg	G	GS	GF	IP	BFP	H	R	ER	HR	SH	SF	HB	TBB	IBB	SO	WP	W	L	Pct	Sv-Op	Hld	Vel	OPS	ERC	ERA
2019	Toledo	AAA	6	5	0	23.1	109	25	19	18	2	0	0	2	13	0	30	9	0	3	.000	0- -	-		.761	5.27	6.94
2019	Det	AL	33	7	9	57.2	276	74	39	37	9	0	3	0	33	1	45	5	0	5	.000	0-1	2	95	.884	6.86	5.77

Juan Soto

Bats: L Throws: L Pos: LF-150   Ht: 6'1" Wt: 185 Born: 10/25/1998 Age: 21

Year	Team	Lg	G	AB	H	2B	3B	HR	(Hm	Rd)	TB	R	RBI	RC	TBB	IBB	SO	HBP	SH	SF	SB	CS	GDP	Avg	OBP	Slg	OPS
2018	Was	NL	116	414	121	25	1	22	(6	16)	214	77	70	73	79	10	99	0	1	0	5	2	9	.292	.406	.517	.923
2019	Was	NL	150	542	153	32	5	34	(18	16)	297	110	110	117	108	3	132	3	0	6	12	1	11	.282	.401	.548	.949
	2 ML YEARS		266	956	274	57	6	56	(24	32)	511	187	180	190	187	13	231	3	1	6	17	3	20	.287	.403	.535	.937

Steven Souza Jr.

Bats: R Throws: R Pos: OF   SOO-zuh   Ht: 6'4" Wt: 225 Born: 4/24/1989 Age: 31

Year	Team	Lg	G	AB	H	2B	3B	HR	(Hm	Rd)	TB	R	RBI	RC	TBB	IBB	SO	HBP	SH	SF	SB	CS	GDP	Avg	OBP	Slg	OPS
2014	Was	NL	21	23	3	0	0	2	(1	1)	9	2	2	1	3	0	7	0	0	0	0	0	1	.130	.231	.391	.622
2015	TB	AL	110	373	84	15	1	16	(6	10)	149	59	40	40	46	0	144	5	1	1	12	6	7	.225	.318	.399	.717
2016	TB	AL	120	430	106	17	1	17	(7	10)	176	58	49	53	31	0	159	4	0	2	7	6	5	.247	.303	.409	.713
2017	TB	AL	148	523	125	21	2	30	(14	16)	240	78	78	85	84	2	179	7	2	1	16	4	9	.239	.351	.459	.810
2018	Ari	NL	72	241	53	15	3	5	(3	2)	89	21	29	29	28	0	75	3	0	0	6	1	4	.220	.309	.369	.678
	5 ML YEARS		471	1590	371	68	7	70	(31	39)	663	218	198	208	192	2	564	20	3	4	41	17	26	.233	.323	.417	.740

Cory Spangenberg

Bats: L Throws: R Pos: 2B-22;3B-6;SS-4;LF-3;PH-2;PR-1   SPAN-jen-burg   Ht: 6'0" Wt: 195 Born: 3/16/1991 Age: 29

Year	Team	Lg	G	AB	H	2B	3B	HR	(Hm	Rd)	TB	R	RBI	RC	TBB	IBB	SO	HBP	SH	SF	SB	CS	GDP	Avg	OBP	Slg	OPS
2019	SnAnt	AAA	113	424	131	28	5	14	(-	-)	211	82	62	84	43	0	136	6	0	3	28	4	3	.309	.378	.498	.876
2014	SD	NL	20	62	18	2	1	2	(1	1)	28	7	9	9	2	0	14	0	1	0	4	2	1	.290	.313	.452	.764
2015	SD	NL	108	303	82	17	5	4	(3	1)	121	38	21	40	28	1	75	2	8	3	9	4	4	.271	.333	.399	.733
2016	SD	NL	14	48	11	1	1	1	(0	1)	17	6	8	7	4	0	13	1	0	0	1	0	0	.229	.302	.354	.656
2017	SD	NL	129	444	117	18	2	13	(6	7)	178	57	49	58	34	1	128	5	2	1	11	3	2	.264	.322	.401	.723
2018	SD	NL	116	298	70	9	4	7	(5	2)	108	35	25	32	25	0	108	2	4	0	6	1	6	.235	.298	.362	.661
2019	Mil	NL	32	95	22	2	2	2	(1	1)	34	11	10	10	6	1	36	0	1	0	3	0	1	.232	.277	.358	.635
	6 ML YEARS		419	1250	320	49	15	29	(16	13)	486	154	119	156	99	3	374	10	16	4	34	10	14	.256	.315	.389	.704

Glenn Sparkman

Pitches: R Bats: B Pos: SP-23; RP-8   Ht: 6'2" Wt: 210 Born: 5/11/1992 Age: 28

Year	Team	Lg	G	GS	GF	IP	BFP	H	R	ER	HR	SH	SF	HB	TBB	IBB	SO	WP	W	L	Pct	Sv-Op	Hld	Vel	OPS	ERC	ERA
2017	Tor	AL	2	0	1	1.0	12	9	7	7	0	0	0	0	1	0	1	0	0	0	-	0-0	0	94	1.924	79.03	63.00
2018	KC	AL	15	3	3	38.1	176	47	20	19	3	0	5	1	15	3	27	3	0	3	.000	0-0	0	94	.816	5.08	4.46
2019	KC	AL	31	23	2	136.0	606	164	96	91	30	1	4	6	41	1	81	6	4	11	.267	0-0	0	93	.876	5.94	6.02
	3 ML YEARS		48	26	6	175.1	794	220	123	117	33	1	9	7	57	4	109	9	4	14	.222	0-0	0	94	.879	6.05	6.01

Gabe Speier

Pitches: L Bats: L Pos: RP-9   Ht: 6'0" Wt: 175 Born: 4/12/1995 Age: 25

Year	Team	Lg	G	GS	GF	IP	BFP	H	R	ER	HR	SH	SF	HB	TBB	IBB	SO	WP	W	L	Pct	Sv-Op	Hld	Vel	OPS	ERC	ERA
2019	NWArk	AA	17	0	12	22.1	101	20	10	6	2	1	2	3	9	0	28	1	1	1	.500	5- -	-	-	.657	3.77	2.42
2019	Omha	AAA	30	0	12	40.0	176	41	29	25	10	0	2	1	17	4	45	2	0	4	.000	1- -	-	-	.848	5.33	5.63
2019	KC	AL	9	0	1	7.1	33	5	6	6	2	0	0	6	6	0	10	1	0	0	-	0-0	1	95	.778	5.10	7.36

George Springer

Bats: R Throws: R Pos: CF-75;RF-59;DH-13;PH-3   Ht: 6'3" Wt: 215 Born: 9/19/1989 Age: 30

Year	Team	Lg	G	AB	H	2B	3B	HR	(Hm	Rd)	TB	R	RBI	RC	TBB	IBB	SO	HBP	SH	SF	SB	CS	GDP	Avg	OBP	Slg	OPS
2014	Hou	AL	78	295	68	8	1	20	(5	15)	138	45	51	45	39	4	114	9	0	2	5	2	4	.231	.336	.468	.804
2015	Hou	AL	102	388	107	19	2	16	(9	7)	178	59	41	60	50	0	109	8	2	3	16	4	4	.276	.367	.459	.826
2016	Hou	AL	162	644	168	29	5	29	(13	16)	294	116	82	100	88	2	178	11	0	1	9	10	12	.261	.359	.457	.815
2017	Hou	AL	140	548	155	29	0	34	(16	18)	286	112	85	99	64	1	111	10	0	4	5	7	11	.283	.367	.522	.889

Year	Team	Lg	G	AB	H	2B	3B	HR	(Hm	Rd)	TB	R	RBI	RC	TBB	IBB	SO	HBP	SH	SF	SB	CS	GDP	Avg	OBP	Slg	OPS
2018	Hou	AL	140	544	144	26	0	22	(12	10)	236	102	71	84	64	0	122	5	0	3	6	4	12	.265	.346	.434	.780
2019	Hou	AL	122	479	140	20	3	39	(18	21)	283	96	96	103	67	1	113	6	0	4	6	2	12	.292	.383	.591	.974
	Postseason		32	130	40	10	0	11	(5	6)	83	24	20	30	17	1	37	0	0	0	1	0	2	.308	.388	.638	1.026
	6 ML YEARS		744	2898	782	131	11	160	(73	87)	1415	530	426	491	372	8	747	50	2	17	47	29	55	.270	.361	.488	.849

Jeffrey Springs

Pitches: L **Bats:** L **Pos:** RP-25   **Ht:** 6'3" **Wt:** 180 **Born:** 9/20/1992 **Age:** 27

			HOW MUCH PITCHED					WHAT HE GAVE UP										THE RESULTS						
Year	Team	Lg	G	GS	GF	IP	BFP	H	R	ER	HR	SH	SF	HB	TBB	IBB	SO	WP	W	L	Pct	Sv-Op	Hld	Vel	OPS	ERC	ERA
2019	Nashv	AAA	6	0	4	7.0	26	6	4	3	1	1	0	0	0	0	12	0	3	0	1.000	0- -	-	-	.760	2.15	3.86
2018	Tex	AL	18	2	4	32.0	141	32	14	12	4	1	0	1	14	1	31	3	1	1	.500	0-1	2	91	.744	4.44	3.38
2019	Tex	AL	25	0	7	32.1	155	38	23	23	4	0	2	0	23	0	32	0	4	1	.800	0-0	1	92	.884	6.57	6.40
	2 ML YEARS		43	2	11	64.1	296	70	37	35	8	1	2	1	37	1	63	3	5	2	.714	0-1	3	92	.816	5.49	4.90

Locke St. John

Pitches: L **Bats:** L **Pos:** RP-7   **Ht:** 6'3" **Wt:** 180 **Born:** 1/31/1993 **Age:** 27

			HOW MUCH PITCHED					WHAT HE GAVE UP										THE RESULTS						
Year	Team	Lg	G	GS	GF	IP	BFP	H	R	ER	HR	SH	SF	HB	TBB	IBB	SO	WP	W	L	Pct	Sv-Op	Hld	Vel	OPS	ERC	ERA
2019	Frisco	AA	22	0	15	29.2	121	21	8	5	2	3	0	1	13	0	42	1	3	2	.600	4- -	-	-	.585	2.62	1.52
2019	Nashv	AAA	17	0	3	19.2	87	19	19	19	4	0	1	0	11	2	23	2	2	2	.500	0- -	-	-	.874	5.41	8.69
2019	Tex	AL	7	0	4	6.2	33	7	4	4	0	0	0	0	4	0	5	0	0	0	-	0-0	2	90	.678	3.97	5.40

Jacob Stallings

Bats: R **Throws:** R **Pos:** C-61;PH-10;PR-1   **Ht:** 6'4" **Wt:** 220 **Born:** 12/22/1989 **Age:** 30

			BATTING																				RUNNING			AVERAGES			
Year	Team	Lg	G	AB	H	2B	3B	HR	(Hm	Rd)	TB	R	RBI	RC	TBB	IBB	SO	HBP	SH	SF	SB	CS	GDP	Avg	OBP	Slg	OPS
2019	Indy	AAA	15	51	14	9	0	2	(-	-)	29	11	7	10	4	0	9	4	0	2	0	0	0	.275	.361	.569	.929
2016	Pit	NL	5	15	6	1	0	0	(0	0)	7	0	2	3	0	0	4	0	0	0	1	0	0	.400	.400	.467	.867
2017	Pit	NL	5	14	5	2	0	0	(0	0)	7	3	3	3	2	1	2	0	0	0	0	0	0	.357	.438	.500	.938
2018	Pit	NL	14	37	8	0	0	0	(0	0)	8	2	5	3	3	0	9	0	0	1	0	0	0	.216	.268	.216	.485
2019	Pit	NL	71	191	50	5	0	6	(1	5)	73	26	13	18	16	5	40	2	1	0	0	0	3	.262	.325	.382	.708
	4 ML YEARS		95	257	69	8	0	6	(1	5)	95	31	23	27	21	6	55	2	1	1	1	0	5	.268	.327	.370	.697

Eric Stamets

Bats: R **Throws:** R **Pos:** SS-15   STAY-mets   **Ht:** 6'0" **Wt:** 190 **Born:** 9/25/1991 **Age:** 28

			BATTING																				RUNNING			AVERAGES			
Year	Team	Lg	G	AB	H	2B	3B	HR	(Hm	Rd)	TB	R	RBI	RC	TBB	IBB	SO	HBP	SH	SF	SB	CS	GDP	Avg	OBP	Slg	OPS
2019	Clmbs	AAA	90	295	72	10	5	6	(-	-)	110	40	38	38	27	0	83	3	0	2	14	1	1	.244	.312	.373	.685
2019	Cle	AL	15	41	2	1	0	0	(0	0)	3	4	2	0	5	0	24	0	1	1	0	0	2	.049	.149	.073	.222

Craig Stammen

Pitches: R **Bats:** R **Pos:** RP-76   STAMM-enn   **Ht:** 6'4" **Wt:** 230 **Born:** 3/9/1984 **Age:** 36

			HOW MUCH PITCHED					WHAT HE GAVE UP										THE RESULTS						
Year	Team	Lg	G	GS	GF	IP	BFP	H	R	ER	HR	SH	SF	HB	TBB	IBB	SO	WP	W	L	Pct	Sv-Op	Hld	Vel	OPS	ERC	ERA
2009	Was	NL	19	19	0	105.2	448	112	67	60	14	4	3	3	24	1	48	7	4	7	.364	0-0	0	89	.774	4.03	5.11
2010	Was	NL	35	19	3	128.0	562	151	78	73	13	5	6	1	41	4	85	3	4	4	.500	0-0	1	90	.814	4.79	5.13
2011	Was	NL	7	0	2	10.1	38	3	1	1	0	0	0	0	4	0	12	1	1	1	.500	0-0	0	91	.272	0.67	0.87
2012	Was	NL	59	0	15	88.1	370	70	27	23	7	5	1	2	36	4	87	3	6	1	.857	1-2	10	92	.636	2.84	2.34
2013	Was	NL	55	0	14	81.2	339	78	30	25	4	8	4	2	27	3	79	2	7	6	.538	0-1	7	92	.682	3.32	2.76
2014	Was	NL	49	0	15	72.2	304	78	34	31	5	3	1	3	14	2	56	1	4	5	.444	0-0	7	92	.708	3.61	3.84
2015	Was	NL	5	0	4	4.0	17	2	0	0	0	0	1	0	3	1	3	0	0	0	-	0-0	2	92	.525	1.66	0.00
2017	SD	NL	60	0	9	80.1	329	68	29	28	12	2	0	2	28	3	74	2	2	3	.400	0-2	11	92	.684	3.46	3.14
2018	SD	NL	73	0	7	79.0	317	65	25	24	3	2	1	3	17	3	88	3	8	3	.727	0-5	23	92	.583	2.17	2.73
2019	SD	NL	76	0	12	82.0	339	80	36	30	13	0	3	2	15	2	73	0	8	7	.533	4-13	31	93	.719	3.51	3.29
	Postseason		6	0	0	7.0	34	8	4	4	1	1	1	3	2	0	5	0	0	0	-	0-0	1	91	.912	6.41	5.14
	10 ML YEARS		438	38	77	732.0	3063	707	327	295	71	29	20	18	209	23	605	22	44	37	.543	5-23	93	91	.705	3.48	3.63

Ryne Stanek

Pitches: R **Bats:** R **Pos:** RP-36; SP-27   **Ht:** 6'4" **Wt:** 225 **Born:** 7/26/1991 **Age:** 28

			HOW MUCH PITCHED					WHAT HE GAVE UP										THE RESULTS						
Year	Team	Lg	G	GS	GF	IP	BFP	H	R	ER	HR	SH	SF	HB	TBB	IBB	SO	WP	W	L	Pct	Sv-Op	Hld	Vel	OPS	ERC	ERA
2017	TB	AL	21	0	4	20.0	95	26	13	13	6	0	1	0	12	2	29	4	0	0	-	0-1	4	98	.985	8.31	5.85
2018	TB	AL	59	29	10	66.1	263	45	23	22	8	0	1	0	27	1	81	5	2	3	.400	0-0	8	98	.618	2.64	2.98
2019	2 Tms		63	27	12	77.0	327	61	39	34	11	0	3	0	39	3	89	5	0	4	.000	1-5	7	98	.688	3.56	3.97
19	TB	AL	41	27	3	55.2	228	44	24	21	7	0	2	0	20	1	61	2	0	2	.000	0-0	2	98	.654	2.93	3.40
19	Mia	NL	22	0	9	21.1	99	17	15	13	4	0	1	0	19	2	28	3	0	2	.000	1-5	5	98	.769	5.31	5.48
	3 ML YEARS		143	56	26	163.1	685	132	75	69	25	0	4	1	78	6	199	14	2	7	.222	1-6	19	98	.702	3.67	3.80

Giancarlo Stanton

Bats: R **Throws:** R **Pos:** LF-10;DH-5;RF-3   john-CAHR-loh   **Ht:** 6'6" **Wt:** 245 **Born:** 11/8/1989 **Age:** 30

Year	Team	Lg	G	AB	H	2B	3B	HR	(Hm	Rd)	TB	R	RBI	RC	TBB	IBB	SO	HBP	SH	SF	SB	CS	GDP	Avg	OBP	Slg	OPS
2010	Fla	NL	100	359	93	21	1	22	(7	15)	182	45	59	56	34	6	123	2	0	1	5	2	7	.259	.326	.507	.833
2011	Fla	NL	150	516	135	30	5	34	(16	18)	277	79	87	81	70	6	166	9	0	6	5	5	11	.262	.356	.537	.893
2012	Mia	NL	123	449	130	30	1	37	(16	21)	273	75	86	79	46	9	143	5	0	1	6	2	5	.290	.361	.608	.969
2013	Mia	NL	116	425	106	26	0	24	(15	9)	204	62	62	66	74	5	140	4	0	1	1	0	10	.249	.365	.480	.845
2014	Mia	NL	145	539	155	31	1	37	(24	13)	299	89	105	109	94	24	170	3	0	2	13	1	16	.288	.395	.555	.950
2015	Mia	NL	74	279	74	12	1	27	(13	14)	169	47	67	54	34	6	95	2	0	3	4	2	5	.265	.346	.606	.952
2016	Mia	NL	119	413	99	20	1	27	(13	14)	202	56	74	56	50	5	140	4	0	2	0	0	6	.240	.326	.489	.815
2017	Mia	NL	159	597	168	32	0	59	(31	28)	377	123	132	117	85	13	163	7	0	3	2	2	13	.281	.376	.631	1.007
2018	NYY	AL	158	617	164	34	1	38	(20	18)	314	102	100	98	70	5	211	8	0	10	5	0	17	.266	.343	.509	.852
2019	NYY	AL	18	59	17	3	0	3	(2	1)	29	8	13	14	12	0	24	0	0	1	0	0	1	.288	.403	.492	.894
	Postseason		5	21	5	0	0	1	(1	0)	8	4	1	1	1	0	7	0	0	0	1	0	1	.238	.273	.381	.654
	10 ML YEARS		1162	4253	1141	239	11	308	(157	151)	2326	686	785	730	569	79	1375	44	0	30	41	14	91	.268	.358	.547	.905

Bubba Starling

Bats: R **Throws:** R **Pos:** CF-36;RF-23;LF-6;PH-2   **Ht:** 6'4" **Wt:** 215 **Born:** 8/3/1992 **Age:** 27

Year	Team	Lg	G	AB	H	2B	3B	HR	(Hm	Rd)	TB	R	RBI	RC	TBB	IBB	SO	HBP	SH	SF	SB	CS	GDP	Avg	OBP	Slg	OPS
2019	Omha	AAA	72	261	81	11	2	7	(-	-)	117	34	38	43	21	0	59	0	0	3	9	3	3	.310	.358	.448	.806
2019	KC	AL	56	186	40	7	0	4	(1	3)	59	26	12	10	9	0	56	1	1	0	2	0	4	.215	.255	.317	.572

Cody Stashak

Pitches: R **Bats:** R **Pos:** RP-17; SP-1   **Ht:** 6'2" **Wt:** 169 **Born:** 6/4/1994 **Age:** 26

Year	Team	Lg	G	GS	GF	IP	BFP	H	R	ER	HR	SH	SF	HB	TBB	IBB	SO	WP	W	L	Pct	Sv-Op	Hld	Vel	OPS	ERC	ERA
2019	Pnscla	AA	19	0	11	28.1	120	28	25	15	4	1	0	2	5	0	40	0	2	3	.400	4--	-	-	.794	3.61	4.76
2019	Roch	AAA	14	2	5	25.0	97	17	5	4	1	0	1	0	4	0	34	0	5	0	1.000	0--	-	-	.510	1.38	1.44
2019	Min	AL	18	1	4	25.0	104	29	9	9	3	0	1	1	1	0	25	0	0	1	.000	0-0	1	92	.773	3.82	3.24

Max Stassi

Bats: R **Throws:** R **Pos:** C-46;1B-3;DH-1;PH-1   STASS-ee   **Ht:** 5'10" **Wt:** 200 **Born:** 3/15/1991 **Age:** 29

Year	Team	Lg	G	AB	H	2B	3B	HR	(Hm	Rd)	TB	R	RBI	RC	TBB	IBB	SO	HBP	SH	SF	SB	CS	GDP	Avg	OBP	Slg	OPS
2013	Hou	AL	3	7	2	0	0	0	(0	0)	2	0	1	0	0	0	2	1	0	0	0	0	1	.286	.375	.286	.661
2014	Hou	AL	7	20	7	2	0	0	(0	0)	9	2	4	4	0	0	6	0	0	0	0	0	0	.350	.350	.450	.800
2015	Hou	AL	11	15	6	0	0	1	(1	0)	9	4	2	3	1	0	5	0	1	0	0	0	1	.400	.438	.600	1.038
2016	Hou	AL	9	13	1	0	0	0	(0	0)	1	1	0	0	0	0	5	0	0	0	0	0	0	.077	.077	.077	.154
2017	Hou	AL	14	24	4	1	0	2	(1	1)	11	5	4	3	6	0	4	0	0	1	0	0	0	.167	.323	.458	.781
2018	Hou	AL	88	221	50	13	0	8	(1	7)	87	28	27	33	23	0	74	6	0	0	0	0	6	.226	.316	.394	.710
2019	2 Tms	AL	51	132	18	1	0	1	(0	1)	22	7	5	2	12	0	49	1	0	2	0	0	3	.136	.211	.167	.378
19	Hou	AL	31	90	15	1	0	1	(0	1)	19	4	3	2	7	0	34	1	0	0	0	0	1	.167	.235	.211	.446
19	LAA	AL	20	42	3	0	0	0	(0	0)	3	3	2	0	5	0	15	0	0	2	0	0	2	.071	.163	.071	.235
	7 ML YEARS		183	432	88	17	0	12	(3	9)	141	47	43	45	42	0	145	8	1	3	0	0	13	.204	.285	.326	.611

Josh Staumont

Pitches: R **Bats:** R **Pos:** RP-16   **Ht:** 6'3" **Wt:** 200 **Born:** 12/21/1993 **Age:** 26

Year	Team	Lg	G	GS	GF	IP	BFP	H	R	ER	HR	SH	SF	HB	TBB	IBB	SO	WP	W	L	Pct	Sv-Op	Hld	Vel	OPS	ERC	ERA
2019	Omha	AAA	32	12	11	51.1	221	31	21	18	4	0	1	3	37	1	74	3	1	5	.167	2--	-	-	.616	3.17	3.16
2019	KC	AL	16	0	7	19.1	88	21	13	8	4	0	0	1	10	1	15	0	0	0	-	0-1	0	96	.870	6.01	3.72

Drew Steckenrider

Pitches: R **Bats:** R **Pos:** RP-15   **Ht:** 6'5" **Wt:** 215 **Born:** 1/10/1991 **Age:** 29

Year	Team	Lg	G	GS	GF	IP	BFP	H	R	ER	HR	SH	SF	HB	TBB	IBB	SO	WP	W	L	Pct	Sv-Op	Hld	Vel	OPS	ERC	ERA
2017	Mia	NL	37	0	7	34.2	151	30	13	9	4	0	1	0	18	1	54	1	1	1	.500	1-1	10	95	.674	3.80	2.34
2018	Mia	NL	71	0	17	64.2	272	55	29	28	7	0	1	2	27	5	74	0	4	4	.500	5-10	19	95	.664	3.39	3.90
2019	Mia	NL	15	0	4	14.1	58	9	10	10	6	0	0	1	5	0	14	0	0	2	.000	0-1	3	95	.778	4.00	6.28
	3 ML YEARS		123	0	28	113.2	481	94	52	47	17	0	2	3	50	6	142	1	5	7	.417	6-12	32	95	.681	3.62	3.72

Robert Stephenson

Pitches: R **Bats:** R **Pos:** RP-57   **Ht:** 6'3" **Wt:** 215 **Born:** 2/24/1993 **Age:** 27

Year	Team	Lg	G	GS	GF	IP	BFP	H	R	ER	HR	SH	SF	HB	TBB	IBB	SO	WP	W	L	Pct	Sv-Op	Hld	Vel	OPS	ERC	ERA
2016	Cin	NL	8	8	0	37.0	170	41	26	25	9	0	0	4	19	1	31	2	2	3	.400	0-0	0	93	.893	6.78	6.08
2017	Cin	NL	25	11	6	84.2	383	81	52	44	12	5	6	2	53	3	86	5	5	6	.455	1-1	0	94	.805	5.06	4.68
2018	Cin	NL	4	3	0	11.2	63	17	12	12	2	0	1	0	12	3	11	2	0	2	.000	0-0	0	93	1.040	9.71	9.26
2019	Cin	NL	57	0	16	64.2	262	43	30	27	9	0	1	0	24	4	81	3	3	2	.600	0-4	11	95	.634	2.33	3.76
	4 ML YEARS		94	22	22	198.0	878	182	120	108	32	5	8	6	108	11	209	12	10	13	.435	1-5	11	94	.786	4.64	4.91

Andrew Stevenson

Bats: L Throws: L Pos: PH-25;LF-5   Ht: 6'0" Wt: 192 Born: 6/1/1994 Age: 26

Year	Team	Lg	G	AB	H	2B	3B	HR	(Hm	Rd)	TB	R	RBI	RC	TBB	IBB	SO	HBP	SH	SF	SB	CS	GDP	Avg	OBP	Slg	OPS
2019	Fresno	AAA	73	302	101	17	8	6	(-	-)	152	50	44	58	24	0	76	1	4	2	10	4	8	.334	.383	.503	.886
2019	Hrsbrg	AA	20	84	21	4	0	1	(-	-)	28	12	5	8	3	0	24	1	0	0	3	0	0	.250	.284	.333	.617
2017	Was	NL	37	57	9	2	0	0	(0	0)	11	5	1	1	7	0	20	1	0	2	1	0	0	.158	.250	.193	.443
2018	Was	NL	57	75	19	2	0	1	(1	0)	24	9	13	11	6	0	23	1	1	3	1	1	0	.253	.306	.320	.626
2019	Was	NL	30	30	11	1	1	0	(0	0)	14	4	0	6	6	0	11	1	0	0	0	1	1	.367	.486	.467	.953
	3 ML YEARS		124	162	39	5	1	1	(1	0)	49	18	14	18	19	0	54	2	3	3	2	2	1	.241	.323	.302	.625

Brock Stewart

Pitches: R Bats: L Pos: RP-13   Ht: 6'3" Wt: 215 Born: 10/3/1991 Age: 28

Year	Team	Lg	G	GS	GF	IP	BFP	H	R	ER	HR	SH	SF	HB	TBB	IBB	SO	WP	W	L	Pct	Sv-Op	Hld	Vel	OPS	ERC	ERA
2019	OkCity	AAA	17	16	0	76.0	365	97	67	62	19	0	3	9	40	0	67	7	5	7	.417	0--	-	-	.981	8.07	7.34
2016	LAD	NL	7	5	0	28.0	126	33	18	18	7	1	0	0	12	1	25	0	2	2	.500	0-0	0	93	.856	6.34	5.79
2017	LAD	NL	17	4	8	34.1	147	28	13	13	4	2	1	1	19	2	29	0	0	0	-	1-1	1	93	.678	3.82	3.41
2018	LAD	NL	9	2	3	17.2	90	23	15	12	4	1	1	2	9	3	14	1	0	1	.000	0-1	0	91	.913	7.13	6.11
2019	2 Tms		13	0	1	25.2	124	37	29	28	11	0	4	3	8	0	19	2	4	0	1.000	0-0	0	92	1.121	9.53	9.82
19	LAD	NL	3	0	1	4.0	21	9	8	8	2	0	2	0	2	0	3	1	0	0	-	0-0	0	93	1.524	18.37	18.00
19	Tor	AL	10	0	0	21.2	103	28	21	20	9	0	2	3	6	0	16	1	4	0	1.000	0-0	0	91	1.044	8.14	8.31
	4 ML YEARS		46	11	12	105.2	487	121	80	71	26	4	6	6	48	6	87	3	6	3	.667	1-2	1	92	.882	6.34	6.05

Christin Stewart

Bats: L Throws: R Pos: LF-89;DH-12;PH-4;PR-1   Ht: 6'0" Wt: 205 Born: 12/10/1993 Age: 26

Year	Team	Lg	G	AB	H	2B	3B	HR	(Hm	Rd)	TB	R	RBI	RC	TBB	IBB	SO	HBP	SH	SF	SB	CS	GDP	Avg	OBP	Slg	OPS
2019	Toledo	AAA	22	83	24	2	0	4	(-	-)	38	14	14	17	18	1	25	1	0	0	1	0	3	.289	.422	.458	.879
2018	Det	AL	17	60	16	1	1	2	(2	0)	25	7	10	13	10	0	13	1	0	1	0	0	1	.267	.375	.417	.792
2019	Det	AL	104	369	86	25	1	10	(3	7)	143	32	40	42	34	3	103	7	0	6	0	1	4	.233	.305	.388	.693
	2 ML YEARS		121	429	102	26	2	12	(5	7)	168	39	50	55	44	3	116	8	0	7	0	1	5	.238	.316	.392	.707

D.J. Stewart

Bats: L Throws: R Pos: RF-26;LF-11;PH-6;DH-3;PR-3   Ht: 6'0" Wt: 230 Born: 11/30/1993 Age: 26

Year	Team	Lg	G	AB	H	2B	3B	HR	(Hm	Rd)	TB	R	RBI	RC	TBB	IBB	SO	HBP	SH	SF	SB	CS	GDP	Avg	OBP	Slg	OPS
2019	Norfolk	AAA	63	230	67	19	2	12	(-	-)	126	42	47	50	38	0	51	4	2	3	5	4	5	.291	.396	.548	.944
2018	Bal	AL	17	40	10	3	0	3	(2	1)	22	8	10	8	4	0	12	2	0	1	2	1	0	.250	.340	.550	.890
2019	Bal	AL	44	126	30	6	0	4	(1	3)	48	15	15	17	14	1	26	1	0	1	1	2	3	.238	.317	.381	.698
	2 ML YEARS		61	166	40	9	0	7	(3	4)	70	23	25	25	18	1	38	3	0	2	3	3	3	.241	.323	.422	.744

Kohl Stewart

Pitches: R Bats: R Pos: RP-7; SP-2   Ht: 6'3" Wt: 195 Born: 10/7/1994 Age: 25

Year	Team	Lg	G	GS	GF	IP	BFP	H	R	ER	HR	SH	SF	HB	TBB	IBB	SO	WP	W	L	Pct	Sv-Op	Hld	Vel	OPS	ERC	ERA
2019	Roch	AAA	20	19	0	91.0	414	90	67	52	10	2	6	11	44	0	80	7	8	6	.571	0--	-	-	.753	4.84	5.14
2018	Min	AL	8	4	0	36.2	159	34	16	15	1	0	0	3	18	0	24	4	2	1	.667	0-0	0	93	.672	3.87	3.68
2019	Min	AL	9	2	5	25.1	109	29	18	18	5	0	0	1	8	0	10	6	2	2	.500	0-0	1	92	.869	5.59	6.39
	2 ML YEARS		17	6	5	62.0	268	63	34	33	6	0	0	4	26	0	34	10	4	3	.571	0-0	1	92	.755	4.57	4.79

Robert Stock

Pitches: R Bats: L Pos: RP-10   Ht: 6'1" Wt: 214 Born: 11/21/1989 Age: 30

Year	Team	Lg	G	GS	GF	IP	BFP	H	R	ER	HR	SH	SF	HB	TBB	IBB	SO	WP	W	L	Pct	Sv-Op	Hld	Vel	OPS	ERC	ERA
2019	ElPaso	AAA	25	3	2	28.1	140	36	14	13	6	0	1	3	19	0	40	5	3	0	1.000	0--	-	-	.901	8.28	4.13
2018	SD	NL	32	0	6	39.2	166	37	13	11	1	1	0	2	13	1	38	3	1	1	.500	0-1	4	98	.615	3.14	2.50
2019	SD	NL	10	0	4	10.2	56	14	14	12	2	0	0	1	8	0	15	4	1	0	1.000	0-1	0	98	.900	8.30	10.13
	2 ML YEARS		42	0	10	50.1	222	51	27	23	3	1	0	3	21	1	53	7	2	1	.667	0-2	4	98	.685	4.10	4.11

Trevor Story

Bats: R Throws: R Pos: SS-144;PH-1   Ht: 6'2" Wt: 214 Born: 11/15/1992 Age: 27

Year	Team	Lg	G	AB	H	2B	3B	HR	(Hm	Rd)	TB	R	RBI	RC	TBB	IBB	SO	HBP	SH	SF	SB	CS	GDP	Avg	OBP	Slg	OPS
2016	Col	NL	97	372	101	21	4	27	(16	11)	211	67	72	67	35	2	130	5	2	1	8	5	5	.272	.341	.567	.909
2017	Col	NL	145	503	120	32	3	24	(13	11)	230	68	82	66	49	4	191	1	7	2	7	2	12	.239	.308	.457	.765
2018	Col	NL	157	598	174	42	6	37	(26	11)	339	88	108	107	47	3	168	7	0	4	27	6	12	.291	.348	.567	.914
2019	Col	NL	145	588	173	38	5	35	(24	11)	326	111	85	113	58	0	174	7	0	3	23	8	3	.294	.363	.554	.917
	Postseason		5	22	7	2	0	1	(0	1)	12	3	1	2	0	0	7	0	0	0	0	0	0	.318	.318	.545	.864
	4 ML YEARS		544	2061	568	133	18	123	(79	44)	1106	334	347	353	189	9	663	21	2	9	65	21	32	.276	.341	.537	.878

Matt Strahm

Pitches: L **Bats:** R **Pos:** RP-30; SP-16 **Ht:** 6'3" **Wt:** 185 **Born:** 11/12/1991 **Age:** 28

Year Team	Lg	HOW MUCH PITCHED					WHAT HE GAVE UP											THE RESULTS								
		G	GS	GF	IP	BFP	H	R	ER	HR	SH	SF	HB	TBB	IBB	SO	WP	W	L	Pct	Sv-Op	Hld	Vel	OPS	ERC	ERA
2016 KC	AL	21	0	1	22.0	88	13	4	3	0	0	1	1	11	1	30	1	2	2	.500	0-0	6	94	.484	1.84	1.23
2017 KC	AL	24	3	3	34.2	154	30	22	21	6	2	0	3	22	2	37	3	2	5	.286	0-0	5	94	.779	5.10	5.45
2018 SD	NL	41	5	5	61.1	245	39	16	14	6	1	1	3	21	1	69	2	3	4	.429	0-0	7	93	.564	2.12	2.05
2019 SD	NL	46	16	4	114.2	487	121	61	60	22	4	1	7	22	4	118	3	6	11	.353	0-1	6	92	.787	4.35	4.71
4 ML YEARS		132	24	13	232.2	974	203	103	98	34	7	3	14	76	8	254	9	13	22	.371	0-1	24	93	.705	3.58	3.79

Dan Straily

Pitches: R **Bats:** R **Pos:** SP-8; RP-6 **Ht:** 6'2" **Wt:** 220 **Born:** 12/1/1988 **Age:** 31

Year Team	Lg	HOW MUCH PITCHED					WHAT HE GAVE UP											THE RESULTS								
		G	GS	GF	IP	BFP	H	R	ER	HR	SH	SF	HB	TBB	IBB	SO	WP	W	L	Pct	Sv-Op	Hld	Vel	OPS	ERC	ERA
2019 Norfolk	AAA	6	6	0	34.0	136	24	9	9	4	1	1	3	8	0	38	0	4	0	1.000	0- -	-	-	.658	2.35	2.38
2019 LV	AAA	6	6	0	33.0	139	33	22	19	5	0	0	0	9	1	30	1	1	4	.200	0- -	-	-	.718	3.85	5.18
2012 Oak	AL	7	7	0	39.1	172	36	19	17	11	1	1	2	16	1	32	0	2	1	.667	0-0	0	91	.803	4.94	3.89
2013 Oak	AL	27	27	0	152.1	640	132	74	67	16	4	5	7	57	0	124	7	10	8	.556	0-0	0	90	.666	3.46	3.96
2014 2 Tms		14	8	0	52.0	231	53	41	39	10	0	1	2	24	1	47	2	1	3	.250	0-0	0	89	.832	5.22	6.75
2015 Hou	AL	4	3	0	16.2	76	16	11	10	2	0	0	1	8	0	14	1	1	0	1.000	0-0	0	89	.747	4.38	5.40
2016 Cin	NL	34	31	0	191.1	792	154	80	80	31	6	3	11	73	4	162	3	14	8	.636	0-0	0	89	.712	3.58	3.76
2017 Mia	NL	33	33	0	181.2	769	176	90	86	31	10	7	5	60	4	170	2	10	9	.526	0-0	0	90	.783	4.20	4.26
2018 Mia	NL	23	23	0	122.1	518	107	62	56	20	4	3	7	52	5	99	1	5	6	.455	0-0	0	90	.754	4.12	4.12
2019 Bal	AL	14	8	2	47.2	236	73	53	52	22	0	3	2	22	0	33	3	2	4	.333	0-0	0	90	1.157	10.98	9.82
14 Oak	AL	7	7	0	38.1	159	33	21	21	9	0	1	1	15	1	34	2	1	2	.333	0-0	0	88	.794	4.31	4.93
14 ChC	NL	7	1	0	13.2	72	20	20	18	1	0	0	1	9	0	13	0	0	1	1.000	0-0	0	90	.917	7.78	11.85
Postseason		1	1	0	6.0	22	4	3	3	1	0	0	1	0	0	8	0	0	0	-	0-0	0	90	.561	1.99	4.50
8 ML YEARS		156	140	2	803.1	3434	747	430	407	143	25	23	37	312	15	681	19	44	40	.524	0-0	0	90	.770	4.34	4.56

Stephen Strasburg

Pitches: R **Bats:** R **Pos:** SP-33 **Ht:** 6'5" **Wt:** 235 **Born:** 7/20/1988 **Age:** 31

Year Team	Lg	HOW MUCH PITCHED					WHAT HE GAVE UP											THE RESULTS								
		G	GS	GF	IP	BFP	H	R	ER	HR	SH	SF	HB	TBB	IBB	SO	WP	W	L	Pct	Sv-Op	Hld	Vel	OPS	ERC	ERA
2010 Was	NL	12	12	0	68.0	274	56	25	22	5	2	2	0	17	0	92	2	5	3	.625	0-0	0	97	.596	2.41	2.91
2011 Was	NL	5	5	0	24.0	88	15	5	4	0	1	1	0	2	0	24	0	1	1	.500	0-0	0	96	.398	0.97	1.50
2012 Was	NL	28	28	0	159.1	653	136	62	56	15	6	4	4	48	1	197	5	15	6	.714	0-0	0	96	.649	2.97	3.16
2013 Was	NL	30	30	0	183.0	731	136	71	61	16	5	1	12	56	1	191	7	8	9	.471	0-0	0	95	.588	2.58	3.00
2014 Was	NL	34	34	0	215.0	868	198	86	75	23	9	4	5	43	4	242	7	14	11	.560	0-0	0	95	.672	3.02	3.14
2015 Was	NL	23	23	0	127.1	523	115	56	49	14	5	1	3	26	0	155	4	11	7	.611	0-0	0	95	.653	2.92	3.46
2016 Was	NL	24	24	0	147.2	598	119	59	59	15	5	1	2	44	1	183	2	15	4	.789	0-0	0	95	.637	2.72	3.60
2017 Was	NL	28	28	0	175.1	701	131	55	49	13	2	4	7	47	5	204	3	15	4	.789	0-0	0	96	.581	2.22	2.52
2018 Was	NL	22	22	0	130.0	544	118	59	54	18	1	5	8	38	2	156	5	10	7	.588	0-0	0	95	.711	3.62	3.74
2019 Was	NL	33	33	0	209.0	841	161	79	77	24	3	4	10	56	4	251	8	18	6	.750	0-0	0	94	.620	2.62	3.32
Postseason		3	3	0	19.0	76	14	4	1	0	2	0	1	4	0	24	0	1	2	.333	0-0	0	96	.474	1.64	0.47
10 ML YEARS		239	239	0	1438.2	5821	1185	557	506	143	39	27	51	377	18	1695	43	112	58	.659	0-0	0	95	.631	2.74	3.17

Chris Stratton

Pitches: R **Bats:** R **Pos:** RP-30; SP-5 **Ht:** 6'2" **Wt:** 211 **Born:** 8/22/1990 **Age:** 29

Year Team	Lg	HOW MUCH PITCHED					WHAT HE GAVE UP											THE RESULTS								
		G	GS	GF	IP	BFP	H	R	ER	HR	SH	SF	HB	TBB	IBB	SO	WP	W	L	Pct	Sv-Op	Hld	Vel	OPS	ERC	ERA
2016 SF	NL	7	0	7	10.0	43	11	4	4	1	0	0	0	5	0	6	0	1	0	1.000	0-0	0	91	.767	5.31	3.60
2017 SF	NL	13	10	1	58.2	256	59	25	24	5	2	3	1	28	0	51	2	4	4	.500	1-2	0	92	.738	4.42	3.68
2018 SF	NL	28	26	1	145.0	625	153	87	82	19	3	6	2	54	1	112	6	10	10	.500	0-0	0	91	.791	4.59	5.09
2019 2 Tms		35	5	7	76.0	344	93	50	47	13	0	1	0	33	1	69	2	1	3	.250	0-0	0	92	.873	6.10	5.57
19 LAA	AL	7	5	0	29.1	144	43	28	28	6	0	1	0	18	0	22	1	0	2	.000	0-0	0	91	1.000	8.90	8.59
19 Pit	NL	28	0	7	46.2	200	50	22	19	7	0	0	0	15	1	47	1	1	1	.500	0-0	0	93	.784	4.50	3.66
4 ML YEARS		83	41	16	289.2	1268	316	166	157	38	5	10	3	120	2	238	10	16	17	.485	1-2	0	91	.802	4.96	4.88

Myles Straw

Bats: R **Throws:** R **Pos:** SS-26;PR-14;CF-11;LF-8;PH-6;2B-4;RF-2;DH-2 **Ht:** 5'10" **Wt:** 180 **Born:** 10/17/1994 **Age:** 25

Year Team	Lg	BATTING																			RUNNING			AVERAGES			
		G	AB	H	2B	3B	HR	(Hm	Rd)	TB	R	RBI	RC	TBB	IBB	SO	HBP	SH	SF	SB	CS	GDP	Avg	OBP	Slg	OPS
2019 RdRck	AAA	66	277	89	11	3	1	(-	-)	109	46	33	47	32	0	50	1	1	2	19	4	5	.321	.391	.394	.785
2018 Hou	AL	9	9	3	0	0	1	(0	0)	6	4	1	2	1	0	1	0	0	0	2	0	0	.333	.400	.667	1.067
2019 Hou	AL	56	108	29	4	2	0	(0	0)	37	27	7	17	19	0	24	0	1	0	8	1	2	.269	.378	.343	.721
Postseason		2	0	0	0	0	0	(0	0)	0	1	0	0	0	0	0	0	0	0	1	0	0	-	-	-	-
2 ML YEARS		65	117	32	4	2	1	(0	1)	43	31	8	19	20	0	24	0	1	0	10	1	2	.274	.380	.368	.747

Hunter Strickland

Pitches: R **Bats:** R **Pos:** RP-28 **Ht:** 6'3" **Wt:** 225 **Born:** 9/24/1988 **Age:** 31

Year Team	Lg	HOW MUCH PITCHED					WHAT HE GAVE UP											THE RESULTS								
		G	GS	GF	IP	BFP	H	R	ER	HR	SH	SF	HB	TBB	IBB	SO	WP	W	L	Pct	Sv-Op	Hld	Vel	OPS	ERC	ERA
2014 SF	NL	9	0	5	7.0	25	5	0	0	0	0	0	0	0	0	9	0	1	0	1.000	1-1	1	98	.440	1.08	0.00
2015 SF	NL	55	0	11	51.1	191	34	14	14	4	0	0	2	10	1	50	1	3	3	.500	0-2	20	97	.543	1.72	2.45
2016 SF	NL	72	0	14	61.0	250	50	21	21	4	0	3	2	19	3	57	3	3	3	.500	3-8	18	97	.589	2.61	3.10
2017 SF	NL	68	0	17	61.1	268	59	20	18	4	1	3	2	29	4	58	3	4	3	.571	1-3	21	96	.702	3.91	2.64

Year Team	Lg	G	GS	GF	IP	BFP	H	R	ER	HR	SH	SF	HB	TBB	IBB	SO	WP	W	L	Pct	Sv-Op	Hld	Vel	OPS	ERC	ERA
2018 SF	NL	49	0	35	45.1	201	43	25	20	5	2	3	1	21	2	37	4	3	5	.375	14-18	0	95	.758	4.03	3.97
2019 2 Tms		28	0	3	24.1	105	22	15	15	6	0	1	3	8	0	18	1	2	1	.667	2-3	10	96	.809	4.72	5.55
19 Sea	AL	4	0	2	3.1	13	2	3	3	1	0	0	1	0	0	3	0	0	1	.000	2-3	0	96	.731	2.70	8.10
19 Was	NL	24	0	1	21.0	92	20	12	12	5	0	1	2	8	0	15	1	2	0	1.000	0-0	10	96	.820	5.05	5.14
Postseason		11	0	5	11.0	43	10	7	7	6	0	0	0	3	0	11	1	1	0	1.000	1-2	1	97	1.052	6.24	5.73
6 ML YEARS		281	0	85	250.1	1040	213	95	88	23	3	10	10	87	10	229	12	16	15	.516	21-35	70	96	.659	3.11	3.16

Ross Stripling

Pitches: R **Bats:** R **Pos:** RP-17; SP-15   **Ht:** 6'2" **Wt:** 220 **Born:** 11/23/1989 **Age:** 30

Year Team	Lg	G	GS	GF	IP	BFP	H	R	ER	HR	SH	SF	HB	TBB	IBB	SO	WP	W	L	Pct	Sv-Op	Hld	Vel	OPS	ERC	ERA
2016 LAD	NL	22	14	4	100.0	419	96	46	44	10	3	1	1	30	3	74	6	5	9	.357	0-0	0	90	.709	3.46	3.96
2017 LAD	NL	49	2	12	74.1	304	69	31	31	10	2	3	0	19	4	74	2	3	5	.375	2-5	4	93	.691	3.29	3.75
2018 LAD	NL	33	21	8	122.0	503	123	42	41	18	2	0	1	22	2	136	3	8	6	.571	0-0	3	92	.722	3.58	3.02
2019 LAD	NL	32	15	4	90.2	370	84	40	35	11	0	4	2	20	0	93	4	4	4	.500	0-0	3	91	.699	3.22	3.47
Postseason		10	0	4	7.1	32	10	5	4	0	0	1	0	2	0	4	0	0	0	-	0-0	0	92	.789	5.10	4.91
4 ML YEARS		136	52	22	387.0	1596	372	159	151	49	7	8	4	91	9	377	15	20	24	.455	2-5	10	91	.708	3.41	3.51

Marcus Stroman

Pitches: R **Bats:** R **Pos:** SP-32   **Ht:** 5'7" **Wt:** 180 **Born:** 5/1/1991 **Age:** 29

Year Team	Lg	G	GS	GF	IP	BFP	H	R	ER	HR	SH	SF	HB	TBB	IBB	SO	WP	W	L	Pct	Sv-Op	Hld	Vel	OPS	ERC	ERA
2014 Tor	AL	26	20	1	130.2	534	125	56	53	7	0	2	3	28	1	111	9	11	6	.647	1-1	0	94	.633	2.93	3.65
2015 Tor	AL	4	4	0	27.0	103	20	5	5	2	0	0	1	6	0	18	2	4	0	1.000	0-0	0	92	.554	2.16	1.67
2016 Tor	AL	32	32	0	204.0	855	209	104	99	21	2	2	4	54	0	166	9	9	10	.474	0-0	0	92	.720	3.81	4.37
2017 Tor	AL	33	33	0	201.0	834	201	82	69	21	0	4	6	62	1	164	3	13	9	.591	0-0	0	92	.715	3.97	3.09
2018 Tor	AL	19	19	0	102.1	449	115	68	63	9	2	3	2	36	2	77	3	4	9	.308	0-0	0	92	.759	4.59	5.54
2019 2 Tms		32	32	0	184.1	774	183	77	66	18	1	2	1	58	1	159	7	10	13	.435	0-0	0	93	.697	3.73	3.22
19 Tor	AL	21	21	0	124.2	513	118	50	41	10	0	1	0	35	0	99	4	6	11	.353	0-0	0	93	.656	3.23	2.96
19 NYM	NL	11	11	0	59.2	261	65	27	25	8	1	1	1	23	1	60	3	4	2	.667	0-0	0	92	.781	4.84	3.77
Postseason		5	5	0	30.2	128	29	16	15	4	0	1	0	7	0	21	2	1	1	.500	0-0	0	93	.690	3.24	4.40
6 ML YEARS		146	140	1	849.1	3549	853	392	355	78	5	13	17	244	3	695	33	51	47	.520	1-1	0	93	.701	3.72	3.76

Pedro Strop

Pitches: R **Bats:** R **Pos:** RP-50   STROPE   **Ht:** 6'1" **Wt:** 220 **Born:** 6/13/1985 **Age:** 35

Year Team	Lg	G	GS	GF	IP	BFP	H	R	ER	HR	SH	SF	HB	TBB	IBB	SO	WP	W	L	Pct	Sv-Op	Hld	Vel	OPS	ERC	ERA
2009 Tex	AL	7	0	3	7.0	30	6	6	6	0	0	0	0	4	0	9	0	0	0	-	0-0	0	95	.679	3.27	7.71
2010 Tex	AL	15	0	5	10.2	60	17	12	12	2	1	0	1	11	0	11	5	0	0	-	0-0	1	95	1.109	11.92	10.13
2011 2 Tms	AL	23	0	6	22.0	90	15	5	5	0	2	1	1	10	0	21	2	2	1	.667	0-2	4	94	.519	2.15	2.05
2012 Bal	AL	70	0	17	66.1	283	52	18	18	2	1	1	4	37	2	58	5	5	2	.714	3-10	24	97	.613	3.22	2.44
2013 2 Tms		66	0	22	57.1	254	45	30	29	5	7	0	6	26	2	66	8	2	5	.286	1-4	17	96	.663	3.21	4.55
2014 ChC	NL	65	0	13	61.0	244	40	19	15	2	0	1	4	25	3	71	6	2	4	.333	2-6	21	95	.535	2.12	2.21
2015 ChC	NL	76	0	12	68.0	270	39	24	22	5	1	3	4	29	6	81	6	2	6	.250	3-5	28	95	.538	1.94	2.91
2016 ChC	NL	54	0	8	47.1	187	27	16	15	4	0	2	4	15	1	60	7	2	2	.500	0-4	21	95	.517	1.78	2.85
2017 ChC	NL	69	0	8	60.1	250	45	22	19	4	2	1	3	26	1	65	7	5	4	.556	0-4	21	96	.619	2.78	2.83
2018 ChC	NL	60	0	20	59.2	240	38	15	15	4	1	1	5	21	3	57	3	6	1	.857	13-17	9	95	.541	2.06	2.26
2019 ChC	NL	50	0	27	41.2	178	33	24	23	6	0	1	5	20	1	49	4	2	5	.286	10-16	6	94	.734	4.01	4.97
11 Tex	AL	11	0	4	9.2	44	7	4	4	0	1	1	1	7	0	9	2	0	1	.000	0-1	0	94	.555	3.34	3.72
11 Bal	AL	12	0	2	12.1	46	8	1	1	0	1	0	0	3	0	12	0	2	0	1.000	0-1	4	95	.483	1.39	0.73
13 Bal	AL	29	0	15	22.1	111	23	19	18	4	4	0	2	15	2	24	5	0	3	.000	0-3	3	96	.861	5.81	7.25
13 ChC	AL	37	0	7	35.0	143	22	11	11	1	3	0	4	11	0	42	3	2	2	.500	1-1	14	96	.520	1.80	2.83
Postseason		22	0	2	19.1	75	9	4	4	1	1	0	4	7	0	14	1	1	0	1.000	0-0	4	95	.524	1.76	1.86
11 ML YEARS		555	0	141	501.1	2086	357	191	179	34	15	11	37	224	19	548	53	28	30	.483	32-68	152	95	.604	2.72	3.21

Garrett Stubbs

Bats: L **Throws:** R **Pos:** C-11;LF-7;PR-4;PH-3;RF-1   **Ht:** 5'10" **Wt:** 175 **Born:** 5/26/1993 **Age:** 27

Year Team	Lg	G	AB	H	2B	3B	HR	(Hm	Rd)	TB	R	RBI	RC	TBB	IBB	SO	HBP	SH	SF	SB	CS	GDP	Avg	OBP	Slg	OPS
2019 RdRck	AAA	63	204	49	11	0	7	(-	-)	81	33	23	30	24	0	38	5	0	2	12	2	6	.240	.332	.397	.729
2019 Hou	AL	19	35	7	3	0	0	(0	0)	10	8	2	1	4	0	7	0	0	0	1	0	1	.200	.282	.286	.568

Daniel Stumpf

Pitches: L **Bats:** L **Pos:** RP-48   **Ht:** 6'2" **Wt:** 208 **Born:** 1/4/1991 **Age:** 29

Year Team	Lg	G	GS	GF	IP	BFP	H	R	ER	HR	SH	SF	HB	TBB	IBB	SO	WP	W	L	Pct	Sv-Op	Hld	Vel	OPS	ERC	ERA
2019 Toledo	AAA	14	0	9	15.1	60	8	2	1	0	0	0	1	4	1	24	0	2	1	.667	4- --	-		.398	1.07	0.59
2016 Phi	NL	7	0	3	5.0	25	9	6	6	1	1	0	0	2	0	2	1	0	0	-	0-0	1	92	1.095	10.22	10.80
2017 Det	AL	55	0	13	37.2	160	37	16	16	5	0	4	2	15	1	33	2	0	1	.000	0-2	9	94	.762	4.48	3.82
2018 Det	AL	56	0	5	38.1	173	44	23	21	5	1	2	0	16	1	37	2	1	5	.167	0-3	11	93	.823	5.12	4.93
2019 Det	AL	48	0	5	29.0	135	35	18	14	5	1	3	0	15	1	28	0	1	1	.500	0-2	5	92	.873	6.24	4.34
4 ML YEARS		166	0	26	110.0	493	125	63	57	16	3	9	2	48	3	100	5	2	7	.222	0-7	26	93	.830	5.39	4.66

Andrew Suarez

Pitches: L **Bats:** L **Pos:** RP-19; SP-2 **Ht:** 6'0" **Wt:** 187 **Born:** 9/11/1992 **Age:** 27

Year Team	Lg	G	GS	GF	IP	BFP	H	R	ER	HR	SH	SF	HB	TBB	IBB	SO	WP	W	L	Pct	Sv-Op	Hld	Vel	OPS	ERC	ERA
2019 Scrmto	AAA	18	15	0	88.0	395	112	57	56	11	2	3	2	33	3	57	3	7	6	.538	0--	-	-	.856	5.91	5.73
2018 SF	NL	29	29	0	160.1	665	163	85	80	23	5	6	3	45	1	130	4	7	13	.350	0-0	0	92	.767	4.15	4.49
2019 SF	NL	21	2	4	32.2	148	39	23	21	7	0	4	1	14	2	25	2	0	2	.000	0-1	1	93	.923	6.27	5.79
2 ML YEARS		50	31	4	193.0	813	202	108	101	30	5	10	4	59	3	155	6	7	15	.318	0-1	1	92	.795	4.49	4.71

Eugenio Suarez

Bats: R **Throws:** R **Pos:** 3B-158;PH-5;DH-1;PR-1   ay-yoo-HAY-nee-   **Ht:** 5'11" **Wt:** 213 **Born:** 7/18/1991 **Age:** 28

Year Team	Lg	G	AB	H	2B	3B	HR	(Hm	Rd)	TB	R	RBI	RC	TBB	IBB	SO	HBP	SH	SF	SB	CS	GDP	Avg	OBP	Slg	OPS
2014 Det	AL	85	244	59	9	1	4	(2	2)	82	33	23	30	22	1	67	5	5	1	3	2	3	.242	.316	.336	.652
2015 Cin	NL	97	372	104	19	2	13	(4	9)	166	42	48	49	17	0	94	3	4	2	4	1	7	.280	.315	.446	.761
2016 Cin	NL	159	565	140	25	2	21	(10	11)	232	78	70	77	51	0	155	8	0	3	11	5	10	.248	.317	.411	.728
2017 Cin	NL	156	534	139	25	2	26	(21	5)	246	87	82	81	84	1	147	9	0	5	4	5	16	.260	.367	.461	.828
2018 Cin	NL	143	527	149	22	2	34	(19	15)	277	79	104	95	64	7	142	9	0	6	1	1	20	.283	.366	.526	.892
2019 Cin	NL	159	575	156	22	2	49	(24	25)	329	87	103	103	70	4	189	11	0	6	3	2	12	.271	.358	.572	.930
Postseason		1	1	0	0	0	0	(0	0)	0	0	0	0	0	0	0	0	0	0	0	0	0	.000	.000	.000	.000
6 ML YEARS		799	2817	747	122	11	147	(80	67)	1332	406	430	435	308	13	794	45	9	23	26	16	68	.265	.345	.473	.817

Jose Suarez

Pitches: L **Bats:** L **Pos:** SP-15; RP-4 **Ht:** 5'10" **Wt:** 225 **Born:** 1/3/1998 **Age:** 22

Year Team	Lg	G	GS	GF	IP	BFP	H	R	ER	HR	SH	SF	HB	TBB	IBB	SO	WP	W	L	Pct	Sv-Op	Hld	Vel	OPS	ERC	ERA
2019 Salt Lk	AAA	7	6	0	32.1	138	24	15	13	3	0	0	2	17	0	31	3	2	1	.667	0--	-	-	.673	3.32	3.62
2019 LAA	AL	19	15	0	81.0	375	100	67	64	23	1	2	10	33	1	72	5	2	6	.250	0-0	0	92	.948	7.55	7.11

Ranger Suarez

Pitches: L **Bats:** L **Pos:** RP-37 **Ht:** 6'1" **Wt:** 180 **Born:** 8/26/1995 **Age:** 24

Year Team	Lg	G	GS	GF	IP	BFP	H	R	ER	HR	SH	SF	HB	TBB	IBB	SO	WP	W	L	Pct	Sv-Op	Hld	Vel	OPS	ERC	ERA
2019 LV	AAA	7	7	0	38.0	162	41	26	24	8	0	2	4	10	0	32	0	2	2	.500	0--	-	-	.874	5.32	5.68
2018 Phi	NL	4	3	0	15.0	69	21	14	9	3	1	0	0	6	1	11	0	1	1	.500	0-0	0	92	.945	7.33	5.40
2019 Phi	NL	37	0	8	48.2	205	52	18	17	6	3	2	1	12	2	42	1	6	1	.857	0-1	6	92	.739	4.07	3.14
2 ML YEARS		41	3	8	63.2	274	73	32	26	9	4	2	1	18	3	53	1	7	2	.778	0-1	6	92	.791	4.78	3.68

Jesus Sucre

Bats: R **Throws:** R **Pos:** C-18;PH-2;1B-1   SUE-cray   **Ht:** 6'0" **Wt:** 200 **Born:** 4/30/1988 **Age:** 32

Year Team	Lg	G	AB	H	2B	3B	HR	(Hm	Rd)	TB	R	RBI	RC	TBB	IBB	SO	HBP	SH	SF	SB	CS	GDP	Avg	OBP	Slg	OPS
2019 Norfolk	AAA	50	184	52	15	0	0	(-	-)	67	20	19	23	12	0	29	2	0	0	0	0	7	.283	.333	.364	.697
2013 Sea	AL	8	26	5	0	0	0	(0	0)	5	1	3	1	2	0	1	0	0	1	0	0	2	.192	.241	.192	.434
2014 Sea	AL	21	61	13	2	0	0	(0	0)	15	4	5	6	0	0	17	0	3	0	0	0	0	.213	.213	.246	.459
2015 Sea	AL	52	127	20	6	0	1	(1	0)	29	9	7	1	6	0	21	0	9	0	0	0	6	.157	.195	.228	.424
2016 Sea	AL	9	25	12	2	0	1	(0	1)	17	4	5	9	2	0	5	2	0	0	0	0	1	.480	.552	.680	1.232
2017 TB	AL	63	176	45	6	0	7	(3	4)	72	20	29	21	7	0	35	3	2	4	2	0	6	.256	.289	.409	.699
2018 TB	AL	73	182	38	5	0	1	(0	1)	46	9	17	9	9	2	29	1	4	2	1	0	4	.209	.247	.253	.500
2019 Bal	AL	21	62	13	2	0	0	(0	0)	15	3	3	4	4	0	13	1	0	0	0	0	1	.210	.269	.242	.511
7 ML YEARS		247	659	146	23	0	10	(4	6)	199	50	69	51	30	2	121	7	18	7	3	0	20	.222	.260	.302	.562

Wander Suero

Pitches: R **Bats:** R **Pos:** RP-78 **Ht:** 6'4" **Wt:** 211 **Born:** 9/15/1991 **Age:** 28

Year Team	Lg	G	GS	GF	IP	BFP	H	R	ER	HR	SH	SF	HB	TBB	IBB	SO	WP	W	L	Pct	Sv-Op	Hld	Vel	OPS	ERC	ERA
2018 Was	NL	40	0	11	47.2	200	43	20	19	4	1	4	8	15	2	47	3	4	1	.800	0-0	2	92	.719	3.38	3.59
2019 Was	NL	78	0	10	71.1	296	64	36	36	5	0	3	3	26	3	81	2	6	9	.400	1-7	19	93	.666	3.34	4.54
2 ML YEARS		118	0	21	119.0	496	107	56	55	9	1	7	7	41	5	128	5	10	10	.500	1-7	21	92	.688	3.35	4.16

Cole Sulser

Pitches: R **Bats:** R **Pos:** RP-7 **Ht:** 6'1" **Wt:** 190 **Born:** 3/12/1990 **Age:** 30

Year Team	Lg	G	GS	GF	IP	BFP	H	R	ER	HR	SH	SF	HB	TBB	IBB	SO	WP	W	L	Pct	Sv-Op	Hld	Vel	OPS	ERC	ERA
2019 Drham	AAA	49	4	14	66.0	273	51	24	24	4	1	0	3	24	0	89	5	6	3	.667	2--	-	-	.593	2.63	3.27
2019 TB	AL	7	0	4	7.1	29	5	0	0	0	0	0	0	3	0	9	0	0	0	-	0-0	0	93	.507	1.90	0.00

Brent Suter

Pitches: L Bats: L Pos: RP-9   SOO-ter   Ht: 6'5" Wt: 195 Born: 8/29/1989 Age: 30

Year	Team	Lg	G	GS	GF	IP	BFP	H	R	ER	HR	SH	SF	HB	TBB	IBB	SO	WP	W	L	Pct	Sv-Op	Hld	Vel	OPS	ERC	ERA
2016	Mil	NL	14	2	4	21.2	91	25	8	8	3	1	0	1	5	0	15	1	2	2	.500	0-0	2	84	.773	4.90	3.32
2017	Mil	NL	22	14	1	81.2	341	83	33	31	8	1	1	2	22	2	64	1	3	2	.600	0-0	0	86	.702	3.75	3.42
2018	Mil	NL	20	18	0	101.1	424	102	55	50	18	5	1	4	19	2	84	1	8	7	.533	0-0	0	87	.754	3.88	4.44
2019	Mil	NL	9	0	0	18.1	65	10	1	1	1	0	0	0	1	0	15	0	4	0	1.000	0-0	2	88	.435	0.88	0.49
4 ML YEARS			65	34	5	223.0	921	220	97	90	30	7	2	7	47	4	178	3	17	11	.607	0-0	4	86	.714	3.61	3.63

Ichiro Suzuki

Bats: L Throws: R Pos: RF-2   EE-chee-row soo-ZOO-kee   Ht: 5'11" Wt: 175 Born: 10/22/1973 Age: 46

Year	Team	Lg	G	AB	H	2B	3B	HR	(Hm	Rd)	TB	R	RBI	RC	TBB	IBB	SO	HBP	SH	SF	SB	CS	GDP	Avg	OBP	Slg	OPS
2001	Sea	AL	157	692	242	34	8	8	(5	3)	316	127	69	124	30	10	53	8	4	4	56	14	3	.350	.381	.457	.838
2002	Sea	AL	157	647	208	27	8	8	(4	4)	275	111	51	110	68	27	62	5	3	5	31	15	8	.321	.388	.425	.813
2003	Sea	AL	159	679	212	29	8	13	(8	5)	296	111	62	107	36	7	69	6	3	1	34	8	3	.312	.352	.436	.788
2004	Sea	AL	161	704	262	24	5	8	(4	4)	320	101	60	125	49	19	63	4	2	3	36	11	6	.372	.414	.455	.869
2005	Sea	AL	162	679	206	21	12	15	(8	7)	296	111	68	109	48	23	66	4	2	6	33	8	5	.303	.350	.436	.786
2006	Sea	AL	161	695	224	20	9	9	(6	3)	289	110	49	107	49	16	71	5	1	2	45	2	2	.322	.370	.416	.786
2007	Sea	AL	161	678	238	22	7	6	(3	3)	292	111	68	128	49	13	77	3	4	2	37	8	7	.351	.396	.431	.827
2008	Sea	AL	162	686	213	20	7	6	(3	3)	265	103	42	100	51	12	65	5	3	4	43	4	8	.310	.361	.386	.747
2009	Sea	AL	146	639	225	31	4	11	(6	5)	297	88	46	111	32	15	71	4	2	1	26	9	1	.352	.386	.465	.851
2010	Sea	AL	162	680	214	30	3	6	(1	5)	268	74	43	96	45	13	86	3	3	1	42	9	3	.315	.359	.394	.754
2011	Sea	AL	161	677	184	22	3	5	(4	1)	227	80	47	80	39	13	69	0	1	4	40	7	11	.272	.310	.335	.645
2012	2 Tms	AL	162	629	178	28	6	9	(6	3)	245	77	55	63	22	5	61	2	5	5	29	7	12	.283	.307	.390	.696
2013	NYY	AL	150	520	136	15	3	7	(5	2)	178	57	35	56	26	4	63	1	6	2	20	4	6	.262	.297	.342	.639
2014	NYY	AL	143	359	102	13	2	1	(1	0)	122	42	22	39	21	1	68	1	2	2	15	3	3	.284	.324	.340	.664
2015	Mia	NL	153	398	91	5	6	1	(1	0)	111	45	21	30	31	1	51	0	5	4	11	5	8	.229	.282	.279	.561
2016	Mia	NL	143	327	95	15	5	1	(1	0)	123	48	22	44	30	1	42	3	3	2	10	2	4	.291	.354	.376	.730
2017	Mia	NL	136	196	50	6	0	3	(0	3)	65	19	20	25	17	1	35	1	1	0	1	1	2	.255	.318	.332	.649
2018	Sea	AL	15	44	9	0	0	0	(0	0)	9	5	0	3	3	0	7	0	0	0	0	0	0	.205	.255	.205	.460
2019	Sea	AL	2	5	0	0	0	0	(0	0)	0	0	0	0	1	0	1	0	0	0	0	0	0	.000	.167	.000	.167
12 Sea		AL	95	402	105	15	5	4	(1	3)	142	49	28	33	17	4	40	0	0	4	15	2	10	.261	.288	.353	.642
12 NYY		AL	67	227	73	13	1	5	(5	0)	103	28	27	30	5	1	21	2	5	1	14	5	2	.322	.340	.454	.794
Postseason			19	78	27	4	0	1	(1	0)	34	10	8	11	7	2	9	0	1	0	4	3	0	.346	.400	.436	.836
19 ML YEARS			2653	9934	3089	362	96	117	(66	51)	3994	1420	780	1457	647	181	1080	55	50	48	509	117	92	.311	.355	.402	.757

Kurt Suzuki

Bats: R Throws: R Pos: C-75;PH-13   Ht: 5'11" Wt: 210 Born: 10/4/1983 Age: 36

Year	Team	Lg	G	AB	H	2B	3B	HR	(Hm	Rd)	TB	R	RBI	RC	TBB	IBB	SO	HBP	SH	SF	SB	CS	GDP	Avg	OBP	Slg	OPS
2007	Oak	AL	68	213	53	13	0	7	(4	3)	87	27	39	33	24	0	39	3	3	5	0	0	4	.249	.327	.408	.735
2008	Oak	AL	148	530	148	25	1	7	(5	2)	196	54	42	66	44	2	69	11	2	1	2	3	20	.279	.346	.370	.716
2009	Oak	AL	147	570	156	37	1	15	(8	7)	240	74	88	77	28	0	59	8	1	7	8	2	14	.274	.313	.421	.734
2010	Oak	AL	131	495	120	18	2	13	(8	5)	181	55	71	54	33	3	49	12	0	4	3	2	22	.242	.303	.366	.669
2011	Oak	AL	134	460	109	26	0	14	(8	6)	177	54	44	42	38	1	64	7	3	7	2	2	14	.237	.301	.385	.686
2012	2 Tms		118	408	96	20	0	6	(3	3)	134	36	43	39	20	3	73	5	4	5	2	0	5	.235	.276	.328	.605
2013	2 Tms		94	285	66	13	1	5	(2	3)	96	25	32	34	22	6	35	3	2	4	2	0	2	.232	.290	.337	.627
2014	Min	AL	131	452	130	34	0	3	(1	2)	173	37	61	65	34	0	46	9	1	7	0	1	9	.288	.345	.383	.727
2015	Min	AL	131	433	104	17	0	5	(3	2)	136	36	50	46	29	4	59	7	6	4	0	0	14	.240	.296	.314	.610
2016	Min	AL	106	345	89	24	1	8	(4	4)	139	34	49	45	18	0	48	5	1	4	0	0	9	.258	.301	.403	.704
2017	Atl	NL	81	276	78	13	0	19	(8	11)	148	38	50	49	17	2	39	13	1	2	0	0	5	.283	.351	.536	.887
2018	Atl	NL	105	347	94	24	0	12	(5	7)	154	45	50	45	22	0	43	13	0	6	0	0	6	.271	.332	.444	.776
2019	Was	NL	85	280	74	11	0	17	(10	7)	136	37	63	53	20	1	36	6	0	3	0	1	10	.264	.324	.486	.809
12 Oak		AL	75	262	57	15	0	1	(1	0)	75	19	18	16	9	0	53	3	2	2	1	0	3	.218	.250	.286	.536
12 Was		NL	43	146	39	5	0	5	(2	3)	59	17	25	23	11	3	20	2	2	3	1	0	2	.267	.321	.404	.725
13 Was		NL	79	252	56	11	1	3	(0	3)	78	19	25	26	20	6	32	3	2	4	2	0	2	.222	.283	.310	.593
13 Oak		AL	15	33	10	2	0	2	(2	0)	18	6	7	8	2	0	3	0	0	0	0	0	0	.303	.343	.545	.888
Postseason			9	25	6	0	0	0	(0	0)	6	0	4	3	2	0	5	0	0	0	0	0	0	.240	.296	.240	.536
13 ML YEARS			1479	5094	1317	275	6	131	(69	62)	1997	552	682	648	349	22	659	102	24	59	19	11	134	.259	.315	.392	.708

Dansby Swanson

Bats: R Throws: R Pos: SS-126;PH-1   Ht: 6'1" Wt: 190 Born: 2/11/1994 Age: 26

Year	Team	Lg	G	AB	H	2B	3B	HR	(Hm	Rd)	TB	R	RBI	RC	TBB	IBB	SO	HBP	SH	SF	SB	CS	GDP	Avg	OBP	Slg	OPS
2016	Atl	NL	38	129	39	7	1	3	(1	2)	57	20	17	17	13	5	34	0	1	2	3	0	2	.302	.361	.442	.803
2017	Atl	NL	144	488	113	23	2	6	(2	4)	158	59	51	55	59	10	120	0	7	1	3	3	7	.232	.312	.324	.636
2018	Atl	NL	136	478	114	25	4	14	(7	7)	189	51	59	59	44	15	122	2	6	3	10	4	5	.238	.304	.395	.699
2019	Atl	NL	127	483	121	26	3	17	(8	9)	204	77	65	61	51	2	124	5	1	5	10	5	7	.251	.325	.422	.748
4 ML YEARS			445	1578	387	81	10	40	(18	22)	608	207	192	192	167	32	400	7	8	14	26	12	21	.245	.318	.385	.703

Erik Swanson

Pitches: R Bats: R Pos: RP-19; SP-8   Ht: 6'3" Wt: 235 Born: 9/4/1993 Age: 26

Year	Team	Lg	G	GS	GF	IP	BFP	H	R	ER	HR	SH	SF	HB	TBB	IBB	SO	WP	W	L	Pct	Sv-Op	Hld	Vel	OPS	ERC	ERA
2019	Tacom	AAA	10	6	0	24.1	111	28	16	15	5	0	0	0	12	0	28	0	0	1	.000	0--	-	-	.855	6.13	5.55
2019	Sea	AL	27	8	7	58.0	245	56	41	37	17	0	1	2	12	1	52	2	1	5	.167	2-2	1	93	.803	4.38	5.74

Anthony Swarzak

Pitches: R Bats: R Pos: RP-59 SWORE-zack **Ht: 6'4" Wt: 215 Born: 9/10/1985 Age: 34**

Year	Team	Lg	G	GS	GF	IP	BFP	H	R	ER	HR	SH	SF	HB	TBB	IBB	SO	WP	W	L	Pct	Sv-Op	Hld	Vel	OPS	ERC	ERA
2009	Min	AL	12	12	0	59.0	268	76	43	41	12	1	1	2	20	0	34	0	3	7	.300	0-0	0	90	.879	6.50	6.25
2011	Min	AL	27	11	2	102.0	441	111	53	49	9	2	3	6	26	1	55	3	4	7	.364	0-0	0	91	.724	4.11	4.32
2012	Min	AL	44	5	9	96.2	413	106	57	54	15	3	6	0	31	8	62	3	3	6	.333	0-1	1	92	.798	4.63	5.03
2013	Min	AL	48	0	8	96.0	387	89	33	31	7	2	5	1	22	1	69	1	3	2	.600	0-2	3	92	.649	2.94	2.91
2014	Min	AL	50	4	11	86.0	378	100	48	44	5	1	2	0	28	5	47	0	3	2	.600	0-1	3	92	.752	4.29	4.60
2015	Cle	AL	10	0	3	13.1	61	18	9	5	1	0	0	0	4	1	13	0	0	0	-	0-0	0	92	.799	5.34	3.38
2016	NYY	AL	26	0	6	31.0	124	28	19	19	10	0	1	1	7	0	31	1	1	2	.333	0-1	1	93	.847	4.51	5.52
2017	2 Tms		70	0	6	77.1	303	58	21	20	6	1	3	2	22	4	91	2	6	4	.600	2-5	27	95	.595	2.29	2.33
2018	NYM	NL	29	0	12	26.1	124	28	18	18	6	0	1	1	14	0	31	2	0	2	.000	4-5	2	94	.861	6.32	6.15
2019	2 Tms		59	0	8	53.1	234	52	30	27	12	0	0	0	27	3	52	1	3	4	.429	4-7	17	93	.792	5.18	4.56
17	CWS	AL	41	0	5	48.1	186	37	12	12	2	0	2	0	13	2	52	2	4	3	.571	1-3	10	94	.555	2.06	2.23
17	Mil	AL	29	0	1	29.0	117	21	9	8	4	1	1	2	9	2	39	0	2	1	.667	1-2	17	95	.660	2.69	2.48
19	Sea	AL	15	0	7	13.2	64	14	11	8	6	0	0	0	8	1	17	1	2	2	.500	3-6	0	94	.933	7.19	5.27
19	Atl	NL	44	0	1	39.2	170	38	19	19	6	0	0	0	19	2	35	1	1	2	.333	1-1	17	93	.739	4.51	4.31
10 ML YEARS			375	32	65	641.0	2725	666	331	308	83	10	22	13	201	23	485	14	26	36	.419	10-22	54	92	.748	4.22	4.32

Blake Swihart

Bats: B Throws: R Pos: PH-18;LF-11;RF-9;C-8;1B-2 SWY-hart **Ht: 6'1" Wt: 200 Born: 4/3/1992 Age: 28**

Year	Team	Lg	G	AB	H	2B	3B	HR	(Hm	Rd)	TB	R	RBI	RC	TBB	IBB	SO	HBP	SH	SF	SB	CS	GDP	Avg	OBP	Slg	OPS
2019	Reno	AAA	28	106	20	2	1	6	(-	-)	42	20	22	12	15	0	31	0	0	1	0	1	6	.189	.287	.396	.683
2015	Bos	AL	84	288	79	17	1	5	(2	3)	113	47	31	34	18	0	77	1	2	0	4	2	8	.274	.319	.392	.712
2016	Bos	AL	19	62	16	0	3	0	(0	0)	22	9	5	8	11	0	17	0	0	1	0	1	0	.258	.365	.355	.720
2017	Bos	AL	6	5	1	0	0	0	(0	0)	1	1	0	1	2	0	3	0	0	0	0	0	0	.200	.429	.200	.629
2018	Bos	AL	82	192	44	10	0	3	(1	2)	63	28	18	17	15	0	57	0	0	4	6	1	4	.229	.285	.328	.613
2019	2 Tms		43	92	15	1	0	4	(2	2)	28	13	13	8	6	0	36	1	0	0	0	0	2	.163	.222	.304	.527
19	Bos	AL	12	26	6	1	0	1	(0	1)	10	4	4	3	2	0	7	1	0	0	0	0	0	.231	.310	.385	.695
19	Ari	NL	31	66	9	0	0	3	(2	1)	18	9	9	5	4	0	29	0	0	0	0	0	2	.136	.186	.273	.458
Postseason			3	3	0	0	0	0	(0	0)	0	0	0	0	0	0	1	0	0	0	0	0	0	.000	.000	.000	.000
5 ML YEARS			234	639	155	28	4	12	(5	7)	227	98	67	68	52	0	190	2	2	1	10	4	14	.243	.301	.355	.656

Noah Syndergaard

Pitches: R Bats: L Pos: SP-32 sin-DER-gard **Ht: 6'6" Wt: 240 Born: 8/29/1992 Age: 27**

Year	Team	Lg	G	GS	GF	IP	BFP	H	R	ER	HR	SH	SF	HB	TBB	IBB	SO	WP	W	L	Pct	Sv-Op	Hld	Vel	OPS	ERC	ERA
2015	NYM	NL	24	24	0	150.0	603	126	60	54	19	5	3	3	31	2	166	6	9	7	.563	0-0	0	97	.645	2.70	3.24
2016	NYM	NL	31	30	0	183.2	744	168	61	53	11	3	4	2	43	2	218	10	14	9	.609	0-0	0	98	.639	2.79	2.60
2017	NYM	NL	7	7	0	30.1	124	29	14	10	0	1	1	1	3	1	34	3	1	2	.333	0-0	0	98	.573	2.13	2.97
2018	NYM	NL	25	25	0	154.1	644	148	55	52	9	3	3	7	39	2	155	2	13	4	.765	0-0	0	97	.651	3.16	3.03
2019	NYM	NL	32	32	0	197.2	825	194	101	94	24	3	8	6	50	2	202	4	10	8	.556	0-0	0	98	.714	3.66	4.28
Postseason			5	4	0	26.0	103	17	7	7	0	1	0	0	11	1	36	1	2	1	.667	0-1	0	98	.505	1.75	2.42
5 ML YEARS			119	118	0	716.0	2940	665	291	263	63	15	19	19	166	9	775	25	47	30	.610	0-0	1	98	.661	3.06	3.31

Jameson Taillon

Pitches: R Bats: R Pos: SP-7 TIE-yohn **Ht: 6'5" Wt: 230 Born: 11/18/1991 Age: 28**

Year	Team	Lg	G	GS	GF	IP	BFP	H	R	ER	HR	SH	SF	HB	TBB	IBB	SO	WP	W	L	Pct	Sv-Op	Hld	Vel	OPS	ERC	ERA
2016	Pit	NL	18	18	0	104.0	418	99	40	39	13	4	1	3	17	1	85	1	5	4	.556	0-0	0	94	.702	3.21	3.38
2017	Pit	NL	25	25	0	133.2	587	152	69	66	11	8	4	4	46	3	125	7	8	7	.533	0-0	0	95	.789	4.61	4.44
2018	Pit	NL	32	32	0	191.0	785	179	69	68	20	4	2	6	46	4	179	2	14	10	.583	0-0	0	95	.681	3.26	3.20
2019	Pit	NL	7	7	0	37.1	158	34	24	17	4	0	1	2	8	1	30	1	2	3	.400	0-0	0	95	.680	2.98	4.10
4 ML YEARS			82	82	0	466.0	1948	464	202	190	48	16	8	15	117	9	419	11	29	24	.547	0-0	0	95	.718	3.60	3.67

Masahiro Tanaka

Pitches: R Bats: R Pos: SP-31; RP-1 mah-sah-HEE-roh tuh-NAH-kah **Ht: 6'3" Wt: 215 Born: 11/1/1988 Age: 31**

Year	Team	Lg	G	GS	GF	IP	BFP	H	R	ER	HR	SH	SF	HB	TBB	IBB	SO	WP	W	L	Pct	Sv-Op	Hld	Vel	OPS	ERC	ERA
2014	NYY	AL	20	20	0	136.1	542	123	47	42	15	2	3	4	21	0	141	4	13	5	.722	0-0	0	91	.657	2.83	2.77
2015	NYY	AL	24	24	0	154.0	609	126	66	60	25	1	8	1	27	0	139	4	12	7	.632	0-0	0	92	.674	2.65	3.51
2016	NYY	AL	31	31	0	199.2	805	179	75	68	22	4	3	3	36	0	165	7	14	4	.778	0-0	0	91	.645	2.80	3.07
2017	NYY	AL	30	30	0	178.1	752	180	100	94	35	1	2	7	41	1	194	7	13	12	.520	0-0	0	92	.771	4.23	4.74
2018	NYY	AL	27	27	0	156.0	635	141	68	65	25	3	2	7	35	0	159	3	12	6	.667	0-0	0	92	.711	3.46	3.75
2019	NYY	AL	32	31	0	182.0	759	186	95	90	28	0	4	2	40	0	149	7	11	9	.550	0-0	0	91	.751	3.89	4.45
Postseason			5	5	0	30.0	112	17	5	5	3	0	0	0	7	0	25	2	3	2	.600	0-0	0	93	.500	1.46	1.50
6 ML YEARS			164	163	0	1006.1	4102	935	451	419	150	11	22	24	200	1	947	32	75	43	.636	0-0	0	91	.704	3.32	3.75

Raimel Tapia

Bats: L **Throws:** L **Pos:** LF-91;PH-38;CF-13;RF-6;PR-1   rye-MELL   **Ht:** 6'3" **Wt:** 185 **Born:** 2/4/1994 **Age:** 26

								BATTING															RUNNING			AVERAGES			
Year	Team	Lg	G	AB	H	2B	3B	HR	(Hm | Rd)	TB	R	RBI	RC	TBB	IBB	SO	HBP	SH	SF				SB	CS	GDP	Avg	OBP	Slg	OPS
2016	Col	NL	22	38	10	0	0	0	(0 | 0)	10	4	3	5	2	0	11	0	0	1				3	0	0	.263	.293	.263	.556
2017	Col	NL	70	160	46	12	2	2	(1 | 1)	68	27	16	20	8	1	36	2	1	0				5	2	3	.288	.329	.425	.754
2018	Col	NL	25	25	5	2	1	1	(0 | 1)	12	6	6	5	2	0	7	0	0	0				0	0	0	.200	.259	.480	.739
2019	Col	NL	138	426	117	23	5	9	(6 | 3)	177	54	44	54	21	0	100	0	0	0				9	3	2	.275	.309	.415	.724
	Postseason		1	1	1	0	0	0	(0 | 0)	1	0	0	1	0	0	0	0	0	0				0	0	0	1.000	1.000	1.000	2.000
	4 ML YEARS		255	649	178	37	8	12	(7 | 5)	267	91	69	84	33	1	154	2	1	1				17	5	5	.274	.311	.411	.722

Stephen Tarpley

Pitches: L **Bats:** R **Pos:** RP-20; SP-1   **Ht:** 6'1" **Wt:** 235 **Born:** 2/17/1993 **Age:** 27

			HOW MUCH PITCHED					WHAT HE GAVE UP										THE RESULTS								
Year	Team	Lg	G	GS	GF	IP	BFP	H	R	ER	HR	SH	SF	HB	TBB	IBB	SO	WP	W	L	Pct	Sv-Op	Hld	Vel	OPS	ERC	ERA
2019	S-WB	AAA	18	2	6	31.2	133	25	15	11	3	1	0	1	13	0	34	3	5	1	.833	3- -	-	-	.634	3.03	3.13
2018	NYY	AL	10	0	3	9.0	40	6	3	3	0	0	0	0	6	0	13	0	0	0	-	0-0	0	93	.506	2.46	3.00
2019	NYY	AL	21	1	3	24.2	120	34	20	19	6	0	0	2	15	1	34	5	1	0	1.000	2-2	2	92	.988	8.99	6.93
	Postseason		1	0	0	1.0	8	4	3	3	0	0	0	0	1	0	1	1	0	0	-	0-0	0	93	1.339	27.72	27.00
	2 ML YEARS		31	1	6	33.2	160	40	23	22	6	0	0	2	21	1	47	5	1	0	1.000	2-2	2	93	.868	6.98	5.88

Dillon Tate

Pitches: R **Bats:** R **Pos:** RP-16   **Ht:** 6'2" **Wt:** 195 **Born:** 5/1/1994 **Age:** 26

			HOW MUCH PITCHED					WHAT HE GAVE UP										THE RESULTS								
Year	Team	Lg	G	GS	GF	IP	BFP	H	R	ER	HR	SH	SF	HB	TBB	IBB	SO	WP	W	L	Pct	Sv-Op	Hld	Vel	OPS	ERC	ERA
2019	Bowie	AA	17	2	12	33.2	137	28	14	13	4	1	0	2	9	2	30	1	2	3	.400	5- -	-	-	.647	2.95	3.48
2019	Bal	AL	16	0	5	21.0	93	18	15	15	3	0	1	5	9	0	20	2	0	2	.000	0-0	1	94	.729	4.64	6.43

Fernando Tatis Jr.

Bats: R **Throws:** R **Pos:** SS-83;PH-1   **Ht:** 6'3" **Wt:** 185 **Born:** 1/2/1999 **Age:** 21

								BATTING															RUNNING			AVERAGES			
Year	Team	Lg	G	AB	H	2B	3B	HR	(Hm	Rd)	TB	R	RBI	RC	TBB	IBB	SO	HBP	SH	SF				SB	CS	GDP	Avg	OBP	Slg	OPS
2016	2 Tms	Low	55	220	60	17	3	4	(-	-)	95	39	25	29	13	0	57	0	1	2				15	3	4	.273	.311	.432	.742
2017	FtWyn	A	117	431	121	26	7	21	(-	-)	224	78	69	90	75	2	124	6	0	6				29	15	6	.281	.390	.520	.910
2017	SnAnt	AA	14	55	14	1	0	1	(-	-)	18	6	6	6	5	2	17	0	0	0				3	0	0	.255	.281	.327	.608
2018	SnAnt	AA	88	353	101	22	4	16	(-	-)	179	77	43	65	33	1	109	6	0	2				16	5	8	.286	.355	.507	.862
2019	SD	NL	84	334	106	13	6	22	(10	12)	197	61	53	73	30	1	110	5	0	3				16	6	4	.317	.379	.590	.969

Mike Tauchman

Bats: L **Throws:** L **Pos:** LF-59;RF-19;CF-14;PH-1;PR-1   **Ht:** 6'2" **Wt:** 220 **Born:** 12/3/1990 **Age:** 29

								BATTING															RUNNING			AVERAGES			
Year	Team	Lg	G	AB	H	2B	3B	HR	(Hm	Rd)	TB	R	RBI	RC	TBB	IBB	SO	HBP	SH	SF				SB	CS	GDP	Avg	OBP	Slg	OPS
2019	S-WB	AAA	28	95	26	10	3	2	(-	-)	48	22	16	20	16	1	16	2	0	1				4	0	1	.274	.386	.505	.891
2017	Col	NL	31	27	6	0	1	0	(0	0)	8	2	2	2	5	0	10	0	0	0				1	2	1	.222	.344	.296	.640
2018	Col	NL	21	32	3	1	0	0	(0	0)	4	5	0	4	4	0	15	0	1	0				1	0	0	.094	.194	.125	.319
2019	NYY	AL	87	260	72	18	1	13	(7	6)	131	46	47	50	34	0	71	1	0	1				6	0	9	.277	.361	.504	.865
	3 ML YEARS		139	319	81	19	2	13	(7	6)	143	53	49	52	43	0	96	1	1	1				8	2	10	.254	.343	.448	.792

Beau Taylor

Bats: L **Throws:** R **Pos:** C-10;PH-1   **Ht:** 5'11" **Wt:** 205 **Born:** 2/13/1990 **Age:** 30

								BATTING															RUNNING			AVERAGES			
Year	Team	Lg	G	AB	H	2B	3B	HR	(Hm	Rd)	TB	R	RBI	RC	TBB	IBB	SO	HBP	SH	SF				SB	CS	GDP	Avg	OBP	Slg	OPS
2019	LsVgs	AAA	62	191	49	13	1	8	(-	-)	88	38	32	39	47	1	70	2	0	4				0	0	4	.257	.408	.461	.869
2019	Buffalo	AAA	10	32	6	2	0	0	(-	-)	8	5	4	2	5	0	8	0	0	2				0	0	0	.188	.282	.250	.532
2018	Oak	AL	7	5	1	1	0	0	(0	0)	2	0	0	0	1	0	2	0	0	0				0	0	0	.200	.333	.400	.733
2019	2 Tms	AL	11	25	4	0	0	2	(1	1)	10	3	2	2	4	0	7	1	0	0				0	0	0	.160	.300	.400	.700
19	Oak	AL	10	23	4	0	0	2	(1	1)	10	3	2	2	4	0	6	1	0	0				0	0	0	.174	.321	.435	.756
19	Tor	AL	1	2	0	0	0	0	(0	0)	0	0	0	0	0	0	1	0	0	0				0	0	0	.000	.000	.000	.000
	2 ML YEARS		18	30	5	1	0	2	(1	1)	12	3	2	2	5	0	9	1	0	0				0	0	0	.167	.306	.400	.706

Chris Taylor

Bats: R **Throws:** R **Pos:** LF-56;SS-39;PH-21;2B-20;CF-20;3B-6;RF-3;PR-2   **Ht:** 6'1" **Wt:** 196 **Born:** 8/29/1990 **Age:** 29

								BATTING															RUNNING			AVERAGES			
Year	Team	Lg	G	AB	H	2B	3B	HR	(Hm	Rd)	TB	R	RBI	RC	TBB	IBB	SO	HBP	SH	SF				SB	CS	GDP	Avg	OBP	Slg	OPS
2014	Sea	AL	47	136	39	8	0	0	(0	0)	47	16	9	18	11	0	39	2	1	1				5	2	3	.287	.347	.346	.692
2015	Sea	AL	37	94	16	3	1	0	(0	0)	21	9	1	1	6	0	31	0	2	0				3	2	0	.170	.220	.223	.443
2016	2 Tms		36	61	13	2	2	1	(0	1)	22	8	7	5	4	1	15	0	0	0				0	0	3	.213	.262	.361	.622
2017	LAD	NL	140	514	148	34	5	21	(7	14)	255	85	72	88	50	0	142	3	0	1				17	4	2	.288	.354	.496	.850
2018	LAD	NL	155	536	136	35	8	17	(10	7)	238	85	63	75	55	0	178	9	0	4				9	6	5	.254	.331	.444	.775
2019	LAD	NL	124	366	96	29	4	12	(8	4)	169	52	52	60	37	3	115	4	2	5				8	0	6	.262	.333	.462	.794
16	Sea	AL	2	3	1	0	0	0	(0	0)	1	0	0	0	0	0	2	0	0	0				0	0	0	.333	.333	.333	.667
16	LAD	NL	34	58	12	2	2	1	(0	1)	21	8	7	5	4	1	13	0	0	0				0	0	3	.207	.258	.362	.620
	Postseason		30	98	26	5	2	4	(2	2)	47	18	10	19	20	0	23	1	0	0				1	1	0	.265	.395	.480	.875
	6 ML YEARS		539	1707	448	111	20	51	(25	26)	752	255	204	247	163	4	520	18	5	11				42	14	19	.262	.331	.441	.772

Josh Taylor

Pitches: L **Bats:** L **Pos:** RP-51; SP-1   **Ht:** 6'5" **Wt:** 225 **Born:** 3/2/1993 **Age:** 27

			HOW MUCH PITCHED					WHAT HE GAVE UP										THE RESULTS						
Year	Team	Lg	G	GS	GF	IP	BFP	H	R	ER	HR	SH	SF	HB	TBB	IBB	SO	WP	W	L	Pct	Sv-Op Hld	Vel	OPS	ERC	ERA
2019	Pwtckt	AAA	20	0	7	23.1	97	18	9	7	2	1	3	1	11	0	32	2	1	1	.500	3- - -	-	.633	3.22	2.70
2019	Bos	AL	52	1	8	47.1	194	40	17	16	5	0	1	2	16	1	62	3	2	2	.500	0-1	4	95	.642	3.22	3.04

Michael A. Taylor

Bats: R **Throws:** R **Pos:** CF-25;PH-16;PR-9;RF-7   **Ht:** 6'4" **Wt:** 212 **Born:** 3/26/1991 **Age:** 29

			BATTING																	RUNNING			AVERAGES			
Year	Team	Lg	G	AB	H	2B	3B	HR	(Hm	Rd)	TB	R	RBI	RC	TBB	IBB	SO	HBP	SH	SF	SB	CS	GDP	Avg	OBP	Slg	OPS
2019	Hrsbrg	AA	57	218	54	16	2	9	(-	-)	101	36	35	33	25	2	69	1	0	3	10	6	4	.248	.324	.463	.787
2014	Was	NL	17	39	8	3	0	1	(0	1)	14	5	5	3	3	0	17	1	0	0	0	2	1	.205	.279	.359	.638
2015	Was	NL	138	472	108	15	2	14	(6	8)	169	49	63	60	35	9	158	1	1	1	16	3	5	.229	.282	.358	.640
2016	Was	NL	76	221	51	11	0	7	(1	6)	83	28	16	20	14	0	77	1	0	1	14	3	2	.231	.278	.376	.654
2017	Was	NL	118	399	108	23	3	19	(11	8)	194	55	53	57	29	3	137	1	1	2	17	7	3	.271	.320	.486	.806
2018	Was	NL	134	353	80	22	3	6	(2	4)	126	46	28	33	29	2	116	1	2	0	24	6	9	.227	.287	.357	.644
2019	Was	NL	53	88	22	7	0	1	(1	0)	32	10	3	7	7	0	34	0	2	0	6	0	0	.250	.305	.364	.669
	Postseason		8	17	5	0	0	2	(1	1)	11	3	8	7	3	0	6	0	0	0	0	0	0	.294	.400	.647	1.047
	6 ML YEARS		536	1572	377	81	8	48	(21	27)	618	193	168	180	117	14	539	5	6	5	77	21	20	.240	.294	.393	.687

Tyrone Taylor

Bats: R **Throws:** R **Pos:** RF-8;PH-5;CF-3;PR-1   **Ht:** 6'0" **Wt:** 185 **Born:** 1/22/1994 **Age:** 26

			BATTING																	RUNNING			AVERAGES			
Year	Team	Lg	G	AB	H	2B	3B	HR	(Hm	Rd)	TB	R	RBI	RC	TBB	IBB	SO	HBP	SH	SF	SB	CS	GDP	Avg	OBP	Slg	OPS
2019	SnAnt	AAA	92	334	90	20	1	14	(-	-)	154	44	59	54	28	0	85	7	1	5	5	0	11	.269	.334	.461	.795
2019	Mil	NL	15	10	4	2	0	0	(0	0)	6	1	1	3	1	0	1	1	0	0	1	0	0	.400	.500	.600	1.100

Julio Teheran

Pitches: R **Bats:** R **Pos:** SP-33   tay-RAHN   **Ht:** 6'2" **Wt:** 205 **Born:** 1/27/1991 **Age:** 29

			HOW MUCH PITCHED					WHAT HE GAVE UP										THE RESULTS						
Year	Team	Lg	G	GS	GF	IP	BFP	H	R	ER	HR	SH	SF	HB	TBB	IBB	SO	WP	W	L	Pct	Sv-Op Hld	Vel	OPS	ERC	ERA
2011	Atl	NL	5	3	0	19.2	87	21	11	11	4	2	1	0	8	0	10	1	1	1	.500	0-0	0	93	.828	5.19	5.03
2012	Atl	NL	2	1	0	6.1	24	5	4	4	0	0	0	0	1	0	5	0	0	0	-	0-0	0	92	.467	1.64	5.68
2013	Atl	NL	30	30	0	185.2	774	173	69	66	22	8	5	13	45	4	170	2	14	8	.636	0-0	0	92	.700	3.45	3.20
2014	Atl	NL	33	33	0	221.0	884	188	82	71	22	13	4	4	51	4	186	1	14	13	.519	0-0	0	90	.639	2.71	2.89
2015	Atl	NL	33	33	0	200.2	843	189	99	90	27	10	3	9	73	3	171	2	11	8	.579	0-0	0	91	.737	4.07	4.04
2016	Atl	NL	30	30	0	188.0	758	157	70	67	22	4	1	9	41	2	167	7	7	10	.412	0-0	0	91	.650	2.79	3.21
2017	Atl	NL	32	32	0	188.1	812	186	103	94	31	7	3	7	72	3	151	6	11	13	.458	0-0	0	91	.772	4.52	4.49
2018	Atl	NL	31	31	0	175.2	724	122	80	77	26	3	5	9	84	3	162	2	9	9	.500	0-0	0	90	.672	3.25	3.94
2019	Atl	NL	33	33	0	174.2	754	148	81	74	22	6	5	14	83	3	162	5	10	11	.476	0-0	0	90	.717	3.99	3.81
	Postseason		2	1	0	4.1	22	9	6	6	1	0	1	0	1	0	7	1	0	1	.000	0-0	0	93	1.105	11.77	12.46
	9 ML YEARS		229	226	0	1360.0	5660	1189	599	554	176	53	27	65	458	22	1184	26	77	73	.513	0-0	0	91	.699	3.52	3.67

Ruben Tejada

Bats: R **Throws:** R **Pos:** 2B-2;3B-2;SS-2;PR-1   **Ht:** 5'11" **Wt:** 200 **Born:** 10/27/1989 **Age:** 30

			BATTING																	RUNNING			AVERAGES			
Year	Team	Lg	G	AB	H	2B	3B	HR	(Hm	Rd)	TB	R	RBI	RC	TBB	IBB	SO	HBP	SH	SF	SB	CS	GDP	Avg	OBP	Slg	OPS
2019	Syrcse	AAA	73	276	90	20	1	6	(-	-)	130	54	42	53	30	0	53	7	0	1	3	3	9	.326	.404	.471	.875
2010	NYM	NL	78	216	46	12	0	1	(0	1)	61	28	15	16	22	3	38	8	6	3	2	2	2	.213	.305	.282	.588
2011	NYM	NL	96	328	93	15	1	0	(0	0)	110	31	36	41	35	3	50	6	4	3	5	1	6	.284	.360	.335	.696
2012	NYM	NL	114	464	134	26	0	1	(0	1)	163	53	25	49	27	0	73	5	3	2	4	4	9	.289	.333	.351	.685
2013	NYM	NL	57	208	42	12	0	0	(0	0)	54	20	10	15	15	0	24	1	3	0	2	1	3	.202	.259	.260	.519
2014	NYM	NL	119	355	84	11	0	5	(1	4)	110	30	34	42	50	11	73	8	4	2	1	2	8	.237	.342	.310	.652
2015	NYM	NL	116	360	94	23	0	3	(2	1)	126	36	28	42	38	5	70	5	2	2	2	1	6	.261	.338	.350	.688
2016	2 Tms		36	66	11	5	0	0	(0	0)	16	9	5	2	7	0	13	1	1	3	0	0	1	.167	.247	.242	.489
2017	Bal	AL	41	113	26	6	0	0	(0	0)	32	17	5	5	8	0	15	2	1	0	0	0	6	.230	.293	.283	.576
2019	NYM	NL	6	9	0	0	0	0	(0	0)	0	1	0	0	0	0	3	0	0	0	0	0	0	.000	.000	.000	.000
16	StL	NL	23	34	6	2	0	0	(0	0)	8	6	3	0	2	0	8	1	0	3	0	0	1	.176	.225	.235	.460
16	SF	NL	13	32	5	3	0	0	(0	0)	8	3	2	2	5	0	5	0	1	0	0	0	0	.156	.270	.250	.520
	Postseason		2	5	0	0	0	0	(0	0)	0	1	0	0	1	0	5	0	0	0	0	0	0	.000	.167	.000	.167
	9 ML YEARS		663	2119	530	110	1	10	(3	7)	672	225	158	212	202	22	359	36	24	15	16	11	41	.250	.324	.317	.641

Rowdy Tellez

Bats: L **Throws:** L **Pos:** 1B-57;DH-45;PH-10   **Ht:** 6'4" **Wt:** 255 **Born:** 3/16/1995 **Age:** 25

			BATTING																	RUNNING			AVERAGES			
Year	Team	Lg	G	AB	H	2B	3B	HR	(Hm	Rd)	TB	R	RBI	RC	TBB	IBB	SO	HBP	SH	SF	SB	CS	GDP	Avg	OBP	Slg	OPS
2019	Buffalo	AAA	26	93	34	9	0	7	(-	-)	64	20	21	26	14	0	25	1	0	1	0	0	1	.366	.450	.688	1.138
2018	Tor	AL	23	70	22	9	0	4	(3	1)	43	10	14	17	2	0	21	0	0	0	0	0	3	.314	.329	.614	.943
2019	Tor	AL	111	370	84	19	0	21	(12	9)	166	49	54	47	29	3	116	7	0	3	1	1	9	.227	.293	.449	.742
	2 ML YEARS		134	440	106	28	0	25	(15	10)	209	59	68	64	31	3	137	7	0	4	1	1	9	.241	.299	.475	.774

Ryan Tepera

Pitches: R **Bats:** R **Pos:** RP-22; SP-1   tuh-PAIR-uh   **Ht:** 6'1" **Wt:** 195 **Born:** 11/3/1987 **Age:** 32

Year	Team	Lg	HOW MUCH PITCHED					WHAT HE GAVE UP										THE RESULTS						
			G	GS	GF	IP	BFP	H	R	ER	HR	SH	SF	HB	TBB	IBB	SO	WP	W	L	Pct	Sv-Op	Hld	Vel	OPS	ERC	ERA
2019	Buffalo	AAA	5	1	0	5.0	23	4	4	2	1	0	0	1	2	0	4	0	0	0	-	0--	-	-	.704	4.15	3.60
2015	Tor	AL	32	0	12	33.0	128	23	14	12	8	0	0	3	6	0	22	2	0	2	.000	1-1	0	95	.670	2.87	3.27
2016	Tor	AL	20	0	13	18.1	85	17	8	6	1	1	0	3	8	1	18	3	0	1	.000	0-0	0	95	.635	3.81	2.95
2017	Tor	AL	73	0	12	77.2	319	57	35	31	7	1	1	8	31	4	81	5	7	1	.875	2-4	17	95	.633	2.94	3.59
2018	Tor	AL	68	0	19	64.2	263	55	27	26	9	0	3	4	24	1	68	5	5	5	.500	7-15	19	95	.738	3.77	3.62
2019	Tor	AL	23	1	7	21.2	91	20	12	12	5	1	2	0	8	2	14	2	0	2	.000	0-0	2	94	.824	4.29	4.98
	Postseason		2	0	1	2.1	14	5	4	4	0	0	3	0	2	0	0	1	0	0	-	0-0	0	93	1.167	12.37	15.43
	5 ML YEARS		216	1	63	215.1	886	172	96	87	30	3	6	18	77	8	203	17	12	11	.522	10-20	38	95	.690	3.40	3.64

Matt Thaiss

Bats: L **Throws:** R **Pos:** 3B-43;1B-13;PH-8   THICE   **Ht:** 6'0" **Wt:** 215 **Born:** 5/6/1995 **Age:** 25

Year	Team	Lg	BATTING																		RUNNING			AVERAGES			
			G	AB	H	2B	3B	HR	(Hm	Rd)	TB	R	RBI	RC	TBB	IBB	SO	HBP	SH	SF	SB	CS	GDP	Avg	OBP	Slg	OPS
2019	Salt Lk	AAA	79	310	85	17	2	14	(-	-)	148	63	49	61	59	0	64	1	0	2	1	0	7	.274	.390	.477	.867
2019	LAA	AL	53	147	31	7	0	8	(8	0)	62	17	23	20	17	0	52	0	0	0	0	0	4	.211	.293	.422	.714

Eric Thames

Bats: L **Throws:** R **Pos:** 1B-105;PH-49;RF-12;DH-3   **Ht:** 6'0" **Wt:** 210 **Born:** 11/10/1986 **Age:** 33

Year	Team	Lg	BATTING																		RUNNING			AVERAGES			
			G	AB	H	2B	3B	HR	(Hm	Rd)	TB	R	RBI	RC	TBB	IBB	SO	HBP	SH	SF	SB	CS	GDP	Avg	OBP	Slg	OPS
2011	Tor	AL	95	362	95	24	5	12	(10	2)	165	58	37	42	23	0	88	5	1	3	2	1	7	.262	.313	.456	.769
2012	2 Tms		86	271	63	12	3	9	(6	3)	108	27	25	25	15	0	87	1	1	2	1	1	7	.232	.273	.399	.672
2017	Mil	NL	138	469	116	26	4	31	(20	11)	243	83	63	77	75	5	163	7	0	0	4	2	6	.247	.359	.518	.877
2018	Mil	NL	96	247	54	10	3	16	(11	5)	118	41	37	40	29	4	97	2	0	0	7	0	3	.219	.306	.478	.783
2019	Mil	NL	149	396	98	23	2	25	(14	11)	200	67	61	64	51	4	140	10	0	2	3	2	0	.247	.346	.505	.851
12	Tor	AL	46	148	36	7	1	3	(1	2)	54	17	11	13	9	0	40	1	0	2	0	1	7	.243	.288	.365	.652
12	Sea	AL	40	123	27	5	2	6	(5	1)	54	10	14	12	6	0	47	0	1	0	1	0	0	.220	.256	.439	.695
	5 ML YEARS		564	1745	426	95	17	93	(61	32)	834	276	223	248	193	13	575	25	2	7	17	6	23	.244	.327	.478	.805

Lane Thomas

Bats: R **Throws:** R **Pos:** CF-19;PH-13;RF-5;PR-5;LF-2   **Ht:** 6'1" **Wt:** 210 **Born:** 8/23/1995 **Age:** 24

Year	Team	Lg	BATTING																		RUNNING			AVERAGES			
			G	AB	H	2B	3B	HR	(Hm	Rd)	TB	R	RBI	RC	TBB	IBB	SO	HBP	SH	SF	SB	CS	GDP	Avg	OBP	Slg	OPS
2019	Memp	AAA	75	265	71	17	2	10	(-	-)	122	42	44	44	32	0	80	4	0	3	11	6	2	.268	.352	.460	.812
2019	StL	NL	34	38	12	0	1	4	(3	1)	26	6	12	12	4	0	8	2	0	0	1	1	1	.316	.409	.684	1.093

Tyler Thornburg

Pitches: R **Bats:** R **Pos:** RP-16   **Ht:** 5'11" **Wt:** 190 **Born:** 9/29/1988 **Age:** 31

Year	Team	Lg	HOW MUCH PITCHED					WHAT HE GAVE UP											THE RESULTS						
			G	GS	GF	IP	BFP	H	R	ER	HR	SH	SF	HB	TBB	IBB	SO	WP	W	L	Pct	Sv-Op	Hld	Vel	OPS	ERC	ERA
2019	OkCity	AAA	12	0	3	12.0	56	11	9	8	3	0	0	1	9	0	15	0	0	0	-	0--	-	-	.853	6.53	6.00
2019	Pwtckt	AAA	11	1	1	10.2	60	17	15	15	5	0	0	0	9	0	13	3	0	2	.000	0--	-	-	1.139	12.69	12.66
2012	Mil	NL	8	3	3	22.0	95	24	11	11	8	1	0	1	7	0	20	1	0	0	-	0-0	0	93	.922	6.44	4.50
2013	Mil	NL	18	7	4	66.2	270	53	17	15	1	4	1	3	26	2	48	2	3	1	.750	0-0	0	92	.575	2.59	2.03
2014	Mil	NL	27	0	4	29.2	131	24	14	14	1	1	1	0	21	0	28	4	3	1	.750	0-0	5	94	.670	3.71	4.25
2015	Mil	NL	24	0	9	34.1	151	31	22	14	7	0	2	3	12	1	34	3	0	2	.000	0-0	1	92	.723	4.20	3.67
2016	Mil	NL	67	0	23	67.0	263	38	19	16	6	0	1	2	25	1	90	4	8	5	.615	13-21	20	94	.541	1.82	2.15
2018	Bos	AL	25	0	9	24.0	107	28	15	15	6	0	1	1	10	0	21	2	2	0	1.000	0-0	3	93	.901	6.56	5.63
2019	Bos	AL	16	0	4	18.2	86	21	16	16	4	0	0	1	10	0	22	1	0	0	-	0-0	0	94	.972	6.51	7.71
	7 ML YEARS		185	10	56	262.1	1103	219	114	101	33	6	6	11	111	4	263	17	16	9	.640	13-21	29	93	.692	3.59	3.47

Trent Thornton

Pitches: R **Bats:** R **Pos:** SP-29; RP-3   **Ht:** 6'0" **Wt:** 195 **Born:** 9/30/1993 **Age:** 26

Year	Team	Lg	HOW MUCH PITCHED					WHAT HE GAVE UP											THE RESULTS						
			G	GS	GF	IP	BFP	H	R	ER	HR	SH	SF	HB	TBB	IBB	SO	WP	W	L	Pct	Sv-Op	Hld	Vel	OPS	ERC	ERA
2019	Tor	AL	32	29	0	154.1	677	156	87	83	24	1	7	5	61	0	149	5	6	9	.400	0-0	0	93	.768	4.60	4.84

Lewis Thorpe

Pitches: L **Bats:** R **Pos:** RP-10; SP-2   **Ht:** 6'1" **Wt:** 218 **Born:** 11/23/1995 **Age:** 24

Year	Team	Lg	HOW MUCH PITCHED					WHAT HE GAVE UP											THE RESULTS						
			G	GS	GF	IP	BFP	H	R	ER	HR	SH	SF	HB	TBB	IBB	SO	WP	W	L	Pct	Sv-Op	Hld	Vel	OPS	ERC	ERA
2019	Roch	AAA	20	19	0	96.1	403	91	51	49	13	3	1	1	25	0	119	5	5	4	.556	0--	0	-	.711	3.45	4.58
2019	Min	AL	12	2	3	27.2	124	38	19	19	7	0	1	0	10	0	31	3	3	2	.600	0-2	0	91	.918	6.41	6.18

Charlie Tilson

Bats: L **Throws:** L **Pos:** RF-30;LF-19;CF-14;PH-5;PR-2   **Ht:** 6'0" **Wt:** 185 **Born:** 12/2/1992 **Age:** 27

Year Team	Lg	G	AB	H	2B	3B	HR	(Hm	Rd)	TB	R	RBI	RC	TBB	IBB	SO	HBP	SH	SF	SB	CS	GDP	Avg	OBP	Slg	OPS
2019 Charllt	AAA	61	236	68	13	2	3	(-	-)	94	36	34	33	19	0	43	2	0	1	4	3	3	.288	.345	.398	.743
2016 CWS	AL	1	2	1	0	0	0	(0	0)	1	0	0	0	0	0	0	0	0	0	0	0	0	.500	.500	.500	1.000
2018 CWS	AL	41	106	28	1	1	0	(0	0)	31	7	11	12	10	0	20	1	2	1	2	3	2	.264	.331	.292	.623
2019 CWS	AL	54	144	33	5	0	1	(0	1)	41	16	12	15	10	1	38	3	0	0	4	0	1	.229	.293	.285	.578
3 ML YEARS		96	252	62	6	1	1	(0	1)	73	23	23	27	20	1	58	4	2	1	6	3	3	.246	.310	.290	.600

Jesus Tinoco

Pitches: R **Bats:** R **Pos:** RP-24   **Ht:** 6'4" **Wt:** 263 **Born:** 4/30/1995 **Age:** 25

Year Team	Lg	G	GS	GF	IP	BFP	H	R	ER	HR	SH	SF	HB	TBB	IBB	SO	WP	W	L	Pct	Sv-Op	Hld	Vel	OPS	ERC	ERA
2019 Albq	AAA	29	0	16	34.0	146	33	17	15	4	0	2	0	18	0	23	1	3	1	.750	1--	-	-	.738	4.68	3.97
2019 Col	NL	24	0	3	36.0	161	36	23	19	12	0	1	1	22	1	28	1	0	3	.000	1-1	2	94	.965	6.94	4.75

Yasmany Tomas

Bats: R **Throws:** R **Pos:** PH-3;DH-1   yahz-MAH-nee toh-MAHS   **Ht:** 6'2" **Wt:** 250 **Born:** 11/14/1990 **Age:** 29

Year Team	Lg	G	AB	H	2B	3B	HR	(Hm	Rd)	TB	R	RBI	RC	TBB	IBB	SO	HBP	SH	SF	SB	CS	GDP	Avg	OBP	Slg	OPS
2019 Reno	AAA	102	405	122	24	3	29	(-	-)	239	63	82	80	22	1	110	3	0	1	2	0	14	.301	.341	.590	.931
2015 Ari	NL	118	406	111	19	3	9	(4	5)	163	40	48	32	17	0	110	2	0	1	5	2	16	.273	.305	.401	.707
2016 Ari	NL	140	530	144	30	1	31	(16	15)	269	72	83	71	31	4	136	1	0	1	2	4	18	.272	.313	.508	.820
2017 Ari	NL	47	166	40	11	1	8	(6	2)	77	19	32	25	13	0	50	0	0	1	0	0	2	.241	.294	.464	.758
2019 Ari	NL	4	6	0	0	0	0	(-	-)	0	0	0	0	0	0	3	0	0	0	0	0	1	.000	.000	.000	.000
4 ML YEARS		309	1108	295	60	5	48	(26	22)	509	131	163	128	61	4	299	3	0	3	7	6	37	.266	.306	.459	.765

Josh Tomlin

Pitches: R **Bats:** R **Pos:** RP-50; SP-1   **Ht:** 6'1" **Wt:** 190 **Born:** 10/19/1984 **Age:** 35

Year Team	Lg	G	GS	GF	IP	BFP	H	R	ER	HR	SH	SF	HB	TBB	IBB	SO	WP	W	L	Pct	Sv-Op	Hld	Vel	OPS	ERC	ERA
2010 Cle	AL	12	12	0	73.0	301	72	38	37	10	3	3	3	19	3	43	1	6	4	.600	0-0	0	89	.773	3.89	4.56
2011 Cle	AL	26	26	0	165.1	662	157	80	78	24	1	3	3	21	2	89	3	12	7	.632	0-0	0	88	.712	3.11	4.25
2012 Cle	AL	21	16	0	103.1	452	126	74	73	18	2	3	3	25	3	56	4	5	8	.385	0-0	0	89	.860	5.34	6.36
2013 Cle	AL	1	0	0	2.0	9	2	0	0	0	0	0	0	0	0	0	0	0	0	-	0-0	0	90	.500	1.68	0.00
2014 Cle	AL	25	16	6	104.0	446	120	66	55	18	1	3	1	14	3	94	6	6	9	.400	0-0	0	89	.781	4.28	4.76
2015 Cle	AL	10	10	0	65.2	251	47	22	22	13	0	0	2	8	0	57	1	7	2	.778	0-0	0	88	.642	2.24	3.02
2016 Cle	AL	30	29	1	174.0	725	187	97	85	36	4	4	3	20	2	118	4	13	9	.591	0-0	0	88	.778	4.06	4.40
2017 Cle	AL	26	26	0	141.0	585	166	80	78	23	0	4	4	14	0	109	1	10	9	.526	0-0	0	88	.807	4.49	4.98
2018 Cle	AL	32	9	19	70.1	321	92	52	48	25	0	2	4	12	1	46	5	2	5	.286	0-0	0	88	.947	6.86	6.14
2019 Atl	NL	51	1	21	79.1	320	82	35	33	14	4	2	0	7	0	51	2	2	1	.667	2-4	7	89	.744	3.53	3.74
Postseason		6	4	2	20.2	81	15	9	9	1	0	0	0	5	0	15	0	3	1	.750	0-0	0	88	.523	1.81	3.92
10 ML YEARS		234	145	47	978.0	4072	1051	544	509	181	15	23	23	140	14	663	27	63	54	.538	2-4	7	88	.782	4.10	4.68

Abraham Toro

Bats: B **Throws:** R **Pos:** 3B-24;PH-3;1B-1;PR-1   **Ht:** 6'1" **Wt:** 190 **Born:** 12/20/1996 **Age:** 23

Year Team	Lg	G	AB	H	2B	3B	HR	(Hm	Rd)	TB	R	RBI	RC	TBB	IBB	SO	HBP	SH	SF	SB	CS	GDP	Avg	OBP	Slg	OPS
2019 CpChr	AA	98	376	115	22	4	16	(-	-)	193	65	70	77	48	2	77	8	0	3	4	1	4	.306	.393	.513	.906
2019 RdRck	AAA	16	66	28	9	0	1	(-	-)	40	17	10	18	10	0	5	2	0	1	0	1	0	.424	.506	.606	1.112
2019 Hou	AL	25	78	17	3	2	2	(1	1)	30	13	9	8	9	0	19	1	0	1	1	1	2	.218	.303	.385	.688

Luis Torrens

Bats: R **Throws:** R **Pos:** C-4;PH-4   **Ht:** 6'0" **Wt:** 175 **Born:** 5/2/1996 **Age:** 24

Year Team	Lg	G	AB	H	2B	3B	HR	(Hm	Rd)	TB	R	RBI	RC	TBB	IBB	SO	HBP	SH	SF	SB	CS	GDP	Avg	OBP	Slg	OPS
2019 Amrillo	AA	97	350	105	23	1	15	(-	-)	175	50	62	66	42	2	67	1	0	4	1	1	15	.300	.373	.500	.873
2017 SD	NL	56	123	20	3	1	0	(0	0)	25	7	7	4	12	3	30	1	3	0	0	0	4	.163	.242	.203	.446
2019 SD	NL	7	14	3	1	0	0	(0	0)	4	2	0	1	2	0	6	0	0	0	0	0	1	.214	.313	.286	.598
2 ML YEARS		63	137	23	4	1	0	(0	0)	29	9	7	5	14	3	36	1	3	0	0	0	5	.168	.250	.212	.462

Carlos Torres

Pitches: R **Bats:** R **Pos:** RP-4   **Ht:** 6'1" **Wt:** 180 **Born:** 10/22/1982 **Age:** 37

Year Team	Lg	G	GS	GF	IP	BFP	H	R	ER	HR	SH	SF	HB	TBB	IBB	SO	WP	W	L	Pct	Sv-Op	Hld	Vel	OPS	ERC	ERA
2019 ElPaso	AAA	15	0	3	25.1	105	21	7	7	2	1	0	1	10	0	23	1	1	1	.500	1--	-	-	.620	3.18	2.49
2019 Toledo	AAA	5	0	2	5.2	19	5	0	0	0	0	0	0	0	0	3	0	0	0	-	0--	-	-	.579	1.77	0.00
2019 Roch	AAA	8	0	3	17.1	77	19	8	8	1	0	3	1	8	0	16	3	4	1	.800	0--	-	-	.810	4.86	4.15
2009 CWS	AL	8	5	2	28.1	130	30	20	19	5	3	3	2	17	2	22	0	1	2	.333	0-0	0	90	.862	6.05	6.04
2010 CWS	AL	5	1	1	13.2	71	23	13	13	2	0	1	0	9	1	13	0	0	1	.000	0-0	0	90	1.041	9.84	8.56
2012 Col	NL	31	0	9	53.0	231	49	31	31	2	6	4	4	26	1	42	6	5	3	.625	0-0	1	91	.723	3.85	5.26
2013 NYM	NL	33	9	6	86.1	352	79	34	33	15	4	1	4	17	1	75	4	4	6	.400	0-0	3	91	.701	3.47	3.44
2014 NYM	NL	73	1	20	97.0	405	89	35	33	11	2	1	2	38	4	96	6	8	6	.571	2-5	12	92	.715	3.77	3.06
2015 NYM	NL	59	0	19	57.2	243	61	32	30	5	1	3	0	18	6	48	5	5	6	.455	0-1	11	92	.743	3.86	4.68

Year	Team	Lg	G	GS	GF	IP	BFP	H	R	ER	HR	SH	SF	HB	TBB	IBB	SO	WP	W	L	Pct	Sv-Op	Hld	Vel	OPS	ERC	ERA
			HOW MUCH PITCHED					**WHAT HE GAVE UP**											**THE RESULTS**								
2016	Mil	NL	72	0	12	82.1	339	65	26	25	8	3	2	4	30	3	78	1	3	3	.500	2-5	20	92	.655	2.94	2.73
2017	Mil	NL	67	0	16	72.2	322	78	37	34	10	2	4	3	33	1	56	4	4	4	.500	1-4	13	94	.785	5.19	4.21
2018	Was	NL	10	0	9	9.2	41	9	7	7	3	0	0	1	3	0	9	0	0	0	-	0-0	0	93	.831	5.23	6.52
2019	Det	AL	4	0	1	6.0	29	9	5	5	2	0	0	1	9	0	8	1	0	0	-	0-0	0	91	.972	8.58	7.50
	10 ML YEARS		362	16	95	506.2	2163	492	240	230	63	21	19	21	192	19	447	27	30	31	.492	5-15	60	92	.743	4.14	4.09

Gleyber Torres

Bats: R **Throws:** R **Pos:** SS-77;2B-65;DH-5;PH-2   **Ht:** 6'1" **Wt:** 200 **Born:** 12/13/1996 **Age:** 23

Year	Team	Lg	G	AB	H	2B	3B	HR	(Hm	Rd)	TB	R	RBI	RC	TBB	IBB	SO	HBP	SH	SF	SB	CS	GDP	Avg	OBP	Slg	OPS
					BATTING																**RUNNING**			**AVERAGES**			
2018	NYY	AL	123	431	117	16	1	24	(13	11)	207	54	77	78	42	3	122	5	1	5	6	2	8	.271	.340	.480	.820
2019	NYY	AL	144	546	152	26	0	38	(20	18)	292	96	90	101	48	3	129	3	1	6	5	2	10	.278	.337	.535	.871
	Postseason		5	16	4	0	0	0	(0	0)	4	1	0	2	2	0	3	0	0	0	0	0	0	.250	.333	.250	.583
	2 ML YEARS		267	977	269	42	1	62	(33	29)	499	150	167	179	90	6	251	8	2	11	11	4	18	.275	.338	.511	.849

Ronald Torreyes

Bats: R **Throws:** R **Pos:** SS-6;2B-1;3B-1;LF-1   tore-RAY-ess   **Ht:** 5'8" **Wt:** 151 **Born:** 9/2/1992 **Age:** 27

Year	Team	Lg	G	AB	H	2B	3B	HR	(Hm	Rd)	TB	R	RBI	RC	TBB	IBB	SO	HBP	SH	SF	SB	CS	GDP	Avg	OBP	Slg	OPS
					BATTING																**RUNNING**			**AVERAGES**			
2019	Roch	AAA	79	308	79	11	1	11	(-	-)	125	48	42	37	12	0	33	4	1	5	2	1	6	.256	.289	.406	.695
2015	LAD	NL	8	6	2	1	0	0	(0	0)	3	1	1	2	1	0	1	0	1	0	0	0	0	.333	.429	.500	.929
2016	NYY	AL	72	155	40	7	4	1	(0	1)	58	20	12	19	10	0	20	1	1	1	2	1	4	.258	.305	.374	.680
2017	NYY	AL	108	315	92	15	1	3	(2	1)	118	35	36	37	11	0	43	1	5	4	2	0	9	.292	.314	.375	.689
2018	NYY	AL	41	100	28	7	1	0	(0	0)	37	9	7	12	2	0	16	0	0	0	0	0	3	.280	.294	.370	.664
2019	Min	AL	7	16	3	0	0	0	(0	0)	3	3	1	0	0	0	3	1	0	0	1	0	0	.188	.235	.188	.423
	Postseason		2	1	0	0	0	0	(0	0)	0	0	0	0	0	0	1	0	0	0	0	0	0	.000	.000	.000	.000
	5 ML YEARS		236	592	165	30	6	4	(2	2)	219	68	57	70	24	0	83	3	7	5	5	1	16	.279	.308	.370	.678

Touki Toussaint

Pitches: R **Bats:** R **Pos:** RP-23; SP-1   TOO-key TOO-sahnt   **Ht:** 6'3" **Wt:** 185 **Born:** 6/20/1996 **Age:** 24

Year	Team	Lg	G	GS	GF	IP	BFP	H	R	ER	HR	SH	SF	HB	TBB	IBB	SO	WP	W	L	Pct	Sv-Op	Hld	Vel	OPS	ERC	ERA
			HOW MUCH PITCHED					**WHAT HE GAVE UP**											**THE RESULTS**								
2019	Gwnntt	AAA	10	10	0	39.2	201	51	34	33	5	0	3	7	28	0	44	3	1	6	.143	0- -	-		.894	8.06	7.49
2018	Atl	NL	7	5	1	29.0	123	18	13	13	1	1	0	2	21	1	32	1	2	1	.667	0-0	0	93	.619	3.05	4.03
2019	Atl	NL	24	1	3	41.2	198	44	28	26	5	2	0	7	26	2	45	6	4	0	1.000	0-0	2	93	.810	6.05	5.62
	Postseason		2	0	0	3.0	13	1	0	0	0	0	0	0	4	0	2	0	1	0	1.000	0-0	0	95	.607	3.31	0.00
	2 ML YEARS		31	6	4	70.2	321	62	41	39	6	3	0	9	47	3	77	7	6	1	.857	0-0	2	93	.737	4.76	4.97

Wilfredo Tovar

Bats: R **Throws:** R **Pos:** SS-31;PR-3   will-FRAY-doe TOE-varr   **Ht:** 5'7" **Wt:** 180 **Born:** 8/11/1991 **Age:** 28

Year	Team	Lg	G	AB	H	2B	3B	HR	(Hm	Rd)	TB	R	RBI	RC	TBB	IBB	SO	HBP	SH	SF	SB	CS	GDP	Avg	OBP	Slg	OPS
					BATTING																**RUNNING**			**AVERAGES**			
2019	Salt Lk	AAA	85	327	105	17	6	4	(-	-)	146	53	57	51	19	0	45	0	0	3	3	5	17	.321	.355	.446	.802
2013	NYM	NL	7	15	3	0	0	0	(0	0)	3	1	2	2	1	1	3	1	2	0	1	0	2	.200	.294	.200	.494
2014	NYM	NL	2	3	0	0	0	0	(0	0)	0	0	0	0	0	0	0	0	0	0	0	0	0	.000	.000	.000	.000
2019	LAA	AL	31	83	16	5	0	0	(0	0)	21	5	5	4	5	0	15	0	0	0	0	0	0	.193	.239	.253	.492
	3 ML YEARS		40	101	19	5	0	0	(0	0)	24	6	7	6	6	1	18	1	2	0	1	0	2	.188	.241	.238	.478

Devon Travis

Bats: R **Throws:** R **Pos:** 2B   DEV-in   **Ht:** 5'9" **Wt:** 190 **Born:** 2/21/1991 **Age:** 29

Year	Team	Lg	G	AB	H	2B	3B	HR	(Hm	Rd)	TB	R	RBI	RC	TBB	IBB	SO	HBP	SH	SF	SB	CS	GDP	Avg	OBP	Slg	OPS
					BATTING																**RUNNING**			**AVERAGES**			
2015	Tor	AL	62	217	66	18	0	8	(4	4)	108	38	35	40	18	0	43	2	0	1	3	1	4	.304	.361	.498	.859
2016	Tor	AL	101	410	123	28	1	11	(2	9)	186	54	50	61	20	0	87	0	1	4	4	1	6	.300	.332	.454	.785
2017	Tor	AL	50	185	48	18	0	5	(2	3)	81	22	24	25	7	0	38	2	1	2	4	2	5	.259	.291	.438	.729
2018	Tor	AL	103	357	83	14	3	11	(6	5)	136	41	44	37	16	1	64	5	0	0	3	2	8	.232	.275	.381	.656
	Postseason		3	12	1	0	0	0	(0	0)	1	2	0	0	0	0	1	0	0	0	0	0	0	.083	.083	.083	.167
	4 ML YEARS		316	1169	320	78	4	35	(14	21)	511	155	153	163	61	1	232	9	2	4	14	6	23	.274	.314	.437	.751

Sam Travis

Bats: R **Throws:** R **Pos:** 1B-29;LF-18;PH-14;DH-8;RF-1;PR-1   **Ht:** 6'0" **Wt:** 205 **Born:** 8/27/1993 **Age:** 26

Year	Team	Lg	G	AB	H	2B	3B	HR	(Hm	Rd)	TB	R	RBI	RC	TBB	IBB	SO	HBP	SH	SF	SB	CS	GDP	Avg	OBP	Slg	OPS
					BATTING																**RUNNING**			**AVERAGES**			
2019	Pwtckt	AAA	68	236	65	14	1	7	(-	-)	102	36	33	39	31	0	62	1	0	0	5	1	5	.275	.362	.432	.794
2017	Bos	AL	33	76	20	6	0	0	(0	0)	26	13	1	5	6	0	23	1	0	0	1	0	2	.263	.325	.342	.667
2018	Bos	AL	19	36	8	3	0	1	(0	1)	14	5	7	3	2	0	10	0	0	0	0	0	1	.222	.263	.389	.652
2019	Bos	AL	59	144	31	4	1	6	(4	2)	55	17	16	15	11	2	36	1	0	1	2	0	6	.215	.274	.382	.656
	3 ML YEARS		111	256	59	13	1	7	(4	3)	95	35	24	23	19	2	69	2	0	1	3	0	9	.230	.288	.371	.659

Blake Treinen

Pitches: R Bats: R Pos: RP-57
TRY-nen
Ht: 6'5" Wt: 225 Born: 6/30/1988 Age: 32

Year Team	Lg	G	GS	GF	IP	BFP	H	R	ER	HR	SH	SF	HB	TBB	IBB	SO	WP	W	L	Pct	Sv-Op	Hld	Vel	OPS	ERC	ERA
2014 Was	NL	15	7	6	50.2	214	57	17	14	1	0	0	2	13	1	30	1	2	3	.400	0-0	0	95	.678	3.86	2.49
2015 Was	NL	60	0	17	67.2	280	62	32	29	4	1	1	2	32	6	65	4	2	5	.286	0-3	10	96	.692	3.76	3.86
2016 Was	NL	73	0	17	67.0	263	51	19	17	5	2	2	0	31	6	63	1	4	1	.800	1-3	22	95	.648	2.92	2.28
2017 2 Tms		72	0	35	75.2	325	80	35	33	6	0	3	5	25	3	74	4	3	6	.333	16-21	10	97	.736	4.24	3.93
2018 Oak	AL	68	0	58	80.1	315	46	12	7	2	1	0	1	21	3	100	6	9	2	.818	38-43	5	97	.417	1.21	0.78
2019 Oak	AL	57	0	35	58.2	266	58	33	32	9	1	1	1	37	1	59	1	6	5	.545	16-21	3	97	.778	5.39	4.91
17 Was	NL	37	0	11	37.2	169	48	24	24	3	0	3	3	13	1	32	1	0	2	.000	3-5	5	97	.832	5.71	5.73
17 Oak	AL	35	0	24	38.0	156	32	11	9	3	0	0	2	12	2	42	3	3	4	.429	13-16	5	97	.633	2.92	2.13
Postseason		4	0	0	4.2	22	5	5	5	1	0	1	1	2	0	5	0	1	1	.500	0-0	0	97	.919	6.25	9.64
6 ML YEARS		345	7	168	400.0	1663	354	148	132	27	5	7	11	159	20	391	17	26	22	.542	71-91	45	96	.652	3.31	2.97

Jose Trevino

Bats: R Throws: R Pos: C-40;PH-1
Ht: 5'11" Wt: 211 Born: 11/28/1992 Age: 27

Year Team	Lg	G	AB	H	2B	3B	HR	Hm	Rd	TB	R	RBI	RC	TBB	IBB	SO	HBP	SH	SF	SB	CS	GDP	Avg	OBP	Slg	OPS
2019 Nashv	AAA	40	146	33	10	0	2	-	-	49	15	22	13	8	0	28	0	0	2	2	0	5	.226	.263	.336	.598
2019 Rngrs	R	11	36	6	1	0	1	-	-	10	3	6	1	2	0	2	0	0	0	0	0	1	.167	.211	.278	.488
2018 Tex	AL	3	8	2	0	0	0	0	0	2	0	3	2	0	0	1	0	0	0	0	0	1	.250	.250	.250	.500
2019 Tex	AL	40	120	31	9	0	2	1	1	46	18	13	11	3	0	27	0	1	2	0	0	6	.258	.272	.383	.655
2 ML YEARS		43	128	33	9	0	2	1	1	48	18	16	13	3	0	28	0	1	2	0	0	7	.258	.271	.375	.646

Lou Trivino

Pitches: R Bats: R Pos: RP-61
Ht: 6'5" Wt: 240 Born: 10/1/1991 Age: 28

Year Team	Lg	G	GS	GF	IP	BFP	H	R	ER	HR	SH	SF	HB	TBB	IBB	SO	WP	W	L	Pct	Sv-Op	Hld	Vel	OPS	ERC	ERA
2018 Oak	AL	69	1	10	74.0	299	53	24	24	8	1	1	2	31	4	82	4	8	3	.727	4-9	23	98	.603	2.76	2.92
2019 Oak	AL	61	0	10	60.0	269	61	40	35	7	2	3	3	31	2	57	7	4	6	.400	0-5	17	97	.782	4.90	5.25
Postseason		1	0	0	3.0	10	1	0	0	0	0	0	0	1	0	4	0	0	0	-	0-0	0	98	.311	0.75	0.00
2 ML YEARS		130	1	20	134.0	568	114	64	59	15	3	4	5	62	6	139	11	12	9	.571	4-14	40	98	.687	3.68	3.96

Nick Tropeano

Pitches: R Bats: R Pos: RP-2; SP-1
TROH-pee-ah-no
Ht: 6'4" Wt: 205 Born: 8/27/1990 Age: 29

Year Team	Lg	G	GS	GF	IP	BFP	H	R	ER	HR	SH	SF	HB	TBB	IBB	SO	WP	W	L	Pct	Sv-Op	Hld	Vel	OPS	ERC	ERA
2019 Salt Lk	AAA	17	15	0	79.2	352	90	55	52	12	0	5	2	31	0	85	3	4	6	.400	0--		-	.840	5.30	5.87
2014 Hou	AL	4	4	0	21.2	91	19	12	11	0	1	1	1	9	1	13	1	1	3	.250	0-0	0	90	.626	2.92	4.57
2015 LAA	AL	8	7	0	37.2	161	40	18	16	2	2	1	0	10	0	38	0	3	2	.600	0-0	0	91	.700	3.53	3.82
2016 LAA	AL	13	13	0	68.1	296	70	27	27	14	1	3	2	31	1	68	4	3	2	.600	0-0	0	91	.843	5.41	3.56
2018 LAA	AL	14	14	0	76.0	316	68	41	40	16	0	2	2	31	2	64	2	5	6	.455	0-0	0	90	.807	4.45	4.74
2019 LAA	AL	3	1	0	13.2	66	18	15	15	6	0	1	2	6	0	10	0	0	1	.000	0-0	0	91	1.061	9.62	9.88
5 ML YEARS		42	39	0	217.1	930	215	113	109	38	4	8	7	87	4	193	7	12	14	.462	0-0	0	91	.800	4.71	4.51

Mike Trout

Bats: R Throws: R Pos: CF-122;DH-12;PH-1
Ht: 6'2" Wt: 235 Born: 8/7/1991 Age: 28

Year Team	Lg	G	AB	H	2B	3B	HR	Hm	Rd	TB	R	RBI	RC	TBB	IBB	SO	HBP	SH	SF	SB	CS	GDP	Avg	OBP	Slg	OPS
2011 LAA	AL	40	123	27	6	0	5	1	4	48	20	16	14	9	0	30	2	0	1	4	0	2	.220	.281	.390	.672
2012 LAA	AL	139	559	182	27	8	30	16	14	315	129	83	127	67	4	139	6	0	7	49	5	7	.326	.399	.564	.963
2013 LAA	AL	157	589	190	39	9	27	13	14	328	109	97	141	110	10	136	9	0	8	33	7	8	.323	.432	.557	.988
2014 LAA	AL	157	602	173	39	9	36	19	17	338	115	111	131	83	6	184	10	0	10	16	2	6	.287	.377	.561	.939
2015 LAA	AL	159	575	172	32	6	41	20	21	339	104	90	131	92	14	158	10	0	5	11	7	11	.299	.402	.590	.991
2016 LAA	AL	159	549	173	32	5	29	14	15	302	123	100	137	116	12	137	11	0	5	30	7	5	.315	.441	.550	.991
2017 LAA	AL	114	402	123	25	3	33	20	13	253	92	72	110	94	15	90	7	0	4	22	4	8	.306	.442	.629	1.071
2018 LAA	AL	140	471	147	24	4	39	17	22	296	101	79	140	122	25	124	10	0	4	24	2	5	.312	.460	.628	1.088
2019 LAA	AL	134	470	137	27	2	45	21	24	303	110	104	132	110	14	120	16	0	4	11	2	5	.291	.438	.645	1.083
Postseason		3	12	1	0	0	1	0	1	4	1	1	0	3	0	2	0	0	0	0	1	0	.083	.267	.333	.600
9 ML YEARS		1199	4340	1324	251	46	285	141	144	2522	903	752	1063	803	100	1118	81	0	48	200	36	57	.305	.419	.581	1.000

Mark Trumbo

Bats: R Throws: R Pos: DH-7;PH-5
Ht: 6'4" Wt: 225 Born: 1/16/1986 Age: 34

Year Team	Lg	G	AB	H	2B	3B	HR	Hm	Rd	TB	R	RBI	RC	TBB	IBB	SO	HBP	SH	SF	SB	CS	GDP	Avg	OBP	Slg	OPS
2019 Norfolk	AAA	12	42	9	3	0	4	-	-	24	5	10	7	6	0	15	0	0	0	0	0	1	.214	.313	.571	.884
2010 LAA	AL	8	15	1	0	0	0	0	0	1	2	2	0	1	0	8	0	0	0	0	0	0	.067	.125	.067	.192
2011 LAA	AL	149	539	137	31	1	29	14	15	257	65	87	69	25	6	120	5	0	4	9	4	17	.254	.291	.477	.768
2012 LAA	AL	144	544	146	19	3	32	12	20	267	66	95	80	36	3	153	4	0	2	4	5	12	.268	.317	.491	.808
2013 LAA	AL	159	620	145	30	2	34	19	15	281	85	100	74	54	6	184	0	0	4	5	2	18	.234	.294	.453	.747
2014 Ari	NL	88	328	77	15	1	14	7	7	136	37	61	44	28	3	89	1	0	5	2	3	4	.235	.293	.415	.707
2015 2 Tms		142	508	133	23	3	22	12	10	228	62	64	58	36	1	132	0	0		12	4	6	.262	.310	.449	.759
2016 Bal	AL	159	613	157	27	1	47	25	22	327	94	108	102	51	1	170	3	0	14	2	0	14	.256	.316	.533	.850
2017 Bal	AL	146	559	131	22	0	23	14	9	222	79	65	57	42	0	149	1	0	1	1	0	13	.234	.289	.397	.686
2018 Bal	AL	90	330	86	12	0	17	6	11	149	41	44	43	24	0	87	2	0	0	0	0	10	.261	.313	.452	.764

Year Team	Lg	G	AB	H	2B	3B	HR	(Hm	Rd)	TB	R	RBI	RC	TBB	IBB	SO	HBP	SH	SF	SB	CS	GDP	Avg	OBP	Slg	OPS
2019 Bal	AL	12	29	5	3	0	0	(0	0)	8	1	3	1	2	0	5	0	0	0	0	0	2	.172	.226	.276	.502
15 Ari	NL	46	174	45	10	3	9	(4	5)	88	23	23	21	10	0	39	0	0	0	0	0	4	.259	.299	.506	.805
15 Sea	AL	96	334	88	13	0	13	(8	5)	140	39	41	37	26	1	93	0	0	1	0	0	8	.263	.316	.419	.735
Postseason		1	4	1	0	0	1	(0	1)	4	1	2	2	0	0	1	0	0	0	0	0	0	.250	.250	1.000	1.250
10 ML YEARS		1097	4085	1018	182	11	218	(109	109)	1876	532	629	528	299	20	1097	16	0	19	23	14	106	.249	.302	.459	.761

Cole Tucker

Bats: B **Throws:** R **Pos:** SS-45;PH-14   **Ht:** 6'3" **Wt:** 205 **Born:** 7/3/1996 **Age:** 23

Year Team	Lg	G	AB	H	2B	3B	HR	(Hm	Rd)	TB	R	RBI	RC	TBB	IBB	SO	HBP	SH	SF	SB	CS	GDP	Avg	OBP	Slg	OPS
2019 Indy	AAA	77	310	81	15	4	8	(-	-)	128	51	28	47	38	1	73	2	3	6	11	3	6	.261	.346	.413	.759
2019 Pit	NL	56	147	31	10	3	2	(1	1)	53	16	13	14	10	1	40	1	1	0	5	0	2	.211	.266	.361	.626

Kyle Tucker

Bats: L **Throws:** R **Pos:** LF-11;RF-11;1B-4;PH-4;PR-3;DH-1   **Ht:** 6'4" **Wt:** 190 **Born:** 1/17/1997 **Age:** 23

Year Team	Lg	G	AB	H	2B	3B	HR	(Hm	Rd)	TB	R	RBI	RC	TBB	IBB	SO	HBP	SH	SF	SB	CS	GDP	Avg	OBP	Slg	OPS
2015 2 Tms	Low	63	232	57	12	2	3	(-	-)	82	30	33	26	16	2	29	1	2	3	18	4	2	.246	.294	.353	.647
2016 2 Tms	Low	117	432	123	25	7	9	(-	-)	189	56	69	70	50	5	81	6	0	9	32	12	8	.285	.360	.438	.798
2017 BuiesCk	A+	48	177	51	12	4	9	(-	-)	98	31	43	38	24	1	45	3	0	2	13	5	1	.288	.379	.554	.932
2017 CpChr	AA	72	287	76	21	1	16	(-	-)	147	39	47	48	22	2	64	5	0	3	8	4	5	.265	.325	.512	.837
2018 Fresno	AAA	100	407	135	27	3	24	(-	-)	240	86	93	96	48	2	84	2	1	6	20	4	11	.332	.400	.590	.989
2019 RdRck	AAA	125	463	123	26	3	34	(-	-)	257	92	97	96	60	1	116	6	0	5	30	5	5	.266	.354	.555	.909
2018 Hou	AL	28	64	9	2	1	0	(0	0)	13	10	4	0	6	0	13	2	0	0	1	1	1	.141	.236	.203	.439
2019 Hou	AL	22	67	18	6	0	4	(1	3)	36	15	11	10	4	1	20	1	0	0	5	0	1	.269	.319	.537	.857
2 ML YEARS		50	131	27	8	1	4	(1	3)	49	25	15	10	10	1	33	3	0	0	6	1	2	.206	.278	.374	.652

Sam Tuivailala

Pitches: R **Bats:** R **Pos:** RP-21; SP-2   TOO-ee-vah-la-la   **Ht:** 6'3" **Wt:** 225 **Born:** 10/19/1992 **Age:** 27

Year Team	Lg	G	GS	GF	IP	BFP	H	R	ER	HR	SH	SF	HB	TBB	IBB	SO	WP	W	L	Pct	Sv-Op	Hld	Vel	OPS	ERC	ERA
2019 2 Tms	Low	8	2	0	7.2	31	6	6	5	2	0	0	0	2	0	9	0	0	2	.000	0- -	-	-	.672	3.29	5.87
2019 Tacom	AAA	6	0	0	5.2	23	5	3	3	1	0	0	0	1	0	5	1	1	0	1.000	0- -	-	-	.670	3.00	4.76
2019 Ark	AA	5	0	0	5.0	17	1	0	0	0	0	0	0	2	0	6	0	0	0	-	0- -	-	-	.243	0.53	0.00
2014 StL	NL	2	0	0	1.0	10	5	4	4	2	0	0	0	2	0	1	0	0	0	-	0-0	0	97	2.075	72.46	36.00
2015 StL	NL	14	0	5	14.2	65	13	5	5	2	0	0	0	8	1	20	3	0	1	.000	0-0	2	96	.744	4.06	3.07
2016 StL	NL	12	0	4	9.0	47	12	6	6	0	0	0	2	6	0	7	1	0	0	-	0-0	0	96	.759	7.05	6.00
2017 StL	NL	37	0	19	42.1	171	35	12	12	4	1	0	2	11	3	34	2	3	3	.500	0-0	1	95	.626	2.69	2.55
2018 2 Tms		36	0	5	37.0	165	41	15	14	3	2	1	2	12	2	30	5	4	3	.571	0-0	4	95	.743	4.29	3.41
2019 Sea	AL	23	2	3	23.0	94	13	6	6	1	0	1	2	11	0	27	1	1	0	1.000	0-1	7	93	.539	2.06	2.35
18 StL	NL	31	0	5	31.2	144	35	14	13	3	2	1	2	11	2	26	4	3	3	.500	0-0	4	95	.736	4.42	3.69
18 Sea	AL	5	0	0	5.1	21	6	1	1	0	0	0	0	1	0	4	1	1	0	1.000	0-0	0	95	.783	3.52	1.69
6 ML YEARS		124	2	36	127.0	552	119	48	47	12	3	2	8	50	6	119	12	8	7	.533	0-1	14	95	.697	3.79	3.33

Troy Tulowitzki

Bats: R **Throws:** R **Pos:** SS-4;PH-1   too-luh-WIT-skee   **Ht:** 6'3" **Wt:** 205 **Born:** 10/10/1984 **Age:** 35

Year Team	Lg	G	AB	H	2B	3B	HR	(Hm	Rd)	TB	R	RBI	RC	TBB	IBB	SO	HBP	SH	SF	SB	CS	GDP	Avg	OBP	Slg	OPS
2006 Col	NL	25	96	23	2	0	1	(0	1)	28	15	6	10	10	3	25	1	1	0	3	0	1	.240	.318	.292	.609
2007 Col	NL	155	609	177	33	5	24	(15	9)	292	104	99	95	57	3	130	9	5	2	7	6	14	.291	.359	.479	.838
2008 Col	NL	101	377	99	24	2	8	(4	4)	151	48	46	42	38	5	56	2	2	2	1	6	16	.263	.332	.401	.732
2009 Col	NL	151	543	161	25	9	32	(17	15)	300	101	92	96	73	4	112	3	0	9	20	11	20	.297	.377	.552	.930
2010 Col	NL	122	470	148	30	3	27	(15	12)	267	89	95	88	48	4	78	5	1	5	11	2	17	.315	.381	.568	.949
2011 Col	NL	143	537	162	36	2	30	(17	13)	292	81	105	101	59	12	79	4	1	5	9	3	16	.302	.372	.544	.916
2012 Col	NL	47	181	52	8	2	8	(3	5)	88	33	27	27	19	1	19	2	0	1	2	2	7	.287	.360	.486	.846
2013 Col	NL	126	446	139	27	0	25	(14	11)	241	72	82	80	57	5	85	4	0	5	1	0	9	.312	.391	.540	.931
2014 Col	NL	91	315	107	18	1	21	(14	7)	190	71	52	70	50	4	57	5	0	5	1	1	4	.340	.432	.603	1.035
2015 2 Tms		128	486	136	27	0	17	(11	6)	214	77	70	69	38	5	114	4	0	4	1	0	17	.280	.337	.440	.777
2016 Tor	AL	131	492	125	21	0	24	(13	11)	218	54	79	71	43	1	101	5	0	4	1	0	14	.254	.318	.443	.761
2017 Tor	AL	66	241	60	10	0	7	(5	2)	91	16	26	21	17	1	40	1	0	1	0	1	10	.249	.300	.378	.678
2019 NYY	AL	5	11	2	1	0	1	(1	0)	6	1	1	1	2	0	4	0	0	0	0	0	0	.182	.308	.545	.853
15 Col	NL	87	323	97	19	0	12	(9	7)	152	46	53	53	24	4	72	1	0	3	0	0	13	.300	.348	.471	.818
15 Tor	AL	41	163	39	8	0	5	(4	1)	62	31	17	16	14	1	42	3	0	1	1	0	4	.239	.317	.380	.697
Postseason		35	136	29	7	1	4	(1	3)	50	11	22	15	8	0	35	1	0	1	0	1	4	.213	.260	.368	.628
13 ML YEARS		1291	4804	1391	264	24	225	(129	96)	2378	762	780	771	511	48	900	47	10	43	57	32	146	.290	.361	.495	.856

Spencer Turnbull

Pitches: R **Bats:** R **Pos:** SP-30   **Ht:** 6'3" **Wt:** 215 **Born:** 9/18/1992 **Age:** 27

Year Team	Lg	G	GS	GF	IP	BFP	H	R	ER	HR	SH	SF	HB	TBB	IBB	SO	WP	W	L	Pct	Sv-Op	Hld	Vel	OPS	ERC	ERA
2018 Det	AL	4	3	0	16.1	69	17	11	11	1	0	0	4	0	15	11	1	0	2	.000	0-0	1	94	.658	3.41	6.06
2019 Det	AL	30	30	0	148.1	656	154	86	76	14	1	4	16	59	1	146	9	3	17	.150	0-0	0	94	.763	4.69	4.61
2 ML YEARS		34	33	0	164.2	725	171	97	87	15	1	4	16	63	1	161	10	3	19	.136	0-0	1	94	.752	4.55	4.76

Justin Turner

Bats: R **Throws:** R **Pos:** 3B-124;PH-13;DH-3;2B-1   **Ht:** 5'11" **Wt:** 202 **Born:** 11/23/1984 **Age:** 35

Year	Team	Lg	G	AB	H	2B	3B	HR	(Hm	Rd)	TB	R	RBI	RC	TBB	IBB	SO	HBP	SH	SF	SB	CS	GDP	Avg	OBP	Slg	OPS
2009	Bal	AL	12	18	3	0	0	0	(0	0)	3	2	3	1	4	0	3	0	0	0	0	0	1	.167	.318	.167	.485
2010	2 Tms		9	17	1	1	0	0	(0	0)	2	1	0	0	1	0	3	0	0	0	0	0	0	.059	.111	.118	.229
2011	NYM	NL	117	435	113	30	0	4	(3	1)	155	49	51	59	39	2	59	10	2	1	7	2	9	.260	.334	.356	.690
2012	NYM	NL	94	171	46	13	1	2	(2	0)	67	20	19	19	9	0	24	4	0	1	1	1	9	.269	.319	.392	.711
2013	NYM	NL	86	200	56	13	1	2	(0	2)	77	12	16	17	11	1	34	1	1	1	0	1	6	.280	.319	.385	.704
2014	LAD	NL	109	288	98	21	1	7	(5	2)	142	46	43	55	28	1	58	4	0	2	6	1	6	.340	.404	.493	.897
2015	LAD	NL	126	385	113	26	1	16	(8	8)	189	55	60	65	36	1	71	13	1	4	5	2	10	.294	.370	.491	.861
2016	LAD	NL	151	556	153	34	3	27	(11	16)	274	79	90	96	48	1	107	10	0	8	4	1	16	.275	.339	.493	.832
2017	LAD	NL	130	457	147	32	0	21	(10	11)	242	72	71	95	59	5	56	19	1	7	7	1	12	.322	.415	.530	.945
2018	LAD	NL	103	365	114	31	1	14	(9	5)	189	62	52	71	47	3	54	12	0	2	2	1	10	.312	.406	.518	.924
2019	LAD	NL	135	479	139	24	0	27	(14	13)	244	80	67	84	51	1	88	14	0	5	2	0	11	.290	.372	.509	.881
10	Bal	AL	5	9	0	0	0	0	(0	0)	0	0	0	0	0	0	3	0	0	0	0	0	0	.000	.000	.000	.000
10	NYM	NL	4	8	1	1	0	0	(0	0)	2	1	0	0	1	0	0	0	0	0	0	0	0	.125	.222	.250	.472
	Postseason		49	179	56	11	1	7	(4	3)	90	22	30	43	25	1	31	8	0	0	4	0	2	.313	.420	.503	.923
	11 ML YEARS		1072	3371	983	225	8	120	(62	58)	1584	478	472	562	333	15	557	87	5	31	34	10	90	.292	.367	.470	.837

Trea Turner

Bats: R **Throws:** R **Pos:** SS-122   TRAY   **Ht:** 6'2" **Wt:** 185 **Born:** 6/30/1993 **Age:** 27

Year	Team	Lg	G	AB	H	2B	3B	HR	(Hm	Rd)	TB	R	RBI	RC	TBB	IBB	SO	HBP	SH	SF	SB	CS	GDP	Avg	OBP	Slg	OPS
2015	Was	NL	27	40	9	1	0	1	(0	1)	13	5	1	2	4	0	12	0	0	0	2	2	0	.225	.295	.325	.620
2016	Was	NL	73	307	105	14	8	13	(7	6)	174	53	40	62	14	0	59	1	0	2	33	6	1	.342	.370	.567	.937
2017	Was	NL	98	412	117	24	6	11	(6	5)	186	75	45	67	30	0	80	4	0	1	46	8	4	.284	.338	.451	.789
2018	Was	NL	162	664	180	27	6	19	(10	9)	276	103	73	105	69	3	132	5	2	0	43	9	7	.271	.344	.416	.760
2019	Was	NL	122	521	155	37	5	19	(11	8)	259	96	57	87	43	2	113	3	0	2	35	5	10	.298	.353	.497	.850
	Postseason		10	43	10	1	0	0	(0	0)	11	6	1	3	3	0	18	0	0	1	3	0	0	.233	.277	.256	.532
	5 ML YEARS		482	1944	566	103	25	63	(34	29)	908	332	216	323	160	5	396	13	2	5	159	30	22	.291	.348	.467	.815

Duane Underwood Jr.

Pitches: R **Bats:** R **Pos:** RP-12   **Ht:** 6'2" **Wt:** 210 **Born:** 7/20/1994 **Age:** 25

			HOW MUCH PITCHED				WHAT HE GAVE UP										THE RESULTS							
Year	Team	Lg	G	GS	GF	IP	BFP	H	R	ER	HR	SH	SF	HB	TBB	IBB	SO	WP	W	L	Pct	Sv-Op	Hld	Vel	OPS	ERC	ERA
2019	Iowa	AAA	33	10	5	81.2	369	84	55	46	8	4	0	3	41	2	95	6	3	7	.300	0- --	-		.737	4.67	5.07
2018	ChC	NL	1	1	0	4.0	16	2	1	1	0	0	0	0	3	0	3	0	0	1	.000	0-0	0	92	.697	3.91	2.25
2019	ChC	NL	12	0	1	11.2	51	13	7	7	2	0	0	1	3	0	13	1	0	0	-	0-0	0	95	.865	5.01	5.40
	2 ML YEARS		13	1	1	15.2	67	15	8	8	3	0	0	1	6	0	16	1	0	1	.000	0-0	0	94	.828	4.72	4.60

Justin Upton

Bats: R **Throws:** R **Pos:** LF-56;DH-5;PH-3   **Ht:** 6'1" **Wt:** 215 **Born:** 8/25/1987 **Age:** 32

Year	Team	Lg	G	AB	H	2B	3B	HR	(Hm	Rd)	TB	R	RBI	RC	TBB	IBB	SO	HBP	SH	SF	SB	CS	GDP	Avg	OBP	Slg	OPS
2007	Ari	NL	43	140	31	8	3	2	(2	0)	51	17	11	13	11	4	37	1	0	0	2	0	3	.221	.283	.364	.647
2008	Ari	NL	108	356	89	19	6	15	(12	3)	165	52	42	47	54	6	121	4	0	3	1	4	3	.250	.353	.463	.816
2009	Ari	NL	138	526	158	30	7	26	(14	12)	280	84	86	94	55	3	137	2	1	4	20	5	10	.300	.366	.532	.899
2010	Ari	NL	133	495	135	27	3	17	(8	9)	219	73	69	73	64	5	152	4	1	7	18	8	20	.273	.356	.442	.799
2011	Ari	NL	159	592	171	39	5	31	(20	11)	313	105	88	103	59	9	126	19	0	4	21	9	8	.289	.369	.529	.898
2012	Ari	NL	150	554	155	24	4	17	(11	6)	238	107	67	82	63	5	121	5	0	6	18	8	7	.280	.355	.430	.785
2013	Atl	NL	149	558	147	27	2	27	(13	14)	259	94	70	84	75	4	161	5	1	4	8	1	12	.263	.354	.464	.818
2014	Atl	NL	154	566	153	34	2	29	(18	11)	278	77	102	84	60	1	171	6	0	8	8	4	10	.270	.342	.491	.833
2015	SD	NL	150	542	136	26	3	26	(15	11)	246	85	81	85	68	5	159	4	0	5	19	5	10	.251	.336	.454	.790
2016	Det	AL	153	570	140	28	2	31	(14	17)	265	81	87	77	50	3	179	4	0	2	9	4	15	.246	.310	.465	.775
2017	2 Tms		152	557	152	44	0	35	(17	18)	301	100	109	109	74	3	180	3	0	1	14	5	9	.273	.361	.540	.901
2018	LAA	AL	145	533	137	18	1	30	(22	8)	247	80	85	79	64	1	176	10	0	6	8	2	12	.257	.344	.463	.808
2019	LAA	AL	63	219	47	8	0	12	(5	7)	91	34	40	30	32	0	78	0	0	5	1	1	5	.215	.309	.416	.724
17	Det	AL	125	459	128	37	0	28	(13	15)	249	81	94	98	57	2	147	3	0	1	10	5	6	.279	.362	.542	.904
17	LAA	AL	27	98	24	7	0	7	(4	3)	52	19	15	11	17	1	33	0	0	0	4	0	3	.245	.357	.531	.887
	Postseason		15	48	11	2	1	2	(0	2)	21	7	4	7	10	0	13	2	0	0	1	0	0	.229	.383	.438	.821
	13 ML YEARS		1697	6208	1651	332	38	298	(171	127)	2953	989	937	960	729	49	1798	67	3	55	147	56	124	.266	.347	.476	.822

Jose Urena

Pitches: R **Bats:** R **Pos:** SP-13; RP-11   oo-RAY-nuh   **Ht:** 6'2" **Wt:** 200 **Born:** 9/12/1991 **Age:** 28

			HOW MUCH PITCHED				WHAT HE GAVE UP										THE RESULTS							
Year	Team	Lg	G	GS	GF	IP	BFP	H	R	ER	HR	SH	SF	HB	TBB	IBB	SO	WP	W	L	Pct	Sv-Op	Hld	Vel	OPS	ERC	ERA
2015	Mia	NL	20	9	4	61.2	274	73	37	36	5	3	5	3	25	2	28	2	1	5	.167	0-1	0	94	.818	5.27	5.25
2016	Mia	NL	28	12	4	83.2	373	91	59	57	11	3	4	6	29	6	58	0	4	9	.308	1-3	1	95	.800	4.70	6.13
2017	Mia	NL	34	28	2	169.2	724	152	77	72	26	5	3	14	64	4	113	5	14	7	.667	0-0	0	95	.735	4.07	3.82
2018	Mia	NL	31	31	0	174.0	712	155	78	77	19	5	4	12	51	8	130	2	9	12	.429	0-0	0	96	.690	3.40	3.98
2019	Mia	NL	24	13	8	84.2	369	99	53	49	13	1	2	2	26	3	62	2	4	10	.286	3-5	0	96	.818	5.16	5.21
	5 ML YEARS		137	93	18	573.2	2452	570	304	291	74	17	18	37	195	23	391	11	32	43	.427	4-9	1	95	.754	4.24	4.57

Richard Urena

Bats: B **Throws:** R **Pos:** SS-13;2B-9;3B-6;PH-4;PR-2;LF-1   oo-RAIN-yuh   **Ht:** 6'0" **Wt:** 195 **Born:** 2/26/1996 **Age:** 24

								BATTING												RUNNING			AVERAGES			
Year Team	Lg	G	AB	H	2B	3B	HR	(Hm Rd)	TB	R	RBI	RC	TBB	IBB	SO	HBP	SH	SF	SB	CS	GDP	Avg	OBP	Slg	OPS
2019 Buffalo	AAA	98	369	101	18	4	6		145	43	52	47	23	1	85	1	4	5	3	2	11	.274	.314	.393	.707
2017 Tor	AL	21	68	14	4	0	1	(1 0)	21	6	4	5	6	0	28	0	1	0	1	0	0	.206	.270	.309	.579
2018 Tor	AL	40	99	29	4	0	1	(0 1)	36	10	6	11	7	0	32	0	2	0	2	1	3	.293	.340	.364	.703
2019 Tor	AL	30	74	18	6	0	0		24	4	4	5	2	0	23	1	3	0	0	0	0	.243	.273	.324	.597
3 ML YEARS		91	241	61	14	0	2	(1 1)	81	20	14	21	15	0	83	1	6	0	3	1	3	.253	.300	.336	.636

Julio Urias

Pitches: L **Bats:** L **Pos:** RP-29; SP-8   oo-ree-AHS   **Ht:** 6'0" **Wt:** 225 **Born:** 8/12/1996 **Age:** 23

		HOW MUCH PITCHED					WHAT HE GAVE UP											THE RESULTS							
Year Team	Lg	G	GS	GF	IP	BFP	H	R	ER	HR	SH	SF	HB	TBB	IBB	SO	WP	W	L	Pct	Sv-Op Hld	Vel	OPS	ERC	ERA
2016 LAD	NL	18	15	1	77.0	336	81	32	29	5	4	1	4	31	0	84	3	5	2	.714	0-0	93	.728	4.37	3.39
2017 LAD	NL	5	5	0	23.1	102	23	15	14	1	2	0	1	14	1	11	1	0	2	.000	0-0	93	.768	4.61	5.40
2018 LAD	NL	3	0	3	4.0	13	1	0	0	0	0	0	0	0	0	7	0	0	0	-	0-0	94	.154	0.14	0.00
2019 LAD	NL	37	8	7	79.2	326	59	28	22	7	0	1	5	27	1	85	2	4	3	.571	4-5	95	.603	2.60	2.49
Postseason		9	1	1	12.0	49	9	6	6	2	0	0	0	5	0	10	0	2	1	.667	0-0	94	.672	3.24	4.50
4 ML YEARS		63	28	11	184.0	777	164	75	65	13	6	2	10	72	2	187	6	9	7	.563	4-5	94	.670	3.46	3.18

Luis Urias

Bats: R **Throws:** R **Pos:** SS-41;2B-26;PH-4;3B-1   oo-REE-ahs   **Ht:** 5'9" **Wt:** 185 **Born:** 6/3/1997 **Age:** 23

								BATTING												RUNNING			AVERAGES			
Year Team	Lg	G	AB	H	2B	3B	HR	(Hm Rd)	TB	R	RBI	RC	TBB	IBB	SO	HBP	SH	SF	SB	CS	GDP	Avg	OBP	Slg	OPS
2015 2 Tms	Low	61	224	67	6	1	0	(- -)	75	34	17	29	21	0	19	12	10	1	8	13	3	.299	.388	.335	.722
2016 Lk Els	A+	120	466	154	26	5	5	(- -)	205	71	52	80	40	1	36	13	8	3	7	13	15	.330	.397	.440	.836
2017 SnAnt	AA	118	442	131	20	4	3	(- -)	168	77	38	74	68	4	65	8	6	2	7	5	9	.296	.398	.380	.778
2018 ElPaso	AAA	120	450	133	30	7	8	(- -)	201	83	45	85	67	0	109	11	3	2	2	1	8	.296	.398	.447	.845
2019 ElPaso	AAA	73	295	93	19	4	19	(- -)	177	62	50	69	36	2	62	6	0	2	7	2	3	.315	.398	.600	.998
2018 SD	NL	12	48	10	1	0	2	(1 1)	17	5	5	6	3	0	10	1	0	1	1	0	0	.208	.264	.354	.618
2019 SD	NL	71	215	48	8	1	4	(1 3)	70	27	24	22	25	0	56	9	0	0	0	1	8	.223	.329	.326	.655
2 ML YEARS		83	263	58	9	1	6	(2 4)	87	32	29	28	28	0	66	10	0	1	1	1	8	.221	.318	.331	.649

Jose Urquidy

Pitches: R **Bats:** R **Pos:** SP-7; RP-2   URR-sha-lah   **Ht:** 6'0" **Wt:** 180 **Born:** 5/1/1995 **Age:** 25

		HOW MUCH PITCHED					WHAT HE GAVE UP											THE RESULTS							
Year Team	Lg	G	GS	GF	IP	BFP	H	R	ER	HR	SH	SF	HB	TBB	IBB	SO	WP	W	L	Pct	Sv-Op Hld	Vel	OPS	ERC	ERA
2019 CpChr	AA	7	6	1	33.0	133	28	18	15	2	0	2	6	2	0	40	1	2	2	.500	0--	-	.613	2.08	4.09
2019 RdRck	AAA	13	12	0	70.0	293	67	37	36	15	1	2	1	16	0	94	2	5	3	.625	0--	-	.746	3.90	4.63
2019 Hou	AL	9	7	0	41.0	167	38	18	18	6	2	0	0	7	0	40	4	2	1	.667	0-0	93	.678	3.05	3.95

Giovanny Urshela

Bats: R **Throws:** R **Pos:** 3B-123;PH-9;DH-3;PR-2;1B-1;LF-1   URR-sha-lah   **Ht:** 6'0" **Wt:** 220 **Born:** 10/11/1991 **Age:** 28

								BATTING												RUNNING			AVERAGES			
Year Team	Lg	G	AB	H	2B	3B	HR	(Hm Rd)	TB	R	RBI	RC	TBB	IBB	SO	HBP	SH	SF	SB	CS	GDP	Avg	OBP	Slg	OPS
2015 Cle	AL	81	267	60	8	1	6	(3 3)	88	25	21	19	18	0	58	2	1	0	0	1	9	.225	.279	.330	.608
2017 Cle	AL	67	156	35	7	0	1	(0 1)	45	14	15	10	8	0	22	0	1	0	0	0	6	.224	.262	.288	.551
2018 Tor	AL	19	43	10	1	0	1	(1 0)	14	7	3	2	2	0	10	1	0	0	0	0	1	.233	.283	.326	.608
2019 NYY	AL	132	442	139	34	0	21	(8 13)	236	73	74	80	25	1	87	5	0	4	1	1	13	.314	.355	.534	.889
Postseason		5	12	2	0	0	0	(0 0)	2	0	1	2	0	0	6	0	0	0	0	0	0	.167	.167	.167	.333
4 ML YEARS		299	908	244	50	1	29	(12 17)	383	119	113	111	53	1	177	8	2	4	1	2	29	.269	.313	.422	.735

Pat Valaika

Bats: R **Throws:** R **Pos:** PH-18;2B-13;SS-7;3B-3;1B-1;DH-1   **Ht:** 5'11" **Wt:** 208 **Born:** 9/9/1992 **Age:** 27

								BATTING												RUNNING			AVERAGES			
Year Team	Lg	G	AB	H	2B	3B	HR	(Hm Rd)	TB	R	RBI	RC	TBB	IBB	SO	HBP	SH	SF	SB	CS	GDP	Avg	OBP	Slg	OPS
2019 Albq	AAA	84	350	112	26	1	22	(- -)	206	60	75	73	27	0	90	0	1	5	5	1	10	.320	.364	.589	.952
2016 Col	NL	13	19	5	1	0	1	(0 1)	9	3	2	1	0	0	8	0	0	0	0	0	0	.263	.263	.474	.737
2017 Col	NL	110	182	47	11	0	13	(9 4)	97	28	40	31	7	0	53	0	5	1	0	0	1	.258	.284	.533	.817
2018 Col	NL	68	122	19	5	0	2	(1 1)	30	8	5	2	9	0	30	0	2	0	0	0	1	.156	.214	.246	.460
2019 Col	NL	40	79	15	5	1	1	(1 0)	25	11	4	8	7	0	34	0	0	0	0	0	1	.190	.256	.316	.572
Postseason		2	2	1	0	0	0	(0 0)	2	0	0	1	0	0	1	0	0	0	0	0	0	.500	.500	1.000	1.500
4 ML YEARS		231	402	86	22	1	17	(11 6)	161	50	51	42	23	0	125	0	7	1	0	0	6	.214	.256	.400	.656

Framber Valdez

Pitches: L **Bats:** L **Pos:** RP-18; SP-8   **Ht:** 5'11" **Wt:** 170 **Born:** 11/19/1993 **Age:** 26

		HOW MUCH PITCHED					WHAT HE GAVE UP											THE RESULTS							
Year Team	Lg	G	GS	GF	IP	BFP	H	R	ER	HR	SH	SF	HB	TBB	IBB	SO	WP	W	L	Pct	Sv-Op Hld	Vel	OPS	ERC	ERA
2019 RdRck	AAA	10	7	2	44.1	180	29	18	16	3	2	0	4	17	0	69	5	5	2	.714	1--	-	.568	2.34	3.25
2018 Hou	AL	8	5	0	37.0	154	22	10	9	3	0	0	4	24	0	34	5	4	1	.800	0-0	92	.595	3.20	2.19
2019 Hou	AL	26	8	7	70.2	329	74	51	46	9	0	4	4	44	0	68	4	4	7	.364	0-0	93	.790	5.65	5.86
2 ML YEARS		34	13	7	107.2	483	96	61	55	12	0	4	8	68	0	102	9	8	8	.500	0-0	93	.728	4.77	4.60

Phillips Valdez

Pitches: R Bats: R Pos: RP-11   Ht: 6'2" Wt: 160 Born: 11/16/1991 Age: 28

			HOW MUCH PITCHED				WHAT HE GAVE UP										THE RESULTS							
Year	Team	Lg	G	GS	GF	IP	BFP	H	R	ER	HR	SH	SF	HB	TBB	IBB	SO	WP	W	L	Pct	Sv-Op	Hld	Vel	OPS	ERC	ERA
2019	Nashv	AAA	26	14	2	78.2	367	87	53	43	10	0	2	11	36	0	65	5	1	7	.125	1--	-	-	.771	5.62	4.92
2019	Tex	AL	11	0	2	16.0	75	17	7	7	3	0	1	2	9	0	18	1	0	0	-	0-0	0	92	.818	6.26	3.94

Breyvic Valera

Bats: B Throws: R Pos: 2B-14;SS-2;3B-1;PR-1   Ht: 5'11" Wt: 160 Born: 1/8/1992 Age: 28

			BATTING																		RUNNING			AVERAGES			
Year	Team	Lg	G	AB	H	2B	3B	HR	(Hm	Rd)	TB	R	RBI	RC	TBB	IBB	SO	HBP	SH	SF	SB	CS	GDP	Avg	OBP	Slg	OPS
2019	Scrmto	AAA	24	74	19	3	0	1	(-	-)	25	10	7	11	16	0	10	1	1	0	2	1	0	.257	.396	.338	.733
2019	S-WB	AAA	83	305	96	18	2	13	(-	-)	157	44	49	60	34	2	34	3	5	1	8	6	6	.315	.388	.515	.903
2017	StL	NL	5	10	1	0	0	0	(0	0)	1	0	0	0	1	0	0	0	0	0	0	0	0	.100	.182	.100	.282
2018	2 Tms		32	64	15	0	1	0	(0	0)	17	8	8	10	7	0	13	0	2	2	1	0	0	.234	.301	.266	.567
2019	2 Tms	AL	17	47	11	2	1	1	(1	0)	18	7	6	8	4	0	7	1	0	0	0	0	1	.234	.308	.383	.691
18	LAD	NL	20	29	5	0	0	0	(0	0)	5	4	4	3	4	0	4	0	1	0	0	0	0	.172	.273	.172	.445
18	Bal	AL	12	35	10	0	1	0	(0	0)	12	4	4	7	3	0	9	0	1	2	1	0	0	.286	.325	.343	.668
19	NYY	AL	12	32	7	1	1	0	(0	0)	10	5	3	5	4	0	5	1	0	0	0	0	0	.219	.324	.313	.637
19	Tor	AL	5	15	4	1	0	1	(1	0)	8	2	3	3	0	0	2	0	0	0	0	0	1	.267	.267	.533	.800
	3 ML YEARS		54	121	27	2	2	1	(1	0)	36	15	14	18	12	0	20	1	2	2	1	0	1	.223	.294	.298	.592

Josh VanMeter

Bats: L Throws: R Pos: LF-47;PH-33;2B-18;1B-17;3B-6;RF-2;DH-2   Ht: 5'11" Wt: 165 Born: 3/10/1995 Age: 25

			BATTING																		RUNNING			AVERAGES			
Year	Team	Lg	G	AB	H	2B	3B	HR	(Hm	Rd)	TB	R	RBI	RC	TBB	IBB	SO	HBP	SH	SF	SB	CS	GDP	Avg	OBP	Slg	OPS
2019	Lsvlle	AAA	49	181	63	14	1	14	(-	-)	121	43	43	49	24	0	37	3	1	2	8	3	3	.348	.429	.669	1.097
2019	Cin	NL	95	228	54	13	1	8	(3	5)	93	33	23	28	29	0	56	2	0	1	9	3	5	.237	.327	.408	.735

Ildemaro Vargas

Bats: B Throws: R Pos: 2B-48;PH-36;3B-14;SS-4;PR-4;LF-1;RF-1   Ht: 6'0" Wt: 170 Born: 7/16/1991 Age: 28

			BATTING																		RUNNING			AVERAGES			
Year	Team	Lg	G	AB	H	2B	3B	HR	(Hm	Rd)	TB	R	RBI	RC	TBB	IBB	SO	HBP	SH	SF	SB	CS	GDP	Avg	OBP	Slg	OPS
2019	Reno	AAA	28	124	50	9	3	2	(-	-)	71	20	24	30	11	0	5	1	0	1	1	1	3	.403	.453	.573	1.025
2017	Ari	NL	12	13	4	1	0	0	(0	0)	5	4	4	2	0	0	3	0	0	0	1	0	1	.308	.308	.385	.692
2018	Ari	NL	14	19	4	0	0	0	(0	1)	7	2	4	4	1	0	4	0	0	0	1	0	1	.211	.250	.368	.618
2019	Ari	NL	92	201	54	9	1	6	(2	4)	83	25	24	26	9	0	24	0	0	1	1	0	6	.269	.299	.413	.712
	3 ML YEARS		118	233	62	10	1	7	(2	5)	95	31	32	32	10	0	31	0	0	1	2	0	8	.266	.295	.408	.703

Jason Vargas

Pitches: L Bats: L Pos: SP-29; RP-1   Ht: 6'0" Wt: 215 Born: 2/2/1983 Age: 37

			HOW MUCH PITCHED				WHAT HE GAVE UP										THE RESULTS							
Year	Team	Lg	G	GS	GF	IP	BFP	H	R	ER	HR	SH	SF	HB	TBB	IBB	SO	WP	W	L	Pct	Sv-Op	Hld	Vel	OPS	ERC	ERA
2005	Fla	NL	17	13	0	73.2	325	71	34	33	4	4	1	4	31	4	59	0	5	5	.500	0-0	0	89	.716	3.68	4.03
2006	Fla	NL	12	5	3	43.0	213	50	39	35	9	4	4	4	30	3	25	2	1	2	.333	0-0	0	88	.952	7.30	7.33
2007	NYM	NL	2	2	0	10.1	51	17	14	14	4	0	0	6	2	1	4	1	0	1	.000	0-0	0	86	.964	8.95	12.19
2009	Sea	AL	23	14	4	91.2	385	98	53	50	16	3	6	3	24	1	54	1	3	6	.333	0-0	0	88	.803	4.64	4.91
2010	Sea	AL	31	31	0	192.2	811	187	86	81	18	4	7	1	54	3	116	1	9	12	.429	0-0	0	87	.699	3.37	3.78
2011	Sea	AL	32	32	0	201.0	857	205	105	95	22	3	4	4	59	4	131	3	10	13	.435	0-0	0	88	.712	3.86	4.25
2012	Sea	AL	33	33	0	217.1	887	201	94	93	35	3	6	3	55	1	141	5	14	11	.560	0-0	0	88	.714	3.57	3.85
2013	LAA	AL	24	24	0	150.0	644	162	68	67	17	3	3	5	46	2	109	0	9	8	.529	0-0	0	87	.758	4.40	4.02
2014	KC	AL	30	30	0	187.0	790	197	82	77	19	3	1	6	41	4	128	1	11	10	.524	0-0	0	87	.713	3.76	3.71
2015	KC	AL	9	9	0	43.0	183	46	20	19	5	0	0	1	12	0	27	0	5	2	.714	0-0	0	88	.740	4.22	3.98
2016	KC	AL	3	3	0	12.0	47	8	3	3	1	0	0	0	3	0	11	0	0	0	-	0-0	0	86	.552	1.73	2.25
2017	KC	AL	32	32	0	179.2	756	181	84	83	27	2	6	5	58	2	134	6	18	11	.621	0-0	0	86	.766	4.33	4.16
2018	NYM	NL	20	20	0	92.0	404	100	60	59	18	5	2	5	30	1	84	0	7	9	.438	0-0	0	86	.819	5.15	5.77
2019	2 Tms	NL	30	29	1	149.2	649	141	84	75	21	6	8	6	63	2	124	5	7	9	.438	0-0	0	84	.751	4.23	4.51
19	NYM	NL	19	18	1	94.1	400	81	45	42	14	2	3	1	39	2	81	3	6	5	.545	0-0	0	85	.712	3.65	4.01
19	Phi	NL	11	11	0	55.1	249	60	39	33	7	4	5	5	24	0	43	2	1	4	.200	0-0	0	84	.814	5.27	5.37
	Postseason		3	3	0	15.1	61	11	6	6	3	0	0	0	6	0	11	1	1	0	1.000	0-0	0	88	.661	3.20	3.52
	14 ML YEARS		298	277	8	1643.0	7002	1664	826	784	216	40	48	47	508	28	1147	25	99	99	.500	0-0	0	87	.744	4.09	4.29

Andrew Vasquez

Pitches: L Bats: L Pos: RP-1   Ht: 6'6" Wt: 228 Born: 9/14/1993 Age: 26

			HOW MUCH PITCHED				WHAT HE GAVE UP										THE RESULTS							
Year	Team	Lg	G	GS	GF	IP	BFP	H	R	ER	HR	SH	SF	HB	TBB	IBB	SO	WP	W	L	Pct	Sv-Op	Hld	Vel	OPS	ERC	ERA
2019	Roch	AAA	15	1	4	18.0	89	17	13	12	1	1	1	1	18	0	27	3	1	2	.333	0--	-	-	.762	5.93	6.00
2019	Pnscla	AA	14	0	3	16.2	83	14	11	10	0	1	0	3	16	1	18	1	1	1	.500	2--	-	-	.688	4.96	5.40
2018	Min	AL	9	0	0	5.0	26	5	4	3	0	0	3	2	2	0	7	0	1	0	1.000	0-0	0	90	.766	5.24	5.40
2019	Min	AL	1	0	0	0.0	3	0	3	3	0	0	0	1	2	0	0	0	0	0	-	0-0	0	85	-	-	-
	2 ML YEARS		10	0	0	5.0	29	5	7	6	0	0	0	4	4	0	7	0	1	0	1.000	0-0	0	89	.829	7.56	10.80

Christian Vazquez

Bats: R Throws: R Pos: C-119;PH-12;DH-11;1B-10;3B-4;2B-2;PR-1   VAZ-kehz   Ht: 5'9" Wt: 195 Born: 8/21/1990 Age: 29

Year	Team	Lg	G	AB	H	2B	3B	HR	(Hm	Rd)	TB	R	RBI	RC	TBB	IBB	SO	HBP	SH	SF	SB	CS	GDP	Avg	OBP	Slg	OPS
2014	Bos	AL	55	175	42	9	0	1	(1	0)	54	15	20	19	19	1	33	0	3	4	0	0	4	.240	.308	.309	.617
2016	Bos	AL	57	172	39	9	1	1	(1	0)	53	21	12	11	10	1	39	2	0	0	0	0	3	.227	.277	.308	.585
2017	Bos	AL	99	324	94	18	2	5	(4	1)	131	43	32	41	17	0	64	3	0	1	7	2	14	.290	.330	.404	.735
2018	Bos	AL	80	251	52	10	0	3	(2	1)	71	24	16	13	13	1	41	4	1	0	4	1	5	.207	.257	.283	.540
2019	Bos	AL	138	482	133	26	1	23	(8	15)	230	66	72	69	33	3	101	0	3	3	4	2	17	.276	.320	.477	.798
	Postseason		14	43	10	1	0	1	(0	1)	14	5	2	2	3	0	10	0	0	0	0	0	0	.233	.283	.326	.608
5 ML YEARS			429	1404	360	72	4	33	(16	17)	539	169	152	153	92	6	278	9	7	8	15	5	43	.256	.305	.384	.689

Felipe Vazquez

Pitches: L Bats: L Pos: RP-56   Ht: 6'2" Wt: 225 Born: 7/5/1991 Age: 28

			HOW MUCH PITCHED					WHAT HE GAVE UP										THE RESULTS							
Year	Team	Lg	G	GS	GF	IP	BFP	H	R	ER	HR	SH	SF	HB	TBB	IBB	SO	WP	W	L	Pct	Sv-Op	Hld	Vel	OPS	ERC	ERA
2015	Was	NL	49	0	17	48.1	189	35	15	15	2	0	1	1	11	2	43	2	2	1	.667	2-3	6	95	.544	1.74	2.79
2016	2 Tms	NL	75	0	11	77.0	327	66	39	35	7	0	2	6	33	3	92	3	1	6	.143	1-4	26	96	.671	3.61	4.09
2017	Pit	NL	73	0	40	75.1	300	47	19	14	4	0	1	4	20	0	88	2	5	3	.625	21-23	14	99	.473	1.61	1.67
2018	Pit	NL	70	0	60	70.0	296	63	24	21	4	0	0	1	24	2	89	3	4	2	.667	37-42	0	98	.618	3.00	2.70
2019	Pit	NL	56	0	47	60.0	236	43	12	11	5	0	1	4	13	0	90	3	5	1	.833	28-31	0	98	.571	2.10	1.65
16	Was	NL	47	0	8	49.2	203	43	26	25	4	0	1	5	15	2	53	1	0	3	.000	1-2	16	95	.673	3.26	4.53
16	Pit	NL	28	0	3	27.1	124	23	13	10	3	0	1	1	18	1	39	2	1	3	.250	0-2	10	97	.666	4.25	3.29
5 ML YEARS			323	0	175	330.2	1348	254	109	96	22	0	5	16	101	7	402	13	17	13	.567	89-103	46	97	.579	2.43	2.61

Vince Velasquez

Pitches: R Bats: R Pos: SP-23; RP-10   Ht: 6'3" Wt: 205 Born: 6/7/1992 Age: 28

			HOW MUCH PITCHED					WHAT HE GAVE UP										THE RESULTS							
Year	Team	Lg	G	GS	GF	IP	BFP	H	R	ER	HR	SH	SF	HB	TBB	IBB	SO	WP	W	L	Pct	Sv-Op	Hld	Vel	OPS	ERC	ERA
2015	Hou	AL	19	7	5	55.2	231	50	28	27	5	0	0	2	21	0	58	3	1	1	.500	0-0	0	95	.720	3.58	4.37
2016	Phi	NL	24	24	0	131.0	551	129	64	60	21	9	5	1	45	1	152	3	8	6	.571	0-0	0	94	.765	4.25	4.12
2017	Phi	NL	15	15	0	72.0	315	74	44	41	15	2	2	2	34	1	68	2	2	7	.222	0-0	0	94	.851	5.58	5.13
2018	Phi	NL	31	30	1	146.2	630	138	83	79	16	7	3	8	59	1	161	9	9	12	.429	0-0	0	94	.747	4.04	4.85
2019	Phi	NL	33	23	2	117.1	516	120	69	64	26	3	3	9	43	2	130	5	7	8	.467	0-0	2	94	.833	5.21	4.91
5 ML YEARS			122	99	8	522.2	2243	511	288	271	83	21	13	23	202	5	569	22	27	34	.443	0-0	2	94	.783	4.51	4.67

Andrew Velazquez

Bats: B Throws: R Pos: 2B-5;3B-4;PH-3;PR-3;CF-2;LF-1   Ht: 5'8" Wt: 170 Born: 7/14/1994 Age: 25

			BATTING																	RUNNING			AVERAGES			
Year	Team	Lg	G	AB	H	2B	3B	HR	(Hm	Rd)	TB	R	RBI	RC	TBB	IBB	SO	HBP	SH	SF	SB	CS	GDP	Avg	OBP	Slg	OPS
2019	Drham	AAA	34	129	35	9	1	4	(-	-)	58	20	16	18	10	0	30	1	1	0	2	4	3	.271	.329	.450	.778
2019	Clmbs	AAA	12	45	11	4	1	0	(-	-)	17	5	5	4	0	0	9	1	0	0	1	1	3	.244	.261	.378	.639
2018	TB	AL	13	10	3	1	0	0	(0	0)	4	3	0	3	1	0	3	1	0	0	1	0	0	.300	.417	.400	.817
2019	2 Tms	AL	15	23	2	2	0	0	(0	0)	4	3	0	0	1	0	13	0	0	0	1	0	0	.087	.125	.174	.299
19	TB	AL	10	12	1	1	0	0	(0	0)	2	2	0	0	0	0	6	0	0	0	0	0	0	.083	.083	.167	.250
19	Cle	AL	5	11	1	1	0	0	(0	0)	2	1	0	0	1	0	7	0	0	0	1	0	0	.091	.167	.182	.348
2 ML YEARS			28	33	5	3	0	0	(0	0)	8	6	0	3	2	0	16	1	0	0	2	0	0	.152	.222	.242	.465

Hector Velazquez

Pitches: R Bats: R Pos: RP-26; SP-8   Ht: 6'0" Wt: 180 Born: 11/26/1988 Age: 31

			HOW MUCH PITCHED					WHAT HE GAVE UP										THE RESULTS							
Year	Team	Lg	G	GS	GF	IP	BFP	H	R	ER	HR	SH	SF	HB	TBB	IBB	SO	WP	W	L	Pct	Sv-Op	Hld	Vel	OPS	ERC	ERA
2019	Pwtckt	AAA	12	0	1	16.1	66	11	6	6	3	0	0	0	11	1	14	1	0	0	-	1--	-	-	.733	4.07	3.31
2017	Bos	AL	8	3	4	24.2	96	21	8	8	4	0	0	0	7	0	19	0	3	1	.750	0-0	0	90	.707	3.39	2.92
2018	Bos	AL	47	8	15	85.0	370	97	35	30	7	0	2	7	26	1	53	4	7	2	.778	0-0	0	91	.766	4.77	3.18
2019	Bos	AL	34	8	11	56.1	247	58	40	34	7	1	3	3	28	0	49	2	1	4	.200	0-1	1	92	.823	5.15	5.43
3 ML YEARS			89	19	30	166.0	713	176	83	72	18	1	5	10	61	1	121	6	11	7	.611	0-1	4	91	.777	4.69	3.90

Pat Venditte

Pitches: B Bats: L Pos: RP-2   ven-DET-ee   Ht: 6'1" Wt: 185 Born: 6/30/1985 Age: 35

			HOW MUCH PITCHED					WHAT HE GAVE UP										THE RESULTS							
Year	Team	Lg	G	GS	GF	IP	BFP	H	R	ER	HR	SH	SF	HB	TBB	IBB	SO	WP	W	L	Pct	Sv-Op	Hld	Vel	OPS	ERC	ERA
2019	Scrmto	AAA	25	1	6	47.1	191	31	19	15	5	0	0	3	17	0	59	0	6	2	.750	0--	-	-	.583	2.39	2.85
2015	Oak	AL	26	0	7	28.2	119	22	14	14	3	1	1	0	12	0	23	0	2	2	.500	0-0	2	85	.679	2.90	4.40
2016	2 Tms	AL	15	0	7	22.0	102	24	18	14	5	0	3	2	11	1	19	0	0	0	-	0-0	1	84	.898	6.23	5.73
2018	LAD	NL	15	0	6	14.0	57	11	4	4	1	0	0	2	3	1	9	0	0	0	-	0-0	0	86	.608	2.50	2.57
2019	SF	NL	2	0	0	3.1	19	4	6	6	1	0	0	3	2	0	2	0	0	0	-	0-0	0	85	.974	11.86	16.20
16	Tor	AL	8	0	3	8.2	44	11	8	5	1	0	2	1	4	0	7	0	0	0	-	0-0	1	84	.796	6.06	5.19
16	Sea	AL	7	0	4	13.1	58	13	10	9	4	0	1	1	7	1	12	0	0	0	-	0-0	0	84	.974	6.34	6.08
4 ML YEARS			58	0	20	68.0	297	61	42	38	10	1	4	7	28	2	53	0	2	2	.500	0-0	3	85	.756	4.19	5.03

Jonny Venters

Pitches: L Bats: L Pos: RP-12   Ht: 6'3" Wt: 200 Born: 3/20/1985 Age: 35

			HOW MUCH PITCHED					WHAT HE GAVE UP										THE RESULTS							
Year	Team	Lg	G	GS	GF	IP	BFP	H	R	ER	HR	SH	SF	HB	TBB	IBB	SO	WP	W	L	Pct	Sv-Op	Hld	Vel	OPS	ERC	ERA
2019	Gwnntt	AAA	7	0	0	7.0	24	3	0	0	0	0	0	0	2	0	6	0	0	0		0- -	-	-	.345	0.90	0.00
2019	Hrsbrg	AA	10	0	1	7.0	34	6	1	1	0	0	0	1	6	0	4	0	0	0		0- -	-	-	.605	4.66	1.29
2010	Atl	NL	79	0	17	83.0	350	61	30	18	1	2	1	8	39	2	93	4	4	4	.500	1-5	24	95	.552	2.64	1.95
2011	Atl	NL	85	0	10	88.0	357	53	19	18	2	7	1	5	43	7	96	4	6	2	.750	5-9	35	95	.508	1.96	1.84
2012	Atl	NL	66	0	12	58.2	262	61	23	21	6	3	0	5	28	3	69	9	5	4	.556	0-3	20	94	.739	4.92	3.22
2018	2 Tms		50	1	10	34.1	145	26	15	14	1	2	1	1	16	3	27	3	5	2	.714	3-4	15	93	.581	2.50	3.67
2019	2 Tms	NL	12	0	3	8.0	49	12	16	11	3	0	0	2	10	1	12	0	0	1	.000	1-2	2	93	1.084	14.26	12.38
18	TB	AL	22	1	6	14.0	58	11	6	6	1	0	0	0	6	1	11	0	1	1	.500	1-1	5	93	.620	2.74	3.86
18	Atl	NL	28	0	4	20.1	87	15	9	8	0	2	1	1	10	2	16	3	4	1	.800	2-3	10	93	.532	2.32	3.54
19	Atl	NL	9	0	2	4.2	31	9	13	9	3	0	0	0	8	0	7	0	0	0		1-2	1	93	1.374	22.56	17.36
19	Was	NL	3	0	1	3.1	18	3	3	2	0	0	0	2	2	1	5	0	0	1	.000	0-0	1	93	.603	4.72	5.40
	Postseason		7	0	0	8.0	31	10	2	2	0	0	0	0	1	0	9	0	0	1	.000	0-0	0	95	.688	4.12	2.25
	5 ML YEARS		292	1	52	272.0	1163	213	103	82	13	14	3	21	136	16	297	20	20	13	.606	10-23	96	94	.606	3.11	2.71

Alex Verdugo

Bats: L Throws: L Pos: CF-61;RF-25;LF-22;PH-17   Ht: 6'0" Wt: 212 Born: 5/15/1996 Age: 24

			BATTING																RUNNING			AVERAGES			
Year	Team	Lg	G	AB	H	2B	3B	HR	(Hm | Rd)	TB	R	RBI	RC	TBB	IBB	SO	HBP	SH	SF	SB	CS	GDP	Avg	OBP	Slg	OPS
2017	LAD	NL	15	23	4	0	0	1	(1 | 0)	7	1	1	0	2	0	4	0	0	0	0	1	1	.174	.240	.304	.544
2018	LAD	NL	37	77	20	6	0	1	(0 | 1)	29	11	4	6	8	0	14	0	1	0	0	0	4	.260	.329	.377	.706
2019	LAD	NL	106	343	101	22	2	12	(5 | 7)	163	43	44	51	26	1	49	2	0	6	4	1	8	.294	.342	.475	.817
	3 ML YEARS		158	443	125	28	2	14	(6 | 8)	199	55	49	57	36	1	67	2	1	6	4	2	13	.282	.335	.449	.784

Drew VerHagen

Pitches: R Bats: R Pos: RP-18; SP-4   verr-HAY-gen   Ht: 6'6" Wt: 230 Born: 10/22/1990 Age: 29

			HOW MUCH PITCHED					WHAT HE GAVE UP										THE RESULTS							
Year	Team	Lg	G	GS	GF	IP	BFP	H	R	ER	HR	SH	SF	HB	TBB	IBB	SO	WP	W	L	Pct	Sv-Op	Hld	Vel	OPS	ERC	ERA
2019	Toledo	AAA	11	11	0	53.0	233	61	29	26	5	0	5	4	13	0	51	0	4	2	.667	0- -	-	-	.776	4.55	4.42
2014	Det	AL	1	1	0	5.0	20	5	3	3	0	0	0	0	3	0	4	0	0	1	.000	0-0	0	91	.753	4.67	5.40
2015	Det	AL	20	0	2	26.1	106	18	6	6	1	1	0	1	14	2	13	1	2	0	1.000	0-1	3	94	.559	2.61	2.05
2016	Det	AL	19	0	4	19.0	90	28	15	15	3	0	1	1	7	1	10	1	1	0	1.000	0-0	2	94	.968	7.50	7.11
2017	Det	AL	24	2	4	34.1	145	42	22	22	10	0	1	1	9	1	25	4	0	3	.000	0-1	5	94	.967	6.43	5.77
2018	Det	AL	41	1	4	56.1	233	46	29	29	6	0	4	3	19	0	53	6	3	3	.500	0-2	3	94	.645	3.09	4.63
2019	Det	AL	22	4	3	58.0	258	70	40	38	9	0	1	4	23	1	51	3	4	3	.571	0-0	1	93	.880	6.13	5.90
	6 ML YEARS		127	8	17	199.0	852	209	115	113	29	1	7	9	75	5	156	15	10	10	.500	0-4	14	94	.800	4.86	5.11

Justin Verlander

Pitches: R Bats: R Pos: SP-34   Ht: 6'5" Wt: 225 Born: 2/20/1983 Age: 37

			HOW MUCH PITCHED					WHAT HE GAVE UP										THE RESULTS							
Year	Team	Lg	G	GS	GF	IP	BFP	H	R	ER	HR	SH	SF	HB	TBB	IBB	SO	WP	W	L	Pct	Sv-Op	Hld	Vel	OPS	ERC	ERA
2005	Det	AL	2	2	0	11.1	54	15	9	9	1	0	0	1	5	0	7	1	0	2	.000	0-0	0	95	.868	6.41	7.15
2006	Det	AL	30	30	0	186.0	776	187	78	75	21	2	4	6	60	1	124	5	17	9	.654	0-0	0	95	.741	4.12	3.63
2007	Det	AL	32	32	0	201.2	866	181	88	82	20	3	1	19	67	3	183	17	18	6	.750	0-0	0	95	.668	3.53	3.66
2008	Det	AL	33	33	0	201.0	880	195	119	108	18	4	6	14	87	8	163	6	11	17	.393	0-0	0	94	.715	4.17	4.84
2009	Det	AL	35	35	0	240.0	982	219	99	92	20	6	4	6	63	5	269	8	19	9	.679	0-0	0	96	.665	3.06	3.45
2010	Det	AL	33	33	0	224.1	925	190	89	84	14	6	8	6	71	0	219	11	18	9	.667	0-0	0	95	.630	2.79	3.37
2011	Det	AL	34	34	0	251.0	969	174	73	67	24	2	3	3	57	0	250	7	24	5	.828	0-0	0	95	.555	1.92	2.40
2012	Det	AL	33	33	0	238.1	956	192	81	70	19	4	3	5	60	2	239	2	17	8	.680	0-0	0	94	.601	2.45	2.64
2013	Det	AL	34	34	0	218.1	925	212	94	84	19	2	6	4	75	1	217	3	13	12	.520	0-0	0	93	.691	3.68	3.46
2014	Det	AL	32	32	0	206.0	893	223	114	104	18	6	5	5	65	1	159	5	15	12	.556	0-0	0	92	.756	4.19	4.54
2015	Det	AL	20	20	0	133.1	535	113	56	50	13	1	6	3	32	1	113	2	5	8	.385	0-0	0	93	.634	2.75	3.38
2016	Det	AL	34	34	0	227.2	903	171	81	77	30	4	7	8	57	1	254	6	16	9	.640	0-0	0	93	.630	2.54	3.04
2017	2 Tms	AL	33	33	0	206.0	849	170	80	77	27	1	4	4	72	4	219	5	15	8	.652	0-0	0	95	.660	3.19	3.36
2018	Hou	AL	34	34	0	214.0	833	156	63	60	28	2	5	8	37	0	290	5	16	9	.640	0-0	0	95	.602	2.16	2.52
2019	Hou	AL	34	34	0	223.0	847	137	66	64	36	0	2	6	42	0	300	4	21	6	.778	0-0	0	95	.579	1.80	2.58
17	Det	AL	28	28	0	172.0	729	153	76	73	23	1	4	3	67	4	176	5	10	8	.556	0-0	0	95	.693	3.67	3.82
17	Hou	AL	5	5	0	34.0	120	17	4	4	4	0	0	1	5	0	43	0	5	0	1.000	0-0	0	95	.464	1.22	1.06
	Postseason		25	24	0	152.1	608	110	57	54	18	1	3	3	46	0	167	8	13	7	.650	0-0	0	95	.599	2.44	3.19
	15 ML YEARS		453	453	0	2982.0	12193	2535	1190	1103	308	43	64	98	850	27	3006	87	225	129	.636	0-0	0	94	.652	2.97	3.33

Thyago Vieira

Pitches: R Bats: R Pos: RP-6   tee-AH-goh   Ht: 6'2" Wt: 210 Born: 7/1/1993 Age: 26

			HOW MUCH PITCHED					WHAT HE GAVE UP										THE RESULTS							
Year	Team	Lg	G	GS	GF	IP	BFP	H	R	ER	HR	SH	SF	HB	TBB	IBB	SO	WP	W	L	Pct	Sv-Op	Hld	Vel	OPS	ERC	ERA
2019	Charllt	AAA	39	0	31	47.1	213	53	33	30	7	3	0	4	22	0	51	5	6	4	.600	8- -	-	-	.854	5.85	5.70
2017	Sea	AL	1	0	1	1.0	3	0	0	0	0	0	0	0	0	0	1	0	0	0		0-0	0	99	.000	0.00	0.00
2018	CWS	AL	16	0	9	17.2	85	21	14	14	4	0	1	3	9	0	15	6	1	1	.500	1-1	1	97	.902	7.34	7.13
2019	CWS	AL	6	0	2	7.0	37	11	8	7	0	0	0	0	5	0	8	0	1	0	1.000	0-0	0	97	.807	7.83	9.00
	3 ML YEARS		23	0	12	25.2	125	32	22	21	4	0	1	3	14	0	24	6	2	1	.667	1-1	1	97	.850	7.00	7.36

Jonathan Villar

Bats: B **Throws:** R **Pos:** 2B-111;SS-97;PR-2;DH-1;PH-1 — vee-YARR — **Ht:** 6'1" **Wt:** 215 **Born:** 5/2/1991 **Age:** 29

								BATTING												RUNNING			AVERAGES			
Year	Team	Lg	G	AB	H	2B	3B	HR	(Hm | Rd)	TB	R	RBI	RC	TBB	IBB	SO	HBP	SH	SF	SB	CS	GDP	Avg	OBP	Slg	OPS
2013	Hou	AL	58	210	51	9	2	1	(0 | 1)	67	26	8	22	24	1	71	0	7	0	18	8	5	.243	.321	.319	.640
2014	Hou	AL	87	263	55	13	2	7	(3 | 4)	93	31	27	24	19	1	80	2	4	1	17	4	4	.209	.267	.354	.620
2015	Hou	AL	53	116	33	7	1	2	(0 | 2)	48	18	11	15	10	0	29	0	1	1	7	2	3	.284	.339	.414	.752
2016	Mil	NL	156	589	168	38	3	19	(6 | 13)	269	92	63	102	79	4	174	2	5	4	62	18	7	.285	.369	.457	.826
2017	Mil	NL	122	403	97	18	1	11	(7 | 4)	150	49	40	45	30	1	132	0	2	1	23	8	4	.241	.293	.372	.665
2018	2 Tms		141	466	121	14	1	14	(6 | 8)	179	54	46	67	41	0	138	5	1	2	35	5	13	.260	.325	.384	.709
2019	Bal	AL	162	642	176	33	5	24	(16 | 8)	291	111	73	100	61	0	176	4	2	4	40	9	8	.274	.339	.453	.792
18	Mil	NL	87	257	67	10	1	6	(2 | 4)	97	26	22	29	19	0	80	2	0	1	14	2	9	.261	.315	.377	.693
18	Bal	AL	54	209	54	4	0	8	(4 | 4)	82	28	24	38	22	0	58	3	1	1	21	3	4	.258	.336	.392	.729
	Postseason		0	0	0	0	0	0	(0 | 0)	0	1	0	0	0	0	0	0	0	0	1	0	0	-	-	-	-
	7 ML YEARS		779	2689	701	132	15	78	(38 | 40)	1097	381	268	375	264	7	800	13	22	13	202	54	44	.261	.328	.408	.736

Meibrys Viloria

Bats: L **Throws:** R **Pos:** C-41;PH-1 — MAY-breez — **Ht:** 5'11" **Wt:** 220 **Born:** 2/15/1997 **Age:** 23

								BATTING												RUNNING			AVERAGES			
Year	Team	Lg	G	AB	H	2B	3B	HR	(Hm	Rd)	TB	R	RBI	RC	TBB	IBB	SO	HBP	SH	SF	SB	CS	GDP	Avg	OBP	Slg	OPS
2019	NWArk	AA	63	220	58	12	0	1	(-	-)	73	21	24	27	24	0	60	3	1	0	2	0	3	.264	.344	.332	.676
2018	KC	AL	10	27	7	2	0	0	(0	0)	9	4	4	3	1	0	9	0	1	0	0	0	1	.259	.286	.333	.619
2019	KC	AL	42	133	28	7	0	1	(0	1)	38	7	15	9	10	0	44	0	1	4	0	1	4	.211	.259	.286	.544
	2 ML YEARS		52	160	35	9	0	1	(0	1)	47	11	19	12	11	0	53	0	2	4	0	1	5	.219	.263	.294	.557

Nick Vincent

Pitches: R **Bats:** R **Pos:** RP-31; SP-1 — **Ht:** 6'0" **Wt:** 185 **Born:** 7/12/1986 **Age:** 33

			HOW MUCH PITCHED					WHAT HE GAVE UP									THE RESULTS							
Year	Team	Lg	G	GS	GF	IP	BFP	H	R	ER	HR	SH	SF	HB	TBB	IBB	SO	WP	W	L	Pct	Sv-Op Hld	Vel	OPS	ERC	ERA
2019	LV	AAA	10	0	5	12.1	48	9	2	2	1	0	0	0	1	0	13	0	0	0	0--	-		.506	1.49	1.46
2012	SD	NL	27	0	3	26.1	105	19	5	5	2	1	0	1	7	0	28	1	2	0	1.000	0-1	5	90	.551	2.13	1.71
2013	SD	NL	45	0	7	46.1	180	33	11	11	1	4	0	2	11	3	49	0	6	3	.667	1-1	10	90	.525	1.67	2.14
2014	SD	NL	63	0	7	55.0	215	44	22	22	5	3	0	2	11	1	62	1	1	2	.333	0-2	20	90	.626	2.39	3.60
2015	SD	NL	26	0	8	23.0	100	25	8	6	0	0	1	0	10	1	22	0	0	1	.000	0-2	0	90	.698	3.95	2.35
2016	Sea	AL	60	0	15	60.1	247	53	26	25	11	1	1	1	15	5	65	0	4	4	.500	3-9	17	90	.700	3.28	3.73
2017	Sea	AL	69	0	7	64.2	262	62	23	23	3	4	4	0	13	5	50	0	3	3	.500	0-2	29	90	.643	2.67	3.20
2018	Sea	AL	62	1	8	56.1	239	50	28	25	7	1	2	3	15	4	56	0	4	4	.500	0-2	15	90	.662	3.11	3.99
2019	2 Tms		32	1	8	44.2	194	47	23	22	8	0	2	4	12	3	47	0	1	4	.200	0-0	1	89	.785	4.63	4.43
19	SF	NL	18	1	4	30.2	138	36	20	19	7	0	1	3	8	2	30	0	1	2	.000	0-0	0	89	.856	5.67	5.58
19	Phi	NL	14	0	4	14.0	56	11	3	3	1	0	1	1	4	1	17	0	1	2	.333	0-0	1	89	.606	2.56	1.93
	8 ML YEARS		384	2	63	376.2	1542	333	146	139	37	14	10	13	94	22	379	2	21	21	.500	4-19	97	90	.654	2.92	3.32

Arodys Vizcaino

Pitches: R **Bats:** R **Pos:** RP-4 — ah-ROH-dis vees-kai-EE-no — **Ht:** 6'0" **Wt:** 245 **Born:** 11/13/1990 **Age:** 29

			HOW MUCH PITCHED					WHAT HE GAVE UP									THE RESULTS							
Year	Team	Lg	G	GS	GF	IP	BFP	H	R	ER	HR	SH	SF	HB	TBB	IBB	SO	WP	W	L	Pct	Sv-Op Hld	Vel	OPS	ERC	ERA
2011	Atl	NL	17	0	2	17.1	77	16	9	9	1	0	0	1	9	1	17	5	1	1	.500	0-2	5	96	.636	3.89	4.67
2014	ChC	NL	5	0	5	5.0	22	5	3	3	1	0	0	0	3	0	4	0	0	0	-	0-0	0	95	.837	5.79	5.40
2015	Atl	NL	36	0	25	33.2	139	27	7	6	1	2	0	0	13	2	37	7	3	1	.750	9-10	3	98	.615	2.42	1.60
2016	Atl	NL	43	0	24	38.2	182	37	25	19	3	1	0	1	26	3	50	3	1	4	.200	10-14	0	97	.685	4.52	4.42
2017	Atl	NL	62	0	28	57.1	235	42	19	18	7	0	1	2	21	1	64	6	5	3	.625	14-17	17	98	.627	2.75	2.83
2018	Atl	NL	39	0	31	38.1	158	30	9	9	4	0	0	2	15	1	40	4	2	2	.500	16-18	1	98	.652	3.09	2.11
2019	Atl	NL	4	0	4	4.0	17	3	1	1	1	0	0	0	3	0	6	0	1	0	1.000	1-2	0	96	.924	5.38	2.25
	Postseason		2	0	2	2.0	8	1	0	0	0	0	0	0	1	0	5	1	0	0	-	1-1	0	97	.393	1.41	0.00
	7 ML YEARS		206	0	119	194.1	830	160	73	65	18	3	1	6	90	8	218	25	13	11	.542	50-63	26	97	.655	3.32	3.01

Daniel Vogelbach

Bats: L **Throws:** R **Pos:** DH-81;1B-57;PH-11 — voh-GULL-bock — **Ht:** 6'0" **Wt:** 250 **Born:** 12/17/1992 **Age:** 27

								BATTING												RUNNING			AVERAGES			
Year	Team	Lg	G	AB	H	2B	3B	HR	(Hm	Rd)	TB	R	RBI	RC	TBB	IBB	SO	HBP	SH	SF	SB	CS	GDP	Avg	OBP	Slg	OPS
2016	Sea	AL	8	12	1	0	0	0	(0	0)	1	0	0	0	1	0	6	0	0	0	0	0	0	.083	.154	.083	.237
2017	Sea	AL	16	28	6	1	0	0	(0	0)	7	0	2	2	3	0	9	0	0	0	0	0	2	.214	.290	.250	.540
2018	Sea	AL	37	87	18	2	0	4	(2	2)	32	9	13	11	13	0	26	2	0	0	0	0	4	.207	.324	.368	.691
2019	Sea	AL	144	462	96	17	0	30	(12	18)	203	73	76	72	92	2	149	2	0	2	0	0	2	.208	.341	.439	.780
	4 ML YEARS		205	589	121	20	0	34	(14	20)	243	82	91	85	109	2	190	4	0	2	0	0	10	.205	.332	.413	.745

Stephen Vogt

Bats: L **Throws:** R **Pos:** C-60;PH-36;LF-7;DH-2;1B-1 — VOTE — **Ht:** 6'0" **Wt:** 225 **Born:** 11/1/1984 **Age:** 35

								BATTING												RUNNING			AVERAGES			
Year	Team	Lg	G	AB	H	2B	3B	HR	(Hm	Rd)	TB	R	RBI	RC	TBB	IBB	SO	HBP	SH	SF	SB	CS	GDP	Avg	OBP	Slg	OPS
2019	Scrmto	AAA	17	58	14	3	0	4	(-	-)	29	9	7	12	14	0	11	0	0	0	0	0	1	.241	.389	.500	.889
2012	TB	AL	18	25	0	0	0	0	(0	0)	0	0	0	0	2	0	2	0	0	0	0	0	0	.000	.074	.000	.074
2013	Oak	AL	47	135	34	6	1	4	(3	1)	54	18	16	15	9	1	28	0	2	2	0	1	2	.252	.295	.400	.695
2014	Oak	AL	84	269	75	10	2	9	(4	5)	116	26	35	38	16	2	39	1	0	1	1	0	2	.279	.321	.431	.752
2015	Oak	AL	136	445	116	21	3	18	(5	13)	197	58	71	75	56	6	97	2	0	8	0	2	9	.261	.341	.443	.783
2016	Oak	AL	137	490	123	30	2	14	(4	10)	199	54	56	51	35	3	83	4	0	3	0	0	6	.251	.305	.406	.711

Year Team	Lg	G	AB	H	2B	3B	HR	(Hm	Rd)	TB	R	RBI	RC	TBB	IBB	SO	HBP	SH	SF	SB	CS	GDP	Avg	OBP	Slg	OPS
2017 2 Tms		99	279	65	15	1	12	(6	6)	118	25	40	33	21	1	56	0	1	2	0	1	2	.233	.285	.423	.708
2019 SF	NL	99	255	67	24	2	10	(3	7)	125	30	40	42	20	1	66	1	0	4	3	1	1	.263	.314	.490	.804
17 Oak	AL	54	157	34	8	1	4	(1	3)	56	12	20	19	16	1	31	0	0	0	0	0	1	.217	.287	.357	.644
17 Mil	NL	45	122	31	7	0	8	(5	3)	62	13	20	14	5	0	25	0	1	0	0	0	0	.254	.281	.508	.789
Postseason		6	19	3	0	1	0	(0	0)	5	2	1	1	2	0	8	0	0	0	0	0	0	.158	.238	.263	.501
7 ML YEARS		620	1898	480	106	11	67	(25	42)	809	211	258	254	159	14	371	8	3	20	4	5	22	.253	.310	.426	.737

Luke Voit

Bats: R **Throws:** R **Pos:** 1B-83;DH-34;PH-2   **Ht:** 6'3" **Wt:** 225 **Born:** 2/13/1991 **Age:** 29

Year Team	Lg	G	AB	H	2B	3B	HR	(Hm	Rd)	TB	R	RBI	RC	TBB	IBB	SO	HBP	SH	SF	SB	CS	GDP	Avg	OBP	Slg	OPS
2017 StL	NL	62	114	28	9	0	4	(4	0)	49	18	18	12	7	0	31	3	0	0	0	0	4	.246	.306	.430	.736
2018 2 Tms		47	143	46	5	0	15	(7	8)	96	30	36	40	17	0	43	1	0	0	0	0	3	.322	.398	.671	1.069
2019 NYY	AL	118	429	113	21	1	21	(7	14)	199	72	62	79	71	2	142	9	0	1	0	0	12	.263	.378	.464	.842
18 StL	NL	8	11	2	0	0	1	(1	0)	5	2	3	2	2	0	4	0	0	0	0	0	0	.182	.308	.455	.762
18 NYY	AL	39	132	44	5	0	14	(6	8)	91	28	33	38	15	0	39	1	0	0	0	0	3	.333	.405	.689	1.095
Postseason		5	17	4	0	1	0	(0	0)	6	2	4	4	4	0	6	0	0	0	0	0	0	.235	.381	.353	.734
3 ML YEARS		227	686	187	35	1	40	(18	22)	344	120	116	131	95	2	216	13	0	1	0	0	19	.273	.371	.501	.873

Edinson Volquez

Pitches: R **Bats:** R **Pos:** RP-7; SP-4   VOHL-kezz   **Ht:** 6'0" **Wt:** 220 **Born:** 7/3/1983 **Age:** 36

		HOW MUCH PITCHED					WHAT HE GAVE UP										THE RESULTS							
Year Team	Lg	G	GS	GF	IP	BFP	H	R	ER	HR	SH	SF	HB	TBB	IBB	SO	WP	W	L	Pct	Sv-Op	Hld	Vel	OPS	ERC	ERA
2005 Tex	AL	6	3	0	12.2	75	25	22	20	3	0	1	2	10	0	11	0	0	4	.000	0-0	0	94	1.155	14.15	14.21
2006 Tex	AL	8	8	0	33.1	164	52	28	27	7	0	1	1	17	0	15	0	1	6	.143	0-0	0	94	.965	9.27	7.29
2007 Tex	AL	6	6	0	34.0	149	34	18	17	4	0	2	2	15	0	29	0	2	1	.667	0-0	0	94	.750	4.63	4.50
2008 Cin	NL	33	32	1	196.0	838	167	82	70	14	6	5	14	93	5	206	10	17	6	.739	0-0	0	94	.681	3.61	3.21
2009 Cin	NL	9	9	0	49.2	218	34	25	24	6	2	1	5	32	0	47	2	4	2	.667	0-0	0	94	.683	3.77	4.35
2010 Cin	NL	12	12	0	62.2	275	59	30	30	6	3	1	3	35	0	67	5	4	3	.571	0-0	0	94	.739	4.60	4.31
2011 Cin	NL	20	20	0	108.2	489	106	72	69	19	5	6	4	65	3	104	5	5	7	.417	0-0	0	94	.833	5.42	5.71
2012 SD	NL	32	32	0	182.2	802	160	88	84	14	5	4	9	105	6	174	9	11	11	.500	0-0	0	94	.706	4.04	4.14
2013 2 Tms		33	32	0	170.1	777	193	114	108	19	9	4	5	77	2	142	16	9	12	.429	0-0	0	92	.804	5.11	5.71
2014 Pit	NL	32	31	0	192.2	809	166	75	65	17	13	6	14	71	6	140	15	13	7	.650	0-0	0	93	.674	3.37	3.04
2015 KC	AL	34	33	0	200.1	850	190	89	79	16	5	7	8	72	1	155	3	13	9	.591	0-0	0	93	.692	3.66	3.55
2016 KC	AL	34	34	0	189.1	853	217	124	113	23	6	6	7	76	1	139	5	10	11	.476	0-0	0	93	.794	5.20	5.37
2017 Mia	NL	17	17	0	92.1	397	78	46	43	8	5	5	3	53	3	81	4	4	8	.333	0-0	0	93	.719	3.93	4.19
2019 Tex	AL	11	4	1	16.0	75	20	12	12	3	0	0	0	12	0	10	3	0	1	.000	0-0	1	93	.935	8.17	6.75
13 SD	NL	27	27	0	142.1	659	168	100	95	14	7	3	3	69	2	116	11	9	10	.474	0-0	0	92	.820	5.45	6.01
13 LAD	NL	6	5	0	28.0	118	25	14	13	5	2	1	0	8	0	26	5	0	2	.000	0-0	0	93	.714	3.45	4.18
Postseason		7	7	0	35.1	154	27	22	21	4	1	3	2	23	2	26	0	1	4	.200	0-0	0	95	.676	3.98	5.35
14 ML YEARS		287	273	2	1540.2	6771	1501	825	761	159	59	49	75	733	27	1320	77	93	88	.514	0-0	1	93	.745	4.42	4.45

Austin Voth

Pitches: R **Bats:** R **Pos:** SP-8; RP-1   **Ht:** 6'2" **Wt:** 201 **Born:** 6/26/1992 **Age:** 28

		HOW MUCH PITCHED					WHAT HE GAVE UP										THE RESULTS							
Year Team	Lg	G	GS	GF	IP	BFP	H	R	ER	HR	SH	SF	HB	TBB	IBB	SO	WP	W	L	Pct	Sv-Op	Hld	Vel	OPS	ERC	ERA
2019 Fresno	AAA	12	12	0	61.1	268	68	34	30	7	0	2	1	15	0	68	6	3	5	.375	0--	-	-	.769	4.13	4.40
2018 Was	NL	4	2	0	12.1	55	12	9	9	3	1	1	0	6	0	11	1	1	1	.500	0-0	0	91	.780	5.19	6.57
2019 Was	NL	9	8	0	43.2	174	33	16	16	5	1	2	3	13	2	44	0	2	1	.667	0-0	0	93	.677	2.74	3.30
2 ML YEARS		13	10	0	56.0	229	45	25	25	8	2	3	3	19	2	55	1	3	2	.600	0-0	0	92	.701	3.25	4.02

Joey Votto

Bats: L **Throws:** R **Pos:** 1B-133;PH-6;DH-4;LF-1   VAH-toe   **Ht:** 6'2" **Wt:** 220 **Born:** 9/10/1983 **Age:** 36

Year Team	Lg	G	AB	H	2B	3B	HR	(Hm	Rd)	TB	R	RBI	RC	TBB	IBB	SO	HBP	SH	SF	SB	CS	GDP	Avg	OBP	Slg	OPS
2007 Cin	NL	24	84	27	7	0	4	(4	0)	46	11	17	17	5	1	15	0	0	0	1	0	0	.321	.360	.548	.907
2008 Cin	NL	151	526	156	32	3	24	(14	10)	266	69	84	91	59	9	102	2	0	2	7	5	7	.297	.368	.506	.874
2009 Cin	NL	131	469	151	38	1	25	(14	11)	266	82	84	99	70	10	106	4	0	1	4	1	8	.322	.414	.567	.981
2010 Cin	NL	150	547	177	36	2	37	(18	19)	328	106	113	132	91	8	125	7	0	3	16	5	11	.324	.424	.600	1.024
2011 Cin	NL	161	599	185	40	3	29	(13	16)	318	101	103	131	110	15	129	4	0	6	8	6	20	.309	.416	.531	.947
2012 Cin	NL	111	374	126	44	0	14	(10	4)	212	59	56	97	94	18	85	5	0	2	5	3	8	.337	.474	.567	1.041
2013 Cin	NL	162	581	177	30	3	24	(11	13)	285	101	73	121	135	19	138	4	0	6	6	3	15	.305	.435	.491	.926
2014 Cin	NL	62	220	56	16	0	6	(6	0)	90	32	23	36	47	2	49	3	0	2	1	1	6	.255	.390	.409	.799
2015 Cin	NL	158	545	171	33	2	29	(14	15)	295	95	80	135	143	15	135	5	0	2	11	3	11	.314	.459	.541	1.000
2016 Cin	NL	158	556	181	34	2	29	(16	13)	306	101	97	130	108	15	120	5	0	8	8	1	16	.326	.434	.550	.985
2017 Cin	NL	162	559	179	34	1	36	(20	16)	323	106	100	139	134	20	83	8	0	6	5	1	16	.320	.454	.578	1.032
2018 Cin	NL	145	503	143	28	2	12	(8	4)	211	67	67	98	108	6	101	9	0	3	2	0	15	.284	.417	.419	.837
2019 Cin	NL	142	525	137	32	1	15	(4	11)	216	79	47	79	76	2	123	4	0	3	5	0	14	.261	.357	.411	.768
Postseason		9	32	8	0	0	0	(0	0)	8	3	1	3	4	0	9	0	0	1	0	0	1	.250	.324	.250	.574
13 ML YEARS		1717	6088	1866	404	20	284	(152	132)	3162	1009	944	1298	1180	140	1311	60	0	44	79	29	146	.307	.421	.519	.941

Michael Wacha

Pitches: R **Bats:** R **Pos:** SP-24; RP-5 — WOCK-uh — **Ht:** 6'6" **Wt:** 215 **Born:** 7/1/1991 **Age:** 28

Year	Team	Lg	G	GS	GF	IP	BFP	H	R	ER	HR	SH	SF	HB	TBB	IBB	SO	WP	W	L	Pct	Sv-Op	Hld	Vel	OPS	ERC	ERA
2013	StL	NL	15	9	2	64.2	260	52	20	20	5	1	3	0	19	0	65	3	4	1	.800	0-1	0	93	.603	2.52	2.78
2014	StL	NL	19	19	0	107.0	447	95	41	38	6	1	2	5	33	0	94	2	5	6	.455	0-0	0	93	.636	3.00	3.20
2015	StL	NL	30	30	0	181.1	762	162	74	68	19	8	3	6	58	4	153	4	17	7	.708	0-0	0	94	.672	3.28	3.38
2016	StL	NL	27	24	1	138.0	606	159	86	78	15	4	5	1	45	6	114	6	7	7	.500	0-0	0	93	.800	4.66	5.09
2017	StL	NL	30	30	0	165.2	701	170	82	76	17	3	4	3	55	3	158	5	12	9	.571	0-0	0	95	.735	4.07	4.13
2018	StL	NL	15	15	0	84.1	355	68	36	30	9	4	5	2	36	0	71	2	8	2	.800	0-0	0	94	.646	3.24	3.20
2019	StL	NL	29	24	0	126.2	562	143	71	67	26	6	3	3	55	4	104	2	6	7	.462	0-0	0	93	.865	5.88	4.76
	Postseason		7	6	1	35.1	144	24	16	16	7	0	0	1	16	4	38	0	4	3	.571	0-0	0	94	.694	3.15	4.08
	7 ML YEARS		165	151	3	867.2	3693	849	410	377	97	27	27	20	301	17	759	24	59	39	.602	0-1	0	94	.722	3.89	3.91

Tyler Wade

Bats: L **Throws:** R **Pos:** 2B-18;LF-14;PR-6;3B-5;SS-4;CF-2;RF-2;DH-2;PH-2 — **Ht:** 6'1" **Wt:** 185 **Born:** 11/23/1994 **Age:** 25

Year	Team	Lg	G	AB	H	2B	3B	HR	(Hm	Rd)	TB	R	RBI	RC	TBB	IBB	SO	HBP	SH	SF	SB	CS	GDP	Avg	OBP	Slg	OPS
2019	S-WB	AAA	79	301	89	19	4	4	(-	-)	128	51	38	47	23	1	76	4	4	2	13	5	2	.296	.352	.425	.777
2017	NYY	AL	30	58	9	4	0	0	(0	0)	13	7	2	1	5	0	19	0	0	0	1	1	2	.155	.222	.224	.446
2018	NYY	AL	36	66	11	4	0	1	(0	1)	18	8	5	4	4	0	23	0	0	0	1	0	1	.167	.214	.273	.487
2019	NYY	AL	43	94	23	3	1	2	(2	0)	34	16	11	12	11	0	28	1	2	0	7	0	0	.245	.330	.362	.692
	3 ML YEARS		109	218	43	11	1	3	(2	1)	65	31	18	17	20	0	70	1	2	0	9	1	3	.197	.268	.298	.566

LaMonte Wade Jr.

Bats: L **Throws:** L **Pos:** CF-14;LF-8;RF-6;PH-5;PR-2;1B-1;DH-1 — **Ht:** 6'1" **Wt:** 205 **Born:** 1/1/1994 **Age:** 26

Year	Team	Lg	G	AB	H	2B	3B	HR	(Hm	Rd)	TB	R	RBI	RC	TBB	IBB	SO	HBP	SH	SF	SB	CS	GDP	Avg	OBP	Slg	OPS
2019	Roch	AAA	77	264	65	12	1	5	(-	-)	94	47	24	44	56	0	48	9	2	3	7	2	8	.246	.392	.356	.748
2019	Min	AL	26	56	11	2	1	2	(1	1)	21	10	5	9	11	0	9	2	0	0	0	1	0	.196	.348	.375	.723

Jacob Waguespack

Pitches: R **Bats:** R **Pos:** SP-13; RP-3 — **Ht:** 6'6" **Wt:** 235 **Born:** 11/5/1993 **Age:** 26

Year	Team	Lg	G	GS	GF	IP	BFP	H	R	ER	HR	SH	SF	HB	TBB	IBB	SO	WP	W	L	Pct	Sv-Op	Hld	Vel	OPS	ERC	ERA
2019	Buffalo	AAA	12	11	0	52.2	236	57	33	31	9	1	3	2	25	0	52	2	2	6	.250	0--	-	-	.816	5.57	5.30
2019	Tor	AL	16	13	0	78.0	335	75	43	38	12	0	0	5	29	0	63	2	5	5	.500	0-0	0	92	.764	4.40	4.38

Adam Wainwright

Pitches: R **Bats:** R **Pos:** SP-31 — **Ht:** 6'7" **Wt:** 235 **Born:** 8/30/1981 **Age:** 38

Year	Team	Lg	G	GS	GF	IP	BFP	H	R	ER	HR	SH	SF	HB	TBB	IBB	SO	WP	W	L	Pct	Sv-Op	Hld	Vel	OPS	ERC	ERA
2005	StL	NL	2	0	1	2.0	9	2	3	3	1	0	0	0	1	0	0	0	0	0	-	0-0	0	91	.958	7.30	13.50
2006	StL	NL	61	0	10	75.0	309	64	26	26	6	4	1	4	22	2	72	3	2	1	.667	3-5	17	91	.644	2.92	3.12
2007	StL	NL	32	32	0	202.0	882	212	93	83	13	9	5	9	70	4	136	6	14	12	.538	0-0	0	89	.721	4.01	3.70
2008	StL	NL	20	20	0	132.0	544	122	51	47	12	6	4	3	34	1	91	3	11	3	.786	0-0	0	90	.688	3.14	3.20
2009	StL	NL	34	**34**	0	**233.0**	970	216	75	68	17	10	5	3	66	1	212	7	**19**	8	.704	0-0	0	91	.646	3.08	2.63
2010	StL	NL	33	33	0	230.1	910	186	68	62	15	13	6	4	56	2	213	2	20	11	.645	0-0	0	91	.604	**2.36**	2.42
2012	StL	NL	32	32	0	198.2	831	196	96	87	15	9	6	6	52	3	184	5	14	13	.519	0-0	0	90	.701	3.41	3.94
2013	StL	NL	34	**34**	0	**241.2**	956	**223**	83	79	15	**13**	2	6	35	2	219	5	**19**	9	.679	0-0	0	91	.636	2.60	2.94
2014	StL	NL	32	32	0	227.0	898	184	64	60	10	8	3	7	50	5	179	4	20	9	.690	0-0	0	90	.580	2.20	2.38
2015	StL	NL	7	4	2	28.0	111	25	7	5	0	2	0	4	4	0	20	0	2	1	.667	0-0	0	90	.590	1.97	1.61
2016	StL	NL	33	33	0	198.2	847	**220**	108	**102**	22	8	9	5	59	4	161	1	13	9	.591	0-0	0	90	.785	4.50	4.62
2017	StL	NL	24	23	0	123.1	526	140	73	70	14	5	1	5	45	4	96	2	12	5	.706	0-0	0	90	.794	4.93	5.11
2018	StL	NL	8	8	0	40.1	181	41	21	20	5	3	2	2	18	1	40	1	2	4	.333	0-0	0	89	.753	4.60	4.46
2019	StL	NL	31	31	0	171.2	745	181	83	80	22	6	5	8	64	7	153	2	14	10	.583	0-0	0	90	.782	4.64	4.19
	Postseason		24	12	9	89.0	361	82	33	30	9	2	2	2	15	0	96	3	4	4	.500	4-5	0	92	.664	2.85	3.03
	14 ML YEARS		383	316	13	2103.2	8739	2012	851	792	167	96	49	62	576	36	1776	41	162	95	.630	3-5	17	90	.685	3.32	3.39

Marcus Walden

Pitches: R **Bats:** R **Pos:** RP-70 — **Ht:** 6'0" **Wt:** 195 **Born:** 9/13/1988 **Age:** 31

Year	Team	Lg	G	GS	GF	IP	BFP	H	R	ER	HR	SH	SF	HB	TBB	IBB	SO	WP	W	L	Pct	Sv-Op	Hld	Vel	OPS	ERC	ERA
2018	Bos	AL	8	0	3	14.2	59	14	7	6	0	0	0	1	3	0	14	2	0	0	-	1-1	0	94	.669	2.79	3.68
2019	Bos	AL	70	0	8	78.0	327	61	38	33	6	1	2	5	32	1	76	6	9	2	.818	2-6	6	94	.642	3.00	3.81
	2 ML YEARS		78	0	13	92.2	386	75	45	39	6	1	2	6	35	1	90	8	9	2	.818	3-7	7	94	.646	2.97	3.79

Mitch Walding

Bats: L **Throws:** R **Pos:** PH-2 — **Ht:** 6'3" **Wt:** 190 **Born:** 9/10/1992 **Age:** 27

Year	Team	Lg	G	AB	H	2B	3B	HR	(Hm	Rd)	TB	R	RBI	RC	TBB	IBB	SO	HBP	SH	SF	SB	CS	GDP	Avg	OBP	Slg	OPS
2019	LV	AAA	90	282	58	11	1	11	(-	-)	104	46	40	41	62	2	133	3	0	3	2	1	4	.206	.351	.369	.720
2018	Phi	NL	13	17	1	0	0	1	(1	0)	4	1	2	1	2	0	12	0	0	0	0	0	1	.059	.158	.235	.393
2019	Phi	NL	2	2	0	0	0	0	(0	0)	0	0	0	0	0	0	2	0	0	0	0	0	0	.000	.000	.000	.000
	2 ML YEARS		15	19	1	0	0	1	(1	0)	4	1	2	1	2	0	14	0	0	0	0	0	1	.053	.143	.211	.353

Christian Walker

Bats: R **Throws:** R **Pos:** 1B-142;PH-13;DH-3   **Ht:** 6'0" **Wt:** 220 **Born:** 3/28/1991 **Age:** 29

					BATTING																		RUNNING			AVERAGES			
Year	Team	Lg	G	AB	H	2B	3B	HR	(Hm	Rd)	TB	R	RBI	RC	TBB	IBB	SO	HBP	SH	SF	SB	CS	GDP	Avg	OBP	Slg	OPS
2014	Bal	AL	6	18	3	1	0	1	(1	0)	7	1	1	1	1	0	9	0	0	0	0	0	0	.167	.211	.389	.599
2015	Bal	AL	7	9	1	0	0	0	(0	0)	1	0	0	1	3	0	4	0	0	0	0	0	0	.111	.333	.111	.444
2017	Ari	NL	11	12	3	1	0	2	(2	0)	10	2	2	2	1	0	5	2	0	0	0	0	0	.250	.400	.833	1.233
2018	Ari	NL	37	49	8	2	0	3	(2	1)	19	6	6	3	3	0	22	1	0	0	1	0	1	.163	.226	.388	.614
2019	Ari	NL	152	529	137	26	1	29	(16	13)	252	86	73	83	67	6	155	6	0	1	8	1	11	.259	.348	.476	.825
	Postseason		2	1	1	0	0	0	(0	0)	1	0	0	1	0	0	0	1	0	0	0	0	0	1.000	1.000	1.000	2.000
	5 ML YEARS		213	617	152	30	1	35	(21	14)	289	95	82	89	75	6	195	9	0	1	9	1	12	.246	.336	.468	.805

Jeremy Walker

Pitches: R **Bats:** R **Pos:** RP-6   **Ht:** 6'5" **Wt:** 205 **Born:** 6/12/1995 **Age:** 25

			HOW MUCH PITCHED					WHAT HE GAVE UP										THE RESULTS								
Year	Team	Lg	G	GS	GF	IP	BFP	H	R	ER	HR	SH	SF	HB	TBB	IBB	SO	WP	W	L	Pct	Sv-Op	Hld	Vel	OPS	ERC	ERA
2019	Missi	AA	21	1	12	58.2	236	56	23	16	2	1	0	1	5	0	57	0	1	6	.143	6--	-	-	.578	2.29	2.45
2019	Gwnntt	AAA	11	0	4	22.2	93	20	10	10	1	0	0	1	6	0	25	1	2	1	.667	1--	-	-	.604	2.75	3.97
2019	Atl	NL	6	0	3	9.1	38	9	2	2	0	0	0	0	4	0	6	0	0	0	-	0-0	0	92	.695	3.50	1.93

Neil Walker

Bats: B **Throws:** R **Pos:** 1B-69;PH-28;3B-26;DH-3;2B-1   **Ht:** 6'3" **Wt:** 210 **Born:** 9/10/1985 **Age:** 34

					BATTING																		RUNNING			AVERAGES			
Year	Team	Lg	G	AB	H	2B	3B	HR	(Hm	Rd)	TB	R	RBI	RC	TBB	IBB	SO	HBP	SH	SF	SB	CS	GDP	Avg	OBP	Slg	OPS
2009	Pit	NL	17	36	7	1	0	0	(0	0)	8	5	0	2	4	0	11	0	0	0	1	0	1	.194	.275	.222	.497
2010	Pit	NL	110	426	126	29	3	12	(5	7)	197	57	66	66	34	1	83	3	2	4	2	3	4	.296	.349	.462	.811
2011	Pit	NL	159	596	163	36	4	12	(4	8)	243	76	83	77	54	5	112	4	0	8	9	6	15	.273	.334	.408	.742
2012	Pit	NL	129	472	132	27	0	14	(7	7)	201	62	69	72	47	1	104	2	1	8	7	5	11	.280	.342	.426	.768
2013	Pit	NL	133	478	120	24	4	16	(8	8)	200	62	53	62	50	4	85	15	5	3	1	2	14	.251	.339	.418	.757
2014	Pit	NL	137	512	139	25	3	23	(10	13)	239	74	76	72	45	2	88	11	1	2	2	2	12	.271	.342	.467	.809
2015	Pit	NL	151	543	146	32	3	16	(8	8)	232	69	71	73	44	5	110	8	0	8	4	1	9	.269	.328	.427	.756
2016	NYM	NL	113	412	116	9	1	23	(10	13)	196	57	55	66	42	3	84	1	0	3	3	1	10	.282	.347	.476	.823
2017	2 Tms	NL	111	385	102	21	2	14	(7	7)	169	59	49	66	55	2	77	5	1	2	0	2	9	.265	.362	.439	.801
2018	NYY	AL	113	347	76	12	1	11	(5	6)	123	48	46	46	42	3	87	5	0	4	0	0	3	.219	.309	.354	.664
2019	Mia	NL	115	337	88	19	1	8	(4	4)	133	37	38	50	42	1	77	1	0	1	3	0	8	.261	.344	.395	.738
17	NYM	NL	73	265	70	13	2	10	(4	6)	117	40	36	46	27	1	47	4	1	2	0	1	4	.264	.339	.442	.780
17	Mil	NL	38	120	32	8	0	4	(3	1)	52	19	13	20	28	1	30	1	0	0	0	1	5	.267	.409	.433	.843
	Postseason		12	35	3	1	0	0	(0	0)	4	1	2	2	2	0	11	1	0	0	0	0	0	.086	.158	.114	.272
	11 ML YEARS		1288	4544	1215	235	22	149	(68	81)	1941	606	606	652	459	27	918	55	10	43	32	22	97	.267	.339	.427	.766

Taijuan Walker

Pitches: R **Bats:** R **Pos:** SP-1   TIE-wahn   **Ht:** 6'4" **Wt:** 235 **Born:** 8/13/1992 **Age:** 27

			HOW MUCH PITCHED					WHAT HE GAVE UP										THE RESULTS								
Year	Team	Lg	G	GS	GF	IP	BFP	H	R	ER	HR	SH	SF	HB	TBB	IBB	SO	WP	W	L	Pct	Sv-Op	Hld	Vel	OPS	ERC	ERA
2013	Sea	AL	3	3	0	15.0	60	11	7	6	0	0	2	0	4	0	12	0	1	0	1.000	0-0	0	95	.546	1.63	3.60
2014	Sea	AL	8	5	2	38.0	160	31	12	11	2	0	0	3	18	1	34	2	2	3	.400	0-0	0	95	.642	3.34	2.61
2015	Sea	AL	29	29	0	169.2	706	163	92	86	25	4	5	9	40	1	157	4	11	8	.579	0-0	0	94	.717	3.74	4.56
2016	Sea	AL	25	25	0	134.1	573	129	75	63	27	3	3	8	37	2	119	4	8	11	.421	0-0	0	94	.767	4.20	4.22
2017	Ari	NL	28	28	0	157.1	684	148	76	61	17	5	8	9	61	7	146	7	9	9	.500	0-0	0	94	.732	3.85	3.49
2018	Ari	NL	3	3	0	13.0	56	15	5	5	1	0	0	0	5	0	9	0	0	0	-	0-0	0	94	.749	4.88	3.46
2019	Ari	NL	1	1	0	1.0	4	1	0	0	0	0	0	0	0	0	1	0	0	0	-	0-0	0	93	.750	1.95	0.00
	Postseason		1	1	0	1.0	9	4	4	4	1	0	0	0	2	1	3	0	0	1	.000	0-0	0	93	1.810	44.27	36.00
	7 ML YEARS		97	94	2	528.1	2243	498	267	232	72	12	18	29	165	11	478	17	31	31	.500	0-0	0	94	.726	3.83	3.95

Chad Wallach

Bats: R **Throws:** R **Pos:** C-14;PH-6;PR-1   **Ht:** 6'3" **Wt:** 230 **Born:** 11/4/1991 **Age:** 28

					BATTING																		RUNNING			AVERAGES			
Year	Team	Lg	G	AB	H	2B	3B	HR	(Hm	Rd)	TB	R	RBI	RC	TBB	IBB	SO	HBP	SH	SF	SB	CS	GDP	Avg	OBP	Slg	OPS
2017	Cin	NL	6	11	1	0	0	0	(0	0)	1	0	0	0	0	0	5	0	0	0	0	0	0	.091	.091	.091	.182
2018	Mia	NL	15	45	8	1	0	1	(1	0)	12	4	5	4	4	0	23	2	1	0	0	0	0	.178	.275	.267	.541
2019	Mia	NL	19	48	12	3	0	1	(1	0)	18	4	3	5	6	0	12	0	0	0	0	0	0	.250	.333	.375	.708
	3 ML YEARS		40	104	21	4	0	2	(2	0)	31	8	8	9	10	0	40	2	1	0	0	0	0	.202	.284	.298	.583

Jared Walsh

Bats: L **Throws:** L **Pos:** 1B-24;PH-7   **Ht:** 6'0" **Wt:** 210 **Born:** 7/30/1993 **Age:** 26

					BATTING																		RUNNING			AVERAGES			
Year	Team	Lg	G	AB	H	2B	3B	HR	(Hm	Rd)	TB	R	RBI	RC	TBB	IBB	SO	HBP	SH	SF	SB	CS	GDP	Avg	OBP	Slg	OPS
2019	Salt Lk	AAA	98	382	124	30	0	36	(-	-)	262	90	86	105	59	0	115	9	0	4	0	0	8	.325	.423	.686	1.109
2019	LAA	AL	34	79	16	5	1	1	(1	0)	26	6	5	8	6	1	35	2	0	0	0	0	0	.203	.276	.329	.605

Donnie Walton

Bats: L Throws: R Pos: SS-5;2B-2   Ht: 5'10" Wt: 184 Born: 5/25/1994 Age: 26

Year	Team	Lg	G	AB	H	2B	3B	HR	(Hm	Rd)	TB	R	RBI	RC	TBB	IBB	SO	HBP	SH	SF	SB	CS	GDP	Avg	OBP	Slg	OPS
																					RUNNING			AVERAGES			
2019	Ark	AA	124	480	144	22	3	11	(-	-)	205	72	50	82	63	0	72	10	2	3	10	13	9	.300	.390	.427	.817
2019	Sea	AL	7	16	3	0	0	0	(0	0)	3	2	2	1	3	0	5	0	0	0	0	1	0	.188	.316	.188	.503

Wei-Chung Wang

Pitches: L Bats: L Pos: RP-25   way-CHUNG WONG   Ht: 6'1" Wt: 160 Born: 4/25/1992 Age: 28

Year	Team	Lg	G	GS	GF	IP	BFP	H	R	ER	HR	SH	SF	HB	TBB	IBB	SO	WP	W	L	Pct	Sv-Op	Hld	Vel	OPS	ERC	ERA
2019	LsVgs	AAA	19	0	8	26.1	116	29	14	14	5	2	0	1	8	1	24	1	1	1	.500	1--	-		.810	4.94	4.78
2014	Mil	NL	14	0	10	17.1	92	30	23	21	6	0	0	1	8	1	13	1	0	0	-	0-0	0	91	1.123	11.03	10.90
2017	Mil	NL	8	0	1	1.1	9	5	2	2	1	0	0	0	0	0	2	0	0	0	-	0-0	0	94	1.444	29.54	13.50
2019	2 Tms		25	0	6	31.0	129	27	13	13	4	0	1	1	14	0	18	0	3	0	1.000	0-0	0	91	.715	4.01	3.77
19	Oak	AL	20	0	5	27.0	110	22	10	10	4	0	1	1	11	0	16	0	1	0	1.000	0-0	0	91	.701	3.67	3.33
19	Pit	NL	5	0	1	4.0	19	5	3	3	0	0	0	0	3	0	2	0	2	0	1.000	0-0	0	92	.796	6.32	6.75
3 ML YEARS			47	0	17	49.2	230	62	38	36	11	0	1	2	22	1	33	1	3	0	1.000	0-0	0	91	.910	6.83	6.52

Taylor Ward

Bats: R Throws: R Pos: LF-9;3B-4;PR-3;DH-2;PH-2   Ht: 6'1" Wt: 200 Born: 12/14/1993 Age: 26

Year	Team	Lg	G	AB	H	2B	3B	HR	(Hm	Rd)	TB	R	RBI	RC	TBB	IBB	SO	HBP	SH	SF	SB	CS	GDP	Avg	OBP	Slg	OPS
2019	Salt Lk	AAA	106	421	129	34	1	27	(-	-)	246	102	71	104	80	1	101	9	0	1	11	5	7	.306	.427	.584	1.011
2018	LAA	AL	40	135	24	3	0	6	(4	2)	45	14	15	14	9	0	45	3	0	0	2	0	0	.178	.245	.333	.578
2019	LAA	AL	20	42	8	3	0	1	(1	0)	14	4	2	2	6	0	23	0	0	0	0	0	1	.190	.292	.333	.625
2 ML YEARS			60	177	32	6	0	7	(5	2)	59	18	17	16	15	0	68	3	0	0	2	0	1	.181	.256	.333	.590

Adam Warren

Pitches: R Bats: R Pos: RP-25   Ht: 6'1" Wt: 224 Born: 8/25/1987 Age: 32

Year	Team	Lg	G	GS	GF	IP	BFP	H	R	ER	HR	SH	SF	HB	TBB	IBB	SO	WP	W	L	Pct	Sv-Op	Hld	Vel	OPS	ERC	ERA
2012	NYY	AL	1	1	0	2.1	17	8	6	6	2	0	0	0	2	0	1	0	0	0	-	0-0	0	92	1.588	33.34	23.14
2013	NYY	AL	34	2	17	77.0	331	80	29	29	10	0	0	2	30	2	64	3	3	2	.600	1-1	1	93	.766	4.60	3.39
2014	NYY	AL	69	0	11	78.2	324	63	27	26	4	5	4	3	24	1	76	4	3	6	.333	3-6	23	94	.615	2.45	2.97
2015	NYY	AL	43	17	5	131.1	534	114	51	48	10	2	2	7	39	1	104	7	7	7	.500	1-1	3	93	.648	3.07	3.29
2016	2 Tms		58	1	7	65.1	277	59	37	34	11	3	2	1	29	6	52	3	7	4	.636	0-3	12	93	.742	4.14	4.68
2017	NYY	AL	46	0	7	57.1	223	35	19	15	4	0	5	1	15	2	54	5	3	2	.600	1-4	11	93	.491	1.53	2.35
2018	2 Tms		47	0	10	51.2	223	48	18	18	6	0	1	2	20	1	52	3	3	2	.600	0-1	4	92	.694	3.82	3.14
2019	SD	NL	25	0	9	28.2	124	28	18	17	9	2	0	1	12	0	25	3	4	1	.800	0-0	3	91	.887	5.72	5.34
16	ChC	NL	29	1	4	35.0	152	31	24	23	7	2	1	0	19	4	27	0	3	2	.600	0-1	6	93	.764	4.53	5.91
16	NYY	AL	29	0	3	30.1	125	28	13	11	4	1	1	1	10	2	25	3	4	2	.667	0-2	6	93	.716	3.71	3.26
18	NYY	AL	24	0	6	30.0	128	26	9	9	3	0	1	1	12	0	37	1	0	1	.000	0-0	2	92	.656	3.43	2.70
18	Sea	AL	23	0	4	21.2	95	22	9	9	3	0	0	1	8	1	15	2	3	1	.750	0-1	2	92	.745	4.37	3.74
Postseason			3	0	0	4.1	16	2	1	0	0	0	0	0	1	0	2	1	0	0	-	0-0	0	91	.321	0.82	2.08
8 ML YEARS			323	21	66	492.1	2053	435	205	193	56	12	14	17	171	13	428	28	30	24	.556	6-16	57	93	.684	3.44	3.53

Art Warren

Pitches: R Bats: B Pos: RP-6   Ht: 6'3" Wt: 230 Born: 3/23/1993 Age: 27

Year	Team	Lg	G	GS	GF	IP	BFP	H	R	ER	HR	SH	SF	HB	TBB	IBB	SO	WP	W	L	Pct	Sv-Op	Hld	Vel	OPS	ERC	ERA
2019	Ark	AA	29	0	22	31.2	128	23	9	6	1	1	0	0	13	0	41	6	2	1	.667	15--	-	-	.555	2.27	1.71
2019	Sea	AL	6	0	2	5.1	21	2	0	0	0	0	0	0	2	0	5	1	1	0	1.000	0-0	1	95	.296	0.81	0.00

Drew Waters

Bats: B Throws: R Pos: CF   Ht: 6'2" Wt: 183 Born: 12/30/1998 Age: 21

Year	Team	Lg	G	AB	H	2B	3B	HR	(Hm	Rd)	TB	R	RBI	RC	TBB	IBB	SO	HBP	SH	SF	SB	CS	GDP	Avg	OBP	Slg	OPS
2017	2 Tms	Low	50	198	55	14	2	4	(-	-)	85	33	24	33	23	0	70	3	0	0	6	3	3	.278	.362	.429	.791
2018	2 Tms	Low	114	460	135	39	9	9	(-	-)	219	72	39	48	29	0	105	7	0	2	23	5	8	.293	.343	.476	.819
2019	Missi	AA	108	420	134	35	9	5	(-	-)	202	63	41	73	28	1	121	4	0	2	13	6	3	.319	.366	.481	.847
2019	Gwnntt	AAA	26	107	29	5	0	2	(-	-)	40	17	11	14	11	0	43	0	0	1	3	0	3	.271	.336	.374	.710

Tony Watson

Pitches: L Bats: L Pos: RP-60   Ht: 6'3" Wt: 218 Born: 5/30/1985 Age: 35

Year	Team	Lg	G	GS	GF	IP	BFP	H	R	ER	HR	SH	SF	HB	TBB	IBB	SO	WP	W	L	Pct	Sv-Op	Hld	Vel	OPS	ERC	ERA
2011	Pit	NL	43	0	6	41.0	174	34	18	18	6	2	1	1	20	4	37	0	2	2	.500	0-1	10	91	.711	3.75	3.95
2012	Pit	NL	68	0	10	53.1	215	37	21	20	5	2	2	1	23	1	53	1	5	2	.714	0-2	16	94	.623	2.62	3.38
2013	Pit	NL	67	0	14	71.2	280	51	19	19	5	3	1	6	12	1	54	2	3	1	.750	2-4	22	94	.544	1.88	2.39
2014	Pit	NL	78	0	3	77.1	305	64	16	14	5	5	3	6	15	0	81	0	10	2	.833	2-9	34	94	.613	2.54	1.63
2015	Pit	NL	77	0	4	75.1	293	55	17	16	3	1	3	4	17	1	62	1	4	1	.800	1-3	41	94	.525	1.92	1.91
2016	Pit	NL	70	0	27	67.2	272	52	26	23	10	4	3	3	20	1	58	0	2	5	.286	15-20	23	93	.672	2.92	3.06
2017	2 Tms	NL	71	0	23	66.2	291	72	26	25	9	5	2	5	20	7	53	0	7	4	.636	10-18	14	94	.764	4.50	3.38
2018	SF	NL	72	0	10	66.0	261	54	19	19	4	3	2	1	14	3	72	0	4	6	.400	0-4	32	92	.599	2.21	2.59

Year Team	Lg	G	GS	GF	IP	BFP	H	R	ER	HR	SH	SF	HB	TBB	IBB	SO	WP	W	L	Pct	Sv-Op	Hld	Vel	OPS	ERC	ERA
2019 SF	NL	60	0	4	54.0	231	56	26	25	9	2	0	5	12	1	41	1	2	2	.500	0-3	25	93	.757	4.36	4.17
17 Pit	NL	47	0	22	46.2	209	57	20	19	7	3	2	3	14	4	35	0	5	3	.625	10-17	6	93	.824	5.45	3.66
17 LAD	NL	24	0	1	20.0	82	15	6	6	2	2	0	2	6	3	18	0	2	1	.667	0-1	8	94	.607	2.52	2.70
Postseason		16	0	0	12.0	48	9	4	3	1	0	0	2	2	0	5	0	2	0	1.000	0-0	4	94	.566	2.43	2.25
9 ML YEARS		606	0	101	573.0	2322	475	188	179	56	27	17	32	153	19	511	5	39	25	.609	30-64	217	93	.640	2.83	2.81

Luke Weaver

Pitches: R Bats: R Pos: SP-12　　　Ht: 6'2" Wt: 170 Born: 8/21/1993 Age: 26

Year Team	Lg	G	GS	GF	IP	BFP	H	R	ER	HR	SH	SF	HB	TBB	IBB	SO	WP	W	L	Pct	Sv-Op	Hld	Vel	OPS	ERC	ERA
2016 StL	NL	9	8	0	36.1	167	46	29	23	7	2	3	2	12	0	45	1	1	4	.200	0-0	0	92	.870	6.23	5.70
2017 StL	NL	13	10	0	60.1	252	59	27	26	7	1	1	1	17	1	72	0	7	2	.778	0-0	0	93	.699	3.66	3.88
2018 StL	NL	30	25	3	136.1	609	150	83	75	19	9	1	3	54	2	121	3	7	11	.389	0-0	0	94	.786	4.93	4.95
2019 Ari	NL	12	12	0	64.1	260	55	22	21	6	0	1	3	14	1	69	0	4	3	.571	0-0	0	94	.645	2.73	2.94
4 ML YEARS		64	55	3	297.1	1288	310	161	145	39	12	6	9	97	4	307	4	19	20	.487	0-0	0	93	.750	4.32	4.39

Jacob Webb

Pitches: R Bats: R Pos: RP-36　　　Ht: 6'1" Wt: 200 Born: 8/15/1993 Age: 26

Year Team	Lg	G	GS	GF	IP	BFP	H	R	ER	HR	SH	SF	HB	TBB	IBB	SO	WP	W	L	Pct	Sv-Op	Hld	Vel	OPS	ERC	ERA
2019 Gwnntt	AAA	10	0	4	10.1	49	9	8	8	1	0	0	0	9	0	12	1	0	1	.000	1--	-	-	.717	5.05	6.97
2019 Atl	NL	36	0	12	32.1	131	24	10	5	4	1	0	1	12	0	28	3	4	0	1.000	2-4	9	95	.661	2.89	1.39

Logan Webb

Pitches: R Bats: R Pos: SP-8　　　Ht: 6'2" Wt: 220 Born: 11/18/1996 Age: 23

Year Team	Lg	G	GS	GF	IP	BFP	H	R	ER	HR	SH	SF	HB	TBB	IBB	SO	WP	W	L	Pct	Sv-Op	Hld	Vel	OPS	ERC	ERA
2019 Rchmd	AA	8	7	0	41.1	179	41	21	10	2	0	0	0	12	0	47	1	1	4	.200	0--	-	-	.649	3.14	2.18
2019 SF	NL	8	8	0	39.2	174	44	25	23	5	0	1	1	14	0	37	4	2	3	.400	0-0	0	93	.795	4.81	5.22

Tyler Webb

Pitches: L Bats: L Pos: RP-65　　　Ht: 6'5" Wt: 230 Born: 7/20/1990 Age: 29

Year Team	Lg	G	GS	GF	IP	BFP	H	R	ER	HR	SH	SF	HB	TBB	IBB	SO	WP	W	L	Pct	Sv-Op	Hld	Vel	OPS	ERC	ERA
2019 Memp	AAA	5	0	1	6.2	28	7	3	2	0	0	0	1	2	0	5	1	0	1	.000	0--	-	-	.677	4.02	2.70
2017 2 Tms	AL	9	0	3	8.0	36	9	5	5	2	0	0	0	5	1	8	0	0	0	-	0-1	0	91	.905	6.96	5.63
2018 2 Tms	NL	22	0	5	20.1	90	22	15	10	3	1	0	1	9	2	15	0	0	1	.000	0-0	0	90	.828	5.17	4.43
2019 StL	NL	65	0	11	55.0	221	33	23	23	7	2	2	2	23	3	48	2	2	1	.667	1-1	8	90	.593	2.29	3.76
17 NYY	AL	7	0	2	6.0	23	3	3	3	1	0	0	0	4	0	5	0	0	0	-	0-0	0	91	.673	3.11	4.50
17 Mil	NL	2	0	1	2.0	13	6	2	2	1	0	0	0	1	1	3	0	0	0	-	0-1	0	92	1.288	21.60	9.00
18 SD	NL	4	0	1	5.0	24	6	7	7	2	0	0	0	3	0	4	0	0	1	.000	0-0	0	89	1.042	8.40	12.60
18 StL	NL	18	0	4	15.1	66	16	8	3	1	1	0	1	6	2	11	0	0	0	-	0-0	0	90	.750	4.17	1.76
3 ML YEARS		96	0	19	83.1	347	64	43	38	12	3	2	3	37	6	71	2	2	2	.500	1-2	8	90	.686	3.32	4.10

Ryan Weber

Pitches: R Bats: R Pos: RP-15; SP-3　　　Ht: 6'1" Wt: 180 Born: 8/12/1990 Age: 29

Year Team	Lg	G	GS	GF	IP	BFP	H	R	ER	HR	SH	SF	HB	TBB	IBB	SO	WP	W	L	Pct	Sv-Op	Hld	Vel	OPS	ERC	ERA
2019 Pwtckt	AAA	16	16	0	78.0	337	86	41	39	9	2	1	3	25	0	63	3	1	5	.167	0--	-	-	.804	4.66	4.50
2015 Atl	NL	5	5	0	28.1	109	25	15	15	3	0	0	2	6	0	19	0	0	3	.000	0-0	0	90	.699	3.26	4.76
2016 Atl	NL	16	2	6	36.1	157	46	22	22	7	1	0	2	5	2	23	1	1	1	.500	0-1	0	91	.877	5.40	5.45
2017 Sea	AL	1	1	0	3.2	14	3	1	1	0	0	0	0	0	0	0	0	0	0	-	0-0	0	90	.500	1.32	2.45
2018 TB	AL	2	0	0	5.1	25	5	5	3	0	0	1	1	2	0	1	0	0	1	.000	0-0	0	89	.701	3.36	5.06
2019 Bos	AL	18	3	8	40.2	181	48	25	23	5	1	0	3	8	0	29	2	2	4	.333	0-0	0	89	.789	4.63	5.09
5 ML YEARS		42	11	14	114.1	486	127	68	64	15	2	1	8	21	2	72	3	3	9	.250	0-1	0	90	.785	4.33	5.04

Allen Webster

Pitches: R Bats: R Pos: RP-12　　　Ht: 6'2" Wt: 200 Born: 2/10/1990 Age: 30

Year Team	Lg	G	GS	GF	IP	BFP	H	R	ER	HR	SH	SF	HB	TBB	IBB	SO	WP	W	L	Pct	Sv-Op	Hld	Vel	OPS	ERC	ERA
2019 Tenn	AA	6	0	0	4.1	24	10	8	8	0	0	0	0	1	0	3	1	0	1	.000	0--	-	-	1.111	10.61	16.62
2013 Bos	AL	8	7	1	30.1	145	37	30	29	7	0	5	2	18	0	23	1	1	2	.333	0-0	0	94	.926	7.56	8.60
2014 Bos	AL	11	11	0	59.0	259	58	35	33	3	0	4	7	28	0	36	2	5	3	.625	0-0	0	92	.736	4.46	5.03
2015 Ari	NL	9	5	1	31.0	142	32	28	20	10	1	1	2	20	1	17	1	1	1	.500	0-0	0	92	.968	7.38	5.81
2018 ChC	NL	3	0	1	3.0	15	2	2	2	1	0	0	2	1	0	3	0	1	0	1.000	0-0	0	95	.750	5.80	6.00
2019 ChC	NL	12	0	6	11.0	52	14	7	6	2	0	0	1	5	2	9	3	0	0	-	1-1	0	94	.885	6.60	4.91
5 ML YEARS		43	23	9	134.1	613	143	102	90	23	1	10	14	72	3	88	7	8	6	.571	1-1	0	93	.847	6.01	6.03

J.B. Wendelken

Pitches: R Bats: R Pos: RP-27   **Ht: 6'1" Wt: 240 Born: 3/24/1993 Age: 27**

Year	Team	Lg	G	GS	GF	IP	BFP	H	R	ER	HR	SH	SF	HB	TBB	IBB	SO	WP	W	L	Pct	Sv-Op	Hld	Vel	OPS	ERC	ERA
2019	LsVgs	AAA	30	1	19	38.2	179	47	26	24	8	0	0	2	19	1	43	3	6	3	.667	3--	-		.893	6.80	5.59
2016	Oak	AL	8	0	3	12.2	64	18	15	14	3	0	0	0	9	0	12	2	0	0	-	0-0	0	93	.931	9.17	9.95
2018	Oak	AL	13	0	3	16.2	62	8	1	1	1	0	0	0	5	0	14	1	0	0	-	0-0	1	95	.438	1.20	0.54
2019	Oak	AL	27	0	4	32.2	131	21	14	13	2	1	1	2	9	2	34	2	3	1	.750	0-1	1	95	.543	1.69	3.58
	3 ML YEARS		48	0	10	62.0	257	47	30	28	6	1	1	2	23	2	60	5	3	1	.750	0-1	2	94	.612	2.69	4.06

Joey Wendle

Bats: L Throws: R Pos: 2B-48;3B-27;SS-10;PH-2;RF-1;PR-1   **Ht: 6'1" Wt: 200 Born: 4/26/1990 Age: 30**

Year	Team	Lg	G	AB	H	2B	3B	HR	(Hm	Rd)	TB	R	RBI	RC	TBB	IBB	SO	HBP	SH	SF	SB	CS	GDP	Avg	OBP	Slg	OPS
2016	Oak	AL	28	96	25	1	0	1	(0	1)	29	11	11	10	6	0	16	0	0	2	2	0	3	.260	.298	.302	.600
2017	Oak	AL	8	13	4	1	0	1	(0	1)	8	3	5	4	1	1	3	0	0	0	0	0	0	.308	.357	.615	.973
2018	TB	AL	139	487	146	33	6	7	(2	5)	212	62	61	70	37	4	96	9	2	10	16	4	11	.300	.354	.435	.789
2019	TB	AL	75	238	55	13	2	3	(2	1)	81	32	19	23	14	0	47	8	0	3	8	3	4	.231	.293	.340	.633
	4 ML YEARS		250	834	230	48	8	12	(4	8)	330	108	96	107	58	5	162	17	2	15	26	7	18	.276	.330	.396	.726

Zack Wheeler

Pitches: R Bats: L Pos: SP-31   **Ht: 6'4" Wt: 195 Born: 5/30/1990 Age: 30**

Year	Team	Lg	G	GS	GF	IP	BFP	H	R	ER	HR	SH	SF	HB	TBB	IBB	SO	WP	W	L	Pct	Sv-Op	Hld	Vel	OPS	ERC	ERA
2013	NYM	NL	17	17	0	100.0	431	90	42	38	10	3	7	4	46	2	84	6	7	5	.583	0-0	0	94	.696	3.88	3.42
2014	NYM	NL	32	32	0	185.1	790	167	84	73	14	5	3	11	79	3	187	9	11	11	.500	0-0	0	95	.678	3.68	3.54
2017	NYM	NL	17	17	0	86.1	386	97	53	50	15	0	1	3	40	1	81	1	3	7	.300	0-0	0	95	.828	5.81	5.21
2018	NYM	NL	29	29	0	182.1	744	150	69	67	14	8	4	9	55	0	179	2	12	7	.632	0-0	0	96	.611	2.81	3.31
2019	NYM	NL	31	31	0	195.1	828	196	93	86	22	8	7	2	50	4	195	5	11	8	.579	0-0	0	97	.694	3.57	3.96
	5 ML YEARS		126	126	0	749.1	3183	700	341	314	75	24	22	29	270	10	726	23	44	38	.537	0-0	0	95	.687	3.69	3.77

Tyler White

Bats: R Throws: R Pos: 1B-56;DH-19;PH-12   **Ht: 5'11" Wt: 225 Born: 10/29/1990 Age: 29**

Year	Team	Lg	G	AB	H	2B	3B	HR	(Hm	Rd)	TB	R	RBI	RC	TBB	IBB	SO	HBP	SH	SF	SB	CS	GDP	Avg	OBP	Slg	OPS
2016	Hou	AL	86	249	54	16	0	8	(2	6)	94	24	28	25	23	1	65	2	0	2	1	0	6	.217	.286	.378	.664
2017	Hou	AL	22	61	17	6	0	3	(3	0)	32	7	10	10	4	0	16	1	0	1	0	1	0	.279	.328	.525	.853
2018	Hou	AL	66	210	58	12	3	12	(9	3)	112	27	42	44	24	0	49	2	0	1	0	1	1	.276	.354	.533	.888
2019	2 Tms		83	240	50	14	0	3	(2	1)	73	18	23	22	36	0	78	0	0	3	0	0	7	.208	.308	.304	.612
19	Hou	AL	71	218	49	14	0	3	(2	1)	72	16	21	22	32	0	74	0	0	3	0	0	7	.225	.320	.330	.650
19	LAD	NL	12	22	1	0	0	0	(0	0)	1	2	2	0	4	0	4	0	0	0	0	0	0	.045	.192	.045	.238
	Postseason		8	13	3	1	0	0	(0	0)	4	0	0	1	3	2	7	2	0	0	0	0	0	.231	.444	.308	.752
	4 ML YEARS		257	760	179	48	3	26	(16	10)	311	76	103	101	87	1	208	5	0	7	1	2	14	.236	.315	.409	.725

Forrest Whitley

Pitches: R Bats: R Pos: P   **Ht: 6'7" Wt: 195 Born: 9/15/1997 Age: 22**

Year	Team	Lg	G	GS	GF	IP	BFP	H	R	ER	HR	SH	SF	HB	TBB	IBB	SO	WP	W	L	Pct	Sv-Op	Hld	Vel	OPS	ERC	ERA
2016	2 Tms	Low	8	6	0	18.2	81	19	12	10	0	0	0	0	6	0	26	2	1	2	.333	0--	-	-	.629	3.10	4.82
2017	2 Tms	Low	19	16	1	77.2	324	70	27	26	4	1	1	4	30	0	117	7	5	4	.556	0--	-	-	.662	3.42	3.01
2018	CpChr	AAA	8	8	0	26.1	108	15	11	11	2	0	1	2	11	0	34	0	2	2	.000	0--	-	-	.504	2.00	3.76
2019	RdRck	AAA	8	5	0	24.1	119	35	33	33	9	1	1	0	15	0	29	1	0	3	.000	0--	-	-	1.149	10.24	12.21
2019	CpChr	AA	6	6	0	22.2	103	18	14	14	2	0	0	3	19	0	36	7	2	2	.500	0--	-	-	.722	5.19	5.56

Rowan Wick

Pitches: R Bats: L Pos: RP-31   **Ht: 6'3" Wt: 235 Born: 11/9/1992 Age: 27**

Year	Team	Lg	G	GS	GF	IP	BFP	H	R	ER	HR	SH	SF	HB	TBB	IBB	SO	WP	W	L	Pct	Sv-Op	Hld	Vel	OPS	ERC	ERA
2019	Iowa	AAA	27	0	16	35.0	138	25	8	7	3	0	0	1	9	2	44	2	1	0	1.000	6--	-	-	.590	2.03	1.80
2018	SD	NL	10	0	3	8.1	38	13	6	6	1	0	0	0	1	0	7	0	0	1	.000	0-0	0	95	.936	6.41	6.48
2019	ChC	NL	31	0	7	33.1	140	22	13	9	0	1	0	3	16	1	35	0	2	0	1.000	2-2	5	96	.528	2.18	2.43
	2 ML YEARS		41	0	10	41.2	178	35	19	15	1	1	0	3	17	1	42	0	2	1	.667	2-2	5	96	.623	2.92	3.24

Brad Wieck

Pitches: L Bats: L Pos: RP-44   **Ht: 6'9" Wt: 255 Born: 10/24/1991 Age: 28**

Year	Team	Lg	G	GS	GF	IP	BFP	H	R	ER	HR	SH	SF	HB	TBB	IBB	SO	WP	W	L	Pct	Sv-Op	Hld	Vel	OPS	ERC	ERA
2019	ElPaso	AAA	14	0	5	17.2	74	16	12	12	5	0	0	0	6	0	34	1	1	1	.500	2--	-	-	.827	4.51	6.11
2019	Iowa	AAA	6	0	1	5.2	23	4	1	1	0	0	0	0	3	0	11	1	1	0	1.000	0--	-	-	.504	2.41	1.59
2018	SD	NL	5	0	0	7.0	24	3	1	1	1	0	0	0	0	0	10	0	0	0	-	0-0	0	92	.417	0.70	1.29
2019	2 Tms	NL	44	0	5	34.2	148	28	23	22	8	0	1	3	13	0	49	1	2	2	.500	0-2	9	94	.748	4.05	5.71
19	SD	NL	30	0	3	24.2	110	26	19	18	7	0	1	1	9	0	31	0	1	1	.000	0-2	8	94	.863	5.62	6.57
19	ChC	NL	14	0	2	10.0	38	2	4	4	1	0	0	2	4	0	18	1	1	1	.667	0-0	1	94	.398	1.14	3.60
	2 ML YEARS		49	0	5	41.2	172	31	24	23	9	0	1	3	13	0	59	1	2	2	.500	0-2	9	94	.699	3.31	4.97

Matt Wieters

Bats: B **Throws:** R **Pos:** C-54;PH-20 — WEE-ters — **Ht:** 6'5" **Wt:** 235 **Born:** 5/21/1986 **Age:** 34

Year	Team	Lg	G	AB	H	2B	3B	HR	(Hm	Rd)	TB	R	RBI	RC	TBB	IBB	SO	HBP	SH	SF	SB	CS	GDP	Avg	OBP	Slg	OPS
2009	Bal	AL	96	354	102	15	1	9	(5	4)	146	35	43	43	28	2	86	1	0	2	0	0	11	.288	.340	.412	.753
2010	Bal	AL	130	446	111	22	1	11	(3	8)	168	37	55	47	47	7	94	2	0	7	0	1	13	.249	.319	.377	.695
2011	Bal	AL	139	500	131	28	0	22	(13	9)	225	72	68	76	48	3	84	2	0	1	1	0	16	.262	.328	.450	.778
2012	Bal	AL	144	526	131	27	1	23	(11	12)	229	67	83	73	60	4	112	4	0	3	3	0	17	.249	.329	.435	.764
2013	Bal	AL	148	523	123	29	0	22	(13	9)	218	59	79	65	43	5	104	0	1	12	2	0	7	.235	.287	.417	.704
2014	Bal	AL	26	104	32	5	0	5	(2	3)	52	13	18	17	6	0	19	0	0	2	0	1	1	.308	.339	.500	.839
2015	Bal	AL	75	258	69	14	1	8	(3	5)	109	24	25	33	21	0	67	0	0	3	0	0	4	.267	.319	.422	.742
2016	Bal	AL	124	423	103	17	1	17	(10	7)	173	48	66	56	32	1	85	5	1	3	1	0	10	.243	.302	.409	.711
2017	Was	NL	123	422	95	20	0	10	(5	5)	145	43	52	41	38	4	94	1	0	4	1	0	14	.225	.288	.344	.632
2018	Was	NL	76	235	56	8	0	8	(7	1)	88	24	30	26	30	3	45	3	1	2	0	1	5	.238	.330	.374	.704
2019	StL	NL	67	168	36	4	0	11	(5	6)	73	15	27	16	12	0	47	1	0	2	1	1	3	.214	.268	.435	.702
	Postseason		12	42	5	1	0	0	(0	0)	6	4	0	1	4	0	10	2	0	0	0	0	0	.119	.229	.143	.372
	11 ML YEARS		1148	3959	989	189	5	146	(77	69)	1626	437	546	493	365	29	837	19	3	41	9	4	101	.250	.313	.411	.724

Aaron Wilkerson

Pitches: R **Bats:** R **Pos:** RP-8 — **Ht:** 6'3" **Wt:** 190 **Born:** 5/24/1989 **Age:** 31

Year	Team	Lg	G	GS	GF	IP	BFP	H	R	ER	HR	SH	SF	HB	TBB	IBB	SO	WP	W	L	Pct	Sv-Op	Hld	Vel	OPS	ERC	ERA
2019	SnAnt	AAA	17	17	0	76.1	314	62	30	29	10	1	1	2	29	0	81	3	8	2	.800	0--	-	-	.674	3.32	3.42
2017	Mil	NL	3	2	1	10.1	37	6	4	4	1	0	0	0	1	0	7	0	1	0	1.000	0-0	0	90	.550	1.20	3.48
2018	Mil	NL	3	1	2	9.0	43	12	10	10	4	0	0	1	3	0	10	0	0	1	.000	0-0	0	89	1.013	8.90	10.00
2019	Mil	NL	8	0	5	16.0	80	25	13	13	4	0	1	0	9	1	11	0	0	0	-	0-0	0	90	1.011	9.52	7.31
	3 ML YEARS		14	3	8	35.1	160	43	27	27	9	0	1	1	13	1	28	0	1	1	.500	0-0	0	90	.901	6.45	6.88

Stevie Wilkerson

Bats: B **Throws:** R **Pos:** CF-72;LF-29;2B-13;PH-11;RF-10;PR-5;DH-1 — **Ht:** 6'1" **Wt:** 195 **Born:** 1/11/1992 **Age:** 28

Year	Team	Lg	G	AB	H	2B	3B	HR	(Hm	Rd)	TB	R	RBI	RC	TBB	IBB	SO	HBP	SH	SF	SB	CS	GDP	Avg	OBP	Slg	OPS
2019	Norfolk	AAA	16	62	20	0	1	2	(-	-)	28	13	10	10	3	0	9	0	2	0	3	0	2	.323	.354	.452	.805
2018	Bal	AL	16	46	8	3	0	0	(0	0)	11	2	3	3	3	0	16	0	0	0	1	0	0	.174	.224	.239	.464
2019	Bal	AL	119	329	74	18	2	10	(6	4)	126	41	35	33	22	0	108	7	1	2	3	3	5	.225	.286	.383	.669
	2 ML YEARS		135	375	82	21	2	10	(6	4)	137	43	38	36	25	0	124	7	1	2	4	3	5	.219	.279	.365	.644

Austen Williams

Pitches: R **Bats:** R **Pos:** RP-2 — **Ht:** 6'3" **Wt:** 220 **Born:** 12/19/1992 **Age:** 27

Year	Team	Lg	G	GS	GF	IP	BFP	H	R	ER	HR	SH	SF	HB	TBB	IBB	SO	WP	W	L	Pct	Sv-Op	Hld	Vel	OPS	ERC	ERA
2019	Hrsbrg	AA	5	0	0	5.1	29	8	6	6	0	1	0	1	3	0	7	2	0	1	.000	0--	-	-	.923	7.24	10.13
2018	Was	NL	10	0	4	9.2	44	10	6	6	5	1	0	0	6	2	8	1	0	1	.000	0-0	0	94	1.075	8.12	5.59
2019	Was	NL	2	0	0	0.1	7	5	6	6	2	0	0	0	1	0	1	0	0	0	-	0-0	0	92	3.024	254.7	162.0
	2 ML YEARS		12	0	4	10.0	51	15	12	12	7	1	0	0	7	2	9	1	0	1	.000	0-0	0	94	1.347	13.67	10.80

Devin Williams

Pitches: R **Bats:** R **Pos:** RP-13 — **Ht:** 6'3" **Wt:** 165 **Born:** 9/21/1994 **Age:** 25

Year	Team	Lg	G	GS	GF	IP	BFP	H	R	ER	HR	SH	SF	HB	TBB	IBB	SO	WP	W	L	Pct	Sv-Op	Hld	Vel	OPS	ERC	ERA
2019	Biloxi	AA	31	0	13	53.1	220	34	16	14	3	1	1	1	29	0	76	7	7	2	.778	4--	-	-	.558	2.49	2.36
2019	Mil	NL	13	0	1	13.2	67	18	9	6	2	1	0	2	6	0	14	1	0	0	-	0-0	2	96	.894	6.97	3.95

Mason Williams

Bats: L **Throws:** R **Pos:** CF-7;LF-2;PR-2;RF-1;DH-1;PH-1 — **Ht:** 6'1" **Wt:** 195 **Born:** 8/21/1991 **Age:** 28

Year	Team	Lg	G	AB	H	2B	3B	HR	(Hm	Rd)	TB	R	RBI	RC	TBB	IBB	SO	HBP	SH	SF	SB	CS	GDP	Avg	OBP	Slg	OPS
2019	Norfolk	AAA	121	442	136	15	3	18	(-	-)	211	62	67	77	46	1	86	0	3	3	4	7	7	.308	.371	.477	.848
2015	NYY	AL	8	21	6	3	0	1	(0	1)	12	3	3	4	1	0	3	0	0	0	0	0	0	.286	.318	.571	.890
2016	NYY	AL	12	27	8	1	0	0	(0	0)	9	4	2	3	1	0	12	0	1	0	0	0	0	.296	.321	.333	.655
2017	NYY	AL	5	16	4	0	0	0	(0	0)	4	3	1	1	1	0	2	0	0	0	2	0	0	.250	.294	.250	.544
2018	Cin	NL	51	123	36	5	1	2	(2	0)	49	10	6	11	7	1	29	0	2	0	1	2	5	.293	.331	.398	.729
2019	Bal	AL	11	30	8	1	0	0	(0	0)	9	4	2	2	3	0	6	0	0	1	1	0	0	.267	.324	.300	.624
	5 ML YEARS		87	217	62	10	1	3	(2	1)	83	24	14	21	13	1	52	0	3	1	4	2	5	.286	.325	.382	.707

Nick Williams

Bats: L **Throws:** L **Pos:** PH-41;LF-23;RF-5;PR-1 — **Ht:** 6'3" **Wt:** 195 **Born:** 9/8/1993 **Age:** 26

Year	Team	Lg	G	AB	H	2B	3B	HR	(Hm	Rd)	TB	R	RBI	RC	TBB	IBB	SO	HBP	SH	SF	SB	CS	GDP	Avg	OBP	Slg	OPS
2019	LV	AAA	48	190	60	15	2	10	(-	-)	109	33	25	40	14	0	52	6	0	0	1	0	1	.316	.381	.574	.955
2017	Phi	NL	83	313	90	14	4	12	(6	6)	148	45	55	47	20	0	97	6	0	4	1	2	8	.288	.338	.473	.811
2018	Phi	NL	140	407	104	12	3	17	(9	8)	173	53	50	50	32	2	111	9	0	0	3	2	4	.256	.324	.425	.749
2019	Phi	NL	67	106	16	4	0	2	(1	1)	26	9	5	1	4	0	43	2	0	0	0	0	1	.151	.196	.245	.442
	3 ML YEARS		290	826	210	30	7	31	(16	15)	347	107	110	98	56	2	251	17	0	4	4	4	13	.254	.313	.420	.733

Taylor Williams

Pitches: R Bats: B Pos: RP-10   Ht: 5'11" Wt: 195 Born: 7/21/1991 Age: 28

Year	Team	Lg	G	GS	GF	IP	BFP	H	R	ER	HR	SH	SF	HB	TBB	IBB	SO	WP	W	L	Pct	Sv-Op	Hld	Vel	OPS	ERC	ERA
2019	SnAnt	AAA	46	0	18	54.0	225	40	24	17	8	3	1	4	21	2	57	2	3	3	.500	6- -	-		.691	3.15	2.83
2017	Mil	NL	5	0	5	4.2	20	4	1	1	0	0	0	0	2	0	4	0	0	0		0-0	-	96	.633	2.67	1.93
2018	Mil	NL	56	0	10	53.0	236	53	28	25	6	4	2	1	25	4	57	4	1	3	.250	0-1	4	96	.747	4.34	4.25
2019	Mil	NL	10	0	4	14.2	73	22	17	16	1	0	0	2	7	2	15	1	1	1	.500	0-1	0	95	.878	7.50	9.82
3 ML YEARS			71	0	19	72.1	329	79	46	42	7	4	2	3	34	6	76	5	2	4	.333	0-2	4	96	.770	4.82	5.23

Trevor Williams

Pitches: R Bats: R Pos: SP-26   Ht: 6'3" Wt: 230 Born: 4/25/1992 Age: 28

Year	Team	Lg	G	GS	GF	IP	BFP	H	R	ER	HR	SH	SF	HB	TBB	IBB	SO	WP	W	L	Pct	Sv-Op	Hld	Vel	OPS	ERC	ERA
2016	Pit	NL	7	1	1	12.2	61	19	13	11	4	0	0	5	0	11	0	1	1	.500	0-1	0	93	1.054	8.89	7.82
2017	Pit	NL	31	25	1	150.1	642	145	73	68	14	8	4	9	52	4	117	2	7	9	.438	0-0	0	92	.715	3.82	4.07
2018	Pit	NL	31	31	0	170.2	701	146	64	59	15	6	4	4	55	3	126	4	14	10	.583	0-0	0	90	.659	3.00	3.11
2019	Pit	NL	26	26	0	145.2	636	162	93	87	27	6	8	7	44	3	113	2	7	9	.438	0-0	0	91	.851	5.11	5.38
4 ML YEARS			95	83	2	479.1	2040	472	243	225	60	20	16	20	156	10	367	8	29	29	.500	0-1	0	91	.748	4.01	4.22

Mac Williamson

Bats: R Throws: R Pos: LF-36;PH-3;RF-2;DH-1;PR-1   Ht: 6'4" Wt: 237 Born: 7/15/1990 Age: 29

Year	Team	Lg	G	AB	H	2B	3B	HR	(Hm	Rd)	TB	R	RBI	RC	TBB	IBB	SO	HBP	SH	SF	SB	CS	GDP	Avg	OBP	Slg	OPS
2019	Scrmto	AAA	23	82	31	4	0	9	(-	-)	62	23	22	26	13	1	25	1	0	2	5	1	1	.378	.459	.756	1.215
2015	SF	NL	10	32	7	0	1	0	(0	0)	9	2	1	1	0	0	8	1	0	1	0	0	1	.219	.235	.281	.517
2016	SF	NL	54	112	25	3	0	6	(1	5)	46	14	15	11	13	0	35	2	0	0	0	1	4	.223	.315	.411	.726
2017	SF	NL	28	68	16	2	0	3	(0	3)	27	8	6	5	5	1	25	0	0	0	1	1	2	.235	.288	.397	.685
2018	SF	NL	28	94	20	4	0	4	(2	2)	36	14	11	9	11	0	27	0	0	0	1	1	1	.213	.295	.383	.678
2019	2 Tms		40	128	20	1	0	4	(3	1)	33	13	17	11	14	0	44	2	0	0	2	1	3	.156	.250	.258	.508
19	SF	NL	15	51	6	1	0	1	(0	1)	10	3	7	4	5	0	18	1	0	0	2	0	2	.118	.211	.196	.407
19	Sea	AL	25	77	14	0	0	3	(3	0)	23	10	10	7	9	0	26	1	0	0	0	1	1	.182	.276	.299	.575
5 ML YEARS			160	434	88	10	1	17	(6	11)	151	51	50	37	43	1	139	5	0	1	4	4	11	.203	.282	.348	.629

Alex Wilson

Pitches: R Bats: R Pos: RP-13   Ht: 6'0" Wt: 220 Born: 11/3/1986 Age: 33

Year	Team	Lg	G	GS	GF	IP	BFP	H	R	ER	HR	SH	SF	HB	TBB	IBB	SO	WP	W	L	Pct	Sv-Op	Hld	Vel	OPS	ERC	ERA
2019	SnAnt	AAA	29	0	8	38.0	152	33	11	9	8	4	1	0	7	1	31	1	4	1	.800	2- -	-		.713	3.16	2.13
2019	Iowa	AAA	10	0	5	12.1	49	12	7	7	2	0	0	1	2	0	11	0	1	2	.333	1- -	-		.763	3.90	5.11
2013	Bos	AL	26	0	9	27.2	127	34	16	15	0	0	1	1	14	1	22	1	1	1	.500	0-0	1	92	.818	5.19	4.88
2014	Bos	AL	18	0	3	28.1	109	20	8	6	3	0	1	2	5	0	19	1	1	0	1.000	0-1	0	93	.624	2.08	1.91
2015	Det	AL	59	1	16	70.0	273	61	19	17	5	2	2	2	11	1	38	2	3	3	.500	2-4	7	92	.609	2.47	2.19
2016	Det	AL	62	0	6	73.0	297	68	26	24	5	0	5	1	21	5	49	2	4	0	1.000	0-4	14	92	.692	3.09	2.96
2017	Det	AL	66	0	11	60.0	260	67	34	30	7	0	2	3	15	5	42	4	2	5	.286	2-7	17	93	.764	4.31	4.50
2018	Det	AL	59	0	13	61.2	245	50	24	23	8	2	2	2	15	2	43	2	2	4	.333	0-4	14	92	.646	2.78	3.36
2019	Mil	NL	13	0	4	11.1	57	15	12	12	3	0	0	0	9	2	13	2	1	1	.500	1-1	1	92	.984	8.80	9.53
7 ML YEARS			303	1	62	332.0	1368	315	139	127	31	4	13	11	90	16	226	14	14	14	.500	5-21	54	92	.699	3.36	3.44

Bobby Wilson

Bats: R Throws: R Pos: C-15   Ht: 6'0" Wt: 230 Born: 4/8/1983 Age: 37

Year	Team	Lg	G	AB	H	2B	3B	HR	(Hm	Rd)	TB	R	RBI	RC	TBB	IBB	SO	HBP	SH	SF	SB	CS	GDP	Avg	OBP	Slg	OPS
2019	Toledo	AAA	28	90	22	2	0	5	(-	-)	39	12	10	13	11	0	25	0	0	0	0	0	1	.244	.327	.433	.760
2008	LAA	AL	7	6	1	0	0	0	(0	0)	1	0	1	0	1	0	3	0	0	0	0	0	0	.167	.286	.167	.452
2009	LAA	AL	12	5	1	1	0	0	(0	0)	2	0	0	0	0	0	1	0	1	0	0	0	1	.200	.200	.400	.600
2010	LAA	AL	40	96	22	6	0	4	(3	1)	40	12	15	12	8	0	23	0	2	0	0	0	3	.229	.288	.417	.705
2011	LAA	AL	57	111	21	8	0	1	(0	1)	32	5	8	7	10	1	16	0	4	2	0	2	2	.189	.252	.288	.540
2012	LAA	AL	75	171	36	5	0	3	(2	1)	50	19	13	13	15	0	33	1	13	1	0	0	7	.211	.277	.292	.569
2014	Ari	NL	2	4	1	0	0	0	(0	0)	1	0	0	0	0	0	0	0	0	0	0	0	0	.250	.250	.250	.500
2015	2 Tms	AL	56	132	25	5	0	1	(1	0)	33	8	14	12	11	0	39	1	2	1	0	1	1	.189	.255	.250	.505
2016	3 Tms	AL	75	228	54	6	0	7	(4	3)	81	25	33	25	11	0	64	1	7	4	0	0	6	.237	.270	.355	.626
2018	Min	AL	47	135	24	8	0	2	(2	0)	38	12	16	10	12	0	37	0	2	2	0	0	6	.178	.242	.281	.523
2019	Det	AL	15	44	4	1	0	0	(0	0)	5	2	2	2	2	0	11	0	1	0	0	0	1	.091	.130	.114	.244
15	TB	AL	25	55	8	0	0	0	(0	0)	8	3	4	2	4	0	20	0	0	0	0	0	0	.145	.203	.145	.349
15	Tex	AL	31	77	17	5	0	1	(1	0)	25	5	10	10	7	0	19	1	2	1	0	1	1	.221	.291	.325	.615
16	Det	AL	5	13	2	0	0	0	(0	0)	2	0	2	1	1	0	3	0	0	0	0	0	1	.154	.200	.154	.354
16	Tex	AL	42	128	32	4	0	3	(2	1)	45	11	22	18	5	0	33	1	4	3	0	0	2	.250	.277	.352	.629
16	TB	AL	28	87	20	2	0	4	(2	2)	34	14	9	6	5	0	28	0	3	0	0	0	3	.230	.272	.391	.663
10 ML YEARS			386	932	189	40	0	18	(12	6)	283	83	102	79	70	1	227	3	32	10	0	3	27	.203	.258	.304	.562

Bryse Wilson

Pitches: R **Bats:** R **Pos:** SP-4; RP-2   **Ht:** 6'1" **Wt:** 225 **Born:** 12/20/1997 **Age:** 22

			HOW MUCH PITCHED						WHAT HE GAVE UP											THE RESULTS						
Year	Team	Lg	G	GS	GF	IP	BFP	H	R	ER	HR	SH	SF	HB	TBB	IBB	SO	WP	W	L	Pct	Sv-Op	Hld	Vel	OPS	ERC	ERA
2016	Braves	R	9	6	0	26.2	101	16	4	2	0	0	0	0	8	0	29	0	1	1	.500	0--	-	-	.431	1.34	0.68
2017	Rome	A	26	26	0	137.0	546	105	45	38	8	3	3	6	37	0	139	6	10	7	.588	0--	-	-	.584	2.31	2.50
2018	Florida	A+	5	5	0	26.2	104	16	4	1	0	0	0	1	7	0	26	0	2	0	1.000	0--	-	-	.439	1.31	0.34
2018	Missi	AA	15	15	0	77.0	335	77	40	34	3	4	3	4	26	2	89	0	3	5	.375	0--	-	-	.662	3.51	3.97
2018	Gwnntt	AAA	5	3	0	22.0	87	20	13	13	6	0	0	0	3	0	28	0	3	0	1.000	0--	-	-	.752	3.62	5.32
2019	Gwnntt	AAA	21	21	0	121.0	504	120	59	46	12	1	5	3	26	1	118	2	10	7	.588	0--	-	-	.690	3.38	3.42
2018	Atl	NL	3	1	2	7.0	33	8	5	5	0	0	1	0	6	2	6	0	1	0	1.000	0-0	0	95	.886	5.54	6.43
2019	Atl	NL	6	4	1	20.0	93	26	18	16	5	2	0	0	10	1	16	1	1	1	.500	0-0	0	95	1.050	7.50	7.20
	2 ML YEARS		9	5	3	27.0	126	34	23	21	5	2	1	0	16	3	22	1	2	1	.667	0-0	0	95	1.011	7.04	7.00

Justin Wilson

Pitches: L **Bats:** L **Pos:** RP-45   **Ht:** 6'2" **Wt:** 205 **Born:** 8/18/1987 **Age:** 32

			HOW MUCH PITCHED						WHAT HE GAVE UP											THE RESULTS						
Year	Team	Lg	G	GS	GF	IP	BFP	H	R	ER	HR	SH	SF	HB	TBB	IBB	SO	WP	W	L	Pct	Sv-Op	Hld	Vel	OPS	ERC	ERA
2012	Pit	NL	8	0	3	4.2	26	10	1	1	0	1	0	0	3	0	7	1	0	0	-	0-0	0	94	1.111	11.83	1.93
2013	Pit	NL	58	0	8	73.2	295	50	17	17	4	3	1	3	28	1	59	5	6	1	.857	0-3	14	95	.543	2.20	2.08
2014	Pit	NL	70	0	15	60.0	256	49	30	28	4	0	0	3	30	5	61	4	3	4	.429	0-3	16	95	.643	3.29	4.20
2015	NYY	AL	74	0	3	61.0	244	49	21	21	3	2	0	2	20	0	66	4	5	0	1.000	0-2	29	95	.602	2.63	3.10
2016	Det	AL	66	0	10	58.2	251	61	29	27	6	1	0	1	17	2	65	4	4	5	.444	1-6	25	95	.708	3.87	4.14
2017	2 Tms		65	0	30	58.0	248	40	23	22	5	0	1	1	35	1	80	4	4	4	.500	13-16	9	96	.633	3.08	3.41
2018	ChC	NL	71	0	12	54.2	236	45	22	21	5	0	1	0	33	1	69	4	4	5	.444	0-3	16	95	.682	3.81	3.46
2019	NYM	NL	45	0	9	39.0	166	33	12	11	4	0	0	2	19	1	44	4	4	2	.667	4-5	9	95	.670	3.78	2.54
17	Det	AL	42	0	26	40.1	157	22	12	12	5	0	1	0	16	0	55	3	3	4	.429	13-15	8	96	.563	1.91	2.68
17	ChC	NL	23	0	4	17.2	91	18	11	10	0	0	0	1	19	1	25	1	1	0	1.000	0-1	1	96	.756	5.98	5.09
	Postseason		6	0	1	5.1	21	3	1	1	0	0	0	0	3	0	4	1	0	0	-	0-0	0	96	.452	1.87	1.69
	8 ML YEARS		457	0	90	409.2	1722	337	155	148	31	7	3	12	185	11	451	30	30	21	.588	18-38	118	95	.643	3.23	3.25

Trey Wingenter

Pitches: R **Bats:** R **Pos:** RP-50; SP-1   **Ht:** 6'7" **Wt:** 200 **Born:** 4/15/1994 **Age:** 26

			HOW MUCH PITCHED						WHAT HE GAVE UP											THE RESULTS						
Year	Team	Lg	G	GS	GF	IP	BFP	H	R	ER	HR	SH	SF	HB	TBB	IBB	SO	WP	W	L	Pct	Sv-Op	Hld	Vel	OPS	ERC	ERA
2018	SD	NL	22	0	5	19.0	81	13	8	8	3	0	1	1	11	0	27	1	0	0	-	0-2	5	97	.647	3.62	3.79
2019	SD	NL	51	1	8	51.0	218	34	32	32	5	1	2	5	28	0	72	4	1	3	.250	1-4	16	96	.633	3.16	5.65
	2 ML YEARS		73	1	13	70.0	299	47	40	40	8	1	3	6	39	0	99	5	1	3	.250	1-6	21	96	.637	3.29	5.14

Jesse Winker

Bats: L **Throws:** L **Pos:** LF-72;PH-23;CF-21;RF-18;DH-1   **Ht:** 6'3" **Wt:** 215 **Born:** 8/17/1993 **Age:** 26

			BATTING																		RUNNING			AVERAGES			
Year	Team	Lg	G	AB	H	2B	3B	HR	(Hm	Rd)	TB	R	RBI	RC	TBB	IBB	SO	HBP	SH	SF	SB	CS	GDP	Avg	OBP	Slg	OPS
2017	Cin	NL	47	121	36	7	0	7	(2	5)	64	21	15	18	15	0	24	0	1	0	1	1	2	.298	.375	.529	.904
2018	Cin	NL	89	281	84	16	0	7	(6	1)	121	38	43	54	49	4	46	2	1	1	0	0	6	.299	.405	.431	.836
2019	Cin	NL	113	338	91	17	2	16	(10	6)	160	51	38	48	38	2	60	8	0	0	0	2	10	.269	.357	.473	.830
	3 ML YEARS		249	740	211	40	2	30	(18	12)	345	110	96	120	102	6	130	10	2	1	1	3	18	.285	.379	.466	.845

Dan Winkler

Pitches: R **Bats:** R **Pos:** RP-27   **Ht:** 6'3" **Wt:** 205 **Born:** 2/2/1990 **Age:** 30

			HOW MUCH PITCHED						WHAT HE GAVE UP											THE RESULTS						
Year	Team	Lg	G	GS	GF	IP	BFP	H	R	ER	HR	SH	SF	HB	TBB	IBB	SO	WP	W	L	Pct	Sv-Op	Hld	Vel	OPS	ERC	ERA
2019	Gwnntt	AAA	18	0	11	16.2	85	16	11	9	1	0	2	1	18	0	20	4	0	1	.000	2--	-	-	.724	6.32	4.86
2019	Scrmto	AAA	12	0	6	14.0	53	6	1	1	1	0	0	2	5	0	9	2	0	1	.000	0--	-	-	.441	1.55	0.64
2015	Atl	NL	2	0	1	1.2	8	2	2	2	2	0	0	0	1	0	2	0	0	0	-	0-0	0	89	1.518	14.99	10.80
2016	Atl	NL	3	0	0	2.1	8	0	0	0	0	0	0	0	1	0	4	0	0	0	-	0-0	0	92	.125	0.20	0.00
2017	Atl	NL	16	0	1	14.1	53	7	4	4	1	1	0	0	6	0	18	0	1	1	.500	0-0	4	94	.511	1.57	2.51
2018	Atl	NL	69	0	11	60.1	255	52	27	23	3	1	1	5	20	1	69	4	4	0	1.000	2-5	23	93	.645	2.99	3.43
2019	Atl	NL	27	0	4	21.2	93	18	14	12	5	0	0	1	11	0	22	1	3	1	.750	0-1	6	93	.804	4.67	4.98
	5 ML YEARS		117	0	16	100.1	417	79	47	41	11	2	1	6	39	1	115	3	8	2	.800	2-6	33	93	.670	3.17	3.68

Patrick Wisdom

Bats: R **Throws:** R **Pos:** 1B-5;3B-4;PH-1   **Ht:** 6'2" **Wt:** 220 **Born:** 8/27/1991 **Age:** 28

			BATTING																		RUNNING			AVERAGES			
Year	Team	Lg	G	AB	H	2B	3B	HR	(Hm	Rd)	TB	R	RBI	RC	TBB	IBB	SO	HBP	SH	SF	SB	CS	GDP	Avg	OBP	Slg	OPS
2019	Nashv	AAA	107	396	95	15	0	31	(-	-)	203	68	74	70	53	3	125	2	1	1	8	2	8	.240	.332	.513	.844
2018	StL	NL	32	50	13	1	0	4	(3	1)	26	11	10	8	6	0	19	2	0	0	2	1	1	.260	.362	.520	.882
2019	Tex	AL	9	26	4	1	0	0	(0	0)	5	1	1	1	1	0	15	0	1	0	0	0	0	.154	.185	.192	.377
	2 ML YEARS		41	76	17	2	0	4	(3	1)	31	12	11	9	7	0	34	2	1	0	2	1	1	.224	.306	.408	.714

Matt Wisler

Pitches: R **Bats:** R **Pos:** RP-36; SP-8   WISS-lurr   **Ht:** 6'3" **Wt:** 215 **Born:** 9/12/1992 **Age:** 27

Year	Team	Lg	G	GS	GF	IP	BFP	H	R	ER	HR	SH	SF	HB	TBB	IBB	SO	WP	W	L	Pct	Sv-Op	Hld	Vel	OPS	ERC	ERA
2015	Atl	NL	20	19	0	109.0	478	119	59	57	16	4	5	4	40	4	72	2	8	8	.500	0-0	0	93	.819	4.91	4.71
2016	Atl	NL	27	26	1	156.2	671	159	90	87	26	2	3	4	49	3	115	5	7	13	.350	1-1	0	93	.756	4.32	5.00
2017	Atl	NL	20	1	8	32.1	153	43	31	30	5	2	3	2	13	0	22	0	0	1	.000	0-0	0	93	.971	6.68	8.35
2018	2 Tms		18	3	3	40.0	166	41	20	19	8	1	3	0	7	0	32	1	1	1	.500	0-1	0	92	.781	3.95	4.28
2019	2 Tms		44	8	7	51.1	224	56	34	32	10	1	1	0	16	0	63	3	3	4	.429	0-3	8	93	.813	4.85	5.61
18	Atl	NL	7	3	1	26.2	112	30	16	16	6	0	1	0	5	0	21	1	1	1	.500	0-0	0	93	.850	4.82	5.40
18	Cin	NL	11	0	2	13.1	54	11	4	3	2	1	2	0	2	0	11	0	0	0	-	0-1	0	92	.633	2.41	2.03
19	SD	NL	21	0	5	29.0	129	34	17	17	5	1	1	0	10	0	34	3	2	2	.500	0-2	4	93	.822	5.35	5.28
19	Sea	AL	23	8	2	22.1	95	22	17	15	5	0	0	0	6	0	29	0	1	2	.333	0-1	4	93	.800	4.21	6.04
5 ML YEARS			129	57	19	389.1	1692	418	234	225	65	10	15	10	125	7	304	11	19	27	.413	1-5	8	93	.803	4.71	5.20

Bobby Witt Jr.

Bats: R **Throws:** R **Pos:** SS   **Ht:** 6'1" **Wt:** 190 **Born:** 6/14/2000 **Age:** 20

							BATTING														RUNNING			AVERAGES			
Year	Team	Lg	G	AB	H	2B	3B	HR	(Hm	Rd)	TB	R	RBI	RC	TBB	IBB	SO	HBP	SH	SF	SB	CS	GDP	Avg	OBP	Slg	OPS
2019	Royals	R	37	164	43	2	5	1	(-	-)	58	30	27	21	13	0	35	1	0	2	9	1	4	.262	.317	.354	.670

Nick Wittgren

Pitches: R **Bats:** R **Pos:** RP-55   **Ht:** 6'2" **Wt:** 216 **Born:** 5/29/1991 **Age:** 29

Year	Team	Lg	G	GS	GF	IP	BFP	H	R	ER	HR	SH	SF	HB	TBB	IBB	SO	WP	W	L	Pct	Sv-Op	Hld	Vel	OPS	ERC	ERA
2016	Mia	NL	48	0	9	51.2	213	50	18	18	6	3	2	1	10	2	42	1	4	3	.571	0-2	6	92	.671	3.21	3.14
2017	Mia	NL	38	0	3	42.1	182	46	22	22	5	0	3	0	13	1	43	2	3	1	.750	0-0	5	92	.800	4.29	4.68
2018	Mia	NL	32	0	6	33.2	148	29	13	11	1	1	1	1	15	3	31	2	2	1	.667	0-0	4	92	.629	2.86	2.94
2019	Cle	AL	55	0	13	57.2	231	47	22	18	10	0	0	0	15	1	60	0	5	1	.833	4-6	12	92	.676	2.99	2.81
4 ML YEARS			173	0	31	185.1	774	172	75	69	22	4	6	2	53	7	176	5	14	6	.700	4-8	27	92	.695	3.32	3.35

Asher Wojciechowski

Pitches: R **Bats:** R **Pos:** SP-16; RP-1   wo-jah-HOW-ski   **Ht:** 6'4" **Wt:** 235 **Born:** 12/21/1988 **Age:** 31

Year	Team	Lg	G	GS	GF	IP	BFP	H	R	ER	HR	SH	SF	HB	TBB	IBB	SO	WP	W	L	Pct	Sv-Op	Hld	Vel	OPS	ERC	ERA
2019	Clmbs	AAA	15	15	0	84.2	347	67	35	34	19	1	2	3	31	0	82	0	8	2	.800	0- -	-		.736	3.78	3.61
2015	Hou	AL	5	3	2	16.1	79	23	13	13	2	0	2	0	7	0	16	1	0	1	.000	0-0	0	91	.965	6.66	7.16
2017	Cin	NL	25	8	2	62.1	279	71	48	45	14	5	2	5	19	1	64	1	4	3	.571	0-0	2	93	.899	5.65	6.50
2019	Bal	AL	17	16	0	82.1	361	80	46	45	17	1	0	9	28	0	80	3	4	8	.333	0-0	0	92	.808	4.81	4.92
3 ML YEARS			47	27	4	161.0	719	174	107	103	33	6	4	14	54	1	160	5	8	12	.400	0-0	2	92	.860	5.32	5.76

Tony Wolters

Bats: L **Throws:** R **Pos:** C-112;PH-9;2B-8;3B-1   WAHL-ters   **Ht:** 5'10" **Wt:** 197 **Born:** 6/9/1992 **Age:** 28

Year	Team	Lg	G	AB	H	2B	3B	HR	(Hm	Rd)	TB	R	RBI	RC	TBB	IBB	SO	HBP	SH	SF	SB	CS	GDP	Avg	OBP	Slg	OPS
2016	Col	NL	71	205	53	15	2	3	(2	1)	81	27	30	30	21	2	53	0	4	0	4	1	1	.259	.327	.395	.723
2017	Col	NL	83	229	55	8	1	0	(0	0)	65	30	16	25	33	9	55	2	2	0	0	1	9	.240	.341	.284	.625
2018	Col	NL	74	182	31	4	4	3	(1	2)	52	19	27	18	26	2	52	3	6	2	2	0	6	.170	.292	.286	.577
2019	Col	NL	121	359	94	17	2	1	(0	1)	118	42	42	42	36	5	68	8	2	6	0	1	9	.262	.337	.329	.666
Postseason			3	3	2	0	0	0	(0	0)	2	0	1	0	0	0	0	0	0	0	0	0	0	.667	.667	.667	1.333
4 ML YEARS			349	975	233	44	9	7	(3	4)	316	118	115	115	116	18	209	16	8	8	6	3	25	.239	.327	.324	.651

Kean Wong

Bats: L **Throws:** R **Pos:** 2B-3;RF-2;PH-2;PR-2   **Ht:** 5'11" **Wt:** 185 **Born:** 4/17/1995 **Age:** 25

Year	Team	Lg	G	AB	H	2B	3B	HR	(Hm	Rd)	TB	R	RBI	RC	TBB	IBB	SO	HBP	SH	SF	SB	CS	GDP	Avg	OBP	Slg	OPS
2019	Drhm	AAA	113	453	139	29	6	10	(-	-)	210	71	63	80	42	1	112	8	2	1	6	3	6	.307	.375	.464	.839
2019	2 Tms	AL	7	18	3	0	0	0	(0	0)	3	2	0	0	0	0	6	0	0	0	0	1	0	.167	.167	.167	.333
19	TB	AL	6	14	3	0	0	0	(0	0)	3	1	0	0	0	0	5	0	0	0	0	1	0	.214	.214	.214	.429
19	LAA	AL	1	4	0	0	0	0	(0	0)	0	1	0	0	0	0	1	0	0	0	0	0	0	.000	.000	.000	.000

Kolten Wong

Bats: L **Throws:** R **Pos:** 2B-147;PH-6   COLT-enn   **Ht:** 5'9" **Wt:** 185 **Born:** 10/10/1990 **Age:** 29

Year	Team	Lg	G	AB	H	2B	3B	HR	(Hm	Rd)	TB	R	RBI	RC	TBB	IBB	SO	HBP	SH	SF	SB	CS	GDP	Avg	OBP	Slg	OPS
2013	StL	NL	32	59	9	1	0	0	(0	0)	10	6	0	0	3	0	12	0	0	0	3	0	2	.153	.194	.169	.363
2014	StL	NL	113	402	100	14	3	12	(10	2)	156	52	42	41	21	3	71	4	5	1	20	4	12	.249	.292	.388	.680
2015	StL	NL	150	557	146	28	4	11	(5	6)	215	71	61	67	36	2	95	15	0	5	15	8	10	.262	.321	.386	.707
2016	StL	NL	121	313	75	7	7	5	(3	2)	111	39	23	36	34	2	52	9	0	5	7	0	3	.240	.327	.355	.682
2017	StL	NL	108	354	101	27	3	4	(3	1)	146	55	42	56	41	11	60	12	1	3	8	2	4	.285	.376	.412	.788
2018	StL	NL	127	353	88	18	2	9	(6	3)	137	41	38	46	31	3	60	14	6	3	6	5	6	.249	.332	.388	.720
2019	StL	NL	148	478	136	25	4	11	(1	10)	202	61	59	81	47	5	83	13	6	5	24	4	2	.285	.361	.423	.784
Postseason			19	49	10	4	1	4	(3	1)	28	5	7	5	1	1	11	0	0	0	2	0	2	.204	.220	.571	.791
7 ML YEARS			799	2516	655	120	23	52	(28	24)	977	325	265	327	213	26	433	67	18	22	83	23	39	.260	.332	.388	.720

Alex Wood

Pitches: L **Bats:** R **Pos:** SP-7   **Ht:** 6'4" **Wt:** 215 **Born:** 1/12/1991 **Age:** 29

Year	Team	Lg	G	GS	GF	IP	BFP	H	R	ER	HR	SH	SF	HB	TBB	IBB	SO	WP	W	L	Pct	Sv-Op	Hld	Vel	OPS	ERC	ERA
2013	Atl	NL	31	11	9	77.2	327	76	29	27	3	6	4	1	27	1	77	4	3	3	.500	0-0	1	92	.670	3.40	3.13
2014	Atl	NL	35	24	2	171.2	694	151	58	53	16	7	3	6	45	1	170	5	11	11	.500	0-0	2	90	.651	3.04	2.78
2015	2 Tms	NL	32	32	0	189.2	801	198	86	81	15	15	3	4	59	4	139	6	12	12	.500	0-0	0	89	.724	3.94	3.84
2016	LAD	NL	14	10	0	60.1	255	56	30	25	5	0	2	3	20	0	66	4	1	4	.200	0-0	0	91	.660	3.49	3.73
2017	LAD	NL	27	25	0	152.1	614	123	50	46	15	4	0	6	38	6	151	2	16	3	**.842**	0-0	1	92	.620	2.58	2.72
2018	LAD	NL	33	27	0	151.2	637	143	70	62	14	3	7	8	40	5	135	2	9	7	.563	0-0	1	90	.664	3.32	3.68
2019	Cin	NL	7	7	0	35.2	153	41	25	23	11	2	0	1	9	0	30	0	1	3	.250	0-0	0	90	.926	6.02	5.80
15	Atl	NL	20	20	0	119.1	509	132	50	47	8	11	1	2	36	2	90	5	7	6	.538	0-0	0	89	.729	4.15	3.54
15	LAD	NL	12	12	0	70.1	292	66	36	34	7	4	2	2	23	2	49	1	5	6	.455	0-0	0	88	.714	3.58	4.35
	Postseason		16	2	4	26.1	110	22	16	12	9	0	0	2	8	3	28	1	1	2	.333	0-0	0	91	.821	4.46	4.10
7 ML YEARS			179	136	11	839.0	3481	788	348	317	79	37	19	29	238	17	768	23	53	43	.552	0-0	5	90	.679	3.38	3.40

Hunter Wood

Pitches: R **Bats:** R **Pos:** RP-34; SP-2   **Ht:** 6'1" **Wt:** 175 **Born:** 8/12/1993 **Age:** 26

Year	Team	Lg	G	GS	GF	IP	BFP	H	R	ER	HR	SH	SF	HB	TBB	IBB	SO	WP	W	L	Pct	Sv-Op	Hld	Vel	OPS	ERC	ERA
2019	Drham	AAA	8	0	4	10.2	53	16	11	9	3	0	0	0	5	0	14	0	1	0	1.000	1--	-	-	.980	8.80	7.59
2017	TB	AL	1	0	1	0.1	1	0	0	0	0	0	0	0	0	0	0	0	0	0	-	0-0	0	90	.000	0.00	0.00
2018	TB	AL	29	8	3	41.0	179	42	17	17	4	1	1	0	18	1	42	0	1	1	.500	0-0	4	94	.727	4.31	3.73
2019	2 Tms	AL	36	2	9	45.1	195	46	20	15	7	0	1	1	12	1	39	5	1	1	.500	1-1	2	94	.721	3.96	2.98
19	TB	AL	19	2	4	29.0	120	26	11	8	4	0	1	1	7	1	24	1	1	1	.500	1-1	1	93	.677	3.20	2.48
19	Cle	AL	17	0	5	16.1	75	20	9	7	3	0	0	0	5	0	15	4	0	0	-	0-0	1	94	.790	5.40	3.86
3 ML YEARS			66	10	13	86.2	375	88	37	32	11	1	2	1	30	2	81	5	2	2	.500	1-1	6	94	.722	4.10	3.32

Brandon Woodruff

Pitches: R **Bats:** L **Pos:** SP-22   **Ht:** 6'4" **Wt:** 215 **Born:** 2/10/1993 **Age:** 27

Year	Team	Lg	G	GS	GF	IP	BFP	H	R	ER	HR	SH	SF	HB	TBB	IBB	SO	WP	W	L	Pct	Sv-Op	Hld	Vel	OPS	ERC	ERA
2017	Mil	NL	8	8	0	43.0	184	43	23	23	5	1	0	3	14	1	32	0	2	3	.400	0-0	0	95	.719	4.16	4.81
2018	Mil	NL	19	4	4	42.1	176	36	18	17	4	0	1	2	14	0	47	1	3	0	1.000	1-1	2	95	.641	3.14	3.61
2019	Mil	NL	22	22	0	121.2	493	109	49	49	12	2	2	5	30	0	143	1	11	3	.786	0-0	0	96	.650	3.13	3.62
	Postseason		4	1	1	12.1	46	7	3	2	0	1	0	2	3	1	20	0	1	1	.500	0-0	0	97	.467	1.44	1.46
3 ML YEARS			49	34	4	207.0	853	188	90	89	21	3	3	10	58	1	222	2	16	6	.727	1-1	2	96	.663	3.34	3.87

Brandon Workman

Pitches: R **Bats:** R **Pos:** RP-73   **Ht:** 6'5" **Wt:** 235 **Born:** 8/13/1988 **Age:** 31

Year	Team	Lg	G	GS	GF	IP	BFP	H	R	ER	HR	SH	SF	HB	TBB	IBB	SO	WP	W	L	Pct	Sv-Op	Hld	Vel	OPS	ERC	ERA
2013	Bos	AL	20	3	5	41.2	180	44	23	23	5	2	1	0	15	1	47	1	6	3	.667	0-1	1	92	.751	4.34	4.97
2014	Bos	AL	19	15	2	87.0	378	88	57	50	11	3	3	1	36	0	70	2	1	10	.091	0-0	1	90	.748	4.43	5.17
2017	Bos	AL	33	0	8	39.2	162	37	17	14	7	2	1	1	11	2	37	1	1	1	.500	0-1	4	92	.782	3.83	3.18
2018	Bos	AL	43	0	4	41.1	167	34	15	15	6	0	3	0	16	0	37	0	6	1	.857	0-0	7	91	.705	3.46	3.27
2019	Bos	AL	73	0	30	71.2	286	29	18	15	1	1	3	2	45	4	104	4	10	1	.909	16-22	15	93	.433	1.47	1.88
	Postseason		10	0	0	9.2	48	14	6	5	2	1	0	0	6	1	7	0	0	1	.000	0-0	1	92	.938	8.49	4.66
5 ML YEARS			188	18	49	281.1	1173	232	130	117	30	8	11	4	123	7	295	8	24	16	.600	16-24	28	92	.674	3.35	3.74

Matt Wotherspoon

Pitches: R **Bats:** R **Pos:** RP-2   **Ht:** 6'2" **Wt:** 215 **Born:** 10/6/1991 **Age:** 28

Year	Team	Lg	G	GS	GF	IP	BFP	H	R	ER	HR	SH	SF	HB	TBB	IBB	SO	WP	W	L	Pct	Sv-Op	Hld	Vel	OPS	ERC	ERA
2019	Norfolk	AAA	33	3	8	65.0	284	65	41	40	10	0	1	5	27	0	67	2	5	2	.714	1--	-	-	.804	4.88	5.54
2019	Bal	AL	2	0	1	4.2	26	10	8	8	2	0	0	1	2	0	2	0	0	0	-	0-0	0	91	1.239	16.54	15.43

Kyle Wright

Pitches: R **Bats:** R **Pos:** SP-4; RP-3   **Ht:** 6'4" **Wt:** 200 **Born:** 10/2/1995 **Age:** 24

Year	Team	Lg	G	GS	GF	IP	BFP	H	R	ER	HR	SH	SF	HB	TBB	IBB	SO	WP	W	L	Pct	Sv-Op	Hld	Vel	OPS	ERC	ERA
2017	2 Tms	Low	9	9	0	17.0	68	11	5	5	0	2	0	1	6	0	18	1	0	1	.000	0--	-	-	.493	1.71	2.65
2018	Missi	AA	20	20	0	109.1	466	103	51	45	6	6	3	0	43	0	105	16	6	8	.429	0--	-	-	.656	3.41	3.70
2018	Gwnntt	AAA	7	4	0	28.2	110	15	9	8	2	1	1	1	8	0	28	4	2	1	.667	0--	-	-	.473	1.37	2.51
2019	Gwnntt	AAA	21	21	0	112.1	476	107	55	52	13	1	3	12	35	0	116	6	11	4	.733	0--	-	-	.727	4.04	4.17
2018	Atl	NL	4	0	1	6.0	28	4	3	3	2	0	0	0	6	0	5	0	0	0	-	0-0	0	94	.812	6.25	4.50
2019	Atl	NL	7	4	2	19.2	93	24	19	19	4	0	0	1	13	1	18	2	0	3	.000	0-0	0	95	.966	7.64	8.69
2 ML YEARS			11	4	3	25.2	121	28	22	22	6	0	0	1	19	1	23	2	0	3	.000	0-0	0	94	.931	7.31	7.71

Steven Wright

Pitches: R Bats: R Pos: RP-6   Ht: 6'2" Wt: 215 Born: 8/30/1984 Age: 35

Year Team	Lg	G	GS	GF	IP	BFP	H	R	ER	HR	SH	SF	HB	TBB	IBB	SO	WP	W	L	Pct	Sv-Op	Hld	Vel	OPS	ERC	ERA
2019 Pwtckt	AAA	5	1	1	9.2	37	6	2	2	1	0	0	0	3	0	4	0	1	0	1.000	0--	-		.537	1.89	1.86
2013 Bos	AL	4	1	2	13.1	59	12	8	8	0	0	0	1	9	0	10	2	2	0	1.000	0-0	0	85	.659	4.22	5.40
2014 Bos	AL	6	1	3	21.0	86	21	8	6	2	0	0	0	4	0	22	1	0	1	.000	0-0	0	84	.632	3.25	2.57
2015 Bos	AL	16	9	3	72.2	310	67	38	33	12	1	1	1	27	0	52	2	5	4	.556	0-0	0	83	.722	3.99	4.09
2016 Bos	AL	24	24	0	156.2	656	138	74	58	12	2	2	8	57	1	127	10	13	6	.684	0-0	0	83	.653	3.34	3.33
2017 Bos	AL	5	5	0	24.0	114	40	24	22	9	0	1	2	5	1	13	1	1	3	.250	0-0	0	84	1.148	10.27	8.25
2018 Bos	AL	20	4	4	53.2	223	41	17	16	5	0	0	2	26	1	42	0	3	1	.750	1-1	2	84	.643	3.23	2.68
2019 Bos	AL	6	0	3	6.1	33	11	6	6	3	0	1	1	4	0	5	0	0	1	.000	0-0	0	83	1.263	14.88	8.53
7 ML YEARS		81	44	15	347.2	1481	330	175	149	43	3	5	15	132	3	271	16	24	16	.600	1-1	2	83	.717	4.06	3.86

Mike Wright Jr.

Pitches: R Bats: R Pos: RP-19   Ht: 6'6" Wt: 215 Born: 1/3/1990 Age: 30

Year Team	Lg	G	GS	GF	IP	BFP	H	R	ER	HR	SH	SF	HB	TBB	IBB	SO	WP	W	L	Pct	Sv-Op	Hld	Vel	OPS	ERC	ERA
2019 Tacom	AAA	15	12	0	58.0	251	61	35	34	4	1	4	2	17	0	56	2	2	5	.286	0--	-	-	.752	3.82	5.28
2015 Bal	AL	12	9	0	44.2	204	52	30	30	9	0	2	5	18	3	26	2	3	5	.375	0-0	0	93	.887	6.20	6.04
2016 Bal	AL	18	12	5	74.2	328	81	53	48	12	1	5	9	26	0	50	2	3	4	.429	0-0	0	93	.850	5.38	5.79
2017 Bal	AL	13	0	4	25.0	109	26	16	16	5	0	1	3	7	0	28	1	0	0	-	0-0	0	94	.830	5.01	5.76
2018 Bal	AL	48	2	16	84.1	388	101	55	52	12	1	6	7	36	1	74	4	4	2	.667	0-0	0	93	.837	6.00	5.55
2019 2 Tms	AL	19	0	9	29.1	147	44	30	26	6	0	2	2	12	1	30	2	0	1	.000	1-2	0	93	.959	8.05	7.98
19 Bal	AL	10	0	4	13.1	66	20	14	14	5	0	1	1	7	0	14	1	0	1	.000	1-2	0	93	1.091	10.62	9.45
19 Sea	AL	9	0	5	16.0	81	24	16	12	1	0	1	1	5	1	16	1	0	0	-	0-0	0	93	.857	6.12	6.75
5 ML YEARS		110	23	34	258.0	1176	304	184	172	44	2	16	26	99	5	208	11	10	12	.455	1-2	1	93	.864	5.98	6.00

Austin Wynns

Bats: R Throws: R Pos: C-25;PH-2;PR-1   Ht: 6'2" Wt: 205 Born: 12/10/1990 Age: 29

Year Team	Lg	G	AB	H	2B	3B	HR	(Hm	Rd)	TB	R	RBI	RC	TBB	IBB	SO	HBP	SH	SF	SB	CS	GDP	Avg	OBP	Slg	OPS
2019 Norfolk	AAA	62	197	52	5	0	3	(-	-)	66	26	25	26	25	0	35	3	2	3	0	0	4	.264	.351	.335	.686
2018 Bal	AL	42	110	28	2	0	4	(1	3)	42	16	11	9	5	0	25	0	3	0	0	0	7	.255	.287	.382	.669
2019 Bal	AL	28	70	15	1	0	1	(0	1)	19	8	5	4	3	0	14	0	1	0	0	0	2	.214	.247	.271	.518
2 ML YEARS		70	180	43	3	0	5	(1	4)	61	24	16	13	8	0	39	0	4	0	0	0	9	.239	.271	.339	.610

Jimmy Yacabonis

Pitches: R Bats: R Pos: RP-25; SP-4   Ht: 6'3" Wt: 205 Born: 3/21/1992 Age: 28

Year Team	Lg	G	GS	GF	IP	BFP	H	R	ER	HR	SH	SF	HB	TBB	IBB	SO	WP	W	L	Pct	Sv-Op	Hld	Vel	OPS	ERC	ERA
2019 Norfolk	AAA	17	0	9	24.0	115	26	15	12	2	2	2	0	15	3	22	1	2	2	.500	2--	-	-	.748	4.87	4.50
2017 Bal	AL	14	0	7	20.2	90	18	10	10	2	0	3	0	14	1	8	1	2	0	1.000	0-0	0	95	.725	4.44	4.35
2018 Bal	AL	12	7	0	40.0	177	40	25	24	8	1	0	5	18	1	33	4	0	2	.000	0-0	0	93	.829	5.57	5.40
2019 Bal	AL	29	4	6	41.0	193	51	32	31	9	0	1	2	24	0	33	4	1	2	.333	0-0	3	94	.953	7.63	6.80
3 ML YEARS		55	11	13	101.2	460	109	67	65	19	1	4	7	56	2	74	9	3	4	.429	0-0	3	94	.862	6.14	5.75

Jordan Yamamoto

Pitches: R Bats: R Pos: SP-15   Ht: 6'0" Wt: 185 Born: 5/11/1996 Age: 24

Year Team	Lg	G	GS	GF	IP	BFP	H	R	ER	HR	SH	SF	HB	TBB	IBB	SO	WP	W	L	Pct	Sv-Op	Hld	Vel	OPS	ERC	ERA
2019 Jaxnvl	AA	12	12	0	65.1	270	53	27	26	7	0	0	7	25	0	64	2	3	5	.375	0--	-	-	.668	3.53	3.58
2019 Mia	NL	15	15	0	78.2	325	54	42	39	11	0	2	5	36	1	82	5	4	5	.444	0-0	0	92	.647	3.10	4.46

Ryan Yarbrough

Pitches: L Bats: R Pos: SP-14; RP-14   Ht: 6'5" Wt: 210 Born: 12/31/1991 Age: 28

Year Team	Lg	G	GS	GF	IP	BFP	H	R	ER	HR	SH	SF	HB	TBB	IBB	SO	WP	W	L	Pct	Sv-Op	Hld	Vel	OPS	ERC	ERA
2019 Drham	AAA	5	4	0	26.0	107	24	11	11	2	0	0	3	3	0	35	2	2	1	.667	0--	-	-	.607	2.84	3.81
2018 TB	AL	38	6	3	147.1	628	140	70	64	18	1	1	8	50	6	128	1	16	6	.727	0-0	0	89	.730	3.86	3.91
2019 TB	AL	28	14	1	141.2	563	121	69	65	15	0	3	9	22	2	117	0	11	6	.647	0-0	0	88	.650	2.60	4.13
2 ML YEARS		66	20	4	289.0	1191	261	139	129	33	1	4	17	70	8	245	1	27	12	.692	0-0	0	89	.692	3.23	4.02

Eric Yardley

Pitches: R Bats: R Pos: RP-10   Ht: 6'0" Wt: 165 Born: 8/18/1990 Age: 29

Year Team	Lg	G	GS	GF	IP	BFP	H	R	ER	HR	SH	SF	HB	TBB	IBB	SO	WP	W	L	Pct	Sv-Op	Hld	Vel	OPS	ERC	ERA
2019 ElPaso	AAA	43	0	16	63.2	261	60	27	20	3	0	0	4	14	1	52	0	0	2	.000	7--	-	-	.649	2.98	2.83
2019 SD	NL	10	0	2	11.2	52	12	5	3	1	2	0	1	3	0	7	0	0	1	.000	0-0	0	86	.668	3.73	2.31

Mike Yastrzemski

Bats: L Throws: L Pos: LF-61;RF-56;PH-12;CF-7   yah-STREHM-skee   Ht: 5'11" Wt: 180 Born: 8/23/1990 Age: 29

Year	Team	Lg	G	AB	H	2B	3B	HR	(Hm	Rd)	TB	R	RBI	RC	TBB	IBB	SO	HBP	SH	SF	SB	CS	GDP	Avg	OBP	Slg	OPS
2019	Scrmto	AAA	40	136	43	11	1	12	(-	-)	92	38	25	36	22	1	36	2	1	2	2	2	3	.316	.414	.676	1.090
2019	SF	NL	107	371	101	22	3	21	(8	13)	192	64	55	61	32	1	107	4	1	3	2	4	4	.272	.334	.518	.852

Kirby Yates

Pitches: R Bats: L Pos: RP-60   Ht: 5'10" Wt: 210 Born: 3/25/1987 Age: 33

Year	Team	Lg	G	GS	GF	IP	BFP	H	R	ER	HR	SH	SF	HB	TBB	IBB	SO	WP	W	L	Pct	Sv-Op	Hld	Vel	OPS	ERC	ERA
2014	TB	AL	37	0	12	36.0	156	33	16	15	4	0	1	3	15	3	42	2	0	2	.000	1-2	0	92	.699	3.94	3.75
2015	TB	AL	20	0	10	20.1	92	23	18	18	10	0	0	1	7	0	21	0	1	0	1.000	0-0	0	92	1.004	7.58	7.97
2016	NYY	AL	41	0	11	41.1	184	41	24	24	5	1	1	4	19	1	50	1	2	1	.667	0-2	2	93	.746	4.77	5.23
2017	2 Tms		62	0	12	56.2	231	44	28	25	12	0	1	2	19	2	88	0	4	5	.444	1-4	20	94	.698	3.42	3.97
2018	SD	NL	65	0	28	63.0	250	41	15	15	6	0	3	4	17	0	90	2	5	3	.625	12-13	16	94	.527	2.00	2.14
2019	SD	NL	60	0	51	60.2	243	41	14	8	2	1	1	7	13	1	101	2	0	5	.000	41-44	0	94	.515	1.72	1.19
17	LAA	AL	1	0	1	1.0	5	2	2	2	2	0	0	0	0	0	1	0	0	0	-	0-0	0	94	2.000	25.07	18.00
17	SD	NL	61	0	12	55.2	226	42	26	23	10	0	1	2	19	2	87	0	4	5	.444	1-4	20	94	.666	3.13	3.72
6 ML YEARS			285	0	124	278.0	1156	223	115	105	39	2	7	21	90	7	392	7	12	16	.429	55-65	38	93	.654	3.21	3.40

Christian Yelich

Bats: L Throws: R Pos: RF-124;LF-6;PH-3;DH-2;CF-1   YELL-itch   Ht: 6'3" Wt: 195 Born: 12/5/1991 Age: 28

Year	Team	Lg	G	AB	H	2B	3B	HR	(Hm	Rd)	TB	R	RBI	RC	TBB	IBB	SO	HBP	SH	SF	SB	CS	GDP	Avg	OBP	Slg	OPS
2013	Mia	NL	62	240	69	12	1	4	(0	4)	95	34	16	35	31	1	66	1	0	1	10	0	4	.288	.370	.396	.766
2014	Mia	NL	144	582	165	30,	6	9	(2	7)	234	94	54	87	70	3	137	3	3	2	21	7	9	.284	.362	.402	.764
2015	Mia	NL	126	476	143	30	2	7	(1	6)	198	63	44	64	47	2	101	2	0	0	16	5	13	.300	.366	.416	.782
2016	Mia	NL	155	578	172	38	3	21	(8	13)	279	78	98	89	72	4	138	4	0	5	9	4	20	.298	.376	.483	.859
2017	Mia	NL	156	602	170	36	2	18	(7	11)	264	100	81	99	80	4	137	6	0	6	16	2	13	.282	.369	.439	.807
2018	Mil	NL	147	574	187	34	7	36	(22	14)	343	118	110	128	68	2	135	7	0	2	22	4	14	.326	.402	.598	1.000
2019	Mil	NL	130	489	161	29	3	44	(27	17)	328	100	97	126	80	16	118	8	0	3	30	2	8	.329	.429	.671	1.100
Postseason			10	36	7	1	0	2	(2	0)	14	7	3	4	11	1	7	0	0	0	2	0	2	.194	.383	.389	.772
7 ML YEARS			920	3541	1067	209	24	139	(67	72)	1741	587	500	628	448	32	832	31	3	19	124	24	81	.301	.383	.492	.874

Gabriel Ynoa

Pitches: R Bats: R Pos: RP-23; SP-13   ee-NOH-uh   Ht: 6'2" Wt: 205 Born: 5/26/1993 Age: 27

Year	Team	Lg	G	GS	GF	IP	BFP	H	R	ER	HR	SH	SF	HB	TBB	IBB	SO	WP	W	L	Pct	Sv-Op	Hld	Vel	OPS	ERC	ERA
2016	NYM	NL	10	3	2	18.1	88	26	13	13	0	0	2	1	7	0	17	0	1	0	1.000	0-0	0	94	.745	5.80	6.38
2017	Bal	AL	9	4	2	34.2	147	39	17	16	5	1	2	1	8	0	26	0	2	3	.400	0-0	0	94	.810	4.60	4.15
2019	Bal	AL	36	13	3	110.2	480	126	77	69	29	0	1	3	26	1	67	4	1	10	.091	0-0	0	94	.858	5.41	5.61
3 ML YEARS			55	20	7	163.2	715	191	107	98	34	1	5	5	41	1	110	4	4	13	.235	0-0	0	94	.836	5.30	5.39

Huascar Ynoa

Pitches: R Bats: R Pos: RP-2   WAH-scar ee-NOH-ah   Ht: 6'3" Wt: 175 Born: 5/28/1998 Age: 22

Year	Team	Lg	G	GS	GF	IP	BFP	H	R	ER	HR	SH	SF	HB	TBB	IBB	SO	WP	W	L	Pct	Sv-Op	Hld	Vel	OPS	ERC	ERA
2019	Missi	AA	6	0	3	13.2	63	17	8	8	2	1	0	0	5	0	15	2	1	2	.333	1--	-	-	.776	5.57	5.27
2019	Gwnntt	AAA	17	14	1	72.2	330	80	47	43	14	0	1	4	34	0	79	3	3	5	.375	0--	-	-	.825	5.85	5.33
2019	Atl	NL	2	0	1	3.0	16	6	6	6	1	0	0	0	1	0	3	0	0	0	-	0-0	0	98	1.171	12.18	18.00

Alex Young

Pitches: L Bats: L Pos: SP-15; RP-2   Ht: 6'2" Wt: 205 Born: 9/9/1993 Age: 26

Year	Team	Lg	G	GS	GF	IP	BFP	H	R	ER	HR	SH	SF	HB	TBB	IBB	SO	WP	W	L	Pct	Sv-Op	Hld	Vel	OPS	ERC	ERA
2019	Reno	AAA	20	8	1	54.2	258	66	38	37	6	2	2	1	26	3	64	6	4	3	.571	0--	-	-	.856	5.48	6.09
2019	Ari	NL	17	15	0	83.1	349	72	40	33	14	3	0	4	27	4	71	2	7	5	.583	0-0	0	89	.710	3.58	3.56

Mark Zagunis

Bats: R Throws: R Pos: PH-22;RF-6;LF-2;PR-1   Ht: 6'0" Wt: 215 Born: 2/5/1993 Age: 27

Year	Team	Lg	G	AB	H	2B	3B	HR	(Hm	Rd)	TB	R	RBI	RC	TBB	IBB	SO	HBP	SH	SF	SB	CS	GDP	Avg	OBP	Slg	OPS
2019	Iowa	AAA	68	255	75	26	1	6	(-	-)	121	35	43	44	24	1	94	4	0	2	6	3	7	.294	.361	.475	.836
2017	ChC	NL	7	14	0	0	0	0	(0	0)	0	0	1	0	4	0	6	0	0	0	2	0	0	.000	.222	.000	.222
2018	ChC	NL	5	5	2	1	0	0	(0	0)	3	0	1	1	1	0	1	0	0	0	0	0	0	.400	.500	.600	1.100
2019	ChC	NL	30	36	9	3	0	0	(0	0)	12	2	5	5	4	0	16	0	0	0	0	0	1	.250	.325	.333	.658
3 ML YEARS			42	55	11	4	0	0	(0	0)	15	2	7	6	9	0	23	0	0	0	2	0	1	.200	.313	.273	.585

Daniel Zamora

Pitches: L **Bats:** L **Pos:** RP-17 **Ht:** 6'3" **Wt:** 195 **Born:** 4/15/1993 **Age:** 27

		HOW MUCH PITCHED					WHAT HE GAVE UP										THE RESULTS					
Year	Team	Lg	G	GS	GF	IP	BFP	H	R	ER	HR	SH	SF	HB	TBB	IBB	SO	WP	W	L	Pct	Sv-Op Hld	Vel	OPS	ERC	ERA
2019	Syrcse	AAA	29	0	7	30.0	117	26	14	14	1	0	0	0	7	0	36	2	2	1	.667	4-- -	-	.591	2.44	4.20
2018	NYM	NL	16	0	4	9.0	36	6	3	3	1	1	0	1	3	1	16	0	1	0	1.000	0-0	5	89	.641	2.45	3.00
2019	NYM	NL	17	0	3	8.2	41	10	5	5	1	0	1	1	5	1	8	0	0	1	.000	0-0	0	89	.861	6.09	5.19
	2 ML YEARS		33	0	7	17.2	77	16	8	8	2	1	1	2	8	2	24	0	1	1	.500	0-0	5	89	.757	4.13	4.08

Seby Zavala

Bats: R **Throws:** R **Pos:** C-3;PH-2 **Ht:** 5'11" **Wt:** 215 **Born:** 8/28/1993 **Age:** 26

						BATTING													RUNNING			AVERAGES			
Year	Team	Lg	G	AB	H	2B	3B	HR	(Hm Rd)	TB	R	RBI	RC	TBB	IBB	SO	HBP	SH	SF	SB	CS	GDP	Avg	OBP	Slg	OPS
2019	Charllt	AAA	82	297	66	14	0	20	(- -)	140	49	45	42	26	0	116	6	0	2	1	1	6	.222	.296	.471	.767
2019	CWS	AL	5	12	1	0	0	0	(0 0)	1	1	0	0	0	0	9	0	0	0	0	0	0	.083	.083	.083	.167

T.J. Zeuch

Pitches: R **Bats:** R **Pos:** SP-3; RP-2 **Ht:** 6'7" **Wt:** 225 **Born:** 8/1/1995 **Age:** 24

			HOW MUCH PITCHED					WHAT HE GAVE UP										THE RESULTS					
Year	Team	Lg	G	GS	GF	IP	BFP	H	R	ER	HR	SH	SF	HB	TBB	IBB	SO	WP	W	L	Pct	Sv-Op Hld	Vel	OPS	ERC	ERA
2019	Buffalo	AAA	13	13	0	78.0	335	70	35	32	6	0	1	8	32	0	39	1	4	3	.571	0-- -	-	.713	3.81	3.69
2019	Tor	AL	5	3	0	22.2	99	22	13	12	2	0	0	0	11	0	20	2	1	2	.333	0-0	0	92	.731	4.15	4.76

Bradley Zimmer

Bats: L **Throws:** R **Pos:** RF-4;PH-3;CF-2;PR-2 **Ht:** 6'5" **Wt:** 220 **Born:** 11/27/1992 **Age:** 27

						BATTING													RUNNING			AVERAGES			
Year	Team	Lg	G	AB	H	2B	3B	HR	(Hm Rd)	TB	R	RBI	RC	TBB	IBB	SO	HBP	SH	SF	SB	CS	GDP	Avg	OBP	Slg	OPS
2017	Cle	AL	101	299	72	15	2	8	(5 3)	115	41	39	37	26	1	99	4	0	3	18	1	5	.241	.307	.385	.692
2018	Cle	AL	34	106	24	5	0	2	(1 1)	35	14	9	9	7	0	44	1	0	0	4	1	1	.226	.281	.330	.611
2019	Cle	AL	9	13	0	0	0	0	(0 0)	0	1	0	0	1	0	7	0	0	0	0	0	0	.000	.071	.000	.071
	3 ML YEARS		144	418	96	20	2	10	(6 4)	150	56	48	46	34	1	150	5	0	3	22	2	6	.230	.293	.359	.652

Kyle Zimmer

Pitches: R **Bats:** R **Pos:** RP-15 **Ht:** 6'3" **Wt:** 225 **Born:** 9/13/1991 **Age:** 28

			HOW MUCH PITCHED					WHAT HE GAVE UP										THE RESULTS					
Year	Team	Lg	G	GS	GF	IP	BFP	H	R	ER	HR	SH	SF	HB	TBB	IBB	SO	WP	W	L	Pct	Sv-Op Hld	Vel	OPS	ERC	ERA
2019	Omha	AAA	37	12	7	54.0	237	46	30	26	6	0	3	1	33	2	52	2	2	4	.333	1-- -	-	.713	4.16	4.33
2019	KC	AL	15	0	3	18.1	102	28	22	22	2	0	0	0	19	0	18	2	0	1	.000	0-0	0	97	.991	10.03	10.80

Ryan Zimmerman

Bats: R **Throws:** R **Pos:** 1B-44;PH-7;DH-3 **Ht:** 6'3" **Wt:** 215 **Born:** 9/28/1984 **Age:** 35

						BATTING													RUNNING			AVERAGES			
Year	Team	Lg	G	AB	H	2B	3B	HR	(Hm Rd)	TB	R	RBI	RC	TBB	IBB	SO	HBP	SH	SF	SB	CS	GDP	Avg	OBP	Slg	OPS
2005	Was	NL	20	58	23	10	0	0	(0 0)	33	6	6	9	3	0	12	0	0	1	0	0	1	.397	.419	.569	.988
2006	Was	NL	157	614	176	47	3	20	(10 10)	289	84	110	101	61	7	120	2	1	4	11	8	15	.287	.351	.471	.822
2007	Was	NL	162	653	174	43	5	24	(11 13)	299	99	91	83	61	3	125	3	0	5	4	1	26	.266	.330	.458	.788
2008	Was	NL	106	428	121	24	1	14	(7 7)	189	51	51	48	31	1	71	3	0	4	1	1	12	.283	.333	.442	.774
2009	Was	NL	157	610	178	37	3	33	(17 16)	320	110	106	96	72	9	119	2	0	9	2	0	22	.292	.364	.525	.888
2010	Was	NL	142	525	161	32	0	25	(9 16)	268	85	85	97	69	6	98	4	0	5	4	1	16	.307	.388	.510	.899
2011	Was	NL	101	395	114	21	2	12	(7 5)	175	52	49	58	41	4	73	1	0	3	3	1	14	.289	.355	.443	.798
2012	Was	NL	145	578	163	36	1	25	(16 9)	276	93	95	84	57	8	116	2	0	4	5	2	20	.282	.346	.478	.824
2013	Was	NL	147	568	156	26	2	26	(7 19)	264	84	79	83	60	2	133	2	0	3	6	0	16	.275	.344	.465	.809
2014	Was	NL	61	214	60	19	1	5	(1 4)	96	26	38	32	22	0	37	0	0	6	0	0	6	.280	.342	.449	.790
2015	Was	NL	95	346	86	25	1	16	(9 7)	161	43	73	49	33	0	79	1	0	10	1	0	13	.249	.308	.465	.773
2016	Was	NL	115	427	93	18	1	15	(9 6)	158	60	46	36	29	1	104	5	0	6	4	1	12	.218	.272	.370	.642
2017	Was	NL	144	524	159	33	0	36	(19 17)	300	90	108	94	44	1	126	3	0	5	1	0	16	.303	.358	.573	.930
2018	Was	NL	85	288	76	21	2	13	(7 6)	140	33	51	41	30	1	55	3	0	2	1	1	10	.264	.337	.486	.824
2019	Was	NL	52	171	44	9	0	6	(2 4)	71	20	27	22	17	0	39	0	0	2	0	0	4	.257	.321	.415	.736
	Postseason		19	62	18	4	0	3	(2 1)	31	5	10	11	5	0	13	0	0	1	1	0	1	.290	.338	.500	.838
	15 ML YEARS		1689	6399	1784	401	22	270	(131 139)	3039	936	1015	933	630	43	1307	31	1	67	43	16	203	.279	.343	.475	.818

Jordan Zimmermann

Pitches: R **Bats:** R **Pos:** SP-23 **Ht:** 6'2" **Wt:** 225 **Born:** 5/23/1986 **Age:** 34

			HOW MUCH PITCHED					WHAT HE GAVE UP										THE RESULTS					
Year	Team	Lg	G	GS	GF	IP	BFP	H	R	ER	HR	SH	SF	HB	TBB	IBB	SO	WP	W	L	Pct	Sv-Op Hld	Vel	OPS	ERC	ERA
2009	Was	NL	16	16	0	91.1	391	95	51	47	10	5	3	4	29	0	92	0	3	5	.375	0-0	0	93	.760	4.25	4.63
2010	Was	NL	7	7	0	31.0	135	31	20	17	8	1	1	2	10	1	27	0	1	2	.333	0-0	0	92	.817	5.02	4.94
2011	Was	NL	26	26	0	161.1	662	154	62	57	12	8	2	7	31	2	124	3	8	11	.421	0-0	0	93	.671	3.02	3.18
2012	Was	NL	32	32	0	195.2	805	186	69	64	18	8	4	8	43	2	153	3	12	8	.600	0-0	0	94	.686	3.22	2.94
2013	Was	NL	32	32	0	213.1	865	192	81	77	19	9	4	7	40	0	161	3	19	9	.679	0-0	0	94	.654	2.79	3.25
2014	Was	NL	32	32	0	199.2	800	185	67	59	13	5	3	6	29	0	182	4	14	5	.737	0-0	0	94	.631	2.64	2.66
2015	Was	NL	33	33	0	201.2	831	204	89	82	24	8	4	2	39	3	164	2	13	10	.565	0-0	0	93	.699	3.63	3.66
2016	Det	AL	19	18	1	105.1	450	118	63	57	14	1	5	2	26	0	66	3	9	7	.563	0-0	0	92	.804	4.48	4.87
2017	Det	AL	29	29	0	160.0	713	204	111	108	29	3	8	7	44	2	103	3	8	13	.381	0-0	0	92	.888	6.00	6.08

			HOW MUCH PITCHED					WHAT HE GAVE UP											THE RESULTS								
Year	Team	Lg	G	GS	GF	IP	BFP	H	R	ER	HR	SH	SF	HB	TBB	IBB	SO	WP	W	L	Pct	Sv-Op	Hld	Vel	OPS	ERC	ERA
2018	Det	AL	25	25	0	131.1	556	140	76	66	28	2	5	2	26	0	111	1	7	8	.467	0-0	0	91	.800	4.42	4.52
2019	Det	AL	23	23	0	112.0	504	145	89	86	19	3	4	6	25	2	82	3	1	13	.071	0-0	0	90	.877	5.74	6.91
	Postseason		3	2	0	12.2	47	10	6	6	1	1	0	0	1	0	11	0	0	1	.000	0-0	0	94	.550	1.80	4.26
	11 ML YEARS		274	273	1	1602.2	6712	1654	778	720	194	53	41	59	342	12	1265	25	95	91	.511	0-0	0	93	.735	3.81	4.04

Ben Zobrist

Bats: B **Throws:** R **Pos:** 2B-32;RF-13;LF-6;PH-5;SS-1;DH-1   ZOH-brist   **Ht:** 6'3" **Wt:** 210 **Born:** 5/26/1981 **Age:** 39

			BATTING																RUNNING			AVERAGES			
Year	Team	Lg	G	AB	H	2B	3B	HR	(Hm | Rd)	TB	R	RBI	RC	TBB	IBB	SO	HBP	SH	SF	SB	CS	GDP	Avg	OBP	Slg	OPS
2006	TB	AL	52	183	41	6	2	2	(2 | 0)	57	10	18	13	10	1	26	0	2	3	2	3	2	.224	.260	.311	.572
2007	TB	AL	31	97	15	2	0	1	(0 | 1)	20	8	9	0	3	0	21	1	2	2	2	0	1	.155	.184	.206	.391
2008	TB	AL	62	198	50	10	2	12	(4 | 8)	100	32	30	31	25	1	37	2	0	2	3	0	4	.253	.339	.505	.844
2009	TB	AL	152	501	149	28	7	27	(18 | 9)	272	91	91	109	91	4	104	2	1	4	17	6	7	.297	.405	.543	.948
2010	TB	AL	151	541	129	28	2	10	(3 | 7)	191	77	75	84	92	1	107	3	7	12	24	3	10	.238	.346	.353	.699
2011	TB	AL	156	588	158	46	6	20	(9 | 11)	276	99	91	100	77	1	128	2	2	5	19	6	9	.269	.353	.469	.822
2012	TB	AL	157	560	151	39	7	20	(8 | 12)	264	88	74	102	97	7	103	3	2	6	14	9	13	.270	.377	.471	.848
2013	TB	AL	157	612	168	36	3	12	(7 | 5)	246	77	71	85	72	4	91	7	1	6	11	3	18	.275	.354	.402	.756
2014	TB	AL	146	570	155	34	3	10	(4 | 6)	225	83	52	75	75	4	84	1	2	6	10	5	8	.272	.354	.395	.749
2015	2 Tms	AL	126	467	129	36	3	13	(5 | 8)	210	76	56	72	62	3	56	1	0	5	3	4	8	.276	.359	.450	.809
2016	ChC	NL	147	523	142	31	3	18	(5 | 13)	233	94	76	81	96	6	82	4	4	4	6	4	17	.272	.386	.446	.831
2017	ChC	NL	128	435	101	20	3	12	(5 | 7)	163	58	50	50	54	2	71	2	2	3	2	2	13	.232	.318	.375	.693
2018	ChC	NL	139	455	139	28	3	9	(2 | 7)	200	67	58	76	55	1	60	2	1	7	3	4	8	.305	.378	.440	.817
2019	ChC	NL	47	150	39	5	0	1	(1 | 0)	47	24	17	18	23	0	24	1	0	2	0	0	6	.260	.358	.313	.671
15	Oak	AL	67	235	63	20	2	6	(2 | 4)	105	39	33	38	33	2	26	0	0	3	1	1	5	.268	.354	.447	.801
15	KC	AL	59	232	66	16	1	7	(3 | 4)	105	37	23	34	29	1	30	1	0	2	2	3	3	.284	.364	.453	.816
	Postseason		64	228	55	17	1	4	(2 | 2)	86	34	14	20	21	2	38	1	1	5	1	0	5	.241	.306	.377	.683
	14 ML YEARS		1651	5880	1566	349	44	167	(73 | 94)	2504	884	768	896	832	35	994	31	26	67	116	49	124	.266	.357	.426	.783

Mike Zunino

Bats: R **Throws:** R **Pos:** C-89;PH-3   zoo-NEE-no   **Ht:** 6'2" **Wt:** 235 **Born:** 3/25/1991 **Age:** 29

			BATTING																RUNNING			AVERAGES			
Year	Team	Lg	G	AB	H	2B	3B	HR	(Hm | Rd)	TB	R	RBI	RC	TBB	IBB	SO	HBP	SH	SF	SB	CS	GDP	Avg	OBP	Slg	OPS
2013	Sea	AL	52	173	37	5	0	5	(3 | 2)	57	22	14	13	16	0	49	3	0	1	1	0	5	.214	.290	.329	.620
2014	Sea	AL	131	438	87	20	2	22	(10 | 12)	177	51	60	39	17	1	158	17	0	4	0	3	12	.199	.254	.404	.658
2015	Sea	AL	112	350	61	11	0	11	(6 | 5)	105	28	28	14	21	0	132	5	8	2	0	1	6	.174	.230	.300	.530
2016	Sea	AL	55	164	34	7	0	12	(9 | 3)	77	16	31	28	21	0	65	6	0	0	0	0	0	.207	.318	.470	.787
2017	Sea	AL	124	387	97	25	0	25	(14 | 11)	197	52	64	55	39	0	160	8	0	1	1	0	8	.251	.331	.509	.840
2018	Sea	AL	113	373	75	18	0	20	(5 | 15)	153	37	44	29	24	0	150	6	0	2	0	0	7	.201	.259	.410	.669
2019	TB	AL	90	266	44	10	1	9	(5 | 4)	83	30	32	18	20	0	98	3	0	0	0	0	4	.165	.232	.312	.544
	7 ML YEARS		677	2151	435	96	3	104	(52 | 52)	849	236	273	196	158	1	812	48	8	11	2	4	42	.202	.271	.395	.665

Fielding Statistics

Andrew Kyne

Cleveland's Roberto Perez turned in one of the finest seasons behind the plate that Baseball Info Solutions has tracked. His 29 Defensive Runs Saved fell just short of Yadier Molina's record of 30, which the Cardinals backstop set in 2013. Prior to this season, Molina had held the top three spots on the all-time list for catcher seasons, having saved 29 runs in 2012 and 26 runs in 2010.

How did Perez arrive at such an impressive DRS total? His performance in pitch framing (11 Strike Zone Runs Saved) and pitch blocking (8 Good Fielding Plays Runs Saved) were significant contributions to that.

The following pages feature this kind of data for 2019 regulars. In addition to basic fielding stats, a breakdown of DRS components can be found.

For catchers like Perez, you'll find the following DRS components: Good Fielding Plays / Defensive Misplays + Errors (GFP/DME), Stolen Bases (SB), Strike Zone (SZ), and Bunts and Adjusted Earned Runs (Other).

All non-catchers are graded on Range & Positioning (R/P) in addition to GFP/DME. Arizona shortstop Nick Ahmed, Milwaukee center fielder Lorenzo Cain, and Los Angeles outfielder/first baseman Cody Bellinger were among the standouts in Range & Positioning this year, which measures how well defenders convert batted balls into outs.

Additionally, outfielders are judged for how well they can throw out runners and deter baserunning advancement (Throws). Washington's Victor Robles and Oakland's Ramon Laureano saved the most runs with their throwing arm in 2019.

All infielders have a component for saving runs on double plays (GDP), and corner infielders have one for saving runs against bunts (Bunts).

First Basemen - Regulars

Player	Tm	G	GS	Inn	PO	A	E	DP	Pct.	Bases Saved	Runs Saved R/P	GFP/ DME	Bunts/ GDP	Total
Olson, Matt	Oak	127	125	1121	1023	90	8	95	.993	+17	12	1	0	13
Walker, Christian	Ari	142	132	1179	1041	139	11	95	.991	+12	9	-1	1	9
Votto, Joey	Cin	133	132	1132	944	118	7	94	.993	+10	7	0	0	7
Freeman, Freddie	Atl	158	157	1366	1296	63	6	128	.996	+5	4	1	0	5
Goldschmidt, Paul	StL	159	155	1370	1256	111	5	145	.996	+5	3	0	1	4
Belt, Brandon	SF	144	123	1155	1017	99	6	108	.995	+3	2	-1	3	4
Cron, C.J.	Min	117	110	993	927	61	8	87	.992	+3	3	-2	2	3
Rizzo, Anthony	ChC	146	144	1227	1140	123	5	120	.996	-1	-1	3	1	3
Thames, Eric	Mil	105	89	782	639	45	3	64	.996	+2	2	-1	1	2
Murphy, Daniel	Col	110	98	884	909	109	9	97	.991	+1	1	0	1	2
Davis, Chris	Bal	97	86	769	671	37	4	86	.994	+1	0	1	-1	0
Gurriel, Yuli	Hou	110	104	895	728	73	3	58	.996	+1	0	0	0	0
Santana, Carlos	Cle	135	135	1186	951	73	10	77	.990	+1	1	0	-2	-1
Pujols, Albert	LAA	98	98	861	719	77	5	70	.994	-4	-3	2	0	-1
Choi, Ji-Man	TB	103	92	842	748	36	6	66	.992	-5	-3	2	0	-1
Hoskins, Rhys	Phi	158	157	1398	1193	122	9	111	.993	-3	-2	-2	2	-2
Smoak, Justin	Tor	89	88	772	686	42	4	64	.995	-4	-3	0	0	-3
Hosmer, Eric	SD	157	155	1356	1128	106	14	82	.989	-2	-1	-2	-1	-4
O'Hearn, Ryan	KC	94	88	766	707	24	4	80	.995	-4	-3	-1	0	-4
Abreu, Jose	CWS	125	125	1104	1012	74	8	128	.993	-5	-4	0	0	-4
Bell, Josh	Pit	134	133	1161	981	96	13	91	.988	-5	-4	-1	0	-5
Alonso, Pete	NYM	156	152	1328	1077	112	12	109	.990	-2	-2	-2	-2	-6

Second Basemen - Regulars

Player	Tm	G	GS	Inn	PO	A	E	DP	Pct.	Range	Bases Saved	Runs Saved R/P	GFP/ DME	GDP	Total
Wong, Kolten	StL	147	134	1195	250	412	9	103	.987	4.98	+18	13	2	-1	14
Sanchez, Yolmer	CWS	149	142	1257	248	416	9	108	.987	4.76	+7	5	2	4	11
Albies, Ozzie	Atl	158	157	1405	273	384	4	117	.994	4.21	+9	7	1	0	8
Hernandez, Cesar	Phi	157	155	1377	271	354	12	97	.981	4.09	+13	10	-2	-2	6
Frazier, Adam	Pit	142	133	1181	222	327	6	78	.989	4.18	+6	4	1	1	6
Rengifo, Luis	LAA	104	90	819	165	218	9	58	.977	4.21	+6	5	-2	0	3
McMahon, Ryan	Col	113	98	860	160	295	13	76	.972	4.76	+3	2	0	1	3
Schoop, Jonathan	Min	113	110	983	166	254	14	62	.968	3.84	+1	1	0	-1	0
Altuve, Jose	Hou	121	119	1024	128	257	11	49	.972	3.38	-1	0	0	-2	-2
Castro, Starlin	Mia	117	115	1013	177	249	9	64	.979	3.79	-3	-2	1	-1	-2
Panik, Joe	TOT	118	104	955	179	261	5	59	.989	4.15	+1	0	0	-3	-3
Dozier, Brian	Was	123	114	1009	145	248	5	61	.987	3.51	-9	-7	2	0	-5
Cano, Robinson	NYM	99	98	804	164	189	5	51	.986	3.95	-11	-8	2	0	-6
Kipnis, Jason	Cle	117	117	1024	150	253	4	51	.990	3.54	-9	-7	1	-1	-7
Gordon, Dee	Sea	111	105	918	190	242	9	63	.980	4.23	-7	-5	-1	-2	-8
Odor, Rougned	Tex	137	134	1188	246	294	15	85	.973	4.09	-11	-8	2	-2	-8
Profar, Jurickson	Oak	124	115	1024	221	245	13	64	.973	4.10	-7	-5	-2	-3	-10

Third Basemen - Regulars

Player	Tm	G	GS	Inn	PO	A	E	DP	Pct.	Range	Bases Saved	Runs Saved R/P	GFP/ DME	Bunts/ GDP	Total
Chapman, Matt	Oak	156	152	1336	146	311	9	27	.981	3.08	+18	14	3	1	18
Donaldson, Josh	Atl	148	148	1297	100	304	13	38	.969	2.80	+17	13	1	1	15
Arenado, Nolan	Col	154	151	1320	111	337	9	43	.980	3.06	+11	8	1	-1	8
Escobar, Eduardo	Ari	144	122	1137	86	219	7	28	.978	2.41	+7	5	2	1	8
Longoria, Evan	SF	119	117	1041	69	233	15	27	.953	2.61	+10	7	-2	2	7
Bregman, Alex	Hou	99	91	806	66	164	8	17	.966	2.57	+9	7	0	0	7
Machado, Manny	SD	119	119	1040	79	187	11	18	.960	2.30	+7	5	1	-1	5
Ramirez, Jose	Cle	126	125	1089	108	222	14	21	.959	2.73	+4	3	-1	1	3
Suarez, Eugenio	Cin	158	151	1309	106	246	17	26	.954	2.42	+4	3	-1	0	2
Rendon, Anthony	Was	146	146	1265	95	249	11	32	.969	2.45	0	0	-1	3	2
Ruiz, Rio	Bal	114	89	843	70	176	8	27	.969	2.63	+1	0	1	1	2
Frazier, Todd	NYM	120	112	997	89	229	12	24	.964	2.87	-3	-3	2	2	1
Carpenter, Matt	StL	107	102	880	55	162	8	16	.964	2.22	+2	1	0	-1	0
Moustakas, Mike	Mil	105	93	799	67	151	11	17	.952	2.46	-2	-2	1	1	0
Seager, Kyle	Sea	104	103	910	64	218	11	23	.962	2.79	-7	-5	2	2	-1
Guerrero Jr., Vladimir	Tor	96	94	824	66	182	17	23	.936	2.71	-1	-1	-2	0	-3
Franco, Maikel	Phi	110	99	925	62	195	8	10	.970	2.50	-7	-5	1	1	-3
Urshela, Giovanny	NYY	123	109	978	59	212	13	20	.954	2.49	-4	-3	-1	0	-4
Cabrera, Asdrubal	TOT	98	91	812	66	174	7	25	.972	2.66	-5	-3	-1	0	-4

Player	Tm	G	GS	Inn	PO	A	E	DP	Pct.	Range	Bases Saved	R/P	GFP/ DME	Bunts/ GDP	Total
Sano, Miguel	Min	91	86	793	52	161	17	14	.926	2.42	-7	-5	1	-1	-5
Devers, Rafael	Bos	152	151	1353	117	292	22	20	.949	2.72	-4	-3	-1	-2	-6
Bryant, Kris	ChC	115	110	939	48	186	13	15	.947	2.24	-7	-5	0	-2	-7
Moncada, Yoan	CWS	129	128	1096	120	256	15	37	.962	3.09	-8	-6	-2	1	-7
Turner, Justin	LAD	124	119	1024	67	219	8	22	.973	2.51	-9	-7	1	-1	-7
Moran, Colin	Pit	121	106	882	62	151	14	20	.938	2.17	-17	-13	1	-1	-13
Dozier, Hunter	KC	100	99	859	66	181	9	21	.965	2.59	-13	-10	-1	-3	-14

Shortstops - Regulars

Player	Tm	G	GS	Inn	PO	A	E	DP	Pct.	Range	Bases Saved	R/P	GFP/ DME	GDP	Total
Ahmed, Nick	Ari	158	155	1381	207	412	13	79	.979	4.03	+24	18	0	0	18
Story, Trevor	Col	144	144	1257	182	416	8	90	.987	4.28	+18	13	2	2	17
Baez, Javier	ChC	129	128	1117	165	366	15	88	.973	4.28	+11	8	3	4	15
Simmons, Andrelton	LAA	102	98	873	137	276	11	56	.974	4.26	+19	15	-1	0	14
DeJong, Paul	StL	157	156	1372	211	435	7	119	.989	4.24	+18	14	-2	2	14
Adames, Willy	TB	152	145	1315	157	388	17	68	.970	3.73	+13	10	2	1	13
Rojas, Miguel	Mia	125	122	1061	178	287	11	75	.977	3.95	+15	12	-1	1	12
Mondesi, Adalberto	KC	100	99	853	147	286	7	66	.984	4.57	+10	8	1	1	10
Seager, Corey	LAD	132	125	1083	138	304	15	59	.967	3.67	+8	6	1	2	9
Lindor, Francisco	Cle	137	137	1196	159	312	10	68	.979	3.54	+7	5	4	0	9
Iglesias, Jose	Cin	144	136	1170	122	324	9	62	.980	3.43	+8	6	1	1	8
Semien, Marcus	Oak	161	161	1435	186	436	12	85	.981	3.90	+15	11	-3	-3	5
Arcia, Orlando	Mil	150	139	1241	208	350	14	79	.976	4.05	+1	1	2	0	3
Polanco, Jorge	Min	142	139	1233	141	343	22	57	.957	3.53	0	0	2	-1	1
Crawford, Brandon	SF	142	137	1233	190	366	16	81	.972	4.06	+2	2	1	-3	0
Galvis, Freddy	TOT	110	106	940	136	293	6	65	.986	4.11	-6	-4	2	0	-2
Swanson, Dansby	Atl	126	123	1091	137	347	12	68	.976	3.99	-5	-3	0	0	-3
Segura, Jean	Phi	142	141	1213	175	351	20	83	.963	3.90	-6	-4	-1	0	-5
Andrus, Elvis	Tex	146	146	1279	205	379	13	80	.978	4.11	-3	-3	-2	-1	-6
Crawford, J.P.	Sea	93	92	806	110	273	12	46	.970	4.27	-7	-5	0	-1	-6
Newman, Kevin	Pit	104	93	824	124	235	10	43	.973	3.92	-10	-7	1	0	-6
Martin Jr., Richie	Bal	117	89	785	108	224	10	47	.971	3.81	-9	-7	0	-1	-8
Anderson, Tim	CWS	122	122	1050	182	324	26	75	.951	4.34	-16	-12	1	2	-9
Turner, Trea	Was	122	122	1065	130	298	13	57	.971	3.62	-13	-10	-1	1	-10
Rosario, Amed	NYM	152	151	1337	161	370	17	72	.969	3.57	-18	-14	-2	0	-16
Bogaerts, Xander	Bos	153	153	1368	165	347	13	70	.975	3.37	-26	-20	0	-1	-21

Left Fielders - Regulars

Player	Tm	G	GS	Inn	PO	A	E	DP	Pct.	Range	Bases Saved	R/P	GFP/ DME	Throws	Total
Peralta, David	Ari	93	91	806	201	3	2	1	.990	2.28	+17	9	-1	2	.10
Brantley, Michael	Hou	120	110	949	159	2	3	0	.982	1.53	+13	8	1	1	10
Grossman, Robbie	Oak	112	90	844	197	2	0	0	1.000	2.12	+13	6	0	-2	4
Ozuna, Marcell	StL	129	129	1112	181	4	4	0	.979	1.50	+7	1	-1	2	2
Soto, Juan	Was	150	150	1327	273	0	2	0	.993	1.85	+12	7	-1	-5	1
Gordon, Alex	KC	146	145	1260	268	7	1	2	.996	1.96	-4	-2	5	-2	1
Pham, Tommy	TB	123	123	1093	158	8	0	0	1.000	1.37	-11	-4	2	3	1
Schwarber, Kyle	ChC	140	137	1157	214	7	6	0	.974	1.72	-11	-6	0	5	-1
Braun, Ryan	Mil	110	108	879	153	6	5	0	.970	1.63	-5	-3	1	0	-2
Stewart, Christin	Det	89	89	767	133	2	5	1	.964	1.58	-1	0	0	-3	-3
Benintendi, Andrew	Bos	131	128	1131	172	7	2	2	.989	1.42	-16	-7	1	3	-3
Rosario, Eddie	Min	124	118	1048	188	7	5	1	.975	1.67	-22	-11	0	5	-6
Jimenez, Eloy	CWS	114	114	968	190	6	3	1	.985	1.82	-12	-6	-1	-4	-11

Center Fielders - Regulars

Player	Tm	G	GS	Inn	PO	A	E	DP	Pct.	Range	Bases Saved	R/P	GFP/ DME	Throws	Total
Robles, Victor	Was	141	135	1199	317	12	6	2	.982	2.47	+18	11	2	9	22
Cain, Lorenzo	Mil	143	133	1177	306	5	2	1	.994	2.38	+31	16	7	-3	20
Bader, Harrison	StL	122	95	910	239	8	4	4	.984	2.44	+22	12	-1	2	13
Kiermaier, Kevin	TB	125	117	1044	250	6	4	1	.985	2.21	+23	10	1	2	13
Hamilton, Billy	TOT	114	89	826	217	3	0	0	1.000	2.40	+18	9	-1	-1	7
Margot, Manuel	SD	135	98	943	249	2	2	0	.992	2.39	+19	10	1	-5	6
DeShields, Delino	Tex	112	94	861	261	2	5	1	.981	2.75	+14	7	1	-2	6
Acuna Jr., Ronald	Atl	100	95	831	206	3	3	0	.986	2.26	+3	2	-1	0	1

Player	Tm	G	GS	Inn	PO	A	E	DP	Pct.	Range	Bases Saved	Runs Saved R/P	GFP/ DME	Throws	Total
Senzel, Nick	Cin	96	92	800	177	4	4	1	.978	2.04	-6	-2	-1	2	-1
Trout, Mike	LAA	122	121	1052	294	5	4	2	.987	2.56	-7	-3	0	2	-1
Bradley Jr., Jackie	Bos	144	137	1247	303	10	4	3	.987	2.26	-15	-8	4	3	-1
Gardner, Brett	NYY	98	94	820	215	2	1	0	.995	2.38	-5	-2	0	0	-2
Pillar, Kevin	TOT	133	130	1170	296	5	4	1	.987	2.32	0	-2	-1	-2	-5
Almora Jr., Albert	ChC	125	80	765	201	3	3	0	.986	2.40	-13	-5	0	0	-5
Laureano, Ramon	Oak	110	104	944	254	8	7	2	.974	2.50	-28	-15	5	5	-5
Smith, Mallex	Sea	106	99	884	246	1	4	1	.984	2.51	-11	-6	-1	-2	-9
Marte, Starling	Pit	130	128	1141	297	8	5	2	.984	2.41	-23	-11	0	2	-9

Right Fielders - Regulars

Player	Tm	G	GS	Inn	PO	A	E	DP	Pct.	Range	Bases Saved	Runs Saved R/P	GFP/ DME	Throws	Total
Judge, Aaron	NYY	92	90	775	177	7	0	0	1.000	2.14	+22	13	3	3	19
Bellinger, Cody	LAD	115	102	911	198	10	2	1	.990	2.05	+23	12	2	5	19
Betts, Mookie	Bos	132	126	1129	274	8	1	0	.996	2.25	+17	10	0	5	15
Harper, Bryce	Phi	152	152	1318	284	13	5	1	.983	2.03	+15	9	-2	2	9
Reddick, Josh	Hou	119	106	932	202	2	4	1	.981	1.97	+10	5	7	-3	9
Garcia, Avisail	TB	92	89	775	143	5	4	0	.974	1.72	+8	5	-1	-1	3
Conforto, Michael	NYM	132	110	1012	242	7	3	1	.988	2.21	-1	0	-2	3	1
Piscotty, Stephen	Oak	90	90	795	168	2	0	0	1.000	1.92	-1	-1	1	1	1
Puig, Yasiel	TOT	146	143	1224	244	8	6	2	.977	1.85	-14	-7	3	4	0
Calhoun, Kole	LAA	150	146	1299	310	7	6	2	.981	2.20	-1	2	-1	-2	-1
Eaton, Adam	Was	139	137	1165	267	3	6	1	.978	2.09	+1	0	-2	0	-2
Yelich, Christian	Mil	124	121	1061	218	7	4	2	.983	1.91	-2	-1	-2	0	-3
Jones, Adam	Ari	130	117	1037	207	2	6	0	.972	1.81	+8	1	-1	-4	-4
Fowler, Dexter	StL	118	80	761	158	5	4	2	.976	1.93	+5	1	-1	-4	-4
Mazara, Nomar	Tex	101	100	878	192	4	1	0	.995	2.01	-4	-2	-2	0	-4
Markakis, Nick	Atl	103	98	869	174	3	1	0	.994	1.83	-2	-1	-1	-4	-6
Blackmon, Charlie	Col	135	134	1178	232	5	4	1	.983	1.81	-6	-5	-1	-2	-8
Castellanos, Nicholas	TOT	137	136	1171	281	6	2	1	.993	2.21	-8	-4	-2	-3	-9

Catchers - Regulars

Player	Tm	G	GS	Inn	PO	A	E	DP	PB	Pct.	SB Att	CS	Pit CS	CS Pct	Cat ERA	Stk Sav	Runs Saved GFP/ DME	SB	SZ	Other	Total
Perez, Roberto	Cle	118	114	994	1082	52	3	12	0	.997	46	17	3	.37	3.60	91	8	2	11	8	29
Hedges, Austin	SD	95	93	813	858	35	11	3	2	.988	31	7	5	.23	4.14	150	-1	0	18	5	22
Posey, Buster	SF	101	96	846	771	46	2	1	1	.998	65	15	9	.23	4.33	72	3	2	9	0	14
Jansen, Danny	Tor	103	94	853	803	47	4	8	4	.995	60	18	1	.30	4.45	44	0	2	5	5	12
Realmuto, J.T.	Phi	133	130	1139	1098	67	9	14	8	.992	86	37	6	.43	4.62	10	4	10	1	-4	11
Zunino, Mike	TB	89	78	690	764	37	6	7	4	.993	41	14	3	.34	3.61	37	1	2	4	2	9
Wolters, Tony	Col	112	102	904	773	75	1	12	4	.999	64	20	3	.31	5.30	-52	7	4	-6	3	8
Maldonado, Martin	TOT	103	98	849	844	35	6	3	6	.993	37	8	2	.22	4.49	-7	6	1	0	1	8
Gomes, Yan	Was	93	90	787	842	41	4	3	10	.995	53	12	6	.23	4.04	-33	4	2	-4	3	5
Vazquez, Christian	Bos	119	103	918	994	71	1	6	9	.999	54	18	4	.33	4.53	56	-4	2	7	0	5
McCann, James	CWS	106	102	905	884	39	7	8	3	.992	50	13	4	.26	4.50	-20	0	3	-2	4	5
Barnhart, Tucker	Cin	102	87	773	812	46	2	2	5	.998	52	11	1	.21	4.17	19	4	-2	2	0	4
Flowers, Tyler	Atl	83	73	679	676	37	3	3	16	.996	46	8	1	.17	4.31	83	-4	0	10	-2	4
Chirinos, Robinson	Hou	112	106	966	1078	51	6	5	4	.995	57	12	0	.21	3.57	-53	10	0	-6	-1	3
Molina, Yadier	StL	111	108	939	916	30	1	5	4	.999	28	6	2	.21	3.81	4	3	-1	0	0	2
Kelly, Carson	Ari	101	85	786	792	49	8	2	4	.991	36	4	11	.11	4.34	11	4	-2	1	-1	2
McCann, Brian	Atl	83	79	678	640	19	3	3	7	.995	43	7	2	.16	4.18	14	-1	-1	2	1	1
Grandal, Yasmani	Mil	137	124	1096	1169	41	8	11	8	.993	95	22	5	.23	4.62	74	1	-3	9	-6	1
Garver, Mitch	Min	82	73	674	690	29	6	4	8	.992	34	3	3	.09	3.89	5	-2	-3	1	4	0
Contreras, Willson	ChC	99	92	812	770	51	12	3	6	.986	52	13	3	.25	3.96	-31	-1	-1	-4	3	-1
Mathis, Jeff	Tex	86	76	651	686	30	6	2	5	.992	58	8	2	.14	4.10	-30	0	-2	-4	5	-1
Sanchez, Gary	NYY	90	86	743	793	32	15	5	7	.982	47	11	0	.23	4.31	-22	0	2	-3	-1	-2
d'Arnaud, Travis	TOT	85	67	627	702	26	3	4	7	.996	45	10	4	.22	4.19	5	-1	0	1	-3	-3
Alfaro, Jorge	Mia	118	112	973	930	55	11	8	11	.989	47	14	2	.30	5.05	16	-3	2	2	-5	-4
Castro, Jason	Min	78	72	631	637	29	1	3	7	.999	35	6	1	.17	4.50	10	-2	-2	1	-4	-7
Severino, Pedro	Bal	89	80	720	655	29	8	5	10	.988	52	10	3	.19	5.53	-67	-5	1	-8	1	-11
Ramos, Wilson	NYM	124	113	1016	1051	50	7	5	10	.994	109	15	2	.14	4.36	-74	-2	-1	-9	-1	-13
Lucroy, Jonathan	TOT	87	75	669	653	44	5	6	7	.993	67	14	4	.21	5.10	-33	-5	-1	-4	-4	-14
Suzuki, Kurt	Was	75	70	628	666	27	3	2	6	.996	48	3	2	.06	4.57	-44	-3	-5	-5	-1	-14
Phegley, Josh	Oak	106	90	824	704	46	2	3	15	.997	69	19	5	.28	4.05	-42	-5	1	-5	-5	-14
Narvaez, Omar	Sea	98	91	816	712	34	6	3	3	.992	66	8	5	.12	5.25	-70	-5	-3	-8	-4	-20
Diaz, Elias	Pit	96	75	707	694	47	12	6	8	.984	56	14	1	.25	5.99	-76	-2	-1	-9	-11	-23

All Other Fielders

Player	Pos	G	GS	Inn	Pct.	DRS
Acuna Jr., R	LF	46	40	333	1.000	3
	RF	35	19	200	1.000	5
Adames, C	2B	4	3	26	1.000	0
	3B	3	2	20	1.000	0
Adams, M	1B	79	71	610	.991	3
Adduci, J	RF	1	1	8	1.000	0
Adrianza, E	1B	20	12	119	.990	-1
	2B	7	7	59	1.000	2
	3B	24	14	148	.955	1
	SS	24	16	152	.959	-2
	LF	1	0	1	-	0
	RF	6	5	38	.667	-1
Aguilar, J	1B	75	65	578	.993	4
	3B	2	0	3	-	0
Alberto, H	2B	90	67	612	.990	5
	3B	66	58	475	.960	-2
	LF	3	1	7	1.000	-1
	RF	1	1	8	1.000	0
Alfaro, J	1B	1	0	1	-	0
Alford, A	LF	6	3	26	1.000	0
	CF	2	2	18	1.000	-1
	RF	5	0	19	.875	0
Allen, A	1B	2	0	5	1.000	0
Allen, G	LF	60	35	361	.989	7
	CF	18	15	133	1.000	-2
	RF	13	8	77	.923	1
Almonte, A	CF	3	1	13	1.000	-1
	RF	9	6	54	.941	2
Alonso, Y	1B	32	31	260	.991	0
Altherr, A	LF	14	3	47	1.000	1
	CF	16	4	52	1.000	0
	RF	6	1	28	.889	-1
Altuve, J	SS	1	0	2	.000	0
Alvarez, Y	LF	10	9	66	.909	1
Anderson, B	3B	67	64	587	.977	8
	RF	55	55	458	.972	5
Andujar, M	3B	4	4	33	.700	-2
Aquino, A	1B	1	0	0	-	0
	RF	54	53	464	.980	3
Arozarena, R	LF	1	0	3	-	0
	CF	5	4	31	1.000	1
	RF	6	0	10	1.000	0
Arraez, L	2B	49	42	390	.974	-8
	3B	17	15	130	1.000	1
	SS	8	3	35	.938	-1
	LF	21	18	161	1.000	0
Arroyo, C	2B	1	1	7	1.000	0
	3B	13	13	112	.938	1
Arteaga, H	2B	2	2	9	1.000	0
	3B	1	0	1	-	0
	SS	36	31	286	.976	-2
Astudillo, W	1B	15	11	103	1.000	0
	2B	2	1	12	1.000	0
	3B	13	11	98	.920	-2
	LF	3	1	9	-	0
	RF	6	3	29	.889	0
Austin, T	1B	23	15	127	.989	-2
	LF	22	16	127	.962	2
	RF	3	1	10	1.000	0
Avelino, A	SS	1	1	8	1.000	0
	LF	1	1	6	1.000	0
Baez, J	3B	1	1	9	1.000	1
Barnes, A	2B	1	1	5	1.000	0
Barnhart, T	1B	3	0	9	1.000	0
Barreto, F	2B	17	13	124	.935	0
	SS	5	1	23	.889	-1
Bauers, J	1B	31	22	213	.990	0
	LF	53	49	404	.988	-3
Beaty, M	1B	35	21	205	.986	-2
	3B	7	7	58	1.000	0
	LF	34	25	234	1.000	1
	RF	2	1	10	1.000	0
Beckham, G	1B	4	1	12	1.000	0
	2B	39	34	312	.992	0
	3B	5	5	44	.909	-1
	SS	18	16	151	.958	-5
Beckham, T	1B	5	4	36	1.000	-1
	2B	8	8	67	.943	-3
	3B	10	9	77	1.000	0
	SS	41	39	344	.932	-8
	LF	13	12	91	1.000	1
Bellinger, C	1B	36	28	230	.995	4

Player	Pos	G	GS	Inn	Pct.	DRS
	CF	25	21	171	.977	3
Belt, B	LF	14	11	81	.944	-4
	RF	1	0	2	-	0
Benintendi, A	CF	12	6	63	1.000	0
Berti, J	3B	20	15	134	1.000	-3
	SS	32	26	242	.981	1
	LF	7	4	32	1.000	1
	CF	21	15	147	.975	-1
	RF	1	0	4	1.000	0
Betts, M	CF	17	16	144	.980	0
Bichette, B	SS	42	42	362	.959	3
Biggio, C	1B	8	2	33	.974	-1
	2B	85	84	735	.989	-1
	LF	1	1	6	1.000	-1
	RF	8	7	61	1.000	-1
Bird, G	1B	10	10	85	1.000	-1
Bishop, B	LF	4	2	20	1.000	2
	CF	20	14	123	1.000	2
	RF	1	0	2	-	0
Blandino, A	1B	3	1	11	1.000	-1
	2B	10	5	50	.962	1
	3B	4	2	19	1.000	0
Bolt, S	CF	3	1	13	1.000	0
	RF	1	1	9	1.000	1
Bonifacio, J	LF	1	1	8	1.000	0
	RF	4	4	33	1.000	-1
Bote, D	2B	50	28	271	.971	4
	3B	67	46	433	.922	0
	SS	9	1	28	.917	0
	RF	1	0	2	1.000	0
Bour, J	1B	37	35	309	.997	0
Bourjos, P	2B	1	0	2	1.000	1
	LF	12	6	65	1.000	0
	CF	11	5	55	1.000	3
Bradley, B	1B	5	5	37	.951	-1
Bradley Jr., J	RF	3	1	13	1.000	0
Brantley, M	RF	9	8	58	1.000	-2
Braun, R	RF	2	2	14	1.000	0
Bregman, A	SS	65	59	495	.986	-2
Brinson, L	CF	60	54	480	.973	-2
	RF	11	10	76	.952	-1
Brito, S	LF	1	0	1	-	0
	CF	4	3	28	1.000	0
	RF	12	8	73	.895	-1
Brosseau, M	1B	1	0	3	1.000	0
	2B	26	21	165	1.000	-3
	3B	18	11	111	.968	0
	LF	5	0	11	1.000	0
	RF	6	0	22	1.000	0
Brown, S	1B	4	1	18	1.000	0
	LF	23	16	153	1.000	5
Broxton, K	LF	21	1	40	1.000	0
	CF	65	51	453	.981	4
	RF	9	4	35	1.000	-1
Bruce, J	1B	16	15	119	.982	-1
	LF	37	37	296	.986	6
	RF	24	20	185	.976	-4
Bryant, K	3B	3	3	27	1.000	0
	LF	23	10	107	1.000	0
	RF	27	19	167	.943	-2
Butera, D	1B	3	0	6	1.000	0
Buxton, B	CF	86	78	692	.991	10
Cabrera, A	1B	3	2	24	1.000	0
	2B	31	29	248	1.000	2
Cabrera, M	LF	24	21	168	1.000	-4
	RF	74	59	515	.989	-11
Cabrera, M	1B	26	26	219	.995	0
Calhoun, K	CF	2	0	8	1.000	1
Calhoun, W	LF	71	69	610	.991	-7
Camargo, J	1B	1	0	1	-	0
	2B	4	3	26	.950	0
	3B	18	9	104	.862	-2
	SS	25	21	193	.989	-2
	LF	11	8	78	.957	1
	RF	5	5	36	1.000	0
Candelario, J	1B	20	18	165	.993	0
	3B	69	68	610	.967	7
Canha, M	1B	15	11	97	1.000	-1
	LF	10	8	71	1.000	0
	CF	56	55	482	.992	-6
	RF	27	25	224	.984	3
Caratini, V	1B	23	11	129	.990	-1

Player	Pos	G	GS	Inn	Pct.	DRS
	3B	2	0	2	1.000	0
Carpenter, M	1B	4	2	19	1.000	1
Casali, C	1B	4	0	6	1.000	0
Castellanos, N	LF	11	4	36	1.000	0
Castro, H	1B	1	1	9	1.000	0
	2B	34	33	296	.963	-4
	3B	10	9	78	.960	-1
	SS	2	2	17	1.000	0
	LF	8	8	71	1.000	1
	CF	30	29	255	.986	-5
	RF	7	5	49	1.000	2
Castro, S	3B	45	42	367	.963	0
	SS	3	2	18	1.000	0
Castro, W	SS	29	28	253	.963	-4
Cave, J	LF	10	7	68	1.000	2
	CF	23	13	146	1.000	-3
	RF	45	34	289	.959	-1
Cervelli, F	1B	3	1	10	1.000	0
Chang, Y	3B	25	21	173	1.000	1
	SS	8	0	18	1.000	0
Chavis, M	1B	49	43	401	.989	1
	2B	45	40	360	.975	-2
	3B	5	2	23	1.000	0
Choo, S	LF	40	39	328	.976	-13
	RF	42	41	361	.973	-3
Collins, Z	1B	1	1	9	1.000	0
Colon, C	2B	3	0	4	1.000	0
Conforto, M	CF	39	33	268	1.000	-4
Contreras, W	1B	2	1	9	1.000	0
	LF	1	0	0	-	-1
	RF	2	1	10	1.000	0
Cooper, G	1B	73	66	561	.994	2
	RF	31	31	248	1.000	0
Cordell, R	LF	2	1	14	1.000	0
	CF	19	13	127	1.000	2
	RF	72	49	458	.972	-4
Cordero, F	CF	5	3	24	1.000	0
	RF	4	1	16	1.000	0
Correa, C	SS	75	75	642	.993	1
Court, R	1B	7	1	21	1.000	0
	LF	3	2	23	.875	-1
	RF	2	2	15	1.000	0
Cowart, K	2B	3	2	20	1.000	0
	3B	6	4	45	1.000	0
Cozart, Z	2B	1	1	7	1.000	0
	3B	31	23	203	.958	4
	SS	5	3	33	.917	0
Cron, K	1B	12	7	64	.983	0
	3B	1	0	2	-	0
Cuevas, N	LF	1	1	3	-	0
Culberson, C	1B	10	1	35	.969	0
	3B	1	0	1	-	0
	SS	7	6	54	.968	0
	LF	36	3	75	1.000	-1
	RF	11	5	61	1.000	2
Cuthbert, C	1B	46	39	349	.983	0
	3B	40	36	319	.916	-5
Dahl, D	LF	39	37	319	.984	-3
	CF	40	36	301	1.000	-4
	RF	24	19	180	.963	-4
d'Arnaud, T	1B	21	16	147	1.000	-2
Davis, C	RF	1	1	8	.500	0
Davis, J	3B	31	27	220	.931	-9
	LF	79	71	585	.980	-11
Davis, J	RF	15	12	101	1.000	-1
Davis, J	LF	1	0	2	1.000	0
	CF	2	0	8	1.000	-1
Davis, J	LF	1	1	7	1.000	0
	CF	33	22	208	.980	-1
	RF	2	1	10	1.000	0
Davis, K	LF	4	4	24	1.000	1
Davis, R	LF	11	0	20	1.000	0
	RF	3	1	12	1.000	0
Davis, T	1B	1	0	2	1.000	0
Daza, Y	LF	3	3	25	1.000	1
	CF	24	19	155	.956	-2
	RF	3	2	15	1.000	1
Dean, A	1B	5	4	32	1.000	0
	LF	44	37	306	.950	-5
	RF	5	5	50	.938	-2
Delmonico, N	1B	1	0	1	-	0
	LF	21	17	142	.970	-2

Player	Pos	G	GS	Inn	Pct.	DRS
Demeritte, T	RF	47	46	412	.990	-8
Descalso, D	1B	1	0	1	-	0
	2B	45	38	302	.980	-4
	3B	3	0	4	-	0
Desmond, I	LF	44	37	332	.984	0
	CF	74	67	609	.969	-19
Devers, R	SS	1	0	2	-	0
Diaz, A	1B	26	18	162	1.000	-1
	2B	25	16	152	1.000	1
	3B	19	15	140	.967	0
	SS	5	2	22	.818	0
	LF	4	3	23	1.000	0
Diaz, I	2B	48	47	418	.952	1
Diaz, Y	1B	22	17	156	.993	1
	3B	50	45	398	.962	-1
Dickerson, A	LF	50	35	336	1.000	0
	RF	1	1	9	-	0
Dickerson, C	LF	65	62	524	.982	-6
Dietrich, D	1B	21	13	119	.985	1
	2B	58	43	355	.994	1
	3B	1	0	1	-	0
	LF	16	9	71	1.000	-2
Difo, W	2B	2	1	10	1.000	0
	3B	6	4	36	.900	-1
	SS	33	30	279	.990	-6
Dixon, B	1B	61	55	485	.991	-1
	2B	3	2	16	.857	0
	3B	4	4	28	.917	-1
	LF	26	19	192	.949	-3
	CF	1	0	3	-	0
	RF	7	6	56	1.000	0
Dozier, H	1B	7	7	62	1.000	-1
	RF	20	17	157	1.000	-1
Drury, B	1B	12	12	109	1.000	-1
	2B	16	12	114	.981	0
	3B	65	59	528	.975	2
	SS	5	3	35	1.000	1
	LF	8	8	67	1.000	0
	RF	18	15	137	1.000	-4
Dubon, M	2B	22	21	192	.973	0
	SS	10	7	61	.963	-1
Duda, L	1B	19	15	138	1.000	-1
Duffy, M	3B	46	41	369	.933	-2
	SS	1	0	5	-	0
Duggar, S	CF	39	34	308	.969	4
	RF	34	33	292	1.000	0
Duvall, A	LF	31	24	229	.957	1
	RF	2	2	10	1.000	0
Dyson, J	LF	16	12	96	.950	2
	CF	103	61	647	.994	5
	RF	21	18	136	1.000	6
Eaton, A	LF	7	6	56	1.000	0
Edman, T	2B	29	23	204	.991	3
	3B	55	41	382	.972	5
	LF	1	0	4	1.000	0
	CF	1	0	1	-	0
	RF	12	11	78	.947	3
Elmore, J	2B	1	0	1	-	0
	3B	4	2	22	.750	-1
	LF	5	4	41	1.000	1
	RF	3	2	22	1.000	0
Encarnacion, E	1B	57	57	489	.996	-1
	2B	1	0	1	-	0
Engel, A	CF	86	65	608	.982	2
Ervin, P	LF	61	33	314	.981	3
	CF	25	17	163	.980	3
	RF	17	2	43	1.000	0
Escobar, E	2B	33	31	237	1.000	-2
Estrada, T	2B	17	10	105	1.000	-1
	SS	9	4	45	.950	0
	LF	2	2	10	1.000	0
	RF	2	0	4	1.000	-1
Farmer, K	1B	18	6	72	.984	0
	2B	41	14	171	.984	1
	3B	12	6	61	1.000	0
	SS	1	0	1	1.000	0
Fisher, D	LF	38	33	289	.966	1
	CF	3	3	25	1.000	-1
	RF	9	5	40	.833	0
Flaherty, R	2B	2	1	11	1.000	0
	3B	11	5	57	1.000	0
Fletcher, D	2B	42	26	239	.990	1

Player	Pos	G	GS	Inn	Pct.	DRS
	3B	90	74	665	.970	5
	SS	39	27	246	.991	1
	LF	21	18	147	1.000	3
	RF	2	0	8	1.000	0
Flores, W	1B	16	4	57	1.000	-1
	2B	64	56	443	.970	-2
Ford, M	1B	29	24	217	.985	-1
Forsythe, L	1B	46	40	348	.994	-5
	2B	8	8	69	1.000	2
	3B	33	28	245	.930	-1
	SS	15	10	105	.952	0
Fowler, D	CF	58	52	377	.988	4
Fraley, J	CF	11	9	76	.941	-3
	RF	1	1	12	1.000	-1
France, T	1B	1	0	1	1.000	0
	2B	21	17	140	1.000	0
	3B	36	28	259	.970	0
Franco, M	1B	2	1	2	1.000	0
Frazier, C	LF	17	14	132	1.000	-2
	RF	36	31	264	.947	-6
Frazier, T	3B	2	2	15	1.000	0
Freeman, M	2B	33	26	248	.981	5
	3B	18	10	109	.914	-1
	SS	9	8	66	.950	0
	LF	6	3	38	1.000	-1
Freese, D	1B	50	37	294	.993	-1
	3B	2	0	2	-	0
Fuentes, J	1B	11	11	96	1.000	1
	3B	2	0	4	-	0
Gallo, J	LF	34	26	242	.985	3
	CF	38	37	310	.965	1
Galloway, I	LF	4	1	15	1.000	0
	CF	13	10	86	1.000	-2
	RF	2	1	10	1.000	0
Galvis, F	2B	32	27	228	.989	-2
Gamel, B	LF	70	36	396	1.000	4
	CF	22	15	137	1.000	0
	RF	23	15	162	.971	1
Garcia, A	1B	5	4	26	1.000	0
Garcia, A	CF	12	10	94	.966	-1
Garcia, G	1B	1	0	1	1.000	0
	2B	74	57	517	.987	2
	3B	13	12	104	.967	-1
	SS	9	4	41	.952	1
	LF	1	0	3	-	0
Garcia, L	2B	2	2	17	1.000	0
	3B	1	1	7	1.000	0
	SS	19	16	147	.944	2
	LF	24	14	131	.957	1
	CF	80	71	573	.972	-6
	RF	45	30	284	.960	-1
Garcia, R	2B	18	14	118	.927	1
	LF	5	1	16	1.000	-1
	RF	1	0	3	-	0
Gardner, B	LF	45	37	348	1.000	7
Garlick, K	LF	12	9	72	1.000	0
	RF	5	0	10	1.000	0
Garneau, D	1B	1	0	1	-	0
Garver, M	1B	1	0	2	1.000	0
Gennett, S	2B	36	34	275	.993	-1
Gerber, M	LF	5	4	31	1.000	0
	RF	5	1	16	1.000	0
Goins, R	2B	2	2	17	1.000	0
	3B	23	21	201	.962	1
	SS	14	9	88	.950	3
	LF	1	0	2	-	0
	RF	7	4	32	1.000	-3
Gomes, Y	1B	1	0	1	1.000	0
Gomez, C	LF	13	1	29	1.000	1
	CF	22	16	134	.973	-4
	RF	7	6	48	1.000	1
Gonzalez, C	LF	20	17	151	1.000	3
	RF	17	15	121	.960	0
Gonzalez, E	3B	16	10	107	.927	2
	SS	26	23	209	.966	3
	LF	4	4	34	1.000	-1
	CF	1	1	9	-	0
Gonzalez, M	1B	21	19	160	.993	-2
	2B	2	2	18	1.000	0
	3B	40	35	292	.990	4
	SS	1	1	9	1.000	0
	LF	18	13	129	1.000	5

Player	Pos	G	GS	Inn	Pct.	DRS
	RF	44	36	327	.970	2
Goodrum, N	1B	18	17	152	.988	0
	2B	22	22	185	.967	-1
	3B	1	1	9	1.000	0
	SS	38	37	327	.952	3
	LF	20	15	155	.970	-6
	CF	8	6	54	.889	0
	RF	5	5	45	1.000	0
Goodwin, B	LF	68	53	508	.962	-6
	CF	39	32	286	1.000	3
	RF	17	16	132	.977	2
Gordon, D	SS	2	2	13	.900	0
Gore, T	LF	9	6	58	1.000	2
	CF	4	3	27	.909	-1
	RF	10	4	47	1.000	1
Gosselin, P	3B	1	0	2	1.000	0
	SS	5	4	42	.933	-2
	LF	6	3	33	1.000	0
Grandal, Y	1B	20	16	143	.992	-3
Granderson, C	LF	85	66	593	1.000	1
	RF	6	1	18	1.000	0
Green, Z	3B	5	4	36	1.000	0
Gregorius, D	SS	80	78	688	.979	-6
Grichuk, R	CF	62	56	487	.992	2
	RF	92	83	725	.994	-10
Grisham, T	LF	17	9	90	1.000	1
	CF	21	14	136	1.000	1
	RF	16	14	112	1.000	3
Grossman, R	CF	1	1	6	1.000	0
	RF	20	13	126	1.000	0
Guillorme, L	2B	8	2	33	.966	1
	3B	5	1	21	1.000	0
	SS	8	5	49	1.000	1
Gurriel, Y	2B	4	2	25	.875	-3
	3B	42	36	328	.967	-1
Gurriel Jr., L	1B	3	1	10	1.000	0
	2B	9	9	75	.917	-1
	LF	63	60	532	1.000	-2
Gutierrez, K	3B	18	18	161	.963	1
Guzman, R	1B	81	72	648	.991	0
Gyorko, J	1B	8	3	37	1.000	0
	2B	3	2	16	1.000	0
	3B	21	10	110	.949	1
Haggerty, S	2B	1	0	1	-	0
	RF	1	0	4	-	0
Hampson, G	2B	50	40	359	.974	-1
	SS	15	10	101	.976	1
	LF	2	2	13	1.000	0
	CF	31	20	189	.981	-3
Haniger, M	CF	24	21	180	1.000	-2
	RF	43	41	359	.991	4
Hanson, A	1B	2	1	10	1.000	0
	2B	8	6	57	1.000	-1
	LF	1	0	1	-	0
	RF	5	4	35	.909	0
Happ, I	1B	7	3	41	1.000	0
	2B	13	9	83	.970	-1
	3B	8	5	54	.955	2
	LF	15	3	44	1.000	1
	CF	13	7	64	1.000	1
	RF	8	1	18	1.000	0
Harrison, J	2B	34	34	306	1.000	0
Haseley, A	LF	22	15	150	.975	6
	CF	40	36	315	1.000	5
	RF	10	8	76	1.000	2
Hays, A	CF	20	15	153	1.000	-1
Healy, R	1B	11	3	38	1.000	0
	3B	44	43	366	.919	-4
Hechavarria, A	2B	29	20	204	.981	1
	3B	6	6	71	1.000	0
	SS	27	18	182	.949	-2
Hedges, A	3B	2	0	3	-	0
Heineman, S	1B	4	4	36	1.000	0
	LF	6	4	39	1.000	1
	CF	9	9	76	1.000	0
	RF	8	4	43	1.000	0
Heredia, G	LF	14	5	61	1.000	1
	CF	41	35	315	.978	-3
	RF	28	15	158	.972	5
Hermosillo, M	LF	14	8	69	1.000	0
	CF	5	4	42	1.000	1
	RF	2	0	4	1.000	0

Player	Pos	G	GS	Inn	Pct.	DRS
Hernandez, G	LF	6	4	44	1.000	0
	CF	2	2	16	1.000	0
	RF	7	6	60	.923	0
Hernandez, K	1B	2	2	16	1.000	0
	2B	85	63	589	.980	3
	3B	1	1	6	1.000	-1
	SS	11	6	67	1.000	1
	LF	10	5	44	1.000	0
	CF	20	16	135	1.000	4
	RF	17	7	66	1.000	1
Hernandez, M	2B	48	29	293	.991	-2
	SS	2	0	3	1.000	0
Hernandez, T	LF	46	38	356	.966	-1
	CF	79	72	636	1.000	-7
Herrera, O	CF	37	32	287	1.000	-3
Herrera, R	2B	1	0	3	1.000	0
	3B	1	0	1	-	0
	SS	1	1	8	1.000	-1
	LF	13	4	55	1.000	-1
	CF	25	10	110	.958	-2
	RF	15	5	60	1.000	-4
Herrmann, C	LF	3	0	8	-	0
Heyward, J	CF	84	74	603	.980	-4
	RF	105	63	619	.982	7
Hicks, A	CF	58	55	499	.991	-1
Hicks, J	1B	29	26	239	.995	-1
Hilliard, S	LF	5	4	36	1.000	-2
	CF	17	11	111	.971	1
	RF	6	3	35	.923	-1
Hiura, K	2B	81	79	679	.949	-4
Hoerner, N	2B	1	1	9	1.000	0
	SS	17	17	151	.972	-2
	CF	1	1	8	1.000	0
Holt, B	1B	11	3	39	1.000	0
	2B	60	56	469	.991	-2
	3B	4	3	22	1.000	0
	SS	6	3	33	1.000	0
	LF	4	3	23	1.000	0
	RF	6	5	56	.929	-1
Inciarte, E	CF	63	57	491	.993	-1
Jackson, D	LF	1	0	1	-	0
	CF	2	1	7	1.000	0
Jankowski, T	LF	2	0	3	-	0
	CF	5	2	24	1.000	1
	RF	5	0	13	1.000	0
Jay, J	LF	13	12	115	1.000	-4
	RF	33	30	249	.977	-4
Joe, C	LF	5	5	33	1.000	2
Jones, A	CF	1	1	8	1.000	0
Jones, J	CF	85	83	726	.980	-13
Joseph, C	2B	13	10	100	.944	0
	3B	3	2	20	1.000	0
	RF	1	0	4	1.000	0
Joyce, M	LF	4	4	29	.750	-1
	RF	33	30	240	.981	-2
Kang, J	3B	44	29	284	.920	-4
	SS	15	10	82	.952	1
Kelly, C	3B	1	0	1	-	0
Kemp, M	LF	17	15	124	1.000	-3
Kemp, T	2B	43	30	307	.992	2
	LF	20	9	103	1.000	5
	CF	12	9	71	1.000	-1
	RF	3	3	23	1.000	0
Kendrick, H	1B	48	35	336	.997	-1
	2B	23	18	166	.987	1
	3B	15	10	99	1.000	-2
Kepler, M	CF	60	53	459	1.000	3
	RF	84	72	652	1.000	4
Kieboom, C	SS	10	10	90	.900	-7
Kiner-Falefa, I	3B	25	23	212	.973	3
Kingery, S	2B	10	6	66	1.000	0
	3B	41	37	306	.962	8
	SS	18	12	119	.967	2
	LF	10	3	39	1.000	0
	CF	65	57	479	.977	0
	RF	1	0	2	-	0
Kinsler, I	2B	72	63	563	.980	1
Knapp, A	1B	1	0	8	1.000	0
Knizner, A	1B	1	0	1	1.000	0
Kolarek, A	1B	3	0	2	1.000	0
Kramer, K	2B	3	0	5	1.000	0
	LF	7	5	44	1.000	0

Player	Pos	G	GS	Inn	Pct.	DRS
	RF	7	6	50	1.000	-1
La Stella, T	1B	3	0	5	1.000	0
	2B	46	43	346	.972	-6
	3B	30	27	235	.980	-2
Lagares, J	CF	125	67	704	.983	-2
LaMarre, R	CF	12	7	58	1.000	-1
	RF	2	0	3	-	0
Lamb, J	1B	24	19	162	.994	0
	3B	36	34	262	.985	-5
Laureano, R	RF	13	11	97	1.000	4
LeMahieu, D	1B	40	28	262	.992	0
	2B	75	66	580	.993	5
	3B	52	47	400	.963	2
Leon, S	1B	1	0	4	1.000	0
Lewis, K	CF	2	1	12	1.000	0
	RF	17	16	149	.974	-2
Leyba, D	2B	8	2	28	.947	0
	3B	1	0	2	1.000	0
	SS	2	1	9	1.000	0
Lin, T	2B	8	4	40	1.000	0
	SS	2	1	10	1.000	0
	CF	1	1	1	-	0
Locastro, T	LF	34	24	222	.982	-1
	CF	20	10	110	1.000	-1
	RF	25	10	129	1.000	4
Long, S	2B	24	24	210	.981	-5
	3B	1	1	8	.667	-1
	LF	16	14	123	1.000	-4
Lopes, T	2B	3	1	8	.800	0
	LF	33	27	227	.978	3
	RF	3	2	24	1.000	0
Lopez, N	2B	76	71	623	.990	3
	SS	33	29	261	.992	0
Lorenzen, M	LF	8	0	9	1.000	0
	CF	18	6	76	1.000	1
	RF	4	0	4	1.000	0
Lowe, B	1B	5	5	38	1.000	0
	2B	69	60	555	.989	5
	LF	2	2	18	1.000	-3
	RF	5	3	34	1.000	0
Lowe, N	1B	21	19	170	.994	0
	3B	4	1	9	1.000	-1
Lucroy, J	1B	9	0	12	1.000	0
Lugo, D	3B	73	70	631	.976	-6
Luplow, J	LF	34	25	204	1.000	-1
	CF	4	3	24	1.000	0
	RF	42	32	294	1.000	1
Lux, G	2B	22	19	178	.970	1
Machado, M	SS	37	35	299	.973	-2
Mahtook, M	LF	1	0	1	-	0
	CF	7	6	58	.889	1
Maldonado, M	1B	1	0	4	1.000	0
Mancini, T	1B	56	51	449	1.000	-1
	LF	6	5	45	1.000	0
	RF	87	78	674	.994	-8
Marisnick, J	CF	109	73	733	.995	5
Markakis, N	LF	9	9	76	1.000	2
Marrero, D	3B	1	0	2	1.000	0
	SS	2	1	9	1.000	0
Marte, K	2B	83	45	462	.990	-1
	SS	11	5	60	1.000	0
	CF	96	89	688	.994	6
Martin, J	LF	12	7	68	1.000	-1
	CF	3	2	23	.900	-2
Martin, L	CF	65	65	565	.993	-1
Martin, R	3B	7	0	13	1.000	1
Martinez, J	LF	15	13	120	.960	-1
	RF	24	24	211	.959	-6
Martinez, J	LF	7	4	39	1.000	0
	RF	75	68	523	.972	-9
Martini, N	LF	26	22	184	1.000	-2
Maybin, C	LF	46	35	326	.969	-5
	CF	3	2	20	1.000	2
	RF	36	26	242	1.000	3
Mayfield, J	2B	5	4	32	1.000	1
	3B	1	0	1	-	0
	SS	21	12	131	.981	1
McBroom, R	1B	6	5	48	1.000	0
	LF	3	2	21	1.000	-1
	RF	12	12	92	1.000	0
McCutchen, A	LF	52	47	402	.988	3
	CF	15	10	93	.964	-1

Player	Pos	G	GS	Inn	Pct.	DRS
McKinney, B	1B	9	1	24	1.000	0
	LF	29	25	224	.975	-2
	RF	43	37	321	.962	1
McMahon, R	1B	19	14	130	.979	3
	3B	22	10	114	1.000	0
McNeil, J	2B	37	24	245	.981	0
	3B	31	16	154	.977	3
	LF	71	45	371	.964	1
	RF	42	38	300	.965	1
Meadows, A	LF	34	32	288	.983	2
	CF	3	0	13	1.000	0
	RF	57	54	472	.989	-8
Mejia, E	2B	1	0	6	1.000	1
	SS	1	0	1	1.000	0
	CF	7	6	46	1.000	-1
Mejia, F	LF	4	3	19	1.000	0
Mejias-Brean, S	1B	5	2	26	1.000	0
	3B	2	2	16	1.000	2
	SS	3	2	19	.875	1
Mendick, D	2B	3	3	25	1.000	0
	3B	3	2	21	1.000	0
	SS	5	3	32	1.000	0
Mercado, O	LF	24	20	180	.879	-1
	CF	82	77	699	.995	9
	RF	9	7	63	.909	-3
Mercer, J	1B	5	5	44	1.000	0
	2B	8	8	67	1.000	-1
	3B	1	0	1	1.000	0
	SS	59	58	510	.968	-9
Merrifield, W	1B	5	4	30	.968	0
	2B	82	76	670	.979	7
	LF	4	4	34	1.000	1
	CF	17	16	131	.979	1
	RF	61	53	466	.991	-3
Miller, B	2B	13	12	93	.935	2
	3B	19	14	108	.941	-3
	SS	1	0	2	1.000	0
	LF	16	12	102	1.000	3
	RF	1	0	2	-	0
Miller, I	LF	2	1	10	1.000	0
	CF	8	1	27	1.000	1
	RF	2	1	10	1.000	0
Molina, Y	1B	4	0	8	1.000	0
	3B	1	0	1	-	0
Moore, D	1B	5	1	14	1.000	0
	2B	18	10	110	1.000	3
	3B	14	5	61	.857	-2
	SS	31	25	239	.967	-5
	LF	31	16	166	.957	5
	CF	4	3	23	1.000	0
	RF	11	7	63	1.000	-1
Morales, K	1B	33	30	270	.987	0
Moran, C	1B	8	4	46	1.000	0
	2B	11	6	61	1.000	0
	LF	2	2	16	1.000	-1
Moreland, M	1B	85	74	664	.995	0
Moroff, M	2B	10	3	36	1.000	0
	3B	2	1	10	1.000	0
	SS	10	3	39	1.000	-2
Morrison, L	1B	3	2	22	1.000	-1
Moustakas, M	2B	47	40	360	.993	0
Mullins II, C	CF	22	18	164	.983	-1
Muncy, M	1B	65	42	403	.995	3
	2B	70	62	520	.973	5
	3B	35	26	234	.929	5
Munoz, Y	2B	4	3	25	1.000	0
	3B	21	11	105	1.000	1
	SS	17	6	72	.977	2
	LF	11	3	47	1.000	-2
	CF	7	4	36	1.000	-3
	RF	12	2	35	1.000	0
Murphy, D	2B	3	0	5	1.000	0
Murphy, T	LF	1	0	1	1.000	0
Myers, W	1B	7	5	43	1.000	0
	3B	2	0	2	-	0
	LF	98	40	492	.991	0
	CF	66	58	426	.976	-10
	RF	5	3	26	.857	1
Naquin, T	LF	15	14	115	1.000	2
	RF	68	60	535	1.000	6
Narvaez, O	2B	1	0	1	1.000	0
Naylor, J	LF	33	29	230	.936	0

Player	Pos	G	GS	Inn	Pct.	DRS
	RF	31	30	228	.936	-3
Negron, K	2B	3	3	26	1.000	0
	3B	4	1	13	1.000	1
	SS	4	1	15	1.000	0
	LF	6	5	30	1.000	1
	CF	8	4	43	1.000	0
	RF	12	7	64	1.000	1
Neuse, S	2B	20	13	114	1.000	2
	3B	5	2	29	.938	1
Newman, K	2B	23	20	158	1.000	2
	3B	6	3	32	.867	0
	LF	2	0	9	1.000	0
Nimmo, B	LF	38	14	158	1.000	-1
	CF	43	38	285	.987	-2
	RF	6	4	38	1.000	2
Nola, A	1B	59	44	405	1.000	-1
	2B	15	13	114	.984	0
	3B	4	1	15	1.000	0
	LF	1	0	1	-	0
	RF	1	1	5	-	0
Noll, J	1B	2	1	9	.833	-1
	3B	1	1	8	1.000	0
Nottingham, J	1B	1	0	2	-	0
Nunez, E	2B	31	21	205	.973	-3
	3B	8	6	60	.923	-6
	SS	6	1	19	1.000	0
Nunez, R	1B	24	21	179	.983	0
	3B	9	8	64	.947	0
	LF	1	0	1	-	0
O'Brien, P	1B	1	0	2	1.000	0
	LF	4	3	27	1.000	-2
	RF	10	10	79	.909	-2
O'Grady, B	1B	2	1	9	1.000	0
	LF	6	1	23	1.000	0
	CF	11	7	56	1.000	-1
O'Hearn, R	LF	2	0	3	-	0
O'Neill, T	LF	33	26	235	.943	0
	CF	3	3	18	.667	0
	RF	8	1	27	1.000	-1
Ortega, R	LF	20	16	156	1.000	0
	CF	3	1	19	1.000	0
	RF	6	1	21	1.000	0
Osuna, J	1B	31	25	231	.987	2
	3B	19	11	103	1.000	0
	LF	2	2	16	.750	0
	RF	23	20	170	.977	-3
Owings, C	2B	25	20	182	1.000	0
	3B	13	9	87	1.000	1
	SS	10	7	60	.964	1
	LF	2	1	5	-	0
	CF	7	6	59	1.000	1
	RF	6	4	37	1.000	0
Palka, D	1B	1	0	6	1.000	0
	RF	23	21	165	1.000	-4
Parker, J	LF	5	3	34	1.000	1
Parra, G	1B	14	12	105	.990	1
	2B	1	0	1	-	0
	3B	1	0	0	-	0
	LF	24	18	174	.978	1
	CF	12	11	82	1.000	1
	RF	34	18	205	1.000	3
Pearce, S	1B	19	15	130	.972	1
	LF	4	3	35	1.000	0
Pederson, J	1B	20	19	149	.962	-3
	LF	84	59	526	.990	6
	CF	2	0	5	1.000	0
	RF	39	30	259	.981	5
Pedroia, D	2B	4	4	28	1.000	-2
Pence, H	LF	16	16	137	1.000	0
	RF	8	7	56	1.000	-4
Peraza, J	2B	78	50	441	.972	1
	3B	5	1	25	1.000	0
	SS	39	22	226	.975	3
	LF	33	13	135	.955	-1
	CF	5	2	18	1.000	0
Perez, H	1B	5	0	9	1.000	0
	2B	45	28	265	.993	3
	3B	14	7	75	1.000	1
	SS	21	10	120	.946	0
	LF	3	0	4	-	0
	RF	7	4	34	1.000	0
Perez, M	1B	2	0	4	1.000	0

Player	Pos	G	GS	Inn	Pct.	DRS
Peterson, D	1B	1	0	1	1.000	0
	LF	9	7	65	1.000	-3
	CF	2	2	18	1.000	-1
	RF	2	2	16	1.000	0
Peterson, J	2B	5	4	40	1.000	0
	3B	9	7	59	.909	-1
	LF	18	12	116	.974	1
	RF	1	0	2	-	0
Phillips, B	LF	3	1	11	1.000	0
	CF	23	17	161	1.000	4
	RF	3	1	12	1.000	1
Pillar, K	RF	27	24	222	.983	2
Pina, M	3B	1	0	0	-	0
Pinder, C	1B	2	1	13	1.000	-1
	2B	21	12	118	.963	-2
	3B	17	8	97	.938	2
	SS	3	0	7	1.000	0
	LF	46	38	305	1.000	7
	CF	5	1	20	1.000	0
	RF	34	22	214	.981	5
Pirela, J	LF	4	4	28	1.000	1
	RF	3	0	9	-	0
Plawecki, K	1B	1	0	2	1.000	0
Polanco, G	RF	36	35	311	.987	-5
Pollock, A	LF	18	18	145	.962	-1
	CF	62	58	510	.989	-9
Posey, B	1B	4	3	24	1.000	0
Prado, M	1B	40	30	275	1.000	1
	3B	22	16	141	.936	2
Profar, J	1B	1	1	9	1.000	0
	LF	7	5	46	1.000	2
Puello, C	LF	12	12	99	1.000	-1
	CF	20	19	148	.983	6
	RF	10	7	65	1.000	1
Pujols, A	3B	1	0	1	-	0
Quinn, R	CF	34	23	235	.984	-1
Ramirez, H	LF	61	47	416	.991	-1
	CF	27	19	162	1.000	-2
	RF	55	34	341	1.000	-2
Ravelo, R	1B	5	5	43	1.000	1
Realmuto, J	1B	4	2	21	1.000	0
Reddick, J	1B	4	0	6	.800	-1
	LF	29	15	151	1.000	0
	CF	9	5	43	1.000	0
Reed, A	1B	4	4	33	.974	0
Reed, M	LF	2	0	6	-	0
	RF	2	2	13	1.000	-1
Rendon, A	2B	1	0	0	-	0
Renfroe, H	LF	67	65	478	.990	7
	CF	4	1	15	1.000	2
	RF	86	45	505	.992	13
Rengifo, L	SS	12	11	83	.938	1
Reyes, F	RF	86	86	661	.971	-11
Reyes, P	2B	7	3	34	.875	0
	3B	2	1	10	.857	0
	SS	2	0	6	1.000	-1
	LF	19	12	107	1.000	1
	CF	11	5	68	1.000	0
	RF	19	7	75	1.000	-5
Reyes, V	LF	21	20	175	1.000	2
	CF	37	35	320	.989	1
	RF	9	8	71	1.000	-1
Reynolds, B	LF	79	68	626	.978	1
	CF	25	25	188	1.000	0
	RF	31	29	241	.983	2
Reynolds, M	1B	32	29	234	.996	1
Rickard, J	LF	26	17	151	.976	2
	CF	16	14	116	.974	2
	RF	25	14	134	1.000	-2
Riddle, J	SS	12	7	71	.917	0
	CF	31	26	235	1.000	0
Riley, A	1B	6	3	41	.972	0
	3B	5	4	38	1.000	0
	LF	58	58	475	.957	4
	RF	2	2	14	1.000	0
Rios, E	1B	12	5	59	1.000	0
	3B	5	2	22	.833	-1
	LF	1	0	1	-	0
Rivera, Y	1B	4	2	28	1.000	0
	2B	2	0	3	1.000	0
	3B	8	5	45	.923	0
	SS	8	3	36	.833	-1

Player	Pos	G	GS	Inn	Pct.	DRS
	CF	1	1	9	1.000	0
	RF	3	1	14	1.000	-1
Robertson, D	2B	26	21	162	.975	2
	3B	43	28	284	.976	1
	SS	16	9	85	.943	-1
Robinson, D	CF	1	0	4	1.000	0
	RF	1	0	1	1.000	0
Robles, V	RF	15	12	110	1.000	2
Rodgers, B	2B	16	13	113	.952	0
	SS	9	5	56	.923	-3
Rodriguez, R	1B	13	12	107	1.000	1
	2B	31	28	252	.983	0
	3B	6	4	32	.833	-3
	SS	20	20	175	.948	-2
	LF	1	1	8	1.000	0
Rodriguez, S	1B	2	0	2	1.000	0
	2B	3	1	11	1.000	0
	3B	24	12	113	1.000	-1
	SS	11	5	78	1.000	2
	LF	8	5	41	1.000	-1
	CF	2	1	12	1.000	0
	RF	4	0	10	1.000	0
Rojas, J	2B	1	0	2	1.000	0
	LF	33	30	276	1.000	2
	RF	6	5	49	1.000	2
Rojas, M	1B	6	1	14	1.000	0
	2B	3	0	6	1.000	0
Rondon, J	1B	1	1	3	1.000	0
	2B	18	14	114	.982	-3
	3B	13	9	90	.964	0
	SS	15	11	96	.951	-2
	LF	2	1	12	1.000	0
Rosario, A	LF	1	0	3	1.000	0
Rosario, E	CF	3	1	9	1.000	0
	RF	11	10	89	1.000	-1
Ruiz, R	1B	12	4	42	1.000	0
	2B	1	0	1	1.000	0
Russell, A	2B	63	39	382	.995	-1
	SS	21	16	144	.924	2
Saladino, T	2B	3	1	12	1.000	1
	3B	6	3	31	1.000	0
	SS	13	9	76	.977	0
	LF	7	3	32	1.000	1
Sanchez, A	1B	1	1	8	1.000	0
	2B	4	0	6	1.000	0
	3B	6	0	12	.857	0
	SS	2	0	5	1.000	0
	LF	1	0	2	-	0
Sandoval, P	1B	23	15	134	.991	2
	3B	45	36	338	.953	-2
Sano, M	1B	9	8	66	.956	-1
Santana, D	1B	44	42	370	.985	1
	2B	17	15	134	.955	2
	3B	8	8	65	.913	1
	SS	9	6	54	.917	-2
	LF	16	8	83	.933	0
	CF	27	22	192	.965	-3
	RF	15	10	100	1.000	0
Santana, D	LF	59	57	510	.920	-10
	RF	42	41	355	.966	-7
Santander, A	LF	40	32	287	1.000	-1
	CF	24	20	156	1.000	-4
	RF	50	37	350	.974	4
Schebler, S	LF	3	0	4	1.000	0
	CF	24	22	193	.982	1
	RF	1	0	2	1.000	0
Schwindel, F	1B	5	4	32	.968	0
Senzel, N	2B	1	0	1	1.000	0
Shaw, C	1B	4	1	12	1.000	0
Shaw, T	1B	6	2	21	1.000	1
	2B	2	0	3	-	0
	3B	71	56	513	.979	3
Shuck, J	LF	7	5	49	1.000	0
	CF	3	1	11	1.000	-1
	RF	10	4	52	1.000	0
Sierra, M	CF	9	8	66	1.000	3
	RF	5	2	21	1.000	-1
Sisco, C	1B	1	0	1	-	0
Skole, M	1B	9	9	78	1.000	-1
Slater, A	1B	8	5	35	1.000	0
	2B	1	0	3	1.000	0
	LF	2	2	16	1.000	0

All Other Fielders

Player	Pos	G	GS	Inn	Pct.	DRS
	RF	46	34	332	.976	1
Smith, D	1B	36	8	118	1.000	1
	LF	32	27	219	.940	-2
	RF	1	0	4	-	-1
Smith, M	LF	5	2	22	1.000	0
	RF	28	23	205	.984	-3
Smith Jr., D	LF	86	82	696	.969	-12
Sogard, E	2B	74	62	572	.979	-4
	3B	6	4	44	1.000	0
	SS	4	3	29	.909	0
	LF	1	1	8	-	0
	RF	6	5	49	1.000	1
Solak, N	2B	5	5	47	1.000	-1
	3B	11	11	97	.889	-3
Solano, D	2B	36	27	251	1.000	2
	3B	2	1	12	1.000	0
	SS	19	14	144	.970	-1
Solarte, Y	2B	10	9	78	1.000	0
	3B	2	0	5	1.000	0
	SS	4	3	24	.900	1
	LF	9	4	43	1.000	1
Soler, J	RF	56	54	447	.971	-8
Sosa, E	2B	4	1	11	1.000	-1
Spangenberg, C	2B	22	14	141	.983	2
	3B	6	3	39	1.000	1
	SS	4	4	21	1.000	0
	LF	3	3	28	1.000	0
Springer, G	CF	75	67	540	1.000	6
	RF	59	39	375	.977	5
Stamets, E	SS	15	14	118	.950	1
Stanton, G	LF	10	10	69	1.000	-1
	RF	3	3	26	.857	0
Starling, B	LF	6	2	26	1.000	-2
	CF	36	34	284	1.000	0
	RF	23	13	134	.968	0
Stassi, M	1B	3	0	5	1.000	0
Stevenson, A	LF	5	3	25	1.000	0
Stewart, D	LF	11	9	72	.909	-1
	RF	26	24	204	.977	-3
Straw, M	2B	4	1	15	1.000	0
	SS	26	14	170	1.000	1
	LF	8	3	35	1.000	2
	CF	11	8	76	1.000	1
	RF	2	1	10	1.000	0
Stubbs, G	LF	7	0	18	1.000	1
	RF	1	0	1	-	0
Sucre, J	1B	1	0	2	1.000	0
Suzuki, I	RF	2	2	10	1.000	1
Swihart, B	1B	2	0	3	1.000	0
	LF	11	5	67	1.000	-3
	RF	9	6	59	1.000	0
Tapia, R	LF	91	78	721	.973	-6
	CF	13	9	84	1.000	1
	RF	6	4	41	1.000	1
Tatis Jr., F	SS	83	82	731	.944	-2
Tauchman, M	LF	59	55	473	1.000	10
	CF	14	11	100	1.000	2
	RF	19	11	122	.970	4
Taylor, C	2B	20	13	119	1.000	0
	3B	6	4	41	.917	1
	SS	39	30	281	.919	-1
	LF	56	30	283	1.000	5
	CF	20	11	111	1.000	1
	RF	3	3	16	.667	0
Taylor, M	CF	25	16	158	.969	0
	RF	7	3	31	1.000	0
Taylor, T	CF	3	0	8	1.000	0
	RF	8	0	16	1.000	0
Tejada, R	2B	2	1	10	1.000	-1
	3B	2	1	8	1.000	0
	SS	2	0	6	1.000	0
Tellez, R	1B	57	57	483	.996	-1
Thaiss, M	1B	13	8	81	1.000	3
	3B	43	31	268	.909	2
Thames, E	RF	12	6	61	1.000	-1
Thomas, L	LF	2	0	4	-	0
	CF	19	4	68	1.000	1
	RF	5	0	10	1.000	0
Tilson, C	LF	19	2	29	1.000	0
	CF	14	12	104	.972	2
	RF	30	27	225	.967	-7
Toro, A	1B	1	0	3	1.000	0

All Other Fielders

Player	Pos	G	GS	Inn	Pct.	DRS
	3B	24	20	187	.962	2
Torres, G	2B	65	64	547	.967	-7
	SS	77	73	660	.961	1
Torreyes, R	2B	1	0	1	1.000	0
	3B	1	1	2	1.000	0
	SS	6	3	34	.933	-3
	LF	1	0	1	-	0
Tovar, W	SS	31	23	207	.989	1
Travis, S	1B	29	20	169	.981	-2
	LF	18	11	112	.964	-1
	RF	1	0	2	1.000	0
Tucker, C	SS	45	36	319	.986	-1
Tucker, K	1B	4	0	14	.929	0
	LF	11	7	66	1.000	0
	RF	11	5	58	1.000	4
Tulowitzki, T	SS	4	4	30	1.000	-1
Turner, J	2B	1	0	1	-	0
Upton, J	LF	56	55	461	.957	-13
Urena, R	2B	9	7	59	1.000	-1
	3B	6	4	35	.917	-1
	SS	13	10	98	.971	0
	LF	1	0	3	1.000	0
Urias, L	2B	26	25	212	.989	4
	3B	1	1	8	1.000	0
	SS	41	39	342	.927	0
Urshela, G	1B	1	0	5	1.000	0
	LF	1	0	1	1.000	0
Valaika, P	1B	1	0	10	1.000	0
	2B	13	11	99	1.000	-1
	3B	3	1	10	1.000	0
	SS	7	3	34	.941	0
Valera, B	2B	14	9	95	1.000	-2
	3B	1	1	9	1.000	0
	SS	2	2	18	1.000	0
VanMeter, J	1B	17	9	80	.985	-1
	2B	18	9	83	1.000	1
	3B	6	2	24	1.000	1
	LF	47	32	270	.951	0
	RF	2	1	7	1.000	0
Vargas, I	2B	48	28	293	.993	1
	3B	14	6	61	.929	-2
	SS	4	1	15	1.000	1
	LF	1	0	4	1.000	0
	RF	1	0	1	-	0
Vazquez, C	1B	10	7	63	.982	0
	2B	2	1	11	1.000	0
	3B	4	0	11	1.000	0
Velasquez, V	LF	1	0	2	1.000	2
Velazquez, A	2B	5	4	37	1.000	1
	3B	4	1	13	.833	0
	LF	1	0	1	-	0
	CF	2	0	4	-	0
Verdugo, A	LF	22	14	128	.957	6
	CF	61	52	476	1.000	3
	RF	25	16	152	.977	4
Villar, J	2B	111	85	733	.978	-11
	SS	97	73	658	.957	0
Vogelbach, D	1B	57	49	422	.995	-4
Vogt, S	1B	1	0	4	1.000	0
	LF	7	5	44	1.000	1
Voit, L	1B	83	81	706	.989	-6
Votto, J	LF	1	0	0	-	0
Wade, T	2B	18	13	122	.985	3
	3B	5	2	32	1.000	0
	SS	4	3	20	1.000	0
	LF	14	9	84	1.000	-2
	CF	2	0	4	1.000	-1
	RF	2	1	10	1.000	0
Wade Jr., L	1B	1	1	9	1.000	-1
	LF	8	4	36	1.000	1
	CF	14	9	72	1.000	-1
	RF	6	1	26	1.000	-1
Walker, N	1B	69	59	532	.996	0
	2B	1	0	1	-	0
	3B	26	20	169	.974	0
Walsh, J	1B	24	21	180	1.000	0
Walton, D	2B	2	1	10	1.000	1
	SS	5	4	37	1.000	-1
Ward, T	3B	4	3	25	.667	-4
	LF	9	7	60	1.000	-2
Wendle, J	2B	48	34	346	1.000	3
	3B	27	22	178	.945	2

All Other Fielders

Player	Pos	G	GS	Inn	Pct.	DRS
	SS	10	8	70	1.000	0
	RF	1	0	1	-	0
White, T	1B	56	45	428	.997	1
Wilkerson, S	2B	12	6	56	.967	-3
	LF	29	15	161	1.000	0
	CF	72	58	524	.993	-5
	RF	10	7	63	.941	-1
Williams, M	LF	2	1	13	1.000	0
	CF	7	7	57	.923	-1
	RF	1	0	2	1.000	0
Williams, N	LF	23	13	144	1.000	-1
	RF	5	2	26	1.000	0
Williamson, M	LF	36	34	308	.972	3
	RF	2	1	10	1.000	2
Winker, J	LF	72	59	487	.971	0
	CF	21	16	132	1.000	-3
	RF	18	11	101	1.000	0
Wisdom, P	1B	5	4	36	.962	0
	3B	4	2	26	1.000	0
Wolters, T	2B	8	0	13	1.000	0
	3B	1	0	1	1.000	0
Wong, Kean	2B	3	2	23	1.000	-1
	RF	2	1	12	1.000	0
Yastrzemski, M	LF	61	42	401	.967	0
	CF	7	2	30	1.000	1
	RF	56	45	390	.990	7
Yelich, C	LF	6	3	31	1.000	1
	CF	1	0	1	1.000	0
Zagunis, M	LF	2	2	13	.750	-2
	RF	6	4	34	1.000	0
Zimmer, B	CF	2	2	13	1.000	1
	RF	4	0	9	-	-1
Zimmerman, R	1B	44	40	346	.991	-1
Zobrist, B	2B	32	23	186	.968	-1
	SS	1	0	2	-	0
	LF	6	2	27	1.000	0
	RF	13	12	86	1.000	1

All Other Catchers

Player	Tm	G	GS	Inn	PO	A	E	DP	PB	Pct.	SB Att	CS	Pit CS	CS Pct	Cat ERA	Stk Sav	GFP/ DME	SB	SZ	Other	Total
Allen, Austin	SD	19	14	128	126	10	1	0	3	.993	9	1	0	.11	6.75	-4	0	0	0	0	0
Astudillo, Willians	Min	21	17	158	159	10	0	2	0	1.000	14	3	0	.21	4.15	-6	-1	0	-1	0	-2
Avila, Alex	Ari	54	49	431	384	29	2	2	2	.995	20	10	1	.50	4.11	4	3	4	0	0	7
Barnes, Austin	LAD	64	61	525	554	12	6	1	2	.990	21	3	2	.14	3.52	38	2	0	5	-1	6
Baron, Steven	Pit	5	2	18	12	0	2	0	0	.857	2	0	0	.00	4.08	0	0	0	0	0	0
Barrera, Tres	Was	1	0	2	0	0	0	0	0	-	0	0	0	-	0.00	0	0	0	0	0	0
Bemboom, Anthony	TOT	25	17	154	162	7	0	0	4	1.000	11	4	2	.36	4.67	6	-1	1	1	0	1
Butera, Drew	Col	14	13	110	99	6	0	0	0	1.000	5	1	1	.20	5.42	-7	1	0	-1	0	0
Caratini, Victor	ChC	59	48	426	460	22	2	1	3	.996	33	4	2	.12	4.48	16	0	0	2	-2	0
Casali, Curt	Cin	67	57	504	572	31	3	4	3	.995	43	9	2	.21	3.73	15	3	0	2	2	7
Castillo, Welington	CWS	48	46	395	354	19	4	4	9	.989	37	7	0	.19	5.63	-61	-1	-1	-7	-1	-10
Castillo, Wilkin	Mia	2	2	18	20	0	0	0	0	1.000	0	0	0	-	4.50	1	0	0	0	-1	-1
Centeno, Juan	Bos	5	3	34	25	5	0	1	2	1.000	5	1	0	.20	4.50	-6	0	0	-1	0	-1
Cervelli, Francisco	TOT	41	38	308	315	18	3	4	6	.991	23	6	2	.26	4.21	3	-1	1	0	2	2
Ciuffo, Nick	TB	3	1	16	21	1	0	0	2	1.000	2	1	0	.50	2.81	0	0	0	0	0	0
Collins, Zack	CWS	10	10	89	75	1	0	0	1	1.000	8	0	1	.00	6.04	-17	-1	-1	-2	0	-4
Davis, Taylor	ChC	6	4	41	53	2	0	0	1	1.000	11	0	0	.00	2.83	1	0	-1	0	0	-1
Dini, Nick	KC	20	17	150	112	12	1	1	1	.992	9	3	1	.33	6.96	-14	-1	1	-2	0	-2
Farmer, Kyle	Cin	15	9	82	78	3	1	0	0	.988	7	1	1	.14	6.72	-1	1	-1	0	0	0
Federowicz, Tim	Tex	29	23	208	203	4	4	0	1	.981	13	3	1	.23	6.74	7	0	0	1	-1	0
Freitas, David	TOT	1	1	9	8	0	0	0	0	1.000	2	0	0	.00	3.00	0	0	0	0	0	0
Gale, Rocky	LAD	4	4	32	37	2	1	0	0	.975	3	1	0	.33	4.50	-1	0	0	0	0	0
Gallagher, Cam	KC	44	36	325	292	8	1	2	1	.997	25	5	0	.20	5.32	16	1	-1	2	-1	1
Garcia, Aramis	SF	11	8	80	90	6	0	2	0	1.000	3	1	0	.33	4.86	9	-1	0	1	0	0
Garneau, Dustin	TOT	34	27	244	239	16	1	0	1	.996	20	5	2	.25	4.24	-3	0	1	0	1	2
Graterol, Juan	Cin	5	5	37	46	1	0	1	1	1.000	2	0	0	.00	5.06	-4	0	0	0	0	0
Greiner, Grayson	Det	58	57	509	478	23	5	2	4	.990	45	7	6	.16	5.09	10	0	-3	1	1	-1
Grullon, Deivy	Phi	2	2	17	21	0	0	0	0	1.000	0	0	0	-	3.71	-2	0	0	0	0	0
Haase, Eric	Cle	8	2	26	27	2	0	0	1	1.000	1	1	0	1.00	7.62	-2	-1	1	0	0	0
Heineman, Tyler	Mia	2	2	23	26	1	0	0	0	1.000	2	1	0	.50	2.31	-1	0	0	0	0	0
Herrmann, Chris	Oak	25	23	201	187	4	2	0	1	.990	7	1	5	.14	3.72	-12	0	-1	-1	0	-2
Hicks, John	Det	60	55	494	477	36	0	3	3	1.000	49	12	4	.24	5.44	-39	0	1	-5	-1	-5
Higashioka, Kyle	NYY	18	14	137	146	8	0	2	0	1.000	15	3	0	.20	4.14	14	0	0	2	0	2
Holaday, Bryan	Mia	38	34	311	288	16	1	2	1	.997	24	4	1	.17	4.37	-36	0	-2	-4	-1	-7
Hundley, Nick	Oak	30	23	195	167	12	0	1	0	1.000	22	4	1	.18	4.98	-9	-1	0	-1	0	-2
Iannetta, Chris	Col	45	37	339	300	16	3	1	2	.991	21	2	2	.10	6.48	-38	-1	-1	-4	-1	-7
Jackson, Alex	Atl	4	4	36	26	3	0	0	0	1.000	0	0	0	-	4.00	0	0	0	0	0	0
Joseph, Caleb	Ari	16	11	97	87	6	1	2	0	.989	5	3	0	.60	4.81	1	0	1	0	0	1
Kiner-Falefa, Isiah	Tex	38	31	281	243	11	1	0	4	.996	15	3	2	.20	5.64	-32	-3	-1	-4	0	-8
Knapp, Andrew	Phi	43	30	297	311	27	3	4	3	.991	23	6	1	.26	4.24	-9	-1	0	-1	1	-1
Knizner, Andrew	StL	16	13	118	121	6	1	3	0	.992	3	2	1	.67	4.96	-25	0	1	-3	0	-2
Kratz, Erik	TOT	17	13	130	141	12	4	1	4	.975	11	3	0	.27	3.12	5	-1	0	0	0	-1
Lavarnway, Ryan	Cin	5	4	42	46	3	1	1	1	.980	6	1	0	.17	4.10	3	0	0	0	0	0
Leon, Sandy	Bos	65	50	465	535	30	3	0	4	.995	32	6	1	.19	4.88	23	-1	-1	3	-1	0
Maile, Luke	Tor	44	41	345	316	28	4	3	4	.989	25	7	5	.28	5.73	20	1	1	2	-1	3
Martin, Russell	LAD	60	52	486	512	29	2	0	7	.996	26	3	2	.12	2.93	16	-1	-1	2	2	2
McGuire, Reese	Tor	30	26	236	226	16	2	1	1	.992	18	4	1	.22	4.61	22	-1	0	3	1	3
Mejia, Francisco	SD	60	52	463	459	24	2	1	1	.996	29	4	1	.14	4.80	18	1	0	2	-3	0
Murphy, John Ryan	TOT	19	17	153	153	9	0	1	0	1.000	4	1	1	.25	3.76	5	2	0	1	0	3
Murphy, Sean	Oak	18	13	131	151	4	1	0	2	.994	6	2	0	.33	2.76	-8	-1	1	-1	0	-1
Murphy, Tom	Sea	67	66	576	499	23	4	3	3	.992	32	12	1	.38	4.70	18	-1	4	2	1	6
Nido, Tomas	NYM	48	38	342	377	12	3	2	2	.992	37	3	0	.08	3.79	5	0	-1	1	1	1
Nola, Austin	Sea	7	4	39	34	2	0	0	1	1.000	3	0	0	.00	4.42	0	0	0	0	0	0
Nottingham, Jacob	Mil	6	0	10	13	0	1	0	0	.929	0	0	0	-	0.00	0	0	0	0	-1	-1
Nunez, Dom	Col	14	10	96	82	7	0	1	2	1.000	9	1	0	.11	5.16	4	1	-1	0	0	0
Perez, Michael	TB	20	15	132	130	12	1	3	0	.993	17	2	2	.12	3.61	6	2	-1	1	0	2
Pina, Manny	Mil	53	38	354	350	15	6	1	2	.984	27	6	1	.22	3.87	29	1	-1	3	3	6
Plawecki, Kevin	Cle	57	46	418	418	19	2	2	1	.995	30	6	1	.20	4.03	37	0	-2	4	-1	1
Read, Raudy	Was	4	2	22	20	1	0	0	0	1.000	1	1	0	1.00	4.91	-4	0	-1	0	0	-1
Rivera, Rene	NYM	8	6	55	65	1	0	0	1	1.000	7	0	0	.00	2.62	-1	-1	0	0	0	-2
Rogers, Jake	Det	34	34	302	287	13	1	0	9	.997	15	4	3	.27	4.98	-1	-1	1	0	2	2
Romine, Austin	NYY	70	62	563	610	26	2	4	6	.997	29	6	4	.21	4.35	5	1	0	1	-1	1
Schwarber, Kyle	ChC	1	0	1	1	0	0	0	0	1.000	0	0	0	-	0.00	0	0	0	0	0	0
Sisco, Chance	Bal	52	45	394	332	9	6	0	1	.983	28	3	2	.11	6.19	-37	-1	-2	-4	-3	-10
Smith, Kevan	LAA	59	46	430	392	22	2	0	1	.995	32	2	3	.06	4.77	-33	-1	-2	-4	1	-6
Smith, Will	LAD	46	45	403	436	20	0	1	2	1.000	25	5	1	.20	3.71	29	1	0	3	-1	3
Stallings, Jacob	Pit	81	53	463	510	24	5	1	4	.991	19	7	1	.37	4.43	28	3	2	5	3	13
Stassi, Max	TOT	46	44	352	370	20	2	3	3	.995	29	4	2	.14	5.09	48	0	-2	6	-1	3
Stubbs, Garrett	Hou	11	6	68	75	3	1	0	0	.987	4	1	0	.25	4.61	-8	-1	0	-1	0	-2
Sucre, Jesus	Bal	18	17	147	111	5	1	4	3	.991	7	3	1	.43	5.94	-18	0	1	-2	0	-1
Swihart, Blake	TOT	8	6	54	55	2	3	0	0	.950	5	1	0	.20	6.17	-6	0	0	-1	0	-1
Taylor, Beau	TOT	10	9	75	68	3	0	0	1	1.000	3	1	2	.33	3.48	3	-2	0	0	0	-2
Torrens, Luis	SD	4	3	28	32	1	0	0	0	1.000	1	0	0	.00	6.43	-1	0	0	0	0	0
Trevino, Jose	Tex	40	32	298	259	13	1	1	1	.996	15	6	1	.40	5.56	0	0	1	0	-1	0
Viloria, Meibrys	KC	41	39	345	294	21	1	2	3	.997	21	8	1	.38	4.85	-22	0	1	-3	1	-1
Vogt, Stephen	SF	60	49	415	415	24	1	0	4	.998	34	5	1	.15	4.55	-10	-1	-3	-1	0	-5
Wallach, Chad	Mia	14	12	119	132	7	1	1	1	.993	5	2	0	.40	3.63	6	-1	0	1	0	0
Wieters, Matt	StL	54	41	387	379	15	2	5	2	.995	19	8	0	.42	3.49	-43	0	2	-5	1	-2
Wilson, Bobby	Det	15	15	128	125	6	0	0	0	1.000	12	1	0	.08	5.85	7	1	-1	1	0	1
Wynns, Austin	Bal	25	20	182	173	12	3	1	2	.984	14	3	0	.21	4.90	-6	0	0	-1	0	0
Zavala, Seby	CWS	3	3	23	22	3	1	0	0	.962	2	1	0	.50	3.91	1	0	0	0	0	0

Runs Saved Multi-Year Summary

John Shirley

Traditionally, baseball statistics valued great hitting and pitching performances, while fielding was a distant afterthought. Runs scored were credited to hitters with statistics such as RBIs, and runs allowed were credited to pitchers with statistics such as ERA. Here at Baseball Info Solutions our premier metric Defensive Runs Saved gives fielding the credit it deserves.

Defensive Runs Saved uses all of our in-depth charting data to estimate how many runs each player saves or costs his team relative to the average player at his position. The next few pages will show you how each player's defensive performance has been trending over the past six seasons.

You will find consistent defensive savants such as Mookie Betts, Kevin Kiermaier, and Andrelton Simmons, who have each saved 10+ runs in every season since 2015. Of these three, Betts saved the most runs this season with 15. But, Kiermaier (13) and Simmons (14) weren't far behind.

You will also find breakout defensive stars such as Nationals center fielder Victor Robles and Indians catcher Roberto Perez. In his first full major league season, Robles was outstanding in the field. He saved 24 runs, the most for any outfielder. Perez had teased his defensive skills as a backup, saving 7, 8, 14, and 4 runs over the last four seasons respectively. This season he played full time and rewarded the Indians' faith in him with an MLB-leading 29 Defensive Runs Saved.

A player must have over 2,500 innings played over the past six seasons or 700 innings in the most recent season at his primary position in order to qualify for this list, and he must have played in the field in multiple seasons. A secondary position is listed if the player has played at a second position over 1,000 innings over six seasons (or 200 innings in the most recent season).

Defensive Runs Saved By Season

Player	YOB	Pos 1	Pos 2	<15	15	16	17	18	19
Abreu, Jose	1987	1B		-10	1	-5	0	-4	-4
Acuna Jr., Ronald	1997	CF	LF					4	9
Adames, Willy	1995	SS						1	13
Adams, Matt	1988	1B		7	5	1	-4	0	3
Ahmed, Nick	1990	SS		2	19	13	3	21	18
Albies, Ozzie	1997	2B					1	8	8
Alfaro, Jorge	1993	C				-1	-5	0	-4
Almora Jr., Albert	1994	CF				3	-2	9	-5
Alonso, Yonder	1987	1B		13	9	-5	-9	4	0
Altuve, Jose	1990	2B		-26	3	-2	3	1	-2
Anderson, Tim	1993	SS				6	-8	0	-9
Andrus, Elvis	1988	SS		18	-1	-3	3	5	-6
Arcia, Orlando	1994	SS				-1	6	4	3
Arenado, Nolan	1991	3B		46	18	20	20	5	8
Avila, Alex	1987	C		0	-7	-1	-4	6	7
Bader, Harrison	1994	CF					3	19	13
Baez, Javier	1992	SS	2B	-4	3	16	5	10	16
Barnhart, Tucker	1991	C		2	-3	-3	11	-7	4
Bell, Josh	1992	1B				-8	6	-9	-5
Bellinger, Cody	1995	RF	1B				7	8	26
Belt, Brandon	1988	1B		14	6	10	10	13	0
Benintendi, Andrew	1994	LF				-1	7	-3	-3
Betts, Mookie	1992	RF	CF	4	10	32	31	20	15
Blackmon, Charlie	1986	CF	RF	-1	-7	-2	-5	-28	-8
Bogaerts, Xander	1992	SS		-17	-1	-10	-11	-19	-21
Bour, Justin	1988	1B		0	-7	0	-2	-3	0
Bradley Jr., Jackie	1990	CF		12	8	11	10	0	-1
Brantley, Michael	1987	LF		-6	-2	1	4	-3	8
Braun, Ryan	1983	LF	RF	-17	-1	6	-5	3	-2
Bregman, Alex	1994	3B	SS			4	-5	-7	5
Bruce, Jay	1987	RF	LF	30	5	-11	6	-4	1
Bryant, Kris	1992	3B			4	10	2	-4	-9
Buxton, Byron	1993	CF			4	3	24	2	10
Cabrera, Asdrubal	1985	SS	3B	-26	-8	-7	-13	-23	-2
Cabrera, Melky	1984	LF	RF	-10	-2	-5	-20	-7	-15
Cabrera, Miguel	1983	1B		-78	4	-6	-8	-2	0
Cain, Lorenzo	1986	CF		58	18	11	5	20	20
Calhoun, Kole	1987	RF		-5	6	2	2	7	0
Cano, Robinson	1982	2B		26	-9	11	0	1	-6
Carpenter, Matt	1985	3B	1B	-8	-10	-5	2	4	1
Castellanos, Nicholas	1992	3B	RF	-31	-9	-11	-21	-19	-9
Castillo, Welington	1987	C		-10	-9	2	-9	-6	-10
Castro, Jason	1987	C		-11	11	4	10	2	-7
Castro, Starlin	1990	2B	3B	-23	-2	-8	-6	0	-2
Cervelli, Francisco	1986	C		10	8	6	-6	-7	2
Chapman, Matt	1993	3B					19	29	18
Chirinos, Robinson	1984	C		-1	0	-1	2	-11	3
Choi, Ji-Man	1991	1B				0	0	0	-1
Choo, Shin-Soo	1982	RF	LF	-20	-11	-4	-6	-5	-16
Conforto, Michael	1993	RF	LF		9	1	-2	-6	-3
Contreras, Willson	1992	C				-1	0	2	-2
Correa, Carlos	1994	SS			0	-3	4	-4	1
Cozart, Zack	1985	SS	3B	39	7	8	2	-6	4
Crawford, Brandon	1987	SS		23	20	20	9	6	0
Crawford, J.P.	1995	SS					6	-5	-6
Cron, C.J.	1990	1B		-5	-5	3	3	-2	3
d'Arnaud, Travis	1989	C		-7	0	-4	-1	-1	-5
Davis, Chris	1986	1B		-20	1	6	-6	-4	0
Davis, Khris	1987	LF		2	-6	-1	-13	-4	1
DeJong, Paul	1993	SS					-1	14	14
DeShields, Delino	1992	CF			-9	0	7	9	6
Desmond, Ian	1985	SS		-24	1	-4	-4	-5	-19
Devers, Rafael	1996	3B					-1	-13	-6
Diaz, Elias	1990	C				0	-3	-2	-23
Dickerson, Corey	1989	LF		-2	-7	2	-1	16	-6
Donaldson, Josh	1985	3B		33	11	2	3	0	15
Dozier, Brian	1987	2B		10	-5	3	-4	-8	-5
Dozier, Hunter	1991	3B				0		-9	-16
Duda, Lucas	1986	1B		-32	4	0	-1	0	-1
Duffy, Matt	1991	3B		-1	9	11		-4	-2
Duvall, Adam	1988	LF		2	-1	16	8	17	1
Dyson, Jarrod	1984	CF		30	11	19	15	9	13
Eaton, Adam	1988	CF	RF	10	-14	20	-5	-6	-1
Encarnacion, Edwin	1983	1B		-72	0	0	-2	0	-2
Engel, Adam	1991	CF					-1	1	2
Escobar, Eduardo	1989	3B		-6	4	-6	-8	-2	6
Flowers, Tyler	1986	C		29	14	2	11	7	4
Forsythe, Logan	1987	2B		-2	6	1	9	-2	-4
Fowler, Dexter	1986	CF	RF	-53	-12	1	-18	-5	0
Franco, Maikel	1992	3B		1	-8	-6	-4	-12	-3
Frazier, Adam	1991	2B				-2	5	7	6
Frazier, Todd	1986	3B		15	6	-2	8	2	1
Freeman, Freddie	1989	1B		1	3	9	1	12	5
Freese, David	1983	3B	1B	-27	-2	5	7	2	-1
Galvis, Freddy	1989	SS	2B	1	-7	-5	-5	7	-4
Garcia, Avisail	1991	RF		-13	-11	1	1	-4	2
Gardner, Brett	1983	LF	CF	87	1	12	20	10	5
Gennett, Scooter	1990	2B		-3	-3	-4	-8	-1	-1
Goldschmidt, Paul	1987	1B		12	18	4	10	6	4
Gomes, Yan	1987	C		30	-1	0	-1	4	5
Gomez, Carlos	1985	CF		78	6	-6	-4	7	-2
Gonzalez, Carlos	1985	RF		18	5	4	-3	-8	3
Gordon, Alex	1984	LF		80	7	4	12	13	1
Gordon, Dee	1988	2B		-25	13	1	3	-7	-8
Grandal, Yasmani	1988	C		14	5	14	17	9	-2
Granderson, Curtis	1981	RF	LF	26	11	3	-3	-5	1
Gregorius, Didi	1990	SS		2	5	-9	1	-2	-6
Grichuk, Randal	1991	RF	CF	4	7	8	6	-1	-8
Grossman, Robbie	1989	LF		3	-1	-21	-3	-4	4
Gurriel, Yuli	1984	1B	3B			0	-5	-3	-4
Hamilton, Billy	1990	CF		15	8	15	9	4	7
Harper, Bryce	1992	RF		18	9	-3	4	-26	9
Harrison, Josh	1987	2B	3B	18	1	8	8	-2	0
Hechavarria, Adeiny	1989	SS	2B	-7	9	9	5	3	-1
Hedges, Austin	1992	C			6	-1	20	12	22
Hernandez, Cesar	1990	2B		-10		-4	-1	-12	6
Herrera, Odubel	1991	CF			10	6	4	-11	-3
Heyward, Jason	1989	RF	CF	78	24	18	18	6	3
Hicks, Aaron	1989	CF		-1	1	4	15	-3	-1
Hoskins, Rhys	1993	1B	LF				-1	-26	-2
Hosmer, Eric	1989	1B		-10	0	-6	-7	8	-4
Hundley, Nick	1983	C		-34	-11	-16	-5	-18	-2
Iannetta, Chris	1983	C		-51	-7	-10	1	-8	-7
Iglesias, Jose	1990	SS		6	-3	3	4	1	8
Inciarte, Ender	1990	CF		20	29	15	5	17	-1
Jansen, Danny	1995	C						-2	12
Jones, Adam	1985	CF	RF	6	4	-10	-12	-25	-4
Jones, JaCoby	1992	CF				1	5	21	-13
Joseph, Caleb	1986	C		14	12	2	9	-1	1
Judge, Aaron	1992	RF				-1	9	14	19
Kelly, Carson	1994	C				0	1	-2	2
Kemp, Matt	1984	RF	LF	-73	-15	-18	-17	-9	-3
Kendrick, Howie	1983	2B	3B	29	-12	-5	-3	-5	-2
Kepler, Max	1993	RF	CF		0	6	5	10	7
Kiermaier, Kevin	1990	CF		14	42	25	22	14	13
Kinsler, Ian	1982	2B		71	19	12	6	10	1
Kipnis, Jason	1987	2B		-13	1	4	-5	-6	-7
Lagares, Juan	1989	CF		54	2	8	15	5	-2
Lamb, Jake	1990	3B		0	7	-8	-13	5	-5
Laureano, Ramon	1994	CF						4	-1
LeMahieu, DJ	1988	2B		37	3	3	8	18	7
Leon, Sandy	1989	C		3	3	-1	15	12	0
Lindor, Francisco	1993	SS			10	17	5	14	9
Longoria, Evan	1985	3B		73	-1	-9	11	7	7
Lucroy, Jonathan	1986	C		92	2	3	-15	-11	-14
Machado, Manny	1992	3B	SS	48	13	16	6	-10	3
Maldonado, Martin	1986	C		27	9	7	21	3	8
Margot, Manuel	1994	CF				4	8	9	6
Marisnick, Jake	1991	CF		22	13	18	2	11	5
Markakis, Nick	1983	RF		5	-6	10	-4	1	-4
Marte, Starling	1988	LF	CF	30	24	17	8	1	-9
Martin, Leonys	1988	CF		29	15	-2	8	3	-1

		Position		DRS By Season					
Player	YOB	1	2	<15	15	16	17	18	19
Martin, Russell	1983	C		105	5	6	3	5	3
Martinez, J.D.	1987	RF	LF	-9	4	-22	-5	-5	-7
Mathis, Jeff	1983	C		55	1	8	6	17	-1
Maybin, Cameron	1987	CF		20	-16	-11	2	6	0
Mazara, Nomar	1995	RF				-5	-6	-4	-4
McCann, Brian	1984	C		37	-4	-5	-8	3	1
McCann, James	1990	C		-1	-6	9	-6	-1	5
McCutchen, Andrew	1986	CF		-18	-8	-28	-14	2	2
McMahon, Ryan	1994	2B					0	3	6
Mercer, Jordy	1986	SS		10	0	-9	-1	-9	-10
Merrifield, Whit	1989	2B	RF			6	5	9	6
Miller, Brad	1989	SS	2B	-8	-20	-17	-4	-3	3
Molina, Yadier	1982	C		153	9	2	7	-1	2
Moncada, Yoan	1995	3B	2B			0	6	-5	-7
Mondesi, Adalberto	1995	SS				-1	-3	6	10
Moran, Colin	1992	3B				1	-1	-8	-13
Moreland, Mitch	1985	1B		-2	2	7	10	0	0
Morrison, Logan	1987	1B		-30	-7	-4	1	3	-1
Moustakas, Mike	1988	3B	2B	10	4	1	-8	2	0
Murphy, Daniel	1985	2B	1B	-20	-5	-11	-15	-19	2
Myers, Wil	1990	1B	LF	-9	-6	7	1	7	-9
Narvaez, Omar	1992	C				-2	-6	-13	-20
Newman, Kevin	1993	SS						-3	-4
Odor, Rougned	1994	2B		-11	-7	-9	3	10	-8
O'Hearn, Ryan	1993	1B						-2	-4
Olson, Matt	1994	1B				0	7	14	13
Ozuna, Marcell	1990	LF	CF	13	-3	-5	10	8	2
Panik, Joe	1990	2B		-1	2	3	-11	-1	-3
Parra, Gerardo	1987	LF	RF	71	-10	-11	5	6	6
Pederson, Joc	1992	CF		0	-3	1	-12	1	8
Pedroia, Dustin	1983	2B		90	-3	12	-2	0	-2
Pence, Hunter	1983	RF		18	0	-3	-3	-4	
Peralta, David	1987	LF	RF	3	-2	3	6	6	10
Perez, Roberto	1988	C		5	7	8	14	4	29
Pham, Tommy	1988	LF	CF	0	3	-4	11	-2	1
Phegley, Josh	1988	C		3	2	-3	3	0	-14
Pillar, Kevin	1989	CF	RF	7	22	21	15	-2	-3
Piscotty, Stephen	1991	RF			-5	3	8	-6	1
Polanco, Gregory	1991	RF		-2	12	2	1	-5	-5
Polanco, Jorge	1993	SS		1	0	-8	-1	-1	1
Pollock, A.J.	1987	CF		21	14	3	8	6	-10
Posey, Buster	1987	C	1B	52	21	24	3	12	14
Prado, Martin	1983	3B	1B	45	10	3	3	3	3
Profar, Jurickson	1993	2B		-4		2	2	-11	-8
Puig, Yasiel	1990	RF		7	2	7	18	6	0
Pujols, Albert	1980	1B		135	4	-4	-1	2	-1
Ramirez, Jose	1992	3B	2B	7	5	-1	5	3	3
Ramos, Wilson	1987	C		24	10	-1	-5	-5	-13
Realmuto, J.T.	1991	C		0	1	-13	-3	-7	11
Reddick, Josh	1987	RF		48	1	6	4	6	8
Rendon, Anthony	1990	3B		5	-1	8	7	-6	2
Reynolds, Mark	1983	1B		-66	-2	4	-4	-6	1
Rivera, Rene	1983	C		28	-6	6	-3	1	-2
Rizzo, Anthony	1989	1B		28	10	11	8	4	3
Robles, Victor	1997	CF					1	1	24
Rojas, Miguel	1989	SS		15	2	0	4	14	12
Rosario, Amed	1995	SS					1	-16	-16
Rosario, Eddie	1991	LF			11	2	-10	5	-8
Ruiz, Rio	1994	3B				0	0	0	2
Russell, Addison	1994	SS	2B		19	19	15	13	1
Sanchez, Gary	1992	C				3	1	6	-2
Sanchez, Yolmer	1992	2B	3B	-2	6	1	15	5	11
Sandoval, Pablo	1986	3B		-1	-11	-1	-7	-4	0
Sano, Miguel	1993	3B			-1	-10	-6	-6	-6
Santana, Carlos	1986	1B		-62	-5	1	8	1	-1
Santana, Domingo	1992	RF	LF	-1	-4	-10	-5	6	-17
Schoop, Jonathan	1991	2B		10	-3	-1	2	4	0
Schwarber, Kyle	1993	LF			-6	0	-9	2	-1
Seager, Corey	1994	SS			2	0	10	-2	9
Seager, Kyle	1987	3B		-2	1	15	-4	-5	-1
Segura, Jean	1990	SS	2B	5	-3	0	-3	5	-5
Semien, Marcus	1990	SS		1	5	-6	-9	9	5
Severino, Pedro	1993	C			0	0	0	1	-11

		Position		DRS By Season					
Player	YOB	1	2	<15	15	16	17	18	19
Shaw, Travis	1990	3B			-1	14	3	8	4
Simmons, Andrelton	1989	SS		88	25	18	32	21	14
Smith, Mallex	1993	CF	RF			7	5	2	-12
Smoak, Justin	1986	1B		-15	4	-5	1	-3	-3
Sogard, Eric	1986	2B		14	6		7	-2	-3
Solarte, Yangervis	1987	3B	2B	-7	-1	-2	1	-11	2
Soto, Juan	1998	LF						-5	1
Springer, George	1989	RF	CF	-2	6	6	-2	-5	11
Stanton, Giancarlo	1989	RF		22	9	4	10	5	-1
Stewart, Christin	1993	LF						-4	-3
Story, Trevor	1992	SS				4	11	1	17
Suarez, Eugenio	1991	3B	SS	-4	-12	1	5	1	2
Suzuki, Kurt	1983	C		-31	-9	-12	4	-7	-14
Swanson, Dansby	1994	SS				0	-7	10	-3
Tapia, Raimel	1994	LF				1	-8	0	-4
Taylor, Michael A.	1991	CF		-1	5	-2	8	10	0
Thames, Eric	1986	1B		-15			-9	-1	1
Trout, Mike	1991	CF		-4	5	6	-6	8	-1
Tulowitzki, Troy	1984	SS		78	5	10	0		-1
Turner, Justin	1984	3B		-12	5	7	6	1	-7
Turner, Trea	1993	SS			2	0	-3	2	-10
Upton, Justin	1987	LF		-12	8	0	8	0	-13
Urshela, Giovanny	1991	3B					0	-3	-4
Vazquez, Christian	1990	C		14		5	12	0	5
Villar, Jonathan	1991	SS	2B	-7	1	0	-1	4	-11
Vogt, Stephen	1984	C		0	-4	-10	-6		-4
Voit, Luke	1991	1B					2	-7	-6
Votto, Joey	1983	1B		33	6	-14	11	9	7
Walker, Christian	1991	1B		-1	0		-1	0	9
Walker, Neil	1985	2B	1B	-10	-2	0	-6	-3	0
Wieters, Matt	1986	C		39	-7	-3	-3	-1	-2
Wolters, Tony	1992	C				5	0	12	8
Wong, Kolten	1990	2B		9	5	4	-1	19	14
Yelich, Christian	1991	LF	RF	12	8	6	-6	4	-1
Zimmerman, Ryan	1984	1B		47	-1	-2	-8	2	-1
Zobrist, Ben	1981	2B	RF	66	-12	-3	1	8	0
Zunino, Mike	1991	C		8	8	8	4	12	9

Injury Information

John Verros

One of the major stories of the 2019 season was the numerous injuries that plagued the Yankees and their unexpected victories in spite of them. The team set a major league record by sending 30 different players to the Injured List, eclipsing a previous major league record of 28. Many of those players sent to the Injured List were major pieces for the club and were gone for large chunks of the season.

Yet the Yankees still emerged from the 162-game regular season with 103 wins and an American League East title. According to the injury data collected here at Baseball Info Solutions, the Yankees led the majors with 2,889 total days missed due to injury. This staggering number failed to impede the club from reaching its regular season goals.

Within the injury section of this year's edition of the Bill James Handbook there are three tables that convey a wide array of information. You can learn about injury severity (we review every potential injury and grade on a 1 to 5 scale with 1 being no visible pain and 5 being extreme pain, with a 3 or higher considered severe), injury events by position (catchers suffer more injuries, pitchers have the highest risk of severe injury) and injury diagnoses (how often an injury occurred, how much time was missed, was surgery needed, was there a recurrence). Note that days missed for injuries from which players typically don't return within a season are not listed.

Among our findings was that hamstring strains result in an average of 22 days missed, that shoulder labrum tears had a 38% recurrence rate, and that six of the nine most common injuries treated with injection had an inflammation diagnosis in 2019.

These are simply a few examples of what our injury data can help illuminate. This data has the potential to be used for things such as the measurement of expected return-to-play times for injured players. The injury data can also provide a way to identify trends that lead to future research endeavors.

Injury Events and Days Missed by Team

Team	Severity Level 1	2	3	4	5	Off Field	Total	IL Stints	IL Days Missed	Total Days Missed
New York Yankees	107	73	46	7	0	28	261	39	2,486	2,889
Los Angeles Angels	96	55	35	8	5	35	234	32	1,264	2,381
San Diego Padres	92	56	26	6	0	29	209	24	1,920	2,225
Tampa Bay Rays	93	79	42	12	0	27	253	30	1,313	2,162
Detroit Tigers	76	57	35	3	0	38	209	26	1,134	2,025
Pittsburgh Pirates	94	74	33	9	6	31	247	34	1,897	2,012
Boston Red Sox	92	68	37	12	0	28	237	23	1,071	1,858
Toronto Blue Jays	84	70	27	6	1	29	217	25	1,417	1,845
Philadelphia Phillies	112	58	21	10	2	25	228	31	1,512	1,721
Seattle Mariners	101	66	16	9	0	27	219	24	1,390	1,711
Miami Marlins	112	76	30	7	0	19	244	25	1,290	1,672
St Louis Cardinals	120	52	44	10	0	16	242	21	823	1,593
Texas Rangers	92	59	38	6	0	21	216	25	1,544	1,575
New York Mets	131	63	43	10	0	26	273	28	1,157	1,553
Colorado Rockies	78	53	41	9	1	21	203	25	917	1,535
Washington Nationals	105	67	37	11	0	22	242	26	1,086	1,491
Chicago White Sox	100	92	33	7	1	23	256	23	1,046	1,488
Arizona Diamondbacks	119	69	30	6	0	19	243	18	1,135	1,483
Milwaukee Brewers	111	62	31	6	1	29	240	19	951	1,475
Oakland Athletics	101	59	38	6	1	28	233	17	1,026	1,444
Chicago Cubs	129	63	21	8	0	36	257	23	1,129	1,396
Minnesota Twins	105	69	40	13	0	31	258	26	675	1,343
Los Angeles Dodgers	131	69	16	9	0	29	254	27	934	1,312
Cleveland Indians	114	48	31	9	1	19	222	18	1,180	1,289
Cincinnati Reds	119	45	27	12	2	33	238	18	624	1,249
Atlanta Braves	94	53	35	4	2	20	208	26	959	1,178
Baltimore Orioles	96	121	37	12	1	28	295	18	748	1,121
Kansas City Royals	93	58	23	4	1	12	191	13	837	929
Houston Astros	104	57	34	6	0	22	223	17	803	863
San Francisco Giants	93	57	13	10	1	23	197	20	619	709

Injury Events by Defensive Position

Position	Total	Severe	Severe Pct	Left Game	Left Game Pct
Catcher	1743	148	8.5%	11	7.4%
Pitcher	288	195	67.7%	78	40.0%
Center Fielder	62	31	50.0%	10	32.3%
Left Fielder	46	22	47.8%	9	40.9%
Right Fielder	42	18	42.9%	10	55.6%
Second Baseman	41	17	41.5%	1	5.9%
Shortstop	35	15	42.9%	9	60.0%
First Baseman	29	13	44.8%	3	23.1%
Third Baseman	20	10	50.0%	4	40.0%

Injuries By Body Part and Diagnosis

Body Part	Diagnosis	Occurences	Avg Days Missed	Recurrence	Surgery	Injection	Season Ending
Head	Concussion	25	18	4%	0%	0%	12%
Nose	Fracture	3	8	0%	0%	0%	0%
Neck	Soreness	18	10	6%	0%	0%	6%
Neck	Strain	3	17	0%	0%	0%	0%
A/C Joint	Sprain	7	12	0%	0%	0%	43%
A/C Joint	Inflammation	5	18	0%	20%	20%	20%
Labrum	Tear	8	-	38%	100%	0%	100%
Rotator Cuff	Inflammation	4	65	0%	0%	25%	0%
Rotator Cuff	Strain	4	63	0%	0%	25%	25%
Shoulder	Inflammation	34	39	0%	3%	6%	29%
Shoulder	Soreness	31	11	3%	0%	3%	13%
Shoulder	Strain	15	38	0%	0%	7%	20%
Shoulder	Fatigue	8	24	0%	0%	0%	25%
Shoulder	Bruise/Contusion	3	8	33%	0%	0%	0%
Biceps	Inflammation	5	32	0%	0%	20%	20%
Biceps	Strain	5	42	0%	0%	0%	60%
Biceps	Soreness	3	6	0%	0%	0%	0%
Elbow	Inflammation	25	44	12%	8%	20%	48%
Elbow	Ulnar Collateral Lig. Injury	16	-	6%	63%	0%	88%
Elbow	Bruise/ Contusion	15	3	0%	0%	0%	13%
Elbow	Soreness	14	19	7%	0%	0%	7%
Elbow	Strain	9	-	0%	11%	11%	78%
Elbow	Ulnar Nerve Injury	6	9	0%	17%	0%	33%
Elbow	Loose Bodies	4	98	25%	100%	0%	0%
Elbow	Bone Spur	4	4	25%	75%	25%	75%
Elbow	Sprain	3	120	0%	0%	0%	33%
Forearm	Strain	26	57	8%	8%	12%	35%
Forearm	Bruise/Contusion	9	1	0%	0%	0%	0%
Forearm	Soreness	7	12	0%	0%	0%	14%
Forearm	Fracture	3	36	0%	33%	0%	67%
Forearm	Inflammation	3	-	0%	0%	0%	100%
Triceps	Strain	3	11	0%	0%	0%	33%
Finger	Blister	13	11	8%	0%	0%	8%
Finger	Fracture	11	24	0%	9%	0%	36%
Finger	Sprain	10	17	0%	0%	0%	10%
Finger	Soreness	9	7	0%	0%	0%	0%
Finger	Bruise/Contusion	8	13	0%	0%	0%	13%
Finger	Laceration	5	11	0%	0%	0%	0%
Finger	Inflammation	3	30	33%	0%	0%	0%
Hand	Bruise/Contusion	34	4	0%	0%	0%	0%
Hand	Soreness	6	18	33%	33%	0%	17%
Hand	Sprain	4	17	0%	0%	0%	25%
Hand	Fracture	4	41	0%	75%	0%	25%
Hand	Blister	3	5	0%	0%	0%	33%
Wrist	Bruise/Contusion	13	9	8%	0%	0%	0%
Wrist	Fracture	9	64	0%	22%	0%	56%
Wrist	Soreness	8	18	25%	0%	13%	13%
Wrist	Sprain	4	7	0%	0%	50%	0%
Wrist	Strain	3	35	33%	0%	0%	0%
Wrist	Inflammation	3	2	33%	0%	0%	33%
Back	Soreness	44	8	5%	0%	0%	7%
Back	Strain	34	49	3%	3%	6%	21%
Back	Muscle Spasm	16	10	0%	0%	0%	0%

Injuries By Body Part and Diagnosis

Body Part	Diagnosis	Occurences	Avg Days Missed	Recurrence	Surgery	Injection	Season Ending
Back	Latissimus Dorsi Strain	15	73	0%	0%	0%	27%
Back	Inflammation	6	21	17%	0%	33%	33%
Back	Trapezius Strain	4	2	25%	0%	0%	25%
Cervical Spine	Strain	3	3	0%	0%	0%	33%
Chest	Bruise/Contusion	3	1	0%	0%	0%	33%
Oblique Muscle	Strain	43	38	0%	0%	2%	19%
Oblique Muscle	Soreness	7	30	14%	0%	14%	43%
Pectoral	Strain	3	61	0%	0%	0%	0%
Ribcage	Bruise/Contusion	5	2	0%	0%	0%	20%
Ribcage	Strain	5	14	0%	0%	0%	20%
Abdomen	Strain	5	21	0%	0%	0%	20%
Groin	Strain	26	19	4%	0%	0%	23%
Groin	Soreness	6	1	0%	0%	0%	33%
Hip	Strain	12	17	0%	8%	8%	25%
Hip	Inflammation	8	12	0%	13%	0%	50%
Hip	Soreness	7	7	0%	0%	0%	0%
Hip	Bruise/Contusion	5	8	20%	0%	0%	20%
Hamstring	Strain	80	22	5%	4%	0%	14%
Hamstring	Soreness	22	3	9%	0%	0%	5%
Quadriceps	Strain	21	28	10%	0%	0%	19%
Quadriceps	Soreness	7	3	0%	0%	0%	0%
Calf	Strain	28	28	7%	0%	4%	14%
Calf	Bruise/Contusion	5	4	0%	0%	0%	0%
Calf	Cramp	5	2	0%	0%	0%	0%
Calf	Soreness	4	2	0%	0%	0%	0%
Knee	Bruise/Contusion	31	3	6%	0%	0%	10%
Knee	Sprain	25	53	0%	28%	0%	40%
Knee	Inflammation	16	23	6%	6%	19%	6%
Knee	Soreness	14	5	21%	0%	7%	7%
Knee	Meniscus Injury	5	102	20%	100%	0%	60%
Shin	Bruise/Contusion	10	12	0%	0%	10%	0%
Ankle	Sprain	33	19	3%	0%	0%	15%
Ankle	Soreness	6	2	0%	0%	0%	0%
Ankle	Bruise/Contusion	5	0	0%	0%	0%	0%
Foot	Bruise/Contusion	20	10	0%	0%	0%	0%
Foot	Soreness	8	5	13%	0%	0%	13%
Foot	Plantar Fasciitis	4	65	25%	0%	0%	25%
Foot	Fracture	3	60	0%	33%	0%	67%
Toe	Bruise/Contusion	6	1	0%	0%	0%	17%
Toe	Fracture	3	36	0%	0%	0%	33%
Other	Illness	67	8	1%	6%	0%	4%

Baserunning

Brian Reiff

There are a fair number of fans out there who lament the loss of baserunning in a game now dominated by strikeouts and home runs. While it's true that stolen base attempts are down from previous seasons, they're not yet at all-time lows, which were reached during the early 1950s. And even if they were, that wouldn't mean that baserunning was gone from the game. Offensive statistics may dominate the conversation, but the next pages show that we have the tools to measure baserunning more deeply than just stolen bases and caught stealings.

The following tables show a whole bunch of statistics that detail a player's or team's performance this season on the basepaths, with the main one to focus on being all the way on the right: Net Gain, which combines all of a baserunner's contributions into one number.

There was a tie atop the player leaderboard this year, as both Jonathan Villar and Christian Yelich finished the season with a Net Gain of plus-43 (a likely welcome change from their early lives when their last names would have put them at the end of any alphabetical list they were on). Both players were balanced in getting to their totals, providing value both through stolen bases and other contributions.

Villar was one of just three players to hit the 40–stolen base mark this season (alongside Mallex Smith and Adalberto Mondesi). He was efficient as well, successfully stealing on over 80 percent of his attempts. That combination of quantity and quality led to his Stolen Base Gain of +22, tied for fifth best in MLB. He rounded out his line by advancing an extra base on at least half his opportunities on each advancement type (First to Third, Second to Home, and First to Home), with the highlight being his 81% second-to-home advancement rate.

Yelich stole only 30 bases (thanks in part to an injury-shortened season), but he had a superior Stolen Base Gain to Villar thanks to a sterling 94% success rate. No other player with three or fewer caught stealings even had 20 stolen bases. His other biggest strength was advancing from first to home on doubles, which he did eight out of 10 times, well above the MLB average rate of 44% since 2002.

On the team leaderboard, the Diamondbacks led MLB in both Baserunning Gain and Stolen Base Gain, leading to a clear finish at the top by 28 bases in Net Gain. It certainly helped to have a combination of Jarrod Dyson and Tim Locastro in the stolen base department, as the two combined to steal 47 bases on 51 attempts.

In fact, the Diamondbacks as a team were successful on 86% of their 102 stolen base attempts, edging out the Dodgers for the highest success rate in the majors. The Diamondbacks were also one of just two teams to finish with a First-to-Third, Second-to-Home and First-to-Home advancement rate in the top half of teams, with the other being the Rockies.

However, the Diamondbacks outperformed the Rockies in Baserunning Gain 62–25 in large part by making only 18 outs while trying to advance, almost exactly half the Rockies' total.

Net Gain is a statistic that measures baserunning production that includes all baserunning advancements on both hits and outs (BR Gain) and stolen bases (SB Gain). It estimates the number of bases a player gained or lost for his team due to his baserunning. BR Gain is the sum of extra baserunning advances a player made over the league average, minus a penalty for the number of BR Outs he made above the league average. SB Gain estimates how many bases each runner gained or lost his team based on his successful and unsuccessful stolen base attempts.

2019 Baserunning

Player	1st to 3rd		2nd to Home		1st to Home		Bases Taken	Out Adv	Doubled Off	BR Outs	GDP	GDP Opps	BR Gain	SB Gain	Net Gain
	Moved	Chances	Moved	Chances	Moved	Chances									
Abreu, Jose	5	30	10	16	4	11	18	6	2	8	24	172	-23	-2	-25
Acuna Jr., Ronald	12	29	16	22	10	14	18	1	1	2	8	97	+18	+19	+37
Adames, Willy	8	29	8	10	5	8	17	2	2	4	9	101	+4	0	+4
Adams, Matt	5	14	1	2	0	3	7	1	1	2	7	71	-2	0	-2
Adrianza, Ehire	5	11	2	6	1	5	10	1	1	2	2	46	+3	-4	-1
Aguilar, Jesus	5	20	3	12	0	7	11	0	1	1	12	77	-7	0	-7
Ahmed, Nick	13	27	11	18	4	9	22	0	0	0	15	112	+18	+4	+22
Alberto, Hanser	10	30	7	17	4	10	18	1	0	1	9	74	+6	-4	+2
Albies, Ozzie	9	27	20	24	7	13	8	6	0	6	2	96	-1	+7	+6
Alfaro, Jorge	5	33	7	12	0	2	14	3	2	5	12	97	-13	-4	-17
Allen, Greg	1	7	4	5	3	4	4	2	0	2	3	46	-2	+4	+2
Almora Jr., Albert	3	10	1	2	3	4	10	2	0	2	8	60	0	0	0
Alonso, Pete	9	33	8	17	4	14	18	1	0	1	13	146	+6	+1	+7
Alonso, Yonder	2	13	3	7	2	2	6	2	1	3	13	44	-16	-2	-18
Altuve, Jose	8	24	9	16	7	12	13	5	1	6	19	109	-16	-4	-20
Alvarez, Yordan	5	18	0	6	2	7	10	1	0	1	9	81	-2	0	-2
Anderson, Brian	8	26	7	12	3	5	10	2	0	3	15	112	-6	+3	-3
Anderson, Tim	12	34	9	15	3	5	15	1	1	2	12	103	+5	+7	+12
Andrus, Elvis	11	24	11	16	2	5	24	3	2	5	16	130	+5	+15	+20
Aquino, Aristides	3	8	1	2	1	2	6	0	0	0	5	42	+4	+7	+11
Arcia, Orlando	7	17	4	7	4	7	21	0	0	0	15	109	+15	-2	+13
Arenado, Nolan	9	37	11	15	10	13	14	2	1	3	14	125	+2	-1	+1
Arraez, Luis	6	23	11	14	2	7	10	0	0	0	2	50	+10	-2	+8
Astudillo, Willians	2	11	5	7	0	2	3	1	0	1	6	31	-6	0	-6
Austin, Tyler	5	8	7	7	1	2	7	0	0	0	2	31	+12	+2	+14
Avila, Alex	2	7	3	8	0	3	7	0	1	1	8	34	-5	+1	-4
Bader, Harrison	7	16	3	9	5	6	13	4	1	5	3	73	+1	+5	+6
Baez, Javier	15	22	15	18	4	7	19	4	1	5	16	111	+8	-3	+5
Barnes, Austin	2	5	5	9	0	2	4	0	0	0	8	41	-2	+3	+1
Barnhart, Tucker	0	10	4	11	1	4	3	2	0	2	5	62	-11	+1	-10
Bauers, Jake	6	23	8	11	2	4	9	2	1	3	3	79	+2	-3	-1
Beaty, Matt	2	7	7	9	1	3	5	1	2	3	6	47	-6	+5	-1
Beckham, Gordon	4	6	6	8	1	3	10	1	1	2	6	35	+3	+1	+4
Beckham, Tim	4	10	3	8	2	5	11	3	1	4	7	60	-5	-5	-10
Bell, Josh	7	35	10	18	5	13	7	6	2	8	11	106	-27	-2	-29
Bellinger, Cody	12	33	7	20	7	10	22	4	1	5	10	131	+4	+5	+9
Belt, Brandon	7	33	6	8	3	13	16	2	0	2	6	119	+7	-2	+5
Benintendi, Andrew	14	35	6	15	6	11	20	1	1	2	6	98	+14	+4	+18
Berti, Jon	5	19	15	22	6	8	7	0	1	1	2	40	+7	+11	+18
Betts, Mookie	16	37	13	24	11	14	26	2	2	4	11	109	+16	+10	+26
Bichette, Bo	1	6	4	5	0	3	3	2	0	2	2	25	-5	-4	-9
Biggio, Cavan	5	19	8	11	1	7	23	1	1	2	0	68	+19	+14	+33
Blackmon, Charlie	6	30	13	21	4	12	26	3	1	4	11	78	+2	-8	-6
Bogaerts, Xander	17	39	16	24	7	15	20	5	0	5	11	144	+9	0	+9
Bote, David	8	20	6	11	3	5	10	0	2	2	11	73	-1	+3	+2
Bradley Jr., Jackie	8	18	9	12	0	5	23	1	1	2	6	107	+19	-4	+15
Brantley, Michael	9	40	8	16	6	13	22	1	0	1	21	159	+1	-1	0
Braun, Ryan	12	22	6	12	2	8	17	2	1	3	15	96	+1	+9	+10
Bregman, Alex	13	41	7	23	5	16	20	4	1	5	9	134	-5	+3	-2
Brinson, Lewis	2	8	3	7	0	2	4	1	1	2	8	49	-9	-1	-10
Broxton, Keon	3	8	4	5	1	1	5	0	0	0	5	53	+6	-2	+4
Bruce, Jay	2	6	3	5	0	2	5	1	0	1	5	53	0	+1	+1
Bryant, Kris	20	34	11	14	6	14	17	2	2	4	10	107	+12	+4	+16
Buxton, Byron	1	4	9	11	0	1	14	3	1	4	3	66	+5	+8	+13
Cabrera, Asdrubal	6	22	4	14	1	10	16	5	0	5	9	104	-10	+4	-6
Cabrera, Melky	7	24	7	13	5	6	8	2	0	2	14	73	-7	+2	-5
Cabrera, Miguel	2	19	3	11	1	13	11	1	0	1	18	117	-15	0	-15
Cain, Lorenzo	11	24	17	20	4	8	12	1	0	1	14	66	+6	+2	+8
Calhoun, Kole	7	27	13	20	6	11	17	2	0	2	14	101	+4	+2	+6
Calhoun, Willie	5	18	6	8	4	10	8	4	0	4	5	65	-4	0	-4
Camargo, Johan	1	12	7	10	0	2	6	0	1	1	5	47	-2	+1	-1
Candelario, Jeimer	10	28	6	9	0	1	15	2	3	5	3	75	+3	+1	+4
Canha, Mark	13	27	11	16	5	10	14	3	0	3	10	93	+6	-1	+5

2019 Baserunning

Player	1st to 3rd Moved	Chances	2nd to Home Moved	Chances	1st to Home Moved	Chances	Bases Taken	Out Adv	Doubled Off	BR Outs	GDP	GDP Opps	BR Gain	SB Gain	Net Gain
Cano, Robinson	1	15	8	15	2	6	7	1	0	1	16	89	-11	0	-11
Caratini, Victor	3	20	5	7	1	2	8	1	1	2	6	40	-4	+1	-3
Carpenter, Matt	4	24	6	15	2	5	10	3	1	4	3	77	-8	+4	-4
Casali, Curt	2	9	2	5	1	3	7	0	0	0	1	42	+6	0	+6
Castellanos, Nicholas	13	41	15	24	4	5	26	6	2	8	12	132	+1	-2	-1
Castillo, Welington	0	9	1	6	0	2	2	2	1	3	8	47	-18	0	-18
Castro, Harold	6	18	6	6	2	4	9	0	1	1	6	58	+6	0	+6
Castro, Jason	2	10	2	6	1	2	3	2	0	2	0	52	-2	0	-2
Castro, Starlin	8	29	7	14	4	8	5	0	1	1	23	131	-15	-2	-17
Cave, Jake	4	14	3	3	2	5	5	1	1	2	5	51	-2	0	-2
Chapman, Matt	15	37	9	11	2	3	14	5	1	6	12	145	0	-1	-1
Chavis, Michael	10	21	6	11	2	8	12	3	0	3	11	82	-1	0	-1
Chirinos, Robinson	1	17	3	8	3	7	16	2	0	2	11	98	-1	-3	-4
Choi, Ji-Man	8	31	7	13	2	5	16	1	0	1	7	100	+9	-4	+5
Choo, Shin-Soo	10	38	11	22	2	11	20	1	1	2	6	83	+4	+13	+17
Conforto, Michael	16	41	12	17	0	3	19	1	2	3	11	121	+10	+3	+13
Contreras, Willson	6	17	6	7	2	8	8	3	2	5	4	64	-7	-3	-10
Cooper, Garrett	2	21	6	12	2	7	6	2	2	4	10	77	-18	0	-18
Cordell, Ryan	5	17	3	8	0	2	5	1	0	1	2	50	0	+1	+1
Correa, Carlos	1	8	2	4	2	4	6	0	0	0	8	71	+1	+1	+2
Crawford, Brandon	9	29	9	13	3	8	15	3	1	4	10	107	0	-1	-1
Crawford, J.P.	2	11	5	11	4	8	15	2	1	3	4	61	+2	-1	+1
Cron, C.J.	9	23	4	10	2	7	16	3	1	4	13	77	-5	0	-5
Cruz, Nelson	7	41	7	13	0	7	13	1	0	1	14	117	-6	-2	-8
Cuthbert, Cheslor	3	13	2	4	4	7	5	1	0	1	14	66	-8	+1	-7
d'Arnaud, Travis	2	13	5	10	3	9	6	3	0	3	4	69	-7	-2	-9
Dahl, David	2	19	12	16	7	9	8	2	1	3	3	80	+2	-4	-2
Davis, Chris	2	12	0	2	0	2	10	1	0	1	6	57	+1	0	+1
Davis, J.D.	6	26	7	13	0	4	13	3	0	3	14	96	-9	+3	-6
Davis, Khris	5	29	9	11	0	6	11	2	0	2	11	100	-4	0	-4
Dean, Austin	4	5	2	4	1	1	3	0	0	0	5	28	+2	-4	-2
DeJong, Paul	9	29	12	20	5	10	14	1	0	1	15	151	+7	-1	+6
Demeritte, Travis	3	11	10	13	1	1	6	1	1	2	3	28	+1	+3	+4
Descalso, Daniel	6	9	2	2	0	3	5	3	0	3	3	28	-3	0	-3
DeShields, Delino	6	17	4	7	2	2	16	1	3	4	8	69	+1	+12	+13
Desmond, Ian	10	27	8	10	3	4	13	1	0	1	12	93	+9	-3	+6
Devers, Rafael	15	31	20	28	8	15	24	6	0	6	8	130	+15	-8	+7
Diaz, Aledmys	4	16	3	5	0	1	8	1	0	1	10	54	-3	+2	-1
Diaz, Elias	5	15	6	9	2	8	9	1	0	1	11	70	-1	0	-1
Diaz, Isan	4	8	0	1	2	4	1	3	1	4	2	38	-9	-6	-15
Diaz, Yandy	6	18	6	12	3	4	8	3	0	3	9	54	-7	-2	-9
Dickerson, Alex	3	8	6	10	0	1	3	0	0	0	5	37	0	-1	-1
Dickerson, Corey	5	13	6	11	1	2	6	4	0	4	4	47	-7	+1	-6
Dietrich, Derek	4	17	5	7	3	4	4	0	1	1	2	45	+2	-1	+1
Dixon, Brandon	5	14	8	11	2	5	13	3	1	4	5	79	+3	+3	+6
Donaldson, Josh	5	36	14	23	0	6	19	5	7	12	13	139	-30	0	-30
Dozier, Brian	10	27	6	9	4	7	11	2	1	3	11	80	-1	-5	-6
Dozier, Hunter	9	23	6	9	4	7	8	2	3	5	9	111	-6	-2	-8
Drury, Brandon	5	15	3	5	0	4	12	0	1	1	6	78	+7	-2	+5
Duffy, Matt	2	10	2	6	0	1	3	2	0	2	4	31	-8	-2	-10
Duggar, Steven	3	8	4	6	0	1	6	1	2	3	1	35	-2	-7	-9
Dyson, Jarrod	14	27	11	16	4	7	16	2	1	3	1	62	+17	+22	+39
Eaton, Adam	20	34	13	18	6	11	28	3	1	4	8	104	+26	+9	+35
Edman, Tommy	6	13	7	9	4	5	12	1	0	1	3	53	+14	+13	+27
Encarnacion, Edwin	8	23	5	11	0	5	7	0	0	0	4	91	+6	-2	+4
Engel, Adam	6	15	4	7	2	2	14	1	1	2	5	50	+8	-3	+5
Ervin, Phillip	4	10	5	7	0	2	8	1	0	1	4	29	+3	-2	+1
Escobar, Eduardo	13	28	7	15	3	7	19	4	0	4	8	161	+12	+3	+15
Farmer, Kyle	1	5	6	6	0	2	8	0	0	0	1	45	+11	+2	+13
Fisher, Derek	3	7	0	2	0	1	3	0	0	0	3	32	+1	+3	+4
Fletcher, David	5	31	11	23	2	10	28	2	1	3	8	99	+5	+2	+7
Flores, Wilmer	4	14	2	6	1	3	5	2	0	2	9	52	-9	0	-9
Flowers, Tyler	4	14	3	4	0	4	10	2	1	3	8	63	-4	0	-4
Forsythe, Logan	1	16	7	13	3	6	11	1	1	2	8	82	-2	+2	0

2019 Baserunning

Player	1st to 3rd Moved	Chances	2nd to Home Moved	Chances	1st to Home Moved	Chances	Bases Taken	Out Adv	Doubled Off	BR Outs	GDP	GDP Opps	BR Gain	SB Gain	Net Gain
Fowler, Dexter	11	30	11	16	1	7	17	7	1	8	6	88	-8	-2	-10
France, Ty	3	9	3	4	0	3	3	1	0	1	8	43	-6	-4	-10
Franco, Maikel	2	13	7	9	1	3	6	1	0	1	14	82	-7	0	-7
Frazier, Adam	12	29	11	19	6	11	13	3	0	3	6	86	+5	-5	0
Frazier, Clint	2	13	3	5	0	1	5	0	0	0	2	49	+4	-3	+1
Frazier, Todd	13	25	6	12	6	9	11	4	0	5	9	89	-2	-3	-5
Freeman, Freddie	13	37	14	22	5	9	19	2	1	3	17	135	+4	0	+4
Freeman, Mike	3	10	3	6	3	4	9	0	0	0	2	45	+10	-3	+7
Freese, David	2	7	4	6	0	0	3	2	1	3	7	43	-10	0	-10
Gallo, Joey	4	8	5	6	3	3	9	0	0	0	0	49	+16	0	+16
Galvis, Freddy	3	16	8	12	5	12	11	1	0	1	14	108	0	0	0
Gamel, Ben	6	18	7	12	3	7	8	0	0	0	0	58	+11	-2	+9
Garcia, Avisail	7	26	5	9	4	5	7	6	2	8	15	107	-25	+2	-23
Garcia, Greg	11	24	8	10	2	4	8	2	1	3	4	58	+3	-4	-1
Garcia, Leury	14	34	20	26	2	9	31	1	4	5	6	97	+21	+5	+26
Gardner, Brett	9	22	5	10	2	5	15	1	1	2	6	101	+10	+6	+16
Garver, Mitch	2	21	5	11	0	6	9	0	0	0	5	65	-1	0	-1
Goins, Ryan	4	13	2	5	0	0	6	0	1	1	7	28	-4	-2	-6
Goldschmidt, Paul	8	27	12	21	9	14	17	0	0	0	11	147	+18	+1	+19
Gomes, Yan	3	15	5	10	1	3	6	2	0	2	7	65	-6	+2	-4
Gonzalez, Erik	3	6	3	4	0	2	1	3	1	4	5	32	-13	+2	-11
Gonzalez, Marwin	3	20	6	11	3	10	7	2	1	3	7	69	-10	+1	-9
Goodrum, Niko	8	18	8	10	6	9	21	0	1	1	7	88	+23	+6	+29
Goodwin, Brian	6	19	6	12	3	6	14	1	1	2	3	79	+9	+1	+10
Gordon, Alex	10	33	14	18	9	14	15	5	0	5	13	95	-3	-1	-4
Gordon, Dee	3	12	3	5	1	4	15	0	2	2	8	96	+6	+12	+18
Grandal, Yasmani	6	31	5	13	2	17	16	2	0	2	16	139	-9	+3	-6
Granderson, Curtis	4	18	2	11	2	9	9	3	0	3	3	38	-10	-6	-16
Gregorius, Didi	4	15	10	12	0	2	7	2	0	2	5	61	+1	0	+1
Greiner, Grayson	1	12	2	4	2	2	4	1	0	1	5	31	-4	0	-4
Grichuk, Randal	5	22	9	13	3	5	13	3	0	3	20	120	-8	0	-8
Grisham, Trent	1	6	4	5	0	2	7	0	1	1	3	33	+2	+1	+3
Grossman, Robbie	6	23	8	11	4	8	9	0	1	1	7	74	+3	+1	+4
Guerrero Jr., Vladimir	5	19	5	10	0	6	15	5	1	6	17	114	-17	-2	-19
Gurriel Jr., Lourdes	3	12	6	7	5	5	6	3	1	4	4	63	-2	-2	-4
Gurriel, Yuli	4	24	9	16	3	8	18	3	1	4	12	121	-3	-1	-4
Guzman, Ronald	0	10	6	11	2	3	8	2	1	3	7	56	-8	-3	-11
Hamilton, Billy	10	18	11	12	2	4	15	2	0	2	1	70	+21	+10	+31
Hampson, Garrett	8	17	7	9	2	2	12	3	0	3	2	50	+9	+9	+18
Haniger, Mitch	4	11	9	12	1	6	10	2	0	2	3	34	+3	+4	+7
Harper, Bryce	7	25	11	24	5	19	21	7	1	8	10	146	-11	+9	-2
Haseley, Adam	3	10	5	10	4	4	8	0	1	1	7	39	+1	+4	+5
Healy, Ryon	1	6	2	9	0	5	6	1	0	1	1	39	-2	0	-2
Hechavarria, Adeiny	3	8	6	8	2	3	3	1	1	2	3	36	-2	+1	-1
Hedges, Austin	4	11	4	6	0	2	2	3	1	4	3	59	-9	+1	-8
Heredia, Guillermo	3	12	4	7	1	1	4	0	0	0	4	42	+2	-2	0
Hernandez, Cesar	8	35	9	19	4	9	24	1	1	2	9	102	+8	+5	+13
Hernandez, Kike	6	18	7	10	5	6	14	2	1	3	9	83	+5	+4	+9
Hernandez, Marco	3	6	2	7	0	1	4	0	0	0	1	31	+3	-3	0
Hernandez, Teoscar	4	18	8	12	1	2	13	2	2	4	8	84	-3	0	-3
Heyward, Jason	14	34	11	19	3	7	26	0	0	0	12	100	+22	+2	+24
Hicks, Aaron	6	13	5	8	3	7	2	1	0	1	2	58	+3	-3	0
Hicks, John	3	9	2	6	0	1	8	4	1	5	7	57	-12	-1	-13
Hiura, Keston	2	13	5	11	2	7	10	3	1	4	6	70	-8	+3	-5
Holt, Brock	3	15	5	8	3	7	5	2	0	2	4	54	-4	+1	-3
Hoskins, Rhys	8	29	9	16	2	11	21	2	0	2	10	125	+7	-2	+5
Hosmer, Eric	8	26	7	14	5	11	14	5	2	7	12	119	-13	-6	-19
Iglesias, Jose	12	30	11	15	4	9	14	3	1	4	17	102	-4	-6	-10
Inciarte, Ender	0	3	7	8	3	4	11	1	0	1	1	40	+12	+5	+17
Jansen, Danny	5	21	7	11	3	8	8	0	1	1	8	80	+1	-2	-1
Jay, Jon	3	10	5	5	0	2	2	1	0	1	1	33	+1	0	+1
Jimenez, Eloy	3	20	9	14	1	5	20	0	0	0	11	97	+12	0	+12
Jones, Adam	4	18	10	11	3	9	14	3	0	4	15	89	-7	0	-7
Jones, JaCoby	1	12	13	13	1	4	17	1	0	1	6	45	+12	+3	+15

2019 Baserunning

Player	1st to 3rd Moved	1st to 3rd Chances	2nd to Home Moved	2nd to Home Chances	1st to Home Moved	1st to Home Chances	Bases Taken	Out Adv	Doubled Off	BR Outs	GDP	GDP Opps	BR Gain	SB Gain	Net Gain
Joyce, Matt	6	16	3	4	2	2	4	1	1	2	3	49	0	0	0
Judge, Aaron	9	30	10	13	1	4	10	1	0	1	11	100	+4	-1	+3
Kelly, Carson	4	15	6	9	0	3	3	0	0	0	11	68	-5	0	-5
Kemp, Tony	4	13	3	8	1	2	8	1	0	1	4	38	+1	-4	-3
Kendrick, Howie	4	17	7	9	1	4	11	2	0	2	11	75	-2	0	-2
Kepler, Max	11	28	7	16	2	10	12	2	1	3	5	90	0	-9	-9
Kiermaier, Kevin	7	19	12	15	1	2	6	1	0	1	8	96	+5	+9	+14
Kiner-Falefa, Isiah	6	13	5	7	0	0	7	0	1	1	9	39	0	+3	+3
Kingery, Scott	11	27	8	14	5	8	14	1	0	1	3	87	+17	+7	+24
Kinsler, Ian	3	8	6	7	1	4	7	1	0	1	5	45	+3	-6	-3
Kipnis, Jason	3	12	7	10	2	7	11	0	0	0	7	88	+8	+3	+11
Knapp, Andrew	2	6	1	2	1	1	4	0	0	0	2	27	+4	0	+4
La Stella, Tommy	3	20	4	5	3	6	14	0	0	0	8	57	+7	0	+7
Lagares, Juan	6	12	5	8	1	2	6	2	1	3	8	47	-6	+2	-4
Lamb, Jake	5	13	2	4	0	1	6	0	0	0	4	56	+6	+1	+7
Laureano, Ramon	8	22	7	10	6	9	11	0	2	2	7	106	+9	+9	+18
LeMahieu, DJ	9	31	14	28	6	11	25	2	1	3	14	103	+4	+1	+5
Lindor, Francisco	3	27	14	22	1	11	17	2	1	3	13	88	-9	+12	+3
Locastro, Tim	1	13	4	7	3	3	10	1	0	1	1	38	+5	+17	+22
Long, Shed	2	6	7	8	1	2	1	0	1	1	1	21	0	-3	-3
Longoria, Evan	5	23	7	8	2	9	12	2	1	3	14	105	-6	+1	-5
Lopes, Tim	2	7	0	3	1	1	2	0	0	0	1	22	0	0	0
Lopez, Nicky	7	22	5	8	3	5	13	3	0	3	5	54	+3	-1	+2
Lowe, Brandon	6	18	7	9	0	1	12	0	0	0	1	65	+17	+5	+22
Lowe, Nate	2	12	5	6	1	1	6	0	1	1	4	47	+3	0	+3
Lucroy, Jonathan	3	19	3	8	0	5	6	2	2	5	17	80	-27	0	-27
Lugo, Dawel	3	9	2	3	1	7	13	1	0	1	8	44	+3	0	+3
Luplow, Jordan	3	13	5	6	3	3	11	0	0	0	7	60	+10	-1	+9
Machado, Manny	10	25	10	17	4	7	21	2	2	4	24	135	-3	-1	-4
Maldonado, Martin	1	15	4	13	1	2	8	2	1	3	11	57	-12	0	-16
Mancini, Trey	7	39	11	17	4	11	20	4	0	4	22	130	-12	+1	-11
Margot, Manuel	7	16	7	13	2	4	21	2	0	2	6	73	+14	+12	+26
Marisnick, Jake	3	11	5	10	0	0	14	2	0	2	6	74	+5	+4	+9
Markakis, Nick	3	25	10	17	5	10	12	3	0	3	11	100	-6	+2	-4
Marte, Ketel	13	30	16	20	4	10	16	1	0	1	7	103	+18	+6	+24
Marte, Starling	7	17	20	24	4	6	12	5	1	6	15	139	-4	+13	+9
Martin Jr., Richie	0	11	6	9	1	4	11	3	1	4	6	61	-7	+8	+1
Martin, Leonys	3	9	7	12	2	6	7	0	0	0	1	32	+7	-6	+1
Martin, Russell	2	10	7	12	1	2	4	1	0	1	1	30	0	+1	+1
Martinez, J.D.	4	24	9	20	3	11	19	0	1	1	19	123	-5	+2	-3
Martinez, Jose	5	26	5	9	2	5	13	1	0	1	14	77	-3	+3	0
Mathis, Jeff	2	10	0	3	0	0	8	1	1	2	2	27	-1	+1	0
Maybin, Cameron	4	11	9	10	1	4	9	1	2	3	5	48	0	-3	-3
Mazara, Nomar	2	15	8	13	1	8	13	2	1	3	5	85	-1	+2	+1
McCann, Brian	2	19	1	5	0	1	5	0	2	2	10	68	-13	0	-13
McCann, James	8	22	8	14	1	5	18	3	0	3	10	84	+3	+2	+5
McCutchen, Andrew	4	18	3	6	2	8	11	0	0	0	1	27	+7	0	+7
McKinney, Billy	4	11	5	9	2	2	5	2	0	2	0	42	+3	-4	-1
McMahon, Ryan	10	27	9	12	4	8	15	4	0	5	14	109	-3	+3	0
McNeil, Jeff	5	26	13	21	2	7	12	6	0	6	5	85	-11	-7	-18
Meadows, Austin	13	33	11	16	5	9	13	6	1	7	3	107	0	-2	-2
Mejia, Francisco	1	7	4	4	1	3	4	1	0	1	6	39	-3	-1	-4
Mercado, Oscar	8	20	12	17	2	3	13	0	2	2	9	81	+7	+7	+14
Mercer, Jordy	3	12	7	11	1	2	8	2	0	2	4	37	-1	0	-1
Merrifield, Whit	9	31	12	21	5	10	16	3	2	5	8	98	-4	0	-4
Molina, Yadier	6	18	7	14	0	6	12	1	1	2	14	89	-6	+6	0
Moncada, Yoan	11	31	13	21	3	6	14	3	1	5	1	98	+6	+4	+10
Mondesi, Adalberto	3	9	8	10	2	2	10	2	0	2	6	98	+8	+29	+37
Moore, Dylan	7	16	9	13	1	1	4	0	1	1	6	47	+1	-7	-6
Morales, Kendrys	2	11	1	7	1	6	0	0	0	0	6	37	-10	0	-10
Moran, Colin	4	18	1	9	5	6	2	1	0	1	13	111	-10	-2	-12
Moreland, Mitch	2	13	4	8	2	5	6	0	1	1	12	71	-7	+1	-6
Moustakas, Mike	5	27	11	15	2	9	12	2	0	2	12	124	-1	+3	+2
Muncy, Max	9	29	7	12	4	11	13	1	3	4	5	115	+2	+2	+4

2019 Baserunning

Player	1st to 3rd Moved	Chances	2nd to Home Moved	Chances	1st to Home Moved	Chances	Bases Taken	Out Adv	Doubled Off	BR Outs	GDP	GDP Opps	BR Gain	SB Gain	Net Gain
Munoz, Yairo	3	9	1	2	0	1	6	1	1	2	5	32	-4	+2	-2
Murphy, Daniel	6	17	9	12	7	14	8	4	0	4	10	88	-5	-1	-6
Murphy, Tom	1	5	5	8	1	2	3	3	1	4	0	48	-6	+2	-4
Myers, Wil	4	15	5	13	2	6	14	1	0	1	12	79	-1	+2	+1
Naquin, Tyler	5	13	6	8	3	4	7	0	1	1	8	37	+1	0	+1
Narvaez, Omar	7	27	7	14	1	11	7	1	1	2	5	79	-6	0	-6
Naylor, Josh	6	14	5	7	0	2	5	1	0	1	4	60	+4	-1	+3
Newman, Kevin	13	29	4	10	4	11	14	5	0	5	5	75	-2	0	-2
Nimmo, Brandon	3	10	2	3	7	10	3	1	1	2	1	36	0	+3	+3
Nola, Austin	2	6	5	8	2	4	18	1	0	1	8	55	+11	+1	+12
Nunez, Eduardo	1	2	0	1	0	0	5	1	0	1	6	35	-2	+3	+1
Nunez, Renato	9	22	7	14	2	3	18	3	0	3	9	112	+9	-1	+8
O'Hearn, Ryan	1	19	5	6	1	2	4	0	0	0	7	65	-2	-2	-4
O'Neill, Tyler	2	7	1	1	0	0	6	0	1	1	3	27	+2	+1	+3
Odor, Rougned	7	19	10	19	2	5	12	1	1	3	4	119	+7	-7	0
Ohtani, Shohei	6	18	11	15	0	3	10	3	0	3	6	107	+3	+6	+9
Olson, Matt	4	21	11	12	0	4	13	3	0	3	11	125	+1	0	+1
Osuna, Jose	0	13	5	9	3	4	6	2	0	2	6	46	-7	0	-7
Owings, Chris	1	2	1	3	0	1	6	0	2	2	2	31	-1	+1	0
Ozuna, Marcell	15	25	12	17	6	10	9	3	0	3	21	120	-2	+8	+6
Panik, Joe	3	28	8	15	4	8	10	2	2	4	6	71	-11	0	-11
Parra, Gerardo	3	8	6	10	2	3	10	3	0	3	7	64	-1	+2	+1
Pederson, Joc	9	26	3	10	1	4	14	0	3	3	4	56	0	-1	-1
Pence, Hunter	5	10	7	7	3	6	9	0	0	0	2	55	+15	+4	+19
Peralta, David	8	19	4	11	1	9	18	0	2	3	9	80	+1	0	+1
Peraza, Jose	10	19	8	10	2	3	9	5	1	6	9	71	-7	-5	-12
Perez, Hernan	2	10	3	5	1	2	7	1	0	1	9	47	-3	+3	0
Perez, Roberto	2	12	2	7	1	7	5	3	1	4	12	91	-19	0	-19
Pham, Tommy	10	28	10	21	8	11	20	8	0	8	22	132	-17	+17	0
Phegley, Josh	1	10	4	11	2	7	6	1	0	1	11	50	-11	-2	-13
Pillar, Kevin	7	14	10	16	13	15	17	1	0	1	15	125	+17	+4	+21
Pina, Manny	1	5	1	2	0	1	3	0	0	0	1	37	+3	0	+3
Pinder, Chad	4	15	3	5	5	6	5	0	0	0	11	90	+2	-2	0
Piscotty, Stephen	4	18	9	11	4	5	6	1	2	3	13	79	-8	+2	-6
Plawecki, Kevin	2	9	0	1	0	2	7	0	0	0	4	31	+3	-2	+1
Polanco, Jorge	14	35	16	20	6	10	23	2	1	3	11	128	+19	-2	+17
Pollock, A.J.	1	6	7	11	2	5	6	0	1	1	7	78	+1	+3	+4
Posey, Buster	7	18	4	11	0	10	10	2	0	2	18	90	-14	0	-14
Prado, Martin	4	15	3	7	1	4	4	0	0	0	10	50	-5	0	-5
Profar, Jurickson	3	18	8	13	4	6	11	1	1	2	12	111	0	+7	+7
Puello, Cesar	2	7	0	0	1	1	3	1	0	1	2	24	-1	0	-1
Puig, Yasiel	6	25	11	16	1	9	12	3	0	3	13	133	-5	+5	0
Pujols, Albert	3	17	4	11	2	6	15	1	0	2	21	105	-11	+3	-8
Ramirez, Harold	5	20	7	11	7	10	10	2	0	2	8	76	+2	0	+2
Ramirez, Jose	9	18	9	13	5	6	18	1	1	2	8	98	+17	+16	+33
Ramos, Wilson	2	27	4	10	0	11	7	0	3	3	16	93	-26	+1	-25
Realmuto, J.T.	14	26	9	16	5	8	13	2	1	3	12	122	+6	+7	+13
Reddick, Josh	4	26	3	9	3	10	18	1	0	2	9	117	+3	+1	+4
Rendon, Anthony	7	33	14	22	3	8	18	0	0	0	13	128	+9	+3	+12
Renfroe, Hunter	4	16	4	8	2	4	4	3	0	3	6	74	-8	+5	-3
Rengifo, Luis	12	28	6	8	7	10	12	1	1	2	6	74	+11	-8	+3
Reyes, Franmil	5	24	8	10	1	2	11	5	0	5	15	87	-14	0	-14
Reyes, Victor	3	8	5	8	4	5	13	3	2	5	5	30	-4	+3	-1
Reynolds, Bryan	13	36	6	10	5	9	14	3	1	4	9	112	+2	-1	+1
Rickard, Joey	4	11	2	3	2	3	1	0	0	0	1	24	+2	0	+2
Riley, Austin	2	10	4	10	3	4	6	1	1	2	4	64	-1	-4	-5
Rizzo, Anthony	13	37	3	14	2	17	21	5	2	7	15	135	-16	+1	-15
Robertson, Daniel	4	15	3	6	0	5	3	0	1	1	10	52	-10	-2	-12
Robles, Victor	7	22	11	19	5	7	13	6	0	6	6	106	-4	+10	+6
Rodriguez, Ronny	2	10	2	3	1	2	9	0	0	0	5	69	+8	+1	+9
Rojas, Josh	3	5	0	2	1	1	5	1	0	1	3	29	+1	0	+1
Rojas, Miguel	7	27	8	14	3	8	10	5	1	6	15	89	-21	-1	-22
Romine, Austin	1	8	2	4	2	2	4	0	0	0	7	49	-1	-1	-2
Rondon, Jose	5	11	0	1	1	2	4	2	0	2	4	34	-3	0	-3

2019 Baserunning

Player	1st to 3rd Moved	Chances	2nd to Home Moved	Chances	1st to Home Moved	Chances	Bases Taken	Out Adv	Doubled Off	BR Outs	GDP	GDP Opps	BR Gain	SB Gain	Net Gain
Rosario, Amed	7	20	11	14	3	6	18	2	0	2	13	138	+11	-1	+10
Rosario, Eddie	11	23	11	17	7	9	15	4	1	5	10	116	+5	+1	+6
Ruiz, Rio	5	16	7	10	1	5	16	3	1	4	12	66	-5	-2	-7
Russell, Addison	2	10	4	4	3	6	8	0	2	3	7	37	-5	+2	-3
Sanchez, Gary	7	17	0	10	2	5	10	1	0	1	3	77	+4	-2	+2
Sanchez, Yolmer	6	30	9	18	4	4	18	0	0	0	7	107	+14	-3	+11
Sandoval, Pablo	3	15	8	15	0	1	6	0	0	0	8	56	-2	+1	-1
Sano, Miguel	6	19	4	7	1	10	6	4	0	4	5	81	-9	-2	-11
Santana, Carlos	8	32	12	17	4	11	22	3	0	3	13	117	+5	+4	+9
Santana, Danny	6	14	12	12	2	7	23	0	1	1	8	92	+23	+9	+32
Santana, Domingo	6	15	4	7	1	4	12	2	0	2	11	95	+1	+2	+3
Santander, Anthony	2	14	2	6	2	4	12	2	0	2	1	81	+7	-3	+4
Schoop, Jonathan	4	10	9	11	4	8	9	2	1	3	13	101	-2	-1	-3
Schwarber, Kyle	7	26	4	9	0	6	14	4	0	4	6	90	-4	-4	-8
Seager, Corey	8	38	14	22	4	8	18	1	0	1	8	114	+12	+1	+13
Seager, Kyle	8	24	8	11	2	3	13	0	2	2	12	107	+5	-2	+3
Segura, Jean	11	24	11	14	4	10	20	3	2	5	11	104	+5	+6	+11
Semien, Marcus	6	26	14	19	4	10	34	3	1	4	11	98	+14	-6	+8
Senzel, Nick	4	12	11	18	4	7	8	4	2	6	6	50	-13	+4	-9
Severino, Pedro	3	13	5	9	0	4	4	1	2	3	5	65	-9	+1	-8
Shaw, Travis	2	10	1	2	3	5	7	1	0	1	5	46	+1	0	+1
Simmons, Andrelton	2	11	8	12	3	10	11	1	1	2	21	87	-13	+6	-7
Sisco, Chance	4	15	4	7	0	3	4	0	0	0	5	35	-1	-2	-3
Slater, Austin	3	9	2	4	3	3	7	1	0	1	1	38	+7	+1	+8
Smith Jr., Dwight	5	16	6	9	1	1	5	4	0	4	8	68	-10	+3	-7
Smith, Dominic	4	11	5	11	1	2	5	1	0	1	5	31	-2	-3	-5
Smith, Kevan	1	7	3	9	1	2	7	1	1	2	8	35	-9	+2	-7
Smith, Mallex	7	18	12	15	4	7	19	1	1	2	7	75	+14	+28	+42
Smith, Will	4	7	2	6	0	2	3	0	2	2	3	28	-5	+2	-3
Smoak, Justin	4	24	5	14	0	5	11	3	2	5	11	82	-20	0	-20
Sogard, Eric	5	19	6	10	3	6	15	1	0	1	4	74	+11	+8	+19
Solak, Nick	1	8	2	3	0	0	1	0	0	0	2	16	-2	+2	0
Solano, Donovan	2	9	7	9	0	1	9	1	0	1	4	36	+4	-2	+2
Soler, Jorge	7	39	11	23	2	4	14	1	0	1	16	133	-4	+1	-3
Soto, Juan	14	41	11	22	9	18	20	6	3	9	11	130	-10	+10	0
Springer, George	9	28	7	12	7	9	19	1	0	1	12	82	+11	+2	+13
Stallings, Jacob	1	10	5	9	2	3	2	0	1	1	3	30	-4	0	-4
Starling, Bubba	6	10	2	3	1	2	5	2	0	2	4	46	+2	+2	+4
Stewart, Christin	3	16	5	13	1	6	8	2	1	3	4	79	-7	-2	-9
Stewart, D.J.	3	7	1	2	0	0	3	1	0	2	3	25	-4	-3	-7
Story, Trevor	12	32	12	15	3	8	26	3	2	5	3	107	+18	+7	+25
Straw, Myles	5	11	7	9	3	4	9	2	0	2	2	16	+6	+6	+12
Suarez, Eugenio	4	26	2	17	1	5	12	7	0	7	12	141	-25	-1	-26
Suzuki, Kurt	4	15	2	5	2	4	8	0	0	0	10	70	+1	-2	-1
Swanson, Dansby	10	23	13	17	9	15	8	0	1	1	7	99	+12	0	+12
Tapia, Raimel	5	21	9	13	1	5	14	5	2	7	2	74	-7	+3	-4
Tatis Jr., Fernando	7	11	11	12	0	2	17	4	1	5	4	62	+7	+4	+11
Tauchman, Mike	8	14	6	10	3	4	11	2	0	2	9	47	+3	+6	+9
Taylor, Chris	5	15	7	11	3	5	9	1	1	2	6	76	+3	+8	+11
Tellez, Rowdy	1	10	8	10	2	6	4	2	2	4	9	66	-14	-1	-15
Thames, Eric	4	24	11	16	1	5	15	0	2	2	0	83	+11	-1	+10
Tilson, Charlie	6	17	2	4	1	2	4	0	0	0	1	29	+5	+4	+9
Torres, Gleyber	6	28	12	19	4	11	14	4	2	6	10	118	-9	+1	-8
Trout, Mike	14	36	13	17	5	11	23	1	2	3	5	123	+22	+7	+29
Turner, Justin	11	28	5	14	0	8	20	2	2	4	11	116	0	+2	+2
Turner, Trea	9	30	13	21	1	6	23	0	2	2	10	78	+8	+25	+33
Upton, Justin	6	13	4	5	1	1	7	1	1	2	5	56	+3	-1	+2
Urias, Luis	2	8	8	9	2	2	4	2	0	2	8	42	-5	-2	-7
Urshela, Giovanny	5	25	9	16	1	6	9	2	0	2	13	96	-9	-1	-10
VanMeter, Josh	2	9	6	7	1	5	1	0	0	0	5	49	-1	+3	+2
Vargas, Ildemaro	3	5	3	6	1	4	8	0	1	1	6	39	+1	+1	+2
Vazquez, Christian	9	19	6	10	1	9	21	2	0	2	17	97	+4	0	+4
Verdugo, Alex	5	14	7	10	3	3	13	1	1	2	8	75	+7	+2	+9
Villar, Jonathan	15	30	13	16	8	13	24	3	1	4	8	110	+21	+22	+43

2019 Baserunning

Player	1st to 3rd Moved	1st to 3rd Chances	2nd to Home Moved	2nd to Home Chances	1st to Home Moved	1st to Home Chances	Bases Taken	Out Adv	Doubled Off	BR Outs	GDP	GDP Opps	BR Gain	SB Gain	Net Gain
Vogelbach, Daniel	5	37	6	13	0	2	10	0	0	0	4	90	+2	0	+2
Vogt, Stephen	1	8	4	6	1	3	2	1	0	1	1	63	+1	+1	+2
Voit, Luke	6	32	6	11	3	11	18	6	1	7	12	117	-14	0	-14
Votto, Joey	8	46	11	23	2	4	16	2	2	4	14	102	-14	+5	-9
Walker, Christian	8	35	12	16	4	7	18	2	1	3	11	101	+4	+6	+10
Walker, Neil	0	14	5	9	4	9	7	1	0	1	8	76	-4	+3	-1
Wendle, Joey	2	8	4	4	5	5	10	1	1	2	4	43	+6	+2	+8
White, Tyler	0	8	1	4	1	4	4	0	0	0	7	55	-4	0	-4
Wilkerson, Stevie	6	16	7	14	2	3	11	3	0	3	5	70	+2	-3	-1
Winker, Jesse	6	17	5	14	0	3	9	4	0	5	10	50	-18	-4	-22
Wolters, Tony	6	16	10	16	4	5	11	3	0	3	9	72	0	-2	-2
Wong, Kolten	13	26	12	16	3	4	11	1	1	2	2	88	+15	+16	+31
Yastrzemski, Mike	6	18	8	12	7	8	9	3	2	5	4	79	0	-6	-6
Yelich, Christian	12	28	12	17	8	10	22	3	1	4	8	113	+17	+26	+43
Zimmerman, Ryan	4	10	4	5	0	0	9	1	0	1	4	38	+6	0	+6
Zobrist, Ben	1	10	2	4	0	4	5	0	1	1	6	36	-6	0	-6
Zunino, Mike	1	11	3	6	1	4	6	0	1	1	4	61	0	0	0

Career Baserunning

Players with 1000 Career Games
(Data goes back to 2002)

Player	1st to 3rd Moved	1st to 3rd Chances	2nd to Home Moved	2nd to Home Chances	1st to Home Moved	1st to Home Chances	Bases Taken	Out Adv	Doubled Off	BR Outs	GDP	GDP Opps	BR Gain	SB Gain	Net Gain
Alonso, Yonder	47	199	51	99	21	63	93	23	12	37	94	663	-93	+6	-87
Altuve, Jose	90	258	115	196	43	75	183	44	10	57	144	988	-47	+106	+59
Andrus, Elvis	180	354	160	214	66	100	267	31	23	55	156	1252	+164	+94	+258
Arenado, Nolan	70	219	77	115	23	48	94	13	7	20	114	890	0	-14	-14
Beckham, Gordon	59	164	84	122	14	37	116	20	13	34	89	673	-4	-5	-9
Belt, Brandon	59	246	75	126	19	60	121	31	6	37	37	847	+14	+5	+19
Blackmon, Charlie	78	264	97	151	34	57	149	22	9	32	41	545	+53	+21	+74
Brantley, Michael	78	276	78	138	37	85	158	15	5	21	113	973	+41	+57	+98
Braun, Ryan	115	338	136	199	56	101	208	32	14	46	174	1480	+55	+95	+150
Bruce, Jay	69	263	86	164	34	72	139	27	8	35	98	1267	+23	-15	+8
Cabrera, Asdrubal	101	328	124	202	38	95	217	57	9	70	163	1371	-44	+26	-18
Cabrera, Melky	114	389	126	212	57	118	222	44	17	63	182	1429	-35	+27	-8
Cabrera, Miguel	140	647	185	342	49	164	265	50	14	66	318	2105	-176	-4	-180
Cain, Lorenzo	91	212	97	141	39	56	142	16	10	26	99	759	+69	+95	+164
Cano, Robinson	124	451	195	314	48	115	256	42	23	66	277	1970	-63	-25	-88
Carpenter, Matt	84	301	94	172	28	66	143	32	12	44	34	674	-1	-9	-10
Castro, Starlin	79	290	102	158	39	82	137	24	12	36	171	1114	-62	-13	-75
Choo, Shin-Soo	108	406	147	233	46	107	246	29	21	50	101	1126	+64	+45	+109
Crawford, Brandon	50	216	85	132	21	45	135	18	4	22	93	957	+40	-25	+15
Cruz, Nelson	65	331	90	159	16	86	160	29	12	41	139	1303	-64	+12	-52
Davis, Chris	54	266	77	147	27	70	116	20	8	30	62	990	+5	-3	+2
Davis, Rajai	73	179	97	140	44	57	180	14	8	22	79	776	+141	+199	+340
Descalso, Daniel	48	138	62	86	15	39	93	8	1	9	33	473	+81	-4	+77
Desmond, Ian	98	250	108	165	40	63	180	23	11	35	132	1096	+70	+69	+139
Donaldson, Josh	66	218	72	115	27	70	144	25	14	39	90	872	-1	+22	+21
Dozier, Brian	97	236	84	131	33	58	128	20	10	31	88	805	+43	+33	+76
Encarnacion, Edwin	95	369	113	192	39	118	166	31	10	41	182	1555	-44	+33	-11
Fowler, Dexter	163	297	118	177	38	68	207	49	28	78	57	818	+62	+13	+75
Frazier, Todd	69	207	60	108	32	62	129	30	10	41	93	895	-12	-2	-14
Freeman, Freddie	80	298	119	187	33	95	161	23	7	30	110	1178	+35	+1	+36
Freese, David	60	255	64	124	15	55	73	24	11	36	135	600	-146	-14	-160
Gardner, Brett	117	289	118	187	46	78	232	21	19	40	55	943	+168	+145	+313
Goldschmidt, Paul	90	287	109	175	47	87	168	10	6	16	110	1104	+105	+61	+166
Gomez, Carlos	73	196	115	152	30	47	119	41	23	64	76	897	-35	+120	+85
Gonzalez, Carlos	72	234	119	183	52	95	159	22	8	30	93	1094	+84	+56	+140
Gordon, Alex	108	381	148	227	57	104	192	23	9	32	110	1182	+89	+23	+112
Granderson, Curtis	122	413	132	248	73	134	219	24	18	42	64	1323	+128	+53	+181
Harper, Bryce	86	218	76	138	59	104	131	39	19	58	76	985	-20	+22	+2
Heyward, Jason	111	304	121	184	50	78	169	21	7	28	86	1060	+123	+32	+155
Hosmer, Eric	74	298	112	178	45	79	139	27	14	43	134	1077	-44	+15	-29
Iannetta, Chris	37	192	57	115	18	57	103	15	6	21	83	794	-21	-9	-30
Jay, Jon	85	273	107	138	35	60	133	21	7	29	90	707	+40	-11	+29
Jones, Adam	102	332	126	186	66	108	199	25	10	37	190	1433	+46	+27	+73
Joyce, Matt	68	211	82	122	32	58	108	14	9	23	71	809	+50	-12	+38
Kemp, Matt	120	330	135	198	42	84	174	48	25	74	179	1442	-65	+57	-8
Kendrick, Howie	128	317	130	211	50	93	181	31	19	52	189	1190	-26	+32	+6
Kinsler, Ian	161	381	216	297	64	117	270	29	23	52	161	1307	+148	+95	+243
Kipnis, Jason	69	235	96	150	31	67	143	12	15	27	75	873	+56	+69	+125
LeMahieu, DJ	60	214	95	155	40	79	139	12	12	24	127	767	-8	-2	-10
Longoria, Evan	82	321	127	197	34	90	172	18	13	32	173	1446	+7	+23	+30
Lowrie, Jed	50	222	79	127	25	72	133	19	3	22	81	866	+31	+1	+32
Lucroy, Jonathan	44	198	64	123	22	64	100	25	11	38	136	870	-119	+12	-107
Machado, Manny	70	211	81	138	26	52	146	25	9	34	132	958	-8	+4	-4
Markakis, Nick	131	563	183	304	54	150	227	29	9	39	209	1647	-25	+4	-21
Martin, Russell	94	362	127	212	43	94	173	31	15	47	190	1270	-69	-1	-70
Martinez, J.D.	53	214	63	129	19	69	114	15	9	24	123	892	-54	+2	-52
Maybin, Cameron	65	171	102	139	41	60	122	15	17	33	83	752	+41	+73	+114
McCann, Brian	50	346	47	148	17	107	121	32	13	46	180	1439	-199	+7	-192
McCutchen, Andrew	104	400	143	218	50	104	161	19	12	32	94	1450	+50	+33	+83
Molina, Yadier	71	380	95	208	19	93	160	30	13	45	254	1483	-204	-8	-212
Morales, Kendrys	63	279	56	118	16	86	111	29	7	37	170	997	-148	-24	-172

414

Career Baserunning
Players with 1000 Career Games
(Data goes back to 2002)

Player	1st to 3rd Moved	1st to 3rd Chances	2nd to Home Moved	2nd to Home Chances	1st to Home Moved	1st to Home Chances	Bases Taken	Out Adv	Doubled Off	BR Outs	GDP	GDP Opps	BR Gain	SB Gain	Net Gain
Moreland, Mitch	33	189	59	107	14	52	83	12	9	22	93	817	-50	+1	-49
Moustakas, Mike	34	217	65	121	13	57	109	23	8	31	96	913	-59	-2	-61
Murphy, Daniel	91	280	101	149	51	92	139	29	9	39	121	1081	+12	+18	+30
Parra, Gerardo	75	225	114	165	31	61	156	44	9	54	110	940	-20	-12	-32
Pedroia, Dustin	92	368	137	217	52	147	191	45	15	62	154	1250	-76	+46	-30
Pence, Hunter	112	356	128	193	75	107	205	20	13	35	149	1330	+101	+10	+111
Posey, Buster	62	267	78	161	30	96	160	15	6	21	148	1018	-28	+5	-23
Prado, Martin	114	326	119	186	36	89	176	32	13	45	171	1077	-26	-16	-42
Pujols, Albert	185	596	215	323	60	162	295	75	23	101	374	2583	-154	+37	-117
Ramirez, Hanley	111	346	153	240	52	95	202	57	16	75	137	1245	-38	+95	+57
Reddick, Josh	77	222	62	105	31	60	137	10	12	24	66	877	+77	+24	+101
Reynolds, Mark	58	263	89	158	24	84	148	21	12	33	117	1143	-15	+2	-13
Rizzo, Anthony	67	251	73	135	21	83	136	37	16	53	98	1104	-70	-9	-79
Rodriguez, Sean	47	135	56	85	17	28	95	14	6	20	57	544	+35	+4	+39
Sandoval, Pablo	44	258	73	137	15	59	137	24	7	31	144	986	-74	-14	-88
Santana, Carlos	83	319	103	172	36	103	163	33	8	43	133	1158	-38	+10	-28
Seager, Kyle	78	219	74	134	21	51	138	27	10	38	96	998	+8	-5	+3
Segura, Jean	76	196	106	144	31	54	158	22	20	43	93	702	+22	+61	+83
Simmons, Andrelton	61	172	78	111	20	54	107	15	7	23	139	800	-28	+17	-11
Smoak, Justin	36	209	53	115	11	64	75	18	6	24	106	846	-100	-3	-103
Stanton, Giancarlo	43	206	73	130	21	60	137	23	4	28	91	1007	+10	+13	+23
Suzuki, Ichiro	170	652	226	357	73	146	323	35	18	54	89	1486	+169	+247	+416
Suzuki, Kurt	69	271	86	167	31	73	119	17	2	20	134	1106	-11	-3	-14
Trout, Mike	158	321	128	182	43	72	183	18	18	37	57	1003	+173	+128	+301
Trumbo, Mark	43	179	59	109	17	53	99	18	6	24	106	797	-39	-5	-44
Tulowitzki, Troy	101	311	107	177	25	67	165	34	17	52	146	1121	-37	-7	-44
Turner, Justin	73	220	72	121	19	58	111	21	5	29	90	821	-7	+14	+7
Upton, Justin	130	362	143	205	61	103	171	24	17	41	124	1430	+94	+35	+129
Votto, Joey	114	477	124	239	40	132	185	46	23	70	146	1455	-131	+21	-110
Walker, Neil	64	244	82	139	37	84	130	13	11	24	97	945	+21	-12	+9
Wieters, Matt	25	199	48	117	11	55	70	15	2	17	101	794	-89	+1	-88
Zimmerman, Ryan	107	350	140	210	54	109	183	26	7	33	203	1506	+29	+11	+40
Zobrist, Ben	129	353	112	194	49	114	229	21	15	36	124	1264	+109	+18	+127

2002-2019 MLB Averages

1st to 3rd	2nd to Home	1st to Home
28%	59%	44%

415

2019 Team Baserunning

Team	1st to 3rd Moved	1st to 3rd Chances	2nd to Home Moved	2nd to Home Chances	1st to Home Moved	1st to Home Chances	Bases Taken	Out Adv	Doubled Off	BR Outs	GDP	GDP Opps	BR Gain	SB Gain	Net Gain
Arizona D-Backs	101	272	100	164	33	83	178	18	6	26	119	1150	+62	+60	+122
Milwaukee Brewers	78	260	90	153	34	94	173	16	7	23	120	1172	+43	+51	+94
Texas Rangers	71	247	102	165	27	76	186	22	13	36	98	1095	+34	+55	+89
St Louis Cardinals	92	280	96	166	38	75	156	26	8	34	110	1162	+19	+58	+77
Philadelphia Phillies	78	254	91	164	35	93	173	22	9	31	97	1111	+34	+42	+76
Washington Nationals	98	305	97	168	34	84	176	28	8	36	116	1133	+13	+58	+71
Cleveland Indians	70	240	103	154	33	87	168	21	8	29	110	1059	+32	+33	+65
Boston Red Sox	109	286	103	180	44	110	201	26	8	34	126	1214	+54	+8	+62
Seattle Mariners	73	252	95	162	25	74	161	17	12	29	83	1078	+39	+21	+60
Los Angeles Dodgers	82	264	93	172	33	78	157	18	18	36	99	1157	+7	+37	+44
Atlanta Braves	82	282	120	181	48	90	145	23	17	40	104	1177	+5	+33	+38
Colorado Rockies	86	289	121	172	48	89	183	35	8	44	111	1087	+25	+9	+34
Chicago White Sox	97	319	101	171	24	64	186	23	12	36	114	1139	+25	+7	+32
Detroit Tigers	70	245	104	163	28	73	185	28	14	42	108	1048	+8	+17	+25
Baltimore Orioles	81	275	85	145	31	71	168	31	6	38	111	1076	-1	+24	+23
Los Angeles Angels	74	287	95	166	34	89	183	17	13	31	142	1194	-5	+25	+20
Oakland Athletics	72	276	100	144	39	82	150	19	8	27	139	1210	+7	+7	+14
Kansas City Royals	76	280	85	148	39	73	138	28	7	35	113	1059	-27	+39	+12
New York Yankees	88	301	115	190	32	91	159	27	8	35	112	1173	0	+11	+11
Tampa Bay Rays	87	301	98	160	42	82	152	33	9	42	114	1207	-15	+20	+5
Houston Astros	71	300	71	154	43	104	202	28	3	33	144	1277	-11	+13	+2
Chicago Cubs	111	280	83	130	31	91	176	27	16	44	127	1103	+1	-3	-2
Minnesota Twins	91	301	108	171	31	100	158	28	10	38	101	1175	+3	-14	-11
San Francisco Giants	70	258	94	146	39	90	136	23	9	32	110	1149	-3	-9	-12
Toronto Blue Jays	57	229	87	141	27	76	145	27	13	40	107	1060	-36	+11	-25
San Diego Padres	79	229	92	140	23	58	136	30	9	39	119	1056	-24	-4	-28
New York Mets	83	294	96	171	30	84	137	27	9	37	129	1173	-55	+2	-53
Pittsburgh Pirates	93	298	96	167	50	96	124	39	7	46	118	1130	-63	+6	-57
Cincinnati Reds	75	265	98	173	24	69	125	31	8	40	111	1076	-62	+4	-58
Miami Marlins	67	272	83	163	38	90	108	25	10	36	139	1084	-108	-5	-113
MLB Totals	2462	8241	2902	4844	1037	2516	4825	763	293	1069	3451	33984			

Stolen Base Attempt Times

Lindsay Zeck

Terrance Gore was the fastest at swiping second base in 2019 with an average time of 3.38 seconds. This is the second time he has claimed the title, the first being in 2016. However, it was Tim Locastro of the Diamondbacks who stole (see what I did there?) the show this season. The rookie not only finished in the top 5 of stolen base attempt times with an average time of 3.49 seconds, but was successful on all 17 of his attempts! The only other player to swipe at least 10 bags without getting caught was fellow rookie Cavan Biggio of the Blue Jays, who stole 14 bases successfully in 2019.

It was the season of speedy rookies. Five of the top 12 speedsters still had their rookie status intact through 2019. These players include: Gore, Locastro, Jon Berti, Nick Senzel, and Victor Robles.

Locastro, along with known speedster Jarrod Dyson, led the Diamondbacks to the second-fastest average stolen base time (3.59 seconds). The fastest team was the Royals (3.53 seconds)—with Adalberto Mondesi leading the way.

Speed, of course, is just one of the elements of a stolen base attempt:

- Biggio was perfect at stealing bases despite finishing 51st in speed (3.64 seconds).
- This year's stolen base champion—Mallex Smith of the Mariners with 46 stolen bases—finished as the 20th fastest.
- Keon Broxton finished with the eighth-fastest average time, but was successful on only 63% of his attempts (10 of 16).
- Elvis Andrus finished with the sixth-most stolen bases (31) despite only eight players with at least six timed attempts being slower than him.

Stolen Base Times - 2B Only

Runner	Timed Attempts	Average
Gore, Terrance	6	3.38
Buxton, Byron	12	3.45
Mondesi, Adalberto	22	3.49
Locastro, Tim	13	3.49
Hamilton, Billy	13	3.51
Dyson, Jarrod	29	3.52
Berti, Jon	14	3.52
Broxton, Keon	8	3.53
Bellinger, Cody	14	3.53
Laureano, Ramon	7	3.54
Robles, Victor	18	3.54
Senzel, Nick	11	3.54
Gardner, Brett	11	3.54
Marisnick, Jake	10	3.54
Story, Trevor	20	3.54
Turner, Trea	26	3.55
Edman, Tommy	9	3.56
Tatis Jr., Fernando	15	3.56
Ohtani, Shohei	10	3.56
Smith, Mallex	36	3.56
Kemp, Tony	8	3.56
Pham, Tommy	11	3.57
Swanson, Dansby	7	3.57
Acuna Jr., Ronald	33	3.59
Kipnis, Jason	6	3.59
Garcia, Leury	14	3.59
Profar, Jurickson	6	3.59
Marte, Starling	17	3.59
DeShields, Delino	16	3.60
Gordon, Dee	15	3.60
Inciarte, Ender	6	3.60
Kiermaier, Kevin	15	3.61
Anderson, Tim	13	3.61
Aquino, Aristides	7	3.61
Lindor, Francisco	15	3.61
Baez, Javier	11	3.61
Hernandez, Teoscar	6	3.61
Moncada, Yoan	10	3.61
Albies, Ozzie	13	3.61
Moore, Dylan	12	3.61
Straw, Myles	6	3.62
Goodrum, Niko	13	3.62
Trout, Mike	6	3.62
Ramirez, Jose	20	3.63
VanMeter, Josh	9	3.63
Lopes, Tim	8	3.63
Allen, Greg	7	3.63
Fletcher, David	8	3.63
Bader, Harrison	6	3.63
Soto, Juan	9	3.63
Biggio, Cavan	8	3.64
Tapia, Raimel	10	3.64
Odor, Rougned	11	3.64
Pillar, Kevin	10	3.64
Merrifield, Whit	10	3.64
Myers, Wil	15	3.65
Simmons, Andrelton	8	3.65
Yelich, Christian	17	3.65
Cain, Lorenzo	16	3.65
Martin, Leonys	6	3.66
Wong, Kolten	17	3.66
Mercado, Oscar	10	3.66
Newman, Kevin	19	3.66
Benintendi, Andrew	7	3.66
Harper, Bryce	9	3.67
Villar, Jonathan	25	3.68
Grossman, Robbie	10	3.68
Rosario, Amed	20	3.68
McNeil, Jeff	6	3.69
Puig, Yasiel	13	3.69
Goodwin, Brian	7	3.69

Runner	Timed Attempts	Average
Dahl, David	7	3.69
Iglesias, Jose	6	3.69
Santana, Danny	13	3.69
Realmuto, J.T.	6	3.69
Wendle, Joey	8	3.70
Meadows, Austin	14	3.71
Eaton, Adam	8	3.71
Freeman, Freddie	6	3.71
Segura, Jean	10	3.72
Margot, Manuel	15	3.72
Betts, Mookie	12	3.73
Hampson, Garrett	12	3.73
Devers, Rafael	12	3.73
Semien, Marcus	13	3.74
Reyes, Victor	9	3.74
Garcia, Avisail	10	3.74
Andrus, Elvis	19	3.76
Kingery, Scott	10	3.76
Heyward, Jason	6	3.77
Parra, Gerardo	7	3.78
Choo, Shin-Soo	6	3.79
Bradley Jr., Jackie	6	3.79
DeJong, Paul	8	3.82
Maybin, Cameron	9	3.83
Santana, Domingo	6	3.84

Pitchers' Repertoires

Lindsay Zeck

Let's talk about two pitchers, Max Scherzer and Stephen Strasburg of the Nationals. Their career stats have been circulating this season for being nearly identical. Take a look:

	ERA	WHIP	K/9	BB/9	H/9	HR/9
Max Scherzer	3.20	1.092	10.6	2.4	7.4	1.0
Stephen Strasburg	3.17	1.086	10.6	2.4	7.4	0.9

It's amazing to see the similarities in their career stats, but here we can look at the pitches they threw this season to see if there are similarities here too.

Both threw fastballs 48 percent of the time, with Scherzer edging out Strasburg in velocity by one mile per hour (94.9 to 93.9). It's in their secondary pitches this season that we begin to see a difference. Scherzer's was the slider which he threw 21% of the time (it was his most effective pitch), whereas Strasburg threw that pitch less than one percent of the time. His secondary pitch was a curveball that he threw 31% of the time with great effectiveness. Scherzer threw a curveball only nine percent of the time. Scherzer and Strasburg align again with their tertiary pitch, the changeup. They threw it 14% and 21% of the time, respectively.

They have both seen a steady decline in their fastball usage. Scherzer threw the heat 72% of the time during his rookie season. Strasburg's usage peaked at 73% in 2011—right after his Tommy John surgery.

Speaking of Tommy John surgery—Scherzer is the only pitcher in the Nationals starting rotation not to have had it. Along with Strasburg, whose season ended abruptly in 2010, Patrick Corbin, Anibal Sanchez, and sometimes starter Erick Fedde have all had the surgery. Corbin and Fedde both went under the knife in 2014.

Scherzer's career numbers give him a good chance at Hall of Fame enshrinement. We'll see if Strasburg can pitch well enough in his 30s to someday share a common bond with Scherzer there too.

Player	Tommy John SX	Fastball Velocity	Fastball	Slider	Change	Cutter	Curve	Splitter	Other
Abad, Fernando	-	93.3	58%	<1%	13%	-	28%	-	
Abreu, Bryan	-	95.1	32%	40%	2%	-	25%	-	
Adam, Jason	-	94.5	61%	-	12%	-	27%	-	
Adams, Austin	-	95.2	37%	63%	-	-	-	-	
Adams, Austin	-	96.2	55%	39%	7%	-	-	-	
Adams, Chance	-	91.8	59%	17%	7%	-	18%	-	
Agrazal, Dario	-	91.2	67%	19%	14%	-	<1%	-	
Alaniz, R.J.	-	93.7	51%	38%	11%	-	-	-	
Albers, Matt	-	92.8	57%	33%	10%	-	-	-	
Alcantara, Sandy	-	95.6	57%	23%	13%	-	7%	-	
Alcantara, Victor	-	93.4	75%	8%	17%	-	-	<1%	
Alexander, Scott	-	92.9	89%	8%	3%	-	-	-	
Alexander, Tyler	-	90.7	55%	18%	11%	16%	-	-	
Allard, Kolby	-	92.5	46%	-	15%	33%	5%	-	
Allen, Cody	Jan `08	92.3	54%	-	-	-	46%	-	
Allen, Logan	-	92.7	48%	23%	21%	-	7%	-	
Almonte, Yency	-	95.7	57%	40%	3%	-	-	-	
Altavilla, Dan	-	96.6	59%	41%	-	-	-	-	
Alvarado, Jose	-	98.2	79%	17%	-	-	4%	-	
Alvarez, Jose	-	91.5	53%	18%	22%	7%	-	-	
Alzolay, Adbert	-	94.4	57%	-	21%	-	22%	-	
Anderson, Brett	July `11	90.8	49%	19%	13%	14%	6%	-	
Anderson, Chase	-	93.4	51%	-	25%	14%	10%	-	
Anderson, Cody	Mar `17	94.4	44%	-	37%	-	19%	-	
Anderson, Drew	Apr `15	92.5	41%	-	4%	29%	26%	-	
Anderson, Justin	-	94.7	47%	52%	-	-	-	<1%	
Anderson, Nick	-	96.1	60%	-	-	-	40%	-	
Anderson, Shaun	-	92.6	58%	30%	9%	-	3%	-	
Anderson, Tanner	-	92.6	69%	19%	9%	2%	-	-	
Anderson, Tyler	-	91.3	48%	-	26%	20%	7%	-	
Andriese, Matt	-	92.5	50%	<1%	37%	-	11%	-	
Arano, Victor	-	93.5	38%	62%	-	-	-	-	
Archer, Chris	-	94.1	50%	36%	12%	-	2%	-	
Armenteros, Rogelio	-	91.0	48%	5%	29%	-	18%	-	
Armstrong, Shawn	-	93.4	59%	-	-	29%	12%	-	
Arrieta, Jake	-	92.5	56%	-	18%	12%	13%	-	
Avila, Pedro	Sept `19	93.6	29%	2%	46%	-	22%	-	
Avilan, Luis	-	90.5	30%	-	58%	-	12%	-	
Baez, Michel	-	96.1	59%	5%	33%	-	3%	-	
Baez, Pedro	-	95.9	51%	18%	32%	-	-	-	
Bailey, Homer	May `15	93.0	51%	13%	-	<1%	9%	26%	
Banda, Anthony	June `18	92.7	56%	-	34%	2%	8%	-	
Banuelos, Manny	Oct `12	91.7	48%	34%	8%	-	10%	-	
Bard, Luke	-	94.2	44%	50%	5%	-	-	-	
Barlow, Scott	June `12	94.1	43%	43%	<1%	-	13%	-	
Barnes, Jacob	-	93.7	48%	<1%	-	52%	-	-	
Barnes, Matt	-	96.7	47%	-	2%	-	51%	-	
Barraclough, Kyle	-	93.5	61%	22%	12%	5%	-	-	
Barrett, Aaron	Sept `15	91.7	71%	28%	1%	-	-	-	
Barrett, Jake	-	92.8	47%	39%	-	-	-	14%	
Barria, Jaime	-	91.7	37%	47%	16%	-	-	-	
Bashlor, Tyler	May `14	95.7	62%	-	12%	-	26%	-	
Bass, Anthony	-	95.4	52%	33%	-	-	-	15%	
Bassitt, Chris	May `16	93.5	65%	14%	8%	-	13%	-	
Bauer, Trevor	-	94.6	42%	14%	8%	16%	20%	-	
Bautista, Gerson	-	97.7	63%	36%	2%	-	-	-	
Bednar, David	-	95.3	43%	-	-	-	22%	34%	

Player	Tommy John SX	Fastball Velocity	Pitch Repertoire						
			Fastball	Slider	Change	Cutter	Curve	Splitter	Other
Bedrosian, Cam	May `11	93.0	48%	51%	-	-	-	1%	
Beede, Tyler	-	94.3	56%	11%	19%	-	14%	-	
Beeks, Jalen	-	92.2	44%	-	32%	6%	19%	-	
Bergen, Travis	Jan `16	90.5	69%	<1%	3%	-	28%	-	
Berrios, Jose	-	92.8	55%	-	16%	-	29%	-	
Bettis, Chad	-	93.0	39%	-	32%	17%	12%	-	
Biagini, Joe	Jan `10	94.0	51%	30%	11%	-	9%	-	
Biddle, Jesse	Oct `15	93.9	55%	20%	-	-	24%	-	
Bieber, Shane	-	93.1	46%	27%	7%	-	20%	-	
Bird, Kyle	-	91.3	52%	47%	<1%	-	-	-	
Blach, Ty	-	90.3	57%	9%	26%	-	9%	-	
Black, Ray	Apr `08	98.2	75%	24%	-	-	<1%	-	
Blackburn, Paul	-	90.6	51%	21%	6%	-	21%	-	
Blazek, Michael	-	95.2	72%	17%	7%	-	3%	-	
Bleier, Richard	-	89.1	65%	6%	5%	24%	-	-	
Blevins, Jerry	-	88.8	43%	-	8%	-	49%	-	
Bolanos, Ronald	-	94.3	63%	13%	5%	-	19%	-	
Borucki, Ryan	Mar `13	92.0	52%	27%	21%	-	-	-	
Boshers, Buddy	-	92.7	40%	-	7%	-	54%	-	
Bowman, Matt	-	92.8	54%	12%	-	18%	-	16%	
Boxberger, Brad	-	90.2	48%	19%	33%	-	-	-	
Boyd, Matthew	-	92.0	54%	36%	6%	-	4%	-	
Brach, Brad	-	93.9	54%	18%	19%	9%	-	-	
Bradford, Chasen	Aug `19	90.5	51%	36%	12%	-	-	-	
Bradley, Archie	-	95.5	70%	-	6%	-	25%	-	
Brasier, Ryan	June `14	96.1	59%	32%	9%	-	-	-	
Brault, Steven	-	92.0	64%	21%	14%	-	1%	-	
Brebbia, John	-	93.5	57%	43%	<1%	-	-	-	
Brennan, Brandon	Aug `13	94.8	52%	6%	42%	-	-	-	
Brewer, Colten	-	93.4	2%	12%	<1%	42%	45%	-	
Brice, Austin	-	93.2	51%	45%	4%	-	-	-	
Brigham, Jeff	July `12	96.6	51%	49%	-	-	-	-	
Britton, Zack	-	94.8	86%	14%	-	-	-	-	
Brooks, Aaron	-	92.0	54%	22%	20%	-	4%	-	
Brosseau, Mike	-	70.5	98%	2%	-	-	-	-	
Buchholz, Clay	-	89.5	34%	-	20%	28%	17%	-	
Buchter, Ryan	-	92.5	64%	-	-	14%	22%	-	
Buehler, Walker	Aug `15	96.6	60%	14%	<1%	13%	12%	-	
Bumgarner, Madison	-	91.4	43%	33%	5%	-	18%	-	
Bummer, Aaron	Aug `15	95.6	76%	7%	<1%	17%	-	-	
Bundy, Dylan	June `13	91.2	50%	23%	17%	-	10%	-	
Burdi, Nick	May `17	96.9	46%	54%	-	-	-	-	
Burke, Brock	-	91.6	62%	23%	16%	-	-	-	
Burnes, Corbin	-	95.2	57%	31%	-	-	8%	4%	
Burr, Ryan	June `19	95.0	58%	16%	-	26%	-	-	
Buttrey, Ty	-	97.1	57%	-	13%	-	30%	-	
Cabrera, Genesis	-	96.3	61%	-	17%	-	22%	-	
Cahill, Trevor	-	91.7	37%	18%	23%	-	22%	-	
Canning, Griffin	-	93.9	42%	29%	13%	-	16%	-	
Carasiti, Matt	-	95.4	58%	-	2%	21%	-	19%	
Carle, Shane	-	94.7	44%	13%	23%	-	19%	-	
Carpenter, David	-	93.4	58%	38%	-	-	-	4%	
Carpenter, Ryan	-	90.0	45%	28%	15%	-	12%	-	
Carrasco, Carlos	Sept `11	93.5	46%	31%	18%	-	4%	-	
Cashner, Andrew	-	93.9	48%	13%	28%	-	11%	-	
Castillo, Diego	-	98.3	49%	51%	-	-	-	-	
Castillo, Luis	-	96.5	51%	17%	33%	-	-	-	
Castro, Miguel	-	97.4	49%	31%	20%	-	-	-	

Player	Tommy John SX	Fastball Velocity	Pitch Repertoire						
			Fastball	Slider	Change	Cutter	Curve	Splitter	Other
Cease, Dylan	July '14	96.5	52%	21%	9%	-	18%	-	
Cessa, Luis	-	94.5	42%	50%	7%	-	<1%	-	
Chacin, Jhoulys	-	90.0	44%	50%	4%	<1%	<1%	2%	
Chafin, Andrew	June '09	93.8	61%	39%	-	-	-	-	
Chapman, Aroldis	-	98.4	69%	31%	<1%	-	-	-	
Chargois, JT	Sept '13	96.1	41%	59%	-	-	-	-	
Chatwood, Tyler	July '14 Jan '06	95.9	71%	-	7%	10%	11%	-	
Chavez, Jesse	-	91.2	45%	<1%	10%	45%	-	-	
Chen, Wei-Yin	Jan '06	91.3	51%	23%	4%	-	22%	-	
Chirinos, Yonny	-	93.9	57%	21%	-	-	-	22%	
Cimber, Adam	-	85.2	68%	32%	-	-	-	-	
Cishek, Steve	-	90.5	59%	40%	<1%	-	-	-	
Cisnero, Jose	May '14	96.4	61%	28%	9%	-	2%	-	
Civale, Aaron	-	92.6	38%	15%	6%	29%	11%	-	
Clarke, Taylor	Jan '13	93.7	53%	25%	12%	-	10%	-	
Clase, Emmanuel	-	99.3	79%	21%	-	-	-	-	
Claudio, Alex	-	85.7	46%	18%	36%	-	-	-	
Clevinger, Mike	Aug '12	95.5	51%	26%	11%	-	12%	-	
Clippard, Tyler	-	90.0	41%	-	31%	4%	4%	21%	
Cobb, Alex	May '15	92.3	48%	-	35%	-	17%	-	
Cole, A.J.	-	94.4	45%	42%	2%	-	11%	-	
Cole, Gerrit	-	97.2	54%	23%	7%	-	15%	-	
Cole, Taylor	-	93.2	42%	23%	31%	-	4%	-	
Collins, Tim	Apr '16 Mar '15	92.2	47%	-	-	32%	21%	-	
Colome, Alex	-	94.4	29%	-	-	71%	-	-	
Conley, Adam	-	95.4	62%	21%	17%	-	-	-	
Coonrod, Sam	Sept '17	96.5	65%	-	18%	-	17%	-	
Corbin, Patrick	Mar '14	91.9	54%	37%	6%	-	4%	-	
Cordero, Jimmy	-	97.5	68%	7%	18%	-	7%	-	
Cortes, Nestor	-	89.6	53%	33%	12%	-	3%	-	
Covey, Dylan	-	94.4	50%	10%	-	22%	-	18%	
Crichton, Stefan	-	93.0	64%	33%	3%	-	-	-	
Crick, Kyle	-	95.3	62%	37%	<1%	-	-	-	
Cueto, Johnny	Aug '18	91.3	51%	2%	18%	22%	6%	-	
Culberson, Charlie	-	89.5	88%	12%	-	-	-	-	
Darvish, Yu	Mar '15	94.2	35%	15%	<1%	35%	7%	8%	
Davies, Zach	-	88.5	53%	<1%	31%	12%	4%	-	
Davis, Austin	-	93.8	58%	24%	18%	-	-	-	
Davis, Rookie	-	91.4	73%	-	-	-	11%	16%	
Davis, Wade	-	93.2	46%	-	-	35%	19%	-	
Dayton, Grant	Aug '17	90.7	77%	-	-	-	23%	-	
De Leon, Jose	Mar '18	92.2	58%	3%	40%	-	-	-	
De Los Santos, Enyel	-	93.3	59%	22%	19%	-	-	-	
deGrom, Jacob	Oct '10	96.9	49%	32%	16%	-	3%	-	
Del Pozo, Miguel	Apr '16	94.7	57%	-	3%	-	40%	-	
DeSclafani, Anthony	-	94.7	56%	26%	5%	-	14%	-	
Despaigne, Odrisamer	-	92.9	54%	11%	7%	20%	8%	-	
Detwiler, Ross	-	91.4	52%	-	16%	19%	14%	-	
Devenski, Chris	-	94.8	44%	19%	37%	-	-	-	
Diaz, Edwin	-	97.5	66%	34%	-	-	-	-	
Diaz, Jairo	Mar '16	97.0	56%	44%	-	-	-	-	
Diaz, Miguel	-	94.8	53%	34%	13%	-	-	-	
Diehl, Phillip	-	91.0	45%	55%	-	-	-	-	
Diekman, Jake	-	95.8	54%	46%	<1%	-	-	-	
Dobnak, Randy	-	92.7	59%	28%	13%	-	-	-	
Dominguez, Seranthony	-	97.4	61%	34%	5%	-	-	-	

Player	Tommy John SX	Fastball Velocity	Fastball	Slider	Change	Cutter	Curve	Splitter	Other
Doolittle, Sean	-	93.5	88%	6%	6%	-	-	-	
Dowdy, Kyle	Jan `14	95.2	67%	14%	5%	-	14%	-	
Drake, Oliver	-	93.6	41%	<1%	-	-	-	58%	
Duffey, Tyler	-	94.0	54%	-	<1%	-	45%	-	
Duffy, Danny	June `12	92.4	53%	26%	12%	-	9%	-	
Dugger, Robert	-	89.9	59%	25%	3%	-	13%	-	
Duke, Zach	Oct `16	88.9	58%	5%	-	31%	7%	-	
Dull, Ryan	-	91.1	54%	40%	6%	-	-	-	
Dunn, Justin	-	92.5	58%	23%	7%	-	12%	-	
Dunn, Mike	-	91.5	47%	44%	-	-	9%	-	
Duplantier, Jon	-	92.2	59%	19%	9%	-	13%	-	
DuRapau, Montana	-	92.3	45%	38%	3%	-	14%	-	
Dyson, Sam	Nov `10	93.9	58%	7%	10%	25%	-	-	
Eades, Ryan	-	91.9	49%	35%	-	-	2%	14%	
Edwards Jr., Carl	-	93.9	75%	-	3%	-	22%	-	
Edwards, Jon	-	93.5	51%	41%	-	-	8%	-	
Eflin, Zach	-	93.6	56%	28%	8%	3%	5%	-	
Eickhoff, Jerad	-	89.5	39%	29%	-	-	32%	-	
Elias, Roenis	-	94.0	57%	4%	30%	-	9%	-	
Eovaldi, Nathan	Aug `16 Jan `07	97.5	43%	3%	-	22%	17%	14%	
Erlin, Robbie	May `16	90.6	51%	<1%	16%	9%	22%	-	
Escobar, Luis	-	95.1	68%	13%	19%	-	-	-	
Eshelman, Tom	-	85.6	46%	21%	18%	-	15%	-	
Estevez, Carlos	-	97.9	69%	27%	4%	-	-	-	
Estrada, Marco	-	87.4	54%	-	30%	11%	5%	-	
Fairbanks, Peter	Jan `17 Jan `11	97.4	44%	56%	-	-	-	-	
Familia, Jeurys	-	96.0	65%	27%	-	-	-	8%	
Faria, Jake	-	93.6	61%	11%	28%	-	-	-	
Farmer, Buck	-	95.1	49%	-	26%	-	25%	-	
Farrell, Luke	-	91.7	52%	35%	-	-	13%	-	
Fedde, Erick	June `14	92.3	55%	20%	7%	18%	-	-	
Feierabend, Ryan	Mar `09	85.6	23%	-	7%	-	2%	-	Knuckleball 68%
Feliz, Michael	-	95.2	73%	20%	6%	-	-	-	
Ferguson, Caleb	May `14	94.5	78%	-	<1%	<1%	22%	-	
Fernandez, Jose	-	92.5	56%	26%	-	18%	-	-	
Fernandez, Junior	-	96.8	42%	27%	32%	-	-	-	
Festa, Matt	-	92.6	53%	40%	-	-	7%	-	
Fiers, Mike	-	90.4	52%	<1%	12%	17%	17%	-	
Fillmyer, Heath	-	92.0	52%	19%	19%	-	10%	-	
Flaherty, Jack	-	93.9	58%	27%	2%	-	12%	-	
Flexen, Chris	July `14	94.3	62%	22%	13%	-	4%	-	
Floro, Dylan	-	93.9	68%	-	4%	29%	-	-	
Flynn, Brian	-	90.5	57%	41%	2%	-	<1%	-	
Foltynewicz, Mike	-	94.9	52%	29%	9%	-	10%	-	
Font, Wilmer	Oct `10	94.3	58%	12%	-	-	19%	10%	
Franco, Enderson	-	95.8	56%	14%	31%	-	-	-	
Frare, Caleb	Dec `12	92.4	60%	40%	-	-	-	-	
Freeland, Kyle	-	91.9	52%	6%	11%	31%	-	-	
Fried, Max	Aug `14	93.8	57%	16%	2%	-	25%	-	
Fry, Jace	June `15 June `12	92.5	25%	49%	7%	-	19%	-	
Fry, Paul	-	90.7	52%	46%	1%	-	-	-	
Fulmer, Carson	-	93.7	44%	-	16%	33%	8%	-	
Gagnon, Drew	-	92.1	54%	8%	33%	-	6%	-	
Gallegos, Giovanny	Jan `11	93.7	55%	44%	<1%	-	-	-	
Gallen, Zac	-	92.9	50%	-	16%	15%	19%	-	

Player	Tommy John SX	Fastball Velocity	Pitch Repertoire						
			Fastball	Slider	Change	Cutter	Curve	Splitter	Other
Gant, John	-	95.9	56%	-	23%	11%	10%	-	
Garcia, Bryan	Feb `18	94.3	52%	31%	17%	-	-	-	
Garcia, Edgar	-	93.9	50%	46%	4%	-	-	-	
Garcia, Jarlin	-	93.3	40%	43%	18%	-	-	-	
Garcia, Luis	-	97.1	47%	34%	-	-	-	19%	
Garcia, Rico	-	90.4	62%	-	27%	-	11%	-	
Garcia, Yimi	Oct `16	94.2	46%	37%	6%	11%	-	-	
Garrett, Amir	-	95.3	43%	57%	-	-	-	-	
Garrett, Reed	-	95.7	65%	7%	-	-	25%	3%	
Garton, Ryan	-	91.6	59%	-	-	24%	17%	-	
Gausman, Kevin	-	94.0	57%	2%	6%	-	<1%	35%	
Gaviglio, Sam	-	89.3	42%	44%	-	-	4%	10%	
Gearrin, Cory	Apr `14	91.3	44%	41%	15%	-	-	-	
German, Domingo	Mar `15	93.6	45%	-	19%	-	36%	-	
Gibaut, Ian	-	95.3	57%	22%	21%	-	-	-	
Gibson, Kyle	Sept `11	93.3	50%	21%	16%	-	12%	-	
Giles, Ken	-	97.0	51%	49%	-	-	-	-	
Gilmartin, Sean	-	89.5	34%	26%	35%	-	4%	-	
Ginkel, Kevin	-	93.5	54%	45%	1%	-	-	-	
Giolito, Lucas	Aug `12	94.3	55%	15%	26%	-	4%	-	
Givens, Mychal	-	95.3	70%	15%	14%	-	-	-	
Glasnow, Tyler	-	97.0	67%	-	4%	-	29%	-	
Godley, Zack	-	90.0	35%	-	6%	17%	42%	-	
Gomez, Jeanmar	-	91.1	51%	20%	23%	-	6%	-	
Gonsolin, Tony	-	93.7	48%	17%	-	-	10%	25%	
Gonzales, Marco	Apr `16	88.9	39%	-	24%	21%	16%	-	
Gonzalez, Chi Chi	July `17	92.2	55%	26%	11%	-	8%	-	
Gonzalez, Gio	-	89.3	51%	-	32%	-	17%	-	
Goody, Nick	Apr `13	92.7	51%	49%	-	-	-	-	
Gordon, Alex	-	78.4	87%	13%	-	-	-	-	
Gott, Trevor	-	94.7	77%	2%	4%	-	18%	-	
Grace, Matt	-	91.3	62%	30%	5%	3%	-	-	
Graterol, Brusdar	Aug `15	99.0	67%	31%	2%	-	-	-	
Gray, Jon	-	96.1	52%	34%	3%	-	11%	-	
Gray, Sonny	-	93.3	47%	22%	6%	<1%	25%	-	
Green, Chad	-	96.5	77%	21%	-	-	-	1%	
Greene, Shane	May `08	92.7	47%	21%	<1%	31%	-	-	
Gregerson, Luke	-	86.9	64%	27%	9%	-	-	-	
Greinke, Zack	-	90.0	46%	16%	22%	-	15%	-	
Grotz, Zac	-	91.9	48%	-	-	8%	3%	40%	
Gsellman, Robert	-	95.4	52%	27%	10%	-	12%	-	
Guduan, Reymin	-	95.7	49%	51%	-	-	-	-	
Guerra, Javier	-	98.0	77%	23%	-	-	-	-	
Guerra, Javy	Jan `05	92.8	59%	25%	9%	-	7%	-	
Guerra, Junior	-	94.7	60%	-	-	-	19%	21%	
Guerrero, Tayron	-	99.0	79%	20%	-	-	-	<1%	
Guerrieri, Taylor	July `13	93.9	45%	-	11%	-	44%	-	
Guilbeau, Taylor	-	94.4	64%	7%	29%	-	-	-	
Gustave, Jandel	June `17	96.1	72%	28%	-	-	-	-	
Hader, Josh	-	95.6	84%	15%	<1%	-	-	-	
Hahn, Jesse	Jan `10	95.1	63%	33%	5%	-	-	-	
Hale, David	-	93.4	60%	18%	21%	-	-	-	
Hall, Matt	-	90.5	66%	7%	3%	-	24%	-	
Hamels, Cole	-	91.4	47%	-	21%	19%	12%	-	
Hammer, J. D.	-	94.4	55%	45%	-	-	-	-	
Hand, Brad	-	92.7	46%	54%	-	-	-	-	
Happ, J.A.	-	91.3	67%	18%	14%	-	<1%	-	
Hardy, Blaine	-	88.2	22%	13%	45%	-	20%	-	

Player	Tommy John SX	Fastball Velocity	Fastball	Slider	Change	Cutter	Curve	Splitter	Other
Harper, Ryne	-	89.4	39%	-	1%	-	60%	-	
Harris, Will	Jan `09	91.3	-	-	-	58%	42%	-	
Hart, Donnie	-	86.8	62%	25%	13%	-	-	-	
Hartlieb, Geoff	-	95.8	70%	21%	9%	-	-	-	
Harvey, Hunter	July `16	98.4	69%	-	-	-	15%	15%	
Harvey, Joe	June `15	95.2	76%	22%	1%	-	-	-	
Harvey, Matt	Oct `13	93.2	47%	28%	10%	-	14%	-	
Heaney, Andrew	July `16	92.5	58%	27%	15%	-	-	-	
Heller, Ben	Apr `18	93.2	49%	43%	8%	-	-	-	
Hellickson, Jeremy	-	88.5	45%	-	23%	18%	13%	-	
Helsley, Ryan	-	97.8	57%	-	3%	32%	9%	-	
Hembree, Heath	-	93.6	70%	16%	-	-	14%	-	
Hendricks, Kyle	-	86.9	62%	-	28%	-	10%	-	
Hendriks, Liam	-	96.5	70%	22%	<1%	-	8%	-	
Herget, Jimmy	-	93.3	55%	39%	6%	-	-	-	
Hernandez, Darwinzon	-	95.5	74%	25%	-	-	<1%	-	
Hernandez, David	Mar `14	93.6	52%	33%	<1%	-	15%	-	
Hernandez, Elieser	-	90.6	55%	33%	11%	-	-	-	
Hernandez, Felix	-	89.6	40%	9%	16%	-	35%	-	
Hernandez, Jonathan	-	96.9	48%	36%	16%	-	-	-	
Herrera, Kelvin	-	96.0	56%	12%	19%	13%	-	-	
Hess, David	-	93.0	59%	25%	12%	-	4%	-	
Hicks, Jordan	June `19	101.2	61%	33%	-	-	-	6%	
Hildenberger, Trevor	-	87.8	37%	26%	37%	-	-	-	
Hill, Rich	June `11	90.3	53%	3%	<1%	<1%	44%	<1%	
Hill, Tim	-	90.2	76%	24%	-	-	-	-	
Hirano, Yoshihisa	-	91.1	48%	-	-	-	<1%	52%	
Hoffman, Jeff	May `14	93.7	59%	<1%	11%	-	29%	-	
Holder, Jonathan	-	92.2	55%	23%	16%	6%	-	-	
Holland, Derek	-	92.4	62%	24%	<1%	-	10%	3%	
Holland, Greg	Oct `15	91.6	47%	43%	-	-	9%	<1%	
Holmes, Clay	Mar `14	94.3	63%	12%	1%	-	24%	-	
Houser, Adrian	July `16	94.4	67%	12%	7%	-	14%	-	
Howard, Sam	-	92.7	44%	56%	-	-	-	-	
Hoyt, James	-	94.0	42%	45%	-	-	-	13%	
Huang, Wei-Chieh	-	92.9	54%	3%	23%	-	21%	-	
Hudson, Dakota	-	93.7	62%	26%	3%	-	10%	-	
Hudson, Daniel	June `13 July `12	96.1	71%	23%	6%	-	-	-	
Hughes, Jared	-	91.3	80%	12%	8%	-	-	-	
Hultzen, Danny	-	93.2	59%	27%	14%	-	-	-	
Hunter, Tommy	-	94.1	53%	-	-	33%	14%	-	
Iglesias, Raisel	-	95.5	47%	31%	22%	-	-	-	
Irvin, Cole	Feb `14	89.8	51%	20%	26%	-	3%	-	
Jackson, Edwin	-	93.4	44%	26%	7%	20%	3%	-	
Jackson, Jay	-	94.4	41%	56%	3%	-	-	-	
Jackson, Luke	-	96.1	38%	53%	<1%	-	9%	-	
James, Josh	-	97.2	63%	20%	14%	-	2%	-	
Jansen, Kenley	-	92.0	88%	12%	-	-	-	-	
Jeffress, Jeremy	-	93.8	64%	-	8%	-	28%	-	
Jennings, Dan	-	91.2	57%	43%	-	-	-	-	
Jerez, Williams	-	94.1	56%	31%	-	-	-	13%	
Jewell, Jake	-	94.4	50%	36%	15%	-	-	-	
Jimenez, Eduardo	June `14	93.4	57%	38%	5%	-	-	-	
Jimenez, Joe	-	95.2	68%	26%	6%	-	-	-	
Johnson, Brian	-	88.9	38%	27%	1%	-	34%	-	
Johnson, D.J.	-	93.5	58%	-	<1%	6%	36%	-	
Jones, Nate	July `14	94.9	59%	39%	2%	-	-	-	

Player	Tommy John SX	Fastball Velocity	Fastball	Slider	Change	Cutter	Curve	Splitter	Other
Junis, Jakob	-	91.5	51%	44%	5%	-	-	-	
Jurado, Ariel	-	92.4	64%	15%	12%	-	9%	-	
Kahnle, Tommy	-	96.5	44%	4%	52%	-	-	-	
Karinchak, James	-	97.1	56%	-	-	-	44%	-	
Karns, Nate	-	90.5	66%	1%	14%	-	19%	-	
Kay, Anthony	Oct `16	93.4	62%	-	19%	-	19%	-	
Kela, Keone	-	96.3	53%	-	3%	-	44%	-	
Keller, Brad	-	93.4	67%	31%	<1%	-	-	1%	
Keller, Kyle	-	94.6	68%	-	-	-	32%	-	
Keller, Mitch	-	95.4	60%	19%	5%	-	17%	-	
Kelley, Shawn	Sept `10 Jan `03	92.0	40%	60%	-	-	-	-	
Kelley, Trevor	-	88.7	60%	21%	2%	17%	-	-	
Kelly, Joe	-	98.0	51%	-	13%	-	36%	-	
Kelly, Merrill	-	91.9	47%	-	13%	19%	21%	-	
Kennedy, Ian	-	94.5	68%	-	2%	15%	15%	-	
Kershaw, Clayton	-	90.4	44%	39%	<1%	-	16%	-	
Keuchel, Dallas	-	88.4	54%	11%	15%	20%	-	-	
Kikuchi, Yusei	-	92.5	49%	28%	-	-	16%	7%	
Kimbrel, Craig	-	96.2	67%	-	-	-	33%	-	
Kingham, Nick	May `15	91.6	49%	1%	17%	14%	19%	-	
Kinley, Tyler	-	95.0	42%	58%	-	-	-	-	
Kintzler, Brandon	-	92.7	73%	10%	17%	-	-	-	
Kittredge, Andrew	-	95.0	58%	37%	5%	-	-	-	
Kline, Branden	Oct `15	96.3	57%	34%	9%	-	<1%	-	
Kluber, Corey	-	91.6	40%	-	9%	29%	23%	-	
Koch, Matt	-	92.4	48%	-	16%	28%	7%	-	
Kolarek, Adam	-	89.3	82%	8%	9%	1%	-	-	
Kuhnel, Joel	-	96.1	61%	33%	6%	-	-	-	
Lakins, Travis	-	93.8	39%	-	4%	37%	19%	-	
Lambert, Peter	-	92.7	53%	13%	21%	-	13%	-	
Lamet, Dinelson	Apr `18	96.1	55%	44%	1%	-	-	-	
Lauer, Eric	-	91.9	53%	6%	4%	22%	15%	-	
Law, Derek	June `14	94.1	37%	31%	13%	-	20%	-	
Leake, Mike	-	88.4	34%	11%	20%	25%	9%	-	
LeBlanc, Wade	-	86.1	28%	<1%	31%	30%	10%	-	
Leclerc, Jose	-	96.8	50%	<1%	37%	-	1%	12%	
Leone, Dominic	-	94.1	48%	15%	1%	36%	-	-	
Lester, Jon	-	90.3	38%	-	12%	35%	15%	-	
Liriano, Francisco	Nov `06	93.0	45%	30%	25%	-	-	-	
Littell, Zack	-	93.9	49%	-	<1%	50%	1%	-	
Loaisiga, Jonathan	May `16	96.9	56%	-	13%	-	31%	-	
Lockett, Walker	-	92.6	56%	-	20%	-	24%	-	
Lopez, Jorge	-	94.2	54%	6%	7%	-	32%	-	
Lopez, Pablo	Nov `13	93.6	59%	-	22%	-	19%	-	
Lopez, Reynaldo	-	95.5	59%	20%	15%	-	7%	-	
Lopez, Yoan	-	96.3	57%	39%	-	-	-	4%	
Lorenzen, Michael	-	96.9	36%	9%	19%	28%	7%	-	
Loup, Aaron	-	91.7	43%	15%	6%	36%	-	-	
Lovelady, Richard	-	93.6	61%	39%	<1%	-	-	-	
Lucas, Josh	Jan `11	90.1	53%	46%	1%	-	-	-	
Lucchesi, Joey	-	90.2	51%	<1%	35%	14%	<1%	-	
Luciano, Elvis	-	94.1	55%	26%	19%	-	-	-	
Lugo, Seth	-	94.4	57%	13%	7%	-	24%	-	
Luzardo, Jesus	Mar `16	96.4	49%	-	20%	-	31%	-	
Lyles, Jordan	-	92.6	52%	9%	7%	<1%	32%	-	
Lynn, Lance	Nov `15	94.2	71%	16%	1%	-	9%	2%	
Lyons, Tyler	-	89.7	40%	49%	10%	-	-	-	

Player	Tommy John SX	Fastball Velocity	Fastball	Slider	Change	Cutter	Curve	Splitter	Other
Maeda, Kenta	-	92.1	37%	31%	24%	<1%	7%	-	
Magill, Matt	May `15	95.2	51%	17%	-	-	31%	-	
Mahle, Tyler	-	93.3	57%	-	-	7%	23%	13%	
Manaea, Sean	-	89.8	64%	21%	15%	-	-	-	
Mantiply, Joe	Mar `18	89.3	52%	31%	17%	-	-	-	
Maples, Dillon	-	96.8	33%	59%	-	-	7%	-	
Margevicius, Nick	-	88.3	54%	25%	8%	-	13%	-	
Markel, Parker	-	95.6	48%	51%	1%	-	-	-	
Marquez, German	-	95.5	52%	20%	3%	-	24%	-	
Marshall, Evan	-	93.6	44%	-	40%	-	17%	-	
Martin, Brett	-	93.9	52%	33%	-	-	15%	-	
Martin, Chris	-	95.7	63%	10%	-	15%	-	12%	
Martin, Corbin	July `19	95.3	63%	7%	11%	-	19%	-	
Martinez, Carlos	-	95.8	50%	28%	18%	3%	-	-	
Marvel, James	May `14	90.5	54%	-	20%	-	26%	-	
Maton, Phil	-	91.0	57%	24%	-	-	19%	-	
Matz, Steven	May `10	93.4	51%	14%	20%	-	15%	-	
May, Dustin	-	96.0	57%	-	1%	31%	11%	-	
May, Trevor	Mar `17	95.6	63%	16%	10%	-	11%	-	
Mayers, Mike	-	94.8	54%	37%	<1%	-	9%	-	
Mayza, Tim	Sept `19	94.2	64%	36%	-	-	-	-	
Mazza, Chris	-	92.1	51%	20%	5%	24%	-	-	
McCarthy, Kevin	-	91.2	59%	6%	22%	12%	-	-	
McClain, Reggie	-	93.8	77%	18%	5%	-	-	-	
McFarland, T.J.	-	89.5	68%	16%	16%	-	-	-	
McGee, Jake	July `08	93.5	80%	20%	-	-	-	-	
McGowin, Kyle	-	91.0	52%	45%	3%	-	-	-	
McHugh, Collin	-	90.8	33%	43%	3%	12%	8%	-	
McKay, Brendan	-	93.7	57%	-	4%	13%	26%	-	
McKay, David	-	93.9	63%	-	-	-	37%	-	
McRae, Alex	-	92.6	57%	20%	10%	-	13%	-	
Means, John	-	91.8	51%	14%	29%	-	6%	-	
Mejia, Adalberto	-	92.8	54%	26%	16%	-	4%	-	
Melancon, Mark	Oct `06	92.1	17%	-	3%	49%	31%	-	
Mella, Keury	-	95.4	63%	17%	19%	-	-	-	
Melville, Tim	Oct `12	89.3	34%	54%	6%	-	6%	-	
Mendez, Yohander	-	93.8	41%	25%	34%	-	-	-	
Menez, Conner	-	91.2	61%	16%	15%	-	8%	-	
Mengden, Daniel	-	91.2	53%	12%	11%	15%	10%	-	
Middleton, Keynan	May `18	94.1	57%	20%	23%	-	-	-	
Mikolas, Miles	-	93.6	52%	24%	1%	-	21%	2%	
Miley, Wade	-	90.5	22%	<1%	20%	48%	9%	-	
Miller, Andrew	-	92.5	39%	61%	-	-	-	-	
Miller, Justin	-	92.2	80%	20%	<1%	-	-	-	
Miller, Shelby	May `17	94.3	70%	-	2%	4%	24%	-	
Mills, Alec	July `13	89.7	54%	11%	19%	-	16%	-	
Milner, Hoby	-	87.6	69%	27%	4%	-	-	-	
Milone, Tommy	-	87.1	44%	11%	38%	-	7%	-	
Minaya, Juan	-	93.4	63%	17%	21%	-	-	-	
Minor, Mike	-	92.6	45%	19%	25%	-	11%	-	Knuckleball <1%
Minter, A.J.	Mar `15	96.0	39%	-	16%	45%	-	-	
Montas, Frankie	-	96.6	57%	25%	-	-	-	18%	
Montero, Rafael	Mar `18	95.8	47%	14%	39%	-	-	-	
Montgomery, Jordan	June `18	91.7	50%	-	18%	-	32%	-	
Montgomery, Mike	-	92.0	43%	-	21%	15%	21%	-	
Moore, Andrew	-	91.2	49%	8%	29%	-	14%	-	
Moore, Matt	Apr `14	93.0	54%	-	12%	19%	15%	-	
Moran, Brian	Apr `14	84.4	56%	44%	-	-	-	-	

427

Player	Tommy John SX	Fastball Velocity	Fastball	Slider	Change	Cutter	Curve	Splitter	Other
Morejon, Adrian	-	96.4	54%	-	6%	-	28%	12%	
Morgan, Adam	-	92.6	28%	38%	20%	-	14%	-	
Morin, Mike	-	91.3	48%	15%	37%	-	-	-	
Moronta, Reyes	Jan `13	97.2	58%	32%	7%	-	3%	-	
Morton, Charlie	June `12	94.4	49%	-	3%	10%	37%	-	
Munoz, Andres	-	99.9	68%	32%	-	-	-	-	
Murphy, John Ryan	-	61.5	100%	-	-	-	-	-	
Musgrave, Harrison	Jan `11	91.3	53%	38%	9%	-	-	-	
Musgrove, Joe	-	92.4	49%	23%	11%	8%	9%	-	
Nelson, Jimmy	-	92.7	52%	27%	<1%	-	20%	-	
Neris, Hector	-	94.6	35%	-	-	-	-	65%	
Neshek, Pat	Nov `08	88.5	38%	62%	<1%	-	-	-	
Neverauskas, Dovydas	-	95.8	57%	-	<1%	21%	22%	-	
Newberry, Jake	-	93.8	53%	45%	3%	-	-	-	
Newcomb, Sean	-	94.4	65%	9%	7%	-	19%	-	
Nicasio, Juan	-	93.6	55%	45%	-	-	-	-	
Noesi, Hector	Jan `07	93.0	44%	30%	9%	-	17%	-	
Nogosek, Stephen	-	95.1	67%	28%	5%	-	-	-	
Nola, Aaron	-	92.9	46%	-	19%	-	35%	-	
Norris, Daniel	-	90.8	52%	23%	19%	-	7%	-	
Norwood, James	-	96.3	64%	18%	-	-	-	19%	
Nova, Ivan	Apr `14	92.4	54%	13%	16%	-	17%	-	
O'Day, Darren	-	86.8	55%	45%	-	-	-	-	
Oberg, Scott	Jan `11	94.4	52%	43%	5%	-	-	-	
Odorizzi, Jake	-	92.9	58%	14%	17%	5%	6%	-	
Oh, Seunghwan	Jan `01	91.1	42%	39%	-	-	14%	5%	
Olson, Tyler	-	87.1	45%	20%	13%	-	22%	-	
Ortiz, Luis	-	94.1	54%	16%	16%	-	14%	-	
Osich, Josh	Jan `10	94.5	17%	-	5%	67%	11%	-	
Osuna, Roberto	July `13	96.7	49%	18%	18%	14%	-	-	
Oswalt, Corey	-	91.6	68%	-	17%	4%	11%	-	
Otero, Dan	Jan `09	89.1	67%	14%	19%	-	-	-	
Ottavino, Adam	May `15	93.9	42%	45%	-	14%	-	-	
Paddack, Chris	Aug `16	93.9	61%	-	29%	-	10%	-	
Pagan, Emilio	-	95.5	61%	36%	-	-	2%	-	
Palumbo, Joseph	Apr `17	94.0	57%	1%	17%	-	25%	-	
Pannone, Thomas	-	89.8	62%	-	15%	<1%	23%	-	
Parker, Blake	-	91.2	48%	-	-	5%	15%	32%	
Parsons, Wes	-	93.7	57%	34%	7%	-	3%	-	
Paxton, James	-	95.5	60%	-	1%	20%	19%	-	
Payamps, Joel	-	92.8	61%	36%	3%	-	-	-	
Payano, Pedro	-	93.6	47%	21%	20%	-	13%	-	
Pazos, James	-	94.3	68%	32%	-	-	-	-	
Peacock, Brad	-	92.2	59%	29%	6%	-	7%	-	
Pena, Felix	-	91.5	49%	-	11%	-	39%	-	
Peralta, Freddy	-	93.6	78%	-	1%	-	21%	-	
Peralta, Wandy	-	95.3	37%	38%	25%	-	-	-	
Peralta, Wily	Jan `07	94.4	55%	30%	-	-	2%	13%	
Perdomo, Luis	-	94.2	55%	34%	11%	-	-	-	
Perez, Cionel	-	95.3	62%	25%	10%	-	2%	-	
Perez, Martin	May `14	94.1	42%	-	22%	31%	5%	-	
Perez, Oliver	-	91.7	51%	49%	-	-	-	-	
Peters, Dillon	July `14	91.1	50%	5%	21%	-	24%	-	
Peterson, Tim	-	90.3	55%	13%	-	-	-	32%	
Petit, Yusmeiro	-	89.2	45%	21%	19%	-	14%	-	
Petricka, Jake	-	93.2	65%	9%	25%	-	-	-	
Phelps, David	Mar `18	92.7	43%	-	<1%	29%	28%	-	
Phillips, Evan	-	94.2	66%	26%	8%	-	-	-	

Player	Tommy John SX	Fastball Velocity	Fastball	Slider	Change	Cutter	Curve	Splitter	Other
Pineda, Michael	July `17	92.6	55%	30%	15%	-	-	-	
Pivetta, Nick	-	94.6	51%	12%	1%	-	35%	-	
Plesac, Zach	Apr `16	94.0	51%	19%	21%	-	10%	-	
Plutko, Adam	-	91.1	54%	24%	11%	-	11%	-	
Poche, Colin	June `14	93.0	89%	10%	-	-	-	2%	
Pomeranz, Drew	-	92.7	61%	-	2%	6%	32%	-	
Ponce de Leon, Daniel	-	93.4	71%	-	7%	14%	8%	-	
Poppen, Sean	-	94.7	57%	39%	4%	-	-	-	
Porcello, Rick	-	90.5	56%	19%	12%	-	13%	-	
Pounders, Brooks	Sept `13	91.7	35%	61%	4%	-	-	-	
Poyner, Bobby	-	89.4	66%	15%	18%	-	<1%	-	
Pressly, Ryan	-	95.6	36%	29%	-	-	35%	-	
Price, David	-	92.0	52%	-	26%	19%	3%	-	
Pruitt, Austin	-	91.9	44%	-	19%	23%	13%	-	
Puk, A.J.	Apr `18	97.1	64%	25%	9%	-	2%	-	
Quantrill, Cal	Mar `15	94.5	57%	21%	18%	-	4%	-	
Quijada, Jose	-	93.3	72%	11%	17%	-	-	-	
Quinn, Roman	-	79.0	100%	-	-	-	-	-	
Quintana, Jose	-	91.4	62%	6%	11%	-	21%	-	
Rainey, Tanner	-	97.8	71%	29%	<1%	-	-	-	
Ramirez, JC	Apr `18	91.0	54%	14%	-	-	31%	<1%	
Ramirez, Neil	-	94.5	56%	31%	-	-	13%	-	
Ramirez, Nick	-	89.8	30%	8%	32%	24%	6%	-	
Ramirez, Noe	-	89.2	28%	37%	34%	-	-	-	
Ramirez, Yefry	-	92.8	53%	14%	29%	-	4%	-	
Ramos, Edubray	-	91.6	37%	54%	8%	-	-	-	
Ray, Robbie	-	92.4	53%	32%	-	-	16%	-	
Reed, Cody	-	94.2	55%	39%	7%	-	-	-	
Reid-Foley, Sean	-	92.6	50%	34%	9%	-	7%	-	
Reininger, Zac	Jan `15	93.9	59%	23%	4%	<1%	13%	-	
Reyes, Alex	Feb `17	96.8	59%	13%	13%	-	15%	-	
Reyes, Gerardo	-	97.0	74%	26%	-	-	-	-	
Rhame, Jacob	-	94.9	68%	10%	22%	-	-	-	
Richard, Clayton	-	90.4	72%	25%	3%	-	-	-	
Richards, Garrett	July `18	95.1	58%	29%	<1%	-	12%	-	
Richards, Trevor	-	90.9	44%	-	38%	11%	7%	-	
Rios, Yacksel	-	96.3	60%	27%	13%	-	-	-	
Roark, Tanner	-	92.1	55%	18%	10%	4%	13%	-	
Robertson, David	Aug `19	91.7	57%	13%	-	-	30%	-	
Robles, Hansel	-	97.1	57%	21%	22%	-	-	-	
Rodgers, Brady	May `17	91.4	53%	28%	12%	-	7%	-	
Rodney, Fernando	Apr `04	93.9	68%	3%	29%	-	-	-	
Rodon, Carlos	May `19	91.5	52%	37%	11%	-	-	-	
Rodriguez, Dereck	-	90.6	48%	14%	21%	-	17%	-	
Rodriguez, Eduardo	-	93.1	55%	4%	24%	18%	-	-	
Rodriguez, Jefry	-	93.5	70%	-	7%	-	23%	-	
Rodriguez, Jose	-	93.4	46%	-	37%	-	17%	-	
Rodriguez, Richard	-	93.2	85%	15%	<1%	-	-	-	
Roe, Chaz	-	92.1	29%	65%	<1%	6%	-	-	
Rogers, Josh	July `19 Apr `13	89.5	53%	22%	23%	-	1%	-	
Rogers, Taylor	-	94.8	50%	46%	-	-	4%	-	
Rogers, Tyler	-	82.4	67%	33%	-	-	-	-	
Romano, Jordan	Mar `15	94.6	64%	36%	-	-	-	-	
Romano, Sal	-	96.0	64%	33%	-	-	3%	-	
Romero, Fernando	July `14	97.0	67%	29%	4%	-	-	-	
Romo, Sergio	-	86.4	24%	60%	16%	-	-	-	
Rondon, Hector	Aug `10	96.7	60%	36%	4%	-	-	-	

Player	Tommy John SX	Fastball Velocity	Fastball	Slider	Change	Cutter	Curve	Splitter	Other
Rosario, Randy	May `14	93.9	70%	30%	-	-	-	-	
Rosenthal, Trevor	Aug `17	98.0	72%	-	3%	25%	-	-	
Ross, Joe	July `17	94.1	63%	21%	8%	-	9%	-	
Ross, Tyson	-	90.0	47%	28%	-	25%	-	-	
Rosscup, Zac	-	92.4	41%	59%	-	-	-	-	
Ruiz, Jose	-	96.4	62%	21%	13%	-	4%	-	
Ryan, Kyle	-	89.6	47%	-	<1%	40%	13%	-	
Ryu, Hyun-Jin	Jan `04	90.6	41%	<1%	27%	19%	12%	-	
Sabathia, CC	-	89.2	16%	30%	12%	42%	-	-	
Sadler, Casey	Oct `15	93.5	38%	31%	3%	-	27%	-	
Sadzeck, Connor	Mar `14	96.0	47%	53%	-	-	-	-	
Salas, Fernando	-	89.7	57%	10%	33%	-	-	-	
Salazar, Danny	Aug `10	86.3	32%	12%	53%	-	3%	-	
Sale, Chris	-	93.2	46%	38%	15%	-	-	-	
Samardzija, Jeff	-	91.9	46%	20%	-	23%	2%	9%	
Sampson, Adrian	July `09	92.5	54%	33%	13%	-	-	-	
Sanchez, Aaron	-	93.6	58%	-	19%	-	23%	-	
Sanchez, Anibal	Jan `03	90.5	35%	3%	28%	27%	6%	-	
Sandoval, Patrick	-	93.0	46%	9%	31%	-	13%	-	
Santana, Dennis	-	92.7	57%	29%	14%	-	-	-	
Santana, Ervin	-	90.1	51%	42%	6%	-	-	-	
Santiago, Hector	-	91.8	60%	16%	19%	2%	3%	-	
Sborz, Josh	-	95.3	64%	28%	-	-	8%	-	
Scherzer, Max	-	94.9	48%	21%	14%	8%	9%	-	
Schlitter, Brian	Jan `11	93.3	83%	5%	2%	10%	-	-	
Schreiber, John	-	91.8	62%	31%	7%	-	-	-	
Schultz, Jaime	Jan `10	95.7	51%	32%	-	-	17%	-	
Scott, Robby	-	87.7	51%	38%	3%	-	8%	-	
Scott, Tanner	-	95.9	59%	41%	-	-	-	-	
Scott, Tayler	-	94.5	57%	43%	-	-	-	-	
Selman, Sam	-	89.9	42%	58%	-	-	-	-	
Senzatela, Antonio	-	93.7	63%	20%	4%	-	10%	3%	
Severino, Luis	-	96.1	57%	27%	16%	-	-	-	
Sewald, Paul	-	91.1	71%	26%	4%	-	-	-	
Shafer, Justin	-	94.3	52%	26%	3%	19%	-	-	
Shaw, Bryan	-	92.5	<1%	9%	7%	75%	8%	-	
Shawaryn, Mike	-	91.9	43%	25%	2%	30%	-	-	
Sheffield, Justus	-	92.8	48%	36%	17%	-	-	-	
Shepherd, Chandler	July `09	92.2	47%	24%	11%	4%	14%	-	
Sherfy, Jimmie	-	92.0	39%	57%	3%	-	-	-	
Shoemaker, Matt	-	90.5	47%	18%	-	-	2%	33%	
Sims, Lucas	-	93.6	51%	17%	6%	-	26%	-	
Sipp, Tony	July `07	90.5	48%	32%	20%	-	-	-	
Skaggs, Tyler	Aug `14	91.4	51%	-	16%	-	34%	-	
Skoglund, Eric	-	89.7	62%	8%	13%	-	17%	-	
Smeltzer, Devin	-	89.1	46%	7%	26%	-	22%	-	
Smith, Burch	Apr `15	92.6	64%	<1%	16%	-	20%	-	
Smith, Caleb	-	91.6	54%	32%	15%	-	-	-	
Smith, Joe	-	88.0	58%	41%	1%	-	-	-	
Smith, Josh A.	Jan `07	91.4	39%	5%	8%	25%	23%	-	
Smith, Josh D.	-	90.5	62%	37%	<1%	-	-	-	
Smith, Will	Mar `17	92.7	47%	44%	2%	-	8%	-	
Smyly, Drew	July `17	91.2	48%	-	5%	18%	29%	-	
Sneed, Cy	-	93.1	42%	12%	12%	29%	6%	-	
Snell, Blake	-	95.6	48%	7%	20%	-	25%	-	
Sobotka, Chad	-	96.1	56%	43%	<1%	-	-	-	
Soria, Joakim	Apr `12 Jan `03	92.7	68%	19%	7%	-	6%	-	

430

Player	Tommy John SX	Fastball Velocity	Fastball	Slider	Change	Cutter	Curve	Splitter	Other
Soroka, Mike	-	92.5	63%	24%	12%	-	-	-	
Soto, Gregory	-	95.4	70%	24%	6%	-	-	-	
Sparkman, Glenn	July `15	93.5	61%	8%	13%	-	19%	-	
Speier, Gabe	Sept `13	94.5	61%	37%	2%	-	-	-	
Springs, Jeffrey	-	92.1	58%	11%	31%	-	-	-	
St. John, Locke	-	89.7	56%	28%	17%	-	-	-	
Stammen, Craig	-	92.8	72%	16%	<1%	-	12%	-	
Stanek, Ryne	-	97.6	56%	22%	-	-	-	23%	
Stashak, Cody	-	91.8	54%	39%	7%	-	-	-	
Staumont, Josh	-	95.9	70%	-	-	-	30%	-	
Steckenrider, Drew	May `13	94.8	62%	38%	-	-	-	-	
Stephenson, Robert	-	95.0	37%	57%	7%	-	-	-	
Stewart, Brock	-	91.6	54%	33%	13%	-	-	-	
Stewart, Kohl	-	91.7	54%	32%	4%	-	9%	-	
Stock, Robert	-	97.9	54%	38%	8%	-	-	-	
Strahm, Matt	July `13	91.5	38%	30%	14%	-	17%	-	
Straily, Dan	-	90.3	52%	20%	24%	-	4%	-	
Strasburg, Stephen	Sept `10	93.9	48%	<1%	21%	-	31%	-	
Stratton, Chris	-	92.2	57%	24%	7%	-	12%	-	
Strickland, Hunter	May `13	95.9	64%	32%	4%	-	-	-	
Stripling, Ross	Apr `14	90.5	39%	18%	15%	-	29%	-	
Stroman, Marcus	-	92.5	39%	2%	5%	24%	30%	-	
Strop, Pedro	-	93.6	37%	40%	-	18%	-		5%
Stumpf, Daniel	-	92.1	53%	38%	9%	-	-	-	
Suarez, Andrew	-	92.8	56%	23%	15%	<1%	5%	-	
Suarez, Jose	-	91.8	47%	3%	31%	-	19%	-	
Suarez, Ranger	-	92.4	53%	21%	27%	-	-	-	
Suero, Wander	-	92.9	<1%	-	21%	72%	7%	-	
Sulser, Cole	Jan `15 Apr `11	93.4	64%	27%	9%	-	-	-	
Suter, Brent	July `18	87.5	78%	-	18%	-	3%	-	
Swanson, Erik	-	92.7	68%	18%	10%	-	-	4%	
Swarzak, Anthony	-	93.4	41%	59%	-	-	-	-	
Syndergaard, Noah	-	97.7	59%	15%	16%	-	10%	-	
Taillon, Jameson	Aug `19 Apr `14	94.8	47%	32%	5%	-	16%	-	
Tanaka, Masahiro	-	91.5	31%	36%	1%	2%	3%	27%	
Tarpley, Stephen	-	92.5	51%	47%	-	-	2%	-	
Tate, Dillon	-	93.7	56%	24%	19%	-	-	-	
Taylor, Josh	-	94.9	61%	38%	-	-	2%	-	
Teheran, Julio	-	89.7	64%	21%	9%	-	6%	-	
Tepera, Ryan	-	93.7	57%	6%	-	31%	-	6%	
Thornburg, Tyler	-	93.7	55%	-	19%	-	26%	-	
Thornton, Trent	-	92.9	47%	15%	9%	16%	13%	-	
Thorpe, Lewis	Apr `15	91.3	50%	21%	12%	-	17%	-	
Tinoco, Jesus	-	93.9	62%	27%	2%	-	8%	-	
Tomlin, Josh	Aug `12	89.3	31%	-	9%	43%	17%	-	
Torres, Carlos	-	91.2	19%	-	-	57%	24%	-	
Toussaint, Touki	-	93.5	49%	-	-	-	27%	23%	
Treinen, Blake	-	96.7	67%	13%	<1%	20%	-	-	
Trivino, Lou	-	97.5	50%	-	5%	34%	11%	-	
Tropeano, Nick	Aug `16	90.8	47%	-	20%	-	24%	9%	
Tuivailala, Sam	-	93.5	62%	20%	-	-	18%	-	
Turnbull, Spencer	-	93.8	65%	20%	3%	-	12%	-	
Underwood Jr., Duane	-	94.8	59%	-	26%	-	15%	-	
Urena, Jose	-	95.9	63%	26%	11%	-	-	-	
Urias, Julio	-	95.2	60%	17%	16%	-	6%	-	
Urquidy, Jose	Jan `17	93.3	47%	17%	26%	-	10%	-	

Player	Tommy John SX	Fastball Velocity	Fastball	Slider	Change	Cutter	Curve	Splitter	Other
Valdez, Framber	-	93.0	61%	-	4%	-	34%	-	
Valdez, Phillips	-	92.3	58%	5%	36%	-	-	-	
Vargas, Jason	Aug `15	84.3	49%	-	35%	-	15%	-	
Vazquez, Felipe	-	98.5	61%	17%	8%	-	14%	-	
Velasquez, Vince	Sept `10	94.1	67%	20%	1%	-	12%	-	
Velazquez, Hector	-	91.6	52%	17%	2%	-	2%	27%	
Venditte, Pat	-	84.7	54%	38%	8%	-	-	-	
Venters, Jonny	Sept `14 May `13 Jan `05	93.1	80%	17%	3%	-	-	-	
VerHagen, Drew	June `08	93.2	53%	31%	<1%	-	16%	-	
Verlander, Justin	-	94.7	50%	28%	4%	-	17%	-	
Vieira, Thyago	-	97.5	68%	26%	-	-	-	6%	
Vincent, Nick	-	89.1	58%	-	4%	38%	<1%	-	
Vizcaino, Arodys	Mar `12	96.0	53%	-	-	-	47%	-	
Volquez, Edinson	Aug `17 Aug `09	93.4	48%	-	37%	-	15%	-	
Voth, Austin	-	92.8	60%	11%	8%	-	20%	-	
Wacha, Michael	-	93.1	51%	-	24%	15%	10%	-	
Waguespack, Jacob	-	91.6	49%	5%	8%	24%	14%	-	
Wainwright, Adam	Feb `11	89.9	38%	-	1%	23%	37%	<1%	
Walden, Marcus	Mar `10	94.2	36%	37%	-	27%	-	-	
Walker, Jeremy	-	92.2	63%	-	<1%	-	36%	-	
Walsh, Jared	Jan `12	90.1	69%	-	11%	-	20%	-	
Wang, Wei-Chung	Jan `11	91.5	44%	37%	16%	-	4%	-	
Warren, Adam	-	91.4	31%	47%	18%	-	4%	-	
Warren, Art	Jan `14	95.1	44%	53%	-	-	3%	-	
Watson, Tony	-	93.0	51%	11%	38%	-	-	-	
Weaver, Luke	-	93.9	52%	-	25%	14%	9%	-	
Webb, Jacob	Apr `15	95.1	54%	33%	12%	-	-	-	
Webb, Logan	June `16	92.9	56%	24%	20%	-	-	-	
Webb, Tyler	Jan `08	89.9	65%	16%	19%	-	-	-	
Weber, Ryan	-	89.4	54%	14%	17%	<1%	15%	-	
Webster, Allen	-	94.4	43%	42%	15%	-	-	-	
Wendelken, J.B.	Oct `16	94.8	60%	5%	17%	-	18%	-	
Wheeler, Zack	Mar `15	96.7	59%	20%	9%	-	10%	2%	
White, Tyler	-	78.1	72%	1%	24%	-	3%	-	
Wick, Rowan	-	95.9	66%	4%	-	2%	28%	-	
Wieck, Brad	Mar `11	93.8	77%	11%	-	-	12%	-	
Wilkerson, Aaron	Aug `11	89.9	50%	17%	15%	-	17%	-	
Wilkerson, Stevie	-	57.8	100%	-	-	-	-	-	
Williams, Devin	Mar `17	96.2	60%	2%	37%	-	-	-	
Williams, Taylor	Aug `15	95.3	63%	31%	6%	-	-	-	
Williams, Trevor	-	91.3	67%	20%	12%	-	<1%	-	
Wilson, Alex	July `07	91.6	46%	-	<1%	54%	-	-	
Wilson, Bryse	-	94.7	72%	12%	13%	-	2%	-	
Wilson, Justin	-	95.1	52%	9%	-	39%	-	-	
Wingenter, Trey	-	95.9	55%	45%	-	-	-	-	
Winkler, Dan	July `14	92.7	21%	21%	6%	52%	-	-	
Wisler, Matt	-	92.8	29%	70%	-	-	<1%	-	
Wittgren, Nick	-	92.3	66%	-	15%	-	19%	-	
Wojciechowski, Asher	-	91.6	54%	25%	2%	19%	-	-	
Wood, Alex	Jan `09	90.0	50%	-	25%	-	25%	-	
Wood, Hunter	-	93.6	56%	-	11%	28%	5%	-	
Woodruff, Brandon	-	96.3	64%	20%	14%	-	2%	-	
Workman, Brandon	June `15	92.9	34%	-	-	19%	47%	-	
Wotherspoon, Matt	-	91.0	62%	21%	17%	-	-	-	
Wright Jr., Mike	-	92.9	58%	1%	5%	36%	-	-	

Player	Tommy John SX	Fastball Velocity	Pitch Repertoire						
			Fastball	Slider	Change	Cutter	Curve	Splitter	Other
Wright, Kyle	-	94.6	54%	26%	8%	-	12%	-	
Wright, Steven	-	82.5	6%	-	-	-	-	-	Knuckleball 94%
Yacabonis, Jimmy	-	93.6	64%	30%	7%	-	-	-	
Yamamoto, Jordan	-	91.5	50%	15%	3%	18%	14%	-	
Yarbrough, Ryan	-	88.2	24%	14%	26%	37%	-	-	
Yardley, Eric	-	86.2	67%	33%	-	-	-	-	
Yates, Kirby	Jan `06	93.5	57%	<1%	-	-	<1%	42%	
Ynoa, Gabriel	-	93.5	56%	27%	13%	-	4%	-	
Ynoa, Huascar	-	97.5	61%	35%	5%	-	-	-	
Young, Alex	-	89.3	36%	23%	20%	-	20%	-	
Zamora, Daniel	-	88.6	24%	73%	2%	-	-	-	
Zeuch, T.J.	-	91.9	52%	20%	20%	-	8%	-	
Zimmer, Kyle	-	96.5	61%	26%	5%	-	8%	-	
Zimmermann, Jordan	Aug `09	90.5	47%	31%	-	-	20%	2%	

Relief Pitching

Mark Simon

This was a great season to be a reliever in that it was easier to find employment than ever before. The average team used 24 relievers this season (not including position players who filled in during blowouts). That's seven more than the average at the start of the decade.

But this was a tough season to be a reliever in terms of performance. Relievers finished the season with a 4.46 ERA, more than half a run higher than at the start of the decade (3.93). By contrast, starters' ERAs went from 4.15 in 2010 to 4.54 now.

You're going to see a lot of names on these lists over the next few pages. Those worth noting include Padres closer Kirby Yates, who finished with 41 saves in 44 opportunities and had a 1.19 ERA, the lowest of anyone with at least 50 relief innings this season. Teammate Craig Stammen wasn't the closer, but he put Yates in position to get those saves, tying Ryan Pressly and Jake Diekman for the MLB lead in holds with 31.

Two of the best relievers in baseball were Yusmeiro Petit of the Athletics and Will Harris of the Astros. Petit had 29 holds and only one blown save. Harris had 26 holds with only one blown. And check out the inherited runners section, where you'll see how Andrew Chafin of the Diamondbacks showed his worth (six runners scoring out of 53 inherited), as did Nick Wittgren of the Indians, who allowed only two of 26 to score.

One thing we'll be keeping a close eye on next season will be the new rule (pending owners' vote) requiring a reliever to pitch to at least three batters or reach the end of an inning upon entering the game. How teams react and adjust to this rule will shape how these numbers look and which names appear in next year's book.

This section gives the usage and performance of each team's bullpen. Many of the stats are described in more detail in the Baseball Glossary at the end of the book.

Arizona Diamondbacks

Pitcher	Pos	T	Rel G	Early Entry	Cons Days	Long	Lev Ind	#	Scrd	Pct	Easy	Reg	Tough	Clean	Win	BS	Holds	Sv/Hld Pct	Opp OPS	Rel ERA
Bradley, Archie	CL	R	65	5	11	15	1.5	25	7	.28	9 - 9	7 - 8	2 - 4	46	0	3	7	.89	.697	3.07
Holland, Greg	CL	R	40	0	8	2	1.8	5	2	.40	13 - 13	4 - 9	0 - 0	28	0	5	0	.77	.687	4.54
Chafin, Andrew	SU	L	77	17	22	2	1.3	53	6	.11	0 - 0	0 - 3	0 - 1	58	0	4	23	.85	.691	3.76
Lopez, Yoan	SU	R	70	12	16	2	1.2	26	7	.27	0 - 1	1 - 2	0 - 1	49	0	3	21	.88	.728	3.41
Hirano, Yoshihisa	SU	R	62	12	10	6	1.5	29	6	.21	1 - 3	0 - 1	0 - 2	40	1	5	15	.76	.723	4.75
Ginkel, Kevin	SU	R	25	5	7	3	1.3	12	2	.17	1 - 1	1 - 1	0 - 0	17	0	0	8	1.00	.532	1.48
McFarland, T.J.	LT	L	51	21	10	11	0.6	32	12	.38	0 - 0	0 - 0	0 - 0	25	0	0	9	1.00	.842	4.82
Scott, Robby	LT	L	11	3	3	1	0.5	5	1	.20	0 - 0	0 - 0	0 - 0	7	0	0	0		.899	4.91
Andriese, Matt	LM	R	54	16	6	18	1.0	25	6	.24	0 - 1	1 - 2	0 - 1	31	0	3	4	.63	.757	4.71
Crichton, Stefan	UR	R	28	7	7	6	0.5	12	4	.33	0 - 0	0 - 0	0 - 0	20	0	0	3	1.00	.578	3.56
Godley, Zack	UR	R	18	5	0	8	0.2	2	0	.00	0 - 0	2 - 2	0 - 0	12	0	0	0	1.00	.711	4.62
Sherfy, Jimmie	UR	R	17	5	3	4	0.8	12	1	.08	0 - 0	0 - 1	1 - 1	11	0	1	0	.50	.867	5.89
Duplantier, Jon	UR	R	12	3	1	8	1.4	0	0	.00	0 - 0	1 - 1	0 - 0	8	0	0	0	1.00	.710	3.42

Atlanta Braves

Pitcher	Pos	T	Rel G	Early Entry	Cons Days	Long	Lev Ind	#	Scrd	Pct	Easy	Reg	Tough	Clean	Win	BS	Holds	Sv/Hld Pct	Opp OPS	Rel ERA
Jackson, Luke	CL	R	71	8	16	10	1.8	26	12	.46	7 - 9	8 - 12	3 - 4	41	1	7	9	.79	.733	3.84
Melancon, Mark	CL	R	23	0	5	2	1.4	2	0	.00	7 - 7	4 - 4	0 - 0	19	0	0	0	1.00	.580	3.86
Newcomb, Sean	SU	L	51	10	9	9	1.2	18	7	.39	1 - 1	0 - 0	0 - 2	34	1	2	16	.89	.661	3.04
Swarzak, Anthony	SU	R	44	7	7	4	1.1	20	6	.30	1 - 1	0 - 0	0 - 0	29	0	0	17	1.00	.739	4.31
Minter, A.J.	SU	L	36	2	7	2	1.4	10	5	.50	3 - 3	1 - 2	1 - 2	21	0	2	5	.83	.857	7.06
Greene, Shane	SU	R	27	0	9	1	1.4	4	4	1.00	0 - 0	1 - 2	0 - 1	18	0	2	10	.85	.736	4.01
Martin, Chris	SU	R	20	0	1	1	1.0	1	1	1.00	0 - 0	0 - 0	0 - 1	15	1	1	6	.86	.589	4.08
Blevins, Jerry	LT	L	45	7	11	3	0.6	21	6	.29	0 - 0	0 - 0	1 - 1	33	0	0	10	1.00	.685	3.90
Biddle, Jesse	LT	L	15	5	2	2	0.9	7	4	.57	0 - 0	0 - 0	0 - 0	7	0	0	0		.882	5.40
Dayton, Grant	LT	L	14	7	3	2	0.3	8	3	.38	0 - 0	0 - 0	0 - 1	9	0	1	1	.50	.824	3.00
Toussaint, Touki	LM	R	23	11	0	12	0.8	13	5	.38	0 - 0	0 - 0	0 - 0	10	0	0	2	1.00	.773	4.24
Tomlin, Josh	UR	R	50	14	4	16	0.7	25	3	.12	0 - 0	2 - 4	0 - 0	32	1	2	7	.82	.740	3.77
Webb, Jacob	UR	R	36	5	7	5	0.9	18	5	.28	1 - 2	1 - 1	0 - 1	27	0	2	9	.85	.661	1.39
Sobotka, Chad	UR	R	32	5	3	8	0.8	19	6	.32	0 - 0	0 - 0	0 - 0	21	0	0	6	1.00	.820	6.21
Winkler, Dan	UR	R	27	5	6	2	1.1	18	4	.22	0 - 0	0 - 1	0 - 0	20	0	1	6	.86	.804	4.98
Parsons, Wes	UR	R	17	8	2	2	0.9	18	7	.39	0 - 0	0 - 0	0 - 0	9	0	0	1	1.00	.745	3.52

Baltimore Orioles

Pitcher	Pos	T	Rel G	Early Entry	Cons Days	Long	Lev Ind	#	Scrd	Pct	Easy	Reg	Tough	Clean	Win	BS	Holds	Sv/Hld Pct	Opp OPS	Rel ERA
Givens, Mychal	CL	R	58	0	9	11	1.7	21	2	.10	4 - 4	3 - 8	4 - 7	38	0	8	7	.69	.722	4.57
Armstrong, Shawn	SU	R	51	15	10	14	1.3	23	9	.39	0 - 2	4 - 5	0 - 2	29	0	5	9	.72	.777	5.13
Fry, Paul	LT	L	66	18	15	13	1.2	43	11	.26	2 - 2	0 - 1	1 - 5	41	0	5	11	.74	.752	5.34
Bleier, Richard	LT	L	52	12	8	6	0.9	34	17	.50	2 - 2	2 - 3	0 - 0	30	0	1	5	.90	.793	5.23
Scott, Tanner	LT	L	28	10	5	6	0.7	12	2	.17	0 - 1	0 - 0	0 - 0	16	1	1	2	.67	.847	4.78
Kline, Branden	LM	R	34	16	1	11	0.8	19	3	.16	0 - 0	0 - 1	0 - 0	18	0	1	5	.83	.860	5.93
Yacabonis, Jimmy	LM	R	25	12	3	11	0.6	13	5	.38	0 - 0	0 - 0	0 - 0	13	0	0	3	1.00	.953	6.75
Phillips, Evan	LM	R	25	13	2	8	0.7	17	9	.53	0 - 0	0 - 0	0 - 0	11	0	0	3	1.00	.821	6.43
Ynoa, Gabriel	LM	R	23	17	4	14	0.6	14	4	.29	0 - 0	0 - 0	0 - 0	9	0	0	0		.787	5.05
Castro, Miguel	UR	R	65	17	12	16	0.8	47	20	.43	1 - 1	0 - 2	1 - 2	37	0	3	9	.79	.712	4.66
Tate, Dillon	UR	R	16	5	2	5	0.8	8	3	.38	0 - 0	0 - 0	0 - 0	9	0	0	1	1.00	.729	6.43
Wright Jr., Mike	UR	R	10	5	1	4	0.4	8	5	.63	0 - 1	1 - 1	0 - 0	3	0	1	0	.50	1.091	9.45

Boston Red Sox

Pitcher	Pos	T	Usage					Inherited Runners			Saves			Relief Results						
			Rel G	Early Entry	Cons Days	Long	Lev Ind	#	Scrd	Pct	Easy	Reg	Tough	Clean	BS Win	BS	Holds	Sv/Hld Pct	Opp OPS	Rel ERA
Workman, Brandon	CL	R	73	6	17	7	2.0	21	2	.10	10 - 10	4 - 8	2 - 4	58	2	6	15	.84	.433	1.88
Barnes, Matt	SU	R	70	2	19	11	1.8	28	7	.25	2 - 2	1 - 8	1 - 2	49	1	8	26	.79	.666	3.78
Brasier, Ryan	SU	R	62	12	21	5	1.3	13	7	.54	4 - 5	3 - 5	0 - 1	42	0	4	9	.80	.722	4.85
Taylor, Josh	LT	L	51	22	11	7	0.9	27	7	.26	0 - 0	0 - 0	0 - 1	36	0	1	4	.80	.638	3.11
Johnson, Brian	LT	L	14	9	4	4	0.8	6	2	.33	0 - 0	0 - 0	0 - 0	8	0	0	0		.976	7.27
Poyner, Bobby	LT	L	12	7	3	1	0.7	5	1	.20	0 - 0	0 - 0	0 - 0	8	0	0	0		.913	8.38
Brewer, Colten	LM	R	58	28	12	10	0.8	38	12	.32	0 - 0	0 - 0	0 - 1	36	0	1	6	.86	.804	4.12
Hernandez, Darwinzon	LM	L	28	11	5	7	0.8	6	2	.33	0 - 0	0 - 0	0 - 0	21	0	0	2	1.00	.721	3.95
Weber, Ryan	LM	R	15	10	2	9	0.5	7	4	.57	0 - 0	0 - 0	0 - 0	7	0	0	0		.707	3.99
Shawaryn, Michael	LM	R	14	8	1	13	0.7	1	0	.00	0 - 0	0 - 0	0 - 0	6	0	0	0		.987	9.74
Walden, Marcus	UR	R	70	28	12	10	1.2	38	12	.32	1 - 2	0 - 2	1 - 2	41	0	4	6	.67	.642	3.81
Hembree, Heath	UR	R	45	14	6	6	0.7	24	5	.21	1 - 1	1 - 2	0 - 0	28	1	1	4	.86	.772	3.86
Velazquez, Hector	UR	R	26	6	5	9	0.5	7	4	.57	0 - 0	0 - 1	0 - 0	14	0	1	1	.50	.815	4.46
Cashner, Andrew	UR	R	19	4	5	5	1.3	0	0	.00	0 - 0	1 - 1	0 - 0	12	0	0	4	1.00	.667	3.86
Smith, Josh A.	UR	R	16	1	3	7	0.4	2	2	1.00	0 - 0	1 - 2	0 - 0	8	0	1	0	.50	.834	4.56
Thornburg, Tyler	UR	R	16	3	3	4	0.2	1	0	.00	0 - 0	0 - 0	0 - 0	7	0	0	0		.972	7.71
Lakins, Travis	UR	R	13	5	1	5	0.9	4	2	.50	0 - 0	0 - 0	0 - 0	6	0	0	1	1.00	.842	5.09
Eovaldi, Nathan	UR	R	11	3	1	3	0.9	1	0	.00	0 - 0	0 - 1	0 - 0	6	0	1	4	.80	.825	5.40
Kelley, Trevor	UR	R	10	4	3	2	1.1	7	2	.29	0 - 0	0 - 0	0 - 0	3	0	0	0		.963	8.64

Chicago Cubs

Pitcher	Pos	T	Usage					Inherited Runners			Saves			Relief Results						
			Rel G	Early Entry	Cons Days	Long	Lev Ind	#	Scrd	Pct	Easy	Reg	Tough	Clean	BS Win	BS	Holds	Sv/Hld Pct	Opp OPS	Rel ERA
Strop, Pedro	CL	R	50	1	8	3	1.2	13	5	.38	7 - 9	3 - 6	0 - 1	33	2	6	6	.73	.734	4.97
Kimbrel, Craig	CL	R	23	0	5	0	1.8	0	0	.00	9 - 9	4 - 7	0 - 0	16	0	3	0	.81	1.019	6.53
Cishek, Steve	SU	R	70	9	23	7	1.6	27	9	.33	3 - 3	3 - 5	1 - 3	50	0	4	11	.82	.642	2.95
Kintzler, Brandon	SU	R	62	8	11	4	1.2	32	7	.22	1 - 1	0 - 0	0 - 2	46	0	2	17	.90	.641	2.68
Ryan, Kyle	LT	L	73	21	16	7	0.9	44	16	.36	0 - 0	0 - 1	0 - 1	46	0	2	14	.88	.669	3.54
Holland, Derek	LT	L	19	4	2	0	0.6	11	5	.45	0 - 0	0 - 0	0 - 1	15	0	1	2	.67	.666	3.29
Rosario, Randy	LT	L	13	3	1	3	0.3	6	4	.67	0 - 0	0 - 0	0 - 1	6	0	1	0	.00	.824	5.91
Brach, Brad	LM	R	42	16	8	9	1.0	22	5	.23	0 - 0	0 - 2	0 - 0	23	0	2	4	.67	.811	6.13
Chatwood, Tyler	LM	R	33	14	2	15	1.0	12	6	.50	1 - 1	1 - 2	0 - 1	19	0	2	3	.71	.666	3.67
Phelps, David	LM	R	24	10	4	2	1.1	20	6	.30	0 - 0	0 - 2	1 - 1	14	0	2	1	.50	.755	3.18
Montgomery, Mike	LM	L	20	6	2	8	0.8	16	7	.44	0 - 0	0 - 0	0 - 1	9	0	1	3	.75	1.004	5.67
Wieck, Brad	LM	L	14	9	4	1	1.3	15	2	.13	0 - 0	0 - 0	0 - 0	9	0	0	1	1.00	.398	3.60
Wick, Rowan	UR	R	31	5	7	8	1.1	16	3	.19	0 - 0	2 - 2	0 - 0	22	0	0	5	1.00	.528	2.43
Edwards Jr., Carl	UR	R	20	4	3	1	1.0	12	8	.67	0 - 0	0 - 2	0 - 0	12	0	2	4	.67	.621	5.87
Maples, Dillon	UR	R	14	4	1	1	0.6	5	0	.00	0 - 0	0 - 0	0 - 0	11	0	0	0		.670	5.40
Underwood Jr., Duane	UR	R	12	6	1	3	0.3	10	3	.30	0 - 0	0 - 0	0 - 0	7	0	0	0		.865	5.40
Webster, Allen	UR	R	12	3	3	2	0.3	11	3	.27	0 - 0	0 - 0	1 - 1	8	0	0	0	1.00	.885	4.91

Chicago White Sox

Pitcher	Pos	T	Usage					Inherited Runners			Saves			Relief Results						
			Rel G	Early Entry	Cons Days	Long	Lev Ind	#	Scrd	Pct	Easy	Reg	Tough	Clean	BS Win	BS	Holds	Sv/Hld Pct	Opp OPS	Rel ERA
Colome, Alex	CL	R	62	0	13	7	1.6	18	6	.33	20 - 20	9 - 11	1 - 2	38	1	3	0	.91	.617	2.80
Bummer, Aaron	SU	L	58	10	8	11	1.5	35	7	.20	0 - 1	1 - 1	0 - 1	42	0	2	27	.93	.520	2.13
Marshall, Evan	SU	R	55	18	9	4	1.3	28	11	.39	0 - 1	0 - 3	0 - 0	41	0	4	19	.83	.669	2.49
Fry, Jace	LT	L	68	27	16	9	0.8	39	9	.23	0 - 0	0 - 0	0 - 2	40	0	2	11	.85	.733	4.75
Osich, Josh	LT	L	57	22	13	14	0.6	45	10	.22	0 - 0	0 - 0	0 - 1	32	0	1	2	.67	.752	4.66
Cordero, Jimmy	LM	R	30	17	5	6	0.8	22	1	.05	0 - 0	0 - 0	0 - 0	22	0	0	4	1.00	.584	2.75
Minaya, Juan	LM	R	22	8	5	7	0.3	14	6	.43	0 - 0	0 - 0	0 - 0	12	0	0	0		.857	3.90
Fulmer, Carson	LM	R	18	9	3	9	0.8	12	5	.42	0 - 0	0 - 0	0 - 0	9	0	0	1	1.00	.742	5.55
Herrera, Kelvin	UR	R	57	2	13	4	0.9	19	12	.63	1 - 2	0 - 0	0 - 1	32	1	2	6	.78	.821	6.14
Ruiz, Jose	UR	R	39	16	4	8	0.7	15	4	.27	0 - 1	0 - 0	0 - 0	19	0	1	1	.50	.932	5.87
Burr, Ryan	UR	R	15	7	0	7	0.5	7	5	.71	0 - 0	0 - 0	0 - 0	7	0	0	0		.733	5.09
Jones, Nate	UR	R	13	4	1	1	0.7	11	3	.27	0 - 0	0 - 0	1 - 1	9	0	0	2	1.00	.793	3.48

Cincinnati Reds

Pitcher	Pos	T	Usage					Inherited Runners			Saves			Relief Results						
			Rel G	Early Entry	Cons Days	Long	Lev Ind	#	Scrd	Pct	Easy	Reg	Tough	Clean	BS Win	BS	Holds	Sv/Hld Pct	Opp OPS	Rel ERA
Iglesias, Raisel	CL	R	68	0	20	8	1.9	16	4	.25	18 - 19	15 - 19	1 - 2	48	0	6	3	.86	.743	4.16
Lorenzen, Michael	SU	R	73	16	15	16	1.2	44	13	.30	1 - 1	5 - 6	1 - 4	46	1	4	21	.88	.644	2.92
Garrett, Amir	SU	L	69	18	13	6	1.4	41	13	.32	0 - 1	0 - 0	0 - 2	45	0	3	22	.88	.695	3.21
Hernandez, David	SU	R	47	6	13	6	1.2	24	9	.38	1 - 1	0 - 2	1 - 2	25	0	3	12	.82	.913	8.02
Duke, Zach	LT	L	30	10	7	2	0.6	13	5	.38	0 - 0	0 - 0	0 - 0	18	0	0	4	1.00	.843	5.01
Hughes, Jared	LM	R	47	15	10	10	0.9	22	9	.41	0 - 0	1 - 2	0 - 1	31	0	2	3	.67	.707	4.10
Peralta, Wandy	LM	R	39	12	7	4	0.7	21	8	.38	0 - 1	0 - 0	0 - 0	26	0	1	2	.67	.893	6.09
Sims, Lucas	LM	R	20	12	1	10	0.8	13	4	.31	0 - 0	0 - 0	0 - 0	13	0	0	3	1.00	.683	3.42
Stephenson, Robert	UR	R	57	18	11	8	0.8	15	4	.27	0 - 0	0 - 3	0 - 1	35	0	4	11	.73	.634	3.76
Bowman, Matt	UR	R	27	8	4	8	0.4	11	4	.36	0 - 0	0 - 0	0 - 0	18	0	0	0		.628	3.66
Gausman, Kevin	UR	R	14	3	1	7	0.9	8	2	.25	0 - 0	0 - 0	0 - 0	8	0	0	2	1.00	.670	3.10
Romano, Sal	UR	R	12	5	1	5	0.3	5	3	.60	0 - 0	2 - 2	0 - 0	5	0	0	1	1.00	1.029	7.71
Kuhnel, Joel	UR	R	11	2	0	1	0.7	5	1	.20	0 - 0	0 - 0	0 - 0	8	0	0	1	1.00	.634	4.66

Cleveland Indians

Pitcher	Pos	T	Usage					Inherited Runners			Saves			Relief Results						
			Rel G	Early Entry	Cons Days	Long	Lev Ind	#	Scrd	Pct	Easy	Reg	Tough	Clean	BS Win	BS	Holds	Sv/Hld Pct	Opp OPS	Rel ERA
Hand, Brad	CL	L	60	1	18	6	1.9	14	0	.00	25 - 27	6 - 9	3 - 3	47	2	5	0	.87	.695	3.30
Cimber, Adam	SU	R	68	14	16	3	1.2	45	11	.24	0 - 0	0 - 0	1 - 3	43	0	2	19	.91	.720	4.45
Perez, Oliver	SU	L	67	14	19	1	1.2	54	17	.31	0 - 0	1 - 1	0 - 4	46	0	4	22	.85	.733	3.98
Wittgren, Nick	SU	R	55	7	6	6	1.1	26	2	.08	0 - 0	3 - 5	1 - 1	37	1	2	12	.89	.676	2.81
Olson, Tyler	LT	L	39	13	9	8	0.6	26	8	.31	0 - 0	0 - 0	0 - 1	26	0	1	1	.50	.809	4.40
Otero, Dan	LM	R	25	12	2	4	0.3	6	3	.50	0 - 0	0 - 0	0 - 0	15	0	0	1	1.00	.879	4.85
Wood, Hunter	LM	R	17	6	1	4	0.4	13	11	.85	0 - 0	0 - 0	0 - 0	9	0	0	1	1.00	.790	3.86
Clippard, Tyler	UR	R	50	13	6	6	0.7	22	7	.32	0 - 0	0 - 0	0 - 0	37	0	0	8	1.00	.594	2.38
Goody, Nick	UR	R	39	11	4	5	1.1	19	9	.47	0 - 0	0 - 0	0 - 0	27	0	0	10	1.00	.690	3.54
Cole, A.J.	UR	R	25	9	4	5	1.0	18	2	.11	1 - 1	0 - 0	0 - 0	15	0	0	0	1.00	.819	3.81
Ramirez, Neil	UR	R	16	6	1	2	0.5	9	2	.22	0 - 0	0 - 0	0 - 0	8	0	0	2	1.00	.938	5.40
Carrasco, Carlos	UR	R	11	4	0	5	0.7	3	0	.00	0 - 1	1 - 1	0 - 0	5	0	1	0	.50	.947	6.60

Colorado Rockies

Pitcher	Pos	T	Usage					Inherited Runners			Saves			Relief Results						
			Rel G	Early Entry	Cons Days	Long	Lev Ind	#	Scrd	Pct	Easy	Reg	Tough	Clean	BS Win	BS	Holds	Sv/Hld Pct	Opp OPS	Rel ERA
Oberg, Scott	SU	R	49	0	11	10	1.6	9	2	.22	2-2	3-5	0-1	37	2	3	8	.81	.569	2.25
McGee, Jake	LT	L	45	10	8	2	0.6	26	17	.65	0-1	0-0	0-1	25	0	2	4	.67	.903	4.35
Dunn, Mike	LT	L	28	7	10	0	0.8	20	7	.35	0-0	0-0	0-1	17	0	1	2	.67	.830	7.13
Pazos, James	LT	L	12	4	3	0	0.8	4	0	.00	0-0	0-0	0-0	10	0	0	3	1.00	.596	1.74
Musgrave, Harrison	LT	L	10	0	2	4	0.9	2	0	.00	0-0	0-0	0-0	8	0	0	0		.648	3.60
Diehl, Phillip	LT	L	10	4	4	2	0.5	4	2	.50	0-0	0-0	0-0	6	0	0	0		.934	7.36
Bettis, Chad	LM	R	36	18	4	12	0.8	16	3	.19	0-0	1-2	0-1	18	0	2	4	.71	.808	5.36
Almonte, Yency	LM	R	28	15	4	8	0.6	15	3	.20	0-0	0-1	0-0	14	0	1	1	.50	.860	5.56
Tinoco, Jesus	LM	R	24	15	3	10	0.5	20	11	.55	0-0	0-0	1-1	8	0	0	2	1.00	.965	4.75
Howard, Sam	LM	L	20	9	2	4	0.7	18	4	.22	0-0	0-0	0-0	11	0	0	0		.895	6.63
Estevez, Carlos	UR	R	71	18	13	14	0.9	38	12	.32	0-0	0-2	0-0	45	0	2	11	.85	.756	3.75
Shaw, Bryan	UR	R	70	21	18	11	1.0	27	16	.59	1-3	0-2	0-1	43	1	5	12	.72	.798	5.38
Diaz, Jairo	UR	R	56	8	14	6	1.2	24	7	.29	2-2	3-5	0-1	38	1	3	7	.80	.745	4.53
Davis, Wade	UR	R	50	2	7	5	1.5	9	1	.11	9-11	6-7	0-0	33	0	3	0	.83	.872	8.65
Johnson, D.J.	UR	R	28	8	6	5	1.1	15	3	.20	0-0	0-0	0-0	17	0	0	4	1.00	.743	5.04
Oh, Seunghwan	UR	R	21	2	3	3	0.8	2	1	.50	0-1	0-0	0-0	10	0	1	3	.75	.983	9.33
Parsons, Wes	UR	R	15	6	1	7	0.8	7	3	.43	0-0	0-0	0-0	7	0	0	1	1.00	.938	6.98

Detroit Tigers

Pitcher	Pos	T	Usage					Inherited Runners			Saves			Relief Results						
			Rel G	Early Entry	Cons Days	Long	Lev Ind	#	Scrd	Pct	Easy	Reg	Tough	Clean	BS Win	BS	Holds	Sv/Hld Pct	Opp OPS	Rel ERA
Greene, Shane	CL	R	38	0	9	2	1.8	0	0	.00	15-17	7-8	0-0	33	0	3	0	.88	.504	1.18
Jimenez, Joe	SU	R	66	0	12	4	1.4	2	0	.00	5-6	4-8	0-0	45	1	5	15	.83	.797	4.37
Stumpf, Daniel	LT	L	48	4	11	0	1.0	32	9	.28	0-0	0-0	0-2	29	0	2	5	.71	.873	4.34
Hardy, Blaine	LT	L	39	12	4	8	0.7	16	7	.44	0-0	0-0	0-0	17	0	0	7	1.00	.751	4.47
Soto, Gregory	LT	L	26	6	2	9	0.8	9	4	.44	0-0	0-0	0-1	16	0	1	2	.67	.835	3.93
Ramirez, Nick	LM	L	46	28	3	25	0.9	29	15	.52	0-0	0-1	0-0	18	0	1	1	.50	.748	4.07
Reininger, Zac	LM	R	24	11	2	6	0.4	13	2	.15	0-0	0-0	0-0	10	0	1	1	1.00	1.188	7.96
VerHagen, Drew	LM	R	18	9	2	9	1.0	10	4	.40	0-0	0-0	0-0	7	0	0	1	1.00	.830	5.87
Hall, Matt	LM	L	16	8	1	10	0.6	10	4	.40	0-0	0-0	0-1	6	0	1	0	.00	.853	7.71
Farmer, Buck	UR	R	72	16	16	6	1.2	44	18	.41	0-0	0-2	0-1	47	1	3	15	.83	.744	3.70
Alcantara, Victor	UR	R	46	10	12	3	0.9	26	13	.50	0-0	0-1	0-2	25	0	3	10	.77	.827	4.85
Cisnero, Jose	UR	R	35	9	4	9	1.0	17	5	.29	0-0	0-0	0-2	19	0	2	4	.67	.805	4.33
McKay, David	UR	R	18	4	1	6	0.8	8	3	.38	0-0	0-0	0-1	10	0	1	1	.50	.647	5.59
Schreiber, John	UR	R	13	4	1	2	0.5	9	2	.22	0-1	0-0	0-0	7	0	1	1	.50	.837	6.23
Garrett, Reed	UR	R	13	2	1	6	0.3	3	0	.00	0-0	0-1	0-0	6	0	1	0	.00	1.144	8.22
Adams, Austin	UR	R	13	3	3	4	0.2	4	2	.50	0-0	0-0	0-0	8	0	0	0		.832	5.14
Rosenthal, Trevor	UR	R	10	0	1	2	0.9	0	0	.00	0-0	0-0	0-0	6	0	0	1	1.00	.504	7.00

Houston Astros

Pitcher	Pos	T	Usage					Inherited Runners			Saves			Relief Results						
			Rel G	Early Entry	Cons Days	Long	Lev Ind	#	Scrd	Pct	Easy	Reg	Tough	Clean	BS Win	BS	Holds	Sv/Hld Pct	Opp OPS	Rel ERA
Osuna, Roberto	CL	R	66	0	20	2	1.9	10	2	.20	28-30	10-12	0-2	52	2	6	0	.86	.555	2.63
Harris, Will	SU	R	68	10	13	1	1.2	27	5	.19	2-2	2-3	0-0	55	0	1	26	.97	.540	1.50
Rondon, Hector	SU	R	61	10	9	2	1.1	14	2	.14	0-1	0-2	0-0	44	1	3	19	.86	.711	2.85
Pressly, Ryan	SU	R	55	0	15	3	1.4	17	4	.24	2-2	0-4	1-2	44	0	5	31	.87	.543	2.32
Valdez, Framber	LT	L	18	9	1	9	0.6	4	1	.20	0-0	0-0	0-0	8	0	0	0		.735	4.63
Devenski, Chris	UR	R	60	14	12	11	0.6	19	4	.21	0-0	0-1	0-0	36	0	1	7	.88	.779	4.84
James, Josh	UR	R	48	12	4	17	1.0	14	6	.43	0-0	1-3	0-0	33	0	2	6	.78	.703	4.77
Smith, Joe	UR	R	28	6	8	1	0.7	11	5	.45	0-0	0-0	0-1	18	0	1	4	.80	.569	1.80
McHugh, Collin	UR	R	27	9	6	8	0.5	5	2	.40	0-0	0-0	0-0	20	0	0	4	1.00	.640	2.67
Biagini, Joe	UR	R	13	4	1	4	0.6	2	0	.00	0-0	0-0	0-0	7	0	0	0		1.118	7.36

Kansas City Royals

Pitcher	Pos	T	Usage					Inherited Runners			Saves			Relief Results						
			Rel G	Early Entry	Cons Days	Long	Lev Ind	#	Scrd	Pct	Easy	Reg	Tough	Clean	BS Win	BS	Holds	Sv/Hld Pct	Opp OPS	Rel ERA
Kennedy, Ian	CL	R	63	2	13	12	1.6	5	1	.20	24 - 26	6 - 8	0 - 0	48	1	4	1	.89	.675	3.41
Diekman, Jake	SU	L	48	3	11	4	1.5	22	5	.23	0 - 1	0 - 1	0 - 0	31	0	2	18	.90	.667	4.75
Lovelady, Richard	LT	L	25	8	5	2	0.8	12	5	.42	0 - 0	0 - 1	0 - 0	12	0	1	2	.67	.952	7.65
Flynn, Brian	LT	L	10	8	0	8	0.9	4	2	.50	0 - 0	0 - 0	0 - 0	3	0	0	0		.820	3.29
Hill, Tim	LM	L	46	21	13	6	0.9	50	16	.32	0 - 0	1 - 1	0 - 1	29	1	1	9	.91	.636	3.63
Lopez, Jorge	LM	R	21	10	2	12	0.6	15	7	.47	0 - 0	1 - 2	0 - 0	7	0	1	0	.50	.780	5.79
Barlow, Scott	UR	R	61	22	9	18	1.2	37	11	.30	0 - 0	1 - 3	0 - 0	33	0	2	14	.88	.735	4.22
McCarthy, Kevin	UR	R	56	18	9	3	1.0	42	16	.38	0 - 0	1 - 4	0 - 1	31	0	4	6	.64	.756	4.48
Peralta, Wily	UR	R	42	2	9	3	1.0	15	4	.27	2 - 2	0 - 1	0 - 2	24	1	3	5	.70	.864	5.80
Boxberger, Brad	UR	R	29	4	6	3	0.9	8	3	.38	0 - 1	0 - 2	1 - 1	20	1	3	0	.25	.751	5.40
Newberry, Jake	UR	R	27	8	4	8	0.6	17	7	.41	0 - 0	0 - 0	0 - 1	15	0	1	4	.80	.849	3.77
Staumont, Josh	UR	R	16	3	1	4	0.8	6	1	.17	0 - 0	0 - 1	0 - 0	8	0	1	0	.00	.870	3.72
Zimmer, Kyle	UR	R	15	6	0	7	0.4	2	2	1.00	0 - 0	0 - 0	0 - 0	7	0	0	0		.991	10.80
Barnes, Jacob	UR	R	15	5	1	1	0.9	8	3	.38	0 - 0	0 - 0	0 - 0	5	0	0	0		.951	8.31

Los Angeles Angels

Pitcher	Pos	T	Usage					Inherited Runners			Saves			Relief Results						
			Rel G	Early Entry	Cons Days	Long	Lev Ind	#	Scrd	Pct	Easy	Reg	Tough	Clean	BS Win	BS	Holds	Sv/Hld Pct	Opp OPS	Rel ERA
Robles, Hansel	CL	R	70	0	19	5	1.5	15	5	.33	13 - 14	10 - 11	0 - 2	55	1	4	2	.86	.602	2.51
Buttrey, Ty	SU	R	72	12	19	12	1.5	35	12	.34	0 - 1	2 - 3	0 - 2	47	0	4	26	.88	.690	3.98
Bedrosian, Cam	SU	R	52	12	10	7	1.2	15	6	.40	1 - 2	0 - 1	0 - 0	38	0	2	15	.89	.630	3.31
Mejia, Adalberto	LT	L	20	7	7	1	1.0	17	6	.35	0 - 0	0 - 0	0 - 0	13	0	0	2	1.00	.625	3.46
Anderson, Justin	LM	L	54	33	9	9	1.0	37	16	.43	1 - 2	0 - 0	0 - 0	32	0	1	11	.92	.778	5.55
Ramirez, Noe	LM	R	44	26	3	13	0.6	18	3	.17	0 - 0	0 - 0	0 - 0	30	0	0	3	1.00	.703	3.64
Cole, Taylor	LM	R	32	13	7	14	0.9	17	4	.24	0 - 0	0 - 0	0 - 0	19	0	0	4	1.00	.738	5.08
Bard, Luke	LM	R	29	18	2	16	0.9	21	7	.33	0 - 0	0 - 1	0 - 0	15	0	1	1	.50	.695	4.89
Cahill, Trevor	LM	R	26	12	2	18	0.8	10	3	.30	0 - 0	0 - 0	0 - 0	12	0	0	0		.864	4.96
Jewell, Jake	LM	R	18	7	4	7	0.3	10	3	.30	0 - 0	0 - 0	0 - 0	9	0	0	1	1.00	.901	6.84
Del Pozo, Miguel	LM	L	17	11	3	0	0.8	13	2	.15	0 - 0	0 - 0	0 - 0	9	0	0	0		.981	10.61
Pena, Felix	LM	R	15	14	0	14	0.7	0	0	.00	0 - 0	0 - 0	0 - 0	3	0	0	1	1.00	.672	4.26
Garcia, Luis	UR	R	62	9	14	8	0.8	26	11	.42	0 - 1	1 - 1	0 - 1	39	0	2	6	.78	.794	4.35
Allen, Cody	UR	R	25	2	4	3	0.7	5	2	.40	3 - 3	0 - 0	1 - 1	16	0	0	0	1.00	1.010	6.26
Middleton, Keynan	UR	R	11	5	1	0	1.1	7	1	.14	0 - 0	0 - 0	0 - 0	9	0	0	0		.564	1.17

Los Angeles Dodgers

Pitcher	Pos	T	Usage					Inherited Runners			Saves			Relief Results						
			Rel G	Early Entry	Cons Days	Long	Lev Ind	#	Scrd	Pct	Easy	Reg	Tough	Clean	BS Win	BS	Holds	Sv/Hld Pct	Opp OPS	Rel ERA
Jansen, Kenley	CL	R	62	0	15	6	2.0	15	5	.33	20 - 23	11 - 16	2 - 2	42	2	8	0	.80	.653	3.71
Baez, Pedro	SU	R	71	15	14	2	1.4	30	10	.33	0 - 1	1 - 4	0 - 2	51	2	6	25	.81	.543	3.10
Urias, Julio	SU	L	29	11	2	16	1.1	3	2	.67	1 - 1	3 - 4	0 - 0	19	1	1	5	.90	.546	2.01
Ferguson, Caleb	LT	L	44	12	7	6	0.5	8	4	.50	0 - 0	0 - 0	0 - 0	31	0	0	4	1.00	.762	4.91
Alexander, Scott	LT	L	28	8	7	0	1.0	18	10	.56	0 - 0	0 - 0	0 - 0	19	0	0	6	1.00	.741	3.63
Kolarek, Adam	LT	L	26	12	8	0	0.9	18	2	.11	0 - 0	0 - 0	0 - 0	22	0	0	3	1.00	.547	0.77
Garcia, Yimi	UR	R	64	21	14	6	0.7	19	6	.32	0 - 0	0 - 2	0 - 1	40	0	3	4	.57	.671	3.61
Kelly, Joe	UR	R	55	17	15	11	1.0	18	7	.39	1 - 1	0 - 3	0 - 2	35	0	5	8	.64	.711	4.56
Floro, Dylan	UR	R	50	15	12	4	1.1	31	12	.39	0 - 0	0 - 1	0 - 2	35	0	3	6	.67	.685	4.24
Sadler, Casey	UR	R	23	4	4	4	0.7	1	1	1.00	1 - 2	0 - 0	0 - 0	18	0	1	2	.75	.703	2.39
Chargois, JT	UR	R	21	3	4	0	0.3	11	7	.64	0 - 0	0 - 0	0 - 0	11	0	0	0		.825	6.33
Stripling, Ross	UR	R	17	3	2	5	0.9	0	0	.00	0 - 0	0 - 0	0 - 0	11	0	0	3	1.00	.670	3.05
Maeda, Kenta	UR	R	11	4	1	2	1.0	1	0	.00	0 - 0	2 - 2	1 - 1	9	0	0	4	1.00	.572	3.24
May, Dustin	UR	R	10	5	1	3	1.5	1	0	.00	0 - 0	0 - 1	0 - 0	8	0	1	4	.80	.667	5.11

Miami Marlins

Pitcher	Pos	T	Usage					Inherited Runners			Saves			Relief Results						
			Rel G	Early Entry	Cons Days	Long	Lev Ind	#	Scrd	Pct	Easy	Reg	Tough	Clean	BS Win	BS	Holds	Sv/Hld Pct	Opp OPS	Rel ERA
Romo, Sergio	CL	R	38	0	13	2	1.6	12	2	.17	10 - 11	7 - 7	0 - 0	26	0	1	1	.95	.673	3.58
Stanek, Ryne	SU	R	22	0	4	4	1.9	8	4	.50	0 - 1	1 - 3	0 - 1	12	0	4	5	.60	.769	5.48
Conley, Adam	LT	L	60	15	13	14	1.0	22	3	.14	2 - 2	0 - 1	0 - 1	34	0	2	6	.80	.908	6.53
Garcia, Jarlin	LT	L	53	11	12	5	0.9	28	6	.21	0 - 0	0 - 0	0 - 1	41	0	1	6	.86	.602	3.02
Quijada, Jose	LT	L	34	8	7	8	0.9	10	0	.00	0 - 0	0 - 1	1 - 1	23	0	1	4	.83	.974	5.76
Moran, Brian	LT	L	10	3	2	1	1.2	7	2	.29	0 - 0	0 - 0	0 - 1	7	0	1	2	.67	.857	4.26
Chen, Wei-Yin	LM	L	45	21	4	23	0.4	14	6	.43	0 - 0	0 - 0	0 - 0	19	0	0	3	1.00	.659	6.59
Anderson, Nick	LM	R	45	11	10	5	1.4	17	3	.18	1 - 1	0 - 1	0 - 0	33	0	1	7	.89	.705	3.92
Brice, Austin	LM	R	36	12	8	12	0.6	16	6	.38	0 - 0	0 - 1	0 - 0	22	0	1	6	.86	.676	3.43
Guerrero, Tayron	UR	R	52	5	12	6	0.6	10	6	.60	0 - 1	0 - 2	0 - 1	32	0	4	6	.60	.804	6.26
Kinley, Tyler	UR	R	52	17	11	9	0.9	27	12	.44	0 - 0	0 - 2	0 - 1	34	0	2	1	.50	.723	3.65
Brigham, Jeff	UR	R	32	9	8	10	0.9	11	4	.36	1 - 1	0 - 1	0 - 0	21	0	1	4	.83	.765	4.46
Steckenrider, Drew	UR	R	15	0	4	2	0.9	0	0	.00	0 - 0	0 - 1	0 - 0	10	0	1	3	.75	.778	6.28
Urena, Jose	UR	R	11	0	2	2	2.2	1	0	.00	2 - 4	1 - 1	0 - 0	7	0	2	0	.60	.907	9.00
Keller, Kyle	UR	R	10	2	1	2	0.6	2	0	.00	0 - 0	0 - 0	0 - 0	7	0	0	0		.715	3.38

Milwaukee Brewers

Pitcher	Pos	T	Usage					Inherited Runners			Saves			Relief Results						
			Rel G	Early Entry	Cons Days	Long	Lev Ind	#	Scrd	Pct	Easy	Reg	Tough	Clean	BS Win	BS	Holds	Sv/Hld Pct	Opp OPS	Rel ERA
Hader, Josh	CL	L	61	0	10	16	1.9	33	8	.24	17 - 17	17 - 22	3 - 5	42	1	7	6	.86	.591	2.62
Claudio, Alex	SU	L	83	35	26	4	1.0	46	13	.28	0 - 0	0 - 1	0 - 2	60	0	3	22	.88	.751	4.06
Guerra, Junior	SU	R	72	23	17	17	1.3	36	15	.42	1 - 1	2 - 7	0 - 3	43	4	8	20	.74	.639	3.55
Jeffress, Jeremy	SU	R	48	12	6	4	1.1	16	2	.13	1 - 3	0 - 1	0 - 0	26	1	3	12	.81	.734	5.02
Pomeranz, Drew	SU	L	24	5	3	3	1.5	13	4	.31	0 - 0	2 - 2	0 - 0	19	0	0	12	1.00	.562	2.31
Peralta, Freddy	LM	R	31	20	1	16	1.0	13	2	.15	0 - 1	1 - 1	0 - 0	18	0	1	5	.86	.691	4.01
Jackson, Jay	LM	R	28	10	6	10	0.5	13	3	.23	0 - 0	0 - 0	0 - 0	20	0	0	2	1.00	.724	4.45
Albers, Matt	UR	R	67	29	13	6	1.4	32	7	.22	1 - 1	2 - 4	1 - 1	45	1	2	10	.88	.728	5.13
Burnes, Corbin	UR	R	28	8	3	9	1.0	12	5	.42	0 - 0	0 - 0	0 - 1	16	0	0	4	1.00	.847	7.76
Barnes, Jacob	UR	R	17	4	3	3	0.3	0	0	.00	0 - 0	0 - 0	0 - 0	11	0	0	1	1.00	.706	5.79
Houser, Adrian	UR	R	17	4	0	9	1.0	7	3	.43	0 - 0	0 - 0	0 - 0	13	0	0	1	1.00	.524	1.47
Black, Ray	UR	R	15	8	2	0	0.6	9	0	.00	0 - 0	0 - 2	0 - 0	12	0	2	2	.50	.802	5.14
Wilson, Alex	UR	R	13	2	3	1	1.2	2	1	.50	0 - 0	1 - 1	0 - 0	8	0	0	1	1.00	.984	9.53
Williams, Devin	UR	R	13	6	0	2	0.4	0	0	.00	0 - 0	0 - 0	0 - 0	6	0	0	2	1.00	.894	3.95
Williams, Taylor	UR	R	10	3	1	5	1.2	3	3	1.00	0 - 0	0 - 1	0 - 0	2	0	1	0	.00	.878	9.82

Minnesota Twins

Pitcher	Pos	T	Usage					Inherited Runners			Saves			Relief Results						
			Rel G	Early Entry	Cons Days	Long	Lev Ind	#	Scrd	Pct	Easy	Reg	Tough	Clean	BS Win	BS	Holds	Sv/Hld Pct	Opp OPS	Rel ERA
Rogers, Taylor	CL	L	60	0	17	11	2.1	19	6	.32	12 - 12	16 - 19	2 - 5	45	1	6	10	.87	.625	2.61
Parker, Blake	CL	R	37	0	8	5	1.7	9	1	.11	5 - 6	4 - 4	1 - 1	28	0	1	9	.95	.773	4.21
May, Trevor	SU	R	65	12	12	8	1.3	22	3	.14	0 - 0	2 - 4	0 - 0	50	0	2	17	.90	.587	2.94
Romo, Sergio	SU	R	27	1	8	0	1.5	8	2	.25	1 - 2	2 - 3	0 - 0	20	0	2	16	.90	.608	3.18
Hildenberger, Trevor	SU	R	22	3	5	1	1.2	23	8	.35	0 - 0	0 - 0	1 - 1	11	0	0	6	1.00	1.033	10.47

Minnesota Twins

Pitcher	Pos	T	Rel G	Early Entry	Cons Days	Long	Lev Ind	#	Scrd	Pct	Easy	Reg	Tough	Clean	BS Win	BS	Holds	Sv/Hld Pct	Opp OPS	Rel ERA
Dyson, Sam	SU	R	12	3	2	1	1.3	2	1	.50	0-0	0-1	0-0	6	1	1	6	.86	.909	7.15
Mejia, Adalberto	LT	L	13	4	2	5	0.9	7	2	.29	0-0	0-1	0-0	5	0	1	2	.67	.894	8.80
Thorpe, Lewis	LT	L	10	5	1	5	1.2	1	0	.00	0-0	0-2	0-0	2	0	2	0	.00	.825	5.68
Stashak, Cody	LM	R	17	8	0	5	0.5	10	4	.40	0-0	0-0	0-0	9	0	0	1	1.00	.764	3.13
Harper, Ryne	UR	R	61	19	12	6	1.0	46	16	.35	1-2	0-0	0-2	40	1	3	12	.81	.709	3.81
Duffey, Tyler	UR	R	58	16	13	11	1.0	24	4	.17	0-1	0-0	0-1	43	1	2	15	.88	.595	2.50
Littell, Zack	UR	R	29	12	5	5	1.0	12	4	.33	0-0	0-1	0-0	23	0	1	1	.50	.708	2.68
Magill, Matt	UR	R	28	3	5	8	0.7	10	2	.20	0-0	0-0	0-0	20	0	0	0		.830	4.45
Morin, Mike	UR	R	23	3	3	3	0.7	11	2	.18	0-0	1-1	0-0	16	0	0	1	1.00	.647	3.18
Romero, Fernando	UR	R	15	1	0	3	0.4	1	0	.00	0-0	0-0	0-0	10	0	0	1	1.00	.914	7.07
Graterol, Brusdar	UR	R	10	1	0	0	1.0	4	3	.75	0-0	0-0	0-0	6	0	0	1	1.00	.714	4.66

New York Mets

Pitcher	Pos	T	Rel G	Early Entry	Cons Days	Long	Lev Ind	#	Scrd	Pct	Easy	Reg	Tough	Clean	BS Win	BS	Holds	Sv/Hld Pct	Opp OPS	Rel ERA
Diaz, Edwin	CL	R	66	0	13	8	1.9	15	8	.53	18-21	8-11	0-1	44	1	7	1	.79	.834	5.59
Lugo, Seth	SU	R	61	5	7	21	1.5	20	3	.15	2-3	4-7	0-1	46	0	5	21	.84	.562	2.70
Wilson, Justin	SU	L	45	4	8	4	1.6	13	5	.38	2-2	1-2	1-1	33	0	1	9	.93	.670	2.54
Avilan, Luis	LT	L	45	11	11	6	0.7	33	6	.18	0-0	0-0	0-0	30	0	0	3	1.00	.782	5.06
Zamora, Daniel	LT	L	17	2	3	0	0.9	16	6	.38	0-0	0-0	0-0	11	0	0	0		.861	5.19
Familia, Jeurys	UR	R	66	9	17	4	1.0	15	5	.33	0-0	0-3	0-1	43	1	4	14	.78	.831	5.70
Gsellman, Robert	UR	R	52	15	9	15	1.1	20	10	.50	0-1	1-3	0-1	26	1	4	7	.67	.766	4.66
Bashlor, Tyler	UR	R	24	5	6	1	0.7	12	4	.33	0-0	0-2	0-1	13	0	3	1	.25	.861	6.95
Gagnon, Drew	UR	R	18	3	1	5	0.6	10	3	.30	0-0	0-1	0-0	10	0	1	0	.00	1.043	8.37
Sewald, Paul	UR	R	17	5	2	5	0.4	5	1	.20	1-1	0-0	0-0	9	0	0	0	1.00	.724	4.58
Brach, Brad	UR	R	16	6	3	0	1.1	10	2	.20	0-0	0-1	0-0	11	0	1	2	.67	.668	3.68
Font, Wilmer	UR	R	12	6	0	7	0.7	8	2	.25	0-0	0-1	0-0	8	0	1	0	.00	.773	3.48

New York Yankees

Pitcher	Pos	T	Rel G	Early Entry	Cons Days	Long	Lev Ind	#	Scrd	Pct	Easy	Reg	Tough	Clean	BS Win	BS	Holds	Sv/Hld Pct	Opp OPS	Rel ERA
Chapman, Aroldis	CL	L	60	0	16	6	1.8	11	2	.18	29-31	7-10	1-1	45	3	5	0	.88	.537	2.21
Ottavino, Adam	SU	R	73	25	14	8	1.5	37	12	.32	1-2	1-6	0-1	55	1	7	28	.81	.624	1.90
Kahnle, Tommy	SU	R	72	20	19	2	1.0	34	7	.21	0-0	0-5	0-0	55	1	5	27	.84	.635	3.67
Britton, Zack	SU	L	66	0	13	3	1.5	19	5	.26	2-3	1-3	0-1	54	1	4	29	.89	.545	1.91
Lyons, Tyler	LT	L	11	4	2	0	0.5	4	0	.00	0-0	0-0	0-0	8	0	0	0		.843	4.15
Cessa, Luis	LM	R	43	21	2	29	0.7	18	5	.28	0-0	1-1	0-0	20	0	0	4	1.00	.751	4.11
Green, Chad	LM	R	39	13	1	16	0.9	19	5	.26	1-1	0-0	1-1	24	0	0	4	1.00	.718	4.35
Cortes, Nestor	LM	L	32	17	1	22	0.7	18	8	.44	0-0	0-0	0-1	11	0	1	1	.50	.834	5.60
Hale, David	LM	R	20	8	1	8	0.5	10	1	.10	0-0	2-2	0-0	11	0	0	0	1.00	.712	3.11
Tarpley, Stephen	LM	L	20	7	3	8	0.6	9	5	.56	0-0	2-2	0-0	10	0	0	2	1.00	.885	5.70
Loaisiga, Jonathan	LM	R	11	7	0	8	0.7	3	2	.67	0-0	0-0	0-1	7	0	1	0	.00	.707	3.20
Holder, Jonathan	UR	R	33	11	4	6	1.0	13	6	.46	0-1	0-0	0-1	18	1	2	4	.67	.764	6.28
Gearrin, Cory	UR	R	18	5	5	2	0.8	4	0	.00	0-0	0-0	0-0	13	0	0	2	1.00	.818	4.50
Adams, Chance	UR	R	13	5	0	8	0.4	6	2	.33	0-0	1-1	0-0	3	0	0	0	1.00	1.068	8.53

Oakland Athletics

Pitcher	Pos	T	Rel G	Early Entry	Cons Days	Long	Lev Ind	#	Scrd	Pct	Easy	Reg	Tough	Clean	BS Win	BS	Holds	Sv/Hld Pct	Opp OPS	Rel ERA
Hendriks, Liam	CL	R	73	10	21	11	1.6	40	16	.40	14 - 14	9 - 13	2 - 5	58	1	7	8	.83	.554	1.63
Treinen, Blake	CL	R	57	3	12	5	1.8	16	5	.31	9 - 9	5 - 8	2 - 4	35	1	5	3	.79	.778	4.91
Petit, Yusmeiro	SU	R	80	34	18	5	1.2	60	14	.23	0 - 0	0 - 0	0 - 1	52	0	1	29	.97	.579	2.71
Soria, Joakim	SU	R	70	1	18	4	1.2	7	0	.00	1 - 2	0 - 4	0 - 0	52	0	5	21	.81	.593	4.24
Trivino, Lou	SU	R	61	7	15	7	1.5	31	11	.35	0 - 1	0 - 2	0 - 2	39	0	5	17	.77	.782	5.25
Diekman, Jake	SU	L	28	5	9	4	1.4	17	5	.29	0 - 0	0 - 0	0 - 0	16	0	0	13	1.00	.668	4.43
Buchter, Ryan	LT	L	64	19	20	6	0.8	36	15	.42	0 - 0	0 - 1	0 - 3	41	0	4	12	.75	.799	2.98
Puk, A.J.	LT	L	10	4	1	4	0.7	3	1	.33	0 - 0	0 - 0	0 - 1	7	0	1	2	.67	.652	3.18
Wang, Wei-Chung	LM	L	20	10	3	8	0.5	19	5	.26	0 - 0	0 - 0	0 - 0	13	0	0	0		.701	3.33
Wendelken, J.B.	UR	R	27	9	3	7	1.0	14	2	.14	0 - 0	0 - 1	0 - 0	19	0	1	1	.50	.543	3.58
Rodney, Fernando	UR	R	17	1	2	2	0.8	4	3	.75	0 - 1	0 - 0	0 - 0	10	0	1	0	.00	.940	9.42

Philadelphia Phillies

Pitcher	Pos	T	Rel G	Early Entry	Cons Days	Long	Lev Ind	#	Scrd	Pct	Easy	Reg	Tough	Clean	BS Win	BS	Holds	Sv/Hld Pct	Opp OPS	Rel ERA
Neris, Hector	CL	R	68	1	15	3	1.8	20	4	.20	15 - 16	9 - 12	4 - 6	50	1	6	2	.83	.613	2.93
Morgan, Adam	SU	L	40	6	14	0	1.4	19	4	.21	0 - 0	0 - 1	0 - 1	34	0	2	19	.90	.621	3.94
Dominguez, Seranthony	SU	R	27	4	8	3	1.4	7	2	.29	0 - 1	0 - 1	0 - 0	20	0	2	9	.82	.725	4.01
Neshek, Pat	SU	R	20	1	5	0	1.2	0	0	.00	3 - 3	0 - 0	0 - 0	13	0	0	6	1.00	.856	5.00
Alvarez, Jose	LT	L	66	18	20	6	1.1	35	11	.31	1 - 1	0 - 0	0 - 2	44	0	2	16	.89	.775	3.47
Davis, Austin	LT	L	14	5	2	7	0.2	0	0	.00	0 - 0	0 - 0	0 - 0	6	0	0	0		.929	6.53
Irvin, Cole	LT	L	13	6	1	5	0.5	5	4	.80	0 - 0	1 - 1	0 - 0	8	0	0	0	1.00	.844	6.00
Garcia, Edgar	LM	R	37	17	5	8	0.4	14	4	.29	0 - 0	0 - 0	0 - 0	23	0	0	2	1.00	.906	5.77
Suarez, Ranger	LM	L	37	17	4	10	0.8	17	5	.29	0 - 0	0 - 1	0 - 0	28	0	1	6	.86	.739	3.14
Hughes, Jared	LM	R	25	11	9	4	1.0	20	7	.35	0 - 0	0 - 0	0 - 1	17	0	1	4	.80	.763	3.91
Nicasio, Juan	UR	R	47	15	11	4	1.0	10	3	.30	0 - 0	0 - 1	1 - 2	33	0	1	10	.92	.810	4.75
Morin, Mike	UR	R	29	7	4	1	1.0	6	1	.17	0 - 0	0 - 0	0 - 1	20	0	1	7	.88	.691	5.79
Parker, Blake	UR	R	21	8	4	3	1.0	5	1	.20	0 - 0	0 - 0	0 - 0	13	0	0	4	1.00	.655	4.50
Ramos, Edubray	UR	R	20	4	7	2	0.6	12	8	.67	0 - 0	0 - 1	0 - 1	11	0	2	2	.50	1.014	5.40
Hammer, J. D.	UR	R	20	6	4	2	0.7	5	3	.60	0 - 1	0 - 0	0 - 0	14	0	1	0	.00	.710	3.79
Pivetta, Nick	UR	R	17	4	2	6	1.1	3	1	.33	0 - 0	0 - 1	0 - 0	9	0	0	1	1.00	.839	4.38
Vincent, Nick	UR	R	14	8	4	1	1.0	7	1	.14	0 - 0	0 - 0	0 - 0	11	0	0	1	1.00	.606	1.93
Velasquez, Vince	UR	R	10	3	1	3	0.9	6	2	.33	0 - 0	0 - 0	0 - 0	5	0	0	2	1.00	.957	4.35

Pittsburgh Pirates

Pitcher	Pos	T	Rel G	Early Entry	Cons Days	Long	Lev Ind	#	Scrd	Pct	Easy	Reg	Tough	Clean	BS Win	BS	Holds	Sv/Hld Pct	Opp OPS	Rel ERA
Vazquez, Felipe	CL	L	56	0	13	7	1.7	16	2	.13	15 - 16	12 - 13	1 - 2	45	0	3	0	.90	.571	1.65
Crick, Kyle	SU	R	52	3	12	6	1.5	9	3	.33	0 - 1	0 - 4	0 - 1	35	1	6	13	.68	.799	4.96
Kela, Keone	SU	R	32	3	4	2	1.4	5	1	.20	1 - 2	0 - 3	0 - 0	25	1	4	6	.64	.606	2.12
Liriano, Francisco	LT	L	69	12	16	9	1.0	30	10	.33	0 - 0	0 - 3	0 - 1	43	0	4	12	.75	.710	3.47
Feliz, Michael	LM	R	57	27	9	8	0.9	29	10	.34	0 - 0	0 - 0	0 - 1	36	0	1	3	.75	.677	3.21
Holmes, Clay	LM	R	35	16	2	17	0.5	18	6	.33	0 - 0	0 - 1	0 - 0	16	0	1	1	.50	.743	5.58
Hartlieb, Geoff	LM	R	29	9	3	12	0.4	17	9	.53	0 - 0	0 - 0	0 - 0	9	0	0	2	1.00	1.020	9.00
Stratton, Chris	LM	R	28	12	3	13	0.5	5	3	.60	0 - 0	0 - 0	0 - 0	17	0	0	0		.784	3.66
Rodriguez, Richard	UR	R	72	22	13	6	1.0	27	9	.33	1 - 2	0 - 2	0 - 1	51	0	4	16	.81	.751	3.72
Markel, Parker	UR	R	15	2	1	5	0.5	7	1	.14	0 - 0	0 - 0	0 - 0	7	0	0	0		.826	5.71
DuRapau, Montana	UR	R	12	5	2	4	0.2	5	3	.60	0 - 0	0 - 0	0 - 0	6	0	0	0		1.018	9.20
Burdi, Nick	UR	R	11	0	1	0	1.3	1	1	1.00	0 - 0	0 - 1	0 - 0	7	0	1	0	.00	.836	9.35
Kingham, Nick	UR	R	10	6	0	7	0.6	7	1	.14	1 - 1	0 - 0	0 - 0	4	0	0	0	1.00	1.022	9.95
Neverauskas, Dovydas	UR	R	10	2	1	2	0.4	4	3	.75	0 - 0	0 - 0	0 - 0	6	0	0	1	1.00	1.081	10.61
Rios, Yacksel	UR	R	10	5	2	2	0.6	7	2	.29	0 - 0	0 - 0	0 - 0	6	0	0	1	1.00	.843	5.23

San Diego Padres

Pitcher	Pos	T	Usage					Inherited Runners			Saves			Relief Results						
			Rel G	Early Entry	Cons Days	Long	Lev Ind	#	Scrd	Pct	Easy	Reg	Tough	Clean	BS Win	BS	Holds	Sv/Hld Pct	Opp OPS	Rel ERA
Yates, Kirby	CL	R	60	0	18	7	2.3	11	2	.18	21 - 22	18 - 18	2 - 4	48	0	3	0	.93	.515	1.19
Stammen, Craig	SU	R	76	11	22	11	1.6	33	8	.24	1 - 2	3 - 9	0 - 2	51	3	9	31	.80	.719	3.29
Wingenter, Trey	SU	R	50	6	8	6	1.2	11	5	.45	0 - 0	1 - 3	0 - 1	34	0	3	16	.85	.632	5.26
Wieck, Brad	SU	L	30	9	6	1	1.1	20	11	.55	0 - 1	0 - 0	0 - 1	17	0	2	8	.80	.863	6.57
Munoz, Andres	SU	R	22	4	4	2	1.2	5	0	.00	1 - 2	0 - 0	0 - 0	17	0	1	8	.90	.611	3.91
Strahm, Matt	LT	L	30	10	6	5	1.2	11	1	.09	0 - 0	0 - 1	0 - 0	22	0	1	6	.86	.643	3.27
Perdomo, Luis	LM	R	46	20	8	14	0.8	30	10	.33	0 - 0	0 - 1	0 - 0	29	0	1	7	.88	.686	4.19
Erlin, Robbie	LM	L	36	17	4	18	0.5	14	1	.07	0 - 0	0 - 1	0 - 0	19	0	1	5	.83	.787	5.40
Warren, Adam	LM	R	25	11	4	11	0.8	12	3	.25	0 - 0	0 - 0	0 - 0	12	0	0	3	1.00	.887	5.34
Baez, Michel	LM	R	23	9	1	5	0.6	9	5	.56	0 - 0	0 - 0	0 - 0	16	0	0	0		.720	3.25
Wisler, Matt	LM	R	21	12	4	10	0.9	17	8	.47	0 - 1	0 - 0	0 - 1	11	0	2	4	.67	.822	5.28
Maton, Phil	LM	R	21	7	4	6	0.5	5	1	.20	0 - 0	0 - 0	0 - 0	7	0	0	2	1.00	.948	7.77
Reyes, Gerardo	UR	R	27	7	6	6	0.5	15	10	.67	0 - 0	0 - 0	0 - 1	13	1	1	1	.50	.738	7.62
Bednar, David	UR	R	13	0	2	0	1.0	2	2	1.00	0 - 0	0 - 0	0 - 0	9	0	0	2	1.00	.876	6.55
Stock, Robert	UR	R	10	5	3	6	0.8	8	2	.25	0 - 0	0 - 1	0 - 0	4	1	1	0	.00	.900	10.13
Yardley, Eric	UR	R	10	8	1	1	0.7	7	4	.57	0 - 0	0 - 0	0 - 0	6	0	0	0		.668	2.31

San Francisco Giants

Pitcher	Pos	T	Usage					Inherited Runners			Saves			Relief Results						
			Rel G	Early Entry	Cons Days	Long	Lev Ind	#	Scrd	Pct	Easy	Reg	Tough	Clean	BS Win	BS	Holds	Sv/Hld Pct	Opp OPS	Rel ERA
Smith, Will	CL	L	63	0	14	6	2.0	9	1	.11	15 - 16	18 - 20	1 - 2	49	4	4	0	.89	.618	2.76
Watson, Tony	SU	L	60	2	11	2	1.6	16	6	.38	0 - 1	0 - 1	0 - 1	41	0	3	25	.89	.757	4.17
Moronta, Reyes	SU	R	56	21	10	10	1.5	23	8	.35	0 - 0	0 - 2	0 - 3	39	0	5	15	.75	.612	2.86
Dyson, Sam	SU	R	49	7	10	0	1.1	14	6	.43	1 - 1	1 - 2	0 - 0	35	0	1	17	.95	.565	2.47
Abad, Fernando	SU	L	21	7	7	1	1.5	20	4	.20	0 - 0	0 - 0	0 - 0	14	0	0	8	1.00	.571	4.15
Rogers, Tyler	SU	R	17	3	4	2	1.2	5	2	.40	0 - 0	0 - 1	0 - 1	13	1	2	5	.71	.463	1.02
Bergen, Travis	LT	L	21	6	5	3	0.3	12	3	.25	0 - 0	0 - 1	0 - 0	15	0	0	0		.823	5.49
Selman, Sam	LT	L	10	6	2	3	0.6	5	1	.20	0 - 0	0 - 1	0 - 0	5	0	1	1	.50	.697	4.35
Gott, Trevor	LM	R	50	28	4	7	0.9	35	7	.20	0 - 1	0 - 0	1 - 1	32	0	1	1	.67	.597	4.44
Holland, Derek	LM	L	24	9	4	10	0.3	12	3	.25	0 - 0	0 - 0	0 - 0	12	0	0	0		.810	5.03
Suarez, Andrew	LM	L	19	8	3	7	0.8	13	4	.31	0 - 1	0 - 0	0 - 0	12	0	1	1	.50	.827	4.37
Vincent, Nick	LM	R	17	8	0	11	0.5	14	5	.36	0 - 0	0 - 0	0 - 0	8	0	0	0		.799	4.85
Melancon, Mark	UR	R	43	7	4	6	1.0	15	4	.27	1 - 1	0 - 0	0 - 0	31	0	0	5	1.00	.724	3.50
Coonrod, Sam	UR	R	33	10	5	2	0.7	15	2	.13	0 - 0	0 - 1	0 - 0	25	0	1	0	.00	.655	3.58
Gustave, Jandel	UR	R	23	8	4	2	0.9	16	5	.31	0 - 0	1 - 1	0 - 1	16	0	1	4	.83	.566	2.96
Rodriguez, Dereck	UR	R	12	4	1	7	0.8	0	0	.00	0 - 0	0 - 0	0 - 0	6	0	0	0		.789	6.53
Anderson, Shaun	UR	R	12	2	2	4	1.1	6	2	.33	0 - 0	2 - 2	0 - 0	7	0	0	1	1.00	.760	6.08
Smith, Burch	UR	R	10	5	1	1	1.1	7	1	.14	0 - 0	0 - 1	0 - 0	7	0	1	0	.00	.711	2.08
Barraclough, Kyle	UR	R	10	1	2	0	1.0	4	1	.25	0 - 0	0 - 0	0 - 1	7	0	1	0	.00	.692	2.25

Seattle Mariners

Pitcher	Pos	T	Usage					Inherited Runners			Saves			Relief Results						
			Rel G	Early Entry	Cons Days	Long	Lev Ind	#	Scrd	Pct	Easy	Reg	Tough	Clean	BS Win	BS	Holds	Sv/Hld Pct	Opp OPS	Rel ERA
Bass, Anthony	SU	R	44	4	5	5	1.4	14	1	.07	1 - 1	2 - 5	2 - 4	30	2	5	6	.69	.560	3.56
Adams, Austin	SU	R	27	8	3	3	1.3	13	4	.31	0 - 0	0 - 1	0 - 1	17	0	2	10	.83	.556	3.07
Tuivailala, Sam	SU	R	21	2	0	2	1.0	4	2	.50	0 - 0	0 - 1	0 - 0	17	0	1	7	.88	.563	2.57
Rosscup, Zac	SU	L	19	2	4	1	1.1	10	2	.20	0 - 0	0 - 0	0 - 1	13	0	1	5	.83	.719	3.21
Guilbeau, Taylor	LT	L	17	4	2	1	0.9	7	3	.43	0 - 0	0 - 0	0 - 2	13	0	2	3	.60	.657	3.65
Biddle, Jesse	LT	L	11	3	0	3	0.6	5	3	.60	0 - 0	0 - 1	0 - 0	4	0	1	1	.50	1.067	9.82
Gearrin, Cory	LM	R	46	17	8	0	1.0	22	6	.27	0 - 0	0 - 0	0 - 0	34	0	0	11	1.00	.667	3.20
Elias, Roenis	LM	L	44	4	11	10	1.5	22	14	.64	8 - 9	5 - 5	1 - 2	25	0	2	1	.88	.686	3.64
Festa, Matt	LM	R	20	3	1	8	0.8	5	2	.40	0 - 1	0 - 0	0 - 1	10	0	2	3	.60	.874	5.64
LeBlanc, Wade	LM	L	18	16	0	17	0.7	7	4	.57	0 - 0	0 - 0	0 - 0	1	0	0	0		.780	4.57
Milone, Tommy	LM	L	17	17	0	17	0.9	10	1	.10	0 - 0	0 - 0	0 - 0	3	0	0	0		.755	4.80
Brennan, Brandon	UR	R	44	13	4	5	1.2	20	8	.40	0 - 0	0 - 2	0 - 0	27	0	2	8	.80	.651	4.56
Magill, Matt	UR	R	22	2	2	2	1.3	0	0	.00	4 - 4	1 - 3	0 - 0	16	0	2	1	.75	.667	3.63
Sadzeck, Connor	UR	R	20	7	1	6	0.4	6	5	.83	0 - 0	1 - 1	0 - 1	13	0	1	1	.67	.672	2.66
Swanson, Erik	UR	R	19	4	2	7	0.6	4	2	.50	0 - 0	2 - 2	0 - 0	14	0	0	1	1.00	.681	3.28
Altavilla, Dan	UR	R	17	5	2	2	1.0	6	6	1.00	0 - 0	0 - 1	0 - 1	11	0	2	1	.33	.613	5.52
Wisler, Matt	UR	R	15	6	1	2	0.9	4	2	.50	0 - 0	0 - 0	0 - 1	5	1	1	4	.80	1.091	10.95
Swarzak, Anthony	UR	R	15	2	2	2	1.5	4	1	.25	2 - 3	0 - 2	1 - 1	8	1	3	0	.50	.933	5.27
Grotz, Zac	UR	R	14	6	0	6	1.0	6	1	.17	0 - 0	0 - 0	0 - 0	6	0	0	1	1.00	.585	4.15
McClain, Reggie	UR	R	12	4	0	5	0.5	3	2	.67	0 - 0	0 - 0	0 - 1	7	0	1	0	.00	.716	5.00
Bradford, Chasen	UR	R	12	4	3	3	0.6	11	1	.09	0 - 0	0 - 0	1 - 1	5	0	0	1	1.00	.898	4.86

St Louis Cardinals

Pitcher	Pos	T	Usage					Inherited Runners			Saves			Relief Results						
			Rel G	Early Entry	Cons Days	Long	Lev Ind	#	Scrd	Pct	Easy	Reg	Tough	Clean	BS Win	BS	Holds	Sv/Hld Pct	Opp OPS	Rel ERA
Martinez, Carlos	CL	R	48	0	18	8	1.9	21	5	.24	12 - 12	10 - 11	2 - 4	35	0	3	3	.90	.590	3.17
Hicks, Jordan	CL	R	29	0	8	5	1.6	8	0	.00	9 - 9	4 - 5	1 - 1	23	0	1	3	.94	.510	3.14
Miller, Andrew	SU	L	73	2	24	1	1.6	44	12	.27	2 - 2	3 - 6	1 - 3	45	1	5	28	.87	.739	4.45
Gant, John	SU	R	64	16	10	12	1.2	29	9	.31	1 - 1	1 - 2	1 - 3	42	1	3	18	.88	.639	3.66
Webb, Tyler	LT	L	65	21	19	6	0.6	30	10	.33	1 - 1	0 - 0	0 - 0	45	0	0	8	1.00	.593	3.76
Cabrera, Genesis	LT	L	11	4	1	2	0.5	5	1	.20	0 - 0	1 - 1	0 - 0	6	0	0	1	1.00	.578	3.75
Helsley, Ryan	LM	R	24	14	3	11	0.6	13	8	.62	0 - 0	0 - 0	0 - 1	12	0	1	1	.50	.734	2.95
Brebbia, John	UR	R	66	15	9	13	0.7	32	8	.25	0 - 0	0 - 1	0 - 0	48	0	1	12	.92	.626	3.59
Gallegos, Giovanny	UR	R	66	19	8	10	0.9	44	7	.16	0 - 0	1 - 3	0 - 1	47	0	3	19	.87	.546	2.31
Leone, Dominic	UR	R	40	10	6	6	0.5	8	2	.25	0 - 0	1 - 2	0 - 0	27	0	1	0	.50	.822	5.53
Mayers, Mike	UR	R	16	6	1	7	0.5	10	2	.20	0 - 0	0 - 0	0 - 0	8	0	0	1	1.00	.888	6.63
Fernandez, Junior	UR	R	13	5	3	2	1.0	9	6	.67	0 - 0	0 - 0	0 - 3	9	0	3	0	.00	.693	5.40

Tampa Bay Rays

Pitcher	Pos	T	Usage					Inherited Runners			Saves			Relief Results						
			Rel G	Early Entry	Cons Days	Long	Lev Ind	#	Scrd	Pct	Easy	Reg	Tough	Clean	BS Win	BS	Holds	Sv/Hld Pct	Opp OPS	Rel ERA
Pagan, Emilio	CL	R	66	10	24	11	1.6	30	9	.30	10 - 12	7 - 11	3 - 5	50	1	8	7	.77	.590	2.31
Roe, Chaz	SU	R	71	24	20	5	1.3	38	10	.26	1 - 1	0 - 3	0 - 1	49	0	4	23	.86	.704	4.06
Castillo, Diego	SU	R	59	11	14	8	1.6	12	1	.08	6 - 7	2 - 3	0 - 0	44	0	2	17	.93	.655	3.08
Poche, Colin	SU	L	51	17	18	13	1.5	30	8	.27	1 - 1	1 - 3	0 - 2	33	1	4	16	.82	.650	4.70
Alvarado, Jose	SU	L	34	1	7	2	2.0	8	1	.13	5 - 6	2 - 3	0 - 0	24	0	2	8	.88	.734	4.55

Tampa Bay Rays

Pitcher	Pos	T	Rel G	Early Entry	Cons Days	Long	Lev Ind	#	Scrd	Pct	Easy	Reg	Tough	Clean	BS Win	BS	Holds	Sv/Hld Pct	Opp OPS	Rel ERA
Anderson, Nick	SU	R	23	5	5	0	1.4	12	4	.33	0 - 1	0 - 0	0 - 2	18	0	3	9	.75	.512	2.11
Kolarek, Adam	LM	L	54	12	19	4	1.1	28	7	.25	1 - 1	0 - 0	0 - 0	36	0	0	14	1.00	.700	3.95
Kittredge, Andrew	LM	R	30	11	7	5	0.7	8	3	.38	0 - 0	0 - 0	0 - 0	19	0	0	2	1.00	.678	3.32
Beeks, Jalen	LM	L	30	24	1	26	0.9	10	2	.20	0 - 0	1 - 1	0 - 0	14	0	0	2	1.00	.746	3.42
Wood, Hunter	LM	R	17	4	1	6	0.7	11	1	.09	0 - 0	1 - 1	0 - 0	12	0	0	1	1.00	.692	2.88
Yarbrough, Ryan	LM	L	14	13	0	13	0.9	4	3	.75	0 - 0	0 - 0	0 - 0	4	0	0	0		.644	3.86
Drake, Oliver	UR	R	50	13	14	13	1.0	20	5	.25	1 - 2	0 - 0	1 - 1	36	1	1	10	.92	.612	3.21
Stanek, Ryne	UR	R	14	4	1	0	0.8	7	4	.57	0 - 0	0 - 0	0 - 0	7	0	0	2	1.00	.903	7.82
Fairbanks, Peter	UR	R	13	6	2	1	1.4	2	2	1.00	2 - 2	0 - 0	0 - 0	8	0	0	3	1.00	.836	5.11
Pruitt, Austin	UR	R	12	7	0	9	0.8	6	2	.33	0 - 0	0 - 0	0 - 0	4	0	0	0		.804	5.40
Font, Wilmer	UR	R	10	4	1	5	0.4	6	3	.50	0 - 0	0 - 0	0 - 0	3	0	0	1	1.00	.806	5.79

Texas Rangers

Pitcher	Pos	T	Rel G	Early Entry	Cons Days	Long	Lev Ind	#	Scrd	Pct	Easy	Reg	Tough	Clean	BS Win	BS	Holds	Sv/Hld Pct	Opp OPS	Rel ERA
Kelley, Shawn	CL	R	51	9	12	2	1.5	24	5	.21	4 - 4	5 - 9	2 - 2	30	0	4	6	.81	.885	4.94
Leclerc, Jose	SU	R	67	3	15	10	1.5	14	4	.29	10 - 12	4 - 6	0 - 0	46	0	4	7	.84	.698	4.43
Martin, Chris	SU	R	38	0	9	3	1.5	4	0	.00	2 - 2	2 - 3	0 - 0	28	0	1	12	.94	.716	3.08
Montero, Rafael	SU	R	22	1	2	6	1.1	5	0	.00	0 - 1	0 - 0	0 - 0	17	0	1	7	.88	.671	2.48
Martin, Brett	LT	L	49	18	6	9	0.7	23	7	.30	0 - 0	0 - 1	0 - 0	27	0	1	4	.80	.728	4.15
Bird, Kyle	LT	L	12	4	1	6	0.3	14	4	.29	0 - 0	0 - 0	1 - 1	6	0	0	0	1.00	.972	7.82
Chavez, Jesse	LM	R	39	14	6	11	1.0	19	8	.42	1 - 1	0 - 0	0 - 1	25	0	1	8	.90	.811	4.13
Springs, Jeffrey	LM	L	25	14	1	13	0.4	13	2	.15	0 - 0	0 - 0	0 - 0	12	0	0	1	1.00	.884	6.40
Sampson, Adrian	LM	R	20	14	2	13	0.7	15	7	.47	0 - 0	0 - 0	0 - 0	6	0	0	0		.839	5.01
Guerrieri, Taylor	LM	R	20	8	2	8	0.4	10	1	.10	0 - 0	0 - 0	0 - 0	11	0	0	3	1.00	.861	5.81
Jurado, Ariel	LM	R	14	9	2	10	0.9	10	3	.30	0 - 0	0 - 0	0 - 0	8	0	0	1	1.00	.699	3.07
Dowdy, Kyle	LM	R	12	7	0	7	0.6	8	6	.75	0 - 0	0 - 0	0 - 1	2	0	1	0	.00	.875	6.98
Clase, Emmanuel	UR	R	20	3	3	2	1.3	8	2	.25	1 - 1	0 - 0	0 - 0	14	0	0	4	1.00	.651	2.42
Gomez, Jeanmar	UR	R	16	7	3	3	0.5	15	6	.40	0 - 0	0 - 0	0 - 0	7	0	0	0		.973	8.22
Valdez, Phillips	UR	R	11	6	3	6	0.4	1	1	1.00	0 - 0	0 - 0	0 - 0	5	0	0	0		.818	3.94
Miller, Shelby	UR	R	11	3	0	5	0.5	5	1	.20	0 - 0	0 - 1	0 - 0	4	0	1	1	.50	.866	6.75

Toronto Blue Jays

Pitcher	Pos	T	Rel G	Early Entry	Cons Days	Long	Lev Ind	#	Scrd	Pct	Easy	Reg	Tough	Clean	BS Win	BS	Holds	Sv/Hld Pct	Opp OPS	Rel ERA
Giles, Ken	CL	R	53	0	7	4	1.8	4	2	.50	15 - 15	7 - 8	1 - 1	43	0	1	0	.96	.574	1.87
Mayza, Tim	LT	L	68	23	19	2	1.0	37	12	.32	0 - 0	0 - 1	0 - 0	42	0	1	18	.95	.741	4.91
Boshers, Buddy	LT	L	27	7	8	3	1.0	16	4	.25	0 - 0	0 - 0	0 - 0	18	0	0	4	1.00	.796	4.26
Gaviglio, Sam	LM	R	52	30	3	31	0.5	20	4	.20	0 - 0	0 - 0	0 - 0	23	0	0	3	1.00	.718	4.61
Biagini, Joe	LM	R	50	7	8	3	1.1	29	6	.21	1 - 2	0 - 1	0 - 0	31	0	2	10	.85	.783	3.78
Hudson, Daniel	LM	R	44	11	8	9	1.3	22	1	.05	0 - 0	1 - 2	1 - 2	31	1	2	8	.83	.663	2.87
Pannone, Thomas	LM	L	30	16	4	12	0.7	16	5	.31	0 - 0	0 - 0	0 - 0	20	0	0	1	1.00	.702	3.54
Luciano, Elvis	LM	R	25	10	2	12	0.2	14	2	.14	0 - 0	0 - 0	0 - 0	12	0	0	0		.847	5.35
Adam, Jason	LM	R	23	10	5	4	1.0	11	3	.27	0 - 0	0 - 0	0 - 0	16	0	1	4	.80	.601	2.91
Law, Derek	UR	R	54	11	12	13	1.2	24	11	.46	1 - 1	3 - 4	1 - 1	31	0	1	8	.93	.786	4.45
Shafer, Justin	UR	R	34	12	3	7	0.8	22	4	.18	1 - 1	0 - 0	0 - 0	20	0	0	3	1.00	.854	3.86
Tepera, Ryan	UR	R	22	2	1	1	1.1	9	2	.22	0 - 0	0 - 0	0 - 0	14	0	0	2	1.00	.751	4.35
Romano, Jordan	UR	R	17	1	0	2	1.1	2	0	.00	0 - 0	0 - 0	0 - 0	7	0	0	5	1.00	.884	7.63
Phelps, David	UR	R	16	1	3	2	0.9	5	0	.00	0 - 0	0 - 2	0 - 0	11	0	2	4	.67	.768	3.86
Guerra, Javy	UR	R	11	1	2	3	0.6	5	4	.80	0 - 0	1 - 1	0 - 0	7	0	0	1	1.00	.714	3.86
Kingham, Nick	UR	R	11	7	0	7	0.7	2	0	.00	0 - 0	0 - 0	0 - 0	6	0	0	0		.866	3.00
Stewart, Brock	UR	R	10	8	1	6	0.6	7	0	.00	0 - 0	0 - 0	0 - 0	3	0	0	0		1.044	8.31

Washington Nationals

Pitcher	Pos	T	Usage					Inherited Runners			Saves			Relief Results						
			Rel G	Early Entry	Cons Days	Long	Lev Ind	#	Scrd	Pct	Easy	Reg	Tough	Clean	BS Win	BS	Holds	Sv/Hld Pct	Opp OPS	Rel ERA
Doolittle, Sean	CL	L	63	0	18	6	1.8	21	8	.38	20 - 22	6 - 7	3 - 6	45	2	6	2	.84	.772	4.05
Hudson, Daniel	CL	R	24	1	8	3	1.2	14	5	.36	2 - 2	4 - 5	0 - 1	19	1	2	3	.82	.593	1.44
Suero, Wander	SU	R	78	13	25	9	1.2	22	8	.36	0 - 0	1 - 5	0 - 2	56	0	6	19	.77	.666	4.54
Rodney, Fernando	SU	R	38	0	13	3	1.4	8	3	.38	2 - 3	0 - 2	0 - 0	29	0	3	17	.86	.676	4.05
Barraclough, Kyle	SU	R	33	0	8	3	1.3	13	11	.85	0 - 0	0 - 0	0 - 2	18	0	2	8	.80	.948	6.66
Strickland, Hunter	SU	R	24	4	8	0	1.2	6	3	.50	0 - 0	0 - 0	0 - 0	14	0	0	10	1.00	.820	5.14
Grace, Matt	LT	L	50	21	11	4	0.6	34	15	.44	0 - 0	0 - 0	0 - 0	25	0	0	4	1.00	.945	6.65
Sipp, Tony	LT	L	36	4	7	0	1.0	21	7	.33	0 - 0	0 - 0	0 - 1	22	0	1	9	.90	.644	4.71
Guerra, Javy	LM	R	40	10	10	12	0.4	22	8	.36	0 - 0	1 - 1	0 - 0	22	0	0	4	1.00	.726	4.86
Rainey, Tanner	UR	R	52	14	15	5	0.9	11	4	.36	0 - 0	0 - 3	0 - 0	37	0	3	9	.75	.696	3.91
Ross, Joe	UR	R	18	5	2	6	1.1	6	0	.00	0 - 1	0 - 1	0 - 0	10	0	2	2	.50	1.067	11.17
Miller, Justin	UR	R	17	4	4	1	0.8	10	6	.60	0 - 1	0 - 0	0 - 0	11	0	1	4	.80	.878	4.02
Rosenthal, Trevor	UR	R	12	0	2	3	0.6	4	1	.25	0 - 0	0 - 0	0 - 0	4	0	0	1	1.00	.938	22.74

Openers

Lindsay Zeck

Having an opener start the game is a pitching strategy that was introduced in 2018 by the Tampa Bay Rays. An opener is a relief pitcher who starts the game, pitches up to two innings, and then has a "starter" come in after him. The second part of this definition is what distinguishes it from a bullpen game in which a team uses only relief pitchers (different sources may have different definitions). By this classification, the first opener was Andrew Kittredge on May 4, 2018. He pitched the first two innings for the Rays against the Toronto Blue Jays and was followed by rookie Ryan Yarbrough who pitched the following five innings.

In 2018, the opener strategy was primarily implemented by the Rays—out of the 63 instances in which a starter was classified as an opener, 39 of them (62%) were Rays pitchers. However, in 2019 we started to see other teams follow suit. Of the 141 times the pitcher who started the game was an opener, the Rays still led with 35 (now down to 25% of league totals), but the Angels and Mariners weren't far behind with 27 and 26, respectively. The Blue Jays (15), Yankees (10), and Rangers (9) also got in on the action, but no other teams had more than three games started with an opener.

Ryne Stanek opened more games than any other player in baseball, and it's not even close. He opened 42 games over the last two seasons, with Diego Castillo of the Rays in second with 12, and Hunter Wood—while on the Rays—and Wilmer Font with the Blue Jays tied for third with 10.

In 2019, Stanek was extremely effective as an opener. In the 22 games he opened, his ERA was an outstanding 2.14. In his 41 non-opener games, his ERA was a 5.40! Now that he's on the Marlins, opens will be hard for him to come by. The Marlins have yet to use an opener.

It will be interesting to see if the opener strategy will continue to pick up steam next season. It's likely that the Rays will continue to use it. Even with Stanek departing the team, they didn't skip a beat the rest of the season. The uncertainty lies with other teams and whether they will be "open" to it.

Opener Usage

By Team			
Team	2018	2019	Total
Tampa Bay Rays	39	35	74
Los Angeles Angels	0	27	27
Seattle Mariners	1	26	27
Toronto Blue Jays	1	15	16
Texas Rangers	3	9	12
New York Yankees	0	10	10
Oakland Athletics	7	3	10
Minnesota Twins	7	0	7
Baltimore Orioles	2	3	5
Pittsburgh Pirates	0	3	3
Houston Astros	1	2	3
San Diego Padres	0	2	2
Los Angeles Dodgers	1	1	2
Washington Nationals	0	1	1
San Francisco Giants	0	1	1
Philadelphia Phillies	0	1	1
Chicago White Sox	0	1	1
Arizona Diamondbacks	0	1	1
Milwaukee Brewers	1	0	1
New York Mets	0	0	0
St Louis Cardinals	0	0	0
Atlanta Braves	0	0	0
Chicago Cubs	0	0	0
Cincinnati Reds	0	0	0
Colorado Rockies	0	0	0
Miami Marlins	0	0	0
Cleveland Indians	0	0	0
Detroit Tigers	0	0	0
Kansas City Royals	0	0	0
Boston Red Sox	0	0	0
Total	63	141	204

Appearances By Pitcher			
Pitcher	2018	2019	Total
Stanek, Ryne	20	22	42
Castillo, Diego	6	6	12
Font, Wilmer	0	10	10
Wood, Hunter	8	2	10
Green, Chad	0	8	8
Wisler, Matt	0	8	8
Hendriks, Liam	6	2	8
Ramirez, Noe	0	7	7
Bedrosian, Cam	0	7	7
Cole, Taylor	0	6	6
Carasiti, Matt	0	5	5
Kittredge, Andrew	1	4	5
Moya, Gabriel	5	0	5
Bard, Luke	0	3	3
Leclerc, Jose	0	3	3
Chavez, Jesse	0	3	3
Romo, Sergio	3	0	3
Gearrin, Cory	0	2	2
Garcia, Luis	0	2	2
Law, Derek	0	2	2
Tuivailala, Sam	0	2	2
Scott, Tayler	0	2	2
Adams, Austin	0	2	2
Yacabonis, Jimmy	0	2	2
DuRapau, Montana	0	2	2
Bautista, Gerson	0	2	2
Dunn, Justin	0	2	2
Vincent, Nick	1	1	2
Sadzeck, Connor	2	0	2

Pitchers Fielding & Holding Runners, and Hitters Pitching

Alex Vigderman

Have you ever had a coworker leave the company, causing everyone else in the group to take on a little extra responsibility to account for the departure? That's what this section is experiencing right now.

This year we're allowing Pitchers Hitting to pursue other opportunities and giving Pitchers Fielding and Hitters Pitching exposure to tasks outside their job descriptions.

Even with all of this, we can still glorify Zack Greinke's multifaceted success this season, because it now covers two sections. In 2019, he was one of the best pitchers in the league, swung a quality bat, and for the twelfth straight year saved at least four runs defensively.

Greinke was tied for the best runs saved total last season but was one of many hurlers looking up at Max Fried of the Braves this year. Fried was one of a trio of Atlanta pitchers who saved at least five runs (along with Dallas Keuchel and Mike Soroka). They became the second trio of pitchers to save at least five runs in a season for the same team, following in the 2005 Giants' footsteps. You can find a player's Defensive Runs Saved in the RS column in the tables that follow.

In terms of controlling the running game, Noah Syndergaard didn't exactly drop the hammer this season. His 42 stolen bases allowed were 18 more than any other pitcher. The next-highest were his teammate Jacob DeGrom (24) and the Cubs' Yu Darvish (24). The Mets as a team yielded 139 stolen bases, a staggering 40 more than any other team.

The Tigers allowed the third-most stolen bases as a team, but that was no fault of Matthew Boyd. He caught five of nine would-be basestealers, all without the help of the catcher.

It was another banner year for position players pitching. Position players threw 93 1/3 innings this season, up from 63 last year and 32 2/3 in 2017.

The player who contributed the most this year was Stevie Wilkerson of the Orioles, who threw 5 1/3 innings, allowing four earned runs and striking out one. His real claim to fame, though, was that he became the first position player to ever record a save, throwing a perfect 16th inning on July 25.

Wilkerson edged out Jared Walsh of the Angels in innings pitched, but Walsh was the more effective of the two. He allowed just one run and struck out five in five innings of work. Of course, that's not a fair fight, because Walsh pitched a fair amount in college and threw an additional 13 innings in Triple-A this year.

Pitchers Fielding and Holding Runners

Pitcher	Inn	PO	A	E	DP	Pct	SBA	CS	PCS	PPO	CS%	RS
Abad, Fernando	13.0	0	0	0	0	-	1	0	0	0	.00	0
Abreu, Bryan	8.2	2	2	0	0	1.000	1	0	0	0	.00	0
Adam, Jason	21.2	3	2	1	1	.833	1	0	0	0	.00	0
Adams, Austin D	16.2	1	3	0	0	1.000	1	0	0	0	.00	0
Adams, Austin L	32.0	2	1	1	1	.750	1	0	0	0	.00	0
Adams, Chance	25.1	0	2	0	0	1.000	0	0	0	0	-	0
Agrazal, Dario	73.1	5	6	1	1	.917	8	3	0	0	.38	0
Alaniz, R.J.	15.2	2	2	1	0	.800	3	1	0	0	.33	0
Albers, Matt	59.2	2	4	0	0	1.000	6	1	0	0	.17	-3
Alcala, Jorge	1.2	0	0	0	0	-	0	0	0	0	-	0
Alcantara, Sandy	197.1	10	20	4	0	.882	14	2	0	0	.14	-2
Alcantara, Victor	42.2	2	6	1	0	.889	5	2	1	0	.40	-1
Alexander, Scott	17.1	2	3	1	0	.833	0	0	0	0	-	0
Alexander, Tyler	53.2	2	2	0	0	1.000	0	0	0	0	-	-2
Allard, Kolby	45.1	2	0	2	0	.500	2	0	0	0	.00	-1
Allen, Cody	23.0	0	0	0	0	-	3	0	0	0	.00	0
Allen, Logan	27.2	1	7	0	1	1.000	1	1	0	0	1.00	1
Almonte, Yency	34.0	2	2	0	0	1.000	4	1	0	0	.25	-1
Altavilla, Dan	14.2	0	4	0	0	1.000	1	0	0	0	.00	0
Alvarado, Jose	30.0	1	4	1	0	.833	1	0	0	0	.00	0
Alvarez, Jose	59.0	5	13	0	0	1.000	3	3	2	0	1.00	1
Alzolay, Adbert	12.1	2	1	1	0	.750	1	0	0	0	.00	0
Anderson, Brett	176.0	5	25	3	1	.909	18	8	5	0	.44	2
Anderson, Chase	139.0	4	15	1	0	.950	14	3	0	0	.21	-1
Anderson, Cody	8.2	0	1	0	0	1.000	0	0	0	0	-	0
Anderson, Drew	6.0	0	1	0	0	1.000	0	0	0	0	-	0
Anderson, Justin	47.0	2	2	0	0	1.000	4	1	0	1	.25	-1
Anderson, Nick	65.0	2	4	1	0	.857	2	1	0	0	.50	1
Anderson, Shaun	96.0	10	14	2	2	.923	5	3	0	0	.60	2
Anderson, Tanner	22.1	3	3	0	0	1.000	2	1	1	0	.50	-1
Anderson, Tyler	20.2	2	1	0	0	1.000	2	0	0	0	.00	-1
Andriese, Matt	70.2	6	12	2	1	.900	9	2	0	0	.22	-2
Arano, Victor	4.2	0	0	0	0	-	1	1	0	0	1.00	0
Araujo, Pedro	0.2	0	0	0	0	-	0	0	0	0	-	0
Archer, Chris	119.2	7	14	1	0	.955	15	6	1	0	.40	0
Armenteros, R.	18.0	1	1	0	0	1.000	0	0	0	0	-	-1
Armstrong, Shawn	58.0	1	2	0	0	1.000	8	1	0	0	.13	-4
Arrieta, Jake	135.2	13	26	3	3	.929	18	6	0	1	.33	2
Avila, Pedro	5.1	1	0	0	0	1.000	0	0	0	0	-	0
Avilan, Luis	32.0	4	3	0	0	1.000	3	0	0	0	.00	0
Baez, Michel	29.2	4	3	0	0	1.000	1	0	0	0	.00	0
Baez, Pedro	69.2	2	6	1	0	.889	6	1	0	0	.17	1
Baez, Sandy	1.0	0	0	0	0	-	0	0	0	0	-	0
Bailey, Homer	163.1	12	14	0	0	1.000	8	3	0	1	.38	1
Banda, Anthony	4.0	0	0	0	0	-	0	0	0	0	-	0
Banuelos, Manny	50.2	2	1	1	1	.750	5	2	0	1	.40	-1
Bard, Luke	49.0	3	1	0	1	1.000	10	2	1	0	.20	-2
Barlow, Scott	70.1	1	6	0	0	1.000	8	1	0	1	.13	-1
Barnes, Jacob	32.2	1	5	0	0	1.000	2	0	0	0	.00	0
Barnes, Matt	64.1	4	2	1	0	.857	6	1	0	0	.17	0
Barnette, Tony	1.1	0	0	0	0	-	0	0	0	0	-	0
Barraclough, Kyle	33.2	3	4	2	0	.778	4	2	0	0	.50	1
Barrett, Aaron	2.1	0	0	0	0	-	0	0	0	0	-	0
Barrett, Jake	3.2	0	0	0	0	-	0	0	0	0	-	0
Barria, Jaime	82.2	4	4	0	0	1.000	1	0	0	1	.00	1
Bashlor, Tyler	22.0	0	0	0	0	-	3	0	0	0	.00	-1
Bass, Anthony	48.0	5	6	0	1	1.000	1	1	0	0	1.00	0
Bassitt, Chris	144.0	5	14	0	3	1.000	12	2	0	0	.17	0
Bauer, Trevor	213.0	12	15	0	1	1.000	18	4	0	0	.22	-2
Bautista, Gerson	9.0	0	0	0	0	-	0	0	0	0	-	0
Bednar, David	11.0	1	1	0	1	1.000	1	0	0	0	.00	0
Bedrosian, Cam	61.1	5	6	0	0	1.000	4	1	0	0	.25	-1
Beede, Tyler	117.0	6	11	1	3	.944	7	2	0	0	.29	-1
Beeks, Jalen	104.1	2	14	0	2	1.000	5	2	1	0	.40	4
Bergen, Travis	19.2	1	1	0	0	1.000	4	1	0	0	.25	0
Berrios, Jose	200.1	12	19	1	0	.969	13	1	1	2	.08	0
Betances, Dellin	0.2	0	0	0	0	-	0	0	0	0	-	0
Bettis, Chad	63.2	7	13	1	2	.952	1	1	0	1	1.00	-1
Biagini, Joe	64.2	0	6	2	0	.750	4	1	0	0	.25	0
Biddle, Jesse	28.0	1	1	3	0	.400	2	0	0	0	.00	-2
Bieber, Shane	214.1	12	14	0	0	1.000	11	4	1	2	.36	0
Bird, Kyle	12.2	0	2	0	0	1.000	4	0	0	0	.00	0
Blach, Ty	27.0	1	3	0	0	1.000	0	0	0	0	-	1
Black, Ray	16.0	1	2	0	0	1.000	1	0	0	0	.00	0
Blackburn, Paul	11.0	1	4	0	0	1.000	5	0	0	0	.00	0
Blazek, Michael	5.0	0	0	0	0	-	0	0	0	0	-	0
Bleier, Richard	55.1	4	8	0	0	1.000	7	1	1	1	.14	-2
Blevins, Jerry	32.1	3	1	1	0	.800	4	0	0	0	.00	-1
Bolanos, Ronald	19.2	2	0	0	0	1.000	0	0	0	0	-	0
Borucki, Ryan	6.2	0	0	0	0	-	0	0	0	0	-	0
Boshers, Buddy	20.0	0	1	0	0	1.000	1	0	0	0	.00	0
Bourque, James	0.2	0	0	0	0	-	0	0	0	0	-	0
Bowman, Matt	32.0	2	8	1	0	.909	5	0	0	0	.00	0
Boxberger, Brad	26.2	3	0	0	0	1.000	4	1	0	0	.25	0
Boyd, Matthew	185.1	7	19	1	0	.963	9	5	5	0	.56	2
Brach, Brad	54.1	5	6	0	1	1.000	3	1	0	0	.33	0
Bradford, Chasen	16.2	2	3	0	1	1.000	0	0	0	0	-	0
Bradley, Archie	71.2	3	1	0	0	1.000	4	1	0	1	.25	-1
Brasier, Ryan	55.2	4	4	1	0	.889	1	0	0	0	.00	0
Brault, Steven	113.1	8	18	0	3	1.000	12	1	0	0	.08	2
Brebbia, John	72.2	1	6	0	0	1.000	2	1	0	0	.50	-1
Brennan, Brandon	47.1	0	5	2	1	.714	6	1	0	0	.17	0
Brewer, Colten	54.2	3	12	0	0	1.000	6	0	0	1	.00	2
Brice, Austin	44.2	2	2	0	0	1.000	2	0	0	0	.00	0
Brigham, Jeff	38.1	0	3	0	0	1.000	4	1	0	0	.25	1
Britton, Zack	61.1	1	10	0	0	1.000	2	1	1	0	.50	1
Brooks, Aaron	110.0	7	8	1	2	.938	8	1	0	0	.13	0
Buchholz, Clay	59.0	7	16	0	2	1.000	5	2	0	0	.40	1
Buchter, Ryan	45.1	3	6	1	0	.900	9	5	3	0	.56	1
Buehler, Walker	182.1	11	17	0	1	1.000	9	1	1	1	.11	-1
Bumgarner, M.	207.2	2	19	1	0	.955	17	3	2	0	.18	1
Bummer, Aaron	67.2	4	12	1	1	.941	2	0	0	0	.00	0
Bundy, Dylan	161.2	10	8	0	1	1.000	13	2	0	0	.15	-1
Burdi, Nick	8.2	0	0	0	0	-	0	0	0	0	-	-1
Burke, Brock	26.2	0	5	0	0	1.000	2	1	0	0	.50	1
Burnes, Corbin	49.0	2	10	2	0	.857	4	0	0	0	.00	0
Burr, Ryan	19.2	1	3	0	0	1.000	0	0	0	0	-	0
Buttrey, Ty	72.1	4	5	0	1	1.000	8	2	0	0	.25	0
Cabrera, Genesis	20.1	0	3	0	0	1.000	2	0	0	0	.00	0
Cahill, Trevor	102.1	9	9	1	0	.947	15	2	1	0	.13	-1
Canning, Griffin	90.1	9	12	2	0	.913	6	0	0	1	.00	1
Carasiti, Matt	9.2	0	1	0	0	1.000	2	1	0	0	.50	0
Carle, Shane	9.1	1	0	0	0	1.000	0	0	0	0	-	-1
Carpenter, David	3.1	1	0	0	0	1.000	0	0	0	0	-	0
Carpenter, Ryan	40.2	1	4	1	0	.833	2	0	0	1	.00	-1
Carrasco, Carlos	80.0	5	6	0	0	1.000	6	3	0	1	.50	1
Cashner, Andrew	150.0	10	17	0	1	1.000	7	5	0	0	.71	-1
Castillo, Diego	68.2	2	6	1	0	.889	3	0	0	0	.00	0
Castillo, Jose	0.2	0	0	0	0	-	0	0	0	0	-	0
Castillo, Luis	190.2	17	30	1	1	.979	10	2	1	0	.20	4
Castro, Miguel	73.1	7	10	1	1	.944	19	1	0	0	.05	-4
Cease, Dylan	73.0	8	6	1	2	.933	1	0	0	0	.00	-2
Cedeno, Xavier	2.0	0	1	0	0	1.000	1	0	0	0	.00	0
Cessa, Luis	81.0	2	9	0	1	1.000	6	2	1	0	.33	0
Chacin, Jhoulys	103.1	10	7	0	2	1.000	7	1	0	0	.14	1
Chafin, Andrew	52.2	7	8	1	2	.938	2	1	1	0	.50	1
Chapman, Aroldis	57.0	1	3	2	0	.667	4	0	0	0	.00	-1
Chargois, JT	21.1	2	0	0	0	1.000	4	0	0	0	.00	-1
Chatwood, Tyler	76.2	7	11	1	1	.947	2	0	0	0	.00	2
Chavez, Jesse	78.0	2	7	0	0	1.000	5	3	0	0	.60	2
Chen, Wei-Yin	68.1	5	7	0	0	1.000	0	0	0	0	-	1
Chirinos, Yonny	133.1	4	10	1	1	.933	9	5	0	0	.56	2
Cimber, Adam	56.2	4	10	2	1	.875	0	0	0	0	-	0
Cishek, Steve	64.0	4	8	1	0	.923	4	1	0	0	.25	-1
Cisnero, Jose	35.1	2	2	0	0	1.000	1	0	0	0	.00	-1
Civale, Aaron	57.2	1	4	1	0	.833	0	0	0	0	-	0
Clarke, Taylor	84.2	4	6	2	0	.833	3	1	0	1	.33	0
Clase, Emmanuel	23.1	0	0	2	0	.000	1	1	0	0	1.00	-1
Claudio, Alex	62.0	4	16	0	2	1.000	5	2	0	0	.40	1
Clevinger, Mike	126.0	12	11	0	0	1.000	14	5	0	1	.36	0
Clippard, Tyler	62.0	2	3	1	0	.833	3	2	0	0	.67	-2
Cobb, Alex	12.1	0	3	0	0	1.000	1	1	0	0	1.00	0

2019 Fielding and Holding Runners

Pitcher	Inn	PO	A	E	DP	Pct	SBA	CS	PCS	PPO	CS%	RS
Cole, A.J.	26.0	0	3	0	0	1.000	2	1	1	0	.50	-1
Cole, Gerrit	212.1	14	12	0	0	1.000	16	5	0	0	.31	-2
Cole, Taylor	51.2	1	10	0	3	1.000	6	1	0	2	.17	0
Collins, Tim	8.2	0	1	0	0	1.000	0	0	0	0	-	0
Colome, Alex	61.0	2	3	1	0	.833	0	0	0	0	-	-1
Conley, Adam	60.2	3	10	0	2	1.000	4	2	0	0	.50	2
Coonrod, Sam	27.2	3	4	0	1	1.000	4	1	0	0	.25	0
Corbin, Patrick	202.0	12	30	0	0	1.000	17	6	4	0	.35	2
Cordero, Jimmy	37.1	2	1	0	0	1.000	4	0	0	0	.00	-1
Cortes, Nestor	66.2	1	5	1	2	.857	0	0	0	0	-	1
Covey, Dylan	58.2	6	2	1	0	.889	9	1	1	0	.11	-3
Crichton, Stefan	30.1	2	4	1	0	.857	0	0	0	0	-	0
Crick, Kyle	49.0	3	6	1	1	.900	7	0	0	0	.00	0
Cueto, Johnny	16.0	1	3	0	0	1.000	1	0	0	0	.00	1
Curtiss, John	2.1	0	1	0	0	1.000	0	0	0	0	-	0
Darvish, Yu	178.2	14	13	1	1	.964	26	2	0	0	.08	-5
Davies, Zach	159.2	11	20	3	2	.912	17	7	2	0	.41	2
Davis, Austin	20.2	1	2	0	0	1.000	3	0	0	0	.00	0
Davis, Rookie	10.2	1	1	0	0	1.000	0	0	0	0	-	0
Davis, Wade	42.2	2	3	1	2	.833	14	0	0	0	.00	-2
Dayton, Grant	12.0	0	1	0	0	1.000	0	0	0	0	-	1
De Jong, Chase	1.0	0	0	0	0	-	0	0	0	0	-	0
De Leon, Jose	4.0	0	0	0	0	-	0	0	0	0	-	0
De Los Santos, E.	11.0	0	0	0	0	-	0	0	0	0	-	0
deGrom, Jacob	204.0	24	17	1	0	.976	28	4	1	0	.14	-4
Del Pozo, Miguel	9.1	1	0	0	0	1.000	3	0	0	0	.00	-1
DeSclafani, A.	166.2	13	14	0	0	1.000	14	3	0	0	.21	0
Despaigne, O.	13.1	0	0	0	0	-	2	2	0	0	1.00	1
Detwiler, Ross	69.2	2	5	0	0	1.000	7	4	1	0	.57	1
Devenski, Chris	69.0	5	5	1	0	.909	15	2	0	1	.13	-1
Diaz, Edwin	58.0	2	3	0	0	1.000	11	0	0	0	.00	-3
Diaz, Jairo	57.2	6	6	2	2	.857	5	1	0	0	.20	0
Diaz, Miguel	6.1	0	0	0	0	-	0	0	0	0	-	0
Diaz, Yennsy	0.2	0	1	0	0	1.000	1	0	0	0	.00	0
Diehl, Phillip	7.1	0	0	0	0	-	0	0	0	0	-	0
Diekman, Jake	62.0	1	5	1	1	.857	2	1	1	0	.50	0
Dobnak, Randy	28.1	2	2	1	0	.800	5	1	0	0	.20	-1
Dominguez, S.	24.2	2	5	0	0	1.000	2	1	0	0	.50	0
Doolittle, Sean	60.0	0	0	0	0	-	3	0	0	0	.00	-1
Dowdy, Kyle	22.1	3	1	0	0	1.000	2	0	0	0	.00	0
Drake, Oliver	56.0	6	2	0	0	1.000	4	3	0	0	.75	0
Duffey, Tyler	57.2	3	8	1	0	.917	1	1	0	0	1.00	0
Duffy, Danny	130.2	1	13	1	1	.933	2	1	0	0	.50	1
Dugger, Robert	34.1	1	2	0	0	1.000	0	0	0	0	-	0
Duke, Zach	23.1	3	3	0	1	1.000	4	0	0	0	.00	0
Dull, Ryan	12.2	1	2	0	0	1.000	0	0	0	0	-	0
Dunn, Justin	6.2	0	1	0	0	1.000	4	0	0	0	.00	-1
Dunn, Mike	17.2	0	1	0	0	1.000	1	1	0	0	1.00	0
Duplantier, Jon	36.2	2	2	0	1	1.000	3	2	1	0	.67	0
DuRapau, M.	17.1	2	1	0	0	1.000	1	1	0	0	1.00	0
Dyson, Sam	62.1	7	7	0	1	1.000	6	2	0	0	.33	-1
Eades, Ryan	11.1	0	1	0	0	1.000	3	0	0	0	.00	0
Edwards, Jon	8.0	1	0	0	0	1.000	0	0	0	0	-	0
Edwards Jr., Carl	17.0	2	2	0	0	1.000	0	0	0	0	-	0
Eflin, Zach	163.1	13	20	1	2	.971	13	4	1	0	.31	-2
Eickhoff, Jerad	58.1	3	7	0	0	1.000	6	3	1	1	.50	2
Elias, Roenis	50.0	1	4	3	0	.625	4	0	0	1	.00	0
Ellis, Chris	1.0	0	0	0	0	-	0	0	0	0	-	0
Eovaldi, Nathan	67.2	8	8	0	2	1.000	3	1	0	1	.33	1
Erlin, Robbie	55.1	4	8	1	0	.923	0	0	0	0	-	-2
Escobar, Luis	5.2	0	2	0	0	1.000	2	0	0	0	.00	0
Eshelman, Tom	36.0	2	2	1	0	.800	0	0	0	0	-	0
Estevez, Carlos	72.0	4	4	1	1	.889	3	1	0	0	.33	-1
Estrada, Marco	23.2	0	1	0	0	1.000	0	0	0	0	-	0
Fairbanks, Peter	21.0	2	0	1	0	.667	2	1	0	0	.50	-1
Familia, Jeurys	60.0	3	5	0	1	1.000	8	2	0	0	.25	-3
Faria, Jake	18.2	0	1	0	0	1.000	1	0	0	0	.00	0
Farmer, Buck	67.2	4	6	2	1	.833	5	1	0	0	.20	-2
Farrell, Luke	13.1	0	1	0	0	1.000	1	1	0	0	1.00	0
Fedde, Erick	78.0	13	12	0	1	1.000	9	3	0	0	.33	0
Feierabend, Ryan	5.2	0	1	0	0	1.000	2	1	1	0	.50	-1
Feliz, Michael	56.1	3	4	2	0	.778	7	2	0	0	.29	-1
Ferguson, Caleb	44.2	1	8	0	0	1.000	2	0	0	0	.00	0

2019 Fielding and Holding Runners

Pitcher	Inn	PO	A	E	DP	Pct	SBA	CS	PCS	PPO	CS%	RS
Fernandez, Jose	3.2	1	1	0	0	1.000	2	0	0	0	.00	1
Fernandez, Junior	11.2	0	0	1	0	.000	2	0	0	0	.00	0
Festa, Matt	22.1	1	3	0	0	1.000	0	0	0	0	-	0
Fiers, Mike	184.2	8	16	2	1	.923	18	5	1	1	.28	1
Fillmyer, Heath	22.1	0	3	0	0	1.000	1	0	0	0	.00	0
Flaherty, Jack	196.1	18	23	0	4	1.000	4	3	0	1	.75	3
Flexen, Chris	13.2	0	1	0	0	1.000	1	0	0	0	.00	0
Floro, Dylan	46.2	5	4	1	1	.900	2	0	0	0	.00	0
Flynn, Brian	29.1	0	6	0	0	1.000	3	1	1	0	.33	1
Foltynewicz, Mike	117.0	3	9	1	0	.923	5	2	0	0	.40	-1
Font, Wilmer	84.1	6	5	0	1	1.000	9	1	0	0	.11	-1
Franco, Enderson	5.1	1	0	0	0	1.000	0	0	0	0	-	0
Frare, Caleb	2.2	0	0	0	0	-	0	0	0	0	-	0
Freeland, Kyle	104.1	3	12	1	1	.938	2	1	1	0	.50	1
Freeman, Sam	2.0	0	0	0	0	-	0	0	0	0	-	0
Fried, Max	165.2	7	34	3	1	.932	6	2	1	4	.33	6
Fry, Jace	55.0	1	8	0	2	1.000	3	1	1	0	.33	1
Fry, Paul	57.1	7	4	0	0	1.000	5	1	1	0	.20	-1
Fulmer, Carson	27.1	1	0	0	0	1.000	3	0	0	0	.00	0
Gagnon, Drew	23.2	3	1	0	0	1.000	3	0	0	0	.00	0
Gallegos, G.	74.0	3	4	1	0	.875	3	1	1	0	.33	1
Gallen, Zac	80.0	4	5	0	0	1.000	11	5	2	0	.45	-1
Gant, John	66.1	5	7	0	0	1.000	1	0	0	0	.00	2
Garcia, Bryan	6.2	1	0	0	0	1.000	0	0	0	0	-	0
Garcia, Edgar	39.0	2	1	0	0	1.000	3	2	0	0	.67	0
Garcia, Jarlin	50.2	1	9	0	0	1.000	2	1	1	0	.50	0
Garcia, Luis	62.0	6	10	1	2	.941	5	0	0	0	.00	-4
Garcia, Rico	6.0	0	0	0	0	-	0	0	0	0	-	0
Garcia, Yimi	62.1	1	2	1	0	.750	2	0	0	0	.00	0
Garrett, Amir	56.0	5	10	1	1	.938	8	1	0	0	.13	2
Garrett, Reed	15.1	0	0	0	0	-	2	1	0	0	.50	0
Garton, Ryan	3.0	1	0	0	0	1.000	0	0	0	0	-	0
Gausman, Kevin	102.1	6	10	3	0	.842	17	4	1	0	.24	-4
Gaviglio, Sam	95.2	4	5	0	1	1.000	7	4	0	0	.57	-2
Gearrin, Cory	55.1	3	7	0	2	1.000	11	0	0	0	.00	0
German, Domingo	143.0	4	12	2	0	.889	5	4	0	0	.80	-3
Gibaut, Ian	14.1	1	1	0	0	1.000	0	0	0	1	-	-1
Gibson, Kyle	160.0	10	14	2	3	.923	9	3	0	1	.33	1
Giles, Ken	53.0	3	2	0	1	1.000	6	1	0	0	.17	-2
Gilmartin, Sean	2.1	0	1	0	0	1.000	0	0	0	0	-	0
Ginkel, Kevin	24.1	1	1	1	0	.667	1	0	0	0	.00	0
Giolito, Lucas	176.2	4	15	0	1	1.000	6	3	0	0	.50	3
Givens, Mychal	63.0	2	4	2	0	.750	12	3	1	1	.25	1
Glasnow, Tyler	60.2	1	5	0	0	1.000	11	2	1	0	.18	-1
Godley, Zack	92.0	10	7	2	0	.895	2	1	0	0	.50	-1
Gomez, Jeanmar	15.1	0	0	0	0	-	1	0	0	0	.00	-1
Gonsolin, Tony	40.0	2	4	1	0	.857	6	1	0	0	.17	0
Gonzales, Marco	203.0	7	23	3	2	.909	9	2	0	0	.22	2
Gonzalez, Chi Chi	63.0	4	10	2	1	.875	2	1	0	0	.50	1
Gonzalez, Gio	87.1	5	12	1	0	.944	9	2	1	0	.22	0
Goody, Nick	40.2	0	1	1	0	.500	2	1	0	0	.50	-1
Gott, Trevor	52.2	2	5	0	0	1.000	5	2	0	0	.40	-1
Grace, Matt	46.2	3	2	2	1	.714	2	1	1	0	.50	-2
Graterol, Brusdar	9.2	1	2	0	0	1.000	0	0	0	0	-	0
Gray, Jon	150.0	18	16	1	0	.971	14	6	0	0	.43	2
Gray, Sonny	175.1	22	19	2	4	.953	19	5	0	0	.26	1
Green, Chad	69.0	0	1	0	0	1.000	8	2	0	0	.25	-2
Greene, Shane	62.2	0	6	2	1	.750	3	0	0	0	.00	-2
Gregerson, Luke	5.2	0	1	0	0	1.000	1	1	0	0	1.00	0
Greinke, Zack	208.2	33	34	1	12	.985	6	4	2	0	.67	4
Grotz, Zac	17.1	0	1	0	0	1.000	3	0	0	0	.00	0
Gsellman, Robert	63.2	2	9	0	2	1.000	4	0	0	0	.00	-1
Guduan, Reymin	5.1	0	0	0	0	-	0	0	0	0	-	0
Guerra, Deolis	0.2	0	0	0	0	-	0	0	0	0	-	0
Guerra, Javier	8.2	1	2	0	0	1.000	0	0	0	0	-	1
Guerra, Javy	67.2	7	3	1	0	.909	2	0	0	0	.00	0
Guerra, Junior	83.2	5	7	0	0	1.000	7	1	0	0	.14	-1
Guerrero, Tayron	46.0	3	2	0	0	1.000	3	1	0	0	.33	-1
Guerrieri, Taylor	26.1	1	0	0	0	1.000	3	1	0	0	.33	-1
Guilbeau, Taylor	12.1	1	2	1	0	.750	1	0	0	0	.00	0
Gustave, Jandel	24.1	0	3	0	0	1.000	0	0	0	0	-	0
Hader, Josh	75.2	2	5	0	0	1.000	2	1	1	0	.50	1
Hahn, Jesse	4.2	0	0	0	0	-	1	0	0	0	.00	0

2019 Fielding and Holding Runners												
Pitcher	Inn	PO	A	E	DP	Pct	SBA	CS	PCS	PPO	CS%	RS
Hale, David	37.2	5	8	0	0	1.000	0	0	0	1	-	2
Hall, Matt	23.1	0	1	0	0	1.000	1	0	0	0	.00	0
Hamels, Cole	141.2	2	18	1	0	.952	12	1	1	1	.08	-1
Hammer, J. D.	19.0	0	2	0	0	1.000	1	0	0	0	.00	0
Hand, Brad	57.1	0	0	0	0	-	2	0	0	0	.00	0
Happ, J.A.	161.1	2	12	1	0	.933	3	1	0	0	.33	-1
Hardy, Blaine	44.1	3	6	0	0	1.000	4	3	3	0	.75	2
Harper, Ryne	54.1	3	3	0	0	1.000	5	1	0	0	.20	0
Harris, Will	60.0	6	10	0	4	1.000	1	1	0	0	1.00	2
Hart, Donnie	7.2	0	1	0	0	1.000	1	1	0	0	1.00	-1
Hartlieb, Geoff	35.0	2	5	0	0	1.000	2	2	0	0	1.00	0
Harvey, Hunter	6.1	0	1	0	0	1.000	0	0	0	0	-	0
Harvey, Joe	18.0	0	1	0	0	1.000	6	1	0	0	.17	-1
Harvey, Matt	59.2	4	6	1	1	.909	5	2	0	0	.40	0
Heaney, Andrew	95.1	4	6	0	1	1.000	4	1	1	0	.25	-1
Hearn, Taylor	0.1	0	0	0	0	-	0	0	0	0	-	0
Heller, Ben	7.1	0	0	0	0	-	1	1	0	0	1.00	-1
Hellickson, Jeremy	39.0	2	7	0	0	1.000	6	0	0	0	.00	1
Helsley, Ryan	36.2	0	3	0	0	1.000	2	0	0	0	.00	-1
Hembree, Heath	39.2	1	1	0	0	1.000	4	1	0	0	.25	0
Hendricks, Kyle	177.0	10	29	2	0	.951	11	6	2	2	.55	1
Hendriks, Liam	85.0	6	6	0	0	1.000	2	1	0	1	.50	1
Herget, Jimmy	6.1	1	0	0	0	1.000	0	0	0	0	-	0
Hernandez, Dar.	30.1	1	4	0	0	1.000	0	0	0	0	-	0
Hernandez, David	42.2	2	2	0	0	1.000	2	0	0	0	.00	0
Hernandez, E.	82.1	0	8	0	0	1.000	1	0	0	0	.00	-1
Hernandez, Felix	71.2	1	5	0	0	1.000	5	1	0	0	.20	-1
Hernandez, J.	16.2	0	0	0	0	-	0	0	0	0	-	0
Herrera, Kelvin	51.1	2	2	0	0	1.000	10	1	0	0	.10	-1
Hess, David	80.0	4	3	1	0	.875	3	1	0	0	.33	-1
Hicks, Jordan	28.2	3	3	0	0	1.000	0	0	0	0	-	-1
Hildenberger, T.	16.1	2	2	0	0	1.000	4	0	0	0	.00	-1
Hill, Rich	58.2	2	8	1	0	.909	5	2	0	0	.40	0
Hill, Tim	39.2	0	5	1	1	.833	3	1	0	0	.33	-2
Hirano, Yoshihisa	53.0	3	7	1	0	.909	1	1	0	0	1.00	0
Hoffman, Jeff	70.0	10	10	1	0	.952	8	2	1	0	.25	1
Holder, Jonathan	41.1	2	3	0	0	1.000	2	0	0	0	.00	0
Holland, Derek	84.1	6	16	1	0	.957	7	2	1	0	.29	0
Holland, Greg	35.2	7	1	0	0	1.000	2	0	0	0	.00	-1
Holmes, Clay	50.0	4	14	1	1	.947	5	1	0	1	.20	1
Houser, Adrian	111.1	8	4	1	0	.923	19	6	0	0	.32	-3
Howard, Sam	19.0	0	3	0	0	1.000	1	0	0	0	.00	0
Hoyt, James	8.1	0	0	0	0	-	1	1	0	0	1.00	0
Huang, Wei-Chieh	5.2	1	0	0	0	1.000	1	1	0	0	1.00	0
Hudson, Dakota	174.2	13	26	2	1	.951	4	1	0	0	.25	3
Hudson, Daniel	73.0	5	8	1	0	.929	6	1	1	0	.17	0
Hughes, Jared	71.1	5	9	0	1	1.000	5	2	1	0	.40	2
Hultzen, Danny	3.1	0	1	1	0	.500	0	0	0	0	-	0
Hunter, Tommy	5.1	2	0	0	0	1.000	1	0	0	0	.00	-1
Iglesias, Raisel	67.0	5	6	1	1	.917	1	1	0	1	1.00	1
Irvin, Cole	41.2	5	2	2	0	.778	0	0	0	0	-	-1
Jackson, Edwin	67.2	5	2	1	0	.875	8	2	1	0	.25	-2
Jackson, Jay	30.1	0	3	0	0	1.000	4	0	0	0	.00	0
Jackson, Luke	72.2	1	5	2	1	.750	7	1	0	0	.14	-4
James, Josh	61.1	1	3	0	1	1.000	10	2	0	0	.20	0
Jansen, Kenley	63.0	7	2	1	0	.900	13	0	0	0	.00	0
Jeffress, Jeremy	52.0	7	9	0	0	1.000	1	1	0	0	1.00	-1
Jennings, Dan	4.2	0	1	0	0	1.000	0	0	0	0	-	0
Jerez, Williams	10.1	1	2	0	0	1.000	1	1	1	0	1.00	-1
Jewell, Jake	26.1	5	2	0	0	1.000	4	0	0	1	.00	-1
Jimenez, Eduardo	10.2	1	0	1	0	.500	0	0	0	0	-	0
Jimenez, Joe	59.2	2	1	1	1	.750	4	2	0	0	.50	-1
Johnson, Brian	40.1	0	1	0	0	1.000	4	1	1	0	.25	-1
Johnson, D.J.	25.0	3	2	0	0	1.000	1	0	0	0	.00	0
Jones, Nate	10.1	0	1	0	0	1.000	1	0	0	0	.00	0
Junis, Jakob	175.1	7	13	1	1	.952	14	1	0	0	.07	-3
Jurado, Ariel	122.1	6	9	2	0	.882	10	3	0	0	.30	-3
Kahnle, Tommy	61.1	4	7	0	1	1.000	3	0	0	0	.00	1
Karinchak, James	5.1	0	0	1	0	.000	1	0	0	0	.00	-1
Karns, Nathan	5.1	0	3	0	0	1.000	1	1	0	0	1.00	0
Kay, Anthony	14.0	0	2	0	0	1.000	0	0	0	0	-	1
Kela, Keone	29.2	1	2	0	0	1.000	0	0	0	0	-	1
Keller, Brad	165.1	3	14	1	1	.944	3	2	0	0	.67	1

2019 Fielding and Holding Runners												
Pitcher	Inn	PO	A	E	DP	Pct	SBA	CS	PCS	PPO	CS%	RS
Keller, Kyle	10.2	0	0	0	0	-	1	0	0	0	.00	0
Keller, Mitch	48.0	3	1	1	0	.800	5	3	0	0	.60	-1
Kelley, Shawn	47.1	6	5	0	2	1.000	2	0	0	0	.00	1
Kelley, Trevor	8.1	0	1	0	0	1.000	1	0	0	0	.00	0
Kelly, Joe	51.1	4	8	4	0	.750	2	0	0	0	.00	1
Kelly, Merrill	183.1	21	14	4	2	.897	5	2	1	0	.40	-3
Kennedy, Ian	63.1	0	5	1	0	.833	2	1	0	0	.50	-1
Kershaw, Clayton	178.1	3	23	0	1	1.000	6	3	2	0	.50	4
Keuchel, Dallas	112.2	3	23	0	4	1.000	1	1	0	0	1.00	5
Kikuchi, Yusei	161.2	10	12	1	1	.957	11	3	2	0	.27	-2
Kimbrel, Craig	20.2	0	1	0	0	1.000	4	2	0	0	.50	0
King, Michael	2.0	0	0	1	0	.000	0	0	0	0	-	-1
Kingham, Nick	55.2	7	5	1	1	.923	5	1	0	0	.20	0
Kinley, Tyler	49.1	4	6	1	0	.909	1	0	0	1	.00	0
Kintzler, Brandon	57.0	11	7	0	2	1.000	1	0	0	1	.00	1
Kittredge, Andrew	49.2	4	4	0	0	1.000	3	2	1	0	.67	0
Kline, Branden	41.0	2	2	0	0	1.000	0	0	0	0	-	-1
Kluber, Corey	35.2	0	3	0	0	1.000	5	2	0	0	.40	-2
Koch, Matt	20.2	2	1	0	0	1.000	1	0	0	0	.00	0
Kolarek, Adam	55.0	5	14	1	0	.950	1	0	0	0	.00	1
Kuhnel, Joel	9.2	0	0	0	0	-	1	0	0	0	.00	0
Lail, Brady	2.2	0	1	0	0	1.000	0	0	0	0	-	0
Lakins, Travis	23.1	4	1	0	0	1.000	1	1	0	0	1.00	0
Lambert, Peter	89.1	14	16	1	3	.968	4	1	1	2	.25	1
Lamet, Dinelson	73.0	6	4	0	0	1.000	7	2	0	0	.29	-1
Lauer, Eric	149.2	11	15	3	1	.897	3	1	0	2	.33	-1
Law, Derek	60.2	3	12	2	0	.882	8	4	1	0	.50	2
Leake, Mike	197.0	20	25	1	4	.978	12	7	0	0	.58	2
LeBlanc, Wade	121.1	7	6	0	1	1.000	3	0	0	0	.00	0
Leclerc, Jose	68.2	7	3	0	0	1.000	5	0	0	0	.00	-2
Leone, Dominic	40.2	1	4	0	0	1.000	1	0	0	0	.00	1
Lester, Jon	171.2	5	5	1	1	.909	16	6	0	0	.38	-4
Liriano, Francisco	70.0	2	13	0	1	1.000	3	0	0	0	.00	4
Littell, Zack	37.0	1	3	0	0	1.000	2	0	1	0	.00	0
Lively, Ben	1.0	0	0	0	0	-	0	0	0	0	-	0
Loaisiga, Jonathan	31.2	1	2	0	1	1.000	4	0	0	0	.00	-1
Lockett, Walker	22.2	1	3	0	0	1.000	2	2	0	0	1.00	-1
Lopez, Jorge	123.2	5	14	0	1	1.000	6	1	0	1	.17	0
Lopez, Pablo	111.1	9	12	0	1	1.000	3	2	0	0	.67	1
Lopez, Reynaldo	184.0	9	13	1	1	.957	17	4	0	1	.24	0
Lopez, Yoan	60.2	5	6	0	1	1.000	4	1	1	0	.25	2
Lorenzen, Michael	83.1	11	12	1	0	.958	6	1	0	0	.17	1
Loup, Aaron	3.1	0	2	0	0	1.000	0	0	0	0	-	1
Lovelady, Richard	20.0	0	2	1	0	.667	0	0	0	0	-	0
Lucas, Josh	15.2	0	2	0	0	1.000	0	0	0	0	-	0
Lucchesi, Joey	163.2	4	17	2	0	.913	7	2	1	0	.29	-4
Luciano, Elvis	33.2	1	3	0	2	1.000	2	0	0	0	.00	0
Lugo, Seth	80.0	12	6	0	0	1.000	4	1	0	0	.25	0
Luzardo, Jesus	12.0	0	1	0	0	1.000	0	0	0	0	-	0
Lyles, Jordan	141.0	6	11	3	1	.850	6	2	1	0	.33	0
Lynn, Lance	208.1	8	6	0	0	1.000	11	3	0	0	.27	-2
Lyons, Tyler	12.2	1	2	0	0	1.000	0	0	0	0	-	0
Maeda, Kenta	153.2	11	18	1	3	.967	8	1	0	0	.13	1
Magill, Matt	50.2	2	4	0	0	1.000	1	0	0	0	.00	0
Mahle, Tyler	129.2	12	13	1	1	.962	5	2	0	0	.40	1
Manaea, Sean	29.2	3	2	0	0	1.000	1	1	0	0	1.00	0
Mantiply, Joe	3.0	2	1	0	0	1.000	0	0	0	0	-	0
Maples, Dillon	11.2	2	3	0	0	1.000	2	1	0	0	.50	0
Margevicius, Nick	57.0	3	6	0	0	1.000	6	0	0	0	.00	1
Markel, Parker	22.0	1	1	0	0	1.000	1	1	0	0	1.00	0
Marquez, German	174.0	17	20	2	0	.949	10	6	1	1	.60	4
Marshall, Evan	50.2	3	3	1	0	.857	3	1	0	0	.33	-1
Martin, Brett	62.1	1	5	0	0	1.000	1	0	0	0	.00	0
Martin, Chris	55.2	0	5	2	0	.714	5	1	1	1	.20	-1
Martin, Corbin	19.1	6	0	1	0	.857	1	0	0	0	.00	0
Martinez, Carlos	48.1	6	7	1	0	.929	2	0	0	0	-	1
Marvel, James	17.1	1	3	0	0	1.000	1	0	0	0	-	1
Maton, Phil	36.2	6	2	1	0	.889	2	0	0	0	-	-1
Matz, Steven	160.1	5	22	0	2	1.000	11	2	0	0	.18	2
May, Dustin	34.2	0	4	0	0	1.000	1	1	0	0	1.00	0
May, Trevor	64.1	2	2	1	0	.800	6	0	0	0	.00	-1
Mayers, Mike	19.0	0	0	0	0	-	1	0	0	0	.00	0
Mayza, Tim	51.1	3	7	2	0	.833	3	0	0	0	.00	0

Pitcher	Inn	PO	A	E	DP	Pct	SBA	CS	PCS	PPO	CS%	RS
				2019 Fielding and Holding Runners								
Mazza, Chris	16.1	1	2	0	0	1.000	1	1	1	0	1.00	1
McCarthy, Kevin	60.1	4	15	0	2	1.000	1	0	0	0	.00	2
McClain, Reggie	21.0	0	2	2	0	.500	5	2	1	0	.40	0
McFarland, T.J.	56.0	5	17	1	1	.957	7	5	3	0	.71	5
McGee, Jake	41.1	3	4	1	0	.875	1	1	1	0	1.00	0
McGowin, Kyle	16.0	2	0	1	0	.667	0	0	0	0		-1
McHugh, Collin	74.2	6	6	1	1	.923	3	0	0	0	.00	0
McKay, Brendan	49.0	2	4	0	0	1.000	2	1	0	0	.50	0
McKay, David	26.1	0	1	0	0	1.000	5	1	0	0	.20	0
McRae, Alex	26.2	3	2	0	0	1.000	1	0	0	0	.00	0
Means, John	155.0	5	10	0	0	1.000	1	1	0	0	1.00	0
Mejia, Adalberto	31.1	0	4	0	0	1.000	0	0	0	0		1
Melancon, Mark	67.1	7	8	0	3	1.000	3	0	0	0	.00	0
Mella, Keury	3.2	0	0	0	0		0	0	0	0		0
Melville, Tim	33.1	2	3	1	0	.833	3	0	0	0	.00	0
Mendez, Y.	4.2	0	2	0	0	1.000	2	2	1	0	1.00	1
Menez, Conner	17.0	2	1	0	0	1.000	2	1	1	0	.50	0
Mengden, Daniel	59.2	2	4	0	0	1.000	4	2	0	0	.50	0
Middleton, Keynan	7.2	0	0	0	0		0	0	0	0		0
Mikolas, Miles	184.0	14	30	0	2	1.000	7	2	0	0	.29	3
Miley, Wade	167.1	7	19	1	1	.963	5	2	1	3	.40	-1
Miller, Andrew	54.2	3	5	0	0	1.000	1	0	0	0	.00	1
Miller, Justin	15.2	0	1	0	0	1.000	3	3	0	0	1.00	1
Miller, Shelby	44.0	1	0	0	0	1.000	8	0	0	0	.00	-2
Mills, Alec	36.0	1	3	0	0	1.000	1	0	0	0	.00	1
Milner, Hoby	3.2	0	0	0	0		0	0	0	0		0
Milone, Tommy	111.2	5	13	1	0	.947	9	2	1	0	.22	0
Minaya, Juan	27.2	1	1	0	0	1.000	0	0	0	0		0
Minor, Mike	208.1	7	21	0	1	1.000	17	4	2	1	.24	1
Minter, A.J.	29.1	0	4	0	0	1.000	6	0	0	0	.00	-2
Montas, Frankie	96.0	2	3	3	0	.625	3	1	0	0	.33	-2
Montero, Rafael	29.0	4	3	0	1	1.000	2	1	0	0	.50	0
Montgomery, J.	4.0	0	0	0	0		0	0	0	0		0
Montgomery, Mike	91.0	5	15	0	0	1.000	15	7	1	1	.47	-2
Moore, Andrew	4.2	0	0	0	0		1	1	0	0	1.00	0
Moore, Matt	10.0	0	3	1	0	.750	0	0	0	0		0
Moran, Brian	6.1	0	1	0	0	1.000	0	0	0	0		0
Morejon, Adrian	8.0	1	2	0	0	1.000	1	0	0	0	.00	0
Morgan, Adam	29.2	1	2	0	0	1.000	3	2	0	0	.67	0
Morin, Mike	50.2	4	5	1	0	.900	2	2	0	1	1.00	2
Moronta, Reyes	56.2	1	1	0	0	1.000	8	0	0	0	.00	-2
Morton, Charlie	194.2	9	6	0	0	1.000	6	3	0	1	.50	-3
Munoz, Andres	23.0	0	1	0	1	1.000	1	0	0	0	.00	0
Musgrave, H.	10.0	3	1	0	0	1.000	0	0	0	0		0
Musgrove, Joe	170.1	30	24	4	0	.931	5	3	1	3	.60	5
Nelson, Jimmy	22.0	1	0	1	0	.500	1	0	0	0	.00	-1
Neris, Hector	67.2	6	6	0	0	1.000	4	2	0	0	.50	1
Neshek, Pat	18.0	1	5	0	1	1.000	0	0	0	0		1
Neverauskas, D.	9.1	1	1	0	0	1.000	1	0	0	0	.00	0
Newberry, Jake	31.0	1	4	0	1	1.000	1	0	0	0	.00	1
Newcomb, Sean	68.1	1	6	1	1	.875	5	1	0	0	.20	0
Nicasio, Juan	47.1	4	7	1	0	.917	6	1	0	0	.17	-3
Noesi, Hector	27.2	1	1	0	0	1.000	1	1	0	0	1.00	0
Nogosek, Stephen	6.2	1	0	0	0	1.000	0	0	0	0		0
Nola, Aaron	202.1	9	27	0	3	1.000	15	8	1	1	.53	5
Norris, Daniel	144.1	6	14	2	0	.909	17	6	3	0	.35	-1
Norwood, James	9.1	0	1	0	0	1.000	0	0	0	1		0
Nova, Ivan	187.0	9	18	1	3	.964	14	4	1	0	.29	0
Oberg, Scott	56.0	2	6	0	0	1.000	4	1	0	0	.25	0
O'Day, Darren	5.1	0	0	0	0		0	0	0	0		0
Odorizzi, Jake	159.0	7	9	0	0	1.000	4	3	0	2	.75	2
Oh, Seunghwan	18.1	1	3	0	0	1.000	0	0	0	0		0
Ohtani, Shohei	0.0	0	0	0	0		0	0	0	0		0
Olson, Tyler	30.2	1	2	0	0	1.000	3	1	0	0	.33	0
O'Rourke, Ryan	1.1	0	0	0	0		1	1	0	0	1.00	0
Ortiz, Luis	3.1	1	0	0	0	1.000	0	0	0	0		0
Osich, Josh	67.2	7	7	0	0	1.000	3	0	0	0	.00	1
Osuna, Roberto	65.0	8	3	1	0	.917	1	0	0	0	.00	0
Oswalt, Corey	6.2	0	0	0	0		0	0	0	0		0
Otero, Dan	29.2	1	3	0	1	1.000	2	1	0	0	.50	0
Ottavino, Adam	66.1	3	3	1	1	.857	16	1	0	0	.06	-4
Paddack, Chris	140.2	8	14	2	0	.917	1	1	0	0	1.00	2
Pagan, Emilio	70.0	2	3	0	0	1.000	2	0	0	0	.00	0

Pitcher	Inn	PO	A	E	DP	Pct	SBA	CS	PCS	PPO	CS%	RS
				2019 Fielding and Holding Runners								
Palumbo, Joseph	16.2	0	2	0	1	1.000	0	0	0	0		0
Pannone, Thomas	73.0	2	3	0	1	1.000	3	0	0	1	.00	0
Parker, Blake	61.1	4	5	0	1	1.000	4	3	0	0	.75	1
Parsons, Wes	34.2	4	6	1	0	.909	6	1	0	0	.17	0
Paxton, James	150.2	2	10	0	0	1.000	11	4	1	0	.36	0
Payamps, Joel	4.0	0	0	0	0		1	0	0	0	.00	0
Payano, Pedro	22.0	0	2	0	1	1.000	1	0	0	0	.00	0
Pazos, James	10.1	0	4	0	0	1.000	3	1	1	0	.33	1
Peacock, Brad	91.2	5	4	2	0	.818	6	1	0	0	.17	1
Pena, Felix	96.1	5	6	3	0	.786	9	3	0	1	.33	-1
Peralta, Freddy	85.0	4	4	0	0	1.000	5	1	0	0	.20	-2
Peralta, Wandy	39.2	8	4	0	0	1.000	2	1	1	0	.50	0
Peralta, Wily	40.1	2	1	0	2	1.000	5	1	0	0	.20	-1
Perdomo, Luis	72.0	6	10	0	0	1.000	8	4	1	0	.50	1
Perez, Cionel	9.0	0	1	0	0	1.000	0	0	0	0		0
Perez, Martin	165.1	9	19	2	0	.933	15	2	1	0	.13	3
Perez, Oliver	40.2	1	3	1	0	.800	3	0	0	0	.00	0
Peters, Dillon	72.0	5	10	0	3	1.000	6	3	3	0	.50	2
Peterson, Tim	7.1	0	0	0	0		1	0	0	0	.00	0
Petit, Yusmeiro	83.0	13	4	0	1	1.000	3	1	0	1	.33	-1
Petricka, Jake	8.0	2	0	0	0	1.000	2	0	0	0	.00	0
Phelps, David	34.1	0	1	0	0	1.000	1	1	0	0	1.00	-1
Phillips, Evan	28.0	0	1	0	0	1.000	1	0	0	0	.00	-1
Pineda, Michael	146.0	5	6	0	0	1.000	9	1	0	0	.11	-3
Pinto, Ricardo	2.1	1	1	0	0	1.000	0	0	0	0		0
Pivetta, Nick	93.2	9	7	0	0	1.000	7	1	0	0	.14	-3
Plesac, Zach	115.2	11	13	2	2	.923	2	1	1	5	.50	3
Plutko, Adam	109.1	10	2	2	0	.857	3	1	0	0	.33	-1
Poche, Colin	51.2	0	1	0	0	1.000	7	1	0	0	.14	-3
Pomeranz, Drew	104.0	2	8	1	0	.909	11	4	1	0	.36	-1
Ponce de Leon, D.	48.2	3	4	0	1	1.000	2	2	1	0	1.00	1
Poppen, Sean	8.1	0	0	0	0		0	0	0	0		0
Porcello, Rick	174.1	16	21	1	1	.974	8	1	0	0	.13	1
Pounders, Brooks	7.1	0	2	0	0	1.000	2	0	0	0	.00	0
Poynter, Bobby	11.2	0	0	0	0		0	0	0	0		0
Pressly, Ryan	54.1	4	6	0	0	1.000	2	0	0	0	.00	1
Price, David	107.1	4	7	0	0	1.000	5	2	0	0	.40	1
Pruitt, Austin	47.0	3	6	0	0	1.000	1	0	0	0	.00	1
Puk, A.J.	11.1	0	1	0	0	1.000	2	0	0	0	.00	-1
Quantrill, Cal	103.0	8	8	1	0	.941	10	0	0	2	.00	-2
Quijada, Jose	29.2	1	2	0	0	1.000	2	0	0	0	.00	0
Quintana, Jose	171.0	15	26	0	1	1.000	11	5	3	1	.45	2
Rainey, Tanner	48.1	1	7	0	0	1.000	4	1	1	0	.25	2
Ramirez, Erasmo	3.0	2	0	0	0	1.000	0	0	0	0		0
Ramirez, JC	8.0	1	1	0	0	1.000	1	0	0	0	.00	0
Ramirez, Neil	25.0	1	1	0	0	1.000	4	0	0	0	.00	0
Ramirez, Nick	79.2	5	10	1	0	.938	8	0	0	0	.00	1
Ramirez, Noe	67.2	8	4	0	0	1.000	7	4	0	0	.57	-1
Ramirez, Yefry	24.1	2	2	1	0	.800	3	1	0	0	.33	-1
Ramos, Edubray	15.0	0	1	0	0	1.000	1	1	0	0	1.00	-1
Ramsey, Matt	1.0	0	0	0	0		0	0	0	0		0
Ray, Robbie	174.1	7	21	2	2	.933	13	3	1	0	.23	2
Reed, Cody	6.1	0	0	0	0		0	0	0	0		0
Reid-Foley, Sean	31.2	0	4	0	0	1.000	2	0	0	0	.00	0
Reininger, Zac	28.0	0	3	0	0	1.000	2	0	0	0	.00	0
Reyes, Alex	3.0	0	0	0	0		0	0	0	0		0
Reyes, Gerardo	26.0	2	2	0	0	1.000	1	0	0	0	.00	0
Rhame, Jacob	6.1	0	2	0	0	1.000	0	0	0	0		0
Richard, Clayton	45.1	5	13	1	1	.947	2	2	2	2	1.00	5
Richards, Garrett	8.2	0	1	0	0	1.000	0	0	0	0		0
Richards, Trevor	135.1	10	14	3	1	.889	8	5	0	0	.63	-3
Rios, Yacksel	13.0	1	1	1	0	.667	0	0	0	0		-1
Roark, Tanner	165.1	11	12	2	1	.920	8	1	0	0	.13	-1
Robertson, David	6.2	1	0	0	0	1.000	0	0	0	0		0
Robles, Hansel	72.2	7	5	1	1	.923	5	2	0	0	.40	-3
Rodgers, Brady	5.0	0	0	0	0		0	0	0	0		0
Rodney, Fernando	47.2	2	3	0	1	1.000	9	3	0	0	.33	-1
Rodon, Carlos	34.2	0	1	0	0	1.000	6	0	0	0	.00	-1
Rodriguez, Dereck	99.0	4	9	0	2	1.000	9	3	1	0	.33	-1
Rodriguez, E.	203.1	2	23	0	1	1.000	9	5	1	0	.56	-1
Rodriguez, Jefry	46.2	2	5	1	2	.875	5	1	1	1	.20	-1
Rodriguez, Jose	19.2	1	2	0	1	1.000	1	0	0	0	.00	0
Rodriguez, R.	65.1	0	4	0	0	1.000	3	1	0	0	.33	1

Pitcher	Inn	PO	A	E	DP	Pct	SBA	CS	PCS	PPO	CS%	RS
Roe, Chaz	51.0	0	3	1	0	.750	11	0	0	0	.00	-3
Rogers, Josh	14.1	0	0	0	0	-	0	0	0	0	-	-1
Rogers, Taylor	69.0	5	9	1	1	.933	0	0	0	0	-	-1
Rogers, Tyler	17.2	1	4	0	0	1.000	0	0	0	0	-	1
Romano, Jordan	15.1	3	2	0	1	1.000	2	0	0	0	.00	0
Romano, Sal	16.1	0	2	0	1	1.000	1	1	0	0	1.00	0
Romero, Fernando	14.0	1	1	0	0	1.000	0	0	0	0	-	0
Romo, Sergio	60.1	0	4	1	0	.800	7	0	0	1	.00	-1
Rondon, Hector	60.2	6	7	0	2	1.000	6	1	0	0	.17	-1
Rosa, Adonis	2.0	1	0	0	0	1.000	0	0	0	0	-	0
Rosario, Randy	14.1	1	3	0	0	1.000	0	0	0	0	-	0
Rosenthal, Trevor	15.1	1	1	1	0	.667	0	0	0	0	-	0
Ross, Joe	64.0	4	11	1	0	.938	1	0	0	0	.00	1
Ross, Tyson	35.1	4	6	1	0	.909	8	3	0	0	.38	0
Rosscup, Zac	18.0	1	3	0	0	1.000	2	1	0	0	.50	0
Ruiz, Jose	40.0	1	5	1	0	.857	4	3	1	0	.75	1
Rumbelow, Nick	1.1	0	0	0	0	-	0	0	0	0	-	0
Rusin, Chris	1.0	0	0	0	0	-	0	0	0	0	-	0
Ryan, Kyle	61.0	5	11	1	1	.941	6	1	0	1	.17	1
Ryu, Hyun-Jin	182.2	7	29	0	1	1.000	2	1	1	1	.50	5
Sabathia, CC	107.1	0	3	2	1	.600	11	2	0	0	.18	-4
Sadler, Casey	46.1	3	9	1	0	.923	2	2	0	0	1.00	1
Sadzeck, Connor	23.2	2	2	0	0	1.000	3	0	0	0	.00	-1
Salas, Fernando	2.2	0	0	0	0	-	0	0	0	0	-	0
Salazar, Danny	4.0	0	0	0	0	-	0	0	0	0	-	0
Sale, Chris	147.1	6	7	0	1	1.000	10	2	0	0	.20	-1
Samardzija, Jeff	181.1	8	9	1	0	.944	18	4	0	0	.22	-3
Sampson, Adrian	125.1	4	17	0	1	1.000	5	2	0	2	.40	2
Sanchez, Aaron	131.1	12	17	0	1	1.000	13	2	0	1	.15	0
Sanchez, Anibal	166.0	17	18	4	0	.897	15	0	0	2	.00	0
Sandoval, Patrick	39.1	2	4	1	0	.857	2	1	0	0	.50	1
Santana, Dennis	5.0	0	0	0	0	-	0	0	0	0	-	0
Santana, Ervin	13.1	2	0	0	1	1.000	1	0	0	0	.00	0
Santiago, Hector	33.2	0	5	0	1	1.000	1	0	0	0	.00	1
Sborz, Josh	9.0	2	0	0	0	1.000	0	0	0	0	-	0
Scherzer, Max	172.1	10	13	1	1	.958	9	1	1	0	.11	-2
Schlitter, Brian	9.2	0	1	0	0	1.000	0	0	0	0	-	0
Schreiber, John	13.0	1	0	0	0	1.000	0	0	0	0	-	0
Schultz, Jaime	5.0	0	0	0	0	-	0	0	0	0	-	0
Scott, Robby	7.1	0	0	0	0	-	1	0	0	0	.00	-1
Scott, Tanner	26.1	0	2	1	0	.667	6	2	1	0	.33	-2
Scott, Tayler	16.1	3	2	1	0	.833	1	0	0	0	.00	0
Selman, Sam	10.1	2	1	0	0	1.000	2	0	0	0	.00	0
Senzatela, Antonio	124.2	10	22	2	2	.941	5	0	0	0	.00	0
Severino, Luis	12.0	0	2	1	0	.667	5	0	0	0	.00	-1
Sewald, Paul	19.2	1	0	0	0	1.000	0	0	0	0	-	0
Shafer, Justin	39.2	2	1	0	0	1.000	2	0	0	0	.00	0
Shaw, Bryan	72.0	6	6	0	0	1.000	6	1	0	0	.17	1
Shawaryn, M.	20.1	0	0	1	0	.000	5	0	0	0	.00	-1
Sheffield, Justus	36.0	1	6	1	1	.875	5	2	1	0	.40	-1
Shepherd, C.	19.0	1	1	0	0	1.000	0	0	0	0	-	0
Sherfy, Jimmie	18.1	0	2	0	0	1.000	2	1	0	0	.50	0
Shoemaker, Matt	28.2	6	4	1	0	.909	2	2	0	0	1.00	1
Shreve, Chasen	2.0	0	0	0	0	-	0	0	0	0	-	0
Sims, Lucas	43.0	2	3	0	0	1.000	5	2	1	0	.40	0
Sipp, Tony	21.0	2	1	1	0	.750	0	0	0	0	-	1
Skaggs, Tyler	79.2	5	7	0	0	1.000	4	2	2	0	.50	1
Skoglund, Eric	21.0	2	4	0	1	1.000	4	1	1	0	.25	1
Slegers, Aaron	3.0	0	0	0	0	-	0	0	0	0	-	0
Smeltzer, Devin	49.0	0	3	0	0	1.000	2	1	1	1	.50	0
Smith, Burch	21.1	1	2	0	0	1.000	0	0	0	0	-	0
Smith, Caleb	153.1	7	12	2	1	.905	11	3	2	0	.27	1
Smith, Joe	25.0	1	1	0	0	1.000	2	0	0	0	.00	0
Smith, Josh A.	31.0	3	1	0	0	1.000	5	1	0	0	.20	-1
Smith, Josh D.	12.2	0	1	0	0	1.000	0	0	0	0	-	0
Smith, Will	65.1	1	3	1	1	.800	2	1	1	0	.50	0
Smyly, Drew	114.0	4	12	0	0	1.000	21	6	5	0	.29	0
Sneed, Cy	21.1	0	1	0	0	1.000	0	0	0	0	-	0
Snell, Blake	107.0	1	14	1	1	.938	24	9	5	0	.38	-2
Sobotka, Chad	29.0	0	0	0	0	-	6	0	0	0	.00	-1
Soria, Joakim	69.0	5	5	0	0	1.000	2	1	1	0	.50	1
Soroka, Mike	174.2	9	27	0	5	1.000	8	2	1	0	.25	5
Soto, Gregory	57.2	1	6	3	1	.700	6	1	0	0	.17	-3

Pitcher	Inn	PO	A	E	DP	Pct	SBA	CS	PCS	PPO	CS%	RS
Sparkman, Glenn	136.0	5	14	0	1	1.000	5	4	0	0	.80	0
Speier, Gabe	7.1	0	2	0	0	1.000	0	0	0	0	-	0
Springs, Jeffrey	32.1	0	1	0	0	1.000	1	0	0	0	.00	0
St. John, Locke	6.2	1	0	0	0	1.000	0	0	0	0	-	0
Stammen, Craig	82.0	6	16	1	1	.957	2	1	1	0	.50	1
Stanek, Ryne	77.0	5	3	0	0	1.000	8	2	0	0	.25	-2
Stashak, Cody	25.0	0	2	0	1	1.000	0	0	0	0	-	0
Staumont, Josh	19.1	1	2	0	0	1.000	1	1	0	0	1.00	0
Steckenrider, D.	14.1	1	0	0	0	1.000	0	0	0	0	-	0
Stephenson, R.	64.2	4	6	4	0	.714	7	1	0	0	.14	0
Stewart, Brock	25.2	1	2	0	0	1.000	2	1	0	0	.50	0
Stewart, Kohl	25.1	1	3	0	0	1.000	6	1	0	0	.17	-1
Stock, Robert	10.2	0	1	0	0	1.000	1	0	0	0	.00	0
Strahm, Matt	114.2	9	11	0	0	1.000	9	1	0	0	.11	0
Straily, Dan	47.2	2	4	1	0	.857	1	1	0	0	1.00	0
Strasburg, S.	209.0	21	24	2	2	.957	18	2	0	0	.11	-1
Stratton, Chris	76.0	7	14	0	1	1.000	5	3	1	0	.60	4
Strickland, Hunter	24.1	2	0	0	0	1.000	4	1	0	0	.25	0
Stripling, Ross	90.2	5	12	1	0	.944	5	3	0	0	.60	2
Stroman, Marcus	184.1	21	30	4	2	.927	19	8	0	2	.42	3
Strop, Pedro	41.2	4	1	1	0	.833	0	0	0	1	-	0
Stumpf, Daniel	29.0	2	1	0	0	1.000	4	1	1	0	.25	0
Suarez, Andrew	32.2	2	1	0	0	1.000	2	1	0	0	.50	0
Suarez, Jose	81.0	4	10	1	0	.933	15	6	4	0	.40	2
Suarez, Ranger	48.2	5	8	0	0	1.000	2	2	0	0	1.00	2
Suero, Wander	71.1	4	7	3	0	.786	9	3	0	2	.33	1
Sulser, Cole	7.1	0	1	0	0	1.000	0	0	0	0	-	0
Suter, Brent	18.1	1	3	1	0	.800	1	1	0	0	1.00	0
Swanson, Erik	58.0	2	3	0	0	1.000	4	0	0	0	.00	-1
Swarzak, Anthony	53.1	0	4	0	0	1.000	3	1	0	0	.33	0
Syndergaard, N.	197.2	14	21	4	4	.897	45	3	0	2	.07	-7
Taillon, Jameson	37.1	1	2	0	0	1.000	4	1	0	0	.25	0
Tanaka, Masahiro	182.0	9	18	2	3	.931	7	5	0	0	.71	2
Tarpley, Stephen	24.2	2	2	0	1	1.000	1	1	1	0	1.00	0
Tate, Dillon	21.0	0	2	0	0	1.000	0	0	0	0	-	0
Taylor, Josh	47.1	0	4	1	0	.800	4	4	2	0	1.00	0
Teheran, Julio	174.2	4	25	0	0	1.000	18	3	0	1	.17	3
Tepera, Ryan	21.2	0	4	1	0	.800	3	1	0	0	.33	1
Thornburg, Tyler	18.2	0	2	0	0	1.000	0	0	0	0	-	0
Thornton, Trent	154.1	6	8	1	1	.933	8	4	1	0	.50	0
Thorpe, Lewis	27.2	0	2	0	0	1.000	2	1	1	0	.50	0
Tinoco, Jesus	36.0	3	2	0	0	1.000	6	3	0	0	.50	0
Tomlin, Josh	79.1	5	11	0	1	1.000	1	1	0	0	1.00	1
Torres, Carlos	6.0	0	0	0	0	-	0	0	0	0	-	0
Toussaint, Touki	41.2	4	4	0	0	1.000	0	0	0	1	-	0
Treinen, Blake	58.2	4	1	0	0	1.000	9	2	0	0	.22	-1
Trivino, Lou	60.0	7	3	1	1	.909	12	3	0	0	.25	-2
Tropeano, Nick	13.2	1	1	0	0	1.000	4	0	1	0	.00	0
Tuivailala, Sam	23.0	0	0	1	0	.000	1	1	0	0	1.00	0
Turnbull, Spencer	148.1	6	13	1	0	.950	19	5	0	0	.26	-1
Underwood Jr., D.	11.2	1	1	0	0	1.000	5	0	0	0	.00	-1
Urena, Jose	84.2	11	8	0	1	1.000	3	1	0	0	.33	1
Urias, Julio	79.2	4	6	4	0	.714	6	2	1	0	.33	0
Urquidy, Jose	41.0	3	3	0	1	1.000	0	0	0	0	-	0
Valdez, Framber	70.2	3	11	1	1	.933	6	0	0	0	.00	-1
Valdez, Phillips	16.0	1	0	0	0	1.000	3	0	0	0	.00	0
Vargas, Jason	149.2	4	17	3	1	.875	17	3	0	1	.18	-1
Vasquez, Andrew	0.0	0	0	0	0	-	0	0	0	0	-	0
Vazquez, Felipe	60.0	0	5	0	0	1.000	1	0	0	0	.00	0
Velasquez, Vince	117.1	14	12	4	4	.867	6	2	0	0	.33	2
Velazquez, Hector	56.1	4	5	1	0	.900	3	3	0	1	1.00	2
Venditte, Pat	3.1	1	0	0	0	1.000	0	0	0	0	-	0
Venters, Jonny	8.0	0	0	0	0	-	0	0	0	0	-	0
VerHagen, Drew	58.0	1	7	0	2	1.000	8	2	0	0	.25	1
Verlander, Justin	223.0	17	10	0	0	1.000	12	3	0	0	.25	2
Vieira, Thyago	7.0	0	1	1	0	.500	0	0	0	0	-	0
Vincent, Nick	44.2	1	2	2	0	.600	1	1	0	0	1.00	0
Vizcaino, Arodys	4.0	0	0	0	0	-	0	0	0	0	-	0
Volquez, Edinson	16.0	3	0	0	1	1.000	1	0	0	0	.00	-1
Voth, Austin	43.2	4	4	0	0	1.000	2	2	1	0	1.00	1
Wacha, Michael	126.2	11	12	1	2	.958	8	3	0	2	.38	0
Waguespack, J.	78.0	2	5	0	0	1.000	5	2	0	0	.40	0
Wainwright, Adam	171.2	15	17	0	1	1.000	8	4	0	0	.50	3

457

Pitcher	Inn	PO	A	E	DP	Pct	SBA	CS	PCS	PPO	CS%	RS
Walden, Marcus	78.0	5	5	1	0	.909	7	1	0	0	.14	0
Walker, Jeremy	9.1	0	1	0	0	1.000	1	1	0	0	1.00	0
Walker, Taijuan	1.0	0	0	0	0	-	0	0	0	0	-	0
Wang, Wei-Chung	31.0	0	5	0	0	1.000	3	2	1	0	.67	2
Warren, Adam	28.2	4	4	0	0	1.000	3	1	1	0	.33	-1
Warren, Art	5.1	0	0	0	0	-	0	0	0	0	-	0
Watson, Tony	54.0	3	9	0	0	1.000	2	1	1	0	.50	0
Weaver, Luke	64.1	5	7	0	0	1.000	0	0	0	0	-	2
Webb, Jacob	32.1	0	1	0	0	1.000	1	0	0	0	.00	-1
Webb, Logan	39.2	0	8	0	1	1.000	3	1	1	0	.33	1
Webb, Tyler	55.0	5	5	0	0	1.000	4	1	1	0	.25	1
Weber, Ryan	40.2	3	9	0	0	1.000	3	1	0	0	.33	1
Webster, Allen	11.0	1	3	0	1	1.000	2	0	0	0	.00	0
Wendelken, J.B.	32.2	1	2	0	0	1.000	1	0	0	0	.00	0
Wheeler, Zack	195.1	13	20	2	0	.943	7	1	0	0	.14	-2
Wick, Rowan	33.1	2	5	0	0	1.000	4	0	0	0	.00	-1
Wieck, Brad	34.2	0	1	1	0	.500	2	1	1	0	.50	-2
Wilkerson, Aaron	16.0	1	1	0	0	1.000	1	1	0	0	1.00	0
Williams, Austen	0.1	0	0	0	0	-	1	0	0	0	.00	0
Williams, Devin	13.2	0	0	0	0	-	2	0	0	0	.00	-1
Williams, Taylor	14.2	4	3	0	0	1.000	1	0	0	0	.00	0
Williams, Trevor	145.2	11	15	1	2	.963	6	2	0	0	.33	0
Wilson, Alex	11.1	0	2	0	0	1.000	1	0	0	0	.00	0
Wilson, Bryse	20.0	0	3	0	0	1.000	2	1	0	0	.50	0
Wilson, Justin	39.0	2	5	0	0	1.000	7	0	0	0	.00	-3
Wingenter, Trey	51.0	0	3	1	1	.750	7	2	1	0	.29	0
Winkler, Dan	21.2	0	1	0	0	1.000	1	1	0	0	1.00	0
Wisler, Matt	51.1	3	4	1	0	.875	4	1	0	0	.25	-1
Wittgren, Nick	57.2	3	7	0	3	1.000	0	0	0	0	-	2
Wojciechowski, A.	82.1	4	2	0	0	1.000	3	0	0	0	.00	0
Wood, Alex	35.2	2	3	0	0	1.000	2	1	0	0	.50	1
Wood, Hunter	45.1	2	2	0	0	1.000	2	0	0	0	.00	-1
Woodruff, Brandon	121.2	7	8	0	1	1.000	11	3	0	1	.27	0
Workman, B.	71.2	4	5	0	1	1.000	12	4	1	0	.33	0
Wotherspoon, M.	4.2	1	1	0	0	1.000	0	0	0	0	-	0
Wright, Kyle	19.2	1	1	0	0	1.000	4	0	0	0	.00	-1
Wright, Steven	6.1	0	1	0	0	1.000	0	0	0	0	-	0
Wright Jr., Mike	29.1	4	1	0	0	1.000	2	2	1	0	1.00	-1
Yacabonis, Jimmy	41.0	2	5	1	1	.875	6	1	1	0	.17	-1
Yamamoto, J.	78.2	5	7	1	1	.923	8	2	0	0	.25	0
Yarbrough, Ryan	141.2	6	13	0	1	1.000	8	3	1	0	.38	0
Yardley, Eric	11.2	1	3	0	1	1.000	0	0	0	0	-	0
Yates, Kirby	60.2	6	5	0	1	1.000	4	1	0	0	.25	0
Ynoa, Gabriel	110.2	7	8	2	0	.882	4	2	0	0	.50	0
Ynoa, Huascar	3.0	1	1	0	0	1.000	0	0	0	0	-	0
Young, Alex	83.1	2	8	0	0	1.000	3	1	1	1	.33	0
Zamora, Daniel	8.2	0	0	0	0	-	0	0	0	0	-	0
Zeuch, T.J.	22.2	0	3	0	0	1.000	0	0	0	0	-	0
Zimmer, Kyle	18.1	0	1	0	0	1.000	3	0	0	0	.00	0
Zimmermann, J.	112.0	7	10	1	1	.944	15	3	0	0	.20	-2

Hitters Pitching

Player	G	W	L	Sv	IP	H	R	ER	BB	SO	ERA	G	W	L	Sv	IP	H	R	ER	BB	SO	ERA
					2019 Pitching											Career Pitching						
Adrianza, Ehire	1	-	-	-	1.0	5	3	3	-	1	27.00	1	0	0	0	1.0	5	3	3	0	1	27.00
Alberto, Hanser	1	-	-	-	1.0	1	2	2	2	-	18.00	1	0	0	0	1.0	1	2	2	2	0	18.00
Altherr, Aaron	1	-	-	-	1.0	2	1	1	-	2	9.00	1	0	0	0	1.0	2	1	1	0	2	9.00
Arteaga, Humberto	1	-	-	-	1.2	2	1	1	1	-	5.40	1	0	0	0	1.2	2	1	1	1	0	5.40
Astudillo, Willians	-	-	-	-	-	-	-	-	-	-		1	0	0	0	1.0	5	5	5	0	0	45.00
Avila, Alex	2	-	-	-	2.0	2	1	1	1	1	4.50	3	0	0	0	4.0	3	1	1	1	1	2.25
Blandino, Alex	-	-	-	-	-	-	-	-	-	-		1	0	0	0	1.0	1	0	0	0	2	0.00
Brantly, Rob	-	-	-	-	-	-	-	-	-	-		1	0	0	0	1.0	1	1	1	0	0	9.00
Brosseau, Mike	3	-	-	-	4.0	5	2	2	-	-	4.50	3	0	0	0	4.0	5	2	2	0	0	4.50
Butera, Drew	-	-	-	-	-	-	-	-	-	-		6	0	0	0	4.1	5	4	4	4	4	8.31
Caratini, Victor	2	-	-	-	2.0	2	2	2	1	-	9.00	4	0	0	0	4.0	5	4	4	1	0	9.00
Culberson, Charlie	2	-	-	-	2.0	2	-	-	2	1	0.00	3	0	0	0	3.0	4	1	1	2	1	3.00
Davis, Chris	1	-	-	-	1.0	2	1	1	-	1	9.00	2	1	0	0	3.0	4	1	1	1	3	3.00
Davis, J.D.	-	-	-	-	-	-	-	-	-	-		3	0	0	0	2.2	2	1	1	1	4	3.38
Davis, Taylor	1	-	-	-	1.0	3	-	-	-	-	0.00	1	0	0	0	1.0	3	0	0	0	0	0.00
Descalso, Daniel	1	-	-	-	1.0	2	2	2	-	-	18.00	6	0	0	0	6.2	6	5	5	1	2	6.75
Desmond, Ian	1	-	-	-	1.0	1	-	-	-	-	0.00	1	0	0	0	1.0	1	0	0	0	0	0.00
Dixon, Brandon	2	-	-	-	2.0	1	2	2	-	1	9.00	4	0	0	0	3.1	1	2	2	0	2	5.40
Dozier, Brian	1	-	-	-	1.0	2	2	2	-	-	18.00	1	0	0	0	1.0	2	2	2	0	0	18.00
Elmore, Jake	-	-	-	-	-	-	-	-	-	-		2	0	0	0	2.0	3	1	1	0	0	4.50
Ervin, Phillip	-	-	-	-	-	-	-	-	-	-		1	0	0	0	0.1	0	0	0	0	0	0.00
Escobar, Eduardo	-	-	-	-	-	-	-	-	-	-		1	0	0	0	1.0	1	0	0	0	0	0.00
Farmer, Kyle	1	-	-	-	1.1	1	-	-	-	-	0.00	1	0	0	0	1.1	1	0	0	0	0	0.00
Federowicz, Tim	1	-	-	-	1.0	3	1	1	-	-	9.00	1	0	0	0	1.0	3	1	1	0	0	9.00
Flaherty, Ryan	-	-	-	-	-	-	-	-	-	-		1	0	0	0	1.0	3	2	2	0	0	18.00
Ford, Mike	1	-	-	-	2.0	6	5	5	-	1	22.50	1	0	0	0	2.0	6	5	5	0	1	22.50
France, Ty	2	-	-	-	2.0	2	1	1	-	-	4.50	2	0	0	0	2.0	2	1	1	0	0	4.50
Freeman, Mike	1	-	-	-	2.0	2	2	2	-	-	9.00	2	0	0	0	3.0	5	3	3	0	0	9.00
Garcia, Greg	-	-	-	-	-	-	-	-	-	-		1	0	0	0	1.0	1	0	0	0	0	0.00
Garcia, Leury	-	-	-	-	-	-	-	-	-	-		2	0	1	0	2.0	2	2	2	2	1	9.00
Garver, Mitch	-	-	-	-	-	-	-	-	-	-		1	0	0	0	1.0	1	0	0	0	0	0.00
Gennett, Scooter	-	-	-	-	-	-	-	-	-	-		1	0	0	0	1.0	2	2	2	1	0	18.00
Goins, Ryan	-	-	-	-	-	-	-	-	-	-		1	0	0	0	1.0	2	0	0	1	0	0.00
Gomez, Carlos	-	-	-	-	-	-	-	-	-	-		1	0	0	0	0.1	0	3	3	4	0	81.00
Gordon, Alex	2	-	-	-	2.1	8	5	5	2	-	19.29	2	0	0	0	2.1	8	5	5	2	0	19.29
Gyorko, Jedd	1	-	-	-	0.1	-	-	-	-	1	0.00	2	0	0	0	1.1	2	1	1	0	1	6.75
Happ, Ian	-	-	-	-	-	-	-	-	-	-		1	0	0	0	1.0	1	0	0	0	0	0.00
Harrison, Josh	-	-	-	-	-	-	-	-	-	-		1	0	0	0	0.1	0	0	0	0	0	0.00
Hernandez, Kike	-	-	-	-	-	-	-	-	-	-		1	0	1	0	0.1	1	3	3	2	0	81.00
Holaday, Bryan	1	-	-	-	0.1	-	-	-	-	-	0.00	4	0	0	0	3.2	4	3	3	0	1	7.36
Jay, Jon	-	-	-	-	-	-	-	-	-	-		1	0	0	0	1.0	1	0	0	0	0	0.00
Joseph, Caleb	2	-	-	-	1.1	-	-	-	-	-	0.00	2	0	0	0	1.1	0	0	0	0	0	0.00
Kingery, Scott	-	-	-	-	-	-	-	-	-	-		1	0	0	0	1.1	4	2	2	0	0	13.50
Kinsler, Ian	1	-	-	-	1.0	1	-	-	2	-	0.00	1	0	0	0	1.0	1	0	0	2	0	0.00
Kratz, Erik	-	-	-	-	-	-	-	-	-	-		5	0	0	0	5.0	8	4	2	1	3	3.60
La Stella, Tommy	-	-	-	-	-	-	-	-	-	-		1	0	0	0	1.1	3	1	1	0	0	6.75
LaMarre, Ryan	-	-	-	-	-	-	-	-	-	-		2	0	0	0	1.2	3	1	1	0	0	5.40
Maile, Luke	2	-	-	-	2.0	1	-	-	-	3	0.00	2	0	0	0	2.0	1	0	0	0	3	0.00
Maldonado, Martin	-	-	-	-	-	-	-	-	-	-		1	0	0	0	1.0	1	0	0	0	0	0.00
Martin, Leonys	-	-	-	-	-	-	-	-	-	-		1	0	0	0	0.2	3	2	2	0	0	27.00
Martin, Russell	4	-	-	-	4.0	2	-	-	-	2	0.00	4	0	0	0	4.0	2	0	0	0	2	0.00
Martini, Nick	1	-	-	-	1.0	-	-	-	2	1	0.00	1	0	0	0	1.0	0	0	0	2	1	0.00
Mathis, Jeff	2	-	-	-	2.0	3	2	2	-	1	9.00	5	0	1	0	5.0	8	5	5	1	2	9.00
Moore, Dylan	1	-	-	-	1.0	5	4	4	2	-	36.00	1	0	0	0	1.0	5	4	4	2	2	36.00
Morales, Kendrys	1	-	-	-	1.0	1	1	1	2	-	9.00	2	0	0	0	2.0	1	1	1	3	0	4.50
Moreland, Mitch	-	-	-	-	-	-	-	-	-	-		2	0	0	0	2.0	2	0	0	0	1	0.00
Murphy, John Ryan	2	-	-	-	3.0	10	9	9	3	-	27.00	2	0	0	0	3.0	10	9	9	3	0	27.00
Murphy, Tom	3	-	-	-	3.0	1	2	2	1	2	6.00	3	0	0	0	3.0	1	2	2	1	2	6.00
Nunez, Eduardo	1	-	-	-	1.0	1	1	1	-	-	9.00	1	0	0	0	1.0	1	1	1	0	0	9.00
Osuna, Jose	2	-	-	-	2.1	3	1	1	-	-	3.86	2	0	0	0	2.1	3	1	1	0	0	3.86
Owings, Chris	1	-	-	-	1.2	6	4	4	1	-	21.60	1	0	0	0	1.2	6	4	4	1	0	21.60
Parra, Gerardo	1	-	-	-	-	1	5	5	4	-		1	0	0	0	0.0	1	5	5	4	0	
Peraza, Jose	2	-	-	-	1.1	1	-	-	-	-	0.00	2	0	0	0	1.1	1	0	0	0	0	0.00
Perez, Hernan	3	-	-	-	3.0	2	1	1	2	1	3.00	7	0	0	0	7.1	10	6	6	4	3	7.36
Peterson, Jace	-	-	-	-	-	-	-	-	-	-		1	0	0	0	1.0	6	4	4	0	1	36.00
Phegley, Josh	-	-	-	-	-	-	-	-	-	-		1	0	0	0	0.2	0	0	0	0	1	0.00
Plawecki, Kevin	2	-	-	-	2.0	-	-	-	-	-	0.00	4	0	0	0	5.0	5	4	4	0	0	7.20
Quinn, Roman	2	-	1	-	3.1	7	3	3	3	1	8.10	3	0	1	0	5.0	13	10	10	5	1	18.00

Hitters Pitching

Player	2019 Pitching											Career Pitching										
	G	W	L	Sv	IP	H	R	ER	BB	SO	ERA	G	W	L	Sv	IP	H	R	ER	BB	SO	ERA
Reed, A.J.	1	-	-	-	1.0	-	-	-	-	-	0.00	1	0	0	0	1.0	0	0	0	0	0	0.00
Reynolds, Mark	1	-	-	-	1.0	2	2	2	1	-	18.00	2	0	0	0	1.1	2	2	2	1	0	13.50
Rizzo, Anthony	-	-	-	-	-	-	-	-	-	-	-	1	0	0	0	0.1	0	0	0	0	0	0.00
Robertson, Daniel	1	-	-	-	1.0	1	-	-	-	-	0.00	2	0	0	0	2.0	1	0	0	0	0	0.00
Rodriguez, Sean	2	-	-	-	1.1	-	-	-	-	1	0.00	2	0	0	0	1.1	0	0	0	0	1	0.00
Romine, Austin	1	-	-	-	1.0	4	3	3	-	-	27.00	1	0	0	0	1.0	4	3	3	0	0	27.00
Rondon, Jose	1	-	-	-	1.0	2	-	-	-	-	0.00	1	0	0	0	1.0	2	0	0	0	0	0.00
Sandoval, Pablo	1	-	-	-	1.0	-	-	-	-	-	0.00	2	0	0	0	2.0	0	0	0	0	0	0.00
Shuck, JB	1	-	-	-	1.0	1	-	-	1	-	0.00	2	0	0	0	2.0	2	1	1	1	0	4.50
Spangenberg, Cory	-	-	-	-	-	-	-	-	-	-	-	2	0	0	0	2.0	4	3	3	3	0	13.50
Stallings, Jacob	1	-	-	-	1.0	-	-	-	-	-	0.00	1	0	0	0	1.0	0	0	0	0	0	0.00
Stassi, Max	1	-	-	-	0.1	-	-	-	-	-	0.00	1	0	0	0	0.1	0	0	0	0	0	0.00
Sucre, Jesus	1	-	-	-	1.0	-	-	-	-	-	0.00	6	0	0	0	5.0	12	8	8	2	0	14.40
Suzuki, Ichiro	-	-	-	-	-	-	-	-	-	-	-	1	0	0	0	1.0	2	1	1	0	0	9.00
Tejada, Ruben	-	-	-	-	-	-	-	-	-	-	-	1	0	0	0	1.0	2	2	2	0	0	18.00
Urena, Richard	1	-	-	-	1.0	4	4	4	1	-	36.00	1	0	0	0	1.0	4	4	4	1	0	36.00
Walsh, Jared	5	-	-	-	5.0	3	1	1	6	5	1.80	5	0	0	0	5.0	3	1	1	6	5	1.80
White, Tyler	4	-	-	-	3.1	7	8	8	5	2	21.60	6	0	0	0	5.1	10	11	11	5	2	18.56
Wilkerson, Stevie	4	-	-	1	5.1	6	4	4	-	1	6.75	4	0	0	1	5.1	6	4	4	0	1	6.75
Zobrist, Ben	1	-	-	-	1.0	-	-	-	2	1	0.00	1	0	0	0	1.0	0	0	0	2	1	0.00

Pitchers Hitting

Alex Vigderman

Have you ever shared a room with your sibling for a while, only to be given your own room and feel overwhelmed by the space? Pitchers hitting now gets its own section for the first time after spending its childhood bunked up with hitters pitching and pitchers fielding.

Now, let's be honest here: with increased specialization early in players' careers, fewer pitchers going deep into games and garnering even two plate appearances, and opposing pitching just flat-out being better, pitchers aren't exactly tearing the cover off the ball as a group. Of the 109 pitchers featured on the 2019 leaderboard that follows, 77 of them had a slugging percentage of .200 or below. But there are some outstanding performers even considering the nature of the position these days.

Pirates lefty Steven Brault went the first 34 plate appearances of his career before his first strikeout, and given that contact ability as a pitcher it's not surprising that he could post a commendable batting average in a given season. That said, a .333 mark that led the position (and with more at-bats than the two guys trailing him) still might make you double-take.

The stick-swinging reputation of Madison Bumgarner has preceded him for years, particularly marked by his duels with Clayton Kershaw where they would trade home runs off each other. Perhaps no season of his career would epitomize that like this one, in which Bumgarner worked nine walks in only 76 plate appearances.

Zack Greinke wasn't a Cy Young frontrunner this year, but this might have been one of his most impressive seasons because of his performance at the plate and with the glove. His .888 OPS easily paced the position, and he stacks up against the best defenders year after year (he saved four runs in 2019). Unfortunately, his being dealt to the Astros during the season deprives us of his stick-swinging services for the foreseeable future.

Pitchers Hitting

Pitchers with 10+ PA or 10+ Total Bases in 2019

Pitcher	B	AB	H	2B	3B	HR	R	RBI	BB	SO	SH	GDP	Avg	OBP	Slg	OPS
Agrazal, Dario	R	22	2	0	0	0	0	2	0	9	1	0	.091	.087	.091	.178
Alcantara, Sandy	R	58	5	1	0	0	2	4	1	46	3	0	.086	.117	.103	.220
Anderson, Chase	R	40	4	1	0	0	1	1	2	24	2	0	.100	.143	.125	.268
Anderson, Shaun	R	25	2	1	0	0	0	0	0	19	2	0	.080	.115	.120	.235
Archer, Chris	R	35	4	0	0	0	1	2	3	19	3	0	.114	.184	.114	.298
Arrieta, Jake	R	45	7	1	0	0	2	4	1	19	4	1	.156	.174	.178	.352
Bauer, Trevor	R	19	3	0	0	0	1	0	2	12	1	0	.158	.238	.158	.396
Beede, Tyler	R	38	4	0	0	0	2	1	3	23	2	0	.105	.171	.105	.276
Brault, Steven	L	42	14	1	0	1	8	2	1	8	7	1	.333	.349	.429	.777
Buehler, Walker	R	59	5	0	0	1	5	2	4	33	3	0	.085	.143	.136	.278
Bumgarner, Madison	R	63	8	0	0	2	4	4	9	40	4	0	.127	.236	.222	.458
Castillo, Luis	R	62	6	1	0	0	3	0	0	32	4	1	.097	.097	.113	.210
Chacin, Jhoulys	R	24	3	0	0	1	2	1	1	10	0	0	.125	.160	.250	.410
Chatwood, Tyler	R	18	3	2	0	0	1	1	1	6	2	0	.167	.211	.278	.488
Clarke, Taylor	R	24	6	0	0	1	2	2	0	10	1	0	.250	.250	.375	.625
Corbin, Patrick	L	65	6	1	0	0	3	4	3	27	4	0	.092	.132	.108	.240
Darvish, Yu	R	56	5	0	0	0	1	3	2	31	3	1	.089	.119	.089	.208
Davies, Zach	R	52	8	2	0	0	3	3	1	25	2	1	.154	.170	.192	.362
deGrom, Jacob	L	65	13	2	0	2	4	6	4	19	1	0	.200	.246	.323	.569
DeSclafani, Anthony	R	55	6	0	0	0	0	1	0	28	2	0	.109	.109	.109	.218
Dugger, Robert	R	11	0	0	0	0	0	0	0	6	0	0	.000	.000	.000	.000
Eflin, Zach	R	50	8	1	0	0	3	2	0	27	2	0	.160	.160	.180	.340
Eickhoff, Jerad	R	14	0	0	0	0	0	0	1	7	4	0	.000	.067	.000	.067
Fedde, Erick	R	15	2	0	0	0	1	0	0	6	5	0	.133	.133	.133	.267
Flaherty, Jack	R	54	10	3	0	0	4	4	2	17	9	0	.185	.211	.241	.451
Foltynewicz, Mike	R	35	2	0	0	0	1	1	0	19	3	1	.057	.057	.057	.114
Freeland, Kyle	L	23	2	0	0	0	1	0	3	15	5	1	.087	.192	.087	.279
Fried, Max	L	56	11	4	0	0	11	4	5	16	4	0	.196	.262	.268	.530
Gallen, Zac	R	19	2	0	0	0	2	1	0	8	5	0	.105	.105	.105	.211
Gausman, Kevin	L	27	1	0	0	0	1	0	0	18	0	1	.037	.037	.037	.074
Godley, Zack	R	19	3	0	0	0	3	2	3	10	1	0	.158	.273	.158	.431
Gonsolin, Tony	R	13	4	0	0	0	2	1	0	4	1	0	.308	.308	.308	.615
Gonzalez, Chi Chi	R	24	1	0	0	0	0	2	0	15	0	0	.042	.042	.042	.083
Gonzalez, Gio	R	25	1	0	0	0	1	0	1	17	2	0	.040	.077	.040	.117
Gray, Jon	R	47	3	0	0	0	1	1	3	22	9	2	.064	.120	.064	.184
Gray, Sonny	R	46	7	0	1	0	3	3	2	19	12	0	.152	.188	.196	.383
Greinke, Zack	R	50	14	4	1	3	7	8	2	12	4	2	.280	.308	.580	.888
Hamels, Cole	L	42	6	1	0	0	1	4	1	15	1	2	.143	.178	.167	.344
Hellickson, Jeremy	R	9	1	0	0	0	3	0	2	4	2	0	.111	.273	.111	.384
Hendricks, Kyle	R	54	8	1	0	0	1	5	2	29	7	1	.148	.193	.167	.360
Hernandez, Elieser	R	19	1	0	0	0	0	0	1	10	4	0	.053	.100	.053	.153
Hill, Rich	L	18	3	1	0	0	0	1	1	9	1	0	.167	.211	.222	.433
Hoffman, Jeff	R	21	5	0	0	0	2	1	0	9	3	0	.238	.238	.238	.476
Holland, Derek	B	14	1	0	0	0	0	0	1	10	1	0	.071	.133	.071	.205
Houser, Adrian	R	22	1	1	0	0	0	0	2	17	3	0	.045	.125	.091	.216
Hudson, Dakota	R	51	4	0	0	0	1	2	0	24	7	1	.078	.096	.078	.175
Keller, Mitch	R	10	0	0	0	0	0	0	0	3	1	1	.000	.000	.000	.000
Kelly, Merrill	R	52	1	0	0	0	3	2	2	25	6	2	.019	.056	.019	.075
Kershaw, Clayton	L	49	5	1	0	0	1	1	1	16	15	0	.102	.120	.122	.242
Keuchel, Dallas	L	38	5	1	0	0	0	2	1	28	2	0	.132	.154	.158	.312
Lambert, Peter	R	28	9	0	0	0	3	2	3	10	3	1	.321	.387	.321	.709
Lamet, Dinelson	R	21	3	0	0	0	1	0	0	11	3	0	.143	.143	.143	.286
Lauer, Eric	R	40	4	2	0	0	1	0	1	23	6	0	.100	.122	.150	.272
Leake, Mike	R	21	1	0	0	0	0	1	1	11	2	0	.048	.091	.048	.139
Lester, Jon	L	48	9	2	0	1	6	6	5	20	0	1	.188	.264	.292	.556
Lopez, Pablo	L	35	6	2	0	0	1	3	0	19	1	0	.171	.171	.229	.400
Lorenzen, Michael	R	48	10	2	0	1	6	6	5	17	0	1	.208	.283	.313	.596
Lucchesi, Joey	L	48	3	0	0	0	0	1	1	36	5	0	.063	.082	.063	.144
Lyles, Jordan	R	45	4	0	0	0	3	4	1	28	1	1	.089	.128	.089	.217
Maeda, Kenta	R	48	12	2	0	0	3	6	0	13	13	0	.250	.250	.292	.542
Mahle, Tyler	R	34	3	1	0	0	4	0	1	19	6	0	.088	.114	.118	.232
Margevicius, Nick	L	15	3	0	0	0	1	0	0	7	2	0	.200	.200	.200	.400
Marquez, German	R	48	11	4	1	0	5	11	0	14	10	1	.229	.229	.354	.583
Matz, Steven	R	57	13	0	0	1	4	1	0	17	4	0	.228	.228	.281	.509
May, Dustin	R	11	1	0	0	0	0	0	0	4	0	0	.091	.091	.091	.182
McKay, Brendan	L	10	2	0	0	1	2	1	1	2	0	1	.200	.273	.500	.773
Mikolas, Miles	R	59	8	1	0	0	1	2	0	27	3	0	.136	.136	.153	.288
Mills, Alec	R	12	1	0	0	0	0	0	0	6	0	0	.083	.083	.083	.167

Pitchers Hitting

Pitchers with 10+ PA or 10+ Total Bases in 2019

Pitcher	B	AB	H	2B	3B	HR	R	RBI	BB	SO	SH	GDP	Avg	OBP	Slg	OPS
Musgrove, Joe	R	51	8	2	1	0	8	3	2	19	8	1	.157	.189	.235	.424
Nola, Aaron	R	59	7	2	0	0	6	2	6	35	5	0	.119	.200	.153	.353
Paddack, Chris	R	42	5	0	0	0	3	2	0	19	4	0	.119	.119	.119	.238
Peralta, Freddy	R	15	2	0	0	0	1	1	0	6	1	0	.133	.133	.133	.267
Pivetta, Nick	R	25	2	0	0	0	1	0	1	19	1	0	.080	.115	.080	.195
Pomeranz, Drew	R	19	0	0	0	0	0	0	0	13	1	1	.000	.000	.000	.000
Ponce de Leon, Daniel	R	9	0	0	0	0	0	0	1	4	2	0	.000	.100	.000	.100
Quantrill, Cal	L	25	2	0	0	0	1	1	1	6	4	0	.080	.115	.080	.195
Quintana, Jose	R	54	5	1	0	0	2	3	0	27	9	1	.093	.093	.111	.204
Ray, Robbie	L	55	4	0	0	0	1	3	0	28	5	2	.073	.073	.073	.145
Richards, Trevor	R	30	3	0	0	0	2	0	2	18	2	0	.100	.156	.100	.256
Roark, Tanner	R	33	5	1	0	1	2	2	0	13	1	0	.152	.152	.273	.424
Rodriguez, Dereck	R	29	5	0	0	0	1	0	0	17	0	0	.172	.172	.172	.345
Ross, Joe	R	19	2	0	0	0	1	0	1	10	0	0	.105	.150	.105	.255
Ryu, Hyun-Jin	R	51	8	1	0	1	3	3	4	23	12	0	.157	.218	.235	.453
Samardzija, Jeff	R	50	6	2	0	0	1	1	0	30	6	0	.120	.120	.160	.280
Sanchez, Anibal	R	52	6	0	0	0	1	1	0	24	4	3	.115	.115	.115	.231
Scherzer, Max	R	55	10	0	0	0	6	2	0	27	6	1	.182	.182	.182	.364
Senzatela, Antonio	R	40	1	0	0	0	2	3	1	24	5	0	.025	.049	.025	.074
Smith, Caleb	R	43	10	2	0	0	2	3	0	15	5	2	.233	.250	.279	.529
Smyly, Drew	L	19	0	0	0	0	1	0	1	9	0	0	.000	.050	.000	.050
Soroka, Mike	R	52	4	0	0	0	2	3	2	22	7	1	.077	.143	.077	.220
Strahm, Matt	R	21	6	2	0	0	1	1	2	12	4	0	.286	.348	.381	.729
Strasburg, Stephen	R	72	12	1	0	1	4	10	3	25	5	0	.167	.200	.222	.422
Stripling, Ross	R	20	3	0	0	0	1	1	2	7	2	1	.150	.227	.150	.377
Stroman, Marcus	R	23	1	0	0	0	2	0	0	13	2	1	.043	.043	.043	.087
Syndergaard, Noah	L	65	6	1	0	2	6	2	3	47	1	1	.092	.132	.200	.332
Teheran, Julio	R	55	6	1	0	0	1	4	0	24	4	0	.109	.107	.127	.234
Urena, Jose	R	19	0	0	0	0	1	0	1	14	2	1	.000	.050	.000	.050
Urias, Julio	L	12	3	0	0	0	0	2	1	4	5	0	.250	.308	.250	.558
Vargas, Jason	L	40	3	0	0	0	0	0	0	22	5	1	.075	.075	.075	.150
Velasquez, Vince	R	30	7	0	0	1	2	3	2	9	4	1	.233	.281	.333	.615
Wacha, Michael	R	36	6	1	0	0	3	3	0	21	3	0	.167	.167	.194	.361
Wainwright, Adam	R	50	8	3	0	0	6	2	2	20	6	0	.160	.189	.220	.409
Weaver, Luke	R	19	2	0	0	1	2	4	0	11	1	0	.105	.100	.263	.363
Webb, Logan	R	9	1	0	0	0	0	0	1	2	1	1	.111	.200	.111	.311
Wheeler, Zack	L	57	12	2	0	1	5	6	2	19	3	0	.211	.262	.298	.561
Williams, Trevor	R	36	6	0	0	0	2	4	2	17	6	0	.167	.211	.167	.377
Woodruff, Brandon	L	45	12	4	0	0	1	4	1	20	3	0	.267	.283	.356	.638
Yamamoto, Jordan	R	21	1	0	0	0	0	1	1	9	4	1	.048	.091	.048	.139
Young, Alex	L	25	1	0	0	0	1	0	0	18	0	0	.040	.040	.040	.080

Career Pitchers Hitting

Active Pitchers with 150+ PAs in their careers

Pitcher	B	AB	H	2B	3B	HR	R	RBI	BB	SO	SH	GDP	Avg	OBP	Slg	OPS
Anderson, Chase	R	264	25	2	0	0	6	10	4	140	28	3	.095	.115	.102	.217
Arrieta, Jake	R	359	60	6	4	6	22	27	14	181	23	5	.167	.198	.256	.455
Bailey, Homer	R	373	61	8	0	0	22	18	11	145	55	11	.164	.190	.185	.375
Bettis, Chad	R	142	8	0	0	0	7	6	13	65	17	1	.056	.135	.056	.192
Bumgarner, Madison	R	594	105	18	0	19	51	62	40	255	40	5	.177	.228	.303	.532
Cahill, Trevor	R	182	22	3	1	0	7	12	5	63	20	2	.121	.144	.148	.293
Cashner, Andrew	R	203	32	2	1	1	16	8	7	84	18	0	.158	.185	.192	.377
Castillo, Luis	R	150	14	2	0	0	7	3	3	66	11	1	.093	.111	.107	.218
Chacin, Jhoulys	R	355	65	8	0	2	16	22	11	86	30	3	.183	.209	.223	.431
Chatwood, Tyler	R	204	42	5	1	0	17	17	8	51	29	1	.206	.236	.240	.476
Cole, Gerrit	R	251	41	2	0	3	17	15	6	112	28	4	.163	.186	.207	.393
Corbin, Patrick	L	357	55	9	3	0	29	23	18	145	31	4	.154	.197	.196	.393
Cueto, Johnny	R	516	53	1	0	0	26	18	14	169	85	6	.103	.128	.105	.232
Davies, Zach	R	181	21	4	0	0	13	7	9	73	28	2	.116	.158	.138	.296
deGrom, Jacob	L	350	66	8	0	3	23	23	17	107	23	8	.189	.226	.237	.463
DeSclafani, Anthony	R	206	27	2	0	1	5	11	5	111	9	2	.131	.151	.155	.306
Eovaldi, Nathan	R	151	12	0	0	0	8	2	6	96	14	0	.079	.115	.079	.194
Foltynewicz, Mike	R	199	14	3	0	0	8	9	1	125	24	2	.070	.075	.085	.160
Godley, Zack	R	141	11	0	0	0	6	5	9	81	20	0	.078	.133	.078	.211
Gonzalez, Gio	R	410	37	7	0	3	16	17	9	190	50	3	.090	.118	.129	.247
Gray, Jon	R	195	17	4	0	1	9	10	11	115	25	2	.087	.136	.123	.259
Greinke, Zack	R	519	117	29	1	9	49	34	26	113	47	8	.225	.263	.337	.600
Hamels, Cole	L	688	116	16	2	2	40	34	19	286	64	8	.169	.195	.206	.401
Happ, J.A.	L	197	20	2	0	1	13	6	10	86	31	1	.102	.145	.127	.272
Harvey, Matt	R	250	27	7	0	1	8	14	4	105	15	10	.108	.122	.148	.270
Hellickson, Jeremy	R	175	25	3	1	0	10	14	11	67	20	1	.143	.201	.171	.372
Hendricks, Kyle	R	306	31	4	0	0	9	15	9	152	26	3	.101	.132	.114	.247
Hill, Rich	L	232	26	5	0	0	4	13	3	101	10	2	.112	.130	.134	.264
Jackson, Edwin	R	297	49	4	0	2	24	13	14	128	23	0	.165	.202	.199	.401
Kennedy, Ian	R	321	42	11	1	1	21	18	33	154	42	3	.131	.213	.181	.394
Kershaw, Clayton	L	662	105	11	1	1	44	37	33	200	108	15	.159	.203	.183	.386
Leake, Mike	R	485	93	18	1	6	46	32	16	196	46	11	.192	.221	.270	.491
Lester, Jon	L	318	34	8	0	3	24	28	19	138	33	6	.107	.156	.160	.317
Liriano, Francisco	L	218	34	3	0	2	7	15	9	85	15	4	.156	.189	.197	.387
Lyles, Jordan	R	217	25	4	0	2	16	15	11	110	14	5	.115	.162	.161	.323
Lynn, Lance	B	278	23	5	0	0	15	5	12	156	35	2	.083	.126	.101	.227
Maeda, Kenta	R	176	27	4	0	1	10	14	1	41	34	3	.153	.158	.193	.351
Marquez, German	R	159	37	6	1	1	14	21	0	46	25	3	.233	.233	.302	.535
Martinez, Carlos	R	225	44	8	0	1	13	23	2	72	17	3	.196	.211	.244	.456
Matz, Steven	R	174	30	3	1	3	8	13	7	49	15	4	.172	.203	.253	.456
Miley, Wade	L	243	37	5	0	1	13	12	10	67	28	4	.152	.186	.185	.371
Minor, Mike	R	210	25	6	0	2	13	10	9	96	16	2	.119	.155	.176	.331
Morton, Charlie	R	266	20	4	0	0	4	6	3	139	37	4	.075	.085	.090	.175
Nelson, Jimmy	R	188	19	2	0	0	3	7	4	113	13	1	.101	.120	.112	.231
Nola, Aaron	R	222	17	4	0	0	10	8	15	129	17	4	.077	.139	.095	.233
Perez, Oliver	L	344	56	2	0	0	14	15	14	116	39	2	.163	.194	.169	.363
Quintana, Jose	L	155	11	1	0	0	4	7	2	84	24	4	.071	.082	.077	.160
Ray, Robbie	L	233	34	6	0	1	11	9	4	115	25	3	.146	.160	.185	.344
Roark, Tanner	R	309	45	8	1	1	12	14	8	114	33	3	.146	.170	.188	.358
Ross, Tyson	R	190	38	2	1	2	14	13	6	78	16	2	.200	.229	.253	.481
Ryu, Hyun-Jin	R	213	38	8	1	1	19	12	12	94	32	1	.178	.226	.239	.465
Samardzija, Jeff	R	350	44	14	0	3	16	22	7	154	33	5	.126	.144	.191	.335
Sanchez, Anibal	R	346	29	1	1	0	8	8	17	169	37	6	.084	.127	.092	.219
Scherzer, Max	R	405	78	6	0	1	31	29	13	133	46	4	.193	.221	.215	.436
Straily, Dan	R	141	10	2	0	0	6	3	13	95	22	2	.071	.155	.085	.240
Strasburg, Stephen	R	435	66	9	0	4	23	29	23	151	55	6	.152	.196	.200	.396
Syndergaard, Noah	L	222	34	7	0	6	14	15	15	144	13	2	.153	.206	.266	.472
Teheran, Julio	R	382	56	6	0	1	10	26	9	112	67	3	.147	.169	.170	.339
Volquez, Edinson	R	308	28	2	0	1	15	9	8	156	45	1	.091	.114	.107	.221
Wacha, Michael	R	248	23	2	0	0	16	16	9	122	29	3	.093	.124	.101	.225
Wainwright, Adam	R	685	136	37	2	10	54	71	24	224	60	9	.199	.225	.302	.527
Wheeler, Zack	L	220	33	7	0	1	12	15	5	89	22	1	.150	.175	.195	.371
Wood, Alex	R	238	23	2	0	0	8	12	9	145	29	3	.097	.130	.105	.235
Zimmermann, Jordan	R	334	56	6	0	1	18	15	10	104	44	2	.168	.191	.195	.385

Lords of the Flies

Alex Vigderman

"I have the power!"
-- Almost every major league hitter in 2019. Or maybe it was He-Man.

You might have noticed while watching games, perusing leaderboards, or watching highlight shows that there was a bit of a spike in home runs this year, even beyond the spike in home runs we saw two years ago.

On a player level, while many were able to parlay this rising tide into some incredible seasons, there were still guys who left some dingers on the table. Diamondbacks third baseman Eduardo Escobar hit 30-plus home runs for the first time in his career. He also had 121 long outs (and was the only player over 100), including 17 of at least 380 feet, the most in the majors.

A few Astros hitters had odd seasons as a part of one of the most productive offenses in recent memory. Alex Bregman and Michael Brantley were two of only four players to hit into at least four outs on balls hit over 400 feet. Bregman and Yuli Gurriel each benefited from the shallow left field fence in Houston, hitting eight and five homers shorter than 360 feet, respectively. Only Joc Pederson, Xander Bogaerts, Brett Gardner, and Eugenio Suarez had as many as five among non-Astros.

In the tables that follow, batted balls are grouped by their distance. Each group includes balls within 10 feet in either direction of the distance listed. For example, the 350 group includes balls hit between 340 and 359 feet. The Long column includes the total long fly ball outs, and the HR column excludes inside-the-park home runs.

Players are included if they hit at least 50 long fly outs or 15 home runs.

Long Outs and Home Runs

Player	Long Out Distances						Home Run Distances					
	330	350	370	390	400+	Long	330	350	370	390	400+	HR
Alonso, Pete	20	10	13	5	1	60	0	2	7	8	36	53
Suarez, Eugenio	13	8	6	3	1	42	1	4	6	13	25	49
Soler, Jorge	9	12	9	12	0	54	1	0	5	9	33	48
Bellinger, Cody	21	19	16	8	2	76	0	3	2	9	33	47
Trout, Mike	15	16	11	4	1	64	0	0	3	9	33	45
Yelich, Christian	9	13	6	6	1	44	0	3	3	9	29	44
Acuna Jr., Ronald	14	16	11	5	1	64	0	0	1	10	30	41
Arenado, Nolan	17	19	21	9	3	83	0	1	4	8	28	41
Cruz, Nelson	10	7	7	5	0	42	0	2	8	3	28	41
Bregman, Alex	12	17	12	11	4	73	0	8	13	11	9	41
Freeman, Freddie	20	18	11	10	0	77	0	0	4	11	23	38
Springer, George	10	8	10	9	2	49	0	1	10	4	23	38
Schwarber, Kyle	16	16	7	2	0	61	0	1	4	13	20	38
Torres, Gleyber	15	8	14	4	0	60	0	3	6	11	18	38
Reyes, Franmil	10	11	11	7	0	49	0	1	4	5	27	37
Bell, Josh	14	10	18	7	2	61	0	2	5	5	25	37
Donaldson, Josh	18	12	8	5	0	60	0	1	2	10	24	37
Chapman, Matt	24	11	9	3	0	58	0	1	5	8	22	36
Martinez, J.D.	17	11	13	6	0	70	0	1	2	14	19	36
Olson, Matt	9	12	9	4	0	44	0	0	6	12	18	36
Pederson, Joc	16	11	8	1	1	47	0	5	4	10	17	36
Kepler, Max	19	14	6	6	1	66	1	3	7	13	12	36
Story, Trevor	24	15	10	3	2	65	0	0	5	7	23	35
Harper, Bryce	19	14	17	5	0	70	0	1	5	7	22	35
Moustakas, Mike	7	23	10	5	0	61	0	2	2	10	21	35
Mancini, Trey	14	15	10	6	0	61	0	0	4	11	20	35
Muncy, Max	8	13	12	10	0	58	0	1	4	11	19	35
Escobar, Eduardo	30	24	24	15	2	121	0	1	8	15	11	35
Sano, Miguel	5	7	3	4	2	25	0	0	3	6	25	34
Sanchez, Gary	8	3	10	5	1	40	0	1	3	5	25	34
Goldschmidt, Paul	19	22	18	6	0	85	1	0	1	9	23	34
Soto, Juan	17	21	14	5	0	69	0	0	7	7	20	34
Encarnacion, Edwin	13	13	5	3	1	44	0	1	6	8	19	34
Rendon, Anthony	15	17	15	10	1	70	0	0	5	14	15	34
Santana, Carlos	12	13	10	7	1	59	1	1	4	14	14	34
Renfroe, Hunter	8	14	8	5	0	45	0	0	5	4	24	33
Calhoun, Kole	14	14	10	2	0	62	0	0	3	9	21	33
Conforto, Michael	15	16	15	2	1	71	1	1	5	6	20	33
Semien, Marcus	26	20	12	5	0	82	0	1	5	8	19	33
Abreu, Jose	11	11	13	7	0	54	0	3	6	5	19	33
Bogaerts, Xander	15	16	12	6	0	66	0	5	2	10	16	33
Meadows, Austin	16	10	12	12	0	66	0	2	4	13	14	33
Blackmon, Charlie	17	14	14	11	2	73	0	1	3	6	22	32
Lindor, Francisco	24	9	17	4	1	69	0	4	2	8	18	32
Devers, Rafael	22	14	8	3	0	58	0	2	7	7	16	32
Machado, Manny	19	17	17	3	1	71	1	0	6	10	15	32
Rosario, Eddie	13	18	12	9	0	80	1	2	6	8	15	32
Nunez, Renato	9	13	7	5	0	54	0	0	2	4	25	31
Bryant, Kris	12	14	9	3	0	54	0	0	5	6	20	31
Jimenez, Eloy	9	10	5	1	0	41	0	2	6	3	20	31
Garver, Mitch	9	6	1	1	0	26	0	2	6	4	19	31
Grichuk, Randal	11	10	10	3	1	57	0	1	5	9	16	31
Marte, Ketel	14	11	7	8	0	59	0	0	8	7	16	31
Altuve, Jose	10	5	10	5	1	45	0	3	4	10	14	31
DeJong, Paul	10	13	16	6	1	67	0	0	3	6	21	30
Odor, Rougned	17	16	13	5	2	64	0	1	6	5	18	30
Vogelbach, Daniel	17	16	6	3	0	54	0	1	7	9	13	30
Gurriel, Yuli	24	12	7	0	1	70	0	5	4	12	9	30
Walker, Christian	12	8	12	6	3	50	0	1	2	6	20	29
Baez, Javier	12	16	3	3	0	49	0	1	7	4	17	29
Ozuna, Marcell	13	12	13	6	0	55	0	1	4	8	16	29
Betts, Mookie	15	27	18	11	2	96	1	3	4	8	13	29
Hoskins, Rhys	19	18	12	7	2	73	0	4	4	10	11	29
Santana, Danny	15	8	7	2	0	40	0	2	2	6	18	28
Grandal, Yasmani	19	12	12	5	2	60	1	0	4	8	15	28
Gardner, Brett	12	6	9	1	0	36	0	5	9	6	8	28
Alvarez, Yordan	4	7	5	2	1	25	1	1	2	3	20	27
Turner, Justin	15	21	14	8	1	80	0	0	3	9	15	27
Castellanos, Nicholas	26	18	15	13	2	91	1	1	3	9	13	27
Judge, Aaron	9	7	7	4	0	33	1	2	8	4	12	27
Rizzo, Anthony	18	10	4	7	0	48	0	1	5	10	11	27
Hernandez, Teoscar	12	11	6	8	0	43	1	1	5	3	16	26
Dozier, Hunter	16	14	7	9	1	59	0	3	4	3	16	26

Long Outs and Home Runs

Player	Long Out Distances						Home Run Distances					
	330	350	370	390	400+	Long	330	350	370	390	400+	HR
Canha, Mark	13	9	3	2	0	35	0	3	6	4	13	26
Bruce, Jay	13	10	7	3	1	42	0	1	5	8	12	26
LeMahieu, DJ	19	17	6	8	1	66	1	3	8	5	9	26
Moncada, Yoan	12	11	5	5	0	45	0	2	2	6	15	25
Cron, C.J.	18	15	6	4	0	55	0	0	5	6	14	25
Thames, Eric	11	10	16	2	1	48	0	1	4	6	14	25
Realmuto, J.T.	19	19	6	4	0	64	0	3	6	5	11	25
Puig, Yasiel	12	17	6	7	0	57	0	1	3	2	18	24
Villar, Jonathan	16	10	7	2	1	48	0	0	3	4	17	24
Choo, Shin-Soo	16	9	11	3	1	46	0	0	2	6	16	24
Laureano, Ramon	13	8	8	3	1	46	0	1	2	5	16	24
McMahon, Ryan	12	11	5	1	0	38	0	0	3	6	15	24
Perez, Roberto	10	7	8	2	0	34	0	1	5	4	14	24
Contreras, Willson	5	9	5	6	0	34	0	0	7	4	13	24
Albies, Ozzie	22	21	13	5	2	82	0	2	5	5	12	24
Pujols, Albert	15	11	12	7	1	58	0	0	7	2	14	23
Davis, Khris	19	19	4	6	0	67	0	2	2	7	12	23
Marte, Starling	13	15	12	4	2	55	0	0	3	9	11	23
Schoop, Jonathan	11	9	7	3	0	40	0	1	2	9	11	23
Ramirez, Jose	21	18	10	2	1	76	0	1	4	7	11	23
Vazquez, Christian	19	18	6	6	0	62	0	3	5	4	10	23
McNeil, Jeff	12	15	9	6	0	57	0	2	3	9	9	23
Galvis, Freddy	15	17	11	7	0	66	0	3	5	8	7	23
Seager, Kyle	16	18	13	5	0	68	0	2	9	6	6	23
Braun, Ryan	14	14	8	4	2	51	0	1	2	4	15	22
Tatis Jr., Fernando	5	8	4	3	0	24	0	2	4	2	14	22
Davis, J.D.	11	8	5	6	1	36	0	0	5	4	13	22
Smoak, Justin	15	15	12	8	0	59	0	0	6	4	12	22
Castro, Starlin	18	23	11	5	0	79	0	1	5	4	12	22
Polanco, Jorge	25	20	18	9	1	95	0	3	1	7	11	22
Hosmer, Eric	14	9	11	2	0	49	0	0	3	9	10	22
Brantley, Michael	18	7	11	5	5	68	0	2	5	5	10	22
Narvaez, Omar	18	11	5	3	0	54	1	2	5	7	7	22
Voit, Luke	11	9	7	1	1	39	0	0	4	2	15	21
Urshela, Giovanny	16	13	9	4	1	56	0	1	3	3	14	21
Yastrzemski, Mike	6	7	6	9	0	35	0	0	2	6	13	21
Tellez, Rowdy	14	6	5	3	0	43	0	2	1	5	13	21
Pillar, Kevin	15	14	13	4	0	70	0	0	1	8	12	21
Santana, Domingo	13	10	4	4	0	41	0	0	4	5	12	21
Pham, Tommy	16	12	7	8	2	56	0	1	3	5	12	21
Bradley Jr., Jackie	4	15	4	6	0	44	0	3	5	2	11	21
Correa, Carlos	9	6	4	4	0	28	0	1	5	6	9	21
Calhoun, Willie	11	7	7	2	0	32	0	2	4	6	9	21
Heyward, Jason	12	15	9	2	0	51	0	3	3	6	9	21
Frazier, Todd	16	13	7	3	1	50	0	1	4	10	6	21
Gurriel Jr., Lourdes	12	8	11	2	0	37	0	1	1	4	14	20
Santander, Anthony	15	12	4	2	1	42	0	0	3	3	14	20
Longoria, Evan	18	11	16	7	0	67	0	0	3	3	14	20
Adames, Willy	9	7	8	10	0	43	2	1	4	1	12	20
Adams, Matt	6	9	7	1	2	32	0	0	0	10	10	20
Anderson, Brian	19	9	3	5	0	49	0	2	3	6	9	20
Dozier, Brian	12	13	12	3	1	54	0	2	2	8	8	20
Profar, Jurickson	9	15	13	3	2	57	0	1	7	8	4	20
Desmond, Ian	10	6	4	3	1	38	0	0	1	3	15	19
Ahmed, Nick	19	11	11	8	3	63	0	1	0	3	15	19
Mazara, Nomar	8	14	10	1	0	44	0	1	3	2	13	19
Garcia, Avisail	7	7	9	6	3	40	0	1	0	6	12	19
Turner, Trea	13	13	9	5	0	55	0	0	2	5	12	19
Hiura, Keston	4	4	5	5	0	19	0	1	2	4	12	19
Seager, Corey	14	18	13	6	0	63	0	1	3	3	12	19
Choi, Ji-Man	10	16	6	5	1	48	0	1	1	8	9	19
Moreland, Mitch	6	8	3	2	0	31	0	2	4	4	9	19
Fowler, Dexter	15	10	14	11	1	55	0	2	4	5	8	19
Dietrich, Derek	2	5	5	4	0	21	1	1	6	3	8	19
Riley, Austin	2	11	5	3	0	28	0	1	1	3	13	18
Chavis, Michael	4	8	4	0	0	22	0	1	1	3	13	18
Ohtani, Shohei	9	11	5	2	0	34	0	0	2	5	11	18
McCann, James	10	5	3	3	0	27	0	1	3	3	11	18
Myers, Wil	8	8	4	6	1	34	0	2	2	4	10	18
Anderson, Tim	18	8	5	4	0	46	0	1	4	3	10	18
Alfaro, Jorge	4	9	7	3	1	34	0	2	4	3	9	18
Kelly, Carson	8	12	10	5	2	44	0	0	2	9	7	18
Kingery, Scott	11	9	12	3	1	47	0	3	4	4	7	18
Cabrera, Asdrubal	15	14	15	3	0	60	0	0	4	8	6	18
Murphy, Tom	7	4	3	2	1	22	0	2	4	6	6	18
Kendrick, Howie	9	6	12	7	0	42	0	0	0	3	14	17

Long Outs and Home Runs

Player	Long Out Distances						Home Run Distances					
	330	350	370	390	400+	Long	330	350	370	390	400+	HR
Franco, Maikel	11	4	11	4	0	36	0	1	0	3	13	17
Swanson, Dansby	14	10	12	5	2	63	0	0	1	6	10	17
Lowe, Brandon	8	3	6	3	1	28	1	0	2	4	10	17
Hernandez, Kike	14	12	9	6	2	54	1	0	2	4	10	17
Pence, Hunter	10	6	2	2	0	27	1	0	3	3	10	17
Robles, Victor	11	10	3	1	2	44	0	0	3	6	8	17
Goodwin, Brian	11	8	9	4	1	41	0	2	1	6	8	17
Chirinos, Robinson	3	4	5	4	3	29	1	1	2	5	8	17
Belt, Brandon	23	21	9	15	4	90	0	3	3	3	8	17
Kipnis, Jason	12	21	9	7	0	68	0	2	4	5	6	17
Suzuki, Kurt	8	10	2	3	0	39	0	3	2	7	5	17
d'Arnaud, Travis	5	11	4	5	0	39	0	1	2	3	10	16
Reynolds, Bryan	16	21	8	1	0	53	0	0	2	5	9	16
Jones, Adam	9	7	11	10	2	50	0	0	4	3	9	16
Biggio, Cavan	10	14	8	10	1	53	0	1	4	4	7	16
Gregorius, Didi	7	6	7	6	0	35	0	1	3	6	6	16
Winker, Jesse	11	6	6	1	0	36	0	4	6	2	4	16
Cooper, Garrett	7	7	4	3	1	24	0	0	1	1	13	15
Guerrero Jr., Vladimir	15	11	11	4	1	54	0	0	0	4	11	15
Haniger, Mitch	1	9	2	4	0	23	0	0	1	5	9	15
Carpenter, Matt	15	15	9	7	0	57	0	0	1	5	9	15
Gonzalez, Marwin	13	12	5	3	0	45	0	0	1	6	8	15
Votto, Joey	22	21	8	6	0	72	0	0	2	5	8	15
Pollock, A.J.	7	2	7	4	0	31	1	0	2	4	8	15
Beckham, Tim	5	6	2	2	0	19	0	0	2	6	7	15
Rosario, Amed	11	15	11	6	1	72	0	1	1	6	7	15
Eaton, Adam	7	13	23	6	0	69	0	3	2	3	7	15
La Stella, Tommy	10	8	8	0	0	39	0	0	4	5	6	15
Arcia, Orlando	22	15	9	8	0	62	0	2	3	4	6	15
Dixon, Brandon	7	6	10	5	4	39	0	1	5	3	6	15
Dahl, David	7	6	8	3	3	37	0	0	1	9	5	15
Drury, Brandon	9	10	10	4	1	41	0	0	2	10	3	15
Mercado, Oscar	23	10	7	5	0	60	1	0	2	9	3	15
Merrifield, Whit	21	16	14	5	0	73	0	0	4	5	5	14
Hernandez, Cesar	14	12	5	5	1	51	0	1	4	4	5	14
Reddick, Josh	14	12	10	4	1	62	0	1	4	5	4	14
Gordon, Alex	25	21	15	8	0	90	0	2	1	3	7	13
Murphy, Daniel	22	10	11	2	3	58	0	1	4	2	6	13
Benintendi, Andrew	19	13	16	5	2	70	0	1	2	5	4	13
Alberto, Hanser	13	13	9	2	0	58	0	0	2	5	5	12
Segura, Jean	10	25	8	3	1	56	0	1	4	2	5	12
Andrus, Elvis	20	17	9	7	0	66	0	1	1	6	4	12
Cabrera, Miguel	15	12	7	9	0	54	0	1	2	5	4	12
Cain, Lorenzo	16	13	5	5	1	56	0	0	2	4	5	11
Crawford, Brandon	11	18	9	6	0	53	0	0	3	3	5	11
Wong, Kolten	20	13	8	3	0	54	0	0	3	4	4	11
Molina, Yadier	12	14	12	7	1	62	0	0	2	3	5	10
Frazier, Adam	18	11	7	5	0	63	0	2	1	2	5	10
Garcia, Leury	11	9	6	2	0	50	0	0	0	3	5	8
Fletcher, David	26	11	8	4	0	66	0	2	1	1	2	6
Rojas, Miguel	19	11	10	2	1	61	0	0	1	1	3	5
Panik, Joe	16	13	18	6	0	66	0	0	2	1	2	5

Hard Hit Balls

Nate Weller

This season, a lot of attention was paid to the gaudy home run totals being posted by teams like the Twins and the numerous league-wide records that were seemingly being broken on a weekly basis. It all prompted plenty of discussions about launch angle, exit velocity, and even the makeup of the ball itself. But one thing was undeniable: players were seemingly hitting the ball harder than ever.

There are numbers outside of home runs that bear that out. The MLB hard-hit rate of 38% was the highest we have ever tracked, three points higher than the previous record which was set only last year. Before 2019, only one player had ever posted a hard-hit rate north of 50%. This year, nine different players accomplished that.

Leading the way was Aaron Judge. In an injury-shortened season, Judge hit the ball hard 128 times, accounting for 54% of his batted-balls. That 54% figure is also the second highest of all-time, trailing only Ryan Howard's 2007 season (55%).

While MLB as a whole was hitting the ball harder than ever, there were also some players who took notable tumbles. Last year's leader, Matt Carpenter, fell out of the top 100 entirely after seeing his hard-hit rate drop by seven percentage points. To make matters worse, his slugging percentage on those balls dropped to .925, well below the league average of 1.111, and almost 300 points lower than his mark from last season. While some of this could just be bad luck, Carpenter has some of the most blatant hitting tendencies in the league and saw a high percentage of extreme shifts and even some four-man outfields.

This section includes a full leaderboard of hard, medium and soft hit rates, reported on a per batted-ball basis, and also includes count and slugging percentage for each. All players with at least 250 plate appearances in 2019 are included.

Hard Hit Balls
Highest Percentage of Hard Hit Balls - Players with 250+ PA in 2019

Player	In Play	Hard		Medium		Soft		Overall			
		Count	SLG	Count	SLG	Count	SLG	Hard Pct	Medium Pct	Soft Pct	SLG
Judge, Aaron	238	128	1.313	88	.345	22	.273	53.8%	37.0%	9.2%	.861
Sano, Miguel	222	117	1.650	85	.306	20	.000	52.7%	38.3%	9.0%	.991
Cruz, Nelson	326	171	1.518	116	.250	39	.154	52.5%	35.6%	12.0%	.898
Gallo, Joey	129	67	1.836	45	.442	17	.118	51.9%	34.9%	13.2%	1.134
Castro, Jason	151	78	1.130	55	.273	18	.059	51.7%	36.4%	11.9%	.691
Alvarez, Yordan	221	113	1.550	86	.349	22	.136	51.1%	38.9%	10.0%	.936
Yelich, Christian	374	190	1.481	130	.273	54	.241	50.8%	34.8%	14.4%	.884
Turner, Justin	395	199	.985	147	.290	49	.184	50.4%	37.2%	12.4%	.626
Olson, Matt	346	174	1.295	118	.288	54	.093	50.3%	34.1%	15.6%	.762
Ohtani, Shohei	278	138	1.059	116	.391	24	.250	49.6%	41.7%	8.6%	.708
Bellinger, Cody	455	224	1.305	171	.281	60	.267	49.2%	37.6%	13.2%	.778
Thames, Eric	258	126	1.250	98	.398	34	.176	48.8%	38.0%	13.2%	.781
Kelly, Carson	236	115	1.132	79	.152	42	.214	48.7%	33.5%	17.8%	.638
Ozuna, Marcell	372	179	1.039	149	.277	44	.068	48.1%	40.1%	11.8%	.620
Harper, Bryce	399	192	1.237	165	.294	42	.214	48.1%	41.4%	10.5%	.739
Goldschmidt, Paul	434	206	1.089	165	.303	63	.206	47.5%	38.0%	14.5%	.659
Donaldson, Josh	396	188	1.277	148	.260	60	.133	47.5%	37.4%	15.2%	.726
Forsythe, Logan	219	104	.806	86	.306	29	.103	47.5%	39.3%	13.2%	.516
VanMeter, Josh	173	82	.902	70	.232	21	.143	47.4%	40.5%	12.1%	.541
Garver, Mitch	226	107	1.710	78	.132	41	.073	47.3%	34.5%	18.1%	.875
Myers, Wil	269	127	1.143	95	.295	47	.217	47.2%	35.3%	17.5%	.682
Reyes, Franmil	345	163	1.375	134	.223	48	.083	47.2%	38.8%	13.9%	.749
Renfroe, Hunter	292	137	1.343	110	.250	45	.111	46.9%	37.7%	15.4%	.752
Freeman, Freddie	472	221	1.145	193	.339	58	.190	46.8%	40.9%	12.3%	.698
Suarez, Eugenio	392	183	1.542	150	.320	59	.136	46.7%	38.3%	15.1%	.852
Soler, Jorge	415	194	1.492	167	.213	54	.222	46.7%	40.2%	13.0%	.815
Hoskins, Rhys	403	186	1.092	154	.333	63	.127	46.2%	38.2%	15.6%	.652
Walker, Christian	375	173	1.227	149	.215	53	.170	46.1%	39.7%	14.1%	.674
Acuna Jr., Ronald	439	202	1.282	175	.276	62	.274	46.0%	39.9%	14.1%	.740
Davis, Khris	337	155	1.000	142	.190	40	.150	46.0%	42.1%	11.9%	.555
Martinez, J.D.	442	203	1.255	194	.307	45	.222	45.9%	43.9%	10.2%	.732
Kingery, Scott	314	144	1.156	126	.389	44	.114	45.9%	40.1%	14.0%	.698
Braun, Ryan	357	163	1.168	133	.242	61	.197	45.7%	37.3%	17.1%	.655
Odor, Rougned	346	158	1.210	126	.230	62	.164	45.7%	36.4%	17.9%	.666
Realmuto, J.T.	423	193	1.085	170	.271	60	.250	45.6%	40.2%	14.2%	.639
Muncy, Max	342	156	1.335	147	.264	39	.154	45.6%	43.0%	11.4%	.743
Kendrick, Howie	290	132	1.108	117	.342	41	.195	45.5%	40.3%	14.1%	.670
Meadows, Austin	399	181	1.276	165	.315	53	.245	45.4%	41.4%	13.3%	.742
Grandal, Yasmani	379	172	1.183	151	.248	56	.054	45.4%	39.8%	14.8%	.642
Bell, Josh	416	189	1.339	172	.262	55	.127	45.4%	41.3%	13.2%	.733
Mazara, Nomar	327	148	1.054	116	.321	63	.161	45.3%	35.5%	19.3%	.626
Dozier, Hunter	380	172	1.300	155	.316	53	.075	45.3%	40.8%	13.9%	.728
Chapman, Matt	439	199	1.286	170	.156	70	.186	45.3%	38.7%	15.9%	.677
Pederson, Joc	341	154	1.351	131	.194	56	.161	45.2%	38.4%	16.4%	.714
Springer, George	370	167	1.392	142	.288	61	.197	45.1%	38.4%	16.5%	.773
Choo, Shin-Soo	399	179	1.117	173	.297	47	.106	44.9%	43.4%	11.8%	.643
Correa, Carlos	207	93	1.489	71	.243	43	.186	44.9%	34.3%	20.8%	.783
Santana, Danny	328	147	1.333	139	.372	42	.238	44.8%	42.4%	12.8%	.783
Rendon, Anthony	468	209	1.267	180	.293	79	.177	44.7%	38.5%	16.9%	.710
Bregman, Alex	479	214	1.184	194	.362	71	.127	44.7%	40.5%	14.8%	.696
Anderson, Brian	348	154	1.144	126	.234	68	.162	44.3%	36.2%	19.5%	.623
Granderson, Curtis	221	98	.959	100	.192	23	.043	44.3%	45.2%	10.4%	.516
Longoria, Evan	346	153	.967	155	.283	38	.237	44.2%	44.8%	11.0%	.581
Hiura, Keston	208	92	1.489	81	.438	35	.200	44.2%	38.9%	16.8%	.865
Story, Trevor	417	184	1.407	182	.331	51	.196	44.1%	43.6%	12.2%	.787
McMahon, Ryan	322	142	1.248	133	.235	47	.191	44.1%	41.3%	14.6%	.675
Cabrera, Miguel	390	172	.853	171	.250	47	.191	44.1%	43.8%	12.1%	.509
Urshela, Giovanny	359	158	1.103	155	.359	46	.196	44.0%	43.2%	12.8%	.665
Hernandez, Teoscar	265	116	1.365	106	.302	43	.186	43.8%	40.0%	16.2%	.746
Trout, Mike	354	155	1.654	153	.278	46	.174	43.8%	43.2%	13.0%	.866
Verdugo, Alex	300	131	.976	117	.278	52	.135	43.7%	39.0%	17.3%	.554
Pollock, A.J.	238	104	1.137	93	.198	41	.244	43.7%	39.1%	17.2%	.615
Alfaro, Jorge	279	122	1.150	107	.318	50	.220	43.7%	38.4%	17.9%	.661
Pham, Tommy	445	194	.959	183	.290	68	.250	43.6%	41.1%	15.3%	.574
Gurriel Jr., Lourdes	232	101	1.384	87	.294	44	.182	43.5%	37.5%	19.0%	.746
Machado, Manny	462	201	1.080	173	.249	88	.149	43.5%	37.4%	19.0%	.590
Jones, JaCoby	205	89	1.148	89	.273	27	.074	43.4%	43.4%	13.2%	.631
Bruce, Jay	231	100	1.381	90	.244	41	.146	43.3%	39.0%	17.7%	.711
La Stella, Tommy	264	114	.982	112	.241	38	.079	43.2%	42.4%	14.4%	.538
Peralta, David	296	128	1.047	118	.322	50	.100	43.2%	39.9%	16.9%	.597
Betts, Mookie	505	217	.967	230	.434	58	.172	43.0%	45.5%	11.5%	.631
Santana, Carlos	467	201	1.209	190	.234	76	.105	43.0%	40.7%	16.3%	.634

Hard Hit Balls
Highest Percentage of Hard Hit Balls - Players with 250+ PA in 2019

Player	In Play	Hard Count	Hard SLG	Medium Count	Medium SLG	Soft Count	Soft SLG	Hard Pct	Medium Pct	Soft Pct	SLG
Lowe, Brandon	184	79	1.423	84	.429	21	.238	42.9%	45.7%	11.4%	.831
Cabrera, Asdrubal	351	150	1.041	158	.277	43	.047	42.7%	45.0%	12.3%	.573
Castellanos, Nicholas	475	203	1.124	212	.376	60	.283	42.7%	44.6%	12.6%	.684
Choi, Ji-Man	309	132	1.125	145	.282	32	.125	42.7%	46.9%	10.4%	.623
Smoak, Justin	309	132	1.069	133	.188	44	.068	42.7%	43.0%	14.2%	.545
Jansen, Danny	270	115	.887	108	.178	47	.087	42.6%	40.0%	17.4%	.466
Reynolds, Bryan	373	159	1.076	153	.421	61	.230	42.6%	41.0%	16.4%	.668
Swanson, Dansby	365	155	1.033	165	.242	45	.156	42.5%	45.2%	12.3%	.568
Pence, Hunter	219	93	1.315	95	.330	31	.194	42.5%	43.4%	14.2%	.728
Yastrzemski, Mike	268	114	1.310	108	.333	46	.196	42.5%	40.3%	17.2%	.727
O'Hearn, Ryan	231	98	1.052	100	.152	33	.121	42.4%	43.3%	14.3%	.528
Kepler, Max	429	182	1.260	163	.181	84	.179	42.4%	38.0%	19.6%	.640
Diaz, Yandy	250	106	1.113	100	.250	44	.091	42.4%	40.0%	17.6%	.593
Calhoun, Kole	392	166	1.295	173	.234	53	.057	42.3%	44.1%	13.5%	.662
Albies, Ozzie	532	225	1.049	228	.283	79	.278	42.3%	42.9%	14.8%	.606
Riley, Austin	168	71	1.464	58	.397	39	.128	42.3%	34.5%	23.2%	.777
Seager, Corey	395	167	1.098	170	.278	58	.155	42.3%	43.0%	14.7%	.604
Lindor, Francisco	507	214	1.181	210	.245	83	.134	42.2%	41.4%	16.4%	.620
Adames, Willy	382	161	.957	170	.355	51	.176	42.1%	44.5%	13.4%	.587
Sanchez, Gary	271	114	1.540	103	.243	54	.148	42.1%	38.0%	19.9%	.770
Arenado, Nolan	503	212	1.297	206	.318	85	.094	42.1%	41.0%	16.9%	.693
Schwarber, Kyle	379	159	1.538	172	.207	48	.125	42.0%	45.4%	12.7%	.753
Alonso, Pete	417	175	1.688	176	.286	66	.091	42.0%	42.2%	15.8%	.841
Semien, Marcus	556	233	1.202	240	.226	83	.108	41.9%	43.2%	14.9%	.618
Castro, Starlin	534	224	.936	225	.262	85	.165	41.9%	42.1%	15.9%	.528
Santana, Domingo	289	121	1.258	130	.287	38	.289	41.9%	45.0%	13.1%	.693
Tatis Jr., Fernando	227	95	1.574	83	.395	49	.347	41.9%	36.6%	21.6%	.879
Marte, Ketel	485	203	1.318	206	.243	76	.289	41.9%	42.5%	15.7%	.698
Molina, Yadier	366	153	.776	159	.290	54	.074	41.8%	43.4%	14.8%	.463
Aguilar, Jesus	240	100	.969	100	.278	40	.050	41.7%	41.7%	16.7%	.524
Brantley, Michael	513	214	1.005	231	.293	68	.132	41.7%	45.0%	13.3%	.568
Flowers, Tyler	168	70	1.232	74	.315	24	.167	41.7%	44.0%	14.3%	.675
DeJong, Paul	440	183	1.160	173	.231	84	.119	41.6%	39.3%	19.1%	.597
Naylor, Josh	190	79	.962	76	.307	35	.086	41.6%	40.0%	18.4%	.540
Carpenter, Matt	293	122	.925	138	.328	33	.242	41.6%	47.1%	11.3%	.568
Tellez, Rowdy	257	107	1.267	110	.229	40	.200	41.6%	42.8%	15.6%	.654
Davis, J.D.	315	131	1.214	148	.308	36	.333	41.6%	47.0%	11.4%	.690
d'Arnaud, Travis	272	113	1.036	107	.308	52	.115	41.5%	39.3%	19.1%	.571
Moustakas, Mike	427	177	1.260	161	.226	89	.124	41.5%	37.7%	20.8%	.635
Votto, Joey	405	168	.867	196	.303	41	.317	41.5%	48.4%	10.1%	.537
Vogt, Stephen	193	80	1.127	94	.297	19	.474	41.5%	48.7%	9.8%	.661
Sandoval, Pablo	210	87	1.306	83	.210	40	.256	41.4%	39.5%	19.0%	.673
Dixon, Brandon	259	107	1.155	109	.431	43	.093	41.3%	42.1%	16.6%	.667
Soto, Juan	416	172	1.292	192	.389	52	.115	41.3%	46.2%	12.5%	.724
Escobar, Eduardo	516	213	1.135	237	.330	66	.197	41.3%	45.9%	12.8%	.642
Gonzalez, Marwin	328	135	.948	152	.291	41	.098	41.2%	46.3%	12.5%	.538
Cron, C.J.	353	145	1.174	149	.264	59	.119	41.1%	42.2%	16.7%	.613
Upton, Justin	146	60	1.190	57	.352	29	.103	41.1%	39.0%	19.9%	.645
Edman, Tommy	265	109	1.000	115	.426	41	.122	41.1%	43.4%	15.5%	.615
Markakis, Nick	361	148	.814	164	.280	49	.224	41.0%	45.4%	13.6%	.490
Winker, Jesse	278	114	1.079	121	.240	43	.186	41.0%	43.5%	15.5%	.576
Pinder, Chad	257	105	1.000	110	.296	42	.146	40.9%	42.8%	16.3%	.561
Cooper, Garrett	272	111	1.145	110	.349	51	.118	40.8%	40.4%	18.8%	.630
Altuve, Jose	422	172	1.181	176	.289	74	.311	40.8%	41.7%	17.5%	.658
Belt, Brandon	403	164	.870	184	.350	55	.145	40.7%	45.7%	13.6%	.531
Rodriguez, Ronny	199	81	1.213	82	.231	36	.167	40.7%	41.2%	18.1%	.624
Abreu, Jose	492	200	1.214	215	.344	77	.117	40.7%	43.7%	15.7%	.662
Calhoun, Willie	258	105	1.288	105	.231	48	.083	40.7%	40.7%	18.6%	.633
Naquin, Tyler	212	86	1.047	85	.378	41	.175	40.6%	40.1%	19.3%	.615
Luplow, Jordan	165	67	1.606	79	.190	19	.158	40.6%	47.9%	11.5%	.756
Hernandez, Kike	321	130	.992	139	.292	52	.058	40.5%	43.3%	16.2%	.536
Senzel, Nick	275	111	1.009	115	.313	49	.265	40.4%	41.8%	17.8%	.584
LeMahieu, DJ	517	209	1.014	234	.392	74	.151	40.4%	45.3%	14.3%	.609
Ramirez, Jose	414	167	1.129	173	.199	74	.176	40.3%	41.8%	17.9%	.566
Beaty, Matt	216	87	.977	92	.250	37	.162	40.3%	42.6%	17.1%	.528
Perez, Roberto	273	110	1.352	122	.226	41	.103	40.3%	44.7%	15.0%	.672
Maldonado, Martin	249	100	.960	108	.217	41	.146	40.2%	43.4%	16.5%	.512
Reyes, Victor	214	86	.976	104	.240	24	.500	40.2%	48.6%	11.2%	.561
Goodrum, Niko	287	115	1.123	132	.305	40	.250	40.1%	46.0%	13.9%	.625
Hosmer, Eric	461	185	1.071	192	.265	84	.202	40.1%	41.6%	18.2%	.577
Blackmon, Charlie	481	193	1.263	213	.389	75	.160	40.1%	44.3%	15.6%	.702
Garcia, Avisail	367	147	1.158	151	.282	69	.232	40.1%	41.1%	18.8%	.624
McCann, Brian	230	92	1.045	95	.215	43	.047	40.0%	41.3%	18.7%	.509

Hard Hit Balls

Highest Percentage of Hard Hit Balls - Players with 250+ PA in 2019

Player	In Play	Hard Count	Hard SLG	Medium Count	Medium SLG	Soft Count	Soft SLG	Hard Pct	Medium Pct	Soft Pct	SLG
Laureano, Ramon	320	128	1.339	140	.293	52	.333	40.0%	43.8%	16.3%	.727
McCann, James	303	121	1.283	140	.336	42	.024	39.9%	46.2%	13.9%	.669
Encarnacion, Edwin	318	127	1.452	129	.260	62	.097	39.9%	40.6%	19.5%	.705
Piscotty, Stephen	277	110	1.028	138	.213	29	.241	39.7%	49.8%	10.5%	.538
Canha, Mark	305	121	1.400	128	.283	56	.143	39.7%	42.0%	18.4%	.700
Mercado, Oscar	365	145	.986	160	.299	60	.138	39.7%	43.8%	16.4%	.548
Torres, Gleyber	423	168	1.349	192	.316	63	.143	39.7%	45.4%	14.9%	.702
Castro, Harold	273	108	.869	138	.286	27	.185	39.6%	50.5%	9.9%	.509
Biggio, Cavan	233	92	1.144	112	.375	29	.241	39.5%	48.1%	12.4%	.658
Polanco, Jorge	524	207	1.005	237	.362	80	.215	39.5%	45.2%	15.3%	.594
Chirinos, Robinson	248	98	1.221	106	.388	44	.140	39.5%	42.7%	17.7%	.672
Guzman, Ronald	173	68	1.254	73	.271	32	.094	39.3%	42.2%	18.5%	.627
Crawford, Brandon	387	152	.845	167	.269	68	.074	39.3%	43.2%	17.6%	.457
Moncada, Yoan	361	142	1.411	175	.413	44	.227	39.3%	48.5%	12.2%	.784
Dickerson, Corey	207	81	1.288	82	.438	44	.205	39.1%	39.6%	21.3%	.721
Pujols, Albert	431	168	1.006	179	.210	84	.119	39.0%	41.5%	19.5%	.499
Gordon, Alex	463	180	.830	216	.299	67	.152	38.9%	46.7%	14.5%	.482
Voit, Luke	288	112	1.241	138	.365	38	.263	38.9%	47.9%	13.2%	.693
Rosario, Eddie	482	187	1.180	221	.256	74	.122	38.8%	45.9%	15.4%	.590
Bogaerts, Xander	498	193	1.243	235	.382	70	.243	38.8%	47.2%	14.1%	.693
Adams, Matt	196	76	1.440	83	.386	37	.108	38.8%	42.3%	18.9%	.738
Dozier, Brian	312	121	1.058	134	.313	57	.175	38.8%	42.9%	18.3%	.576
Desmond, Ian	327	127	1.230	147	.352	53	.113	38.8%	45.0%	16.2%	.654
Dietrich, Derek	178	69	1.485	67	.179	42	.071	38.8%	37.6%	23.6%	.655
Zunino, Mike	168	65	1.123	68	.088	35	.114	38.7%	40.5%	20.8%	.494
Puig, Yasiel	426	165	1.209	175	.243	86	.174	38.7%	41.1%	20.2%	.602
Schoop, Jonathan	318	123	1.301	120	.269	75	.173	38.7%	37.7%	23.6%	.647
Gurriel, Yuli	505	195	1.135	220	.329	90	.167	38.6%	43.6%	17.8%	.611
Andrus, Elvis	514	198	.845	244	.259	72	.153	38.5%	47.5%	14.0%	.468
Vogelbach, Daniel	315	121	1.378	133	.233	61	.131	38.4%	42.2%	19.4%	.649
Merrifield, Whit	558	214	.986	267	.325	77	.260	38.4%	47.8%	13.8%	.569
Drury, Brandon	308	118	1.060	115	.219	75	.147	38.3%	37.3%	24.4%	.521
Hicks, Aaron	152	58	1.386	60	.276	34	.088	38.2%	39.5%	22.4%	.658
Bader, Harrison	233	89	.977	106	.356	38	.105	38.2%	45.5%	16.3%	.552
Jimenez, Eloy	336	128	1.370	147	.363	61	.213	38.1%	43.8%	18.2%	.719
Benintendi, Andrew	409	156	.876	198	.454	55	.204	38.1%	48.4%	13.4%	.581
Galvis, Freddy	415	158	1.058	202	.358	55	.127	38.1%	48.7%	13.3%	.592
Cano, Robinson	324	123	.992	144	.270	57	.123	38.0%	44.4%	17.6%	.520
Davis, Chris	171	65	1.095	87	.279	19	.368	38.0%	50.9%	11.1%	.595
Taylor, Chris	258	98	1.186	124	.378	36	.257	38.0%	48.1%	14.0%	.673
Seager, Kyle	309	117	1.086	157	.333	35	.171	37.9%	50.8%	11.3%	.599
Hicks, John	211	80	1.213	90	.236	41	.073	37.9%	42.7%	19.4%	.576
Santander, Anthony	298	113	1.204	128	.298	57	.140	37.9%	43.0%	19.1%	.616
Murphy, Tom	174	66	1.677	79	.342	29	.103	37.9%	45.4%	16.7%	.803
Gamel, Ben	209	79	.857	100	.440	30	.200	37.8%	47.8%	14.4%	.560
Mondesi, Adalberto	291	110	1.057	123	.429	58	.241	37.8%	42.3%	19.9%	.624
Turner, Trea	410	155	1.078	185	.413	70	.243	37.8%	45.1%	17.1%	.635
Goodwin, Brian	288	109	1.290	129	.331	50	.280	37.8%	44.8%	17.4%	.683
Profar, Jurickson	387	146	.966	156	.240	85	.129	37.7%	40.3%	22.0%	.490
Marte, Starling	451	170	1.059	195	.391	86	.202	37.7%	43.2%	19.1%	.609
Devers, Rafael	530	200	1.280	236	.369	94	.160	37.7%	44.5%	17.7%	.681
Maybin, Cameron	167	63	1.365	70	.329	34	.265	37.7%	41.9%	20.4%	.707
Jones, Adam	387	146	.972	177	.278	64	.188	37.7%	45.7%	16.5%	.523
Ahmed, Nick	456	172	1.091	208	.262	76	.132	37.7%	45.6%	16.7%	.549
Ervin, Phillip	175	66	1.156	74	.392	35	.200	37.7%	42.3%	20.0%	.636
McNeil, Jeff	436	164	1.146	223	.329	49	.204	37.6%	51.1%	11.2%	.623
Candelario, Jeimer	237	89	.888	101	.270	47	.149	37.6%	42.6%	19.8%	.479
Walker, Neil	261	98	.753	121	.421	42	.214	37.5%	46.4%	16.1%	.512
Fowler, Dexter	350	131	1.047	157	.312	62	.258	37.4%	44.9%	17.7%	.577
McKinney, Billy	182	68	1.269	81	.218	33	.121	37.4%	44.5%	18.1%	.596
Baez, Javier	377	141	1.450	168	.371	68	.250	37.4%	44.6%	18.0%	.752
Flores, Wilmer	235	88	1.023	109	.306	38	.158	37.4%	46.4%	16.2%	.551
Rizzo, Anthony	429	160	1.250	190	.250	79	.244	37.3%	44.3%	18.4%	.624
Grichuk, Randal	425	158	1.236	185	.315	82	.195	37.2%	43.5%	19.3%	.634
Mercer, Jordy	199	74	1.027	79	.329	46	.217	37.2%	39.7%	23.1%	.563
Cuthbert, Cheslor	242	90	.811	107	.336	45	.178	37.2%	44.2%	18.6%	.483
Pillar, Kevin	529	197	.932	225	.305	107	.159	37.2%	42.5%	20.2%	.506
Mancini, Trey	464	172	1.404	219	.302	73	.233	37.1%	47.2%	15.7%	.702
Martinez, Jose	254	94	.989	124	.320	36	.139	37.0%	48.8%	14.2%	.544
Contreras, Willson	260	96	1.516	108	.299	56	.286	36.9%	41.5%	21.5%	.744
Panik, Joe	397	146	.662	177	.254	74	.111	36.8%	44.6%	18.6%	.376
Kipnis, Jason	381	140	.993	186	.225	55	.204	36.7%	48.8%	14.4%	.508
Nunez, Renato	402	147	1.290	173	.292	82	.146	36.6%	43.0%	20.4%	.626

Hard Hit Balls
Highest Percentage of Hard Hit Balls - Players with 250+ PA in 2019

Player	In Play	Hard Count	Hard SLG	Medium Count	Medium SLG	Soft Count	Soft SLG	Hard Pct	Medium Pct	Soft Pct	SLG
McCutchen, Andrew	164	60	1.283	83	.229	21	.190	36.6%	50.6%	12.8%	.610
Conforto, Michael	405	148	1.370	202	.307	55	.182	36.5%	49.9%	13.6%	.678
Cain, Lorenzo	460	168	.799	217	.286	75	.213	36.5%	47.2%	16.3%	.458
Dahl, David	271	99	1.309	136	.481	36	.167	36.5%	50.2%	13.3%	.742
Berti, Jon	184	67	.955	81	.407	36	.222	36.4%	44.0%	19.6%	.568
Bote, David	212	77	1.221	104	.255	31	.258	36.3%	49.1%	14.6%	.610
Bradley Jr., Jackie	344	123	1.174	166	.366	55	.111	35.8%	48.3%	16.0%	.614
Bryant, Kris	400	143	1.366	190	.407	67	.179	35.8%	47.5%	16.8%	.711
Stewart, Christin	272	97	1.031	131	.294	44	.159	35.7%	48.2%	16.2%	.538
Prado, Martin	207	74	.575	98	.281	35	.086	35.7%	47.3%	16.9%	.353
Posey, Buster	336	120	.731	171	.318	45	.178	35.7%	50.9%	13.4%	.446
Rojas, Miguel	427	152	.752	214	.278	61	.200	35.6%	50.1%	14.3%	.435
Nimmo, Brandon	132	47	1.348	66	.281	19	.056	35.6%	50.0%	14.4%	.633
Kemp, Tony	203	72	.929	101	.263	30	.069	35.5%	49.8%	14.8%	.470
Lucroy, Jonathan	245	87	.859	115	.228	43	.116	35.5%	46.9%	17.6%	.430
Shaw, Travis	141	50	.960	65	.185	26	.077	35.5%	46.1%	18.4%	.440
Moreland, Mitch	226	80	1.367	120	.336	26	.115	35.4%	53.1%	11.5%	.674
Holt, Brock	206	73	.757	103	.412	30	.300	35.4%	50.0%	14.6%	.515
Buxton, Byron	206	73	1.333	91	.427	42	.119	35.4%	44.2%	20.4%	.685
Haniger, Mitch	167	59	1.492	73	.310	35	.114	35.3%	43.7%	21.0%	.691
Heyward, Jason	406	143	1.141	191	.243	72	.167	35.2%	47.0%	17.7%	.546
White, Tyler	165	58	.873	84	.262	23	.130	35.2%	50.9%	13.9%	.451
Sogard, Eric	339	119	1.034	160	.329	60	.153	35.1%	47.2%	17.7%	.544
Ramirez, Harold	331	116	1.035	156	.288	59	.186	35.0%	47.1%	17.8%	.530
Guerrero Jr., Vladimir	375	131	.992	166	.358	78	.167	34.9%	44.3%	20.8%	.539
Castillo, Welington	158	55	1.340	71	.310	32	.094	34.8%	44.9%	20.3%	.615
Ruiz, Rio	285	99	.990	130	.281	56	.107	34.7%	45.6%	19.6%	.493
Arraez, Luis	300	104	.816	159	.354	37	.083	34.7%	53.0%	12.3%	.481
Grossman, Robbie	336	116	.696	167	.313	53	.264	34.5%	49.7%	15.8%	.437
Phegley, Josh	258	89	.966	123	.331	46	.130	34.5%	47.7%	17.8%	.514
Gregorius, Didi	273	94	1.215	124	.211	55	.073	34.4%	45.4%	20.1%	.528
Suzuki, Kurt	247	85	1.205	113	.250	49	.163	34.4%	45.7%	19.8%	.557
Moran, Colin	353	121	1.076	177	.354	55	.182	34.3%	50.1%	15.6%	.573
Simmons, Andrelton	361	124	.815	167	.228	70	.086	34.3%	46.3%	19.4%	.402
Gardner, Brett	386	132	1.351	175	.364	79	.089	34.2%	45.3%	20.5%	.645
Beckham, Tim	202	69	1.478	86	.314	47	.234	34.2%	42.6%	23.3%	.693
Eaton, Adam	472	161	.963	219	.314	92	.244	34.1%	46.4%	19.5%	.526
Osuna, Jose	217	74	1.155	102	.307	41	.146	34.1%	47.0%	18.9%	.559
Wong, Kolten	406	138	.927	184	.331	84	.205	34.0%	45.3%	20.7%	.511
Nola, Austin	177	60	1.237	79	.333	38	.237	33.9%	44.6%	21.5%	.617
Tauchman, Mike	190	64	1.250	97	.427	29	.345	33.7%	51.1%	15.3%	.693
Barnhart, Tucker	235	79	1.101	117	.267	39	.053	33.6%	49.8%	16.6%	.515
Chavis, Michael	220	74	1.351	100	.400	46	.304	33.6%	45.5%	20.9%	.700
Vazquez, Christian	387	130	1.134	208	.383	49	.146	33.6%	53.7%	12.7%	.604
Caratini, Victor	188	63	1.274	98	.292	27	.074	33.5%	52.1%	14.4%	.589
Margot, Manuel	313	105	1.019	145	.246	63	.190	33.5%	46.3%	20.1%	.497
Moore, Dylan	155	52	1.288	68	.338	35	.176	33.5%	43.9%	22.6%	.623
Frazier, Todd	341	114	1.237	159	.283	68	.176	33.4%	46.6%	19.9%	.581
Rosario, Amed	497	166	1.025	259	.322	72	.225	33.4%	52.1%	14.5%	.541
Lugo, Dawel	217	72	.873	112	.312	33	.242	33.2%	51.6%	15.2%	.488
Kinsler, Ian	205	68	.940	88	.250	49	.204	33.2%	42.9%	23.9%	.466
Franco, Maikel	331	110	1.101	144	.218	77	.104	33.2%	43.5%	23.3%	.485
Severino, Pedro	235	78	1.224	111	.273	46	.109	33.2%	47.2%	19.6%	.552
Arcia, Orlando	393	130	.872	186	.273	77	.182	33.1%	47.3%	19.6%	.449
Segura, Jean	507	168	.880	234	.305	105	.240	33.1%	46.2%	20.7%	.481
Kiermaier, Kevin	345	114	1.035	164	.325	67	.119	33.0%	47.5%	19.4%	.519
Alonso, Yonder	224	74	1.082	110	.156	40	.125	33.0%	49.1%	17.9%	.455
Wilkerson, Stevie	224	74	1.247	114	.268	36	.139	33.0%	50.9%	16.1%	.570
Gomes, Yan	231	76	1.160	115	.235	40	.200	32.9%	49.8%	17.3%	.530
Duggar, Steven	186	61	.966	91	.267	34	.235	32.8%	48.9%	18.3%	.486
Hernandez, Cesar	516	169	.922	238	.314	109	.202	32.8%	46.1%	21.1%	.488
Rengifo, Luis	268	87	.988	137	.281	44	.182	32.5%	51.1%	16.4%	.492
Anderson, Tim	391	126	1.224	194	.415	71	.282	32.2%	49.6%	18.2%	.650
Reddick, Josh	445	143	.894	226	.317	76	.132	32.1%	50.8%	17.1%	.471
Garcia, Greg	231	74	.986	110	.271	47	.170	32.0%	47.6%	20.3%	.482
Fletcher, David	534	171	.684	269	.326	94	.266	32.0%	50.4%	17.6%	.430
Wendle, Joey	194	62	.758	101	.245	31	.323	32.0%	52.1%	16.0%	.424
Ramos, Wilson	407	130	.961	203	.313	74	.135	31.9%	49.9%	18.2%	.488
Peraza, Jose	320	102	.673	154	.359	64	.109	31.9%	48.1%	20.0%	.409
Hedges, Austin	206	65	1.154	93	.154	48	.170	31.6%	45.1%	23.3%	.478
Marisnick, Jake	200	63	1.270	93	.400	44	.091	31.5%	46.5%	22.0%	.609
Diaz, Elias	251	79	.684	105	.317	67	.104	31.5%	41.8%	26.7%	.377
Bauers, Jake	260	81	1.200	131	.240	48	.229	31.2%	50.4%	18.5%	.537

Hard Hit Balls

Highest Percentage of Hard Hit Balls - Players with 250+ PA in 2019

Player	In Play	Hard		Medium		Soft		Overall			
		Count	SLG	Count	SLG	Count	SLG	Hard Pct	Medium Pct	Soft Pct	SLG
Locastro, Tim	170	53	.784	74	.243	43	.326	31.2%	43.5%	25.3%	.429
Parra, Gerardo	218	68	1.077	117	.265	33	.182	31.2%	53.7%	15.1%	.498
Allen, Greg	183	57	.893	95	.312	31	.034	31.1%	51.9%	16.9%	.449
Cabrera, Melky	338	105	.952	152	.250	81	.163	31.1%	45.0%	24.0%	.448
DeShields, Delino	267	83	.901	148	.305	36	.229	31.1%	55.4%	13.5%	.482
Iglesias, Jose	437	134	.962	217	.276	86	.221	30.7%	49.7%	19.7%	.472
Almora Jr., Albert	284	87	1.023	129	.266	68	.119	30.6%	45.4%	23.9%	.466
Martin, Leonys	161	49	1.306	80	.169	32	.125	30.4%	49.7%	19.9%	.513
Murphy, Daniel	368	112	.982	194	.428	62	.131	30.4%	52.7%	16.8%	.544
Hampson, Garrett	215	65	1.190	102	.250	48	.313	30.2%	47.4%	22.3%	.545
Tapia, Raimel	326	98	1.010	172	.384	56	.214	30.1%	52.8%	17.2%	.543
Wolters, Tony	299	90	.591	161	.353	48	.234	30.1%	53.8%	16.1%	.405
Frazier, Adam	484	144	.882	251	.372	89	.136	29.8%	51.9%	18.4%	.482
Narvaez, Omar	339	101	1.250	176	.351	62	.177	29.8%	51.9%	18.3%	.586
Smith Jr., Dwight	280	82	1.099	141	.365	57	.140	29.3%	50.4%	20.4%	.535
Dyson, Jarrod	317	93	.761	155	.288	69	.203	29.3%	48.9%	21.8%	.408
Villar, Jonathan	472	137	1.412	232	.366	103	.155	29.0%	49.2%	21.8%	.624
Garcia, Leury	452	129	.921	259	.360	64	.188	28.5%	57.3%	14.2%	.498
Crawford, J.P.	268	76	1.000	131	.364	61	.119	28.4%	48.9%	22.8%	.489
Sanchez, Yolmer	389	106	.724	203	.354	80	.177	27.2%	52.2%	20.6%	.420
Newman, Kevin	434	116	.948	230	.410	88	.193	26.7%	53.0%	20.3%	.510
Smith, Mallex	372	98	.907	181	.324	93	.269	26.3%	48.7%	25.0%	.463
Lopez, Nicky	331	84	.759	183	.260	64	.143	25.4%	55.3%	19.3%	.376
Robles, Victor	417	104	1.301	212	.363	101	.212	24.9%	50.8%	24.2%	.564
Martin Jr., Richie	205	51	1.184	106	.225	48	.208	24.9%	51.7%	23.4%	.457
Alberto, Hanser	480	118	.949	278	.326	84	.241	24.6%	57.9%	17.5%	.466
Lagares, Juan	186	45	1.136	107	.276	34	.147	24.2%	57.5%	18.3%	.459
Hamilton, Billy	234	55	.528	117	.430	62	.161	23.5%	50.0%	26.5%	.380
Gordon, Dee	341	75	.877	194	.316	72	.246	22.0%	56.9%	21.1%	.425
All MLB	125736	47785	1.111	56551	.297	21400	.168	38.0%	45.0%	17.0%	.585

Pinch Hitting

Mark Simon

Pinch-hitters combined to hit .222/.314/.394 in 2019.

Don't scoff at that. Pinch-hitting is hard and that's actually a good season for them. Not surprisingly, the power numbers improved considerably over years past, just as they improved for just about everyone else.

Giants fan favorite Pablo Sandoval was the premier pinch-hitter in 2019, hitting .375 with an MLB-leading 18 hits. He's fit into that role nicely the last two seasons. He was 8-for-28 (.286) in that role in 2018.

Jose Osuna of the Pirates hit as many home runs as a pinch-hitter as he did when he otherwise played. His five pinch-hit homers led the majors. Gerardo Parra, Charlie Culberson, Tyler Austin, and Osuna all tied for the MLB lead with 10 pinch-hit RBIs. Austin filled the role in a big way for the Brewers in September, helping their chase for the NL Wild Card with a pinch-hit home run against the Cubs and a game-winning sacrifice fly against the Marlins.

Another of the most valuable pinch-hitters in 2019 was Howie Kendrick, who was great both when he started and when he came off the bench for the Nationals. Kendrick hit .361 as a pinch-hitter with 13 hits and 7 RBI. Kendrick has almost as any pinch-hits this season as he had in the first 13 years of his career (14).

The most frequently used pinch-hitters were both Braves: Matt Joyce and Culberson. Culberson had more success, hitting .283 with 10 RBI in 53 at-bats. Joyce batted .216 with six RBI.

The person for whom pinch-hitting was hardest was Reds catcher Tucker Barnhart, who was 0-for-21. Cubs outfielder Kyle Schwarber also struggled, going 0-for-12. Also of note was Mark Reynolds, who was 2-for-38 for the Rockies.

We should give props to one of 2018's top pinch-hitters, Tommy La Stella, who carried that success with the Cubs over into 2019, hitting .295 with 16 home runs for the Angels until his season was essentially ended by a fractured tibia.

You don't have to be a great pinch-hitter to be impactful. Hunter Renfroe was 4-for-19 as a pinch-hitter, but two of those hits were home runs, including a walk-off grand slam against Dodgers closer Kenley Jansen.

The following pages in this section feature pinch-hitting records for every batter with at least 10 pinch-hit plate appearances or pinch total bases in 2019, as well as career totals for every active player with at least 100 pinch-hit plate appearances.

Pinch Hitting

Pinch Hitters with 10+ PAs or 10+ Total Bases in 2019

Batter	B	AB	H	2B	3B	HR	RBI	TBB	IBB	SO	GDP	Avg	OBP	Slg	OPS
Adams, Matt	L	33	3	1	0	2	2	0	0	19	1	.091	.091	.303	.394
Adrianza, Ehire	B	10	4	1	1	0	1	1	0	2	0	.400	.455	.700	1.155
Aguilar, Jesus	R	37	9	2	0	2	7	5	0	15	2	.243	.318	.459	.778
Alfaro, Jorge	R	12	1	0	0	0	1	0	0	8	0	.083	.143	.083	.226
Allen, Austin	L	15	4	3	0	0	2	1	0	6	0	.267	.313	.467	.779
Allen, Greg	B	10	3	1	0	0	5	4	1	3	0	.300	.529	.400	.929
Almora Jr., Albert	R	19	2	0	0	1	2	1	1	4	0	.105	.190	.263	.454
Alonso, Yonder	L	44	9	4	0	1	4	4	1	9	4	.205	.271	.364	.634
Altherr, Aaron	R	19	2	1	0	1	3	1	0	8	0	.105	.143	.316	.459
Austin, Tyler	R	47	10	2	1	4	10	7	0	19	1	.213	.309	.553	.862
Bader, Harrison	R	10	1	0	0	0	0	0	0	3	0	.100	.182	.100	.282
Barnes, Austin	R	10	2	0	0	0	2	2	0	3	2	.200	.333	.200	.533
Barnhart, Tucker	L	21	0	0	0	0	1	3	0	8	1	.000	.125	.000	.125
Beaty, Matt	L	30	8	1	0	1	6	2	0	7	0	.267	.313	.400	.713
Belt, Brandon	L	16	3	0	0	2	3	3	1	2	0	.188	.316	.563	.878
Blandino, Alex	R	8	2	0	0	0	0	2	0	5	0	.250	.400	.250	.650
Bote, David	R	23	7	3	0	0	4	4	0	7	1	.304	.407	.435	.842
Bour, Justin	L	13	3	1	0	0	2	0	0	7	1	.231	.231	.308	.538
Braun, Ryan	R	28	4	1	0	0	1	1	0	7	1	.143	.194	.179	.372
Bruce, Jay	L	19	3	0	0	2	4	1	0	5	2	.158	.200	.474	.674
Cabrera, Melky	B	37	10	5	0	0	8	7	2	3	5	.270	.386	.405	.792
Camargo, Johan	B	38	10	3	0	4	9	1	0	9	1	.263	.282	.658	.940
Canha, Mark	R	8	1	0	0	1	2	1	0	2	0	.125	.300	.500	.800
Caratini, Victor	B	19	8	1	0	2	7	3	0	5	0	.421	.522	.789	1.311
Carpenter, Matt	L	16	4	1	0	1	5	4	0	5	0	.250	.381	.500	.881
Casali, Curt	R	14	2	1	0	0	1	3	0	8	0	.143	.278	.214	.492
Choi, Ji-Man	L	12	2	0	0	0	1	7	2	6	0	.167	.500	.167	.667
Cron, Kevin	R	21	4	1	0	2	2	2	0	9	1	.190	.292	.524	.815
Culberson, Charlie	R	53	15	2	2	2	10	4	0	13	2	.283	.333	.509	.843
Cuthbert, Cheslor	R	8	1	0	0	1	2	2	0	2	1	.125	.300	.500	.800
d'Arnaud, Travis	R	12	3	1	0	0	2	0	0	2	0	.250	.231	.333	.564
Davis, Chris	L	10	0	0	0	0	1	1	0	6	0	.000	.091	.000	.091
Davis, J.D.	R	33	8	1	0	1	6	2	0	12	2	.242	.286	.364	.649
Davis, Rajai	R	16	3	1	0	1	7	1	0	2	0	.188	.235	.438	.673
Daza, Yonathan	R	15	4	0	1	0	0	1	0	2	0	.267	.313	.400	.713
Dean, Austin	R	15	5	1	0	0	0	0	0	5	1	.333	.333	.400	.733
Descalso, Daniel	L	31	2	0	0	0	1	3	0	12	0	.065	.143	.065	.207
Desmond, Ian	R	19	2	0	0	2	3	2	0	7	2	.105	.217	.421	.638
Diaz, Elias	R	10	3	1	0	0	0	0	0	3	0	.300	.300	.400	.700
Dickerson, Alex	L	24	6	0	0	0	5	4	0	8	1	.250	.345	.250	.595
Dickerson, Corey	L	14	5	3	0	0	5	1	1	3	0	.357	.400	.571	.971
Dietrich, Derek	L	29	4	1	0	2	4	4	1	10	0	.138	.324	.379	.704
Dozier, Brian	R	12	4	1	0	0	0	2	0	2	1	.333	.429	.417	.845
Duvall, Adam	R	8	1	0	0	0	0	0	0	2	0	.125	.300	.125	.425
Dyson, Jarrod	L	8	2	0	0	1	2	4	0	1	0	.250	.500	.625	1.125
Edman, Tommy	B	13	3	0	1	1	3	0	0	3	0	.231	.286	.615	.901
Ervin, Phillip	R	27	8	0	2	2	6	2	0	8	0	.296	.345	.667	1.011
Farmer, Kyle	R	37	10	3	0	1	6	1	0	12	0	.270	.289	.432	.722
Flores, Wilmer	R	21	4	1	0	0	2	2	0	7	0	.190	.261	.238	.499
Ford, Mike	L	11	5	1	0	2	3	1	0	3	0	.455	.500	1.091	1.591
Fowler, Dexter	B	9	3	0	0	1	2	2	0	1	0	.333	.455	.667	1.121
France, Ty	R	20	7	1	0	0	3	1	0	6	1	.350	.381	.400	.781
Franco, Maikel	R	13	3	1	0	1	2	1	0	3	0	.231	.286	.538	.824
Frazier, Adam	L	12	5	3	0	0	3	1	0	1	0	.417	.462	.667	1.128
Frazier, Todd	R	11	3	2	0	0	0	1	0	5	0	.273	.333	.455	.788
Freeman, Mike	L	9	1	0	0	0	2	1	0	7	0	.111	.250	.111	.361
Freese, David	R	30	12	4	0	2	3	6	0	5	3	.400	.500	.733	1.233
Freitas, David	R	13	1	0	0	0	0	3	0	5	1	.077	.250	.077	.327
Fuentes, Josh	R	12	1	0	0	0	0	0	0	6	0	.083	.083	.083	.167
Gamel, Ben	L	36	7	2	0	1	6	3	0	11	0	.194	.250	.333	.583
Garcia, Greg	L	36	10	2	0	0	3	8	0	10	0	.278	.435	.333	.768
Garcia, Robel	B	9	1	0	0	0	0	1	0	6	0	.111	.200	.111	.311
Garlick, Kyle	R	15	3	2	0	0	0	3	0	6	0	.200	.333	.333	.667
Garver, Mitch	R	9	0	0	0	0	0	5	0	3	0	.000	.357	.000	.357
Goins, Ryan	L	10	2	1	0	0	0	1	0	3	0	.200	.273	.300	.573
Goodwin, Brian	L	18	5	0	0	1	6	3	1	7	0	.278	.381	.444	.825
Gosselin, Phil	R	32	10	1	0	0	3	2	0	11	0	.313	.353	.344	.697
Granderson, Curtis	L	46	9	1	0	4	4	11	1	7	1	.196	.351	.478	.829

Pinch Hitting
Pinch Hitters with 10+ PAs or 10+ Total Bases in 2019

Batter	B	AB	H	2B	3B	HR	RBI	TBB	IBB	SO	GDP	Avg	OBP	Slg	OPS
Grisham, Trent	L	10	0	0	0	0	0	2	0	4	0	.000	.167	.000	.167
Grossman, Robbie	B	21	5	1	1	1	7	4	0	3	1	.238	.360	.524	.884
Guillorme, Luis	L	19	5	1	0	1	3	3	0	6	0	.263	.364	.474	.837
Gyorko, Jedd	R	31	5	0	0	1	3	4	0	8	0	.161	.257	.258	.515
Hampson, Garrett	R	15	3	2	0	0	1	2	0	7	0	.200	.294	.333	.627
Happ, Ian	B	16	6	1	0	2	4	2	0	6	0	.375	.421	.813	1.234
Hechavarria, Adeiny	R	18	5	0	0	2	5	2	0	3	1	.278	.333	.611	.944
Hernandez, Kike	R	20	6	0	0	2	8	1	1	6	0	.300	.318	.600	.918
Hernandez, Marco	L	17	6	2	0	1	1	0	0	4	0	.353	.389	.647	1.036
Herrera, Rosell	B	21	6	1	0	2	3	3	0	9	1	.286	.375	.619	.994
Hicks, John	R	11	3	0	0	2	5	0	0	4	0	.273	.273	.818	1.091
Holt, Brock	L	8	5	1	0	0	3	3	0	2	0	.625	.667	.750	1.417
Jankowski, Travis	L	9	1	0	0	0	0	1	0	2	0	.111	.200	.111	.311
Jones, Adam	R	11	5	0	3	5	2	1	4	0	.455	.538	1.273	1.811
Joseph, Corban	L	10	2	1	0	0	0	1	0	1	0	.200	.273	.300	.573
Joyce, Matt	L	74	16	3	0	2	6	11	0	20	2	.216	.318	.338	.655
Kang, Jung Ho	R	15	1	0	0	0	1	0	0	7	-- 0	.067	.063	.067	.129
Kelly, Carson	R	14	2	1	0	0	1	1	0	4	0	.143	.200	.214	.414
Kemp, Tony	L	31	9	0	1	2	7	5	0	7	0	.290	.421	.548	.969
Kendrick, Howie	R	36	13	3	0	2	7	4	0	7	0	.361	.415	.611	1.026
Kinsler, Ian	R	17	3	0	0	0	0	2	0	9	0	.176	.263	.176	.440
Knapp, Andrew	B	32	7	1	0	0	2	2	0	11	1	.219	.265	.250	.515
Lagares, Juan	R	11	1	0	0	0	0	2	0	5	0	.091	.231	.091	.322
Lamb, Jake	L	22	7	1	0	1	6	2	0	4	0	.318	.375	.500	.875
Leyba, Domingo	B	12	2	0	0	0	0	3	0	6	0	.167	.333	.167	.500
Locastro, Tim	R	14	2	0	0	0	0	2	0	4	0	.143	.368	.143	.511
Longoria, Evan	R	11	1	0	0	0	1	1	0	1	1	.091	.167	.091	.258
Lowe, Nate	L	10	1	0	0	0	2	0	0	6	0	.100	.091	.100	.191
Luplow, Jordan	R	19	5	0	1	0	3	2	0	8	2	.263	.333	.368	.702
Margot, Manuel	R	20	5	2	0	1	2	2	0	5	0	.250	.318	.500	.818
Martin, Russell	R	16	1	0	0	0	1	3	0	6	1	.063	.250	.063	.313
Martinez, Jose	R	38	8	1	1	1	8	4	0	11	2	.211	.286	.368	.654
McKinney, Billy	L	8	2	1	0	0	1	4	0	5	0	.250	.500	.375	.875
McMahon, Ryan	L	13	3	1	0	2	6	0	0	6	0	.231	.231	.769	1.000
Mejia, Francisco	B	18	6	4	0	0	3	0	0	5	0	.333	.368	.556	.924
Miller, Brad	L	31	7	0	1	1	3	3	0	9	0	.226	.314	.387	.701
Moran, Colin	L	20	6	0	0	3	9	3	0	6	0	.300	.391	.750	1.141
Moreland, Mitch	L	11	4	1	0	1	5	3	0	3	0	.364	.500	.727	1.227
Morrison, Logan	L	23	5	0	0	2	3	2	0	7	1	.217	.280	.478	.758
Munoz, Yairo	R	36	7	1	0	0	0	1	0	8	1	.194	.216	.222	.438
Murphy, Daniel	L	25	5	2	0	0	7	1	0	11	0	.200	.231	.280	.511
Myers, Wil	R	23	5	0	0	3	4	2	0	11	0	.217	.280	.609	.889
Narvaez, Omar	L	20	6	0	0	0	0	1	1	6	0	.300	.333	.300	.633
Naylor, Josh	L	27	5	1	0	2	8	2	0	6	0	.185	.233	.444	.678
Nunez, Eduardo	R	12	3	0	0	1	4	1	0	0	0	.250	.308	.500	.808
Nunez, Renato	R	10	1	0	0	1	1	3	0	3	0	.100	.308	.400	.708
O'Grady, Brian	L	12	2	1	0	1	2	0	0	6	0	.167	.167	.500	.667
O'Hearn, Ryan	L	9	2	1	0	1	2	3	1	3	0	.222	.417	.667	1.083
Ohtani, Shohei	L	11	4	0	0	0	1	4	0	4	0	.364	.533	.364	.897
O'Neill, Tyler	R	16	2	1	0	0	0	1	0	9	1	.125	.176	.188	.364
Ortega, Rafael	L	9	3	2	0	0	1	1	0	2	0	.333	.400	.556	.956
Osuna, Jose	R	29	10	3	0	5	10	0	0	4	1	.345	.345	.966	1.310
Panik, Joe	L	25	6	1	0	0	2	2	0	3	1	.240	.296	.280	.576
Parra, Gerardo	L	47	9	3	0	0	10	2	0	10	1	.191	.240	.255	.495
Pederson, Joc	L	29	7	1	0	2	5	3	0	7	0	.241	.313	.483	.795
Pence, Hunter	R	13	3	0	0	1	4	1	0	5	0	.231	.286	.462	.747
Peraza, Jose	R	18	3	0	0	1	3	5	0	4	0	.167	.375	.333	.708
Perez, Hernan	R	17	3	2	0	1	1	2	0	5	0	.176	.263	.471	.734
Pina, Manny	R	17	3	0	0	1	2	2	0	11	0	.176	.333	.353	.686
Pinder, Chad	R	23	5	0	0	2	6	1	0	8	0	.217	.269	.478	.747
Posey, Buster	R	10	2	1	0	0	2	1	0	0	1	.200	.273	.300	.573
Prado, Martin	R	43	9	2	0	0	3	5	0	12	1	.209	.286	.256	.542
Quinn, Roman	B	8	2	1	0	0	0	2	0	1	0	.250	.400	.375	.775
Ramirez, Harold	R	13	2	1	0	0	0	1	0	5	0	.154	.214	.231	.445
Ramos, Wilson	R	20	8	0	0	0	4	3	1	5	1	.400	.500	.400	.900
Ravelo, Rangel	R	20	5	2	0	1	5	2	0	6	1	.250	.318	.500	.818
Realmuto, J.T.	R	12	2	0	0	1	3	0	0	4	0	.167	.167	.417	.583
Renfroe, Hunter	R	19	4	1	0	2	6	2	0	5	0	.211	.286	.579	.865
Reyes, Franmil	R	14	3	0	0	2	4	3	1	4	2	.214	.353	.643	.996

Pinch Hitting
Pinch Hitters with 10+ PAs or 10+ Total Bases in 2019

Batter	B	AB	H	2B	3B	HR	RBI	TBB	IBB	SO	GDP	Avg	OBP	Slg	OPS
Reyes, Pablo	R	20	6	2	0	1	5	5	0	5	0	.300	.440	.550	.990
Reynolds, Mark	R	38	2	0	0	1	3	8	0	19	0	.053	.217	.132	.349
Rickard, Joey	R	11	2	0	0	0	1	0	0	4	0	.182	.182	.182	.364
Riddle, J.T.	L	12	4	1	0	1	1	1	0	4	0	.333	.385	.667	1.051
Riley, Austin	R	9	2	2	0	0	2	1	0	4	0	.222	.300	.444	.744
Rios, Edwin	L	14	3	1	0	2	3	3	0	9	0	.214	.353	.714	1.067
Rivera, Yadiel	R	8	2	1	0	0	1	4	0	4	0	.250	.500	.375	.875
Rodriguez, Ronny	R	12	2	0	0	0	1	0	0	6	0	.167	.167	.167	.333
Rodriguez, Sean	R	26	4	0	0	1	3	4	0	13	1	.154	.258	.269	.527
Ruiz, Rio	L	21	4	0	0	1	3	2	0	7	0	.190	.250	.333	.583
Sanchez, Adrian	R	17	5	0	0	0	1	1	0	6	0	.294	.333	.294	.627
Sandoval, Pablo	B	48	18	8	0	2	6	2	1	12	2	.375	.400	.667	1.067
Santana, Danny	B	9	3	0	1	2	5	2	1	3	0	.333	.500	1.222	1.722
Schwarber, Kyle	L	12	0	0	0	0	0	2	0	5	0	.000	.143	.000	.143
Shaw, Chris	L	11	0	0	0	0	0	1	0	6	0	.000	.083	.000	.083
Shaw, Travis	L	11	3	0	0	1	2	6	0	6	0	.273	.556	.545	1.101
Slater, Austin	R	17	6	3	0	1	7	4	0	7	0	.353	.500	.706	1.206
Smith, Dominic	L	28	8	2	0	2	6	8	0	6	1	.286	.459	.571	1.031
Smith Jr., Dwight	L	10	3	0	0	0	1	0	0	4	0	.300	.364	.300	.664
Sogard, Eric	L	12	1	0	0	0	1	1	0	2	1	.083	.154	.083	.237
Solano, Donovan	R	30	9	0	1	0	2	3	0	10	1	.300	.364	.367	.730
Stallings, Jacob	R	10	6	1	0	0	2	0	0	2	0	.600	.600	.700	1.300
Stevenson, Andrew	L	19	8	1	1	0	0	5	0	7	1	.421	.560	.579	1.139
Suzuki, Kurt	R	12	3	1	0	1	6	0	0	3	1	.250	.308	.583	.891
Swihart, Blake	B	15	2	0	0	0	2	2	0	8	1	.133	.278	.133	.411
Tapia, Raimel	L	36	10	1	0	4	9	2	0	11	1	.278	.316	.639	.955
Taylor, Chris	R	17	6	1	1	1	5	4	2	5	0	.353	.476	.706	1.182
Taylor, Michael A.	R	12	5	3	0	0	1	3	0	3	0	.417	.533	.667	1.200
Tellez, Rowdy	L	9	2	0	0	2	4	1	1	3	0	.222	.300	.889	1.189
Thames, Eric	L	40	8	1	0	2	6	9	0	18	0	.200	.347	.375	.722
Thomas, Lane	R	12	4	0	0	3	6	1	0	2	1	.333	.385	1.083	1.468
Travis, Sam	R	10	3	2	1	0	1	4	2	2	1	.300	.500	.700	1.200
Tucker, Cole	B	11	5	1	2	0	2	2	0	4	0	.455	.571	.909	1.481
Turner, Justin	R	10	1	0	0	1	3	2	0	2	0	.100	.308	.400	.708
Valaika, Pat	R	14	3	1	0	1	2	3	0	5	1	.214	.353	.500	.853
VanMeter, Josh	L	27	5	2	0	0	2	4	0	12	1	.185	.333	.259	.593
Vargas, Ildemaro	B	36	10	1	0	2	6	0	0	6	1	.278	.278	.472	.750
Vazquez, Christian	R	12	4	0	0	2	2	0	0	2	1	.333	.333	.833	1.167
Verdugo, Alex	L	15	5	0	0	1	2	1	1	2	0	.333	.353	.533	.886
Vogelbach, Daniel	L	10	3	2	0	0	6	1	0	3	0	.300	.364	.500	.864
Vogt, Stephen	L	29	7	4	0	1	5	5	1	10	0	.241	.343	.483	.826
Walker, Christian	R	11	3	0	0	2	5	2	0	4	0	.273	.385	.818	1.203
Walker, Neil	B	23	7	2	0	2	5	5	0	5	0	.304	.429	.652	1.081
White, Tyler	R	10	2	0	0	0	0	2	0	1	0	.200	.333	.200	.533
Wieters, Matt	B	14	2	0	0	1	2	3	0	4	0	.143	.333	.357	.690
Wilkerson, Stevie	B	11	4	1	1	0	0	0	0	3	0	.364	.364	.636	1.000
Williams, Nick	L	39	5	1	0	0	1	1	0	18	0	.128	.171	.154	.325
Winker, Jesse	L	19	2	0	0	1	1	4	0	7	1	.105	.261	.263	.524
Yastrzemski, Mike	L	12	4	1	0	1	4	0	0	5	0	.333	.333	.667	1.000
Zagunis, Mark	R	17	3	0	0	0	3	4	0	12	0	.176	.333	.176	.510

Career Pinch Hitting
Active Pinch Hitters with 100+ PAs in their careers

Batter	B	AB	H	2B	3B	HR	RBI	TBB	IBB	SO	GDP	Avg	OBP	Slg	OPS
Adams, Matt	L	217	55	10	0	11	49	11	3	75	4	.253	.290	.452	.742
Aguilar, Jesus	R	122	27	6	0	5	18	14	0	44	6	.221	.302	.393	.696
Almora Jr., Albert	R	101	19	3	0	1	14	3	1	17	5	.188	.215	.248	.462
Alonso, Yonder	L	130	31	10	0	2	12	19	3	28	5	.238	.336	.362	.697
Bour, Justin	L	86	21	3	0	5	22	12	0	28	2	.244	.340	.453	.793
Culberson, Charlie	R	138	32	3	3	6	27	6	0	39	6	.232	.265	.428	.693
Davis, Rajai	R	129	25	7	1	1	12	17	2	33	2	.194	.291	.287	.577
Descalso, Daniel	L	279	56	9	1	6	34	30	1	81	1	.201	.286	.305	.590
Dickerson, Corey	L	96	21	7	1	0	9	6	4	29	1	.219	.265	.313	.577
Dietrich, Derek	L	112	22	9	1	5	18	8	1	39	2	.196	.318	.429	.747
Duda, Lucas	L	85	18	7	0	4	17	14	0	29	0	.212	.327	.435	.762
Forsythe, Logan	R	92	19	5	0	2	12	11	0	29	3	.207	.302	.326	.628
Fowler, Dexter	B	88	22	5	1	3	11	15	0	30	1	.250	.365	.432	.797
Freese, David	R	125	37	9	1	4	18	28	5	36	5	.296	.426	.480	.906
Garcia, Greg	L	183	47	7	0	2	15	33	0	54	3	.257	.387	.328	.715
Gennett, Scooter	L	93	15	3	0	3	20	7	3	30	2	.161	.218	.290	.508
Gosselin, Phil	R	164	41	7	0	1	11	12	1	51	2	.250	.298	.311	.609
Grandal, Yasmani	B	85	18	3	0	3	16	19	0	36	3	.212	.356	.353	.709
Granderson, Curtis	L	146	36	3	0	8	18	34	3	38	1	.247	.387	.432	.818
Gyorko, Jedd	R	98	21	5	0	2	12	12	1	27	2	.214	.295	.327	.621
Harrison, Josh	R	113	19	2	1	3	14	4	0	21	2	.168	.202	.283	.485
Hernandez, Kike	R	149	32	8	0	6	19	17	3	46	1	.215	.292	.389	.681
Hundley, Nick	R	93	20	3	0	2	20	5	1	32	0	.215	.257	.312	.569
Iannetta, Chris	R	83	21	3	0	4	12	15	1	31	1	.253	.379	.434	.812
Jay, Jon	L	151	42	3	1	3	19	14	1	37	7	.278	.358	.371	.729
Joyce, Matt	L	274	57	15	1	8	39	55	3	83	9	.208	.340	.358	.698
Kendrick, Howie	R	91	27	6	0	2	13	8	0	20	4	.297	.353	.429	.782
La Stella, Tommy	L	162	45	14	0	1	23	26	1	27	5	.278	.391	.383	.773
McCann, Brian	L	110	19	5	0	3	12	12	4	32	2	.173	.266	.300	.566
Moreland, Mitch	L	95	28	5	0	4	23	14	2	24	3	.295	.391	.474	.865
Murphy, Daniel	L	137	33	6	2	4	28	10	2	33	3	.241	.289	.401	.690
Osuna, Jose	R	104	21	5	0	7	14	1	0	21	8	.202	.217	.452	.669
Parra, Gerardo	L	195	46	9	1	2	28	11	2	45	5	.236	.282	.323	.605
Pearce, Steve	R	120	23	8	1	1	11	13	1	40	4	.192	.279	.300	.579
Pederson, Joc	L	95	17	4	0	4	10	19	0	31	0	.179	.313	.347	.660
Perez, Hernan	R	100	20	5	1	1	8	7	0	26	4	.200	.252	.300	.552
Prado, Martin	R	103	27	7	0	2	20	18	2	21	2	.262	.371	.388	.759
Reynolds, Mark	R	144	27	4	0	7	23	21	1	54	7	.188	.302	.361	.663
Rodriguez, Sean	R	153	23	2	0	5	19	23	0	70	2	.150	.280	.261	.542
Sandoval, Pablo	B	114	36	13	0	3	22	8	3	32	4	.316	.363	.509	.872
Shuck, JB	L	108	24	2	1	0	7	14	0	20	4	.222	.315	.259	.574
Solano, Donovan	R	112	26	0	3	0	9	5	0	28	2	.232	.283	.286	.569
Suzuki, Ichiro	L	242	63	6	1	2	22	21	2	42	1	.260	.325	.318	.643
Thames, Eric	L	94	15	2	1	3	10	16	0	44	1	.160	.282	.298	.580
Turner, Justin	R	172	45	10	0	6	38	16	1	34	8	.262	.325	.424	.749
Valaika, Pat	R	101	28	11	0	5	20	5	0	38	3	.277	.308	.535	.843
Vogt, Stephen	L	95	17	6	1	2	11	17	3	28	0	.179	.298	.326	.625

Manufactured Runs, Productive Outs & Unproductive Outs

Brian Reiff

Past iterations of this section have called attention to the fact that manufactured runs in MLB have been steadily decreasing. In each of 2015, 2016, 2017 and 2018, MLB set a record low for manufactured runs, at least since BIS began tracking the stat in 2002.

A new record low was set again in 2019, unsurprisingly. In 2019, MLB manufactured 3,984 runs, a 2% decrease from 2018. That aligns closely with previous seasons, which each saw between a 1 and 2% drop.

Let's add some context. The Boston Red Sox manufactured 170 runs this season, more than any other team in MLB. If you take your 2019 *Bill James Handbook* off the shelf, brush off some of the dust and open to this section, you'll see that two teams surpassed that mark in the 2018 season, and not by insignificant margins—the Chicago Cubs led the way with 199 manufactured runs in 2018, nearly 20% more than the Red Sox's total.

On the other end, the Cincinnati Reds trailed MLB in manufactured runs last year with 108. This year, the Detroit Tigers barely broke 100, an admittedly arbitrary threshold but significant in this base-10 society we find ourselves in (my apologies to any binary enthusiasts reading this).

For those curious, the definitions for each of Manufactured Runs, Productive Outs and Unproductive Outs, while mostly intuitive, can be found in the glossary at the end of this book. Player and team leaderboards can be found by turning the page.

Players with the most Manufactured Runs, Productive Outs, & Unproductive Outs

Manufactured Runs		Productive Outs		Unproductive Outs	
Acuna Jr., Ronald	32	Abreu, Jose	43	DeJong, Paul	108
Villar, Jonathan	32	Andrus, Elvis	41	Alonso, Pete	104
Smith, Mallex	31	Gordon, Alex	36	Escobar, Eduardo	103
Garcia, Leury	30	Rosario, Eddie	34	Goldschmidt, Paul	95
Devers, Rafael	27	Brantley, Michael	33	Abreu, Jose	95
Turner, Trea	26	Bell, Josh	32	Chapman, Matt	94
Betts, Mookie	25	Soto, Juan	32	Suarez, Eugenio	91
Eaton, Adam	24	Marte, Starling	31	Hoskins, Rhys	88
Albies, Ozzie	23	Seager, Corey	31	Moustakas, Mike	87
Trout, Mike	22	Ahmed, Nick	30	Grichuk, Randal	87
Bogaerts, Xander	21	Mazara, Nomar	30	Mancini, Trey	86
Dyson, Jarrod	21	Perez, Roberto	29	Soler, Jorge	86
Freeman, Freddie	21	Escobar, Eduardo	29	Bogaerts, Xander	86
Robles, Victor	21	Arcia, Orlando	29	Odor, Rougned	85
Ramirez, Jose	20	Hosmer, Eric	29	Castellanos, Nicholas	85
Marte, Starling	20	Rendon, Anthony	28	Polanco, Jorge	85
Frazier, Adam	20	Pillar, Kevin	28	Devers, Rafael	82
Semien, Marcus	19	Cabrera, Asdrubal	28	Donaldson, Josh	82
Hernandez, Cesar	19	Panik, Joe	28	Santana, Carlos	81
Muncy, Max	19	Castro, Starlin	27	Story, Trevor	81
Bader, Harrison	19	Hernandez, Cesar	27	Rosario, Amed	81
Choo, Shin-Soo	19	Bregman, Alex	26	Rendon, Anthony	80
Baez, Javier	19	Kipnis, Jason	26	Harper, Bryce	80
Story, Trevor	18	Arenado, Nolan	26	Pillar, Kevin	80
Wong, Kolten	18	Freeman, Freddie	26	Brantley, Michael	77
Sanchez, Yolmer	18	Bradley Jr., Jackie	25	Pham, Tommy	77
Bellinger, Cody	18	Villar, Jonathan	25	Machado, Manny	77
Lindor, Francisco	18	Ramos, Wilson	25	Bregman, Alex	77
Harper, Bryce	18	Wong, Kolten	25	Davis, Khris	76
Polanco, Jorge	18	Markakis, Nick	25	Realmuto, J.T.	76
Anderson, Tim	18	Bogaerts, Xander	25	Puig, Yasiel	75
Rosario, Amed	18	Devers, Rafael	25	Dozier, Hunter	75
Newman, Kevin	17	Crawford, Brandon	25	Moran, Colin	74
Tatis Jr., Fernando	17	Bellinger, Cody	25	Freeman, Freddie	74
Castellanos, Nicholas	17	Eaton, Adam	25	Castro, Starlin	74
Heyward, Jason	17	Marte, Ketel	24	Grandal, Yasmani	74
Cain, Lorenzo	17	Rojas, Miguel	24	Torres, Gleyber	73
Seager, Corey	17	Swanson, Dansby	24	Marte, Starling	73
Santana, Danny	17	Guerrero Jr., Vladimir	24	Bryant, Kris	73
Pillar, Kevin	17	Pham, Tommy	24	Ohtani, Shohei	72
Gurriel, Yuli	17	Segura, Jean	24	Garcia, Avisail	72
Pham, Tommy	17	Frazier, Adam	24	Cruz, Nelson	72
Ahmed, Nick	16	Profar, Jurickson	23	Martinez, J.D.	72
Andrus, Elvis	16	Santander, Anthony	23	Bradley Jr., Jackie	71
Margot, Manuel	16	Lindor, Francisco	23	Gardner, Brett	71
Adames, Willy	16	Harper, Bryce	23	Yelich, Christian	71
Vazquez, Christian	16	Machado, Manny	23	Walker, Christian	71
Donaldson, Josh	16	Wolters, Tony	23	Eaton, Adam	71
Mancini, Trey	16	Sanchez, Yolmer	23	Trout, Mike	71
Segura, Jean	16	Mondesi, Adalberto	23	Altuve, Jose	71
Edman, Tommy	16				

Manufactured Runs, Productive Outs, & Unproductive Outs Produced by Team

Team	Manufactured Runs	Productive Outs	Unproductive Outs
Arizona Diamondbacks	144	241	712
Atlanta Braves	152	238	721
Baltimore Orioles	144	218	685
Boston Red Sox	170	227	767
Chicago White Sox	148	211	717
Chicago Cubs	126	212	647
Cincinnati Reds	116	189	679
Cleveland Indians	144	246	689
Colorado Rockies	136	254	690
Detroit Tigers	100	195	766
Houston Astros	128	229	756
Kansas City Royals	132	212	690
Los Angeles Dodgers	144	252	709
Los Angeles Angels	131	205	696
Miami Marlins	120	231	639
Milwaukee Brewers	106	191	755
Minnesota Twins	126	209	721
New York Yankees	122	192	708
New York Mets	114	214	696
Oakland Athletics	123	191	747
Philadelphia Phillies	130	209	725
Pittsburgh Pirates	148	271	693
San Diego Padres	138	209	671
San Francisco Giants	112	230	701
Seattle Mariners	122	187	749
St Louis Cardinals	159	227	694
Tampa Bay Rays	129	225	762
Texas Rangers	161	231	710
Toronto Blue Jays	107	183	714
Washington Nationals	152	240	691

Manufactured Runs, Productive Outs, & Unproductive Outs Allowed by Team

Team	Manufactured Runs	Productive Outs	Unproductive Outs
Arizona Diamondbacks	121	232	651
Atlanta Braves	143	220	709
Baltimore Orioles	154	223	727
Boston Red Sox	124	211	765
Chicago White Sox	143	211	734
Chicago Cubs	152	235	691
Cincinnati Reds	119	221	648
Cleveland Indians	94	157	721
Colorado Rockies	160	285	695
Detroit Tigers	161	248	739
Houston Astros	98	195	646
Kansas City Royals	148	234	763
Los Angeles Dodgers	107	187	649
Los Angeles Angels	127	209	740
Miami Marlins	145	224	675
Milwaukee Brewers	127	224	709
Minnesota Twins	143	214	747
New York Yankees	103	173	717
New York Mets	125	219	750
Oakland Athletics	111	218	726
Philadelphia Phillies	139	250	687
Pittsburgh Pirates	140	224	733
San Diego Padres	148	234	697
San Francisco Giants	139	212	727
Seattle Mariners	165	239	679
St Louis Cardinals	109	203	685
Tampa Bay Rays	129	176	712
Texas Rangers	153	221	778
Toronto Blue Jays	142	241	746
Washington Nationals	115	229	654

Managers Record

Mark Simon

Nowadays, the statistics by which we can evaluate a manager are just as much a means to evaluate a front office, since with many teams the making of a lineup and in-game decision making process is the product of discussions held between the manager, his coaching staff, and his bosses well before gametime.

However, it is the manager who gets the credit or blame as the public face of the team's decision-making structure. With that in mind, we can take a look at which managers make use of different approaches and tactics the most and least.

Indians manager Terry Francona was given a roster that allowed for a lineup with the platoon advantage 73% of the time. That was the highest platoon advantage rate in baseball, 16 percentage points above the major league average.

On the mound, this was a year of heavy bullpen usage. No one used his bullpen more than Red Sox manager Alex Cora, whose team utilized 632 relievers, including 134 instances in which he used one on consecutive days (third to Kevin Cash's and Dave Martinez's 136). In the NL, Bud Black's Rockies struggled with their starting pitchers all season, forcing him to use relievers 590 times, most in the league, two more than Craig Counsell and the Brewers. Also of note: A.J. Hinch and the Astros didn't issue an intentional walk all season, the first time that's happened since intentional walks began being tracked in 1955.

This section has career data for each recent manager in the majors as well as a look at the league as a whole. You'll see a good mix of old school and new school approaches indicative of the different ways that teams and their managers operate as the game evolves.

Brad Ausmus

Year	Team	Lg	G	LUp	PL%	PH	PR	DS	Quick	Slow	LO	RCD	LS	Rel	SBA	SacA	RM	PO	#	Good	NG	Bomb	W	L	Pct
2014	Tigers	AL	162	103	.51	79	43	44	28	55	**43**	99	1	473	147	32	144	13	34	17	17	5	90	72	.556
2015	Tigers	AL	161	122	.47	83	38	50	33	59	30	131	4	505	134	37	161	7	32	18	14	7	74	87	.460
2016	Tigers	AL	161	111	.48	89	31	50	41	37	18	93	4	476	87	21	95	3	25	12	13	4	86	75	.534
2017	Tigers	AL	162	131	.50	103	30	24	28	52	17	97	6	510	99	16	104	3	**42**	**26**	16	8	64	**98**	.395
2019	Angels	AL	162	153	.57	98	27	**44**	34	29	0	105	5	589	85	4	78	1	11	5	6	4	72	90	.444
	162-Game Average			124	.50	91	34	43	33	47	22	105	4	512	111	22	117	5	29	16	13	6	77	85	.475

Dusty Baker

Year	Team	Lg	G	LUp	PL%	PH	PR	DS	Quick	Slow	LO	RCD	LS	Rel	SBA	SacA	RM	PO	#	Good	NG	Bomb	W	L	Pct
1994	Giants	NL	115	76	.53	177	16	9	29	25	2	86	12	288	154	88		78	40	24	16	8	55	60	.478
1995	Giants	NL	144	97	.41	230	36	13	32	50	8	90	8	381	184	101		77	51	32	19	14	67	77	.465
1996	Giants	NL	162	129	.51	250	17	15	24	58	15	94	8	425	166	103		96	60	37	23	15	68	94	.420
1997	Giants	NL	162	114	.71	212	17	22	46	25	17	132	4	481	170	85		93	57	36	21	12	90	72	.556
1998	Giants	NL	163	130	.62	224	20	12	43	38	8	113	5	433	153	111		41	68	42	26	9	89	74	.546
1999	Giants	NL	162	119	.62	233	16	16	30	51	27	111		450	165	113		40	41	25	16	10	86	76	.531
2000	Giants	NL	162	82	.56	233	26	22	38	50	25	91	3	384	118	86		37	26	17	9	2	97	65	.599
2001	Giants	NL	162	122	.48	261	22	19	40	48	10	114	4	439	99	95		45	49	33	16	6	90	72	.556
2002	Giants	NL	162	118	.43	223	32	38	29	56	**53**	106	8	417	95	89	42	41	44	28	16	10	95	66	.590
2003	Cubs	NL	162	114	.49	272	25	43	24	58	**65**	111	3	420	104	93	31	24	36	23	13	4	88	74	.543
2004	Cubs	NL	162	113	.44	254	16	19	37	41	42	129	8	460	94	108	71	**62**	33	22	11	7	89	73	.549
2005	Cubs	NL	162	121	.59	240	21	29	40	46	36	103	2	457	104	88	107	**70**	48	27	21	7	79	83	.488
2006	Cubs	NL	162	133	.56	271	9	26	45	39	22	**165**	2	**542**	170	108	139	46	44	28	16	11	66	**96**	.407
2008	Reds	NL	162	119	.58	285	28	27	20	**63**	39	124	2	507	132	100	101	37	40	28	12	4	74	88	.457
2009	Reds	NL	162	130	.45	252	15	35	30	**62**	**35**	115	1	478	136	120	118	23	36	29	7	4	78	84	.481
2010	Reds	NL	162	120	.46	258	19	49	36	41	22	140	0	502	136	91	157	13	32	22	10	9	91	71	.562
2011	Reds	NL	162	**142**	.42	240	29	42	34	51	20	115	0	501	147	102	226	33	47	26	21	5	79	83	.488
2012	Reds	NL	162	121	.43	201	19	39	33	39	30	78	4	425	114	**108**	148	19	33	22	11	3	97	65	.599
2013	Reds	NL	162	95	.54	236	20	27	39	40	14	90	3	461	102	**110**	157	**21**	28	23	5	3	90	72	.556
2016	Nationals	NL	162	112	.57	220	20	27	35	45	21	119	4	508	160	59	161	3	43	28	15	9	95	67	.586
2017	Nationals	NL	162	124	.59	241	33	26	22	53	**27**	90	2	487	138	57	113	3	39	29	10	6	97	65	.599
	162-Game Average			118	.52	243	22	27	35	48	26	112	4	459	138	98	121	44	43	28	15	8	85	77	.525

Rocco Baldelli

Year	Team	Lg	G	LUp	PL%	PH	PR	DS	Quick	Slow	LO	RCD	LS	Rel	SBA	SacA	RM	PO	#	Good	NG	Bomb	W	L	Pct
2019	Twins	AL	162	145	.62	84	24	35	42	43	1	94	**16**	524	49	16	56	4	10	9	1	1	101	61	.623
	162-Game Average			145	.62	84	24	35	42	43	1	94	16	524	49	16	56	4	10	9	1	1	101	61	.623

Jeff Banister

Year	Team	Lg	G	LUp	PL%	PH	PR	DS	Quick	Slow	LO	RCD	LS	Rel	SBA	SacA	RM	PO	#	Good	NG	Bomb	W	L	Pct
2015	Rangers	AL	162	127	.57	94	51	46	40	47	11	122	0	498	140	**66**	158	5	29	19	10	5	88	74	.543
2016	Rangers	AL	162	124	.55	84	**58**	38	47	44	7	85	1	479	135	26	136	3	16	5	11	**8**	95	67	.586
2017	Rangers	AL	162	134	.54	66	40	20	39	40	6	71	7	464	157	35	153	0	22	9	13	10	78	84	.481
2018	Rangers	AL	152	122	.61	74	40	21	29	44	1	61	3	465	108	42	135	1	22	13	9	5	64	88	.421
	162-Game Average			129	.57	81	48	32	39	44	6	86	3	484	137	43	148	2	23	12	11	7	83	79	.512

Rod Barajas

Year	Team	Lg	G	LUp	PL%	PH	PR	DS	Quick	Slow	LO	RCD	LS	Rel	SBA	SacA	RM	PO	#	Good	NG	Bomb	W	L	Pct
2019	Padres	NL	8	8	.69	28	2	1	5	0	0	4	0	34	4	2	8	0	0	0	0	0	1	7	.125
	162-Game Average			162	.69	567	41	20	101	0	0	81	0	689	81	41	162	0	0	0	0	0	20	142	.123

David Bell

Year	Team	Lg	G	LUp	PL%	PH	PR	DS	Quick	Slow	LO	RCD	LS	Rel	SBA	SacA	RM	PO	#	Good	NG	Bomb	W	L	Pct
2019	Reds	NL	162	140	.55	319	28	46	36	43	9	104	10	535	118	44	111	1	31	25	6	5	75	87	.463
	162-Game Average			140	.55	319	28	46	36	43	9	104	10	535	118	44	111	1	31	25	6	5	75	87	.463

Bud Black

Year	Team	Lg	G	LUp	PL%	PH	PR	DS	Quick	Slow	LO	RCD	LS	Rel	SBA	SacA	RM	PO	#	Good	NG	Bomb	W	L	Pct
2007	Padres	NL	163	115	.62	279	18	13	63	28	13	122	0	485	79	85	73	56	48	28	20	11	89	74	.546
2008	Padres	NL	162	113	.63	286	25	20	55	36	17	109	0	491	53	75	78	31	61	30	31	17	63	99	.389
2009	Padres	NL	162	137	.64	264	8	34	50	37	8	118	5	527	111	99	84	55	58	42	16	6	75	87	.463
2010	Padres	NL	162	135	.61	285	16	45	55	33	10	132	7	499	174	99	135	31	51	35	16	8	90	72	.556
2011	Padres	NL	162	140	.58	288	20	43	40	36	10	110	2	490	214	69	184	41	56	31	25	13	71	91	.438
2012	Padres	NL	162	132	.74	280	26	35	45	43	11	126	5	529	201	89	162	21	48	34	14	7	76	86	.469
2013	Padres	NL	162	145	.66	271	24	37	35	46	4	102	1	488	152	78	122	12	31	20	11	8	76	86	.469
2014	Padres	NL	162	157	.74	313	23	29	49	33	13	104	1	481	125	74	116	15	32	24	8	4	77	85	.475
2015	Padres	NL	65	50	.54	113	6	6	8	25	3	40	0	199	54	24	46	2	15	11	4	0	32	33	.492
2017	Rockies	NL	162	111	.51	261	19	14	44	34	4	100	2	549	93	76	149	4	20	14	6	3	87	75	.537
2018	Rockies	NL	163	126	.56	276	20	19	29	49	5	103	1	518	128	65	137	2	24	16	8	5	91	72	.558
2019	Rockies	NL	162	141	.60	305	8	13	27	58	1	114	3	590	102	71	96	5	33	21	12	3	71	91	.438
	162-Game Average			132	.62	282	19	27	44	41	9	112	2	512	130	79	121	24	42	27	15	7	79	83	.488

Bruce Bochy

Year	Team	Lg	G	LUp	PL%	PH	PR	DS	Quick	Slow	LO	RCD	LS	Rel	SBA	SacA	RM	PO	#	Good	NG	Bomb	W	L	Pct
1995	Padres	NL	144	96	.59	262	30	23	44	41	17	38	3	337	170	68		38	37	19	18	11	70	74	.486
1996	Padres	NL	162	114	.52	289	29	15	51	33	10	67	12	411	164	73		65	47	29	18	12	91	71	.562
1997	Padres	NL	162	111	.60	291	26	9	45	45	3	81	11	426	200	84		58	37	20	17	11	76	86	.469
1998	Padres	NL	162	108	.65	280	62	44	44	45	9	81	12	369	116	84		27	45	31	14	10	98	64	.605
1999	Padres	NL	162	137	.60	298	51	21	44	36	4	68	5	403	241	60		29	48	29	19	13	74	88	.457
2000	Padres	NL	162	134	.52	285	44	14	41	47	14	105	5	443	184	52		27	50	21	29	11	76	86	.469
2001	Padres	NL	162	116	.60	255	54	27	32	47	6	85	10	422	173	43		23	54	31	23	13	79	83	.488
2002	Padres	NL	162	123	.66	259	44	56	39	40	17	106	4	459	115	63	74	14	61	38	23	14	66	96	.407
2003	Padres	NL	162	134	.58	339	20	29	34	43	16	100	4	473	115	63	41	6	52	33	19	12	64	98	.395
2004	Padres	NL	162	96	.54	261	28	47	47	32	15	76	3	437	77	75	96	14	39	24	15	10	87	75	.537
2005	Padres	NL	162	128	.58	285	31	49	46	36	23	87	1	456	143	89	111	16	45	33	12	8	82	80	.506
2006	Padres	NL	162	111	.60	264	64	48	43	42	24	111	2	475	154	77	110	21	63	43	20	10	88	74	.543
2007	Giants	NL	162	128	.72	264	50	45	26	50	36	132	2	496	152	86	119	10	41	29	12	3	71	91	.438
2008	Giants	NL	162	134	.68	274	32	39	24	59	42	97	6	478	154	77	155	5	59	40	19	8	72	90	.444
2009	Giants	NL	162	134	.65	231	21	52	42	40	32	84	8	457	106	93	118	5	49	32	17	10	88	74	.543
2010	Giants	NL	162	126	.55	224	45	70	29	37	40	118	12	477	87	102	144	12	58	41	17	8	92	70	.568
2011	Giants	NL	162	138	.62	245	49	42	38	38	44	108	3	480	136	79	175	11	46	36	10	6	86	76	.531
2012	Giants	NL	162	112	.75	220	32	55	22	50	31	136	9	526	157	87	176	15	42	30	12	5	94	68	.580
2013	Giants	NL	162	109	.70	263	19	45	33	52	23	143	4	524	93	78	164	7	64	46	18	6	76	86	.469
2014	Giants	NL	162	131	.66	236	29	64	45	41	19	102	1	475	83	53	147	12	35	25	10	9	88	74	.543
2015	Giants	NL	162	124	.63	230	12	21	45	32	11	137	2	557	129	54	173	8	28	20	8	3	84	78	.519
2016	Giants	NL	162	121	.66	268	7	29	31	42	28	148	4	575	115	54	178	6	30	25	5	4	87	75	.537
2017	Giants	NL	162	136	.61	298	22	12	22	59	20	93	2	502	110	51	135	3	42	29	13	11	64	98	.395
2018	Giants	NL	162	140	.59	305	16	30	36	38	6	100	0	549	111	43	139	2	37	25	12	5	73	89	.451
2019	Giants	NL	162	141	.67	362	11	25	34	43	4	94	2	587	75	37	101	4	26	16	10	4	77	85	.475
	162-Game Average			124	.62	273	33	37	38	43	20	100	5	474	135	69	131	18	46	30	16	9	80	82	.494

Aaron Boone

Year	Team	Lg	G	LUp	PL%	PH	PR	DS	Quick	Slow	LO	RCD	LS	Rel	SBA	SacA	RM	PO	#	Good	NG	Bomb	W	L	Pct
2018	Yankees	AL	162	137	.54	71	14	24	45	32	3	75	5	508	84	17	113	3	9	4	5	3	100	62	.617
2019	Yankees	AL	162	155	.48	57	24	32	43	27	1	80	5	545	77	19	81	2	12	9	3	1	103	59	.636
	162-Game Average			146	.51	64	19	28	44	30	2	78	5	527	81	18	97	3	11	7	4	2	102	61	.626

Mickey Callaway

Year	Team	Lg	G	LUp	PL%	PH	PR	DS	Quick	Slow	LO	RCD	LS	Rel	SBA	SacA	RM	PO	#	Good	NG	Bomb	W	L	Pct
2018	Mets	NL	162	151	.58	258	17	30	41	43	11	72	10	501	110	39	119	6	32	17	15	9	77	85	.475
2019	Mets	NL	162	132	.50	273	42	65	35	57	16	87	6	502	83	42	102	10	40	27	13	6	86	76	.531
	162-Game Average			142	.54	266	30	48	38	50	14	80	8	502	97	41	111	8	36	22	14	8	82	81	.503

Kevin Cash

Year	Team	Lg	G	LUp	PL%	PH	PR	DS	Quick	Slow	LO	RCD	LS	Rel	SBA	SacA	RM	PO	#	Good	NG	Bomb	W	L	Pct
2015	Rays	AL	162	137	.62	219	23	38	72	33	10	134	3	530	132	27	173	2	23	17	6	3	80	82	.494
2016	Rays	AL	162	142	.55	103	11	28	42	52	18	100	8	485	97	24	146	12	25	16	9	4	68	94	.420
2017	Rays	AL	162	126	.57	123	21	24	39	47	16	89	9	511	122	24	143	12	37	25	12	8	80	82	.494

Year	Team	Lg	G	LUp	PL%	PH	PR	DS	Quick	Slow	LO	RCD	LS	Rel	SBA	SacA	RM	PO	#	Good	NG	Bomb	W	L	Pct
				LINEUPS		SUBSTITUTION			PITCHER USAGE						TACTICS				INTENTIONAL BB				RESULTS		
2018	Rays	AL	162	151	.58	109	25	33	50	18	5	115	10	553	**179**	37	**190**	2	**34**	20	14	9	90	72	.556
2019	Rays	AL	162	152	.59	131	31	43	**50**	18	0	**136**	6	603	131	11	166	3	27	14	13	8	96	66	.593
162-Game Average				142	.58	137	22	33	51	34	10	115	7	536	132	25	164	6	29	18	11	6	83	79	.512

Terry Collins

Year	Team	Lg	G	LUp	PL%	PH	PR	DS	Quick	Slow	LO	RCD	LS	Rel	SBA	SacA	RM	PO	#	Good	NG	Bomb	W	L	Pct
				LINEUPS		SUBSTITUTION			PITCHER USAGE						TACTICS				INTENTIONAL BB				RESULTS		
1994	Astros	NL	115	74	.54	185	20	13	6	6	0	37	4	268	168	90		37	28	17	11	5	66	49	.574
1995	Astros	NL	144	106	.49	302	38	11	15	7	8	100	8	394	236	97		44	39	27	12	8	76	68	.528
1996	Astros	NL	162	111	.41	257	30	38	13	12	9	70	10	371	243	94		35	42	30	12	6	82	80	.506
1997	Angels	AL	162	117	.70	86	34	22	10	16	15	67	8	400	198	55		60	25	13	12	4	84	78	.519
1998	Angels	AL	162	119	.57	100	64	33	15	11	28	86	11	415	138	69		38	16	6	10	4	85	77	.525
1999	Angels	AL	133	113	.56	93	26	16	10	16	10	68	2	315	93	39		7	10	1	9	3	51	82	.383
2011	Mets	NL	162	121	.68	247	18	28	32	44	23	126	5	514	165	48	151	9	48	35	13	9	77	85	.475
2012	Mets	NL	162	**141**	.69	**329**	16	38	39	36	19	113	0	505	117	75	149		29	18	11	3	74	88	.457
2013	Mets	NL	162	132	.61	266	12	33	33	42	15	131	**4**	**535**	149	67	128	3	38	30	8	3	74	88	.457
2014	Mets	NL	162	135	.55	247	17	26	28	46	23	111	6	489	135	73	119	2	38	23	15	4	79	83	.488
2015	Mets	NL	162	138	.52	255	15	40	47	36	6	119	8	485	76	49	117	1	43	33	10	6	90	72	.556
2016	Mets	NL	162	129	.68	292	17	50	53	33	6	141	4	538	60	55	80	6	39	26	13	9	87	75	.537
2017	Mets	NL	162	**149**	.66	247	20	32	25	54	8	**127**	6	568	81	52	97	3	51	27	**24**	**14**	70	92	.432
162-Game Average				128	.59	239	27	31	26	29	14	104	6	467	150	73	120	20	36	23	13	6	80	82	.494

Alex Cora

Year	Team	Lg	G	LUp	PL%	PH	PR	DS	Quick	Slow	LO	RCD	LS	Rel	SBA	SacA	RM	PO	#	Good	NG	Bomb	W	L	Pct
				LINEUPS		SUBSTITUTION			PITCHER USAGE						TACTICS				INTENTIONAL BB				RESULTS		
2018	Red Sox	AL	162	134	.55	96	22	31	**58**	44	5	101	4	535	156	8	183	1	8	4	4	1	**108**	54	.667
2019	Red Sox	AL	162	135	.57	123	29	18	45	**52**	16	134	3	**632**	98	26	140	2	22	14	8	6	84	78	.519
162-Game Average				135	.56	110	26	25	52	48	11	118	4	584	127	17	162	2	15	9	6	4	96	66	.593

Craig Counsell

Year	Team	Lg	G	LUp	PL%	PH	PR	DS	Quick	Slow	LO	RCD	LS	Rel	SBA	SacA	RM	PO	#	Good	NG	Bomb	W	L	Pct
				LINEUPS		SUBSTITUTION			PITCHER USAGE						TACTICS				INTENTIONAL BB				RESULTS		
2015	Brewers	NL	137	106	.54	247	14	30	30	47	3	85	1	424	99	56	106	2	30	26	4	3	61	76	.445
2016	Brewers	NL	162	123	.55	284	4	22	40	41	1	115	3	513	**237**	71	160	0	33	16	17	8	73	89	.451
2017	Brewers	NL	162	123	.53	285	18	44	58	35	5	124	5	550	169	56	159	0	45	30	15	9	86	76	.531
2018	Brewers	NL	163	137	.54	288	17	77	**64**	29	0	105	**18**	559	156	38	**148**	1	34	22	12	7	**96**	67	.589
2019	Brewers	NL	162	134	.64	317	14	56	**60**	26	1	97	**17**	588	126	29	78	3	28	22	6	2	89	73	.549
162-Game Average				128	.56	293	14	47	52	36	2	108	9	543	162	52	134	1	35	24	11	6	83	79	.512

John Farrell

Year	Team	Lg	G	LUp	PL%	PH	PR	DS	Quick	Slow	LO	RCD	LS	Rel	SBA	SacA	RM	PO	#	Good	NG	Bomb	W	L	Pct
				LINEUPS		SUBSTITUTION			PITCHER USAGE						TACTICS				INTENTIONAL BB				RESULTS		
2011	Blue Jays	AL	162	131	.43	64	**48**	22	40	41	26	62	3	474	183	40	181	22	28	17	11	5	81	81	.500
2012	Blue Jays	AL	162	131	.50	94	30	16	49	44	7	84	3	495	164	46	211	15	20	11	9	7	73	89	.451
2013	Red Sox	AL	162	126	.68	93	41	20	28	46	34	71	4	450	142	32	147	5	10	5	5	3	**97**	65	.599
2014	Red Sox	AL	162	**145**	.55	101	24	17	29	53	28	107	1	493	88	26	124	4	19	11	8	2	71	91	.438
2015	Red Sox	AL	114	96	.56	55	18	20	26	28	6	62	1	326	63	27	105	2	12	6	6	1	50	64	.439
2016	Red Sox	AL	162	118	.53	110	28	11	34	51	26	79	2	463	107	15	169	10	16	8	8	3	93	69	.574
2017	Red Sox	AL	162	137	.54	95	39	17	30	**63**	**33**	97	4	515	137	20	131	2	18	13	5	1	93	69	.574
162-Game Average				132	.54	91	34	18	35	49	24	84	3	480	132	31	159	7	18	11	8	3	83	79	.512

Terry Francona

Year	Team	Lg	G	LUp	PL%	PH	PR	DS	Quick	Slow	LO	RCD	LS	Rel	SBA	SacA	RM	PO	#	Good	NG	Bomb	W	L	Pct
				LINEUPS		SUBSTITUTION			PITCHER USAGE						TACTICS				INTENTIONAL BB				RESULTS		
1997	Phillies	NL	162	98	.66	288	19	28	28	54	22	102	9	409	148	91		30	42	23	19	9	68	94	.420
1998	Phillies	NL	162	84	.53	256	20	19	34	57	20	88	7	385	142	85		16	27	10	17	8	75	87	.463
1999	Phillies	NL	162	85	.51	239	13	31	29	41	16	111	7	441	160	81		27	24	14	10	6	77	85	.475
2000	Phillies	NL	162	108	.53	278	17	14	38	43	25	102	5	414	132	89		16	32	22	10	7	65	97	.401
2004	Red Sox	AL	162	141	.65	116	65	**58**	41	48	32	105	8	437	98	18	91	28	28	22	6	4	98	64	.605
2005	Red Sox	AL	162	104	.67	110	46	37	25	55	30	99	3	442	57	21	79	11	28	18	10	5	95	67	.586
2006	Red Sox	AL	162	116	.59	93	**54**	49	36	44	13	94	9	454	74	33	98	16	25	11	14	7	86	76	.531
2007	Red Sox	AL	162	109	.60	84	34	23	41	35	32	89	4	451	120	45	90	14	20	14	6	4	**96**	66	.593
2008	Red Sox	AL	162	131	.59	62	40	40	50	30	20	90	**11**	466	155	40	87	8	17	10	7	4	95	67	.586
2009	Red Sox	AL	162	113	.58	85	47	28	36	50	30	68	6	463	165	29	68	9	24	15	9	6	95	67	.586
2010	Red Sox	AL	162	**143**	.62	125	34	34	32	**63**	**49**	92	3	443	85	36	125	26	30	17	13	4	89	73	.549
2011	Red Sox	AL	162	123	.67	89	44	11	**52**	46	27	94	4	444	144	29	163	34	11	6	5	2	90	72	.556

Year	Team	Lg	G	LUp	PL%	PH	PR	DS	Quick	Slow	LO	RCD	LS	Rel	SBA	SacA	RM	PO	#	Good	NG	Bomb	W	L	Pct
2013	Indians	AL	162	121	.75	78	45	24	47	34	18	122	2	540	153	41	158	5	26	15	11	6	92	70	.568
2014	Indians	AL	162	133	.78	123	16	24	37	37	18	150	7	573	131	58	128	3	51	29	22	13	85	77	.525
2015	Indians	AL	161	127	.75	138	21	13	40	36	23	85	8	476	114	63	87	4	27	20	7	5	81	80	.503
2016	Indians	AL	161	101	.73	114	27	29	47	39	18	103	3	504	165	44	126	2	34	22	12	7	94	67	.584
2017	Indians	AL	162	131	.73	93	43	50	48	31	20	106	4	497	111	35	95	2	15	11	4	3	102	60	.630
2018	Indians	AL	162	105	.75	97	74	42	29	48	23	121	10	508	171	44	152	6	29	19	10	6	91	71	.562
2019	Indians	AL	162	132	.73	101	25	15	30	44	29	89	9	522	138	57	100	2	19	11	8	7	93	69	.574
162-Game Average				116	.65	135	37	30	38	44	24	100	6	467	130	49	110	14	27	16	11	6	88	74	.543

Ron Gardenhire

Year	Team	Lg	G	LUp	PL%	PH	PR	DS	Quick	Slow	LO	RCD	LS	Rel	SBA	SacA	RM	PO	#	Good	NG	Bomb	W	L	Pct
2002	Twins	AL	161	111	.69	141	36	42	54	25	10	84	1	435	141	48	44	11	24	16	8	4	94	67	.584
2003	Twins	AL	162	126	.63	144	50	26	49	33	13	85	2	399	138	59	37	14	35	16	19	6	90	72	.556
2004	Twins	AL	162	131	.59	129	45	29	56	21	20	106	4	435	162	66	121	18	27	15	12	7	92	70	.568
2005	Twins	AL	162	135	.58	104	45	26	50	21	5	87	1	396	146	59	138	16	38	28	10	3	83	79	.512
2006	Twins	AL	162	97	.62	93	36	21	60	31	3	82	5	421	143	48	130	11	25	14	11	4	96	66	.593
2007	Twins	AL	162	139	.63	104	42	25	45	30	8	99	4	438	142	45	148	11	33	14	19	9	79	83	.488
2008	Twins	AL	163	103	.64	109	26	12	47	29	5	115	3	485	144	73	143	17	38	25	13	8	88	75	.540
2009	Twins	AL	163	129	.63	83	54	34	43	25	12	115	3	480	117	62	100	21	20	9	11	6	87	76	.534
2010	Twins	AL	162	112	.62	86	55	30	57	28	5	106	1	465	96	47	140	14	19	12	7	4	94	68	.580
2011	Twins	AL	162	150	.58	93	48	21	34	44	17	82	1	457	131	44	170	5	37	21	16	9	63	99	.389
2012	Twins	AL	162	121	.62	64	45	24	42	31	4	82	1	499	172	49	207	10	43	27	16	6	66	96	.407
2013	Twins	AL	162	139	.66	103	42	28	41	43	6	78	1	511	85	37	137	14	31	13	18	7	66	96	.407
2014	Twins	AL	162	132	.64	97	44	23	40	40	2	82	2	491	135	31	149	5	24	11	13	6	70	92	.432
2018	Tigers	AL	162	144	.56	75	60	8	40	39	1	99	3	542	100	25	121	6	20	11	9	7	64	98	.395
2019	Tigers	AL	161	155	.48	68	42	7	45	46	2	87	0	577	77	19	93	7	24	13	11	6	47	114	.292
162-Game Average				128	.61	100	45	24	47	32	8	93	2	469	129	47	125	12	29	16	13	6	79	83	.488

John Gibbons

Year	Team	Lg	G	LUp	PL%	PH	PR	DS	Quick	Slow	LO	RCD	LS	Rel	SBA	SacA	RM	PO	#	Good	NG	Bomb	W	L	Pct
2004	Blue Jays	AL	50	36	.68	42	3	2	16	8	7	22	1	130	34	2	47	21	11	5	6	3	20	30	.400
2005	Blue Jays	AL	162	124	.66	148	11	37	55	18	9	77	12	432	107	28	128	45	29	13	16	9	80	82	.494
2006	Blue Jays	AL	162	120	.53	112	32	40	59	33	17	94	16	482	98	20	127	40	56	32	24	12	87	75	.537
2007	Blue Jays	AL	162	131	.46	139	48	33	45	37	31	75	9	420	79	35	99	37	34	17	17	6	83	79	.512
2008	Blue Jays	AL	74	60	.48	53	15	18	12	20	12	43	0	205	70	23	39	10	26	16	10	6	35	39	.473
2013	Blue Jays	AL	162	136	.63	124	31	24	55	44	14	69	2	487	153	41	160	4	33	17	16	6	74	88	.457
2014	Blue Jays	AL	162	128	.72	202	41	49	45	37	20	73	8	449	99	49	161	6	23	17	6	2	83	79	.512
2015	Blue Jays	AL	162	129	.48	97	41	47	46	37	13	85	6	469	111	45	152	2	20	10	10	3	93	69	.574
2016	Blue Jays	AL	162	141	.44	90	37	54	39	30	6	98	6	487	78	33	109	1	10	6	4	3	89	73	.549
2017	Blue Jays	AL	162	136	.56	126	39	33	41	33	8	100	4	578	77	35	132	4	25	14	11	5	76	86	.469
2018	Blue Jays	AL	162	154	.59	128	38	28	27	49	2	111	3	590	77	8	120	6	19	13	6	4	73	89	.451
162-Game Average				133	.56	129	34	37	45	35	14	87	7	484	101	33	130	18	29	16	13	6	81	81	.500

Joe Girardi

Year	Team	Lg	G	LUp	PL%	PH	PR	DS	Quick	Slow	LO	RCD	LS	Rel	SBA	SacA	RM	PO	#	Good	NG	Bomb	W	L	Pct
2006	Marlins	NL	162	117	.50	250	44	66	46	40	28	76	3	438	168	97	108	42	58	37	21	7	78	84	.481
2008	Yankees	AL	162	114	.63	97	37	42	60	37	12	88	10	475	157	38	173	36	37	22	15	8	89	73	.549
2009	Yankees	AL	162	106	.73	97	61	42	36	45	27	88	13	461	139	44	83	33	28	14	14	9	103	59	.636
2010	Yankees	AL	162	114	.72	117	44	31	43	39	33	76	3	430	133	47	152	20	37	26	11	6	95	67	.586
2011	Yankees	AL	162	94	.69	72	41	53	51	36	21	88	2	465	193	50	151	26	43	30	13	4	97	65	.599
2012	Yankees	AL	162	107	.70	149	33	48	37	53	21	115	7	485	120	47	145	10	32	17	15	4	95	67	.586
2013	Yankees	AL	162	141	.59	119	15	29	42	50	23	82	4	428	146	49	131	4	34	20	14	6	85	77	.525
2014	Yankees	AL	162	142	.74	100	27	33	51	28	10	95	7	475	138	44	132	8	23	10	13	9	84	78	.519
2015	Yankees	AL	162	126	.79	118	50	57	48	34	9	80	10	497	88	32	92	6	16	8	8	4	87	75	.537
2016	Yankees	AL	162	143	.72	85	32	48	53	44	8	99	7	483	94	35	89	3	15	9	6	4	84	78	.519
2017	Yankees	AL	162	140	.56	112	22	10	49	29	9	79	7	477	112	28	117	3	18	11	7	4	91	71	.562
162-Game Average				122	.67	120	37	42	47	40	18	88	7	465	135	46	125	17	31	19	12	6	90	72	.556

Fredi Gonzalez

Year	Team	Lg	G	LUp	PL%	PH	PR	DS	Quick	Slow	LO	RCD	LS	Rel	SBA	SacA	RM	PO	#	Good	NG	Bomb	W	L	Pct
2007	Marlins	NL	162	96	.50	284	29	34	38	56	20	138	5	560	139	91	79	22	60	36	24	16	71	91	.438
2008	Marlins	NL	161	106	.51	255	38	49	38	39	8	120	3	511	104	61	75	17	66	42	24	14	84	77	.522
2009	Marlins	NL	162	97	.58	281	28	49	48	26	12	116	0	530	110	86	88	20	60	38	22	15	87	75	.537

Year	Team	Lg	G	LUp	PL%	PH	PR	DS	Quick	Slow	LO	RCD	LS	Rel	SBA	SacA	RM	PO	#	Good	NG	Bomb	W	L	Pct
2010	Marlins	NL	70	31	.41	104	12	16	14	13	11	35	1	193	56	33	64	10	18	11	7	5	34	36	.486
2011	Braves	NL	162	119	.60	260	27	29	53	36	21	144	0	510	121	95	139	19	73	49	24	13	89	73	.549
2012	Braves	NL	162	108	.61	268	18	27	50	34	9	115	4	460	133	67	116	20	40	28	12	11	94	68	.580
2013	Braves	NL	162	115	.50	214	40	51	50	42	8	124	2	466	95	79	94	11	35	26	9	4	96	66	.593
2014	Braves	NL	162	103	.45	206	34	34	27	41	20	122	3	472	128	70	106	23	36	24	12	8	79	83	.488
2015	Braves	NL	162	140	.61	255	21	31	35	55	7	136	0	532	102	80	135	4	45	35	10	5	67	95	.414
2016	Braves	NL	37	34	.73	58	9	11	9	9	3	33	1	131	26	20	36	0	15	11	4	2	9	28	.243
	162-Game Average			110	.54	252	30	38	41	41	14	125	2	504	117	79	108	17	52	35	17	11	82	80	.506

Andy Green

Year	Team	Lg	G	LUp	PL%	PH	PR	DS	Quick	Slow	LO	RCD	LS	Rel	SBA	SacA	RM	PO	#	Good	NG	Bomb	W	L	Pct
2016	Padres	NL	162	130	.56	249	29	25	46	53	6	119	4	510	170	48	138	3	44	26	18	9	68	94	.420
2017	Padres	NL	162	138	.55	238	10	38	45	43	5	101	2	517	122	63	119	2	28	18	10	4	71	91	.438
2018	Padres	NL	162	146	.62	264	21	38	45	49	5	84	6	535	131	49	109	0	28	17	11	6	66	96	.407
2019	Padres	NL	154	139	.45	263	11	51	52	31	0	99	5	509	103	42	93	0	19	14	5	3	69	85	.448
	162-Game Average			140	.54	257	18	38	48	45	4	102	4	524	133	51	116	1	30	19	11	6	69	93	.426

Chip Hale

Year	Team	Lg	G	LUp	PL%	PH	PR	DS	Quick	Slow	LO	RCD	LS	Rel	SBA	SacA	RM	PO	#	Good	NG	Bomb	W	L	Pct
2015	Diamondbacks	NL	162	130	.48	270	14	35	49	35	5	103	8	550	176	67	146	5	45	35	10	6	79	83	.488
2016	Diamondbacks	NL	162	139	.45	266	10	30	27	66	7	130	5	575	168	51	120	0	57	41	16	8	69	93	.426
	162-Game Average			135	.46	268	12	33	38	51	6	117	7	563	172	59	133	3	51	38	13	7	74	88	.457

A.J. Hinch

Year	Team	Lg	G	LUp	PL%	PH	PR	DS	Quick	Slow	LO	RCD	LS	Rel	SBA	SacA	RM	PO	#	Good	NG	Bomb	W	L	Pct
2009	Diamondbacks	NL	133	115	.63	222	10	13	24	50	24	61	5	392	113	64	41	5	24	12	12	6	58	75	.436
2010	Diamondbacks	NL	79	56	.53	120	7	4	12	40	21	39	1	207	58	19	51	7	19	9	10	9	31	48	.392
2015	Astros	AL	162	151	.63	122	40	37	33	41	19	97	0	482	169	31	128	6	17	11	6	2	86	76	.531
2016	Astros	AL	162	143	.55	118	35	27	42	35	9	87	1	500	146	38	137	5	19	11	8	6	84	78	.519
2017	Astros	AL	162	144	.56	73	29	39	57	35	3	83	8	519	140	21	148	6	17	12	5	3	101	61	.623
2018	Astros	AL	162	144	.54	92	34	39	31	35	10	80	4	510	97	9	154	2	4	3	1	0	103	59	.636
2019	Astros	AL	162	134	.46	81	41	26	38	30	7	92	2	492	94	15	96	0	0	0	0	0	107	55	.660
	162-Game Average			141	.56	131	31	29	38	42	15	85	3	492	130	31	120	5	16	9	7	4	90	72	.556

Clint Hurdle

Year	Team	Lg	G	LUp	PL%	PH	PR	DS	Quick	Slow	LO	RCD	LS	Rel	SBA	SacA	RM	PO	#	Good	NG	Bomb	W	L	Pct
2002	Rockies	NL	140	100	.52	274	28	41	33	45	17	104	3	437	139	46	50	13	38	22	16	11	67	73	.479
2003	Rockies	NL	162	108	.47	317	17	32	35	40	5	87	4	500	100	82	26	16	51	31	20	13	74	88	.457
2004	Rockies	NL	162	131	.57	289	18	35	36	63	20	74	1	473	77	128	67	12	84	54	30	12	68	94	.420
2005	Rockies	NL	162	135	.60	273	21	40	42	60	17	89	2	459	97	114	119	22	54	28	26	15	67	95	.414
2006	Rockies	NL	162	111	.49	259	17	22	34	52	17	107	2	499	135	156	114	28	81	45	36	23	76	86	.469
2007	Rockies	NL	163	96	.51	283	32	29	45	37	13	112	1	529	131	112	109	26	61	30	31	14	90	73	.552
2008	Rockies	NL	162	131	.49	253	20	31	40	43	16	85	2	485	178	111	116	43	49	31	18	6	74	88	.457
2009	Rockies	NL	46	42	.60	73	8	10	11	14	3	31	0	135	45	26	34	3	11	8	3	1	18	28	.391
2011	Pirates	NL	162	134	.60	278	26	63	58	27	1	134	3	549	160	101	173	20	65	39	26	13	72	90	.444
2012	Pirates	NL	162	133	.55	270	26	60	50	33	3	74	2	483	125	82	120	17	30	18	12	3	79	83	.488
2013	Pirates	NL	162	127	.51	289	24	61	61	25	7	76	3	465	136	83	172	20	26	22	4	2	94	68	.580
2014	Pirates	NL	162	123	.50	322	28	38	47	40	7	91	0	442	151	85	187	24	43	26	17	7	88	74	.543
2015	Pirates	NL	162	108	.50	269	48	76	39	40	9	124	1	500	143	81	173	9	38	31	7	3	98	64	.605
2016	Pirates	NL	162	125	.41	293	39	73	57	36	1	119	4	525	155	55	154	9	28	15	13	6	78	83	.484
2017	Pirates	NL	162	138	.51	277	23	37	42	39	6	110	8	502	103	59	124	7	32	17	15	7	75	87	.463
2018	Pirates	NL	161	128	.62	267	14	27	44	38	1	88	6	480	108	45	119	2	43	32	11	5	82	79	.509
2019	Pirates	NL	161	131	.67	281	30	38	40	49	0	85	7	548	93	60	117	16	22	15	7	5	69	92	.429
	162-Game Average			124	.53	283	26	44	44	42	9	99	3	497	129	88	122	18	47	29	18	9	79	83	.488

Brandon Hyde

Year	Team	Lg	G	LUp	PL%	PH	PR	DS	Quick	Slow	LO	RCD	LS	Rel	SBA	SacA	RM	PO	#	Good	NG	Bomb	W	L	Pct
2011	Marlins	NL	1	1	.44	0	0	0	0	0	1	1	0	3	0	0	1	0	1	1	0	0	0	1	.000
2019	Orioles	AL	162	150	.70	126	26	42	30	35	1	73	11	533	114	34	82	0	11	5	6	4	54	108	.333
	162-Game Average			150	.69	125	26	42	30	35	2	74	11	533	113	34	82	0	12	6	6	4	54	108	.333

Gabe Kapler

Year	Team	Lg	G	LINEUPS		SUBSTITUTION			PITCHER USAGE						TACTICS				INTENTIONAL BB				RESULTS		
				LUp	PL%	PH	PR	DS	Quick	Slow	LO	RCD	LS	Rel	SBA	SacA	RM	PO	#	Good	NG	Bomb	W	L	Pct
2018	Phillies	NL	162	138	.66	295	22	38	38	38	3	117	11	596	95	46	65	0	35	25	10	5	80	82	.494
2019	Phillies	NL	162	106	.55	312	11	21	28	48	3	121	9	564	96	50	69	0	38	31	7	4	81	81	.500
	162-Game Average			122	.61	304	17	30	33	43	3	119	10	580	96	48	67	0	37	28	9	5	81	82	.497

Torey Lovullo

Year	Team	Lg	G	LINEUPS		SUBSTITUTION			PITCHER USAGE						TACTICS				INTENTIONAL BB				RESULTS		
				LUp	PL%	PH	PR	DS	Quick	Slow	LO	RCD	LS	Rel	SBA	SacA	RM	PO	#	Good	NG	Bomb	W	L	Pct
2015	Red Sox	AL	48	40	.58	17	17	4	9	16	10	28	0	149	35	10	32	0	5	3	2	1	28	20	.583
2017	Diamondbacks	NL	162	129	.55	254	28	36	34	45	6	116	2	513	133	50	85	3	45	32	13	6	93	69	.574
2018	Diamondbacks	NL	162	144	.66	258	13	32	31	45	2	143	2	573	104	60	92	3	43	29	14	4	82	80	.506
2019	Diamondbacks	NL	162	126	.66	256	21	46	32	38	0	105	9	557	102	49	105	5	38	19	19	8	85	77	.525
	162-Game Average			133	.62	238	24	36	32	44	5	119	4	544	113	51	95	3	40	25	15	6	87	75	.537

Pete Mackanin

Year	Team	Lg	G	LINEUPS		SUBSTITUTION			PITCHER USAGE						TACTICS				INTENTIONAL BB				RESULTS		
				LUp	PL%	PH	PR	DS	Quick	Slow	LO	RCD	LS	Rel	SBA	SacA	RM	PO	#	Good	NG	Bomb	W	L	Pct
2005	Pirates	NL	26	24	.52	54	1	5	11	4	1	22	0	94	19	19	20	2	5	2	3	1	12	14	.462
2007	Reds	NL	80	57	.59	130	10	26	20	22	9	58	3	266	62	44	36	12	18	10	8	3	41	39	.513
2015	Phillies	NL	88	82	.76	143	2	16	25	26	5	58	4	278	70	48	93	9	12	7	5	2	37	51	.420
2016	Phillies	NL	162	144	.64	260	14	46	44	44	4	128	2	505	141	61	138	17	30	19	11	10	71	91	.438
2017	Phillies	NL	162	135	.66	236	11	21	37	44	3	114	2	506	84	40	91	0	39	24	15	4	66	96	.407
	162-Game Average			138	.65	257	12	36	43	44	7	119	3	516	118	66	118	13	33	19	13	6	71	91	.438

Joe Maddon

Year	Team	Lg	G	LINEUPS		SUBSTITUTION			PITCHER USAGE						TACTICS				INTENTIONAL BB				RESULTS		
				LUp	PL%	PH	PR	DS	Quick	Slow	LO	RCD	LS	Rel	SBA	SacA	RM	PO	#	Good	NG	Bomb	W	L	Pct
1996	Angels	AL	22	19	.64	21	5	0	7	6	6	10	3	48	11	20		6	4	3	1	1	8	14	.364
1998	Angels	AL	8	4	.57	2	4	0	1	5	3	5	3	12	2	7		0	1	0	1	0	6	2	.750
1999	Angels	AL	29	19	.58	29	4	1	6	0	4	20	0	85	23	12		7	3	1	2	1	19	10	.655
2006	Devil Rays	AL	162	145	.54	81	26	51	41	39	16	79	10	444	186	51	132	48	39	19	20	13	61	101	.377
2007	Devil Rays	AL	162	122	.53	80	19	16	31	56	19	113	1	483	179	40	118	50	31	18	13	4	66	96	.407
2008	Rays	AL	162	115	.69	133	16	39	48	37	14	112	7	448	192	31	113	26	29	15	14	8	97	65	.599
2009	Rays	AL	162	123	.66	140	21	18	28	51	23	139	3	510	255	29	99	15	22	10	12	7	84	78	.519
2010	Rays	AL	162	129	.67	174	31	18	41	34	26	135	2	491	219	45	166	12	34	28	6	3	96	66	.593
2011	Rays	AL	162	130	.67	137	16	31	34	36	47	112	6	438	217	42	187	4	38	23	15	6	91	71	.562
2012	Rays	AL	162	151	.62	156	37	52	43	38	33	123	3	472	178	40	181	7	35	25	10	6	90	72	.556
2013	Rays	AL	163	147	.64	193	27	56	52	38	16	111	6	485	111	26	117	6	38	21	17	11	92	71	.564
2014	Rays	AL	162	130	.58	171	23	15	44	35	26	110	3	494	90	54	143	2	27	20	7	3	77	85	.475
2015	Cubs	NL	162	119	.60	288	22	32	41	31	14	129	2	552	132	48	180	3	38	22	16	10	97	65	.599
2016	Cubs	NL	162	130	.62	236	19	35	56	29	13	100	3	503	100	54	111	6	24	19	5	3	103	58	.640
2017	Cubs	NL	162	143	.65	296	7	51	47	30	10	85	3	531	93	54	122	1	29	18	11	7	92	70	.568
2018	Cubs	NL	163	152	.61	280	18	48	41	44	5	120	2	600	104	56	130	1	33	25	8	6	95	68	.583
2019	Cubs	NL	162	140	.56	244	15	43	40	41	7	103	4	576	69	46	87	3	16	11	5	3	84	78	.519
	162-Game Average			133	.62	185	22	35	42	38	20	112	4	499	150	46	135	14	31	19	11	6	88	74	.543

Dave Martinez

Year	Team	Lg	G	LINEUPS		SUBSTITUTION			PITCHER USAGE						TACTICS				INTENTIONAL BB				RESULTS		
				LUp	PL%	PH	PR	DS	Quick	Slow	LO	RCD	LS	Rel	SBA	SacA	RM	PO	#	Good	NG	Bomb	W	L	Pct
2018	Nationals	NL	162	125	.61	295	23	24	31	62	22	123	4	562	152	55	91	3	37	24	13	6	82	80	.506
2019	Nationals	NL	162	106	.49	253	15	19	32	41	13	136	8	530	145	77	82	0	41	31	10	6	93	69	.574
	162-Game Average			116	.55	274	19	23	32	52	18	130	6	546	149	66	87	2	39	28	12	6	88	75	.540

Mike Matheny

Year	Team	Lg	G	LINEUPS		SUBSTITUTION			PITCHER USAGE						TACTICS				INTENTIONAL BB				RESULTS		
				LUp	PL%	PH	PR	DS	Quick	Slow	LO	RCD	LS	Rel	SBA	SacA	RM	PO	#	Good	NG	Bomb	W	L	Pct
2012	Cardinals	NL	162	122	.62	286	37	33	53	37	8	118	5	506	128	95	144	16	28	13	15	7	88	74	.543
2013	Cardinals	NL	162	89	.56	237	30	41	42	49	25	114	4	483	67	73	125	6	26	20	6	6	97	65	.599
2014	Cardinals	NL	162	119	.56	258	21	35	53	32	17	119	5	485	89	81	155	10	35	20	15	7	90	72	.556
2015	Cardinals	NL	162	135	.52	274	46	41	51	29	11	142	8	515	107	60	168	15	37	29	8	3	100	62	.617
2016	Cardinals	NL	162	146	.50	284	39	42	42	39	8	95	2	481	61	56	107	21	35	19	16	8	86	76	.531
2017	Cardinals	NL	162	144	.45	295	21	30	45	34	5	106	8	546	112	68	125	8	50	33	17	11	83	79	.512
2018	Cardinals	NL	93	69	.47	140	13	34	20	22	3	61	5	321	55	38	57	1	24	13	11	6	47	46	.505
	162-Game Average			125	.53	270	31	39	47	37	12	115	6	508	94	72	134	12	36	22	13	7	90	72	.556

Don Mattingly

Year	Team	Lg	G	LINEUPS		SUBSTITUTION			PITCHER USAGE						TACTICS				INTENTIONAL BB				RESULTS		
				LUp	PL%	PH	PR	DS	Quick	Slow	LO	RCD	LS	Rel	SBA	SacA	RM	PO	#	Good	NG	Bomb	W	L	Pct
2011	Dodgers	NL	161	140	.57	233	29	44	45	40	30	86	1	461	166	93	181	13	48	27	21	12	82	79	.509
2012	Dodgers	NL	162	127	.59	247	22	43	51	39	20	118	2	506	148	105	153	8	62	38	24	15	86	76	.531
2013	Dodgers	NL	162	145	.55	210	18	47	40	30	18	118	3	504	106	99	131	10	44	28	16	7	92	70	.568
2014	Dodgers	NL	162	124	.51	237	17	62	49	31	15	107	5	496	188	67	168	2	35	20	15	8	94	68	.580
2015	Dodgers	NL	161	136	.70	276	20	45	50	30	13	119	1	508	93	67	136	2	32	18	14	5	91	70	.565
2016	Marlins	NL	161	111	.48	281	28	69	48	35	10	145	1	559	99	63	101	3	62	42	20	14	79	82	.491
2017	Marlins	NL	162	98	.52	271	9	20	43	34	4	120	5	580	121	66	125	2	59	39	20	12	77	85	.475
2018	Marlins	NL	161	137	.46	283	19	53	47	43	2	114	0	546	76	45	121	1	73	40	33	19	63	98	.391
2019	Marlins	NL	162	143	.43	293	24	25	34	48	3	112	1	539	85	49	124	0	52	33	19	9	57	105	.352
	162-Game Average			129	.53	260	21	45	45	37	13	116	2	524	121	73	138	4	52	32	20	11	80	82	.494

Bob Melvin

Year	Team	Lg	G	LINEUPS		SUBSTITUTION			PITCHER USAGE						TACTICS				INTENTIONAL BB				RESULTS		
				LUp	PL%	PH	PR	DS	Quick	Slow	LO	RCD	LS	Rel	SBA	SacA	RM	PO	#	Good	NG	Bomb	W	L	Pct
2003	Mariners	AL	162	111	.62	81	62	33	27	46	43	56	6	366	145	44	37	5	24	14	10	4	93	69	.574
2004	Mariners	AL	162	151	.59	109	66	26	26	63	43	82	5	414	152	56	123	24	32	18	14	8	63	99	.389
2005	Diamondbacks	NL	162	120	.68	310	26	38	26	56	36	123	11	458	93	93	101	30	43	27	16	9	77	85	.475
2006	Diamondbacks	NL	162	114	.72	278	11	35	37	42	15	86	0	461	106	83	61	30	44	28	16	8	76	86	.469
2007	Diamondbacks	NL	162	146	.57	243	11	61	35	42	31	96	2	469	133	74	70	25	38	30	8	4	90	72	.556
2008	Diamondbacks	NL	162	134	.57	263	27	30	41	39	16	102	0	444	81	87	79	28	41	27	14	9	82	80	.506
2009	Diamondbacks	NL	29	29	.62	47	6	8	7	4	3	17	0	91	29	17	13	3	3	1	2	2	12	17	.414
2011	Athletics	AL	99	87	.71	33	13	17	24	23	18	59	2	283	103	34	87	23	9	5	4	3	47	52	.475
2012	Athletics	AL	162	132	.71	111	17	18	63	29	5	93	2	462	154	41	116	30	34	21	13	6	94	68	.580
2013	Athletics	AL	162	133	.77	166	14	35	48	28	7	84	7	447	102	32	74	8	23	18	5	3	96	66	.593
2014	Athletics	AL	162	137	.77	187	38	44	45	30	11	101	2	441	103	28	91	16	28	20	8	5	88	74	.543
2015	Athletics	AL	162	137	.65	161	24	35	53	36	10	100	10	487	107	17	130	20	19	8	11	8	68	94	.420
2016	Athletics	AL	162	141	.64	135	28	39	55	36	7	96	3	492	73	19	79	5	28	14	14	8	69	93	.426
2017	Athletics	AL	162	137	.60	126	19	32	39	46	5	117	4	525	79	16	85	9	17	12	5	4	75	87	.463
2018	Athletics	AL	162	121	.55	138	16	23	49	22	1	115	9	578	56	10	74	8	19	14	5	3	97	65	.599
2019	Athletics	AL	162	138	.53	117	11	34	36	30	4	123	10	547	70	10	72	4	19	12	7	4	97	65	.599
	162-Game Average			133	.64	169	26	34	41	39	17	98	5	471	107	45	87	18	28	18	10	6	83	79	.512

Paul Molitor

Year	Team	Lg	G	LINEUPS		SUBSTITUTION			PITCHER USAGE						TACTICS				INTENTIONAL BB				RESULTS		
				LUp	PL%	PH	PR	DS	Quick	Slow	LO	RCD	LS	Rel	SBA	SacA	RM	PO	#	Good	NG	Bomb	W	L	Pct
2015	Twins	AL	162	124	.59	75	34	27	51	27	7	123	4	520	108	44	132	5	34	20	14	8	83	79	.512
2016	Twins	AL	162	148	.61	72	25	18	33	57	4	117	4	533	123	47	157	5	26	13	13	8	59	103	.364
2017	Twins	AL	162	137	.71	104	22	31	54	32	4	95	8	520	123	46	164	4	37	19	18	11	85	77	.525
2018	Twins	AL	162	145	.70	102	21	23	35	43	14	104	3	566	74	21	134	5	34	18	16	11	78	84	.481
	162-Game Average			139	.65	88	26	25	43	40	7	110	5	535	107	40	147	5	33	18	15	10	76	86	.469

Charlie Montoyo

Year	Team	Lg	G	LINEUPS		SUBSTITUTION			PITCHER USAGE						TACTICS				INTENTIONAL BB				RESULTS		
				LUp	PL%	PH	PR	DS	Quick	Slow	LO	RCD	LS	Rel	SBA	SacA	RM	PO	#	Good	NG	Bomb	W	L	Pct
2019	Blue Jays	AL	162	158	.59	79	25	15	47	26	1	87	10	591	71	18	86	6	25	20	5	0	67	95	.414
	162-Game Average			158	.59	79	25	15	47	26	1	87	10	591	71	18	86	6	25	20	5	0	67	95	.414

Bryan Price

Year	Team	Lg	G	LINEUPS		SUBSTITUTION			PITCHER USAGE						TACTICS				INTENTIONAL BB				RESULTS		
				LUp	PL%	PH	PR	DS	Quick	Slow	LO	RCD	LS	Rel	SBA	SacA	RM	PO	#	Good	NG	Bomb	W	L	Pct
2014	Reds	NL	162	130	.54	220	21	33	35	37	26	82	3	428	174	87	135	9	33	21	12	5	76	86	.469
2015	Reds	NL	162	118	.57	263	16	26	42	48	15	102	2	521	172	63	144	28	42	29	13	7	64	98	.395
2016	Reds	NL	162	109	.52	230	17	23	37	39	10	67	3	484	190	81	163	26	31	23	8	5	68	94	.420
2017	Reds	NL	162	94	.57	241	13	25	37	42	7	64	13	504	159	68	128	17	37	23	14	7	68	94	.420
2018	Reds	NL	18	18	.60	29	2	1	2	7	0	10	1	61	10	8	13	3	8	6	2	1	3	15	.167
	162-Game Average			114	.55	239	17	26	37	42	14	79	5	486	171	75	142	20	37	25	12	6	68	94	.420

Tom Prince

Year	Team	Lg	G	LINEUPS		SUBSTITUTION			PITCHER USAGE						TACTICS				INTENTIONAL BB				RESULTS		
				LUp	PL%	PH	PR	DS	Quick	Slow	LO	RCD	LS	Rel	SBA	SacA	RM	PO	#	Good	NG	Bomb	W	L	Pct
2019	Pirates	NL	1	1	.25	1	0	0	0	0	0	0	0	2	0	0	0	0	0	0	0	0	0	1	.000
	162-Game Average			162	.25	162	0	0	0	0	0	0	0	324	0	0	0	0	0	0	0	0	0	162	.000

Rick Renteria

Year	Team	Lg	G	LUp	PL%	PH	PR	DS	Quick	Slow	LO	RCD	LS	Rel	SBA	SacA	RM	PO	#	Good	NG	Bomb	W	L	Pct
2014	Cubs	NL	162	137	.63	275	9	20	50	42	12	103	1	537	105	77	106	5	37	23	14	8	73	89	.451
2017	White Sox	AL	162	150	.57	86	26	9	31	58	6	108	2	520	102	47	133	1	36	19	17	9	67	95	.414
2018	White Sox	AL	162	142	.60	90	30	25	18	66	9	99	5	553	139	28	126	10	25	15	10	6	62	100	.383
2019	White Sox	AL	161	143	.66	87	27	27	32	48	7	91	4	536	91	35	103	5	30	16	14	5	72	89	.447
162-Game Average				143	.61	135	23	20	33	54	9	100	3	537	109	47	117	5	32	18	14	7	69	93	.426

Jim Riggleman

Year	Team	Lg	G	LUp	PL%	PH	PR	DS	Quick	Slow	LO	RCD	LS	Rel	SBA	SacA	RM	PO	#	Good	NG	Bomb	W	L	Pct
1994	Padres	NL	117	93	.63	184	28	19	11	5	3	53	10	273	116	80		52	62	34	28	11	47	70	.402
1995	Cubs	NL	144	92	.56	196	9	30	15	8	13	119	12	414	142	90		53	68	45	23	12	73	71	.507
1996	Cubs	NL	162	87	.54	326	34	21	17	11	7	114	11	439	158	79		65	55	33	22	10	76	86	.469
1997	Cubs	NL	162	127	.50	280	40	44	13	5	2	113	9	441	176	103		74	51	38	13	6	68	94	.420
1998	Cubs	NL	163	104	.60	273	26	35	16	14	20	133	6	449	109	89		26	48	22	26	15	90	73	.552
1999	Cubs	NL	162	122	.61	312	25	30	16	19	8	105	4	441	104	94		20	48	21	27	15	67	95	.414
2008	Mariners	AL	90	70	.60	75	30	22	21	25	19	50	4	272	57	27	88	10	25	17	8	3	36	54	.400
2009	Nationals	NL	75	60	.51	115	15	33	24	16	4	63	6	250	59	44	36	8	33	17	16	8	33	42	.440
2010	Nationals	NL	162	131	.58	271	33	67	50	32	9	101	5	494	151	101	158	13	57	37	20	10	69	93	.426
2011	Nationals	NL	75	59	.58	105	22	23	24	15	2	54	5	220	80	47	89	3	22	16	6	3	38	37	.507
2018	Reds	NL	144	113	.65	215	16	34	31	40	4	93	15	483	100	68	138	10	52	30	22	9	64	80	.444
162-Game Average				118	.58	262	31	40	26	21	10	111	10	465	139	91	151	37	58	34	23	11	74	88	.457

Dave Roberts

Year	Team	Lg	G	LUp	PL%	PH	PR	DS	Quick	Slow	LO	RCD	LS	Rel	SBA	SacA	RM	PO	#	Good	NG	Bomb	W	L	Pct
2015	Padres	NL	1	1	.63	3	0	0	0	1	0	2	0	3	1	1	0	0	1	1	0	0	0	1	.000
2016	Dodgers	NL	162	120	.69	325	11	26	60	26	6	143	5	606	71	45	120	2	51	36	15	10	91	71	.562
2017	Dodgers	NL	162	147	.64	345	10	30	82	22	3	104	18	536	105	45	97	3	33	23	10	6	104	58	.642
2018	Dodgers	NL	163	155	.67	362	16	51	64	29	3	112	9	593	99	51	87	0	39	26	13	5	92	71	.564
2019	Dodgers	NL	162	139	.62	309	13	16	57	28	2	108	9	545	67	61	44	3	24	12	12	8	106	56	.654
162-Game Average				140	.65	335	12	31	66	26	3	117	10	569	85	51	87	2	37	24	12	7	98	64	.605

Mike Scioscia

Year	Team	Lg	G	LUp	PL%	PH	PR	DS	Quick	Slow	LO	RCD	LS	Rel	SBA	SacA	RM	PO	#	Good	NG	Bomb	W	L	Pct
2000	Angels	AL	162	75	.62	110	41	4	56	42	6	95	9	441	145	63		40	44	28	16	7	82	80	.506
2001	Angels	AL	162	130	.62	118	30	8	29	41	5	81	9	384	168	66		50	47	22	25	12	75	87	.463
2002	Angels	AL	162	102	.64	162	57	26	36	33	34	88	8	400	168	62	52	30	24	15	9	3	99	63	.611
2003	Angels	AL	162	130	.64	134	54	40	50	48	11	60	4	375	190	64	79	25	38	26	12	3	77	85	.475
2004	Angels	AL	162	126	.57	94	32	44	37	40	22	61	11	343	189	70	229	33	27	18	9	3	92	70	.568
2005	Angels	AL	162	124	.65	92	37	37	47	37	24	88	9	379	218	58	160	43	24	15	9	4	95	67	.586
2006	Angels	AL	162	114	.63	103	45	38	38	49	21	99	9	380	205	37	166	22	27	18	9	6	89	73	.549
2007	Angels	AL	162	127	.66	103	26	19	39	40	14	94	4	396	194	41	166	44	22	12	10	5	94	68	.580
2008	Angels	AL	162	125	.63	74	30	36	37	48	21	87	1	383	177	39	151	31	32	22	10	6	100	62	.617
2009	Angels	AL	162	123	.62	80	26	37	47	47	33	91	1	434	211	55	137	40	35	22	13	6	97	65	.599
2010	Angels	AL	162	133	.59	96	31	23	41	52	48	76	0	410	156	58	223	28	33	17	16	8	80	82	.494
2011	Angels	AL	162	129	.64	88	14	24	31	37	55	57	8	386	187	69	212	46	34	25	9	5	86	76	.531
2012	Angels	AL	162	121	.55	73	33	47	37	47	31	96	8	444	167	61	236	33	20	11	9	7	89	73	.549
2013	Angels	AL	162	118	.56	88	26	39	31	44	29	130	8	496	116	48	205	41	36	19	17	11	78	84	.481
2014	Angels	AL	162	125	.58	123	46	59	49	39	22	141	0	543	120	35	189	14	41	31	10	6	98	64	.605
2015	Angels	AL	162	125	.53	117	62	73	38	38	12	145	4	518	86	41	168	15	45	34	11	9	85	77	.525
2016	Angels	AL	162	133	.45	98	54	57	47	32	12	99	2	527	107	38	211	14	27	19	8	5	74	88	.457
2017	Angels	AL	162	116	.52	109	38	24	57	26	4	92	8	543	180	23	208	11	25	14	11	7	80	82	.494
2018	Angels	AL	162	132	.50	114	33	34	58	19	3	102	7	601	111	16	134	3	17	9	8	1	80	82	.494
162-Game Average				121	.59	104	38	35	42	40	21	94	5	441	163	50	172	30	31	20	12	6	87	75	.537

Scott Servais

Year	Team	Lg	G	LUp	PL%	PH	PR	DS	Quick	Slow	LO	RCD	LS	Rel	SBA	SacA	RM	PO	#	Good	NG	Bomb	W	L	Pct
2016	Mariners	AL	162	114	.72	166	33	43	42	38	8	93	7	476	84	36	79	1	30	16	14	6	86	76	.531
2017	Mariners	AL	162	120	.52	93	29	18	55	32	3	98	7	527	124	26	99	4	28	15	13	7	78	84	.481
2018	Mariners	AL	162	124	.54	103	42	28	44	42	3	122	3	537	116	43	91	7	21	15	6	4	89	73	.549
2019	Mariners	AL	162	153	.58	82	33	35	33	37	4	58	3	538	162	17	100	7	25	11	14	5	68	94	.420
162-Game Average				128	.59	111	34	31	44	37	5	93	5	520	122	31	92	5	26	14	12	6	80	82	.494

Mike Shildt

Year	Team	Lg	G	LUp	PL%	PH	PR	DS	Quick	Slow	LO	RCD	LS	Rel	SBA	SacA	RM	PO	#	Good	NG	Bomb	W	L	Pct
2018	Cardinals	NL	69	58	.49	117	22	30	21	11	1	44	3	244	40	29	82	0	25	16	9	2	41	28	.594
2019	Cardinals	NL	162	97	.48	268	30	44	47	33	9	111	10	542	145	57	154	2	41	29	12	4	91	71	.562
	162-Game Average			109	.48	270	36	52	48	31	7	109	9	551	130	60	166	1	46	32	15	4	93	69	.574

Buck Showalter

Year	Team	Lg	G	LUp	PL%	PH	PR	DS	Quick	Slow	LO	RCD	LS	Rel	SBA	SacA	RM	PO	#	Good	NG	Bomb	W	L	Pct
1994	Yankees	AL	113	79	.59	95	31	3	24	30	0	38	7	241	95	34		22	24	13	11	4	70	43	.619
1995	Yankees	AL	145	107	.68	124	30	20	29	42	37	57	6	302	80	27		29	21	14	7	1	79	65	.549
1998	Diamondbacks	NL	162	124	.62	252	17	15	34	40	7	43	6	368	111	68		13	32	16	16	9	65	97	.401
1999	Diamondbacks	NL	162	97	.63	220	20	17	37	48	25	74	3	382	176	75		15	48	29	19	8	100	62	.617
2000	Diamondbacks	NL	162	99	.60	250	32	11	46	26	18	74	12	390	141	89		10	53	28	25	16	85	77	.525
2003	Rangers	AL	162	133	.61	88	51	41	35	33	12	93	7	494	90	35	80	12	45	24	21	14	71	91	.438
2004	Rangers	AL	162	120	.64	86	15	24	53	30	12	82	10	468	105	30	88	5	29	19	10	3	89	73	.549
2005	Rangers	AL	162	98	.59	57	22	11	42	39	17	79	8	454	82	11	103	5	31	10	21	16	79	83	.488
2006	Rangers	AL	162	95	.57	39	34	22	41	27	10	85	4	489	77	30	72	8	18	11	7	5	80	82	.494
2010	Orioles	AL	57	42	.74	20	11	13	23	9	10	24	1	144	38	13	31	1	10	9	1	1	34	23	.596
2011	Orioles	AL	162	117	.53	60	39	27	43	40	14	61	2	478	106	32	133	6	42	31	11	5	69	93	.426
2012	Orioles	AL	162	120	.62	78	28	31	37	42	10	88	0	492	87	46	145	6	36	25	11	5	93	69	.574
2013	Orioles	AL	162	100	.65	90	23	21	31	39	19	84	4	473	108	37	104	4	32	11	21	13	85	77	.525
2014	Orioles	AL	162	120	.49	77	29	51	37	34	17	89	2	479	64	50	101	10	25	16	9	4	96	66	.593
2015	Orioles	AL	162	145	.60	89	21	35	35	41	6	76	8	453	69	26	95	10	27	12	15	8	81	81	.500
2016	Orioles	AL	162	125	.53	74	31	33	36	50	16	68	9	443	32	21	55	10	23	13	10	5	89	73	.549
2017	Orioles	AL	162	115	.44	95	31	40	27	57	21	93	3	492	45	19	40	8	21	15	6	5	75	87	.463
2018	Orioles	AL	162	152	.55	98	30	31	27	47	7	58	8	490	103	23	75	2	29	21	8	6	47	115	.290
	162-Game Average			117	.59	112	29	26	38	40	15	75	6	445	95	39	91	10	32	19	14	8	82	80	.506

Brian Snitker

Year	Team	Lg	G	LUp	PL%	PH	PR	DS	Quick	Slow	LO	RCD	LS	Rel	SBA	SacA	RM	PO	#	Good	NG	Bomb	W	L	Pct
2016	Braves	NL	124	85	.62	214	8	14	31	36	7	96	1	456	83	64	118	7	40	23	17	10	59	65	.476
2017	Braves	NL	162	108	.58	268	38	16	31	52	8	101	1	530	108	76	139	3	39	27	12	9	72	90	.444
2018	Braves	NL	162	103	.65	254	24	21	50	39	8	92	2	553	126	59	137	7	43	32	11	5	90	72	.556
2019	Braves	NL	162	95	.60	265	20	33	44	35	1	96	6	575	117	34	91	3	33	27	6	3	97	65	.599
	162-Game Average			104	.61	266	24	22	41	43	6	102	3	561	115	62	129	5	41	29	12	7	84	78	.519

Robin Ventura

Year	Team	Lg	G	LUp	PL%	PH	PR	DS	Quick	Slow	LO	RCD	LS	Rel	SBA	SacA	RM	PO	#	Good	NG	Bomb	W	L	Pct
2012	White Sox	AL	162	75	.48	72	64	23	39	34		104	4	466	152	42	174	13	29	17	12	7	85	77	.525
2013	White Sox	AL	162	116	.47	76	47	33	24	52	38	133	0	470	147	24	132	15	24	12	12	4	63	99	.389
2014	White Sox	AL	162	115	.55	85	49	44	26	59	29	96	5	453	121	26	150	28	42	25	17	5	73	89	.451
2015	White Sox	AL	162	114	.57	118	29	35	16	66	43	94	3	414	110	39	146	18	34	21	13	8	76	86	.469
2016	White Sox	AL	162	116	.56	53	27	13	29	58	29	128	4	481	113	37	148	10	30	18	12	2	78	84	.481
	162-Game Average			107	.53	81	43	30	27	56	35	111	3	457	129	34	150	17	32	19	13	5	75	87	.463

Don Wakamatsu

Year	Team	Lg	G	LUp	PL%	PH	PR	DS	Quick	Slow	LO	RCD	LS	Rel	SBA	SacA	RM	PO	#	Good	NG	Bomb	W	L	Pct
2009	Mariners	AL	162	138	.51	58	31	19	50	27	18	76	1	410	122	61	91	4	13	3	10	6	85	77	.525
2010	Mariners	AL	112	93	.61	49	21	12	37	21	20	39	2	254	129	40	124	17	25	11	14	7	42	70	.375
2018	Rangers	AL	10	10	.59	7	2	1	5	0	0	8	0	41	1	0	3	0	1	0	1	1	3	7	.300
	162-Game Average			137	.55	65	31	18	52	27	22	70	2	402	144	58	124	12	22	8	14	8	74	88	.457

Walt Weiss

Year	Team	Lg	G	LUp	PL%	PH	PR	DS	Quick	Slow	LO	RCD	LS	Rel	SBA	SacA	RM	PO	#	Good	NG	Bomb	W	L	Pct
2013	Rockies	NL	162	136	.56	260	18	32	50	42	0	96	2	503	144	80	149	15	52	28	24	7	74	88	.457
2014	Rockies	NL	162	134	.51	270	12	26	40	49	2	119	0	547	133	69	140	11	32	16	16	7	66	96	.407
2015	Rockies	NL	162	122	.56	262	9	36	45	47	2	125	1	584	140	58	138	13	42	26	16	6	68	94	.420
2016	Rockies	NL	162	120	.58	255	7	32	32	57	7	120	2	533	105	69	154	3	38	24	14	7	75	87	.463
	162-Game Average			128	.55	262	12	32	42	49	3	115	1	542	131	69	145	11	41	24	18	7	71	91	.438

Chris Woodward

Year	Team	Lg	G	LINEUPS		SUBSTITUTION			PITCHER USAGE						TACTICS				INTENTIONAL BB				RESULTS		
				LUp	PL%	PH	PR	DS	Quick	Slow	LO	RCD	LS	Rel	SBA	SacA	RM	PO	#	Good	NG	Bomb	W	L	Pct
2019	Rangers	AL	162	150	.62	82	14	19	32	48	24	70	2	499	169	19	115	0	11	4	7	5	78	84	.481
	162-Game Average			150	.62	82	14	19	32	48	24	70	2	499	169	19	115	0	11	4	7	5	78	84	.481

Ned Yost

Year	Team	Lg	G	LINEUPS		SUBSTITUTION			PITCHER USAGE						TACTICS				INTENTIONAL BB				RESULTS		
				LUp	PL%	PH	PR	DS	Quick	Slow	LO	RCD	LS	Rel	SBA	SacA	RM	PO	#	Good	NG	Bomb	W	L	Pct
2003	Brewers	NL	162	97	.44	304	22	39	23	59	18	90	6	460	138	85	40	23	43	28	15	9	68	94	.420
2004	Brewers	NL	161	131	.60	283	25	20	39	41	27	63	2	423	178	79	108	8	27	16	11	8	67	94	.416
2005	Brewers	NL	162	99	.46	259	18	35	26	41	42	71	2	395	113	89	97	50	52	23	29	10	81	81	.500
2006	Brewers	NL	162	106	.48	238	12	14	33	44	18	77	4	427	108	80	82	16	34	14	20	12	75	87	.463
2007	Brewers	NL	162	109	.60	259	11	41	37	42	18	117	7	492	128	74	94	19	37	28	9	9	83	79	.512
2008	Brewers	NL	150	74	.48	217	5	16	37	39	23	69	5	399	141	61	105	31	30	17	13	7	83	67	.553
2010	Royals	AL	127	80	.57	56	25	6	22	39	20	65	0	332	127	40	128	18	25	16	9	5	55	72	.433
2011	Royals	AL	162	87	.58	36	28	16	42	42	21	56	7	420	211	65	203	19	42	27	15	5	71	91	.438
2012	Royals	AL	162	118	.57	60	34	15	48	37	10	108	1	500	170	37	149	25	44	29	15	11	72	90	.444
2013	Royals	AL	162	127	.60	79	48	39	43	44	21	72	2	427	185	48	168	25	12	9	5	5	86	76	.531
2014	Royals	AL	162	101	.52	51	63	46	37	51	26	93	1	451	189	45	159	3	14	7	7	3	89	73	.549
2015	Royals	AL	162	83	.57	40	40	26	51	42	13	90	3	493	138	45	126	5	10	7	3	1	95	67	.586
2016	Royals	AL	162	108	.54	50	38	12	49	44	10	85	2	472	156	55	130	0	8	6	2	2	81	81	.500
2017	Royals	AL	162	86	.53	48	29	25	53	31	2	120	0	538	122	20	110	0	24	14	10	6	80	82	.494
2018	Royals	AL	162	150	.58	48	7	12	32	52	6	75	0	483	155	42	136	1	28	15	13	7	58	104	.358
2019	Royals	AL	162	132	.56	58	25	16	30	52	5	85	3	520	156	32	92	0	25	15	10	5	59	103	.364
	162-Game Average			107	.54	133	27	24	38	45	18	85	3	461	154	57	123	15	30	17	12	7	77	85	.475

Categories of this record are Games Managed (G), Number of Different Lineups Used (LUp), the percentage of players who had the platoon advantage at the start of the game (PL%), Pinch Hitters Used (PH), Pinch Runners Used (PR), Defensive Substitutes Used (DS), Quick Hooks (Quick), Slow Hooks (Slow), Long Outings by Starting Pitchers (LO), Relievers Used on Consecutive Days (RCD), Long Saves (LS), Relievers Used (Rel), Stolen Base Attempts (SBA), Sacrifice Bunt Attempts (SacA), Runners Moving with the Pitch (RM), Pitchouts ordered (PO), Intentional Walks issued (#), Intentional Walks resulting in a Good Outcome (Good), Intentional Walks resulting Not in a Good Outcome (NG), Intentional Walks Blowing Up on the Manager (Bomb), Wins (W), Losses (L), and Winning Percentage (Pct).

2019 American League Managers

Manager	G	LUp	PL%	PH	PR	DS	Quick	Slow	LO	RCD	LS	Rel	SBA	SacA	RM	PO	#	Good	NG	Bomb	W	L	Pct
Brandon Hyde, Bal	162	150	.70	126	26	42	30	35	1	73	11	533	114	34	82	0	11	5	6	4	54	108	.333
Alex Cora, Bos	162	135	.57	123	29	18	45	52	16	134	3	632	98	26	140	2	22	14	8	6	84	78	.519
Terry Francona, Cle	162	132	.73	101	25	15	30	44	29	89	9	522	138	57	100	2	19	11	8	7	93	69	.574
Rick Renteria, CWS	161	143	.66	87	27	27	32	48	7	91	4	536	91	35	103	5	30	16	14	5	72	89	.447
Ron Gardenhire, Det	161	155	.48	68	42	7	45	46	2	87	0	577	77	19	93	7	24	13	11	6	47	114	.292
A.J. Hinch, Hou	162	134	.46	81	41	26	38	30	7	92	2	492	94	15	96	0	0	0	0	0	107	55	.660
Ned Yost, KC	162	132	.56	58	25	16	30	52	5	85	3	520	156	32	92	0	25	15	10	5	59	103	.364
Brad Ausmus, LAA	162	153	.57	98	27	44	34	29	0	105	5	589	85	4	78	1	11	5	6	4	72	90	.444
Rocco Baldelli, Min	162	145	.62	84	24	35	42	43	1	94	16	524	49	16	56	4	10	9	1	1	101	61	.623
Aaron Boone, NYY	162	155	.48	57	24	32	43	27	1	80	5	545	77	19	81	2	12	9	3	1	103	59	.636
Bob Melvin, Oak	162	138	.53	117	11	34	36	30	4	123	10	547	70	10	72	4	19	12	7	4	97	65	.599
Scott Servais, Sea	162	153	.57	82	33	35	33	37	4	58	3	538	162	17	100	7	25	11	14	7	68	94	.420
Kevin Cash, TB	162	152	.59	131	31	43	50	18	0	136	6	603	131	11	166	3	27	14	13	8	96	66	.593
Chris Woodward, Tex	162	150	.62	82	14	19	32	48	24	70	2	499	169	19	115	0	11	4	7	5	78	84	.481
Charlie Montoyo, Tor	162	158	.59	79	25	15	47	26	1	87	10	591	71	18	86	6	25	20	5	0	67	95	.414
162-Game Average		146	.58	92	27	27	38	38	7	94	6	550	106	22	97	3	18	11	7	4	80	82	.494

2019 National League Managers

Manager	G	LUp	PL%	PH	PR	DS	Quick	Slow	LO	RCD	LS	Rel	SBA	SacA	RM	PO	#	Good	NG	Bomb	W	L	Pct
Torey Lovullo, Ari	162	126	.66	256	21	46	32	38	0	105	9	557	102	49	105	5	38	19	19	8	85	77	.525
Brian Snitker, Atl	162	95	.60	265	20	33	44	35	1	96	6	575	117	34	91	3	33	27	6	3	97	65	.599
Joe Maddon, ChC	162	140	.56	244	15	43	40	41	7	103	4	576	69	46	87	3	16	11	5	3	84	78	.519
David Bell, Cin	162	140	.55	319	28	46	36	43	9	104	10	535	118	44	111	1	31	25	6	5	75	87	.463
Bud Black, Col	162	141	.60	305	8	13	27	58	1	114	3	590	102	71	96	5	33	21	12	3	71	91	.438
Dave Roberts, LAD	162	139	.62	309	13	16	57	28	2	108	9	545	67	61	44	3	24	12	12	8	106	56	.654
Don Mattingly, Mia	162	143	.43	293	24	25	34	48	3	112	1	539	85	49	124	0	52	33	19	9	57	105	.352
Craig Counsell, Mil	162	134	.64	317	14	56	60	26	1	97	17	588	126	29	78	3	28	22	6	2	89	73	.549
Mickey Callaway, NYM	162	132	.50	273	42	65	35	57	16	87	6	502	83	42	102	10	40	27	13	6	86	76	.531
Gabe Kapler, Phi	162	106	.55	312	11	21	28	48	3	121	9	564	96	50	69	0	38	31	7	4	81	81	.500
Clint Hurdle, Pit	161	131	.67	281	30	38	40	49	0	85	7	548	93	60	117	16	22	15	7	5	69	92	.429
Andy Green, SD	154	139	.45	263	11	51	52	31	0	99	5	509	103	42	93	0	19	14	5	3	69	85	.448
Bruce Bochy, SF	162	141	.67	362	11	25	34	43	4	94	2	587	75	37	101	4	26	16	10	4	77	85	.475
Mike Shildt, StL	162	97	.48	268	30	44	47	33	9	111	10	542	145	57	154	2	41	29	12	4	91	71	.562
Dave Martinez, Was	162	106	.49	253	15	19	32	41	13	136	8	530	145	77	82	0	41	31	10	6	93	69	.574
162-Game Average		128	.56	289	20	36	40	41	5	105	7	554	102	50	97	4	32	22	10	5	82	80	.506

Manager	G	LUp	PL%	PH	PR	DS	Quick	Slow	LO	RCD	LS	Rel	SBA	SacA	RM	PO	#	Good	NG	Bomb	W	L	Pct
Tom Prince, Pit	1	1	.25	1	0	0	0	0	0	0	0	2	0	0	0	0	0	0	0	0	0	1	.000
Rod Barajas, SD	8	8	.69	28	2	1	5	0	0	4	0	34	4	2	8	0	0	0	0	0	1	7	.125

Ballparks and Park Indices

Joe Rosales

Recent seasons have seen new team and league-wide home run records broken…and then broken again. This past season not only continued the trend, but even seemed to accelerate it. The 2019 Twins, Yankees, Astros, and Dodgers now represent the four highest single-season team home run totals ever. However, Giants fans might be forgiven if they didn't entirely notice how extreme things had gotten. There were more home runs hit than usual at Oracle Park in 2019, but the 161 balls that cleared the fence are still second to the 164 that did so in 2004. Furthermore, only one ballpark had fewer balls reach the seats in 2019, Kansas City's Kauffman Stadium (160)—although there were also two inside the park home runs at Kauffman this year, so more total home runs than at Oracle.

As a consequence of Oracle Park's unique attributes, it garnered a home run park index of 69 in 2019, the lowest in Major League Baseball. Given that 100 represents the average ballpark, this means that San Francisco suppressed home runs by 31 percent. Things were slightly better for right-handed batters than for left-handed batters, as the home run park index for righties was 74 and just 60 for lefties, but both were still the lowest in the National League (and lefties was the lowest in all of MLB). And things look pretty similar over the course of the last three years combined, where Oracle's home run park index is just 59 for lefties, 74 for righties, and 68 overall, all the lowest in baseball.

In Bill's article on the aesthetics of the game earlier in this book, he makes the point that the essence of baseball—and what makes it fun to watch—is the contest between fielder and baserunner after the ball is put in play. At this current point in the history of the game where the "three true outcomes" of home runs, strikeouts, and walks are as frequent as they've ever been, the best place to still see some action may be in parks like San Francisco and Kansas City. At Kauffman Stadium in particular this year, there were fewer home runs (index of 73), fewer strikeouts (85), and fewer walks (90) than in the average ballpark, while there were more hits (109), doubles (117), and triples (126)—plus those two inside the park home runs.

Arizona Diamondbacks - Chase Field Surface: FieldTurf
LF: 330   CF: 407   RF:334

| | 2019 Season | | | | | | | 2018-2019 | | | | | | |
| | Home Games | | | Away Games | | | | Home Games | | | Away Games | | | |
	D'Backs	Opp	Total	D'Backs	Opp	Total	Index	D'Backs	Opp	Total	D'Backs	Opp	Total	Index
G	81	81	162	81	81	162		162	162	324	162	162	324	
Avg	.249	.252	.250	.255	.251	.253	99	.245	.244	.245	.242	.247	.244	100
AB	2751	2870	5621	2882	2698	5580	101	5451	5697	11148	5642	5366	11008	101
R	399	370	769	414	373	787	98	758	698	1456	748	689	1437	101
H	684	724	1408	735	676	1411	100	1338	1389	2727	1364	1324	2688	101
2B	143	146	289	145	143	288	100	255	288	543	292	260	552	97
3B	24	19	43	16	10	26	164	58	32	90	32	16	48	185
HR	97	110	207	123	110	233	88	177	201	378	219	193	412	91
BB	280	237	517	260	279	539	95	572	504	1076	528	534	1062	100
SO	656	753	1409	704	674	1378	102	1365	1496	2861	1455	1379	2834	100
Foul Outs	51	60	111	49	68	117	94	108	107	215	89	110	199	107
E	42	59	101	44	39	83	122	80	113	193	81	81	162	119
E-Infield	18	27	45	18	17	35	129	33	47	80	32	32	64	125
LHB-Avg	.255	.253	.254	.238	.248	.243	105	.252	.240	.246	.223	.245	.233	105
LHB-HR	40	43	83	45	45	90	91	70	79	149	87	73	160	92
RHB-Avg	.244	.251	.248	.268	.253	.261	95	.241	.246	.244	.257	.248	.252	97
RHB-HR	57	67	124	78	65	143	86	107	122	229	132	120	252	89

Atlanta Braves - SunTrust Park
LF: 335   CF: 400   RF:325

| | 2019 Season | | | | | | | 2017-2019 | | | | | | |
| | Home Games | | | Away Games | | | | Home Games | | | Away Games | | | |
	Braves	Opp	Total	Braves	Opp	Total	Index	Braves	Opp	Total	Braves	Opp	Total	Index
G	81	81	162	81	81	162		243	243	486	243	243	486	
Avg	.262	.257	.259	.254	.254	.254	102	.260	.252	.256	.258	.247	.252	101
AB	2679	2814	5493	2881	2743	5624	98	8126	8451	16577	8600	8062	16662	99
R	433	367	800	422	376	798	100	1170	1145	2315	1176	1076	2252	103
H	701	724	1425	731	697	1428	100	2116	2130	4246	2216	1990	4206	101
2B	140	142	282	137	111	248	116	415	461	876	465	366	831	106
3B	15	10	25	14	13	27	95	39	36	75	45	49	94	80
HR	131	97	228	118	106	224	104	286	262	548	303	286	589	94
BB	318	264	582	301	284	585	102	804	859	1663	800	908	1708	98
SO	716	698	1414	751	695	1446	100	1914	2036	3950	2027	2038	4065	98
Foul Outs	42	49	91	61	52	113	82	146	150	296	149	156	305	98
E	41	61	102	37	44	81	126	137	168	305	118	142	260	117
E-Infield	24	23	47	10	13	23	204	58	71	129	48	48	96	134
LHB-Avg	.263	.252	.259	.266	.248	.258	100	.266	.244	.257	.266	.239	.254	101
LHB-HR	48	40	88	43	40	83	113	123	111	234	130	109	239	99
RHB-Avg	.260	.260	.260	.243	.258	.251	104	.254	.257	.256	.249	.252	.251	102
RHB-HR	83	57	140	75	66	141	99	163	151	314	173	177	350	90

Baltimore Orioles - Oriole Park at Camden Yards
LF: 333   CF: 410   RF:318

| | 2019 Season | | | | | | | 2017-2019 | | | | | | |
| | Home Games | | | Away Games | | | | Home Games | | | Away Games | | | |
	Orioles	Opp	Total	Orioles	Opp	Total	Index	Orioles	Opp	Total	Orioles	Opp	Total	Index
G	81	81	162	81	81	162		243	243	486	243	243	486	
Avg	.248	.280	.265	.245	.261	.253	105	.254	.270	.262	.243	.274	.258	102
AB	2740	2946	5686	2856	2751	5607	101	8253	8710	16963	8500	8201	16701	102
R	359	532	891	370	449	819	109	1093	1350	2443	1001	1364	2365	103
H	680	826	1506	699	718	1417	106	2100	2350	4450	2065	2251	4316	103
2B	134	168	302	118	143	261	114	384	447	831	379	482	861	95
3B	16	11	27	9	20	29	92	25	34	59	27	48	75	77
HR	114	175	289	99	130	229	124	349	425	774	284	356	640	119
BB	227	266	493	235	295	530	92	664	837	1501	612	892	1504	98
SO	665	628	1293	770	620	1390	92	1979	1863	3842	2280	1821	4101	92
Foul Outs	61	74	135	59	64	123	108	190	208	398	181	185	366	107
E	54	58	112	54	56	110	102	144	142	286	162	141	303	94
E-Infield	18	21	39	14	21	35	111	51	57	108	63	46	109	99
LHB-Avg	.243	.264	.253	.231	.246	.238	107	.231	.269	.254	.217	.264	.245	104
LHB-HR	43	62	105	43	50	93	114	95	166	261	80	149	229	113
RHB-Avg	.252	.291	.273	.255	.272	.263	104	.264	.270	.267	.253	.282	.266	100
RHB-HR	71	113	184	56	80	136	131	254	259	513	204	207	411	123

Boston Red Sox - Fenway Park
LF: 310 CF: 420 RF:302

| | 2019 Season | | | | | | | 2017-2019 | | | | | | |
| | Home Games | | | Away Games | | | | Home Games | | | Away Games | | | |
	Red Sox	Opp	Total	Red Sox	Opp	Total	Index	Red Sox	Opp	Total	Red Sox	Opp	Total	Index
G	79	79	158	83	83	166		241	241	482	245	245	490	
Avg	.274	.245	.259	.265	.258	.262	99	.275	.244	.260	.256	.244	.250	104
AB	2747	2771	5518	3023	2889	5912	98	8329	8506	16835	8733	8316	17049	100
R	431	410	841	470	418	888	100	1286	1081	2367	1276	1062	2338	103
H	753	678	1431	801	745	1546	97	2290	2079	4369	2234	2033	4267	104
2B	201	168	369	144	151	295	134	571	456	1027	431	387	818	127
3B	15	13	28	12	13	25	120	46	37	83	31	47	78	108
HR	112	93	205	133	122	255	86	287	271	558	334	315	649	87
BB	287	319	606	303	286	589	110	840	788	1628	890	794	1684	98
SO	659	820	1479	723	813	1536	103	1849	2407	4256	2010	2364	4374	99
Foul Outs	36	47	83	70	46	116	77	135	142	277	210	172	382	73
E	53	47	100	35	56	91	115	154	170	324	118	154	272	121
E-Infield	24	20	44	19	23	42	110	63	71	134	50	62	112	122
LHB-Avg	.271	.249	.261	.260	.244	.253	103	.262	.251	.257	.250	.240	.246	104
LHB-HR	40	41	81	53	48	101	86	103	99	202	148	106	254	79
RHB-Avg	.277	.242	.258	.269	.265	.267	97	.285	.241	.261	.260	.246	.253	103
RHB-HR	72	52	124	80	74	154	86	184	172	356	186	209	395	93

Chicago Cubs - Wrigley Field
LF: 355 CF: 400 RF:353

| | 2019 Season | | | | | | | 2017-2019 | | | | | | |
| | Home Games | | | Away Games | | | | Home Games | | | Away Games | | | |
	Cubs	Opp	Total	Cubs	Opp	Total	Index	Cubs	Opp	Total	Cubs	Opp	Total	Index
G	81	81	162	81	81	162		244	244	488	243	243	486	
Avg	.262	.239	.250	.244	.263	.253	99	.262	.242	.252	.249	.244	.246	102
AB	2649	2773	5422	2812	2719	5531	98	8024	8347	16371	8557	8075	16632	98
R	422	316	738	392	401	793	93	1243	1034	2277	1154	1023	2177	104
H	693	663	1356	685	714	1399	97	2105	2023	4128	2128	1967	4095	100
2B	138	121	259	132	144	276	96	407	383	790	423	353	776	103
3B	17	13	30	9	12	21	146	56	34	90	33	36	69	133
HR	123	87	210	133	108	241	89	318	266	584	328	280	608	98
BB	309	245	554	272	289	561	101	909	868	1777	870	842	1712	105
SO	669	751	1420	791	693	1484	98	1996	2153	4149	2253	2063	4316	98
Foul Outs	30	35	65	47	54	101	66	99	98	197	155	151	306	65
E	53	39	92	64	36	100	92	158	148	306	158	163	321	95
E-Infield	20	18	38	25	17	42	90	54	65	119	63	63	126	94
LHB-Avg	.264	.241	.254	.236	.277	.255	100	.264	.245	.256	.244	.245	.245	105
LHB-HR	52	25	77	64	38	102	82	152	89	241	176	108	284	88
RHB-Avg	.259	.238	.248	.250	.254	.252	98	.261	.241	.249	.253	.242	.247	101
RHB-HR	71	62	133	69	70	139	93	166	177	343	152	172	324	106

Chicago White Sox - Guaranteed Rate Field
LF: 330 CF: 400 RF:335

| | 2019 Season | | | | | | | 2017-2019 | | | | | | |
| | Home Games | | | Away Games | | | | Home Games | | | Away Games | | | |
	White Sox	Opp	Total	White Sox	Opp	Total	Index	White Sox	Opp	Total	White Sox	Opp	Total	Index
G	80	80	160	81	81	162		242	242	484	243	243	486	
Avg	.256	.252	.254	.265	.274	.270	94	.252	.248	.250	.254	.267	.260	96
AB	2650	2764	5414	2879	2702	5581	98	8035	8370	16405	8530	8072	16602	99
R	335	417	752	373	415	788	97	1022	1224	2246	1048	1276	2324	97
H	679	697	1376	764	741	1505	93	2021	2073	4094	2166	2153	4319	95
2B	121	118	239	139	160	299	82	373	365	738	402	480	882	85
3B	5	5	10	15	14	29	36	45	24	69	52	51	103	68
HR	90	141	231	92	97	189	126	271	376	647	279	300	579	113
BB	190	305	495	188	277	465	110	608	932	1540	596	935	1531	102
SO	743	684	1427	806	628	1434	103	2243	2009	4252	2297	1755	4052	106
Foul Outs	44	57	101	61	64	125	83	168	205	373	160	180	340	111
E	57	60	117	60	53	113	105	174	172	346	171	144	315	110
E-Infield	25	30	55	26	17	43	130	91	74	165	69	67	136	122
LHB-Avg	.236	.238	.237	.248	.272	.260	91	.246	.235	.240	.250	.265	.258	93
LHB-HR	26	51	77	18	36	54	155	91	147	238	74	128	202	123
RHB-Avg	.269	.262	.266	.276	.276	.276	96	.254	.257	.256	.256	.268	.261	98
RHB-HR	64	90	154	74	61	135	114	180	229	409	205	172	377	107

Cincinnati Reds - Great American Ballpark
LF: 328   CF: 404   RF:325

| | 2019 Season | | | | | | | 2017-2019 | | | | | | |
| | Home Games | | | Away Games | | | | Home Games | | | Away Games | | | |
	Reds	Opp	Total	Reds	Opp	Total	Index	Reds	Opp	Total	Reds	Opp	Total	Index
G	79	79	158	83	83	166		241	241	482	245	245	490	
Avg	.252	.232	.242	.236	.238	.237	102	.254	.248	.251	.247	.262	.254	99
AB	2601	2690	5291	2849	2705	5554	100	8018	8374	16392	8448	8101	16549	101
R	341	357	698	360	354	714	103	1128	1192	2320	1022	1207	2229	106
H	655	625	1280	673	645	1318	102	2039	2077	4116	2083	2126	4209	99
2B	111	131	242	124	129	253	100	357	444	801	378	422	800	101
3B	5	6	11	22	13	35	33	42	32	74	48	36	84	89
HR	114	111	225	113	103	216	109	329	373	702	289	317	606	117
BB	239	273	512	253	263	516	104	851	858	1709	765	841	1606	107
SO	703	795	1498	733	757	1490	106	2122	2193	4315	2019	1917	3936	111
Foul Outs	52	64	116	56	51	107	114	158	186	344	153	134	287	121
E	42	37	79	49	50	99	84	119	115	234	148	134	282	84
E-Infield	13	16	29	15	21	36	85	47	45	92	55	59	114	82
LHB-Avg	.255	.232	.241	.218	.259	.240	100	.268	.253	.260	.254	.279	.266	98
LHB-HR	33	64	97	44	47	91	101	130	203	333	130	159	289	116
RHB-Avg	.250	.233	.242	.246	.223	.235	103	.244	.244	.244	.241	.249	.245	100
RHB-HR	81	47	128	69	56	125	116	199	170	369	159	158	317	118

Cleveland Indians - Progressive Field
LF: 325   CF: 405   RF:325

| | 2019 Season | | | | | | | 2017-2019 | | | | | | |
| | Home Games | | | Away Games | | | | Home Games | | | Away Games | | | |
	Indians	Opp	Total	Indians	Opp	Total	Index	Indians	Opp	Total	Indians	Opp	Total	Index
G	81	81	162	81	81	162		243	243	486	243	243	486	
Avg	.246	.238	.242	.253	.242	.248	97	.259	.238	.249	.255	.241	.248	100
AB	2620	2752	5372	2805	2697	5502	98	8023	8341	16364	8508	8052	16560	99
R	382	321	703	387	336	723	97	1231	930	2161	1174	939	2113	102
H	644	654	1298	710	654	1364	95	2080	1987	4067	2170	1937	4107	99
2B	137	169	306	149	146	295	106	448	468	916	468	420	888	104
3B	5	9	14	13	11	24	60	25	26	51	41	29	70	74
HR	107	113	220	116	94	210	107	309	306	615	342	264	606	103
BB	273	228	501	290	222	512	100	875	600	1475	846	663	1509	99
SO	654	790	1444	678	718	1396	106	1780	2429	4209	1894	2237	4131	103
Foul Outs	57	58	115	66	72	138	85	152	148	300	188	186	374	81
E	35	53	88	48	35	83	106	107	172	279	135	113	248	113
E-Infield	14	20	34	15	18	33	103	44	65	109	50	58	108	101
LHB-Avg	.239	.237	.238	.258	.238	.250	95	.263	.251	.258	.256	.244	.251	103
LHB-HR	55	54	109	69	43	112	99	176	159	335	187	127	314	107
RHB-Avg	.254	.238	.245	.246	.246	.246	100	.255	.228	.239	.254	.238	.245	98
RHB-HR	52	59	111	47	51	98	117	133	147	280	155	137	292	98

Colorado Rockies - Coors Field
LF: 347   CF: 415   RF:350

| | 2019 Season | | | | | | | 2017-2019 | | | | | | |
| | Home Games | | | Away Games | | | | Home Games | | | Away Games | | | |
	Rockies	Opp	Total	Rockies	Opp	Total	Index	Rockies	Opp	Total	Rockies	Opp	Total	Index
G	81	81	162	81	81	162		243	243	486	244	244	488	
Avg	.300	.296	.298	.230	.256	.243	123	.295	.278	.287	.235	.248	.241	119
AB	2852	2989	5841	2808	2703	5511	106	8322	8635	16957	8413	8058	16471	103
R	500	544	1044	335	414	749	139	1433	1363	2796	1006	1097	2103	134
H	855	885	1740	647	691	1338	130	2457	2404	4861	1973	2002	3975	123
2B	178	190	368	145	135	280	124	500	508	1008	396	375	771	127
3B	30	28	58	11	16	27	203	93	86	179	28	56	84	207
HR	132	144	276	92	126	218	119	361	343	704	265	301	566	121
BB	269	294	563	220	295	515	103	794	830	1624	721	816	1537	103
SO	671	649	1320	832	615	1447	86	1955	1995	3950	2353	1948	4301	89
Foul Outs	43	36	79	75	50	125	60	120	114	234	175	165	340	67
E	50	61	111	47	47	94	118	130	160	290	118	136	254	115
E-Infield	18	23	41	16	21	37	111	49	66	115	40	62	102	113
LHB-Avg	.311	.281	.297	.243	.267	.254	117	.308	.270	.289	.237	.254	.245	118
LHB-HR	65	53	118	41	51	92	120	149	131	280	100	124	224	123
RHB-Avg	.288	.308	.299	.218	.247	.233	129	.285	.284	.285	.232	.244	.238	119
RHB-HR	67	91	158	51	75	126	119	212	212	424	165	177	342	119

Detroit Tigers - Comerica Park
LF: 345 CF: 420 RF:330

| | 2019 Season | | | | | | | 2017-2019 | | | | | | |
| | Home Games | | | Away Games | | | | Home Games | | | Away Games | | | |
	Tigers	Opp	Total	Tigers	Opp	Total	Index	Tigers	Opp	Total	Tigers	Opp	Total	Index
G	81	81	162	80	80	160		243	243	486	242	242	484	
Avg	.246	.285	.266	.235	.263	.249	107	.257	.272	.265	.236	.272	.254	104
AB	2759	2989	5748	2790	2675	5465	104	8271	8726	16997	8328	8064	16392	103
R	285	506	791	297	409	706	111	1031	1331	2362	916	1274	2190	107
H	678	851	1529	655	704	1359	111	2126	2370	4496	1968	2195	4163	108
2B	138	156	294	154	159	313	89	449	437	886	416	446	862	99
3B	29	28	57	12	16	28	194	69	67	136	42	46	88	149
HR	64	145	209	85	105	190	105	237	352	589	234	332	566	100
BB	183	277	460	208	259	467	94	651	769	1420	671	796	1467	93
SO	769	685	1454	826	683	1509	92	2002	1881	3883	2247	1904	4151	90
Foul Outs	66	65	131	57	46	103	121	203	237	440	151	157	308	138
E	64	41	105	46	45	91	114	144	127	271	145	138	283	95
E-Infield	24	16	40	18	16	34	116	61	58	119	58	53	111	107
LHB-Avg	.248	.283	.268	.247	.275	.262	103	.248	.266	.259	.239	.278	.261	99
LHB-HR	15	45	60	21	31	52	105	60	132	192	59	131	190	92
RHB-Avg	.245	.286	.265	.230	.257	.243	109	.261	.275	.268	.235	.269	.251	107
RHB-HR	49	100	149	64	74	138	105	177	220	397	175	201	376	105

Houston Astros - Minute Maid Park
LF: 315 CF: 409 RF:326

| | 2019 Season | | | | | | | 2017-2019 | | | | | | |
| | Home Games | | | Away Games | | | | Home Games | | | Away Games | | | |
	Astros	Opp	Total	Astros	Opp	Total	Index	Astros	Opp	Total	Astros	Opp	Total	Index
G	81	81	162	81	81	162		240	240	480	246	246	492	
Avg	.284	.219	.251	.265	.222	.244	103	.271	.220	.245	.270	.232	.252	97
AB	2735	2790	5525	2878	2671	5549	100	7961	8168	16129	8716	8134	16850	98
R	489	322	811	431	318	749	108	1249	916	2165	1364	958	2322	96
H	776	612	1388	762	593	1355	102	2157	1794	3951	2352	1889	4241	95
2B	160	98	258	163	135	298	87	445	335	780	502	448	950	86
3B	13	9	22	15	12	27	82	23	33	56	43	32	75	78
HR	150	132	282	138	98	236	120	356	320	676	375	254	629	112
BB	318	220	538	327	228	555	97	839	675	1514	880	730	1610	98
SO	579	881	1460	587	790	1377	106	1637	2558	4195	1813	2393	4206	104
Foul Outs	50	49	99	69	61	130	76	170	154	324	206	156	362	94
E	29	48	77	42	34	76	101	113	149	262	120	142	262	103
E-Infield	9	18	27	16	19	35	77	42	65	107	45	67	112	98
LHB-Avg	.293	.202	.240	.277	.207	.237	101	.270	.207	.233	.262	.221	.239	98
LHB-HR	40	63	103	37	43	80	122	93	140	233	101	114	215	110
RHB-Avg	.279	.233	.258	.259	.234	.248	104	.272	.229	.252	.273	.241	.259	97
RHB-HR	110	69	179	101	55	156	119	263	180	443	274	140	414	114

Kansas City Royals - Kauffman Stadium
LF: 330 CF: 410 RF:330

| | 2019 Season | | | | | | | 2017-2019 | | | | | | |
| | Home Games | | | Away Games | | | | Home Games | | | Away Games | | | |
	Royals	Opp	Total	Royals	Opp	Total	Index	Royals	Opp	Total	Royals	Opp	Total	Index
G	80	80	160	82	82	164		242	242	484	244	244	488	
Avg	.255	.279	.268	.239	.268	.253	106	.258	.270	.264	.243	.273	.258	102
AB	2672	2870	5542	2824	2706	5530	103	8055	8559	16614	8482	8200	16682	100
R	337	461	798	354	408	762	107	1009	1264	2273	1022	1229	2251	102
H	682	801	1483	674	724	1398	109	2079	2309	4388	2063	2238	4301	103
2B	150	163	313	131	136	267	117	442	441	883	382	403	785	113
3B	21	17	38	19	11	30	126	52	58	110	41	46	87	127
HR	61	101	162	101	120	221	73	216	290	506	294	332	626	81
BB	215	278	493	241	304	545	90	642	806	1448	631	844	1475	99
SO	614	599	1213	791	631	1422	85	1745	1785	3530	2136	1818	3954	90
Foul Outs	60	49	109	48	51	99	110	186	164	350	165	180	345	102
E	38	47	85	35	48	83	105	103	126	229	126	141	267	86
E-Infield	20	15	35	15	17	32	112	54	48	102	54	60	114	90
LHB-Avg	.247	.295	.274	.220	.263	.242	113	.259	.279	.270	.237	.267	.252	107
LHB-HR	16	47	63	26	48	74	84	96	114	210	120	130	250	84
RHB-Avg	.260	.266	.263	.250	.271	.260	101	.258	.263	.260	.248	.277	.262	99
RHB-HR	45	54	99	75	72	147	68	120	176	296	174	202	376	80

Los Angeles Angels - Angel Stadium of Anaheim
LF: 330   CF: 400   RF:330

	2019 Season							2018-2019						
	Home Games			Away Games				Home Games			Away Games			
	Angels	Opp	Total	Angels	Opp	Total	Index	Angels	Opp	Total	Angels	Opp	Total	Index
G	79	79	158	83	83	166		160	160	320	164	164	328	
Avg	.248	.248	.248	.246	.260	.253	98	.243	.242	.242	.246	.261	.253	96
AB	2672	2803	5475	2870	2772	5642	102	5318	5580	10898	5696	5440	11136	100
R	385	411	796	384	457	841	99	740	766	1506	750	824	1574	98
H	663	695	1358	705	722	1427	100	1290	1349	2639	1401	1421	2822	96
2B	137	132	269	131	152	283	98	259	249	508	258	291	549	95
3B	11	10	21	10	18	28	77	19	18	37	25	29	54	70
HR	112	129	241	108	138	246	101	226	238	464	208	234	442	107
BB	288	288	576	298	288	586	101	553	558	1111	547	564	1111	102
SO	627	733	1360	649	671	1320	106	1252	1459	2711	1324	1331	2655	104
Foul Outs	58	47	105	61	52	113	96	128	105	233	133	118	251	95
E	51	44	95	41	55	96	104	90	85	175	78	98	176	102
E-Infield	21	21	42	19	29	48	92	46	32	78	32	45	77	104
LHB-Avg	.244	.239	.242	.243	.265	.253	95	.237	.233	.235	.231	.265	.249	94
LHB-HR	64	47	111	43	49	92	120	102	88	190	66	83	149	125
RHB-Avg	.251	.254	.253	.248	.257	.253	100	.246	.248	.247	.254	.258	.256	96
RHB-HR	48	82	130	65	89	154	89	124	150	274	142	151	293	98

Los Angeles Dodgers - Dodger Stadium
LF: 330   CF: 395   RF:330

	2019 Season							2017-2019						
	Home Games			Away Games				Home Games			Away Games			
	Dodgers	Opp	Total	Dodgers	Opp	Total	Index	Dodgers	Opp	Total	Dodgers	Opp	Total	Index
G	81	81	162	81	81	162		244	244	488	243	243	486	
Avg	.264	.217	.240	.251	.229	.240	100	.253	.222	.237	.252	.232	.242	98
AB	2668	2736	5404	2825	2651	5476	99	7983	8295	16278	8490	8034	16524	98
R	441	271	712	445	342	787	90	1205	835	2040	1255	968	2223	91
H	704	595	1299	710	606	1316	99	2017	1841	3858	2138	1865	4003	96
2B	142	114	256	160	125	285	91	438	356	794	472	354	826	98
3B	7	4	11	13	20	33	34	23	16	39	50	53	103	38
HR	143	103	246	136	82	218	114	377	286	663	358	262	620	109
BB	287	167	454	320	225	545	84	881	573	1454	1022	683	1705	87
SO	627	793	1420	729	726	1455	99	2032	2375	4407	2140	2258	4398	102
Foul Outs	48	56	104	48	43	91	116	148	177	325	158	163	321	103
E	45	36	81	61	38	99	82	138	123	261	156	115	271	96
E-Infield	20	12	32	25	20	45	71	55	49	104	69	52	121	86
LHB-Avg	.275	.219	.250	.263	.232	.249	100	.259	.224	.243	.252	.240	.247	98
LHB-HR	83	38	121	81	38	119	108	201	111	312	190	96	286	112
RHB-Avg	.253	.217	.232	.240	.226	.232	100	.248	.221	.233	.251	.227	.239	98
RHB-HR	60	65	125	55	44	99	123	176	175	351	168	166	334	106

Miami Marlins - Marlins Park
LF: 340   CF: 416   RF:335

	2019 Season							2017-2019						
	Home Games			Away Games				Home Games			Away Games			
	Marlins	Opp	Total	Marlins	Opp	Total	Index	Marlins	Opp	Total	Marlins	Opp	Total	Index
G	81	81	162	81	81	162		240	240	480	245	245	490	
Avg	.245	.242	.243	.236	.248	.242	100	.248	.241	.244	.249	.267	.258	95
AB	2724	2807	5531	2788	2666	5454	101	8068	8321	16389	8534	8138	16672	100
R	326	415	741	289	393	682	109	965	1083	2048	1017	1356	2373	88
H	667	678	1345	659	662	1321	102	1999	2006	4005	2127	2172	4299	95
2B	124	152	276	141	129	270	101	327	420	747	431	450	881	86
3B	13	17	30	5	10	15	197	38	47	85	35	40	75	115
HR	68	105	173	78	131	209	82	216	253	469	252	368	620	77
BB	204	315	519	191	300	491	104	686	910	1596	650	937	1587	102
SO	730	716	1446	739	662	1401	102	1967	1996	3963	2168	1833	4001	101
Foul Outs	41	85	126	45	62	107	116	139	207	346	159	183	342	103
E	41	47	88	53	58	111	79	112	153	265	138	161	299	90
E-Infield	9	15	24	24	24	48	50	35	66	101	57	65	122	85
LHB-Avg	.205	.242	.230	.220	.273	.256	90	.238	.241	.239	.258	.279	.270	89
LHB-HR	18	42	60	15	59	74	76	67	109	176	74	150	224	80
RHB-Avg	.255	.241	.249	.240	.230	.236	106	.253	.241	.247	.245	.257	.250	99
RHB-HR	50	63	113	63	72	135	84	149	144	293	178	218	396	75

Milwaukee Brewers - Miller Park
LF: 344   CF: 400   RF:345

	2019 Season							2017-2019						
	Home Games			Away Games			Index	Home Games			Away Games			Index
	Brewers	Opp	Total	Brewers	Opp	Total		Brewers	Opp	Total	Brewers	Opp	Total	
G	81	81	162	81	81	162		246	246	492	241	241	482	
Avg	.252	.227	.239	.241	.265	.253	95	.250	.238	.244	.249	.250	.249	98
AB	2677	2765	5442	2865	2777	5642	96	8126	8440	16566	8425	7996	16421	99
R	388	370	758	381	396	777	98	1165	1072	2237	1090	1050	2140	102
H	675	628	1303	691	736	1427	91	2031	2005	4036	2096	1999	4095	97
2B	134	115	249	145	132	277	93	397	388	785	401	374	775	100
3B	9	15	24	8	21	29	86	32	45	77	31	60	91	84
HR	126	115	241	124	110	234	107	361	302	663	331	281	612	107
BB	324	273	597	305	297	602	103	875	846	1721	838	830	1668	102
SO	770	825	1595	793	672	1465	113	2318	2291	4609	2274	1980	4254	107
Foul Outs	50	71	121	59	61	120	105	138	198	336	144	168	312	107
E	44	54	98	53	37	90	109	179	159	338	141	130	271	122
E-Infield	20	29	49	18	12	30	163	79	69	148	59	53	112	129
LHB-Avg	.260	.229	.245	.248	.272	.258	95	.263	.235	.248	.248	.260	.254	98
LHB-HR	72	44	116	71	48	119	99	183	124	307	156	123	279	110
RHB-Avg	.246	.226	.235	.235	.261	.249	94	.241	.240	.240	.249	.242	.246	98
RHB-HR	54	71	125	53	62	115	115	178	178	356	175	158	333	105

Minnesota Twins - Target Field
LF: 339   CF: 411   RF:328

	2019 Season							2017-2019						
	Home Games			Away Games			Index	Home Games			Away Games			Index
	Twins	Opp	Total	Twins	Opp	Total		Twins	Opp	Total	Twins	Opp	Total	
G	81	81	162	81	81	162		241	241	482	245	245	490	
Avg	.264	.262	.263	.276	.251	.264	100	.265	.262	.263	.255	.257	.256	103
AB	2795	2936	5731	2937	2735	5672	101	8146	8577	16723	8669	8241	16910	101
R	442	394	836	497	360	857	98	1256	1166	2422	1236	1151	2387	103
H	737	770	1507	810	686	1496	101	2159	2247	4406	2211	2121	4332	103
2B	168	153	321	150	129	279	114	473	452	925	448	392	840	111
3B	12	12	24	11	11	22	108	49	31	80	27	44	71	114
HR	137	98	235	170	100	270	86	332	303	635	347	317	664	97
BB	283	227	510	242	225	467	108	869	758	1627	783	750	1533	107
SO	644	776	1420	690	687	1377	102	1902	2073	3975	2102	1933	4035	100
Foul Outs	64	53	117	67	74	141	82	191	151	342	207	192	399	87
E	44	42	86	67	51	118	73	129	122	251	157	150	307	83
E-Infield	19	17	36	27	30	57	63	49	46	95	66	75	141	68
LHB-Avg	.273	.270	.271	.272	.245	.260	104	.270	.260	.266	.258	.259	.259	103
LHB-HR	53	29	82	71	36	107	77	169	113	282	166	136	302	96
RHB-Avg	.255	.257	.256	.280	.255	.267	96	.259	.264	.262	.251	.256	.254	103
RHB-HR	84	69	153	99	64	163	92	163	190	353	181	181	362	97

New York Mets - Citi Field
LF: 335   CF: 408   RF:330

	2019 Season							2017-2019						
	Home Games			Away Games			Index	Home Games			Away Games			Index
	Mets	Opp	Total	Mets	Opp	Total		Mets	Opp	Total	Mets	Opp	Total	
G	81	81	162	81	81	162		243	243	486	243	243	486	
Avg	.250	.239	.244	.264	.263	.263	93	.235	.243	.239	.259	.271	.265	90
AB	2688	2803	5491	2936	2798	5734	96	7978	8416	16394	8624	8354	16978	97
R	380	340	720	411	397	808	89	998	1044	2042	1204	1263	2467	83
H	671	670	1341	774	735	1509	89	1873	2041	3914	2233	2266	4499	87
2B	123	136	259	157	151	308	88	361	363	724	470	443	913	82
3B	5	7	12	12	12	24	52	30	28	58	49	38	87	69
HR	126	97	223	116	107	223	104	302	285	587	334	324	658	92
BB	254	241	495	262	259	521	99	769	769	1538	842	808	1650	97
SO	669	835	1504	715	685	1400	112	1973	2343	4316	2106	1997	4103	109
Foul Outs	54	53	107	42	49	91	123	213	171	384	169	146	315	126
E	49	44	93	50	45	95	98	134	124	258	145	130	275	94
E-Infield	17	13	30	27	17	44	68	46	58	104	77	48	125	83
LHB-Avg	.258	.253	.255	.260	.263	.261	98	.236	.250	.243	.259	.268	.263	92
LHB-HR	43	43	86	53	37	90	104	140	116	256	177	127	304	89
RHB-Avg	.244	.231	.237	.266	.263	.264	90	.234	.237	.235	.259	.273	.266	88
RHB-HR	83	54	137	63	70	133	105	162	169	331	157	197	354	96

New York Yankees - Yankee Stadium
LF: 318   CF: 408   RF:314

	2019 Season Home Games			Away Games			Index	2017-2019 Home Games			Away Games			Index
	Yankees	Opp	Total	Yankees	Opp	Total		Yankees	Opp	Total	Yankees	Opp	Total	
G	81	81	162	81	81	162		243	243	486	243	243	486	
Avg	.263	.234	.248	.271	.262	.267	93	.263	.233	.248	.256	.242	.249	99
AB	2651	2754	5405	2932	2781	5713	95	8044	8341	16385	8648	8205	16853	97
R	440	316	756	503	423	926	82	1344	983	2327	1308	1085	2393	97
H	698	644	1342	795	730	1525	88	2115	1945	4060	2215	1988	4203	97
2B	114	125	239	176	152	328	77	358	377	735	467	436	903	84
3B	8	5	13	9	13	22	62	29	14	43	34	29	63	70
HR	143	114	257	163	134	297	91	427	312	739	387	305	692	110
BB	264	246	510	305	261	566	95	913	747	1660	897	758	1655	103
SO	687	804	1491	750	730	1480	106	2033	2452	4485	2211	2276	4487	103
Foul Outs	53	53	106	54	56	110	102	159	156	315	184	157	341	95
E	46	46	92	56	43	99	93	144	161	305	147	152	299	102
E-Infield	19	11	30	21	13	34	88	57	63	120	57	60	117	103
LHB-Avg	.229	.243	.238	.255	.260	.258	92	.251	.233	.242	.247	.244	.246	98
LHB-HR	35	42	77	48	46	94	89	129	117	246	115	103	218	119
RHB-Avg	.276	.228	.253	.278	.264	.272	93	.269	.233	.251	.261	.241	.252	100
RHB-HR	108	72	180	115	88	203	92	298	195	493	272	202	474	106

Oakland Athletics - RingCentral Coliseum
LF: 330   CF: 400   RF:330

	2019 Season Home Games			Away Games			Index	2017-2019 Home Games			Away Games			Index
	Athletics	Opp	Total	Athletics	Opp	Total		Athletics	Opp	Total	Athletics	Opp	Total	
G	79	79	158	83	83	166		241	241	482	245	245	490	
Avg	.248	.236	.242	.250	.249	.249	97	.248	.239	.243	.250	.254	.252	97
AB	2621	2745	5366	2940	2796	5736	98	8013	8436	16449	8591	8159	16750	100
R	391	301	692	454	379	833	87	1177	1015	2192	1220	1165	2385	93
H	649	647	1296	735	695	1430	95	1989	2015	4004	2146	2074	4220	96
2B	147	126	273	145	123	268	109	491	409	900	428	408	836	110
3B	13	8	21	10	15	25	90	31	36	67	27	34	61	112
HR	119	85	204	138	116	254	86	339	270	609	379	325	704	88
BB	290	227	517	288	250	538	103	858	707	1565	835	746	1581	101
SO	593	671	1264	745	628	1373	98	1977	1963	3940	2233	1775	4008	100
Foul Outs	78	83	161	63	68	131	131	230	241	471	188	167	355	135
E	40	52	92	40	51	91	106	139	139	278	151	133	284	100
E-Infield	17	20	37	16	21	37	105	59	53	112	64	59	123	93
LHB-Avg	.214	.239	.230	.256	.245	.249	92	.233	.238	.236	.262	.247	.253	93
LHB-HR	28	41	69	36	54	90	75	100	116	216	124	132	256	85
RHB-Avg	.262	.232	.249	.248	.252	.250	100	.255	.240	.248	.244	.260	.251	99
RHB-HR	91	44	135	102	62	164	93	239	154	393	255	193	448	90

Philadelphia Phillies - Citizens Bank Park
LF: 329   CF: 401   RF:329

	2019 Season Home Games			Away Games			Index	2017-2019 Home Games			Away Games			Index
	Phillies	Opp	Total	Phillies	Opp	Total		Phillies	Opp	Total	Phillies	Opp	Total	
G	81	81	162	81	81	162		242	242	484	244	244	488	
Avg	.253	.259	.256	.239	.263	.251	102	.247	.252	.250	.239	.264	.252	99
AB	2730	2862	5592	2841	2709	5550	101	8064	8514	16578	8466	8107	16573	101
R	410	392	802	364	402	766	105	1148	1123	2271	993	1181	2174	105
H	690	740	1430	679	712	1391	103	1994	2145	4139	2027	2144	4171	100
2B	151	112	263	160	137	297	88	410	395	805	429	442	871	92
3B	12	12	24	14	11	25	95	47	39	86	45	44	89	97
HR	123	132	255	92	126	218	116	330	349	679	245	301	546	124
BB	293	268	561	269	278	547	102	835	776	1611	803	797	1600	101
SO	709	701	1410	744	691	1435	98	2150	2265	4415	2240	1901	4141	107
Foul Outs	84	66	150	57	34	91	164	215	182	397	181	151	332	120
E	50	60	110	47	54	101	109	146	150	296	156	132	288	104
E-Infield	21	26	47	15	15	30	157	50	61	111	53	49	102	110
LHB-Avg	.253	.268	.261	.248	.262	.255	102	.250	.263	.257	.249	.272	.260	99
LHB-HR	49	63	112	45	50	95	120	127	170	297	113	138	251	122
RHB-Avg	.253	.252	.252	.233	.263	.248	102	.246	.243	.244	.232	.258	.245	100
RHB-HR	74	69	143	47	76	123	113	203	179	382	132	163	295	126

Pittsburgh Pirates - PNC Park
LF: 325　　CF: 399　　RF:320

| | 2019 Season | | | | | | | 2017-2019 | | | | | | |
| | Home Games | | | Away Games | | | | Home Games | | | Away Games | | | |
	Pirates	Opp	Total	Pirates	Opp	Total	Index	Pirates	Opp	Total	Pirates	Opp	Total	Index
G	80	80	160	82	82	164		240	240	480	245	245	490	
Avg	.262	.264	.263	.267	.271	.269	98	.257	.257	.257	.251	.264	.258	100
AB	2753	2891	5644	2904	2757	5661	102	8045	8515	16560	8517	8194	16711	101
R	377	451	828	381	460	841	101	1026	1118	2144	1092	1217	2309	95
H	722	764	1486	775	747	1522	100	2071	2188	4259	2138	2167	4305	101
2B	166	203	369	149	148	297	125	431	528	959	423	430	853	113
3B	20	16	36	18	18	36	100	56	32	88	56	59	115	77
HR	69	119	188	94	122	216	87	206	285	491	265	312	577	86
BB	229	305	534	196	279	475	113	731	804	1535	687	788	1475	105
SO	563	722	1285	650	721	1371	94	1694	2022	3716	1961	2019	3980	94
Foul Outs	43	44	87	60	46	106	82	134	133	267	152	144	296	91
E	60	54	114	61	64	125	93	162	143	305	163	167	330	94
E-Infield	24	25	49	23	23	46	109	74	59	133	70	65	135	101
LHB-Avg	.286	.274	.280	.281	.284	.282	99	.276	.268	.271	.264	.274	.269	101
LHB-HR	37	49	86	41	59	100	90	95	135	230	104	141	245	95
RHB-Avg	.243	.258	.251	.255	.261	.258	97	.246	.249	.247	.243	.257	.250	99
RHB-HR	32	70	102	53	63	116	85	111	150	261	161	171	332	79

San Diego Padres - PETCO Park
LF: 336　　CF: 396　　RF:322

| | 2019 Season | | | | | | | 2017-2019 | | | | | | |
| | Home Games | | | Away Games | | | | Home Games | | | Away Games | | | |
	Padres	Opp	Total	Padres	Opp	Total	Index	Padres	Opp	Total	Padres	Opp	Total	Index
G	81	81	162	81	81	162		240	240	480	246	246	492	
Avg	.227	.241	.234	.248	.261	.254	92	.231	.246	.239	.240	.264	.252	95
AB	2612	2819	5431	2779	2732	5511	99	7784	8366	16150	8449	8249	16698	99
R	312	368	680	370	421	791	86	917	1091	2008	986	1281	2267	91
H	593	680	1273	688	714	1402	91	1796	2061	3857	2025	2180	4205	94
2B	96	151	247	128	151	279	90	322	429	751	379	431	810	96
3B	10	9	19	14	13	27	71	43	31	74	42	46	88	87
HR	101	101	202	118	114	232	88	268	282	550	302	344	646	88
BB	256	239	495	248	224	472	106	765	758	1523	670	778	1448	109
SO	773	729	1502	808	746	1554	98	2194	2104	4298	2409	2095	4504	99
Foul Outs	51	47	98	68	47	115	86	172	135	307	189	145	334	95
E	50	53	103	66	40	106	97	160	128	288	169	133	302	98
E-Infield	20	14	34	17	15	32	106	55	40	95	56	51	107	91
LHB-Avg	.236	.241	.239	.251	.278	.266	90	.240	.251	.246	.232	.275	.254	97
LHB-HR	18	35	53	23	48	71	74	72	102	174	84	139	223	81
RHB-Avg	.223	.242	.232	.246	.250	.248	93	.226	.243	.235	.244	.257	.250	94
RHB-HR	83	66	149	95	66	161	95	196	180	376	218	205	423	91

San Francisco Giants - Oracle Park
LF: 339　　CF: 399　　RF:309

| | 2019 Season | | | | | | | 2017-2019 | | | | | | |
| | Home Games | | | Away Games | | | | Home Games | | | Away Games | | | |
	Giants	Opp	Total	Giants	Opp	Total	Index	Giants	Opp	Total	Giants	Opp	Total	Index
G	81	81	162	81	81	162		243	243	486	243	243	486	
Avg	.229	.242	.236	.248	.257	.252	93	.241	.248	.245	.244	.265	.254	96
AB	2725	2885	5610	2854	2712	5566	101	8167	8627	16794	8504	8145	16649	101
R	271	373	644	407	400	807	80	908	1041	1949	1012	1207	2219	88
H	623	699	1322	709	696	1405	94	1967	2141	4108	2071	2156	4227	97
2B	138	108	246	162	136	298	82	419	402	821	426	430	856	95
3B	17	20	37	9	17	26	141	53	71	124	31	66	97	127
HR	63	98	161	104	129	233	69	171	232	403	257	333	590	68
BB	224	243	467	251	276	527	88	680	745	1425	710	794	1504	94
SO	720	738	1458	715	630	1345	108	1984	2016	4000	2122	1855	3977	100
Foul Outs	45	48	93	57	50	107	86	149	146	295	159	164	323	91
E	50	43	93	40	42	82	113	136	116	252	138	135	273	92
E-Infield	20	15	35	19	24	43	81	62	51	113	65	60	125	90
LHB-Avg	.227	.237	.231	.253	.246	.250	92	.240	.246	.243	.251	.266	.258	94
LHB-HR	30	26	56	57	42	99	60	80	68	148	128	116	244	59
RHB-Avg	.231	.246	.239	.243	.263	.254	94	.241	.249	.246	.237	.264	.251	98
RHB-HR	33	72	105	47	87	134	74	91	164	255	129	217	346	74

Seattle Mariners - T-Mobile Park
LF: 331   CF: 405   RF:326

| | 2019 Season | | | | | | | 2017-2019 | | | | | | |
| | Home Games | | | Away Games | | | | Home Games | | | Away Games | | | |
	Mariners	Opp	Total	Mariners	Opp	Total	Index	Mariners	Opp	Total	Mariners	Opp	Total	Index
G	81	81	162	81	81	162		243	243	486	243	243	486	
Avg	.235	.254	.244	.240	.272	.256	96	.247	.246	.246	.253	.267	.260	95
AB	2680	2867	5547	2820	2785	5605	99	8017	8497	16514	8547	8202	16749	99
R	367	438	805	391	455	846	95	1036	1133	2169	1149	1243	2392	91
H	629	727	1356	676	757	1433	95	1979	2089	4068	2164	2190	4354	93
2B	123	144	267	131	192	323	84	366	398	764	425	489	914	85
3B	8	9	17	20	15	35	49	33	24	57	44	35	79	73
HR	107	134	241	132	126	258	94	288	347	635	327	345	672	96
BB	297	251	548	291	254	545	102	748	703	1451	757	692	1449	102
SO	817	653	1470	764	586	1350	110	2087	2034	4121	1982	1777	3759	111
Foul Outs	53	65	118	57	56	113	106	148	196	344	171	192	363	96
E	65	41	106	67	44	111	95	164	126	290	159	143	302	96
E-Infield	23	16	39	29	19	48	81	73	47	120	70	44	114	105
LHB-Avg	.229	.257	.241	.248	.262	.253	95	.243	.248	.245	.254	.270	.260	94
LHB-HR	49	45	94	61	49	110	83	106	120	226	131	125	256	91
RHB-Avg	.241	.251	.247	.231	.277	.258	96	.250	.245	.247	.253	.266	.260	95
RHB-HR	58	89	147	71	77	148	103	182	227	409	196	220	416	99

St Louis Cardinals - Busch Stadium
LF: 336   CF: 400   RF:335

| | 2019 Season | | | | | | | 2017-2019 | | | | | | |
| | Home Games | | | Away Games | | | | Home Games | | | Away Games | | | |
	Cardinals	Opp	Total	Cardinals	Opp	Total	Index	Cardinals	Opp	Total	Cardinals	Opp	Total	Index
G	81	81	162	81	81	162		243	243	486	243	243	486	
Avg	.250	.226	.238	.241	.251	.246	97	.251	.240	.245	.249	.252	.250	98
AB	2631	2716	5347	2818	2673	5491	97	7948	8340	16288	8469	8062	16531	99
R	388	294	682	376	368	744	92	1098	971	2069	1186	1087	2273	91
H	659	613	1272	678	671	1349	94	1998	2000	3998	2110	2031	4141	97
2B	113	116	229	133	130	263	89	360	369	729	418	381	799	93
3B	14	7	21	10	12	22	98	32	33	65	29	43	72	92
HR	89	93	182	121	98	219	85	262	255	517	349	263	612	86
BB	285	249	534	276	296	572	96	833	760	1593	846	871	1717	94
SO	648	686	1334	772	713	1485	92	1945	2036	3981	2203	2051	4254	95
Foul Outs	66	46	112	54	49	103	112	159	165	324	149	139	288	114
E	37	58	95	29	58	87	109	148	140	288	145	159	304	95
E-Infield	15	22	37	12	25	37	100	54	59	113	54	70	124	91
LHB-Avg	.271	.231	.248	.244	.252	.248	100	.257	.247	.251	.245	.261	.255	98
LHB-HR	21	45	66	34	40	74	92	69	131	200	89	121	210	94
RHB-Avg	.241	.222	.232	.239	.251	.244	95	.249	.234	.242	.251	.244	.248	98
RHB-HR	68	48	116	87	58	145	82	193	124	317	260	142	402	81

Tampa Bay Rays - Tropicana Field Surface: FieldTurf
LF: 315   CF: 404   RF:322

| | 2019 Season | | | | | | | 2017-2019 | | | | | | |
| | Home Games | | | Away Games | | | | Home Games | | | Away Games | | | |
	Rays	Opp	Total	Rays	Opp	Total	Index	Rays	Opp	Total	Rays	Opp	Total	Index
G	81	81	162	81	81	162		240	240	480	246	246	492	
Avg	.249	.222	.236	.258	.239	.248	95	.252	.224	.238	.253	.244	.248	96
AB	2743	2798	5541	2885	2733	5618	99	7944	8163	16107	8637	8232	16869	98
R	366	307	673	403	349	752	89	1076	901	1977	1103	1105	2208	92
H	684	621	1305	743	653	1396	93	1999	1827	3826	2183	2007	4190	94
2B	142	132	274	149	132	281	99	367	367	734	424	429	853	90
3B	14	16	30	15	10	25	122	54	35	89	50	28	78	120
HR	99	90	189	118	91	209	92	271	259	530	324	279	603	92
BB	271	215	486	271	238	509	97	830	678	1508	797	779	1576	100
SO	753	847	1600	740	774	1514	107	2167	2295	4462	2252	2099	4351	107
Foul Outs	65	68	133	63	51	114	118	184	210	394	190	171	361	114
E	33	37	70	54	47	101	69	104	136	240	168	133	301	82
E-Infield	13	19	32	26	13	39	82	42	62	104	72	42	114	94
LHB-Avg	.252	.215	.234	.262	.229	.247	95	.254	.208	.233	.257	.235	.247	94
LHB-HR	45	34	79	52	32	84	93	122	85	207	143	100	243	88
RHB-Avg	.247	.226	.236	.255	.245	.250	95	.250	.233	.241	.250	.249	.249	97
RHB-HR	54	56	110	66	59	125	90	149	174	323	181	179	360	95

Texas Rangers - Rangers Ballpark in Arlington
LF: 332   CF: 400   RF:325

| | 2019 Season | | | | | | | 2017-2019 | | | | | | |
| | Home Games | | | Away Games | | | | Home Games | | | Away Games | | | |
	Rangers	Opp	Total	Rangers	Opp	Total	Index	Rangers	Opp	Total	Rangers	Opp	Total	Index
G	81	81	162	81	81	162		243	243	486	243	243	486	
Avg	.262	.277	.270	.234	.261	.247	109	.261	.276	.269	.227	.258	.242	111
AB	2762	2952	5714	2778	2677	5455	105	8146	8739	16885	8277	8013	16290	104
R	454	482	936	356	396	752	124	1335	1398	2733	1011	1144	2155	127
H	723	817	1540	651	698	1349	114	2125	2410	4535	1883	2064	3947	115
2B	160	156	316	136	154	290	104	432	496	928	385	426	811	110
3B	17	17	34	7	15	22	148	42	54	96	27	35	62	149
HR	114	125	239	109	116	225	101	345	366	711	309	311	620	111
BB	279	304	583	255	279	534	104	884	844	1728	749	789	1538	108
SO	725	704	1429	853	675	1528	89	2128	1822	3950	2427	1785	4212	90
Foul Outs	57	55	112	49	49	98	109	151	186	337	168	169	337	96
E	62	73	135	43	65	108	125	180	178	358	153	147	300	119
E-Infield	26	32	58	18	22	40	145	68	74	142	61	66	127	112
LHB-Avg	.260	.271	.265	.240	.259	.248	107	.257	.271	.263	.224	.252	.236	112
LHB-HR	81	48	129	75	35	110	108	223	122	345	193	98	291	115
RHB-Avg	.263	.281	.273	.229	.262	.247	111	.265	.279	.273	.231	.261	.248	110
RHB-HR	33	77	110	34	81	115	94	122	244	366	116	213	329	107

Toronto Blue Jays - Rogers Centre Surface: FieldTurf
LF: 328   CF: 400   RF:328

| | 2019 Season | | | | | | | 2017-2019 | | | | | | |
| | Home Games | | | Away Games | | | | Home Games | | | Away Games | | | |
	Blue Jays	Opp	Total	Blue Jays	Opp	Total	Index	Blue Jays	Opp	Total	Blue Jays	Opp	Total	Index
G	81	81	162	81	81	162		243	243	486	243	243	486	
Avg	.230	.258	.244	.243	.261	.252	97	.241	.256	.249	.240	.265	.252	99
AB	2697	2907	5604	2796	2683	5479	102	8024	8616	16640	8445	8218	16663	100
R	359	430	789	367	398	765	103	1052	1209	2261	1076	1235	2311	98
H	619	751	1370	680	699	1379	99	1931	2206	4137	2024	2180	4204	98
2B	129	163	292	141	177	318	90	436	492	928	423	483	906	103
3B	12	9	21	9	14	23	89	24	35	59	18	46	64	92
HR	136	134	270	111	94	205	129	356	343	699	330	296	626	112
BB	253	300	553	256	304	560	97	739	851	1590	811	853	1664	96
SO	720	707	1427	794	625	1419	98	2011	2102	4113	2217	1900	4117	100
Foul Outs	71	71	142	44	73	117	119	207	198	405	185	211	396	102
E	46	34	80	50	47	97	82	144	121	265	145	130	275	96
E-Infield	18	14	32	25	14	39	82	52	52	104	68	50	118	88
LHB-Avg	.225	.259	.243	.245	.255	.250	97	.242	.243	.242	.238	.255	.247	98
LHB-HR	60	65	125	45	43	88	144	137	129	266	120	123	243	109
RHB-Avg	.232	.258	.245	.242	.266	.253	97	.240	.265	.252	.240	.273	.255	99
RHB-HR	76	69	145	66	51	117	118	219	214	433	210	173	383	113

Washington Nationals - Nationals Park
LF: 336   CF: 403   RF:335

| | 2019 Season | | | | | | | 2017-2019 | | | | | | |
| | Home Games | | | Away Games | | | | Home Games | | | Away Games | | | |
	Nationals	Opp	Total	Nationals	Opp	Total	Index	Nationals	Opp	Total	Nationals	Opp	Total	Index
G	81	81	162	81	81	162		243	243	486	243	243	486	
Avg	.274	.253	.263	.256	.234	.245	107	.275	.247	.261	.248	.236	.242	108
AB	2710	2852	5562	2802	2639	5441	102	8200	8435	16635	8382	7955	16337	102
R	453	384	837	420	340	760	110	1283	1092	2375	1180	986	2166	110
H	743	722	1465	717	618	1335	110	2259	2083	4342	2080	1877	3957	110
2B	163	149	312	135	132	267	114	482	423	905	411	374	785	113
3B	13	9	22	14	9	23	94	36	30	66	47	37	84	77
HR	130	112	242	101	90	191	124	333	325	658	304	264	568	114
BB	301	254	555	283	263	546	99	900	737	1637	857	762	1619	99
SO	635	773	1408	673	738	1411	98	1887	2267	4154	2037	2118	4155	98
Foul Outs	73	59	132	66	66	132	98	192	173	365	189	220	409	88
E	42	43	85	45	43	88	97	113	139	252	124	125	249	101
E-Infield	18	20	38	25	16	41	93	46	56	102	58	38	96	106
LHB-Avg	.275	.278	.276	.247	.237	.242	114	.282	.257	.269	.253	.236	.245	110
LHB-HR	44	55	99	38	32	70	135	135	145	280	143	103	246	112
RHB-Avg	.274	.236	.255	.260	.232	.247	103	.271	.240	.255	.245	.236	.241	106
RHB-HR	86	57	143	63	58	121	117	198	180	378	161	161	322	115

2019 American League Ballpark Index Rankings

Home Park	Avg	AB	R	H	2B	3B	HR	BB	SO	FO	E	E-Inf	LHB Avg	LHB HR	RHB Avg	RHB HR
Rangers (Rangers Ballpark in Arlington)	109	105	124	114	104	148	101	104	89	109	125	145	107	108	111	94
Tigers (Comerica Park)	107	104	111	111	89	194	105	94	92	121	114	116	103	105	109	105
Orioles (Oriole Park at Camden Yards)	105	101	109	106	114	92	124	92	92	108	102	111	107	114	104	131
Astros (Minute Maid Park)	103	100	108	102	87	82	120	97	106	76	101	77	101	122	104	119
Royals (Kauffman Stadium)	106	103	107	109	117	126	73	90	85	110	105	112	113	84	101	68
Blue Jays (Rogers Centre)	97	102	103	99	90	89	129	97	98	119	82	82	97	144	97	118
Red Sox (Fenway Park)	99	98	100	97	134	120	86	110	103	77	115	110	103	86	97	86
Angels (Angel Stadium of Anaheim)	98	102	99	100	98	77	101	101	106	96	104	92	95	120	100	89
Twins (Target Field)	100	101	98	101	114	108	86	108	102	82	73	63	104	77	96	92
Indians (Progressive Field)	97	98	97	95	106	60	107	100	106	85	106	103	95	99	100	117
White Sox (Guaranteed Rate Field)	94	98	97	93	82	36	126	110	103	83	105	130	91	155	96	114
Mariners (T-Mobile Park)	96	99	95	95	84	49	94	102	110	106	95	81	95	83	96	103
Rays (Tropicana Field)	95	99	89	93	99	122	92	97	107	118	69	82	95	93	95	90
Athletics (RingCentral Coliseum)	97	98	87	95	109	90	86	103	98	131	106	105	92	75	100	93
Yankees (Yankee Stadium)	93	95	82	88	77	62	91	95	106	102	93	88	92	89	93	92

2019 National League Ballpark Index Rankings

Home Park	Avg	AB	R	H	2B	3B	HR	BB	SO	FO	E	E-Inf	LHB Avg	LHB HR	RHB Avg	RHB HR
Rockies (Coors Field)	123	106	139	130	124	203	119	103	86	60	118	111	117	120	129	119
Nationals (Nationals Park)	107	102	110	110	114	94	124	99	98	98	97	93	114	135	103	117
Marlins (Marlins Park)	100	101	109	102	101	197	82	104	102	116	79	50	90	76	106	84
Phillies (Citizens Bank Park)	102	101	105	103	88	95	116	102	98	164	109	157	102	120	102	113
Reds (Great American Ballpark)	102	100	103	102	100	33	109	104	106	114	84	85	100	101	103	116
Pirates (PNC Park)	98	102	101	100	125	100	87	113	94	82	93	109	99	90	97	85
Braves (SunTrust Park)	102	98	100	100	116	95	104	102	100	82	126	204	100	113	104	99
Diamondbacks (Chase Field)	99	101	98	100	100	164	88	95	102	94	122	129	105	91	95	86
Brewers (Miller Park)	95	96	98	91	93	86	107	103	113	105	109	163	95	99	94	115
Cubs (Wrigley Field)	99	98	93	97	96	146	89	101	98	66	92	90	100	82	98	93
Cardinals (Busch Stadium)	97	97	92	94	89	98	85	96	92	112	109	100	100	92	95	82
Dodgers (Dodger Stadium)	100	99	90	99	91	34	114	84	99	116	82	71	100	108	100	123
Mets (Citi Field)	93	96	89	89	88	52	104	99	112	123	98	68	98	104	90	105
Padres (PETCO Park)	92	99	86	91	90	71	88	106	98	86	97	106	90	74	93	95
Giants (AT&T Park)	93	101	80	94	82	141	69	88	108	86	113	81	92	60	94	74

2019 AL Home Runs			2019 AL LHB Home Runs			2019 AL RHB Home Runs	
Home Park	Index		Home Park	Index		Home Park	Index
Blue Jays	129		White Sox	155		Orioles	131
White Sox	126		Blue Jays	144		Astros	119
Orioles	124		Astros	122		Blue Jays	118
Astros	120		Angels	120		Indians	117
Indians	107		Orioles	114		White Sox	114
Tigers	105		Rangers	108		Tigers	105
Rangers	101		Tigers	105		Mariners	103
Angels	101		Indians	99		Rangers	94
Mariners	94		Rays	93		Athletics	93
Rays	92		Yankees	89		Yankees	92
Yankees	91		Red Sox	86		Twins	92
Twins	86		Royals	84		Rays	90
Red Sox	86		Mariners	83		Angels	89
Athletics	86		Twins	77		Red Sox	86
Royals	73		Athletics	75		Royals	68

2019 NL Home Runs			2019 NL LHB Home Runs			2019 NL RHB Home Runs	
Home Park	Index		Home Park	Index		Home Park	Index
Nationals	124		Nationals	135		Dodgers	123
Rockies	119		Phillies	120		Rockies	119
Phillies	116		Rockies	120		Nationals	117
Dodgers	114		Braves	113		Reds	116
Reds	109		Dodgers	108		Brewers	115
Brewers	107		Mets	104		Phillies	113
Mets	104		Reds	101		Mets	105
Braves	104		Brewers	99		Braves	99
Cubs	89		Cardinals	92		Padres	95
Padres	88		Diamondbacks	91		Cubs	93
Diamondbacks	88		Pirates	90		Diamondbacks	86
Pirates	87		Cubs	82		Pirates	85
Cardinals	85		Marlins	76		Marlins	84
Marlins	82		Padres	74		Cardinals	82
Giants	69		Giants	60		Giants	74

2019 AL Avg	
Home Park	Index
Rangers	109
Tigers	107
Royals	106
Orioles	105
Astros	103
Twins	100
Red Sox	99
Angels	98
Indians	97
Blue Jays	97
Athletics	97
Mariners	96
Rays	95
White Sox	94
Yankees	93

2019 AL LHB Avg	
Home Park	Index
Royals	113
Rangers	107
Orioles	107
Twins	104
Red Sox	103
Tigers	103
Astros	101
Blue Jays	97
Indians	95
Angels	95
Mariners	95
Rays	95
Athletics	92
Yankees	92
White Sox	91

2019 AL RHB Avg	
Home Park	Index
Rangers	111
Tigers	109
Astros	104
Orioles	104
Royals	101
Angels	100
Athletics	100
Indians	100
Blue Jays	97
Red Sox	97
White Sox	96
Mariners	96
Twins	96
Rays	95
Yankees	93

2019 NL Avg	
Home Park	Index
Rockies	123
Nationals	107
Braves	102
Phillies	102
Reds	102
Marlins	100
Dodgers	100
Diamondbacks	99
Cubs	99
Pirates	98
Cardinals	97
Brewers	95
Giants	93
Mets	93
Padres	92

2019 NL LHB Avg	
Home Park	Index
Rockies	117
Nationals	114
Diamondbacks	105
Phillies	102
Dodgers	100
Reds	100
Braves	100
Cubs	100
Cardinals	100
Pirates	99
Mets	98
Brewers	95
Giants	92
Marlins	90
Padres	90

2019 NL RHB Avg	
Home Park	Index
Rockies	129
Marlins	106
Braves	104
Nationals	103
Reds	103
Phillies	102
Dodgers	100
Cubs	98
Pirates	97
Cardinals	95
Diamondbacks	95
Brewers	94
Giants	94
Padres	93
Mets	90

2019 AL Doubles	
Home Park	Index
Red Sox	134
Royals	117
Orioles	114
Twins	114
Athletics	109
Indians	106
Rangers	104
Rays	99
Angels	98
Blue Jays	90
Tigers	89
Astros	87
Mariners	84
White Sox	82
Yankees	77

2019 AL Triples	
Home Park	Index
Tigers	194
Rangers	148
Royals	126
Rays	122
Red Sox	120
Twins	108
Orioles	92
Athletics	90
Blue Jays	89
Astros	82
Angels	77
Yankees	62
Indians	60
Mariners	49
White Sox	36

2019 AL Errors	
Home Park	Index
Rangers	125
Red Sox	115
Tigers	114
Athletics	106
Indians	106
Royals	105
White Sox	105
Angels	104
Orioles	102
Astros	101
Mariners	95
Yankees	93
Blue Jays	82
Twins	73
Rays	69

2019 NL Doubles	
Home Park	Index
Pirates	125
Rockies	124
Braves	116
Nationals	114
Marlins	101
Reds	100
Diamondbacks	100
Cubs	96
Brewers	93
Dodgers	91
Padres	90
Cardinals	89
Phillies	88
Mets	88
Giants	82

2019 NL Triples	
Home Park	Index
Rockies	203
Marlins	197
Diamondbacks	164
Cubs	146
Giants	141
Pirates	100
Cardinals	98
Phillies	95
Braves	95
Nationals	94
Brewers	86
Padres	71
Mets	52
Dodgers	34
Reds	33

2019 NL Errors	
Home Park	Index
Braves	126
Diamondbacks	122
Rockies	118
Giants	113
Cardinals	109
Phillies	109
Brewers	109
Mets	98
Padres	97
Nationals	97
Pirates	93
Cubs	92
Reds	84
Dodgers	82
Marlins	79

2017-2019 American League Ballpark Index Rankings

Home Park	TOTALS												LHB		RHB	
	Avg	AB	R	H	2B	3B	HR	BB	SO	FO	E	E-Inf	Avg	HR	Avg	HR
Rangers (Rangers Ballpark in Arlington)	111	104	127	115	110	149	111	108	90	96	119	112	112	115	110	107
Tigers (Comerica Park)	104	103	107	108	99	149	100	93	90	138	95	107	99	92	107	105
Red Sox (Fenway Park)	104	100	103	104	127	108	87	98	99	73	121	122	104	79	103	93
Twins (Target Field)	103	101	103	103	111	114	97	107	100	87	83	68	103	96	103	97
Royals (Kauffman Stadium)	102	100	102	103	113	127	81	99	90	102	86	90	107	84	99	80
Orioles (Oriole Park at Camden Yards)	102	102	103	103	95	77	119	98	92	107	94	99	104	113	100	123
Indians (Progressive Field)	100	99	102	99	104	74	103	99	103	81	113	101	103	107	98	98
Yankees (Yankee Stadium)	99	97	97	97	84	70	110	103	103	95	102	103	98	119	100	106
Blue Jays (Rogers Centre)	99	100	98	98	103	92	112	96	100	102	96	88	98	109	99	113
Astros (Minute Maid Park)	97	98	96	95	86	78	112	98	104	94	103	98	98	110	97	114
Athletics (RingCentral Coliseum)	97	100	93	96	110	112	88	101	100	135	100	93	93	85	99	90
White Sox (Guaranteed Rate Field)	96	99	97	95	85	68	113	102	106	111	110	122	93	123	98	107
Rays (Tropicana Field)	96	98	92	94	90	120	92	100	107	114	82	94	94	88	97	95
Angels (Angel Stadium of Anaheim)[1]	96	100	98	96	95	70	107	102	104	95	102	104	94	125	96	98
Mariners (T-Mobile Park)	95	99	91	93	85	73	96	102	111	96	96	105	94	91	95	99

2017-2019 National League Ballpark Index Rankings

Home Park	TOTALS												LHB		RHB	
	Avg	AB	R	H	2B	3B	HR	BB	SO	FO	E	E-Inf	Avg	HR	Avg	HR
Rockies (Coors Field)	119	103	134	123	127	207	121	103	89	67	115	113	118	123	119	119
Nationals (Nationals Park)	108	102	110	110	113	77	114	99	98	88	101	106	110	112	106	115
Cubs (Wrigley Field)	102	98	104	100	103	133	98	105	98	65	95	94	105	88	101	106
Braves (SunTrust Park)	101	99	103	101	106	80	94	98	98	98	117	134	101	99	102	90
Diamondbacks (Chase Field)[1]	100	101	101	101	97	185	91	100	100	107	119	125	105	92	97	89
Pirates (PNC Park)	100	101	95	100	113	77	86	105	94	91	94	101	101	95	99	79
Phillies (Citizens Bank Park)	99	101	105	100	92	97	124	101	107	120	104	110	99	122	100	126
Reds (Great American Ballpark)	99	101	106	99	101	89	117	107	111	121	84	82	98	116	100	118
Cardinals (Busch Stadium)	98	99	91	97	93	92	86	94	95	114	95	91	98	94	98	81
Dodgers (Dodger Stadium)	98	98	91	96	98	38	109	87	102	103	96	86	98	112	98	106
Brewers (Miller Park)	98	99	102	97	100	84	107	102	107	107	122	129	98	110	98	105
Giants (AT&T Park)	96	101	88	97	95	127	68	94	100	91	92	90	94	59	98	74
Padres (PETCO Park)	95	99	91	94	96	87	88	109	99	95	98	91	97	81	94	91
Marlins (Marlins Park)	95	100	88	95	86	115	77	102	101	103	90	85	89	80	99	75
Mets (Citi Field)	90	97	83	87	82	69	92	97	109	126	94	83	92	89	88	96

2017-2019 AL Home Runs		2017-2019 AL LHB Home Runs		2017-2019 AL RHB Home Runs	
Home Park	Index	Home Park	Index	Home Park	Index
Orioles	119	Angels[1]	125	Orioles	123
White Sox	113	White Sox	123	Astros	114
Astros	112	Yankees	119	Blue Jays	113
Blue Jays	112	Rangers	115	White Sox	107
Rangers	111	Orioles	113	Rangers	107
Yankees	110	Astros	110	Yankees	106
Angels[1]	107	Blue Jays	109	Tigers	105
Indians	103	Indians	107	Mariners	99
Tigers	100	Twins	96	Angels[1]	98
Twins	97	Tigers	92	Indians	98
Mariners	96	Mariners	91	Twins	97
Rays	92	Rays	88	Rays	95
Athletics	88	Athletics	85	Red Sox	93
Red Sox	87	Royals	84	Athletics	90
Royals	81	Red Sox	79	Royals	80

2017-2019 NL Home Runs		2017-2019 NL LHB Home Runs		2017-2019 NL RHB Home Runs	
Home Park	Index	Home Park	Index	Home Park	Index
Phillies	124	Rockies	123	Phillies	126
Rockies	121	Phillies	122	Rockies	119
Reds	117	Reds	116	Reds	118
Nationals	114	Dodgers	112	Nationals	115
Dodgers	109	Nationals	112	Cubs	106
Brewers	107	Brewers	110	Dodgers	106
Cubs	98	Braves	99	Brewers	105
Braves	94	Pirates	95	Mets	96
Mets	92	Cardinals	94	Padres	91
Diamondbacks[1]	91	Diamondbacks[1]	92	Braves	90
Padres	88	Mets	89	Diamondbacks[1]	89
Pirates	86	Cubs	88	Cardinals	81
Cardinals	86	Padres	81	Pirates	79
Marlins	77	Marlins	80	Marlins	75
Giants	68	Giants	59	Giants	74

1. 2018-2019 only

2017-2019 AL Avg	
Home Park	Index
Rangers	111
Tigers	104
Red Sox	104
Twins	103
Royals	102
Orioles	102
Indians	100
Yankees	99
Blue Jays	99
Astros	97
Athletics	97
White Sox	96
Rays	96
Angels[1]	96
Mariners	95

2017-2019 AL LHB Avg	
Home Park	Index
Rangers	112
Royals	107
Red Sox	104
Orioles	104
Twins	103
Indians	103
Tigers	99
Yankees	98
Blue Jays	98
Astros	98
Angels[1]	94
Mariners	94
Rays	94
Athletics	93
White Sox	93

2017-2019 AL RHB Avg	
Home Park	Index
Rangers	110
Tigers	107
Red Sox	103
Twins	103
Orioles	100
Yankees	100
Royals	99
Blue Jays	99
Athletics	99
Indians	98
White Sox	98
Astros	97
Rays	97
Angels[1]	96
Mariners	95

2017-2019 NL Avg	
Home Park	Index
Rockies	119
Nationals	108
Cubs	102
Braves	101
Diamondbacks[1]	100
Pirates	100
Phillies	99
Reds	99
Cardinals	98
Dodgers	98
Brewers	98
Giants	96
Padres	95
Marlins	95
Mets	90

2017-2019 NL LHB Avg	
Home Park	Index
Rockies	118
Nationals	110
Diamondbacks[1]	105
Cubs	105
Pirates	101
Braves	101
Phillies	99
Cardinals	98
Dodgers	98
Reds	98
Brewers	98
Padres	97
Giants	94
Mets	92
Marlins	89

2017-2019 NL RHB Avg	
Home Park	Index
Rockies	119
Nationals	106
Braves	102
Cubs	101
Phillies	100
Reds	100
Pirates	99
Marlins	99
Giants	98
Brewers	98
Cardinals	98
Dodgers	98
Diamondbacks[1]	97
Padres	94
Mets	88

2017-2019 AL Doubles	
Home Park	Index
Red Sox	127
Royals	113
Twins	111
Rangers	110
Athletics	110
Indians	104
Blue Jays	103
Tigers	99
Orioles	95
Angels[1]	95
Rays	90
Astros	86
Mariners	85
White Sox	85
Yankees	84

2017-2019 AL Triples	
Home Park	Index
Rangers	149
Tigers	149
Royals	127
Rays	120
Twins	114
Athletics	112
Red Sox	108
Blue Jays	92
Astros	78
Orioles	77
Indians	74
Mariners	73
Yankees	70
Angels[1]	70
White Sox	68

2017-2019 AL Errors	
Home Park	Index
Red Sox	121
Rangers	119
Indians	113
White Sox	110
Astros	103
Yankees	102
Angels[1]	102
Athletics	100
Blue Jays	96
Mariners	96
Tigers	95
Orioles	94
Royals	86
Twins	83
Rays	82

2017-2019 NL Doubles	
Home Park	Index
Rockies	127
Pirates	113
Nationals	113
Braves	106
Cubs	103
Reds	101
Brewers	100
Dodgers	98
Diamondbacks[1]	97
Padres	96
Giants	95
Cardinals	93
Phillies	92
Marlins	86
Mets	82

2017-2019 NL Triples	
Home Park	Index
Rockies	207
Diamondbacks[1]	185
Cubs	133
Giants	127
Marlins	115
Phillies	97
Cardinals	92
Reds	89
Padres	87
Brewers	84
Braves	80
Pirates	77
Nationals	77
Mets	69
Dodgers	38

2017-2019 NL Errors	
Home Park	Index
Brewers	122
Diamondbacks[1]	119
Braves	117
Rockies	115
Phillies	104
Nationals	101
Padres	98
Dodgers	96
Cubs	95
Cardinals	95
Pirates	94
Mets	94
Giants	92
Marlins	90
Reds	84

Lefty/Righty Statistics

Nate Weller

In this era of baseball specialization, lefty-righty splits are usually of great significance. Teams look for edges wherever they can find them.

There weren't many edges to be found against Christian Yelich, who hit a remarkable .358/.455/.734 against right-handed pitchers. That's an 1.189 OPS (the best in MLB by 65 points!). Left-handed pitchers had at least a slight chance against him. He hit "only" .277/.381/.555 against them (his OPS was sixth-best for a left-handed hitter against lefties).

What made left-handed swinging Yordan Alvarez a rookie phenom was that there was almost no drop-off for him against left-handed pitching. He slashed .317/.424/.658 against righties (his on-base and slugging percentage trailed only Yelich and Mike Trout) and .307/.389/.649 versus lefties (he had the highest OPS for a left-handed hitter against left-handed pitching).

On the other side of things, there were a few notable reverse splits in 2019. Kevin Kiermaier struggled mightily against right-handed pitching, hitting .197 in 325 at-bats, but raked against lefties, hitting .311 in 122 at-bats. On the other side of the plate, Kiermaier's teammate, Willy Adames, hit .292 in 349 at-bats against righties and only .181 in 182 at-bats against lefties.

On the pitching side, the stats reflect the performance of opposing batters. Generally speaking, pitchers fared better against same-handed hitters, but some of the best pitchers in the league were able to dominate regardless of the handedness of the batter.

Few were more dominant than Justin Verlander, who faced a fairly even split of righties and lefties and shut down both, allowing opposing righties to hit only .182, and opposing lefties to hit .163. Both of the batting averages, by lefties and righties, were the lowest of his 15-year career.

Tyler Clippard and his great changeup allowed the lowest batting average to opposing batters of the opposite handedness, holding lefties to a .123 batting average. Against same-side hitters, Clippard allowed a still-impressive batting average of .227.

The following pages include platoon splits for all hitters with at least 20 plate appearances and pitchers with at least 20 batters faced in 2019. It contains batting average, on-base percentage and slugging percentage along with a count of at-bats, hits, doubles, triples, home runs, RBI, walks and strikeouts for hitters against both right and left-handed pitchers.

Justin Time

Justin Verlander's slider was an incredible pitch in 2019. He led all pitchers in outs recorded (276) and lowest batting average against it (.114), and ranked second to Max Scherzer in strike percentage and second to Will Smith in chase percentage (minimum 400 sliders thrown). Verlander's slider ranked second to Gerrit Cole's fastball in terms of run value per FanGraphs pitch value stats.

Batters vs. Left-Handed and Right-Handed Pitchers

Batter	vs	Avg	AB	H	2B	3B	HR	RBI	BB	SO	OBP	Slg
Abreu, Jose	L	.360	164	59	11	0	9	31	12	31	.418	.591
Bats Right	R	.257	470	121	27	1	24	92	24	121	.299	.472
Acuna Jr., Ronald	L	.270	126	34	2	1	10	24	15	38	.361	.540
Bats Right	R	.282	500	141	20	1	31	77	61	150	.366	.512
Adames, Cristhian	L	.222	9	2	1	0	0	0	1	3	.300	.333
Bats Both	R	.385	13	5	0	0	0	2	1	5	.429	.385
Adames, Willy	L	.181	182	33	5	0	8	15	13	55	.235	.341
Bats Right	R	.292	349	102	20	1	12	37	33	98	.358	.458
Adams, Matt	L	.210	62	13	3	0	4	14	1	20	.222	.452
Bats Left	R	.230	248	57	11	0	16	42	19	95	.289	.468
Adrianza, Ehire	L	.269	52	14	0	1	2	5	6	11	.350	.423
Bats Both	R	.273	150	41	8	2	3	17	14	29	.349	.413
Aguilar, Jesus	L	.236	123	29	4	0	4	13	18	32	.329	.366
Bats Right	R	.236	191	45	8	0	8	37	25	49	.323	.403
Ahmed, Nick	L	.312	141	44	15	1	6	24	16	23	.377	.560
Bats Right	R	.234	415	97	18	5	13	58	36	90	.295	.395
Alberto, Hanser	L	.398	221	88	11	2	5	20	6	25	.414	.534
Bats Right	R	.238	303	72	10	0	7	31	10	25	.269	.340
Albies, Ozzie	L	.389	149	58	9	1	11	33	6	20	.414	.685
Bats Both	R	.267	491	131	34	7	13	53	48	92	.334	.444
Alfaro, Jorge	L	.286	112	32	5	0	6	20	3	38	.322	.491
Bats Right	R	.254	319	81	9	1	12	37	19	116	.308	.401
Alford, Anthony	L	.000	13	0	0	0	0	0	0	7	.000	.000
Bats Right	R	.333	15	5	0	0	1	1	1	4	.412	.533
Allen, Austin	L	.100	10	1	0	0	0	1	0	4	.100	.100
Bats Left	R	.236	55	13	4	0	0	2	6	17	.311	.309
Allen, Greg	L	.186	70	13	2	0	0	3	2	14	.208	.214
Bats Both	R	.248	161	40	7	3	4	24	9	39	.322	.404
Almonte, Abraham	L	.333	3	1	0	0	0	0	2	0	.600	.333
Bats Both	R	.286	28	8	3	1	1	4	5	8	.394	.571
Almora Jr., Albert	L	.213	108	23	1	0	2	8	5	21	.254	.278
Bats Right	R	.247	231	57	10	1	10	24	11	41	.279	.429
Alonso, Pete	L	.240	150	36	8	1	14	35	24	57	.354	.587
Bats Right	R	.266	447	119	22	1	39	85	48	126	.359	.582
Alonso, Yonder	L	.254	63	16	5	0	4	14	7	14	.338	.524
Bats Left	R	.183	229	42	8	0	6	23	32	56	.284	.297
Altherr, Aaron	L	.150	20	3	2	0	0	1	1	6	.190	.250
Bats Right	R	.049	41	2	0	0	1	2	2	19	.111	.122
Altuve, Jose	L	.331	130	43	10	1	11	22	9	16	.380	.677
Bats Right	R	.286	370	106	17	2	20	52	32	66	.343	.505
Alvarez, Yordan	L	.307	114	35	12	0	9	25	14	30	.389	.649
Bats Left	R	.317	199	63	14	0	18	53	38	64	.424	.658
Anderson, Brian	L	.232	112	26	5	0	6	12	6	30	.301	.438
Bats Right	R	.271	347	94	28	1	14	54	38	84	.355	.478
Anderson, Tim	L	.326	144	47	9	0	5	17	6	28	.351	.493
Bats Right	R	.339	354	120	23	0	13	39	9	81	.360	.514
Andrus, Elvis	L	.275	182	50	9	2	4	22	12	30	.318	.412
Bats Right	R	.275	418	115	18	2	8	50	22	66	.311	.385
Andujar, Miguel	L	.000	11	0	0	0	0	0	0	3	.000	.000
Bats Right	R	.167	36	6	0	0	0	1	1	8	.184	.167
Aquino, Aristides	L	.265	49	13	3	0	4	10	4	17	.333	.571
Bats Right	R	.256	156	40	5	0	15	37	12	43	.310	.577
Arcia, Orlando	L	.240	121	29	3	1	4	10	11	24	.304	.380
Bats Right	R	.217	373	81	13	0	11	49	32	85	.276	.340
Arenado, Nolan	L	.315	162	51	7	1	13	30	27	29	.416	.611
Bats Right	R	.315	426	134	24	1	28	88	35	64	.364	.573
Arozarena, Randy	L	.333	3	1	1	0	0	0	0	1	.500	.667
Bats Right	R	.294	17	5	0	0	1	2	2	3	.368	.471
Arraez, Luis	L	.274	84	23	2	0	0	8	18	9	.398	.298
Bats Left	R	.355	242	86	18	1	4	20	18	20	.399	.488
Arroyo, Christian	L	.240	25	6	1	0	0	1	3	9	.321	.280
Bats Right	R	.200	25	5	1	0	2	6	2	9	.286	.480
Arteaga, Humberto	L	.250	36	9	1	0	0	2	2	6	.308	.278
Bats Right	R	.174	86	15	3	0	0	2	6	22	.237	.209
Astudillo, Williams	L	.250	52	13	1	0	1	5	1	3	.273	.327
Bats Right	R	.275	138	38	8	0	3	16	4	5	.309	.399
Austin, Tyler	L	.228	92	21	4	0	6	16	17	36	.345	.467
Bats Right	R	.129	62	8	1	1	3	8	7	31	.217	.323
Avila, Alex	L	.219	32	7	2	0	1	7	3	11	.306	.375
Bats Left	R	.205	132	27	6	0	8	17	33	57	.364	.432
Bader, Harrison	L	.177	96	17	6	1	4	10	9	31	.255	.385
Bats Right	R	.215	251	54	8	2	8	29	37	86	.334	.359
Baez, Javier	L	.304	102	31	4	2	8	17	8	30	.348	.618
Bats Right	R	.275	429	118	34	2	21	68	20	126	.307	.510
Barnes, Austin	L	.194	62	12	4	0	1	8	5	17	.271	.306
Bats Right	R	.207	150	31	8	1	4	17	18	39	.302	.353
Barnhart, Tucker	L	.133	45	6	1	0	0	3	6	14	.235	.156
Bats Left	R	.247	271	67	13	0	11	37	38	69	.343	.417
Barreto, Franklin	L	.148	27	4	0	0	2	5	0	10	.148	.370
Bats Right	R	.100	30	3	2	0	0	0	1	13	.129	.167
Bauers, Jake	L	.231	117	27	4	0	5	14	9	36	.289	.393
Bats Left	R	.224	255	57	12	1	7	29	36	79	.322	.361
Beaty, Matt	L	.125	32	4	1	0	0	3	1	6	.176	.156
Bats Left	R	.286	217	62	18	1	9	43	16	27	.338	.502
Beckham, Gordon	L	.158	57	9	1	1	0	0	4	17	.226	.211
Bats Right	R	.235	166	39	12	1	6	15	9	51	.287	.428
Beckham, Tim	L	.280	93	26	4	0	4	15	6	34	.330	.452
Bats Right	R	.218	211	46	17	1	11	32	15	68	.276	.464
Bell, Josh	L	.224	143	32	5	0	9	25	17	42	.313	.448
Bats Both	R	.297	384	114	32	3	28	91	57	76	.387	.615
Bellinger, Cody	L	.280	193	54	7	0	18	44	34	38	.386	.596
Bats Left	R	.317	366	116	27	3	29	71	61	70	.416	.645
Belt, Brandon	L	.211	133	28	7	0	3	12	23	40	.333	.331
Bats Left	R	.242	393	95	25	3	14	45	60	87	.341	.427
Bemboom, Anthony	L	.200	5	1	0	0	1	2	1	1	.333	.800
Bats Left	R	.122	49	6	1	0	0	2	0	20	.122	.143
Benintendi, Andrew	L	.269	160	43	12	0	5	27	21	43	.358	.438
Bats Left	R	.265	381	101	28	5	8	41	38	97	.336	.428
Berti, Jon	L	.269	52	14	2	0	4	5	5	15	.345	.538
Bats Right	R	.275	204	56	12	1	2	19	19	58	.349	.373
Betts, Mookie	L	.271	166	45	13	0	6	13	30	22	.381	.458
Bats Right	R	.304	431	131	27	5	23	67	67	79	.395	.550
Bichette, Bo	L	.368	57	21	5	0	4	6	5	14	.413	.667
Bats Right	R	.288	139	40	13	0	7	15	9	36	.336	.532
Biggio, Cavan	L	.237	118	28	5	1	3	10	23	41	.368	.373
Bats Left	R	.233	236	55	12	1	13	38	48	82	.361	.458
Bird, Greg	L	.250	8	2	0	0	1	1	1	3	.333	.625
Bats Left	R	.148	27	4	0	0	0	0	5	13	.281	.148
Bishop, Braden	L	.083	24	2	0	0	0	0	1	8	.120	.083
Bats Right	R	.125	32	4	0	0	0	4	2	13	.176	.125
Blackmon, Charlie	L	.307	215	66	15	1	14	29	12	42	.359	.581
Bats Left	R	.318	365	116	27	6	18	57	28	62	.368	.573
Blandino, Alex	L	.269	26	7	1	0	0	1	7	8	.412	.308
Bats Right	R	.200	10	2	0	0	1	2	3	6	.438	.500
Bogaerts, Xander	L	.291	165	48	13	0	10	37	18	35	.359	.552
Bats Right	R	.316	449	142	39	0	23	80	58	87	.393	.557
Bonifacio, Jorge	L	.455	11	5	2	0	0	2	1	4	.500	.636
Bats Right	R	.222	9	2	1	0	0	1	0	3	.222	.333
Bote, David	L	.218	78	17	6	0	2	9	9	25	.311	.372
Bats Right	R	.271	225	61	11	0	9	32	35	68	.380	.440
Bour, Justin	L	.167	24	4	1	0	0	1	4	9	.310	.208
Bats Left	R	.173	127	22	4	0	8	25	13	43	.248	.394
Bourjos, Peter	L	.077	26	2	0	0	0	0	0	9	.077	.077
Bats Right	R	.111	18	2	1	0	0	2	1	6	.150	.167
Bradley, Bobby	L	.167	12	2	2	0	0	2	1	5	.231	.333
Bats Left	R	.182	33	6	3	0	1	2	3	15	.250	.364
Bradley Jr., Jackie	L	.213	164	35	8	0	4	16	16	56	.305	.335
Bats Left	R	.230	330	76	20	3	17	46	40	99	.324	.464
Brantley, Michael	L	.282	163	46	8	0	3	22	15	27	.353	.387
Bats Left	R	.323	412	133	32	2	19	68	36	39	.380	.549
Braun, Ryan	L	.287	157	45	13	1	10	25	16	27	.360	.573
Bats Right	R	.285	302	86	18	1	12	50	18	78	.334	.470
Bregman, Alex	L	.350	163	57	14	1	16	38	28	23	.443	.742
Bats Right	R	.274	391	107	23	1	25	74	91	60	.415	.529
Brinson, Lewis	L	.200	55	11	2	0	0	5	6	16	.297	.236
Bats Right	R	.164	171	28	7	1	0	10	7	58	.214	.216
Brito, Socrates	L	.000	2	0	0	0	0	0	0	0	.000	.000
Bats Left	R	.081	37	3	0	1	0	2	4	17	.171	.135
Brosseau, Mike	L	.300	70	21	2	0	4	10	3	17	.329	.500
Bats Right	R	.242	62	15	5	0	2	6	4	22	.309	.419
Brown, Seth	L	.214	14	3	0	0	0	1	0	4	.214	.214
Bats Left	R	.311	61	19	8	2	0	12	7	19	.391	.508
Broxton, Keon	L	.193	88	17	2	0	3	6	10	44	.276	.318
Bats Right	R	.147	116	17	2	0	3	10	10	60	.217	.241
Bruce, Jay	L	.211	71	15	3	0	6	16	8	18	.291	.507
Bats Left	R	.218	239	52	14	0	20	43	11	64	.252	.527
Bryant, Kris	L	.295	105	31	6	1	9	20	23	28	.426	.629
Bats Right	R	.279	438	122	29	0	22	57	51	117	.370	.495
Butera, Drew	L	.160	25	4	2	0	0	3	4	8	.267	.240
Bats Right	R	.167	18	3	1	0	0	0	0	6	.167	.222
Buxton, Byron	L	.317	63	20	6	0	3	11	5	16	.368	.556
Bats Right	R	.245	208	51	24	4	7	35	14	52	.298	.500

Batters vs. Left-Handed and Right-Handed Pitchers

Batter	vs	Avg	AB	H	2B	3B	HR	RBI	BB	SO	OBP	Slg
Cabrera, Asdrubal	L	.265	117	31	8	0	3	23	19	20	.357	.410
Bats Both	R	.258	330	85	17	1	15	68	38	83	.337	.452
Cabrera, Melky	L	.270	126	34	6	0	3	16	1	14	.276	.389
Bats Both	R	.286	252	72	16	1	4	31	16	27	.331	.405
Cabrera, Miguel	L	.340	97	33	9	0	4	20	13	22	.414	.557
Bats Right	R	.268	396	106	12	0	8	39	35	86	.329	.359
Cain, Lorenzo	L	.264	159	42	7	0	6	14	16	30	.326	.421
Bats Right	R	.258	403	104	23	0	5	34	34	76	.324	.352
Calhoun, Kole	L	.212	165	35	5	0	10	27	23	44	.312	.424
Bats Left	R	.240	387	93	24	1	23	47	47	118	.330	.486
Calhoun, Willie	L	.225	102	23	5	1	7	15	7	19	.279	.500
Bats Left	R	.290	207	60	9	0	14	33	16	34	.345	.536
Camargo, Johan	L	.215	65	14	5	1	2	11	6	18	.282	.415
Bats Both	R	.240	167	40	7	0	5	21	9	25	.278	.371
Candelario, Jeimer	L	.193	83	16	4	0	1	8	11	26	.295	.277
Bats Both	R	.206	252	52	13	2	7	24	32	73	.309	.357
Canha, Mark	L	.221	131	29	4	1	8	15	23	27	.350	.450
Bats Right	R	.297	279	83	12	2	18	43	44	80	.418	.548
Cano, Robinson	L	.215	107	23	2	0	2	7	6	24	.280	.290
Bats Left	R	.272	283	77	26	0	11	32	19	45	.318	.481
Caratini, Victor	L	.250	40	10	3	0	1	4	6	10	.375	.400
Bats Both	R	.270	204	55	8	0	10	30	23	49	.342	.456
Carpenter, Matt	L	.217	83	18	4	0	2	7	16	25	.343	.337
Bats Left	R	.228	333	76	16	2	13	39	47	104	.332	.405
Casali, Curt	L	.241	83	20	1	0	4	12	13	22	.337	.398
Bats Right	R	.258	124	32	8	0	4	20	12	37	.326	.419
Castellanos, Nicholas	L	.370	108	40	13	0	8	19	10	16	.425	.713
Bats Right	R	.272	507	138	45	3	19	54	31	127	.318	.485
Castillo, Welington	L	.222	81	18	8	0	2	14	6	27	.289	.395
Bats Right	R	.201	149	30	4	0	10	27	10	47	.255	.430
Castro, Harold	L	.212	66	14	0	0	0	5	2	18	.235	.212
Bats Left	R	.309	288	89	10	4	5	33	7	68	.321	.424
Castro, Jason	L	.125	40	5	0	0	0	3	5	19	.222	.125
Bats Left	R	.254	197	50	9	0	13	27	28	69	.354	.497
Castro, Starlin	L	.323	164	53	7	0	9	21	8	28	.351	.530
Bats Right	R	.252	472	119	24	4	13	65	20	83	.283	.403
Castro, Willi	L	.250	20	5	1	0	1	3	2	6	.318	.450
Bats Both	R	.225	80	18	5	1	0	5	4	28	.276	.313
Cave, Jake	L	.283	46	13	3	0	3	6	3	20	.320	.543
Bats Left	R	.250	152	38	8	2	5	19	18	51	.360	.428
Cervelli, Francisco	L	.156	32	5	1	0	1	3	3	13	.229	.281
Bats Right	R	.229	109	25	7	1	2	9	10	28	.323	.367
Chang, Yu-Cheng	L	.115	26	3	0	0	0	1	6	9	.281	.115
Bats Right	R	.213	47	10	2	1	1	5	5	13	.288	.362
Chapman, Matt	L	.234	154	36	8	1	11	25	23	35	.335	.513
Bats Right	R	.254	429	109	28	2	25	66	50	112	.344	.503
Chavis, Michael	L	.226	106	24	3	0	8	17	3	37	.261	.481
Bats Right	R	.266	241	64	7	1	10	41	28	90	.347	.427
Chirinos, Robinson	L	.274	84	23	8	0	3	17	27	32	.439	.476
Bats Right	R	.227	282	64	14	1	14	41	24	93	.315	.433
Choi, Ji-Man	L	.210	81	17	3	0	2	6	11	22	.309	.321
Bats Left	R	.274	329	90	17	2	17	57	53	86	.377	.492
Choo, Shin-Soo	L	.229	166	38	4	0	6	19	14	53	.317	.361
Bats Left	R	.280	397	111	27	2	18	42	64	112	.393	.494
Collins, Zack	L	.136	22	3	0	0	0	2	2	11	.240	.136
Bats Left	R	.203	64	13	3	1	3	10	12	28	.329	.422
Conforto, Michael	L	.241	174	42	7	0	6	26	15	50	.316	.385
Bats Left	R	.264	375	99	22	1	27	66	69	99	.382	.544
Contreras, Willson	L	.320	75	24	3	1	6	14	9	21	.400	.627
Bats Right	R	.260	285	74	15	1	18	50	29	81	.343	.509
Cooper, Garrett	L	.220	109	24	2	0	5	13	6	26	.265	.376
Bats Right	R	.305	272	83	14	1	10	37	27	84	.375	.474
Cordell, Ryan	L	.216	97	21	3	0	2	7	6	33	.260	.309
Bats Right	R	.225	120	27	5	0	5	17	13	36	.314	.392
Correa, Carlos	L	.308	65	20	4	1	3	12	13	12	.423	.538
Bats Right	R	.270	215	58	12	0	18	47	22	63	.337	.577
Court, Ryan	L	.267	15	4	1	0	0	4	0	7	.267	.333
Bats Right	R	.111	9	1	0	0	1	1	1	4	.200	.444
Cowart, Kaleb	L	.333	3	1	0	0	0	0	0	0	.333	.333
Bats Both	R	.136	22	3	3	0	0	1	1	7	.174	.273
Cozart, Zack	L	.119	42	5	0	0	0	3	4	7	.200	.119
Bats Right	R	.127	55	7	2	0	0	4	1	9	.158	.164
Crawford, Brandon	L	.236	140	33	7	1	1	9	7	28	.277	.321
Bats Left	R	.225	360	81	17	1	10	50	46	89	.313	.361
Crawford, J.P.	L	.160	106	17	2	0	0	10	16	26	.268	.179
Bats Left	R	.255	239	61	19	4	7	36	27	57	.333	.456
Cron, C.J.	L	.326	129	42	7	0	11	31	10	27	.385	.636
Bats Right	R	.225	329	74	17	0	14	47	19	80	.281	.404
Cron, Kevin	L	.222	18	4	1	0	1	5	1	9	.250	.444
Bats Right	R	.208	53	11	3	0	5	11	3	19	.276	.547
Cruz, Nelson	L	.322	115	37	5	0	16	29	20	29	.424	.783
Bats Right	R	.307	339	104	21	0	25	79	36	102	.381	.590
Culberson, Charlie	L	.321	53	17	3	1	2	10	1	11	.333	.528
Bats Right	R	.220	82	18	2	1	3	10	5	33	.270	.378
Cuthbert, Cheslor	L	.317	82	26	6	0	5	17	5	18	.364	.573
Bats Right	R	.220	227	50	8	0	4	23	14	49	.269	.308
Dahl, David	L	.319	116	37	13	2	3	15	7	38	.357	.543
Bats Left	R	.295	258	76	15	3	12	46	21	72	.351	.516
d'Arnaud, Travis	L	.276	134	37	7	0	10	27	13	32	.333	.552
Bats Right	R	.235	217	51	9	0	6	42	19	53	.299	.359
Davis, Chris	L	.131	61	8	0	0	2	3	7	30	.232	.230
Bats Left	R	.191	246	47	9	0	10	33	32	109	.286	.350
Davis, J.D.	L	.312	141	44	8	0	8	17	14	28	.374	.539
Bats Right	R	.305	269	82	14	1	14	40	24	69	.366	.520
Davis, Jaylin	L	.154	13	2	0	0	0	0	2	4	.267	.154
Bats Right	R	.172	29	5	0	0	1	3	1	7	.250	.276
Davis, Jonathan	L	.273	22	6	0	0	0	1	4	7	.407	.273
Bats Right	R	.148	61	9	1	0	2	5	1	17	.209	.262
Davis, Khris	L	.285	130	37	0	0	11	25	19	28	.380	.538
Bats Right	R	.197	351	69	11	0	12	48	28	118	.258	.330
Davis, Rajai	L	.267	15	4	1	0	1	7	0	2	.267	.533
Bats Right	R	.100	10	1	1	0	0	1	1	3	.182	.200
Daza, Yonathan	L	.188	32	6	0	0	0	2	3	4	.250	.188
Bats Right	R	.215	65	14	1	1	0	1	4	17	.261	.262
Dean, Austin	L	.242	62	15	4	0	2	4	3	18	.277	.403
Bats Right	R	.216	116	25	10	0	4	17	6	29	.252	.405
DeJong, Paul	L	.221	113	25	7	0	3	10	15	33	.315	.363
Bats Right	R	.236	470	111	24	1	27	68	47	116	.318	.464
Delmonico, Nicky	L	.222	9	2	0	0	0	0	0	5	.222	.222
Bats Left	R	.204	54	11	2	0	1	6	4	20	.271	.296
Demeritte, Travis	L	.244	45	11	4	0	0	0	3	15	.292	.333
Bats Right	R	.218	124	27	3	2	3	10	11	48	.285	.347
Descalso, Daniel	L	.167	18	3	1	0	0	1	2	4	.238	.222
Bats Left	R	.173	150	26	4	1	2	14	21	53	.275	.253
DeShields, Delino	L	.274	124	34	8	2	4	14	8	37	.323	.468
Bats Right	R	.236	233	55	7	2	0	18	30	63	.326	.283
Desmond, Ian	L	.297	182	54	14	2	14	38	15	38	.350	.626
Bats Right	R	.226	261	59	17	2	6	27	19	81	.282	.375
Devers, Rafael	L	.269	208	56	15	0	7	29	6	42	.301	.442
Bats Left	R	.330	439	145	39	4	25	86	42	77	.388	.608
Diaz, Aledmys	L	.215	65	14	3	1	3	11	11	7	.325	.431
Bats Right	R	.297	145	43	9	0	6	29	15	21	.371	.483
Diaz, Elias	L	.268	82	22	6	0	0	5	5	13	.307	.341
Bats Right	R	.231	221	51	8	0	2	23	18	43	.292	.294
Diaz, Isan	L	.100	40	4	0	1	1	4	4	14	.182	.225
Bats Left	R	.194	139	27	5	1	4	19	15	45	.280	.331
Diaz, Yandy	L	.311	103	32	5	1	7	16	14	25	.393	.583
Bats Right	R	.245	204	50	15	0	7	22	21	36	.313	.422
Dickerson, Alex	L	.190	21	4	1	1	0	2	1	5	.227	.333
Bats Left	R	.288	153	44	12	2	6	26	12	37	.345	.510
Dickerson, Corey	L	.271	59	16	4	0	3	15	2	15	.290	.492
Bats Left	R	.313	201	63	24	2	9	44	14	41	.355	.587
Dietrich, Derek	L	.160	25	4	1	0	0	1	0	9	.222	.200
Bats Left	R	.190	226	43	7	2	19	42	28	65	.338	.491
Difo, Wilmer	L	.321	28	9	0	0	1	2	1	8	.345	.429
Bats Both	R	.233	103	24	2	0	1	6	11	21	.307	.282
Dini, Nick	L	.250	28	7	2	0	1	5	2	6	.290	.429
Bats Right	R	.143	28	4	1	0	1	1	2	12	.250	.286
Dixon, Brandon	L	.278	97	27	6	1	3	13	4	31	.308	.454
Bats Right	R	.238	294	70	14	3	12	39	17	105	.285	.429
Donaldson, Josh	L	.215	121	26	7	0	7	15	32	42	.395	.446
Bats Right	R	.271	428	116	26	0	30	79	68	113	.375	.542
Dozier, Brian	L	.280	118	33	8	0	7	19	18	28	.375	.525
Bats Right	R	.221	298	66	12	0	13	31	43	77	.327	.393
Dozier, Hunter	L	.281	121	34	4	2	8	20	17	33	.370	.545
Bats Right	R	.279	402	112	25	8	18	64	38	115	.342	.515
Drury, Brandon	L	.231	143	33	8	1	3	10	5	39	.257	.364
Bats Right	R	.211	275	58	13	0	12	31	20	74	.264	.389
Dubon, Mauricio	L	.267	30	8	2	0	2	2	1	7	.290	.533
Bats Right	R	.276	76	21	3	0	2	7	4	13	.313	.395
Duda, Lucas	L	.095	21	2	1	0	0	1	2	4	.174	.143
Bats Left	R	.190	84	16	3	0	4	14	9	28	.271	.369

Batters vs. Left-Handed and Right-Handed Pitchers

Batter	vs	Avg	AB	H	2B	3B	HR	RBI	BB	SO	OBP	Slg
Duffy, Matt	L	.164	55	9	4	0	0	3	9	13	.288	.236
Bats Right	R	.304	92	28	4	0	1	9	10	16	.379	.380
Duggar, Steven	L	.207	87	18	2	0	0	5	5	35	.250	.230
Bats Left	R	.247	174	43	10	2	4	23	11	43	.292	.397
Duvall, Adam	L	.333	39	13	2	1	4	8	3	9	.386	.744
Bats Right	R	.235	81	19	2	0	6	11	4	30	.279	.481
Dyson, Jarrod	L	.326	46	15	0	0	0	1	3	12	.380	.326
Bats Left	R	.218	354	77	11	2	7	26	44	74	.304	.319
Eaton, Adam	L	.290	138	40	7	3	2	10	12	28	.359	.428
Bats Left	R	.276	428	118	18	4	13	39	53	78	.366	.428
Edman, Tommy	L	.321	84	27	4	3	4	11	5	14	.380	.583
Bats Both	R	.298	242	72	13	4	7	25	11	47	.339	.471
Elmore, Jake	L	.150	20	3	1	0	0	3	0	1	.150	.200
Bats Right	R	.259	27	7	0	0	0	1	2	7	.310	.259
Encarnacion, Edwin	L	.245	106	26	4	0	11	22	21	22	.375	.594
Bats Right	R	.244	312	76	14	0	23	64	37	81	.332	.510
Engel, Adam	L	.313	83	26	6	1	2	9	5	22	.360	.482
Bats Right	R	.201	144	29	4	1	4	17	9	56	.272	.326
Ervin, Phillip	L	.349	86	30	4	4	4	13	8	19	.411	.628
Bats Right	R	.227	150	34	7	3	3	10	10	44	.285	.373
Escobar, Eduardo	L	.298	191	57	12	2	11	35	8	35	.327	.555
Bats Both	R	.256	445	114	17	8	24	83	42	95	.318	.492
Estrada, Thairo	L	.154	13	2	0	0	0	1	2	5	.267	.154
Bats Right	R	.275	51	14	3	0	3	11	1	10	.302	.510
Farmer, Kyle	L	.274	62	17	4	0	3	12	5	16	.338	.484
Bats Right	R	.207	121	25	2	0	6	15	5	43	.248	.372
Federowicz, Tim	L	.200	25	5	1	0	0	1	0	4	.200	.240
Bats Right	R	.140	50	7	1	0	4	6	5	27	.218	.400
Fisher, Derek	L	.245	49	12	0	1	3	9	7	14	.339	.469
Bats Left	R	.155	97	15	4	0	4	8	14	43	.261	.320
Flaherty, Ryan	L	.000	4	0	0	0	0	0	0	1	.000	.000
Bats Left	R	.176	17	3	2	0	0	1	0	6	.176	.294
Fletcher, David	L	.276	181	50	9	1	3	12	21	11	.350	.387
Bats Right	R	.296	415	123	21	3	3	37	34	53	.350	.383
Flores, Wilmer	L	.337	104	35	8	0	7	17	4	12	.367	.615
Bats Right	R	.304	161	49	10	0	2	20	11	19	.358	.404
Flowers, Tyler	L	.155	84	13	3	2	1	8	13	32	.273	.274
Bats Right	R	.262	187	49	8	1	10	26	18	73	.341	.476
Ford, Mike	L	.333	33	11	1	0	7	11	3	4	.389	1.000
Bats Left	R	.236	110	26	6	0	5	14	14	24	.339	.427
Forsythe, Logan	L	.184	114	21	8	1	1	11	16	39	.285	.298
Bats Right	R	.251	203	51	9	0	6	28	28	61	.347	.384
Fowler, Dexter	L	.213	108	23	3	0	4	13	18	27	.331	.352
Bats Both	R	.245	379	93	21	1	15	54	56	115	.350	.425
Fraley, Jake	L	.111	9	1	0	0	0	0	0	4	.111	.111
Bats Left	R	.161	31	5	2	0	0	1	0	10	.188	.226
France, Ty	L	.236	55	13	3	0	4	9	1	18	.263	.509
Bats Right	R	.233	129	30	5	1	3	15	8	31	.306	.357
Franco, Maikel	L	.245	102	25	4	0	6	18	14	15	.333	.461
Bats Right	R	.230	287	66	13	0	11	38	22	46	.283	.390
Frazier, Adam	L	.259	143	37	8	2	1	11	9	22	.307	.364
Bats Left	R	.285	411	117	25	5	9	39	31	53	.346	.436
Frazier, Clint	L	.196	56	11	3	0	4	9	5	19	.262	.464
Bats Right	R	.290	169	49	11	0	8	29	11	51	.335	.497
Frazier, Todd	L	.294	126	37	7	0	8	21	13	30	.373	.540
Bats Right	R	.234	321	75	12	2	13	46	27	76	.311	.405
Freeman, Freddie	L	.255	161	41	6	0	8	24	11	44	.309	.441
Bats Left	R	.310	436	135	28	2	30	97	76	83	.416	.589
Freeman, Mike	L	.304	56	17	2	0	2	9	4	22	.355	.446
Bats Left	R	.264	121	32	6	0	2	15	18	39	.366	.364
Freese, David	L	.287	101	29	8	0	5	11	16	30	.385	.515
Bats Right	R	.361	61	22	5	0	6	18	7	14	.435	.738
Fuentes, Josh	L	.130	23	3	1	0	0	1	0	11	.130	.174
Bats Right	R	.281	32	9	0	0	3	6	1	9	.303	.563
Gallagher, Cam	L	.222	36	8	3	0	1	6	3	10	.293	.389
Bats Right	R	.244	90	22	4	0	2	6	8	18	.320	.356
Gallo, Joey	L	.333	75	25	7	0	8	22	11	34	.427	.747
Bats Left	R	.217	166	36	8	1	14	27	41	80	.372	.530
Galloway, Isaac	L	.067	15	1	0	0	0	0	0	5	.067	.067
Bats Right	R	.205	39	8	1	0	0	1	0	12	.205	.231
Galvis, Freddy	L	.283	180	51	13	0	4	19	3	38	.295	.422
Bats Both	R	.249	377	94	15	1	19	51	25	107	.296	.446
Gamel, Ben	L	.354	65	23	3	0	1	8	12	22	.456	.446
Bats Left	R	.220	246	54	15	0	6	25	28	82	.303	.354
Garcia, Aramis	L	.120	25	3	0	0	1	1	4	11	.241	.240
Bats Right	R	.176	17	3	1	0	1	4	0	10	.176	.412

Batter	vs	Avg	AB	H	2B	3B	HR	RBI	BB	SO	OBP	Slg
Garcia, Avisail	L	.265	162	43	7	1	7	19	14	40	.328	.451
Bats Right	R	.291	327	95	18	1	13	53	17	85	.334	.471
Garcia, Greg	L	.200	35	7	0	0	0	3	6	10	.317	.200
Bats Left	R	.254	276	70	13	4	4	28	47	73	.370	.373
Garcia, Leury	L	.311	183	57	13	1	3	14	6	34	.344	.443
Bats Both	R	.264	394	104	14	2	5	26	15	105	.294	.348
Garcia, Robel	L	.111	18	2	0	1	1	2	2	11	.200	.389
Bats Both	R	.241	54	13	2	1	4	9	5	24	.300	.537
Gardner, Brett	L	.212	132	28	6	1	5	17	9	32	.268	.386
Bats Left	R	.265	359	95	20	6	23	57	43	76	.346	.546
Garlick, Kyle	L	.267	30	8	3	0	3	5	3	12	.333	.667
Bats Right	R	.222	18	4	1	0	0	1	2	7	.300	.278
Garneau, Dustin	L	.300	30	9	2	0	1	5	4	6	.400	.467
Bats Right	R	.214	56	12	3	0	2	9	6	16	.323	.375
Garver, Mitch	L	.321	106	34	6	1	12	23	19	27	.434	.736
Bats Right	R	.249	205	51	10	0	19	44	22	60	.326	.576
Gennett, Scooter	L	.172	29	5	0	0	1	2	0	8	.167	.276
Bats Left	R	.240	104	25	7	0	1	9	2	33	.266	.337
Gerber, Mike	L	.000	6	0	0	0	0	0	0	4	.000	.000
Bats Left	R	.056	18	1	1	0	0	0	2	11	.150	.111
Goins, Ryan	L	.406	32	13	0	1	2	6	3	7	.472	.656
Bats Left	R	.205	112	23	6	0	0	4	14	37	.294	.259
Goldschmidt, Paul	L	.269	104	28	2	1	9	24	22	24	.394	.567
Bats Right	R	.258	493	127	23	0	25	73	56	142	.335	.456
Gomes, Yan	L	.261	69	18	3	0	4	13	15	15	.400	.478
Bats Right	R	.212	245	52	13	0	8	30	23	69	.289	.363
Gomez, Carlos	L	.238	21	5	1	0	0	1	2	3	.385	.286
Bats Right	R	.185	65	12	2	0	3	9	5	27	.239	.354
Gonzalez, Carlos	L	.114	35	4	0	0	0	0	5	16	.225	.114
Bats Left	R	.227	110	25	3	0	3	10	13	36	.310	.336
Gonzalez, Erik	L	.333	48	16	2	0	0	1	2	11	.360	.375
Bats Right	R	.213	94	20	2	1	1	5	7	26	.272	.287
Gonzalez, Marwin	L	.300	120	36	5	0	5	12	3	22	.323	.467
Bats Both	R	.249	305	76	14	0	10	43	28	76	.322	.393
Goodrum, Niko	L	.361	97	35	6	3	1	8	9	21	.411	.515
Bats Both	R	.215	326	70	21	2	11	37	37	117	.296	.393
Goodwin, Brian	L	.263	95	25	8	1	4	15	5	29	.320	.495
Bats Left	R	.261	318	83	21	2	13	32	33	100	.328	.462
Gordon, Alex	L	.248	153	38	8	0	3	22	13	31	.331	.359
Bats Left	R	.273	403	110	23	1	10	54	38	69	.350	.409
Gordon, Dee	L	.326	92	30	1	1	1	11	2	13	.344	.391
Bats Left	R	.259	301	78	11	5	2	23	16	48	.292	.349
Gore, Terrance	L	.450	20	9	1	0	0	0	3	4	.542	.500
Bats Right	R	.161	31	5	1	1	0	1	3	14	.235	.258
Gosselin, Phil	L	.296	27	8	0	0	0	1	3	7	.367	.296
Bats Right	R	.237	38	9	3	0	0	6	0	9	.237	.316
Grandal, Yasmani	L	.258	155	40	7	1	11	25	37	43	.397	.529
Bats Both	R	.240	358	86	19	1	17	52	72	96	.372	.441
Granderson, Curtis	L	.245	49	12	6	1	1	12	8	11	.350	.469
Bats Left	R	.172	268	46	11	0	11	22	33	87	.267	.336
Gregorius, Didi	L	.216	88	19	2	1	6	20	5	13	.266	.466
Bats Left	R	.246	236	58	12	1	10	41	12	40	.280	.432
Greiner, Grayson	L	.139	36	5	0	0	2	5	2	13	.184	.306
Bats Right	R	.215	172	37	5	1	3	14	11	57	.265	.308
Grichuk, Randal	L	.250	188	47	9	3	9	26	16	46	.311	.473
Bats Right	R	.224	398	89	20	2	22	54	19	117	.265	.450
Grisham, Trent	L	.219	32	7	1	1	1	4	3	14	.306	.406
Bats Left	R	.234	124	29	5	1	5	20	17	34	.333	.411
Grossman, Robbie	L	.173	52	9	1	1	1	9	6	12	.259	.288
Bats Both	R	.250	368	92	20	2	5	29	53	74	.344	.356
Guerrero Jr., Vladimir	L	.215	130	28	5	0	4	15	15	23	.297	.346
Bats Right	R	.293	334	98	21	2	11	54	31	68	.355	.467
Guillorme, Luis	L	.333	6	2	0	0	0	0	0	2	.333	.333
Bats Left	R	.236	55	13	4	0	1	3	7	12	.323	.364
Gurriel, Yuli	L	.241	158	38	15	1	7	23	18	12	.322	.481
Bats Right	R	.320	406	130	25	1	24	81	19	53	.352	.564
Gurriel Jr., Lourdes	L	.300	110	33	7	0	11	20	4	33	.330	.664
Bats Right	R	.265	204	54	12	2	9	30	16	53	.326	.475
Gutierrez, Kelvin	L	.348	23	8	0	1	1	3	2	7	.400	.565
Bats Right	R	.220	50	11	2	0	0	8	3	17	.259	.260
Guzman, Ronald	L	.134	67	9	5	0	2	9	10	26	.238	.299
Bats Left	R	.249	189	47	15	0	8	27	22	61	.335	.455
Gyorko, Jedd	L	.135	37	5	1	0	0	2	4	9	.220	.162
Bats Right	R	.200	55	11	0	0	2	7	5	15	.267	.309
Hamilton, Billy	L	.184	103	19	6	1	0	5	14	30	.280	.262
Bats Both	R	.235	213	50	8	1	0	10	18	57	.293	.282

Batters vs. Left-Handed and Right-Handed Pitchers

Batter	vs	Avg	AB	H	2B	3B	HR	RBI	BB	SO	OBP	Slg
Hampson, Garrett	L	.243	111	27	4	2	4	11	8	26	.294	.423
Bats Right	R	.250	188	47	5	2	4	16	16	62	.306	.362
Haniger, Mitch	L	.263	57	15	3	0	4	10	10	20	.391	.526
Bats Right	R	.206	189	39	10	1	11	22	20	61	.290	.444
Hanson, Alen	L	.190	21	4	0	0	0	2	1	9	.217	.190
Bats Both	R	.136	22	3	0	0	0	2	2	8	.240	.136
Happ, Ian	L	.233	30	7	2	1	1	4	3	11	.303	.467
Bats Both	R	.273	110	30	5	0	10	26	12	28	.341	.591
Harper, Bryce	L	.283	187	53	11	0	15	44	22	53	.366	.583
Bats Left	R	.249	386	96	25	1	20	70	77	125	.375	.474
Harrison, Josh	L	.167	24	4	1	0	1	1	0	6	.167	.333
Bats Right	R	.177	113	20	6	1	0	7	6	21	.228	.248
Haseley, Adam	L	.212	52	11	2	0	0	8	3	16	.281	.250
Bats Left	R	.282	170	48	12	0	5	18	11	44	.337	.441
Hays, Austin	L	.120	25	3	1	0	0	2	2	5	.185	.160
Bats Right	R	.419	43	18	5	0	4	11	5	8	.479	.814
Healy, Ryon	L	.200	45	9	5	0	0	5	5	13	.275	.311
Bats Right	R	.250	124	31	11	0	7	21	8	27	.294	.508
Hechavarria, Adeiny	L	.261	46	12	2	0	4	8	3	6	.306	.565
Bats Right	R	.236	157	37	10	1	5	25	11	42	.297	.408
Hedges, Austin	L	.143	70	10	2	0	1	9	9	30	.265	.214
Bats Right	R	.186	242	45	7	0	10	27	18	79	.248	.339
Heineman, Scott	L	.200	30	6	1	0	0	2	4	9	.294	.233
Bats Right	R	.222	45	10	5	0	2	5	5	11	.314	.467
Heredia, Guillermo	L	.281	114	32	11	0	3	13	8	29	.339	.456
Bats Right	R	.156	90	14	2	0	2	7	10	31	.267	.244
Hermosillo, Michael	L	.000	7	0	0	0	0	1	1	4	.273	.000
Bats Right	R	.172	29	5	1	1	0	2	4	15	.314	.276
Hernandez, Cesar	L	.263	171	45	9	0	1	16	12	22	.308	.333
Bats Both	R	.286	441	126	22	3	13	55	33	78	.342	.438
Hernandez, Gorkys	L	.042	24	1	1	0	0	1	2	6	.115	.083
Bats Right	R	.240	25	6	0	2	0	1	3	8	.310	.400
Hernandez, Kike	L	.263	156	41	4	0	7	21	16	28	.335	.423
Bats Right	R	.221	258	57	15	1	10	43	20	69	.285	.403
Hernandez, Marco	L	.320	50	16	3	0	0	3	1	13	.346	.380
Bats Left	R	.214	98	21	4	0	2	8	2	29	.245	.316
Hernandez, Teoscar	L	.246	142	35	7	2	8	25	21	49	.341	.493
Bats Right	R	.222	275	61	12	0	18	40	24	104	.287	.462
Herrera, Odubel	L	.280	25	7	1	0	0	5	0	4	.269	.320
Bats Left	R	.208	101	21	9	1	1	11	11	29	.292	.347
Herrera, Rosell	L	.125	32	4	0	0	1	2	2	9	.176	.219
Bats Both	R	.233	73	17	6	0	1	9	9	18	.333	.356
Herrmann, Chris	L	.200	10	2	0	0	0	1	0	2	.200	.200
Bats Left	R	.203	74	15	3	0	1	7	9	27	.289	.284
Heyward, Jason	L	.205	112	23	4	0	2	11	8	29	.258	.295
Bats Left	R	.264	401	106	16	4	19	51	60	81	.365	.466
Hicks, Aaron	L	.266	79	21	3	0	2	8	4	23	.298	.380
Bats Both	R	.218	142	31	7	0	10	28	27	49	.339	.479
Hicks, John	L	.241	83	20	4	0	3	9	6	34	.289	.398
Bats Right	R	.199	236	47	11	0	10	26	7	75	.222	.373
Higashioka, Kyle	L	.267	15	4	2	0	1	3	0	5	.267	.600
Bats Right	R	.195	41	8	3	0	2	8	0	21	.190	.415
Hilliard, Sam	L	.267	15	4	0	0	2	3	5	5	.450	.667
Bats Left	R	.274	62	17	4	2	5	10	4	18	.328	.645
Hiura, Keston	L	.240	75	18	6	0	1	6	7	27	.313	.360
Bats Right	R	.322	239	77	17	2	18	43	18	80	.385	.636
Hoerner, Nico	L	.273	11	3	0	0	1	5	0	1	.250	.545
Bats Right	R	.284	67	19	1	1	2	12	3	10	.314	.418
Holaday, Bryan	L	.258	31	8	2	0	0	3	3	7	.314	.323
Bats Right	R	.286	84	24	4	0	4	9	8	14	.355	.476
Holt, Brock	L	.224	58	13	3	0	0	6	5	12	.281	.276
Bats Left	R	.318	201	64	11	2	3	25	23	45	.394	.438
Hoskins, Rhys	L	.261	138	36	9	1	9	27	45	38	.444	.536
Bats Right	R	.215	432	93	24	4	20	58	71	135	.335	.428
Hosmer, Eric	L	.231	156	36	9	1	1	16	11	33	.280	.321
Bats Left	R	.276	463	128	20	1	21	83	29	130	.321	.460
Hundley, Nick	L	.118	17	2	0	0	1	2	0	4	.167	.294
Bats Right	R	.226	53	12	3	1	1	3	2	14	.255	.377
Iannetta, Chris	L	.190	58	11	3	0	2	6	14	23	.342	.345
Bats Right	R	.244	86	21	7	0	4	15	4	31	.286	.465
Iglesias, Jose	L	.270	122	33	2	1	3	13	6	14	.310	.377
Bats Right	R	.293	382	112	19	2	8	46	14	56	.320	.416
Inciarte, Ender	L	.273	44	12	3	0	0	3	6	11	.360	.341
Bats Left	R	.239	155	37	8	2	5	21	20	30	.339	.413
Jankowski, Travis	L	.000	2	0	0	0	0	0	0	0	.000	.000
Bats Left	R	.200	20	4	0	0	0	0	2	4	.273	.200

Batter	vs	Avg	AB	H	2B	3B	HR	RBI	BB	SO	OBP	Slg
Jansen, Danny	L	.224	116	26	6	0	6	15	12	25	.297	.431
Bats Right	R	.199	231	46	6	1	7	28	19	54	.271	.325
Jay, Jon	L	.263	57	15	1	0	0	4	3	10	.323	.281
Bats Left	R	.269	108	29	7	0	0	5	5	20	.304	.333
Jimenez, Eloy	L	.259	135	35	6	0	7	20	11	45	.322	.459
Bats Right	R	.270	333	90	12	2	24	59	19	89	.313	.535
Jones, Adam	L	.261	157	41	11	1	4	22	10	33	.306	.420
Bats Right	R	.259	328	85	14	0	12	45	21	68	.317	.412
Jones, JaCoby	L	.200	60	12	4	0	1	2	4	18	.246	.317
Bats Right	R	.244	238	58	15	3	10	24	23	76	.326	.458
Joseph, Caleb	L	.333	6	2	0	0	0	2	0	2	.333	.333
Bats Right	R	.188	32	6	2	0	0	1	1	8	.235	.250
Joseph, Corban	L	.500	2	1	0	0	0	0	0	1	.500	.500
Bats Left	R	.145	62	9	3	0	1	7	3	11	.182	.242
Joyce, Matt	L	.273	22	6	2	0	0	1	4	6	.385	.364
Bats Left	R	.298	178	53	8	0	7	22	34	39	.410	.461
Judge, Aaron	L	.343	99	34	7	0	8	19	22	28	.467	.657
Bats Right	R	.247	279	69	11	1	19	36	42	113	.349	.498
Kang, Jung Ho	L	.160	75	12	2	1	3	7	1	34	.171	.333
Bats Right	R	.175	97	17	5	0	7	17	10	26	.257	.443
Kelly, Carson	L	.356	87	31	9	0	6	18	16	22	.462	.667
Bats Right	R	.203	227	46	10	0	12	29	32	57	.303	.405
Kemp, Matt	L	.286	14	4	1	0	1	3	1	4	.333	.571
Bats Right	R	.174	46	8	1	0	0	2	0	15	.170	.196
Kemp, Tony	L	.237	38	9	1	2	1	7	2	4	.295	.447
Bats Left	R	.208	207	43	8	2	7	22	21	43	.291	.367
Kendrick, Howie	L	.376	117	44	10	0	6	26	8	18	.421	.615
Bats Right	R	.327	217	71	13	1	11	36	19	31	.381	.548
Kepler, Max	L	.293	147	43	7	0	9	36	13	24	.356	.524
Bats Left	R	.236	377	89	25	0	27	54	47	75	.328	.517
Kieboom, Carter	L	.143	7	1	0	0	0	0	1	2	.250	.143
Bats Right	R	.125	32	4	0	0	2	2	3	14	.200	.313
Kiermaier, Kevin	L	.311	122	38	7	0	3	17	5	28	.341	.443
Bats Left	R	.197	325	64	13	7	11	38	21	76	.254	.382
Kiner-Falefa, Isiah	L	.209	67	14	3	1	0	6	3	17	.254	.284
Bats Right	R	.252	135	34	9	0	1	15	11	32	.320	.341
Kingery, Scott	L	.293	123	36	10	1	7	13	5	40	.318	.561
Bats Right	R	.245	335	82	24	3	12	42	29	107	.314	.442
Kinsler, Ian	L	.206	68	14	2	0	3	5	8	16	.295	.368
Bats Right	R	.221	190	42	10	0	6	17	11	38	.271	.368
Kipnis, Jason	L	.245	155	38	6	0	3	15	9	26	.291	.342
Bats Left	R	.244	303	74	17	1	14	50	31	62	.311	.446
Knapp, Andrew	L	.250	32	8	2	0	0	2	4	11	.333	.313
Bats Both	R	.202	104	21	7	0	2	6	14	40	.314	.327
Knizner, Andrew	L	.200	10	2	0	0	0	1	0	2	.200	.200
Bats Right	R	.233	43	10	2	0	2	6	4	12	.313	.419
Kramer, Kevin	L	.100	10	1	0	0	0	0	0	4	.100	.100
Bats Left	R	.188	32	6	1	0	0	5	6	13	.300	.219
Kratz, Erik	L	.200	10	2	2	0	0	1	1	2	.273	.400
Bats Right	R	.077	39	3	0	0	1	2	1	12	.143	.154
La Stella, Tommy	L	.265	83	22	2	0	3	7	5	8	.315	.398
Bats Left	R	.306	209	64	6	0	13	37	15	20	.358	.522
Lagares, Juan	L	.238	80	19	7	0	1	11	6	24	.291	.363
Bats Right	R	.202	178	36	5	1	4	16	16	51	.274	.309
LaMarre, Ryan	L	.308	13	4	0	0	2	3	0	2	.308	.769
Bats Right	R	.100	10	1	0	0	0	0	3	3	.308	.100
Lamb, Jake	L	.304	23	7	1	0	3	5	5	8	.429	.739
Bats Left	R	.177	164	29	7	2	3	25	27	47	.308	.299
Laureano, Ramon	L	.296	125	37	9	0	6	17	5	31	.326	.512
Bats Right	R	.285	309	88	20	0	18	50	22	92	.345	.524
LeMahieu, DJ	L	.375	160	60	11	0	10	31	17	23	.435	.631
Bats Right	R	.310	442	137	22	2	16	71	29	67	.352	.477
Leon, Sandy	L	.187	75	14	0	0	3	9	2	18	.208	.307
Bats Both	R	.196	97	19	3	0	2	10	11	29	.282	.289
Lewis, Kyle	L	.158	19	3	0	0	1	2	1	11	.200	.316
Bats Right	R	.308	52	16	5	0	5	11	2	18	.327	.692
Leyba, Domingo	L	.333	3	1	0	0	0	0	0	1	.333	.333
Bats Both	R	.273	22	6	2	1	0	5	4	8	.370	.455
Lin, Tzu-Wei	L	.286	7	2	1	0	0	0	1	3	.375	.429
Bats Left	R	.154	13	2	1	0	0	1	1	3	.214	.231
Lindor, Francisco	L	.258	198	51	11	0	8	24	23	32	.341	.434
Bats Both	R	.298	400	119	29	2	24	50	23	66	.333	.560
Locastro, Tim	L	.225	80	18	4	2	1	5	7	21	.354	.363
Bats Right	R	.265	132	35	8	0	0	12	7	23	.359	.326
Long, Shed	L	.333	36	12	4	1	1	2	5	6	.415	.583
Bats Left	R	.241	116	28	8	0	4	13	11	34	.307	.414

Batters vs. Left-Handed and Right-Handed Pitchers

Batter	vs	Avg	AB	H	2B	3B	HR	RBI	BB	SO	OBP	Slg
Longoria, Evan	L	.286	140	40	7	1	6	24	18	27	.373	.479
Bats Right	R	.240	313	75	12	1	14	45	25	85	.303	.419
Lopes, Tim	L	.319	47	15	3	0	1	4	6	9	.396	.447
Bats Right	R	.234	64	15	4	0	0	8	9	20	.333	.297
Lopez, Nicky	L	.267	105	28	5	0	1	6	5	16	.306	.343
Bats Left	R	.230	274	63	17	2	1	24	13	35	.265	.318
Lowe, Brandon	L	.242	66	16	2	0	3	9	2	36	.265	.409
Bats Left	R	.278	230	64	15	2	14	42	23	77	.355	.543
Lowe, Nate	L	.292	24	7	2	0	2	5	3	10	.393	.625
Bats Left	R	.258	128	33	6	0	5	14	10	40	.312	.422
Lucroy, Jonathan	L	.227	97	22	2	0	3	10	6	19	.269	.340
Bats Right	R	.235	196	46	8	1	5	26	21	32	.321	.362
Lugo, Dawel	L	.232	69	16	2	0	1	5	2	19	.253	.304
Bats Right	R	.250	204	51	9	4	5	21	6	40	.277	.407
Luplow, Jordan	L	.320	128	41	10	1	14	30	26	32	.439	.742
Bats Right	R	.216	97	21	5	0	1	8	7	29	.274	.299
Lux, Gavin	L	.083	12	1	0	0	1	1	0	4	.083	.333
Bats Left	R	.270	63	17	4	1	1	8	7	20	.343	.413
Machado, Manny	L	.315	127	40	6	1	13	27	18	26	.404	.685
Bats Right	R	.239	460	110	15	1	19	58	47	102	.315	.400
Mahtook, Mikie	L	.000	3	0	0	0	0	0	0	1	.000	.000
Bats Right	R	.000	20	0	0	0	0	0	2	10	.091	.000
Maile, Luke	L	.057	35	2	0	0	1	3	3	12	.132	.143
Bats Right	R	.190	84	16	2	1	1	6	5	21	.236	.274
Maldonado, Martin	L	.229	105	24	7	0	4	8	8	35	.281	.410
Bats Right	R	.206	228	47	12	0	8	19	24	51	.298	.364
Mancini, Trey	L	.277	191	53	15	0	12	26	22	47	.365	.545
Bats Right	R	.297	411	122	23	2	23	71	41	96	.363	.530
Margot, Manuel	L	.330	103	34	8	0	2	7	16	24	.420	.466
Bats Right	R	.200	295	59	11	3	10	30	22	64	.260	.359
Marisnick, Jake	L	.225	102	23	8	0	4	14	6	36	.288	.422
Bats Right	R	.237	190	45	8	3	6	20	11	59	.289	.405
Markakis, Nick	L	.245	102	25	8	1	0	16	9	12	.310	.343
Bats Left	R	.298	312	93	17	1	9	46	38	47	.371	.446
Marte, Ketel	L	.333	165	55	11	1	12	31	7	22	.368	.630
Bats Both	R	.327	404	132	25	8	20	61	46	64	.396	.577
Marte, Starling	L	.269	134	36	8	2	6	16	2	28	.281	.493
Bats Right	R	.304	405	123	23	4	17	66	23	66	.362	.506
Martin, Jason	L	.400	5	2	0	0	0	0	0	1	.400	.400
Bats Left	R	.226	31	7	2	0	0	2	4	9	.314	.290
Martin, Leonys	L	.155	71	11	3	0	1	4	5	25	.221	.239
Bats Left	R	.218	165	36	4	0	8	15	16	53	.299	.388
Martin, Russell	L	.218	55	12	1	0	3	5	9	14	.348	.400
Bats Right	R	.221	154	34	4	0	3	15	21	46	.333	.305
Martin Jr., Richie	L	.243	148	36	4	1	3	13	9	36	.298	.345
Bats Right	R	.170	135	23	4	2	3	10	5	47	.217	.296
Martinez, J.D.	L	.404	141	57	9	1	19	40	25	31	.494	.887
Bats Right	R	.272	434	118	24	1	17	65	47	107	.344	.449
Martinez, Jose	L	.329	70	23	4	0	5	15	8	15	.397	.600
Bats Right	R	.254	264	67	9	2	5	27	27	67	.325	.360
Martini, Nick	L	.000	18	0	0	0	0	1	2	8	.095	.000
Bats Left	R	.280	75	21	4	1	1	6	12	18	.386	.400
Mathis, Jeff	L	.149	67	10	2	0	1	4	5	24	.208	.224
Bats Right	R	.161	161	26	7	0	1	8	10	63	.209	.224
Maybin, Cameron	L	.231	78	18	6	0	3	14	10	23	.318	.423
Bats Right	R	.311	161	50	11	0	8	18	20	49	.387	.528
Mayfield, Jack	L	.208	24	5	3	0	1	3	1	7	.240	.458
Bats Right	R	.125	40	5	2	0	1	2	0	9	.125	.250
Mazara, Nomar	L	.220	127	28	2	1	6	20	5	33	.252	.394
Bats Left	R	.288	302	87	25	0	13	46	23	75	.344	.500
McBroom, Ryan	L	.280	25	7	3	0	0	1	3	8	.357	.400
Bats Right	R	.300	50	15	2	0	0	5	4	17	.364	.340
McCann, Brian	L	.171	35	6	2	0	0	4	5	7	.268	.229
Bats Left	R	.260	242	63	7	0	12	41	26	46	.331	.438
McCann, James	L	.295	122	36	12	0	4	17	13	36	.372	.492
Bats Right	R	.265	317	84	14	1	14	43	17	101	.311	.448
McCutchen, Andrew	L	.294	51	15	4	1	0	4	12	11	.429	.412
Bats Right	R	.244	168	41	8	0	10	25	31	44	.362	.470
McGuire, Reese	L	.238	21	5	0	0	1	3	2	5	.304	.381
Bats Left	R	.316	76	24	7	0	4	8	5	13	.358	.566
McKinney, Billy	L	.196	51	10	1	0	3	6	1	18	.226	.392
Bats Left	R	.220	200	44	13	1	9	22	18	55	.285	.430
McMahon, Ryan	L	.257	152	39	5	0	10	28	9	56	.298	.487
Bats Left	R	.247	328	81	17	1	14	55	47	104	.342	.433
McNeil, Jeff	L	.312	141	44	10	0	3	16	9	20	.378	.447
Bats Left	R	.320	369	118	28	1	20	59	26	55	.387	.564

Batter	vs	Avg	AB	H	2B	3B	HR	RBI	BB	SO	OBP	Slg
Meadows, Austin	L	.275	167	46	8	3	9	32	9	53	.316	.521
Bats Left	R	.298	363	108	21	4	24	57	45	78	.384	.576
Mejia, Erick	L	.333	9	3	1	0	0	2	1	2	.400	.444
Bats Both	R	.154	13	2	0	0	0	2	3	5	.294	.154
Mejia, Francisco	L	.279	61	17	3	0	1	4	4	10	.323	.377
Bats Both	R	.261	165	43	8	2	7	18	9	46	.313	.461
Mejias-Brean, Seth	L	.222	9	2	1	0	0	0	1	2	.300	.333
Bats Right	R	.238	21	5	1	0	2	5	2	7	.304	.571
Mendick, Danny	L	.235	17	4	0	0	0	1	0	8	.235	.235
Bats Right	R	.364	22	8	0	0	2	3	1	3	.391	.636
Mercado, Oscar	L	.263	156	41	9	0	7	21	12	33	.320	.455
Bats Right	R	.273	282	77	16	3	8	33	16	51	.317	.436
Mercer, Jordy	L	.328	61	20	5	0	3	9	1	9	.339	.557
Bats Right	R	.251	195	49	11	0	6	13	12	48	.301	.400
Merrifield, Whit	L	.280	193	54	14	1	8	28	14	32	.327	.487
Bats Right	R	.311	488	152	27	9	8	46	31	94	.357	.453
Miller, Brad	L	.158	19	3	0	0	1	5	3	7	.273	.316
Bats Left	R	.274	135	37	6	1	12	20	12	38	.338	.600
Molina, Yadier	L	.320	75	24	5	0	2	11	9	5	.395	.467
Bats Right	R	.259	344	89	19	0	8	46	14	53	.292	.384
Moncada, Yoan	L	.299	154	46	15	2	4	25	9	49	.345	.500
Bats Both	R	.322	357	115	19	3	21	54	31	105	.377	.569
Mondesi, Adalberto	L	.256	133	34	4	1	3	16	3	37	.266	.368
Bats Both	R	.266	282	75	16	9	6	46	16	95	.302	.450
Moore, Dylan	L	.224	76	17	6	0	3	8	8	25	.330	.421
Bats Right	R	.199	171	34	8	2	6	20	17	68	.290	.374
Morales, Kendrys	L	.200	25	5	0	0	0	2	6	5	.364	.200
Bats Both	R	.193	145	28	2	1	2	10	20	21	.304	.262
Moran, Colin	L	.273	77	21	4	0	2	11	1	18	.282	.403
Bats Left	R	.278	389	108	26	1	11	69	29	99	.329	.434
Moreland, Mitch	L	.204	54	11	3	0	1	7	5	18	.283	.315
Bats Left	R	.262	244	64	14	1	18	51	29	56	.338	.549
Moroff, Max	L	.000	10	0	0	0	0	0	1	4	.091	.000
Bats Both	R	.182	22	4	1	0	1	4	1	12	.217	.364
Morrison, Logan	L	.000	5	0	0	0	0	0	0	1	.000	.000
Bats Left	R	.233	30	7	1	0	2	3	3	9	.303	.467
Moustakas, Mike	L	.276	163	45	9	0	11	27	13	27	.343	.534
Bats Left	R	.244	360	88	21	1	24	60	40	71	.323	.508
Mullins II, Cedric	L	.067	15	1	0	0	0	0	2	5	.176	.067
Bats Both	R	.102	49	5	0	2	0	4	2	9	.182	.184
Muncy, Max	L	.268	157	42	6	1	11	38	19	52	.365	.529
Bats Left	R	.242	330	80	16	0	24	60	71	97	.377	.509
Munoz, Yairo	L	.282	39	11	1	0	0	2	4	11	.349	.308
Bats Right	R	.263	133	35	6	1	2	11	3	26	.283	.368
Murphy, Daniel	L	.320	122	39	11	1	3	17	11	27	.381	.500
Bats Left	R	.263	316	83	24	0	10	61	21	47	.307	.434
Murphy, John Ryan	L	.125	24	3	1	0	2	3	3	12	.222	.417
Bats Right	R	.205	39	8	2	0	2	4	3	16	.262	.410
Murphy, Sean	L	.278	18	5	2	0	0	3	2	5	.350	.389
Bats Right	R	.229	35	8	3	0	4	5	4	11	.325	.657
Murphy, Tom	L	.347	118	41	6	1	11	25	11	37	.408	.695
Bats Right	R	.211	142	30	6	0	7	15	8	50	.252	.401
Myers, Wil	L	.233	86	20	1	1	7	15	18	39	.365	.512
Bats Right	R	.241	349	84	21	0	11	38	33	129	.309	.395
Naquin, Tyler	L	.286	63	18	2	0	4	10	4	14	.329	.508
Bats Left	R	.289	211	61	17	0	6	24	10	52	.324	.455
Narvaez, Omar	L	.227	75	17	1	0	2	10	18	10	.379	.320
Bats Left	R	.289	353	102	11	0	20	45	29	82	.346	.490
Naylor, Josh	L	.292	48	14	3	0	0	4	2	8	.320	.354
Bats Left	R	.239	205	49	12	0	8	28	23	56	.314	.415
Negron, Kristopher	L	.176	34	6	0	0	1	3	3	10	.243	.265
Bats Right	R	.302	43	13	1	0	1	5	2	16	.333	.395
Neuse, Sheldon	L	.212	33	7	2	0	0	4	2	13	.250	.273
Bats Right	R	.304	23	7	1	0	0	3	2	6	.360	.348
Newman, Kevin	L	.286	126	36	5	2	1	5	9	12	.348	.381
Bats Right	R	.316	367	116	15	4	11	59	19	50	.355	.469
Nido, Tomas	L	.194	36	7	1	0	2	2	3	9	.256	.389
Bats Right	R	.190	100	19	4	0	2	12	4	28	.221	.290
Nimmo, Brandon	L	.375	40	15	4	0	3	10	7	14	.490	.700
Bats Left	R	.182	159	29	7	1	5	19	39	57	.347	.333
Nola, Austin	L	.256	78	20	5	1	5	14	12	15	.356	.538
Bats Right	R	.275	160	44	7	0	5	17	11	48	.335	.413
Nunez, Dom	L	.000	2	0	0	0	0	0	0	1	.000	.000
Bats Left	R	.189	37	7	3	0	2	4	3	16	.244	.432
Nunez, Eduardo	L	.200	70	14	2	0	2	10	4	12	.240	.314
Bats Right	R	.247	97	24	5	0	0	10	0	15	.245	.299

Batters vs. Left-Handed and Right-Handed Pitchers

Batter	vs	Avg	AB	H	2B	3B	HR	RBI	BB	SO	OBP	Slg
Nunez, Renato	L	.270	200	54	9	0	13	38	14	44	.326	.510
Bats Right	R	.229	341	78	15	0	18	52	30	99	.302	.431
O'Brien, Peter	L	.067	15	1	0	0	0	0	0	7	.067	.067
Bats Right	R	.222	27	6	1	0	1	4	4	12	.344	.370
Odor, Rougned	L	.236	165	39	14	0	9	32	21	57	.330	.485
Bats Left	R	.190	357	68	16	1	21	61	31	121	.260	.417
O'Grady, Brian	L	.400	5	2	1	0	0	0	0	2	.400	.600
Bats Left	R	.162	37	6	1	1	2	3	4	15	.279	.405
O'Hearn, Ryan	L	.170	53	9	1	0	1	3	7	20	.262	.245
Bats Left	R	.200	275	55	12	1	13	35	32	79	.285	.393
Ohtani, Shohei	L	.282	103	29	4	2	3	13	10	37	.348	.447
Bats Left	R	.288	281	81	16	3	15	49	23	73	.341	.527
Olson, Matt	L	.223	157	35	7	0	11	27	9	41	.289	.478
Bats Left	R	.288	326	94	19	0	25	64	42	97	.380	.577
O'Neill, Tyler	L	.269	26	7	1	0	0	0	3	12	.345	.308
Bats Right	R	.261	115	30	5	0	5	16	7	41	.303	.435
Ortega, Rafael	L	.083	12	1	0	0	0	0	0	3	.083	.083
Bats Left	R	.224	76	17	3	0	2	10	8	19	.298	.342
Osuna, Jose	L	.228	92	21	4	0	2	9	6	16	.276	.337
Bats Right	R	.284	169	48	16	0	8	27	12	32	.328	.521
Owings, Chris	L	.164	67	11	3	0	1	6	7	37	.253	.254
Bats Right	R	.124	113	14	3	1	2	8	7	41	.182	.221
Ozuna, Marcell	L	.217	83	18	4	0	6	20	6	24	.270	.482
Bats Right	R	.249	402	100	19	1	23	69	56	90	.341	.473
Palka, Daniel	L	.091	11	1	0	0	0	1	0	3	.091	.091
Bats Left	R	.110	73	8	0	0	2	3	8	32	.207	.192
Panik, Joe	L	.289	97	28	6	0	1	10	11	10	.372	.381
Bats Left	R	.232	341	79	15	2	4	29	32	37	.298	.323
Parra, Gerardo	L	.226	62	14	4	1	1	6	3	13	.279	.371
Bats Left	R	.236	212	50	10	0	8	42	16	46	.297	.396
Pearce, Steve	L	.200	40	8	1	0	1	3	2	16	.238	.300
Bats Right	R	.163	49	8	3	0	0	6	5	15	.250	.224
Pederson, Joc	L	.224	49	11	2	0	0	1	1	15	.240	.265
Bats Left	R	.252	401	101	14	3	36	73	49	96	.349	.571
Pedroia, Dustin	L	.000	3	0	0	0	0	0	0	0	.000	.000
Bats Right	R	.118	17	2	0	0	0	1	1	2	.167	.118
Pence, Hunter	L	.327	110	36	8	1	8	22	8	23	.378	.636
Bats Right	R	.278	176	49	9	0	10	37	18	46	.345	.500
Peralta, David	L	.248	113	28	7	1	2	15	11	31	.323	.381
Bats Left	R	.286	269	77	22	2	10	42	24	56	.351	.494
Peraza, Jose	L	.287	108	31	8	1	1	6	8	13	.336	.407
Bats Right	R	.220	268	59	10	1	5	27	9	45	.265	.321
Perez, Hernan	L	.257	113	29	7	0	5	9	4	23	.280	.451
Bats Right	R	.202	119	24	4	0	3	9	7	43	.246	.311
Perez, Michael	L	.273	11	3	1	0	0	0	0	5	.273	.364
Bats Left	R	.200	35	7	4	0	0	2	8	14	.364	.314
Perez, Roberto	L	.264	129	34	2	1	9	19	20	43	.360	.504
Bats Right	R	.227	260	59	7	0	15	44	25	84	.301	.427
Peterson, Dustin	L	.375	8	3	1	0	0	1	2	3	.545	.500
Bats Right	R	.194	36	7	3	0	0	5	0	11	.194	.278
Peterson, Jace	L	.227	22	5	0	0	1	2	3	4	.346	.364
Bats Left	R	.218	78	17	3	1	1	9	3	20	.244	.321
Pham, Tommy	L	.340	159	54	13	0	3	12	37	35	.467	.478
Bats Right	R	.248	408	101	20	2	18	56	44	88	.326	.439
Phegley, Josh	L	.284	95	27	8	0	5	20	3	11	.320	.526
Bats Right	R	.219	219	48	10	0	7	42	12	52	.266	.361
Phillips, Brett	L	.200	10	2	1	0	0	0	2	3	.333	.300
Bats Left	R	.127	55	7	1	0	2	6	8	20	.231	.255
Pillar, Kevin	L	.278	162	45	12	0	9	29	8	15	.305	.519
Bats Right	R	.252	449	113	25	3	12	59	10	74	.280	.401
Pina, Manny	L	.319	72	23	6	0	4	10	7	25	.395	.569
Bats Right	R	.151	86	13	2	0	3	15	9	25	.245	.279
Pinder, Chad	L	.252	163	41	9	0	7	27	12	39	.313	.436
Bats Right	R	.230	178	41	12	0	6	20	8	49	.268	.399
Piscotty, Stephen	L	.360	86	31	5	0	6	17	5	17	.391	.628
Bats Right	R	.214	271	58	12	1	7	27	24	67	.283	.343
Plawecki, Kevin	L	.200	50	10	3	0	1	7	3	11	.245	.320
Bats Right	R	.231	108	25	7	0	2	10	9	20	.306	.352
Polanco, Gregory	L	.229	35	8	0	0	2	5	2	12	.289	.400
Bats Left	R	.246	118	29	8	1	4	12	10	37	.305	.432
Polanco, Jorge	L	.270	196	53	10	1	6	24	10	43	.305	.423
Bats Both	R	.306	435	133	30	6	16	55	50	73	.378	.513
Pollock, A.J.	L	.323	99	32	3	0	6	18	6	22	.370	.535
Bats Right	R	.239	209	50	12	1	9	29	17	52	.308	.435
Posey, Buster	L	.230	126	29	11	0	0	9	4	14	.258	.317
Bats Right	R	.269	279	75	13	0	7	29	30	57	.346	.391

Batter	vs	Avg	AB	H	2B	3B	HR	RBI	BB	SO	OBP	Slg
Prado, Martin	L	.268	97	26	5	0	0	7	7	9	.311	.320
Bats Right	R	.209	148	31	4	0	2	8	5	32	.234	.277
Profar, Jurickson	L	.305	105	32	7	0	3	17	13	17	.378	.457
Bats Both	R	.192	354	68	17	2	17	50	35	58	.278	.395
Puello, Cesar	L	.245	49	12	3	0	2	9	5	14	.413	.429
Bats Right	R	.250	76	19	2	0	2	9	5	24	.313	.355
Puig, Yasiel	L	.279	136	38	6	0	5	23	14	30	.357	.434
Bats Right	R	.263	419	110	24	2	19	61	30	103	.317	.465
Pujols, Albert	L	.261	165	43	9	0	11	37	14	22	.315	.515
Bats Right	R	.236	326	77	13	0	12	56	29	46	.299	.387
Quinn, Roman	L	.191	47	9	1	0	2	6	8	14	.309	.340
Bats Both	R	.230	61	14	2	1	2	5	4	20	.288	.393
Ramirez, Hanley	L	.176	17	3	1	0	0	3	2	7	.263	.235
Bats Right	R	.188	32	6	0	0	2	5	6	10	.316	.375
Ramirez, Harold	L	.263	118	31	6	0	2	11	5	30	.298	.364
Bats Right	R	.281	303	85	14	3	9	39	13	61	.318	.436
Ramirez, Jose	L	.269	156	42	9	0	7	24	15	14	.326	.462
Bats Both	R	.248	326	81	24	3	16	59	37	60	.327	.488
Ramos, Wilson	L	.346	107	37	4	0	5	20	15	15	.423	.523
Bats Right	R	.270	366	99	15	0	9	53	29	54	.329	.385
Ravelo, Rangel	L	.167	6	1	0	0	0	1	1	1	.286	.167
Bats Right	R	.212	33	7	2	0	2	6	2	11	.250	.455
Realmuto, J.T.	L	.276	145	40	12	0	8	22	9	34	.323	.524
Bats Right	R	.275	393	108	24	3	17	61	32	89	.329	.481
Reddick, Josh	L	.309	110	34	5	0	5	10	6	18	.345	.491
Bats Left	R	.266	391	104	14	3	9	46	30	48	.312	.386
Reed, A.J.	L	.250	4	1	0	0	0	0	0	2	.250	.250
Bats Left	R	.125	40	5	0	0	1	4	4	19	.200	.200
Rendon, Anthony	L	.316	136	43	9	1	10	26	26	27	.433	.618
Bats Right	R	.320	409	131	35	2	24	100	54	59	.404	.592
Renfroe, Hunter	L	.239	113	27	3	1	11	19	17	31	.331	.575
Bats Right	R	.208	327	68	16	0	22	45	29	123	.274	.459
Rengifo, Luis	L	.223	121	27	5	1	2	10	9	31	.278	.331
Bats Both	R	.246	236	58	13	2	5	23	31	62	.342	.381
Reyes, Franmil	L	.280	125	35	9	0	7	23	17	39	.361	.520
Bats Right	R	.238	369	88	10	0	30	58	30	117	.292	.509
Reyes, Pablo	L	.259	58	15	4	2	1	11	3	16	.295	.448
Bats Right	R	.165	85	14	3	0	1	8	10	20	.260	.235
Reyes, Victor	L	.292	72	21	3	2	0	6	3	18	.320	.389
Bats Both	R	.309	204	63	13	3	3	19	11	46	.341	.446
Reynolds, Bryan	L	.264	144	38	10	0	5	17	9	36	.318	.438
Bats Both	R	.334	347	116	27	4	11	51	37	85	.401	.530
Reynolds, Mark	L	.169	71	12	5	0	2	9	12	29	.286	.324
Bats Right	R	.172	64	11	2	0	2	11	10	28	.295	.297
Rickard, Joey	L	.256	82	21	2	1	2	7	12	30	.365	.378
Bats Right	R	.198	86	17	7	1	1	3	6	20	.258	.337
Riddle, J.T.	L	.240	25	6	3	0	3	7	1	6	.269	.720
Bats Left	R	.178	107	19	3	0	3	5	4	36	.221	.290
Riley, Austin	L	.262	65	17	4	0	7	15	8	28	.338	.646
Bats Right	R	.215	209	45	7	1	11	34	8	80	.260	.416
Rios, Edwin	L	.286	7	2	1	0	0	0	1	3	.375	.429
Bats Left	R	.275	40	11	1	1	4	8	8	18	.396	.650
Rivera, Yadiel	L	.214	28	6	1	0	0	3	3	12	.290	.250
Bats Right	R	.156	32	5	1	0	0	0	3	8	.229	.188
Rizzo, Anthony	L	.250	124	31	5	0	6	30	15	20	.371	.435
Bats Left	R	.307	388	119	24	3	21	64	56	66	.416	.546
Robertson, Daniel	L	.250	84	21	3	0	1	7	10	27	.344	.321
Bats Right	R	.187	123	23	6	1	1	12	14	32	.291	.276
Robles, Victor	L	.248	137	34	9	1	3	13	8	32	.346	.394
Bats Right	R	.257	409	105	24	2	14	52	27	108	.319	.428
Rodgers, Brendan	L	.208	24	5	0	0	0	4	2	9	.269	.208
Bats Right	R	.231	52	12	2	0	0	3	2	18	.273	.269
Rodriguez, Ronny	L	.239	67	16	4	1	3	13	3	20	.268	.463
Bats Right	R	.215	209	45	8	2	11	30	10	62	.247	.431
Rodriguez, Sean	L	.227	66	15	2	0	3	7	10	26	.346	.394
Bats Right	R	.217	46	10	3	0	1	5	9	15	.351	.348
Rogers, Jake	L	.286	21	6	1	0	2	3	3	11	.375	.619
Bats Right	R	.088	91	8	2	0	2	5	10	40	.186	.176
Rojas, Josh	L	.290	31	9	3	0	0	5	5	11	.389	.387
Bats Left	R	.196	107	21	4	0	2	11	13	30	.289	.290
Rojas, Miguel	L	.297	138	41	6	0	3	14	10	11	.347	.406
Bats Right	R	.278	345	96	23	1	2	32	22	51	.325	.368
Romine, Austin	L	.309	68	21	5	0	2	8	4	11	.347	.471
Bats Right	R	.269	160	43	7	0	6	27	6	39	.293	.425
Rondon, Jose	L	.250	76	19	3	0	2	6	5	14	.296	.368
Bats Right	R	.134	67	9	0	0	1	3	6	24	.227	.179

Batters vs. Left-Handed and Right-Handed Pitchers

Batter	vs	Avg	AB	H	2B	3B	HR	RBI	BB	SO	OBP	Slg
Rosario, Amed	L	.311	148	46	12	1	6	18	12	32	.360	.527
Bats Right	R	.280	468	131	18	6	9	54	19	92	.311	.402
Rosario, Eddie	L	.281	153	43	11	0	5	27	8	23	.315	.451
Bats Left	R	.274	409	112	17	1	27	82	14	63	.294	.518
Ruiz, Rio	L	.250	68	17	3	0	1	11	4	18	.288	.338
Bats Left	R	.228	302	69	10	2	11	35	36	70	.310	.384
Russell, Addison	L	.192	52	10	2	0	2	6	9	19	.306	.346
Bats Right	R	.252	163	41	2	1	7	17	11	39	.309	.405
Saladino, Tyler	L	.111	18	2	0	0	1	4	1	9	.158	.278
Bats Right	R	.128	47	6	0	0	1	4	4	17	.212	.191
Sanchez, Adrian	L	.250	8	2	0	0	0	1	1	2	.333	.250
Bats Right	R	.217	23	5	0	0	0	0	0	8	.217	.217
Sanchez, Gary	L	.200	95	19	4	0	7	14	11	39	.296	.463
Bats Right	R	.243	301	73	8	1	27	63	29	86	.322	.545
Sanchez, Yolmer	L	.292	120	35	7	1	1	10	10	24	.346	.392
Bats Both	R	.239	376	90	13	3	1	33	34	93	.309	.298
Sandoval, Pablo	L	.313	48	15	4	0	3	9	3	12	.353	.583
Bats Both	R	.259	224	58	19	0	11	32	15	55	.305	.491
Sano, Miguel	L	.284	109	31	5	1	11	24	12	41	.355	.651
Bats Right	R	.232	271	63	14	1	23	55	43	118	.343	.546
Santana, Carlos	L	.324	185	60	9	0	11	40	34	34	.428	.551
Bats Both	R	.260	388	101	21	1	23	53	74	74	.381	.497
Santana, Danny	L	.276	145	40	8	1	9	27	10	51	.325	.531
Bats Both	R	.286	329	94	15	5	19	54	15	100	.323	.535
Santana, Domingo	L	.238	122	29	5	0	8	19	20	48	.345	.475
Bats Right	R	.258	329	85	15	1	13	50	30	116	.322	.429
Santander, Anthony	L	.272	136	37	4	0	9	28	7	37	.310	.500
Bats Both	R	.254	244	62	16	1	11	31	12	49	.290	.463
Schebler, Scott	L	.154	13	2	0	0	1	2	0	2	.154	.385
Bats Left	R	.118	68	8	2	0	1	5	14	25	.268	.191
Schoop, Jonathan	L	.277	112	31	5	0	9	23	10	36	.354	.563
Bats Right	R	.249	321	80	18	1	14	36	10	80	.285	.442
Schwarber, Kyle	L	.229	109	25	4	1	6	18	11	36	.306	.450
Bats Left	R	.255	420	107	25	2	32	74	59	120	.348	.552
Seager, Corey	L	.240	167	40	8	0	6	24	14	44	.308	.395
Bats Left	R	.289	322	93	36	1	13	63	30	54	.348	.528
Seager, Kyle	L	.285	130	37	6	0	11	25	14	27	.361	.585
Bats Left	R	.217	263	57	13	1	12	38	30	59	.301	.411
Segura, Jean	L	.289	135	39	17	1	6	18	9	17	.342	.563
Bats Right	R	.277	441	122	20	3	6	42	21	56	.316	.376
Semien, Marcus	L	.309	178	55	14	3	7	22	25	24	.394	.539
Bats Right	R	.276	479	132	29	4	26	70	62	78	.360	.516
Senzel, Nick	L	.316	95	30	5	3	3	16	8	15	.371	.526
Bats Right	R	.236	280	66	15	1	9	26	22	86	.296	.393
Severino, Pedro	L	.273	143	39	7	0	8	25	10	33	.323	.490
Bats Right	R	.228	162	37	6	0	5	19	19	40	.319	.358
Shaw, Travis	L	.102	49	5	1	0	0	2	0	17	.137	.122
Bats Left	R	.171	181	31	4	0	7	14	36	72	.315	.309
Shuck, JB	L	.267	15	4	0	1	0	1	0	4	.267	.400
Bats Left	R	.188	32	6	0	0	0	1	8	6	.366	.188
Sierra, Magneuris	L	1.000	2	2	0	0	0	0	0	0	1.000	1.000
Bats Left	R	.316	38	12	1	1	0	1	2	7	.350	.395
Simmons, Andrelton	L	.303	99	30	4	0	4	7	9	7	.367	.465
Bats Right	R	.251	299	75	15	0	3	33	15	30	.289	.331
Sisco, Chance	L	.105	19	2	0	0	0	0	3	9	.292	.105
Bats Left	R	.223	148	33	7	0	8	20	19	52	.339	.432
Skole, Matt	L	.250	8	2	0	0	0	1	0	4	.250	.250
Bats Left	R	.203	64	13	2	0	0	5	7	27	.278	.234
Slater, Austin	L	.275	80	22	6	2	2	10	11	19	.363	.475
Bats Right	R	.205	88	18	3	1	3	11	11	40	.307	.364
Smith, Dominic	L	.303	33	10	1	0	2	7	3	7	.361	.515
Bats Left	R	.278	144	40	9	0	9	18	16	37	.354	.528
Smith, Kevan	L	.338	68	23	8	0	1	12	8	11	.410	.500
Bats Right	R	.203	123	25	4	0	4	8	8	26	.263	.333
Smith, Mallex	L	.264	148	39	5	2	1	8	14	37	.339	.345
Bats Left	R	.213	362	77	14	7	5	29	28	104	.283	.331
Smith, Will	L	.211	57	12	2	0	3	7	5	25	.281	.404
Bats Right	R	.274	113	31	7	0	12	35	13	27	.364	.655
Smith Jr., Dwight	L	.212	99	21	5	0	3	17	9	32	.282	.354
Bats Left	R	.252	258	65	11	3	10	36	17	50	.302	.434
Smoak, Justin	L	.220	132	29	7	0	3	16	20	22	.331	.341
Bats Both	R	.202	282	57	9	0	19	45	59	84	.347	.436
Sogard, Eric	L	.279	104	29	6	0	6	12	11	22	.345	.510
Bats Left	R	.295	292	86	17	2	7	28	27	41	.356	.438
Solak, Nick	L	.319	47	15	5	1	3	8	7	9	.418	.660
Bats Right	R	.275	69	19	1	0	2	9	8	20	.375	.377
Solano, Donovan	L	.339	115	39	3	1	3	12	8	23	.382	.461
Bats Right	R	.320	100	32	10	0	1	11	2	26	.333	.450
Solarte, Yangervis	L	.176	34	6	1	0	0	2	2	4	.222	.206
Bats Both	R	.231	39	9	4	0	1	5	2	12	.268	.410
Soler, Jorge	L	.259	143	37	8	1	9	30	19	45	.352	.517
Bats Right	R	.267	446	119	25	0	39	87	54	133	.354	.585
Soto, Juan	L	.285	186	53	12	3	6	33	28	43	.371	.478
Bats Left	R	.281	356	100	20	2	28	77	80	89	.416	.584
Spangenberg, Cory	L	.176	17	3	0	1	1	2	0	9	.176	.471
Bats Left	R	.244	78	19	2	1	1	8	6	27	.298	.333
Springer, George	L	.272	125	34	3	1	8	18	24	32	.399	.504
Bats Right	R	.299	354	106	17	2	31	78	43	81	.377	.621
Stallings, Jacob	L	.340	47	16	3	0	3	6	1	8	.367	.596
Bats Right	R	.236	144	34	2	0	3	7	15	32	.313	.313
Stamets, Eric	L	.091	11	1	1	0	0	0	2	5	.231	.182
Bats Right	R	.033	30	1	0	0	0	2	3	19	.118	.033
Stanton, Giancarlo	L	.286	14	4	2	0	1	1	3	8	.412	.643
Bats Right	R	.289	45	13	1	0	2	12	9	16	.400	.444
Starling, Bubba	L	.185	54	10	2	0	1	2	3	12	.241	.278
Bats Right	R	.227	132	30	5	0	3	10	6	44	.261	.333
Stassi, Max	L	.028	36	1	0	0	0	0	6	15	.167	.028
Bats Right	R	.177	96	17	1	0	1	5	6	34	.229	.219
Stevenson, Andrew	L	1.000	1	1	0	0	0	0	0	0	1.000	1.000
Bats Left	R	.345	29	10	1	1	0	0	6	11	.472	.448
Stewart, Christin	L	.236	72	17	5	0	1	6	5	19	.309	.347
Bats Left	R	.232	297	69	20	1	9	34	29	84	.304	.397
Stewart, D.J.	L	.333	42	14	2	0	0	2	3	6	.378	.381
Bats Left	R	.190	84	16	4	0	4	13	11	20	.289	.381
Story, Trevor	L	.314	172	54	14	1	9	24	13	49	.369	.564
Bats Right	R	.286	416	119	24	4	26	61	45	125	.360	.550
Straw, Myles	L	.294	34	10	3	0	0	3	6	5	.400	.382
Bats Right	R	.257	74	19	1	2	0	4	13	19	.368	.324
Stubbs, Garrett	L	.375	8	3	2	0	0	2	1	0	.444	.625
Bats Left	R	.148	27	4	1	0	0	0	3	7	.233	.185
Suarez, Eugenio	L	.276	123	34	4	0	11	24	30	49	.417	.577
Bats Right	R	.270	452	122	18	2	38	79	40	140	.340	.571
Sucre, Jesus	L	.217	23	5	0	0	0	0	1	4	.250	.217
Bats Right	R	.205	39	8	2	0	0	3	3	9	.279	.256
Suzuki, Kurt	L	.343	67	23	4	0	4	20	3	9	.375	.582
Bats Right	R	.239	213	51	7	0	13	43	17	27	.308	.455
Swanson, Dansby	L	.293	99	29	2	1	4	16	9	19	.349	.455
Bats Right	R	.240	384	92	24	2	13	49	42	105	.320	.414
Swihart, Blake	L	.111	18	2	0	0	0	0	2	7	.200	.111
Bats Both	R	.176	74	13	1	0	4	13	4	29	.228	.351
Tapia, Raimel	L	.277	101	28	1	1	3	9	3	35	.298	.396
Bats Left	R	.274	325	89	22	4	6	35	18	65	.312	.422
Tatis Jr., Fernando	L	.419	62	26	2	1	5	12	15	19	.542	.726
Bats Right	R	.294	272	80	11	5	17	41	15	91	.332	.559
Tauchman, Mike	L	.357	70	25	9	0	1	13	11	16	.446	.529
Bats Left	R	.247	190	47	9	1	12	34	23	55	.329	.495
Taylor, Beau	L	.000	2	0	0	0	0	0	0	0	.333	.000
Bats Left	R	.174	23	4	0	0	2	2	4	7	.296	.435
Taylor, Chris	L	.255	141	36	14	1	7	24	19	42	.342	.518
Bats Right	R	.267	225	60	15	3	5	28	18	73	.327	.427
Taylor, Michael A.	L	.278	36	10	3	0	1	3	3	13	.333	.444
Bats Right	R	.231	52	12	4	0	0	0	4	21	.286	.308
Tellez, Rowdy	L	.270	115	31	10	0	6	23	8	37	.317	.513
Bats Left	R	.208	255	53	9	0	15	31	21	79	.283	.420
Thaiss, Matt	L	.227	22	5	1	0	1	6	2	7	.292	.409
Bats Left	R	.208	125	26	6	0	7	17	15	45	.293	.424
Thames, Eric	L	.200	50	10	1	0	2	6	9	19	.339	.340
Bats Left	R	.254	346	88	22	2	23	55	42	121	.348	.529
Thomas, Lane	L	.364	11	4	0	1	1	3	0	2	.364	.818
Bats Right	R	.296	27	8	0	0	3	9	4	6	.424	.630
Tilson, Charlie	L	.130	23	3	0	0	0	1	2	7	.200	.130
Bats Left	R	.248	121	30	5	0	1	11	8	31	.311	.314
Toro, Abraham	L	.087	23	2	0	0	0	0	2	6	.192	.087
Bats Both	R	.273	55	15	3	2	2	9	7	13	.349	.509
Torres, Gleyber	L	.286	140	40	9	0	9	23	15	37	.359	.543
Bats Right	R	.276	406	112	17	0	29	67	33	92	.329	.532
Tovar, Wilfredo	L	.233	43	10	3	0	0	4	4	6	.298	.302
Bats Right	R	.150	40	6	2	0	0	1	1	9	.171	.200
Travis, Sam	L	.221	95	21	2	0	5	14	8	21	.279	.400
Bats Right	R	.204	49	10	2	1	1	2	3	15	.264	.347
Trevino, Jose	L	.333	39	13	5	0	1	7	1	8	.341	.538
Bats Right	R	.222	81	18	4	0	1	6	2	19	.238	.309

Batters vs. Left-Handed and Right-Handed Pitchers

Batter	vs	Avg	AB	H	2B	3B	HR	RBI	BB	SO	OBP	Slg
Trout, Mike	L	.266	143	38	10	1	10	26	38	39	.429	.559
Bats Right	R	.303	327	99	17	1	35	78	72	81	.442	.682
Trumbo, Mark	L	.158	19	3	3	0	0	3	1	3	.200	.316
Bats Right	R	.200	10	2	0	0	0	0	1	2	.273	.200
Tucker, Cole	L	.191	47	9	3	0	1	8	4	19	.255	.319
Bats Both	R	.220	100	22	7	3	1	5	6	21	.271	.380
Tucker, Kyle	L	.296	27	8	3	0	1	5	0	6	.321	.519
Bats Left	R	.250	40	10	3	0	3	6	4	14	.318	.550
Turner, Justin	L	.288	160	46	11	0	12	23	15	35	.358	.581
Bats Right	R	.292	319	93	13	0	15	44	36	53	.378	.473
Turner, Trea	L	.316	117	37	9	0	2	6	10	23	.367	.444
Bats Right	R	.292	404	118	28	5	17	51	33	90	.349	.512
Upton, Justin	L	.136	66	9	4	0	2	12	11	31	.253	.288
Bats Right	R	.248	153	38	4	0	10	28	21	47	.333	.471
Urena, Richard	L	.231	26	6	3	0	0	1	2	6	.286	.346
Bats Both	R	.250	48	12	3	0	0	3	0	17	.265	.313
Urias, Luis	L	.351	57	20	3	0	2	12	2	14	.383	.509
Bats Right	R	.177	158	28	5	1	2	12	23	42	.312	.259
Urshela, Giovanny	L	.303	142	43	10	0	8	23	6	28	.333	.542
Bats Right	R	.320	300	96	24	0	13	51	19	59	.365	.530
Valaika, Pat	L	.238	42	10	4	1	1	3	4	19	.304	.452
Bats Right	R	.135	37	5	1	0	0	1	3	15	.200	.162
Valera, Breyvic	L	.267	15	4	1	0	0	2	0	4	.313	.333
Bats Both	R	.219	32	7	1	1	1	4	4	3	.306	.406
VanMeter, Josh	L	.125	24	3	2	0	0	1	3	8	.250	.208
Bats Left	R	.250	204	51	11	1	8	22	26	48	.336	.431
Vargas, Ildemaro	L	.340	53	18	3	0	5	17	1	3	.340	.679
Bats Both	R	.243	148	36	6	1	1	7	8	21	.282	.318
Vazquez, Christian	L	.285	158	45	10	0	11	28	13	26	.337	.557
Bats Right	R	.272	324	88	16	1	12	44	20	75	.312	.438
Verdugo, Alex	L	.327	101	33	6	2	2	9	5	16	.358	.485
Bats Left	R	.281	242	68	16	0	10	35	21	33	.336	.471
Villar, Jonathan	L	.264	227	60	9	1	9	25	16	66	.310	.432
Bats Both	R	.280	415	116	24	4	15	48	45	110	.354	.465
Viloria, Meibrys	L	.125	32	4	0	0	0	3	2	15	.171	.125
Bats Left	R	.238	101	24	7	0	1	12	8	29	.286	.337
Vogelbach, Daniel	L	.161	124	20	4	0	5	17	20	40	.288	.315
Bats Left	R	.225	338	76	13	0	25	59	72	109	.359	.485
Vogt, Stephen	L	.222	45	10	3	0	2	8	1	15	.234	.422
Bats Left	R	.271	210	57	21	2	8	32	19	51	.330	.505
Voit, Luke	L	.250	108	27	5	0	5	13	16	33	.354	.435
Bats Right	R	.268	321	86	16	1	16	49	55	109	.386	.474
Votto, Joey	L	.243	152	37	7	0	1	10	22	44	.347	.309
Bats Left	R	.268	373	100	25	1	14	37	54	79	.361	.453
Wade, Tyler	L	.278	18	5	2	0	0	2	1	6	.316	.389
Bats Left	R	.237	76	18	1	1	2	9	10	22	.333	.355
Wade Jr., LaMonte	L	.000	7	0	0	0	0	0	1	2	.300	.000
Bats Left	R	.224	49	11	2	1	2	5	10	7	.356	.429
Walker, Christian	L	.241	145	35	8	0	6	14	28	40	.368	.421
Bats Right	R	.266	384	102	18	1	23	59	39	115	.340	.497
Walker, Neil	L	.275	51	14	3	0	0	5	6	5	.351	.333
Bats Both	R	.259	286	74	16	1	8	33	36	72	.343	.406
Wallach, Chad	L	.308	13	4	1	0	0	0	3	4	.438	.385
Bats Right	R	.229	35	8	2	0	1	3	3	8	.289	.371
Walsh, Jared	L	.250	8	2	2	0	0	1	0	2	.250	.500
Bats Left	R	.197	71	14	3	1	1	4	6	33	.278	.310
Ward, Taylor	L	.167	12	2	0	0	0	1	2	7	.286	.167
Bats Right	R	.200	30	6	3	0	1	1	4	16	.294	.400
Wendle, Joey	L	.130	54	7	1	0	0	4	4	15	.203	.148
Bats Left	R	.261	184	48	12	2	3	15	10	32	.319	.397
White, Tyler	L	.146	89	13	3	0	1	8	14	32	.260	.213
Bats Right	R	.245	151	37	11	0	2	15	22	46	.337	.358
Wieters, Matt	L	.195	41	8	1	0	4	7	3	17	.267	.512
Bats Both	R	.220	127	28	3	0	7	20	9	30	.268	.409
Wilkerson, Stevie	L	.154	117	18	5	0	1	9	9	47	.242	.222
Bats Both	R	.264	212	56	13	2	9	26	13	61	.311	.472
Williams, Mason	L	.222	9	2	0	0	0	0	1	3	.300	.222
Bats Left	R	.286	21	6	1	0	0	2	2	3	.333	.333
Williams, Nick	L	.118	17	2	1	0	0	2	0	9	.118	.176
Bats Left	R	.157	89	14	3	0	2	3	4	34	.211	.258
Williamson, Mac	L	.133	30	4	0	0	0	2	2	13	.188	.133
Bats Right	R	.163	98	16	1	0	4	15	12	31	.268	.296
Wilson, Bobby	L	.000	7	0	0	0	0	0	1	1	.125	.000
Bats Right	R	.108	37	4	1	0	0	2	1	10	.132	.135
Winker, Jesse	L	.163	43	7	0	0	0	2	6	6	.280	.163
Bats Left	R	.285	295	84	17	2	16	36	32	54	.368	.519

Batter	vs	Avg	AB	H	2B	3B	HR	RBI	BB	SO	OBP	Slg
Wisdom, Patrick	L	.125	8	1	0	0	0	0	1	5	.222	.125
Bats Right	R	.167	18	3	1	0	0	1	0	10	.167	.222
Wolters, Tony	L	.280	107	30	10	0	0	12	13	20	.369	.374
Bats Left	R	.254	252	64	7	2	1	30	23	48	.324	.310
Wong, Kolten	L	.288	111	32	4	0	3	11	5	18	.333	.405
Bats Left	R	.283	367	104	21	4	8	48	42	65	.369	.428
Wynns, Austin	L	.188	16	3	1	0	0	1	1	1	.235	.250
Bats Right	R	.222	54	12	0	0	1	4	2	13	.250	.278
Yastrzemski, Mike	L	.329	82	27	7	0	4	12	5	20	.382	.561
Bats Left	R	.256	289	74	15	3	17	43	27	87	.321	.505
Yelich, Christian	L	.277	173	48	10	1	12	24	25	37	.381	.555
Bats Left	R	.358	316	113	19	2	32	73	55	81	.455	.734
Zagunis, Mark	L	.278	18	5	2	0	0	3	2	5	.350	.389
Bats Right	R	.222	18	4	1	0	0	2	2	11	.300	.278
Zimmerman, Ryan	L	.367	49	18	3	0	2	8	4	12	.415	.551
Bats Right	R	.213	122	26	6	0	4	19	13	27	.285	.361
Zobrist, Ben	L	.190	21	4	0	0	0	1	7	4	.393	.190
Bats Both	R	.271	129	35	5	0	1	16	16	20	.351	.333
Zunino, Mike	L	.154	91	14	1	0	2	11	10	34	.238	.231
Bats Right	R	.171	175	30	9	1	7	21	10	64	.229	.354
AL	L	.258	-	-	-	-	-	-	-	-	.328	.444
	R	.251	-	-	-	-	-	-	-	-	.320	.437
NL	L	.257	-	-	-	-	-	-	-	-	.327	.437
	R	.249	-	-	-	-	-	-	-	-	.321	.429
MLB	L	.258	-	-	-	-	-	-	-	-	.328	.441
	R	.250	-	-	-	-	-	-	-	-	.321	.433

Pitchers vs. Left-Handed and Right-Handed Batters

Pitcher	vs	Avg	AB	H	2B	3B	HR	RBI	BB	SO	OBP	Slg
Abad, Fernando	L	.172	29	5	0	0	1	2	1	8	.200	.276
Throws Left	R	.235	17	4	0	0	1	5	2	1	.316	.412
Abreu, Bryan	L	.071	14	1	0	0	0	0	0	6	.071	.071
Throws Right	R	.200	15	3	1	0	0	1	3	7	.333	.267
Adam, Jason	L	.133	30	4	0	0	0	1	5	5	.308	.133
Throws Right	R	.244	45	11	4	0	1	7	5	13	.308	.400
Adams, Austin D	L	.267	30	8	2	0	2	5	8	7	.421	.533
Throws Right	R	.278	36	10	3	0	2	9	5	7	.357	.528
Adams, Austin L	L	.149	47	7	3	0	1	6	5	24	.226	.277
Throws Right	R	.200	65	13	2	0	3	6	11	29	.325	.369
Adams, Chance	L	.319	47	15	5	0	3	8	6	7	.407	.617
Throws Right	R	.375	64	24	7	0	4	18	5	16	.429	.672
Agrazal, Dario	L	.238	147	35	4	0	7	20	10	27	.313	.408
Throws Right	R	.329	143	47	9	2	8	20	8	14	.378	.587
Alaniz, R.J.	L	.269	26	7	2	0	2	5	3	4	.345	.577
Throws Right	R	.324	37	12	3	0	1	10	4	9	.381	.486
Albers, Matt	L	.286	63	18	4	0	4	17	13	7	.425	.540
Throws Right	R	.220	159	35	7	0	4	17	16	50	.290	.340
Alcantara, Sandy	L	.253	403	102	17	2	16	53	49	72	.333	.424
Throws Right	R	.226	340	77	26	0	7	32	32	79	.308	.365
Alcantara, Victor	L	.241	58	14	5	0	1	8	5	5	.308	.379
Throws Right	R	.295	105	31	5	0	7	24	10	19	.362	.543
Alexander, Scott	L	.364	33	12	1	0	2	13	2	4	.400	.576
Throws Left	R	.143	35	5	2	1	0	2	5	5	.268	.257
Alexander, Tyler	L	.239	46	11	1	0	2	5	1	11	.286	.391
Throws Left	R	.318	179	57	12	3	7	23	6	36	.339	.536
Allard, Kolby	L	.296	54	16	2	1	0	7	6	10	.387	.370
Throws Left	R	.275	131	36	5	1	3	15	13	23	.338	.397
Allen, Cody	L	.244	41	10	1	0	5	10	11	14	.396	.634
Throws Right	R	.264	53	14	5	1	4	8	9	15	.371	.623
Allen, Logan	L	.357	28	10	3	0	2	4	2	5	.438	.679
Throws Left	R	.321	81	26	7	1	2	16	11	12	.398	.506
Almonte, Yency	L	.347	49	17	5	0	2	7	6	9	.418	.571
Throws Right	R	.242	91	22	7	0	5	15	8	20	.307	.484
Altavilla, Dan	L	.188	16	3	1	0	1	8	0	5	.188	.438
Throws Right	R	.176	34	6	1	0	0	6	12	13	.383	.206
Alvarado, Jose	L	.194	36	7	1	0	0	2	8	13	.333	.222
Throws Left	R	.282	78	22	3	1	2	13	19	26	.418	.423
Alvarez, Jose	L	.236	110	26	4	0	4	16	6	22	.277	.382
Throws Left	R	.328	122	40	6	0	4	15	12	29	.385	.475
Alzolay, Adbert	L	.321	28	9	2	0	2	7	4	3	.406	.607
Throws Right	R	.182	22	4	0	0	2	3	5	10	.357	.455
Anderson, Brett	L	.221	172	38	6	0	3	13	12	19	.280	.308
Throws Left	R	.280	510	143	27	2	17	57	37	71	.329	.441
Anderson, Chase	L	.189	233	44	12	3	6	20	21	57	.265	.343
Throws Right	R	.280	293	82	17	3	17	42	29	67	.353	.532
Anderson, Cody	L	.235	17	4	2	0	1	5	5	3	.435	.529
Throws Right	R	.421	19	8	2	0	0	4	3	6	.500	.526
Anderson, Drew	L	.300	10	3	0	0	0	0	3	2	.462	.300
Throws Right	R	.214	14	3	0	0	1	5	3	4	.353	.429
Anderson, Justin	L	.238	84	20	9	0	4	19	16	29	.356	.488
Throws Right	R	.227	97	22	7	1	2	18	16	31	.339	.381
Anderson, Nick	L	.250	112	28	9	1	4	17	11	48	.317	.455
Throws Right	R	.183	131	24	2	1	4	8	7	62	.234	.305
Anderson, Shaun	L	.292	178	52	13	0	7	23	17	26	.357	.483
Throws Right	R	.289	204	59	11	1	6	32	21	44	.357	.441
Anderson, Tanner	L	.360	50	18	1	0	4	13	4	11	.407	.620
Throws Right	R	.255	47	12	1	0	0	2	3	7	.300	.277
Anderson, Tyler	L	.348	23	8	0	0	3	8	4	8	.429	.739
Throws Left	R	.368	68	25	8	1	5	18	7	15	.421	.735
Andriese, Matt	L	.228	114	26	8	2	4	18	15	31	.321	.439
Throws Right	R	.286	161	46	9	0	4	21	12	48	.339	.416
Archer, Chris	L	.235	204	48	7	2	12	30	27	66	.333	.466
Throws Right	R	.260	254	66	11	0	13	37	28	77	.332	.457
Armenteros, Rogelio	L	.303	33	10	1	0	0	4	1	8	.324	.333
Throws Right	R	.189	37	7	1	0	1	5	4	10	.268	.297
Armstrong, Shawn	L	.209	86	18	2	0	2	11	12	20	.310	.302
Throws Right	R	.324	148	48	11	1	6	27	17	43	.400	.534
Arrieta, Jake	L	.317	249	79	11	1	14	35	32	43	.393	.538
Throws Right	R	.252	278	70	11	0	7	30	19	67	.313	.367
Avila, Pedro	L	.222	9	2	0	0	0	0	2	3	.364	.222
Throws Right	R	.182	11	2	0	0	0	1	0	2	.250	.182
Avilan, Luis	L	.102	49	5	1	0	1	3	5	17	.185	.184
Throws Left	R	.373	75	28	4	0	4	16	9	13	.460	.587
Baez, Michel	L	.212	52	11	4	0	3	10	8	10	.323	.462
Throws Right	R	.233	60	14	3	0	0	5	6	18	.324	.283
Baez, Pedro	L	.176	119	21	6	1	2	9	8	29	.234	.294
Throws Right	R	.172	128	22	2	0	4	17	15	40	.274	.281
Bailey, Homer	L	.216	328	71	14	1	12	36	27	82	.277	.375
Throws Right	R	.299	304	91	10	2	9	37	26	67	.357	.434
Banuelos, Manny	L	.321	56	18	5	0	2	4	10	14	.424	.518
Throws Left	R	.296	142	42	4	0	10	30	23	30	.393	.535
Bard, Luke	L	.290	69	20	4	0	4	16	6	15	.355	.522
Throws Right	R	.189	111	21	2	0	4	16	7	25	.260	.315
Barlow, Scott	L	.288	104	30	7	1	3	16	15	34	.388	.462
Throws Right	R	.209	163	34	9	3	3	22	22	58	.305	.356
Barnes, Jacob	L	.228	57	13	2	0	0	4	10	12	.343	.263
Throws Right	R	.291	79	23	4	1	7	23	12	20	.376	.633
Barnes, Matt	L	.174	92	16	2	0	3	15	22	50	.345	.293
Throws Right	R	.232	151	35	7	0	5	16	16	60	.304	.377
Barraclough, Kyle	L	.235	51	12	2	0	3	8	8	12	.339	.451
Throws Right	R	.295	88	26	5	0	6	22	13	28	.394	.557
Barria, Jaime	L	.242	157	38	8	1	6	23	15	41	.308	.420
Throws Right	R	.305	177	54	15	1	18	36	12	34	.352	.706
Bashlor, Tyler	L	.233	30	7	0	0	2	9	7	8	.368	.433
Throws Right	R	.259	54	14	2	0	4	9	10	12	.375	.519
Bass, Anthony	L	.165	79	13	3	1	2	6	6	21	.221	.304
Throws Right	R	.191	89	17	1	0	3	10	11	22	.287	.303
Bassitt, Chris	L	.209	278	58	10	2	14	37	29	82	.291	.410
Throws Right	R	.251	267	67	11	1	7	23	18	59	.316	.378
Bauer, Trevor	L	.247	364	90	16	4	20	52	41	101	.339	.478
Throws Right	R	.216	436	94	27	3	14	49	41	152	.294	.388
Bautista, Gerson	L	.167	18	3	0	0	1	5	0	3	.158	.333
Throws Right	R	.476	21	10	2	1	1	6	9	4	.633	.810
Bednar, David	L	.261	23	6	2	0	1	3	3	8	.333	.478
Throws Right	R	.235	17	4	1	0	2	7	2	6	.316	.647
Bedrosian, Cam	L	.172	116	20	2	1	3	7	15	34	.273	.284
Throws Right	R	.241	116	28	3	1	4	24	7	30	.294	.388
Beede, Tyler	L	.272	213	58	12	2	9	28	25	42	.354	.474
Throws Right	R	.271	255	69	7	0	13	33	21	71	.330	.451
Beeks, Jalen	L	.318	110	35	7	0	3	13	14	20	.406	.464
Throws Left	R	.268	299	80	20	0	9	40	26	69	.334	.425
Bergen, Travis	L	.192	26	5	2	0	1	5	1	4	.250	.385
Throws Left	R	.265	49	13	5	0	3	9	8	14	.368	.551
Berrios, Jose	L	.247	388	96	21	1	12	44	28	99	.306	.399
Throws Right	R	.254	386	98	14	2	14	39	23	96	.299	.409
Bettis, Chad	L	.300	110	33	9	1	5	17	14	22	.384	.536
Throws Right	R	.302	149	45	8	1	5	24	7	20	.350	.470
Biagini, Joe	L	.320	103	33	7	0	10	22	10	23	.381	.680
Throws Right	R	.253	150	38	8	1	4	14	16	37	.329	.400
Biddle, Jesse	L	.404	47	19	2	0	2	11	7	8	.491	.574
Throws Left	R	.299	77	23	4	1	3	20	15	18	.421	.494
Bieber, Shane	L	.228	382	87	17	0	18	33	20	127	.271	.414
Throws Right	R	.231	428	99	20	1	13	37	20	132	.271	.374
Bird, Kyle	L	.227	22	5	0	0	1	3	7	5	.452	.364
Throws Left	R	.231	26	6	0	0	4	11	8	5	.412	.692
Blach, Ty	L	.471	34	16	3	1	4	18	3	3	.514	.971
Throws Left	R	.341	88	30	7	0	4	14	14	17	.431	.557
Black, Ray	L	.292	24	7	0	1	2	2	4	4	.393	.625
Throws Right	R	.194	36	7	0	0	3	5	5	14	.310	.444
Blackburn, Paul	L	.423	26	11	2	1	2	7	2	5	.448	.808
Throws Right	R	.333	24	8	1	0	1	6	2	3	.407	.500
Blazek, Michael	L	.200	10	2	1	0	1	4	3	0	.385	.600
Throws Right	R	.364	11	4	0	0	0	0	2	0	.462	.364
Bleier, Richard	L	.222	99	22	5	0	1	13	2	18	.250	.303
Throws Left	R	.355	121	43	14	1	5	27	6	12	.392	.612
Blevins, Jerry	L	.180	61	11	3	0	1	6	7	20	.261	.279
Throws Left	R	.233	60	14	3	0	4	12	9	17	.347	.483
Bolanos, Ronald	L	.250	40	10	3	1	2	6	7	10	.354	.525
Throws Right	R	.206	34	7	3	0	1	4	5	9	.325	.382
Borucki, Ryan	L	.571	7	4	1	0	0	1	2	0	.667	.714
Throws Left	R	.407	27	11	5	0	2	9	4	6	.484	.815
Boshers, Buddy	L	.257	35	9	2	0	2	6	6	11	.366	.486
Throws Left	R	.250	44	11	3	0	1	4	4	15	.327	.386
Bowman, Matt	L	.283	53	15	5	0	0	7	7	11	.361	.377
Throws Right	R	.174	69	12	3	0	2	7	6	14	.237	.304
Boxberger, Brad	L	.222	54	12	2	0	1	6	9	15	.344	.315
Throws Right	R	.265	49	13	3	1	2	10	8	12	.362	.490
Boyd, Matthew	L	.231	134	31	5	0	7	14	6	44	.286	.425
Throws Left	R	.250	587	147	31	2	32	83	44	194	.305	.474
Brach, Brad	L	.403	72	29	5	3	2	10	13	8	.500	.639
Throws Right	R	.211	133	28	3	0	2	20	18	52	.297	.278

Pitchers vs. Left-Handed and Right-Handed Batters

Pitcher	vs	Avg	AB	H	2B	3B	HR	RBI	BB	SO	OBP	Slg
Bradford, Chasen	L	.280	25	7	1	0	3	6	2	2	.321	.680
Throws Right	R	.256	39	10	2	0	3	4	2	9	.293	.538
Bradley, Archie	L	.267	116	31	9	2	2	18	17	44	.361	.431
Throws Right	R	.231	156	36	6	0	3	17	19	43	.330	.327
Brasier, Ryan	L	.247	93	23	7	0	6	20	14	23	.351	.516
Throws Right	R	.231	121	28	3	0	3	14	7	38	.277	.331
Brault, Steven	L	.250	104	26	5	0	3	13	8	30	.304	.385
Throws Left	R	.270	337	91	24	1	12	44	45	70	.368	.454
Brebbia, John	L	.225	89	20	5	1	3	14	12	29	.337	.404
Throws Right	R	.212	184	39	7	0	3	15	15	58	.270	.299
Brennan, Brandon	L	.242	66	16	4	0	3	15	12	17	.354	.439
Throws Right	R	.175	103	18	4	0	3	10	12	30	.256	.301
Brewer, Colten	L	.244	86	21	2	1	2	12	11	27	.337	.360
Throws Right	R	.299	127	38	10	0	4	23	23	25	.404	.472
Brice, Austin	L	.246	69	17	3	0	3	13	10	15	.366	.420
Throws Right	R	.192	104	20	2	0	4	13	8	31	.274	.327
Brigham, Jeff	L	.220	59	13	1	1	3	11	8	16	.313	.424
Throws Right	R	.267	86	23	2	0	5	11	6	23	.319	.465
Britton, Zack	L	.158	57	9	2	0	0	5	9	25	.269	.193
Throws Left	R	.191	152	29	4	0	3	12	23	28	.299	.276
Brooks, Aaron	L	.283	219	62	9	4	11	32	20	39	.352	.511
Throws Right	R	.258	217	56	17	0	10	34	14	43	.321	.475
Buchholz, Clay	L	.310	129	40	10	0	8	22	8	23	.355	.574
Throws Right	R	.302	106	32	12	0	5	18	8	16	.348	.557
Buchter, Ryan	L	.238	105	25	4	1	5	17	7	33	.289	.438
Throws Left	R	.274	62	17	4	0	3	9	16	17	.420	.484
Buehler, Walker	L	.216	352	76	17	3	8	31	23	109	.267	.349
Throws Right	R	.231	333	77	12	2	12	36	14	106	.269	.387
Bumgarner, Madison	L	.200	175	35	9	0	4	15	6	52	.235	.320
Throws Left	R	.258	605	156	32	5	26	76	37	151	.307	.456
Bummer, Aaron	L	.178	90	16	2	0	1	5	4	21	.213	.233
Throws Left	R	.188	144	27	2	0	3	13	20	39	.299	.264
Bundy, Dylan	L	.274	310	85	19	0	12	37	24	60	.329	.452
Throws Right	R	.239	318	76	21	1	17	46	34	102	.315	.472
Burdi, Nick	L	.188	16	3	0	1	0	1	2	11	.278	.313
Throws Right	R	.381	21	8	2	0	1	4	1	6	.409	.619
Burke, Brock	L	.391	23	9	0	0	1	4	2	3	.462	.522
Throws Left	R	.256	82	21	6	0	5	15	9	11	.333	.512
Burnes, Corbin	L	.398	83	33	7	0	8	22	17	19	.500	.771
Throws Right	R	.287	129	37	4	0	9	28	3	51	.303	.527
Burr, Ryan	L	.294	34	10	1	1	0	5	2	10	.333	.382
Throws Right	R	.171	41	7	2	0	3	8	6	10	.265	.439
Buttrey, Ty	L	.228	123	28	5	1	3	13	13	43	.309	.358
Throws Right	R	.263	156	41	5	0	5	25	10	41	.318	.391
Cabrera, Genesis	L	.500	20	10	0	0	1	4	2	4	.542	.650
Throws Left	R	.203	64	13	4	0	1	8	9	15	.311	.313
Cahill, Trevor	L	.296	179	53	17	2	11	26	12	34	.352	.598
Throws Right	R	.256	227	58	7	2	14	35	27	47	.336	.489
Canning, Griffin	L	.204	162	33	4	2	8	23	20	45	.299	.401
Throws Right	R	.263	179	47	13	2	6	19	10	51	.316	.458
Carasiti, Matt	L	.200	10	2	0	0	1	4	2	3	.308	.500
Throws Right	R	.333	27	9	2	0	1	2	3	7	.400	.519
Carle, Shane	L	.211	19	4	1	0	1	4	5	3	.423	.421
Throws Right	R	.389	18	7	2	1	2	7	4	3	.522	.944
Carpenter, Ryan	L	.378	45	17	5	0	3	13	1	6	.391	.689
Throws Left	R	.326	135	44	9	1	9	25	12	19	.384	.607
Carrasco, Carlos	L	.274	146	40	8	1	9	17	9	43	.318	.527
Throws Right	R	.301	173	52	15	1	9	29	7	53	.330	.555
Cashner, Andrew	L	.223	265	59	13	3	4	22	28	51	.298	.340
Throws Right	R	.279	305	85	14	2	15	48	30	57	.347	.485
Castillo, Diego	L	.271	96	26	3	0	4	8	10	32	.340	.427
Throws Right	R	.205	161	33	6	2	4	17	16	49	.295	.342
Castillo, Luis	L	.209	358	75	17	1	13	33	45	123	.308	.372
Throws Right	R	.194	330	64	12	0	9	35	34	103	.270	.312
Castro, Miguel	L	.258	93	24	3	0	3	18	20	16	.386	.387
Throws Right	R	.218	179	39	9	0	7	36	21	55	.293	.385
Cease, Dylan	L	.285	144	41	10	0	9	21	18	35	.372	.542
Throws Right	R	.257	144	37	3	2	6	23	17	46	.333	.431
Cessa, Luis	L	.278	126	35	5	1	4	15	12	31	.343	.429
Throws Right	R	.223	179	40	8	0	10	23	19	44	.300	.436
Chacin, Jhoulys	L	.283	184	52	11	2	11	35	27	31	.377	.543
Throws Right	R	.278	227	63	9	0	14	32	19	70	.339	.502
Chafin, Andrew	L	.258	124	32	4	0	3	10	8	39	.313	.363
Throws Left	R	.256	78	20	0	0	3	12	10	29	.341	.372
Chapman, Aroldis	L	.163	49	8	3	0	0	6	5	23	.236	.224
Throws Left	R	.192	156	30	4	0	3	11	20	62	.285	.276

Pitcher	vs	Avg	AB	H	2B	3B	HR	RBI	BB	SO	OBP	Slg
Chargois, JT	L	.235	17	4	2	0	0	3	3	6	.348	.353
Throws Right	R	.283	60	17	2	1	4	17	2	22	.308	.550
Chatwood, Tyler	L	.306	121	37	6	0	3	16	17	33	.393	.430
Throws Right	R	.176	159	28	4	0	5	16	20	41	.284	.296
Chavez, Jesse	L	.248	129	32	7	0	4	16	8	34	.303	.395
Throws Right	R	.281	178	50	13	2	8	31	14	38	.340	.511
Chen, Wei-Yin	L	.301	103	31	6	0	7	24	5	22	.348	.563
Throws Left	R	.316	177	56	14	2	8	28	13	41	.368	.554
Chirinos, Yonny	L	.189	227	43	9	3	7	22	18	56	.248	.348
Throws Right	R	.255	271	69	10	0	16	34	10	58	.289	.469
Cimber, Adam	L	.296	54	16	5	0	3	11	5	10	.387	.556
Throws Right	R	.244	164	40	5	1	3	17	14	31	.304	.341
Cishek, Steve	L	.216	88	19	2	0	4	12	16	26	.358	.375
Throws Right	R	.206	141	29	4	0	3	12	13	31	.285	.298
Cisnero, Jose	L	.298	57	17	4	1	2	11	11	16	.423	.509
Throws Right	R	.228	79	18	3	1	3	10	8	24	.303	.405
Civale, Aaron	L	.235	81	19	10	1	1	7	6	24	.272	.420
Throws Right	R	.203	123	25	5	1	3	10	10	22	.269	.333
Clarke, Taylor	L	.252	163	41	10	1	11	27	21	31	.342	.528
Throws Right	R	.274	164	45	7	3	12	25	9	37	.320	.573
Clase, Emmanuel	L	.227	44	10	3	1	1	4	2	10	.277	.409
Throws Right	R	.233	43	10	3	0	1	4	4	11	.298	.372
Claudio, Alex	L	.218	119	26	7	0	4	15	9	23	.301	.378
Throws Left	R	.274	113	31	8	1	4	17	15	21	.357	.469
Clevinger, Mike	L	.219	237	52	15	0	5	20	28	74	.301	.346
Throws Right	R	.198	222	44	9	1	5	13	9	95	.236	.315
Clippard, Tyler	L	.123	106	13	1	2	3	9	8	31	.210	.255
Throws Right	R	.227	110	25	10	0	5	15	7	33	.292	.455
Cobb, Alex	L	.292	24	7	0	0	3	4	1	0	.320	.667
Throws Right	R	.412	34	14	5	0	6	9	1	8	.429	1.088
Cole, A.J.	L	.317	41	13	4	0	2	5	1	11	.326	.561
Throws Right	R	.273	66	18	5	0	2	11	7	19	.338	.439
Cole, Gerrit	L	.175	383	67	15	1	17	37	30	182	.235	.352
Throws Right	R	.198	379	75	15	0	12	23	18	144	.238	.332
Cole, Taylor	L	.256	90	23	5	0	1	9	14	24	.362	.344
Throws Right	R	.310	113	35	10	1	1	25	10	26	.365	.442
Collins, Tim	L	.286	14	4	2	0	1	1	2	0	.375	.643
Throws Left	R	.250	20	5	1	0	0	1	1	4	.273	.300
Colome, Alex	L	.190	100	19	6	0	3	14	8	30	.248	.340
Throws Right	R	.192	120	23	4	2	4	16	15	25	.283	.358
Conley, Adam	L	.336	107	36	10	2	1	12	9	19	.398	.495
Throws Left	R	.286	140	40	7	1	9	25	20	34	.377	.543
Coonrod, Sam	L	.207	29	6	1	0	1	4	10	4	.425	.345
Throws Right	R	.200	65	13	1	0	2	6	5	16	.288	.308
Corbin, Patrick	L	.190	137	26	2	0	2	6	13	60	.260	.248
Throws Left	R	.235	609	143	35	1	22	67	57	178	.300	.404
Cordero, Jimmy	L	.163	49	8	2	0	1	5	9	12	.305	.265
Throws Right	R	.217	83	18	3	1	3	5	2	19	.253	.386
Cortes, Nestor	L	.344	90	31	5	0	6	18	7	23	.394	.600
Throws Left	R	.249	177	44	4	0	10	27	21	46	.327	.441
Covey, Dylan	L	.385	109	42	7	0	6	27	19	19	.477	.615
Throws Right	R	.243	136	33	6	0	6	23	9	22	.302	.419
Crichton, Stefan	L	.146	41	6	1	0	2	6	4	15	.239	.317
Throws Right	R	.236	72	17	2	0	1	9	4	18	.286	.306
Crick, Kyle	L	.210	81	17	3	1	3	10	12	24	.347	.383
Throws Right	R	.235	102	24	3	0	7	21	23	37	.383	.471
Cueto, Johnny	L	.280	25	7	2	1	3	7	2	5	.333	.800
Throws Right	R	.129	31	4	1	0	0	2	7	8	.289	.161
Darvish, Yu	L	.243	342	83	13	3	19	40	23	101	.301	.465
Throws Right	R	.181	315	57	10	1	14	32	33	128	.266	.352
Davies, Zach	L	.254	307	78	14	3	12	40	26	45	.315	.436
Throws Right	R	.258	299	77	13	2	8	28	25	57	.312	.395
Davis, Austin	L	.269	26	7	1	0	1	2	5	10	.387	.423
Throws Left	R	.273	55	15	2	0	5	11	9	14	.403	.582
Davis, Rookie	L	.300	20	6	3	0	2	6	5	4	.423	.750
Throws Right	R	.300	20	6	1	0	1	2	3	6	.391	.500
Davis, Wade	L	.280	75	21	6	1	0	13	13	17	.393	.387
Throws Right	R	.300	100	30	3	0	7	19	16	25	.402	.540
Dayton, Grant	L	.250	16	4	0	0	2	4	2	4	.333	.625
Throws Left	R	.258	31	8	0	0	2	3	2	10	.303	.452
De Leon, Jose	L	.143	7	1	0	0	0	1	2	3	.333	.143
Throws Right	R	.222	9	2	0	0	0	1	1	4	.417	.222
De Los Santos, Enyel	L	.500	8	4	0	0	2	4	2	1	.600	1.250
Throws Right	R	.273	33	9	0	0	2	4	3	8	.333	.455
deGrom, Jacob	L	.213	314	67	8	1	9	25	29	102	.288	.331
Throws Right	R	.202	431	87	20	0	10	29	15	153	.232	.318

Pitchers vs. Left-Handed and Right-Handed Batters

Pitcher	vs	Avg	AB	H	2B	3B	HR	RBI	BB	SO	OBP	Slg
Del Pozo, Miguel	L	.353	17	6	1	0	0	1	5	6	.478	.412
Throws Left	R	.222	18	4	0	0	3	7	3	5	.333	.722
DeSclafani, Anthony	L	.246	317	78	16	1	17	42	39	81	.331	.464
Throws Right	R	.230	318	73	12	0	12	29	10	86	.257	.381
Despaigne, Odrisamer	L	.476	21	10	2	0	2	6	2	1	.542	.857
Throws Right	R	.368	38	14	3	1	1	8	5	6	.432	.579
Detwiler, Ross	L	.265	68	18	4	0	4	14	2	10	.292	.500
Throws Left	R	.318	214	68	9	1	16	37	25	36	.394	.593
Devenski, Chris	L	.273	139	38	8	0	7	19	14	40	.348	.482
Throws Right	R	.237	131	31	5	3	6	23	7	32	.275	.458
Diaz, Edwin	L	.193	88	17	3	0	5	10	13	45	.294	.398
Throws Right	R	.299	137	41	7	0	10	31	9	54	.358	.569
Diaz, Jairo	L	.216	102	22	6	0	2	15	13	25	.304	.333
Throws Right	R	.281	121	34	7	3	5	20	6	38	.323	.512
Diaz, Miguel	L	.625	8	5	2	1	0	2	0	1	.700	1.125
Throws Right	R	.222	18	4	1	0	1	3	1	3	.263	.444
Diehl, Phillip	L	.200	15	3	2	0	0	2	2	5	.333	.333
Throws Left	R	.412	17	7	3	0	1	5	0	3	.412	.765
Diekman, Jake	L	.224	85	19	6	0	0	10	16	21	.362	.294
Throws Left	R	.210	143	30	6	1	3	17	23	63	.347	.329
Dobnak, Randy	L	.175	57	10	2	0	0	3	1	9	.203	.211
Throws Right	R	.321	53	17	1	0	1	4	4	14	.390	.396
Dominguez, Seranthony	L	.372	43	16	1	1	2	8	3	9	.426	.581
Throws Right	R	.151	53	8	1	0	1	5	9	20	.274	.226
Doolittle, Sean	L	.221	77	17	3	3	2	10	2	23	.241	.416
Throws Left	R	.279	165	46	7	0	9	24	13	43	.339	.485
Dowdy, Kyle	L	.214	28	6	1	0	1	4	7	7	.351	.357
Throws Right	R	.333	60	20	3	0	3	16	11	10	.444	.533
Drake, Oliver	L	.147	102	15	2	0	1	2	2	33	.163	.196
Throws Right	R	.216	97	21	6	0	8	18	17	37	.339	.526
Duffey, Tyler	L	.196	102	20	3	0	4	9	5	28	.245	.343
Throws Right	R	.205	117	24	3	0	4	12	9	54	.268	.333
Duffy, Danny	L	.257	113	29	8	0	4	17	14	30	.354	.434
Throws Left	R	.249	385	96	20	1	17	48	32	85	.313	.439
Dugger, Robert	L	.300	60	18	5	1	2	12	13	8	.449	.517
Throws Right	R	.214	70	15	3	0	4	12	4	17	.260	.429
Duke, Zach	L	.250	52	13	4	0	3	10	11	14	.385	.500
Throws Left	R	.250	32	8	1	0	1	4	7	4	.400	.375
Dull, Ryan	L	.400	25	10	2	0	2	5	5	4	.516	.720
Throws Right	R	.417	36	15	8	0	3	12	2	11	.436	.889
Dunn, Justin	L	.000	4	0	0	0	0	0	8	1	.667	.000
Throws Right	R	.133	15	2	0	0	0	2	1	4	.167	.133
Dunn, Mike	L	.212	33	7	1	1	2	14	2	10	.231	.485
Throws Left	R	.313	32	10	2	0	2	4	4	5	.389	.563
Duplantier, Jon	L	.250	60	15	4	0	0	5	11	20	.375	.317
Throws Right	R	.308	78	24	5	0	2	12	7	14	.389	.449
DuRapau, Montana	L	.400	35	14	5	0	3	13	7	8	.500	.800
Throws Right	R	.295	44	13	1	1	1	8	2	14	.354	.432
Dyson, Sam	L	.225	89	20	3	0	3	8	5	23	.281	.360
Throws Right	R	.234	141	33	6	1	3	16	8	32	.280	.355
Eades, Ryan	L	.333	12	4	1	0	0	0	5	2	.556	.417
Throws Right	R	.226	31	7	2	0	2	6	1	8	.250	.484
Edwards, Jon	L	.222	9	2	1	0	0	0	2	2	.462	.333
Throws Right	R	.158	19	3	1	0	2	3	4	3	.304	.526
Edwards Jr., Carl	L	.222	18	4	0	0	1	6	8	4	.464	.389
Throws Right	R	.178	45	8	1	0	2	9	5	15	.260	.333
Eflin, Zach	L	.268	280	75	17	0	17	44	34	56	.348	.511
Throws Right	R	.268	362	97	17	0	11	38	14	73	.303	.406
Eickhoff, Jerad	L	.308	78	24	5	1	10	21	7	15	.372	.782
Throws Right	R	.236	144	34	6	0	8	16	11	36	.295	.444
Elias, Roenis	L	.368	57	21	1	0	5	18	9	11	.455	.649
Throws Left	R	.181	138	25	6	0	5	21	9	36	.235	.333
Eovaldi, Nathan	L	.266	124	33	5	0	12	24	18	34	.363	.597
Throws Right	R	.285	137	39	8	0	4	19	17	36	.368	.431
Erlin, Robbie	L	.333	96	32	2	0	2	9	6	24	.379	.417
Throws Left	R	.296	135	40	9	0	4	24	9	28	.333	.452
Escobar, Luis	L	.556	9	5	1	0	0	2	2	1	.667	.667
Throws Right	R	.385	13	5	1	0	1	3	2	1	.438	.692
Eshelman, Tom	L	.241	58	14	2	0	4	12	6	9	.318	.483
Throws Right	R	.359	92	33	4	0	8	17	5	13	.388	.663
Estevez, Carlos	L	.287	122	35	11	0	5	24	14	24	.353	.500
Throws Right	R	.222	158	35	9	0	7	20	9	57	.268	.411
Estrada, Marco	L	.146	41	6	0	2	3	7	1	7	.186	.463
Throws Right	R	.315	54	17	3	0	4	6	7	4	.413	.593
Fairbanks, Peter	L	.182	44	8	4	0	0	5	2	17	.217	.273
Throws Right	R	.378	45	17	3	0	5	11	8	11	.472	.778

Pitcher	vs	Avg	AB	H	2B	3B	HR	RBI	BB	SO	OBP	Slg
Familia, Jeurys	L	.312	93	29	3	1	3	15	19	23	.430	.462
Throws Right	R	.248	133	33	11	0	4	16	23	40	.367	.421
Faria, Jake	L	.302	43	13	4	0	1	5	8	11	.404	.465
Throws Right	R	.395	38	15	3	0	4	6	4	8	.465	.789
Farmer, Buck	L	.270	100	27	7	2	1	15	11	22	.342	.410
Throws Right	R	.232	151	35	7	1	7	28	13	51	.306	.430
Farrell, Luke	L	.167	18	3	0	0	2	3	1	5	.200	.500
Throws Right	R	.115	26	3	0	1	1	4	2	7	.179	.308
Fedde, Erick	L	.333	150	50	9	1	6	21	16	19	.393	.527
Throws Right	R	.217	143	31	7	0	5	15	17	22	.309	.371
Feierabend, Ryan	L	.571	7	4	0	0	0	4	0	2	.571	.571
Throws Left	R	.333	21	7	2	0	2	3	1	2	.364	.714
Feliz, Michael	L	.194	98	19	5	1	4	11	16	27	.304	.388
Throws Right	R	.227	110	25	2	0	7	21	11	46	.309	.436
Ferguson, Caleb	L	.194	72	14	4	0	4	8	10	22	.306	.417
Throws Left	R	.263	95	25	6	0	3	17	17	32	.390	.421
Fernandez, Jose	L	.333	6	2	1	0	0	2	2	1	.444	.500
Throws Left	R	.400	10	4	1	0	1	2	3	1	.571	.800
Fernandez, Junior	L	.100	10	1	0	0	0	0	5	4	.471	.100
Throws Right	R	.235	34	8	0	0	2	9	1	12	.297	.412
Festa, Matt	L	.214	28	6	2	0	1	6	7	8	.371	.393
Throws Right	R	.255	55	14	3	2	4	11	5	13	.328	.600
Fiers, Mike	L	.248	335	83	13	1	11	25	23	63	.296	.391
Throws Right	R	.239	348	83	6	1	19	46	30	63	.312	.425
Fillmyer, Heath	L	.333	39	13	3	0	2	11	7	7	.429	.564
Throws Right	R	.288	52	15	2	0	4	10	5	8	.367	.558
Flaherty, Jack	L	.202	357	72	12	0	14	30	30	97	.263	.353
Throws Right	R	.182	347	63	12	1	11	29	25	134	.249	.317
Flexen, Chris	L	.158	19	3	2	0	0	2	9	4	.429	.263
Throws Right	R	.324	37	12	4	0	1	9	4	6	.381	.514
Floro, Dylan	L	.339	59	20	4	0	2	10	8	15	.426	.508
Throws Right	R	.211	123	26	4	1	2	20	6	27	.252	.309
Flynn, Brian	L	.298	47	14	3	0	0	5	6	10	.389	.362
Throws Left	R	.358	67	24	6	0	2	14	11	12	.451	.537
Foltynewicz, Mike	L	.228	206	47	9	2	11	25	17	42	.289	.451
Throws Right	R	.258	240	62	10	2	12	33	20	63	.318	.467
Font, Wilmer	L	.248	129	32	11	0	8	23	17	44	.333	.519
Throws Right	R	.238	193	46	15	1	9	26	12	51	.292	.466
Franco, Enderson	L	.200	10	2	0	0	1	1	0	1	.200	.500
Throws Right	R	.222	9	2	1	0	0	0	1	3	.300	.333
Freeland, Kyle	L	.298	84	25	4	0	3	10	4	21	.330	.452
Throws Left	R	.295	342	101	17	7	22	67	35	58	.360	.579
Fried, Max	L	.231	143	33	7	0	4	15	10	45	.290	.364
Throws Left	R	.281	501	141	26	0	17	56	37	128	.333	.435
Fry, Jace	L	.193	83	16	6	0	0	10	19	30	.352	.265
Throws Left	R	.235	119	28	4	0	7	15	24	38	.368	.445
Fry, Paul	L	.250	100	25	5	0	6	18	13	21	.359	.480
Throws Left	R	.244	119	29	6	1	1	11	16	34	.343	.336
Fulmer, Carson	L	.241	29	7	1	0	2	9	5	6	.353	.483
Throws Right	R	.244	78	19	2	0	3	15	15	19	.374	.385
Gagnon, Drew	L	.432	44	19	1	0	7	14	2	5	.468	.932
Throws Right	R	.234	64	15	5	0	4	15	5	12	.300	.500
Gallegos, Giovanny	L	.149	114	17	6	0	4	11	8	43	.211	.307
Throws Right	R	.186	145	27	4	1	5	11	8	50	.237	.331
Gallen, Zac	L	.207	150	31	9	1	5	10	16	48	.292	.380
Throws Right	R	.217	143	31	7	0	3	12	20	48	.319	.329
Gant, John	L	.221	77	17	6	0	3	11	17	18	.362	.416
Throws Right	R	.215	158	34	5	1	1	15	17	42	.291	.278
Garcia, Bryan	L	.273	11	3	0	0	0	0	2	4	.385	.273
Throws Right	R	.353	17	6	2	0	1	8	3	3	.450	.647
Garcia, Edgar	L	.313	48	15	3	0	5	12	10	13	.424	.688
Throws Right	R	.242	95	23	2	0	6	12	16	32	.348	.453
Garcia, Jarlin	L	.247	77	19	3	1	0	6	5	13	.289	.312
Throws Left	R	.194	108	21	2	0	4	12	11	26	.279	.324
Garcia, Luis	L	.260	100	26	1	0	5	13	19	25	.375	.420
Throws Right	R	.255	137	35	4	0	8	25	14	32	.344	.460
Garcia, Rico	L	.400	10	4	2	0	1	2	3	0	.538	.900
Throws Right	R	.333	15	5	1	0	2	5	2	2	.412	.800
Garcia, Yimi	L	.171	82	14	2	1	7	8	4	21	.218	.476
Throws Right	R	.182	143	26	7	0	8	17	10	45	.258	.399
Garrett, Amir	L	.202	94	19	3	0	2	11	17	42	.342	.298
Throws Left	R	.221	113	25	6	0	5	14	18	36	.333	.407
Garrett, Reed	L	.286	21	6	3	0	1	2	7	5	.464	.571
Throws Right	R	.429	42	18	5	0	2	12	6	5	.510	.690
Gausman, Kevin	L	.265	181	48	11	0	8	33	21	59	.337	.459
Throws Right	R	.295	220	65	11	1	7	32	11	55	.339	.450

Pitchers vs. Left-Handed and Right-Handed Batters

Pitcher	vs	Avg	AB	H	2B	3B	HR	RBI	BB	SO	OBP	Slg
Gaviglio, Sam	L	.277	148	41	13	0	5	20	12	29	.329	.466
Throws Right	R	.206	214	44	5	0	13	29	10	59	.251	.411
Gearrin, Cory	L	.276	76	21	3	1	3	11	10	14	.368	.461
Throws Right	R	.252	135	34	4	1	2	12	15	33	.338	.341
German, Domingo	L	.242	310	75	15	0	20	40	23	87	.301	.484
Throws Right	R	.210	238	50	12	0	10	24	16	66	.265	.387
Gibaut, Ian	L	.185	27	5	2	0	0	3	5	9	.303	.259
Throws Right	R	.292	24	7	2	0	1	7	5	7	.419	.500
Gibson, Kyle	L	.288	316	91	14	3	11	46	29	71	.358	.456
Throws Right	R	.262	321	84	16	1	12	45	27	89	.320	.430
Giles, Ken	L	.174	92	16	3	0	4	8	7	36	.232	.337
Throws Right	R	.202	99	20	7	0	1	5	10	47	.275	.303
Ginkel, Kevin	L	.200	40	8	1	0	2	3	2	16	.238	.375
Throws Right	R	.152	46	7	2	0	0	3	7	12	.264	.196
Giolito, Lucas	L	.172	308	53	13	1	11	28	26	106	.237	.328
Throws Right	R	.235	332	78	15	3	13	38	31	122	.305	.416
Givens, Mychal	L	.267	90	24	3	2	7	18	13	29	.352	.578
Throws Right	R	.179	140	25	1	1	6	13	13	57	.258	.329
Glasnow, Tyler	L	.155	97	15	1	1	1	3	6	37	.202	.216
Throws Right	R	.212	118	25	4	0	3	6	8	39	.262	.322
Godley, Zack	L	.282	188	53	13	3	7	29	19	39	.346	.495
Throws Right	R	.259	166	43	7	1	7	30	23	31	.364	.440
Gomez, Jeanmar	L	.154	13	2	1	0	1	2	2	3	.250	.462
Throws Right	R	.412	51	21	6	0	1	15	4	7	.456	.588
Gonsolin, Tony	L	.182	77	14	4	0	2	7	8	20	.259	.312
Throws Right	R	.174	69	12	5	0	2	8	7	17	.256	.333
Gonzales, Marco	L	.302	205	62	12	0	8	35	11	29	.341	.478
Throws Left	R	.251	589	148	38	3	15	55	45	118	.305	.402
Gonzalez, Chi Chi	L	.250	108	27	8	1	5	13	22	21	.374	.481
Throws Right	R	.242	132	32	5	0	6	22	11	25	.306	.417
Gonzalez, Gio	L	.147	68	10	2	1	1	2	7	16	.227	.250
Throws Left	R	.257	257	66	12	5	8	32	30	62	.334	.436
Goody, Nick	L	.226	53	12	3	0	2	7	10	14	.344	.396
Throws Right	R	.188	96	18	2	1	5	17	12	36	.275	.385
Gott, Trevor	L	.208	72	15	3	0	0	11	5	19	.253	.250
Throws Right	R	.220	118	26	2	1	4	16	12	38	.299	.356
Grace, Matt	L	.322	87	28	4	0	3	17	2	25	.352	.471
Throws Left	R	.317	104	33	9	0	8	26	8	10	.360	.635
Graterol, Brusdar	L	.214	14	3	0	0	1	4	2	2	.333	.429
Throws Right	R	.318	22	7	1	0	0	2	0	8	.318	.364
Gray, Jon	L	.272	265	72	17	4	8	36	37	69	.361	.457
Throws Right	R	.248	302	75	17	1	11	28	19	81	.298	.421
Gray, Sonny	L	.196	281	55	8	2	8	26	34	94	.290	.324
Throws Right	R	.196	341	67	13	2	9	29	34	111	.273	.326
Green, Chad	L	.246	126	31	6	2	4	15	8	54	.307	.421
Throws Right	R	.248	141	35	8	0	6	16	11	44	.310	.433
Greene, Shane	L	.266	94	25	3	0	4	11	8	29	.337	.426
Throws Right	R	.154	136	21	4	0	4	13	9	35	.211	.272
Gregerson, Luke	L	.364	11	4	0	0	0	3	1	1	.417	.364
Throws Right	R	.467	15	7	2	0	0	1	0	1	.467	.600
Greinke, Zack	L	.221	375	83	18	0	10	30	17	85	.257	.349
Throws Right	R	.235	392	92	19	2	11	40	13	102	.262	.378
Grotz, Zac	L	.154	26	4	0	0	0	1	1	7	.185	.154
Throws Right	R	.270	37	10	3	0	0	6	7	11	.391	.351
Gsellman, Robert	L	.283	92	26	9	0	2	19	12	24	.377	.446
Throws Right	R	.248	153	38	9	1	5	19	11	36	.312	.418
Guduan, Reymin	L	.375	8	3	1	0	1	4	1	0	.444	.875
Throws Left	R	.357	14	5	0	0	2	5	3	6	.444	.786
Guerra, Javier	L	.211	19	4	1	0	2	4	1	3	.238	.579
Throws Right	R	.231	13	3	1	0	1	2	2	3	.333	.538
Guerra, Javy	L	.268	112	30	5	1	5	18	7	21	.308	.464
Throws Right	R	.239	155	37	8	1	5	23	10	36	.289	.400
Guerra, Junior	L	.178	129	23	5	1	3	13	27	32	.327	.302
Throws Right	R	.206	170	35	7	0	8	26	9	45	.253	.388
Guerrero, Tayron	L	.264	72	19	4	0	4	16	16	21	.413	.486
Throws Right	R	.232	99	23	4	0	3	19	20	22	.371	.364
Guerrieri, Taylor	L	.304	46	14	0	2	2	7	8	16	.429	.522
Throws Right	R	.226	53	12	4	1	1	8	14	11	.388	.396
Guilbeau, Taylor	L	.227	22	5	0	1	1	6	1	4	.292	.455
Throws Left	R	.200	25	5	0	0	1	3	2	3	.259	.320
Gustave, Jandel	L	.242	33	8	3	0	0	1	4	6	.324	.333
Throws Right	R	.189	53	10	1	0	1	10	5	8	.246	.264
Hader, Josh	L	.143	63	9	2	1	5	6	2	34	.182	.444
Throws Left	R	.158	202	32	5	1	10	26	18	104	.238	.342
Hahn, Jesse	L	.000	5	0	0	0	0	0	5	1	.500	.000
Throws Right	R	.438	16	7	2	0	1	6	1	6	.471	.750

Pitcher	vs	Avg	AB	H	2B	3B	HR	RBI	BB	SO	OBP	Slg
Hale, David	L	.274	62	17	7	1	0	6	3	6	.303	.419
Throws Right	R	.256	86	22	5	1	2	8	4	17	.297	.407
Hall, Matt	L	.310	29	9	2	1	1	10	5	8	.429	.552
Throws Left	R	.279	68	19	1	0	3	10	10	19	.372	.426
Hamels, Cole	L	.265	117	31	3	0	3	14	10	26	.331	.368
Throws Left	R	.259	425	110	25	0	14	43	46	117	.335	.416
Hammer, J. D.	L	.208	24	5	2	0	1	1	4	4	.321	.417
Throws Right	R	.222	45	10	1	1	1	9	8	9	.340	.356
Hand, Brad	L	.196	56	11	1	0	0	4	6	21	.286	.214
Throws Left	R	.258	163	42	12	0	6	17	12	63	.320	.442
Happ, J.A.	L	.228	158	36	4	0	6	15	11	40	.285	.367
Throws Left	R	.268	463	124	23	1	28	66	38	100	.327	.503
Hardy, Blaine	L	.235	51	12	2	1	7	11	6	11	.305	.725
Throws Left	R	.230	113	26	3	1	3	15	7	18	.270	.354
Harper, Ryne	L	.265	102	27	7	1	3	19	5	30	.299	.441
Throws Right	R	.250	108	27	4	0	4	17	5	20	.282	.398
Harris, Will	L	.207	121	25	1	0	2	4	3	34	.226	.264
Throws Right	R	.183	93	17	2	0	4	11	11	28	.269	.333
Hart, Donnie	L	.214	14	3	0	0	0	0	1	2	.267	.214
Throws Left	R	.091	11	1	0	0	0	0	3	1	.286	.091
Hartlieb, Geoff	L	.394	71	28	4	2	7	28	5	16	.423	.803
Throws Right	R	.312	77	24	6	0	1	15	13	22	.402	.429
Harvey, Hunter	L	.143	7	1	1	0	0	0	3	3	.400	.286
Throws Right	R	.133	15	2	0	1	1	1	1	8	.188	.467
Harvey, Joe	L	.091	22	2	0	0	1	3	7	7	.300	.227
Throws Right	R	.348	46	16	1	1	2	10	6	10	.444	.543
Harvey, Matt	L	.295	105	31	10	2	5	19	18	20	.397	.571
Throws Right	R	.258	124	32	5	0	8	19	11	19	.324	.492
Heaney, Andrew	L	.321	84	27	1	0	6	13	6	25	.374	.548
Throws Left	R	.231	286	66	14	0	14	35	24	93	.302	.427
Heller, Ben	L	.250	8	2	0	0	0	0	3	2	.455	.250
Throws Right	R	.250	16	4	1	0	1	1	0	7	.250	.500
Hellickson, Jeremy	L	.329	73	24	6	0	6	14	9	11	.398	.658
Throws Right	R	.264	87	23	4	0	3	15	11	19	.354	.414
Helsley, Ryan	L	.231	65	15	4	1	3	12	7	14	.301	.462
Throws Right	R	.257	74	19	5	0	2	6	5	18	.304	.405
Hembree, Heath	L	.222	63	14	4	3	4	11	8	17	.310	.571
Throws Right	R	.225	89	20	4	0	3	8	10	29	.324	.371
Hendricks, Kyle	L	.237	317	75	23	1	7	30	19	84	.287	.382
Throws Right	R	.260	358	93	16	1	12	36	13	66	.293	.411
Hendriks, Liam	L	.257	152	39	7	1	4	19	10	56	.309	.395
Throws Right	R	.145	152	22	9	0	1	14	11	68	.200	.224
Herget, Jimmy	L	.364	11	4	0	0	2	3	1	0	.417	.909
Throws Right	R	.333	12	4	2	0	0	3	2	0	.429	.500
Hernandez, Darwinzon	L	.089	45	4	2	0	0	1	9	31	.255	.133
Throws Left	R	.319	72	23	8	0	1	8	17	26	.462	.472
Hernandez, David	L	.351	74	26	9	1	5	23	6	28	.402	.703
Throws Right	R	.273	99	27	4	2	2	16	14	25	.357	.414
Hernandez, Elieser	L	.260	146	38	10	1	11	24	17	36	.341	.568
Throws Right	R	.226	168	38	8	1	9	19	9	49	.296	.446
Hernandez, Felix	L	.294	119	35	10	1	6	20	14	27	.373	.546
Throws Right	R	.289	173	50	13	0	11	29	11	30	.347	.555
Hernandez, Jonathan	L	.241	29	7	1	0	2	5	7	7	.378	.483
Throws Right	R	.200	35	7	0	0	1	4	6	12	.317	.286
Herrera, Kelvin	L	.296	81	24	3	0	2	14	10	16	.370	.407
Throws Right	R	.283	127	36	7	1	6	28	13	37	.352	.496
Hess, David	L	.266	124	33	7	0	5	16	16	26	.357	.444
Throws Right	R	.300	203	61	10	2	23	53	14	42	.342	.709
Hicks, Jordan	L	.250	36	9	3	0	1	4	7	12	.386	.417
Throws Right	R	.113	62	7	0	0	1	3	4	19	.167	.161
Hildenberger, Trevor	L	.333	24	8	4	0	0	5	2	5	.370	.500
Throws Right	R	.423	52	22	4	0	2	17	5	10	.492	.615
Hill, Rich	L	.192	52	10	1	0	1	4	5	15	.263	.269
Throws Left	R	.233	163	38	6	0	9	16	13	57	.304	.436
Hill, Tim	L	.186	59	11	1	0	0	8	5	11	.262	.203
Throws Left	R	.238	84	20	4	0	4	18	8	28	.326	.429
Hirano, Yoshihisa	L	.250	88	22	1	0	4	14	10	28	.323	.398
Throws Right	R	.248	117	29	8	0	3	16	12	33	.331	.393
Hoffman, Jeff	L	.243	140	34	8	0	7	14	19	42	.335	.450
Throws Right	R	.326	132	43	10	1	14	35	15	26	.404	.735
Holder, Jonathan	L	.262	65	17	3	1	2	10	7	19	.342	.431
Throws Right	R	.252	103	26	4	0	6	22	4	27	.287	.466
Holland, Derek	L	.192	99	19	2	0	1	7	12	22	.286	.242
Throws Left	R	.288	219	63	12	1	19	56	33	60	.385	.612
Holland, Greg	L	.180	61	11	2	0	2	10	12	22	.315	.311
Throws Right	R	.215	65	14	4	0	3	6	12	19	.329	.415

Pitchers vs. Left-Handed and Right-Handed Batters

Pitcher	vs	Avg	AB	H	2B	3B	HR	RBI	BB	SO	OBP	Slg
Holmes, Clay	L	.266	79	21	5	1	1	9	19	18	.420	.392
Throws Right	R	.209	115	24	4	0	4	22	17	38	.345	.348
Houser, Adrian	L	.277	184	51	9	4	6	25	23	54	.357	.467
Throws Right	R	.217	230	50	5	0	8	25	14	63	.273	.343
Howard, Sam	L	.265	34	9	0	0	2	6	5	11	.375	.441
Throws Left	R	.286	42	12	3	0	3	11	5	12	.388	.571
Hoyt, James	L	.333	15	5	0	1	2	2	2	4	.412	.867
Throws Right	R	.067	15	1	0	0	0	0	0	6	.067	.067
Huang, Wei-Chieh	L	.167	12	2	2	0	0	1	2	1	.286	.333
Throws Right	R	.429	14	6	2	0	0	4	3	1	.556	.571
Hudson, Dakota	L	.260	312	81	26	0	11	35	55	62	.369	.449
Throws Right	R	.232	340	79	11	0	11	39	31	74	.308	.362
Hudson, Daniel	L	.205	117	24	10	0	3	10	12	22	.280	.368
Throws Right	R	.213	150	32	7	0	5	19	15	49	.292	.360
Hughes, Jared	L	.193	83	16	2	0	2	10	9	12	.269	.289
Throws Right	R	.238	172	41	10	0	11	34	18	42	.318	.488
Iglesias, Raisel	L	.241	108	26	7	0	7	15	9	33	.299	.500
Throws Right	R	.240	146	35	6	1	5	19	12	56	.304	.397
Irvin, Cole	L	.365	52	19	3	0	2	8	3	11	.397	.538
Throws Left	R	.236	110	26	5	0	5	23	10	20	.311	.418
Jackson, Edwin	L	.326	141	46	13	2	9	31	17	21	.406	.638
Throws Right	R	.373	158	59	12	1	14	44	15	31	.426	.728
Jackson, Jay	L	.250	40	10	3	0	3	12	8	15	.373	.550
Throws Right	R	.174	69	12	1	0	3	6	10	32	.288	.319
Jackson, Luke	L	.157	108	17	3	0	5	13	9	44	.222	.324
Throws Right	R	.331	178	59	6	0	5	31	17	62	.396	.449
James, Josh	L	.193	109	21	2	0	6	18	21	49	.328	.376
Throws Right	R	.212	118	25	5	1	4	16	14	51	.311	.373
Jansen, Kenley	L	.198	131	26	8	0	5	19	9	39	.255	.374
Throws Right	R	.229	109	25	4	1	4	13	7	41	.287	.394
Jeffress, Jeremy	L	.281	89	25	6	0	2	11	7	17	.333	.416
Throws Right	R	.259	112	29	4	0	3	15	10	29	.346	.375
Jennings, Dan	L	.231	13	3	0	0	0	2	4	5	.444	.231
Throws Left	R	.455	11	5	0	0	1	6	3	4	.571	.727
Jerez, Williams	L	.375	16	6	1	0	1	4	3	1	.474	.625
Throws Left	R	.261	23	6	1	1	1	2	6	8	.414	.522
Jewell, Jake	L	.326	43	14	3	1	3	9	4	10	.383	.651
Throws Right	R	.237	59	14	0	0	5	12	4	13	.313	.492
Jimenez, Eduardo	L	.150	20	3	1	0	0	3	2	3	.227	.200
Throws Right	R	.375	24	9	3	0	1	3	3	5	.444	.625
Jimenez, Joe	L	.262	103	27	4	1	5	13	13	38	.350	.466
Throws Right	R	.228	127	29	8	0	8	11	10	44	.300	.480
Johnson, Brian	L	.232	56	13	4	1	1	4	5	11	.295	.393
Throws Left	R	.357	112	40	13	0	5	24	18	20	.446	.607
Johnson, D.J.	L	.267	45	12	4	0	0	4	6	15	.353	.356
Throws Right	R	.229	48	11	1	1	1	9	13	9	.415	.354
Jones, Nate	L	.154	13	2	0	0	0	0	2	5	.267	.154
Throws Right	R	.308	26	8	0	0	2	6	5	5	.438	.538
Junis, Jakob	L	.298	372	111	23	2	13	57	31	90	.359	.476
Throws Right	R	.250	324	81	14	0	18	38	27	74	.317	.460
Jurado, Ariel	L	.281	228	64	18	3	7	39	17	32	.337	.478
Throws Right	R	.324	259	84	17	2	14	45	19	49	.363	.568
Kahnle, Tommy	L	.209	115	24	4	0	6	17	10	48	.278	.400
Throws Right	R	.191	110	21	4	1	3	13	10	40	.262	.327
Karinchak, James	L	.091	11	1	0	0	0	2	0	7	.083	.091
Throws Right	R	.222	9	2	1	0	0	0	1	1	.300	.333
Karns, Nathan	L	.000	8	0	0	0	0	0	0	4	.000	.000
Throws Right	R	.538	13	7	1	0	0	0	3	1	.647	.615
Kay, Anthony	L	.182	11	2	1	0	0	1	1	5	.250	.273
Throws Left	R	.283	46	13	2	0	0	6	4	8	.353	.326
Kela, Keone	L	.200	40	8	4	0	1	2	8	8	.333	.375
Throws Right	R	.164	67	11	5	0	2	6	3	25	.211	.328
Keller, Brad	L	.251	311	78	8	4	7	27	45	70	.350	.370
Throws Right	R	.243	313	76	11	6	8	41	25	52	.307	.393
Keller, Kyle	L	.200	10	2	0	0	0	0	3	3	.429	.200
Throws Right	R	.115	26	3	0	0	3	3	5	8	.281	.462
Keller, Mitch	L	.380	92	35	7	0	3	18	8	27	.431	.554
Throws Right	R	.322	115	37	10	3	3	18	8	38	.363	.539
Kelley, Shawn	L	.374	91	34	9	1	6	18	7	13	.424	.692
Throws Right	R	.214	98	21	2	0	6	11	4	30	.250	.418
Kelley, Trevor	L	.333	9	3	1	0	2	3	1	2	.364	1.111
Throws Right	R	.273	22	6	3	0	0	7	4	4	.345	.409
Kelly, Joe	L	.247	85	21	4	0	3	11	12	29	.347	.400
Throws Right	R	.241	116	28	6	0	3	15	10	33	.313	.371
Kelly, Merrill	L	.274	325	89	18	3	9	33	31	62	.337	.431
Throws Right	R	.247	384	95	20	1	20	57	26	96	.295	.461

Pitcher	vs	Avg	AB	H	2B	3B	HR	RBI	BB	SO	OBP	Slg
Kennedy, Ian	L	.226	124	28	4	0	4	10	10	40	.289	.355
Throws Right	R	.298	121	36	3	0	2	15	7	33	.336	.372
Kershaw, Clayton	L	.208	144	30	8	1	5	13	9	40	.258	.382
Throws Left	R	.225	510	115	15	2	23	44	32	149	.273	.398
Keuchel, Dallas	L	.189	74	14	4	1	2	7	6	25	.268	.351
Throws Left	R	.281	360	101	10	3	14	39	33	66	.353	.442
Kikuchi, Yusei	L	.263	133	35	8	1	8	18	7	27	.305	.519
Throws Left	R	.304	527	160	33	5	28	78	43	89	.359	.545
Kimbrel, Craig	L	.233	43	10	2	0	4	9	3	16	.306	.558
Throws Right	R	.289	38	11	3	0	5	6	9	14	.426	.763
Kingham, Nick	L	.355	110	39	9	2	7	24	11	20	.413	.664
Throws Right	R	.328	119	39	13	0	4	17	14	26	.398	.538
Kinley, Tyler	L	.243	70	17	5	0	2	15	14	17	.365	.400
Throws Right	R	.234	111	26	2	0	3	13	22	29	.363	.333
Kintzler, Brandon	L	.163	80	13	4	1	1	7	7	17	.247	.275
Throws Right	R	.256	129	33	5	2	4	14	6	31	.297	.419
Kittredge, Andrew	L	.317	63	20	3	1	3	11	6	17	.375	.540
Throws Right	R	.237	131	31	2	0	4	12	6	41	.275	.344
Kline, Branden	L	.217	60	13	2	0	5	12	10	14	.324	.500
Throws Right	R	.310	100	31	8	0	4	15	9	20	.373	.510
Kluber, Corey	L	.286	63	18	6	0	3	15	9	16	.378	.524
Throws Right	R	.306	85	26	5	0	1	11	6	22	.366	.400
Koch, Matt	L	.400	45	18	6	0	5	15	2	3	.460	.867
Throws Right	R	.262	42	11	2	0	3	7	2	6	.326	.524
Kolarek, Adam	L	.178	107	19	3	0	2	12	3	26	.221	.262
Throws Left	R	.282	103	29	5	1	5	13	13	19	.362	.495
Kuhnel, Joel	L	.267	15	4	1	0	1	3	2	4	.353	.533
Throws Right	R	.182	22	4	0	0	0	1	3	5	.280	.182
Lakins, Travis	L	.231	39	9	0	1	0	1	7	11	.362	.282
Throws Right	R	.280	50	14	8	0	1	11	3	7	.309	.500
Lambert, Peter	L	.339	168	57	16	3	8	32	18	26	.411	.613
Throws Right	R	.305	203	62	13	2	10	35	18	31	.367	.537
Lamet, Dinelson	L	.242	149	36	9	0	6	20	14	52	.321	.423
Throws Right	R	.208	125	26	5	0	6	16	16	53	.301	.392
Lauer, Eric	L	.331	151	50	12	0	6	23	12	24	.384	.530
Throws Left	R	.247	438	108	23	0	14	52	39	114	.312	.395
Law, Derek	L	.237	118	28	8	1	3	16	21	34	.350	.398
Throws Right	R	.275	120	33	7	1	5	24	19	33	.385	.475
Leake, Mike	L	.296	426	126	29	2	19	50	20	73	.340	.507
Throws Right	R	.275	367	101	16	1	22	56	7	54	.289	.504
LeBlanc, Wade	L	.276	116	32	10	0	9	22	6	29	.311	.595
Throws Left	R	.296	382	113	23	2	19	59	25	63	.340	.516
Leclerc, Jose	L	.267	116	31	11	1	4	23	18	37	.366	.483
Throws Right	R	.158	133	21	5	1	3	13	21	63	.296	.278
Leone, Dominic	L	.243	70	17	4	0	3	9	14	22	.365	.429
Throws Right	R	.256	86	22	5	0	6	21	8	24	.319	.523
Lester, Jon	L	.319	163	52	9	2	4	22	10	35	.366	.472
Throws Left	R	.286	535	153	26	3	22	65	42	130	.339	.469
Liriano, Francisco	L	.194	72	14	4	0	2	8	13	22	.326	.333
Throws Left	R	.246	187	46	11	0	6	25	22	41	.329	.401
Littell, Zack	L	.255	55	14	4	0	1	8	5	13	.317	.382
Throws Right	R	.247	81	20	4	1	3	8	4	19	.282	.432
Loaisiga, Jonathan	L	.321	56	18	2	0	2	8	4	16	.371	.464
Throws Right	R	.210	62	13	5	0	4	10	12	21	.325	.484
Lockett, Walker	L	.429	42	18	1	0	1	6	4	8	.478	.524
Throws Right	R	.283	53	15	4	1	5	8	2	8	.321	.679
Lopez, Jorge	L	.332	244	81	16	1	15	47	22	55	.390	.590
Throws Right	R	.241	245	59	10	1	12	41	20	54	.312	.437
Lopez, Pablo	L	.303	218	66	15	2	9	32	17	45	.365	.514
Throws Right	R	.217	207	45	8	1	6	27	10	50	.272	.353
Lopez, Reynaldo	L	.290	355	103	18	3	16	50	45	76	.370	.493
Throws Right	R	.267	374	100	26	0	19	62	20	93	.313	.489
Lopez, Yoan	L	.211	90	19	4	0	6	11	4	17	.245	.456
Throws Right	R	.246	134	33	7	2	5	15	13	25	.305	.440
Lorenzen, Michael	L	.195	128	25	6	1	4	16	13	39	.278	.352
Throws Right	R	.240	179	43	6	0	5	20	15	46	.297	.358
Lovelady, Richard	L	.341	44	15	1	1	0	6	4	13	.408	.409
Throws Left	R	.366	41	15	7	0	2	10	4	4	.413	.683
Lucas, Josh	L	.222	18	4	0	0	1	3	5	3	.360	.389
Throws Right	R	.244	41	10	2	0	1	7	2	13	.273	.366
Lucchesi, Joey	L	.221	140	31	6	0	4	13	16	37	.301	.350
Throws Left	R	.236	479	113	26	3	19	56	40	121	.295	.422
Luciano, Elvis	L	.268	56	15	6	0	3	8	15	10	.423	.536
Throws Right	R	.280	75	21	5	0	1	9	9	17	.375	.387
Lugo, Seth	L	.167	120	20	4	1	4	8	8	41	.225	.317
Throws Right	R	.211	171	36	6	0	4	20	8	63	.261	.316

Pitchers vs. Left-Handed and Right-Handed Batters

Pitcher	vs	Avg	AB	H	2B	3B	HR	RBI	BB	SO	OBP	Slg
Luzardo, Jesus	L	.071	14	1	0	0	0	0	1	5	.133	.071
Throws Left	R	.143	28	4	2	0	1	1	2	11	.226	.321
Lyles, Jordan	L	.277	220	61	14	4	13	36	31	57	.367	.555
Throws Right	R	.220	318	70	14	1	12	29	24	89	.275	.384
Lynn, Lance	L	.267	412	110	25	3	6	40	41	97	.332	.386
Throws Right	R	.219	389	85	17	3	15	44	18	149	.264	.393
Lyons, Tyler	L	.286	21	6	0	0	3	5	1	11	.318	.714
Throws Left	R	.259	27	7	4	0	1	6	4	6	.375	.519
Maeda, Kenta	L	.247	279	69	13	2	11	40	30	65	.324	.427
Throws Right	R	.158	285	45	8	2	11	27	21	104	.219	.316
Magill, Matt	L	.280	82	23	8	0	3	11	11	20	.358	.488
Throws Right	R	.231	121	28	7	1	4	15	9	44	.295	.405
Mahle, Tyler	L	.282	234	66	11	1	15	41	21	53	.345	.530
Throws Right	R	.252	278	70	10	0	10	26	13	76	.294	.396
Manaea, Sean	L	.211	38	8	1	0	1	1	1	10	.250	.316
Throws Left	R	.129	62	8	2	0	2	3	6	20	.217	.258
Maples, Dillon	L	.083	12	1	0	0	0	0	5	4	.353	.083
Throws Right	R	.179	28	5	0	0	2	3	5	14	.378	.393
Margevicius, Nick	L	.390	82	32	11	1	5	20	2	10	.419	.732
Throws Left	R	.263	156	41	8	0	7	22	17	32	.339	.449
Markel, Parker	L	.279	43	12	4	0	3	5	8	15	.404	.581
Throws Right	R	.298	47	14	3	0	3	16	9	9	.431	.553
Marquez, German	L	.264	329	87	18	4	15	42	20	72	.308	.480
Throws Right	R	.254	342	87	9	0	14	43	15	103	.291	.404
Marshall, Evan	L	.221	68	15	4	0	0	3	10	12	.321	.279
Throws Right	R	.233	116	27	4	0	5	19	14	29	.313	.397
Martin, Brett	L	.269	104	28	2	0	3	17	8	27	.325	.375
Throws Left	R	.288	153	44	12	0	4	22	10	35	.331	.444
Martin, Chris	L	.202	99	20	2	0	5	9	1	35	.208	.374
Throws Right	R	.291	110	32	5	0	4	13	4	30	.313	.445
Martin, Corbin	L	.268	41	11	4	0	2	4	7	10	.375	.512
Throws Right	R	.308	39	12	1	0	6	7	5	9	.386	.795
Martinez, Carlos	L	.237	76	18	4	0	1	12	9	24	.322	.329
Throws Right	R	.208	101	21	2	0	1	8	9	29	.286	.257
Marvel, James	L	.250	32	8	2	0	2	3	3	3	.351	.500
Throws Right	R	.405	42	17	7	0	2	12	3	6	.444	.714
Maton, Phil	L	.293	58	17	5	0	1	10	5	12	.359	.431
Throws Right	R	.236	89	21	5	1	6	11	7	21	.299	.517
Matz, Steven	L	.270	126	34	7	1	5	17	11	29	.345	.460
Throws Left	R	.258	500	129	25	3	22	64	41	124	.318	.452
May, Dustin	L	.346	52	18	4	0	1	12	4	14	.404	.481
Throws Right	R	.188	80	15	2	0	1	3	1	18	.226	.250
May, Trevor	L	.185	124	23	4	0	5	12	7	37	.235	.339
Throws Right	R	.182	110	20	3	0	3	9	19	42	.306	.291
Mayers, Mike	L	.333	30	10	2	1	2	9	5	8	.444	.667
Throws Right	R	.239	46	11	3	1	1	5	6	8	.327	.413
Mayza, Tim	L	.211	95	20	7	0	4	11	13	23	.312	.411
Throws Left	R	.248	101	25	6	0	4	17	14	32	.333	.426
Mazza, Chris	L	.296	27	8	4	0	0	4	3	4	.406	.444
Throws Right	R	.351	37	13	5	1	0	6	2	7	.405	.541
McCarthy, Kevin	L	.297	91	27	8	0	2	16	13	9	.374	.451
Throws Right	R	.277	148	41	11	0	2	25	8	29	.321	.392
McClain, Reggie	L	.273	33	9	4	0	0	6	8	2	.415	.394
Throws Right	R	.265	49	13	3	0	2	10	5	9	.333	.449
McFarland, T.J.	L	.292	120	35	6	1	3	22	9	22	.336	.433
Throws Left	R	.343	105	36	7	1	3	14	11	13	.410	.514
McGee, Jake	L	.235	68	16	2	1	3	16	4	15	.267	.426
Throws Left	R	.326	95	31	6	1	8	20	7	20	.390	.663
McGowin, Kyle	L	.333	33	11	1	0	3	7	1	7	.343	.636
Throws Right	R	.306	36	11	1	0	4	12	3	11	.375	.667
McHugh, Collin	L	.174	132	23	6	1	6	19	18	45	.278	.371
Throws Right	R	.264	148	39	13	1	6	20	12	37	.321	.486
McKay, Brendan	L	.220	50	11	5	0	0	6	2	8	.250	.320
Throws Left	R	.284	148	42	10	1	8	22	14	48	.344	.527
McKay, David	L	.244	45	11	5	0	0	5	7	14	.358	.356
Throws Right	R	.173	52	9	0	0	3	9	10	20	.306	.346
McRae, Alex	L	.358	53	19	2	0	5	14	7	7	.443	.679
Throws Right	R	.283	60	17	4	0	4	13	9	12	.394	.550
Means, John	L	.184	141	26	8	2	3	9	7	35	.223	.333
Throws Left	R	.249	449	112	25	1	20	59	31	86	.303	.443
Mejia, Adalberto	L	.261	46	12	4	0	1	13	8	12	.364	.413
Throws Left	R	.273	77	21	4	1	3	15	13	18	.378	.468
Melancon, Mark	L	.278	97	27	4	1	0	10	9	25	.340	.340
Throws Right	R	.265	166	44	5	0	4	16	9	43	.309	.367
Melville, Tim	L	.269	67	18	4	0	4	10	9	12	.354	.507
Throws Right	R	.281	57	16	1	0	5	8	5	12	.339	.561
Mendez, Yohander	L	.333	9	3	0	0	2	4	1	5	.400	1.000
Throws Left	R	.143	7	1	0	0	0	1	4	3	.455	.143
Menez, Conner	L	.182	22	4	0	0	1	3	3	7	.280	.318
Throws Left	R	.243	37	9	2	0	3	7	9	15	.383	.541
Mengden, Daniel	L	.320	128	41	12	1	4	15	21	21	.416	.523
Throws Right	R	.173	104	18	4	0	3	9	6	21	.216	.298
Middleton, Keynan	L	.000	6	0	0	0	0	0	2	2	.250	.000
Throws Right	R	.200	20	4	2	0	0	2	5	4	.360	.300
Mikolas, Miles	L	.284	335	95	20	1	11	39	23	72	.336	.448
Throws Right	R	.261	375	98	13	5	16	48	9	72	.288	.451
Miley, Wade	L	.207	145	30	3	0	7	16	14	33	.284	.372
Throws Left	R	.267	501	134	22	2	16	53	47	107	.332	.415
Miller, Andrew	L	.213	94	20	0	0	4	13	14	39	.333	.340
Throws Left	R	.236	106	25	2	0	7	21	13	31	.344	.453
Miller, Justin	L	.250	20	5	0	0	2	4	1	4	.286	.550
Throws Right	R	.289	38	11	0	0	3	8	3	7	.372	.526
Miller, Shelby	L	.256	78	20	3	0	3	16	13	15	.359	.410
Throws Right	R	.362	105	38	6	0	5	28	16	15	.449	.562
Mills, Alec	L	.321	56	18	4	1	2	3	6	13	.433	.536
Throws Right	R	.167	78	13	1	0	3	9	5	29	.235	.295
Milone, Tommy	L	.248	125	31	10	0	9	17	7	36	.291	.544
Throws Left	R	.238	298	71	19	1	15	36	16	58	.276	.460
Minaya, Juan	L	.279	43	12	5	0	0	2	6	9	.367	.395
Throws Right	R	.275	69	19	6	1	4	16	6	18	.351	.565
Minor, Mike	L	.249	185	46	6	0	7	23	13	49	.303	.395
Throws Left	R	.242	594	144	22	0	23	55	55	151	.310	.396
Minter, A.J.	L	.260	50	13	3	0	1	8	6	14	.339	.380
Throws Left	R	.324	71	23	6	0	2	12	17	21	.456	.493
Montas, Frankie	L	.231	199	46	14	1	4	16	12	62	.274	.372
Throws Right	R	.229	166	38	9	0	4	18	11	41	.291	.355
Montero, Rafael	L	.111	54	6	1	1	1	2	2	16	.143	.222
Throws Right	R	.327	52	17	2	0	4	6	3	18	.386	.596
Montgomery, Mike	L	.452	84	38	7	1	4	20	4	13	.484	.702
Throws Left	R	.273	275	75	16	0	14	38	30	56	.349	.484
Moore, Andrew	L	.375	8	3	1	0	1	1	1	1	.444	.875
Throws Right	R	.273	11	3	1	0	1	2	0	1	.273	.636
Moore, Matt	L	.000	1	0	0	0	0	0	0	0	.000	.000
Throws Left	R	.097	31	3	0	0	0	0	1	9	.125	.097
Moran, Brian	L	.182	11	2	0	0	1	3	1	5	.308	.455
Throws Left	R	.308	13	4	1	1	0	2	1	5	.400	.538
Morejon, Adrian	L	.412	17	7	4	0	0	5	0	3	.412	.647
Throws Left	R	.364	22	8	2	0	1	3	3	6	.440	.591
Morgan, Adam	L	.143	49	7	1	1	0	2	4	17	.250	.204
Throws Left	R	.224	58	13	2	0	4	11	6	12	.297	.466
Morin, Mike	L	.225	80	18	4	0	0	6	6	11	.295	.275
Throws Right	R	.248	113	28	6	0	6	18	4	15	.283	.460
Moronta, Reyes	L	.227	75	17	3	0	0	6	13	18	.352	.267
Throws Right	R	.180	133	24	6	0	4	18	20	52	.292	.316
Morton, Charlie	L	.227	366	83	18	3	11	47	29	136	.299	.383
Throws Right	R	.202	351	71	15	3	4	17	28	104	.266	.296
Munoz, Andres	L	.220	41	9	3	0	1	5	5	13	.304	.366
Throws Right	R	.159	44	7	3	0	1	3	6	17	.260	.295
Musgrave, Harrison	L	.250	20	5	1	1	0	3	1	6	.286	.400
Throws Left	R	.211	19	4	0	0	0	1	6	6	.385	.211
Musgrove, Joe	L	.270	319	86	27	5	11	44	15	65	.314	.489
Throws Right	R	.239	343	82	21	0	10	41	24	92	.291	.388
Nelson, Jimmy	L	.333	42	14	2	2	1	4	9	13	.462	.548
Throws Right	R	.250	44	11	2	1	3	14	8	13	.377	.545
Neris, Hector	L	.167	108	18	2	0	5	12	15	37	.272	.324
Throws Right	R	.201	134	27	5	0	5	13	9	52	.275	.351
Neshek, Pat	L	.308	26	8	0	1	2	4	1	5	.333	.615
Throws Right	R	.300	50	15	1	0	3	4	1	4	.308	.500
Neverauskas, Dovydas	L	.158	19	3	1	0	0	3	3	6	.292	.211
Throws Right	R	.500	24	12	5	0	2	9	4	4	.586	.958
Newberry, Jake	L	.354	48	17	5	1	4	9	5	8	.415	.750
Throws Right	R	.174	69	12	3	0	3	10	11	21	.286	.348
Newcomb, Sean	L	.250	76	19	0	0	2	8	9	23	.345	.329
Throws Left	R	.230	183	42	10	1	6	18	20	42	.306	.393
Nicasio, Juan	L	.279	68	19	5	0	2	9	11	18	.375	.441
Throws Right	R	.309	123	38	8	1	2	16	10	27	.368	.439
Noesi, Hector	L	.227	44	10	2	1	2	10	7	13	.327	.455
Throws Right	R	.317	63	20	4	2	5	15	7	11	.394	.683
Nogosek, Stephen	L	.500	12	6	2	0	2	4	1	2	.538	1.167
Throws Right	R	.316	19	6	0	0	0	2	1	4	.333	.316
Nola, Aaron	L	.240	333	80	15	3	11	38	39	105	.325	.402
Throws Right	R	.227	422	96	19	0	16	42	41	124	.307	.386

Pitchers vs. Left-Handed and Right-Handed Batters

Pitcher	vs	Avg	AB	H	2B	3B	HR	RBI	BB	SO	OBP	Slg
Norris, Daniel	L	.260	104	27	4	2	5	12	7	25	.325	.481
Throws Left	R	.279	456	127	24	2	20	53	31	100	.324	.471
Norwood, James	L	.200	10	2	0	0	0	0	3	1	.385	.200
Throws Right	R	.269	26	7	1	1	1	3	5	10	.387	.500
Nova, Ivan	L	.293	379	111	26	0	17	45	23	57	.335	.496
Throws Right	R	.313	364	114	18	0	13	48	24	57	.365	.470
Oberg, Scott	L	.225	89	20	0	0	3	9	14	28	.330	.326
Throws Right	R	.173	110	19	2	1	2	10	9	30	.233	.264
O'Day, Darren	L	.200	5	1	1	0	0	0	0	1	.333	.400
Throws Right	R	.143	14	2	2	0	0	0	1	5	.200	.286
Odorizzi, Jake	L	.277	289	80	15	2	8	34	26	91	.335	.426
Throws Right	R	.194	304	59	14	0	8	21	27	87	.266	.319
Oh, Seunghwan	L	.343	35	12	0	0	1	6	1	7	.361	.429
Throws Right	R	.362	47	17	1	0	5	10	5	9	.423	.702
Olson, Tyler	L	.245	49	12	6	0	0	9	7	14	.333	.367
Throws Left	R	.306	72	22	4	0	3	12	9	14	.398	.486
Osich, Josh	L	.171	111	19	5	0	5	16	4	30	.200	.351
Throws Left	R	.297	145	43	8	0	10	26	11	31	.344	.559
Osuna, Roberto	L	.150	120	18	2	1	3	10	8	39	.214	.258
Throws Right	R	.231	117	27	3	0	5	12	4	34	.256	.385
Oswalt, Corey	L	.500	12	6	2	0	1	6	4	2	.625	.917
Throws Right	R	.188	16	3	2	0	0	5	2	3	.278	.313
Otero, Dan	L	.271	48	13	3	0	1	5	2	6	.300	.396
Throws Right	R	.367	79	29	4	0	5	12	1	10	.383	.608
Ottavino, Adam	L	.241	79	19	3	0	3	14	15	21	.361	.392
Throws Right	R	.177	158	28	6	1	2	11	25	67	.292	.266
Paddack, Chris	L	.211	266	56	13	1	12	30	18	69	.264	.402
Throws Right	R	.198	258	51	8	0	11	25	13	84	.246	.357
Pagan, Emilio	L	.179	84	15	2	1	6	11	10	33	.271	.440
Throws Right	R	.179	168	30	4	2	6	17	3	63	.193	.333
Palumbo, Joseph	L	.267	15	4	0	0	3	7	2	5	.353	.867
Throws Left	R	.309	55	17	6	0	4	10	6	16	.397	.636
Pannone, Thomas	L	.224	85	19	2	0	4	10	7	20	.295	.388
Throws Left	R	.269	201	54	14	1	9	38	24	49	.357	.483
Parker, Blake	L	.260	96	25	3	0	3	11	12	23	.345	.385
Throws Right	R	.215	130	28	4	0	10	19	10	42	.280	.477
Parsons, Wes	L	.255	47	12	1	0	4	9	12	9	.407	.532
Throws Right	R	.270	74	20	2	1	2	17	17	17	.406	.405
Paxton, James	L	.266	143	38	7	0	2	8	9	46	.314	.357
Throws Left	R	.234	427	100	23	2	21	55	46	140	.308	.445
Payano, Pedro	L	.255	47	12	6	0	1	7	6	8	.340	.447
Throws Right	R	.359	39	14	1	0	2	2	9	9	.490	.538
Pazos, James	L	.200	20	4	0	0	1	1	2	8	.273	.350
Throws Left	R	.200	15	3	1	0	0	0	2	2	.294	.267
Peacock, Brad	L	.279	165	46	12	1	11	24	16	40	.348	.564
Throws Right	R	.179	179	32	8	1	4	18	15	56	.251	.302
Pena, Felix	L	.260	173	45	12	0	10	23	19	46	.345	.503
Throws Right	R	.181	193	35	7	0	6	26	15	55	.248	.311
Peralta, Freddy	L	.219	128	28	5	1	3	11	23	50	.338	.344
Throws Right	R	.280	211	59	14	1	12	41	14	65	.329	.526
Peralta, Wandy	L	.237	76	18	4	0	5	20	6	19	.299	.487
Throws Left	R	.293	75	22	2	0	6	11	10	13	.376	.560
Peralta, Wily	L	.304	69	21	5	0	6	22	8	12	.383	.638
Throws Right	R	.289	83	24	3	0	1	6	11	12	.372	.361
Perdomo, Luis	L	.288	104	30	6	1	3	17	7	17	.333	.452
Throws Right	R	.229	170	39	7	0	3	24	11	38	.284	.324
Perez, Cionel	L	.300	10	3	0	0	1	2	1	1	.364	.600
Throws Left	R	.286	28	8	2	0	2	8	1	6	.310	.571
Perez, Martin	L	.228	136	31	6	0	1	14	9	28	.291	.294
Throws Left	R	.293	523	153	30	0	22	82	58	107	.360	.476
Perez, Oliver	L	.207	87	18	2	0	3	11	7	26	.274	.333
Throws Left	R	.286	70	20	12	0	2	14	5	22	.346	.543
Peters, Dillon	L	.232	82	19	5	0	3	7	9	12	.315	.402
Throws Left	R	.313	211	66	19	2	15	39	17	43	.372	.635
Peterson, Tim	L	.200	10	2	0	0	0	1	2	0	.333	.200
Throws Right	R	.294	17	5	1	0	1	4	5	3	.478	.529
Petit, Yusmeiro	L	.218	124	27	5	2	6	19	5	27	.244	.435
Throws Right	R	.176	170	30	5	1	5	13	5	44	.199	.306
Petricka, Jake	L	.250	8	2	0	0	0	0	5	0	.538	.250
Throws Right	R	.190	21	4	3	0	0	3	1	3	.217	.333
Phelps, David	L	.273	44	12	0	2	3	6	5	14	.347	.568
Throws Right	R	.226	84	19	2	1	2	9	12	22	.327	.345
Phillips, Evan	L	.286	42	12	5	0	0	4	11	13	.436	.405
Throws Right	R	.286	70	20	3	0	2	17	9	27	.393	.414
Pineda, Michael	L	.260	246	64	9	1	7	21	7	51	.277	.390
Throws Right	R	.247	312	77	17	1	16	40	21	89	.301	.462

Pitcher	vs	Avg	AB	H	2B	3B	HR	RBI	BB	SO	OBP	Slg
Pivetta, Nick	L	.261	176	46	9	3	10	21	24	40	.348	.517
Throws Right	R	.294	194	57	9	2	10	35	15	49	.352	.515
Plesac, Zach	L	.216	185	40	9	1	7	16	19	37	.296	.389
Throws Right	R	.253	245	62	16	1	12	28	21	51	.315	.473
Plutko, Adam	L	.283	212	60	12	1	10	31	15	26	.333	.491
Throws Right	R	.252	218	55	15	0	12	22	11	52	.294	.486
Poche, Colin	L	.167	66	11	3	0	3	11	7	26	.276	.348
Throws Left	R	.190	116	22	3	1	6	17	12	46	.277	.388
Pomeranz, Drew	L	.230	122	28	5	0	5	18	7	45	.273	.393
Throws Left	R	.274	281	77	9	3	16	38	37	92	.364	.498
Ponce de Leon, Daniel	L	.164	67	11	3	0	0	6	14	29	.313	.209
Throws Right	R	.234	107	25	4	0	6	11	12	23	.317	.439
Poppen, Sean	L	.111	9	1	1	0	0	2	4	3	.385	.222
Throws Right	R	.409	22	9	2	1	1	5	1	6	.435	.727
Porcello, Rick	L	.284	349	99	22	5	13	52	26	66	.341	.487
Throws Right	R	.273	363	99	21	0	18	54	19	77	.311	.479
Pounders, Brooks	L	.222	9	2	0	0	1	3	2	1	.417	.556
Throws Right	R	.333	21	7	1	1	0	2	0	4	.333	.476
Poyner, Bobby	L	.235	17	4	1	1	0	5	2	3	.350	.412
Throws Left	R	.231	26	6	1	0	2	5	3	8	.310	.500
Pressly, Ryan	L	.124	97	12	1	0	2	5	5	40	.165	.196
Throws Right	R	.250	100	25	5	0	4	13	7	32	.299	.420
Price, David	L	.263	76	20	5	1	0	6	3	17	.317	.355
Throws Left	R	.257	346	89	23	1	15	49	29	111	.314	.460
Pruitt, Austin	L	.209	91	19	4	0	2	9	9	24	.277	.319
Throws Right	R	.326	86	28	6	1	5	14	3	15	.344	.593
Puk, A.J.	L	.385	13	5	1	0	0	1	1	3	.429	.462
Throws Left	R	.172	29	5	0	0	1	2	4	10	.273	.276
Quantrill, Cal	L	.290	241	70	15	2	10	34	24	43	.354	.494
Throws Right	R	.217	166	36	3	1	5	21	4	46	.243	.337
Quijada, Jose	L	.260	50	13	1	1	7	12	8	18	.403	.740
Throws Left	R	.222	63	14	5	0	3	8	18	26	.395	.444
Quintana, Jose	L	.253	150	38	11	0	1	20	5	32	.277	.347
Throws Left	R	.290	528	153	32	2	19	68	41	120	.336	.466
Rainey, Tanner	L	.261	69	18	6	0	4	14	19	28	.420	.522
Throws Right	R	.139	101	14	1	1	2	8	19	46	.298	.228
Ramirez, JC	L	.286	14	4	1	1	0	2	0	2	.286	.500
Throws Right	R	.222	18	4	3	0	1	3	1	2	.300	.556
Ramirez, Neil	L	.295	44	13	3	0	4	11	7	9	.392	.636
Throws Right	R	.255	51	13	3	0	3	8	8	15	.344	.490
Ramirez, Nick	L	.231	104	24	3	1	2	17	12	22	.308	.337
Throws Left	R	.255	204	52	13	2	9	38	23	52	.330	.471
Ramirez, Noe	L	.212	85	18	4	2	3	10	4	16	.264	.412
Throws Right	R	.243	169	41	7	0	6	16	16	63	.317	.391
Ramirez, Yefry	L	.333	45	15	4	0	3	11	8	14	.439	.622
Throws Right	R	.288	52	15	4	0	1	8	8	13	.403	.423
Ramos, Edubray	L	.368	19	7	1	0	2	6	2	2	.429	.737
Throws Right	R	.286	42	12	1	1	3	9	5	9	.375	.571
Ray, Robbie	L	.209	153	32	9	2	4	12	11	52	.271	.373
Throws Left	R	.241	489	118	24	3	26	71	73	183	.341	.462
Reed, Cody	L	.231	13	3	0	0	0	0	0	6	.231	.231
Throws Left	R	.273	11	3	0	0	0	1	1	1	.333	.273
Reid-Foley, Sean	L	.274	62	17	6	0	2	8	11	14	.400	.468
Throws Right	R	.250	64	16	2	0	3	8	10	14	.347	.422
Reininger, Zac	L	.333	42	14	5	0	3	6	12	6	.473	.667
Throws Right	R	.375	80	30	10	2	8	18	4	11	.400	.850
Reyes, Gerardo	L	.250	52	13	2	1	3	13	5	15	.350	.500
Throws Right	R	.229	48	11	2	1	0	9	6	23	.304	.313
Rhame, Jacob	L	.000	9	0	0	0	0	0	6	4	.400	.000
Throws Right	R	.273	11	3	2	0	1	4	3	1	.429	.727
Richard, Clayton	L	.212	33	7	0	0	1	2	3	5	.316	.303
Throws Left	R	.317	145	46	11	1	8	29	15	17	.387	.572
Richards, Garrett	L	.190	21	4	2	1	0	4	4	8	.320	.381
Throws Right	R	.462	13	6	1	1	2	4	2	3	.533	1.154
Richards, Trevor	L	.252	218	55	10	1	8	27	30	48	.345	.417
Throws Right	R	.247	292	72	15	2	11	33	26	79	.313	.425
Rios, Yacksel	L	.364	22	8	3	0	3	10	3	4	.423	.909
Throws Right	R	.276	29	8	1	0	1	5	5	8	.421	.414
Roark, Tanner	L	.289	315	91	18	2	15	39	31	76	.373	.502
Throws Right	R	.262	340	89	18	1	13	39	20	82	.305	.435
Robertson, David	L	.235	17	4	1	0	0	0	1	5	.278	.294
Throws Right	R	.400	10	4	0	0	1	4	5	1	.600	.700
Robles, Hansel	L	.226	124	28	7	0	2	12	6	40	.258	.331
Throws Right	R	.217	138	30	4	0	4	11	10	35	.268	.333
Rodgers, Brady	L	.182	11	2	1	0	0	1	1	3	.250	.273
Throws Right	R	.455	11	5	0	0	4	9	2	1	.538	1.545

Pitchers vs. Left-Handed and Right-Handed Batters

Pitcher	vs	Avg	AB	H	2B	3B	HR	RBI	BB	SO	OBP	Slg
Rodney, Fernando	L	.287	94	27	2	0	3	15	14	25	.380	.404
Throws Right	R	.250	88	22	6	0	2	19	14	24	.353	.386
Rodon, Carlos	L	.077	13	1	1	0	0	2	2	6	.222	.154
Throws Left	R	.256	125	32	6	1	4	16	15	40	.336	.416
Rodriguez, Dereck	L	.250	172	43	12	0	10	30	24	32	.345	.494
Throws Right	R	.288	226	65	9	2	11	37	12	39	.326	.491
Rodriguez, Eduardo	L	.264	163	43	3	0	9	28	14	48	.335	.448
Throws Left	R	.250	607	152	27	2	15	56	61	165	.320	.376
Rodriguez, Jefry	L	.237	76	18	7	0	4	14	12	16	.333	.487
Throws Right	R	.294	102	30	6	0	1	9	9	17	.348	.382
Rodriguez, Jose	L	.261	23	6	0	0	2	2	4	4	.370	.522
Throws Right	R	.220	50	11	1	0	3	4	7	9	.316	.420
Rodriguez, Richard	L	.294	109	32	3	0	8	20	11	27	.366	.541
Throws Right	R	.221	149	33	2	0	6	15	12	36	.280	.356
Roe, Chaz	L	.227	44	10	1	0	1	5	9	18	.370	.318
Throws Right	R	.258	151	39	9	0	2	25	22	47	.351	.358
Rogers, Josh	L	.235	17	4	0	0	0	2	1	2	.316	.235
Throws Left	R	.333	42	14	3	0	7	12	5	3	.440	.905
Rogers, Taylor	L	.273	66	18	1	0	1	3	4	25	.333	.333
Throws Left	R	.208	192	40	8	0	7	22	7	65	.251	.359
Rogers, Tyler	L	.136	22	3	0	0	0	1	2	6	.240	.136
Throws Right	R	.209	43	9	3	0	0	2	1	10	.227	.279
Romano, Jordan	L	.192	26	5	0	0	1	4	5	10	.344	.308
Throws Right	R	.333	36	12	1	0	3	7	4	11	.442	.611
Romano, Sal	L	.387	31	12	7	0	2	7	3	10	.457	.806
Throws Right	R	.278	36	10	1	0	2	8	5	6	.357	.472
Romero, Fernando	L	.429	21	9	3	0	1	4	4	3	.520	.714
Throws Right	R	.256	39	10	1	0	1	2	7	15	.383	.359
Romo, Sergio	L	.242	99	24	4	0	2	15	11	22	.313	.343
Throws Right	R	.205	127	26	7	1	5	13	6	38	.248	.394
Rondon, Hector	L	.219	96	21	6	1	6	14	8	21	.306	.490
Throws Right	R	.259	135	35	8	0	4	12	12	27	.318	.407
Rosario, Randy	L	.150	20	3	2	0	1	4	2	4	.227	.400
Throws Left	R	.316	38	12	2	0	1	5	3	9	.366	.447
Rosenthal, Trevor	L	.174	23	4	1	0	0	4	12	8	.513	.217
Throws Right	R	.233	30	7	0	0	0	7	14	9	.467	.233
Ross, Joe	L	.314	118	37	7	0	4	14	22	27	.430	.475
Throws Right	R	.272	136	37	12	0	3	23	11	30	.333	.426
Ross, Tyson	L	.254	71	18	1	1	3	14	4	11	.299	.423
Throws Right	R	.324	71	23	5	0	4	11	14	14	.435	.563
Rosscup, Zac	L	.200	35	7	0	0	1	7	11	14	.391	.286
Throws Left	R	.375	40	15	4	0	1	6	8	12	.479	.550
Ruiz, Jose	L	.273	55	15	4	0	0	6	8	14	.365	.345
Throws Right	R	.366	112	41	6	0	6	22	16	21	.447	.580
Ryan, Kyle	L	.226	93	21	3	1	0	8	9	24	.291	.280
Throws Left	R	.256	133	34	2	0	5	18	20	34	.353	.383
Ryu, Hyun-Jin	L	.199	171	34	4	0	6	16	3	43	.211	.327
Throws Left	R	.245	514	126	31	0	11	33	21	120	.280	.370
Sabathia, CC	L	.198	91	18	2	0	7	14	7	26	.270	.451
Throws Left	R	.284	331	94	21	0	20	48	32	81	.348	.529
Sadler, Casey	L	.241	87	21	2	0	4	7	6	15	.313	.402
Throws Right	R	.230	87	20	3	1	1	8	7	16	.292	.322
Sadzeck, Connor	L	.135	37	5	0	0	2	4	8	15	.289	.297
Throws Right	R	.245	53	13	4	0	1	7	7	12	.355	.377
Sale, Chris	L	.247	89	22	6	1	1	6	4	28	.295	.371
Throws Left	R	.216	467	101	24	1	23	68	33	190	.282	.420
Samardzija, Jeff	L	.233	339	79	12	6	17	44	32	75	.303	.454
Throws Right	R	.216	338	73	12	3	11	26	17	65	.258	.367
Sampson, Adrian	L	.274	223	61	13	3	8	34	19	46	.331	.466
Throws Right	R	.324	293	95	25	3	21	56	17	55	.377	.645
Sanchez, Aaron	L	.279	272	76	14	2	13	45	32	68	.359	.489
Throws Right	R	.277	249	69	15	0	7	38	36	47	.383	.422
Sanchez, Anibal	L	.248	298	74	20	1	11	35	29	60	.315	.433
Throws Right	R	.226	349	79	18	2	11	33	29	74	.292	.384
Sandoval, Patrick	L	.306	36	11	3	0	3	6	5	8	.390	.639
Throws Left	R	.218	110	24	6	0	3	12	14	34	.310	.355
Santana, Dennis	L	.571	7	4	0	1	0	2	1	2	.667	.857
Throws Right	R	.154	13	2	0	0	1	2	3	4	.333	.385
Santana, Ervin	L	.300	30	9	3	0	3	7	3	3	.353	.700
Throws Right	R	.385	26	10	4	1	3	7	3	2	.433	.962
Santiago, Hector	L	.317	41	13	2	0	3	7	7	11	.417	.585
Throws Left	R	.293	99	29	10	0	5	15	15	29	.383	.545
Sborz, Josh	L	.333	15	5	2	0	2	7	2	4	.389	.867
Throws Right	R	.250	20	5	2	0	0	0	2	3	.318	.350
Scherzer, Max	L	.255	298	76	24	0	11	30	23	102	.317	.446
Throws Right	R	.193	352	68	19	0	7	22	10	141	.220	.307

Pitcher	vs	Avg	AB	H	2B	3B	HR	RBI	BB	SO	OBP	Slg
Schlitter, Brian	L	.308	13	4	2	0	0	4	3	2	.438	.462
Throws Right	R	.333	24	8	1	0	0	2	1	4	.360	.375
Schreiber, John	L	.304	23	7	0	0	1	4	2	8	.360	.435
Throws Right	R	.290	31	9	1	0	2	7	2	11	.353	.516
Schultz, Jaime	L	.286	7	2	0	0	1	2	1	1	.375	.714
Throws Right	R	.333	12	4	2	0	0	1	2	2	.429	.500
Scott, Robby	L	.294	17	5	2	0	1	2	2	5	.368	.588
Throws Left	R	.250	12	3	1	0	0	0	5	4	.471	.333
Scott, Tanner	L	.188	48	9	2	0	2	5	9	17	.328	.354
Throws Left	R	.358	53	19	3	0	2	11	10	20	.469	.528
Scott, Tayler	L	.371	35	13	3	0	2	12	4	7	.436	.629
Throws Right	R	.419	43	18	1	0	4	14	7	7	.537	.721
Selman, Sam	L	.150	20	3	0	0	1	2	4	7	.292	.300
Throws Left	R	.200	15	3	1	0	1	2	2	3	.368	.467
Senzatela, Antonio	L	.327	251	82	20	0	11	47	32	36	.403	.538
Throws Right	R	.300	263	79	18	2	8	33	25	40	.366	.475
Severino, Luis	L	.148	27	4	1	0	0	2	4	12	.281	.185
Throws Right	R	.143	14	2	0	0	0	0	2	5	.250	.143
Sewald, Paul	L	.200	20	4	2	0	0	1	3	8	.304	.300
Throws Right	R	.259	54	14	4	0	3	7	0	14	.268	.500
Shafer, Justin	L	.265	68	18	6	1	4	11	15	19	.398	.559
Throws Right	R	.264	87	23	6	1	2	11	10	20	.347	.425
Shaw, Bryan	L	.200	120	24	3	3	2	17	13	24	.289	.325
Throws Right	R	.290	155	45	12	1	10	36	16	34	.366	.574
Shawaryn, Michael	L	.250	32	8	0	0	4	11	8	13	.405	.625
Throws Right	R	.346	52	18	6	0	1	8	5	16	.443	.519
Sheffield, Justus	L	.207	29	6	1	0	2	3	6	8	.378	.448
Throws Left	R	.328	116	38	9	1	3	16	12	29	.395	.500
Shepherd, Chandler	L	.267	30	8	1	0	1	4	1	9	.313	.400
Throws Right	R	.326	46	15	2	1	4	8	5	8	.404	.674
Sherfy, Jimmie	L	.259	27	7	2	0	1	3	2	10	.333	.444
Throws Right	R	.327	49	16	2	0	3	6	3	12	.365	.551
Shoemaker, Matt	L	.189	37	7	2	0	1	1	6	11	.302	.324
Throws Right	R	.148	61	9	1	1	2	4	3	13	.200	.295
Sims, Lucas	L	.172	64	11	3	0	3	11	12	20	.312	.359
Throws Right	R	.222	90	20	4	1	5	12	7	37	.283	.456
Sipp, Tony	L	.255	47	12	3	0	1	7	2	8	.283	.383
Throws Left	R	.219	32	7	1	0	0	4	7	10	.359	.250
Skaggs, Tyler	L	.213	75	16	3	0	2	3	5	18	.272	.333
Throws Left	R	.251	227	57	10	1	7	32	23	60	.320	.396
Skoglund, Eric	L	.333	15	5	0	0	1	3	3	1	.444	.533
Throws Left	R	.338	74	25	8	1	4	18	6	3	.386	.635
Smeltzer, Devin	L	.316	38	12	3	0	1	1	4	10	.395	.474
Throws Left	R	.252	151	38	5	3	7	18	8	28	.289	.464
Smith, Burch	L	.308	39	12	3	1	2	7	4	6	.372	.590
Throws Right	R	.275	51	14	2	0	1	7	10	14	.403	.373
Smith, Caleb	L	.211	133	28	6	0	4	15	12	34	.279	.346
Throws Left	R	.227	440	100	23	2	29	62	48	134	.308	.486
Smith, Joe	L	.229	35	8	2	0	2	5	4	10	.308	.457
Throws Right	R	.196	56	11	2	0	0	6	1	12	.211	.232
Smith, Josh A.	L	.327	55	18	1	0	5	12	5	8	.393	.618
Throws Right	R	.247	73	18	3	0	5	12	3	21	.295	.493
Smith, Josh D.	L	.304	23	7	3	0	0	7	5	5	.452	.435
Throws Left	R	.154	26	4	1	1	0	3	6	9	.333	.269
Smith, Will	L	.157	70	11	0	1	1	6	1	42	.167	.229
Throws Left	R	.212	165	35	4	1	9	15	20	54	.297	.412
Smyly, Drew	L	.287	101	29	6	1	12	26	11	20	.357	.723
Throws Left	R	.276	352	97	17	3	20	48	44	100	.358	.511
Sneed, Cy	L	.310	42	13	3	0	1	5	1	11	.326	.452
Throws Right	R	.289	45	13	2	0	4	10	4	12	.347	.600
Snell, Blake	L	.329	70	23	5	0	3	10	4	24	.365	.529
Throws Left	R	.222	329	73	13	0	11	33	36	123	.300	.362
Sobotka, Chad	L	.295	44	13	2	0	1	6	6	16	.380	.409
Throws Right	R	.221	68	15	2	0	5	14	13	22	.369	.471
Soria, Joakim	L	.230	126	29	4	1	5	18	7	34	.279	.397
Throws Right	R	.175	126	22	2	0	4	7	13	45	.255	.286
Soroka, Mike	L	.282	277	78	11	0	9	28	19	44	.331	.419
Throws Right	R	.203	370	75	10	2	5	24	22	98	.256	.281
Soto, Gregory	L	.294	68	20	2	0	0	6	7	14	.355	.324
Throws Left	R	.314	172	54	12	2	9	32	26	31	.400	.564
Sparkman, Glenn	L	.280	286	80	18	2	18	49	28	47	.348	.545
Throws Right	R	.313	268	84	16	0	12	41	13	34	.350	.507
Speier, Gabe	L	.250	12	3	1	0	1	3	2	4	.357	.583
Throws Left	R	.133	15	2	0	0	1	1	4	6	.316	.333
Springs, Jeffrey	L	.356	45	16	5	0	0	6	8	9	.444	.467
Throws Left	R	.262	84	22	6	1	4	15	15	23	.370	.500

Pitchers vs. Left-Handed and Right-Handed Batters

Pitcher	vs	Avg	AB	H	2B	3B	HR	RBI	BB	SO	OBP	Slg
St. John, Locke	L	.375	8	3	0	0	0	2	2	2	.500	.375
Throws Left	R	.190	21	4	3	0	0	3	2	3	.261	.333
Stammen, Craig	L	.203	143	29	10	0	4	15	8	31	.248	.357
Throws Right	R	.290	176	51	7	1	9	22	7	42	.317	.494
Stanek, Ryne	L	.197	122	24	4	1	7	17	17	39	.295	.418
Throws Right	R	.227	163	37	9	0	4	22	22	50	.314	.356
Stashak, Cody	L	.366	41	15	4	0	0	5	0	8	.381	.463
Throws Right	R	.233	60	14	4	1	3	6	1	17	.242	.483
Staumont, Josh	L	.263	38	10	4	0	1	3	3	5	.317	.447
Throws Right	R	.282	39	11	2	0	3	8	7	10	.404	.564
Steckenrider, Drew	L	.130	23	3	0	0	2	2	2	10	.200	.391
Throws Right	R	.207	29	6	0	0	4	8	3	4	.303	.621
Stephenson, Robert	L	.214	98	21	7	1	4	12	17	31	.330	.429
Throws Right	R	.159	138	22	8	1	5	17	7	50	.199	.341
Stewart, Brock	L	.361	61	22	4	0	7	15	3	9	.388	.770
Throws Right	R	.313	48	15	4	1	4	14	5	10	.386	.688
Stewart, Kohl	L	.242	33	8	1	0	3	8	4	2	.324	.545
Throws Right	R	.313	67	21	5	1	2	8	4	8	.361	.507
Stock, Robert	L	.381	21	8	2	0	0	2	3	6	.458	.476
Throws Right	R	.231	26	6	1	0	2	9	5	9	.375	.500
Strahm, Matt	L	.274	124	34	8	0	5	12	10	31	.343	.460
Throws Left	R	.264	329	87	19	1	17	45	12	87	.298	.483
Straily, Dan	L	.281	89	25	5	2	6	15	14	16	.380	.584
Throws Right	R	.400	120	48	8	0	16	39	8	17	.438	.867
Strasburg, Stephen	L	.192	344	66	8	3	11	35	29	112	.259	.328
Throws Right	R	.224	424	95	17	2	13	40	27	139	.280	.366
Stratton, Chris	L	.300	130	39	7	1	5	18	22	29	.401	.485
Throws Right	R	.300	180	54	14	1	8	33	11	40	.339	.522
Strickland, Hunter	L	.342	38	13	5	0	5	12	5	2	.422	.868
Throws Right	R	.164	55	9	1	0	1	4	3	16	.233	.236
Stripling, Ross	L	.249	181	45	11	0	6	21	14	49	.298	.409
Throws Right	R	.239	163	39	12	1	5	12	6	44	.273	.417
Stroman, Marcus	L	.291	374	109	19	1	11	36	27	80	.339	.436
Throws Right	R	.220	337	74	13	1	7	34	31	79	.286	.326
Strop, Pedro	L	.203	74	15	4	1	2	8	12	21	.322	.365
Throws Right	R	.231	78	18	5	0	4	13	8	28	.330	.449
Stumpf, Daniel	L	.255	55	14	2	0	2	9	5	17	.306	.400
Throws Left	R	.344	61	21	4	1	3	12	10	11	.431	.590
Suarez, Andrew	L	.259	54	14	4	0	0	3	5	12	.317	.333
Throws Left	R	.333	75	25	6	1	7	21	9	13	.398	.720
Suarez, Jose	L	.202	84	17	6	0	3	10	6	29	.281	.381
Throws Left	R	.339	245	83	11	0	20	52	27	43	.417	.629
Suarez, Ranger	L	.213	61	13	3	0	1	6	3	14	.258	.311
Throws Left	R	.310	126	39	5	0	5	16	9	28	.353	.468
Suero, Wander	L	.279	129	36	6	0	0	12	12	34	.338	.326
Throws Right	R	.207	135	28	8	0	5	17	14	47	.292	.378
Sulser, Cole	L	.125	8	1	1	0	0	1	0	4	.125	.250
Throws Right	R	.222	18	4	0	0	0	1	3	5	.333	.222
Suter, Brent	L	.235	17	4	0	0	1	1	0	5	.235	.412
Throws Left	R	.128	47	6	2	1	0	0	1	10	.146	.213
Swanson, Erik	L	.267	105	28	6	1	9	18	7	21	.316	.600
Throws Right	R	.224	125	28	4	0	8	21	5	31	.260	.448
Swarzak, Anthony	L	.271	70	19	2	1	5	13	12	27	.378	.543
Throws Right	R	.241	137	33	2	0	7	17	15	25	.316	.409
Syndergaard, Noah	L	.266	350	93	18	2	13	44	21	78	.310	.440
Throws Right	R	.248	408	101	19	2	11	47	29	124	.299	.385
Taillon, Jameson	L	.216	74	16	4	1	2	13	7	15	.289	.378
Throws Right	R	.247	73	18	5	1	2	7	1	15	.267	.425
Tanaka, Masahiro	L	.285	354	101	26	4	15	41	25	65	.331	.508
Throws Right	R	.237	359	85	17	0	13	42	15	84	.270	.393
Tarpley, Stephen	L	.200	40	8	1	0	1	3	5	18	.289	.300
Throws Left	R	.413	63	26	5	0	5	14	10	16	.507	.730
Tate, Dillon	L	.185	27	5	1	0	2	8	3	4	.313	.444
Throws Right	R	.255	51	13	2	0	1	8	6	16	.361	.353
Taylor, Josh	L	.203	69	14	1	0	2	6	4	24	.247	.304
Throws Left	R	.245	106	26	4	0	3	12	12	38	.331	.368
Teheran, Julio	L	.215	265	57	9	1	9	28	45	66	.342	.358
Throws Right	R	.239	380	91	24	1	13	48	38	96	.318	.411
Tepera, Ryan	L	.290	31	9	1	1	3	5	7	5	.421	.677
Throws Right	R	.224	49	11	3	0	2	8	1	9	.231	.408
Thornburg, Tyler	L	.217	23	5	2	0	1	3	4	5	.357	.435
Throws Right	R	.308	52	16	8	1	3	13	6	17	.379	.673
Thornton, Trent	L	.248	310	77	19	3	13	39	31	78	.321	.455
Throws Right	R	.270	293	79	10	1	11	43	30	71	.336	.423
Thorpe, Lewis	L	.364	22	8	2	0	0	4	4	7	.444	.455
Throws Left	R	.330	91	30	9	1	3	12	6	24	.371	.549

Pitcher	vs	Avg	AB	H	2B	3B	HR	RBI	BB	SO	OBP	Slg
Tinoco, Jesus	L	.310	58	18	3	0	7	13	14	6	.438	.724
Throws Right	R	.228	79	18	5	1	5	15	8	22	.307	.506
Tomlin, Josh	L	.250	124	31	3	3	6	16	3	25	.264	.468
Throws Right	R	.279	183	51	7	1	8	19	4	26	.294	.459
Torres, Carlos	L	.231	13	3	0	0	1	1	0	4	.286	.462
Throws Right	R	.429	14	6	1	0	1	4	1	4	.467	.714
Toussaint, Touki	L	.390	59	23	7	0	4	13	9	13	.493	.712
Throws Right	R	.202	104	21	2	0	1	12	17	32	.336	.250
Treinen, Blake	L	.254	114	29	6	0	5	15	16	27	.351	.439
Throws Right	R	.259	112	29	3	0	4	19	21	32	.373	.393
Trivino, Lou	L	.267	116	31	10	0	4	21	14	24	.344	.457
Throws Right	R	.263	114	30	6	0	3	13	17	33	.368	.395
Tropeano, Nick	L	.333	27	9	1	0	2	8	3	4	.424	.593
Throws Right	R	.300	30	9	1	0	4	7	3	6	.364	.733
Tuivailala, Sam	L	.185	27	5	1	0	0	1	9	9	.395	.222
Throws Right	R	.151	53	8	2	1	1	6	2	18	.196	.283
Turnbull, Spencer	L	.298	302	90	17	3	7	36	28	64	.370	.444
Throws Right	R	.234	274	64	17	1	7	39	31	82	.328	.380
Underwood Jr., Duane	L	.357	14	5	2	1	1	6	2	4	.438	.857
Throws Right	R	.242	33	8	2	0	1	4	1	9	.286	.394
Urena, Jose	L	.319	160	51	12	0	8	29	14	24	.371	.544
Throws Right	R	.270	178	48	10	0	5	20	12	38	.321	.410
Urias, Julio	L	.198	101	20	5	2	3	9	12	33	.299	.376
Throws Left	R	.203	192	39	4	1	4	17	15	52	.268	.297
Urquidy, Jose	L	.179	78	14	2	0	3	7	3	22	.210	.321
Throws Right	R	.300	80	24	6	0	3	9	4	18	.333	.488
Valdez, Framber	L	.197	71	14	4	0	1	14	19	23	.366	.296
Throws Left	R	.291	206	60	9	1	8	33	25	45	.373	.461
Valdez, Phillips	L	.292	24	7	2	0	3	6	3	6	.357	.750
Throws Right	R	.256	39	10	0	0	0	1	6	12	.383	.256
Vargas, Jason	L	.254	126	32	14	0	3	14	12	28	.329	.437
Throws Left	R	.248	440	109	20	1	18	58	51	96	.326	.420
Vazquez, Felipe	L	.191	47	9	3	1	1	4	3	25	.283	.362
Throws Left	R	.199	171	34	6	0	4	10	10	65	.246	.304
Velasquez, Vince	L	.266	199	53	9	3	10	27	21	54	.336	.492
Throws Right	R	.259	259	67	13	1	16	38	22	76	.334	.502
Velazquez, Hector	L	.238	101	24	8	1	5	20	16	24	.339	.485
Throws Right	R	.309	110	34	6	1	2	13	12	25	.386	.436
Venters, Jonny	L	.294	17	5	1	0	1	3	6	6	.500	.529
Throws Left	R	.350	20	7	0	0	2	7	4	6	.480	.650
VerHagen, Drew	L	.311	103	32	7	2	3	17	14	22	.395	.505
Throws Right	R	.299	127	38	8	0	6	21	9	29	.360	.504
Verlander, Justin	L	.163	406	66	14	4	17	31	25	171	.221	.342
Throws Right	R	.182	390	71	14	3	19	31	17	129	.216	.379
Vieira, Thyago	L	.385	13	5	1	0	0	2	4	5	.529	.462
Throws Right	R	.316	19	6	0	0	0	1	1	3	.350	.316
Vincent, Nick	L	.250	60	15	5	1	1	6	7	15	.348	.417
Throws Right	R	.276	116	32	3	0	7	18	5	32	.312	.483
Volquez, Edinson	L	.222	27	6	1	0	1	4	3	4	.300	.370
Throws Right	R	.389	36	14	2	0	2	8	9	6	.511	.611
Voth, Austin	L	.263	76	20	6	2	1	7	8	14	.329	.434
Throws Right	R	.165	79	13	3	0	4	5	5	30	.239	.354
Wacha, Michael	L	.259	189	49	11	1	8	24	26	40	.358	.455
Throws Right	R	.309	304	94	14	0	18	49	29	64	.364	.533
Waguespack, Jacob	L	.208	130	27	5	1	4	13	16	30	.299	.354
Throws Right	R	.281	171	48	12	1	8	24	13	33	.346	.503
Wainwright, Adam	L	.288	292	84	17	2	14	43	45	62	.380	.503
Throws Right	R	.262	370	97	21	1	8	35	19	91	.310	.389
Walden, Marcus	L	.198	116	23	7	0	3	16	13	36	.275	.336
Throws Right	R	.222	171	38	10	1	3	24	19	40	.318	.345
Walker, Jeremy	L	.286	7	2	0	0	0	1	0	1	.286	.286
Throws Right	R	.259	27	7	3	0	0	2	4	5	.355	.370
Wang, Wei-Chung	L	.220	50	11	0	0	1	9	6	9	.298	.280
Throws Left	R	.254	63	16	5	0	3	8	8	9	.347	.476
Warren, Adam	L	.163	43	7	1	0	1	4	6	12	.265	.256
Throws Right	R	.318	66	21	2	1	8	13	6	13	.384	.742
Warren, Art	L	.286	7	2	0	0	0	0	0	3	.286	.286
Throws Right	R	.000	12	0	0	0	0	0	2	2	.143	.000
Watson, Tony	L	.359	64	23	3	0	2	15	5	9	.414	.500
Throws Left	R	.223	148	33	3	2	7	13	7	32	.277	.412
Weaver, Luke	L	.225	129	29	7	0	2	9	8	35	.286	.326
Throws Right	R	.230	113	26	9	0	4	12	6	34	.267	.416
Webb, Jacob	L	.179	39	7	1	0	0	3	5	13	.289	.205
Throws Right	R	.218	78	17	7	0	4	12	7	15	.282	.462
Webb, Logan	L	.247	89	22	6	0	2	9	9	21	.316	.382
Throws Right	R	.319	69	22	3	2	3	13	5	16	.368	.551

Pitchers vs. Left-Handed and Right-Handed Batters

Pitcher	vs	Avg	AB	H	2B	3B	HR	RBI	BB	SO	OBP	Slg
Webb, Tyler	L	.157	102	16	3	1	2	8	11	26	.252	.265
Throws Left	R	.189	90	17	2	1	5	13	12	22	.279	.400
Weber, Ryan	L	.317	82	26	6	2	4	13	6	13	.385	.585
Throws Right	R	.253	87	22	5	0	1	9	2	16	.270	.345
Webster, Allen	L	.267	15	4	0	0	0	1	4	2	.421	.267
Throws Right	R	.323	31	10	3	0	2	8	1	7	.364	.613
Wendelken, J.B.	L	.160	50	8	1	0	1	5	6	10	.250	.240
Throws Right	R	.191	68	13	5	1	1	9	3	24	.243	.338
Wheeler, Zack	L	.275	316	87	12	1	12	41	32	85	.341	.434
Throws Right	R	.245	444	109	21	0	10	48	18	110	.274	.360
Wick, Rowan	L	.226	53	12	4	0	0	7	8	14	.339	.302
Throws Right	R	.149	67	10	2	0	0	4	8	21	.260	.179
Wieck, Brad	L	.265	49	13	4	0	4	18	1	12	.288	.592
Throws Left	R	.183	82	15	3	0	4	9	12	37	.302	.366
Wilkerson, Aaron	L	.412	34	14	2	0	3	7	7	5	.512	.735
Throws Right	R	.306	36	11	2	0	1	9	2	6	.333	.444
Williams, Devin	L	.269	26	7	1	0	1	4	4	6	.387	.423
Throws Right	R	.344	32	11	4	0	1	3	2	8	.400	.563
Williams, Taylor	L	.385	26	10	2	0	0	7	4	3	.500	.462
Throws Right	R	.316	38	12	2	0	1	11	3	12	.366	.447
Williams, Trevor	L	.335	239	80	20	2	10	42	23	34	.391	.561
Throws Right	R	.247	332	82	20	3	17	48	21	79	.298	.479
Wilson, Alex	L	.357	14	5	1	0	1	4	5	3	.526	.643
Throws Right	R	.294	34	10	2	0	2	5	4	10	.368	.529
Wilson, Bryse	L	.316	38	12	4	1	3	9	7	7	.422	.711
Throws Right	R	.326	43	14	6	0	2	6	3	9	.370	.605
Wilson, Justin	L	.217	46	10	2	0	0	3	11	17	.368	.261
Throws Left	R	.232	99	23	3	0	4	10	8	27	.303	.384
Wingenter, Trey	L	.140	93	13	2	1	1	13	12	36	.264	.215
Throws Right	R	.236	89	21	6	0	4	15	16	36	.355	.438
Winkler, Dan	L	.222	27	6	1	0	1	5	4	8	.344	.370
Throws Right	R	.222	54	12	3	1	4	13	7	14	.311	.537
Wisler, Matt	L	.257	70	18	7	1	5	15	7	19	.325	.600
Throws Right	R	.279	136	38	6	0	5	24	9	44	.322	.434
Wittgren, Nick	L	.241	83	20	4	0	5	11	7	23	.300	.470
Throws Right	R	.203	133	27	7	0	5	9	8	37	.248	.368
Wojciechowski, Asher	L	.253	150	38	5	4	10	19	14	33	.345	.540
Throws Right	R	.243	173	42	12	0	7	26	14	47	.307	.434
Wood, Alex	L	.296	27	8	2	0	2	4	1	7	.321	.593
Throws Left	R	.289	114	33	7	0	9	16	8	23	.341	.588
Wood, Hunter	L	.257	74	19	2	0	1	12	7	8	.325	.324
Throws Right	R	.255	106	27	4	1	6	16	5	31	.288	.481
Woodruff, Brandon	L	.265	211	56	9	1	8	27	18	67	.332	.431
Throws Right	R	.218	243	53	6	0	4	18	12	76	.259	.292
Workman, Brandon	L	.132	106	14	3	0	1	9	21	48	.277	.189
Throws Right	R	.116	129	15	4	0	0	6	24	56	.258	.147
Wotherspoon, Matt	L	.429	14	6	0	0	0	4	1	0	.467	.429
Throws Right	R	.444	9	4	1	0	2	7	1	2	.545	1.222
Wright, Kyle	L	.361	36	13	4	1	1	8	3	6	.410	.611
Throws Right	R	.256	43	11	2	0	3	7	10	12	.407	.512
Wright, Steven	L	.250	12	3	0	0	2	4	2	1	.333	.750
Throws Right	R	.533	15	8	1	0	1	1	2	4	.611	.800
Wright Jr., Mike	L	.319	47	15	3	0	1	4	8	10	.429	.447
Throws Right	R	.345	84	29	9	0	5	29	4	20	.374	.631
Yacabonis, Jimmy	L	.281	57	16	2	1	4	9	8	10	.369	.561
Throws Right	R	.321	109	35	10	0	5	25	16	23	.414	.550
Yamamoto, Jordan	L	.152	125	19	2	0	6	14	17	38	.265	.312
Throws Right	R	.223	157	35	11	0	5	22	19	44	.315	.389
Yarbrough, Ryan	L	.231	130	30	10	1	4	16	9	30	.292	.415
Throws Left	R	.228	400	91	21	2	11	46	11	87	.258	.373
Yardley, Eric	L	.188	16	3	0	0	0	0	0	2	.188	.188
Throws Right	R	.300	30	9	1	0	1	6	3	5	.382	.433
Yates, Kirby	L	.197	122	24	8	0	2	10	8	54	.311	.311
Throws Right	R	.172	99	17	3	0	0	5	5	47	.245	.202
Ynoa, Gabriel	L	.274	219	60	10	2	17	37	15	33	.319	.571
Throws Right	R	.286	231	66	14	0	12	29	11	34	.327	.502
Young, Alex	L	.167	90	15	4	0	3	5	10	20	.250	.311
Throws Left	R	.253	225	57	12	0	11	35	17	51	.317	.453
Zamora, Daniel	L	.294	17	5	2	0	0	6	3	5	.409	.412
Throws Left	R	.294	17	5	1	0	1	3	2	3	.368	.529
Zeuch, T.J.	L	.286	42	12	1	0	0	2	8	10	.400	.310
Throws Right	R	.217	46	10	6	0	2	9	3	10	.265	.478
Zimmer, Kyle	L	.286	35	10	1	0	1	7	4	8	.359	.400
Throws Right	R	.375	48	18	7	1	1	12	15	10	.524	.625
Zimmermann, Jordan	L	.346	237	82	18	2	12	44	18	35	.399	.591
Throws Right	R	.275	229	63	11	5	7	40	7	47	.300	.459

Pitcher	vs	Avg	AB	H	2B	3B	HR	RBI	BB	SO	OBP	Slg
AL	L	.251	-	-	-	-	-	-	-	-	.324	.434
	R	.257	-	-	-	-	-	-	-	-	.324	.447
NL	L	.254	-	-	-	-	-	-	-	-	.333	.439
	R	.247	-	-	-	-	-	-	-	-	.313	.421
MLB	L	.253	-	-	-	-	-	-	-	-	.328	.436
	R	.252	-	-	-	-	-	-	-	-	.319	.434

2019 Leader Boards

John Shirley

You may have heard this one before, but let us remind you again: Mike Trout is good at baseball. Analytics and numbers aren't needed to see this. His talent is undeniable to even the least knowledgeable baseball fan. However, his numbers are pretty eye-popping too.

Despite playing only 134 games last season, Trout still finished second in the AL with 45 home runs. He led the AL in On Base Percentage (.438), Slugging, Intentional Walks, At Bats per Home Run (10.4), and Runs Created per 27 Outs at home (10.6) and on the road (10.0).

Trout excelled early in the season with an AL-leading 1.098 OPS during the first half. He then "fell off" all the way to a still-highly-impressive 1.054 OPS during the second half of the season, good for fourth during this stretch. Over the full season he crushed fastballs (1.052 OPS), changeups (1.455 OPS), and sliders (1.054 OPS).

You will find Trout's name all over the Bill James leader boards as well. He led the AL in Offensive Winning % (.815), Isolated Power (.353), Secondary Average (.611), and Runs Created per 27 Outs (10.3). He was also in the top 10 in Power / Speed Number (17.7) and Speed Score (6.99).

Some other fun facts you'll find as you go through the leader boards include:
- Christian Yelich was Trout's NL equivalent among the Bill James metrics. He finished first in Offensive Winning % (.808), Isolated Power (.342), Secondary Average (.566), and Runs Created per 27 Outs (9.9).
- Justin Verlander was the only pitcher to achieve a Game Score of at least 100 (September 1st vs. Toronto). He struck out 14 and was one walk away from a perfect game. His Houston teammate Gerrit Cole was the only pitcher to achieve a game score of at least 100 last season.
- Noah Syndergaard allowed the most stolen bases (42), 18 more than any other pitcher in MLB.
- Adalberto Mondesi had an impressive 12 steals of third, five more than any other player in MLB.

2019 American League Batting Leaders

Batting Average		On Base Percentage		Slugging Average		Home Runs	
(minimum 502 PA)		(minimum 502 PA)		(minimum 502 PA)			
Anderson, Tim	.335	Trout, Mike	.438	Trout, Mike	.645	Soler, Jorge	48
LeMahieu, DJ	.327	Bregman, Alex	.423	Cruz, Nelson	.639	Trout, Mike	45
Moncada, Yoan	.315	Santana, Carlos	.397	Bregman, Alex	.592	Bregman, Alex	41
Brantley, Michael	.311	Cruz, Nelson	.392	Springer, George	.591	Cruz, Nelson	41
Devers, Rafael	.311	Betts, Mookie	.391	Soler, Jorge	.569	Springer, George	39
Cruz, Nelson	.311	Bogaerts, Xander	.384	Meadows, Austin	.558	Torres, Gleyber	38
Bogaerts, Xander	.309	Springer, George	.383	Martinez, J.D.	.557	Chapman, Matt	36
Alberto, Hanser	.305	Martinez, J.D.	.383	Bogaerts, Xander	.555	Kepler, Max	36
Martinez, J.D.	.304	Voit, Luke	.378	Devers, Rafael	.555	Martinez, J.D.	36
Merrifield, Whit	.302	LeMahieu, DJ	.375	Altuve, Jose	.550	Olson, Matt	36

Games		Plate Appearances		At Bats		Hits	
Merrifield, Whit	162	Semien, Marcus	747	Merrifield, Whit	681	Merrifield, Whit	206
Semien, Marcus	162	Merrifield, Whit	735	Semien, Marcus	657	Devers, Rafael	201
Soler, Jorge	162	Villar, Jonathan	714	Devers, Rafael	647	LeMahieu, DJ	197
Villar, Jonathan	162	Betts, Mookie	706	Villar, Jonathan	642	Bogaerts, Xander	190
Abreu, Jose	159	Polanco, Jorge	704	Abreu, Jose	634	Semien, Marcus	187
Santana, Carlos	158	Devers, Rafael	702	Polanco, Jorge	631	Polanco, Jorge	186
Bregman, Alex	156	Bogaerts, Xander	698	Bogaerts, Xander	614	Abreu, Jose	180
Chapman, Matt	156	Abreu, Jose	693	LeMahieu, DJ	602	Brantley, Michael	179
Devers, Rafael	156	Bregman, Alex	690	Mancini, Trey	602	Betts, Mookie	176
Bogaerts, Xander	155	Santana, Carlos	686	Andrus, Elvis	600	Villar, Jonathan	176

Singles		Doubles		Triples		Total Bases	
Merrifield, Whit	139	Devers, Rafael	54	Dozier, Hunter	10	Devers, Rafael	359
LeMahieu, DJ	136	Bogaerts, Xander	52	Merrifield, Whit	10	Semien, Marcus	343
Fletcher, David	133	Semien, Marcus	43	Mondesi, Adalberto	10	Bogaerts, Xander	341
Alberto, Hanser	125	Merrifield, Whit	41	Smith, Mallex	9	Soler, Jorge	335
Garcia, Leury	123	Benintendi, Andrew	40	Gardner, Brett	7	Bregman, Alex	328
Andrus, Elvis	122	Betts, Mookie	40	Kiermaier, Kevin	7	Mancini, Trey	322
Anderson, Tim	117	Brantley, Michael	40	Meadows, Austin	7	Martinez, J.D.	320
Polanco, Jorge	117	Gurriel, Yuli	40	Polanco, Jorge	7	Abreu, Jose	319
Brantley, Michael	115	Lindor, Francisco	40	Semien, Marcus	7	Merrifield, Whit	315
Villar, Jonathan	114	Polanco, Jorge	40	2 tied with	6	Betts, Mookie	313

Runs Scored		RBI		Walks		Strikeouts	
Betts, Mookie	135	Abreu, Jose	123	Bregman, Alex	119	Odor, Rougned	178
Devers, Rafael	129	Bogaerts, Xander	117	Trout, Mike	110	Soler, Jorge	178
Semien, Marcus	123	Soler, Jorge	117	Santana, Carlos	108	Villar, Jonathan	176
Bregman, Alex	122	Devers, Rafael	115	Betts, Mookie	97	Choo, Shin-Soo	165
Villar, Jonathan	111	Bregman, Alex	112	Vogelbach, Daniel	92	Santana, Domingo	164
Bogaerts, Xander	110	Rosario, Eddie	109	Semien, Marcus	87	Grichuk, Randal	163
Santana, Carlos	110	Cruz, Nelson	108	Pham, Tommy	81	Calhoun, Kole	162
Trout, Mike	110	Martinez, J.D.	105	Smoak, Justin	79	Sano, Miguel	159
LeMahieu, DJ	109	Gurriel, Yuli	104	Choo, Shin-Soo	78	Bradley Jr., Jackie	155
Polanco, Jorge	107	Trout, Mike	104	Bogaerts, Xander	76	Moncada, Yoan	154

2019 American League Batting Leaders

Intentional Walks	
Trout, Mike	14
Santana, Carlos	12
Lindor, Francisco	9
Martinez, J.D.	9
Cruz, Nelson	8
Calhoun, Kole	7
Devers, Rafael	7
Olson, Matt	7
Betts, Mookie	6
Meadows, Austin	6

BA Bases Loaded (minimum 10 PA)	
LeMahieu, DJ	.667
Urshela, Giovanny	.625
Smith, Mallex	.583
Brantley, Michael	.556
Santana, Danny	.556
Beckham, Tim	.500
Betts, Mookie	.500
Galvis, Freddy	.500
Reddick, Josh	.500
Trout, Mike	.500

Sacrifice Hits	
Garcia, Leury	11
DeShields, Delino	8
Mercado, Oscar	7
Perez, Roberto	7
Sanchez, Yolmer	7
Cordell, Ryan	6
Freeman, Mike	6
Jay, Jon	5
Kipnis, Jason	5
Martin Jr., Richie	5

Sacrifice Flies	
Abreu, Jose	10
Andrus, Elvis	10
Betts, Mookie	9
Reddick, Josh	9
Bregman, Alex	8
Laureano, Ramon	8
Pujols, Albert	8
Choi, Ji-Man	7
Polanco, Jorge	7
14 tied with	6

BA Close & Late (minimum 50 PA)	
Anderson, Tim	.385
Bogaerts, Xander	.374
Rosario, Eddie	.358
Arraez, Luis	.346
Brantley, Michael	.338
Vazquez, Christian	.337
Andrus, Elvis	.333
Canha, Mark	.333
McCann, James	.333
Gordon, Alex	.329

Batting Average w/ RISP (minimum 100 PA)	
LeMahieu, DJ	.392
Cabrera, Miguel	.369
Cruz, Nelson	.368
d'Arnaud, Travis	.348
Alvarez, Yordan	.344
Torres, Gleyber	.344
Brantley, Michael	.343
Rosario, Eddie	.340
Martinez, J.D.	.338
Abreu, Jose	.337

SLG vs. LHP (minimum 125 PA)	
Martinez, J.D.	.887
Cruz, Nelson	.783
Bregman, Alex	.742
Luplow, Jordan	.742
Garver, Mitch	.736
Murphy, Tom	.695
Altuve, Jose	.677
Alvarez, Yordan	.649
Cron, C.J.	.636
LeMahieu, DJ	.631

SLG vs. RHP (minimum 377 PA)	
Trout, Mike	.682
Springer, George	.621
Devers, Rafael	.608
Cruz, Nelson	.590
Soler, Jorge	.585
Meadows, Austin	.576
Moncada, Yoan	.569
Gurriel, Yuli	.564
Lindor, Francisco	.560
Bogaerts, Xander	.557

Leadoff Hitters OBP (minimum 150 PA)	
Springer, George	.385
Meadows, Austin	.382
Betts, Mookie	.375
LeMahieu, DJ	.372
Fletcher, David	.371
Choo, Shin-Soo	.368
Alberto, Hanser	.364
Semien, Marcus	.363
Bichette, Bo	.361
Sogard, Eric	.359

Cleanup Hitters SLG (minimum 150 PA)	
Olson, Matt	.723
Soler, Jorge	.610
Encarnacion, Edwin	.598
Brantley, Michael	.567
Martinez, J.D.	.553
Canha, Mark	.543
Dozier, Hunter	.543
Pujols, Albert	.500
Sanchez, Gary	.497
Rosario, Eddie	.492

BA vs. LHP (minimum 125 PA)	
Martinez, J.D.	.404
Alberto, Hanser	.398
LeMahieu, DJ	.375
Abreu, Jose	.360
Bregman, Alex	.350
Murphy, Tom	.347
Pham, Tommy	.340
Altuve, Jose	.331
Anderson, Tim	.326
Cron, C.J.	.326

BA vs. RHP (minimum 377 PA)	
Devers, Rafael	.330
Brantley, Michael	.323
Moncada, Yoan	.322
Gurriel, Yuli	.320
Bogaerts, Xander	.316
Merrifield, Whit	.311
LeMahieu, DJ	.310
Cruz, Nelson	.307
Polanco, Jorge	.306
Betts, Mookie	.304

Home BA (minimum 251 PA)	
LeMahieu, DJ	.338
Bogaerts, Xander	.337
Devers, Rafael	.318
Cabrera, Miguel	.315
Betts, Mookie	.314
Brantley, Michael	.312
Gurriel, Yuli	.311
Moncada, Yoan	.309
Abreu, Jose	.309
Merrifield, Whit	.307

Away BA (minimum 251 PA)	
Alberto, Hanser	.345
Anderson, Tim	.345
Martinez, J.D.	.333
Polanco, Jorge	.324
Moncada, Yoan	.321
LeMahieu, DJ	.318
Bregman, Alex	.315
Brantley, Michael	.311
Devers, Rafael	.304
Urshela, Giovanny	.304

OBP vs. LHP (minimum 125 PA)	
Martinez, J.D.	.494
Pham, Tommy	.467
Bregman, Alex	.443
Luplow, Jordan	.439
LeMahieu, DJ	.435
Garver, Mitch	.434
Trout, Mike	.429
Santana, Carlos	.428
Cruz, Nelson	.424
Abreu, Jose	.418

OBP vs. RHP (minimum 377 PA)	
Trout, Mike	.442
Bregman, Alex	.415
Betts, Mookie	.395
Bogaerts, Xander	.393
Choo, Shin-Soo	.393
Devers, Rafael	.388
Voit, Luke	.386
Meadows, Austin	.384
Santana, Carlos	.381
Cruz, Nelson	.381

2019 American League Batting Leaders

Stolen Bases		Caught Stealing		Highest SB Success Pct		Lowest SB Success Pct	
				(minimum 20 SBA)		(minimum 20 SBA)	
Smith, Mallex	46	Merrifield, Whit	10	Pham, Tommy	86.2	Moore, Dylan	55.0
Mondesi, Adalberto	43	Moore, Dylan	9	Mondesi, Adalberto	86.0	Odor, Rougned	55.0
Villar, Jonathan	40	Odor, Rougned	9	Ramirez, Jose	85.7	Merrifield, Whit	66.7
Andrus, Elvis	31	Smith, Mallex	9	Smith, Mallex	83.6	Garcia, Leury	75.0
Pham, Tommy	25	Villar, Jonathan	9	Villar, Jonathan	81.6	Anderson, Tim	77.3
DeShields, Delino	24	Andrus, Elvis	8	Gordon, Dee	81.5	Santana, Danny	77.8
Ramirez, Jose	24	Devers, Rafael	8	Lindor, Francisco	81.5	Hamilton, Billy	78.3
Gordon, Dee	22	Semien, Marcus	8	DeShields, Delino	80.0	Kiermaier, Kevin	79.2
Lindor, Francisco	22	Meadows, Austin	7	Andrus, Elvis	79.5	Andrus, Elvis	79.5
Santana, Danny	21	Mondesi, Adalberto	7	Kiermaier, Kevin	79.2	DeShields, Delino	80.0

Steals of Third		Grounded Into DP		Grounded Into DP Pct		Hit By Pitch	
				(minimum 50 GIDP Ops)			
Mondesi, Adalberto	12	Abreu, Jose	24	Biggio, Cavan	0.00	Gordon, Alex	19
Pham, Tommy	7	Mancini, Trey	22	Castro, Jason	0.00	Canha, Mark	18
Smith, Mallex	7	Pham, Tommy	22	Moncada, Yoan	1.02	Choo, Shin-Soo	18
Choo, Shin-Soo	6	Brantley, Michael	21	Santander, Anthony	1.23	Trout, Mike	16
Merrifield, Whit	6	Pujols, Albert	21	Lowe, Brandon	1.54	Abreu, Jose	13
Villar, Jonathan	6	Simmons, Andrelton	21	Hamilton, Billy	1.64	Chirinos, Robinson	13
Andrus, Elvis	4	Grichuk, Randal	20	Meadows, Austin	2.80	Bradley Jr., Jackie	12
DeShields, Delino	4	Altuve, Jose	19	Odor, Rougned	3.36	Olson, Matt	12
Gore, Terrance	4	Martinez, J.D.	19	Hicks, Aaron	3.45	3 tied with	11
Lindor, Francisco	4	Cabrera, Miguel	18	Pence, Hunter	3.64		

Pitches Seen		At Bats Per Home Run		Highest GB/FB Ratio		Lowest GB/FB Ratio	
		(minimum 502 PA)		(minimum 502 PA)		(minimum 502 PA)	
Semien, Marcus	2965	Trout, Mike	10.4	Garcia, Leury	2.33	Trout, Mike	0.49
Bregman, Alex	2915	Cruz, Nelson	11.1	Pham, Tommy	2.15	Polanco, Jorge	0.66
Betts, Mookie	2909	Soler, Jorge	12.3	LeMahieu, DJ	1.91	Bregman, Alex	0.69
Bogaerts, Xander	2862	Springer, George	12.3	Andrus, Elvis	1.84	Olson, Matt	0.70
Villar, Jonathan	2843	Olson, Matt	13.4	Anderson, Tim	1.76	Nunez, Renato	0.70
Chapman, Matt	2805	Bregman, Alex	13.5	Smith, Mallex	1.70	Ramirez, Jose	0.71
Santana, Carlos	2793	Torres, Gleyber	14.4	Choo, Shin-Soo	1.69	Betts, Mookie	0.72
Merrifield, Whit	2773	Kepler, Max	14.6	Villar, Jonathan	1.56	Odor, Rougned	0.73
Polanco, Jorge	2771	Jimenez, Eloy	15.1	Adames, Willy	1.54	Vogelbach, Daniel	0.74
Soler, Jorge	2750	Vogelbach, Daniel	15.4	Altuve, Jose	1.53	Kepler, Max	0.78

Pitches Per Plate App		Pct Pitches Taken		Best BPS on OutZ		Worst BPS on OutZ	
(minimum 502 PA)		(minimum 1500 Pitches)		(minimum 502 PA)		(minimum 502 PA)	
Vogelbach, Daniel	4.54	Forsythe, Logan	67.3	Gurriel, Yuli	.747	Adames, Willy	.247
Gardner, Brett	4.33	Vogelbach, Daniel	65.9	Trout, Mike	.689	Calhoun, Kole	.252
Meadows, Austin	4.23	Garver, Mitch	65.0	Alberto, Hanser	.684	Davis, Khris	.285
Bregman, Alex	4.23	Bregman, Alex	64.9	Merrifield, Whit	.647	Soler, Jorge	.294
Santana, Domingo	4.20	Biggio, Cavan	63.9	Bregman, Alex	.645	Kepler, Max	.299
Chapman, Matt	4.19	Fletcher, David	63.7	Altuve, Jose	.644	Choo, Shin-Soo	.320
Olson, Matt	4.18	Trout, Mike	63.2	Rosario, Eddie	.639	Vogelbach, Daniel	.332
Trout, Mike	4.18	Betts, Mookie	61.7	Bogaerts, Xander	.636	Pham, Tommy	.340
Springer, George	4.14	Grossman, Robbie	61.6	Brantley, Michael	.634	Kipnis, Jason	.368
Betts, Mookie	4.12	Pham, Tommy	61.6	Devers, Rafael	.605	Santana, Domingo	.370

2019 American League Batting Leaders

Best OPS vs Fastballs
(minimum 251 PA)

Springer, George	1.144
Cruz, Nelson	1.095
Canha, Mark	1.060
Soler, Jorge	1.055
Trout, Mike	1.052
Bogaerts, Xander	1.039
Mancini, Trey	1.029
Bregman, Alex	1.026
Gardner, Brett	.998
Semien, Marcus	.982

Best OPS vs Curveballs
(minimum 50 PA)

Benintendi, Andrew	1.476
Bregman, Alex	1.304
Olson, Matt	1.220
Villar, Jonathan	1.160
Gurriel, Yuli	1.144
Santana, Carlos	1.089
Nunez, Renato	1.053
Urshela, Giovanny	.996
LeMahieu, DJ	.989
Meadows, Austin	.940

Best OPS vs Changeups
(minimum 50 PA)

Trout, Mike	1.455
Martinez, J.D.	1.392
Mazara, Nomar	1.195
Cruz, Nelson	1.178
LeMahieu, DJ	1.115
Devers, Rafael	1.111
Alvarez, Yordan	1.054
Santana, Carlos	1.034
Abreu, Jose	1.021
Torres, Gleyber	.985

Best OPS vs Sliders
(minimum 32 PA)

Alvarez, Yordan	1.361
Gregorius, Didi	1.206
Santana, Danny	1.186
McKinney, Billy	1.070
Trout, Mike	1.054
Guzman, Ronald	1.051
Gurriel Jr., Lourdes	1.045
Springer, George	1.043
Schoop, Jonathan	1.029
Reyes, Franmil	1.017

OPS
(minimum 502 PA)

Trout, Mike	1.083
Cruz, Nelson	1.031
Bregman, Alex	1.015
Springer, George	.974
Bogaerts, Xander	.939
Martinez, J.D.	.939
Soler, Jorge	.922
Meadows, Austin	.922
Devers, Rafael	.916
2 tied with	.915

OPS First Half
(minimum 260 PA)

Trout, Mike	1.098
Gallo, Joey	1.060
Springer, George	.973
Santana, Carlos	.958
Bregman, Alex	.927
Devers, Rafael	.923
Cruz, Nelson	.921
Bogaerts, Xander	.919
Martinez, J.D.	.918
Moncada, Yoan	.908

OPS Second Half
(minimum 201 PA)

Cruz, Nelson	1.147
Bregman, Alex	1.134
Soler, Jorge	1.076
Trout, Mike	1.054
Alvarez, Yordan	1.044
Semien, Marcus	1.018
Gurriel, Yuli	1.005
Altuve, Jose	.995
Betts, Mookie	.992
Meadows, Austin	.982

OPS by Catchers
(minimum 251 PA)

Garver, Mitch	1.032
Narvaez, Omar	.889
Murphy, Tom	.874
Vazquez, Christian	.840
McCann, James	.819
Sanchez, Gary	.816
d'Arnaud, Travis	.788
Chirinos, Robinson	.787
Castro, Jason	.762
Perez, Roberto	.761

OPS by First Basemen
(minimum 251 PA)

Gurriel, Yuli	.900
Olson, Matt	.896
Santana, Carlos	.874
Choi, Ji-Man	.862
Abreu, Jose	.856
Voit, Luke	.825
Moreland, Mitch	.816
Pujols, Albert	.799
Cron, C.J.	.749
Guzman, Ronald	.728

OPS by Second Basemen
(minimum 251 PA)

Altuve, Jose	.912
Lowe, Brandon	.879
LeMahieu, DJ	.850
Sogard, Eric	.807
Villar, Jonathan	.801
Torres, Gleyber	.796
Biggio, Cavan	.793
Merrifield, Whit	.793
Schoop, Jonathan	.782
Odor, Rougned	.736

OPS by Third Basemen
(minimum 251 PA)

Bregman, Alex	.936
Devers, Rafael	.913
Moncada, Yoan	.907
Sano, Miguel	.905
Urshela, Giovanny	.890
Dozier, Hunter	.855
Chapman, Matt	.848
Guerrero Jr., Vladimir	.821
Seager, Kyle	.790
Ramirez, Jose	.790

OPS by Shortstops
(minimum 251 PA)

Bregman, Alex	1.134
Torres, Gleyber	.954
Bogaerts, Xander	.940
Correa, Carlos	.926
Semien, Marcus	.892
Anderson, Tim	.865
Polanco, Jorge	.845
Lindor, Francisco	.836
Villar, Jonathan	.764
Adames, Willy	.734

OPS by Left Fielders
(minimum 251 PA)

Gurriel Jr., Lourdes	.912
Brantley, Michael	.896
Pham, Tommy	.854
Jimenez, Eloy	.842
Calhoun, Willie	.837
Santana, Domingo	.788
Rosario, Eddie	.780
Benintendi, Andrew	.763
Gordon, Alex	.748
Stewart, Christin	.737

OPS by Center Fielders
(minimum 251 PA)

Trout, Mike	1.112
Springer, George	1.009
Hernandez, Teoscar	.861
Laureano, Ramon	.855
Buxton, Byron	.827
Gardner, Brett	.819
Jones, JaCoby	.745
Bradley Jr., Jackie	.737
Marisnick, Jake	.717
Mercado, Oscar	.712

OPS by Right Fielders
(minimum 251 PA)

Betts, Mookie	.916
Judge, Aaron	.906
Mancini, Trey	.895
Kepler, Max	.885
Garcia, Avisail	.863
Mazara, Nomar	.803
Calhoun, Kole	.799
Castellanos, Nicholas	.777
Grichuk, Randal	.740
Piscotty, Stephen	.719

OPS by Designated Hitters
(minimum 125 PA)

Alvarez, Yordan	1.042
Cruz, Nelson	1.030
Soler, Jorge	.991
Encarnacion, Edwin	.929
Martinez, J.D.	.884
Voit, Luke	.879
Meadows, Austin	.871
Smoak, Justin	.854
Ohtani, Shohei	.845
Choo, Shin-Soo	.828

2019 American League Batting Leaders

OPS Batting Left vs. LHP (minimum 125 PA)	
Alvarez, Yordan	1.038
Seager, Kyle	.945
Kepler, Max	.880
Meadows, Austin	.837
Tellez, Rowdy	.831
Odor, Rougned	.815
Benintendi, Andrew	.796
Kiermaier, Kevin	.784
Olson, Matt	.767
Rosario, Eddie	.766

OPS Batting Left vs. RHP (minimum 377 PA)	
Devers, Rafael	.996
Meadows, Austin	.960
Moncada, Yoan	.945
Brantley, Michael	.928
Lindor, Francisco	.893
Gardner, Brett	.892
Polanco, Jorge	.891
Choo, Shin-Soo	.886
Santana, Carlos	.879
Choi, Ji-Man	.869

OPS Batting Right vs. LHP (minimum 125 PA)	
Martinez, J.D.	1.381
Cruz, Nelson	1.207
Bregman, Alex	1.186
Luplow, Jordan	1.181
Garver, Mitch	1.170
Murphy, Tom	1.103
LeMahieu, DJ	1.066
Altuve, Jose	1.057
Cron, C.J.	1.020
Abreu, Jose	1.009

OPS Batting Right vs. RHP (minimum 377 PA)	
Trout, Mike	1.124
Springer, George	.999
Cruz, Nelson	.971
Bogaerts, Xander	.950
Betts, Mookie	.945
Bregman, Alex	.945
Soler, Jorge	.939
Gurriel, Yuli	.916
Mancini, Trey	.893
Semien, Marcus	.876

OPS vs. LHP (minimum 125 PA)	
Martinez, J.D.	1.381
Cruz, Nelson	1.207
Bregman, Alex	1.186
Luplow, Jordan	1.181
Garver, Mitch	1.170
Murphy, Tom	1.103
LeMahieu, DJ	1.066
Altuve, Jose	1.057
Alvarez, Yordan	1.038
Cron, C.J.	1.020

OPS vs. RHP (minimum 377 PA)	
Trout, Mike	1.124
Springer, George	.999
Devers, Rafael	.996
Cruz, Nelson	.971
Meadows, Austin	.960
Bogaerts, Xander	.950
Betts, Mookie	.945
Bregman, Alex	.945
Moncada, Yoan	.945
Soler, Jorge	.939

RC Per 27 Outs vs. LHP (minimum 125 PA)	
Martinez, J.D.	14.4
LeMahieu, DJ	10.9
Cruz, Nelson	10.9
Garver, Mitch	10.9
Murphy, Tom	10.8
Luplow, Jordan	10.5
Bregman, Alex	10.4
Cron, C.J.	9.0
Santana, Carlos	8.9
Trout, Mike	8.8

RC Per 27 Outs vs. RHP (minimum 377 PA)	
Trout, Mike	10.8
Springer, George	8.0
Moncada, Yoan	7.9
Meadows, Austin	7.8
Devers, Rafael	7.7
Cruz, Nelson	7.5
Bregman, Alex	7.5
Betts, Mookie	7.5
Brantley, Michael	7.4
Polanco, Jorge	7.3

Highest RBI % (minimum 502 PA)	
Cruz, Nelson	48.65
Trout, Mike	47.21
LeMahieu, DJ	45.01
Bregman, Alex	44.37
Springer, George	43.86
Kepler, Max	43.19
Meadows, Austin	42.97
Semien, Marcus	42.57
Soler, Jorge	42.45
Rosario, Eddie	42.05

Lowest RBI % (minimum 502 PA)	
Smith, Mallex	22.74
Garcia, Leury	22.98
Sanchez, Yolmer	24.16
Adames, Willy	27.15
Fletcher, David	29.27
Reddick, Josh	29.82
Pham, Tommy	30.28
Bradley Jr., Jackie	30.53
Grichuk, Randal	30.83
Alberto, Hanser	30.89

Highest Strikeout per PA (minimum 502 PA)	
Santana, Domingo	.323
Odor, Rougned	.306
Santana, Danny	.295
Voit, Luke	.278
Moncada, Yoan	.275
Davis, Khris	.274
Bradley Jr., Jackie	.273
Vogelbach, Daniel	.267
Jimenez, Eloy	.266
2 tied with	.262

Lowest Strikeout per PA (minimum 502 PA)	
Alberto, Hanser	.091
Fletcher, David	.098
Brantley, Michael	.104
Gurriel, Yuli	.106
Bregman, Alex	.120
Reddick, Josh	.120
Pujols, Albert	.125
LeMahieu, DJ	.137
Ramirez, Jose	.137
Semien, Marcus	.137

Home Runs At Home	
Chapman, Matt	21
Cruz, Nelson	21
Soler, Jorge	21
Trout, Mike	21
Torres, Gleyber	20
6 tied with	19

Home Runs Away	
Soler, Jorge	27
Bregman, Alex	25
Trout, Mike	24
Olson, Matt	23
Springer, George	21
Cruz, Nelson	20
Meadows, Austin	20
Rosario, Eddie	20
Sano, Miguel	20
3 tied with	19

Longest Avg Home Run (min 10 over the wall)	
Chavis, Michael	419
Trout, Mike	419
Gallo, Joey	418
Guerrero Jr., Vladimir	418
Sanchez, Gary	417
Mazara, Nomar	416
Sano, Miguel	415
Garcia, Avisail	415
Castro, Jason	415
Soler, Jorge	414

Shortest Avg Home Run (min 10 over the wall)	
Sogard, Eric	378
Goodrum, Niko	381
Tauchman, Mike	381
Cabrera, Asdrubal	381
Gardner, Brett	382
Bregman, Alex	382
Phegley, Josh	382
McKinney, Billy	383
Maldonado, Martin	383
Seager, Kyle	383

2019 American League Batting Leaders

Under Age 26: AB Per HR
(minimum 502 PA)

Olson, Matt	13.4
Bregman, Alex	13.5
Torres, Gleyber	14.4
Jimenez, Eloy	15.1
Meadows, Austin	16.1
Odor, Rougned	17.4
Nunez, Renato	17.5
Lindor, Francisco	18.7
Devers, Rafael	20.2
Moncada, Yoan	20.4

Under Age 26: OPS
(minimum 502 PA)

Bregman, Alex	1.015
Meadows, Austin	.922
Devers, Rafael	.916
Moncada, Yoan	.915
Olson, Matt	.896
Torres, Gleyber	.871
Lindor, Francisco	.854
Jimenez, Eloy	.828
Benintendi, Andrew	.774
Guerrero Jr., Vladimir	.772

Under Age 26: RC/27 Outs
(minimum 502 PA)

Bregman, Alex	8.3
Meadows, Austin	7.1
Moncada, Yoan	7.0
Devers, Rafael	6.9
Olson, Matt	6.7
Torres, Gleyber	6.5
Benintendi, Andrew	5.7
Fletcher, David	5.5
Lindor, Francisco	5.3
Nunez, Renato	5.1

Longest Home Run

Mazara, Nomar, 6/21	505
Mazara, Nomar, 3/28	482
Sano, Miguel, 9/17	482
Sanchez, Gary, 6/21	481
Bradley Jr., Jackie, 8/27	478
Alvarez, Yordan, 7/19	474
Broxton, Keon, 5/24	474
Correa, Carlos, 8/10	474
Cruz, Nelson, 7/25	473
Trout, Mike, 5/18	473

Swing and Miss %
(minimum 1500 Pitches Seen)

Mondesi, Adalberto	37.9
Davis, Chris	37.7
Sano, Miguel	37.3
Judge, Aaron	36.2
Dixon, Brandon	34.6
Voit, Luke	34.2
Davis, Khris	34.0
Hernandez, Teoscar	33.6
Chirinos, Robinson	33.0
Bradley Jr., Jackie	32.1

Highest First Swing %
(minimum 502 PA)

Garcia, Avisail	43.8
Voit, Luke	41.3
Rosario, Eddie	39.4
Davis, Khris	39.2
Altuve, Jose	38.9
Kepler, Max	38.5
Alberto, Hanser	37.8
Devers, Rafael	37.4
Jimenez, Eloy	37.0
Benintendi, Andrew	36.9

Lowest First Swing %
(minimum 502 PA)

Fletcher, David	8.1
Bogaerts, Xander	13.1
Gardner, Brett	13.3
Trout, Mike	14.4
Ramirez, Jose	14.5
Meadows, Austin	14.6
Pujols, Albert	14.7
Betts, Mookie	15.1
Vogelbach, Daniel	16.7
Bregman, Alex	16.8

Home RC Per 27 Outs
(minimum 251 PA)

Trout, Mike	10.6
LeMahieu, DJ	9.4
Bogaerts, Xander	8.5
Santana, Danny	8.2
Semien, Marcus	8.2
Gurriel, Yuli	8.0
Cruz, Nelson	7.9
Betts, Mookie	7.8
Choo, Shin-Soo	7.4
Chapman, Matt	7.2

Road RC Per 27 Outs
(minimum 251 PA)

Trout, Mike	10.0
Bregman, Alex	9.4
Martinez, J.D.	9.2
Olson, Matt	9.0
Springer, George	8.2
Santana, Carlos	7.7
Meadows, Austin	7.5
Polanco, Jorge	7.3
Moncada, Yoan	7.2
Soler, Jorge	7.0

Lead Changing RBI

Santana, Carlos	39
Abreu, Jose	37
Devers, Rafael	37
Soler, Jorge	33
Bogaerts, Xander	32
Bregman, Alex	32
Dozier, Hunter	32
Gurriel, Yuli	32
Mancini, Trey	32
Olson, Matt	32

2019 National League Batting Leaders

Batting Average (minimum 502 PA)		On Base Percentage (minimum 502 PA)		Slugging Average (minimum 502 PA)		Home Runs	
Yelich, Christian	.329	Yelich, Christian	.429	Yelich, Christian	.671	Alonso, Pete	53
Marte, Ketel	.329	Rendon, Anthony	.412	Bellinger, Cody	.629	Suarez, Eugenio	49
Rendon, Anthony	.319	Bellinger, Cody	.406	Rendon, Anthony	.598	Bellinger, Cody	47
McNeil, Jeff	.318	Rizzo, Anthony	.405	Marte, Ketel	.592	Yelich, Christian	44
Arenado, Nolan	.315	Soto, Juan	.401	Arenado, Nolan	.583	Acuna Jr., Ronald	41
Blackmon, Charlie	.314	Freeman, Freddie	.389	Alonso, Pete	.583	Arenado, Nolan	41
Reynolds, Bryan	.314	Marte, Ketel	.389	Blackmon, Charlie	.576	Freeman, Freddie	38
Newman, Kevin	.308	McNeil, Jeff	.384	Suarez, Eugenio	.572	Schwarber, Kyle	38
Bellinger, Cody	.305	Bryant, Kris	.382	Bell, Josh	.569	Bell, Josh	37
Turner, Trea	.298	Grandal, Yasmani	.380	Story, Trevor	.554	Donaldson, Josh	37

Games		Plate Appearances		At Bats		Hits	
Castro, Starlin	162	Acuna Jr., Ronald	715	Albies, Ozzie	640	Albies, Ozzie	189
Alonso, Pete	161	Hoskins, Rhys	705	Castro, Starlin	636	Marte, Ketel	187
Goldschmidt, Paul	161	Albies, Ozzie	702	Escobar, Eduardo	636	Arenado, Nolan	185
Hernandez, Cesar	161	Escobar, Eduardo	699	Acuna Jr., Ronald	626	Blackmon, Charlie	182
Albies, Ozzie	160	Alonso, Pete	693	Hosmer, Eric	619	Rosario, Amed	177
Hoskins, Rhys	160	Freeman, Freddie	692	Rosario, Amed	616	Freeman, Freddie	176
Hosmer, Eric	160	Goldschmidt, Paul	682	Hernandez, Cesar	612	Acuna Jr., Ronald	175
DeJong, Paul	159	Harper, Bryce	682	Alonso, Pete	597	Rendon, Anthony	174
Suarez, Eugenio	159	Castro, Starlin	676	Freeman, Freddie	597	Story, Trevor	173
3 tied with	158	2 tied with	667	Goldschmidt, Paul	597	Castro, Starlin	172

Singles		Doubles		Triples		Total Bases	
Rosario, Amed	125	Rendon, Anthony	44	Escobar, Eduardo	10	Bellinger, Cody	351
Hernandez, Cesar	123	Seager, Corey	44	Marte, Ketel	9	Alonso, Pete	348
Castro, Starlin	115	Albies, Ozzie	43	Albies, Ozzie	8	Arenado, Nolan	343
Albies, Ozzie	114	Blackmon, Charlie	42	Blackmon, Charlie	7	Marte, Ketel	337
Newman, Kevin	114	Baez, Javier	38	Eaton, Adam	7	Blackmon, Charlie	334
Arenado, Nolan	111	McNeil, Jeff	38	Edman, Tommy	7	Suarez, Eugenio	329
Eaton, Adam	111	Story, Trevor	38	Ervin, Phillip	7	Freeman, Freddie	328
Hosmer, Eric	111	5 tied with	37	Frazier, Adam	7	Yelich, Christian	328
3 tied with	110			Rosario, Amed	7	Rendon, Anthony	326
				4 tied with	6	Story, Trevor	326

Runs Scored		RBI		Walks		Strikeouts	
Acuna Jr., Ronald	127	Rendon, Anthony	126	Hoskins, Rhys	116	Suarez, Eugenio	189
Bellinger, Cody	121	Freeman, Freddie	121	Grandal, Yasmani	109	Acuna Jr., Ronald	188
Rendon, Anthony	117	Alonso, Pete	120	Soto, Juan	108	Alonso, Pete	183
Freeman, Freddie	113	Arenado, Nolan	118	Donaldson, Josh	100	Harper, Bryce	178
Blackmon, Charlie	112	Escobar, Eduardo	118	Harper, Bryce	99	Story, Trevor	174
Story, Trevor	111	Bell, Josh	116	Bellinger, Cody	95	Hoskins, Rhys	173
Soto, Juan	110	Bellinger, Cody	115	Muncy, Max	90	Myers, Wil	168
Bryant, Kris	108	Harper, Bryce	114	Freeman, Freddie	87	Goldschmidt, Paul	166
Alonso, Pete	103	Soto, Juan	110	Conforto, Michael	84	Hosmer, Eric	163
Eaton, Adam	103	Suarez, Eugenio	103	Belt, Brandon	83	McMahon, Ryan	160

2019 National League Batting Leaders

Intentional Walks		BA Bases Loaded		Sacrifice Hits		Sacrifice Flies	
		(minimum 10 PA)					
Bellinger, Cody	21	Ramos, Wilson	.611	Kershaw, Clayton	15	Ahmed, Nick	12
Franco, Maikel	19	Iglesias, Jose	.571	Maeda, Kenta	13	Escobar, Eduardo	10
Yelich, Christian	16	Parra, Gerardo	.571	Gray, Sonny	12	Castro, Starlin	9
Bell, Josh	13	Rizzo, Anthony	.571	Ryu, Hyun-Jin	12	Rendon, Anthony	9
Arenado, Nolan	11	Murphy, Daniel	.556	Marquez, German	10	Arenado, Nolan	8
Freeman, Freddie	11	Conforto, Michael	.545	Eaton, Adam	9	Realmuto, J.T.	8
Harper, Bryce	11	Acuna Jr., Ronald	.500	Flaherty, Jack	9	Bell, Josh	7
Kelly, Carson	10	Dickerson, Corey	.500	Gray, Jon	9	12 tied with	6
Rendon, Anthony	8	Nimmo, Brandon	.500	Quintana, Jose	9		
2 tied with	7	Pillar, Kevin	.500	Musgrove, Joe	8		

BA Close & Late		Batting Average w/ RISP		SLG vs. LHP		SLG vs. RHP	
(minimum 50 PA)		(minimum 100 PA)		(minimum 125 PA)		(minimum 377 PA)	
Yelich, Christian	.443	Blackmon, Charlie	.385	Machado, Manny	.685	Yelich, Christian	.734
Edman, Tommy	.397	Rendon, Anthony	.365	Albies, Ozzie	.685	Bellinger, Cody	.647
Walker, Neil	.367	Freeman, Freddie	.363	Marte, Ketel	.630	Bell, Josh	.615
Cooper, Garrett	.362	Harper, Bryce	.357	Bryant, Kris	.629	Rendon, Anthony	.592
Iglesias, Jose	.360	McNeil, Jeff	.350	Desmond, Ian	.626	Freeman, Freddie	.589
Davis, J.D.	.358	Taylor, Chris	.341	Rendon, Anthony	.618	Soto, Juan	.584
Kendrick, Howie	.356	Albies, Ozzie	.338	Kendrick, Howie	.615	Alonso, Pete	.582
Hiura, Keston	.354	Rojas, Miguel	.337	Arenado, Nolan	.611	Marte, Ketel	.577
Soto, Juan	.349	Bell, Josh	.336	Bellinger, Cody	.596	Arenado, Nolan	.573
Castro, Starlin	.340	Baez, Javier	.333	Alonso, Pete	.587	Blackmon, Charlie	.573

Leadoff Hitters OBP		Cleanup Hitters SLG		BA vs. LHP		BA vs. RHP	
(minimum 150 PA)		(minimum 150 PA)		(minimum 125 PA)		(minimum 377 PA)	
Winker, Jesse	.387	Bellinger, Cody	.632	Albies, Ozzie	.389	Yelich, Christian	.358
McNeil, Jeff	.386	Arenado, Nolan	.621	Kendrick, Howie	.376	Reynolds, Bryan	.334
Tatis Jr., Fernando	.386	Baez, Javier	.570	Marte, Ketel	.333	Marte, Ketel	.327
McCutchen, Andrew	.378	Bell, Josh	.564	Castro, Starlin	.323	Rendon, Anthony	.320
Newman, Kevin	.374	Soto, Juan	.551	Murphy, Daniel	.320	McNeil, Jeff	.320
Blackmon, Charlie	.368	Donaldson, Josh	.523	Dahl, David	.319	Bellinger, Cody	.318
Acuna Jr., Ronald	.364	Rizzo, Anthony	.519	Turner, Trea	.316	Blackmon, Charlie	.318
Turner, Trea	.355	Murphy, Daniel	.509	Rendon, Anthony	.316	Newman, Kevin	.316
Garcia, Greg	.346	Moustakas, Mike	.505	Machado, Manny	.315	Arenado, Nolan	.315
Berti, Jon	.343	Hoskins, Rhys	.501	Arenado, Nolan	.315	Freeman, Freddie	.310

Home BA		Away BA		OBP vs. LHP		OBP vs. RHP	
(minimum 251 PA)		(minimum 251 PA)		(minimum 125 PA)		(minimum 377 PA)	
Blackmon, Charlie	.379	Newman, Kevin	.350	Hoskins, Rhys	.444	Yelich, Christian	.455
Rizzo, Anthony	.354	Reynolds, Bryan	.335	Rendon, Anthony	.433	Bellinger, Cody	.417
Arenado, Nolan	.351	McNeil, Jeff	.325	Bryant, Kris	.426	Freeman, Freddie	.416
Marte, Ketel	.347	Rosario, Amed	.323	Kendrick, Howie	.421	Rizzo, Anthony	.416
Yelich, Christian	.347	Iglesias, Jose	.322	Suarez, Eugenio	.417	Soto, Juan	.416
Story, Trevor	.328	Rendon, Anthony	.321	Arenado, Nolan	.416	Rendon, Anthony	.404
Rendon, Anthony	.317	Turner, Justin	.321	Albies, Ozzie	.414	Reynolds, Bryan	.401
Soto, Juan	.311	Wong, Kolten	.316	Machado, Manny	.404	Marte, Ketel	.396
McNeil, Jeff	.310	Freeman, Freddie	.313	Grandal, Yasmani	.397	Bell, Josh	.387
Albies, Ozzie	.310	Marte, Ketel	.313	Donaldson, Josh	.395	McNeil, Jeff	.387

2019 National League Batting Leaders

Stolen Bases			Caught Stealing			Highest SB Success Pct (minimum 20 SBA)			Lowest SB Success Pct (minimum 20 SBA)	
Acuna Jr., Ronald	37		Rosario, Amed	10		Yelich, Christian	93.8		Rosario, Amed	65.5
Turner, Trea	35		Acuna Jr., Ronald	9		Dyson, Jarrod	88.2		Newman, Kevin	66.7
Dyson, Jarrod	30		Robles, Victor	9		Turner, Trea	87.5		Cain, Lorenzo	69.2
Yelich, Christian	30		Cain, Lorenzo	8		Wong, Kolten	85.7		Myers, Wil	69.6
Robles, Victor	28		Newman, Kevin	8		Berti, Jon	85.0		Tatis Jr., Fernando	72.7
Marte, Starling	25		Story, Trevor	8		Margot, Manuel	83.3		Story, Trevor	74.2
Wong, Kolten	24		Baez, Javier	7		Marte, Starling	80.6		Bellinger, Cody	75.0
Story, Trevor	23		Myers, Wil	7		Acuna Jr., Ronald	80.4		Robles, Victor	75.7
Margot, Manuel	20		5 tied with	6		Robles, Victor	75.7		Acuna Jr., Ronald	80.4
Rosario, Amed	19					Bellinger, Cody	75.0		Marte, Starling	80.6

Steals of Third			Grounded Into DP			Grounded Into DP Pct (minimum 50 GIDP Ops)			Hit By Pitch	
Yelich, Christian	7		Machado, Manny	24		Gamel, Ben	0.00		Rizzo, Anthony	27
Robles, Victor	6		Castro, Starlin	23		Thames, Eric	0.00		Dietrich, Derek	25
Acuna Jr., Ronald	4		Ozuna, Marcell	21		Vogt, Stephen	1.59		Robles, Victor	25
Arcia, Orlando	4		Posey, Buster	18		Dyson, Jarrod	1.61		Locastro, Tim	22
Bader, Harrison	4		Freeman, Freddie	17		Albies, Ozzie	2.08		Alonso, Pete	21
Margot, Manuel	4		Iglesias, Jose	17		Wong, Kolten	2.27		McNeil, Jeff	21
Ozuna, Marcell	4		Baez, Javier	16		Tapia, Raimel	2.70		Marte, Starling	16
13 tied with	3		Cano, Robinson	16		Story, Trevor	2.80		Bryant, Kris	15
			Grandal, Yasmani	16		Kingery, Scott	3.45		Anderson, Brian	14
			Ramos, Wilson	16		Dahl, David	3.75		Turner, Justin	14

Pitches Seen			At Bats Per Home Run (minimum 502 PA)			Highest GB/FB Ratio (minimum 502 PA)			Lowest GB/FB Ratio (minimum 502 PA)	
Hoskins, Rhys	3223		Yelich, Christian	11.1		Ramos, Wilson	3.26		Hoskins, Rhys	0.58
Acuna Jr., Ronald	3048		Alonso, Pete	11.3		Hosmer, Eric	2.42		Belt, Brandon	0.58
Goldschmidt, Paul	2888		Suarez, Eugenio	11.7		Iglesias, Jose	2.16		Rendon, Anthony	0.72
Soto, Juan	2791		Bellinger, Cody	11.9		Cain, Lorenzo	2.08		Escobar, Eduardo	0.73
Harper, Bryce	2787		Pederson, Joc	12.5		Segura, Jean	1.91		Bellinger, Cody	0.74
Alonso, Pete	2762		Muncy, Max	13.9		McMahon, Ryan	1.82		Story, Trevor	0.79
Freeman, Freddie	2750		Schwarber, Kyle	13.9		Marte, Starling	1.79		Moustakas, Mike	0.79
Donaldson, Josh	2742		Bell, Josh	14.2		Newman, Kevin	1.74		Arenado, Nolan	0.80
Grandal, Yasmani	2733		Arenado, Nolan	14.3		Crawford, Brandon	1.70		Bryant, Kris	0.83
Suarez, Eugenio	2728		Donaldson, Josh	14.8		Hernandez, Cesar	1.69		Turner, Justin	0.84

Pitches Per Plate App (minimum 502 PA)			Pct Pitches Taken (minimum 1500 Pitches)			Best BPS on OutZ (minimum 502 PA)			Worst BPS on OutZ (minimum 502 PA)	
Hoskins, Rhys	4.57		Garcia, Greg	65.8		Turner, Trea	.714		Walker, Christian	.251
Muncy, Max	4.38		Grandal, Yasmani	61.5		Yelich, Christian	.695		DeJong, Paul	.267
Grandal, Yasmani	4.32		Hoskins, Rhys	60.8		Arenado, Nolan	.651		Crawford, Brandon	.269
Acuna Jr., Ronald	4.26		Dozier, Brian	60.7		Realmuto, J.T.	.623		Cain, Lorenzo	.310
Soto, Juan	4.24		Granderson, Curtis	60.2		Baez, Javier	.618		Seager, Corey	.340
Goldschmidt, Paul	4.24		Muncy, Max	59.9		Marte, Ketel	.612		Ozuna, Marcell	.348
Fowler, Dexter	4.21		Gamel, Ben	59.9		Bellinger, Cody	.603		Arcia, Orlando	.350
McMahon, Ryan	4.17		Carpenter, Matt	59.4		Newman, Kevin	.597		McMahon, Ryan	.353
Schwarber, Kyle	4.16		Soto, Juan	59.2		Pillar, Kevin	.595		Grandal, Yasmani	.355
Donaldson, Josh	4.16		Bader, Harrison	58.6		Albies, Ozzie	.576		Soto, Juan	.356

2019 National League Batting Leaders

Best OPS vs Fastballs (minimum 251 PA)		Best OPS vs Curveballs (minimum 50 PA)		Best OPS vs Changeups (minimum 50 PA)		Best OPS vs Sliders (minimum 32 PA)	
Rendon, Anthony	1.125	Baez, Javier	1.132	Yelich, Christian	1.258	Nimmo, Brandon	1.209
Yelich, Christian	1.068	Freeman, Freddie	1.122	Moustakas, Mike	1.089	Caratini, Victor	1.197
Bellinger, Cody	1.066	Blackmon, Charlie	1.108	Alonso, Pete	1.079	Blackmon, Charlie	1.148
Muncy, Max	1.053	Soto, Juan	1.104	Story, Trevor	1.059	Hiura, Keston	1.125
Marte, Ketel	1.033	Rendon, Anthony	1.102	Sandoval, Pablo	1.006	Rizzo, Anthony	1.114
Bell, Josh	1.009	McNeil, Jeff	1.090	Soto, Juan	.980	Tatis Jr., Fernando	1.077
Alonso, Pete	1.007	Arenado, Nolan	1.068	Bellinger, Cody	.975	Bell, Josh	1.054
Freeman, Freddie	1.006	Acuna Jr., Ronald	1.067	Conforto, Michael	.961	Anderson, Brian	1.048
Soto, Juan	.991	Marte, Ketel	.969	Desmond, Ian	.920	Puig, Yasiel	1.048
Suarez, Eugenio	.988	Walker, Christian	.938	McNeil, Jeff	.878	Hernandez, Cesar	1.021

OPS (minimum 502 PA)		OPS First Half (minimum 260 PA)		OPS Second Half (minimum 201 PA)		OPS by Catchers (minimum 251 PA)	
Yelich, Christian	1.100	Yelich, Christian	1.140	Marte, Ketel	1.081	Contreras, Willson	.901
Bellinger, Cody	1.035	Bellinger, Cody	1.124	Suarez, Eugenio	1.081	Grandal, Yasmani	.864
Rendon, Anthony	1.010	Bell, Josh	1.024	Yelich, Christian	1.034	Kelly, Carson	.844
Marte, Ketel	.981	Blackmon, Charlie	1.010	Rendon, Anthony	1.023	Realmuto, J.T.	.832
Arenado, Nolan	.962	Alonso, Pete	1.006	Hiura, Keston	1.006	Suzuki, Kurt	.806
Soto, Juan	.949	Rendon, Anthony	.997	Castellanos, Nicholas	1.002	Ramos, Wilson	.773
Alonso, Pete	.941	Freeman, Freddie	.978	Schwarber, Kyle	.997	Alfaro, Jorge	.760
Blackmon, Charlie	.940	Bryant, Kris	.955	Arenado, Nolan	.995	Barnhart, Tucker	.745
Freeman, Freddie	.938	Soto, Juan	.943	Davis, J.D.	.979	McCann, Brian	.745
Bell, Josh	.936	Arenado, Nolan	.939	Turner, Justin	.971	Flowers, Tyler	.738

OPS by First Basemen (minimum 251 PA)		OPS by Second Basemen (minimum 251 PA)		OPS by Third Basemen (minimum 251 PA)		OPS by Shortstops (minimum 251 PA)	
Alonso, Pete	.944	Hiura, Keston	.936	Rendon, Anthony	1.010	Tatis Jr., Fernando	.972
Freeman, Freddie	.937	Muncy, Max	.858	Arenado, Nolan	.966	Story, Trevor	.916
Bell, Josh	.928	Albies, Ozzie	.851	Suarez, Eugenio	.939	Baez, Javier	.860
Rizzo, Anthony	.925	Wong, Kolten	.779	Donaldson, Josh	.904	Turner, Trea	.850
Thames, Eric	.896	Dozier, Brian	.770	Turner, Justin	.887	Seager, Corey	.820
Cooper, Garrett	.837	Frazier, Adam	.745	Bryant, Kris	.861	Newman, Kevin	.812
Goldschmidt, Paul	.823	Hernandez, Cesar	.741	Escobar, Eduardo	.825	DeJong, Paul	.765
Walker, Christian	.822	Cano, Robinson	.728	Moustakas, Mike	.815	Rosario, Amed	.758
Hoskins, Rhys	.814	McMahon, Ryan	.726	Anderson, Brian	.812	Ahmed, Nick	.750
Murphy, Daniel	.806	Hernandez, Kike	.687	Machado, Manny	.792	Swanson, Dansby	.749

OPS by Left Fielders (minimum 251 PA)		OPS by Center Fielders (minimum 251 PA)		OPS by Right Fielders (minimum 251 PA)		OPS by Pitchers (minimum 50 PA)	
Davis, J.D.	.968	Marte, Ketel	1.095	Yelich, Christian	1.125	Greinke, Zack	.898
Soto, Juan	.949	Acuna Jr., Ronald	.864	Bellinger, Cody	1.063	Marquez, German	.596
Dickerson, Corey	.902	Marte, Starling	.847	Blackmon, Charlie	.948	Lester, Jon	.567
Pederson, Joc	.902	Desmond, Ian	.800	Harper, Bryce	.876	Maeda, Kenta	.565
Braun, Ryan	.890	Pollock, A.J.	.792	Reyes, Franmil	.857	Wheeler, Zack	.561
Schwarber, Kyle	.873	Pillar, Kevin	.760	Heyward, Jason	.851	deGrom, Jacob	.558
Reynolds, Bryan	.870	Robles, Victor	.756	Conforto, Michael	.845	Matz, Steven	.537
Ozuna, Marcell	.805	Senzel, Nick	.752	Martinez, Jose	.805	Fried, Max	.523
Peralta, David	.793	Cain, Lorenzo	.699	Eaton, Adam	.792	Ryu, Hyun-Jin	.462
Tapia, Raimel	.706	Heyward, Jason	.696	Markakis, Nick	.789	Flaherty, Jack	.451

2019 National League Batting Leaders

OPS Batting Left vs. LHP (minimum 125 PA)		OPS Batting Left vs. RHP (minimum 377 PA)		OPS Batting Right vs. LHP (minimum 125 PA)		OPS Batting Right vs. RHP (minimum 377 PA)	
Bellinger, Cody	.982	Yelich, Christian	1.189	Albies, Ozzie	1.099	Rendon, Anthony	.996
Harper, Bryce	.949	Bellinger, Cody	1.061	Machado, Manny	1.089	Alonso, Pete	.941
Blackmon, Charlie	.940	Freeman, Freddie	1.005	Bryant, Kris	1.055	Arenado, Nolan	.937
Yelich, Christian	.936	Bell, Josh	1.002	Rendon, Anthony	1.050	Donaldson, Josh	.917
Dahl, David	.900	Soto, Juan	1.000	Kendrick, Howie	1.036	Story, Trevor	.911
Muncy, Max	.893	Marte, Ketel	.976	Arenado, Nolan	1.027	Suarez, Eugenio	.911
Murphy, Daniel	.881	Rizzo, Anthony	.962	Marte, Ketel	.998	Acuna Jr., Ronald	.878
Moustakas, Mike	.876	McNeil, Jeff	.951	Suarez, Eugenio	.994	Marte, Starling	.868
Soto, Juan	.850	Blackmon, Charlie	.940	Hoskins, Rhys	.980	Bryant, Kris	.866
McNeil, Jeff	.825	Reynolds, Bryan	.931	Desmond, Ian	.977	Turner, Trea	.864

OPS vs. LHP (minimum 125 PA)		OPS vs. RHP (minimum 377 PA)		RC Per 27 Outs vs. LHP (minimum 125 PA)		RC Per 27 Outs vs. RHP (minimum 377 PA)	
Albies, Ozzie	1.099	Yelich, Christian	1.189	Albies, Ozzie	11.9	Yelich, Christian	12.2
Machado, Manny	1.089	Bellinger, Cody	1.061	Bryant, Kris	9.7	Rendon, Anthony	8.9
Bryant, Kris	1.055	Freeman, Freddie	1.005	Marte, Ketel	8.8	Bell, Josh	8.8
Rendon, Anthony	1.050	Bell, Josh	1.002	Rendon, Anthony	8.6	Freeman, Freddie	8.8
Kendrick, Howie	1.036	Soto, Juan	1.000	Hoskins, Rhys	8.5	Soto, Juan	8.6
Arenado, Nolan	1.027	Rendon, Anthony	.996	Kendrick, Howie	8.2	Bellinger, Cody	8.3
Marte, Ketel	.998	Marte, Ketel	.973	Acuna Jr., Ronald	8.2	Rizzo, Anthony	8.2
Suarez, Eugenio	.994	Rizzo, Anthony	.962	Goldschmidt, Paul	8.1	Marte, Ketel	8.0
Bellinger, Cody	.982	McNeil, Jeff	.951	Arenado, Nolan	8.0	McNeil, Jeff	8.0
Hoskins, Rhys	.980	Alonso, Pete	.941	Machado, Manny	8.0	Arenado, Nolan	7.6

Highest RBI % (minimum 502 PA)		Lowest RBI % (minimum 502 PA)		Highest Strikeout per PA (minimum 502 PA)		Lowest Strikeout per PA (minimum 502 PA)	
Yelich, Christian	46.34	Cain, Lorenzo	24.84	McMahon, Ryan	.297	Newman, Kevin	.117
Rendon, Anthony	46.24	Eaton, Adam	27.04	Suarez, Eugenio	.285	Rojas, Miguel	.118
Freeman, Freddie	45.76	Votto, Joey	27.06	Baez, Javier	.278	Segura, Jean	.118
Bell, Josh	44.36	Rojas, Miguel	28.54	Story, Trevor	.265	Frazier, Adam	.123
Arenado, Nolan	44.03	Frazier, Adam	28.67	Alonso, Pete	.264	Iglesias, Jose	.132
Harper, Bryce	43.95	Belt, Brandon	28.82	Acuna Jr., Ronald	.263	McNeil, Jeff	.132
Bellinger, Cody	43.66	Arcia, Orlando	28.89	Harper, Bryce	.261	Ramos, Wilson	.132
Alonso, Pete	43.60	Crawford, Brandon	30.51	Walker, Christian	.257	Rendon, Anthony	.133
Acuna Jr., Ronald	43.02	Segura, Jean	31.38	Schwarber, Kyle	.256	Marte, Ketel	.137
Blackmon, Charlie	42.83	Hernandez, Cesar	31.50	Muncy, Max	.253	Pillar, Kevin	.137

Home Runs At Home		Home Runs Away		Longest Avg Home Run (min 10 over the wall)		Shortest Avg Home Run (min 10 over the wall)	
Alonso, Pete	27	Alonso, Pete	26	Desmond, Ian	425	Winker, Jesse	378
Bellinger, Cody	27	Suarez, Eugenio	25	Acuna Jr., Ronald	418	Barnhart, Tucker	380
Yelich, Christian	27	Acuna Jr., Ronald	23	Cooper, Garrett	418	Wieters, Matt	385
Pederson, Joc	24	Muncy, Max	22	McMahon, Ryan	415	Suzuki, Kurt	386
Story, Trevor	24	Moustakas, Mike	21	Alonso, Pete	414	Edman, Tommy	387
Suarez, Eugenio	24	Arenado, Nolan	20	Story, Trevor	414	Murphy, Daniel	388
Blackmon, Charlie	22	Bell, Josh	20	Renfroe, Hunter	413	Segura, Jean	389
Donaldson, Josh	22	Bellinger, Cody	20	Bader, Harrison	412	Hoskins, Rhys	389
Freeman, Freddie	22	DeJong, Paul	20	Blackmon, Charlie	412	Ramirez, Harold	389
Arenado, Nolan	21	Schwarber, Kyle	20	Bell, Josh	411	Iglesias, Jose	389

2019 National League Batting Leaders

Under Age 26: AB Per HR
(minimum 502 PA)

Alonso, Pete	11.3
Bellinger, Cody	11.9
Acuna Jr., Ronald	15.3
Soto, Juan	15.9
Marte, Ketel	17.8
McMahon, Ryan	20.0
Seager, Corey	25.7
Albies, Ozzie	26.7
Swanson, Dansby	28.4
Reynolds, Bryan	30.7

Under Age 26: OPS
(minimum 502 PA)

Bellinger, Cody	1.035
Marte, Ketel	.981
Soto, Juan	.949
Alonso, Pete	.941
Acuna Jr., Ronald	.883
Reynolds, Bryan	.880
Albies, Ozzie	.852
Seager, Corey	.817
McMahon, Ryan	.779
Rosario, Amed	.755

Under Age 26: RC/27 Outs
(minimum 502 PA)

Marte, Ketel	8.3
Bellinger, Cody	8.2
Soto, Juan	7.7
Acuna Jr., Ronald	7.0
Reynolds, Bryan	6.8
Albies, Ozzie	6.6
Alonso, Pete	6.6
Seager, Corey	5.9
McMahon, Ryan	4.9
Robles, Victor	4.9

Longest Home Run

Ravelo, Rangel, 9/12	487
Desmond, Ian, 6/10	486
Arenado, Nolan, 9/10	482
Marte, Ketel, 6/2	482
McMahon, Ryan, 6/27	479
Iannetta, Chris, 6/2	476
Alonso, Pete, 7/17	474
Bell, Josh, 4/7	474
Happ, Ian, 8/5	474
3 tied with	473

Swing and Miss %
(minimum 1500 Pitches Seen)

Alfaro, Jorge	37.6
Baez, Javier	34.8
Harper, Bryce	33.2
Myers, Wil	32.2
Contreras, Willson	32.0
Thames, Eric	31.7
McMahon, Ryan	31.2
Kingery, Scott	31.0
Taylor, Chris	30.9
Renfroe, Hunter	29.7

Highest First Swing %
(minimum 502 PA)

McNeil, Jeff	47.7
Baez, Javier	44.3
Albies, Ozzie	43.1
Ramos, Wilson	43.1
Harper, Bryce	41.8
Crawford, Brandon	41.6
Moran, Colin	40.8
Seager, Corey	39.9
McMahon, Ryan	39.1
Freeman, Freddie	37.6

Lowest First Swing %
(minimum 502 PA)

Eaton, Adam	16.3
Hoskins, Rhys	17.6
DeJong, Paul	20.2
Grandal, Yasmani	20.3
Segura, Jean	20.5
Rizzo, Anthony	20.9
Frazier, Adam	21.5
Cain, Lorenzo	21.7
Muncy, Max	22.0
Pederson, Joc	22.1

Home RC Per 27 Outs
(minimum 251 PA)

Yelich, Christian	11.7
Rizzo, Anthony	10.8
Blackmon, Charlie	10.3
Arenado, Nolan	9.3
Soto, Juan	9.2
Story, Trevor	9.1
Marte, Ketel	9.0
Rendon, Anthony	9.0
Bellinger, Cody	8.3
Donaldson, Josh	8.0

Road RC Per 27 Outs
(minimum 251 PA)

Rendon, Anthony	8.8
Bell, Josh	8.4
Freeman, Freddie	8.2
Wong, Kolten	8.2
Yelich, Christian	8.1
McNeil, Jeff	8.1
Bellinger, Cody	8.0
Alonso, Pete	7.6
Marte, Ketel	7.6
Muncy, Max	7.4

Lead Changing RBI

Rendon, Anthony	43
Freeman, Freddie	40
Suarez, Eugenio	38
Bell, Josh	37
Alonso, Pete	36
Arenado, Nolan	34
Bellinger, Cody	33
Castro, Starlin	33
Harper, Bryce	32
Muncy, Max	32

2019 American League Pitching Leaders

Earned Run Average (minimum 162 IP)		Winning Percentage (minimum 15 Decisions)		Opponent Batting Average (minimum 162 IP)		Baserunners Per 9 IP (minimum 162 IP)	
Cole, Gerrit	2.50	German, Domingo	.818	Verlander, Justin	.172	Verlander, Justin	7.47
Verlander, Justin	2.58	Cole, Gerrit	.800	Cole, Gerrit	.186	Cole, Gerrit	8.18
Morton, Charlie	3.05	Fiers, Mike	.789	Giolito, Lucas	.205	Bieber, Shane	9.74
Bieber, Shane	3.28	Verlander, Justin	.778	Morton, Charlie	.215	Giolito, Lucas	9.78
Giolito, Lucas	3.41	Clevinger, Mike	.765	Bieber, Shane	.230	Morton, Charlie	10.31
Minor, Mike	3.59	Rodriguez, Eduardo	.760	Fiers, Mike	.243	Fiers, Mike	11.11
Lynn, Lance	3.67	Morton, Charlie	.727	Lynn, Lance	.243	Tanaka, Masahiro	11.28
Berrios, Jose	3.68	Paxton, James	.714	Minor, Mike	.244	Lynn, Lance	11.32
Rodriguez, Eduardo	3.81	Miley, Wade	.700	Keller, Brad	.247	Berrios, Jose	11.41
Anderson, Brett	3.89	Pineda, Michael	.688	Boyd, Matthew	.247	Minor, Mike	11.45

Games		Games Started		Complete Games		Shutouts	
Petit, Yusmeiro	80	Gonzales, Marco	34	Bieber, Shane	3	Bieber, Shane	2
Diekman, Jake	76	Nova, Ivan	34	Giolito, Lucas	3	Giolito, Lucas	2
Hendriks, Liam	75	Rodriguez, Eduardo	34	Leake, Mike	2	11 tied with	1
Farmer, Buck	73	Verlander, Justin	34	Minor, Mike	2		
Ottavino, Adam	73	7 tied with	33	Nova, Ivan	2		
Workman, Brandon	73			Verlander, Justin	2		
Buttrey, Ty	72			13 tied with	1		
Kahnle, Tommy	72						
3 tied with	71						

Wins		Losses		No Decisions		Wild Pitches	
Verlander, Justin	21	Turnbull, Spencer	17	Stanek, Ryne	26	Lynn, Lance	18
Cole, Gerrit	20	Lopez, Reynaldo	15	Kikuchi, Yusei	15	Cahill, Trevor	14
Rodriguez, Eduardo	19	Bundy, Dylan	14	Thornton, Trent	15	Barnes, Matt	13
German, Domingo	18	Junis, Jakob	14	Fiers, Mike	14	Fiers, Mike	13
Gonzales, Marco	16	Keller, Brad	14	Green, Chad	14	Castro, Miguel	11
Lynn, Lance	16	Sanchez, Aaron	14	Miley, Wade	13	Snell, Blake	11
Morton, Charlie	16	Gonzales, Marco	13	Norris, Daniel	13	5 tied with	9
4 tied with	15	Norris, Daniel	13	Perez, Martin	13		
		Zimmermann, Jordan	13	Tanaka, Masahiro	12		
		3 tied with	12	4 tied with	11		

Strikeouts		Walks Allowed		Intentional Walks Allowed		Hit Batters	
Cole, Gerrit	326	Rodriguez, Eduardo	75	Herrera, Kelvin	6	Turnbull, Spencer	16
Verlander, Justin	300	Keller, Brad	70	McCarthy, Kevin	6	Bauer, Trevor	14
Bieber, Shane	259	Minor, Mike	68	Hand, Brad	5	Bassitt, Chris	13
Lynn, Lance	246	Sanchez, Aaron	68	Hendriks, Liam	5	Sale, Chris	13
Morton, Charlie	240	Perez, Martin	67	7 tied with	4	Morton, Charlie	12
Boyd, Matthew	238	Lopez, Reynaldo	65			Diekman, Jake	11
Giolito, Lucas	228	Bauer, Trevor	63			Junis, Jakob	11
Sale, Chris	218	Miley, Wade	61			Sanchez, Aaron	11
Rodriguez, Eduardo	213	Thornton, Trent	61			3 tied with	10
Minor, Mike	200	2 tied with	59				

2019 American League Pitching Leaders

Runs Allowed	
Lopez, Reynaldo	119
Porcello, Rick	114
Kikuchi, Yusei	109
Junis, Jakob	108
Nova, Ivan	107
Gonzales, Marco	106
Perez, Martin	104
Boyd, Matthew	101
Gibson, Kyle	99
Sparkman, Glenn	96

Hits Allowed	
Nova, Ivan	225
Gonzales, Marco	210
Lopez, Reynaldo	203
Porcello, Rick	198
Kikuchi, Yusei	195
Lynn, Lance	195
Rodriguez, Eduardo	195
Berrios, Jose	194
Junis, Jakob	192
Minor, Mike	190

Doubles Allowed	
Gonzales, Marco	50
Lopez, Reynaldo	44
Nova, Ivan	44
Porcello, Rick	43
Tanaka, Masahiro	43
Lynn, Lance	42
Kikuchi, Yusei	41
Bundy, Dylan	40
Sampson, Adrian	38
3 tied with	37

Home Runs Allowed	
Boyd, Matthew	39
Kikuchi, Yusei	36
Verlander, Justin	36
Lopez, Reynaldo	35
Happ, J.A.	34
Bieber, Shane	31
Junis, Jakob	31
Porcello, Rick	31
5 tied with	30

Run Support Per Nine IP (minimum 162 IP)	
Rodriguez, Eduardo	7.88
Perez, Martin	7.68
Cole, Gerrit	7.50
Porcello, Rick	7.49
Bailey, Homer	6.45
Anderson, Brett	6.09
Gonzales, Marco	6.07
Berrios, Jose	6.06
Miley, Wade	5.97
Lynn, Lance	5.79

% Pitches In Strike Zone (minimum 162 IP)	
Giolito, Lucas	46.0
Lopez, Reynaldo	45.8
Fiers, Mike	44.6
Cole, Gerrit	44.3
Porcello, Rick	44.2
Verlander, Justin	44.2
Morton, Charlie	44.0
Anderson, Brett	43.9
Lynn, Lance	42.8
Gonzales, Marco	42.0

Pitches Per Start (minimum 30 GS)	
Lynn, Lance	107.7
Minor, Mike	104.9
Rodriguez, Eduardo	102.8
Cole, Gerrit	101.9
Verlander, Justin	101.4
Bieber, Shane	100.5
Berrios, Jose	97.9
Boyd, Matthew	97.4
Lopez, Reynaldo	95.8
Morton, Charlie	95.1

Pitches Per Batter (minimum 162 IP)	
Anderson, Brett	3.58
Tanaka, Masahiro	3.67
Berrios, Jose	3.72
Nova, Ivan	3.73
Gonzales, Marco	3.73
Perez, Martin	3.76
Junis, Jakob	3.80
Keller, Brad	3.82
Fiers, Mike	3.85
Porcello, Rick	3.85

Quality Starts	
Cole, Gerrit	26
Verlander, Justin	26
Bieber, Shane	24
Berrios, Jose	21
Lynn, Lance	20
Fiers, Mike	19
Gonzales, Marco	19
Morton, Charlie	19
Anderson, Brett	17
Giolito, Lucas	17

Batters Faced	
Lynn, Lance	875
Gonzales, Marco	866
Minor, Mike	863
Bieber, Shane	859
Rodriguez, Eduardo	859
Verlander, Justin	847
Berrios, Jose	842
Cole, Gerrit	817
Lopez, Reynaldo	809
Nova, Ivan	806

Innings Pitched	
Verlander, Justin	223.0
Bieber, Shane	214.1
Cole, Gerrit	212.1
Lynn, Lance	208.1
Minor, Mike	208.1
Rodriguez, Eduardo	203.1
Gonzales, Marco	203.0
Berrios, Jose	200.1
Morton, Charlie	194.2
Nova, Ivan	187.0

Most Pitches in a Game	
Fiers, Mike	131
Bauer, Trevor	127
Minor, Mike	126
Bauer, Trevor	123
Bauer, Trevor	122
Bailey, Homer	121
5 tied with	120

Stolen Bases Allowed	
Castro, Miguel	18
Ottavino, Adam	15
Snell, Blake	15
Turnbull, Spencer	14
7 tied with	13

Caught Stealing Off	
Snell, Blake	9
Anderson, Brett	8
Montgomery, Mike	7
Norris, Daniel	6
Stroman, Marcus	6
Suarez, Jose	6
11 tied with	5

Stolen Base Pct Allowed (minimum 162 IP)	
Tanaka, Masahiro	28.6
Keller, Brad	33.3
Boyd, Matthew	44.4
Rodriguez, Eduardo	44.4
Giolito, Lucas	50.0
Morton, Charlie	50.0
Anderson, Brett	55.6
Miley, Wade	60.0
Bailey, Homer	62.5
Bieber, Shane	63.6

Pickoffs	
Plesac, Zach	6
Anderson, Brett	5
Boyd, Matthew	5
Snell, Blake	5
Miley, Wade	4
Richard, Clayton	4
Suarez, Jose	4
8 tied with	3

2019 American League Pitching Leaders

Strikeouts Per 9 IP
(minimum 162 IP)

Cole, Gerrit	13.82
Verlander, Justin	12.11
Giolito, Lucas	11.62
Boyd, Matthew	11.56
Morton, Charlie	11.10
Bieber, Shane	10.88
Lynn, Lance	10.63
Rodriguez, Eduardo	9.43
Berrios, Jose	8.76
Minor, Mike	8.64

Opp On-Base Percentage
(minimum 162 IP)

Verlander, Justin	.219
Cole, Gerrit	.237
Bieber, Shane	.271
Giolito, Lucas	.273
Morton, Charlie	.283
Lynn, Lance	.300
Tanaka, Masahiro	.300
Boyd, Matthew	.301
Berrios, Jose	.302
Fiers, Mike	.304

Opp Slugging Average
(minimum 162 IP)

Morton, Charlie	.340
Cole, Gerrit	.343
Verlander, Justin	.361
Giolito, Lucas	.373
Keller, Brad	.381
Lynn, Lance	.390
Rodriguez, Eduardo	.391
Bieber, Shane	.393
Minor, Mike	.395
Bailey, Homer	.403

Opponent OPS
(minimum 162 IP)

Cole, Gerrit	.579
Verlander, Justin	.579
Morton, Charlie	.623
Giolito, Lucas	.646
Bieber, Shane	.663
Lynn, Lance	.689
Minor, Mike	.704
Berrios, Jose	.707
Keller, Brad	.711
Fiers, Mike	.712

Home Runs Per Nine IP
(minimum 162 IP)

Morton, Charlie	0.69
Keller, Brad	0.82
Lynn, Lance	0.91
Gonzales, Marco	1.02
Anderson, Brett	1.02
Rodriguez, Eduardo	1.06
Bailey, Homer	1.16
Berrios, Jose	1.17
Giolito, Lucas	1.22
Cole, Gerrit	1.23

Batting Average vs. LHB
(minimum 125 BF)

Workman, Brandon	.132
Osuna, Roberto	.150
Verlander, Justin	.163
Giolito, Lucas	.172
Bedrosian, Cam	.172
McHugh, Collin	.174
Cole, Gerrit	.175
Means, John	.184
May, Trevor	.185
Chirinos, Yonny	.189

Batting Average vs. RHB
(minimum 225 BF)

Verlander, Justin	.182
Odorizzi, Jake	.194
Cole, Gerrit	.198
Clevinger, Mike	.198
Bauer, Trevor	.199
Morton, Charlie	.202
Gaviglio, Sam	.206
German, Domingo	.210
Sale, Chris	.216
Lynn, Lance	.219

Opp BA w/ RISP
(minimum 125 BF)

Cole, Gerrit	.173
Morton, Charlie	.179
Bundy, Dylan	.209
Minor, Mike	.214
Thornton, Trent	.215
Keller, Brad	.216
Bassitt, Chris	.221
Paxton, James	.224
Lynn, Lance	.230
Boyd, Matthew	.231

OBP vs. Leadoff Hitter
(minimum 150 BF)

Verlander, Justin	.198
Bieber, Shane	.228
Cole, Gerrit	.247
Perez, Martin	.273
Lynn, Lance	.274
Means, John	.277
Tanaka, Masahiro	.284
Happ, J.A.	.291
Pineda, Michael	.291
Gonzales, Marco	.294

Strikeouts / Walks Ratio
(minimum 162 IP)

Verlander, Justin	7.14
Cole, Gerrit	6.79
Bieber, Shane	6.48
Boyd, Matthew	4.76
Morton, Charlie	4.21
Lynn, Lance	4.17
Giolito, Lucas	4.00
Berrios, Jose	3.82
Tanaka, Masahiro	3.73
Porcello, Rick	3.18

Highest GB/FB Ratio
(minimum 162 IP)

Anderson, Brett	2.15
Keller, Brad	1.72
Miley, Wade	1.67
Perez, Martin	1.64
Morton, Charlie	1.60
Nova, Ivan	1.52
Rodriguez, Eduardo	1.49
Tanaka, Masahiro	1.45
Bailey, Homer	1.30
Bieber, Shane	1.25

Lowest GB/FB Ratio
(minimum 162 IP)

Lopez, Reynaldo	0.79
Boyd, Matthew	0.79
Verlander, Justin	0.80
Giolito, Lucas	0.84
Porcello, Rick	0.92
Minor, Mike	1.00
Cole, Gerrit	1.02
Fiers, Mike	1.03
Lynn, Lance	1.05
Gonzales, Marco	1.07

Sacrifice Flies Allowed

Gonzales, Marco	9
Jurado, Ariel	9
Bundy, Dylan	7
Lopez, Jorge	7
Pineda, Michael	7
Thornton, Trent	7
Berrios, Jose	6
Castro, Miguel	6
Lynn, Lance	6
Minor, Mike	6

Sacrifice Hits Allowed

Jurado, Ariel	5
Norris, Daniel	5
Anderson, Brett	4
Boyd, Matthew	4
Farmer, Buck	4
Fiers, Mike	4
Odorizzi, Jake	4
13 tied with	3

GIDP Induced

Nova, Ivan	30
Minor, Mike	23
Gonzales, Marco	22
Keller, Brad	22
Rodriguez, Eduardo	20
Duffy, Danny	18
Lopez, Reynaldo	18
5 tied with	17

GIDP Per Nine IP
(minimum 162 IP)

Nova, Ivan	1.44
Keller, Brad	1.20
Minor, Mike	0.99
Gonzales, Marco	0.98
Rodriguez, Eduardo	0.89
Lopez, Reynaldo	0.88
Anderson, Brett	0.87
Fiers, Mike	0.83
Junis, Jakob	0.77
Tanaka, Masahiro	0.74

2019 American League Pitching Leaders

Saves			Blown Saves			Save Pct (minimum 20 Save Ops)			Save Opportunities	
Osuna, Roberto	38		Barnes, Matt	8		Giles, Ken	95.8		Osuna, Roberto	44
Chapman, Aroldis	37		Givens, Mychal	8		Colome, Alex	90.9		Chapman, Aroldis	42
Hand, Brad	34		Pagan, Emilio	8		Kennedy, Ian	88.2		Hand, Brad	39
Colome, Alex	30		Hendriks, Liam	7		Chapman, Aroldis	88.1		Rogers, Taylor	36
Kennedy, Ian	30		Ottavino, Adam	7		Greene, Shane	88.0		Kennedy, Ian	34
Rogers, Taylor	30		Osuna, Roberto	6		Hand, Brad	87.2		Colome, Alex	33
Hendriks, Liam	25		Rogers, Taylor	6		Osuna, Roberto	86.4		Hendriks, Liam	32
Giles, Ken	23		Workman, Brandon	6		Robles, Hansel	85.2		Pagan, Emilio	28
Robles, Hansel	23		11 tied with	5		Rogers, Taylor	83.3		Robles, Hansel	27
Greene, Shane	22					Hendriks, Liam	78.1		Greene, Shane	25

Easy Saves			Regular Saves			Tough Saves			Holds Adjusted Saves % (minimum 20 Save Ops + Holds)	
Chapman, Aroldis	29		Rogers, Taylor	16		Givens, Mychal	4		Harris, Will	96.8
Osuna, Roberto	28		Osuna, Roberto	10		Hand, Brad	3		Petit, Yusmeiro	96.7
Hand, Brad	25		Robles, Hansel	10		Pagan, Emilio	3		Giles, Ken	95.8
Kennedy, Ian	24		Colome, Alex	9		Bass, Anthony	2		Parker, Blake	95.0
Colome, Alex	20		Hendriks, Liam	9		Hendriks, Liam	2		Diekman, Jake	93.9
Giles, Ken	15		Chapman, Aroldis	7		Kelley, Shawn	2		Bummer, Aaron	93.3
Greene, Shane	15		Giles, Ken	7		Rogers, Taylor	2		Castillo, Diego	92.6
Hendriks, Liam	14		Greene, Shane	7		Treinen, Blake	2		Cimber, Adam	90.9
Robles, Hansel	13		Pagan, Emilio	7		Workman, Brandon	2		Colome, Alex	90.9
Rogers, Taylor	12		2 tied with	6		24 tied with	1		2 tied with	90.5

Relief Wins			Relief Losses			Relief Games			Holds	
Workman, Brandon	10		Fry, Paul	9		Petit, Yusmeiro	80		Diekman, Jake	31
Walden, Marcus	9		Buttrey, Ty	7		Diekman, Jake	76		Pressly, Ryan	31
Pena, Felix	8		Castillo, Diego	7		Hendriks, Liam	73		Britton, Zack	29
Yarbrough, Ryan	8		Diekman, Jake	7		Ottavino, Adam	73		Petit, Yusmeiro	29
9 tied with	6		Jimenez, Joe	7		Workman, Brandon	73		Ottavino, Adam	28
			Milone, Tommy	7		Buttrey, Ty	72		Bummer, Aaron	27
			Brennan, Brandon	6		Farmer, Buck	72		Kahnle, Tommy	27
			Farmer, Buck	6		Kahnle, Tommy	72		Barnes, Matt	26
			Givens, Mychal	6		Roe, Chaz	71		Buttrey, Ty	26
			Trivino, Lou	6		4 tied with	70		Harris, Will	26

Relief Innings			Inherited Runners Scrd % (minimum 30 IR)			Relief Opp On Base Pct (minimum 50 IP)			Relief Opp Slugging Avg (minimum 50 IP)	
Gaviglio, Sam	95.2		Biagini, Joe	19.4		Petit, Yusmeiro	.218		Workman, Brandon	.166
Beeks, Jalen	92.0		Bummer, Aaron	20.0		Pagan, Emilio	.221		Bummer, Aaron	.252
LeBlanc, Wade	84.2		Kahnle, Tommy	20.6		Pressly, Ryan	.233		Britton, Zack	.254
Hendriks, Liam	83.0		Osich, Josh	22.2		Osuna, Roberto	.234		Chapman, Aroldis	.263
Petit, Yusmeiro	83.0		Fry, Jace	23.1		Harris, Will	.246		Harris, Will	.294
Cessa, Luis	81.0		Petit, Yusmeiro	23.3		Hendriks, Liam	.247		Hendriks, Liam	.307
Milone, Tommy	80.2		Cimber, Adam	24.4		Clippard, Tyler	.252		Ottavino, Adam	.308
Ramirez, Nick	79.2		Fry, Paul	25.6		Giles, Ken	.255		Pressly, Ryan	.310
Walden, Marcus	78.0		Diekman, Jake	25.6		Drake, Oliver	.256		Diekman, Jake	.316
Castro, Miguel	73.1		Roe, Chaz	26.3		Duffey, Tyler	.257		May, Trevor	.316

2019 American League Pitching Leaders

Relief Opp BA Vs LHB (minimum 50 AB)	
Clippard, Tyler	.108
Montero, Rafael	.111
Pressly, Ryan	.124
Workman, Brandon	.132
McHugh, Collin	.140
Drake, Oliver	.147
Osuna, Roberto	.150
Britton, Zack	.158
Wendelken, J.B.	.160
Bass, Anthony	.165

Relief Opp BA Vs RHB (minimum 50 AB)	
Workman, Brandon	.116
Greene, Shane	.118
Leclerc, Jose	.137
Hendriks, Liam	.140
Pena, Felix	.161
Soria, Joakim	.169
McKay, David	.173
Newberry, Jake	.174
Elias, Roenis	.174
Brennan, Brandon	.175

Relief Opp Batting Average (minimum 50 IP)	
Workman, Brandon	.123
Clippard, Tyler	.173
Pagan, Emilio	.179
Drake, Oliver	.181
Poche, Colin	.181
Britton, Zack	.182
Bummer, Aaron	.184
May, Trevor	.184
Chapman, Aroldis	.185
Pressly, Ryan	.188

Relief Earned Run Average (minimum 50 IP)	
Harris, Will	1.50
Hendriks, Liam	1.63
Giles, Ken	1.87
Workman, Brandon	1.88
Ottavino, Adam	1.90
Britton, Zack	1.91
Bummer, Aaron	2.13
Chapman, Aroldis	2.21
Pagan, Emilio	2.31
Pressly, Ryan	2.32

Rel OBP 1st Batter Faced (minimum 40 BF)	
Clippard, Tyler	.120
Pressly, Ryan	.145
Devenski, Chris	.150
Harris, Will	.164
Hudson, Daniel	.182
Gaviglio, Sam	.192
Bummer, Aaron	.207
Duffey, Tyler	.207
Osich, Josh	.211
Bedrosian, Cam	.212

Rel Opp BA w/ Runners On (minimum 50 IP)	
Workman, Brandon	.137
Chapman, Aroldis	.142
Giles, Ken	.151
Cessa, Luis	.167
Ottavino, Adam	.169
Givens, Mychal	.173
Rondon, Hector	.174
Osuna, Roberto	.176
Clippard, Tyler	.181
Bummer, Aaron	.181

Relief Opp BA w/ RISP (minimum 50 IP)	
May, Trevor	.113
Chapman, Aroldis	.130
Giles, Ken	.130
Duffey, Tyler	.148
Pressly, Ryan	.150
Britton, Zack	.158
Workman, Brandon	.167
Ottavino, Adam	.171
Castillo, Diego	.175
Harris, Will	.178

Fastest Avg Fastball-Relief (minimum 50 IP)	
Chapman, Aroldis	98.4
Castillo, Diego	98.2
Trivino, Lou	97.5
Castro, Miguel	97.4
James, Josh	97.2
Robles, Hansel	97.1
Buttrey, Ty	97.1
Garcia, Luis	97.1
Giles, Ken	97.0
Leclerc, Jose	96.8

Fastest Average Fastball (minimum 162 IP)	
Cole, Gerrit	97.2
Lopez, Reynaldo	95.5
Verlander, Justin	94.7
Morton, Charlie	94.4
Giolito, Lucas	94.3
Lynn, Lance	94.2
Perez, Martin	94.1
Keller, Brad	93.4
Bieber, Shane	93.1
Rodriguez, Eduardo	93.1

Slowest Average Fastball (minimum 162 IP)	
Gonzales, Marco	88.9
Fiers, Mike	90.4
Porcello, Rick	90.5
Miley, Wade	90.5
Anderson, Brett	90.8
Tanaka, Masahiro	91.5
Junis, Jakob	91.5
Boyd, Matthew	92.0
Nova, Ivan	92.4
Minor, Mike	92.6

Pitches 100+ Velocity	
Chapman, Aroldis	198
Clase, Emmanuel	125
Castillo, Diego	73
Cole, Gerrit	55
Alvarado, Jose	51
Cordero, Jimmy	50
Eovaldi, Nathan	41
Rosenthal, Trevor	31
Graterol, Brusdar	23
James, Josh	22

Pitches 95+ Velocity	
Cole, Gerrit	1739
Lopez, Reynaldo	1362
Paxton, James	1247
Lynn, Lance	1124
Green, Chad	971
Verlander, Justin	929
Hudson, Daniel	844
Bauer, Trevor	837
Hendriks, Liam	833
Clevinger, Mike	827

Pitches Less Than 80 MPH	
Morton, Charlie	943
Sanchez, Aaron	788
Boyd, Matthew	748
LeBlanc, Wade	681
Bauer, Trevor	659
Smyly, Drew	595
Font, Wilmer	582
Romo, Sergio	563
Milone, Tommy	550
Yarbrough, Ryan	537

Lowest % Fastballs (minimum 162 IP)	
Miley, Wade	21.8
Tanaka, Masahiro	30.5
Gonzales, Marco	39.3
Perez, Martin	42.3
Minor, Mike	44.6
Bieber, Shane	45.6
Anderson, Brett	48.6
Morton, Charlie	49.0
Verlander, Justin	49.9
Bailey, Homer	50.6

Highest % Fastballs (minimum 162 IP)	
Lynn, Lance	71.4
Keller, Brad	66.8
Lopez, Reynaldo	58.6
Porcello, Rick	56.5
Berrios, Jose	55.3
Giolito, Lucas	55.0
Rodriguez, Eduardo	54.6
Nova, Ivan	54.2
Cole, Gerrit	54.0
Boyd, Matthew	53.8

Highest % Curveballs (minimum 162 IP)	
Morton, Charlie	37.3
Berrios, Jose	28.9
Bieber, Shane	20.2
Verlander, Justin	17.5
Fiers, Mike	17.4
Nova, Ivan	16.8
Gonzales, Marco	16.0
Cole, Gerrit	15.4
Porcello, Rick	12.6
Minor, Mike	11.4

2019 American League Pitching Leaders

Highest % Changeups		Highest % Sliders		Balks		Strikeout/Hit Ratio	
(minimum 162 IP)		(minimum 162 IP)				(minimum 50 IP)	
Giolito, Lucas	26.1	Junis, Jakob	43.8	Boyd, Matthew	4	Workman, Brandon	3.59
Minor, Mike	24.6	Tanaka, Masahiro	36.2	Chirinos, Yonny	3	Giles, Ken	2.31
Gonzales, Marco	23.9	Boyd, Matthew	36.2	Cole, Gerrit	3	Cole, Gerrit	2.30
Rodriguez, Eduardo	23.5	Keller, Brad	31.4	Richard, Clayton	3	Chapman, Aroldis	2.24
Perez, Martin	22.1	Verlander, Justin	28.4	10 tied with	2	Verlander, Justin	2.19
Miley, Wade	20.2	Bieber, Shane	26.8			Poche, Colin	2.18
Nova, Ivan	16.2	Cole, Gerrit	23.2			James, Josh	2.17
Berrios, Jose	15.9	Lopez, Reynaldo	20.0			Barnes, Matt	2.16
Lopez, Reynaldo	14.8	Minor, Mike	19.4			Pagan, Emilio	2.13
Anderson, Brett	13.4	Anderson, Brett	18.7			Hendriks, Liam	2.03

Opp OPS vs Fastballs		Opp OPS vs Curveballs		Opp OPS vs Changeups		Opp OPS vs Sliders	
(minimum 251 BF)		(minimum 100 BF)		(minimum 100 BF)		(minimum 64 BF)	
Cole, Gerrit	.565	Workman, Brandon	.447	Kahnle, Tommy	.468	Petit, Yusmeiro	.339
Giolito, Lucas	.622	Stroman, Marcus	.481	Miley, Wade	.524	Verlander, Justin	.428
Bassitt, Chris	.623	Fiers, Mike	.517	Minor, Mike	.524	Giles, Ken	.437
Odorizzi, Jake	.656	Morton, Charlie	.519	Pineda, Michael	.548	Hendriks, Liam	.442
Bieber, Shane	.675	Verlander, Justin	.519	Yarbrough, Ryan	.570	Pressly, Ryan	.442
Berrios, Jose	.703	Bauer, Trevor	.567	Milone, Tommy	.586	Clevinger, Mike	.504
Bailey, Homer	.706	Paxton, James	.605	Giolito, Lucas	.613	Ottavino, Adam	.506
Pineda, Michael	.706	Barnes, Matt	.614	Anderson, Brett	.623	Taylor, Josh	.510
Chirinos, Yonny	.710	Cole, Gerrit	.615	Sanchez, Aaron	.633	Brasier, Ryan	.516
4 tied with	.711	Pena, Felix	.622	Sale, Chris	.634	Castro, Miguel	.522

Earned Runs	
Lopez, Reynaldo	110
Porcello, Rick	107
Junis, Jakob	102
Kikuchi, Yusei	98
Nova, Ivan	98
Boyd, Matthew	94
Perez, Martin	94
Sparkman, Glenn	91
Gonzales, Marco	90
Tanaka, Masahiro	90

Hits Per Nine Innings	
(minimum 162 IP)	
Verlander, Justin	5.53
Cole, Gerrit	6.02
Giolito, Lucas	6.67
Morton, Charlie	7.12
Bieber, Shane	7.81
Fiers, Mike	8.09
Minor, Mike	8.21
Keller, Brad	8.38
Lynn, Lance	8.42
Rodriguez, Eduardo	8.63

2019 National League Pitching Leaders

Earned Run Average (minimum 162 IP)	
Ryu, Hyun-Jin	2.32
deGrom, Jacob	2.43
Soroka, Mike	2.68
Flaherty, Jack	2.75
Gray, Sonny	2.87
Scherzer, Max	2.93
Kershaw, Clayton	3.03
Corbin, Patrick	3.25
Buehler, Walker	3.26
Strasburg, Stephen	3.32

Winning Percentage (minimum 15 Decisions)	
Buehler, Walker	.778
Soroka, Mike	.765
Kershaw, Clayton	.762
Strasburg, Stephen	.750
Fried, Max	.739
Ryu, Hyun-Jin	.737
Marquez, German	.706
Hudson, Dakota	.696
Corbin, Patrick	.667
Castillo, Luis	.652

Opponent Batting Average (minimum 162 IP)	
Flaherty, Jack	.192
Gray, Sonny	.196
Castillo, Luis	.202
deGrom, Jacob	.207
Strasburg, Stephen	.210
Darvish, Yu	.213
Scherzer, Max	.222
Kershaw, Clayton	.222
Buehler, Walker	.223
Samardzija, Jeff	.225

Baserunners Per 9 IP (minimum 162 IP)	
Flaherty, Jack	9.03
deGrom, Jacob	9.04
Ryu, Hyun-Jin	9.26
Kershaw, Clayton	9.49
Scherzer, Max	9.61
Buehler, Walker	9.72
Strasburg, Stephen	9.78
Gray, Sonny	10.11
Samardzija, Jeff	10.27
Soroka, Mike	10.36

Games	
Claudio, Alex	83
Suero, Wander	78
Chafin, Andrew	77
Stammen, Craig	76
Lorenzen, Michael	73
Miller, Andrew	73
Ryan, Kyle	73
Guerra, Junior	72
Hughes, Jared	72
Rodriguez, Richard	72

Games Started	
Bumgarner, Madison	34
Nola, Aaron	34
Corbin, Patrick	33
Flaherty, Jack	33
Ray, Robbie	33
Strasburg, Stephen	33
Teheran, Julio	33
8 tied with	32

Complete Games	
Alcantara, Sandy	2
Buehler, Walker	2
Eflin, Zach	2
12 tied with	1

Shutouts	
Alcantara, Sandy	2
Corbin, Patrick	1
Eflin, Zach	1
Hendricks, Kyle	1
Marquez, German	1
Matz, Steven	1
Mikolas, Miles	1
Ryu, Hyun-Jin	1
Syndergaard, Noah	1
Vargas, Jason	1

Wins	
Strasburg, Stephen	18
Fried, Max	17
Hudson, Dakota	16
Kershaw, Clayton	16
Castillo, Luis	15
Buehler, Walker	14
Corbin, Patrick	14
Ryu, Hyun-Jin	14
Wainwright, Adam	14
4 tied with	13

Losses	
Alcantara, Sandy	14
Kelly, Merrill	14
Mikolas, Miles	14
Eflin, Zach	13
Iglesias, Raisel	12
Mahle, Tyler	12
Musgrove, Joe	12
Richards, Trevor	12
Samardzija, Jeff	12
7 tied with	11

No Decisions	
Darvish, Yu	17
Anderson, Chase	16
Bumgarner, Madison	16
Nola, Aaron	15
Davies, Zach	14
Flaherty, Jack	14
Syndergaard, Noah	14
6 tied with	13

Wild Pitches	
Marquez, German	14
Darvish, Yu	11
Fried, Max	11
Quintana, Jose	11
Kelly, Joe	10
Andriese, Matt	9
Beede, Tyler	9
Guerrero, Tayron	9
3 tied with	8

Strikeouts	
deGrom, Jacob	255
Strasburg, Stephen	251
Scherzer, Max	243
Corbin, Patrick	238
Ray, Robbie	235
Flaherty, Jack	231
Darvish, Yu	229
Nola, Aaron	229
Castillo, Luis	226
Buehler, Walker	215

Walks Allowed	
Hudson, Dakota	86
Ray, Robbie	84
Teheran, Julio	83
Alcantara, Sandy	81
Nola, Aaron	80
Castillo, Luis	79
Corbin, Patrick	70
Gray, Sonny	68
Wainwright, Adam	64
Vargas, Jason	63

Intentional Walks Allowed	
Sanchez, Anibal	10
Hudson, Dakota	8
Matz, Steven	7
Wainwright, Adam	7
Conley, Adam	6
Richards, Trevor	6
9 tied with	5

Hit Batters	
Teheran, Julio	14
Mikolas, Miles	12
Darvish, Yu	11
Lopez, Pablo	11
Nola, Aaron	11
Agrazal, Dario	10
Bumgarner, Madison	10
Strasburg, Stephen	10
8 tied with	9

2019 National League Pitching Leaders

Runs Allowed	
Lester, Jon	101
Syndergaard, Noah	101
Quintana, Jose	100
Bumgarner, Madison	99
Senzatela, Antonio	99
Musgrove, Joe	98
Marquez, German	96
Kelly, Merrill	95
Alcantara, Sandy	94
2 tied with	93

Hits Allowed	
Lester, Jon	205
Wheeler, Zack	196
Syndergaard, Noah	194
Mikolas, Miles	193
Bumgarner, Madison	191
Quintana, Jose	191
Kelly, Merrill	184
Wainwright, Adam	181
Alcantara, Sandy	179
Nola, Aaron	176

Doubles Allowed	
Musgrove, Joe	48
Alcantara, Sandy	43
Quintana, Jose	43
Scherzer, Max	43
Bumgarner, Madison	41
Williams, Trevor	40
Hendricks, Kyle	39
4 tied with	38

Home Runs Allowed	
Darvish, Yu	33
Smith, Caleb	33
Bumgarner, Madison	30
Ray, Robbie	30
DeSclafani, Anthony	29
Kelly, Merrill	29
Marquez, German	29
Eflin, Zach	28
Kershaw, Clayton	28
Samardzija, Jeff	28

Run Support Per Nine IP (minimum 162 IP)	
Fried, Max	7.50
Kershaw, Clayton	7.17
Ray, Robbie	6.97
Lester, Jon	6.92
Marquez, German	6.41
Quintana, Jose	6.32
Sanchez, Anibal	6.24
Hudson, Dakota	6.08
Buehler, Walker	6.07
Strasburg, Stephen	5.73

% Pitches In Strike Zone (minimum 162 IP)	
Marquez, German	45.7
Buehler, Walker	45.4
Wheeler, Zack	44.6
Scherzer, Max	44.4
Musgrove, Joe	43.6
Hendricks, Kyle	43.3
Mikolas, Miles	43.0
Syndergaard, Noah	42.8
Darvish, Yu	42.7
Wainwright, Adam	42.1

Pitches Per Start (minimum 30 GS)	
deGrom, Jacob	103.0
Strasburg, Stephen	102.5
Wheeler, Zack	101.9
Corbin, Patrick	100.0
Castillo, Luis	98.7
Lester, Jon	98.2
Nola, Aaron	98.0
Syndergaard, Noah	96.7
Alcantara, Sandy	96.6
Flaherty, Jack	96.3

Pitches Per Batter (minimum 162 IP)	
Marquez, German	3.63
Eflin, Zach	3.65
Soroka, Mike	3.65
Alcantara, Sandy	3.69
Hendricks, Kyle	3.70
Musgrove, Joe	3.70
Ryu, Hyun-Jin	3.74
Syndergaard, Noah	3.75
Mikolas, Miles	3.75
Hudson, Dakota	3.76

Quality Starts	
Corbin, Patrick	24
deGrom, Jacob	23
Kershaw, Clayton	22
Ryu, Hyun-Jin	22
Strasburg, Stephen	22
Bumgarner, Madison	20
Castillo, Luis	20
Flaherty, Jack	20
3 tied with	18

Batters Faced	
Nola, Aaron	852
Bumgarner, Madison	844
Strasburg, Stephen	841
Alcantara, Sandy	838
Corbin, Patrick	835
Wheeler, Zack	828
Syndergaard, Noah	825
deGrom, Jacob	804
Castillo, Luis	781
Kelly, Merrill	777

Innings Pitched	
Strasburg, Stephen	209.0
Bumgarner, Madison	207.2
deGrom, Jacob	204.0
Nola, Aaron	202.1
Corbin, Patrick	202.0
Syndergaard, Noah	197.2
Alcantara, Sandy	197.1
Flaherty, Jack	196.1
Wheeler, Zack	195.1
Castillo, Luis	190.2

Most Pitches in a Game	
Wainwright, Adam	126
Matz, Steven	120
Scherzer, Max	120
Castillo, Luis	119
Wacha, Michael	119
Corbin, Patrick	118
Davies, Zach	118
Flaherty, Jack	118
Wheeler, Zack	118
5 tied with	117

Stolen Bases Allowed	
Syndergaard, Noah	42
Darvish, Yu	24
deGrom, Jacob	24
Strasburg, Stephen	16
Sanchez, Anibal	15
Teheran, Julio	15
5 tied with	14

Caught Stealing Off	
Nola, Aaron	8
Davies, Zach	7
Archer, Chris	6
Arrieta, Jake	6
Corbin, Patrick	6
Gray, Jon	6
Hendricks, Kyle	6
Houser, Adrian	6
Lester, Jon	6
Marquez, German	6

Stolen Base Pct Allowed (minimum 162 IP)	
Flaherty, Jack	25.0
Marquez, German	40.0
Musgrove, Joe	40.0
Hendricks, Kyle	45.5
Nola, Aaron	46.7
Kershaw, Clayton	50.0
Ryu, Hyun-Jin	50.0
Wainwright, Adam	50.0
Quintana, Jose	54.5
Kelly, Merrill	60.0

Pickoffs	
Fried, Max	5
Corbin, Patrick	4
Hendricks, Kyle	4
Musgrove, Joe	4
Quintana, Jose	4
Lambert, Peter	3
McFarland, T.J.	3
22 tied with	2

2019 National League Pitching Leaders

Strikeouts Per 9 IP (minimum 162 IP)	
Scherzer, Max	12.69
Ray, Robbie	12.13
Darvish, Yu	11.54
deGrom, Jacob	11.25
Strasburg, Stephen	10.81
Castillo, Luis	10.67
Buehler, Walker	10.61
Corbin, Patrick	10.60
Flaherty, Jack	10.59
Gray, Sonny	10.52

Opp On-Base Percentage (minimum 162 IP)	
Flaherty, Jack	.256
deGrom, Jacob	.257
Ryu, Hyun-Jin	.263
Scherzer, Max	.266
Buehler, Walker	.268
Kershaw, Clayton	.269
Strasburg, Stephen	.271
Gray, Sonny	.281
Samardzija, Jeff	.281
Darvish, Yu	.284

Opp Slugging Average (minimum 162 IP)	
deGrom, Jacob	.323
Gray, Sonny	.325
Flaherty, Jack	.335
Soroka, Mike	.340
Castillo, Luis	.343
Strasburg, Stephen	.349
Ryu, Hyun-Jin	.359
Buehler, Walker	.368
Scherzer, Max	.371
Corbin, Patrick	.375

Opponent OPS (minimum 162 IP)	
deGrom, Jacob	.580
Flaherty, Jack	.591
Gray, Sonny	.605
Strasburg, Stephen	.620
Ryu, Hyun-Jin	.622
Soroka, Mike	.628
Castillo, Luis	.633
Buehler, Walker	.636
Scherzer, Max	.637
Kershaw, Clayton	.664

Home Runs Per Nine IP (minimum 162 IP)	
Soroka, Mike	0.72
Ryu, Hyun-Jin	0.84
deGrom, Jacob	0.84
Gray, Sonny	0.87
Scherzer, Max	0.94
Hendricks, Kyle	0.97
Buehler, Walker	0.99
Wheeler, Zack	1.01
Strasburg, Stephen	1.03
Castillo, Luis	1.04

Batting Average vs. LHB (minimum 125 BF)	
Yamamoto, Jordan	.152
Lugo, Seth	.167
Neris, Hector	.167
Baez, Pedro	.176
Guerra, Junior	.178
Anderson, Chase	.189
Corbin, Patrick	.190
Strasburg, Stephen	.192
Lorenzen, Michael	.195
Gray, Sonny	.196

Batting Average vs. RHB (minimum 225 BF)	
Maeda, Kenta	.158
Darvish, Yu	.181
Flaherty, Jack	.182
Scherzer, Max	.193
Castillo, Luis	.194
Gray, Sonny	.196
Paddack, Chris	.198
deGrom, Jacob	.202
Soroka, Mike	.203
Samardzija, Jeff	.216

Opp BA w/ RISP (minimum 125 BF)	
Gray, Sonny	.160
deGrom, Jacob	.183
Gray, Jon	.184
Ryu, Hyun-Jin	.186
Darvish, Yu	.194
DeSclafani, Anthony	.195
Anderson, Chase	.200
Castillo, Luis	.204
Buehler, Walker	.208
Sanchez, Anibal	.212

OBP vs. Leadoff Hitter (minimum 150 BF)	
Lucchesi, Joey	.216
Ryu, Hyun-Jin	.219
Strasburg, Stephen	.231
Maeda, Kenta	.238
Greinke, Zack	.240
Corbin, Patrick	.244
Hendricks, Kyle	.246
deGrom, Jacob	.248
Flaherty, Jack	.254
Scherzer, Max	.263

Strikeouts / Walks Ratio (minimum 162 IP)	
Scherzer, Max	7.36
Ryu, Hyun-Jin	6.79
Buehler, Walker	5.81
deGrom, Jacob	5.80
Marquez, German	5.00
Bumgarner, Madison	4.72
Hendricks, Kyle	4.69
Kershaw, Clayton	4.61
Mikolas, Miles	4.50
Strasburg, Stephen	4.48

Highest GB/FB Ratio (minimum 162 IP)	
Hudson, Dakota	2.67
Fried, Max	2.41
Castillo, Luis	2.07
Soroka, Mike	2.02
Ryu, Hyun-Jin	1.98
Strasburg, Stephen	1.78
Wainwright, Adam	1.70
Marquez, German	1.69
Nola, Aaron	1.68
Gray, Sonny	1.63

Lowest GB/FB Ratio (minimum 162 IP)	
Bumgarner, Madison	0.86
Samardzija, Jeff	0.88
Teheran, Julio	0.96
Sanchez, Anibal	0.97
Ray, Robbie	1.00
Flaherty, Jack	1.03
Scherzer, Max	1.07
DeSclafani, Anthony	1.12
Kelly, Merrill	1.18
Hendricks, Kyle	1.19

Sacrifice Flies Allowed	
Quintana, Jose	13
Corbin, Patrick	8
Syndergaard, Noah	8
Vargas, Jason	8
Williams, Trevor	8
Hudson, Dakota	7
Mikolas, Miles	7
Wheeler, Zack	7
4 tied with	6

Sacrifice Hits Allowed	
Ray, Robbie	11
Corbin, Patrick	8
Hendricks, Kyle	8
Ryu, Hyun-Jin	8
Wheeler, Zack	8
Davies, Zach	7
Gausman, Kevin	7
Gray, Jon	7
Holland, Derek	7
12 tied with	6

GIDP Induced	
Alcantara, Sandy	23
Mikolas, Miles	23
Soroka, Mike	23
Hudson, Dakota	20
Brault, Steven	18
Bumgarner, Madison	18
Lester, Jon	18
4 tied with	17

GIDP Per Nine IP (minimum 162 IP)	
Soroka, Mike	1.19
Mikolas, Miles	1.13
Alcantara, Sandy	1.05
Hudson, Dakota	1.03
Lester, Jon	0.94
Kershaw, Clayton	0.86
Ryu, Hyun-Jin	0.84
Eflin, Zach	0.83
Fried, Max	0.81
Castillo, Luis	0.80

2019 National League Pitching Leaders

Saves

Yates, Kirby	41
Hader, Josh	37
Iglesias, Raisel	34
Smith, Will	34
Jansen, Kenley	33
Doolittle, Sean	29
Neris, Hector	28
Vazquez, Felipe	28
Diaz, Edwin	26
Martinez, Carlos	24

Blown Saves

Stammen, Craig	9
Guerra, Junior	8
Jansen, Kenley	8
Diaz, Edwin	7
Hader, Josh	7
Jackson, Luke	7
7 tied with	6

Save Pct
(minimum 20 Save Ops)

Yates, Kirby	93.2
Vazquez, Felipe	90.3
Smith, Will	89.5
Martinez, Carlos	88.9
Bradley, Archie	85.7
Iglesias, Raisel	85.0
Hader, Josh	84.1
Doolittle, Sean	82.9
Neris, Hector	82.4
Jansen, Kenley	80.5

Save Opportunities

Hader, Josh	44
Yates, Kirby	44
Jansen, Kenley	41
Iglesias, Raisel	40
Smith, Will	38
Doolittle, Sean	35
Neris, Hector	34
Diaz, Edwin	33
Vazquez, Felipe	31
Martinez, Carlos	27

Easy Saves

Yates, Kirby	21
Doolittle, Sean	20
Jansen, Kenley	20
Diaz, Edwin	18
Iglesias, Raisel	18
Hader, Josh	17
Neris, Hector	15
Smith, Will	15
Vazquez, Felipe	15
Holland, Greg	13

Regular Saves

Smith, Will	18
Yates, Kirby	18
Hader, Josh	17
Iglesias, Raisel	15
Vazquez, Felipe	12
Jansen, Kenley	11
Martinez, Carlos	10
Neris, Hector	9
Diaz, Edwin	8
Jackson, Luke	8

Tough Saves

Neris, Hector	4
Doolittle, Sean	3
Hader, Josh	3
Jackson, Luke	3
Bradley, Archie	2
Jansen, Kenley	2
Martinez, Carlos	2
Yates, Kirby	2
22 tied with	1

Holds Adjusted Saves %
(minimum 20 Save Ops + Holds)

Dyson, Sam	95.0
Yates, Kirby	93.2
Morgan, Adam	90.5
Vazquez, Felipe	90.3
Kintzler, Brandon	90.0
Martinez, Carlos	90.0
Smith, Will	89.5
Bradley, Archie	89.3
Watson, Tony	89.3
3 tied with	88.0

Relief Wins

Gant, John	11
Guerra, Junior	9
Jackson, Luke	9
Albers, Matt	8
Stammen, Craig	8
Baez, Pedro	7
Gott, Trevor	7
Lugo, Seth	7
7 tied with	6

Relief Losses

Iglesias, Raisel	12
Conley, Adam	11
Suero, Wander	9
Crick, Kyle	7
Diaz, Edwin	7
Lopez, Yoan	7
Moronta, Reyes	7
Stammen, Craig	7
5 tied with	6

Relief Games

Claudio, Alex	83
Suero, Wander	78
Chafin, Andrew	77
Stammen, Craig	76
Lorenzen, Michael	73
Miller, Andrew	73
Ryan, Kyle	73
Guerra, Junior	72
Hughes, Jared	72
Rodriguez, Richard	72

Holds

Stammen, Craig	31
Miller, Andrew	28
Baez, Pedro	25
Watson, Tony	25
Chafin, Andrew	23
Claudio, Alex	22
Garrett, Amir	22
Lopez, Yoan	21
Lorenzen, Michael	21
Lugo, Seth	21

Relief Innings

Guerra, Junior	83.2
Lorenzen, Michael	83.1
Stammen, Craig	82.0
Lugo, Seth	80.0
Tomlin, Josh	76.1
Hader, Josh	75.2
Gallegos, Giovanny	74.0
Brebbia, John	72.2
Jackson, Luke	72.2
2 tied with	72.0

Inherited Runners Scrd %
(minimum 30 IR)

Chafin, Andrew	11.3
Gallegos, Giovanny	15.9
Avilan, Luis	18.2
Gott, Trevor	20.0
Albers, Matt	21.9
Brach, Brad	21.9
Kintzler, Brandon	21.9
Hader, Josh	24.2
Stammen, Craig	24.2
Brebbia, John	25.0

Relief Opp On Base Pct
(minimum 50 IP)

Hader, Josh	.225
Gallegos, Giovanny	.226
Garcia, Yimi	.244
Lugo, Seth	.246
Yates, Kirby	.252
Dyson, Sam	.254
Vazquez, Felipe	.254
Baez, Pedro	.255
Stephenson, Robert	.257
Smith, Will	.261

Relief Opp Slugging Avg
(minimum 50 IP)

Yates, Kirby	.262
Baez, Pedro	.287
Oberg, Scott	.291
Moronta, Reyes	.298
Dyson, Sam	.311
Gott, Trevor	.316
Lugo, Seth	.316
Vazquez, Felipe	.317
Garcia, Jarlin	.319
Gallegos, Giovanny	.320

2019 National League Pitching Leaders

Relief Opp BA Vs LHB
(minimum 50 AB)

Strahm, Matt	.137
Hader, Josh	.143
Wingenter, Trey	.143
Gallegos, Giovanny	.149
Urias, Julio	.153
Webb, Tyler	.157
Smith, Will	.157
Jackson, Luke	.157
Kintzler, Brandon	.163
2 tied with	.167

Relief Opp BA Vs RHB
(minimum 50 AB)

Hicks, Jordan	.113
Rainey, Tanner	.139
Wick, Rowan	.149
Dominguez, Seranthony	.151
Hader, Josh	.158
Stephenson, Robert	.159
Chatwood, Tyler	.161
Kela, Keone	.164
Houser, Adrian	.167
Pomeranz, Drew	.167

Relief Opp Batting Average
(minimum 50 IP)

Hader, Josh	.155
Gallegos, Giovanny	.170
Webb, Tyler	.172
Baez, Pedro	.174
Garcia, Yimi	.178
Stephenson, Robert	.182
Yates, Kirby	.186
Neris, Hector	.186
Lugo, Seth	.192
Guerra, Junior	.194

Relief Earned Run Average
(minimum 50 IP)

Yates, Kirby	1.19
Vazquez, Felipe	1.65
Oberg, Scott	2.25
Gallegos, Giovanny	2.31
Dyson, Sam	2.47
Hader, Josh	2.62
Kintzler, Brandon	2.68
Lugo, Seth	2.70
Smith, Will	2.76
Moronta, Reyes	2.86

Rel OBP 1st Batter Faced
(minimum 40 BF)

Lugo, Seth	.197
Gallegos, Giovanny	.197
Floro, Dylan	.200
Garrett, Amir	.203
Stephenson, Robert	.214
Anderson, Nick	.222
Blevins, Jerry	.222
Lorenzen, Michael	.222
Smith, Will	.222
Guerra, Javy	.225

Rel Opp BA w/ Runners On
(minimum 50 IP)

Garcia, Yimi	.141
Yates, Kirby	.141
Gallegos, Giovanny	.161
Baez, Pedro	.165
Hader, Josh	.167
Vazquez, Felipe	.173
Smith, Will	.174
Stephenson, Robert	.178
Cishek, Steve	.183
Feliz, Michael	.184

Relief Opp BA w/ RISP
(minimum 50 IP)

Gallegos, Giovanny	.125
Vazquez, Felipe	.125
Oberg, Scott	.137
Hader, Josh	.148
Yates, Kirby	.148
Garcia, Yimi	.154
Neris, Hector	.161
Newcomb, Sean	.163
Jansen, Kenley	.171
3 tied with	.176

Fastest Avg Fastball-Relief
(minimum 50 IP)

Vazquez, Felipe	98.5
Kelly, Joe	98.0
Estevez, Carlos	97.9
Diaz, Edwin	97.5
Moronta, Reyes	97.2
Diaz, Jairo	97.0
Lorenzen, Michael	96.9
Lopez, Yoan	96.3
Jackson, Luke	96.1
Familia, Jeurys	96.0

Fastest Average Fastball
(minimum 162 IP)

Syndergaard, Noah	97.7
deGrom, Jacob	96.9
Wheeler, Zack	96.7
Buehler, Walker	96.6
Castillo, Luis	96.5
Alcantara, Sandy	95.6
Marquez, German	95.5
Scherzer, Max	94.9
DeSclafani, Anthony	94.7
Darvish, Yu	94.2

Slowest Average Fastball
(minimum 162 IP)

Hendricks, Kyle	86.9
Teheran, Julio	89.7
Wainwright, Adam	89.9
Lucchesi, Joey	90.2
Lester, Jon	90.3
Kershaw, Clayton	90.4
Sanchez, Anibal	90.5
Ryu, Hyun-Jin	90.6
Quintana, Jose	91.4
Bumgarner, Madison	91.4

Pitches 100+ Velocity

Guerrero, Tayron	273
Hicks, Jordan	247
Munoz, Andres	180
Vazquez, Felipe	132
Black, Ray	62
Estevez, Carlos	58
Helsley, Ryan	42
Diaz, Edwin	36
Syndergaard, Noah	36
Rosenthal, Trevor	31

Pitches 95+ Velocity

Syndergaard, Noah	1823
Wheeler, Zack	1809
Buehler, Walker	1686
deGrom, Jacob	1559
Castillo, Luis	1506
Alcantara, Sandy	1391
Woodruff, Brandon	1168
Gray, Jon	1147
Marquez, German	1036
Scherzer, Max	873

Pitches Less Than 80 MPH

Vargas, Jason	1938
Wainwright, Adam	1060
Hendricks, Kyle	881
Quintana, Jose	741
Nola, Aaron	687
Fried, Max	667
Bauer, Trevor	659
Smyly, Drew	595
Ryu, Hyun-Jin	591
Lucchesi, Joey	570

Lowest % Fastballs
(minimum 162 IP)

Darvish, Yu	34.9
Sanchez, Anibal	35.4
Lester, Jon	38.4
Wainwright, Adam	38.5
Ryu, Hyun-Jin	40.5
Bumgarner, Madison	43.1
Kershaw, Clayton	44.0
Samardzija, Jeff	45.6
Nola, Aaron	46.2
Kelly, Merrill	46.7

Highest % Fastballs
(minimum 162 IP)

Teheran, Julio	63.8
Soroka, Mike	63.4
Hendricks, Kyle	62.2
Quintana, Jose	61.8
Hudson, Dakota	61.7
Buehler, Walker	60.3
Syndergaard, Noah	59.2
Wheeler, Zack	59.0
Flaherty, Jack	58.2
Alcantara, Sandy	57.0

Highest % Curveballs
(minimum 162 IP)

Wainwright, Adam	36.8
Nola, Aaron	35.2
Strasburg, Stephen	30.6
Fried, Max	24.7
Gray, Sonny	24.6
Marquez, German	24.1
Mikolas, Miles	21.4
Kelly, Merrill	21.4
Quintana, Jose	20.9
Bumgarner, Madison	18.3

2019 National League Pitching Leaders

Highest % Changeups
(minimum 162 IP)

Lucchesi, Joey	34.7
Castillo, Luis	32.5
Hendricks, Kyle	28.0
Sanchez, Anibal	28.0
Ryu, Hyun-Jin	27.5
Strasburg, Stephen	20.7
Nola, Aaron	18.5
Syndergaard, Noah	16.1
deGrom, Jacob	16.0
Scherzer, Max	14.5

Highest % Sliders
(minimum 162 IP)

Kershaw, Clayton	39.1
Corbin, Patrick	37.0
Bumgarner, Madison	33.4
Ray, Robbie	31.7
deGrom, Jacob	31.5
Flaherty, Jack	27.5
Hudson, Dakota	25.8
DeSclafani, Anthony	25.6
Soroka, Mike	24.2
Mikolas, Miles	23.6

Balks

Castillo, Luis	3
Jansen, Kenley	3
Sanchez, Anibal	3
Senzatela, Antonio	3
Andriese, Matt	2
Lopez, Pablo	2
Mikolas, Miles	2
Neris, Hector	2
51 tied with	1

Strikeout/Hit Ratio
(minimum 50 IP)

Hader, Josh	3.37
Yates, Kirby	2.46
Wingenter, Trey	2.12
Gallegos, Giovanny	2.11
Smith, Will	2.09
Vazquez, Felipe	2.09
Neris, Hector	1.98
Stephenson, Robert	1.88
Lugo, Seth	1.86
Garrett, Amir	1.77

Opp OPS vs Fastballs
(minimum 251 BF)

Flaherty, Jack	.556
Buehler, Walker	.573
deGrom, Jacob	.582
Woodruff, Brandon	.585
Kershaw, Clayton	.595
Scherzer, Max	.618
Paddack, Chris	.631
Ryu, Hyun-Jin	.650
Houser, Adrian	.658
Teheran, Julio	.659

Opp OPS vs Curveballs
(minimum 100 BF)

Greinke, Zack	.244
Gray, Sonny	.417
Strasburg, Stephen	.486
Marquez, German	.540
Nola, Aaron	.633
Hill, Rich	.644
Bumgarner, Madison	.649
Lauer, Eric	.652
Mikolas, Miles	.655
Wainwright, Adam	.672

Opp OPS vs Changeups
(minimum 100 BF)

Baez, Pedro	.470
Ryu, Hyun-Jin	.512
Castillo, Luis	.514
Gonzalez, Gio	.524
Strasburg, Stephen	.524
Hamels, Cole	.536
deGrom, Jacob	.563
Davies, Zach	.587
Lucchesi, Joey	.592
Greinke, Zack	.612

Opp OPS vs Sliders
(minimum 64 BF)

Scherzer, Max	.383
Brigham, Jeff	.407
Stephenson, Robert	.444
Gallegos, Giovanny	.467
Strop, Pedro	.468
Liriano, Francisco	.472
Romo, Sergio	.493
Smith, Will	.494
Brebbia, John	.502
Lamet, Dinelson	.504

Earned Runs

Syndergaard, Noah	94
Senzatela, Antonio	93
Marquez, German	92
Bumgarner, Madison	90
Kelly, Merrill	90
Quintana, Jose	89
Nola, Aaron	87
Williams, Trevor	87
Wheeler, Zack	86
3 tied with	85

Hits Per Nine Innings
(minimum 162 IP)

Flaherty, Jack	6.19
Gray, Sonny	6.26
Castillo, Luis	6.56
deGrom, Jacob	6.79
Strasburg, Stephen	6.93
Darvish, Yu	7.05
Kershaw, Clayton	7.32
Scherzer, Max	7.52
Corbin, Patrick	7.53
Samardzija, Jeff	7.54

2019 American League Fielding Leaders

2B Pivot % (minimum 98 G)	
Sanchez, Yolmer	0.734
Schoop, Jonathan	0.730
Rengifo, Luis	0.661
Villar, Jonathan	0.643
Gordon, Dee	0.621
Kipnis, Jason	0.614
Altuve, Jose	0.586
Odor, Rougned	0.570
Profar, Jurickson	0.552

SS Pivot % (minimum 98 G)	
Galvis, Freddy	0.673
Simmons, Andrelton	0.651
Mondesi, Adalberto	0.627
Semien, Marcus	0.622
Andrus, Elvis	0.618
Lindor, Francisco	0.611
Adames, Willy	0.610
Anderson, Tim	0.540
Bogaerts, Xander	0.514
Martin Jr., Richie	0.500

Highest Pct CS by Catchers (minimum 600 INN or 50 SBA)	
Perez, Roberto	37.0
Zunino, Mike	34.1
Vazquez, Christian	33.3
Jansen, Danny	30.0
Phegley, Josh	27.5
McCann, James	26.0
Sanchez, Gary	23.4
Lucroy, Jonathan	22.2
Maldonado, Martin	22.2
Chirinos, Robinson	21.1

Lowest Pct CS by Catchers (minimum 600 INN or 50 SBA)	
Garver, Mitch	8.8
Narvaez, Omar	12.1
Mathis, Jeff	13.8
Castro, Jason	17.1
Severino, Pedro	19.2
Chirinos, Robinson	21.1
Lucroy, Jonathan	22.2
Maldonado, Martin	22.2
Sanchez, Gary	23.4
McCann, James	26.0

2B Double Play % (minimum 98 G)	
Rengifo, Luis	0.636
Sanchez, Yolmer	0.598
Kipnis, Jason	0.542
Odor, Rougned	0.540
Villar, Jonathan	0.520
Schoop, Jonathan	0.519
Gordon, Dee	0.513
Profar, Jurickson	0.508
Altuve, Jose	0.469

3B Double Play % (minimum 98 G)	
Ruiz, Rio	0.543
Moncada, Yoan	0.479
Seager, Kyle	0.478
Ramirez, Jose	0.415
Urshela, Giovanny	0.413
Bregman, Alex	0.405
Chapman, Matt	0.400
Dozier, Hunter	0.362
Devers, Rafael	0.218

SS Double Play % (minimum 98 G)	
Mondesi, Adalberto	0.663
Simmons, Andrelton	0.662
Adames, Willy	0.648
Lindor, Francisco	0.606
Semien, Marcus	0.591
Andrus, Elvis	0.589
Galvis, Freddy	0.576
Anderson, Tim	0.568
Martin Jr., Richie	0.526
Bogaerts, Xander	0.508

Errors	
Anderson, Tim	26
Devers, Rafael	22
Polanco, Jorge	22
Torres, Gleyber	20
Villar, Jonathan	20
Sano, Miguel	19
Adames, Willy	17
Guerrero Jr., Vladimir	17
5 tied with	15

Fielding Errors	
Devers, Rafael	14
Anderson, Tim	13
Guerrero Jr., Vladimir	13
Cuthbert, Cheslor	11
Sano, Miguel	11
Urshela, Giovanny	11
Odor, Rougned	10
Villar, Jonathan	10
5 tied with	9

Throwing Errors	
Anderson, Tim	13
Polanco, Jorge	13
Torres, Gleyber	13
Adames, Willy	12
Profar, Jurickson	11
Villar, Jonathan	10
Sanchez, Gary	9
6 tied with	8

Range Factor for 2B (minimum 98 games)	
Sanchez, Yolmer	4.76
Villar, Jonathan	4.37
Gordon, Dee	4.23
Rengifo, Luis	4.21
Profar, Jurickson	4.10
Odor, Rougned	4.09
Schoop, Jonathan	3.84
Kipnis, Jason	3.54
Altuve, Jose	3.38

Range Factor for 3B (minimum 98 games)	
Moncada, Yoan	3.09
Chapman, Matt	3.08
Seager, Kyle	2.79
Ramirez, Jose	2.73
Devers, Rafael	2.72
Ruiz, Rio	2.63
Dozier, Hunter	2.59
Bregman, Alex	2.57
Urshela, Giovanny	2.49

Range Factor for SS (minimum 98 games)	
Mondesi, Adalberto	4.57
Anderson, Tim	4.34
Simmons, Andrelton	4.26
Galvis, Freddy	4.18
Andrus, Elvis	4.11
Semien, Marcus	3.90
Martin Jr., Richie	3.81
Adames, Willy	3.73
Lindor, Francisco	3.54
Polanco, Jorge	3.53

2019 National League Fielding Leaders

2B Pivot %			SS Pivot %			Highest Pct CS by Catchers			Lowest Pct CS by Catchers	
(minimum 98 G)			(minimum 98 G)			(minimum 600 INN or 50 SBA)			(minimum 600 INN or 50 SBA)	
Castro, Starlin	0.729		Swanson, Dansby	0.706		Realmuto, J.T.	43.0		Suzuki, Kurt	6.3
Frazier, Adam	0.683		DeJong, Paul	0.697		Wolters, Tony	31.3		Kelly, Carson	11.1
Albies, Ozzie	0.679		Seager, Corey	0.647		Alfaro, Jorge	29.8		Ramos, Wilson	13.8
Dozier, Brian	0.641		Ahmed, Nick	0.643		Contreras, Willson	25.0		McCann, Brian	16.3
McMahon, Ryan	0.639		Rojas, Miguel	0.635		Diaz, Elias	25.0		Flowers, Tyler	17.4
Panik, Joe	0.600		Story, Trevor	0.617		Grandal, Yasmani	23.2		Barnhart, Tucker	21.2
Hernandez, Cesar	0.593		Segura, Jean	0.606		Posey, Buster	23.1		Molina, Yadier	21.4
Wong, Kolten	0.581		Baez, Javier	0.597		Gomes, Yan	22.6		Hedges, Austin	22.6
Cano, Robinson	0.574		Arcia, Orlando	0.597		Hedges, Austin	22.6		Gomes, Yan	22.6
			Newman, Kevin	0.561		Molina, Yadier	21.4		Posey, Buster	23.1

2B Double Play %			3B Double Play %			SS Double Play %	
(minimum 98 G)			(minimum 98 G)			(minimum 98 G)	
Castro, Starlin	0.592		Moran, Colin	0.528		DeJong, Paul	0.669
Albies, Ozzie	0.565		Donaldson, Josh	0.478		Baez, Javier	0.649
Cano, Robinson	0.562		Arenado, Nolan	0.464		Seager, Corey	0.640
McMahon, Ryan	0.534		Frazier, Todd	0.449		Swanson, Dansby	0.621
Frazier, Adam	0.503		Escobar, Eduardo	0.444		Iglesias, Jose	0.617
Wong, Kolten	0.503		Longoria, Evan	0.424		Segura, Jean	0.614
Dozier, Brian	0.500		Rendon, Anthony	0.410		Story, Trevor	0.613
Hernandez, Cesar	0.486		Bryant, Kris	0.382		Rojas, Miguel	0.600
Panik, Joe	0.483		Moustakas, Mike	0.378		Ahmed, Nick	0.582
			Carpenter, Matt	0.368		Rosario, Amed	0.566

Errors			Fielding Errors			Throwing Errors	
Segura, Jean	20		Crawford, Brandon	12		Tatis Jr., Fernando	14
Tatis Jr., Fernando	18		Rosario, Amed	11		Baez, Javier	12
Rosario, Amed	17		Hiura, Keston	10		Moustakas, Mike	11
Suarez, Eugenio	17		Hosmer, Eric	10		Segura, Jean	11
Crawford, Brandon	16		McMahon, Ryan	10		Realmuto, J.T.	9
Hiura, Keston	16		Moran, Colin	10		Contreras, Willson	8
McMahon, Ryan	16		7 tied with	9		Grandal, Yasmani	8
5 tied with	15					Hedges, Austin	8
						Machado, Manny	8
						Suarez, Eugenio	8

Range Factor for 2B			Range Factor for 3B			Range Factor for SS	
(minimum 98 games)			(minimum 98 games)			(minimum 98 games)	
Wong, Kolten	4.98		Arenado, Nolan	3.06		Baez, Javier	4.28
McMahon, Ryan	4.76		Frazier, Todd	2.87		Story, Trevor	4.28
Albies, Ozzie	4.21		Donaldson, Josh	2.80		DeJong, Paul	4.24
Frazier, Adam	4.18		Longoria, Evan	2.61		Crawford, Brandon	4.06
Panik, Joe	4.15		Turner, Justin	2.51		Arcia, Orlando	4.05
Hernandez, Cesar	4.09		Franco, Maikel	2.50		Ahmed, Nick	4.03
Cano, Robinson	3.95		Moustakas, Mike	2.46		Swanson, Dansby	3.99
Castro, Starlin	3.79		Rendon, Anthony	2.45		Rojas, Miguel	3.95
Dozier, Brian	3.51		Suarez, Eugenio	2.42		Newman, Kevin	3.92
			Escobar, Eduardo	2.41		Segura, Jean	3.90

2019 Active Career Batting Leaders

Batting Average		On Base Percentage		Slugging Average		Home Runs	
(minimum 1000 PA)		(minimum 1000 PA)		(minimum 1000 PA)			
Cabrera, Miguel	.315	Votto, Joey	.421	Trout, Mike	.581	Pujols, Albert	656
Altuve, Jose	.315	Trout, Mike	.419	Bellinger, Cody	.559	Cabrera, Miguel	477
Suzuki, Ichiro	.311	Soto, Juan	.403	Judge, Aaron	.558	Encarnacion, Edwin	414
Votto, Joey	.307	Judge, Aaron	.394	Pujols, Albert	.549	Cruz, Nelson	401
Trout, Mike	.305	Cabrera, Miguel	.392	Stanton, Giancarlo	.547	Braun, Ryan	344
Blackmon, Charlie	.304	Goldschmidt, Paul	.391	Arenado, Nolan	.546	Granderson, Curtis	344
Cano, Robinson	.302	Nimmo, Brandon	.387	Cabrera, Miguel	.543	Cano, Robinson	324
LeMahieu, DJ	.302	Harper, Bryce	.385	Martinez, J.D.	.537	Bruce, Jay	312
Posey, Buster	.302	Bryant, Kris	.385	Story, Trevor	.537	Stanton, Giancarlo	308
Yelich, Christian	.301	Bregman, Alex	.384	Soto, Juan	.535	2 tied with	298

Games		At Bats		Hits		Total Bases	
Pujols, Albert	2823	Pujols, Albert	10687	Pujols, Albert	3202	Pujols, Albert	5863
Suzuki, Ichiro	2653	Suzuki, Ichiro	9934	Suzuki, Ichiro	3089	Cabrera, Miguel	4857
Cabrera, Miguel	2400	Cabrera, Miguel	8949	Cabrera, Miguel	2815	Cano, Robinson	4170
Cano, Robinson	2185	Cano, Robinson	8502	Cano, Robinson	2570	Suzuki, Ichiro	3994
Markakis, Nick	2117	Markakis, Nick	8172	Markakis, Nick	2355	Braun, Ryan	3462
Granderson, Curtis	2057	Kinsler, Ian	7423	Kinsler, Ian	1999	Markakis, Nick	3462
Molina, Yadier	1983	Granderson, Curtis	7236	Molina, Yadier	1963	Encarnacion, Edwin	3434
Encarnacion, Edwin	1916	Jones, Adam	7009	Cabrera, Melky	1962	Granderson, Curtis	3368
Kinsler, Ian	1888	Molina, Yadier	6970	Jones, Adam	1939	Cruz, Nelson	3274
Cabrera, Melky	1887	Encarnacion, Edwin	6881	Braun, Ryan	1933	Kinsler, Ian	3268

Doubles		Triples		Runs Scored		RBI	
Pujols, Albert	661	Suzuki, Ichiro	96	Pujols, Albert	1828	Pujols, Albert	2075
Cabrera, Miguel	577	Granderson, Curtis	95	Cabrera, Miguel	1429	Cabrera, Miguel	1694
Cano, Robinson	562	Fowler, Dexter	82	Suzuki, Ichiro	1420	Cano, Robinson	1272
Markakis, Nick	499	Gardner, Brett	68	Kinsler, Ian	1243	Encarnacion, Edwin	1242
Kinsler, Ian	416	Gordon, Dee	54	Cano, Robinson	1234	Braun, Ryan	1128
Votto, Joey	404	Pence, Hunter	54	Granderson, Curtis	1217	Cruz, Nelson	1119
Braun, Ryan	401	Andrus, Elvis	48	Markakis, Nick	1104	Markakis, Nick	1031
Zimmerman, Ryan	401	Braun, Ryan	48	Encarnacion, Edwin	1080	McCann, Brian	1018
Pedroia, Dustin	394	McCutchen, Andrew	48	Braun, Ryan	1066	Longoria, Evan	1015
Cabrera, Melky	383	Blackmon, Charlie	47	Ramirez, Hanley	1049	Zimmerman, Ryan	1015

Walks		Intentional Walks		Hit By Pitch		Strikeouts	
Pujols, Albert	1322	Pujols, Albert	311	Choo, Shin-Soo	150	Reynolds, Mark	1927
Votto, Joey	1180	Cabrera, Miguel	234	Rizzo, Anthony	145	Granderson, Curtis	1916
Cabrera, Miguel	1135	Suzuki, Ichiro	181	Dietrich, Derek	118	Davis, Chris	1835
Santana, Carlos	944	Votto, Joey	140	Gordon, Alex	118	Upton, Justin	1798
Granderson, Curtis	924	Cano, Robinson	111	Gomez, Carlos	112	Cabrera, Miguel	1761
Encarnacion, Edwin	887	Goldschmidt, Paul	105	Marte, Starling	111	Kemp, Matt	1600
Markakis, Nick	881	Trout, Mike	100	Jay, Jon	109	Cruz, Nelson	1567
Choo, Shin-Soo	855	Harper, Bryce	81	Martin, Russell	107	Choo, Shin-Soo	1546
Zobrist, Ben	832	Longoria, Evan	81	Pujols, Albert	107	Bruce, Jay	1535
McCutchen, Andrew	823	Freeman, Freddie	80	Jones, Adam	103	Gordon, Alex	1498

2019 Active Career Batting Leaders

Sacrifice Hits		Sacrifice Flies		Stolen Bases		Seasons Played	
Kershaw, Clayton	108	Pujols, Albert	114	Suzuki, Ichiro	509	Pujols, Albert	19
Andrus, Elvis	100	Longoria, Evan	86	Davis, Rajai	415	Sabathia, CC	19
Cueto, Johnny	85	Cabrera, Miguel	84	Gordon, Dee	330	Suzuki, Ichiro	19
Teheran, Julio	67	Markakis, Nick	73	Andrus, Elvis	302	Cabrera, Miguel	17
Gardner, Brett	64	Kemp, Matt	72	Hamilton, Billy	299	Jackson, Edwin	17
Hamels, Cole	64	Molina, Yadier	70	Ramirez, Hanley	281	Perez, Oliver	17
Wainwright, Adam	60	Zimmerman, Ryan	67	Gomez, Carlos	268	Rodney, Fernando	17
Bailey, Homer	55	Zobrist, Ben	67	Gardner, Brett	267	Granderson, Curtis	16
Jay, Jon	55	Encarnacion, Edwin	65	Altuve, Jose	254	Greinke, Zack	16
Strasburg, Stephen	55	Cabrera, Melky	64	Dyson, Jarrod	250	Molina, Yadier	16

At Bats Per Home Run (minimum 1000 AB)		Grounded Into DP		Highest SB Success Pct (minimum 100 SBA)		Lowest SB Success Pct (minimum 100 SBA)	
Gallo, Joey	12.0	Pujols, Albert	395	Dyson, Jarrod	85.0	Odor, Rougned	56.4
Judge, Aaron	12.9	Cabrera, Miguel	318	Trout, Mike	84.7	Bruce, Jay	61.9
Sanchez, Gary	13.3	Cano, Robinson	277	Turner, Trea	84.1	Castro, Starlin	63.6
Stanton, Giancarlo	13.8	Molina, Yadier	254	Mondesi, Adalberto	84.0	Parra, Gerardo	64.0
Olson, Matt	14.3	Markakis, Nick	209	Yelich, Christian	83.8	Molina, Yadier	64.1
Bellinger, Cody	14.4	Zimmerman, Ryan	203	Betts, Mookie	83.4	Frazier, Todd	66.1
Muncy, Max	14.6	Jones, Adam	190	Pollock, A.J.	81.8	LeMahieu, DJ	66.1
Schwarber, Kyle	14.7	Martin, Russell	190	Gardner, Brett	81.4	Martin, Russell	66.4
Davis, Khris	14.8	Kendrick, Howie	189	Cain, Lorenzo	81.4	Puig, Yasiel	67.5
Renfroe, Hunter	14.9	Encarnacion, Edwin	182	Suzuki, Ichiro	81.3	Bourjos, Peter	68.0

Strikeouts / Walks Ratio (minimum 1000 AB)		At Bats Per GIDP (minimum 1000 AB)		OPS (minimum 1000 PA)		Secondary Average (minimum 1000 PA)	
Pujols, Albert	.967	Moncada, Yoan	261.4	Trout, Mike	1.000	Trout, Mike	.507
Pedroia, Dustin	1.048	Gallo, Joey	220.5	Judge, Aaron	.952	Judge, Aaron	.493
Santana, Carlos	1.073	Buxton, Byron	156.3	Votto, Joey	.941	Gallo, Joey	.485
Votto, Joey	1.111	Hamilton, Billy	155.9	Soto, Juan	.937	Soto, Juan	.461
Bregman, Alex	1.112	DeShields, Delino	128.8	Cabrera, Miguel	.935	Bellinger, Cody	.449
Panik, Joe	1.155	Carpenter, Matt	119.3	Bellinger, Cody	.928	Hoskins, Rhys	.447
Zobrist, Ben	1.195	Granderson, Curtis	113.1	Pujols, Albert	.927	Muncy, Max	.444
Ramirez, Jose	1.199	Suzuki, Ichiro	108.0	Goldschmidt, Paul	.916	Harper, Bryce	.435
Betts, Mookie	1.251	Albies, Ozzie	106.9	Bregman, Alex	.911	Stanton, Giancarlo	.422
La Stella, Tommy	1.267	Eaton, Adam	104.3	Stanton, Giancarlo	.905	Goldschmidt, Paul	.420

Highest Strikeout per PA (minimum 1000 PA)		Lowest Strikeout per PA (minimum 1000 PA)		Plate Appearances		At Bats Per RBI (minimum 1000 AB)	
Broxton, Keon	.386	Simmons, Andrelton	.089	Pujols, Albert	12231	Pujols, Albert	5.2
Gallo, Joey	.380	Panik, Joe	.094	Suzuki, Ichiro	10734	Cabrera, Miguel	5.3
Sano, Miguel	.363	Pedroia, Dustin	.097	Cabrera, Miguel	10236	Aguilar, Jesus	5.3
Zunino, Mike	.342	Suzuki, Ichiro	.101	Cano, Robinson	9264	Sanchez, Gary	5.3
Davis, Chris	.329	Molina, Yadier	.102	Markakis, Nick	9180	Arenado, Nolan	5.4
Happ, Ian	.325	Pujols, Albert	.105	Granderson, Curtis	8306	Stanton, Giancarlo	5.4
Santana, Domingo	.320	Brantley, Michael	.106	Kinsler, Ian	8299	Bellinger, Cody	5.5
Hernandez, Teoscar	.318	Gurriel, Yuli	.107	Encarnacion, Edwin	7945	Encarnacion, Edwin	5.5
Judge, Aaron	.316	Shuck, JB	.110	Molina, Yadier	7655	Cruz, Nelson	5.6
Taylor, Michael A.	.316	Altuve, Jose	.114	Cabrera, Melky	7527	Correa, Carlos	5.6

2019 Active Career Pitching Leaders

Earned Run Average (minimum 750 IP)		Winning Percentage (minimum 100 Decisions)		Opponent Batting Average (minimum 750 IP)		Baserunners Per 9 IP (minimum 750 IP)	
Kershaw, Clayton	2.44	Kershaw, Clayton	.695	Clippard, Tyler	.197	Kershaw, Clayton	9.20
deGrom, Jacob	2.62	Strasburg, Stephen	.659	Kershaw, Clayton	.208	deGrom, Jacob	9.64
Sale, Chris	3.03	Scherzer, Max	.656	Sale, Chris	.218	Sale, Chris	9.85
Bumgarner, Madison	3.13	Price, David	.652	Darvish, Yu	.218	Kluber, Corey	10.08
Hendricks, Kyle	3.14	Cole, Gerrit	.644	deGrom, Jacob	.221	Strasburg, Stephen	10.09
Clippard, Tyler	3.14	Lester, Jon	.638	Scherzer, Max	.222	Scherzer, Max	10.16
Kluber, Corey	3.16	Tanaka, Masahiro	.636	Strasburg, Stephen	.222	Clippard, Tyler	10.25
Strasburg, Stephen	3.17	Verlander, Justin	.636	Hill, Rich	.224	Bumgarner, Madison	10.30
Scherzer, Max	3.20	Wainwright, Adam	.630	Verlander, Justin	.228	Tanaka, Masahiro	10.37
Cole, Gerrit	3.22	Kluber, Corey	.628	Nola, Aaron	.232	Hendricks, Kyle	10.40

Games		Games Started		Complete Games		Shutouts	
Rodney, Fernando	951	Sabathia, CC	560	Sabathia, CC	38	Kershaw, Clayton	15
Smith, Joe	782	Verlander, Justin	453	Verlander, Justin	26	Sabathia, CC	12
Clippard, Tyler	751	Greinke, Zack	447	Hernandez, Felix	25	Hernandez, Felix	11
Soria, Joakim	710	Hamels, Cole	421	Kershaw, Clayton	25	Santana, Ervin	11
Romo, Sergio	708	Hernandez, Felix	418	Wainwright, Adam	22	Wainwright, Adam	10
Perez, Oliver	670	Lester, Jon	411	Santana, Ervin	21	Verlander, Justin	9
Robertson, David	661	Santana, Ervin	384	Cueto, Johnny	17	Cueto, Johnny	8
Gregerson, Luke	646	Scherzer, Max	356	Hamels, Cole	17	Holland, Derek	8
Albers, Matt	616	Kershaw, Clayton	344	Kluber, Corey	17	Vargas, Jason	8
Sipp, Tony	616	Porcello, Rick	339	Price, David	17	3 tied with	7

Wins		Losses		Innings Pitched		Batters Faced	
Sabathia, CC	251	Sabathia, CC	161	Sabathia, CC	3577.1	Sabathia, CC	14989
Verlander, Justin	225	Hernandez, Felix	136	Verlander, Justin	2982.0	Verlander, Justin	12193
Greinke, Zack	205	Jackson, Edwin	133	Greinke, Zack	2872.0	Greinke, Zack	11729
Lester, Jon	190	Verlander, Justin	129	Hernandez, Felix	2729.2	Hernandez, Felix	11284
Scherzer, Max	170	Santana, Ervin	127	Hamels, Cole	2694.2	Hamels, Cole	11101
Hernandez, Felix	169	Greinke, Zack	123	Lester, Jon	2537.2	Lester, Jon	10595
Kershaw, Clayton	169	Hamels, Cole	121	Santana, Ervin	2421.1	Santana, Ervin	10205
Hamels, Cole	163	Porcello, Rick	118	Scherzer, Max	2290.0	Scherzer, Max	9278
Wainwright, Adam	162	Liriano, Francisco	114	Kershaw, Clayton	2274.2	Kershaw, Clayton	8958
Price, David	150	2 tied with	108	Wainwright, Adam	2103.2	Wainwright, Adam	8739

Strikeouts		Walks Allowed		Hit Batters		Wild Pitches	
Sabathia, CC	3093	Sabathia, CC	1099	Sabathia, CC	123	Hernandez, Felix	156
Verlander, Justin	3006	Verlander, Justin	850	Morton, Charlie	117	Jackson, Edwin	108
Scherzer, Max	2692	Lester, Jon	820	Hernandez, Felix	105	Liriano, Francisco	100
Greinke, Zack	2622	Liriano, Francisco	816	Cueto, Johnny	104	Cahill, Trevor	97
Hamels, Cole	2558	Hernandez, Felix	805	Santana, Ervin	102	Santana, Ervin	97
Hernandez, Felix	2524	Gonzalez, Gio	796	Hamels, Cole	100	Kershaw, Clayton	88
Kershaw, Clayton	2464	Jackson, Edwin	779	Sale, Chris	98	Verlander, Justin	87
Lester, Jon	2355	Hamels, Cole	766	Verlander, Justin	98	Greinke, Zack	86
Sale, Chris	2007	Perez, Oliver	754	Scherzer, Max	85	Volquez, Edinson	77
Price, David	1981	Santana, Ervin	754	2 tied with	84	Kennedy, Ian	76

2019 Active Career Pitching Leaders

Saves			Save Pct			Home Runs Allowed			Strikeouts Per 9 IP	
			(minimum 50 Save Ops)						(minimum 750 IP)	
Kimbrel, Craig	346		Kimbrel, Craig	90.3		Sabathia, CC	382		Darvish, Yu	11.12
Rodney, Fernando	327		Chapman, Aroldis	89.5		Santana, Ervin	322		Ray, Robbie	11.09
Jansen, Kenley	301		Britton, Zack	89.5		Hamels, Cole	310		Sale, Chris	11.08
Chapman, Aroldis	273		Jansen, Kenley	88.8		Verlander, Justin	308		Miller, Andrew	10.65
Soria, Joakim	221		Davis, Wade	88.4		Greinke, Zack	292		Strasburg, Stephen	10.60
Holland, Greg	206		Giles, Ken	88.4		Hernandez, Felix	264		Scherzer, Max	10.58
Melancon, Mark	194		Holland, Greg	88.0		Lester, Jon	258		deGrom, Jacob	10.25
Osuna, Roberto	154		Diaz, Edwin	87.7		Porcello, Rick	255		Cole, Gerrit	10.06
Allen, Cody	153		Iglesias, Raisel	87.5		Scherzer, Max	254		Clippard, Tyler	9.98
Britton, Zack	145		Allen, Cody	86.9		Jackson, Edwin	249		Archer, Chris	9.83

Opp On-Base Percentage			Opp Slugging Average			Hits Per Nine Innings			Home Runs Per Nine IP	
(minimum 750 IP)			(minimum 750 IP)			(minimum 750 IP)			(minimum 750 IP)	
Kershaw, Clayton	.262		Kershaw, Clayton	.318		Clippard, Tyler	6.38		Kershaw, Clayton	0.68
deGrom, Jacob	.271		deGrom, Jacob	.334		Kershaw, Clayton	6.79		Martinez, Carlos	0.70
Sale, Chris	.273		Rodney, Fernando	.346		Sale, Chris	7.25		Rodney, Fernando	0.70
Strasburg, Stephen	.279		Sale, Chris	.351		Darvish, Yu	7.28		Wainwright, Adam	0.71
Kluber, Corey	.280		Strasburg, Stephen	.352		deGrom, Jacob	7.30		Ross, Tyson	0.73
Scherzer, Max	.280		Martinez, Carlos	.353		Scherzer, Max	7.40		Morton, Charlie	0.76
Clippard, Tyler	.280		Clippard, Tyler	.355		Strasburg, Stephen	7.41		Richards, Garrett	0.76
Tanaka, Masahiro	.283		Richards, Garrett	.356		Hill, Rich	7.44		deGrom, Jacob	0.78
Bumgarner, Madison	.284		Gray, Sonny	.359		Verlander, Justin	7.65		Gonzalez, Gio	0.78
Petit, Yusmeiro	.286		Miller, Andrew	.363		Arrieta, Jake	7.77		Lynn, Lance	0.81

Strikeouts / Walks Ratio			Stolen Base Pct Allowed			GIDP Induced			GIDP Per Nine IP	
(minimum 750 IP)			(minimum 750 IP)						(minimum 750 IP)	
Sale, Chris	5.37		Cueto, Johnny	42.7		Sabathia, CC	316		Chatwood, Tyler	1.39
Kluber, Corey	5.00		Miley, Wade	46.0		Hernandez, Felix	270		Perez, Martin	1.30
Tomlin, Josh	4.74		Greinke, Zack	50.3		Lester, Jon	233		Gibson, Kyle	1.16
Tanaka, Masahiro	4.74		LeBlanc, Wade	50.8		Greinke, Zack	220		Richard, Clayton	1.15
deGrom, Jacob	4.72		Kershaw, Clayton	51.9		Hamels, Cole	215		Keuchel, Dallas	1.11
Strasburg, Stephen	4.50		Tomlin, Josh	52.2		Wainwright, Adam	210		Albers, Matt	1.09
Pineda, Michael	4.47		Lynn, Lance	52.5		Porcello, Rick	206		Stroman, Marcus	1.08
Scherzer, Max	4.36		Eovaldi, Nathan	54.8		Leake, Mike	189		Duke, Zach	1.07
Kershaw, Clayton	4.27		Duke, Zach	56.9		Santana, Ervin	184		Martinez, Carlos	1.05
Cole, Gerrit	4.24		2 tied with	58.3		Liriano, Francisco	181		Anderson, Brett	1.04

Complete Game %			Quality Start Pct			Walks Per 9 IP			Games Finished	
(minimum 100 GS)			(minimum 100 GS)			(minimum 750 IP)				
Kluber, Corey	0.08		deGrom, Jacob	74.9		Tomlin, Josh	1.29		Rodney, Fernando	590
Kershaw, Clayton	0.07		Kershaw, Clayton	73.8		Tanaka, Masahiro	1.79		Kimbrel, Craig	466
Wainwright, Adam	0.07		Sale, Chris	69.8		Zimmermann, Jordan	1.92		Jansen, Kenley	443
Sale, Chris	0.07		Cole, Gerrit	68.2		Kluber, Corey	1.96		Chapman, Aroldis	411
Sabathia, CC	0.07		Verlander, Justin	67.3		Leake, Mike	1.98		Soria, Joakim	403
Carrasco, Carlos	0.06		Bumgarner, Madison	66.1		Pineda, Michael	2.02		Melancon, Mark	334
Hernandez, Felix	0.06		Scherzer, Max	65.7		Hunter, Tommy	2.02		Holland, Greg	320
Keuchel, Dallas	0.06		Price, David	65.3		Hendricks, Kyle	2.03		Allen, Cody	291
Cueto, Johnny	0.06		Kluber, Corey	64.5		Sale, Chris	2.07		Cishek, Steve	283
Verlander, Justin	0.06		Greinke, Zack	64.2		Bumgarner, Madison	2.09		Robertson, David	276

2019 American League Bill James Leaders

Top Game Scores

Pitcher	Date	Opp	IP	H	R	ER	BB	SO	GS
Verlander, Justin, Hou	9/1	Tor	9.0	0	0	0	1	14	100
Bieber, Shane, Cle	7/24	Tor	9.0	1	0	0	1	10	94
Giolito, Lucas, CWS	8/21	Min	9.0	3	0	0	0	12	93
Sale, Chris, Bos	6/5	KC	9.0	3	0	0	0	12	93
Bieber, Shane, Cle	5/19	Bal	9.0	5	0	0	0	15	92
Tanaka, Masahiro, NYY	6/17	TB	9.0	2	0	0	1	10	92
Cole, Gerrit, Hou	9/8	Sea	8.0	1	1	1	0	15	91
Fiers, Mike, Oak	5/7	Cin	9.0	0	0	0	2	6	91
Sale, Chris, Bos	8/8	LAA	8.0	2	0	0	0	13	91
Kikuchi, Yusei, Sea	8/18	Tor	9.0	2	0	0	1	8	90
Leake, Mike, Sea	7/19	LAA	9.0	1	0	0	1	6	90

Worst Game Scores

Pitcher	Date	Opp	IP	H	R	ER	BB	SO	GS
Tanaka, Masahiro, NYY	7/25	Bos	3.1	12	12	12	3	4	-11
Jackson, Edwin, Tor	5/31	Col	2.1	10	10	10	3	4	-2
Fiers, Mike, Oak	9/9	Hou	1.0	9	9	9	0	1	0
Bailey, Homer, Oak	7/22	Hou	2.0	8	9	9	3	2	3
Cobb, Alex, Bal	4/20	Min	2.2	10	9	9	0	2	4
Banuelos, Manny, CWS	5/4	Bos	2.2	10	9	9	0	3	5
Gonzales, Marco, Sea	6/2	LAA	4.2	9	10	10	3	2	5
Hernandez, Felix, Sea	9/8	Hou	2.0	7	11	7	2	1	5
Nova, Ivan, CWS	4/23	Bal	4.0	11	9	9	3	4	5
Cease, Dylan, CWS	8/29	Min	2.0	10	8	8	1	3	6
McHugh, Collin, Hou	4/21	Tex	3.1	8	10	9	1	1	6
Nova, Ivan, CWS	5/17	Tor	3.0	8	9	8	4	1	6

Runs Created

Semien, Marcus	136
Trout, Mike	132
Bregman, Alex	126
Bogaerts, Xander	124
LeMahieu, DJ	122
Devers, Rafael	119
Betts, Mookie	118
Martinez, J.D.	117
Merrifield, Whit	114
Santana, Carlos	114

Runs Created Per 27 Outs

Trout, Mike	10.3
Bregman, Alex	8.3
Cruz, Nelson	8.3
Springer, George	7.7
LeMahieu, DJ	7.7
Bogaerts, Xander	7.5
Semien, Marcus	7.4
Martinez, J.D.	7.4
Santana, Carlos	7.1
Meadows, Austin	7.1

Offensive Winning %

Trout, Mike	.815
Cruz, Nelson	.744
LeMahieu, DJ	.742
Bregman, Alex	.729
Semien, Marcus	.710
Springer, George	.702
Meadows, Austin	.697
Santana, Carlos	.678
Bogaerts, Xander	.678
Torres, Gleyber	.677

Secondary Average
(minimum 502 PA)

Trout, Mike	.611
Bregman, Alex	.520
Cruz, Nelson	.452
Springer, George	.451
Soler, Jorge	.433
Vogelbach, Daniel	.431
Santana, Carlos	.429
Betts, Mookie	.419
Meadows, Austin	.392
Semien, Marcus	.385

Isolated Power
(minimum 502 PA)

Trout, Mike	.353
Cruz, Nelson	.328
Soler, Jorge	.304
Springer, George	.299
Bregman, Alex	.296
Olson, Matt	.277
Meadows, Austin	.268
Kepler, Max	.267
Chapman, Matt	.257
Torres, Gleyber	.256

Power / Speed Number
(minimum 502 PA)

Villar, Jonathan	30.0
Lindor, Francisco	26.1
Santana, Danny	24.0
Ramirez, Jose	23.5
Pham, Tommy	22.8
Betts, Mookie	20.6
Choo, Shin-Soo	18.5
Merrifield, Whit	17.8
Trout, Mike	17.7
Meadows, Austin	17.6

Speed Scores

Smith, Mallex	8.41
Gardner, Brett	7.90
Villar, Jonathan	7.60
Gordon, Dee	7.54
Betts, Mookie	7.50
Garcia, Leury	7.41
Ramirez, Jose	7.25
Merrifield, Whit	7.09
Lindor, Francisco	7.06
Trout, Mike	6.99

Cheap Wins

Cashner, Andrew	5
Porcello, Rick	5
Gonzales, Marco	4
Happ, J.A.	4
11 tied with	3

Tough Losses

Lynn, Lance	7
Stroman, Marcus	6
Verlander, Justin	6
Bieber, Shane	5
Boyd, Matthew	5
Turnbull, Spencer	5
Bundy, Dylan	4
Giolito, Lucas	4
Keller, Brad	4
Sale, Chris	4

2019 National League Bill James Leaders

Top Game Scores

Pitcher	Date	Opp	IP	H	R	ER	BB	SO	GS
Marquez, German, Col	4/14	SF	9.0	1	0	0	0	9	94
Strasburg, Stephen, Was	8/31	Mia	8.0	2	0	0	0	14	92
Alcantara, Sandy, Mia	5/19	NYM	9.0	2	0	0	1	8	90
Buehler, Walker, LAD	6/21	Col	9.0	3	2	2	0	16	89
Peralta, Freddy, Mil	4/3	Cin	8.0	2	0	0	0	11	89
Young, Alex, Ari	9/7	Cin	8.0	2	0	0	1	12	89
Buehler, Walker, LAD	8/3	SD	9.0	5	1	1	0	15	88
Ryu, Hyun-Jin, LAD	5/12	Was	8.0	1	0	0	1	9	88
Syndergaard, Noah, NYM	5/2	Cin	9.0	4	0	0	1	10	88
Flaherty, Jack, StL	9/3	SF	8.0	1	0	0	1	8	87
Strasburg, Stephen, Was	4/21	Mia	8.0	2	0	0	2	11	87

Worst Game Scores

Pitcher	Date	Opp	IP	H	R	ER	BB	SO	GS
Marquez, German, Col	7/15	SF	2.2	11	11	11	0	3	-5
Margevicius, Nick, SD	6/16	Col	1.1	11	9	9	1	1	-4
Anderson, Chase, Mil	8/18	Was	2.1	9	10	10	2	1	-2
Lopez, Pablo, Mia	5/10	NYM	3.0	10	10	10	2	3	0
Brault, Steven, Pit	9/13	ChC	2.2	8	10	10	3	2	1
Gausman, Kevin, Atl	5/29	Was	1.0	8	8	8	2	1	4
Lester, Jon, ChC	8/6	Oak	4.0	10	11	9	3	6	5
Hamels, Cole, ChC	8/14	Phi	2.0	9	8	8	2	2	6
Lambert, Peter, Col	8/7	Hou	3.0	7	9	9	4	1	6
Fedde, Erick, Was	7/30	Atl	3.2	9	9	9	4	4	7
Syndergaard, Noah, NYM	8/28	ChC	3.0	9	10	9	1	5	7

Runs Created

Rendon, Anthony	130
Freeman, Freddie	126
Yelich, Christian	126
Harper, Bryce	125
Bellinger, Cody	124
Arenado, Nolan	123
Acuna Jr., Ronald	122
Marte, Ketel	121
Soto, Juan	117
Blackmon, Charlie	115

Runs Created Per 27 Outs

Yelich, Christian	9.9
Rendon, Anthony	8.8
Marte, Ketel	8.3
Bellinger, Cody	8.2
Rizzo, Anthony	7.8
Arenado, Nolan	7.7
Soto, Juan	7.7
McNeil, Jeff	7.7
Freeman, Freddie	7.6
Harper, Bryce	7.6

Offensive Winning %

Yelich, Christian	.808
Bellinger, Cody	.763
Rendon, Anthony	.763
Marte, Ketel	.753
McNeil, Jeff	.739
Rizzo, Anthony	.734
Bell, Josh	.717
Harper, Bryce	.712
Freeman, Freddie	.710
Soto, Juan	.709

Secondary Average
(minimum 502 PA)

Yelich, Christian	.566
Bellinger, Cody	.522
Soto, Juan	.487
Muncy, Max	.458
Donaldson, Josh	.452
Harper, Bryce	.449
Alonso, Pete	.446
Grandal, Yasmani	.444
Hoskins, Rhys	.435
Rendon, Anthony	.435

Isolated Power
(minimum 502 PA)

Yelich, Christian	.342
Bellinger, Cody	.324
Alonso, Pete	.323
Suarez, Eugenio	.301
Bell, Josh	.292
Pederson, Joc	.289
Schwarber, Kyle	.282
Rendon, Anthony	.279
Arenado, Nolan	.269
Soto, Juan	.266

Power / Speed Number
(minimum 502 PA)

Acuna Jr., Ronald	38.9
Yelich, Christian	35.7
Story, Trevor	27.8
Turner, Trea	24.6
Marte, Starling	24.0
Bellinger, Cody	22.7
Robles, Victor	21.2
Harper, Bryce	21.0
Albies, Ozzie	18.5
Soto, Juan	17.7

Speed Scores

Turner, Trea	7.79
Marte, Starling	7.46
Acuna Jr., Ronald	7.33
Eaton, Adam	7.31
Story, Trevor	7.29
Kingery, Scott	7.22
Margot, Manuel	7.21
Marte, Ketel	7.19
Albies, Ozzie	7.19
Baez, Javier	7.06

Cheap Wins

Arrieta, Jake	4
Hudson, Dakota	4
Senzatela, Antonio	4
8 tied with	3

Tough Losses

Gray, Sonny	7
Alcantara, Sandy	5
Bumgarner, Madison	5
Flaherty, Jack	5
Gallen, Zac	5
Mikolas, Miles	5
Scherzer, Max	5
Teheran, Julio	5
8 tied with	4

Additional Bill James Leaders

AL Batters Win Shares

Semien, Marcus	36
LeMahieu, DJ	33
Trout, Mike	33
Bregman, Alex	31
Torres, Gleyber	28
Polanco, Jorge	26
Betts, Mookie	25
Bogaerts, Xander	25
Chapman, Matt	25
Springer, George	25

NL Batters Win Shares

Yelich, Christian	33
Bellinger, Cody	31
Rendon, Anthony	31
Albies, Ozzie	29
Marte, Ketel	29
Acuna Jr., Ronald	28
Freeman, Freddie	28
Harper, Bryce	27
Donaldson, Josh	25
Rizzo, Anthony	25

AL Pitchers Win Shares

Verlander, Justin	23
Cole, Gerrit	22
Bieber, Shane	19
Lynn, Lance	18
Minor, Mike	18
Morton, Charlie	18
Hendriks, Liam	17
5 tied with	15

NL Pitchers Win Shares

deGrom, Jacob	21
Strasburg, Stephen	19
Ryu, Hyun-Jin	18
Flaherty, Jack	17
Gray, Sonny	17
Soroka, Mike	17
Castillo, Luis	16
Corbin, Patrick	16
Hader, Josh	16
Scherzer, Max	16

Career Batters Win Shares

Pujols, Albert	487
Cabrera, Miguel	402
Cano, Robinson	344
Suzuki, Ichiro	324
Votto, Joey	309
Trout, Mike	299
McCutchen, Andrew	277
Molina, Yadier	277
Braun, Ryan	276
Kinsler, Ian	250

Career Pitchers Win Shares

Sabathia, CC	242
Verlander, Justin	237
Greinke, Zack	224
Kershaw, Clayton	201
Hamels, Cole	189
Hernandez, Felix	188
Scherzer, Max	185
Lester, Jon	175
Wainwright, Adam	151
2 tied with	144

AL Component ERA
(minimum 162 IP)

Verlander, Justin	1.80
Cole, Gerrit	2.02
Morton, Charlie	2.67
Giolito, Lucas	2.75
Bieber, Shane	2.94
Lynn, Lance	3.41
Berrios, Jose	3.69
Fiers, Mike	3.76
Minor, Mike	3.78
Tanaka, Masahiro	3.89

NL Component ERA
(minimum 162 IP)

deGrom, Jacob	2.21
Flaherty, Jack	2.31
Ryu, Hyun-Jin	2.45
Gray, Sonny	2.57
Scherzer, Max	2.58
Strasburg, Stephen	2.62
Buehler, Walker	2.66
Kershaw, Clayton	2.86
Soroka, Mike	2.86
Castillo, Luis	2.94

Highest Avg Game Score
(minimum 30 GS)

Verlander, Justin	66.62
Cole, Gerrit	66.33
Bieber, Shane	59.70
Morton, Charlie	59.12
Lynn, Lance	56.73
Minor, Mike	55.97
Odorizzi, Jake	54.80
Berrios, Jose	54.22
Rodriguez, Eduardo	53.88
Boyd, Matthew	53.44

AL Lowest Avg Game Score
(minimum 30 GS)

Kikuchi, Yusei	44.53
Porcello, Rick	46.09
Nova, Ivan	46.24
Lopez, Reynaldo	46.79
Junis, Jakob	47.61
Happ, J.A.	48.70
Turnbull, Spencer	48.93
Bundy, Dylan	49.57
Anderson, Brett	49.77
Bailey, Homer	50.39

AL Lowest Offensive Win %

Garcia, Leury	.348
Sanchez, Yolmer	.362
Smith, Mallex	.368
Grichuk, Randal	.377
Bradley Jr., Jackie	.384
Andrus, Elvis	.401
Adames, Willy	.407
Davis, Khris	.432
Profar, Jurickson	.432
Alberto, Hanser	.433

Highest Avg Game Score
(minimum 30 GS)

deGrom, Jacob	63.66
Flaherty, Jack	61.42
Strasburg, Stephen	60.12
Gray, Sonny	59.19
Buehler, Walker	58.50
Castillo, Luis	58.28
Corbin, Patrick	58.12
Darvish, Yu	56.87
Nola, Aaron	55.06
Bumgarner, Madison	54.97

NL Lowest Avg Game Score
(minimum 30 GS)

Lester, Jon	47.94
Quintana, Jose	48.13
Wainwright, Adam	50.26
Davies, Zach	50.52
Musgrove, Joe	50.65
Kelly, Merrill	50.78
Matz, Steven	50.97
Fried, Max	51.17
Mikolas, Miles	51.31
Hudson, Dakota	51.72

NL Lowest Offensive Win %

Arcia, Orlando	.294
Cain, Lorenzo	.369
Castro, Starlin	.410
Crawford, Brandon	.426
Swanson, Dansby	.438
Iglesias, Jose	.443
McMahon, Ryan	.443
Jones, Adam	.448
Rojas, Miguel	.463
Ahmed, Nick	.464

Win Shares

Brian Reiff

Everybody loves a good surprise.

One example might be winning the lottery. You may claim that it wasn't a surprise, that you knew playing the birthday of your father's brother's nephew's cousin's former roommate was always going to win, but you'd be lying to yourself.

There are also things that are not at all surprising. One of those things is Mike Trout being good at baseball. He's led MLB in Win Shares four of the last six years, with fellow AL West player Jose Altuve surpassing him the other two times. Therefore, it's not at all surprising that, for a seventh consecutive season, the (as-of-yet unreal) Win Shares trophy is staying in the division. What may be surprising is its recipient.

Marcus Semien led the way in 2019 with 36 Win Shares, three more than any of his competitors (Trout, Christian Yelich and DJ LeMahieu all had 33). It was a career year for the shortstop, who accumulated more Win Shares this season than in his previous two combined and increased his career total (dating back to 2013) by 50%.

Eight other players had at least 29 Win Shares, the threshold set forth by this book's namesake to designate MVP candidates: Trout, LeMahieu and Alex Bregman from the AL, and Yelich, Cody Bellinger, Anthony Rendon, Ketel Marte and Ozzie Albies from the NL.

Putting in the effort

Phillies outfielder Bryce Harper led right fielders in catches made that required him to slide, dive or jump. His 30 were one better than Giants outfielder Kevin Pillar.

Pillar has the most over the last five seasons with 117, which helps validate his nickname, "Superman."

WIN SHARES BY YEAR

Player	<10	10	11	12	13	14	15	16	17	18	19	Career
Abreu, Jose						29	27	20	24	17	20	137
Acuna Jr., Ronald										19	28	47
Adames, Willy										8	15	23
Adams, Matt				1	12	15	3	9	11	8	6	65
Adrianza, Ehire					0	1	3	1	6	7	7	25
Aguilar, Jesus						0	1	0	9	19	7	36
Ahmed, Nick						1	8	3	4	15	17	48
Albers, Matt	6	5	3	6	5	1	6	0	10	0	4	46
Alberto, Hanser							1	1		0	12	14
Albies, Ozzie									8	18	29	55
Alcantara, Sandy									0	2	12	14
Alfaro, Jorge								0	5	12	10	27
Allen, Cody				1	8	14	12	14	11	7	0	67
Almora Jr., Albert								5	11	13	3	32
Alonso, Pete											24	24
Alonso, Yonder		0	4	17	12	6	8	12	17	12	1	89
Altuve, Jose			2	17	11	30	27	36	35	23	17	198
Alvarez, Yordan											14	14
Anderson, Brett	8	9	4	3	0	3	8	0	1	3	11	50
Anderson, Brian									2	27	13	42
Anderson, Chase						6	5	6	14	8	7	46
Anderson, Nick											8	8
Anderson, Tim								10	7	13	19	49
Andrus, Elvis	17	20	18	23	15	13	21	26	25	7	17	202
Aquino, Aristides										0	8	8
Archer, Chris				0	10	11	14	8	10	6	3	62
Arcia, Orlando								4	18	5	12	39
Arenado, Nolan					9	12	26	26	26	28	24	151
Arraez, Luis											14	14
Arrieta, Jake		5	5	0	3	12	27	16	11	8	6	93
Avila, Alex	3	7	27	15	6	14	6	2	13	3	6	102
Avilan, Luis				4	10	2	3	2	4	3	2	30
Bader, Harrison									2	13	9	24
Baez, Javier						2	1	14	15	24	19	75
Baez, Pedro						2	4	6	6	4	8	30
Bailey, Homer	7	5	5	12	11	8	0	0	1	0	10	59
Barnes, Matt						0	1	5	7	7	7	27
Barnhart, Tucker						1	4	12	14	9	9	49
Bassitt, Chris							2	4	0	3	9	18
Bauer, Trevor				0	0	5	8	11	12	18	11	65
Beaty, Matt											9	9
Beckham, Gordon	12	11	14	13	7	5	3	3	0	1	2	71
Beckham, Tim						0	5	5	20	6	9	45
Bell, Josh								3	16	15	24	58
Bellinger, Cody									23	19	31	73
Belt, Brandon			5	17	24	5	20	24	12	14	15	136
Benintendi, Andrew								4	19	24	15	62
Berrios, Jose								0	10	12	13	35
Betances, Dellin			0		0	14	14	12	9	9	0	58
Bettis, Chad					0	0	7	10	2	5	2	26
Bieber, Shane										7	19	26
Biggio, Cavan											14	14
Blackmon, Charlie			1	1	7	16	20	22	33	25	21	146
Blevins, Jerry	4	3	2	7	5	2	2	6	5	2	3	41
Bogaerts, Xander					1	7	22	19	16	27	25	117
Bote, David										6	9	15
Bour, Justin						3	12	11	17	14	1	58
Bourjos, Peter		3	16	5	4	7	2	5	3	0	0	45
Boxberger, Brad				2	1	8	8	1	3	6	1	30
Boyd, Matthew							0	5	4	8	10	27
Brach, Brad			0	3	1	5	9	12	11	4	2	47
Bradley, Archie							0	6	12	7	9	34
Bradley Jr., Jackie					1	5	10	19	14	16	10	75
Brantley, Michael	3	5	11	18	21	31	21	1	10	16	21	158
Braun, Ryan	81	25	37	28	9	17	20	20	9	15	15	276
Bregman, Alex								10	23	36	31	100
Britton, Zack			6	3	1	17	15	19	6	5	9	81
Bruce, Jay	16	18	22	18	21	10	10	18	21	10	5	167
Bryant, Kris							30	32	26	15	23	126
Buchholz, Clay	9	18	6	9	12	2	8	5	0	10	0	79
Buehler, Walker									0	10	13	23
Bumgarner, Madison	1	8	12	11	12	16	17	19	8	9	11	124

WIN SHARES BY YEAR

Player	<10	10	11	12	13	14	15	16	17	18	19	Career
Bummer, Aaron									1	1	10	12
Bundy, Dylan				0				7	11	3	6	27
Buxton, Byron							2	5	14	1	11	33
Cabrera, Asdrubal	37	9	25	19	12	15	11	21	17	20	16	202
Cabrera, Melky	44	8	19	25	7	19	16	20	16	6	6	186
Cabrera, Miguel	165	30	38	32	37	28	26	25	7	5	9	402
Cahill, Trevor	7	16	9	11	6	0	2	5	3	5	2	66
Cain, Lorenzo		6	0	7	12	19	27	13	24	25	11	144
Calhoun, Kole				0	8	20	21	19	17	8	14	107
Calhoun, Willie									1	1	8	10
Camargo, Johan									7	16	5	28
Canha, Mark							12	0	1	12	19	44
Cano, Robinson	80	34	30	34	35	34	21	28	23	18	7	344
Carpenter, Matt			0	9	35	27	30	21	20	28	11	181
Carrasco, Carlos	0	3	5		0	12	14	12	18	15	3	82
Cashner, Andrew		2	1	2	10	9	3	2	13	2	7	51
Castellanos, Nicholas					0	13	13	15	18	26	16	101
Castillo, Luis									6	6	16	28
Castillo, Welington		1	0	4	10	12	10	14	14	2	5	72
Castro, Jason			4	8	18	10	7	9	12	1	7	76
Castro, Starlin		12	25	23	7	20	13	15	13	18	11	157
Cervelli, Francisco	3	7	4	0	3	7	17	9	6	19	3	78
Chacin, Jhoulys	0	10	12	4	15	2	2	5	10	12	0	72
Chapman, Aroldis		2	4	21	12	13	13	15	9	12	10	111
Chapman, Matt									11	25	25	61
Chatwood, Tyler			3	3	11	1		11	8	2	6	45
Chavez, Jesse	4	0	0	0	3	7	6	3	3	12	5	43
Chavis, Michael											8	8
Chen, Wei-Yin				12	7	12	14	2	2	3	0	52
Chirinos, Robinson			1		0	11	4	6	10	13	11	56
Chirinos, Yonny										5	9	14
Choi, Ji-Man								0	1	6	14	21
Choo, Shin-Soo	44	27	8	25	31	9	25	5	17	15	18	224
Cishek, Steve		1	6	10	14	10	3	11	6	10	8	79
Claudio, Alex						1	1	5	12	5	4	28
Clevinger, Mike								2	11	17	14	44
Clippard, Tyler	7	9	13	11	10	10	9	7	3	7	6	92
Cobb, Alex				3	6	13	13	0	12	3	0	50
Cole, Gerrit					8	7	18	6	10	16	22	87
Colome, Alex					1	2	6	12	12	9	12	54
Conforto, Michael							8	6	20	21	20	75
Contreras, Willson								9	17	14	13	53
Cooper, Garrett									1	1	9	11
Corbin, Patrick				4	13		5	5	11	15	16	69
Correa, Carlos							18	26	26	12	13	95
Cozart, Zack			1	11	12	8	4	12	19	2	1	70
Crawford, Brandon			5	13	11	22	20	21	13	18	13	136
Crawford, J.P.									2	5	10	17
Cron, C.J.						8	9	14	10	12	12	65
Cruz, Nelson	30	19	16	17	16	22	26	21	24	22	22	235
Cueto, Johnny	13	12	12	21	5	22	12	19	6	4	0	126
Dahl, David									6	9	12	27
d'Arnaud, Travis					1	8	11	3	10	1	15	49
Darvish, Yu				14	18	10		8	12	1	9	72
Davies, Zach							2	8	13	1	11	35
Davis, Chris	15	1	4	19	33	12	27	17	8	2	1	140
Davis, J.D.									1	1	14	16
Davis, Khris					6	12	11	15	20	23	8	95
Davis, Rajai	23	14	6	11	6	14	6	13	3	2	1	99
Davis, Wade	2	8	6	7	2	15	19	11	12	12	0	94
deGrom, Jacob						11	15	11	11	20	21	89
DeJong, Paul									13	16	20	49
Descalso, Daniel		1	10	5	11	3	1	8	9	12	2	62
DeSclafani, Anthony						0	7	7		3	10	27
DeShields, Delino							16	2	10	6	10	44
Desmond, Ian	2	11	16	18	25	19	12	22	7	12	8	152
Devenski, Chris								11	10	3	3	27
Devers, Rafael									7	9	24	40
Diaz, Aledmys								18	4	12	7	41
Diaz, Edwin								8	10	18	3	39
Dickerson, Corey					4	15	8	9	18	16	10	80
Diekman, Jake				1	3	4	4	7	2	4	3	28
Dietrich, Derek					5	6	6	15	12	16	9	69

Player	<10	10	11	12	13	14	15	16	17	18	19	Career
Donaldson, Josh		0		8	32	27	32	28	25	7	25	184
Doolittle, Sean				5	8	11	2	4	11	12	9	62
Dozier, Brian				4	19	19	24	24	26	15	11	142
Dozier, Hunter								0		1	16	17
Drury, Brandon							0	9	12	0	4	25
Duda, Lucas		0	11	13	8	25	17	3	11	7	0	95
Duffy, Danny			1	2	3	12	7	15	10	6	7	63
Duffy, Matt					2	22	5			18	4	51
Duke, Zach	37	1	4	2	2	7	5	8	1	4	1	72
Dunn, Mike	0	2	5	0	7	6	3	4	5	0	0	32
Duvall, Adam						0	2	16	12	5	4	39
Dyson, Jarrod		2	2	8	7	9	6	12	8	4	10	68
Dyson, Sam				0	0	4	9	14	5	8	7	47
Eaton, Adam			2	5	20	24	24	5	12	16		108
Edman, Tommy											12	12
Eflin, Zach								0	0	6	9	15
Encarnacion, Edwin	54	8	11	31	22	19	24	19	18	14	18	238
Eovaldi, Nathan			2	3	5	4	9	6	5		1	35
Escobar, Eduardo			0	2	2	13	14	7	14	20	22	94
Estrada, Marco	0	0	4	8	7	5	12	12	7	3	0	58
Familia, Jeurys				0	0	9	15	16	2	9	1	52
Fiers, Mike			0	8	0	7	9	7	3	12	12	58
Flaherty, Jack									0	9	17	26
Flaherty, Ryan				2	7	9	4	4	1	2	0	29
Fletcher, David										8	18	26
Flores, Wilmer					2	7	16	9	8	11	8	61
Flowers, Tyler	0	0	3	3	3	10	7	10	12	7	6	61
Foltynewicz, Mike						0	0	6	5	14	5	30
Forsythe, Logan			3	8	3	4	16	16	10	9	7	76
Fowler, Dexter	15	13	16	15	13	16	22	22	16	3	17	168
Franco, Maikel						1	13	17	6	13	7	57
Frazier, Adam								5	13	12	15	45
Frazier, Clint									3	0	9	12
Frazier, Todd			3	13	15	20	13	15	13	12	18	122
Freeland, Kyle									11	21	0	32
Freeman, Freddie		0	19	18	35	28	22	28	22	26	28	226
Freese, David	1	8	13	19	9	12	15	14	15	10	7	123
Fried, Max									1	2	12	15
Gallegos, Giovanny									0	1	9	10
Gallo, Joey							2	0	16	13	11	42
Galvis, Freddy				3	4	2	15	16	18	14	12	84
Gamel, Ben								1	13	9	7	30
Gant, John								1	0	6	8	15
Garcia, Avisail				1	5	4	10	11	22	6	13	72
Garcia, Greg						0	2	7	6	3	11	29
Garcia, Leury					2	1	1	1	8	9	8	30
Gardner, Brett	12	17	16	2	22	19	19	17	19	13	17	173
Garver, Mitch									1	11	18	30
Gausman, Kevin					1	6	5	12	9	9	1	43
Gearrin, Cory			0	2	2		0	4	9	5	3	25
Gennett, Scooter					9	14	7	11	17	20	2	80
German, Domingo									1	1	9	11
Gibson, Kyle					0	8	12	4	7	13	7	51
Giles, Ken						7	11	6	12	5	11	52
Giolito, Lucas								0	4	1	15	20
Givens, Mychal							4	7	10	5	5	31
Glasnow, Tyler								1	1	4	8	14
Goins, Ryan					2	2	12	3	12	1	3	35
Goldschmidt, Paul			6	17	36	20	35	25	29	25	21	214
Gomes, Yan					2	14	18	5	4	12	9	72
Gomez, Carlos	21	4	7	12	21	27	14	11	11	6	2	136
Gonzales, Marco						2	0		1	10	11	24
Gonzalez, Carlos	15	25	20	15	15	5	18	18	8	14	1	154
Gonzalez, Gio	2	15	15	17	11	8	9	6	17	8	4	114
Gonzalez, Marwin				2	2	6	8	7	26	13	12	76
Goodwin, Brian								1	6	6	10	23
Gordon, Alex	29	3	24	20	21	26	16	9	6	11	13	178
Gordon, Dee			6	3	2	22	26	7	18	11	10	105
Grandal, Yasmani				11	4	12	15	19	12	17	24	114
Granderson, Curtis	91	16	26	21	4	17	29	13	13	11	3	244
Gray, Jon							1	9	10	7	12	39
Gray, Sonny					5	13	16	0	10	6	17	67
Greene, Shane						4	0	3	9	5	11	32

Player	<10	10	11	12	13	14	15	16	17	18	19	Career
Gregerson, Luke	5	9	4	9	7	8	11	10	3	0	0	66
Gregorius, Didi				0	10	9	17	16	18	21	11	102
Greinke, Zack	63	11	10	16	17	15	26	10	18	17	21	224
Grichuk, Randal						1	12	13	7	13	8	54
Grossman, Robbie					7	10	0	10	10	13	11	61
Guerra, Junior							0	10	1	5	9	25
Guerrero Jr., Vlad											11	11
Gurriel, Yuli								2	18	19	20	59
Gurriel Jr., Lourdes										8	9	17
Gyorko, Jedd					12	11	11	12	15	13	1	75
Hader, Josh									6	14	16	36
Hamels, Cole	51	16	17	18	13	15	12	16	10	12	9	189
Hamilton, Billy					2	15	5	9	10	8	3	52
Hand, Brad			1	0	1	3	1	8	14	12	11	51
Haniger, Mitch								3	12	28	7	50
Happ, Ian									12	12	7	31
Happ, J.A.	17	6	1	5	3	7	10	18	10	14	6	97
Harper, Bryce					21	19	38	20	22	23	27	179
Harris, Will				0	5	1	9	11	5	5	10	46
Harrison, Josh			5	4	3	25	12	15	15	9	1	89
Harvey, Matt					5	14		14	2	0	5	40
Healy, Ryon								11	12	9	4	36
Hechavarria, Adeiny				3	5	13	13	9	9	5	8	65
Hellickson, Jeremy		3	15	11	4	1	5	12	5	5	0	61
Hendricks, Kyle						7	8	17	11	13	12	68
Hendriks, Liam				0	0	0	5	3	5	1	17	31
Hernandez, Cesar					3	1	12	24	18	22	16	96
Hernandez, David	3	6	10	9	3		1	5	7	7	0	51
Hernandez, Felix	69	23	16	15	16	22	14	8	4	1	0	188
Hernandez, Kike						5	9	2	9	13	12	50
Hernandez, Teoscar								2	3	11	12	28
Herrera, Kelvin			0	10	5	10	8	13	7	7	1	61
Herrera, Odubel						16	25	10	14	2		67
Heyward, Jason		23	11	22	14	23	21	12	14	16	13	169
Hicks, Aaron					4	4	11	4	11	22	7	63
Hill, Rich	19	1	1	3	0	1	4	12	11	7	5	64
Hiura, Keston											12	12
Holland, Derek	2	3	14	8	13	4	2	4	0	10	0	60
Holland, Greg		0	9	11	18	15	7		12	5	4	81
Holt, Brock				3	1	12	14	6	2	11	8	57
Hoskins, Rhys									10	22	18	50
Hosmer, Eric			13	10	18	14	22	17	30	16	17	157
Hudson, Dakota										3	12	15
Hudson, Daniel	1	9	16	0		0	4	4	3	2	11	50
Hughes, Jared			0	6	1	6	7	4	7	11	5	47
Hundley, Nick	13	10	12	2	10	6	7	6	5	6	1	78
Hunter, Tommy	8	10	3	4	10	8	4	3	8	6	1	65
Iannetta, Chris	33	3	16	8	10	17	8	5	10	5	2	117
Iglesias, Jose			0	1	13		12	13	11	15	12	77
Iglesias, Raisel							4	7	14	11	9	45
Inciarte, Ender						10	15	14	22	17	7	85
Jackson, Luke							0	0	2	2	10	14
Jansen, Danny										3	9	12
Jansen, Kenley		6	6	15	16	11	12	17	19	10	10	122
Jay, Jon		8	13	15	17	16	3	12	12	11	4	111
Jeffress, Jeremy	1	1	0	1	3	7	10	4	16	2		45
Jennings, Dan				2	2	3	6	5	5	0		26
Jimenez, Eloy											12	12
Jones, Adam	23	15	16	26	23	25	15	18	18	11	9	199
Jones, Nate				9	4	0	2	10	1		3	30
Joseph, Caleb						7	12	2	8	4	1	34
Joyce, Matt	7	10	19	13	11	10	1	11	14	3	8	107
Judge, Aaron								0	29	19	16	64
Kang, Jung Ho							17	11		0	1	29
Kela, Keone							8	2	6	8	4	28
Keller, Brad										12	9	21
Kelley, Shawn	3	2	2	2	4	3	4	8	0	4	5	37
Kelly, Carson								0	1	0	11	12
Kelly, Joe				5	9	5	6	2	7	5	3	42
Kelly, Merrill											8	8
Kemp, Matt	58	15	37	21	6	20	18	16	6	17	0	214
Kendrick, Howie	45	19	18	16	13	27	18	11	10	2	12	191
Kennedy, Ian	2	11	20	11	2	9	4	14	3	4	10	90

Player	<10	10	11	12	13	14	15	16	17	18	19	Career
Kepler, Max							0	8	12	13	19	52
Kershaw, Clayton	17	15	23	19	22	22	21	16	19	12	15	201
Keuchel, Dallas				0	3	16	22	6	13	11	7	78
Kiermaier, Kevin					0	9	19	13	13	7	11	72
Kimbrel, Craig		4	17	18	17	16	11	9	19	14	0	125
Kingery, Scott										8	12	20
Kinsler, Ian	77	13	22	15	20	24	21	29	12	13	4	250
Kintzler, Brandon		0	1	2	8	4	0	7	11	4	7	44
Kipnis, Jason			6	24	27	10	22	19	9	17	13	147
Kluber, Corey			0	1	9	21	14	20	23	20	1	109
La Stella, Tommy						9	3	4	5	2	8	31
Lagares, Juan					7	15	13	2	2	3	2	44
Lamb, Jake						1	9	16	17	4	4	51
Laureano, Ramon										9	17	26
Leake, Mike		7	9	8	12	10	10	5	8	8	8	85
LeBlanc, Wade	2	6	2	4	0	2		4	4	10	3	37
Leclerc, Jose								1	4	12	8	25
LeMahieu, DJ			0	6	8	9	14	22	20	19	33	131
Leon, Sandy				0	0	1	3	12	9	6	3	34
Lester, Jon	44	17	14	8	12	18	13	18	9	14	8	175
Lindor, Francisco							14	21	27	30	19	111
Liriano, Francisco	22	14	4	4	12	7	12	6	2	4		93
Longoria, Evan	43	28	25	14	24	21	18	20	18	7	14	232
Lorenzen, Michael							2	4	6	7	12	31
Lowe, Brandon										6	14	20
Lowrie, Jed	8	8	5	11	23	11	6	8	22	29	0	131
Lucchesi, Joey										6	8	14
Lucroy, Jonathan		4	15	15	19	26	10	22	11	10	5	137
Lugo, Seth								6	3	8	12	29
Luplow, Jordan									1	1	9	11
Lyles, Jordan			0	1	2	6	1	2	1	4	8	25
Lynn, Lance			2	11	7	16	12		11	6	18	83
Machado, Manny				7	20	12	27	28	19	28	18	159
Maeda, Kenta								11	7	5	10	33
Maldonado, Martin			0	7	3	4	5	7	11	11	6	54
Manaea, Sean								7	8	9	4	28
Mancini, Trey								1	19	6	17	43
Margot, Manuel								1	13	10	9	33
Marisnick, Jake					2	5	9	3	6	5	7	37
Markakis, Nick	71	22	19	16	11	20	20	17	14	22	11	243
Marquez, German								1	11	16	13	41
Marte, Ketel							9	7	6	16	29	67
Marte, Starling				5	20	17	20	17	10	21	21	131
Martin, Leonys			0	1	14	14	5	13	1	9	3	60
Martin, Russell	72	9	14	12	16	22	17	15	7	8	7	199
Martinez, Carlos					1	4	14	16	12	10	9	66
Martinez, J.D.			6	7	3	19	25	17	20	33	22	152
Martinez, Jose								1	10	20	8	39
Matz, Steven							4	9	0	4	8	25
Maybin, Cameron	5	8	17	13	0	5	16	14	10	9	8	105
Mazara, Nomar								16	16	10	10	52
McCann, Brian	81	19	23	12	16	19	21	12	7	5	7	222
McCann, James						0	10	9	10	6	11	51
McCutchen, Andrew	18	22	28	40	34	33	35	17	22	20	8	277
McGee, Jake		0	2	8	5	15	7	4	7	0	2	50
McHugh, Collin				0	0	13	13	8	4	9	4	51
McMahon, Ryan									0	4	11	15
McNeil, Jeff										11	24	35
Meadows, Austin										5	23	28
Means, John										0	10	10
Melancon, Mark	1	2	10	0	15	15	17	16	3	3	8	90
Mercado, Oscar											14	14
Mercer, Jordy				2	13	10	8	13	12	9	5	72
Merrifield, Whit								8	21	22	21	72
Mikolas, Miles				2	0	0				17	8	27
Miley, Wade			2	14	10	7	9	3	4	7	11	67
Miller, Andrew	4	0	2	4	2	9	13	19	11	3	4	71
Miller, Brad					10	11	15	15	6	5	6	68
Miller, Shelby				2	10	10	11	1	1	0	0	35
Milone, Tommy			2	10	6	5	8	1	0	0	4	36
Minor, Mike			0	3	7	13	3		11	11	18	66
Molina, Yadier	75	17	18	29	29	19	16	21	19	18	16	277
Moncada, Yoan								0	6	13	23	42

Player	<10	10	11	12	13	14	15	16	17	18	19	Career
Mondesi, Adalberto								2	1	8	12	23
Montas, Frankie								0	0	3	8	11
Montgomery, Mike							2	7	10	6	3	28
Moore, Matt			1	8	13	1	1	10	1	0	1	36
Morales, Kendrys	27	8		14	17	2	21	15	10	9	1	124
Moran, Colin								0	1	13	14	28
Moreland, Mitch		6	8	9	10	3	16	10	12	12	8	94
Morrison, Logan		9	11	4	7	11	9	9	16	3	0	79
Morton, Charlie	4	0	8	0	6	4	2	1	10	13	18	66
Moustakas, Mike			4	14	5	9	21	1	15	19	19	107
Muncy, Max							1	2		21	22	46
Murphy, Daniel	16		14	20	22	21	19	31	27	10	9	189
Murphy, Tom							2	2	0	1	10	15
Myers, Wil					14	6	9	19	19	10	10	87
Naquin, Tyler								13	0	5	8	26
Narvaez, Omar								3	7	10	14	34
Nelson, Jimmy					1	0	8	4	13		0	26
Neris, Hector						0	2	11	11	3	13	40
Neshek, Pat	15	0	1	3	2	13	4	5	11	4	1	59
Newman, Kevin										1	16	17
Nicasio, Juan			4	2	4	3	3	5	10	0	2	33
Nimmo, Brandon								2	6	22	8	38
Nola, Aaron							4	3	12	22	14	55
Nova, Ivan		2	11	5	13	0	2	8	8	6	9	64
Nunez, Eduardo		2	8	4	6	3	6	15	18	7	1	70
Nunez, Renato								0	1	5	11	17
Oberg, Scott							3	1	3	9	10	26
O'Day, Darren	11	9	0	10	8	10	12	3	6	1	1	71
Odor, Rougned						11	16	18	8	13	13	79
Odorizzi, Jake				0	1	7	11	11	7	7	12	56
Oh, Seunghwan								16	5	9	0	30
Ohtani, Shohei										20	12	32
Olson, Matt								0	9	19	21	49
Osuna, Roberto							11	15	13	8	14	61
Otero, Dan					0	5	9	0	1	2	1	32
Ottavino, Adam			0	5	7	6	4	5	3	14	8	52
Owings, Chris					2	8	6	11	9	3	2	41
Ozuna, Marcell					8	19	10	15	29	19	14	114
Paddack, Chris											10	10
Pagan, Emilio									4	3	15	22
Panik, Joe						10	17	13	15	6	11	72
Parker, Blake				0	4	0		1	10	7	5	27
Parra, Gerardo	9	6	19	9	15	6	14	2	9	12	7	108
Paxton, James					3	5	3	5	11	11	9	47
Peacock, Brad		2		2	2	0	1	12	5	6		30
Pearce, Steve	6	1	0	6	4	19	5	9	7	12	0	69
Pederson, Joc						0	15	19	7	11	17	69
Pedroia, Dustin	70	12	27	17	25	17	12	21	15	0	0	216
Pence, Hunter	54	21	24	18	25	26	7	15	13	3	12	218
Peralta, David						7	20	2	16	23	13	81
Peralta, Wily				3	5	12	3	4	0	4	1	32
Peraza, Jose							0	7	5	14	5	31
Perez, Hernan				0	1	0	4	11	9	7	2	34
Perez, Martin				1	8	2	3	9	9	1	6	39
Perez, Oliver	42	0		3	4	5	2	2	2	5	4	69
Perez, Roberto						2	7	5	8	2	18	42
Peterson, Jace						1	14	9	3	4	2	33
Petit, Yusmeiro	7			0	2	4	3	2	10	8	10	46
Pham, Tommy						0	7	4	21	17	17	66
Phegley, Josh					2	0	8	1	2	2	10	25
Phelps, David					7	3	4	3	12	4	3	36
Pillar, Kevin					1	1	15	15	9	11	16	68
Pina, Manny				0	0			2	12	8	5	27
Pinder, Chad								1	7	8	8	24
Pineda, Michael			10			8	7	6	5		9	45
Piscotty, Stephen							11	22	7	21	7	68
Plesac, Zach											9	9
Polanco, Gregory						8	17	14	6	18	2	65
Polanco, Jorge						1	1	8	14	11	26	61
Pollock, A.J.				2	14	10	27	1	15	13	10	92
Pomeranz, Drew			1	4	0	5	5	12	15	0	4	46
Porcello, Rick	13	5	8	7	9	13	5	19	8	12	6	105
Posey, Buster	0	20	9	38	24	30	29	24	22	15	12	223

	WIN SHARES BY YEAR											
Player	<10	10	11	12	13	14	15	16	17	18	19	Career
Prado, Martin	24	22	12	23	15	15	17	22	1	3	1	155
Pressly, Ryan					4	2	3	6	3	8	9	35
Price, David	7	17	13	19	12	16	19	14	7	14	6	144
Profar, Jurickson				0	5			6	1	16	10	38
Puig, Yasiel					17	27	9	10	17	11	16	107
Pujols, Albert	315	32	26	25	10	19	18	17	7	8	10	487
Quintana, Jose				9	13	12	15	15	10	9	6	89
Ramirez, Erasmo				2	2	0	10	6	6	0	0	26
Ramirez, Hanley	118	22	10	17	23	18	7	17	5	5	0	242
Ramirez, Harold											9	9
Ramirez, Jose					1	7	4	22	28	29	17	108
Ramos, Wilson		3	13	3	8	10	11	24	6	19	15	112
Ray, Robbie						0	6	7	17	7	8	45
Realmuto, J.T.						1	10	19	19	25	22	96
Reddick, Josh	0	1	7	16	13	13	17	12	21	10	12	122
Rendon, Anthony					12	26	9	22	29	22	31	151
Renfroe, Hunter								2	9	12	11	34
Rengifo, Luis											8	8
Reyes, Franmil										8	13	21
Reynolds, Bryan											19	19
Reynolds, Mark	51	16	16	12	11	7	7	9	14	5	1	149
Richards, Garrett			0	1	6	13	14	2	2	4	0	42
Richards, Trevor										3	8	11
Rivera, Rene	4		2		2	14	5	6	7	3	1	44
Rizzo, Anthony			0	12	14	28	32	29	25	22	25	187
Roark, Tanner					7	15	4	17	7	8	8	66
Robertson, David	5	4	11	7	12	12	13	10	13	9	0	96
Robles, Hansel							3	6	3	3	15	30
Robles, Victor									1	2	15	18
Rodney, Fernando	32	6	1	19	11	10	4	7	10	7	3	110
Rodon, Carlos							9	8	3	6	1	27
Rodriguez, Eduardo							8	4	8	10	15	45
Rodriguez, Sean	3	9	10	8	4	6	2	13	2	2	3	62
Rogers, Taylor								4	7	8	13	32
Rojas, Miguel						1	4	3	8	13	12	41
Romo, Sergio	8	8	9	11	9	8	5	4	4	7	11	84
Rondon, Hector					2	11	16	7	4	7	5	52
Rosario, Amed									2	14	19	35
Rosario, Eddie							12	5	14	16	17	64
Rosenthal, Trevor					2	7	11	14	1	7	0	42
Ross, Tyson		0	3	0	5	13	12	0	0	8	0	41
Ruiz, Rio								1	2	0	8	11
Rusin, Chris				0	3	0	4	6	11	1	0	25
Russell, Addison							3	18	17	10	5	53
Ryu, Hyun-Jin					13	9		0	7	7	18	54
Sabathia, CC	141	20	19	14	8	0	5	11	11	10	3	242
Salazar, Danny						4	4	14	10	5	0	37
Sale, Chris		5	11	19	15	17	15	17	20	18	7	144
Samardzija, Jeff	3	0	7	8	7	11	6	11	8	0	11	72
Sanchez, Aaron						6	6	17	1	4	2	36
Sanchez, Anibal	16	11	10	10	17	8	5	1	1	10	11	100
Sanchez, Gary							0	11	16	8	15	50
Sanchez, Yolmer						1	7	3	14	15	15	55
Sandoval, Pablo	33	9	23	18	22	21	6	0	2	6	8	148
Sano, Miguel							16	11	14	4	17	62
Santana, Carlos		7	22	21	26	22	13	19	17	19	24	190
Santana, Danny						18	3	1	3	0	15	40
Santana, Domingo						0	6	7	21	4	11	49
Santana, Ervin	46	14	14	2	14	9	7	11	17	0	0	134
Santander, Anthony									0	1	9	10
Santiago, Hector			1	7	8	5	11	7	2	5	0	46
Schebler, Scott							1	7	9	8	1	26
Scherzer, Max	13	13	10	14	20	18	18	20	21	22	16	185
Schoop, Jonathan					0	6	9	18	26	8	9	76
Schwarber, Kyle							10	0	10	15	18	53
Seager, Corey							6	29	31	4	20	90
Seager, Kyle			3	24	23	28	17	30	20	14	11	170
Segura, Jean				4	21	13	12	23	16	24	15	128
Semien, Marcus					2	7	10	21	11	21	36	108
Senzel, Nick											8	8
Severino, Luis							5	1	16	16	1	39
Shaw, Bryan			3	4	7	8	7	7	7	0	5	48
Shaw, Travis							7	12	22	21	3	65

	WIN SHARES BY YEAR											
Player	<10	10	11	12	13	14	15	16	17	18	19	Career
Shoemaker, Matt					1	11	5	9	4	1	3	34
Simmons, Andrelton				8	19	13	14	14	24	22	6	120
Smith, Caleb									0	3	8	11
Smith, Joe	11	3	8	6	9	14	8	4	6	4	3	76
Smith, Mallex								6	6	18	8	38
Smith, Will					2	3	4	7	3	10	14	43
Smith, Will											10	10
Smith Jr., Dwight									1	2	8	11
Smoak, Justin		7	10	9	12	4	10	4	23	21	10	110
Smyly, Drew					6	10	10	5	4		3	38
Snell, Blake								5	6	22	6	39
Sogard, Eric			0	1	1	10	7	8	8	1	15	51
Solano, Donovan				8	9	10	1	1			10	39
Solarte, Yangervis						16	18	16	16	6	1	73
Soler, Jorge						4	10	7	0	6	18	45
Soria, Joakim	42	15	7		2	6	10	5	6	8	5	106
Soroka, Mike										1	17	18
Soto, Juan										15	24	39
Spangenberg, Cory						2	10	1	16	6	2	37
Springer, George						10	13	23	24	19	25	114
Stammen, Craig	3	3	2	9	7	4	1		7	10	9	55
Stanton, Giancarlo		13	19	19	15	31	14	12	29	18	3	173
Story, Trevor								13	13	26	22	74
Straily, Dan				2	7	1	0	9	7	4	0	30
Strasburg, Stephen		5	2	14	11	13	8	11	17	7	19	107
Strickland, Hunter						2	5	7	7	4	1	26
Stroman, Marcus						9	3	10	16	2	14	54
Strop, Pedro	0	0	3	10	5	6	8	5	7	12	4	60
Suarez, Eugenio						9	10	16	16	21	21	93
Suzuki, Ichiro	238	23	15	11	10	8	4	10	5	0	0	324
Suzuki, Kurt	41	10	8	10	6	14	8	7	12	10	11	137
Swanson, Dansby								4	10	15	15	44
Swarzak, Anthony		0	4	2	8	3	0	1	11	0	3	32
Syndergaard, Noah							9	18	2	11	9	49
Taillon, Jameson								6	6	14	1	27
Tanaka, Masahiro						12	10	18	8	11	7	66
Tatis Jr., Fernando											18	18
Tauchman, Mike									0	0	12	12
Taylor, Chris						5	1	1	23	17	13	60
Taylor, Michael A.						1	14	4	14	5	0	38
Teheran, Julio			0	0	12	15	8	13	7	9	11	75
Tejada, Ruben			3	11	14	4	15	11	0	1	0	59
Thames, Eric			7	3					15	9	13	47
Tomlin, Josh		4	9	0	0	2	6	10	6	0	6	43
Torres, Carlos		0	0	3	4	7	2	8	4	0	0	28
Torres, Gleyber										19	28	47
Treinen, Blake						4	3	8	7	19	4	45
Trout, Mike			3	38	40	40	42	35	29	39	33	299
Trumbo, Mark		0	14	19	14	8	10	22	5	6	0	98
Tulowitzki, Troy	58	25	25	5	21	16	14	18	4	0		186
Turner, Justin	0	0	15	4	3	18	18	25	24	19	20	146
Turner, Trea							0	17	17	25	19	78
Upton, Justin	28	14	26	16	21	21	21	14	22	17	4	204
Urias, Julio								5	0	0	9	14
Urshela, Giovanny								3	1	0	21	25
Vargas, Jason	8	10	8	11	7	10	3	1	12	0	6	76
Vazquez, Christian						4		3	11	4	15	37
Vazquez, Felipe							5	4	17	12	13	51
Verdugo, Alex									0	1	11	12
Verlander, Justin	60	17	27	23	14	8	8	20	17	20	23	237
Villar, Jonathan					3	5	4	24	8	15	19	78
Vincent, Nick				3	6	4	1	5	6	4	2	31
Vizcaino, Arodys			1			0	6	2	10	7	1	27
Vogelbach, Daniel								0	0	2	12	14
Vogt, Stephen					0	4	8	18	9	6	11	56
Voit, Luke									2	10	17	29
Volquez, Edinson	20	3	0	6	0	11	13	5	3		0	61
Votto, Joey	46	33	33	27	30	8	33	33	33	22	11	309
Wacha, Michael					4	7	14	2	8	6	4	45
Wainwright, Adam	54	20		9	16	23	3	10	6	1	9	151
Walker, Christian							0	0	0	0	16	16
Walker, Neil	0	16	20	21	20	21	22	19	16	9	7	171
Walker, Taijuan					1	3	6	5	11	1	0	27

	WIN SHARES BY YEAR											
Player	<10	10	11	12	13	14	15	16	17	18	19	Career
Warren, Adam				0	6	8	9	3	7	5	1	39
Watson, Tony			3	5	8	11	12	9	7	9	3	67
Wendle, Joey								2	1	19	5	27
Wheeler, Zack					5	8			1	11	12	37
Wieters, Matt	9	12	23	23	19	5	7	16	7	7	5	133
Wilson, Alex					1	3	8	7	4	5	0	28
Wilson, Justin				0	8	2	7	5	10	4	6	42
Winker, Jesse									3	12	8	23
Wittgren, Nick								5	2	2	8	17
Wolters, Tony								5	5	3	10	23
Wong, Kolten					1	10	18	9	14	12	24	88
Wood, Alex					4	13	8	2	15	6	0	48
Woodruff, Brandon									2	3	11	16
Workman, Brandon					2	0			3	5	15	25
Yarbrough, Ryan										9	9	18
Yastrzemski, Mike											14	14
Yates, Kirby						2	0	1	4	12	14	33
Yelich, Christian					8	22	15	21	23	34	33	156
Zimmerman, Ryan	76	23	15	22	23	8	10	3	18	7	3	208
Zimmermann, Jordan	3	1	11	15	15	16	11	4	3	5	0	84
Zobrist, Ben	38	21	28	27	26	18	17	19	9	19	3	225
Zunino, Mike					2	11	5	8	14	7	5	52

Instant Replay

Alex Vigderman

It seems like instant replay is now integrated enough that nobody's bothering to argue about it much anymore. Which is great, because we need more time to argue about robot umpires and whether to ban the shift.

Instant replay might not be getting as much air time as it did because there are simply fewer reviews. This season there were 1,348 reviews made, compared to 1,375 in 2018. The good news is that umpires are overturning fewer calls: the overturn rate dropped from 48 to 45 percent.

There are a few more categories of replay than we had last year, so the type of reviews can be discussed in more detail.

Will the extension of netting down the lines make fan interference, and its reviews, an endangered species? There were 27 such reviews in 2019, with five being overturned. It's hard to imagine seeing that total next season.

How valuable is it to make violations of the home plate collision rule reviewable? There were 27 reviews with that pretense in 2019, with only one being overturned—and that one didn't even involve a catcher.

The most eagle-eyed team in terms of calling for reviews in 2019 was the Rangers, who led MLB in net overturned calls. They issued the fourth-most challenges (tied with the Blue Jays and Marlins) and got calls overturned at the third-highest rate. Perhaps they intimidated their opponents into poor decisions themselves, because the overturn rate against them was the seventh-lowest in the league.

In terms of judiciousness, the Yankees reigned supreme, challenging the fewest plays of anyone, but posting an overturn rate just shy of 70%. They barely missed having their third straight season above the 70% mark, which shows incredible consistency.

2019 Instant Replay Summary

Replay Type	Total Replays	Overturned	Percent
Tag Play	521	210	40.3
Force Play	492	296	60.2
Hit By Pitch	86	37	43.0
Fair or Foul	66	10	15.2
Boundary Call (Home Run)	55	18	32.7
Fan Interference	27	5	18.5
Home Plate Collision	27	1	3.7
Trap or Catch	21	7	33.3
Slide Interference	15	2	13.3
Rules Check	10	1	10.0
Stadium Boundary	8	6	75.0
Runner Placement	7	3	42.9
Timing Play	4	2	50.0
Missed Base	4	0	0.0
Record Keeping	3	1	33.3
Passed Runner	1	1	100.0
Tag-Up Play	1	0	0.0

2019 Challenges

Team	Challenges	Overturned	Pct	Opponent Challenges	Overturned	Pct	Net
Texas Rangers	49	31	63.3	30	12	40.0	19
Philadelphia Phillies	55	27	49.1	38	14	36.8	13
Los Angeles Dodgers	37	19	51.4	34	9	26.5	10
Toronto Blue Jays	49	21	42.9	36	14	38.9	7
Boston Red Sox	38	23	60.5	46	17	37.0	6
Cincinnati Reds	46	20	43.5	34	15	44.1	5
Kansas City Royals	32	23	71.9	31	19	61.3	4
Miami Marlins	49	23	46.9	38	20	52.6	3
Tampa Bay Rays	56	22	39.3	41	20	48.8	2
Houston Astros	41	20	48.8	38	19	50.0	1
Chicago Cubs	37	16	43.2	43	16	37.2	0
Minnesota Twins	47	16	34.0	30	16	53.3	0
Washington Nationals	35	16	45.7	39	16	41.0	0
New York Yankees	23	16	69.6	37	17	45.9	-1
Arizona Diamondbacks	39	21	53.8	46	22	47.8	-1
Detroit Tigers	39	16	41.0	32	18	56.3	-2
Cleveland Indians	30	16	53.3	43	18	41.9	-2
Milwaukee Brewers	31	17	54.8	41	19	46.3	-2
St Louis Cardinals	41	16	39.0	40	18	45.0	-2
New York Mets	39	15	38.5	36	18	50.0	-3
Atlanta Braves	37	17	45.9	53	20	37.7	-3
Baltimore Orioles	34	12	35.3	35	15	42.9	-3
Los Angeles Angels	33	17	51.5	40	21	52.5	-4
Seattle Mariners	37	16	43.2	36	20	55.6	-4
San Diego Padres	55	22	40.0	41	27	65.9	-5
Chicago White Sox	29	13	44.8	37	18	48.6	-5
Pittsburgh Pirates	44	17	38.6	50	23	46.0	-6
Colorado Rockies	39	19	48.7	47	27	57.4	-8
Oakland Athletics	33	13	39.4	45	22	48.9	-9
San Francisco Giants	28	15	53.6	45	25	55.6	-10

Introduction to the 2020 Projections for Hitters

Bill James

Every year in this space, we make a list of all of the hitters in the major leagues and project, God-like, what each hitter's stats are going to be the next year. Then a year later, in this space, I have to look over the results and confess in a servile manner to all of the terrible mistakes that we made the previous year. It's a plum assignment.

In last year's book we projected the 2019 batting stats for 413 players who did play in the majors in 2019. Of those 413 players, 89 did clearly better than we had projected that they would do, 141 did clearly worse, and 183 did more or less what we said they would do—understanding, of course, that were you to study the projections and put players into one of those three classes, your count would no doubt be different than mine. But we'll start with the good ones.

Among the 413 projections printed here last year, two of the most accurate were for Ryan Braun and Jake Marisnick:

Ryan Braun

Act/Proj	G	AB	R	H	D	T	HR	RBI	BB	SO	SB	Avg	Slg
Actual	144	459	70	131	31	2	22	75	34	105	11	.285	.505
Projected	133	475	70	131	29	3	23	74	43	102	12	.276	.495

Jake Marisnick

Act/Proj	G	AB	R	H	D	T	HR	RBI	BB	SO	SB	Avg	Slg
Actual	120	292	46	68	16	3	10	34	17	95	10	.233	.411
Projected	115	278	41	61	13	2	10	31	18	95	8	.219	.388

Many of the highest-scoring projections are for players who had limited playing time, because it is not that hard to guess right when a player has fewer at bats. As he gets more playing time, it is harder to stay on target—just like firing a arrow at a target. The further the arrow travels, the less likely it is to stay exactly on target. But some other players for whom we had good projections include Kris Bryant, Delino DeShields, Todd Frazier, Colin Moran, Nolan Arenado, JD Martinez, Robinson Chirinos and Juan Soto:

Kris Bryant

Act/Proj	G	AB	R	H	D	T	HR	RBI	BB	SO	SB	Avg	Slg
Actual	147	543	108	153	35	1	31	77	74	145	4	.282	.521
Projected	150	573	102	158	36	3	30	89	81	160	5	.276	.506

Delino DeShields

Act/Proj	G	AB	R	H	D	T	HR	RBI	BB	SO	SB	Avg	Slg
Actual	118	357	42	89	15	4	4	32	38	100	24	.249	.347
Projected	115	351	59	83	15	2	3	26	45	96	20	.236	.316

Todd Frazier

Act/Proj	G	AB	R	H	D	T	HR	RBI	BB	SO	SB	Avg	Slg
Actual	133	447	63	112	19	2	21	67	40	106	1	.251	.443
Projected	132	439	59	100	20	1	21	62	51	117	7	.228	.421

Colin Moran

Act/Proj	G	AB	R	H	D	T	HR	RBI	BB	SO	SB	Avg	Slg
Actual	149	466	46	129	30	1	13	80	30	117	0	.277	.429
Projected	144	458	50	123	22	1	13	67	43	106	0	.269	.406

Nolan Arenado

Act/Proj	G	AB	R	H	D	T	HR	RBI	BB	SO	SB	Avg	Slg
Actual	155	588	102	185	31	2	41	118	62	93	3	.315	.583
Projected	159	614	100	185	44	4	40	117	63	118	2	.301	.581

JD Martinez

Act/Proj	G	AB	R	H	D	T	HR	RBI	BB	SO	SB	Avg	Slg
Actual	146	575	98	175	33	2	36	105	72	138	2	.304	.557
Projected	146	555	93	163	38	2	36	109	58	154	4	.294	.564

Robinson Chirinos

Act/Proj	G	AB	R	H	D	T	HR	RBI	BB	SO	SB	Avg	Slg
Actual	114	366	57	87	22	1	17	58	51	125	1	.238	.443
Projected	115	386	52	82	18	1	17	54	43	136	1	.212	.396

Juan Soto

Act/Proj	G	AB	R	H	D	T	HR	RBI	BB	SO	SB	Avg	Slg
Actual	150	542	110	153	32	5	34	110	108	132	12	.282	.548
Projected	148	540	101	148	34	1	30	107	104	127	7	.274	.507

Nolan Arenado, of course, is easy to project because he puts up the same numbers every year. Todd Frazier and JD Martinez are not as easy because they have been up and down some, and Colin Moran and Juan Soto are not as easy because they don't have long track records, but we happened to guess about right; our formulas guessed about right. We had 183 "good" projections; of course, they're not all THAT good. Our projections for Brian Anderson and Nick Markakis represent the bottom boundary of what we would consider to be good projections:

Brian Anderson

Act/Proj	G	AB	R	H	D	T	HR	RBI	BB	SO	SB	Avg	Slg
Actual	126	459	57	120	33	1	20	66	44	114	5	.261	.468
Projected	156	569	81	150	30	3	15	72	60	137	2	.264	.406

Nick Markakis

Act/Proj	G	AB	R	H	D	T	HR	RBI	BB	SO	SB	Avg	Slg
Actual	116	414	61	118	25	2	9	62	47	59	2	.285	.420
Projected	158	591	72	165	36	1	10	71	65	91	1	.279	.394

We got some parts of that right, some parts of it wrong; any worse than that and we wouldn't consider it to be a good projection. Moving on now to the second group of players, the six players who performed most dramatically better than we had expected that they would were Jorge Soler, Renato Nunez, Hunter Dozier, Ryan McMahon, Christian Vazquez and Trey Mancini:

Jorge Soler

Act/Proj	G	AB	R	H	D	T	HR	RBI	BB	SO	SB	Avg	Slg
Actual	162	589	95	156	33	1	48	117	73	178	3	.265	.569
Projected	79	219	27	51	12	0	10	31	28	73	2	.233	.425

Renato Nunez

Act/Proj	G	AB	R	H	D	T	HR	RBI	BB	SO	SB	Avg	Slg
Actual	151	541	72	132	24	0	31	90	44	143	1	.244	.460
Projected	73	227	26	52	11	0	10	27	17	68	0	.229	.410

Hunter Dozier

Act/Proj	G	AB	R	H	D	T	HR	RBI	BB	SO	SB	Avg	Slg
Actual	139	523	75	146	29	10	26	84	55	148	2	.279	.522
Projected	95	337	37	73	19	1	9	32	31	118	2	.217	.359

Ryan McMahon

Act/Proj	G	AB	R	H	D	T	HR	RBI	BB	SO	SB	Avg	Slg
Actual	141	480	70	120	22	1	24	83	56	160	5	.250	.450
Projected	93	187	20	45	10	1	6	23	14	58	1	.241	.401

Christian Vazquez

Act/Proj	G	AB	R	H	D	T	HR	RBI	BB	SO	SB	Avg	Slg
Actual	138	482	66	133	26	1	23	72	33	101	4	.276	.477
Projected	84	230	25	59	12	1	2	21	16	43	3	.257	.343

Trey Mancini

Act/Proj	G	AB	R	H	D	T	HR	RBI	BB	SO	SB	Avg	Slg
Actual	154	602	106	175	38	2	35	97	63	143	1	.291	.535
Projected	122	398	48	104	19	2	17	48	30	108	0	.261	.447

All of these players had what we could comfortably call breakout seasons. They all started hitting well early in the season, and, because they were hitting well, they got more playing time than we had expected them to get, and then they continued hitting all season, so they wound up with big numbers compared to our projections. No excuses; we were just wrong.

You can notice something else here, if you want to. Four of the six top over-achieving players played for two teams which lost 100 games apiece. You might think that, when you have dramatically over-achieving players, they might contribute to the team having a good season, but it doesn't happen that way because it is much easier to grab un-expected playing time on a bad team than it is on a good team. There were good teams, however, which had several over-achievers versus our projections. On the Minnesota Twins Miguel Sano, Max Kepler, Mitch Garver and Nelson Cruz all performed substantially better than our projections. On the Oakland A's, Matt Chapman, Ramon Laureano, Mark Canha and Marcus Semien all played much better than we had projected; on the Astros, Michael Brantley, Alex Bregman, and George Springer. Several players on the Yankees played well that we hadn't made projections for, at all, while Brett Gardner and DJ LeMahieu beat the numbers we had sketched out for them. Max Muncy beat his projections big-time for the second straight season, and Cody Bellinger was great:

Max Muncy

Act/Proj	G	AB	R	H	D	T	HR	RBI	BB	SO	SB	Avg	Slg
Actual	141	487	101	122	22	1	35	98	90	149	4	.251	.515
Projected	132	475	66	110	21	2	27	66	74	148	3	.232	.455

Cody Bellinger

Act/Proj	G	AB	R	H	D	T	HR	RBI	BB	SO	SB	Avg	Slg
Actual	156	558	121	170	34	3	47	115	95	108	15	.305	.629
Projected	155	548	86	142	27	4	32	89	72	153	13	.259	.498

Obviously we're not shocked that Cody Bellinger took a step forward after an off-season as a 22-year-old, but you can't project those things. SOME 22-year-olds step forward as 23-year-olds; some don't. You don't really know who will and who won't until it happens, so you project SOME improvement for all of them. Should probably give you Peter Alonso:

Peter Alonso

Act/Proj	G	AB	R	H	D	T	HR	RBI	BB	SO	SB	Avg	Slg
Actual	161	597	103	155	30	2	53	120	72	183	1	.260	.583
Projected	127	456	66	111	24	1	26	80	60	152	0	.243	.471

OK, the final group is hitters who hit far WORSE than we thought they would.   When a player dramatically underachieves vs. our projection, it is usually because he was injured.   This apparently is most common among New Yorkers:

Giancarlo Stanton

Act/Proj	G	AB	R	H	D	T	HR	RBI	BB	SO	SB	Avg	Slg
Actual	18	59	8	17	3	0	3	13	12	24	0	.288	.492
Projected	154	574	98	149	29	1	42	107	77	186	4	.260	.533

Miguel Andujar

Act/Proj	G	AB	R	H	D	T	HR	RBI	BB	SO	SB	Avg	Slg
Actual	12	47	1	6	0	0	0	1	1	11	0	.128	.128
Projected	149	545	68	157	40	2	22	87	28	96	3	.288	.490

Jed Lowrie

Act/Proj	G	AB	R	H	D	T	HR	RBI	BB	SO	SB	Avg	Slg
Actual	9	7	0	0	0	0	0	0	1	4	0	.000	.000
Projected	148	548	70	143	35	2	16	71	63	112	0	.261	.420

Matt Kemp was injured early in the season and then released:

Matt Kemp

Act/Proj	G	AB	R	H	D	T	HR	RBI	BB	SO	SB	Avg	Slg
Actual	20	60	4	12	2	0	1	5	1	19	0	.200	.283
Projected	146	543	69	150	32	1	24	87	39	138	1	.276	.471

Kyle Tucker actually hit about as well as we thought that he would, but couldn't get into the lineup until the Astros had run away and hid from everyone.

Kyle Tucker

Act/Proj	G	AB	R	H	D	T	HR	RBI	BB	SO	SB	Avg	Slg
Actual	22	67	15	18	6	0	4	11	4	20	5	.269	.537
Projected	146	503	77	133	30	3	24	82	48	129	13	.264	.479

Bo Bichette actually hit quite a bit better than we thought he would, but didn't get the playing time that we had projected for him:

Bo Bichette

Act/Proj	G	AB	R	H	D	T	HR	RBI	BB	SO	SB	Avg	Slg
Actual	46	196	32	61	18	0	11	21	14	50	4	.311	.571
Projected	144	522	74	132	33	7	10	63	43	131	22	.253	.400

Many different people have worked to develop the complex network of formulas that we use to make these projections, but this type of error happens because of me. My very strong opinion is that, for young players just coming out of the minors, if they MIGHT play regularly, we should project that they WILL play regularly. I am always surrounded by colleagues who would prefer to project young players who might play into a 150-at-bat type role, but I just can't stand to do that. If you project a player into 150 at bats, no matter who he is he's going to wind up projected for 4 to 6 homers, 20 RBI, no triples, 8 to 10 doubles. Everybody looks the same. It doesn't really tell you what the young player can do. I would much rather present a batting line like we did for Bichette or Tucker and be wrong than present some neutered version of it which doesn't tell the reader what kind of player the young man will be. In 20-some years of doing this we must have had 50 collaborators in creating the projections, of whom not a single one agreed with me about this or even understood what I was saying, but my name is on the book, so people are nice enough to go along with me. Thank you for reading.

2020 Hitter Projections

Hitter	Team	Age	G	AB	H	2B	3B	HR	R	RBI	RC	RC27	BB	SO	SB	CS	SB%	Avg	OBP	Slg	OPS
Abreu, Jose	CWS	33	152	594	163	35	2	28	79	101	91	5.5	40	138	2	1	.67	.274	.334	.481	.815
Acuna Jr., Ronald	Atl	22	156	595	171	30	3	37	106	93	117	7.0	68	171	30	8	.79	.287	.368	.534	.903
Adames, Willy	TB	24	152	531	134	24	3	17	70	58	69	4.5	54	157	5	3	.63	.252	.325	.405	.730
Adams, Matt	Was	31	111	277	66	15	1	16	36	47	38	4.7	20	86	0	0	.00	.238	.294	.473	.767
Adrianza, Ehire	Min	30	107	288	76	16	2	6	39	32	37	4.5	25	64	2	1	.67	.264	.333	.396	.729
Aguilar, Jesus	TB	30	111	370	89	17	0	17	45	58	49	4.6	40	105	0	0	.00	.241	.320	.424	.744
Ahmed, Nick	Ari	30	148	529	133	30	4	16	65	64	67	4.3	43	111	6	4	.60	.251	.313	.414	.726
Alberto, Hanser	Bal	27	132	470	131	20	2	10	50	47	55	4.2	14	52	3	3	.50	.279	.304	.394	.698
Albies, Ozzie	Atl	23	150	597	170	38	7	20	94	73	96	5.8	47	111	14	3	.82	.285	.342	.472	.814
Alfaro, Jorge	Mia	27	128	425	103	17	2	14	43	54	46	3.7	22	156	3	2	.60	.242	.297	.391	.688
Allen, Austin	SD	26	48	156	41	11	0	8	19	22	24	5.4	12	43	0	0	.00	.263	.320	.487	.807
Allen, Greg	Cle	27	62	164	41	7	2	3	23	15	19	4.0	12	43	6	1	.86	.250	.324	.372	.696
Almora Jr., Albert	ChC	26	129	333	86	17	2	8	42	35	39	4.1	18	61	2	1	.67	.258	.298	.393	.692
Alonso, Pete	NYM	25	161	585	146	30	2	49	94	122	109	6.4	74	183	1	1	.50	.250	.353	.559	.911
Alonso, Yonder	Col	33	103	264	69	14	1	10	36	39	39	5.2	31	60	0	0	.00	.261	.343	.436	.779
Altuve, Jose	Hou	30	145	569	173	35	4	22	92	74	102	6.6	49	90	11	4	.73	.304	.365	.496	.861
Alvarez, Yordan	Hou	23	143	509	143	33	0	41	90	118	113	8.0	77	153	2	0	1.00	.281	.379	.587	.966
Anderson, Brian	Mia	27	150	570	149	33	3	20	78	78	82	5.0	59	142	4	2	.67	.261	.346	.435	.781
Anderson, Tim	CWS	27	147	577	163	29	3	17	80	60	78	4.8	21	142	17	4	.81	.282	.311	.432	.743
Andrus, Elvis	Tex	31	152	601	169	34	4	12	81	67	82	4.8	41	99	22	8	.73	.281	.331	.411	.742
Andujar, Miguel	NYY	25	141	527	147	37	2	18	64	77	76	5.2	27	98	2	1	.67	.279	.319	.459	.778
Aquino, Aristides	Cin	26	135	481	111	19	2	36	61	76	69	4.8	35	165	7	1	.88	.231	.290	.503	.793
Arcia, Orlando	Mil	25	143	413	98	18	2	11	43	44	44	3.6	32	93	7	4	.64	.237	.294	.370	.664
Arenado, Nolan	Col	29	158	608	189	41	3	43	102	122	136	8.4	63	107	3	3	.50	.311	.379	.600	.980
Arraez, Luis	Min	23	135	488	156	26	1	5	69	46	77	6.0	50	47	5	2	.71	.320	.384	.408	.792
Arroyo, Christian	Cle	25	41	134	34	8	0	4	16	18	16	4.1	9	33	1	1	.50	.254	.310	.403	.713
Astudillo, Willians	Min	28	72	219	64	11	0	8	26	28	31	5.1	6	11	1	1	.50	.292	.326	.452	.778
Austin, Tyler	Mil	28	62	113	24	6	1	5	15	16	14	4.0	12	44	1	0	1.00	.212	.294	.416	.710
Avila, Alex	Ari	33	71	195	42	8	0	8	22	23	25	4.3	39	82	1	1	.50	.215	.349	.379	.728
Bader, Harrison	StL	26	124	351	82	16	2	14	54	41	44	4.2	35	117	9	3	.75	.234	.321	.410	.731
Baez, Javier	ChC	27	153	567	151	33	4	30	86	94	86	5.3	32	169	12	5	.71	.266	.310	.497	.807
Barnes, Austin	LAD	30	61	190	44	10	1	6	26	21	23	4.1	23	49	3	1	.75	.232	.327	.389	.717
Barnhart, Tucker	Cin	29	118	359	88	18	1	9	33	41	44	4.2	43	83	1	1	.50	.245	.329	.376	.705
Barreto, Franklin	Oak	24	87	234	52	11	2	8	31	26	26	3.6	18	87	5	1	.83	.222	.289	.389	.678
Bart, Joey	SF	23	65	215	51	9	2	16	26	35	34	5.3	19	75	0	0	.00	.237	.299	.521	.820
Bauers, Jake	Cle	24	105	321	75	18	1	9	43	40	39	4.1	41	94	6	3	.67	.234	.324	.380	.704
Beaty, Matt	LAD	27	110	301	86	21	1	9	37	43	46	5.6	22	45	3	0	1.00	.286	.345	.452	.796
Beckham, Gordon	Det	33	46	133	33	7	0	3	16	13	15	3.9	11	31	1	0	1.00	.248	.315	.368	.683
Beckham, Tim	Sea	30	101	360	82	18	2	13	43	42	40	3.7	26	116	2	2	.50	.228	.285	.397	.683
Bell, Josh	Pit	27	154	535	141	31	4	27	79	91	91	6.0	73	117	1	2	.33	.264	.355	.488	.843
Bellinger, Cody	LAD	24	157	574	163	32	4	45	103	110	130	8.1	88	134	14	3	.82	.284	.382	.589	.971
Belt, Brandon	SF	32	124	396	102	25	3	14	55	50	62	5.4	60	103	3	2	.60	.258	.359	.442	.801
Benintendi, Andrew	Bos	25	149	571	157	39	5	16	86	83	90	5.6	67	130	13	4	.76	.275	.356	.445	.801
Berti, Jon	Mia	30	95	306	73	11	4	5	43	27	34	3.7	29	81	14	4	.78	.239	.317	.350	.666
Betts, Mookie	Bos	27	152	604	181	46	5	28	120	91	125	7.7	82	99	18	3	.86	.300	.387	.531	.918
Bichette, Bo	Tor	22	147	580	154	40	6	23	83	73	89	5.3	46	148	21	6	.78	.266	.323	.474	.797
Biggio, Cavan	Tor	25	139	499	120	24	4	26	80	85	87	6.0	102	173	16	2	.89	.240	.374	.461	.834
Bird, Greg	NYY	27	62	194	43	10	0	10	24	27	26	4.4	25	59	0	0	.00	.222	.317	.428	.745
Blackmon, Charlie	Col	33	154	621	191	36	8	33	112	83	122	7.3	50	123	5	3	.63	.308	.369	.551	.919
Bogaerts, Xander	Bos	27	153	596	168	43	2	23	94	97	100	6.1	64	121	6	2	.75	.282	.356	.477	.833
Bote, David	ChC	27	101	253	61	12	1	9	33	33	33	4.4	30	79	3	1	.75	.241	.333	.403	.736
Bour, Justin	LAA	32	97	279	64	12	0	15	35	44	39	4.7	38	82	1	0	1.00	.229	.324	.434	.758
Bradley Jr., Jackie	Bos	30	147	504	120	29	4	17	71	65	65	4.4	54	150	8	3	.73	.238	.324	.413	.737
Brantley, Michael	Hou	33	147	574	175	37	2	19	82	85	100	6.5	52	70	5	1	.83	.305	.369	.476	.844
Braun, Ryan	Mil	36	141	486	134	30	2	23	72	75	79	5.8	41	110	10	3	.77	.276	.338	.488	.826
Bregman, Alex	Hou	26	159	590	170	44	3	35	111	109	128	7.9	102	93	7	2	.78	.288	.402	.551	.953
Brinson, Lewis	Mia	26	63	136	28	6	1	4	14	15	13	3.1	10	47	2	0	1.00	.206	.275	.353	.628
Brosseau, Mike	TB	26	51	170	44	11	1	9	24	29	27	5.5	14	45	1	0	1.00	.259	.330	.494	.824
Brown, Seth	Oak	27	76	224	50	13	2	9	28	36	26	4.0	17	79	2	0	1.00	.223	.284	.420	.704
Bruce, Jay	Phi	33	99	297	71	16	1	18	39	50	43	4.9	27	78	1	1	.50	.239	.305	.481	.786
Bryant, Kris	ChC	28	144	545	149	34	2	31	99	84	102	6.6	77	151	4	2	.67	.273	.379	.514	.893
Buxton, Byron	Min	26	125	403	99	24	5	14	61	50	54	4.5	29	120	19	3	.86	.246	.303	.434	.737
Cabrera, Asdrubal	Was	34	130	441	119	27	2	17	60	64	67	5.4	42	98	2	1	.67	.270	.339	.456	.795
Cabrera, Melky	Pit	35	85	279	81	17	1	6	32	36	39	5.2	17	36	1	0	1.00	.290	.333	.423	.756
Cabrera, Miguel	Det	37	108	348	100	19	0	11	41	48	55	5.7	40	77	0	0	.00	.287	.364	.437	.801
Cain, Lorenzo	Mil	34	148	547	151	29	3	12	79	52	76	4.9	51	107	16	5	.76	.276	.344	.406	.750
Calhoun, Kole	LAA	32	148	492	117	24	2	22	73	62	67	4.6	56	134	3	1	.75	.238	.322	.429	.751
Calhoun, Willie	Tex	25	131	461	120	25	1	25	61	66	71	5.4	40	80	1	0	1.00	.260	.325	.482	.806
Camargo, Johan	Atl	26	110	308	84	20	1	9	39	43	43	5.0	24	67	1	0	1.00	.273	.329	.432	.761
Candelario, Jeimer	Det	26	111	364	85	22	2	13	46	46	47	4.4	44	103	2	1	.67	.234	.326	.412	.738
Canha, Mark	Oak	31	132	445	109	25	2	21	70	63	65	5.2	52	119	2	1	.67	.245	.342	.452	.794
Cano, Robinson	NYM	37	128	495	132	28	1	16	64	63	67	4.8	38	85	0	0	.00	.267	.325	.424	.750
Caratini, Victor	ChC	26	92	270	73	15	1	9	32	36	40	5.2	27	62	1	0	1.00	.270	.346	.433	.779
Carlson, Dylan	StL	21	139	476	122	28	6	22	83	65	78	5.7	55	137	12	0	1.00	.256	.341	.479	.820
Carpenter, Matt	StL	34	139	459	113	30	2	19	76	57	72	5.4	77	133	4	2	.67	.246	.362	.444	.806
Casali, Curt	Cin	31	77	225	53	10	0	7	23	29	26	4.0	25	63	0	0	.00	.236	.320	.373	.693
Castellanos, Nicholas	ChC	28	157	624	175	47	5	26	82	87	102	5.9	47	154	2	2	.50	.280	.336	.497	.833
Castro, Welington	CWS	33	88	282	65	13	0	12	27	40	32	3.8	19	87	0	0	.00	.230	.286	.404	.690
Castro, Harold	Det	26	118	415	106	15	2	6	40	38	40	3.4	15	97	5	2	.71	.255	.283	.345	.628

582

2020 Hitter Projections

Hitter	Team	Age	G	AB	H	2B	3B	HR	R	RBI	RC	RC27	BB	SO	SB	CS	SB%	Avg	OBP	Slg	OPS
Castro, Jason	Min	33	78	222	48	11	0	8	28	25	25	3.8	28	79	0	0	.00	.216	.310	.374	.683
Castro, Starlin	Mia	30	155	609	170	32	2	18	70	75	82	4.8	34	118	3	2	.60	.279	.320	.427	.747
Castro, Willi	Det	23	118	429	108	22	5	10	56	50	52	4.2	29	126	9	2	.82	.252	.313	.396	.709
Cave, Jake	Min	27	88	247	62	13	3	8	34	30	32	4.5	20	82	2	1	.67	.251	.315	.425	.740
Cervelli, Francisco	Atl	34	75	260	63	13	1	5	31	29	30	4.0	33	71	1	1	.50	.242	.346	.358	.703
Cespedes, Yoenis	NYM	34	130	511	135	29	3	26	75	81	79	5.4	40	129	4	2	.67	.264	.323	.485	.808
Chapman, Matt	Oak	27	149	561	139	35	3	33	92	85	92	5.6	68	158	1	1	.50	.248	.338	.497	.835
Chavis, Michael	Bos	24	131	512	118	22	1	28	71	81	66	4.4	46	183	3	1	.75	.230	.301	.441	.743
Chirinos, Robinson	Hou	36	112	370	78	17	1	16	52	51	43	3.8	45	130	1	1	.50	.211	.318	.392	.710
Chisenhall, Lonnie	Pit	31	76	218	56	14	1	6	26	30	28	4.5	17	50	2	1	.67	.257	.316	.413	.729
Choi, Ji-Man	TB	29	121	389	96	22	1	15	46	58	56	5.0	57	109	2	2	.50	.247	.350	.424	.774
Choo, Shin-Soo	Tex	37	151	555	142	27	2	21	86	63	83	5.2	78	160	10	3	.77	.256	.362	.425	.787
Collins, Zack	CWS	25	55	164	35	8	0	7	21	24	21	4.3	30	70	0	0	.00	.213	.338	.390	.729
Conforto, Michael	NYM	27	152	555	139	30	2	33	87	92	95	5.9	83	155	5	2	.71	.250	.357	.490	.847
Contreras, Willson	ChC	28	129	457	117	26	2	22	60	71	70	5.3	50	123	2	2	.50	.256	.342	.466	.808
Cooper, Garrett	Mia	29	78	216	57	11	0	7	25	28	29	4.7	18	60	0	0	.00	.264	.329	.412	.741
Cordell, Ryan	CWS	28	62	137	28	6	1	4	14	15	12	2.9	10	45	2	1	.67	.204	.264	.350	.614
Cordero, Franchy	SD	25	62	202	45	8	4	7	25	21	23	3.8	16	84	4	1	.80	.223	.283	.406	.689
Correa, Carlos	Hou	25	120	460	124	28	2	24	70	83	81	6.2	59	118	3	1	.75	.270	.356	.496	.852
Cozart, Zack	LAA	34	107	362	90	18	3	10	47	38	45	4.3	32	65	1	0	1.00	.249	.318	.398	.716
Crawford, Brandon	SF	33	151	531	133	30	3	12	61	65	65	4.2	52	125	3	2	.60	.250	.323	.386	.709
Crawford, J.P.	Sea	25	120	417	94	20	4	8	51	43	46	3.6	53	104	6	3	.67	.225	.319	.350	.669
Cron, C.J.	Min	27	126	418	108	23	1	21	50	68	59	5.0	28	105	1	1	.50	.258	.319	.469	.788
Cron, Kevin	Ari	27	54	175	41	9	0	13	23	33	27	5.3	18	59	0	0	.00	.234	.316	.509	.825
Cruz, Nelson	Min	39	145	542	149	25	1	37	83	103	100	6.6	61	148	1	1	.50	.275	.358	.530	.887
Culberson, Charlie	Atl	31	87	157	36	7	1	4	16	18	15	3.3	9	45	1	1	.50	.229	.275	.363	.639
Cuthbert, Cheslor	KC	27	76	245	59	12	1	7	22	29	28	3.9	18	59	1	0	1.00	.241	.298	.384	.682
Dahl, David	Col	26	116	410	112	26	5	17	62	60	63	5.5	28	119	5	3	.63	.273	.324	.485	.810
Dalbec, Bobby	Bos	25	63	202	45	8	1	13	27	34	29	4.9	26	81	1	0	1.00	.223	.326	.465	.792
d'Arnaud, Travis	TB	31	94	303	74	16	1	11	39	45	38	4.3	25	69	0	0	.00	.244	.306	.413	.719
Davis, Chris	Bal	34	75	183	36	7	0	9	22	24	20	3.5	23	78	0	0	.00	.197	.293	.383	.676
Davis, J.D.	NYM	27	112	335	91	19	1	16	44	52	53	5.7	31	90	2	1	.67	.272	.339	.478	.816
Davis, Khris	Oak	32	121	392	93	18	1	22	57	66	55	4.8	40	122	0	0	.00	.237	.316	.457	.772
Dean, Austin	Mia	26	94	309	85	18	2	12	40	45	47	5.4	25	74	2	1	.67	.275	.333	.463	.796
DeJong, Paul	StL	26	146	538	139	31	2	29	83	84	80	4.9	50	153	6	4	.60	.249	.323	.468	.791
Demeritte, Travis	Det	25	129	477	105	26	3	22	69	63	61	4.2	53	184	5	2	.71	.220	.305	.426	.730
Descalso, Daniel	ChC	33	100	227	53	11	2	6	30	27	29	4.3	34	70	2	1	.67	.233	.336	.379	.715
DeShields, Delino	Tex	27	108	327	78	14	3	5	49	28	38	3.9	39	93	19	5	.79	.239	.325	.346	.671
Desmond, Ian	Col	34	132	455	118	23	4	18	65	65	64	4.9	36	126	7	3	.70	.259	.319	.446	.765
Devers, Rafael	Bos	23	152	605	171	42	3	29	102	103	102	6.0	51	127	7	6	.54	.283	.341	.506	.847
Diaz, Aledmys	Hou	29	96	282	71	17	1	10	37	36	37	4.5	22	47	2	1	.67	.252	.315	.426	.740
Diaz, Elias	Pit	29	97	280	72	14	0	4	28	31	30	3.7	19	53	0	0	.00	.257	.307	.350	.657
Diaz, Isan	Mia	24	145	519	120	25	4	23	76	74	70	4.5	63	175	5	3	.63	.231	.323	.428	.750
Diaz, Yandy	TB	28	98	346	93	17	2	8	46	36	49	5.0	46	77	2	1	.67	.269	.356	.399	.755
Dickerson, Alex	SF	30	88	280	72	17	3	8	38	38	37	4.7	23	65	1	0	1.00	.257	.325	.425	.750
Dickerson, Corey	Phi	31	130	494	132	34	4	20	65	69	72	5.1	30	112	3	2	.60	.267	.312	.474	.785
Dietrich, Derek	Cin	30	120	385	90	20	3	17	57	49	49	4.3	33	109	1	1	.50	.234	.333	.434	.766
Difo, Wilmer	Was	28	117	359	89	14	3	5	48	31	39	3.7	30	86	8	1	.89	.248	.309	.345	.655
Dixon, Brandon	Det	28	123	421	99	22	2	15	47	51	47	3.7	23	151	5	2	.71	.235	.281	.404	.685
Donaldson, Josh	Atl	34	145	534	137	30	1	31	92	90	95	6.2	88	146	3	1	.75	.256	.367	.490	.857
Dozier, Brian	Was	33	134	411	101	23	2	20	63	54	62	5.2	52	101	5	2	.71	.246	.336	.457	.794
Dozier, Hunter	KC	28	142	521	125	30	4	20	62	66	68	4.5	51	163	3	2	.60	.240	.311	.428	.739
Drury, Brandon	Tor	27	114	314	75	19	1	11	32	36	38	4.1	23	85	0	0	.00	.239	.297	.411	.708
Dubon, Mauricio	SF	25	114	412	110	20	2	11	51	39	51	4.4	24	75	10	4	.71	.267	.311	.405	.716
Duda, Lucas	Atl	34	67	160	35	9	0	8	18	23	20	4.2	18	53	0	0	.00	.219	.309	.425	.734
Duffy, Matt	TB	29	80	236	65	11	1	3	27	26	29	4.4	20	45	2	1	.67	.275	.340	.369	.708
Duggar, Steven	SF	26	111	319	79	14	3	6	42	32	38	4.1	30	102	4	3	.57	.248	.314	.386	.700
Duvall, Adam	Atl	31	99	294	70	16	1	20	41	53	43	5.0	24	88	1	1	.50	.238	.307	.503	.810
Dyson, Jarrod	Ari	35	119	381	92	13	5	5	58	29	43	3.8	40	77	23	5	.82	.241	.320	.341	.661
Eaton, Adam	Was	31	145	550	155	29	5	13	94	53	83	5.4	61	108	12	4	.75	.282	.367	.424	.791
Edman, Tommy	StL	25	92	327	95	21	4	8	48	33	49	5.5	22	67	12	2	.86	.291	.343	.437	.780
Encarnacion, Edwin	NYY	37	139	515	128	21	1	35	84	98	88	5.9	73	128	1	0	1.00	.249	.350	.497	.847
Engel, Adam	CWS	28	92	225	48	10	2	5	26	20	20	2.9	15	73	5	2	.71	.213	.278	.342	.620
Ervin, Phillip	Cin	27	131	376	90	18	4	12	48	46	47	4.2	37	105	9	3	.75	.239	.321	.404	.725
Escobar, Eduardo	Ari	31	155	596	156	35	6	27	78	91	89	5.2	47	129	4	3	.57	.262	.320	.477	.798
Farmer, Kyle	Cin	29	87	189	46	11	1	5	19	22	21	3.8	12	49	2	1	.67	.243	.299	.392	.691
Fisher, Derek	Tor	26	56	141	31	6	1	6	21	18	18	4.2	19	53	4	1	.80	.220	.317	.404	.721
Fletcher, David	LAA	26	154	566	160	32	3	6	75	49	73	4.6	44	69	8	3	.73	.283	.338	.382	.719
Flores, Wilmer	Ari	28	110	359	102	21	1	14	43	53	54	5.5	22	47	0	0	.00	.284	.332	.465	.798
Flowers, Tyler	Atl	34	86	288	65	12	1	10	34	37	33	3.8	30	101	0	0	.00	.226	.318	.378	.697
Ford, Mike	NYY	27	89	268	67	14	0	17	40	43	45	5.3	36	62	0	0	.00	.250	.347	.493	.840
Forsythe, Logan	Tex	33	77	231	58	12	1	6	30	26	30	4.6	29	64	1	0	1.00	.251	.342	.390	.732
Fowler, Dexter	StL	34	129	390	95	19	3	13	58	44	54	4.8	57	110	5	2	.71	.244	.347	.408	.755
France, Ty	SD	25	89	293	80	17	1	15	41	49	46	5.5	21	69	1	2	.33	.273	.351	.491	.842
Franco, Maikel	Phi	27	96	304	77	15	1	15	35	46	43	4.9	24	51	0	0	.00	.253	.310	.457	.767
Frazier, Adam	Pit	28	145	508	142	30	5	8	69	51	68	4.8	42	77	5	4	.56	.280	.343	.406	.748
Frazier, Clint	NYY	25	74	208	49	13	1	8	29	25	24	4.2	18	65	2	1	.67	.236	.303	.423	.726
Frazier, Todd	NYM	34	134	442	102	20	1	21	61	62	57	4.3	47	113	3	2	.60	.231	.317	.423	.740
Freeman, Freddie	Atl	30	156	599	180	42	3	31	101	103	124	7.7	85	135	6	3	.67	.301	.395	.536	.930
Freeman, Mike	Cle	32	73	175	39	7	1	3	21	15	17	3.2	16	51	1	0	1.00	.223	.295	.326	.621
Freese, David	LAD	37	86	247	63	12	0	9	33	34	33	4.7	26	69	0	0	.00	.255	.338	.413	.751

583

2020 Hitter Projections

Hitter	Team	Age	G	AB	H	2B	3B	HR	R	RBI	RC	RC27	BB	SO	SB	CS	SB%	Avg	OBP	Slg	OPS
Gallagher, Cam	KC	27	61	159	37	7	0	3	13	16	15	3.3	13	32	0	0	.00	.233	.299	.333	.632
Gallo, Joey	Tex	26	146	509	106	24	2	40	87	93	82	5.2	86	229	6	3	.67	.208	.328	.499	.827
Galvis, Freddy	Cin	30	152	589	143	30	4	17	68	67	67	3.9	37	147	6	3	.67	.243	.290	.394	.684
Gamel, Ben	Mil	28	121	343	87	18	3	6	47	35	41	4.2	34	94	4	2	.67	.254	.325	.376	.701
Garcia, Avisail	TB	29	128	466	124	22	2	17	60	65	62	4.7	31	122	7	4	.64	.266	.320	.431	.751
Garcia, Greg	SD	30	112	247	60	11	1	3	31	21	28	3.8	36	64	1	1	.50	.243	.351	.332	.683
Garcia, Leury	CWS	29	124	431	112	18	3	7	57	38	46	3.7	19	107	10	4	.71	.260	.299	.364	.663
Gardner, Brett	NYY	36	145	528	130	23	5	18	86	59	71	4.6	60	117	11	3	.79	.246	.329	.411	.740
Garver, Mitch	Min	29	109	371	94	22	1	23	57	62	62	5.8	43	105	0	0	.00	.253	.336	.504	.840
Goins, Ryan	CWS	32	71	172	37	8	1	3	17	17	15	2.9	15	51	1	1	.50	.215	.282	.326	.607
Goldschmidt, Paul	StL	32	160	602	169	33	2	33	98	98	116	6.9	94	169	7	2	.78	.281	.382	.507	.889
Gomes, Yan	Was	32	102	340	80	18	1	13	41	47	41	4.1	27	96	1	0	1.00	.235	.303	.409	.712
Gonzalez, Carlos	ChC	34	87	252	65	14	1	9	34	30	35	4.8	24	71	1	1	.50	.258	.325	.429	.753
Gonzalez, Erik	Pit	28	82	180	41	8	2	3	19	16	16	3.0	8	55	3	1	.75	.228	.265	.344	.609
Gonzalez, Marwin	Min	31	131	438	117	25	1	15	56	60	61	4.9	37	104	2	1	.67	.267	.331	.432	.763
Goodrum, Niko	Det	28	123	432	103	24	4	13	56	49	54	4.2	41	138	10	3	.77	.238	.307	.403	.710
Goodwin, Brian	LAA	29	88	245	56	14	1	9	31	28	29	4.0	23	78	4	1	.80	.229	.300	.404	.704
Gordon, Alex	KC	36	133	419	107	21	1	11	52	49	53	4.4	42	94	4	2	.67	.255	.339	.389	.728
Gordon, Dee	Sea	32	130	460	126	15	6	3	59	30	50	3.8	19	74	24	8	.75	.274	.308	.352	.661
Grandal, Yasmani	Mil	31	145	504	121	26	1	27	71	75	82	5.5	90	143	3	2	.60	.240	.360	.456	.816
Granderson, Curtis	Mia	39	82	186	40	9	1	7	27	20	22	3.9	26	56	1	1	.50	.215	.318	.387	.705
Gregorius, Didi	NYY	30	129	496	129	24	3	21	68	74	67	4.7	31	77	4	2	.67	.260	.310	.448	.758
Greiner, Grayson	Det	27	49	109	24	4	0	3	9	11	11	3.2	10	36	0	0	.00	.220	.292	.339	.631
Grichuk, Randal	Tor	28	134	450	108	27	3	26	60	64	62	4.7	29	133	2	1	.67	.240	.293	.487	.780
Grisham, Trent	Mil	23	87	296	71	14	2	14	41	45	45	5.2	47	90	4	1	.80	.240	.350	.443	.792
Grossman, Robbie	Oak	30	119	339	85	19	1	6	44	34	43	4.4	50	77	5	3	.63	.251	.350	.366	.716
Guerrero Jr., Vladimir	Tor	21	147	531	158	32	2	27	69	95	100	6.9	55	94	1	1	.50	.298	.368	.518	.886
Gurriel Jr., Lourdes	Tor	26	136	512	133	30	2	27	69	87	72	4.9	25	132	6	4	.60	.260	.305	.484	.789
Gurriel, Yuli	Hou	36	146	552	155	37	1	21	74	89	82	5.3	30	70	4	2	.67	.281	.325	.466	.790
Guzman, Ronald	Tex	25	78	226	55	12	1	9	29	30	30	4.5	23	69	1	1	.50	.243	.321	.425	.746
Gyorko, Jedd	LAD	31	72	209	51	9	0	9	24	28	27	4.4	21	52	2	1	.67	.244	.316	.416	.732
Hamilton, Billy	Atl	29	81	225	55	9	3	1	32	14	24	3.6	20	57	15	3	.83	.244	.306	.324	.631
Hampson, Garrett	Col	25	104	302	74	13	3	7	38	24	37	4.1	26	82	15	2	.88	.245	.307	.377	.684
Haniger, Mitch	Sea	29	121	446	111	24	2	21	65	62	66	5.1	49	126	5	1	.83	.249	.334	.453	.787
Happ, Ian	ChC	25	117	349	78	16	1	17	52	51	47	4.5	48	127	6	1	.86	.223	.323	.421	.744
Harper, Bryce	Phi	27	155	574	149	35	1	37	106	105	114	6.9	114	171	14	5	.74	.260	.387	.517	.904
Harrison, Josh	Det	32	96	337	89	18	2	7	42	32	40	4.2	18	65	6	2	.75	.264	.315	.392	.707
Haseley, Adam	Phi	24	141	491	125	26	1	17	68	59	66	4.7	47	129	7	0	1.00	.255	.331	.415	.746
Hayes, Ke'Bryan	Pit	23	134	485	123	31	4	13	64	56	66	4.7	50	125	9	1	.90	.254	.330	.414	.744
Hays, Austin	Bal	24	132	475	117	26	2	23	63	66	62	4.5	25	134	9	1	.90	.246	.291	.455	.746
Healy, Ryon	Sea	28	121	411	104	22	1	17	47	56	53	4.5	24	99	0	0	.00	.253	.297	.436	.733
Hechavarria, Adeiny	Atl	31	77	230	60	11	2	4	28	25	26	4.0	13	46	2	1	.67	.261	.303	.378	.682
Hedges, Austin	SD	27	97	277	58	12	1	11	27	36	28	3.3	20	88	1	0	1.00	.209	.270	.379	.649
Heredia, Guillermo	TB	29	73	176	42	8	0	3	22	15	18	3.4	17	41	1	1	.50	.239	.323	.335	.658
Hermosillo, Michael	LAA	25	60	105	20	4	1	4	14	12	10	3.0	10	42	2	1	.67	.190	.286	.362	.648
Hernandez, Cesar	Phi	30	158	612	166	26	5	12	84	58	82	4.7	66	123	11	5	.69	.271	.347	.389	.736
Hernandez, Kike	LAD	28	124	370	92	20	2	16	51	48	52	4.9	38	85	3	1	.75	.249	.324	.443	.767
Hernandez, Marco	Bos	27	54	134	34	7	1	2	17	12	14	3.5	5	37	1	1	.50	.254	.286	.366	.651
Hernandez, Teoscar	Tor	27	131	468	105	23	3	24	66	62	60	4.3	44	164	7	3	.70	.224	.295	.440	.735
Heyward, Jason	ChC	30	141	476	123	23	3	13	67	57	64	4.7	55	91	5	2	.71	.258	.340	.401	.741
Hicks, Aaron	NYY	30	119	437	105	21	2	19	71	59	63	4.9	64	115	6	3	.67	.240	.340	.428	.768
Hicks, John	Det	30	95	291	68	14	1	10	31	35	31	3.6	15	94	1	1	.50	.234	.274	.392	.665
Hilliard, Sam	Col	26	90	292	60	12	3	14	39	38	33	3.7	26	121	8	2	.80	.205	.275	.411	.686
Hiura, Keston	Mil	23	144	522	138	33	3	28	74	74	83	5.5	41	163	12	5	.71	.264	.332	.500	.832
Hoerner, Nico	ChC	23	91	292	81	17	2	6	42	34	40	4.9	20	43	5	0	1.00	.277	.328	.411	.739
Holaday, Bryan	Mia	32	68	174	40	9	0	4	14	19	18	3.4	14	34	0	0	.00	.230	.298	.351	.649
Holt, Brock	Bos	32	94	273	71	14	2	4	38	28	34	4.3	30	65	2	1	.67	.260	.342	.370	.712
Hoskins, Rhys	Phi	27	148	541	127	31	2	31	85	92	89	5.5	95	156	3	2	.60	.235	.359	.471	.830
Hosmer, Eric	SD	30	154	527	137	27	1	17	67	75	69	4.6	47	127	2	2	.50	.260	.323	.412	.735
Iglesias, Jose	Cin	30	132	460	120	26	2	7	53	47	50	3.8	23	64	6	4	.60	.261	.303	.372	.675
Inciarte, Ender	Atl	29	127	472	129	22	4	7	67	41	60	4.5	41	75	15	6	.71	.273	.337	.381	.718
India, Jonathan	Cin	23	105	369	88	9	0	13	73	49	49	4.5	62	106	8	0	1.00	.238	.374	.369	.743
Jackson, Alex	Atl	24	70	219	43	9	1	16	27	37	25	3.7	15	100	0	0	.00	.196	.276	.466	.741
Jansen, Danny	Tor	25	97	304	74	17	1	13	37	41	41	4.7	32	65	1	1	.50	.243	.329	.434	.764
Jay, Jon	CWS	35	67	157	41	7	1	1	20	12	16	3.6	10	31	1	1	.50	.261	.322	.338	.659
Jimenez, Eloy	CWS	23	147	548	154	28	3	33	78	93	94	6.2	37	143	0	0	.00	.281	.331	.524	.855
Jones, Adam	Ari	34	139	504	130	25	1	18	63	64	62	4.3	27	101	2	1	.67	.258	.304	.419	.722
Jones, JaCoby	Det	28	99	281	63	14	2	8	35	27	30	3.5	22	96	6	2	.75	.224	.294	.374	.668
Jones, Nolan	Cle	22	39	131	27	6	1	8	25	19	19	4.8	22	59	1	0	1.00	.206	.325	.450	.775
Joyce, Matt	Atl	35	112	272	66	15	1	9	41	33	38	4.8	44	68	1	1	.50	.243	.352	.404	.757
Judge, Aaron	NYY	28	133	495	129	24	1	33	90	80	93	6.6	84	185	4	2	.67	.261	.373	.513	.886
Kelly, Carson	Ari	25	111	338	81	17	0	15	41	45	47	4.7	44	79	0	0	.00	.240	.334	.423	.757
Kemp, Tony	ChC	28	110	293	80	13	3	5	40	30	39	4.7	29	48	7	3	.70	.273	.347	.389	.736
Kendrick, Howie	Was	36	118	409	125	24	2	14	60	56	69	6.3	31	73	4	2	.67	.306	.360	.477	.837
Kepler, Max	Min	27	142	521	131	31	4	28	89	80	84	5.5	62	103	2	2	.50	.251	.338	.488	.825
Kieboom, Carter	Was	22	135	492	122	25	2	17	69	67	68	4.7	61	152	4	0	1.00	.248	.340	.411	.751
Kiermaier, Kevin	TB	30	110	355	86	16	5	10	47	37	42	4.0	25	86	13	4	.76	.242	.299	.400	.699
Kiner-Falefa, Isiah	Tex	25	80	223	56	11	1	2	24	20	23	3.6	18	45	3	1	.75	.251	.321	.336	.657
Kingery, Scott	Phi	26	140	468	114	27	3	16	63	48	58	4.2	31	141	13	3	.81	.244	.298	.417	.714
Kinsler, Ian	SD	38	90	263	66	14	1	8	37	27	32	4.2	20	46	4	2	.67	.251	.311	.403	.714
Kipnis, Jason	Cle	33	108	379	97	23	2	13	47	47	53	4.8	37	81	5	2	.71	.256	.327	.430	.757

584

2020 Hitter Projections

Hitter	Team	Age	G	AB	H	2B	3B	HR	R	RBI	RC	RC27	BB	SO	SB	CS	SB%	Avg	OBP	Slg	OPS
Kirilloff, Alex	Min	22	120	447	121	21	1	20	61	60	66	5.3	31	106	6	0	1.00	.271	.325	.456	.781
Knapp, Andrew	Phi	28	72	170	37	9	1	3	19	16	17	3.3	20	61	0	0	.00	.218	.307	.335	.643
Knizner, Andrew	StL	25	74	212	57	10	0	7	26	25	29	4.8	17	43	2	0	1.00	.269	.335	.415	.750
La Stella, Tommy	LAA	31	116	401	108	18	1	14	51	51	56	5.0	37	52	0	0	.00	.269	.337	.424	.761
Lagares, Juan	NYM	31	93	202	47	10	1	3	26	18	19	3.2	13	52	3	1	.75	.233	.286	.337	.622
Lamb, Jake	Ari	29	80	217	53	12	2	10	31	34	33	5.3	30	66	1	0	1.00	.244	.344	.456	.800
Laureano, Ramon	Oak	25	144	490	131	30	3	22	77	67	77	5.5	41	146	14	3	.82	.267	.336	.476	.812
LeMahieu, DJ	NYY	31	149	604	177	32	3	16	93	72	92	5.5	52	99	5	3	.63	.293	.352	.435	.787
Leon, Sandy	Bos	30	60	126	26	5	0	3	13	13	11	2.8	10	35	0	0	.00	.206	.270	.317	.588
Lewis, Kyle	Sea	24	125	470	113	28	1	19	66	72	63	4.6	51	181	2	0	1.00	.240	.316	.426	.742
Lindor, Francisco	Cle	26	155	636	181	40	4	32	103	86	113	6.4	58	106	21	6	.78	.285	.348	.511	.859
Locastro, Tim	Ari	27	87	208	53	12	2	4	34	16	26	4.3	14	45	9	1	.90	.255	.349	.389	.738
Long, Shed	Sea	24	118	430	101	18	4	13	56	50	50	3.9	42	138	6	4	.60	.235	.307	.386	.693
Longoria, Evan	SF	34	135	481	124	26	2	18	57	65	65	4.7	37	110	2	1	.67	.258	.319	.432	.751
Lopez, Nicky	KC	25	89	271	73	11	2	3	33	22	32	4.2	23	35	4	1	.80	.269	.331	.358	.689
Lowe, Brandon	TB	25	136	478	119	28	3	26	67	84	73	5.3	47	169	7	2	.78	.249	.325	.483	.808
Lowe, Nate	TB	24	118	412	108	24	0	21	65	67	70	6.0	61	117	1	0	1.00	.262	.364	.473	.837
Lowrie, Jed	NYM	36	118	437	106	25	1	11	55	50	53	4.2	50	98	0	0	.00	.243	.323	.380	.703
Lucroy, Jonathan	ChC	34	93	288	75	15	1	7	32	34	37	4.5	27	48	0	1	.00	.260	.330	.392	.723
Lugo, Dawel	Det	25	130	459	119	23	4	9	51	50	51	3.9	18	92	4	1	.80	.259	.292	.386	.677
Luplow, Jordan	Cle	26	124	415	103	24	3	21	65	58	65	5.3	52	111	5	3	.63	.248	.340	.472	.813
Lux, Gavin	LAD	22	142	490	138	26	6	25	86	69	91	6.7	57	141	8	1	.89	.282	.358	.512	.870
Machado, Manny	SD	27	160	625	168	32	2	35	85	93	104	5.9	66	126	6	3	.67	.269	.342	.494	.837
Madrigal, Nick	CWS	23	134	487	147	29	4	4	87	48	74	5.7	43	25	21	0	1.00	.302	.363	.402	.766
Maile, Luke	Tor	29	51	102	21	5	0	2	9	9	9	2.8	8	28	1	0	1.00	.206	.270	.314	.584
Maldonado, Martin	Hou	33	113	338	73	15	0	11	38	33	33	3.3	27	92	0	0	.00	.216	.291	.358	.649
Mancini, Trey	Bal	28	149	539	147	29	3	28	75	76	89	5.9	48	136	1	0	1.00	.273	.339	.494	.832
Margot, Manuel	SD	25	135	417	103	21	5	10	52	40	50	4.1	33	86	16	6	.73	.247	.305	.393	.699
Marisnick, Jake	Hou	29	111	275	61	13	2	9	42	31	28	3.4	17	92	7	2	.78	.222	.279	.382	.661
Markakis, Nick	Atl	36	130	471	133	29	1	9	60	60	68	5.2	53	73	1	1	.50	.282	.359	.406	.764
Marte, Ketel	Ari	26	146	534	155	31	7	19	77	65	90	6.2	48	85	8	2	.80	.290	.352	.481	.833
Marte, Starling	Pit	31	141	559	160	32	5	19	86	73	84	5.4	31	110	24	8	.75	.286	.340	.463	.804
Martin Jr., Richie	Bal	25	90	212	49	8	2	4	24	18	21	3.3	15	59	7	2	.78	.231	.294	.344	.639
Martin, Russell	LAD	37	77	220	47	8	0	7	30	26	24	3.5	32	63	1	1	.50	.214	.329	.345	.675
Martinez, J.D.	Bos	32	151	578	172	38	2	37	97	110	120	7.7	66	153	3	1	.75	.298	.373	.562	.936
Martinez, Jose	StL	31	128	411	116	23	1	12	51	56	62	5.4	41	92	3	1	.75	.282	.350	.431	.781
Mathis, Jeff	Tex	37	57	148	28	7	1	2	12	12	11	2.3	11	54	0	0	.00	.189	.245	.291	.536
Maybin, Cameron	NYY	33	105	295	73	15	1	7	42	31	37	4.2	35	80	9	4	.69	.247	.331	.376	.708
Mazara, Nomar	Tex	25	135	491	131	27	2	21	63	77	73	5.2	40	120	3	1	.75	.267	.328	.458	.787
McCann, James	CWS	30	117	393	93	18	1	12	41	46	42	3.7	26	117	2	1	.67	.237	.292	.379	.672
McCutchen, Andrew	Phi	33	148	556	142	30	2	24	88	76	88	5.5	87	139	7	4	.64	.255	.363	.446	.809
McGuire, Reese	Tor	25	71	204	47	9	1	6	22	23	22	3.7	19	48	2	1	.67	.230	.302	.373	.675
McKinney, Billy	Tor	25	63	143	33	7	2	6	17	18	19	4.4	14	40	0	0	.00	.231	.304	.434	.737
McMahon, Ryan	Col	25	140	476	117	25	2	22	60	74	67	4.9	49	154	4	1	.80	.246	.319	.445	.764
McNeil, Jeff	NYM	28	141	537	162	34	4	22	85	76	94	6.5	40	81	6	3	.67	.302	.370	.503	.873
Meadows, Austin	TB	25	138	494	130	31	5	25	73	74	79	5.6	44	115	10	4	.71	.263	.330	.498	.828
Mejia, Francisco	SD	24	79	259	66	14	2	9	30	31	33	4.5	16	62	1	0	1.00	.255	.311	.429	.739
Mercado, Oscar	Cle	25	139	515	135	27	3	15	77	55	69	4.6	41	122	22	6	.79	.262	.325	.414	.739
Mercer, Jordy	Det	33	125	449	117	26	2	11	50	47	56	4.4	35	92	1	1	.50	.261	.321	.401	.722
Merrifield, Whit	KC	31	160	646	183	41	5	13	88	63	91	5.0	45	121	21	8	.72	.283	.335	.423	.757
Miller, Brad	Phi	30	87	214	49	10	2	11	28	30	30	4.6	25	69	2	1	.67	.229	.313	.449	.761
Molina, Yadier	StL	37	116	429	116	23	1	11	46	56	54	4.5	26	69	5	2	.71	.270	.320	.406	.725
Moncada, Yoan	CWS	25	151	540	139	27	5	23	80	73	80	5.2	56	179	10	4	.71	.257	.331	.454	.784
Mondesi, Adalberto	KC	24	114	425	106	19	8	13	56	56	55	4.4	22	137	37	5	.88	.249	.288	.424	.711
Moore, Dylan	Sea	27	62	154	32	7	1	4	17	16	14	3.0	14	46	5	3	.63	.208	.291	.344	.635
Moran, Colin	Pit	27	139	461	124	25	1	14	49	66	63	4.8	38	113	0	0	.00	.269	.329	.419	.747
Moreland, Mitch	Bos	34	117	368	89	21	1	16	49	59	50	4.7	38	95	1	0	1.00	.242	.318	.435	.753
Mountcastle, Ryan	Bal	23	135	541	144	29	3	25	72	77	76	5.0	24	162	2	0	1.00	.266	.302	.470	.772
Moustakas, Mike	Mil	31	145	547	140	30	1	32	71	83	85	5.4	48	103	3	1	.75	.256	.323	.490	.813
Mullins II, Cedric	Bal	25	75	214	51	10	2	6	32	20	26	4.1	18	49	8	1	.89	.238	.303	.388	.691
Muncy, Max	LAD	29	145	499	121	22	1	30	81	79	83	5.7	83	154	3	1	.75	.242	.357	.471	.828
Munoz, Yairo	StL	25	61	129	33	6	1	3	15	15	15	3.9	8	31	4	2	.67	.256	.304	.388	.692
Murphy, Daniel	Col	35	130	447	135	32	2	16	66	73	77	6.4	34	69	2	1	.67	.302	.355	.490	.845
Murphy, Sean	Oak	25	104	302	70	19	1	13	44	41	39	4.4	29	85	1	0	1.00	.232	.310	.430	.740
Murphy, Tom	Sea	29	71	242	54	13	1	11	24	29	28	3.8	16	94	1	0	1.00	.223	.277	.421	.698
Myers, Wil	SD	29	149	450	107	26	2	19	62	58	62	4.7	52	155	15	4	.79	.238	.319	.431	.751
Naquin, Tyler	Cle	29	83	218	59	11	2	7	27	26	30	4.8	15	50	3	2	.60	.271	.323	.436	.759
Narvaez, Omar	Sea	28	126	419	112	17	1	16	50	46	62	5.3	51	91	0	0	.00	.267	.351	.427	.778
Naylor, Josh	SD	23	88	277	75	15	1	10	36	39	42	5.3	30	57	1	1	.50	.271	.344	.440	.785
Neuse, Sheldon	Oak	25	52	114	27	5	0	3	12	14	12	3.6	9	40	0	0	.00	.237	.298	.360	.658
Newman, Kevin	Pit	26	144	518	142	26	4	9	68	52	65	4.4	34	77	14	7	.67	.274	.326	.392	.718
Nido, Tomas	NYM	26	68	189	41	9	0	4	17	22	16	2.8	10	50	0	0	.00	.217	.260	.328	.588
Nimmo, Brandon	NYM	27	117	364	85	19	3	11	54	39	49	4.5	61	118	6	3	.67	.234	.357	.393	.750
Nola, Austin	Sea	30	77	265	63	14	1	5	30	30	29	3.7	26	66	2	1	.67	.238	.315	.355	.670
Nunez, Renato	Bal	26	135	480	113	23	1	27	59	71	64	4.5	38	134	1	1	.50	.235	.301	.456	.757
Odor, Rougned	Tex	26	142	501	117	26	3	26	71	75	64	4.3	39	147	10	7	.59	.234	.298	.453	.751
O'Hearn, Ryan	KC	26	105	349	75	18	2	15	37	46	42	4.0	39	111	0	0	.00	.215	.297	.407	.704
Ohtani, Shohei	LAA	25	110	375	104	22	3	20	57	66	66	6.3	37	110	11	3	.79	.277	.345	.512	.857
Olson, Matt	Oak	26	151	539	130	29	0	35	78	89	86	5.4	66	159	1	0	1.00	.241	.334	.490	.824
O'Neill, Tyler	StL	25	65	163	38	7	1	10	24	28	23	4.8	14	63	2	0	1.00	.233	.298	.472	.770
Osuna, Jose	Pit	27	93	221	57	16	1	8	31	32	30	4.8	16	49	1	1	.50	.258	.314	.448	.762

2020 Hitter Projections

Hitter	Team	Age	G	AB	H	2B	3B	HR	R	RBI	RC	RC27	BB	SO	SB	CS	SB%	Avg	OBP	Slg	OPS
Ozuna, Marcell	StL	29	147	557	157	27	2	29	77	92	95	6.1	54	126	8	3	.73	.282	.347	.494	.841
Pache, Cristian	Atl	21	51	179	46	13	2	7	22	26	26	5.2	14	55	2	0	1.00	.257	.314	.469	.784
Palka, Daniel	CWS	28	60	167	36	7	1	8	22	23	20	3.9	18	59	1	1	.50	.216	.296	.413	.709
Panik, Joe	NYM	29	125	400	106	21	2	7	47	37	50	4.4	37	46	3	1	.75	.265	.333	.380	.713
Paredes, Isaac	Det	21	99	316	89	17	0	9	38	44	47	5.4	35	53	2	0	1.00	.282	.362	.421	.783
Parra, Gerardo	Was	33	100	239	65	13	1	6	31	30	31	4.5	15	49	5	3	.63	.272	.323	.410	.733
Pederson, Joc	LAD	28	142	412	101	21	2	29	65	62	71	5.9	55	108	2	2	.50	.245	.345	.517	.862
Pedroia, Dustin	Bos	36	45	132	37	7	0	2	17	14	17	4.6	13	19	1	1	.50	.280	.345	.379	.724
Pence, Hunter	Tex	37	108	325	85	15	2	12	46	49	44	4.7	26	80	4	2	.67	.262	.320	.431	.751
Peralta, David	Ari	32	138	530	151	32	6	19	70	74	86	5.9	45	117	2	1	.67	.285	.348	.475	.823
Peraza, Jose	Cin	26	139	448	123	19	4	7	53	39	53	4.2	21	65	13	5	.72	.275	.317	.382	.699
Perez, Hernan	Mil	29	90	240	59	12	1	7	26	24	27	3.8	12	57	7	2	.78	.246	.282	.392	.673
Perez, Roberto	Cle	31	117	398	85	17	1	17	45	58	46	3.9	49	134	0	0	.00	.214	.304	.389	.694
Perez, Salvador	KC	30	120	461	122	26	1	22	49	67	63	4.8	17	93	1	0	1.00	.265	.301	.469	.770
Pham, Tommy	TB	32	139	515	138	25	4	18	84	65	82	5.6	71	132	18	5	.78	.268	.363	.437	.800
Phegley, Josh	Oak	32	89	243	56	14	1	8	29	36	26	3.7	15	55	0	0	.00	.230	.289	.395	.684
Phillips, Brett	KC	26	45	137	26	4	2	4	17	14	14	3.2	18	58	4	0	1.00	.190	.288	.336	.624
Pillar, Kevin	SF	31	149	530	142	34	2	15	65	59	67	4.4	22	87	11	4	.73	.268	.305	.425	.729
Pina, Manny	Mil	33	81	260	63	14	1	9	28	32	32	4.2	20	65	1	0	1.00	.242	.306	.408	.714
Pinder, Chad	Oak	28	108	284	71	16	1	11	36	35	36	4.4	18	81	0	0	.00	.250	.306	.430	.736
Piscotty, Stephen	Oak	29	120	398	103	25	1	14	51	52	55	4.9	37	91	2	1	.67	.259	.331	.432	.763
Plawecki, Kevin	Cle	29	61	173	41	9	0	4	18	20	18	3.6	14	37	0	0	.00	.237	.309	.358	.667
Polanco, Gregory	Pit	28	123	394	96	25	3	14	56	53	54	4.7	42	102	9	3	.75	.244	.320	.429	.749
Polanco, Jorge	Min	26	149	581	161	35	5	19	78	76	88	5.4	52	110	6	4	.60	.277	.340	.453	.792
Pollock, A.J.	LAD	32	110	407	110	25	3	18	62	52	64	5.5	32	90	8	2	.80	.270	.333	.479	.812
Posey, Buster	SF	33	111	410	118	24	1	10	50	53	62	5.5	42	64	1	0	1.00	.288	.360	.424	.784
Profar, Jurickson	Oak	27	142	479	119	29	3	19	64	63	69	5.0	52	82	8	1	.89	.248	.333	.441	.774
Puello, Cesar	Mia	29	47	95	22	4	0	2	11	10	10	3.5	9	29	1	0	1.00	.232	.330	.337	.667
Puig, Yasiel	Cle	29	150	534	142	29	3	24	76	79	82	5.4	51	122	15	6	.71	.266	.337	.466	.803
Pujols, Albert	LAA	40	119	380	97	15	0	16	41	59	50	4.6	29	56	2	0	1.00	.255	.311	.421	.732
Quinn, Roman	Phi	27	57	120	28	4	2	2	17	10	13	3.7	11	37	7	1	.88	.233	.303	.350	.653
Ramirez, Harold	Mia	25	127	404	112	22	2	9	46	48	52	4.6	22	93	4	2	.67	.277	.326	.408	.734
Ramirez, Jose	Cle	27	150	572	160	42	4	27	91	87	106	6.6	68	83	25	6	.81	.280	.360	.509	.869
Ramos, Wilson	NYM	32	129	459	121	20	0	15	46	63	59	4.6	36	79	1	0	1.00	.264	.320	.405	.725
Realmuto, J.T.	Phi	29	141	537	146	34	3	21	80	75	80	5.3	39	119	7	2	.78	.272	.328	.464	.792
Reddick, Josh	Hou	33	136	448	122	21	3	13	59	56	62	4.9	39	68	4	2	.67	.272	.331	.420	.750
Rendon, Anthony	Was	30	151	566	173	44	3	29	100	104	120	7.9	74	96	5	2	.71	.306	.394	.548	.942
Renfroe, Hunter	SD	28	134	440	102	23	1	27	56	65	60	4.6	34	140	3	1	.75	.232	.291	.473	.764
Rengifo, Luis	LAA	23	108	247	60	11	3	6	34	26	30	4.2	28	60	3	2	.60	.243	.327	.385	.712
Reyes, Franmil	Cle	24	150	500	126	23	1	34	73	86	81	5.6	51	159	0	0	.00	.252	.322	.506	.828
Reyes, Pablo	Pit	26	68	155	38	8	1	6	20	19	20	4.4	14	38	3	2	.60	.245	.312	.426	.738
Reyes, Victor	Det	25	133	424	119	23	4	9	55	50	56	4.7	20	94	12	3	.80	.281	.315	.417	.732
Reynolds, Bryan	Pit	25	147	528	149	33	4	20	83	76	87	6.0	56	139	5	3	.63	.282	.358	.473	.831
Rickard, Joey	SF	29	58	144	36	9	1	3	19	14	18	4.2	14	36	2	1	.67	.250	.325	.389	.714
Riddle, J.T.	Mia	28	75	186	45	9	1	5	21	21	20	3.6	10	45	1	1	.50	.242	.284	.382	.666
Riley, Austin	Atl	23	129	448	116	25	2	33	68	84	77	6.0	36	156	0	0	.00	.259	.322	.545	.867
Rizzo, Anthony	ChC	30	155	574	165	35	3	28	91	102	108	6.8	79	98	5	3	.63	.287	.396	.505	.901
Robert, Luis	CWS	22	138	481	124	26	7	26	87	73	75	5.4	26	145	19	0	1.00	.258	.308	.503	.811
Robertson, Daniel	TB	26	82	207	48	9	1	4	24	20	22	3.6	26	58	1	1	.50	.232	.335	.343	.678
Robles, Victor	Was	23	155	548	143	34	4	18	84	66	75	4.7	40	133	24	8	.75	.261	.337	.436	.773
Rodgers, Brendan	Col	23	66	208	51	10	1	7	24	26	25	4.1	14	58	1	0	1.00	.245	.305	.404	.709
Rodriguez, Ronny	Det	28	92	282	68	13	2	12	32	36	33	3.9	12	77	4	2	.67	.241	.275	.429	.704
Rogers, Jake	Det	25	84	245	48	9	1	12	34	36	27	3.5	29	99	1	0	1.00	.196	.294	.388	.682
Rojas, Josh	Ari	26	105	366	99	25	4	14	57	54	63	6.0	46	87	15	3	.83	.270	.357	.475	.832
Rojas, Miguel	Mia	31	142	488	129	24	1	6	52	46	53	3.8	32	67	7	5	.58	.264	.317	.355	.672
Romine, Austin	NYY	31	75	230	55	11	0	6	25	34	23	3.4	13	55	1	1	.50	.239	.283	.365	.648
Rosario, Amed	NYM	24	147	556	152	27	7	12	70	62	71	4.5	30	118	18	8	.69	.273	.315	.412	.727
Rosario, Eddie	Min	28	149	582	161	32	3	29	85	90	88	5.4	28	107	5	3	.63	.277	.311	.491	.802
Ruiz, Keibert	LAD	21	45	140	38	5	0	3	15	15	17	4.3	11	15	0	0	.00	.271	.333	.371	.705
Ruiz, Rio	Bal	26	99	312	73	15	1	9	34	40	35	3.9	31	79	0	0	.00	.234	.305	.375	.680
Russell, Addison	ChC	26	121	382	91	20	2	15	51	53	49	4.4	37	102	3	1	.75	.238	.315	.419	.734
Sanchez, Gary	NYY	27	117	432	103	20	0	31	63	76	67	5.3	43	127	1	0	1.00	.238	.317	.500	.817
Sanchez, Jesus	Mia	22	125	425	104	19	1	15	49	62	52	4.2	36	122	3	0	1.00	.245	.308	.400	.708
Sanchez, Yolmer	CWS	28	140	467	112	22	4	5	52	44	46	3.3	36	111	6	4	.60	.240	.301	.336	.637
Sandoval, Pablo	SF	33	61	165	40	9	0	5	19	20	19	3.9	11	37	0	0	.00	.242	.294	.388	.682
Sano, Miguel	Min	27	112	388	89	19	1	28	60	71	63	5.5	54	162	0	0	.00	.229	.327	.500	.827
Santana, Carlos	Cle	34	153	537	135	29	2	26	84	83	90	5.8	97	102	3	1	.75	.251	.369	.458	.827
Santana, Danny	Tex	29	121	430	112	24	5	18	66	57	60	4.8	23	131	14	5	.74	.260	.304	.465	.769
Santana, Domingo	Sea	27	113	344	83	17	1	14	45	48	47	4.6	43	132	5	2	.71	.241	.331	.419	.749
Santander, Anthony	Bal	25	113	370	92	21	2	17	44	52	48	4.5	20	86	2	1	.67	.249	.293	.454	.747
Schoop, Jonathan	Min	28	137	488	124	27	4	23	64	76	64	4.5	23	126	1	1	.50	.254	.299	.455	.754
Schwarber, Kyle	ChC	27	150	515	125	24	2	34	80	85	87	5.8	78	162	2	2	.50	.243	.348	.495	.843
Seager, Corey	LAD	26	141	530	150	39	2	22	83	80	90	6.1	51	112	2	1	.67	.283	.352	.489	.840
Seager, Kyle	Sea	32	132	465	114	26	1	21	58	68	63	4.7	45	101	2	2	.50	.245	.318	.441	.759
Segura, Jean	Phi	30	149	604	173	34	4	12	86	60	81	4.9	33	85	13	5	.72	.286	.331	.416	.746
Semien, Marcus	Oak	29	154	615	164	36	4	24	93	78	96	5.5	70	118	9	4	.69	.267	.344	.455	.799
Senzel, Nick	Cin	25	115	399	105	22	3	14	58	47	57	4.9	35	113	13	5	.72	.263	.327	.439	.766
Severino, Pedro	Bal	26	82	251	58	10	0	9	24	29	27	3.7	20	59	2	1	.67	.231	.296	.378	.674
Shaw, Travis	Mil	30	103	294	67	15	1	14	38	41	39	4.5	36	85	2	1	.67	.228	.318	.429	.747
Sierra, Magneuris	Mia	24	111	415	103	16	5	4	48	24	42	3.4	21	95	16	3	.84	.248	.288	.340	.627
Simmons, Andrelton	LAA	30	149	563	156	29	2	10	65	62	71	4.5	38	57	12	4	.75	.277	.327	.389	.716

2020 Hitter Projections

Hitter	Team	Age	G	AB	H	2B	3B	HR	R	RBI	RC	RC27	BB	SO	SB	CS	SB%	Avg	OBP	Slg	OPS
Sisco, Chance	Bal	25	94	270	63	13	0	11	37	36	34	4.2	29	93	0	0	.00	.233	.330	.404	.734
Slater, Austin	SF	27	100	313	80	18	1	10	39	41	44	4.8	36	100	4	1	.80	.256	.344	.415	.759
Smith Jr., Dwight	Bal	27	74	183	44	9	1	6	22	23	22	4.1	16	42	2	1	.67	.240	.308	.399	.707
Smith, Dominic	NYM	25	77	171	41	9	0	6	21	21	20	4.0	14	45	1	1	.50	.240	.301	.398	.699
Smith, Kevan	LAA	32	97	338	84	16	1	7	33	37	37	3.8	23	65	2	0	1.00	.249	.308	.364	.672
Smith, Mallex	Sea	27	123	391	98	16	6	4	53	30	45	3.9	35	98	31	8	.79	.251	.322	.353	.675
Smith, Will	LAD	25	120	424	97	20	1	30	62	81	66	5.2	51	138	3	0	1.00	.229	.323	.493	.816
Smoak, Justin	Tor	33	130	424	102	22	0	23	56	65	66	5.3	66	116	0	0	.00	.241	.348	.455	.803
Sogard, Eric	TB	33	97	258	63	12	1	5	33	23	30	3.9	28	46	4	1	.80	.244	.323	.357	.680
Solak, Nick	Tex	25	139	496	130	20	2	27	77	74	78	5.5	51	143	7	2	.78	.262	.343	.474	.817
Solano, Donovan	SF	32	115	294	78	16	1	4	29	31	29	3.9	15	59	1	1	.50	.265	.305	.367	.673
Soler, Jorge	KC	28	154	557	139	31	1	37	77	98	95	5.9	71	175	3	1	.75	.250	.343	.508	.851
Soto, Juan	Was	21	150	537	153	35	3	36	105	115	124	8.4	109	127	11	1	.92	.285	.407	.562	.970
Souza Jr., Steven	Ari	31	78	259	63	13	2	11	35	35	37	4.9	32	86	6	2	.75	.243	.333	.436	.770
Spangenberg, Cory	Mil	29	57	159	38	7	2	3	19	15	17	3.6	12	53	3	1	.75	.239	.297	.365	.661
Springer, George	Hou	30	143	562	152	28	2	35	104	91	102	6.4	74	136	6	4	.60	.270	.363	.514	.878
Stallings, Jacob	Pit	30	79	248	62	15	0	6	31	29	28	3.9	16	57	0	0	.00	.250	.306	.383	.689
Stanton, Giancarlo	NYY	30	140	524	132	26	1	37	89	99	92	6.1	70	179	2	1	.67	.252	.346	.517	.863
Starling, Bubba	KC	27	105	307	67	13	1	6	33	26	27	2.9	19	93	4	1	.80	.218	.268	.326	.594
Stassi, Max	LAA	29	63	134	26	5	0	4	15	13	11	2.7	12	47	0	0	.00	.194	.270	.321	.591
Stewart, Christin	Det	26	130	459	107	22	2	19	53	62	60	4.4	53	138	1	1	.50	.233	.322	.420	.742
Stewart, D.J.	Bal	26	94	316	75	17	1	14	45	47	44	4.7	39	84	5	2	.71	.237	.332	.430	.763
Story, Trevor	Col	27	154	590	161	39	5	37	91	95	108	6.5	56	184	18	6	.75	.273	.342	.544	.886
Straw, Myles	Hou	25	56	133	35	4	1	0	21	10	15	4.0	16	31	8	1	.89	.263	.347	.308	.655
Suarez, Eugenio	Cin	28	157	575	147	27	2	36	83	94	96	5.8	69	174	3	2	.60	.256	.346	.497	.843
Suzuki, Kurt	Was	36	85	300	80	17	0	12	35	49	42	4.9	20	41	0	0	.00	.267	.329	.443	.773
Swanson, Dansby	Atl	26	143	514	130	27	3	16	69	66	69	4.6	55	131	9	4	.69	.253	.330	.411	.740
Tapia, Raimel	Col	26	85	191	50	11	2	4	24	19	23	4.3	10	45	4	1	.80	.262	.302	.403	.705
Tatis Jr., Fernando	SD	21	152	565	154	23	8	37	106	88	102	6.3	53	191	23	8	.74	.273	.343	.538	.882
Tauchman, Mike	NYY	29	82	206	48	10	2	5	26	23	24	3.8	22	50	4	2	.67	.233	.310	.374	.684
Taylor, Chris	LAD	29	119	398	103	26	4	11	58	46	56	4.9	40	120	8	3	.73	.259	.333	.427	.760
Taylor, Michael A.	Was	29	87	200	45	11	1	6	26	22	22	3.7	18	75	8	2	.80	.225	.292	.380	.672
Tellez, Rowdy	Tor	25	117	309	73	18	0	15	36	44	41	4.5	29	89	1	1	.50	.236	.310	.440	.750
Thaiss, Matt	LAA	25	66	175	40	9	1	7	22	23	22	4.2	21	49	1	1	.50	.229	.315	.411	.726
Thames, Eric	Mil	33	137	410	97	22	3	26	68	59	66	5.5	55	147	3	1	.75	.237	.338	.495	.833
Thomas, Lane	StL	24	67	179	41	8	2	7	23	28	22	4.2	18	64	4	1	.80	.229	.310	.413	.723
Tilson, Charlie	CWS	27	49	132	31	5	1	1	14	11	12	3.0	9	30	2	1	.67	.235	.289	.311	.599
Toro, Abraham	Hou	23	130	451	127	32	5	16	70	76	78	6.2	54	110	3	1	.75	.282	.368	.481	.850
Torres, Gleyber	NYY	23	144	521	148	26	2	34	80	96	97	6.7	52	128	6	3	.67	.284	.354	.537	.891
Travis, Devon	Tor	29	48	153	40	8	1	4	19	18	18	4.2	8	29	2	1	.67	.261	.302	.405	.708
Travis, Sam	Bos	26	57	161	38	8	0	4	19	18	18	3.8	15	46	2	0	1.00	.236	.305	.360	.665
Trevino, Jose	Tex	27	58	175	39	8	0	3	16	18	14	2.7	8	37	1	1	.50	.223	.257	.320	.577
Trout, Mike	LAA	28	144	521	154	31	4	43	111	101	138	9.7	116	135	15	3	.83	.296	.435	.618	1.053
Trumbo, Mark	Bal	34	73	239	58	11	0	12	30	33	31	4.5	19	68	0	0	.00	.243	.301	.439	.740
Tucker, Cole	Pit	23	56	179	42	8	2	4	24	16	20	3.8	18	49	4	1	.80	.235	.312	.369	.680
Tucker, Kyle	Hou	23	142	492	122	28	4	30	78	85	80	5.6	49	140	19	1	.95	.248	.324	.496	.820
Turner, Justin	LAD	35	130	474	139	30	1	23	74	70	87	6.7	51	85	2	1	.67	.293	.378	.506	.885
Turner, Trea	Was	27	144	591	167	33	6	20	97	65	97	5.9	52	129	37	6	.86	.283	.345	.460	.805
Upton, Justin	LAA	32	145	501	120	25	1	27	76	83	74	5.0	62	168	5	2	.71	.240	.329	.455	.784
Urias, Luis	SD	23	104	360	89	18	3	11	50	37	48	4.6	43	92	3	1	.75	.247	.342	.406	.748
Urshela, Giovanny	NYY	28	120	428	110	23	1	13	51	52	51	4.2	24	83	1	1	.50	.257	.303	.407	.709
VanMeter, Josh	Cin	25	95	297	75	18	2	13	37	39	45	5.2	32	77	8	2	.80	.253	.329	.458	.787
Vargas, Ildemaro	Ari	28	83	206	54	10	1	3	23	18	23	3.9	11	22	2	0	1.00	.262	.303	.364	.667
Varsho, Daulton	Ari	23	115	418	101	20	2	18	87	64	58	4.7	41	84	13	0	1.00	.242	.320	.428	.748
Vazquez, Christian	Bos	29	132	471	124	26	1	14	57	56	60	4.5	32	97	4	1	.80	.263	.314	.412	.726
Verdugo, Alex	LAD	24	106	350	98	20	1	10	39	40	50	5.2	30	54	4	2	.67	.280	.340	.429	.769
Villar, Jonathan	Bal	29	151	540	141	25	3	19	78	61	77	4.9	53	155	31	8	.79	.261	.331	.424	.755
Viloria, Meibrys	KC	23	68	224	48	11	0	1	18	31	18	2.6	23	75	1	1	.50	.214	.290	.277	.567
Vogelbach, Daniel	Sea	27	136	485	111	22	1	26	65	78	74	5.1	87	142	0	0	.00	.229	.348	.439	.788
Vogt, Stephen	SF	35	78	198	47	12	1	7	22	26	24	4.2	18	46	1	1	.50	.237	.304	.414	.718
Voit, Luke	NYY	29	115	391	103	20	2	18	57	57	63	5.7	51	117	0	0	.00	.263	.359	.463	.821
Votto, Joey	Cin	36	146	506	143	30	2	18	79	65	92	6.6	95	113	4	1	.80	.283	.402	.457	.858
Walker, Christian	Ari	29	144	504	120	25	2	24	67	69	68	4.6	49	154	5	2	.71	.238	.313	.438	.752
Walker, Neil	Mia	34	102	280	70	13	1	8	36	33	36	4.4	32	64	1	0	1.00	.250	.333	.389	.723
Walsh, Jared	LAA	26	88	212	49	12	0	13	30	32	31	4.9	23	84	0	0	.00	.231	.318	.472	.790
Waters, Drew	Atl	21	49	169	38	12	1	3	25	18	17	3.4	12	64	3	0	1.00	.225	.280	.361	.641
Wendle, Joey	TB	30	111	342	86	20	3	5	42	34	37	3.7	19	75	8	3	.73	.251	.304	.371	.676
White, Evan	Sea	24	110	407	109	16	1	28	69	70	67	5.9	30	126	1	0	1.00	.268	.324	.518	.843
White, Tyler	LAD	29	69	159	40	8	0	6	20	23	22	4.8	20	43	0	0	.00	.252	.343	.415	.758
Wieters, Matt	StL	34	72	227	52	10	0	8	22	29	25	3.7	20	55	1	1	.50	.229	.297	.379	.676
Wilkerson, Stevie	Bal	28	70	153	35	7	1	5	19	17	16	3.5	10	47	2	1	.67	.229	.289	.386	.675
Williams, Nick	Phi	26	74	160	38	7	1	6	20	18	18	3.8	9	52	1	1	.50	.238	.291	.406	.697
Williamson, Mac	Sea	29	46	91	20	4	0	4	12	13	10	3.8	8	30	1	0	1.00	.220	.297	.396	.693
Winker, Jesse	Cin	26	120	398	109	22	1	13	51	49	61	5.5	51	74	0	0	.00	.274	.365	.432	.797
Wolters, Tony	Col	28	100	266	65	13	2	2	29	27	28	3.6	29	57	1	1	.50	.244	.330	.331	.661
Wong, Kolten	StL	29	145	487	131	26	4	11	64	56	67	4.8	46	86	16	4	.80	.269	.349	.407	.756
Yastrzemski, Mike	SF	29	126	434	103	24	4	18	62	56	57	4.5	42	132	3	2	.60	.237	.312	.435	.747
Yelich, Christian	Mil	28	149	576	171	36	4	35	102	98	125	8.0	80	139	24	4	.86	.297	.389	.556	.945
Zimmer, Bradley	Cle	27	54	178	38	8	1	5	23	19	19	3.4	18	71	6	1	.86	.213	.300	.354	.654

587

2020 Hitter Projections

PLAYER			BATTING												BASERUNNING			AVERAGES			
Hitter	Team	Age	G	AB	H	2B	3B	HR	R	RBI	RC	RC27	BB	SO	SB	CS	SB%	Avg	OBP	Slg	OPS
Zimmerman, Ryan	Was	35	70	224	59	14	1	10	30	37	34	5.4	20	51	0	0	.00	.263	.327	.469	.795
Zobrist, Ben	ChC	39	111	359	94	19	2	8	53	41	49	4.8	50	57	1	1	.50	.262	.355	.393	.748
Zunino, Mike	TB	29	92	250	51	11	0	12	28	34	26	3.4	20	93	0	0	.00	.204	.276	.392	.668

Introduction to the Pitcher's Projections

Bill James

My first comment about the Pitcher Projections is that I personally had nothing to do with creating them. I don't mean this in the sense of "I'm not taking responsibility for these things," because actually, I'd be happy to take responsibility for them; it seems to me that they are pretty good. I just don't want to take credit for somebody else's work.

Pitchers used to be evaluated based on their season's work in a highly aggregated form. If you think of small units of performance, like pitches and at bats, that is the un-aggregated end of the spectrum, and if you look at end results like wins, losses and runs, things which rely on many of the smallest units being put together, that would be the aggregated end. Pitchers used to pitch 250, 300 innings a year sometimes. In the modern world there are lots of innings being diverted to guys who just pitch 50 innings a year, and pitchers are evaluated now by components. We measure the speed of every pitch; we measure the break. We understand, now, that wins and losses and runs allowed are end products and involve a lot of luck and input from the teammates, so we don't pay as much attention to them.

Roundabout way of 'splaining it, but that's why I'm not involved in the process. When I was young, to predict what pitchers would do, you had to try to predict wins, losses and ERA. That was pretty much impossible, frankly, so I refused to have anything to do with it. John Dewan started the process when I wouldn't, and, because he started it, he's always been in charge of the process. It's gotten to be dramatically more accurate, over the years, so. . .here we are.

The pitcher projections will be published at the end of this article, and you can study them at your leisure or, if you are reading this book for your college class, you can study them when you have to get ready for the test. What we do here in the intro is to review last season's projections.

In 2019 there were 418 pitchers for whom we published a projection in last year's handbook, and who pitched in the majors in 2019. Of those 418 projections, there were 199 that I would say were on target, 158 which were too optimistic—that is, the pitcher did not pitch as much or as well as we suggested that he would—and 61 which were too pessimistic; that is, the pitcher did better than we thought. The reason that the over/underachieved ratio is imbalanced is that a substantial number of pitchers get hurt every year, and, when a pitcher gets hurt, he has a disappointing season probably 99% of the time. There were a handful of major league pitchers last year who had injuries but had good seasons anyway. Mike Clevinger had a couple of stints on the Injured List with a bad back and a sprained ankle, but he had a good year anyway.

Eight pitchers who did about what we expected them to do would be Jared Hughes (Cincinnati-Philadelphia), Roberto Osuna (Houston), Brad Keller (Royals), Madison Bumgarner (you probably know who Madison Bumgarner pitches for), Clayton Kershaw (uh. . .), Jon Gray (Rockies), Brad Hand (Cleveland) and Eric Lauer (San Diego):

Jared Hughes

Act/Proj	G	GS	IP	H	HR	BB	SO	W	L	Sv	ERA
Actual	72	0	71.3	57	13	27	54	5	5	1	4.04
Projected	69	0	74.0	65	6	25	54	4	4	0	3.88

Roberto Osuna

Act/Proj	G	GS	IP	H	HR	BB	SO	W	L	Sv	ERA
Actual	66	0	65.0	45	8	12	73	4	3	38	2.63
Projected	69	0	69.0	55	6	12	75	5	3	36	2.97

Brad Keller

Act/Proj	G	GS	IP	H	HR	BB	SO	W	L	Sv	ERA
Actual	28	28	165.3	154	15	70	122	7	14	0	4.19
Projected	29	29	166.0	180	11	65	123	7	11	0	4.28

Madison Bumgarner

Act/Proj	G	GS	IP	H	HR	BB	SO	W	L	Sv	ERA
Actual	34	34	207.7	191	30	43	203	9	9	0	3.90
Projected	31	31	197.0	186	23	52	181	11	11	0	3.74

Clayton Kershaw

Act/Proj	G	GS	IP	H	HR	BB	SO	W	L	Sv	ERA
Actual	29	28	178.3	145	28	41	189	16	5	0	3.03
Projected	28	28	188.0	159	20	33	192	14	7	0	3.14

Jon Gray

Act/Proj	G	GS	IP	H	HR	BB	SO	W	L	Sv	ERA
Actual	26	25	150.0	147	19	56	150	11	8	0	3.84
Projected	30	30	174.0	181	22	56	181	11	9	0	4.04

Brad Hand

Act/Proj	G	GS	IP	H	HR	BB	SO	W	L	Sv	ERA
Actual	60	0	57.3	53	6	18	84	6	4	34	3.30
Projected	71	0	72.0	59	9	25	91	5	3	31	3.47

Eric Lauer

Act/Proj	G	GS	IP	H	HR	BB	SO	W	L	Sv	ERA
Actual	30	29	149.7	158	20	51	138	8	10	0	4.45
Projected	27	27	141.0	152	18	57	127	6	10	0	4.50

If a pitcher has more value than our projections suggested, that would mean either that he pitched better than expected or that he pitched more than expected, or some combination of the two. To get to the top level of the over-achievers category, it's almost always a combination. Only one pitcher surpassed expectations by a wide enough margin to make the top of the category with level playing time. Dakota Hudson (Cardinals) switched from middle relief to a starting role, led the National League in walks, but had a great year:

Dakota Hudson

Act/Proj	G	GS	IP	H	HR	BB	SO	W	L	Sv	ERA
Actual	33	32	174.7	160	22	86	136	16	7	1	3.35
Projected	60	0	65.0	63	2	26	47	4	3	0	3.95

He's the only one of the top over-achievers who has that story. Liam Hendriks, Brandon Workman, Daniel Hudson and Emilio Pagan moved into late-inning relief roles and had seasons way above what could have been expected based on previous seasons:

Liam Hendriks

Act/Proj	G	GS	IP	H	HR	BB	SO	W	L	Sv	ERA
Actual	75	2	85.0	61	5	21	124	4	4	25	1.80
Projected	29	15	31.0	29	3	9	36	2	1	0	3.44

Brandon Workman

Act/Proj	G	GS	IP	H	HR	BB	SO	W	L	Sv	ERA
Actual	73	0	71.7	29	1	45	104	10	1	16	1.88
Projected	44	0	47.0	40	7	16	45	3	2	0	3.83

Daniel Hudson

Act/Proj	G	GS	IP	H	HR	BB	SO	W	L	Sv	ERA
Actual	69	1	73.0	56	8	27	71	9	3	8	2.47
Projected	46	0	49.0	44	6	22	48	3	2	0	4.13

Emilio Pagan

Act/Proj	G	GS	IP	H	HR	BB	SO	W	L	Sv	ERA
Actual	66	0	70.0	45	12	13	96	4	2	20	2.31
Projected	49	0	56.0	46	8	16	60	4	3	0	3.52

Ian Kennedy, a struggling starter over the previous two seasons, moved into a similar role and at least posted 30 saves:

Ian Kennedy

Act/Proj	G	GS	IP	H	HR	BB	SO	W	L	Sv	ERA
Actual	63	0	63.3	64	6	17	73	3	2	30	3.41
Projected	30	30	163.0	170	32	57	141	6	12	0	4.67

Domingo German in 2018 was 2-6 with a 5.57 ERA, so we had projected him for only 47 innings in 2019. He pitched three times that many and won a marginally incredible 18 games, although he actually had a higher ERA than we had projected:

Domingo German

Act/Proj	G	GS	IP	H	HR	BB	SO	W	L	Sv	ERA
Actual	27	24	143.0	125	30	39	153	18	4	0	4.03
Projected	13	8	47.0	43	7	17	53	3	2	0	3.85

His story is similar to that of Jordan Lyles, Mike Soroka, Hyun-Jin Ryu and Chris Bassitt, except more extreme:

Jordan Lyles

Act/Proj	G	GS	IP	H	HR	BB	SO	W	L	Sv	ERA
Actual	28	28	141.0	131	25	55	146	12	8	0	4.15
Projected	34	3	69.0	72	10	25	60	3	4	0	4.50

Mike Soroka

Act/Proj	G	GS	IP	H	HR	BB	SO	W	L	Sv	ERA
Actual	29	29	174.7	153	14	41	142	13	4	0	2.68
Projected	18	18	93.0	92	7	24	82	6	4	0	3.67

Hyun-Jin Ryu

Act/Proj	G	GS	IP	H	HR	BB	SO	W	L	Sv	ERA
Actual	29	29	182.7	160	17	24	163	14	5	0	2.32
Projected	20	20	120.0	122	19	31	116	7	6	0	4.02

Chris Bassitt

Act/Proj	G	GS	IP	H	HR	BB	SO	W	L	Sv	ERA
Actual	28	25	144.0	125	21	47	141	10	5	0	3.81
Projected	12	4	47.0	50	4	18	43	2	3	0	4.31

Homer Bailey and Lance Lynn are veteran starting pitchers who just had much better seasons than we had any reason to explain:

Homer Bailey

Act/Proj	G	GS	IP	H	HR	BB	SO	W	L	Sv	ERA
Actual	31	31	163.3	162	21	53	149	13	9	0	4.57
Projected	36	10	108.0	144	20	38	77	4	8	0	5.67

Lance Lynn

Act/Proj	G	GS	IP	H	HR	BB	SO	W	L	Sv	ERA
Actual	33	33	208.3	195	21	59	246	16	11	0	3.67
Projected	30	27	159.0	153	21	72	148	9	8	0	4.31

And one major league pitcher pitched no more than we had expected—but had 85 more strikeouts and 26 fewer walks than we had projected:

Lucas Giolito

Act/Proj	G	GS	IP	H	HR	BB	SO	W	L	Sv	ERA
Actual	29	29	176.7	131	24	57	228	14	9	0	3.41
Projected	31	31	176.0	181	24	83	143	7	13	0	4.76

Our final group of pitchers is those who did much less than we had projected. It is a very large group, 158 pitchers, the great majority of whom were either injured or pitched badly early in the season and were sent somewhere to reflect on their sins. I'll just show you the stats for three or four of them, and list the names of some others:

Kyle Freeland

Act/Proj	G	GS	IP	H	HR	BB	SO	W	L	Sv	ERA
Actual	22	22	104.3	126	25	39	79	3	11	0	6.73
Projected	33	33	214.0	221	24	77	172	13	11	0	4.25

Luis Severino

Act/Proj	G	GS	IP	H	HR	BB	SO	W	L	Sv	ERA
Actual	3	3	12.0	6	0	6	17	1	1	0	1.50
Projected	32	32	195.0	174	19	52	219	14	7	0	3.34

Tyler Anderson

Act/Proj	G	GS	IP	H	HR	BB	SO	W	L	Sv	ERA
Actual	5	5	20.7	33	8	11	23	0	3	0	11.76
Projected	29	29	161.0	167	25	53	147	9	9	0	4.28

Corey Kluber

Act/Proj	G	GS	IP	H	HR	BB	SO	W	L	Sv	ERA
Actual	7	7	35.7	44	4	15	38	2	3	0	5.80
Projected	31	31	212.0	180	24	40	224	15	8	0	3.21

Other pitchers who had intensely disappointing seasons include but are not limited to Jordan Zimmermann, Kevin Gausman, Chris Archer, Zack Godley, Dellin Betances, Taijuan Walker, Jeremy Hellickson, Felix Hernandez, Wei-Yin Chen, Jhoulys Chacin, Carlos Carrasco, Craig Kimbrel, Matt Harvey, Alex Cobb, Marco Estrada, Wade Davis, Jameson Taillon, Dennis Santana, Alex Wood, Matt Hall, and Alex Reyes.

We can't foresee injuries. Truth be told, we can't foresee anything. If I could foresee the future, I wouldn't have gone to see Yentl or that game that Tampa Bay beat the Red Sox 16-5 in 38-degree weather back in 2012.

We're not really trying to predict the future here; what we really do is (a) look at everything that the player has done in the past, (b) try to normalize that by removing from the record those things that resulted from luck or abnormalities rather than ability, (c) gently modify that standard of performance for the changes that occur with aging, (d) assemble whatever information we can find about the intentions of each team, and (e) project each player's and each pitcher's current skills, as best we can, into a role that fits on the team. We get a lot of things wrong and a few things right, but we appreciate your interest in our work.

2020 Pitcher Projections

PLAYER			HOW MUCH			WHAT HE WILL GIVE UP					THE RESULTS				
Pitcher	Team	Age	G	GS	IP	H	HR	BB	SO	HB	W	L	Pct	Sv	BR/9	ERA
Adam, Jason	Tor	28	44	0	43	34	6	20	48	4	3	2	.600	0	12.1	4.04
Adams, Chance	NYY	25	19	0	32	31	5	16	30	2	2	2	.500	0	13.8	4.78
Agrazal, Dario	Pit	25	16	16	86	102	15	18	60	7	4	6	.400	0	13.3	5.02
Akin, Keegan	Bal	25	30	30	154	149	18	79	164	4	7	10	.412	0	13.6	4.38
Albers, Matt	Mil	37	62	0	51	49	9	21	47	3	3	3	.500	0	12.9	4.59
Alcantara, Sandy	Mia	24	31	31	199	194	24	85	158	11	9	13	.409	0	13.1	4.55
Alcantara, Victor	Det	27	39	0	38	43	5	15	28	2	1	3	.250	0	14.2	4.97
Alexander, Scott	LAD	30	53	0	54	51	4	22	41	1	3	3	.500	0	12.3	4.15
Alexander, Tyler	Det	25	13	13	69	92	12	14	62	4	2	5	.286	0	14.3	5.22
Allard, Kolby	Tex	22	30	30	153	183	19	55	130	4	7	10	.412	0	14.2	4.89
Allen, Logan	Cle	23	27	27	167	169	25	67	155	11	9	10	.474	0	13.3	4.61
Almonte, Yency	Col	26	39	0	44	44	7	22	39	3	2	2	.500	0	14.1	4.91
Alvarado, Jose	TB	25	33	0	31	23	2	19	38	0	2	1	.667	5	12.2	3.62
Alvarez, Jose	Phi	31	68	0	56	58	6	18	49	1	3	3	.500	0	12.4	4.20
Alzolay, Adbert	ChC	25	10	10	52	49	8	26	60	3	3	3	.500	0	13.5	4.50
Anderson, Brett	Oak	32	28	28	161	185	19	43	89	3	8	10	.444	0	12.9	4.76
Anderson, Chase	Mil	32	29	29	151	140	28	53	129	7	8	8	.500	0	11.9	4.47
Anderson, Ian	Atl	22	12	12	64	58	8	35	77	1	4	3	.571	0	13.2	4.15
Anderson, Justin	LAA	27	55	0	55	45	7	36	65	3	3	3	.500	0	13.7	4.42
Anderson, Nick	TB	29	66	0	64	51	9	20	97	2	5	2	.714	5	10.3	3.15
Anderson, Shaun	SF	25	33	10	80	88	10	28	67	1	4	5	.444	0	13.2	4.56
Anderson, Tyler	Col	30	11	11	60	65	10	21	56	1	3	3	.500	0	13.1	4.65
Andriese, Matt	Ari	30	50	0	72	75	10	23	73	2	4	4	.500	0	12.5	4.25
Arano, Victor	Phi	25	53	0	53	44	7	16	60	1	4	2	.667	0	10.4	3.54
Archer, Chris	Pit	31	26	26	140	145	21	54	158	4	7	8	.467	0	13.1	4.37
Armstrong, Shawn	Bal	29	54	0	57	57	6	27	63	3	3	4	.429	0	13.7	4.34
Arrieta, Jake	Phi	34	28	28	162	163	22	59	133	8	8	10	.444	0	12.8	4.50
Avilan, Luis	NYM	30	59	0	40	39	4	18	42	3	2	2	.500	0	13.5	4.28
Baez, Michel	SD	24	44	0	39	35	4	19	45	4	2	2	.500	0	13.4	4.16
Baez, Pedro	LAD	32	66	0	67	51	9	24	66	3	5	3	.625	0	10.5	3.78
Bailey, Homer	Oak	34	29	29	169	198	28	57	140	6	8	11	.421	0	13.9	5.04
Banuelos, Manny	CWS	29	12	3	32	39	5	17	30	2	1	2	.333	0	16.3	5.63
Bard, Luke	LAA	29	31	2	51	59	9	20	52	4	2	3	.400	0	14.6	5.12
Barlow, Scott	KC	27	65	0	76	70	10	35	85	4	4	5	.444	0	12.9	4.21
Barnes, Jacob	KC	30	37	0	35	37	4	16	33	0	2	2	.500	0	13.6	4.63
Barnes, Matt	Bos	30	67	0	64	49	7	33	97	2	4	3	.571	0	11.8	3.40
Barraclough, Kyle	SF	30	40	0	38	31	4	24	46	2	2	2	.500	0	13.5	4.15
Barria, Jaime	LAA	23	22	17	100	108	20	29	87	4	5	6	.455	0	12.7	4.77
Bass, Anthony	Sea	32	50	0	53	52	6	17	47	1	3	3	.500	24	11.9	4.12
Bassitt, Chris	Oak	31	28	22	137	138	19	48	129	13	7	8	.467	0	13.1	4.47
Bauer, Trevor	Cin	29	30	30	191	159	23	72	228	13	11	10	.524	0	11.5	3.72
Bednar, David	SD	25	29	0	31	27	4	11	43	1	2	1	.667	0	11.3	3.55
Bedrosian, Cam	LAA	28	62	0	60	53	6	22	61	2	4	3	.571	0	11.6	3.84
Beede, Tyler	SF	27	26	25	129	136	19	61	129	8	6	9	.400	0	14.3	4.85
Beeks, Jalen	TB	26	31	4	100	102	13	40	96	5	5	6	.455	0	13.2	4.50
Berrios, Jose	Min	26	32	32	204	189	26	61	202	11	13	10	.565	0	11.5	3.97
Betances, Dellin	NYY	32	37	0	37	24	3	17	61	3	3	1	.750	0	10.7	2.87
Bettis, Chad	Col	31	26	3	49	58	8	17	32	2	2	3	.400	0	14.1	5.24
Biagini, Joe	Hou	30	49	0	54	58	8	21	46	2	3	3	.500	0	13.5	4.75
Bieber, Shane	Cle	25	32	32	209	190	25	38	237	5	14	9	.609	0	10.0	3.42
Bielak, Brandon	Hou	24	6	6	32	28	4	13	30	1	2	1	.667	0	11.8	4.13
Blach, Ty	Bal	29	10	9	44	58	6	14	28	1	2	3	.400	0	14.9	5.42
Bleier, Richard	Bal	33	57	0	62	73	5	11	32	3	3	4	.429	5	12.6	4.50
Blevins, Jerry	Atl	36	46	0	33	29	4	16	38	2	2	2	.500	0	12.8	4.12
Boshers, Buddy	Tor	32	54	0	40	39	5	17	42	2	2	2	.500	0	13.1	4.28
Bowman, Matt	Cin	29	26	0	34	31	3	15	30	1	2	2	.500	0	12.4	4.14
Boyd, Matthew	Det	29	29	29	172	167	31	51	190	8	8	11	.421	0	11.8	4.16
Brach, Brad	NYM	34	52	0	50	47	4	23	53	1	3	3	.500	0	12.8	3.99
Bradford, Chasen	Sea	30	42	0	45	51	6	12	30	2	2	3	.400	0	13.0	4.80
Bradley, Archie	Ari	27	66	0	72	64	7	31	81	3	4	4	.500	31	12.3	3.88
Brasier, Ryan	Bos	32	56	0	50	46	7	16	52	2	3	2	.600	0	11.5	4.01
Brault, Steven	Pit	28	26	23	135	139	16	70	118	8	6	9	.400	0	14.5	4.84
Brebbia, John	StL	30	59	0	63	55	8	21	72	3	4	3	.571	0	11.3	3.74
Brennan, Brandon	Sea	28	41	0	43	44	4	20	42	1	2	3	.400	0	13.6	4.30
Brewer, Colten	Bos	27	46	0	41	46	4	21	41	2	2	2	.500	0	15.1	4.83
Brice, Austin	Mia	28	27	0	31	29	4	11	30	3	1	2	.333	0	12.5	4.36
Brigham, Jeff	Mia	28	33	0	37	32	4	14	38	2	2	2	.500	6	11.7	3.97
Britton, Zack	NYY	32	66	0	64	49	3	30	55	2	4	3	.571	0	11.4	3.75
Brooks, Aaron	Bal	30	28	20	123	154	25	36	89	6	4	9	.308	0	14.3	5.49
Brown, Zack	Mil	25	9	9	46	51	6	22	40	2	2	3	.400	0	14.7	4.99
Buchholz, Clay	Tor	35	15	15	81	86	15	24	57	2	4	5	.444	0	12.4	4.84
Buchter, Ryan	Oak	33	55	0	48	39	7	22	49	2	3	3	.500	0	11.8	4.09
Buehler, Walker	LAD	25	31	31	198	162	22	50	230	7	15	7	.682	0	10.0	3.33
Bukauskas, J.B.	Ari	23	6	6	31	31	4	21	37	0	2	2	.500	0	15.1	4.79
Bumgarner, Madison	SF	30	32	32	205	195	29	50	193	9	11	12	.478	0	11.2	3.99
Bummer, Aaron	CWS	26	61	0	75	66	5	29	69	3	4	4	.500	0	11.8	3.83
Bundy, Dylan	Bal	27	28	28	168	176	33	57	167	7	7	11	.389	0	12.9	4.69
Burke, Brock	Tex	23	26	26	155	149	16	55	152	9	9	9	.500	0	12.4	4.05
Burnes, Corbin	Mil	25	31	0	33	35	5	13	38	1	2	2	.500	0	13.4	4.37

2020 Pitcher Projections

PLAYER			HOW MUCH			WHAT HE WILL GIVE UP					THE RESULTS				
Pitcher	Team	Age	G	GS	IP	H	HR	BB	SO	HB	W	L	Pct	Sv	BR/9	ERA
Buttrey, Ty	LAA	27	68	0	69	67	7	28	79	4	4	4	.500	0	12.9	3.99
Cahill, Trevor	LAA	32	38	15	118	122	20	50	102	6	6	7	.462	0	13.6	4.89
Canning, Griffin	LAA	24	15	15	80	69	9	26	86	5	5	4	.556	0	11.3	3.71
Carrasco, Carlos	Cle	33	27	25	151	141	21	35	172	5	10	7	.588	0	10.8	3.69
Cashner, Andrew	Bos	33	36	18	116	122	16	46	79	4	6	7	.462	0	13.3	4.85
Castillo, Diego	TB	26	64	10	75	56	7	26	88	4	5	3	.625	0	10.3	3.37
Castillo, Jose	SD	24	43	0	43	29	4	17	61	3	3	2	.600	0	10.3	3.12
Castillo, Luis	Cin	27	29	29	186	156	24	69	205	7	11	10	.524	0	11.2	3.77
Castro, Miguel	Bal	25	61	0	67	61	9	35	56	2	3	4	.429	0	13.2	4.57
Cease, Dylan	CWS	24	28	28	160	163	20	73	183	5	8	10	.444	0	13.6	4.36
Cessa, Luis	NYY	28	42	0	82	81	13	28	73	2	5	4	.556	0	12.2	4.34
Chacin, Jhoulys	Bos	32	27	27	143	148	21	57	120	8	8	8	.500	0	13.4	4.72
Chafin, Andrew	Ari	30	73	0	50	46	5	20	59	2	3	2	.600	0	12.2	3.83
Chapman, Aroldis	NYY	32	55	0	54	35	3	24	80	2	4	2	.667	35	10.2	2.90
Chatwood, Tyler	ChC	30	40	3	77	71	8	47	67	4	4	4	.500	0	14.3	4.68
Chavez, Jesse	Tex	36	41	6	55	61	10	15	49	2	3	3	.500	0	12.8	4.67
Chen, Wei-Yin	Mia	34	42	0	71	78	12	21	60	3	3	5	.375	0	12.9	4.69
Chirinos, Yonny	TB	26	31	23	149	143	21	34	126	4	9	8	.529	0	10.9	4.03
Cimber, Adam	Cle	29	63	0	55	53	6	15	41	4	3	3	.500	0	11.8	4.23
Cishek, Steve	ChC	34	61	0	55	43	5	23	52	6	3	3	.500	0	11.8	3.96
Cisnero, Jose	Det	31	48	0	48	48	6	26	54	3	2	3	.400	0	14.4	4.69
Civale, Aaron	Cle	25	29	29	164	162	20	41	138	5	10	8	.556	0	11.4	4.07
Clarke, Taylor	Ari	27	8	8	45	45	7	16	36	2	2	3	.400	0	12.6	4.50
Clase, Emmanuel	Tex	22	47	0	46	46	3	11	45	1	3	2	.600	0	11.3	3.63
Claudio, Alex	Mil	28	77	0	56	55	5	16	39	4	3	3	.500	0	11.9	4.16
Clevinger, Mike	Cle	29	27	27	178	145	20	63	207	3	12	8	.600	0	10.7	3.52
Clippard, Tyler	Cle	35	56	0	60	46	10	19	65	4	4	3	.571	0	10.4	3.73
Cobb, Alex	Bal	32	28	28	150	188	28	40	99	4	6	11	.353	0	13.9	5.31
Cole, A.J.	Cle	28	31	0	32	36	6	13	33	1	2	2	.500	0	14.1	4.92
Cole, Gerrit	Hou	29	32	32	209	155	27	55	285	5	17	6	.739	0	9.3	3.03
Cole, Taylor	LAA	30	42	5	52	55	6	21	54	2	3	3	.500	0	13.5	4.42
Colome, Alex	CWS	31	58	0	60	54	7	21	55	2	3	3	.500	26	11.6	4.05
Conley, Adam	Mia	30	55	0	57	63	9	25	46	3	2	4	.333	0	14.4	5.13
Coonrod, Sam	SF	27	52	0	43	41	5	23	41	4	2	3	.400	0	14.2	4.71
Corbin, Patrick	Was	30	31	31	199	191	27	66	222	4	13	9	.591	0	11.8	3.94
Cordero, Jimmy	CWS	28	51	0	63	62	6	30	55	4	3	4	.429	0	13.7	4.50
Cortes, Nestor	NYY	25	39	0	66	61	9	25	64	2	4	3	.571	0	12.0	4.19
Cotton, Jharel	Oak	28	24	6	61	57	12	22	61	1	3	3	.500	0	11.8	4.35
Covey, Dylan	CWS	28	14	8	45	52	7	18	35	1	2	3	.400	0	14.2	5.10
Crichton, Stefan	Ari	28	36	0	38	37	4	12	36	2	2	2	.500	0	12.1	3.96
Crick, Kyle	Pit	27	57	0	57	51	6	34	63	6	3	4	.429	0	14.4	4.50
Cueto, Johnny	SF	34	30	30	177	173	21	51	148	9	9	10	.474	0	11.8	4.17
Darvish, Yu	ChC	33	28	28	175	147	28	59	212	10	11	8	.579	0	11.1	3.78
Davies, Zach	Mil	27	28	28	141	147	19	45	96	4	8	8	.500	0	12.5	4.57
Davis, Wade	Col	34	44	0	37	35	5	19	39	2	2	2	.500	5	13.6	4.50
De Leon, Jose	TB	27	8	8	43	40	7	22	54	4	2	3	.400	0	13.8	4.50
De Los Santos, Enyel	Phi	24	26	26	149	148	23	58	130	8	8	9	.471	0	12.9	4.62
deGrom, Jacob	NYM	32	31	31	202	169	21	48	239	6	14	8	.636	0	9.9	3.27
DeSclafani, Anthony	Cin	30	30	30	178	177	35	50	172	4	9	11	.450	0	11.7	4.35
Detwiler, Ross	CWS	34	12	8	51	63	11	18	35	2	2	4	.333	0	14.6	5.65
Devenski, Chris	Hou	29	58	0	67	59	10	19	71	3	5	3	.625	0	10.9	3.84
Diaz, Edwin	NYM	26	60	0	53	39	7	18	87	3	4	2	.667	27	10.2	2.97
Diaz, Jairo	Col	29	60	0	68	64	6	25	72	3	5	3	.625	4	12.2	3.89
Diekman, Jake	Oak	33	74	0	58	45	4	34	74	8	3	3	.500	0	13.5	3.86
Dobnak, Randy	Min	25	10	10	53	48	4	12	44	2	4	2	.667	0	10.5	3.65
Dominguez, Seranthony	Phi	25	51	0	52	36	4	21	63	3	4	2	.667	0	10.4	3.32
Doolittle, Sean	Was	33	55	0	52	44	8	12	59	1	4	2	.667	27	9.9	3.51
Drake, Oliver	TB	33	58	0	63	54	8	23	78	1	4	3	.571	5	11.1	3.67
Duffey, Tyler	Min	29	64	0	62	61	10	18	72	2	4	3	.571	0	11.8	4.00
Duffy, Danny	KC	31	26	26	150	155	23	51	133	7	7	10	.412	0	14.3	4.53
Dugger, Robert	Mia	24	21	21	110	126	20	43	102	9	4	8	.333	0	14.6	5.20
Dunn, Justin	Sea	24	29	29	158	173	21	66	177	9	7	11	.389	0	14.1	4.59
Duplantier, Jon	Ari	25	24	4	40	34	2	24	41	3	2	2	.500	0	13.7	4.10
Edwards Jr., Carl	SD	28	47	0	45	31	4	27	54	2	3	2	.600	0	12.0	3.73
Eflin, Zach	Phi	26	32	32	179	190	27	52	145	8	9	11	.450	0	12.6	4.53
Eovaldi, Nathan	Bos	30	22	22	117	121	20	42	112	3	6	7	.462	0	12.8	4.58
Erlin, Robbie	SD	29	40	0	59	69	7	12	51	1	3	3	.500	0	12.5	4.27
Estevez, Carlos	Col	27	64	0	68	69	10	25	74	2	4	3	.571	0	12.7	4.24
Familia, Jeurys	NYM	30	64	0	70	66	4	39	75	3	4	4	.500	0	13.9	4.12
Farmer, Buck	Det	29	70	0	69	77	9	28	66	3	3	5	.375	0	14.1	4.77
Fedde, Erick	Was	27	20	10	75	89	10	28	59	2	4	4	.500	0	14.3	4.98
Feliz, Michael	Pit	27	56	0	55	53	8	26	70	2	3	3	.500	0	13.3	4.26
Ferguson, Caleb	LAD	23	49	0	50	40	6	21	63	3	3	2	.600	0	11.5	3.70
Fiers, Mike	Oak	35	30	30	167	172	31	48	122	9	8	10	.444	0	12.3	4.75
Flaherty, Jack	StL	24	33	33	209	156	26	64	244	9	15	9	.625	0	9.9	3.39
Floro, Dylan	LAD	29	42	0	40	42	5	13	34	1	2	2	.500	0	12.6	4.28
Foltynewicz, Mike	Atl	28	29	29	174	159	23	61	163	6	11	8	.579	0	11.7	4.07
Font, Wilmer	Tor	30	39	15	71	72	13	23	74	2	4	4	.500	0	12.3	4.38
Freeland, Kyle	Col	27	19	19	93	105	14	35	73	2	5	5	.500	0	13.7	4.94
Fried, Max	Atl	26	31	29	167	168	18	64	176	8	10	8	.556	0	12.9	4.18
Fry, Jace	CWS	26	67	0	55	47	5	34	68	2	3	3	.500	0	13.6	4.02

597

2020 Pitcher Projections

Pitcher	Team	Age	G	GS	IP	H	HR	BB	SO	HB	W	L	Pct	Sv	BR/9	ERA
Fry, Paul	Bal	27	66	0	53	55	5	26	56	5	2	4	.333	0	14.6	4.59
Fulmer, Carson	CWS	26	21	2	31	32	5	20	31	2	1	2	.333	0	15.7	5.38
Fulmer, Michael	Det	27	10	10	52	53	6	15	41	2	2	3	.400	0	12.1	4.27
Gallegos, Giovanny	StL	28	65	0	72	51	8	17	88	2	5	3	.625	5	8.8	3.00
Gallen, Zac	Ari	24	27	27	152	129	20	51	170	6	10	7	.588	0	11.0	3.72
Gant, John	StL	27	64	0	65	62	7	29	57	1	4	3	.571	0	12.7	4.24
Garcia, Edgar	Phi	23	32	0	38	30	7	18	45	1	2	2	.500	0	11.6	4.05
Garcia, Jarlin	Mia	27	60	0	52	51	7	19	39	2	2	4	.333	0	12.5	4.42
Garcia, Luis	LAA	33	59	0	60	61	8	29	55	4	3	4	.429	0	14.1	4.80
Garcia, Yimi	LAD	29	62	0	62	53	15	13	62	6	4	3	.571	0	10.5	4.19
Garrett, Amir	Cin	28	65	0	51	45	7	26	58	2	3	3	.500	0	12.9	4.24
Gausman, Kevin	Cin	29	38	11	91	89	14	28	91	3	5	5	.500	0	11.9	4.16
Gaviglio, Sam	Tor	30	49	6	87	91	14	23	74	3	5	5	.500	0	12.1	4.40
Gearrin, Cory	NYY	34	66	0	58	56	6	24	49	5	3	3	.500	0	13.2	4.42
German, Domingo	NYY	27	26	26	161	148	29	50	173	7	10	8	.556	0	11.5	4.08
Gibson, Kyle	Min	32	30	30	169	185	25	63	154	6	9	10	.474	0	13.5	4.71
Gilbert, Logan	Sea	23	24	24	135	121	10	51	149	11	7	8	.467	0	12.2	3.75
Giles, Ken	Tor	29	53	0	54	45	6	16	74	1	4	2	.667	31	10.3	3.23
Ginkel, Kevin	Ari	26	48	0	48	29	5	16	69	1	4	1	.800	4	8.6	2.71
Giolito, Lucas	CWS	25	30	30	195	171	27	78	213	9	10	11	.476	0	11.9	4.02
Givens, Mychal	Bal	30	59	0	63	52	8	25	76	3	4	3	.571	31	11.4	3.74
Glasnow, Tyler	TB	26	25	25	136	104	16	61	167	3	9	6	.600	0	11.1	3.59
Godley, Zack	Tor	30	26	4	74	79	10	31	64	4	4	5	.444	0	13.9	4.74
Gonsolin, Tony	LAD	26	17	9	63	51	8	26	64	3	4	3	.571	0	11.4	3.95
Gonzales, Marco	Sea	28	32	32	204	216	25	53	156	7	10	13	.435	0	12.2	4.31
Gonzalez, Chi Chi	Col	28	13	11	59	65	8	25	45	2	3	3	.500	0	14.0	4.96
Gonzalez, Gio	Mil	34	27	27	143	134	17	60	129	3	8	8	.500	0	12.4	4.24
Goody, Nick	Cle	28	47	0	46	40	10	22	57	2	2	3	.400	0	12.5	4.50
Gore, MacKenzie	SD	21	22	22	129	133	23	52	154	6	6	8	.429	0	13.3	4.54
Gossett, Daniel	Oak	27	8	8	43	43	5	15	36	1	2	3	.400	0	12.3	4.30
Gott, Trevor	SF	27	37	0	39	37	3	14	40	3	2	2	.500	8	12.5	3.88
Grace, Matt	Was	31	33	0	31	36	4	8	23	1	2	2	.500	0	13.1	4.65
Graterol, Brusdar	Min	21	50	0	50	41	4	21	50	4	3	2	.600	0	11.9	3.81
Gray, Jon	Col	28	26	26	159	165	22	55	161	5	10	8	.556	0	12.7	4.33
Gray, Sonny	Cin	30	29	29	178	149	21	71	192	7	10	9	.526	0	11.5	3.84
Green, Chad	NYY	29	52	10	74	64	9	20	98	3	5	3	.625	0	10.6	3.35
Greene, Shane	Atl	31	70	0	68	59	9	23	70	4	4	3	.571	6	11.4	3.91
Greinke, Zack	Hou	36	32	32	198	187	32	37	176	3	14	8	.636	0	10.3	3.91
Gsellman, Robert	NYM	26	57	0	62	65	6	22	54	4	3	4	.429	0	13.2	4.36
Guerra, Javier	SD	24	32	0	32	24	10	20	32	0	1	2	.333	0	12.4	5.06
Guerra, Javy	Was	34	49	0	56	58	8	20	48	1	3	3	.500	0	12.7	4.50
Guerra, Junior	Mil	35	71	0	82	73	13	35	74	3	5	5	.500	0	12.2	4.40
Guerrero, Tayron	Mia	29	41	0	37	37	5	25	36	3	1	3	.250	0	15.8	5.23
Guerrieri, Taylor	Tex	27	28	0	41	45	5	20	37	3	2	3	.400	0	14.9	5.05
Guilbeau, Taylor	Sea	27	38	0	39	39	3	15	38	3	2	2	.500	0	13.2	4.16
Gustave, Jandel	SF	27	44	0	48	45	4	21	37	2	2	3	.400	0	12.8	4.35
Hader, Josh	Mil	26	59	0	73	44	11	28	120	3	6	2	.750	34	9.2	2.86
Hall, Matt	Det	26	30	0	46	50	5	20	52	2	2	3	.400	0	14.1	4.41
Hamels, Cole	ChC	36	29	29	153	149	21	60	147	10	9	8	.529	0	12.9	4.42
Hand, Brad	Cle	30	60	0	63	49	7	21	86	5	4	3	.571	36	10.7	3.29
Happ, J.A.	NYY	37	29	29	176	171	29	54	158	6	10	9	.526	0	11.8	4.28
Hardy, Blaine	Det	33	37	10	74	74	10	20	57	1	4	5	.444	0	11.6	4.18
Harper, Ryne	Min	31	51	0	45	48	4	12	47	1	3	2	.600	0	12.2	3.93
Harris, Will	Hou	35	64	0	59	50	6	14	61	1	4	2	.667	4	9.9	3.38
Hartlieb, Geoff	Pit	26	34	0	38	42	3	18	42	1	2	2	.500	0	14.4	4.50
Harvey, Hunter	Bal	25	40	0	42	50	11	17	46	3	1	4	.200	0	15.0	5.68
Harvey, Matt	Oak	31	11	11	57	67	10	20	44	2	2	4	.333	0	14.1	5.21
Hatch, Thomas	Tor	25	7	7	34	37	6	14	30	3	2	2	.500	0	14.3	5.16
Heaney, Andrew	LAA	29	24	24	131	130	26	37	148	7	7	7	.500	0	12.0	4.26
Hearn, Taylor	Tex	25	27	27	140	124	17	67	154	7	8	8	.500	0	12.7	4.14
Helsley, Ryan	StL	25	57	0	68	58	9	31	69	1	4	3	.571	0	11.9	4.09
Hendricks, Kyle	ChC	30	28	28	173	165	20	38	144	7	11	8	.579	0	10.9	3.94
Hendriks, Liam	Oak	31	72	0	81	65	7	22	107	2	6	3	.667	27	9.9	3.03
Hernandez, Darwinzon	Bos	23	35	7	74	63	6	67	113	9	4	4	.500	0	16.9	4.69
Hernandez, Elieser	Mia	25	23	23	126	113	21	43	135	12	6	8	.429	0	12.0	4.19
Hernandez, Felix	Sea	34	17	17	85	92	15	32	69	7	3	6	.333	0	13.9	5.08
Hernandez, Jonathan	Tex	23	34	0	35	40	5	18	35	2	1	3	.250	0	15.4	5.15
Herrera, Kelvin	CWS	30	55	0	53	55	9	18	52	1	2	4	.333	5	12.6	4.50
Hess, David	Bal	26	19	6	51	57	10	19	44	1	2	4	.333	0	13.6	5.12
Hill, Rich	LAD	40	15	15	78	63	10	26	88	5	5	3	.625	0	10.8	3.69
Hill, Tim	KC	30	61	0	56	57	6	17	54	3	3	3	.500	5	12.4	4.12
Hirano, Yoshihisa	Ari	36	50	0	46	42	7	18	47	2	3	3	.500	0	12.1	4.22
Hoffman, Jeff	Col	27	17	17	82	89	14	35	81	5	4	5	.444	0	14.2	4.94
Holder, Jonathan	NYY	27	32	0	35	33	4	9	38	1	2	2	.500	0	11.1	3.69
Holland, Derek	ChC	33	50	5	63	65	11	30	57	3	3	4	.429	0	14.0	5.00
Holmes, Clay	Pit	27	35	0	52	57	4	34	50	5	2	4	.333	0	16.6	5.20
Honeywell, Brent	TB	25	31	18	103	111	12	30	116	3	6	5	.545	0	12.6	4.02
Houck, Tanner	Bos	24	25	5	42	50	4	22	40	6	2	3	.400	0	16.7	5.36
Houser, Adrian	Mil	27	27	27	151	152	19	51	148	8	9	8	.529	0	12.6	4.23
Howard, Sam	Col	27	32	0	31	32	4	13	30	2	2	2	.500	0	13.6	4.65
Howard, Spencer	Phi	23	24	24	120	82	9	40	152	7	9	4	.692	0	9.7	3.02

598

2020 Pitcher Projections

Pitcher	Team	Age	G	GS	IP	H	HR	BB	SO	HB	W	L	Pct	Sv	BR/9	ERA
Hudson, Dakota	StL	25	31	31	178	171	14	82	135	10	10	10	.500	0	13.3	4.41
Hudson, Daniel	Was	33	60	0	63	57	8	26	60	5	4	3	.571	7	12.6	4.24
Hughes, Jared	Phi	34	75	0	78	71	10	28	57	4	4	4	.500	0	11.9	4.33
Hultzen, Danny	ChC	30	32	0	30	19	0	18	43	6	2	1	.667	0	12.9	3.32
Hunter, Tommy	Phi	33	58	0	58	54	6	13	51	2	4	3	.571	0	10.7	3.76
Iglesias, Raisel	Cin	30	67	0	65	55	9	22	78	2	4	3	.571	36	10.9	3.64
Irvin, Cole	Phi	26	26	26	130	144	19	31	97	4	7	8	.467	0	12.4	4.54
Jackson, Edwin	Det	36	13	7	50	62	10	23	37	2	1	4	.200	0	15.7	5.94
Jackson, Jay	Mil	32	42	0	42	31	5	17	56	2	3	2	.600	0	10.7	3.37
Jackson, Luke	Atl	28	67	0	70	64	8	32	90	3	5	3	.625	6	12.7	3.88
James, Josh	Hou	27	57	0	50	38	5	24	71	3	4	2	.667	4	11.7	3.45
Jansen, Kenley	LAD	32	58	0	62	48	8	14	77	3	5	2	.714	32	9.4	3.17
Jewell, Jake	LAA	27	23	0	34	39	5	14	31	3	2	2	.500	0	14.8	5.16
Jimenez, Joe	Det	25	59	0	56	52	7	22	73	3	3	3	.500	30	12.4	3.88
Johnson, Brian	Bos	29	30	10	59	69	10	28	50	1	3	4	.429	0	14.9	5.34
Johnson, DJ	Col	30	33	0	32	35	3	14	38	2	2	2	.500	0	14.3	4.36
Junis, Jakob	KC	27	30	30	176	192	31	51	163	12	8	12	.400	0	13.0	4.71
Jurado, Ariel	Tex	24	28	15	115	144	16	29	76	4	5	8	.385	0	13.9	5.05
Kahnle, Tommy	NYY	30	66	0	57	47	6	23	78	2	4	2	.667	0	11.4	3.42
Karinchak, James	Cle	24	53	0	53	31	4	34	111	0	4	2	.667	0	11.0	2.50
Kay, Anthony	Tor	25	27	27	148	147	17	71	148	11	8	9	.471	0	13.9	4.53
Kela, Keone	Pit	27	54	0	53	41	7	20	66	2	3	3	.500	29	10.7	3.61
Keller, Brad	KC	24	29	29	170	176	14	69	128	7	8	11	.421	0	13.3	4.45
Keller, Kyle	Mia	27	42	0	53	44	8	26	68	2	3	3	.500	0	12.2	3.95
Keller, Mitch	Pit	24	27	27	141	143	14	53	162	6	8	8	.500	0	12.9	3.99
Kelley, Shawn	Tex	36	50	0	45	48	12	11	42	1	2	3	.400	0	12.0	4.80
Kelly, Joe	LAD	32	52	0	48	41	4	22	53	3	3	2	.600	0	12.4	3.84
Kelly, Merrill	Ari	31	29	29	178	184	34	57	150	2	9	11	.450	0	12.3	4.63
Kennedy, Ian	KC	35	57	0	60	61	11	20	57	2	3	4	.429	33	12.5	4.58
Kershaw, Clayton	LAD	32	29	28	181	152	25	37	186	2	13	7	.650	0	9.5	3.48
Keuchel, Dallas	Atl	32	30	30	180	186	19	58	140	6	11	9	.550	0	12.5	4.31
Kikuchi, Yusei	Sea	29	29	29	154	189	34	48	110	6	5	12	.294	0	14.2	5.58
Kimbrel, Craig	ChC	32	61	0	59	38	8	27	90	4	4	2	.667	33	10.5	3.21
Kinley, Tyler	Mia	29	64	0	61	57	7	40	65	1	3	4	.429	0	14.5	4.57
Kintzler, Brandon	ChC	35	51	0	47	46	4	12	35	3	3	2	.600	0	11.7	4.10
Kittredge, Andrew	TB	30	48	5	53	50	5	15	61	2	4	2	.667	0	11.4	3.58
Kline, Branden	Bal	28	35	0	40	43	7	19	39	1	2	3	.400	0	14.2	4.96
Kluber, Corey	Cle	34	32	32	202	172	25	47	213	6	14	9	.609	0	10.0	3.52
Knebel, Corey	Mil	28	31	0	30	19	3	14	45	1	2	1	.667	0	10.2	3.05
Kolarek, Adam	LAD	31	76	0	45	42	2	15	38	3	3	2	.600	0	12.0	3.90
Kopech, Michael	CWS	24	24	24	129	118	12	67	163	12	7	8	.467	0	13.7	4.09
Kremer, Dean	Bal	24	25	25	133	153	18	52	142	2	6	9	.400	0	14.0	4.67
Kuhl, Chad	Pit	27	21	21	113	122	15	43	101	5	6	7	.462	0	13.5	4.62
Lakins, Travis	Bos	26	20	5	32	33	3	16	28	2	2	2	.500	0	14.3	4.64
Lambert, Peter	Col	23	23	23	109	122	16	31	78	4	6	6	.500	0	13.0	4.71
Lamet, Dinelson	SD	27	27	27	144	114	18	62	189	8	9	7	.563	0	11.5	3.63
Lauer, Eric	SD	25	28	28	149	155	20	55	136	6	8	9	.471	0	13.0	4.47
Law, Derek	Tor	29	62	0	67	67	8	31	71	2	4	4	.500	6	13.4	4.37
Leake, Mike	Ari	32	29	29	188	217	28	32	122	9	9	11	.450	0	12.4	4.64
LeBlanc, Wade	Sea	35	25	3	95	107	17	24	72	1	4	7	.364	0	12.5	4.74
Leclerc, Jose	Tex	26	64	0	65	41	5	38	92	4	4	3	.571	30	11.5	3.29
Leone, Dominic	StL	28	36	0	37	33	6	16	41	1	2	2	.500	0	12.2	4.15
Lester, Jon	ChC	36	30	30	172	186	24	55	156	5	10	10	.500	0	12.9	4.45
Liriano, Francisco	Pit	36	54	0	56	58	8	30	50	3	3	4	.429	0	14.6	5.06
Littell, Zack	Min	24	52	0	55	58	7	22	54	2	3	3	.500	0	13.4	4.50
Lopez, Jorge	KC	27	34	20	125	148	21	50	107	8	5	9	.357	0	14.8	5.33
Lopez, Pablo	Mia	24	29	29	151	151	21	41	133	12	7	10	.412	0	12.3	4.35
Lopez, Reynaldo	CWS	26	31	31	181	180	29	67	162	7	8	12	.400	0	12.6	4.53
Lopez, Yoan	Ari	27	64	0	56	51	10	21	49	1	3	3	.500	0	11.7	4.36
Lorenzen, Michael	Cin	28	68	0	82	73	8	30	75	3	5	4	.556	6	11.6	3.93
Loup, Aaron	SD	32	50	0	31	31	2	12	35	4	2	2	.500	0	13.6	4.06
Lowther, Zac	Bal	24	29	29	176	157	15	93	180	6	9	11	.450	0	13.1	4.12
Lucchesi, Joey	SD	27	28	28	160	148	24	55	157	4	9	9	.500	0	11.6	4.11
Lugo, Seth	NYM	30	57	0	81	74	10	20	88	3	5	4	.556	8	10.8	3.66
Luzardo, Jesus	Oak	22	18	18	100	88	10	27	111	3	6	5	.545	0	10.6	3.47
Lyles, Jordan	Mil	29	28	28	151	147	27	59	150	4	8	8	.500	0	12.5	4.47
Lynn, Lance	Tex	33	31	31	205	205	27	73	217	9	11	12	.478	0	12.6	4.17
Maeda, Kenta	LAD	32	39	23	150	127	22	49	161	5	10	6	.625	0	10.9	3.82
Magill, Matt	Sea	30	51	0	52	52	8	22	58	2	2	3	.400	6	13.2	4.42
Mahle, Tyler	Cin	25	20	20	105	107	17	35	102	5	5	6	.455	0	12.6	4.46
Manaea, Sean	Oak	28	28	28	165	144	21	41	152	8	10	8	.556	0	10.5	3.80
Markel, Parker	Pit	29	31	0	37	28	3	24	52	4	2	2	.500	0	13.6	3.82
Marquez, German	Col	25	27	27	175	178	26	44	181	7	11	8	.579	0	11.8	4.05
Marshall, Evan	CWS	30	61	0	57	61	6	23	50	1	3	4	.429	0	13.4	4.50
Martin, Brett	Tex	25	50	0	64	87	6	20	68	2	3	4	.429	0	15.3	4.86
Martin, Chris	Atl	34	57	0	54	51	7	6	60	1	4	2	.667	0	9.7	3.40
Martin, Corbin	Ari	24	6	6	34	30	4	14	36	1	2	2	.500	0	11.9	3.91
Martinez, Carlos	StL	28	65	0	53	45	5	21	54	3	3	3	.500	36	11.7	3.84
Marvel, James	Pit	26	7	7	34	35	3	12	27	3	2	2	.500	0	13.2	4.37
Maton, Phil	Cle	27	27	0	36	33	5	13	42	2	2	2	.500	0	12.0	3.91
Matz, Steven	NYM	29	30	30	170	174	27	56	159	8	9	10	.474	0	12.6	4.48

2020 Pitcher Projections

Pitcher	Team	Age	G	GS	IP	H	HR	BB	SO	HB	W	L	Pct	Sv	BR/9	ERA
May, Dustin	LAD	22	23	23	128	116	8	34	122	14	9	5	.643	0	11.5	3.71
May, Trevor	Min	30	64	0	71	59	10	30	85	3	5	3	.625	4	11.7	3.86
McCarthy, Kevin	KC	28	66	0	71	78	7	23	48	2	3	5	.375	0	13.1	4.50
McCullers Jr., Lance	Hou	26	24	24	134	116	11	54	149	7	10	5	.667	0	11.9	3.73
McFarland, T.J.	Ari	31	52	0	57	64	6	20	36	1	3	4	.429	0	13.4	4.74
McGee, Jake	Col	33	44	0	41	47	8	13	34	2	2	2	.500	0	13.6	5.05
McHugh, Collin	Hou	33	32	3	59	54	8	20	63	3	4	3	.571	0	11.7	4.01
McKay, Brendan	TB	24	26	26	138	109	13	41	175	4	10	6	.625	0	10.0	3.19
McKay, David	Det	25	36	0	39	30	4	23	55	5	2	2	.500	0	13.4	3.85
McKenzie, Triston	Cle	22	24	24	136	103	16	46	127	6	9	6	.600	0	10.3	3.70
Means, John	Bal	27	29	29	173	194	24	43	135	7	8	11	.421	0	12.7	4.55
Medina, Adonis	Phi	23	23	23	118	139	14	46	87	16	5	8	.385	0	15.3	5.30
Mejia, Adalberto	LAA	27	36	0	33	33	4	14	30	1	2	2	.500	0	13.1	4.37
Melancon, Mark	Atl	35	65	0	65	68	5	18	61	2	4	3	.571	34	12.2	3.93
Melville, Tim	Col	30	13	13	66	76	14	30	56	4	3	4	.429	0	15.0	5.59
Menez, Conner	SF	25	18	5	43	39	5	21	53	3	2	3	.400	0	13.2	4.09
Mengden, Daniel	Oak	27	17	10	73	70	9	23	57	2	4	4	.500	0	11.7	4.19
Middleton, Keynan	LAA	26	42	0	43	37	5	20	42	1	3	2	.600	0	12.1	4.04
Mikolas, Miles	StL	31	29	29	179	185	23	31	134	10	11	9	.550	0	11.4	4.15
Miley, Wade	Hou	33	31	31	166	178	24	63	134	6	10	9	.526	0	13.4	4.77
Miller, Andrew	StL	35	70	0	54	40	6	22	70	6	4	2	.667	5	11.3	3.54
Mills, Alec	ChC	28	33	5	67	72	9	23	63	3	4	4	.500	0	13.2	4.50
Milone, Tommy	Sea	33	17	8	58	63	13	13	49	1	2	4	.333	0	11.9	4.74
Minor, Mike	Tex	32	29	29	206	199	32	65	189	8	11	12	.478	0	11.9	4.25
Minter, A.J.	Atl	26	38	0	38	38	3	17	46	1	2	2	.500	0	13.3	3.91
Montas, Frankie	Oak	27	27	27	160	160	19	49	155	6	9	9	.500	0	12.1	4.08
Montero, Rafael	Tex	29	56	0	54	61	7	22	57	2	3	3	.500	0	14.2	4.67
Montgomery, Mike	KC	30	24	24	121	133	14	44	87	7	5	8	.385	0	13.7	4.76
Moore, Matt	Det	31	18	18	96	115	17	34	78	4	3	7	.300	0	14.3	5.25
Morgan, Adam	Phi	30	46	0	40	40	6	13	39	2	2	2	.500	0	12.4	4.28
Morin, Mike	Phi	29	62	0	60	61	7	14	43	3	3	3	.500	0	11.7	4.18
Morrow, Brandon	ChC	35	36	0	37	40	5	11	36	1	2	2	.500	0	12.6	4.38
Morton, Charlie	TB	36	30	30	185	150	17	61	215	14	12	8	.600	0	10.9	3.50
Munoz, Andres	SD	21	55	0	56	37	5	29	78	6	4	2	.667	0	11.6	3.44
Musgrove, Joe	Pit	27	28	28	158	163	21	36	143	8	9	9	.500	0	11.8	4.13
Nelson, Jimmy	Mil	31	21	21	101	95	14	50	113	8	6	6	.500	0	13.6	4.46
Neris, Hector	Phi	31	63	0	65	54	10	24	84	4	4	3	.571	14	11.4	3.74
Neshek, Pat	Phi	39	33	0	31	31	4	5	23	0	2	2	.500	0	10.5	3.87
Newcomb, Sean	Atl	27	58	1	64	57	6	32	63	2	4	3	.571	0	12.8	4.13
Nicasio, Juan	Phi	33	35	0	35	37	4	12	36	2	2	2	.500	0	13.1	4.37
Nix, Jacob	SD	24	15	15	86	76	8	17	67	5	5	4	.556	0	10.3	3.72
Noesi, Hector	Mia	33	23	7	55	56	15	18	54	2	2	4	.333	0	12.4	4.99
Nola, Aaron	Phi	27	32	32	201	175	22	69	219	8	13	10	.565	0	11.3	3.73
Norris, Daniel	Det	27	29	28	86	102	13	29	77	2	3	6	.333	0	13.9	4.87
Nova, Ivan	CWS	33	33	33	176	204	31	41	113	8	7	12	.368	0	12.9	4.99
Oaks, Trevor	KC	27	6	6	34	40	2	11	22	1	2	2	.500	0	13.8	4.63
Oberg, Scott	Col	30	57	0	59	54	5	21	58	1	4	3	.571	26	11.6	3.76
O'Day, Darren	Atl	37	33	0	32	24	4	10	40	3	2	1	.667	0	10.4	3.39
Odorizzi, Jake	Min	30	30	30	166	155	25	60	169	5	10	8	.556	0	11.9	4.14
Osich, Josh	CWS	31	56	0	58	64	10	21	51	1	2	4	.333	0	13.3	4.89
Osuna, Roberto	Hou	25	62	0	63	49	6	11	70	3	5	2	.714	37	9.0	3.09
Otero, Dan	Cle	35	48	0	47	54	7	6	29	1	3	3	.500	0	11.7	4.41
Ottavino, Adam	NYY	34	67	0	62	42	7	34	80	3	4	3	.571	0	11.5	3.55
Paddack, Chris	SD	24	31	31	179	138	27	38	194	8	12	8	.600	0	9.3	3.42
Pagan, Emilio	TB	29	66	0	74	53	11	20	92	2	5	3	.625	23	9.1	3.24
Palumbo, Joseph	Tex	25	24	24	123	110	22	60	159	7	6	7	.462	0	13.0	4.32
Pannone, Thomas	Tor	26	33	7	71	69	13	27	69	4	4	4	.500	0	12.7	4.57
Parker, Blake	Phi	35	62	0	68	61	11	23	74	3	4	4	.500	0	11.5	4.01
Parsons, Wes	Col	27	37	0	46	50	4	22	40	2	3	2	.600	0	14.5	4.70
Paxton, James	NYY	31	29	29	166	150	21	52	194	2	11	7	.611	0	11.1	3.67
Peacock, Brad	Hou	32	24	15	93	82	13	36	103	4	6	4	.600	0	11.8	4.01
Pearson, Nate	Tor	23	25	25	138	109	16	46	141	6	9	7	.563	0	10.5	3.64
Pena, Felix	LAA	30	25	5	63	59	10	23	64	4	3	4	.429	0	12.3	4.22
Peralta, Freddy	Mil	24	38	9	69	55	8	32	95	2	5	3	.625	0	11.6	3.55
Peralta, Wandy	SF	28	40	0	32	34	3	14	24	1	2	2	.500	0	13.8	4.64
Perdomo, Luis	SD	27	50	0	73	79	10	24	58	3	4	5	.444	0	13.1	4.63
Perez, Martin	Min	29	31	29	164	186	22	64	121	4	8	10	.444	0	13.9	4.94
Perez, Oliver	Cle	38	67	0	39	37	4	12	44	4	2	2	.500	0	12.2	3.85
Peters, Dillon	LAA	27	24	24	129	155	23	44	106	6	6	9	.400	0	14.3	5.27
Peterson, David	NYM	24	6	6	32	41	4	12	33	2	1	2	.333	0	15.5	5.21
Petit, Yusmeiro	Oak	35	74	0	79	66	11	14	67	0	5	4	.556	0	9.1	3.61
Phelps, David	ChC	33	54	0	42	38	5	20	45	1	3	2	.600	0	12.6	4.10
Pineda, Michael	Min	31	21	21	125	131	22	28	118	4	7	7	.500	0	11.7	4.25
Pivetta, Nick	Phi	27	33	6	70	66	10	28	75	3	4	4	.500	0	12.5	4.18
Plesac, Zach	Cle	25	30	30	177	152	20	50	151	6	11	9	.550	0	10.6	3.82
Plutko, Adam	Cle	28	26	26	137	141	24	39	107	3	7	8	.467	0	12.0	4.53
Poche, Colin	TB	26	60	0	63	46	8	22	95	3	5	2	.714	5	10.1	3.09
Pomeranz, Drew	Mil	31	58	0	60	54	10	28	68	2	3	3	.500	3	12.6	4.28
Ponce de Leon, Daniel	StL	28	13	13	73	56	6	37	72	5	5	3	.625	0	12.1	3.88
Porcello, Rick	Bos	31	32	32	177	191	28	43	151	9	10	10	.500	0	12.4	4.48
Pressly, Ryan	Hou	31	56	0	57	45	7	16	71	1	4	2	.667	0	9.8	3.32

2020 Pitcher Projections

Pitcher	Team	Age	G	GS	IP	H	HR	BB	SO	HB	W	L	Pct	Sv	BR/9	ERA
Price, David	Bos	34	27	27	151	148	21	43	160	6	10	7	.588	0	11.7	3.99
Pruitt, Austin	TB	30	16	3	63	69	10	15	55	1	3	4	.429	0	12.1	4.43
Puk, A.J.	Oak	25	25	25	134	128	14	56	180	5	8	7	.533	0	12.7	3.81
Quantrill, Cal	SD	25	28	28	141	157	19	43	120	5	7	9	.438	0	13.1	4.57
Quijada, Jose	Mia	24	39	0	33	28	6	20	42	3	1	2	.333	0	13.9	4.64
Quintana, Jose	ChC	31	30	30	165	173	21	51	147	4	10	9	.526	0	12.4	4.28
Rainey, Tanner	Was	27	58	0	58	42	7	46	84	3	4	3	.571	0	14.1	4.11
Ramirez, Nick	Det	30	51	0	80	82	10	34	72	2	3	6	.333	0	13.3	4.50
Ramirez, Noe	LAA	30	49	7	62	56	11	21	70	4	4	3	.571	0	11.8	4.08
Ramirez, Yefry	Pit	26	19	0	33	32	5	18	37	2	2	2	.500	0	14.2	4.78
Ray, Robbie	Ari	28	30	30	155	131	26	75	204	5	9	8	.529	0	12.3	4.01
Reed, Cody	Cin	27	34	0	35	37	5	15	35	2	2	2	.500	0	13.9	4.76
Reid-Foley, Sean	Tor	24	16	16	85	85	14	49	91	6	4	6	.400	0	14.8	5.03
Reyes, Alex	StL	25	10	10	54	42	5	37	68	3	3	3	.500	0	13.7	4.10
Reyes, Gerardo	SD	27	33	0	33	26	4	14	43	3	2	2	.500	0	11.7	3.64
Richard, Clayton	Tor	36	9	9	41	49	6	15	26	2	2	3	.400	0	14.5	5.27
Richards, Garrett	SD	32	21	21	114	101	12	54	127	2	7	6	.538	0	12.4	3.95
Richards, Trevor	TB	27	28	23	131	126	17	50	124	5	7	7	.500	0	12.4	4.26
Roark, Tanner	Oak	33	29	29	165	173	24	52	141	10	8	10	.444	0	12.8	4.53
Robertson, David	Phi	35	62	0	58	41	6	25	74	1	4	3	.571	27	10.4	3.35
Robles, Hansel	LAA	29	64	0	70	64	11	25	70	2	4	4	.500	34	11.7	4.15
Rodney, Fernando	Was	43	45	0	45	44	5	27	47	2	2	3	.400	0	14.6	4.70
Rodriguez, Dereck	SF	28	28	17	106	109	17	36	84	4	5	7	.417	0	12.7	4.67
Rodriguez, Eduardo	Bos	27	31	31	199	184	25	72	209	7	12	10	.545	0	11.9	4.00
Rodriguez, Jefry	Cle	26	13	6	34	31	4	17	28	1	2	2	.500	0	13.0	4.37
Rodriguez, Richard	Pit	30	65	0	60	56	8	20	62	3	3	3	.500	5	11.9	4.01
Roe, Chaz	TB	33	70	0	51	44	4	24	60	3	3	3	.500	0	12.5	3.86
Rogers, Taylor	Min	29	56	0	64	56	6	15	74	4	4	3	.571	32	10.5	3.39
Rogers, Tyler	SF	29	54	0	58	51	3	23	48	3	3	3	.500	0	12.1	3.92
Romero, Fernando	Min	25	31	0	33	36	3	16	32	3	2	2	.500	0	15.0	4.78
Romo, Sergio	Min	37	69	0	62	58	11	18	61	2	4	3	.571	0	11.3	4.17
Rondon, Hector	Hou	32	58	0	61	59	10	19	55	2	4	3	.571	0	11.8	4.28
Ross, Joe	Was	27	24	10	68	79	9	24	57	4	4	4	.500	0	14.2	4.90
Ross, Tyson	Det	33	14	14	73	84	10	34	53	4	3	5	.375	0	15.0	5.30
Ruiz, Jose	CWS	25	32	0	37	39	4	20	37	2	2	2	.500	0	14.8	4.74
Ryan, Kyle	ChC	28	71	0	61	59	7	28	55	2	3	3	.500	0	13.1	4.43
Ryu, Hyun-Jin	LAD	33	27	27	173	167	23	31	154	4	12	7	.632	0	10.5	3.85
Sadler, Casey	LAD	29	32	0	41	44	5	11	36	3	3	2	.600	0	12.7	4.28
Sadzeck, Connor	Sea	28	49	0	50	53	8	26	54	4	2	4	.333	0	14.9	5.04
Salazar, Danny	Cle	30	26	22	128	117	20	63	149	5	7	7	.500	0	13.0	4.33
Sale, Chris	Bos	31	28	28	162	128	19	37	223	12	12	6	.667	0	9.8	3.12
Samardzija, Jeff	SF	35	29	29	179	172	27	49	141	6	9	11	.450	0	11.4	4.24
Sampson, Adrian	Tex	28	32	8	88	107	15	22	66	5	4	6	.400	0	13.7	5.07
Sanchez, Anibal	Was	36	26	26	149	158	27	51	128	4	8	8	.500	0	12.9	4.74
Sanchez, Sixto	Mia	21	24	24	142	155	13	34	130	4	7	9	.438	0	12.2	4.04
Sandoval, Patrick	LAA	23	13	13	57	58	6	27	65	1	3	3	.500	0	13.6	4.19
Santana, Edgar	Pit	28	52	0	53	57	6	14	46	2	3	3	.500	0	12.4	4.25
Santiago, Hector	CWS	32	25	3	55	57	12	28	50	2	2	4	.333	0	14.2	5.32
Scherzer, Max	Was	35	31	31	202	154	24	47	266	9	16	7	.696	0	9.4	3.08
Scott, Tanner	Bal	25	32	0	32	30	2	18	41	1	2	2	.500	0	13.8	3.95
Senzatela, Antonio	Col	25	22	22	109	129	15	43	72	4	6	6	.500	0	14.5	5.20
Severino, Luis	NYY	26	30	30	182	159	19	48	212	6	13	8	.619	0	10.5	3.45
Shafer, Justin	Tor	27	42	0	50	46	6	24	47	2	3	3	.500	0	13.0	4.33
Shaw, Bryan	Col	32	61	0	62	68	9	26	53	2	3	4	.429	0	13.9	4.87
Sheffield, Justus	Sea	24	31	31	177	181	24	84	176	5	8	12	.400	0	13.7	4.61
Shepherd, Chandler	Bal	27	9	9	49	63	9	18	45	2	2	4	.333	0	15.2	5.51
Shoemaker, Matt	Tor	33	24	24	138	135	21	39	120	6	8	8	.500	0	11.7	4.23
Sims, Lucas	Cin	26	37	4	58	52	10	29	69	4	3	4	.429	0	13.2	4.50
Skoglund, Eric	KC	27	11	7	42	53	8	13	28	2	1	4	.200	0	14.6	5.47
Smeltzer, Devin	Min	24	15	8	65	67	10	15	59	3	4	3	.571	0	11.8	4.23
Smith, Caleb	Mia	28	29	29	161	141	27	63	178	7	8	10	.444	0	11.8	4.11
Smith, Joe	Hou	36	46	0	43	38	6	10	43	2	3	2	.600	0	10.5	3.78
Smith, Josh A.	Bos	32	20	0	34	42	6	11	32	2	2	2	.500	0	14.6	5.29
Smith, Will	SF	30	60	0	63	45	7	20	87	0	4	3	.571	32	9.3	3.01
Smyly, Drew	Phi	31	26	26	131	136	31	55	140	2	6	8	.429	0	13.3	4.98
Snell, Blake	TB	27	28	28	163	132	17	65	202	1	11	7	.611	0	10.9	3.45
Sobotka, Chad	Atl	26	31	0	30	25	4	17	39	3	2	2	.500	0	13.5	4.20
Soria, Joakim	Oak	36	63	0	62	54	7	19	69	2	4	3	.571	0	10.9	3.61
Soroka, Mike	Atl	22	28	28	178	168	16	42	151	7	12	8	.600	0	11.0	3.81
Soto, Gregory	Det	25	32	6	51	63	9	27	46	2	2	4	.333	0	16.2	5.83
Sparkman, Glenn	KC	28	30	27	146	182	26	40	93	5	5	11	.313	0	14.0	5.34
Springs, Jeffrey	Tex	27	27	0	36	39	4	17	45	1	2	2	.500	0	14.3	4.38
Stammen, Craig	SD	36	71	0	81	76	10	19	74	2	5	4	.556	0	10.8	3.82
Stanek, Ryne	Mia	28	62	0	70	57	8	35	83	1	4	4	.500	0	12.0	3.81
Stashak, Cody	Min	26	42	1	44	43	6	8	53	1	3	2	.600	0	10.6	3.57
Staumont, Josh	KC	26	25	0	32	28	4	24	39	2	1	2	.333	0	15.2	4.64
Steckenrider, Drew	Mia	29	55	0	51	40	7	21	58	2	3	3	.500	0	11.1	3.82
Stephenson, Robert	Cin	27	57	0	62	50	10	32	69	1	3	4	.429	0	12.0	4.17
Strahm, Matt	SD	28	57	9	94	90	16	25	99	6	5	5	.500	0	11.6	4.09
Strasburg, Stephen	Was	31	31	31	195	165	22	56	225	9	14	8	.636	0	10.6	3.52
Stratton, Chris	Pit	29	35	0	54	65	7	22	45	1	2	4	.333	0	14.7	5.08

2020 Pitcher Projections

Pitcher	Team	Age	G	GS	IP	H	HR	BB	SO	HB	W	L	Pct	Sv	BR/9	ERA
Strickland, Hunter	Was	31	48	0	43	43	6	17	36	2	2	2	.500	0	13.0	4.61
Stripling, Ross	LAD	30	34	16	113	107	15	26	114	2	8	5	.615	0	10.8	3.76
Stroman, Marcus	NYM	29	31	31	181	179	18	58	155	3	10	10	.500	0	11.9	4.06
Strop, Pedro	ChC	35	50	0	41	31	4	17	43	4	3	2	.600	7	11.4	3.85
Suarez, Andrew	SF	27	36	0	47	56	6	16	35	1	2	3	.400	0	14.0	4.89
Suarez, Jose	LAA	22	23	15	100	107	15	40	97	8	5	6	.455	0	14.0	4.82
Suarez, Ranger	Phi	24	54	0	67	72	7	20	54	3	4	4	.500	0	12.8	4.37
Suero, Wander	Was	28	75	0	68	65	6	24	71	4	5	3	.625	0	12.3	3.89
Suter, Brent	Mil	30	47	5	76	76	9	15	66	2	5	4	.556	0	11.0	3.92
Swanson, Erik	Sea	26	35	7	61	60	12	18	62	2	3	4	.429	11	11.8	4.28
Swarzak, Anthony	Atl	34	57	0	51	48	8	21	51	1	3	3	.500	0	12.4	4.33
Syndergaard, Noah	NYM	27	31	31	194	190	18	49	198	6	12	9	.571	0	11.4	3.73
Tanaka, Masahiro	NYY	31	29	29	181	185	30	40	157	5	11	9	.550	0	11.4	4.22
Tate, Dillon	Bal	26	29	0	39	42	5	14	32	4	2	3	.400	0	13.8	4.85
Taylor, Josh	Bos	27	62	0	56	60	5	25	65	3	3	3	.500	0	14.1	4.26
Teheran, Julio	Atl	29	30	30	161	139	24	70	144	10	9	8	.529	0	12.2	4.36
Thornton, Trent	Tor	26	31	29	164	174	22	53	154	6	9	9	.500	0	12.8	4.40
Thorpe, Lewis	Min	24	18	2	40	42	6	11	47	0	2	2	.500	0	11.9	3.94
Tinoco, Jesus	Col	25	36	0	52	59	12	23	42	1	3	3	.500	0	14.4	5.54
Tomlin, Josh	Atl	35	48	0	54	63	11	6	37	1	3	3	.500	0	11.7	4.67
Toussaint, Touki	Atl	24	26	5	48	44	5	28	53	5	3	3	.500	0	14.4	4.50
Treinen, Blake	Oak	32	52	0	51	46	5	23	52	1	3	3	.500	5	12.4	3.95
Trivino, Lou	Oak	28	48	0	48	43	4	21	47	2	3	3	.500	0	12.4	3.99
Tuivailala, Sam	Sea	27	38	0	39	34	4	15	39	2	2	2	.500	0	11.8	3.99
Turnbull, Spencer	Det	27	30	30	158	166	13	61	158	15	7	10	.412	0	13.8	4.33
Urena, Jose	Mia	28	60	0	65	66	9	22	47	4	3	5	.375	30	12.7	4.64
Urias, Julio	LAD	23	36	6	68	54	5	25	71	3	5	3	.625	0	10.9	3.48
Urquidy, Jose	Hou	25	26	26	131	120	22	26	151	1	10	5	.667	0	10.1	3.58
Valdez, Framber	Hou	26	26	15	98	94	10	48	113	7	6	5	.545	0	13.7	4.22
Vargas, Jason	Phi	37	30	30	157	162	29	62	128	6	8	10	.444	0	13.2	4.90
Velasquez, Vince	Phi	28	30	30	152	149	27	59	164	8	8	9	.471	0	12.8	4.44
Velazquez, Hector	Bos	31	30	3	43	44	5	18	33	2	2	2	.500	0	13.4	4.61
VerHagen, Drew	Det	29	25	4	94	109	13	34	85	5	4	7	.364	0	14.2	4.88
Verlander, Justin	Hou	37	32	32	218	157	32	48	271	7	17	7	.708	0	8.8	3.13
Vincent, Nick	Phi	33	35	0	43	40	6	10	42	2	3	2	.600	0	10.9	3.85
Voth, Austin	Was	28	11	9	56	59	8	19	52	2	3	3	.500	0	12.9	4.42
Wacha, Michael	StL	28	26	26	124	132	19	50	105	3	6	7	.462	0	13.4	4.79
Waguespack, Jacob	Tor	26	28	28	151	172	21	66	134	7	7	10	.412	0	14.6	5.01
Wainwright, Adam	StL	38	30	30	163	176	20	60	138	7	9	9	.500	0	13.4	4.61
Walden, Marcus	Bos	31	70	0	74	75	5	31	65	4	4	4	.500	0	13.4	4.26
Walker, Taijuan	Ari	27	14	14	80	77	12	28	70	4	4	5	.444	0	12.3	4.39
Warren, Adam	SD	32	38	0	43	38	7	17	39	2	2	3	.400	0	11.9	4.32
Watson, Tony	SF	35	49	0	43	41	5	11	36	3	2	3	.400	0	11.5	4.14
Weaver, Luke	Ari	26	28	28	149	142	17	44	152	4	9	8	.529	0	11.5	3.85
Webb, Jacob	Atl	26	36	0	34	27	5	17	35	1	2	2	.500	0	11.9	4.04
Webb, Logan	SF	23	15	15	71	78	8	24	70	2	3	5	.375	0	13.2	4.38
Webb, Tyler	StL	29	67	0	58	54	7	22	54	2	3	3	.500	0	12.1	4.15
Weber, Ryan	Bos	29	23	0	39	48	4	11	28	2	2	2	.500	0	14.1	4.85
Wheeler, Zack	NYM	30	30	30	188	187	23	56	183	5	11	10	.524	0	11.9	4.03
Wick, Rowan	ChC	27	45	0	50	40	4	23	54	2	3	2	.600	0	11.7	3.72
Wieck, Brad	ChC	28	41	0	32	26	4	13	48	1	2	1	.667	0	11.3	3.35
Williams, Trevor	Pit	28	28	28	158	165	20	51	122	6	8	9	.471	0	12.6	4.47
Wilson, Bryse	Atl	22	10	10	54	59	7	16	53	1	3	3	.500	0	12.7	4.33
Wilson, Justin	NYM	32	55	0	50	44	5	25	60	1	3	2	.600	3	12.6	3.83
Wingenter, Trey	SD	26	56	0	57	37	7	29	77	5	4	3	.571	0	11.2	3.54
Wisler, Matt	Sea	27	45	12	78	88	12	21	73	1	4	5	.444	0	12.7	4.44
Wittgren, Nick	Cle	29	54	0	67	54	9	16	55	1	3	3	.500	0	11.6	4.19
Wojciechowski, Asher	Bal	31	24	23	119	126	29	44	111	8	5	9	.357	0	13.5	5.18
Wood, Alex	Cin	29	15	15	81	80	11	23	73	4	4	5	.444	0	11.9	4.14
Wood, Hunter	Cle	26	42	0	47	49	8	17	48	1	2	3	.400	0	12.8	4.50
Woodruff, Brandon	Mil	27	30	30	162	150	18	51	174	7	10	8	.556	0	11.6	3.82
Workman, Brandon	Bos	31	70	0	71	48	7	35	87	2	5	3	.625	35	10.8	3.47
Wright, Kyle	Atl	24	7	7	35	34	4	14	34	2	2	2	.500	0	12.9	4.24
Wright, Steven	Bos	35	20	8	51	55	6	20	35	3	3	3	.500	0	13.8	4.86
Yamamoto, Jordan	Mia	24	31	31	166	151	25	77	171	14	7	11	.389	0	13.1	4.47
Yarbrough, Ryan	TB	28	28	19	155	149	19	35	137	9	9	8	.529	0	11.2	3.96
Yates, Kirby	SD	33	68	0	67	48	7	19	101	6	5	3	.625	38	9.8	2.96
Ynoa, Gabriel	Bal	27	36	14	96	117	16	24	60	3	4	7	.364	0	13.5	5.11
Young, Alex	Ari	26	26	26	146	147	19	55	131	6	8	9	.471	0	12.8	4.41
Zeuch, T.J.	Tor	24	24	24	122	130	11	47	78	7	6	7	.462	0	13.6	4.69
Zimmer, Kyle	KC	28	31	0	32	35	4	23	30	1	1	2	.333	0	16.6	5.49
Zimmermann, Jordan	Det	34	24	24	125	158	24	30	92	5	4	10	.286	0	13.9	5.30

Career Targets

Andrew Kyne

Bill James devised "The Favorite Toy" to estimate a player's probability of breaking a record or reaching a milestone.

In last year's *Handbook*, the highest probability of such an event belonged to Albert Pujols, who was projected to have a 97% chance to someday reach 2,000 career runs batted in. With 1,982 RBI entering the season, Pujols was very likely to not only reach the milestone, but to do so early in 2019. Sure enough, he notched his 2,000th with a solo home run on May 9 in Detroit.

This year, the highest probability of reaching a career batting target belongs to another generational talent, Miguel Cabrera. He is now estimated to have a 75% chance of reaching 3,000 hits. Although his power numbers were limited this season, Cabrera still hit for a .282 average and added 139 hits to his career ledger. He now sits 185 hits shy of 3,000.

Some records may never be broken, and the rest of the batting targets feature many longshots. But an obvious player to keep an eye on is Mike Trout, whose name can be found in several places in this section. After hitting a career-best 45 home runs in 2019, Trout is now projected to have a 43% chance to hit 500 home runs, a 29% chance to hit 600 home runs, and a 14% chance to hit more than 762 home runs, the all-time record.

Additionally, BIS has developed a system, separate from The Favorite Toy, that estimates the likelihood that a pitcher will throw a no-hitter. Gerrit Cole is currently the most likely to do so at an astonishing 62%, far ahead of any other pitcher. This season, Cole had two outings in which he allowed only one hit and three outings in which he allowed two hits. He also found his strikeout touch with the Astros, recording double-digit strikeouts in 21 starts this year.

A couple new names to watch on the most likely no-hitter list are Lucas Giolito (27%) and Luis Castillo (21%). Young pitchers Jack Flaherty (23%) and Blake Snell (23%) were featured on last year's list as well.

Justin Verlander, Cole's teammate in Houston, was listed as having a 32% chance at a future no-hitter in last year's *Handbook*. Verlander held the Blue Jays without a hit on September 1 for the third no-hitter of his career. Only Nolan Ryan and Sandy Koufax have thrown more than three career no-hitters. With a 26% chance of another, it's possible that Verlander could join them.

3,000 Hits	
% chance to reach milestone	
Pujols, Albert	done
Suzuki, Ichiro	done
Cabrera, Miguel	75%
Markakis, Nick	30%
Cano, Robinson	26%
Castro, Starlin	25%
Altuve, Jose	24%
Freeman, Freddie	23%
Andrus, Elvis	20%
Hosmer, Eric	20%
Arenado, Nolan	19%
Machado, Manny	17%
Yelich, Christian	16%
Betts, Mookie	15%
Bogaerts, Xander	15%
Castellanos, Nicholas	15%
Lindor, Francisco	13%
Jones, Adam	12%
Trout, Mike	12%
LeMahieu, DJ	10%
Segura, Jean	9%
Harper, Bryce	9%
Albies, Ozzie	7%
Bregman, Alex	7%
Bellinger, Cody	7%
Devers, Rafael	6%
Rizzo, Anthony	6%
Benintendi, Andrew	5%
Story, Trevor	4%
Rendon, Anthony	4%
Goldschmidt, Paul	4%
Blackmon, Charlie	3%
Baez, Javier	2%
Ramirez, Jose	2%
Martinez, J.D.	2%
Turner, Trea	2%
Marte, Ketel	2%
Rosario, Amed	1%
Acuna Jr., Ronald	1%
Rosario, Eddie	< 1%
Semien, Marcus	< 1%
Brantley, Michael	< 1%
Anderson, Tim	< 1%
Suarez, Eugenio	< 1%

Career Targets

762 Home Runs
% chance to break record

Trout, Mike	14%
Bellinger, Cody	6%
Arenado, Nolan	1%
Alonso, Pete	< 1%

2,298 RBI
% chance to break record

Pujols, Albert	7%
Arenado, Nolan	3%
Harper, Bryce	< 1%

2,296 Runs Scored
% chance to break record

Betts, Mookie	11%
Trout, Mike	6%
Lindor, Francisco	1%

4,257 Hits
% chance to break record

900 Home Runs
% chance to reach milestone

2,000 RBI
% chance to reach milestone

Pujols, Albert	done
Arenado, Nolan	15%
Harper, Bryce	11%
Freeman, Freddie	7%
Bogaerts, Xander	5%
Bellinger, Cody	5%
Trout, Mike	4%
Machado, Manny	4%
Bregman, Alex	2%
Rizzo, Anthony	< 1%

6,857 Total Bases
% chance to break record

Lindor, Francisco	< 1%
Arenado, Nolan	< 1%
Trout, Mike	< 1%

4,000 Hits
% chance to reach milestone

800 Home Runs
% chance to reach milestone

Trout, Mike	10%
Bellinger, Cody	3%

600 Home Runs
% chance to reach milestone

Pujols, Albert	done
Trout, Mike	29%
Arenado, Nolan	21%
Suarez, Eugenio	16%
Harper, Bryce	16%
Machado, Manny	15%
Bellinger, Cody	13%
Lindor, Francisco	11%
Alonso, Pete	11%
Yelich, Christian	10%

793 Doubles
% chance to break record

Castellanos, Nicholas	16%
Bogaerts, Xander	14%
Betts, Mookie	11%
Lindor, Francisco	7%
Devers, Rafael	6%
Bregman, Alex	5%
Albies, Ozzie	2%
Ramirez, Jose	2%
Rendon, Anthony	2%
Freeman, Freddie	1%

Most Likely No-Hitter
% chance to reach milestone

Cole, Gerrit	62%
Ray, Robbie	32%
Sale, Chris	29%
Giolito, Lucas	27%
Verlander, Justin	26%
Snell, Blake	23%
Flaherty, Jack	23%
Scherzer, Max	22%
Castillo, Luis	21%
Darvish, Yu	21%

700 Home Runs
% chance to reach milestone

Pujols, Albert	24%
Trout, Mike	19%
Bellinger, Cody	8%
Arenado, Nolan	8%
Harper, Bryce	6%
Alonso, Pete	5%
Machado, Manny	5%
Suarez, Eugenio	4%
Acuna Jr., Ronald	1%
Lindor, Francisco	< 1%

500 Home Runs
% chance to reach milestone

Pujols, Albert	done
Cabrera, Miguel	68%
Encarnacion, Edwin	66%
Trout, Mike	43%
Arenado, Nolan	32%
Martinez, J.D.	31%
Cruz, Nelson	29%
Stanton, Giancarlo	27%
Harper, Bryce	26%
Machado, Manny	24%

1,000 Stolen Bases
% chance to reach milestone

The 300-Win Candidates

Nate Weller

Historically, how many wins a player accumulated has acted as a barometer for how good of a pitcher they were. But as analytics has continued to evolve, statistics such as FIP have taken over the space formerly filled by wins to help us gauge how good a pitcher really is.

You don't have to look any further than last season when Jacob deGrom won the Cy Young Award despite barely winning more games than he lost. His 10 wins were the lowest total for a Cy Young winning starting pitcher. It was further proof that win totals continue to be weighted less and less.

But with all of that said, there is still something special and prestigious about joining the 300-win club. And with the continued emergence of bullpenning and an increased emphasis on pitch count, reaching the milestone is harder than ever.

Justin Verlander was the only pitcher to gain a lot of momentum this season, seeing his odds increase from 25 to 54 percent. But even still, Verlander would need to maintain his current Established Win Level of 19.1 for four more seasons in order to make it, which is a tall task for *anyone*, let alone a pitcher entering his age-37 season.

Including Verlander, only 11 pitchers in total are given more than a puncher's chance at joining the club. Even Max Scherzer, who finds himself among the betting favorites for the NL Cy Young Award, saw his chances of reaching 300 wins more than cut in half.

Zack Greinke, who was a big mover last year, saw only a small uptick in his odds despite winning 18 games this year. Jon Lester and Clayton Kershaw did just enough this season to maintain a glimmer of hope, but are given only three and two percent chances to make it respectively.

A handful of other players fell off the board entirely. Corey Kluber and David Price were both given more than a one percent chance last season but didn't make the cut this year. CC Sabathia ranked as the fifth most likely to reach the milestone at this time last year, but after racking up only five wins in his farewell tour, Sabathia will finish his career 49 wins short.

A few young pitchers are making their first appearances. After a Cy Young–caliber season, Gerrit Cole now ranks as the fourth most likely to get to 300. The only other pitcher under 30 to make the cut is Madison Bumgarner, though he's hanging on by a thread after only nine wins in 2019.

Pitchers on Course For 300 Wins

Name	2019 Age	R/L	W	L	EWL	Momentum	Chance
Verlander, Justin	36	R	225	129	19.1	.855	54%
Greinke, Zack	35	R	205	123	15.3	.744	16%
Scherzer, Max	34	R	170	89	13.9	.820	16%
Cole, Gerrit	28	R	94	52	18.5	.774	6%
Sabathia, CC	38	L	251	161	6.7	.634	4%
Porcello, Rick	30	R	149	118	13.0	.740	3%
Lester, Jon	35	L	190	108	13.1	.668	3%
Kershaw, Clayton	31	L	169	74	13.6	.671	2%
Wainwright, Adam	37	R	162	95	10.8	.663	1%
Lynn, Lance	32	R	98	68	14.0	.724	1%
Strasburg, Stephen	30	R	112	58	15.9	.698	1%
Leake, Mike	31	R	105	98	10.2	.706	<1%
Hamels, Cole	35	L	163	121	8.4	.712	<1%
Bumgarner, Madison	29	L	119	92	9.8	.745	<1%

EWL: Established Win Level

Baseball Glossary

% Inherited Scored
The percentage of inherited baserunners a relief pitcher allows to score.

% Pitches Taken
The percentage of pitches that a batter does not swing at out of the total number of pitches thrown to him.

1st Batter Average
The Batting Average that a relief pitcher allows to the first batter he faces when he enters a game.

1st Batter OBP
The On-Base Percentage that a relief pitcher allows to the first batter he faces when he enters a game.

1st to 3rd (Baserunning)
"Moved" is the number of times a runner goes from 1st base to 3rd base on a SINGLE. "Chances" are the number of times a runner is on 1st base and a batter is credited with a SINGLE.

1st to Home (Baserunning)
"Moved" is the number of times a runner goes from 1st base to home on a DOUBLE. "Chances" are the number of times a runner is on 1st base and a batter is credited with a DOUBLE.

2nd to Home (Baserunning)
"Moved" is the number of times a runner goes from 2nd base to home on a SINGLE. "Chances" are the number of times a runner is on 2nd base and a batter is credited with a SINGLE.

Active Career Batting Leaders
A list of batting leaders among active (appearing in the most recent season) players. An active player is eligible when he meets the minimum requirements for the following categories:

> 1,000 At Bats—Batting Average, On-Base Percentage, Slugging Average, At
> Bats Per HR, At Bats Per GDP, At Bats Per RBI, Strikeout to Walk Ratio
> 100 Stolen Base Attempts—Stolen Base Success Percentage

Active Career Pitching Leaders
A list of pitching leaders among active (appearing in the most recent season) players. An active player is eligible when he meets the minimum requirements for the following categories:

> 750 Innings Pitched—Earned Run Average, Opponent Batting Average, all "Per
> 9 Innings" categories, Strikeout to Walk Ratio
> 250 Games Started—Complete Game Frequency
> 100 Decisions—Win-Loss Percentage

BA w/ RISP
The Batting Average allowed by a pitcher while pitching with runners in scoring position.

Base Taken

A player is credited with a Base Taken whenever he moves up a base on a Wild Pitch, Passed Ball, Balk, Sacrifice Fly, or Defensive Indifference.

Batting Average

Hits divided by at bats.

Batting Average on Balls in Play (BABIP)

Hits in play divided by balls in play. Home runs are not counted as balls in play.

Batting Average Plus Slugging (BPS)

Batting Average plus Slugging Average. Used in Leader Boards on out-of-zone pitches (OutZ).

Blown Save

When a relief pitcher enters a game in a Save Situation (see definition for Save Situation) and allows the other team to score the tying or go-ahead run.

Bomb (Intentional Walk)

An Intentional Walk is counted as a "Bomb" if
1. The next batter, after the IBB, does not ground into a double play, and
2. Multiple runs are scored in the inning, after the intentional walk.

BR Gain (Baserunning)

BR Gain (or Loss if a negative number) is the total of all the types of extra baserunning advances minus the (triple) penalty for all the BR Outs compared with what would be expected based on the MLB averages.

BR Outs (Baserunning)

BR Outs include the sum of Outs Advancing, Doubled Offs, and when a runner is tagged out on the bases when another runner moves up on a Wild Pitch, Passed Ball, or scores on a Sacrifice Fly.

BS Win

A Blown Save Win is a "win" credited to a reliever who has blown a save opportunity.

Career Targets

This method, also called the Favorite Toy, is a way to estimate the probability that a player will achieve a specific career goal. In this example, 3,000 hits will be used. The four components of the formula are:

1. Needed Hits. This is the number of Hits (or any statistic) that a player needs to reach a desired goal.

2. Years Remaining. This is the estimated number of years remaining in the player's career. It is determined using the player's age (on June 30th of the previous year; after a given season ends, use the season when making the calculation). The formula is (42 - age) divided by two. This means a player who is 20 years old will have 11 remaining seasons, a player who is 25 years old will have 8.5 remaining seasons and a player who is 35 years old will have 3.5 remaining seasons. If the player is a catcher, then multiply his remaining seasons by .7. The only stipulation is that years remaining must always be greater than or equal to 1.5.

3. Established Hit Level. The Established Hit Level is a weighted average of the player's hits over the past three seasons. To calculate the Established Hit Level after a given season is complete, add (Hits from two

years ago), (Hits from last year multiplied by two), and (Hits from this year multiplied by three), then divide by six. If the Established Hit Level is less than 75% of the most recent performance, then the Established Hit Level is equal to .75 times the most recent performance.

4. Projected Remaining Hits. This is calculated by multiplying Years Remaining by the Established Hit Level.

The probability of achieving the specified goal is found by dividing Projected Remaining Hits by Needed Hits, then subtracting .5. The maximum that any player has of achieving a goal is .85 raised to the power of (Need Hits / Established Hit Level). This prevents the possibility of a player reaching a goal from being higher than 100 percent, which is impossible.

Catcher Pickoffs (CPO, CPkof)
The number of baserunners thrown out when a catcher throws to a base with a leading baserunner, and the runner is tagged out attempting to return to the base. Catcher pickoffs are not an official statistic and are not counted toward Caught Stealing totals.

Catcher's ERA
The ERA for a catcher is equal to the ERA of pitchers pitching while the catcher is playing behind the plate. It is calculated exactly like ERA for pitchers. Take the number of earned runs allowed while the catcher is playing, multiply it by 9 and then divide it by the total number of defensive innings that the catcher was behind the plate.

Cheap Win
A starting pitcher who wins the game with a game score under 50 gets credit for a cheap win. See Game Score.

Clean Outing
A Clean Outing is a game in which the reliever is not charged with a run (earned or otherwise) AND does not allow an inherited runner to score.

Cleanup Slugging Average
The Slugging Average of a batter when he bats in the cleanup spot, or fourth, in the batting order.

Close and Late
A situation in a game that is very similar to a Save Situation. The following requirements are necessary for a Close and Late game:
1. The game is in the seventh inning or later AND
2. The batting team is either leading by one run or tied OR
3. The tying run is on base, at bat, or on deck.

Component ERA (ERC)
A statistic that estimates what a pitcher's ERA should have been, based on his pitching performance. The ERC formula is calculated as follows:

1. Subtract the pitcher's Home Runs Allowed from his Hits Allowed.
2. Multiply Step 1 by 1.255.
3. Multiply his Home Runs Allowed by four.

4. Add Steps 2 and 3 together.
5. Multiply Step 4 by .89.
6. Add his Walks and Hit Batsmen.
7. Multiply Step 6 by .475.
8. Add Steps 5 and 7 together.

This yields the pitcher's total base estimate (PTB), which is:

$$PTB = 0.89 \times (1.255 \times (H - HR) + 4 \times HR) + 0.475 \times (BB + HB)$$

For those pitchers for whom there is intentional walk data, use this formula instead:

$$PTB = 0.89 \times (1.255 \times (H - HR) + 4 \times HR) + 0.56 \times (BB + HB - IBB)$$

9. Add Hits and Walks and Hit Batsmen.
10. Multiply Step 9 by PTB.
11. Divide Step 10 by Batters Facing Pitcher. If BFP data is unavailable, approximate it by multiplying Innings Pitched by 2.9, then adding Step 9.
12. Multiply Step 11 by 9.
13. Divide Step 12 by Innings Pitched.
14. Subtract .56 from Step 13.

This is the pitcher's ERC, which is:

$$\frac{(H + BB + HB) \times PTB}{BFP \times IP} \times 9 - 0.56$$

If the result after Step 13 is less than 2.24, adjust the formula as follows:

$$\frac{(H + BB + HB) \times PTB}{BFP \times IP} \times 9 \times 0.75$$

Consecutive Days
A count of how many times the pitcher was used after having pitched on the previous day or (in a few cases) in an earlier game on the same day.

Defensive Misplay
Any play which is not an error (or a passed ball) on which the fielder surrenders a base advance or the opportunity to make an out when a better play or a different play would have or might have gotten the out or prevented the advancement.

Defensive Runs Saved
Defensive Runs Saved (Runs Saved, for short) is the innovative metric introduced by John Dewan in *The Fielding Bible—Volume II* and modified in *The Fielding Bible—Volume III* and *The Fielding Bible—Volume IV.* The Runs Saved value indicates how many runs a player saved or cost his team in the field compared to the average player at his position. A player of zero Runs Saved is about average; a positive number of runs saved indicates above-average defense, below-average fielders post negative Runs Saved totals. There are eight components of Runs Saved:

Range and Positioning Runs Saved (all positions except Catcher)
Adjusted Earned Runs Saved (Catchers)
Strike Zone Runs Saved (Catchers)
Stolen Base Runs Saved (Catchers, Pitchers)
Bunt Runs Saved (Corner Infielders, Pitchers, Catchers)
Double Play Runs Saved (Infielders)
Outfield Arm Runs Saved (Outfielders)
Good Play/Misplay Runs Saved (All Positions)

Double Play %
Successful Double Plays divided by the number of Double Play opportunities. This statistic includes both the fielder who started the play and the pivot man.

Double Play Opportunity
A fielder is considered to have a double play opportunity when a ground ball is hit with a runner on first base and less than 2 outs and that fielder is involved in the play. This is used to calculate Double Play % and Pivot %.

Doubled Off
A runner is Doubled Off when he is out for failing to get back to his base before he, or the base, is tagged after a ball hit in the air is caught.

Early Entry
A count of the number of times the reliever entered the game in the sixth inning or earlier.

Earned Run Average
The number of earned runs that a pitcher surrenders per nine innings that he pitches. It is calculated by multiplying the total earned runs allowed by nine and dividing by the total number of innings pitched.

Easy Save
This label is used to separate Saves by difficulty level (Easy or Tough). A Save is considered Easy if the relief pitcher enters the game, pitches one inning or less, and the first batter he faces does not at least represent the tying run.

Fielding Percentage
The percent of plays a player makes in the field without making an error out of his total opportunities. Calculated by dividing (Putouts plus Assists) by (Putouts plus Assists plus Errors).

Games Finished
The relief pitcher who is in the game for each team when the game ends is credited with a Game Finished.

Game Score
To determine the starting pitcher's Game Score:
Start with 50.
Add 1 point for each out recorded by the starting pitcher.
Add 2 points for each inning the pitcher completes after the fourth inning.
Add 1 point for each strikeout.
Subtract 2 points for each hit allowed.

Subtract 4 points for each earned run allowed.
Subtract 2 points for an unearned run.
Subtract 1 point for each walk.

GDP
Grounded into Double Play.

GDP Opportunity
This is a situation where the batter has a chance to ground into a double play. It occurs with at least a runner on first base and less than two outs.

Good Fielding Play
A Good Fielding Play is a play that is made when it is not clear whether or not the play can be made. It is a play that is made when, had the play not been made, no one would have faulted the fielder for not making it.

Ground / Fly Ratio (Grd/Fly, GB/FB)
Calculated for both batters and pitchers. For batters, it is the number of groundballs hit divided by the number of flyballs hit. For pitchers, it is exactly the same but uses the number of groundballs and flyballs allowed. Every fair batted ball is included except for bunts and line drives.

Hall of Fame Monitor
Updated in the 2018 Handbook, the Hall of Fame Monitor was invented by Bill James as a quantitative measure of a player's likelihood of induction into the Hall of Fame. Accomplishments like career statistical benchmarks, championship seasons, and awards are all assigned point values, and each player is put on a scale where anyone from 70-130 is a plausible Hall of Famer, and over 130 is a sure-fire candidate.

Hall of Fame Value (HOF-V)
Introduced by Bill James in the 2019 Handbook, a player's Hall of Fame Value is determined by taking his Wins Above Replacement (according to Baseball Reference), multiplying it by four, and adding it to his Win Shares. Catchers receive a multiplier bonus according to how much they caught in their career: 20% for a full career, 10% for half a career, and so on. A score of 500 indicates that the player is worthy of Hall of Fame candidacy (independent of his likelihood of being selected).

Hold
A relief pitcher is given a Hold anytime he enters the game in a Save Situation (see definition for Save Situation), records one out or more, and exits the game without giving up the lead. If the pitcher finishes the game, then he will only earn credit for a Save. He cannot receive credit for both a Hold and a Save.

Holds Adjusted Save Percentage (same as Save/Hold Percentage)
Holds plus Saves divided by Holds plus Saves Opportunities.

Inherited Runner
Any runner who was on base at the time a relief pitcher enters the game.

Isolated Power
Slugging Average minus Batting Average.

K/BB Ratio
Strikeouts divided by Walks.

Leadoff On-Base Percentage
The On-Base Percentage of a batter when he bats leadoff, or first, in the batting order.

Leverage Index
Leverage is the amount of swing in the possible change in win probability, compared to the average swing in all situations. The average swing value, by definition, is indexed to 1.00.

If the score of the game is 12-0 or 14-1 the possible changes in win probability will be very close to negligible. Whether the pitcher gives up a home run or gets a double play ball doesn't really change the outcome of the game. There won't be much swing in either direction for the probability of the win. But in the late innings of a close game, the change in win probability among the various events will have rather wild swings. With a runner on first, two outs, down by one, and in the bottom of the ninth, the game can hinge on one swing of the bat. A home run and an out will both end the game, but with different outcomes for the teams involved. The Leverage Index we use (LI) was developed at the website Tangotiger.net, and compiled at the website FanGraphs.com.

Long Outing
A Long Outing is one in which the starting pitcher throws more than 110 pitches. Prior to 2002, we used 120 pitches as the cutoff in the Manager's Record section.

Long Save
A Long Save is when the pitcher credited with a save pitches more than one inning.

Manufactured Runs
1. A run that scores without a hit, or a run on which the only hit(s) is/are infield hits, is always scored as a Manufactured Run.
2. A run which is driven in by a home run is never scored a Manufactured Run, under any circumstance.
3. A run which is driven in by a double or a triple is scored as a Manufactured Run only if *two* of the four bases result from advancing on one of these four acts: a sacrifice bunt, a stolen base, a hit and run, or a bunt single.
4. Otherwise, a run is considered to be a Manufactured Run if two of the four bases do not result from the runner being forced along by a walk, a hit batsman, or a safe hit reaching the outfield.
5. A forceout or fielder's choice which does not improve the position of the base runners should not be counted as contributing toward a Manufactured Run. Advancing on a forceout or a fielder's choice DOES count toward a manufactured run, if the play is one which improves the position of the baserunners.
6. A base "gained" on a double play does not count as a contribution to a Manufactured Run. A run scored on a double play is a Manufactured Run only if two of the OTHER bases are not attributable to forced advancement.

Net Gain
Net Gain is a statistic that measures baserunning production that includes all baserunning advancements on both hits and outs (BR Gain) and stolen bases (SB Gain).

Not Good Outcome (Intentional Walk)

A Not Good Outcome (NG) for an Intentional Walk occurs when one run scored in the inning after the intentional walk (and the next batter after the intentional walk did not ground into a double play).

Offensive Winning Percentage (OWP)

A player's Offensive Winning Percentage is the winning percentage of a hypothetical team which has an offense consisting of nine of that player, and pitching and defense which is average for the player's league. It is calculated by taking the square of RC/27 (see the definition for Runs Created per 27 Outs), dividing it by the sum of the square of RC/27 and the square of the average runs scored per game in the league.

On-Base Percentage

(Hits plus Walks plus Hit by Pitcher) divided by (At Bats plus Walks plus Hit by Pitcher plus Sacrifice Flies).

$$\frac{H + BB + HBP}{AB + BB + HBP + SF}$$

On-Base Plus Slugging (OPS)

On-Base Percentage plus Slugging Average

$$\frac{H + BB + HBP}{AB + BB + HBP + SF} + \frac{TB}{AB}$$

Opponent Batting Average

Hits Allowed divided by (Batters Faced minus Walks minus Hit Batsmen minus Sacrifice Hits minus Sacrifice Flies minus Catcher's Interference). The denominator is intended to replicate the number of at-bats against a pitcher.

$$\frac{H}{BFP - BB - HBP - SH - SF - CI}$$

Opposition OPS

The OPS of the hitters facing the pitcher.

Out Advancing

A runner is out advancing when he is tagged out attempting to score from 2nd base on a single or from 1st base on a double, or attempting to go from 1st base to 3rd base on a single.

Park Index

To calculate the park index for home runs in a given ballpark, we take the total home runs of both the home team and its opponents at the ballpark and compare it to the total home runs of the home team and its opponents in other games. We then divide each of those totals by the at-bats in the equivalent situations, so that if there are more at-bats in either situation, the index is not skewed. The result is then multiplied by 100 to yield the familiar form.

The park indices for doubles, triples, walks, strikeouts and home runs by lefties and righties are determined like home runs above—relative to at-bats. Indices of at-bats, runs, hits, errors and infield fielding errors (E-

Infield) are calculated relative to games. The three batting average indices are calculated as is, since these are already relative to at-bats.

PCS (Pitchers' Caught Stealing)
The number of runners officially scored as Caught Stealing where the pitcher initiated the play. PCS plays are often referred to as pickoffs, but differ when the runner breaks towards the next base instead of returning to the base he was on. Pickoffs, which aren't an official statistic, involve the pitcher throwing to the base the runner was leading from, and the runner is out trying to return there.

Pitcher Pickoffs (PPO, PPkof)
The number of baserunners thrown out when a pitcher throws to a base with a leading baserunner, and the runner is tagged out attempting to return to the base. PPO is not an official statistic and does not count toward Caught Stealing totals.

Pivot %
Successful Double Plays turned by pivot man divided by the number of Double Play opportunities with that pivot man involved.

Plate Appearances
At Bats plus Total Walks plus Hit By Pitches plus Sacrifice Hits plus Sacrifice Flies plus Times Reached on Defensive Interference.

Platoon Advantage %
Platoon Advantage % is the percentage of players in the starting lineup who have the platoon advantage (i.e. bats right against a left-handed pitcher or bats left against a right-hander) against the starting pitcher; e.g. if the opposing starting pitcher is right handed and the batting team has six left-handed batters in its lineup, the platoon advantage for that game would be 67%.

Power/Speed Number
A single number that reflects a combination of power and speed. To calculate the Power/Speed Number, multiply Home Runs by Stolen Bases by two, and divide by the sum of Home Runs and Stolen Bases.

$$\frac{2 \times HR \times SB}{HR + SB}$$

Productive Out
An out made by the batter which advances at least one runner. See also Unproductive Out.

Quality Start
A game where the starting pitcher pitches for at least six innings and allows no more than three earned runs.

Quality Start Percentage
Quality Starts divided by Games Started (see the definition for Quality Start).

Quick Hooks
Used in the Manager's Record. For Quick Hooks and Slow Hooks a score is calculated for each game that is the sum of the number of Pitches plus 10 times the number of Runs Allowed. The bottom 25% of scores in the league are considered to be Quick Hooks.

Range and Positioning System

Formerly called the Plus/Minus System, the Range and Positioning System is a method for evaluating defensive play on batted balls. It is made possible by a game scoring system in which each batted ball is rated for type (line drive, grounder, etc.), velocity within its type (based on hang time for flyballs and time to the infielder or through the infield on groundballs), and location on the field. A player gets credit (a "plus" number) if he makes a play that at least one other player at his position missed during the season and he loses credit (a "minus" number") if he misses a play that at least one player made. The size of the credits are proportional to the percentage of times all players make the play. All plays for each player at his position are summed to get his total Plays Saved for the season. A total of zero would be average and any other number would approximate how many plays more or less the player made than the average player at the position for the number of chances the player had to field batted balls.

Range Factor

The number of Successful Chances (Putouts plus Assists) times nine divided by the number of Defensive Innings Played.

RBI %

The percentage of all potential runs driven in by a certain hitter. Simply put, it's RBIs divided by RBI Opportunities. RBI Opportunities are defined as RBI plus a weighted total of baserunners who the hitter failed to drive in. Any plays where the batter reached safely and no outs were recorded aren't counted as missed opportunities. They are defined like so:

> 1.00 for each runner on third base with less than 2 outs, plus
> .70 for each runner on third base with 2 outs, plus
> .70 for each runner on second base, plus
> .40 for each runner on first base, plus
> .10 for each bases-empty plate appearance.

Regular Saves

Any save which does not meet the definition either of an Easy Save or a Tough Save is a "Regular" Save.

Run Support Per 9 IP

The total number of runs scored by a pitcher's team while he is in the game multiplied by nine and divided by total Innings Pitched.

Runs Created

"Runs Created" is an estimate of the number of a team's runs which are created by each individual hitter. There are many different formulas for estimating runs created. . .did you want the one that involves swinging a dead cat in the cemetery under a full moon? Yeah, I don't blame you. . .worm-eaten persimmons are so hard to find in the modern world.

This is the one we use now; it is complicated enough. First, there is an "A" Factor in the formula, a "B" Factor, and a "C" factor. The "A" Factor, which represents the number of times the hitter is on base, is Hits, Plus Walks, Plus Hit Batsmen, Minus Caught Stealing, Minus Grounded Into Double Play. The "B" Factor, which represents the hitter's ability to advance other runners, is 1.125 times the player's Singles, plus 1.69 times his Doubles, plus 3.02 times his Triples, plus 3.73 times his Home Runs, plus .29 times his Walks and Hit Batsmen, not counting intentional walks, plus .492 times Sacrifice Hits, Sacrifice Flies and Stolen Bases, minus .04 times Strikeouts. The "C" Factor, which represents opportunities, is At Bats, Plus Walks, Plus Hit By Pitch, Plus Sacrifice Hits, Plus Sacrifice Flies.

Having made these initial calculations of the A, B and C factors, we then change the "A" factor to "A plus 2.4 times C".

We change the "B" factor to "B plus 3 times C".

We change the "C" factor to "9 times C".

Multiply A times B, divide by the new C ("9 times C"), and subtract .90 times by the original C.

This is our first, temporary estimate of the player's runs created. What we have done here is to ask these questions:

1. How many runs would a team probably score that consisted of eight "ordinary" type of hitters, plus this particular hitter?
2. How many of those runs would be created by the eight ordinary type of hitters?
3. What is the difference and thus, how many runs did our player create?

To estimate this, we have placed our player in the context of eight hitters with a .300 on base percentage (2.4 divided by 8) and a .375 advancement percentage (3 divided by 8). For each trip through the batting order, the eight ordinary-type hitters would produce 9/10 of a run (2.4 times 3, divided by 8). The "9" in the denominator is eight ordinary hitters plus our man. The "-.9" being subtracted at the end is the runs created by the "ordinary" hitters. In essence, we have placed the hitter in a neutral solution, measured the neutral solution without our hitter, measured it with our hitter, and then estimated the contribution of this hitter as being the difference between the two.

We're not quite done. After that, we adjust the player's runs created estimate for his performance in two "run-sensitive" situations. Suppose that a player whose overall batting average is .250, has batted 100 times with runners in scoring position, and has gone 30-for-100. That's five hits better than expected, 30 hits where we would have expected 25. His team will score an extra five runs because he has done that, and so we increase the player's runs created estimate by five runs. If the player has hit poorly with runners in scoring position, we decrease it by the shortfall in the same way.

Suppose that a player has batted 250 times with runners on base, 250 times with the bases empty, and that he has hit 20 home runs overall. We would expect him to have hit 10 with men on base, 10 with the bases empty, right?

Suppose that he didn't. Suppose that he hit 12 with the bases empty, 8 with men on base. His team would score two runs less than expected because he did this, and we would thus penalize him two runs for the shortfall.

This is our second runs created estimate the player's runs created, adjusted for his batting performance in run sensitive situations.

Suppose, however, that we figure the runs created for all of the individuals on a team, and we add them up, and it doesn't match the runs actually scored by the team? What if the formulas say that the team should have scored 800 runs, but they actually scored 820?

Then obviously, the formulas missed. We're trying to measure the runs ACTUALLY created by each hitter as best we can, in the real world, not the theoretical impact of some combination of singles, doubles, triples and walks. If the actual number is different than the estimates, we have to adjust the estimates to fit the facts. In this case—820 runs scored with only 800 runs created— we would multiply each runs created estimate by 820/800, or 1.025. Then we round it off to an integer, and that's the player's estimated runs created.

Let go of that cat, Arthur. Heck, the moon isn't full for three weeks, anyway.

Runs Created per 27 Outs (RC/27)

This statistic estimates the number of runs per game that a team made up of nine of the same player would score. To calculate RC/27, multiply Runs Created by league outs per team game, divide the result by outs made by the player (the sum of at bats plus sacrifice hits plus sacrifice flies plus caught stealing plus grounded into double plays, minus hits). The formula written out is:

$$\frac{\frac{RC \times 3 \times LgIP}{2 \times LgG}}{AB - H + SH + SF + CS + GDP}$$

Runs Saved

See Defensive Runs Saved.

Save Opportunities

The sum of Saves and Blown Saves (see Save Situation).

Save/Hold Percentage (same as Holds Adjusted Saves Percentage)

The sum of Saves and Holds, divided by the sum of Saves, Holds, and Blown Saves.

For several years we figured "Save Percentage", which is simply Saves divided by Save Opportunities, and this stat had some currency in the game. But the Save Percentage severely discriminates against middle relievers, who have no real chance to be credited with the Save, since they will be taken out of the game and replaced by the Closer even if they throw 110 miles an hour and strike out everybody they see. Middle relievers typically have Save Percentages of zero, even if they pitch well. The Save/Hold Percentage is a much more realistic evaluation of a pitcher's success in Save situations.

Save Percentage

A pitcher's Saves divided by the total number of Save Situations he faces (see definition for Save Situation).

Save Situation

A relief pitcher is in a Save Situation when he enters the game with his team in the lead, has the opportunity to finish the game, is not the winning pitcher of record at the time, and meets any one of the three following conditions:

1.The pitcher's team is leading by no more than three runs and the pitcher has the chance to pitch for at least one inning,

OR

2.The pitcher enters the game with the potential tying run on base, at bat, or on deck,

OR

3. The pitcher pitches three or more effective innings regardless of the lead. The determination of a save in this situation is made by the official scorer.

It is not possible to have more than one save credited to a single team in a game.

SB Gain (Baserunning)

Stolen Base attempts must be successful greater than about two thirds of the time to have a positive result on the number of runs scored. SB gain is therefore the number of bases stolen minus two times the number of caught stealing (SB Gain = SB - 2CS). For example, a runner steals 30 bases and is caught stealing 7 times. His SB Gain would be 30 - 2 * 7 = +16. Another runner steals 10 bases and is caught stealing 6 times. His SB Gain (actually a loss) would be 10 - 2 * 6 = -2.

SB Success Percentage

Stolen Bases divided by the number of Stolen Base attempts (Stolen Bases plus Caught Stealing).

$$\frac{SB}{SB + CS}$$

Secondary Average

A number meant to reflect everything else except for batting average. A player will have a high Secondary Average if he hits for power, takes walks and steals bases. It is calculated with the following formula:

$$\frac{TB - H + BB + SB}{AB}$$

Similarity Score

A number which reflects the similarity between two different statistical lines, either for a player or for a team. A score of 1,000 means that the statistical lines are identical.

Slow Hooks

Used in the Manager's Record. For Quick Hooks and Slow Hooks a score is calculated for each game that is the sum of the number of Pitches plus 10 times the number of Runs Allowed. The top 25% of scores in the league are considered to be Slow Hooks.

Slugging Average

Total Bases divided by At Bats.

Slugging Average on Balls in Play (SlgBIP)

Total bases gained on balls in play divided by balls in play. Home runs are not counted as balls in play.

Speed Score

Speed score is an estimate of a player's running speed, based on six indicators of running speed found in his batting and fielding records. Those six indicators are stolen base success rate, the frequency of stolen base attempts, triples, grounding into double plays, runs scored as a percentage of times on base, and defensive position and range.

The full process of estimating Speed Scores is long and complex, and can be found on Bill James Online or by contacting Baseball Info Solutions.

Total Bases (TB)

Hits plus Doubles plus (2 times Triples) plus (3 times Home Runs).

$$H + 2B + (2 \times 3B) + (3 \times HR)$$

Tough Loss

A starting pitcher who loses the game with a game score (see definition for Game Score) over 50 gets credit for a tough loss.

Tough Save

This label is used to separate Saves by difficulty level (Easy or Tough). A Save is considered Tough if the relief pitcher enters the game with the tying run on base.

Total Chances (TC)

The number of plays in which a defensive player participated, determined as Assists + Putouts + Errors.

Unproductive Out

An out made by the batter with runners on base that fails to advance any baserunner or results in a weaker baserunner configuration than before. Excludes the third out of an inning. See also Productive Out.

Win Probability

The probability of a team winning the game determined at any time during the game based on the score, inning, outs and base situation.

Win Shares

Win Shares are a system devised by Bill James for valuing a player's overall contribution to his team over a season. This allows us to more effectively compare players across positions, even between pitchers and position players. The use of the word "shares" is important, because they are split up among players based on how many wins a team actually earns. For each win, a team has three Win Shares to allocate among its players. Those shares are then allocated according to how much each player contributed to the team's run scoring and prevention.

Winning Percentage

Wins divided by (Wins plus Losses).

Minor League Abbreviation Key

Abbreviation	Team	Level	League	MLB Affiliate	First Year	Last Year
Abrdn	Aberdeen IronBirds	A-	New York-Penn League	Baltimore Orioles	2015	2019
Akron	Akron RubberDucks	AA	Eastern League	Cleveland Indians	2015	2019
Albq	Albuquerque Isotopes	AAA	Pacific Coast League	Colorado Rockies	2015	2019
Altna	Altoona Curve	AA	Eastern League	Pittsburgh Pirates	2015	2019
Amrillo	Amarillo Sod Poodles	AA	Texas League	San Diego Padres	2019	2019
Angels	AZL Angels	R	Arizona League	Los Angeles Angels	2015	2019
Ark	Arkansas Travelers	AA	Texas League	Los Angeles Angels	2015	2016
Ark	Arkansas Travelers	AA	Texas League	Seattle Mariners	2017	2019
As	AZL Athletics	R	Arizona League	Oakland Athletics	2015	2018
AsGold	AZL Athletics Gold	R	Arizona League	Oakland Athletics	2019	2019
AsGrn	AZL Athletics Green	R	Arizona League	Oakland Athletics	2019	2019
Ashvll	Asheville Tourists	A	South Atlantic League	Colorado Rockies	2015	2019
Astros	GCL Astros	R	Gulf Coast League	Houston Astros	2015	2019
Auburn	Auburn Doubledays	A-	New York-Penn League	Washington Nationals	2015	2019
Augsta	Augusta GreenJackets	A	South Atlantic League	San Francisco Giants	2015	2019
B Jays	GCL Blue Jays	R	Gulf Coast League	Toronto Blue Jays	2015	2019
Batvia	Batavia Muckdogs	A-	New York-Penn League	Miami Marlins	2015	2019
Beloit	Beloit Snappers	A	Midwest League	Oakland Athletics	2015	2019
BG	Bowling Green Hot Rods	A	Midwest League	Tampa Bay Rays	2015	2019
Billings	Billings Mustangs	R+	Pioneer League	Cincinnati Reds	2015	2019
Biloxi	Biloxi Shuckers	AA	Southern League	Milwaukee Brewers	2015	2019
Bklyn	Brooklyn Cyclones	A-	New York-Penn League	New York Mets	2015	2019
Bkrsfld	Bakersfield Blaze	A+	California League	Seattle Mariners	2015	2016
Bluefld	Bluefield Blue Jays	R+	Appalachian League	Toronto Blue Jays	2015	2019
Bnghtn	Binghamton Mets	AA	Eastern League	New York Mets	2015	2016
Bnghtn	Binghamton Rumble Ponies	AA	Eastern League	New York Mets	2017	2019
Boise	Boise Hawks	A-	Northwest League	Colorado Rockies	2015	2019
Bowie	Bowie Baysox	AA	Eastern League	Baltimore Orioles	2015	2019
Bradtn	Bradenton Marauders	A+	Florida State League	Pittsburgh Pirates	2015	2019
Braves	GCL Braves	R	Gulf Coast League	Atlanta Braves	2015	2019
BrewersB	AZL Brewers Blue	R	Arizona League	Milwaukee Brewers	2019	2019
Brewrs	AZL Brewers	R	Arizona League	Milwaukee Brewers	2015	2018
BrewrsGold	AZL Brewers Gold	R	Arizona League	Milwaukee Brewers	2019	2019
Brham	Birmingham Barons	AA	Southern League	Chicago White Sox	2015	2019
Brstol	Bristol Pirates	R+	Appalachian League	Pittsburgh Pirates	2015	2019
BrvdCt	Brevard Co. Manatees	A+	Florida State League	Milwaukee Brewers	2015	2016
Buffalo	Buffalo Bisons	AAA	International League	Toronto Blue Jays	2015	2019
BuiesCk	Buies Creek Astros	A+	Carolina League	Houston Astros	2017	2018
Burlgtn	Burlington IA Bees	A	Midwest League	Los Angeles Angels	2015	2019
Burlgtn	Burlington NC Royals	R+	Appalachian League	Kansas City Royals	2015	2019
Cards	GCL Cardinals	R	Gulf Coast League	St Louis Cardinals	2015	2019
Carlina	Carolina Mudcats	A+	Carolina League	Atlanta Braves	2015	2016
Carlina	Carolina Mudcats	A+	Carolina League	Milwaukee Brewers	2017	2019
Charllt	Charlotte NC Knights	AAA	International League	Chicago White Sox	2015	2019
Charltt	Charlotte FL Stone Crabs	A+	Florida State League	Tampa Bay Rays	2015	2019
Chatt	Chattanooga Lookouts	AA	Southern League	Minnesota Twins	2015	2018
Chatt	Chattanooga Lookouts	AA	Southern League	Cincinnati Reds	2019	2019
Clinton	Clinton LumberKings	A	Midwest League	Seattle Mariners	2015	2018
Clinton	Clinton LumberKings	A	Midwest League	Miami Marlins	2019	2019
Clmbs	Columbus Clippers	AAA	International League	Cleveland Indians	2015	2019
Clrwtr	Clearwater Threshers	A+	Florida State League	Philadelphia Phillies	2015	2019
ColSpr	Colorado Spr. Sky Sox	AAA	Pacific Coast League	Milwaukee Brewers	2015	2018
Columb	Columbia Fireflies	A	South Atlantic League	New York Mets	2016	2019
Conn	Connecticut Tigers	A-	New York-Penn League	Detroit Tigers	2015	2019
CpChr	Corpus Christi Hooks	AA	Texas League	Houston Astros	2015	2019
Crpds	Cedar Rapids Kernels	A	Midwest League	Minnesota Twins	2015	2019
CtnSC	Charleston RiverDogs	A	South Atlantic League	New York Yankees	2015	2019
Cubs	AZL Cubs	R	Arizona League	Chicago Cubs	2015	2018
Cubs2	AZL Cubs2	R	Arizona League	Chicago Cubs	2018	2019
Danvle	Danville Braves	R+	Appalachian League	Atlanta Braves	2015	2019
Dayton	Dayton Dragons	A	Midwest League	Cincinnati Reds	2015	2019
Dbcks	AZL D-backs	R	Arizona League	Arizona Diamondbacks	2015	2019

623

Minor League Abbreviation Key

Abbreviation	Team	Level	League	MLB Affiliate	First Year	Last Year
Ddgrs	AZL Dodgers	R	Arizona League	Los Angeles Dodgers	2015	2018
Ddgrs	AZL Dodgers 1	R	Arizona League	Los Angeles Dodgers	2019	2019
Ddgrs2	AZL Dodgers 2	R	Arizona League	Los Angeles Dodgers	2019	2019
Dlmrva	Delmarva Shorebirds	A	South Atlantic League	Baltimore Orioles	2015	2019
Dnedin	Dunedin Blue Jays	A+	Florida State League	Toronto Blue Jays	2015	2019
Drham	Durham Bulls	AAA	International League	Tampa Bay Rays	2015	2019
DwnEast	Down East Wood Ducks	A+	Carolina League	Texas Rangers	2017	2019
Dytona	Daytona Tortugas	A+	Florida State League	Cincinnati Reds	2015	2019
Elizab	Elizabethton Twins	R+	Appalachian League	Minnesota Twins	2015	2019
ElPaso	El Paso Chihuahuas	AAA	Pacific Coast League	San Diego Padres	2015	2019
Erie	Erie SeaWolves	AA	Eastern League	Detroit Tigers	2015	2019
Eugene	Eugene Emeralds	A-	Northwest League	Chicago Cubs	2015	2019
Everett	Everett AquaSox	A-	Northwest League	Seattle Mariners	2015	2019
Faytvll	Fayetteville Woodpeckers	A+	Carolina League	Houston Astros	2019	2019
Florida	Florida Fire Frogs	A+	Florida State League	Atlanta Braves	2017	2019
Frdrck	Frederick Keys	A+	Carolina League	Baltimore Orioles	2015	2019
Fresno	Fresno Grizzlies	AAA	Pacific Coast League	Houston Astros	2015	2018
Fresno	Fresno Grizzlies	AAA	Pacific Coast League	Washington Nationals	2019	2019
Frisco	Frisco RoughRiders	AA	Texas League	Texas Rangers	2015	2019
FtMyrs	Fort Myers Miracle	A+	Florida State League	Minnesota Twins	2015	2019
FtWyn	Fort Wayne TinCaps	A	Midwest League	San Diego Padres	2015	2019
GdJunc	Grand Junction Rockies	R+	Pioneer League	Colorado Rockies	2015	2019
Giants	AZL Giants	R	Arizona League	San Francisco Giants	2015	2018
Giants Blk	AZL Giants Black	R	Arizona League	San Francisco Giants	2019	2019
Giants Orng	AZL Giants Orange	R	Arizona League	San Francisco Giants	2018	2019
Gr Falls	Great Falls Voyagers	R+	Pioneer League	Chicago White Sox	2015	2019
Grnsbr	Greensboro Grasshoppers	A	South Atlantic League	Miami Marlins	2015	2018
Grnsbr	Greensboro Grasshoppers	A	South Atlantic League	Pittsburgh Pirates	2019	2019
Grnvlle	Greeneville Astros	R+	Appalachian League	Houston Astros	2015	2019
Grnvlle	Greenville Drive	A	South Atlantic League	Boston Red Sox	2015	2019
Gt Lks	Great Lakes Loons	A	Midwest League	Los Angeles Dodgers	2015	2019
Gwnntt	Gwinnett Braves	AAA	International League	Atlanta Braves	2015	2017
Gwnntt	Gwinnett Stripers	AAA	International League	Atlanta Braves	2018	2019
Helena	Helena Brewers	R+	Pioneer League	Milwaukee Brewers	2015	2018
Hgrstn	Hagerstown Suns	A	South Atlantic League	Washington Nationals	2015	2019
Hi Dsrt	High Desert Mavericks	A+	California League	Texas Rangers	2015	2016
HiroCrp	Hiroshima Carp	IND	Independent League	Independent	2015	2015
Hkry	Hickory Crawdads	A	South Atlantic League	Texas Rangers	2015	2019
Hlsbro	Hillsboro Hops	A-	Northwest League	Arizona Diamondbacks	2015	2019
Hrsbrg	Harrisburg Senators	AA	Eastern League	Washington Nationals	2015	2019
Hrtfrd	Hartford Yard Goats	AA	Eastern League	Colorado Rockies	2016	2019
HudVal	Hudson Valley Renegades	A-	New York-Penn League	Tampa Bay Rays	2015	2019
Idaho	Idaho Falls Chukars	R+	Pioneer League	Kansas City Royals	2015	2019
Indians	AZL Indians Blue	R	Arizona League	Cleveland Indians	2019	2019
Indians2	AZL Indians2	R	Arizona League	Cleveland Indians	2018	2018
IndiansR	AZL Indians Red	R	Arizona League	Cleveland Indians	2019	2019
Indns	AZL Indians	R	Arizona League	Cleveland Indians	2015	2018
Indy	Indianapolis Indians	AAA	International League	Pittsburgh Pirates	2015	2019
InldEm	Inland Empire 66ers	A+	California League	Los Angeles Angels	2015	2019
Iowa	Iowa Cubs	AAA	Pacific Coast League	Chicago Cubs	2015	2019
Jacksn	Jackson Generals	AA	Southern League	Seattle Mariners	2015	2016
Jacksn	Jackson Generals	AA	Southern League	Arizona Diamondbacks	2017	2019
Jaxnvl	Jacksonville Suns	AA	Southern League	Miami Marlins	2015	2016
Jaxnvl	Jacksonville Jumbo Shrimp	AA	Southern League	Miami Marlins	2017	2019
Jhscty	Johnson City Cardinals	R+	Appalachian League	St Louis Cardinals	2015	2019
Jupiter	Jupiter Hammerheads	A+	Florida State League	Miami Marlins	2015	2019
Kane	Kane County Cougars	A	Midwest League	Arizona Diamondbacks	2015	2019
Knapol	Kannapolis Intimidators	A	South Atlantic League	Chicago White Sox	2015	2019
Kngspt	Kingsport Mets	R+	Appalachian League	New York Mets	2015	2019
Lakwd	Lakewood BlueClaws	A	South Atlantic League	Philadelphia Phillies	2015	2019
Lancst	Lancaster JetHawks	A+	California League	Houston Astros	2015	2016
Lancst	Lancaster JetHawks	A+	California League	Colorado Rockies	2017	2019
Lk Cty	Lake County Captains	A	Midwest League	Cleveland Indians	2015	2019
Lk Els	Lake Elsinore Storm	A+	California League	San Diego Padres	2015	2019

Minor League Abbreviation Key

Abbreviation	Team	Level	League	MLB Affiliate	First Year	Last Year
Lkland	Lakeland Flying Tigers	A+	Florida State League	Detroit Tigers	2015	2019
Lnsng	Lansing Lugnuts	A	Midwest League	Toronto Blue Jays	2015	2019
Lowell	Lowell Spinners	A-	New York-Penn League	Boston Red Sox	2015	2019
LsVgs	Las Vegas 51s	AAA	Pacific Coast League	New York Mets	2015	2018
LsVgs	Las Vegas Aviators	AAA	Pacific Coast League	Oakland Athletics	2019	2019
Lsvlle	Louisville Bats	AAA	International League	Cincinnati Reds	2015	2019
LV	Lehigh Valley IronPigs	AAA	International League	Philadelphia Phillies	2015	2019
Lxngtn	Lexington Legends	A	South Atlantic League	Kansas City Royals	2015	2019
Lynbrg	Lynchburg Hillcats	A+	Carolina League	Cleveland Indians	2015	2019
Mdest	Modesto Nuts	A+	California League	Colorado Rockies	2015	2016
Mdest	Modesto Nuts	A+	California League	Seattle Mariners	2017	2019
Mdlnd	Midland RockHounds	AA	Texas League	Oakland Athletics	2015	2019
Memp	Memphis Redbirds	AAA	Pacific Coast League	St Louis Cardinals	2015	2019
Mets	GCL Mets	R	Gulf Coast League	New York Mets	2015	2019
MhVlly	Mahoning Valley Scrappers	A-	New York-Penn League	Cleveland Indians	2015	2019
Missi	Mississippi Braves	AA	Southern League	Atlanta Braves	2015	2019
Mobile	Mobile BayBears	AA	Southern League	Arizona Diamondbacks	2015	2016
Mobile	Mobile BayBears	AA	Southern League	Los Angeles Angels	2017	2019
Mont	Montgomery Biscuits	AA	Southern League	Tampa Bay Rays	2015	2019
Mrlns	GCL Marlins	R	Gulf Coast League	Miami Marlins	2015	2019
MrtlBh	Myrtle Beach Pelicans	A+	Carolina League	Chicago Cubs	2015	2019
Ms	AZL Mariners	R	Arizona League	Seattle Mariners	2015	2019
Msoula	Missoula Osprey	R+	Pioneer League	Arizona Diamondbacks	2015	2019
Nashv	Nashville Sounds	AAA	Pacific Coast League	Oakland Athletics	2015	2018
Nashv	Nashville Sounds	AAA	Pacific Coast League	Texas Rangers	2019	2019
Nats	GCL Nationals	R	Gulf Coast League	Washington Nationals	2015	2019
NewOr	New Orleans Zephyrs	AAA	Pacific Coast League	Miami Marlins	2015	2016
NewOr	New Orleans Baby Cakes	AAA	Pacific Coast League	Miami Marlins	2017	2019
Nexen	Nexen Heroes	IND	Independent League	Independent	2015	2015
Nham	New Hampshire Fisher Cats	AA	Eastern League	Toronto Blue Jays	2015	2019
Nippon	Hokkaido Nippon Ham Fighters	IND	Independent League	Independent	2015	2015
Norfolk	Norfolk Tides	AAA	International League	Baltimore Orioles	2015	2019
NWArk	NW Arkansas Naturals	AA	Texas League	Kansas City Royals	2015	2019
NwBrit	New Britain Rock Cats	AA	Eastern League	Colorado Rockies	2015	2015
Ogden	Ogden Raptors	R+	Pioneer League	Los Angeles Dodgers	2015	2019
OkCity	Oklahoma City Dodgers	AAA	Pacific Coast League	Los Angeles Dodgers	2015	2019
Omha	Omaha Storm Chasers	AAA	Pacific Coast League	Kansas City Royals	2015	2019
Orem	Orem Owlz	R+	Pioneer League	Los Angeles Angels	2015	2019
Orioles	GCL Orioles	R	Gulf Coast League	Baltimore Orioles	2015	2019
Padres	AZL Padres	R	Arizona League	San Diego Padres	2015	2019
Padres2	AZL Padres2	R	Arizona League	San Diego Padres	2017	2019
Peoria	Peoria Chiefs	A	Midwest League	St Louis Cardinals	2015	2019
Phillies	GCL Phillies	R	Gulf Coast League	Philadelphia Phillies	2015	2019
PhilliesW	GCL Phillies West	R	Gulf Coast League	Philadelphia Phillies	2016	2019
Pirates	GCL Pirates	R	Gulf Coast League	Pittsburgh Pirates	2015	2019
PlmBh	Palm Beach Cardinals	A+	Florida State League	St Louis Cardinals	2015	2019
Pnscla	Pensacola Blue Wahoos	AA	Southern League	Cincinnati Reds	2015	2018
Pnscla	Pensacola Blue Wahoos	AA	Southern League	Minnesota Twins	2019	2019
Portlnd	Portland ME Sea Dogs	AA	Eastern League	Boston Red Sox	2015	2019
Prnctn	Princeton Rays	R+	Appalachian League	Tampa Bay Rays	2015	2019
Ptomc	Potomac Nationals	A+	Carolina League	Washington Nationals	2015	2019
Pulski	Pulaski Yankees	R+	Appalachian League	New York Yankees	2015	2019
Pwtckt	Pawtucket Red Sox	AAA	International League	Boston Red Sox	2015	2019
QuadC	Quad Cities River Bandits	A	Midwest League	Houston Astros	2015	2019
Rays	GCL Rays	R	Gulf Coast League	Tampa Bay Rays	2015	2019
Rchmd	Richmond Flying Squirrels	AA	Eastern League	San Francisco Giants	2015	2019
RckyMt	Rocky Mountain Vibes	R+	Pioneer League	Milwaukee Brewers	2019	2019
Rcuca	Rancho Cucamonga Quakes	A+	California League	Los Angeles Dodgers	2015	2019
Rdng	Reading Fightin Phils	AA	Eastern League	Philadelphia Phillies	2015	2019
RdRck	Round Rock Express	AAA	Pacific Coast League	Texas Rangers	2015	2018
RdRck	Round Rock Express	AAA	Pacific Coast League	Houston Astros	2019	2019
Reds	AZL Reds	R	Arizona League	Cincinnati Reds	2015	2019
RedSx	GCL Red Sox	R	Gulf Coast League	Boston Red Sox	2015	2019
Reno	Reno Aces	AAA	Pacific Coast League	Arizona Diamondbacks	2015	2019

Minor League Abbreviation Key

Abbreviation	Team	Level	League	MLB Affiliate	First Year	Last Year
Rngrs	AZL Rangers	R	Arizona League	Texas Rangers	2015	2019
Roch	Rochester Red Wings	AAA	International League	Minnesota Twins	2015	2019
Rome	Rome Braves	A	South Atlantic League	Atlanta Braves	2015	2019
Royals	AZL Royals	R	Arizona League	Kansas City Royals	2015	2019
Salem	Salem Red Sox	A+	Carolina League	Boston Red Sox	2015	2019
Salt Lk	Salt Lake City Bees	AAA	Pacific Coast League	Los Angeles Angels	2015	2019
Savann	Savannah Sand Gnats	A	South Atlantic League	New York Mets	2015	2015
Sbend	South Bend Cubs	A	Midwest League	Chicago Cubs	2015	2019
Scrmto	Sacramento River Cats	AAA	Pacific Coast League	San Francisco Giants	2015	2019
SlKzr	Salem-Keizer Volcanoes	A-	Northwest League	San Francisco Giants	2015	2019
SnAnt	San Antonio Missions	AA	Texas League	San Diego Padres	2015	2018
SnAnt	San Antonio Missions	AAA	Pacific Coast League	Milwaukee Brewers	2019	2019
SnJos	San Jose Giants	A+	California League	San Francisco Giants	2015	2019
Spkane	Spokane Indians	A-	Northwest League	Texas Rangers	2015	2019
Sprgfld	Springfield Cardinals	AA	Texas League	St Louis Cardinals	2015	2019
Stcktn	Stockton Ports	A+	California League	Oakland Athletics	2015	2019
StCol	State College Spikes	A-	New York-Penn League	St Louis Cardinals	2015	2019
Stluci	St. Lucie Mets	A+	Florida State League	New York Mets	2015	2019
StnIld	Staten Island Yankees	A-	New York-Penn League	New York Yankees	2015	2019
S-WB	Scranton WB RailRiders	AAA	International League	New York Yankees	2015	2019
Syrcse	Syracuse Chiefs	AAA	International League	Washington Nationals	2015	2018
Syrcse	Syracuse Mets	AAA	International League	New York Mets	2019	2019
Tacom	Tacoma Rainiers	AAA	Pacific Coast League	Seattle Mariners	2015	2019
Tampa	Tampa Yankees	A+	Florida State League	New York Yankees	2015	2017
Tampa	Tampa Tarpons	A+	Florida State League	New York Yankees	2018	2019
Tenn	Tennessee Smokies	AA	Southern League	Chicago Cubs	2015	2019
Tigers	GCL Tigers	R	Gulf Coast League	Detroit Tigers	2015	2019
TigersW	GCL Tigers West	R	Gulf Coast League	Detroit Tigers	2016	2019
Toledo	Toledo Mud Hens	AAA	International League	Detroit Tigers	2015	2019
TriCity	Tri-City NY ValleyCats	A-	New York-Penn League	Houston Astros	2015	2019
TriCity	Tri-City WA Dust Devils	A-	Northwest League	San Diego Padres	2015	2019
Trntn	Trenton Thunder	AA	Eastern League	New York Yankees	2015	2019
Tulsa	Tulsa Drillers	AA	Texas League	Los Angeles Dodgers	2015	2019
Twins	GCL Twins	R	Gulf Coast League	Minnesota Twins	2015	2019
Vancvr	Vancouver Canadians	A-	Northwest League	Toronto Blue Jays	2015	2019
Visalia	Visalia Rawhide	A+	California League	Arizona Diamondbacks	2015	2019
Vrmnt	Vermont Lake Monsters	A-	New York-Penn League	Oakland Athletics	2015	2019
Wilmg	Wilmington Blue Rocks	A+	Carolina League	Kansas City Royals	2015	2019
WinSa	Winston-Salem Dash	A+	Carolina League	Chicago White Sox	2015	2019
Wisc	Wisconsin Timber Rattlers	A	Midwest League	Milwaukee Brewers	2015	2019
Wmich	West Michigan Whitecaps	A	Midwest League	Detroit Tigers	2015	2019
Wmspt	Williamsport Crosscutters	A-	New York-Penn League	Philadelphia Phillies	2015	2019
Wsox	AZL White Sox	R	Arizona League	Chicago White Sox	2015	2019
WV	West Virginia Power	A	South Atlantic League	Pittsburgh Pirates	2015	2018
WV	West Virginia Power	A	South Atlantic League	Seattle Mariners	2019	2019
WV	West Virginia Black Bears	A-	New York-Penn League	Pittsburgh Pirates	2015	2019
Yanks1	GCL Yankees	R	Gulf Coast League	New York Yankees	2015	2019
Yanks2	GCL Yankees2	R	Gulf Coast League	New York Yankees	2015	2019

Baseball Info Solutions

Since the company's founding, analytics' place in sports has changed a lot, but Baseball Info Solutions (BIS) has remained true to its objective. The company's mission is to provide the most accurate, in-depth, and timely professional baseball and football data, including cutting-edge research and analysis, striving to educate professional teams and the public about sports analytics. BIS is thrilled to work with the majority of teams in Major League Baseball as a part of that goal. It also operates as Sports Info Solutions, delivering NFL and college football advanced data to broadcasters, NFL teams and directly to the public.

It all begins with the data collection operation. BIS's staff of operations analysts does excellent work in organizing the ever-expanding crew of highly trained video scouts, and together they record data from every Major League Baseball and Nippon Professional Baseball game, as well as many minor league games. That data covers everything from basic box score data to pitch locations, types, and velocities to batted ball hang times, defensive shifts, and much more. BIS collects a lot of data that cannot be found any place else. BIS video scouts log 10–12 hours on every game capturing the most in-depth information possible.

The data itself is valuable to many clients, but BIS's research and development department creates analytics and undertakes research projects with the data to help it reach its full potential utility. Their most well-known endeavor is the Defensive Runs Saved statistic, which estimates how many runs fielders save their teams because of a variety of skills such as range, throwing, prevention of stolen bases, pitch framing, and many other factors. Recent R&D department innovations include applying internally collected infielder positioning data to make enhancements to DRS and the creation of a pitch predicting tool.

John Dewan co-founded BIS in 2002, having already spent a couple of decades in the industry at the forefront of the sabermetric movement. He got his start in the field as the Executive Director of Project Scoresheet, which was a Bill James-led effort to comprehensively collect baseball data. This led to the incorporation and development of STATS Inc. from a bedroom office to its sale to News Corp in 2000. Without those efforts, many of the statistics and analytics that we all take for granted may not even be available at all.

If you would like to contact Baseball Info Solutions for data inquiries, potential job openings, or additional information, you can reach us at:

Baseball Info Solutions
41 S. 2nd Street
Coplay, PA 18037
610-261-2370
www.baseballinfosolutions.com

Acknowledgments

While *The Bill James Handbook* is in its 31st year, its production is somewhat analogous to a "routine double play" in that many little things need to go right and be handled with care in order to finish the job seamlessly. An incredible number of people dedicate countless hours to all aspects of the book, from the data collection to the final editing phase, and we do it on an accelerated timeline so that as soon as the World Series is over, the book is on shelves by November 1. We'd like to take a moment to extend our thanks to all those involved.

First of all, thank you to the man that started it all, Bill James. From the original Baseball Abstracts that he began publishing in 1977 through today, he has continued to ask prescient and evocative questions that challenge assumptions and inspire new approaches.

John and Sue Dewan are the CEO and Director of Human Resources of Baseball Info Solutions, respectively, as well as the primary owners of the company. They started BIS in 2002 along with the late Steve Moyer, who also deserves great thanks for his everlasting contributions. In addition to his nominal title, John is deeply engaged with the baseball research department, providing guidance and oversight to the company's new initiatives as well as editorial final approval on everything that makes it into the *Handbook*. Sue, meanwhile, serves as the often-hidden backbone of the company, and she is a passionate advocate for each and every member of our consistently growing team.

Rob Dougherty is the President of Baseball Info Solutions, responsible for leading the strategic vision and overseeing the day-to-day operations of the organization. With extensive experience in sports data and journalism, he ascended to the role of President after serving as the Vice President of Information Technology and Finance, and prior to that the Director of IT. He sets the high-level vision for the book process and handles coordination with the publisher, amongst other responsibilities.

Joe Rosales serves as the point person for the production of *The Bill James Handbook*. He oversees the process from start to finish, and along with a few specific people deserves an extra tip of the cap. Jon Vrecsics leads the overwhelming stat-checking process with incredible attention to detail. Will Creager coordinates the technical aspects of the book's production. And it would be more efficient to list the aspects of the book that Brian Reiff isn't involved with than to enumerate his contributions.

At the core of this book is the data the we collect, and our Operations Department deserves thanks for their unparalleled data collection efforts and industry-leading accuracy. The aforementioned Jon Vrecsics took over as Director of Operations this year, and his vast experience has led to a seamless transition from his predecessor Tim Kwilos, who still serves vital functions in a consulting role. The rest of the Baseball Operations department includes Dan Casey, Todd Radcliffe, James Mehall, Nathan Phares, Jason Paff, Michael Churchward, Josh Hofer, Ted Baarda, Nathan Cooper, Noah Gatsik, Cole Ratliff, Justin Stine, and John Verros.

We should clarify for those who haven't heard that our company has expanded to also cover NFL and NCAA football, and we now alternatively go by the name Sports Info Solutions. Our very talented Director of Football and Research Matt Manocherian brings several years of relevant hands-on NFL experience to SIS, and his overall contributions to the company are far too numerous to list here in their entirety. He, along with Football Operations Coordinator Dan Foehrenbach, lead our growing football footprint as we work to fulfill our mission to educate both the teams and public about another sport that we believe can be improved by applying advanced analytics.

The people that transfer the raw data that Ops collects into the advanced metrics and analytics that you know and love are the Research and Development Department. The department is overseen by Matt Manocherian, but don't be fooled—Lead Researcher and Strategic Advisor Joe Rosales is the key figure at the head of all baseball-related research initiatives. Immense praise is due for Lindsay Zeck, Alex Vigderman, Brian Reiff, Mark Simon, Andrew Kyne, John Shirley, Nate Weller, Bryce Rossler, and intern Jon Becker, the R&D staff responsible for creating the bulk of the statistics and content found in the handbook. Check out SportsInfoSolutionsBlog.com for more of their baseball and football research all year long!

The SIS Information Technology Department is constantly behind the scenes making our clients happy and making everything that we do possible. Director of IT Patrick Coyle leads a team featuring Craig Saboe, Tricia Wilson, Brandyn Bechtel, Will Creager, Ben Stanczak, Tim Paul, and intern Dominic Cuoci. While keeping the Handbook on track, they also work tirelessly to ensure that we keep pace with the myriad needs of our clients during the company's busiest time of year when the Handbook overlaps with postseason baseball and the second month of the football season.

Corey March is in charge of our Business Development initiatives, fostering our relationships with clients and building new avenues for expanded business with the help of Patrick Rowley and intern Kyle Rodemann. Carol Olsen leads our office management, covering countless tasks that keep us running on a day-to-day basis, and Melanie Milbauer is our HR Specialist. They both work tirelessly to make sure that we all stay comfortable and happy during the heavy crunch of this time of year. Additionally, our Accountant/Bookkeeper Kelly Pohl recently joined the team, and if you are reading this, she has successfully made sure that we paid all our bills in time to get this made.

We are especially grateful to all of our outstanding team of Video Scouts. Their dedication and attention to detail provide the foundation of our business.

Senior Video Scouts are full-time employees who contribute to multiple operations within the company. They include Evan Butler, Kerby Callison, Jeff Dean, Ken Gaffney, Segev Goldberg, Ben Hrkach, Kyle Price, Nick Rabasco, Bryce Rossler, David Salway, John Todd, and Dan Wallie.

Our Video Scout Associates have spent multiple seasons with us, and they include Dominic Asta, Brett Bittiger, Mitch Glessner, Will Hoefer, Quinn Ireland, Michael Kogler, Shawn Larner, Glen Mueller, Matt Noskow, Austin Schied, and Harris Yudin.

Our Video Scouts are made up of Christian Beyer, Logan Boling, Arthur Bonser, Charles Book, William Clarke, Jacob Claspille, E. Joseph Conklin, Samuel Danes, Alexander Davy, Matthew Dell' Agnese, Brian Devine, Corey Eiferman, Eric Fitch, Matthew Freedman, Alex Gaffney, Christopher Glahn, Max Glasser, Luke Glavin, Max Gordon, Colin Grant, Maxwell Greenfield, Bryan Guo, Joseph Hirsch, Jeffrey Jackson, Matt Johnson, Matthew Kolln, Johnny Kraft, Seunghwan Kwon, Corey Leaden, Edward Lehr, Mark Lyman, Thomas Maguire, Joey Mahon, David Mandelberg, Tim Mansfield, Stephen Marciello, James McIntyre, Franklin Miller, Joshua Osburn, Ryan Otis, Chance Peacock, Macabee Pereira, Brandon Phillips, Francis Pinckney, Luke Porter, Kory Reinsfelder, Dominick Ricotta, Zachary Ripple, Brandon Ruud, Kyle Saathoff, Daniel Sarna, Max Schell, Tony Shields, Clayton Sisler, Brandon Stone, Robert Taylor, Brandon Tew, Christian

Tinory, David Tofani, Grant VanLiew, Dylan Vosk, Sam Weber, Chris Weikel, Caleb Whittemore, and Joseph Wittreich.

We also thank our Video Editors Brendon Baker, Jessica Carnivale, Kevin Engel, Jeff Israel, Alek Kawczynski, Jonah King, Luke Leon, Austin Major, Duane Mills, Chris Ranalli, Anthony Strasser, and Beau Yaremko.

Our partners at ACTA Publications include President Greg Pierce, Tom Wright, Mary Eggert, Mary Rickey, Abby Pierce, Brian Tobin, Mary Doyle, Isz and Patricia Lynch.

Thank you to our friends in the baseball industry who have helped us over the years. They include Andy Andres, David Appelman, Scott Bush, Jim Callis, Dave Cameron, Chris Dial, Greg Dreyfuss, Rylan Edwards, Tony Farwell, Sean Forman, Peter Gammons, Vince Genarro, Marshall Greenhut, Jason Grey, Ben Jedlovec, Christina Kahrl, Eric Karabell, Brian Kenny, Peter Kreutzer, Michael Lehrer, Ben Lindbergh, Rob Mains, Gene McCaffrey, Bob Meyerhoff, Mike Murphy, Noel Nash, Rob Neyer, Alex Patton, Mike Phillips, David Pinto, Joe Posnanski, Adam Richman, Hal Richman, Meg Rowley, Travis Sawchik, Bret Sayre, Peter Schoenke, Ron Shandler, Joe Sheehan, John Sickels, Chris Singleton, Dave Studenmund, Jeff Sullivan, Tom Tango, Hans Van Slooten, Mark Watson, Rick Wilton, and Don Zminda. We would also like to thank Steve Ruskowski for his assistance in stat-checking.

There are too many people too thank for making this book possible to fit them all in this section, but you know who you are, and we extend our sincerest gratitude for your help.

Most importantly, thank you to all of our readers. You inspire us and empower us to continue to dive deeper, and we're thrilled that you keep coming back to learn more about the game that we all love.